HOLY BIBLE

MODERN
ENGLISH
VERSION

PASSIO

MEV Economy Bible
Published by Passio
Charisma Media/Charisma House Book Group
600 Rinehart Road
Lake Mary, Florida 32746
www.charismahouse.com

Published in cooperation with Hudson Bible.

Like all translations of the Bible, this translation of the Scriptures is subject to human limitations and imperfections. Recognizing these limitations, the publisher sought God's guidance and wisdom throughout this project. Our prayer is that He will use this translation for the benefit of the church and His kingdom. Should a mistake be found, please feel free to contact the publisher.

16 17 18 19 — 9 8 7 6 5 4 3 2

Printed in the United States of America

CONTENTS

To Her Majesty Elizabeth II, by the Grace of God, of the United Kingdom of Great Britain and Northern Ireland, and of Her Other Realms and Territories, Queen, Head of the Commonwealth, Defender of the Faith.

The translators of the Bible wish grace, mercy, and peace through Jesus Christ our Lord.

PREFACE TO
THE READER

In January 1604, King James I convened the Hampton Court Conference at the Hampton Court Palace. Meeting with King James I were two parties representing the Church of England. One party comprised the Archbishop of Canterbury, John Whitgift, and eight bishops who represented the episcopacy, supported by eight deans and one archdeacon. The second party comprised several Anglicans who were moderate Puritans led by John Rainolds, who was the president of Corpus Christi College, Oxford. The conference comprised three meetings over a period of three days.

The conference was called in response to a series of requests for reform set down in the Millenary Petition by the Puritans, a document that contained the signatures of one thousand Puritan ministers. The petition detailed complaints about the terms *absolution* and *confirmation*, water baptism administered by women rather than by ministers, excommunication for "trifles and twelvepenny matters" and ecclesiastical discipline administered by governmental authority, and various other issues.

King James I persuaded the bishops that only ministers should administer baptisms. He also abolished excommunication for "trifles and twelvepenny matters," though he maintained that bishops should not be the sole administers of ecclesiastical discipline and that the trial policies of the commissaries' court should be reviewed by the Lord Chancellor and Lord Chief Justice. The King alleviated many of the Puritans' concerns and brought much peace between the two parties.

Trouble mounted for the Puritans when Archbishop John Whitgift died soon after the conference. Richard Bancroft was appointed to the See of Canterbury, and due to the King's concerns, the Puritan ministers were expected to adhere to each of the Thirty-Nine Articles that upheld the hierarchical nature of the Church of England, which the Puritans sought to abolish.

But the major outcome of the conference was that King James I commissioned a new translation of the Holy Bible into the English vernacular, which became the predecessor to the Modern English Version. The translation was to be pleasing both to the episcopacy and to the moderate Puritans who emphasized that man should be able to study the Holy Bible, not only with the help of the ministers but also privately. The translation became known as the Authorized Version because only this translation would be authorized to be read in the Church of England once it replaced portions of the Great Bible inserted in the 1662 edition of the *Book of Common Prayer*. In some parts of the world it is known as the King James Version. The translation enabled King James I to broaden his support in the Church and among the populace. It demonstrated his moderate and inclusive approach to concerns in the Church.

King James I gave certain instructions to the translators: The new translation would contain no marginal notes, it would conform to the ecclesiology of the Church of England, the translation of certain words should reflect old ecclesiastical words such as "church" and were not to be translated as "congregation," and the new translation would reflect the episcopal structure of the Church of England and traditional beliefs about ordained clergy.

He also required the Church to use the Bishop's Bible as the primary guide for the translation and retain the familiar names of the biblical characters. However, for additional textual support, he permitted the Church to use the Tyndale Bible, the Coverdale Bible, Matthew's Bible, the Great Bible, and the Geneva Bible. This instruction is the basis for the statement in the flyleaf of the Authorized Version: "translated out of the original tongues, and with the former translations diligently compared and revised, by His Majesty's special command." William Tyndale's translation from the Greek text, now known as the Textus Receptus, comprises eighty percent of the King James Version New Testament. The King James Version Old Testament is based on the Jacob ben Hayyim edition of the Masoretic Text.

Forty-seven scholars represented the Church of England, both Puritans and High Churchmen, including the Anglican scholar Sir Henry Savile, who was not a clergyman. They formed six committees: two at the University of Oxford, two at the University of Cambridge, and two at the Collegiate Church of St. Peter at Westminster, popularly known as Westminster Abbey. The King's printer printed forty unbound copies of the 1602 Bishop's Bible for the committees. This meant that the scholars could record their agreed-upon changes in the margins for the printer to insert into the text. The committees were assigned various sections of Scriptures. They then compared their drafts and revised them until they achieved consistency in the translation.

The Anglican clergy working on the King James Version stated their purpose: not to make a new translation, but to make a good one better. They also wanted to make the Bible more known and accessible to the people. Thus they produced the King James Version in 1611.

Later, the University of Oxford produced a standard text of the King James Version, known as the 1769 Oxford Update and edited by Dr. Benjamin Blayney. Dr. Blayney standardized the punctuation and spelling to update the King James Version. The 1769 Oxford Update is the edition commonly used today.

The King James Version has been the standard version for Protestants throughout the English-speaking world for over four hundred years now. Its flowing language, prose rhythm, and powerful and majestic style made it a literary classic, with many of its phrases and expressions embedded in contemporary English.

Today, realizing the need to update the King James Version for the twenty-first century, forty-seven scholars serving as professors, or chaplains to the Armed Forces of Her Majesty Queen Elizabeth II and to the United States Armed Forces, comprising the Committee on Bible Translation under the leadership of the senior editorial advisor Dr. Stanley M. Horton and the chief editor Dr. James F. Linzey, have joined forces to produce a more updated edition of the King James Version called the Modern English Version, which is based on a modern English vernacular.

The Modern English Version is a translation of the Textus Receptus and the Jacob ben Hayyim edition of the Masoretic Text, using the King James Version as the base manuscript. The Committee on Bible Translation adhered to the principle of formal equivalence, the meaning of which is to be as literal as proper English syntax and grammar will allow. At times it is impossible to translate every word or thought from Greek into English with proper syntax or a modern English vernacular. In such instances, it is important to realize certain words may go untranslated. For example, the Semitism in Matthew 11:4 transliterated as, "*kai apokritheis Ho Iesous eipen autois*," is translated in the King James Version as "Jesus answered and said unto them." This is not an effective rendition in the modern English vernacular due to the redundant speech, nor is it translated literally in the King James Version. So, to translate the Greek into the modern English vernacular, the phrase is translated as "Jesus answered them." Additionally, the original translators of the King James Version did not translate the Greek "*Ho*," translated as "the," nor did they translate "*apokritheis*" literally as "answering." Their goal was to use proper English grammar and syntax in the modern English vernacular of their day. Yet, by leaving certain terms untranslated in this update, it may appear that a Greek text other than the Textus Receptus may have been used. Such is not the case. A different English rendering is being used to re-translate the Textus Receptus while updating the King James Version manuscript.

When using the Textus Receptus as the base text for a contemporary English translation, the translators cannot use archaic, non-standard, purely literalistic English, nor fail to use what is known today about linguistics and ancient literary and cultural understandings in contemporary English translations. The original translators of the King James Version had this same approach for their own cultural and linguistic setting.

The original motive for creating this translation was to provide an update by military chaplains for the troops so they could understand the King James Version better. This project grew larger than anticipated in the search for academically qualified scholars when the chaplains "enlisted" the help of those who were not chaplains to get the job done, and when an unexpected publishing opportunity was offered. The target audience grew from the military to the entire English-speaking world. The translators began their work on June 2, 2005; they completed the New Testament on October 25, 2011, and the Old Testament on May 28, 2014.

The forty-seven American and English translators, being in great Christian unity and cooperation, who have a personal relationship with God through Jesus Christ and who have formed an interdenominational translation committee, represent churches such as the Baptist Union of Great Britain, Charismatic Episcopal Church, Central Church of the Nazarene, Church of Christ, Church of England, Church of God, Elim Church, Evangelical Lutheran Church of America, Free Methodist Church of North America, General Council of the Assemblies of God, International Church of the Foursquare Gospel, Methodist Church of Great Britain, Methodist Episcopal Church, Presbyterian Church of America, Reformed Presbyterian Church of North America, Southern Baptist Convention, United Church of Christ, United Methodist Church, and the United Reformed Church. The translators represent a cross section of the English-speaking Church. So it is their prayer that the Modern English Version will please the entire English-speaking world.

As professors or graduates of some of the world's leading colleges, seminaries, and universities, they represent institutions such as the Assemblies of God Theological Seminary, the College of William and Mary, Evangel University, Fuller Theological Seminary, Geneva College, Golden Gate Baptist Theological Seminary, Gordon-Conwell Theological Seminary, Harvard University, Hebrew Union College, Midwestern Baptist Theological Seminary, New Orleans Baptist Theological Seminary, Oklahoma Baptist University, Oral Roberts University, the Oxford Centre for Hebrew and Jewish Studies, Pentecostal Theological Seminary, Princeton Theological Seminary, Reformed Presbyterian Theological Seminary, Saint Leo University, the Southern Baptist Theological Seminary, Southwestern Baptist Theological Seminary, Stanford University, the University of Notre Dame, Vanguard University of Southern California, Westminster Seminary California, Westminster Theological Seminary, and Yale University. The translators are devoted to making a good translation better and ensuring that the Modern English Version is an accurate and responsible update of the King James Version.

The work of translating Scripture has always been an important part of Christian missions. Due to the work of missionary Bible translators, the complete Bible is available in over four hundred languages today. Missionaries normally have not used ancient Greek, Hebrew, or Aramaic texts in translation work. Instead, they usually have relied on the King James Version. In like manner, the Modern English Version is useful to continue translation work on the mission field. The Modern English Version is a translator's Bible for missions work to provide the Word of God to all English-speaking people and the entire world.

Compare the original Tyndale Translation with the updates of the following passage:

For when the worlde thorow wysdome knew not God in ye wysdome of God: it pleased God thorow folisshnes of preachinge to save them yt beleve (1Co 1:21, Tyndale Translation, 1534).

For after that, in the wisedom of God, the world by wisedome knew not God, it pleased God by the foolishnesse of preaching, to saue them that beleeue (1Co 1:21, KJV, 1611).

For after that in the wisdom of God the world by wisdom knew not God, it pleased God by the foolishness of preaching to save them that believe (1Co 1:21, KJV, 1769).

For since, in the wisdom of God, the world through wisdom did not know God, it pleased God through the foolishness of the message preached to save those who believe (1Co 1:21, NKJV, 1982).

For since, in the wisdom of God, the world through its wisdom did not know God, it pleased God through the foolishness of preaching to save those who believe (1Co 1:21, MEV, 2014).

The clergymen and scholars comprising the Committee on Bible Translation offer up to God the Modern English Version, the inspired Word of God, in the spirit of praise and gratitude, for the purpose of making disciples and teaching all nations in the name of the Father and of the Son and of the Holy Spirit.

The Committee on Bible Translation

COMMITTEE ON BIBLE TRANSLATION

THE
OLD TESTAMENT

GENESIS

The Creation

1 In the beginning God created the heavens and the earth. [2] The earth was formless and void, [1] darkness was over the surface of the deep, and the Spirit of God was moving[2] over the surface of the water.

[3] God said, "Let there be light," and there was light. [4] God saw that the light was good, and God separated the light from the darkness. [5] God called the light Day, and the darkness He called Night. So the evening and the morning were the first day.

[6] Then God said, "Let there be an expanse in the midst of the waters, and let it separate the waters from the waters." [7] So God made the expanse and separated the waters which were under the expanse from the waters which were above the expanse. And it was so. [8] God called the expanse Heaven. So the evening and the morning were the second day.

[9] Then God said, "Let the waters under the heavens be gathered together into one place, and let the dry land appear." And it was so. [10] God called the dry land Earth, and the gathering together of the waters He called Seas. Then God saw that it was good.

[11] Then God said, "Let the earth produce vegetation:[3] plants yielding seed and fruit trees on the earth yielding fruit after their kind with seed in them." And it was so. [12] The earth produced vegetation, plants yielding seed after their kind and trees yielding fruit with seed in them after their kind. And God saw that it was good. [13] So the evening and the morning were the third day.

[14] And God said, "Let there be lights in the expanse of the heavens to separate the day from the night, and let them be signs to indicate seasons, and days, and years. [15] Let them be lights in the expanse of the heavens to give light on the earth." And it was so. [16] God made two great lights: the greater light to rule the day and the lesser light to rule the night. He made the stars also. [17] Then God set them in the expanse of the heavens to give light on the earth, [18] to rule over the day and over the night, and to divide the light from the darkness. Then God saw that it was good. [19] So the evening and the morning were the fourth day.

[20] Then God said, "Let the waters swarm with swarms of living creatures and let the birds fly above the earth in the open expanse of the heavens." [21] So God created great sea creatures and every living thing that moves, with which the waters swarmed, according to their kind, and every winged bird according to its kind. And God saw that it was good. [22] Then God blessed them, saying, "Be fruitful and multiply and fill the waters in the seas, and let the birds multiply on the earth." [23] So the evening and the morning were the fifth day.

[24] Then God said, "Let the earth bring forth living creatures according to their kinds: livestock, and creeping things, and beasts of the earth according to their kinds." And it was so. [25] So God made the beasts of the earth according to their kind, and the livestock according to their kind, and everything that creeps on the earth according to its kind. And God saw that it was good.

[26] Then God said, "Let us make man in our image, after our likeness, and let them have dominion over the fish of the sea, and over the birds of the air, and over the livestock, and over all the earth, and over every creeping thing that creeps on the earth."

[27] So God created man in His own image;
    in the image of God He created him;
    male and female He created them.

[28] God blessed them and said to them, "Be fruitful and multiply, and replenish the earth and subdue it. Rule over the fish of the sea and over the birds of the air and over every living thing that moves on the earth."

[29] Then God said, "See, I have given you every plant yielding seed which is on the face of all the earth and every tree which has fruit yielding seed. It shall be food for you. [30] To every beast of the earth and to every bird of the air and to everything that creeps on the earth which has the breath of life in it, I have given every green plant for food." And it was so.

[31] God saw everything that He had made, and indeed it was very good. So the evening and the morning were the sixth day.

2 So the heavens and the earth, and all their hosts, were finished.

[2] On the seventh day God completed His work which He had done, and He rested on the seventh day from all His work which He had done. [3] Then God blessed the seventh day and made it holy, because on it He had rested from all His work which He had created and made.

Adam and Eve

[4] This is the account[4] of the heavens and the earth when they were created.

In the day that the Lord God made the earth and the heavens, [5] no shrub of the field was yet on the earth, and no plant of the field had yet sprouted, for the Lord God had not caused it to rain on the earth, and there was no man to cultivate the ground. [6] But a mist[5] arose from the earth and watered the whole surface of the ground. [7] Then the Lord God formed man from the dust of the ground and breathed into his nostrils the breath of life, and man became a living being.

[8] The Lord God planted a garden in the east, in Eden, and there He placed the man whom He had formed. [9] Out of the ground the Lord God made to grow every tree that is pleasant to the sight and good for food. The tree of life was also in the midst of the garden, along with the tree of knowledge of good and evil.

[10] A river flowed out of Eden to water the garden, and from there it parted and became four rivers. [11] The name of the first is Pishon; it encompasses the whole land of Havilah, where there is gold. [12] The gold of that land is good; bdellium and the onyx stone are there. [13] The name of the second river is Gihon; it encompasses the whole land of Cush. [14] The name of the third river is Tigris; it goes toward the east of Assyria. The fourth river is the Euphrates.

[15] The Lord God took the man and put him in the garden of Eden to till it and to keep it. [16] And the Lord God commanded the man, saying, "Of every tree of the garden you may freely eat, [17] but of the tree of the knowledge of good and evil you shall not eat, for in the day that you eat from it you will surely die."

[18] Then the Lord God said, "It is not good that the man should be alone. I will make him a helper suitable for him."

[19] Out of the ground the Lord God formed every beast of the field and every bird of the sky, and brought them to the man to see what he would call them. Whatever the man called every living creature, that was its name. [20] The man gave names to all the livestock, to the birds of the sky, and to every beast of the field, but for Adam[6] there was not found a helper suitable for him.

[21] So the Lord God caused a deep sleep to fall on Adam, and he slept. Then He took one of his ribs and closed up the place with flesh. [22] Then the rib which the Lord God had taken from man, He made into a woman, and He brought her to the man. [23] Then Adam said,

"This is now bone of my bones
    and flesh of my flesh;
she will be called Woman,
    for she was taken out of Man."

[1]2 Or a waste and emptiness.   [2]2 Or hovering.   [3]11 Or grass.   [4]4 Lit. These are the generations.   [5]6 Or flow.   [6]20 MT the man, or the Adam.

²⁴ Therefore a man will leave his father and his mother and be joined to his wife, and they will become one flesh.

²⁵ They were both naked, the man and his wife, and were not ashamed.

The Fall

3 Now the serpent was more subtle than any beast of the field which the Lord God had made. And he said to the woman, "Has God said, 'You shall not eat of any tree of the garden'?"

² And the woman said to the serpent, "We may eat of the fruit from the trees of the garden; ³ but from the fruit of the tree which is in the midst of the garden, God has said, 'You will not eat of it, nor will you touch it, or else you will die.' "

⁴ Then the serpent said to the woman, "You surely will not die! ⁵ For God knows that on the day you eat of it your eyes will be opened and you will be like God, knowing good and evil."

⁶ When the woman saw that the tree was good for food, that it was pleasing to the eyes and a tree desirable to make one wise, she took of its fruit and ate; and she gave to her husband with her, and he ate. ⁷ Then the eyes of both were opened, and they knew that they were naked. So they sewed fig leaves together and made coverings for themselves.

⁸ Then they heard the sound of the Lord God walking in the garden in the cool of the day, and the man and his wife hid themselves from the presence of the Lord God among the trees of the garden. ⁹ The Lord God called to the man and said to him, "Where are you?"

¹⁰ He said, "I heard Your voice in the garden and was afraid because I was naked, so I hid myself."

¹¹ And He said, "Who told you that you were naked? Have you eaten from the tree of which I commanded you not to eat?"

¹² The man said, "The woman whom You gave to be with me, she gave me *fruit* of the tree, and I ate."

¹³ Then the Lord God said to the woman, "What have you done?" And the woman said, "The serpent deceived me, and I ate."

¹⁴ The Lord God said to the serpent: "Because you have done this,

You are cursed above all livestock,
    and above every beast of the field;
you will go on your belly,
    and you will eat dust
    all the days of your life.
¹⁵ I will put enmity
    between you and the woman,
    and between your offspring and her offspring;
he will bruise your head,
    and you will bruise his heel."

¹⁶ To the woman He said,

"I will greatly multiply your pain in childbirth,
    and in pain you will bring forth children;
your desire will be for your husband,
    and he will rule over you."

¹⁷ And to Adam He said, "Because you have listened to the voice of your wife and have eaten from the tree about which I commanded you, saying, 'You shall not eat of it,'

Cursed is the ground on account of you;
    in hard labor you will eat of it
    all the days of your life.
¹⁸ Thorns and thistles it will bring forth for you,
    and you will eat the plants of the field.
¹⁹ By the sweat of your face
    you will eat bread
until you return to the ground,
    because out of it you were taken;
for you are dust,
    and to dust you will return."

²⁰ The man called his wife's name Eve because she was the mother of all the living.

²¹ The Lord God made garments of skins for both Adam and his wife and clothed them. ²² The Lord God said, "The man has become like one of us, knowing good and evil. And now, he might reach out his hand, and take also from the tree of life, and eat, and live forever"— ²³ therefore the Lord God sent him out from the garden of Eden, to till the ground from which he was taken. ²⁴ He drove the man out, and at the east of the garden of Eden He placed the cherubim and a flaming sword which turned in every direction, to guard the way to the tree of life.

Cain and Abel

4 Adam had relations with his wife Eve, and she conceived, gave birth to Cain and said, "I have gotten a man with the help of the Lord." ² Then she gave birth again to his brother Abel.

And Abel was a keeper of flocks, but Cain was a tiller of the ground. ³ In the course of time Cain brought an offering to the Lord of the fruit of the ground. ⁴ Abel also brought the first-born of his flock and of their fat portions. And the Lord had respect for Abel and for his offering, ⁵ but for Cain and for his offering, He did not have respect. And Cain was very angry and his countenance fell.

⁶ The Lord said to Cain, "Why are you angry? Why is your countenance fallen? ⁷ If you do well, shall you not be accepted?¹ But if you do not do well, sin is crouching at the door. It desires to dominate you, but you must rule over it."

⁸ Cain told Abel his brother. And it came about, when they were in the field, that Cain rose up against his brother Abel and killed him.

⁹ The Lord said to Cain, "Where is Abel your brother?"

He said, "I do not know. Am I my brother's keeper?"

¹⁰ And then He said, "What have you done? The voice of your brother's blood is crying out to Me from the ground. ¹¹ Now you are cursed from the ground which opened its mouth to receive your brother's blood from your hand. ¹² From now on when you till the ground, it will not yield for you its best. You will be a fugitive and a wanderer on the earth."

¹³ Then Cain said to the Lord, "My punishment is more than I can bear. ¹⁴ You have driven me out this day from the face of the earth, and from your face will I be hidden; and I will be a fugitive and a vagabond in the earth, and it will happen that anyone who finds me will kill me."

¹⁵ So the Lord said to him, "Therefore whoever kills Cain, vengeance will be taken on him sevenfold." Then the Lord put a mark upon Cain, so that no one finding him would kill him. ¹⁶ Then Cain went out from the presence of the Lord and settled in the land of Nod, east of Eden.

¹⁷ Cain had relations with his wife, and she conceived and gave birth to Enoch. He built a city and called the name of the city after the name of his son, Enoch. ¹⁸ To Enoch was born Irad, and Irad was the father of Mehujael, and Mehujael was the father of Methushael, and Methushael was the father of Lamech.

¹⁹ Lamech took two wives. The name of one was Adah, and the name of the other Zillah. ²⁰ Adah gave birth to Jabal. He was the father of those who dwell in tents and have livestock. ²¹ His brother's name was Jubal. He was the father of all those who play the harp and flute. ²² Zillah gave birth to Tubal-Cain, a forger of every tool of bronze and iron. The sister of Tubal-Cain was Naamah.

²³ Lamech said to his wives:

"Adah and Zillah, hear my voice,
    you wives of Lamech, and listen to my speech.
For I have killed a man for wounding me,
    a young man who hurt me.
²⁴ If Cain will be avenged sevenfold,
    then truly Lamech seventy-sevenfold."

²⁵ Adam had relations with his wife again, and she had another son and called his name Seth, for she said, "God has granted me

---

¹ 7 Or *uplifted.*

another offspring instead of Abel because Cain killed him." ²⁶ To Seth also was born a son, and he called his name Enosh.

At that time men began to call on the name of the LORD.

Adam's Descendants

5 This is the book of the generations of Adam.

In the day when God created man, He made him in the likeness of God. ² He created them male and female. He blessed them and called them Mankind in the day when they were created.

³ Adam lived a hundred and thirty years and became the father of a son in his own likeness, after his own image, and called his name Seth. ⁴ The days of Adam after he became the father of Seth were eight hundred years, and he had other sons and daughters. ⁵ So all the days that Adam lived were nine hundred and thirty years, and he died.

⁶ Seth lived one hundred and five years and became the father of Enosh. ⁷ Seth lived after the birth of Enosh eight hundred and seven years and had other sons and daughters. ⁸ So all the days of Seth were nine hundred and twelve years, and he died.

⁹ Enosh lived ninety years and became the father of Kenan. ¹⁰ Enosh lived after the birth of Kenan eight hundred and fifteen years and had other sons and daughters. ¹¹ So all the days of Enosh were nine hundred and five years, and he died.

¹² Kenan lived seventy years and became the father of Mahalalel. ¹³ Kenan lived after the birth of Mahalalel eight hundred and forty years and had other sons and daughters. ¹⁴ So all the days of Kenan were nine hundred and ten years, and he died.

¹⁵ Mahalalel lived sixty-five years and became the father of Jared. ¹⁶ Mahalalel lived after the birth of Jared eight hundred and thirty years and had other sons and daughters. ¹⁷ So all the days of Mahalalel were eight hundred and ninety-five years, and he died.

¹⁸ Jared lived one hundred and sixty-two years and became the father of Enoch. ¹⁹ Jared lived after the birth of Enoch eight hundred years and had other sons and daughters. ²⁰ So all the days of Jared were nine hundred and sixty-two years, and he died.

²¹ Enoch lived sixty-five years and became the father of Methuselah. ²² Enoch walked with God after the birth of Methuselah for three hundred years and had other sons and daughters. ²³ So all the days of Enoch were three hundred and sixty-five years. ²⁴ Enoch walked with God, and then he was no more because God took him.

²⁵ Methuselah lived one hundred and eighty-seven years and became the father of Lamech. ²⁶ Methuselah lived after the birth of Lamech seven hundred and eighty-two years and had other sons and daughters. ²⁷ So all the days of Methuselah were nine hundred and sixty-nine years, and he died.

²⁸ Lamech lived one hundred and eighty-two years and had a son. ²⁹ He named his son Noah, saying, "This one will comfort us concerning our work and the toil of our hands because of the ground which the LORD has cursed." ³⁰ Lamech lived after the birth of Noah five hundred and ninety-five years and had other sons and daughters. ³¹ So all the days of Lamech were seven hundred and seventy-seven years, and he died.

³² Noah was five hundred years old and became the father of Shem, Ham, and Japheth.

Man's Wickedness

6 When men began to multiply on the face of the earth and daughters were born to them, ² the sons of God saw that the daughters of men were fair and took as wives any they chose. ³ The LORD said, "My Spirit will not always strive with man, for he is flesh; yet his days will be a hundred and twenty years."

⁴ The Nephilim were on the earth in those days, and also after that, when the sons of God came in to the daughters of men, and they bore children to them. These were the mighty men who were of old, men of renown.

⁵ The LORD saw that the wickedness of man was great on the earth, and that every intent of the thoughts of his heart was continually only evil. ⁶ The LORD was sorry that He had made man on the earth, and it grieved Him in His heart. ⁷ So the LORD said, "I will destroy man, whom I have created, from the face of the earth—both man and beast, and the creeping things, and the birds of the sky, for I am sorry that I have made them." ⁸ But Noah found grace in the eyes of the LORD.

Noah and the Flood

⁹ These are the generations of Noah.

Noah was a just man and blameless among his contemporaries. Noah walked with God. ¹⁰ Noah had three sons: Shem, Ham, and Japheth.

¹¹ The earth was corrupt before God and filled with violence. ¹² God looked on the earth and saw it was corrupt, for all flesh had corrupted their way on the earth. ¹³ So God said to Noah, "The end of all flesh is come before Me, for the earth is filled with violence because of them. Now I will destroy them with the earth. ¹⁴ Make an ark of cypress wood for yourself. Make rooms in the ark, and cover it inside and out with pitch. ¹⁵ And this is how you must make it: The length of the ark will be three hundred cubits, the width of it fifty cubits, and the height of it thirty cubits.¹ ¹⁶ Make an opening² one cubit³ below the top of the ark all around; and you must set the door of the ark on the side. Make it with a lower, a second, and a third story. ¹⁷ I will bring a flood of waters on the earth to destroy all flesh, wherever there is the breath of life under heaven, and everything that is on the earth will die. ¹⁸ But I will establish My covenant with you; you must go into the ark—you, and your sons, and your wife, and your sons' wives with you. ¹⁹ Bring every living thing of all flesh, two of every kind, into the ark to keep them alive with you. They shall be male and female. ²⁰ Two of every kind of bird, of every kind of animal, and of every kind of creeping thing of the earth will come to you to be kept alive. ²¹ Also, take with you of every kind of food that is eaten and gather it to yourself, and it will be for food for you and for them."

²² Noah did this; he did all that God commanded him.

7 The LORD said to Noah, "You and your entire household go into the ark, for you alone I have seen to be righteous before Me among this generation. ² Take with you seven each of every clean animal, the male and its female, and two each of every unclean animal, the male and its female, ³ and seven each of birds of the air, the male and female, to keep offspring alive on the face of all the earth. ⁴ In seven days I will cause it to rain on the earth for forty days and forty nights, and every living thing that I have made I will destroy from the face of the earth."

⁵ And Noah did according to all that the LORD commanded him. ⁶ Noah was six hundred years old when the floodwaters came upon the earth. ⁷ And Noah went with his sons and his wife and his sons' wives into the ark because of the floodwaters. ⁸ Everything that creeps on the land from clean and unclean animals and birds ⁹ came in two by two, male and female, to Noah into the ark, as God had commanded Noah. ¹⁰ After seven days, the waters of the flood were on the earth.

¹¹ In the six hundredth year of Noah's life, in the second month, on the seventeenth day of the month, the same day, all the fountains of the great deep burst open and the floodgates of the heavens were opened. ¹² The rain fell upon the earth for forty days and forty nights.

¹³ On the very same day Noah and the sons of Noah, Shem, Ham, and Japheth, and Noah's wife, and the three wives of his sons with them, entered the ark. ¹⁴ They and every wild animal according to its kind, and all the livestock according to their kind, and every creeping thing that creeps on the earth according to its kind, and every bird according to its kind, every bird of every sort, ¹⁵ went with Noah into the ark, two by two of all flesh in which was the breath of life. ¹⁶ So they went in, male and female of all flesh, just as God had commanded him; then the LORD shut him in.

---

¹⁷ The flood was on the earth forty days, and the water increased and lifted up the ark, so that it rose up above the earth. ¹⁸ The water prevailed and increased greatly upon the earth, and the ark floated on the surface of the water. ¹⁹ The water prevailed exceedingly on the earth, and all the high mountains that were under the whole heaven were covered. ²⁰ The waters prevailed upward and the mountains were covered fifteen cubits deep.¹ ²¹ All flesh that moved on the earth died: birds and livestock and beasts, and every creeping thing that crept on the earth, and every man. ²² All in whose nostrils was the breath of life, all that was on the dry land, died. ²³ So He blotted out every living thing which was on the face of the ground, both man and animals and the creeping things and the birds of the heavens. They were blotted out from the earth, and only Noah and those who were with him in the ark remained alive.

²⁴ The waters prevailed on the earth for one hundred and fifty days.

The Flood Recedes

8 God remembered Noah and every living thing and all the livestock that were with him in the ark. So God made a wind to pass over the earth, and the water receded. ² Also the fountains of the deep and the floodgates of heaven were closed, and the rain from the heavens was restrained. ³ The water receded steadily from the earth, and after the end of one hundred and fifty days the waters decreased. ⁴ The ark rested in the seventh month, on the seventeenth day of the month, on the mountains of Ararat. ⁵ The water continually decreased until the tenth month. In the tenth month, on the first day of the month, the tops of the mountains became visible.

⁶ Then at the end of forty days, Noah opened the window of the ark which he had made, ⁷ and he sent forth a raven, which went to and fro until the waters were dried up on the earth. ⁸ Then he sent out a dove to see if the waters had subsided from the face of the ground. ⁹ But the dove found no rest for the sole of her foot, so she returned to him into the ark, for the waters were on the surface of all the earth. Then he put forth his hand, and took her, and brought her into the ark to himself. ¹⁰ He waited yet another seven days, and again he sent out the dove from the ark. ¹¹ The dove came to him in the evening, and in her mouth there was a freshly plucked olive leaf. So Noah knew that the waters had receded from the earth. ¹² He waited another seven days and sent out the dove again, but it did not return to him again.

¹³ So in the six hundred and first year, in the first month, the first day of the month, the waters were dried up from the earth; and Noah removed the covering of the ark, and looked, and saw the surface of the ground was dry. ¹⁴ In the second month, on the twenty-seventh day of the month, the earth was dry.

¹⁵ Then God spoke to Noah, saying, ¹⁶ "Go out of the ark, you and your wife, and your sons and your sons' wives with you. ¹⁷ Bring out with you every living thing of all flesh that is with you, birds and animals, and every creeping thing that creeps on the earth, so that they may breed abundantly on the earth and be fruitful and multiply on the earth."

¹⁸ So Noah and his sons and his wife and his sons' wives went out. ¹⁹ Every beast, every creeping thing, every bird, and everything that moves on the earth, according to their families, went out of the ark. ²⁰ Then Noah built an altar to the LORD and took of every clean animal and of every clean bird and offered burnt offerings on the altar. ²¹ The LORD smelled a soothing aroma; and the LORD said in His heart, "I will never again curse the ground because of man, for the inclination of man's heart is evil from his youth, nor will I again destroy every living thing as I have done.

²² While the earth remains,
seedtime and harvest,
cold and heat,
summer and winter,
and day and night
will not cease."

The Noahic Covenant

9 Then God blessed Noah and his sons and said to them, "Be fruitful and multiply and fill the earth. ² Every beast of the earth and every bird of the sky and all that moves on the earth and all the fish of the sea will fear you and be terrified of you. They are given into your hand. ³ Every moving thing that lives will be food for you. I give you everything, just as I gave you the green plant.

⁴ "Only you shall not eat flesh with its life, *that is*, its blood. ⁵ But for your own lifeblood I will surely require a reckoning; from every animal will I require it; of man, too, will I require a reckoning for human life, of every man for that of his fellow man.

⁶ Whoever sheds the blood of man,
    by man shall his blood be shed;
for God made man
    in His own image.

⁷ And as for you, be fruitful and multiply; increase abundantly in the earth and multiply in it."

⁸ Again God spoke to Noah and to his sons with him, saying, ⁹ "As for Me, I establish My covenant with you, and with your descendants after you; ¹⁰ and with every living creature that is with you, the birds, the livestock, and every beast of the earth with you; of all that comes out of the ark, every beast of the earth. ¹¹ I establish My covenant with you. Never again shall all flesh be cut off by the waters of a flood. Never again shall there be a flood to destroy the earth."

¹² Then God said, "This is the sign of the covenant which I am making between Me and you and every living creature that is with you, for all future generations. ¹³ I have set My rainbow in the cloud, and it shall be a sign of a covenant between Me and the earth. ¹⁴ When I bring a cloud over the earth, the rainbow will be seen in the cloud; ¹⁵ then I will remember My covenant, which is between Me and you and every living creature of all flesh, and the waters will never again become a flood to destroy all flesh. ¹⁶ The rainbow will appear in the cloud, and I will see it and remember the everlasting covenant between God and every living creature of all flesh that is on the earth."

¹⁷ So God said to Noah, "This is the sign of the covenant that I have established between Me and all flesh that is on the earth."

The Sons of Noah

¹⁸ The sons of Noah who went forth from the ark were Shem, Ham, and Japheth. Ham was the father of Canaan. ¹⁹ These were the three sons of Noah, and from them the whole earth was populated.

²⁰ Noah began to be a man of the soil, and he planted a vineyard. ²¹ Then he drank some of the wine and became drunk, and lay uncovered in his tent. ²² And Ham, the father of Canaan, saw the nakedness of his father, and told his two brothers outside. ²³ So Shem and Japheth took a garment, and laid it upon both their shoulders, and went backward, and covered the nakedness of their father. Their faces were turned away, and they did not see their father's nakedness.

²⁴ When Noah awoke from his wine and knew what his younger son had done to him, ²⁵ he said,

"Canaan be cursed!
    He will be a servant of servants
    to his brothers."

²⁶ He also said,

"Blessed be the LORD God of Shem,
    and let Canaan be his servant.
²⁷ May God enlarge Japheth,
    and may he dwell in the tents of Shem,
    and may Canaan be his servant."

²⁸ Noah lived after the flood three hundred and fifty years. ²⁹ All the days of Noah were nine hundred and fifty years, and then he died.

---

¹ 20 About 23 feet, or 6.8 meters.

The Table of Nations

10 Now these are the generations of Shem, Ham, and Japheth, the sons of Noah. And sons were born to them after the flood.

The Japhethites
1Ch 1:5–7
2 The sons of Japheth were
Gomer, Magog, Madai, Javan, Tubal, Meshek, and Tiras.
3 The sons of Gomer were
Ashkenaz, Riphath, and Togarmah.
4 The sons of Javan were
Elishah, Tarshish, the Kittites, and the Rodanites. 5 From these the coastlands of the nations were divided¹ into their lands, everyone according to his tongue, according to their families, by their nations.

The Hamites
1Ch 1:8–16
6 The sons of Ham were
Cush, Egypt, Put, and Canaan.
7 The sons of Cush were
Seba, Havilah, Sabtah, Raamah, and Sabteka;
and the sons of Raamah were
Sheba and Dedan.

8 Cush was the father of Nimrod. He became a mighty one on the earth. 9 He was a mighty hunter before the Lord. Therefore it is said, "Even like Nimrod the mighty hunter before the Lord." 10 The beginning of his kingdom was Babel,² Uruk, Akkad, and Kalneh in the land of Shinar. 11 From that land he went to Assyria and built Nineveh, the city Rehoboth Ir, and Calah, 12 and Resen between Nineveh and Calah (that is the principal city).

13 Egypt was the father of
the Ludites, Anamites, Lehabites, Naphtuhites, 14 Pathrusites, Kasluhites (from whom came the Philistines), and Caphtorites.
15 Canaan was the father of
Sidon his firstborn and Heth, 16 and the Jebusites, Amorites, Girgashites, 17 Hivites, Arkites, Sinites, 18 Arvadites, Zemarites, and the Hamathites.

Later the families of the Canaanites spread abroad. 19 The border of the Canaanites was from Sidon toward Gerar to Gaza, and then to Sodom, Gomorrah, Admah, Zeboyim, as far as Lasha.
20 These are the sons of Ham, according to their families, according to their languages, in their lands and in their nations.

The Semites
Ge 11:10–27; 1Ch 1:17–27
21 To Shem, who was the father of all the children of Eber, whose older brother was Japheth,³ were sons born also.

22 The sons of Shem were
Elam, Ashur, Arphaxad, Lud, and Aram.
23 The sons of Aram were
Uz, Hul, Gether, and Meshek.
24 Arphaxad was the father of Shelah,
and Shelah was the father of Eber.
25 To Eber were born two sons.
The name of one was Peleg, for in his days the earth was divided; his brother's name was Joktan.
26 Joktan was the father of
Almodad, Sheleph, Hazarmaveth, Jerah, 27 Hadoram, Uzal, Diklah, 28 Obal, Abimael, Sheba, 29 Ophir, Havilah, and Jobab. All these were the sons of Joktan.

30 Their dwelling place was from Mesha all the way to Sephar, the hill country of the east.

31 These are the sons of Shem, by their families and their language, in their lands and their nations.

32 These are the families of the sons of Noah, according to their generations, in their nations. From these were the nations divided in the earth after the flood.

The Tower of Babel

11 Now the whole earth had one language and the same words. 2 As the people journeyed from the east, they found a plain in the land of Shinar and settled there.
3 They said to each other, "Let us make bricks and bake them thoroughly." And they had brick for stone and tar for mortar. 4 Then they said, "Come, let us build us a city and a tower, whose top will reach to heaven, and let us make a name for ourselves; otherwise we will be scattered abroad over the face of the whole earth."
5 But the Lord came down to see the city and the tower that the sons of men built. 6 The Lord said, "The people are one and they have one language, and this is only the beginning of what they will do; now nothing that they propose to do will be impossible for them. 7 Come, let us go down and there confuse their language, so that they may not understand one another's speech."
8 So the Lord scattered them abroad from there over the face of all the earth, and they stopped building the city. 9 Therefore the name of it was called Babel, because there the Lord confused the language of all the earth. From there the Lord scattered them abroad over the face of all the earth.

Shem's Descendants
Ge 10:21–31; 1Ch 1:17–27
10 These are the generations of Shem.

Shem was a hundred years old, and two years after the flood he became the father of Arphaxad. 11 Shem lived after the birth of Arphaxad five hundred years, and had other sons and daughters.
12 Arphaxad lived thirty-five years, and became the father of Shelah. 13 Arphaxad lived after the birth of Shelah four hundred and three years, and had other sons and daughters.
14 Shelah lived thirty years, and became the father of Eber. 15 Shelah lived after the birth of Eber four hundred and three years, and had other sons and daughters.
16 Eber lived thirty-four years, and became the father of Peleg. 17 Eber lived after the birth of Peleg four hundred and thirty years, and had other sons and daughters.
18 Peleg lived thirty years, and became the father of Reu. 19 Peleg lived after the birth of Reu two hundred and nine years, and had other sons and daughters.
20 Reu lived thirty-two years, and became the father of Serug. 21 Reu lived after the birth of Serug two hundred and seven years, and had other sons and daughters.
22 Serug lived thirty years, and became the father of Nahor. 23 Serug lived after the birth of Nahor two hundred years, and had other sons and daughters.
24 Nahor lived twenty-nine years, and became the father of Terah. 25 Nahor lived after the birth of Terah one hundred and nineteen years, and had other sons and daughters.
26 Now Terah lived seventy years, and became the father of Abram, Nahor, and Haran.

Terah's Descendants
27 These are the generations of Terah.

Terah became the father of Abram, Nahor, and Haran, and Haran became the father of Lot. 28 Haran died before his father Terah in the land of his birth, in Ur of the Chaldeans. 29 Abram and Nahor took wives. The name of Abram's wife was Sarai, and the name of Nahor's wife, Milkah, the daughter of Haran, the father of Milkah and the father of Iskah. 30 But Sarai was barren; she had no child.
31 Terah took his son Abram and his grandson Lot, son of Haran, and his daughter-in-law Sarai, his son Abram's wife, and they went

---

¹ 5 Or *separated themselves.* ² 10 Or *Babylon.* ³ 21 Or *the older brother of Japheth.*

out together from Ur of the Chaldeans to go into the land of Canaan; but when they came to Harran, they settled there.

[32] The days of Terah were two hundred and five years, and Terah died in Harran.

The Call of Abram

12 Now the LORD said to Abram, "Go from your country, your family, and your father's house to the land that I will show you.

[2] I will make of you a great nation;
　　I will bless you
　and make your name great,
　　so that you will be a blessing.
[3] I will bless them who bless you
　　and curse him who curses you,[1]
　and in you all families of the earth
　　will be blessed."

[4] So Abram departed, as the LORD had spoken to him, and Lot went with him. Abram was seventy-five years old when he departed from Harran. [5] Abram took Sarai his wife, Lot his brother's son, and all their possessions that they had accumulated, and the people that they had acquired in Harran, and they set out for the land of Canaan. They came to the land of Canaan.

[6] Then Abram passed through the land to the place of Shechem, to the oak of Moreh. The Canaanites were in the land at that time. [7] The LORD appeared to Abram and said, "To your descendants I will give this land." So he built an altar to the LORD, who had appeared to him.

[8] From there he continued on to a mountain to the east of Bethel and pitched his tent, having Bethel on the west and Ai on the east. There he built an altar to the LORD and called on the name of the LORD. [9] Then Abram continued his journey toward the Negev.

Abram in Egypt

Ge 20:1–18; 26:1–11

[10] Now there was a famine in the land, so Abram went down to Egypt to live there, for the famine was severe in the land. [11] When he was getting near to Egypt, he said to Sarai his wife, "I know you are a beautiful woman. [12] Therefore, when the Egyptians see you, they will say, 'This is his wife.' They will then kill me, but they will let you live. [13] Say you are my sister so that I may be treated well for your sake. Then my life will be spared because of you."

[14] So when Abram entered Egypt, the Egyptians saw that Sarai was very beautiful. [15] The princes of Pharaoh saw her and commended her to Pharaoh, and she was taken into Pharaoh's house. [16] He treated Abram well for her sake and he had sheep and livestock, male and female donkeys, male and female servants, and camels.

[17] But the LORD afflicted Pharaoh and his house with great plagues because of Abram's wife, Sarai. [18] So Pharaoh called Abram, and said, "What have you done to me? Why did you not tell me that she was your wife? [19] Why did you say, 'She is my sister'? I might have taken her as my wife. Now here is your wife; take her and leave." [20] Pharaoh commanded his men concerning him, and they sent him away with his wife and all that he had.

Abram and Lot

13 So Abram went up from Egypt to the Negev, he and his wife and all that he had, and Lot with him. [2] Abram was very wealthy in livestock, in silver and in gold.

[3] He continued on his journey from the Negev and came to Bethel, to the place where his tent had been at the beginning, between Bethel and Ai, [4] to the place where he first made an altar. There Abram called on the name of the LORD.

[5] Now Lot, who went with Abram, also had flocks and herds and tents. [6] But the land was not able to support them both dwelling together because their possessions were so great. [7] And there was strife between the herdsmen of Abram's livestock and the herdsmen of Lot's livestock. The Canaanites and the Perizzites dwelled in the land at that time.

[8] So Abram said to Lot, "Let there be no strife, I ask you, between me and you, and between my herdsmen and your herdsmen, for we are close relatives. [9] Is not the whole land before you? Please separate from me. If you will go to the left, then I will go to the right, or if you take the right, then I will go to the left."

[10] Lot lifted up his eyes, and looked at all the valley of the Jordan, that it was well watered everywhere like the garden of the LORD, like the land of Egypt as you go to Zoar. This was before the LORD destroyed Sodom and Gomorrah. [11] Then Lot chose for himself the entire valley of the Jordan and journeyed east, and the two of them separated from each other. [12] Abram dwelled in the land of Canaan, and Lot dwelled in the cities of the valley and pitched his tent as far as Sodom. [13] Now the men of Sodom were exceedingly wicked and sinners against the LORD.

[14] After Lot had departed from him, the LORD said to Abram, "Lift up now your eyes, and look from the place where you are, northward and southward and eastward and westward. [15] All the land that you see I will give to you and to your descendants forever. [16] I will make your descendants like the dust of the earth, so that if a man could number the dust of the earth, then your descendants could also be numbered. [17] Arise, and walk throughout the land across its length and its width, for I will give it to you."

[18] So Abram moved his tent and came and settled by the oaks of Mamre, which are in Hebron, and built an altar to the LORD there.

Abram Rescues Lot

14 In the days that Amraphel was king of Shinar, Arioch king of Ellasar, Kedorlaomer king of Elam, and Tidal king of Goyim, [2] they made war with Bera king of Sodom, Birsha king of Gomorrah, Shinab king of Admah, Shemeber king of Zeboyim, and the king of Bela (that is, Zoar). [3] All these were joined together in the Valley of Siddim (that is, the Dead Sea). [4] For twelve years they had served Kedorlaomer, but in the thirteenth year they rebelled.

[5] In the fourteenth year, Kedorlaomer and the kings who were with him came and defeated the Rephaites in Ashteroth Karnaim, the Zuzites in Ham, and the Emites in Shaveh Kiriathaim, [6] and the Horites in their hill country of Seir, as far as El Paran, which is by the wilderness. [7] Then they turned back and came to En Mishpat (that is, Kadesh) and conquered all the country of the Amalekites and also the Amorites who lived in Hazezon Tamar.

[8] Then the king of Sodom, the king of Gomorrah, the king of Admah, the king of Zeboyim, and the king of Bela (that is, Zoar) came out, and they joined together in battle in the Valley of Siddim [9] against Kedorlaomer, the king of Elam, Tidal king of Goyim, Amraphel king of Shinar, and Arioch king of Ellasar—four kings against five. [10] Now the Valley of Siddim was full of tar pits, and as the kings of Sodom and Gomorrah fled, some fell in them, and the rest fled to the hill country. [11] Then they took all the possessions of Sodom and Gomorrah, and all their provisions, and departed. [12] They also took Lot, Abram's brother's son, who lived in Sodom, and his possessions, and went their way.

[13] Then one who had escaped came and told Abram the Hebrew, who was living near the oaks of Mamre the Amorite, brother of Eshkol and Aner, and these were allies with Abram. [14] When Abram heard that his relative was taken captive, he armed his three hundred and eighteen trained servants born in his own house, and pursued them as far as Dan. [15] During the night he divided his men to attack them and defeated them, and pursued them as far as Hobah, which is north of Damascus. [16] He brought back all the possessions, along with his relative Lot and his possessions, and also the women and the people.

Melchizedek Blesses Abram

[17] After his return from the defeat of Kedorlaomer and the kings who had joined with him, the king of Sodom went out to meet him in the Valley of Shaveh (that is, the King's Valley).

---

1 3 Or treats you lightly.

¹⁸ Then Melchizedek king of Salem brought out bread and wine. He was the priest of God Most High. ¹⁹ And he blessed him and said,

"Blessed be Abram by God Most High,
Creator¹ of heaven and earth;
²⁰ and blessed be God Most High,
who has delivered your enemies into your hand."

Then Abram gave him a tenth of everything.
²¹ The king of Sodom said to Abram, "Give me the people and take the goods for yourself."
²² But Abram said to the king of Sodom, "I have lifted up my hand to the Lord, God Most High, the Possessor of heaven and earth, ²³ that I will take nothing that is yours, not a thread or a sandal strap; lest you say, 'I have made Abram rich.' ²⁴ I will accept only that which my men have eaten and the portion that belongs to the men who went with me, Aner, Eshkol, and Mamre. Let them take their portion."

The Abrahamic Covenant

15 After this the word of the Lord came to Abram in a vision, saying,

"Do not fear, Abram.
I am your shield,
your exceedingly great reward.²"

² But Abram said, "Lord God, what will You give me, seeing I am childless and the heir of my house is Eliezer of Damascus?" ³ Abram said, "Since You have not given me any children, my heir is a servant born in my house."
⁴ Then the word of the Lord came to him, saying, "This man will not be your heir, but a son that is from your own body will be your heir." ⁵ He brought him outside and said, "Look up toward heaven and count the stars, if you are able to count them." And He said to him, "So will your descendants be."
⁶ Abram believed the Lord, and He credited it to him as righteousness.
⁷ He also said to him, "I am the Lord who brought you out of Ur of the Chaldeans to give you this land to possess³ it."
⁸ But Abram said, "Lord God, how may I know that I will possess it?"
⁹ So He said to him, "Bring Me a three-year-old heifer, a three-year-old female goat, a three-year-old ram, a turtledove, and a young pigeon."
¹⁰ Then Abram brought all of these to Him and cut them in two and laid each piece opposite the other, but he did not cut the birds in half. ¹¹ When the birds of prey came down on the carcasses, Abram drove them away.
¹² As the sun was going down, a deep sleep fell on Abram, and terror and a great darkness fell on him. ¹³ Then He said to Abram, "Know for certain that your descendants will live as strangers in a land that is not theirs, and they will be enslaved and mistreated for four hundred years. ¹⁴ But I will judge the nation that they serve, and afterward they will come out with great possessions. ¹⁵ As for you, you will go to your fathers in peace and you will be buried at a good old age. ¹⁶ In the fourth generation, your descendants will return here, for the iniquity of the Amorites is not yet complete."
¹⁷ When the sun went down and it was dark, a smoking fire pot with a flaming torch passed between these pieces. ¹⁸ On that same day the Lord made a covenant with Abram, saying, "To your descendants I have given this land, from the river of Egypt to the great Euphrates River— ¹⁹ the land of the Kenites, the Kenizzites, the Kadmonites, ²⁰ the Hittites, the Perizzites, the Rephaites, ²¹ the Amorites, the Canaanites, the Girgashites, and the Jebusites."

The Birth of Ishmael

16 Now Sarai, Abram's wife, had borne him no children, and she had a maidservant, an Egyptian, whose name was Hagar. ² So Sarai said to Abram, "The Lord has prevented me from

having children. Please go in to my maid; it may be that I will obtain children through her."
Abram listened to Sarai. ³ So after Abram had been living for ten years in the land of Canaan, Sarai, his wife, took Hagar her maid, the Egyptian, and gave her to her husband Abram to be his wife. ⁴ He went in to Hagar, and she conceived.
When she saw that she had conceived, she began to despise her mistress. ⁵ Then Sarai said to Abram, "May the wrong done to me be on you! I gave my maid into your arms; and when she saw that she had conceived, I became despised in her eyes. May the Lord judge between you and me."
⁶ But Abram said to Sarai, "Indeed, your maid is in your power; do to her as you please." Then Sarai dealt harshly with her, and she fled from her presence.
⁷ The angel of the Lord found her by a spring of water in the wilderness. It was the spring on the way to Shur. ⁸ And he said, "Hagar, Sarai's maid, where have you come from and where are you going?"
And she said, "I am fleeing from the presence of my mistress Sarai."
⁹ Then the angel of the Lord said to her, "Return to your mistress, and submit yourself to her authority." ¹⁰ The angel of the Lord also said to her, "I will multiply your descendants exceedingly so that they will be too many to count."
¹¹ Then the angel of the Lord said to her,

"You are pregnant
and will bear a son.
You shall call his name Ishmael,
because the Lord has heard your affliction.
¹² He will be a wild man;
his hand will be against every man,
and every man's hand will be against him.
And he will dwell
in the presence of all his brothers."

¹³ Then she called the name of the Lord that spoke to her, "You are the God who sees," for she said, "Have I now looked on Him who sees me?" ¹⁴ Therefore the well was called Beer Lahai Roi. It is between Kadesh and Bered.
¹⁵ So Hagar bore Abram a son, and Abram called the son she bore Ishmael. ¹⁶ Abram was eighty-six years old when Hagar bore Ishmael to Abram.

The Covenant of Circumcision

17 When Abram was ninety-nine years old, the Lord appeared to him and said, "I am Almighty God. Walk before Me and be blameless. ² And I will make My covenant between you and Me and will exceedingly multiply you."
³ Abram fell on his face and God said to him, ⁴ "As for Me, My covenant is with you, and you shall be the father of a multitude of nations. ⁵ No longer will your name be called Abram, but your name will be Abraham, for I have made you the father of a multitude of nations. ⁶ I will make you exceedingly fruitful; and I will make nations of you, and kings will come from you. ⁷ I will establish My covenant between Me and you and your descendants after you throughout their generations for an everlasting covenant, to be God to you and your descendants after you. ⁸ All the land of Canaan, where you now live as strangers, I will give to you and to your descendants for an everlasting possession, and I will be their God."
⁹ Then God said to Abraham, "As for you, you shall keep My covenant, you and your descendants after you throughout their generations. ¹⁰ This is My covenant, which you shall keep, between Me and you and your descendants after you; every male among you shall be circumcised. ¹¹ You shall circumcise the flesh of your foreskins, and it shall be a sign of the covenant between Me and you. ¹² Every male throughout every generation that is eight days old shall be circumcised, whether born in your household or bought with money from a foreigner who is not your descendant. ¹³ He who is born in your house and he who is bought with your money

---

¹ 19 Or Possessor.   ² 1 Or your reward will be great.   ³ 7 Or inherit.

must be circumcised. My covenant shall be in your flesh as an everlasting covenant. [14] Any uncircumcised male whose flesh of his foreskin is not circumcised shall be cut off from his people. He has broken My covenant."

[15] Then God said to Abraham, "As for Sarai your wife, you will not call her name Sarai, but her name will be Sarah. [16] I will bless her and also give you a son by her. I will bless her, and she will be the mother of nations. Kings of peoples will come from her."

[17] Then Abraham fell on his face and laughed and said in his heart, "Shall a child be born to a man that is a hundred years old? Shall Sarah, who is ninety years old, bear a child?" [18] Abraham said to God, "Oh, that Ishmael might live before You!"

[19] Then God said, "No, but your wife Sarah will bear you a son, and you will call his name Isaac. I will establish My covenant with him as an everlasting covenant and with his descendants after him. [20] And as for Ishmael, I have heard you. I have blessed him, and will make him fruitful and will multiply him exceedingly. He will be the father of twelve princes, and I will make him a great nation. [21] But I will establish My covenant with Isaac, whom Sarah will bear to you at this set time next year." [22] Then He stopped talking with Abraham, and God went up from him.

[23] Then Abraham took Ishmael, his son, and all that were born in his house, and all that were bought with his money, every male among the men of Abraham's household, and circumcised the flesh of their foreskins that very same day as God had said to him. [24] Abraham was ninety-nine years old when he was circumcised in the flesh of his foreskin. [25] His son, Ishmael, was thirteen years old when he was circumcised in the flesh of his foreskin. [26] Abraham and Ishmael were circumcised on the same day. [27] All the men born in Abraham's household or bought from foreigners were circumcised with him.

Isaac's Birth Foretold

18 The LORD appeared to Abraham near the great oak trees of Mamre while he sat in the tent door in the heat of the day. [2] Abraham lifted up his eyes and looked and saw three men standing across from him. When he saw them, he ran from the tent door to meet them and bowed himself toward the ground.

[3] He said, "My Lord, if I have found favor in Your sight, do not pass by Your servant. [4] Please let a little water be brought and wash your feet and rest yourselves under the tree. [5] I will bring a piece of bread so that you may refresh yourselves. After that you may pass on, now that you have come to your servant."

And they said, "So do, as you have said."

[6] So Abraham hurried into the tent to Sarah, and said, "Quickly prepare three measures[f] of fine flour, knead it, and make cakes."

[7] Then Abraham ran to the herd and took a choice and tender calf and gave it to a servant, who hurried to prepare it. [8] He then brought butter and milk and the calf that he had prepared and set it before them; and he stood by them under the tree while they ate.

[9] They said to him, "Where is Sarah your wife?"

And he said, "There, in the tent."

[10] One of them said, "I will certainly return to you about this time next year, and Sarah your wife will have a son."

And Sarah heard it in the tent door, which was behind him. [11] Now Abraham and Sarah were old and very advanced in age, and Sarah was well past childbearing. [12] Therefore Sarah laughed to herself, saying, "After I am so old and my lord is old also, shall I have pleasure?"

[13] Then the LORD said to Abraham, "Why did Sarah laugh and say, 'Shall I surely bear a child when I am old?' [14] Is anything too difficult for the LORD? At the appointed time I will return to you, at this time next year, and Sarah will have a son."

[15] Then Sarah denied it, saying, "I did not laugh," because she was afraid.

But He said, "Yes, you did laugh."

Sodom and Gomorrah

[16] Then the men rose up and looked toward Sodom, and Abraham went with them to see them on their way. [17] Then the LORD said,

"Should I hide from Abraham what I am doing, [18] since Abraham will surely become a great and mighty nation, and all the nations of the earth will be blessed in him? [19] I chose him, and he will instruct his children and his household after him to keep the way of the LORD by doing righteousness and justice, so that the LORD may bring to Abraham what He promised him."

[20] Then the LORD said, "Because the outcry against Sodom and Gomorrah is great, and because their sin is very grave, [21] I will go down and see if what they have done is as bad as the outcry that has come to Me. If not, I will know."

[22] The men turned away from there and went toward Sodom, but Abraham remained standing before the LORD. [23] Then Abraham drew near and said, "Shall You also destroy the righteous with the wicked? [24] What if there are fifty righteous in the city? Shall You also destroy, and not spare the place, for the fifty righteous who are in it? [25] Far be it from You to do such a thing as this, to slay the righteous with the wicked, so that the righteous should be treated like the wicked; far be it from You. Should not the Judge of all the earth do right?"

[26] So the LORD said, "If I find in Sodom fifty righteous within the city, then I will spare the entire place for their sakes."

[27] Then Abraham answered and said, "I who am but dust and ashes have taken it upon myself to speak to the Lord. [28] Suppose there were five less than the fifty righteous. Will You destroy all the city for lack of five?"

And He said, "If I find forty-five there, I will not destroy it."

[29] And he spoke to Him yet again and said, "Suppose there will be forty found there?"

So He said, "I will not do it for the sake of forty."

[30] Then he said to Him, "Let not the Lord be angry, and I will speak. Suppose there will be thirty found there?"

Again He said, "I will not do it if I find thirty there."

[31] He said, "Behold, I have undertaken to speak to the Lord. Suppose twenty are found there?"

He said, "I will not destroy it for the sake of twenty."

[32] Then he said, "Let not the Lord be angry, and I will speak only once more. Suppose ten will be found there?"

Then He said, "I will not destroy it for the sake of ten."

[33] So the LORD went His way as soon as He had stopped speaking to Abraham, and Abraham returned to his place.

Sodom and Gomorrah Destroyed

19 Now the two angels came to Sodom in the evening, and Lot was sitting at the gate of Sodom. When Lot saw them he rose up to meet them, and he bowed himself with his face toward the ground. [2] Then he said, "Here, my lords, please turn in to your servant's house and spend the night and wash your feet; and then you may rise early and go on your way."

They said, "No, we will stay in the open square all night."

[3] But he strongly insisted, so they turned aside with him and entered his house. Then he made them a feast and baked unleavened bread, and they ate. [4] Before they lay down, the men of the city, the men of Sodom, both old and young, all the people from every quarter, surrounded the house. [5] They then called to Lot and said to him, "Where are the men who came to you tonight? Bring them out to us, so that we may have relations with them."

[6] So Lot went out through the door to them and shut the door behind him. [7] Then he said, "Please, my brothers, do not act so wickedly. [8] Look, I have two daughters who have not been with a man. Please, let me bring them out to you, and you may do to them as you wish. Only do nothing to these men, for they have come under the shelter of my roof."

[9] But they replied, "Stand back!" Also, they said, "This man came here as an alien, and he keeps acting like a judge. We will deal worse with you than with them." So they pressed hard against Lot, and came close to breaking down the door.

[10] But the men reached out their hands and pulled Lot into the house with them and shut the door. [11] Then they struck the men that were at the door of the house, both small and great, with blindness so that they wore themselves out groping for the door.

---

[f] 6 Likely about 36 pounds, or 16 kilograms.

12 Then the men said to Lot, "Have you anyone else here? Sons-in-law, sons, daughters, or anyone you have in the city, take them out of this place! 13 For we are about to destroy this place, because the outcry against its people has grown great before the presence of the LORD, and the LORD has sent us to destroy it."

14 So Lot went out and spoke to his sons-in-law, who had married his daughters, and said, "Get up, get out of this place, for the LORD will destroy this city!" But to his sons-in-law he seemed to be joking.

15 When the morning dawned, the angels urged Lot, saying, "Arise, take your wife and your two daughters who are here. Otherwise you will be consumed in the punishment of the city."

16 And while he lingered, the men took hold of his and his wife's hands, along with the hands of his two daughters, the LORD being merciful to him, and brought him out and set him outside the city. 17 When they had brought them out, one of them said to them, "Escape for your lives! Do not look behind you or stay anywhere in the plain. Escape to the mountain, lest you be destroyed."

18 Then Lot said to them, "Please, no, my lords! 19 Your servant has found grace in your eyes, and you have shown your mercy, which you have shown to me by saving my life. However, I cannot escape to the mountain. Otherwise some evil will overtake me, and I will die. 20 Look, this city is close enough to flee to, and it is a little one. Please, let me escape there (is it not a little one?), and my life will be saved."

21 He said to him, "I have granted your request in this matter also. I will not overthrow this city of which you have spoken. 22 Hurry, escape there, for I cannot do anything until you arrive there." Therefore the name of the city was called Zoar.

23 The sun had risen over the land when Lot entered Zoar. 24 Then the LORD rained brimstone and fire on Sodom and Gomorrah. It was from the LORD out of heaven. 25 So He overthrew those cities, all the valley, all the inhabitants of the cities, and what grew on the ground. 26 But his wife, behind him, looked back, and she became a pillar of salt.

27 Now Abraham got up early in the morning and went to the place where he stood before the LORD. 28 Then he looked toward Sodom and Gomorrah, and toward all the land of the valley, and he saw the smoke of the land going up like the smoke of a furnace.

29 So it was that when God destroyed the cities of the valley, God remembered Abraham, and sent Lot out of the middle of the destruction, when He overthrew the cities in which Lot lived.

Lot and His Daughters

30 Then Lot left Zoar, and lived in the mountains, along with his two daughters who were with him, for he was afraid to dwell in Zoar. He and his two daughters lived in a cave. 31 And the firstborn said to the younger, "Our father is old, and there is no man on the earth to have relations with us after the manner of all the earth. 32 Let us make our father drink wine and let us lie with him, so that we may preserve the lineage of our father."

33 So they made their father drink wine that night, and the firstborn went in and had relations with her father. He did not know when she lay down or when she arose.

34 On the next day the firstborn said to the younger, "Indeed, last night I had relations with my father. Let us make him drink wine tonight also, so that you may go in and have relations with him, so that we may preserve the lineage of our father." 35 So they made their father drink wine that night also. Then the younger arose and lay down with him, and he did not know when she lay down or when she arose.

36 Therefore both the daughters of Lot were pregnant by their father. 37 The firstborn bore a son and called his name Moab. He is the father of the Moabites to this day. 38 The younger also gave birth to a son and called his name Ben-Ammi. He is the father of the Ammonites to this day.

Abraham and Abimelek

Ge 12:10–20; 26:1–11

20 Abraham journeyed from there toward the Negev, settled between Kadesh and Shur, and then he sojourned in Gerar.

2 Then Abraham said about Sarah his wife, "She is my sister." So Abimelek, king of Gerar, sent for her and took Sarah.

3 But God came to Abimelek in a dream by night and said to him, "You are a dead man because of the woman whom you have taken, for she is a man's wife."

4 Abimelek had not gone near her, and he said, "Lord, will You slay a righteous nation? 5 Did he not say to me, 'She is my sister,' and did not even she herself say, 'He is my brother'? In the integrity of my heart and innocence of my hands I have done this."

6 And God said to him in a dream, "Yes, I know that you did this in the integrity of your heart. For I also kept you from sinning against Me. Therefore, I did not let you touch her. 7 Therefore return the man's wife, for he is a prophet and he will pray for you. Moreover, you will live. However, if you do not return her, know that you will surely die, you and all who are yours."

8 So Abimelek rose early in the morning, and called all his servants and told them all these things, and the men were very afraid. 9 Then Abimelek called Abraham and said to him, "What have you done to us? How have I offended you that you would bring on me and on my kingdom a great sin? You have done things to me that should not have been done." 10 Then Abimelek said to Abraham, "What were you thinking of, that you did this thing?"

11 Abraham said, "Because I thought, surely there is no fear of God in this place, and they will slay me because of my wife. 12 Still, indeed, she is my sister. She is the daughter of my father, but not the daughter of my mother. She became my wife. 13 When God caused me to travel from my father's house, I said to her, 'This is your kindness which you must show me: Every place where we go, say concerning me, He is my brother.' "

14 Then Abimelek took sheep, oxen, and male and female servants, and gave them to Abraham, and returned his wife Sarah to him. 15 Abimelek said, "My land is before you; settle wherever it pleases you."

16 To Sarah he said, "I have given your brother a thousand shekels of silver.*1* It is a sign of your innocence in the eyes of all who are with you, and before everyone you are vindicated."

17 So Abraham prayed to God, and God healed Abimelek, his wife, and his female servants. Then they bore children. 18 For the LORD had closed up all the wombs of the house of Abimelek because of Sarah, Abraham's wife.

The Birth of Isaac

21 The LORD visited Sarah as He had said, and the LORD did for Sarah as He had spoken. 2 For Sarah conceived and bore Abraham a son in his old age, at the set time that God had spoken to him. 3 Abraham called the name of his son who was born to him, whom Sarah bore to him, Isaac. 4 Then Abraham circumcised his son Isaac when he was eight days old, as God had commanded him. 5 Now Abraham was one hundred years old when his son Isaac was born to him.

6 And Sarah said, "God has made me laugh. All who hear will laugh with me." 7 Also she said, "Who would have said to Abraham that Sarah would nurse children? Yet I have borne him a son in his old age."

Hagar and Ishmael Depart

8 So the child grew and was weaned. Then Abraham made a great feast the same day that Isaac was weaned. 9 Sarah saw the son of Hagar the Egyptian, whom she had borne to Abraham, mocking. 10 Therefore she said to Abraham, "Throw out this slave woman and her son, for the son of this slave woman shall not be heir with my son, Isaac."

11 This matter was very displeasing in Abraham's sight because of his son. 12 But God said to Abraham, "Do not be upset concerning the boy and your slave wife. Whatever Sarah has said to you, listen to what she says, for in Isaac your descendants will be called. 13 Yet I will also make a nation of the son of the slave woman, because he is your offspring."

14 So Abraham rose up early in the morning, and took bread and a skin of water and gave it to Hagar, putting it on her shoulder, and

---

1 16 About 25 pounds, or 12 kilograms.

sent her away with the child. So she departed and wandered in the Wilderness of Beersheba.

[15] When the water in the skin was gone, she placed the child under one of the shrubs. [16] Then she went and sat down across from him at a distance of about a bowshot, for she said to herself, "Let me not see the death of the child." She sat across from him, and lifted up her voice and wept.

[17] And God heard the boy's voice. Then the angel of God called to Hagar out of heaven and said to her, "What is the matter with you, Hagar? Do not be afraid, for God has heard the voice of the boy where he is. [18] Arise, pick up the boy and hold him in your hands, for I will make him a great nation."

[19] Then God opened her eyes, and she saw a well of water. And she went and filled the skin with water and gave the boy a drink.

[20] God was with the boy; and he grew and lived in the wilderness and became an archer. [21] He lived in the Wilderness of Paran, and his mother found a wife for him out of the land of Egypt.

The Treaty With Abimelek

[22] Now it came to pass at that time that Abimelek and Phicol, the commander of his army, spoke to Abraham, saying, "God is with you in all that you do. [23] Now therefore, swear to me by God that you will not deal deceitfully with me, or with my children, or with my descendants. Instead, according to the kindness that I have shown to you, you will show to me and to the land where you have lived."

[24] Abraham said, "I will swear."

[25] Then Abraham complained to Abimelek about a well of water that Abimelek's servants had violently seized. [26] And Abimelek said, "I do not know who has done this. You did not tell me, and I have not heard of it until today."

[27] So Abraham took sheep and oxen and gave them to Abimelek, and the two of them made a covenant. [28] Then Abraham set seven ewe lambs of the flock by themselves. [29] And Abimelek said to Abraham, "What is the meaning of these seven ewe lambs that you have set by themselves?"

[30] And he said, "You shall take these seven ewe lambs from my hand so that they may be a witness that I have dug this well."

[31] Therefore he called that place Beersheba, because the two of them swore an oath there.

[32] Thus they made a covenant at Beersheba. Then Abimelek rose with Phicol, the commander of his army, and they returned to the land of the Philistines. [33] Abraham planted a tamarisk tree in Beersheba, and there he called on the name of the Lord, the Everlasting God. [34] Abraham stayed in the land of the Philistines many days.

The Sacrifice of Isaac

22 After these things God tested Abraham and said to him, "Abraham!"

And he said, "Here I am."

[2] Then He said, "Take your son, your only son Isaac, whom you love, and go to the land of Moriah, and offer him there as a burnt offering on one of the mountains of which I will tell you."

[3] So Abraham rose up early in the morning and saddled his donkey, and took two of his young men with him and Isaac his son; and he split the wood for the burnt offering, and arose and went to the place that God had told him. [4] Then on the third day Abraham lifted up his eyes and saw the place from a distance. [5] Abraham said to his young men, "Stay here with the donkey. The boy and I will go over there and worship and then return to you."

[6] So Abraham took the wood of the burnt offering and laid it on Isaac his son; and he took the fire in his hand and the knife. So the two of them walked on together. [7] But Isaac spoke to Abraham his father and said, "My father!"

And he said, "Here I am, my son."

Then he said, "Here is the fire and the wood, but where is the lamb for the burnt offering?"

[8] Abraham said, "My son, God will provide for Himself the lamb for a burnt offering." So the two of them went together.

[9] Then they came to the place that God had told him. So Abraham built an altar there and arranged the wood; and he bound Isaac his son and laid him on the altar, on the wood. [10] Then Abraham stretched out his hand and took the knife to slay his son. [11] But the angel of the Lord called to him out of heaven and said, "Abraham, Abraham!"

And he said, "Here I am."

[12] Then He said, "Do not lay your hands on the boy or do anything to him, because now I know that you fear God, seeing you have not withheld your only son from Me."

[13] Then Abraham lifted up his eyes and looked, and behind him was a ram caught in a thicket by his horns. So Abraham went and took the ram and offered him up as a burnt offering in the place of his son. [14] Abraham called the name of that place The Lord Will Provide, as it is said to this day, "In the mount of the Lord it will be provided."

[15] Then the angel of the Lord called to Abraham out of heaven a second time, [16] and said, "By Myself I have sworn, says the Lord, because you have done this thing, and have not withheld your son, your only son, [17] I will indeed bless you and I will indeed multiply your descendants as the stars of the heavens and as the sand that is on the seashore. Your descendants will possess the gate of their enemies. [18] Through your offspring all the nations of the earth will be blessed, because you have obeyed My voice."

[19] So Abraham returned to his young men, and they arose and went together to Beersheba. Then Abraham lived at Beersheba.

Sons of Nahor

[20] After these things Abraham was told, "Milkah has also borne children to your brother Nahor: [21] Uz his firstborn, Buz his brother, Kemuel the father of Aram, [22] Kesed, Hazo, Pildash, Jidlaph, and Bethuel." [23] Bethuel became the father of Rebekah. Milkah gave birth to these eight to Nahor, Abraham's brother. [24] His concubine, whose name was Reumah, also bore Tebah, Gaham, Tahash, and Maakah.

The Death of Sarah

23 Sarah lived one hundred and twenty-seven years. These were the years of the life of Sarah. [2] Then Sarah died in Kiriath Arba (that is, Hebron) in the land of Canaan, and Abraham went in to mourn for Sarah and to weep for her.

[3] Then Abraham stood up from before his dead and spoke to the Hittites,[1] saying, [4] "I am a stranger and a foreigner among you. Give me property for a burying place among you, that I may bury my dead out of my sight."

[5] So the Hittites answered Abraham, [6] "Hear us, my lord. You are a mighty prince among us. Bury your dead in the choicest of our burial places. None of us will withhold from you his burial place that you may bury your dead."

[7] Then Abraham stood up and bowed himself to the people of the land, the Hittites. [8] He spoke with them, saying, "If it be your wish that I bury my dead out of my sight, hear me and entreat Ephron the son of Zohar for me, [9] that he may give me the cave of Machpelah, which he owns, at the end of his field. Let him give it to me in your presence for the full price for a burial site."

[10] Now Ephron was sitting among the Hittites; and Ephron the Hittite answered Abraham in the presence of all the Hittites, all who went in at the gate of his city, saying, [11] "No, my lord. Hear me: I give you the field and the cave that is in it. I give it to you in the presence of the sons of my people. Bury your dead."

[12] Then Abraham bowed before the people of the land. [13] Then he spoke to Ephron in the hearing of the people of the land, saying, "Indeed, if you will give it, please hear me. I will give you money for the field; take it from me and I will bury my dead there."

[14] Then Ephron answered Abraham, saying to him, [15] "My lord, listen to me. The land is worth four hundred shekels of silver.[2] What is that between me and you? So bury your dead."

[16] Abraham listened to Ephron; and Abraham weighed out for Ephron four hundred shekels of silver, the price that he had

---

[1] 3 Or *the sons of Heth*; also in vv. 5, 7, 10, 16, 18, and 20.   [2] 15 About 10 pounds, or 4.6 kilograms.

named in the hearing of the Hittites, according to the standard commercial measure.

[17] So the field of Ephron, which was in Machpelah, which was before Mamre, the field and the cave that was in it, and all the trees that were in the field that were within all the surrounding borders were deeded [18] to Abraham as a possession in the presence of the Hittites, before all who went in at the gate of his city. [19] After this, Abraham buried Sarah his wife in the cave of the field of Machpelah before Mamre (that is, Hebron) in the land of Canaan. [20] So the field and the cave that was in it were deeded to Abraham by the Hittites as property for a burial place.

Isaac and Rebekah

24 Now Abraham was old, well advanced in age; and the LORD had blessed Abraham in all things. [2] So Abraham said to his servant, the oldest of his household, who was in charge over all that he had, "Please, place your hand under my thigh, [3] and I will make you swear by the LORD, the God of heaven and the God of the earth, that you will not take a wife for my son from the daughters of the Canaanites, among whom I live. [4] But you shall go to my country and to my family, and take a wife for my son Isaac."

[5] Then the servant said to him, "Perhaps the woman will not be willing to follow me to this land. Must I take your son back to the land from which you came?"

[6] Abraham said to him, "See to it that you do not take my son back there. [7] The LORD God of heaven, who took me from my father's family and from the land of my relatives, and who spoke to me and swore to me, saying, 'To your descendants I will give this land,' He shall send His angel before you and you shall take a wife for my son from there. [8] If the woman is not willing to follow you, then you will be free from my oath. Only do not take my son back there." [9] So the servant put his hand under the thigh of Abraham his master and swore to him concerning this matter.

[10] Then the servant took ten of his master's camels and departed, for all the goods of his master were in his hand. And he arose and went to the city of Nahor in Aram Naharaim. [11] He made his camels kneel down outside the city by a well of water in the evening when the women came out to draw water.

[12] Then he said, "O LORD, the God of my master Abraham, please let me have success this day and show kindness to my master Abraham. [13] See, here I stand by the well of water, and the daughters of the men of the city are coming out to draw water. [14] Let it be that the young woman to whom I shall say, 'Please lower your pitcher, that I may drink,' and she shall say, 'Drink, and I will give your camels water also'—let her be the one that You have appointed for Your servant Isaac. Then I will know that You have shown kindness to my master."

[15] Before he had finished speaking, Rebekah, who was born to Bethuel, son of Milkah, the wife of Nahor, Abraham's brother, came out with a pitcher on her shoulder. [16] The young woman was very beautiful to look at, a virgin, and no man had ever been with her. She went down to the well and filled her pitcher and came up.

[17] Then the servant ran to meet her and said, "Please let me drink a little water from your pitcher."

[18] So she said, "Drink, my lord." Then she quickly let down her pitcher to her hand and gave him a drink.

[19] When she had finished giving him a drink, she said, "I will draw water for your camels also, until they have finished drinking." [20] Then she quickly emptied her pitcher into the trough and ran to the well to draw water and drew for all his camels. [21] The man, gazing at her, remained silent, trying to discern whether the LORD had made his journey a success or not.

[22] When the camels had finished drinking, the man took a gold nose ring of half a shekel weight[1] and two bracelets for her wrists of ten shekels weight[2] in gold, [23] and said, "Whose daughter are you? Please tell me, is there room in your father's house for us to lodge?"

[24] She said to him, "I am the daughter of Bethuel the son of Milkah, whom she bore to Nahor." [25] Again she said to him, "We have both straw and provision enough, and room in which to lodge."

[26] Then the man bowed down his head and worshipped the LORD. [27] And he said, "Blessed be the LORD God of my master Abraham, who has not forsaken His mercy and His truth toward my master. As for me, the LORD led me to the house of my master's relatives."

[28] So the young woman ran and told her mother's household of these things. [29] Now Rebekah had a brother whose name was Laban, and Laban ran out to the man at the well. [30] When he saw the nose ring and bracelets on his sister's hands and when he heard the words of Rebekah his sister, saying, "This is what the man said to me," he went to the man who stood by the camels at the well. [31] And he said, "Come in, blessed of the LORD. Why do you stand outside? I have prepared the house and a place for the camels."

[32] So the man came to the house. Then he unloaded his camels and gave straw and provision to the camels and water to wash his feet and the feet of the men who were with him. [33] He then set food before him to eat, but he said, "I will not eat until I have told about my errand."

And he said, "Speak on."

[34] So he said, "I am Abraham's servant. [35] The LORD has greatly blessed my master, and he has become wealthy. He has given him flocks and herds, and silver and gold, and male and female servants, and camels and donkeys. [36] Sarah my master's wife bore a son to my master when she was old, and he has given to him all that he has. [37] My master made me swear, saying, 'You must not take a wife for my son from the daughters of the Canaanites, in whose land I live. [38] But you shall go to my father's house, and to my relatives, and take a wife for my son.'

[39] "So I said to my master, 'Perhaps the woman will not follow me.'

[40] "Then he said to me, 'The LORD, before whom I walk, will send His angel with you and prosper your way, and you will take a wife for my son from my relatives and from my father's house. [41] You will be free from my oath, when you come to my family, if they will not give her to you; then you will be released from my oath.'

[42] "So today I came to the well and said, 'O LORD, the God of my master Abraham, if You will now give me success in my task; [43] I am standing by the well of water, and let it be that when the virgin comes forth to draw water, and I say to her, "Please give me a little water from your pitcher to drink," [44] and she says to me, "Drink, and I will also draw for your camels," let her be the woman whom the LORD has appointed for my master's son.'

[45] "Before I had finished speaking in my heart, there was Rebekah coming out with her pitcher on her shoulder; and she went down to the well and drew water. Then I said to her, 'Please let me drink.'

[46] "She then quickly let down her pitcher from her shoulder and said, 'Drink, and I will give your camels a drink also.' So I drank, and she gave the camels a drink also.

[47] "Then I asked her, 'Whose daughter are you?'

"And she said, 'The daughter of Bethuel, Nahor's son, whom Milkah bore for him.'

"So I put the nose ring on her nose and the bracelets on her wrists. [48] And I bowed down my head and worshipped the LORD, and blessed the LORD God of my master Abraham, who had led me in the right way to take the daughter of my master's brother for his son. [49] And now if you will deal kindly and truly with my master, tell me; and if not, tell me, so that I may turn to the right hand or to the left."

[50] Then Laban and Bethuel answered and said, "This thing comes from the LORD; we cannot speak to you bad or good. [51] Here is Rebekah before you; take her and go, and let her be the wife of your master's son, as the LORD has spoken."

[52] When Abraham's servant heard their words, he worshipped the LORD, bowing himself to the earth. [53] Then the servant brought out jewels of silver and gold, and clothing and gave them to Rebekah. He also gave precious things to her brother and to her mother. [54] Then they ate and drank, he and the men who were with him, and stayed all night.

The next morning they arose, and he said, "Send me away to my master."

---

[1] 22 About ⅓ ounce, or 5.7 grams.   [2] 22 About 4 ounces, or 115 grams.

55 But her brother and her mother said, "Let the young woman remain with us a few days, at least ten; after that she may go."

56 So he said to them, "Do not delay me, seeing the Lord has given me success. Let me go that I may go to my master."

57 They said, "We will call the girl and ask her." 58 Then they called Rebekah and said to her, "Will you go with this man?"

And she said, "I will go."

59 So they sent away Rebekah their sister and her nurse, and Abraham's servant and his men. 60 They blessed Rebekah and said to her,

"May you, our sister, become the mother
   of thousands of ten thousands;
and may your descendants possess
   the gate of those who hate them."

61 Then Rebekah and her maids arose and they rode on the camels and followed the man. So the servant took Rebekah and went his way.

62 Now Isaac came from the way of Beer Lahai Roi, for he lived in the Negev. 63 Isaac went out in the evening to meditate in the field; and he lifted up his eyes and looked, and surely the camels were coming. 64 And Rebekah lifted up her eyes, and when she saw Isaac, she dismounted from her camel 65 and said to the servant, "Who is this man walking in the field to meet us?"

The servant said, "It is my master." Therefore she took a veil and covered herself.

66 Then the servant told Isaac all the things he had done. 67 So Isaac brought her into the tent of his mother Sarah; and he took Rebekah and she became his wife and he loved her. So Isaac was comforted after his mother's death.

The Death of Abraham
1Ch 1:32–33

25 Then Abraham took another wife, whose name was Keturah. 2 And she bore to him Zimran, Jokshan, Medan, Midian, Ishbak, and Shuah. 3 Jokshan was the father of Sheba and Dedan. The descendants of Dedan were the Ashurites, the Letushites, and the Leummites. 4 The sons of Midian were Ephah, Epher, Hanok, Abida, and Eldaah. All these were the children of Keturah.

5 Abraham gave all that he had to Isaac. 6 But to the sons of his concubines Abraham gave gifts, and while he was still living, he sent them away from his son Isaac eastward to the east country.

7 These are the years of Abraham's life that he lived: one hundred and seventy-five years. 8 Then Abraham breathed his last and died at a good old age, an old man and full of years; and he was gathered to his people. 9 His sons Isaac and Ishmael buried him in the cave of Machpelah, in the field of Ephron the son of Zohar the Hittite, east of Mamre, 10 the field that Abraham purchased from the sons of Heth. There Abraham was buried with his wife Sarah. 11 After the death of Abraham, God blessed his son Isaac. Isaac lived at Beer Lahai Roi.

Sons of Ishmael
1Ch 1:29–31

12 These are the generations of Ishmael, Abraham's son, whom Hagar the Egyptian, Sarah's maidservant, bore to Abraham.

13 These are the names of the sons of Ishmael, by their names, according to their generations: the firstborn of Ishmael, Nebaioth, and then Kedar, Adbeel, Mibsam, 14 Mishma, Dumah, Massa, 15 Hadad, Tema, Jetur, Naphish, and Kedemah. 16 These were the sons of Ishmael, and these were their names, by their towns and their settlements, twelve princes according to their peoples. 17 These were the years of the life of Ishmael: one hundred and thirty-seven years. He breathed his last and died; and he was gathered to his people. 18 They lived from Havilah as far as Shur, which is east of Egypt, as you go toward Assyria. He died in the presence of all his relatives.

The Births of Jacob and Esau

19 These are the generations of Isaac, Abraham's son.

Abraham was the father of Isaac. 20 Isaac was forty years old when he took Rebekah as his wife, the daughter of Bethuel the Syrian of Paddan Aram, the sister to Laban the Syrian.

21 Now Isaac pleaded with the Lord for his wife, because she was barren; and the Lord granted his plea, and Rebekah his wife conceived. 22 But the children struggled together within her, and she said, "If all is well, why am I like this?" So she went to inquire of the Lord.

23 Then the Lord said to her,

"Two nations are in your womb,
   and two peoples will be separated from your body;
one people will be stronger than the other,
   and the older will serve the younger."

24 Now when the time of her delivery came, there were twins in her womb. 25 The first came out red all over, like a hairy garment, and they called his name Esau. 26 After that his brother came out, and his hand took hold of Esau's heel, so he was named Jacob. Isaac was sixty years old when she bore them.

27 So the boys grew. Esau was a cunning hunter, a man of the field, while Jacob was a calm man, living in tents. 28 Isaac loved Esau, because he ate of his game, but Rebekah loved Jacob.

Esau Sells His Birthright

29 Now Jacob cooked a stew; and Esau came in from the field and he was famished. 30 So Esau said to Jacob, "Please feed me some of that red stew, for I am famished." Therefore his name was called Edom.

31 Then Jacob said, "First sell me your birthright."

32 Esau said, "Look, I am about to die; of what use is the birthright to me?"

33 Then Jacob said, "Swear to me this day." So he swore to him, and he sold his birthright to Jacob.

34 Then Jacob gave Esau bread and lentil stew. Then he ate and drank, arose, and went his way.

Thus Esau despised his birthright.

Isaac and Abimelek
Ge 12:10–20; 20:1–18

26 There was a famine in the land, in addition to the first famine that was during the days of Abraham. Isaac went to Abimelek king of the Philistines in Gerar. 2 The Lord appeared to him and said, "Do not go down to Egypt. Live in the land of which I will tell you. 3 Sojourn in this land, and I will be with you and will bless you; for I will give to you and all your descendants all these lands, and I will fulfill the oath which I swore to Abraham your father. 4 I will make your descendants multiply as the stars of the heavens and will give your descendants all these lands. By your descendants all the nations of the earth will be blessed,[1] 5 because Abraham obeyed Me and kept My charge, My commandments, My statutes, and My laws." 6 So Isaac lived in Gerar.

7 The men of the place asked him about his wife. And he said, "She is my sister," for he was afraid to say, "She is my wife," *thinking*, "The men of the place might kill me on account of Rebekah, because she is beautiful in appearance."

8 When he had been there a long time, Abimelek the king of the Philistines looked out of a window and saw Isaac caressing Rebekah his wife. 9 Abimelek summoned Isaac and said, "She is surely your wife, so how is it you said, 'She is my sister'?"

Then Isaac said to him, "Because I said, 'I might die on account of her.' "

10 Abimelek said, "What is this you have done to us? One of the people might have easily lain with your wife, and you might have brought guilt upon us!"

11 Abimelek charged all his people, saying, "He who touches this man or his wife will surely be put to death."

---

1 4 Or will bless themselves.

[12] Then Isaac sowed in that land and reaped in the same year a hundredfold; the LORD blessed him. [13] The man became rich and continued to prosper until he became very wealthy. [14] For he had possessions of flocks and herds and a great number of servants so that the Philistines envied him. [15] For the Philistines had stopped up all the wells which his father's servants had dug in the days of Abraham his father by filling them with dirt.

[16] Abimelek said to Isaac, "Go away from us, for you are much more powerful than we are."

[17] So Isaac departed from there and pitched his tent in the Valley of Gerar and settled there. [18] Isaac dug again the wells of water, which they had dug in the days of Abraham his father, for the Philistines had stopped them up after the death of Abraham. He called their names after the names his father had called them.

[19] But when Isaac's servants dug in the valley and found a well of running water there, [20] the herdsmen of Gerar contended with Isaac's herdsmen, saying, "The water is ours." So he called the name of the well Esek, because they contended with him. [21] They dug another well and quarreled over that also. So he called the name of it Sitnah. [22] Then he moved away from there and dug another well, and they did not quarrel over it. So he called the name of it Rehoboth, for he said, "For now the LORD has made room for us, and we will be fruitful in the land."

[23] He went up from there to Beersheba. [24] The LORD appeared to him that same night and said, "I am the God of Abraham your father. Do not fear, for I am with you. I will bless you and multiply your descendants for the sake of My servant Abraham."

[25] He built an altar there, called on the name of the LORD, and pitched his tent there. And there Isaac's servants dug a well.

[26] Then Abimelek went to him from Gerar, along with Ahuzzath, one of his friends, and Phicol the commander of his army. [27] Isaac said to them, "Why have you come to me, since you hate me and have sent me away from you?"

[28] And they said, "We saw plainly that the LORD was with you. So we said, 'Let there now be an oath between us, between you and us, and let us make a covenant with you, [29] so that you will do us no harm, just as we have not touched you, and have done you nothing but good and have sent you away in peace. You are now the blessed of the LORD.' "

[30] Then he made them a feast, and they ate and drank. [31] They rose up early in the morning and swore an oath with one another. Isaac sent them away, and they departed from him in peace.

[32] That same day Isaac's servants came and told him about the well that they had dug and said to him, "We have found water." [33] And he called it Shibah. Therefore, the name of the city is Beersheba to this day.

[34] Esau was forty years old when he took as wives Judith the daughter of Beeri the Hittite, and Basemath the daughter of Elon the Hittite, [35] and they brought grief to Isaac and to Rebekah.

Isaac Blesses Jacob

27 When Isaac was old and his eyes were so weak that he could not see, he called Esau his oldest son and said to him, "My son."

And he answered him, "Here I am."

[2] He said, "I am old. I do not know the day of my death. [3] Therefore, please take your weapons, your quiver and your bow, and go out to the field and hunt game for me. [4] And prepare for me savory food, such as I love, and bring it to me that I may eat, so that my soul may bless you before I die."

[5] Rebekah was listening when Isaac spoke to Esau his son. So when Esau went to the field to hunt for wild game and bring it back, [6] Rebekah said to her son Jacob, "I heard your father speak to your brother Esau, saying, [7] 'Bring me wild game, and prepare for me savory food, that I may eat and bless you in the presence of the LORD before my death.' [8] Now therefore, my son, listen to me as I command you. [9] Go now to the flock, and get me two choice young goats, so that I may prepare from them savory food for your father, such as he loves. [10] Then you will take it to your father, so that he may eat and so that he may bless you before his death."

[11] But Jacob said to his mother Rebekah, "Look, my brother Esau is a hairy man, and I am a man of smooth *skin*. [12] Perhaps my father will feel me, and I will seem to him as a deceiver, and I will bring a curse on myself and not a blessing."

[13] His mother said to him, "Let your curse be upon me, my son. Only listen to me and go get them for me."

[14] He went and got them and brought them to his mother. Then his mother prepared savory food such as his father loved. [15] Then Rebekah took the best clothes belonging to her older son Esau, which were with her in the house, and put them on Jacob her younger son. [16] Then she put the skins of the young goats on his hands and on the smooth part of his neck. [17] She put the savory food and the bread, which she had prepared, into the hands of her son Jacob.

[18] He came to his father and said, "My father."

And he said, "Here I am. Who are you, my son?"

[19] And Jacob said to his father, "I am Esau your firstborn. I have done just as you asked me. Please arise, sit and eat of my wild game, so that your soul may bless me."

[20] Isaac said to his son, "How is it that you have found it so quickly, my son?"

And he said, "Because the LORD your God brought it to me."

[21] Isaac said to Jacob, "Please come near, so that I may feel you, my son, whether you are really my son Esau or not."

[22] Jacob went near to his father Isaac, and he felt him and said, "The voice is the voice of Jacob, but the hands are the hands of Esau." [23] He did not recognize him because his hands were hairy, just like his brother Esau's hands; so he blessed him. [24] He asked, "Are you really my son Esau?"

And he said, "I am."

[25] He said, "Bring it near to me, and I will eat of my son's wild game, so that my soul may bless you."

And he brought it near to him, and he ate. He also brought him wine, and he drank. [26] His father Isaac said to him, "Come near now and kiss me, my son."

[27] He came near and kissed him; and he smelled the smell of his clothing and blessed him and said,

"See, the smell of my son
  is like the smell of the field
  which the LORD has blessed.
[28] Therefore, may God give you of the dew of heaven
  and the fatness of the earth,
  and plenty of grain and new wine.
[29] Let peoples serve you,
  and nations bow down to you.
Be master over your brothers,
  and let your mother's sons bow down to you.
Cursed be everyone who curses you,
  and blessed be those who bless you!"

[30] As soon as Isaac had finished blessing Jacob, and Jacob had barely gone out from the presence of his father Isaac, Esau his brother came in from his hunting. [31] He also had prepared savory food and brought it to his father, and said to his father, "Let my father arise and eat of his son's wild game, so that your soul may bless me."

[32] Isaac his father said to him, "Who are you?"

And he said, "I am your son, your firstborn, Esau."

[33] Then Isaac trembled violently, and said, "Who? Where then is he who hunted game and brought it to me? I ate all of it before you came, and I have blessed him. Yes, and he shall be blessed."

[34] When Esau heard the words of his father, he cried with a great and exceedingly bitter cry, and said to his father, "Bless me, even me also, O my father!"

[35] He said, "Your brother came deceitfully and has taken away your blessing."

[36] Esau said, "Is he not rightly named Jacob? For he has supplanted me these two times. He took away my birthright, and now he has taken away my blessing." And he said, "Have you not reserved a blessing for me?"

[37] Then Isaac answered and said to Esau, "I have made him your lord, and I have given to him all his brothers as servants; and I have sustained him with grain and new wine. What can I now do for you, my son?" [38] And Esau said to his father, "Do you have only one blessing, my father? Bless me, even me also; O my father!" Then Esau lifted up his voice and wept. [39] Isaac his father answered and said to him,

"Your dwelling shall be
    away from the fatness of the earth
    and away from the dew of heaven from above.
[40] You will live by your sword
    and will serve your brother.
When you become restless,
    you will break his yoke
    from your neck."

Jacob Escapes From Esau

[41] So Esau hated Jacob because of the blessing with which his father blessed him. And Esau said in his heart, "The days of mourning for my father are at hand; then I will kill my brother Jacob." [42] These words of Esau her older son were told to Rebekah; and she sent and called Jacob her younger son, and said to him, "Your brother Esau consoles himself regarding you by planning to kill you. [43] Now therefore, my son, listen to me and get up and flee to Laban, my brother in Harran. [44] Stay with him a few days until your brother's fury subsides, [45] until your brother's anger against you turns away, and he forgets what you have done to him. Then I will send and get you from there. Why should I lose both of you in one day?" [46] Then Rebekah said to Isaac, "I am tired of my life because of the daughters of Heth. If Jacob takes a wife from the daughters of Heth, such as these who are of the daughters of the land, what good will my life be to me?"

28 Then Isaac called Jacob and blessed him. Then he charged him and said to him, "You must not take a wife of the daughters of Canaan. [2] Arise, go to Paddan Aram to the house of Bethuel your mother's father, and take for yourself a wife from there, from the daughters of Laban your mother's brother. [3] May God Almighty bless you and make you fruitful and multiply you, so that you may become a multitude of people. [4] May He give you the blessing of Abraham, to you and your descendants with you, that you may inherit the land where you are a stranger, which God gave to Abraham." [5] Then Isaac sent Jacob away, and he went to Paddan Aram to Laban, the son of Bethuel the Syrian, the brother of Rebekah, Jacob's and Esau's mother.

[6] Esau saw that Isaac had blessed Jacob and sent him away to Paddan Aram to take for himself a wife from there, and that as he blessed him he gave him a charge, saying, "You must not take a wife of the daughters of Canaan," [7] and that Jacob obeyed his father and his mother and had gone to Paddan Aram. [8] Esau saw that the daughters of Canaan did not please Isaac his father. [9] So Esau went to Ishmael and took as his wife Mahalath the daughter of Ishmael, Abraham's son, the sister of Nebaioth, in addition to the wives he had.

Jacob's Dream at Bethel

[10] Then Jacob went out from Beersheba and went toward Harran. [11] He came to a certain place and stayed there all night, because the sun had set. He took one of the stones of that place and put it under his head, and lay down in that place to sleep. [12] He dreamed and saw a ladder set up on the earth with the top of it reaching to heaven. The angels of God were ascending and descending on it. [13] The LORD stood above it and said, "I am the LORD God of Abraham your father and the God of Isaac. The land on which you lie, to you will I give it and to your descendants. [14] Your descendants will be like the dust of the earth, and you will spread abroad to the west and to the east and to the north and to the south, and in you and in your descendants all the

families of the earth will be blessed. [15] Remember, I am with you, and I will protect you wherever you go, and I will bring you back to this land. For I will not leave you until I have done what I promised you."

[16] Jacob awoke out of his sleep, and he said, "Surely the LORD is in this place, and I did not know it." [17] He was afraid and said, "How awesome is this place! This is none other but the house of God, and this is the gate of heaven." [18] So Jacob rose up early in the morning and took the stone that he had put under his head, set it up as a pillar, and poured oil on top of it. [19] He called the name of that place Bethel, but previously the name of the city was called Luz. [20] Jacob vowed a vow, saying, "If God will be with me and will protect me in this way that I go, and will give me bread to eat and clothing to put on, [21] so that I return to my father's house in peace, then the LORD will be my God. [22] Then this stone, which I have set for a pillar, will be the house of God, and from all that You give me I will surely give a tenth to You."

Jacob Meets Rachel

29 Then Jacob went on his journey and came into the land of the people of the east. [2] As he looked, he saw a well in the field and three flocks of sheep lying by it, for out of that well the flocks were watered. A large stone was on the well's opening. [3] When all the flocks were gathered there, the shepherds rolled the stone from the well's opening, watered the sheep, then put the stone back on the well's opening in its place.

[4] Jacob said to them, "My brothers, where are you from?"

And they said, "We are from Harran."

[5] Then he said to them, "Do you know Laban the son of Nahor?"

And they said, "We know him."

[6] He said to them, "Is he well?"

And they said, "He is well, and here is Rachel his daughter coming with the sheep."

[7] He said, "Since it is yet midday, it is not the time that the livestock should be gathered together. Water the sheep, and go and feed them."

[8] They said, "We cannot until all the flocks are gathered together and the stone is rolled from the well's opening. Then we may water the sheep."

[9] While he was still speaking with them, Rachel came with her father's sheep, for she kept them. [10] When Jacob saw Rachel the daughter of Laban his mother's brother and the sheep of Laban his mother's brother, Jacob went near and rolled the stone from the well's opening and watered the flock of Laban his mother's brother. [11] Jacob kissed Rachel and wept aloud. [12] Jacob told Rachel that he was her father's relative and that he was Rebekah's son. Then she ran and told her father.

[13] When Laban heard the news of Jacob his sister's son, he ran to meet him and embraced him and kissed him and brought him to his house. Then Jacob told Laban all these things. [14] Laban said to him, "Surely you are my bone and my flesh."

And he stayed with him for a month. [15] Laban said to Jacob, "Since you are my relative, should you therefore serve me for nothing? Tell me, what shall your wages be?"

Jacob Marries Leah and Rachel

[16] Now Laban had two daughters. The name of the older was Leah, and the name of the younger was Rachel. [17] Leah's eyes were tender, but Rachel was beautiful in form and appearance. [18] Jacob loved Rachel, so he said, "I will serve you seven years for Rachel your younger daughter."

[19] Laban said, "It is better that I give her to you than that I should give her to another man. Stay with me." [20] So Jacob served seven years for Rachel, and they seemed to him but a few days because of the love he had for her.

[21] Then Jacob said to Laban, "Give me my wife, for my days are fulfilled, so that I may have relations with her."

[22] Laban gathered together all the men of the place and prepared a feast. [23] But in the evening he took Leah his daughter and brought her to Jacob, and Jacob had relations with her. [24] Laban gave Zilpah his maid to his daughter Leah for a maidservant.

²⁵ In the morning Jacob discovered it was Leah, and he said to Laban, "What is this you have done to me? Did I not serve you for Rachel? Why then have you tricked me?"

²⁶ Then Laban said, "It is not the custom in our country to marry off the younger before the firstborn. ²⁷ Fulfill the period of seven days for this one, and we will give you the other also in return for serving me another seven years."

²⁸ Jacob did so and completed her week. Then Laban gave him Rachel his daughter as his wife also. ²⁹ Laban gave Bilhah his maidservant to Rachel his daughter to be her maid. ³⁰ So Jacob also had relations with Rachel, and he loved Rachel more than Leah and served Laban another seven years.

Jacob's Children

³¹ When the LORD saw that Leah was unloved, He opened her womb, but Rachel was barren. ³² Leah conceived and gave birth to a son, and she called his name Reuben, for she said, "Surely the LORD has looked upon my affliction. Now therefore my husband will love me."

³³ She conceived again and gave birth to a son and said, "Because the LORD has heard that I was unloved, He has therefore given me this son also." Then she called his name Simeon.

³⁴ She conceived again and gave birth to a son and said, "Now this time my husband will be joined to me, because I have borne him three sons." Therefore his name was called Levi.

³⁵ She conceived again and gave birth to a son, and she said, "Now I will praise the LORD!" Therefore she called his name Judah. Then she stopped giving birth.

30 When Rachel saw that she could not give Jacob children, she became jealous of her sister. She said to Jacob, "Give me children, or I will die."

² Jacob became angry with Rachel and said, "Am I in the place of God, who has withheld from you the fruit of the womb?"

³ Then she said, "Here is my maid Bilhah. Have relations with her so that she may bear *a child* on my knees,¹ so that I may also have children through her."

⁴ So she gave him Bilhah her maidservant as a wife, and Jacob had relations with her. ⁵ Bilhah conceived and gave Jacob a son. ⁶ Rachel said, "God has vindicated me, and He has also heard my voice and has given me a son." Therefore she called his name Dan.

⁷ Bilhah, Rachel's maid, conceived again and gave Jacob a second son. ⁸ Then Rachel said, "With great wrestling have I wrestled with my sister, and I have prevailed." So she called his name Naphtali.

⁹ When Leah saw that she had stopped having children, she took Zilpah her maid and gave her to Jacob as a wife. ¹⁰ Zilpah, Leah's maid, gave Jacob a son. ¹¹ Then Leah said, "How fortunate!" So she called his name Gad.

¹² Zilpah, Leah's maid, gave Jacob a second son. ¹³ Then Leah said, "Happy am I, for women will call me happy." So she called his name Asher.

¹⁴ At the time of the wheat harvest, Reuben went and found mandrakes in the field and brought them to his mother Leah. Then Rachel said to Leah, "Please give me some of your son's mandrakes."

¹⁵ Leah said to her, "Is it a small matter that you have taken my husband? Would you take away my son's mandrakes also?"

So Rachel said, "All right, he may lie with you tonight in exchange for your son's mandrakes."

¹⁶ When Jacob came out of the field in the evening, Leah went out to meet him and said, "You must sleep with me, because I have paid for you with my son's mandrakes." And he slept with her that night.

¹⁷ God listened to Leah, and she conceived and gave Jacob a fifth son. ¹⁸ Leah said, "God has given me my reward because I have given my maid to my husband." So she called his name Issachar.

¹⁹ Leah conceived again and gave Jacob a sixth son. ²⁰ Leah said, "God has given me a good gift. Now my husband will dwell with me, because I have given him six sons." So she called his name Zebulun.

²¹ Afterwards she gave birth to a daughter and called her name Dinah.

²² Then God remembered Rachel, and God listened to her and opened her womb. ²³ She conceived and gave birth to a son and said, "God has taken away my reproach." ²⁴ And she called his name Joseph, saying, "The LORD will add to me another son."

Jacob's Agreement With Laban

²⁵ When Rachel had given birth to Joseph, Jacob said to Laban, "Send me away, so that I may go to my own place, to my country. ²⁶ Give me my wives and my children, for whom I have served you, and let me go. For you know the service that I have given you."

²⁷ Laban said to him, "If I have found favor in your eyes, please stay. For I have learned by divination that the LORD has blessed me on account of you." ²⁸ He said, "Name me your wages, and I will give it."

²⁹ Jacob said to him, "You know how I have served you, and how your livestock have fared with me. ³⁰ For you had little before I came, and it is now increased to a multitude. The LORD has blessed you since I came, and now when may I also provide for my own house?"

³¹ Laban said, "What may I give you?"

And Jacob said, "You may not give me anything, but if you will do this *one* thing for me, I will continue to feed and keep your flock. ³² I will pass through all your flock today, removing from it all the speckled and spotted sheep, and every brown sheep from among the lambs, and the spotted and speckled among the goats. These shall be my wages. ³³ So my integrity will answer for me in time to come. When you come to examine my wages, every one that is not speckled and spotted among the goats, and brown among the sheep that are with me will be considered stolen."

³⁴ Laban said, "Agreed. Let it be according to your word." ³⁵ He removed that day the male goats that were striped and spotted and all the female goats that were speckled and spotted, every one that had some white in it, and all the brown ones among the sheep, and gave them into the care of his sons. ³⁶ He put three days' journey between himself and Jacob, and Jacob fed the rest of Laban's flocks.

³⁷ Then Jacob took rods of fresh-cut poplar, almond, and plane trees, and peeled white streaks in them, exposing the white which was in the rods. ³⁸ He set the rods which he had peeled before the flocks in the troughs, that is, the watering places, where the flocks came to drink, so that they would mate when they came to drink. ³⁹ The flocks mated before the rods and gave birth to *young* that were striped, speckled, and spotted. ⁴⁰ Jacob separated the lambs and made the flocks face toward the striped and all the brown in the flock of Laban. He put his own flocks by themselves and did not put them with Laban's sheep. ⁴¹ Whenever the stronger sheep mated, Jacob laid the rods before the eyes of the sheep in the troughs, so that they might mate among the rods. ⁴² But when the livestock were feeble, he did not put them in. So the weaker were Laban's and the stronger Jacob's. ⁴³ The man became exceedingly prosperous and had many sheep and female servants and male servants and camels and donkeys.

Jacob Flees From Laban

31 Now *Jacob* heard the words of Laban's sons, saying, "Jacob has taken away all that was our father's, and he has gotten all his wealth from what was our father's." ² Jacob saw the look of Laban and saw he was not congenial toward him as before.

³ Then the LORD said to Jacob, "Return to the land of your fathers, to your family, and I will be with you."

⁴ So Jacob sent and called Rachel and Leah to the field where his flock was, ⁵ and said to them, "I see your father's demeanor, that it is not congenial toward me as before; but the God of my father has been with me. ⁶ You know that with all my strength I have served your father. ⁷ Your father has deceived me and changed my wages ten times, but God did not allow him to hurt me. ⁸ If he said, 'The speckled will be your wages,' then all the flock produced speckled. If he said, 'The striped will be your pay,' then all the flock produced striped. ⁹ In this way God has taken away your father's flock and given them to me.

¹⁰ "When the livestock conceived, I lifted up my eyes and saw in a dream that the male goats mating with the flock were striped, speckled, and spotted. ¹¹ The angel of God spoke to me in a dream, saying,

---

¹ 3 Meaning "on my behalf."

'Jacob.' And I said, 'Here I am.' ¹² He said, 'Now lift up your eyes and see all the male goats which mate with the flock are striped, speckled, and spotted, for I have seen all that Laban has done to you. ¹³ I am the God of Bethel, where you anointed the pillar, where you vowed a vow to Me. Now arise, and get out of this land, and return to the land of your family.' "

¹⁴ Rachel and Leah answered him, "Is there any portion or inheritance left for us in our father's house? ¹⁵ Are we not seen by him as foreigners? For he has sold us and has completely spent our money also. ¹⁶ For all the riches which God has taken from our father are ours and our children's. Now then, whatever God has said to you, do it."

¹⁷ Then Jacob rose up and set his sons and his wives on camels. ¹⁸ Then he carried away all his livestock and all his goods which he had obtained, his acquired livestock which he had gotten in Paddan Aram, in order to go to Isaac his father in the land of Canaan. ¹⁹ When Laban went to shear his sheep, Rachel stole the household idols that were her father's. ²⁰ Jacob also deceived Laban the Syrian by not telling him that he was fleeing. ²¹ So Jacob fled with all that he had, and he rose up and passed over the river and headed toward the mountains of Gilead.

Laban Pursues Jacob

²² Laban was told on the third day that Jacob had fled. ²³ He took his kinsmen with him and pursued him for seven days until he caught up with him in the mountains of Gilead. ²⁴ But God came to Laban the Syrian in a dream by night and said to him, "Take care that you speak to Jacob neither good nor bad."

²⁵ Then Laban overtook Jacob. Now Jacob had pitched his tent on the mountain, and Laban with his kinsmen pitched in the mountains of Gilead. ²⁶ Laban said to Jacob, "What have you done that you have stolen away without my knowing and carried away my daughters like captives taken with the sword? ²⁷ Why did you flee away secretly and sneak away from me and not tell me? I would have sent you away with joy and with songs, with the tambourine and harp. ²⁸ And why did you not permit me to kiss my sons and my daughters farewell? You have acted foolishly in so doing. ²⁹ It is in my power to do you harm, but the God of your father spoke to me last night, saying, 'Take care that you not speak to Jacob either good or bad.' ³⁰ Now you surely have gone away because you longed desperately after your father's house, yet why have you stolen my gods?"

³¹ Then Jacob answered and said to Laban, "Because I was afraid, for I thought that you would take your daughters from me by force. ³² But anyone with whom you find your gods, let him not live. In the presence of our kinsmen, point out what I have that is yours and take it." For Jacob did not know that Rachel had stolen them.

³³ So Laban went into Jacob's tent and into Leah's tent and into the two female servants' tents, but he did not find them. Then he went out of Leah's tent and entered into Rachel's tent. ³⁴ Now Rachel had taken the household idols and put them in the camel's saddle and sat on them. Laban searched the entire tent, but could not find them.

³⁵ She said to her father, "Let not my lord be displeased that I cannot rise before you, for the manner of women is on me." So he searched, but he did not find the household idols.

³⁶ Then Jacob became angry and berated Laban. And Jacob asked Laban, "What is my offense? What is my sin that you have so hotly pursued after me? ³⁷ You have searched all my things, and yet what have you found of all your household things? Set it here before my kinsmen and your kinsmen, so that they may judge between us both.

³⁸ "This twenty years I have been with you. Your ewes and your female goats have not miscarried their young, and the male goats of your flock I have not eaten. ³⁹ That which was torn by beasts I did not bring to you. I bore the loss of it. You required it from my hand *whether it* was stolen by day or stolen by night. ⁴⁰ It was like this with me: In the day the heat consumed me and the frost by night, and my sleep fled from my eyes. ⁴¹ I have been twenty years in your house. I served you fourteen years for your two daughters and six years for your flock, and you have changed my wages ten times. ⁴² If the God of my father, the God of Abraham and the Fear

of Isaac, had not been with me, surely you would have sent me away empty now. God has seen my affliction and the labor of my hands and rebuked you last night."

Laban's Covenant With Jacob

⁴³ Laban answered and said to Jacob, "These daughters are my daughters, and these children are my children, and the flocks are my flocks, and all that you see is mine. But what can I do this day to my daughters or to their children whom they have borne? ⁴⁴ Now therefore come, let us make a covenant, you and I, and let it be as a witness between you and me."

⁴⁵ So Jacob took a stone and set it up for a pillar. ⁴⁶ Jacob said to his kinsmen, "Gather stones." So they took stones and made a pile, and they ate there on the pile. ⁴⁷ And Laban called it Jegar Sahadutha, but Jacob called it Galeed.

⁴⁸ Laban said, "This pile is a witness between me and you this day." Therefore its name was called Galeed, ⁴⁹ and Mizpah, for he said, "May the Lᴏʀᴅ watch between you and me, when we are apart from one another. ⁵⁰ If you mistreat my daughters, or if you take other wives beside my daughters, although no one else is with us, remember that God is witness between you and me."

⁵¹ Then Laban said to Jacob, "See this pile and see this pillar which I have thrown between you and me. ⁵² This heap is a witness, and this pillar is a witness, so that I will not cross over this pile to you and so that you will not pass over this pile and this pillar to me for harm. ⁵³ The God of Abraham, the God of Nahor, and the God of their father, judge between us."

Then Jacob vowed by the Fear of his father Isaac. ⁵⁴ Then Jacob offered a sacrifice on the mountain and called his kinsmen to eat bread. And they ate bread and stayed all night on the mountain.

⁵⁵ Early in the morning Laban rose up, kissed his grandchildren and his daughters, and blessed them. Then Laban departed and returned to his place.

Jacob Prepares to Meet Esau

32 Jacob went on his way, and the angels of God met him. ² When Jacob saw them, he said, "This is God's camp." So he called the name of that place Mahanaim.

³ Jacob sent messengers before him to his brother Esau in the land of Seir, the country of Edom. ⁴ He commanded them, saying, "This is what you must say to my lord Esau: This is what your servant Jacob says, 'I have sojourned with Laban and stayed there until now. ⁵ I have oxen and donkeys, flocks, and male servants and female servants, and I am sending *this message* to tell my lord, so that I may find favor in your sight.' "

⁶ The messengers returned to Jacob, saying, "We went to your brother Esau. He is coming to meet you, and what is more, four hundred men are with him."

⁷ Then Jacob was very afraid and distressed, and he divided the people that were with him, along with the flocks and herds and the camels, into two groups. ⁸ He said, "If Esau comes to the one camp and attacks it, then the other camp which is left may escape."

⁹ And Jacob said, "O God of my father Abraham and God of my father Isaac, the Lᴏʀᴅ who said to me, 'Return to your country and to your relatives, and I will prosper you,' ¹⁰ I am not worthy of all the lovingkindness and of all the faithfulness which You have shown to Your servant. For with my staff I crossed over this Jordan, and now I have become two encampments. ¹¹ Deliver me, I pray, from the hand of my brother, from the hand of Esau. For I fear him, that he will come and attack me and the mothers with the children. ¹² You said, 'I will surely prosper you and make your descendants as the sand of the sea, which is too many to be counted.' "

¹³ So he spent the night there. Then he selected from what he had with him a gift for his brother Esau: ¹⁴ two hundred female goats and twenty male goats, two hundred ewes and twenty rams, ¹⁵ thirty female camels with their colts, forty cows and ten bulls, twenty female donkeys and ten male donkeys. ¹⁶ He gave them to his servants, every drove by itself, and said to his servants, "Pass over before me, and keep a distance between each drove."

¹⁷ He commanded the one leading, saying, "When my brother Esau meets you and asks you, saying, 'To whom do you belong, and where are you going, and to whom do these *animals* belong?'

[18] then you are to say, 'They belong to your servant Jacob. They are a gift sent to my lord Esau, and he is also behind us.' "

[19] Likewise he commanded the second and the third and all that followed the droves, saying, "This is what you are to say to Esau when you find him. [20] Moreover, say, 'Your servant Jacob is behind us.' " For he said, "I will appease him with the gift that goes before me, and then I will see his face. Perhaps he will accept me." [21] So the gift went before him, but he lodged that night in the encampment.

Jacob Wrestles With God

[22] The same night he arose and took his two wives, his two female servants, and his eleven sons, and crossed over the ford of the Jabbok. [23] He took them and sent them across the stream along with all that he had. [24] Jacob was left alone, and a man wrestled with him there until daybreak. [25] When the man saw that He did not prevail against Jacob, He touched the socket of his thigh, so the socket of Jacob's thigh was dislocated, as he wrestled with Him. [26] Then He said, "Let Me go, for the day breaks."

But Jacob said, "I will not let You go, unless You bless me."

[27] So He said to him, "What is your name?"

And he said, "Jacob."

[28] Then the man said, "Your name will no more be called Jacob, but Israel. For you have fought with God and with men, and have prevailed."

[29] Then Jacob asked Him, "Tell me, I pray You, Your name."

But He said, "Why do you ask Me My name?" Then He blessed him there.

[30] Jacob called the name of the place Peniel, saying, "I have seen God face to face, and my life has been preserved."

[31] As he crossed over Peniel, the sun rose over him, and he was limping on his thigh. [32] Therefore to this day the children of Israel do not eat the sinew which is attached to the socket of the thigh, because He touched the socket of Jacob's thigh in the sinew of the hip.

Jacob Meets Esau

33 Then Jacob looked up and saw Esau coming and four hundred men with him. So he divided the children among Leah, Rachel, and the two female servants. [2] He put the female servants and their children in front, then Leah and her children next, and then Rachel and Joseph last. [3] He went on before them, bowing himself to the ground seven times, until he came near to his brother.

[4] But Esau ran to meet him and embraced him and fell on his neck and kissed him, and they wept. [5] When Esau looked up and saw the women and the children, he said, "Who are those with you?"

Jacob said, "The children whom God has graciously given your servant."

[6] Then the female servants came near, they and their children, and they bowed down. [7] Leah also with her children came near and bowed themselves. Afterward Joseph and Rachel came near, and they bowed themselves.

[8] Esau said, "What do you mean by all this company that I met?"

Jacob answered, "These are to find favor in the sight of my lord."

[9] Esau said, "I have enough, my brother. Keep what you have for yourself."

[10] Jacob said, "No, I pray you, if I have now found favor in your sight, then receive my gift from my hand. For I have seen your face, and it is as though I have seen the face of God, with you having received me favorably. [11] Please take my blessing that has been brought to you, because God has dealt graciously with me and because I have plenty." So he urged him, and he took it.

[12] Then Esau said, "Let us journey on our way, and I will go ahead of you."

[13] But Jacob said to him, "My lord knows that the children are weak, and the flocks and herds with young are with me. If they are driven hard one day, all the flock will die. [14] Please let my lord pass over before his servant, and I will lead on slowly, according to the pace of the livestock that goes before me and the pace the children will be able to endure, until I come to my lord at Seir."

[15] So Esau said, "Let me leave some of the people that are with me with you."

But Jacob said, "What need is there? Let me find favor in the sight of my lord."

[16] So Esau returned that day making his way back to Seir. [17] But Jacob journeyed to Sukkoth and built himself a house and made booths for his livestock. Therefore the name of the place is called Sukkoth.

[18] Jacob came peacefully to the city of Shechem, which is in the land of Canaan, on his way from Paddan Aram, and camped before the city. [19] He bought a parcel of a field, where he had pitched his tent, from the children of Hamor, Shechem's father, for a hundred pieces [1] of silver. [20] He erected an altar there and called it El Elohe Israel.

Dinah Is Defiled

34 Now Dinah, the daughter of Leah, whom she bore to Jacob, went out to see the daughters of the land. [2] When Shechem, the son of Hamor the Hivite, prince of the land, saw her, he took her and lay with her and defiled her. [3] He was very smitten by Dinah the daughter of Jacob, and he loved the girl and spoke kindly to her. [4] Shechem spoke to his father Hamor, saying, "Get me this girl for *my* wife."

[5] Now Jacob heard that Shechem had violated his daughter Dinah, but his sons were with his livestock in the field, so Jacob held his peace until they came.

[6] Hamor the father of Shechem went out to Jacob to commune with him. [7] The sons of Jacob came out of the field when they heard it, and the men were grieved and were very disturbed, because Shechem had disgraced Israel by lying with Jacob's daughter, a thing that should not be done.

[8] Hamor spoke with them, saying, "The soul of my son Shechem longs for your daughter. I pray that you will give her to him to marry. [9] Make marriages with us, and give your daughters to us, and take our daughters for yourselves. [10] You may dwell with us, and the land will be before you. Dwell and trade in it and get possessions in it."

[11] Shechem said to her father and to her brothers, "Let me find favor in your eyes, and whatever you say to me I will give. [12] You can make the dowry and gift I must bring high, and I will give according to what you say to me. Just give me the girl to marry."

[13] The sons of Jacob answered Shechem and Hamor his father deceitfully, because he had defiled Dinah their sister. [14] They said to them, "We cannot do this. To give our sister to one who is uncircumcised would be a disgrace to us. [15] But we will consent to you in this: If you will become as we are, that is, every one of your males be circumcised, [16] then we will give our daughters to you, and we will take your daughters to us, and we will dwell with you, and we will become one people. [17] But if you will not listen to us and be circumcised, then we will take our daughter, and we will leave."

[18] Their words pleased Hamor and Shechem, Hamor's son. [19] The young man did not delay to do the thing, because he wanted Jacob's daughter. Now he was more respected than all the household of his father. [20] So Hamor and Shechem his son came to the gate of their city, and they spoke with the men of their city, saying, [21] "These men are at peace with us. Therefore let them dwell in the land and trade in it. For the land is large enough for them. Let us take their daughters as our wives, and let us give them our daughters. [22] Only on this condition will the men consent to dwell with us and be one people: if every male among us will be circumcised as they are circumcised. [23] Will not their livestock and their possessions and every animal of theirs be ours? Only, let us agree with them, and they will dwell with us."

[24] All who went out of the gate of his city listened to Hamor and Shechem his son, and every male was circumcised, all who went out of the gate of his city.

[25] On the third day, when they were in pain, two of Jacob's sons, Simeon and Levi, Dinah's brothers, took their swords and went to the unsuspecting city and killed all the males. [26] They killed Hamor

---

[1] 19 Heb. *a hundred qesitahs*; a *qesitah* was a coin of unknown weight and value.

and Shechem his son with the edge of the sword and took Dinah out of the house of Shechem and departed. [27] The sons of Jacob came upon the slain and looted the city, because they had defiled their sister. [28] They took their flocks and their herds, their donkeys and whatever was in the city and in the fields. [29] They took captive and looted all their wealth, all their little ones, and their wives, even all that was in each house. [30] Then Jacob said to Simeon and Levi, "You have brought trouble on me by making me revolting among the inhabitants of the land, among the Canaanites and the Perizzites. Our being few in number, they will gather themselves together against me and slay me, and I will be destroyed, both I and my household." [31] But they said, "Should he treat our sister like a prostitute?"

Jacob Returns to Bethel

35 Then God said to Jacob, "Arise, go up to Bethel, dwell there, and there make an altar to God, who appeared to you when you fled from the face of Esau your brother."

[2] So Jacob said to his household and to all who were with him, "Put away the foreign gods that are among you. Purify yourselves and change your clothes. [3] Let us arise and go up to Bethel, and there I will make an altar to God, who answered me in the day of my distress and has been with me wherever I have gone." [4] So they gave Jacob all the foreign gods which were in their possession and all their earrings which were in their ears, and Jacob hid them under the oak which was near Shechem. [5] As they traveled, the terror of God was on the cities that were around them, and they did not pursue the sons of Jacob.

[6] So Jacob came to Luz (that is, Bethel), which is in the land of Canaan, he and all the people who were with him. [7] There he built an altar and called the place El Bethel, because God had appeared to him there when he fled from his brother.

[8] Now Deborah, Rebekah's nurse, died and was buried beneath Bethel under the oak. So it was called Allon Bakuth.

[9] God appeared to Jacob again when he came out of Paddan Aram and blessed him. [10] God said to him, "Your name is Jacob. Your name shall not be called Jacob any more, but Israel shall be your name." So He called his name Israel.

[11] God said to him, "I am God Almighty. Be fruitful and multiply. A nation and a company of nations will come from you, and kings shall come forth from you. [12] The land that I gave Abraham and Isaac, I will give to you, and to your descendants after you I will give the land." [13] Then God went up from him in the place where He had spoken with him.

[14] Jacob set up a pillar in the place where He had spoken with him, a pillar of stone, and he poured out a drink offering on it, and he poured oil on it *too*. [15] So Jacob called the name of the place where God had spoken with him Bethel.

The Deaths of Rachel and Isaac
1Ch 2:1–2

[16] They journeyed from Bethel, and when they were still some distance from Ephrath, Rachel went into labor, and she had a difficult labor. [17] When she was in hard labor, the midwife said to her, "Do not fear. You will have this son also." [18] As her soul was departing (for she died), she called his name Ben-Oni, but his father called him Benjamin.

[19] Rachel died and was buried on the way to Ephrath, which is Bethlehem. [20] Jacob set a pillar on her grave. It is the pillar of Rachel's grave to this day.

[21] Israel journeyed and pitched his tent beyond the tower of Eder. [22] When Israel lived in that land, Reuben went and lay with Bilhah, his father's concubine, and Israel heard about it.

Now the sons of Jacob were twelve:
[23] The sons of Leah were
Reuben, Jacob's firstborn,
and Simeon and Levi and Judah and Issachar and Zebulun.
[24] The sons of Rachel were
Joseph and Benjamin.
[25] And the sons of Bilhah, Rachel's maidservant, were
Dan and Naphtali.

[26] And the sons of Zilpah, Leah's maidserva...
Gad and Asher.
These are the sons of Jacob, which were bo...
dan Aram.

[27] Jacob came back to Isaac his father in Mam...
(which is Hebron), where Abraham and Isaac had sojourned.
[28] Now the days of Isaac were one hundred and eighty years. [29] And Isaac breathed his last and died and was gathered to his people, being old and full of days, and his sons Esau and Jacob buried him.

Esau's Descendants
1Ch 1:35–42

36 Now these are the generations of Esau, who is Edom.

[2] Esau took his wives from the daughters of Canaan: Adah the daughter of Elon the Hittite, and Oholibamah the daughter of Anah the daughter of Zibeon the Hivite, [3] and Basemath, Ishmael's daughter, sister of Nebaioth.

[4] Adah bore to Esau Eliphaz, and Basemath bore Reuel, [5] and Oholibamah bore Jeush, Jalam, and Korah. These are the sons of Esau, who were born to him in the land of Canaan.

[6] Then Esau took his wives, his sons, his daughters, and all the people of his house, his livestock, all his animals, and all his property that he had acquired in the land of Canaan, and he moved to a land some distance from his brother Jacob. [7] For their possessions were too great for them to dwell together, and the land where they were foreigners could not sustain them because of their livestock. [8] So Esau settled in the hill country of Seir. Esau is Edom.

[9] These are the generations of Esau the father of the Edomites in the hill country of Seir.

[10] These are the names of Esau's sons:
Eliphaz the son of Adah the wife of Esau, and Reuel the son of Basemath the wife of Esau.
[11] The sons of Eliphaz were
Teman, Omar, Zepho, Gatam, and Kenaz.
[12] Timna was a concubine to Eliphaz, Esau's son, and she bore to Eliphaz Amalek. These were the sons of Adah, Esau's wife.
[13] These are the sons of Reuel:
Nahath, Zerah, Shammah, and Mizzah. These were the sons of Basemath, Esau's wife.
[14] These were the sons of Oholibamah, the daughter of Anah the daughter of Zibeon, Esau's wife: she bore to Esau Jeush, Jalam, and Korah.

The Chiefs of Edom

[15] These were chiefs of the sons of Esau.
The sons of Eliphaz the firstborn son of Esau were
Chief Teman, Chief Omar, Chief Zepho, Chief Kenaz,
[16] Chief Korah, Chief Gatam, and Chief Amalek. These are the chiefs who came from Eliphaz in the land of Edom. These were the sons of Adah.
[17] These were the sons of Reuel Esau's son:
Chief Nahath, Chief Zerah, Chief Shammah, and Chief Mizzah. These are the chiefs who came from Reuel in the land of Edom. These were the sons of Basemath, Esau's wife.
[18] These were the sons of Oholibamah, Esau's wife:
Chief Jeush, Chief Jalam, and Chief Korah. These were the chiefs who came from Oholibamah, the daughter of Anah, Esau's wife.
[19] These were the sons of Esau, who is Edom, and these were their chiefs.

The Sons of Seir

[20] These were the sons of Seir the Horite, who inhabited the land: Lotan, Shobal, Zibeon, Anah, [21] Dishon, Ezer, and Dishan. These were the chiefs of the Horites, the children of Seir in the land of Edom.

_e children of Lotan were
  Hori and Homam, and Lotan's sister was Timna.
²³ The children of Shobal were these:
  Alvan, Manahath, Ebal, Shepho, and Onam.
²⁴ These were the children of Zibeon:
  Aiah and Anah. This was the Anah who found the water
  in the wilderness as he fed the donkeys of Zibeon, his father.
²⁵ The children of Anah were these:
  Dishon and Oholibamah, the daughter of Anah.
²⁶ These are the children of Dishon:
  Hemdan, Eshban, Ithran, and Keran.
²⁷ The children of Ezer were these:
  Bilhan, Zaavan, and Akan.
²⁸ The children of Dishan were these:
  Uz and Aran.
²⁹ These were the chiefs that came from the Horites:
  Chief Lotan, Chief Shobal, Chief Zibeon, Chief Anah,
    ³⁰ Chief Dishon, Chief Ezer, and Chief Dishan. These are
  the chiefs who came from Hori, among their chiefs in the
  land of Seir.

The Kings of Edom
1Ch 1:43–54
³¹ These were the kings who reigned in the land of Edom before there reigned any king over the children of Israel.
³² Bela the son of Beor reigned in Edom, and the name of his city was Dinhabah.
³³ Bela died, and Jobab the son of Zerah of Bozrah reigned in his stead.
³⁴ Jobab died, and Husham of the land of Temani reigned in his stead.
³⁵ Husham died, and Hadad the son of Bedad, who defeated Midian in the field of Moab, reigned in his stead, and the name of his city was Avith.
³⁶ Hadad died, and Samlah of Masrekah reigned in his stead.
³⁷ Samlah died, and Shaul of Rehoboth by the river reigned in his stead.
³⁸ Shaul died, and Baal-Hanan the son of Akbor reigned in his stead.
³⁹ Baal-Hanan the son of Akbor died, and Hadad reigned in his stead, and the name of his city was Pau. His wife's name was Mehetabel, the daughter of Matred, the daughter of Me-Zahab.

⁴⁰ These are the names of the chiefs who came from Esau, according to their families, according to their places, by their names: Chief Timnah, Chief Alvah, Chief Jetheth, ⁴¹ Chief Oholibamah, Chief Elah, Chief Pinon, ⁴² Chief Kenaz, Chief Teman, Chief Mibzar, ⁴³ Chief Magdiel, and Chief Iram. These were the chiefs of Edom, according to their settlements in the land of their possession.

Esau *was* the father of the Edomites.

Joseph's Dreams
37 Now Jacob lived in the land where his father was a foreigner, in the land of Canaan.

² These are the *generations* of Jacob.

Joseph, being seventeen years old, was feeding the flock with his brothers, and the boy was with the sons of Bilhah and with the sons of Zilpah, his father's wives. Joseph brought back a bad report about them to their father.
³ Now Israel loved Joseph more than all his sons, because he was the son of his old age, and he made him a coat of many colors.[1]
⁴ But when his brothers saw that their father loved him more than all his brothers, they hated him and could not speak peaceably to him.
⁵ Now Joseph dreamed a dream, and when he told it to his brothers, they hated him even more. ⁶ He said to them, "Please listen to this dream which I have dreamed. ⁷ We were binding sheaves in the field. All of a sudden my sheaf rose up and stood upright, and your sheaves stood around it and bowed down to my sheaf."

⁸ His brothers said to him, "Will you really reign over us, or will you really have dominion over us?" So they hated him even more because of his dreams and his words.

⁹ Then he dreamed another dream and told it to his brothers and said, "I have dreamed another dream. The sun and the moon and eleven stars were bowing to me."

¹⁰ But when he told it to his father and his brothers, his father rebuked him and said to him, "What is this dream that you have dreamed? Will I and your mother and your brothers really come to bow down ourselves to you to the ground?" ¹¹ So his brothers were jealous of him, but his father kept the matter *in mind*.

Joseph Sold Into Slavery
¹² Now his brothers went to feed their father's flock in Shechem. ¹³ Israel said to Joseph, "Are not your brothers feeding the flock in Shechem? Come, and I will send you to them."

He answered, "Here I am."

¹⁴ Israel said to him, "Please go and see if it is well with your brothers and well with the flocks, and bring back word to me." So he sent him out of the Valley of Hebron, and he came to Shechem.

¹⁵ A certain man found him wandering in the field. The man asked him, "What are you looking for?"

¹⁶ And he said, "I am looking for my brothers. Please tell me where they are feeding their flocks."

¹⁷ The man said, "They have departed from here. I heard them say, 'Let us go to Dothan.'"

So Joseph went after his brothers and found them in Dothan.

¹⁸ When they saw him some distance away, before he came near to them, they conspired against him to kill him.

¹⁹ They said one to another, "The master of dreams comes!
²⁰ Come now, let us kill him and throw him into some pit, and we will say, 'Some evil beast has devoured him.' Then we will see what will become of his dreams."

²¹ But when Reuben heard it, he rescued him out of their hands, saying, "Let us not kill him." ²² Reuben said to them, "Shed no blood, but throw him into this pit here in the wilderness, but lay no hand on him," so that he might rescue him out of their hands and deliver him to his father again.

²³ When Joseph came to his brothers, they stripped Joseph of his coat—his coat of many colors that he had on. ²⁴ And they took him and threw him into a pit. The pit was empty, and there was no water in it.

²⁵ Then they sat down to eat. And looking up, they saw a caravan of Ishmaelites coming from Gilead, with their camels bearing spices, balm, and myrrh, carrying it down to Egypt.

²⁶ Then Judah said to his brothers, "What profit is it if we kill our brother and cover up his blood? ²⁷ Come, let us sell him to the Ishmaelites, and let us not lay our hand on him, for he is our brother and our own flesh." So his brothers agreed.

²⁸ Then when the Midianite merchants passed by, they drew Joseph up and lifted him out of the pit and sold Joseph to the Ishmaelites for twenty shekels of silver.[2] They took Joseph to Egypt.

²⁹ When Reuben returned to the pit and saw that Joseph was not in the pit, he tore his clothes. ³⁰ He returned to his brothers, and said, "The boy is not *there*, and I, where can I go?"

³¹ They took Joseph's coat and killed a young goat and dipped the coat in the blood. ³² Then they took the coat of many colors and brought it to their father and said, "This we have found. Do you know whether it is your son's coat or not?"

³³ He knew it and said, "It is my son's coat. A wild beast has devoured him. Joseph has without a doubt been torn into pieces."

³⁴ Jacob tore his clothes and put sackcloth on his waist and mourned for his son many days. ³⁵ All his sons and all his daughters rose up to comfort him, but he refused to be comforted. And he said, "For I will go down into the grave mourning for my son." So his father wept for him.

---

[1] 3 From the Septuagint, a cloak with long sleeves, a full-length cloak, or an embroidered cloak, showing favoritism.   [2] 28 About 8 ounces, or 230 grams.

[36] Meanwhile the Midianites sold him in Egypt to Potiphar, an officer of Pharaoh and captain of the guard.

Judah and Tamar

38 At that time Judah left his brothers and visited a certain Adullamite, whose name was Hirah. [2] There Judah saw the daughter of a certain Canaanite, whose name was Shua, and he took her and had relations with her. [3] She conceived and bore a son, and he called his name Er. [4] She conceived again and bore a son, and she called his name Onan. [5] She again conceived and bore a son and called his name Shelah. He was at Kezib when she bore him.

[6] Judah took a wife for Er his firstborn, whose name was Tamar. [7] But Er, Judah's firstborn, was wicked in the sight of the LORD, so the LORD killed him. [8] Then Judah said to Onan, "Go have relations with your brother's wife, and marry her, and raise up descendants for your brother." [9] But Onan knew that the descendant would not be his, so when he had relations with his brother's wife, he let his semen go on the ground, so that he would not give a descendant to his brother. [10] What he did displeased the LORD; therefore He killed him also.

[11] Then Judah said to Tamar, his daughter-in-law, "Remain a widow at your father's house until Shelah my son grows up." For he thought, "He may die also, just as his brothers did." So Tamar went and lived in her father's house.

[12] As time went on, the daughter of Shua, Judah's wife, died. After Judah was consoled, he went up to his sheepshearers in Timnah, he and his friend Hirah the Adullamite.

[13] It was told to Tamar, "Your father-in-law is going up to Timnah to shear his sheep." [14] She took off her widow's clothing, covered herself with a veil, wrapped herself up, and sat in an open place, which is by the road to Timnah. For she saw that Shelah was grown, and she was not given to him as *his* wife.

[15] When Judah saw her, he thought she was a prostitute, because she had covered her face. [16] He turned to her by the road and said, "Come now, let me have relations with you" (for he did not know that she was his daughter-in-law).

And she said, "What will you give me, so that you may have relations with me?"

[17] And he said, "I will send you a young goat from the flock."

And she said, "Will you give me a pledge, until you send it?"

[18] And he said, "What pledge should I give you?"

And she said, "Your signet, your bracelets, and your staff that is in your hand." So he gave them to her and had relations with her, and she conceived by him. [19] She arose and went away, and taking off her veil, she put on her widow's clothing.

[20] Judah sent the young goat by his friend the Adullamite to receive his pledge from the woman's hand, but he could not find her. [21] Then he asked the men of the place, "Where is the cult prostitute who was at Enaim by the road?"

And they said, "There was no prostitute in this place."

[22] So he returned to Judah and said, "I cannot find her. Also, the men of the place said there was no cult prostitute in this place."

[23] Judah replied, "Let her keep them for herself, or we shall be laughed at. I sent this young goat, and you did not find her."

[24] After about three months, it was told Judah, "Tamar your daughter-in-law has turned to prostitution, and what is more, as a result of prostitution she is pregnant."

Then Judah said, "Bring her forth, and let her be burned!"

[25] When she was brought forth, she sent *word* to her father-in-law, saying, "By the man to whom these belong am I with child." And she said, "Please identify whose these are—the signet and bracelet and staff."

[26] Judah recognized them and said, "She has been more righteous than I, because I did not give her to Shelah my son." He did not have relations with her again.

[27] When it was time for her to give birth, there were twins in her womb. [28] While she was giving birth, one put out his hand, and the midwife took and tied on his hand a scarlet thread, saying, "This one came out first." [29] But as he drew back his hand, his brother came out. Then she said, "How have you made a breach for yourself?" Therefore his name was called Perez. [30] Afterward his brother came out, the one that had the scarlet thread on his hand, and his name was called Zerah.

Joseph and Potiphar's Wife

39 Now Joseph was brought down to Egypt, and Potiphar, an officer of Pharaoh, captain of the guard, an Egyptian, bought him from the Ishmaelites who had brought him down there.

[2] The LORD was with Joseph, so that he became a prosperous man. He was in the house of his master, the Egyptian. [3] His master saw that the LORD was with him and that the LORD made all that he did to prosper. [4] Joseph found favor in his sight and served him. So he made him overseer over his house, and all that he had he put under his charge. [5] From the time that he had made him overseer in his house and over all that he had, the LORD blessed the Egyptian's house on account of Joseph. So the blessing of the LORD was on all that he had in the house and in the field. [6] So he left all that he had in Joseph's charge, and he had no concerns regarding anything except the food he ate.

Now Joseph was handsome and well-built. [7] After a time, his master's wife took notice of Joseph and said, "Lie with me."

[8] But he refused and said to his master's wife, "My master does not concern himself with *anything* concerning me in the house, and he has committed all that he has to my charge. [9] There is none greater in this house than I. He has kept nothing back from me but you, because you are his wife. How then can I do this great wickedness and sin against God?" [10] She spoke to Joseph every day, but he did not listen to her about lying with her or being with her.

[11] But it happened one day that Joseph went into the house to do his work, and none of the men of the house was there. [12] She caught him by his clothing, saying, "Lie with me." But he left his clothing in her hand and fled and got outside.

[13] When she saw that he had left his clothing in her hand and had fled outside, [14] she called to the men of her house and spoke to them, saying, "See, he has brought in a Hebrew among us to humiliate us. He came in to me to lie with me, and I cried out with a loud voice. [15] When he heard that I lifted up my voice and cried out, he left his clothing with me, fled, and got outside."

[16] She laid up his clothing next to her until his master came home. [17] She spoke to him using these words, saying, "The Hebrew servant, whom you have brought to us, came in to me to mock me. [18] When I lifted up my voice and cried out, he left his clothing with me and fled outside."

[19] When his master heard the words of his wife, which she spoke to him, saying, "This is what your servant did to me," he became enraged. [20] Joseph's master took him and put him into the prison, a place where the king's prisoners were confined.

So he was there in the prison. [21] But the LORD was with Joseph and showed him mercy and gave him favor in the sight of the keeper of the prison. [22] The keeper of the prison committed all the prisoners that were in the prison to the charge of Joseph. So whatever they did there, he was the one responsible for it. [23] The keeper of the prison did not concern himself with anything that was under Joseph's charge because the LORD was with him. And whatever he did, the LORD made it to prosper.

Joseph Interprets Dreams

40 Sometime after this, the cupbearer of the king of Egypt and his baker offended their lord, the king of Egypt. [2] Pharaoh was angry with his two officials, with the chief of the cupbearers and with the chief of the bakers. [3] So he put them in confinement in the house of the captain of the guard, in the prison, the place where Joseph was confined. [4] The captain of the guard charged Joseph with them, and he attended to them.

They continued to be in confinement for some time. [5] Then the cupbearer and the baker for the king of Egypt, who were confined in the prison, both had a dream the same night, each man with his own dream and each dream with its *own* interpretation.

[6] Joseph came in to them in the morning and looked at them and realized they were sad. [7] So he asked Pharaoh's officials who were with him in the care of his lord's house, saying, "Why do you look so sad today?"

[8] And they said to him, "We have dreamed a dream, and there is no interpreter for it."

Then Joseph said to them, "Do not interpretations belong to God? Please tell them to me."

[9] The chief cupbearer told his dream to Joseph and said to him, "In my dream, a vine was in front of me. [10] And in the vine there were three branches. As it budded, its blossoms shot forth and its clusters brought forth ripe grapes. [11] Pharaoh's cup was in my hand, and I took the grapes, and pressed them into Pharaoh's cup, and I put the cup into Pharaoh's hand."

[12] Joseph said to him, "This is the interpretation of it. The three branches are three days. [13] Within three days Pharaoh will lift up your head and restore you to your place, and you will deliver Pharaoh's cup into his hand in the same way you did before when you were his cupbearer. [14] But remember me when it is well with you, and show kindness, I pray you, to me, and make mention of me to Pharaoh, and get me out of this house. [15] For I was indeed kidnapped out of the land of the Hebrews, and I have done nothing that they should put me in the dungeon."

[16] When the chief baker saw that the interpretation was good, he said to Joseph, "I also was in my dream, and I had three white baskets on my head. [17] In the uppermost basket there was all manner of baked goods for Pharaoh, and the birds ate them out of the basket on my head."

[18] Joseph answered and said, "This is the interpretation: The three baskets are three days. [19] Within three days Pharaoh will lift your head from off you and will hang you on a tree, and the birds will eat your flesh from you."

[20] It happened on the third day, which was Pharaoh's birthday, that he made a feast for all his servants. He lifted up the heads of the chief cupbearer and the chief baker among his servants. [21] He restored the chief cupbearer to his position again, and he put the cup into Pharaoh's hand. [22] However, he hanged the chief baker, just as Joseph had interpreted to them.

[23] Yet, the chief cupbearer did not remember Joseph, but forgot him.

Pharaoh's Dreams

41 After two whole years, Pharaoh had a dream that he was standing by the Nile. [2] Seven fine-looking and fattened cows suddenly came up out of the river, and they grazed in the meadow. [3] Then seven other cows came up after them out of the river, ugly and gaunt, and stood by the other cows on the riverbank. [4] The ugly and gaunt cows ate up the seven fine-looking and fattened cows. Then Pharaoh awoke.

[5] He slept and dreamed a second time. Seven ears of grain suddenly came up on one stalk, plump and good. [6] Then seven thin ears, scorched by the east wind, sprang up after them. [7] The seven thin ears devoured the seven plump and full ears. Then Pharaoh awoke and realized it was a dream.

[8] In the morning his spirit was troubled, and he sent and called for all the magicians of Egypt and all its wise men. Pharaoh told them his dreams, but there was no one who could interpret them to Pharaoh.

[9] Then the chief cupbearer spoke to Pharaoh, saying, "Today I remember my offenses. [10] Pharaoh was angry with his servants and put me in confinement in the captain of the guard's house, both me and the chief baker. [11] And we had a dream in the same night, he and I. We, each of us, dreamed according to the interpretation of his *own* dream. [12] A young Hebrew man was with us there, a servant to the captain of the guard. We told him and he interpreted our dreams for us. To each man he interpreted according to his *own* dream. [13] It happened just as he interpreted. He restored me to my position, and the baker was hanged."

[14] So Pharaoh sent and called for Joseph, and they brought him hastily out of the dungeon. He shaved himself, changed his clothes, and came to Pharaoh.

[15] Pharaoh said to Joseph, "I have dreamed a dream, and there is no one who can interpret it. I have heard it said of you that you can understand a dream to interpret it."

[16] Joseph answered Pharaoh, saying, "It is not in me. God will give Pharaoh a favorable answer."

[17] Then Pharaoh said to Joseph, "In my dream, I stood on the bank of the Nile. [18] And suddenly there came up out of the river seven cows, fattened and fine-looking, and they grazed in the reeds. [19] Then seven other cows came up after them, poor and very ugly and gaunt. I have never seen such ugliness in all the land of Egypt. [20] And the gaunt and ugly cows ate up the first seven fat cows. [21] And when they had eaten them up, no one would have known that they had eaten them, for they were still as ugly as before. Then I awoke.

[22] "I also saw in my dreams seven ears *of grain*, full and good, suddenly come up on one stalk. [23] Then seven ears, thin and scorched by the east wind, sprang up after them. [24] And the thin ears swallowed the seven good ears. So I told this to the magicians, but there was no one who could explain it to me."

[25] Then Joseph said to Pharaoh, "The dreams of Pharaoh are *one and the same*. God has shown Pharaoh what He is about to do. [26] The seven good cows are seven years, and the seven good ears are seven years. The dreams are one. [27] The seven gaunt and ugly cows that came up after them are seven years, and the seven empty ears scorched by the east wind will be seven years of famine.

[28] "It is as I have spoken to Pharaoh. God has shown Pharaoh what He is about to do. [29] Seven years of great abundance will come throughout all the land of Egypt. [30] However, there will arise after them seven years of famine. All the abundance will be forgotten in the land of Egypt, and the famine will consume the land. [31] The abundance will be unknown in the land because of the famine following, for it will be very severe. [32] The reason the dream was repeated to Pharaoh twice is because the matter is established by God, and God will soon bring it to pass.

[33] "Now, therefore, let Pharaoh seek out a man *who is* discerning and wise and set him over the land of Egypt. [34] Let Pharaoh do this, and let him appoint officials over the land and collect the fifth part of the produce of the land of Egypt in the seven abundant years. [35] Let them gather all the food from those good years that come and lay up grain under the authority of Pharaoh, and let them keep food in the cities. [36] This food will be for a reserve for the land for the seven years of famine which will be in the land of Egypt, so that the land does not perish during the famine."

Joseph Rises to Power

[37] The counsel seemed good to Pharaoh and to all of his servants. [38] Pharaoh said to his servants, "Can we find anyone like this man, in whom is the Spirit of God?"

[39] And Pharaoh said to Joseph, "Since God has shown you all this, there is no one as discerning and wise as you. [40] You will be over my house, and according to your word all my people will be ruled. Only in regard to the throne will I be greater than you."

[41] Then Pharaoh said to Joseph, "See, I have set you over all the land of Egypt." [42] Pharaoh took off his ring from his hand and put it on Joseph's hand and arrayed him in clothes of fine linen and put a gold chain around his neck. [43] Then he had him ride in the second chariot which was his, and they cried out before him, "Bow the knee!" So he set him over all the land of Egypt.

[44] Pharaoh said to Joseph, "I am Pharaoh, and without your consent no man will lift up his hand or foot in all the land of Egypt." [45] Pharaoh called Joseph's name Zaphenath-Paneah, and he gave him a wife, Asenath the daughter of Potiphera priest of On.[1] And Joseph went out over all the land of Egypt.

[46] Joseph was thirty years old when he stood before Pharaoh, the king of Egypt. And Joseph went out from the presence of Pharaoh and went throughout all the land of Egypt. [47] In the seven abundant years the earth brought forth plentifully. [48] So he gathered up all the food of the seven years which was in the land of Egypt and laid up the food in the cities. He put in every city the food of the fields which surrounded the city. [49] Joseph gathered great quantities of grain as the sand of the sea until he stopped measuring it, for it was beyond measure.

[50] Before the years of famine came, two sons were born to Joseph, whom Asenath, the daughter of Potiphera priest of On, bore to him.

---

[1] 45 *On* is also called *Heliopolis*.

[51] Joseph called the name of the firstborn Manasseh, "For God," he said, "has made me forget all my trouble and all my father's house." [52] The name of the second he called Ephraim, *saying*, "For God has caused me to be fruitful in the land of my affliction."

[53] The seven years of abundance that were in the land of Egypt ended. [54] The seven years of famine began to come, just as Joseph had said. The famine was in all lands, but there was food in all the land of Egypt. [55] When all the land of Egypt was hungry, the people cried to Pharaoh for food, and Pharaoh said to all the Egyptians, "Go to Joseph. Do whatever he says to you."

[56] The famine was over all the face of the earth, so Joseph opened all the storehouses and sold to the Egyptians, and the famine was severe throughout the land of Egypt. [57] Moreover, all countries came to Egypt to Joseph to buy grain, because the famine was so severe in all the lands.

Joseph's Brothers Go to Egypt

42 Now when Jacob saw that there was grain in Egypt, Jacob said to his sons, "Why do you look at one another?" [2] And he said, "I have heard that there is grain in Egypt. Go down there and buy *some* for us, so that we may live and not die."

[3] Joseph's ten brothers went down to buy grain in Egypt. [4] But Jacob did not send Benjamin, Joseph's brother, with his brothers for he said, "Perhaps some harm might happen to him." [5] Thus the sons of Israel came to buy grain among those who came, for the famine was in the land of Canaan.

[6] Now Joseph was the governor over the land, and it was he who sold to all the people of the land. So Joseph's brothers came and bowed themselves down before him with their faces to the ground. [7] Joseph saw his brothers, and he recognized them, but he pretended to be a stranger to them and spoke harshly to them. He said to them, "From where do you come?"

And they said, "From the land of Canaan to buy food."

[8] Joseph knew his brothers, but they did not know him. [9] Joseph also remembered the dreams that he had dreamed of them. He said to them, "You are spies! You came to see the nakedness of the land!"

[10] They said to him, "No, my lord, your servants have come only to buy food. [11] We are all one man's sons. We are honest men. Your servants are not spies."

[12] But he said to them, "No, you have come to see the nakedness of the land!"

[13] They said, "Your servants are twelve brothers, the sons of one man in the land of Canaan. The youngest is with our father today, and one is no longer living."

[14] Joseph said to them, "It is as I said to you, 'You are spies!' [15] Here is how you will be tested. By the life of Pharaoh, you will not leave here unless your youngest brother comes here. [16] Send one of you, and let him get your brother, and you will be kept in prison, so that your words may be tested, whether there be any truth in you. Or else, by the life of Pharaoh, you are surely spies." [17] He put them all together in custody for three days.

[18] Joseph said to them the third day, "Do this and live, for I fear God. [19] If you are honest men, let one of your brothers be confined in your prison house. The rest of you go and carry grain for the famine of your households. [20] Nevertheless, bring your youngest brother to me so that your words may be verified and you shall not die." And they did so.

[21] Then they said one to another, "We are guilty concerning our brother, because we saw the anguish of his soul when he pleaded with us, but we would not listen. Therefore, this distress has come upon us."

[22] Reuben answered them, saying, "Did I not speak to you, saying, 'Do not sin against the boy'; and you would not listen? Therefore, his blood is now required of us." [23] They did not know that Joseph understood them, for he spoke to them through an interpreter.

[24] He turned himself away from them and wept, but then turned back to them again and spoke with them. Then he took Simeon from them and bound him before their eyes.

[25] Joseph then gave the command to fill their sacks with grain and to restore every man's money to his sack and to give them provisions for the way. And it was done for them.

Joseph's Brothers Return Home

[26] They loaded their donkeys with the grain and departed from there.

[27] As one of them opened his sack to give his donkey feed in the lodging place, he saw his money. It was in the mouth of his sack. [28] And he said to his brothers, "My money has been returned. Here it is in my sack!"

Then their hearts sank, and they were afraid, saying to one another, "What is this that God has done to us?"

[29] They came to Jacob their father in the land of Canaan and told him all that had happened to them, saying, [30] "The man, the lord of the land, spoke harshly to us and took us for spies of the country. [31] And we said to him, 'We are honest men. We are not spies. [32] We are twelve brothers, *all* sons of our father. One is no longer living, and the youngest is with our father today in the land of Canaan.'

[33] "The man, the lord of the country, said to us, 'Here is how I may know that you are honest men. Leave one of your brothers here with me, take food for the famine of your households, and be gone. [34] But bring your youngest brother back to me. Then I will know that you are not spies, but that you are honest men. Then I will deliver your brother to you, and you may trade in the land.' "

[35] As they emptied their sacks, every man's bundle of money was in his sack. When both they and their father saw the bundles of money, they were afraid. [36] Then Jacob their father said to them, "You have bereaved me of my children! Joseph is no more, Simeon is no more, and you will take Benjamin away. All these things are against me."

[37] Reuben spoke to his father, saying, "Kill my two sons if I fail to bring him to you. Put him in my hands, and I will bring him back to you."

[38] But Jacob said, "My son must not go down with you, for his brother is dead, and he alone is left. If harm should happen to him on the journey you are to make, then you will bring down my gray hairs with sorrow to the grave."

Joseph's Brothers Return With Benjamin

43 Now the famine was severe in the land. [2] When they had eaten up the grain which they had brought out of Egypt, their father said to them, "Go back and buy us a little food."

[3] Judah spoke to him, saying, "The man solemnly warned us, saying, 'You will not see my face unless your brother is with you.' [4] If you will send our brother with us, we will go down and buy food for you. [5] But if you will not send him, we will not go down. For the man said to us, 'You will not see my face unless your brother is with you.' "

[6] Israel said, "Why did you treat me so badly as to tell the man that you had *another* brother?"

[7] And they said, "The man asked us directly about ourselves and our family, saying, 'Is your father still alive? Do you have another brother?' So we answered his questions. How could we even know that he would say, 'Bring your brother down'?"

[8] And Judah said to Israel his father, "Send the boy with me, and we will arise and go, so that we may live and not die, both we and you, and also our little ones. [9] I will be a surety for him. You may hold me personally responsible for him. If I fail to bring him back to you and set him before you, then let me bear the blame forever. [10] For if we had not delayed, we could have returned twice."

[11] Their father Israel said to them, "If it must be so, do this. Take some of the best fruits in the land in your bags, and carry down a present for the man: a little balm and a little honey, spices, and myrrh, pistachio nuts and almonds. [12] Take double the money with you, along with the money that was brought back in the mouths of your sacks. Carry it with you again. Perhaps it was a mistake. [13] Also, take your brother and arise, return to the man. [14] And may God Almighty give you mercy before the man, so that he may send away your other brother, along with Benjamin. As for me, if I am bereaved, I am bereaved."

[15] The men took the gift, and they took double the money with them, along with Benjamin. Then they went on their way down to Egypt and stood before Joseph. [16] When Joseph saw Benjamin with them, he said to the house steward, "Bring these men home,

slaughter an animal and prepare it, for these men will dine with me at noon."

¹⁷ The man did as Joseph ordered, so the man brought the men into Joseph's house. ¹⁸ The men were afraid because they were brought into Joseph's house. They said, "We have been brought in because of the money that was returned in our sacks the first time, so that he may seek occasion against us and fall upon us and take us for slaves with our donkeys."

The Feast With Joseph

¹⁹ They approached the steward of Joseph's house, and they spoke with him at the entrance of the house. ²⁰ They said, "My lord, we indeed came down the first time to buy food. ²¹ When we came to the lodging place, we opened our sacks and realized every man's money was in the mouth of his sack, our money in full weight. So we have brought it again with us. ²² We have also brought additional money with us to buy food. We cannot tell who put our money in our sacks."

²³ He said, "Be at peace; do not be afraid. Your God and the God of your father has given you treasure in your sacks. I had your money." Then he brought Simeon out to them.

²⁴ The man brought the men into Joseph's house and gave them water to wash their feet and gave feed to their donkeys. ²⁵ Then they made ready the gift for Joseph's coming at noon, for they heard that they would be eating a meal there.

²⁶ When Joseph came home, they brought into the house to him the present that they had with them and bowed themselves to him to the ground. ²⁷ He asked them about their well-being and said, "Is your father well, the old man of whom you spoke? Is he still alive?"

²⁸ And they answered, "Your servant our father is in good health. He is still alive." And they bowed down their heads and prostrated themselves.

²⁹ He lifted up his eyes and saw his brother Benjamin, his mother's son, and said, "Is this your younger brother of whom you spoke to me?" And he said, "God be gracious to you, my son." ³⁰ Joseph hurried *out*, for he was deeply moved over his brother and sought a place to weep. So he entered into his chamber and wept there.

³¹ Then he washed his face and came out. Controlling himself, he said, "Serve the food."

³² They served him by himself and them by themselves and the Egyptians who ate with him by themselves, because the Egyptians could not eat a meal with the Hebrews, for that is an abomination to the Egyptians. ³³ They sat before him, the firstborn according to his birthright and the youngest according to his youth, and the men looked at one another in astonishment. ³⁴ He gave them portions from his own table, but Benjamin's serving was five times more than any of theirs. So they drank and feasted with him.

Joseph Detains Benjamin

44 Then he commanded the steward of his house, saying, "Fill the men's sacks with food, as much as they can carry, and put every man's money in the mouth of his sack. ² Put my cup, the silver cup, in the mouth of the sack of the youngest, along with his grain money." And he did according to what Joseph had spoken.

³ As soon as the morning was light, the men were sent away, they and their donkeys. ⁴ When they were gone out of the city, but not yet far off, Joseph said to his steward, "Get up, follow after the men. When you overtake them, say to them, 'Why have you rewarded evil for good? ⁵ Is this not the one from which my lord drinks and uses as he practices divination? You have done evil in doing this.' "

⁶ So he overtook them, and he spoke to them these same words. ⁷ They said to him, "Why does my lord say these words? Far be it from your servants that they should do such a thing. ⁸ Look, we brought back to you from the land of Canaan the money that we found in the top of our sacks. Why then would we steal silver or gold from your lord's house? ⁹ Whichever of your servants is found with it shall die, and the rest of us will become my lord's slaves."

¹⁰ He said, "Now let it also be according to your words. He with whom it is found shall be my slave, and you will be blameless."

¹¹ Then every man hurriedly took down his sack to the ground, and every man opened his sack. ¹² He searched, beginning with the oldest and ending with the youngest. The cup was found in Benjamin's sack. ¹³ Then they tore their clothes, and every man loaded his donkey and returned to the city.

¹⁴ When Judah and his brothers came to Joseph's house, he was still there; and they fell to the ground before him. ¹⁵ Joseph said to them, "What deed is this that you have done? Did you not know that such a man as I can certainly practice divination?"

¹⁶ And Judah said, "What shall we say to my lord? What shall we speak? Or how shall we clear ourselves? God has found out the iniquity of your servants. Here we are, my lord's servants, both we and he also in whose possession the cup was found."

¹⁷ But he said, "Far be it from me that I should do so. The man in whose possession the cup was found shall be my slave; but as for you, go up in peace to your father."

Judah's Plea for Benjamin

¹⁸ Then Judah approached him and said, "O my lord, please let your servant speak a word in my lord's ears, and do not be angry with your servant, for you are equal to Pharaoh. ¹⁹ My lord asked his servants, saying, 'Have you a father or a brother?' ²⁰ And we said to my lord, 'We have a father, an old man, and a young brother, the child of his old age. His brother is dead, and he alone is left of his mother, and his father loves him.'

²¹ "You said to your servants, 'Bring him down to me, so that I may set my eyes on him.' ²² We said to my lord, 'The boy cannot leave his father, for if he should leave his father, his father would die.' ²³ You said to your servants, 'Unless your youngest brother comes down with you, you will not see my face again.' ²⁴ When we went back to your servant, my father, we told him the words of my lord.

²⁵ "Our father said, 'Go again and buy us a little food.' ²⁶ We said, 'We cannot go down. If our youngest brother is with us, then we will go down, for we may not see the man's face, unless our youngest brother is with us.'

²⁷ "Your servant, my father, said to us, 'You know that my wife bore me two sons. ²⁸ And the one went out from me, and I said, "Surely he was torn in pieces," and I have not seen him since. ²⁹ And if you take this one also from me and he is harmed, you will bring down my gray hairs with sorrow to the grave.'

³⁰ "Now therefore when I come to your servant, my father, and the boy is not with us, as his life is bound up in the boy's life, ³¹ when he sees that the boy is not with us, he will die, and your servants will bring down the gray hairs of your servant, our father, with sorrow to the grave. ³² For your servant became surety for the boy to my father, saying, 'If I fail to bring him to you, then I shall bear the blame to my father forever.'

³³ "Now therefore, please let your servant stay as a slave to my lord instead of the boy, and let the boy go up with his brothers. ³⁴ For how can I go up to my father if the boy is not with me, lest perhaps I see the evil that would find my father?"

Joseph Reveals His Identity

45 Then Joseph could not restrain himself before all who stood by him, and he cried out, "Make every man go out from me." So no man stood with him when Joseph made himself known to his brothers. ² He wept so loudly that the Egyptians and the house of Pharaoh heard about it.

³ Joseph said to his brothers, "I am Joseph. Is my father still alive?" But his brothers could not answer him, for they were dismayed in his presence.

⁴ Joseph said to his brothers, "Please come near to me," and they came near. Then he said, "I am your brother, Joseph, whom you sold into Egypt. ⁵ Now do not be upset or angry with yourselves because you sold me here, for God sent me before you to preserve life. ⁶ For these two years the famine has been in the land, and there are still five years in which there will be neither plowing nor harvesting. ⁷ God sent me ahead of you to preserve you *as* a remnant on the earth and to save your lives by a great deliverance.

⁸ "So now it was not you who sent me here, but God. He has made me a father to Pharaoh and lord of his entire household and a ruler throughout all the land of Egypt. ⁹ Hurry and go up

to my father and say to him, 'This is what your son Joseph says, "God has made me lord of all Egypt. Come down to me; do not delay. ¹⁰ And you will dwell in the land of Goshen, and you will be near me, you and your children and your children's children, along with your flocks, your herds, and all that you have. ¹¹ I will provide for you there, for there are still five years of famine *to come, lest* you and your household, and all that you have, come to poverty." '

¹² "Your eyes and the eyes of my brother Benjamin see that it is my mouth that is speaking to you. ¹³ You must tell my father of all my glory in Egypt and of all that you have seen, and you must hurry and bring my father down here."

¹⁴ Then he fell on his brother Benjamin's neck and wept, and Benjamin wept on his neck. ¹⁵ Moreover he kissed all his brothers and wept on them. After that his brothers talked with him.

¹⁶ When the news reached Pharaoh's palace that Joseph's brothers had come, it pleased Pharaoh and his servants. ¹⁷ Pharaoh said to Joseph, "Say to your brothers, 'Do this. Load your animals and go to the land of Canaan. ¹⁸ Get your father and your households and come to me, and I will give you the best of the land of Egypt, and you shall eat the fat of the land.'

¹⁹ "You are also commanded to say, 'Do this: Take your wagons out of the land of Egypt for your little ones and for your wives, and get your father and come. ²⁰ Also do not concern yourself with your goods, for the best of all the land of Egypt is yours.' "

²¹ So the sons of Israel did so, and Joseph gave them wagons, according to the commandment of Pharaoh, and gave them provisions for the journey. ²² To each of them he gave a change of clothes, but he gave to Benjamin three hundred shekels of silver¹ and five changes of clothes. ²³ To his father he sent the following: ten donkeys loaded with the best things of Egypt and ten female donkeys loaded with grain and bread and provisions for his father on the journey. ²⁴ So he sent his brothers away, and they departed. He said to them, "Do not quarrel on the way."

²⁵ They went up out of Egypt and came to the land of Canaan to Jacob their father. ²⁶ They told him, "Joseph is still alive, and he is governor over all the land of Egypt." And Jacob's heart stood still because he could not believe them. ²⁷ They told him all the words of Joseph, which he had said to them, and when he saw the wagons that Joseph had sent to carry him, the spirit of their father Jacob revived. ²⁸ Then Israel said, "Enough! Joseph my son is still alive. I will go and see him before I die."

Jacob's Journey to Egypt

46 So Israel set out with all that he had and came to Beersheba and offered sacrifices to the God of his father Isaac. ² God spoke to Israel in visions of the night and said, "Jacob, Jacob."

And he said, "Here I am."

³ Then He said, "I am God, the God of your father. Do not be afraid to go down to Egypt, for I will make you into a great nation there. ⁴ I will go down with you to Egypt, and I will also surely bring you back again. And Joseph's own hand shall close your eyes."

⁵ Jacob arose from Beersheba, and the sons of Israel carried Jacob their father and their little ones and their wives in the wagons that Pharaoh had sent to carry him. ⁶ They took their livestock and their possessions that they had acquired in the land of Canaan, and came to Egypt, Jacob and all his descendants with him. ⁷ He brought with him to Egypt his sons and his sons' sons, his daughters and his sons' daughters, and all his descendants.

⁸ These were the names of the sons of Israel, Jacob and his sons, who came to Egypt:

Reuben, Jacob's firstborn.
⁹ The sons of Reuben were
    Hanok, Pallu, Hezron, and Karmi.
¹⁰ The sons of Simeon were
    Jemuel, Jamin, Ohad, Jakin, Zohar, and Shaul the son of a Canaanite woman.

¹¹ The sons of Levi were
    Gershon, Kohath, and Merari.
¹² The sons of Judah were
    Er, Onan, Shelah, Perez, and Zerah (but Er and Onan died in the land of Canaan).
    The sons of Perez were
      Hezron and Hamul.
¹³ The sons of Issachar were
    Tola, Puah, Job, and Shimron.
¹⁴ The sons of Zebulun were
    Sered, Elon, and Jahleel.
¹⁵ These were the sons of Leah, whom she bore to Jacob in Paddan Aram, with his daughter Dinah. All his sons and his daughters *numbered* thirty-three.

¹⁶ And the sons of Gad were
    Zephon, Haggi, Shuni, Ezbon, Eri, Arodi, and Areli.
¹⁷ The sons of Asher were
    Imnah, Ishvah, Ishvi, Beriah,
    and Serah their sister.
    The sons of Beriah:
      Heber and Malkiel.
¹⁸ These were the sons of Zilpah, whom Laban gave to Leah his daughter; and these she bore to Jacob, sixteen in all.

¹⁹ The sons of Rachel, Jacob's wife, were
    Joseph and Benjamin. ²⁰ To Joseph in the land of Egypt were born Manasseh and Ephraim, whom Asenath the daughter of Potiphera, the priest of On, bore to him.
²¹ The sons of Benjamin were
    Bela, Beker, Ashbel, Gera, Naaman, Ehi, Rosh, Muppim, Huppim, and Ard.
²² These were the sons of Rachel who were born to Jacob, fourteen in all.

²³ The son of Dan was
    Hushim.
²⁴ The sons of Naphtali:
    Jahziel,² Guni, Jezer, and Shillem.³
²⁵ These were the sons of Bilhah, whom Laban gave to Rachel his daughter, and she bore these to Jacob, seven in all.

²⁶ All those who came with Jacob to Egypt, who were direct descendants, besides the wives of Jacob's sons, were sixty-six in all. ²⁷ And the sons of Joseph, who were born to him in Egypt, were two. All those of the house of Jacob who came to Egypt were seventy.

Jacob Settles in Goshen

²⁸ Now he sent Judah ahead of him to Joseph to get directions to Goshen. And they came into the land of Goshen. ²⁹ Joseph readied his chariot and went up to Goshen to meet Israel his father. As soon as he appeared to him, he fell on his neck and wept on his neck a long time.

³⁰ Israel said to Joseph, "Now let me die, since I have seen your face, because you are still alive."

³¹ Joseph said to his brothers and to his father's household, "I will go up and tell Pharaoh and say to him, 'My brothers and my father's household, who were in the land of Canaan, have come to me. ³² The men are shepherds; their work has been to feed livestock, and they have brought their flocks and their herds and all that they have.' ³³ When Pharaoh calls you and asks, 'What is your occupation?' ³⁴ you shall say, 'Your servants have been keepers of livestock from our youth even until now, both we and our fathers,' so that you may dwell in the land of Goshen, because every shepherd is an abomination to the Egyptians."

47 Then Joseph went and told Pharaoh, "My father and my brothers and their flocks and their herds and all that they possess have come from the land of Canaan and are *now* in the land of Goshen." ² He took five men from among his brothers and presented them before Pharaoh.

¹22 About 7½ pounds, or 3.5 kilograms.   ²24 *Jahzeel* in Nu 26:48.   ³24 *Shallum* in 1Ch 7:13.

³ Pharaoh asked his brothers, "What is your occupation?" And they said to Pharaoh, "Your servants are shepherds, both we and also our fathers." ⁴ They said to Pharaoh, "We have come to sojourn in the land, for your servants have no pasture for their flocks, because the famine is severe in the land of Canaan. Now therefore, please allow your servants to dwell in the land of Goshen."

⁵ Pharaoh spoke to Joseph, saying, "Your father and your brothers have come to you. ⁶ The land of Egypt is before you. Have your father and your brothers dwell in the best of the land. Have them dwell in the land of Goshen, and if you know any capable men among them, then put them in charge over my livestock."

⁷ Then Joseph brought in Jacob his father and presented him to Pharaoh, and Jacob blessed Pharaoh. ⁸ Pharaoh said to Jacob, "How old are you?"

⁹ And Jacob said to Pharaoh, "The days of the years of my pilgrimage are one hundred and thirty years. My days of the years of my life have been few and evil, and they have not attained to the days of the years of the lives of my fathers in the days of their pilgrimage." ¹⁰ And Jacob blessed Pharaoh and went out from his presence.

¹¹ So Joseph settled his father and his brothers and gave them a possession in the land of Egypt, in the best *part* of the land, in the land of Rameses, as Pharaoh had commanded. ¹² Joseph provided food for his father, his brothers, and his father's entire household, according to the number *of their* children.

Joseph and the Famine

¹³ There was no food in all the land, for the famine was very severe, so that the land of Egypt and all the land of Canaan languished because of the famine. ¹⁴ Joseph gathered up all the money that was found in the land of Egypt and in the land of Canaan for the grain that they bought, and Joseph brought the money into Pharaoh's house. ¹⁵ When the money was all spent in the land of Egypt and in the land of Canaan, all the Egyptians came to Joseph and said, "Give us food, for why should we die in your presence? For our money is gone."

¹⁶ Joseph said, "Give your livestock, and I will give you *food* for your livestock, if *your* money is gone." ¹⁷ They brought their livestock to Joseph, and Joseph gave them food in exchange for the horses, the flocks, the herds, and the donkeys; and he fed them with food in exchange for all their livestock for that year.

¹⁸ When that year was ended, they came to him the second year and said to him, "We will not hide it from our lord, that our money is all spent. Our lord also has our herds of livestock. There is nothing left in the sight of my lord but our bodies and our lands. ¹⁹ Why should we die before your eyes, both we and our land? Buy us and our land for food, and we and our land will be slaves to Pharaoh. Also give us seed, so that we may live and not die, so that the land will not be desolate."

²⁰ So Joseph bought all the land of Egypt for Pharaoh, for every Egyptian man sold his field because the famine was severe on them. So the land became Pharaoh's. ²¹ As for the people, he removed them to cities from one end of the borders of Egypt to the other end. ²² Only the land of the priests he did not buy; for the priests had an allotment from Pharaoh, and they lived off their allotment that Pharaoh gave them. Therefore they did not sell their lands.

²³ Then Joseph said to the people, "I have bought you and your land today for Pharaoh; here is seed for you so you may sow the land. ²⁴ At the harvest, you must give a fifth part to Pharaoh and four parts will be your own, as seed for the field and for your food and for those of your households and for food for your little ones."

²⁵ They said, "You have saved our lives. Let us find grace in the sight of my lord, and we will be Pharaoh's slaves."

²⁶ So Joseph made it a law over the land of Egypt to this day, that Pharaoh should have the fifth part, except from the land of the priests, which did not become Pharaoh's.

Jacob's Request of Joseph

²⁷ Israel lived in the land of Egypt, in the land of Goshen, and they had possessions there and grew and became very numerous.

²⁸ And Jacob lived in the land of Egypt seventeen years, so the years of Jacob's life were one hundred and forty-seven years. ²⁹ When the time drew near when Israel would die, he called his son Joseph and said to him, "If now I have found grace in your sight, please put your hand under my thigh and deal kindly and truly with me. Please do not bury me in Egypt, ³⁰ but let me lie with my fathers. Carry me out of Egypt and bury me in their burial place."

And he said, "I will do as you have said."

³¹ And he said, "Swear to me," and he swore to him. Then Israel bowed himself at the head of his bed.

Jacob Blesses Joseph's Sons

48 After these things, Joseph was told, "Your father is sick." So he took his two sons Manasseh and Ephraim with him. ² When Jacob was told, "Your son Joseph is coming to you," Israel strengthened himself and sat up in the bed.

³ Jacob said to Joseph, "God Almighty appeared to me at Luz in the land of Canaan, and blessed me. ⁴ And He said to me, 'I will make you fruitful and multiply you, and I will make you into a multitude of people and will give this land to your descendants after you for an everlasting possession.'

⁵ "Now your two sons, Ephraim and Manasseh, who were born to you in the land of Egypt before I came to you in Egypt, are mine; as Reuben and Simeon, they shall be mine. ⁶ Any children you have after them will be yours and will be called by the names of their brothers in their inheritance. ⁷ As for me, when I came from Paddan, Rachel died beside me in the land of Canaan on the way, when there was still some distance to get to Ephrath, and I buried her there on the way to Ephrath (that is, Bethlehem)."

⁸ Then Israel saw Joseph's sons and said, "Whose are these?"

⁹ And Joseph said to his father, "They are my sons, whom God has given me in this place."

And he said, "Please bring them to me, and I will bless them." ¹⁰ Now the eyes of Israel were dim with age, so that he could not see. So Joseph brought them near to him, and he kissed them and embraced them.

¹¹ Israel said to Joseph, "I never thought I would see your face, but here God has also shown me your children."

¹² So Joseph took them from beside his knees, and he bowed down with his face to the ground. ¹³ Joseph took them both, Ephraim in his right hand toward Israel's left hand, and Manasseh in his left hand toward Israel's right hand, and brought them near him. ¹⁴ Israel stretched out his right hand and laid it on Ephraim's head, who was the younger, and his left hand on Manasseh's head, crossing his hands, for Manasseh was the firstborn.

¹⁵ He blessed Joseph and said,

"God, before whom my fathers
    Abraham and Isaac walked,
the God who fed me
    all my life long to this day,
¹⁶ the angel who redeemed me from all evil,
    bless the boys;
let them be called by my name,
    and the name of my fathers, Abraham and Isaac;
and let them grow into a multitude
    in the midst of the earth."

¹⁷ When Joseph saw that his father laid his right hand on the head of Ephraim, it displeased him, and he took hold of his father's hand to remove it from Ephraim's head to Manasseh's head. ¹⁸ Joseph said to his father, "Not so, my father, for this one is the firstborn. Put your right hand on his head."

¹⁹ His father refused and said, "I know it, my son, I know it. He will also become a people, and he will also be great, but truly his younger brother shall be greater than he, and his descendants will become a multitude of nations." ²⁰ He blessed them that day, saying,

"By you Israel will bless, saying,
    'May God make you like Ephraim and Manasseh.' "

So he set Ephraim before Manasseh.

²¹ Israel said to Joseph, "I am about to die, but God will be with you and return you again to the land of your fathers. ²² Moreover, I have given to you one portion more than your brothers, which I took out of the hand of the Amorites with my sword and my bow."

Jacob Blesses His Sons

Dt 33:1–29

49 Jacob called to his sons and said, "Gather yourselves together, so that I may tell you what will befall you in the last days.

² Gather yourselves together and hear, sons of Jacob,
    and listen to your father Israel.

³ Reuben, you are my firstborn,
    my might and the beginning of my strength,
    the excellency of dignity, and the excellency
        of power.
⁴ Unstable as water, you shall not excel,
    because you went up to your father's bed;
    then you defiled it—he went up to my couch.

⁵ Simeon and Levi are brothers;
    weapons of violence are their swords.
⁶ Let my soul not enter into their council;
    let my glory not be united with their assembly;
for in their anger they killed men
    and in their self-will they hamstrung oxen.
⁷ Cursed be their anger, for it is fierce;
    and their wrath, for it is cruel!
I will divide them in Jacob
    and scatter them in Israel.

⁸ Judah, your brothers shall praise you;
    your hand shall be on the neck of your enemies;
    your father's sons will bow down before you.
⁹ Judah is a lion's cub;
    from the prey, my son, you have gone up.
He crouches and lies down like a lion;
    and as a lion, who dares rouse him?
¹⁰ The scepter shall not depart from Judah,
    nor a lawgiver from between his feet,
until Shiloh comes;
    and to him will be the obedience of the people.
¹¹ He tethers his foal to the vine,
    and his colt to the choicest vine;
he washes his garments in wine,
    his clothes in the blood of grapes.
¹² His eyes are darker than wine,
    and his teeth whiter than milk.

¹³ Zebulun shall dwell at the haven of the sea;
    and he shall be a haven of ships.
    His border shall be at Sidon.

¹⁴ Issachar is a strong donkey,
    lying down between two burdens;
¹⁵ he saw that a resting place was good,
    and that the land was pleasant;
so he bowed his shoulder to bear the burden
    and became a slave to forced labor.

¹⁶ Dan shall judge his people
    as one of the tribes of Israel.
¹⁷ Dan shall be a serpent by the road,
    a viper on the path,
that bites the horse's heels
    so that its rider will fall backward.

¹⁸ I wait for Your salvation, O LORD!

¹⁹ Gad shall be attacked by raiding bands,
    but he shall raid at their heels.

²⁰ Asher's food shall be rich,
    and he shall yield royal delicacies.

²¹ Naphtali is a doe set loose;
    he gives beautiful words.

²² Joseph is a fruitful bough,
    a fruitful bough by a spring,
    whose branches run over the wall.
²³ The archers bitterly attacked him,
    they shot at him and hated him.
²⁴ But his bow remained firm.
    His arms were agile
because of the hands of the Mighty One of Jacob,
    because of the Shepherd, the Rock of Israel,
²⁵ because of the God of your father who will help you,
    and by the Almighty who will bless you
with blessings from heaven above,
    blessings from the deep that lies beneath,
    the blessings of the breasts and the womb.
²⁶ The blessings of your father have surpassed
    the blessings of my fathers,
    up to the utmost bound of the everlasting hills.
They will be on the head of Joseph,
    and on the crown of the head of him who was set apart
        from his brothers.

²⁷ Benjamin is a ravenous wolf;
    in the morning he devours the prey,
    and at night he divides the spoil."

²⁸ These are all the twelve tribes of Israel, and this is what their father said to them when he blessed them. He blessed them, each with the blessing appropriate to him.

The Death of Jacob

²⁹ Then he charged them and said to them, "I am about to be gathered to my people. Bury me with my fathers in the cave that is in the field of Ephron the Hittite, ³⁰ in the cave that is in the field of Machpelah, which is before Mamre in the land of Canaan, which Abraham bought along with the field from Ephron the Hittite as a burial place. ³¹ They buried Abraham and Sarah his wife there. They buried Isaac and Rebekah his wife there, and I buried Leah there. ³² The field and the cave that is there were purchased from the children of Heth."

³³ When Jacob finished instructing his sons, he drew his feet into the bed, breathed his last, and was gathered to his people.

The Burial of Jacob

50 Then Joseph fell on his father's face and wept over him and kissed him. ² Joseph commanded his servants the physicians to embalm his father. So the physicians embalmed Israel. ³ Forty days were required for him, for such is the time required for those who are embalmed. Then the Egyptians mourned for him seventy days.

⁴ When the days of his mourning were past, Joseph spoke to the household of Pharaoh, saying, "If now I have found favor in your eyes, speak to Pharaoh, saying, ⁵ 'My father made me swear, saying, "I am about to die. Bury me in my tomb which I dug for myself in the land of Canaan." Now therefore please let me go up and bury my father, and then I will return.'"

⁶ Pharaoh said, "Go up and bury your father, as he made you swear to do."

⁷ Joseph went up to bury his father, and all the servants of Pharaoh went up with him too, the elders of his household and all the elders of the land of Egypt, ⁸ all the house of Joseph and his brothers and his father's household. They left only their little ones and their flocks and their herds in the land of Goshen. ⁹ Both the chariot and horsemen also went up with him. It was a very great comp

[10] When they came to the threshing floor of Atad, which is beyond the Jordan, they mourned with a great and very sorrowful lamentation. He observed seven days of mourning for his father. [11] When the inhabitants of the land, the Canaanites, saw the mourning at the threshing floor of Atad, they said, "This is a grievous mourning for the Egyptians." Therefore the place was called Abel Mizraim, which is beyond the Jordan.

[12] So his sons did with him just as he had commanded them. [13] For his sons carried him into the land of Canaan and buried him in the cave of the field of Machpelah, near Mamre, which Abraham bought with the field as a burial site from Ephron the Hittite. [14] After he had buried his father, Joseph returned to Egypt, he and his brothers and all who went up with him to bury his father.

Joseph Reassures His Brothers

[15] When Joseph's brothers saw that their father was dead, they said, "Perhaps Joseph will hate us and will certainly pay us back for all the wrong we did to him." [16] So they sent a message to Joseph, saying, "Your father gave this command before he died: [17] 'Say to Joseph, "I beg you, forgive the transgressions of your brothers and their sin. For they did evil to you." ' Now, please forgive the transgressions of the servants of the God of your father." And Joseph wept when they spoke to him.

[18] Then his brothers also went and fell down before his face and said, "We are your servants."

[19] Joseph said to them, "Do not be afraid, for am I in the place of God? [20] But as for you, you intended to harm me, but God intended it for good, in order to bring it about as it is this day, to save many lives. [21] So now, do not fear. I will provide for you and your little ones." So he comforted them and spoke kindly to them.

The Death of Joseph

[22] Joseph stayed in Egypt, he and his father's household, and Joseph lived one hundred and ten years. [23] Joseph saw Ephraim's children to the third generation. Also, the children of Makir, the son of Manasseh, were brought up on Joseph's knees.

[24] Joseph said to his brothers, "I am about to die. God will surely come to you and bring you out of this land to the land of which He swore to Abraham, to Isaac, and to Jacob." [25] Then Joseph made the sons of Israel swear, saying, "God will surely visit you, and you shall carry up my bones from here."

[26] So Joseph died at the age of one hundred and ten years old, and they embalmed him, and he was put in a coffin in Egypt.

EXODUS

Israel Oppressed

1 Now these are the names of the sons of Israel, which came into Egypt (each man and his household came with Jacob): [2] Reuben, Simeon, Levi, and Judah; [3] Issachar, Zebulun, and Benjamin; [4] Dan, Naphtali, Gad, and Asher. [5] All the people who came from the seed of Jacob were seventy people, but Joseph was in Egypt *already*.

[6] Joseph died, as did all his brothers, and all that generation. [7] Nevertheless, the sons of Israel were fruitful, and increased abundantly, and multiplied, and became exceedingly mighty,[1] so that the land was filled with them.

[8] Now there rose up a new king over Egypt, who did not know Joseph. [9] He said to his people, "Surely, the people of the sons of Israel are more numerous and powerful than we. [10] Come, let us deal wisely with them, lest they multiply, and it come to pass that when any war breaks out, they also join our enemies, and fight against us, and escape from the land."

[11] Therefore they set taskmasters over them to afflict them with their labor. They built for Pharaoh storage cities: Pithom and Rameses. [12] But the more they afflicted them, the more they multiplied and grew so that as a result they abhorred the sons of Israel. [13] The Egyptians made the children of Israel to serve with rigor, [14] and they made their lives bitter with hard service—in mortar and in brick, and in all manner of service in the field, all their service in which they made them serve was with rigor.

[15] The king of Egypt spoke to the Hebrew midwives, of which the name of one was Shiphrah, and the name of the other Puah, [16] and he said, "When you perform the office of a midwife to the Hebrew women and see them on the stools, if it is a son, then you must kill him, but if it is a daughter, then she may live." [17] However, the midwives feared God, and did not do as the king of Egypt commanded them, but kept the male children alive. [18] The king of Egypt called for the midwives and said to them, "Why have you done this thing and preserved the male children's lives?"

[19] The midwives said to Pharaoh, "Because the Hebrew women are not like the Egyptian women, for they are vigorous and give birth before the midwives come to them."

[20] Therefore God dealt well with the midwives, and the people multiplied and grew very mighty. [21] So it happened that because the midwives feared God, He gave them families.

[22] Pharaoh charged all his people, saying, "You must cast every son that is born into the river, and you must preserve every daughter's life."

The Birth of Moses

2 Now a man of the house of Levi went and married a daughter of Levi. [2] And the woman conceived and bore a son, and when she saw him, that he was a beautiful child, she hid him three months. [3] When she could no longer hide him, she took for him a container *made* of bulrushes and daubed it with tar and with pitch. She then put the child in it and set it in the reeds by the river's bank. [4] Then his sister stood afar off so that she might know what would happen to him.

[5] The daughter of Pharaoh came down to wash herself at the river while her maidens walked along by the river's side, and when she saw the container among the reeds, she sent her maid, and she retrieved it. [6] When she opened it, she saw the child. He was crying. She had compassion on him and said, "This is one of the Hebrews' children."

[7] Then his sister said to Pharaoh's daughter, "Shall I go and call for you a nursing woman of the Hebrew women so that she may nurse the child for you?"

[8] And Pharaoh's daughter said to her, "Go." So the young girl went and called the child's mother. [9] Pharaoh's daughter said to her, "Take this child away, and nurse him for me, and I will give you your wages." So the woman took the child and nursed him. [10] Now the child grew, and she brought him to Pharaoh's daughter, and he became her son. And she called his name Moses and said, "Because I drew him out of the water."

[11] In those days, when Moses was grown, he went out to his brothers and looked on their burdens; and he saw an Egyptian striking a Hebrew, one of his brothers. [12] He looked this way and that way, and when he saw no one, he killed the Egyptian and hid

---

[1] 7 Or *numerous*; also in v. 20.

him in the sand. ¹³ When he went out the next day, two men of the Hebrews struggled with each other; and he said to him that did the wrong, "Why do you strike your companion?"

¹⁴ He said, "Who made you a prince and a judge over us? Do you intend to kill me as you killed the Egyptian?" Moses feared and said, "Surely this thing is known."

Moses Flees to Midian

¹⁵ Now when Pharaoh heard this thing, he sought to slay Moses. But Moses fled from the presence of Pharaoh and settled in the land of Midian, and he dwelled by a well. ¹⁶ Now the priest of Midian had seven daughters, and they came and drew water, and filled the troughs to water their father's flock. ¹⁷ Then shepherds came and drove them away, but Moses stood up and helped them, and watered their flock.

¹⁸ When they came to Reuel their father, he said, "Why is it you have come *back* so soon today?"

¹⁹ And they said, "An Egyptian delivered us out of the hand of the shepherds and also drew water for us and watered the flock."

²⁰ He said to his daughters, "So where is he? Why is it that you have left the man? Call him so that he may eat bread."

²¹ Moses was content to dwell with the man, and he gave Zipporah, his daughter, to Moses. ²² Then she gave birth to a son, and he called his name Gershom, for he said, "I have been a sojourner in a foreign land."

²³ In the passing of time the king of Egypt died. And the children of Israel sighed because of the bondage, and they cried out, and their cry came up to God on account of the bondage. ²⁴ God heard their groaning, and God remembered His covenant with Abraham, Isaac, and Jacob. ²⁵ God looked on the children of Israel, and God had concern for them.

Moses at the Burning Bush

3 Now Moses kept the flock of Jethro his father-in-law, the priest of Midian, and he led the flock to the far side of the desert and came to the mountain of God, to Horeb. ² The angel of the LORD appeared to him in a flame of fire from the midst of a bush, and he looked, and the bush burned with fire, but the bush was not consumed. ³ So Moses said, "I will now turn aside and see this great sight, why the bush is not burnt."

⁴ When the LORD saw that he turned aside to see, God called to him from out of the midst of the bush and said, "Moses, Moses." And he said, "Here am I."

⁵ He said, "Do not approach here. Remove your sandals from off your feet, for the place on which you are standing is holy ground." ⁶ Moreover He said, "I am the God of your father, the God of Abraham, the God of Isaac, and the God of Jacob." And Moses hid his face, for he was afraid to look upon God.

⁷ The LORD said, "I have surely seen the affliction of My people who are in Egypt and have heard their cry on account of their taskmasters, for I know their sorrows. ⁸ Therefore, I have come down to deliver them out of the hand of the Egyptians, and to bring them up out of that land to a good and spacious land, to a land flowing with milk and honey, to the place of the Canaanites, the Hittites, the Amorites, the Perizzites, the Hivites, and the Jebusites. ⁹ Now therefore, the cry of the children of Israel has come to Me. Moreover, I have also seen the oppression with which the Egyptians are oppressing them. ¹⁰ Come now therefore, and I will send you to Pharaoh so that you may bring forth My people, the children of Israel, out of Egypt."

¹¹ Moses said to God, "Who am I that I should go to Pharaoh and that I should bring forth the children of Israel out of Egypt?"

¹² And He said, "Certainly I will be with you, and this will be a sign to you, that I have sent you: When you have brought forth the people out of Egypt, all of you shall serve God on this mountain."

¹³ Moses said to God, "I am going to the children of Israel and will say to them, 'The God of your fathers has sent me to you.' When they say to me, 'What is His name?' what shall I say to them?"

¹⁴ And God said to Moses, "I AM WHO I AM,"¹ and He said, "You will say this to the children of Israel, 'I AM has sent me to you.' "

¹⁵ God, moreover, said to Moses, "Thus you will say to the children of Israel, 'The LORD, the God of your fathers, the God of Abraham, the God of Isaac, and the God of Jacob, has sent me to you. This is My name forever, and this is My memorial to all generations.'

¹⁶ "Go, and gather the elders of Israel together, and say to them, 'The LORD, the God of your fathers, the God of Abraham, of Isaac, and of Jacob, appeared to me, saying, "I am indeed concerned about you and what has been done to you in Egypt. ¹⁷ Therefore, I said, I will bring you up out of the affliction of Egypt to the land of the Canaanites, the Hittites, the Amorites, the Perizzites, the Hivites, and the Jebusites, to a land flowing with milk and honey." '

¹⁸ "They shall listen to your voice, and you shall come, you and the elders of Israel, to the king of Egypt, and you must say to him, 'The LORD, the God of the Hebrews has met with us. Therefore, now, let us go, we ask you, three days' journey into the wilderness so that we may sacrifice to the LORD our God.' ¹⁹ However, I know that the king of Egypt will not let you go, no, not even under a forceful hand. ²⁰ So I will stretch out My hand and strike Egypt with all My wonders which I will perform in its midst, and after that he will let you go.

²¹ "I will give this people favor in the sight of the Egyptians, and it will come to pass, that, when you go, you will not go empty-handed. ²² But every woman will borrow of her neighbor, and of her that sojourns in her house, articles of silver, and articles of gold, and clothing, and you will put them on your sons, and on your daughters—in this way you will plunder the Egyptians."

Moses' Miraculous Signs

4 And Moses answered and said, "But they will not believe me, nor listen to my voice. For they will say, 'The LORD has not appeared to you.' "

² The LORD said to him, "What is that in your hand?" And he said, "A rod."

³ He said, "Throw it on the ground." And he threw it on the ground, and it became a serpent. Then Moses fled from it. ⁴ Then the LORD said to Moses, "Put forth your hand and take it by the tail." And he put forth his hand, and caught it, and it became a rod in his hand. ⁵ "*This is so* that they may believe that the LORD, the God of their fathers, the God of Abraham, the God of Isaac, and the God of Jacob, has appeared to you."

⁶ The LORD said furthermore to him, "Now put your hand into your bosom." He put his hand into his bosom, and when he took it out, his hand was as leprous as snow.

⁷ He said, "Put your hand into your bosom again." So he put his hand into his bosom again and brought it out of his bosom, and it was restored like his other flesh.

⁸ "If they will not believe you, nor listen to the voice of the first sign, then they may believe the voice of the latter sign. ⁹ But if they will not believe also these two signs or listen to your voice, then you shall take water from the river and pour it on the dry land, and the water which you take out of the river will become blood on the dry land."

¹⁰ Then Moses said to the LORD, "O my Lord, I am not eloquent, neither before nor since You have spoken to Your servant. But I am slow of speech, and of a slow tongue."

¹¹ The LORD said to him, "Who has made man's mouth? Or who made the dumb, or deaf, or the seeing, or the blind? Have not I, the LORD? ¹² Now therefore go, and I will be with your mouth and teach you what you must say."

¹³ He said, "O my Lord, send, I pray, by the hand of whomever else You will send."

¹⁴ The anger of the LORD was inflamed against Moses, and He said, "Is not Aaron the Levite your brother? I know that he can speak well. And also, he comes out to meet you, and when he sees you, he will be glad in his heart. ¹⁵ You shall speak to him and put the words in his mouth, and I will be with your mouth, and with his mouth, and will teach you what you must do. ¹⁶ What's more, he will be your spokesman to the people, and he will be as a mouth for you, and you will be as God to him. ¹⁷ You must take this rod in your hand, with which you will perform the signs."

---

¹ 14 The Heb. *to be*, related to the covenantal name of God translated *Lord*.

Moses Returns to Egypt

[18] Moses went and returned to Jethro his father-in-law and said to him, "Please let me go and return to my brothers who are in Egypt, and see whether they be yet alive."

And Jethro said to Moses, "Go in peace."

[19] The LORD said to Moses in Midian, "Go, return to Egypt, for all the men are dead who sought your life." [20] Moses took his wife and his sons and set them on a donkey, and he returned to the land of Egypt. And Moses took the rod of God in his hand.

[21] The LORD said to Moses, "When you go to return into Egypt, see that you do all those wonders before Pharaoh, which I have put in your hand, but I will harden his heart, so that he shall not let the people go. [22] You shall say to Pharaoh, 'Thus says the LORD: Israel is My son, even My firstborn. [23] So I say to you, "Let My son go, that he may serve Me. And if you refuse to let him go, I will slay your son, even your firstborn." ' "

[24] At a lodging place on the way, the LORD met him and sought to kill him. [25] Then Zipporah took a sharp stone, and cut off the foreskin of her son, and threw it at his feet, and said, "Surely a bloody husband are you to me." [26] So He let him go. Then she said, "A bloody husband *you are*, because of the circumcision."

[27] Now the LORD said to Aaron, "Go into the wilderness to meet Moses." So he went, and met him at the mount of God, and kissed him. [28] Moses told Aaron all the words of the LORD who had sent him, and all the signs which He had commanded him.

[29] Moses and Aaron went and gathered together all the elders of the children of Israel. [30] And Aaron spoke all the words which the LORD had spoken to Moses and did the signs in the sight of the people. [31] And the people believed. And when they heard that the LORD had visited the children of Israel and that He had looked on their affliction, they bowed down and worshipped.

Bricks Without Straw

5 And afterward Moses and Aaron went in and said to Pharaoh, "Thus says the LORD, the God of Israel, 'Let My people go, that they may hold a feast to Me in the wilderness.' "

[2] And Pharaoh said, "Who is the LORD that I should obey His voice to let Israel go? I do not know the LORD, nor will I let Israel go."

[3] They said, "The God of the Hebrews has met with us. Let us go, we pray you, three days' journey into the wilderness, and sacrifice to the LORD our God, lest He fall upon us with pestilence or with the sword."

[4] But the king of Egypt said to them, "Why do you, Moses and Aaron, take the people from their work? Get back to your labor." [5] Pharaoh said, "Look, the people of the land now are numerous, and you make them rest from their labor."

[6] Pharaoh commanded the same day the taskmasters of the people and their officers, saying, [7] "You shall no more give the people straw to make brick, as before. Let them go and gather straw for themselves. [8] However, the quota of the bricks, which they were making previously, you shall lay upon them. You shall not diminish any of it. For they are idle. Therefore they cry out, saying, 'Let us go and sacrifice to our God.' [9] Let there be more work laid upon the men so that they may labor therein, and let them not regard deceptive words."

[10] The taskmasters of the people and their officers went out, and they spoke to the people, saying, "Thus says Pharaoh, 'I will not give you straw. [11] Go, get straw where you can find it, yet nothing of your work shall be diminished.' " [12] So the people scattered abroad throughout all the land of Egypt to gather stubble for straw. [13] The taskmasters pushed them, saying, "Fulfill your works, your daily tasks, just as when there was straw." [14] The officers of the children of Israel, which Pharaoh's taskmasters had set over them, were beaten and were asked, and demanded, "Why have you not fulfilled your task in making brick both yesterday and today, as previously?"

[15] Then the officers of the children of Israel came and cried to Pharaoh, saying, "Why do you deal this way with your servants? [16] There is no straw being given to your servants, and they say to us, 'Make brick.' And indeed, your servants are beaten, but the fault is in your *own* people."

[17] But he said, "You are slackers! Slackers! Therefore you say, 'Let us go and do sacrifice to the LORD.' [18] Go therefore now and work, for there shall be no straw given you, yet shall you deliver the quota of bricks."

[19] The officers of the children of Israel saw that they were in trouble, after it was said, "You shall not diminish anything from your bricks of your daily task." [20] Then they met Moses and Aaron, who stood in the way, as they came forth from Pharaoh. [21] And they said to them, "May the LORD look on you and judge, because you have made our scent stink in the estimation of Pharaoh and in the estimation of his servants, to put a sword in their hand to slay us."

God Promises Deliverance

[22] Moses returned to the LORD, and said, "Lord, why have You caused trouble for this people? Why is it that You have sent me? [23] For since I came to Pharaoh to speak in Your name, he has done evil to this people; neither have You delivered Your people at all."

6 Then the LORD said to Moses, "Now you shall see what I will do to Pharaoh, for with a strong hand shall he let them go, and with a strong hand shall he drive them out of his land."

[2] Then God spoke to Moses, and said to him, "I am the LORD, [3] and I appeared to Abraham, to Isaac, and to Jacob, by the name of God Almighty, but by My name, The LORD, I was not known to them. [4] I have also established My covenant with them, to give them the land of Canaan, the land of their pilgrimage, wherein they sojourned. [5] I have also heard the groaning of the children of Israel, whom the Egyptians keep in bondage, and I have remembered My covenant.

[6] "Therefore say to the children of Israel: 'I am the LORD, and I will bring you out from under the burdens of the Egyptians, and I will rid you out of their bondage, and I will redeem you with a stretched-out arm and with great judgments. [7] And I will take you to Me for a people, and I will be to you a God. And you shall know that I am the LORD your God, who brings you out from under the burdens of the Egyptians. [8] I will bring you into the land, which I swore to give to Abraham, to Isaac, and to Jacob, and I will give it to you for a heritage. I am the LORD.' "

[9] Moses spoke so to the children of Israel, but they did not listen to Moses on account of *their* anguish of spirit and for cruel bondage.

[10] The LORD spoke to Moses, saying, [11] "Go in, tell Pharaoh king of Egypt to let the children of Israel go out of his land."

[12] Moses spoke before the LORD, saying, "The children of Israel have not listened to me. How then shall Pharaoh listen to me, as I am of uncircumcised lips?"

[13] And the LORD spoke to Moses and to Aaron, and gave them a command for the children of Israel, and for Pharaoh, king of Egypt, to bring the children of Israel out of the land of Egypt.

The Genealogy of Moses and Aaron

[14] These are the heads of their fathers' houses:

The sons of Reuben the firstborn of Israel: Hanok, Pallu, Hezron, and Karmi. These are the families of Reuben.

[15] The sons of Simeon: Jemuel, Jamin, Ohad, Jakin, Zohar, and Shaul the son of a Canaanite woman. These are the families of Simeon.

[16] These are the names of the sons of Levi according to their generations: Gershon, Kohath, and Merari, and the years of the life of Levi were one hundred and thirty-seven years.

[17] The sons of Gershon: Libni, and Shimei, according to their families.

[18] The sons of Kohath: Amram, Izhar, Hebron, and Uzziel, and the years of the life of Kohath were one hundred and thirty-three years.

[19] The sons of Merari: Mahli and Mushi.

These are the families of Levi according to their generations.

[20] Now Amram married Jochebed his father's sister, and she bore him Aaron and Moses. And the years of the life of Amram were one hundred and thirty-seven years.

[21] The sons of Izhar: Korah, Nepheg, and Zikri.

[22] The sons of Uzziel: Mishael, Elzaphan, and Sithri.

[23] Aaron took to himself Elisheba, daughter of Amminadab, sister of Nahshon, to wife; and she bore him Nadab, Abihu, Eleazar, and Ithamar.

[24] The sons of Korah: Assir, Elkanah, and Abiasaph. These are the families of the Korahites.

²⁵ Eleazar, Aaron's son, married one of the daughters of Putiel, and she bore him Phinehas.

These are the heads of the fathers of the Levites according to their families.

²⁶ It was that Aaron and Moses to whom the LORD said, "Bring out the children of Israel from the land of Egypt according to their armies." ²⁷ They are the ones who spoke to Pharaoh king of Egypt to bring out the children of Israel from Egypt. It was that Moses and Aaron.

Aaron to Speak for Moses
²⁸ On the day when the LORD spoke to Moses in the land of Egypt, ²⁹ the LORD spoke to Moses, saying, "I am the LORD. Speak to Pharaoh the king of Egypt all that I say to you."

³⁰ However, Moses said before the LORD, "Listen! I am unskilled in speech, so how will Pharaoh listen to me?"

7 So the LORD said to Moses, "See, I have made you a god to Pharaoh, and Aaron your brother will be your prophet. ² You shall speak all that I command you, and Aaron your brother shall tell Pharaoh to send the children of Israel out of his land. ³ But I will harden Pharaoh's heart and multiply My signs and My wonders in the land of Egypt. ⁴ Nevertheless, Pharaoh will not listen to you, so that I may lay My hand upon Egypt and bring forth My armies and My people, the children of Israel, out of the land of Egypt by great judgments. ⁵ And the Egyptians shall know that I am the LORD when I stretch forth My hand upon Egypt and bring out the children of Israel from among them."

⁶ So Moses and Aaron did it. Just as the LORD commanded them, so they did. ⁷ Moses was eighty years old, and Aaron was eighty-three years old when they spoke to Pharaoh.

Aaron's Rod Becomes a Snake
⁸ Now the LORD spoke to Moses and to Aaron, saying, ⁹ "When Pharaoh shall speak to you, saying, 'Show a miracle,' then you shall say to Aaron, 'Take your rod, and throw it before Pharaoh,' and it shall become a serpent."

¹⁰ So Moses and Aaron went to Pharaoh, and they did what the LORD had commanded. And Aaron threw down his rod before Pharaoh and before his servants, and it became a serpent. ¹¹ Then Pharaoh also called the wise men and the sorcerers. Then the magicians of Egypt likewise performed with their secret arts. ¹² For every man threw down his rod, and they became serpents. But Aaron's rod swallowed up their rods. ¹³ Nonetheless, Pharaoh's heart hardened so that he would not listen to them, just as the LORD had said.

The First Plague: Waters Turn to Blood
¹⁴ The LORD said to Moses, "Pharaoh's heart is hardened. He refuses to let the people go. ¹⁵ Go to Pharaoh in the morning as he goes out to the water, and you shall stand by the river's bank to meet him. You must take the rod which was turned to a serpent in your hand. ¹⁶ Then you are to say to him, 'The LORD, the God of the Hebrews, has sent me to you, saying, "Let My people go, so that they may serve Me in the wilderness." But up to this point you have not listened! ¹⁷ Thus says the LORD, "In this you shall know that I am the LORD: Indeed, I will strike the waters of the Nile with the rod that is in my hand, and they shall be turned to blood. ¹⁸ And the fish that are in the river shall die, and the river shall stink so that the Egyptians shall be weary of drinking the river's water." ' "

¹⁹ Then the LORD spoke to Moses, "Say to Aaron, 'Take your rod, and stretch out your hand over the waters of Egypt, over their rivers, over their canals, over their ponds, and over all their pools of water, so that they may become blood. And there will be blood throughout all the land of Egypt, both in vessels of wood, and in vessels of stone.' "

²⁰ Moses and Aaron did so, just as the LORD commanded. And he lifted up the rod and struck the waters that were in the river, in the sight of Pharaoh, and in the sight of his servants, and all the waters that were in the river were turned to blood. ²¹ The fish that were in the river died, the river stank, and the Egyptians could not drink of the water of the river. Blood was everywhere throughout the land of Egypt.

²² Nevertheless, the magicians of Egypt did the same with their secret arts, and Pharaoh's heart was hardened, and he did not listen to them, as the LORD had said. ²³ Then Pharaoh turned and went into his house, and he did not concern himself with this either. ²⁴ So all the Egyptians dug around about the river for water to drink, because they could not drink of the water of the river.

²⁵ Seven days passed after the LORD had struck the river.

The Second Plague: Frogs
8 Then the LORD said to Moses, "Go to Pharaoh and say to him, 'Thus says the LORD: Let My people go, so that they may serve Me. ² But if you refuse to let them go, then I will plague all your borders with frogs. ³ And the river will swarm with frogs, which shall go up and come into your house, and into your bedchamber, and on your bed, and into the houses of your servants, and on your people, and into your ovens, and into your kneading troughs. ⁴ So the frogs shall come upon you, upon your people, and upon all your servants.' "

⁵ Then the LORD said to Moses, "Say to Aaron, 'Stretch forth your hand with your rod over the streams, over the rivers, and over the ponds, and cause frogs to come up on the land of Egypt.' "

⁶ Aaron stretched out his hand over the waters of Egypt, and the frogs came up, and covered the land of Egypt. ⁷ The magicians did the same with their secret arts and brought up frogs upon the land of Egypt.

⁸ Then Pharaoh called for Moses and Aaron, and said, "Entreat the LORD, that He may take away the frogs from me, and from my people, and I will let the people go, so that they may sacrifice to the LORD."

⁹ Moses said to Pharaoh, "Glory yourself over me: When shall I entreat for you, your servants, and your people, to destroy the frogs from you and your houses, that they may remain in the river only?"

¹⁰ And he said, "Tomorrow."

Then he said, "Be it according to your word, in order that you may know that there is no one like the LORD our God. ¹¹ The frogs shall depart from you, and from your houses, from your servants, and from your people. They shall remain in the river only."

¹² Moses and Aaron went out from Pharaoh, and Moses cried out to the LORD concerning the frogs which he had brought against Pharaoh. ¹³ Then the LORD did according to the word of Moses. And the frogs died out of the houses, the villages, and the fields. ¹⁴ So they gathered them together in heaps, and the land stank. ¹⁵ But when Pharaoh saw that there was relief, he hardened his heart and did not listen to them, as the LORD had said.

The Third Plague: Gnats
¹⁶ Then the LORD said to Moses, "Say to Aaron, 'Stretch out your rod, and strike the dust of the land, so that it may become gnats throughout all the land of Egypt.' " ¹⁷ They did so, for Aaron stretched out his hand with his rod and smote the dust of the earth, and it became gnats on man and on beast. All the dust of the land became gnats throughout all the land of Egypt. ¹⁸ Then the magicians tried with their secret arts to bring forth gnats, but they could not, so there were gnats upon man and beast.

¹⁹ Then the magicians said to Pharaoh, "This is the finger of God." Nevertheless, Pharaoh's heart was hardened, and he did not listen to them, just as the LORD had said.

The Fourth Plague: Flies
²⁰ So the LORD said to Moses, "Rise up early in the morning and stand before Pharaoh as he comes forth to the water and say to him, 'Thus says the LORD: Let My people go, so that they may serve Me. ²¹ Otherwise, if you will not let My people go, indeed I will send swarms of flies on you, and on your servants, and on your people, and into your houses. And the houses of the Egyptians shall be full of swarms of flies and also the ground wherever they are.

²² " 'I will in that day set apart the land of Goshen, in which My people dwell, so that no swarms of flies shall be there, in order that you may know that I am the LORD in the midst of the earth.

²³ I will put a division between My people and your people. Tomorrow this sign will happen.' "

²⁴ The Lᴏʀᴅ did so, and great swarms *of flies* came into the house of Pharaoh, and into his servants' houses, and into all the land of Egypt. The land was corrupted because of the swarms *of flies*.

²⁵ Pharaoh called for Moses and Aaron, and said, "Go, sacrifice to your God in the land."

²⁶ Moses said, "It is not right to do so, for what we shall sacrifice to the Lᴏʀᴅ our God would be an abomination to the Egyptians. If we shall sacrifice what is an abomination of the Egyptians before their eyes, will they not stone us? ²⁷ We will go three days' journey into the wilderness, and then we will sacrifice to the Lᴏʀᴅ our God, as He shall command us."

²⁸ Pharaoh said, "I will let you go, that you may sacrifice to the Lᴏʀᴅ your God in the wilderness. Only you shall not go very far away. Make entreaty for me."

²⁹ Moses said, "Indeed, I am leaving you, and I will plead with the Lᴏʀᴅ that the swarms *of flies* may depart from Pharaoh, from his servants, and from his people tomorrow. But let not Pharaoh deal deceitfully any more by not letting the people go to sacrifice to the Lᴏʀᴅ."

³⁰ Moses went away from Pharaoh and entreated the Lᴏʀᴅ. ³¹ Then the Lᴏʀᴅ did according to the word of Moses, and He removed the swarms *of flies* from Pharaoh, from his servants, and from his people. Not one remained. ³² Nevertheless, Pharaoh hardened his heart at this time also, nor would he let the people go.

The Fifth Plague: Livestock Die

9 Then the Lᴏʀᴅ said to Moses, "Go to Pharaoh, and speak to him, 'Thus says the Lᴏʀᴅ, the God of the Hebrews: Let My people go, so that they may serve Me. ² For if you refuse to let *them* go and continue holding them, ³ indeed, the hand of the Lᴏʀᴅ will be upon your livestock which are in the field, upon the horses, upon the donkeys, upon the camels, upon the oxen, and upon the sheep. There shall be a very grievous pestilence. ⁴ The Lᴏʀᴅ shall separate between the livestock of Israel and the livestock of Egypt, and nothing shall die of all that belongs to the children of Israel.' "

⁵ So the Lᴏʀᴅ appointed a set time, saying, "Tomorrow the Lᴏʀᴅ shall do this thing in the land." ⁶ Then the Lᴏʀᴅ did this thing the next day, so that all the livestock of Egypt died, but not one of the livestock of the children of Israel died. ⁷ Pharaoh sent, and there was not one of the livestock of the children of Israel dead. And the heart of Pharaoh was hardened, so that he did not let the people go.

The Sixth Plague: Boils

⁸ Then the Lᴏʀᴅ said to Moses and to Aaron, "Take for yourselves handfuls of ashes from a kiln, and let Moses toss it toward the heavens in the sight of Pharaoh. ⁹ It shall become fine dust over all the land of Egypt and shall be a boil breaking forth with blisters upon man and beast, throughout all the land of Egypt."

¹⁰ So they took the ashes from a kiln and stood before Pharaoh. Then Moses tossed it up toward the heavens, and it became a boil breaking forth with blisters upon man and beast. ¹¹ The magicians could not stand before Moses because of the boils, for the boils were upon the magicians and upon all the Egyptians. ¹² Moreover, the Lᴏʀᴅ hardened the heart of Pharaoh, so that he did not listen to them, just as the Lᴏʀᴅ had spoken to Moses.

The Seventh Plague: Hail

¹³ Then the Lᴏʀᴅ said to Moses, "Rise up early in the morning, and stand before Pharaoh, and say to him, 'Thus says the Lᴏʀᴅ, the God of the Hebrews: Let My people go, so that they may serve Me. ¹⁴ For I will at this time send all My plagues upon you and your servants and your people, so that you may know that there is none like Me in all the earth. ¹⁵ For by now I could have stretched out My hand, so that I might strike you and your people with pestilence, and you would be cut off from the earth. ¹⁶ But, indeed, for this cause I have raised you up, in order to show in you My power and so that My name may be declared throughout all the earth. ¹⁷ Still, you exalt yourself against My people by forbidding them to go. ¹⁸ Certainly, tomorrow about this time I will cause it to rain a very severe hail, such as has not happened in Egypt since

it was founded until now. ¹⁹ Send therefore now and bring your livestock and all that you have in the field to safety. Every man and beast which shall be found in the field and not brought home when the hail comes down upon them will die.' "

²⁰ He that feared the word of the Lᴏʀᴅ among the servants of Pharaoh made his servants and his livestock flee into the houses. ²¹ But he that failed to regard the word of the Lᴏʀᴅ left his servants and his livestock in the field.

²² So the Lᴏʀᴅ said to Moses, "Stretch forth your hand toward the heavens, so that there may be hail in all the land of Egypt, upon man and beast, and upon every herb of the field, throughout the land of Egypt." ²³ Moses stretched forth his rod toward the heavens, and the Lᴏʀᴅ sent thunder and hail, and fire ran along upon the ground. So the Lᴏʀᴅ rained hail upon the land of Egypt. ²⁴ So there was hail, and fire mingled with the hail. It was so severe that there had been none like it in all the land of Egypt since it became a nation. ²⁵ The hail struck all the land of Egypt, all that was in the field, both man and beast, and the hail struck every herb of the field and broke every tree of the field. ²⁶ Only in the land of Goshen, where the children of Israel *were*, was there no hail.

²⁷ Then Pharaoh sent and called for Moses and Aaron, and said to them, "I have sinned this time. The Lᴏʀᴅ is righteous, and I and my people are wicked. ²⁸ Entreat the Lᴏʀᴅ, for there has been enough of God's mighty thunder and hail, and I will let you go, and you shall stay no longer."

²⁹ Moses said to him, "As soon as I am gone out of the city, I will spread out my hands to the Lᴏʀᴅ. The thunder shall cease, and there shall no longer be any more hail, so that you may know that the earth is the Lᴏʀᴅ's. ³⁰ But as for you and your servants, I know that you will not yet fear the Lᴏʀᴅ God."

³¹ Now the flax and the barley were struck, for the barley was in the ear, and the flax was in bud. ³² But the wheat and the spelt were not struck, for they grow up later.

³³ So Moses went out of the city from Pharaoh and spread out his hands to the Lᴏʀᴅ, and the thunders and hail ceased, and the rain was no longer poured upon the earth. ³⁴ However, when Pharaoh saw that the rain and the hail and the thunders were ceased, he sinned yet more, and hardened his heart, he and his servants. ³⁵ The heart of Pharaoh hardened, and he would not let the children of Israel go, just as the Lᴏʀᴅ had spoken by Moses.

The Eighth Plague: Locusts

10 Then the Lᴏʀᴅ said to Moses, "Go to Pharaoh, for I have hardened his heart and the heart of his servants, that I might show these signs of Mine before him, ² in order that you may tell in the hearing of your son, and of your son's son, what things I have done in Egypt, and My signs which I have done among them, that you may know that I am the Lᴏʀᴅ."

³ Moses and Aaron came to Pharaoh and said to him, "Thus says the Lᴏʀᴅ, the God of the Hebrews, 'How long will you refuse to humble yourself before Me? Let My people go, that they may serve Me. ⁴ For if you refuse to let My people go, indeed, tomorrow I will bring locusts into your territory. ⁵ And they shall cover the face of the earth, such that no one will be able to see the earth. What's more, they shall eat the remainder of that which has escaped—that which remains to you from the hail—and shall eat every tree which grows for you out of the field. ⁶ And they shall fill your houses, and the houses of all your servants, and the houses of all the Egyptians—which neither your fathers, nor your fathers' fathers have seen since the day that they were on the earth until this day.' " And he turned and went out from Pharaoh.

⁷ Then Pharaoh's servants said to him, "How long shall this man be a snare to us? Let the men go, so that they may serve the Lᴏʀᴅ their God. Do you not yet know that Egypt is destroyed?"

⁸ So Moses and Aaron were brought back to Pharaoh, and he said to them, "Go, serve the Lᴏʀᴅ your God! But who are the ones that shall go?"

⁹ And Moses said, "We will go with our young and our old, with our sons and our daughters, with our flocks and our herds will we go, for *we must hold* a feast to the Lᴏʀᴅ."

¹⁰ Then he said to them, "The Lᴏʀᴅ indeed be with you when I let you and your little ones go. Beware, for evil is before you.

¹¹ Not so! Go now, you that are men, and serve the Lord, for that is what you desire." Then they were driven out from Pharaoh's presence.

¹² Then the Lord said to Moses, "Stretch out your hand over the land of Egypt for the locusts, so that they may come up upon the land of Egypt and eat every herb of the land, even all that the hail has left."

¹³ So Moses stretched forth his rod over the land of Egypt; then the Lord brought an east wind upon the land all that day and all that night. And when it was morning, the east wind brought the locusts. ¹⁴ The locusts went up over all the land of Egypt and settled down in all the territory of Egypt. They were very grievous. Never before had there been such locusts as they, nor would there be such ever again. ¹⁵ For they covered the face of the whole earth, so that the land was darkened, and they ate every herb of the land, and all the fruit of the trees which the hail had left. As a result, nothing green remained there in the trees or herbs of the field, through all the land of Egypt.

¹⁶ Then Pharaoh called for Moses and Aaron in haste and said, "I have sinned against the Lord, your God, and against you. ¹⁷ Now therefore please forgive my sin only this once, and entreat the Lord your God, so that He may take away from me this death only."

¹⁸ So he went out from Pharaoh and prayed to the Lord. ¹⁹ Then the Lord turned a mighty strong west wind, which took away the locusts and threw them into the Red Sea. Not one locust remained in all the territory of Egypt. ²⁰ But the Lord hardened Pharaoh's heart, so that he would not let the children of Israel go.

The Ninth Plague: Darkness

²¹ Then the Lord said to Moses, "Stretch out your hand toward the heavens, so that there may be darkness over the land of Egypt, a darkness *which* may be felt." ²² So Moses stretched forth his hand toward the heavens, and there was a thick darkness in all the land of Egypt for three days. ²³ They did not see one another; nor did anyone rise from his place for three days. But all the children of Israel had light in their dwellings.

²⁴ Then Pharaoh called to Moses and said, "Go, serve the Lord. Only let your flocks and your herds be detained. Even let your little ones also go with you."

²⁵ But Moses said, "You must also give us sacrifices and burnt offerings, so that we may sacrifice to the Lord our God. ²⁶ Our livestock will go with us also. Not a hoof will be left behind, for we must take of them to serve the Lord our God. And we do not know with what we must serve the Lord, until we get there."

²⁷ But the Lord hardened Pharaoh's heart, and he would not let them go. ²⁸ So Pharaoh said to him, "Get away from me! Watch yourself, do not see my face anymore; for in the day you see my face you shall die."

²⁹ Then Moses said, "As you wish. I will never see your face again."

Warning of the Final Plague

11 Now the Lord said to Moses, "I will still bring one plague more upon Pharaoh, and upon Egypt. Afterwards he will let you go from here. When he lets you go, he shall surely thrust you out from here altogether. ² Speak now in the hearing of the people, and let every man borrow of his neighbor and every woman of her neighbor, articles of silver and articles of gold." ³ Then the Lord gave the people favor in the sight of the Egyptians. Moreover, the man Moses was very great in the land of Egypt, in the sight of Pharaoh's servants, and in the sight of the people.

⁴ Moses said, "Thus says the Lord, 'About midnight I will go out into the midst of Egypt, ⁵ and all the firstborn in the land of Egypt shall die, from the firstborn of Pharaoh who sits on his throne, even to the firstborn of the maidservant that is behind the mill, as well as all the firstborn of beasts. ⁶ Then there shall be a great cry throughout all the land of Egypt, such as there has never been, nor shall ever be again. ⁷ But against any of the children of Israel a dog will not even move his tongue, against man or beast, in order that you may know how that the Lord distinguishes between Egypt and Israel.' ⁸ Then all these your servants shall come down to me and bow themselves to me, saying, 'Get out, and all the people

who follow you!' After that I will go out." And he went out from Pharaoh in great anger.

⁹ Then the Lord said to Moses, "Pharaoh shall not listen to you so that My wonders may be multiplied in the land of Egypt." ¹⁰ So Moses and Aaron did all these wonders before Pharaoh, and the Lord hardened Pharaoh's heart, and he would not let the children of Israel go out of his land.

The Passover Instituted
Lev 23:4–8; Nu 28:16–25; Dt 16:1–8

12 Now the Lord spoke to Moses and Aaron in the land of Egypt, saying: ² This month shall be the beginning of months to you. It shall be the first month of the year to you. ³ Speak to all the congregation of Israel, saying: On the tenth day of this month every man shall take a lamb, according to the house of their fathers, a lamb for a household. ⁴ And if the household be too little for the lamb, let him and his neighbor next to his house take it according to the number of the persons; according to what each man shall eat, divide the lamb. ⁵ Your lamb shall be without blemish, a male of the first year. You shall take it out from the sheep, or from the goats. ⁶ You shall keep it up until the fourteenth day of the same month, and then the whole assembly of the congregation of Israel shall kill it in the evening. ⁷ They shall take some of the blood and put it on the two side posts and on the upper doorpost of the houses in which they shall eat it. ⁸ They shall eat the flesh on that night, roasted with fire, and they shall eat it with unleavened bread and bitter herbs. ⁹ Do not eat it raw, nor boiled at all with water, but roasted with fire, its head with its legs and its entrails. ¹⁰ And you shall let nothing of it remain until the morning, but that of it which remains until the morning you shall burn with fire. ¹¹ In this way shall you eat it: with your waist girded, your sandals on your feet, and your staff in your hand. So you shall eat it in haste. It is the Lord's Passover.

¹² For I will pass through the land of Egypt this night and will smite all the firstborn in the land of Egypt, both man and beast, and against all the gods of Egypt I will execute judgment. I am the Lord. ¹³ The blood shall be to you for a sign on the houses where you are. And when I see the blood, I will pass over you, and the plague shall not be upon you to destroy *you* when I smite the land of Egypt.

¹⁴ This day shall be a memorial to you, and you shall keep it as a feast to the Lord. Throughout your generations you shall keep it a feast by an eternal ordinance. ¹⁵ Seven days you shall eat unleavened bread. On the first day you shall put away leaven out of your houses, for whoever eats leavened bread from the first day until the seventh day, that person shall be cut off from Israel. ¹⁶ On the first day there shall be a holy convocation, and on the seventh day there shall be a holy convocation for you. No manner of work shall be done on them; but that which every man must eat—that only may be prepared for you.

¹⁷ You shall observe the Feast of Unleavened Bread. For on this very day I brought your armies out of the land of Egypt. Therefore you shall observe this day throughout your generations as an ordinance forever. ¹⁸ In the first *month*, on the fourteenth day of the month at evening, you shall eat unleavened bread until the twenty-first day of the month at evening. ¹⁹ Seven days shall there be no leaven found in your houses, for whoever eats that which is leavened, that person shall be cut off from the congregation of Israel, whether he be a stranger or born in the land. ²⁰ You shall eat nothing leavened. In all your dwellings you shall eat unleavened bread.

²¹ Then Moses called for all the elders of Israel and said to them, "Draw out and take for yourselves a lamb according to your families and kill the Passover *lamb*. ²² You shall take a bunch of hyssop, and dip it in the blood that is in the basin, and apply the lintel and the two side posts with the blood that is in the basin, and none of you shall go out from the door of his house until the morning. ²³ For the Lord will pass through to kill the Egyptians. And when He sees the blood upon the lintel and on the two side posts, the Lord will pass over the door and will not permit the destroyer to come to your houses to kill *you*.

²⁴ "And you shall observe this thing as an ordinance to you and to your sons forever. ²⁵ When you enter the land which the Lord will give you, according as He has promised, that you shall observe this service. ²⁶ And when your children shall say to you, 'What does

this service mean to you?' [27] that you shall say, 'It is the sacrifice of the LORD's Passover, who passed over the houses of the children of Israel in Egypt, when He smote the Egyptians, and delivered our households.'" And the people bowed down and worshipped. [28] Then the children of Israel went and did *so*. Just as the LORD had commanded Moses and Aaron, so they did.

The Tenth Plague: Death of the Firstborn

[29] At midnight the LORD smote all the firstborn in the land of Egypt, from the firstborn of Pharaoh that sat on his throne to the firstborn of the captive who was in the dungeon and all the firstborn of livestock. [30] Pharaoh rose up in the night, he and all his servants and all the Egyptians, and there was a great cry in Egypt, for there was not a house where there was not someone dead.

The Exodus

[31] Then he called for Moses and Aaron at night and said, "Rise up, and get out from among my people, both you and the children of Israel, and go, serve the LORD, as you have said. [32] Also take your flocks and your herds, as you have said, and be gone, and bless me also."

[33] The Egyptians urged the people, so that they might send them out of the land in haste, for they said, "We all will be dead." [34] So the people took their dough before it was leavened, *with* their kneading troughs being bound up in their clothes on their shoulders. [35] Now the children of Israel did according to the word of Moses, and they requested of the Egyptians articles of silver and articles of gold, and clothing. [36] And the LORD gave the people favor in the sight of the Egyptians, so that they gave them *what they requested*. Thus they plundered the Egyptians.

[37] Then the children of Israel journeyed from Rameses to Sukkoth, about six hundred thousand men on foot, besides children. [38] A mixed multitude also went up with them along with flocks and herds, a large amount of livestock. [39] They baked unleavened cakes of the dough which they brought forth out of Egypt, for it was not leavened because they were driven out of Egypt and could not linger, nor had they prepared for themselves any food.

[40] Now the sojourning of the children of Israel who lived in Egypt was four hundred and thirty years. [41] And at the end of the four hundred and thirty years, on the very day, all the hosts of the LORD went out from the land of Egypt. [42] It is a night to be observed to the LORD for bringing them out from the land of Egypt. This is that night for the LORD to be observed by all the children of Israel in their generations.

The Ordinance of Passover

[43] So the LORD said to Moses and Aaron: This is the ordinance of the Passover:

No foreigner may eat of it. [44] But every man's servant bought with money, when you have circumcised him, may eat it. [45] A foreigner or a hired servant shall not eat it.

[46] In one house shall it be eaten. You shall not carry any of the flesh outside of the house, nor shall you break a bone of it. [47] All the congregation of Israel shall keep it.

[48] Now when a stranger sojourns with you and keeps the Passover to the LORD, let all his males be circumcised, and then let him come near and keep it. And he shall be as one that is born in the land. However, no uncircumcised person shall eat of it. [49] The same law shall apply to him that is a native and to the stranger who sojourns among you.

[50] So all the children of Israel did it. They did just as the LORD commanded Moses and Aaron. [51] And that same day the LORD brought the children of Israel out of the land of Egypt by their hosts.

Consecration of the Firstborn

13 Then the LORD spoke to Moses, saying: [2] Sanctify unto Me all the firstborn, the firstborn of every womb among the children of Israel, both of man and of beast. It is Mine.

The Feast of Unleavened Bread

[3] Moses said to the people, "Remember this day, in which you came out from Egypt, out of the house of bondage, for by strength of hand the LORD brought you out from this place. Nothing leavened shall be eaten. [4] On this day, you are going out, in the month of Aviv. [5] It shall be when the LORD brings you into the land of the Canaanites and the Hittites and the Amorites and the Hivites and the Jebusites, which He swore to your fathers to give you, a land flowing with milk and honey, that you shall keep this ceremony in this month. [6] Seven days you shall eat unleavened bread, and on the seventh day shall be a feast to the LORD. [7] Unleavened bread shall be eaten seven days. And there shall be no leavened bread seen among you, nor shall there be leaven seen among you in all your borders. [8] You shall declare to your son on that day, saying, 'This is done because of that which the LORD did for me when I came forth out of Egypt.' [9] It shall be as a sign to you on your hand and as a memorial on your forehead, in order that the LORD's law may be in your mouth. For with a strong hand the LORD brought you out of Egypt. [10] You shall, therefore, keep this ordinance at its appointed time from year to year.

The Law of the Firstborn

[11] "It shall be when the LORD brings you into the land of the Canaanites, just as He swore to you and to your fathers, and shall give it you, [12] that you shall set apart to the LORD the first offspring of every womb and the first offspring of every beast which you have. The males shall be the LORD's. [13] But every first offspring of a donkey you shall redeem with a lamb. And if you do not redeem it, then you shall break its neck, and all the firstborn of man among your sons you shall redeem.

[14] "It shall be when your son asks you in time to come, saying, 'What is this?' that you shall say to him, 'With a strong hand the LORD brought us out from Egypt, from the house of bondage. [15] And when Pharaoh stubbornly refused to let us go, that the LORD killed all the firstborn in the land of Egypt, both the firstborn of man, and the firstborn of beast. Therefore, I sacrifice to the LORD the first male offspring of every womb, but all the firstborn of my sons I redeem.' [16] It shall be as a sign on your hand and as frontlets on your forehead, for with a strong hand the LORD brought us out of Egypt."

The Route of the Exodus

[17] Now when Pharaoh had let the people go, God did not lead them through the way of the land of the Philistines, although it was nearby. For God said, "Lest the people change their minds when they see war, and they return to Egypt." [18] Therefore, God led the people around, *through* the way of the wilderness to the Red Sea, and the children of Israel went up prepared for war out of the land of Egypt.

[19] Moses took the bones of Joseph with him, for he had made the children of Israel solemnly swear, saying, "God will surely attend to you, and you shall carry my bones away from here with you."

[20] They took their journey from Sukkoth and camped in Etham, on the edge of the wilderness. [21] The LORD went before them by day in a pillar of cloud to lead them *along* the way, and by night in a pillar of fire, to give them light, so that they might travel by day and by night. [22] He did not remove the pillar of cloud by day or the pillar of fire by night from before the people.

Crossing the Red Sea

14 Now the LORD spoke to Moses, saying: [2] Speak to the children of Israel, so that they turn and camp before Pi Hahiroth, between Migdol and the sea, before Baal Zephon. Opposite it you shall camp by the sea. [3] For Pharaoh will say of the children of Israel, "They are confused in the land. The wilderness has shut them in." [4] So I will harden Pharaoh's heart, so that he shall pursue them. And I will be honored because of Pharaoh and because of all his army, so that the Egyptians may know that I am the LORD. And they did so.

[5] When it was told the king of Egypt that the people fled, the heart of Pharaoh and of his servants was turned against the people, and they said, "Why have we done this, that we have let Israel go from serving us?" [6] So he made ready his chariot and took his people with him. [7] And he took six hundred select chariots, and all the chariots of Egypt, and officers over every one of them. [8] The LORD hardened the heart of Pharaoh king of Egypt, and he pursued

after the children of Israel. However, the children of Israel went out with confidence. [9] But the Egyptians pursued after them, all the horses and chariots of Pharaoh, and his horsemen, and his army, and overtook them camping by the sea, beside Pi Hahiroth, before Baal Zephon.

[10] When Pharaoh drew near, the children of Israel lifted up their eyes, and indeed, the Egyptians were marching after them, and they were extremely terrified, so the children of Israel cried out to the LORD. [11] Then they said to Moses, "Is it because there were no graves in Egypt that you have taken us away to die in the wilderness? Why have you dealt with us in this way, bringing us out of Egypt? [12] Is not this the word that we spoke to you in Egypt, saying, 'Let us alone, that we may serve the Egyptians'? For it would have been better for us to serve the Egyptians than to die in the wilderness."

[13] But Moses said to the people, "Fear not! Stand firm! And see the salvation of the LORD, which He will show you today. For the Egyptians whom you have seen today, you shall never see again. [14] The LORD shall fight for you, while you hold your peace."

[15] The LORD said to Moses, "Why do you cry out to Me? Speak to the children of Israel, so that they go forward. [16] And as for you, lift up your rod, and stretch out your hand over the sea, and divide it; then the children of Israel shall go on dry ground through the midst of the sea. [17] As for Me, surely, I will harden the hearts of the Egyptians, so that they shall follow them, and I will be honored through Pharaoh, through all his army, his chariots, and his horsemen. [18] Then the Egyptians shall know that I am the LORD when I am honored through Pharaoh, his chariots, and his horsemen."

[19] Then the angel of God, which went before the camp of Israel, moved and went behind them, and the pillar of the cloud moved before them and stood behind them. [20] So it came between the camp of the Egyptians and the camp of Israel, and there was a cloud and darkness to them, but it gave light by night. Therefore, the one did not come near the other the entire night.

[21] Then Moses stretched out his hand over the sea, and the LORD caused the sea to go back by a strong east wind all that night, and made the sea dry land, so that the waters were divided. [22] The children of Israel went into the midst of the sea on the dry ground, and the waters were a wall unto them on their right hand, and on their left.

[23] Then the Egyptians pursued and went in after them into the midst of the sea, even all Pharaoh's horses, his chariots, and his horsemen. [24] And in the morning watch the LORD looked down on the army of the Egyptians through the pillar of fire and of the cloud and threw the camp of the Egyptians into confusion. [25] He removed their chariot wheels, so that they drove them with difficulty, and the Egyptians said, "Let us flee from the face of Israel, for the LORD is fighting for them against Egypt."

[26] Then the LORD said to Moses, "Stretch out your hand over the sea, so that the waters may come back upon the Egyptians, upon their chariots, and their horsemen." [27] So Moses stretched forth his hand over the sea, and the sea returned to its normal place when the morning appeared, while the Egyptians fled against it, so the LORD overthrew the Egyptians in the midst of the sea. [28] The waters returned and covered the chariots, and the horsemen, and all the host of Pharaoh that came into the sea after them. There remained not so much as one of them.

[29] But the children of Israel walked on dry land in the midst of the sea. And the waters were a wall to them on their right hand and on their left. [30] Thus the LORD saved Israel that day from the hand of the Egyptians, and Israel saw the Egyptians dead upon the seashore. [31] When Israel saw the great power which the LORD used upon the Egyptians, the people feared the LORD, and they believed in the LORD and in His servant Moses.

A Song of Moses

15 Then Moses and the children of Israel sang this song to the LORD and spoke, saying:

"I will sing to the LORD,
    for He has triumphed gloriously!

He has thrown the horse and his rider
    into the sea!
[2] The LORD is my strength and song,
    and He has become my salvation.
He is my God, and I will praise Him;
    my father's God, and I will exalt Him.
[3] The LORD is a man of war;
    the LORD is His name.
[4] Pharaoh's chariots and his army
    He has thrown into the sea;
his chosen captains also
    are drowned in the Red Sea.
[5] The depths have covered them;
    they sank to the bottom like a stone.

[6] "Your right hand, O LORD,
    is glorious in power.
Your right hand, O LORD,
    shatters the enemy.
[7] In the greatness of Your excellence,
    You overthrow those who rise up against You.
You send out Your wrath;
    it consumes them like stubble.
[8] With the blast of Your nostrils
    the waters were gathered together.
The flowing waters stood upright as a heap;
    and the depths were congealed in the heart of the sea.

[9] "The enemy said,
    'I will pursue. I will overtake.
I will divide the spoil;
    my lust shall be satisfied upon them.
I will draw my sword,
    my hand shall destroy them.'
[10] You blew with Your wind,
    and the sea covered them;
they sank like lead
    in the mighty waters.

[11] "Who is like You, O LORD, among the gods?
    Who is like You,
        glorious in holiness,
        fearful in praises,
        doing wonders?
[12] You stretched out Your right hand,
    and the earth swallowed them.

[13] "In Your mercy You have led
    the people whom You have redeemed;
You have guided them by Your strength
    to Your holy dwelling.
[14] The peoples have heard and are afraid;
    sorrow has taken hold on the inhabitants of Philistia.
[15] Then the chiefs of Edom were amazed;
    the mighty men of Moab, trembling takes hold of them;
all the inhabitants of Canaan are melted away.
[16]   Fear and dread fall upon them;
by the greatness of Your arm
    they are as still as a stone,
until Your people pass over, O LORD,
    until the people whom You have purchased pass over.
[17] You shall bring them in, and plant them
    on the mountain of Your inheritance,
in the place, O LORD, which You have made for Your dwelling,
    in the sanctuary, O LORD, which Your hands have established.
[18] The LORD will reign
    forever and ever."

[19] For the horses of Pharaoh went in with his chariots and with his horsemen into the sea, and the LORD brought back the waters of the sea upon them, but the children of Israel walked on dry land in the midst of the sea.

The Song of Miriam

²⁰ Miriam the prophetess, the sister of Aaron, took a timbrel in her hand, and all the women went out after her with timbrels and with dancing. ²¹ Miriam answered them,

"Sing to the Lord,
   for He triumphed gloriously!
The horse and his rider
   He has hurled into the sea."

The Waters of Marah and Elim

²² Then Moses led Israel from the Red Sea, and they went out into the Wilderness of Shur, and they went three days in the wilderness and found no water. ²³ When they came to Marah, they could not drink of the waters of Marah, for they were bitter. Therefore, the name of it was called Marah. ²⁴ So the people murmured against Moses, saying, "What shall we drink?"

²⁵ And he cried to the Lord, and the Lord showed him a tree. When he had thrown *it* into the waters, the waters were made sweet. There He made for them a statute and an ordinance, and there He tested them. ²⁶ He said, "If you diligently listen to the voice of the Lord your God, and do what is right in His sight, and give ear to His commandments, and keep all His statutes, I will not afflict you with any of the diseases with which I have afflicted the Egyptians. For I am the Lord who heals you."

²⁷ Then they came to Elim, where there were twelve wells of water and seventy palm trees, and they camped there by the waters.

Bread and Quail

16 Then they set out from Elim, and all the congregation of the children of Israel came to the Wilderness of Sin, which is between Elim and Sinai, on the fifteenth day of the second month after their departing out of the land of Egypt. ² The whole congregation of the children of Israel murmured against Moses and Aaron in the wilderness. ³ Now the children of Israel said to them, "Would to God we had died by the hand of the Lord in the land of Egypt, when we sat by the pots of meat, when we ate bread to the full, for you have brought us forth into this wilderness to kill this whole assembly with hunger."

⁴ Then the Lord said to Moses, "Indeed, I will rain bread from heaven for you. And the people shall go out and gather a certain amount every day, that I may test them, whether they will walk in My law or not. ⁵ And it shall come to pass that on the sixth day they shall prepare that which they bring in, and it will be twice as much as they gather daily."

⁶ So Moses and Aaron said to all the children of Israel, "At evening, you shall know that the Lord has brought you out from the land of Egypt. ⁷ And in the morning you shall see the glory of the Lord, because He hears your murmurings against the Lord. And what are we that you murmur against us?" ⁸ Then Moses said, "This will happen when the Lord gives you meat to eat in the evening and bread in the morning to satisfy, for the Lord hears your murmurings which you murmur against Him. And what are we? Your murmurings are not against us, but against the Lord."

⁹ Then Moses said to Aaron, "Say to all the congregation of the children of Israel, 'Come near before the Lord, for He has heard your murmurings.' "

¹⁰ So as Aaron spoke to the whole congregation of the children of Israel, they looked toward the wilderness, and indeed, the glory of the Lord appeared in the cloud.

¹¹ Then the Lord spoke to Moses, saying, ¹² "I have heard the murmurings of the children of Israel. Speak to them, saying, '*In* the evening you shall eat meat, and in the morning you shall be filled with bread. And you shall know that I am the Lord your God.' "

¹³ So in the evening the quail came up and covered the camp, and in the morning a layer of dew was surrounding the camp. ¹⁴ When the layer of dew evaporated, on the surface of the wilderness there lay a small flaky thing, as fine as the frost on the ground. ¹⁵ When the children of Israel saw it, they said one to another, "What is it?" For they did not know what it was.

And Moses said to them, "This is the bread which the Lord has given you to eat. ¹⁶ This is what the Lord has commanded, 'Every man is to gather of it according to what he will eat, an omer¹ for every man, according to the number of your people. Every man should take for them for whoever lives in his tent.' "

¹⁷ The children of Israel did so, and gathered, some more, some less. ¹⁸ When they measured it with an omer, he that gathered much had nothing left over, and he that gathered little had no lack. They gathered every man according what he could eat.

¹⁹ Moses said to them, "Let no man leave any of it until the morning."

²⁰ However, they did not listen to Moses, and some of them left part of it until the morning, and it bred worms, and stank, and Moses was angry with them.

²¹ So they gathered it every morning, every man according to what he could eat. And when the sun got hot, it melted. ²² Now on the sixth day they gathered twice as much bread, two omers² per man, and then all the leaders of the congregation came and told Moses. ²³ He said to them, "This is what the Lord has said, 'Tomorrow is the Sabbath, a holy Sabbath to the Lord. Bake that which you will bake today, and boil that you will boil, and all that which remains over lay up for yourselves to be kept until the morning.' "

²⁴ So they laid it up until the morning, just as Moses commanded, and it did not stink, nor was there any worm in it. ²⁵ Moses said, "Eat it today, for today is a Sabbath to the Lord. Today you will not find it in the field. ²⁶ Six days you shall gather it, but on the seventh day, the Sabbath, there will be none."

²⁷ It happened that some of the people went out on the seventh day to gather, but they found nothing. ²⁸ Then the Lord said to Moses, "How long will you refuse to keep My commandments and My instructions? ²⁹ See, the Lord has given you the Sabbath; therefore He gives you bread for two days on the sixth day. Every man remain in his place. Let no man go out of his place on the seventh day." ³⁰ So the people rested on the seventh day.

³¹ The house of Israel named it manna, and it was like coriander seed and was white, and its taste was like wafers made with honey. ³² Then Moses said, "This is what the Lord has commanded, 'Fill an omer of it to be kept for your generations *to come,* so that they may see the bread that I fed you in the wilderness, when I brought you forth from the land of Egypt.' "

³³ Moses said to Aaron, "Take a pot and put an omer full of manna in it, and place it before the Lord, to be kept for generations *to come.*"

³⁴ As the Lord commanded Moses, so Aaron placed it before the testimony, to be kept. ³⁵ The children of Israel ate manna forty years, until they came to an inhabited land. They ate the manna until they came to the border of the land of Canaan.

³⁶ Now an omer is one-tenth of an ephah.

Water From the Rock

17 All the congregation of the children of Israel journeyed from the Wilderness of Sin, from place to place, according to the commandment of the Lord, and pitched in Rephidim, but there was no water for the people to drink. ² Therefore the people contended with Moses and said, "Give us water so that we may drink."

And Moses said to them, "Why do you contend with me? Why do you test the Lord?"

³ But the people thirsted there for water, and the people murmured against Moses, and said, "Why is it that you have brought us up out of Egypt, to kill us and our children and our livestock with thirst?"

⁴ Then Moses cried out to the Lord, saying, "What shall I do to this people? They are almost ready to stone me."

⁵ The Lord said to Moses, "Pass over before the people, and take with you some of the elders of Israel. And take in your hand your rod with which you struck the Nile, and go. ⁶ Indeed, I will stand before you there on the rock in Horeb, and you shall strike the rock, and there water shall come out of it, so that the people may drink." Then Moses did so in the sight of the elders of Israel. ⁷ He called the

---

¹16 Likely about 3 pounds, or 1.4 kilograms; and in vv. 18, 32, 33, and 36.   ²22 Likely about 6 pounds, or 2.8 kilograms.

name of the place Massah, and Meribah, because of the contending of the children of Israel, and because they tested the LORD, saying, "Is the LORD among us, or not?"

The Amalekites Defeated

[8] Then Amalek came and fought with Israel in Rephidim. [9] So Moses said to Joshua, "Choose men for us and go out, fight against Amalek. Tomorrow I will stand on the top of the hill with the rod of God in my hand." [10] So Joshua did as Moses had said to him and fought against Amalek. And Moses, Aaron, and Hur went up to the top of the hill. [11] Now when Moses held up his hand, Israel prevailed, but when he let down his hand, Amalek prevailed. [12] But Moses' hands became heavy. So they took a stone, and put it under him, and he sat on it. And Aaron and Hur supported his hands, one on one side, and the other on the other side. And his hands were steady until the going down of the sun. [13] So Joshua laid low Amalek and his people with the edge of the sword.

[14] Then the LORD said to Moses, "Write this as a memorial in a book and rehearse it to Joshua, for I will utterly wipe out the remembrance of Amalek from under heaven."

[15] Then Moses built an altar and called the name of it, The LORD Is My Banner; [16] for he said, "For the LORD has sworn that the LORD will have war with Amalek from generation to generation."

Jethro Counsels Moses

18 Jethro, the priest of Midian, Moses' father-in-law, heard of all that God had done for Moses, and for Israel His people, and that the LORD had brought Israel out of Egypt.

[2] Then Jethro, Moses' father-in-law, took Zipporah, Moses' wife, after he had sent her back, [3] and her two sons, one of whom was named Gershom; for he said, "I have been a sojourner in a foreign land." [4] And the name of the other was Eliezer, for *he said*, "The God of my father was my help, and He delivered me from the sword of Pharaoh."

[5] Then Jethro, Moses' father-in-law, came with his sons and his wife to Moses in the wilderness, where he camped at the mountain of God. [6] And he said to Moses, "I, your father-in-law, Jethro, am coming to you, and your wife, and her two sons with her."

[7] Then Moses went out to meet his father-in-law, and bowed down and kissed him; and they asked each other of the other's welfare, and then they went into the tent. [8] Moses told his father-in-law all that the LORD had done to Pharaoh and to the Egyptians for Israel's sake, and all the hardships that had come on them along the way, and how the LORD delivered them.

[9] Jethro rejoiced because of all the goodness which the LORD had done for Israel, whom He had delivered out of the hand of the Egyptians. [10] Jethro said, "The LORD be blessed, who has delivered you out of the hand of the Egyptians, and out of the hand of Pharaoh, who has delivered the people from under the hand of the Egyptians. [11] Now I know that the LORD is greater than all gods, for in the matter in which they treated the *people* insolently, *He was* above them." [12] Then Jethro, Moses' father-in-law, took a burnt offering and sacrifices for God, and Aaron and all the elders of Israel came to eat bread with Moses' father-in-law before God.

[13] On the next day, Moses sat to judge the people, and the people stood around Moses from the morning until the evening. [14] When Moses' father-in-law saw all that he was doing for the people, he said, "What is this thing that you are doing for the people? Why are you sitting by yourself while all the people stand around you from morning until evening?"

[15] Then Moses said to his father-in-law, "Because the people come to me to inquire of God. [16] When they have a dispute, it comes to me, and I judge between a man and his neighbor, and I make known the statutes of God and His laws."

[17] Moses' father-in-law said to him, "What you are doing is not good. [18] You will surely wear yourself out, both you, and these people who are with you, for this thing is too heavy for you. You are not able to do it by yourself. [19] Now listen to me, I will advise you, and may God be with you: You be a representative for the people to God

so that you may bring *their* disputes to God. [20] And you shall teach them the statutes and laws and shall show them the way in which they must walk and the work that they must do. [21] Moreover, you shall choose out of all the people capable men who fear God, men of truth, hating dishonest gain, and place *these men* over them, to be rulers of thousands, rulers of hundreds, rulers of fifties, and rulers of tens. [22] Let them judge the people at all times, and let it be that every difficult matter they shall bring to you, but every small matter they shall judge, so that it will be easier for you, and they will bear *the burden* with you. [23] If you shall do this thing and God commands you *so*, then you will be able to endure, and all these people also will go to their place in peace."

[24] So Moses listened to his father-in-law and did everything that he had said. [25] Moses chose capable men out of all Israel and made them heads over the people, rulers of thousands, rulers of hundreds, rulers of fifties, and rulers of tens. [26] They judged the people at all times. They brought the difficult cases to Moses, but they judged every small matter themselves.

[27] Moses sent out his father-in-law, and he went his way to his own land.

Israel at Mount Sinai

19 In the third month after the children of Israel had gone forth out of the land of Egypt, on the same day they came into the Wilderness of Sinai. [2] When they set out from Rephidim, they came to the Wilderness of Sinai and camped in the wilderness. Israel camped there before the mountain.

[3] Moses went up to God, and the LORD called to him from the mountain, saying, "Thus you shall say to the house of Jacob and tell the children of Israel: [4] 'You have seen what I did to the Egyptians, and how I lifted you up on eagles' wings, and brought you to Myself. [5] Now therefore, if you will faithfully obey My voice and keep My covenant, then you shall be My special possession out of all the nations, for all the earth is Mine. [6] And you will be to Me a kingdom of priests and a holy nation.' These are the words which you shall speak to the children of Israel."

[7] So Moses came and called for the elders of the people and laid before them all these words which the LORD commanded him. [8] Then all the people answered together and said, "All that the LORD has spoken we will do." And Moses brought back the words of the people to the LORD.

[9] The LORD said to Moses, "Indeed, I am going to come to you in a thick cloud, so that the people may hear when I speak with you and always believe in you." Then Moses told the words of the people to the LORD.

[10] The LORD said to Moses, "Go to the people and sanctify them today and tomorrow, and have them wash their clothes, [11] and be ready for the third day, for on the third day the LORD will come down in the sight of all the people on Mount Sinai. [12] You shall set boundaries for the people all around, saying, 'Take heed to yourselves so that you not go up onto the mountain or touch its border. Whoever touches the mountain will surely be put to death. [13] No hand will touch him, but he shall surely be stoned or shot through, whether it be beast or man. He shall not live.' When the trumpet sounds a long *blast*, they shall come up to the mountain."

[14] So Moses went down from the mountain to the people and sanctified the people, and they washed their clothes. [15] He said to the people, "Be ready for the third day. Do not go near *your* wives."

[16] So on the third day, in the morning, there was thunder and lightning, and a thick cloud on the mountain, and the sound of an exceedingly loud trumpet. All the people who were in the camp trembled. [17] Then Moses brought the people out of the camp to meet with God, and they stood at the foot of the mountain. [18] Now Mount Sinai was completely covered in smoke because the LORD had descended upon it in fire, and the smoke ascended like the smoke of a furnace, and the whole mountain shook violently. [19] When the sound of the trumpet grew louder and louder, Moses spoke, and God answered him with a voice.[1]

[20] The LORD came down on Mount Sinai, on the top of the mountain. And the LORD called Moses up to the top of the mountain, and

---

[1] 19 Or thunder.

Moses went up. [21] Then the LORD said to Moses, "Go down, warn the people, lest they force their way to the LORD to look, and many of them perish. [22] Let the priests also, which come near to the LORD, sanctify themselves, lest the LORD break through against them."

[23] Moses said to the LORD, "The people cannot come up to Mount Sinai, for You warned us, saying, 'Set boundaries around the mountain, and sanctify it.' "

[24] Then the LORD said to him, "Go, get down, and come up, you and Aaron with you, but do not let the priests and the people force their way through to come up to the LORD, lest He break through against them."

[25] So Moses went down to the people and spoke to them.

The Ten Commandments
Dt 5:6–21

20 Now God spoke all these words, saying:

[2] I am the LORD your God, who brought you out of the land of Egypt, out of the house of bondage.
[3] You shall have no other gods before Me.
[4] You shall not make for yourself any graven idol, or any likeness of anything that is in heaven above, or that is in the earth beneath, or that is in the water below the earth. [5] You shall not bow down to them or serve them; for I, the LORD your God, am a jealous God, visiting the iniquity of the fathers on the children to the third and fourth generation of them who hate Me, [6] and showing lovingkindness to thousands of them who love Me and keep My commandments.
[7] You shall not take the name of the LORD your God in vain, for the LORD will not hold guiltless anyone who takes His name in vain.
[8] Remember the Sabbath day and keep it holy. [9] Six days you shall labor and do all your work, [10] but the seventh day is a Sabbath to the LORD your God. On it you shall not do any work, you, or your son, or your daughter, or your male servant, or your female servant, or your livestock, or your sojourner who is within your gates. [11] For in six days the LORD made heaven and earth, the sea, and all that is in them, and rested on the seventh day. Therefore the LORD blessed the Sabbath day and made it holy.
[12] Honor your father and your mother, that your days may be long in the land which the LORD your God is giving you.
[13] You shall not murder.
[14] You shall not commit adultery.
[15] You shall not steal.
[16] You shall not bear false witness against your neighbor.
[17] You shall not covet your neighbor's house; you shall not covet your neighbor's wife, or his manservant, or his maidservant, or his ox, or his donkey, or anything that is your neighbor's.

[18] All the people witnessed the thunder and the lightning and the sound of the trumpet and the mountain smoking; and when the people saw it, they trembled and stood at a distance. [19] They said to Moses, "You speak to us, and we will listen, but do not let God speak to us, lest we die."

[20] Moses said to the people, "Do not fear, for God has come to test you, so that the fear of Him may be before you so that you do not sin."

[21] The people stood a distance away as Moses drew near to the thick darkness where God was.

The Law About the Altar
[22] Then the LORD said to Moses: Thus you shall say to the children of Israel, "You yourselves have seen that I have spoken to you from heaven. [23] You shall not make gods of silver alongside Me or make gods of gold for yourselves.

[24] "You shall make an altar of earth for Me and on it you shall sacrifice your burnt offerings and your peace offerings, your sheep, and your oxen. In every place where I cause My name to be honored, I will come to you and bless you. [25] If you will make Me an altar of stone, you shall not build it of cut stones, for if you use your tool on it, you will have polluted it. [26] And you shall not go up by steps to My altar, so that your nakedness will not be exposed on it."

The Law About Servants
Dt 15:12–18; Lev 25:39–55

21 Now these are the judgments which you will set before them.

[2] If you buy a Hebrew servant, he will serve for six years, but in the seventh he shall go out free without paying anything. [3] If he came in by himself, he shall go out by himself. If he is married, then his wife will go out with him. [4] If his master gives him a wife, and she bears him sons or daughters, the wife and her children shall belong to her master, and he will go out by himself.

[5] However, if the servant plainly says, "I love my master, my wife, and my children. I will not go out free," [6] then his master will bring him to the judges, then he shall also bring him to the door or to the doorpost, and his master shall bore his ear through with an awl, and he shall serve him forever.

[7] If a man sells his daughter to be a female servant, she shall not go out as the male servants do. [8] If she does not please her master, who has betrothed her to himself, then he shall let her be redeemed. He has no authority to sell her to a foreign nation, because he has dealt deceitfully with her. [9] If he has designated her for his son, then he shall deal with her according to the customary rights of daughters. [10] If he marries another wife, then he must not diminish *the first one's* food, her clothing, or her marital rights. [11] If he does not provide these three for her, then she shall go out free, without paying money.

The Law About Violence
[12] He that strikes a man so that he dies shall surely be put to death. [13] However, if it was not premeditated, but God let *him* fall into his hand, then I will appoint you a place where he may flee. [14] But if a man willfully comes upon his neighbor in order to kill him cunningly, then you must take him from My altar, that he may die.
[15] He who strikes his father or his mother shall surely be put to death.
[16] He who kidnaps a man and sells him, or if he is found in his possession, shall surely be put to death.
[17] He who curses his father or his mother shall surely be put to death.
[18] If men fight and one strikes the other with a stone or with his fist, and he does not die, but must remain in bed, [19] and then if he gets up and walks around on his staff, then he who struck him shall go unpunished. Only he must pay for his loss of time and shall see to it that he is thoroughly healed.
[20] If a man strikes his male servant or his female servant with a rod so that he *or she* dies at his hand, then he shall surely be punished. [21] Nevertheless, if he survives for a day or two, then he shall not be punished, for it is his money.
[22] If men fight and hurt a pregnant woman so that her child is born prematurely,[1] yet there is no serious injury, then he shall be surely punished in accordance with what the woman's husband demands of him, and he shall pay as the judges determine. [23] But if there is any serious injury, then you shall give life for life, [24] eye for eye, tooth for tooth, hand for hand, foot for foot, [25] burn for burn, wound for wound, bruise for bruise.
[26] If a man strikes the eye of his male servant or the eye of his female servant so that it is destroyed, then he must let him go free on account of his eye. [27] If he knocks out his male servant's tooth or his female servant's tooth, then he shall let him *or her* go free on account of *the* tooth.

Laws About Property
[28] If an ox gores a man or a woman to death, then the ox must surely be stoned and its flesh must not be eaten, but the owner of the ox will be acquitted. [29] But if the ox has had the habit of goring, and the owner has been made aware of it, and he has not kept it in, and it has killed a man or a woman, then the ox shall be stoned and its

---

[1] 22 Or she has a miscarriage.

owner also shall be put to death. [30] If a ransom is set for him, then he shall give for the ransom of his life whatever is demanded of him. [31] Whether it gored a son or gored a daughter, it will be done to him according to this rule. [32] If the ox gores a male servant or a female servant, then its owner shall give thirty shekels[1] of silver to their master, and the ox must be stoned.

[33] If a man opens a pit or if a man digs a pit and does not cover it, and an ox or a donkey falls into it, [34] the owner of the pit must make restitution. He must give money to their owner, and the dead animal will be his.

[35] If one man's ox hurts another's so that it dies, then they shall sell the live ox and divide its proceeds and divide the dead ox also. [36] Or if it be known that the ox has had the habit of goring and its owner has not kept it in, then he shall surely pay ox for ox and the dead *animal* will become his own.

Laws About Restitution

22 If a man steals an ox or a sheep and kills it or sells it, then he shall repay five oxen for an ox, and four sheep for a sheep.

[2] If a thief is caught breaking in and is struck so that he dies, then there will be no blood guilt for him. [3] If the sun has risen on him, then there is blood guilt for him.

He must make full restitution. If he has nothing, then he will be sold for his theft. [4] If the stolen item is in fact found alive in his possession, whether it be an ox, or donkey, or sheep, then he shall repay double.

[5] If a man causes a field or vineyard to be eaten and puts out his beast so that it feeds in another man's field, he must make restitution of the best of his own field and of the best of his own vineyard.

[6] If fire breaks out and catches in thorn bushes, so that stacked grain or the standing grain or the field are consumed, then he who started the fire must surely make restitution.

[7] If a man gives his neighbor money or items to be kept *for him*, and it is stolen from the man's house, if the thief is caught, he must repay double. [8] If the thief is not caught, then the owner of the house will be brought before the judges to determine if he has laid his hand on his neighbor's goods. [9] For any kind of trespass, whether it be for an ox, for a donkey, for a sheep, for clothing, or for any type of lost thing, where another says it is his, the case of both parties shall come before the judges. And whoever the judges find guilty will pay double to his neighbor.

[10] If a man gives his neighbor a donkey, or an ox, or a sheep, or any beast to keep *for him*, and it dies, or is injured, or is driven away while no one sees it, [11] then there will be an oath before the Lord between both of them that he has not laid his hand upon his neighbor's property. And its owner must accept this, and he will not have to make restitution. [12] However, if it was stolen from him, he shall make restitution to its owner. [13] If it is torn in pieces, then let him bring it as evidence, and he will not have to repay for that which was torn.

[14] If a man borrows anything from his neighbor, and it is hurt or dies when the owner was not with it, then he shall surely make restitution. [15] But if the owner was with it, he shall not make restitution. If it was a hired thing, it came with his hire.

Moral and Ceremonial Laws

[16] If a man seduces a virgin who is not engaged and has relations with her, he must surely endow her to be his wife. [17] If her father absolutely refuses to give her to him, he must pay money according to the dowry of virgins.

[18] You must not allow a sorceress to live.

[19] Whoever has relations with a beast must surely be put to death.

[20] He who sacrifices to any god other than the Lord alone shall be utterly destroyed.

[21] You must neither wrong a foreigner nor oppress him, for you were foreigners in the land of Egypt.

[22] You shall not afflict any widow or orphan. [23] If you afflict them in any way and they cry at all to Me, I will surely hear their cry. [24] And My anger will burn, and I will kill you with the sword,

and your wives will become widows, and your children fatherless.

[25] If you lend money to any of My people who is poor among you, do not be a creditor to him, and do not charge him interest. [26] If you take your neighbor's garment as a pledge, you shall return it to him before the sun goes down, [27] for that is his only covering; it is his garment for his body. In what else will he sleep? And when he cries out to Me, I will hear, for I am gracious.

[28] You shall not curse God or curse the ruler of your people.

[29] You must not delay to offer the first of your harvest and of your vats.

You must give to Me the firstborn of your sons. [30] Likewise you must do the same with your oxen and with your sheep. Seven days it shall remain with its mother, but on the eighth day you must give it to Me.

[31] You will be holy men to Me; therefore you must not eat any flesh that is torn by beasts in the field. You must throw it to the dogs.

Laws of Justice and Mercy

23 You must not give a false report. Do not join your hand with the wicked to be a malicious witness.

[2] You must not follow the masses to do evil, and do not testify in a dispute that agrees with the crowd to pervert *justice*. [3] You must not show partiality to a poor man in his dispute.

[4] If you meet your enemy's ox or his donkey going astray, you shall surely return it to him. [5] If you see the donkey of someone who hates you lying under its burden, you must not ignore it; you must surely help with him.

[6] You shall not turn justice away from your poor in his dispute. [7] Keep far away from a false charge, and do not kill the innocent and the righteous, for I will not justify the wicked.

[8] You shall not take a bribe, for a bribe blinds those who see and subverts the words of the righteous.

[9] Also you shall not oppress a foreigner, for you know the life of a foreigner, seeing you were foreigners in the land of Egypt.

The Laws of Sabbaths

[10] You shall sow your land for six years and shall gather in its produce, [11] but in the seventh year you shall let it rest and lie fallow, so that the poor of your people may eat, and what they leave the beasts of the field may eat. You shall do likewise with your vineyard and with your olive grove.

[12] For six days you are to do your work, but on the seventh day you must cease, so that your ox and your donkey may rest, and the son of your female servant and the foreigner may refresh themselves.

[13] In all things that I have said to you, watch yourselves, and do not mention the name of other gods, nor let *them* be heard from your mouth.

The Three Annual Feasts

[14] Three times in the year you must celebrate a feast to Me.

[15] You shall observe the Feast of Unleavened Bread. For seven days you shall eat unleavened bread, as I commanded you, in the appointed time of the month Aviv, for in it you came out from Egypt.

No one shall appear before Me empty-handed.

[16] You shall observe the Feast of Harvest, the first fruits of your labors, which you have sown in the field.

You shall observe the Feast of Ingathering at the end of the year, when you have gathered in the fruit of your labors from the field.

[17] Three times in the year all your males shall appear before the Lord God.

[18] You shall not offer the blood of My sacrifice with leavened bread, nor shall the fat of My sacrifice remain until the morning.

[19] The first of the first fruits of your land you shall bring into the house of the Lord your God.

You shall not boil a young goat in its mother's milk.

The Angel Prepares the Way

[20] Indeed, I am going to send an angel before you to guard you along the way and to bring you into the place which I have

---

[1] 32 About 12 ounces, or 345 grams.

prepared. [21] Be on guard before him and obey his voice. Do not provoke him, for he will not pardon your transgressions, for My name is in him. [22] But if you diligently obey his voice and do all that I say, then I will be an enemy to your enemies and an adversary to your adversaries. [23] For My angel will go before you and bring you to the Amorites, and the Hittites, and the Perizzites, and the Canaanites, the Hivites, and the Jebusites, and I will completely destroy them. [24] You must not bow down to their gods, or serve them, or do according to their practices, but you shall utterly overthrow them and break down their images in pieces. [25] You shall serve the LORD your God, and He shall bless your bread and your water, and I will remove sickness from your midst. [26] No one shall be miscarrying or be barren in your land. I will fulfill the number of your days.

[27] I will send My fear before you, and I will throw into panic all the people to whom you shall come. I will make all your enemies turn their backs to you. [28] I will send hornets before you which shall drive out the Hivite, the Canaanite, and the Hittite from before you. [29] I will not drive them out before you in one year, lest the land become desolate and the beasts of the field multiply against you. [30] Little by little I will drive them out before you, until you become fruitful and inherit the land.

[31] I will set your boundaries from the Red Sea to the sea of the Philistines, and from the desert to the River;[1] for I will deliver the inhabitants of the land into your hand, and you will drive them out before you. [32] You must not make a covenant with them or with their gods. [33] They shall not live in your land, lest they cause you to sin against Me, for if you serve their gods, it will surely be a snare to you.

The Covenant Confirmed

24 Then He said to Moses, "Come up to the LORD, you, and Aaron, Nadab, and Abihu, and seventy of the elders of Israel, and you shall worship from a distance. [2] Moses alone shall come near the LORD, but they shall not come near, nor may the people go up with him."

[3] Moses came and told the people all the words of the LORD and all the ordinances. Then all the people answered with one voice and said, "All the words which the LORD has said we will do." [4] Moses wrote all the words of the LORD, and rose up early in the morning, and built an altar at the foot of the mountain with twelve pillars for the twelve tribes of Israel. [5] He sent young Israelite men who offered burnt offerings and sacrificed peace offerings of young bulls to the LORD. [6] Moses took half of the blood and put it in basins, and half of the blood he sprinkled on the altar. [7] He took the Book of the Covenant and read in the hearing of the people, and they said, "All that the LORD has said we will do, and we will be obedient." [8] So Moses took the blood, and sprinkled it on the people, and said, "This is the blood of the covenant, which the LORD has made with you in accordance with all these words."

Moses on Mount Sinai

[9] Then Moses went up with Aaron, Nadab, and Abihu, and seventy of the elders of Israel, [10] and they saw the God of Israel, and under His feet there was something like a paved work of sapphire stone as clear as the sky itself. [11] He did not lay His hand upon the nobles of the children of Israel. Also they saw God, and they ate and they drank.

[12] The LORD said to Moses, "Come up to Me to the mountain and stay there, and I will give you the stone tablets with law and the commandments which I have written, so that you may teach them."

[13] Moses rose up with Joshua his attendant, and Moses went up to the mountain of God. [14] He said to the elders, "Wait for us in this place until we return to you. Aaron and Hur are with you. Whoever has any matters of dispute let him come to them."

[15] Moses went up to the mountain, and the cloud covered the mountain. [16] The glory of the LORD rested on Mount Sinai, and the cloud covered it for six days. And on the seventh day He called to Moses from the midst of the cloud. [17] Now the appearance of the glory of the LORD was like a consuming fire on the top of the mountain to the eyes of the children of Israel. [18] Moses went into the midst of the cloud and went up to the mountain. And Moses was on the mountain for forty days and forty nights.

Offerings for the Tabernacle
Ex 35:4–9

25 The LORD said to Moses: [2] Tell the children of Israel to bring Me an offering. From every man who gives willingly with his heart you shall receive My offering. [3] This is the offering which you shall take from them: gold, silver, and bronze, [4] blue, purple, scarlet, fine linen, goats' hair, [5] rams' skins dyed red, porpoise skins, acacia wood, [6] oil for the light, spices for anointing oil and for fragrant incense, [7] onyx stones, and stones to be set in the ephod and in the breastplate.

[8] Let them make Me a sanctuary that I may dwell among them. [9] According to all that I show you—the pattern of the tabernacle and the pattern of all its furniture—you shall make it just so.

The Ark of the Covenant
Ex 37:1–9

[10] They shall make an ark of acacia wood two and a half cubits long, and one and a half cubits wide, and one and a half cubits high.[2] [11] You shall overlay it with pure gold, inside and out shall you overlay it, and you shall make a gold border around it. [12] You shall cast four gold rings for it and put them on the four feet with two rings on the one side of it and two rings on the other side of it. [13] You shall make poles of acacia wood and overlay them with gold. [14] You shall put the poles into the rings on the sides of the ark in order to carry the ark with them. [15] The poles must remain in the rings of the ark. They must not be removed from it. [16] You shall put into the ark the testimony which I shall give you.

[17] You shall make a mercy seat of pure gold, two and a half cubits long and one and a half cubits wide. [18] You shall make two cherubim of gold, make them of hammered work at the two ends of the mercy seat. [19] Make one cherub on the one end and the other cherub on the other end. From the mercy seat you shall make the cherubim on its two ends. [20] The cherubim shall stretch forth their wings upward, covering the mercy seat with their wings and facing one another. The faces of the cherubim are to face toward the mercy seat. [21] You shall put the mercy seat above upon the ark, and in the ark you shall put the testimony that I will give you. [22] I will meet with you there, and I will meet with you from above the mercy seat, from between the two cherubim which are upon the ark of the testimony. I will speak with you all that I will command you for the children of Israel.

The Table for the Showbread
Ex 37:10–16

[23] You shall also make a table of acacia wood, two cubits long, one cubit wide, and a half cubit high.[3] [24] You shall overlay it with pure gold and make a gold border around it. [25] You shall make a border around it of a handbreadth, and you shall make a gold molding for the frame all around. [26] You shall make four gold rings for it and put the rings on the four corners that are on its four feet. [27] The rings shall be close to the frame to provide places for the poles to carry the table. [28] You shall make the poles of acacia wood and overlay them with gold, so that the table may be carried with them. [29] You shall make the dishes, its spoons, its pitchers, and its bowls with which to pour drink offerings. You shall make them of pure gold. [30] You shall set the showbread on the table before Me always.

The Gold Lampstand
Ex 37:17–24

[31] You shall make a lampstand of pure gold. The lampstand and its base and its shaft are to be made of hammered metal. Its cups, its buds, and its flowers shall be of one piece. [32] Six branches shall go out from its sides, three branches of the lampstand from its one side and three branches of the lampstand from its other side. [33] Three cups shall be made shaped like almond *flowers* with buds

---

*1 31 Euphrates River.   2 10 About 3¾ feet long and 2¼ feet wide and high, or 1.1 meters long and 68 centimeters wide and high; similarly in v. 17.
3 23 About 3 feet long, 1½ feet wide, and 2¼ feet high, or 90 centimeters long, 45 centimeters wide, and 68 centimeters high.*

and blossoms on one branch, and three cups made like almond *flowers* in the other branch, with buds and blossoms, and the same for the six branches that come out of the lampstand. [34] On the lampstand shall be four cups shaped like almond *flowers*, with their buds and their blossoms. [35] There shall be a bud under two branches of the same, and a bud under two branches of the same, and a bud under *the next* two branches of the same, according to the six branches that proceed out of the lampstand. [36] Their buds and their branches shall be of the same *piece*, all of it shall be one hammered work of pure gold.

[37] You shall make its seven lamps, and they shall light its lamps so that they may give light to the area in front of it. [38] Its snuffers and their snuff dishes shall be of pure gold. [39] It shall be made from a talent[1] of pure gold along with all these utensils. [40] See that you make them according to their pattern which was shown to you on the mountain.

The Tabernacle
Ex 36:8–38

26 Moreover you shall make the tabernacle with ten curtains of fine twisted linen, and blue, and purple, and scarlet. Make them with cherubim, the work of a skilled workman. [2] The length of each curtain shall be twenty-eight cubits, and the width of each curtain four cubits.[2] All of the curtains shall have the same measurements. [3] Five curtains shall be joined together, one to another. And the other five curtains are to be joined, one to another. [4] You shall make loops of blue on the edge of the end curtain in one set, and likewise you shall make *loops* in the outermost edge of the end curtain in the second set. [5] You shall make fifty loops in the one curtain, and you shall make fifty loops in the edge of the curtain that is in the second set. The loops are to be opposite to one another. [6] You shall make fifty clasps of gold and join the curtains together with the clasps so that the tabernacle shall be one unit.

[7] You shall make curtains of goats' hair to be a covering upon the tabernacle. You shall make eleven curtains. [8] The length of each curtain shall be thirty cubits, and the width of each curtain four cubits,[3] and the eleven curtains shall all have the same measure. [9] You shall join five curtains by themselves, and six curtains by themselves. You shall double over the sixth curtain at the front of the tabernacle. [10] You shall make fifty loops on the edge of the end curtain in one set and fifty loops on the edge of the curtain that joins the second set. [11] You shall make fifty bronze clasps, and put the clasps into the loops, and join the tent together so that it may be one unit. [12] The part that remains of the curtains of the tent, the half curtain that remains, shall hang over the back of the tabernacle. [13] A cubit[4] on the one side and a cubit on the other side of that which remains in the length of the curtains of the tent shall hang over the sides of the tabernacle on this side and on that side to cover it. [14] You shall make a covering for the tent out of rams' skins dyed red and a covering above of porpoise skins.

[15] You shall make boards for the tabernacle of acacia wood, standing upright. [16] Ten cubits[5] shall be the length of each board, and a cubit and a half shall be the width of each board. [17] There shall be two tenons for each board, fitted to one another. You shall make all the boards of the tabernacle in this way. [18] You shall make the boards for the tabernacle, twenty boards for the south side. [19] You shall make forty sockets of silver under the twenty boards, two sockets under one board for its two tenons and two sockets under another board for its two tenons. [20] For the second side of the tabernacle, on the north side, there shall be twenty boards, [21] and their forty sockets of silver, two sockets under one board, and two sockets under another board. [22] For the back of the tabernacle, to the west, you shall make six boards. [23] You shall make two boards for the corners of the tabernacle at the back. [24] They shall be doubled together beneath and finished together at the top of it into one ring. So it shall be for both of them. They shall form

the two corners. [25] There shall be eight boards with their sockets of silver, sixteen sockets, two sockets under one board and two sockets under another board.

[26] You shall make bars of acacia wood, five for the boards of the one side of the tabernacle, [27] and five bars for the boards of the other side of the tabernacle, and five bars for the boards of the side of the tabernacle for the back to the west. [28] The middle bar in the center of the boards shall reach from end to end. [29] You shall overlay the boards with gold and make their rings of gold to provide places for the bars, and you shall overlay the bars with gold.

[30] You shall set up the tabernacle according to the plan which you have been shown on the mountain.

[31] You shall make a veil of blue, and purple, and scarlet, and fine twined linen. It shall be made with cherubim, the skillful work of a workman. [32] You shall hang it on four pillars of acacia wood overlaid with gold. Their hooks *also* shall be of gold on four sockets of silver. [33] You shall hang up the veil under the clasps, so that you may bring in the ark of the testimony within the veil; and the veil shall serve for you as a partition between the holy place and the Most Holy. [34] You shall put the mercy seat on the ark of the testimony in the Most Holy. [35] You shall set the table outside the veil, and the lampstand opposite the table on the side of the tabernacle toward the south, and you shall put the table on the north side.

[36] You shall make a screen for the doorway of the tent of blue, and purple, and scarlet, and fine twined linen, the work of an embroiderer. [37] You shall make five pillars of acacia wood for the screen and overlay them with gold, with their hooks also made of gold, and you shall cast five sockets of bronze for them.

The Altar of Burnt Offering
Ex 38:1–7

27 You shall make an altar of acacia wood, five cubits long and five cubits wide.[6] The altar shall be square, and its height shall be three cubits.[7] [2] You shall make its horns on its four corners. Its horns shall be part of it, and you shall overlay it with bronze. [3] You shall make its pots for its ashes, and its shovels, and its basins, and its meat hooks, and its fire pans. You shall make all of its vessels out of bronze. [4] You shall make a grating for it, a network of bronze, and on the net you shall make four bronze rings at its four corners. [5] You shall put it under the ledge of the altar beneath, so that the net will reach halfway up the altar. [6] You shall make poles for the altar, poles of acacia wood, and overlay them with bronze. [7] The poles shall be put into the rings, so that the poles shall be on the two sides of the altar when carrying it. [8] You shall make it hollow with boards. Just as it was shown you on the mountain, so shall they make it.

The Court of the Tabernacle
Ex 38:9–20

[9] You shall make the court of the tabernacle. On the south side there shall be curtains for the court of fine twined linen one hundred cubits long[8] for one side; [10] and it *shall have* twenty pillars with twenty bronze sockets. The hooks of the pillars and their bands shall be of silver. [11] Likewise for the north side in length there shall be curtains one hundred cubits long, and its twenty pillars and their twenty sockets of bronze. The hooks of the pillars and their bands *shall be* of silver.

[12] For the width of the court on the west side shall be curtains of fifty cubits[9] with their ten pillars and their ten sockets. [13] The width of the court on the east side shall be fifty cubits. [14] The curtains on one side of the gate shall be fifteen cubits[10] with their three pillars and their three sockets. [15] On the other side shall be curtains fifteen cubits with their three pillars and their three sockets.

[16] For the gate of the court there shall be a curtain of twenty cubits,[11] of blue, and purple, and scarlet, and fine twined linen, the work of an embroiderer, with their four pillars and their four

---

[1] 39 About 75 pounds, or 34 kilograms.   [2] 2 About 42 feet long and 6 feet wide, or 13 meters long and 1.8 meters wide.
[3] 8 About 45 feet long and 6 feet wide, or 13.5 meters long and 1.8 meters wide.   [4] 13 About 18 inches, or 45 centimeters.
[5] 16 About 15 feet long and 2¼ feet wide, or 4.5 meters long and 68 centimeters wide.   [6] 1 About 7½ feet, or 2.3 meters long and wide.
[7] 1 About 4½ feet, or 1.4 meters.   [8] 9 About 150 feet, or 45 meters; and in v. 11.   [9] 12 About 75 feet, or 23 meters; and in v. 13.   [10] 14 About 23 feet, or
6.8 meters; and in v. 15.   [11] 16 About 30 feet, or 9 meters.

sockets. [17] All the pillars around about the court shall be furnished with silver bands. Their hooks shall be of silver, and their sockets of bronze. [18] The length of the court shall be one hundred cubits, and the width fifty[1] throughout, and the height five cubits[2] of fine twisted linen, and their sockets of bronze. [19] All the utensils of the tabernacle used in all its service, and all its tent pegs, and all the tent pegs of the court shall be of bronze.

The Oil for the Lamp
Lev 24:1–3

[20] You shall command the children of Israel that they bring you pure oil of olive pressed for the light, to cause the lamp to burn continually. [21] In the tent of meeting, outside the veil which is before the testimony, Aaron and his sons shall arrange it from evening to morning before the LORD. It shall be a perpetual statute for the children of Israel for generations to come.

The Priestly Garments

28 And bring near to yourself Aaron, your brother, and his sons with him from among the children of Israel, so that they may minister to Me as priests—Aaron, Nadab and Abihu, Eleazar and Ithamar, Aaron's sons. [2] You shall make holy garments for your brother Aaron, for glory and for beauty. [3] You shall speak to all who are specially skilled, whom I have filled with the spirit of wisdom, that they may make Aaron's garments to consecrate him, that he may minister to Me as a priest. [4] These are the garments which they shall make: a breastplate, and an ephod, and a robe, and an embroidered coat, a turban, and a sash. They shall make holy garments for Aaron your brother and his sons, that he may minister to Me as priest. [5] They shall take the gold, the blue, the purple, and the scarlet, and fine linen.

The Ephod
Ex 39:2–7

[6] They shall make the ephod of gold, of blue, and of purple, of scarlet, and fine twined linen, the work of a skilled workman. [7] It shall have the two shoulder pieces attached to its two corners, so it shall be joined together. [8] The skillfully woven waistband of the ephod, which is on it, shall be of the same workmanship, of the same material: of gold, of blue and purple, and scarlet, and fine twisted linen.

[9] You shall take two onyx stones and engrave on them the names of the children of Israel, [10] six of their names on one stone, and the other six names of the rest on the other stone, according to their birth. [11] With the work of an engraver in stone, like the engravings of a signet, you shall engrave the two stones with the names of the children of Israel. You shall set them in filigree of gold. [12] You shall put the two stones on the shoulders of the ephod as stones of memorial for the children of Israel, and Aaron shall bear their names before the LORD on his two shoulders as a memorial. [13] You shall make filigree settings of gold, [14] and two chains of pure gold. You shall make them of twisted cord and fasten the braided chains to the filigree settings.

The Breastplate
Ex 39:8–21

[15] You shall make the breastplate of judgment, the work of a skillful workman. You shall make it in the same manner as the ephod. Of gold, of blue, and of purple, and of scarlet, and of fine twisted linen you shall make it. [16] It is to be square when doubled: a span[3] in length and a span in width. [17] You shall set in it four rows of stones. The first row shall be a sardius, a topaz, and a carbuncle; [18] the second row an emerald, a sapphire, and a diamond; [19] the third row a jacinth, an agate, and an amethyst; [20] and the fourth row a beryl, an onyx, and a jasper. They shall be set in gold filigree. [21] The stones shall be according to the names of the children of Israel, twelve, according to their names, each like the engravings of a signet, every one according to his name for the twelve tribes.

[22] You shall make for the breastplate braided chains of pure gold. [23] You shall make on the breastplate two rings of gold and shall put the two rings on the two ends of the breastplate. [24] You shall put the two braided chains of gold on the two rings which are on the ends of the breastplate. [25] You shall fasten the other two ends of the two braided chains in the two filigree settings and put them on the front of the shoulder pieces of the ephod. [26] You shall make two rings of gold and shall put them on the two ends of the breastplate, on the edge of it which is toward the inner side of the ephod. [27] You shall make two other rings of gold and shall put them on the two shoulder pieces of the ephod underneath toward the front, close to the place where it is joined above the skillfully woven waistband of the ephod. [28] They shall bind the breastplate by its rings to the rings of the ephod with a blue cord, so that it may be above the skillfully woven waistband of the ephod, and so that the breastplate will not come loose from the ephod.

[29] Aaron shall bear the names of the children of Israel on the breastplate of judgment over his heart when he goes into the holy place, as a memorial before the LORD continually. [30] You shall put the Urim and the Thummim in the breastplate of judgment, and they shall be over Aaron's heart when he goes in before the LORD. And Aaron shall bear the judgment of the children of Israel over his heart before the LORD continually.

Other Priestly Garments
Ex 39:22–31

[31] You shall make the robe of the ephod completely blue. [32] There shall be a hole at the top of it, in the middle of it. Around its opening it shall have a binding of woven work, like the opening of a coat of mail, so that it will not be torn. [33] You shall make on its hem pomegranates of blue, and of purple, and of scarlet, all around its hem, and bells of gold between them all around: [34] a golden bell and a pomegranate, a golden bell and a pomegranate, all around on the hem of the robe. [35] It shall be on Aaron when he ministers. And its sound shall be heard when he goes into the holy place before the LORD, and when he comes out, so that he does not die.

[36] You shall make a plate of pure gold and engrave on it, like the engravings of a signet,

HOLINESS TO THE LORD.

[37] You shall put it on a blue cord, so that it may be upon the turban. It is to be on the front of the turban. [38] It shall be on Aaron's forehead, so that Aaron may bear the iniquity of the holy things which the children of Israel shall consecrate in regard to all their holy gifts. And it shall always be on his forehead, so that they may be accepted before the LORD.

[39] You shall embroider the tunic of fine linen, and you shall make the turban of fine linen, and you shall make the sash, the work of an embroiderer. [40] For Aaron's sons you shall make tunics. You shall make sashes for them, and you shall make caps for them, for glory and for beauty. [41] You shall put them on Aaron your brother, and on his sons with him, and shall anoint them, and consecrate them, and sanctify them, that they may minister to Me as priests. [42] You shall make linen undergarments for them to cover their naked skin. They shall reach from the waist to the thighs. [43] They shall be on Aaron and on his sons when they come into the tent of meeting or when they come near to the altar to minister in the holy place, so that they may not bear iniquity and die.

It shall be a perpetual statute to him and his descendants after him.

Consecration of the Priests
Lev 8:1–36

29 Now this is the thing that you shall do to them to consecrate them, to minister as priests to Me: Take one young bull and two rams without blemish, [2] and unleavened bread, and unleavened cakes mixed with oil, and unleavened wafers anointed with oil—you shall make them of wheat flour. [3] You shall put them

---

[1] 18 About 150 feet long and 75 feet wide, or 45 meters long and 23 meters wide.　　[2] 18 About 7½ feet, or 2.3 meters.
[3] 16 About 9 inches, or 23 centimeters.

into one basket and bring them in the basket with the bull and the two rams. [4] Then you shall bring Aaron and his sons to the door of the tent of meeting and wash them with water. [5] You shall take the garments and clothe Aaron *with* the tunic and the robe of the ephod and the ephod and the breastplate, and gird him with the skillfully woven band of the ephod. [6] And you shall put the turban on his head and put the holy crown on the turban. [7] Then shall you take the anointing oil and pour it on his head and anoint him. [8] You shall bring his sons and put tunics on them. [9] You shall gird them with sashes, Aaron and his sons, and put the headbands on them, and the priest's office shall be theirs for a perpetual statute. Thus you shall consecrate Aaron and his sons.

[10] Then you shall bring a bull before the tent of meeting, and Aaron and his sons shall put their hands on the head of the bull. [11] You shall kill the bull before the Lord by the door of the tent of meeting. [12] You shall take of the blood of the bull, and put it on the horns of the altar with your finger, and pour all the blood beside the bottom of the altar. [13] You shall take all the fat that covers the entrails, and the lobe that is above the liver, and the two kidneys, and the fat that is on them, and burn them on the altar. [14] But the flesh of the bull, its skin, and its dung, you shall burn with fire outside the camp. It is a sin offering.

[15] You shall also take one ram, and Aaron and his sons shall put their hands on the head of the ram. [16] You shall slay the ram, and you shall take its blood and sprinkle it around on the altar. [17] Then you shall cut the ram in pieces, and wash its entrails and its legs, and put *them* with its pieces and its head. [18] You shall burn the whole ram on the altar. It is a burnt offering to the Lord. It is a soothing aroma, an offering made by fire to the Lord.

[19] Then you shall take the other ram, and Aaron and his sons shall put their hands on the head of the ram. [20] You shall kill the ram and take some of its blood and put it on the tip of the right ear of Aaron, and on the tip of the right ear of his sons, and on the thumb of their right hand, and on the great toe of their right foot, and sprinkle the blood around on the altar. [21] You shall take some of the blood that is on the altar and some of the anointing oil and sprinkle it on Aaron and on his garments, and on his sons, and on the garments of his sons with him. So he and his garments shall be consecrated, along with his sons and his sons' garments with him.

[22] Also you shall take the fat and the rump of the ram, and the fat that covers the entrails and the lobe above the liver, and the two kidneys, and the fat that is on them and the right shoulder (for it is a ram of consecration), [23] and one loaf of bread, and one cake of oiled bread, and one wafer out of the basket of the unleavened bread that is before the Lord. [24] And you shall put all of these in the hands of Aaron and in the hands of his sons, and shall wave them for a wave offering before the Lord. [25] Then you shall take them from their hands and burn them on the altar for a burnt offering, for a soothing aroma before the Lord. It is an offering made by fire to the Lord. [26] You shall take the breast of Aaron's ram of consecration, and wave it as a wave offering before the Lord, and it shall be your portion.

[27] You shall consecrate the breast of the wave offering that is waved and the thigh of the priest's portion that is contributed from the ram of the consecration, from that which was for Aaron and from that which was for his sons. [28] It shall be for Aaron and his sons by a statute forever, for it is a contribution. It shall be a contribution from the children of Israel from their peace offerings, their contributions to the Lord.

[29] The holy garments belonging to Aaron are to belong to his sons after him, so that they may be anointed in them and be consecrated in them. [30] The son that is priest in his stead shall put them on seven days when he comes into the tent of meeting to minister in the holy place.

[31] You shall take the ram of the consecration and boil its flesh in a holy place. [32] Aaron and his sons shall eat the flesh of the ram and the bread that is in the basket by the door of the tent of meeting. [33] They shall eat those things by which the atonement was made in order to consecrate and sanctify them, but no one else shall eat

them, because they are holy. [34] If any of the flesh from the consecrations or from the bread remain until the morning, then you shall burn the remainder with fire. It shall not be eaten, because it is holy.

[35] Thus shall you do to Aaron and his sons according to all that I have commanded you. You shall consecrate them for seven days. [36] Every day you must offer a bull as a sin offering for atonement, and you must cleanse the altar when you make atonement for it. You must anoint it to consecrate it. [37] For seven days you must make atonement for the altar and consecrate it, and then the altar will be most holy, and whatever touches the altar will be holy.

The Daily Offerings

[38] Now this is what you are to offer on the altar: two one-year-old lambs every day, continually. [39] The one lamb you must offer in the morning, and the other lamb you must offer at sundown. [40] And with the first lamb *will be* a tenth *of an ephah*[1] of flour mingled with the fourth part of a hin[2] of beaten oil, and the fourth part of a hin of wine for a drink offering. [41] The other lamb you must offer at sundown and must offer with it the same grain offering and the same drink offering as in the morning, for a soothing aroma, an offering made by fire to the Lord.

[42] This will be a continual burnt offering throughout your generations at the door of the tent of meeting before the Lord, where I will meet with you, to speak to you there. [43] I will meet there with the children of Israel, and it will be consecrated by My glory. [44] I will sanctify the tent of meeting and the altar. I will also sanctify both Aaron and his sons to minister as priests to Me. [45] I will dwell among the children of Israel and will be their God. [46] Then they will know that I am the Lord their God who brought them out of the land of Egypt, so that I may dwell among them. I am the Lord their God.

The Altar of Incense

Ex 37:25–28

30 Also, you must make an altar for burning incense. You must make it of acacia wood. [2] It must be a cubit in length, and its width a cubit. It will be square. Its height will be two cubits; [3] the horns shall be of one piece with it. [3] You must overlay it with pure gold, its top, its sides all around, and its horns; and you must make a molding of gold all around it. [4] You must make two golden rings for it under its molding. You must make *them* on its two sides, on opposite sides of it, and they will be holders for the poles with which to carry it. [5] Then you must make the poles of acacia wood and overlay them with gold. [6] You must put it before the veil that is by the ark of the testimony, in front of the mercy seat that is over the testimony, where I will meet with you.

[7] Aaron must burn sweet incense on it. Every morning, when he trims the lamps, he must burn incense. [8] When Aaron lights the lamps at sundown, he must burn incense on it. It is to be a perpetual incense before the Lord throughout your generations. [9] You must offer no strange incense on it, nor burnt sacrifice, nor grain offering, and you must not pour out a drink offering on it. [10] Aaron must make atonement on its horns once a year with the blood of the sin offering of atonement. Once a year he must make atonement on it throughout your generations. It is most holy to the Lord.

The Atonement Money

[11] The Lord spoke to Moses, saying: [12] When you take the census of the children of Israel according to their number, then each man is to pay a ransom for his life to the Lord when you count them, so that there be no plague among them when you number them. [13] This is what everyone who is counted must give: half a shekel according to the shekel of the sanctuary[4] (a shekel is twenty gerahs). The half shekel will be the offering to the Lord. [14] Everyone who is counted, from twenty years old and above, must give an offering to the Lord. [15] The rich must not give more and the poor must not give less than half a shekel when they give the offering to the Lord, to make atonement for your lives. [16] You must take the atonement money of the children of Israel and give it for the service of the tent

---

[1] 40 Likely about 3½ pounds, or 1.6 kilograms.　[2] 40 Likely about 1 quart, or 1 liter.　[3] 2 About 1½ feet long and wide and 3 feet high, or 45 centimeters long and wide and 90 centimeters high.　[4] 13 About ⅕ ounce, or 5.8 grams; and in v. 15.

of meeting, so that it may be a memorial to the children of Israel before the Lord, to make atonement for your lives.

The Bronze Basin

[17] The Lord spoke to Moses, saying: [18] You must also make a basin of bronze, with its base also of bronze, for washing, and you must put it between the tent of meeting and the altar, and you must put water in it. [19] For Aaron and his sons must wash their hands and their feet from it. [20] When they go into the tent of meeting, or when they come near the altar to minister by burning incense as an offering made by fire to the Lord, they must wash with water so that they will not die. [21] So they must wash their hands and their feet, so that they will not die. And it will be a perpetual statute for them, even to him and to his seed throughout their generations.

The Anointing Oil

[22] Moreover the Lord spoke to Moses, saying: [23] Take for yourself choice spices: five hundred shekels[1] of pure myrrh, half as much sweet-smelling cinnamon (two hundred and fifty shekels[2]), two hundred and fifty shekels of sweet-smelling cane, [24] five hundred shekels of cassia, according to the shekel of the sanctuary, and a hin[3] of olive oil. [25] And you must make with it a holy anointing oil, a perfumed compound, the work of a perfumer. It will be a holy anointing oil. [26] And you must anoint the tent of meeting with it, along with the ark of the testimony, [27] and the table and all its utensils, and the lampstand and its utensils, and the altar of incense, [28] and the altar of burnt offering with all its utensils, and the basin and its stand. [29] You must consecrate them, so that they may be most holy. Whatever touches them must be holy.

[30] You must anoint Aaron and his sons and consecrate them, so that they may minister as priests to Me. [31] You must speak to the children of Israel, saying, "This will be a holy anointing oil to Me throughout your generations. [32] It must not be poured out on anyone's body, nor shall you make any other like it in composition. It is holy, and it will be holy to you. [33] Whoever makes anything like it or whoever puts any of it on a layman will be cut off from his people."

The Incense

[34] Then the Lord said to Moses: Take for yourself sweet spices, stacte and onycha and galbanum, sweet spices with pure frankincense of equal amounts. [35] You shall make of these an incense, a compound expertly blended, mingled with salt, pure and holy. [36] You must beat some of it very fine and put part of it before the testimony in the tent of meeting where I will meet with you. It will be most holy to you. [37] As for the perfume which you will make, you may not make *it* for yourselves using the same recipe. It must be holy for the Lord to you. [38] Whoever makes anything like it in order to use it as perfume must be cut off from his people.

The Tabernacle Artisans

Ex 35:30–35

31 Now the Lord spoke to Moses, saying: [2] See, I have called by name Bezalel the son of Uri, the son of Hur, of the tribe of Judah. [3] I have filled him with the Spirit of God in wisdom, in understanding, in knowledge, and in all manner of craftsmanship [4] to devise artistic works for work with gold, with silver, and with bronze, [5] and in the cutting of stones for settings, and in carving of wood, to work in all manner of craftsmanship. [6] I, indeed, have given him Oholiab, the son of Ahisamak, of the tribe of Dan, and I have given skill to all who are specially skilled, that they may make everything that I have commanded you: [7] the tent of meeting, the ark of the testimony, and the mercy seat that is on it, and all the furniture of the tent, [8] the table and its utensils, and the pure lampstand with all its utensils, and the altar of incense, [9] the altar of burnt offering with all its utensils, and the basin and its stand, [10] the woven garments, the holy garments for Aaron the priest and the garments of his sons, to minister as priests, [11] the anointing oil and sweet incense for the holy place. They must make *them* according to all that I have commanded you.

The Sabbath Law

[12] The Lord spoke to Moses, saying: [13] Speak also to the children of Israel, saying, "You must surely keep My Sabbaths, for it is a sign between Me and you throughout your generations, that you may know that I am the Lord who sanctifies you.

[14] "You shall keep the Sabbath, for it is holy to you. Everyone who defiles it will surely be put to death. For whoever does any work on it, that person will be cut off from among his people. [15] Six days may work be done, but on the seventh is the Sabbath of complete rest, holy to the Lord. Whoever does any work on the Sabbath day will surely be put to death. [16] Therefore the children of Israel must keep the Sabbath, to observe the Sabbath throughout their generations, for a perpetual covenant. [17] It is a sign between Me and the children of Israel forever, for in six days the Lord made heaven and earth, but on the seventh day He rested and was refreshed."

[18] When He had made an end of communing with him on Mount Sinai, He gave Moses the two tablets of testimony, tablets of stone, written with the finger of God.

The Golden Calf

32 Now when the people saw that Moses delayed coming down from the mountain, the people gathered themselves together around Aaron and said to him, "Come, make us gods which will go before us. As for this Moses, the man who brought us up out of the land of Egypt, we do not know what has become of him."

[2] Aaron said to them, "Break off the gold earrings that are in the ears of your wives, your sons, and your daughters, and bring *them* to me." [3] So all the people broke off the gold earrings that were in their ears and brought *them* to Aaron. [4] He received *them* from their hand, and fashioned it with an engraving tool, and made it into a molded calf. Then they said, "This is your god, O Israel, who brought you up from the land of Egypt."

[5] When Aaron saw *it*, he built an altar before it. And Aaron made a proclamation and said, "Tomorrow will be a feast to the Lord." [6] So they rose up early on the next day, and offered burnt offerings, and brought peace offerings. And the people sat down to eat and to drink, and rose up to play.

[7] The Lord spoke to Moses, "Go, and get down, for your people, whom you brought out of the land of Egypt, have corrupted *themselves*. [8] They have quickly turned aside from the way which I commanded them. They have made for themselves a molded calf, and have worshipped it, and have sacrificed to it, and said, 'This is your god, O Israel, which has brought you up from the land of Egypt.' "

[9] Then the Lord said to Moses, "I have seen this people, and certainly, it is a stiff-necked people. [10] Now therefore let Me alone, so that My wrath may burn against them and I may destroy them. And I will make of you a great nation."

[11] But Moses sought the favor of the Lord his God, and said, "Lord, why does Your wrath burn against Your people, whom You have brought forth from the land of Egypt with great power and with a mighty hand? [12] Why should the Egyptians speak, saying, 'With evil *intent* He brought them out, to kill them in the mountains and to destroy them from the face of the earth'? Turn from Your fierce wrath and relent of this harm against Your people. [13] Remember Abraham, Isaac, and Israel, Your servants, to whom You swore by Yourself, and said to them, 'I will multiply your descendants as the stars of the heavens, and all this land that I have spoken of will I give to your descendants, and they will inherit *it* forever.' " [14] Then the Lord relented of the harm which He said He would do to His people.

[15] Moses turned and went down from the mountain with the two tablets of testimony in his hand. The tablets were written on both their sides. They were written on one side and on the other. [16] The tablets were God's work, and the writing was God's writing, engraved on the tablets.

[17] When Joshua heard the noise of the people as they shouted, he said to Moses, "There is a sound of war in the camp."

---

[1] 23 About 12½ pounds, or 5.8 kilograms; and in v. 24.   [2] 23 About 6¼ pounds, or 2.9 kilograms.   [3] 24 Likely about 1 gallon, or 3.8 liters.

¹⁸ But he said:

"It is not the sound of those who shout for victory,
nor is it the sound of those who cry because of being
overcome,
but I hear the sound of singing."

¹⁹ As soon as he came near the camp, he saw the calf and the dancing, and Moses' anger burned, so he threw the tablets from his hands and shattered them at the bottom of the mountain. ²⁰ Then he took the calf which they had made and burned it in the fire, ground it to powder, and scattered it on the water, and made the children of Israel drink it.

²¹ Moses said to Aaron, "What did this people do to you, that you have brought so great a sin upon them?"

²² Aaron said, "Do not let the anger of my lord burn. You know that the people are set on evil. ²³ For they said to me, 'Make a god for us which will go before us, for this Moses, the man that brought us up from the land of Egypt, we do not know what has become of him.' ²⁴ I said to them, 'Whoever has any gold, let them break it off.' So they gave it to me, and then I threw it into the fire, and this calf came out.'"

²⁵ Now when Moses saw the people were in a frenzy, for Aaron had let them get completely out of control, causing derision from their enemies, ²⁶ then Moses stood in the gate of the camp and said, "Whoever is on the Lord's side, come to me." And all the Levites gathered themselves together around him.

²⁷ He said to them, "Thus says the Lord, the God of Israel, 'Every man fasten his sword on his side, and go back and forth from gate to gate throughout the camp, and let every man kill his brother, and every man his friend, and every man his neighbor.'" ²⁸ The Levites did according to the word of Moses, and about three thousand men of the people died that day. ²⁹ For Moses had said, "Consecrate yourselves today to the Lord, that He may bestow a blessing on you this day, for every man opposes his son and his brother."

³⁰ On the next day Moses said to the people, "You have committed a great sin, and now I will go up to the Lord. Perhaps I can make atonement for your sin."

³¹ Then Moses returned to the Lord and said, "Oh, this people has committed a great sin and have made a god of gold for themselves. ³² Yet now, if You will, forgive their sin, but if not, I pray, blot me out of Your book which You have written."

³³ Then the Lord said to Moses, "Whoever has sinned against Me, I will blot him out of My book. ³⁴ So go now, lead the people to the place of which I have spoken to you. Indeed, My angel will go before you. Nevertheless in the day when I punish, I will indeed punish them for their sin."

³⁵ And the Lord plagued the people because they had made the calf, the one that Aaron made.

The Command to Leave Sinai

33 Then the Lord said to Moses, "Depart, go up from here, you and the people whom you have brought up from the land of Egypt, to the land which I swore to Abraham, Isaac, and Jacob, saying, 'To your descendants I will give it.' ² I will send an angel before you, and I will drive out the Canaanite, the Amorite, the Hittite, the Perizzite, the Hivite, and the Jebusite. ³ Go up to a land flowing with milk and honey. However, I will not go up in your midst, for you are a stiff-necked people, and I might destroy you on the way."

⁴ When the people heard this disturbing word, they mourned. And no one put on his ornaments. ⁵ For the Lord had said to Moses, "Say to the children of Israel, 'You are a stiff-necked people. If I went up among you for one moment, I might destroy you. Now therefore, take off your ornaments, so that I may know what I will do to you.'" ⁶ The children of Israel stripped themselves of their ornaments by Mount Horeb.

The Tent of Meeting

⁷ Moses took the tent and pitched it outside the camp, a good distance from the camp, and called it the tent of meeting. And anyone who sought the Lord would go out to the tent of meeting which was outside the camp. ⁸ So whenever Moses went out to the tent, all the people would rise up and stand, every man at the entrance of his tent, and gaze after Moses until he entered the tent. ⁹ And whenever Moses entered the tent, the pillar of cloud descended and stood at the entrance of the tent, and the Lord spoke with Moses. ¹⁰ When all the people saw the pillar of cloud standing at the entrance of the tent, all the people rose up and worshipped, every man at the entrance of his tent. ¹¹ The Lord spoke to Moses face to face, just as a man speaks to his friend. When he returned to the camp, his servant Joshua, the son of Nun, a young man, did not depart from the tent.

The Glory of God

¹² Moses said to the Lord, "See, You say to me, 'Bring up this people,' but You have not let me know whom You will send with me. Yet You have said, 'I know you by name, and you have also found grace in My sight.' ¹³ Now therefore, I pray You, if I have found favor in Your sight, show me now Your way, that I may know You, and that I may find favor in Your sight. Consider too that this nation is Your people."

¹⁴ And He said, "My Presence will go with you, and I will give you rest."

¹⁵ Then he said to Him, "If Your Presence does not go with us, do not bring us up from here. ¹⁶ For how will it be known that I have found favor in Your sight, I and Your people? Is it not by Your going with us, so that we will be distinguished, I and Your people, from all the people who are on the face of the earth?"

¹⁷ The Lord said to Moses, "I will do this thing of which you have spoken, for you have found favor in My sight, and I know you by name."

¹⁸ Then Moses said, "I pray, show me Your glory."

¹⁹ Then He said, "I will make all My goodness pass before you, and I will proclaim the name of the Lord before you. I will be gracious to whom I will be gracious and will show mercy on whom I will show mercy." ²⁰ He said, "You cannot see My face, for no man can see Me and live."

²¹ Then the Lord said, "Indeed, there is a place by Me. You must stand on the rock. ²² While My glory passes by, I will put you in a cleft of the rock and will cover you with My hand while I pass by. ²³ Then I will take away My hand, and you will see My back, but My face may not be seen."

The New Stone Tablets

34 Now the Lord said to Moses, "Cut out for yourself two tablets of stone like the first, and I will write on these tablets the words that were on the first tablets, which you broke. ² Be ready in the morning, and come up in the morning to Mount Sinai, and present yourself there to Me on the top of the mountain. ³ No one is to come up with you. Do not let anyone be seen anywhere on the mountain, and the flocks or herds may not graze in front of the mountain."

⁴ So he cut out two tablets of stone like the first, and Moses rose up early in the morning and went up to Mount Sinai, just as the Lord had commanded him, and took in his hand the two tablets of stone. ⁵ Then the Lord descended in the cloud, and stood with him there, and proclaimed the name of the Lord. ⁶ The Lord passed by before him, and proclaimed, "The Lord, the Lord God, merciful and gracious, slow to anger, and abounding in goodness and truth, ⁷ keeping mercy for thousands, forgiving iniquity and transgression and sin, but who will by no means clear the guilty, visiting the iniquity of fathers on the children and on the children's children, to the third and the fourth generation."

⁸ Moses made haste and bowed to the ground and worshipped. ⁹ He said, "If now I have found favor in Your sight, O Lord, let my Lord, I pray, go among us, for we are a stiff-necked people. Pardon our iniquity and our sin, and take us for your inheritance."

The Covenant Renewed

¹⁰ Then He said: Indeed, I am going to make a covenant before all your people. I will do wonders such as have not been done in all the earth nor in any nation. And all the people among whom you live will see the work of the Lord, for it is a fearful thing that I will do with you. ¹¹ Obey what I command you this day. Indeed, I am going to drive out before you the Amorite, the Canaanite,

the Hittite, the Perizzite, the Hivite, and the Jebusite. [12] Watch yourself so that you make no covenant with the inhabitants of the land where you are going, lest it become a snare in your midst. [13] But you shall destroy their altars, break their *sacred* pillars, and cut down their Asherah poles[1] [14] (for you shall not worship any other god, for the LORD, whose name is Jealous, is a jealous God), [15] lest you make a covenant with the inhabitants of the land, and they prostitute themselves with their gods, and sacrifice to their gods, and someone invites you to eat of his sacrifice. [16] And then you take of their daughters for your sons, and their daughters prostitute themselves after their gods. They will make your sons prostitute themselves after their gods.

[17] You shall make no molded gods for yourselves.

[18] You shall keep the Feast of Unleavened Bread. For seven days you are to eat unleavened bread, as I commanded you, in the month of Aviv, for in the month of Aviv you came out of Egypt.

[19] Every firstborn of the womb belongs to Me, and every firstborn male among your livestock, whether ox or sheep. [20] But you must redeem with a lamb the firstborn of a donkey, and if you fail to redeem him, then you must break his neck. You must redeem all the firstborn of your sons.

No one may appear before Me empty-handed.

[21] You shall work six days, but on the seventh day you must rest. Even at the time of plowing and harvest you must rest.

[22] You must observe the Feast of Weeks, the first fruits of the wheat harvest, and the Feast of Ingathering at the end of the year. [23] Three times in the year all your males must appear before the Lord GOD, the God of Israel. [24] For I will drive out the nations before you and enlarge your borders. No man will covet your land when you go up to appear before the LORD your God three times in the year.

[25] You must not offer the blood of My sacrifice with leaven, nor is the sacrifice of the Feast of the Passover to be left until the following morning.

[26] The first of the first fruits of your land you must bring to the house of the LORD your God.

You must not boil a young goat in its mother's milk.

[27] Then the LORD said to Moses: Write down these words, for in accordance with these words I have made a covenant with you and with Israel. [28] So he was there with the LORD forty days and forty nights. He did not eat bread or drink water. And He wrote on the tablets the words of the covenant, the Ten Commandments.

Moses' Radiant Face

[29] When Moses came down from Mount Sinai with the two tablets of testimony in the hands of Moses, when he came down from the mountain, Moses did not know that the skin of his face shone while he talked with Him. [30] So when Aaron and all the children of Israel saw Moses, amazingly, the skin of his face shone, and they were afraid to come near him. [31] But Moses called to them, and Aaron and all the rulers of the congregation returned to him, and Moses spoke to them. [32] Afterward all the children of Israel drew near, and he commanded them all that the LORD had spoken to him on Mount Sinai.

[33] When Moses finished speaking with them, he put a veil over his face. [34] But whenever Moses went in before the LORD to speak with Him, he took the veil off until he came out. Then he came out and spoke to the children of Israel what he had been commanded. [35] The children of Israel saw the face of Moses, that the skin of Moses' face shone, and then Moses put the veil over his face again until he went in to speak with Him.

Sabbath Regulations

35 Moses gathered all the congregation of the children of Israel together, and said to them: These are the things the LORD has commanded you to do. [2] Six days shall work be done, but on the seventh day you shall have a holy day, a Sabbath of rest to the LORD. Whoever does any work on it must be put to death. [3] You must not kindle fire in any of your dwellings on the Sabbath day.

Offerings for the Tabernacle
Ex 25:1–7; 39:32–41

[4] Moses said to all the congregation of the children of Israel: This is the thing which the LORD commanded, saying: [5] Take from among you an offering to the LORD. Whoever is of a willing heart, let him bring it as an offering to the LORD: gold, silver, and bronze, [6] and blue, purple, and scarlet, fine linen, goats' hair, [7] rams' skins dyed red, and porpoise skins, and acacia wood, [8] oil for the light, and spices for anointing oil, and for the fragrant incense, [9] onyx stones, and gemstones to be set for the ephod and for the breastplate.

[10] Every skilled craftsman among you shall come and make all that the LORD has commanded: [11] the tabernacle with its tent and its covering, its hooks and its boards, its bars, its pillars, and its sockets; [12] the ark with its poles, the mercy seat, and the veil that conceals it; [13] the table with its poles, and all its utensils, and the showbread; [14] the lampstand also for the light and its utensils and its lamps, and the oil for the light; [15] and the incense altar with its poles, and the anointing oil and the fragrant incense, and the hanging for the door at the entrance of the tabernacle; [16] the altar of burnt offering with its bronze grating, its poles, and all its utensils, the basin and its stand; [17] the hangings of the court, its pillars and their sockets, and the curtain for the gate of the court; [18] the pegs of the tabernacle and the pegs of the court and their cords; [19] the woven garments for serving in the holy place, the holy garments for Aaron the priest and the garments of his sons, to minister as priests.

[20] Then all the congregation of the children of Israel departed from the presence of Moses. [21] Everyone whose heart stirred him and everyone whose spirit was willing came and brought the LORD's offering for the work of the tent of meeting and for all its service and for the holy garments. [22] They came, both men and women, as many as had willing hearts, and brought brooches, earrings, rings and bracelets, all kinds of gold jewelry, and everyone that offered an offering of gold to the LORD. [23] Everyone who had blue, purple, and scarlet, and fine linen, and goats' hair, and red skins of rams, and porpoise skins, brought them. [24] Everyone who was making a contribution of silver and bronze brought the LORD's offering, and everyone who had acacia wood for any work of the service brought it. [25] All the women that were skilled spun with their hands and brought what they had spun, both of blue, purple, and scarlet, and of fine linen. [26] All the women whose hearts stirred them to action and were skilled spun goats' hair. [27] The leaders brought onyx stones and gemstones to be set for the ephod and for the breastplate, [28] and spice and oil for the light, and for the anointing oil, and for the fragrant incense. [29] The children of Israel brought a willing offering to the LORD, every man and woman whose heart was willing to bring *material* for all the work which the LORD had commanded through Moses to be made.

Bezalel and Oholiab
Ex 31:2–6

[30] Moses said to the children of Israel: See, the LORD has called by name Bezalel the son of Uri, the son of Hur, of the tribe of Judah. [31] And He has filled him with the Spirit of God, in wisdom, in understanding, and in knowledge, and in all manner of craftsmanship, [32] to design artistic works, to work in gold, in silver, and in bronze, [33] and in the cutting of stones for settings and in the carving of wood in order to make every manner of artistic work. [34] He also has put in his heart to teach, both he and Oholiab, the son of Ahisamak, of the tribe of Dan. [35] He has filled them with skill to do all manner of work as craftsmen; as designers; as embroiderers in blue, in purple, in scarlet, and in fine linen; and as weavers: as craftsmen of every work and artistic designers.

36 So Bezalel and Oholiab, and every skilled person, in whom the LORD has put skill and understanding to know how to do all manner of work for the service of the sanctuary, are to do the work according to all that the LORD has commanded.

[2] Moses called Bezalel and Oholiab and every skilled person in whom the LORD had put wisdom, everyone whose heart stirred him to come to the work to do it. [3] They received from Moses all the offerings which the children of Israel had brought to do the work

---

[1] 13 Carved images of a female deity.

of the service of the sanctuary, and they *continued* to bring to him freewill offerings every morning. [4] And all the skilled men who were doing all the work of the sanctuary came from the work they were doing, [5] and they said to Moses, "The people are bringing much more than is needed for the service of the work which the LORD commanded *us* to do."

[6] So Moses issued a command, and they circulated a proclamation throughout the camp, saying, "Let no man or woman do any more work for the offering of the sanctuary." So the people were restrained from bringing *any more*. [7] For the material they had was sufficient for all the work and more than enough to do it.

Construction of the Tabernacle
Ex 26:1–37

[8] Every skilled man among those who were doing the work made the tabernacle with ten curtains of fine twisted linen, and blue, and purple, and scarlet, with cherubim that were the work of skillful workmen. [9] The length of each curtain was twenty-eight cubits, and the width of each curtain four cubits.[1] All of the curtains were the same size. [10] He joined the five curtains to one another, and the other five curtains he joined to one another. [11] He made loops of blue on the edge of the outermost curtain in the first set. He did likewise along the edge of the outermost curtain in the second set. [12] He made fifty loops in the one curtain and made fifty loops on the edge of the curtain which was in the second set. The loops were opposite one another. [13] He made fifty gold clasps and joined the curtains to one another with the clasps, so that the tabernacle was a unit.

[14] He made curtains of goats' hair for a tent over the tabernacle. He made eleven curtains in all. [15] The length of each curtain was thirty cubits, and the width of each curtain was four cubits.[2] The eleven curtains were all the same size. [16] He joined five curtains by themselves and six curtains by themselves. [17] He made fifty loops on the outermost edge of the curtain in the *first* set, and he made fifty loops on the edge of the curtain which joined the second set. [18] He made fifty bronze clasps to join the tent together, so that it would be one unit. [19] He made a covering for the tent out of rams' skins dyed red and a covering of porpoise skins above.

[20] Then he made boards for the tabernacle out of acacia wood, standing upright. [21] The length of each board was ten cubits, and the width of each board was one and a half cubits.[3] [22] Each board had two tenons, equally distant from each other. He did this for all the boards of the tabernacle. [23] He made boards for the tabernacle: twenty boards for the south side. [24] He made forty sockets of silver under the twenty boards; two sockets under one board for its two tenons and two sockets under another board for its two tenons. [25] For the other side of the tabernacle, which is toward the north corner, he made twenty boards, [26] and their forty sockets of silver: two sockets under one board, and two sockets under another board. [27] For the back of the tabernacle westward he made six boards. [28] He made two boards for the corners of the tabernacle at the back. [29] They were doubled beneath and joined together at the top in one ring. He did this with both of them in both the corners. [30] There were eight boards with their sockets of silver, sixteen sockets, two under every board.

[31] He made bars of acacia wood, five for the boards of one side of the tabernacle, [32] and five bars for the boards of the other side of the tabernacle, and five bars for the boards of the tabernacle for the back to the west. [33] He made the middle bar to pass through the boards from the one end to the other. [34] He overlaid the boards with gold, and made their rings of gold to be places for the bars, and overlaid the bars with gold.

[35] He made a veil of blue and purple, and scarlet, and fine twined linen. He made cherubim, the work of a skillful designer. [36] He made four pillars of acacia wood and overlaid them with gold with their hooks of gold, and he cast four sockets of silver for them. [37] He made

a hanging for the tabernacle entrance of blue, purple, scarlet, and fine twisted linen, the work of an embroiderer. [38] And he made its five pillars with their hooks, and he overlaid their tops and their bands with gold, but their five sockets were of bronze.

Making the Ark of the Covenant
Ex 25:10–20

37 Now Bezalel made the ark of acacia wood. Its length was two and a half cubits, and its width a cubit and a half, and its height a cubit and a half.[4] [2] He overlaid it with pure gold, inside and out, and made a gold molding for it all around. [3] He cast four rings of gold for it on its four feet, with two rings on one side and two rings on the other side of it. [4] He made poles of acacia wood and overlaid them with gold. [5] He put the poles into the rings on the sides of the ark to carry the ark.

[6] He made the mercy seat of pure gold, two and a half cubits long and one and a half cubits wide. [7] He made two cherubim of gold. He made them of hammered metal on the two ends of the mercy seat: [8] one cherub on one end, and one cherub on the other end. Of one piece with the mercy seat he made the cherubim on its two ends. [9] The cherubim spread out their wings upward, covering the mercy seat with their wings, with their faces toward each other. The faces of the cherubim were looking toward the mercy seat.

Making the Table for the Showbread
Ex 25:23–29

[10] He made the table of acacia wood, two cubits long and a cubit wide and a cubit and a half high.[5] [11] And he overlaid it with pure gold and made a gold molding for it all around. [12] Also he made a rim for it of a handbreadth[6] all around, and he made a gold molding for the rim all around. [13] He cast four rings of gold for it and put the rings on the four corners that were on its four feet. [14] Close by the rim were the rings, the holders for the poles to carry the table. [15] He made the poles of acacia wood and overlaid them with gold, to carry the table. [16] He made the utensils which were on the table, its dishes and its pans and its bowls and its jars, to be used in pouring out offerings, of pure gold.

Making the Lampstand
Ex 25:31–39

[17] Then he made the lampstand of pure gold. He made it of hammered work, its base and its shaft. Its cups, its buds, and its blossoms were of the same *piece*. [18] Six branches were extending from its sides, three branches of the lampstand from one side of it, and three branches of the lampstand from the other side of it. [19] Three cups shaped like almond flowers, a bulb and a flower were on the first branch, and three cups shaped like almond flowers, a bulb and a flower were on the next branch, and the same for the six branches going out of the lampstand. [20] In the lampstand there were four cups made like almond flowers, its bulbs and its flowers. [21] And a bulb was under the first two branches from it, and a bulb under the next two branches from it, and a bulb under the third two branches from it, according to the six branches coming out of it. [22] Their bulbs and their branches were of the same *piece*. All of it was one hammered work of pure gold. [23] He made its seven lamps with its snuffers and its trays of pure gold. [24] He made it and all of its utensils from a talent[7] of pure gold.

Making the Altar of Incense
Ex 30:1–5

[25] He made the incense altar of acacia wood. Its length was a cubit, and the width a cubit, a square, and two cubits high.[8] Its horns were of the same *piece*. [26] He overlaid it with pure gold, its top, its sides all around, and its horns. He also made a gold molding for it all around. [27] He also made two rings of gold for it under its molding, on its two sides, on opposite sides, to be places

---

[1] 9 About 42 feet long and 6 feet wide, or 13 meters long and 1.8 meters wide.   [2] 15 About 45 feet long and 6 feet wide, or 14 meters long and 1.8 meters wide.   [3] 21 About 15 feet long and 2¼ feet wide, or 4.5 meters long and 68 centimeters wide.   [4] 1 About 3¾ feet long and 2¼ feet wide and high, or 1.1 meters long and 68 centimeters wide and high; similarly in v. 6.   [5] 10 About 3 feet long, 1½ feet wide, and 2¼ feet high, or 90 centimeters long, 45 centimeters wide, and 68 centimeters high.   [6] 12 About 3 inches, or 7.5 centimeters.   [7] 24 About 75 pounds, or 34 kilograms.   [8] 25 About 1½ feet long and wide and 3 feet high, or 45 centimeters long and wide and 90 centimeters high.

for the poles to carry it. ²⁸ He made the poles of acacia wood and overlaid them with gold.

²⁹ He made the holy anointing oil and the pure incense of sweet spices, according to the work of a perfumer.

Making the Altar of Burnt Offering
Ex 27:1–8

38 He made the altar of burnt offering of acacia wood. It was five cubits¹ long and five cubits wide. It was square, and it was three cubits high.² ² He made its horns on its four corners. The horns were part of the same *piece*, and he overlaid it with bronze. ³ He made all the utensils of the altar, the pots, and the shovels, and the basins, the flesh hooks, and the fire pans. He made all its utensils of bronze. ⁴ He made for the altar a bronze grating, a network beneath, under its ledge, reaching halfway up. ⁵ He cast four rings for the four ends of the bronze grating to provide places for the poles. ⁶ He made the poles of acacia wood and overlaid them with bronze. ⁷ He put the poles into the rings on the sides of the altar with which to carry it. He made *the altar* hollow, out of boards.

Making the Bronze Basin
⁸ He made the basin of bronze with its base of bronze from the mirrors of the women who served at the entrance of the tent of meeting.

Making the Court of the Tabernacle
Ex 27:9–19

⁹ He made the courtyard: On the south side southward the hangings of the courtyard were of fine twisted linen, one hundred cubits;³ ¹⁰ their twenty pillars and their twenty bases were of bronze. The hooks of the pillars and their bands *were* of silver. ¹¹ For the north side the hangings were one hundred cubits; their twenty pillars and their twenty sockets *were* of bronze. The hooks of the pillars and their bands *were* of silver.

¹² For the west side the hangings were fifty cubits⁴ *with* their ten pillars and their ten sockets. The hooks of the pillars and their bands *were* of silver. ¹³ For the east side eastward, fifty cubits. ¹⁴ The hangings of one side of the gate were fifteen cubits⁵ *with* their three pillars and their three sockets, ¹⁵ and also for the other side of the court gate. On both sides of the gate of the courtyard the hangings *were* fifteen cubits *with* their three pillars and their three sockets. ¹⁶ All the hangings of the courtyard all around were of fine twisted linen. ¹⁷ The sockets for the pillars were of bronze, the hooks of the pillars and their bands *were* of silver, and the overlaying of their tops of silver, and all the pillars of the courtyard were furnished with silver bands.

¹⁸ The screen for the gate of the courtyard was embroidered of blue, and purple, and scarlet, and fine twisted linen. Its length was twenty cubits,⁶ and its height was five cubits,⁷ corresponding to the hangings of the courtyard. ¹⁹ Their four pillars and their four sockets *were* of bronze. Their hooks and their bands *were* of silver, and the overlaying of their tops and their bands *were* of silver. ²⁰ All the tent pegs of the tabernacle and of the courtyard all around were bronze.

The Inventory of the Tabernacle
²¹ This is the inventory of the tabernacle, the tabernacle of testimony, as it was counted according to the commandment of Moses for the service of the Levites by the hand of Ithamar, son of Aaron the priest. ²² Bezalel, the son of Uri the son of Hur of the tribe of Judah, made all that the LORD commanded Moses. ²³ With him was Oholiab the son of Ahisamak, of the tribe of Dan, an engraver and designer, an embroiderer in blue and purple and scarlet yarns, and fine linen. ²⁴ All the gold that was used for the work, in all the work of the sanctuary, even the gold of the wave offering, was twenty-nine talents, and seven hundred and thirty shekels,⁸ according to the shekel of the sanctuary.

²⁵ The silver of those who were numbered of the congregation was one hundred talents,⁹ and a thousand, seven hundred and seventy-five shekels,¹⁰ according to the shekel of the sanctuary; ²⁶ a bekah for every man, that is, half a shekel,¹¹ according to the shekel of the sanctuary, for everyone who was numbered, from twenty years old and upward, for six hundred and three thousand, five hundred and fifty men. ²⁷ The hundred talents of silver were for casting the sockets of the sanctuary and the sockets of the veil—a hundred sockets of the hundred talents, a talent for a socket. ²⁸ Of the one thousand seven hundred seventy-five shekels, he made hooks for the pillars and overlaid their tops and made bands for them.

²⁹ The bronze of the wave offering was seventy talents and two thousand four hundred shekels.¹² ³⁰ With it he made the sockets for the door of the tent of meeting, and the bronze altar and its bronze grating, and all the utensils of the altar, ³¹ and the sockets of the courtyard all around, and the sockets of the courtyard gate, and all the tent pegs of the tabernacle, and all the tent pegs of the courtyard all around.

Making the Priestly Garments

39 Now from the blue, purple, and scarlet they made woven garments for serving in the holy place and made the holy garments for Aaron, just as the LORD commanded Moses.

Making the Ephod
Ex 28:6–14

² He made the ephod of gold, blue, purple, and scarlet, and fine twisted linen. ³ Then they hammered the gold into thin sheets and cut it into threads to work them into the blue, the purple, the scarlet, and the fine linen, with skillful work. ⁴ They made shoulder pieces for it, in order to attach it together. It was joined by the two edges together. ⁵ The skillfully woven waistband of his ephod that was on it was like it, of the same material, of gold, blue, purple, and scarlet, and fine twisted linen, just as the LORD commanded Moses.

⁶ They set the onyx stones enclosed in gold filigree settings; they were engraved like the engravings of a signet, according to the names of the children of Israel. ⁷ And he put them on the shoulder pieces of the ephod, to be stones for a memorial to the children of Israel, just as the LORD commanded Moses.

Making the Breastplate
Ex 28:15–28

⁸ He made the breastplate, the work of a skillful workman, like the workmanship of the ephod: of gold, blue, purple, and scarlet, and fine twisted linen. ⁹ It was square. They made the breastplate folded double, a span¹³ long and a span wide when doubled. ¹⁰ They set in it four rows of stones. A row of sardius, topaz, and carbuncle was the first row; ¹¹ the second row, an emerald, a sapphire, and a diamond; ¹² the third row, a jacinth, an agate, and an amethyst; ¹³ and the fourth row, a beryl, an onyx, and a jasper. They were enclosed in settings of gold filigree. ¹⁴ The stones were corresponding to the names of the children of Israel, twelve, corresponding to their names, *like* the engravings of a signet, each with its name, corresponding to the twelve tribes.

¹⁵ They made on the breastplate braided chains like cords of pure gold. ¹⁶ They made two gold filigree settings and two gold rings and put the two rings in the two ends of the breastplate. ¹⁷ They put the two braided chains of gold in the two rings on the ends of the breastplate. ¹⁸ The *other* two ends of the two braided chains they fastened in the two filigree *settings* and put them on the shoulder pieces of the ephod at the front of it. ¹⁹ They made two rings of gold and put them on the two ends of the breastplate, on the edge of it which was on the inner side of the ephod. ²⁰ They made two other golden rings and put them on the two sides of the ephod underneath, toward the front of it, over against where it joined, above

---

¹ 1 About 7½ feet, or 2.3 meters long and wide.   ² 1 About 4½ feet, or 1.4 meters.   ³ 9 About 150 feet, or 45 meters.   ⁴ 12 About 75 feet, or 23 meters.   ⁵ 14 About 22 feet, or 6.8 meters.   ⁶ 18 About 30 feet, or 9 meters.   ⁷ 18 About 7½ feet, or 2.3 meters.   ⁸ 24 A little over a ton, or 1 metric ton.   ⁹ 25 About 3¾ tons, or 3.4 metric tons; and in v. 27.   ¹⁰ 25 About 44 pounds, or 20 kilograms; and in v. 28.   ¹¹ 26 About ⅓ ounce, or 5.7 grams.   ¹² 29 About 2½ tons, or 2.4 metric tons.   ¹³ 9 About 9 inches, or 23 centimeters.

the waistband of the ephod. [21] They bound the breastplate by its rings to the rings of the ephod with a blue cord, so that it might be above the waistband of the ephod, and that the breastplate might not come loose from the ephod, just as the LORD commanded Moses.

Making Other Priestly Garments
Ex 28:31–43

[22] Then he made the robe of the ephod of woven work, all of blue. [23] There was an opening in the middle of the robe, like the opening of a coat of mail, with a band all around the opening so that it should not be torn. [24] They made on the hems of the robe pomegranates of blue, purple, and scarlet, and twisted linen. [25] They made bells of pure gold and put the bells between the pomegranates all around on the hem of the robe. [26] There was a bell and a pomegranate, a bell and a pomegranate, all around about the hem of the robe to be used in service, just as the LORD commanded Moses.

[27] They made tunics of finely woven linen for Aaron and his sons, [28] and the turban of fine linen, and the decorated caps of fine linen, and linen breeches of fine twisted linen. [29] The sash was of fine twisted linen and blue, purple, and scarlet, the work of an embroiderer, just as the LORD commanded Moses.

[30] They made the plate of the holy crown of pure gold and wrote on it an inscription, like the engravings of a signet:

HOLINESS TO THE LORD.

[31] They attached to it a blue cord, to fasten it to the turban above, just as the LORD commanded Moses.

The Work Completed
Ex 35:10–19

[32] Thus all the work of the tabernacle of the tent of meeting was finished, and the children of Israel did according to all that the LORD commanded Moses—so they did. [33] They brought the tabernacle to Moses, the tent and all its furnishings: its clasps, its boards, its bars, and its pillars, and its sockets; [34] and the covering of rams' skins dyed red, and the covering of porpoise skins, and the screening veil; [35] the ark of the testimony and its poles and the mercy seat; [36] the table, and all its utensils, and the showbread; [37] the pure gold lampstand, with its arrangement of lamps, and all its utensils, and the oil for the light; [38] and the gold altar, and the anointing oil, and the fragrant incense, and the curtain for the entrance to the tent; [39] the bronze altar, and its bronze grating, its poles and all its utensils, the basin and its stand; [40] the hangings of the courtyard, its pillars, and its sockets, and the curtain for the courtyard gate, its cords, and its pegs, and all the utensils for the service of the tabernacle, for the tent of meeting; [41] the woven garments of service to do service in the holy place, and the holy garments for Aaron the priest and his sons' garments, to minister as priests.

[42] The children of Israel did all the work according to all that the LORD commanded Moses. [43] Moses looked over all the work, and indeed they had done it; as the LORD had commanded, so they had done. Then Moses blessed them.

The Tabernacle Erected

40 Now the LORD spoke to Moses, saying: [2] On the first day of the first month you shall set up the tabernacle of the tent of meeting. [3] You shall put the ark of the testimony in it and screen the ark with the veil. [4] You shall bring in the table and arrange the things that are to be arranged on it, and you shall bring in the lampstand and set up its lamps. [5] You shall set the gold altar of incense before the ark of the testimony and put the curtain for the entrance to the tabernacle.

[6] You shall set the altar of the burnt offering in front of the entrance of the tabernacle of the tent of meeting. [7] You shall set the basin between the tent of meeting and the altar and put water in it. [8] You shall set up the courtyard around it and hang up the curtain at the courtyard gate.

[9] You shall take the anointing oil and anoint the tabernacle and all that is in it and shall consecrate it and all its furnishings, and it shall be holy. [10] Then you shall anoint the altar of the burnt offering and all its utensils, and consecrate the altar, and the altar shall be most holy. [11] You shall anoint the basin and its stand, and consecrate it.

[12] Then you shall bring Aaron and his sons to the entrance of the tent of meeting and wash them with water. [13] You shall put the holy garments on Aaron and anoint him and consecrate him, so that he may minister to Me as a priest. [14] You shall bring his sons and clothe them with tunics. [15] Then you shall anoint them just as you anointed their father, so that they may minister to Me as priests, for their anointing will surely be an everlasting priesthood throughout their generations. [16] Thus Moses did. According to all that the LORD commanded him, so he did.

[17] In the first month of the second year, on the first day of the month, the tabernacle was erected. [18] Moses erected the tabernacle and fastened its sockets, and set up its boards, and inserted its bars, and erected its pillars. [19] Then he spread the tent over the tabernacle and put the covering of the tent on top of it, just as the LORD commanded Moses.

[20] He took the testimony and put it into the ark, attached the poles to the ark, and put the mercy seat on top of the ark. [21] And he brought the ark into the tabernacle, and set up the veil of the screening, and screened the ark of the testimony, just as the LORD commanded Moses.

[22] Then he put the table in the tent of meeting on the north side of the tabernacle outside the veil. [23] He set the bread in order on it before the LORD, just as the LORD had commanded Moses.

[24] And he put the lampstand in the tent of meeting, opposite the table, on the south side of the tabernacle. [25] He lighted the lamps before the LORD, just as the LORD commanded Moses.

[26] Then he put the gold altar in the tent of meeting before the veil. [27] And he burned fragrant incense on it, just as the LORD commanded Moses. [28] Then he set up the curtain at the entrance of the tabernacle.

[29] He put the altar of burnt offering by the entrance of the tabernacle of the tent of meeting and offered on it the burnt offering and the grain offering, just as the LORD commanded Moses.

[30] Then he set the basin between the tent of meeting and the altar and put water in it for washing. [31] It was there Moses and Aaron and his sons washed their hands and their feet. [32] Whenever they went into the tent of meeting, and whenever they came near the altar, they washed, just as the LORD commanded Moses.

[33] He erected the courtyard all around the tabernacle and the altar, and set up the curtain of the courtyard gate. So Moses finished the work.

The Glory of the LORD

[34] Then the cloud covered the tent of meeting, and the glory of the LORD filled the tabernacle. [35] Moses was not able to enter into the tent of meeting because the cloud settled on it, and the glory of the LORD filled the tabernacle.

[36] When the cloud was lifted up from over the tabernacle, the children of Israel would set out in all their journeys. [37] But if the cloud was not lifted up, then they did not set out until the day that it was lifted. [38] For the cloud of the LORD was on the tabernacle by day, and fire was on it by night, in the sight of all the house of Israel, throughout all their journeys.

LEVITICUS

The Burnt Offering

1 And the LORD called Moses and spoke to him from the tent of meeting, saying: ² Speak to the children of Israel and say to them: When an individual among you brings an offering to the LORD, you shall bring your offering from the livestock, either from the herd or from the flock.

³ If his offering is a burnt sacrifice, and it is from the herd, he shall offer a male without blemish. At the door of the tent of meeting, he shall offer it of his own free will before the LORD. ⁴ Then he shall lay his hand on the head of the burnt offering, and it shall be accepted for him to make atonement¹ for him. ⁵ And he shall slaughter the bull before the LORD, and the sons of Aaron, the priests, shall bring the blood and sprinkle the blood on all the sides of the altar that is at the door of the tent of meeting. ⁶ Then he shall skin the burnt offering and cut it up into parts. ⁷ The sons of Aaron the priest shall put fire on the altar and arrange the wood on the fire. ⁸ Then the priests, the sons of Aaron, shall arrange the parts, with the head and the fat, on the wood that is on the fire that is on the altar. ⁹ But he shall wash its entrails and its legs in water, and the priest shall burn everything on the altar. It is a burnt sacrifice, a food offering made by fire, which is a pleasing aroma for the LORD.

¹⁰ If his gift for a burnt offering is from the flocks, whether from the sheep or from the goats, he shall bring a male without blemish. ¹¹ He shall slaughter it at the north side of the altar before the LORD. And the sons of Aaron, the priests, shall sprinkle its blood on all the sides of the altar. ¹² He shall cut it up into parts, with its head and its fat, and the priest shall arrange them on the wood that is on the fire that is on the altar. ¹³ But he shall wash the entrails and the legs with water. The priest shall bring it all and burn it on the altar. It is a burnt sacrifice, a food offering made by fire, which is a pleasing aroma for the LORD.

¹⁴ If his offering to the LORD is a burnt sacrifice of birds, then he shall bring his offering from turtledoves or from young pigeons. ¹⁵ The priest shall bring it to the altar, wring off its head, and burn it on the altar. Its blood shall be drained out on the side of the altar. ¹⁶ He shall remove its entrails with its feathers and throw it to the east side of the altar to the place of the ashes. ¹⁷ And he shall split it open by its wings, but not tear it in two. The priest shall burn it on the altar on the wood that is on the fire. It is a burnt sacrifice, a food offering made by fire, which is a pleasing aroma for the LORD.

The Grain Offering

2 When a person offers a grain offering to the LORD, his offering shall be of wheat flour. He shall pour olive oil on it and put frankincense on it. ² And he shall bring it to the sons of Aaron, the priests, and he shall scoop out a handful of the flour and its oil, along with all its frankincense. And the priest shall burn this memorial portion on the altar, a food offering made by fire, which is a pleasing aroma for the LORD. ³ And the remainder of the grain offering shall belong to Aaron and to his sons, which is a most holy part of the food offerings to the LORD made by fire.

⁴ When you bring an oven-baked grain offering, it shall be unleavened cakes of fine flour mixed with oil or unleavened wafers spread with oil. ⁵ If your offering is grain on a griddle, it shall be of unleavened wheat flour mixed with olive oil. ⁶ Break it into pieces and pour oil on it. It is a grain offering. ⁷ If your offering is grain in a skillet, it shall be made of wheat flour in olive oil. ⁸ You shall bring the grain offering that is made of these things to the LORD, and when it is presented to the priest, he shall take it to the altar. ⁹ The priest shall remove a memorial portion from the grain offering and burn it on the altar, a food offering made by fire, which is a pleasing aroma for the LORD. ¹⁰ The remainder of the grain offering shall belong to Aaron and to his sons, which is a most holy part of the food offerings to the LORD made by fire.

¹¹ No grain offering that you bring to the LORD shall be made with leaven, for you shall not burn leaven nor any honey as a food offering by fire to the LORD. ¹² As an offering of first fruits, you may offer them to the LORD, but they shall not be offered on the altar for a pleasing aroma. ¹³ You shall season all your grain offerings with salt. You shall not fail to use the salt of the covenant of your God on your grain offering. With all your offerings you shall offer salt.

¹⁴ If you offer a grain offering of your first fruits to the LORD, you shall offer for the grain offering of your first fruits fresh ripe grain roasted by fire, coarsely ground new grain. ¹⁵ You shall put olive oil on it and frankincense on it. It is a grain offering. ¹⁶ The priest shall burn its memorial portion and some of its coarsely ground new grain and oil, along with all its frankincense as a food offering made by fire to the LORD.

The Peace Offering

3 If his offering is a peace sacrifice, and if he is offering from the herd, whether male or female, then he shall offer it without blemish before the LORD. ² He shall lay his hand on the head of his offering and slaughter it at the door of the tent of meeting, and the sons of Aaron, the priests, shall sprinkle the blood on the sides of the altar. ³ He shall offer from the peace sacrifice, as a food offering made by fire to the LORD, the fat that covers the entrails and all the fat that is on the entrails, ⁴ and the two kidneys with the fat that is above them, which is on the loins, and the appendage on the liver which he shall remove with the kidneys. ⁵ Then the sons of Aaron shall burn it on the altar on the burnt sacrifice that is on the wood that is on the fire, as a food offering made by fire, which is a pleasing aroma for the LORD.

⁶ If his offering for a peace sacrifice to the LORD is from the flock, male or female, he shall offer it without blemish. ⁷ If he is offering a sheep for his offering, he shall offer it before the LORD. ⁸ He shall lay his hand upon the head of his offering and slaughter it before the tent of meeting, and the sons of Aaron shall sprinkle its blood on the sides of the altar. ⁹ He shall offer from the peace sacrifice, a food offering made by fire for the LORD, its fat, and the whole fatty tail which he shall remove close to the backbone, and the fat that covers the entrails, and all the fat that is on the entrails, ¹⁰ and the two kidneys with the fat that is above them, which is on the loins, and the appendage on the liver which he shall remove with the kidneys. ¹¹ The priest shall burn it on the altar as a food offering made by fire for the LORD.

¹² If his offering is a goat, he shall offer it before the LORD. ¹³ He shall lay his hand on its head and slaughter it before the tent of meeting, and the sons of Aaron shall sprinkle its blood on the sides of the altar. ¹⁴ He shall offer from it as his offering, an offering made by fire for the LORD, the fat that covers the entrails and all the fat that is on the entrails, ¹⁵ and the two kidneys with the fat that is above them, which is on the loins, and the appendage on the liver which he shall remove with the kidneys. ¹⁶ The priest shall burn them on the altar as a food offering made by fire for a pleasing aroma. All the fat belongs to the LORD.

¹⁷ As a continual statute for your generations in all your settlements, you shall not eat any fat or any blood.

The Sin Offering

4 And the LORD spoke to Moses, saying: ² Speak to the children of Israel, saying: When a person sins unintentionally against any of the commandments of the LORD that should not be done, and he violates one of them, ³ if the anointed priest sins, so as to bring guilt on the people, he shall bring for his sin that he has committed a bull without blemish to the LORD for a sin offering. ⁴ He shall bring the bull to the opening of the tent of meeting before the LORD, and he shall lay his hand on the bull's head and slaughter the bull before the LORD. ⁵ The anointed priest shall take some of the bull's blood and bring it into the tent of meeting. ⁶ The priest shall dip his finger in the blood and sprinkle some of the blood seven times before the LORD in front of the veil of the sanctuary. ⁷ Then the priest

---

¹ 4 To appease wrath, remove sin, and reconcile with God.

shall put some of the blood on the horns of the altar of fragrant incense before the Lord which is in the tent of meeting, and shall pour *the rest of* the blood of the bull at the base of the altar of the burnt offering which is at the door of the tent of meeting. [8] Then he shall remove all the fat of the bull that is for the sin offering—the fat that covers the entrails—and all the fat that is on the entrails, [9] and the two kidneys with the fat that is above them, which is on the loins, and the appendage on the liver which he shall remove with the kidneys, [10] just as these are removed from the bull of the peace sacrifice, and the priest shall burn them on the altar of the burnt offering. [11] The skin of the bull, and all its flesh, with its head, its legs, its entrails, and its dung, [12] all *the rest of* the bull, he shall bring outside the camp to a *ritually* clean[1] place at the ash pile and burn it on wood with fire. It shall be burned on the ash heap.

[13] If the whole congregation of Israel commits an unintentional sin, and the matter is hidden from the eyes of the assembly, and they do any one of the things that by the commandments of the Lord should not be done, and they are *found* guilty, [14] and the sin that they committed against *the commandment* becomes known, the congregation shall offer a bull for a sin offering, and they will bring it before the tent of meeting. [15] The elders of the congregation shall lay their hands on the head of the bull before the Lord, and the bull will be slaughtered before the Lord. [16] The anointed priest shall bring some of the bull's blood to the tent of meeting. [17] And the priest shall dip his finger in some of the blood and sprinkle it seven times before the Lord in front of the veil. [18] He shall put some of the blood on the horns of the altar that is before the Lord, which is in the tent of meeting, and he shall pour all *the rest* of the blood at the base of the altar of the burnt offering that is at the opening of the tent of meeting. [19] He shall remove all the fat from it and burn it on the altar. [20] He shall do to this bull just as he did to the bull of the sin offering; this is what he will do to it. And the priest shall make atonement for them, and they shall be forgiven. [21] He shall bring the bull outside the camp, and he shall burn it just as he burned the first bull. It is the sin offering of the congregation.

[22] Whenever a leader sins, and he does unintentionally any one of the things that by the commandments of the Lord his God should not be done and is *found* guilty, [23] or his sin that he committed was made known to him, he shall bring as his offering a male goat without blemish, [24] and he shall lay his hand on the head of the goat, and he shall slaughter it in the place where they slaughter the burnt offering before the Lord. It is a sin offering. [25] The priest shall take some of the blood of the sin offering on his finger and put it on the horns of the altar of the burnt offering, and he shall pour out its blood at the base of the altar of the burnt offering. [26] And he shall burn all its fat on the altar, like the fat of the peace sacrifice, and the priest shall make atonement for him for his sin, and he shall be forgiven.

[27] If any one of the common people should sin unintentionally by doing one of the things that by the commandments of the Lord should not be done, and is *found* guilty, [28] or his sin that he committed was made known to him, he shall bring as his offering a female goat without blemish, for his sin that he committed. [29] He shall lay his hand on the head of the sin offering, and he shall slaughter the sin offering in the place of the burnt offering. [30] The priest shall take some of its blood on his finger and put it on the horns of the altar of the burnt offering, and he shall pour out *the rest of* its blood at the base of the altar. [31] And he shall remove all its fat, just as the fat is removed from the peace sacrifice, and the priest shall burn it on the altar for a pleasing aroma to the Lord, and the priest shall make atonement for him, and he shall be forgiven.

[32] And if he brings a sheep for a sin offering, he shall bring a female without blemish, [33] and lay his hand on the head of the sin offering, and he shall slaughter it for a sin offering in the place where they slaughter the burnt offering. [34] The priest shall take

some of the blood of the sin offering on his finger and put it on the horns of the altar of the burnt offering, and all the *rest of* its blood he shall pour out at the base of the altar. [35] And he shall remove all the fat, just as the fat of the sheep is removed from the peace sacrifice, and the priest shall burn it on the altar as a food offering to the Lord made by fire. And the priest shall make atonement for his sin that he committed, and he shall be forgiven.

The Guilt Offering

5 When a person sins in hearing the spoken oath, and he is a witness, whether he saw or knew *about the incident,* if he does not report it, he bears guilt.

[2] Or *when* a person touches any *ceremonially* unclean thing, whether it is a carcass of unclean wildlife, or a carcass of an unclean domesticated animal, or the carcass of an unclean crawling thing, and he did not realize it, then he has become unclean and guilty.

[3] Or when he touches human uncleanness, any uncleanness by which he may become *ceremonially* unclean, and he did not realize it, when he realizes it, then he shall be guilty.

[4] Or when a person swears by speaking rashly with his lips to do evil or to do good, anything that a man may speak rashly by oath, and he did not realize it, but when he realizes it, then he has become guilty of any of these things.

[5] When he becomes guilty of one of these things, he shall confess that he has sinned in that thing. [6] And he shall bring his guilt offering to the Lord for his sin which he has committed, a female from the flock, a lamb or goat, for a sin offering. And the priest shall make atonement for him concerning his sin.

[7] If he cannot afford an animal, then he shall bring for his guilt offering, on account of the sin that he committed, two turtledoves or two pigeons to the Lord, one for a sin offering and one for a burnt offering. [8] He shall bring them to the priest who shall offer the one for the sin offering first. He will wring off its head at its neck, but he shall not sever it. [9] Then he shall sprinkle some of the blood of the sin offering on the side of the altar, and the rest of the blood shall be poured out at the base of the altar. It is a sin offering. [10] But the second he shall treat as a burnt offering according to the regulation. The priest shall make atonement for him for his sin that he committed, and he shall be forgiven.

[11] But if he cannot afford to bring two turtledoves or two pigeons, he shall bring for his offering *for the sin* that he committed one-tenth of an ephah[2] of wheat flour for a sin offering. He shall not place olive oil on it, nor shall he put frankincense on it, for it is a sin offering. [12] Then he shall bring it to the priest, and *the priest* shall scoop out a handful from it as a memorial portion and burn it on the altar as a food offering to the Lord made by fire. It is a sin offering. [13] The priest shall make atonement for him concerning his sin that he committed from any of these *offenses,* and he shall be forgiven. The *remainder* will belong to the priest, like the grain offering.

Offerings With Restitution

[14] The Lord spoke to Moses, saying: [15] When a person acts unfaithfully and sins unintentionally in regard to the holy things of the Lord, then for his restitution offering to the Lord he shall bring a ram without blemish from the flock—*or its equivalent,* in your estimation, *in* silver shekels (using the sanctuary shekel[3])—for a guilt offering. [16] And he shall repay *the sin* that he committed with regard to the holy thing and shall add a fifth to it and give it to the priest. The priest shall make atonement for him with the ram of the guilt offering, and he shall be forgiven.

[17] If a person sins unintentionally and does any one of the things that by commandments of the Lord should not be done and he is *found* guilty, he shall bear his iniquity. [18] He shall bring to the priest a ram without blemish from the flock—or its equivalent value[4]—for a guilt offering. The priest shall make atonement for him concerning his error that he made unintentionally, and he shall be forgiven. [19] It is a guilt offering: He has indeed incurred guilt before the Lord.

---

[1] 12 "Clean" and "unclean" refer to ceremonial aspects of places, objects, or people.   [2] 11 Likely about 3½ pounds, or 1.6 kilograms.
[3] 15 About ⅖ ounce, or 12 grams.   [4] 18 This is a shorthand version of the full formula found in Lev 5:15.

6 And the Lord spoke to Moses, saying: [2] When a person sins and acts unfaithfully against the Lord by lying to another concerning *something left in* storage, or entrusted *to him*, or theft, or by extorting his neighbor, [3] or by finding a lost item and lying about it, and he swears falsely concerning one of all the things that a man may do to sin in these things, [4] when he sins and he is *found* guilty, he shall return whatever he stole, or whatever he extorted, or whatever was left in storage with him, or the lost item which he found, [5] or about which he swore falsely, then he shall repay it in full and shall add one-fifth to it. He shall give it to whom it belongs on the day that he is found guilty. [6] And he shall bring his guilt offering to the Lord, a ram without blemish from the flock—or its equivalent value[1]—for a guilt offering to the priest. [7] And the priest shall make atonement for him before the Lord, and he shall be forgiven for anything he may have done to incur guilt.

The Law of the Burnt Offering

[8] The Lord spoke to Moses, saying: [9] Command Aaron and his sons, saying: This is the law for the burnt offering. The burnt offering shall be on the hearth upon the altar all night until the morning, and the fire of the altar shall be kept burning on it. [10] The priest shall put on his linen robe, and his linen undergarments on his body. Then he shall remove the ashes from the fire of the burnt offering on the altar, and he shall put them beside the altar. [11] Then he shall take off his garments and put on other garments, and he shall bring the ashes outside the camp to a clean place. [12] The fire on the altar shall be kept burning on it. It shall not go out. The priest shall feed it with wood every morning. He will arrange the burnt offering on it, and he shall burn the fat of the peace offerings on it. [13] A perpetual fire shall be kept burning on the altar. It shall never go out.

The Law of the Grain Offering

[14] This is the law of the grain offering. The sons of Aaron shall offer it before the Lord on the altar. [15] He shall take from it a handful of the flour of the grain offering, and of the oil and all the frankincense which is on the grain offering, and shall burn it on the altar for a pleasing aroma as a memorial to the Lord. [16] Aaron and his sons shall eat the remainder of it; it shall be eaten without leaven in a holy place. They shall eat it in the court of the tent of meeting. [17] It shall not be baked with leaven. I have given it to them for their portion of My food offerings made by fire. It is most holy, as is the sin offering and as is the guilt offering. [18] All the males among the children of Aaron shall eat of it. It shall be a perpetual statute in your generations concerning the food offerings of the Lord made by fire. Everyone who touches them shall become holy.

[19] The Lord spoke to Moses, saying: [20] This is the offering of Aaron and of his sons which they shall offer to the Lord in the day when he is anointed: a tenth part of an ephah[2] of wheat flour for a regular grain offering, half of it in the morning and half at night. [21] It shall be made on a griddle with olive oil. When it is well mixed, you shall bring it; and the baked pieces of the grain offering you shall offer as a pleasing aroma to the Lord. [22] The priest from among the sons of Aaron who is anointed to succeed him shall offer it. It is a perpetual statute to the Lord. It shall be completely burned up. [23] For every grain offering for the priest shall be completely burned up. It shall not be eaten.

The Law of the Sin Offering

[24] The Lord spoke to Moses, saying: [25] Speak to Aaron and to his sons, saying: This is the law of the sin offering: In the place where the burnt offering is killed shall the sin offering also be killed before the Lord. It is most holy. [26] The priest who offers it for sin shall eat it. In a holy place it shall be eaten in the court of the tent of meeting. [27] Whatever touches its flesh shall be holy, and when blood is sprinkled on any garment, you shall wash it in a holy place. [28] And the clay vessel where it is boiled shall be broken, and if it is boiled in a bronze pot, it shall be both scoured and rinsed in water. [29] All the males among the priests shall eat *from this offering*. It is most holy. [30] Any sin offering where blood is brought into the tent of meeting to make atonement in the holy place shall not be eaten. It shall be burned up in the fire.

The Law of the Guilt Offering

7 Likewise this is the law of the guilt offering. It is most holy. [2] In the place where they kill the burnt offering they shall kill the guilt offering, and its blood shall he sprinkle on the sides of the altar. [3] He shall offer all the fat. The fatty tail and the fat that covers the entrails, [4] and the two kidneys and the fat that is on them, which is on the loins, and the appendage that is above the liver, along with the kidneys, he shall take away. [5] And the priest shall burn them on the altar for a food offering made by fire to the Lord. It is a guilt offering. [6] Every male among the priests shall eat from it. It shall be eaten in a holy place. It is most holy.

[7] As the sin offering, so is the guilt offering; there is one law for them: the priest who makes atonement shall have it. [8] The priest who offers anyone's burnt offering shall have for himself the skin of the burnt offering that he has offered. [9] Every grain offering that is baked in the oven and all that is prepared in a pan or griddle shall be for the priest who offers it. [10] And every grain offering, *whether* mixed with oil or dry, shall be equally shared among all the sons of Aaron.

The Law of Peace Offerings

[11] This is the law of the sacrifice of peace offerings that a person shall offer to the Lord. [12] If he gives it as a thanksgiving *offering*, then he shall offer with the thanksgiving sacrifice unleavened cakes mixed with oil, and unleavened wafers smeared with oil, and cakes of wheat flour mixed with olive oil. [13] Besides the cakes, he shall offer for his offering leavened bread with the sacrifice of his thanksgiving peace offerings. [14] From this he shall offer one loaf from each offering, as a gift to the Lord. It shall be for the priest who sprinkles the blood of the peace offerings. [15] The flesh of the sacrifice of his peace offerings for thanksgiving shall be eaten the same day that it is offered; he shall not leave any of it until the morning.

[16] But if the sacrifice of his offering is a vow or a voluntary offering, it shall be eaten the same day that he offers his sacrifice, and on the next day also the remainder of it can be eaten. [17] But the remainder of the flesh of the sacrifice on the third day shall be burned up with fire. [18] If any of the flesh of the sacrifice of his peace offerings is eaten at all on the third day, the one eating shall not be accepted, nor shall it be imputed to him who offers it. It shall be contaminated, and the one who eats of it shall bear his iniquity.

[19] The flesh that touches any unclean thing shall not be eaten. It shall be burned up with fire. And as for the *other* flesh, all who are *ritually* clean can eat of it. [20] But the person who eats of the flesh of the sacrifice of peace offerings that belong to the Lord, and who has any uncleanness on him, that individual shall be cut off from his people. [21] Moreover the person who shall touch any unclean thing, whether the uncleanness of man or any unclean beast or any detestable unclean creature, and then eats of the flesh of the sacrifice of the peace offering that belongs to the Lord, that individual shall be cut off from his people.

Eating Fat and Blood Forbidden

[22] The Lord spoke to Moses, saying: [23] Speak to the children of Israel, saying: You shall not eat any fat of an ox, a sheep, or a goat. [24] The fat of an animal that dies of itself and the fat of that which is torn by beasts may be used in any other way, but you shall certainly not eat of it. [25] For whoever eats the fat of an animal that is a food offering made by fire to the Lord, that individual shall be cut off from his people. [26] Moreover you shall not eat any manner of blood, whether from a fowl or animal, in any of your dwellings. [27] Whoever eats any manner of blood, that individual shall be cut off from his people.

The Priests' Share

[28] The Lord spoke to Moses, saying: [29] Speak to the children of Israel, saying: He who offers the sacrifice of his peace offerings to

---

[1] 6 Shorthand version of the full formula found in Lev 5:15.   [2] 20 Likely about 3½ pounds, or 1.6 kilograms.

the Lord shall bring his sacrifice to the Lord from his peace offerings. ³⁰ His own hands shall bring the food offerings of the Lord made by fire, the fat with the breast that the breast may be waved for a wave offering before the Lord. ³¹ The priest shall burn the fat on the altar, but the breast shall be for Aaron and his sons. ³² The right thigh you shall give to the priest for a contribution offering for the sacrifice of your peace offerings. ³³ The one among the sons of Aaron who offers the blood of the peace offerings and the fat shall have the right thigh for his portion. ³⁴ For the breast that is waved and the thigh that is contributed I have taken from the children of Israel, from the sacrifices of their peace offerings, and have given them to Aaron the priest and to his sons as a perpetual portion from the children of Israel.

³⁵ This is the consecrated portion for Aaron and his sons, from the food offerings of the Lord made by fire, in the day when *Moses* presented them to minister as priests before the Lord, ³⁶ which the Lord commanded that they be given this, in the day that he anointed them, from the children of Israel as a perpetual portion throughout their generations.

³⁷ This is the law of the burnt offering, of the grain offering, and of the sin offering, and of the guilt offering, and of the ordinations, and of the sacrifice of the peace offerings, ³⁸ which the Lord commanded Moses on Mount Sinai, in the day that He commanded the children of Israel to offer their offerings to the Lord in the Wilderness of Sinai.

The Consecration of Aaron and His Sons
Ex 29:1–37

8 And the Lord spoke to Moses, saying: ² Take Aaron and his sons with him, and the garments, and the anointing oil, and a bull for the sin offering, and two rams, and a basket of unleavened bread, ³ and gather all the congregation together at the entrance of the tent of meeting. ⁴ And Moses did as the Lord commanded him, and the assembly was gathered together at the entrance of the tent of meeting.

⁵ Moses said to the congregation, "This is the thing which the Lord commanded to be done." ⁶ Moses brought Aaron and his sons and washed them with water. ⁷ Then he put the tunic on him, and tied the sash around him, and clothed him with the robe, and put the ephod upon him, and he girded him with the decorative band of the ephod and bound the ephod to him. ⁸ He put the breastplate on him. He also put the Urim and the Thummim in the breastplate. ⁹ Then he put the turban upon his head. Also on the turban at the front he put the golden plate, the holy crown, as the Lord commanded Moses.

¹⁰ Moses took the anointing oil, and anointed the tabernacle and all that was in it, and sanctified them. ¹¹ He sprinkled oil on the altar seven times and anointed the altar and all its vessels, both the laver and its stand, to sanctify them. ¹² Then he poured some of the anointing oil on the head of Aaron and anointed him to sanctify him. ¹³ Moses brought the sons of Aaron and put tunics on them, and girded them with sashes, and put headbands on them, as the Lord commanded Moses.

¹⁴ He brought the bull for the sin offering, and Aaron and his sons laid their hands on the head of the bull for the sin offering. ¹⁵ He slaughtered it, and Moses took the blood, and put it on the horns of the altar around it with his finger, and purified the altar, and poured the blood at the base of the altar, and sanctified it to make reconciliation on it. ¹⁶ He took all the fat that was on the entrails, and the appendage above the liver, and the two kidneys with their fat, and Moses burned them on the altar. ¹⁷ But the bull, and its hide, its flesh, and its refuse he burned with fire outside the camp, as the Lord commanded Moses.

¹⁸ Then he brought the ram for the burnt offering, and Aaron and his sons laid their hands on the head of the ram. ¹⁹ He killed it, and Moses sprinkled the blood on the sides of the altar. ²⁰ He cut the ram into pieces, and Moses burned the head, the pieces, and the fat. ²¹ He washed the entrails and the legs in water, and Moses burned the whole ram on the altar. It was a burnt offering for a pleasing aroma, and a food offering made by fire to the Lord, as the Lord commanded Moses.

²² Next he brought the other ram, the ram of consecration, and Aaron and his sons laid their hands on the head of the ram. ²³ He slaughtered it, and Moses took some of its blood and put it on the tip of the right ear of Aaron, and on the thumb of his right hand, and on the big toe of his right foot. ²⁴ He brought the sons of Aaron, and Moses put some of the blood on the tips of their right ears, and on the thumbs of their right hands, and on the big toes of their right feet. Then Moses sprinkled the blood on the sides of the altar. ²⁵ He took the fat, and the fatty tail, and all the fat that was on the entrails, and the appendage above the liver, and the two kidneys, and their fat, and the right thigh, ²⁶ and out of the basket of unleavened bread that was before the Lord he took one unleavened cake, and a cake of oiled bread, and one wafer and put them on the fat and on the right thigh. ²⁷ And he put all *these* on the hands of Aaron and on the hands of his sons and waved them for a wave offering before the Lord. ²⁸ Then Moses took them from off their hands and burned them on the altar with the burnt offering. This was a consecration for a pleasing aroma, an offering made by fire to the Lord. ²⁹ Moses took the breast and waved it for a wave offering before the Lord. This part of the ram of consecration was for Moses, as the Lord commanded Moses.

³⁰ Then Moses took some of the anointing oil and some of the blood which was on the altar and sprinkled it on Aaron, and on his garments, and on his sons, and on the garments of his sons with him and sanctified Aaron, and his garments, and his sons, and the garments of his sons with him.

³¹ Moses said to Aaron and to his sons, "Boil the flesh at the entrance of the tent of meeting and eat it there with the bread that is in the basket of consecrations just as I commanded, saying, 'Aaron and his sons shall eat it.' ³² That which remains of the flesh and of the bread you shall burn up. ³³ You shall not go out of the door of the tent of meeting for seven days, until the days of your consecration are at an end, for your consecration will take seven days. ³⁴ As he has done this day, so the Lord has commanded what is to be done to make atonement for you. ³⁵ Therefore you shall abide at the entrance of the tent of meeting day and night for seven days and keep the charge of the Lord that you do not die, for so I have been commanded."

³⁶ So Aaron and his sons did all things which the Lord commanded by the hand of Moses.

The Priestly Ministry Begins

9 And it came to pass on the eighth day that Moses called Aaron and his sons and the elders of Israel. ² Then he said to Aaron, "Take a young calf for a sin offering and a ram for a burnt offering, without blemish, and offer them before the Lord. ³ To the children of Israel you shall speak, saying, 'Take a male goat for a sin offering, and a calf and a lamb—both a year old without blemish—for a burnt offering, ⁴ also an ox and a ram for peace offerings to sacrifice before the Lord, and a grain offering mixed with oil. For today the Lord will appear to you.' "

⁵ They brought that which Moses commanded before the tent of meeting, and the entire congregation drew near and stood before the Lord. ⁶ Moses said, "This is the thing which the Lord commanded that you should do; then the glory of the Lord shall appear to you."

⁷ Then Moses said to Aaron, "Go to the altar, and offer your sin offering and your burnt offering, and make atonement for yourself and for the people, and offer the sacrifice of the people, and make atonement for them, as the Lord commanded."

⁸ Aaron therefore went to the altar and slaughtered the calf of the sin offering which was for himself. ⁹ The sons of Aaron brought the blood to him, and he dipped his finger in the blood, and put it on the horns of the altar, and poured out the blood at the base of the altar. ¹⁰ But the fat, the kidneys, and the appendage above the liver of the sin offering he burned on the altar, as the Lord commanded Moses. ¹¹ The flesh and the hide he burned with fire outside the camp.

¹² He slaughtered the burnt offering, and the sons of Aaron presented the blood to him, which he sprinkled on the sides of the altar. ¹³ They presented the burnt offering to him, with its pieces, and the head, and he burned them on the altar. ¹⁴ He then washed the entrails and the legs and burned them with the burnt offering on the altar.

¹⁵ He brought the people's offering, and took the goat which was the sin offering for the people, and slaughtered it, and offered it for sin as the first offering.

¹⁶ And he brought the burnt offering and offered it according to its regulation. ¹⁷ Then he brought the grain offering, took a handful of it, and burned it on the altar, besides the burnt sacrifice of the morning.

¹⁸ He slaughtered the ox and the ram as a sacrifice of peace offerings for the people, and the sons of Aaron presented the blood to him, which he sprinkled on the sides of the altar, ¹⁹ and the fat of the ox and of the ram, the fatty tail, and that which covers the entrails, and the kidneys, and the appendage above the liver. ²⁰ They put the fat pieces on the breasts, and he burned the fat on the altar. ²¹ But the breasts and the right thigh Aaron waved for a wave offering before the LORD just as Moses commanded.

²² Aaron lifted up his hand toward the people, and blessed them, and came down from offering the sin offering, the burnt offering, and peace offerings.

²³ Moses and Aaron went into the tent of meeting, and when they came out they blessed the people, and the glory of the LORD appeared to all the people. ²⁴ A fire came out from before the LORD, and it consumed the burnt offering and the fat that were on the altar. When all the people saw this, they shouted and fell on their faces.

The Death of Nadab and Abihu

10 Now Nadab and Abihu, the sons of Aaron, each took his censer and put fire in it, and put incense on it, and offered strange fire before the LORD, which He did not command them *to do*. ² Then a fire came out from the LORD and devoured them, and they died before the LORD. ³ Then Moses said to Aaron, "This is what the LORD spoke, saying:

'I will be sanctified
    by those who come near Me;
and before all the people
    I will be glorified.' "

And Aaron held his peace.

⁴ Moses called Mishael and Elzaphan, the sons of Uzziel the uncle of Aaron, and said to them, "Come near, and carry your brothers from before the sanctuary out of the camp." ⁵ So they went near, and carried them in their tunics out of the camp as Moses had said.

⁶ Moses said to Aaron, and to Eleazar and Ithamar his sons, "Do not let your hair be loosely disheveled, nor rend your clothes, lest you die, and lest wrath come upon all the people. Instead, let your brothers, the whole house of Israel, mourn the burning which the LORD has caused. ⁷ You shall not go out from the entrance of the tent of meeting, lest you die, for the anointing oil of the LORD is upon you." And they did according to the word of Moses.

⁸ The LORD spoke to Aaron, saying: ⁹ Do not drink wine nor strong drink, you or your sons with you, when you go into the tent of meeting, lest you die. It shall be a perpetual statute throughout your generations, ¹⁰ so that you may differentiate between what is holy and common and between what is unclean and clean. ¹¹ And so you may teach the children of Israel all the statutes that the LORD has spoken to them by the hand of Moses.

¹² Moses spoke to Aaron, and to Eleazar and Ithamar, his sons who were left: Take the grain offering that remains of the food offerings of the LORD made by fire and eat it without leaven beside the altar. For it is most holy. ¹³ And you shall eat it in a holy place, because it is your due and your sons' due from the food sacrifices of the LORD made by fire. For so I have been commanded. ¹⁴ The breast that is waved and the thigh that is contributed you shall eat in a clean place, you, and your sons, and your daughters with you, for they are your due and your sons' due which are given out of the sacrifices of peace offerings of the children of Israel. ¹⁵ The thigh that is contributed and the breast that is waved they shall bring with the fat pieces of the food offerings made by fire to wave them as a wave offering before the LORD, and it shall be yours and your sons' with you as a perpetual statute, as the LORD has commanded.

¹⁶ Moses diligently sought the goat of the sin offering and saw it was burned up. And he was angry with Eleazar and Ithamar, the sons of Aaron who were left alive, saying, ¹⁷ "Why have you not eaten the sin offering in the sacred area, knowing that it is most holy and God has given it to you to bear the iniquity of the congregation to make atonement for them before the LORD? ¹⁸ Its blood was not brought into the inner part of the sanctuary. Indeed you should have eaten it in the sanctuary as I commanded."

¹⁹ Aaron said to Moses, "Today they have offered their sin offering and their burnt offering before the LORD, and such things have happened to me! If I had eaten the sin offering today, should it have been accepted in the sight of the LORD?" ²⁰ And when Moses heard that, he approved.

Clean and Unclean Foods

Dt 14:3–20

11 The LORD spoke to Moses and Aaron, saying to them: ² Speak to the children of Israel, saying: These are the living things which you shall eat among all the animals that are on the earth. ³ Whatever animal has a parted hoof (that is, split-hoofed), and chews the cud among the animals, that one you shall eat.

⁴ Nevertheless these you shall not eat of those that chew the cud or of those that have a divided hoof: The camel, because it chews the cud but does not have a divided hoof, is unclean to you; ⁵ the rock badger, because it chews the cud but does not have a divided hoof, is unclean to you; ⁶ the hare, because it chews the cud but does not have a divided hoof, is unclean to you; ⁷ the pig, though it does have a divided hoof (that is, split-hoofed), yet it does not chew the cud, is unclean to you; ⁸ you shall not eat of their flesh, and their carcasses you must not touch; they are unclean to you.

⁹ These you shall eat of all that are in the waters: Whatever has fins and scales in the waters, in the seas and in the rivers, these you shall eat; ¹⁰ all that do not have fins and scales in the seas and in the rivers, from all that move in the waters and from any living thing that is in the waters, they are detestable to you; ¹¹ they shall be detestable to you. You shall not eat of their flesh, and you shall detest their carcasses. ¹² Whatever has no fins or scales in the waters is detestable to you.

¹³ These you shall detest among the birds; they shall not be eaten; they are detestable: the griffon vulture, the bearded vulture, and the black vulture, ¹⁴ the kite, and buzzard of any kind, ¹⁵ the raven of any kind, ¹⁶ and the eagle owl, the short-eared and long-eared owls, and the hawk of any kind, ¹⁷ and the little owl, the cormorant, and the screech owl, ¹⁸ and the white owl, the scops owl, and the osprey, ¹⁹ and the stork, the heron of any kind, the hoopoe, and the bat.

²⁰ All flying insects that walk, moving on all fours, shall be detestable to you. ²¹ Yet these you may eat of every flying insect that creeps on all fours: those that have jointed legs above their feet with which to hop on the ground. ²² Even of these you may eat: the locust of any kind, the bald locust of any kind, the cricket of any kind, and the grasshopper of any kind. ²³ But all other flying insects that have four feet shall be detestable to you.

²⁴ And by these you shall be unclean. Whoever touches the carcass of these shall be unclean until the evening.

Unclean Animals

²⁵ Whoever carries any of the carcasses of these shall wash his clothes and be unclean until the evening. ²⁶ The carcass of every animal that divides the hoof but is not completely split-hoofed nor chews the cud is unclean to you. Everyone who touches them shall be unclean. ²⁷ Whatever animal that walks on its paws, among all manner of animals that go on all fours, those are unclean to you. Whoever touches their carcass shall be unclean until the evening. ²⁸ He who carries the carcass of these shall wash his clothes and be unclean until the evening; they are unclean to you.

²⁹ These also shall be unclean to you among the crawling things that move on the ground: the mole rat, the mouse, and the great lizard of any kind, ³⁰ and the gecko, the lizard, the wall gecko, the sand lizard, and the chameleon. ³¹ These are unclean to you among all that crawl. Whoever touches them when they are dead shall be unclean until the evening. ³² And anything on which any of them falls when they are dead shall be unclean, whether it be an article of wood or clothing or a skin or a sack, any article that is used for any purpose. It must be put in water. And it shall be

unclean until the evening; then it shall be clean. ³³ Every clay vessel into which any of these falls, everything in it shall be unclean, and you shall break it. ³⁴ Any food in it that may be eaten on which water is poured shall be unclean, and any drink that may be drunk in every such vessel shall be unclean. ³⁵ Everything on which any part of their carcass falls shall be unclean; whether it is an oven or stove, it shall be broken to pieces. They are unclean and shall be unclean to you. ³⁶ Nevertheless a fountain or cistern where there is plenty of water shall be clean, but whoever touches their carcass shall be unclean. ³⁷ If any part of their carcass falls on any grain seed that is to be sown, it shall be clean. ³⁸ But if any water is put on the seed, and any part of their carcass fall on it, it shall be unclean to you.

³⁹ If any animal from which you may eat dies, whoever touches the carcass shall be unclean until the evening. ⁴⁰ And the person who eats of the carcass shall wash his clothes and be unclean until the evening. The person who carries the carcass shall wash his clothes and be unclean until the evening.

⁴¹ Every crawling thing that moves on the ground shall be detestable. It shall not be eaten. ⁴² Whatever goes on its belly, and whatever goes on all fours, or whatever has many feet from any crawling things that move on the earth, you shall not eat them for they are detestable. ⁴³ You shall not make yourselves detestable with any crawling thing that moves, nor shall you make yourselves unclean with them, that you should thereby be defiled by them. ⁴⁴ For I am the LORD your God. You shall therefore sanctify yourselves, and you shall be holy, for I am holy. Neither shall you defile yourselves with any manner of crawling thing that moves on the ground. ⁴⁵ For I am the LORD who brings you up out of the land of Egypt to be your God. Therefore you shall be holy, for I am holy.

⁴⁶ This is the law for the animals, and the fowls, and every living creature that moves in the waters, and every creature that crawls on the ground, ⁴⁷ to differentiate between the unclean and the clean, and between the animal that may be eaten and the animal that may not be eaten.

Purification After Childbirth

12 Then the LORD spoke to Moses, saying: ² Speak to the children of Israel, saying: If a woman has conceived and bears a male child, then she shall be unclean seven days, as in the days of her *monthly* menstruation she shall be unclean. ³ On the eighth day the flesh of his foreskin shall be circumcised. ⁴ And she shall then continue in the blood of her purifying for thirty-three days. She shall not touch anything holy, nor come into the sanctuary until the days of her purifying are fulfilled. ⁵ But if she gives birth to a female child, then she shall be unclean for two weeks as in her monthly menstruation, and she shall continue in the blood of her purifying for sixty-six days.

⁶ When the days of her purifying are fulfilled, whether for a son or for a daughter, she shall bring a year-old lamb for a burnt offering, and a young pigeon or a turtledove for a sin offering, to the entrance of the tent of meeting, ⁷ who shall offer it before the LORD and make atonement for her. Then she shall be cleansed from the issue of her blood.

This is the law for the woman who has given birth to a male or a female child. ⁸ If she cannot afford a lamb, then she shall bring two turtledoves or two pigeons, one for the burnt offering and the other for a sin offering, and the priest shall make atonement for her, and she shall be clean.

The Law Concerning Leprosy

13 And the LORD spoke to Moses and Aaron, saying: ² When a man has on the skin of his body a swelling, a scab, or spot, and it turns on the skin of his body like a mark of a leprous sore, then he shall be brought to Aaron the priest or to one of his sons the priests. ³ And the priest shall examine the mark on the skin of the body, and when the hair on the diseased area is white, and the mark appears to be deeper than the skin of his body, then it is a leprous sore. So the priest shall look on him and pronounce him unclean. ⁴ If the spot is white on the skin of his body, and it appears to be no deeper than the skin, and the hair is not white, then the priest shall isolate the person who has the mark for

seven days. ⁵ Then the priest shall examine him on the seventh day, and if the mark is still visible, and the mark has not spread into the skin, then the priest shall isolate him for seven days more. ⁶ And the priest shall examine him again on the seventh day, and if the mark has faded and not spread into the skin, then the priest shall pronounce him clean; it is only a scab, and he shall wash his clothes and be clean. ⁷ But if the scab spreads in the skin after he has been seen by the priest for his cleansing, he shall be seen by the priest again. ⁸ And if the priest sees that the scab has spread in the skin, then the priest shall pronounce him unclean. It is leprosy.

⁹ When a person has leprosy, then it shall be reported to the priest. ¹⁰ And the priest shall examine him, and if there is a white swelling in the skin, and it has turned the hair white, and there is raw flesh in the swelling, ¹¹ it is a recurring leprosy in the skin of his body, and the priest shall pronounce him unclean, but he shall not isolate him, for he is unclean.

¹² If the leprosy breaks out all over the skin, and the disease covers all the skin of the person who has the disease from his head to his feet, wherever the priest looks, ¹³ then the priest shall examine, and if the leprosy has covered all his body, he shall pronounce him clean from the disease. It has all turned white, and he is clean. ¹⁴ But when raw flesh appears on him, he shall be unclean. ¹⁵ The priest shall see the raw flesh and pronounce him to be unclean, for the raw flesh is unclean. It is leprosy. ¹⁶ Or if the raw flesh turns again, and it is changed to white, then he shall come to the priest. ¹⁷ And the priest shall see him, and if the disease is changed to white, then the priest shall pronounce him clean who has the disease. He is clean.

¹⁸ And when the skin has a boil, and it is healed, ¹⁹ and in the place of the boil there is a white swelling or a reddish-white spot, then it will be shown to the priest. ²⁰ And if the priest sees it, and it is deeper than the skin, and the hair has turned white, then the priest shall pronounce him unclean. It is a leprous sore that has broken out in the boil. ²¹ But if the priest looks at it, and there are no white hairs in it, and if it is not deeper than the skin but has faded, then the priest shall isolate the person for seven days. ²² If it spreads around the skin, then the priest shall pronounce him unclean. It is a leprous sore. ²³ But if the spot stays in its place and does not spread, then it is the scar of a boil, and the priest shall pronounce him clean.

²⁴ Or if there is some of the skin on the body where there is a burn, and the raw flesh that has a burn becomes a reddish or white spot, ²⁵ then the priest shall examine it, and if the hair in the spot has turned white, and it is deeper than the skin, then it is a leprous disease broken out from the burn. Therefore the priest shall pronounce him unclean. It is a leprous sore. ²⁶ But if the priest looks at it, and there is no white hair in the spot, and it is no deeper than the other skin and is faded, then the priest shall isolate him for seven days. ²⁷ And the priest shall examine him on the seventh day, and if it has spread around the skin, then the priest shall pronounce him unclean. It is a leprous sore. ²⁸ If the spot stays in its place and it does not spread in the skin, but is faded, then it is a swelling from the burn, and the priest shall pronounce him clean, for it is a scar from the burn.

²⁹ If a man or woman has a sore on the head or in the beard, ³⁰ then the priest shall examine the sore, and if it is deeper than the skin and there is in it a yellow thin hair, then the priest shall pronounce him unclean. It is a scaly leprosy of the head or beard. ³¹ If the priest examines the scaly sore, and it is no deeper than the skin, and there is no black hair in it, then the priest shall isolate the person with the scale for seven days. ³² And on the seventh day the priest shall examine the sore, and if the scale has not spread, and there is no yellow hair in it, and the scale is not deeper than the skin, ³³ then he shall shave, but the scale he shall not shave, and the priest shall isolate the person with the scale another seven days. ³⁴ And on the seventh day the priest shall examine the scale. If the scale has not spread in the skin and is no deeper than the skin, the priest shall pronounce him clean. He shall wash his clothes and be clean. ³⁵ But if the scale spreads over the skin after his cleansing, ³⁶ then the priest shall examine him. If the scale has spread over the skin, the priest

shall not look for yellow hair. He is unclean. [37] But if the scale appears not to have changed and there is black hair growing in it, then the scale is healed. He is clean and the priest shall pronounce him clean.

[38] If a man or a woman has spots on the skin of the body, even white bright spots, [39] then the priest shall examine, and if the bright spots on the skin of the body are a faded white, then it is just a rash that has broken out on the skin. He is clean.

[40] When a man has lost hair from his head, then he is bald. He is still clean. [41] And when a man has lost hair from his forehead, then he is bald on the forehead. He is still clean. [42] But if there is on the bald head or bald forehead a reddish-white sore, it is a leprous disease breaking out on his bald head or his bald forehead. [43] Then the priest shall examine it. If the diseased swelling is reddish-white on his bald head or on his bald forehead, resembling a leprous disease in the skin of the body, [44] he is leprous. He is unclean. The priest shall pronounce him unclean. His disease is on his head.

[45] The man who has the leprous disease shall have torn clothes and disheveled hair; and he shall cover his mustache and shall cry, "Unclean, unclean." [46] All the days that he has the disease, he shall be defiled. He is unclean. He shall dwell alone, and he shall live outside the camp.

The Law About Leprous Garments

[47] If a garment has a leprous disease, whether it is a wool or a linen garment, [48] whether it is in the warp or woof of the linen or wool fabric, or in the leather or anything made of leather, [49] and if the disease is greenish or reddish in the garment, or in the leather, or in the warp or woof, or in anything made of leather, it is a leprous disease and shall be shown to the priest. [50] And the priest shall examine the disease, and isolate the infected article for seven days. [51] And he shall examine the disease on the seventh day. If the disease has spread in the garment, either in the warp or in the woof, or in the leather, or in any work that is made of leather, this is a spreading leprous disease. It is unclean. [52] He shall therefore burn that garment, whether warp or woof, wool or linen, or anything of leather that has the disease, for it is a spreading leprous disease. It shall be burned in the fire.

[53] If the priest examines *it*, and the disease has not spread in the garment, either in the warp or the woof, or in anything of leather, [54] then the priest shall command that they wash the article in which the disease appears, and he shall isolate it for seven days more. [55] The priest shall examine the infected article after it has been washed. If the infected spot has not changed its color, even if the disease has not spread, it is unclean. You shall burn it in the fire, whether the leprous spot is on the inside or on the outside of the article. [56] If the priest examines and the disease has faded after washing it, he shall tear the spot out of the garment, or out of the leather, or out of the warp or the woof. [57] If it still appears in the garment, either in the warp or in the woof, or in anything of leather, it is spreading. You shall burn in the fire that in which the disease appears. [58] The garment that you have washed, either in the warp or woof, or anything of leather, if the disease is gone from it, then it shall be washed a second time and shall be clean.

[59] This is the law of the leprous disease in a garment of wool or linen, either in the warp or woof, or anything of leather to determine if it is clean or unclean.

The Law for Cleansing Lepers

14 The LORD spoke to Moses, saying: [2] This shall be the law of the leper in the day of his cleansing: It shall be reported to the priest, [3] and the priest shall go out of the camp, and the priest shall examine him and see if the disease is healed in the leprous person. [4] Then the priest shall command that two live clean birds and cedar wood and scarlet fabric and hyssop be brought for him who is to be cleansed. [5] The priest shall command that one of the birds be slaughtered in a clay vessel over running water. [6] As for the living bird, he shall take it, the cedar wood, the scarlet, and the hyssop, and shall dip them and the living bird in the blood of the bird that was killed over the running water. [7] Then he shall

sprinkle *it* seven times on him who is to be cleansed from leprosy, and he shall pronounce him clean and shall let the living bird loose into the open field.

[8] He that is to be cleansed shall wash his clothes, and shave off all his hair, and wash himself in water, so that he may be clean. After that he shall come into the camp and shall stay outside of his tent seven days. [9] But it shall be on the seventh day that he shall shave all his hair off his head and his beard and his eyebrows, all his hair he shall shave off, and he shall wash his clothes. Also he shall wash his body in water, and he shall be clean.

[10] On the eighth day he shall take two male lambs without blemish, and one ewe lamb a year old without blemish, and three-tenths of an *ephah¹* of wheat flour mixed with oil for a grain offering, and one log of oil. [2] [11] The priest who makes him clean shall present the man who is to be made clean and those things before the LORD at the entrance of the tent of meeting.

[12] Then the priest shall take one male lamb and offer it for a guilt offering, along with the log of oil, and wave them for a wave offering before the LORD. [13] Then he shall slaughter the lamb in the place where they kill the sin offering and the burnt offering in the holy sanctuary. For as the sin offering is the priest's, so is the guilt offering. It is most holy. [14] And the priest shall take some of the blood of the guilt offering, and the priest shall put it on the tip of the right ear of him who is to be cleansed, and on the thumb of his right hand, and on the big toe of his right foot. [15] And the priest shall take some of the log of oil and pour it into the palm of his own left hand. [16] Then the priest shall dip his right finger in the oil that is in his left hand, and shall sprinkle from the oil with his finger seven times before the LORD. [17] And some of the rest of the oil that is in his hand the priest shall put on the tip of the right ear of him who is to be cleansed, and on the thumb of his right hand, and on the big toe of his right foot, and on the blood of the guilt offering. [18] And the rest of the oil that is in the priest's hand he shall pour upon the head of him who is to be cleansed, and the priest shall make atonement for him-before the LORD.

[19] The priest shall offer the sin offering, and make atonement for him who is to be cleansed from his *ceremonial* uncleanness, and afterward he shall kill the burnt offering. [20] Then the priest shall offer the burnt offering and the grain offering on the altar, and the priest shall make atonement for him, and he shall be clean.

[21] But if he is poor and cannot afford so much, then he shall take one male lamb for a guilt offering to be waved to make atonement for him, and one-tenth of an *ephah³* of wheat flour mixed with oil for a grain offering, and a log of oil, [22] and two turtledoves or two pigeons, such as he is able to afford. The one shall be a sin offering and the other a burnt offering.

[23] He shall bring them on the eighth day for his cleansing to the priest at the entrance of the tent of meeting before the LORD. [24] The priest shall take the lamb of the guilt offering, along with the log of oil, and the priest shall wave them for a wave offering before the LORD. [25] Then he shall kill the lamb of the guilt offering; and the priest shall take some of the blood of the guilt offering and put it on the tip of the right ear of him who is to be cleansed and on the thumb of his right hand and on the big toe of his right foot. [26] Next the priest shall pour some of the oil into the palm of his own left hand, [27] and the priest shall sprinkle with his right finger some of the oil that is in his left hand seven times before the LORD. [28] Then the priest shall put some of the oil that is in his hand on the tip of the right ear of him who is to be cleansed, and on the thumb of his right hand, and on the big toe of his right foot on the place of the blood of the guilt offering. [29] The rest of the oil that is in the priest's hand he shall pour on the head of him who is to be cleansed to make atonement for him before the LORD. [30] He shall offer one of the turtledoves or the pigeons, such as he can afford, [31] even such as he is able to get, one for a sin offering and the other for a burnt offering, along with the grain offering, and the priest shall make atonement for him who is to be cleansed before the LORD.

[32] This is the law for a person who has a leprous sore who cannot afford the offerings for his cleansing.

---

¹ *10* Likely about 11 pounds, or 5 kilograms. ² *10* About ½ quart, or 0.3 liter; and in vv. 12, 15, 21, and 24. ³ *21* Likely about 3½ pounds, or 1.6 kilograms.

The Law About Leprous Houses

33 The Lord spoke to Moses and to Aaron, saying: 34 When you have come into the land of Canaan, which I am giving to you for a possession, and I put a leprous disease in a house of the land of your possession, 35 then he who owns the house shall come and tell the priest, "It seems to me there is some disease in the house." 36 Then the priest shall command that they empty the house before the priest goes into it to examine the disease, so that all that is in the house is not made unclean. Afterwards, the priest shall go in to examine the house. 37 He shall examine the disease and see if the disease is in the walls of the house with greenish or reddish spots, which appear to go deeper than the wall. 38 Then the priest shall go out to the door of the house and close off the house seven days. 39 The priest shall return on the seventh day and shall examine and see if the disease has spread in the walls of the house. 40 Then the priest shall command that they take away the stones in which the disease appears and throw them into an unclean place outside the city. 41 And he shall cause the house to be scraped all around, and they shall pour out the plaster that they scrape off outside the city into an unclean place. 42 And they shall take other stones and put them in the place of those stones, and he shall take other plaster and shall plaster the house.

43 If the disease comes again and breaks out in the house after he has taken away the stones and after he has scraped the house and after it is plastered, 44 then the priest shall come and examine and see if the disease has spread in the house. If the disease has spread in the house, it is a persistent leprosy in the house; it is unclean. 45 He shall break down the house, the stones and the timber, and all the plaster of the house, and he shall carry them out of the city into an unclean place.

46 Moreover, he who goes into the house while it is closed off shall be unclean until the evening. 47 And he who sleeps in the house shall wash his clothes, and he who eats in the house shall wash his clothes.

48 If the priest comes in and examines it and sees the disease has not spread in the house after the house was plastered, then the priest shall pronounce the house clean, because the disease is healed. 49 He shall take two birds, and cedar wood, and scarlet, and hyssop to cleanse the house. 50 Then he shall kill one of the birds in a clay vessel over running water. 51 He shall take the cedar wood, and the hyssop, and the scarlet, and the living bird, and dip them in the blood of the slain bird, and in the running water, and sprinkle the house seven times. 52 Then he shall cleanse the house with the blood of the bird, and with the running water, and with the living bird, and with the cedar wood, and with the hyssop, and with the scarlet. 53 But he shall let the living bird loose outside the city into the open fields and make atonement for the house, and it shall be clean.

54 This is the law for all manner of leprous sore and scale, 55 and for the disease of a garment, or of a house, 56 and for a swelling, or for a scab, or for a spot, 57 to discern when it is unclean and when it is clean.

This is the law of leprosy.

The Law About Bodily Discharges

15 Then the Lord spoke to Moses and to Aaron, saying: 2 Speak to the children of Israel, and say to them: When any man has a discharge out of his body, his discharge is unclean. 3 This is the instruction for his uncleanness in his discharge, whether the discharge from his body flows or his body is stopped up by his discharge, it is his uncleanness.

4 Every bed on which the man with the discharge lies shall be unclean, and everything on which he sits shall be unclean. 5 Whoever touches the bed shall wash his clothes, and bathe himself in water, and be unclean until the evening. 6 And whoever sits on anything where the man sat who has the discharge shall wash his clothes, and bathe himself in water, and be unclean until the evening.

7 And whoever touches the body of him who has the discharge shall wash his clothes, and bathe himself in water, and be unclean until the evening.

8 If the man with the discharge spits on someone who is clean, then he shall wash his clothes, and bathe himself in water, and be unclean until the evening.

9 Any saddle on which the man with a discharge rides shall be unclean. 10 Whoever touches anything that was under him shall be unclean until the evening, and he who carries any of those things shall wash his clothes, and bathe himself in water, and be unclean until the evening.

11 Whomever he who has the discharge touches, and has not rinsed his hands in water, he shall wash his clothes and bathe in water, and be unclean until evening.

12 The earthen vessel that he who has the discharge touches shall be broken, and every vessel of wood shall be rinsed in water.

13 When he who has a discharge is cleansed of his issue, then he shall count to himself seven days for his cleansing, and wash his clothes, and bathe his body in running water, and shall be clean. 14 On the eighth day he shall take two turtledoves or two pigeons and come before the Lord at the entrance of the tent of meeting and give them to the priest. 15 And the priest shall offer them, one for a sin offering and the other for a burnt offering, and the priest shall make atonement for him before the Lord for his discharge.

16 If any man has a seminal emission, then he shall wash all his body in water and be unclean until the evening. 17 Every garment and all leather on which there is seminal emission shall be washed with water and be unclean until the evening. 18 If a man lies with a woman, and there is an emission of semen, they shall both bathe themselves in water and be unclean until the evening.

19 If a woman has a discharge, and the discharge from her body is blood, she shall be set apart for seven days; and whoever touches her shall be unclean until the evening.

20 Everything that she lies on in her menstrual impurity shall be unclean. Also, everything that she sits on shall be unclean. 21 Whoever touches her bed shall wash his clothes and bathe himself in water, and be unclean until the evening. 22 Whoever touches anything on which she sits shall wash his clothes and bathe himself in water, and be unclean until the evening. 23 Whether it is the bed or anything on which she sits, when he touches it he shall be unclean until the evening.

24 If any man lies with her, and her menstrual impurity is on him, he shall be unclean seven days, and every bed where he lies shall be unclean.

25 If a woman has a discharge of blood for many days, not at the time of her menstrual impurity, or if she has a discharge beyond the time of her impurity, all the days of the discharge she shall be in uncleanness, as in the days of her impurity. She shall be unclean. 26 Every bed that she lies on all the days of her discharge shall be for impurity, and whatever she sits on shall be unclean, as the uncleanness of her menstrual impurity. 27 Whoever touches those things shall be unclean and shall wash his clothes and bathe himself in water and be unclean until the evening.

28 But if she is cleansed of her discharge, then she shall count to herself seven days, and after that she shall be clean. 29 On the eighth day she shall take two turtledoves or two pigeons and bring them to the priest at the entrance of the tent of meeting. 30 The priest shall offer one for a sin offering and the other for a burnt offering, and the priest shall make atonement for her before the Lord for her unclean discharge.

31 Thus you shall separate the children of Israel from their uncleanness, so that they do not die in their uncleanness by defiling My tabernacle that is among them.

32 This is the law for him who has a discharge and for him who has a seminal emission and thus becomes unclean, 33 and for her who is sick from her menstruation, and for him who has a discharge, for anyone male or female, and for the man who lies with a woman who is unclean.

The Day of Atonement

Lev 23:26–32; Nu 29:7–11

16 The Lord spoke to Moses after the death of the two sons of Aaron, when they drew near to the Lord and died. 2 The Lord said to Moses: Speak to Aaron your brother so that he does not come at any time into the Holy Place within the veil before the mercy seat, which is on the ark, so that he will not die, for I will appear in the cloud on the mercy seat.

³ Thus Aaron shall come into the Holy Place with a young bull for a sin offering and a ram for a burnt offering. ⁴ He shall put on the holy linen tunic, and he shall have the linen undergarment on his body, and shall be girded with a linen sash, and shall be wearing the linen turban. These are holy garments. Therefore he shall wash his body in water and then put them on. ⁵ He shall take from the congregation of the children of Israel two male goats for a sin offering and one ram for a burnt offering.

⁶ Aaron shall offer his bull for the sin offering, which is for himself, and make atonement for himself and for his house. ⁷ Then he shall take the two goats and present them before the LORD at the entrance of the tent of meeting. ⁸ Aaron shall cast lots for the two goats: one lot for the LORD and the other lot for the scapegoat. ⁹ Aaron shall bring the goat on which the lot of the LORD falls and offer him for a sin offering. ¹⁰ But the goat on which the lot falls to be the scapegoat shall be presented alive before the LORD to make atonement with it, that it may be sent away as a scapegoat into the wilderness.

¹¹ Aaron shall bring the bull of the sin offering, which is for himself, and shall make atonement for himself, and for his house, and shall kill the bull of the sin offering for himself. ¹² And he shall take a censer full of burning coals of fire from the altar before the LORD, and two handfuls of sweet incense beaten small, and bring it within the veil. ¹³ And he shall put the incense on the fire before the LORD, that the cloud of the incense may cover the mercy seat that is over the testimony, so that he does not die. ¹⁴ And he shall take of the blood of the bull, and sprinkle it with his finger on the mercy seat on the eastern side, and before the mercy seat he shall sprinkle from the blood with his finger seven times.

¹⁵ Then he shall kill the goat of the sin offering, which is for the people, and bring its blood within the veil, and do with that blood as he did with the blood of the bull, and sprinkle it over and in front of the mercy seat. ¹⁶ And he shall make atonement for the Holy Place, because of the uncleanness of the children of Israel and because of their transgressions in all their sins, and so he shall do for the tent of meeting that remains among them in the midst of their uncleanness. ¹⁷ There shall be no man in the tent of meeting when he goes in to make atonement in the Holy Place, until he comes out and has made atonement for himself, and for his household, and for all the congregation of Israel.

¹⁸ Then he shall go out to the altar that is before the LORD and make atonement for it, and he shall take some of the blood of the bull and some of the blood of the goat, and put it on the horns of the altar all around. ¹⁹ He shall sprinkle from the blood on it with his finger seven times, and cleanse it, and consecrate it from the uncleanness of the children of Israel.

²⁰ When he has made an end of atonement for the Holy Place, and the tent of meeting, and the altar, then he shall bring the live goat. ²¹ And Aaron shall lay both his hands on the head of the live goat, and confess over it all the iniquities of the children of Israel, and all their transgressions in all their sins, putting them on the head of the goat, and shall send it away by the hand of a designated man into the wilderness. ²² And the goat shall bear on it all their iniquities to a desolate land, and he shall let the goat go free in the wilderness.

²³ Then Aaron shall come into the tent of meeting, and shall take off the linen garments which he put on when he went into the Holy Place, and shall leave them there. ²⁴ And he shall wash his body with water in a holy place, and put on his garments, and come out, and offer his burnt offering, and the burnt offering of the people, and make atonement for himself and for the people. ²⁵ The fat of the sin offering he shall burn on the altar.

²⁶ He who releases the goat as the scapegoat shall wash his clothes, and bathe his body in water, and afterward come into the camp. ²⁷ The bull for the sin offering and the goat for the sin offering, whose blood was brought in to make atonement in the Holy Place, shall be carried outside the camp. They shall burn in the fire their hides, their flesh, and their refuse. ²⁸ He who burns them shall wash his clothes, and bathe his body in water, and afterward he shall come into the camp.

²⁹ This shall be a perpetual statute for you so that in the seventh month, on the tenth day of the month, you shall humble yourselves,

and do no work of any kind, whether it is the native citizen or the stranger who sojourns among you. ³⁰ For on that day the priest shall make atonement for you to cleanse you, so that you may be clean from all your sins before the LORD. ³¹ It shall be a sabbath, a solemn rest for you, and you shall humble yourselves. It is a perpetual statute. ³² The priest, who is anointed and consecrated to minister as a priest in the place of his father, shall make atonement, and shall put on the linen garments, the holy garments. ³³ And he shall make atonement for the Holy Sanctuary, for the tent of meeting, and for the altar, and he shall make atonement for the priests, and for all the people of the congregation.

³⁴ This shall be a perpetual statute for you to make atonement for the children of Israel for all their sins once a year.

And Moses did as the LORD commanded him.

The Law About Eating Blood

17 And the LORD spoke to Moses, saying: ² Speak to Aaron, and to his sons, and to all the children of Israel, and say to them: This is the thing which the LORD has commanded, saying: ³ If anyone of the house of Israel *ritually* slaughters an ox, a lamb, or goat in the camp, or slaughters it outside of the camp, ⁴ and does not bring it to the entrance of the tent of meeting to offer it as a gift to the LORD before the tabernacle of the LORD, then blood guilt shall be accounted to that man. He has shed blood, and that man shall be cut off from among his people. ⁵ This is so that the children of Israel may bring their sacrifices which they offer in the open field, even that they may bring them to the LORD at the entrance of the tent of meeting, to the priest, and offer them for peace offerings to the LORD. ⁶ The priest shall sprinkle the blood on the altar of the LORD at the entrance of the tent of meeting, and burn the fat for a pleasing aroma to the LORD. ⁷ They shall no more offer their sacrifices to goat demons, after whom they have acted like whores. This shall be a perpetual statute for them throughout their generations.

⁸ You shall say to them: Any man from the house of Israel, or from the foreigners who sojourn among you, who offers a burnt offering or sacrifice, ⁹ and does not bring it to the entrance of the tent of meeting to offer it to the LORD, even that man shall be cut off from among his people.

¹⁰ Whoever from the house of Israel, or from the strangers who sojourn among you, who eats any manner of blood, I will set My face against that person who eats blood, and will cut him off from among his people. ¹¹ For the life of the flesh is in the blood, and I have given it to you on the altar to make atonement for your lives; for it is the blood that makes atonement for the soul. ¹² Therefore I said to the children of Israel: No person among you shall eat blood, nor shall any stranger who sojourns among you eat blood. ¹³ Whoever from the children of Israel, or from the foreigners who sojourn among you, who hunts and catches any wild animal or fowl that may be eaten, he shall even pour out the blood and cover it with dirt. ¹⁴ For the life of every creature is its blood; in its blood is its life. Therefore I said to the children of Israel: You shall not eat the blood of any creature, for the life of every creature is its blood. Whoever eats it shall be cut off.

¹⁵ Every person who eats that which died of itself, or that which was torn by animals, whether he is a native citizen or a foreigner, he shall both wash his clothes and bathe himself in water, and be unclean until the evening. Then he shall be clean. ¹⁶ But if he does not wash them or bathe his body, then he shall bear his iniquity.

Laws on Immoral Relations

18 The LORD spoke to Moses, saying: ² Speak to the children of Israel, and say to them: I am the LORD your God. ³ After the practices of the land of Egypt, from where you lived, you shall not follow, and after the practices of the land of Canaan, to where I will bring you, you shall not follow; nor shall you walk in their ordinances. ⁴ You shall follow My decrees and keep My ordinances to walk in them: I am the LORD your God. ⁵ You shall therefore keep My statutes and My judgments, which if a man does them, then he shall live by them: I am the LORD.

⁶ None of you shall approach any of his near relatives to have relations: I am the LORD.

[7] You shall not have relations with your father or have relations with your mother. She is your mother. You shall not have relations with her.

[8] You shall not have relations with your father's wife, for this exposes your father's nakedness.

[9] You shall not have relations with your sister, whether your father's or mother's daughter, whether raised in the family or another home.

[10] You shall not have relations with your son's daughter or your daughter's daughter, for this exposes your own nakedness.

[11] You shall not have relations with your father's wife's daughter who is raised in your father's family, for she is your sister.

[12] You shall not have relations with your father's sister, for she is your father's relative.

[13] You shall not have relations with your mother's sister, for she is your mother's relative.

[14] You shall not expose the nakedness of your father's brother. You shall not approach his wife for relations; she is your aunt.

[15] You shall not have relations with your daughter-in-law, for she is your son's wife—you shall not have relations with her.

[16] You shall not have relations with your brother's wife, for this exposes your brother's nakedness.

[17] You shall not have relations with a woman and her daughter, nor shall you have her son's daughter or her daughter's daughter, for this exposes the woman's nakedness. They are all near relatives. It is depravity.

[18] And you shall not have a woman as a rival wife, who is the sister of your other wife, for this is to expose her nakedness while her sister, your other wife, is still alive.

[19] Also you shall not approach a woman to have relations as long as she is in her menstrual uncleanness.

[20] Moreover, you shall not have relations with your neighbor's wife to defile yourself with her.

[21] You shall not let any of your children be offered through the fire to Molek, and so profane the name of your God: I am the LORD.

[22] You shall not lie with a man as one does with a woman. It is an abomination.

[23] You shall not lie with an animal to defile yourself, nor shall any woman lie with an animal. It is a perversion.

[24] Do not defile yourselves in any of these ways, for in these practices the nations I am casting out before you have defiled themselves. [25] And the land has become defiled; therefore I have punished its iniquity, and the land has vomited out her inhabitants. [26] But you shall therefore keep My statutes and My decrees, and you shall not commit any of these abominations, either the native citizen or any foreigner who sojourns among you [27] (for the people of the land, who were before you, committed all of these abominations, and the land became defiled), [28] lest the land vomit you out also when you defile it, as it vomited out the nations that were before you.

[29] For whoever shall commit any of these abominations, those persons who commit them shall be cut off from among their people. [30] Therefore you shall keep My ordinances, that you do not commit any one of these abominable customs which were committed before you, so that you do not defile yourselves by them: I am the LORD your God.

Moral and Ceremonial Laws

19 And the LORD spoke to Moses, saying: [2] Speak to all the congregation of the children of Israel, and say to them: You shall be holy, for I the LORD your God am holy.

[3] Every one of you shall revere his mother and his father, and you will keep My Sabbaths: I am the LORD your God.

[4] Do not turn to idols, nor make for yourselves cast metal gods: I am the LORD your God.

[5] When you offer a sacrifice of peace offerings to the LORD, you shall offer it so that you might be accepted. [6] It shall be eaten the same day you offer it or on the next day, and if any remains until the third day, it shall be burned in the fire. [7] If it is eaten at all on the third day, then it is contaminated. It shall not be accepted. [8] Therefore everyone who eats it shall bear his iniquity, because he has defiled what is holy of the LORD, and that person shall be cut off from among his people.

[9] When you reap the harvest of your land, you shall not reap up to the edge of your field, nor shall you gather the gleanings of your harvest. [10] You shall not glean bare your vineyard, nor shall you gather every fallen grape of your vineyard. You shall leave them for the poor and stranger: I am the LORD your God.

[11] You shall not steal, nor deal falsely, nor lie to one another.

[12] You shall not swear falsely by My name, and so defile the name of your God: I am the LORD.

[13] You shall not defraud your neighbor or rob him. The wages of him who is hired shall not stay with you all night until the morning.

[14] You shall not curse the deaf, nor put a stumbling block before the blind, but you shall fear your God: I am the LORD.

[15] You shall do no unrighteousness in a court. You shall not be partial to the poor, nor honor the person who is great, but in righteousness you shall judge your neighbor.

[16] You shall not go around as a slanderer among your people, nor shall you stand by while the life of your neighbor is in danger: I am the LORD.

[17] You shall not hate your brother in your heart. You shall surely reason honestly with your neighbor, and not suffer sin because of him.

[18] You shall not take vengeance, nor bear any grudge against the children of your people, but you shall love your neighbor as yourself: I am the LORD.

[19] You shall keep My statutes.

You shall not let your livestock breed with a different kind.

You shall not sow your field with mixed seed, nor shall your garment be mixed into two types of fabric.

[20] Whoever lies with a slave woman who is betrothed to another man and not yet ransomed or given freedom, compensation will be made. They shall not be put to death, because she was not free. [21] He shall bring his guilt offering to the LORD at the entrance of the tent of meeting, a ram for a guilt offering. [22] The priest shall make atonement for him with the ram of the guilt offering before the LORD for his sin which he has done, and he will be forgiven for the sin that he has committed.

[23] When you come into the land and plant any kind of tree for food, then you shall count the fruit as forbidden. [1] Three years it shall be forbidden to you. It shall not be eaten. [24] But in the fourth year all the fruit shall be holy and an offering of praise to the LORD. [25] And in the fifth year you shall eat of the fruit that it may yield an increase to you: I am the LORD your God.

[26] You shall not eat anything with the blood in it, nor shall you practice divination or fortune-telling.

[27] You shall not round the corners of the hair on your head, nor shall you mar the edges of your beard.

[28] You shall not make any cuttings in your flesh for the dead nor make any tattoo marks on yourselves: I am the LORD.

[29] Do not prostitute your daughter and cause her to be defiled, lest the land fall into whoredom and become full of wickedness.

[30] You shall keep My Sabbaths and revere My sanctuary: I am the LORD.

[31] Do not turn to spirits through mediums or necromancers. Do not seek after them to be defiled by them: I am the LORD your God.

[32] You shall rise up before a gray head, and honor the face of an old man, and fear your God: I am the LORD.

[33] When a foreigner sojourns with you in your land, you shall not do him wrong. [34] The foreigner who dwells with you shall be to you as one born among you, and you shall love him as yourself for you were foreigners in the land of Egypt: I am the LORD your God.

[35] You shall do no unrighteousness in judgment regarding measures in length, weight, or quantity. [36] You shall have honest balances, honest weights, an honest ephah, [2] and an honest hin: [3] I am the LORD your God, who brought you out of the land of Egypt.

[37] Therefore you shall observe all My statutes and all My judgments and do them: I am the LORD.

---

[1] 23 Or *uncircumcised*.   [2] 36 A dry measure of about ⅗ of a bushel, or 22 liters.   [3] 36 A liquid measure of about 1 gallon, or 3.8 liters.

Penalties for Violating the Law

20 Then the Lord spoke to Moses, saying: [2] Again, you shall say to the children of Israel: Whoever from the children of Israel or from the foreigners who sojourn in Israel who gives any of his children to Molek, he shall surely be put to death. The people of the land shall stone him. [3] I will set My face against that man and will cut him off from among his people, because he has given some of his descendants to Molek to defile My sanctuary and to defile My holy name. [4] If the people of the land in any way hide their eyes from the man when he gives of his children to Molek and do not put him to death, [5] then I will set My face against that man and against his family; and I will cut them off from their people, both him and those who follow after him as whores after Molek.

[6] The person who turns to spirits through mediums and necromancers in order to whore after them, I will even set My face against that person and will cut him off from among his people.

[7] Consecrate yourselves therefore, and be holy, for I am the Lord your God. [8] You shall keep My statutes, and do them; I am the Lord who sanctifies you.

[9] For anyone who curses his father or his mother shall be surely put to death. He has cursed his father or his mother, and his blood guilt shall be upon him.

[10] If a man commits adultery with another man's wife, even he who commits adultery with his neighbor's wife, the adulterer and the adulteress shall surely be put to death.

[11] If a man lies with his father's wife, he has exposed his father's nakedness. Both of them shall surely be put to death. Their blood guilt shall be upon them.

[12] If a man lies with his daughter-in-law, both of them shall surely be put to death. They have committed a perversion. Their blood guilt shall be upon them.

[13] If a man lies with another man as with a woman, both of them have committed an abomination. They shall surely be put to death. Their blood guilt shall be upon them.

[14] If a man lies with a woman and also her mother, it is wickedness. Both he and they shall be burned with fire, so that there is no wickedness among you.

[15] If a man lies with an animal, he shall surely be put to death, and you shall kill the animal.

[16] If a woman approaches an animal and lies with it, you shall kill the woman and the animal. They shall surely be put to death. Their blood guilt shall be upon them.

[17] If a man lies with his sister, whether the daughter of his father or mother, they have exposed each other's nakedness; it is a wicked thing and they shall be cut off from the sight of their people. He has exposed his sister's nakedness, and he shall bear his iniquity.

[18] If a man lies with a woman during her menstrual period and exposes her nakedness, her fountain of blood is then exposed. Both of them shall be cut off from among their people.

[19] You shall not have relations with your mother's sister or your father's sister, for this is to expose the nakedness of one's relative. They shall bear their iniquity.

[20] If a man lies with his uncle's wife, he has exposed his uncle's nakedness. They shall bear their sin. They shall die childless.

[21] If a man lies with his brother's wife, it is impurity. He has exposed his brother's nakedness. They shall be childless.

[22] You shall therefore keep all My statutes and all My decrees and do them, so that the land to where I am bringing you will not vomit you out. [23] You shall not walk in the customs of the nation that I am driving out before you, for they committed all these things, and therefore I abhorred them. [24] But I have said to you: You shall inherit their land, and I will give it to you to possess it, a land that flows with milk and honey. I am the Lord your God, who has separated you from other peoples.

[25] You shall therefore make distinction between the clean animal from the unclean, and the unclean fowl from the clean, and you shall not make yourselves detestable by animal, or by fowl, or by any manner of living thing that crawls on the ground, which I have separated from you as unclean. [26] You shall be holy unto Me; for I the Lord am holy and have separated you from other peoples, that you should be Mine.

[27] A man or woman who speaks to spirits as a medium or necromancer shall surely be put to death. They shall stone them. Their blood guilt shall be upon them.

Rules for Priestly Conduct

21 Then the Lord said to Moses: Speak to the priests, the sons of Aaron, and say to them: None shall make himself unclean for the dead among his people, [2] but for his closest relatives, that is, for his mother, his father, his son, his daughter, his brother, [3] and his virgin sister (who is near him because she has not had a husband), for her he may be made unclean. [4] And he shall not make himself unclean as a husband among his people *because of the dead* and so defile himself.

[5] They shall not make bald areas on their heads, nor shall they shave off the edges of their beards, nor make any cuts in their flesh. [6] They shall be holy unto their God, and not profane the name of their God; for they offer the offerings of the Lord made by fire, and the food of their God. Therefore they shall be holy.

[7] They shall not take a wife who is a whore or has been defiled, nor shall they take a woman divorced from her husband, for he is holy unto his God. [8] You shall sanctify him, for he offers the food of your God. He shall be holy to you, for I the Lord, who sanctifies you, am holy.

[9] The daughter of any priest, if she defiles herself by being a whore, she also defiles her father. She shall be burned with fire.

[10] He who is the high priest among his brothers, on whose head the anointing oil was poured and who is consecrated to wear the garments, shall not dishevel his hair, nor tear his clothes; [11] nor shall he approach any dead body, nor make himself unclean, even for his father or his mother; [12] nor shall he go out of the sanctuary, so as not to defile the sanctuary of his God, for the consecration of the anointing oil of his God is upon him: I am the Lord.

[13] He shall take a wife in her virginity. [14] A widow, or a divorced woman, or a defiled woman, or a prostitute, these he shall not marry. But he shall take for a wife a virgin of his own people, [15] so that he does not defile his offspring among his people, for I am the Lord who sanctifies him.

[16] The Lord spoke to Moses, saying: [17] Speak to Aaron, saying: None of your offspring in their generations who has any blemish may approach to offer the food of his God. [18] For whoever has a blemish, he shall not approach, whether a blind or lame man, or one who has a physical flaw on his face or a limb that is too long, [19] or a man who has a broken foot or broken hand, [20] or a hunchback, or a dwarf, or who has a defect in his eye, or eczema or scabs, or is a eunuch. [21] No man who has a blemish from the offspring of Aaron the priest shall come near to offer the food offerings of the Lord made by fire. He has a blemish; he shall not come near to offer the bread of his God. [22] He shall eat the food of his God, both of the most holy and of the holy. [23] Only he shall not go in through the veil or come to the altar, because he has a blemish, so that he does not defile My sanctuaries, for I am the Lord who sanctifies them.

[24] Moses spoke this to Aaron, and to his sons, and to all the children of Israel.

Holy Offerings

22 And the Lord spoke to Moses, saying: [2] Speak to Aaron and to his sons that they should be very respectful with the holy things of the children of Israel, and that they do not defile My holy name with those things which the people have consecrated to Me: I am the Lord.

[3] Say to them: Whoever from your offspring through your generations approaches the holy things, which the children of Israel have dedicated to the Lord, while he has uncleanness, that person shall be cut off from My presence: I am the Lord.

[4] If a man of the offspring of Aaron is a leper or has a discharge, he shall not eat of the holy offerings until he is clean. And whoever touches anything that is unclean by contact with the dead or a man who had an emission of semen, [5] or whoever touches any crawling thing whereby he may be made unclean, or a man from whom he may receive uncleanness, whatever uncleanness he has, [6] the person who has touched any such thing shall be unclean until

evening, and shall not eat of the holy things unless he washes his body with water. [7] When the sun goes down, he shall be clean, and afterward he shall eat of the holy things, because it is his food. [8] That which dies of itself or is torn by animals he shall not eat, becoming unclean by it: I am the Lord.

[9] They shall therefore keep My ordinance, lest they bear sin from it and therefore die if they defile it: I am the Lord who sanctifies them.

[10] There shall be no outsider[1] who eats of a holy thing, whether a foreign guest of the priest or a hired servant, he shall not eat of a holy offering. [11] But if a priest buys a person with his money, the person acquired shall eat of it, and he that is born in his house shall eat of his food. [12] If the priest's daughter marries an outsider, she may not eat of an offering of the holy things. [13] But if the priest's daughter is a widow or divorced, and has no child and has returned to her father's house as in her youth, she may eat of her father's food; but no outsider may eat of it.

[14] If a man eats the holy thing unwittingly, then he shall add a fifth of the value to it and shall give the holy thing to the priest. [15] They shall not defile the holy things of the children of Israel, which they offer to the Lord, [16] and cause them to suffer and to bear the iniquity of guilt when they eat their holy things, for I am the Lord who sanctifies them.

Acceptable Offerings

[17] The Lord spoke to Moses, saying: [18] Speak to Aaron, and to his sons, and to all the children of Israel, and say to them: Whoever from the house of Israel or from the foreigners in Israel who offers his burnt offering for any vows or freewill offerings that he offers to the Lord, [19] then if it is to be accepted for you, the offering shall be a male without blemish, a bull, sheep, or goat. [20] But whatever has a blemish you shall not offer, for it shall not be acceptable for you. [21] Whoever offers a sacrifice of peace offerings to the Lord to fulfill his vow or a freewill offering, whether from the herd or flock, to be accepted it shall be perfect, with no blemish on it. [22] Blind, or disabled, or maimed, or having an ulcer or eczema or scabs, you shall not offer these to the Lord, nor make a food offering by fire on the altar to the Lord. [23] A herd animal or a flock animal that has a limb that is too long or short you may offer for a freewill offering, but for a vow it shall not be accepted. [24] You shall not offer to the Lord an animal that is bruised or crushed or torn or cut; nor shall you make any offering of them in your land. [25] Nor from a foreigner shall you offer an animal as the food of your God, because a blemish is in them from their mutilation. They shall not be accepted for you.

[26] The Lord spoke to Moses, saying: [27] When an ox, or a sheep, or a goat is born, then it shall be seven days with its mother, and from the eighth day and thereafter it shall be accepted for a food offering made by fire to the Lord. [28] But you shall not slaughter on the same day an ox or a sheep and her young.

[29] When you offer a sacrifice of thanksgiving to the Lord, offer it so that it may be accepted. [30] On the same day it shall be eaten. You shall leave none of it until the next day: I am the Lord.

[31] Therefore you shall keep My commandments and do them: I am the Lord. [32] You shall not defile My holy name, but I will be sanctified among the children of Israel: I am the Lord who sanctifies you, [33] who brought you out of the land of Egypt, to be your God: I am the Lord.

The Appointed Feasts

23 And the Lord spoke to Moses, saying: [2] Speak to the children of Israel, and say to them: Concerning the feasts of the Lord that you shall proclaim to be holy convocations, these are My appointed feasts.

The Sabbath

[3] For six days work shall be done, but the seventh day is the Sabbath of complete rest, a holy convocation. You shall do no work. It is the Sabbath of the Lord in all your dwellings.

The Passover and the Feast of Unleavened Bread
Ex 12:14–20; Nu 28:16–25; Dt 16:1–8

[4] These are the appointed feasts of the Lord, holy convocations which you shall proclaim in their appointed times. [5] On the fourteenth day of the first month at evening is the Lord's Passover. [6] On the fifteenth day of the same month is the Feast of Unleavened Bread to the Lord. For seven days you must eat unleavened bread. [7] On the first day you shall have a holy convocation. You shall do no regular work. [8] But you shall offer a food offering made by fire to the Lord for seven days. On the seventh day is a holy convocation. You shall do no regular work.

Offering the First Fruits

[9] The Lord spoke to Moses, saying: [10] Speak to the children of Israel, and say to them: When you have come into the land that I am giving to you and reap its harvest, then you shall bring a sheaf bundle of the first fruits of your harvest to the priest. [11] And he shall wave the sheaf before the Lord so that you may be accepted. On the day after the Sabbath the priest shall wave it. [12] You shall offer that day when you wave the sheaf a year-old male lamb without blemish for a burnt offering to the Lord. [13] The grain offering shall be two-tenths of an ephah[2] of wheat flour mixed with oil, a food offering made by fire to the Lord for a pleasing aroma; its drink offering shall be of wine, a fourth of a hin.[3] [14] You shall eat neither bread nor grain, parched or fresh, until the same day that you have brought an offering to your God. It shall be a perpetual statute throughout your generations in all your dwellings.

The Feast of Weeks
Nu 28:26–31; Dt 16:9–12

[15] You shall count seven full weeks from the next day after the Sabbath, from the day that you brought the sheaf bundle of the wave offering. [16] You shall count fifty days to the day after the seventh Sabbath; then you shall offer a new grain offering to the Lord. [17] You shall bring out of your habitations two wave loaves of two-tenths of an ephah. They shall be of wheat flour, baked with leaven. They are the first fruits to the Lord. [18] You shall offer with the bread seven lambs without blemish of the first year, one bull, and two rams. They shall be for a burnt offering to the Lord, with their grain offering and their drink offerings, that is, a food offering made by fire, of a pleasing aroma to the Lord. [19] Then you shall sacrifice one male goat for a sin offering, and two lambs of the first year for a sacrifice of peace offerings. [20] The priest shall wave them with the bread of the first fruits for a wave offering before the Lord with the two lambs. They shall be holy to the Lord for the priest. [21] You shall make a proclamation on the same day and shall hold a holy convocation. You shall do no regular work. It shall be a perpetual statute in all your dwellings throughout your generations.

[22] When you reap the harvest of your land, you shall not reap your field up to the edge, nor shall you gather any gleaning of your harvest. You shall leave them to the poor and to the foreigner: I am the Lord your God.

The Feast of Trumpets
Nu 29:1–6

[23] The Lord spoke to Moses, saying: [24] Speak to the children of Israel, saying: In the seventh month, on the first day of the month, you shall have a sabbath, a memorial with the blowing of trumpets, a holy convocation. [25] You shall do no regular work, and you shall offer a food offering made by fire to the Lord.

The Day of Atonement
Lev 16:2–34; Nu 29:7–11

[26] The Lord spoke to Moses, saying: [27] Also on the tenth day of this seventh month there shall be the Day of Atonement. It shall be a holy convocation to you, and you shall humble yourselves, and offer a food offering made by fire to the Lord. [28] You shall do no work on that same day, for it is the Day of Atonement to make atonement for you before the Lord your God. [29] For whoever is

---

[1] 10 Or *stranger*.   [2] 13 Likely about 7 pounds, or 3.2 kilograms; and in v. 17.   [3] 13 About 1 quart, or 1 liter.

not humbled on that same day, he shall be cut off from among his people. [30] And whoever does any work in that same day, that person I will destroy from among his people. [31] You shall do no manner of work. It shall be a perpetual statute throughout your generations in all your dwellings. [32] It shall be to you a sabbath of complete rest, and you shall afflict your souls. On the ninth day of the month starting at the evening, from evening to evening, you shall celebrate your sabbath.

The Feast of Tabernacles
Nu 29:12–39; Dt 16:13–17

[33] The Lord spoke to Moses, saying: [34] Speak to the children of Israel, saying: The fifteenth day of this seventh month shall be the Feast of Tabernacles for seven days to the Lord. [35] On the first day shall be a holy convocation. You shall do no regular work. [36] For seven days you shall offer food offerings made by fire to the Lord. On the eighth day it shall be a holy convocation to you, and you shall offer a food offering made by fire to the Lord. It is a solemn assembly, and you shall do no regular work.

[37] These are the appointed feasts of the Lord, which you shall proclaim to be holy convocations, to offer a food offering made by fire to the Lord, burnt offerings and grain offerings, sacrifices and drink offerings, each on its proper day, [38] besides the Sabbaths of the Lord, besides your gifts, besides all your vows, and besides all your freewill offerings which you give to the Lord.

[39] On the fifteenth day of the seventh month, when you have gathered in the produce of the land, you shall keep a feast to the Lord for seven days. On the first day shall be a sabbath, and on the eighth day shall be a sabbath. [40] You shall take on the first day the branches of majestic trees—branches of palm trees, branches of leafy trees, and willows from a brook, and you shall rejoice before the Lord your God for seven days. [41] You shall keep it as a feast to the Lord for seven days in the year. It shall be a perpetual statute in your generations. You shall celebrate it in the seventh month. [42] You shall dwell in booths for seven days. All who are native children of Israel shall dwell in booths, [43] that your generations may know that I made the children of Israel dwell in booths when I brought them out of the land of Egypt: I am the Lord your God.

[44] Moses declared to the children of Israel the feasts of the Lord.

The Tabernacle Lamps
Ex 27:20–21

24 And the Lord spoke to Moses, saying: [2] Command the children of Israel that they bring to you pure olive oil beaten for the lamp, to cause the lamps to burn continually. [3] Outside the veil of the sanctuary, in the tent of meeting, Aaron shall arrange it continually, from the evening until the morning before the Lord. It shall be a perpetual statute in your generations. [4] He shall arrange the lamps continually on the pure *gold* lampstand before the Lord.

The Bread of the Tabernacle

[5] You shall take wheat flour and bake twelve cakes. Two-tenths of an ephah[1] shall be in each cake. [6] You shall set them in two rows, six in a row, on the pure *gold* table before the Lord. [7] You shall put pure frankincense on each row, so that it may be on the bread for a memorial, a food offering made by fire to the Lord. [8] Every Sabbath he shall set it in order continually before the Lord, with the portion taken from the children of Israel by a perpetual covenant. [9] It shall be for Aaron and his sons, and they shall eat it in a holy place, for it is most holy to him of the food offerings of the Lord made by fire by a perpetual statute.

The Punishment for Blasphemy

[10] The son of an Israelite woman, whose father was an Egyptian, went out among the children of Israel, and this son of the Israelite woman and a man of Israel fought together in the camp. [11] And the Israelite woman's son blasphemed the name of the Lord and cursed. And they brought him to Moses. (His mother's name was Shelomith, the daughter of Dibri, of the tribe of Dan.) [12] And they put him in custody, so that the words of the Lord might be shown to them.

[13] The Lord spoke to Moses, saying: [14] Bring outside the camp him who has cursed, and let all who heard him lay their hands on his head, and let the entire congregation stone him. [15] You shall speak to the children of Israel, saying: Whoever curses his God shall bear his sin. [16] Whoever blasphemes the name of the Lord, he shall surely be put to death, and the entire congregation shall certainly stone him. The foreigner as well as the native in the land, when he blasphemes the name, then he shall be put to death.

[17] Whoever kills any man shall surely be put to death. [18] Whoever kills an animal shall make restitution, animal for animal. [19] If anyone causes injury to his neighbor, as he has done, so shall it be done to him, [20] fracture for fracture, eye for eye, tooth for tooth; as he has caused an injury to another, so shall it be done to him. [21] Whoever kills an animal shall make restitution. And whoever kills a man shall be put to death. [22] You shall have one manner of law for the foreigner as for the native, for I am the Lord your God.

[23] So Moses spoke to the children of Israel, and they brought outside the camp him who had cursed, and stoned him. And the children of Israel did as the Lord commanded Moses.

The Sabbath Year

25 Then the Lord spoke to Moses on Mount Sinai, saying: [2] Speak to the children of Israel, and say to them: When you come into the land that I give you, the land shall keep a sabbath to the Lord. [3] For six years you shall sow your field, and six years you shall prune your vineyard and gather in its fruit, [4] but in the seventh year there shall be a sabbath of complete rest for the land, a sabbath for the Lord. You shall neither sow your field nor prune your vineyard. [5] That which grows by itself from your harvest you shall not reap, nor gather the grapes of your unpruned vines, for it is a year of complete rest for the land. [6] The sabbath produce of the land shall be food for you: for you, and for your male and female servants, and for your hired servant, and for your stranger who sojourns with you, [7] and for your livestock, and for the wild animals in your land, shall all its increase be food.

The Year of Jubilee
Dt 15:1–11; Ex 21:2–11; Dt 15:12–18

[8] You shall count seven *sabbath* weeks of years, seven times seven years, and the time of the seven sabbaths of years shall be to you forty-nine years. [9] Then you shall sound the horn blasts on the tenth day of the seventh month. On the Day of Atonement you shall make the sound of the horn throughout all your land. [10] You shall consecrate the fiftieth year, and proclaim liberty throughout all the land to all the inhabitants. It shall be a Jubilee to you, and each of you shall return to his possession, and every person shall return to his family. [11] That fiftieth year will be a Jubilee for you. You shall neither sow nor reap that which grows by itself, nor gather the grapes of your unpruned vines. [12] For it is the Jubilee. It shall be holy to you. You shall eat the produce of the field.

[13] In the Year of Jubilee you shall return to your property.

[14] If you sell anything to your neighbor or buy anything from your neighbor, you shall not oppress one another. [15] According to the number of years after the Jubilee you shall pay your neighbor, and according to the number of years of the crops he shall sell to you. [16] According to the increase of years you shall increase the price, and according to the decrease of years you shall diminish the price of it. For he shall sell to you according to the number of years of crops. [17] You shall not therefore oppress one another, but you shall fear your God. For I am the Lord your God.

[18] Therefore you shall do My statutes, and keep My decrees, and do them, and you shall dwell securely in the land. [19] The land shall yield its fruit, and you shall eat your fill and live securely in it. [20] If you shall say, "What shall we eat in the seventh year, if we shall not sow nor gather in our crop?" [21] then I will command My blessing upon you in the sixth year, and it shall bring forth produce for three years. [22] You shall sow in the eighth year, and eat yet of old crops until the ninth year until its crops come in for you.

---

[1] 5 Likely about 7 pounds, or 3.2 kilograms.

Redemption of Property

²³ The land shall not be permanently sold, for the land is Mine. For you are foreigners and sojourners with Me. ²⁴ In all the land of your possession you shall grant a redemption for the land.

²⁵ If your brother becomes poor and has sold some of his possession, then his nearest redeemer will come to redeem it, and buy back that which his brother sold. ²⁶ If the man has none to redeem it, but he himself is able to redeem it, ²⁷ then let him count the years since the sale and pay back the balance to the man to whom he sold it, so that he may return to his property. ²⁸ But if he is not able to restore it to himself, then that which he sold shall remain in the hand of him who has bought it until the Year of Jubilee, and in the Jubilee it shall be released, and he shall return to his possession.

²⁹ If a man sells a house in a walled city, then he may redeem it within a year after it is sold, within a full year he may have the right to buy it back. ³⁰ If it is not redeemed within the time of a full year, then the house that is in the walled city shall be given permanently to him who bought it throughout his generations. It shall not be returned in the Jubilee. ³¹ But the houses of the villages that have no wall around them shall be counted as the fields of the land. They may be redeemed, and they shall be returned in the Jubilee.

³² For the cities of the Levites, they may redeem at any time the houses in the cities that they possess. ³³ If a Levite purchases back the house that was sold in the city of his possession, then it shall be returned in the Jubilee. For the houses of the cities of the Levites are their possession among the children of Israel. ³⁴ But the fields of the land of their cities may not be sold, for they are their perpetual possession.

Helping the Poor

³⁵ If your brother becomes poor and cannot maintain himself with you, then you shall support him as if he were a foreigner or a sojourner, so that he may live with you. ³⁶ Take no usury or interest from him; but fear your God, so that your brother may live with you. ³⁷ You shall not lend him your money at interest, nor lend him your food for profit. ³⁸ I am the LORD your God, who brought you out of the land of Egypt, to give you the land of Canaan and to be your God.

The Law About Slavery

³⁹ If your brother who dwells near you becomes poor and sells himself to you, you shall not compel him to serve as a bondservant. ⁴⁰ But as a hired servant and as a sojourner he shall be with you. He shall serve you until the Year of Jubilee. ⁴¹ And then he shall depart from you, both he and his children with him, and he shall return to his own family and to the possession of his fathers. ⁴² For they are My servants, whom I brought out of the land of Egypt. They shall not be sold as slaves. ⁴³ You shall not rule over him with harshness, but you shall fear your God.

⁴⁴ Both your male and female slaves, whom you may have, they shall be bought from the nations that are around you. ⁴⁵ Moreover of the foreigners who sojourn among you and of their families who are with you, who were born in your land, you may also buy from them, and they may be your possession. ⁴⁶ You may take them as an inheritance for your children after you, for their possession. They shall be your slaves forever. But over your brothers, the children of Israel, you shall not rule over one another with rigor.

⁴⁷ If a sojourner or foreigner becomes rich by you, and your brother who dwells beside him becomes poor and sells himself to the foreigner or sojourner with you, or to a member of the stranger's family, ⁴⁸ then after he is sold he may be redeemed again. One of his brothers may redeem him, ⁴⁹ or either his uncle or his cousin may redeem him, or any who is near of kin to him of his family may redeem him. Or if he is able, he may redeem himself. ⁵⁰ He shall calculate with him who bought him from the year that he was sold to the Year of Jubilee, and the price of his sale shall be according to the number of years, according to the time of a hired servant. ⁵¹ If there are still many years left *until the Jubilee*, he shall pay the price proportionately for his redemption as some of the price that he was bought for. ⁵² If there remain but a few years

until the Year of Jubilee, then he shall calculate and pay the price proportionately for his redemption according to his years of service. ⁵³ As a yearly hired servant he shall be treated, and the other shall not rule harshly over him in your sight.

⁵⁴ If he is not redeemed in these years, then he shall go out in the Year of Jubilee, both he and his children with him. ⁵⁵ For to Me the children of Israel are servants. They are My servants whom I brought out of the land of Egypt: I am the LORD your God.

Rewards for Obedience

26 You shall not make for yourselves idols; neither set up a carved image nor a standing stone, nor shall you set up any sculpted stone in your land to bow down to it, for I am the LORD your God.

² You shall keep My Sabbaths and reverence My sanctuary: I am the LORD.

³ If you walk in My statutes and keep My commandments and do them, ⁴ then I will give you rain in due season, and the land shall yield its increase, and the trees of the field shall yield their fruit. ⁵ Your threshing shall last till the grape harvest, and the grape harvest shall last till the time for sowing, and you shall eat your bread till you are full and dwell in your land safely.

⁶ I will give peace in the land, and you shall lie down *for sleep*, and none shall make you afraid; I will remove harmful beasts from the land, and the sword shall not go through your land. ⁷ You shall chase your enemies, and they shall fall before you by the sword. ⁸ Five of you shall chase a hundred, and a hundred of you shall put ten thousand to flight, and your enemies shall fall before you by the sword.

⁹ I will turn toward you and make you fruitful and multiply you, and I will confirm My covenant with you. ¹⁰ You shall eat the old harvest long stored, and clear out the old to make way for the new. ¹¹ I will set My tabernacle among you, and I shall not abhor you. ¹² I will walk among you, and I will be your God, and you shall be My people. ¹³ I am the LORD your God, who brought you out of the land of Egypt, that you should not be their slaves, and I have broken the bars of your yoke and made you walk upright.

Punishment for Disobedience

¹⁴ But if you will not listen to Me, and will not do all these commandments, ¹⁵ if you despise My statutes, or if you abhor My judgments, so that you will not do all My commandments, but you break My covenant, ¹⁶ then I will do this to you: I will visit you with terror, with wasting disease, and with a fever that shall consume the eyes and cause sorrow of heart, and you shall sow your seed in vain, for your enemies shall eat it. ¹⁷ I will set My face against you, and you shall be slain before your enemies. They that hate you shall reign over you, and you shall flee when none pursues you.

¹⁸ If you will not yet listen to Me after all this, then I will punish you seven times more for your sins. ¹⁹ I will break the pride of your power, and I will make your heaven as iron and your land as bronze. ²⁰ Your strength shall be spent in vain, for your land shall not yield her increase, nor shall the trees of the land yield their fruits.

²¹ If you continue to walk contrary to Me and will not listen to Me, I will bring seven times more plagues upon you according to your sins. ²² I will also send wild beasts among you, which shall rob you of your children, destroy your livestock, and make you few in number. And your roads shall be desolate.

²³ And if by these things you are not turned to Me, but walk contrary to Me, ²⁴ then I will also walk contrary to you and will punish you yet seven times for your sins. ²⁵ I will bring a sword upon you that shall extract vengeance for My covenant. And when you are gathered together within your cities, I will send pestilence among you, and you shall be delivered into the hand of the enemy. ²⁶ When I have broken the supply of your bread, ten women shall bake your bread in one oven, and they shall ration your bread again by weight, and you shall eat and not be satisfied.

²⁷ If you will not listen to Me for all this, but walk contrary to Me, ²⁸ then I will walk contrary to you also in fury, and I Myself will chastise you seven times for your sins. ²⁹ You shall eat the flesh of your sons and the flesh of your daughters. ³⁰ I will destroy your high

places, and cut down your images, and cast your funeral offerings on the lifeless forms of your idols, and I shall abhor you. 31 I will make your cities a waste and bring your sanctuaries to desolation, and I will not smell the savor of your fragrant offerings. 32 I will bring the land into desolation, and your enemies that dwell there shall be astonished at it. 33 I will scatter you among the nations and I will draw out a sword after you. And your land shall be desolate and your cities a waste. 34 Then the land shall enjoy its sabbaths as long as it lies desolate, while you are in your enemies' land; then the land shall rest and enjoy its sabbaths. 35 As long as it lies desolate it shall rest because it did not rest during your sabbaths when you lived upon it.

36 And on those who are left alive of you I will send faintness into their hearts in the lands of their enemies; and the sound of a shaken leaf shall make them flee, and they shall flee as from a sword, and they shall fall when no one pursues. 37 They shall fall one upon one another, as to escape before the sword, though no one pursues, and you shall have no power to stand before your enemies. 38 You shall perish among the nations, and the land of your enemies shall consume you. 39 And those who are left of you shall rot away in their iniquity in your enemies' lands, and also because of the iniquities of their fathers, they shall rot away with them.

40 But if they confess their iniquity, and the iniquity of their fathers, with their treachery that they committed against Me, and also that they have walked contrary to Me, 41 and that I also have walked contrary to them and have brought them into the land of their enemies; if then their uncircumcised hearts are humbled, and they then accept the punishment of their iniquity, 42 then will I remember My covenant with Jacob, and also My covenant with Isaac, and also My covenant with Abraham, and I will remember the land. 43 But the land shall be abandoned by them, and enjoy its sabbaths while it lies desolate without them. They shall make amends for their iniquity, because they despised My judgments and because they abhorred My statutes. 44 Yet for all that, when they are in the land of their enemies, I will not cast them away, nor will I abhor them to destroy them utterly and to break My covenant with them, for I am the LORD their God. 45 But for their sake I will remember the covenant with their fathers, whom I brought out of the land of Egypt in the sight of the nations, that I might be their God: I am the LORD.

46 These are the statutes and judgments and laws that the LORD made between Himself and the children of Israel on Mount Sinai by the hand of Moses.

Laws About Vows

27 And the LORD spoke to Moses, saying: 2 Speak to the children of Israel, and say to them: When a man makes a special vow to the LORD based on the equivalent value[1] of persons, 3 then the equivalent value of a male from twenty to sixty years old shall be fifty shekels[2] of silver, according to the sanctuary shekel.[3] 4 If the person is a female, then the equivalent value shall be thirty shekels.[4] 5 If the person is five to twenty years old, then the equivalent value shall be twenty shekels[5] for a male and ten shekels[6] for a female. 6 If the person is one month to five years old, then the equivalent value shall be five shekels[7] for a male and three shekels[8] of silver for a female. 7 If the person is sixty years old or older, then the equivalent value shall be fifteen shekels[9] for a male and ten shekels for a female. 8 But if he is too poor *to afford* the equivalent value, then he shall present himself before the priest and the priest shall set his value. According to what the person making the vow can afford, so the priest shall set his value.

9 And if it be an animal, of which men bring an offering to the LORD, all that any man gives of such to the LORD shall be holy. 10 He shall not exchange it nor substitute it, good for bad or bad for good. If he in fact substitutes an animal for another, then both it and its substitute shall be holy. 11 If it is any sort of unclean animal that is not permitted as an offering to the LORD, then he shall present the animal before the priest. 12 And the priest shall set its value, whether good or bad; according to the equivalent value set by the priest, so shall it be. 13 But if he plans on redeeming it, then he shall add one-fifth to the equivalent value.

14 When a man consecrates his house as holy to the LORD, then the priest shall set its value, whether good or bad, according to the equivalent value set by the priest, so shall it be established. 15 If he who consecrates the house should redeem it, then he shall add one-fifth to its equivalent value, and it shall be his.

16 If a man shall consecrate to the LORD some of his land, then the equivalent value shall be according to the seed *needed to sow it*: fifty shekels of silver per homer[10] of barley seed. 17 If he consecrates his field from the Year of Jubilee, the equivalent value shall stay fixed, 18 but if he consecrates his field after the Jubilee, then the priest shall calculate for him the price according to the years that remain until the *next* Year of Jubilee, and the equivalent value shall be reduced. 19 And if he who consecrated the field plans on redeeming it, then he shall add one-fifth to the equivalent value, and it will be established as his. 20 If he does not redeem the field, but rather sells the field to another man, it may not be redeemed again. 21 But when the field is released in the Jubilee, it shall be holy to the LORD as a devoted field; it shall become the possession of the priest.

22 If a man consecrates to the LORD a field that he purchased, which is not part of his land property, 23 then the priest shall calculate for him the amount of the valuation, up to the Year of Jubilee, and he shall give your valuation on that day as a holy thing to the LORD. 24 In the Year of Jubilee the field shall return to the one from whom it was bought, to him to whom the property of land belongs. 25 All your estimations shall be according to the shekel of the sanctuary: Twenty gerahs[11] shall be one shekel.

26 A firstborn of animals, which as firstborn belongs to the LORD, no man may consecrate; whether ox or sheep, it is the LORD's. 27 If it is among the unclean animals, then he shall ransom it at the equivalent value and shall add one-fifth to it, but if it is not redeemed, then it shall be sold at the equivalent value.

28 Anything that a man shall devote to the LORD from all that he has, whether human, animal, or land, shall not be sold or redeemed. Every devoted thing is most holy to the LORD.

29 No one devoted of men, who shall be doomed to death, shall be redeemed; he shall surely be put to death.

30 Any tithe of the land, whether seed of the land or fruit of the trees, belongs to the LORD. It is holy to the LORD. 31 If a man plans on redeeming some of his tithe, he shall add one-fifth to it. 32 Any tithe of herd or flock, all that passes under the *counting* staff, the tenth one shall be holy to the LORD. 33 A person shall not differentiate between good or bad, nor shall he make a substitute for it, but if he does, then both it and its substitute shall be holy. It shall not be redeemed.

34 These are the commandments that the LORD commanded Moses for the children of Israel on Mount Sinai.

---

[1] *2* Shorthand for the formula in Lev 5:15. [2] *3* About 1¼ pounds, or 575 grams; and in v. 16. [3] *3* About ⅖ ounce, or 12 grams; and in v. 25.
[4] *4* About 12 ounces, or 345 grams. [5] *5* About 8 ounces, or 230 grams. [6] *5* About 4 ounces, or 115 grams; and in v. 7. [7] *6* About 2 ounces, or 58 grams.
[8] *6* About 1¼ ounces, or 35 grams. [9] *7* About 6 ounces, or 175 grams. [10] *16* Likely about 300 pounds, or 135 kilograms.
[11] *25* About 1/50 ounce or 0.6 gram.

Israel's First Census

1 And the Lord spoke to Moses in the Wilderness of Sinai in the tent of meeting on the first day of the second month in the second year after they went out from the land of Egypt, saying: ² Take the sum of all the congregation of the children of Israel, after their families, by the house of their fathers, with the number of their names, every male by their polls, ³ from twenty years old and upward, all who are able to go out to war in Israel. You and Aaron will number them by their armies. ⁴ With you there will be a man of every tribe, each one the head of his father's house. ⁵ These are the names of the men who will stand with you:

of the tribe of Reuben, Elizur the son of Shedeur;
⁶ of Simeon, Shelumiel the son of Zurishaddai;
⁷ of Judah, Nahshon the son of Amminadab;
⁸ of Issachar, Nethanel the son of Zuar;
⁹ of Zebulun, Eliab the son of Helon;
¹⁰ of the children of Joseph:
    of Ephraim, Elishama the son of Ammihud;
    of Manasseh, Gamaliel the son of Pedahzur;
¹¹ of Benjamin, Abidan the son of Gideoni;
¹² of Dan, Ahiezer the son of Ammishaddai;
¹³ of Asher, Pagiel the son of Okran;
¹⁴ of Gad, Eliasaph the son of Deuel;
¹⁵ of Naphtali, Ahira the son of Enan.

¹⁶ These were the renowned of the congregation, leaders of the tribes of their fathers, heads of thousands in Israel.

¹⁷ Moses and Aaron took these men who had been mentioned by name, ¹⁸ and they assembled all the congregation on the first day of the second month, and they declared their pedigrees according to their families, by the house of their fathers, according to the number of the names, from twenty years old and upward, by their polls. ¹⁹ As the Lord commanded Moses, so he numbered them in the Wilderness of Sinai.

²⁰ The children of Reuben, the oldest son of Israel,
by their generations, after their families, by the house of their fathers, according to the number of the names, by their polls, every male from twenty years old and upward, all who were able to go out to war, ²¹ those who were numbered of them, even of the tribe of Reuben, were forty-six thousand five hundred.

²² Of the children of Simeon,
by their generations, after their families, by the house of their fathers, those who were numbered of them, according to the number of the names, by their polls, every male from twenty years old and upward, all who were able to go out to war, ²³ those who were numbered of them, even of the tribe of Simeon, were fifty-nine thousand three hundred.

²⁴ Of the children of Gad,
by their generations, after their families, by the house of their fathers, according to the number of the names, from twenty years old and upward, all who were able to go out to war, ²⁵ those who were numbered of them, even of the tribe of Gad, were forty-five thousand six hundred and fifty.

²⁶ Of the children of Judah,
by their generations, after their families, by the house of their fathers, according to the number of the names, from twenty years old and upward, all who were able to go out to war, ²⁷ those who were numbered of them, even of the tribe of Judah, were seventy-four thousand six hundred.

²⁸ Of the children of Issachar,
by their generations, after their families, by the house of their fathers, according to the number of the names, from twenty years old and upward, all who were able to go out to war, ²⁹ those who were numbered of them, even of the tribe of Issachar, were fifty-four thousand four hundred.

³⁰ Of the children of Zebulun,
by their generations, after their families, by the house of their fathers, according to the number of the names, from twenty years old and upward, all who were able to go out to war, ³¹ those who were numbered of them, even of the tribe of Zebulun, were fifty-seven thousand four hundred.

³² Of the children of Joseph,
namely, of the children of Ephraim,
by their generations, after their families, by the house of their fathers, according to the number of the names, from twenty years old and upward, all who were able to go out to war, ³³ those who were numbered of them, even of the tribe of Ephraim, were forty thousand five hundred.
³⁴ Of the children of Manasseh,
by their generations, after their families, by the house of their fathers, according to the number of the names, from twenty years old and upward, all who were able to go out to war, ³⁵ those who were numbered of them, even of the tribe of Manasseh, were thirty-two thousand two hundred.

³⁶ Of the children of Benjamin,
by their generations, after their families, by the house of their fathers, according to the number of the names, from twenty years old and upward, all who were able to go out to war, ³⁷ those who were numbered of them, even of the tribe of Benjamin, were thirty-five thousand four hundred.

³⁸ Of the children of Dan,
by their generations, after their families, by the house of their fathers, according to the number of the names, from twenty years old and upward, all who were able to go out to war, ³⁹ those who were numbered of them, even of the tribe of Dan, were sixty-two thousand seven hundred.

⁴⁰ Of the children of Asher,
by their generations, after their families, by the house of their fathers, according to the number of the names, from twenty years old and upward, all who were able to go out to war, ⁴¹ those who were numbered of them, even of the tribe of Asher, were forty-one thousand five hundred.

⁴² Of the children of Naphtali,
by their generations, after their families, by the house of their fathers, according to the number of the names, from twenty years old and upward, all who were able to go out to war, ⁴³ those who were numbered of them, even of the tribe of Naphtali, were fifty-three thousand four hundred.

⁴⁴ These are those who were numbered, which Moses and Aaron numbered, and the leaders of Israel, being twelve men. Each one was for the house of his fathers. ⁴⁵ So were all those who were numbered of the children of Israel, by the house of their fathers, from twenty years old and upward, all who were able to go out to war in Israel. ⁴⁶ Even all they who were numbered were six hundred and three thousand five hundred and fifty.

⁴⁷ But the Levites after the tribe of their fathers were not numbered among them. ⁴⁸ For the Lord had spoken to Moses, saying: ⁴⁹ Only you will not number the tribe of Levi, nor take the census of them among the children of Israel, ⁵⁰ but you will appoint the Levites over the tent of the testimony, and over all its vessels, and

over all things that belong to it. They will carry the tabernacle, and all its vessels, and they will minister to it, and will camp around the tabernacle. [51] When the tabernacle sets out, the Levites will take it down, and when the tabernacle is to be set up, the Levites will set it up, and the foreigner that approaches will be put to death. [52] The children of Israel will pitch their tents, every man by his own camp, and every man by his own standard, throughout their armies. [53] But the Levites will camp around the tabernacle of the testimony, so there will be no wrath on the congregation of the children of Israel. And the Levites will keep the charge of the tabernacle of the testimony.

[54] Thus the children of Israel did according to all that the LORD commanded Moses.

Tribes and Leaders by Armies

2 And the LORD spoke to Moses and to Aaron, saying: [2] Every man of the children of Israel will camp by his own standard, with the ensign of his father's house. Facing the tent of meeting they will camp.

[3] On the east side toward the rising of the sun the standard of the camp of Judah will camp throughout their armies, and Nahshon the son of Amminadab will be captain of the children of Judah. [4] His host, and those who were numbered of them, were seventy-four thousand six hundred.

[5] Those who camp next to him will be the tribe of Issachar, and Nethanel the son of Zuar will be captain of the children of Issachar. [6] His host, and those who were numbered of them, were fifty-four thousand four hundred.

[7] Then comes the tribe of Zebulun, and Eliab the son of Helon will be captain of the children of Zebulun. [8] His host, and those who were numbered of them, were fifty-seven thousand four hundred.

[9] All who were numbered throughout the armies in the camp of Judah were one hundred and eighty-six thousand four hundred. They will march out first.

[10] On the south side will be the standard of the camp of Reuben according to their armies, and the captain of the children of Reuben will be Elizur the son of Shedeur. [11] His host, and those who were numbered of them, were forty-six thousand five hundred.

[12] Those who camp by him will be the tribe of Simeon, and the captain of the children of Simeon will be Shelumiel the son of Zurishaddai. [13] His host, and those who were numbered of them, were fifty-nine thousand three hundred.

[14] Then comes the tribe of Gad, and the captain of the sons of Gad will be Eliasaph the son of Reuel. [15] His host, and those who were numbered of them, were forty-five thousand six hundred and fifty.

[16] All who were numbered in the camp of Reuben were one hundred and fifty-one thousand four hundred and fifty, throughout their armies. And they will set out in the second rank.

[17] Then the tent of meeting will set out with the camp of the Levites in the middle of the camp. As they camp, so they will set out, every man in his place by their standards.

[18] On the west side will be the standard of the camp of Ephraim according to their armies, and the captain of the sons of Ephraim will be Elishama the son of Ammihud. [19] His host, and those who were numbered of them, were forty thousand five hundred.

[20] By him will be the tribe of Manasseh, and the captain of the children of Manasseh will be Gamaliel the son of Pedahzur. [21] His host, and those who were numbered of them, were thirty-two thousand two hundred.

[22] Then comes the tribe of Benjamin, and the captain of the sons of Benjamin will be Abidan the son of Gideoni. [23] His host, and those who were numbered of them, were thirty-five thousand four hundred.

[24] All who were numbered of the camp of Ephraim were one hundred and eight thousand one hundred, throughout their armies. And they will go out in the third rank.

[25] The standard of the camp of Dan will be on the north side by their armies, and the captain of the children of Dan will be Ahiezer the son of Ammishaddai. [26] His host, and those who were numbered of them, were sixty-two thousand seven hundred.

[27] Those who camp by him will be the tribe of Asher, and the captain of the children of Asher will be Pagiel the son of Okran. [28] His host, and those who were numbered of them, were forty-one thousand five hundred.

[29] Then the tribe of Naphtali, and the captain of the children of Naphtali will be Ahira the son of Enan. [30] His host, and those who were numbered of them, were fifty-three thousand four hundred.

[31] All they who were numbered in the camp of Dan were one hundred and fifty-seven thousand six hundred. They will set out in the back with their standards.

[32] These are those who were numbered of the children of Israel by the house of their fathers. All those who were numbered of the camps throughout their hosts were six hundred and three thousand five hundred and fifty. [33] But the Levites were not numbered among the children of Israel, as the LORD commanded Moses.

[34] The children of Israel did according to all that the LORD commanded Moses. So they camped by their standards, and so they set out, each one after his family, according to their fathers' houses.

The Sons of Aaron

3 These also are the generations of Aaron and Moses in the day that the LORD spoke with Moses in Mount Sinai. [2] These are the names of the sons of Aaron: Nadab the firstborn, and Abihu, Eleazar, and Ithamar. [3] These are the names of the sons of Aaron, the priests who were anointed, whom he consecrated to minister as priests. [4] Nadab and Abihu died before the LORD when they brought strange fire before the LORD in the Wilderness of Sinai, and they had no children, and Eleazar and Ithamar ministered as priests in the sight of Aaron their father.

Duties of the Levites

[5] The LORD spoke to Moses, saying: [6] Bring the tribe of Levi near, and present them before Aaron the priest, and they will minister to him. [7] They will keep his directives, and serve the whole congregation before the tent of meeting, to do the service of the tabernacle. [8] They will keep all the instruments of the tent of meeting, and attend to the needs of the children of Israel, to do the service of the tabernacle. [9] You will give the Levites to Aaron and to his sons. They are wholly given to him from the children of Israel. [10] You will appoint Aaron and his sons, and they will attend to their priesthood, and the foreigner that approaches will be put to death.

[11] The LORD spoke to Moses, saying: [12] I Myself have taken the Levites from among the children of Israel instead of all the firstborn that open the womb among the children of Israel. Therefore the Levites will be Mine [13] because all the firstborn are Mine, for on the day that I struck all the firstborn in the land of Egypt I set apart to Me all the firstborn in Israel, both man and beast. They will be Mine. I am the LORD.

A Census of the Levites

[14] The LORD spoke to Moses in the Wilderness of Sinai, saying: [15] Number the children of Levi after the house of their fathers, by their families. You will number every male from a month old and older. [16] Moses numbered them according to the word of the LORD, as he was commanded.

[17] These were the sons of Levi by their names:
Gershon, and Kohath, and Merari.

[18] These are the names of the sons of Gershon by their families: Libni and Shimei;

[19] the sons of Kohath by their families:
Amram, and Izhar, Hebron, and Uzziel;

[20] the sons of Merari by their families:
Mahli and Mushi.

These are the families of the Levites according to the house of their fathers.

[21] From Gershon was the family of the Libnites and the family of the Shimeites. These are the families of the Gershonites. [22] Those who were numbered of them, according to the number of all the males, from a month old and older, those who were numbered of them were seven thousand five hundred. [23] The families of the Gershonites were to camp behind the west side of the tabernacle. [24] The chief of the house of the father of the Gershonites was Eliasaph the son of Lael. [25] The charge of the sons of Gershon in the tent of meeting *included* the tabernacle, and the tent, its covering, and the hanging for the door of the tent of meeting, [26] the hangings of the court, the curtain for the opening of the court that is around the tabernacle and the altar, and its cords—all the service pertaining to these.

[27] Of Kohath was the family of the Amramites, and the family of the Izharites, and the family of the Hebronites, and the family of the Uzzielites. These are the families of the Kohathites. [28] The number of all the males, from a month old and older, were eight thousand six hundred, keeping the guard of the sanctuary. [29] The families of the sons of Kohath were to camp on the south side of the tabernacle. [30] The chief of the house of the father of the families of the Kohathites was Elizaphan the son of Uzziel. [31] Their duty included the ark, and the table, and the lampstand, and the altars, and the vessels of the sanctuary they minister with, and the hanging, and all its service. [32] Eleazar the son of Aaron the priest was to be chief over the leaders of the Levites and to have the oversight of those who kept the guard of the sanctuary.

[33] Of Merari was the family of the Mahlites and the family of the Mushites. These are the families of Merari. [34] Those who were numbered of them, according to the number of all the males from a month old and older, were six thousand two hundred. [35] The chief of the house of the father of the families of Merari was Zuriel the son of Abihail. These were to camp on the north side of the tabernacle. [36] Under the oversight and guard of the sons of Merari were the frames of the tabernacle, the bars, the pillars, the sockets, all their accessories, all the service pertaining to these, [37] and the pillars of the court all around, with their sockets, and pins, and cords.

[38] But those who were to camp before the tabernacle toward the east, even before the tent of meeting on the east side, were Moses, and Aaron and his sons, keeping the guard of the sanctuary for the guard of the children of Israel, and the foreigner who approached was to be put to death.

[39] All who were numbered of the Levites, which Moses and Aaron numbered at the commandment of the LORD, throughout their families, all the males from a month old and older, were twenty-two thousand.

The Redemption of the Firstborn

[40] The LORD said to Moses: Number all the firstborn of the males of the children of Israel from a month old and older and take the number of their names. [41] You will take the Levites for Me (I am the LORD) instead of all the firstborn among the children of Israel, and the livestock of the Levites instead of all the firstborn among the livestock of the children of Israel.

[42] Moses numbered, as the LORD commanded him, all the firstborn among the children of Israel. [43] All the firstborn males, by the number of names, from a month old and upward, of those who were numbered of them, were twenty-two thousand two hundred and seventy-three.

[44] The LORD spoke to Moses, saying: [45] Take the Levites instead of all the firstborn among the children of Israel, and the livestock of the Levites instead of their livestock, and the Levites will be Mine. I am the LORD. [46] For those who are to be redeemed of the two hundred and seventy-three of the firstborn of the children of Israel, which are more than the Levites, [47] you will take five shekels[1] apiece by the poll; according to the shekel of the sanctuary you will take them (the shekel is twenty gerahs). [48] And you will give the money, by which the number of them is to be redeemed, to Aaron and to his sons.

[49] Moses took the redemption money of those who were over and above those who were redeemed by the Levites. [50] Of the firstborn of the children of Israel he took the money, one thousand three hundred and sixty-five shekels,[2] after the shekel of the sanctuary. [51] And Moses gave the money of those who were redeemed to Aaron and to his sons, according to the word of the LORD, as the LORD commanded Moses.

Duties of the Kohathites

4 And the LORD spoke to Moses and to Aaron, saying: [2] Take the sum of the sons of Kohath from among the sons of Levi, after their families, by the house of their fathers, [3] from thirty years old and older, even to fifty years old, all that enter into the host, to do the work in the tent of meeting.

[4] This will be the service of the sons of Kohath in the tent of meeting, concerning the holiest things. [5] And when the camp sets out, Aaron will come, and his sons, and they will take down the covering curtain, and cover the ark of the testimony with it, [6] and will put on it the covering of porpoise skins, and will spread over it a cloth completely of blue, and will put in its poles.

[7] Upon the table of showbread they will spread a cloth of blue, and put the dishes on it, and the spoons, and the bowls, and covers to cover it, and the showbread will be on it. [8] And they will spread on them a cloth of scarlet, and cover the same with a covering of porpoise skins, and will put in its poles.

[9] They will take a cloth of blue, and cover the lampstand of the light, and its lamps, and its tongs, and its snuff dishes, and all its oil vessels, with which they minister to it. [10] And they will put it and all its vessels within a covering of porpoise skins and will put it on a carrying pole.

[11] Upon the golden altar they will spread a cloth of blue, and cover it with a covering of porpoise skins, and will put in its poles. [12] And they will take all the instruments of ministry, with which they minister in the sanctuary, and put them in a cloth of blue, and cover them with a covering of porpoise skins, and will put them on a carrying pole.

[13] And they will take away the ashes from the altar and spread a purple cloth on it. [14] They shall put on it all the instruments with which they minister there, the censers, the flesh hooks, the shovels, the basins, all the utensils of the altar. And they will spread on it a covering of porpoise skins and insert its poles.

[15] When Aaron and his sons have finished covering the sanctuary, and all the instruments of the sanctuary, as the camp is to set out, after that, the sons of Kohath will come to carry it. But they will not touch any holy thing, lest they die. These things are the burden of the sons of Kohath in the tent of meeting.

[16] To the office of Eleazar, Aaron the priest's son, pertains the oil for the light, and the sweet incense, and the daily grain offering, and the anointing oil, and the oversight of all the tabernacle, and of all that is in it, in the sanctuary, and in the instruments thereof.

[17] The LORD spoke to Moses and to Aaron, saying: [18] Do not cut the tribe of the families of the Kohathites from among the Levites. [19] But do this to them, that they may live and not die, when they approach the most holy things. Aaron and his sons will go in, and appoint each one to his service and to his burden. [20] But they will not go in to see when the holy things are covered, lest they die.

Duties of the Gershonites

[21] The LORD spoke to Moses, saying: [22] Take also the sum of the sons of Gershon, throughout the houses of their fathers, by their families. [23] From thirty years old and older to fifty years old you will number them, all that enter in to perform the service, to do the work in the tent of meeting.

[24] This is the service of the families of the Gershonites, to serve, and to work. [25] And they will carry the curtains of the tabernacle, and the tent of meeting, its covering, and the covering of the porpoise skins that is on it, and the hanging for the door of the tent of meeting, [26] and the hangings of the courtyard, and the hanging for

---

[1] 47 About 2 ounces, or 58 grams.   [2] 50 About 35 pounds, or 16 kilograms.

the opening of the gate of the courtyard, which is by the tabernacle and by the altar all around, and their cords, and all the instruments of their service, and all that is made for them. So they will serve. [27] At the appointment of Aaron and his sons will be all the service of the sons of the Gershonites, in all their burdens, and in all their service. And you shall assign to them all their tasks as their duty. [28] This is the service of the families of the sons of Gershon in the tent of meeting. And their charge will be under the hand of Ithamar the son of Aaron the priest.

Duties of the Merarites

[29] As for the sons of Merari, you will number them by their families, by the house of their fathers. [30] From thirty years old and older, even to fifty years old, you will number them, everyone who enters into the service, to do the work of the tent of meeting. [31] This is the charge of their burden, according to all their service in the tent of meeting. The boards of the tabernacle, and its bars thereof, and its pillars, and its sockets, [32] and the pillars of the court round about, and their sockets, and their pins, and their cords, with all their instruments, and with all their service, and by name you will list the instruments of the charge of their burden. [33] This is the service of the families of the sons of Merari, according to all their service, in the tent of meeting, under the hand of Ithamar the son of Aaron the priest.

Census of the Levites

[34] Moses, Aaron, and the leaders of the congregation numbered the sons of the Kohathites by their families, and by the house of their fathers, [35] from thirty years old and older to fifty years old, everyone who entered into the service, for the work in the tent of meeting. [36] And those who were numbered by their families were two thousand seven hundred and fifty. [37] These were the ones listed of the families of the Kohathites, all who might do service in the tent of meeting, which Moses and Aaron numbered according to the commandment of the LORD by the hand of Moses. [38] Those who were numbered of the sons of Gershon, throughout their families, and by the house of their fathers, [39] from thirty years old and older to fifty years old, everyone who entered into the service, for the work in the tent of meeting, [40] even those who were numbered of them, throughout their families, by the house of their fathers, were two thousand six hundred and thirty. [41] These were the ones listed by the families of the sons of Gershon, of all who might do service in the tent of meeting, whom Moses and Aaron numbered according to the commandment of the LORD. [42] Those who were numbered of the families of the sons of Merari, throughout their families, by the house of their fathers, [43] from thirty years old and older to fifty years old, everyone who entered into the service, for the work in the tent of meeting, [44] even those who were numbered by their families, were three thousand two hundred. [45] These were the ones listed of the families of the sons of Merari, whom Moses and Aaron numbered according to the word of the LORD by the hand of Moses. [46] All those who were numbered of the Levites, whom Moses, Aaron, and the leaders of Israel numbered, by their families, and by the house of their fathers, [47] from thirty years old and older to fifty years old, everyone who came to do the service of the ministry, and the service of the work in the tent of meeting, [48] even those who were numbered were eight thousand five hundred and eighty. [49] According to the commandment of the LORD they were numbered by the hand of Moses, each according to his service, and according to his burden.

Thus they were numbered by him, as the LORD commanded Moses.

The Unclean

5 And the LORD spoke to Moses, saying: [2] Command the children of Israel that they put out of the camp every leper, and everyone who has a discharge, and whoever is defiled by the dead. [3] Both male and female you will put out. You will put them outside the camp, so they do not defile their camps in the midst of which I dwell.

[4] The children of Israel did so, and put them outside the camp. As the LORD spoke to Moses, so the children of Israel did.

Restitution for Wrongs

[5] The LORD spoke to Moses, saying: [6] Tell the children of Israel: When a man or woman commits any sin against another, acting unfaithfully against the LORD, that person is guilty, [7] and shall confess his sin which he has committed, and he will repay his offense with its principal, and add to it one-fifth, and give it to him who was wronged. [8] But if the man has no relative to repay the offense to, let the offense be repaid to the LORD, even to the priest, beside the ram of the atonement, whereby an atonement will be made for him. [9] Every offering of all the holy things of the children of Israel, which they bring to the priest, will be his. [10] Every man's holy things will be his. Whatever any man gives the priest, it will be his.

The Test for Adultery

[11] The LORD spoke to Moses, saying: [12] Speak to the children of Israel and say to them: If any man's wife goes astray, and acts treacherously against him, [13] and a man lies with her carnally, and it is hidden from the eyes of her husband, and it is concealed though she has defiled herself, and there is no witness against her, nor is she caught in the act, [14] and if the spirit of jealousy comes on him, and he is jealous of his wife who has defiled herself, or if the spirit of jealousy comes on him and he is jealous of his wife, though she has not defiled herself, [15] then the man shall bring his wife to the priest and he shall bring her offering for her, a tenth of an ephah[1] of barley flour. He shall pour no oil on it nor put frankincense on it, for it is a grain offering of jealousy, a grain offering of remembrance, bringing iniquity to remembrance.

[16] The priest will bring her near, and set her before the LORD. [17] And the priest will take holy water in an earthen vessel, and the priest will take some of the dust that is on the floor of the tabernacle and put it into the water. [18] And the priest will set the woman before the LORD, and uncover the woman's head, and put the memorial offering in her hands, which is the grain offering of jealousy, and the priest will have in his hand the bitter water that causes the curse. [19] And the priest will charge her by an oath, and say to the woman, "If no man has lain with you, and if you have not gone astray to impurity with another instead of your husband, be free from this bitter water that causes the curse. [20] But if you have gone astray to another instead of your husband, and if you are defiled, and a man besides your husband has lain with you"— [21] then the priest will charge the woman with an oath of cursing, and the priest will say to the woman, "The LORD make you a curse and an oath among your people, when the LORD makes your thigh rot and your belly swell. [22] And this water that causes the curse will go into your bowels, to make your belly swell and your thigh rot."

And the woman will say, "Amen, amen."

[23] The priest will write these curses in a book, and he will wash them out with the bitter water. [24] And he will cause the woman to drink the bitter water that causes the curse. And the water that causes the curse will enter into her and become bitter. [25] Then the priest will take the grain offering of jealousy out of the woman's hand and will wave the offering before the LORD and offer it on the altar. [26] And the priest will take a handful of the offering, the memorial portion, and burn it on the altar, and afterward will cause the woman to drink the water. [27] When he has made her to drink the water, then it will be that, if she is defiled and has acted treacherously against her husband, the water that causes the curse will enter into her, and become bitter, and her belly will swell, and her thigh will rot, and the woman will be a curse among her people. [28] If the woman is not defiled, but is clean, then she will be free and will conceive offspring.

[29] This is the law of jealousies, when a wife goes astray to another instead of her husband, and is defiled, [30] or when the spirit of jealousy comes on him, and he is jealous over his wife, and will set the woman before the LORD, and the priest will perform on her all this law. [31] Then the man will be guiltless from iniquity, and this woman will bear her iniquity.

---

[1] 15 Likely about 3½ pounds, or 1.6 kilograms.

The Nazirite Vow

6 And the Lord spoke to Moses, saying: [2] Speak to the children of Israel and say to them: When either a man or woman will make a hard vow, the vow of a Nazirite, to separate themselves to the Lord, [3] he will separate himself from wine and strong drink and will drink no vinegar of wine, or vinegar of strong drink. Neither shall he drink any juice of grapes, nor eat fresh or dry grapes. [4] All the days of his separation he will eat nothing that is made of the grapevine, from the seed to the skin.

[5] All the days of the vow of his separation no razor will come on his head until the days are fulfilled in which he separates himself to the Lord. He will be holy and will let the locks of the hair of his head grow. [6] All the days that he separates himself to the Lord he will not approach a dead body. [7] He will not defile himself for his father or for his mother, for his brother or for his sister if they die because the separation of his God is on his head. [8] All the days of his separation he is holy to the Lord.

[9] If any man dies very suddenly beside him, and he has defiled his consecrated head, then he will shave his head in the day of his cleansing, on the seventh day will he shave it. [10] On the eighth day he will bring two turtledoves or two young pigeons to the priest, to the door of the tent of meeting. [11] And the priest will offer one as a sin offering and the other as a burnt offering and make an atonement for him, since he sinned because of the dead, and will sanctify his head that same day. [12] He will consecrate to the Lord the days of his separation and bring a male lamb in its first year as a guilt offering. But the previous days will be lost because his separation was defiled.

[13] This is the law of the Nazirite. When the days of his separation are fulfilled, he will be brought to the door of the tent of meeting. [14] And he will offer his offering to the Lord, one male lamb a year old without blemish as a burnt offering, one ewe lamb a year old without blemish as a sin offering, one ram without blemish as a peace offering, [15] a basket of unleavened bread, loaves of fine flour mixed with oil, unleavened wafers anointed with oil, and their grain offering with their drink offerings.

[16] The priest will bring them before the Lord and will offer his sin offering and his burnt offering. [17] And he will offer the ram as a sacrifice of a peace offering to the Lord with the basket of unleavened bread. The priest will offer also his grain offering and his drink offering.

[18] The Nazirite will shave his consecrated head at the door of the tent of meeting, and will take the hair from his consecrated head and put it in the fire which is under the sacrifice of the peace offerings. [19] The priest will take the cooked shoulder of the ram, and one unleavened cake out of the basket, and one unleavened wafer and will put them on the hands of the Nazirite, after he has shaved his consecrated hair. [20] And the priest will wave them as a wave offering before the Lord. This is holy for the priest, with the breast waved and the shoulder offered. And after that the Nazirite may drink wine.

[21] This is the law of the Nazirite who has vowed to the Lord, his offering for his separation, besides whatever else his hand is able to provide. According to the vow which he spoke, so he must do, according to the law of his separation.

The Priestly Blessing

[22] The Lord spoke to Moses, saying: [23] Speak to Aaron and to his sons, saying, This is how you will bless the children of Israel, saying to them,

[24] The Lord bless you
    and keep you;
[25] the Lord make His face to shine upon you,
    and be gracious unto you;
[26] the Lord lift His countenance upon you,
    and give you peace.

[27] They will put My name upon the children of Israel, and I will bless them.

Offerings at the Tabernacle's Dedication

7 And it was on the day that Moses had fully set up the tabernacle and anointed it and sanctified it and all its instruments, both the altar and all its vessels, and anointed them, and sanctified them, [2] that the leaders of Israel, heads of their fathers' houses, who were the leaders of the tribes, and were over them who were counted, made an offering. [3] And they brought their offering before the Lord, six covered wagons, and twelve oxen, a wagon for two of the leaders, and for each one an ox. And they brought them before the tabernacle.

[4] The Lord spoke to Moses, saying: [5] Accept these things from them, that they may be used in the service of the tent of meeting. Give them to the Levites, to each man according to his service. [6] Moses took the wagons and the oxen and gave them to the Levites. [7] Two wagons and four oxen he gave to the sons of Gershon, according to their service. [8] And four wagons and eight oxen he gave to the sons of Merari, according to their service, under the hand of Ithamar the son of Aaron the priest. [9] But to the sons of Kohath he gave none because the service of the sanctuary belonging to them was that that they should carry on their shoulders.

[10] The leaders brought their dedication offerings when the altar was anointed, and offered their offerings before the altar. [11] The Lord said to Moses: They will offer their offering, each leader on his day, for the dedicating of the altar.

[12] He that offered his offering the first day was Nahshon the son of Amminadab, of the tribe of Judah.

[13] And his offering was one silver charger, the weight of which was one hundred and thirty shekels,[1] one silver bowl of seventy shekels,[2] after the shekel of the sanctuary, both of them full of fine flour mixed with oil as a grain offering; [14] one spoon of ten shekels[3] of gold, full of incense; [15] one young bull, one ram, and one male lamb in its first year as a burnt offering; [16] one goat kid as a sin offering; [17] and as a sacrifice of peace offerings, two oxen, five rams, five male goats, and five male lambs in their first year. This was the offering of Nahshon the son of Amminadab.

[18] On the second day Nethanel the son of Zuar, leader of Issachar, presented an offering.

[19] He offered as his offering one silver charger, the weight of which was one hundred and thirty shekels, one silver bowl of seventy shekels, after the shekel of the sanctuary, both of them full of fine flour mingled with oil as a grain offering; [20] one spoon of ten shekels of gold, full of incense; [21] one young bull, one ram, and one male lamb in its first year as a burnt offering; [22] one goat kid as a sin offering; [23] and as a sacrifice of peace offerings, two oxen, five rams, five male goats, and five male lambs in their first year. This was the offering of Nethanel the son of Zuar.

[24] On the third day Eliab the son of Helon, leader of the children of Zebulun, presented an offering.

[25] And his offering was one silver charger, the weight of which was one hundred and thirty shekels, one silver bowl of seventy shekels, after the shekel of the sanctuary, both of them full of fine flour mixed with oil as a grain offering; [26] one spoon of ten shekels of gold, full of incense; [27] one young bull, one ram, one male lamb in its first year as a burnt offering; [28] one goat kid as a sin offering; [29] and as a sacrifice of peace offerings, two oxen, five rams, five male goats, five male lambs in their first year. This was the offering of Eliab the son of Helon.

[30] On the fourth day Elizur the son of Shedeur, leader of the children of Reuben, presented an offering.

[31] And his offering was one silver charger, the weight of which was one hundred and thirty shekels, one silver bowl of seventy shekels, after the shekel of the sanctuary, both of

---

[1] 13 About 3¼ pounds, or 1.5 kilograms; and throughout this chapter.   [2] 13 About 1¾ pounds, or 800 grams; and throughout this chapter.
[3] 14 About 4 ounces, or 115 grams; and throughout this chapter.

them full of fine flour mixed with oil as a grain offering; [32] one spoon of ten shekels of gold, full of incense; [33] one young bull, one ram, one male lamb in its first year as a burnt offering; [34] one goat kid as a sin offering; [35] and as a sacrifice of peace offerings, two oxen, five rams, five male goats, five male lambs in their first year. This was the offering of Elizur the son of Shedeur.

[36] On the fifth day Shelumiel the son of Zurishaddai, leader of the children of Simeon, presented an offering. [37] And his offering was one silver charger, the weight of which was one hundred and thirty shekels, one silver bowl of seventy shekels, after the shekel of the sanctuary, both of them full of fine flour mixed with oil as a grain offering; [38] one spoon of ten shekels of gold, full of incense; [39] one young bull, one ram, one male lamb in its first year, as a burnt offering; [40] one goat kid as a sin offering; [41] and as a sacrifice of peace offerings, two oxen, five rams, five male goats, five male lambs in their first year. This was the offering of Shelumiel the son of Zurishaddai.

[42] On the sixth day Eliasaph the son of Deuel, leader of the children of Gad, presented an offering. [43] And his offering was one silver charger, the weight of which was one hundred and thirty shekels, one silver bowl of seventy shekels, after the shekel of the sanctuary, both of them full of fine flour mixed with oil as a grain offering; [44] one spoon of ten shekels of gold, full of incense; [45] one young bull, one ram, one male lamb in its first year as a burnt offering; [46] one goat kid as a sin offering; [47] and as a sacrifice of peace offerings, two oxen, five rams, five male goats, five male lambs in their first year. This was the offering of Eliasaph the son of Deuel.

[48] On the seventh day Elishama the son of Ammihud, leader of the children of Ephraim, presented an offering. [49] And his offering was one silver charger, the weight of which was one hundred and thirty shekels, one silver bowl of seventy shekels, after the shekel of the sanctuary, both of them full of fine flour mixed with oil as a grain offering; [50] one spoon of ten shekels of gold, full of incense; [51] one young bull, one ram, one male lamb in its first year as a burnt offering; [52] one goat kid as a sin offering; [53] and as a sacrifice of peace offerings, two oxen, five rams, five male goats, five male lambs in their first year. This was the offering of Elishama the son of Ammihud.

[54] On the eighth day Gamaliel the son of Pedahzur, leader of the children of Manasseh, presented an offering. [55] And his offering was one silver charger, the weight of which was one hundred and thirty shekels, one silver bowl of seventy shekels, after the shekel of the sanctuary, both of them full of fine flour mixed with oil as a grain offering; [56] one spoon of ten shekels of gold, full of incense; [57] one young bull, one ram, and one male lamb in its first year as a burnt offering; [58] one goat kid as a sin offering; [59] and as a sacrifice of peace offerings, two oxen, five rams, five male goats, five male lambs in their first year. This was the offering of Gamaliel the son of Pedahzur.

[60] On the ninth day Abidan the son of Gideoni, leader of the children of Benjamin, presented an offering. [61] And his offering was one silver charger, the weight of which was one hundred and thirty shekels, one silver bowl of seventy shekels, after the shekel of the sanctuary, both of them full of fine flour mixed with oil as a grain offering; [62] one spoon of ten shekels of gold, full of incense; [63] one young bull, one ram, and one male lamb in its first year as a burnt offering; [64] one goat kid as a sin offering; [65] and as a sacrifice of peace offerings, two oxen, five rams, five male

goats, and five male lambs in their first year. This was the offering of Abidan the son of Gideoni.

[66] On the tenth day Ahiezer the son of Ammishaddai, leader of the children of Dan, presented an offering. [67] And his offering was one silver charger, the weight of which was one hundred and thirty shekels, one silver bowl of seventy shekels, after the shekel of the sanctuary, both of them full of fine flour mixed with oil as a grain offering; [68] one spoon of ten shekels of gold, full of incense; [69] one young bull, one ram, and one male lamb in its first year as a burnt offering; [70] one goat kid as a sin offering; [71] and as a sacrifice of peace offerings, two oxen, five rams, five male goats, and five male lambs in their first year. This was the offering of Ahiezer the son of Ammishaddai.

[72] On the eleventh day Pagiel the son of Okran, leader of the children of Asher, presented an offering. [73] And his offering was one silver charger, the weight of which was one hundred and thirty shekels, one silver bowl of seventy shekels, after the shekel of the sanctuary, both of them full of fine flour mixed with oil as a grain offering; [74] one spoon of ten shekels of gold, full of incense; [75] one young bull, one ram, and one male lamb in its first year as a burnt offering; [76] one goat kid as a sin offering; [77] and as a sacrifice of peace offerings, two oxen, five rams, five male goats, and five male lambs in their first year. This was the offering of Pagiel the son of Okran.

[78] On the twelfth day Ahira the son of Enan, leader of the children of Naphtali, presented an offering. [79] And his offering was one silver charger, the weight of which was one hundred and thirty shekels, one silver bowl of seventy shekels, after the shekel of the sanctuary, both of them full of fine flour mixed with oil as a grain offering; [80] one spoon of ten shekels of gold, full of incense; [81] one young bull, one ram, and one male lamb in its first year as a burnt offering; [82] one goat kid as a sin offering; [83] and as a sacrifice of peace offerings, two oxen, five rams, five male goats, and five male lambs in their first year. This was the offering of Ahira the son of Enan.

[84] This was the dedication of the altar, in the day when it was anointed, by the leaders of Israel: twelve silver plates, twelve silver bowls, and twelve gold spoons, [85] each silver plate weighing one hundred and thirty shekels, each bowl seventy. All the silver vessels weighed two thousand four hundred shekels, [1] according to the shekel of the sanctuary. [86] The gold spoons were twelve, full of incense, weighing ten shekels apiece, according to the shekel of the sanctuary. All the gold of the spoons was one hundred and twenty shekels. [2] [87] All the oxen for the burnt offering were twelve bulls, twelve rams, twelve male lambs in their first year, with their grain offering, and twelve goat kids for a sin offering. [88] And all the oxen for the sacrifice of the peace offerings were twenty-four bulls, the rams sixty, the goats sixty, the one-year-old lambs sixty. This was the dedication of the altar after it was anointed.

[89] And then Moses went into the tent of meeting to speak with Him, and he heard the voice of One speaking to him from the mercy seat that was on the ark of the testimony, from between the two cherubim, and He spoke to him.

The Seven Lamps

8 And the LORD spoke to Moses, saying: [2] Speak to Aaron and say to him: When you set up the lamps, the seven lamps will give light before the lampstand.

[3] Aaron did so. He lit the lamps before the lampstand, as the LORD commanded Moses. [4] And this was the work of the lampstand: hammered gold, to its shaft, to its flowers was beaten work. According to the pattern which the LORD had shown Moses, so he made the lampstand.

---

[1] 85 About 60 pounds, or 28 kilograms.　[2] 86 About 3 pounds, or 1.4 kilograms.

Consecrating the Levites

[5] The LORD spoke to Moses, saying: [6] Take the Levites from among the children of Israel and cleanse them. [7] Thus you will do to them to cleanse them: Splash purifying water on them, and let them shave their whole body, and let them wash their clothes, and so make themselves clean. [8] Then let them take a young bull with its grain offering, also fine flour mixed with oil, and you will take another young bull as a sin offering. [9] You will bring the Levites before the tent of meeting. And you will gather the whole assembly of the children of Israel together. [10] And you will bring the Levites before the LORD. And the children of Israel will put their hands on the Levites. [11] And Aaron will offer the Levites before the LORD as a wave offering of the children of Israel, that they may do the service of the LORD.

[12] The Levites will lay their hands on the heads of the bulls, and you will offer one as a sin offering and the other as a burnt offering to the LORD, to make an atonement for the Levites. [13] You will set the Levites before Aaron and before his sons, and offer them as a wave offering to the LORD. [14] Thus will you separate the Levites from among the children of Israel, and the Levites will be Mine.

[15] And afterwards the Levites will go in to do the service of the tent of meeting, and you will cleanse them and offer them as a wave offering. [16] For they are completely set aside for Me by the children of Israel. Instead of all who open the womb, instead of the firstborn of all the children of Israel, I have taken them for Myself. [17] For all the firstborn of the children of Israel are Mine, both man and animal. On the day that I struck every firstborn in the land of Egypt I sanctified them for Myself. [18] I have taken the Levites instead of all the firstborn of the children of Israel. [19] I have given the Levites as a gift to Aaron and to his sons from among the children of Israel, to serve the service of the children of Israel in the tent of meeting and to make an atonement for the children of Israel, so there will be no plague among the children of Israel when the children of Israel approach the sanctuary.

[20] Moses and Aaron and all the congregation of the children of Israel did to the Levites; according to all that the LORD commanded Moses concerning the Levites, so the children of Israel did to them. [21] The Levites cleansed themselves from sin, and they washed their clothes, and Aaron offered them as a wave offering before the LORD, and Aaron made an atonement for them to cleanse them. [22] And after that the Levites went in to do their service in the tent of meeting before Aaron and before his sons. As the LORD had commanded Moses concerning the Levites, so they did to them.

[23] The LORD spoke to Moses, saying: [24] This is what belongs to the Levites: From twenty-five years old and older they will go in to do their duty concerning the service of the tent of meeting. [25] And from the age of fifty years they will cease doing their duty concerning its service and will serve no more. [26] But *they* will minister with their brothers in the tent of meeting, to attend to their needs, but will not do the work. Thus you will do to the Levites concerning their duties.

The Passover at Sinai

9 And the LORD spoke to Moses in the Wilderness of Sinai, in the first month of the second year after they came out of the land of Egypt, saying: [2] Let the children of Israel also keep the Passover at its appointed time. [3] On the fourteenth day of this month, at evening, you will keep it at its appointed time. According to all its rites and according to all its ceremonies, you will keep it.

[4] Moses spoke to the children of Israel, that they should keep the Passover. [5] They kept the Passover on the fourteenth day of the first month at evening in the Wilderness of Sinai. According to all that the LORD commanded Moses, so the children of Israel did.

[6] There were men who were unclean by the dead body of a man, so they could not keep the Passover on that day, and they came before Moses and before Aaron on that day. [7] And those men said to him, "We are defiled by the dead body of a man. Why are we kept back, that we may not offer an offering of the LORD at its appointed time among the children of Israel?"

[8] And Moses said to them, "Stand still, and I will hear what the LORD will command concerning you."

[9] The LORD spoke to Moses, saying: [10] Speak to the children of Israel, saying: If any man of you or of your posterity is unclean because of a dead body, or is far off on a journey, he will still keep the Passover to the LORD. [11] The fourteenth day of the second month at evening they will keep it, and eat it with unleavened bread and bitter herbs. [12] They will leave none of it until the morning, nor break any of its bones. According to all the ordinances of the Passover they will keep it. [13] But the man who is ceremonially clean, and is not on a journey, and fails to keep the Passover, even the same person will be cut off from his people. Because he did not bring the offering of the LORD at its appointed time, that man will bear his sin.

[14] If a stranger will sojourn among you and will keep the Passover to the LORD, according to the ordinance of the Passover, and according to the manner of it, so he will do. You will have one ordinance both for the resident alien and for the natural born citizen of the land.

The Cloud and the Fire

[15] And on the day that the tabernacle was erected, the cloud covered the tabernacle, the tent of the testimony, and at evening there was over the tabernacle the appearance of fire until the morning. [16] So it was always. The cloud covered it by day, and the appearance of fire by night. [17] When the cloud was lifted up from over the tabernacle, then after it the children of Israel journeyed, and in the place where the cloud settled, there the children of Israel camped. [18] At the commandment of the LORD the children of Israel journeyed, and at the commandment of the LORD they camped. As long as the cloud dwelt over the tabernacle they camped. [19] When the cloud remained many days over the tabernacle, then the children of Israel kept the charge of the LORD and did not journey. [20] When the cloud remained a few days over the tabernacle, according to the commandment of the LORD they dwelt in their tents, and according to the commandment of the LORD they journeyed. [21] When the cloud dwelt from evening until morning and the cloud was lifted up in the morning, then they journeyed. Whether it was by day or by night that the cloud was lifted up, they journeyed. [22] Whether it was two days, or a month, or a long time that the cloud dwelt over the tabernacle, the children of Israel dwelt in their tents and did not journey. But when it was lifted up they journeyed. [23] At the command of the LORD they camped, and at the command of the LORD they journeyed. They kept the charge of the LORD at the command of the LORD by the hand of Moses.

The Silver Trumpets

10 And the LORD spoke to Moses, saying: [2] Make for yourself two silver trumpets. Of a hammered work you will make them, and you will use them for summoning of the assembly and directing the breaking up of the camps. [3] When they blow both of them, all the assembly will assemble themselves to you at the door of the tent of meeting. [4] If they blow only one, then the leaders, who are heads of the thousands of Israel, will gather themselves to you. [5] When you blow an alarm, then the camps that lie on the east will set out. [6] When you blow an alarm the second time, then the camps that lie on the south will set out. They will blow an alarm for their setting out. [7] But when the assembly is to be gathered together, you will blow, but you will not sound an alarm.

[8] The sons of Aaron, the priests, will blow the trumpets, and they will be to you as an ordinance forever throughout your generations. [9] And if you go to war in your land against the enemy that oppresses you, then you will blow an alarm with the trumpets, and you will be remembered before the LORD your God, and you will be saved from your enemies. [10] Also in the day of your gladness, and at your appointed days, and in the beginnings of your months, you shall blow the trumpets over your burnt offerings, and over the sacrifices of your peace offerings that they may be a memorial for you before your God. I am the LORD your God.

The Departure From Sinai

[11] And it was on the twentieth day of the second month, in the second year, that the cloud was lifted up from over the tabernacle of the testimony. [12] The children of Israel set out from the Wilderness of Sinai. And the cloud dwelt in the Wilderness of Paran. [13] And they set out for the first time at the command of the LORD by the hand of Moses.

¹⁴ And the standard of the camp of the sons of Judah set out first by their armies, and over his armies was Nahshon the son of Amminadab. ¹⁵ Over the armies of the tribe of the children of Issachar was Nethanel the son of Zuar. ¹⁶ Over the armies of the tribe of the children of Zebulun was Eliab the son of Helon. ¹⁷ The tabernacle was taken down, and the sons of Gershon and the sons of Merari set out, carrying the tabernacle.

¹⁸ The standard of the camp of Reuben set out by their armies, and over his armies was Elizur the son of Shedeur. ¹⁹ Over the armies of the tribe of the children of Simeon was Shelumiel the son of Zurishaddai. ²⁰ Over the armies of the tribe of the children of Gad was Eliasaph the son of Deuel. ²¹ The Kohathites set out, carrying the sanctuary, and they set up the tabernacle before they came.

²² The standard of the camp of the children of Ephraim set out by their armies, and over his armies was Elishama the son of Ammihud. ²³ Over the armies of the tribe of the children of Manasseh was Gamaliel the son of Pedahzur. ²⁴ Over the armies of the tribe of the children of Benjamin was Abidan the son of Gideoni.

²⁵ Then the standard of the camp of the children of Dan set out, which was the rear guard of all the camps by their armies, and over his armies was Ahiezer the son of Ammishaddai. ²⁶ Over the armies of the tribe of the children of Asher was Pagiel the son of Okran. ²⁷ Over the armies of the tribe of the children of Naphtali was Ahira the son of Enan. ²⁸ This was the order of march of the children of Israel, company by company, when they set out.

²⁹ Moses said to Hobab, the son of Reuel the Midianite, Moses' father-in-law, "We are setting out to the place of which the LORD said, 'I will give it to you.' Come with us, and we will do good to you because the LORD has spoken good concerning Israel."

³⁰ Hobab said to him, "I will not go. But I will depart to my own land, and to my kindred."

³¹ So Moses said, "Please do not leave us, because you know where to camp in the wilderness, and you may be our eyes. ³² Moreover, if you go with us, then it will be that whatever good the LORD will do for us, we will likewise do for you."

³³ They set out three days from the mountain of the LORD, and the ark of the covenant of the LORD went before them the three days' journey, to find a resting place for them. ³⁴ And the cloud of the LORD was over them by day when they set out from of the camp.

³⁵ And it was, when the ark set out, that Moses said,

"Rise up, O LORD,
     and let Your enemies be scattered,
     and let them that hate You flee before You."

³⁶ And when it rested, he said,

"Return, O LORD,
     to the multitude of thousands of Israel."

Complaints in the Desert

11 Now when the people complained openly before the LORD, the LORD heard, and His anger burned. Then the fire of the LORD burned among them and consumed the outskirts of the camp. ² And the people cried out to Moses, and Moses prayed to the LORD, and the fire was quenched. ³ He called the name of the place Taberah because the fire of the LORD burned among them.

⁴ The mixed multitude that was among them lusted, and the children of Israel wept again and said, "Who will give us meat to eat? ⁵ We remember the fish, which we ate in Egypt for free, the cucumbers, and the melons, and the leeks, and the onions, and the garlic. ⁶ But now our life is dried up. There is nothing at all except this manna before our eyes."

⁷ The manna was as coriander seed, and it looked like bdellium. ⁸ The people went about and gathered it, and ground it in mills or beat it in a mortar, and boiled it in pots, and made cakes of it, and the taste of it was like the taste of cakes baked in oil. ⁹ When the dew fell on the camp at night, the manna fell on it.

¹⁰ Then Moses heard the people weep throughout their families, every man in the opening of his tent, and the anger of the LORD

burned greatly. Moses was also displeased. ¹¹ Moses said to the LORD, "Why have You hurt Your servant? And why have I not found favor in Your eyes, that You lay the burden of all this people on me? ¹² Have I conceived all this people? Have I given them birth, that You should say to me, 'Carry them in your bosom, as a nurse bears the nursing child,' to the land which You swore to their fathers? ¹³ Where am I to get meat to give to all these people? For they weep to me, saying, 'Give us meat, that we may eat.' ¹⁴ I am not able to bear all these people alone, because the burden is too heavy for me. ¹⁵ If You do this to me, please kill me at once, if I have found favor in Your eyes, and do not let me see my misery."

The Seventy Elders

¹⁶ Then the LORD said to Moses, "Gather to Me seventy men of the elders of Israel, whom you know to be the elders of the people, and officers over them, and bring them to the tent of meeting, that they may take a stand there with you. ¹⁷ And I will come down, and I will speak with you there, and I will take of the Spirit which is on you and will put it on them, and they will bear the burden of the people with you, and you will not bear it by yourself.

¹⁸ "And say to the people: Consecrate yourselves for tomorrow, and you shall eat meat, for you have wept in the hearing of the LORD, saying, 'Who will give us meat to eat? For it was better for us in Egypt.' Therefore the LORD will give you meat, and you shall eat. ¹⁹ You shall eat, not one day, or two days, or five days, or ten days, or twenty days, ²⁰ but a whole month, until it comes out at your nostrils, and it will be nauseating to you because you rejected the LORD who is among you and have wept before Him, saying, 'Why did we come out of Egypt?' "

²¹ And Moses said, "The people I am with number six hundred thousand foot soldiers, and You have said, 'I will give them meat that they may eat a whole month.' ²² Will the flocks and the herds be slaughtered for them, to satisfy them? Or will all the fish of the sea be gathered together for them, to satisfy them?"

²³ And the LORD said to Moses, "Is the hand of the LORD shortened? Now you will see if My word will happen to you or not."

²⁴ Moses went out, and he spoke to the people the words of the LORD and gathered the seventy men of the elders of the people and set them around the tabernacle. ²⁵ And the LORD came down in a cloud, and spoke to him, and took of the Spirit that was on him, and gave it to the seventy elders, and when the Spirit rested on them, they prophesied, but did not do it again.

²⁶ But two men remained in the camp. The name of one was Eldad, and the name of the other, Medad. And the Spirit rested on them. They were among those listed, but they had not gone out to the tent, and so they prophesied in the camp. ²⁷ And a young man ran and told Moses and said, "Eldad and Medad prophesy in the camp."

²⁸ Then Joshua the son of Nun, the assistant of Moses from his youth, answered and said, "My lord Moses, forbid them."

²⁹ Moses said to him, "Are you jealous for my sake? Oh, that all the people of the LORD were prophets, and that the LORD would put His Spirit upon them!" ³⁰ And Moses returned to the camp, he and the elders of Israel.

The LORD Sends Quail

³¹ Now a wind from the LORD started up, and it swept quail from the sea and let them fall beside the camp, about a day's journey on this side and a day's journey on the other side, around the camp, and about two cubits¹ above the ground. ³² And the people stayed up all that day, all night, and all the next day, and gathered the quail. Those who gathered least gathered ten homers.² And they spread them out for themselves all around the camp. ³³ While the meat was between their teeth, before it was chewed, the anger of the LORD burned against the people, and the LORD struck the people with a very great slaughter. ³⁴ And he called the name of that place Kibroth Hattaavah because there they buried the people who had the craving.

³⁵ The people journeyed from Kibroth Hattaavah to Hazeroth, and they camped at Hazeroth.

---

¹ 31 About 3 feet, or 90 centimeters.   ² 32 Likely about 1¾ tons, or 1.6 metric tons.

Miriam and Aaron Oppose Moses

12 And Miriam and Aaron spoke against Moses because of the Cushite woman whom he married, for he had married a Cushite woman. ² They said, "Has the LORD spoken only by Moses? Has He not spoken also by us?" And the LORD heard it.

³ (Now the man Moses was very humble, more than all the men on the face of the earth.)

⁴ And the LORD spoke at once to Moses and to Aaron and to Miriam, "Come out, you three, to the tent of meeting." And those three came out. ⁵ The LORD came down in a pillar of cloud, and stood in the opening of the tabernacle, and called Aaron and Miriam, and they both came forward. ⁶ He said, "Hear now My word.

If there is a prophet among you,
  I the LORD will make Myself known to him in a vision,
  and I will speak to him in a dream.
⁷ Not so with My servant Moses;
  he is entrusted with all My house.
⁸ Face to face I speak with him clearly,
  and not in riddles,
  and the likeness of the LORD will he behold.
Then why were you not afraid
  to speak against My servant, against Moses?"

⁹ And the anger of the LORD burned against them, and He set out. ¹⁰ When the cloud went away from over the tabernacle, Miriam became leprous as snow, and Aaron turned toward Miriam and saw that she was leprous. ¹¹ Aaron said to Moses, "Alas, my lord, do not lay the sin on us, which we have done foolishly, and which we have sinned. ¹² Do not let her be as dead, who when he goes out of his mother's womb half his flesh is eaten."

¹³ And Moses cried out to the LORD, saying, "O God, heal her, I pray!"

¹⁴ But the LORD said to Moses, "If her father had but spit in her face, would she not be ashamed seven days? Let her be shut out of the camp seven days, and afterward she may be received again." ¹⁵ Miriam was shut out from the camp seven days, and the people did not set out until Miriam was brought in again.

¹⁶ Afterward the people set out from Hazeroth and camped in the Wilderness of Paran.

Spying in Canaan

13 And the LORD spoke to Moses, saying, ² "Send men that they may explore the land of Canaan, which I am giving to the children of Israel. Of every tribe of their fathers you will send a man, each one a chief among them."

³ And Moses sent them from the Wilderness of Paran according to the LORD. All those men were heads of the children of Israel. ⁴ These were their names:

of the tribe of Reuben, Shammua the son of Zakkur;
⁵ of the tribe of Simeon, Shaphat the son of Hori;
⁶ of the tribe of Judah, Caleb the son of Jephunneh;
⁷ of the tribe of Issachar, Igal the son of Joseph;
⁸ of the tribe of Ephraim, Hoshea the son of Nun;
⁹ of the tribe of Benjamin, Palti the son of Raphu;
¹⁰ of the tribe of Zebulun, Gaddiel the son of Sodi;
¹¹ of the tribe of Joseph, namely, of the tribe of Manasseh, Gaddi the son of Susi;
¹² of the tribe of Dan, Ammiel the son of Gemalli;
¹³ of the tribe of Asher, Sethur the son of Michael;
¹⁴ of the tribe of Naphtali, Nahbi the son of Vophsi;
¹⁵ of the tribe of Gad, Geuel the son of Maki.

¹⁶ These are the names of the men whom Moses sent to explore the land. And Moses called Hoshea the son of Nun Joshua.

¹⁷ Moses sent them to explore the land of Canaan and said to them, "Go up to this southland, and go up into the mountain. ¹⁸ And see what the land is, and the people that dwell in it, whether they are strong or weak, few or many; ¹⁹ and what the land is that they dwell in, whether it is good or bad, and what cities are that they dwell in, whether in tents, or in fortifications; ²⁰ and what the land is, whether it is fat or lean, whether there is wood in it or not. And you be courageous and bring some of the fruit of the land." Now the time was the time of the first ripe grapes.

²¹ So they went up and explored the land from the Wilderness of Zin to Rehob, near Lebo Hamath. ²² They went up by the Negev and came to Hebron where Ahiman, Sheshai, and Talmai, the children of Anak, were (now Hebron was built seven years before Zoan in Egypt). ²³ And they came to the Valley of Eshkol, and cut down from there a branch with one cluster of grapes, and they carried it on a pole between two of them, and they brought some of the pomegranates and of the figs. ²⁴ The place was called the Valley of Eshkol because of the cluster of grapes which the children of Israel cut down from there. ²⁵ They returned from exploring the land after forty days.

The Spies' Report

²⁶ And they returned and came to Moses and to Aaron and to all the assembly of the children of Israel, to the Wilderness of Paran, to Kadesh, and brought back word to them and to the entire assembly and showed them the fruit of the land. ²⁷ They reported to him and said, "We came to the land where you sent us, and surely it flows with milk and honey, and this is the fruit of it. ²⁸ However, the people are strong that dwell in the land, and the cities are fortified and very great, and also we saw the children of Anak there. ²⁹ The Amalekites dwell in the land of the Negev, and the Hittites, and the Jebusites, and the Amorites dwell in the mountains, and the Canaanites dwell by the sea and by the edge of the Jordan."

³⁰ Caleb silenced the people before Moses and said, "Let us go up at once and possess it, for we are able to overcome it."

³¹ But the men that went up with him said, "We are not able to go up against the people because they are stronger than we." ³² They gave the children of Israel a bad report of the land which they had spied out, saying, "The land through which we have gone as spies is a land that devours its inhabitants, and all the people whom we saw in it are men of great stature. ³³ And there we saw the giants, the sons of Anak, which come from the giants, and in our eyes we were like grasshoppers, and so we were in their eyes."

Israel Refuses to Enter Canaan

14 And the whole assembly lifted up their voices and cried, and the people wept that night. ² All the children of Israel grumbled against Moses and against Aaron, and the whole assembly said to them, "O that we had died in the land of Egypt! Or that we had died in this wilderness! ³ And why has the LORD brought us to this land to fall by the sword, that our wives and our children should become prey? Is it not better for us to return to Egypt?" ⁴ And they said one to another, "Let us select a leader, and let us return to Egypt."

⁵ Then Moses and Aaron fell on their faces before all the congregation of the assembly of the children of Israel. ⁶ Joshua the son of Nun, and Caleb the son of Jephunneh, from the ones who explored the land, tore their clothes. ⁷ And they spoke to all the assembly of the children of Israel, saying, "The land which we passed through to explore it is a very, very good land. ⁸ If the LORD delights in us, then He will bring us into this land and give it to us, a land which flows with milk and honey. ⁹ Only do not rebel against the LORD, nor fear the people of the land because they are bread for us. Their defense is gone from them, and the LORD is with us. Do not fear them."

¹⁰ But all the assembly said, "Stone them with stones." And the glory of the LORD appeared at the tent of meeting before all the children of Israel. ¹¹ The LORD said to Moses, "How long will this people disgrace Me? And how long will they not believe Me, in spite of all the signs which I have done among them? ¹² I will strike them with the pestilence, and disinherit them, and will make from you a nation greater and mightier than they."

Moses Intercedes for the People

¹³ Moses said to the LORD, "Then the Egyptians will hear of it, for by Your power You brought this people up from among them, ¹⁴ and they will say to the inhabitants of this land that they heard that You, LORD, are among this people, that You, LORD, are seen face to face, and Your cloud stands over them, and in the pillar of cloud

You go before them by day and by a pillar of fire at night. ¹⁵ Now if You kill all this people as one man, then the nations which have heard the fame of You will speak, saying, ¹⁶ "The Lᴏʀᴅ was not able to bring this people into the land which He swore to them, so He slaughtered them in the wilderness.'

¹⁷ "So now, I pray, let the power of my Lord be great, just as You have spoken, saying, ¹⁸ "The Lᴏʀᴅ is slow to anger and abounding in mercy, forgiving iniquity and transgression; but He will by no means clear the guilty, visiting the iniquity of the fathers upon the children to the third and fourth generation.' ¹⁹ Pardon the iniquity of this people, I pray, according to the greatness of Your grace, just as You have pardoned this people, from Egypt even until now."

²⁰ The Lᴏʀᴅ said, "I have forgiven according to your word. ²¹ But truly as I live, all the earth will be filled with the glory of the Lᴏʀᴅ. ²² Because all those men seeing My glory and My signs which I did in Egypt and in the wilderness, and have tempted Me now these ten times, and have not listened to My voice, ²³ surely they will not see the land which I swore to their fathers, nor will any of them who disgraced Me see it. ²⁴ But My servant Caleb, because he had a different spirit with him and followed Me fully, I will bring him into the land where he went, and his seed will possess it. ²⁵ Now the Amalekites and the Canaanites lived in the valley. Tomorrow you will turn, and you will set out for the wilderness by the way of the Red Sea."

Death of Rebels Predicted

²⁶ The Lᴏʀᴅ spoke to Moses and to Aaron, saying: ²⁷ How long will this evil assembly be murmuring against Me? I have heard the murmurings of the children of Israel which they murmur against Me. ²⁸ Say to them, "As I live," says the Lᴏʀᴅ, "just as you have spoken in My ears, so I will do to you: ²⁹ In this wilderness your corpses will fall, and all who were numbered of you, according to your whole number, from twenty years old and upward, who have murmured against Me, ³⁰ you will not go into the land which I swore by My hand to cause you to dwell in it, except Caleb the son of Jephunneh and Joshua the son of Nun. ³¹ But your children, whom you said would be a prey, I will bring them in and they will know the land, which you rejected. ³² But as for you, your corpses will fall in this wilderness. ³³ Your children will be shepherds in the wilderness forty years, and they will suffer for your fornications, until your corpses are in the wilderness. ³⁴ According to the number of the days in which you spied out the land, forty days, a year for each day you will bear your iniquity, forty years, and you will know My displeasure." ³⁵ I the Lᴏʀᴅ have spoken. I will surely do this to all this evil assembly gathered against Me. In this wilderness they will be finished, and there they will die.

³⁶ The men whom Moses sent to explore the land, who returned and made all the assembly murmur against him by bringing up an evil report about the land, ³⁷ the men who brought an evil report about the land, died by the pestilence before the Lᴏʀᴅ. ³⁸ But Joshua the son of Nun and Caleb the son of Jephunneh, from the men that went to explore the land, lived.

Defeat in Battle

³⁹ Moses spoke these words to all the children of Israel, and the people mourned greatly. ⁴⁰ They rose up early in the morning, and they went up to the top of the mountain, saying, "Here we are. We will go up to the place which the Lᴏʀᴅ has promised, for we have sinned."

⁴¹ Moses said, "Why do you now transgress the commandment of the Lᴏʀᴅ? This will not prosper. ⁴² Do not go up, for the Lᴏʀᴅ is not among you; do not let yourselves be defeated by your enemies. ⁴³ For the Amalekites and the Canaanites are there before you, and you will fall by the sword because you are turned from the Lᴏʀᴅ, and the Lᴏʀᴅ will not be with you."

⁴⁴ But they presumed to go up to the top of the mountain. But the ark of the covenant of the Lᴏʀᴅ and Moses did not depart from the midst of the camp. ⁴⁵ Then the Amalekites and the Canaanites who dwelt on that mountain went down and defeated them, pursuing them as far as Hormah.

Laws of Grain and Drink Offerings

15 And the Lᴏʀᴅ spoke to Moses, saying: ² Speak to the children of Israel, and say to them: When you come into the land of your dwelling, which I am giving to you, ³ when you make an offering by fire to the Lᴏʀᴅ, a burnt offering, or a sacrifice in performing a vow, or as a freewill offering, or in your appointed feasts, to make a pleasing aroma to the Lᴏʀᴅ, of the herd or of the flock, ⁴ then he who brings his offering to the Lᴏʀᴅ will bring a grain offering of a tenth of an ephah¹ of flour mixed with the fourth part of a hin² of oil. ⁵ One-fourth of a hin of wine as a drink offering you will prepare with the burnt offering or sacrifice, for each lamb.

⁶ Or for a ram, you will make a grain offering of two-tenths of an ephah³ of flour mixed with one-third of a hin⁴ of oil. ⁷ As a drink offering you will offer one-third of a hin of wine, as a pleasing aroma to the Lᴏʀᴅ.

⁸ When you prepare a bull as a burnt offering, or as a sacrifice in performing a vow, or as a peace offering to the Lᴏʀᴅ, ⁹ then shall be brought with the bull a grain offering of three-tenths of an ephah⁵ of flour mixed with one-half a hin⁶ of oil. ¹⁰ You will bring as a drink offering one-half a hin of wine, as a fire offering, as a pleasing aroma to the Lᴏʀᴅ. ¹¹ Thus it will be done for one herd animal, or for one ram, or for a flock animal, whether from the sheep or from the goats. ¹² According to the number that you will make, so you will do for every one according to their number.

¹³ Every native Israelite will do these things in this manner, in offering a fire offering as a pleasing aroma to the Lᴏʀᴅ. ¹⁴ A foreigner who lives with you, or who resides among you throughout your generations, and would present a fire offering, a pleasing aroma to the Lᴏʀᴅ, shall do as you do. ¹⁵ One ordinance will be for you of the assembly and for the foreigner who lives with you, an ordinance forever throughout your generations. As you are, so will the foreigner be before the Lᴏʀᴅ. ¹⁶ One law and one justice will be for you and for the foreigner who lives with you.

¹⁷ The Lᴏʀᴅ spoke to Moses, saying: ¹⁸ Speak to the children of Israel, and say to them: When you come into the land where I bring you, ¹⁹ then it will be, when you eat of the bread of the land you will offer up an offering to the Lᴏʀᴅ. ²⁰ From the first of your dough you will offer a cake as an offering. As you make the offering of the threshing floor, so will you offer it. ²¹ Of the first of your dough you will give to the Lᴏʀᴅ an offering throughout your generations.

Laws About Unintentional Sins

²² If you have erred and not observed all these commandments which the Lᴏʀᴅ has spoken to Moses, ²³ even all that the Lᴏʀᴅ has commanded you by the hand of Moses, from the day that the Lᴏʀᴅ commanded Moses and onward through your generations, ²⁴ then it will be, if it is committed by ignorance without the knowledge of the assembly, that all the assembly will offer one young bull as a burnt offering, as a pleasing aroma to the Lᴏʀᴅ, with its grain offering and its drink offering, according to the rule, and one kid of the goats as a sin offering. ²⁵ The priest will make atonement for all the assembly of the children of Israel, and it will be forgiven them because it is ignorance, and they will bring their offering, a sacrifice made by fire to the Lᴏʀᴅ, and their sin offering before the Lᴏʀᴅ, for their ignorance. ²⁶ And it will be forgiven all the assembly of the children of Israel and the foreigner who lives among them, because all the people were in ignorance.

²⁷ If a person sins unintentionally, then he will bring a year-old female goat as a sin offering. ²⁸ The priest will make an atonement for the person who sins unintentionally, when he sins by ignorance before the Lᴏʀᴅ, to make an atonement for him; and it will be forgiven him. ²⁹ You shall have one law for the person who acts through ignorance, for the natural-born citizen among the children of Israel and foreigner who lives in your midst.

Laws About Intentional Sins

³⁰ But the person who acts by a high hand, the natural-born citizen or the foreigner, the same reviles the Lᴏʀᴅ, and that person will be cut off from among his people. ³¹ Because he has despised the

---

14 Likely about 3½ pounds, or 1.6 kilograms.   *24* About 1 quart, or 1 liter; and in v. 5.   *36* Likely about 7 pounds, or 3.2 kilograms.
46 About 1⅓ quarts, or 1.3 liters; and in v. 7.   *59* Likely about 11 pounds, or 5 kilograms.   *69* About 2 quarts, or 1.9 liters; and in v. 10.

word of the Lord and has broken His commandment, that person will be totally cut off. His iniquity will be on him.

The Sabbath-Breaker Executed

[32] While the children of Israel were in the wilderness, they found a man who gathered sticks on the Sabbath day. [33] The ones who found him gathering sticks brought him to Moses and Aaron and to all the assembly. [34] They put him in confinement because it was not declared what should be done to him. [35] The Lord said to Moses, "The man will surely die. All the assembly will stone him with stones outside the camp." [36] All the assembly brought him outside the camp and stoned him with stones, and he died as the Lord commanded Moses.

Tassels on Garments

[37] The Lord spoke to Moses, saying: [38] Speak to the children of Israel, and tell them to make for themselves tassels on the corners of their garments throughout the generations to come, and they will put a ribbon of blue on the corners of their garments. [39] And it will be for you a tassel, and you will see it, and you will remember all the commandments of the Lord, and you will do them, and you will not follow the lust of your own heart and your own eyes. [40] So shall you remember and do all My commandments, and be holy to your God. [41] I am the Lord your God who brought you out of the land of Egypt, to be your God: I am the Lord your God.

Opposition to Moses and Aaron

16 Now Korah the son of Izhar, the son of Kohath, the son of Levi, and Dathan and Abiram the sons of Eliab, and On the son of Peleth, sons of Reuben, took men, [2] and they rose up before Moses and men of the children of Israel, two hundred and fifty chiefs of the assembly, famous in the assembly, well-known men. [3] They assembled against Moses and against Aaron, and said to them, "You take too much upon yourselves, seeing all the congregation are holy, every one of them, and the Lord is among them. So why do you exalt yourselves above the assembly of the Lord?"

[4] And when Moses heard it, he fell on his face, [5] and he spoke to Korah and to all his company, saying, "In the morning the Lord will show who is His and who is holy, and He will bring him to come near to Him. Whom He has chosen He will bring near to Him. [6] Do this: Take censers, Korah and all his company; [7] put fire in them, and put incense in them before the Lord tomorrow, and it will be that the man whom the Lord chooses, he will be holy. You take too much upon yourselves, sons of Levi."

[8] Moses said to Korah, "Listen, please, sons of Levi. [9] Does it seem a small thing to you that the God of Israel has separated you from the assembly of Israel to bring you near to Himself to do the service of the tabernacle of the Lord, and to stand before the assembly to minister to them? [10] And He has brought you near to Him, and all your brothers, the sons of Levi, with you, and you also seek the priesthood? [11] Therefore both you and all your company are gathered together against the Lord, and who is Aaron that you murmur against him?"

[12] And Moses sent for Dathan and Abiram the sons of Eliab, who said, "We will not come up. [13] Is it a small thing that you have brought us up out of a land that flows with milk and honey to kill us in the wilderness because you make yourself a prince over us? [14] Moreover you have not brought us into a land that flows with milk and honey nor given us inheritance of fields and vineyards. Will you put out the eyes of these men? We will not come up."

[15] Moses was very angry and said to the Lord, "Do not respect their offering. I have not taken one donkey from them, nor have I hurt one of them."

[16] Moses said to Korah, "You and all your company be before the Lord, you and them and Aaron, tomorrow. [17] Let each man take his censer and put incense in it, and each of you bring his censer before the Lord, two hundred and fifty censers. Also you and Aaron shall each bring his censer." [18] Every man took his censer and put fire in it, and laid incense on it, and stood at the door of the tent of meeting with Moses and Aaron. [19] Korah gathered all the assembly against them to the door of the tent of meeting, and the glory of the Lord appeared to all the assembly. [20] The Lord spoke to Moses and to Aaron, saying: [21] Separate yourselves from among this assembly, that I may consume them in a moment.

[22] They fell on their faces and said, "O God, the God of the spirits of all flesh, will one man sin and You will be angry with all the assembly?"

[23] And the Lord spoke to Moses, saying: [24] Speak to the assembly, saying: Get up from around the tents of Korah, Dathan, and Abiram.

[25] Moses rose up and went to Dathan and Abiram, and the elders of Israel followed him. [26] He spoke to the assembly, saying, "Depart now from the tents of these wicked men, and touch nothing of theirs, lest you be swept away for all their sins." [27] So they got up from the tents of Korah, Dathan, and Abiram, on every side, and Dathan and Abiram came out and stood in the opening of their tents, and their wives, and their sons, and their children.

[28] Moses said, "By this you will know that the Lord has sent me to do all these works, because I have not done them of my own mind. [29] If these men die the common death of all men, or if they are visited after the visitation of all men, then the Lord has not sent me. [30] But if the Lord makes a new thing, and the earth opens its mouth and swallows them with all that belongs to them, and they go down alive into the pit, then you will know that these men have despised the Lord."

[31] So it was, when he finished speaking all these words, that the ground that was under them split open. [32] And the earth opened its mouth and swallowed them, and their houses, and all the men that belonged to Korah, and all his goods. [33] And they and all that belonged to them went down alive into the pit, and the earth closed on them, and they perished from among the assembly. [34] All Israel that was around them fled at their cry because they said, "The earth will swallow us also."

[35] A fire went out from the Lord and consumed the two hundred and fifty men that offered incense.

[36] The Lord spoke to Moses, saying: [37] Tell Eleazar the son of Aaron the priest to take up the censers out of the blaze, for they are holy. Then scatter the fire far and wide. [38] As for the censers of these men who have sinned at the cost of their own lives, make them into hammered plates as a covering for the altar, for they presented them before the Lord and they are holy. They shall be a sign to the children of Israel.

[39] So Eleazar the priest took the bronze censers, which those who were burned had offered, and they were hammered out as a covering on the altar, [40] to be a memorial to the children of Israel, that no outsider, who is not of the descendants of Aaron, shall approach to offer incense before the Lord, that he might not become like Korah and his company, as the Lord has said to him through Moses.

The People Complain

[41] But the next day all the assembly of the children of Israel murmured against Moses and against Aaron, saying, "You have killed the people of the Lord."

[42] When the assembly was gathered against Moses and Aaron, they looked toward the tent of meeting. The cloud covered it, and the glory of the Lord appeared. [43] Moses and Aaron went before the tent of meeting. [44] And the Lord spoke to Moses, saying, [45] "Get up from among this assembly, that I may destroy them in a moment." And they fell on their faces.

[46] Moses said to Aaron, "Take a censer and put fire in it from off the altar, and put in incense, and go quickly to the assembly, and make an atonement for them, because wrath has gone out from the Lord. The plague has begun." [47] Aaron took it as Moses commanded and ran into the midst of the assembly, where the plague had begun among the people. He put in incense and made an atonement for the people. [48] He stood between the dead and the living, and the plague was stopped. [49] Now those who died in the plague were fourteen thousand seven hundred, besides those that died concerning the thing of Korah. [50] Aaron returned to Moses, to the door of the tent of meeting, and the plague was stopped.

The Budding of Aaron's Rod

17 And the Lord spoke to Moses, saying: [2] Speak to the children of Israel, and take from them a rod, a rod for the house of their fathers, from all their leaders according to the house of their fathers, twelve rods. Write each man's name on his rod. ³ You will write the name of Aaron on the rod of Levi, because one rod will be for each father's house. ⁴ You will lay them in the tent of meeting before the testimony, where I will meet with you. ⁵ It will be that the rod of the man whom I choose will bud. Thus I will rid myself of the complaints of the children of Israel, that they have been making against you.

⁶ Moses spoke to the children of Israel, and each one of their leaders gave him a rod, one for each leader, according to their fathers' houses, even twelve rods, and the rod of Aaron was among their rods. ⁷ Moses laid the rods before the LORD in the tent of witness.

⁸ When Moses went into the tent of witness the next day, the rod of Aaron, for the house of Levi, had sprouted. It brought forth buds, produced blossoms, and yielded almonds. ⁹ Moses brought out all the rods from before the LORD to all the children of Israel, and they looked, and each man took his rod.

¹⁰ The LORD said to Moses, "Return the rod of Aaron before the testimony, to be kept for a warning to rebels, that you may put an end to their complaints before Me, or else they will die." ¹¹ Moses did so. As the LORD commanded him, so he did.

¹² The children of Israel spoke to Moses, saying, "Behold, we expire, we perish, we all perish. ¹³ Anyone approaching the tabernacle of the LORD will die. Are we all to perish?"

Duties of Priests and Levites

18 And the LORD said to Aaron: You and your sons and your father's house with you will bear the iniquity of the sanctuary, and you and your sons with you will bear the iniquity of your priesthood. ² Your brothers also of the tribe of Levi, the tribe of your father, bring with you, and let them be joined with you, and minister to you. But you and your sons with you will minister before the tent of witness. ³ They will perform duties for you and for the whole tent; but they will not come near the vessels of the sanctuary or the altar, so that neither they nor you die. ⁴ They will be joined to you and perform the duties of the tent of meeting, for all the service of the tent; no foreigner will come near you.

⁵ You yourselves will perform the duties of the sanctuary and the duties of the altar, so that wrath may never come upon the children of Israel again. ⁶ I Myself have taken your brothers, the Levites, from among the children of Israel; they are given to you as a gift from the LORD to perform the service of the tent of meeting. ⁷ And you and your sons with you will attend to your priesthood for everything at the altar, and within the veil, and you will serve. I have given your priesthood to you as a gift service, and the foreigner that comes near will be put to death.

Offerings for Priests and Levites

⁸ The LORD spoke to Aaron: I have certainly given you the charge of the offerings made to Me, all the hallowed gifts of the children of Israel. To you and to your sons have I given them as a portion, as an ordinance forever. ⁹ This will be yours of the most holy things, reserved from the fire: All of their offerings, all of their grain offerings and all of their sin offerings, and all of their guilt offerings, which they render to Me, will be most holy for you and for your sons. ¹⁰ In a most holy place shall you eat it; every male shall eat it. It shall be holy to you.

¹¹ This is yours: the offering of their gift, with all the wave offerings of the children of Israel. I have given them to you and to your sons and to your daughters with you, as an eternal statute. Everyone who is clean in your house will eat of it.

¹² All the best of the oil, and all the best of the wine, and of the wheat, the first fruits of what they will offer to the LORD, those have I given to you. ¹³ The first ripe fruit of all which is in their land, which they will bring to the LORD, will be yours. Everyone who is clean in your house will eat of it.

¹⁴ Everything devoted in Israel will be yours. ¹⁵ Everything that opens the womb of all flesh, which they bring to the LORD, whether it is of men or animals, will be yours. However, you will surely redeem the firstborn of man, and the firstborn of unclean beasts you will redeem. ¹⁶ Their redemption price, reckoned from one month of age, is five shekels,¹ after the shekel of the sanctuary, which is twenty gerahs.

¹⁷ But the firstborn of a herd animal, or the firstborn of a sheep, or the firstborn of a goat, you will not redeem. They are holy. You will splash their blood on the altar and will burn their fat as a fire offering, as a pleasing aroma to the LORD. ¹⁸ Their flesh will be yours, as the wave breast and as the right shoulder are yours. ¹⁹ All the offerings of the holy things which the children of Israel offer to the LORD I have given to you, and to your sons and your daughters with you, as an eternal statute. It is a covenant of salt forever before the LORD, to you and to your seed with you.

²⁰ The LORD said to Aaron: You will not have an inheritance in their land, nor will you have any territory among them. I am your territory and your inheritance among the children of Israel.

Tithes for Supporting the Levites

²¹ I have given the children of Levi all the tithes in Israel for an inheritance, for their service, which they serve, even the service of the tent of meeting. ²² Hereafter, the children of Israel shall not come near the tent of meeting, lest they bear sin and die. ²³ But the Levites will do the service of the tent of meeting, and they will bear their iniquity. It will be an eternal statute throughout your generations, that among the children of Israel they have no inheritance. ²⁴ But the tithes of the children of Israel, which they offer as an offering to the LORD, I have given to the Levites to inherit. Therefore I have said to them, among the children of Israel they will have no inheritance.

The Tithe of the Levites

²⁵ The LORD spoke to Moses, saying: ²⁶ You will speak to the Levites, and say to them: When you take from the children of Israel the tithes that I have given you from them for your inheritance, then you will offer up an offering of it to the LORD, even one-tenth of the tithe. ²⁷ And this offering will be counted to you, as though it was the grain of the threshing floor, and as the fullness of the winepress. ²⁸ Thus you also will set apart an offering to the LORD from all the tithes which you receive from the children of Israel. Out of them you will give the offering of the LORD to Aaron the priest. ²⁹ Out of all your gifts you shall present every offering due to the LORD, from all the best of them, the consecrated part of them.

³⁰ You will say to them: When you have offered the best from it, then it will be counted to the Levites as the increase of the threshing floor, and as the increase of the winepress. ³¹ You will eat it in every place, you and your households, because it is your reward for your service in the tent of meeting. ³² You will bear no sin because of it, when you have offered the best of it. The holy things of the children of Israel you will not pollute, and you will not die.

Laws of Purification

19 And the LORD spoke to Moses and to Aaron, saying: ² This is the statute of the law which the LORD has commanded, saying: Tell the children of Israel that they will bring you a healthy red heifer, which has no blemish, and on which a yoke has never gone, ³ and you will give it to Eleazar the priest, and he will bring it outside the camp, and it will be slaughtered before him. ⁴ And Eleazar the priest will take from its blood with his finger and sprinkle some of its blood directly before the tent of meeting seven times. ⁵ Then it will be burned in his sight. Its hide and its flesh and its blood, with her dung, will be burned. ⁶ And the priest will take cedar wood, and hyssop, and scarlet and throw it into the midst of the burning of the heifer. ⁷ Then the priest will wash his clothes, and he will bathe his body in water, and afterward he will come into the camp, and the priest will be unclean until evening. ⁸ He who burns it will wash his clothes in water, and bathe his body in water, and will be unclean until evening.

⁹ A man who is clean will gather the ashes of the heifer and deposit them outside the camp in a clean place, and it will be guarded for the assembly of the children of Israel for water of purification. It is for purifying from sin. ¹⁰ He that gathers the ashes of the heifer will wash his clothes and be unclean until evening, and it will be

---

¹ 16 About 2 ounces, or 58 grams.

for the children of Israel and for the foreigner that lives among them, for an eternal statute.

[11] He that touches the dead body of any man will be unclean seven days. [12] He will make himself clean on the third day, and on the seventh day he will be clean. But if he does not make himself clean on the third day, then the seventh day he will not be clean. [13] Whoever touches the body of any man that is dead and does not purify himself defiles the tabernacle of the Lord, and that person will be cut off from Israel. Because the water of purification was not sprinkled on him, he will be unclean. His uncleanness is still on him.

[14] This is the law, when a man dies in a tent. Each person who comes into the tent and all that is in the tent will be unclean seven days. [15] Every open vessel which has no covering fastened on it is unclean.

[16] Whoever in the field touches one that is slain with a sword, or a dead body, or a bone of a man, or a grave will be unclean seven days.

[17] For an unclean person they will take from the ashes of the burnt sin offering, and running water will be on it in a vessel. [18] A clean person will take hyssop, and dip it in the water, and splash it on the tent, and on all the vessels, and on the people who were there, and on him that touched a bone, or one slain, or one dead, or a grave. [19] The clean person will splash on the unclean person on the third day and on the seventh day. And on the seventh day he shall purify himself, wash his clothes, and bathe in water; and he will be clean at evening. [20] But the man who is unclean and does not purify himself, that person will be cut off from among the assembly because he has defiled the sanctuary of the Lord. The water of purification has not been sprinkled on him. He is unclean. [21] It will be an eternal statute to them.

He that sprinkles the water of purification will wash his clothes, and he that touches the water of purification will be unclean until evening. [22] Whatever the unclean person touches will be unclean, and the person that touches it will be unclean until evening.

Moses Strikes the Rock

20 Then the children of Israel, the whole assembly, came to the Wilderness of Zin in the first month, and the people dwelt in Kadesh, and Miriam died there and was buried there.

[2] And there was no water for the assembly, and they gathered themselves together against Moses and against Aaron. [3] The people argued with Moses, and spoke, saying, "O that we had died when our brothers died before the Lord! [4] And why have you brought up the assembly of the Lord into this wilderness, that we and our livestock should die here? [5] And why have you brought us up from Egypt, to bring us into this evil place? It is no place of seed, or of figs, or of vines, or of pomegranates. Nor is there any water to drink."

[6] Moses and Aaron went from the presence of the assembly to the door of the tent of meeting, and they fell on their faces, and the glory of the Lord appeared to them. [7] The Lord spoke to Moses, saying: [8] Take the rod, and gather the assembly together, you and Aaron your brother, and speak to the rock before their eyes, and it will give its water, and you will bring out to them water from the rock; so you will give the assembly and their livestock drink.

[9] So Moses took the rod from before the Lord, as He commanded him. [10] Moses and Aaron gathered the assembly before the rock, and he said to them, "Hear now, you rebels. Will we bring out water from this rock for you?" [11] And Moses lifted up his hand, and he struck the rock twice with his rod, and plenty of water came out, and the assembly drank, and their livestock.

[12] The Lord spoke to Moses and Aaron, "Because you did not believe in Me, to sanctify Me in the eyes of the children of Israel, therefore you will not bring this assembly into the land which I have given them."

[13] This is the water of Meribah because the children of Israel argued with the Lord, and He was sanctified among them.

Edom Denies Israel Passage

[14] Moses sent messengers from Kadesh to the king of Edom,

"Thus says your brother Israel: You know all the hardship that has found us, [15] how our fathers went down into Egypt,

and we lived in Egypt a long time, and the Egyptians distressed us and our fathers. [16] And when we cried out to the Lord, He heard our voice and sent an angel and brought us out of Egypt.

"And here we are in Kadesh, a city on the edge of your territory. [17] Please let us pass through your land. We will not pass through the fields or the vineyards, or drink of the water of the wells. We will travel the king's highway. We will not turn to the right hand nor the left, until we have passed through your territory."

[18] Edom said to him,

"You will not pass through me, lest with the sword I come out against you."

[19] The children of Israel said to him,

"We will travel the highway, and if we and our livestock drink of your water, then we will pay for it. I will only go through on my feet without doing anything else."

[20] He said,

"You will not go through."

And Edom came out against them with many people and with a strong hand. [21] Edom refused to give Israel passage through his territory, so Israel turned away from him.

The Death of Aaron

[22] They journeyed from Kadesh, and the children of Israel, even the whole assembly, came to Mount Hor. [23] The Lord spoke to Moses and Aaron in Mount Hor, by the border of the land of Edom, saying, [24] "Aaron will be gathered to his people because he will not enter into the land which I have given to the children of Israel because you rebelled against Me at the water of Meribah. [25] Take Aaron and Eleazar his son, and bring them up to Mount Hor, [26] and strip Aaron of his garments, and put them on Eleazar his son, and Aaron will be gathered to his people, and he will die there."

[27] Moses did as the Lord commanded, and they went up onto Mount Hor in the sight of all the assembly. [28] Moses stripped Aaron of his garments and put them on Eleazar his son. And Aaron died there on the top of the mountain, and Moses and Eleazar came down from the mountain. [29] When all the assembly saw that Aaron was dead, they wept for Aaron thirty days, all the house of Israel.

Arad Destroyed

21 When King Arad the Canaanite, who lived in the Negev, heard that Israel came by the way of Atharim, he fought against Israel and took some of them captive. [2] Israel vowed a vow to the Lord and said, "If You will indeed deliver this people into my hand, then I will utterly destroy their cities." [3] The Lord listened to the voice of Israel and delivered up the Canaanites, and they utterly destroyed them and their cities, and he called the name of the place Hormah.

The Bronze Serpent

[4] They journeyed from Mount Hor by the way of the Red Sea, to go around the land of Edom, and the soul of the people was very discouraged because of the way. [5] The people spoke against God and against Moses, "Why have you brought us up from Egypt to die in the wilderness? For there is no bread or water, and our soul loathes this worthless manna."

[6] So the Lord sent poisonous serpents among the people, and they bit the people, and many children of Israel died. [7] So the people came to Moses and said, "We have sinned for we have spoken against the Lord and against you. Pray to the Lord, and He will take away the serpents from us." And Moses prayed for the people.

[8] The Lord said to Moses, "Make a poisonous serpent, and put it on a pole, and it will be, that everyone who is bitten, when he looks at it, will live." [9] Moses made a bronze serpent and put it on

a pole, and if a serpent had bitten any man, when he looked at the bronze serpent he lived.

The Journey to Moab

[10] The children of Israel set out and camped in Oboth. [11] They journeyed from Oboth and camped at Iye Abarim in the wilderness, which is before Moab toward the sunrise. [12] From there they journeyed and camped in the Valley of Zered. [13] From there they journeyed and camped on the other side of Arnon, which is in the wilderness that comes out of the borders of the Amorites, for Arnon is the border of Moab, between Moab and the Amorites. [14] Therefore it is said in the Book of the Wars of the LORD:

"Zahab in Suphah, and in the brooks
   of Arnon, [15] and at the stream of the brooks
   that goes down to the dwelling of Ar,
   and lies on the border of Moab."

[16] From there they went to Beer. That is the well of which the LORD spoke to Moses, "Gather the people together, and I will give them water."

[17] Then Israel sang this song:

"Spring up, O well!
   sing to it—
[18] the leaders dug the well;
   the nobles of the people dug,
   by the lawgiver, with their staffs."

And from the wilderness they went to Mattanah, [19] and from Mattanah to Nahaliel, and from Nahaliel to Bamoth, [20] and from Bamoth in the valley that is in the country of Moab to the top of Pisgah, which looks toward Jeshimon.

King Sihon Defeated

[21] Israel sent messengers to Sihon king of the Amorites, saying,

[22] "Let me pass through your land. We will not turn into the fields nor into the vineyards. We will not drink of the waters of the well. But we will go along by the king's highway until we are past your borders."

[23] Sihon would not allow Israel to pass through his border. But Sihon gathered all his people together and went out against Israel into the wilderness, and he came to Jahaz and fought against Israel. [24] Israel defeated him with the edge of the sword and possessed his land from Arnon to Jabbok, all the way to the children of Ammon, because the border of the children of Ammon was strong. [25] Israel took all these cities, and Israel lived in all the cities of the Amorites, in Heshbon, and in all its villages. [26] Because Heshbon was the city of Sihon the king of the Amorites, who had fought against the former king of Moab and taken all his land out of his hand, to Arnon. [27] Therefore they that speak in proverbs say:

"Come into Heshbon; let it be built,
   and let the city of Sihon be established,
[28] because a fire went out of Heshbon,
   a flame from the city of Sihon;
it has devoured Ar of Moab
   and the masters of the high places of Arnon.
[29] Woe to you, Moab!
   You have perished, O people of Chemosh!
He has made his sons fugitives,
   and his daughters captives,
   to Sihon king of the Amorites.

[30] "We have overthrown them;
   Heshbon is perished to Dibon,
and we have desolated them to Nophah,
   which reaches to Medeba."

[31] Thus Israel lived in the land of the Amorites.

King Og Defeated

[32] Moses sent to spy out Jazer, and they took its villages and drove out the Amorites who were there. [33] They turned and went up by the way of Bashan, and Og the king of Bashan went out against them, he and all his people, to the battle at Edrei.

[34] The LORD said to Moses, "Do not fear him because into your hand I have given him, and all his people, and his land, and you will do to him as you did to Sihon king of the Amorites, who dwelt at Heshbon."

[35] So they killed him, and his sons, and all his people, until there was not a survivor left to him alive, and they possessed his land.

Balak Summons Balaam

22 Then the children of Israel set out and camped in the plains of Moab on the other side of the Jordan from Jericho. [2] Balak the son of Zippor saw all that Israel had done to the Amorites. [3] Moab was very afraid of the people because they were many, and Moab was distressed because of the children of Israel.

[4] Moab said to the elders of Midian, "Now this company will lick up all that are around us, as the ox licks up the grass of the field."

And Balak the son of Zippor was king of the Moabites at that time. [5] He sent messengers to Balaam the son of Beor at Pethor, which is by the Euphrates in the land of the sons of his people, to call him, saying,

"A people went out from Egypt. They cover the face of the earth, and they dwell next to me. [6] And now, please come curse this people for me because they are too mighty for me. Perhaps I will prevail, and we will defeat them, and I will drive them out of the land because I know that he whom you bless is blessed, and he whom you curse is cursed."

[7] The elders of Moab and the elders of Midian went with the divination payments in their hand, and they came to Balaam and spoke to him the words of Balak.

[8] He said to them, "Lodge here tonight, and I will bring you word again, as the LORD will speak to me." And the leaders of Moab dwelt with Balaam.

[9] God came to Balaam and said, "Who are these men with you?"

[10] And Balaam said to God, "Balak the son of Zippor, king of Moab, has sent word to me, saying, [11] 'A people went out of Egypt who covers the face of the earth. Now come, curse them for me. Perhaps I will be able to battle them and drive them out.' "

[12] God said to Balaam, "You will not go with them. You will not curse the people because they are blessed."

[13] So Balaam rose up in the morning and said to the princes of Balak, "Go to your land because the LORD refuses to let me to go with you."

[14] The princes of Moab rose up, and they went to Balak and said, "Balaam refuses to come with us."

[15] Again Balak sent officials, more numerous and more honorable than they. [16] They came to Balaam and said to him,

"Thus says Balak the son of Zippor, 'Please, let nothing hold you back from coming to me, [17] because I will promote you to very great honor, and anything you say to me I will do. Come please, curse this people for me.' "

[18] Balaam answered the servants of Balak, "If Balak gave me his house full of silver and gold, I am not able to go beyond the command of the LORD my God, to do less or more. [19] Now please remain here tonight, that I may know what more the LORD will say to me."

[20] God came to Balaam at night and said to him, "If the men come to call you, rise up and go with them. But surely the word which I will say to you, that will you do."

Balaam, the Donkey, and the Angel

[21] Balaam rose up in the morning, and saddled his donkey, and went with the princes of Moab. [22] The anger of God was inflamed because he went, and the angel*f* of the LORD stood in the way as

an adversary against him. Now he was riding on his donkey, and his two servants were with him. [23] The donkey saw the angel of the LORD standing in the way, and His sword was drawn in His hand, so the donkey turned out of the way and went into the field. Balaam struck the donkey to turn her onto the road.

[24] But the angel of the LORD stood in a narrow path of the vineyards, a wall on this side and a wall on that side. [25] When the donkey saw the angel of the LORD, she threw herself into the wall and crushed the foot of Balaam against the wall, and he struck her again.

[26] The angel of the LORD went further and stood in a narrow place where there was no way to turn either to the right hand or to the left. [27] When the donkey saw the angel of the LORD, she fell down under Balaam, and the anger of Balaam was inflamed, and he struck the donkey with a staff. [28] Then the LORD opened the mouth of the donkey, and she said to Balaam, "What have I done to you, that you have struck me these three times?"

[29] And Balaam said to the donkey, "You have mocked me. O that there was a sword in my hand, for now I would kill you."

[30] The donkey said to Balaam, "Am I not your donkey, whom you have ridden since I became yours, to this day? Do I normally do this to you?"

And he said, "No."

[31] Then the LORD opened the eyes of Balaam, and he saw the angel of the LORD standing in the way, and His sword was drawn in His hand, and he bowed his head and fell flat on his face.

[32] The angel of the LORD said to him, "Why have you struck your donkey these three times? I have come out to oppose you, because your way is perverse before Me. [33] And the donkey saw Me and turned from Me these three times. If she had not turned from Me, surely by now I would have slain you and saved her alive."

[34] Balaam said to the angel of the LORD, "I have sinned because I did not know that You stood in the way against me. Now therefore, if it displeases You, I will return."

[35] The angel of the LORD said to Balaam, "Go with the men. But only speak the word that I tell you to speak." So Balaam went with the leaders of Balak.

[36] When Balak heard that Balaam had come, he went out to meet him in a city of Moab which is on the border of Arnon, which is at the furthest end of the border. [37] Balak said to Balaam, "Did I not earnestly send to summon you? Why did you not come to me? Indeed am I not able to honor you?"

[38] And Balaam said to Balak, "I have come to you now. But am I able to speak just anything? The word God puts in my mouth is what I will speak."

[39] Balaam went with Balak, and they came to Kiriath Huzoth. [40] Balak offered oxen and sheep and sent them to Balaam and to the officials who were with him.

Balaam's First Prophecy

[41] It came to pass on the next day that Balak took Balaam and brought him up to Bamoth Baal, and from there he saw the extent of the people.

23 And Balaam said to Balak, "Build for me seven altars, and prepare for me seven oxen and seven rams." [2] Balak did as Balaam had spoken, and Balak and Balaam offered on every altar a bull and a ram.

[3] Balaam said to Balak, "Stand by your burnt offering, and I will go. Perhaps the LORD will come to meet me, and whatever He shows me I will tell you." And he went to a high place.

[4] God met Balaam, and he said to Him, "I have prepared seven altars, and I have offered on every altar a bull and a ram."

[5] The LORD put a word in the mouth of Balaam and said, "Return to Balak, and thus you will speak."

[6] So he returned to Balak, who was standing by his burnt offering with all the princes of Moab. [7] Then Balaam uttered his oracle, saying:

"Balak has brought me from Aram,
the king of Moab from the mountains of the east,

saying, 'Come, curse Jacob for me,
and come, defy Israel!'
[8] How will I curse
whom God has not cursed?
Or how will I defy
whom the LORD has not defied?
[9] For from the top of the rocks I see him,
and from the hills I behold him;
there, the people will dwell alone
and will not be counted among the nations.
[10] Who can count the dust of Jacob
and the number of the fourth part of Israel?
Let me die the death of the righteous,
and let my last end be like his!"

[11] And Balak said to Balaam, "What have you done to me? I brought you to curse my enemies, but now you have certainly blessed them."

[12] He answered and said, "Must I not take heed to speak what the LORD puts in my mouth?"

Balaam's Second Prophecy

[13] And Balak said to him, "Please come with me to another place from where you may see them. You will see part of them, but will not see them all. Curse them for me from there." [14] He brought him into the field of Zophim, to the top of Pisgah, and built seven altars and offered a bull and a ram on each altar.

[15] He said to Balak, "Stand here by your burnt offerings while I meet the LORD over there."

[16] The LORD met Balaam and put a word in his mouth and said, "Go again to Balak, and thus you will speak."

[17] When he came to him, he was standing by his burnt offerings with the princes of Moab. And Balak said to him, "What has the LORD spoken?"

[18] And he took up his parable and said:

"Rise up, Balak, and hear!
Listen to me, you son of Zippor!
[19] God is not a man, that He should lie,
nor a son of man, that He should repent.
Has He spoken, and will He not do it?
Or has He spoken, and will He not make it good?
[20] See, I have received a commandment to bless,
and He has blessed, and I cannot reverse it.

[21] "He has not beheld iniquity in Jacob,
nor has He seen perverseness in Israel.
The LORD his God is with him,
and the shout of a king is among them.
[22] God, who brings them out of Egypt,
has strength like a wild ox.
[23] Surely there is no enchantment against Jacob,
nor is there any divination against Israel.
For this time it will be said of Jacob and of Israel,
'See what God has done!'
[24] A people rises up as a great lion;
and lifts itself up like a lion;
it shall not lie down until it eats the prey
and drinks the blood of the slain."

[25] Balak said to Balaam, "Do not curse them at all, nor bless them at all."

[26] But Balaam answered and said to Balak, "Did I not tell you, saying, 'All that the LORD speaks, I must do'?"

Balaam's Third Prophecy

[27] And Balak said to Balaam, "Please come. I will bring you to another place. Perhaps it will please God that you may curse them for me from there." [28] Balak brought Balaam to the top of Peor, which looks toward Jeshimon.

---

[1] 22 At times the Lord speaks directly through an angel (cf. the story of the burning bush in Ex 3:2–4).

²⁹ Balaam said to Balak, "Build for me seven altars, and prepare for me seven bulls and seven rams." ³⁰ Balak did as Balaam said and offered a bull and a ram on each altar.

24 And when Balaam saw that it pleased the LORD to bless Israel, he did not go as other times to seek for enchantments, but he set his face toward the wilderness. ² Balaam lifted up his eyes, and he saw Israel dwelling in their tents by their tribes, and the Spirit of God came on him. ³ He took up his proverb and said:

"Balaam the son of Beor has said,
    and the man whose eyes are open has said,
⁴ he has said, who heard the words of God,
    who saw the vision of the Almighty,
    falling into a trance, but having his eyes open:

⁵ "How lovely are your tents, O Jacob,
    and your tabernacles, O Israel!

⁶ "Like palm trees are they spread out,
    like gardens by the river's side,
like the aloe plant, which the LORD has planted,
    and like cedar trees beside the waters.
⁷ He will pour the water out of his buckets,
    and his seed will be in many waters.

"His king will be higher than Agag,
    and his kingdom will be exalted.

⁸ "God brings him out of Egypt;
    he has the horns of a wild ox;
he will eat up the nations, his enemies,
    and will break their bones,
    and pierce them through with his arrows.
⁹ He crouches, he lies down as a lion, and as a lion,
    who will stir him up?

"Blessed is he who blesses you,
    and cursed is he who curses you."

¹⁰ The anger of Balak was inflamed against Balaam, and he struck his hands together. And Balak said to Balaam, "I called you to curse my enemies, and indeed, you have certainly blessed them these three times. ¹¹ Now flee to your own place. I thought to promote you to great honor. But certainly, the LORD has kept you back from honor." ¹² Balaam said to Balak, "Did I not speak to your messengers which you sent to me, saying, ¹³ 'If Balak would give me his house full of silver and gold, I cannot go beyond the mouth of the LORD, to do either good or bad of my own mind. But what the LORD speaks, I will speak'? ¹⁴ And now, I am going to my people. Come, I will advise you what this people will do to your people in the latter days."

Balaam's Fourth Prophecy
¹⁵ He took up his parable and said:

"The oracle of Balaam the son of Beor,
    and the oracle of the man whose eyes are open;
¹⁶ the oracle of the one hearing the words of God,
    and knowing the knowledge of the Most High,
who sees the vision of the Almighty,
    falling into a trance, but having his eyes open:

¹⁷ "I will see him, but not now;
    I will behold him, but not near;
a star will come out of Jacob,
    and a scepter will rise out of Israel,
and will crush the borderlands of Moab,
    and destroy all the children of Sheth.
¹⁸ Edom will be a possession,
    and Seir, a possession of its enemies,
    while Israel does valiantly.

¹⁹ One out of Jacob shall have dominion,
    and destroy the survivors of the city."

²⁰ Then he looked on Amalek; he took up his proverb and said:

"Amalek was the first of the nations,
    but his end will be that he perishes forever."

²¹ He looked on the Kenites and took up his proverb and said:

"Strong is your dwelling place,
    and you put your nest in a rock;
²² nevertheless the Kenite will be wasted.
    How long until Ashur carries you away captive?"

²³ He took up his proverb and said:

"Alas, who will live when God does this?
²⁴ And ships will come from the coasts of Cyprus
    and will afflict Ashur and will afflict Eber,
    and he also will perish forever."

²⁵ Balaam rose up and went and returned to his place, and Balak also went his way.

Moab Seduces Israel
25 While Israel dwelt in Shittim, the people began to commit harlotry with the women of Moab. ² They called the people to the sacrifices of their gods, and the people ate and bowed down to their gods. ³ Israel joined himself to the Baal of Peor, and the anger of the LORD was inflamed against Israel. ⁴ The LORD said to Moses, "Take all the chiefs of the people and hang them before the LORD in the sun, that the fierce anger of the LORD turn from Israel." ⁵ Moses said to the judges of Israel, "Kill each of the men who have aligned themselves with the Baal of Peor." ⁶ Behold, one of the children of Israel came and brought to his brothers a Midianite woman in the sight of Moses and in the sight of all the assembly of the children of Israel, who were weeping before the door of the tent of meeting. ⁷ When Phinehas the son of Eleazar, the son of Aaron the priest, saw it, he rose up from among the assembly and took a spear in his hand, ⁸ and he went after the man of Israel into the tent, and thrust both of them through, the man of Israel and the woman through her belly. So the plague was stopped from the children of Israel. ⁹ Those that died in the plague were twenty-four thousand.

¹⁰ The LORD spoke to Moses, saying, ¹¹ "Phinehas the son of Eleazar, the son of Aaron the priest, has turned My wrath away from the children of Israel, because he was zealous for My sake among them, so I did not exterminate the children of Israel in My zeal. ¹² Therefore say, 'I hereby grant him My covenant of peace. ¹³ And it will be for him and his seed after him, even the covenant of an everlasting priesthood, because he was zealous for his God and made an atonement for the children of Israel.' " ¹⁴ Now the name of the slain Israelite who was slain with the Midianite woman was Zimri the son of Salu, a leader of a chief house among the Simeonites. ¹⁵ The name of the Midianite woman that was slain was Kozbi the daughter of Zur. He was chief over a people and of a father's house in Midian. ¹⁶ The LORD spoke to Moses, saying, ¹⁷ "Be hostile to the Midianites, and defeat them, ¹⁸ because they have been hostile to you with their wiles, with which they have deceived you in the matter of Peor and in the matter of Kozbi the daughter of a leader of Midian, their sister, who was slain on the day of the plague because of Peor."

The Second Census
26 After the plague, the LORD spoke to Moses and to Eleazar the son of Aaron the priest, saying, ² "Take the count of all the assembly of the children of Israel from twenty years old and older, throughout their fathers' houses, all that are able to go to war in Israel." ³ Moses and Eleazar the priest spoke with them

in the plains of Moab by Jordan near Jericho, saying, [4] "Take the count of the people from twenty years old and older," as the LORD commanded Moses.

The children of Israel, who went out of the land of Egypt, were these:

[5] Reuben, the oldest son of Israel. The children of Reuben:
of Hanok, from whom comes the family of the Hanokites;
of Pallu, the family of the Palluites;
[6] of Hezron, the family of the Hezronites;
of Karmi, the family of the Karmites.
[7] These are the families of the Reubenites: those who were counted were forty-three thousand seven hundred and thirty.

[8] The son of Pallu was Eliab. [9] The sons of Eliab were Nemuel, and Dathan, and Abiram. This is that Dathan and Abiram, called out from the assembly, who argued against Moses and against Aaron in the company of Korah when they argued against the LORD. [10] And the earth opened its mouth and swallowed them with Korah when that company died, when the fire devoured two hundred and fifty men, and they became a sign. [11] But the children of Korah did not die.

[12] The sons of Simeon by their families were:
of Nemuel, the family of the Nemuelites;
of Jamin, the family of the Jaminites;
of Jakin, the family of the Jakinites;
[13] of Zerah, the family of the Zerahites;
of Shaul, the family of the Shaulites.
[14] These are the families of the Simeonites: twenty-two thousand two hundred.

[15] The children of Gad by their families were:
of Zephon, the family of the Zephonites;
of Haggi, the family of the Haggites;
of Shuni, the family of the Shunites;
[16] of Ozni, the family of the Oznites;
of Eri, the family of the Erites;
[17] of Arodi, the family of the Arodites;
of Areli, the family of the Arelites.
[18] These are the families of the children of Gad according to those by their count: forty thousand five hundred.

[19] The sons of Judah were Er and Onan, and Er and Onan died in the land of Canaan.
[20] The sons of Judah after their families were:
of Shelah, the family of the Shelanites;
of Perez, the family of the Perezites;
of Zerah, the family of the Zerahites.
[21] The sons of Perez were:
of Hezron, the family of the Hezronites;
of Hamul, the family of the Hamulites.
[22] These are the families of Judah by their count: seventy-six thousand five hundred.

[23] The sons of Issachar by their families were:
of Tola, the family of the Tolaites;
of Puah, the family of the Puites;
[24] of Jashub, the family of the Jashubites;
of Shimron, the family of the Shimronites.
[25] These are the families of Issachar by their count: sixty-four thousand three hundred.

[26] The sons of Zebulun by their families were:
of Sered, the family of the Seredites;
of Elon, the family of the Elonites;
of Jahleel, the family of the Jahleelites.
[27] These are the families of the Zebulunites by their count: sixty thousand five hundred.

[28] The sons of Joseph according to their families, by Manasseh and Ephraim, were:

[29] The sons of Manasseh:
of Makir, the family of the Makirites, and Makir begot Gilead;
of Gilead, the family of the Gileadites.
[30] These are the sons of Gilead:
of Iezer, the family of the Iezerites;
of Helek, the family of the Helekites;
[31] and of Asriel, the family of the Asrielites;
and of Shechem, the family of the Shechemites;
[32] and of Shemida, the family of the Shemidaites;
and of Hepher, the family of the Hepherites.
[33] Zelophehad the son of Hepher had no sons, but daughters, and the names of the daughters of Zelophehad were Mahlah, Noah, Hoglah, Milkah, and Tirzah.
[34] These are the families of Manasseh, and those who were numbered of them were fifty-two thousand seven hundred.

[35] These are the sons of Ephraim according to their families:
of Shuthelah, the family of the Shuthelahites;
of Beker, the family of the Bekerites;
of Tahan, the family of the Tahanites.
[36] These are the sons of Shuthelah:
of Eran, the family of the Eranites.
[37] These are the families of the sons of Ephraim by their count: thirty-two thousand five hundred.

These are the sons of Joseph by their families.

[38] The sons of Benjamin by their families were:
of Bela, the family of the Belaites;
of Ashbel, the family of the Ashbelites;
of Ahiram, the family of the Ahiramites;
[39] of Shupham, the family of the Shuphamites;
of Hupham, the family of the Huphamites.
[40] The sons of Bela were Ard and Naaman:
of Ard, the family of the Ardites;
and of Naaman, the family of the Naamites.
[41] These are the sons of Benjamin by their families, and by their count: forty-five thousand six hundred.

[42] These are the sons of Dan according to their families:
of Shuham, the family of the Shuhamites.
These are the families of Dan after their families. [43] All the families of the Shuhamites, by their count, were sixty-four thousand four hundred.

[44] The sons of Asher by their families were:
of Imnah, the family of the Imnites;
of Ishvi, the family of the Ishvites;
of Beriah, the family of the Beriites.
[45] Of the sons of Beriah were:
of Heber, the family of the Heberites;
of Malkiel, the family of the Malkielites.
[46] The name of the daughter of Asher was Serah.
[47] These are the families of the sons of Asher by their count: fifty-three thousand four hundred.

[48] Of the sons of Naphtali by their families were:
of Jahzeel, the family of the Jahzeelites;
of Guni, the family of the Gunites;
[49] of Jezer, the family of the Jezerites;
of Shillem, the family of the Shillemites.
[50] These are the families of Naphtali according to their families; those who were numbered of them were forty-five thousand four hundred.

[51] These were the counted of the children of Israel: six hundred and one thousand, seven hundred and thirty.

[52] The LORD spoke to Moses, saying: [53] To these the land will be divided for an inheritance by the number of names. [54] To a large tribe you shall give a large inheritance, and to small tribe you shall

give a small inheritance. To each one his inheritance will be given according to those who were numbered of him. [55] But the land will be divided by lot. By the names of the tribes of their fathers they will inherit. [56] According to the lot his possession will be divided between large and small.

[57] These are those counted of the Levites by their families:
of Gershon, the family of the Gershonites;
of Kohath, the family of the Kohathites;
of Merari, the family of the Merarites.
[58] These are the families of the Levites:
the family of the Libnites,
the family of the Hebronites,
the family of the Mahlites,
the family of the Mushites,
the family of the Korahites.
And Kohath begot Amram. [59] And the name of the wife of Amram was Jochebed, the daughter of Levi, whom her mother bore to Levi in Egypt, and she bore to Amram Aaron and Moses and Miriam their sister. [60] To Aaron was born Nadab, and Abihu, Eleazar, and Ithamar. [61] Nadab and Abihu died when they offered foreign fire before the LORD.

[62] Those who were numbered of them were twenty-three thousand, each male from a month old and older; for they were not counted among the children of Israel, because there was no inheritance given them among the children of Israel.

[63] These were counted by Moses and Eleazar the priest, who counted the children of Israel in the plains of Moab by Jordan near Jericho. [64] But among these there was not a man counted by Moses and Aaron the priest when they counted the children of Israel in the Wilderness of Sinai [65] because the LORD had said of them, "They will surely die in the wilderness." And there was not a man left of them, except Caleb the son of Jephunneh and Joshua the son of Nun.

Laws of Inheritance
Nu 36:1–12

27 Then came near the daughters of Zelophehad, the son of Hepher, the son of Gilead, the son of Makir, the son of Manasseh, of the families of Manasseh the son of Joseph, and these are the names of his daughters: Mahlah, Noah, Hoglah, Milkah, and Tirzah. [2] They stood before Moses, and before Eleazar the priest, and before the leaders and all the assembly by the door of the tent of meeting, saying, [3] "Our father died in the wilderness, and he was not in the company of them that gathered against the LORD, in the company of Korah, but died in his own sin and had no sons. [4] Why should the name of our father diminish from among his family, because he has no son? Give to us a possession among the brothers of our father."

[5] Moses brought their case before the LORD. [6] The LORD spoke to Moses, saying: [7] The daughters of Zelophehad speak right. You will certainly give them an inheritance among their father's brothers, and you will cause the inheritance of their father to pass on to them.

[8] You will speak to the children of Israel, saying, "If a man dies, and has no son, then you will cause his inheritance to pass on to his daughter. [9] If he has no daughter, then you will give his inheritance to his brothers. [10] If he has no brothers, then you will give his inheritance to his father's brothers. [11] If his father has no brothers, then you will give his inheritance to his closest kinsman in his family, and he will possess it. And it will be for the children of Israel a statute of judgment, as the LORD commanded Moses."

Joshua to Succeed Moses

[12] The LORD said to Moses, "Go up into this mountain of Abarim, and see the land which I have given to the children of Israel. [13] When you have seen it, you also will be gathered to your people as Aaron your brother was gathered. [14] For you rebelled against My commandment in the Wilderness of Zin when the congregation argued against Me. You did not show My holiness at the waters before their eyes." (These are the waters of Meribah in Kadesh in the Wilderness of Zin.)

[15] Moses spoke to the LORD, saying, [16] "Let the LORD, the God of the spirits of all flesh, appoint a man over the assembly [17] who will go out before them, and who will go in before them, and who will lead them out, and who will bring them in, so the assembly of the LORD will not be like sheep who do not have a shepherd."

[18] The LORD said to Moses, "Take Joshua the son of Nun, a man in whom is the Spirit, and lay your hand on him, [19] and cause him to stand before Eleazar the priest and before all the assembly, and command in their sight. [20] You will put some of your majesty on him, in order that all the assembly of the children of Israel will listen. [21] He will stand before Eleazar the priest, who will ask for him about the judgment of the Urim before the LORD. At his word will they go out, and at his word they will come in, both he and all the children of Israel with him, even all the assembly."

[22] Moses did as the LORD commanded him, and he took Joshua, and he caused him to stand before Eleazar the priest and before all the assembly. [23] And he laid his hands on him and commanded him as the LORD spoke by the hand of Moses.

Daily Offerings

28 And the LORD spoke to Moses, saying: [2] Command the children of Israel and say to them: My offering, My bread for My sacrifices made by fire, as a pleasing aroma to Me, you will guard to offer to Me at their time. [3] You will say to them: This is the fire offering which you will bring near to the LORD: two male lambs in their first year, without blemish, day by day, as a regular burnt offering. [4] The one lamb you will offer in the morning, and the other lamb you will offer at evening, [5] and one-tenth of an ephah[1] of flour as a grain offering, mingled with one-fourth of a hin[2] of beaten oil. [6] It is a regular burnt offering, which was ordained at Mount Sinai as a pleasing aroma, a sacrifice made by fire to the LORD. [7] Its drink offering will be one-fourth of a hin for the one lamb. In a holy place you will pour the strong wine to the LORD as a drink offering. [8] The other lamb you will offer at evening. As the morning grain offering and its drink offering, you will offer it as an offering made by fire, a pleasing aroma to the LORD.

Sabbath Offerings

[9] On the Sabbath day two lambs in their first year, without blemish, and two-tenths of an ephah[3] of flour as a grain offering, mixed with oil, and its drink offering— [10] this is the burnt offering of every Sabbath, in addition to the regular burnt offering and its drink offering.

Monthly Offerings

[11] At the beginnings of your months you will offer a burnt offering to the LORD: two young bulls, one ram, seven lambs in their first year, without blemish; [12] three-tenths of an ephah[4] of flour as a grain offering, mixed with oil, for one bull; and two-tenths of an ephah of flour as a grain offering, mixed with oil, for one ram; [13] and one-tenth of an ephah of flour mixed with oil as a grain offering for one lamb; as a burnt offering of a pleasing aroma, a sacrifice made by fire to the LORD. [14] Their drink offerings will be one-half a hin[5] of wine for a bull, and one-third of a hin[6] for a ram, and one-fourth of a hin for a lamb. This is the burnt offering of each month throughout the months of the year. [15] Also one male goat as a sin offering to the LORD shall be offered, besides the regular burnt offering and its drink offering.

Passover Offerings
Ex 12:14–20; Lev 23:4–8; Dt 16:1–8

[16] On the fourteenth day of the first month is the Passover of the LORD. [17] On the fifteenth day of this month is the feast. Unleavened bread will be eaten for seven days. [18] On the first day there will be

---

[1] 5 Likely about 3½ pounds, or 1.6 kilograms; and in vv. 13, 21, and 29.　*[2] 5* About 1 quart, or 1 liter; and in vv. 7 and 14.
[3] 9 Likely about 7 pounds, or 3.2 kilograms; and in vv. 12, 20, and 28.　*[4] 12* Likely about 11 pounds, or 5 kilograms; and in vv. 20 and 28.
[5] 14 About 2 quarts, or 1.9 liters.　*[6] 14* About 1⅓ quarts, or 1.3 liters.

a holy convocation. You will not do any ordinary work, [19] but you will offer a sacrifice made by fire as a burnt offering to the LORD: two young bulls, and one ram, and seven lambs in their first year. Be sure they are without blemish. [20] And their grain offering will be of flour mixed with oil. Three-tenths of an ephah you will offer for a bull, and two-tenths of an ephah for a ram. [21] One-tenth of an ephah you will offer for each of the seven lambs, [22] and one goat as a sin offering, to make an atonement for you. [23] You will offer these in addition to the burnt offering in the morning, which is for a regular burnt offering. [24] The same way you will offer daily, throughout the seven days, the food of the sacrifice made by fire, as a pleasing aroma to the LORD. It will be offered in addition to the regular burnt offering and its drink offering. [25] And on the seventh day you will have a holy assembly. You will not do any ordinary work.

Offerings at the Feast of Weeks
Lev 23:15–22; Dt 16:9–12
[26] And on the day of the first fruits, when you bring a new grain offering to the LORD at your Feast of Weeks, you will have a holy assembly. You will do no ordinary work. [27] But you will offer the burnt offering as a pleasing aroma to the LORD: two young bulls, one ram, and seven lambs in their first year; [28] and their grain offering of flour mixed with oil, three-tenths of an ephah for one bull, two-tenths of an ephah for one ram, [29] one-tenth of an ephah for each of the seven lambs; [30] and one goat, to make an atonement for you. [31] Make sure they are without blemish. You will offer them with their drink offerings, besides the regular burnt offering and its grain offering.

Offerings at the Feast of Trumpets
Lev 23:23–25
29 In the seventh month, on the first day of the month, you will have a holy assembly. You will do no ordinary work. It is a day of blowing the trumpets for you. [2] You will offer a burnt offering as a pleasing aroma to the LORD: one young bull, one ram, and seven lambs in their first year, without blemish; [3] their grain offering will be of flour mixed with oil, three-tenths of an ephah[1] for a bull, and two-tenths of an ephah[2] for a ram, [4] and one-tenth of an ephah[3] for one lamb, for the seven lambs; [5] also one goat as a sin offering, to make an atonement for you; [6] besides the burnt offering of the month and its grain offering, and the daily burnt offering and its grain offering, and their drink offerings, according to their rule, as a pleasing aroma, a sacrifice made by fire to the LORD.

Offerings on the Day of Atonement
Lev 16:2–34; 23:26–32
[7] You will have a holy assembly on the tenth day of this seventh month, and you will afflict yourselves. You will not do any work on it. [8] But you will offer a burnt offering to the LORD as a pleasing aroma: one young bull, one ram, and seven lambs in their first year. Be sure they are without blemish. [9] Their grain offering will be of flour mixed with oil, three-tenths of an ephah for the bull, and two-tenths of an ephah for one ram, [10] and one-tenth of an ephah for each of the seven lambs; [11] also one goat as a sin offering in addition to the sin offering of atonement, and the regular burnt offering, and its grain offering, and their drink offerings.

Offerings at the Feast of Tabernacles
Lev 23:33–43; Dt 16:13–17
[12] On the fifteenth day of the seventh month you will have a holy convocation. You will do no ordinary work, and you will keep a feast to the LORD seven days. [13] And you will offer a burnt offering, a sacrifice made by fire, as a pleasing aroma to the LORD: thirteen young bulls, two rams, and fourteen lambs in their first year, without blemish. [14] And their grain offering will be of flour mixed with oil, three-tenths of an ephah to a bull, and two-tenths of an ephah to each ram of the two rams, [15] and one-tenth to each lamb of the fourteen lambs; [16] and one goat as a sin offering in addition to the regular burnt offering, its grain offering, and its drink offering.

[17] On the second day present twelve young bulls, two rams, fourteen lambs in their first year without blemish, [18] and their grain offering and their drink offerings, for the bulls, for the rams, and for the lambs, by their number according to the ordinance; [19] also one goat as a sin offering, besides the regular burnt offering, and its grain offering, and their drink offerings.

[20] On the third day present eleven bulls, two rams, fourteen lambs in their first year without blemish, [21] and their grain offering and their drink offerings, for the bulls, for the rams, and for the lambs, by their number according to the ordinance; [22] also one goat as a sin offering, besides the regular burnt offering, and its grain offering, and its drink offering.

[23] On the fourth day present ten bulls, two rams, and fourteen lambs in their first year without blemish, [24] and their grain offering and their drink offerings, for the bulls, for the rams, and for the lambs, by their number according to the ordinance; [25] also one goat as a sin offering in addition to the regular burnt offering, its grain offering, and its drink offering.

[26] On the fifth day present nine bulls, two rams, and fourteen lambs in their first year without blemish, [27] and their grain offering and their drink offerings, for the bulls, for the rams, and for the lambs, by their number according to the ordinance; [28] also one goat as a sin offering in addition to the regular burnt offering, and its grain offering, and its drink offering.

[29] On the sixth day present eight bulls, two rams, and fourteen lambs in their first year without blemish, [30] and their grain offering and their drink offerings, for the bulls, for the rams, and for the lambs, by their number according to the ordinance; [31] also one goat as a sin offering in addition to the regular burnt offering, its grain offering, and its drink offering.

[32] On the seventh day present seven bulls, two rams, and fourteen lambs in their first year without blemish, [33] and their grain offering and their drink offerings, for the bulls, for the rams, and for the lambs, by their number according to the ordinance; [34] also one goat as a sin offering in addition to the regular burnt offering, its grain offering, and its drink offering.

[35] On the eighth day you will have a solemn assembly. You will do no ordinary work on it. [36] But you will offer a burnt offering, a sacrifice made by fire as a pleasing aroma to the LORD: one bull, one ram, seven lambs in their first year, without blemish. [37] Their grain offering and their drink offerings, for the bull, for the ram, and for the lambs, will be according to their number, according to the rule; [38] also one goat as a sin offering in addition to the regular burnt offering, and its grain offering, and its drink offering.

[39] These things you will do to the LORD in your set feasts in addition to your vows and your freewill offerings, as your burnt offerings, and as your grain offerings, and as your drink offerings, and as your peace offerings.

[40] Moses told the children of Israel everything, according to all that the LORD commanded Moses.

The Law About Vows
30 And Moses spoke to the heads of the tribes of the children of Israel, saying: This is the thing that the LORD has commanded. [2] If a man vows a vow to the LORD, or swears an oath to bind himself with a bond, he will not break his word. He will do according to all that proceeds out of his mouth.

[3] If a woman makes a vow to the LORD, and binds herself by a bond, while in her father's house in her youth, [4] and her father hears her vow and her bond with which she has bound herself, and her father is silent to her, then all her vows will stand, and every bond with which she has bound herself will stand. [5] But if her father restrains her in the day he hears, none of her vows or her bonds with which she has bound herself will stand, and the LORD will forgive her, because her father restrained her.

[6] If she had a husband when she vowed, or uttered anything out of her lips with which she bound herself, [7] and her husband heard it and was silent to her in the day that he heard it, then her vows will stand, and her bonds with which she bound herself will stand.

---

1 3 Likely about 11 pounds, or 5 kilograms; and in vv. 9 and 14. *2 3* Likely about 7 pounds, or 3.2 kilograms; and in vv. 9 and 14. *3 4* Likely about 3½ pounds, or 1.6 kilograms; and in vv. 10 and 15.

[8] But if her husband restrains her on the day that he heard it, then he will make her vow which she vowed and that which she uttered with her lips, with which she bound herself, of no effect, and the LORD will forgive her.

[9] But every vow of a widow and of her that is divorced, with which she has bound herself, will stand against her.

[10] If she vowed in her husband's house, or bound herself by a bond with an oath, [11] and her husband heard it and was silent to her and did not restrain her, then all her vows will stand, and every bond with which she bound herself will stand. [12] But if her husband has clearly voided them on the day he heard them, then whatever proceeded out of her lips concerning her vows, or concerning the bond of herself, will not stand. Her husband has voided them, and the LORD will forgive her. [13] Every vow, and every binding oath to afflict her soul, her husband may establish, or her husband may nullify. [14] But if her husband says nothing to her from day to day, then he confirms all her vows, or all her pledges, which bind her. He confirms them because he said nothing to her on the day that he heard them. [15] But if he clearly makes them void after he has heard them, then he will bear her iniquity.

[16] These are the statutes which the LORD commanded Moses, between a man and his wife, and between the father and his daughter, while she is still young and in her father's house.

Vengeance on the Midianites

31 And the LORD spoke to Moses, saying, [2] "Avenge the children of Israel on the Midianites. Afterward you will be gathered to your people."

[3] Moses spoke to the people, saying, "Arm some of your men for war, and let them go against the Midianites to give the vengeance of the LORD against Midian. [4] A thousand from each tribe, throughout all the tribes of Israel, you will send to the war." [5] So there were delivered from the thousands of Israel a thousand of each tribe, twelve thousand armed for war. [6] Moses sent them to the war, a thousand from each tribe, with Phinehas the son of Eleazar the priest, with the holy vessels and the trumpets to sound the alarm in his hand.

[7] They waged war against the Midianites, as the LORD commanded Moses, and they killed every male. [8] They killed the kings of Midian, in addition to the rest of those who were killed: Evi, and Rekem, and Zur, and Hur, and Reba, five kings of Midian. Balaam the son of Beor they also killed with the sword. [9] The children of Israel returned with the women of Midian and their children and took their livestock, and all their flocks, and all their wealth for plunder. [10] They burned with fire all their cities in which they lived and all their camps. [11] They took all the plunder and all the prey of men and of beasts. [12] They brought the captives, the prey, and the plunder to Moses, to Eleazar the priest, to the assembly of the children of Israel, and to the camp on the plains of Moab, which are by Jordan across from Jericho.

[13] Moses and Eleazar the priest and all the leaders of the assembly went to meet them outside the camp. [14] Moses was angry with the officers of the army, with the captains over thousands, and captains over hundreds, who came from the battle.

[15] Moses said to them, "Have you saved all the women alive? [16] These caused the children of Israel, through the word of Balaam, to act unfaithfully against the LORD concerning the thing of Peor, and there was a plague among the assembly of the LORD. [17] So now kill every male among the little ones, and kill every woman who has known a man by lying with him. [18] But keep alive for yourselves all the young girls who have not known a man by lying with him.

[19] "And you stay outside the camp seven days. Whoever has killed any person and whoever has touched any slain, purify both yourselves and your captives on the third day and on the seventh day. [20] Purify all your clothes, and all that is made of skins, and all work of goats' hair, and all things made of wood."

[21] Eleazar the priest said to the fighting men of Israel who went to the battle, "This is the ordinance of the law which the LORD commanded Moses: [22] Only the gold, and the silver, the bronze, the iron, the tin, and the lead, [23] everything that can go through the fire, you will make it go through the fire, and it will be clean, but some of it will be purified with the water of purification, and all that cannot pass through the fire you will make go through the water. [24] You will wash your clothes on the seventh day, and you will be clean, and afterward you will come into the camp."

Dividing the Plunder

[25] The LORD spoke to Moses, saying, [26] "Take the count of the plunder that was taken, of man and of beast, you and Eleazar the priest, and the chief of the fathers of the assembly. [27] And divide the prey into two parts between those that took the war on themselves, who went out to battle, and between all the assembly. [28] And levy a tribute to the LORD from the fighting men of Israel who went out to battle: one person out of five hundred, of the people and of the oxen, and of the donkeys, and of the sheep; [29] take it from their half, and give it to Eleazar the priest as an offering to the LORD. [30] Of the half of the children of Israel, you will take one portion of fifty, of the people, of the oxen, of the donkeys, and of the flocks, of all manner of beasts, and give them to the Levites, who keep the guard of the tabernacle of the LORD." [31] Moses and Eleazar the priest did as the LORD commanded Moses.

[32] The plunder, being the rest of the prey, which the fighting men of Israel had caught, was six hundred and seventy-five thousand sheep, [33] seventy-two thousand oxen, [34] and sixty-one thousand donkeys, [35] and thirty-two thousand people in all, of women who had not known a man by lying with him.

[36] The half, which was the portion of those that went out to war, was three hundred and thirty-seven thousand five hundred sheep.

[37] And the LORD's tribute of the sheep was six hundred and seventy-five.

[38] The oxen were thirty-six thousand, of which the LORD's tribute was seventy-two.

[39] The donkeys were thirty thousand five hundred, of which the LORD's tribute was sixty-one.

[40] The people were sixteen thousand, of which the LORD's tribute was thirty-two people.

[41] Moses gave the tribute which was the LORD's offering to Eleazar the priest, as the LORD commanded Moses.

[42] Of the half of the children of Israel, which Moses divided from the men who fought, [43] the half belonging to the assembly was three hundred and thirty-seven thousand five hundred sheep, [44] thirty-six thousand oxen, [45] thirty thousand five hundred donkeys, [46] and sixteen thousand people. [47] From the half of the children of Israel Moses took one out of fifty, of man and of beast, and gave them to the Levites, who kept the guard of the tabernacle of the LORD, as the LORD commanded Moses.

[48] The officers who were over thousands of the army, the captains of thousands, and captains of hundreds, came near to Moses, [49] and they said to Moses, "Your servants have taken the count of the fighting men of Israel who are in our hand, and not a man of us is missing. [50] We have brought an offering for the LORD, what every man has gotten of jewels of gold, chains, and bracelets, rings, earrings, and pendants, to make an atonement for ourselves before the LORD."

[51] Moses and Eleazar the priest took the gold from them, all in the form of fashioned articles. [52] All the gold of the offering that they offered up to the LORD, of the captains of thousands and of the captains of hundreds, was sixteen thousand seven hundred and fifty shekels.[1] [53] The fighting men of Israel had taken plunder, each man for himself. [54] And Moses and Eleazar the priest took the gold of the captains of thousands and of hundreds and brought it into the tent of meeting as a memorial for the children of Israel before the LORD.

The Tribes Settling in Gilead

32 Now the children of Reuben and the children of Gad had a very great number of livestock, and when they saw the land of Jazer and the land of Gilead was a place for livestock, [2] the children of Gad and the children of Reuben came and spoke to Moses, and to Eleazar the priest, and to the leaders of the assembly, saying, [3] "Ataroth, and Dibon, and Jazer, and Nimrah, and Heshbon, and Elealeh, and Sebam, and Nebo, and Beon, [4] the land which the LORD defeated before the assembly of Israel is a land for livestock,

---

[1] 52 About 420 pounds, or 190 kilograms.

and your servants have livestock." [5] And they said, "If we have found mercy in your sight, let this land be given to your servants for a possession, and do not take us over the Jordan."

[6] Moses said to the children of Gad and to the children of Reuben, "Will your brothers go to war, and you will dwell here? [7] And why would you discourage the hearts of the children of Israel from going over into the land which the LORD has given to them? [8] Thus your fathers did, when I sent them from Kadesh Barnea to see the land. [9] When they went up to the Valley of Eshkol and saw the land, they discouraged the hearts of the children of Israel so they would not go into the land which the LORD had given them. [10] And the anger of the LORD was inflamed on that day, and He swore, saying, [11] 'Surely none of the men who came up out of Egypt, from twenty years old and older, will see the ground which I swore to Abraham, to Isaac, and to Jacob, because they did not completely follow Me, [12] except Caleb the son of Jephunneh the Kenizzite, and Joshua the son of Nun, because they completely followed the LORD.' [13] The anger of the LORD was inflamed against Israel, and He made them wander in the wilderness forty years, until all the generation that did evil in the eyes of the LORD was finished.

[14] "Behold, you have risen up in your fathers' place, an increase of sinful men, to increase more the burning anger of the LORD toward Israel. [15] If you turn away from following Him, He will again abandon them in the wilderness, and you will destroy all this people."

[16] They approached him and said, "We will build sheepfolds here for our livestock and cities for our children. [17] But we ourselves will be armed, ready before the children of Israel, until we have brought them to their place. Our little ones will dwell in the fortified cities because of the inhabitants of the land. [18] We will not return to our houses until all the children of Israel have inherited their inheritance. [19] We will not inherit with them on the other side of the Jordan or beyond, because our inheritance fell to us on this side of the Jordan to the east."

[20] Moses said to them, "If you will do this thing, if you will be armed before the LORD for war, [21] and all of you, each armed, will go over the Jordan before the LORD until He has driven out His enemies from before Him [22] and the land is subdued before the LORD, then after that you will return and be exempt before the LORD and before Israel, and this land will be your possession before the LORD.

[23] "But if you will not do so, you have sinned against the LORD, and be sure your sin will find you out. [24] Build for yourselves cities for your children and folds for your sheep, and do that which has proceeded out of your mouth."

[25] The children of Gad and the children of Reuben spoke to Moses, saying, "Your servants will do as my lord commands. [26] Our children, our wives, our flocks, and all our livestock will be there in the cities of Gilead, [27] but your servants will cross over, each man armed for war, before the LORD to battle, as my lord says."

[28] So Moses commanded Eleazar the priest, and Joshua the son of Nun, and the chief fathers of the tribes of the children of Israel. [29] And Moses said to them, "If the children of Gad and the children of Reuben will cross over the Jordan with you, each man armed for battle before the LORD, and the land will be subdued before you, you are to give them the land of Gilead as a possession. [30] But if they do not cross over with you armed, they will have possessions among you in the land of Canaan."

[31] The children of Gad and the children of Reuben answered, saying, "As the LORD has said to your servants, so we will do. [32] We will cross over, armed before the LORD into the land of Canaan, so the possession of our inheritance on this side of the Jordan may be ours."

[33] Moses gave to the children of Gad, to the children of Reuben, and to half the tribe of Manasseh the son of Joseph, the kingdom of Sihon king of the Amorites and the kingdom of Og king of Bashan, the land with the cities within the borders, the cities of the surrounding land.

[34] The children of Gad built Dibon and Ataroth and Aroer, [35] Atroth Shophan and Jazer and Jogbehah, [36] Beth Nimrah and Beth Haran, fortified cities, and folds for sheep. [37] And the children of Reuben built Heshbon and Elealeh and Kiriathaim, [38] Nebo and Baal Meon (their names being changed) and Sibmah; and they named the other cities which they built.

[39] The children of Makir the son of Manasseh went to Gilead and captured it and drove out the Amorites who were in it. [40] Moses gave Gilead to Makir the son of Manasseh, and he lived in it. [41] Jair the son of Manasseh went and captured its small towns and called them Havvoth Jair. [42] Nobah went and captured Kenath and its villages and called it Nobah, after his own name.

Recounting Israel's Journey

33 These are the journeys of the children of Israel, who went out of the land of Egypt with their armies under the hand of Moses and Aaron. [2] Moses recorded the starting points of their journeys at the command of the LORD. These are their journeys according to their starting points.

[3] They set out from Rameses in the first month, on the fifteenth day of the first month. On the day after the Passover the children of Israel went out with a high hand in the sight of all the Egyptians, [4] because the Egyptians buried all their firstborn, whom the LORD had killed among them. Upon their gods the LORD executed judgments.

[5] The children of Israel set out from Rameses and camped in Sukkoth.

[6] They set out from Sukkoth and camped in Etham, which is on the edge of the wilderness.

[7] They set out from Etham and turned to Pi Hahiroth, which is before Baal Zephon, and they camped before Migdol.

[8] They set out from before Pi Hahiroth, and passed through the midst of the sea into the wilderness, and went three days' journey in the Wilderness of Etham, and camped in Marah.

[9] They set out from Marah, and came to Elim, and in Elim were twelve fountains of water and seventy palm trees, and they camped there.

[10] They set out from Elim and camped by the Red Sea.

[11] They set out from the Red Sea and camped in the Wilderness of Sin.

[12] They set out from the Wilderness of Sin and camped in Dophkah.

[13] They set out from Dophkah and camped in Alush.

[14] They set out from Alush and camped at Rephidim, where there was no water for the people to drink.

[15] They set out from Rephidim and camped in the Wilderness of Sinai.

[16] They set out from the Wilderness of Sinai and camped at Kibroth Hattaavah.

[17] They set out from Kibroth Hattaavah and camped at Hazeroth.

[18] They set out from Hazeroth and camped in Rithmah.

[19] They set out from Rithmah and camped at Rimmon Perez.

[20] They set out from Rimmon Perez and camped in Libnah.

[21] They set out from Libnah and camped at Rissah.

[22] They set out from Rissah and camped in Kehelathah.

[23] They set out from Kehelathah and camped at Mount Shepher.

[24] They set out from Mount Shepher and camped in Haradah.

[25] They set out from Haradah and camped in Makheloth.

[26] They set out from Makheloth and camped at Tahath.

[27] They set out from Tahath and camped at Terah.

[28] They set out from Terah and camped in Mithkah.

[29] They went from Mithkah and camped in Hashmonah.

[30] They set out from Hashmonah and camped at Moseroth.

[31] They set out from Moseroth and camped in Bene Jaakan.

[32] They set out from Bene Jaakan and camped at Hor Haggidgad.

[33] They set out from Hor Haggidgad and camped in Jotbathah.

[34] They set out from Jotbathah and camped at Abronah.

[35] They set out from Abronah and camped at Ezion Geber.

[36] They set out from Ezion Geber and camped in the Wilderness of Zin, which is Kadesh.

[37] They set out from Kadesh and camped at Mount Hor, at the edge of the land of Edom. [38] Aaron the priest went up onto Mount Hor at the word of the LORD and died there in the fortieth year after the children of Israel came out of the land of Egypt, in the first day of the fifth month. [39] Aaron was one hundred and twenty-three years old when he died on Mount Hor.

[40] King Arad the Canaanite, who lived in the south in the land of Canaan, heard of the coming of the children of Israel.

[41] They set out from Mount Hor and camped in Zalmonah.

[42] They set out from Zalmonah and camped in Punon.

[43] They set out from Punon and camped in Oboth.

[44] They set out from Oboth and camped in Iye Abarim, on the border of Moab.

[45] They set out from Iye Abarim and camped in Dibon Gad.

[46] They set out from Dibon Gad and camped in Almon Diblathaim.

[47] They set out from Almon Diblathaim and camped in the mountains of Abarim, before Nebo.

[48] They set out from the mountains of Abarim and camped in the plains of Moab near Jordan of Jericho. [49] They camped by Jordan, from Beth Jeshimoth to Abel Shittim in the plains of Moab.

Instructions for Conquering Canaan

[50] The LORD spoke to Moses in the plains of Moab by Jordan near Jericho, saying: [51] Speak to the children of Israel, and say to them: When you are crossing over Jordan into the land of Canaan, [52] then you will drive out all the inhabitants of the land from before you, and destroy all their carved images, and destroy all their molded images, and destroy all their high places, [53] and you will drive out the inhabitants of the land and dwell in it, because I have given you the land to inherit it. [54] You will possess the land by lot for an inheritance among your families, and to the larger you will give the larger inheritance, and to the smaller you will give the smaller inheritance. Every man's inheritance will be in the place where his lot falls. By the tribes of your fathers you will inherit.

[55] But if you do not drive out the inhabitants of the land from before you, then those whom you let remain will be like thorns in your eyes and thorns in your sides. They will show hostility to you in the land in which you live. [56] And what I had planned to do to them, I will do to you.

The Borders of Canaan

34 And the LORD spoke to Moses, saying: [2] Command the children of Israel, and say to them: When you are going into the land of Canaan, this is the land that will fall to you for an inheritance, the land of Canaan with its borders.

[3] Then your south side will be from the Wilderness of Zin along by the border of Edom, and your south border will be the end of the Dead Sea to the east. [4] And your border will turn from the south to the Ascent of Akrabbim, and continue to Zin, and the end of it will be from the south to Kadesh Barnea. Then it will continue to Hazar Addar, and pass on to Azmon. [5] And the border will circle around from Azmon to the Brook of Egypt, and the end of it will be at the *Mediterranean* Sea.

[6] For the western border, you will have the *Mediterranean* Sea and its coastline. This will be your western border.

[7] This will be your northern border: From the *Mediterranean* Sea you will mark a line to Mount Hor; [8] from Mount Hor you will mark a line of your border to Lebo Hamath, and the limits of the border will be to Zedad. [9] And the border will go on to Ziphron, and the limits of it will be at Hazar Enan. This will be your northern border.

[10] You will mark a line for your eastern border from Hazar Enan to Shepham. [11] And the border will go down from Shepham to Riblah, on the east side of Ain, and the border will go down and will reach the side of the Sea of Kinnereth to the east. [12] And the border will go down to the Jordan, and the limits of it will be at the Dead Sea.

This will be your land with its borders all around.

[13] Moses commanded the children of Israel, saying: This is the land which you will possess by lot, which the LORD commanded to give to the nine tribes, and to the half-tribe [14] because the tribe of the children of Reuben by the house of their fathers and the tribe of the children of Gad by the house of their fathers have received their inheritance, and half the tribe of Manasseh has received their inheritance. [15] The two tribes and the half-tribe have received their inheritance on this side of the Jordan near Jericho to the east, toward the sunrise.

The Leaders to Divide the Land

[16] The LORD spoke to Moses, saying: [17] These are the names of the men who will divide the land for you: Eleazar the priest and Joshua the son of Nun. [18] You will take one leader of each tribe to divide the land by inheritance. [19] These are the names of the men:

of the tribe of Judah,
　Caleb the son of Jephunneh;
[20] of the tribe of the children of Simeon,
　Shemuel the son of Ammihud;
[21] of the tribe of Benjamin,
　Elidad the son of Kislon;
[22] the leader of the tribe of the children of Dan,
　Bukki the son of Jogli;
[23] the leader of the children of Joseph, for the tribe of the
　children of Manasseh,
　Hanniel the son of Ephod;
[24] the leader of the tribe of the children of Ephraim,
　Kemuel the son of Shiphtan;
[25] the leader of the tribe of the children of Zebulun,
　Elizaphan the son of Parnak;
[26] the leader of the tribe of the children of Issachar,
　Paltiel the son of Azzan;
[27] the leader of the tribe of the children of Asher,
　Ahihud the son of Shelomi;
[28] the leader of the tribe of the children of Naphtali,
　Pedahel the son of Ammihud.

[29] These are the ones whom the LORD commanded to divide the inheritance among the children of Israel in the land of Canaan.

The Levites' Cities

Dt 4:41–43; 19:1–14; Jos 20:1–9

35 And the LORD spoke to Moses in the plains of Moab by Jordan near Jericho, saying: [2] Command the children of Israel, and they will give to the Levites of the inheritance of their possession cities to dwell in, and you will give the Levites pasturelands around the city. [3] The cities will be for them to dwell in, and their pasturelands will be for their livestock, and for their property, and for all their animals.

[4] The pasturelands of the cities, which you will give to the Levites, will reach from the wall of the city and beyond one thousand cubits[1] all around. [5] You will measure from without the city on the east side two thousand cubits,[2] and on the south side two thousand cubits, and on the west side two thousand cubits, and on the north side two thousand cubits, and the city will be in the middle. This will be for them the pasturelands of the cities.

Cities of Refuge

[6] Among the cities which you will give to the Levites there will be six cities of refuge, which you will appoint for the manslayer, that he may flee there, and to them you will add forty-two cities. [7] So all the cities which you will give to the Levites will be forty-eight cities. You will give them with their pasturelands. [8] The cities which you shall give shall be from the possession of the children of Israel. From the larger tribes you shall give many, and from the smaller tribes you shall give few. Each tribe, in proportion to the inheritance that it receives, shall give of its cities to the Levites.

[9] The LORD spoke to Moses, saying: [10] Speak to the children of Israel and say to them: When you are crossing over the Jordan into the land of Canaan, [11] then you shall designate cities as your cities of refuge, so that a manslayer who unintentionally kills a person may flee there. [12] The cities will be for you a refuge from the avenger, so that the manslayer does not die until he stands trial before the assembly. [13] The cities which you designate shall be your six cities of refuge. [14] You will give three cities across the Jordan, and three cities you will give in the land of Canaan, which will be cities of refuge. [15] For the children of Israel, and for the stranger, and for the foreign sojourner

---

[1] 4　About 1,500 feet, or 450 meters.　　[2] 5　About 3,000 feet, or 900 meters.

among them will be six cities. These will be for a refuge. Everyone that unintentionally kills any person may flee there.

¹⁶ If he strikes him with an instrument of iron, so that he dies, he is a murderer. The murderer shall surely be put to death. ¹⁷ If he strikes him with a stone in hand, by which he could die, and he dies, he is a murderer. The murderer shall surely be put to death. ¹⁸ Or if he strikes him with a weapon of wood in hand, by which he could die, and he dies, he is a murderer. The murderer shall surely be put to death. ¹⁹ The avenger of blood himself will slay the murderer. When he meets him, he will slay him. ²⁰ But if he pushed him out of hatred, or threw something at him, lying in wait, so he dies, ²¹ or in hatred struck him with his hand, so he died, he that struck him shall surely be put to death, because he is a murderer. The avenger of blood will slay the murderer when he meets him.

²² But if he pushed him suddenly without hatred, or threw anything at him without lying in wait, ²³ or used a stone that may cause death, unintentionally throwing it at him, resulting in death, though they were not enemies, and was not trying to harm him, ²⁴ then the assembly will judge between the manslayer and the avenger of blood according to these judgments. ²⁵ And the assembly will deliver the manslayer out of the hand of the avenger of blood, and the assembly will restore him to the city of his refuge where he fled, and he will dwell in it until the death of the high priest, who was anointed with the holy oil.

²⁶ But if the manslayer will go out at any time beyond the border of the city of his refuge where he fled, ²⁷ and the avenger of blood finds him outside the borders of the city of his refuge, and the avenger of blood kills the manslayer, he will not be guilty of blood, ²⁸ because the manslayer should have remained in the city of his refuge until the death of the high priest. But after the death of the high priest the manslayer may return to the land of his possession.

²⁹ So these things will be for a statute of judgment to you throughout your generations in all your dwelling places.

³⁰ Whoever kills a person, the murderer will be put to death by the testimony of witnesses, but one witness will not testify against a person for death.

³¹ And you will not take a ransom for the life of a murderer who is guilty of death, but he will surely be put to death.

³² You will not take a ransom for him who fled to the city of his refuge, that he should come out again to dwell in the land, until the death of the priest.

³³ So you will not defile the land which you are in, because blood defiles the land, and the land cannot be cleansed of the blood that is shed in it, except by the blood of him that shed it. ³⁴ So do not defile the land which you are dwelling in, where I am residing, because I the Lord am residing among the children of Israel.

Marriage of Female Heirs
Nu 27:1–11

36 And the chief fathers of the families of the children of Gilead the son of Makir, the son of Manasseh, of the families of the sons of Joseph, came near, and spoke before Moses and before the leaders, the chief fathers of the children of Israel. ² And they said, "The Lord commanded my lord to give the land for an inheritance by lot to the children of Israel, and my lord was commanded by the Lord to give the inheritance of Zelophehad our brother to his daughters. ³ If they are married to any of the sons of the other tribes of the children of Israel, then their inheritance will be taken from the inheritance of our fathers and will be added to the inheritance of the tribe to which they are married, so will it be taken from the lot of our inheritance. ⁴ When the jubilee of the children of Israel happens, then their inheritance will be added to the inheritance of the tribe to which they are married, so their inheritance will be taken away from the inheritance of the tribe of our fathers."

⁵ Moses commanded the children of Israel according to the word of the Lord, saying: "The tribe of the sons of Joseph has spoken right. ⁶ This is the thing which the Lord commands concerning the daughters of Zelophehad, saying, 'Let them marry whom they think best. But they may marry only within a clan of their father's tribe. ⁷ So the inheritance of the children of Israel will not turn from tribe to tribe, because every one of the children of Israel will keep the inheritance of the tribe of his fathers. ⁸ Every daughter that possesses an inheritance in any tribe of the children of Israel will be wife to one of the families of the tribe of her father, so every man of the children of Israel may enjoy the inheritance of his fathers. ⁹ Thus no inheritance will turn from one tribe to another tribe, but every tribe of the children of Israel will keep its own inheritance.' "

¹⁰ Just as the Lord commanded Moses, thus the daughters of Zelophehad did, ¹¹ for Mahlah, Tirzah, Hoglah, Milkah, and Noah, the daughters of Zelophehad, were married to their uncles' sons. ¹² And they were married into the families of the sons of Manasseh the son of Joseph, and their inheritance remained in the tribe of the family of their father.

¹³ These are the commandments and the judgments which the Lord commanded by the hand of Moses to the children of Israel in the plains of Moab by Jordan near Jericho.

DEUTERONOMY

The Command to Leave Horeb

1 These are the words which Moses spoke to all Israel on the other side of the Jordan in the wilderness, in the plain opposite Suph, between Paran and Tophel and Laban and Hazeroth and Dizahab. ² (It is an eleven-day *journey* from Horeb by the way of Mount Seir to Kadesh Barnea.)

³ In the fortieth year, in the eleventh month, on the first day of the month, Moses spoke to the children of Israel, according to all that the Lord had commanded him *to give* to them. ⁴ *It was* after he had slain Sihon the king of the Amorites, who lived in Heshbon, and Og the king of Bashan, who lived at Ashtaroth in Edrei.

⁵ Across the Jordan, in the land of Moab, Moses began to declare this law, saying: ⁶ The Lord our God spoke to us in Horeb, saying, "You have dwelt long enough at this mountain. ⁷ Turn, and take your journey, and go to the mountains of the Amorites, and to all their neighbors, in the plain, in the mountains

and in the lowland, in the Negev and by the seacoast, to the land of the Canaanites and to Lebanon, as far as the great river, the River Euphrates. ⁸ See, I have set the land before you. Go in and possess the land which the Lord swore to your fathers, Abraham, Isaac, and Jacob, to give to them and to their descendants after them."

Leaders Appointed

⁹ I spoke to you at that time, saying, "I am not able to bear you by myself. ¹⁰ The Lord your God has multiplied you, and surely you are this day as numerous as the stars of heaven. ¹¹ May the Lord, the God of your fathers, make you a thousand times more numerous and bless you, just as He has promised you! ¹² How can I myself bear your load and your burden and your strife? ¹³ Choose wise, discerning, and knowing men, among your tribes, and I will appoint them as leaders over you."

[14] You answered me, and said, "The thing which you have said is good for us to do."

[15] So I took the leaders of your tribes, wise and well-known men, and appointed them as leaders over you, leaders over thousands, and leaders over hundreds, and leaders over fifties, and leaders over tens, and officers among your tribes. [16] I charged your judges at that time, saying, "Hear the issues between your countrymen, and judge righteously between every man and his fellow countryman, and the foreigner that is with him. [17] You shall not show partiality in judgment, but you shall hear the small as well as the great. You shall not be afraid in any man's presence, for the judgment is God's. The case that is too hard for you, you shall bring it to me, and I will hear it." [18] At that time, I commanded you all the things you should do.

Israel Sends Spies

[19] When we departed from Horeb, we went through all that great and terrible wilderness, which you saw by the way of the mountain of the Amorites, as the LORD our God commanded us, and we came to Kadesh Barnea. [20] I said to you, "You have come to the mountains of the Amorites, which the LORD our God is giving to us. [21] See, the LORD your God has set the land before you. Go up and possess it, just as the LORD, the God of your fathers, spoke to you. Do not fear or be discouraged."

[22] So all of you came near to me and said, "Let us send men before us, so that they shall scout out the land, and bring back to us word concerning what way we should go up and into what cities we shall come."

[23] The thing pleased me, and I took twelve men from you, one out of each tribe. [24] They turned and went up into the hill country and came to the Valley of Eshkol and scouted it out. [25] They took the fruit of the land in their hands, and brought it down to us, and brought us word again, and said, "It is a good land which the LORD our God is giving us."

Israel Rebels

[26] Yet you were not willing to go up, but rebelled against the commandment of the LORD your God. [27] You murmured in your tents, and said, "Because the LORD hates us, He has brought us out of the land of Egypt to deliver us into the hand of the Amorites to destroy us. [28] Where shall we go up? Our brothers have discouraged our hearts, saying, 'The people are greater and taller than we. The cities are great and walled up to heaven. And moreover, we have seen the sons of the Anakites there.'"

[29] Then I said to you, "Do not be terrified, or afraid of them. [30] The LORD your God who goes before you, He shall fight for you, just as all that He did for you in Egypt before your eyes, [31] and in the wilderness, where you saw how the LORD your God carried you, as a man carries his son, in all the way that you went, until you came to this place."

[32] Yet in this thing you did not believe the LORD your God, [33] who went in the way before you, to find you a place to pitch your tents, in fire by night and in a cloud by day, to show you by what way you should go.

[34] The LORD heard the sound of your words, and was angry, and vowed, saying, [35] "Not one of these men of this evil generation will see the good land which I swore to give to your fathers. [36] The exception will be Caleb the son of Jephunneh. He shall see it, and to him I will give the land upon which he has walked, and to his children, because he has wholly followed the LORD."

[37] Also the LORD was angry with me on your account, saying, "You also shall not go in. [38] But Joshua the son of Nun, who stands before you, he shall go in. Encourage him, for he will cause Israel to inherit it. [39] Moreover, your little ones, who you said would be a prey, and your children, who in that day had no knowledge between good and evil, they shall go in, and to them will I give it, and they shall possess it. [40] But as for you, turn around, and take your journey into the wilderness by the way of the Red Sea."

[41] Then you answered and said to me, "We have sinned against the LORD. We will go up and fight, just as the LORD our God com-

manded us." So each of you girded on his weapons of war and you thought it easy to go up into the hill country.

[42] Then the LORD said to me, "Tell them, 'Do not go up nor fight, for I am not among you; lest you be defeated before your enemies.'"

[43] So I spoke to you, but you would not listen. Instead, you rebelled against the commandment of the LORD and went presumptuously up into the hill country. [44] The Amorites, who lived in the hill country, came out against you, and chased you as bees do, and destroyed you in Seir as far as Hormah. [45] Then you returned and wept before the LORD, but the LORD would neither listen to your voice nor give ear to you. [46] So you dwelt in Kadesh many days, according to the days you dwelt there.

The Wilderness Years

2 Then we turned, and set out toward the wilderness by the way of the Red Sea, as the LORD spoke to me, and we circled Mount Seir for many days.

[2] Then the LORD spoke to me, saying, [3] "You have circled this mountain long enough. Now turn north. [4] Command the people, saying: You are to pass through the territory of your brothers the children of Esau, who dwell in Seir, and they shall be afraid of you. So carefully watch yourselves. [5] Do not provoke them, for I will not give you any of their land, no, not so much as a footprint, because I have given Mount Seir to Esau for a possession. [6] You may buy food from them with money so that you may eat, and you may also buy water from them with money so that you may drink.

[7] "For the LORD your God has blessed you in all the works of your hands. He knows your wanderings through this great wilderness. These forty years the LORD your God has been with you. You have lacked nothing."

[8] So we passed by our brothers, the children of Esau, who lived in Seir, through the way of the plain from Elath and from Ezion Geber, and we turned and passed by the way of the Wilderness of Moab.

[9] The LORD said to me, "Do not harass the Moabites, nor contend with them in battle, for I will not give you any of their land for a possession, because I have given Ar to the children of Lot as a possession."

[10] (The Emites lived there in times past, a people as great and as many and as tall as the Anakites. [11] These people, as well as the Anakites, also were regarded as giants,[1] but the Moabites call them Emites. [12] The Horites also formerly lived in Seir, but the children of Esau dispossessed and destroyed them, and settled there in their place, just as Israel did to the land of its possession, which the LORD gave to them.)

[13] "Cross over the Zered Valley." So we went over the Zered Valley. [14] Now the length of time it took for us to come to Kadesh Barnea until we crossed over the brook Zered was thirty-eight years, until all the generation of the men of war perished from among the army, just as the LORD swore to them. [15] For indeed the hand of the LORD was against them, to destroy them from among their midst, until they were gone.

[16] So it came to pass, when all the men of war were gone and dead from among the people, [17] then the LORD spoke to me, saying, [18] "Today, you are to pass over through Ar, the border of Moab. [19] When you come close to the Ammonites, do not harass them or provoke them, for I will not give you any of the land of the Ammonites as a possession, because I have given it to the children of Lot for a possession."

[20] (That also is considered the land of giants. Giants formerly lived there, but the Ammonites call them Zamzummites. [21] They were a great people, as numerous and tall as the Anakites. But the LORD destroyed them before *the Ammonites*. Then they dispossessed them and lived in their place, [22] just as He had done *for* the children of Esau, who lived in Seir, when He destroyed the Horites from before them, and they dispossessed them, and lived in their place even to this day. [23] And the Avvites, who lived in villages as far as Gaza, the Caphtorites, who came out of Caphtor, destroyed them, and lived in their place.)

---

[1] 11 *Rephaites*, English trans. of Heb. *Rephaim*, also 2:20; 3:11; Jos 13:12; 17:15.

King Sihon Defeated

24 "Arise, set out, and cross the River Arnon. See, I have given Sihon the Amorite, king of Heshbon, and his land into your hand. Begin to possess it and contend with him in battle. 25 This day I will begin to put the dread of you and the fear of you on the nations that are under the whole heaven, who shall hear the report of you, and shall tremble, and be in anguish because of you."

26 I sent messengers out of the Wilderness of Kedemoth to Sihon, king of Heshbon, with words of peace, saying, 27 "Let me pass through your land. I will only go on the main road. I will not turn aside to the right or the left. 28 You shall sell me food for money so that I may eat, and give me water for money so that I may drink, only allow me to pass through on foot, 29 just as the children of Esau who dwell in Seir and the Moabites who dwell in Ar did for me, until I pass over the Jordan into the land which the LORD our God is giving us." 30 But Sihon, king of Heshbon, would not let us pass by him, for the LORD your God hardened his spirit and made his heart obstinate, so that He might deliver him into your hand as he is to this day.

31 The LORD said to me, "See, I have begun to give Sihon and his land to you. Begin to possess it, so that you may inherit his land."

32 Then Sihon came out against us, he and all his people, to fight at Jahaz. 33 Then the LORD our God delivered him over to us, and we struck him down with his sons and all his people. 34 We took all his cities at that time and utterly destroyed the men, the women, and the children of every city. We left no survivors. 35 We took only the livestock for plunder and the spoils of the cities which we took. 36 From Aroer, which is on the bank of the River Arnon, and from the city that is in the valley, all the way to Gilead, there was not one city too strong for us. The LORD our God delivered all to us. 37 Only you did not come near the land of the Ammonites, nor to any place on the River Jabbok, nor to the cities in the hill country, nor to any place the LORD our God had forbidden us.

King Og Defeated

3 Then we turned and went up the way to Bashan, and Og, the king of Bashan, came out against us, he and all his people, to battle at Edrei. 2 Then the LORD said to me, "Do not fear him, for I will deliver him and all his people and his land into your hand; and you shall do to him as you did to Sihon, king of the Amorites, who lived at Heshbon."

3 So the LORD, our God, delivered Og, the king of Bashan, with all his people, into our hands also, and we struck him down until there was no survivor remaining. 4 We took all his cities at that time. There was not a city which we did not take from them: sixty cities, all the region of Argob, the kingdom of Og in Bashan. 5 All these cities were fortified with high walls, gates, and bars, besides a great many rural towns. 6 We utterly destroyed them, as we did to Sihon, king of Heshbon, utterly destroying the men, women, and children of every city. 7 But we took all the livestock and the spoil of the cities as plunder for ourselves.

8 So at that time we took from the hand of the two kings of the Amorites the land that was across the Jordan, from the River Arnon to Mount Hermon 9 (the Sidonians call Hermon Sirion, and the Amorites call it Senir), 10 all the cities of the plain, and all Gilead, and all Bashan, as far as Salekah and Edrei, cities of the kingdom of Og in Bashan. 11 For only Og, king of Bashan, remained of the remnant of the giants. (Notably, his bedstead was a bedstead of iron. Is it not in Rabbah of the children of Ammon? It is nine cubits long and four cubits wide, t according to the cubit of a man.)

Division of the Land

12 This is the land which we possessed at that time from Aroer, which is by the River Arnon, and half the hill country of Gilead and its cities I gave to the Reubenites and to the Gadites. 13 The rest of Gilead, and all Bashan, the kingdom of Og, I gave to the half-tribe of Manasseh. (All the region of Argob, with all Bashan, was called the land of giants. 14 Jair, the son of Manasseh, took all the region of Argob, that is, Bashan, as far as the border of the Geshurites and the Maakathites, and called the villages after his own name,

Havvoth Jair, as it is to this day.) 15 I gave Gilead to Makir. 16 To the Reubenites and to the Gadites I gave the territory from Gilead even as far as the stream bed of the River Arnon, half the valley as the border to the River Jabbok, which is the border of the Ammonites; 17 the plain also, with the Jordan as the border, from Kinnereth as far as the east side of the Sea of the Arabah (that is, the Dead Sea), below the slopes of Pisgah.

18 Then I commanded you at that time, saying, "The LORD your God has given you this land to possess it. All you men of valor shall pass over armed before your brothers, the children of Israel. 19 But your wives and your little ones, and your livestock (for I know that you have much livestock) shall remain in your cities which I have given you 20 until the LORD has given rest to your brothers, as well as to you, and until they also possess the land which the LORD your God has given them beyond the Jordan. Then each of you shall return to his possession which I have given you."

Moses Forbidden to Cross the Jordan

21 I commanded Joshua at that time, saying, "Your eyes have seen all that the LORD your God has done to these two kings. So shall the LORD do to all the kingdoms where you pass. 22 Do not fear them, for the LORD your God, He shall fight for you."

23 I pleaded with the LORD at that time, saying, 24 "O LORD God, You have begun to show Your servant Your greatness, and Your mighty hand, for what god is there in heaven or in earth that can do according to Your works and according to Your might? 25 Let me, I pray, go over and see the good land that is beyond the Jordan, that good hill country, and Lebanon."

26 But the LORD was angry with me because of you and would not listen to me, and the LORD said to me, "Enough of that! Speak to Me no more of this matter. 27 Get up to the top of Pisgah and lift up your eyes to the west and north and south and east, and see it with your eyes, for you shall not cross over this Jordan. 28 But charge Joshua and encourage him and strengthen him, for he shall cross over before this people, and he shall cause them to inherit the land which you will see." 29 So we remained in the valley over against Beth Peor.

Moses Commands Obedience

4 Now therefore, listen, O Israel, to the statutes and to the judgments which I am teaching you to do, so that you may live; and go in and possess the land which the LORD, the God of your fathers, is giving you. 2 You shall not add to the word which I am commanding you, nor shall you take anything from it, so that you may keep the commandments of the LORD your God which I command you.

3 Your eyes have seen what the LORD did at Baal Peor; for the LORD your God has destroyed from among you all the men who followed Baal of Peor. 4 But you who held fast to the LORD your God are alive to this day, every one of you.

5 See, I have taught you statutes and judgments, just as the LORD my God commanded me, that you should do so in the land where you are entering to possess it. 6 Therefore, keep and do them, for this is your wisdom and your understanding in the sight of the nations which shall hear all these statutes, and say, "Surely this great nation is a wise and understanding people." 7 For what nation is there so great, who has a god so near to it as the LORD our God is in all things whenever we call on Him? 8 And what nation is there so great that has statutes and judgments so righteous as all this law, which I am setting before you today?

9 Only give heed to yourself and keep your soul diligently, lest you forget the things which your eyes have seen and lest they depart from your heart all the days of your life; but teach them to your sons, and your grandsons. 10 Especially concerning the day you stood before the LORD your God at Horeb, when the LORD said to me, "Gather the people together to Me, so that I will let them hear My words so that they may learn to fear Me all the days they shall live on the earth, and so that they may teach their children." 11 Then you came near and stood at the foot of the mountain, and the mountain burned with fire up to the midst of heaven, with darkness, a cloud, a thick cloud. 12 Then the LORD spoke to you out of the midst of the

---

t 11 About 14 feet long and 6 feet wide, or 4 meters long and 1.8 meters wide.

fire. You heard the sound of the words but saw no form—only a voice was heard. [13] He declared to you His covenant, which He commanded you to perform, even the Ten Commandments, and He wrote them on two tablets of stone. [14] The Lord commanded me at that time to teach you statutes and judgments, so that you might do them in the land which you are crossing over to possess.

Idolatry Forbidden

[15] Give good care to yourselves, for you saw no form on the day that the Lord spoke to you in Horeb from the midst of the fire, [16] lest you corrupt yourselves and make a graven image for yourselves in the form of any figure, the likeness of male or female, [17] the likeness of any beast that is on the earth, the likeness of any winged fowl that flies in the air, [18] the likeness of anything that creeps on the ground, the likeness of any fish that is in the waters beneath the earth. [19] And *beware*, lest you lift up your eyes to heaven, and when you see the sun, and the moon, and the stars, even all the host of heaven, you are led astray and worship them, and serve them, that which the Lord your God has allotted to all nations under the whole heaven. [20] But the Lord has taken you and brought you out of the iron furnace, from Egypt, to be to Him a people of inheritance, as you are today.

[21] Furthermore, the Lord was angry with me because of you and swore that I should not cross over the Jordan, and that I would not go into that good land which the Lord your God is giving you for an inheritance. [22] So I must die in this land. I shall not cross over the Jordan, but you shall go over and possess that good land. [23] Watch yourselves, so that you do not forget the covenant of the Lord your God, which He made with you, and make yourself a graven image or the likeness of anything as the Lord your God has forbidden you. [24] For the Lord your God is a consuming fire. He is a jealous God.

[25] When you produce children and grandchildren and you have remained a long time in the land, and you corrupt yourselves and make a graven image, or the likeness of anything, and do evil in the sight of the Lord your God, to provoke Him to anger, [26] I call heaven and earth to witness against you today, that you will surely and suddenly perish from off the land that you are going across the Jordan to possess. You will not prolong your days on it, but shall be completely destroyed. [27] The Lord shall scatter you among the peoples, and you shall be left few in number among the nations where the Lord shall lead you. [28] There you will serve gods, the work of men's hands, wood and stone, which neither see nor hear nor eat nor smell. [29] But if from there you will seek the Lord your God, you will find Him, if you seek Him with all your heart and with all your soul. [30] When you are in distress and all these things come upon you, even in the latter days, if you turn to the Lord your God and shall be obedient to His voice [31] (for the Lord your God is a merciful God), He will not abandon you or destroy you or forget the covenant of your fathers which He swore to them.

[32] Indeed, ask about the days that are past, which were before you, since the day that God created man[1] on the earth, and ask from one end of heavens to the other, whether there has ever been any such thing as this great thing, or has *anything* like it ever been heard? [33] Has a people ever heard the voice of God speaking out of the midst of the fire, as you have heard, and lived? [34] Or has God ever tried to take for Himself a nation from the midst of another nation, by trials, by signs, and by wonders, and by war, and by a mighty hand, and by a stretched-out arm, and by great terrors, according to all that the Lord your God did for you in Egypt before your eyes? [35] To you it was shown so that you might know that the Lord, He is God. There is no one else besides Him. [36] Out of heaven He let you hear His voice so that He might instruct you, and on earth He showed you His great fire, and you heard His words out of the midst of the fire. [37] Because He loved your fathers, therefore He chose their descendants after them and personally brought you out of Egypt with His mighty power [38] to drive out nations from before you greater and mightier than you are, to bring you in, to give you their land for an inheritance, as it is today.

[39] Know therefore today, and consider it in your heart, that the Lord, He is God in heaven above and on the earth below. There is no other. [40] Therefore, you shall keep His statutes and His commandments which I command you this day, so that it may go well with you and with your children after you, and so that you may prolong your days in the land, which the Lord your God gives you, forever.

Cities of Refuge

Nu 35:6–34; Dt 19:1–14; Jos 20:1–9

[41] Then Moses set apart three cities across the Jordan, toward the east, [42] that the manslayer might flee there, that is, anyone who killed his neighbor unintentionally without hating him in time past could flee to one of these cities and live: [43] Bezer in the wilderness in the plateau of the Reubenites, and Ramoth in Gilead of the Gadites, and Golan in Bashan of the Manassites.

Introduction to the Law

[44] This is the law which Moses set before the children of Israel. [45] These are the testimonies, and the statutes, and the ordinances which Moses spoke to the children of Israel, after they came out of Egypt, [46] on this side of the Jordan, in the valley over against Beth Peor, in the land of Sihon, king of the Amorites, who lived at Heshbon, whom Moses and the children of Israel struck down, after they had come out of Egypt. [47] They possessed his land, and the land of Og, king of Bashan, the two kings of the Amorites, who were across the Jordan toward the east, [48] from Aroer, which is by the edge of the River Arnon, even as far as Mount Sion (that is, Hermon), [49] with all the Arabah across the Jordan to the east, even to the sea of the Arabah, under the slopes of Pisgah.

The Ten Commandments

Ex 20:1–17

5 Then Moses called all Israel and said to them: Hear, O Israel, the statutes and ordinances which I am speaking in your hearing today, so that you may learn them, and keep, and do them. [2] The Lord our God made a covenant with us in Horeb. [3] The Lord did not make this covenant with our fathers, but with us, we who are living now and here today. [4] The Lord talked with you face to face on the mountain from the midst of the fire. [5] I stood between the Lord and you at that time to declare to you the word of the Lord; for you were afraid because of the fire and would not go up to the mountain. He said:

[6] I am the Lord, your God, who brought you out of the land of Egypt, from the house of bondage.

[7] You shall have no other gods before Me.

[8] You shall not make yourself any graven image, or any likeness of anything that is in heaven above, or that is in the earth beneath, or that is in the waters beneath the earth; [9] you shall not bow down to them, nor serve them. For I, the Lord your God, am a jealous God, visiting the iniquity of the fathers on the children, and on the third and fourth generations of those who hate Me, [10] but showing mercy to thousands of them that love Me and keep My commandments.

[11] You shall not take the name of the Lord your God in vain, for the Lord will not exonerate anyone who takes His name in vain.

[12] Keep the Sabbath day, to keep it holy, just as the Lord your God has commanded you. [13] Six days you shall labor and do all your work, [14] but the seventh day is the Sabbath of the Lord your God. On it you shall not do any work: you, nor your son, nor your daughter, nor your male servant, nor your female servant, nor your ox, nor your donkey, nor any of your livestock, nor the foreigner that is within your gates, so that your male servant and your female servant may rest as well as you. [15] Remember that you were a servant in the land of Egypt, and that the Lord your God brought you out from there with a mighty hand and by an outstretched arm; therefore your God commanded you to keep the Sabbath day.

[16] Honor your father and your mother, just as the Lord your God has commanded you, that your days may be prolonged, and that it may go well with you in the land which the Lord your God is giving you.

---

[1] 32 Or Adam.

[17] You shall not murder.

[18] You shall not commit adultery.

[19] You shall not steal.

[20] You shall not bear false witness against your neighbor.

[21] You shall not covet your neighbor's wife, nor shall you covet your neighbor's house, his field, his male servant, his female servant, his ox, his donkey, or anything that belongs to your neighbor.

[22] These are the words the LORD spoke to all your assembly at the mountain out from the midst of the fire, the cloud, and the thick darkness with a great voice, and He added no more. He wrote them on two tablets of stone and gave them to me.

[23] When you heard the voice out of the midst of the darkness, while the mountain did burn with fire, you came near to me, all the heads of your tribes, and your elders. [24] You said, "See, the LORD our God has shown us His glory and His greatness, and we have heard His voice from the midst of the fire. We have seen this day that God speaks with man, yet he lives. [25] Now, therefore, why should we die? For this great fire will consume us. If we hear the voice of the LORD our God any more, then we will die. [26] For who is there of all flesh who has heard the voice of the living God speaking out of the midst of the fire, as we have, and lived? [27] Go near and hear all that the LORD our God will say. Then speak to us all that the LORD our God will speak to you, and we will hear and do it."

[28] The LORD heard the sound of your words when you spoke to me, and the LORD said to me, "I have heard the sound of the words of this people which they have spoken to you. They have done well in all that they have spoken. [29] O that there were such a heart in them that they would fear Me and always keep all My commandments, that it might be well with them and with their children forever!

[30] "Go say to them, 'Return to your tents.' [31] But as for you, stand here by Me, so that I may speak to you all the commandments, and the statutes, and the ordinances which you shall teach them, that they may keep them in the land which I am giving them to possess."

[32] Therefore, be careful to do as the LORD your God has commanded you. You shall not turn aside to the right hand or to the left. [33] You shall walk in all the ways which the LORD your God has commanded you, so that you may live and that it may be well with you, and that you may prolong *your* days in the land which you shall possess.

The Greatest Commandment

6 Now these are the commandments, the statutes, and the ordinances which the LORD your God commanded to teach you, so that you may observe them in the land which you are crossing over to possess, [2] so that you might fear the LORD your God in order to keep all His statutes and His commandments which I command you—you, and your son, and your grandson—all the days of your life, so that your days may be prolonged. [3] Hear therefore, O Israel, and be careful to do it, so that it may be well with you and so that you may multiply greatly, as the LORD the God of your fathers has promised you in the land that flows with milk and honey.

[4] Hear, O Israel: The LORD is our God. The LORD is one! [5] And you shall love the LORD your God with all your heart and with all your soul and with all your might. [6] These words, which I am commanding you today, shall be in your heart. [7] You shall teach them diligently to your children and shall talk of them when you sit in your house, and when you walk by the way, and when you lie down, and when you rise up. [8] You shall bind them as a sign on your hand, and they shall be as frontlets between your eyes. [9] You shall write them on the doorposts of your house and on your gates.

[10] Then it shall be when the LORD your God brings you into the land which He swore to your fathers, to Abraham, Isaac, and Jacob, to give you great and fine cities, which you did not build, [11] and houses full of all good things which you did not fill, and hewn cisterns which you did not dig, vineyards and olive trees which you did not plant, and you eat and are full, [12] then beware lest you forget the LORD who brought you out of the land of Egypt, out of the house of bondage.

[13] You shall fear the LORD your God and serve Him and shall swear by His name. [14] You shall not go after other gods, the gods of the people which surround you [15] (for the LORD your God is a jealous God among you). Otherwise the anger of the LORD your God will be inflamed against you and destroy you from off the face of the earth. [16] You shall not tempt the LORD your God, as you tempted *Him* in Massah. [17] You shall diligently keep the commandments of the LORD your God, and His testimonies and His statutes which He has commanded you. [18] You shall do what is right and good in the sight of the LORD that it may be well with you and that you may go in and possess the good land which the LORD swore to your fathers, [19] to drive out all your enemies before you, just as the LORD has spoken.

[20] When your son asks you in time to come, saying, "What do the testimonies and the statutes and the judgments mean which the LORD our God has commanded you?" [21] then you shall say to your son, "We were slaves of Pharaoh in Egypt, and the LORD brought us out of Egypt with a mighty hand. [22] And the LORD showed great and devastating signs and wonders upon Egypt, upon Pharaoh, and upon all his household before our eyes. [23] He brought us out from there, so that He might bring us in, to give us the land which He swore to our fathers. [24] The LORD commanded us to do all these statutes, to fear the LORD our God, for our good always, that He might preserve us, as He has to this day. [25] It will be our righteousness if we are careful to keep all these commandments before the LORD our God, just as He has commanded us."

The Chosen People

7 When the LORD your God brings you into the land which you are entering to possess and has driven out many nations before you, the Hittites and the Girgashites and the Amorites and the Canaanites and the Perizzites and the Hivites and the Jebusites, seven nations greater and mightier than you, [2] and when the LORD your God delivers them before you and you strike them down, then you must utterly destroy them. You shall make no covenant with them nor show mercy to them. [3] What is more, you shall not intermarry with them. You shall not give your daughters to their sons or take their daughters for your sons. [4] For they will turn your sons away from following Me to serve other gods. Then the anger of the LORD will be inflamed against you, and He will quickly destroy you: [5] But this is how you shall deal with them: You shall destroy their altars and break down their images and cut down their Asherim[1] and burn their graven images with fire. [6] For you are a holy people to the LORD your God. The LORD your God has chosen you to be His special people, treasured above all peoples who are on the face of the earth.

[7] The LORD did not set His love on you nor choose you because you were more in number than any of the peoples, for you were the fewest of all the peoples. [8] But it is because the LORD loved you and because He kept the oath which He swore to your fathers. The LORD brought you out with a mighty hand and redeemed you out of the house of slavery, from the hand of Pharaoh, king of Egypt. [9] Know therefore that the LORD your God, He is God, the faithful God, who keeps covenant and mercy with them who love Him and keep His commandments to a thousand generations, [10] yet He repays those who hate Him to their face, to destroy them. He will not be slack with him who hates Him. He will repay him to his face. [11] Therefore keep the commandments and the statutes and the judgments which I command you today, by doing them.

[12] If you listen to these judgments, keep them, and do them, then the LORD your God shall keep with you the covenant and the mercy which He swore to your fathers. [13] He will love you and bless you and multiply you. He will also bless the fruit of your womb and the fruit of your land, your grain, and your wine, and your oil, the increase of your herd and the young of your flock, in the land which He swore to your fathers to give you. [14] You shall be blessed above all peoples. There will not be male or female barren among you or among your livestock. [15] The LORD will take away from you all sickness, and will afflict you with none of the evil diseases of Egypt, which you know, but will lay them on all those who hate you.

---

[15] Or *groves*, referring to wooden symbols of a female deity.

[16] You must consume all the peoples whom the Lord your God will deliver to you. Your eye shall have no pity on them, nor shall you serve their gods, for that will be a snare to you.

[17] If you say in your heart, "These nations are greater than I—how can I dispossess them?" [18] you shall not be afraid of them. You must surely remember what the Lord your God did to Pharaoh and to all Egypt, [19] the great trials which your eyes saw, and the signs, and the wonders, and the mighty hand, and the stretched-out arm, by which the Lord your God brought you out. So the Lord your God will do to all the peoples of whom you are afraid. [20] Moreover the Lord your God will send the hornet among them, until they who are left and hide themselves from you perish. [21] You must not be frightened of them, for the Lord your God is among you, a great and awesome God. [22] The Lord your God will drive out those nations before you, little by little. You will not be able to destroy them all at once, lest the beasts of the field become too numerous for you. [23] But the Lord your God will deliver them to you and will throw them into a great confusion until they are destroyed. He will deliver their kings into your hand so that you may erase their names from under heaven. No man will be able to stand before you until you have destroyed them. [25] You must burn the graven images of their gods with fire. You must not desire the silver or gold that is on them nor take any of it, lest you be snared by them, for it is an abomination to the Lord your God. [26] You shall not bring an abomination into your house, lest you become cursed like it, but you must absolutely detest and abhor it, for it is a cursed thing.

Remember the Lord Your God

8 You must carefully keep all the commandments that I am commanding you today, so that you may live, and multiply, and go in and possess the land which the Lord swore to your fathers. [2] You must remember that the Lord your God led you all the way these forty years in the wilderness, to humble you, and to prove you, to know what was in your heart, whether you would keep His commandments or not. [3] He humbled you and let you suffer hunger, and fed you with manna, which you did not know, nor did your fathers know, that He might make you know that man does not live by bread alone; but man lives by every word that proceeds out of the mouth of the Lord. [4] Your clothing did not wear out on you, nor did your feet swell these forty years. [5] You must also consider in your heart that, as a man disciplines his son, so the Lord your God disciplines you.

[6] Therefore you must keep the commandments of the Lord your God, to walk in His ways and to fear Him. [7] For the Lord your God is bringing you into a good land, a land of brooks of water, of fountains and springs that flow out of valleys and hills, [8] a land of wheat, barley, vines, fig trees, and pomegranates, a land of olive oil and honey, [9] a land where you may eat bread without scarcity, in which you will not lack anything, a land whose stones are iron, and out of whose hills you may dig copper.

[10] When you have eaten and are full, then you shall bless the Lord your God for the good land which He has given you. [11] Beware that you do not forget the Lord your God by not keeping His commandments, and His judgments, and His statutes, which I am commanding you today. [12] Otherwise, when you have eaten and are full and have built and occupied good houses, [13] and when your herds and your flocks multiply, and your silver and your gold multiply, and all that you have multiplies, [14] then your heart will become proud and you will forget the Lord your God who brought you out of the land of Egypt, from the house of slavery, [15] who led you through that great and terrible wilderness, where there were fiery serpents and scorpions and drought, where there was no water, who brought forth for you water out of the rock of flint, [16] who fed you in the wilderness with manna, which your fathers did not know, that He might humble you and that He might prove you, to do good for you in the end. [17] Otherwise, you may say in your heart, "My power and the might of my hand have gained me this wealth." [18] But you must remember the Lord your God, for it is He who gives you the ability to get wealth, so that He may establish His covenant which He swore to your fathers, as it is today.

[19] If you ever forget the Lord your God and go after other gods and serve them and worship them, then I testify against you today that you will surely perish. [20] Just like the nations which the Lord will destroy before you, so shall you perish because you would not be obedient to the voice of the Lord your God.

Not Because of Righteousness

9 Hear, O Israel! You are to cross over the Jordan today, to go in to possess nations greater and mightier than you, great cities fortified up to heaven, [2] a great and tall people, the children of the Anakites, whom you know and of whom you have heard *it* said, "Who can stand before the children of Anak?" [3] Understand therefore today that the Lord your God is He who goes over before you as a consuming fire. He shall destroy them and shall bring them down before you, so that you drive them out and destroy them quickly, as the Lord has spoken to you.

[4] Do not say in your heart, after the Lord your God has driven them out before you, "On account of my righteousness the Lord has brought me in to possess this land," but it is because of the wickedness of these nations the Lord is driving them out before you. [5] It is not because of your righteousness or the uprightness of your heart that you enter to possess their land, but because of the wickedness of these nations that the Lord your God drives them out before you, and that He may fulfill the word which the Lord swore to your fathers, Abraham, Isaac, and Jacob. [6] Understand, therefore, that the Lord your God is not giving you this good land to possess on account of your righteousness, for you are a stubborn people.

The Golden Calf

[7] Remember, and do not forget how you provoked the Lord your God to wrath in the wilderness. From the day that you departed out of the land of Egypt until you came to this place, you have been rebellious against the Lord. [8] Also in Horeb you provoked the Lord to wrath, so that the Lord was angry enough with you to destroy you. [9] When I went up into the mountain to receive the tablets of stone, the tablets of the covenant which the Lord made with you, then I remained on the mountain forty days and forty nights. I did not eat bread or drink water. [10] The Lord delivered to me two tablets of stone, written with the finger of God, and on them was written all the words which the Lord spoke to you at the mountain out of the midst of the fire on the day of the assembly.

[11] At the end of forty days and forty nights, the Lord gave me the two tablets of stone, the tablets of the covenant. [12] Then the Lord said to me, "Arise, go down from here quickly, for your people whom you brought out of Egypt have corrupted themselves. They are quickly turned aside from the way which I commanded them. They have made a molded image for themselves."

[13] Furthermore the Lord spoke to me, saying, "I have seen this people, and indeed, they are a stubborn people. [14] Let Me alone, so that I may destroy them and blot out their name from under heaven, and I will make of you a nation mightier and greater than they."

[15] So I returned and came down from the mount, and the mount burned with fire, and the two tablets of the covenant were in my two hands. [16] I looked, and indeed, you had sinned against the Lord your God and had made yourselves a molded calf. You had quickly turned aside out of the way which the Lord had commanded you. [17] I took the two tablets and threw them out of my two hands and broke them before your eyes.

[18] I fell down before the Lord, as at the first, forty days and forty nights. I did not eat bread or drink water because of all your sins which you committed, doing what was wicked in the sight of the Lord to provoke Him to anger. [19] For I was afraid of the anger and hot displeasure with which the Lord was wrathful against you to destroy you. But the Lord listened to me at that time also. [20] The Lord was angry enough with Aaron to destroy him, so I also prayed for Aaron at the same time. [21] I took your sin, the calf which you had made, and burned it with fire, and crushed it, and ground it very small until it was as small as dust. Then I threw the dust into the brook that descended down from the mountain.

[22] Also at Taberah and at Massah and at Kibroth Hattaavah you provoked the Lord to wrath.

[23] Likewise when the Lord sent you from Kadesh Barnea, saying, "Go up and possess the land which I have given you," then you rebelled against the commandment of the Lord your God, and you

did not believe Him or listen to His voice. [24] You have been rebellious against the LORD from the day I knew you.

[25] So I fell down before the LORD forty days and forty nights; I fell down because the LORD had said He would destroy you. [26] I prayed therefore to the LORD, and said, "O Lord GOD, do not destroy Your people, Your inheritance, which You have redeemed through Your greatness, which You have brought out of Egypt with a mighty hand. [27] Remember Your servants, Abraham, Isaac, and Jacob. Do not look at the stubbornness of this people or at their wickedness or their sin. [28] Otherwise, the land from which You brought us may say, 'Because the LORD was not able to bring them into the land which He promised them and because He hated them, He has brought them out to slay them in the wilderness.' [29] Yet they are Your people, Your inheritance, whom You brought out by Your mighty power and by Your stretched-out arm."

The Second Pair of Tablets

10 At that time the LORD said to me, "Cut out for yourself two tablets of stone like the first and come up to Me onto the mountain and make an ark of wood for yourself. [2] I will write on the tablets the words that were on the first tablets which you broke, and you shall put them in the ark."

[3] So I made an ark of acacia wood and cut out two tablets of stone just like the first and went up onto the mountain with the two tablets in my hand. [4] He wrote on the tablets just like the first writing, the Ten Commandments which the LORD spoke to you at the mountain out of the midst of the fire on the day of the assembly, and the LORD gave them to me. [5] I turned around and came down from the mountain and put the tablets in the ark which I had made, and there they are, just as the LORD commanded me.

[6] (The children of Israel set out from Beeroth of the sons of Jaakan to Moserah. There Aaron died and was buried, and his son Eleazar ministered in the priest's office in his place. [7] From there they journeyed to Gudgodah, and from Gudgodah to Jotbathah, a land of rivers of waters. [8] At that time the LORD set apart the tribe of Levi to carry the ark of the covenant of the LORD, to stand before the LORD to minister to Him, and to bless in His name, to this day. [9] Therefore, Levi has no portion or inheritance with his brothers. The LORD is his inheritance, just as the LORD your God promised him.)

[10] As for me, I stayed on the mountain like the first time, forty days and forty nights, and the LORD listened to me at that time also. The LORD was not willing to destroy you. [11] The LORD said to me, "Arise, take your journey before the people, so that they may go in and possess the land which I swore to give to their fathers."

The Essence of the Law

[12] Now, Israel, what does the LORD your God require of you, but to fear the LORD your God, to walk in all His ways, and to love Him, and to serve the LORD your God with all your heart and with all your soul, [13] to keep the commandments of the LORD and His statutes which I am commanding you today for your good?

[14] Indeed, heaven and the highest heavens belong to the LORD your God, also the earth with all that is in it. [15] The LORD delighted only in your fathers, to love them; and He chose their descendants after them, *even* you above all people, as *it* is today. [16] Therefore, circumcise your heart, and do not be stubborn anymore. [17] For the LORD your God is the God of gods and Lord of lords, the great, the mighty, and the fearsome God who is unbiased and takes no bribe. [18] He executes the judgment of the orphan and the widow and loves the foreigner, giving him food and clothing. [19] Therefore, love the foreigner, for you were foreigners in the land of Egypt. [20] You must fear the LORD your God. You must serve Him and cling to Him, and swear by His name. [21] He is your praise, and He is your God, who has done for you these great and fearsome things which your eyes have seen. [22] Your fathers went down into Egypt with seventy people, and now the LORD your God has made you as numerous as the stars of heaven.

Love and Obey

11 You must love the LORD your God and keep His charge, His statutes, His ordinances, and His commandments always. [2] Know this day that I am not speaking with your children who

have not known and who have not seen the discipline of the LORD your God, His greatness, His mighty hand, and His outstretched arm, [3] and His signs and His works which He did in the midst of Egypt to Pharaoh, the king of Egypt, and to all his land, [4] and what He did to the army of Egypt, to their horses, and to their chariots, when He made the water of the Red Sea to flow over them as they pursued after you, and how the LORD utterly destroyed them, [5] and what He did to you in the wilderness until you came to this place, [6] and what He did to Dathan and Abiram, the sons of Eliab, the son of Reuben, when the earth opened its mouth and swallowed them up, their households, their tents, and everything that was in their possession, in the midst of all Israel. [7] But your eyes have seen all the great deeds of the LORD which He did.

[8] Therefore you must keep all the commandments which I am commanding you today, so that you may be strong and go in and possess the land which you are going to possess; [9] and that you may prolong your days in the land which the LORD swore to your fathers to give to them and to their descendants, a land flowing with milk and honey. [10] For the land which you are entering to possess is not like the land of Egypt from where you came, where you sowed your seed and watered it with your foot like a vegetable garden, [11] but the land, which you are entering to possess, is a land of hills and valleys and drinks water from the rain of heaven, [12] a land for which the LORD your God cares. The eyes of the LORD your God are always on it, from the beginning of the year even to the end of the year.

[13] It will be, if you will diligently obey My commandments which I am commanding you today, to love the LORD your God, and to serve Him with all your heart and with all your soul, [14] then I will give you the rain of your land in its season, the early rain and the latter rain, that you may gather in your grain and your wine and your oil. [15] I will provide grass in your fields for your livestock, that you may eat and be full.

[16] Take heed to yourselves that your heart be not deceived, and you turn away and serve other gods and worship them. [17] Then the LORD's wrath will be inflamed against you, and He will shut up the heavens so that there will be no rain and the land will not yield its fruit, and you will quickly perish from the good land which the LORD is giving you. [18] Therefore you must fix these words of mine in your heart and in your soul, and bind them as a sign on your hand, so that they may be as frontlets between your eyes. [19] You shall teach them to your children, speaking of them when you sit in your house and when you walk by the way, when you lie down, and when you rise up. [20] You shall write them on the doorposts of your house and on your gates, [21] so that your days and the days of your children may be multiplied in the land which the LORD swore to your fathers to give them, as long as the days of heaven on the earth.

[22] For if you diligently keep all these commandments which I am commanding you to do—to love the LORD your God, to walk in all His ways, and to hold fast to Him— [23] then the LORD will drive out all these nations from before you, and you will dispossess nations greater and mightier than you. [24] Every place where the soles of your feet tread will be yours. Your border will be from the wilderness to Lebanon, from the river, the River Euphrates, as far as the *Mediterranean* Sea. [25] No man will be able to resist you, for the LORD your God shall lay the fear of you and the dread of you on all the land where you shall tread, just as He has spoken to you.

[26] See, I am setting before you today a blessing and a curse: [27] the blessing if you obey the commandments of the LORD your God, which I am commanding you today, [28] and the curse, if you will not obey the commandments of the LORD your God, but turn from the way which I am commanding you today, to go after other gods which you have not known. [29] Now it shall be, when the LORD your God has brought you into the land which you are entering to possess, that you shall put the blessing on Mount Gerizim and the curse on Mount Ebal. [30] Are they not on the other side of the Jordan, west where the sun goes down, in the land of the Canaanites, who dwell in the plain opposite Gilgal, beside the oaks of Moreh? [31] For you will cross over the Jordan to go in to possess the land which the LORD your God is giving you, and you will possess it, and dwell in it. [32] You must be careful to do all the statutes and judgments which I am setting before you today.

The One Place of Worship

12 These are the statutes and judgments which you shall be careful to observe in the land, which the Lord, the God of your fathers, has given you to possess, all the days that you live on the earth. [2] You must utterly destroy all the places where the nations which you will possess served their gods, on the high mountains, and on the hills, and under every green tree. [3] And you shall overthrow their altars, and break their pillars, and burn their Asherah poles[1] with fire, and you shall cut down the engraved images of their gods, and eliminate their names out of that place.

[4] You shall not act this way toward the Lord your God. [5] But you must seek only the place which the Lord your God shall choose out of all your tribes to establish His name, and there you must go. [6] There you shall bring your burnt offerings, your sacrifices, your tithes, the offerings of your hand, your vows, your freewill offerings, and the firstborn of your herds and of your flocks. [7] There you must eat before the Lord your God, and you shall rejoice in all that you put your hand to, you and your households, where the Lord your God has blessed you.

[8] You are not to do all the things that we are doing here today, where every man does whatever is right in his own eyes. [9] For you have not yet come to the rest and to the inheritance which the Lord your God has given you. [10] But when you cross the Jordan, and dwell in the land which the Lord your God has given you to inherit, and when He gives you rest from all your enemies round about, so that you dwell in safety, [11] then there will be a place which the Lord your God will choose to cause His name to dwell. There you must bring all that I command you: your burnt offerings, and your sacrifices, your tithes, the offering of your hand, and all your choice vows which you vow to the Lord. [12] You will rejoice before the Lord your God, you, your sons, your daughters, your male servants, your female servants, and the Levite who is within your gates, for he has no portion or inheritance with you. [13] Be careful that you do not offer your burnt offerings in every place that you see. [14] Rather, in the place which the Lord will choose in one of your tribes, there you must offer your burnt offerings, and there you must do all that I command you.

[15] Notwithstanding, you may kill and eat meat within all your gates, whatever your heart desires, according to the blessing of the Lord your God which He has given you. The unclean and the clean may eat of it, of the gazelle and of the deer, [16] only you must not eat the blood. You shall pour it on the ground like water. [17] You may not eat within your gates the tithe of your grain, your wine, your oil, the firstborn of your herds or of your flock, any of your vows which you vow, your freewill offerings, or the offering of your hand. [18] Rather you must eat them before the Lord your God in the place which the Lord your God will choose—you, your son, your daughter, your male servant, your female servant, and the Levite that is within your gates—and you shall rejoice before the Lord your God in all that you undertake to do. [19] Take heed to yourself that you do not forsake the Levite as long as you live on the earth.

[20] When the Lord your God shall enlarge your border as He has promised you, and you say, "I will eat meat," because you desire to eat meat, then you may eat as much meat as your heart desires. [21] If the place which the Lord your God has chosen to put His name is too far from you, then you shall kill of your herd and of your flock, which the Lord has given you, as I have commanded you, and you must eat in your gates whatever your heart desires. [22] Even as the gazelle and the deer are eaten, so you shall eat them. The unclean and the clean shall eat of them alike. [23] Only be sure that you do not eat the blood. For the blood is the life, and you may not eat the life with the meat. [24] You must not eat it. You must pour it on the ground like water. [25] You must not eat it, so that it may go well with you and with your children after you, when you do that which is right in the sight of the Lord.

[26] You shall take only your holy things which you have, along with your vows, and go to the place which the Lord shall choose. [27] You must offer your burnt offerings, the meat and the blood, on the altar of the Lord your God; and the blood of your sacrifices will be poured out on the altar of the Lord your God, and you shall eat the meat. [28] Observe and hear all these words which I command

you, so that it may go well with you and with your children after you forever, when you do that which is good and right in the sight of the Lord your God.

[29] When the Lord your God shall cut off the nations from before you, where you go to possess them, and you dispossess them, and dwell in their land, [30] take heed to yourself so that you are not ensnared by following them, after they have been destroyed before you, and that you not inquire after their gods, saying, "How did these nations serve their gods? Even so I will do likewise." [31] You shall not do so to the Lord your God, for every abomination to the Lord, which He hates, they have done to their gods. They have even burned their sons and their daughters in the fire to their gods.

[32] Whatever I command you, be careful to do it. You shall not add to it or take away from it.

Idolatry

13 If a prophet or a dreamer of dreams arises among you and gives you a sign or a wonder, [2] and the sign or the wonder comes to pass concerning that which he spoke to you, saying, "Let us go after other gods," which you have not known, "and let us serve them," [3] you must not listen to the words of that prophet or that dreamer of dreams, for the Lord your God is testing you, to know whether you love the Lord your God with all your heart and with all your soul. [4] You must follow after the Lord your God, fear Him, and keep His commandments, obey His voice, and you must serve Him, and cling to Him. [5] That prophet or that dreamer of dreams must be put to death because he has spoken in order to turn you away from the Lord your God, who brought you out of the land of Egypt and redeemed you out of the house of bondage, to entice you away from the way in which the Lord your God commanded you to walk. So you must put the evil away from your midst.

[6] If your brother, the son of your mother, or your son, or your daughter, or your beloved wife, or your friend, who is as your own soul, entices you secretly, saying, "Let us go and serve other gods," which you have not known, neither you nor your fathers, [7] namely, of the gods of the people who are all around you, near you or far away from you, from one end of the earth to the other end of the earth, [8] you shall not consent to him or listen to him, neither should your eye pity him, nor shall you spare or conceal him, [9] but you must surely kill him. Your hand must be first upon him to put him to death, and afterwards, the hand of all the people. [10] You shall stone him with stones so that he dies because he has sought to entice you away from the Lord your God who brought you out of the land of Egypt, from the house of bondage. [11] All Israel shall hear and fear and no more do any such wickedness as this among you.

[12] If you hear it said in one of your cities, in which the Lord your God has given you to dwell, saying, [13] "Certain men, the sons of wickedness, are gone out from among you and have seduced the inhabitants of their city, saying, 'Let us go and serve other gods,'" which you have not known, [14] then you shall inquire, search out, and ask diligently. If it be true and certain that such an abomination has been among you, [15] you shall surely put the inhabitants of that city to the sword, utterly destroying it, all that is in it and its livestock—with the edge of the sword. [16] You must gather all the spoils of it into the middle of the street and burn the city with fire along with all the spoils within it for the Lord your God, and it will be a heap forever. It must not be rebuilt. [17] Nothing of the cursed thing there must cling to your hand, so that the Lord may turn from the fierceness of His anger and show you mercy, have compassion on you, and multiply you, just as He swore to your fathers, [18] if you listen to the voice of the Lord your God, to keep all His commandments which I command you today, and do that which is right in the eyes of the Lord your God.

Clean and Unclean Food

Lev 11:1–23

14 You are the sons of the Lord your God. You shall not cut yourselves or make any baldness between your eyes for the dead. [2] For you are a holy people to the Lord your God, and the Lord

13 Wooden symbols of a female deity.

has chosen you to be a peculiar people to Himself, treasured above all the nations that are on the earth.

[3] You must not eat any detestable thing. [4] These are the animals which you may eat: the ox, the sheep, and the goat, [5] the deer, the gazelle, the fallow deer, the wild goat, and the ibex, and the antelope, and the mountain sheep. [6] You may eat every animal with divided hooves, with the hoof divided into two parts, and that chews the cud. [7] Nevertheless, you may not eat of these that chew the cud, or of them that divide the hoof: the camel, the rabbit, and the coney. For they chew the cud, but their hoof is not divided, therefore they are unclean to you. [8] The pig is unclean to you because it divides the hoof, yet it does not chew the cud. You must not eat of their flesh or touch their dead carcass.

[9] These you shall eat of all that are in the water: All that have fins and scales you may eat. [10] Whatever does not have fins and scales you may not eat. It is unclean to you.

[11] You may eat of all clean birds. [12] However, these are the ones which you cannot eat: the eagle, the vulture, the buzzard, [13] the red kite, the falcon, and the kite after its kind, [14] every raven after its kind, [15] and the ostrich, the owl, the seagull, and the hawk after its kind, [16] the little owl, and the great owl, and the white owl, [17] the pelican, the carrion vulture, and the cormorant, [18] the stork, and the heron after its kind, and the hoopoe, and the bat.

[19] Every creeping thing that flies is unclean to you. They must not be eaten. [20] You may eat all the clean birds.

[21] You must not eat of anything that dies of itself, but you may give it to the foreigner that is in your gates, so that he may eat it, or you may sell it to a foreigner, for you are a holy people to the LORD your God.

You shall not boil a young goat in its mother's milk.

Tithes

[22] You must be certain to tithe all the produce of your seed, so that the field produces year by year. [23] You must eat before the LORD your God, in the place in which He shall choose to place His name, the tithe of your grain, of your wine, of your oil, and of the firstborn of your herds and of your flocks so that you may learn to always fear the LORD your God. [24] If the distance is too long for you, so that you are not able to carry it, because the place is too far from you, where the LORD your God shall choose to set His name, when the LORD your God blesses you, [25] then you shall exchange it for money and bind up the money in your hand and go to the place which the LORD your God shall choose. [26] Then you may spend that money for whatever your heart desires, for oxen, or for sheep, or for wine, or for strong drink, or for whatever your heart desires, and you may eat there before the LORD your God, and you shall rejoice, you, and your household, [27] and the Levite that is within your gates. You must not forsake him, for he has no portion or inheritance with you.

[28] At the end of three years you must bring forth all the tithe of your produce the same year and lay it up within your gates. [29] Then the Levite (because he has no portion or inheritance with you), the foreigner, the fatherless, and the widow, who are within your gates, shall come and shall eat and be satisfied, so that the LORD your God may bless you in all the work of your hand which you do.

The Sabbatical Year
Lev 25:8–38

15 At the end of every seven years you shall grant a relinquishing *of debts*. [2] This is the manner of the relinquishing: Every creditor that has loaned anything to his neighbor shall relinquish it. He shall not exact it of his neighbor, or of his brother, because it is called the LORD's relinquishment. [3] You may collect it from a foreigner, but that which your brother has that is yours your hand shall release. [4] However, there will be no poor among you, for the LORD will greatly bless you in the land which the LORD your God has given you for an inheritance to possess, [5] if only you carefully obey the voice of the LORD your God, by carefully observing all these commandments which I command you today. [6] For the LORD your God will bless you, just as He promised you, and you will lend to many nations, but you

shall not borrow. You will reign over many nations, but they will not reign over you.

[7] If there be among you a poor man, one of your brothers within any of your gates in your land which the LORD your God has given you, you must not harden your heart or shut your hand from your poor brother. [8] But you shall open your hand wide to him and must surely lend him what is sufficient for his need, in that which he lacks. [9] Beware lest there be a wicked thought in your heart, saying, "The seventh year, the year of release, is at hand," and your eye be evil against your poor brother and you give him nothing, and he cry out to the LORD against you, and it become sin in you. [10] You must surely give to him, and your heart shall not be grieved when you give to him, because in this thing the LORD your God will bless you in all your works, and in all that you put your hand to do. [11] For the poor will never cease from being in the land. Therefore, I command you, saying, "You shall open your hand wide to your brother, to your poor and needy in your land."

Freeing Servants
Ex 21:2–6; Lev 25:38–55

[12] If your brother, a Hebrew man, or a Hebrew woman, is sold to you and serves you six years, then in the seventh year you must let him go free from you. [13] When you send him out free from you, you must not let him go away empty-handed. [14] You shall supply him liberally out of your flock, out of your floor, and out of your winepress. From that with which the LORD your God has blessed you, you shall give to him. [15] You shall remember that you were a slave in the land of Egypt and the LORD your God redeemed you. Therefore, I command this to you today.

[16] It shall be, if he says to you, "I will not go away from you," because he loves you and your house, because he is well off with you, [17] then you must take an awl and pierce it through his ear into the door, and he shall be your servant forever. And you shall also do likewise to your female servant.

[18] It will not seem difficult for you when you send him away free from you, for he has been worth a double hired servant[1] in serving you six years. Then the LORD your God will bless you in all that you do.

The Firstborn Animals

[19] You must sanctify all the firstborn males that come out of your herd and flock to the LORD your God. You must do no work with the firstborn of your bulls or shear the firstborn of your sheep. [20] You shall eat it before the LORD your God year by year in the place where the LORD shall choose, you and your household. [21] If there is any defect in it, if it is lame or blind or has a serious defect, you shall not sacrifice it to the LORD your God. [22] You shall eat it within your gates. The unclean and the clean person alike shall eat it, as if it were a gazelle or a deer. [23] Only you must not eat its blood. You shall pour it on the ground like water.

The Passover
Ex 12:14–20; Lev 23:4–8; Nu 28:16–25

16 Observe the month of Aviv[2] and keep the Passover to the LORD your God, for in the month of Aviv the LORD your God brought you out of Egypt by night. [2] Therefore, you must sacrifice the Passover to the LORD your God, from the flock or the herd, in the place where the LORD shall choose to place His name. [3] You must not eat leavened bread with it. For seven days you must eat unleavened bread, the bread of affliction, for you came out of the land of Egypt in a hurry, so that you may remember all the days of your life the day when you came out of the land of Egypt. [4] There must not be any leavened bread seen with you within all your borders for seven days, nor may any of the meat which you sacrificed in the evening on the first day remain overnight until morning.

[5] You may not sacrifice the Passover within any of your gates that the LORD your God has given you. [6] But at the place where the LORD your God chooses to place His name, there you shall sacrifice the Passover in the evening at sunset, at the time that you came out of Egypt. [7] You shall roast and eat it in the place where the LORD your

---

[1] 18 Or *double the amount.*   [2] 1 March-April in the modern calendar.

God will choose, and you must return in the morning, and go to your tents. [8] For six days you must eat unleavened bread, and on the seventh day there shall be a solemn assembly to the LORD your God. You must do no work *on that day*.

The Feast of Weeks
Lev 23:15–22; Nu 28:26–31

[9] You must count seven weeks for yourself. Begin counting the seven weeks from the time you begin to put the sickle to the standing grain. [10] You must keep the Feast of Weeks to the LORD your God with a tribute of a freewill offering from your hand, which you must give to the LORD your God, in proportion to how much the LORD your God has blessed you. [11] You shall rejoice before the LORD your God—you, your son, your daughter, your male servant, your female servant, the Levite who is within your gates, the foreigner, the orphan, and the widow who are among you—in the place where the LORD your God has chosen to place His name. [12] You must remember that you were a slave in Egypt, and you must be careful to observe these statutes.

The Feast of Tabernacles
Lev 23:33–43; Nu 29:12–39

[13] You shall observe the Feast of Tabernacles seven days after you have gathered in your threshing floor and your winepress, [14] and you shall rejoice in your feast, you, your son, your daughter, your male servant, your female servant, the Levite, the foreigner, the orphan, and the widow who are within your gates. [15] You are to celebrate the festival for seven days to the LORD your God in the place where the LORD your God will choose, because the LORD your God will bless you in all your produce, and in all the works of your hands. Therefore, you will indeed rejoice.

[16] Three times a year all your males must appear before the LORD your God in the place where He will choose: at the Feast of Unleavened Bread, at the Feast of Weeks, and at the Feast of Tabernacles, and they must not appear before the LORD empty. [17] Every man must give as he is able, in proportion to the blessing of the LORD your God, which He has given you.

Judges

[18] You must appoint judges and officers in all your gates, which the LORD your God gives you, throughout your tribes, and they shall judge the people with righteous judgment. [19] You must not pervert judgment nor show partiality. You must not accept a bribe, for a bribe blinds the eyes of the wise and perverts the words of the righteous. [20] You must follow that which is altogether just, so that you may live and inherit the land which the LORD your God is giving you.

Idolatry Forbidden

[21] You must not plant for yourself an Asherah[1] of any trees near the altar of the LORD your God, which you make for yourself. [22] You shall not set up for yourself any image, which the LORD your God hates.

17 You must not sacrifice to the LORD your God any bull or sheep that has a blemish or any defect, for that is detestable to the LORD your God. [2] If there be found among you, within any of your gates which the LORD your God gives you, man or woman, who has acted wickedly in the sight of the LORD your God, by transgressing His covenant, [3] and has gone and served other gods and worshipped them, either the sun, or moon, or any of the host of heaven, which I have not commanded, [4] and if it is told to you, and you have heard of it, and investigated diligently, and it is true, and the matter is certain that such a detestable thing has happened in Israel, [5] then you must bring forth that man or that woman who has committed that wicked thing to your gates, that very man or woman, and stone them with stones until they die. [6] On the testimony of two or three witnesses he that is to die must be put to death, but on the testimony of one witness he cannot be put to death. [7] The hands of the witnesses shall be first against him to put him to death, and afterward the hands of all the people. So you shall purge the evil from among you.

Courts of Law

[8] If there arises a matter too difficult for you in judgment, between one kind of bloodshed and another, between one kind of lawsuit and another, and between one kind of assault and another, matters of controversy within your gates, then you must arise and go up to the place where the LORD your God shall choose. [9] You must go to the Levitical priests or to the judge in *office* those days, and inquire, and they will show you the verdict of judgment. [10] You shall do according to the verdict which they declare to you from the place where the LORD will choose to show you, and you must be careful to do all that they instruct you to do. [11] You must do according to the terms of the law which they instruct you and according to the verdict which they tell you. You must not deviate from the sentence which they show you, to the right or to the left. [12] The man who acts presumptuously and does not listen to the priest who stands to minister before the LORD your God, or to the judge—that man must die, and you must purge the evil from Israel. [13] Then all the people will hear, and fear, and not act presumptuously again.

Appointing a King

[14] When you have come into the land which the LORD your God gives you and possess it and dwell there and then say, "I will set a king over me just like all the nations that are around me," [15] you must set a king over you whom the LORD your God will choose. You must select a king over you who is from among your brothers. You may not select a foreigner over you who is not your countryman. [16] What is more, he shall not accumulate horses for himself or cause the people to return to Egypt in order that he accumulate horses, for as the LORD has said to you, "You must not go back that way ever again." [17] He shall not acquire many wives for himself, lest his heart turn away; nor shall he acquire for himself excess silver and gold. [18] It must be, when he sits on the throne of his kingdom, that he shall write a copy of this law for himself on a scroll before the priests, the Levites, [19] It must be with him, and he must read it all the days of his life so that he may learn to fear the LORD his God, and carefully observe all the words of this law and these statutes, and do them, [20] that his heart will not be lifted up above his brothers and so that he may not turn aside from the commandment, to the right or to the left, to the end, so that he may prolong his days in his kingdom, he and his children, in the midst of Israel.

Provision for Priests and Levites

18 The Levitical priests and all the tribe of Levi will not have any portion or inheritance with Israel. They must eat the offerings of the LORD made by fire and His portion. [2] They will have no inheritance among their brothers. The LORD is their inheritance, just as He has said to them.

[3] This shall be the priest's due from the people, from them that offer a sacrifice, whether it be an ox or sheep: they shall give to the priest the shoulder, the two cheeks, and the stomach. [4] You must give him the first fruit of your grain, of your wine, and of your oil, and the first of the fleece of your sheep also. [5] For the LORD your God has chosen him out of all your tribes to stand to minister in the name of the LORD, him and his sons forever.

[6] If a Levite comes from any of your gates out of all Israel, where he lives, and comes with all the desire of his mind to the place where the LORD shall choose, [7] then he shall minister in the name of the LORD his God, as all his brothers the Levites do, who stand there before the LORD. [8] They must have the same portions to eat, besides any profits he may receive from the sale of his father's inheritance.

A Call to Holiness

[9] When you enter into the land which the LORD your God gives you, you must not learn to practice the abominations of those nations. [10] There must not be found among you anyone who makes his son or his daughter pass through the fire, or who uses divination, or uses witchcraft, or an interpreter of omens, or a sorcerer, [11] or one who casts spells, or a spiritualist, or an occultist, or a necromancer. [12] For all that do these things are an abomination

---

[1] 21 Wooden symbol of a female deity.

to the Lord, and because of these abominations the Lord your God will drive them out from before you. [13] You must be blameless before the Lord your God.

The Prophet

[14] For these nations, which you shall possess, listened to soothsayers and to diviners, but as for you, the Lord your God has not permitted you to do so. [15] The Lord your God will raise up for you a prophet from the midst of you, of your brothers, like me. You must listen to him. [16] This is according to all that you desired of the Lord your God in Horeb on the day of the assembly, saying, "Let me not hear again the voice of the Lord my God, nor let me see this great fire anymore, so that I do not die."

[17] The Lord said to me, "They have done well in what they have said. [18] I will raise up a prophet from among their brothers, like you, and will put My words in his mouth, and he will speak to them all that I command him. [19] It will be that whoever will not listen to My words which he will speak in My name, I will require it of him. [20] But the prophet, who presumes to speak a word in my name, which I have not commanded him to speak, or who shall speak in the name of other gods—that prophet shall die."

[21] And you may say in your heart, "How can we know the word which the Lord has not spoken?" [22] When a prophet speaks in the name of the Lord, if the thing does not occur or come to pass, that is the thing which the Lord has not spoken; the prophet has spoken it presumptuously. You shall not be afraid of him.

Cities of Refuge

Nu 35:6–34; Dt 4:41–43; Jos 20:1–9

19 When the Lord your God has cut off the nations, whose land the Lord your God is giving you, and you dispossess them, and dwell in their cities, and in their houses, [2] you shall set apart three cities for yourselves in the midst of your land, which the Lord your God is giving you to possess. [3] You shall prepare a roadway for yourself, and divide the territory of your land into three parts, which the Lord your God is giving you to inherit, so that every manslayer may flee there.

[4] This is the word concerning the manslayer who will flee there, so that he may live: Whoever kills his neighbor unintentionally, whom he did not hate previously, [5] like when a man goes into the forest with his neighbor to cut wood, and his hand raises the axe to cut down the tree, and the axe head slips from the handle and lands on his neighbor causing him to die, then he may flee to one of those cities, and live. [6] Otherwise the avenger of blood might, while he is angry, pursue the manslayer and overtake him (because the way is long) and kill him, even though he was not worthy of death (since he did not hate him previously). [7] Therefore, i command you, saying, "You shall set apart three cities for yourselves."

[8] If the Lord your God enlarges your borders as He promised your fathers, and gives you all the land which He promised to give to your fathers, [9] and if you will carefully keep all these commandments, which I command you today, to love the Lord your God, and to always walk in His ways, then you must add three cities more for yourself, besides these three. [10] Then innocent blood will not be shed in your land, which the Lord your God is giving you for an inheritance, and blood guiltiness be on you.

[11] But if any man hates his neighbor, and lies in wait for him, and rises up against him, and mortally strikes him, causing him to die, and flees to one of these cities, [12] then the elders of his city must send and fetch him from there, and deliver him to the hand of the avenger of blood, so that he may die. [13] Your eye must not pity him, but you must remove the guilt of innocent blood from Israel, so that it may go well with you.

[14] You shall not remove your neighbor's landmark, which they of old time have set in your inheritance, which you shall inherit in the land that the Lord your God is giving you to possess.

Witnesses

[15] A single witness must not rise up against a man on account of any iniquity or any sin that he sins. At the testimony of two witnesses or at the testimony of three witnesses shall the matter be established.

[16] If a false witness rises up against any man to testify against him to accuse him of doing wrong, [17] then both the men between whom the controversy is must stand before the Lord, before the priests and the judges, who are in *office* those days. [18] The judges will thoroughly investigate, and if the witness is a false witness and has testified falsely against his brother, [19] then you must do to him as he conspired to have done to his brother. In this way you must remove the evil from among you. [20] Those who remain will hear and fear, and will never again commit any such evil among you. [21] You must not show pity. But life will be for life, eye for eye, tooth for tooth, hand for hand, foot for foot.

Rules of Warfare

20 When you go out to battle against your enemies, and see horses, and chariots, and a people that outnumber you, do not be afraid of them, for the Lord your God is with you, who brought you up out of the land of Egypt. [2] It will be, when you approach the battle, that the priest will approach and speak to the people, [3] and he shall say to them, "Hear, O Israel, you approach today to do battle against your enemies. Do not be fainthearted. Do not fear, and do not tremble or be terrified because of them. [4] For the Lord your God is He that goes with you, to fight for you against your enemies, to save you."

[5] The officers will speak to the people, saying, "What man is there who has built a new house and has not dedicated it? Let him go and return to his house, lest he die in the battle, and another man dedicate it. [6] What man is there who has planted a vineyard, and has not yet eaten of it? Let him also go and return to his house, lest he die in the battle, and another man eat of it. [7] What man is there who is engaged to a woman but has not married her? Let him go and return to his house, lest he die in the battle, and another man take her." [8] The officers are to speak further to the people, and they shall say, "What man is there that is fearful and fainthearted? Let him go and return to his house, lest his brother's heart faint as well as his heart." [9] It will be, when the officers have made an end of speaking to the people, that they must make captains of the armies to lead the people.

[10] When you come near to a city to fight against it, then proclaim peace to it. [11] It shall be, if it gives you a reply of peace and opens to you, then it must be that all the people that are found within shall become slaves to you and they shall serve you. [12] If it will not make peace with you but makes war against you, then you are to besiege it. [13] And when the Lord your God has delivered it into your hands, you are to slay every male there with the edge of the sword. [14] But the women, and the little ones, and the livestock, and all that is in the city, all the spoil within, you are to take to yourself, and you will eat the spoil of your enemies, which the Lord your God has given you. [15] Thus you are to do to all the cities which are far away, which are not the cities of these nearby nations.

[16] But of the cities of these people, which the Lord your God is giving you for an inheritance, you must not leave alive anything that breathes. [17] But you shall completely destroy them: namely, the Hittites, and the Amorites, the Canaanites, and the Perizzites, the Hivites, and the Jebusites, just as the Lord your God has commanded you, [18] so that they do not teach you to participate in all their abominations, which they have done to their gods, causing you to sin against the Lord your God.

[19] When you lay siege to a city for a long time, in making war against it in order to take it, you shall not destroy the trees there by chopping them down with an axe, for you may eat from them, and you shall not cut them down. For the tree of the field is not a man in which to lay siege. [20] However, you may destroy and cut down only the trees which you know are not fruit trees, so that you may build siege engines against the city that makes war with you until it falls.

Atonement for Unsolved Murders

21 If someone is found slain in the land which the Lord your God is giving you to possess, lying in the field, and it is not known who has slain him, [2] then your elders and your judges are to come forth, and they must measure *how far* it is to the cities which are around him who was slain. [3] And it must be, that the city which is closest to the slain man, that is, the elders of that city shall take a heifer which has not been worked, that has never pulled in yoke, [4] and the elders of that city must bring down the heifer to a valley with flowing water, which is neither plowed nor sown, and shall break the heifer's neck there in the valley. [5] Then the priests, the sons of Levi, must come near, for the LORD your God has chosen them to minister to Him, and to bless in the name of the LORD, and by their word every controversy and every assault will be settled. [6] And all the elders of that city, which is nearest to the slain man, shall wash their hands over the heifer whose neck was broken in the valley. [7] Then they must answer and say, "Our hands have not shed this blood, and our eyes have not seen it. [8] Be merciful, O LORD, to Your people Israel, whom You have redeemed, and lay not innocent blood in the midst of Your people Israel." And the blood guilt will be forgiven them. [9] In this way you are to remove the guilt of innocent blood from among you when you do that which is right in the eyes of the LORD.

Marrying Female Captives

[10] When you go forth to war against your enemies, and the LORD your God has delivered them into your hands, and you have taken them captive, [11] and you see among the captives a beautiful woman, and have a desire for her to have her as your wife, [12] then you are to bring her home to your house, and she is to shave her head and trim her nails. [13] She must also discard the clothing of her captivity and shall remain in your house, and mourn her father and her mother for a full month. After that you may have relations with her, and be her husband, and she will be your wife. [14] It will be, if you are not pleased with her, then you must let her go wherever she pleases, but you may not sell her at all for money, nor are you to make merchandise of her, because you have humbled her.

The Right of the Firstborn

[15] If a man has two wives, one beloved and another unloved, and both have borne him children, both the loved one and the unloved one, and if the firstborn son is hers that is unloved, [16] then it must be, when he gives his sons the inheritance which he has, that he may not make the firstborn son of the loved come before the son of the unloved, who was indeed the firstborn. [17] On the contrary, he must acknowledge the son of the unloved for the firstborn, by giving him a double portion of all that he has, for he is the beginning of his strength. The right of the firstborn is his.

Dealing With a Rebellious Son

[18] If a man has a stubborn and rebellious son, who will not obey the voice of his father or the voice of his mother, and who, when they have disciplined him, will not listen to them, [19] then his father and his mother are to lay hold of him and bring him out to the elders of his city, to the gate of his city. [20] They shall say to the elders of his city, "This son of ours is stubborn and rebellious. He will not listen to us. He is a glutton and a drunkard." [21] Then all the men of his city must stone him with stones, until he dies. In this way you are to remove the evil from among you, and all Israel shall hear and fear.

Various Laws

[22] If a man has committed a sin worthy of death and is executed, and you hang him on a tree, [23] then his body must not remain all night on the tree, but you must bury him that day (for he that is hanged is accursed of God) so that your land may not be defiled, which the LORD your God is giving you for an inheritance.

22 You must not see your brother's ox or his sheep go astray and hide yourself from them. You must certainly bring them back to your brother. [2] If your brother is not near you or if you do not know him, then you are to bring it to your own house, and it will be with you until your brother seeks after it. Then you must return it to him. [3] In the same way, you must do so with his donkey, with his clothing, and with anything lost by your brother which he has lost and you have found. You must not hide yourself *from him*.

[4] You are not to see your brother's donkey or his ox fall down by the way and hide yourself from them. You certainly must help him to lift them up.

[5] A woman must not wear man's clothing, nor is a man to put on a woman's clothing. For all that do so are abominations to the LORD your God.

[6] If you happen to notice a bird's nest along the way, in any tree or on the ground, whether they be young ones or eggs, and the mother is sitting on the young or on the eggs, you are not to take the mother from the young. [7] You must certainly let the mother go, but you may take the young for yourself, so that it may be well with you, and that you may prolong your days.

[8] When you build a new house, you must make a guard rail for your roof so that you bring no blood guilt on your house, should anyone fall from there.

[9] You must not sow your vineyard with two kinds of seeds, or the fruit of your seed which you have sown and the fruit of your vineyard will be defiled.

[10] You must not plow with an ox and a donkey together.

[11] You must not wear clothing made of a material of wool and linen together.

[12] You must make tassels on the four quarters of your clothing with which you cover yourself.

Laws About Marriage

[13] If any man takes a wife and has sexual relations with her and then rejects her, [14] and accuses her of impropriety and publicly defames her, saying, "I married this woman, but when I had sexual relations with her, I found her not to be a virgin," [15] then the father and mother of the girl must produce *evidence* of the girl's virginity to the elders of the city at the gate. [16] The girl's father must say to the elders, "I gave my daughter to this man to wife, and he has rejected her. [17] What is more, he has accused her of impropriety, saying, 'I did not find your daughter to be a virgin.' However, this is the evidence of my daughter's virginity." And they shall spread the cloth before the elders of the city. [18] The elders of that city must take that man and punish him, [19] and they must fine him a hundred *shekels[1]* of silver and give them to the father of the girl, because he has publicly humiliated a virgin of Israel. Then she is to remain his wife. He may not divorce her all his days.

[20] But if the accusation is true, and the evidence of virginity does not exist for the girl, [21] then they shall bring the girl out to the door of her father's house, and the men of her city shall stone her with stones until she dies, because she has brought disgrace into Israel, to act like a whore in her father's house. In this way you may purge the evil from among you.

[22] If a man is discovered lying with a married woman, then both of them must die, both the man that lay with the woman, and the woman. In this way you may purge the evil from Israel.

[23] If a girl who is a virgin is engaged to a man, and *another* man finds her in the city and has sexual relations with her, [24] then you must bring them both out to the gate of that city and you must stone them with stones until they die, the girl because she did not cry out even though in the city, and the man because he has violated his neighbor's wife. In this way you may purge the evil from among you.

[25] But if a man finds an engaged girl in the field, and the man forces her and rapes her, then only the man that raped her shall die. [26] However, you are to do nothing to the girl. There is no sin worthy of death in the girl, for just as when a man rises against his neighbor and murders him, so is this matter. [27] For he found her in the field, the engaged girl cried out, but there was no one to save her.

[28] If a man finds a girl who is a virgin who is not engaged and seizes her and lies with her and they are discovered, [29] then the man who lay with her must give fifty shekels[2] of silver to the girl's father, and she shall be his wife because he has violated her. He may not divorce her all his days.

[30] A man must not marry his father's wife and in this way dishonor his father.

---

[1] 19 About 2½ pounds, or 1.2 kilograms.   [2] 29 About 1¼ pounds, or 575 grams.

Exclusion From the Assembly

23 No one who is emasculated or has his male organ cut off may enter the assembly of the Lord.

[2] No one of illegitimate birth may enter the assembly of the Lord. Even to his tenth generation no one *related to him* may enter the assembly of the Lord.

[3] No Ammonite or Moabite may enter the assembly of the Lord. Even to their tenth generation they may not enter the assembly of the Lord forever, [4] because they refused you bread and water on the way, when you came from out of Egypt and because they hired Balaam, the son of Beor of Pethor of Mesopotamia, against you to curse you. [5] Nevertheless, the Lord your God would not listen to Balaam. Instead the Lord your God turned the curse into a blessing on you because the Lord your God loves you. [6] You are not ever to seek their peace nor their prosperity all your days.

[7] You are not to abhor an Edomite, for he is your brother. You shall not abhor an Egyptian, because you were a foreigner in his land. [8] The children who are born of them may enter the assembly of the Lord in their third generation.

Uncleanness in the Camp

[9] When the army goes out against your enemies, then keep yourself from every wicked thing. [10] If there be among you any man who is not clean because of a nocturnal emission, then he must leave the camp. He may not re-enter the camp. [11] And it must be that when evening comes, he must wash himself with water, and at sunset he may re-enter the camp.

[12] You must also have a place outside the camp where one may go outside. [13] You must have a spade among your equipment, and it must be, when you relieve yourself outside, you must dig there and turn and cover up your excrement. [14] For the Lord your God walks in the midst of your camp, to deliver you, and to defeat your enemies before you. Therefore, your camp must be holy, so that He does not see any indecent thing among you, and turn away from you.

Various Laws

[15] You must not deliver *back* to his master a slave who has escaped from his master to you. [16] He is to dwell with you, even among you, in a place which he shall choose in one of your towns, where he prefers. You must not oppress him.

[17] There must never be a cult prostitute among the daughters of Israel nor a cult prostitute among the sons of Israel. [18] You must never bring the wage of a prostitute or the wage of a dog into the house of the Lord your God for any vow, for both of these are abominations to the Lord your God.

[19] You must not charge interest on a loan to your brother: interest on money, interest on food, or on anything that may be lent with interest. [20] You may charge interest to a foreigner, but to your brother you may not lend with interest so that the Lord your God may bless you in all to which you set your hand in the land which you are entering to possess.

[21] When you make a vow to the Lord your God, you must not be slow to pay it, for the Lord your God will surely require it of you, and it would be a sin to you. [22] But if you refrain from making a vow, it will not be a sin to you. [23] That which goes out of your lips you must keep and do, even a freewill offering, just as you have vowed to the Lord your God, what you have promised with your mouth.

[24] When you go into your neighbor's vineyard, you may eat grapes to your fill at your own pleasure, but you may not put any in your basket. [25] When you enter into the standing grain of your neighbor, you may pluck the ears with your hand, but you may not use a sickle on your neighbor's standing grain.

Laws About Marriage and Divorce

24 When a man takes a wife and marries her, and it happens that she finds no favor in his eyes because he has found some indecency in her, then let him write her a bill of divorce and put it in her hand and send her out of his house. [2] When she departs out of his house, she may go and be another man's wife. [3] If the second husband rejects her and writes her a bill of divorce and puts it in her hand and sends her out of his house, or if the second husband who took her to be his wife dies, [4] her first husband,

who sent her away, may not take her again to be his wife, since she is defiled, for that is abomination before the Lord, and you must not bring sin on the land, which the Lord your God is giving you for an inheritance.

[5] When a man has taken a new wife, he shall not go out to war or be charged with any business; he is to be free at home one year, and must bring joy to his wife which he has taken.

Various Laws

[6] No man shall take a lower or upper millstone as a pledge, for he would be taking a man's life as a pledge.

[7] If a man is found kidnapping any of his brothers of the children of Israel, and makes property of him or sells him, then that kidnapper must die, and you must remove the evil from among you.

[8] Be careful with an outbreak of leprosy, that you diligently observe and do according to all that the Levitical priests instruct you. As I have commanded them, so you must carefully do. [9] Remember what the Lord your God did to Miriam on the way, after you came out of Egypt.

[10] When you do lend your brother anything, you may not go into his house to take his pledge. [11] You must stand outside, and the man to whom you lend must bring the pledge outside to you. [12] If the man is poor, you may not sleep with his pledge. [13] In any case, you must return the pledge to him when the sun goes down, so that he may sleep in his own cloak and bless you, and it will be righteousness to you before the Lord your God.

[14] You may not oppress a hired servant that is poor and needy, whether he is one of your brothers or one of your foreigners who are in your land within your towns. [15] You must give him his wages on that very day before the sun sets, for he is poor, and sets his heart on it, lest he cry against you to the Lord, and it be a sin to you.

[16] Fathers may not be put to death for the sons, nor shall sons be put to death for their fathers. Every man shall be put to death for his own sin.

[17] You must not pervert the justice of the foreigner or of the fatherless, nor take a widow's cloak as a pledge. [18] On the contrary, you must remember that you were a slave in Egypt and the Lord your God redeemed you there. Therefore, I command you to do this.

[19] Whenever you reap your harvest in your field and have forgotten a sheaf in the field, you may not go back to get it. It will be for the foreigner, for the fatherless, and for the widow, so that the Lord your God may bless you in all the work of your hands. [20] When you beat your olive tree, you may not go over the boughs again. It will be for the foreigner, for the fatherless, and for the widow. [21] When you gather the grapes of your vineyard, you shall not glean it again. It will be for the foreigner, for the fatherless, and for the widow. [22] You must remember that you were a slave in the land of Egypt. Therefore I command you to do this thing.

25 If there is a controversy between men, they are to go to court for judgment, so that the judges may judge them. Then they shall justify the righteous and condemn the wicked. [2] It must be, if the wicked man is worthy to be beaten, then the judge must make him lie down and be beaten in his presence, with the number of strikes his guilt deserves. [3] He may give him forty stripes, but no more, lest, if he should exceed and beat him more with numerous stripes, then your brother may appear contemptible to you.

[4] You must not muzzle the ox when he treads out the grain.

Levirate Marriage

[5] If brothers dwell together, and one of them dies without having had a child, the wife of the deceased may not marry outside *the family* to a stranger. Her husband's brother must go to her and take her to himself as a wife and perform the duty of a husband's brother to her. [6] It shall be, that the firstborn whom she bears shall continue in the name of his brother who is deceased, so that his name will not be blotted out of Israel.

[7] If the man does not want to take his brother's wife, then let his brother's wife go up to the gate to the elders and say, "My husband's brother refuses to raise up his brother's name in Israel. He will not perform the duty of my husband's brother." [8] Then the elders of his city shall call him, and speak to him, and if he persists and says, "I do not want to take her," [9] then his brother's wife must come to him

in the presence of the elders and remove his sandal from his foot, and spit in his face, and answer and say, "So shall it be done to that man who will not build up his brother's house." [10] His name will be called in Israel, "The house of him who has his sandal removed."

Various Laws

[11] When a man and his brother fight one another, and the wife of the one draws near in order to deliver her husband out of the hand of him who fights him, and reaches out her hand and seizes him by the private parts, [12] then you must cut off her hand. You must not pity her.

[13] You must not have in your bag different weights, a large and a small. [14] You must not have in your house differing measures, a large and a small. [15] But you must have a perfect and just weight—a perfect and just measure you must have, so that your days may be lengthened in the land which the Lord your God is giving you. [16] For all who do such things and all who act unjustly are an abomination to the Lord your God.

[17] Remember what Amalek did to you by the road when you were coming out of Egypt, [18] how he met you by the way and attacked at your rear all that were stragglers behind you, when you were exhausted and weary. He did not fear God. [19] Therefore it shall be, when the Lord your God has given you rest from all your surrounding enemies, in the land which the Lord your God is giving you for an inheritance to possess, that you must blot out the remembrance of Amalek from under heaven. You must not forget it.

First Fruits and Tithes

26 And it must be, when you come into the land which the Lord your God is giving you for an inheritance, and you possess it, and dwell in it, [2] that you shall take from the first of all the produce of the ground which you shall bring from your land that the Lord your God is giving you, and put it in a basket and go to the place where the Lord your God chooses to make His name abide. [3] You shall go to the priest in office at that time and say to him, "I profess this day to the Lord your God that I have come into the land which the Lord promised to our fathers to give us." [4] The priest will take the basket out of your hand and set it down before the altar of the Lord your God. [5] Then you must answer and say before the Lord your God, "A wandering Aramean[1] was my father, and he went down into Egypt, and sojourned there *with only* a few in number, but there he became a great, mighty, and populous nation. [6] However, the Egyptians mistreated and afflicted us, and laid upon us harsh labor. [7] And when we cried to the Lord God of our fathers, the Lord heard our voice, and looked on our affliction, our labor, and our oppression. [8] And the Lord brought us forth out of Egypt with a mighty hand and with an outstretched arm and with great terror, and with signs and wonders. [9] Then He brought us into this place, and has given us this land, a land that flows with milk and honey. [10] Now, indeed, I have brought the first fruits of the land, which you, O Lord, have given me." Then you must set it before the Lord your God and worship before the Lord your God. [11] You must rejoice in every good thing which the Lord your God has given to you and your house, you, and the Levite, as well as the foreigner who is among you.

[12] When you have finished tithing all the tithes of your income the third year, which is the year of tithing, and have given it to the Levite, the foreigner, the orphan, and the widow, that they may eat within your towns and be satisfied, [13] then you shall say before the Lord your God, "I have removed the sacred things out of my house and also have given them to the Levite, and to the foreigner, to the orphan, and to the widow, according to all Your commandments which You have commanded me. I have not transgressed Your commandments or forgotten them. [14] I have not eaten anything when in mourning, nor have I removed anything while unclean, nor offered anything to the dead. I have listened to the voice of the Lord my God and have done according to all that You have commanded me. [15] Look down from Your holy habitation, from heaven, and bless Your people Israel and the land which You have given us, as You swore to our fathers, a land flowing with milk and honey."

An Exhortation to Obey

[16] Today the Lord your God has commanded you to do these statutes and judgments. You must therefore keep and do them with all your heart and with all your soul. [17] You have affirmed today that the Lord is your God and vowed to walk in His ways, and to keep His statutes, and His commandments, and His judgments, and to listen to His voice. [18] And the Lord has affirmed today that you are His special people, just as He has promised you, and that you should keep all His commandments. [19] He will exalt you above all nations which He has made, in praise, and in name, and in honor; and that you may be a holy people to the Lord your God, just as He has spoken.

The Altar on Mount Ebal

27 Then Moses and the elders of Israel commanded the people, saying: Keep all the commandments which I am commanding you today. [2] On the day when you cross over the Jordan into the land which the Lord your God is giving you, you must set up for yourself great stones, and cover them with plaster. [3] Then you must write all the words of this law on them, when you cross over, so that you may enter into the land which the Lord your God is giving you, a land flowing with milk and honey, just as the Lord God of your fathers promised you. [4] Therefore, when you cross over the Jordan, you shall set up these stones, which I am commanding you today, on Mount Ebal, and you shall cover them with plaster. [5] There you must build an altar to the Lord your God, an altar of stones. You must not use any iron tool on them. [6] You must build the altar of the Lord your God with whole stones, and you must offer burnt offerings on it to the Lord your God. [7] You must offer peace offerings and eat there, and rejoice before the Lord your God. [8] You must write all the words of this law very clearly on the stones.

[9] Moses and the Levitical priests spoke to all Israel, saying: Be silent and listen, O Israel. Today you have become the people of the Lord your God. [10] Therefore, you must obey the voice of the Lord your God and do His commandments and His statutes, which I am commanding you today.

[11] Moses commanded the people the same day, saying:

[12] These shall stand on Mount Gerizim to bless the people when you cross over the Jordan: Simeon, Levi, Judah, Issachar, Joseph, and Benjamin. [13] And these must stand on Mount Ebal for the curse: Reuben, Gad, Asher, Zebulun, Dan, and Naphtali.

[14] The Levites will answer and say to all the men of Israel with a loud voice:

[15] "Cursed is the man who makes any graven or molded image, an abomination to the Lord, the work of the hands of the craftsman, and puts it in a secret place." And all the people shall answer and say, "Amen."

[16] "Cursed is he who disrespects his father or his mother." And all the people shall say, "Amen."

[17] "Cursed is he who removes his neighbor's landmark." And all the people shall say, "Amen."

[18] "Cursed is he who misleads the blind man on the road." And all the people shall say, "Amen."

[19] "Cursed is he who perverts justice for the foreigner, orphan, and widow." And all the people shall say, "Amen."

[20] "Cursed is he who lies with his father's wife, for he dishonors his father." And all the people shall say, "Amen."

[21] "Cursed is he who lies with any kind of beast." And all the people shall say, "Amen."

[22] "Cursed is he who lies with his sister, the daughter of his father, or the daughter of his mother." And all the people shall say, "Amen."

[23] "Cursed is he who lies with his mother-in-law." And all the people shall say, "Amen."

[24] "Cursed is he who strikes down his neighbor secretly." And all the people shall say, "Amen."

[25] "Cursed is he who receives pay to slay an innocent person." And all the people shall say, "Amen."

[26] "Cursed is he who does not confirm all the words of this law by doing them." And all the people shall say, "Amen."

1 5 Rebekah, Jacob's mother, was an Aramean.

Blessings for Obedience

28 Now it will be, if you will diligently obey the voice of the LORD your God, being careful to do all His commandments which I am commanding you today, then the LORD your God will set you high above all the nations of the earth. [2] And all these blessings will come on you and overtake you if you listen to the voice of the LORD your God.

[3] You will be blessed in the city and blessed in the field.

[4] Your offspring will be blessed, and the produce of your ground, and the offspring of your livestock, the increase of your herd and the flocks of your sheep.

[5] Your basket and your kneading bowl will be blessed.

[6] You will be blessed when you come in and blessed when you go out.

[7] The LORD will cause your enemies who rise up against you to be defeated before you; they will come out against you one way and flee before you seven ways.

[8] The LORD will command the blessing on you in your barns and in all that you set your hand to do, and He will bless you in the land which the LORD your God is giving you.

[9] The LORD will establish you as a holy people to Himself, just as He swore to you, if you will keep the commandments of the LORD your God and walk in His ways. [10] All people of the earth shall see that you are called by the name of the LORD, and they shall be afraid of you. [11] The LORD will make you overflow in prosperity, in the offspring of your body, in the offspring of your livestock, and in the produce of your ground, in the land which the LORD swore to your fathers to give you.

[12] The LORD will open up to you His good treasure, the heavens, to give the rain to your land in its season and to bless all the work of your hand. You will lend to many nations, but you will not borrow. [13] The LORD will make you the head and not the tail; you will only be above and you will not be beneath, if you listen to the commandments of the LORD your God, which I am commanding you today, to observe and to do them. [14] Also, you shall not turn aside from any of the words which I am commanding you today, to the right hand or to the left, to go after other gods to serve them.

Warnings Against Disobedience

[15] But it will happen, if you will not listen to the voice of the LORD your God, by being careful to do all His commandments and His statutes which I am commanding you today, that all these curses will come upon you and overtake you.

[16] You will be cursed in the city and cursed in the field.

[17] Your basket and your kneading bowl will be cursed.

[18] Your offspring will be cursed along with the fruit of your land, the produce of your herd, and the flocks of your sheep.

[19] You will be cursed when you come in and cursed when you go out.

[20] The LORD will send cursing, vexation, and rebuke on you in all that you set your hand to do, until you are destroyed and until you perish quickly because of the wickedness of your doings, by which you have forsaken Me. [21] The LORD will make pestilence cling to you until it has consumed you from the land, which you are going to possess. [22] The LORD will strike you with a wasting disease, with a fever, with an inflammation, with an extreme heat, with the sword, with blight, and with mildew, and they shall pursue you until you perish. [23] The heavens which are over your head will be bronze, and the earth that is under you will be iron. [24] The LORD will make the rain of your land powder and dust. It will come from heaven down on you until you are destroyed.

[25] The LORD will cause you to be defeated before your enemies, and you will go out one way against them and flee seven ways before them, and will become *an object* of terror to all the kingdoms of the earth. [26] Your carcass will be meat for all the fowls of the air and beasts of the earth, and no man will frighten them away. [27] The LORD will strike you with the boils of Egypt and with tumors, eczema, and with the itch, from which you cannot be healed. [28] The LORD will strike you with madness, and blindness, and bewilderment of heart. [29] You will grope at noon, as the blind man gropes in darkness, and you will not prosper in your ways. You will only be oppressed and continually robbed, and no man will save you.

[30] You will be engaged to a woman and another man shall rape her. You will build a house, but you will not dwell in it. You will plant a vineyard, but you will not gather its grapes. [31] Your ox will be killed before your eyes, and you will not eat of it. Your donkey will be violently taken away from before you and will not be returned to you. Your sheep will be given to your enemies, and you will have no one to rescue them. [32] Your sons and your daughters will be given to another people. Your eyes will look and fail with longing for them all day long, but there will be nothing you can do. [33] A nation that you do not know will consume the produce of your land and all your labors, and you will be nothing but oppressed and crushed all the time. [34] You will go insane because of what your eyes will see. [35] The LORD will strike you in the knees and legs with sore boils that cannot be healed, from the sole of your foot to the top of your head.

[36] The LORD will bring you and your king, which you will set over you, to a nation which neither you nor your fathers have known, and there you will serve other gods, wood and stone. [37] You will become a horror, a proverb, and an object of ridicule among all nations where the LORD shall lead you.

[38] You will carry a lot of seed out into the field but will gather but little in, for the locust will consume it. [39] You will plant vineyards and dress them, but will neither drink of the wine nor gather the grapes, for worms will eat them. [40] You will have olive trees throughout all your coasts, but you will not anoint yourself with the oil, for your olive will drop off. [41] You will give birth to sons and daughters, but you will not enjoy them, for they will go into captivity. [42] The locust will consume all of your trees and fruit of your land.

[43] The foreigner who resides with you will get up higher and higher, and you will go down lower and lower. [44] He will lend to you, but you will not lend to him. He will be the head, but you will be the tail.

[45] Moreover, all of these curses will come on you and will pursue you and overtake you, until you are destroyed, because you did not obey the voice of the LORD your God, by keeping His commandments and His statutes which He commanded you. [46] They will be a perpetual sign and wonder in regard to you and your descendants, [47] because you did not serve the LORD your God with joy and with gladness of heart, for the abundance of all things. [48] Therefore, you will serve your enemies whom the LORD will send against you, in hunger, thirst, nakedness, and need of all things, and He will put a yoke of iron on your neck until He has destroyed you.

[49] The LORD will bring a nation against you from far away, from the end of the earth, as swift as the eagle flies, a nation whose language you will not understand, [50] a nation with a fierce countenance, which will not respect the old or show favor to the young. [51] They will eat the offspring of your livestock and the produce of your land, until you are destroyed. They will leave you no grain, wine, or oil, or the offspring of your herd or the offspring of your sheep, until they have destroyed you. [52] He will lay siege on you in all your towns until your high and fortified walls in which you trusted come down throughout all your land, and he will lay siege on you in all your towns throughout all your land which the LORD your God has given you.

[53] You will eat the offspring of your own body, the flesh of your sons and of your daughters, which the LORD your God has given you, during the siege and distress in which your enemies will persecute you. [54] The man who is tender among you, and very delicate, his eye shall be hostile toward his brother and toward his beloved wife and toward the rest of his children who remain, [55] so that he will not give to any of them any of the flesh of his children which he will eat, because he has nothing left to him because of the siege and the distress by which your enemies will persecute you in all your towns. [56] The tender and delicate woman among you, who would not venture to set the sole of her foot on the ground *because of her* delicateness and tenderness, will be hostile toward her beloved husband, and toward her son and her daughter, [57] and toward her afterbirth that comes out from between her legs, and toward her

children whom she will bear. For she will secretly eat them because of lack during the siege and distress in which your enemy will persecute you in your towns.

⁵⁸ If you are not careful to observe all the words of this law that are written in this book so that you may fear this glorious and fearful name, the Lᴏʀᴅ your God, ⁵⁹ then the Lᴏʀᴅ will bring extraordinary plagues on you and your descendants, even great long-lasting plagues, and severe and long-lasting sicknesses. ⁶⁰ Moreover, He will bring all the diseases of Egypt upon you, which you were afraid of, and they will cling to you. ⁶¹ Also every sickness and every plague which is not written in the Book of the Law will the Lᴏʀᴅ bring upon you until you are destroyed. ⁶² You will be left few in number, whereas you were as numerous as the stars of heaven, because you would not obey the voice of the Lᴏʀᴅ your God. ⁶³ It will be that as the Lᴏʀᴅ rejoiced over you to do you good and to multiply you, so the Lᴏʀᴅ will take pleasure over you to destroy you and to bring you to nothing. You will be plucked from off the land which you go to possess.

⁶⁴ The Lᴏʀᴅ will scatter you among all the peoples, from the one end of the earth to the other, and there you will serve other gods, wood and stone, which neither you nor your fathers have known. ⁶⁵ Among these nations you will find no ease, nor will the sole of your foot have rest. But there the Lᴏʀᴅ will give you a trembling heart, failing of eyes, and despair of soul. ⁶⁶ Your life shall hang in doubt before you. You will be in dread day and night and will have no assurance of your life. ⁶⁷ In the morning you will say, "Would to God it were evening!" And at evening you will say, "Would to God it were morning!" because of the fear of your heart and because of the sights your eyes will see. ⁶⁸ The Lᴏʀᴅ will bring you into Egypt again with ships, by the way by which I spoke to you, "You will not see it ever again." And there you will be sold to your enemies as male and female slaves, but no one will buy you.

Renewal of the Covenant

29 These are the words of the covenant which the Lᴏʀᴅ commanded Moses to make with the children of Israel in the land of Moab, besides the covenant which He made with them in Horeb.

² Moses proclaimed to all Israel, and said to them:

You have seen all that the Lᴏʀᴅ did before your eyes in the land of Egypt, to Pharaoh and all his servants and to all his land— ³ the great temptations which your eyes have seen, those signs and great wonders. ⁴ Yet to this day the Lᴏʀᴅ has not given you a heart to know, eyes to see, and ears to hear. ⁵ I have led you forty years in the wilderness. Your clothes have not worn out on you, and your sandal has not worn out on your foot. ⁶ You have not eaten bread, nor have you drunk wine or strong drink, so that you might know that I am the Lᴏʀᴅ your God.

⁷ When you came to this place, Sihon, the king of Heshbon, and Og, the king of Bashan, came out against us to battle, and we defeated them. ⁸ We took their land and gave it as an inheritance to the Reubenites, the Gadites, and to half of the tribe of Manasseh. ⁹ Therefore, keep the words of this covenant and do them, so that you may prosper in all you do. ¹⁰ Today all of you stand before the Lᴏʀᴅ your God, the heads of your tribes, your elders, and your officers, with all the men of Israel, ¹¹ your little ones, your wives, and your foreigners who are in your camp, from the one who chops your wood to the one who draws your water— ¹² so that you should enter into a covenant with the Lᴏʀᴅ your God, and into His oath, which the Lᴏʀᴅ your God is making with you today. ¹³ Today He will establish that you are His people and that He is your God, just as He has said to you and He has sworn to your fathers, to Abraham, to Isaac, and to Jacob. ¹⁴ It is not with you alone that I am making this covenant and this oath, ¹⁵ but with him who stands here with us today before the Lᴏʀᴅ our God, and with him who is not here with us today ¹⁶ (for you know that we lived in the land of Egypt and how we came through the nations which you passed by, ¹⁷ and you have seen their abominations and their idols of wood and stone, of silver and gold, which were among them); ¹⁸ lest there be among you a man or woman or family or tribe whose heart turns away today from the Lᴏʀᴅ our God to go

and serve the gods of these nations, and lest there be among you a root bearing poisonous and bitter fruit; ¹⁹ and it happens that, when he hears the words of this covenant, he blesses himself in his heart, saying, "I shall have peace, even though I walk in the stubbornness of my heart," thus destroying the watered ground with the dry. ²⁰ The Lᴏʀᴅ will not spare him; rather the anger of the Lᴏʀᴅ and His jealousy will smolder against that man. All the curses that are written in this book will rest on him, and the Lᴏʀᴅ will blot out his name from under heaven. ²¹ The Lᴏʀᴅ will single him out for disaster out of all the tribes of Israel, according to all the curses of the covenant that are written in this Book of the Law.

²² The generation to come, your children who will rise up after you and the foreigner who will come from a far land, when they see the plagues of that land, and the sicknesses which the Lᴏʀᴅ has laid on it, will say, ²³ "The whole land is brimstone and salt, a burning waste, unsown and unproductive, and no grass grows there, like the overthrow of Sodom and Gomorrah, Admah and Zeboyim, which the Lᴏʀᴅ overthrew in His anger and wrath." ²⁴ All nations will say, "Why has the Lᴏʀᴅ done such to this land? What does the heatedness of this great anger mean?"

²⁵ Then men will say, "Because they have forsaken the covenant of the Lᴏʀᴅ God of their fathers, which He made with them when He brought them out of the land of Egypt. ²⁶ For they went and served other gods, and worshipped them, gods which they did not know and which He had not given to them. ²⁷ The anger of the Lᴏʀᴅ burned against this land, bringing on it all the curses that are written in this book. ²⁸ The Lᴏʀᴅ rooted them out of their land in anger and in wrath and in great indignation, and threw them into another land, as it is today."

²⁹ The secret things belong to the Lᴏʀᴅ our God, but those things which are revealed belong to us and to our children forever, so that we may keep all the words of this law.

The Promise of Restoration

30 When all these things happen to you, the blessing and the curse, which I have set before you, and you remember them among all the nations, where the Lᴏʀᴅ your God has driven you, ² then you must return to the Lᴏʀᴅ your God and obey His voice according to all that I am commanding you today, you and your children, with all your heart, and with all your soul. ³ Then the Lᴏʀᴅ your God will overturn your captivity and have compassion on you and will return and gather you from all the nations, where the Lᴏʀᴅ your God has scattered you. ⁴ If any of you are driven out to the outmost parts of heaven, from there will the Lᴏʀᴅ your God gather you, and from there He will get you. ⁵ The Lᴏʀᴅ your God will bring you to the land which your fathers possessed, and you shall possess it. He will prosper you and multiply you more than your fathers. ⁶ The Lᴏʀᴅ your God will circumcise your heart and the heart of your descendants to love the Lᴏʀᴅ your God with all your heart and with all your soul, so that you may live. ⁷ The Lᴏʀᴅ your God will put all these curses on your enemies, on them who hate you, who persecuted you. ⁸ You will return and obey the voice of the Lᴏʀᴅ, and obey all His commandments which I am commanding you today. ⁹ The Lᴏʀᴅ your God will make you prosper in every work of your hand, in the offspring of your body, and in the offspring of your livestock, and in the produce of your land, for good. For the Lᴏʀᴅ will once again rejoice over you for good, just as He rejoiced over your fathers, ¹⁰ if you obey the voice of the Lᴏʀᴅ your God, by keeping His commandments and His statutes which are written in this Book of the Law, and if you return to the Lᴏʀᴅ your God with all your heart and with all your soul.

The Choice of Life or Death

¹¹ This commandment which I am commanding you today is not hidden from you, nor is it far off. ¹² It is not in heaven, that you should say, "Who will go up for us to heaven and bring it to us, so that we may hear it and do it?" ¹³ It is not beyond the sea, so that you should say, "Who shall go over the sea for us and bring it to us, so that we may hear it and do it?" ¹⁴ But the word is very near to you, in your mouth, and in your heart, so that you may do it.

[15] See, today I have set before you life and prosperity, and death and disaster. [16] What I am commanding you today is to love the LORD your God, to walk in His ways, and to keep His commandments and His statutes and His judgments, so that you may live and multiply. Then the LORD your God will bless you in the land which you go to possess.

[17] But if your heart turns away, so that you do not obey, but are drawn away, and worship other gods and serve them, [18] then I declare to you today that you will surely perish and that you will not prolong your days in the land which you are crossing the Jordan to go in and possess.

[19] I call heaven and earth to witnesses against you this day, that I have set before you life and death, blessing and curse. Therefore choose life, that both you and your descendants may live; [20] that you may love the LORD your God, that you may obey His voice, and that you may cling to Him, for He is your life and the length of your days; and that you may dwell in the land that the LORD swore to your fathers, to Abraham, Isaac, and Jacob, to give them.

Joshua to Succeed Moses

31 Then Moses went and spoke these words to all Israel. [2] He said to them, "I am a hundred and twenty years old today. I can no longer come and go. Also, the LORD has said to me, 'You may not cross over the Jordan.' [3] The LORD your God will cross over before you. He will destroy these nations before you, you will possess them, and Joshua will cross over before you, just as the LORD has said. [4] The LORD will do to them as He did to Sihon and to Og, the kings of the Amorites, and to their land, which He destroyed. [5] The LORD will give them up before you, so that you may do to them according to all the commandments which I have commanded you. [6] Be strong and of a good courage. Fear not, nor be afraid of them, for the LORD your God, it is He who goes with you. He will not fail you, nor forsake you."

[7] Moses called to Joshua, and said to him in the sight of all Israel, "Be strong and of good courage, for you must go with this people to the land which the LORD has sworn to their fathers to give them, and you will enable them to inherit it. [8] The LORD, He goes before you. He will be with you. He will not fail you nor forsake you. Do not fear, nor be dismayed."

[9] Moses wrote this law and delivered it to the priests, the sons of Levi who bore the ark of the covenant of the LORD, and to all the elders of Israel. [10] Moses commanded them, saying, "At the end of every seven years, at the time of the year of the cancellation of debts, at the Feast of Tabernacles, [11] when all Israel has come to appear before the LORD your God in the place which He will choose, you must read this law before all Israel in their hearing. [12] Gather the people together, men, women, children, and your foreigner who is within your towns, so that they may hear and learn and fear the LORD your God, and observe to do all the words of this law. [13] Their children, who have not known *it*, may hear and learn to fear the LORD your God, as long as you live in the land which you cross the Jordan to possess."

Prediction of Israel's Rebellion

[14] The LORD said to Moses, "Indeed, your days draw near when you must die. Call Joshua, and present yourselves in the tent of meeting, so that I may commission him." So Moses and Joshua went, and presented themselves in the tent of meeting.

[15] The LORD appeared in the tent in a pillar of cloud, and the pillar of cloud stood over the door of the tent. [16] The LORD said to Moses, "You are about to lie down with your fathers, and this people will rise up and begin to prostitute themselves after the gods of the foreigners of the land, where they are going to be among them, and will forsake Me and break My covenant which I have made with them. [17] Then My anger will burn against them on that day, and I will forsake them, and I will hide My face from them, and they will be devoured, and many disasters and troubles will befall them, so that they will say in that day, 'Have not these disasters come upon us because our God is not among us?' [18] And I will surely hide My face in that day for all the evil things which they shall have done, in that they turned to other gods.

[19] "Now therefore write yourself this song and teach it to the children of Israel. Put it on their mouths, so that this song may be a witness for Me against the children of Israel. [20] For when I have brought them into the land which I swore to their fathers, flowing with milk and honey, and they have eaten, and filled themselves, and become fat, then they will turn to other gods, and serve them, and provoke Me, and break My covenant. [21] Then when many disasters and troubles have fallen on them, this song will testify against them as a witness, for it must not be forgotten from the mouths of their descendants. For I know their intention which they are developing even now, before I have brought them into the land which I promised." [22] Therefore, Moses wrote this song the same day, and taught it to the children of Israel.

[23] He gave Joshua, the son of Nun, an exhortation, and said, "Be strong and of a good courage, for you will bring the children of Israel into the land which I swore to them, and I will be with you."

[24] When Moses had finished writing the words of this law in a book, until they were completed, [25] then Moses commanded the Levites, who bore the ark of the covenant of the LORD, saying, [26] "Take this Book of the Law, and put it inside the ark of the covenant of the LORD your God, so that it may be there for a witness against you. [27] For I know your rebellion and your stiff neck. Even now, while I am yet alive with you today, you have been rebellious against the LORD. How much more after my death? [28] Gather to me all the elders of your tribes, and your officers, so that I may speak these words in their hearing and call heaven and earth to witness against them. [29] For I know that after my death you will utterly corrupt yourselves and turn aside from the way which I have commanded you, and disaster will befall you in the latter days, because you will do evil in the sight of the LORD, to provoke Him to anger through the work of your hands."

The Song of Moses

[30] Moses spoke the words of this song until they were finished, in the hearing of all the assembly of Israel:

32 Give ear, O heavens, and I will speak;
  hear, O earth, the words of my mouth.
[2] My teaching will drop like the rain,
  my sayings will distill as the dew,
  as the droplets on the grass,
  and as the showers on the herb.

[3] For I will proclaim the name of the Lord:
  Ascribe greatness to our God!
[4] He is the Rock; His work is perfect;
  for all His ways are just.
  He is a God of faithfulness and without injustice;
  righteous and upright is He.

[5] They have acted corruptly to Him;
  they are not His children, but blemished;
  they are a perverse and crooked generation.
[6] Is this how you repay the LORD,
  you foolish and unwise people?
  Is He not your father, who has bought you?
  Has He not made you, and established you?

[7] Remember the days of old,
  consider the years of previous generations.
  Ask your father, and he will show you;
  your elders, and they will tell you:
[8] When the Most High gave the nations their inheritance,
  when He separated the sons of man, [t]
  He set the boundaries of the peoples
  according to the number of the children of Israel.
[9] For the LORD's portion is His people;
  Jacob is the allotment of His inheritance.

---

[t] 18 Or *Adam.*

¹⁰ He found him in a desert land
    and in the howling waste of a wilderness;
He led him about, He instructed him,
    He protected him like the pupil of His eye.
¹¹ Like an eagle stirs up her nest,
    that flutters over her young,
He spread out his wings and took him;
    He lifted him on His pinions;
¹² the LORD alone guided him,
    and there was no foreign god with him.

¹³ He made him ride on the high places of the earth,
    and he ate of the produce of the fields;
He made him suck honey out of the rock
    and oil out of the flinty rock,
¹⁴ butter from the herd,
    and milk from the flock,
along with the fat of lambs,
and rams of the breed from Bashan,
    and goats,
    with the best of the kernels of wheat;
you drank the pure blood of the grape.

¹⁵ But Jeshurun grew fat and kicked;
    you grew fat, you grew thick;
    you are covered with fat.
Then he forsook God who made him,
    and devalued the Rock of his salvation.
¹⁶ They made Him jealous with strange gods;
    with abominations they provoked Him to anger.
¹⁷ They sacrificed to demons, not to God,
    to gods whom they knew not,
    to new gods that recently came along,
    whom your fathers did not fear.
¹⁸ You have forgotten the Rock who begot you;
    you are unmindful, and have forgotten the God who
        gave you birth.

¹⁹ When the LORD saw it, He despised them,
    because of the provocation of His sons and daughters.
²⁰ He said: I will hide My face from them;
    I will see what their end will be,
for they are a very perverse generation,
    children in whom there is no loyalty.
²¹ They have made Me jealous with that which is not God;
    they have provoked Me to anger with their empty things.
And I will make them jealous of those who are not
        a people;
    I will provoke them to anger with a foolish nation.
²² For a fire has been inflamed by My anger,
    and it will burn to the lowest part of Sheol,¹
and shall consume the earth and its produce,
    and ignite the foundations of the mountains.

²³ I will heap misfortunes on them;
    I will use My arrows on them.
²⁴ They will be starved by famine,
    and consumed by plague and bitter destruction;
I will also send the teeth of beasts upon them,
    with the poison of crawling creatures in the dust.
²⁵ The sword outside and terror within will destroy both the
        young man and the virgin,
    the infant along with the man of gray hair.
²⁶ I said, "I want to cut them into pieces,
    I will cause the memory of them to disappear from
        among men,"
²⁷ however, I feared the wrath of the enemy,
    that their adversaries would misunderstand
and say, "Our hand is victorious,
    and the LORD has not done all this."

²⁸ For they are a nation devoid of counsel;
    there is no understanding in them.
²⁹ Would that they were wise,
    so that they understood this,
    so that they would comprehend their future!
³⁰ How should one chase a thousand,
    and two put ten thousand to flight,
unless their Rock had sold them,
    and the LORD had given them up?
³¹ For their rock is not as our Rock;
    even our enemies themselves concede this.
³² For their vine is from the vine of Sodom
    and from the fields of Gomorrah;
their grapes are grapes of poison;
    their clusters are bitter.
³³ Their wine is the poison of dragons
    and the deadly venom of cobras.

³⁴ Is not this laid up in store with Me
    and sealed up among My treasures?
³⁵ Vengeance is Mine, and recompense;
    their foot will slip in due time;
for the day of their calamity is at hand,
    and the things to come hasten upon them.

³⁶ For the LORD will judge His people,
    and relent in regard to His servants,
when He sees that their power is gone
    and there is no one left, whether restrained or free.
³⁷ He will say: Where are their gods,
    their rock in whom they trusted,
³⁸ which ate the fat of their sacrifices
    and drank the wine of their drink offerings?
Let them rise up and help you
    and be your protection.

³⁹ See now that I, even I, am He,
    and there is no god besides Me;
I kill, and I make alive;
    I wound, and I heal;
    there is no one who can deliver out of My hand.
⁴⁰ For I lift up My hand to heaven,
    and say: As I live forever,
⁴¹ if I sharpen My flashing sword
    and My hand takes hold on judgment,
I will render vengeance on My enemies
    and will repay those who hate Me.
⁴² I will make My arrows drunk with blood,
    and My sword shall devour flesh,
with the blood of the slain and of the captives,
    from the heads of the leaders of the enemies.

⁴³ Rejoice, O you nations, with His people;
    for He will avenge the blood of His servants
and will render vengeance on His adversaries
    and will be merciful to His land and people.

⁴⁴ Moses came and spoke all the words of this song in the hearing of the people, he, with Joshua, the son of Nun. ⁴⁵ When Moses finished speaking all these words to all Israel, ⁴⁶ he said to them, "Set your hearts on all the words which I testify among you today, which you shall command your children to be careful to observe, all the words of this law. ⁴⁷ For it is no idle word for you, because it is your life, and by this word you will prolong your days in the land which you cross over the Jordan to possess."

Moses to Die on Mount Nebo

⁴⁸ The LORD spoke to Moses that same day, saying, ⁴⁹ "Go up to this mountain of the Abarim, to Mount Nebo, which is in the land of Moab opposite Jericho, and look at the land of Canaan, which I

---

¹ 22 Or *the lowest depths of the earth* or *underworld.*

am giving to the children of Israel for a possession. [50] Die on the mount where you go up, and be gathered to your people, just as Aaron, your brother, died on Mount Hor and was gathered to his people, [51] because you trespassed against Me among the children of Israel at the waters of Meribah Kadesh, in the Wilderness of Zin, because you did not treat Me as holy in the midst of the children of Israel. [52] Nevertheless, you will see the land before you, but you may not go there, to the land which I am giving to the children of Israel."

Moses Blesses Israel
Ge 49:1–28

33 Now this is the blessing with which Moses, the man of God, blessed the children of Israel before his death. [2] He said:

The Lord came from Sinai and rose up from Seir to them;
　He shone forth from Mount Paran,
and He came with ten thousands of holy ones;
　from His right hand went a fiery law[1] for them.
[3] Surely, He loved the people;
　all His holy ones are in Your hand,
and they sit down at Your feet;
　everyone receives Your words.
[4] Moses decreed us a law,
　the inheritance of the assembly of Jacob.
[5] He was king over Jeshurun,
　when the heads of the people and the tribes of Israel were
　　gathered together.

[6] Let Reuben live, and not die,
　and let not his men be few.

[7] This is the blessing to Judah. He said:

Listen, O Lord, to the voice of Judah,
　and bring him to his people;
may his hands contend for them,
　and may You help him against his enemies.

[8] Of Levi he said:

Let Your Thummim and Your Urim be with Your
　　godly one,
whom You tested at Massah,
　and with whom You contended at the waters
　　of Meribah,
[9] who said to his father and to his mother,
　"I have not seen him,"
and he did not acknowledge his brothers
　or know his own children,
for they have kept Your word
　and guarded Your covenant.
[10] They will teach Jacob Your judgments
　and Israel Your law.
They will put incense before You
　and the whole burnt offerings on your altar.
[11] Bless, O Lord, his substance,
　and accept the work of his hands;
run through the loins of them that rise against him
　and of them that hate him,
　so that they rise never again.

[12] Of Benjamin he said:

The beloved of the Lord
　will dwell in safety by Him,
and the Lord will protect him all day long;
　he will dwell between His shoulders.

[13] Of Joseph he said:

May his land be blessed of the Lord,
　from the harvest of the heavens,
　by the dew,
　and by the deep crouching beneath,
[14] by the precious fruits brought forth by the sun,
　and by the choice things put forth by the moon,
[15] by the finest things of the ancient mountains,
　and by the choice things of the everlasting hills,
[16] by the best things of the earth and its fullness,
　and by the goodwill of Him who dwelt in the bush.
May the blessing rest on the head of Joseph,
　on top of the head of him who was separated from
　　his brothers.
[17] His glory is like the firstborn of his bull,
　and his horns are like the horns of a wild ox;
with them he will push the peoples together to the ends of
　　the earth;
they are the ten thousands of Ephraim,
　and they are the thousands of Manasseh.

[18] Of Zebulun he said:

Rejoice, Zebulun, in your going outside,
　and Issachar in your tents.
[19] They will call the peoples to the mountain;
　there they will offer sacrifices of righteousness,
for they will draw out the abundance of the seas
　and the treasures hid in the sand.

[20] Of Gad he said:

Blessed be he who enlarges Gad;
　he dwells as a lion
　and tears an arm and the crown of a head.
[21] He provided the first part for himself,
　because there, in a portion of the ruler, he was seated.
He came with the heads of the people.
　He executed the justice of the Lord,
　and His ordinances with Israel.

[22] Of Dan he said:

Dan is a lion's whelp;
　he will leap forth from Bashan.

[23] Of Naphtali he said:

O Naphtali, satisfied with favor
　and full with the blessing of the Lord,
　possess the west and the south.

[24] Of Asher he said:

May Asher be blessed with children;
　may he be acceptable to his brothers,
　and may he dip his foot in oil.[2]
[25] Your sandals will be iron and brass;
　according to your days, so shall be your strength.

[26] There is none like the God of Jeshurun,
　who rides through the heavens to help you,
　and in His majesty through the skies.
[27] The eternal God is your refuge,
　and underneath you are the everlasting arms;
He will drive out the enemy before you,
　and will say, "Destroy them."
[28] Israel dwells in safety;
　the fountain of Jacob will be secluded
in a land of grain and new wine;
　its heavens will rain down dew.

---

[1] 2 Or *flashing lightning.*　[2] 24 A metaphor depicting prosperity.

²⁹ Blessed are you, O Israel!
  Who is like you,
    a people saved by the Lord,
  the shield of your help,
    who is the sword of your majesty!
  Your enemies will cringe before you,
    and you will tread upon their high places.

The Death of Moses

34 Moses went up from the plains of Moab to Mount Nebo, to the top of Pisgah, which is opposite Jericho. Then the Lord showed him all the land—from Gilead to Dan, ² and all Naphtali and the land of Ephraim and Manasseh, and all the land of Judah, to the *Mediterranean* Sea, ³ and the Negev and the plain of the valley of Jericho, the city of palm trees, as far as Zoar. ⁴ The Lord said to him, "This is the land which I swore to Abraham, to Isaac, and to Jacob, saying, 'I will give it to your descendants.' I have caused you to see it with your eyes, but you will not cross over there."

⁵ So Moses, the servant of the Lord, died there in the land of Moab, according to the word of the Lord. ⁶ He buried him in a valley in the land of Moab, opposite Beth Peor, but no man knows of his burial place to this day. ⁷ Moses was a hundred and twenty years old when he died. His eye was not dim, nor was his vitality diminished. ⁸ The children of Israel wept for Moses in the plains of Moab thirty days. Then the days of weeping and mourning for Moses were ended.

⁹ Now Joshua, the son of Nun, was full of the spirit of wisdom, for Moses had laid his hands on him. And the children of Israel listened to him and did as the Lord commanded Moses.

¹⁰ Since then there has not arisen a prophet in Israel like Moses, whom the Lord knew face to face, ¹¹ in all the signs and wonders which the Lord sent him to do in the land of Egypt, to Pharaoh, to all his servants, and to all his land, ¹² and by all that mighty power and by all the great terror which Moses displayed in the sight of all Israel.

JOSHUA

The Lord Commissions Joshua

1 Now after the death of Moses the servant of the Lord, the Lord spoke to Joshua son of Nun, the assistant of Moses: ² "Moses My servant is dead, so now get up and cross over the Jordan—you and all this people—to the land that I am giving to the children of Israel. ³ I have given you every place that the sole of your foot shall tread, as I said to Moses. ⁴ From the wilderness and this Lebanon, as far as the great river, the River Euphrates, all the land of the Hittites, and to the *Mediterranean* Sea toward the setting of the sun will be your territory. ⁵ No man will be able to stand against you all the days of your life. As I was with Moses, I will be with you. I will not abandon you. I will not leave you.

⁶ "Be strong and courageous, for you shall provide the land that I swore to their fathers to give them as an inheritance for this people. ⁷ Be strong and very courageous, in order to act carefully in accordance with all the law that My servant Moses commanded you. Do not turn aside from it to the right or the left, so that you may succeed wherever you go. ⁸ This Book of the Law must not depart from your mouth. Meditate on it day and night so that you may act carefully according to all that is written in it. For then you will make your way successful, and you will be wise. ⁹ Have not I commanded you? Be strong and courageous. Do not be afraid or dismayed, for the Lord your God is with you wherever you go."

Joshua Takes Command

¹⁰ Then Joshua commanded the officers of the people, ¹¹ "Pass through the midst of the camp and command the people, 'Prepare food, for in three days you will cross the Jordan to go to take possession of the land that the Lord your God is giving you to possess.' "

¹² To the Reubenites, the Gadites, and to the half-tribe of Manasseh, Joshua said, ¹³ "Remember the word that Moses the servant of the Lord commanded you: 'The Lord your God has given you a place for rest and will give this land.' ¹⁴ Your wives, your children, and your livestock may live in the land that Moses gave you on the east side of the Jordan. But you must cross over with your brothers fully armed, your mighty men of valor, and help them, ¹⁵ until the Lord has given your brothers rest, as He has given you, and they also have possessed the land that the Lord your God is giving to them. Then you may return to your own land and possess what Moses the servant of the Lord gave you *on the east* side of the Jordan where the sun rises."

¹⁶ They answered Joshua, "All that you command us we will do, and wherever you send us we will go. ¹⁷ Just as we obeyed Moses in all things, we will obey you. May the Lord your God be with you, as He was with Moses! ¹⁸ Whoever rebels against your command and disobeys your words, in all that you command him, shall be put to death. Only be strong and courageous."

Rahab and the Spies

2 Then Joshua son of Nun sent two men out from Shittim to spy, saying, "Go see the land, especially Jericho." So they went, and they came to the house of a prostitute named Rahab. They spent the night there.

² The king of Jericho was told, "Israelite men came here tonight to spy out the land." ³ So the king of Jericho sent orders to Rahab, "Bring out the men who came to you, who have entered your house, for they came to spy out the whole land."

⁴ Now the woman had taken the two men and had hidden them. She said, "Yes, the men came to me, but I did not know where they were from. ⁵ The men went out when it was time to shut the gate at dark. I do not know where the men went. Chase after them quickly, for you can overtake them." ⁶ Yet she had brought them up to the roof. She hid them in the stalks of flax that she had spread out on the roof. ⁷ So the men chased after them on the road to the Jordan as far as the fords. They shut the gate as soon as the pursuers went out after them.

⁸ Before the spies went to sleep, Rahab went up to them on the roof. ⁹ She said to the men, "I know that the Lord has given you the land, for dread from you has fallen upon us, and all the inhabitants of the land melt *in terror* before you. ¹⁰ For we heard how the Lord dried up the waters of the Red Sea before you when you came out of Egypt, and what you did to Sihon and Og, the two kings of the Amorites who were on the other side of the Jordan, whom you completely destroyed. ¹¹ Our hearts melted when we heard *these things*, and no man had any breath in him because of you, for the Lord your God is God in heaven above and on earth below.

¹² "So now, since I have acted faithfully toward you, please swear to me by the Lord that you will also act faithfully toward my father's house. Please give me a firm pledge ¹³ that you will spare my father, my mother, my brothers, my sisters, and all whom they own, and that you will deliver our lives from death."

¹⁴ The men said to her, "Our lives for yours; if you do not report us, then when the Lord gives us the land, we will act faithfully and kindly with you."

¹⁵ Then Rahab lowered them by a rope through the window, for her home was set into the wall where she lived. ¹⁶ She said to them, "Go to the hill country so that the pursuers do not find you. Hide there three days until the pursuers return. After that, you can go on your way."

¹⁷ The men said to her, "We will be free from this oath that you have made us swear, ¹⁸ unless, when we come into the land, you tie this red cord to the window through which you let us down. You must bring your father, your mother, your brothers, and all who belong to your father's household into your home. ¹⁹ Anyone who comes out of the doors of your house into the street is responsible for his own blood, and we will be innocent. Yet for anyone who stays with you inside the house, we are responsible for his blood if someone should lay a hand on him. ²⁰ But if you tell about this business of ours, then we will be released from the oath that you have made us swear."

²¹ She said, "Let it be so, according to your words."

Then she sent them off, and they departed. Then she tied the red cord in the window.

²² They went and came to the hill country. They stayed there three days, until the pursuers returned. The pursuers had sought them all along the way but had not found them. ²³ So the two men returned. They descended from the hill country. They crossed the river, came to Joshua son of Nun, and told him all that they had discovered. ²⁴ They said to Joshua, "The Lᴏʀᴅ has surely given the whole land into our hands! Indeed, all the inhabitants of the land melt *in terror* before us."

Israel Crossing the Jordan

3 In the morning Joshua got up early; then he and all the children of Israel set out from Shittim and came to the Jordan. They stayed there before crossing over. ² After three days the officers went through the camp. ³ They commanded the people, "When you see the ark of the covenant of the Lᴏʀᴅ your God and the Levite priests carrying it, then you shall set out from where you are and go behind it. ⁴ There must be a distance of two thousand cubits*ᵗ* between you and it. Do not draw closer to it, in order that you may know the way you should go. For you have not passed this way before."

⁵ Joshua said to the people, "Consecrate yourselves, for tomorrow the Lᴏʀᴅ will perform wondrous deeds among you."

⁶ Joshua said to the priests, "Pick up the ark of the covenant, and proceed ahead of the people." So they picked up the ark of the covenant and went in front of the people.

⁷ The Lᴏʀᴅ said to Joshua, "Today I will begin to honor you in the sight of all Israel, so that they may know that just as I was with Moses, so I will be with you. ⁸ You shall command the priests who carry the ark of the covenant, 'When you come to the bank of the Jordan, stand still in the river.'"

⁹ So Joshua said to the children of Israel, "Draw near and hear the words of the Lᴏʀᴅ your God." ¹⁰ And Joshua said, "By this you will know that the living God is among you, and that He will thoroughly drive out the Canaanites, the Hittites, the Hivites, the Perizzites, the Girgashites, the Amorites, and the Jebusites from before you. ¹¹ See, the ark of the covenant of the Lᴏʀᴅ of all the earth is passing before you into the Jordan. ¹² Now select twelve men from the tribes of Israel, one man per tribe. ¹³ When the soles of the feet of the priests who bear the ark of the Lᴏʀᴅ, the Lord of all the earth, touch the water of the Jordan, the water of the Jordan that flows from upstream will be cut off and pile up."

¹⁴ When the people set out from their tents to cross over the Jordan, the priests were carrying the ark of the covenant before the people. ¹⁵ When the carriers of the ark came to the Jordan, the feet of the priests carrying the ark dipped into the edge of the water. (Now the Jordan overflows its banks all the days of the harvest.) ¹⁶ Then the water that flows down from upstream stood still and rose up in a heap very far away at Adam, the city beside Zarethan. The water that flows down toward the Sea of Arabah (the Dead Sea) stopped and was cut off. The people crossed over opposite Jericho. ¹⁷ The priests carrying the ark of the covenant of the Lᴏʀᴅ

stood firmly on dry ground in the middle of the Jordan, and all Israel crossed over on dry ground until the entire people completed crossing over the Jordan.

Twelve Memorial Stones

4 When the entire people had completed crossing over the Jordan, the Lᴏʀᴅ said to Joshua, ² "Take twelve men from among the people, one man per tribe. ³ Command them: 'Pick up twelve stones from the middle of the Jordan, from the place where the feet of the priests are standing; bring them over with you, and set them in the place you will camp tonight.'"

⁴ So Joshua summoned the twelve men he had appointed from among the children of Israel, one man per tribe. ⁵ Then Joshua said to them, "Cross over before the ark of the Lᴏʀᴅ your God into the middle of the Jordan. Each of you lift up a stone upon your shoulder, one for each of the tribes of the children of Israel, ⁶ so that this will be a sign among you. When your children ask, 'What do these stones mean to you?' ⁷ you will answer them that the waters of the Jordan were cut off before the ark of the covenant of the Lᴏʀᴅ. When it crossed the Jordan, the waters of the Jordan were cut off. These stones will be a memorial for the children of Israel continually."

⁸ Then the children of Israel did as Joshua commanded and picked up twelve stones from the middle of the Jordan, one for each of the tribes of the children of Israel, as the Lᴏʀᴅ had spoken to Joshua. They crossed over with them to the settlement and set them there. ⁹ Joshua also set twelve stones in the middle of the Jordan at the place where the feet of the priests who carried the ark of the covenant were standing. The stones are there to this day.

¹⁰ The priests who were carrying the ark stood in the middle of the Jordan until everything was completed that the Lᴏʀᴅ had commanded Joshua to say to the people, according to all that Moses had commanded Joshua. The people quickly crossed over. ¹¹ When all the people had finished crossing over, the ark of the Lᴏʀᴅ and the priests crossed over in the presence of the people. ¹² The Reubenites, the Gadites, and the half-tribe of Manasseh crossed over in battle formation in front of the children of Israel, according to what Moses had said to them. ¹³ About forty thousand battle-ready men crossed over before the Lᴏʀᴅ for battle on the plains of Jericho.

¹⁴ On that day, the Lᴏʀᴅ honored Joshua in the sight of all Israel. They feared him as they had feared Moses, all the days of his life.

¹⁵ The Lᴏʀᴅ spoke to Joshua, ¹⁶ "Command the priests carrying the ark of the testimony: 'Come up out of the Jordan!'"

¹⁷ So Joshua commanded the priests, "Come up out of the Jordan!"

¹⁸ Then when the priests who were carrying the ark of the covenant of the Lᴏʀᴅ came up from the middle of the Jordan and the soles of the priests' feet touched the dry ground, the waters of the Jordan returned to their place and overflowed all its banks as before.

¹⁹ Now the people came up from the Jordan on the tenth day of the first month, and they camped at Gilgal, on the eastern border of Jericho. ²⁰ Joshua set up in Gilgal those twelve stones that they took from the Jordan. ²¹ He said to the children of Israel, "When your children someday ask their parents, 'What do these stones mean?' ²² then you shall explain to your children, 'Israel crossed over the Jordan here on dry ground!' ²³ For the Lᴏʀᴅ your God dried up the waters of the Jordan before you until you crossed over, as the Lᴏʀᴅ your God did to the Red Sea when He dried it up before us until we crossed over, ²⁴ so that all the peoples of the earth might know the hand of the Lᴏʀᴅ, that it is mighty, and you would fear the Lᴏʀᴅ your God always."

5 When all the kings of the Amorites west of the Jordan and of the Canaanites by the sea *to the east* heard that the Lᴏʀᴅ had dried up the waters of the Jordan before the children of Israel while they crossed over, their hearts melted, and there was no longer any breath in them because of the children of Israel.

Circumcision and Passover at Gilgal

² At that time the Lᴏʀᴅ said to Joshua, "Make flint knives and circumcise the children of Israel a second time." ³ So Joshua made

flint knives and circumcised the children of Israel at the Hill of the Foreskins called Gibeath Haaraloth. 4 Now this is the reason why Joshua circumcised them: All the males who came out of Egypt who were men of fighting age had died in the wilderness along the way after leaving Egypt. 5 All of the people who had come out were circumcised, but all the people born in the wilderness along the way after leaving Egypt were not circumcised. 6 The children of Israel had traveled forty years in the wilderness until all the people, the men of fighting age who came out of Egypt, died, because they did not obey the Lord. The Lord had sworn not to let them see the land that He had sworn to their fathers to give to us, a land flowing with milk and honey. 7 Yet He raised up their descendants in their place. These men Joshua circumcised, for they were uncircumcised. They had not been circumcised along the way. 8 So when the entire people was completely circumcised, they stayed where they were in the camp until they healed.

9 The Lord said to Joshua, "Today I have rolled away the disgrace of Egypt from upon you." So the name of that place is called Gilgal even to this day.

10 The children of Israel camped in Gilgal and kept the Passover on the fourteenth day of the month in the evening on the plains of Jericho. 11 The day after the Passover, they ate of the produce of the land, unleavened bread, and roasted grain. 12 The manna stopped the day after they ate from the produce of the land, and the children of Israel no longer had manna. That year they ate what the land of Canaan yielded.

The Fall of Jericho

13 Now when Joshua was by Jericho, he looked up and saw a man standing in front of him. In His hand was His drawn sword. Joshua went to Him and said, "Are You for us or for our enemies?"

14 He said, "Neither, for I am the commander of the army of the Lord. Now I have come." Then Joshua fell with his face to the ground and worshipped. Then he said, "What does my Lord wish to say to His servant?"

15 The commander of the army of the Lord said to Joshua, "Remove your sandals from your feet, for the place where you are standing is holy." So Joshua did this.

6 Now Jericho was tightly secured before the children of Israel. There was no one leaving or entering.

2 The Lord said to Joshua, "See, I have given Jericho, its king, and mighty men of valor into your hand. 3 All the men of fighting age shall march around the city. Circle the city once. Do this for six days. 4 Seven priests shall carry seven ram's horn trumpets before the ark. On the seventh day, march around the city seven times, with the priests blowing the trumpets. 5 When they blow a long blast on the ram's horn and when you hear the trumpet sound, all the people shall shout a loud battle cry. The walls of the city will fall down, and the people will go up, every man straight ahead."

6 So Joshua son of Nun summoned the priests and said to them, "Take up the ark of the covenant. Seven priests bearing seven ram's horn trumpets shall be in front of the ark of the Lord." 7 He said to the people, "Advance and march around the city. Let the armed men pass on before the ark of the Lord."

8 So when Joshua had spoken to the people, the seven priests bearing seven ram's horn trumpets before the Lord advanced and blew their trumpets. The ark of the covenant of the Lord went after them. 9 The armed men went before the priests blowing the trumpets, and the rear guard went after the ark while the trumpets were blowing. 10 Now Joshua had commanded the people, "Do not shout a battle cry, and do not let your voices be heard. Do not let a word come out of your mouths until the time I say to you, 'Shout the battle cry!' Then shout." 11 So he had the ark of the Lord circle the city once. Then they came into the camp and spent the night there.

12 Then Joshua got up early in the morning, and the priests picked up the ark of the Lord. 13 Seven priests bearing seven ram's horn trumpets before the ark of the Lord moved on, blowing their trumpets continually. The armed men went before them, and the rear guard went after the ark of the Lord while the trumpets were blowing. 14 The second day they circled the city once, and they returned to the camp. They did this for six days.

15 Then on the seventh day they got up early as dawn was breaking and circled the city in this way seven times. Only on that day did they circle the city seven times. 16 On the seventh time, the priests blew the trumpets and Joshua said to the people, "Shout the battle cry, for the Lord has given you the city! 17 The city and all that is in it are dedicated to the Lord for destruction. Only Rahab the prostitute may live, she, and all who are with her in her house, for she hid the messengers we sent. 18 As for you, keep yourselves from that which is dedicated for destruction, lest you be destroyed. If you take from that which is dedicated for destruction, you will set the Israelite camp for destruction and bring trouble upon it. 19 All the silver, gold, and bronze and iron articles are set apart for the Lord. They will go into the treasury of the Lord."

20 So the people shouted, and they blew the trumpets. When the people heard the trumpet sound, they shouted a loud battle cry, and the wall fell down. So the people went up into the city, one man after the other, and they captured it. 21 They destroyed all that was in the city: man and woman, young and old, and oxen, sheep, and donkey with the edge of the sword.

22 Yet to the two men who had spied out the land, Joshua said, "Enter the prostitute's house, and bring out the woman and everyone who belongs to her, as you swore to her." 23 So the young men who had been spies entered and brought out Rahab, her father, her mother, her brothers, everyone who belonged to her, and her whole extended family. They brought them out and placed them outside of the camp of Israel.

24 They burned the city and everything in it with fire. Only the silver, the gold, the bronze and iron articles they gave to the treasury of the house of the Lord. 25 Yet Rahab the prostitute, her father's family, and everyone who belonged to her, Joshua let live. They live among Israel to this day because she hid the messengers Joshua sent to spy on Jericho.

26 At that time Joshua made them swear, "Cursed before the Lord will be the man who arises and rebuilds this city of Jericho.

He will establish it
    at the cost of his firstborn
and erect its gates
    at the cost of his youngest child."

27 So the Lord was with Joshua, and he became famous throughout the land.

Achan's Sin

7 Yet the children of Israel violated their obligations with regard to the things dedicated for destruction. Achan, son of Karmi, son of Zimri, son of Zerah, from the tribe of Judah took from the things dedicated for destruction, and the anger of the Lord burned against the children of Israel.

2 Joshua sent men from Jericho to Ai (which is near Beth Aven, east of Bethel) and said to them, "Go up and spy on the land." So the men went up and spied on Ai.

3 Then they returned to Joshua and said to him, "All the people need not go up. Let about two or three thousand men go up and strike Ai. Since they are so few, all the people need not weary themselves." 4 So about three thousand men went up from among the people there, but they fled from before the men of Ai. 5 The men of Ai struck down thirty-six men and pursued them from the gate to Shebarim. They struck them down on the mountainside, and the hearts of the people melted like water.

6 Then Joshua ripped his clothes. He and the Israelite elders fell on their faces to the ground in front of the ark of the Lord until evening and threw dirt upon their heads. 7 Joshua said, "O Lord God, why did You bring this people across the Jordan to give us into the hands of the Amorites to destroy us? If only we had been content to dwell on the other side of the Jordan! 8 O my Lord, what should I say now that Israel has fled before its enemies? 9 The Canaanites and all the inhabitants of the land may hear, turn on us, and cut off our name from the earth. What will You do for Your great name?"

10 Then the Lord said to Joshua, "Stand up! Why have you fallen on your face? 11 Israel has sinned, and they have broken

My covenant that I commanded them. They took from the things dedicated for destruction. They have stolen, acted deceitfully, and put them among their own possessions. [12] Therefore the children of Israel cannot stand before their enemies. They turn their backs to their enemies because they have become dedicated for destruction. I will not be with you anymore if you do not destroy the things dedicated for destruction in your midst.

[13] "Get up! Consecrate the people and say, 'Consecrate yourselves for tomorrow, for thus says the Lord, the God of Israel: "Things dedicated for destruction are in your midst, O Israel. You are not able to stand before your enemies until you remove the things dedicated for destruction from your midst."

[14] " 'In the morning you will be brought forward by tribes, and the tribe that the Lord selects by lot shall come forward by clans. The clan that the Lord selects by lot shall come forward by households, and the household that the Lord selects by lot shall come forward man by man. [15] And he who is taken with the things dedicated for destruction shall be burned with fire, he and all who belong to him, for he broke the covenant of the Lord and has done a disgraceful action in Israel.' "

[16] So Joshua got up early in the morning and brought forward Israel by their tribes. The tribe of Judah was selected. [17] He brought forward the clans of Judah, and the clan of the Zerahites was selected. He brought forward the clan of the Zerahites man by man, and Zimri was selected. [18] He brought forward the household of Zimri man by man, and Achan son of Karmi, son of Zimri, son of Zerah, from the tribe of Judah, was selected.

[19] Then Joshua said to Achan, "O my son, give glory to the Lord, the God of Israel, and give Him praise! Tell me what you have done! Do not hold back anything from me."

[20] Achan answered Joshua and said, "Indeed, I sinned against the Lord, the God of Israel. This is what I did: [21] When I saw among the plundered goods a beautiful robe from Babylon, two hundred shekels of silver,[1] and a gold bar weighing fifty shekels,[2] I coveted them, so I took them. They are hidden in the ground in my tent. The silver is underneath them."

[22] So Joshua sent messengers, and they ran to the tent. There it all was hidden in the ground with the silver underneath. [23] They took it from the tent and brought it to Joshua and all the children of Israel. They spread it out before the Lord.

[24] Then Joshua, and all Israel with him, took Achan son of Zerah, the silver, the robe, the gold bar, his sons, his daughters, his oxen, his donkeys, his sheep, his tent, and all he had, and brought them up to the Valley of Achor. [25] Then Joshua said, "Why have you brought trouble on us? The Lord will trouble you today!"

So all Israel stoned him. They burned them with fire and stoned them with stones. [26] Then they erected over him a large pile of stones, which is still there today. So the Lord turned from His burning anger. Therefore the name of the place is called the Valley of Achor to this day.

Ai Destroyed

8 Then the Lord said to Joshua, "Do not be afraid or dismayed. Take all the fighting men with you. Arise, and go up to Ai. See, I have given the king of Ai, his people, his city, and his land into your hand. [2] Do to Ai and its king what you did to Jericho and its king, except you may plunder its spoils and its livestock. Now set an ambush for the city behind it."

[3] So Joshua and all the fighting men arose to go up to Ai. Joshua chose thirty thousand men, mighty men of valor, and sent them out at night. [4] He commanded them, "You shall ambush the city from behind. Do not go very far from the city. All of you be ready. [5] I and all the people who are with me will approach the city. When they come out to engage us as before, we will flee from them. [6] They will come after us until we have lured them away from the city, for they will think, 'They are fleeing from us as before!' So we will flee from them. [7] Then you shall rise up for the ambush and take possession of the city. The Lord your God will give it into your hands. [8] When you have seized the city, set it on fire. Act according to the word of the Lord. See, I have commanded you."

[9] So Joshua sent them out. They went to the place of ambush and took up a position between Bethel and Ai, westward of Ai, and Joshua spent the night among the people.

[10] Joshua got up early in the morning and mustered the people. He and the elders of Israel went up before the people to Ai. [11] All the fighting men who were with him went up and drew near to the city. They camped north of Ai, and there was a valley between them and Ai. [12] He took about five thousand men and set them in ambush between Bethel and Ai, westward of the city. [13] So they stationed the people, all the army that was on the north of the city, and its rear guard on the west of the city, and Joshua spent that night in the midst of the valley.

[14] When the king of Ai saw this, the men of the city hurriedly got up early and went out to engage Israel in battle at the assembly point near the Arabah. Yet he did not know that there was an ambush for him behind the city. [15] So Joshua and all Israel allowed themselves to be beaten before them, and they fled in the direction of the wilderness. [16] All the people who were in Ai were assembled to pursue them, so they pursued Joshua and were drawn away from the city. [17] Not a man was left in Ai or Bethel who did not go out after Israel. They left the city wide open, and they pursued Israel.

[18] The Lord said to Joshua, "Point toward Ai with the sword that is in your hand, for I will give it into your hand." So Joshua pointed toward the city with the sword in his hand. [19] When his hand pointed, the men in ambush got up quickly from their place and ran. They came into the city, captured it, and quickly set the city on fire.

[20] The men of Ai turned around and looked, and there from the city came smoke rising to the sky! They could not flee in any direction, and the people who had fled into the wilderness had turned back toward their pursuers. [21] When Joshua and all Israel saw that the ambush had captured the city and that smoke rose from it, they turned and struck down the men of Ai. [22] Then the men in the city came out to engage them in battle, so they were now in the middle, with Israel on each side. Israel struck them down until neither survivors nor escapees were left. [23] They took the king of Ai alive and brought him to Joshua.

[24] When Israel completed killing all the inhabitants of Ai in the open wilderness where they had pursued them, and when all of them had finally fallen by the edge of the sword, all Israel returned to Ai and struck it with the edge of the sword. [25] All who had fallen that day, men and women, numbered twelve thousand, all the people of Ai. [26] Joshua did not draw back his hand with the stretched-out sword until he destroyed all the inhabitants of Ai. [27] Israel plundered only the livestock and the spoil of that city for themselves, according to the word of the Lord that He had commanded Joshua.

[28] Joshua burned Ai and made it a heap forever, a desolation to this day. [29] The king of Ai hanged on a tree until evening. At sunset, Joshua commanded that the people take down the body from the tree and throw it down at the city gate. They erected a large heap of stones over it that remains to this day.

The Covenant Renewal at Mount Ebal

[30] Then Joshua built an altar to the Lord God of Israel on Mount Ebal, [31] as Moses the servant of the Lord had commanded the children of Israel. As is written in the Book of the Law of Moses, it was "an altar of uncut stones not shaped by iron tools." They sacrificed burnt offerings to the Lord on it, as well as peace offerings. [32] There in the presence of the children of Israel he wrote a copy of the Law of Moses on the stones. [33] All Israel, resident alien and native alike, with its elders, officials, and judges, were standing on either side of the ark in front of the Levite priests carrying the ark of the covenant of the Lord, half in front of Mount Gerizim and half in front of Mount Ebal, as Moses the servant of the Lord had commanded from the beginning, in order to bless the people of Israel.

[34] After this, Joshua read out all the words of the law, both blessing and curse, according to all that is written in the Book of the Law. [35] There was not a word from all that Moses had commanded that Joshua did not read out before the whole assembly of Israel,

---

[1] 21 About 5 pounds, or 2.3 kilograms.   [2] 21 About 1¼ pounds, or 575 grams.

with the women, the children, and the resident aliens who were among them.

The Gibeonite Deception

9 When all the kings west of the Jordan in the hill country, in the low country, and along all the coast of the *Mediterranean* Sea toward Lebanon—the Hittite, the Amorite, the Canaanite, the Perizzite, the Hivite, and the Jebusite kings—heard this, [2] they gathered together as one to wage war against Joshua and Israel.

[3] But when the inhabitants of Gibeon heard what Joshua had done to Jericho and Ai, [4] they acted craftily, and took old sacks on their donkeys, and old wineskins, torn and mended, [5] old and patched sandals on their feet, and old garments on themselves. All the bread of their provision was dry and crumbly. [6] They went to Joshua at the Gilgal settlement and said to him and the children of Israel, "We have come from a distant land. Now make a pact with us."

[7] Then the children of Israel said to these Hivites, "Perhaps you live among us, so how could we make a pact with you?"

[8] Yet they said to Joshua, "We are your slaves."

Joshua said to them, "Who are you, and where do you come from?"

[9] They said to him, "We, your slaves, have come from a very distant land because of the name of the Lord your God, for we heard news of Him and all He did in Egypt [10] and all that He did to the two Amorite kings on the other side of the Jordan, King Sihon of Heshbon and King Og of Bashan in Ashtaroth. [11] So our elders and all the inhabitants of our country said to us, 'Take food provisions for the journey and go to meet them. Say to them, "We are your slaves. So now, make a pact with us." ' [12] This bread of ours was hot as we took it from our homes on the day we left to come to you, but now, see, it is dry and crumbly. [13] These wineskins that we filled were new, but see, they are ripped open. These clothes and sandals wore out due to the very long journey."

[14] So the men *examined* some of the food provisions, but they did not ask the Lord about it. [15] Joshua made peace with them and made a covenant with them to let them live, and the leaders of the congregation swore an oath to them.

[16] Three days after they had made a covenant with them, they heard that they were neighbors to them and lived among them. [17] So the children of Israel set out and came to their cities on the third day. Their cities were Gibeon, Kephirah, Beeroth, and Kiriath Jearim. [18] Now the children of Israel did not attack them, for the leaders of the congregation had sworn an oath to them by the Lord, the God of Israel, so the congregation murmured against the leaders.

[19] Yet all the leaders said to the whole congregation, "We swore to them by the Lord God of Israel, so now we may not harm them. [20] This is what we will do to them. We will let them live so that wrath will not come upon us due to the oath that we swore to them." [21] The leaders of the congregation also said to them, "Let them live!" So they became woodcutters and water carriers for the whole congregation, as the leaders told them.

[22] Joshua met them and said, "Why did you trick us, saying, 'We are very distant from you,' but you are living in our midst? [23] Therefore now you are cursed, and you will always be slaves, cutting wood and carrying water for the house of my God."

[24] They answered Joshua, "It was told to your slaves that the Lord your God commanded Moses His servant to give you all the land and to destroy all the inhabitants of the land before you. So we were very afraid for our lives, and we did this thing. [25] Now here we are, in your hands. Do to us whatever is good and right in your eyes."

[26] Thus he did to them, and delivered them from the hand of the children of Israel; and they did not kill them. [27] That day he made them woodcutters and water carriers for the congregation and the altar of the Lord, even to this day, at the place He would choose.

The Sun Stands Still

10 Now when King Adoni-Zedek of Jerusalem heard that Joshua captured Ai and destroyed it, doing to Ai and its king as he had done to Jericho and its king, and how the inhabitants of Gibeon had made peace with Israel and were among them, [2] he *and his people* were very afraid. Gibeon was a large city, like one of the royal cities. It was larger than Ai, and all its men were warriors. [3] So King Adoni-Zedek of Jerusalem sent this message to King Hoham of Hebron, King Piram of Jarmuth, King Japhia of Lachish, and King Debir of Eglon: [4] "Come and help me! Let us attack Gibeon, for it has made peace with Joshua and all the children of Israel."

[5] So the five kings of the Amorites—the kings of Jerusalem, Hebron, Jarmuth, Lachish, and Eglon—and all their armies gathered, advanced, and camped against Gibeon. Then they waged war against it.

[6] The men of Gibeon sent this message to Joshua at the Gilgal settlement: "Do not abandon your slaves. Come up to us quickly. Save us! Help us! For all the Amorite kings living in the hill country have gathered against us."

[7] So Joshua went up from Gilgal, he and all the people of war with him, and all the mighty men of valor. [8] The Lord said to Joshua, "Do not be afraid of them, for I have given them into your hand. Not a single man can stand before you."

[9] Then Joshua came upon them suddenly, having marched all night from Gilgal. [10] The Lord panicked them before Israel. They struck them with overwhelming force at Gibeon, then Israel pursued them on the road that rises to Beth Horon and struck them down as far as Azekah and Makkedah. [11] As they fled from Israel on the downslope from Beth Horon, the Lord hurled large hailstones down upon them from the sky as far as Azekah. They died, and *in fact* more died from the hailstones than the children of Israel killed with the sword.

[12] On the day the Lord gave over the Amorites to the children of Israel, Joshua spoke to the Lord and said in full view of Israel:

"Sun, stand still over Gibeon;
    and moon, in the Valley of Aijalon."
[13] So the sun stood still,
    and the moon stood in place
    until the people brought vengeance on their enemies.

Is this not written in the book of Jashar?

The sun stood still in the middle of the sky and did not set for about a full day. [14] There has not been a day like this either before or after it, when the Lord obeyed a man, for the Lord waged war for Israel.

[15] Then Joshua, and all Israel with him, returned to the settlement at Gilgal.

The Execution of Five Amorite Kings

[16] Yet these five kings fled and hid themselves in the cave at Makkedah. [17] Joshua was told, "The five kings have been found hiding themselves in the cave at Makkedah." [18] So Joshua said, "Roll large stones over the mouth of the cave, and station men to stand guard over it. [19] As for you, do not stop pursuing your enemies, but attack them from behind. Do not let them go back to their cities, for the Lord your God has given them into your hand."

[20] When Joshua and the children of Israel had finished striking them with overwhelming force until they were completely defeated, the survivors escaped from them and went back to their fortified cities. [21] Then all the people returned safely to Joshua at the Makkedah settlement, and no one spoke against any of the children of Israel.

[22] Joshua said, "Open the mouth of the cave, and bring out to me those five kings from the cave." [23] They did this, and they brought out those five kings from the cave: the kings of Jerusalem, Hebron, Jarmuth, Lachish, and Eglon. [24] When they brought out those five kings to Joshua, he called out to all the men of Israel and the army commanders, "Come here and place your feet on the necks of these kings." So they came near and placed their feet on their necks.

[25] Then Joshua said to them, "Do not be afraid or dismayed. Be strong and courageous! For this is what the Lord will do to all your enemies against whom you fight." [26] After that, Joshua struck them down, killed them, and hung them on five trees. They were hanging on the trees until evening.

[27] At sundown Joshua commanded men to take them down from the trees and throw them into the cave in which they had hidden themselves. Over the mouth of the cave he placed large stones, which remain to this day.

Southern Cities Conquered

²⁸ Joshua took Makkedah that day and struck it and its king with the edge of the sword. He destroyed it and all life within it. He did not leave any survivors. He did to the king of Makkedah just as he did to the king of Jericho. ²⁹ Then Joshua passed from Makkedah to Libnah with all of Israel, and they fought against Libnah. ³⁰ The LORD gave Libnah and its king into the hand of Israel, and they struck all who lived in it with the edge of the sword. There were no survivors left. They did to its king what they had done to the king of Jericho. ³¹ Then Joshua passed from Libnah to Lachish with all of Israel, camped against it, and waged war against it. ³² The LORD gave Lachish into the hand of Israel. They captured it on the second day and struck all who lived in it with the edge of the sword, just as they had done to Libnah. ³³ King Horam of Gezer came up to help Lachish, but Joshua attacked him and his people until he did not have a single survivor left. ³⁴ From Lachish, Joshua and all of Israel passed to Eglon. They camped against it and waged war against it. ³⁵ They captured it that day and struck it with the edge of the sword. All who lived in it were destroyed that day, just as Israel had done to Lachish. ³⁶ Then Joshua and all of Israel went up from Eglon to Hebron and waged war against it. ³⁷ They captured it and struck its king, and all who lived in it, and its *surrounding* towns with the edge of the sword. No survivor was left. Just as they had done to Eglon, they destroyed it and all who lived in it.

³⁸ Then Joshua and all of Israel turned to Debir and waged war against it. ³⁹ They captured it, its king, and all its *surrounding* towns and struck them with the edge of the sword. They destroyed all who lived in them, and no survivor was left. As he had done to Hebron, so he did to Debir and its king as they had done to Libnah and its king. ⁴⁰ So Joshua attacked the whole land: the hill country, the Negev, the lowlands, the mountain slopes, and all their kings. No survivor was left. He destroyed all who breathed, as the LORD God of Israel had commanded. ⁴¹ Joshua attacked the land from Kadesh Barnea to Gaza and the land of Goshen as far as Gibeon. ⁴² Joshua captured all these kings and their land in one campaign because the LORD God of Israel waged war for Israel. ⁴³ Then Joshua and all of Israel returned to the settlement at Gilgal.

Northern Kings Defeated

11 When King Jabin of Hazor heard these things, he sent word to King Jobab of Madon, the king of Shimron, the king of Akshaph, ² and the kings of the northern hill country, the Arabah south of Kinnereth, the low country, and the heights of Dor in the west, ³ to the Canaanites in the east and in the west, the Amorites, the Hittites, the Perizzites, the Jebusites in the hill country, and the Hivites at Mount Hermon in the land of Mizpah. ⁴ So these kings went out with all their armies, people as numerous as *grains of sand* on the seashore, with a large number of horses and chariots. ⁵ These kings all met and camped together at the waters of Merom in order to wage war against Israel.

⁶ The LORD said to Joshua, "Do not be afraid of them, for about this time tomorrow I will make them dead before Israel. Hamstring their horses and burn their chariots with fire." ⁷ So Joshua and all his fighting forces came upon them by surprise at the waters of Merom and fell upon them. ⁸ The LORD gave them into the hand of Israel. They struck them down and pursued them all the way to Greater Sidon, Misrephoth Maim, and Mizpah Valley to the east. They struck them down until no survivor remained. ⁹ Joshua did to them as the LORD had said. He hamstrung their horses and burned their chariots with fire.

¹⁰ At that time Joshua turned, captured Hazor, and struck down its king with the sword. Hazor was formerly the head of all these kingdoms. ¹¹ They struck all who lived in them with the edge of the sword, destroying them. No one who breathed was left, and he burned Hazor with fire. ¹² Joshua captured all these kings and their towns. He struck them with the edge of the sword, destroying them, as Moses the servant of the LORD had commanded. ¹³ However, Israel did not burn any of the cities that stood on mounds except Hazor. Joshua burned it.

¹⁴ The children of Israel plundered all the goods and the livestock of these cities, but they struck all the people with the edge of the sword until they destroyed them. They did not spare anyone who breathed. ¹⁵ As the LORD commanded Moses His servant, so Moses commanded Joshua, and Joshua did it. He did not ignore a word of all that the LORD commanded Moses.

¹⁶ So Joshua took all that land: the hill country, the Negev, all the land of Goshen, the lowland, the Arabah, the hill country of Israel and its lowland. ¹⁷ From Mount Halak to Seir, and as far as Baal Gad in the Lebanon Valley under Mount Hermon: All their kings he captured, struck down, and killed. ¹⁸ Joshua engaged all those kings in battle for a long time. ¹⁹ There was no city that made peace with the children of Israel except the Hivites living in Gibeon. They conquered all of them ²⁰ because the LORD hardened their hearts to engage Israel in battle. They destroyed them without mercy, to put them to death, as the LORD had commanded Moses.

²¹ At that time Joshua came and wiped out the Anakites from the hill country: from Hebron, from Debir, from Anab, from all the hill country of Judah, and from all the hill country of Israel. Joshua utterly destroyed them and their cities. ²² No Anakites were left in the land of the children of Israel, but they did remain in Gaza, Gath, and Ashdod. ²³ So Joshua took the whole land according to all that the LORD had said to Moses. Joshua gave it to Israel as an inheritance according to their allotted portions by their tribes. Then the land rested from war.

The List of Defeated Kings

12 These are the kings on the east side of the Jordan, from the River Arnon to Mount Hermon and all the eastern Arabah, whom the children of Israel struck down to take over their land: ² Sihon king of the Amorites, who lived at Heshbon and ruled from Aroer, which is on the bank of River Arnon, and from the middle of the valley as far as the River Jabbok, which is the border of the Ammonites, that is, half of Gilead, ³ and the Arabah to the Sea of Galilee eastward, and toward Beth Jeshimoth, to the Sea of Arabah, the Dead Sea, southward below the slopes of Pisgah; ⁴ and Og king of Bashan, one of the remnant of the giants, who lived at Ashtaroth and at Edrei ⁵ and ruled over Mount Hermon, Salekah, and all of Bashan to the border of the Geshurites and the Maakathites, and over half of Gilead to the border of Sihon king of Heshbon.

⁶ Moses the servant of the LORD and the children of Israel struck them down, and the servant of the LORD Moses gave their land to Reuben, Gad, and the half-tribe of Manasseh.

⁷ These are the kings of the land whom Joshua and the children of Israel defeated on the west side of the Jordan, from Baal Gad in the Valley of Lebanon to Mount Halak, that rises toward Seir. Joshua gave their land to the tribes of Israel according to their allotted portions as an inheritance, ⁸ in the hill country, in the lowland, in the Arabah, in the slopes, in the wilderness, and in the Negev—the land of the Hittites, the Amorites, the Canaanites, the Perizzites, the Hivites, and the Jebusites:

⁹ The king of Jericho, one;
the king of Ai, which is beside Bethel, one;
¹⁰ the king of Jerusalem, one;
the king of Hebron, one;
¹¹ the king of Jarmuth, one;
the king of Lachish, one;
¹² the king of Eglon, one;
the king of Gezer, one;
¹³ the king of Debir, one;
the king of Geder, one;
¹⁴ the king of Hormah, one;
the king of Arad, one;
¹⁵ the king of Libnah, one;
the king of Adullam, one;
¹⁶ the king of Makkedah, one;
the king of Bethel, one;
¹⁷ the king of Tappuah, one;
the king of Hepher, one;

¹⁸ the king of Aphek, one;
the king of Lasharon, one;
¹⁹ the king of Madon, one;
the king of Hazor, one;
²⁰ the king of Shimron Meron, one;
the king of Akshaph, one;
²¹ the king of Taanach, one;
the king of Megiddo, one;
²² the king of Kedesh, one;
the king of Jokneam in Carmel, one;
²³ the king of Dor in Naphoth Dor, one;
the king of the people in Gilgal, one;
²⁴ the king of Tirzah, one—thirty-one kings in all.

Land Still to be Taken

13 Now Joshua was old and well advanced in years. The LORD said to him, "You are old and advanced in years, but very much of the land still remains to be possessed.

² "This is the land that remains: all the districts of the Philistines and those of the Geshurites ³ (from the Shihor east of Egypt northward to the boundary of Ekron, which is counted as Canaanite; the cities of the five Philistine governors: Gaza, Ashdod, Ashkelon, Gath, and Ekron), and also the Avvites' lands. ⁴ Also remaining in the south is all the land of the Canaanites, Arah owned by the Sidonians, as far as Aphek at the Amorite boundary, ⁵ the land of the Gebalites and all Lebanon to the east, and from Baal Gad at the foot of Mount Hermon to Lebo Hamath.

⁶ "I will drive out from before the children of Israel all the inhabitants of the hill country from Lebanon to Misrephoth Maim and all the Sidonians. Be sure to divide these lands by lot as an inheritance for Israel as I have commanded you. ⁷ So now, divide this land as an inheritance for the nine tribes and the half-tribe of Manasseh."

Division of the Land East of the Jordan River

⁸ *With the other half-tribe of Manasseh,* Reuben and Gad took their inheritance that Moses gave to them on the east side of the Jordan, as Moses the servant of the LORD had given them: ⁹ from Aroer on the bank of the River Arnon, the city in the middle of the valley, all the plain from Medeba to Dibon, ¹⁰ all the cities of King Sihon of the Amorites who reigned in Heshbon, and the land up to the Ammonite border. ¹¹ *Moses had also given them* Gilead, the territory of the Geshurites and Maakathites, all of Mount Hermon, and all of Bashan as far as Salekah, ¹² and in Bashan all the kingdom of Og, one of the last remnant of the giants, who reigned in Ashtaroth and Edrei. Moses struck them down and took their lands. ¹³ Yet the children of Israel did not drive out the Geshurites or the Maakathites, and Geshur and Maakah live among Israel until this day.

¹⁴ However Moses did not give an inheritance to the tribe of Levi. The burnt offerings of the LORD God of Israel are their inheritance, as He said to them.

¹⁵ Moses assigned land to the tribe of the Reubenites according to their clans. ¹⁶ Their territory was from Aroer on the edge of the Arnon Valley, the city in the middle of the valley, all the plain of Medeba, ¹⁷ Heshbon and all its towns in the plain: Dibon, Bamoth Baal, Beth Baal Meon, ¹⁸ Jahaz, Kedemoth, Mephaath, ¹⁹ Kiriathaim, Sibmah, Zereth Shahar on the hill of the valley, ²⁰ Beth Peor, the slopes of Pisgah, Beth Jeshimoth, ²¹ all the cities of the plain, and the whole kingdom of King Sihon of the Amorites, who reigned in Heshbon. Moses struck him down along with the leaders of Midian, Evi, Rekem, Zur, Hur, and Reba, who were princes of Sihon who lived in the land. ²² The children of Israel killed Balaam son of Beor, who practiced divination, with the sword along with the rest of the slain. ²³ The border of the Reubenites was the banks of the Jordan. This was the inheritance of the Reubenites according to their clans: those towns and their settlements.

²⁴ Moses assigned land to the tribe of Gad for the Gadites according to their clans. ²⁵ Their territory was Jazer, all the cities of Gilead, and half of the Ammonite land as far as Aroer, which is east of Rabbah, ²⁶ from Heshbon to Ramath Mizpah, Betonim, and from Mahanaim to the territory of Debir. ²⁷ In the valley were Beth Haram, Beth Nimrah, Sukkoth, and Zaphon, the rest of the kingdom of King Sihon of Heshbon, the Jordan as its boundary to the lower Sea of Galilee to the east of the Jordan. ²⁸ This was the inheritance of the Gadites according to their clans: those towns and their settlements.

²⁹ Moses assigned land to the half-tribe of Manasseh for the descendants of Manasseh according to their clans. ³⁰ Their territory was from Mahanaim, through all of Bashan, all the kingdom of King Og of Bashan, all the sixty villages of Jair that are in Bashan, ³¹ half of Gilead, Ashtaroth, and Edrei: cities of the kingdom of Og in Bashan. This was for the descendants of Makir son of Manasseh, half of the descendants of Makir by their clans.

³² This is the territory Moses assigned in the desert plains of Moab, on the eastern side of Jericho and the Jordan. ³³ Yet Moses did not assign land to the tribe of Levi as an inheritance. The LORD God of Israel was their inheritance, as He said to them.

Division of the Land West of the Jordan

14 These are the territories that the children of Israel inherited in the land of Canaan, which Eleazar the priest, Joshua son of Nun, and the family leaders of the Israelite tribes assigned to them. ² Their inheritance fell to them by lot, as the LORD commanded through Moses, for the nine and a half tribes. ³ For Moses had assigned the inheritance of two and a half tribes on the other side of the Jordan, but he had not assigned an inheritance among them to the Levites. ⁴ The descendants of Joseph were two tribes: Manasseh and Ephraim. They did not give territory to the Levites in the land, but only towns in which to live, along with the pastures, livestock, and property. ⁵ Just as the LORD had commanded Moses, so the children of Israel did when they divided the land.

Hebron Given to Caleb

⁶ The descendants of Judah approached Joshua at Gilgal, and Caleb son of Jephunneh the Kenizzite said to him, "You know what the LORD said to Moses the man of God about you and me at Kadesh Barnea. ⁷ I was forty years old when Moses the servant of the LORD sent me from Kadesh Barnea to spy on the land, and I brought word back to him as it was in my heart. ⁸ My companions who went up with me made the hearts of the people melt, but I wholeheartedly followed after the LORD my God. ⁹ On that day Moses swore an oath, 'The land on which your foot treads shall be your inheritance, for your descendants perpetually, because you completely followed after the LORD my God.'

¹⁰ "Now, the LORD has kept me alive, just as He said, for forty-five years, since the LORD spoke this word to Moses while Israel wandered in the wilderness. Now, here I am this day, eighty-five years old. ¹¹ I am still just as strong today as I was on the day that Moses sent me. My strength now is just like my strength then, both for battle and for going out and returning. ¹² So now, give me this hill country that the LORD spoke about on that day. That day you heard that the Anakites live there in large, fortified cities. Perhaps the LORD will be with me, and I will drive them out, as the LORD said."

¹³ Then Joshua blessed him and gave Hebron to Caleb son of Jephunneh as an inheritance. ¹⁴ Therefore Hebron became an inheritance of Caleb son of Jephunneh the Kenizzite until this day because he completely followed after the LORD, the God of Israel. ¹⁵ The former name of Hebron was Kiriath Arba. Arba was the greatest man among the Anakites.

Then the land had rest from war.

Allotment for Judah
Jdg 1:11–15

15 The allotment for the tribe of Judah, by their clans, stretches southward to the border of Edom, to the Zin wilderness in the south.

[2] Their southern border runs from the southern tip of the Salt Sea, [3] to south of the Ascent of Akrabbim, crosses to Zin, rises south of Kadesh Barnea, crosses to Hezron, then rises to Addar, turns toward Karka, [4] then crosses to Azmon, goes out to the Brook of Egypt, and then to the sea. This is your southern border.

[5] The eastern border is the Salt Sea up to the mouth of the Jordan. The northern border runs from the northern extremity of the Dead Sea at the mouth of the Jordan River, [6] then rises to Beth Hoglah, crosses north of Beth Arabah, rises to the Stone of Bohan son of Reuben, [7] and rises to Debir from the Achor Valley, turns northward to Gilgal opposite the Ascent of Adummim south of the valley, and crosses to the waters of En Shemesh and onward to En Rogel. [8] The border rises to Valley of Ben Hinnom, to the southern slope of the Jebusites (that is, Jerusalem), then rises to the top of the hill west of the Valley of Ben Hinnom, at the northern end of the Valley of Rephaim. [9] The border turns from the top of the hill to the waters of Nephtoah and goes out to the cities of Mount Ephron, then turns to Baalah (that is, Kiriath Jearim). [10] The border turns west of Baalah to Mount Seir, crosses to the northern slope of Mount Jearim (that is, Kesalon), descends to Beth Shemesh, and crosses to Timnah. [11] The border goes out to the northern slope of Ekron, turns to Shikkeron, crosses to Mount Baalah, goes out to Jabneel, and ends at the sea.

[12] The western border was the coastline of the *Mediterranean* Sea.

These were the borders surrounding the tribe of Judah according to their clans.

[13] According to the word of the Lord to Joshua, Caleb son of Jephunneh was given an allotment among the tribe of Judah: Kiriath Arba (that is, Hebron). Arba was the father of Anak. [14] Caleb drove out from there three Anakites: Sheshai, Ahiman, and Talmai, descendants of Anak. [15] He went up from there against the inhabitants of Debir. Before the name of Debir was Kiriath Sepher. [16] Caleb said, "I will give my daughter Aksah in marriage to whoever attacks Kiriath Sepher and captures it." [17] Othniel son of Kenaz, the brother of Caleb, captured it, so Caleb gave him Aksah his daughter in marriage.

[18] When she came to Othniel, she urged him to ask her father for a field. She dismounted from her donkey, and Caleb said to her, "What can I do for you?"

[19] She answered, "Please give me a blessing. Since you have given me land in the Negev, now give me springs of water." So he gave her the upper and lower springs.

[20] This is the inheritance of the tribe of Judah according to their clans.

[21] The cities at the southern extremity of the tribe of Judah toward the border with Edom were Kabzeel, Eder, Jagur, [22] Kinah, Dimonah, Adadah, [23] Kedesh, Hazor, Ithnan, [24] Ziph, Telem, Bealoth, [25] Hazor Hadattah, Kerioth Hezron (that is, Hazor), [26] Amam, Shema, Moladah, [27] Hazar Gaddah, Heshmon, Beth Pelet, [28] Hazar Shual, Beersheba, Biziothiah, [29] Baalah, Iyim, Ezem, [30] Eltolad, Kesil, Hormah, [31] Ziklag, Madmannah, Sansannah, [32] Lebaoth, Shilhim, Ain, and Rimmon. The cities numbered twenty-nine with their villages.

[33] In the lowland were Eshtaol, Zorah, Ashnah, [34] Zanoah, En Gannim, Tappuah, Enam, [35] Jarmuth, Adullam, Sokoh, Azekah, [36] Shaaraim, Adithaim, Gederah (Gederothaim): fourteen cities with their villages.

[37] *Also there were* Zenan, Hadashah, Migdal Gad, [38] Dilean, Mizpah, Joktheel, [39] Lachish, Bozkath, Eglon, [40] Kabbon, Lahmas, Kitlish, [41] Gederoth, Beth Dagon, Naamah, and Makkedah: sixteen cities with their villages.

[42] *Also there were* Libnah, Ether, Ashan, [43] Iphtah, Ashnah, Nezib, [44] Keilah, Akzib, and Mareshah: nine cities with their villages.

[45] *Also there were* Ekron, its towns and villages; [46] from Ekron to the sea, all the land near Ashdod and their villages, [47] Ashdod, its towns and villages, Gaza, its towns and villages, as far as the Brook of Egypt and the *Mediterranean* Sea with its coast.

[48] In the hill country were Shamir, Jattir, Sokoh, [49] Dannah, Kiriath Sannah (that is, Debir), [50] Anab, Eshtemoh, Anim, [51] Goshen, Holon, and Giloh: eleven cities with their villages.

[52] *Also there were* Arab, Dumah, Eshan, [53] Janim, Beth Tappuah, Aphekah, [54] Humtah, Kiriath Arba (that is, Hebron), and Zior: nine cities with their villages.

[55] *Also there were* Maon, Carmel, Ziph, Juttah, [56] Jezreel, Jokdeam, Zanoah, [57] Kain, Gibeah, and Timnah: ten cities with their villages.

[58] *Also there were* Halhul, Beth Zur, Gedor, [59] Maarath, Beth Anoth, and Eltekon: six cities with their villages.

[60] *Also there were* Kiriath Baal (that is, Kiriath Jearim) and Rabbah: two cities with their villages.

[61] In the wilderness were Beth Arabah, Middin, Sekakah, [62] Nibshan, City of Salt, and En Gedi: six cities with their villages.

[63] The people of Judah were not able to drive out the Jebusites living in Jerusalem, so the Jebusites live with the people of Judah in Jerusalem to this day.

Allotment for Ephraim and Manasseh

16 The allotment of land for the descendants of Joseph was from the Jordan by Jericho then east into the wilderness, rising from Jericho to the hill country of Bethel. [2] It goes out from Bethel to Luz and passes to the border of Arkite territory at Ataroth. [3] It goes down westward to the territory of the Japhletites, to the border of lower Beth Horon and Gezer, and then goes out to the sea.

[4] So the descendants of Joseph, Manasseh and Ephraim, took their inheritance.

[5] The territory of the Ephraimites, according to their clans, was as follows. The border of their inheritance on the east was Ataroth Addar as far as upper Beth Horon. [6] The border goes out toward the sea with Mikmethath on the north. It turns eastward toward Taanath Shiloh and passes it on the east toward Janoah. [7] It descends from Janoah to Ataroth and to Naarah, touches Jericho, and extends to the Jordan. [8] From Tappuah the border goes west to the Kanah Ravine and out to the sea. This is the inheritance of the tribe of the Ephraimites according to their clans. [9] The other cities for the Ephraimites were in the middle of the inheritance of the descendants of Manasseh, all the cities and their villages.

[10] They did not drive out the Canaanites who lived in Gezer, so the Canaanites live in the midst of Ephraim until this day performing heavy labor as slaves.

17 Then allotment was made to the tribe of Manasseh, for he was the firstborn of Joseph. To Makir the firstborn of Manasseh, the father of Gilead, were allotted Gilead and Bashan, because he was a warrior. [2] And allotments were made to the rest of the tribe of Manasseh, according to their families: Abiezer, Helek, Asriel, Shechem, Hepher, and Shemida; these were the male descendants of Manasseh son of Joseph, according to their families.

[3] Yet Zelophehad, son of Hepher, son of Gilead, son of Makir, son of Manasseh had no sons, only daughters. These were his daughters' names: Mahlah, Noah, Hoglah, Milkah, and Tirzah. [4] They approached Eleazar the priest, Joshua son of Nun, and the leaders, saying, "The Lord commanded Moses to give us an inheritance among our relatives." So Joshua gave them an inheritance among their fathers' relatives according to the word of the Lord. [5] Therefore Manasseh received ten regions, apart from the lands of Gilead and Bashan on the east side of the Jordan, [6] because the daughters of Manasseh received an inheritance among his sons, and the rest of the people of Manasseh received the land of Gilead.

[7] The boundary of Manasseh was from Asher to Mikmethath east of Shechem, and it runs south toward the inhabitants of En Tappuah. [8] Now Manasseh owned the land of Tappuah, but Tappuah on the border of Manasseh belonged to the Ephraimites. [9] Then the border descended to the Kanah Ravine, southward to the brook. These cities of Ephraim are among the cities of Manasseh. The border of Manasseh was on the north side of the brook, and it ended at the sea. [10] The land belonging to Ephraim was to the south, and the land belonging to Manasseh to the north. The *Mediterranean*

Sea was the boundary of this territory, which bordered Asher in the north and Issachar in the east.

[11] In Issachar and Asher, Manasseh was assigned districts: Beth Shan, Ibleam, Dor, Endor, Taanach, Megiddo, Naphoth, and their respective villages.

[12] Yet the sons of Manasseh could not take possession of those cities, because the Canaanites were determined to live in that land. [13] But when the children of Israel became strong, they put the Canaanites to hard labor as slaves, but they did not actually drive them out.

[14] The descendants of Joseph said to Joshua, "Why have you assigned us a single allotment, a single portion? We are a numerous people, as the Lord has blessed us."

[15] Joshua said to them, "If you are a numerous people, go up to the forests and clear out a place there for yourselves in the land of the Perizzites and the giants, since the hill country of Ephraim is too small for you."

[16] The descendants of Joseph said, "The hill country is not enough for us, and all the Canaanites living in the plains have iron chariots, both those in Beth Shan and the Jezreel Valley."

[17] Joshua said to Ephraim and Manasseh, the descendants of Joseph, "You are a numerous people who have great strength. There will not be only one allotment for you. [18] The hill country shall be yours. Although it is a forest you shall clear it and own it to its borders. You shall drive out the Canaanites, even though they have iron chariots and are strong."

Dividing the Rest of the Land

18 The whole congregation of the children of Israel assembled at Shiloh and set up the tent of meeting there. The land was subdued before them. [2] Yet seven tribes among the children of Israel remained who had not yet received their inheritance.

[3] So Joshua said to the children of Israel, "How long will you delay going in to possess the land that the Lord, the God of your fathers, has given you? [4] Select three men from each tribe, and I will send them out; and they will rise and go throughout the land, and describe it according to their inheritance, and they will come back to me. [5] They shall divide it into seven portions. Judah will stay in their territory in the south, and the house of Joseph will stay in their territory in the north. [6] So describe the land in seven portions and return to me. Then I will cast lots for you here before the Lord our God. [7] Yet there is no portion for the Levites among you, for the priesthood of the Lord is their inheritance. Gad, Reuben, and the half-tribe of Manasseh have acquired their inheritance on the east side of the Jordan, which Moses the servant of the Lord gave them."

[8] So the men got up and left. Joshua commanded those who were leaving to survey the land, saying, "Go and walk back and forth throughout the land. Write a description of it, then return to me. Here in Shiloh I will cast lots for you before the Lord." [9] The men went and passed through the land. In a book they wrote a description of it by cities in seven portions, and they came back to Joshua at the Shiloh settlement. [10] Joshua cast lots for them in Shiloh before the Lord. There Joshua apportioned the land for the children of Israel according to their divisions.

The Allotment for Benjamin

[11] The lot of the tribe of Benjamin, according to their clans, came up. The territory allotted to it fell between Judah and Joseph.

[12] Their northern border goes from the Jordan up the northern slope of Jericho. It runs westward into the hill country and extends to the wilderness of Beth Aven. [13] The border passes from there southward toward Luz, to the slope of Luz (that is, Bethel), and descends to Ataroth Addar on the hill south of lower Beth Horon.

[14] On the western side, the border turns south from the hill that lies to the south near Beth Horon, and it extends to Kiriath Baal (that is, Kiriath Jearim), a city belonging to Judah. This is the western border.

[15] The southern border starts from Kiriath Jearim and goes out westward to the spring of the waters of Nephtoah. [16] The border then descends to the foot of the mountain that lies by the Valley of Ben Hinnom, which is at the north end of the Valley of Rephaim.

It descends from the Hinnom Valley to the slope of the Jebusites, then down to En Rogel. [17] The border runs north and goes out to En Shemesh and Geliloth, which is opposite the Ascent of Adummim, and descends to the Stone of Bohan the son of Reuben. [18] It passes toward the slope north of the Beth Arabah and descends to the Arabah. [19] The border passes north of the slope of Beth Hoglah, and it runs out to the northern tip of the Dead Sea at the southern end of the Jordan. This is the southern border.

[20] The Jordan forms the eastern boundary.

This is the inheritance of the tribe of Benjamin, according to their clans, by its boundaries all around.

[21] The cities belonging to the tribe of Benjamin, according to their clans, were Jericho, Beth Hoglah, Emek Keziz, [22] Beth Arabah, Zemaraim, Bethel, [23] Avvim, Parah, Ophrah, [24] Kephar Ammoni, Ophni, and Geba: twelve cities with their villages.

[25] Also there were Gibeon, Ramah, Beeroth, [26] Mizpah, Kephirah, Mozah, [27] Rekem, Irpeel, Taralah, [28] Zelah, Haeleph, the Jebusite city (that is, Jerusalem), Gibeah, and Kiriath: fourteen cities with their villages.

This is the inheritance of the tribe of Benjamin according to their clans.

Allotment for Simeon
1Ch 4:28–33

19 The second lot came out for Simeon, for the tribe of Simeon according to their clans. Their inheritance was within the inheritance of the tribe of Judah. [2] Their inheritance was Beersheba, Sheba, Moladah, [3] Hazar Shual, Balah, Ezem, [4] Eltolad, Bethul, Hormah, [5] Ziklag, Beth Markaboth, Hazar Susah, [6] Beth Lebaoth, and Sharuhen: thirteen cities and their villages;

[7] Ain, Rimmon, Ether, and Ashan: four cities and their villages; [8] and all the villages that were around these cities as far as Baalath Beer, Ramah of the Negev.

This was the inheritance of the tribe of Simeon according to their clans. [9] Simeon received a portion of the inheritance of Judah, for the inheritance of Judah was too large for them, so Simeon inherited land in the midst of the inheritance of Judah.

Allotment for Zebulun

[10] The third lot came up for Zebulun according to their clans. Their territory extended to Sarid, [11] and their border ascended westward to Maralah, reaching Dabbesheth and the valley east of Jokneam. [12] From Sarid the border turned east to the border of Kisloth Tabor, out to Daberath, and up to Japhia. [13] From there it passes east to Gath Hepher and Eth Kazin. It turns out to Rimmon and turns toward Neah. [14] The boundary turns north to Hannathon and extends to the Valley of Iphtah El; [15] and Kattath, Nahalal, Shimron, Idalah, and Bethlehem: twelve cities and their villages.

[16] This was the inheritance of the tribe of Zebulun according to their clans: these cities and their villages.

Allotment for Issachar

[17] The fourth lot came out for Issachar, for the tribe of Issachar according to their clans. [18] Their territory included Jezreel, Kesulloth, Shunem, [19] Hapharaim, Shion, Anaharath, [20] Rabbith, Kishion, Ebez, [21] Remeth, En Gannim, En Haddah, and Beth Pazzez. [22] The border touches Tabor, Shahazumah, and Beth Shemesh, then extends to the Jordan: sixteen cities and their villages.

[23] This is the inheritance of the tribe of Issachar according to their clans: the cities and their villages.

Allotment for Asher

[24] The fifth lot came out for the tribe of Asher according to their clans. [25] Their territory included Helkath, Hali, Beten, Akshaph, [26] Allammelek, Amad, and Mishal. On the west their border touches Carmel and Shihor Libnath. [27] Then it turns eastward, goes to Beth Dagon, and touches Zebulun and the Valley of Iphtah El northward to Beth Emek and Neiel; then it continues in the north to Kabul, [28] Abdon, Rehob, Hammon, Kanah, as far as Greater Sidon. [29] Then the border turned to Ramah, reaching the fortified city of Tyre. Then

the border turned to Hosah, and ended at the *Mediterranean* Sea by the region of Akzib, [30] Ummah, Aphek, and Rehob: twenty-two cities and their villages.

[31] This is the inheritance of the tribe of Asher according to their clans: these cities and their villages.

Allotment for Naphtali

[32] The sixth lot came out for the tribe of Naphtali according to their clans.

[33] Their border runs from Heleph, from the oak of Zaanannim, to Adami Nekeb and Jabneel, as far as Lakkum, and extends to the Jordan. [34] The border turns west to Aznoth Tabor, goes out from there to Hukkok, and touches Zebulun on the south, Asher on the west, and Judah at the Jordan on the east. [35] Their fortified cities were Ziddim, Zer, Hammath, Rakkath, Kinnereth, [36] Adamah, Ramah, Hazor, [37] Kedesh, Edrei, En Hazor, [38] Iron, Migdal El, Horem, Beth Anath, and Beth Shemesh: nineteen cities and their villages.

[39] This is the inheritance of the tribe of Naphtali according to their clans: the cities and their villages.

Allotment for Dan

[40] The seventh lot came out for the tribe of Dan according to their clans. [41] The territory of their inheritance included Zorah, Eshtaol, Ir Shemesh, [42] Shaalabbin, Aijalon, Ithlah, [43] Elon, Timnah, Ekron, [44] Eltekeh, Gibbethon, Baalath, [45] Jehud, Bene Berak, Gath Rimmon, [46] Me Jarkon, and Rakkon, along with the territory near Joppa.

[47] Yet the tribe of Dan lost their territory, so they went up to wage war against Leshem and captured it. They attacked it with the edge of the sword, took possession of it, and settled there. They called Leshem Dan after the name of Dan their father.

[48] This is the inheritance of the tribe of Dan according to their clans: these cities and their villages.

The Allotment for Joshua

[49] When they had finished allotting the land according to its boundaries, the children of Israel gave an inheritance among them to Joshua son of Nun. [50] According to the word of the LORD, they gave him the city for which he asked: Timnath Serah in the hill country of Ephraim. He built up the city and lived in it.

[51] These are the inheritances that Eleazar the priest, Joshua son of Nun, and the family leaders of the Israelite tribes assigned by lot in Shiloh before the LORD at the entrance of the tent of meeting. So they completed dividing the land.

Cities of Refuge
Nu 35:9–34; Dt 4:41–43; 19:1–14

20 Then the LORD said to Joshua, [2] "Say to the children of Israel, 'Choose refuge cities, as I told you through Moses, [3] so that anyone who kills a person without intent and unknowingly may flee there. They shall be your refuge from the avenger of blood.

[4] " 'The refugee can flee to one of these cities then stand at the entrance of the city gate and tell his case to the city elders. They will take him into the city and give him a place to stay, and he will live with them. [5] When the avenger of blood comes after him, they shall not hand over the manslayer to him, for he struck down his neighbor unintentionally with no premeditated malice. [6] He shall live in that city until he stands before the congregation for judgment, until the death of the high priest serving at that time. Then the manslayer may return to his home and to his city from which he had fled.' "

[7] They selected Kedesh in Galilee in the hill country of Naphtali, Shechem in the hill country of Ephraim, and Kiriath Arba (that is, Hebron) in the hill country of Judah. [8] Across the Jordan east of Jericho, they selected Bezer in the wilderness plain from the tribe of Reuben, Ramoth in Gilead from the tribe of Gad, and Golan in Bashan from the tribe of Manasseh. [9] These were the cities designated for all the children of Israel and resident foreigners living among them, to which anyone who killed someone inadvertently could flee and not die at the hand of the avenger of blood until he stood before the congregation.

Cities for the Levites
1Ch 6:54–80

21 The family leaders of the Levites approached Eleazar the priest, Joshua son of Nun, and the family leaders of the Israelite tribes. [2] At Shiloh in the land of Canaan they said to them, "Through Moses the LORD commanded that we be given cities in which to live and grazing lands for our livestock." [3] So according to the word of the LORD, out of their inheritance the children of Israel gave the Levites these cities and their grazing lands.

[4] The lot came out for the clans of the Kohathites, so the Levites who were descendants of Aaron received an allotment of thirteen cities from the tribes of Judah, Simeon, and Benjamin. [5] The remaining descendants of Kohath received an allotment of ten cities from the clans of the tribes of Ephraim, Dan, and the half-tribe of Manasseh.

[6] The descendants of Gershon received an allotment of thirteen cities from the clans of the tribes of Issachar, Asher, Naphtali, and the half-tribe of Manasseh in Bashan.

[7] Descendants of Merari by their clans received an allotment of twelve cities from the tribes of Reuben, Gad, and Zebulun.

[8] The children of Israel allotted the Levites these cities and their grazing lands, as the LORD commanded through Moses.

[9] From the tribes of Judah and Simeon they assigned the following cities with these names. [10] They were assigned to the descendants of Aaron, to the clans of the Kohathites of the tribe of Levi, for theirs was the first lot.

[11] They assigned them Kiriath Arba (Arba was the father of Anak), which is Hebron, in the hill country of Judah, and the grazing lands around it. [12] (Now they had assigned the city's fields and its surrounding villages to Caleb son of Jephunneh as his property.)

[13] So to the descendants of Aaron the priest they assigned Hebron (a refuge city for people who committed manslaughter), Libnah with its pastures, [14] Jattir, Eshtemoa, [15] Holon, Debir, [16] Ain, Juttah, and Beth Shemesh, together with the grazing lands of each: nine cities from these two tribes.

[17] From the tribe of Benjamin *they assigned* Gibeon, Geba, [18] Anathoth, and Almon, together with the grazing lands of each: four cities.

[19] Altogether the descendants of Aaron received thirteen cities and their grazing lands.

[20] The rest of the Levites from the clans of the descendants of Kohath received cities allotted from the tribe of Ephraim. [21] They assigned them Shechem (a refuge city for people who committed manslaughter) in the hill country of Ephraim, Gezer, [22] Kibzaim, and Beth Horon, together with the grazing lands of each: four cities.

[23] From the tribe of Dan *they assigned* Eltekeh, Gibbethon, [24] Aijalon, and Gath Rimmon, together with the grazing lands of each: four cities.

[25] From the half-tribe of Manasseh they assigned Taanach and Gath Rimmon, together with the grazing lands of each: two cities.

[26] Altogether the rest of the clans of the descendants of Kohath received ten cities and their grazing lands.

[27] From the half-tribe of Manasseh *they assigned* to the descendants of Gershon (one of the Levite clans): Golan in Bashan (a refuge city for people who committed manslaughter) and Be Eshterah, together with the grazing lands of each: two cities.

[28] From the tribe of Issachar *they assigned* Kishion, Daberath, [29] Jarmuth, and En Gannim, together with the grazing lands of each: four cities.

[30] From the tribe of Asher *they assigned* Mishal, Abdon, [31] Helkath, and Rehob, together with the grazing lands of each: four cities.

[32] From the tribe of Naphtali *they assigned* Kedesh in Galilee (a refuge city for people who committed manslaughter), Hammoth Dor, and Kartan, together with the grazing lands of each: three cities.

[33] Altogether the Gershonites according to their clans received thirteen cities and their grazing lands.

³⁴ From the tribe of Zebulun *they assigned* to the descendants of Merari (the remaining Levites): Jokneam, Kartah, ³⁵ Dimnah, and Nahalal, together with the grazing lands of each: four cities.

³⁶ From the tribe of Reuben *they assigned* Bezer, Jahaz, ³⁷ Kedemoth, and Mephaath, together with the grazing lands of each: four cities.

³⁸ From the tribe of Gad *they assigned* Ramoth in Gilead (a refuge city for people who committed manslaughter), Mahanaim, ³⁹ Heshbon, and Jazer, together with the grazing lands of each: four cities in all.

⁴⁰ So twelve cities were allotted for the descendants of Merari according to their clans (the remaining Levite clans).

⁴¹ Altogether the Levites received forty-eight cities and their grazing lands within the possessions of the children of Israel. ⁴² Each of these cities had grazing lands surrounding them. It was this way with all these cities.

⁴³ The Lᴏʀᴅ gave Israel all the land that He swore to give to their fathers. They took possession of it and lived in it. ⁴⁴ The Lᴏʀᴅ gave them rest all around, according to all that He swore to their fathers. Not a man among their enemies stood before them, and the Lᴏʀᴅ delivered all their enemies into their hands. ⁴⁵ Not a single word of all the good things that the Lᴏʀᴅ had spoken to the children of Israel failed. They all came to pass.

The Eastern Tribes Return Home

22 Then Joshua summoned the Reubenites, the Gadites, and the half-tribe of Manasseh. ² He said to them, "You have done everything that Moses the servant of the Lᴏʀᴅ commanded you and have obeyed me in everything that I have commanded you. ³ You have not left your brothers these many days down to this day, and you have observed the obligations of the commandment of the Lᴏʀᴅ your God. ⁴ Now the Lᴏʀᴅ your God has given rest to your brothers, as He had said to them. So now, turn and go to your homes, to the land of your possession, which Moses the servant of the Lᴏʀᴅ gave you on the other side of the Jordan. ⁵ Only carefully obey the commandment and the law that Moses the servant of the Lᴏʀᴅ commanded you: to love the Lᴏʀᴅ your God, to walk in all His ways, to obey His commandments, to cling to Him, and to serve Him with all your heart and soul."

⁶ Joshua blessed them and sent them off, and they went to their tents. ⁷ Moses had assigned land in Bashan to half the tribe of Manasseh, and to the other half Joshua assigned land among their brothers on the west side of the Jordan. When Joshua sent them also to their homes and blessed them, ⁸ he said, "Return home with great wealth, much livestock, silver, gold, copper, iron, and great quantities of clothing. Divide the spoil of your enemies among your brothers."

⁹ So the Reubenites, Gadites, and the half-tribe of Manasseh left the children of Israel at Shiloh in the land of Canaan to go to the land of Gilead, the land of their possession, according to the word of the Lᴏʀᴅ through Moses.

¹⁰ The tribes of Reuben, Gad, and the half-tribe of Manasseh came near the Jordan in the land of Canaan and built a very large altar by the Jordan. ¹¹ The children of Israel heard someone say, "The tribes of Reuben, Gad, and the half-tribe of Manasseh have built an altar by the land of Canaan by the Jordan on the Israelite side." ¹² When the children of Israel heard this, they assembled the whole congregation of the children of Israel at Shiloh to go up against them in war.

¹³ Then the children of Israel sent Phinehas, son of Eleazar the priest, to the sons of Reuben, to the sons of Gad, and to the half-tribe of Manasseh, into the land of Gilead, ¹⁴ and with him ten chiefs, one chief each for each father's household of every tribe of Israel; and each one of them was the head of his father's house among the thousands of Israel.

¹⁵ They came to the tribes of Reuben, Gad, and the half-tribe of Manasseh in the land of Gilead and said to them, ¹⁶ "The whole congregation of the Lᴏʀᴅ says, 'What is this trespass you have committed against the God of Israel? Today you have turned from following the Lᴏʀᴅ by building yourselves an altar to rebel against

Him! ¹⁷ Is the sin of Peor, from which we have still not purified ourselves even today, not enough for us, which brought a plague upon the congregation of the Lᴏʀᴅ ¹⁸ that today you have turned away from following the Lᴏʀᴅ?

"'If today you are rebelling against the Lᴏʀᴅ, then tomorrow He will be angry with the whole congregation of Israel! ¹⁹ If indeed your own land is unclean, then cross over to the land of the Lᴏʀᴅ where the tabernacle of the Lᴏʀᴅ stands and take land among us. Yet do not rebel against the Lᴏʀᴅ or rebel against us by building an altar other than the altar of the Lᴏʀᴅ our God. ²⁰ Did not Achan son of Zerah commit a trespass in the things under the ban, and wrath fall on all the congregation of Israel? And that man did not perish alone in his iniquity.' "

²¹ Then the tribes of Reuben, Gad, and the half-tribe of Manasseh answered and said to the heads of the Israelite clans, ²² "The Lᴏʀᴅ God of gods, the Lᴏʀᴅ God of gods, He knows, and may Israel know—if we *have acted* in rebellion or disloyalty against the Lᴏʀᴅ, do not spare us today. ²³ If we have built an altar to turn away from following the Lᴏʀᴅ, to offer burnt offerings and grain offerings or make peace offerings upon it, may the Lᴏʀᴅ Himself demand *an account*.

²⁴ "We did this deed because we were worried that in the future your descendants might say, 'What have you to do with the Lᴏʀᴅ God of Israel? ²⁵ The Lᴏʀᴅ made the Jordan a boundary between us and you, the descendants of Reuben and Gad. You have no share in the Lᴏʀᴅ!' In this way your descendants might make our descendants to stop worshipping the Lᴏʀᴅ.

²⁶ "So we said to each other, 'Let us build this altar, not for burnt offering or sacrifice,' ²⁷ but as a witness for us, for you, and for the generations after us, that we may perform the service of the Lᴏʀᴅ before Him with our burnt offerings, sacrifices, and peace offerings, and in the future your descendants will not be able to say to our descendants, 'You have no share in the Lᴏʀᴅ!' '

²⁸ "Therefore we said, 'In the future, if they say this to us or to our descendants, we will say, "Look at the replica of the altar of the Lᴏʀᴅ that our fathers made, not for burnt offerings or sacrifices, but as a witness between you and us." '

²⁹ "God forbid that we should rebel against the Lᴏʀᴅ by turning from following the Lᴏʀᴅ today by building an altar for burnt offerings, grain offerings, and sacrifices other than the altar of the Lᴏʀᴅ God that stands before His tabernacle!"

³⁰ When Phinehas the priest, the leaders of the congregation, and the heads of the Israelite clans who were with him heard what the descendants of Reuben, Gad, and Manasseh said, it pleased them. ³¹ Phinehas son of Eleazar the priest said to the descendants of Reuben, Gad, and Manasseh, "Today we know that the Lᴏʀᴅ is in our midst because you did not violate your obligations to the Lᴏʀᴅ in this *matter*. Indeed, you have delivered the children of Israel from the judgment of the Lᴏʀᴅ."

³² Then Phinehas son of Eleazar the priest and the leaders returned from *meeting* the descendants of Reuben and Gad in the land of Gilead to the children of Israel in the land of Canaan. They brought back a report. ³³ This report was good in the eyes of the children of Israel, and the children of Israel blessed God. They decided not to make war against the descendants of Reuben and Gad to ruin the land in which they lived.

³⁴ The descendants of Reuben and Gad named the altar *Witness*, "For it is a witness between us that the Lᴏʀᴅ is God."

Joshua's Charge to the Leaders

23 A long time later, after the Lᴏʀᴅ had given Israel rest from all their enemies around them, Joshua was old and advanced in years. ² Joshua called for all Israel, their elders, clan heads, judges, and officials, and said to them, "I am old and advanced in years. ³ You have seen all that the Lᴏʀᴅ your God did to all these peoples before you, for it is the Lᴏʀᴅ your God who has waged war for you. ⁴ See, I have allotted to you as an inheritance *the land of* these peoples who remain, along with *the land of* the peoples whom I defeated, from the Jordan to the *Mediterranean* Sea in the west. ⁵ The Lᴏʀᴅ your God will drive them out and dispossess them from before you, and you will inherit their land, as the Lᴏʀᴅ your God told you.

⁶ "Now be very strong to observe and enact all that is written in the Book of the Law of Moses, so that you do not deviate from it to the right or the left. ⁷ Do not assimilate with these peoples remaining among you. Do not invoke the names of their gods, nor swear by, serve, or worship them. ⁸ Instead, cling to the Lord your God, as you have done until today.

⁹ "For the Lord has dispossessed before you great and mighty peoples, and as for you, not a single man has been able to stand against you until today. ¹⁰ One man from among you can make a thousand flee, for it is the Lord your God who wages war for you, as He told you. ¹¹ Now be careful, therefore, to love the Lord your God! ¹² "For if you should turn and cling to the remainder of these peoples who are left with you, and you intermarry and assimilate with them, and they with you, ¹³ know for certain that the Lord your God will no longer drive out these nations from before you. But they shall be snares and traps to you, a whip on your sides and thorns in your eyes, until you perish from off this good ground that the Lord your God has given you.

¹⁴ "Now, I am going the way of all the earth. You know in all your hearts and souls that not a single word has failed out of all the good things that the Lord your God has said concerning you. All came true for you. Not a single word among them failed. ¹⁵ So just as every good thing that the Lord your God said to you came to be, even so the Lord can bring every bad thing upon you until He has destroyed you from this good land that the Lord your God gave you. ¹⁶ If you break the covenant of the Lord your God that He commanded you, and go and serve other gods and worship them, the anger of the Lord will burn against you, and you will quickly perish from the good land that He gave you."

Covenant Renewed at Shechem

24 Joshua called for all the Israelite tribes at Shechem and summoned the elders, clan heads, judges, and officials of Israel. They presented themselves before God.

² Joshua said to all the people, "Thus says the Lord God of Israel: Long ago your fathers—Terah father of Abraham and Nahor—lived beyond the Euphrates¹ and served other gods. ³ I took your father Abraham from beyond the Euphrates,² brought him through all the land of Canaan, and gave him many descendants. To him I gave Isaac. ⁴ To Isaac I gave Jacob and Esau, and to Esau I gave Mount Seir for his inheritance, but Jacob and his descendants went down into Egypt.

⁵ "I sent Moses and Aaron, I struck Egypt down with all I did in their midst, and afterward I brought you out. ⁶ I brought your fathers out of Egypt, then you came to the sea. The Egyptians pursued your fathers with chariots and horsemen to the Red Sea. ⁷ *Your fathers* cried out to the Lord, and He placed darkness between you and the Egyptians. He made the sea come upon them and cover them. Your own eyes saw what I did to Egypt, and you lived in the wilderness a long time.

⁸ "I brought you to the land of the Amorites who lived on the other side of the Jordan. They waged war against you, but I gave them into your hand so that you might inherit their land, and I destroyed them before you. ⁹ Then Balak son of Zippor, king of Moab, arose and waged war against Israel. He called for Balaam son of Beor to curse you, ¹⁰ but I refused to listen to Balaam. Therefore he blessed you still, and I delivered you out of his hand.

¹¹ "You crossed the Jordan and came to Jericho. The leaders of Jericho, along with the Amorites, Perizzites, Canaanites, Hittites,

Girgashites, Hivites, and Jebusites, waged war against you, but I gave them into your hand. ¹² I sent the hornet and drove out the two Amorite kings from before you, but not with your sword or your bow. ¹³ I gave you a land for which you did not work, and cities that you did not build. You live in them, and you are eating from the produce of vineyards and olive groves you did not plant.

¹⁴ "Now fear the Lord, and serve Him with sincerity and faithfulness. Put away the gods your fathers served beyond the River³ and in Egypt. Serve the Lord. ¹⁵ If it is displeasing to you to serve the Lord, then choose today whom you will serve, if it should be the gods your fathers served beyond the River⁴ or the gods of the Amorites' land where you are now living. Yet as for me and my house, we will serve the Lord."

¹⁶ The people answered and said, "God forbid that we forsake the Lord and serve other gods! ¹⁷ For it is the Lord our God who brought us and our fathers out from slavery in the land of Egypt and performed these great signs in our sight and guarded us all the way that we went and among all the peoples through whom we passed. ¹⁸ The Lord drove out before us all the people, even the Amorites, who lived in the land. So we will indeed serve the Lord, for He is our God."

¹⁹ Then Joshua said to the people, "You are not able to serve the Lord, for He is a holy God. He is a jealous God, and He will not forgive your transgressions nor your sins. ²⁰ If you forsake the Lord and serve foreign gods, then He will turn, bring disaster upon you, and finish you off, after having been good to you."

²¹ The people said to Joshua, "No, we will serve the Lord!"

²² Joshua said to the people, "You are witnesses against yourselves, that you have chosen the Lord, to serve Him."

Then they said, "We are witnesses."

²³ "Now then," he said, "put away the foreign gods in your midst, and stretch out your hearts to the Lord God of Israel!"

²⁴ The people said to Joshua, "It is the Lord our God we will serve, and His voice that we will obey."

²⁵ So that day Joshua made a covenant for the people and established regulations and laws for them at Shechem. ²⁶ Joshua wrote these words in the Book of the Law of God. He took a large stone and set it up under the oak by the sanctuary of the Lord.

²⁷ Joshua said to all the people, "See, this stone will be a witness for us, for it has heard all the words of the Lord that He spoke to us. It will be a witness for us, lest you deny your God."

²⁸ Then Joshua sent the people away, each man to his inheritance.

Joshua's Death and Burial

²⁹ After these events took place, Joshua son of Nun, the servant of the Lord, died at the age of one hundred and ten. ³⁰ They buried him in the territory of his inheritance in Timnath Serah, which is in the hill country of Ephraim north of Mount Gaash.

³¹ Israel served the Lord all the days of Joshua and of the elders who outlived Joshua and had known all the deeds that the Lord had done for Israel.

³² They buried the bones of Joseph, which the children of Israel had brought out of Egypt, in Shechem in the part of the field that Jacob bought from the descendants of Hamor the father of Shechem for one hundred pieces of silver.⁵ It became an inheritance of the descendants of Joseph.

³³ Eleazar son of Aaron died, and they buried him at Gibeah, the town of Phinehas his son, which was in the hill country of Ephraim.

---

¹ 2 Euphrates River.   ² 3 Euphrates River.   ³ 14 Euphrates River.   ⁴ 15 Euphrates River.
⁵ 32 Heb. *a hundred kesitahs*; a kesitah was a coin of unknown weight and value.

JUDGES

Israel Fights Remaining Canaanites

1 After the death of Joshua, the children of Israel inquired of the LORD, "Who should go up against the Canaanites first, in order to wage war against them?" ² The LORD said, "Judah shall go up. Indeed, I have given the land into their hands."

³ Then the men of Judah said to Simeon, their brothers, "Come up with us into our allotted territory. We will wage war against the Canaanites. Likewise we will go with you into your allotted territory." So Simeon went with them.

⁴ Then Judah went up, and the LORD gave the Canaanites and Perizzites into their hands. They struck down ten thousand men in Bezek. ⁵ They found Adoni-Bezek in Bezek and fought against him. They struck down the Canaanites and Perizzites. ⁶ Yet Adoni-Bezek fled, and they chased after him, seized him, and cut off his thumbs and big toes.

⁷ Adoni-Bezek said, "Seventy kings whose thumbs and big toes were cut off once collected scraps of food under my table. Just as I have done, so God has repaid me." They brought him to Jerusalem, and he died there.

⁸ Then Judah waged war against Jerusalem. They captured it, struck it with the edge of the sword, and set the city up in flames.

⁹ Afterwards, Judah went down to wage war against the Canaanites living in the hill country, the Negev, and the lowlands. ¹⁰ Judah went against the Canaanites living in Hebron (previously the name of Hebron was Kiriath Arba) and they struck down Sheshai, Ahiman, and Talmai. ¹¹ From there they went against the inhabitants of Debir (previously the name of Debir was Kiriath Sepher).

¹² Caleb said, "He who attacks Kiriath Sepher and takes it, I will give him my daughter Aksah as wife." ¹³ Othniel son of Kenaz, the younger brother of Caleb, captured it. So Caleb gave him Aksah his daughter in marriage.

¹⁴ When she came to Othniel, she urged him to ask her father for a field. As she dismounted from her donkey, Caleb said to her, "What can I do for you?"

¹⁵ She answered, "Please give me a special gift. Since you have given me land in the Negev, now give me springs of water." So Caleb gave her the upper and lower springs.

¹⁶ The descendants of Moses' father-in-law, the Kenite, went up with the descendants of Judah from the City of Palms to the Negev near Arad. Then they went and lived with the people.

¹⁷ But Judah went with his brother Simeon and struck down the Canaanites living in Zephath and utterly destroyed it. So now they call the city Hormah. ¹⁸ Then Judah captured Gaza, Ashkelon, Ekron, and the territory belonging to each of these cities.

¹⁹ The LORD was with Judah, and they took the hill country but could not drive out the inhabitants of the coastal plain, for they had iron chariots. ²⁰ They gave Hebron to Caleb, as Moses had said, and he drove out the three sons of Anak. ²¹ However, the tribe of Benjamin did not drive out the Jebusites living in Jerusalem, so the Jebusites live with the tribe of Benjamin in Jerusalem to this day.

²² The descendants of Joseph went up against Bethel, and the LORD was with them. ²³ The descendants of Joseph sent spies into Bethel (the former name of the city was LUZ). ²⁴ The spies saw a man coming out of the city and said to him, "Please show us the entrance to the city, and we will deal kindly with you." ²⁵ So he showed them an entrance to the city. They struck the city with the edge of the sword, but they let the man and his extended family go. ²⁶ The man went to the land of the Hittites. He built a city and named it LUZ, and that is its name to this day.

²⁷ Manasseh did not drive out the inhabitants of Beth Shan, Taanach, Dor, Ibleam, Megiddo, or their daughter villages, for the Canaanites were determined to live in that land. ²⁸ When the children of Israel became strong, they put the Canaanites to hard labor as slaves, but they did not actually drive them out. ²⁹ Ephraim did not drive out the inhabitants of Gezer, so the Canaanites lived among them in Gezer. ³⁰ Zebulun did not drive out the inhabitants of Kitron and Nahalol, so the Canaanites lived among them and became slave laborers. ³¹ Asher did not drive out the inhabitants of Akko, Sidon, Ahlab, Akzib, Helbah, Aphek, or Rehob. ³² Asher lived among the Canaanites, the inhabitants of the land, for they did not drive them out. ³³ Naphtali did not drive out the inhabitants of Beth Shemesh or Beth Anath, so they live among the Canaanites, the inhabitants of the land. The *Canaanites* of Beth Shemesh and Beth Anath became slave laborers for them. ³⁴ The Amorites pushed the tribe of Dan into the hill country, for they would not let them come down to the coastal plain. ³⁵ The Amorites were determined to live in Mount Heres, Aijalon, and Shaalbim, but the hand of the descendants of Joseph was heavy *on them*, and they became slave laborers. ³⁶ The border of the Amorites was from the Ascent of Akrabbim to Sela and beyond.

The Angel of the LORD at Bokim

2 The angel¹ of the LORD went up from Gilgal to Bokim and said, "I brought you up from Egypt and brought you into the land that I promised your fathers. I said, 'I will never break My covenant with you, ² but you must not make a pact with the inhabitants of this land, and you must tear down their altars.' Yet you have not obeyed Me. What is this you have done? ³ So now I say, 'I will not drive them out before you. They will be thorns in your sides, and their gods will be a snare to you.'"

⁴ When the angel of the LORD spoke these words to all the children of Israel, the people raised their voices and wept aloud. ⁵ They named that place Bokim and sacrificed to the LORD there.

The Death of Joshua

⁶ When Joshua dismissed the people, each Israelite went to his inheritance to possess the land. ⁷ So the people served the LORD all the days of Joshua, and all the days of the elders who outlived Joshua, who had seen all the great works that the LORD had done for Israel.

⁸ Joshua, the son of Nun, the servant of the LORD, died at the age of one hundred and ten. ⁹ They buried him in the territory of his inheritance in Timnath Heres, in the hill country of Ephraim, north of Mount Gaash.

¹⁰ That entire generation passed away, and after them grew up a generation who did not know the LORD or the deeds that He had done for Israel.

Israel's Unfaithfulness

¹¹ The children of Israel did evil in the sight of the LORD and served the Baals. ¹² They abandoned the LORD God of their fathers, who brought them out of the land of Egypt. They followed after other gods, the gods of the peoples around them. They worshipped them and provoked the LORD to anger. ¹³ They abandoned the LORD and served Baal and the Ashtoreths. ¹⁴ The anger of the LORD burned against Israel, and He gave them into the hands of those who plundered them; and He sold them into the hands of their enemies around them, so that they were no longer able to stand against their enemies. ¹⁵ Whenever they marched out, the hand of the LORD was against them to bring disaster, as the LORD had said and as He had sworn to them. They were in great distress.

¹⁶ Then the LORD raised up judges who delivered them from the hand of those who plundered them. ¹⁷ Yet they would not listen to their judges, for they prostituted themselves to other gods and worshipped them. They quickly turned aside from the path their fathers had walked, who had obeyed the commandments of the LORD. They did not do *as their fathers had done*. ¹⁸ When the LORD raised up judges for them, the LORD was with the judge and delivered them from the hand of their enemies all the days of the judge; for their groaning before their oppressors and tormentors grieved the LORD. ¹⁹ When the judge died, the people turned back and acted more wickedly than their fathers, pursuing other gods

to serve and worship them. They would not give up their practices and obstinate ways.

[20] The anger of the LORD burned against Israel, and He said, "Because this nation has violated My covenant that I commanded their fathers and has not heeded My voice, [21] I will no longer drive out from before them any of the nations that Joshua left when he died, [22] so that through them I may test Israel and see whether or not they will keep the ways of the LORD, to walk in them as their fathers did." [23] So the LORD left those nations, not hurrying to drive them out; and He did not deliver them into the hand of Joshua.

3 Now these are the nations that the LORD left to test those in Israel who had not experienced war in Canaan [2] (so that *later* generations of the children of Israel who did not know *war* before might know it, to teach them how to fight): [3] the five Philistine lords, all the Canaanites, the Sidonians, and the Hivites living on Mount Lebanon, from Mount Baal Hermon to Lebo Hamath. [4] They were to test Israel, in order to know if they would obey the commandments of the LORD, which He commanded their fathers by the hand of Moses. [5] The children of Israel lived among the Canaanites, Hittites, Amorites, Perizzites, Hivites, and Jebusites. [6] They took their daughters for themselves as wives, and gave their own daughters to their sons, and served their gods.

Othniel

[7] The children of Israel did what was evil in the sight of the LORD. They forgot the LORD their God and served the Baals and the Asherahs. [8] The anger of the LORD burned against Israel, and He sold them into the hands of Cushan-Rishathaim, king of Mesopotamia. The children of Israel served Cushan-Rishathaim for eight years. [9] Then the children of Israel cried out to the LORD, and the LORD raised up a deliverer in order to save the children of Israel—Othniel son of Kenaz, the younger brother of Caleb. [10] The Spirit of the LORD came on him, and he judged Israel. He went out to battle, and the LORD gave Cushan-Rishathaim, king of Mesopotamia, into his hands, so that *Othniel* overpowered Cushan-Rishathaim. [11] The land rested forty years, then Othniel son of Kenaz died.

Ehud

[12] Then the children of Israel once more did what was evil in the sight of the LORD, so the LORD strengthened King Eglon of Moab against Israel because they had done what was evil in the sight of the LORD. [13] Eglon joined forces with the Ammonites and Amalekites; then he went and attacked Israel and took possession of the City of Palms. [14] The children of Israel served King Eglon of Moab for eighteen years.

[15] Then the children of Israel cried out to the LORD, and the LORD raised up a deliverer—Ehud son of Gera the Benjamite, a left-handed man. The children of Israel sent a tribute payment by him to King Eglon of Moab. [16] Ehud made a cubit-long[1] two-edged sword for himself and strapped it onto his right thigh under his cloak. [17] He brought the tribute payment to King Eglon of Moab. Now Eglon was a very fat man. [18] When Ehud finished offering the tribute payment, he sent away the people who carried it. [19] But he himself turned back from the stone idols that were at Gilgal, and said, "I have a secret message for you, O king."

And he said, "Keep silence!" And all who attended him departed from him.

[20] Ehud approached him as he was sitting alone in his cool upper chamber. Ehud said, "I have a message from God for you." And *Eglon* rose from his seat. [21] Then Ehud reached with his left hand, drew the sword from his right thigh, and plunged it into the belly of *Eglon*. [22] The hilt went in after the blade and the fat closed over the blade and his entrails came out, for he did not pull the sword out of the belly of Eglon. [23] Then Ehud went out to the entrance hall and closed the doors of the upper chamber on him and locked them.

[24] When he went out, the servants of *Eglon* came. They looked and noticed the doors of the upper chamber were locked. They thought, "Surely he is attending to his needs in the cool chamber." [25] They waited until they were embarrassed, but he still did not open

the doors of the upper chamber. So they took a key and opened it. There, fallen dead on the floor, was their lord.

[26] Yet Ehud escaped while they were waiting. He passed the sacred stones and escaped to Seirah. [27] Upon his arrival, he blew a ram's horn trumpet in the hill country of Ephraim. Then the children of Israel went down with him from the hill country, and he led them. [28] He said to them, "Follow me, for the LORD has given your enemies the Moabites into your hands." They followed him, and they captured the Jordan fords leading to Moab. They did not let anyone cross. [29] They struck down about ten thousand Moabites, all strong and valorous men, and not a single man escaped. [30] So Moab was humbled under the hand of Israel that day, and the land had peace for eighty years.

Shamgar

[31] After *Ehud* was Shamgar son of Anath. He struck down six hundred Philistine men with an ox goad. He also saved Israel.

Deborah

4 When Ehud was dead, the children of Israel once more did what was evil in the sight of the LORD. [2] The LORD sold them into the hands of King Jabin of Canaan, who ruled in Hazor. The commander of his army was Sisera. He lived in Harosheth Haggoyim. [3] The children of Israel cried out to the LORD, for *Sisera* had nine hundred iron chariots and had forcefully oppressed the children of Israel for twenty years.

[4] Now Deborah, the wife of Lappidoth, was a prophetess. She judged Israel at that time. [5] She would sit under the palm tree of Deborah between Ramah and Bethel in the hill country of Ephraim. The children of Israel would go up to her for *her to render* judgment. [6] She sent for Barak son of Abinoam from Kedesh in Naphtali and said to him, "The LORD God of Israel commands you, 'Go and deploy troops at Mount Tabor, and take ten thousand men from the tribes of Naphtali and Zebulun with you. [7] I will draw Sisera, the commander of the army of Jabin, with his chariots and large army to you at the River Kishon and give him into your hands.' "

[8] Barak said to her, "If you will go with me, then I will go, but if you will not go with me, then I will not go."

[9] She said, "I will indeed go with you. However, the way you are going will gain you no glory, for the LORD will deliver Sisera into the hand of a woman." Then Deborah got up and went with Barak to Kedesh. [10] Barak called Zebulun and Naphtali to Kedesh. Ten thousand men went up on foot with him, and Deborah went up with him *also*.

[11] Now Heber the Kenite had moved away from the Kenites, who were descendants of Hobab, Moses' father-in-law. He pitched his tent at the oak in Zaanannim, near Kedesh.

[12] Then they told Sisera that Barak son of Abinoam had gone up to Mount Tabor. [13] So Sisera summoned all his nine hundred iron chariots and all the people with him, from Harosheth Haggoyim to the River Kishon.

[14] Then Deborah said to Barak, "Get up, for this is the day that the LORD has given Sisera into your hands. Has not the LORD gone out before you?" So Barak went down from Mount Tabor with ten thousand men behind him. [15] The LORD routed Sisera and all of his chariots and all of his army with the edge of the sword in front of Barak. Sisera dismounted his chariot and fled on foot.

[16] Barak chased after the chariots and the army as far as Harosheth Haggoyim. The whole army of Sisera fell by the edge of the sword. Not a single man survived. [17] Sisera fled on foot to the tent of Jael, the wife of Heber the Kenite, for there was peace between King Jabin of Hazor and the family of Heber the Kenite.

[18] Jael went out to meet Sisera and said to him, "Turn aside, my lord. Turn aside to me. Do not be afraid." So he turned aside to her into the tent, and she covered him with a rug.

[19] He said to her, "Please give me a little water to drink, for I am thirsty." So she opened a leather milk container, gave it to him to drink, and covered him.

[20] He said to her, "Stand in the entrance to the tent, and if anyone comes and asks you, 'Is there a man here?' then you say, 'No.' "

---

[1] 16 About 18 inches, or 45 centimeters.

21 Then Jael the wife of Heber took a tent peg and a hammer in her hand and went quietly to him, for he was fast asleep and tired. She drove the tent peg into his temple, and it went down into the ground, so he died.

22 Now as Barak had been chasing Sisera, Jael came out to meet him and said, "Come, and I will show you the man whom you seek." When he came in, there was Sisera fallen dead with a tent peg in his temple.

23 So God humbled King Jabin of Canaan before the children of Israel that day. 24 The children of Israel grew more and more powerful over King Jabin of Canaan until he was no more.

The Song of Deborah

5 On that day, Deborah and Barak son of Abinoam sang:

2 "When the leaders in Israel lead,
　　when the people freely volunteer,
　　　bless the Lord!

3 "Hear, O kings! Listen, O rulers!
　　I will sing to the Lord;
　　I will sing praise to the Lord God of Israel.

4 "Lord, when You went out from Seir,
　　when You marched from the land of Edom,
　the ground shook and the skies poured,
　　indeed, the dense clouds poured water.
5 The mountains quaked before the Lord,
　　this very Sinai, before the Lord God of Israel.

6 "In the days of Shamgar son of Anath,
　　in the days of Jael, *main* roads were abandoned
　　and travelers used roundabout paths.
7 Village life ceased. It ceased
　　until I, Deborah, arose;
　　I arose *like* a mother in Israel.
8 They were choosing new gods,
　　and warfare was at the city gates,
　but not a shield or spear was to be seen
　　among forty thousand in Israel.
9 My heart is with the rulers of Israel
　　who offered themselves willingly among the people.
　　Bless the Lord!

10 "You who ride on white donkeys,
　　you who sit in judges' attire,
　　you who walk on the road,
11 consider the voice of those who distribute water among the
　　　watering places.
　　There they tell of the righteous deeds of the Lord,
　　the righteous deeds of villagers in Israel.

　"Then the people of the Lord
　　go down to the gates.
12 Awake, awake, Deborah!
　　Awake, awake, sing a song!
　Stand up, Barak,
　　and capture your prisoners, son of Abinoam!

13 "The survivors
　　came down to the nobles;
　the people of the Lord
　　came down for me against the mighty.
14 Some came from Ephraim, whose roots were in Amalek,
　　following you, Benjamin, with your people.
　From Makir rulers came down,
　　and from Zebulun those who carry the staff of a scribe.
15 The princes of Issachar were with Deborah,
　　and Issachar was with Barak;
　they were sent into the valley on foot.
　Among the clans of Reuben
　　there was great resolve of heart.

16 Why do you sit among the sheepfolds
　　to hear playing of pipes for the flocks?
　In the clans of Reuben
　　there was much searching of heart.
17 Gilead stayed beyond the Jordan.
　　As for Dan, why did he stay with the ships?
　Asher stayed by the seacoast
　　and settled by its bays.
18 Zebulun is a people who risked their lives to the
　　　point of death,
　　Naphtali also, on the heights of the battlefield.

19 "Kings came to wage war.
　　The kings of Canaan waged war
　in Taanach, by the waters of Megiddo;
　　they took no money as profit.
20 From the heavens the stars fought,
　　from their courses they fought against Sisera.
21 The torrent of Kishon swept them away,
　　that ancient torrent, the torrent of Kishon.
　My soul, march on in strength!
22 Then horses' hooves pounded,
　　the galloping, galloping of his steeds.
23 Curse Meroz, said the angel of the Lord,
　　curse its inhabitants,
　for they did not come to the aid of the Lord,
　　to the aid of the Lord against the mighty warriors.

24 "Most blessed of women is Jael,
　　the wife of Heber the Kenite,
　　most blessed of tent-dwelling women.
25 He asked for water, she gave him milk.
　　In a magnificent bowl she brought cream.
26 Her hand on a tent peg,
　　her right hand on a workman's hammer;
　she struck Sisera, she crushed his skull,
　　she shattered and pierced his temple.
27 Between her feet he sank, he fell, he lay;
　　between her feet he sank, he fell;
　　where he sank, there he fell, overpowered.

28 "The mother of Sisera looked through the window,
　　and cried out through the lattice,
　'Why is his chariot so late?
　　Why is the sound of his war chariots so delayed?'
29 Her wise attendants answered her,
　　indeed, she replied to herself,
30 'Are they not finding and dividing the spoils:
　　a girl or two for each man;
　dyed garments as plunder for Sisera,
　　dyed and embroidered garments,
　two pieces of dyed embroidery for the neck of
　　　the looter?'

31 "May all Your enemies perish like this, O Lord!
　　But may those who love Him rise like the sun
　　when it rises in full strength."

Then the land was at peace for forty years.

Gideon

6 The children of Israel did evil in the sight of the Lord, so the Lord gave them into the hands of Midian for seven years. 2 The hands of Midian dominated Israel, and because of Midian the children of Israel made hiding places for themselves in the mountains, caves, and strongholds. 3 Whenever Israel would plant crops, the Midianites, Amalekites, and the people from the east would come up against them. 4 Then they would make camp by them and ruin crops of the land all the way to Gaza. They did not leave any provisions behind in Israel—neither sheep, nor cattle, nor donkeys. 5 For they came with their livestock and tents like a swarm of locusts. They and their camels were too numerous to count, and they came

into the land to destroy it. [6] Israel was made weak before Midian and cried out to the Lord.

[7] When the children of Israel cried out to the Lord because of Midian, [8] the Lord sent them a prophet who said, "Thus says the Lord God of Israel: I brought you up from Egypt and out of that place of slavery. [9] I delivered you from the hands of Egypt and all your oppressors. I drove them out from before you and gave you their land. [10] I said to you, 'I am the Lord your God. Do not worship the gods of the Amorites in whose land you are living.' But you have disobeyed Me."

[11] Now the angel[1] of the Lord came and sat under the oak tree in Ophrah belonging to Joash the Abiezrite. Gideon his son was threshing wheat in a winepress to hide it from the Midianites. [12] The angel of the Lord appeared and said to him, "The Lord is with you, O mighty man of valor."

[13] Then Gideon said to him, "O my lord, if the Lord is with us, then why has all this happened to us? Where are all His miracles that our fathers told us about? They said, 'Did not the Lord bring us out of Egypt?' Yet now the Lord has forsaken us and delivered us into the hands of the Midianites."

[14] Then the Lord turned to him and said, "Go in this strength of yours. Save Israel from the control of Midian. Have I not sent you?"

[15] And he said to Him, "O my Lord, how can I save Israel? Indeed my clan is the weakest in Manasseh, and I am the youngest in my father's house."

[16] Then the Lord said to him, "But I will be with you, and you will strike the Midianites as one man."

[17] And he said to Him, "If I have found favor in Your sight, give me a sign that it is You who are speaking with me. [18] Please do not depart from here until I come to You and bring out my gift and set it before You."

And He said, "I will stay until you return."

[19] So Gideon went and prepared a young goat and unleavened bread from an ephah of flour. He put the meat in a basket, and he put the broth in a pot, and brought them out and offered them to Him under the oak.

[20] And the angel of God said to him, "Take the meat and the unleavened bread, lay them on this rock, and pour out the broth." And so he did. [21] The angel of the Lord reached out the tip of the staff that was in His hand and touched the meat and unleavened flatbread. Fire rose out of the rock and consumed the meat and unleavened bread. Then the angel of the Lord departed from his sight. [22] Then Gideon perceived that it was indeed the angel of the Lord. So Gideon said, "Alas, O Lord God! I have seen the angel of the Lord face to face."

[23] Then the Lord said to him, "Peace be with you. Do not be afraid. You will not die."

[24] Then Gideon built an altar for the Lord there and called it The Lord Is Peace. Even to this day it stands in Ophrah of the Abiezrites.

[25] That night the Lord said to him, "Take a bull from your father's herd and a second bull seven years old. Tear down your father's Baal altar and cut down the Asherah pole beside it. [26] Then build an altar to the Lord your God on top of this stronghold in an orderly way. Take the second bull and offer it as a burnt offering with the wood of the Asherah pole that you will cut down."

[27] So Gideon took ten men from among his slaves and did as the Lord had told him, but because he was too afraid of *the rest of* his father's household and the men of the city to do it by day, he did it at night.

[28] When the men of the city got up early in the morning, the altar of Baal was torn down, the Asherah pole beside it was cut down, and the second bull had been offered on the *new* altar that had been built.

[29] They said to each other, "Who has done this?"

When they had inquired and asked, they responded, "Gideon son of Joash has done this."

[30] Then the men of the city said to Joash, "Bring out your son so that he may die, for he tore down the altar of Baal and cut down the Asherah pole beside it."

[31] Joash then said to all who stood against him, "Would you plead for Baal? Would you save him? Whoever fights for him will be killed by morning. If *Baal* is a god, let him fight for himself, for someone has torn down his altar." [32] Therefore on that day he called him Jerub-Baal, saying, "Let Baal fight him, for he tore down the altar *of Baal*."

[33] All the Midianites, Amalekites, and the people from the east gathered together, and they crossed over, and camped in the Valley of Jezreel. [34] The Spirit of the Lord enveloped Gideon. He blew a ram's horn trumpet, and the Abiezrites assembled behind him. [35] He sent messengers throughout all of Manasseh and they assembled behind him as well. He *also* sent messengers to Asher, Zebulun, and Naphtali, so *these tribes* came up to meet them.

[36] Gideon said to God, "If You will use my hands to save Israel, as You have said— [37] I am placing a fleece of wool on the threshing floor. If there is dew on the fleece only and all of the ground remains dry, then I will know that You will save Israel with my hands, as You have said." [38] So it happened. He got up early the next morning and squeezed the fleece. Enough dew poured out of the fleece to fill a bowlful of water.

[39] Then Gideon said to God, "Do not let Your anger burn against me as I speak only one *more* time. Please let me perform a test with the fleece one *more* time. Please, let the fleece be the only *thing* dry, and let there be dew on all of the ground." [40] So God did this during that night. Only the fleece was dry, and the dew was on all the ground.

Gideon Defeats the Midianites

7 Then Jerub-Baal (that is, Gideon) and all the people who were with him got up early and set up camp at Harod Spring. There was a camp of Midianites to the north of them in the valley near the hill of Moreh. [2] The Lord said to Gideon, "You have too many people with you for Me to give the Midianites into their hands, lest Israel glorify themselves over Me, saying, 'Our own power saved us.' [3] So now, call out so the people can hear, 'Whoever is afraid or anxious may turn back and leave Mount Gilead.' " So twenty-two thousand from among the people turned back, and ten thousand were left.

[4] But the Lord said to Gideon, "There are still too many people. Bring them down to the water, and I will test them for you there. When I say to you, 'This one will go with you,' he will go with you. Everyone about whom I will say, 'This one will not go with you,' will not go."

[5] So he brought the people down to the water, and the Lord said to Gideon, "You shall set apart by himself everyone who laps the water with his tongue like dogs; likewise, everyone who kneels down to drink." [6] The number of those who lapped, putting their hands to their mouths, was three hundred. The rest of the people had knelt to drink water.

[7] The Lord said to Gideon, "With three hundred men who lapped *to drink,* I will save you and give the Midianites into your hands. *All the rest* of the people should go home." [8] So the *three hundred men* took provisions and ram's horn trumpets in their hands. Gideon sent all the *other* Israelite men to their tents, but he kept the three hundred men.

Now the Midianite camp was below him in the valley. [9] That night the Lord said to him, "Get up and go down into the camp, for I have given it into your hands. [10] Yet if you are afraid to go down, then go down to the camp with Purah your servant. [11] Listen to what they say, and afterward you will be emboldened to go down to the camp." So he and Purah his servant went down near the edge of the camp. [12] Now the Midianites, Amalekites, and the Kedemites covered the valley like locusts; and their camels could not be counted, *for they were* as numerous as *grains of* sand on the seashore.

[13] Gideon came and overheard one man who was telling his dream to another. The man said, "Listen to a dream I had. I saw a dry cake of barley bread rolling into the Midianite camp. It rolled up to a tent and struck it. It fell, turned upside down, and collapsed."

[14] The other man responded, "This is none other than the sword of Gideon son of Joash the Israelite. God has given Midian and the whole camp into his hands."

---

[1] 11 At times the Lord speaks directly through an angel (cf. the story of the burning bush in Ex 3:2–4).

¹⁵ When Gideon heard the telling of the dream and its interpretation, he worshipped, returned to the camp of Israel, and said, "Get up, for the LORD has given the Midianite camp into your hands." ¹⁶ He divided the three hundred men into three combat units. He gave all of them ram's horn trumpets, empty jars, and torches within the jars.

¹⁷ He said to them, "Look at me and do likewise. Watch, and when I come to the perimeter of the camp, do as I do. ¹⁸ When I and all who are with me blow the horn, then you will blow the horns all around the camp and shout, 'For the LORD and for Gideon!' "

¹⁹ So Gideon and a hundred men with him went to the edge of the camp at the start of the middle night watch, just as they were setting the watch. Then they blew the horns and smashed the jars in their hands. ²⁰ The three combat units blew the horns and broke the jars. They held the torches in their left hands and the horns for blowing in their right hands. They called out, "A sword for the LORD and for Gideon!" ²¹ Every man stood in his place all around the camp, but the men in the camp ran, shouted, and fled.

²² When they blew the three hundred horns, the LORD turned every man's sword against his fellow man throughout the camp. The *Midianite* camp fled to Beth Shittah in the direction of Zererah, up to the border of Abel Meholah, near Tabbath. ²³ The men of Israel from Naphtali, Asher, and all of Manasseh were summoned, and they chased after the Midianites. ²⁴ Now Gideon sent messengers throughout the hill country of Ephraim, saying, "Come down to engage Midian in battle. Take control of the water *ways* as far as Beth Barah and the Jordan."

All the men of Ephraim were summoned, and they took control of the water *ways* as far as Beth Barah and the Jordan. ²⁵ They captured Oreb and Zeeb, the two Midianite commanders. They killed Oreb at the rock of Oreb and killed Zeeb at the winepress of Zeeb. They chased after the Midianites and brought the heads of Oreb and Zeeb to Gideon on the other side of the Jordan.

Zebah and Zalmunna

8 Then the men of Ephraim said to him, "What have you done to us by not calling us to go and wage war against Midian?" They argued heatedly with him.

² He said to them, "What have I done now compared to you? Are not the gleanings of the grapes of Ephraim better than the harvest of Abiezer? ³ It was into your hands that God gave the Midianite commanders, Oreb and Zeeb. What was I able to do compared to you?" When *Gideon* said this, their anger against him cooled down.

⁴ Then Gideon came to the Jordan and crossed over, he and the three hundred men who were with him, exhausted but still pursuing. ⁵ He said to the men of Sukkoth, "Please give some loaves of bread to the people who are following me, for they are exhausted, and I am pursuing Zebah and Zalmunna, kings of Midian."

⁶ The officials of Sukkoth said, "Are the hands of Zebah and Zalmunna already in your hands that we should give bread to your army?"

⁷ So Gideon said, "Because of this, when the LORD gives Zebah and Zalmunna into my hands, I will tear your bodies with desert thorns and briers."

⁸ He went up from there to Peniel and spoke to them in the same way. The men of Peniel answered him just as the men of Sukkoth had. ⁹ So he also said to the men of Peniel, "When I return safely, I will tear down this tower."

¹⁰ Now Zebah and Zalmunna were in Karkor with their armies, about fifteen thousand survivors; they were all who were left of all the army of the Kedemites, for one hundred twenty thousand armsbearing men had fallen. ¹¹ Gideon went up on the route of the tent dwellers east of Nobah and Jogbehah and attacked the camp while the army was off guard. ¹² Zebah and Zalmunna fled, and Gideon chased after them. He captured Zebah and Zalmunna, the two kings of Midian, and the entire army was terrified.

¹³ Gideon son of Joash returned from battle by the Pass of Heres. ¹⁴ He captured a young man from among the men of Sukkoth and asked him to write the *names of* the leaders and elders of Sukkoth, seventy-seven men. ¹⁵ Then he came to the men of

Sukkoth and said, "Here are Zebah and Zalmunna, about whom you taunted me. You said, 'Have you subjugated Zebah and Zalmunna that we should give bread to your weary army?' " ¹⁶ He took the city elders and disciplined the men of Sukkoth with thorns and briers of the wilderness. ¹⁷ He tore down the tower of Peniel and killed the men of the city.

¹⁸ Then he said to Zebah and Zalmunna, "What kind of men did you kill at Tabor?"

They said, "They were like you. Each one looked like the son of a king."

¹⁹ He said, "They were my brothers, the sons of my mother. As the LORD lives, if you had allowed them to live, I would not kill you." ²⁰ Gideon said to his firstborn Jether, "Rise and kill them!" Yet the young man did not draw his sword because he was afraid, for he was still a young man.

²¹ Then Zebah and Zalmunna said, "You get up and attack us, for a man is judged by his strength." So Gideon got up and killed Zebah and Zalmunna and took the crescent-shaped ornaments that were on the necks of their camels.

Gideon's Ephod

²² Then the men of Israel said to Gideon, "Rule over us, you, and your son, and your grandson, for you have saved us from the hands of Midian."

²³ Gideon said to them, "I will not rule over you, and my son will not rule over you. The LORD will rule over you." ²⁴ Gideon continued, "I have a request to make of you, that each man would give me an earring from his spoils." (*Their enemy* had golden earrings because they were Ishmaelites.)

²⁵ They said, "We will certainly give them." So they spread out a cloak, and each man threw a ring of his spoils there. ²⁶ The weight of the golden earrings that he requested was seventeen hundred gold shekels.[1] This was in addition to the crescent-shaped ornaments, jewelry, and purple clothing worn by the kings of Midian, as well as the chains hanging on the necks of their camels. ²⁷ Gideon used these things to make an ephod. He put it in his city, in Ophrah, and all Israel prostituted themselves to it there. It became a snare to Gideon and his family.

²⁸ The Midianites were humbled before the children of Israel and did not lift their heads high again. The land had peace for forty years in the days of Gideon.

The Death of Gideon

²⁹ Jerub-Baal son of Joash went to his house and lived there. ³⁰ Gideon had seventy sons, for he had many wives. ³¹ His concubine who lived in Shechem also bore him a son, and he named him Abimelek. ³² Gideon son of Joash died at a good old age, and he was buried in the tomb of his father Joash in Ophrah of the Abiezrites.

³³ After Gideon died, the children of Israel turned again to prostitute themselves with the Baals. They made Baal-Berith their god. ³⁴ The children of Israel did not remember the LORD their God, who had delivered them from the hands of their enemies around them, ³⁵ and they did not keep faith with the family of Jerub-Baal (that is, Gideon), for all the good he had done for Israel.

Abimelek

9 Abimelek son of Jerub-Baal went to Shechem, to his mother's brothers. He spoke to them and to the house of his mother's father saying, ² "Please say in the hearing of all of the leaders of Shechem, 'Which is better for you, to have all seventy sons of Jerub-Baal rule over you, or for one man to rule over you? Remember that I am your own flesh and bone.' "

³ So his mother's brothers spoke all these things about him in the hearing of all the leaders of Shechem, and their hearts inclined toward Abimelek, for they said, "He is our brother." ⁴ They gave him seventy silver coins[2] from the temple of Baal-Berith. Abimelek hired unprincipled and undisciplined men, and they followed him. ⁵ He went to his father's house at Ophrah and killed his brothers, the seventy sons of Jerub-Baal, on a single stone. Yet Jotham, the youngest son of Jerub-Baal, survived because he hid himself. ⁶ All the leaders

---

[1] 26 About 43 pounds, or 20 kilograms.   [2] 4 About 1¾ pounds, or 800 grams.

of Shechem and everyone from Beth Millo gathered together by the oak near the pillar in Shechem to make Abimelek king.

⁷ When Jotham heard this, he went and stood on the top of Mount Gerizim. He raised his voice and called out, saying to them, "Listen to me, leaders of Shechem, so that God may listen to you! ⁸ The trees once went out to anoint a king over them. They said to the olive tree, 'Rule over us!'

⁹ "Yet the olive tree said to them, 'Should I stop making oil, by which God and men are honored, to go and sway over the trees?'

¹⁰ "So the trees said to the fig tree, 'You come and rule over us.'

¹¹ "Yet the fig tree said to them, 'Should I stop making my sweet aroma and my fruit, to go and sway over the trees?'

¹² "So the trees said to the grapevine, 'You come and rule over us.'

¹³ "Yet the grapevine said to them, 'Should I stop making my fresh wine, which cheers God and men, to go and sway over the trees?'

¹⁴ "So the trees said to the thorn bush, 'You come and rule over us.'

¹⁵ "The thorn bush said to the trees, 'If you really want to anoint me king over you, then come and take refuge in my shade. If not, let fire come out from the thorn bush and consume the cedars of Lebanon!'

¹⁶ "Now then, did you show good faith and integrity when you made Abimelek king? Did you deal well with Jerub-Baal and his family? Did you do to him as his actions deserved, ¹⁷ considering that my father waged war for you, risked his life for you, and delivered you from the hands of Midian? ¹⁸ Yet you have taken a stand against my father's family today. You killed his seventy sons, each on a single stone. You made Abimelek, son of his slave woman, king over the leaders of Shechem because he is your brother. ¹⁹ So if you did show good faith and integrity in what you did with Jerub-Baal and his family today, then rejoice in Abimelek, and may he also rejoice in you. ²⁰ If not, let fire come out from Abimelek and consume the leaders of Shechem and Beth Millo, and let fire come out from the leaders of Shechem and from Beth Millo and consume Abimelek!"

²¹ Then Jotham ran away and fled. He went to Beer and lived there because of Abimelek his brother.

The Downfall of Abimelek

²² After Abimelek ruled over Israel for three years, ²³ God sent an evil spirit between Abimelek and the leaders of Shechem, and the leaders of Shechem dealt treacherously with Abimelek, ²⁴ so that the violence done to the seventy sons of Jerub-Baal and their blood might come back upon Abimelek their brother, who killed them, and upon the leaders of Shechem, who empowered him to kill his brothers. ²⁵ The leaders of Shechem set ambushes against him on the hilltops and robbed all who passed by them on the road. This was told to Abimelek.

²⁶ Gaal, the son of Ebed, and his brothers came *to Shechem*, and the leaders of Shechem trusted him. ²⁷ They went out to the field, gathered and trod their grapes, and had a celebration. They went to the temple of their god and ate, drank, and cursed Abimelek. ²⁸ Gaal son of Ebed said, "Who is Abimelek, and who is Shechem, that we should serve him? Is he not the son of Jerub-Baal, and *is not* Zebul his officer? Serve the sons of Hamor, the father of Shechem. Why should we serve *Abimelek*? ²⁹ If only this people were under my command, I would get rid of Abimelek." So he said to Abimelek, "Muster your army and come out!"

³⁰ Then Zebul the city ruler heard the words of Gaal son of Ebed and he burned with anger. ³¹ He secretly sent messengers to Abimelek, saying, "Gaal, the son of Ebed, and his brothers have come to Shechem and are fortifying the city against you. ³² So now, get up at night, you and the people with you, and lie in wait in the field. ³³ In the morning at sunrise, get up early and attack the city. He and the people with him will come out to you, then you can do to them as you find opportunity."

³⁴ So Abimelek and all the people who were with him got up at night and lay in wait by Shechem in four companies. ³⁵ When Gaal son of Ebed went out and stood at the entrance of the city gate, then Abimelek and the people who were with him got up from their hiding places.

³⁶ Gaal saw these people and said to Zebul, "Look, people are coming down from the hilltops."

Zebul said to him, "The shadows of the hills look like men to you."

³⁷ Gaal spoke again and said, "Look, people are coming down the middle of the land, and a company is coming by way of the Diviner's Oak."

³⁸ Then Zebul said to him, "Where is your mouth now, which said, 'Who is Abimelek, that we should serve him?' Are not these the people you dismissed out of hand? Go now, I pray, and fight against them."

³⁹ So Gaal went out before the leaders of Shechem and fought Abimelek. ⁴⁰ Abimelek chased him, and Gaal fled from him. Many fell wounded at the entrance of the gate. ⁴¹ Abimelek stayed in Arumah, and Zebul drove out Gaal and his brothers from living in Shechem.

⁴² The next day the people went out into the field, and this was told to Abimelek. ⁴³ So he took the people and divided them into three companies, and they laid in wait in the field. When the people came out from the city, he rose up against them and struck them down. ⁴⁴ Abimelek and the company that was with him rushed forward and stood at the entrance of the city gate. The two other combat units attacked everyone in the field and struck them down. ⁴⁵ Abimelek fought against the city all that day. He captured the city and killed the people inside it; he tore down the city and spread salt over it.

⁴⁶ When the leaders of the Tower of Shechem heard this, they entered the fortified temple of El-Berith. ⁴⁷ Abimelek was told that all the leaders of the Tower of Shechem had gathered together. ⁴⁸ So Abimelek and all the people who were with him went up Mount Zalmon. He took an axe in his hand and cut off a tree branch, lifted it, and carried it on his shoulder. Then he said to the men who were with him, "What you have seen me do, hurry and do the same." ⁴⁹ So everyone likewise cut off a branch and followed Abimelek. They placed them on the fortification and set the fortification on fire over them. So all the people of the Tower of Shechem died, about a thousand men and women.

⁵⁰ Then Abimelek went to Thebez and encamped against Thebez and captured it. ⁵¹ But there was a fortified tower within the city, so all of the men and women and the leaders of the city fled there. They shut themselves in and went up to the top of the tower. ⁵² Abimelek came to the tower and fought against it. But as he drew near to the tower entrance to burn it with fire, ⁵³ a certain woman dropped an upper millstone on the head of Abimelek, and it crushed his skull. ⁵⁴ Urgently he called to the young man who carried his gear and said to him, "Draw your sword and kill me, so that people may not say about me, 'A woman killed him.'" So the young man pierced him through, and he died. ⁵⁵ Then the men of Israel saw that Abimelek was dead, so everyone went home.

⁵⁶ Thus God repaid the wickedness of Abimelek, which he committed against his father by killing his seventy brothers. ⁵⁷ God also repaid the evil deeds of the men of Shechem, and the curse of Jotham son of Jerub-Baal came upon them.

Tola

10 After the death of Abimelek, Tola the son of Puah, the son of Dodo, a man of Issachar, arose to save Israel. He lived in Shamir, in the hill country of Ephraim. ² He judged Israel for twenty-three years. Then he died and was buried in Shamir.

Jair

³ After him Jair the Gileadite arose and judged Israel for twenty-two years. ⁴ He had thirty sons who rode thirty donkeys and owned thirty cities that are in the land of Gilead. They are called Havvoth Jair to this day. ⁵ Jair died and was buried in Kamon.

Jephthah

⁶ Again the children of Israel did evil in the sight of the LORD. They worshipped the Baals, the Ashtoreths, and the gods of Syria, Sidon, Moab, the Ammonites, and the Philistines. They abandoned the LORD and did not serve Him. ⁷ The anger of the LORD burned against Israel,

and He sold them into the hands of the Philistines and the Ammonites. [8] They brutally oppressed the children of Israel that year. For eighteen years *they oppressed* all the children of Israel beyond the Jordan in the land of the Amorites in Gilead. [9] The Ammonites also crossed over the Jordan to wage war against Judah, Benjamin, and Ephraim, so that Israel was greatly distressed. [10] Then the children of Israel cried out to the Lord, "We have sinned against You, for we have abandoned our God and worshipped the Baals."

[11] The Lord said to the children of Israel, "Did I not deliver you from Egypt, the Amorites, the Ammonites, the Philistines, [12] the Sidonians, the Amalekites, and the Maonites when they oppressed you? You cried out to Me, and I saved you from their hands. [13] Yet you have abandoned Me and worshipped other gods. Therefore I will not save you again. [14] Go and cry out to the gods that you have chosen. Let them save you in your time of distress."

[15] Then the children of Israel said to the Lord, "We have sinned. Do to us whatever seems good in Your sight. Please, just deliver us today." [16] They removed the foreign gods from among them and worshipped the Lord, and He could no longer endure the suffering of Israel.

[17] The Ammonites had been called out and set up camp in Gilead. The children of Israel assembled and set up camp in Mizpah. [18] The commanders of Gilead said to each other, "Who is the man who will begin to fight against the Ammonites? He will be the ruler of all the inhabitants of Gilead."

11 Now Jephthah the Gileadite was a mighty man of valor, but he was the son of a prostitute. Gilead was the father of Jephthah. [2] Gilead's wife also bore him sons. His wife's sons grew up and drove Jephthah away. They said to him, "You will not inherit anything from our father's house because you are the son of another woman." [3] So Jephthah fled from his brothers and lived in the land of Tob. Men of ill repute gathered around Jephthah and went out with him.

[4] Some time passed, then the Ammonites waged war with Israel. [5] When the Ammonites waged war with Israel, the elders of Gilead went to bring Jephthah back from the land of Tob. [6] They said to Jephthah, "Come and be our leader so that we may fight the Ammonites."

[7] Jephthah said to the elders of Gilead, "Did you not hate me and drive me out of my father's house? Why have you come to me now that you are in trouble?"

[8] The elders of Gilead said to Jephthah, "Even so, we have turned to you. Come with us and fight the Ammonites. You will be ruler over all the inhabitants of Gilead."

[9] Jephthah said to the elders of Gilead, "If you bring me back to wage war against the Ammonites, and the Lord gives them to me, then I will be your ruler."

[10] The elders of Gilead said to Jephthah, "May the Lord be a witness between us if we do not act according to your word." [11] So Jephthah went with the elders of Gilead. The people set him over them as ruler and leader. And Jephthah spoke all his words before the Lord in Mizpah.

[12] Jephthah sent messengers to the Ammonite king to say, "What *problem* is there between you and me, that you have come to me to wage war in my land?"

[13] The Ammonite king said to the messengers of Jephthah, "Because when Israel came up from Egypt, they took my land, from the Arnon to the Jabbok and as far as the Jordan. Now return it peacefully."

[14] Again Jephthah sent messengers to the Ammonite king, [15] and said to him,

"Jephthah says this: Israel did not take the land of Moab, nor the Ammonite land; [16] for when Israel came up from Egypt, they went into the desert as far as the Red Sea and came to Kadesh. [17] Then Israel sent messengers to the king of Edom, saying, 'Please let us pass through your land.' Yet the king of Edom would not listen. They also sent messengers to the king of Moab, but he was unwilling. So Israel stayed at Kadesh. [18] They went into the wilderness, around the lands of Edom and Moab. They went east of the land of Moab and set up camp on the other side of the River Arnon. They did not cross the boundary of Moab, for the River Arnon was the boundary of Moab.

[19] "Then Israel sent messengers to Sihon king of the Amorites, who ruled in Heshbon. Israel said to him, 'Please let us pass through your land to our home.' [20] Yet Sihon did not trust Israel to pass through his territory, so Sihon gathered all his people and set up camp in Jahaz to fight with Israel.

[21] "The Lord God of Israel gave Sihon and all his people into the hands of Israel, and they struck them down. So Israel took possession of all the land of the Amorites who lived in that land. [22] They took possession of all of the territory of the Amorites, from the Arnon to the Jabbok and from the desert to the Jordan.

[23] "Now that the Lord God of Israel has driven out the Amorites from before His people Israel, should you take it? [24] Will you not take possession of whatever Chemosh your god gives you? So everything that the Lord our God possesses before us, we will take possession of it. [25] Now are you really better than Balak son of Zippor, the king of Moab? Did he ever contend with Israel or wage war with them? [26] Israel has lived in Heshbon and its nearby towns, in Aroer and its nearby towns, and in all the cities along the banks of the River Arnon for three hundred years. Why did you not take them back during that time? [27] So I have not sinned against you, but it is you who are doing evil to me by waging war against me. May the Lord, the Judge, judge today between the children of Israel and the Ammonites."

[28] Yet the Ammonite king would not listen to the message that Jephthah had sent him.

[29] Then the Spirit of the Lord came on Jephthah and he passed through Gilead and Manasseh, and passed through Mizpah of Gilead, and went on to the Ammonites. [30] Jephthah made a vow to the Lord, "If You will indeed give the Ammonites into my hands, [31] then whatever comes out from the door of my house to meet me, when I return safely from the Ammonites, will surely be the Lord's, and I will offer it up as a burnt offering."

[32] So Jephthah crossed over to the Ammonites to wage war against them, and the Lord gave them into his hands. [33] He struck them down from Aroer to Minnith, twenty cities, and as far as Abel Keramim. The defeat was very severe, and the Ammonites were humbled before the children of Israel.

[34] When Jephthah went to his house at Mizpah, there was his daughter coming out to meet him, dancing with a tambourine. She was his only child. Other than her, he had neither son nor daughter. [35] When he saw her, he ripped up his clothes and said, "Alas, my daughter! You have brought utter disaster to me. You are my undoing, for I have given my word to the Lord, and I cannot take it back."

[36] She said to him, "My father, you have opened your mouth to the Lord. Do to me what has come out of your mouth, because the Lord worked vengeance upon your enemies, the Ammonites." [37] Then she said to her father, "Let this be done for me: Give me two months, and I and my friends will wander the hill country and mourn over my virginity."

[38] He said, "Go," and he sent her away for two months. She and her friends went and mourned over her virginity in the hill country. [39] At the end of two months she returned to her father, and he did to her according to the vow that he had made. She had not ever slept with a man.

So it became a custom in Israel [40] that the women of Israel would commemorate the daughter of Jephthah the Gileadite for four days each year.

Jephthah and Ephraim

12 The men of Ephraim gathered together and crossed over to Zaphon. They said to Jephthah, "Why did you go to wage war with the Ammonites and not call us to go with you? We will burn down your house right on top of you."

[2] Jephthah said to them, "My people and I were in a very great conflict with the Ammonites. I called you, but you did not save me from their hands. [3] When I saw that you were not going to save me, I took my life in my own hands and crossed over to the Ammonites. Then the Lord gave them into my hands. Now why have you come up to me today to wage war against me?"

⁴ Then Jephthah assembled all the men of Gilead and fought with Ephraim. The men of Gilead struck Ephraim down, for they had said, "You Gileadites are fugitives in Ephraim, living in Ephraim and Manasseh." ⁵ Gilead captured the fords of the Jordan River leading to Ephraim. Whenever an Ephraimite fugitive would say, "Let me cross," the Gileadite men would say to him, "Are you an Ephraimite?" If he said, "No," ⁶ then they would say to him, "Say, 'Shibboleth'!" Yet he would say, "Sibboleth," for he could not pronounce it *correctly*. Then they would grab him and kill him at the Jordan fords. During that time forty-two thousand from Ephraim fell.

⁷ Jephthah judged Israel for six years. When Jephthah the Gileadite died, he was buried among the cities of Gilead.

Ibzan, Elon, and Abdon

⁸ After him, Ibzan of Bethlehem judged Israel. ⁹ He had thirty sons, and he gave thirty daughters in marriage outside his clan; and he brought thirty daughters from outside for his sons. He judged Israel for seven years. ¹⁰ Then Ibzan died and was buried in Bethlehem.

¹¹ After him, Elon the Zebulunite judged Israel. He judged Israel for ten years. ¹² Elon the Zebulunite died and was buried in Aijalon in the land of Zebulun.

¹³ After him, Abdon son of Hillel the Pirathonite judged Israel. ¹⁴ He had forty sons and thirty grandsons who rode seventy donkeys. He judged Israel for eight years. ¹⁵ Abdon son of Hillel the Pirathonite died and was buried in Pirathon in the land of Ephraim, in the Amalekite hill country.

The Birth of Samson

13 Again the children of Israel did evil in the sight of the Lord, so the Lord gave them into the hands of the Philistines for forty years.

² There was a certain man from Zorah, from the tribe of Dan. His name was Manoah. His wife was infertile and had borne no children. ³ The angel of the Lord appeared to the woman and said to her, "Indeed, you are infertile and have borne no children, yet you will conceive and bear a son. ⁴ Now be careful, I pray, that you drink no wine or strong drink and that you do not eat anything ritually unclean. ⁵ For you will conceive and bear a son. No razor may touch his head, for the boy will be a Nazirite to God from the womb. He will begin to save Israel from the hand of the Philistines."

⁶ Then the woman went to her husband and said, "A man of God came to me. He looked like a very fearsome angel of God. I did not ask him where he was from, and he did not tell me his name. ⁷ He said to me, 'You will conceive and bear a son. So now, do not drink wine or strong drink, and do not eat anything ritually unclean, for the boy will be a Nazirite to God from the womb until the day he dies.' "

⁸ Then Manoah prayed to the Lord, "O my Lord, let the man of God whom You sent come again to us, so that he can teach us what we should do for the boy who will be born."

⁹ God listened to the voice of Manoah, and the angel of God came again to the woman. She was sitting in the field; but her husband Manoah was not with her. ¹⁰ The woman hurried and ran to tell her husband, "The man who came to me the other day has appeared to me."

¹¹ So Manoah got up and went after his wife. He came to the man and said to him, "Are you the man who spoke to my wife?" He said, "I am."

¹² Then Manoah said, "Now may your words come true! What will be the boy's way of life and his work?"

¹³ The angel of the Lord said to Manoah, "Your wife must observe everything that I said to her. ¹⁴ She must not consume anything that grows on the vine. She must not drink wine or strong drink, and she must not eat anything ritually unclean. She must observe everything that I commanded her."

¹⁵ Manoah said to the angel of the Lord, "Please let us detain you, and let us prepare a young goat for you."

¹⁶ The angel of the Lord said to Manoah, "If I stay, I will not eat your food, but if you want to make an offering to the Lord,

you should offer it." (For Manoah did not know that he was an angel of the Lord.)

¹⁷ Manoah said to the angel of the Lord, "What is your name, so that we can honor you when your words come true?"

¹⁸ The angel of the Lord said to him, "Why do you ask my name? It is too wonderful." ¹⁹ Manoah took the young goat and the grain offering and offered them to the Lord upon a rock. Then he did a wondrous thing while Manoah and his wife watched. ²⁰ When the flame went up from the altar toward the heavens, the angel of the Lord went up in the flames from the altar. Seeing this, Manoah and his wife fell face down on the ground. ²¹ The angel of the Lord did not appear again to Manoah and his wife. Then Manoah knew that he was an angel of the Lord.

²² Manoah said to his wife, "We are certainly going to die, for we have seen God."

²³ Yet his wife said to him, "If the Lord wanted to kill us, He would not have taken the burnt offering and grain offering from us. He would not have shown us these things, nor let us hear things such as these at this time."

²⁴ So the woman bore a son, and she called him Samson. The boy grew, and the Lord blessed him. ²⁵ The Spirit of the Lord began to move upon him at Mahaneh Dan, between Zorah and Eshtaol.

Samson's Wedding

14 Samson went down to Timnah and saw a woman from the daughters of the Philistines. ² He came back up and told his father and mother, "I have seen a woman in Timnah from the daughters of the Philistines; now get her for me as a wife."

³ His father and mother said to him, "Are there no women among your relatives, or all of our people, that you are intending to take a wife from among the uncircumcised Philistines?"

Yet Samson said to his father, "Get her for me, for she pleases me well." ⁴ His father and mother did not know that this was from the Lord, for He was seeking an opportunity *to act* against the Philistines. At that time the Philistines were ruling over Israel.

⁵ Samson went down with his father and mother to Timnah. As they came to the vineyards of Timnah, suddenly a young lion came roaring toward him. ⁶ Then the Spirit of the Lord came mightily upon him, and though unarmed, he tore the lion in two as one might tear a young goat in two. However, he did not tell his father and his mother what he had done. ⁷ So Samson went down and spoke with the woman, and she pleased Samson.

⁸ After a while, when he returned to take her, he turned aside to see the carcass of the lion. And a swarm of bees and honey were in the carcass of the lion. ⁹ He scooped it out into his hands and ate it as he went along. He came to his father and mother and gave some to them, and they also ate. Yet he did not tell them he had scooped the honey out of a lion's carcass.

¹⁰ Then his father went down to the woman. Samson put on a feast there, for this is what young men would do. ¹¹ When *the Philistines* saw him, they brought thirty companions to be with him.

¹² Samson said to them, "Let me tell you a riddle. If you can explain it to me within the seven days of the feast, then I will find thirty linen robes and thirty sets of clothes to give you. ¹³ However, if you are not able to explain it to me, then you will give me thirty linen robes and thirty sets of clothes."

They said to him, "Tell us your riddle, so we can hear it."

¹⁴ He said to them,

"Out of the eater came something to eat,
  and out of the strong came something sweet."

They could not explain the riddle after three days.

¹⁵ On the fourth day they said to Samson's wife, "Trick your groom into telling us the riddle, or we will burn you and your father's house with fire. Have you invited us to steal what we have? Is that not so?"

¹⁶ So Samson's wife wept all over him and said, "You must hate me. You do not love me. You have told a riddle to the young men and did not tell it to me."

Then he said to her, "I have not told it to my father and mother. Why should I tell it to you?" ¹⁷ She wept on him for the seven days of the feast, then on the seventh day he told it to her because she had nagged him. Then she explained the riddle to her people.

[18] So on the seventh day before sunset, the men of the city said to Samson,

"What is sweeter than honey,
    and what is stronger than a lion?"

Then he said to them,

"If you had not plowed with my heifer,
    you would not have solved my riddle."

[19] Then the Spirit of the LORD mightily came upon him, and he went down to Ashkelon and struck down thirty of their men. He took their clothes and gave them to the ones who had explained the riddle. His anger burned and he went up to his father's house. [20] So Samson's wife was given to his companion, who had been his best man.

Samson's Revenge

15 After a while, during the wheat harvest, Samson went to visit his wife, *taking* a young goat. He said, "I'm going in to my wife in her bedroom," but her father would not let him go in.

[2] Her father said, "I thought that you thoroughly hated her, so I gave her to your best man. Is not her younger sister better than she? Please, let her be your wife instead."

[3] Samson said to them, "This time I cannot be blamed by the Philistines when I do them harm." [4] Samson went and caught three hundred foxes. He took torches and turned the foxes tail to tail and put a torch between each pair of tails. [5] He set fire to the torches and sent the foxes into standing grain of the Philistines. He burned the harvested grain, standing grain, vineyards, and olive trees.

[6] The Philistines asked, "Who did this?" They said, "Samson, the son-in-law of the Timnite, because the *Timnite* took the bride of *Samson* and gave her to his best man."

So the Philistines went up and burned her and her father with fire. [7] Samson said to them, "Because you have done this, I will take revenge on you, and afterwards I will stop." [8] He struck them down with a mighty blow, then went to live in a cave in Etam Rock.

[9] Then the Philistines went up and set up camp in Judah. They deployed against Lehi. [10] The men of Judah said, "Why have you come up against us?"

They said, "It is to take Samson prisoner that we have come up, to do to him what he did to us."

[11] So three thousand men from Judah went to the cave in Etam Rock and said to Samson, "Do you not know that the Philistines are ruling us? Why have you done this to us?"

He said to them, "As they did to me, so I have done to them."

[12] They said to him, "We have come to take you prisoner, to give you into the hands of the Philistines."

Samson said to them, "Swear to me that you will not attack me."

[13] They said to him, "No, we will bind you securely and give you into their hands, but we will not kill you." They bound him with two new ropes and took him away from the rock. [14] He came to Lehi, and the Philistines shouted as they approached him. Then the Spirit of the LORD came mightily upon him. The ropes on his arms became like burned flax and the ties on his hands dissolved. [15] Then he found a fresh jawbone of a donkey, reached out his hand and took it, and with it struck down a thousand men.

[16] Samson said,

"With a jawbone of a donkey,
    heaps upon heaps.
With a jawbone of a donkey
    I have slain a thousand men."

[17] When he finished speaking, he threw the jawbone away and called that place Ramath Lehi.

[18] He was very thirsty, and he called out to the LORD, "You gave this great deliverance through Your servant, but now may I die of thirst and fall into the hands of the uncircumcised?" [19] So God split open the basin at Lehi, and water flowed out of it. He drank, was refreshed, and revived. Because of this he called the place En Hakkore, which is in Lehi to this day.

[20] Samson judged Israel for twenty years in the days of the Philistines.

Samson and Delilah

16 Samson went to Gaza. There he saw a prostitute and spent the night with her. [2] The people of Gaza *were told*, "Samson has come here!" So they surrounded him and laid in wait for him all night at the city gate. They kept quiet all night, thinking, "In the morning light we will kill him."

[3] Samson lay until midnight, then at midnight he got up. He grabbed the doors of the city gate and the two gateposts and pulled them out along with the bar. He put them on his shoulder and brought them to the top of the mountain near Hebron.

[4] After this Samson loved a woman in the Valley of Sorek, whose name was Delilah. [5] The Philistine rulers came up to her and said, "Trick him! Find out about how his strength is so great and how we can overcome him, bind him, and humiliate him. Each one of us will give you eleven hundred silver coins.*"

[6] So Delilah said to Samson, "Please tell me how your strength is so great and how you could be bound in order to be subdued."

[7] Samson said to her, "If they bind me with seven fresh bowstrings that have not been dried, then I will become weak and be like an ordinary man."

[8] So the Philistine rulers brought her seven fresh bowstrings that had not been dried, and she bound him with them. [9] They lay in wait in her inner room. She said to him, "The Philistines are upon you, Samson." Then he split apart the bowstrings like a single thread is split apart at the touch of fire. So the source of his strength did not become known.

[10] Delilah said to Samson, "You have deceived me. You have told me lies. Now, please tell me how you can be bound."

[11] He said to her, "If they bind me with new ropes that have never been used, then I will become weak and be like an ordinary man."

[12] So Delilah took new ropes and bound him with them. Then she said to him, "The Philistines are upon you, Samson." For men were lying in wait, remaining in the room. But he split apart the ropes on his arms like a thread.

[13] Delilah said to Samson, "Up to now you have deceived me. You have told me lies. Tell how you can be bound."

He said to her, "If you weave seven locks of my hair into the fabric on the loom *and fasten it with the pin, then I will become weak and be like an ordinary man*." [14] So Delilah lulled him to sleep and wove seven locks of his hair into the fabric on the loom. She fastened it with the pin and said to him, "The Philistines are upon you, Samson." He awakened from his sleep and tore away from the loom pin and the fabric.

[15] She said to him, "How can you say, 'I love you,' when your heart is not with me? You have deceived me these three times and have not told me how your strength is so great." [16] Every day she nagged him with her words and pleaded with him until he was tired to death.

[17] So he told her all his secrets and said to her, "No razor has touched my head, for I have been a Nazirite to God from my mother's womb. If I were shaven, my strength would leave me, and I would become weak and be like all other men."

[18] Delilah saw that he had told her all his secrets, so she sent for the Philistine rulers, saying, "Come up this time, for he has told me all his secrets." So the Philistine rulers came up to her and brought the money in their hands. [19] Delilah lulled Samson to sleep on her knees and called for a man to shave off the seven locks of his hair. Then she began to humiliate him, and his strength left him.

[20] She said, "The Philistines are upon you, Samson."

---

[15] About 28 pounds, or 13 kilograms.

Then he awakened from his sleep and thought, "I will go out as before and shake myself free *of them*." He did not know that the Lord had left him.

[21] The Philistines seized him and gouged out his eyes. They took him down to Gaza, bound him with bronze chains, and he ground grain in prison. [22] Yet after it had been shaven, the hair on his head began to grow back.

The Death of Samson

[23] The Philistine rulers gathered to offer a great sacrifice to Dagon their god and to celebrate. They said, "Our god has given Samson our enemy into our hands."

[24] The people saw him and praised their god, for they said,

"Our god has given into our hands
    our enemy,
the one who ruined our land
    and killed many of us."

[25] When their hearts were merry, they said, "Call for Samson, so he can entertain us." So they called for Samson from the prison, and he entertained them.

They placed him between the pillars. [26] Samson said to the young man who held his hand, "Let me rest and touch the pillars on which the temple is set, then I can lean against them." [27] The temple was full of men and women, and all the Philistine rulers were there. There were about three thousand men and women on the roof watching Samson entertain. [28] Samson called out to the Lord, "Lord God, remember me, I pray! Please strengthen me just this once, God, so that I may get full revenge on the Philistines for my two eyes!" [29] Then Samson grasped the two middle pillars on which the temple was set and leaned against them, one with his right hand and one with his left. [30] Samson said, "Let me die with the Philistines!" He pushed with all his strength, and the temple fell upon the rulers and all the people who were in it. At his death he killed more than he had killed in his life.

[31] Then his brothers and all his family came down, carried him, brought him up, and buried him between Zorah and Eshtaol in the grave of his father Manoah. He had judged Israel for twenty years.

Micah's Idols

17 There was a man from the hill country of Ephraim whose name was Micah. [2] He said to his mother, "The eleven hundred *shekels* of silver[1] that were taken from you, on which you put a curse, even speaking the curse in my ears—here is the silver with me. I took it."

Then his mother said, "May the Lord bless my son!"

[3] Then he returned the eleven hundred silver coins to his mother. His mother said, "I certainly consecrated the silver to the Lord, for my son to make a carved idol and a metal idol, so now I return it to you."

[4] When he returned the silver to his mother, she took two hundred *shekels* of silver[2] and gave them to a silversmith to make a carved idol and a metal idol. And they were put in the house of Micah.

[5] This man Micah owned a shrine. He made an ephod and household idols, and he hired one of his sons to be a priest for him. [6] In those days there was no king in Israel. Everyone did what was right in his eyes.

[7] There was a young man from Bethlehem in Judah. He was a Levite from Judah, and he stayed as a resident foreigner there. [8] The man went from the city of Bethlehem in Judah to stay wherever he could find *a place*. He came to the hill country of Ephraim, to the house of Micah, to do his work.

[9] Micah said to him, "Where do you come from?"

He said to him, "I am a Levite from Bethlehem in Judah, and I am going to stay wherever I can find *a place*."

[10] Micah said to him, "Live with me, and be a father and a priest for me. I will give you ten silver coins[3] a year, a set of clothes, and food." So the Levite went in. [11] The Levite decided to live with the

man, and the young man became like one of his sons. [12] Micah ordained the Levite, and the young man became his priest and lived in the house of Micah. [13] Then Micah said, "Now I know that the Lord will do good for me, for I have a Levite to be my priest."

The Danites Settle in Laish

18 In those days there was no king in Israel.

And in those days the tribe of the Danites was looking for an inheritance in which to live, for no territory had come into their possession among the tribes of Israel up to that time. [2] So the children of Dan sent out from their families five valorous men from Zorah and Eshtaol in order to spy out and explore the land. They said to them, "Go, explore the land."

They came to the hill country of Ephraim, to the house of Micah, and they spent the night there. [3] When they were at the house of Micah, they noticed the speech of the young Levite. They turned aside and said to him, "Who brought you here? What are you doing in this place? What is your business here?"

[4] He told them what Micah had done for him, saying, "He hired me, and I became his priest."

[5] They said to him, "Please ask God if we may know whether our mission will be a success as we go to do it."

[6] The priest said to them, "Go in peace. The Lord is watching the way you are going."

[7] The five men went away and came to Laish. They saw the people who were there, living securely according to the culture of the Sidonians. There were no rulers in the land who might put them to shame for anything. They were far from the Sidonians and had no ties with anyone.

[8] When they came back to their brothers in Zorah and Eshtaol, their brothers asked them, "What do you have to say?"

[9] They said, "Get up! Let us go up against them, for we have seen the land. It is very good. You are silent, but do not hesitate to go to take the land. [10] When you go, you will come to a secure people and to an expansive land. For God has given it into your hands: a place where there is no lack of anything on the earth."

[11] So six hundred fully armed men set out from the family of the Danites, from Zorah and Eshtaol. [12] They went up and set up camp in Kiriath Jearim in Judah. Therefore they call that place Mahaneh Dan to this day. It is west of Kiriath Jearim. [13] From there they passed the hill country of Ephraim and came to the house of Micah.

[14] The five men who went to spy out the land of Laish said to their brothers, "Did you know that in these houses are an ephod, household idols, a carved image, and a metal idol? Now think about what to do." [15] So they turned aside there and came to the house of the young Levite, to the house of Micah, and greeted him. [16] The six hundred men armed with their weapons of war, who were the children of Dan, stood at the entrance to the gate. [17] The five men who went to spy out the land went in and took the carved idol, ephod, household idols, and the metal idol. The priest was standing at the entrance to the gate with the six hundred fully armed men.

[18] When these men went into the house of Micah and took the carved idol, ephod, household idols, and the metal idol, the priest said to them, "What are you doing?"

[19] They said to him, "Quiet! Put your hand over your mouth and go with us. Be a father and priest for us. Is it better to be a priest for one man's house or for a tribe and a family in Israel?" [20] So the priest's heart was glad. He took the ephod, the household idols, and the carved image and went among the people. [21] So they turned and left, putting the children, livestock, and valuables in front of them.

[22] They had gone far from the house of Micah, but the neighbors of Micah assembled and caught up to the children of Dan. [23] They called out to the children of Dan. So they turned and said to Micah, "What is wrong that have you assembled together?"

[24] He said, "You took the gods that I made, and the priest, and then you left. What do I have left? So what is this that you say to me, 'What is wrong?'"

[25] The children of Dan said to him, "Do not let us hear your voice again. Otherwise bitter men might meet you and you will forfeit your life and the lives of your family." [26] So the children of Dan

[1] 2 About 28 pounds, or 13 kilograms.   [2] 4 About 5 pounds, or 2.3 kilograms.   [3] 10 About 4 ounces, or 115 grams.

went their way. And when Micah saw that they were too strong for him, he turned and went back to his house. ²⁷ They took what Micah had made and his priest, and came to Laish to a quiet and secure people. They struck them down with the edge of the sword and burned the city with fire. ²⁸ There was no one to save them because the city was far from Sidon and had no contact with anyone. It was in the valley by Beth Rehob.

They rebuilt the city and lived there. ²⁹ They called the city Dan, after their father Dan, who was born to Israel (Laish was the former name of the city). ³⁰ The children of Dan set up the carved idol for themselves. Jonathan the son of Gershom, the son of Manasseh, and his sons were priests to the tribe of Dan until the time of exile from the land. ³¹ So they displayed Micah's graven image that he had made, for the whole time that the house of God was in Shiloh.

A Levite and His Concubine

19 In those days, when there was no king in Israel, there was a certain Levite living as resident foreigner in a remote part of the hill country of Ephraim. He took a concubine for himself from Bethlehem in Judah. ² Yet his concubine became angry with him and went away from him to her father's house at Bethlehem in Judah. She was there for four months. ³ Her husband got up and went after her in order to speak tenderly to her and bring her back. His servant and two donkeys were with him. When he came to her father's house, the girl's father saw him and was happy to meet with him. ⁴ His father-in-law, the girl's father, prevailed upon him to stay with him for three days. So they ate and drank and spent the night there.

⁵ On the fourth day they woke up early in the morning. He got ready to go, but the girl's father said to his son-in-law, "Strengthen yourself with a little food, and then you can go." ⁶ So the two of them sat down to eat and drink together. Then the girl's father said to the man, "Please spend the night and let your heart be merry." ⁷ The man got up to go, but his father-in-law urged him until he turned back and spent the night there. ⁸ He got up early in the morning on the fifth day to go. The girl's father said, "Please, strengthen yourself and wait until later in the day." So the two of them ate.

⁹ Then the man got up to go: he, his concubine, and his servant. His father-in-law, the girl's father, said to him, "Look! It is getting dark. Spend the night! Settle in and spend the night here, let your heart be merry. You can get up early tomorrow and go home." ¹⁰ Yet the man did not want to spend the night, so he got up and left and approached Jebus (that is, Jerusalem). Two saddled donkeys and his concubine were with him.

¹¹ When they were near Jebus, it was getting very late. The servant said to his master, "Come, let us turn aside to this Jebusite city and spend the night in it."

¹² His master said to him, "We must not turn aside to a city of foreigners, who are not children of Israel. We will continue on to Gibeah." ¹³ He said to his servant, "Come, let us go to one of these places. We will spend the night in Gibeah or Ramah." ¹⁴ They continued and went on. The sun went down when they were near Gibeah in Benjamin. ¹⁵ So they turned aside there to go and spend the night in Gibeah. They went in and sat in the city square, but no one took them in to spend the night.

¹⁶ Just then, an old man came in at evening time from his work in the field. The man was from the hill country of Ephraim and lived as a resident foreigner in Gibeah, but the townspeople were Benjamites. ¹⁷ He looked up and saw the traveler in the city square. The old man said, "Where are you going, and where do you come from?"

¹⁸ He said to him, "We are traveling from Bethlehem in Judah to a remote part of the hill country of Ephraim. I am from there. I went to Bethlehem in Judah, and now I am going to the house of the LORD. No one has taken me into his home. ¹⁹ Yet there is enough straw and fodder for our donkeys, with bread and wine for me, your maidservant, and the young man who is with your servant. We do not lack anything."

²⁰ The old man said, "Do not worry. I will take care of whatever you need. Just do not spend the night in the city square." ²¹ So he brought him into his house and gave food to his donkeys. They washed their feet, ate, and drank.

²² While they were enjoying themselves, the men of the city, who were wicked men, surrounded the house and pounded on the door. They said to the old man, the master of the house, "Bring out the man who came to your house, so we can have relations with him."

²³ The master of the house went out to them and said, "No, my brothers, do not commit this evil act, not after this man has come into my house. Do not commit this disgrace. ²⁴ Here are my virgin daughter and the man's concubine. Let me bring them out to you. Ravish them and do to them what you please. But do not commit this vile act against this man."

²⁵ The men were unwilling to listen to him, so the man seized his concubine and brought her out to them in the street. They knew her and abused her all night until morning. As the dawn began to break, they let her go. ²⁶ The woman came back at daybreak and fell down at the door of the man's house where her master was, *lying there* until it was light.

²⁷ Her master got up in the morning and opened the doors of the house. He went out to go on his way, but there was the woman, his concubine, fallen at the door of the house with her hands on the threshold. ²⁸ He said to her, "Get up, let us be going," but there was no answer. So the man put her on a donkey and went home.

²⁹ When he got home, he took a knife and seized his concubine, then cut her body into twelve pieces. Then he sent her throughout all the territory of Israel. ³⁰ Everyone who saw this said, "Nothing like this has been done or seen since the day the children of Israel came out of the land of Egypt until today. Consider it, take counsel, and speak up!"

The Children of Israel Punish the Benjamites

20 All the children of Israel from Dan to Beersheba, and *also from* the land of Gilead, went out and gathered together in an assembly as one man before the LORD at Mizpah. ² The leaders of all the people from all the tribes of Israel presented themselves in an assembly of the people of God, who numbered four hundred thousand infantrymen bearing swords. ³ (The Benjamites heard that the children of Israel had gone up to Mizpah.) The children of Israel said, "Tell how this evil happened!"

⁴ So the Levite, the husband of the murdered woman, answered, "My concubine and I came to Gibeah, in Benjamin, to spend the night. ⁵ Then the leaders of Gibeah rose up against me. At night they surrounded the house where I was staying. They wanted to kill me; instead they ravished my concubine so that she died. ⁶ I seized my concubine, cut her into pieces, and sent her throughout all the territory of Israel, because they committed an infamous and disgraceful act in Israel. ⁷ Now, all of you are children of Israel. Give your advice and counsel here."

⁸ All the people arose as one man and said, "Not a man among us will go to his tent, and no one will turn aside to his house. ⁹ Now this is what we will do to Gibeah. We will go against it by lot. ¹⁰ We will take ten men out of every hundred, from every tribe of Israel, a hundred from every thousand, and a thousand from every ten thousand, to bring provisions for the troops. Then when they come to Gibeah in Benjamin, they may repay them for all the evil that they committed in Israel." ¹¹ So all the men of Israel gathered at the city, united like one man.

¹² The tribes of Israel sent men throughout the whole tribe of Benjamin, saying, "What is this evil that has been committed among you? ¹³ Now hand over the wicked men in Gibeah, so that we can kill them and purge the evil from Israel."

Yet the Benjamites were not willing to listen to their fellow children of Israel. ¹⁴ The Benjamites gathered from their cities at Gibeah in order to go out and wage war against the children of Israel. ¹⁵ That day, the Benjamites mustered twenty-six thousand armed men from the cities and seven hundred specially chosen men from Gibeah. ¹⁶ Out of all these people there were seven hundred specially chosen men who were left-handed, all of whom could sling a stone at a hair and not miss.

¹⁷ The men of Israel, apart from Benjamin, gathered four hundred thousand armed men who drew the sword; all of them were men of war.

¹⁸ The children of Israel arose, went up to Bethel, and asked God, "Who should go up first to wage war against the Benjamites?"

The Lord said, "Judah first."

[19] The children of Israel got up in the morning and camped against Gibeah. [20] The men of Israel went out for battle with Benjamin, and the men of Israel lined up for battle at Gibeah. [21] Then the Benjamites came out from Gibeah and struck twenty-two thousand Israelite men down to the ground. [22] The people, the men of Israel, rallied and lined up for battle again in the place where they had lined up on the first day. [23] Then the children of Israel went up and wept before the Lord until evening. They asked the Lord, "Should we advance and fight our brother-tribesmen the Benjamites again?"

The Lord said, "Advance against them."

[24] So the children of Israel advanced against the Benjamites for the second day. [25] And on the second day, the Benjamites went out from Gibeah to meet them and again struck eighteen thousand men down to the ground, every one of them armed.

[26] Then all the children of Israel, all the people, went up to Bethel where they wept and sat before the Lord. They fasted that day until evening and offered burnt offerings and peace offerings before the Lord. [27] The children of Israel asked the Lord (because the ark of the covenant of God was there in those days, [28] and Phinehas the son of Eleazar, the son of Aaron, stood before it then), "Should we go out again to wage war with our brother-tribesmen the Benjamites, or should we not?"

The Lord said, "Go up, for tomorrow I will give them into your hands."

[29] So Israel set an ambushing force around Gibeah. [30] The children of Israel went up against the Benjamites on the third day and lined up at Gibeah as before. [31] The Benjamites went out to engage the people and were drawn away from the city. They began to strike the people down as before. On the main roads that go up to Bethel and Gibeah and in the field, they struck down about thirty children of Israel. [32] The Benjamites said, "They are struck down before us like at the beginning." But the children of Israel said, "Let us retreat and draw them away from the city toward the main roads."

[33] So all the men of Israel rose up out of their place and assumed their battle positions at Baal Tamar. Then the men of Israel in ambush charged out of their places, out of the meadows of Gibeah. [34] Ten thousand specially chosen men from all of Israel came against Gibeah. The battle was fierce, and the Benjamites did not know that disaster was upon them. [35] The Lord defeated Benjamin before Israel, and that day the children of Israel struck down twenty-five thousand one hundred Benjamites, every one of them armed. [36] The Benjamites saw that they were defeated.

Now the men of Israel had withdrawn from Benjamin, because they relied on the men in ambush whom they had set against Gibeah. [37] So the ambushing force rushed on and attacked Gibeah. They struck down the whole city with the edge of the sword. [38] The men of Israel had made an agreement with the ambushing force that when they sent up a large amount of smoke from the city, [39] the children of Israel would turn around in battle.

When the Benjamites had begun to strike the children of Israel down, about thirty men, they said, "Surely they are struck down before us like at the beginning." [40] Yet when the smoke began to rise up from the city in a column, the Benjamites looked behind them and suddenly noticed the whole city going up in smoke to the sky. [41] Then the men of Israel turned around, and the men of Benjamin were horrified because they saw that disaster had come on them. [42] So they fled from the men of Israel toward the direction of the wilderness, but the battle overtook them. Whoever came out of the cities destroyed them in their midst. [43] They surrounded the Benjamites, chased them without rest, and trampled them down near Gibeah toward the east. [44] Eighteen thousand men from Benjamin fell; all these were men of valor. [45] The rest turned and fled toward the wilderness to Rimmon Rock, and they cut down five thousand men on the main roads. They pursued them relentlessly until they reached Gidom and killed two thousand of them.

[46] So the Benjamites who fell that day numbered twenty-five thousand, every one of them armed, valorous men. [47] However,

six hundred men turned and fled toward the wilderness, to Rimmon Rock. They dwelled at Rimmon Rock for four months. [48] Yet the men of Israel turned back against the Benjamites and struck them with the edge of the sword—city inhabitants, animals, and everything that could be found. Indeed, they set on fire every city that could be found.

Wives for the Benjamites

21 In Mizpah the men of Israel had taken an oath: "No one among us will give his daughter to a Benjamite as his wife."

[2] So the people came to Bethel and sat there before God until evening. They raised their voices and wept, sobbing loudly. [3] They said, "Why, Lord God of Israel, has this happened in Israel, that today a tribe is missing from Israel?"

[4] In the morning the people got up early and built an altar there. They offered burnt offerings and peace offerings.

[5] The children of Israel said, "Who from all the tribes of Israel did not go up with the assembly to the Lord?" For they vowed a solemn oath regarding whoever did not go up to the Lord at Mizpah stating, "He must be killed."

[6] The children of Israel lamented for Benjamin their brother, and said, "One tribe is cut off from Israel today. [7] What can we do to find wives for those who are left? For we swore by the Lord not to give them our daughters as wives." [8] So they said, "Is there anyone from among the tribes of Israel who did not go up to the Lord at Mizpah?" Then they learned that no one from the camp of Jabesh Gilead had come to the assembly. [9] When the people were counted, indeed, there was not a man there from among the inhabitants of Jabesh Gilead.

[10] So the assembly sent twelve thousand valorous men there and commanded them, "Go and strike down the inhabitants of Jabesh Gilead with the edge of the sword, including women and children. [11] This is what you will do: You will kill every man and every woman who has slept with a man." [12] So among the inhabitants of Jabesh Gilead they found four hundred young virgins who had never slept with a man, and they brought them to the camp at Shiloh in the land of Canaan.

[13] Then the whole assembly sent *someone* to speak to the Benjamites who were at Rimmon Rock, and they declared peace. [14] So the Benjamites returned at that time, and they gave to them the women who were still alive from among the women of Jabesh Gilead. Yet they did not find enough for them.

[15] The people felt sorry for Benjamin, for the Lord had made a gap among the tribes of Israel. [16] The elders of the assembly said, "What can we do to find wives for those who are left? The Benjamite women were destroyed." [17] They said, "*There must be* an inheritance for the remnant of Benjamin, so that a tribe will not be wiped out from Israel. [18] Yet we cannot give them our daughters for wives, for the children of Israel swore, 'Cursed be anyone who gives a wife to Benjamin.'" [19] They said, "Wait! There is an annual festival of the Lord in Shiloh, which is north of Bethel, east of the main road that goes up from Bethel to Shechem, and south of Lebonah."

[20] So they commanded the Benjamites, "Go and hide in the vineyards. [21] Watch, and then when the daughters of Shiloh come out to dance in the dances, come out from the vineyards and have every man grab a wife for himself from among the daughters of Shiloh. Then go to the land of Benjamin. [22] When their fathers or their brothers come to us to complain, we will say to them, 'Be favorable to them for our sakes, because we did not take for each man a wife in the battle; for you have not given women to them at the time, thereby making yourselves guilty.'"

[23] So the Benjamites did this. They carried away wives for each man from among the dancers that they caught. Then they returned to their inheritance, rebuilt the cities, and lived in them.

[24] At that time, the children of Israel departed from there each man to his tribe and to his family. They went out from there to their own inheritance.

[25] In those days there was no king in Israel; everyone did what was right in his own eyes.

RUTH

Naomi Loses

1 In the days when the judges ruled, there was a famine in the land. And a man from Bethlehem in Judah went to live in the land of Moab, he and his wife and his two sons. [2] The name of the man was Elimelek, the name of his wife was Naomi, and the names of his two sons were Mahlon and Kilion. They were Ephrathites from Bethlehem in Judah. And they went to Moab and lived there.

[3] Now Elimelek, the husband of Naomi, died, so she was left alone with her two sons. [4] They took Moabite wives for themselves; the name of one was Orpah and the name of the other Ruth. They lived there about ten years. [5] Then Mahlon and Kilion also died, and Naomi was left without her two sons and her husband.

[6] So she got up with her daughters-in-law to return from the land of Moab, for in the land of Moab, she had heard that the Lord had visited His people by giving them food. [7] She set out from the place where she had been, with her two daughters-in-law, and they went on their way to return to the land of Judah.

[8] Then Naomi said to her two daughters-in-law, "Go, return each to her mother's house. May the Lord deal kindly with you, as you have dealt with your deceased husbands and with me. [9] May the Lord grant that you each find rest in the house of *another* husband."

Then she kissed them, and they raised their voices and wept aloud. [10] They said to her, "We will return with you to your people."

[11] But Naomi said, "Turn back, my daughters. Why would you go with me? Are there sons in my womb, who could become your husbands? [12] Turn back, my daughters! Go, for I am too old to have a husband. Even if I thought that there was still hope for me, that I could have a husband tonight and give birth to sons, [13] would you wait until they were grown? Would you refrain from getting married? No, my daughters. It is much more bitter for me than for you, for the hand of the Lord has turned against me."

[14] Then they raised their voices and wept aloud once more. Orpah kissed her mother-in-law, but Ruth clung to her.

[15] Naomi said, "Look, your sister-in-law has returned to her people and her gods. Return with her!"

[16] But Ruth said, "Do not urge me to leave you or to turn back from following you. For wherever you go, I will go, and wherever you stay, I will stay. Your people shall be my people and your God my God. [17] Where you die, I will die, and there I will be buried. May the Lord do thus to me, and worse, if anything but death separates you and me!" [18] When Naomi saw that she was determined to go with her, she said no more to her.

[19] So they both went on until they came to Bethlehem. When they came to Bethlehem, the whole town was stirred because of them, and the women asked, "Is this Naomi?"

[20] But she said to them, "Do not call me Naomi. Call me Mara, because the Almighty has brought great bitterness to me. [21] I was full when I left, but the Lord has caused me to return empty. Why should you call me Naomi when the Lord has opposed me? The Almighty has brought misfortune upon me!"

[22] So Naomi returned from the land of Moab with Ruth the Moabite, her daughter-in-law. They came to Bethlehem at the start of the *spring* barley harvest.

Ruth Meets Boaz

2 Now Naomi had a relative of her husband, a man of prominence and means from the clan of Elimelek. His name was Boaz.

[2] Ruth the Moabitess said to Naomi, "Please let me go into the field and glean among the heads of grain behind anyone in whose eyes I may find favor."

Naomi said to her, "Go, my daughter." [3] So she went to glean in the field behind the harvesters. She happened to come to a part of the field belonging to Boaz, who was from the clan of Elimelek.

[4] Just then Boaz came from Bethlehem and said to the harvesters, "May the Lord be with you!"

And they said to him, "May the Lord bless you."

[5] Then Boaz said to his servant who was in charge of his harvesters, "Whose young woman is this?"

[6] So the servant who was in charge of his harvesters answered, "She is the young Moabitess woman who came back with Naomi from the land of Moab. [7] She said, 'Please let me glean and gather *grain* among the bundles behind the harvesters.' So she came and has remained from morning until now, though she rested a little while in the house."

[8] Then Boaz said to Ruth, "Listen, my daughter. Do not go to glean in another field and leave this one. Stay close to my young women. [9] Keep your eyes on the field in which they reap and follow after them. I have commanded the men not to touch you. When you are thirsty, go to the vessels and drink from what the young men have drawn."

[10] So she fell on her face, bowed down to the ground, and said to him, "Why have I found favor in your eyes, that you should acknowledge me, a foreigner?"

[11] Boaz answered and said to her, "I have been told all that you have done for your mother-in-law after the death of your husband, and how you left your father and mother and your homeland and came to a people you did not know before. [12] May the Lord reward your deeds. May you have a full reward from the Lord, the God of Israel, under whose wings you have come to take refuge."

[13] Then she said, "May I find favor in your eyes, my lord, for you have comforted me and have spoken kindly to your servant, though I am not like one of your servant girls."

[14] At mealtime Boaz said to her, "Come over here, and eat some bread, and dip your piece in the vinegar."

So she sat down beside the harvesters, and he passed her some roasted grain. She ate and was full and had some left over. [15] When she got up to glean, Boaz commanded his young men, "Let her glean even among the bundles, and do not harm her. [16] Also pull out some *grain* for her from the bundles and leave it so that she may glean it, and do not rebuke her."

[17] So she gleaned in the field until evening. Then she beat out what she had gleaned, and it was about an ephah [f] of barley. [18] She took it up and went into the city, and her mother-in-law saw what she had gleaned. She drew *it* out and gave her what she had left, after she had been satisfied.

[19] Her mother-in-law said to her, "Where did you glean today, and where did you work? May he who took notice of you be blessed."

So she told her mother-in-law with whom she had worked, and said, "The name of the man with whom I worked today is Boaz."

[20] Then Naomi said to her daughter-in-law, "May he be blessed of the Lord who has not withdrawn His kindness to the living and to the dead." Naomi said to her, "This man is a close relative of ours, one of our redeeming relatives."

[21] Then Ruth the Moabitess said, "He even told me, 'You should stay close to my servants until they have finished all my harvest.'"

[22] Naomi said to Ruth her daughter-in-law, "It is better, my daughter, that you go with his young women, for in someone else's field you might be harmed."

[23] So she stayed close to the young women of Boaz to glean until the end of barley harvest and wheat harvest. And she lived with her mother-in-law.

Ruth's Redemption

3 One day Naomi her mother-in-law said to her, "My daughter, why should I not find a home that will be good for you? [2] Now is not Boaz our relative, with whose young women you have been

---

[f] 17 Likely about 30 pounds, or 13 kilograms.

working? Tonight he winnows barley on the threshing floor. [3] Now wash and anoint yourself, and put on your best clothes. Then go down to the threshing floor, but do not let the man know you are there until he has finished eating and drinking. [4] When he lies down, notice the place where he is lying. Go in and uncover his feet and lie down. He will tell you what you will do."

[5] She said to her, "All that you say to me I will do." [6] So she went down to the threshing floor and did all that her mother-in-law had instructed.

[7] When Boaz had eaten and drunk and his heart was merry, he went to lie down at the end of the heap of grain. Then Ruth came softly, uncovered his feet, and lay down. [8] At midnight, the man was startled and rolled over; and there, a woman was lying at his feet.

[9] He said, "Who are you?"

And she answered, "I am Ruth, your maidservant. Spread your cloak over me, for you are a redeeming kinsman."

[10] He said, "May you be blessed of the Lord, my daughter. You have shown your last act of kindness to be greater than the first, because you have not pursued young men, whether poor or rich. [11] So now, my daughter, do not worry. All that you ask me, I will do for you. All of my fellow townsmen know that you are a woman of noble character. [12] Now it is true that I am a redeeming kinsman. Yet there is another redeemer closer than I am. [13] Stay here tonight, and in the morning if he wants to redeem you, very well. Let him do so. Yet if he does not want to redeem you, then I will redeem you. I will, as the Lord lives! Sleep here until morning."

[14] So she lay at his feet until morning, but she arose before one could recognize another. Then he said, "It must not be known that a woman came to the threshing floor."

[15] He said, "Bring me the shawl you have on you, and hold it." So she held it, and he poured six measures of barley into it and placed it on her. Then she went into the city.

[16] When Ruth came to her mother-in-law, Naomi said, "How did it go, my daughter?"

Then she told her all that Boaz had done for her. [17] She said, "He gave me these six ephahs of barley, for he said to me, 'Do not return to your mother-in-law empty-handed.'"

[18] Then Naomi said, "Wait here, my daughter, until you learn what happens. For the man will not rest until the matter is settled today."

Boaz Marries Ruth

4 So Boaz went up to the gate and sat down there. And now the redeemer of whom he had spoken passed by, and Boaz said, "Come over, friend, and sit here." So he went over and sat down.

[2] Then Boaz took ten men from among the elders of the town and said, "Sit here." So they sat down. [3] He said to the redeemer, "Naomi, who has come back from the land of Moab, must sell the plot of land belonging to our brother Elimelek. [4] I thought I should inform you and say, 'Buy it in the presence of those sitting here and in the presence of the elders of my people. If you want to redeem it, redeem it. But if you will not redeem it, tell me so

that I know, for there is no one prior to you to redeem it, and I am next after you.'"

So he said, "I will redeem it."

[5] Then Boaz said, "On the day you buy the field from the hand of Naomi, you also acquire Ruth the Moabitess, the wife of the deceased, to perpetuate the name of the deceased through his inheritance."

[6] The redeemer replied, "I am not able to redeem it for myself lest I ruin my own inheritance. Take my redemption rights for yourself, for I cannot do it."

[7] (Now this was the custom in ancient times in Israel for redeeming and exchanging: to confirm a transaction, a man would remove his sandal and give it to his neighbor. This was a binding act in Israel.)

[8] Therefore the redeemer said to Boaz, "Buy it yourself," and he removed his sandal.

[9] Then Boaz said to the elders and all the people, "You are witnesses today that I have bought everything that belonged to Elimelek, Kilion, and Mahlon from Naomi. [10] Moreover I have also acquired Ruth the Moabitess, the wife of Mahlon, to be my wife, in order to preserve the name of the deceased man for his inheritance, so that his name will not be cut off from among his brothers or from his town. You are witnesses this day."

[11] Then all the people who were at the gate, along with the elders, said, "We are witnesses. May the Lord make the woman who is coming to your house like Rachel and Leah, who together built up the house of Israel. May you do well in Ephrathah and be famous in Bethlehem! [12] May your house be like the house of Perez, whom Tamar bore to Judah, through the offspring that the Lord will give you by this young woman."

The Genealogy of David

[13] So Boaz took Ruth, and she became his wife. When they came together, the Lord enabled her to conceive, and she bore a son. [14] Then the women said to Naomi, "Blessed be the Lord, who has not left you without a redeemer. May he become famous in Israel! [15] He will be a comfort for your soul and support you in your old age. For your daughter-in-law, who loves you and who is better to you than seven sons, has given birth to him."

[16] Then Naomi took the child, laid him on her lap, and became his nurse. [17] The neighbor women gave him a name, saying, "A son has been born to Naomi!" And they named him Obed. He was the father of Jesse, the father of David.

[18] Now these are the descendants of Perez:

Perez was the father of Hezron,
[19] Hezron the father of Ram,
Ram the father of Amminadab,
[20] Amminadab the father of Nahshon,
Nahshon the father of Salmon,
[21] Salmon the father of Boaz,
Boaz the father of Obed,
[22] Obed the father of Jesse,
and Jesse the father of David.

1 Samuel

The Birth of Samuel

1 Now there was a certain man from Ramathaim Zuphim, in the hill country of Ephraim, and his name was Elkanah, the son of Jeroham, the son of Elihu, the son of Tohu, the son of Zuph, an Ephraimite. [2] And he had two wives; the name of one was Hannah and the name of the second was Peninnah. Now Peninnah had children, but Hannah had no children.

[3] This man went up out of his city annually to worship and to sacrifice to the LORD of Hosts in Shiloh. And there the two sons of Eli, Hophni and Phinehas, were priests to the LORD. [4] When the day came that Elkanah sacrificed, he gave portions to Peninnah his wife and to all her sons and her daughters. [5] But to Hannah he gave a double portion because he loved Hannah, but the LORD had closed her womb. [6] Now her rival provoked her greatly, making her miserable because the LORD had closed her womb. [7] Thus it was yearly, when she went up to the house of the LORD, that she provoked her. So Hannah wept and did not eat. [8] Then said Elkanah her husband to her, "Hannah, why are you weeping? And why do you not eat? Why is your heart grieved? Am I not better to you than ten sons?"

[9] So Hannah arose after they had eaten in Shiloh and after they had drunk. Now Eli the priest was sitting on a seat by the door of the tabernacle of the LORD. [10] And she was bitter, and prayed to the LORD, and wept severely. [11] So she made a vow and said, "O LORD of Hosts, if You will indeed look on the affliction of Your maidservant, and remember me and not forget Your maidservant, but will give to Your maidservant a baby boy, then I will give him to the LORD all the days of his life, and no razor shall touch his head." [1]

[12] And as she was praying before the LORD, Eli watched her mouth. [13] Now Hannah was speaking in her heart. Her lips were moving, but her voice was not heard. Therefore Eli thought she was drunk. [14] So Eli said to her, "How long will you be drunk? Put away your wine from you."

[15] And Hannah answered and said, "No, my lord, I am a woman of sorrow. I have drunk neither wine nor strong drink, but have poured out my soul before the LORD. [16] Do not consider your handmaid to be a sinful woman, for out of the abundance of my concern and provocation I have spoken until now."

[17] Then Eli answered and said, "Go in peace, and the God of Israel grant you your request that you have asked of Him."

[18] And she said, "Let your handmaid find grace in your sight." So the woman went her way and ate, and her face was not sad as before.

[19] They rose up in the morning early and worshipped before the LORD. And they returned and came to their house to Ramah. And Elkanah knew Hannah his wife, and the LORD remembered her. [20] And it came to pass that Hannah conceived and bore a son. And she called his name Samuel saying, "Because I have asked him of the LORD."

The Dedication of Samuel

[21] Then the man Elkanah and all his house went up to offer to the LORD the yearly sacrifice and his vow. [22] But Hannah did not go, for she said to her husband, "I will not go up until the child is weaned, and then I will bring him, that he may appear before the LORD and live there forever."

[23] So Elkanah her husband said to her, "Do what seems good to you. Wait until you have weaned him; only may the LORD establish His word." So the woman remained, and nursed her son until she weaned him.

[24] When she had weaned him, she took him up with her with three bulls, one ephah [2] of flour, and a bottle of wine. And she brought him to the house of the LORD in Shiloh, though the boy was young. [25] Then they slaughtered a bull, and they brought the boy to Eli. [26] And she said, "Oh, my lord! As you live, my lord, I am the woman that stood by you here praying to the LORD. [27] For this boy I prayed, and the LORD has given me my petition which I asked of Him.

[28] Therefore also I have let the LORD have him. As long as he lives he will be dedicated to the LORD." And he worshipped the LORD there.

The Prayer of Hannah

2 Hannah prayed, saying:

"My heart rejoices in the LORD;
    my horn is exalted in the LORD.
My mouth is bold against my enemies,
    because I rejoice in Your salvation.

[2] "There is none holy as the LORD,
    for there is none besides You,
    and there is no rock like our God.

[3] "Do not multiply proud speech,
    nor let arrogance come out of your mouth,
for the LORD is the God of knowledge,
    and by Him actions are examined.

[4] "The bows of the mighty are broken,
    but those who stumbled are girded with strength.
[5] Those that were full have hired out themselves for bread,
    and those that were hungry ceased *to hunger*.
Even the barren has borne seven,
    and she that has many children wastes away.

[6] "The LORD kills and makes alive;
    He brings down to the grave and brings up.
[7] The LORD makes poor and makes rich;
    He brings low and lifts up.
[8] He raises up the poor out of the dust
    and lifts up the oppressed from the dunghill
to make them sit with princes
    and inherit a throne of glory.

"For the pillars of the earth belong to the LORD,
    and He has set the world upon them.
[9] He will guard the feet of His saints,
    but the wicked will be silent in darkness.

"For by strength shall no man prevail.
[10]   The adversaries of the LORD will be broken to pieces;
He will thunder against them out of heaven.
    The LORD will judge the ends of the earth.

"He will give strength to His king
    and exalt the horn of His anointed."

[11] Then Elkanah went to Ramah to his house. And the boy ministered to the LORD before Eli the priest.

Wicked Sons of Eli

[12] Now the sons of Eli were corrupt. They did not know the LORD. [13] The priest's custom with the people was that when any man offered a sacrifice, the priest's servant came while the flesh was cooking with a three-pronged fork in his hand. [14] And he struck it into the pan, or kettle, or cauldron, or pot, *and* all that the fork brought up the priest took for himself. This they did in Shiloh to all the children of Israel who came there. [15] Even before they burned the fat, the priest's servant would come and say to the man sacrificing, "Give meat for the priest to roast. For he will not take boiled meat from you, but only raw."

[16] If any man said to him, "Let them first burn the fat and then take as much as you wish," then he would answer him, "No, but you will give it *to me now*, and if not, I will take *it* by force."

---

1 11 Hannah dedicates Samuel as a lifetime Nazirite (see Nu 6:2–21).   *2 24* Likely about 36 pounds, or 16 kilograms.

[17] Therefore the sin of the young men was very great before the LORD. For the men treated the offering of the LORD with contempt.

God Blesses Hannah

[18] But Samuel ministered before the LORD, as a boy, wearing a linen ephod. [19] Now his mother would make him a little coat and brought it to him every year when she came up with her husband to offer the yearly sacrifice. [20] And Eli would bless Elkanah and his wife and say, "The LORD give you offspring from this woman for the sake of the request which was made to the LORD." Then they would return to their home. [21] The LORD visited Hannah, so that she conceived and bore three sons and two daughters. And the boy Samuel grew before the LORD.

Eli Confronts Hophni and Phinehas

[22] Now Eli was very old, and he heard all that his sons were doing to all Israel, even that they lay with the women who served at the doorway of the tent of meeting. [23] He said to them, "Why are you doing these things? For I am hearing of your evil dealings from all these people. [24] No, my sons! Truly, it is not a good report that I hear the people of the LORD spreading. [25] If one man sins against another, God will judge him, but if a man sins against the LORD, who will intercede for him?" But they did not listen to the voice of their father, because the LORD desired to kill them.

[26] Now the boy Samuel was growing both in stature and favor with the LORD and also with men.

God's Case Against the House of Eli

[27] A man of God came to Eli and said to him, "Thus says the LORD, 'Did I *not* plainly reveal Myself to the house of your father, when they were in Egypt in Pharaoh's house? [28] And choose him out of all the tribes of Israel to be My priest, to offer upon My altar, to burn incense, to wear an ephod before Me? And I gave to the house of your father all the offerings made by fire by the children of Israel? [29] Why do you kick at My sacrifice and at My offering, which I have commanded in My dwelling, and honor your sons above Me, to make yourselves fat with the best of all the offerings of Israel My people?'

[30] "Therefore the LORD God of Israel says, 'I surely said that your house, and the house of your father, should walk before Me forever,' but now the LORD says, 'Far be it from Me *to do so*, for those who honor Me, I will honor, and those that despise Me will be humbled. [31] The days are coming when I will cut off your authority and the strength of your father's house, so there shall not be an old man in your house. [32] You shall see the distress of *My* dwelling, despite all the good which will be done for Israel. And there shall not be an elderly man in your house perpetually. [33] Yet the one I do not cut off from My altar will be spared so your eyes will not stop *weeping* or your soul grieving. All the increase of your house will die in their prime.

[34] "This will be the sign to you which will come upon your two sons, Hophni and Phinehas: In one day, they will both die. [35] And I will raise up for Myself a faithful priest; what is in My heart and in My soul he will do *it*. And I will build him a sure house, and it will walk before My anointed forever. [36] But it will be that everyone who is left in your house will come and bow down to him for a piece of silver and a morsel of bread, and will say, Please attach me to one of the priestly offices, that I may eat a piece of bread.' "

God Calls Samuel

3 Now the boy Samuel was ministering to the LORD before Eli. And the word of the LORD was rare in those days. There was no vision coming forth.

[2] At that time, Eli was lying down in his place (now his eyes had begun to grow weak that he could not see), [3] and the lamp of God had not yet gone out, and Samuel was lying down in the house of the LORD where the ark of God was.

[4] Then the LORD called to Samuel, and he answered, "Here I am." [5] He ran to Eli and said, "Here I am, for you called me." And he said, "I did not call. Return, lie down again." And he went and lay down.

[6] The LORD called Samuel again. So Samuel arose and went to Eli, and said, "Here I am, for you called me."

And he answered, "I did not call, my son. Return, lie down again."

[7] Now Samuel did not yet know the LORD, nor had the word of the LORD been revealed to him.

[8] The LORD again called Samuel a third time. So he arose and went to Eli and said, "Here I am, for you called me."

Then Eli understood that the LORD was calling to the boy. [9] Therefore Eli said to Samuel, "Go, lie down. And it will be, if He calls you, that you will say, 'Speak, LORD, for Your servant listens.' " So Samuel went and lay down in his place.

[10] The LORD came and stood, and He called as at other times, "Samuel, Samuel."

Then Samuel said, "Speak, for Your servant listens."

[11] The LORD said to Samuel, "See, I am doing something in Israel which will make both ears ring of every one that hears it. [12] In that day I will bring about against Eli everything which I have spoken with regard to his house, from beginning to end. [13] For I told him that I will judge his house forever, for the guilt which he knew, because his sons are cursed, and he did not rebuke them. [14] Therefore I have sworn to the house of Eli that the iniquity of Eli's house shall not be atoned for with sacrifice nor offering forever."

[15] Samuel lay until the morning; then he opened the doors of the house of the LORD. Now Samuel feared to report the vision to Eli. [16] Then Eli called Samuel, and said, "Samuel, my son."

And he answered, "Here I am."

[17] He said, "What is the thing that the LORD has spoken to you? Do not hide it from me. Thus may God do so to you, and more also, if you hide from me a word out of all the things that He spoke to you." [18] Samuel told him everything, and did not hide from him a thing. And he said, "It is the LORD; let Him do what is good in His eyes."

[19] And Samuel grew, and the LORD was with him and did not let any of his words fall to the ground. [20] All Israel from Dan even to Beersheba knew that Samuel was proven to be a prophet of the LORD. [21] And the LORD appeared again in Shiloh. For the LORD revealed Himself to Samuel in Shiloh by the word of the LORD.

4 And the word of Samuel came to all Israel.

The Ark of God Captured

And Israel went out to battle against the Philistines and they made camp beside Ebenezer, and the Philistines encamped in Aphek. [2] The Philistines arrayed themselves in a battle line against Israel, and when the battle was over, Israel was beaten before the Philistines, who struck down on the field of battle about four thousand men. [3] When the people came into the camp, the elders of Israel said, "Why has the LORD struck us today before the Philistines? Let us bring the ark of the covenant of the LORD out of Shiloh to us, that it might come among us and rescue us out of the hand of our enemies."

[4] So the people sent to Shiloh, that they might bring from there the ark of the covenant of the LORD of Hosts, who dwells above the cherubim. And the two sons of Eli, Hophni and Phinehas, were there with the ark of the covenant of God.

[5] When the ark of the covenant of the LORD came into the camp, all Israel shouted with a great shout, so that the ground was in an uproar. [6] When the Philistines heard the sound of the shout, they said, "What does this great shout in the camp of the Hebrews mean?" Then they understood that the ark of the LORD had come into the camp.

[7] The Philistines were afraid, when they said, "God is come into the camp." And they said, "Woe to us! For this has never happened *to us* before. [8] Woe to us! Who will deliver us out of the hand of these mighty gods? These are the gods that struck the Egyptians with every plague in the wilderness. [9] Be strong and be men, O Philistines, lest you be servants to the Hebrews, as they have been to you. Now be men and fight."

[10] So the Philistines fought and Israel was beaten. And they fled every man into his tent. It was a very great defeat, for there fell of Israel thirty thousand foot soldiers. [11] Now the ark of God was taken, and the two sons of Eli, Hophni and Phinehas, died.

[12] There ran a man of Benjamin from the battle line, and he came to Shiloh the same day with his clothes torn and with dust upon his head. [13] When he came, Eli was sitting on a seat by the

wayside watching. For his heart feared for the ark of God. Now the man came to tell *it* in the city, and all the city cried out.

[14] When Eli heard the noise of the crying, he said, "What does the noise of this tumult mean?"

And the man hurriedly came and told Eli. [15] Now Eli was ninety-eight years old, and his eyes were dim, so that he could not see. [16] The man said to Eli, "I am he that came out of the army, and I fled today out of the battle line."

And he said, "What is the word, my son?"

[17] The messenger answered and said, "Israel has fled before the Philistines, and there also has been a great slaughter among the people. Your two sons also, Hophni and Phinehas, are dead. And the ark of God is taken."

[18] When he mentioned the ark of God, Eli fell from off the seat backward by the side of the gate. And his neck broke and he died, for he was an old and heavy man. And he had judged Israel forty years.

[19] His daughter-in-law, Phinehas' wife, was pregnant, about to give birth. And when she heard the news that the ark of God was taken, and that her father-in-law and her husband were dead, she kneeled down and gave birth, for her pains came upon her. [20] About the time of her death the women that stood by her said to her, "Do not fear, for you have borne a son." But she did not answer or regard it.

[21] She named the child Ichabod, saying, "The glory is departed from Israel," because the ark of God was taken, and because of her father-in-law and her husband. [22] She said, "The glory is departed from Israel, for the ark of God is taken."

The Philistines and the Ark

5 Now the Philistines took the ark of God, and brought it from Ebenezer to Ashdod. [2] When the Philistines took the ark of God, they brought it into the house of Dagon and set it by Dagon. [3] When the Ashdodites arose early in the morning, Dagon had fallen upon his face to the ground before the ark of the LORD. And they took Dagon and set him in his place again. [4] When they arose early on the next morning, again Dagon was fallen upon his face to the ground before the ark of the LORD, and the head of Dagon and both the palms of his hands were cut off upon the threshold. Only the *torso* of Dagon was left to him. [5] Therefore neither the priests of Dagon, nor any coming into Dagon's house, tread on the threshold of Dagon in Ashdod to this day.

[6] But the hand of the LORD was heavy upon the Ashdodites. He desolated them and struck them with tumors, even Ashdod and its territories. [7] When the men of Ashdod saw that it was so, they said, "The ark of the God of Israel cannot remain with us. For His hand is heavy upon us and upon Dagon our god." [8] So they sent and gathered all the lords of the Philistines unto them, and said, "What shall we do with the ark of the God of Israel?"

And they answered, "Let the ark of the God of Israel be carried around to Gath." And they carried the ark of the God of Israel *there*.

[9] It happened that after they had carried it about, the hand of the LORD was against the city with a very great destruction. And He struck the men of the city, both small and great. And tumors broke out on them. [10] Therefore they sent the ark of God to Ekron.

And it came about that as the ark of God came to Ekron, that the Ekronites cried out, saying, "They have brought about the ark of the God of Israel to slay us and our people." [11] So they sent and gathered together all the lords of the Philistines, and said, "Send away the ark of the God of Israel, and let it go again to His own place that He might not kill me and my people," for there was a deadly destruction throughout all the city. The hand of God was very heavy there. [12] The men that did not die were plagued with the tumors. And the cry of the city went up to heaven.

The Ark Returned to Israel

6 Now the ark of the LORD had been in the country of the Philistines seven months. [2] The Philistines called for the priests and the diviners, saying, "What shall we do with the ark of the LORD? Tell us how we should send it to its place."

[3] They said, "If you send away the ark of the God of Israel, do not send it empty. But return to Him a guilt offering. Then you will be healed, and it will be known to you why His hand is not removed from you."

[4] Then said they, "What will be the guilt offering which we will return to Him?"

They answered, "Five golden tumors and five golden mice according to the number of the lords of the Philistines. For one plague was on you all, and on your lords. [5] Therefore you will make images of your tumors and images of your mice that ravage the land. And you will give glory to the God of Israel. Perhaps He will lighten His hand from off you, even from off your gods and from off your land. [6] Why then do you harden your hearts, as the Egyptians and Pharaoh hardened their hearts? When He dealt severely with them, did they not let the people go, and they departed?

[7] "Now therefore make a new cart, and take two milk cows on which there has never been a yoke. Then tie the cows to the cart and bring their calves home, away from them. [8] Then take the ark of the LORD and set it on the cart. And put the images of gold, which you return to Him for a guilt offering, in a box by the side. And send it away, that it may go. [9] See, if it goes up by the way of His own territory to Beth Shemesh, then He has done us this great evil. But if not, then we will know that it is not His hand that struck us; it was by chance that it happened to us."

[10] The men did so. And they took two milk cows, tied them to the cart, and shut up their calves at home. [11] And they set the ark of the LORD on the cart, as well as the box with the mice of gold and the images of their tumors. [12] Then the cows took the straight way to the way of Beth Shemesh, and went along the highway, lowing as they went. They did not turn aside to the right hand or to the left with the lords of the Philistines walking after them to the border of Beth Shemesh.

[13] Now Beth Shemesh was reaping their wheat harvest in the valley. And they lifted up their eyes and saw the ark, and they rejoiced to see it. [14] The cart came into the field of Joshua, the Beth Shemite, and stood there where there was a great stone. And they split the wood of the cart, and offered the cows as a burnt offering to the LORD. [15] The Levites took down the ark of the LORD and the box that was with it, where the articles of gold were, and put them on the great stone. And the men of Beth Shemesh offered burnt offerings and made sacrifices the same day to the LORD. [16] When the five lords of the Philistines had seen it, they returned to Ekron the same day.

[17] These are the golden tumors which the Philistines returned for a guilt offering to the LORD: for Ashdod one, for Gaza one, for Ashkelon one, for Gath one, for Ekron one. [18] And the golden mice, according to the number of all the cities of the Philistines belonging to the five lords, both of fortified cities, and of country villages. And the great stone, where they set the ark of the LORD, *is a witness* to this day in the field of Joshua, the Beth Shemite.

[19] Then He struck the men of Beth Shemesh, because they had looked into the ark of the LORD. He struck fifty thousand and seventy men. And the people lamented, because the LORD had struck the people with a great slaughter. [20] The men of Beth Shemesh said, "Who is able to stand before the LORD, this holy God? And to whom will He go up from us?"

[21] And they sent messengers to the inhabitants of Kiriath Jearim, saying, "The Philistines have brought back the ark of the LORD. Come down, and take it up to you."

7 So the men of Kiriath Jearim came and took up the ark of the LORD. And they brought it into the house of Abinadab on the hill, and sanctified Eleazar his son to keep the ark of the LORD. [2] And from the day the ark resided in Kiriath Jearim, the days increased to twenty years.

Samuel Judges Israel

And all the house of Israel lamented after the LORD. [3] Samuel spoke to all the house of Israel, saying, "If you are returning to the LORD with all your heart, then put away the foreign gods and Ashtoreths from your midst. And make firm your hearts unto the LORD, and serve Him only. Then He will deliver you out of the hand of the Philistines." [4] So the children of Israel put away the Baals and Ashtoreths and served the LORD only.

[5] Then Samuel said, "Gather all Israel to Mizpah, and I will pray to the LORD for you." [6] They gathered together to Mizpah. And they drew water and poured it out before the LORD. And they fasted

on that day, and said there, "We have sinned against the Lord." So Samuel judged the children of Israel in Mizpah.

[7] When the Philistines heard that the children of Israel were gathered together to Mizpah, the lords of the Philistines went up against Israel. And when the children of Israel heard it, they were afraid of the Philistines. [8] The children of Israel said to Samuel, "Do not stop crying unto the Lord our God for us, that He might save us out of the hand of the Philistines." [9] Samuel took a suckling lamb, and offered it for a burnt offering unto the Lord. And Samuel cried to the Lord for Israel and the Lord heard him.

[10] As Samuel was offering up the burnt offering, the Philistines drew near to battle against Israel, but the Lord thundered with a great thunder on that day against the Philistines, and confused them. So they were beaten before Israel. [11] Israel's fighting men went out of Mizpah, and pursued the Philistines, and struck them, as far as below Beth Kar.

[12] Then Samuel took a stone and set it between Mizpah and Shen. And he called its name Ebenezer[1] saying, "Thus far the Lord has helped us."

[13] So the Philistines were subdued, and they did not again come into the territory of Israel. And the hand of the Lord was against the Philistines all the days of Samuel. [14] The cities which the Philistines had taken from Israel were restored to Israel, from Ekron even to Gath. And Israel rescued their territory out of the hands of the Philistines. And there was peace between Israel and the Amorites.

[15] So Samuel judged Israel all the days of his life. [16] He went annually in a circuit to Bethel, and Gilgal, and Mizpah. And he judged Israel in all those places. [17] But his return was to Ramah, for his house was there and there he judged Israel. And there he built an altar to the Lord.

Israel Demands a King

8 And it came about when Samuel was old, that he installed his sons as judges for Israel. [2] Now the name of his firstborn son was Joel, and the name of his second son was Abijah. They were judging in Beersheba. [3] But his sons did not walk in his way, for they followed after unlawful gain, and they took bribes, and they perverted justice.

[4] And all the elders of Israel gathered together and they came to Samuel at Ramah. [5] They said to him, "You are old and your sons do not walk in your ways. Now, install for us a king to govern us like all the nations."

[6] But the thing was evil in the eyes of Samuel, because they said, "Give us a king to govern us." And Samuel prayed to the Lord. [7] The Lord said to Samuel, "Obey the voice of the people in relation to all that they say to you. For it is not you they have rejected, but Me they have rejected from reigning over them. [8] Just as all the deeds which they have done to Me, from the day I brought them up from Egypt even to this day, in that they have forsaken Me and have served other gods, so they are doing also to you now. [9] Now then, obey their voice. Only you will testify against them and proclaim to them the judgment concerning the king who will reign over them."

[10] So Samuel said all the words of the Lord to the people who were asking from him a king. [11] And he said, "This will be the judgment concerning the king who will reign over you: Your sons he will take in order to place them for himself in his chariots and as his horsemen, and they will run before his chariot, [12] and in order to assign for himself captains of thousands and captains of fifties, and to plow his ground, and to gather in his harvest, and to make his weapons of war and the equipment of his chariots. [13] And your daughters he will take for perfumers, and cooks, and bakers. [14] And your choicest fields, and vineyards, and olive groves he will take and give them to his servants. [15] And of your seed fields and your vineyards he will take a tenth of their harvest and will give it to his high officials and to his servants. [16] And your menservants and your maidservants, and the best of your young men and asses he will take and make do his work. [17] Your flocks he will take a tenth of, but you will be his for slaves. [18] And you will cry out in that day because of your king, whom you have chosen for yourselves, but the Lord will not answer you in that day."

[19] But the people refused to obey the voice of Samuel. And they said, "No! But surely a king will be over us! [20] So that we also will be like all the nations! And so that our king will govern us, and will go out before us, and will fight our battles."

[21] And after Samuel heard all the words of the people, he spoke them in the hearing of the Lord. [22] And the Lord said to Samuel, "Obey their voice, and make for them a king."

So Samuel said to Israel's fighting men, "Go every man to his city."

Samuel Anoints Saul

9 Now there was a man of Benjamin, whose name was Kish, the son of Abiel, the son of Zeror, the son of Bekorath, the son of Aphiah, a Benjamite, a mighty man of power. [2] He had a son, whose name was Saul, a choice and handsome man, and there was not a better looking man among the children of Israel. From his shoulders and up he was taller than any of the people.

[3] Now the donkeys of Kish, the father of Saul, were lost. And Kish said to his son Saul, "Take now one of the servants with you, and arise, go find the donkeys." [4] He passed through the mountains of Ephraim, and passed through the land of Shalisha, but they did not find them. And they passed through the land of Shaalim, but they were not there. Then he passed through the land of the Benjamites, but they did not find them.

[5] When they came to the land of Zuph, Saul said to his servant that was with him, "Come, and let us return lest my father stop caring about the donkeys and worry about us."

[6] He said to him, "Look, there is in this city a man of God, and he is highly respected. All that he speaks surely comes about. Now let us go there. Perhaps he can show us the way that we should go."

[7] Then Saul said to his servant, "But listen, if we go, what will we bring the man? For the bread is gone from our satchels, and there is no present to bring to the man of God. What do we have?"

[8] And the servant answered Saul again, and said, "Look, I have here in my hand a quarter of a shekel[2] of silver. I will give it to the man of God, to tell us our way." [9] (Formerly in Israel, when a man went to inquire of God, thus he said, "Come, and let us go to the seer." For he that is now called a prophet was formerly called a seer.)

[10] Then Saul said to his servant, "Well said. Come, let us go." So they went to the city where the man of God was.

[11] As they went up the hill to the city, they found young women going out to draw water and said to them, "Is the seer here?"

[12] And they answered them and said, "He is. See, he is ahead of you. Hurry now, for today he came to the city, because there is a sacrifice for the people in the high place today. [13] As soon as you come into the city, you will find him before he goes up to the high place to eat. For the people will not eat until he comes, because he must bless the sacrifice. Afterwards those invited will eat. Now therefore, go up, for about this time of the day you will find him there."

[14] So they went up into the city. And when they entered, Samuel was coming toward them to go up to the high place.

[15] Now the Lord had revealed in the ear of Samuel one day before Saul came, saying, [16] "Tomorrow about this time I will send you a man out of the land of Benjamin. And you will anoint him to be leader over My people Israel, that he may save My people out of the hand of the Philistines. For I have looked upon My people, because their cry has come unto Me."

[17] When Samuel saw Saul, the Lord said to him, "Here is the man of whom I spoke to you! This one will rule over My people."

[18] Then Saul drew near to Samuel in the gate, and said, "Tell me, please, where is the seer's house?"

[19] Samuel answered Saul, and said, "I am the seer. Go up before me to the high place, for you will eat with me today. And tomorrow I will let you go, and will tell you then all that is in your heart. [20] As for your donkeys that were lost three days ago, do not your worry about them for they have been found. And on whom is all the desire of Israel? Is it not on you and on all your father's house?"

[21] And Saul answered and said, "Am not I a Benjamite, of the smallest of the tribes of Israel? And my family the least of all the families of the tribe of Benjamin? Why do you speak to me this way?"

---

[1] 12 Lit. Stone of help.   [2] 8 About 1/10 ounce, or 3 grams.

22 And Samuel took Saul and his servant, and brought them into the hall, and gave them a place at the head of those invited, which were about thirty men. 23 Samuel said to the cook, "Bring the portion which I gave you, of which I said to you, 'Set it aside.' "

24 Then the cook took up the thigh and what was on it and set it before Saul. And Samuel said, "Here is what was set aside. Set it before you and eat, because it has been kept for you until this time, since I said I have invited the people." So Saul ate with Samuel that day.

25 When they had come down from the high place into the city, *Samuel* spoke with Saul up on the roof. 26 They arose early, and it was at the rising of the dawn that Samuel called to Saul on the roof, saying, "Get up, that I may send you away." So Saul arose, and both he and Samuel went to the street. 27 As they were going down to the outskirts of the city, Samuel said to Saul, "Tell the servant to pass on before us." So he passed on. "But you stand still and I will proclaim to you the word of God."

10 Then Samuel took a vial of oil and poured it upon his head. And he kissed him and said, "Has not the LORD anointed you over His inheritance as ruler? 2 When you have departed from me today, you will find two men by Rachel's tomb in the territory of Benjamin at Zelzah. And they will say to you, 'The donkeys which you went to look for have been found. And now, your father has stopped caring about the donkeys, and worries for you, saying, "What will I do for my son?" '

3 "Then you will go forward from there, and you will come to the plain of Tabor. And there you will meet three men going up to God to Bethel: one carrying three kids, another carrying three loaves of bread, and another carrying a bottle of wine. 4 And they will greet you and give you two loaves of bread, which you will receive from their hands.

5 "After that you will come to the hill of God, where the garrison of the Philistines is. And when you come there to the city, you will meet a group of prophets coming down from the high place with a harp, a tambourine, a flute, and a lyre before them. And they will prophesy. 6 And the Spirit of the LORD will come upon you, and you will prophesy with them. And you will be turned into another man. 7 And it will be when these signs come to you, do for yourself what the occasion requires; for God is with you.

8 "Then you will go down before me to Gilgal. And listen, I will be coming down to you, *in order* to offer burnt offerings, *and* to offer sacrifices of peace offerings. Seven days you will wait, until I come to you. Then I will make known to you what you will do."

9 And it happened, that when he turned his back to go from Samuel, that God gave him another heart. And all those signs came to pass that day. 10 When they came to the hill, a group of prophets met him. And the Spirit of God came upon him, and he prophesied among them. 11 So when all who previously knew him saw that he prophesied among the prophets, the people said one to another, "What is this that has come upon the son of Kish? Is Saul also among the prophets?"

12 And a man from there answered and said, "But who is their father?" Therefore it became a proverb, "Is Saul also among the prophets?" 13 When he had finished prophesying, he came to the high place.

14 And Saul's uncle said to him and to his servant, "Where did you go?"

And he said, "To seek the donkeys. And when we saw that *they were* nowhere *around*, we went to Samuel."

15 Saul's uncle said, "Please tell me what Samuel said to you."

16 Saul said to his uncle, "He told us plainly that the donkeys were found." But the matter of the kingdom, of which Samuel had spoken, he did not mention.

Saul Proclaimed King

17 Therefore Samuel called the people together unto the LORD at Mizpah. 18 And he said to the children of Israel, "Thus says the LORD, the God of Israel, 'I brought up Israel out of Egypt, and delivered you out of the hand of the Egyptians, and out of the hand of all kingdoms, and of them that oppressed you.' 19 But you have today rejected your God, who saves you from all your troubles and your distresses. And you have said to Him, 'No, but set a king over us.' Now therefore present yourselves before the LORD by your tribes, and by your clans."

20 So Samuel brought near all the tribes of Israel and the tribe of Benjamin was taken. 21 Then he brought near the tribe of Benjamin by its families. And the family of Matri was chosen. Then Saul the son of Kish was taken. But when they sought him, he could not be found. 22 Therefore they inquired again of the LORD, "Has the man come here yet?"

And the LORD answered, "He has hidden himself among the equipment."

23 So they ran and took him from there. When he stood among the people, he was taller than any of the people from his shoulders and upward. 24 Then Samuel said to all the people, "Do you see him whom the LORD has chosen? Truly there is none like him among all the people."

And all the people shouted and said, "*Long* live the king."

25 Samuel told the people the ordinances of the kingdom, and wrote them in a book, and laid them up before the LORD. And Samuel sent all the people away, every man to his house.

26 Saul also went home to Gibeah. And there went with him *a band of* valiant *men* whose hearts God had touched. 27 But some worthless men said, "How will this man save us?" And they despised him, and did not bring him a present. But he remained silent.

Saul Rescues Jabesh Gilead

11 Then Nahash the Ammonite came up, and encamped against Jabesh Gilead. And all the men of Jabesh said to Nahash, "Make a covenant with us, and we will serve you."

2 Nahash the Ammonite answered them, "On this *condition* will I make a covenant with you, that I may pluck out all your right eyes. So I will inflict it as a reproach upon all Israel."

3 The elders of Jabesh said to him, "Give us seven days, that we may send messengers to all the territory of Israel. And *then* if there is no one to rescue us, we will come out to you."

4 So the messengers came to Gibeah of Saul, and spoke the words in the ears of the people. And all the people lifted up their voices, and wept. 5 Now Saul *was* coming out of the field after the cattle, and Saul said, "Why are the people weeping?" And they reported to him the words of the men of Jabesh.

6 The Spirit of God came strongly upon Saul when he heard these words, and he became very angry. 7 He took a yoke of oxen, and hewed them in pieces. And he sent them throughout all the territory of Israel by the hands of messengers, saying, "Whoever does not come out after Saul and after Samuel, so will it be done to his oxen." And the fear of the LORD fell on the people, and they came out as one man. 8 When he numbered them in Bezek, the children of Israel were three hundred thousand, and the men of Judah thirty thousand.

9 They said to the messengers that came, "Thus will you say to the men of Jabesh Gilead, 'Tomorrow, by the time the sun is hot, you will have help.' " And the messengers came and reported it to the men of Jabesh and they were glad. 10 Therefore the men of Jabesh said, "Tomorrow we will come out to you, and you may do to us all that seems good to you."

11 On the next day Saul put the people in three companies. And they came into the midst of the camp in the morning and struck down the Ammonites until the heat of the day. Those surviving were scattered, so that *even* two of them were not left together.

Saul Confirmed as King

12 The people said to Samuel, "Who said, 'Shall Saul reign over us?' Bring the men, that we may put them to death."

13 Saul said, "There will not be a man put to death this day. For today the LORD has worked deliverance in Israel."

14 Then Samuel said to the people, "Come, and let us go to Gilgal and renew the kingdom there." 15 All the people went to Gilgal and there they made Saul king before the LORD in Gilgal. And there they made sacrifices of peace offerings before the LORD. And there Saul and all Israel's fighting men rejoiced greatly.

Samuel's Farewell Address

12 Then Samuel said to all Israel: "I have listened to your voice in all that you said to me, and have made a king over you. [2] And now, see, the king walks before you, but I am old and gray-headed. As for my sons, they are with you. But I have walked before you from my childhood to this day. [3] Behold, here I am. Witness against me before the Lord and before His anointed. Whose ox have I taken? Or whose donkey have I taken? Or whom have I defrauded? Whom have I oppressed? Or from whose hand have I received any bribe to blind my eyes with? Indeed I will restore it you."

[4] They said, "You have not defrauded us, nor oppressed us. Neither have you taken anything from any man's hand."

[5] He said to them, "The Lord is witness against you, and His anointed is witness this day, that you have not found anything in my hand."

And they answered, "*He is* witness."

[6] Samuel said to the people: "It is the Lord that prepared Moses and Aaron, and that brought your fathers up out of the land of Egypt. [7] Now therefore stand still that I may reason with you before the Lord, concerning all the righteous acts of the Lord, which He did for you and your fathers.

[8] "When Jacob went into Egypt and your fathers cried out to the Lord, the Lord sent Moses and Aaron who brought forth your fathers out of Egypt and made them dwell in this place.

[9] "When they forgot the Lord their God, He sold them into the hand of Sisera, captain of the host of Hazor, and into the hand of the Philistines, and into the hand of the king of Moab. And they fought against them. [10] They cried to the Lord, and said, 'We have sinned, because we have forsaken the Lord and have served the Baals and the Ashtoreths. But now deliver us out of the hand of our enemies, and we will serve You.' [11] The Lord sent Jerub-Baal, Bedan, *1* Jephthah, and Samuel. And He delivered you out of the hand of your enemies on every side, and you dwelled in safety.

[12] "When you saw that Nahash, king of the Ammonites, came against you, you said to me, 'No, but a king will reign over us,' when the Lord your God was your king. [13] Now therefore, look at the king whom you have chosen and for whom you have asked! And see that the Lord has set a king over you. [14] If you will fear the Lord, and serve Him, and obey His voice, and not rebel against the commandment of the Lord, then both you and the king that reigns over you will continue following the Lord your God. [15] But if you will not obey the voice of the Lord, but rebel against the commandment of the Lord, then will the hand of the Lord be against you, *as it was* against your fathers.

[16] "Even now, take your stand and see this great thing which the Lord is doing before your eyes. [17] Is it not the wheat harvest today? I will call to the Lord. And He will send thunder and rain, that you may know and see that your wickedness is great, which you have done in the sight of the Lord, by asking for yourselves a king."

[18] So Samuel called to the Lord. And the Lord sent thunder and rain that day, and all the people greatly feared the Lord and Samuel.

[19] All the people said to Samuel, "Pray for your servants to the Lord your God, that we will not die, for we have added to all our sins this evil, to ask for ourselves a king."

[20] Samuel said to the people, "Do not fear. You have done all this wickedness, only do not turn aside from following the Lord, and serve the Lord with all your heart. [21] But do not turn aside, for *then you would be going* after empty things which cannot profit or deliver, for they are nothing. [22] As befits His great name, the Lord will not abandon His people. For it has pleased the Lord to make you His people. [23] Moreover as for me, God forbid that I should sin against the Lord in ceasing to pray for you. But I will teach you the good and the right way. [24] Fear the Lord; serve Him in truth with all your heart, and consider what great things He has done for you. [25] But if you still do wickedly, both you and your king will be swept away."

Saul Fails His Commission

13 Saul was *thirty* years old when he began to reign, and he reigned *forty*-two years over Israel.*2*

[2] Saul chose for himself three thousand men of Israel. Two thousand were with Saul in Mikmash and in mountains of Bethel, and a thousand were with Jonathan in Gibeah of Benjamin. The rest of the people he sent each to his tent.

[3] Jonathan struck the garrison of the Philistines that was in Geba, and the Philistines heard of it. And Saul blew the trumpet throughout all the land, saying, "Let the Hebrews hear." [4] All Israel heard that Saul had struck the garrison of the Philistines, and that Israel had become odious to the Philistines. And the people were called together after Saul to Gilgal.

[5] The Philistines gathered together to fight with Israel, thirty thousand chariots and six thousand horsemen, with people like the sand which is on the seashore in multitude. And they came up and camped in Mikmash, east of Beth Aven. [6] When Israel's fighting men saw that they were in a strait (for the people were distressed), then the people hid themselves in caves, in hollows, *among* rocks, and in cellars and cisterns. [7] *Some* of the Hebrews went over Jordan to the land of Gad and Gilead.

But *as for* Saul, he was still in Gilgal, and all the people followed him, trembling. [8] He waited seven days, according to the set time that Samuel *had appointed*. But Samuel did not come to Gilgal, and the people were scattered from him. [9] Saul said, "Bring here to me the burnt offering and the peace offerings." Then he offered the burnt offering. [10] When he finished offering the burnt offering, Samuel came. And Saul went out to meet him to greet him.

[11] Samuel said, "What have you done?"

And Saul said, "Because I saw that the people were scattered from me, and that you did not come to the appointed assembly days, and the Philistines are gathering themselves together at Mikmash, [12] therefore I said, 'The Philistines will come down now upon me to Gilgal, and I have not *yet* appeased the face of the Lord.' So I forced myself, and offered the burnt offering."

[13] Samuel said to Saul, "You have done foolishly. You have not kept the commandment of the Lord your God, which He commanded you. Truly now, the Lord would have established your kingdom over Israel forever. [14] But now your kingdom will not continue. The Lord has sought for Himself a man after His own heart and the Lord has commanded him to be prince over His people, because you have not kept that which the Lord commanded you."

[15] Samuel arose, and went up from Gilgal to Gibeah of Benjamin. And Saul numbered the people that were present with him, about six hundred men.

Israel Unarmed

[16] Now Saul, and Jonathan his son, and the people that were with them, were staying in Gibeah of Benjamin, but the Philistines encamped in Mikmash. [17] Then raiders came out of the camp of the Philistines in three companies. One company turned to the way that leads to Ophrah, to the land of Shual. [18] And another company turned the way to Beth Horon. And another company turned to the way of the border that looks to the Valley of Zeboyim toward the wilderness.

[19] Now there was no blacksmith found throughout all the land of Israel. For the Philistines said, "Lest the Hebrews make for themselves swords or spears." [20] So all the children of Israel went down to the Philistines, to sharpen every man his plow-point, his axe, his adze and his hoe. [21] The sharpening *charge* was two-thirds of a shekel*3* for plow-points, axes, pitchforks, and adzes, and to fix an ox-goad.

[22] So it came to pass on the day of battle, that neither sword nor spear were found in the hand of any of the people who were with Saul and Jonathan. But they were found *in the hand of* Saul and Jonathan his son.

[23] And the garrison of the Philistines had marched out to the ravine of Mikmash.

---

1 11 Perhaps *Barak* here (see LXX). *2* 1 Lit. "The son of a year was Saul in his ruling and two years he ruled over Israel." Most translations read in Saul's age and length of reign from external evidence (Josephus) or from the New Testament (Paul, who mentions a forty-year reign for Saul in Ac 13:21). *3* 21 About ¼ ounce, or 8 grams.

Jonathan Defeats the Philistines

14 A day came that Jonathan, the son of Saul, said to the young man that bore his armor, "Come, and let us cross over to the Philistine garrison which is on the other side." But he did not tell his father.

2 Now Saul was staying on the outskirts of Gibeah under the pomegranate tree which is in Migron. And the people that were with him *were* about six hundred men. 3 And Ahijah, the son of Ahitub, Ichabod's brother, the son of Phinehas, the son of Eli, the priest of the LORD in Shiloh, was wearing the ephod. But the people did not know that Jonathan had gone.

4 Between the passages, by which Jonathan sought to go over to the Philistines' garrison, there was a sharp rock on the one side, and a sharp rock on the other side. And the name of the one was Bozez, and the name of the other Seneh. 5 The crag of the one rose north opposite Mikmash, and the other faced southward opposite Geba.

6 Jonathan said to the young man bearing his armor, "Come, and let us cross over to the garrison of these uncircumcised. Perhaps the LORD will work for us. For the LORD is not limited to save by many or by few."

7 His armor bearer said to him, "Do all that is in your heart. Turn yourself, *and* I *will be* with you according to your heart."

8 Then Jonathan said, "Now we will cross over to *these* men, and we will reveal ourselves to them. 9 If they say to us, 'Wait until we come to you,' then we will stand still in our place, and we will not go up to them. 10 But if they say, 'Come up to us,' then we will go up, for the LORD has delivered them into our hand, and this will be a sign to us."

11 So the two of them revealed themselves to the garrison of the Philistines. And the Philistines said, "Look, the Hebrews are coming out of the caves where they have hidden themselves." 12 The men of the garrison answered Jonathan and his armor bearer, and said, "Come up to us, and we will teach you something."

So Jonathan said to his armor bearer, "Come up after me. For the LORD has delivered them into the hand of Israel."

13 Jonathan climbed up upon his hands and upon his feet with his armor bearer behind him. And they fell before Jonathan. And his armor bearer was dealing death blows after him. 14 That first slaughter, which Jonathan and his armor bearer made, was about twenty men within about a half-acre field.

15 There was trembling in the camp, in the field, and among all the people. The garrison and the raiders also trembled, and the ground quaked. It was the fear of God.

16 The watchmen of Saul in Gibeah of Benjamin looked, and behold, the multitude melted away, and they went even here *and there.* 17 Then Saul said to the people that were with him, "Number now, and see who has gone from us." And when they had numbered, Jonathan nor his armor bearer *were there.*

18 Saul said to Ahijah, "Bring here the ark of God." For the ark of God was at that time with the children of Israel. 19 It came to pass, while Saul talked to the priest, that the noise which was in the camp of the Philistines went on and increased. So Saul said to the priest, "Withdraw your hand."

20 Saul and all the people who were with him assembled, and they went to the battle. And every man's sword was against his fellow, so that there was very great confusion. 21 Even the Hebrews who were with the Philistines the days before, who went up with them into the camp from the country round about, even they also turned to be with the children of Israel that were with Saul and Jonathan. 22 Also all of Israel's fighting men, who had hidden themselves in mountains of Ephraim, heard that the Philistines fled, and even they followed hard after them in the battle. 23 So the LORD saved Israel that day, and the battle passed beyond Beth Aven.

Saul's Rash Oath

24 Now Israel's fighting men were distressed that day. For Saul had placed the people under a curse, saying, "Cursed is the man that eats any food before it is evening, and I have been avenged on my enemies." So none of the people tasted any food.

25 All *the people* of the land came to the forest, and there was honey on the ground. 26 When the people came into the forest *there was* flowing honey. But no man put his hand to his mouth, because the people feared the oath. 27 But Jonathan had not heard when his father made the people swear. Therefore he put forward the end of the rod that was in his hand, and dipped it in the honeycomb. Then he put his hand to his mouth, and his eyes were brightened. 28 Then one of the people answered, and said, "Your father surely made the people swear, saying, 'Cursed is the man that eats any food this day.'" And the people were weary.

29 Then said Jonathan, "My father has troubled the land. See how my eyes have brightened, because I tasted a little of this honey. 30 How much more, if the people had surely eaten freely today of the spoil of their enemies which they found? But now the defeat of the Philistines has not been great."

31 And they struck the Philistines that day from Mikmash to Aijalon, and the people were very weary. 32 The people rushed upon the spoil; they took sheep, oxen, and calves and slew them on the ground. And the people ate *them* with the blood. 33 Then they reported to Saul, saying, "Look, the people are sinning against the LORD by eating the blood."

And he said, "You have dealt faithlessly. Roll a great stone to me this day." 34 Saul said, "Disperse yourselves among the people, and say to them, 'Bring to me here every man his ox or sheep. And slaughter them here, and eat. But you shall not sin against the LORD by eating with the blood.'"

And all the people brought every man his ox with him that night, and slew *them* there. 35 And Saul built an altar to the LORD. It was the first altar that he built to the LORD.

36 Saul said, "Let us go down after the Philistines by night and plunder them until the morning light. And let us not leave a man of them."

And they said, "Do whatever seems good to you."

Then the priest said, "Let us draw near here to God."

37 Saul asked of God, "Shall I go down after the Philistines? Will You deliver them into the hand of Israel?" But He did not answer him that day.

38 Saul said, "Come here, all you leaders of the people, and observe and see how this sin has come about this day. 39 For, as the LORD lives, who saves Israel, even if it is in Jonathan my son, he will surely die." But there was not one who answered him from among all the people.

40 Then he said to all Israel, "You will be on one side, and I and Jonathan my son will be on the other side."

And the people said to Saul, "Do what seems good to you."

41 Therefore Saul said to the LORD, the God of Israel, "Give a perfect lot." And Saul and Jonathan were taken, but the people escaped. 42 Saul said, "Cast lots between me and Jonathan my son." And Jonathan was taken.

43 Then Saul said to Jonathan, "Tell me what you have done."

And Jonathan told him, and said, "I indeed tasted a little honey with the end of the staff that was in my hand. Here I am. I must die."

44 Saul said, "May God do so *to me* and more also, for you will surely die, Jonathan."

45 The people said to Saul, "Will Jonathan die, who has worked this great salvation in Israel? God forbid. As the LORD lives, there will not one hair of his head fall to the ground. For he has worked with God this day." So the people rescued Jonathan, and he did not die.

46 Then Saul went up from following the Philistines, and the Philistines went to their own place.

47 So Saul took the kingdom over Israel and fought against all his enemies on every side, against Moab, and against the Ammonites, against Edom and against the kings of Zobah, and against the Philistines. Whatever place he turned himself, he defeated *them.* 48 He gathered an army, and struck the Amalekites, and delivered Israel out of the hand of its plunderers.

Saul's Family

49 Now the sons of Saul were Jonathan, Ishvi, and Malki-Shua. And the names of his two daughters were Merab, the firstborn, and Michal, the youngest. 50 And the name of the wife of Saul was Ahinoam, the daughter of Ahimaaz. And the name of the captain of his army was Abner, the son of Ner, the uncle of Saul. 51 Kish was the father of Saul, and Ner the father of Abner was the son of Abiel.

52 There was strong war against the Philistines all the days of Saul, and when Saul saw any strong man, or any valiant man, he took him into his service.

The LORD Rejects Saul

15 Samuel said to Saul, "The LORD sent me to anoint you to be king over His people, over Israel. Now therefore listen to the voice of the words of the LORD. 2 Thus says the LORD of Hosts, 'I remember what Amalek did to Israel, how he laid wait for him in the way, when he came up from Egypt. 3 Now go and strike Amalek, and utterly destroy all that they have, and do not have compassion on them but put to death both man and woman, child and infant, ox and sheep, camel and donkey.' "

4 So Saul summoned the people together, and numbered them in Telaim, two hundred thousand foot soldiers and ten thousand men of Judah. 5 Then Saul came to the city of Amalek and laid an ambush in the valley. 6 Saul said to the Kenites, "Go, depart, go down from among the Amalekites, lest I destroy you with them. For you showed kindness to all the children of Israel when they came up out of Egypt." So the Kenites departed from among the Amalekites.

7 Then Saul struck the Amalekites from Havilah until you come to Shur, which is near Egypt. 8 He took Agag the king of the Amalekites alive and utterly destroyed all the people with the edge of the sword. 9 But Saul and the people spared Agag, and the best of the sheep, oxen, fatlings, and lambs. And of all that was good, they were not willing to utterly destroy them. But everything that was despised and weak, that they completely destroyed.

10 Then came the word of the LORD to Samuel, saying, 11 "I regret that I have set up Saul to be king because he has turned back from following Me, and he has not carried out My words." And it grieved Samuel, and he cried to the LORD all night.

12 When Samuel rose early to meet Saul in the morning, it was told Samuel, saying, "Saul came to Carmel and set himself up a monument. Then he turned and has passed on down to Gilgal."

13 Samuel came to Saul. And Saul said to him, "Blessed are you of the LORD. I have carried out the word of the LORD."

14 Then Samuel said, "Then what is the sound of this flock of sheep in my ears? And the sound of the cattle which I am hearing?"

15 And Saul said, "They have brought them from the Amalekites. For the people spared the best of the sheep and oxen, to sacrifice to the LORD your God, and the rest we have utterly destroyed."

16 Then Samuel said to Saul, "Stop, and I will tell you what the LORD spoke to me this night."

And he said to him, "Speak."

17 Samuel said, "When you were little in your own sight, were you not made the head of the tribes of Israel, and the LORD anointed you king over Israel? 18 And the LORD sent you on a journey, and said, 'Go and utterly destroy the sinners, the Amalekites, and fight against them until they are destroyed.' 19 Why then did you not obey the voice of the LORD? And why did you rush upon the spoil and do evil in the sight of the LORD?"

20 And Saul said to Samuel, "I have obeyed the voice of the LORD. And I have followed in the way which the LORD sent me, and have brought Agag the king of Amalek, and have utterly destroyed the Amalekites. 21 But the people took from the plunder sheep and oxen, the first fruits of the banned things to sacrifice to the LORD your God in Gilgal."

22 Samuel said,

"Does the LORD delight in burnt offerings and sacrifices
    as much as in obeying the voice of the LORD?
Obedience is better than sacrifice,
    a listening ear than the fat of rams.
23 For rebellion is as the sin of witchcraft,
    and stubbornness is as iniquity and idolatry.
Because you have rejected the word of the LORD,
    He has also rejected you from being king."

24 Saul said to Samuel, "I have sinned. For I have transgressed the commandment of the LORD, and your words, because I feared the people, and obeyed their voice. 25 Now therefore, please pardon my sin and return with me, that I may worship the LORD."

26 Samuel said to Saul, "I will not return with you. For you have rejected the word of the LORD, and the LORD has rejected you from being king over Israel."

27 As Samuel turned about to go, he seized the edge of his robe and it tore. 28 Samuel said to him, "The LORD has torn the kingdom of Israel from you this day, and has given it to a neighbor of yours who is better than you. 29 Also the Strength of Israel will not lie nor repent. For He is not a man, that He should repent."

30 Then he said, "I have sinned, yet please honor me before the elders of my people, and before Israel, and turn back with me, that I may worship the LORD your God." 31 So Samuel turned back after Saul, and Saul worshipped the LORD.

32 Then Samuel said, "Bring me Agag the king of the Amalekites." And Agag came to him reluctantly. But Agag said, "Surely the bitterness of death is past."

33 Samuel said,

"As your sword has made women childless,
    so will your mother be childless among women."

And Samuel hacked Agag in pieces before the LORD in Gilgal.

34 Then Samuel went to Ramah, and Saul went up to his house to Gibeah of Saul. 35 Now Samuel did not see Saul up to the day of his death. But Samuel mourned for Saul and the LORD regretted that he had made Saul king over Israel.

Samuel Anoints David as King

16 The LORD said to Samuel, "How long will you mourn for Saul, since I have rejected him from ruling over Israel? Fill your horn with oil and go. I will send you to Jesse the Bethlehemite, for I have chosen a king for Myself *from* among his sons."

2 Samuel said, "How can I go? If Saul hears it, he will kill me." And the LORD said, "Take a heifer with you and say, 'I have come to sacrifice to the LORD.' 3 Call Jesse to the sacrifice, and I will show you what you will do. And you will anoint for Me *him* whom I tell to you."

4 Samuel did that which the LORD spoke, and came to Bethlehem. The elders of the town trembled at his coming, and said, "Do you come in peace?"

5 And he said, "I have come in peace to sacrifice to the LORD. Consecrate yourselves, and come with me to the sacrifice." And he consecrated Jesse and his sons and called them to the sacrifice.

6 When they came, he looked on Eliab, and said, "Surely the anointed of the LORD is before Him."

7 But the LORD said to Samuel, "Do not look on his appearance or on the height of his stature, because I have rejected him. For the LORD sees not as man sees. For man looks on the outward appearance, but the LORD looks on the heart."

8 Then Jesse called Abinadab, and made him pass before Samuel. And he said, "Neither has the LORD chosen this *one*." 9 Then Jesse made Shammah to pass by. And he said, "Neither has the LORD chosen this *one*." 10 So Jesse made seven of his sons pass before Samuel. And Samuel said to Jesse, "The LORD has not chosen these."

11 Samuel said to Jesse, "Are *these* all your young men?"

And he said, "There remains yet the youngest, and *there* he is shepherding the flock."

Then Samuel said to Jesse, "Send and bring him, for we will not sit down until he comes here."

12 So he sent and brought him in. Now he was ruddy with beautiful eyes and a good appearance.

And the LORD said, "Arise, anoint him, for this is he."

13 Then Samuel took the horn of oil, and anointed him in the midst of his brothers. And the Spirit of the LORD came on David from that day forward. So Samuel arose and went to Ramah.

David Serves Saul

14 Now the Spirit of the LORD departed from Saul and an evil spirit from the LORD terrified him.

15 So the servants of Saul said to him, "See, an evil spirit from God troubles you. 16 Let our lord now tell your servants, who are before you, *that* they might seek out a man experienced in playing the lyre. And it will come to pass, when the evil spirit

from God is on you, that he will play with his hand, and you will be well."

¹⁷ Saul said to his servants, "Find me now a man that can play well, and bring him to me."

¹⁸ Then one from the servants answered, and said, "I have seen a son of Jesse the Bethlehemite, who is experienced in playing music, a mighty man of valor, a man of battle, and skillful in words, even a man of fine appearance. And the Lᴏʀᴅ is with him."

¹⁹ Therefore Saul sent messengers to Jesse, and said, "Send me David your son, who is with the sheep." ²⁰ Jesse took a donkey laden with bread, a bottle of wine, and a young goat and he sent them with his son David to Saul.

²¹ David came to Saul, and stood before him. And Saul loved him greatly and he became his armor bearer. ²² Saul sent to Jesse, saying, "Let David stand before me, for he has found favor in my sight."

²³ It happened that when the evil spirit from God came on Saul, David would take the lyre in his hand and play. So Saul was refreshed and was well, and the evil spirit departed from him.

David and Goliath

17 Now the Philistines gathered their armies for battle, and were gathered at Sokoh, which belongs to Judah. And they camped between Sokoh and Azekah in Ephes Dammim. ² Saul and Israel's fighting men were gathered, and they camped in the Valley of Elah. And they drew up in battle order to meet the Philistines. ³ Now the Philistines were standing at *the base of* the mountain on the one side, and Israel was standing at *the base of* the mountain on the other side, and the valley was between them.

⁴ There went out a champion from the camp of the Philistines, Goliath was his name, from Gath, whose height was six cubits and a span.¹ ⁵ He had a helmet of bronze on his head, and he was armed with a coat of mail. Now the weight of the bronze coat was five thousand shekels.² ⁶ He had greaves of bronze on his legs and a bronze javelin between his shoulders. ⁷ The staff of his spear was like a weaver's beam. His iron spearhead weighed six hundred shekels.³ And a shield-bearer was walking before him.

⁸ He stood and called out to the ranks of Israel, "Why have you come out to line up for battle? Am not I the Philistine, and you the servants of Saul? Choose for yourselves a man and let him come down to me. ⁹ If he is able to fight with me and to strike me down, then we will be your servants. But if I prevail against him and strike him down, then you will be our servants and will serve us." ¹⁰ The Philistine said, "I defy the battle lines of Israel this day. Give me a man, and let us fight together." ¹¹ When Saul and all Israel heard these words of the Philistine, they were filled with terror and were greatly afraid.

¹² Now David was the son of that Ephrathite of Bethlehem in Judah whose name was Jesse, who had eight sons. And the man was old in the days of Saul *and* advanced in years. ¹³ The three eldest sons of Jesse went and followed Saul to the battle. And the names of his three sons that went to the battle were Eliab the firstborn, and next to him Abinadab, and the third was Shammah. ¹⁴ As for David, he was the youngest. The three eldest followed Saul, ¹⁵ but David would go back and forth from Saul to shepherd his father's flock in Bethlehem.

¹⁶ The Philistine stepped forward morning and evening and took his stand *daily* for forty days.

¹⁷ Then Jesse said to David his son, "Take now for your brothers an ephah⁴ of this parched grain and these ten loaves and run to the camp to your brothers. ¹⁸ Carry these ten cheeses to the captain of their thousand, and look into your brothers' health, and bring back news of them." ¹⁹ Now Saul, and they, and all Israel's fighting men were in the Valley of Elah fighting with the Philistines.

²⁰ So David rose up early in the morning and left the flock with a keeper. And he carried away *the food* and went as Jesse had commanded him. And when he came to the encampment, the army was going out to the battle line, and they shouted a war cry. ²¹ And Israel and the Philistines ordered themselves in battle lines, army against army. ²² David left his things with the

keeper of the equipment, and he ran to the battle line. And he went and greeted his brothers. ²³ As he was speaking with them, the champion, Goliath, the Philistine from Gath, was going up from the battle line of the Philistines. And he spoke these same words and David heard them. ²⁴ When all Israel's fighting men saw the man, they fled from him, and were very afraid.

²⁵ The men of Israel said, "Have you seen this man who has come up? Surely he has come up to defy Israel, and it will be that the man who kills him, the king will enrich him with great riches, will give him his daughter, and will make his father's house exempt *from taxes* in Israel."

²⁶ David spoke to the men that stood by him, saying, "What will be done for the man that kills this Philistine and takes away *this* reproach from Israel? For who is this uncircumcised Philistine that he should defy the armies of the living God?"

²⁷ And the people answered him in the same way, saying, "So will it be done to the man who kills him."

²⁸ Eliab his eldest brother heard when he spoke to the men. And Eliab's anger was kindled against David, and he said, "Why have you come down here? And with whom have you left those few sheep in the wilderness? I know your pride and the evil of your heart. For you have come down that you might see the battle."

²⁹ David said, "What have I done now? Was it not *only* a word?" ³⁰ And he turned from him toward another and spoke in the same way. And the people answered him again as at the first. ³¹ When the words which David spoke were heard, they reported them to Saul and he sent for him.

³² David said to Saul, "Let no man's heart fail because of him. Your servant will go and fight with this Philistine."

³³ Saul said to David, "You are not able to go against this Philistine to fight with him. For you are but a youth, and he has been a man of war from his youth."

³⁴ David said to Saul, "Your servant was a shepherd for my father's flock, and the lion came and the bear, and took a lamb out of the flock. ³⁵ And I went out after him, and struck him, and delivered it out of his mouth. And when he arose against me, I took hold of his beard, struck him, and killed him. ³⁶ Your servant slew both the lion and the bear. And this uncircumcised Philistine will be as one of them, because he has reviled the armies of the living God." ³⁷ David said, "The Lᴏʀᴅ who delivered me out of the paw of the lion and out of the paw of the bear, He will deliver me out of the hand of this Philistine."

And Saul said to David, "Go, and the Lᴏʀᴅ be with you."

³⁸ Saul clothed David with his armor. And he put a helmet of bronze on his head. He also clothed him with a coat of mail. ³⁹ David secured his sword to his armor and tried to walk, but he was not used to it, for he had not tested *them*.

And David said to Saul, "I cannot walk with these, for I have not tested *them*." So David took them off. ⁴⁰ He took his staff in his hand and chose for himself five smooth stones out of the brook. And he put them in his shepherd's bag, even in a pouch. And his sling was in his hand. Then he drew near to the Philistine.

⁴¹ The Philistine came walking and drew near to David, and the man bearing the shield *went* before him. ⁴² When the Philistine looked and saw David, he despised him. For he was a youth and ruddy with a handsome appearance. ⁴³ The Philistine said to David, "Am I a dog, that you come to me with sticks?" Then the Philistine cursed David by his gods. ⁴⁴ The Philistine said to David, "Come to me, and I will give your flesh to the birds of the heavens and to the beasts of the field."

⁴⁵ Then David said to the Philistine, "You come to me with a sword, a spear, and a shield, but I come to you in the name of the Lᴏʀᴅ of Hosts, the God of the armies of Israel, whom you have reviled. ⁴⁶ This day will the Lᴏʀᴅ deliver you into my hand. And I will strike you down and cut off your head. Then I will give the corpses of the Philistine camp this day to the birds of the air and to the beasts of the earth so that all the earth may know that there is a God in Israel. ⁴⁷ And then all this assembly will know that it is not by sword and spear that the Lᴏʀᴅ saves. For the battle belongs

---

¹ ⁴ About 9 feet 9 inches, or 3 meters.   ² ⁵ About 125 pounds, or 58 kilograms.   ³ ⁷ About 15 pounds, or 6.9 kilograms.
⁴ ¹⁷ Likely about 36 pounds, or 16 kilograms.

to the LORD, and He will give you into our hands."

⁴⁸ When the Philistine arose and came near to meet David, David hurried and ran toward the battle line to meet the Philistine. ⁴⁹ David put his hand in his bag and took from there a stone. And he slung it and struck the Philistine in his forehead. Therefore the stone sunk into his forehead and he fell upon his face to the ground. ⁵⁰ So David prevailed over the Philistine with a sling and with a stone. And he struck down the Philistine and slew him, but there was no sword in the hand of David.

⁵¹ Therefore David ran and stood over the Philistine. Then he took his sword and drew it from out of its sheath, and he finished him off and he cut off his head with it.

When the Philistines saw their champion was dead, they fled. ⁵² And the fighting men of Israel and Judah arose and shouted. And they pursued the Philistines from the entrance of the Valley of Elah as far as the gates of Ekron. So the Philistine dead lay slain on the road to Shaaraim as far as Gath and Ekron. ⁵³ Then the children of Israel returned from chasing after the Philistines and they plundered their tents.

⁵⁴ David took the head of the Philistine and brought it to Jerusalem, but he put his armor in his tent.

⁵⁵ When Saul saw David going out against the Philistine, he said to Abner, the commander of the army, "Whose son is this youth, Abner?"

And Abner said, "As your soul lives, O king, I do not know."

⁵⁶ The king said, "Inquire whose son the young man is."

⁵⁷ So when David returned from slaying the Philistine, Abner took him and brought him before Saul with the Philistine's head in his hand.

⁵⁸ Saul said to him, "Whose son are you, young man?"

And David answered, "I am the son of your servant, Jesse the Bethlehemite."

Saul Fears David

18 When he had finished speaking to Saul, the soul of Jonathan was bound to the soul of David, so that Jonathan loved him as his own soul. ² And Saul took him that day and would not permit him to return home to his father's house. ³ Then Jonathan and David made a covenant because he loved him as his own soul. ⁴ So Jonathan stripped himself of the robe that was on him and gave it to David, even his garments, his sword, his bow, and his belt.

⁵ David went out wherever Saul sent him, and he was successful. So Saul set him over the men of war, and it was pleasing in the sight of all the people and also in the sight of the servants of Saul.

⁶ When they came home, as David was returning from slaying the Philistine, the women came out from all cities of Israel to meet King Saul, singing and dancing, with tambourines, with joy, and with musical instruments. ⁷ The dancing women sang and said,

"Saul has slain his thousands,
    and David his ten thousands."

⁸ Saul became very angry, and this saying was displeasing to him. Therefore he said, "They have ascribed to David ten thousands, but to me they have ascribed thousands. Now what remains for him to have but the kingdom?" ⁹ So Saul was suspicious of David from that day and forward.

¹⁰ It came to pass the following day, that an evil spirit from God came upon Saul, so that he raved in the midst of the house. And David was playing *the lyre*, as at other times. Now there was a spear in Saul's hand. ¹¹ And Saul threw the spear. For he said, "I will pin David to the wall." But David avoided him two times.

¹² Saul was afraid of David because the LORD was with him but had departed from Saul. ¹³ Therefore Saul removed him from his presence and placed him as his captain over a thousand. And he went out and came in before the people. ¹⁴ David was successful in all his ways and the LORD was with him. ¹⁵ When Saul saw that he was very successful, he was afraid of him. ¹⁶ Now all Israel and Judah loved David, because he went out and came in before them.

David Marries Michal

¹⁷ Saul said to David, "Behold my elder daughter Merab, I will give her to you as *your* wife. Only be valiant for me, and fight the battles of the LORD." For Saul said, "Let not my hand be against him, but let the hand of the Philistines be against him."

¹⁸ But David said to Saul, "Who am I? And what is my life, or my father's family in Israel, that I should be son-in-law to the king?" ¹⁹ So when it was time that Merab, daughter of Saul, should have been given to David, she was given to Adriel the Meholathite for a wife.

²⁰ Now Michal, daughter of Saul, loved David and they told Saul, and the thing pleased him. ²¹ Saul said, "I will give her to him that she may be a snare to him, and so that the hand of the Philistines may be against him." Therefore Saul said to David, "For a second time, you may be my son-in-law today."

²² Saul commanded his servants, saying, "Speak to David in secret saying, 'Listen, the king delights in you and all his servants love you. Now therefore become the king's son-in-law.' "

²³ So the servants of Saul spoke these words in the ears of David. And David said, "Does it seem to you a light thing to be a king's son-in-law, seeing that I am a poor man, and lightly esteemed?"

²⁴ And the servants of Saul reported to him saying, "According to these words, David spoke." ²⁵ Saul said, "Thus will you say to David, 'The king does not desire any dowry but a hundred foreskins of the Philistines, to be avenged of the king's enemies.' " But Saul thought to make David fall by the hand of the Philistines.

²⁶ When his servants told David these words, it pleased David well to be the king's son-in-law. Now the days had not expired; ²⁷ therefore David arose and went, he and his men, and killed two hundred men of the Philistines. Then David brought their foreskins and they gave them in full to the king, that he might be the king's son-in-law. And Saul gave him Michal his daughter for a wife.

²⁸ When Saul saw and knew that the LORD was with David, and that Michal, his daughter, loved him, ²⁹ Saul was yet the more afraid of David, and Saul became the enemy of David continually.

³⁰ Then the commanders of the Philistines went out *to make war*. And when they went out David was more successful than all the servants of Saul, so that his name was highly honored.

Saul Tries to Kill David

19 And Saul spoke to Jonathan, his son, and to all his servants, that they should kill David. But Jonathan, Saul's son, delighted very much in David. ² Jonathan told David, saying, "My father Saul seeks to kill you. Therefore, be on guard in the morning; stay in a secret place and hide yourself. ³ And I will go out and stand beside my father in the field where you are. Then I will speak about you to my father, and what I observe I will report to you."

⁴ Jonathan spoke positively of David to Saul his father and said to him, "Do not let the king sin against his servant, against David, because he has not sinned against you, and because his deeds have been very good toward you. ⁵ For he took his life in his hand and struck down the Philistine, and the LORD made a great salvation for all Israel. You saw it and rejoiced. Now why then would you sin against innocent blood, to kill David without cause?"

⁶ So Saul listened to the voice of Jonathan and Saul vowed, "As the LORD lives, he will not be killed."

⁷ Jonathan called David, and Jonathan reported to him all these words. Then Jonathan brought David to Saul, and he was in his presence as previously.

⁸ Then there was war again, and David went out and fought with the Philistines. He slew them with a great slaughter and they fled from him.

⁹ Now an evil spirit from the LORD was upon Saul as he was sitting in his house with his spear in his hand. And David was playing *the lyre*. ¹⁰ Then Saul sought to pin David to the wall with the spear, but he escaped from Saul's presence. He struck the spear into the wall. But David fled and escaped that night.

¹¹ Saul also sent messengers to the house of David, to watch him and to slay him in the morning. But Michal, wife of David, told him, saying, "If you do not save your life tonight, tomorrow you will be dead." ¹² So Michal let David down through a window, and he went and fled to safety. ¹³ Michal took an idol and laid it

in the bed, and put a braided goat hair pillow for its head and covered it with clothes.

[14] When Saul sent messengers to take David, she said, "He is sick." [15] Saul sent the messengers *again* to see David, saying, "Bring him up to me in the bed, that I may kill him." [16] When the messengers came in, there was the idol in the bed with a goat hair pillow for its head.

[17] Saul said to Michal, "Why have you betrayed me and sent away my enemy, so that he escaped?"

And Michal said to Saul, "He said to me, 'Let me go. Why should I kill you?' "

[18] Now David fled, and he escaped and came to Samuel at Ramah. And he reported to him all that Saul had done to him. And he and Samuel went and stayed in Naioth. [19] It was told Saul, saying, "David is at Naioth in Ramah." [20] Then Saul sent messengers to take David, but when they saw the company of the prophets prophesying and Samuel taking his stand over them, the Spirit of God came upon the messengers of Saul and they also prophesied. [21] When it was reported to Saul, he sent other messengers. And they also prophesied. So Saul sent messengers again a third time, and they too prophesied. [22] Then he also went to Ramah and came to the great well that is in Seku. And he asked and said, "Where are Samuel and David?"

And one said, "*They are* at Naioth in Ramah.

[23] He went there to Naioth in Ramah, and the Spirit of God came upon him also. And he went on and he prophesied until he came to Naioth in Ramah. [24] He stripped off his clothes and he also prophesied before Samuel. And he lay down naked all that day and all that night. Therefore they say, "Is Saul also among the prophets?"

David and Jonathan

20 David fled from Naioth in Ramah, and came and said before Jonathan, "What have I done? What is my offense? And what is my sin before your father, that he seeks my life?"

[2] And he said to him, "Far from it! You shall not die. Look, my father does nothing either great or small that he does not reveal to me. Why would my father hide this thing from me? It is not so."

[3] David vowed again and said, "Your father certainly knows that I have found favor in your sight. And he says, 'Do not let Jonathan know this, lest he be distressed.' However, as the LORD lives and as your soul lives, *there is* but a step between me and death."

[4] Jonathan said to David, "Whatever you say, I will do it for you."

[5] David said to Jonathan, "Tomorrow is the New Moon, and I should not fail to sit with the king to eat. But let me go that I may hide myself in the field until the evening of the third day. [6] If your father misses me at all, then say, 'David asked for leave from me that he might run to Bethlehem his city, for there is a yearly sacrifice there for all the family.' [7] If he says, 'Good,' it will be well for your servant. But if he gets angry, know that evil is determined by him. [8] Therefore deal kindly with your servant, for you have brought your servant into a covenant of the LORD with you. But if there is *any* guilt in me, kill me yourself. For why should you bring me to your father?"

[9] Then Jonathan said, "Far be it from you. For if I indeed knew that my father had determined evil against you, would I not tell it you?"

[10] David said to Jonathan, "Who will tell me? Or what if your father answers you roughly?"

[11] So Jonathan said to David, "Come, let us go out into the field." And the two of them went out to the field.

[12] Then Jonathan said to David, "The LORD God of Israel *is witness*. When I have sounded out my father about this time tomorrow, *or by* the third day, and if he is favorable toward David, then will I not send and reveal it to you? [13] May the LORD do so to Jonathan and much more. If it pleases my father to do you evil, then I will reveal it you and send you away that you may go in peace. And may the LORD be with you as He has been with my father. [14] And if I live, not only will you show me the kindness of the LORD, that I shall not die, [15] but you will not cut off your faithfulness from my house forever, even when the LORD has cut off each one of the enemies of David from the face of the earth."

[16] So Jonathan made a covenant with the house of David *saying*, "May the LORD require it at the hand of the enemies of David." [17] Jonathan made David swear again, because he loved him. For he loved him as he loved his own soul.

[18] Then Jonathan said to David, "Tomorrow is the New Moon, and you will be missed, because your seat will be empty. [19] When you have stayed three days, you will surely go down and come to the place where you hid yourself on the day *this* happened, and wait *there* beside the stone Ezel. [20] And I will shoot three arrows to its side, as though I shot at a target. [21] Then I will send a boy, saying, 'Go, find the arrows.' If I expressly say to the boy, 'See, the arrows are on this side of you, take them,' then come, for it will be safe for you. And as the LORD lives, it is nothing *of concern.* [22] But if I say to the young man, 'See, the arrows are beyond you,' go, for the LORD has sent you away. [23] As for the matter *upon* which you and I have spoken, the LORD is between you and me forever."

[24] So David hid himself in the field. And when the New Moon appeared, the king sat down over food to eat. [25] Now the king sat on his seat, as at other times, even on a seat by the wall. Then Jonathan arose and Abner sat by Saul's side, but David's place was empty. [26] Nevertheless Saul did not say anything that day. For he thought, "Something has happened. He is not clean; surely he is not clean." [27] It happened on the following day, which was the second day of the month, that David's place remained empty. So Saul said to Jonathan his son, "Why has the son of Jesse not come to eat food either yesterday or today?"

[28] And Jonathan answered Saul, "David earnestly asked leave from me to go to Bethlehem. [29] And he said, 'Please let me go, for our family has a sacrifice in the city and my brother has commanded me *to come.* Now, if I have found favor in your sight, please let me leave and see my brothers.' This is why he has not come to the king's table."

[30] Then Saul was angry with Jonathan and he said to him, "You son of a perverse rebellious woman, do I not know that you are choosing the son of Jesse to your own shame, and to the shame of your mother's nakedness? [31] For as long as the son of Jesse lives on the earth, neither you nor your kingdom will be established. Now, send and bring him to me, for he is a dead man."

[32] Jonathan answered Saul his father and said to him, "Why should he be killed? What has he done?" [33] So Saul cast a spear at him to strike him. Therefore Jonathan knew that his father was determined to kill David.

[34] And Jonathan arose from the table in fierce anger and did not eat food on the second day of the month. For he was grieved for David, because his father had dishonored him.

[35] In the morning Jonathan went out to the field at the time appointed with David, and a little boy was with him. [36] And he said to his boy, "Run, find the arrows which I shoot." He ran, and he shot the arrow over him. [37] When the boy came to the place of the arrow which Jonathan had shot, Jonathan called after the boy and said, "Is not the arrow beyond you?" [38] Then Jonathan cried after the boy, "Hurry quickly! Do not stay!" And Jonathan's boy gathered up the arrow and came to his master. [39] But the boy did not know anything. Only Jonathan and David knew the matter. [40] Jonathan gave his weapons to his boy and said to him, "Go, carry *them* to the city."

[41] When the boy had gone, David arose from the south side *of the stone,* and fell on his face to the ground, and bowed himself three times. They kissed one another and wept together, but David *wept* more.

[42] Jonathan said to David, "Go in peace, since the two of us swore in the name of the LORD, saying, 'The LORD will be between me and you, and between my descendants and your descendants forever.' " So he arose and departed, but Jonathan went into the city.

David at Nob

21 Then David came to Nob to Ahimelek the priest. And Ahimelek trembled coming to meet David and said to him, "Why are you alone and no man is with you?"

[2] And David said to Ahimelek the priest, "The king commanded me a matter and said to me, 'Let no man know anything of the business which I am sending you and what I have commanded you.' But *to* the young men I made known a certain place *to meet.*

³ Now therefore what is in your hand? Give me five loaves of bread in my hand, or whatever can be found."

⁴ The priest answered David and said, "There is no common bread at hand. But there is holy bread, if the young men have indeed been kept from women."

⁵ David answered the priest and said to him, "Indeed women have been kept from us. As previously, when I went out the vessels of the young men were holy even *if* it was an ordinary journey. How much more then today will their vessels be holy?" ⁶ So the priest gave him holy *bread*. For there was no bread there but the showbread that was removed from before the Lord, in order to place hot bread *there* on the day when it was taken away.

⁷ Now a certain man of the servants of Saul was there that day, detained before the Lord. And his name was Doeg, the Edomite, chief of the shepherds of Saul.

⁸ David said to Ahimelek, "Is there not a spear or a sword here at hand? For neither my sword nor my weapons did I bring with me, because the king's business was urgent."

⁹ The priest said, "The sword of Goliath the Philistine, whom you struck down in the Valley of Elah, is here, wrapped in a cloth behind the ephod. If you will take that, take it. For there is none other but that here."

And David said, "There is none like it. Give it me."

David Flees to Gath

¹⁰ David arose and fled that day from Saul. And he went to Achish the king of Gath. ¹¹ The servants of Achish said to him, "Is this not David the king of the land? Did they not sing with dances for him, saying,

'Saul has slain his thousands,
    and David his ten thousands'?"

¹² And David took these words to heart and greatly feared Achish the king of Gath. ¹³ Therefore he changed his behavior before them and pretended to be insane in their hands. And he scratched on the doors of the gate and let his spittle run down his beard.

¹⁴ Then said Achish to his servants, "You see the man is acting like a madman. Why then have you brought him to me? ¹⁵ Am I one who lacks lunatics, that you brought this one to behave as a madman in my presence? Will this man come into my house?"

David Protects His Parents

22 David departed from there and escaped to the cave of Adullam. And when his brothers and all his father's house heard it, they went down to him there. ² There gathered to him every one that was in distress, and every one in debt, and every one that was discontented. So he became captain over them. Now there were with him about four hundred men.

³ Then David went from there to Mizpah of Moab. And he said to the king of Moab, "Please let my father and my mother come forth and be with you until I know what God will do for me." ⁴ He brought them before the king of Moab, and they lived with him all the while that David was in the stronghold.

⁵ The prophet Gad said to David, "Do not remain in the stronghold. Go to the land of Judah." So David went and came to the forest of Hereth.

Saul Kills the Priests of Nob

⁶ When Saul heard that David and the men who were with him were discovered, Saul was sitting in Gibeah under the tamarisk tree on the hill with his spear in his hand. And all his servants were standing about him. ⁷ Saul said to his servants that stood about him, "Hear now, Benjamites! Will the son of Jesse give every one of you fields and vineyards? Will he appoint you all as captains of thousands and captains of hundreds? ⁸ You have all conspired against me, and no one revealed to me that my son made a covenant with the son of Jesse. And not one of you is grieved for me and revealed it to me that my son raised up my servant against me to ambush me as at this day."

⁹ Then Doeg the Edomite, who was chief over the servants of Saul, answered and said, "I saw the son of Jesse coming to Nob, to Ahimelek the son of Ahitub. ¹⁰ And he inquired of the Lord for him and gave him provisions. And he gave him the sword of Goliath the Philistine."

¹¹ So the king sent to summon Ahimelek the priest, the son of Ahitub, and all his father's house, the priests that were in Nob. And they all came to the king. ¹² Saul said, "Hear now, son of Ahitub!" And he answered, "Here I am, my lord."

¹³ Saul said to him, "Why have you conspired against me, you and the son of Jesse, in that you gave him bread and a sword, and have inquired of God for him, that he should rise against me to ambush *me*, as at this day?"

¹⁴ Then Ahimelek answered the king and said, "And who is as faithful among all your servants as David, who is the king's son-in-law, chief of your bodyguard, and is honored in your house? ¹⁵ Did I *just* today begin to inquire of God for him? Far be it from me! Let not the king assign any blame to his servant, or to all the house of my father. For your servant has known nothing of all this matter, whether small or great."

¹⁶ The king said, "You will surely die, Ahimelek, you and all your father's house."

¹⁷ The king said to the guards standing near him, "Turn and kill the priests of the Lord, because their hand is with David. And because they knew that he was fleeing and did not reveal it to me."

But the servants of the king would not put forth their hand to attack the priests of the Lord.

¹⁸ The king said to Doeg, "You turn and fall upon the priests." And Doeg the Edomite turned and struck the priests and killed on that day eighty-five men who wore a linen ephod. ¹⁹ And Nob, the city of the priests, he struck with the edge of the sword. Both men and women, children and babies, oxen, donkeys, and sheep, *he struck* with the edge of the sword.

David, Protector of the Priestly Line

²⁰ But one of the sons of Ahimelek the son of Ahitub, named Abiathar, escaped and fled after David. ²¹ Abiathar reported to David that Saul had killed the priests of the Lord. ²² David said to Abiathar, "I knew it that day when Doeg the Edomite was there, that he would surely tell Saul. I have caused the death of all the persons of your father's house. ²³ Remain with me. Do not fear. For the one who seeks my life seeks your life, but you are safe with me."

David Saves Keilah

23 Then they told David, "Listen, the Philistines are fighting against Keilah, and they are looting the threshing floors." ² Therefore David inquired of the Lord, saying, "Shall I go and attack these Philistines?"

And the Lord said to David, "Go and attack the Philistines, and rescue Keilah."

³ The men of David said to him, "We are afraid here in Judah. How much more then, if we go down to Keilah against the armies of the Philistines?"

⁴ Then David again inquired of the Lord. And the Lord answered him and said, "Arise, go down to Keilah because I am giving the Philistines into your hand." ⁵ Then David and his men went to Keilah. He fought with the Philistines and carried off their livestock, and he struck them with a great slaughter. So David rescued the inhabitants of Keilah. ⁶ When Abiathar the son of Ahimelek fled to David at Keilah, he came down with the ephod in his hand.

Saul Pursues David

⁷ It was reported to Saul that David had come to Keilah. And Saul said, "God has delivered him into my hand. For he is shut in, by entering into a town that has gates and bars." ⁸ Then Saul summoned all the people together for war, to go down to Keilah to besiege David and his men.

⁹ David found out that Saul was planning evil against him. So he said to Abiathar the priest, "Bring the ephod near." ¹⁰ And David said, "O Lord, God of Israel, Your servant has certainly heard that Saul seeks to come to Keilah, to destroy the city on account of me. ¹¹ Will the leaders of Keilah deliver me into his hand? Will Saul come down, as Your servant has heard? O Lord, God of Israel, please tell Your servant."

And the Lord said, "He will come down."

¹² Then said David, "Will the men of Keilah deliver me and my men into the hand of Saul?"

And the Lord said, "They will deliver you."

¹³ So David and his men, which were about six hundred, arose and left Keilah. And they went wherever they could go. Now it was told Saul that David had escaped from Keilah. So he halted the expedition.

¹⁴ And David remained in the wilderness in strongholds, and dwelled in mountains in the Wilderness of Ziph. Saul sought him every day, but God did not give him into his hand.

¹⁵ Now David saw that Saul had come out to seek his life. And David was in the Wilderness of Ziph in Horesh. ¹⁶ Jonathan, the son of Saul, arose and went to David at Horesh. And he strengthened his hand in God. ¹⁷ He said to him, "Do not fear, for the hand of Saul my father will not find you. You will be king over Israel, and I will be next to you. Saul my father knows this." ¹⁸ The two of them made a covenant before the Lord. And David stayed in Horesh, but Jonathan went to his house.

¹⁹ Then the Ziphites went up to Saul to Gibeah saying, "Is David not hiding himself with us in strongholds in Horesh, on the hill of Hakilah, which is south of Jeshimon? ²⁰ Now, O king, come down according to all the desire of your soul to come down. And our part will be to deliver him into the king's hand."

²¹ Saul said, "Blessed are you of the Lord. For you have had compassion on me. ²² Please go, make sure again. Investigate and see the place where his foot *rests*, and who has seen him there. For it has been said to me that he is very cunning. ²³ So look and learn about all the hiding places where he hides himself. And come to me with certainty, and I will go with you. And it will be that if he is in the land, then I will track him throughout all the clans of Judah."

²⁴ So they arose and went to Ziph before Saul. But David and his men were in the Wilderness of Maon, in the desert south of Jeshimon. ²⁵ Saul and his men went to seek *him*, but they told David. Therefore he came down to the Rock, and lived in the Wilderness of Maon. And when Saul heard *that*, he pursued after David in the Wilderness of Maon.

²⁶ Saul went on this side of the mountain and David and his men on that side of the mountain. And David hurried to get away from Saul. Now Saul and his men were closing in on David and his men to capture them. ²⁷ But a messenger came to Saul saying, "Hurry and go! For the Philistines have invaded the land." ²⁸ So Saul returned from pursuing after David, and he went against the Philistines. Therefore they called that place the Rock of Escape. ²⁹ David then went up from there and lived in the strongholds of En Gedi.

David Spares Saul's Life

24 When Saul had returned from following the Philistines, it was reported to him, saying, "David is in the Wilderness of En Gedi." ² Then Saul took three thousand chosen men out of all Israel and went to seek David and his men in front of the rocks of the wild goats.

³ He came to the sheep pens by the way and a cave was there. And Saul went in to relieve himself. Now David and his men were sitting in the rear of the cave. ⁴ The men of David said to him, "This is the day of which the Lord said to you, 'I am giving your enemy into your hand. You may do with him as seems good in your eyes.' " Then David arose and secretly cut off the corner of Saul's robe.

⁵ Afterward David's heart troubled him because he had cut off a corner of Saul's robe. ⁶ He said to his men, "The Lord forbid that I should do this thing to my lord, the Lord's anointed, to stretch out my hand against him. For he is anointed of the Lord." ⁷ So David dispersed his men by *these* words and did not let them rise against Saul. And Saul arose from the cave and went on his way.

⁸ David arose afterward and went out from the cave. And he called after Saul saying, "My lord the king!" And when Saul looked behind him, David had bowed down with his face to the ground and paid homage. ⁹ David said to Saul, "Why do you listen to the words of men saying, 'David seeks your harm'? ¹⁰ This day you have seen with your own eyes that the Lord delivered you today into my hand in the cave. So that some said to kill you, but *my eye* had compassion on you. And I said, 'I will not put forth my hand

against my lord, for he is anointed of the Lord.' ¹¹ See, my father! Look at the corner of your robe in my hand. Indeed, I cut off the corner of your robe, but I did not kill you. Observe and see that there is no evil or rebellion in my hand. I have not sinned against you, but you are lying in wait for my life to take it. ¹² The Lord will judge between me and you, and the Lord will avenge me on you, but my hand will not be against you. ¹³ As the proverb of the ancients says, 'From the wicked comes forth wickedness,' but my hand will not be against you.

¹⁴ "After whom has the king of Israel come out? After whom are you pursuing? After a dead dog? A single flea? ¹⁵ May the Lord be judge, and decide between me and you. And may He see and plead my case, and deliver me out of your hand."

¹⁶ When David finished speaking these words to Saul, Saul said, "Is this your voice, my son David?" And Saul lifted up his voice and wept. ¹⁷ And he said to David, "You are more righteous than I. For you have rewarded me with good, while I have rewarded you with evil. ¹⁸ And you have shown today that you have dealt well with me, when the Lord delivered me into your hand and you did not kill me. ¹⁹ For if a man finds his enemy, will he let him safely go away? Therefore may the Lord reward you well for what you have done for me this day. ²⁰ Now, listen, I know that you will surely be king and that the kingdom of Israel will be established in your hand. ²¹ Therefore swear to me now by the Lord that you will not cut off my descendants after me and that you will not destroy my name out of my father's household."

²² So David swore to Saul and Saul went home. But David and his men went up to the stronghold.

Death of Samuel

25 Now Samuel died. And all the children of Israel gathered together and mourned him, and they buried him at his home in Ramah. Then David arose and went down to the Wilderness of Paran.

David, Nabal, and Abigail

² Now there was a man in Maon whose work was in Carmel. He was a rich man with three thousand sheep and a thousand goats, and he was shearing his sheep in Carmel. ³ The man's name was Nabal and the name of his wife Abigail. She was a woman of good understanding and beautiful, but the man was harsh and evil in his actions and he was a Calebite.

⁴ David heard in the wilderness that Nabal was shearing his sheep. ⁵ So David sent out ten young men, and David said to the young men, "Go up to Carmel, and go to Nabal and greet him in my name. ⁶ And thus you shall say to him who lives *in prosperity*, 'Peace be to you and peace to your house, and to all that you have, peace.

⁷ " 'I have heard that you have shearers. Now your shepherds were with us. We did not harm them nor did they miss anything all the days they were in Carmel. ⁸ Ask your young men and they will tell you. Therefore let *my* young men find favor in your eyes, for we have come on a good day. Please give whatever you find at hand to your servants, and to your son David.' "

⁹ When David's young men came, they spoke to Nabal according to all these words in the name of David, then they waited.

¹⁰ And Nabal answered David's servants, and said, "Who is David? And who is the son of Jesse? Today many servants are breaking away each one from his master. ¹¹ Should I then take my bread, and my water, and my meat, that which I have killed for my shearers, and give it to men whose origins are unknown?"

¹² So David's young men turned themselves around and went back. And they came and reported to him all these words. ¹³ David said to his men, "Each man strap on his sword." And each man strapped on his sword. David also put on his sword, and four hundred men went up after David. But two hundred stayed with the baggage.

¹⁴ Now one of the young men told Abigail, Nabal's wife, "Listen, David sent messengers out of the wilderness to bless our master; and he railed against them. ¹⁵ But the men were very good to us, and we were not harmed, nor did we miss anything, all the days we went about with them in the field. ¹⁶ They were a wall to us both by

night and day, all the days we were with them keeping the flocks. [17] Now therefore know and consider what you will do, for evil is determined against our master and against all his household. He is such a worthless man that *one* cannot speak to him." [18] Then Abigail hurried and took two hundred loaves, two bottles of wine, five prepared sheep, five measures[1] of roasted grain, a hundred clusters of raisins, and two hundred cakes of figs, and she loaded them on donkeys. [19] And she said to her servants, "Go on before me. See, I will be coming after you." But she did not tell her husband Nabal.

[20] And as she was riding on the donkey and going down into the cover of the mountain, David and his men were coming down to meet her and she met them. [21] Now David had said, "Surely in vain have I guarded all that this *man* has in the wilderness, so that nothing was missed of all that belonged to him. And he has returned me evil for good. [22] So may God do unto the enemies of David and more also, if by morning I leave *even* one male of all who belong to him."

[23] When Abigail saw David, she hurriedly got down from the donkey and fell before David upon her face. And she bowed herself to the ground. [24] So she fell at his feet and said, "Against me alone, my lord, is the guilt. Please let your handmaid speak in your ears, and hear the words of your handmaid. [25] Please do not let my lord set his heart against this worthless man, against Nabal. For as his name is, so is he, Nabal is his name and folly is with him. But I, your handmaid, did not see the young men of my lord, whom you sent. [26] Now my lord, as the LORD lives, and as your soul lives, because the LORD has restrained you from coming in bloodshed and from avenging yourself with your own hand, now let your enemies, and those seeking to do evil to my lord, be as Nabal. [27] Now let this blessing which your maidservant has brought to my lord be given to the young men who follow my lord.

[28] "Please forgive the transgression of your handmaid, for the LORD will certainly make my lord a sure house, because my lord fights the battles of the LORD, and evil will not be found in you all your days. [29] Even *if* a man rises to pursue you and to seek your life, the life of my lord will be bound in the bundle of the living with the LORD your God. But the lives of your enemies He will sling out, as from the hollow of a sling. [30] It will be, when the LORD does for my lord according to all the good that He has spoken concerning you and has appointed you ruler over Israel, [31] that this will be no grief to you, nor an offense of heart to my lord, either that you have shed blood without cause, or that my lord has avenged himself. But when the LORD has dealt well with my lord, then remember your handmaid."

[32] David said to Abigail, "Blessed be the LORD, God of Israel, who sent you this day to meet me. [33] And blessed is your discretion, and blessed are you who have kept me this day from coming to shed blood and from avenging myself with my own hand. [34] For as the LORD, the God of Israel lives, who has restrained me from injuring you, if you had not hurried to come and meet me, surely there would not have been left *even* one male to Nabal by the morning light."

[35] So David received from her hand what she had brought him and said to her, "Go up in peace to your house. See, I have obeyed your voice, and have granted your request."

[36] Abigail came to Nabal, and he was feasting in his house, like the feast of a king. And Nabal's heart was merry within him, for he was very drunk. Therefore she told him nothing until the morning light. [37] But in the morning when the wine was gone out of Nabal, his wife told him these things. And his heart died within him, and he became as a stone. [38] And about ten days after that, the LORD struck Nabal and he died.

[39] When David heard that Nabal was dead, he said, "Blessed is the LORD, who has defended the cause of my reproach from the hand of Nabal, and has kept his servant from evil. For the LORD has returned the wickedness of Nabal upon his own head."

And David sent and spoke with Abigail, to take her as his wife. [40] When the servants of David came to Abigail at Carmel, they spoke to her, saying, "David has sent us to you to take you as his wife."

[41] She arose, and bowed herself on her face to the ground, and said, "Here is your handmaid, a servant to wash the feet of the servants of my lord." [42] Abigail hurriedly arose and rode on a donkey with her five young women who attended her. And she went after the messengers of David and became his wife. [43] David also took Ahinoam of Jezreel. So both of them were his wives. [44] But Saul had given Michal his daughter, David's wife, to Paltiel the son of Laish who was from Gallim.

David Again Spares Saul's Life

26 Then the Ziphites came to Saul at Gibeah, saying, "Is David not hiding himself on the hill of Hakilah, which is before Jeshimon?"

[2] Then Saul arose and went down to the Wilderness of Ziph, having three thousand chosen men of Israel with him, to seek David in the Wilderness of Ziph. [3] Saul camped on the hill of Hakilah, which is before Jeshimon, by the road. But David stayed in the wilderness, when he saw that Saul came after him into the wilderness. [4] And David sent out spies and knew that Saul had certainly come.

[5] So David arose and came to the place where Saul had camped. And David saw the place where Saul was lying down and Abner son of Ner, the commander of his army. Saul was lying down in the encampment, while the people encamped around him.

[6] Then David answered and said to Ahimelek the Hittite, and to Abishai the son of Zeruiah, brother of Joab, saying, "Who will go down with me to Saul to the camp?"

And Abishai said, "I will go down with you."

[7] So David and Abishai came to the people by night while Saul lay sleeping within the circle of the camp. And his spear was stuck in the ground at his head, and Abner and the people were lying all around him.

[8] Then Abishai said to David, "God has today delivered your enemy into your hand. Now please let me strike him with the spear through to the ground with one stroke, and I will not strike him a second time."

[9] David said to Abishai, "Do not destroy him. For who can stretch out his hand against the LORD's anointed and remain unpunished?" [10] David said, "As the LORD lives, the LORD will strike him, or his day will come to die, or he will go down into battle and perish. [11] The LORD forbid that I should stretch out my hand against the LORD's anointed, but now please take the spear that is at his head and the jug of water, and let us go."

[12] So David took the spear and the jug of water from Saul's head and they went away. No one saw, no one knew, and no one awoke, for they were all asleep, because a deep sleep from the LORD had fallen upon them.

[13] Then David went over to the other side and stood on the top of a hill at a distance. A great space was between them. [14] And David called to the people and to Abner the son of Ner, saying, "Will you not answer, Abner?"

Then Abner answered and said, "Who are you that calls to the king?"

[15] And David said to Abner, "Are you not a man? And who is like to you in Israel? Why then have you not guarded your lord the king? For one of the people came in to destroy the king your lord. [16] This thing is not good which you have done. As the LORD lives, you are worthy of death because you have not guarded your master, the LORD's anointed. And now, see where is the king's spear? And the jug of water that was at his head?"

[17] Saul knew David's voice, and said, "Is this your voice, my son David?"

And David said, "It is my voice, my lord king." [18] He said, "Why is my lord pursuing after his servant? For what have I done? Or what evil is in my hand? [19] Now please let my lord king hear the words of his servant. If the LORD has stirred you up against me, let Him accept an offering. But if it was the sons of men, cursed are they before the LORD. For they have driven me today from having a share in the inheritance of the LORD, saying, 'Go, serve other gods.' [20] Now do not let my blood fall to the ground away from the presence of

---

[1] 18 Likely about 60 pounds, or 27 kilograms.

the LORD. Truly the king of Israel has come out to seek a single flea, as when one pursues a partridge in the mountains."

21 Then said Saul, "I have sinned. Return, my son David, for I will not harm you again, because my soul was precious in your eyes this day. I have acted foolishly and have seriously gone astray."

22 David answered and said, "See, the king's spear! Let one of the young men come over and get it. 23 The LORD requites to every man his right conduct and loyalty. So the LORD gave you into my hand today, but I am not willing to stretch my hand against the LORD's anointed. 24 As your life was highly valued in my eyes this day, so may my life be highly valued in the eyes of the LORD, and may He rescue me out of all distress."

25 Then Saul said to David, "Blessed are you, my son David. You will do great things, and will surely prevail."

So David went on his way, and Saul returned to his place.

David With the Philistines

27 Then David said in his heart, "Now I will perish one day by the hand of Saul. There is nothing better for me than that I should escape to the land of the Philistines. Then Saul will despair of continually seeking me within all the territory of Israel. So will I escape out of his hand."

2 David arose and passed over with the six hundred men that were with him to Achish, the son of Maok, king of Gath. 3 And David lived with Achish at Gath, he and his men, each man with his household, even David with his two wives, Ahinoam the Jezreelitess, and Abigail the Carmelitess, Nabal's widow. 4 It was reported to Saul that David had fled to Gath, so he no longer sought him.

5 David said to Achish, "If I have now found favor in your eyes, let them give me a place in one of the cities in the countryside, that I may dwell there. For why should your servant dwell in the royal city with you?"

6 Then Achish gave him Ziklag that day. Therefore Ziklag has belonged to the kings of Judah to this day. 7 The number of days that David lived in the country of the Philistines was a year and four months.

8 David and his men went up and invaded the Geshurites, the Girzites, and the Amalekites. For they were inhabitants of the land from of old, as you come to Shur, even to the land of Egypt. 9 So David would strike the land and would not leave either man or woman alive. And he would take the sheep, the cattle, the donkeys, the camels, and the garments. And then he came back to Achish.

10 Then Achish would say, "Where have you made a raid today?" And David would say, "Against the Negev of Judah," or "Against the Negev of the Jerahmeelites," or "Against the Negev of the Kenites." 11 Now David would leave neither a man nor a woman alive, to bring tidings to Gath, saying, "Lest they should tell on us, saying, 'Thus David has done.' " This was his practice all the days which he lived in the country of the Philistines. 12 And Achish believed David, saying, "He has surely become a stench to his people Israel. Therefore he will be my servant forever."

28 And it came about in those days, that the Philistines gathered their armies together for war to fight with Israel. And Achish said to David, "Know assuredly that you will go out with me to battle, you and your men."

2 David said to Achish, "Surely you will know what your servant can do."

And Achish said to David, "Therefore I will appoint you my bodyguard for life."

The Medium of Endor

3 Now Samuel died and all Israel mourned him, and they buried him in Ramah, his own city. And Saul had removed the mediums and the necromancers from the land.

4 Then the Philistines gathered themselves together. And they came and camped in Shunem. So Saul gathered all Israel together, and they camped in Gilboa. 5 When Saul saw the camp of the Philistines, he was afraid and his heart trembled greatly. 6 Saul inquired of the LORD, but the LORD did not answer him by dreams, or by lots, or by prophets. 7 Then said Saul to his servants, "Seek for me a woman who is a medium, that I may go to her and inquire of her."

And his servants said to him, "There is woman medium in Endor."

8 So Saul disguised himself, put on other clothes, and he went with two of his men. And they came to the woman by night and he said, "Please divine for me by a spirit, and bring up for me whom I will name to you."

9 The woman said to him, "Listen, you know what Saul has done, how he has eliminated the mediums and necromancers from the land. Now why are you laying a trap for my life to cause my death?"

10 Saul swore to her by the LORD, saying, "As the LORD lives, no punishment will happen to you for this thing."

11 Then said the woman, "Whom shall I bring up for you?"

And he said, "Bring up Samuel for me."

12 When the woman saw Samuel, she cried out with a loud voice. And the woman said to Saul, "Why have you deceived me? For you are Saul."

13 The king said to her, "Do not be afraid. What did you see?"

And the woman said to Saul, "I saw a divine being ascending out of the earth."

14 He said to her, "What is his appearance?"

And she said, "An old man is coming up, and he is covered with a robe."

And Saul perceived that it was Samuel. And he kneeled with his face to the ground and bowed himself.

15 Samuel said to Saul, "Why have you roused me to bring me up?"

And Saul answered, "I am greatly distressed, for the Philistines make war against me, and God has departed from me and does not answer me any longer by prophets or by dreams. Therefore I have called you that you might make known to me what I should do."

16 Then said Samuel, "Why then do you ask me, since the LORD has departed from you and has become your enemy? 17 The LORD has done for Himself as He spoke by me. The LORD has torn the kingdom from your hand and has given it to your neighbor, David. 18 As you did not obey the voice of the LORD and did not carry out His fierce wrath against Amalek, therefore the LORD has done this thing to you this day. 19 And moreover, the LORD will deliver Israel with you into the hand of the Philistines, and tomorrow you and your sons will be with me. The LORD will also deliver the army of Israel into the hand of the Philistines."

20 Saul immediately fell full length upon the ground because he greatly feared the words of Samuel. Also there was no strength in him, for he had eaten no bread all day and all night.

21 The woman came to Saul and saw that he was terrified. And she said to him, "Listen, your handmaid has obeyed your voice. I have taken my life in my hand and have listened to your words which you spoke to me. 22 Now therefore you also, please obey the voice of your maidservant and let me set before you a piece of bread, and eat so that you may have strength when you go on your way."

23 But he refused and said, "I will not eat."

But his servants, and also the woman, urged him and he listened to them. So he arose from the ground and sat on the bed.

24 Now the woman had a fattened calf in the house, and she hurried and killed it, and took flour, and kneaded it, and baked unleavened bread from it. 25 She brought it before Saul and his servants, and they ate. Then they arose and went away that night.

Philistines Reject David

29 Now the Philistines gathered together all their armies to Aphek, and the children of Israel were camping by the spring which is in Jezreel. 2 The lords of the Philistines were advancing by hundreds and by thousands, and David and his men were advancing in the rear with Achish. 3 Then the princes of the Philistines said, "What are these Hebrews *doing here*?"

And Achish said to the princes of the Philistines, "Is this not David, the servant of Saul, king of Israel, who has been with me these days, or *rather* these years? And I have found no fault in him since the day of his desertion to this day."

4 But the princes of the Philistines became angry with him. And the princes of the Philistines said to him, "Make this man return

and let him go again to his place which you have appointed him. He will not go down with us in battle, lest he might be an adversary to us in the battle. For with what could he make himself acceptable to his master, if not with the heads of these men? [5] Is this not David, whom they sing for in dances saying,

'Saul has slain his thousands,
and David his ten thousands'? "

[6] Then Achish called David and said to him, "As the Lord lives, you have been upright, and your going out and your coming in with me in the camp has been pleasing in my sight. For I have not found evil in you since the day of your coming to me to this day. However, you are not acceptable in the eyes of the lords. [7] Therefore now, return and go in peace, that you do not displease the lords of the Philistines."

[8] David said to Achish, "But what have I done? And what have you found in your servant, from the day which I came before you to this day, that I may not come and fight against the enemies of my lord the king?"

[9] And Achish answered and said to David, "I know that you are pleasing in my sight like an angel of God. However the lords of the Philistines have said, 'He shall not go up with us in battle.' [10] Therefore rise up early in the morning with your master's servants who have come with you. And when you have risen early in the morning and it is light, then depart."

[11] So David and his men rose early to depart in the morning *and* return to the land of the Philistines. But the Philistines went up to Jezreel.

David Defeats the Amalekites

30 Now when David and his men came to Ziklag on the third day, the Amalekites had raided the south as far as Ziklag. They had struck Ziklag and burned it with fire. [2] They had taken as captives all the women who were there. They did not kill anyone, but carried them off and went on their way.

[3] David and his men came to the city, and they found it burned with fire, and their wives, their sons, and their daughters taken captive. [4] So David and the people that were with him lifted up their voice and wept until they had no strength in them to weep. [5] Now David's two wives were taken captive, Ahinoam the Jezreelitess and Abigail the wife of Nabal the Carmelite. [6] David was greatly distressed, for the people talked of stoning him, because all the people were bitter in spirit, each over his sons and daughters. But David encouraged himself in the Lord his God.

[7] And David said to Abiathar the priest, the son of Ahimelek, "Please bring the ephod to me." So Abiathar brought the ephod to David. [8] David inquired at the Lord, saying, "Should I pursue after this raiding party? Will I overtake them?"

And He answered him, "Pursue *them*, for you will surely overtake them and will surely recover *all*."

[9] So David went, he and the six hundred men who were with him. And they came to the brook Besor, where those that were left behind remained. [10] But David pursued, he and four hundred men, for two hundred who were too exhausted to cross over the brook Besor remained behind.

[11] They found an Egyptian in the field and took him to David. He gave him bread and he ate, and they made him drink water. [12] And they gave him a part of a cake of figs and two cakes of raisins. When he had eaten, his spirit came back to him, for he had not eaten bread or drunk any water for three days and three nights.

[13] Then David said to him, "To whom do you belong? And where are you from?"

And he said, "I am a young man of Egypt, servant to an Amalekite. And my master left me, because three days ago I fell sick. [14] We raided the south of the Kerethites, the south of Judah, and the south of Caleb. And we burned Ziklag with fire."

[15] David said to him, "Will you bring me down to this raiding party?"

And he said, "Swear to me by God that you will neither kill me, nor deliver me into the hand of my master, and I will bring you down to this raiding party."

[16] When he brought him down, they were spread out over all the land, eating, drinking, and dancing, because of all the great spoil which they had taken from the land of the Philistines and from the land of Judah. [17] David struck them from twilight until the evening of the next day, and no man escaped except four hundred young men who rode on camels and fled. [18] So David recovered all that the Amalekites had taken, and David rescued his two wives. [19] Now there was nothing missing, from the smallest *thing* to the greatest, neither sons, nor daughters, or plunder, or anything which they had taken. David brought back all *of it*. [20] And David took all the flocks and the herds, *which* they drove before the *other* livestock. And they said, "This is David's spoil."

[21] Then David came to the two hundred men, who were too exhausted to follow David, whom they left at the brook Besor. And they went out to meet David and the people who were with him. And when David came near to the people, he greeted them. [22] Then all the wicked and worthless ones from the men who went with David answered and said, "Because they did not go with us, we will not give them anything from the spoil that we have rescued, except to every man his wife and his children, that they may lead them away and depart."

[23] Then David said, "You will not do so, my brothers, with what the Lord has given us, for He has preserved us, and has delivered into our hand the raiding party that came against us. [24] And who will listen to you in this matter? Indeed as the share *is* of the one going down to battle, so *will be* the share of the one staying with the equipment. They will share equally." [25] So it was so from that day forward, that he set it *as* a statute and an ordinance for Israel to this day.

[26] When David came to Ziklag, he sent part of the spoil to his friends, the elders of Judah, saying, "Here is a gift to you from the spoil of the enemies of the Lord": [27] to those who were in Bethel, in Ramoth of the Negev, and in Jattir; [28] to those who were in Aroer, Siphmoth, Eshtemoa, [29] and in Rakal; to those who were in the cities of the Jerahmeelites and the Kenites; [30] to those who were in Hormah, Bor Ashan, Athak [31] and in Hebron; and to those who were in all the other places where David and his men had roamed.

The House of Saul, Dead and Buried

2Sa 1:4–12; 1Ch 10:1–12

31 Now the Philistines were fighting against Israel, and Israel's fighting men fled before the Philistines and they fell slain on Mount Gilboa. [2] The Philistines overtook Saul and his sons. And the Philistines killed his sons, Jonathan, Abinadab, and Malki-Shua, Saul's sons. [3] The battle was heavy against Saul. The archers found him, and he was severely wounded by the archers.

[4] Then Saul said to his armor bearer, "Draw your sword and thrust me through with it, lest these uncircumcised come and thrust me through and abuse me."

But his armor bearer would not, for he was very afraid. Therefore Saul took his sword and fell upon it. [5] When his armor bearer saw that Saul was dead, he also fell upon his sword and died with him. [6] So Saul died with his three sons and his armor bearer, together *with* all his men on that same day.

[7] When Israel's fighting men who were on the other side of the valley, and those who were on the other side of the Jordan, saw that Israel's fighting men fled and that Saul and his sons were dead, they abandoned the cities and fled. So the Philistines came and lived in them.

[8] The following day, when the Philistines came to strip the dead, they found Saul and his three sons fallen on Mount Gilboa. [9] They cut off his head, stripped off his armor, and sent *them* into the land of the Philistines round about, to make it known in the house of their idols and among their people. [10] They put his armor in the house of Ashtoreth, and they fastened his body to the wall of Beth Shan.

[11] When the inhabitants of Jabesh Gilead heard what the Philistines had done to Saul, [12] all the valiant men arose and went all night, and they took the body of Saul and the bodies of his sons from the wall of Beth Shan, and they came to Jabesh and burned them there. [13] Then they took their bones and buried them under the tamarisk tree at Jabesh, and they *mourned*, fasting seven days.

The Death of Saul

1Sa 31:1–13; 1Ch 10:1–13

1 After the death of Saul, when David had returned from the slaughter of the Amalekites, David had remained two days in Ziklag. [2] On the third day, a man came from the camp of Saul with his clothes torn and dirt upon his head. As he approached David, he fell to the ground prostrate.

[3] David asked him, "Where have you come from?"

He responded, "I fled from the camp of Israel."

[4] David said to him, "Tell me, what is the report?"

So he reported, "The people fled from battle. Many of the people have fallen and died; even Saul and his son Jonathan are dead."

[5] Then David asked the young man who was reporting to him, "How do you know that Saul and his son Jonathan are dead?"

[6] The young man who was reporting to him answered, "I happened to be on Mount Gilboa when, in front of me, Saul was leaning on his spear with the chariots and horsemen drawing close. [7] When he turned around, he noticed me. He summoned me, and I responded, 'Here I am.'

[8] "He asked me, 'Who are you?'

"I answered, 'I am an Amalekite.'

[9] "Then he said to me, 'Stand over me and kill me, for I have been mortally wounded, yet I am still alive.'

[10] "So I stood beside him and killed him because I knew that he could not live after he had fallen. Then I took the crown that was on his head and the armlet that was on his arm, and I have brought them here to my lord."

[11] Then David took hold of his clothes and tore them, *as did* all of the men who were with him. [12] They mourned and wept and fasted until evening for Saul, Jonathan his son, the people of the LORD, and the house of Israel, because they had fallen by the sword.

[13] Then David asked the young man who was reporting to him, "Where are you from?"

He responded, "I am the son of one who sought refuge, an Amalekite."

[14] David said to him, "How is it that you did not fear raising your hand to destroy the anointed of the LORD?"

[15] Then David called to one of the young men and said, "Step forward and execute him." So he struck him and killed him. [16] But David said to him, "Your blood is upon your own head, since your mouth has testified against you, saying, 'I put an end to the anointed of the LORD.'"

The Lament of David

[17] Then David recited this lament over Saul and Jonathan his son, [18] and he told them to teach the sons of Judah the Song of the Bow. It is written in the book of Jashar:

[19] Your splendor, O Israel, has been slain upon your hills.
How the mighty ones have fallen.

[20] Do not report it in Gath,
do not announce it in the streets of Ashkelon,
lest the daughters of the Philistines rejoice,
or the daughters of the uncircumcised exult.

[21] O mountains of Gilboa,
may there be no rain or dew upon you
or your bountiful fields;
for there the shield of the mighty was defiled!
The shield of Saul *is* no longer anointed with oil.

[22] From the blood of the slain,
from the fat of mighty,
the bow of Jonathan did not turn back,
nor did the sword of Saul return empty.

[23] Saul and Jonathan,
beloved and delightful,
neither in life nor death will they be separated.
They were swifter than eagles,
they were stronger than lions.

[24] O daughters of Israel, weep over Saul,
who clothed you in scarlet and jewels,
who adorned your garments with gold jewelry.

[25] How the mighty ones have fallen in the midst of battle!
Jonathan was slain on your high places.

[26] I am distressed for you, my brother Jonathan;
you were very dear to me;
your love was more remarkable than the love of women.

[27] How the mighty have fallen,
and the weapons of war have perished.

David Anointed King Over Judah

2 After this, David consulted the LORD, asking, "Shall I go to one of the cities of Judah?"

The LORD responded to him, "Go up."

David asked, "Where should I go?"

And He said, "Hebron."

[2] So David went up there, along with his two wives, Ahinoam the Jezreelitess, and Abigail the widow of Nabal the Carmelite. [3] And David brought the men who were with him, each man with his household, and they lived in the cities of Hebron. [4] Then the men of Judah came and there anointed David as king over the house of Judah, and they informed David that it was the men of Jabesh Gilead who had buried Saul.

[5] So David sent messengers to the men of Jabesh Gilead saying, "May you be blessed by the LORD, you who have shown this loyalty to your lord Saul by burying him. [6] Now may the LORD show you loyalty and faithfulness, even as I deal kindly with you who have done this thing. [7] Now may your hands be strong and may you be courageous, since your lord Saul is dead and the house of Judah has anointed me as king over them."

War Between the Houses of David and Saul

1Ch 3:1–4

[8] However, Abner the son of Ner, commander of the army of Saul, had taken Ish-Bosheth the son of Saul and brought him over to Mahanaim. [9] He installed him as king over Gilead, the Ashurites, Jezreel, Ephraim, and Benjamin, over Israel in its entirety.

[10] Ish-Bosheth the son of Saul was forty years old when he began to reign over Israel, and he ruled for two years. However, the house of Judah followed David. [11] The length of time during which David was king in Hebron over the house of Judah was seven years and six months.

[12] Abner the son of Ner, with the servants of Ish-Bosheth the son of Saul, went out from Mahanaim toward Gibeon. [13] And Joab the son of Zeruiah, with the servants of David, went out in order to meet together at the pool of Gibeon. They sat down, one group on one side of the pool and the other group on the side of the pool opposite them.

[14] Abner suggested to Joab, "Let the young men come forward and compete before us."

And Joab replied, "Let them come."

[15] So they stepped forward and were counted, twelve from Benjamin and Ish-Bosheth and twelve from the servants of David. [16] Each one grabbed his opponent by the head and thrust his sword in his opponent's side; so they fell down together. Therefore that place was called Helkath Hazzurim, which is at Gibeon.

[17] The fighting was very fierce that day, but Abner and the men of Israel were defeated by the servants of David.

[18] Now the three sons of Zeruiah were there: Joab, Abishai, and Asahel; and Asahel was as fast as a wild gazelle. [19] So Asahel pursued Abner, and as he went, he did not turn to the right hand or to the

left from following Abner. [20] Abner looked behind him and said, "Is that you, Asahel?"

He answered, "It is I."

[21] Abner said to him, "Turn aside to your right or left, overtake one of the young men, and take his equipment for yourself," but Asahel was not willing to desist.

[22] Abner continued still to reason with Asahel, "Abandon your pursuit. Why should I strike you down? How then could I show my face to your brother Joab?"

[23] But he refused to desist. So Abner struck him in the abdomen with the butt of his spear, so that the spear came out of his back. He fell there and died on the spot. When all of the others came to the place where Asahel fell and died, they halted.

[24] But Joab and Abishai pursued Abner. As the sun was setting, they came to the hill of Ammah, which is next to Giah on the way to the Wilderness of Gibeon. [25] The sons of Benjamin gathered to the rear of Abner into a single formation, and they took their stand atop one of the hills.

[26] Abner called to Joab, "Must the sword consume forever? Do you not understand that a bitter taste will result in the end? How long will you refuse to command the people to withdraw from chasing their brothers?"

[27] Joab responded, "As God lives, I assure you that if you had not said this, the people would have each pursued his brother throughout the night."

[28] So Joab blew a trumpet, and all the people stood still. They pursued Israel no longer, nor did they continue to fight anymore.

[29] So Abner and his men traveled through the Arabah all that night, crossed the Jordan, and marched all morning until they returned to Mahanaim.

[30] Joab refrained from pursuing Abner, but instead mustered all of the people. There were nineteen men besides Asahel missing from among the servants of David. [31] But the servants of David routed Benjamin and the men of Abner; three hundred and sixty of their men died. [32] They carried Asahel back and interred him in his father's tomb, which was at Bethlehem. Then Joab and his men traveled throughout the night and reached Hebron at dawn.

3 The struggle between the house of Saul and the house of David endured, but David grew stronger as Saul became weaker. [2] Sons were born to David in Hebron:

his firstborn was Amnon, by Ahinoam the Jezreelitess;
[3] and his second, Kileab, by Abigail the widow of Nabal, the Carmelite;
and the third, Absalom the son of Maakah the daughter of Talmai, the king of Geshur;
[4] and the fourth, Adonijah the son of Haggith;
and the fifth, Shephatiah the son of Abital;
[5] and the sixth, Ithream, was born to Eglah, the wife of David.

These were born to David in Hebron.

Abner Defects to David

[6] While there was war between the house of Saul and the house of David, Abner was strengthening himself in the house of Saul. [7] Now Saul had a concubine whose name was Rizpah, the daughter of Aiah, and Ish-Bosheth said to Abner, "Why have you gone in to my father's concubine?"

[8] Abner became very angry over the words of Ish-Bosheth. He said, "Am I a dog's head that belongs to Judah? Each day I show loyalty to the house of Saul your father, to his brothers, and to his friends by not allowing you to fall into the hand of David. Yet today you are charging me with guilt concerning this woman. [9] May God do so to Abner, and more also, for as the LORD has sworn to David, this I will do for him, [10] to transfer the kingdom from the house of Saul and to establish the throne of David over Israel and Judah, from Dan to Beersheba." [11] And he could not offer a response to Abner, for fear of him.

[12] So Abner sent messengers to David on his behalf saying, "To whom does the land belong? Make your covenant with me, and my hand will be with you to bring over all of Israel to you."

[13] He responded, "Very well, I will make a covenant with you, but I require one thing from you: you will not see my face unless you bring Michal the daughter of Saul with you when you come to see me." [14] Then David sent messengers to Ish-Bosheth the son of Saul, saying, "Give me my wife Michal, to whom I was betrothed for one hundred Philistine foreskins."

[15] So Ish-Bosheth sent for her, and he took her from her husband, Paltiel the son of Laish. [16] But her husband went with her, weeping as he went, as far as Bahurim. Then Abner said to him, "Go. Return." So he turned back.

[17] Abner had a word with the elders of Israel, "In days past, you were seeking David as king over you. [18] So do it now, because the LORD said to David: By the hand of David, I will save My people Israel from the hand of the Philistines and from the hand of every enemy."

[19] Abner also spoke privately with Benjamin. Then Abner went to tell David privately at Hebron all that was received favorably by Israel and the entire house of Benjamin. [20] So Abner, along with twenty men, went to David at Hebron, and David held a festival for Abner and the men who were with him. [21] Abner said to David, "Let me arise, go, and gather all Israel to my lord the king, so that they may make a covenant with you, that you may rule over all that your heart desires." So David sent Abner away, and he went peaceably.

Joab Murders Abner

[22] Now the servants of David and Joab came from a raid and brought much plunder with them, but Abner was no longer with David at Hebron, because he had sent him away in peace. [23] When Joab and the whole of the army that was with him arrived, they reported to Joab, "Abner the son of Ner came to the king and he sent him away peaceably."

[24] So Joab went to the king and said, "What have you done? Abner came to you. Why is it that you sent him away? Now he is long gone. [25] You know that Abner the son of Ner came to deceive you, to learn of your coming and going, to discern all that you are doing."

[26] When Joab left David, he sent messengers after Abner, and they brought him back from the well of Sirah. However, David was not aware of this. [27] So Abner returned to Hebron, and Joab pulled him aside in the gateway so as to speak with him undisturbed. There he struck him in the midsection so that he died on account of the blood of Asahel, his brother.

[28] Afterward when David heard of this, he said, "My kingdom and I are forever blameless before the LORD for the blood of Abner the son of Ner. [29] May it fall upon the head of Joab and upon all his father's house. May the house of Joab never be without one who has a discharge, or who is a leper, or who leans on a staff, or who falls by the sword, or who lacks food."

[30] So Joab and his brother Abishai killed Abner, because he killed Asahel their brother at Gibeon in the battle.

[31] David said to Joab and all of the people with him, "Tear your clothes, put on sackcloth, and mourn before Abner." As for King David, he followed behind the bier. [32] When they buried Abner at Hebron, the king raised his voice and wept at the grave of Abner, and all of the people wept.

[33] Then, the king lamented for Abner, saying,

"Should Abner have died as a fool dies?
[34]   Your hands were not bound,
         and your feet were not put in fetters;
     as a man falls before the wicked, so you have fallen."

And all of the people continued to weep over him.

[35] Then all of the people came to persuade David to eat food while it was still day. But David took an oath, saying, "May God do to me, and more also, if I taste food or anything else before the sun sets." [36] All of the people recognized this, and it pleased them, as everything that the king did was pleasing to all of the people. [37] That very day, all of the people, all of Israel, understood that it was not *ordered* from the king to have Abner the son of Ner killed.

[38] David said to his servant, "Do you not understand that a great leader has fallen this day in Israel? [39] Today, I am weak, even if an anointed king, and these men, the sons of Zeruiah, are too strong for me. May the LORD repay the evildoer according to his wickedness."

Ish-Bosheth Murdered

4 When the son of Saul heard that Abner had died in Hebron, his courage failed, and all of Israel was disheartened. ² Now the son of Saul had two men who were leaders of raiding bands. The name of one was Baanah and the name of the other Rekab, both sons of Rimmon the Beerothite, from among the sons of Benjamin. Now Beeroth is also regarded as part of Benjamin, ³ because the Beerothites fled to Gittaim and have been sojourners there until this day.

⁴ Now Jonathan the son of Saul had a son with crippled feet. He was five years old when the report of Saul and Jonathan came from Jezreel. His nurse picked him up and fled, but in her haste to escape, he fell and became lame. His name was Mephibosheth.

⁵ The sons of Rimmon the Beerothite, Rekab and Baanah, went out and came to the house of Ish-Bosheth in the heat of the day, as he was resting in his bed at midday. ⁶ They entered the house as if to get wheat and stabbed him in the abdomen. Then Rekab and his brother Baanah fled to safety.

⁷ When they entered the house, he was lying on his bed in his bedroom; they struck him, killed him, and beheaded him. Then they took his head and traveled by way of the Arabah all night. ⁸ They brought the head of Ish-Bosheth to David in Hebron and said to the king, "Here is the head of Ish-Bosheth the son of Saul, your enemy who sought your life. This day, the Lord has given retribution against Saul and his descendent to my lord the king."

⁹ David answered Rekab and his brother Baanah, the sons of Rimmon the Beerothite, "As the Lord, who has delivered my life from every distress, lives, ¹⁰ when one reported to me that Saul was dead, although he was a bearer of good news in his own eyes, I seized him and killed him at Ziklag, which was my reward for his message. ¹¹ How much more so, when guilty men have slain an innocent man in his own house on his own bed, should I not now require his blood from your hand and wipe you from the earth?"

¹² David then gave orders to the young men. They killed them, cut off their hands and feet, and hung them at the pool in Hebron, but they took the head of Ish-Bosheth and buried it in the grave of Abner at Hebron.

David Anointed King Over Israel
1Ch 11:1–3

5 All of the tribes of Israel came to David at Hebron and said, "We are your bone and flesh. ² Previously, when Saul was king over us, you were the one leading Israel out and in. Also, the Lord said to you: You will shepherd My people Israel, and you will be ruler over Israel."

³ So all of the elders of Israel came to the king at Hebron, and King David made a covenant with them before the Lord at Hebron. They anointed David king over Israel.

⁴ David was thirty years old when he began to reign, and he reigned forty years. ⁵ He reigned over Judah from Hebron for seven years and six months, and he reigned over all of Israel and Judah from Jerusalem for thirty-three years.

David Conquers Jerusalem
1Ch 3:5–9; 11:4–9; 14:1–7

⁶ The king and his men went to Jerusalem against the Jebusites, who were living in the land. They said to David, "You will not enter here; even the blind and the lame will turn you away"—thinking, "David cannot enter here." ⁷ Nevertheless, David overthrew the stronghold of Zion, which is now the City of David.

⁸ David said on that day, "Whoever defeats the Jebusites, let him go through the water shaft to reach the lame and the blind, who are despised by David." Therefore, it is said, "The blind and lame shall not come into the house."

⁹ So David occupied the stronghold, and he called it the City of David. He built on all sides from the terraces inward. ¹⁰ David went on and became great, because the Lord, the God of Hosts, was with him.

¹¹ King Hiram of Tyre sent messengers to David with cedar wood, carpenters, and stonemasons, and they built a house for David.

¹² Then David understood that the Lord had appointed him king over Israel, and that He had exalted his kingdom for the sake of His people Israel.

¹³ David took more concubines and wives in Jerusalem, after having come from Hebron, and they bore him more sons and daughters. ¹⁴ These are the names of the children born to him in Jerusalem: Shammua, Shobab, Nathan, Solomon, ¹⁵ Ibhar, Elishua, Nepheg, Japhia, ¹⁶ Elishama, Eliada, and Eliphelet.

David Defeats the Philistines
1Ch 14:8–17

¹⁷ When the Philistines heard that they had anointed David king over Israel, all of the Philistines went up to search for David, but David heard about this and went down to the stronghold. ¹⁸ Now the Philistines had come and were spread out in the Valley of Rephaim. ¹⁹ So David asked the Lord, "Shall I go up against the Philistines? Will You give them into my hand?"

The Lord said to David, "Go up, because I will certainly give them into your hand."

²⁰ So David came to Baal Perazim, and David defeated them there. He said, "The Lord has breached my enemies before me like bursting tides." Therefore, he named that place Baal Perazim. ²¹ The Philistines abandoned their idols there, and David and his men carried them away.

²² Once again, the Philistines went up and spread out in the Valley of Rephaim. ²³ When David inquired of the Lord, He said, "You shall not go up. Circle around behind them and come against them opposite the trees. ²⁴ When you hear the sound of marching in the tops of the trees, pay attention, because at that point the Lord is going before you to defeat the army of the Philistines." ²⁵ So David did just as the Lord commanded, and he defeated the Philistines from Geba as far as Gezer.

The Ark Brought to Jerusalem
1Ch 13:1–14; 15:25–16:3

6 Again David gathered all of the chosen men in Israel, thirty thousand. ² David and all of the people who were with him arose and went from Baalah of Judah to bring up the ark of God, so named for the name of the Lord of Hosts who sits enthroned among the cherubim that are upon it. ³ They loaded the ark of God on a new cart and brought it from the house of Abinadab, which was on the hill. Uzzah and Ahio the sons of Abinadab were driving the new cart. ⁴ They brought it with the ark of God from the house of Abinadab on the hill, and Ahio was walking in front of the ark. ⁵ Meanwhile, David and the entire house of Israel were celebrating before the Lord with all sorts of instruments made of fir wood, on harps, on stringed instruments, on tambourines, on sistrums, and on cymbals.

⁶ When they came to the threshing floor of Nakon, Uzzah reached out and took hold of the ark of God, because the oxen had stumbled. ⁷ The Lord became angry against Uzzah, and God struck him down on the spot for his irreverence. He died there beside the ark of God.

⁸ David became angry because of the outburst of the Lord against Uzzah; that place is called Perez Uzzah to this day.

⁹ David feared the Lord that day, and he thought, "How can the ark of the Lord come to me?" ¹⁰ So David did not allow the ark of the Lord to be brought to him in the City of David. Instead, David redirected it to the house of Obed-Edom the Gittite. ¹¹ The ark of the Lord remained at the house of Obed-Edom the Gittite for three months, and the Lord blessed Obed-Edom and his entire household.

¹² When it was reported to King David, "The Lord has blessed Obed-Edom and everything that belongs to him, for the sake of the ark of God," David went and brought up the ark of God from the house of Obed-Edom to the City of David with rejoicing. ¹³ When those who were carrying the ark of the Lord had taken six steps, David would sacrifice an ox and a fattened steer. ¹⁴ David danced before the Lord with all of his might, and he wore a linen ephod. ¹⁵ So David and the whole house of Israel escorted the ark of the Lord with shouting and the sound of the horn.

¹⁶ When the ark of the Lord entered the City of David, Michal the daughter of Saul looked down from the window, and upon

seeing King David leaping and dancing before the Lord, she thought contemptuously of him in her mind.

[17] They brought the ark of the Lord and set it in its place inside the tent that David had erected for it. Then David offered burnt offerings and peace offerings before the Lord. [18] When David had finished offering the burnt offerings and peace offerings, he blessed the people before the Lord of Hosts. [19] He distributed to all of the people, the entire multitude of Israel, both men and women, one bread cake, one date cake, and one raisin cake to each one. Then all of the people left, each to his household.

[20] David returned to bless his household, but Michal the daughter of Saul came out to meet him. She said, "How the king of Israel has dignified himself today, exposing himself this day in the sight of his servant's slave girls like one of the rabble might shamelessly expose himself."

[21] Then David responded to Michal, "It was before the Lord, who chose me over your father and over everyone in his household, to appoint me ruler over the people of the Lord, over Israel. I was celebrating before the Lord. [22] I will humble myself even more than this and be abased in my own eyes. But by the maidservants, of whom you have spoken, I will be held in honor."

[23] Michal the daughter of Saul had no children to the day of her death.

God's Covenant With David
1Ch 17:1–15

7 Now when the king settled into his house and the Lord had given him rest from all of his enemies on all sides, [2] the king said to Nathan the prophet, "I am dwelling in a cedar house, but the ark of God is sitting in a tent."

[3] Nathan said to the king, "Go, do all that is in your heart because the Lord is with you."

[4] That night the word of the Lord came to Nathan:

[5] Go and say to My servant David: Thus says the Lord: Do you intend to build a house for Me in which I will dwell? [6] I have not dwelt in a house since the day I brought the sons of Israel from Egypt until this day. I have been moving about with a tent as My dwelling. [7] Wherever I have moved with all the sons of Israel, have I ever spoken a word to anyone from the tribes of Israel, whom I commanded to shepherd My people Israel, saying, "Why have you not built Me a house of cedar?"

[8] Now therefore, you will say to My servant David: Thus says the Lord of Hosts: I took you from the pasture, from following after the sheep, to be ruler over My people Israel. [9] I have been with you wherever you have gone, and I have cut off all of your enemies before you. I will make your name great, like the great ones across the land. [10] Moreover, I will appoint a place for My people Israel. I will plant them, and they will dwell in that very place. They will be restless no longer, and the unjust will no longer oppress them, as in former times, [11] ever since the day in which I appointed judges over My people Israel. I will give you rest from all of your enemies.

The Lord declares to you that He will instead bring about a house for you. [12] When your days are complete and you lie down with your fathers, I will raise up after you an offspring from your body, and I will establish his rule. [13] He will build a house for My name, and I will establish his royal throne forever. [14] I will be a father to him, and he will be a son to Me. When he goes astray, I will correct him with the rod of men and afflictions of the sons of men. [15] My commitment will not abandon him, as I removed it from Saul, whom I deposed before you. [16] Your house and dominion will endure before Me forever, and your throne will be established by the Lord forever.

[17] So Nathan spoke to David in accordance with all of these words and the entirety of this vision.

The Prayer of David
1Ch 17:16–27

[18] Then King David went in and sat before the Lord. He said,

"Who am I, O Lord God, and what is my house that You have brought me this far? [19] Yet this was comparatively insignificant in Your sight, Lord God, for You have also spoken about Your servant's house into the distant future. Is this Your manner with man, Lord God?

[20] "What more can David say to You? You know Your servant, Lord God. [21] Because of Your word, according to Your will, You have done all of this greatness to inform Your servant.

[22] "Therefore You are great, Lord God. There is none like You, and there is no God except You, according to everything that we have heard with our ears. [23] And who is like Your people, like Israel—a single nation in the land, whom God went to redeem as a people for Himself, making a name for Himself by doing great and awesome things for Your land, before Your people whom You redeemed for Yourself from Egypt, a nation and its gods. [24] You established Your people Israel as Your own people forever, and You, Lord, became their God.

[25] "Now, Lord God, confirm forever the word that You spoke regarding Your servant and his house and do as You have spoken. [26] May Your name be magnified forever by saying, 'The Lord of Hosts is God over Israel,' and may the house of Your servant David be established before You.

[27] "For You, O Lord of Hosts, God of Israel, have revealed a word to Your servant, saying, 'I will build you a house.' Therefore, Your servant has found the courage to pray this prayer to You. [28] Now, Lord God, You are God, and Your words are true. You have spoken this good message to Your servant. [29] Now, be resolved and bless Your servant's dynastic house, so that it may stand before You forever. You, Lord God, have spoken, and with Your blessing, the house of Your servant will be blessed forever."

David's Victories
1Ch 18:1–13

8 Afterward, David defeated the Philistines and subdued them, and David took Metheg Ammah from the hand of the Philistines.

[2] He also defeated Moab. He measured them with a length of rope, forcing them to lie down on the ground. He measured two lengths of rope to be put to death, but the entirety of one length he allowed to live. So the Moabites became subject to David, bearing tribute.

[3] David also defeated Hadadezer the son of Rehob, king of Zobah, when he went to restore his authority over the River Euphrates. [4] David seized from him one thousand seven hundred horsemen and twenty thousand foot soldiers, and David hamstrung all of the chariot horses, save those for one hundred chariots.

[5] The Arameans of Damascus came to help Hadadezer king of Zobah, but David defeated twenty-two thousand men of the Arameans. [6] David put garrisons in Aram of Damascus; and the Arameans became servants who bore tribute to David. The Lord helped David wherever he went.

[7] David took the shields of gold that were issued to the servants of Hadadezer and brought them to Jerusalem. [8] From Betah [f] and Berothai, cities of Hadadezer, King David took great quantities of bronze.

[9] When Toi king of Hamath heard that David had defeated the entire army of Hadadezer, [10] Toi sent his son Joram to King David to greet him and bless him on account of his fighting with Hadadezer and his defeat of him, for Hadadezer was an opponent of Toi. Joram brought with him implements of silver, gold, and bronze, [11] which King David dedicated to the Lord along with the silver and gold that he dedicated from all of the nations that he had subdued, [12] that is, from Aram, [g] Moab, the Ammonites, the Philistines, Amalek, and the plunder from Hadadezer the son of Rehob, king of Zobah.

[13] So David made a name for himself upon his return from defeating eighteen thousand Arameans [3] in the Valley of Salt.

---

[f] 8 Tibhath in 1Ch 18:8.   [2] 12 Possibly Edom. Cf. 2Sa 8:14, 1Ch 18:11–13, LXX and Syriac mss. See also note for v. 13.
[3] 13 Possibly Edomites. Cf. 2Sa 8:14, 1Ch 18:11–13, LXX and Syriac mss.

[14] He set up garrisons in Edom. Throughout all of Edom, he set up garrisons, and all of Edom became subject to David. The LORD helped David wherever he went.

David's Officials
1Ch 18:14–17

[15] David reigned over all of Israel, and he administered fair judgments to all of his people. [16] Joab the son of Zeruiah was over the army. Jehoshaphat the son of Ahilud was secretary. [17] Zadok the son of Ahitub and Ahimelek the son of Abiathar were priests. Seraiah was scribe. [18] Benaiah the son of Jehoiada was in charge of the Kerethites and Pelethites. The sons of David were chief ministers.

David's Kindness to Mephibosheth

9 David said, "Is there still anyone left from the house of Saul to whom I may show kindness on behalf of Jonathan?"

[2] Now there was a servant from the house of Saul whose name was Ziba. So they summoned him to David. The king said to him, "Are you Ziba?"

He replied, "I am your servant."

[3] The king said, "Is there no one else from the house of Saul to whom I may show the kindness of God?"

Ziba responded to the king, "There is still a son of Jonathan who is crippled in both feet."

[4] The king said to him, "Where is he?"

Ziba told the king, "He is at the house of Makir the son of Ammiel at Lo Debar."

[5] So King David sent for and brought him from the house of Makir the son of Ammiel, from Lo Debar.

[6] Mephibosheth the son of Jonathan the son of Saul came to David and fell upon his face and bowed down. Then David said, "Mephibosheth," and he responded, "I am your servant."

[7] David said to him, "Do not be afraid, for I will certainly show you kindness on account of Jonathan, your father. I will return to you every field of Saul, your father, and you will eat at my table perpetually."

[8] He bowed low and said, "What is your servant that you should be concerned for a dead dog like me?"

[9] The king summoned Ziba the servant of Saul, and he said to him, "All that belonged to Saul and to all his house, I have given to the son of your master. [10] You will work the ground for him—you, your sons, and your servants. You will bring in the produce so that the son of your master will have food to eat; but Mephibosheth, the son of your master, will always eat at my table." Now Ziba had fifteen sons and twenty servants.

[11] Ziba said to the king, "Everything that my lord the king has commanded his servant, your servant will do." So Mephibosheth ate at the table of David like one of the sons of the king.

[12] Now Mephibosheth had a young son whose name was Mika, and all who dwelled in the house of Ziba were servants to Mephibosheth. [13] So Mephibosheth lived in Jerusalem, because he ate continually at the table of the king. Now he was lame in both of his feet.

David Defeats the Ammonites and Arameans
1Ch 19:1–19

10 After this, the king of the Ammonites died, and Hanun his son reigned in his stead. [2] David said, "I will show kindness to Hanun the son of Nahash, as his father showed kindness to me." So David sent a message by way of his servants to comfort him concerning his father, and the servants of David went to the land of the Ammonites.

[3] But the Ammonite officials said to Hanun, their lord, "Has David honored your father in your eyes by sending comforters to you? Was it not in an effort to search out the city, to scout it in order to overthrow it, that he sent his servants to you?" [4] So Hanun seized the servants of David, shaved half of the beard of each, cut their robes in half so that they were exposed, and sent them away.

[5] When they reported what had happened to David, he sent messengers to meet them, because the men were severely ashamed. The king instructed them, "Remain at Jericho until your beards have regrown, then return."

[6] When the Ammonites saw that they had become odious to David, the Ammonites sent and hired the Arameans of Beth Rehob and the Arameans of Zobah, twenty thousand foot soldiers, and from the king of Maakah, one thousand men, and from Tob, twelve thousand men.

[7] When David heard of it, he sent Joab and all the army with the warriors. [8] The Ammonites came out and drew up in battle formation at the entrance of the gate. But the Arameans of Zobah, Rehob, Tob, and Maakah were by themselves in the open field.

[9] When Joab saw that the battlefronts were both before and behind him, he selected some from the best men in Israel and lined them up opposite Aram. [10] The remainder of the people he placed under the charge of Abishai his brother, and lined them up opposite the Ammonites. [11] Then he said, "If Aram starts to prevail over me, you shall help me, but if the Ammonites begin to prevail over you, then I will come to help you. [12] Be strong and let us fight with resolve for the sake of our people and the cities of our God. May the LORD do what seems good to Him."

[13] Joab advanced the people that were with him to fight against Aram, and they retreated from before him. [14] When the Ammonites realized that Aram had fled, they retreated from before Abishai and entered the city. Then Joab turned away from fighting against the Ammonites, and he came to Jerusalem.

[15] When Aram saw that they had been defeated by Israel, they assembled together. [16] Hadadezer sent for and summoned the Arameans who were beyond the River,[*] and they came to Helam. Shobak the commander of the army of Hadadezer led them.

[17] When David was informed of this, he assembled all of Israel. They crossed over the Jordan and came to Helam. Aram was drawn up in formation opposite David, and they fought against him. [18] Aram retreated before Israel. David killed seven hundred charioteers, forty thousand horsemen from Aram, and wounded Shobak the commander of the army so that he died there. [19] When all of the kings who were subject to Hadadezer realized that they were being defeated by Israel, they made peace with Israel and became subject to them.

From then on, Aram was fearful of further helping the Ammonites.

David and Bathsheba

11 In the spring of the year, the time when the kings go out to battle, David sent out Joab and his officers, and all of Israel with him. They brought to ruin the Ammonites and besieged Rabbah, but David remained in Jerusalem.

[2] One evening when David arose from his bed and was walking on the roof of the king's house, from the roof he saw a woman bathing; and the woman was very beautiful. [3] So, David sent someone to inquire about the woman. And it was asked, "Is this not Bathsheba the daughter of Eliam, the wife of Uriah the Hittite?" [4] So David sent messengers, and took her; and she came to him, and he lay with her. When she had purified herself from her uncleanness, she returned to her house. [5] The woman conceived. So she sent a message and reported to David, "I am pregnant."

[6] Then David sent an order to Joab, "Send Uriah the Hittite to me." So, Joab sent Uriah to David. [7] When Uriah came to him, David asked about the welfare of Joab, the people, and the fighting. [8] Then David said to Uriah, "Go down to your house. Wash your feet." So Uriah left the house of the king, and a gift from the king followed him. [9] But Uriah slept at the entrance of the house of the king with all of the servants of his lord; he did not go down to his house.

[10] When they reported to David, saying, "Uriah did not go down to his house," David said to Uriah, "Have you not come from a journey? Why did you not go down to your house?"

[11] Uriah responded to David, "The ark, Israel, and Judah dwell in makeshift shelters. My lord Joab and the officers of my lord are camping in the open field. But I may enter my house to eat, to drink, and to sleep with my wife? As you live and as your soul lives, I will not do this thing!"

---

[*] 16 Euphrates River.

[12] So David said to Uriah, "Remain here another day, and I will send you back tomorrow." Uriah remained in Jerusalem that day and the following day. [13] Now David invited him to eat in his presence, and he drank until he got Uriah drunk. In the evening, he went to lie down in his lodging with the servants of his lord, but he did not go down to his house.

[14] That morning, David wrote a message to Joab and sent it by way of Uriah. [15] He wrote in the message, "Send Uriah to the front of the line where the fighting is heaviest then withdraw from him, so that he may be struck down and die."

[16] So as Joab was besieging the city, he stationed Uriah in a place where he knew fierce men were. [17] When the men of the city came out, they fought with Joab, and some people among those who served David fell; Uriah the Hittite died among them.

[18] Joab sent word to inform David of all of the events of the battle. [19] He instructed the messenger, "When you finish telling the king all the details of the battle, [20] if his anger rises and he says to you, 'Why did you approach so near to the city? Did you not know that they might shoot from the city wall? [21] Who killed Abimelek the son of Jerub-Besheth? Did not a woman throw an upper millstone on him from the city wall so that he died at Thebez? Why did you approach so near to the city wall?' You shall then say, 'Additionally your servant Uriah the Hittite is dead.' "

[22] So the messenger departed and came to report to David everything that Joab had sent with him. [23] The messenger reported to David, "The men prevailed over us when they came out against us in the open field, but we drove them back to the entrance of the gate. [24] Then the archers shot at your servants from upon the city wall, and some of those who serve the king are dead. Even your servant Uriah the Hittite died."

[25] So David replied to the messenger, "Thus you shall report to Joab, 'Do not allow this thing to dismay you, for the sword devours one as well as another. Sustain your attack against the city and bring it to ruin.' Encourage him with this reply."

[26] When the wife of Uriah heard that her husband was dead, she mourned for her husband. [27] When the time of mourning was concluded, David sent for her and brought her to his house. She became his wife and bore him a son. But the thing that David had done was displeasing to the Lord.

Nathan Rebukes David

1Ch 20:1–3

12 The Lord sent Nathan to David. He came to him and said, "There were two men in a certain city. One was wealthy, but the other was poor. [2] The wealthy man had a very large flock and herd, [3] but the poor man had nothing except a single small ewe lamb that he had acquired. He nourished it and raised it together with himself and his sons. From his crumbs, it would eat; from his cup, it would drink; and in his arms it would lie. It was like a daughter to him.

[4] "There came a visitor to the wealthy man, but he was unwilling to take from his own flock or herd to prepare a meal for the wanderer who had come to him. Instead he took the poor man's ewe lamb and prepared food for the wanderer who had come to him."

[5] David became very angry because of this man. He said to Nathan, "As the Lord lives, the man who did this deserves to die. [6] And he shall restore the lamb fourfold, because he did this thing, and because he had no pity."

[7] Then Nathan told David, "You are this man! Thus says the Lord, the God of Israel: I anointed you as king over Israel and I rescued you from the hand of Saul. [8] I gave to you your master's house and your master's wives into your arms, and I gave to you the house of Israel and Judah. If this were too little, I would have continued to do for you much more. [9] Why have you despised the word of the Lord by doing evil in His sight? You struck down Uriah the Hittite with the sword, and you took his wife as a wife for yourself. You killed him with the sword of the Ammonites. [10] Now the sword will never depart from your house, because you have despised Me and have taken the wife of Uriah the Hittite to be your wife.

[11] "Thus says the Lord: See, I will raise up trouble against you from within your own house. I will take your wives before your eyes and will give them to your neighbor, and he will lie with your wives in broad daylight. [12] Although you did it secretly, I will do this thing before all of Israel, and under the sun."

[13] Then David said to Nathan, "I have sinned against the Lord." Nathan said to David, "Now the Lord has put away your sin; you shall not die. [14] Nevertheless, because by this deed you have utterly scorned the Lord, the child who is born to you shall die."

[15] Then Nathan went to his house. The Lord struck the child that the wife of Uriah had born for David, and he became sick. [16] David entreated God on behalf of the child. He fasted for a period, and he would go in and lie throughout the night on the ground. [17] The elders of his house stood beside him to rouse him from the ground, but he was not willing, nor would he consume food with them.

[18] The child died on the seventh day, and the servants of David were afraid to tell him that the child had died. They said, "When the child was alive, we would speak to him, but he would not acknowledge our voices. Now how can we say to him, 'The child is dead'? He may do harm."

[19] When David noticed that his servants were whispering to one another, he perceived that the child was dead. So he asked his servants, "Is the child dead?"

They said, "He is dead."

[20] So David arose from the ground, washed, anointed himself, and changed his garments. Then he entered the house of the Lord and worshipped. He then went in to his own house. When he asked, they set down food for him and ate.

[21] His servants said to him, "What is this thing you have done? You fasted and wept for the sake of the living child, but when the child died, you arose and ate food."

[22] He explained, "As long as the child was alive, I fasted and wept because I thought, 'Who knows? The Lord may be gracious to me, so that the child may live.' [23] But now he is dead. Why should I fast? Am I able to bring him back again? I will go to him, but he will not return to me."

The Birth of Solomon

[24] Then David comforted Bathsheba, his wife. He went to her and lay with her, so that she conceived a son. They named him Solomon, and the Lord loved him. [25] So He sent a word by way of the prophet Nathan that he should be named Jedidiah for the sake of the Lord.

[26] Now Joab fought against Rabbah of the Ammonites and assumed control of the royal city. [27] So Joab sent messengers to David and reported, "I have fought against Rabbah, and I have occupied the water supply of the city. [28] Now gather the remainder of the people, lay siege to the city, and take it. Otherwise, I myself will capture the city, and it will be called by my name."

[29] So David gathered all of the people and they went to Rabbah, fought against it, and took it. [30] David took the crown of their king from his head, and its weight was a talent[1] of gold and precious stone. It was placed upon the head of David. He brought out large quantities of plunder from the city. [31] He brought out the people who were in it, and he put them to work with saws, and iron picks, and iron axes, and sent them to work in the brick kiln. Thus he did to all of the cities of the Ammonites. Then David and all of the people returned to Jerusalem.

Amnon and Tamar

13 After this, Absalom the son of David had a beautiful sister whose name was Tamar, and Amnon the son of David fell in love with her.

[2] It depressed Amnon to the point of falling ill that Tamar his sister was a virgin, but it was impossible for Amnon to pursue her.

[3] Now Amnon had a friend whose name was Jonadab the son of Shimeah, the brother of David, and Jonadab was a very crafty individual. [4] He asked him, "Why are you, the son of the king, so sullen morning after morning? Will you not tell me?"

Amnon told him, "I am in love with Tamar, the sister of Absalom my brother."

[1] 30 About 75 pounds, or 34 kilograms.

⁵ Jonadab instructed him, "Lie down on your bed and pretend to be ill. When your father comes to see you, say to him, 'Please allow Tamar, my sister, to come and prepare some food for me. She should make the food here, so that when I see it, I may eat it from her hand.' "

⁶ So Amnon lay down and pretended to be ill. When the king came to see him, Amnon said to the king, "Please let my sister Tamar come here to make a couple of cakes, so that I may be nourished from her hand."

⁷ Then David sent word to Tamar at the house, "Please go to the house of Amnon your brother, and prepare food for him." ⁸ So Tamar went to the house of Amnon her brother, where he was lying. She took the dough, kneaded it, and made the cakes before him. Then she baked them. ⁹ Then she took the baking tray and served the cakes to him, but he refused to eat.

Amnon said, "Send everyone away." So they all left him. ¹⁰ Then Amnon said to Tamar, "Bring the food into the bedroom that I may eat from your hand." So Tamar took the cakes that she had made and brought them in the bedroom to Amnon her brother. ¹¹ When she brought them close for him to eat, he took hold of her and said, "Come, lie with me, my sister."

¹² She pled with him, "No, my brother, do not violate me, for such a thing is not to be done in Israel. Do not carry out this awful thing. ¹³ As for me, where could I escape my disgrace? And you would be like one of the fools in Israel. Now, please speak to the king, for he will not withhold me from you." ¹⁴ But he refused to listen to her. So, being stronger than her, he overpowered her and lay with her.

¹⁵ Then Amnon hated her greatly, so that the hatred with which he hated her was greater than the love with which he had loved her. And Amnon said to her, "Get up, go away."

¹⁶ She said to him, "No, because this great offense of dismissing me is worse than the other which you did to me."

But he refused to listen to her. ¹⁷ He called his personal servant and said, "Send this woman out from me, and secure the door behind her." ¹⁸ Now she was wearing a long robe, because the virgin daughters of the king were clothed in such garments. So his servant put her out and secured the door behind her. ¹⁹ So Tamar put ashes on her head and tore the long robe that she was wearing. She put her hand on her head and left, wailing as she went.

²⁰ Absalom her brother said to her, "Has Amnon your brother been with you? Keep silent for now, my sister. He is your brother. Do not take this thing to heart." So Tamar stayed in the house of Absalom, her brother, a desolate woman.

²¹ When King David heard about these things, he was very angry. ²² And Absalom would not speak with Amnon, either pleasantly or angrily; but Absalom hated Amnon because he had raped his sister Tamar.

Absalom Kills Amnon

²³ Two full years later, the sheepshearers of Absalom were in Baal Hazor, near Ephraim, and Absalom invited all of the sons of the king. ²⁴ Then Absalom came to the king and requested, "Your servant has sheepshearers; will the king and his servants kindly go with your servant?"

²⁵ The king said to Absalom, "No, my son, we must not all go or we will be a burden to you." When he urged him, he refused to go, but gave him his blessing.

²⁶ Absalom said, "If not, allow my brother Amnon to go with us."

But the king replied to him, "Why should he go with you?" ²⁷ But Absalom urged him until he sent Amnon and all of the king's sons along with him.

²⁸ Now, Absalom had commanded his servant, "Look for Amnon to become carefree on account of the wine. Then I will say to you, 'Strike Amnon, and kill him.' Do not be afraid, for am not I myself commanding you? Be strong and brave." ²⁹ So, the servants of Absalom did to Amnon that which Absalom had commanded. Then the sons of the king arose, each mounting his mule, and fled.

³⁰ While they were on the way, the report reached David: "Absalom struck down all of the sons of the king, and there is not one of them remaining." ³¹ Then the king arose, tore his garments,

and lay on the ground, while all of his servants who were standing nearby tore their garments.

³² But Jonadab, the son of David's brother Shimeah, said, "My lord should not think that they have killed all of the servants who are the king's sons. Amnon alone is dead, for this has been determined from the day he raped Tamar, his sister, by the very declaration of Absalom. ³³ Now, my lord the king should not take this matter to heart, thinking that all of the king's sons are dead. Instead Amnon alone is dead."

³⁴ Absalom fled.

Now when the servant who was keeping watch looked up, he saw many people coming on the road beyond him, around the hill. ³⁵ So Jonadab said to the king, "See, the king's sons are coming. As your servant spoke, so it is."

³⁶ As soon as he had finished speaking, the sons of the king arrived, lifted their voices, and wept. The king and all of his servants also wept loudly.

³⁷ Now Absalom fled and went to Talmai the son of Ammihud, king of Geshur, but David mourned over his son every day.

³⁸ When Absalom fled and went to Geshur, he was there for three years. ³⁹ Then King David longed to go out to Absalom, for he was consoled over the death of Amnon.

Absalom Returns to Jerusalem

14 Now Joab the son of Zeruiah recognized that the king's mind was on Absalom. ² So Joab sent a request to Tekoa and brought from there a wise woman. He instructed her, "Act as if you are observing mourning rites. Put on mourning garments, and do not anoint yourself with oil, but act like a woman who has been mourning over the dead like this for many days. ³ Then come to the king and speak to him in this manner." Thus Joab put the words in her mouth.

⁴ As the Tekoan woman spoke to the king, she fell on her face toward the ground and bowed low. Then she said, "Help me, O king."

⁵ The king said to her, "What troubles you?"

She responded, "Alas, I am a widow, and my husband is dead. ⁶ Furthermore, your servant had two sons. The two of them were fighting in the field, but there was no one to separate them. One struck the other and killed him. ⁷ Now the entire family has risen up against your maidservant, and they said, 'Deliver him who struck his brother, so that we may kill him for the life of his brother whom he killed, and we will destroy the heir also.' So they will extinguish my remaining ember, and leave my husband neither name nor remnant on the face of the earth."

⁸ Then the king said to the woman, "Go to your house, and I will give orders concerning you."

⁹ The Tekoan woman responded to the king, "May guilt rest upon me and the house of my father, my lord the king, and may the king and his throne be blameless."

¹⁰ The king said, "Whoever speaks to you, bring him to me, and he will not cause you harm again."

¹¹ Then she said, "May the king remember the Lᴏʀᴅ your God so that the avenger of blood will not continue to destroy, lest they exterminate my son."

He said, "As the Lᴏʀᴅ lives, not one hair of your son will fall to the ground."

¹² Then the woman said, "Allow your servant to speak a word to my lord the king."

So he said, "Speak."

¹³ The woman said, "Why have you planned like this against the people of God? The king's speaking this word is like a self-conviction, for the king has not brought back his own banished one. ¹⁴ We will surely die and are like water spilled on the ground, which cannot be gathered up again. Yet God does not take away a life; He devises plans so that His banished ones will not be cast out from Him.

¹⁵ "So now I have come to speak to my lord the king about this matter because the people have made me afraid. So, I thought, 'I will speak to the king. Perhaps the king will perform the request of his servant. ¹⁶ For the king may accept my request to deliver his servant from the hand of the man who would destroy me and my son from the inheritance of God.'

[17] "So, your servant thought, 'May the word of my lord the king provide rest. For like the angel of God, my lord the king discerns good from evil. May the LORD your God be with you.' "

[18] Then the king answered and said to the woman, "Please do not conceal from me anything that I ask you."

The woman said, "May my lord the king please speak."

[19] The king said, "Is the hand of Joab with you in all of this?"

The woman answered and said, "As your soul lives, my lord the king, there is no turning right or left from anything that you spoke, my lord the king, for your servant Joab is the very one who commanded me and placed all of these words in my mouth. [20] In order to change this situation, your servant Joab did this thing; but my lord is wise, as with the wisdom of the angel of God, so as to discern everything happening in the land."

[21] Then the king said to Joab, "This is what I will do. Go and bring back the young man Absalom."

[22] Then Joab fell with his face to ground and bowed low and blessed the king. Joab said, "Today your servant knows that I have found favor in your eyes, my lord the king, since the king has granted the request of his servant."

[23] Then Joab arose and went to Geshur, and he brought Absalom to Jerusalem. [24] The king said, "Let him turn to his own house. He shall not come into my presence." So Absalom turned to his house and did not come into the king's presence.

David Forgives Absalom

[25] In all of Israel, there was no man as handsome as Absalom. From the sole of his foot to the top of his head, there was not a blemish on him. [26] When he cut the hair of his head (and at the end of every year he cut it, for it was heavy on him), he weighed the hair from his head at two hundred shekels,[1] according to the king's standard.

[27] There were born to Absalom three sons and one daughter whose name was Tamar. She was a beautiful woman.

[28] Absalom lived in Jerusalem for two full years without coming into the king's presence. [29] Then Absalom sent a message to Joab, requesting that he send him to the king, but he was not willing to come to him. So he sent a second message, but still he was not willing to come. [30] Then he said to his servants, "See, Joab's field is next to mine, and he has barley there. Go, set it on fire." So the servants of Absalom set the field on fire.

[31] Then Joab arose, came to Absalom at his house, and said to him, "Why have your servants set my plot of land on fire?"

[32] Absalom said to Joab, "I sent a message to you, saying: Come, so that I may send you to the king, asking, 'Why have I come from Geshur? It would be better for me to be there still.' Now, let me go before the king, and if there is still guilt with me, may he put me to death."

[33] So Joab came and reported this to him. Then he summoned Absalom. So he came to the king, bowed low to him, his face on the ground before the king; then the king kissed Absalom.

Absalom's Conspiracy

15 After this Absalom acquired for himself a chariot, horses, and fifty men to run before him. [2] Absalom would go early and stand beside the way into the gate. When any man who had a dispute concerning which he had come to the king for a judgment approached, Absalom would call to him and say, "Which city are you from?" And he would say, "Your servant is from one of the tribes of Israel." [3] Then Absalom would say to him, "Look, your claim is good and right, but there is no one to hear you on behalf of the king." [4] Absalom would continue, "If I were appointed a judge in the land, then every man who had a claim could come and I would give him justice."

[5] When a man would approach to bow before him, he would reach out, embrace him, and kiss him. [6] Absalom acted this way toward every Israelite who came to the king for a judgment. So Absalom stole the hearts of the men of Israel.

[7] After forty years, Absalom said to the king, "Please allow me to go fulfill my vow that I made to the LORD in Hebron. [8] For your servant made a vow when I was dwelling in Geshur in Aram, saying: If indeed the LORD will bring me back to Jerusalem, then I will serve the LORD."

[9] The king said to him, "Go in peace." So he arose and went to Hebron.

[10] But Absalom sent scouts throughout all of the tribes of Israel, saying, "When you hear the sound of the horn, say: Absalom has become king in Hebron." [11] Now two hundred men went with Absalom from Jerusalem, invited and unsuspecting; they did not know anything. [12] Absalom sent for Ahithophel the Gilonite, the advisor of David, from his city Giloh, while he was offering the sacrifices. Now the conspiracy was strong, for the number of people with Absalom was continually growing.

David Flees Jerusalem

[13] A messenger came to David and said, "The hearts of the men of Israel are following Absalom."

[14] David said to all of his servants who were with him in Jerusalem, "Get up. We must flee or there will be no escape from Absalom for us. Hurry up and leave, or he will soon reach us and bring disaster upon us, striking the city with the edge of the sword."

[15] The king's servants said to the king, "Whatever our lord the king decides, we are your servants."

[16] So the king left with his entire house after him, but he left behind ten women, concubines, to watch over the house. [17] So the king left with all of the people after him, and they came to a stop at the furthest house. [18] Now all his servants passed on beside him, all the Kerethites, all the Pelethites, and all the Gittites, six hundred men who had followed him from Gath, passed on before the king.

[19] The king said to Ittai the Gittite, "Why are you also going with us? Go back and dwell with the king, for you are a foreigner and, moreover, exiled from your own place. [20] You came only yesterday. Shall I cause you to go roaming around with us today? I am going where I go. Go back, and take back your brothers with you. Mercy and truth be with you."

[21] Ittai answered the king and said, "As the LORD lives and as lives my lord the king, only in the place where my lord the king is, whether for death or for life, there alone will your servant be."

[22] So David said to Ittai, "Go on, pass by." So Ittai the Gittite passed by, along with all of his men and all of the children and elderly who were with him.

[23] The whole land wept with a loud voice as all the people passed by. Now the king was crossing over the brook Kidron, and all of the people were crossing over on the road to the wilderness.

[24] And also Zadok and all of the Levites with him were carrying the ark of the covenant of God. They set down the ark of God, and Abiathar came up until all of the people had finished passing from the city.

[25] The king said to Zadok, "Take the ark of God back to the city. If I have found favor in the eyes of the LORD, He will bring me back and allow me to see both it and its resting place. [26] But if He should say now, 'I take no delight in you,' here I am. May He do to me what seems good to Him."

[27] The king also said to Zadok the priest, "Are you not a seer? Return to the city in peace with your two sons, your son Ahimaaz and Jonathan the son of Abiathar. [28] I will wait at the fords of the wilderness until word from you comes to inform me." [29] So Zadok and Abiathar returned the ark of God to Jerusalem, and they remained there.

[30] David went up the ascent of the Mount of Olives, weeping as he went. His head was covered and he went barefoot. Then all of the people who were with him each covered his head and went up, weeping as they went. [31] Now it was reported to David that Ahithophel was conspiring with Absalom, and David said, "O LORD, make the advice of Ahithophel folly."

[32] When David came to the summit where he would worship God, Hushai the Arkite approached him with his coat torn and dirt on his head. [33] David said to him, "If you pass on with me, you will be a burden to me. [34] But if you return to the city, you may say to Absalom, 'I am your servant, O king, as I was a servant of your

---

[1] 26 About 5 pounds, or 2.3 kilograms.

father. As I was then, so now I am your servant,' so as to counter the advice of Ahithophel. [35] Will not Zadok and Abiathar the priests be with you there? You shall report everything that you hear from the king's house to Zadok and Abiathar the priests. [36] Their two sons Ahimaaz the son of Zadok and Jonathan the son of Abiathar will be there with them. You shall send word of everything that you hear to me by their hand."

[37] So Hushai, the friend of David, came to the city as Absalom entered Jerusalem.

David and Ziba

16 When David had passed a little beyond the summit, Ziba the servant of Mephibosheth met him, with a couple of saddled donkeys carrying two hundred loaves of bread, one hundred clusters of raisins, one hundred summer fruits, and one skin of wine.

[2] The king said to Ziba, "Why do you have these things?"

Ziba replied, "The donkeys are for the household of the king to ride. The bread and the summer fruit are for the servants to eat. The wine is for those who become weary in the wilderness to drink."

[3] The king said, "And where is your master's son?"

Ziba said to the king, "He is staying in Jerusalem, for he said, 'Today they will return to me the house of Israel and my father's kingdom.'"

[4] Then David said to Ziba, "Everything that belonged to Mephibosheth is now yours."

Ziba replied, "I bow before you. May I find favor in your sight, my lord the king."

Shimei Curses David

[5] When King David came to Bahurim, a man of the family of the house of Saul came out. His name was Shimei son of Gera, and he came out continuously cursing. [6] He threw stones at David and all of the servants of King David, as well as all of the people and all of the warriors who were at his right and left. [7] Shimei said when he cursed: "Come out! Come out! You bloodthirsty man, you scoundrel! [8] The Lord has returned upon you all the blood of the house of Saul, in whose place you have reigned. And the Lord has given the kingdom into the hand of your son Absalom. You are taken in your own evil, because you are a man of blood."

[9] Then Abishai the son of Zeruiah said to the king, "How can this dead dog curse my lord the king! Let me go over and remove his head."

[10] The king responded, "What do you have against me, sons of Zeruiah? Suppose that he curses because the Lord has said to him, 'Curse David.' Who shall then say, 'Why do you do so?'"

[11] David then said to Abishai and to all of his servants, "My son who came from my own body seeks my life, and now also this Benjamite. Leave him alone and let him curse if the Lord has so instructed him. [12] Perhaps today the Lord will look upon my guilt and return kindness instead of his cursing."

[13] So David and his men continued on the road, and Shimei went along on the hillside beside them, cursing, throwing stones, and flinging dust at them as he went. [14] The king and all of the people who were with him arrived at their destination exhausted, but he refreshed himself there.

The Advice of Ahithophel and Hushai

[15] Now Absalom and all of the Israelite people entered Jerusalem, and Ahithophel was with him. [16] When Hushai the Arkite, the friend of David, came to Absalom, Hushai said to Absalom, "Long live the king! Long live the king!"

[17] Then Absalom said to Hushai, "Is this the extent of your commitment to your friend? Why have you not gone with your friend?"

[18] Hushai said to Absalom, "No! For whom the Lord, this people, and all men of Israel have chosen, his I will be and with him I will remain. [19] Furthermore, whom shall I serve? Should it not be his son? As I served your father, so shall I be with you."

[20] Absalom said to Ahithophel, "Give your advice. What shall we do?"

[21] Ahithophel said to Absalom, "Lie with your father's concubines, whom he left to watch over the palace. When all Israel hears that you have made yourself abhorred by your father, then the hands of all who are with you will be strong." [22] So they set up a tent for Absalom on the roof, and Absalom went in to his father's concubines in the sight of all of Israel.

[23] In those days, the advice that Ahithophel gave was as when one inquired a word from God. Such was all of the advice of Ahithophel, whether that which he gave to David or to Absalom.

17 Ahithophel also said to Absalom, "Let me choose twelve thousand men so that I may arise and pursue David tonight. [2] I will overtake him while he is weary and weak and strike him with terror; all of the people who are with him will flee. Then I will strike only the king, [3] and I will return all of the people to you. When all return except the man whom you are seeking, all of the people will be at peace." [4] The advice pleased Absalom and all of the elders of Israel.

[5] So Absalom said, "Summon Hushai the Arkite so that we may hear what he has to say as well." [6] When Hushai came to Absalom, Absalom said to him, "This is what Ahithophel had advised. Should we do this thing? If not, you should tell us."

[7] Hushai said to Absalom, "At this time, the advice that Ahithophel has given is not good. [8] Moreover, Hushai said, "You know that your father and his men are warriors, and they have been provoked like a bear robbed of her cubs. Your father is a veteran of warfare. He will not spend the night with the people. [9] Even now, he has hidden himself in a ravine or some other place, and when one of them falls in the first attack, whoever hears will say, 'It was a defeat for the people who follow Absalom.' [10] Then even the valiant one, whose heart is like that of a lion, will completely despair, for all of Israel knows that your father is a warrior, and those who are with him are brave.

[11] "Therefore my advice is for all of Israel, from Dan to Beersheba, to be completely gathered to you like the multitude of the sand along the shoreline and for you to go to battle in person. [12] We will come upon him in one of the places where he may be found, and we will fall upon him like the dew upon the ground. Neither he nor any of the men who are with him will remain, not a single one. [13] If he withdraws into a city, then all of Israel will bring ropes to that city. We will raze it until it is a valley, until there cannot be found there even a pebble."

[14] Then Absalom and all of the men of Israel said, "The advice of Hushai the Arkite is better than the advice of Ahithophel." For the Lord had decided to undermine the prudent advice of Ahithophel, so that the Lord might bring calamity to Absalom.

Hushai Warns David to Escape

[15] Then Hushai said to Zadok and Abiathar the priests, "Ahithophel advised Absalom and the elders of Israel to do one thing, but I advised them to do another thing. [16] Now quickly send someone to report to David, 'Do not spend the night at the fords of the wilderness, but instead cross over. Otherwise, the king and all of the people who are with him will be swallowed up.'"

[17] Now Jonathan and Ahimaaz were waiting at En Rogel. A servant girl would go report to them, and they would go report to King David, because they could not be seen entering the city. [18] But a young man saw them and reported this to Absalom. So the two of them went quickly and came to the house of a man in Bahurim. He had a well in his courtyard, and they went down into it. [19] The wife took a covering and spread it over the opening of the well. Then she scattered grain over it so that nothing could be discerned.

[20] The servants of Absalom came to the woman at the house and said, "Where are Ahimaaz and Jonathan?"

She said, "They crossed over the brook of water." When they searched, they could not find them. So they returned to Jerusalem.

[21] After they left, they came up from the well, went, and reported to King David. They said to David, "Arise and quickly cross over the water because thus has Ahithophel advised against you." [22] So David and all of the people who were with him arose and crossed over the Jordan. By daybreak, there was not one left who had not crossed over the Jordan.

[23] When Ahithophel realized that his advice was not followed, he saddled his donkey and returned to his house in his own city. He gave instruction to his household, then he hanged himself and died; he was interred in the tomb of his father.

Absalom's Death

²⁴ David came to Mahanaim as Absalom crossed the Jordan, he and every Israelite with him. ²⁵ Now Absalom had placed Amasa over the army in the place of Joab. Now Amasa was the son of a man named Jether the Ishmaelite, who went in to Abigail the daughter of Nahash and sister of Zeruiah, the mother of Joab. ²⁶ Israel and Absalom camped in the land of Gilead.

²⁷ When David came to Mahanaim, Shobi the son of Nahash from Rabbah of the Ammonites, Makir the son of Ammiel from Lo Debar, and Barzillai the Gileadite from Rogelim ²⁸ brought bedding, metal bowls, ceramic vessels, wheat, barley, flour, roasted grain, beans, lentils, ²⁹ honey, curds, sheep, and cheese from the livestock for David and the people who were with him to eat and use. For they said, "The people are hungry, exhausted, and thirsting in the wilderness."

18 David mustered the people who were with him, and he set over them commanders of thousands and commanders of hundreds. ² Then David dispatched the people, one-third under the command of Joab, one-third under the command of Abishai the son of Zeruiah and brother of Joab, and one-third under the command of Ittai the Gittite. Then David said to the people, "I myself will go out with you."

³ But the people said, "You should not go, for if we retreat, they will not be concerned about us. Even if half of us die, they will not be concerned about us. But now you are worth ten thousand of us. Therefore, it would be better to assist us from the city."

⁴ The king said to them, "I will do what seems best to you."

So the king stood beside the gate while all of the people went out by hundreds and thousands. ⁵ The king commanded Joab, Abishai, and Ittai, "Deal gently with the young man Absalom." All of the people heard the king instruct the commanders concerning Absalom.

⁶ So the people went out toward Israel in the field, but the fighting occurred in the forest of Ephraim. ⁷ The people of Israel were defeated there by the servants of David. That day the defeat was extensive, twenty thousand men. ⁸ The fighting spread across the land, and the people consumed by the forest were more numerous than those consumed by the sword that day.

⁹ Absalom was encountered by some of the servants of David. Now Absalom was riding on his mule. When the mule went under the branches of a very large tree, his head was caught in the tree. He was left in midair while the mule that was under him kept going. ¹⁰ One man saw him and reported it to Joab, saying, "I saw Absalom hanging in a tree."

¹¹ Joab said to the man who was reporting to him, "What? You saw him? Why did you not strike him on the spot, sending him to the ground? I would have given you ten shekels¹ of silver and a belt."

¹² The man said to Joab, "Not even if I had felt the weight of a thousand shekels² of silver in my hand would I have laid a hand on the king's son. In our hearing the king commanded you, Abishai, and Ittai saying: Beware lest anyone touch the young man Absalom! ¹³ Otherwise, I would have worked falsehood against my own life. For nothing is hidden from the king, and you yourself would have set yourself against me."

¹⁴ Then Joab said, "I will not waste any more time with you." He took three spears in his hand and thrust them into the heart of Absalom while he was still alive in the midst of the tree. ¹⁵ Then ten young men, armor bearers for Joab, gathered around and struck down Absalom, killing him.

¹⁶ When Joab blew the horn, the people returned from pursuing Israel, for Joab held back the people. ¹⁷ Then they took Absalom, disposed of him in a large pit in the forest, and piled over him a very large heap of stones. Then all Israel fled, everyone to his home.

¹⁸ Now Absalom in his lifetime had taken and set up for himself a memorial stone in the Valley of the King, for he said, "I have no son by whom my name may be remembered." So he named the memorial stone after himself; and to this day, it is called the monument of Absalom.

David Mourns

¹⁹ Then Ahimaaz the son of Zadok said, "Allow me to run and bring the news to the king that the Lᴏʀᴅ has delivered him from the hand of his enemies."

²⁰ But Joab said to him, "You will not be a man who bears news today; you may bear news another day. Today you will not bear news because the king's son is dead."

²¹ Then Joab said to the Cushite, "Go, report to the king what you have seen." The Cushite bowed to Joab, then ran off.

²² Ahimaaz again said to Joab, "Whatever may happen, let me run also, after the Cushite."

Then Joab said, "Why is it that you want to run, my son? There is no messenger's reward for you to obtain."

²³ "Whatever happens, I want to run."

So he said to him, "Run." So Ahimaaz ran by way of the plain and passed the Cushite.

²⁴ Now David was sitting between the two gates when the watchman went up to the roof of the gate, to the city wall. He lifted his eyes and saw a man running by himself. ²⁵ The watchman called and told the king.

The king said, "If he is alone, there is news in his mouth." And he came ever closer.

²⁶ Then the watchman saw another man running. The watchman called to the gatekeeper and said, "Look there is another man running alone."

The king said, "He also is bringing news."

²⁷ The watchman said, "I think that the running of the first one is like the running of Ahimaaz."

The king said, "He is a good man and comes with good news."

²⁸ Then Ahimaaz called to the king and said, "All is well." He bowed down to the ground before the king and said, "Blessed be the Lᴏʀᴅ your God who has handed over the men who raised their hand against my lord the king."

²⁹ The king said, "Is it well for the young man Absalom?"

Ahimaaz said, "I saw a great commotion when Joab sent the servant of the king, your servant, but I do not know what it was."

³⁰ The king said, "Step aside and stand here." So he stepped aside and stood in position.

³¹ Then the Cushite came and said, "Good news for my lord the king, for today the Lᴏʀᴅ has delivered you from those who rose up against you."

³² The king said to the Cushite, "Is it well for the young man Absalom?"

The Cushite said, "May the enemies of my lord the king and all who would rise up against you to do harm become as the young man is."

³³ The king was deeply moved and went up to the upper chamber of the gate and wept. As he went he said, "O my son Absalom, my son, my son Absalom! If only I could have given my death in your stead, Absalom, my son, my son!"

19 It was reported to Joab that the king was weeping and mourning over Absalom. ² The victory that day was turned into mourning for all of the people, for the people heard that day, "The king is grieving for his son." ³ So the people entered the city by stealth that day, as a people who have been disgraced steal away when they flee from battle. ⁴ The king covered his face and called with a loud voice, "My son Absalom, my son, my son!"

⁵ Then Joab came to the king in his house and said, "Today you have shamed the faces of all of your servants who saved your life today, as well as the lives of your sons and daughters, the lives of your wives, and the lives of your concubines, ⁶ by loving those who hated you and hating those who love you. You have shown today that commanders and servants are nothing to you. I know that if Absalom were alive instead today and all of us were dead, then this would be right in your eyes. ⁷ Now go out and speak reassuringly to your servants, for I swear by the Lᴏʀᴅ that if you do not go out, no man will stay with you this night, and this will be worse for you than any calamity that has come against you from your youth until now."

¹11 About 4 ounces, or 115 grams.   ²12 About 25 pounds, or 12 kilograms.

[8] So the king arose and took his seat in the gate, and the people were all told, "The king is sitting in the gate." So all the people came before the king, but the children of Israel had fled, each to his tent.

David Returns to Jerusalem

[9] Now all of the people began to quarrel throughout all of the tribes of Israel, saying, "The king delivered us from the hand of our enemies, and he saved us from the hand of the Philistines, but now he has fled from the land on account of Absalom. [10] But Absalom, whom we anointed over us, has died in battle. Now why are you idle to bring back the king?"

[11] Then David sent word to Zadok and Abiathar the priests, saying, "Speak to the elders of Israel, saying, 'Why are you last to bring the king back to his house when the word of all Israel has come to the king, to his house? [12] You are my brother. You are my bone and my flesh. Why are you last to bring back the king?' [13] Say to Amasa, 'Are you not my bone and my flesh? May God do to me, and more so, if you are not commander of the army before me from now on in the place of Joab.'"

[14] He swayed the heart of every man of Judah as though they were one man, and they sent a message to the king: "Return, you and all of your servants."

[15] So the king returned and came as far as the Jordan, and Judah came to Gilgal to meet the king and bring the king across the Jordan. [16] Shimei the son of Gera, the Benjamite who was from Bahurim, hastened to go down with the men of Judah to meet King David. [17] With him were a thousand men from Benjamin. And Ziba, the servant of the house of Saul, with his fifteen sons and twenty servants, rushed down to the Jordan before the king. [18] They crossed the ford to bring the household of the king across and to do what was pleasing in his eyes.

Shimei the son of Gera fell before the king as he was crossing the Jordan, [19] and he said to the king, "Do not regard me as guilty, my lord, or remember how your servant went astray the day when my lord the king went out from Jerusalem. May the king not take it to heart. [20] For your servant knows that I have sinned. Therefore, I have come this day, first from all of the house of Joseph, to go down to meet my lord the king."

[21] Abishai the son of Zeruiah answered, "Shall not Shimei be put to death for this, because he cursed the anointed of the LORD?" [22] David said, "What do you sons of Zeruiah have against me that you should become an adversary to me today? Should any man in Israel be put to death today? For do I not know that today I am king over Israel?" [23] The king said to Shimei, "You will not die." The king gave him his oath.

[24] Then Mephibosheth the son of Saul went down to meet the king. He had neither dressed his feet, nor trimmed his mustache, nor washed his clothes from the day the king left until the day he came back in peace. [25] When he came from Jerusalem to meet the king, the king said to him, "Why did you not go with me, Mephibosheth?" [26] He said, "My lord, O king, my servant deceived me. For your servant said, 'I will saddle the mule for myself in order to ride on it and go with the king,' because your servant is lame. [27] But he has slandered your servant to my lord the king. Still my lord the king is as the angel of God, so do what seems best to you. [28] For all my father's house were but dead men before my lord the king. Yet you set your servant among those who eat at your table. What right do I have to cry out any more to the king?"

[29] The king said to him, "Why do you still speak of your affairs? I say that you and Ziba shall divide the field." [30] Mephibosheth said to the king, "Let him even take everything, since my lord the king has come safely to his house."

[31] Now Barzillai the Gileadite had come down from Rogelim in order to see the king across the Jordan. [32] Barzillai was very old, eighty years old. But he sustained the king during his stay in Mahanaim, for he was a very rich man. [33] The king said to Barzillai, "Cross over with me and I will sustain you with me in Jerusalem."

[34] Barzillai said to the king, "How many days are left in my life that I should go up with the king to Jerusalem? [35] I am now eighty years old. Can I discern what is pleasant from what is harmful? Can your servant taste what I eat and what I drink? Can I still hear the voices of men and women who sing? Why, then, should your servant be a burden to my lord the king? [36] Your servant is merely crossing over the Jordan with the king. Why should the king repay me with this reward? [37] Now allow your servant to return, that I may die in my own city with the grave of my father and my mother. But here is your servant Kimham. He will cross over with my lord the king. Do for him what seems best to you."

[38] The king said, "Kimham will cross over with me, and I will do for him what seems best to you. Whatever you require of me, I will do for you."

[39] All of the people crossed over the Jordan. And when the king had crossed over, the king kissed Barzillai and blessed him and he returned to his own place.

[40] The king passed on to Gilgal, and Kimham went on with him; all of the people of Judah and half of the people of Israel passed on with the king.

[41] Now all of the men of Israel were coming to the king and said to the king, "Why have our brothers, the men of Judah, stolen you away and brought the king and his household across the Jordan, and all of the men of David with him?"

[42] All of the men of Judah answered the men of Israel, "Because the king is our close relative. Why are you angry over this matter? Have we eaten at all at the king's expense? Has he given any gift to us?"

[43] And the men of Israel answered the men of Judah and said, "We have ten shares in the king. Therefore we also have more claim on David than you. Why then did you treat us with contempt? Were we not the first to advise bringing back our king?"

But the words of the men of Judah were harsher than the words of the men of Israel.

Sheba Rebels Against David

20 There happened to be a worthless man there whose name was Sheba the son of Bikri, a Benjamite. He sounded the trumpet and said,

"We have no share in David,
    nor do we have an inheritance in the son of Jesse;
every man to his tents, O Israel."

[2] So every man of Israel withdrew from following David and followed after Sheba the son of Bikri, but the men of Judah stayed with their king, from the Jordan as far as Jerusalem.

[3] When the king came to his house in Jerusalem, he took the ten women, the concubines whom he had left to keep watch over the house, and he placed them in custody. He provided for them but did not go in to them. They were shut up until the day of their deaths, living as in widowhood.

[4] Then the king said to Amasa, "Summon for me the men of Judah in three days, then present yourself here." [5] So Amasa went to summon Judah, but he delayed beyond the deadline determined for him.

[6] So David said to Abishai, "Now Sheba the son of Bikri will cause more harm for us than Absalom. You take your lord's servants and pursue after him. Otherwise, he will find fortified cities and escape from our sight." [7] The men of Joab went out after him, along with the Kerethites, the Pelethites, and all of the warriors; and they went out from Jerusalem to pursue after Sheba the son of Bikri.

[8] When they were at the large stone which is in Gibeon, Amasa came to meet them. Now Joab was dressed in his battle armor, and fastened on it was a belt with a sword in its sheath at the waist. As he went forward, it fell out.

[9] Joab said to Amasa, "Is it well with you, my brother?" and he took Amasa by the beard with his right hand to kiss him. [10] Amasa was not on guard against the sword in the hand of Joab, and he struck him in the midsection spilling his entrails on the ground. He died without being struck a second time. Then Joab and Abishai his brother pursued after Sheba the son of Bikri.

[11] Now one of the young men of Joab stood by him and said, "Whoever favors Joab and whoever is for David, *let him* follow Joab." [12] Now Amasa was wallowing in his own blood in the middle

of the path. When the man saw that all of the people stood still, he moved Amasa from the path to the field and threw a covering over him, when he observed that everyone who passed by would stop. [13] Once he removed him from the path, all of the men passed by, following Joab in pursuit of Sheba the son of Bikri.

[14] He passed through all of the tribes of Israel toward Abel Beth Maakah, also passing by all of the Bikrites. Once assembled, they also came after him. [15] They came and besieged him in Abel Beth Maakah. They constructed a siege ramp against the city, standing it against the rampart. As all of the people who were with Joab were battering the city wall in order to bring it down, [16] a wise woman called from the city, "Listen! Listen! Say to Joab, 'Come closer so that I may speak with you.' " [17] When he came near, the woman said, "Are you Joab?"

He said, "I am."

She said to him, "Listen to the words of your servant," and he said, "I'm listening."

[18] She said, "In former times, they would say, 'Let them inquire carefully in Abel,' and thus they would resolve an issue. [19] I am a trustworthy and faithful one of Israel. You are attempting to destroy a city, even a mother, in Israel. Why do you swallow up the inheritance of the LORD?"

[20] Joab responded, "Far be it, far be it from me to swallow up or destroy. [21] That is not true. But a man from the hill country of Ephraim, Sheba the son of Bikri by name, has lifted his hand against King David. Only deliver him, and I will depart from the city."

And the woman said to Joab, "His head will be thrown to you over the wall."

[22] The woman, with her wisdom, came to all of the people in the city, and they cut off the head of Sheba the son of Bikri. When they threw it to Joab, he blew the horn, and they dispersed from the city, each going to his own tent. Joab returned to Jerusalem to the king.

David's Officials

[23] Now Joab was over the entire army of Israel. Benaiah the son of Jehoiada was over the Kerethites and Pelethites. [24] Adoniram was over conscripted labor. Jehoshaphat the son of Ahilud was secretary. [25] Sheva was scribe. Zadok and Abiathar were priests, [26] and also Ira the Jairite was priest to David.

David Avenges the Gibeonites

21 Now there was a famine in the days of David for three years, year after year; and David called upon the LORD. The LORD said, "There is blood guilt upon Saul and upon his house because he put the Gibeonites to death."

[2] So the king summoned the Gibeonites and spoke to them. Now the Gibeonites were not from the children of Israel. Instead they were a remnant of the Amorites. Although the children of Israel had made a pact with them, Saul attempted to destroy them in his zeal for the people of Israel and Judah. [3] David said to the Gibeonites, "What must I do for you, and with what may I appease you that you may bless the inheritance of the LORD?"

[4] The Gibeonites said to him, "We have no concern for silver or gold from Saul or his household, nor is it for us to put any man in Israel to death."

He said to them, "What are you saying I should do for you?"

[5] They said to the king, "Regarding the man who put an end to us and planned to exterminate us from the entire territory of Israel, [6] let seven of his male descendants be handed over to us, and we will hang them before the LORD at Gibeah of Saul, the chosen one of the LORD."

The king said, "I will hand them over."

[7] But the king spared Mephibosheth the son of Jonathan, the son of Saul on account of the oath of the LORD that was between them, between David and Jonathan the son of Saul. [8] So the king took the two sons of Rizpah the daughter of Aiah, Armoni and Mephibosheth, whom she had born to Saul, and the five sons of Michal the daughter of Saul, whom she had born to Adriel the son of Barzillai the Meholathite. [9] He delivered them into the hands of the Gibeonites, and they hanged them on the mountain before the LORD; the seven of them fell together. They were put to death in the first days of harvest, in the beginning of the barley harvest.

[10] Rizpah the daughter of Aiah took sackcloth and spread it for herself on the rock, from the beginning of the harvest until the rains poured on them from heaven. She did not allow the birds of the air to rest on them by day nor the animals of the field by night. [11] When it was reported to David that which Rizpah the daughter of Aiah, the concubine of Saul, had done, [12] David went and took the bones of Saul and the bones of Jonathan his son from the men of Jabesh Gilead who had secretly taken them from the plaza in Beth Shan, where the Philistines had hung them the day the Philistines struck down Saul on Gilboa. [13] He brought up the bones of Saul and the bones of Jonathan his son from there, and they gathered the bones of those who had been hanged.

[14] They interred the bones of Saul and Jonathan his son in the land of Benjamin at Zela, in the tomb of Kish, his father. They did everything that the king commanded. After that God was entreated regarding the land.

Wars With the Philistines

1Ch 20:4–8

[15] Now once again there was a battle between the Philistines and Israel. So David went down and his servants with him to fight the Philistines, and David grew weary. [16] Now Ishbi-Benob, who was among the descendants of the giant and was girded with new weaponry, had a spear weighing three hundred bronze shekels and had said that he would strike David down. [17] But Abishai the son of Zeruiah came to his aid. He struck down the Philistine and killed him. Then the men of David made an oath with him, saying, "You shall no longer come out with us to battle, so that you do not extinguish the lamp of Israel."

[18] Now afterwards there was again a battle with the Philistines at Gob. Then Sibbekai the Hushathite struck down Saph, who was among the descendants of the giant.

[19] Once again, there was a battle with the Philistines at Gob. On this occasion, Elhanan the son of Jaare-Oregim the Bethlehemite struck down Goliath the Gittite, whose spear shaft was like a weaver's beam.

[20] Once again, there was war at Gath. There was a man of stature who had six fingers on each hand and six toes on each foot, twenty-four in number. Now he also was born to the giant. [21] When he taunted Israel, Jonathan the son of Shimeah, the brother of David, struck him down.

[22] Now these four were born to the giant in Gath, and they fell by the hand of David and by the hand of his servants.

David's Song of Deliverance

Ps 18:1–50

22 Now on the day the LORD delivered him from the hand of all of his enemies and from the hand of Saul, David spoke to the LORD the words of this song. [2] He said:

The LORD is my rock and my fortress and my deliverer;
[3]   the God of my strength, in whom I will trust;
    my shield and the horn of my salvation,
  my fortress and my sanctuary;
    my Savior, You save me from violence.

[4] I call upon the LORD, who is praiseworthy,
    and I am saved from my enemies.
[5] When the waves of death encompassed me,
    the currents of destruction made me afraid.
[6] The ropes of Sheol were wrapped around me;
    the snares of death were opposite me.

[7] In my distress I called on the LORD,
    and cried out to my God;
  from His temple He heard my voice.
    My cry *reached* His ears.
[8] Then the earth quaked and trembled;
    the foundations of the heavens rumbled and shook,
    because He was angry.
[9] Smoke rose from His nostrils,
    devouring fire from His mouth;
    coals blazed forth from Him.

10 He bowed the heaven as He came down,
    with thick darkness under His feet.
11 He rode upon a cherub as He flew,
    and appeared upon the wings of the wind.
12 He made darkness canopies around Him,
    dark waters and thick clouds of the skies.
13 From the brightness before Him
    embers of fire are kindled.
14 The Lord thundered from heaven,
    and the Most High uttered His voice.
15 He sent out arrows and dispersed them;
    with lightning He sent them into confusion.
16 The channels of the sea appeared,
    the foundations of the world were exposed
    with the rebuke of the Lord,
        from the blast of breath from His nostrils.

17 He reached from on high and took me;
    He drew me out of mighty waters.
18 He rescued me from my strong enemy,
    from those who hate me;
    for they were stronger than I.
19 They confronted me in the day of my disaster,
    but the Lord was my support.
20 He brought me to the open expanse;
    He rescued me, for He delighted in me.

21 The Lord did for me according to my righteousness;
    according to the cleanness of my hands He
        recompensed me.
22 For I have kept the ways of the Lord,
    and I have not become guilty against my God.
23 For all His judgments are before me,
    and I have not abandoned His statutes.
24 I am blameless toward Him,
    and I have kept myself from guilt.
25 The Lord has recompensed me according to
        my righteousness,
    according to my cleanness in His sight.

26 With the faithful You prove Yourself faithful;
    with the blameless You prove Yourself blameless;
27 with the pure You show Yourself pure;
    but with the perverse You show Yourself shrewd.
28 You deliver a humble people;
    but Your eyes are upon the exalted to bring them down.
29 For You are my lamp, O Lord;
    the Lord illuminates my darkness.
30 For by You I can run *over* a channel;
    by my God I can leap over a wall.

31 As for God, His way is perfect;
    the word of the Lord is proven;
    He is a shield
    for all who take refuge in Him.
32 For who is God except the Lord?
    And who is a rock except our God?
33 God is my strong fortress,
    and He sets the blameless on His way.
34 He makes my feet like hinds' *feet*;
    He sets me on my high places.
35 He trains my hand for battle,
    so that my arm may bend a bow of bronze.
36 You have given me a shield of Your salvation,
    and Your humility has made me great.
37 You widen my stride under me,
    and my feet do stagger.

38 I pursued my enemies and destroyed them;
    I did not turn back until they were consumed.

39 I consumed them and shattered them so that they did
        not rise;
    they fell under my feet.
40 You girded me with strength for the battle;
    You subjugated under me those who rose up against me.
41 You caused my enemies to retreat from me;
    I destroyed those who hated me.
42 They looked, but there was no one to save them,
    to the Lord, but He did not respond.
43 I crushed them like the dust of the land,
    like the mud of the streets, I ground them and stamped
        them down.

44 You have also delivered me from the strivings of my people;
    You have kept me as the head of the nations.
    A people whom I have not known will serve me.
45   Foreigners submit to me, cringing;
    as soon as they hear, they obey me.
46 Foreigners lose heart;
    they gird themselves as they leave their fortresses.

47 The Lord lives; blessed be my rock.
    May the God of the rock of my salvation be exalted,
48 the God who gave me retribution
    and brought down peoples under me,
49   who brought me out from my enemies.
    You exalted me above those who rose up against me;
    You delivered me from violent ones.
50 Therefore, I praise You, O Lord, among the nations;
    I sing praises to Your name.

51 He is a tower of salvation for His king,
    and He acts faithfully toward His anointed,
    toward David and his descendants forever.

David's Last Words

23 Now these are the last words of David:

    The oracle of David the son of Jesse,
        the oracle of the man who was raised on high,
    the anointed of the God of Jacob,
        and the favorite psalmist of Israel:

2 The Spirit of the Lord spoke by me,
    and His word was on my tongue.
3 The God of Israel said,
    the Rock of Israel spoke to me:
    He who rules over man justly,
    who rules in the fear of God,
4 is like the light of the morning *when* the sun rises,
    a morning with no clouds,
    gleaming after the rain
        like grass from the land.

5 Is not my house like this with God?
    For He made an everlasting covenant with me,
    ordered in all things and secure.
    For *this is* all my salvation and all *my* desire;
    will He not make *it* flourish?
6 But the worthless individual is like a thorn tossed away,
        all of them,
    for they cannot be taken with the hand.
7 But the man who touches them
    must have an iron *implement* and the shaft of a spear,
    and they must be burned with fire on the spot.

David's Mighty Warriors
1Ch 11:10–41
8 These are the names of the warriors whom David had:
Josheb-Basshebeth, a Tahkemonite, was head of the three.¹ He

---

¹ 8 Or *captains*, or *thirty*. Cf. 1Ch 11:11.

was also known as Adino the Eznite, on account of eight hundred slain on one occasion.

[9] After him was Eleazar the son of Dodai the son of Ahohi. He was among the three warriors with David when they defied the Philistines who were gathered together there to fight when the men of Israel withdrew. [10] He arose and attacked the Philistines until his hand grew weary and stuck to the sword. The LORD brought about a great victory that day, and the people returned only to plunder. [11] After him was Shammah the son of Agee the Hararite. The Philistines had gathered into a troop, where the plot of the field was full of lentils, and the people fled before the Philistines. [12] He took his stand in the midst of the plot of land, defended it, and defeated the Philistines. The LORD brought about a great victory.

[13] Then three[1] of the thirty chief men went down and came to David at the cave of Adullam during the harvest. Now the Philistine army was in the Valley of Rephaim. [14] At that time, David was in the stronghold while the Philistine garrison was at Bethlehem. [15] David said longingly, "O that someone would give me a drink of water from the well in Bethlehem by the gate!" [16] The three warriors breached the Philistine camp and drew up water from the well in Bethlehem by the gate, and they brought it to David. However, he was not willing to drink it, so he poured it out as a drink offering to the LORD. [17] He said, "Far be it from me, O LORD, to drink this, the blood of the men who risked their lives." So he was not willing to drink it.

These things the three warriors did.

[18] Now Abishai, the brother of Joab and son of Zeruiah, was chief of the thirty.[2] He wielded his spear against three hundred men and killed them, and won a name beside the three. [19] Was he more honored than the three? He became their commander, but he did not attain to the three. [20] And Benaiah the son of Jehoiada was a valiant man of Kabzeel, who had done great acts. He struck down two sons of Ariel of Moab. He also went down and killed a lion in the middle of a pit on a snowy day. [21] He struck down an Egyptian, an impressive man. Now the Egyptian had a spear in his hand, but Benaiah went down to him with a staff, seized the spear from the Egyptian, and killed him with his own spear. [22] These things Benaiah the son of Jehoiada did and won for himself a name alongside the three. [23] He was more honored than the thirty, but he did not attain to the three. So David set him over his bodyguard.

[24] Among the thirty were
  Asahel the brother of Joab,
  Elhanan the son of Dodo of Bethlehem,
  [25] Shammah the Harodite,
  Elika the Harodite,
  [26] Helez the Paltite,
  Ira the son of Ikkesh the Tekoite,
  [27] Abiezer the Anathothite,
  Mebunnai the Hushathite,
  [28] Zalmon the Ahohite,
  Maharai the Netophathite,
  [29] Heled the son of Baanah the Netophathite,
  Ithai the son of Ribai from Gibeah of Benjamin,
  [30] Benaiah the Pirathonite,
  Hiddai from the brooks of Gaash,
  [31] Abi-Albon the Arbathite,
  Azmaveth the Barhumite,
  [32] Eliahba the Shaalbonite,
  of the sons of Jashen,
  Jonathan,
  [33] Shammah the Hararite,
  Ahiam the son of Sharar the Hararite,
  [34] Eliphelet the son of Ahasbai, the son of the Maakathite,
  Eliam the son of Ahithophel the Gilonite,
  [35] Hezro the Carmelite,
  Paarai the Arbite,
  [36] Igal the son of Nathan from Zobah,

the son of Hagri,
  [37] Zelek the Ammonite,
  Naharai the Beerothite, the armor bearer of Joab the son of Zeruiah,
  [38] Ira the Ithrite,
  Gareb the Ithrite,
  [39] and Uriah the Hittite.
There were thirty-seven in all.

David's Census of Israel and Judah
1Ch 21:1–17

24 Again the LORD became angry against Israel, and He incited David against them, saying, "Go and count the people of Israel and Judah."

[2] The king said to Joab the commander of the army who was with him, "Go throughout all of the tribes of Israel, from Dan to Beersheba, and muster the people so that I may know the number of the people."

[3] Joab said to the king, "May the LORD your God add to the people however many they are one hundred times over in the sight of my lord the king. But why does my lord the king so desire this thing?"

[4] However, the king's word prevailed against Joab and the commanders of the army. So Joab and the commanders of the army went out from before the king to register the people of Israel.

[5] They crossed the Jordan and camped at Aroer, south of the city, in the middle of the ravine of Gad toward Jazer. [6] They went toward Gilead to the land of Tahtim Hodshi. Then they went toward Dan Jaan and around to Sidon. [7] They went to the fortress of Tyre and all of the towns of the Hivites and Canaanites. They went to the Negev and Beersheba.

[8] They went throughout the entire land, and after nine months and twenty days, they came to Jerusalem.

[9] Joab gave the count of the census of the people to the king. There were eight hundred thousand capable men who could draw a sword in Israel, and the men of Judah were five hundred thousand.

Judgment for David's Sin

[10] Now the heart of David struck him after he had counted the people. David said to the LORD, "I have sinned greatly by what I have done. Now may the LORD take away the iniquity of your servant, for I have behaved very foolishly."

[11] When David arose in the morning, the word of the LORD came to the prophet Gad, the seer for David, saying, [12] "Go and speak to David: Thus says the LORD: Three options I am laying before you. Choose for yourself one of them, and I will do this to you."

[13] So Gad came to David and told him. He said to him, "Shall seven years of famine come to you in your land? Or shall you flee three months before your enemies while they pursue you? Or shall there be three days of plague in your land? Now consider and advise what answer I shall return to Him who sent me."

[14] David said to Gad, "I am very distressed. Let us fall by the hand of the LORD, for His mercy is great. May I not fall by the hand of man."

[15] So the LORD sent a plague upon Israel from the morning until the appointed time. Seventy thousand men from the people died, from Dan to Beersheba. [16] When the angel stretched out his hand toward Jerusalem to destroy it, the LORD relented from the calamity. He said to the angel who was annihilating the people, "Enough! Now stay your hand." The angel of the LORD was at the threshing floor of Araunah the Jebusite.

[17] On seeing the angel who was striking down the people, David said to the LORD, "I am the one who has sinned and I am the one who has done wrong. These sheep, what have they done? Please, let your hand be against me and against the house of my father."

David Builds an Altar
1Ch 21:18–26

[18] Gad came to David that day and said to him, "Go up and erect an altar to the LORD on the threshing floor of Araunah the

---

[1] 13 Text reads *thirty*, but *three* has been translated here on the basis of other textual witnesses and Masoretic marginal notation. Cf. 22:16.
[2] 18 Or *another three*, Cf. 11:20.

Jebusite." ¹⁹ So David went up according to the word of Gad, as the Lᴏʀᴅ commanded. ²⁰ When Araunah looked and saw the king and his servants coming toward him, he went out and bowed low to the king with his face on the ground.

²¹ Araunah said, "Why has my lord the king come to his servant?"

David replied, "To purchase the threshing floor from you in order to build an altar to the Lᴏʀᴅ, so that the plague may be averted from the people."

²² Araunah said to David, "Let my lord the king take and offer up what seems good to him. Here are the oxen for the burnt of-fering and the threshing sledges and yokes of the oxen for wood. ²³ Everything, O king, Araunah gives to the king." Araunah also said to the king, "May the Lᴏʀᴅ your God be favorable toward you."

²⁴ However, the king said to Araunah, "No, for I will certainly purchase from you for a fair price. I will not offer up to the Lᴏʀᴅ burnt offerings that cost me nothing."

So David purchased the threshing floor and the oxen for fifty shekels¹ of silver. ²⁵ David built an altar to the Lᴏʀᴅ there and offered burnt offerings and peace offerings. Then the land pleaded with the Lᴏʀᴅ, and the plague was averted from Israel.

1 Kings

Adonijah Seeks Kingship

1 Now King David was old and advanced in years, and they covered him with clothes, but he could not get warm. ² There-fore his servants said to him, "Let a young virgin be found for my lord the king, and let her stand before the king and care for him, and let her lie by your side so that my lord the king may keep warm."

³ So they searched for a beautiful young woman throughout the land of Israel and found Abishag, a Shunammite, and brought her to the king. ⁴ She was very beautiful and cared for the king and ministered to him, but the king did not know her intimately.

⁵ Then Adonijah the son of Haggith exalted himself, saying, "I will be king," and he assembled chariots and horsemen and fifty men to run before him. ⁶ His father had not confronted him at any time by asking, "Why have you done this?" He also was a very attractive man, and he was born next after Absalom.

⁷ He conferred with Joab the son of Zeruiah and with Abiathar the priest, and they agreed to help him. ⁸ But Zadok the priest and Benaiah the son of Jehoiada and Nathan the prophet and Shimei and Rei and David's mighty men did not join Adonijah.

⁹ Adonijah slaughtered sheep and oxen and fat cattle by the Stone of Zoheleth, which is by En Rogel, and invited all his brothers, the king's sons, and all the men of Judah, the king's servants. ¹⁰ But he did not invite Nathan the prophet, Benaiah, the mighty men, or his brother Solomon.

¹¹ Therefore Nathan spoke to Bathsheba the mother of Solomon, saying, "Have you not heard that Adonijah the son of Haggith reigns and David our lord does not know it? ¹² Now please come and let me give you some advice, so that you may save your own life as well as that of your son Solomon. ¹³ Go to King David and say to him, 'Did not you, my lord, O king, swear to your handmaid, saying: Assuredly Solomon your son shall reign after me, and he shall sit upon my throne? Why then does Adonijah reign?' ¹⁴ Then while you are still there talking with the king, I will come in and confirm your words."

¹⁵ So Bathsheba went to the king's chamber. Now the king was very old, and Abishag the Shunammite ministered to him. ¹⁶ Bath-sheba bowed and prostrated herself before the king.

And the king said, "What do you want?"

¹⁷ And she said to him, "My lord, you swore by the Lᴏʀᴅ your God to your handmaid, saying: Assuredly Solomon your son shall reign after me, and he shall sit upon my throne. ¹⁸ But Adonijah reigns, and now, my lord, O king, you are unaware. ¹⁹ He has slain oxen and fat cattle and sheep in abundance and has invited all the sons of the king and Abiathar the priest and Joab the commander of the army, but he has not invited your servant Solomon. ²⁰ And you, my lord, O king, all the eyes of Israel are upon you that you should tell them who shall sit on the throne of my lord the king after him. ²¹ Otherwise it shall be that when my lord the king sleeps with his fathers, I and my son Solomon shall be considered offenders."

²² While she was still talking with the king, Nathan the prophet also came in. ²³ The king was told, "Nathan the prophet is here," and when he entered the king's presence, he bowed himself before the king with his face to the ground.

²⁴ Nathan said, "My lord, O king, have you said, 'Adonijah shall reign after me, and he shall sit upon my throne'? ²⁵ For he has gone down this day and has slain oxen, fat cattle, and sheep in abundance and has invited all the king's sons, the commanders of the guard, and Abiathar the priest, and they eat and drink with him, saying, 'God save King Adonijah!' ²⁶ But he has not invited me, your servant, or Zadok the priest or Benaiah the son of Jehoiada or your servant Solomon. ²⁷ Is this thing done by my lord the king, and you have not let your servants know who should sit on the throne of my lord the king after him?"

Solomon Becomes King
1Ch 29:21–25

²⁸ Then King David answered and said, "Call Bathsheba to me." And she came into the king's presence and stood before the king.

²⁹ The king vowed, "As the Lᴏʀᴅ lives, who has redeemed my soul out of all distress, ³⁰ even as I swore to you by the Lᴏʀᴅ God of Israel, saying, 'Assuredly Solomon your son shall reign after me, and he shall sit upon my throne in my stead,' even so will I certainly do this day."

³¹ Then Bathsheba bowed with her face to the ground in rever-ence to the king and said, "Let my lord King David live forever."

³² King David said, "Call Zadok the priest, Nathan the prophet, and Benaiah the son of Jehoiada for me." So they came before the king. ³³ And the king said to them, "Take with you the servants of your lord, and cause Solomon my son to ride upon my own mule, and bring him down to Gihon. ³⁴ And let Zadok the priest and Nathan the prophet there anoint him king over Israel, and blow the trumpet and say, 'God save King Solomon!' ³⁵ Then you shall come up after him. And he shall come and sit on my throne, for he will be king in my place as I have appointed him to be ruler over Israel and over Judah."

³⁶ Benaiah the son of Jehoiada answered the king and said, "Amen! May the Lᴏʀᴅ, the God of my lord the king, also say so! ³⁷ As the Lᴏʀᴅ has been with my lord the king, may He also be with Solomon and make his throne greater than the throne of my lord King David."

³⁸ So Zadok the priest, Nathan the prophet, Benaiah the son of Jehoiada, and the Kerethites and the Pelethites went down and had Solomon ride on King David's mule and brought him to Gi-hon. ³⁹ Zadok the priest took a horn of oil out of the tabernacle and anointed Solomon. Then they blew the trumpet, and all the

¹ 24 About 1.25 pounds, or 575 grams.

people said, "God save King Solomon!" [40] All the people came up to see him and played flutes and greatly rejoiced, so that the earth shook at the sound.

[41] Adonijah and all the guests that were with him heard the commotion as they were finishing their meal, and when Joab heard the sound of the trumpet, he said, "Why is the city so loud and in an uproar?"

[42] While he was speaking, Jonathan the son of Abiathar the priest came. Adonijah said to him, "Come in, for you are a valiant man and bring good tidings."

[43] Jonathan answered Adonijah, saying, "Surely our lord King David has made Solomon king. [44] The king has sent with him Zadok the priest, Nathan the prophet, Benaiah the son of Jehoiada, and the Kerethites, and the Pelethites. And they had him ride on the king's mule. [45] And Zadok the priest and Nathan the prophet have anointed him king in Gihon, and they have come up from their rejoicing, so that the city is in an uproar. This is the noise that you heard. [46] Also Solomon sits on the throne of the kingdom. [47] Moreover, the king's servants came to bless our lord King David, saying, 'May God make the name of Solomon better than your name and make his throne greater than your throne.' And the king bowed himself upon the bed. [48] The king also said, 'Blessed be the LORD God of Israel, who has given one to sit on my throne this day so that I could see with my own eyes.' "

[49] All the guests that were with Adonijah were afraid and rose up and went on their way. [50] Adonijah feared Solomon. So he got up and went to the altar and held on to its horns. [51] Then Solomon was told, "Adonijah fears King Solomon, for he has caught hold of the horns on the altar, saying 'Let King Solomon swear to me today that he will not slay his servant with the sword.' "

[52] And Solomon said, "If he will show himself a worthy man, not one of his hairs will fall to the ground, but if wickedness is found in him, he shall die." [53] So King Solomon sent for him, and they brought him down from the altar, and he came and bowed himself to King Solomon. And Solomon said to him, "Go to your house."

David's Charge to Solomon

1Ch 29:26–28

2 Now it was coming close to the day of David's death, and he gave his son Solomon a charge, saying:

[2] "I am going the way of all the earth. Be strong, and show yourself to be a man. [3] And keep the charge of the LORD your God, walking in His ways, keeping His statutes, His commandments, His judgments, and His testimonies, as it is written in the Law of Moses, that you may prosper in all that you do and wherever you turn, [4] that the LORD may carry out His word that He spoke concerning me, saying, 'If your children take heed to their way, to walk before Me in faithfulness with all their hearts and with all their souls, you shall not fail to have a man on the throne of Israel.'

[5] "Moreover, you know also what Joab the son of Zeruiah did to me, what he did to the two commanders of the army of Israel, to Abner the son of Ner and to Amasa the son of Jether, whom he killed, shedding the blood of war in a time of peace. He spilled their blood on the belt that was around his waist and on the shoes of his feet. [6] Do the right thing according to your wisdom, and do not let his gray head go down to the grave in peace.

[7] "But show kindness to the sons of Barzillai the Gileadite, and let them eat at your table, for with such loyalty they supported me when I fled from your brother Absalom.

[8] "There is also with you Shimei the son of Gera, a Benjamite from Bahurim, who cursed me with a grievous curse in the day when I went to Mahanaim. But when he came down to meet me at the Jordan, I swore to him by the LORD, saying, 'I will not put you to death with the sword.' [9] Now therefore do not hold him guiltless, for you are a wise man and know what you ought to do to him. Bring his gray head down to the grave with blood."

[10] So David slept with his fathers and was buried in the City of David. [11] David reigned over Israel forty years. He reigned seven years in Hebron and thirty-three years in Jerusalem. [12] So Solomon sat upon the throne of his father David, and his kingdom was firmly established.

The Throne of Solomon Established

[13] Then Adonijah the son of Haggith came to Bathsheba the mother of Solomon. And she said, "Do you come in peace?"

And he said, "*I come* peaceably." [14] Then he said, "I have something to say to you."

And she said, "Speak."

[15] He said, "You know that the kingdom was mine and that all Israel viewed me as the king. However, the kingdom has become my brother's, for it was given to him by the LORD. [16] And now I ask one petition of you; do not deny me."

She said to him, "Keep speaking."

[17] And he said, "Please speak to Solomon the king, for he will not refuse you, that he may give me Abishag the Shunammite as a wife."

[18] Bathsheba said, "Very well, I will speak to the king on your behalf."

[19] So Bathsheba went to King Solomon to speak to him on behalf of Adonijah. The king rose up to meet her and bowed to her. Then he sat down on his throne and had a seat placed at his right hand for her to sit upon. [20] Then she said, "I desire one small petition of you. Please do not deny me."

And the king said to her, "Ask, my mother, for I will not refuse you."

[21] She said, "Let Abishag the Shunammite be given as a wife to Adonijah your brother."

[22] King Solomon answered his mother, "Now why do you ask Abishag the Shunammite for Adonijah? Ask for him the kingdom also, for he is my elder brother. Ask not only for him, but also for Abiathar the priest, and for Joab the son of Zeruiah."

[23] Then King Solomon swore by the LORD, saying, "May God do so to me and more also if this word does not cost Adonijah his life. [24] Now therefore as the LORD lives, who has established me and set me on the throne of David my father and who has made me a house as He promised, Adonijah shall be put to death this day." [25] So King Solomon dispatched Benaiah the son of Jehoiada, and he executed him.

[26] The king said to Abiathar the priest, "Go to Anathoth, to your own fields, for you are worthy of death. But I will not at this time put you to death, because you bore the ark of the Lord GOD before David my father and because you shared in all the hardships my father endured." [27] So Solomon expelled Abiathar from being priest to the LORD, thus fulfilling the word of the LORD that He had spoken concerning the house of Eli in Shiloh.

[28] Then word came to Joab, for Joab had followed Adonijah, though he did not support Absalom. And Joab fled to the tabernacle of the LORD and caught hold of the horns of the altar. [29] King Solomon was told that Joab had fled to the tabernacle of the LORD and was by the altar. Then Solomon sent Benaiah the son of Jehoiada, saying, "Go and execute him."

[30] So Benaiah came to the tabernacle of the LORD and said to him, "Thus says the king, 'Come forth.' "

And he said, "No, I will die here."

And Benaiah told the king all Joab said.

[31] The king said to him, "Do as he has said, strike him down and bury him, and thus take away from me and my father's house the guilt for the blood Joab shed without cause. [32] The LORD shall return his blood upon his own head, for he attacked two men more righteous and better than he—Abner the son of Ner, commander of the army of Israel, and Amasa the son of Jether, commander of the army of Judah—and killed them with the sword when my father David was unaware. [33] Therefore their blood shall return upon the head of Joab and upon the head of his seed forever, but upon David and upon his seed and upon his house and upon his throne shall the peace of the LORD rest forever."

[34] So Benaiah the son of Jehoiada went up and attacked and killed him, and he was buried in his own house in the wilderness. [35] The king put Benaiah the son of Jehoiada over the army in place of Joab and put Zadok the priest in the place of Abiathar.

[36] The king sent and called for Shimei and said to him, "Build a house for yourself in Jerusalem, and dwell there, and never leave the city. [37] For on the day you go out and pass over the Kidron

Valley, know for certain that you will surely die. Your blood shall be on your own head."

38 Shimei said to the king, "What you say is good. As my lord the king has said, so will your servant do." And Shimei lived in Jerusalem many days.

39 It came about that at the end of three years, two servants of Shimei ran away to Achish son of Maakah king of Gath. And they told Shimei, saying, "Your servants are in Gath." 40 Shimei arose, saddled his donkey, and went to Gath to Achish to look for his servants. And Shimei went and brought his servants from Gath.

41 Solomon was told that Shimei had gone from Jerusalem to Gath and had returned. 42 The king sent and called for Shimei and said to him, "Did I not make you swear by the LORD and warned you, saying, 'Know for certain that on the day you go out and walk abroad anywhere, you shall surely die'? And you said to me, 'What you say is good; I will obey.' 43 Why then have you not kept the oath of the LORD and the commandment that I gave you?"

44 The king also said to Shimei, "You know all the wickedness in your heart and what you did to David my father. Therefore the LORD shall return your wickedness on your own head. 45 But King Solomon shall be blessed, and the throne of David shall be established before the LORD forever."

46 So the king commanded Benaiah the son of Jehoiada, who went out and attacked him so that he died.

And the kingdom was established in the hand of Solomon.

Solomon Asks for Wisdom
2Ch 1:2–13

3 Solomon made a treaty with Pharaoh king of Egypt. He married Pharaoh's daughter and brought her to the City of David until he finished building his palace, the house of the LORD, and the wall around Jerusalem. 2 The people were sacrificing at the high places, because no house had yet been built for the name of the LORD. 3 Solomon loved the LORD, walking in the statutes of his father David, though he sacrificed and burned incense at the high places.

4 The king went to Gibeon to sacrifice there, for that was the great high place, and he offered a thousand burnt offerings on that altar. 5 While he was in Gibeon, the LORD appeared to Solomon in a dream at night, and He said, "Ask what you want from Me."

6 Solomon answered, "You have shown great mercy to your servant David my father, because he walked before You in faithfulness, righteousness, and uprightness of heart toward You. And You have shown him great kindness in giving him a son to sit on his throne this day.

7 "Now, O LORD, my God, You have made Your servant king in place of my father David, and I am still a little child and do not know how to go out or come in. 8 And Your servant is in the midst of Your people whom You have chosen, a great people, so numerous that they cannot be numbered or counted. 9 Give Your servant therefore an understanding heart to judge Your people, that I may discern between good and bad, for who is able to judge among so great a people?"

10 It pleased the Lord that Solomon had asked this. 11 God said to him, "Because you have asked this and have not asked for yourself long life or riches or the lives of your enemies, but have asked for yourself wisdom so that you may have discernment in judging, 12 I now do according to your words. I have given you a wise and an understanding heart, so that there has never been anyone like you in the past, and there shall never arise another like you. 13 I have also given you what you have not asked, both riches and honor, so that no kings will compare to you all of your days. 14 If you will walk in My ways, keeping My statutes and My commandments as your father David did, then I will lengthen your days." 15 Solomon awoke and found it was a dream.

Then he came to Jerusalem and stood before the ark of the covenant of the LORD and offered up burnt offerings and peace offerings and made a feast for all of his servants.

The Wisdom of Solomon
16 At that time, two women who were prostitutes came and stood before the king. 17 The first woman said, "O my lord, this woman and I live in the same house, and I bore a child with her in the house. 18 Three days after I gave birth, she also had a child, and we were together. There was no one else with us in the house, only the two of us were in the house.

19 "Then this woman's child died during the night because she rolled over on it. 20 She got up at midnight and took my son from beside me while your servant slept and laid him at her bosom and laid her dead child at my bosom. 21 When I rose in the morning to feed my child, it was dead. But when I looked closely in the morning *light*, I recognized that it was not my son whom I bore."

22 The other woman said, "No, the living is my son, and the dead is your son."

And she said, "No, the dead is your son, and the living is my son." Thus they spoke before the king.

23 Then the king said, "One says, 'This is my son who lives, and your son is the dead,' and the other says, 'No, but your son is dead, and my son is the living.' "

24 So the king said, "Bring me a sword." And they brought a sword before the king. 25 The king said, "Divide the living child in two, and give half to the one and half to the other."

26 Then the woman whose child was the living one spoke to the king, for she yearned with compassion for her son, and she said, "O my lord, give her the living child, and do not kill it."

But the other said, "Let it be neither mine nor yours and divide it."

27 Then the king answered and said, "Give her the living child, and do not slay it. She is its mother."

28 All Israel heard of the king's judgment, and they feared the king, for they saw that the wisdom of God was in him, to execute sound judgment.

The Court of Solomon

4 So King Solomon was king over all Israel. 2 These were the officials in his court:

Azariah the son of Zadok was the priest.
3 Elihoreph and Ahijah, the sons of Shisha, were secretaries. Jehoshaphat the son of Ahilud was the recorder;
4 Benaiah the son of Jehoiada was over the army. Zadok and Abiathar were priests.
5 Azariah the son of Nathan was over the officers, and Zabud the son of Nathan was principal officer and the king's friend.
6 Ahishar was over the household, and Adoniram the son of Abda was over the forced labor.

7 Solomon had twelve officers over all Israel who made provision for the king and his household. Each man was assigned a month to make provision. 8 These are their names:

the son of Hur in Mount Ephraim;
9 the son of Deker in Makaz and in Shaalbim and Beth Shemesh and Elon Bethhanan;
10 the son of Hesed in Arubboth (to him belonged Sokoh and all the land of Hepher);
11 the son of Abinadab in all the region of Dor (he had Taphath the daughter of Solomon as his wife);
12 Baana the son of Ahilud in Taanach, Megiddo, and all Beth Shan that is by Zarethan beneath Jezreel, and from Beth Shan to Abel Meholah as far as the other side of Jokmeam;
13 the son of Geber in Ramoth Gilead (to him pertained the towns of Jair the son of Manasseh which are in Gilead, and also the region of Argob which is in Bashan, sixty great cities with walls and iron bars);
14 Ahinadab the son of Iddo in Mahanaim;
15 Ahimaaz in Naphtali (he had taken Basemath the daughter of Solomon as his wife);
16 Baana the son of Hushai in Asher and in Aloth;
17 Jehoshaphat the son of Paruah in Issachar;
18 Shimei the son of Ela in Benjamin;
19 Geber the son of Uri in the country of Gilead, the country of Sihon king of the Amorites and of Og king of Bashan. He was the only officer who was in that region.

The Wealth of Solomon

20 Judah and Israel had a large populace, as numerous as the sand by the sea. They ate and drank and were happy. 21 Solomon reigned over all kingdoms from the River[1] to the land of the Philistines and to the border of Egypt. The people brought presents and served Solomon all the days of his life.

22 Solomon's provision for one day was thirty kors[2] of fine flour and sixty kors[3] of meal, 23 ten fat oxen and twenty pasture-fed cattle, a hundred sheep in addition to deer, roebucks, gazelle, and fatted poultry. 24 For he had dominion over all the region on this side of the River[4] from Tiphsah to Gaza, over all the kings on this side of the River,[5] and he had peace on all borders of his land. 25 Judah and Israel lived safely, every man under his vine and under his fig tree, from Dan to Beersheba all the days of Solomon.

26 Solomon had forty thousand stalls of horses for his chariots and twelve thousand horsemen.

27 Those officers made provision for King Solomon and for all who came to King Solomon's table, every man in his month, and they lacked nothing. 28 Barley also and straw for the horses and dromedaries were brought to the place where the officers were, every man according to his charge.

29 God gave Solomon wisdom and great depth of understanding as well as compassion, as vast as the sand on the seashore. 30 Solomon's wisdom excelled the wisdom of all the people of the East country and all the wisdom of Egypt. 31 For he was wiser than all other men, wiser than Ethan the Ezrahite, Heman, Kalkol, and Darda, the sons of Mahol; his fame spread throughout all the surrounding nations. 32 He spoke three thousand proverbs, and his songs numbered a thousand and five. 33 He spoke of trees, from the cedar tree that is in Lebanon to the hyssop that springs out of the wall. He also spoke of beasts and of fowl and of insects and fish. 34 People from all over came to hear the wisdom of Solomon, from all kings of the earth, who had heard of his wisdom.

Plans to Build the Temple

2Ch 2:1–18

5 Now Hiram king of Tyre sent his servants to Solomon, for he had heard that they had anointed him king in place of his father, and Hiram had always loved David. 2 And Solomon sent *word* to Hiram, saying,

3 "You know how David my father was unable to build a house for the name of the LORD his God because of the wars all around him, until the LORD put his enemies under his feet. 4 But now the LORD my God has given me peace on every side, so that there is neither adversary nor misfortune. 5 So know that I plan to build a house to honor the name of the LORD my God, just as the LORD spoke to my father David, saying, 'Your son, whom I will set on your throne after you, shall build a house to honor My name.'

6 "Now therefore command that cedar trees from Lebanon be cut down for me, and my servants shall be with your servants, and I will pay your servants whatever you command, for you know that there are none among my people who can cut timber like the Sidonians."

7 When Hiram heard the words of Solomon, he rejoiced greatly and said, "Blessed be the LORD this day, who has given David a wise son over this great people."

8 Hiram sent to Solomon, saying,

"I have considered the things which you contacted me about, and I will do all you asked concerning timber of cedar and fir. 9 My servants shall bring them down from Lebanon to the sea, and I will send them by sea in floats to the place that you shall

name and will cause them to be discharged into your care there, and in return you will meet my wishes by giving food for my household."

10 So Hiram gave Solomon cedar trees and fir trees as he desired. 11 Solomon gave Hiram twenty thousand kors[6] of wheat for his household and twenty baths[7] of pure oil. This is what Solomon gave to Hiram each year. 12 The LORD gave Solomon wisdom, as He promised, and there was peace between Hiram and Solomon as they made a treaty together.

13 King Solomon drafted men from all Israel, totaling thirty thousand men. 14 He sent them to Lebanon in turns, ten thousand a month, with each spending a month in Lebanon and two months at home. Adoniram administered the labor force. 15 Solomon had seventy thousand porters and eighty thousand stonecutters in the mountains, 16 not counting the chief of Solomon's officers who were over the work, three thousand three hundred, who ruled over the people who did the work. 17 At the king's command, they quarried out great, costly stones in order to lay the foundation of the house with dressed stones. 18 Solomon's builders and Hiram's builders, along with the stonemasons, cut them and prepared timber and stones to build the house.

Solomon Builds the Temple

2Ch 3:1–14

6 In the four hundred and eightieth year after the children of Israel came out of the land of Egypt, in the fourth year of Solomon's reign over Israel, in the month Ziv (which is the second month), he began to build the house of the LORD.

2 The house which King Solomon built for the LORD had a length of sixty cubits, a width of twenty cubits, and a height of thirty cubits.[8] 3 The porch in front of the temple was twenty cubits[9] in length, the same as the width of the house, and ten cubits[10] deep in front of the house. 4 He made beveled windows for the house. 5 He also built a structure against the wall of the house, running around the walls of the house, both of the temple and of the inner sanctuary, and he made side chambers all around. 6 The lowest story was five cubits[11] broad, the middle one was six cubits[12] broad, and the third was seven cubits[13] broad. For around the outside of the house, he made offsets on the wall so that the supporting beams should not be inserted into the walls of the house.

7 The house was built of stone prepared at the quarry, so that neither hammer nor axe nor any tool of iron was heard in the house while it was being built.

8 The door for the middle chamber was in the right side of the house, and it had winding stairs into the middle chamber and out of the middle into the third. 9 So he built the house and finished it and covered it with beams and boards of cedar. 10 Then he built chambers against the whole house, five cubits high, and they rested on the house with timber of cedar.

11 Now the word of the LORD came to Solomon, saying, 12 "Concerning this house which you are building, if you will walk in My statutes and execute My judgments and keep all My commandments and walk in them, then I will carry out My word with you, which I spoke to David your father, 13 and I will dwell among the people of Israel and will not forsake My people Israel."

14 So Solomon built the house and finished it. 15 He built the interior walls of the house with boards of cedar. From the floor of the house to the ceiling, he covered them on the inside with wood; and he covered the floor of the house with planks of fir. 16 He lined twenty cubits on the sides of the house, both the floor and the walls, with boards of cedar, and he even lined them within, even the inner sanctuary and the Most Holy Place. 17 The house, that is, the nave in front of the inner sanctuary, was forty cubits[14] long. 18 The cedar of the house within had carvings of gourds and open flowers. All was cedar. There was no stone seen.

---

1 21 Euphrates River.   2 22 Likely about 5½ tons, or 5 metric tons.   3 22 Likely about 11 tons, or 10 metric tons.   4 24 Euphrates River.
5 24 Euphrates River.   6 11 Likely about 3,600 tons, or 3,250 metric tons.   7 11 About 120,000 gallons, or 440,000 liters.   8 2 About 90 feet long,
30 feet wide, and 45 feet high, or 27 meters long, 9 meters wide, and 14 meters high.   9 3 About 30 feet, or 9 meters; and in vv. 16 and 20.
10 3 About 15 feet, or 4.5 meters; and in vv. 23–26.   11 6 About 7½ feet, or 2.3 meters; and in vv. 10 and 24.   12 6 About 9 feet, or 2.7 meters.
13 6 About 11 feet, or 3.2 meters.   14 17 About 60 feet, or 18 meters.

[19] He prepared the inner sanctuary in the inner part of the house in order to set there the ark of the covenant of the LORD. [20] The inner sanctuary was twenty cubits long, twenty cubits wide, and twenty cubits high. He overlaid it with pure gold. He also overlaid the altar of cedar. [21] So Solomon overlaid the interior of the house with pure gold, and he made a partition with gold chains in front of the inner sanctuary, and he overlaid it with gold. [22] He overlaid the whole house with gold as well as the whole altar that was by the inner sanctuary.

[23] Within the inner sanctuary, he made two cherubim from olive wood, each ten cubits high. [24] One wing of the cherub was five cubits, and the other wing was also five cubits. From the furthest part of the one wing to the furthest part of the other was ten cubits. [25] The other cherub was ten cubits. Both the cherubim were the same shape and size. [26] The height of the one cherub was ten cubits, and so was that of the other cherub. [27] He set the cherubim within the inner sanctuary, and they stretched forth the wings of the cherubim, so that the wing of the one touched the one wall and the wing of the other cherub touched the other wall, and their wings touched one another in the middle of the house. [28] He overlaid the cherubim with gold.

[29] He carved all the walls of the house with carved figures of cherubim and palm trees and open flowers both inside and out. [30] He overlaid the floor of the house with gold, both inside and out.

[31] For the entrance to the inner sanctuary, he made doors of olive wood; the lintel and doorposts were five-sided. [32] The two doors were also made of olive wood. He carved on them cherubim, palm trees, and open flowers, overlaid them with gold, and spread gold upon the cherubim and upon the palm trees. [33] So also he made for the entrance to the nave four-sided posts of olive wood. [34] The two doors were made from fir tree, with two leaves of each door folding. [35] He carved on them cherubim and palm trees and open flowers and covered them with gold fitted upon the carved work.

[36] He built the inner court with three rows of hewed stone and a row of cedar beams.

[37] In the fourth year, in the month Ziv, the foundation of the house of the LORD was laid, [38] and in the eleventh year, in the month Bul (which is the eighth month), the house was completely finished. All the details and plans were met. So he took seven years to build it.

Solomon's Palace Built

7 Solomon was building his own house for thirteen years, and he finished all his house. [2] He built the House of the Forest of Lebanon. Its length was a hundred cubits, and its width was fifty cubits, and its height was thirty cubits,[1] built on four rows of cedar pillars with cedar beams upon the pillars. [3] It was covered with cedar over the top of the beams, which sat upon forty-five pillars, fifteen in a row. [4] There were window frames in three rows and window opposite window in three tiers. [5] All the doors and posts were rectangular with the openings facing each other in three tiers.

[6] He made a porch of pillars with a length of fifty cubits and a breadth of thirty cubits.[2] There was a porch in front with pillars, and a canopy in front of them.

[7] Then he made a porch for the throne, from which he would judge, and called it the Hall of Judgment. It was covered with cedar from one side of the floor to the other. [8] His own house where he lived, in the other court back of the hall, was similar in style. Solomon also made a house like this for Pharaoh's daughter, whom he had taken as a wife.

[9] All these were built with costly stones, cut to size and sawed with saws on the inside and outside, from the foundation up to the coping, throughout the outside toward the great court. [10] The foundation was of large, costly stones, stones of ten[3] and eight[4] cubits in size. [11] Above were costly stones cut to size, along with cedars. [12] The great court was enclosed with three rows of hewed stones and a row of cedar beams. So were the inner court of the house of the LORD and the porch of the house.

The Furnishings of the Temple

2Ch 4:2–5:1

[13] Now King Solomon sent and called Huram out of Tyre. [14] He was the son of a widow from the tribe of Naphtali, and his father was a man of Tyre who worked in bronze, and he was filled with wisdom and understanding and skill to make all sorts of items in bronze. So he came to King Solomon and performed all his work.

[15] He cast two pillars of bronze eighteen cubits high each and twelve cubits[5] in circumference. [16] He made two capitals of cast bronze to set on the tops of the pillars. The height of the one capital was five cubits,[6] and the height of the other capital was five cubits. [17] He made lattices of checker work with wreaths of chainwork for the capitals on top of the pillars: seven for one capital and seven for the other. [18] Likewise he made pomegranates in two rows around the one latticework to cover the capital that was on the top of the pillar, and he did the same for the other capital. [19] The capitals that were on top of the pillars in the porch were four cubits[7] high and in the shape of lilies. [20] The capitals on top of the two pillars also had pomegranates above, by the convex surface which was next to the latticework. There were two hundred pomegranates in rows encircling each capital. [21] He set up the pillars in the porch of the temple. He set up the right pillar and called it Jakin, and he set up the left pillar and called it Boaz. [22] The tops of the pillars were in the shape of lilies. This completed the work on the pillars.

[23] He made a cast metal sea, ten cubits from one side to the other. It was round and had a height of five cubits, and a line of thirty cubits[8] encircled it. [24] Under the brim all the way around there were gourds, ten in a cubit. When it was cast, the gourds were placed in two rows going all the way around it.

[25] It stood on top of twelve oxen with three facing north, three facing toward the west, three facing toward the south, and three facing toward the east. The sea was set on them, and their hindquarters were turned inward. [26] It was a hand-breadth[9] thick, and the brim was made similar to the brim of a cup, like a lily blossom. It could hold two thousand baths.[10]

[27] He made ten stands out of bronze, each measuring four cubits long, four cubits wide, and three cubits high.[11] [28] The work of the stands looked like this: They had panels, and the panels were set in the frames. [29] And on the panels that were set in the frames were lions, oxen, and cherubim. On the frames both above and below the lions and oxen, there were wreaths of beveled work. [30] Every stand had four bronze wheels and axles of bronze, and at the four corners were supports for a basin. The supports were cast with wreaths at the side of each. [31] Its opening was within a crown that projected upward one cubit. Its opening was round, like the work of a pedestal, a cubit and a half deep.[12] At its opening there were engravings, and its panels were four-sided, not round. [32] Underneath the panels were four wheels, and the axles of the wheels were joined to the stand, and the height of a wheel was a cubit and a half. [33] The wheels worked like chariot wheels in that their axles and rims and spokes and hubs were all cast metal.

[34] There were four supports for the four corners of each stand, and the supports were part of one piece with the stand itself. [35] On the top of the stand, there was a round band half a cubit[13] high, and on the top of the stand its stays and its panels were of one piece with it. [36] On the surface of its stays and on its panels, he engraved cherubim, lions, and palm trees, according to the space of each, with wreaths all around. [37] In this way he made the ten stands, with them all having the same shape, measure, and size.

[38] Then he made ten basins of bronze, with each basin able to hold forty baths,[14] each being four cubits. Upon every one of the

---

[1] 2 About 150 feet long, 75 feet wide and 45 feet high, or 45 meters long, 23 meters wide and 14 meters high. [26] 6 About 75 feet long and 45 feet wide, or 23 meters long and 14 meters wide. [3] 10 About 15 feet, or 4.5 meters; and in v. 23. [4] 10 About 12 feet, or 3.6 meters. [5] 15 About 27 feet high and 18 feet in circumference, or 8.1 meters high and 5.4 meters in circumference. [6] 16 About 7½ feet, or 2.3 meters; and in v. 23. [7] 19 About 6 feet, or 1.8 meters; and in v. 38. [8] 23 About 45 feet, or 14 meters. [9] 26 About 3 inches, or 7.5 centimeters. [10] 26 About 12,000 gallons, or 44,000 liters. [11] 27 About 6 feet long and wide and 4½ feet high, or 1.8 meters long and wide and 1.4 meters high. [12] 31 About 2¼ feet, or 68 centimeters; and in v. 32. [13] 35 About 9 inches, or 23 centimeters. [14] 38 About 240 gallons, or 880 liters.

ten stands sat one basin. [39] He put five stands on the right side of the house, and five on the left side of the house. He set the sea on the right side of the house toward the southeast. [40] Huram also made the pots, the shovels, and the basins.

So Huram finished all the work in making items for King Solomon for use in the house of the Lord: [41] the two pillars, the two bowls of the capitals that were on the top of the two pillars, the two latticeworks to cover the two bowls of the capitals that were upon the top of the pillars; [42] and the four hundred pomegranates for the two latticeworks, two rows of pomegranates for each latticework, to cover the two bowls of the capitals that were on the pillars; [43] the ten stands and ten basins on the stands; [44] one sea and twelve oxen under the sea; [45] the pots, the shovels, and the basins.

All these vessels that Huram made for King Solomon for the house of the Lord were of burnished bronze. [46] In the plain of the Jordan the king cast them, in the clay ground between Sukkoth and Zarethan. [47] Solomon left all the vessels unweighed because there were so many. The weight of the bronze was also never measured.

[48] Solomon made all the vessels that were needed for the house of the Lord: the altar of gold, the table of gold on which was showbread, [49] the candlesticks of pure gold, five on the right side and five on the left before the inner sanctuary; the flowers, the lamps, and the tongs, of gold; [50] the cups, snuffers, basins, dishes for incense, fire pans, of pure gold; the sockets for the doors of the innermost part of the house, the Most Holy Place, and for the doors of the nave of the temple, of gold.

[51] All the work that King Solomon made for the house of the Lord was completed. And Solomon brought in the things which David his father had dedicated—the silver, the gold, and the cups—and he put them among the treasures of the house of the Lord.

The Ark Brought to the Temple
2Ch 5:2–6:11

8 Then Solomon assembled the elders of Israel and all the heads of the tribes, the chief of the fathers of the children of Israel, before King Solomon in Jerusalem, so that they could ensure that the ark of the covenant of the Lord would be brought out of the City of David in Zion. [2] All the men of Israel assembled themselves before King Solomon at the feast in the month Ethanim, which is the seventh month.

[3] All the elders of Israel came, and the priests carried the ark. [4] The priests and Levites brought up the ark of the Lord, the tabernacle of the congregation, and all the holy implements that were in the tabernacle. [5] King Solomon and all the congregation of Israel who were assembled before him stood together in front of the ark, sacrificing so many sheep and oxen that they could not be told or numbered.

[6] The priests brought in the ark of the covenant of the Lord to its place in the inner sanctuary of the house, to the Most Holy Place under the wings of the cherubim. [7] For the cherubim spread forth their two wings over the place of the ark and covered the ark and the poles from above. [8] The poles were so long that the ends of the poles could be seen out in the holy place in front of the inner sanctuary, but they could not be seen from outside, and they are there to this day. [9] There was nothing in the ark except for the two tablets of stone that Moses put there at Horeb when the Lord made a covenant with the children of Israel after they had come out of the land of Egypt.

[10] And when the priests came out of the holy place, the cloud filled the house of the Lord, [11] so that the priests could not continue to minister because of the cloud, for the glory of the Lord filled the house of the Lord.

[12] Then Solomon spoke, saying, "The Lord said that He would dwell in the thick darkness. [13] I have surely built You a house to dwell in, a settled place for You to abide in forever."

[14] Then the king turned around and blessed all the congregation of Israel (and all the congregation of Israel stood), [15] and he said,

"Blessed be the Lord God of Israel, who spoke with His mouth to my father David and has with His hand fulfilled His word, saying, [16] 'Since the day that I brought forth My people Israel out of Egypt, I chose no city from any tribe of Israel to build a house where My name might be praised, but I chose David to be over My people Israel.'

[17] "My father David had it in mind to build a house for the name of the Lord God of Israel. [18] The Lord said to my father David, 'Whereas it was in your heart to build a house for My name, you had good intentions. [19] Nevertheless, you shall not build the house, but your son who will come out of your loins, he shall build the house for My name.'

[20] "The Lord has fulfilled His word that He spoke, and I have been elevated to the position of my father David, to sit on the throne of Israel as the Lord promised, and have built a house for the name of the Lord God of Israel. [21] I have set a place there for the ark, which houses the covenant of the Lord which He made with our fathers when He brought them out of the land of Egypt."

Solomon's Prayer of Dedication
2Ch 6:12–40

[22] Then Solomon stood in front of the altar of the Lord in the presence of all the congregation of Israel and spread his hands toward heaven. [23] and he said,

"Lord God of Israel, there is no God like You in heaven above or on earth below who keeps covenant and mercy with Your servants who walk before You with all their hearts, [24] who have kept what You promised Your servant David my father. You spoke also with Your mouth and have fulfilled it with Your hand, as it is this day.

[25] "Therefore, Lord God of Israel, now keep what You promised Your servant David my father, saying, 'You will not fail to have a man sit before Me on the throne of Israel, so long as your sons take heed to their way, that they walk before Me as you have walked before Me.' [26] Now, O God of Israel, let Your word, I pray, be fulfilled, which You spoke to Your servant David my father.

[27] "But will God indeed dwell on the earth? See, heaven and the heaven of heavens cannot contain You. How much less can this house that I have built? [28] Yet give consideration to the prayer of Your servant and to his supplication, O Lord my God; listen to the cry and to the prayer which Your servant prays before You today, [29] that Your eyes may be upon this house night and day, even toward the place of which You have said, 'My name shall be there,' that You may listen to the prayer which Your servant shall make toward this place. [30] Please listen to the supplication of Your servant and of Your people Israel when they pray toward this place. May You hear in heaven, Your dwelling place, and when You hear, forgive.

[31] "If any man sins against his neighbor, and an oath be laid upon him to cause him to swear, and the oath comes before Your altar in this house, [32] then may You hear in heaven and act and judge Your servants, condemning the wicked, bringing his way on his own head, and justifying the righteous, giving him according to his righteousness.

[33] "When Your people Israel are defeated by their enemies, because they have sinned against You, and they turn back to You and call upon Your name and pray and make supplication to You in this house, [34] then may You hear in heaven and forgive the sin of Your people Israel and bring them again to the land which You gave to their fathers.

[35] "When heaven is shut up, and there is no rain, because they have sinned against You, if they pray toward this place and call upon Your name and turn from their sin when You afflict them, [36] then may You hear in heaven and forgive the sin of Your servants and Your people Israel, that You may teach them the good way in which they should walk and give rain upon Your land which You have given to Your people as an inheritance.

[37] "When there is famine in the land, if there is plague, blight, mildew, locust, or grasshopper; if their enemy besieges them in the land of their cities; whatever plague, whatever sickness there is; [38] whatever prayer, whatever supplication is

made by anyone, or by all Your people Israel, each knowing the affliction of his own heart, and spreading his hands toward this house; [39] then hear in heaven Your dwelling place, and forgive, and act, and render to everyone according to all his ways, whose hearts You know—for only You know the hearts of the sons of men— [40] so that they may fear You all the days that they live in the land that You gave to our fathers.

[41] "Also concerning the foreigner who is not of Your people Israel and comes from a far country for Your name's sake [42] (for they will hear of Your great name and of Your strong hand and of Your outstretched arm), when he comes and prays toward this house, [43] may You hear in heaven, Your dwelling place, and do all that the foreigner asks of You, so all people of the earth will know Your name, to fear You as Your people Israel do, and that they may know that this house, which I have built, is called by Your name.

[44] "If Your people go out to battle against their enemy wherever You send them, and they pray to the Lord toward the city which You have chosen and toward the house that I have built for Your name, [45] then may You hear their prayer and supplication in heaven and maintain their cause.

[46] "If they sin against You (for there is no man who does not sin), and You get angry with them and hand them over to the enemy so that they are carried away as captives to the land of the enemy, far or near, [47] yet when they come to their senses while in the land where they were carried captives, and repent and make supplication to You, saying, 'We have sinned and have acted perversely and have committed wickedness,' [48] and so return to You with all their hearts and with all their souls in the land of their enemies, who carried them away as captives, and pray to You toward their land, which You gave to their fathers, the city which You have chosen and the house which I have built for Your name, [49] then may You hear their prayers and supplications in heaven, Your dwelling place, and maintain their cause, [50] and forgive Your people who have sinned against You and all their transgressions which they committed against You and grant them compassion before those who carried them away as captives, so they will have compassion on them. [51] For they are Your people and Your inheritance whom You brought forth out of Egypt from the midst of the furnace of iron.

[52] "Let Your eyes be open to the supplication of Your servant and to the supplication of Your people Israel, to listen to them regarding all for which they call upon You. [53] For You did call them out from among all the people of the earth to be Your inheritance, as You spoke by the hand of Moses Your servant when You brought our fathers out of Egypt, O Lord God."

[54] Now when Solomon finished praying this prayer and making supplication to the Lord, he arose from before the altar of the Lord, from kneeling on his knees with his hands spread up to heaven. [55] He stood up and blessed all the congregation of Israel with a loud voice, saying,

[56] "Blessed be the Lord who has given rest to His people Israel according to all that He promised. Not one word of His promises which He gave by the hand of Moses His servant has failed. [57] The Lord our God be with us, as He was with our fathers. Let Him neither leave us nor forsake us, [58] that He may incline our hearts to Him, to walk in all His ways and to keep His commandments, statutes, and judgments, which He commanded our fathers. [59] And let these my words, with which I have made supplication before the Lord, be close to the Lord our God day and night, that He will maintain the cause of His servant and the cause of His people Israel at all times as the situation demands, [60] so that all the people of the earth may know that the Lord is God and that there is none else. [61] Let your hearts, therefore, be perfect with the Lord our God, to walk in His statutes and keep His commandments, as at this day."

The Dedication of the Temple
2Ch 7:1–10

[62] The king and all Israel with him offered sacrifices before the Lord. [63] Solomon offered a sacrifice of peace offerings, which he offered to the Lord, twenty-two thousand oxen and a hundred and twenty thousand sheep. So the king and all the children of Israel dedicated the house of the Lord.

[64] The same day the king consecrated the middle of the court that was in front of the house of the Lord, for there he offered burnt offerings and meat offerings and the fat of the peace offerings, because the bronze altar that was before the Lord was too little to receive the burnt offerings and meat offerings and the fat of the peace offerings.

[65] At that time, Solomon held a feast for all Israel, a great congregation, from the entry of Lebo Hamath to the Brook of Egypt, before the Lord our God, seven days and *another* seven days, a total of fourteen days. [66] On the eighth day he sent the people away, and they blessed the king and went to their tents rejoicing in their hearts for all the goodness that the Lord had done for David His servant and for Israel His people.

The Lord Appears to Solomon
2Ch 7:11–22

9 When Solomon had finished building the house of the Lord and the king's house and all else he desired, [2] the Lord appeared to Solomon a second time, as He had appeared to him at Gibeon. [3] The Lord said to him,

"I have heard your prayer and supplication, which you made before Me. I have consecrated this house which you built by putting My name there forever. And My eyes and My heart shall be there perpetually.

[4] "If you will walk before Me, as your father David walked, in integrity of heart and uprightness, so that you are obedient to do all that I have commanded you, and will keep My statutes and My judgments, [5] then I will establish the throne of your kingdom upon Israel forever, just as I promised to your father David, saying, 'You shall not fail to have a man upon the throne of Israel.'

[6] "But if you and your sons turn in any way from following Me and do not keep My commandments and My statutes which I have set before you, but go and serve other gods and worship them, [7] then I will cut Israel out of the land which I have given them, and I will cast this house, which I have consecrated for My name, out of My sight, and Israel shall be a proverb and a byword among all people. [8] And everyone who passes by this high house will be astonished and will hiss, and they shall say, 'Why has the Lord done this to this land, and to this house?' [9] And they will answer, 'Because they forsook the Lord their God, who brought their fathers out of the land of Egypt, and took hold of other gods and have worshipped and served them. That is why the Lord has brought all this disaster upon them.'"

Solomon's Other Activities
2Ch 8:1–18

[10] When twenty years had passed since Solomon had built the two houses, the house of the Lord and the king's house [11] (now Hiram the king of Tyre had furnished Solomon with cedar and fir trees, along with gold, as he had requested), King Solomon gave Hiram twenty cities in the land of Galilee. [12] Hiram came out from Tyre to see the cities Solomon had given him, and he was not pleased with them. [13] He said, "What cities are these which you have given me, my brother?" And he called them the land of Kabul to this day. [14] Hiram sent to the king one hundred and twenty talents *[i]* of gold.

[15] This is the account of the forced labor which King Solomon conscripted to build the house of the Lord and his own house, Millo, the wall of Jerusalem, Hazor, Megiddo, and Gezer. [16] For Pharaoh, king of Egypt, had gone up against and conquered Gezer and burned it with fire and slain the Canaanites that lived in the city and given it as a present to his daughter, Solomon's wife. [17] Solomon built Gezer and Lower Beth Horon [18] and Baalath and Tadmor in the wilderness, in the land, [19] and all the storage cities that Solomon

---

[i] 14 About 4½ tons, or 4 metric tons.

had, cities for his chariots and cities for his horsemen and all that which Solomon desired to build in Jerusalem and in Lebanon and in all the land of his dominion.

[20] All the people who were left of the Amorites, Hittites, Perizzites, Hivites, and Jebusites, who were not children of Israel, [21] the descendants of those who were left in the land and whom the people of Israel were not able to utterly destroy, were conscripted by Solomon for slave labor to this day. [22] But Solomon did not make any children of Israel into slaves, but instead used them as men of war, as his servants, his leaders, his captains, rulers of his chariots, and his horsemen. [23] These were the chief officers over Solomon's work, five hundred and fifty, who ruled over the people who did the labor.

[24] But Pharaoh's daughter moved out of the City of David to her house which Solomon had built for her, and he then built Millo.

[25] Three times a year Solomon offered burnt offerings and peace offerings on the altar that he built to the LORD, and he burned incense on the altar that was before the LORD. So he finished the house.

[26] King Solomon built a fleet of ships in Ezion Geber, which is beside Elath on the shore of the Red Sea in the land of Edom. [27] Hiram sent shipmen who had knowledge of the sea to serve alongside Solomon's men. [28] They went to Ophir and acquired four hundred and twenty talents[1] of gold there and brought it to King Solomon.

The Queen of Sheba
2Ch 9:1–12

10 Now when the queen of Sheba heard of Solomon's fame connected to the name of the LORD, she came to test him with hard questions. [2] She came to Jerusalem with a very great retinue, with camels bearing spices, and very much gold, and precious stones; and when she came to Solomon, she told him all that was on her mind. [3] Solomon answered all her questions; there was not anything too difficult for the king which he could not answer. [4] When the queen of Sheba observed Solomon's wisdom and the house he had built [5] and the meat of his table and the sitting of his servants and the attendance of his ministers and their clothing and his cupbearers and his entryway by which he went up to the house of the LORD, it took her breath away.

[6] She said to the king, "What I heard in my own land about your acts and your wisdom was true! [7] I did not believe it until I came and saw it with my own eyes! In fact, I was not even told half. Your wisdom and prosperity are greater than the stories I heard! [8] Happy are your men, and happy are these your servants who stand continually before you and hear your wisdom! [9] Blessed be the LORD your God, who delighted in you and set you on the throne of Israel, because the LORD loved Israel forever; therefore He made you king in order to execute judgment and justice."

[10] She gave the king a hundred and twenty talents[2] of gold and a great amount of spices and precious stones. No one gave as many spices as the queen of Sheba gave to King Solomon.

[11] The ships of Hiram, which brought gold from Ophir, also brought from Ophir a large quantity of almug wood and precious stones. [12] The king made pillars for the house of the LORD out of the almug trees and harps also and psalteries for singers for the king's house. Never before had such almug wood *been brought*, nor has any such been seen to this day.

[13] King Solomon gave to the queen of Sheba all she desired, no matter what she asked for, in addition to what Solomon gave her from his royal bounty. So she turned and went to her own country, she and her servants.

Solomon's Wealth
2Ch 1:14–17; 9:13–28

[14] Now the weight of gold that came to Solomon in one year was six hundred and sixty-six talents[3] of gold. [15] In addition, he collected from the merchantmen and the traffic of the spice merchants and from all the kings of Arabia and the governors of the country.

[16] King Solomon made two hundred large shields of beaten gold made of six hundred shekels[4] of gold each. [17] He made three

hundred shields of beaten gold with three pounds[5] of gold in each shield. And the king put them in the House of the Forest of Lebanon.

[18] The king also made a great throne of ivory and overlaid it with the best gold. [19] The throne had six steps, and the back of the throne was round, and there were armrests on either side of the seat with two lions standing beside the armrests. [20] Twelve lions stood on the sides of the six steps, and there was no other like it in any kingdom. [21] All of King Solomon's drinking cups were made of gold, and all the cups of the House of the Forest of Lebanon were made of pure gold. None were made of silver, for it was not considered valuable in the days of Solomon. [22] For the king had ships at sea at Tarshish with the ships of Hiram. Every three years the ships of Tarshish came bringing gold, silver, ivory, apes, and peacocks.

[23] So King Solomon exceeded all the kings of the earth in terms of riches and wisdom. [24] All the earth came to Solomon to hear his wisdom, which God had put in his heart. [25] Everyone brought an annual tribute in the form of presents, silver and gold cups, garments, armor, spices, horses, and mules.

[26] Solomon gathered together chariots and horsemen. He had one thousand four hundred chariots and twelve thousand horsemen whom he stationed in the cities for chariots and with the king at Jerusalem. [27] The king made silver to be in Jerusalem as plentiful as stones, and he made cedars to be as plentiful as sycamore trees in the valley. [28] Solomon had horses brought out of Egypt along with linen yarn. The king's merchants received the linen yarn at a price. [29] He brought chariots from Egypt at a price of six hundred shekels of silver and a horse for a hundred and fifty.[6] And he exported them to all the kings of the Hittites and the kings of Aram, by their means.

Solomon's Apostasy

11 But King Solomon loved many foreign women in addition to the daughter of Pharaoh, women of the Moabites, Ammonites, Edomites, Sidonians, and Hittites, [2] from the nations which the LORD warned the children of Israel about, saying, "You shall not go in to them, nor shall they come in to you, for they will surely turn your heart away toward their gods." Solomon clung to these in love. [3] He had seven hundred wives who were princesses and three hundred concubines, and his wives turned his heart away. [4] For when Solomon was old, his wives turned his heart away after other gods, and his heart was not perfect with the LORD his God as the heart of David his father had been. [5] For Solomon went after Ashtoreth, the goddess of the Sidonians, and after Molek, the abomination of the Ammonites. [6] Solomon did what was evil in the sight of the LORD and did not fully follow the LORD as his father David had done.

[7] Then Solomon built a high place for Chemosh, the abomination of Moab, in the hill that is close to Jerusalem, and for Molek, the abomination of the children of Ammon. [8] He did the same for all his foreign wives, who burned incense and sacrificed to their gods.

[9] The LORD was angry with Solomon because he turned his heart away from the LORD God of Israel, who had appeared to him twice, [10] and had warned him about this, that he should not follow other gods, but he was disobedient to the LORD's command. [11] Therefore the LORD said to Solomon, "Since you have done this and have not kept My covenant and statutes, which I commanded you, I will surely take the kingdom from you and give it to your servant. [12] I will not do this in your lifetime for your father David's sake, but I will tear it out of the hand of your son. [13] However, I will not take the whole kingdom away, but will preserve one tribe for your son for David My servant's sake and for the sake of Jerusalem which I chose."

Solomon's Adversaries

[14] The LORD stirred up an adversary against Solomon, Hadad the Edomite. He was a prince of Edom. [15] For when David was in Edom, and Joab the commander of the army had gone to bury the slain, he had killed every male in Edom [16] (for six months Joab stayed there with his men until he had killed every male in Edom). [17] But Hadad fled to Egypt, he and some Edomites who served his father, Hadad still being a small child. [18] They set out from Midian and

---

[1] 28 About 16 tons, or 14 metric tons.   [2] 10 About 4½ tons, or 4 metric tons.   [3] 14 About 25 tons, or 23 metric tons.
[4] 16 About 15 pounds, or 6.9 kilograms; and in v. 29.   [5] 17 About 3¾ tons, or 1.7 kilograms, or if double minas, about 7½ pounds, or 3.5 kilograms.
[6] 29 About 3¾ pounds, or 1.7 kilograms.

went to Paran, and they gathered men from Paran and then arrived in Egypt and presented him before Pharaoh king of Egypt, who gave him a house and provisions and land.

¹⁹ Pharaoh had great affection for Hadad, so much so that he gave him his sister-in-law, the sister of Tahpenes the queen, as a wife. ²⁰ Tahpenes' sister gave birth to his son, Genubath, whom Tahpenes weaned in Pharaoh's house. Genubath lived in Pharaoh's house among the sons of Pharaoh.

²¹ When Hadad heard in Egypt that David slept with his fathers and that Joab, the commander of the army, was dead, he said to Pharaoh, "Allow me to depart and go to my own country."

²² Then Pharaoh said to him, "But what have you lacked with me that you want to go to your own country?"

And he answered, "Nothing, however let me go anyway."

²³ God stirred up another adversary against him, Rezon the son of Eliada, who fled from his lord Hadadezer, king of Zobah. ²⁴ He gathered a group of men and became leader over a band when David killed the men of Zobah, and they fled to Damascus and lived and reigned there. ²⁵ He was an enemy of Israel all the days of Solomon in addition to the troubles caused by Hadad, and he hated Israel and reigned over Aram.

Jeroboam's Rebellion

²⁶ Jeroboam the son of Nebat, an Ephraimite of Zeredah, who was Solomon's servant and whose mother's name was Zeruah, a widow woman, even he lifted up his hand against the king.

²⁷ This is what led to his rebellion against the king. Solomon built Millo and repaired the wall of the City of David his father. ²⁸ Jeroboam was a mighty man of valor, and when Solomon saw that the young man was industrious, he made him ruler over all the labor force of the house of Joseph.

²⁹ At that time, when Jeroboam went out of Jerusalem, the prophet Ahijah the Shilonite found him along the way, and he had dressed himself in a new garment, and the two *of them* were alone in the field. ³⁰ Ahijah took off the new garment that he wore and tore it into twelve pieces, ³¹ and he said to Jeroboam: Take ten pieces, for thus says the Lᴏʀᴅ, the God of Israel, "See, I will tear the kingdom out of the hand of Solomon and will give ten tribes to you ³² (but he shall have one tribe for My servant David's sake and for the sake of Jerusalem, the city which I have chosen out of all the tribes of Israel), ³³ because they have forsaken Me and have worshipped Ashtoreth the goddess of the Sidonians, Chemosh the god of the Moabites, and Molek the god of the children of Ammon and have not walked in My ways and have not done that which is right in My eyes, to keep My statutes and judgments, as his father David had done.

³⁴ "However, I will not take the whole kingdom out of his hand, but I will make him prince all the days of his life for David My servant's sake, whom I chose, because he kept My commandments and My statutes. ³⁵ But I will take the kingdom out of his son's hand and will give ten tribes to you. ³⁶ To his son will I give one tribe, so that My servant David will always have a light before Me in Jerusalem, the city in which I have chosen to put My name. ³⁷ I will take you, and you shall reign according to all that your soul desires and shall be king over Israel. ³⁸ It shall be, if you will listen to all that I command you and will walk in My ways and do what is right in My sight to keep My statutes and My commandments, as David My servant did, I will be with you and build you a sure house, as I built for David, and will give Israel to you. ³⁹ I will thus afflict the seed of David, but not forever."

⁴⁰ Solomon therefore sought to kill Jeroboam. And Jeroboam arose and fled to Egypt to Shishak, king of Egypt, and he stayed in Egypt until the death of Solomon.

The Death of Solomon

2Ch 9:29–31

⁴¹ The rest of the acts of Solomon and all that he did and his wisdom, are they not written in the book of the acts of Solomon? ⁴² And the time that Solomon reigned in Jerusalem over all Israel was forty years. ⁴³ Solomon slept with his fathers and was buried in the City of David his father, and his son Rehoboam reigned after him.

Israel Rebels Against Rehoboam

2Ch 10:1–11:4

12 And Rehoboam went to Shechem, for all Israel had gone to Shechem to make him king. ² When Jeroboam the son of Nebat, who was still in Egypt, heard of it (for he had fled from King Solomon and stayed in Egypt), ³ they called and sent *for* him. And Jeroboam and all the congregation of Israel came and spoke to Rehoboam, saying, ⁴ "Your father made our yoke unbearable. Now, therefore, make the grievous service to your father and the heavy yoke he put upon us lighter, and we will serve you."

⁵ He said to them, "Depart for three days, and then come back to me." And the people departed.

⁶ King Rehoboam consulted with the old men who advised his father Solomon while he was still alive and asked, "How do you advise me to answer the people?"

⁷ And they spoke to him, saying, "If you will be a servant to this people this day and will serve them and answer them and speak kind words to them, they will be your servants forever."

⁸ But he rejected the advice that the old men gave him and consulted with the young men who grew up with him and who stood before him, ⁹ and he said to them, "What advice do you give on how we should answer this people, who have spoken to me saying, 'Make the yoke your father put on us lighter'?"

¹⁰ And the young men who grew up with him said, "Thus shall you answer this people who said to you, 'Your father made our yoke heavy, but make it lighter for us'; thus shall you say to them, 'My little finger will be thicker than my father's loins! ¹¹ Whereas my father loaded you with a heavy yoke, I will add to your burden. My father chastised you with whips, but I will chastise you with scorpions!' "

¹² So Jeroboam and all the people came to Rehoboam on the third day, just as the king had appointed, saying, "Come to me again the third day." ¹³ The king answered the people roughly and forsook the counsel the old men gave him, ¹⁴ and instead spoke to them following the advice of the young men. He said, "My father made your yoke heavy, and I will add to your burden. My father chastised you with whips, but I will chastise you with scorpions." ¹⁵ Thus the king did not listen to the people, for the cause was from the Lᴏʀᴅ, that He might fulfill His saying, which the Lᴏʀᴅ spoke by Ahijah the Shilonite to Jeroboam the son of Nebat.

¹⁶ So when all Israel saw that the king did not listen to them, the people responded to the king, saying,

"What portion do we have in David?
    We also do not have an inheritance in the son of Jesse.
To your tents, O Israel,
    and see to your own house, David!"

So the people of Israel departed to their tents. ¹⁷ But the people of Israel living in the cities of Judah were ruled over by Rehoboam.

¹⁸ Then King Rehoboam sent Adoniram, who was in charge of the forced labor, and all Israel stoned him to death. As a result, King Rehoboam quickly mounted his chariot and fled to Jerusalem. ¹⁹ So Israel rebelled against the house of David, *and it remains so* even to this day.

²⁰ When all Israel heard that Jeroboam had returned, they sent and called him before the congregation and made him king over all Israel. Only the tribe of Judah followed the house of David.

²¹ When Rehoboam arrived at Jerusalem, he assembled all the house of Judah along with the tribe of Benjamin, a hundred and eighty thousand chosen men who were warriors, to fight against the house of Israel and to bring the kingdom back to Rehoboam the son of Solomon.

²² But the word of God came to Shemaiah the man of God, saying: ²³ Speak to Rehoboam the son of Solomon, king of Judah, and to all the house of Judah and Benjamin and to the remnant of the people, saying, ²⁴ "Thus says the Lᴏʀᴅ: You shall not go up, nor fight against your brothers the children of Israel. Every man is to return to his house, for this thing is from Me." They listened therefore to the word of the Lᴏʀᴅ and turned to depart, according to the word of the Lᴏʀᴅ.

Jeroboam's Golden Calves

²⁵ Then Jeroboam built Shechem in Mount Ephraim and lived there and went out from there and built Peniel.

²⁶ Jeroboam said in his heart, "The kingdom will return to the house of David. ²⁷ If this people go up to do sacrifice in the house of the LORD at Jerusalem, then shall the heart of this people turn again to their lord, even to Rehoboam king of Judah, and they shall kill me and go again to Rehoboam king of Judah."

²⁸ At that point, the king got some advice and made two golden calves and said to the people, "It is too difficult for you to go up to Jerusalem. Here are your gods, O Israel, which brought you up out of the land of Egypt." ²⁹ He set one in Bethel, and he put the other in Dan. ³⁰ This was a sin, for the people went to worship before the one, even all the way in Dan.

³¹ He also made houses on high places and appointed priests from among all the people who were not Levites. ³² Jeroboam ordained a feast in the eighth month, on the fifteenth day of the month, like the feast in Judah, and he offered *sacrifice* on the altar. He did this in Bethel, sacrificing to the calves that he had made, and he stationed in Bethel the priests of the high places he had made. ³³ So he made offerings on the altar that he had made in Bethel on the fifteenth day of the eighth month, a holiday he imagined in his own heart, and ordained a feast for the children of Israel, and he sacrificed on the altar and burned incense.

The Man of God From Judah

13 A man of God came out of Judah to Bethel by the word of the LORD while Jeroboam stood by the altar to burn incense. ² He cried against the altar by the word of the LORD and said, "O altar, altar, thus says the LORD: 'A child named Josiah will be born in the house of David, and he will sacrifice upon you the priests of the high places who burn incense on you, and these men's bones shall be burned upon you.' " ³ He gave a sign the same day, saying, "This is the sign that the LORD has spoken: 'The altar will be torn apart, and the ashes that are upon it will be poured out.' "

⁴ When King Jeroboam heard the saying of the man of God who had cried against the altar in Bethel, he reached out his hand from the altar, saying, "Arrest him!" And the hand that he put forth against him dried up so that he could not pull it back in again. ⁵ The altar also was torn, and the ashes poured out from the altar, just as the man of God had said it would as a sign of the LORD.

⁶ The king answered and said to the man of God, "Seek the face of the LORD your God, and pray for me, that my hand will be healed." And the man of God interceded with the LORD, and the king's hand was healed and became as it was before.

⁷ The king said to the man of God, "Come home with me and refresh yourself, and I will give you a reward."

⁸ The man of God said to the king, "If you were to give me half your house, I would not go with you, nor will I eat bread nor drink water in this place, ⁹ for so I was commanded by the word of the LORD, saying: You shall eat no bread, nor drink water nor return by the same way that you came." ¹⁰ So he went another way and did not return by the same way he came to Bethel.

¹¹ Now there lived an old prophet in Bethel, and his sons came and told him all that the man of God had done that day in Bethel. They also told their father the words that he had spoken to the king. ¹² Their father said to them, "What way did he go?" For his sons had seen the way the man of God who came from Judah had gone. ¹³ He said to his sons, "Saddle my donkey." So they saddled the donkey for him, and he rode on it. ¹⁴ He went after the man of God and found him sitting under an oak, and he said to him, "Are you the man of God who came from Judah?"

And he said, "I am."

¹⁵ Then he said to him, "Come home with me and eat bread."

¹⁶ He said, "I may not return with you or go in with you, nor will I eat bread nor drink water with you in this place, ¹⁷ for I was commanded by the word of the LORD: You shall eat no bread *and* drink no water there nor return by the way you came."

¹⁸ He said to him, "I am a prophet like you, and an angel spoke to me by the word of the LORD, saying, 'Bring him back with you into your house so that he may eat bread and drink water.' " But

he had lied to him. ¹⁹ So he went back with him to his house and ate bread and drank water.

²⁰ Then as they sat at the table, the word of the LORD came to the prophet who brought him back, ²¹ and he cried out to the man of God who came from Judah, saying, "Thus says the LORD: Since you have disobeyed the mouth of the LORD and have not kept the commandment that the LORD your God commanded you, ²² but instead came back and have eaten bread and drunk water in the place of which the LORD told you to eat no bread and drink no water, your carcass will not be buried in the tomb of your fathers!"

²³ After he had eaten bread and had drunk, he saddled the donkey for the prophet whom he had brought back. ²⁴ As he was going, a lion met him on the way and killed him, and his body was thrown in the road, and both the donkey and lion stood by it. ²⁵ Some men passed by and saw the body thrown in the road with the lion standing by the body, and they came and told the story in the city where the old prophet lived.

²⁶ When the prophet who brought him back from the way heard about it, he said, "It is the man of God who was disobedient to the word of the LORD, and thus the LORD has delivered him to the lion, which has torn and slain him, according to the word of the LORD that He spoke to him."

²⁷ He said to his sons, "Saddle my donkey," and they saddled it. ²⁸ He then went and found his body thrown in the road, and the donkey and the lion were still standing by the body. The lion had not eaten the body nor attacked the donkey. ²⁹ The prophet picked up the body of the man of God and laid it on his donkey and brought it back. The old prophet came to the city to mourn and to bury him. ³⁰ He laid his body in his own tomb, and they mourned over him, saying, "Alas, my brother!"

³¹ And after he had buried him, he said to his sons, "When I am dead, bury me in the grave in which the man of God is buried; lay my bones beside his bones. ³² For the saying that he cried out by the word of the LORD against the altar in Bethel and against all the houses of the high places that are in the cities of Samaria shall surely come to pass."

³³ After this event Jeroboam did not turn from his evil ways, but made priests for the high places again from among all the people. Any who would, he consecrated to be priests of the high places. ³⁴ This matter became sin to the house of Jeroboam, so as to cut it off and to destroy it from the face of the earth.

Ahijah Prophesies Against Jeroboam

14 At that time, Jeroboam's son Abijah became sick. ² Jeroboam said to his wife, "Please get up and disguise yourself, so that you will not be recognized as the wife of Jeroboam, and go to Shiloh. There you will find Ahijah the prophet, who told me that I would be king over this people. ³ Take ten loaves, cakes, and a jar of honey, and go to him. He will tell you what will happen to our child." ⁴ Jeroboam's wife did so and arose and went to Shiloh, to the house of Ahijah.

But Ahijah could not see, for in his old age he had gone blind. ⁵ The LORD said to Ahijah, "The wife of Jeroboam has come to ask you about her son, for he is sick. You shall say thus and thus to her, for when she comes, she will be disguised as another woman."

⁶ And so when Ahijah heard the sound of her feet as she came in the door, he said, "Come in, wife of Jeroboam. Why do you disguise yourself as another? I have been sent to you with bad news. ⁷ Go tell Jeroboam, 'Thus says the LORD God of Israel: I raised you up from among the people and made you prince over My people Israel, ⁸ and took the kingdom away from the house of David and gave it you. Yet you have not been as My servant David, who kept My commandments and who followed Me with all his heart to do only that which was right in My eyes, ⁹ but you have sinned more than all who were before you, for you have gone and made other gods and molded images and provoked Me to anger and have cast Me behind your back.

¹⁰ " 'Therefore I will bring disaster upon the house of Jeroboam and will cut off from Jeroboam all males, both slave and free in Israel, and will take away the remnant of the house of Jeroboam, as a man takes away refuse until it is all gone. ¹¹ Descendants of Jeroboam who die in the city will be eaten by dogs, and those who

die in the field will be eaten by the birds of the air, for the Lord has spoken it.'

12 "Arise therefore and go to your own house. When your feet enter the city, the child will die. 13 All Israel will mourn for him and bury him, for he alone from the house of Jeroboam will come to the grave, because in him there is found some good thing toward the Lord God of Israel.

14 "Moreover the Lord will raise up a king over Israel who will destroy the house of Jeroboam this day and from now on. 15 For the Lord will smite Israel, as a reed is shaken in the water, and He will uproot Israel from this good land, which he gave to their fathers, and will scatter them beyond the river, because they have made their Asherah poles, provoking the Lord to anger. 16 He shall give Israel up because of the sins of Jeroboam who sinned and who led Israel to sin."

17 Jeroboam's wife arose and departed and came to Tirzah. As she arrived at the threshold of the door, the child died, 18 and they buried him, and all Israel mourned for him, according to the word of the Lord, which He spoke by the hand of His servant Ahijah the prophet.

19 The rest of the acts of Jeroboam, how he waged war and how he reigned, are written in the book of the chronicles of the kings of Israel. 20 Jeroboam reigned twenty-two years, and then he slept with his fathers, and Nadab, his son, reigned in his stead.

Rehoboam, King of Judah
2Ch 12:9–16

21 Rehoboam the son of Solomon reigned in Judah. Rehoboam was forty-one years old when he began to reign, and he reigned seventeen years in Jerusalem, the city which the Lord had chosen out of all the tribes of Israel to put His name there. And his mother's name was Naamah, an Ammonitess.

22 Judah did evil in the sight of the Lord, and the people provoked Him to jealousy with the sins they committed, even worse than their fathers had done. 23 For they also built high places and images and Asherah poles on every high hill and under every green tree. 24 There were also male cult prostitutes in the land, and they did according to all the abominations of the nations that the Lord cast out before the children of Israel.

25 In the fifth year of King Rehoboam, Shishak king of Egypt came up against Jerusalem. 26 He took away all the treasures of the house of the Lord and the treasures of the king's house, even all the shields of gold which Solomon had made. 27 King Rehoboam replaced them with bronze shields and committed them to the hands of the chief of the guard who guarded the king's house. 28 And whenever the king entered the house of the Lord, the guards carried them and brought them back into the guard chamber.

29 Now the rest of the acts of Rehoboam and all that he did, are they not written in the book of the chronicles of the kings of Judah? 30 There was war between Rehoboam and Jeroboam all their days. 31 Rehoboam slept with his fathers and was buried with his fathers in the City of David. And his mother's name was Naamah, an Ammonitess. And Abijah his son reigned in his stead.

Abijah, King of Judah
2Ch 13:1–2; 13:22–14:1

15 Now in the eighteenth year of King Jeroboam the son of Nebat, Abijah became king over Judah. 2 He reigned three years in Jerusalem. His mother's name was Maakah, the daughter of Abishalom.

3 He walked in all the sins of his father that he had done before him, and his heart was not wholly devoted to the Lord his God as the heart of his father David had been. 4 Nevertheless, for David's sake, the Lord his God gave him a lamp in Jerusalem, to set up his son after him and to establish Jerusalem, 5 because David did that which was right in the eyes of the Lord and did not turn aside from anything that He commanded him all the days of his life, except in the matter involving Uriah the Hittite.

6 The war begun between Rehoboam and Jeroboam continued all the days of his life. 7 Now the rest of the acts of Abijah and all that he did, are they not written in the book of the chronicles of the kings of Judah? And there was war between Abijah and Jeroboam.

8 Abijah slept with his fathers, and they buried him in the City of David, and Asa his son reigned in his place.

Asa, King of Judah
2Ch 14:2–3; 15:16–17:1

9 In the twentieth year of Jeroboam king of Israel, Asa became king over Judah. 10 He reigned forty-one years in Jerusalem, and his grandmother's name was Maakah, the daughter of Abishalom.

11 Asa did what was right in the eyes of the Lord, just as his father David had done. 12 He expelled the male cult prostitutes from the land and removed all the idols that his fathers had made. 13 In addition he even deposed his grandmother Maakah as queen, because she had made an idol in a grove. Asa destroyed her idol and burned it by the Kidron brook. 14 But the high places were not all removed, even though Asa's heart was wholly devoted to the Lord all his days. 15 He brought into the house of the Lord the things that both his father and he himself had dedicated, the silver and gold and cups.

16 There was war between Asa and Baasha king of Israel all their days. 17 Baasha king of Israel went up against Judah and fortified Ramah so he could prevent anyone from going out or coming in to Asa king of Judah.

18 Then Asa took all the silver and the gold that were left in the treasures of the house of the Lord, as well as the treasures of the king's house, and delivered them into the hand of his servants, and he sent them to Ben-Hadad, the son of Tabrimmon, the son of Hezion, king of Aram, who lived at Damascus, saying, 19 "There is a treaty between me and you and between my father and your father. I have sent to you a present of silver and gold. Come and break your treaty with Baasha king of Israel, so he will depart from me."

20 So Ben-Hadad listened to King Asa and sent the commanders of his armies against the cities of Israel and conquered Ijon, Dan, Abel Beth Maakah, and all Kinnereth, along with all the land of Naphtali. 21 When Baasha heard about it, he halted the fortification of Ramah and moved to Tirzah. 22 Then King Asa made a proclamation throughout all Judah—none was exempted—and they took away the stones of Ramah and the timber with which Baasha had built, and King Asa used them to build Geba of Benjamin as well as Mizpah.

23 The rest of all the acts of Asa and all his might and all that he did and the cities that he built, are they not written in the book of the chronicles of the kings of Judah? When he was old, he got a disease in his feet. 24 Asa then slept with his fathers and was buried with them in the city of his father David, and Jehoshaphat his son reigned in his place.

Nadab, King of Israel

25 Nadab the son of Jeroboam began to reign over Israel in the second year of Asa king of Judah and reigned over Israel two years. 26 He did evil in the sight of the Lord and walked in the way of his father and in his sin with which he made Israel to sin.

27 Baasha the son of Ahijah of the house of Issachar conspired against him, and Baasha killed him at Gibbethon, which belonged to the Philistines, for Nadab and all Israel laid siege to Gibbethon. 28 It was in the third year of Asa king of Judah that Baasha killed him and took his throne.

29 When he became king, Baasha killed all the house of Jeroboam. No one from Jeroboam's family was left breathing. He completely destroyed them, according to the word of the Lord which He spoke by His servant Ahijah the Shilonite, 30 because of the sins of Jeroboam which he sinned and which he made Israel sin, by his provocation with which he provoked the Lord God of Israel to anger.

31 Now the rest of the acts of Nadab and all that he did, are they not written in the book of the chronicles of the kings of Israel? 32 And there was war between Asa and Baasha king of Israel all their days.

Baasha, King of Israel

33 In the third year of Asa king of Judah, Baasha the son of Ahijah began to reign over all Israel in Tirzah, *and he did so* twenty-four

years. ³⁴ He did evil in the sight of the LORD and walked in the way of Jeroboam and in his sin with which he made Israel to sin.

16 Then the word of the LORD came to Jehu the son of Hanani against Baasha, saying, ² "I exalted you out of the dust and made you prince over My people Israel, and you have walked in the way of Jeroboam and have made My people Israel to sin, to provoke Me to anger with their sins. ³ See, I will take away the posterity of Baasha and the posterity of his house and will make your house like the house of Jeroboam the son of Nebat. ⁴ Those from the house of Baasha who die in the city will be eaten by dogs, and those who die in the fields will be eaten by the birds of the air."

⁵ Now the rest of the acts of Baasha and what he did and his might, are they not written in the book of the chronicles of the kings of Israel? ⁶ So Baasha slept with his fathers and was buried in Tirzah, and Elah his son reigned in his place.

⁷ And so it was by the hand of the prophet Jehu the son of Hanani that the word of the LORD came against Baasha and his house, for all the evil that he did in the sight of the LORD in provoking Him to anger with the work of his hands because he acted like the house of Jeroboam and also because he killed it.

Elah, King of Israel

⁸ In the twenty-sixth year of Asa king of Judah, Elah the son of Baasha began to reign over Israel in Tirzah, *and he did so* two years.

⁹ His servant Zimri, commander of half his chariots, conspired against him, and when he was in Tirzah, drinking himself drunk in the house of Arza, manager of his house in Tirzah, ¹⁰ Zimri went in and smote him and killed him. This took place in the twenty-seventh year of Asa king of Judah, and Zimri reigned in his place.

¹¹ When he began to reign, as soon as he was seated on his throne, he executed all the household of Baasha. He left no males, neither of his relatives nor of his friends. ¹² Thus Zimri destroyed all the house of Baasha, according to the word of the LORD which He spoke against Baasha by Jehu the prophet, ¹³ because of all the sins of Baasha and the sins of Elah his son, by which they sinned and by which they made Israel to sin in provoking the LORD God of Israel to anger with their vanities.

¹⁴ Now the rest of the acts of Elah and all that he did, are they not written in the book of the chronicles of the kings of Israel?

Zimri, King of Israel

¹⁵ In the twenty-seventh year of Asa king of Judah, Zimri reigned seven days in Tirzah. Now the troops were encamped against Gibbethon, which belonged to the Philistines. ¹⁶ The troops who were encamped heard how Zimri had conspired and had slain the king. As a result, all Israel made Omri, the commander of the army, king over Israel that day in the camp. ¹⁷ Omri went up from Gibbethon and all Israel with him, and they besieged Tirzah. ¹⁸ When Zimri saw that the city had fallen, he went into the citadel of the king's house and burned the king's house over him with fire, and he died, ¹⁹ because of his sins which he sinned in doing evil in the sight of the LORD, in walking in the way of Jeroboam and in his sin which he did to make Israel to sin.

²⁰ Now the rest of the acts of Zimri and his treason, are they not written in the book of the chronicles of the kings of Israel?

Omri, King of Israel

²¹ Then the people of Israel were divided into two parts. Half of the people followed Tibni the son of Ginath to make him king, and half followed Omri. ²² But the people who followed Omri defeated the people who followed Tibni, the son of Ginath. So Tibni died, and Omri reigned.

²³ In the thirty-first year of Asa king of Judah, Omri began to reign over Israel, *and he did so* twelve years. He reigned six years in Tirzah. ²⁴ He bought the hill of Samaria from Shemer for two talents^f of silver. He fortified the hill and named the city he built after the name of Shemer, owner of the hill, calling it "Samaria."

²⁵ But Omri did evil in the eyes of the LORD and did worse than all who preceded him, ²⁶ for he walked in all the ways of Jeroboam

the son of Nebat and in his sin with which he made Israel to sin to provoke the LORD God of Israel to anger with their vanities.

²⁷ Now the rest of the acts Omri performed and his might that he showed, are they not written in the book of the chronicles of the kings of Israel? ²⁸ So Omri slept with his fathers and was buried in Samaria, and Ahab his son reigned in his place.

Ahab Reigns in Israel

²⁹ In the thirty-eighth year of Asa king of Judah, Ahab the son of Omri began to reign over Israel, and Ahab the son of Omri reigned over Israel in Samaria twenty-two years. ³⁰ Ahab the son of Omri did more evil in the sight of the LORD than all who were before him. ³¹ The sins of Jeroboam the son of Nebat were seen as minor for him to walk in, for he took Jezebel the daughter of Ethbaal, king of the Sidonians, as his wife and went and served Baal and worshipped him. ³² He raised an altar for Baal in the house of Baal, which he had built in Samaria. ³³ Ahab made an Asherah and did more to provoke the LORD God of Israel to anger than all the kings of Israel who preceded him.

³⁴ In his days, Hiel the Bethelite built Jericho. He laid the foundation at the expense of his firstborn Abiram and set up the gates at the cost of the life of his youngest son Segub, according to the word of the LORD, which He spoke by Joshua the son of Nun.

Elijah's Prediction of Drought

17 Now Elijah the Tishbite, who was one of the inhabitants of Gilead, said to Ahab, "As the LORD God of Israel lives before whom I stand, there will not be dew or rain these years except by my word."

² The word of the LORD came to him, saying, ³ "Go from here and turn eastward and hide by the Kerith brook, which is east of the Jordan. ⁴ You shall drink from the brook, and I have commanded the ravens to feed you there."

⁵ So he went and did according to the word of the LORD, for he went and lived by the Kerith brook, which is east of the Jordan. ⁶ The ravens brought him bread and meat in the morning and bread and meat in the evening, and he drank from the brook.

The Widow of Zarephath

⁷ After some time, the brook dried up because there had been no rain in the land. ⁸ The word of the LORD came to him, saying, ⁹ "Arise, go to Zarephath, which belongs to Sidon, and live there. I have commanded a widow there to provide for you." ¹⁰ So he got up and went to Zarephath, and when he came to the gate of the city, a widow was there gathering sticks. He called to her and said, "Please get a small cup of water for me to drink." ¹¹ As she was going to get it, he called to her and said, "Please bring me a morsel of bread in your hand."

¹² She said, "As the LORD your God lives, I do not have bread, but only a handful of meal in a barrel and a little oil in a jar. I am gathering two sticks, that I can go in and make it for me and my son, so we may eat it and die."

¹³ Elijah said to her, "Do not fear; go and do as you have said, but make a little cake for me first, and bring it to me, and afterward, make some for your son and you, ¹⁴ for thus says the LORD God of Israel: The barrel of meal will not run out, nor will the jar of oil empty, until the day that the LORD sends rain upon the earth."

¹⁵ She went and did what Elijah told her to do, and she, he, and her household ate many days. ¹⁶ The barrel of meal did not run out, nor did the jar of oil empty, according to the word of the LORD, which He spoke by Elijah.

¹⁷ Later on, the son of the woman, the mistress of the house, became terribly sick, so much so that he had no breath left in him. ¹⁸ She said to Elijah, "What do I have to do with you, O you man of God? Have you come to remind me of my sin and to kill my son?"

¹⁹ And he said to her, "Give me your son," and he took him out of her arms and carried him up to a loft where he slept and laid him on his own bed. ²⁰ He cried to the LORD and said, "O LORD, my God, have You brought tragedy upon the widow with whom I live by killing her son?" ²¹ And he stretched himself upon the child three

^f 24 About 150 pounds, or 68 kilograms.

times and cried to the Lord and said, "O Lord, my God, I pray that You let this child's soul come into him again."

[22] The Lord heard the voice of Elijah, and the soul of the child came into him again, and he was revived. [23] Elijah took the child and brought him down out of the chamber into the house and returned him to his mother, and Elijah said, "See, your son lives!"

[24] The woman said to Elijah, "Now, because of this, I know that you are a man of God, and that the word of the Lord in your mouth is truth!"

Elijah Confronts Ahab

18 After many days, in the third year, the word of the Lord came to Elijah, saying, "Go and present yourself to Ahab, and I will send rain upon the earth." [2] Elijah went to show himself to Ahab.

And there was a great famine in Samaria. [3] Ahab called Obadiah, who was the governor of his house. (Now Obadiah feared the Lord greatly. [4] When Jezebel killed the prophets of the Lord, Obadiah took a hundred prophets and hid them in groups of fifty in a cave and fed them with bread and water.) [5] And Ahab said to Obadiah, "Go into the land, to all the springs of water and to all the brooks. Perhaps we will find grass to save the horses and mules, so that we do not lose all the beasts." [6] So they divided the land between them to search throughout it. Ahab went one way by himself, and Obadiah went another way by himself.

[7] As Obadiah was going along, he met Elijah, and he recognized him and fell on his face and said, "Is that you, my lord Elijah?"

[8] And he answered him, "I am. Go, tell your lord, 'Elijah is here.' "

[9] He said, "What evil have I done that you would hand your servant into the hand of Ahab to put me to death? [10] As the Lord your God lives, there is no nation or kingdom where my lord has not looked for you, and when they said, 'He is not here,' he made the kingdom and nation swear that they could not find you, [11] and now you say, 'Go, tell your lord, "Elijah is here!" ' [12] As soon as I am gone from you, the Spirit of the Lord will carry you to a place I do not know, and so when I come and tell Ahab and he cannot find you, he will execute me. But I, your servant, have feared the Lord since my youth. [13] Were you not told what I did when Jezebel killed the prophets of the Lord, how I hid a hundred men of the Lord's prophets in groups of fifty in a cave and fed them with bread and water? [14] And now you say, 'Go, tell your lord, "Elijah is here," ' and he will execute me."

[15] Elijah said, "As the Lord of Hosts lives, before whom I stand, I will surely show myself to him today."

Elijah and the Prophets of Baal

[16] So Obadiah went to meet Ahab and told him. And Ahab went to meet Elijah. [17] When Ahab saw Elijah, Ahab said to him, "Are you he that troubles Israel?"

[18] And he answered, "I have not troubled Israel, but you and your father's house, in that you have forsaken the commandments of the Lord and you have followed the Baals. [19] Now send word out and gather for me all Israel on Mount Carmel, along with the four hundred and fifty prophets of Baal and the four hundred prophets of Asherah who eat at Jezebel's table."

[20] So Ahab called out all the children of Israel and gathered the prophets together on Mount Carmel. [21] Elijah came to all the people and said, "How long will you stay between two opinions? If the Lord is God, follow Him, but if Baal, then follow him."

And the people did not say a word.

[22] Then Elijah said to the people, "I alone remain a prophet of the Lord, but Baal's prophets number four hundred and fifty men. [23] Therefore, let them give us two bulls, and let them choose one bull for themselves and cut it in pieces and lay it on some wood, but do not light a fire under it, and I will prepare the other bull, lay it on some wood, and not light a fire underneath it. [24] And you call on the name of your gods, and I will call on the name of the Lord, and the God that answers by fire, let Him be God."

And all the people answered and said, "It is well spoken."

[25] Elijah said to the prophets of Baal, "Choose one bull for yourselves and prepare it first, for there are many of you, and call on the name of your god, but do not light a fire underneath."

[26] They took the bull which was given to them, and they prepared it and called on the name of Baal from morning until noon, saying, "O Baal, hear us." But there was no voice, and no one answered. And they leaped upon the altar which was made.

[27] By noon, Elijah mocked them, saying, "Cry out loud, for he is a god. Either he is talking or is gone away or is on a journey, or perhaps he is asleep and needs to be awakened." [28] They cried out loud and cut themselves with knives and spears according to their custom until the blood gushed out on them. [29] And as midday passed, they prophesied until the time of the offering of the evening sacrifice. But there was no voice. No one answered; no one paid attention.

[30] Elijah said to all the people, "Come near to me." And all the people came near to him. And he repaired the altar of the Lord that was broken down. [31] Elijah took twelve stones, according to the number of the tribes of the sons of Jacob, to whom the word of the Lord came saying, "Israel shall be your name," [32] and he built an altar in the name of the Lord with stones, and he made a trench around the altar, so deep that it could contain two seahs[1] of seed. [33] He arranged the wood and cut the bull in pieces and laid him on the wood and said, "Fill four barrels with water, and pour it on the burnt sacrifice and on the wood."

[34] He said, "Do it a second time," and they did it a second time. And he said, "Do it a third time," and they did it the third time. [35] The water ran all around the altar and also filled the trench with water.

[36] At the time of the offering of the evening sacrifice, Elijah the prophet came near and said, "The Lord, God of Abraham, Isaac, and of Israel, let it be known this day that You are God in Israel and that I am Your servant and that I have done all these things at Your word. [37] Hear me, O Lord, hear me, so that this people may know that You are the Lord God and that You have turned their hearts back again."

[38] Then the fire of the Lord fell and consumed the burnt sacrifice and the wood and the stones and the dust and licked up the water that was in the trench.

[39] When all the people saw it, they fell on their faces and said, "The Lord, He is God! The Lord, He is God!"

[40] Elijah said to them, "Arrest the prophets of Baal, and do not let one of them escape." And they arrested them, and Elijah brought them down to the Kishon brook and executed them there.

End of the Drought

[41] Elijah said to Ahab, "Get up, eat and drink, for there is a sound of a heavy rainfall." [42] So Ahab got up to eat and drink. And Elijah went up to the top of Carmel, and he threw himself down on the ground and put his face between his knees.

[43] And he said to his servant, "Go up now, and look toward the sea."

And he went up and looked and said, "There is nothing."

And he said, "Go again," seven times.

[44] On the seventh time, he said, "A small cloud as small as a man's hand is rising out of the sea."

And he said, "Go up and say to Ahab, 'Mount your chariot and get down, so that the rain does not stop you.' "

[45] In the meantime, the sky turned black with clouds and wind, and there was a great rain. And Ahab rode and went to Jezreel. [46] The hand of the Lord was on Elijah, and he girded up his loins and ran ahead of Ahab to the entrance of Jezreel.

Elijah Flees From Jezebel

19 And Ahab told Jezebel all that Elijah had done and how he had executed all the prophets with the sword. [2] Then Jezebel sent a messenger to Elijah, saying, "So let the gods do to me and more also, if I do not make your life as the life of one of them by tomorrow about this time."

---

[1] 32 Likely about 24 pounds, or 11 kilograms.

³ When he saw that she was serious, he arose and ran for his life to Beersheba, which belongs to Judah, and left his servant there. ⁴ But he went a day's journey into the wilderness and came and sat down under a juniper tree and asked that he might die, saying, "It is enough! Now, O LORD, take my life, for I am not better than my fathers."

⁵ As he lay and slept under the juniper tree, an angel touched him and said to him, "Arise and eat." ⁶ He looked, and there was a cake baked on coals and a jar of water at his head. And he ate and drank and then lay down again.

⁷ The angel of the LORD came again a second time and touched him and said, "Arise and eat, because the journey is too great for you." ⁸ He arose and ate and drank and went in the strength of that food forty days and forty nights to Horeb, the mountain of God.

Elijah Hears the LORD

⁹ He came to a cave and camped there, and the word of the LORD came to him, and He said to him, "Why are you here, Elijah?"

¹⁰ And he said, "I have been very zealous for the LORD, Lord of Hosts, for the children of Israel have forsaken Your covenant, thrown down Your altars, and killed Your prophets with the sword, and I alone am left, and they seek to take my life."

¹¹ He said, "Go and stand on the mountain before the LORD."

And, behold, the LORD passed by, and a great and strong wind split the mountains and broke in pieces the rocks before the LORD, but the LORD was not in the wind. And after the wind, an earthquake came, but the LORD was not in the earthquake. ¹² And after the earthquake, a fire came, but the LORD was not in the fire, and after the fire, a still, small voice. ¹³ When Elijah heard it, he wrapped his face in his cloak and went out and stood in the entrance to the cave.

And a voice came to him and said, "Why are you here, Elijah?"

¹⁴ And he said, "I have been very zealous for the LORD, Lord of Hosts, because the children of Israel have forsaken Your covenant, thrown down Your altars, and killed your prophets with the sword, and I alone am left, and they seek to take my life."

¹⁵ The LORD said to him, "Go, return on the road through the Wilderness of Damascus, and when you arrive, anoint Hazael to be king over Aram. ¹⁶ And you shall anoint Jehu, the son of Nimshi, to be king over Israel, and you shall anoint Elisha, the son of Shaphat of Abel Meholah, to be prophet in your place. ¹⁷ He who escapes the sword of Hazael will be killed by Jehu, and he who escapes the sword of Jehu will be killed by Elisha. ¹⁸ Still, I have preserved seven thousand men in Israel for Myself, all of whose knees have not bowed to Baal and whose mouths have not kissed him."

The Call of Elisha

¹⁹ So he departed from there and found Elisha the son of Shaphat, who was plowing with twelve yoke of oxen before him and he with the twelfth, and Elijah passed by him and threw his cloak on him. ²⁰ He left the oxen and ran after Elijah and said, "Please let me kiss my father and mother, and then I will follow you."

And he said to him, "Go back, for what have I done to you?"

²¹ So he returned from following him and took a yoke of oxen and sacrificed them and boiled their flesh with the yokes from the oxen and gave it to the people, and they ate. Then he got up and went after Elijah and ministered to him.

Ben-Hadad Attacks Samaria

20 Now Ben-Hadad the king of Aram gathered his army together. Thirty-two kings were with him, with horses and chariots, and he went up and besieged Samaria and fought against it. ² He sent messengers into the city to Ahab king of Israel and said to him, "Thus says Ben-Hadad: ³ Your silver and gold is mine, as are your most attractive wives and children."

⁴ The king of Israel answered, "My lord, O king, just as you have said, I and all that I own are yours."

⁵ The messengers came again and said, "Thus says Ben-Hadad: Although I have said that you must give me your silver and gold, your wives and your children, ⁶ instead I will send my servants tomorrow about this time, and they will search your house and the houses of your servants, and whatever is precious to you, they

will put it in their hands and take it away."

⁷ Then the king of Israel called all the elders of the land and said, "Please notice how this man is looking for trouble, for he has demanded I give him my wives and children and my silver and gold, and I have not denied his request."

⁸ All the elders and all the people said to him, "Do not listen to him or consent to his demands."

⁹ Therefore he said to the messengers of Ben-Hadad, "Tell my lord the king: I will comply with the first request of your servant, but this thing I will not do." And the messengers departed and brought him word again.

¹⁰ Then Ben-Hadad sent *messengers* to him and said, "The gods do to me and then some if the dust of Samaria shall suffice for handfuls for all the people who follow me."

¹¹ The king of Israel answered, "Tell him: Let not he who puts on *his armor* boast himself as he who takes *it* off."

¹² When Ben-Hadad heard this message as he was drinking with the kings in the pavilions, he said to his servants, "Station yourselves!" And they stationed themselves against the city.

Ahab Defeats Ben-Hadad

¹³ Then a prophet came to Ahab king of Israel, saying, "Thus says the LORD: Have you seen this great multitude? See, I will deliver it into your hand this day, and you shall know that I am the LORD."

¹⁴ Ahab asked, "By whom?"

And he said, "Thus says the LORD: By the young leaders of the provinces."

Then he said, "Who shall order the battle?"

And he answered, "You."

¹⁵ Then he counted the young leaders of the provinces, and they were two hundred and thirty-two, and after them he counted all the people, all the children of Israel, and had seven thousand.

¹⁶ They went out at noon. But Ben-Hadad and the thirty-two kings who helped him were getting drunk in the pavilions. ¹⁷ The young leaders of the provinces went out first.

Ben-Hadad sent out scouts, and they told him, "Men from Samaria have come out."

¹⁸ He said, "If they have come out peacefully, take them alive, and if they have come out for battle, take them alive."

¹⁹ So these young leaders of the provinces came out of the city, followed by the army. ²⁰ Each one killed his man, and the Arameans fled with Israel pursuing them, but Ben-Hadad, the king of Aram, escaped on a horse with the horsemen. ²¹ The king of Israel went out and attacked the horses and chariots and killed a great number of Arameans.

²² The prophet came to the king of Israel and said, "Go, strengthen yourself and prepare, and see what you do, for next year the king of Aram will come up against you."

²³ The servants of the king of Aram said to him, "Their gods are gods of the hills. That is why they were stronger than us, but if we fight against them in the plain, we will surely be stronger than they. ²⁴ Do this: Dismiss the kings, each from his position, and put commanders in their places, ²⁵ and assemble an army like the army that you lost, horse for horse and chariot for chariot, and we will fight them in the plain and will surely be stronger than they." And he listened to their advice and followed it.

²⁶ The next year Ben-Hadad assembled the Arameans and went up to Aphek to fight against Israel. ²⁷ The children of Israel were assembled and were all present, and they went against them, and the children of Israel camped in front of them like two little flocks of kids, while the Arameans filled the country.

²⁸ A man of God came and spoke to the king of Israel and said, "Thus says the LORD: Because the Arameans have said, 'The LORD is God of the hills, but He is not God of the valleys,' I will deliver all this great multitude into your hand, and you will know that I am the LORD."

²⁹ They camped opposite each other for seven days, and on the seventh day, the battle was joined. The children of Israel killed a hundred thousand Aramean footmen in one day. ³⁰ But the rest fled into the city of Aphek, where a wall fell on twenty-seven thousand of the men who were left. And Ben-Hadad fled and came into the city into an inner chamber.

³¹ His servants said to him, "We have heard that the kings of the house of Israel are merciful kings. Please let us put sackcloth on our loins and ropes on our heads and go out to the king of Israel. Perhaps he will spare your life."

³² So they girded sackcloth on their loins and put ropes on their heads and came to the king of Israel and said, "Your servant Ben-Hadad says, 'Please let me live.' "

And he said, "Is he still alive? He is my brother!"

³³ Now the men were diligently looking for a positive sign and quickly took hold of it, and they said, "Your brother Ben-Hadad!"

Then he said, "Go. You bring him." Then Ben-Hadad came to him and got into the chariot.

³⁴ Ben-Hadad said to him, "I will restore the cities which my father took from your father, and you shall make streets for yourself in Damascus, as my father made in Samaria."

Then Ahab said, "I will send you away with this covenant." So he made a covenant with him and sent him away.

A Prophet Condemns Ahab

³⁵ Speaking in the word of the LORD, a certain man of the sons of the prophets said to his neighbor, "Strike me, please." But the man refused to strike him.

³⁶ Then he said to him, "Because you have not obeyed the voice of the LORD, as soon as you leave me, a lion will kill you." And as soon as he left him, a lion found and killed him.

³⁷ Then he found another man and said, "Strike me, please." And the man struck him so that he was wounded. ³⁸ So the prophet departed and waited for the king and disguised himself with ashes on his face. ³⁹ As the king passed by, he cried to the king and said, "Your servant went out into the midst of the battle, and a man turned aside and brought a man to me and said, 'Keep this man, and if by any means he goes missing, then your life shall be given for his life, or else you shall pay a talent¹ of silver.' ⁴⁰ As your servant was busy here and there, he disappeared."

And the king of Israel said to him, "So shall your judgment be; you have decided it yourself."

⁴¹ He quickly took the ashes away from his face, and the king of Israel recognized him as one of the prophets. ⁴² He said to him, "Thus says the LORD, 'Because you have let go out of your hand a man whom I had appointed to utter destruction, you shall pay for his life with your life and his people with your people.' " ⁴³ The king of Israel went to his house in Samaria angry and depressed.

Naboth's Vineyard

21 Now Naboth the Jezreelite had a vineyard in Jezreel right by the palace of Ahab king of Samaria. ² And after this Ahab spoke to Naboth, saying, "Give me your vineyard, so that I can have it for a garden of herbs, because it is near to my house, and I will give you a better vineyard for it, or if you prefer, I will give you its worth in money."

³ Naboth said to Ahab, "The LORD forbid that I should give you the inheritance of my fathers."

⁴ Ahab returned home angry and depressed because of the answer Naboth the Jezreelite had given him, for he had said, "I will not give you the inheritance of my fathers." He lay down on his bed and sulked and would not eat any bread.

⁵ But Jezebel his wife came to him and said, "Why is your spirit so sad that you refuse to eat bread?"

⁶ And he said to her, "Because I spoke to Naboth the Jezreelite and said to him, 'Give me your vineyard for money; or else, if you prefer, I will give you another vineyard for it.' And he answered, 'I will not give you my vineyard.' "

⁷ Jezebel his wife said to him, "Are you not the governor of the kingdom of Israel? Get up and eat bread, and let your heart be happy, for I will get the vineyard of Naboth the Jezreelite for you."

⁸ So she wrote letters in Ahab's name and sealed them with his seal and sent the letters to the elders and to the nobles that were in the city where Naboth lived. ⁹ In the letters she wrote,

"Proclaim a fast, and set Naboth on high among the people, ¹⁰ and set two men, sons of Belial,² before him, to bear witness against him, saying, 'You blasphemed God and the king.' And then carry him out and stone him, so that he will die."

¹¹ The men of his city, the elders and the nobles who lived in his city, did as Jezebel had sent word to them, as it was written in the letters that she had sent to them. ¹² They proclaimed a fast and set Naboth on high among the people. ¹³ Two men, children of Belial, came in and sat in front of him, and the men of Belial witnessed against Naboth in the presence of the people, saying, "Naboth blasphemed God and the king." Then they carried him out of the city and stoned him to death. ¹⁴ Then they sent word to Jezebel, saying, "Naboth has been stoned and is dead."

¹⁵ When Jezebel heard that Naboth had been stoned and was dead, she said to Ahab, "Arise, take possession of the vineyard of Naboth the Jezreelite, which he refused to sell to you for money, for Naboth is not alive, but dead." ¹⁶ When Ahab heard that Naboth was dead, he got up to go down to the vineyard of Naboth the Jezreelite, to take possession of it.

The LORD Condemns Ahab

¹⁷ The word of the LORD came to Elijah the Tishbite, saying: ¹⁸ Arise, go down to meet Ahab, king of Israel, who is in Samaria. He is now in the vineyard of Naboth, where he has gone down to possess it. ¹⁹ You shall speak to him, saying, "Thus says the LORD: Have you killed and also taken possession?" And you shall speak to him, saying, "Thus says the LORD: In the place where dogs licked the blood of Naboth, dogs will lick your own blood!"

²⁰ Ahab said to Elijah, "Have you found me, my enemy?"

And he answered, "I have found you, because you have sold yourself to work evil in the sight of the LORD. ²¹ 'See, I will bring disaster upon you and will take away your posterity and will cut off all your males, both free and slave, who are left in Israel, ²² and will make your house like the house of Jeroboam the son of Nebat and like the house of Baasha the son of Ahijah, for the provocation with which you have provoked Me to anger and made Israel to sin.'

²³ "The LORD also spoke of Jezebel, saying, 'The dogs will eat Jezebel by the wall of Jezreel.'

²⁴ "Those who from Ahab's family who die in the city will be eaten by dogs, and those who die in the field will be eaten by birds of the air."

²⁵ But there were none compared to Ahab, who sold himself to evil deeds in the sight of the LORD, which Jezebel his wife stirred up. ²⁶ He performed the most abominable act in following idols like the Amorites, whom the LORD cast out before the children of Israel.

²⁷ When Ahab heard those words, he tore his clothes and put on sackcloth on his flesh and fasted and lay in sackcloth and walked meekly.

²⁸ The word of the LORD came to Elijah the Tishbite, saying, ²⁹ "See how Ahab humbles himself before Me? Because he humbles himself before Me, I will not bring the disaster during his lifetime, but during his son's lifetime I will bring the disaster on his household."

Micaiah Prophesies Against Ahab
2Ch 18:1–27

22 And there were three years without war between Aram and Israel. ² In the third year, Jehoshaphat king of Judah went to visit the king of Israel. ³ The king of Israel said to his servants, "You know that Ramoth in Gilead is ours, but we have done nothing to take it out of the hand of the king of Aram!"

⁴ And he said to Jehoshaphat, "Will you go with me to battle Ramoth Gilead?"

And Jehoshaphat said to the king of Israel, "I am as you are, my people as your people, my horses as your horses." ⁵ Jehoshaphat said to the king of Israel, "Please ask for a word from the LORD today."

⁶ Then the king of Israel gathered the prophets together, approximately four hundred men, and said to them, "Shall I go against Ramoth Gilead to battle, or shall I wait?"

---

¹ *39* About 75 pounds, or 34 kilograms.   ² *10* Or, *evil men.*

And they said, "Go up, for the Lord shall deliver it into the hand of the king."

[7] Jehoshaphat said, "Is there not a prophet of the Lord here whom we can ask?"

[8] And the king of Israel said to Jehoshaphat, "There is still one man, Micaiah the son of Imlah, by whom we can inquire of the Lord. But I hate him because he never prophesies good for me, but always evil."

And Jehoshaphat said, "Let not the king say so."

[9] Then the king of Israel called an officer and said, "Quickly, bring Micaiah the son of Imlah."

[10] The king of Israel and Jehoshaphat the king of Judah *each* put on his robes and sat on his throne at the entrance of the gate of Samaria, and all the prophets prophesied before them. [11] Zedekiah the son of Kenaanah made horns of iron and said, "Thus says the Lord: With these you shall push the Arameans until you have consumed them."

[12] All the prophets prophesied similarly, saying, "Go up to Ramoth Gilead and prosper, for the Lord will deliver it into the king's hand."

[13] The servant who had gone to get Micaiah spoke to him, saying, "See here, the words of the prophets unanimously declare success for the king. Please let your word be like the word of one of them, and speak that which is good."

[14] Micaiah said, "As the Lord lives, I will speak whatever the Lord says to me."

[15] So he came to the king. And the king said to him, "Micaiah, shall we go against Ramoth Gilead to battle, or shall we wait?"

And he answered him, "Go and prosper, for the Lord will deliver it into the hand of the king."

[16] The king said to him, "How many times must I admonish you to tell me only the truth in the name of the Lord?"

[17] And he said, "I saw all Israel scattered upon the hills, as sheep without a shepherd, and the Lord said, 'These have no master. Let every man return to his own house in peace.' "

[18] The king of Israel said to Jehoshaphat, "Did I not tell you that he would not prophesy good concerning me, but evil?"

[19] And he said, "Hear, therefore, the word of the Lord: I saw the Lord sitting on His throne, and all the host of heaven standing beside Him on His right hand and on His left. [20] The Lord said, 'Who will persuade Ahab so that he will go up and die at Ramoth Gilead?'

"And one said this, and another said that. [21] Then a spirit came forth and stood before the Lord and said, 'I will persuade him.'

[22] "The Lord said to him, 'How?'

"And he said, 'I will go and be a lying spirit in the mouth of all his prophets.'

"And He said, 'You will be successful and persuade him. Go forth, and do so.'

[23] "Now therefore, the Lord has put a lying spirit in the mouths of all your prophets here, and He has spoken evil concerning you!"

[24] Then Zedekiah the son of Kenaanah walked up and struck Micaiah on the cheek and said, "Which way did the spirit of the Lord go from me in order to speak to you?"

[25] And Micaiah said, "You will see in that day, when you go into an inner chamber to hide."

[26] The king of Israel said, "Take Micaiah back to Amon the governor of the city and to Joash the king's son, [27] and say, 'Thus says the king: Put this man in the prison, and feed him with reduced rations of bread and water until I return safely.' "

[28] Micaiah said, "If you return safely, the Lord has not spoken through me." And he said, "Listen, all you people!"

Ahab Dies in Battle
2Ch 18:28–34

[29] So the king of Israel and Jehoshaphat the king of Judah went up to Ramoth Gilead. [30] The king of Israel said to Jehoshaphat,

"I will disguise myself and enter into the battle, but you wear your robes." And the king of Israel disguised himself and went into the battle.

[31] But the king of Aram ordered his thirty-two commanders who had control over his chariots, saying, "Fight neither against small nor great, but only against the king of Israel." [32] So when the commanders of the chariots saw Jehoshaphat, they said, "Surely it is the king of Israel." And they turned aside to fight against him, and Jehoshaphat cried out. [33] When the commanders of the chariots realized that it was not the king of Israel, they turned away from pursuing him.

[34] A certain man drew a bow at random and struck the king of Israel between the joints of the armor, and because of this, he said to the driver of his chariot, "Turn around and carry me out of the battle, for I am wounded." [35] The battle intensified that day, and the king was propped up in his chariot against the Arameans and died that evening, and the blood ran out of the wound into the floor of the chariot. [36] A proclamation went throughout the army as the sun was setting, saying, "Every man is to return to his city, and every man is to return to his own country."

[37] So the king died and was brought to Samaria, and they buried him there. [38] The chariot was washed in the pool of Samaria, and the dogs licked up the king's blood, and they washed his armor according to the word which the Lord spoke.

[39] Now the rest of the acts of Ahab and all that he did and the ivory house that he built and all the cities that he built, are they not written in the book of the chronicles of the kings of Israel? [40] So Ahab slept with his fathers. And Ahaziah his son reigned in his place.

Jehoshaphat, King of Judah
2Ch 20:31–21:1

[41] Jehoshaphat the son of Asa began to reign over Judah in the fourth year of Ahab king of Israel. [42] Jehoshaphat was thirty-five years old when he began to reign, and he reigned twenty-five years in Jerusalem. His mother's name was Azubah, the daughter of Shilhi. [43] He walked in all the ways of Asa his father. He did not turn aside, doing that which was right in the eyes of the Lord. Nevertheless, the high places were not taken down, and the people continued to offer *sacrifices* and burn incense there. [44] So Jehoshaphat made peace with the king of Israel.

[45] Now the rest of the acts of Jehoshaphat and the strength he showed and how he warred, are they not written in the book of the chronicles of the kings of Judah? [46] And he exterminated from the land the remnant of the male cult prostitutes who remained in the days of his father Asa. [47] At that time there was no king in Edom, and a regent sat in the king's place.

[48] Jehoshaphat made ships of Tarshish to go to Ophir for gold, but they never made it there, for the ships were broken at Ezion Geber. [49] Then Ahaziah the son of Ahab said to Jehoshaphat, "Let my servants go with your servants in the ships." But Jehoshaphat did not agree.

[50] Jehoshaphat slept with his fathers and was buried with his fathers in the City of David his father, and Jehoram his son reigned in his place.

Ahaziah, King of Israel

[51] Ahaziah the son of Ahab began to reign over Israel in Samaria the seventeenth year of Jehoshaphat king of Judah, and he reigned two years over Israel. [52] He did evil in the sight of the Lord and walked in the way of his father and in the way of his mother and in the way of Jeroboam the son of Nebat who made Israel sin, [53] for he served Baal and worshipped him and provoked the Lord God of Israel to anger, according to all that his father had done.

2 KINGS

God Judges Ahaziah

1 Then Moab rebelled against Israel after the death of Ahab. [2] Ahaziah fell down through a lattice in his upper chamber that was in Samaria and became ill. So he sent messengers and said to them, "Go, inquire of Baal-Zebub the god of Ekron whether I will recover from this illness."

[3] But the angel of the LORD said to Elijah the Tishbite, "Arise, go up to meet the messengers of the king of Samaria, and say to them, 'Is it because there is not a God in Israel, that you go to inquire of Baal-Zebub the god of Ekron?' [4] Therefore thus says the LORD, 'You will not come down from the bed on which you have gone up but will surely die.' " Then Elijah departed.

[5] When the messengers returned to the king, he said to them, "Why have you returned?"

[6] And they said to him, "A man came up to meet us and said to us, 'Go, return to the king that sent you and say to him: Thus says the LORD: Is it because there is no God in Israel that you are sending to inquire of Baal-Zebub the god of Ekron? Therefore you will not come down from the bed on which you have gone up, but you will surely die.' "

[7] He said to them, "What sort of man was he who came up to meet you and told you these things?"

[8] They answered him, "He was a hairy man with a leather belt around his waist."

He said, "It was Elijah the Tishbite."

[9] Then the king sent to him a captain of fifty with his fifty men. He went up to Elijah, and there he was, sitting on the top of a hill, and he said to him, "Man of God, the king says, 'Come down.' "

[10] But Elijah answered the captain of fifty: "If I am a man of God, then let fire come down from heaven and consume you and your fifty men." Then fire came down from heaven and consumed him and his fifty men.

[11] Again the king sent to him another captain of fifty with his fifty men. He said, "Man of God, thus says the king: Come down quickly."

[12] Elijah answered them, "If I am a man of God, let fire come down from heaven and consume you and your fifty men." Then the fire of God came down from heaven and consumed him and his fifty men.

[13] Then again the king sent a third captain of fifty with his fifty men. The third captain of fifty went up, came and fell on his knees before Elijah, and pleaded with him, "Man of God, may my life and the life of these fifty servants of yours be precious in your sight. [14] See, fire came down from heaven and consumed the two captains of the former fifties with their fifty men. May my life now be precious in your sight."

[15] Then the angel of the LORD said to Elijah, "Go down with him. Do not be afraid of him." So he arose and went down with him to the king.

[16] Then he said to him, "Thus says the LORD: Have you sent messengers to inquire of Baal-Zebub the god of Ekron, because there is no God in Israel to inquire of His word? Therefore you will not come down from the bed on which you have gone up, but you will surely die." [17] So he died according to the word of the LORD which Elijah had spoken.

Then Jehoram[1] reigned in his place in the second year of Jehoram son of Jehoshaphat, king of Judah, because he had no son. [18] Now the rest of the acts of Ahaziah which he did, are they not written in the book of the chronicles of the kings of Israel?

Elijah Ascends to Heaven

2 Then when the LORD was about to take Elijah up to heaven by a whirlwind, Elijah went with Elisha from Gilgal. [2] Elijah said to Elisha, "Tarry here, I ask you, for the LORD has sent me to Bethel."

But Elisha said to him, "As the LORD lives, and as you live, I will not leave you." So they went down to Bethel.

[3] The sons of the prophets who were at Bethel came out to Elisha and said to him, "Do you know that today the LORD is taking away your master from you?"

And he said, "Yes, I know. Keep silent."

[4] Elijah said to him, "Elisha, stay here, for the LORD has sent me to Jericho."

And he said, "As the LORD lives, and as you live, I will not leave you." So they entered Jericho.

[5] The sons of the prophets who were at Jericho approached Elisha and said to him, "Do you know that today the LORD is taking away your master from you?"

And he said, "Yes, I know. Keep silent."

[6] Then Elijah said to him, "Stay here, for the LORD has sent me to the Jordan."

And he said, "As the LORD lives, and as you live, I will not leave you." And the two of them went on.

[7] Fifty men of the sons of the prophets went and stood at a distance, and the two of them stood by the Jordan. [8] Then Elijah took his robe and rolled it up and struck the water, and it was divided from one side to the other. Then the two of them crossed on dry ground.

[9] And as they were crossing, Elijah said to Elisha, "Ask for something, and I will do it for you before I am taken away from you."

And Elisha said, "Let a double portion of your spirit be upon me."

[10] He said, "You have asked for a difficult thing, but if you see me when I am taken from you, it will happen to you. If not, it will not."

[11] As they continued walking and talking, a chariot of fire and horses of fire separated the two of them, and Elijah went up by a whirlwind into heaven. [12] Elisha was watching and crying, "My father, my father, the chariot of Israel and its horsemen!" And he did not see him again. Then he grabbed his own clothes and tore them in two pieces.

[13] He picked up the robe of Elijah that fell from him, and he returned and stood on the bank of the Jordan. [14] And he took the robe of Elijah that fell from him, and struck the water, and said, "Where is the LORD, God of Elijah?" When he had struck the water, it parted from one side to the other, and Elisha crossed over.

[15] When the sons of the prophets who were at Jericho saw him from far off, they said, "The spirit of Elijah rests on Elisha." And they came to meet him and bowed down to the ground before him. [16] They said to him, "Look now, there are fifty strong men with your servants. Let them go and look for your master. Perhaps the Spirit of the LORD has lifted him up and thrown him on some mountain or into some valley."

He said, "Do not send them."

[17] When they urged him until he was ashamed, he said, "Send them." So they sent fifty men, and they searched for three days but did not find him. [18] When they returned to him (for he had stayed at Jericho), he said to them, "Did I not say to you, do not go?"

Elisha Performs Miracles

[19] Now the men of the city said to Elisha, "The location of this city is good, as my lord sees, but the water is bad, and the land is unfruitful."

[20] He said, "Bring me a new bowl and put salt in it." So they brought it to him.

[21] He went out to the spring of water and threw the salt into it and said, "Thus says the LORD: I have healed this water. No more death or unfruitfulness will come from it." [22] So the waters have been healthy until this day, according to the word that Elisha spoke.

[23] He went up from there to Bethel, and going up on the way, little boys came out of the city and made fun of him and said to him, "Go up, you bald head! Go up, you bald head!" [24] He turned around, saw them, and cursed them in the name of the LORD. Then

---

[1] **17** *Joram* in 1Ch 3:11; 26:24.

two she-bears came out of the woods and ripped open forty-two of the boys. [25] He went from there to Mount Carmel, and from there he returned to Samaria.

Jehoram Reigns Over Israel

3 Now Jehoram son of Ahab reigned over Israel in Samaria in the eighteenth year of Jehoshaphat king of Judah and reigned twelve years. [2] He did evil in the sight of the LORD, but not like his father and mother, for he removed the pillar of Baal that his father had made. [3] Nevertheless he clung to the sins of Jeroboam the son of Nebat, who had caused Israel to sin. He did not depart from them.

[4] Now Mesha king of Moab was a sheep-breeder and gave back to the king of Israel a hundred thousand lambs and the wool of a hundred thousand rams. [5] But when Ahab died, the king of Moab rebelled against the king of Israel. [6] King Jehoram went out of Samaria at that time and mustered all Israel. [7] He went and sent to Jehoshaphat the king of Judah, saying, "The king of Moab has rebelled against me. Will you go with me to Moab to battle?"

He said, "I will go up. I am as you are, my people as your people, and my horses as your horses."

[8] Then he said, "Which way should we go up?"

And he said, "The way through the Wilderness of Edom."

[9] So the king of Israel, the king of Judah, and the king of Edom went, and they marched around seven days. But there was no water for the camp or for the livestock that followed them.

[10] The king of Israel said, "Alas! The LORD has called these three kings to give them into the hand of Moab!"

[11] But Jehoshaphat said, "Is there a prophet of the LORD here, through whom we may inquire of the LORD?"

Then one of the king of Israel's servants answered, "Elisha the son of Shaphat, who poured water on the hands of Elijah, is here."

[12] Jehoshaphat said, "The word of the LORD is with him." So the king of Israel and Jehoshaphat and the king of Edom went down to him.

[13] Elisha said to the king of Israel, "What have I to do with you? Go to your father's prophets, or to your mother's prophets."

Then the king of Israel said to him, "No. The LORD has called these three kings to deliver them into the hand of Moab."

[14] Elisha said, "As the LORD of Hosts lives, before whom I stand, surely, were it not for my regard for Jehoshaphat the king of Judah, I would not look at you nor see you. [15] Now bring me a musician."

And when the musician played, the hand of the LORD came upon him. [16] He said, "Thus says the LORD, 'Make this valley full of pools.' [17] For thus says the LORD, 'You will not see wind; nor will you see rain, yet that valley will be filled with water, that you may drink, both you and your livestock, and your cattle.' [18] This is an easy thing in the sight of the LORD, and He will give the Moabites into your hand. [19] You will strike every fortified city and every choice city, and will cut down every good tree, and stop every spring of water, and you will ruin every good piece of land with stones."

[20] So in the morning as the offering was offered up, suddenly water flowed from the way of Edom, and the land was filled with water.

[21] And when all the Moabites heard that the kings had come up to fight against them, all who were able to bear arms and older were summoned and stood at the border. [22] They got up early in the morning, and the sun shone on the water, and the Moabites saw the water opposite them was as red as blood. [23] Then they said, "This is blood. The kings have surely fought together; and they have killed one another. Now therefore, Moab, to the spoil!"

[24] When they came to the camp of Israel, the children of Israel arose and struck the Moabites, so that they ran from them. And they went forward into their land, killing the Moabites. [25] They demolished the cities, and on every good piece of land every man threw a stone and filled it with stones, and they stopped every spring of water and cut down every good tree. Only in Kir Hareseth did the stones in the wall remain, until the slingers surrounded it and struck it.

[26] When the king of Moab saw that the battle was overwhelming him, he took with him seven hundred swordsmen to break through to the king of Edom, but they were unable. [27] Then he took his firstborn son, who would have reigned in his place, and offered him for a burnt offering on the wall. And great wrath came upon Israel, and they departed from him and returned to their own land.

The Widow's Olive Oil

4 Now one of the wives of the sons of the prophets cried to Elisha, "Your servant my husband is dead, and you know that your servant feared the LORD, but a creditor has come to take my two sons as slaves."

[2] Elisha said to her, "What shall I do for you? Tell me, what do you have in the house?"

She said, "Your servant has nothing in the house except a jar of oil."

[3] Then he said, "Go, ask for vessels from all your neighbors, empty vessels and not just a few. [4] Then go in, shut the door behind you and your sons, and pour the oil into all these vessels. When each is full, set it aside."

[5] So she left him and shut the door behind her and her sons, and they kept bringing vessels to her, and she kept pouring. [6] When the vessels were full, she said to her son, "Bring me another vessel."

But he said to her, "There is not another vessel." And the oil ceased.

[7] Then she went and told the man of God. And he said, "Go, sell the oil, and pay your debt, and you and your children can live on the rest."

Elisha Raises the Shunammite's Son

[8] One day Elisha passed through Shunem, and a noble woman was there who urged him to eat a meal. So whenever he passed through, he stopped there to eat a meal. [9] And she said to her husband, "I know that he is a holy man of God regularly passing through near us. [10] Let us make a little walled upper room and put for him there a bed, a table, a chair, and a lamp, so when he comes to us he can stay there."

[11] One day he came by there, and he turned aside to the upper room and lay down. [12] He said to Gehazi his servant, "Call this Shunammite woman." So he called her and she stood before him. [13] He said to him, "Say to her, Look, you have gone to all this trouble for us. What may be done for you? Would you have a word spoken on your behalf to the king, or to the captain of the army?"

And she answered, "I am living among my people."

[14] He said, "What may be done for her?"

And Gehazi said, "Actually, she has no son, and her husband is old."

[15] He said, "Call her." When he had called her, she stood in the entrance. [16] He said, "At this season, when it is time, you will embrace a son."

And she said, "No, my lord, man of God, do not lie to your servant."

[17] But the woman conceived and bore a son at that season, at the time that Elisha had told her.

[18] When the child was older, he went out one day to his father with the reapers. [19] He said to his father, "My head, my head!"

And he said to a servant, "Carry him to his mother." [20] When he had taken him and brought him to his mother, the boy sat on her knees until noon, and died. [21] She went up, and laid him down on the bed of the man of God, shut the door on him, and went out.

[22] Then she called to her husband, "Send me one of the servants and one of the donkeys, so that I may run to the man of God and return."

[23] He said, "Why are you going to him today? It is neither New Moon nor Sabbath."

She said, "It will be all right."

[24] Then she saddled the donkey and said to her servant, "Lead on, and do not hold back for me unless I tell you." [25] So she went and came to the man of God at Mount Carmel.

And when the man of God saw her far off, he said to Gehazi his servant, "Look, over there is the Shunammite woman. [26] Now run to meet her, and say to her, Are you all right? Is your husband all right? Is the child all right?"

And she said, "It is all right."

[27] When she came to the man of God at the mountain, she grabbed his feet. Gehazi approached to push her away. But the

man of God said, "Let her alone, for she is in bitter distress, and the LORD has hidden it from me and has not told me."

28 Then she said, "Did I ask for a son from my lord? Did I not say, Do not give me false hope?"

29 Then he said to Gehazi, "Prepare yourself, take my staff in your hand, and go. If you find anyone, do not greet him, and if anyone greets you, do not answer him, and lay my staff on the face of the boy."

30 Then the boy's mother said, "As the LORD lives, and as you live, I will not leave without you." And he got up and followed her.

31 Gehazi passed through ahead of them and laid the staff on the face of the boy, but there was no sound or response. So he returned to meet him and told him, "The boy is not awake."

32 When Elisha came into the house, he saw that the boy was dead, lying on his bed. 33 So he went in, and shut the door on the two of them, and prayed to the LORD. 34 He went up and lay on the child, put his face on his face, and his eyes on his eyes, and his hands on his hands. Then he bent over the child, and the child's flesh warmed. 35 Then he got down, walked once back and forth in the house, and went up, and bent over him; the boy sneezed seven times, and the boy opened his eyes.

36 Then Elisha called Gehazi and said, "Call the Shunammite woman." So he called her, and she came to him. Then he said, "Pick up your son." 37 Then she came in, fell at his feet, and bowed down to the ground. Then she picked up her son and went out.

Elisha Purifies the Deadly Stew

38 When Elisha returned to Gilgal, there was a famine in the land. The sons of the prophets were sitting before him, and he said to his servant, "Put on the big cooking pot, and boil some stew for the sons of the prophets."

39 One went out into the field to gather herbs. He found a wild vine and gathered from it wild gourds, filling his clothes, and came and split them into the pot of stew, but they did not recognize them. 40 So they poured it out for the men to eat. But as they were eating the stew, they cried out, "Man of God, there is death in the pot." They could not eat it.

41 But he said, "Then bring flour." He threw it into the pot and said, "Pour it for the people and let them eat." And there was nothing bad in the pot.

Elisha Feeds One Hundred Men

42 A man came from Baal Shalishah, and he brought the man of God food from the first fruits—twenty loaves of barley and fresh ears of grain—in his sack. And Elisha said, "Give it to the people and let them eat."

43 But his servant said, "How can I set this before a hundred men?"

He said, "Give it to the people and let them eat, for thus says the LORD, 'They will eat and have some left.' " 44 So he set it before them, they ate, and some was left over, according to the word of the LORD.

Naaman Healed of Leprosy

5 Now Naaman, captain of the army of the king of Aram, was a great man before his master and held favor because by him the LORD had given deliverance to Aram. He was also a mighty warrior, but he had leprosy.

2 The Arameans had gone out raiding and had taken captive a little girl from the land of Israel, and she waited on the wife of Naaman. 3 She said to her mistress, "If only my lord were before the prophet who is in Samaria! Then he would take away his leprosy from him."

4 So Naaman went in and told his lord, "Thus and so spoke the girl from the land of Israel." 5 The king of Aram said, "Go, and I will send a letter to the king of Israel." So he went and took with him ten talents[1] of silver, six thousand shekels[2] of gold, and ten sets of clothes. 6 He brought the letter to the king of Israel, which read, "Now when this letter comes to you, know that I have sent Naaman my servant to you, that you may take away from him his leprosy."

7 When the king of Israel had read the letter, he tore his clothes and said, "Am I God, to kill and to give life, that this man sends a man to me to take away his leprosy? But consider, and see how he is seeking a quarrel with me."

8 But when Elisha the man of God heard that the king of Israel had torn his clothes, he sent word to the king, saying, "Why have you torn your clothes? Let him come to me, and he will know that there is a prophet in Israel." 9 So Naaman came with his horses and chariot and stood at the entrance to the house of Elisha. 10 Elisha sent a messenger to him, saying, "Go and wash seven times in the Jordan, and your flesh will be returned and cleansed."

11 But Naaman became angry and went away and said to himself, "Surely he could have come out, and stood and called on the name of the LORD his God, and waved his hand over the infected area, and taken away the leprosy. 12 Are not Abana and Pharpar, rivers of Damascus, better than all the waters of Israel? Could I not wash in them and be clean?" So he turned and went away in a rage.

13 But his servants approached and spoke to him, "My father, if the prophet had told you to do some great thing, would you not have done it? How much more when he said to you, 'Wash and be clean'?" 14 So he went down and dipped himself in the Jordan seven times, according to the word of the man of God, and his flesh returned like the flesh of a little boy, and he was clean.

15 Then he returned to the man of God, he and all his company. He came and stood before him, and he said, "Now I know that there is no God in all the land, except in Israel. Now take a gift from your servant."

16 But he said, "As the LORD lives, before whom I stand, I will take no gift." He urged him to take it, but he refused.

17 Then Naaman said, "If not, let two mule loads of dirt be given to your servant, for your servant will no longer offer a burnt offering or sacrifice to any god, except the LORD. 18 But may the LORD pardon your servant on one account: When my master enters the house of Rimmon to worship, and he leans on my hand, and I bow down in the house of Rimmon, when I do bow down in the house of Rimmon, may the LORD pardon your servant on this one account."

19 He said to him, "Go in peace." So he departed from him a short distance.

Gehazi's Greed

20 Then Gehazi the servant of Elisha the man of God said, "My master has spared Naaman the Aramean by not taking from his hands what he brought. As the LORD lives, I will run after him and take something from him."

21 So Gehazi pursued Naaman. Then Naaman saw him running after him, jumped down from the chariot to meet him, and said, "Is everything all right?"

22 And he said, "Everything is all right. My master has sent me and says, 'Even now two servants from Ephraim, from the sons of the prophets, have come to me. Give them a talent[3] of silver and two changes of clothes.' "

23 Naaman said, "Please, take two talents." He urged him and tied up two talents of silver in two bags with two changes of clothes and gave them to two of his servants, who carried them before Gehazi. 24 When he came to Ophel, he took them from their hand and put them away in the house. Then he sent the men away, and they departed.

25 Then he entered and stood before his master. And Elisha said to him, "Where have you come from, Gehazi?"

And he said, "Your servant went here and there."

26 He said to him, "Did my heart not go with you when the man turned from his chariot to meet you? Is it a time to take money, and to take garments, olives and vineyards, sheep and oxen, male and female servants? 27 The leprosy of Naaman will cling to you and to your descendants forever." So he went out from his presence, leprous like snow.

The Floating Axe Head

6 Now the sons of the prophets said to Elisha, "Look, the place where we are living with you is too small for us. 2 Let us go to

---

[1] 5 About 750 pounds, or 340 kilograms.   [2] 5 About 150 pounds, or 69 kilograms.   [3] 22 About 75 pounds, or 34 kilograms.

the Jordan and take from there one beam per man, and let us make for ourselves a place to live there."

And Elisha said, "Go."

³ Then one of them said, "Please come with your servants." And he said, "I will come." ⁴ So he went with them.

And they came to the Jordan and cut down trees. ⁵ But as one was cutting down a tree, the axe head fell into the water. He cried, "Ah, master! It was borrowed."

⁶ Then the man of God said, "Where did it fall?" When he showed him the place, he cut off a stick, and threw it in there, and he made the iron float. ⁷ So Elisha said, "Pick it up." And he reached out his hand and took it.

The Blinded Arameans Captured

⁸ Then the king of Aram was fighting against Israel, and he took counsel with his servants, saying, "At such and such a place will be my camp."

⁹ But the man of God sent word to the king of Israel, saying, "Take care not to pass through this place, for the Arameans are marching down there." ¹⁰ The king of Israel sent word to the place of which the man of God spoke. He warned him and was on his guard there more than once.

¹¹ The mind of the king of Aram was troubled by this, so he called his servants and said to them, "Will you not tell me who among us sides with the king of Israel?"

¹² Then one of his servants said, "No one, my lord, O king. Elisha, the prophet who is in Israel, tells the king of Israel the words that you speak in your bedroom."

¹³ He said, "Go and see where he is, so that I may send for him and take him." And it was told to him, "He is in Dothan." ¹⁴ So he sent horses, chariots, and a great army there. They came by night and surrounded the city.

¹⁵ When a servant of the man of God rose early in the morning and went out, a force surrounded the city both with horses and chariots. And his servant said to him, "Alas, my master! What will we do?"

¹⁶ And he said, "Do not be afraid, for there are more with us than with them."

¹⁷ Then Elisha prayed, "Lord, open his eyes and let him see." So the Lord opened the eyes of the young man, and he saw that the mountain was full of horses and chariots of fire surrounding Elisha.

¹⁸ When they came down to him, Elisha prayed to the Lord, "Strike this people with blindness." And He struck them with blindness according to the word of Elisha.

¹⁹ Elisha said to them, "This is not the way, and this is not the city. Follow me, and let me bring you to the man whom you seek." But he led them to Samaria.

²⁰ When they entered Samaria, Elisha said, "Lord, open the eyes of these men and let them see." And the Lord opened their eyes, and they saw that they were in the middle of Samaria.

²¹ The king of Israel said to Elisha when he saw them, "My father, shall I kill them? Shall I kill them?"

²² And he said, "You shall not kill them. Did you capture with your sword and with your bow those whom you want to kill? Set bread and water before them, and let them eat and drink and then go to their master." ²³ So he prepared for them a great banquet. When they had eaten and had drunk, he sent them away, and they went to their master. So the Aramean raiders did not enter into the land of Israel again.

Ben-Hadad Besieges Samaria

²⁴ After this, Ben-Hadad king of Aram gathered all his army, went up, and besieged Samaria. ²⁵ There was a great famine in Samaria, and they besieged it until a donkey's head was sold for eighty shekels¹ of silver, and one-fourth of a kab² of dove droppings for five shekels³ of silver.

²⁶ As the king of Israel was walking across the city wall, a woman cried out to him, "Help, my lord king."

²⁷ He said, "If the Lord will not help you, how can I help you? From the threshing floor or from the winepress?" ²⁸ And the king said to her, "What is wrong with you?"

And she said, "This woman said to me, 'Give your son and let us eat him today, and we will eat my son tomorrow.' ²⁹ So we boiled my son and ate him. The next day I said to her, 'Give your son, that we may eat him.' But she has hidden her son."

³⁰ When the king heard the words of the woman, he tore his clothes. And since he was walking across the city wall, the people saw that he had sackcloth on his body underneath. ³¹ Then he said, "So may God do to me, and even more, if the head of Elisha the son of Shaphat stands on his shoulders after today."

³² Now Elisha was sitting in his house, and the elders were sitting with him. The king sent a messenger, but before the messenger came to him, Elisha said to the elders, "Are you aware that this son of a murderer has sent a man to take off my head? When the messenger enters, shut the door and hold it against him. Is not the sound of his master's feet behind him?"

³³ And while he was speaking with them, the messenger came down to him, and then the king said, "This calamity is of the Lord! Why should I hope in the Lord any longer?"

7 Then Elisha said, "Hear the word of the Lord: Thus says the Lord: Tomorrow about this time a measure⁴ of fine flour will be sold for a shekel,⁵ and two measures⁶ of barley for a shekel, at the gate of Samaria."

² Then an officer on whose hand the king leaned answered the man of God, "If the Lord were to make windows in heaven, could this thing happen?"

And he said, "You will see it with your eyes, but you will not eat from it."

The Arameans Flee

³ There were four leprous men at the entry of the gate, and they said to one another, "Why are we sitting here until we die? ⁴ If we say, 'Let us enter the city,' the famine is in the city, and we shall die there. But if we sit here, we die also. Now come, let us fall into the camp of the Arameans. If they spare our lives, we will live, and if they kill us, we will die."

⁵ So they rose at twilight to enter the camp of the Arameans. When they came to the edge of the camp of the Arameans, there was no one there. ⁶ For the Lord had caused the Aramean camp to hear the sound of chariots, horses, even the sound of a large army, so that they said to one another, "Listen, the king of Israel has hired the kings of the Hittites and the kings of the Egyptians to come against us." ⁷ So they got up and ran away in the twilight and abandoned their tents, their horses, and their donkeys. The camp remained just as it was, and they ran for their lives.

⁸ When these leprous men came to the edge of the camp, they went into one tent. They ate and drank, carried off silver, gold, and clothes, and went and hid them. Then they went back, entered another tent, and carried off things from there and went and hid them.

⁹ Then they said to one another, "We are not doing right today. This is a day of good news. If we are silent and wait until the morning light, we will be found guilty. Let us go now and enter the city and tell the king's household."

¹⁰ So they went and called to the gatekeepers of the city, and they told them, "We came to the camp of the Arameans, and there was no one there. There was no sound of a man's voice, only horses tied, donkeys tied, and the tents as they were." ¹¹ Then the gatekeepers called out and told the king's household inside.

¹² The king got up in the night and said to his servants, "I will show you what the Arameans have done to us. They know that we are starving, so they left the camp to hide themselves in the field, saying, 'When they come out of the city, we will capture them alive and get into the city.' "

¹³ One of his servants answered, "Let some men take five of the remaining horses, since those remaining will suffer the fate of the

---

¹25 About 2 pounds, or 920 grams. ²25 Likely about ¼ pound, or 100 grams. ³25 About 2 ounces, or 58 grams.
⁴1 Likely about 12 pounds, or 5.5 kilograms of flour, and in vv. 16 and 18. ⁵1 About ⅜ ounce, or 12 grams, and in vv. 16 and 18.
⁶1 Likely about 20 pounds, or 9 kilograms of barley, and in vv. 16 and 18.

whole multitude of Israel that have perished already; so let us send them and see."

14 So they took two chariots with horses, and the king sent them after the army of the Arameans, saying, "Go and see." 15 So they went after them to the Jordan, and the whole way was full of clothes and vessels, which the Arameans had thrown away in their haste. Then the messengers returned and told the king. 16 Then the people went out and looted the camp of the Arameans. So a measure of fine flour was sold for a shekel, and two measures of barley for a shekel, according to the word of the Lord.

17 The king had appointed the officer on whose hand he leaned to have charge over the gate, and the people trampled him in the gate, and he died, just as the man of God had said when the king came down to him. 18 Then the man of God had spoken to the king, saying, "Two seahs of barley shall be sold for a shekel, and a seah of fine flour for a shekel, about this time tomorrow at the gate of Samaria."

19 The officer had answered the man of God, "If the Lord should make windows in heaven, could such a thing happen?" And he had said, "You shall see it with your own eyes, but you shall not eat of it." 20 So it happened to him, for the people trampled him in the gate, and he died.

The Shunammite's Land Restored

8 Then Elisha spoke to the woman whose son he had restored to life, "Get up and go, you and your household, and sojourn wherever you can, for the Lord has called for a famine, and it will come on the land for seven years." 2 So the woman got up and did according to the word of the man of God. She went with her household and sojourned in the land of the Philistines for seven years.

3 At the end of seven years, the woman returned from the land of the Philistines, and she went forth to appeal to the king for her house and her field. 4 Now the king was talking with Gehazi the servant of the man of God, saying, "Tell me all the great things that Elisha has done." 5 As he was telling the king how he had restored a dead body to life, the woman whose son he had restored to life started appealing to the king for her house and her land.

Gehazi said, "My lord king, this is the woman, and this is her son whom Elisha restored to life." 6 When the king questioned the woman, she told him.

So the king appointed to her an official, saying, "Restore all that was hers and all the proceeds of the field from the day that she abandoned the land until now."

Ben-Hadad Is Murdered

7 Then Elisha came to Damascus while Ben-Hadad the king of Aram was ill, and he was told, "The man of God has come here." 8 The king said to Hazael, "Take a present with you and go to meet the man of God. Inquire of the Lord through him, saying, 'Will I recover from this illness?'"

9 So Hazael went to meet him and took a present with him, all sorts of good things from Damascus, forty camel loads. He came and stood before him and said, "Your son Ben-Hadad king of Aram has sent me to you, asking, 'Will I recover from this illness?'" 10 And Elisha said to him, "Go, say to him, 'You will certainly recover,' but the Lord has shown me that he will certainly die." 11 Hazael stared at him until he was ashamed. Then the man of God wept.

12 Hazael said, "Why are you weeping, my lord?"

He said, "Because I know the evil that you will do to the children of Israel. You will set their fortresses on fire. You will kill their young men with the sword. You will smash their children and rip open their pregnant women."

13 Hazael said, "What? Is your servant a dog that he should do this great thing?"

And Elisha said, "The Lord has shown me that you will be king over Aram."

14 Then he left Elisha and went to his master, who said to him, "What did Elisha say to you?" And he said, "He told me that you would surely recover." 15 But the next day he took a blanket, dipped it in water, and spread it on his face, so that he died. And Hazael reigned in his place.

Jehoram, King of Judah
2Ch 21:5–20

16 In the fifth year of Joram the son of Ahab, king of Israel, Jehoram the son of Jehoshaphat, king of Judah, became king. 17 He was thirty-two years old when he became king, and he reigned eight years in Jerusalem. 18 He walked in the way of the kings of Israel, just as the house of Ahab had done, for the daughter of Ahab was his wife. He did evil in the sight of the Lord. 19 Yet the Lord was not willing to destroy Judah, for the sake of His servant David, since He promised to give a lamp to him and his sons perpetually.

20 In his days Edom rebelled against the rule of Judah, and they put a king over themselves. 21 So Jehoram crossed over to Zair, all his chariots with him, and he rose at night and struck Edom and the captains of their chariots who had surrounded him. But the people fled to their tents. 22 So Edom has been in rebellion against the rule of Judah until this day. Libnah rebelled at the same time.

23 The rest of the deeds of Jehoram and all that he did, are they not written in the book of the annals of the kings of Judah? 24 So Jehoram slept with his fathers and was buried with his fathers in the City of David. Ahaziah his son reigned in his place.

Ahaziah, King of Judah
2Ch 22:1–6

25 In the twelfth year of Joram the son of Ahab, king of Israel, Ahaziah the son of Jehoram, king of Judah, became king. 26 Ahaziah was twenty-two years old when he became king. He reigned one year in Jerusalem. His mother's name was Athaliah, the daughter of Omri, king of Israel. 27 He walked in the way of the house of Ahab and did evil in the sight of the Lord, as the house of Ahab did, for he was the son-in-law of the house of Ahab.

28 He went with Joram the son of Ahab to the war against Hazael king of Aram at Ramoth Gilead, and the Arameans struck Joram. 29 King Joram returned to be healed in Jezreel of the wounds which the Arameans had inflicted on him at Ramah when he fought against Hazael king of Aram.

And Ahaziah the son of Jehoram, king of Judah, went down to see Joram the son of Ahab in Jezreel because he was ill.

Jehu Anointed King of Israel

9 Then Elisha the prophet called one of the sons of the prophets, "Prepare yourself. Take this flask of oil in your hand, and go to Ramoth Gilead. 2 When you get there, look for Jehu the son of Jehoshaphat, the son of Nimshi. Go in and make him rise from among his brothers, and bring him into an inner chamber. 3 Then take the flask of oil, pour it on his head, and say, 'Thus says the Lord: I have anointed you king over Israel.' Then open the door and flee. Do not wait."

4 So the young man, the prophet, went to Ramoth Gilead. 5 When he arrived, the commanders of the army were sitting, and he said, "I have a word for you, Commander."

Jehu said, "Which one of us?"

And he said, "For you, Commander."

6 So he arose, went into the house, poured the oil on his head, and said to him, "Thus says the Lord, God of Israel: I am anointing you king over the people of the Lord, over Israel. 7 You will strike the house of Ahab your master, and I will avenge the blood of my servants the prophets and the blood of all the servants of the Lord from the hand of Jezebel. 8 The whole house of Ahab will perish, and I will cut off from Ahab all the males in Israel, both imprisoned and free. 9 I will make the house of Ahab like the house of Jeroboam son of Nebat and like the house of Baasha the son of Ahijah. 10 Dogs will eat Jezebel in the territory of Jezreel, and no one will bury her." Then he opened the door and fled.

11 When Jehu had returned to his master's servants, one said to him, "Is all well? Why did this madman come to you?"

And he said to them, "You know this man and his babble."

12 They said, "A lie! Tell us."

Then he said, "Thus and thus he spoke to me, saying, 'Thus says the Lord: I am anointing you king over Israel.'"

13 Then they hurried. Each took his clothes, put them under him on the bare stairs, and blew a horn, saying, "Jehu is king."

Joram of Israel Killed

2Ch 22:7–9

[14] So Jehu the son of Jehoshaphat, the son of Nimshi, conspired against Joram. Joram had been guarding Ramoth Gilead, he and all Israel, because of Hazael king of Aram. [15] But King Joram had returned to be healed in Jezreel from the wounds with which the Arameans had stricken him when he fought with Hazael king of Aram. So Jehu said, "If this be your minds, let no fugitive exit the city to go tell Jezreel." [16] Then Jehu rode in a chariot and went to Jezreel, for Joram lay there. Ahaziah king of Judah had come down to see Joram.

[17] A watchman was standing on the tower in Jezreel, and he saw the company of Jehu as he was coming and said, "I see a company." And Joram said, "Take a horseman and send him to meet them, and let him say, 'Is it peace?' "

[18] So the horseman went to meet him and said, "Thus says the king, 'Is it peace?' "

But Jehu said, "What have you to do with peace? Circle in behind me."

So the watchman reported, "The messenger came to them, but he is not returning."

[19] Then he sent out a second horseman, who came to them and said, "Thus says the king, 'Is it peace?' "

Again, Jehu said, "What have you to do with peace? Circle in behind me."

[20] The watchman reported, "He came to them, but he is not returning. The driving is like the driving of Jehu the son of Nimshi, for he drives furiously."

[21] Then Joram said, "Hitch my chariot." So his chariot was hitched, and Joram king of Israel and Ahaziah king of Judah went out, each in his chariot. They went out to meet Jehu and found him on the property of Naboth the Jezreelite. [22] When Joram saw Jehu he said, "Is it peace, Jehu?"

And he said, "What peace, so long as the harlotries of your mother Jezebel and her sorceries are so many?"

[23] Then Joram turned the reins, fled, and said to Ahaziah, "There is treachery, Ahaziah."

[24] Jehu drew a bow with his full strength and shot Joram between his shoulder blades. The arrow went out at his heart, and he kneeled down in his chariot. [25] Then Jehu said to Bidkar his officer, "Lift him up and throw him on the property of the field of Naboth the Jezreelite. Remember when you and I were riding together after Ahab his father and the LORD pronounced this oracle about him: [26] 'Surely I have seen yesterday the blood of Naboth and his sons, declares the LORD, and I will pay you back on this property, declares the LORD.' Now lift him up and throw him onto the property, according to the word of the LORD."

Ahaziah of Judah Killed

[27] But when Ahaziah the king of Judah saw this, he fled on the path to the garden house. Jehu chased after him and said, "Shoot him too." So they shot him on the ascent to Gur, which is by Ibleam. And he fled to Megiddo and died there. [28] His servants carried him in a chariot to Jerusalem and buried him in his tomb with his fathers in the City of David. [29] In the eleventh year of Joram the son of Ahab, Ahaziah became king over Judah.

Jezebel Executed

[30] When Jehu came to Jezreel, Jezebel heard about it. She put black paint on her eyes, adorned her head, and looked down through the window. [31] As Jehu entered in at the gate, she said, "Is everything all right, Zimri, murderer of his master?"

[32] And he lifted up his face toward the window and said, "Who is on my side? Who?" And two or three eunuchs looked down to him. [33] He said, "Drop her down." So they dropped her down and some of her blood splattered on the wall and on the horses. Then he trampled her.

[34] Then he entered, ate and drank, and said, "Attend to that cursed woman and bury her, for she is a king's daughter." [35] So they went to bury her, but they found nothing of her except a skull, the feet, and the palms of her hands. [36] They returned and told Jehu, and he said, "This is the word of the LORD, which He spoke by His

servant Elijah the Tishbite, saying, 'On the property of Jezreel dogs will eat the flesh of Jezebel. [37] The corpse of Jezebel will be like dung in the field on the property of Jezreel, so that they cannot say, This is Jezebel.' "

Ahab's Seventy Sons Killed

10 Now Ahab had seventy sons in Samaria. So Jehu wrote letters and sent them to Samaria to the captains of Jezreel, to the elders, and to the guardians of the sons of Ahab, saying, [2] "Now as soon as this letter comes to you—since you are with your master's sons, chariots, horses, a fortified city, and weapons— [3] select the best and most fitting of your master's sons, put him on his father's throne, and fight for your master's house."

[4] But they were extremely afraid and said, "Two kings could not stand before him. How can we stand?"

[5] So he who was over the house, and he who was over the city, the elders, and the guardians sent word to Jehu, saying, "We are your servants, and everything you say to us we will do. We will not appoint a man king. Do what is good in your eyes."

[6] Then he wrote a second letter to them, saying, "If you belong to me and will obey me, take the heads of your master's sons and come to me at Jezreel at this time tomorrow."

Now the king's sons, seventy men, were with the great men of the city who brought them up. [7] When the letter came to them, they took the king's sons, slaughtered all seventy, put their heads in baskets, and sent them to him in Jezreel. [8] So the messenger came and told him, saying, "They have brought the heads of the king's sons."

Then he said, "Put them in two heaps at the entry of the gate until morning."

[9] When morning came, he went out and stood and said to all the people, "You are innocent. I conspired against my master and killed him, but who struck all these? [10] Know then that the words of the LORD which He spoke about the house of Ahab will not fall to the ground. The LORD has done that which He spoke by His servant Elijah." [11] So Jehu struck all that remained of the house of Ahab in Jezreel and all his great men, his confidants, and his priests, until he left him no survivor.

Ahaziah's Forty-Two Brothers Killed

[12] Then he got up and went to Samaria. When he was at Beth Eked of the Shepherds on the way, [13] Jehu found the brothers of Ahaziah king of Judah and said, "Who are you?"

And they said, "We are brothers of Ahaziah, and we have come down to visit the sons of the king and the sons of the queen mother."

[14] He said, "Capture them alive." So they took them alive and slaughtered them at the pit of Beth Eked, forty-two men. Not a man of them remained.

[15] Then he left there and found Jehonadab son of Rekab coming to meet him. He greeted him and said to him, "Is your heart right with me, as my heart is with yours?"

And Jehonadab said, "It is."

"If it is, give me your hand." So he gave him his hand, and he pulled him up to him into the chariot. [16] He said, "Come with me, and see my zeal for the LORD." So he made him ride in his chariot.

[17] Then he came to Samaria and struck all that remained to Ahab in Samaria until he exterminated them, according to the word of the LORD which He spoke to Elijah.

Worshippers of Baal Killed

[18] Then Jehu gathered all the people and said to them, "Ahab served Baal a little, but Jehu will serve him much. [19] Now call to me all the prophets of Baal, all his worshippers, and all his priests. Let none go unaccounted for, because I have a great sacrifice for Baal. All who are not accounted for will not live." But Jehu did it with cunning in order to destroy the servants of Baal.

[20] Jehu said, "Sanctify a festive assembly for Baal." So they proclaimed it. [21] Jehu sent word through all Israel, and all the worshippers of Baal came. Not a man remained who did not come. They came into the house of Baal, and the house of Baal was full from one end to the other. [22] He said to the one in charge of the wardrobe, "Bring out garments for all the worshippers of Baal." So he brought them garments.

²³ Then Jehu and Jehonadab the son of Rekab went into the house of Baal and said to the worshippers of Baal, "Search and see that there are no worshippers of the LORD here with you and only worshippers of Baal." ²⁴ Then they went to offer sacrifices and burnt offerings, but Jehu put eighty men outside and said, "If any of the men whom I have brought into your hands escapes, the one who lets him go will die in his place."

²⁵ As soon as he had finished making the burnt offering, Jehu said to the guards and the officers, "Go in. Kill them. No one comes out." So they struck them with the edge of the sword. The guards and the officers threw them out and went to the city of the house of Baal. ²⁶ They brought out the sacred pillar from the house of Baal and burned it. ²⁷ They broke down the sacred pillar of Baal, and tore down the house of Baal and made it a latrine to this day.

²⁸ So Jehu exterminated Baal from Israel. ²⁹ But from the sins of Jeroboam son of Nebat, who caused Israel to sin, Jehu did not turn aside (that is, the golden calves that were in Bethel and Dan).

³⁰ And the LORD said to Jehu, "Because you have done well by doing what is right in My sight, and have done to the house of Ahab all that was in My heart, four generations of your sons will sit on the throne of Israel." ³¹ But Jehu was not careful to walk in the law of the LORD God of Israel with all his heart. He did not turn aside from the sins of Jeroboam, who caused Israel to sin.

The Death of Jehu

³² In those days the LORD began to trim off parts of Israel, and Hazael struck them in all the territory of Israel: ³³ from the Jordan eastward, all the land of Gilead, the Gadites, the Reubenites, the Manassites from Aroer, which is by the River Arnon, even Gilead and Bashan.

³⁴ Now the rest of the deeds of Jehu, all he did and all his power, are they not written in the book of the annals of the kings of Israel? ³⁵ So Jehu slept with his fathers, and they buried him in Samaria. Jehoahaz his son became king in his place. ³⁶ The days that Jehu reigned over Israel in Samaria were twenty-eight years.

Athaliah Reigns in Judah
2Ch 22:10–23:21

11 Now when Athaliah the mother of Ahaziah saw that her son was dead, she rose up and destroyed all the royal descendants. ² But Jehosheba, the daughter of King Joram, sister of Ahaziah, took Joash¹ the son of Ahaziah, and stole him away from among the king's sons who were being murdered; and they hid him and his nurse in the bedroom, from Athaliah, so that he was not killed. ³ He was with her, hidden in the house of the LORD for six years, while Athaliah reigned over the land.

Joash Anointed King of Judah

⁴ But in the seventh year Jehoiada sent word and took the captains of hundreds from the Carites and the guards and brought them to him in the house of the LORD. He made a covenant with them, put them under oath in the house of the LORD, and then showed them the king's son. ⁵ He commanded them, saying, "This is the thing that you shall do: One-third of your unit, those who come on duty on the Sabbath, will guard the king's house. ⁶ One-third will be at the gate of Sur, and one-third will be at the gate behind the guards. You will take turns guarding the house. ⁷ Two of your companies from all who go out on the Sabbath will keep watch over the house of the LORD for the king. ⁸ You will encircle the king, each man with his weapons in his hand, and the one that comes within the ranks must be killed. They must be with the king when he goes out and comes in."

⁹ The captains of hundreds did according to everything that Jehoiada the priest commanded. Each took his men, those who came on duty on the Sabbath, with those that went off duty on the Sabbath, and came to Jehoiada the priest. ¹⁰ And the priest gave to the captains of hundreds spears and shields which belonged to King David that were in the house of the LORD. ¹¹ The guards

stood, each with his weapons in his hand, from the south side of the house to the north side of the house, along the altar and the house, surrounding the king.

¹² Then he brought out the king's son and put the crown on him and gave him the testimony. They made him king and anointed him. Then they clapped their hands and said, "Live, O king!"

The Death of Athaliah

¹³ Then Athaliah heard the sound of the guards and the people, so she came to the people in the house of the LORD. ¹⁴ Then she looked, and the king was standing by a pillar according to custom, the captains and the trumpeters by the king, and all the people of the land were rejoicing and blowing trumpets. So Athaliah tore her clothes and cried, "Conspiracy, conspiracy!"

¹⁵ But Jehoiada the priest commanded the captains of hundreds, those appointed over the forces, "Bring her out of the house to the ranks, and kill with the sword whoever follows her." For the priest had said, "Let her not be killed in the house of the LORD." ¹⁶ So they laid hands on her, and she came through the horses' entrance into the king's house. Then she was put to death there.

¹⁷ Jehoiada made a covenant between the LORD and the king and the people, that they should be the people of the LORD, and also between the king and the people. ¹⁸ Then all the people of the land entered the house of Baal and broke down its altars. His images they thoroughly broke in pieces, and they killed Mattan the priest of Baal before the altars.

The priest put appointees over the house of the LORD. ¹⁹ He took the captains of hundreds, the Carites, the guards, and all the people of the land. Then they brought down the king from the house of the LORD and marched through the gate of the guards to the king's house. Then he sat on the throne of the kings. ²⁰ All the people of the land rejoiced, and the city was quiet. They had killed Athaliah with the sword at the king's house.

²¹ Jehoash² was seven years old when he became king.

Jehoash Repairs the Temple
2Ch 24:1–27

12 In the seventh year of Jehu, Jehoash became king. He reigned forty years in Jerusalem. His mother's name was Zibiah of Beersheba. ² Jehoash did what was right in the sight of the LORD all his days because Jehoiada the priest instructed him. ³ However, the high places were not taken away. The people still sacrificed and made offerings in the high places.

⁴ Now Jehoash said to the priests, "All the consecrated money that is brought into the house of the LORD, the money for which each man is currently assessed, and all the money that is brought voluntarily to the house of the LORD, ⁵ let the priests receive it, each from his donor, and repair the damages to the house wherever damages are found."

⁶ But in the twenty-third year of King Jehoash the priests had not repaired the damages to the house. ⁷ Then King Jehoash called for Jehoiada the priest and the other priests and said to them, "Why have you not repaired the damages to the house? So now money will no longer be taken from your donors. You will give it over for the damages to the house." ⁸ The priests agreed that they should take no more money from the people, nor repair the damages of the house.

⁹ So Jehoiada the priest took a chest, made a hole in its lid, and set it beside the altar on the right side as one enters the house of the LORD. The priests guarding the threshold put there all the money that was brought into the house of the LORD. ¹⁰ Whenever they saw that there was much money in the chest, the king's scribe and the high priest went up, emptied it, and counted the money that was found in the house of the LORD. ¹¹ They gave the money that was weighed out into the hands of the workers who were appointed to the house of the LORD. Then they paid it out to the carpenters and builders working on the house of the LORD, ¹² to the masons and stonecutters, and to buy timber and cut stone to repair the damages to the house of the LORD, that is, whatever went out for repairs to the house.

---

¹2 An alternate spelling of *Jehoash.*   ²21 An alternate spelling of *Joash.*

13 But for the house of the LORD silver bowls, snuffers, sprinkling basins, trumpets, and all the gold and silver vessels were not made with any of the money that was brought into the house of the LORD, 14 for they gave it to the workmen, and they repaired the house of the LORD with it. 15 They did not settle accounts with the men in whose hand they gave the money to give to the workmen, for they dealt faithfully. 16 The money from the guilt offerings and the money from the sin offerings were not brought into the house of the LORD. It belonged to the priests.

Hazael Threatens Jerusalem

17 Then Hazael king of Aram went up, fought against Gath, and seized it. Then Hazael set his face to go up to Jerusalem. 18 So Jehoash king of Judah took all the consecrated things that Jehoshaphat, Jehoram, and Ahaziah, his fathers, kings of Judah, had dedicated and his own consecrated things, all the gold that was found in the treasuries of the house of the LORD and in the king's house, and sent it to Hazael king of Aram. Then Hazael went away from Jerusalem.

The Death of Joash

19 Now the rest of the deeds of Joash, and all that he did, are they not written in the book of the annals of the kings of Judah? 20 His servants rose up, made a conspiracy, and struck Joash in the house of Millo, which goes down to Silla. 21 Jozabad the son of Shimeath and Jehozabad the son of Shomer, his servants, struck him, and he died. They buried him with his fathers in the City of David. Then Amaziah his son reigned in his place.

Jehoahaz, King of Israel

13 In the twenty-third year of Joash the son of Ahaziah, king of Judah, Jehoahaz the son of Jehu reigned over Israel in Samaria for seventeen years. 2 He did evil in the sight of the LORD and followed the sins of Jeroboam the son of Nebat, who caused Israel to sin. He did not turn aside from them. 3 The anger of the LORD was kindled against Israel, so He gave them into the hand of Hazael king of Aram and into the hand of Ben-Hadad the son of Hazael all their days.

4 But Jehoahaz appeased the LORD, and the LORD listened to him. For He saw the oppression of Israel, because the king of Aram oppressed them. 5 So the LORD gave Israel a savior, so that they got out from under the hand of Aram. Then the children of Israel dwelt in their tents as before. 6 Nevertheless, they did not turn aside from the sins of the house of Jeroboam, who caused Israel to sin, but walked in them. The Asherah pole also stood in Samaria.

7 So Jehoahaz had only fifty horsemen, ten chariots, and ten thousand footmen left, for the king of Aram had destroyed them and made them like the dust at threshing.

8 Now the rest of the deeds of Jehoahaz, all that he did and his power, are they not written in the book of the annals of the kings of Israel? 9 And Jehoahaz slept with his fathers, and they buried him in Samaria. Joash his son reigned in his place.

Jehoash, King of Israel

10 In the thirty-seventh year of Joash king of Judah, Jehoash the son of Jehoahaz reigned over Israel in Samaria for sixteen years. 11 He did evil in the sight of the LORD. He did not turn aside from all the sins of Jeroboam the son of Nebat, who caused Israel to sin, but he walked in them.

12 The rest of the deeds of Joash, all that he did and his power with which he fought against Amaziah king of Judah, are they not written in the book of the annals of the kings of Israel? 13 So Joash slept with his fathers, and Jeroboam sat on his throne. Joash was buried in Samaria with the kings of Israel.

The Death of Elisha

14 Now Elisha had become sick with the illness of which he would die. So Joash the king of Israel went down to him and wept before him, and said, "My father, my father, the chariot of Israel and its horsemen."

15 Elisha said to him, "Take a bow and arrows." So he took a bow and arrows. 16 Then he said to the king of Israel, "Draw the bow." So he drew it. Elisha put his hands on the king's hands.

17 Then he said, "Open the east window." So he opened it. Then Elisha said, "Shoot." So he shot. Then he said, "The arrow of the deliverance of the LORD, and the arrow of deliverance from Aram; for you must strike Aram in Aphek until you have destroyed them." 18 Then he said, "Take the arrows." So he took them. Then he said to the king of Israel, "Strike the ground." So he struck it three times and stood there. 19 Then the man of God was angry with him and said, "You should have struck it five or six times. Then you would have stricken Aram until you had finished them. Now you will strike Aram just three times."

20 So Elisha died, and they buried him. Now Moabite raiders would enter the land in the spring. 21 As they were burying a man, they saw raiders. So they threw the man into the tomb of Elisha. When the man touched the bones of Elisha, he came to life and stood on his feet.

Israel Recaptures Cities from Aram

22 Now Hazael king of Aram oppressed Israel all the days of Jehoahaz. 23 But the LORD was gracious to them and had compassion on them. He turned toward them because of His covenant with Abraham, Isaac, and Jacob, and would not yet destroy them or cast them from His presence.

24 Then Hazael king of Aram died and Ben-Hadad his son reigned in his place. 25 And Jehoash the son of Jehoahaz took back the cities from Ben-Hadad the son of Hazael that had been taken from Jehoahaz his father in war. Three times Joash struck him and recovered the cities of Israel.

Amaziah, King of Judah

2Ch 25:1—26:2

14 In the second year of Joash son of Jehoahaz, king of Israel, Amaziah the son of Joash, king of Judah, became king. 2 He was twenty-five years old when he became king and reigned twenty-nine years in Jerusalem. His mother's name was Jehoaddan from Jerusalem. 3 He did what was right in the sight of the LORD, only not like David his father. He did everything that Joash his father did. 4 But he did not remove the high places. Still the people sacrificed and made offerings on the high places.

5 As soon as he seized the kingdom, he killed his servants who had killed his father, the king. 6 But he did not kill the children of the murderers, according to what is written in the Book of the Law of Moses, in which the LORD commanded, "Fathers must not be put to death for the children, nor the children be put to death for the fathers. Rather, a man should be put to death for his own sin."

7 He struck ten thousand Edomites in the Valley of Salt and captured Sela in battle. He called it Joktheel, as it is to this day.

8 Then Amaziah sent messengers to Jehoash son of Jehoahaz, son of Jehu, king of Israel, saying, "Come, let us look one another in the face."

9 Then Jehoash the king of Israel sent word to Amaziah king of Judah, saying, "The thorn bush in Lebanon sent to the cedar in Lebanon, saying, 'Give your daughter to my son for a wife.' But a wild animal passed through in Lebanon and trampled the thorn bush. 10 You have indeed struck Edom, and your heart has lifted you up. Enjoy respect and sit at home. Why stir up trouble and fall, you and Judah with you?"

11 But Amaziah would not listen. So Jehoash king of Israel went up, and he and Amaziah king of Judah looked one another in the face at Beth Shemesh, which belongs to Judah. 12 Judah was beaten before Israel, and every man fled to his tent. 13 Jehoash king of Israel captured Amaziah king of Judah, the son of Jehoash, the son of Ahaziah, at Beth Shemesh. Then he came to Jerusalem and breached the wall of Jerusalem from the Gate of Ephraim to the Corner Gate, four hundred cubits.¹ 14 He took all the gold and silver, all the vessels found in the house of the LORD and in the treasuries of the king's house, and hostages, and then returned to Samaria.

---

¹ 13 About 600 feet, or 180 meters.

¹⁵ Now the rest of the deeds Jehoash did, his power and how he fought with Amaziah king of Judah, are they not written in the book of the annals of the kings of Israel? ¹⁶ So Jehoash slept with his fathers and was buried in Samaria with the kings of Israel. Jeroboam his son reigned in his place.

¹⁷ Amaziah the son of Joash king of Judah lived fifteen years after the death of Jehoash son of Jehoahaz, king of Israel. ¹⁸ And the rest of the deeds of Amaziah, are they not written in the book of the annals of the kings of Judah?

¹⁹ They made a conspiracy against him in Jerusalem, and he fled to Lachish. But they sent after him to Lachish, and killed him there. ²⁰ They carried him on horses, and he was buried in Jerusalem with his fathers in the City of David.

²¹ All the people of Judah took Azariah, who was sixteen years old, and made him king instead of his father Amaziah. ²² He built Elath and restored it to Judah after the king slept with his fathers.

Jeroboam II, King of Israel

²³ In the fifteenth year of Amaziah the son of Joash, king of Judah, Jeroboam the son of Joash, king of Israel, became king in Samaria for forty-one years. ²⁴ He did evil in the sight of the LORD. He did not turn aside from all the sins of Jeroboam the son of Nebat, who caused Israel to sin. ²⁵ He restored the border of Israel from the entrance of Lebo Hamath to the Sea of the Arabah, according to the word of the LORD God of Israel, which He spoke by His servant Jonah the son of Amittai, the prophet, who was from Gath Hepher.

²⁶ For the LORD saw the very bitter affliction of Israel. There was no one left, imprisoned or free, and no helper for Israel. ²⁷ The LORD had not said that He would wipe out the name of Israel from under heaven, so He saved them by the hand of Jeroboam son of Joash.

²⁸ Now the rest of the deeds of Jeroboam, all that he did and his power, how he fought, and how he recovered for Israel Damascus and Hamath, which had belonged to Judah, are they not written in the book of the annals of the kings of Israel? ²⁹ Jeroboam slept with his fathers, with the kings of Israel. Zechariah his son reigned in his place.

Azariah, King of Judah

2Ch 26:3–23

15 In the twenty-seventh year of Jeroboam king of Israel, Azariah son of Amaziah, king of Judah, became king. ² He was sixteen years old when he became king, and he reigned fifty-two years in Jerusalem. His mother's name was Jekoliah from Jerusalem. ³ He did what was right in the sight of the LORD, according to all that his father Amaziah had done. ⁴ But the high places were not removed. The people continued sacrificing and making offerings on the high places.

⁵ The LORD afflicted the king, and he was leprous until the day of his death. He lived in a separate house. Jotham the king's son was in charge of the house, judging the people of the land.

⁶ Now the rest of the deeds of Azariah, and all that he did, are they not written in the book of the annals of the kings of Judah? ⁷ So Azariah slept with his fathers, and they buried him with his fathers in the City of David. Jotham his son reigned in his place.

Zechariah, King of Israel

⁸ In the thirty-eighth year of Azariah king of Judah, Zechariah the son of Jeroboam became king of Israel in Samaria for six months. ⁹ He did evil in the sight of the LORD, as his fathers had done. He did not turn aside from the sins of Jeroboam the son of Nebat, who caused Israel to sin.

¹⁰ Shallum the son of Jabesh conspired against him, struck him at Ibleam, and killed him. Then Shallum reigned in his place. ¹¹ Now the rest of the deeds of Zechariah are written in the book of the annals of the kings of Israel. ¹² This was the word of the LORD which He spoke to Jehu, "Your sons will sit on the throne of Israel to the fourth generation." And it was so.

Shallum, King of Israel

¹³ Shallum son of Jabesh became king in the thirty-ninth year of Uzziah king of Judah. He reigned for a month in Samaria. ¹⁴ Then Menahem son of Gadi went up from Tirzah, entered Samaria, and struck Shallum son of Jabesh in Samaria and killed him. Then Menahem reigned in his place.

¹⁵ Now the rest of the deeds of Shallum and the conspiracy he made are written in the book of the annals of the kings of Israel. ¹⁶ Then Menahem struck Tiphsah and all who were in it, and the territories around Tirzah. Because they did not open up the city to him, he attacked it. Then he split open all its pregnant woman.

Menahem, King of Israel

¹⁷ In the thirty-ninth year of Azariah king of Judah, Menahem son of Gadi became king over Israel for ten years in Samaria. ¹⁸ He did evil in the sight of the LORD. He did not turn aside all his days from the sins of Jeroboam the son of Nebat, who caused Israel to sin.

¹⁹ Pul the king of Assyria came against the land, and Menahem gave Pul a thousand talents¹ of silver, that he might help him strengthen his control of the kingdom. ²⁰ Menahem exacted the money from Israel, from all the very wealthy men, fifty shekels² of silver each, to give to the king of Assyria. So the king of Assyria left and did not stay there in the land.

²¹ The rest of the deeds of Menahem, and all that he did, are they not written in the book of the annals of the kings of Israel? ²² And Menahem slept with his fathers, and Pekahiah his son reigned in his place.

Pekahiah, King of Israel

²³ In the fiftieth year of Azariah king of Judah, Pekahiah the son of Menahem became king over Israel in Samaria for two years. ²⁴ He did evil in the sight of the LORD. He did not turn aside from the sins of Jeroboam the son of Nebat, who caused Israel to sin. ²⁵ But Pekah son of Remaliah, his officer, conspired against him and struck him in Samaria, in the palace of the king's house, with Argob, Arieh, and fifty men of the Gileadites with him. He killed him and reigned in his place.

²⁶ Now the rest of the deeds of Pekahiah and all that he did are written in the book of the annals of the kings of Israel.

Pekah, King of Israel

²⁷ In the fifty-second year of Azariah king of Judah, Pekah son of Remaliah became king over Israel in Samaria for twenty years. ²⁸ He did evil in the sight of the LORD. He did not turn aside from the sins of Jeroboam son of Nebat, who caused Israel to sin.

²⁹ In the days of Pekah king of Israel, Tiglath-Pileser king of Assyria came and took Ijon, Abel Beth Maakah, Janoah, Kedesh, Hazor, Gilead, Galilee, and all the land of Naphtali, and then exiled them to Assyria. ³⁰ Then Hoshea son of Elah made a conspiracy against Pekah son of Remaliah and struck and killed him. Then he reigned in his place in the twentieth year of Jotham son of Uzziah.

³¹ The rest of the deeds of Pekah and all that he did are written in the book of the annals of the kings of Israel.

Jotham, King of Judah

2Ch 27:1–9

³² In the second year of Pekah son of Remaliah, king of Israel, Jotham son of Uzziah, king of Judah, became king. ³³ He was twenty-five years old when he became king, and he reigned sixteen years in Jerusalem. His mother's name was Jerusha daughter of Zadok. ³⁴ He did what was right in the sight of the LORD. He did according to all that his father Uzziah had done. ³⁵ Only he did not remove the high places. The people continued sacrificing and making offerings on the high places. He built the upper gate of the house of the LORD.

³⁶ Now the rest of the deeds of Jotham, and all that he did, are they not written in the book of the annals of the kings of Judah? ³⁷ In those days the LORD began to send Rezin king of Aram and Pekah son of Remaliah against Judah. ³⁸ Jotham slept with his

---

¹19 About 38 tons, or 34 metric tons.   ²20 About 1¼ pounds, or 575 grams.

fathers and was buried with his fathers in the City of David his father. Then Ahaz his son reigned in his place.

Ahaz, King of Judah
2Ch 28:1–27

16 In the seventeenth year of Pekah son of Remaliah, Ahaz son of Jotham, king of Judah, became king. [2] Ahaz was twenty years old when he became king, and he reigned for sixteen years in Jerusalem. He did not do what was right in the sight of the Lord his God like David his father. [3] He walked in the way of the kings of Israel and even made his son pass through the fire according to the abominations of the nations whom the Lord dispossessed before the children of Israel. [4] He sacrificed and made offerings on the high places, on the hills, and under every green tree.

[5] Then Rezin king of Aram and Pekah son of Remaliah, king of Israel, came up to Jerusalem to battle, and they besieged Ahaz but could not subdue him. [6] At that time Rezin king of Aram recovered Elath for Aram and expelled the Judeans from Elath. The Edomites came to Elath and live there to this day.

[7] So Ahaz sent messengers to Tiglath-Pileser king of Assyria, saying, "I am your servant and your son. Come up and save me from the hand of the king of Aram and from the hand of the king of Israel, who are rising up against me." [8] Then Ahaz took the silver and gold that was found in the house of the Lord and in the treasures of the king's house, and sent a present to the king of Assyria. [9] So the king of Assyria listened to him. The king of Assyria went up to Damascus, captured it, exiled the people to Kir, and killed Rezin.

[10] Then King Ahaz went to Damascus to meet Tiglath-Pileser king of Assyria and saw an altar that was in Damascus. King Ahaz sent to Uriah the priest a pattern of the altar and model of it, according to the manner of its construction. [11] Uriah the priest built an altar according to all that King Ahaz had sent from Damascus. Thus Uriah the priest worked until King Ahaz came from Damascus. [12] When the king came back from Damascus and saw the altar, the king approached the altar and made offerings on it. [13] He offered his burnt offering and his grain offering, poured out his libations, and sprinkled the blood of his peace offerings upon the altar. [14] And the bronze altar that was before the Lord he moved from the front of the house, from between the altar and the house of the Lord. He put it on the north side of the new altar.

[15] Then King Ahaz commanded Uriah the priest, "Upon the great altar offer the morning burnt offering, the evening grain offering, the king's burnt offering, and his grain offering with the burnt offering of all the people of the land, their grain offering, and their libations. Sprinkle on it all the blood of the burnt offering and all the blood of the sacrifice, and the bronze altar will be for me to inquire by." [16] So Uriah the priest did everything that King Ahaz commanded.

[17] King Ahaz cut off the bases of the stands and removed the basin from them. He took down the sea from off the bronze oxen that were under it and put it on stone pavement. [18] The structure for the Sabbath that they had built in the house and the king's outer entrance he removed from the house of the Lord for the king of Assyria.

[19] Now the rest of the deeds of Ahaz that he did, are they not written in the book of the annals of the kings of Judah? [20] Ahaz slept with his fathers and was buried with his fathers in the City of David. Then Hezekiah his son reigned in his place.

Hoshea, King of Israel
2Kgs 18:9–12

17 In the twelfth year of Ahaz king of Judah, Hoshea son of Elah became king in Samaria over Israel for nine years. [2] He did evil in the sight of the Lord, only not as the kings of Israel who were before him. [3] Shalmaneser king of Assyria came up against him. Hoshea became his servant and gave him gifts. [4] But the king of Assyria found conspiracy in Hoshea, for he had sent messengers to So king of Egypt and offered up no gift to the king of Assyria as he had done year by year. So the king of Assyria detained him, and then put him in prison.

Israel Exiled to Assyria
[5] Then the king of Assyria went throughout all the land, went up to Samaria, and besieged it for three years. [6] In the ninth year of Hoshea, the king of Assyria seized Samaria and exiled Israel to Assyria. He put them in Halah, in Habor by the River of Gozan, and in the cities of the Medes.

[7] This happened because the children of Israel had sinned against the Lord their God, who had brought them up from the land of Egypt from under the hand of Pharaoh king of Egypt. They had feared other gods [8] and walked in the statutes of the nations, whom the Lord dispossessed before the children of Israel, and walked in the statutes which the kings of Israel had made. [9] The children of Israel ascribed things to the Lord their God that were not so, and they built for themselves high places in all their cities from the watchtower to the fortified city. [10] They set up standing stones and Asherah poles on every high hill and under every green tree. [11] There they burned incense on all the high places, as the nations did whom the Lord had carried away before them. And they did wicked things to provoke the Lord to anger, [12] for they served idols, of which the Lord had said to them, "You shall not do this thing." [13] But the Lord warned Israel and Judah by all the prophets and by all the seers, saying, "Turn from your evil ways, and keep My commandments and My statutes, according to all the law which I commanded your fathers and which I sent to you by My servants the prophets."

[14] But they would not listen. They stiffened their necks, like the neck of their fathers, who did not believe in the Lord their God. [15] They rejected His statutes and His covenant that He had made with their fathers and the decrees He had given them. They followed idols, and became idolaters, and followed the surrounding nations, concerning whom the Lord commanded them, that they should not do like them.

[16] They forsook all the commandments of the Lord their God, made themselves cast images (two calves), made an Asherah pole, worshipped all the host of heaven, and served Baal. [17] They caused their sons and daughters to pass through the fire, used divination and omens, and sold themselves to do evil in the sight of the Lord to anger Him.

[18] Therefore the Lord was very angry with Israel and removed them from His presence. None remained except the tribe of Judah. [19] Judah also did not keep the commandments of the Lord their God, but walked in the statutes of Israel which they made. [20] The Lord rejected all the seed of Israel, afflicted them, and gave them into the hand of plunderers until He had cast them out of His presence.

[21] For He had torn Israel from the house of David, and they made Jeroboam the son of Nebat king. Jeroboam diverted Israel from following the Lord and caused them to sin greatly. [22] For the children of Israel walked in all the sins which Jeroboam committed. They did not turn aside from them [23] until the Lord removed Israel from His presence as He had said by all His servants the prophets. So Israel was exiled from their land to Assyria until this day.

Assyria Resettles Samaria
[24] Then the king of Assyria brought people from Babylon, Kuthah, Avva, Hamath, and Sepharvaim and put them in the cities of Samaria instead of the children of Israel. They possessed Samaria and lived in its cities. [25] Right at the beginning of their settling there, they did not fear the Lord, so the Lord sent lions among them, and they killed some of them. [26] So they said to the king of Assyria, "The nations which you have exiled and settled in the cities of Samaria do not know the law of the god of the land. Therefore He has sent lions among them; they are killing them, because they do not know the requirements of the god of the land."

[27] Then the king of Assyria commanded, "Escort back one of the priests whom you exiled from there and let him go and dwell there. Let him teach them the law of the god of the land." [28] Then one of the priests whom they had exiled from Samaria came and lived in Bethel. He taught them how they should fear the Lord.

[29] But each nation was making its own gods, and they put them in the houses of the high places that the people of Samaria had made, each nation in the cities where they were living. [30] The men of Babylon made Sukkoth Benoth, the men of Kuthah made Nergal, the men of Hamath made Ashima, [31] the

Avvites made Nibhaz and Tartak. The Sepharvites were burning their children in fire to Adrammelek and Anammelek, the gods of Sepharvaim. [32] They feared the Lord and made from amongst themselves priests of the high places, who were working for them in the houses of the high places. [33] They feared the Lord, and they were serving their own gods, after the manner of the nations whom they exiled from there.

[34] To this day they continue to practice their former customs. They do not fear the Lord, nor are they doing according to the statutes, requirements, the law or commandment that the Lord commanded the children of Jacob, whom He named Israel. [35] The Lord had made a covenant and commanded them, saying, "You shall not fear other gods, nor bow yourselves to them. You shall not serve them or sacrifice to them. [36] Rather, the Lord, who brought you up out of the land of Egypt with great power and an outstretched arm, Him you shall fear, to Him you shall bow down, and to Him you shall sacrifice. [37] The statutes, the ordinances, the law, and the commandment, which He wrote for you, you shall observe to do forever. And you shall not fear other gods. [38] The covenant that I have made with you, you shall not forget. You shall not fear other gods. [39] Rather the Lord your God you shall fear, and He will deliver you from the hand of all your enemies."

[40] But they did not listen; rather they were practicing their former customs. [41] So these nations feared the Lord and were serving their carved images, both their children and their grandchildren, as their fathers did, and so they are doing to this day.

Hezekiah, King of Judah
2Ch 29:1–2; 31:1, 20–21; 2Ki 17:3–7

18 In the third year of Hoshea son of Elah, king of Israel, Hezekiah the son of Ahaz, king of Judah, became king. [2] He was twenty-five years old when he became king, and he reigned twenty-nine years in Jerusalem. His mother's name was Abi daughter of Zechariah. [3] He did what was right in the sight of the Lord, according to everything that David his father had done. [4] He removed the high places, broke down the sacred pillars, cut down the Asherah poles, and crushed the bronze serpent that Moses had made, for until those days the children of Israel had made offerings to it. They called it Nehushtan.

[5] He trusted in the Lord God of Israel. Afterwards, there was no one like him among all the kings of Judah or among those who were before him. [6] He clung to the Lord. He did not depart from following him, but kept His commandments, which the Lord commanded Moses. [7] The Lord was with him. Wherever he went, he prospered. He rebelled against the king of Assyria and did not serve him. [8] He struck the Philistines as far as Gaza and its territory, from watchtower to fortified city.

[9] In the fourth year of King Hezekiah, which was the seventh year of Hoshea son of Elah, king of Israel, Shalmaneser king of Assyria came up against Samaria and besieged it. [10] He seized it at the end of three years. In the sixth year of Hezekiah, that is, the ninth year of Hoshea king of Israel, Samaria was taken. [11] Then the king of Assyria exiled Israel to Assyria and put them in Halah and in Habor by the River of Gozan and in the cities of the Medes, [12] because they did not obey the voice of the Lord their God, but transgressed His covenant and all that Moses the servant of the Lord commanded, and would not obey or do them.

Sennacherib Invades Judah
Isa 36:1–22; 2Ch 32:9–19

[13] In the fourteenth year of King Hezekiah, Sennacherib king of Assyria came up against all the fortified cities of Judah and captured them. [14] Hezekiah king of Judah sent word to the king of Assyria at Lachish, saying, "I have done wrong; turn away from me. I will bear whatever you put on me." So the king of Assyria required of Hezekiah king of Judah three hundred talents[1] of silver and thirty talents[2] of gold. [15] So Hezekiah gave him all the silver that

was found in the house of the Lord and in the treasuries of the king's house.

[16] At that time Hezekiah cut off the gold from the doors of the temple of the Lord and from the doorposts that Hezekiah king of Judah had overlaid and gave it to the king of Assyria.

[17] Then the king of Assyria sent the Tartan,[3] the Rabsaris,[4] and the Rabshakeh[5] from Lachish to King Hezekiah with a great army against Jerusalem. So they went up and came to Jerusalem. When they went up, they came and stood by the conduit of the upper pool, which is on the highway of the Fuller's Field. [18] Then they called to the king, and Eliakim the son of Hilkiah, who was over the household, Shebna the scribe, and Joah the son of Asaph, the recorder, came out to them.

[19] Then the Rabshakeh said to them, "Speak to Hezekiah:

"Thus says the great king, the king of Assyria: What is the basis of your confidence? [20] You speak empty words concerning counsel and strength for the war. Now on whom do you trust, that you have rebelled against me? [21] Now, look! You trust in the staff of this bruised reed, on Egypt, on which if a man leans, it will enter his hand and pierce it. So is Pharaoh king of Egypt to all who trust in him. [22] But if you say to me, 'We trust in the Lord our God,' is it not He, whose high places and altars Hezekiah has removed, saying to Judah and to Jerusalem, 'You shall worship before this altar in Jerusalem'? [23] "Now, make a wager with my lord king of Assyria. I will give you two thousand horses if you are able to set riders on them. [24] How can you turn away one official of the least of my master's servants and put your trust on Egypt for chariots and horsemen? [25] Have I come up apart from the will of the Lord against this place to destroy it? The Lord said to me, Go up against this land and destroy it."

[26] Then Eliakim the son of Hilkiah, Shebna, and Joah said to the Rabshakeh, "Speak to your servants in Aramaic, for we understand it. Do not speak with us in the language of Judah in earshot of the people who are on the wall."

[27] But the Rabshakeh said to them, "Has my master sent me to speak these words to your master and to you, and not to the men sitting on the wall, who are about to eat their own dung and drink their own urine with you?"

[28] Then the Rabshakeh stood and called with a loud voice in the language of Judah, "Hear the word of the great king, the king of Assyria. [29] Thus says the king: 'Do not let Hezekiah deceive you, for he is not able to deliver you from my hand. [30] Do not let Hezekiah make you trust in the Lord, saying, The Lord will surely deliver us, and this city will not be given into the hand of the king of Assyria.'

[31] "Do not listen to Hezekiah, for thus says the king of Assyria: 'Submit to me; come out to me, so that every man may eat from his own vine and his own fig tree and drink water from his own cistern, [32] until I come and take you to a land like your own land, a land of grain and wine, a land of bread and vineyards, a land of olive oil and honey, that you may live and not die.'

"Do not listen to Hezekiah when he leads you astray saying, The Lord will deliver us. [33] Has any of the gods of the nations at all delivered its land from the hand of the king of Assyria? [34] Where are the gods of Hamath and Arpad? Where are the gods of Sepharvaim, Hena, and Ivvah? Have they delivered Samaria from my hand? [35] Who among all the gods of the lands have delivered their land out of my hand, that the Lord should deliver Jerusalem from my hand?"

[36] But the people were silent and answered him not a word, for the king's command was, "Do not answer him."

[37] Then Eliakim son of Hilkiah, who was over the household, Shebna the scribe, and Joah the son of Asaph, the recorder, came to Hezekiah with their clothes torn and told him the words of the Rabshakeh.

---

[1] 14 About 11 tons, or 10 metric tons.   [2] 14 About 1 ton, or 1 metric ton.   [3] 17 Possibly *Commander in Chief*.
[4] 17 Possibly *Chief of Staff*.   [5] 17 Possibly *Commanding General*.

Hezekiah Consults Isaiah
Isa 37:1–13

19 When King Hezekiah heard it, he tore his clothes, covered himself with sackcloth, and entered the house of the Lord. [2] He sent Eliakim, who was over the household, Shebna the scribe, and the elders of the priests, covered with sackcloth, to Isaiah the prophet, the son of Amoz. [3] They said to him, "Thus says Hezekiah: This day is a day of distress, chastisement, and disgrace, for children have come to the mouth of the womb, but there is no strength to birth them. [4] Perhaps the Lord your God will hear all the words of the Rabshakeh, whom the king of Assyria, his master, has sent to taunt the living God and will rebuke the words that the Lord your God has heard, and you might lift up a prayer for the remnant that are left."

[5] When the servants of King Hezekiah came to Isaiah, [6] Isaiah said to them, "Thus shall you say to your master, 'Thus says the Lord: Do not be afraid of the words that you have heard, with which the servants of the king of Assyria have blasphemed Me. [7] I am putting a spirit in him, and he will hear a report and return to his own land. Then I will cause him to fall by the sword in his own land.'"

Sennacherib Defies the Lord

[8] Then the Rabshakeh returned and found the king of Assyria warring against Libnah, for he had heard that he had departed from Lachish.

[9] When the king heard concerning Tirhakah king of Cush, "He has come out to fight against you," he sent messengers to Hezekiah, saying, [10] "Thus you shall speak to Hezekiah king of Judah, saying: Do not let your God in whom you trust deceive you, saying: Jerusalem will not be given into the hand of the king of Assyria. [11] You have heard what the kings of Assyria have done to all lands by annihilating them. Will you be delivered? [12] Have the gods of the nations delivered them, the nations that my fathers destroyed, Gozan, Harran, Rezeph, and the sons of Eden who were in Tel Assar? [13] Where is the king of Hamath, the king of Arpad, the king of the city of Sepharvaim, of Hena, and Ivvah?"

Hezekiah's Prayer
Isa 37:14–20

[14] Hezekiah received the letter from the hand of the messengers and read it. Then Hezekiah went up to the house of the Lord and spread it before the Lord. [15] Then Hezekiah prayed before the Lord and said, "O Lord, God of Israel, who sits on the cherubim, You alone are God over all the kingdoms of the earth. You have made the sky and the earth. [16] Incline, O Lord, Your ear and hear. Open, O Lord, Your eyes and see. Hear the words of Sennacherib, which he sent to taunt the living God.

[17] "Surely, O Lord, the kings of Assyria have annihilated the nations and their lands [18] and have put their gods in the fire, for they were no gods but the work of men's hands, wood and stone; thus they have been destroyed. [19] So now, O Lord our God, save us from his hand, that all the kingdoms of the earth may know that You, O Lord, are God alone."

Isaiah Prophesies Sennacherib's Fall
Isa 37:21–38; 2Ch 32:20–21

[20] Then Isaiah son of Amoz sent word to Hezekiah, saying, "Thus says the Lord God of Israel: That which you have prayed to Me concerning Sennacherib king of Assyria I have heard. [21] This is the word that the Lord has spoken concerning him:

She despises you, she ridicules you—
   virgin daughter of Zion.
Behind you, she shakes her head—
   daughter of Jerusalem.
[22] Whom have you taunted and blasphemed?
   And against whom have you raised a voice
and lifted your eyes upward?
   Against the Holy One of Israel.
[23] By your messengers
   you have taunted the Lord,

and have said,
   'With my many chariots
I have gone up the height of the mountains,
   to farthest reaches of Lebanon,
and I will cut down its tallest cedars,
   its choicest junipers.
I will enter its most remote canopies of night,
   its dense forest.
[24] I have dug *wells*
   and drunk foreign waters,
and I dried up with the sole of my foot
   all the streams of Egypt.'

[25] "Have you not heard?
   Long ago I arranged it,
in ancient times I formed it;
   now I bring it to pass,
that you will turn impregnable cities
   into desolate heaps of stones.
[26] Their inhabitants are powerless;
   they are terrified and ashamed.
They are like grass of the field
   and new vegetation,
grass on the roof tops,
   scorched before it stands.

[27] "But I know your dwelling place,
   your going out and your coming in,
   and your raging against Me.
[28] Because you have raged against Me,
   and your self-assuredness has come up to My ears,
I will put My hook in your nose
   and My bridle on your lips,
and I will turn you back
   on the way by which you came.

[29] "This will be the sign to you:

This year you will eat what grows itself,
   and in the second year the same.
Then in the third year sow, reap,
   and plant vineyards, and eat their fruits.
[30] The spared of the house of Judah who remain
   will again take root below, and bear fruit above.
[31] For from Jerusalem a remnant will go forth,
   and escapees from Mount Zion.

"The zeal of the Lord of Hosts will do this.

[32] "Therefore thus says the Lord concerning the king of Assyria:

He will not enter this city,
   shoot an arrow there,
approach it with shield,
   or heap up a siege ramp against it.
[33] By the way that he came, he will return;
   he will not enter this city,
   declares the Lord.
[34] For I will protect this city to save it,
   for My own sake and for the sake of David
   My servant."

The Death of Sennacherib

[35] On that night the angel of the Lord went out and struck one hundred and eighty-five thousand in the camp of the Assyrians. When others woke up early in the morning, these were all dead bodies. [36] So Sennacherib king of Assyria departed and stayed in Nineveh.

[37] As he was worshipping in the house of Nisrok his god, Adrammelek and Sharezer his sons struck him with the sword, and they escaped into the land of Ararat. Esarhaddon his son reigned in his place.

Hezekiah's Life Extended

2Ch 32:24–26; Isa 38:1–8

20 In those days Hezekiah became ill and was near death. The prophet Isaiah son of Amoz came to him, and said to him, "Thus says the Lord: Set your house in order, for you shall die and not live."

² Then he turned his face toward the wall and prayed to the Lord, saying, ³ "Please, O Lord, remember how I have walked before You faithfully and with an undivided heart and have done what is good in Your sight." And Hezekiah wept bitterly.

⁴ Now before Isaiah had come out of the middle courtyard, the word of the Lord came to him, saying, ⁵ "Turn back and say to Hezekiah the leader of My people: Thus says the Lord, the God of David your father: I have heard your prayer; I have seen your tears. I will heal you. On the third day you shall go up to the house of the Lord. ⁶ I will add to your days fifteen years, and I will deliver you and this city from the hand of the king of Assyria. I will defend this city for My own sake and for the sake of David My servant."

⁷ Then Isaiah said, "Take a cake of figs." So they took it and laid it on the boil, and he recovered.

⁸ Hezekiah said to Isaiah, "What will be the sign that the Lord will heal me, and that I should go up to the house of the Lord on the third day?"

⁹ Isaiah said, "This is the sign to you from the Lord, that the Lord will do the thing that He has spoken: Should the shadow walk forward ten steps or go back ten steps?"

¹⁰ And Hezekiah answered, "It is an easy thing for the shadow to stretch ten steps, so let it go back ten steps."

¹¹ Isaiah the prophet called to the Lord, and He made the shadow go back ten steps on the stairs of Ahaz.

Envoys From Babylon

Isa 39:1–8; 2Ch 32:32–33

¹² At that time Marduk-Baladan son of Baladan, king of Babylon, sent letters and a gift to Hezekiah, for he had heard that Hezekiah had been ill. ¹³ Hezekiah welcomed them and showed them all the treasure house, the silver, the gold, the spices, the fine oil, all the armory, and all that was found in his storehouses. There was nothing in his house nor in all his dominion that Hezekiah did not show them.

¹⁴ Then Isaiah the prophet came to King Hezekiah and said to him, "What did these men say? From where did they come to you?"

Hezekiah said, "They came from a distant land, from Babylon."

¹⁵ He said, "What have they seen in your house?"

Hezekiah said, "They have seen everything in my house. There is nothing in my storehouses that I did not show them."

¹⁶ Isaiah said to Hezekiah, "Hear the word of the Lord: ¹⁷ The days are coming when everything that is in your house and that your fathers have stored up until this day will be carried off to Babylon. Nothing will be left, says the Lord. ¹⁸ Some of your sons who go out from you, who will be born to you, will be taken away. They will be eunuchs in the palace of the king of Babylon."

¹⁹ Then Hezekiah said to Isaiah, "The word of the Lord that you have spoken is good." And he said, "Why not, if there is peace and security in my days?"

The Death of Hezekiah

²⁰ The rest of the deeds of Hezekiah, all his power, how he made a pool and a conduit and brought water into the city, are they not written in the book of the annals of the kings of Judah? ²¹ Hezekiah slept with his fathers, and Manasseh his son reigned in his place.

Manasseh, King of Judah

2Ch 33:1–20

21 Manasseh was twelve years old when he became king, and he reigned fifty-five years in Jerusalem. His mother's name was Hephzibah. ² He did evil in the sight of the Lord, according to the abominations of the nations whom the Lord dispossessed before the children of Israel. ³ He went back and rebuilt the high places that Hezekiah his father had

destroyed. He erected altars for Baal, made an Asherah pole as Ahab king of Israel had done, and worshipped all the host of heaven and served them. ⁴ He built altars in the house of the Lord, of which the Lord had said, "In Jerusalem I will put My name." ⁵ He built altars for all the host of heaven in the two courts of the house of the Lord. ⁶ He made his son pass through the fire, was conjuring and seeking omens, and dealt with mediums and soothsayers. He did much evil in the sight of the Lord, provoking Him to anger.

⁷ He put a carved image of Asherah that he had made in the house of which the Lord said to David and to Solomon his son, "In this house and in Jerusalem, which I have chosen out of all tribes of Israel, I will put My name forever. ⁸ I will not make the feet of Israel to wander homeless from the land that I gave to their fathers, if only they will be careful to do according to all that I have commanded them and according to all the law that My servant Moses commanded them." ⁹ But they did not listen. Manasseh led them to do more evil than the nations whom the Lord had destroyed before the children of Israel.

¹⁰ The Lord spoke by His servants the prophets, saying, ¹¹ "Because Manasseh king of Judah has done these abominations, things more evil than all that the Amorites did, and has also caused Judah to sin with his idols, ¹² therefore thus says the Lord God of Israel: I am bringing evil on Jerusalem and Judah, such evil that the ears of whoever hears about it will tingle. ¹³ I will stretch over Jerusalem the measuring line of Samaria and the level of the house of Ahab, and I will wipe out Jerusalem as one wipes out a bowl, wiping it and turning it upside down. ¹⁴ I will disregard the remnant of My inheritance and give them into the hand of their enemies. They shall become plunder and spoil for all their enemies, ¹⁵ because they have done evil in My sight and have provoked Me to anger, since the day their fathers came out of Egypt, even to this day."

¹⁶ Moreover, Manasseh shed innocent blood very much, until he had filled Jerusalem from one end to the other; besides his sin he caused Judah to sin by doing evil in the sight of the Lord.

¹⁷ Now the rest of the deeds of Manasseh, all that he did, and his sin that he committed, are they not written in the book of the annals of the kings of Judah? ¹⁸ Manasseh slept with his fathers, and was buried in the garden of his house, in the garden of Uzza. Amon his son reigned in his place.

Amon, King of Judah

2Ch 33:21–25

¹⁹ Amon was twenty-two years old when he became king. He reigned two years in Jerusalem. His mother's name was Meshullemeth, daughter of Haruz of Jotbah. ²⁰ He did evil in the sight of the Lord, as his father Manasseh had done. ²¹ He walked in all the ways that his father walked, served the idols that his father served, and worshipped them. ²² He abandoned the Lord God of his fathers, and he did not walk in the way of the Lord.

²³ The servants of Amon conspired against him and killed the king in his house. ²⁴ But the people of the land struck all those who conspired against King Amon, and the people of the land made Josiah his son king in his place.

²⁵ Now the rest of the deeds of Amon that he did, are they not written in the book of the annals of the kings of Judah? ²⁶ And he was buried in his tomb in the garden of Uzza, and Josiah his son reigned in his place.

Josiah, King of Judah

2Ch 34:1–28

22 Josiah was eight years old when he became king, and he reigned thirty-one years in Jerusalem. His mother's name was Jedidah daughter of Adaiah from Bozkath. ² He did what was right in the sight of the Lord and walked in all the ways of David his father. He did not turn aside to the right hand or to the left.

The Book of the Law Found

³ In the eighteenth year of King Josiah the king sent Shaphan son of Azaliah, son of Meshullam, the scribe, to the house of the Lord,

saying, [4] "Go up to Hilkiah the high priest, and have him prepare the money that has been brought to the house of the LORD, which the keepers of the threshold have gathered from the people. [5] Let them deliver it to the hand of the appointed workers of the house of the LORD, and let them give it to the workers who are in the house of the LORD to repair the damages to the house, [6] that is, to the carpenters, the builders, and the masons to buy timber and cut stone to repair the house. [7] But there need be no settling of accounts with them concerning the money that was given to their hand, because they are behaving honestly."

[8] Hilkiah the high priest said to Shaphan the scribe, "I have found the Book of the Law in the house of the LORD." Hilkiah gave the book to Shaphan, and he read it. [9] Then Shaphan the scribe came to the king and brought the king a report. He said, "Your servants have emptied the money that was found in the house and have given it into the hand of the appointed workers of the house of the LORD." [10] Shaphan the scribe informed the king, saying, "Hilkiah the priest has given me a book." So Shaphan read it before the king.

[11] When the king had heard the words of the Book of the Law, he tore his clothes. [12] Then the king commanded Hilkiah the priest, Ahikam son of Shaphan, Akbor son of Micaiah, Shaphan the scribe, and Asaiah, a servant of the king, saying, [13] "Go, inquire of the LORD for me, for the people, and for all Judah concerning the words of this book that has been found, for great is the wrath of the LORD that is kindled against us, because our fathers have not obeyed the words of this book by doing according to all that is written concerning us."

[14] So Hilkiah the priest, Ahikam, Akbor, Shaphan, and Asaiah went to Huldah the prophetess, wife of Shallum, son of Tikvah, son of Harhas, keeper of the wardrobe (she lived in Jerusalem in the second quarter), and they spoke with her.

[15] She said to them, "Thus says the LORD God of Israel: Tell the man that sent you to Me, [16] Thus says the LORD: See, I will bring evil on this place and on its inhabitants—all the words of the book that the king of Judah has read. [17] Because they have forsaken Me and have made offerings to other gods, so that they have provoked Me to anger with all the works of their hands, therefore My wrath will be kindled against this place, and it will not be quenched. [18] But to the king of Judah who sent you to inquire of the LORD, thus shall you say to him, Thus says the LORD God of Israel with regard to the words you have heard: [19] Because your heart was timid, and you humbled yourself before the LORD when you heard what I spoke against this place and against its inhabitants, that they should become a desolation and a curse, and you have torn your clothes and wept before Me, I also have heard you, declares the LORD. [20] Therefore, I will gather you to your fathers, and you will be gathered to your grave in peace. Your eyes will not see all the evil which I am about to bring upon this place."

Then they brought the king a report.

Josiah Renews the Covenant

2Ch 34:3–33; 35:1–36:1

23 Then the king sent them away and they gathered all the elders of Judah and Jerusalem to him. [2] The king went up to the house of the LORD, and all the men of Judah and all the inhabitants of Jerusalem with him, the priests, the prophets, and all the people, both small and great. He read in their hearing all the words of the Book of the Covenant that was found in the house of the LORD. [3] The king stood by a pillar and made a covenant before the LORD to follow the LORD, to keep His commandments, His testimonies, and His statutes with all his heart and all his soul, to perform the words of this covenant that were written in this book. All the people agreed with the covenant.

[4] The king commanded Hilkiah the high priest, the priests of the second order, and the keepers of the threshold to bring out of the temple of the LORD all the implements that were made for Baal, for Asherah, and for all the host of heaven. Then he burned them outside Jerusalem in the fields of Kidron and carried their ashes to Bethel. [5] Then he removed the idolatrous priests whom the kings of Judah had ordained to burn incense on the

high places at the cities of Judah and around Jerusalem; those also who burned incense to Baal, to the sun, to the moon, to the constellations, and to all the host of heaven. [6] He brought out the Asherah from the house of the LORD to the outside of Jerusalem, to the Kidron Valley. Then he burned it at the Kidron Valley, crushed it to dust, and threw its dust upon the graves of the people. [7] He tore down the houses of the male cult prostitutes that were in the house of the LORD, where the women were weaving hangings for the Asherah.

[8] He brought all the priests out of the cities of Judah and defiled the high places where the priests had made offerings, from Geba to Beersheba. He broke down the high places of the gates at the entry of the gates of Joshua the governor of the city, which were on the left at the gate of the city. [9] However the priests of the high places did not go up to the altar of the LORD in Jerusalem. Instead they ate unleavened bread among their fellow priests.

[10] He defiled Topheth, which is in the Valley of Ben Hinnom, so that no man would make his son or his daughter pass through the fire to Molek. [11] He removed the horses that the kings of Judah had given to the sun, at the entry of the house of the LORD, by the hall of Nathan-Melek the eunuch, which was in the vestibule. The chariots of the sun he burned with fire.

[12] The altars that were on the roof of the upper chamber of Ahaz, which the kings of Judah had made, and the altars which Manasseh had made in the two courts of the house of the LORD the king tore down and banished from there and threw their dust into the Kidron Valley. [13] The high places east of Jerusalem, south of the Mount of Corruption, which Solomon the king of Israel had built for Ashtoreth the abomination of the Sidonians, for Chemosh the abomination of the Moabites, and for Molek the abomination of the Ammonites, the king defiled. [14] He broke the standing stones, cut down the Asherah poles, and filled their sites with human bones.

[15] Moreover, the altar that was at Bethel and the high place which Jeroboam the son of Nebat, who made Israel sin, had made, both that altar and the high place he tore down. Then he burned the high place and crushed it to powder, and he burned the Asherah. [16] As Josiah turned, he saw the tombs that were there on the mount. He took the bones out of the tombs and burned them on the altar and defiled it, according to the word of the LORD that the man of God proclaimed, the one who announced these things.

[17] Then he said, "What is this monument that I see?"

The men of the city said to him, "It is the tomb of the man of God who came from Judah and proclaimed these things that you have done against the altar of Bethel."

[18] He said, "Let him rest. No one shall disturb his bones." So they let his bones alone, with the bones of the prophet who came out of Samaria.

[19] Moreover, all the houses of the high places that were in the cities of Samaria, which the kings of Israel had made to provoke the LORD to anger, Josiah removed. He did to them just as he had done in Bethel. [20] He slaughtered on the altars all the priests of the high places who were there, and burned human bones on them. Then he returned to Jerusalem.

[21] The king commanded all the people, "Keep the Passover to the LORD your God as it is written in this Book of the Covenant." [22] For such a Passover had not been kept from the days of the judges who judged Israel, nor in all the days of the kings of Israel and the kings of Judah. [23] But in the eighteenth year of King Josiah, this Passover was kept to the LORD in Jerusalem.

[24] Moreover, Josiah disposed of the mediums, the soothsayers, the teraphim, the idols, and all the abominations that were seen in the land of Judah and in Jerusalem, so that he established the words of the law that were written in the book that Hilkiah the priest found in the house of the LORD. [25] Now there had been no king like him before or after, who turned to the LORD with all his heart, with all his soul, and with all his might, according to all the Law of Moses.

[26] However, the LORD did not turn from the fierceness of His great wrath, by which His anger was kindled against Judah, because of all the provocations with which Manasseh had provoked Him. [27] The LORD said, "I will also remove Judah from before Me, as I have

removed Israel. I will reject this city that I have chosen, Jerusalem, and the house of which I said, My name shall be there."

Josiah Dies in Battle

²⁸ Now the rest of the deeds of Josiah, and all that he did, are they not written in the book of the annals of the kings of Judah? ²⁹ In his days Pharaoh Necho, king of Egypt, went up against the king of Assyria to the River Euphrates. King Josiah went to meet him, but he killed him at Megiddo when he had seen him. ³⁰ His servants carried him dead in a chariot from Megiddo, brought him to Jerusalem, and buried him in his own tomb. The people of the land took Jehoahaz the son of Josiah, anointed him, and made him king in place of his father.

Jehoahaz, King of Judah
2Ch 36:2–4

³¹ Jehoahaz was twenty-three years old when he became king, and he reigned three months in Jerusalem. His mother's name was Hamutal daughter of Jeremiah of Libnah. ³² He did evil in the sight of the LORD, according to all that his fathers had done. ³³ Pharaoh Necho imprisoned him at Riblah in the land of Hamath, so that he might not reign in Jerusalem, and imposed tribute on the land of a hundred talents¹ of silver and a talent² of gold. ³⁴ Pharaoh Necho made Eliakim son of Josiah king in place of Josiah his father and changed his name to Jehoiakim. He took Jehoahaz away and went to Egypt, and he died there. ³⁵ Jehoiakim gave the silver and gold to Pharaoh, but he taxed the land to give the money according to Pharaoh's demand. According to an assessed amount, he exacted the silver and gold from the people of the land to give to Pharaoh Necho.

Jehoiakim, King of Judah
2Ch 36:5–8

³⁶ Jehoiakim was twenty-five years old when he became king. He reigned eleven years in Jerusalem. His mother's name was Zebidah daughter of Pedaiah of Rumah. ³⁷ He did evil in the sight of the LORD, according to all that his fathers had done.

Judah Overrun by Enemies

24 In his days Nebuchadnezzar king of Babylon came up, and Jehoiakim became his servant for three years. Then he turned and rebelled against him. ² The LORD sent against him bands of Chaldeans, bands of Arameans, bands of Moabites, and bands of Ammonites. He sent them against Judah to destroy it, according to the word of the LORD that He spoke by His servants the prophets. ³ Surely at the decree of the LORD this came upon Judah, to remove them from before Him, for the sins of Manasseh, according to all that he had done, ⁴ and also for the innocent blood that he had shed, for he filled Jerusalem with innocent blood, and the LORD was not willing to pardon.

⁵ Now the rest of the deeds of Jehoiakim and all that he did, are they not written in the book of the annals of the kings of Judah? ⁶ So Jehoiakim slept with his fathers, and Jehoiachin his son reigned in his place.

⁷ The king of Egypt did not come again from his land, for the king of Babylon had taken over from the Brook of Egypt to the River Euphrates all that belonged to the king of Egypt.

Jehoiachin, King of Judah
2Ch 36:9–10

⁸ Jehoiachin was eighteen years old when he became king. He reigned in Jerusalem three months. His mother's name was Nehushta daughter of Elnathan of Jerusalem. ⁹ He did evil in the sight of the LORD, according to all that his father had done.

¹⁰ At that time the servants of Nebuchadnezzar king of Babylon came up against Jerusalem, and the city was under siege. ¹¹ Nebuchadnezzar king of Babylon came up to the city while his servants were besieging it, ¹² and Jehoiachin king of Judah went out to the king of Babylon, he, his mother, his servants, his princes, and his eunuchs. The king of Babylon took him in the eighth year of his reign.

The Captivity of Jerusalem

¹³ He brought out from there all the treasures of the house of the LORD and the treasures of the king's house, and cut in pieces all the implements of gold in the temple of the LORD, which Solomon king of Israel had made, just as the LORD had spoken. ¹⁴ He exiled all Jerusalem, all the princes, and all the mighty men of valor, ten thousand captives, and all the craftsmen and smiths. No one remained, except the poorest people of the land.

¹⁵ He exiled Jehoiachin in Babylon. The king's mother, the king's wives, his eunuchs, and the elite of the land he took into exile from Jerusalem to Babylon. ¹⁶ All the fighting men, seven thousand, the craftsmen and smiths, one thousand, all those strong and fit for war the king of Babylon brought them into exile in Babylon. ¹⁷ The king of Babylon made Mattaniah, the uncle of Jehoiachin, king in his place and changed his name to Zedekiah.

Zedekiah, King of Judah
2Ch 36:11–16; Jer 52:1–3

¹⁸ Zedekiah was twenty-one years old when he became king. He reigned eleven years in Jerusalem. His mother's name was Hamutal daughter of Jeremiah of Libnah. ¹⁹ He did evil in the sight of the LORD, according to all that Jehoiakim had done. ²⁰ Because of the anger of the LORD this happened in Jerusalem and Judah until He threw them out from His presence. But Zedekiah rebelled against the king of Babylon.

The Fall and Exile of Judah
Jer 39:1–10; 40:7–9; 41:1–18; 52:4–27; 2Ch 36:17–20

25 In the ninth year of his reign, in the tenth month, on the tenth day of the month, Nebuchadnezzar king of Babylon came, he and all his army, against Jerusalem, and set up camp near it. They built siege mounds against it all around. ² The city came under siege until the eleventh year of King Zedekiah. ³ On the ninth day of the fourth month the famine was severe in the city, and there was no food for the people of the land. ⁴ The city was breached, and all the fighting men fled by night by the way of the gate between the two walls, which is by the king's garden, though the Chaldeans were all around the city. They went along the way of the Arabah. ⁵ Then the army of the Chaldeans pursued the king and overtook him in the plains of Jericho. All his army deserted him. ⁶ So they captured the king and brought him up to the king of Babylon at Riblah, and they passed sentence upon him. ⁷ They slaughtered the sons of Zedekiah before his eyes, and put out the eyes of Zedekiah. They bound him with bronze fetters and brought him to Babylon.

⁸ In the fifth month, on the seventh day of the month (that was the nineteenth year of King Nebuchadnezzar, king of Babylon), Nebuzaradan, the captain of the bodyguard, a servant of the king of Babylon, came to Jerusalem. ⁹ He burned the house of the LORD, the king's house, and all the houses of Jerusalem. Every great house he burned with fire. ¹⁰ All the army of the Chaldeans who were with the captain of the guard tore down the walls of Jerusalem all around. ¹¹ The rest of the people who remained in the city, the deserters who had defected to the king of Babylon, and the rest of the crowd Nebuzaradan the captain of the bodyguard took into exile. ¹² But the captain of the bodyguard left some of the poor of the land to be vinedressers and farmers.

¹³ The bronze pillars that were in the house of the LORD, the stands, and the bronze sea that were in the house of the LORD the Chaldeans broke in pieces, and carried their bronze to Babylon. ¹⁴ The pots, the shovels, the snuffers, the incense bowls, and all the bronze implements which were used in service they took away. ¹⁵ The fire pans and sprinkling basins that were fine gold and fine silver the captain of the bodyguard took.

¹⁶ The two pillars, the one sea, and the stands, which Solomon had made for the house of the LORD—the bronze of all these implements was beyond weight. ¹⁷ The height of the one pillar was eighteen cubits,³ and a bronze capital was on it. The height of the capital was three cubits.⁴ Latticework and pomegranates, all

---

¹ 33 About 3¾ tons, or 3.4 metric tons.   ² 33 About 75 pounds, or 34 kilograms.   ³ 17 About 27 feet, or 8.1 meters.   ⁴ 17 About 4½ feet, or 1.4 meters.

of bronze, were on the capital all around. The second pillar with its latticework was like it.

[18] The captain of the bodyguard took Seraiah the chief priest, Zephaniah the second priest, and the three keepers of the threshold. [19] From the city he took a eunuch who was an officer over the fighting men, five men of the king's council who were found in the city, the chief scribe of the army who mustered the people of the land, and sixty men from the people of the land who were found in the city. [20] Nebuzaradan captain of the bodyguard took them, and brought them to the king of Babylon at Riblah. [21] Then the king of Babylon struck them down and killed them at Riblah in the land of Hamath.

Thus he exiled Judah from their land.

Gedaliah, Governor of Judah

[22] Over the people who remained in the land of Judah, whom Nebuchadnezzar king of Babylon had left, he appointed Gedaliah the son of Ahikam, the son of Shaphan. [23] When all the captains of the armies, they and their men, heard that the king of Babylon had appointed Gedaliah, they came to Gedaliah at Mizpah, that is, Ishmael son of Nethaniah, Johanan son of Kareah, Seraiah son of Tanhumeth the Netophathite, and Jaazaniah son of the Maakathite,

they and their men. [24] Gedaliah swore to them and to their men, and said to them, "Do not be afraid of being the servants of the Chaldeans. Live in the land and serve the king of Babylon, and it will go well for you."

[25] But in the seventh month, Ishmael the son of Nethaniah, the son of Elishama, of the royal line, came with ten men and struck down Gedaliah. He died along with the Judeans and Chaldeans who were with him at Mizpah. [26] Then all the people, both small and great, and the captains of the armies arose and went to Egypt, for they were afraid of the Chaldeans.

Jehoiachin Released from Prison
Jer 52:31–34

[27] In the thirty-seventh year of the exile of Jehoiachin king of Judah, in the twelfth month, on the twenty-seventh day of the month, Awel-Marduk king of Babylon, in the year that he became king, released Jehoiachin king of Judah from prison. [28] He spoke kindly to him, and gave him a throne above the thrones of the kings that were with him in Babylon. [29] He changed his prison garments, and he ate food continually before him all the days of his life. [30] His allowance was a regular allowance given him by the king every day, all the days of his life.

1 CHRONICLES

The Generations From Adam to Abraham

1 Adam, Seth, Enosh; [2] Kenan, Mahalalel, Jared; [3] Enoch, Methuselah, Lamech;

[4] Noah,
    Shem, Ham, and Japheth.

Japhethites
Ge 10:2–5

[5] The sons of Japheth *were*
    Gomer, Magog, Madai, Javan, Tubal, Meshek,
    and Tiras.
[6] The sons of Gomer *were*
    Ashkenaz, Riphath, and Togarmah.
[7] The sons of Javan *were*
    Elishah, Tarshish, the Kittites, and
    the Rodanites.

Hamites
Ge 10:6–20

[8] The sons of Ham *were*
    Cush, Egypt, Put, and Canaan.
[9] The sons of Cush *were*
    Seba, Havilah, Sabta, Raamah, and Sabteka.
The sons of Raamah *were*
    Sheba and Dedan.
[10] Cush became the father of
    Nimrod, who began to be mighty on the earth.
[11] Egypt became the father of
    the Ludites, Anamites, Lehabites, and Naphtuhites, [12] Pathrusites, Kasluhites (from whom came the Philistines), and the Caphtorites.
[13] Canaan became the father of
    Sidon, his firstborn, and Heth [14] and the Jebusites,
    the Amorites, the Girgashites, [15] the Hivites, the Arkites,
    the Sinites, [16] the Arvadites, the Zemarites, and the
    Hamathites.

Semites
Ge 10:21–31; 11:10–27

[17] The sons of Shem *were*
    Elam, Ashur, Arphaxad, Lud, Aram,
    Uz, Hul, Gether, and Meshek.
[18] Arphaxad became the father of Shelah,
    and Shelah became the father of Eber.
[19] Two sons were born to Eber:
    The name of one *was* Peleg, for in his days the earth was
    divided, and the name of his brother *was* Joktan.
[20] Joktan became the father of
    Almodad, Sheleph, Hazarmaveth, and Jerah,
    [21] Hadoram, Uzal, and Diklah, [22] Ebal, Abimael,
    Sheba, [23] Ophir, Havilah, and Jobab. All these *were*
    the sons of Joktan.

    [24] Shem, Arphaxad, Shelah,
    [25] Eber, Peleg, Reu,
    [26] Serug, Nahor, Terah,
    [27] and Abram, who is Abraham.

The Generations of Abraham

[28] The sons of Abraham *were*
    Isaac and Ishmael.

Descendants of Hagar
Ge 25:12–16

[29] These *are* their generations:
    The firstborn of Ishmael *was* Nebaioth, then Kedar, Adbeel,
    Mibsam, [30] Mishma, Dumah, Massa, Hadad, Tema, [31] Jetur,
    Naphish, and Kedemah. These *were* the sons of Ishmael.

Descendants of Keturah
Ge 25:1–4

[32] The sons of Keturah, Abraham's concubine:
    She bore Zimran, Jokshan, Medan, Midian, Ishbak,
    and Shuah.

The sons of Jokshan *were*
Sheba and Dedan.
[33] The sons of Midian *were*
Ephah, Epher, Hanok, Abida, and Eldaah.
All these *were* the sons of Keturah.

Descendants of Sarah
Ge 36:10–14
[34] Abraham *also* became the father of Isaac.
The sons of Isaac *were*
Esau and Israel.

[35] The sons of Esau *were*
Eliphaz, Reuel, Jeush, Jalam, and Korah.
[36] The sons of Eliphaz *were*
Teman, Omar, Zephi, Gatam, Kenaz, Timna,
and Amalek.
[37] The sons of Reuel *were*
Nahath, Zerah, Shammah, and Mizzah.

Descendants of Esau in Edom
Ge 36:20–43
[38] The sons of Seir *were*
Lotan, Shobal, Zibeon, Anah, Dishon, Ezer,
and Dishan.
[39] The sons of Lotan *were*
Hori and Homam; the sister of Lotan *was* Timna.
[40] The sons of Shobal *were*
Alian, Manahath, Ebal, Shepho, and Onam.
The sons of Zibeon *were*
Aiah and Anah.
[41] The son of Anah *was*
Dishon.
The sons of Dishon *were*
Hamran, Eshban, Ithran, and Keran.
[42] The sons of Ezer *were*
Bilhan, Zaavan, and Jaakan.
The sons of Dishan *were*
Uz and Aran.

[43] These *are* the kings who reigned in the land of Edom before
any king reigned *over* the children of Israel:
Bela the son of Beor (the name of his city *was* Dinhabah).
[44] When Bela died, Jobab the son of Zerah from Bozrah reigned
in his place.
[45] When Jobab died, Husham from the land of the Temanites
reigned in his place.
[46] When Husham died, Hadad the son of Bedad, the one who
struck Midian in the open field of Moab, reigned in his
place (the name of his city *was* Avith).
[47] When Hadad died, Samlah from Masrekah reigned in his
place.
[48] When Samlah died, Shaul from Rehoboth on the River
reigned in his place.
[49] When Shaul died, Baal-Hanan the son of Akbor reigned in
his place.
[50] When Baal-Hanan died, Hadad reigned in his place (the name
of his city *was* Pai, and the name of his wife *was* Mehetabel,
the daughter of Matred, the daughter of Me-Zahab). [51] Then
Hadad died.

The tribal chiefs of Edom *were*
Chief Timnah, Chief Alvah, Chief Jetheth, [52] Chief Oholibamah, Chief Elah, Chief Pinon, [53] Chief Kenaz, Chief Teman,
Chief Mibzar, [54] Chief Magdiel, and Chief Iram. These *were*
the chiefs of Edom.

Sons of Israel
Ge 35:23–26; Ru 4:18–22; Mt 1:3–6
2 These *are* the sons of Israel:
Reuben, Simeon, Levi, Judah, Issachar, Zebulun, [2] Dan,
Joseph, Benjamin, Naphtali, Gad, and Asher.

From Judah to David
[3] The sons of Judah *were*
Er, Onan, and Shelah: *These* three were born to him by
the daughter of Shua the Canaanitess. Now Er, the firstborn
of Judah, was evil in the sight of the Lord, and He put him
to death. [4] Then Tamar his daughter-in-law bore Perez and
Zerah for him. In all, Judah had five sons.

[5] The sons of Perez *were*
Hezron and Hamul.
[6] The sons of Zerah *were*
Zimri, Ethan, Heman, Kalkol, and Dara, five of them in all.
[7] The sons of Karmi *were*
Achar, the troubler of Israel, who acted unfaithfully in
regard to the ban.
[8] The son of Ethan *was*
Azariah.
[9] Now the sons of Hezron, who were born to him, *were*
Jerahmeel, Ram, and Kelubai.

Sons of Ram
[10] Ram became the father of
Amminadab, and Amminadab became the father of
Nahshon, a leader of the sons of Judah. [11] Nahshon became
the father of Salma, and Salma became the father of Boaz.
[12] Boaz
became the father of Obed, and Obed became the father
of Jesse.
[13] Now Jesse became the father of
his firstborn Eliab, and Abinadab the second, and Shimea
the third, [14] Nethanel the fourth, Raddai the fifth, [15] Ozem
the sixth, David the seventh; [16] their sisters were Zeruiah
and Abigail. The sons of Zeruiah *were* Abishai, Joab, and
Asahel, three *in all*. [17] Abigail bore Amasa: the father of
Amasa was Jether the Ishmaelite.

Sons of Caleb
[18] Caleb the son of Hezron had *children* with his wife Azubah
and with Jerioth. These are her sons: Jesher, Shobab, and
Ardon. [19] Now Azubah died, and Caleb took Ephrath *as a
wife*. She bore Hur for him. [20] Hur became the father of
Uri, and Uri became the father of Bezalel.
[21] Afterward Hezron had relations with the daughter of
Makir, the father of Gilead, whom he took *as a wife*
when he was sixty years old, and she bore Segub for him.
[22] Segub became the father of Jair, who had twenty-three
cities in the land of Gilead. [23] He took Geshur and Aram,
the towns of Jair, from them, with Kenath and its villages,
sixty towns. All these were descendants of Makir, the father
of Gilead.

[24] After the death of Hezron in Caleb Ephrathah, Hezron's wife
Abijah bore him Ashhur the father of Tekoa.

Sons of Jerahmeel
[25] Now the sons of Jerahmeel the firstborn of Hezron were
Ram the firstborn, Bunah, Oren, Ozem, and Ahijah.
[26] Jerahmeel also had another wife. Her name was Atarah,
and she was the mother of Onam.
[27] The sons of Ram the firstborn of Jerahmeel were
Maaz, Jamin, and Eker.
[28] The sons of Onam were
Shammai and Jada.
And the sons of Shammai *were*
Nadab and Abishur.
[29] The name of the wife of Abishur *was* Abihail. She bore him
Ahban and Molid.
[30] The sons of Nadab *were*
Seled and Appaim, but Seled died without children.
[31] The son of Appaim *was*
Ishi. The son of Ishi *was* Sheshan,
and the son of Sheshan *was* Ahlai.

³² The sons of Jada the brother of Shammai *were*
    Jether and Jonathan, but Jether died without children.
³³ The sons of Jonathan *were*
    Peleth and Zaza.
These were the sons of Jerahmeel.
³⁴ Now Sheshan had no children except daughters,
    but he did have a servant, an Egyptian, whose name *was*
    Jarha. ³⁵ Sheshan gave *one of* his daughters to Jarha his
    servant *as a wife*, and she bore him Attai.
³⁶ Attai became the father of Nathan,
    and Nathan became the father of Zabad.
³⁷ Zabad became the father of Ephlal,
    and Ephlal became the father of Obed.
³⁸ Obed became the father of Jehu,
    and Jehu became the father of Azariah.
³⁹ Azariah became the father of Helez,
    and Helez became the father of Eleasah.
⁴⁰ Eleasah became the father of Sismai,
    and Sismai became the father of Shallum.
⁴¹ Shallum became the father of Jekamiah,
    and Jekamiah became the father of Elishama.

Caleb's Clans

⁴² Now the sons of Caleb the brother of Jerahmeel *were*
    Mesha his firstborn, who was the father of Ziph, and the
    sons of Mareshah the father of Hebron.
⁴³ The sons of Hebron *were*
    Korah, Tappuah, Rekem, and Shema. ⁴⁴ Shema became
    the father of Raham, the father of Jorkeam, and Rekem
    became the father of Shammai. ⁴⁵ The son of Shammai
    was Maon, and Maon was the father of Beth Zur.
⁴⁶ Ephah, Caleb's concubine, bore Haran, Moza, and Gazez,
    and Haran became the father of Gazez.
⁴⁷ The sons of Jahdai *were*
    Regem, Jotham, Geshan, Pelet, Ephah, and Shaaph.
⁴⁸ Maakah, Caleb's concubine, bore Sheber and Tirhanah.
    ⁴⁹ She also bore Shaaph the father of Madmannah, Sheva
    the father of Makbenah, and the father of Gibea. The
    daughter of Caleb was Aksah.
⁵⁰ These were the sons of Caleb the son of Hur, the firstborn of
    Ephrathah:
    Shobal the father of Kiriath Jearim, ⁵¹ Salma the father of
    Bethlehem, and Hareph the father of Beth Gader.
⁵² Now sons were *born* to Shobal the father of Kiriath Jearim:
    Haroeh *and* half of the Manahathites. ⁵³ The families of
    Kiriath Jearim *were* the Ithrites, the Puthites, the Shuma-
    thites, and the Mishraites. From these the Zorathites and
    the Eshtaolites went forth.
⁵⁴ The sons of Salma *were*
    Bethlehem, the Netophathites, Atroth Beth Joab, and half of
    the Manahathites, the Zorites. ⁵⁵ The families of the scribes
    who lived at Jabez *were* the Tirathites, the Shimeathites,
    and the Sucathites. They are the Kenites who came from
    Hammath, the father of the house of Rekab.

The Generations of David
2Sa 3:2–5; 5:14–16; 1Ch 14:4–7

3 Now these were the sons of David, who were born to him in
Hebron:
    The firstborn *was* Amnon by Ahinoam the Jezreelitess;
    the second, Daniel by Abigail the Carmelitess;
    ² the third *was* Absalom the son of Maakah, the daughter
    of Talmai king of Geshur;
    the fourth, Adonijah the son of Haggith;
    ³ the fifth, Shephatiah by Abital;
    the sixth, Ithream by Eglah his wife.
⁴ Six *sons* were born to him in Hebron, and he reigned
    there seven years and six months.
He also reigned thirty-three years in Jerusalem. ⁵ Now these were
born to him in Jerusalem:

Shimea, Shobab, Nathan, and Solomon, four sons
    by Bathsheba the daughter of Ammiel; ⁶ then Ibhar,
    Elishama, Eliphelet, ⁷ Nogah, Nepheg, Japhia, ⁸ Elishama,
    Eliada, and Eliphelet, nine. ⁹ These *were* all the sons of
    David, besides the sons of the concubines, and Tamar
    their sister.

The Kings of Judah

¹⁰ Solomon's son *was* Rehoboam;
    Abijah *was* his son,
    Asa his son,
    Jehoshaphat his son,
    ¹¹ Joram¹ his son,
    Ahaziah his son,
    Joash his son,
    ¹² Amaziah his son,
    Azariah his son,
    Jotham his son,
    ¹³ Ahaz his son,
    Hezekiah his son,
    Manasseh his son,
    ¹⁴ Amon his son,
    and Josiah his son.
¹⁵ The sons of Josiah *were*
    the firstborn Johanan,
    the second Jehoiakim,
    the third Zedekiah,
    and the fourth Shallum.
¹⁶ The sons of Jehoiakim *were*
    Jeconiah his son
    and Zedekiah his son.

The Post-Exilic Royal Line

¹⁷ The sons of Jeconiah *were* Assir,
    Shealtiel his son, ¹⁸ Malkiram, Pedaiah, Shenazzar,
    Jekamiah, Hoshama, and Nedabiah.
¹⁹ The sons of Pedaiah *were*
    Zerubbabel and Shimei,
and the sons of Zerubbabel *were*
    Meshullam and Hananiah,
    and Shelomith *was* their sister;
    ²⁰ and Hashubah, Ohel, Berekiah, Hasadiah, *and* Jushab-
    Hesed, five.
²¹ The sons of Hananiah *were*
    Pelatiah and Jeshaiah, the sons of Rephaiah, the sons of
    Arnan, the sons of Obadiah, and the sons of Shekaniah.
²² The sons of Shekaniah *were*
    Shemaiah and the sons of Shemaiah:
    Hattush, Igal, Bariah, Neariah, and Shaphat, six *in all*.
²³ The sons of Neariah *were*
    Elioenai, Hizkiah, and Azrikam, three *in all*.
²⁴ The sons of Elioenai *were*
    Hodaviah, Eliashib, Pelaiah, Akkub, Johanan, Delaiah, and
    Anani, seven *in all*.

Other Sons of Judah

4 The sons of Judah *were*
Perez, Hezron, Karmi, Hur, and Shobal.
² Reaiah the son of Shobal became the father of Jahath, and
    Jahath became the father of Ahumai and Lahad. These *are*
    the families of the Zorathites.
³ These *were the sons of* the father of Etam:
    Jezreel, Ishma, and Idbash. The name of their sister *was*
    Hazzelelponi. ⁴ Penuel *was* the father of Gedor, and Ezer
    was the father of Hushah.
These *were* the sons of Hur, the firstborn of Ephrathah, the
    father of Bethlehem.
⁵ Ashhur the father of Tekoa *had* two wives: Helah and Naarah.
⁶ Naarah bore him Ahuzzam, Hepher, Temeni, and Haahash-
    tari. These *were* the sons of Naarah.

---

¹ 11 *Jehoram* in 2Ki 1:17; 8:16.

7 The sons of Helah *were*

Zereth, Zohar, and Ethnan. 8 Koz became the father of Anub and Hazzobebah and the families of Aharhel the son of Harum.

9 Now Jabez was more honorable than his brothers, and his mother called his name Jabez, saying, "Because I bore *him* in hardship." 10 Then Jabez called on the God of Israel, saying, "Oh, that You would indeed bless me and enlarge my territory, that Your hand might be with me, and that You would keep *me* from evil, that *it* may not bring me hardship!" So God granted what he asked.

11 Kelub the brother of Shuhah became the father of Mehir, who *was* the father of Eshton. 12 Eshton became the father of Beth Rapha, Paseah, and Tehinnah the father of Ir Nahash. These *were* the men of Rekah.

13 The sons of Kenaz *were*

Othniel and Seraiah,

and the sons of Othniel *were*

Hathath *and Meonothai.* 14 Meonothai became the father of Ophrah,

and Seraiah became the father of Joab,

the father of Ge Harashim, for they were craftsmen.
15 The sons of Caleb the son of Jephunneh *were*

Iru, Elah, and Naam,

and the son of Elah *was*

Kenaz.
16 The sons of Jehallelel *were*

Ziph, Ziphah, Tiria, and Asarel.
17 The sons of Ezrah *were*

Jether, Mered, Epher, and Jalon, and *Mered's wife* bore Miriam, Shammai, and Ishbah the father of Eshtemoa. 18 His Judean wife bore Jered the father of Gedor, Heber the father of Soko, and Jekuthiel the father of Zanoah. So these were the sons of Bithiah the daughter of Pharaoh, whom Mered took.
19 The sons of his wife Hodiah, the sister of Naham, *were* the father of Keilah the Garmite and Eshtemoa the Maakathite.
20 The sons of Shimon *were*

Amnon, Rinnah, Ben-Hanan, and Tilon.

And the sons of Ishi *were*

Zoheth and Ben-Zoheth.
21 The sons of Shelah the son of Judah *were*

Er the father of Lekah, Laadah the father of Mareshah, the families of the house of workers of fine linen at Beth Ashbea; 22 Jokim, the men of Kozeba, Joash, Saraph, who was lord in Moab, and Jashubi Lehem (these records are ancient). 23 They *were* the potters, those dwelling at Netaim and Gederah (they dwelt there with the king for his work).

Sons of Simeon
Jos 19:2–10

24 The sons of Simeon *were*

Nemuel, Jamin, Jarib, Zerah, Shaul,
25 Shallum his son, Mibsam his son, *and* Mishma his son.
26 The sons of Mishma *were*

Hammuel his son, Zakkur his son, *and* Shimei his son.
27 Shimei had sixteen sons and six daughters, but his brothers did not have many sons, nor did all their family multiply as much as the sons of Judah. 28 Now they dwelt in Beersheba, Moladah, and Hazar Shual 29 as *well as* in Bilhah, Ezem, Tolad, 30 Bethuel, Hormah, Ziklag, 31 Beth Markaboth, Hazar Susim, Beth Biri, and Shaaraim. These *were* their cities until the reign of David. 32 Their villages *were* Etam, Ain, Rimmon, Token, and Ashan, five cities *in all,* 33 and all the villages that *were* around these cities as far as Baal. Such *are* their inhabited cities, and those registered to them *were* 34 Meshobab, Jamlech, and Joshah the son of Amaziah; 35 Joel, and Jehu the son of Joshibiah, the son of Seraiah, the son of Asiel;

36 Elioenai, Jaakobah, Jeshohaiah, Asaiah, Adiel, Jesimiel, Benaiah; 37 Ziza the son of Shiphi, the son of Allon, the son of Jedaiah, the son of Shimri, the son of Shemaiah.

38 These mentioned by name *were* leaders in their families, and their fathers' houses increased greatly. 39 They went to the entrance of Gedor, as far as the east side of the valley, to seek pasture for their flocks. 40 There they found rich, good pasture, and the land was wide, quiet, and peaceful; for former inhabitants there belonged to Ham.

41 In the days of Hezekiah king of Judah, those written by name came and attacked their tents, *along with* the Meunites who were found there, and utterly destroyed them until this day. Then they dwelt there in their place because *there was* pasture for their flocks there. 42 Now *some* of them, *namely* five hundred men from the sons of Simeon, went to Mount Seir with Pelatiah, Neariah, Rephaiah, and Uzziel, the sons of Ishi, as their captains. 43 *Then* they struck down the rest of the Amalekites who had escaped. So they have dwelt there until this day.

Sons of Reuben

5 Now the sons of Reuben the firstborn of Israel (for he was the firstborn, but since he defiled his father's bed, his birthright was given to the sons of Joseph the son of Israel, so that the genealogy is not listed according to the birthright; 2 though Judah prevailed over his brothers and a ruler came from him, yet the birthright belonged to Joseph), 3 the sons of Reuben the firstborn of Israel *were*

Hanok, Pallu, Hezron, and Karmi.
4 The sons of Joel *were*

Shemaiah his son, Gog his son,

Shimei his son, 5 Micah his son,

Reaiah his son, Baal his son,
6 and Beerah his son, whom Tiglath-Pileser the king of Assyria led into exile. He was a leader of the Reubenites.
7 His brothers according to their families by the registration of their generations *were* ·

Jeiel, the first, and Zechariah; 8 Bela the son of Azaz, the son of Shema, the son of Joel, who dwelt in Aroer, even as far as Nebo and Baal Meon. 9 And he dwelt toward the east as far as the entrance to the wilderness from the Euphrates, for their cattle were abundant in the land of Gilead.
10 Now in the days of Saul, they made war with the Hagrites, who fell by their hand, and they dwelt in their tents over all the eastern plains of Gilead.

Sons of Gad

11 The sons of Gad dwelt opposite them in the land of Bashan as far as Salekah.
12 Joel *was* the first, Shapham the second, with Janai and Shaphat in Bashan.
13 Their brothers of their father's house *were*

Michael, Meshullam, Sheba, Jorai, Jakan, Zia, and Eber, seven *in all.*
14 These *are* the sons of Abihail, the son of Huri, the son of Jaroah, the son of Gilead, the son of Michael, the son of Jeshishai, the son of Jahdo, the son of Buz;
15 Ahi the son of Abdiel, the son of Guni, *was* the head of their father's house.
16 They dwelt in Gilead in Bashan, and in its towns, and in all the outlands of Sharon to *the edge of* their borders.
17 All of them were registered *by genealogy* in the days of Jotham king of Judah and in the days of Jeroboam king of Israel.

18 The sons of Reuben, and the Gadites, and the half-tribe of Manasseh *numbered* forty-four thousand seven hundred and sixty valiant men, men able to bear shield and sword, to shoot with a bow, and *who were* skillful in battle, who went to war. 19 They made war with the Hagrites, *namely* Jetur, Naphish, and Nodab. 20 They were helped against them, and the Hagrites and all who *were* with them were delivered into their hand, for they cried to God in the battle, and He heard their prayer because they trusted in Him. 21 They captured their livestock:

fifty thousand of their camels, two hundred and fifty thousand sheep, two thousand donkeys, and one hundred thousand men. [22] So many fell slain, because the war was of God. And they dwelt in their place until the exile.

The Half-Tribe of Manasseh

[23] The children of the half-tribe of Manasseh *also* dwelt in the land. They increased from Bashan as far as Baal Hermon and Senir, even to Mount Hermon.

[24] These were the heads of their fathers' houses: Epher, Ishi, Eliel, Azriel, Jeremiah, Hodaviah, and Jahdiel, mighty men of valor, men of reputation, *and* heads of their fathers' houses. [25] They were unfaithful to the God of their fathers and played the harlot after the gods of the peoples of the land, whom God had wiped out before them. [26] So the God of Israel stirred up the spirit of Pul the king of Assyria, *even* the spirit of Tiglath-Pileser king of Assyria, and he led the Reubenites, the Gadites, and the half-tribe of Manasseh into exile and brought them to Halah, Habor, Hara, and to the river of Gozan to this day.

Sons of Levi

6 The sons of Levi *were* Gershon, Kohath, and Merari.
[2] The sons of Kohath *were* Amram, Izhar, Hebron, and Uzziel.
[3] The children of Amram *were* Aaron, Moses, and Miriam.

The sons of Aaron *were* Nadab, Abihu, Eleazar, and Ithamar. [4] Eleazar became the father of Phinehas, Phinehas the father of Abishua, [5] Abishua the father of Bukki, and Bukki the father of Uzzi. [6] Uzzi became the father of Zerahiah, and Zerahiah the father of Meraioth. [7] Meraioth became the father of Amariah, and Amariah father of Ahitub. [8] Ahitub became the father of Zadok, and Zadok father of Ahimaaz. [9] Ahimaaz became the father of Azariah, and Azariah father of Johanan. [10] Johanan became the father of Azariah (he was the one who ministered as a priest in the temple that Solomon built in Jerusalem). [11] Azariah became the father of Amariah, and Amariah father of Ahitub. [12] Ahitub became the father of Zadok, and Zadok the father of Shallum. [13] Shallum became the father of Hilkiah, and Hilkiah the father of Azariah. [14] Azariah became the father of Seraiah, and Seraiah of Jehozadak. [15] Jehozadak went *into exile* when the Lord led Judah and Jerusalem into exile by the hand of Nebuchadnezzar.

[16] The sons of Levi *were* Gershom, Kohath, and Merari.
[17] These *are* the names of the sons of Gershom: Libni and Shimei.
[18] The sons of Kohath *were* Amram, Izhar, Hebron, and Uzziel.
[19] The sons of Merari *were* Mahli and Mushi.

Now these *are* the families of the Levites according to their fathers.
[20] Of Gershom *were* Libni his son, Jahath his son, Zimmah his son, [21] Joah his son, Iddo his son, Zerah his son, and Jeatherai his son.
[22] The sons of Kohath *were* Amminadab his son, Korah his son, Assir his son, [23] Elkanah his son,

Ebiasaph his son, Assir his son, [24] Tahath his son, Uriel his son, Uzziah his son, and Shaul his son.
[25] The sons of Elkanah *were* Amasai and Ahimoth.
[26] As for Elkanah, the sons of Elkanah *were* Zophai his son, Nahath his son, [27] Eliab his son, Jeroham his son, and Elkanah his son.
[28] The sons of Samuel *were* the firstborn Joel and Abijah.
[29] The sons of Merari *were* Mahli, Libni his son, Shimei his son, Uzzah his son, [30] Shimea his son, Haggiah his son, *and* Asaiah his son.

The Temple Musicians

Jos 21:4–39

[31] These *are* the ones whom David appointed over the service of song in the house of the Lord, after the ark rested *there*. [32] Now they were ministering before the dwelling place of the tabernacle of meeting with singing until Solomon had built the house of the Lord in Jerusalem, and they were arranged by their order according to their service.

[33] These *are* the ones standing in order with their sons.

Of the sons of the Kohathites *were*
Heman the singer,
the son of Joel, the son of Samuel,
[34] the son of Elkanah, the son of Jeroham,
the son of Eliel, the son of Toah,
[35] the son of Zuph, the son of Elkanah,
the son of Mahath, the son of Amasai,
[36] the son of Elkanah, the son of Joel,
the son of Azariah, the son of Zephaniah,
[37] the son of Tahath, the son of Assir,
the son of Ebiasaph, the son of Korah,
[38] the son of Izhar, the son of Kohath,
the son of Levi, the son of Israel.
[39] His brother Asaph, the one standing at his right hand, was
Asaph the son of Berekiah, the son of Shimea,
[40] the son of Michael, the son of Baaseiah,
the son of Malkijah, [41] the son of Ethni,
the son of Zerah, the son of Adaiah,
[42] the son of Ethan, the son of Zimmah,
the son of Shimei, [43] the son of Jahath,
the son of Gershom, the son of Levi.
[44] Of the sons of Merari, their brothers, *standing* on the left hand *was*
Ethan the son of Kishi, the son of Abdi,
the son of Malluk, [45] the son of Hashabiah,
the son of Amaziah, the son of Hilkiah,
[46] the son of Amzi, the son of Bani,
the son of Shemer, [47] the son of Mahli,
the son of Mushi, the son of Merari,
the son of Levi.

[48] Their brothers the Levites also *were* appointed for all kinds of service to the tabernacle of the house of God. [49] But Aaron and his sons were making sacrifices on the altar of the burnt offering and on the altar of incense for all the work of the Most Holy Place and to make atonement for Israel, according to all that Moses the servant of God had commanded.

[50] Now these *are* the sons of Aaron:
Eleazar his son, Phinehas his son,
Abishua his son, [51] Bukki his son,
Uzzi his son, Zerahiah his son,
[52] Meraioth his son, Amariah his son,
Ahitub his son, [53] Zadok his son,
and Ahimaaz his son.

[54] And these *are* their dwelling places according to their walled settlements in their territory, for they were given to them, *namely* to the sons of Aaron and to the families of the Kohathites, by lot.

[55] They gave them Hebron in the land of Judah, and its surrounding outlands. [56] But the open fields of the city, and its villages, they gave to Caleb the son of Jephunneh.

[57] To the sons of Aaron they gave the cities of Judah with the cities of refuge: Hebron and Libnah with its outlands, Jattir and Eshtemoa with their outlands, [58] Hilen with its outlands, Debir with its outlands, [59] Ashan with its outlands, and Beth Shemesh with its outlands. [60] From the tribe of Benjamin, *they gave* Geba with its outlands, Alemeth with its outlands, and Anathoth with its outlands.

All their cities throughout their families *were* thirteen.

[61] To the sons of Kohath, those remaining from the family of *that* tribe, *they gave* ten cities by lot from half the tribe of Manasseh. [62] To the sons of Gershon, throughout their families, *they gave* from the tribe of Issachar, from the tribe of Asher, from the tribe of Naphtali, and from the tribe of Manasseh in Bashan, thirteen cities *in all*. [63] To the sons of Merari, throughout their families, *they gave* by lot from the tribe of Reuben, from the tribe of Gad, and from the tribe of Zebulun, twelve cities *in all*.

[64] Thus, the sons of Israel gave cities with their outlands to the Levites. [65] They gave by lot from the tribe of the sons of Judah, and from the tribe of the sons of Simeon, and from the tribe of the sons of Benjamin, these cities, which are called by *their* names.

[66] Then some from the families of the sons of Kohath *received* cities for their territory from the tribe of Ephraim. [67] They gave to them with the cities of refuge: Shechem in the mountains of Ephraim with its outlands, Gezer with its outlands, [68] Jokmeam with its outlands, Beth Horon with its outlands, [69] Aijalon with its outlands, and Gath Rimmon with its outlands. [70] Also the half-tribe of Manasseh *gave* Aner with its outlands and Bileam with its outlands for the remaining family of the sons of Kohath.

[71] To the sons of Gershom, the family of the half-tribe of Manasseh *gave* Golan in Bashan with its outlands and Ashtaroth with its outlands. [72] From the tribe of Issachar, *they received* Kedesh with its outlands, Daberath with its outlands, [73] Ramoth with its outlands, and Anem with its outlands. [74] From the tribe of Asher, *they received* Mashal with its outlands, Abdon with its outlands, [75] Hukok with its outlands, and Rehob with its outlands. [76] From the tribe of Naphtali, *they received* Kedesh in Galilee with its outlands, Hammon with its outlands, and Kiriathaim with its outlands.

[77] To the remaining sons of Merari, the tribe of Zebulun *gave* Rimmono with its outlands and Tabor with its outlands. [78] Then on the other side of the Jordan *opposite* Jericho, to the east of the Jordan, from the tribe of Reuben *they were given* Bezer in the wilderness with its outlands, Jahzah with its outlands, [79] Kedemoth with its outlands, and Mephaath with its outlands. [80] And from the tribe of Gad, *they received* Ramoth in Gilead with its outlands, Mahanaim with its outlands, [81] Heshbon with its outlands, and Jazer with its outlands.

Sons of Issachar

7 Now the sons of Issachar *were*
Tola, Puah, Jashub, and Shimron, four *in all*.
[2] The sons of Tola *were*
Uzzi, Rephaiah, Jeriel, Jahmai, Ibsam, and Samuel. *They were* heads of their father's house. The sons of Tola were mighty men of valor in their generations. Their number in the days of David *was* twenty-two thousand six hundred.
[3] The son of Uzzi was
Izrahiah,
and the sons of Izrahiah were

Michael, Obadiah, Joel, and Ishiah, five chiefs in all. [4] With them, by their generations, after the house of their fathers, *were* thirty-six thousand troops of war, battle-ready, for they had many wives and sons.
[5] Now their brothers from all the families of Issachar *were* mighty men of valor, in all eighty-seven thousand registered by genealogy.

Sons of Benjamin
[6] Benjamin *had*
Bela, Beker, and Jediael, three *sons in all*.
[7] The sons of Bela *were* five:
Ezbon, Uzzi, Uzziel, Jerimoth, and Iri. *They were* heads of their fathers' houses, mighty men of valor, and registered by their genealogies, twenty-two thousand and thirty-four *in number*.
[8] The sons of Beker *were*
Zemirah, Joash, Eliezer, Elioenai, Omri, Jeremoth, Abijah, Anathoth, and Alemeth. All these *are* the sons of Beker.
[9] Now their registration according to their generations, heads of their fathers' houses, mighty men of valor, *was* twenty thousand two hundred.
[10] The son of Jediael was
Bilhan,
along with the sons of Bilhan:
Jeush, Benjamin, Ehud, Kenaanah, Zethan, Tarshish, and Ahishahar. [11] All these sons of Jediael *were* heads of their fathers' houses, mighty men of valor, *numbering* seventeen thousand two hundred soldiers, ready to go out to war for battle.
[12] And the Shuppites and Huppites *were* the sons of Ir; the Hushites the sons of Aher.

Sons of Naphtali
[13] The sons of Naphtali *were*
Jahziel, Guni, Jezer, and Shallum, descendants of Bilhah.

Sons of Manasseh
[14] The sons of Manasseh *were*
Asriel, whom his Aramean concubine bore. She *also* bore Makir the father of Gilead. [15] Now Makir took a wife for Huppim and Shuppim, whose sister's name was Maakah.
The name of the second was Zelophehad, and Zelophehad had daughters.
[16] Maakah the wife of Makir bore a son, and she called his name Peresh. His brother's name *was* Sheresh, and his sons *were* Ulam and Rakem.
[17] The son of Ulam was
Bedan.
These *were* the sons of Gilead, the son of Makir, the son of Manasseh. [18] His sister Hammoleketh bore Ishhod, Abiezer, and Mahlah.
[19] The sons of Shemida were
Ahian, Shechem, Likhi, and Aniam.

Sons of Ephraim
[20] The sons of Ephraim *were*
Shuthelah, Bered his son,
Tahath his son, Eleadah his son,
Tahath his son, [21] Zabad his son,
Shuthelah his son, and Ezer and Elead, whom the men of Gath born in that land killed because they came down to take their livestock. [22] Ephraim their father mourned many days, and his brothers came to comfort him. [23] Then he went in to his wife, and she conceived and bore a son, so he called his name Beriah, because evil had been in his house [24] (his daughter was Sheerah, who built *both* Lower and Upper Beth Horon as well as Uzzen Sheerah).
[25] Rephah *was* also his son, *as were* Resheph,
Telah his son, Tahan his son,

[26] Ladan his son, Ammihud his son,
Elishama his son, [27] Nun his son,
and Joshua his son.

[28] Their possessions and settlements were Bethel and its towns, and to the east Naaran, and to the west Gezer with its towns, Shechem and its towns, and Ayyah and its towns; [29] also along the borders of the Manassites, Beth Shan and its towns, Taanach and its towns, Megiddo and its towns, and Dor and its towns. In these lived the sons of Joseph the son of Israel.

Sons of Asher

[30] Now the children of Asher *were*
Imnah, Ishvah, Ishvi, Beriah, and their sister Serah.
[31] The sons of Beriah *were*
Heber and Malkiel, who was the father of Birzaith.
[32] Heber became the father of Japhlet, Shomer, Hotham, and their sister Shua.
[33] The sons of Japhlet *were*
Pasak, Bimhal, and Ashvath.
These *were* the children of Japhlet.
[34] The sons of Shomer *were*
Ahi, Rohgah, Hubbah, and Aram.
[35] The sons of his brother Helem *were*
Zophah, Imna, Shelesh, and Amal.
[36] The sons of Zophah *were*
Suah, Harnepher, Shual, Beri, Imrah, [37] Bezer, Hod, Shamma, Shilshah, Ithran, and Beera.
[38] The sons of Jether *were*
Jephunneh, Pispah, and Ara.
[39] The sons of Ulla *were*
Arah, Hanniel, and Rizia.

[40] All these *were* the children of Asher, heads of their fathers' houses, choice men, mighty men of valor, and heads of the leaders. They were registered by their genealogy among the army fit for war. Their number *was* twenty-six thousand men.

The Generations of Benjamin
1Ch 9:34–44

8 Now Benjamin became the father of Bela his firstborn, Ashbel the second, Aharah the third,
[2] Nohah the fourth, and Rapha the fifth.
[3] The sons of Bela were
Addar, Gera, Abihud, [4] Abishua, Naaman, Ahoah, [5] Gera, Shephuphan, and Huram.
[6] These *are* the sons of Ehud, who *were* the heads of the fathers' *houses* to those dwelling in Geba, and who exiled them to Manahath.
[7] So he exiled Naaman, Ahijah, and Gera and *then* became the father of Uzza and Ahihud.
[8] Shaharaim had *sons* in the country of Moab after he had sent away his wives Hushim and Baara. [9] He had *sons* with his wife Hodesh, *namely* Jobab, Zibia, Mesha, Malkam, [10] Jeuz, Sakia, and Mirmah. These *were* his sons, heads of the fathers' *houses*. [11] He also had sons by Hushim: Abitub and Elpaal.
[12] The sons of Elpaal *were*
Eber, Misham, Shemed (he built Ono and Lod with its towns), [13] Beriah, and Shema, who were heads of the fathers' *houses* to those dwelling in Aijalon *and* who drove out the inhabitants of Gath,
[14] *as well as* Ahio, Shashak, Jeremoth, [15] Zebadiah, Arad, Eder, [16] Michael, Ishpah, and Joha, the sons of Beriah.
[17] Zebadiah, Meshullam, Hizki, Heber, [18] Ishmerai, Izliah, and Jobab *were* the sons of Elpaal.
[19] Jakim, Zikri, Zabdi, [20] Elienai, Zillethai, Eliel, [21] Adaiah, Beraiah, and Shimrath *were* the sons of Shimei.
[22] Ishpan, Eber, Eliel, [23] Abdon, Zikri, Hanan, [24] Hananiah, Elam, Anthothijah, [25] Iphdeiah, and Penuel *were* the sons of Shashak.
[26] Shamsherai, Shehariah, Athaliah, [27] Jaareshiah, Elijah, and Zikri *were* the sons of Jeroham.

[28] These *were* heads of the fathers' houses according to their generations, chief men who dwelt in Jerusalem.

[29] The father of Gibeon dwelt in Gibeon,
and Maakah *was* his wife's name. [30] His firstborn son *was* Abdon, *along with* Zur, Kish, Baal, Nadab, [31] Gedor, Ahio, and Zeker. [32] Mikloth also became the father of Shimeah. Now these also dwelt in Jerusalem with their own families near their brothers.
[33] Ner became the father of Kish; Kish the father of Saul;
Saul the father of Jonathan, Malki-Shua, Abinadab, and Esh-Baal.
[34] Jonathan's son *was*
Merib-Baal, and Merib-Baal became the father of Micah.
[35] The sons of Micah *were*
Pithon, Melek, Tarea, and Ahaz.
[36] Ahaz became the father of Jehoaddah, and Jehoaddah became the father of Alemeth, Azmaveth, and Zimri. Zimri became the father of Moza, [37] and Moza became the father of Binea. Now Raphah *was* his son, Eleasah his son, *and* Azel his son.
[38] Azel had six sons, and their names *were*
Azrikam, Bokeru, Ishmael, Sheariah, Obadiah, and Hanan. All these *were* the sons of Azel.
[39] The sons of his brother Eshek *were*
Ulam his firstborn, Jeush the second, and Eliphelet the third. [40] The sons of Ulam *were* mighty men of valor, *even* archers, and had many sons and grandsons, one hundred and fifty *in all*.
These *were* all the sons of Benjamin.

9 So all Israel was registered by genealogies, and these were written in the book of the kings of Israel. And Judah was led into exile to Babylon for their unfaithfulness.
[2] Now the first ones to dwell in their possessions in their cities *were* children of Israel, priests, Levites, and temple servants.

A Post-Exilic Genealogy
Ne 11:3–19

[3] Some of the sons of Judah dwelt in Jerusalem *alongside* some of the sons of Benjamin, Ephraim, and Manasseh:
[4] Uthai the son of Ammihud, the son of Omri, the son of Imri, the son of Bani, of the sons of Perez the son of Judah;
[5] of the Shilonites:
Asaiah the firstborn and his sons;
[6] of the sons of Zerah:
Jeuel and their brothers, six hundred and ninety.
[7] *Those* of the sons of Benjamin *were*
Sallu the son of Meshullam, the son of Hodaviah, the son of Hassenuah;
[8] Ibneiah the son of Jeroham; Elah the son of Uzzi, the son of Mikri; Meshullam the son of Shephatiah, the son of Reuel, the son of Ibnijah;
[9] and their brothers according to their generations, nine hundred and fifty-six. All these men were heads of families according to their fathers' houses.
[10] *Those* of the priests *were*
Jedaiah, Jehoiarib, Jakin;
[11] Azariah the son of Hilkiah, the son of Meshullam, the son of Zadok, the son of Meraioth, the son of Ahitub, the head official of the house of God;
[12] Adaiah the son of Jeroham, the son of Pashhur, the son of Malkijah; Maasai the son of Adiel, the son of Jahzerah, the son of Meshullam, the son of Meshillemith, the son of Immer;
[13] and their brothers, heads of the houses of their fathers, one thousand seven hundred and sixty very able men for the work of the service of the house of God.
[14] *Those* of the Levites *were*
Shemaiah the son of Hasshub, the son of Azrikam, the son of Hashabiah, of the sons of Merari; [15] Bakbakkar, Heresh, Galal, and Mattaniah the son of Mika, the son of Zikri, the

son of Asaph; [16] Obadiah the son of Shemaiah, the son of Galal, the son of Jeduthun; Berekiah the son of Asa, the son of Elkanah, who lived in the villages of the Netophathites.

[17] Now the gatekeepers *were*

Shallum, Akkub, Talmon, Ahiman, and their brothers (Shallum was the head *officer* [18] who until then *had served* at the king's eastern gate). They *were* the gatekeepers for the camps of the Levites. [19] Shallum the son of Kore, the son of Ebiasaph, the son of Korah, and his brothers from his father's house, the Korahites, *were* over the work of the service, gatekeepers of the tabernacle. Their fathers had been over the camp of the LORD, guards at the entrance. [20] Phinehas the son of Eleazar was the official over them in previous *times, and* the LORD *was* with him. [21] Zechariah the son of Meshelemiah was gatekeeper at the entrance to the tent of meeting.

[22] All those chosen as gatekeepers *were* two hundred and twelve. They were registered by their genealogy in their villages. *Now* David and Samuel the seer established them in their trusted offices. [23] So they and their sons *were* in charge of the gates of the house of the LORD, *that is,* the house of the tabernacle, as guards. [24] The gatekeepers were on four sides: east, west, north, and south. [25] Their brothers in their villages *were* to come for seven days from time to time *to serve* with them. [26] For in their trusted offices the four main gatekeepers who were Levites *had charge* over the chambers and treasuries of the house of God. [27] They spent the night around the house of God, for the watch was entrusted to them, and they were responsible for opening *it* every morning.

[28] Some of them were in charge of the vessels of service, that they should bring them in and out by number. [29] Some *others were* appointed over the furnishings and all the implements of the sanctuary as well as the fine flour, the wine, the oil, the frankincense, and the spices. [30] And some of the sons of the priests mixed the ointment of the spices. [31] Mattithiah, one of the Levites (he *was* the firstborn of Shallum the Korahite), was entrusted with making the flat cakes. [32] *Others* of the sons of the Kohathites and from their brothers *were given charge* over the showbread to prepare *it* every Sabbath.

[33] Now these *are* the singers, heads of the fathers' houses of the Levites, who stayed in the *temple* chambers, free *from other service,* because they *were occupied* with the work day and night. [34] These *were* the heads of the fathers' houses of the Levites according to their generations, leaders, who dwelt in Jerusalem.

The Genealogy of Saul
1Ch 8:28–38

[35] Now Jeiel the father of Gibeon, whose wife's name was Maakah, dwelt in Gibeon. [36] His firstborn son *was* Abdon, then Zur, Kish, Baal, Ner, Nadab, [37] Gedor, Ahio, Zechariah, and Mikloth. [38] Mikloth became the father of Shimeam. These also dwelt in Jerusalem with their own families near their brothers.

[39] Ner became the father of Kish; Kish the father of Saul; Saul the father of Jonathan, Malki-Shua, Abinadab, and Esh-Baal.

[40] The son of Jonathan *was* Merib-Baal, and Merib-Baal became the father of Micah. [41] The sons of Micah *were*

Pithon, Melek, Tahrea, and Ahaz.

[42] Ahaz became the father of Jarah, and Jarah the father of Alemeth, Azmaveth, and Zimri. Zimri became the father of Moza, [43] and Moza became the father of Binea, Rephaiah his son, Eleasah his son, *and* Azel his son.

[44] Azel had six sons, and these *were* their names:

Azrikam, Bokeru, Ishmael, Sheariah, Obadiah, and Hanan. These *were* the sons of Azel.

The Death of Saul
1Sa 31:1–13; 2Sa 1:4–12

10 Now *when* the Philistines fought against Israel, every Israelite *fighter* fled before the Philistines, and the slain fell on Mount Gilboa. [2] But the Philistines pursued Saul and his sons and struck down Saul's sons Jonathan, Abinadab, and Malki-Shua. [3] As the battle with Saul became heavy, the archers' bows found *their target* and mortally wounded him.

[4] So Saul said to his armor bearer, "Draw your sword and pierce me through lest these uncircumcised *Philistines* come and make a fool of me."

But his armor bearer was unwilling to do it because he was overwhelmed with fear, so Saul took the sword and fell on it *himself.* [5] When the armor bearer saw that Saul was dead, he too fell on his sword and died. [6] Thus, Saul and his three sons, *namely* all his house, died together.

[7] Now *when* all the children of Israel in the valley saw that they had fled *the battlefield,* and Saul and his sons were dead, they abandoned their cities and escaped, *leaving* the Philistines to come and dwell in them.

[8] The next day, *when* the Philistines came to pillage the slain, they found Saul and his sons fallen on Mount Gilboa. [9] So they stripped *Saul,* removed his head and his armor, and circulated the news of his demise throughout the land of the Philistines to their idols *as well as* the people. [10] Then they placed his armor in the temple of their gods, while his head they impaled in the house of Dagon.

[11] Now all Jabesh Gilead heard about everything the Philistines did to Saul, [12] so their valiant men rose up and carried the body of Saul and the bodies of his sons to Jabesh. They buried their bones under the oak in Jabesh and fasted, *mourning* seven days.

[13] So Saul died because of his unfaithful deeds against the LORD, because of his failure to keep the word of the LORD, and because he sought to consult a spirit *of divination* [14] but did not seek the LORD. So He killed him and turned the kingdom over to David the son of Jesse.

David, King of Israel
2Sa 5:1–10

11 Then all Israel assembled before David at Hebron, saying, "We are your *own people, even* your flesh and blood. [2] Also from times past until now, even when Saul was king, you were the one who led Israel going out and coming in, and the LORD your God said to you, Indeed, you will shepherd My people Israel as the ruler of Israel."

[3] Then all the elders of Israel came to King David at Hebron, and he made a covenant with them there before the LORD. So they anointed David king over Israel according to the word of the LORD *delivered* by Samuel.

David Conquers Jerusalem

[4] Now David and all Israel *with him* went to Jerusalem (that is, Jebus, since the Jebusites still dwelt there in the land). [5] And the Jebusites said to David, "You will not come here," but he captured the stronghold of Zion (it is the City of David).

[6] Now David had said, "Whoever strikes Jebus first will be the commander and leader *of the army,*" so Joab, the son of Zeruiah, went up first and became the commander.

[7] Then David dwelt in the stronghold, which is why they called it the City of David, [8] and he fortified the city all around from the Millo encircling *the stronghold,* while Joab preserved the rest of the city. [9] So David kept on going, becoming greater *and greater,* and the LORD of Hosts was with him.

David's Mighty Men
2Sa 23:8–39

[10] Now these *are* the heads of the mighty men whom David had, who strengthened him in his kingdom, along with all Israel, to establish him as king according to the word of the LORD to Israel. [11] These *make up* the number of the mighty men who *fought* for David:

Jashobeam, the son of Hakmoni, the head of the thirty, who lifted his spear *in triumph* over three hundred slain at one time.

[12] After him was Eleazar, the son of Dodai the Ahohite, who was among the three mighty men. [13] He was with David at Pas Dammim when the Philistines were gathered there for battle. There was a piece of ground full of barley. Now the men fled from the

Philistines. ¹⁴ But they stood their ground in the middle of the field, defended it, and killed the Philistines; and the Lᴏʀᴅ saved them by a great victory.

¹⁵ Now three of the thirty captains climbed down the rock to David at the cave of Adullam while the camp of the Philistines was set up in the Valley of Rephaim. ¹⁶ (At that time, David was in the stronghold, but a garrison of the Philistines was in Bethlehem.) ¹⁷ Now David was overcome with longing and said, "Who will get me a drink of water from the well of Bethlehem by the gate?" ¹⁸ These three broke through the Philistine camp, drew water from the well of Bethlehem by the gate, and carried *it* back to David. However, he was not willing to drink it but poured out *the water* to the Lᴏʀᴅ. ¹⁹ For he said, "Far be it from me before my God to do this. Should I drink the life blood of these men who put their lives in jeopardy? For at the risk of their lives they brought it." Therefore he would not drink it.

The three mighty men did these things.

²⁰ Also Abishai himself, the brother of Joab, was a captain of the three who lifted his spear *in triumph* over three hundred slain and was given a name among the three. ²¹ He was honored as a leader by the second *company* of the three, but he did not attain to the *first* three.

²² Benaiah son of Jehoiada was the son of a valiant man from Kabzeel, who had done many deeds. He killed two Moabite warriors. Indeed, once he went down into a well and struck a lion on a snowy day. ²³ And he killed an Egyptian, a man of great stature, five cubits¹ tall. The Egyptian had in his hand a spear like a weaver's beam, and he went down to him with a staff, wrested the spear from the Egyptian's hand, and killed him with his own spear. ²⁴ Benaiah, the son of Jehoiada, did these things, and won a name among the three mighty men. ²⁵ Out of the thirty *captains*, he himself was honored, and although he did not attain to the three, David set him over his guard.

²⁶ Now the *other* mighty men of valor of the army *were*
Asahel the brother of Joab,
Elhanan the son of Dodo of Bethlehem,
²⁷ Shammoth the Harorite,
Helez the Pelonite,
²⁸ Ira the son of Ikkesh the Tekoite,
Abiezer the Anathothite,
²⁹ Sibbekai the Hushathite,
Ilai the Ahohite,
³⁰ Maharai the Netophathite,
Heled the son of Baanah, the Netophathite,
³¹ Ithai the son of Ribai of Gibeah in Benjamin,
Benaiah the Pirathonite,
³² Hurai from the rivers of Gaash,
Abiel the Arbathite,
³³ Azmaveth the Baharumite,
Eliahba the Shaalbonite,
³⁴ the sons of Hashem the Gizonite,
Jonathan the son of Shagee, the Hararite,
³⁵ Ahiam the son of Sakar, the Hararite,
Eliphal the son of Ur,
³⁶ Hepher the Mekerathite,
Ahijah the Pelonite,
³⁷ Hezro the Carmelite,
Naarai the son of Ezbai,
³⁸ Joel the brother of Nathan,
Mibhar the son of Hagri,
³⁹ Zelek the Ammonite,
Naharai the Berothite, the armor bearer of Joab, the son of Zeruiah,
⁴⁰ Ira the Ithrite,
Gareb the Ithrite,
⁴¹ Uriah the Hittite,
Zabad the son of Ahlai,
⁴² Adina the son of Shiza, the Reubenite, a captain of the Reubenites, and thirty with him,

⁴³ Hanan the son of Maakah,
Joshaphat the Mithnite,
⁴⁴ Uzzia the Ashterathite,
Shama and Jeiel the sons of Hotham, the Aroerite,
⁴⁵ Jediael the son of Shimri and
Joha his brother, the Tizite,
⁴⁶ Eliel the Mahavite,
and Jeribai and Joshaviah the sons of Elnaam,
Ithmah the Moabite,
⁴⁷ Eliel, Obed, and Jaasiel the Mezobaite.

The Mighty Men Join David

12 Now these are the men who came to David at Ziklag, while he yet kept himself away from Saul the son of Kish. They *were* among the brave men, helpers in the war. ² They were armed with bows, and could use both the right hand and the left in hurling stones and shooting arrows out of a bow. They were Saul's brothers of Benjamin.

³ The chief was Ahiezer, then Joash, the sons of Shemaah the Gibeathite; Jeziel and Pelet the sons of Azmaveth; Berakah, and Jehu the Anathothite; ⁴ and Ishmaiah the Gibeonite, a brave warrior among the thirty, and over the thirty; Jeremiah, Jahaziel, Johanan, and Jozabad the Gederathite; ⁵ and Eluzai, Jerimoth, Bealiah, Shemariah, and Shephatiah the Haruphite; ⁶ and Elkanah, Ishiah, Azarel, Joezer, and Jashobeam the Korahites; ⁷ and Joelah and Zebadiah, the sons of Jeroham of Gedor.

⁸ From the Gadites mighty men of valor, men of the war battalion, who could handle shield and sword, whose faces were like the faces of lions, and who were as swift as the gazelles on the mountains, separated themselves for David in the stronghold in the wilderness:
⁹ Ezer the captain,
Obadiah the second, Eliab the third,
¹⁰ Mishmannah the fourth, Jeremiah the fifth,
¹¹ Attai the sixth, Eliel the seventh,
¹² Johanan the eighth, Elzabad the ninth,
¹³ Jeremiah the tenth, Makbannai the eleventh.

¹⁴ These *were* from Gad, captains of the battalions. One of the least *of them* was as a hundred and the greatest as a thousand. ¹⁵ These were the ones who crossed over the Jordan during the first month when it had overflowed its banks and caused the valley dwellers to flee to the east and to the west.

¹⁶ Some of the sons of Benjamin and Judah came to the stronghold of David. ¹⁷ So David went out before them and said to them, "If you have come in peace to help me, then I will *have* a heart united with *yours*, but if to betray me to my adversaries, when *there is* no violence in my hand, may the God of our fathers see, and may He decide *between us*."

¹⁸ Then the Spirit came upon Amasai the captain of the officers, *and he said,*

"*We are* for you, David,
  and with you, son of Jesse.
Peace, peace to you,
  and peace to the one helping you,
    for your God helps you."

So David welcomed them and appointed them as captains of the troops.

¹⁹ Now some from Manasseh joined forces with David when he came with the Philistines for battle against Saul, but they did not help them. For after taking counsel, the lords of the Philistines sent him away, saying, "*It will be* our heads if he falls *back* to his lord Saul." ²⁰ As he went to Ziklag, these men of Manasseh deserted to join him: Adnah, Jozabad, Jediael, Michael, Jozabad, Elihu, and Zillethai, chiefs of thousands in Manasseh. ²¹ So they helped David against the bands *of raiders* because all of them were mighty men of valor and commanders in the army. ²² For at *that* time, day by day, they came to help David until *they became* a great camp like the camp of God.

David's Army at Hebron

23 Now these *make up* the number of the leaders equipped for the battalion who came to David at Hebron in order to turn the kingdom of Saul over to him, as the mouth of the LORD *had spoken*.

24 The sons of Judah who carried shields and spears: six thousand eight hundred equipped for war.

25 From the sons of Simeon, mighty men of valor, fit for war: seven thousand one hundred.

26 From the sons of the Levites: four thousand six hundred.

27 Jehoiada *was* the principal leader of the Aaronites, and *he brought* with him three thousand seven hundred,

28 while Zadok, a brave young warrior, *brought* twenty-two leaders from the house of his father.

29 From the sons of Benjamin, the brothers of Saul: three thousand (up to that time the greater number of them were keeping *their loyalty* with the house of Saul).

30 From the sons of Ephraim: twenty thousand eight hundred mighty men of valor, men of reputation in the house of their fathers.

31 From the half-tribe of Manasseh: eighteen thousand who were marked by name to come and crown David king.

32 From the sons of Issachar, those having understanding of times and what Israel should do: two hundred of their captains with all their brothers at their command.

33 Of Zebulun, fifty thousand seasoned troops, equipped for battle with all the weapons of war, to help David with singleness of purpose. From Zebulun, those going out to war, equipped for battle with all the weapons of war, to help David with an undivided heart: fifty thousand.

34 From Naphtali: one thousand leaders and thirty-seven thousand with shields and spears.

35 From the Danites, competent for battle: twenty-eight thousand six hundred.

36 From Asher, those going out to war, arranged for battle: forty thousand.

37 Also from the other side of the Jordan, from the Reubenites, the Gadites, and half of the tribe of Manasseh with all their battle array: one hundred and twenty thousand.

38 All these *made up* the men of war, arranged in ranks, *who* came to Hebron with a sincere heart to make David king over all Israel, along with the all the rest of Israel *who* with one heart *came* to make David king. 39 Now *all these* were there with David three days, eating and drinking, for their brothers had made provisions for them, 40 and also the ones who were as near to them as Issachar, Zebulun, and Naphtali were bringing bread on donkeys, on camels, on mules, and on oxen, food of fine flour, fig cakes, raisins, wine, oil, herds, and flocks in abundance, for there was joy in Israel.

The Ark
2Sa 6:1–11

13 So David conferred with the captains of the thousands and of the hundreds *and* with every leader. 2 Then he said to all the assembly of Israel, "If it seems good to you and to the LORD our God, let us send word to the rest of our brothers throughout all the land of Israel along with the priests and the Levites in their cities, that they might join us here. 3 Then let us bring the ark of the LORD our God back to us, for we did not seek it during the days of Saul." 4 Then all the assembly agreed to do it because the thing *seemed* right in the eyes of all the people.

5 So David assembled all Israel, from Shihor in Egypt as far as the entrance to Hamath, in order to bring the ark of God from Kiriath Jearim. 6 And he went up with all Israel to Baalah, *that is*, to Kiriath Jearim, which belongs to Judah, to bring up the ark of God, the LORD who dwells between the cherubim, where *His* name is called.

7 They transported the ark of God on a new cart from the house of Abinadab with Uzzah and Ahio driving the cart 8 while David and all Israel played *music* before God with all their might, *performing* songs on lyres, harps, tambourines, cymbals, and trumpets.

9 When they had come as far as the threshing floor of Kidon, Uzzah stretched out his hand to take hold of the ark because the oxen had stumbled *on the path*. 10 Then the anger of the LORD burned against Uzzah, and He struck him because he reached his hand out to touch the ark. Thus, *Uzzah* died there before God.

11 Now David was angry because the LORD struck out against Uzzah, so he called that place Perez Uzzah, *as it is* to this day.

12 David was afraid of God that day, saying, "How can I *ever* bring the ark of God to myself?" 13 So David *stopped moving* the ark of God to himself in the City of David and diverted it to the house of Obed-Edom the Gittite, 14 and *while* the ark of God stayed in his house three months, the LORD blessed the house of Obed-Edom and all he had.

David Established at Jerusalem
2Sa 5:11–25; 1Ch 3:5–8

14 Then Hiram the king of Tyre sent messengers to David with cedar wood, stonemasons, and carpenters to build a palace for him. 2 So David knew that the LORD had established him as king over Israel because his kingdom was highly exalted for the sake of His people Israel.

3 Now David took more wives in Jerusalem, and David became the father of more sons and daughters. 4 These are the names of the children who were born to him in Jerusalem: Shammua, Shobab, Nathan, Solomon, 5 Ibhar, Elishua, Elpelet, 6 Nogah, Nepheg, Japhia, 7 Elishama, Beeliada, and Eliphelet.

David Defeats the Philistines

8 Now *when* the Philistines heard that David had been anointed king over all Israel, all the Philistines went up to seek out David, but David heard and went out to them. 9 So the Philistines came and raided the Valley of Rephaim. 10 Then David inquired of the LORD, saying, "Should I go up against the Philistines? Will You give them into my hand?"

The LORD answered, "Go up *against them*, and I will give them into your hand."

11 And they went up to Baal Perazim, and David struck them down there. Then David said, "God broke through my enemies by my hand as the breaking through of waters." Therefore they named that place Baal Perazim. 12 They abandoned their gods there, and David said *that* they should be burned with fire.

13 Now the Philistines raided the valley once more. 14 And David again inquired of God, and God *answered* him: "Do not go up after them, but turn around behind them and come to them in front of the balsam trees. 15 Whenever you hear the sound of marching in the tops of the balsam trees, you will advance the battle, for God has gone out before you to strike the camp of the Philistines." 16 David did just as God commanded him, and they struck the camp of the Philistines from Gibeon as far as Gezer.

17 So the fame of David went out in all the lands, and the LORD put the dread of him on all the nations.

The Ark Brought to Jerusalem
2Sa 6:12–19

15 So David built houses for himself in the City of David, and he prepared a place for the ark of God and pitched a tent for it. 2 Then David said, "No one may carry the ark of God except the Levites since the LORD chose them to carry the ark of the LORD and to minister before Him always."

3 David assembled all Israel to Jerusalem in order to bring up the ark of the LORD to the place he had prepared for it. 4 And David gathered *representatives* of the sons of Aaron and the Levites, *as follows*:

5 from the sons of Kohath,
    Uriel the leader and one hundred and twenty of his
    brothers;
6 from the sons of Merari,
    Asaiah the leader and two hundred and twenty of his
    brothers;
7 from the sons of Gershom,
    Joel the leader and one hundred and thirty of his brothers;
8 from the sons of Elizaphan,
    Shemaiah the leader and two hundred of his brothers;
9 from the sons of Hebron,
    Eliel the leader and eighty of his brothers;

[10] from the sons of Uzziel,
Amminadab the leader and one hundred and twelve of his
brothers.
[11] Then David called for Zadok and Abiathar the priests and for the
Levites: Uriel, Asaiah, Joel, Shemaiah, Eliel, and Amminadab. [12] He
said to them, "You are the captains of the fathers' houses for the
Levites. Consecrate yourselves, you and your brothers, so you may
bring up the ark of the Lord, the God of Israel, to *the place* I have
prepared for it [13] because *on* the first *attempt* without you the Lord
struck out against us since we did not seek Him properly.".[14] So the
priests and the Levites consecrated themselves to bring up the ark of
the Lord, the God of Israel. [15] The sons of the Levites lifted up the ark
of God just as Moses commanded, with the poles on their shoulders,
according to the word of the Lord.
[16] Then David told the leaders of the Levites to position their
brothers the singers with musical instruments, harps, lyres, and
cymbals to resound with joyful songs.
[17] So the Levites placed Heman the son of Joel, and from his
brothers, Asaph the son of Berekiah, and from their brothers the
sons of Merari, Ethan the son of Kushaiah, [18] and with them their
brothers of the second rank: Zechariah, Ben, Jaaziel, Shemiramoth,
Jehiel, Unni, Eliab, Benaiah, Maaseiah, Mattithiah, Eliphelehu, Mikneiah, Obed-Edom, and Jeiel, the gatekeepers.
[19] So the singers, Heman, Asaph, and Ethan, *were directed* to
sound cymbals of brass. [20] Zechariah, Aziel, Shemiramoth, Jehiel,
Unni, Eliab, Maaseiah, and Benaiah *were to accompany* with
harps on Alamoth. [21] Mattithiah, Eliphelehu, Mikneiah, Obed-
Edom, Jeiel, and Azaziah *were to lead* with lyres on the Sheminith. [22] Kenaniah, leader of the Levites, *was to conduct* the music
because he *was* skillful.
[23] Berekiah and Elkanah were gatekeepers for the ark. [24] Shebaniah, Joshaphat, Nethanel, Amasai, Zechariah, Benaiah, and Eliezer,
the priests, *were assigned* to sound trumpets before the ark of God.
Obed-Edom and Jehiah were gatekeepers for the ark.
[25] So David, the elders of Israel, and the leaders of the thousands
went to bring up the ark of the covenant of the Lord from the house
of Obed-Edom with rejoicing. [26] Since God helped the Levites who
carried the ark of the covenant of the Lord, they sacrificed seven
bulls and seven rams. [27] Now David was clothed in a fine linen robe,
as were the Levites who carried the ark, the singers, and Kenaniah,
the conductor of singing and singers. David *himself* wore a linen
ephod. [28] So all Israel brought up the ark of the covenant of the
Lord with a shout and with the sound of the ram's horn and with
trumpets and cymbals, making music on harps and lyres.
[29] Now as the ark of the covenant of the Lord was entering the
City of David, Michal the daughter of Saul was looking down from
the window, and when she saw King David dancing and spinning,
she despised him in her heart.

The Ark Set in the Tent

16 So they brought in the ark of God, placed it in the midst of
the tent that David had erected for it, and drew near to God
with burnt offerings and peace offerings. [2] When David had finished
offering the burnt offerings and the peace offerings, he blessed the
people in the name of the Lord. [3] Then he distributed to all the children of Israel, both men and women, a loaf of bread, a piece of meat,
and a raisin cake for each.
[4] And he appointed some of the Levites to minister before the ark
of the Lord, to commemorate, to thank, and to praise the Lord God
of Israel: [5] Asaph the chief, and next to him Zechariah, then Jeiel,
Shemiramoth, Jehiel, Mattithiah, Eliab, Benaiah, and Obed-Edom:
Jeiel with stringed instruments and harps, but Asaph made music
with the cymbals. [6] Moreover, Benaiah and Jahaziel the priests
sounded trumpets continually before the ark of the covenant of God.

David's Psalm of Thanksgiving

Ps 96:1–13; 105:1–15; 106:1, 47–48
[7] On that day then, David delivered for the first time this psalm of
thanksgiving to the Lord into the hand of Asaph and his brothers:

[8] Give thanks to the Lord, call on His name;
make known His deeds among the peoples.

[9] Sing to Him, sing praise to Him,
recount all His wonders.
[10] Glory in His holy name;
let the heart of those who seek the Lord rejoice.
[11] Seek the Lord and His strength;
seek His face continually.

[12] Remember His wonders which He has done,
His wonders and the judgments of His mouth,
[13] O seed of Israel, His servant,
O sons of Jacob, His chosen.
[14] He is the Lord our God;
His judgments are in all the earth.

[15] Remember His covenant forever,
the word He commanded for a thousand generations,
[16] that He made with Abraham,
even His oath to Isaac.
[17] He confirmed it to Jacob as a statute,
to Israel *for* an everlasting covenant,
[18] saying, "To you I will give the land of Canaan
as the portion of your inheritance."

[19] When you were few in number,
few indeed, and strangers *there*,
[20] when they wandered from nation to nation,
from one kingdom to another,
[21] He allowed no man to oppress them;
He rebuked kings on their account,
[22] saying, "Do not touch My anointed,
and do My prophets no harm."

[23] Sing to the Lord, all the earth.
Proclaim good tidings of His salvation from day to day.
[24] Declare His glory among the nations,
His wonders among all the peoples.

[25] For great is the Lord and greatly to be praised.
He is to be feared above all gods.
[26] For all the gods of the peoples are idols,
but the Lord made the heavens.
[27] Honor and majesty are before Him;
strength and joy are in His place.
[28] Give to the Lord, O families of the peoples,
give to the Lord glory and strength.
[29] Give to the Lord the glory due His name;
bring an offering and come before Him,
bow down to the Lord in holy array.
[30] Tremble before Him, all the earth.
The world also is firmly established; it shall not be moved.

[31] Let the heavens rejoice, and let the earth be glad.
Let them say among the nations, "The Lord is King."
[32] Let the sea roar, and all its fullness.
Let the field rejoice, and all that is in it.
[33] Then the trees of the forest will ring out before the Lord,
for He is coming to judge the earth.

[34] Oh, give thanks to the Lord, for *He is* good;
for His mercy endures forever.
[35] Now say, "Save us, O God of our salvation,
and gather us and deliver us from the nations,
that we may give thanks to Your holy name,
to glory in Your praise.
[36] Blessed is the Lord, the God of Israel,
from everlasting to everlasting."

Then all the people said, "Amen," and "Praise the Lord."

Worship Before the Ark

[37] So he left Asaph and his brothers before the ark of the covenant of the Lord to minister before the ark regularly, as each

day required, [38] and also Obed-Edom and his sixty-eight brothers, while Obed-Edom, the son of Jeduthun, and Hosah were to be gatekeepers.

[39] And he left Zadok the priest and his priestly brothers before the tabernacle of the LORD at the high place that was at Gibeon [40] to offer burnt offerings to the LORD on the altar of burnt offering continually, morning and evening, according to all that was written in the Law of the LORD, which He commanded Israel.

[41] With them were Heman and Jeduthun and the rest who were chosen, who were marked by name to give thanks to the LORD, for His mercy endures forever. [42] Heman and Jeduthun had with them trumpets and cymbals to sound aloud and instruments for sacred song. The sons of Jeduthun were appointed to the gate.

[43] Then all the people departed, each man to his house, and David returned to bless his house.

The Davidic Covenant
2Sa 7:1–17

17 Now it happened as David dwelt in his house that he said to Nathan the prophet, "Here I am dwelling in a house of cedar while the ark of the LORD is under curtains."

[2] So Nathan said to David, "Do all that is in your heart, for God is with you."

[3] But it happened on that same night that the word of the LORD came to Nathan, saying,

[4] Go and tell David My servant: Thus says the LORD: You will not build a house for Me to dwell in, [5] for I have not dwelt in a house since the day when I brought Israel up *even* until this day, but I have gone from tent to tent and from tabernacle *to tabernacle*. [6] Wherever I have gone in all Israel, have I ever spoken a word to the any of the judges of Israel that I commanded to shepherd My people, saying, Why have you not built Me a house of cedar?

[7] And now say this to My servant David: Thus says the LORD of Hosts: I took you from the pasture, from following after the flock, to be ruler over My people Israel, [8] and I have been with you wherever you went, and I have cut off all your enemies from before you. Also I will make your name like the names of the greatest on earth. [9] And I will appoint a place for My people Israel, and I will plant them there where they will dwell securely and tremble no more, *so that* the sons of wickedness will not oppress them just as before [10] from the time when I commanded the judges of My people Israel. I will subdue all your enemies.

And I declare to you the LORD will build a house for you. [11] Then it will be when your days are full and you go to your fathers, I will raise up your seed after you from your own sons. His kingdom I will establish. [12] He is the one who will build Me a house, and I will establish his throne forever. [13] I will be a father to him, and he will be a son to Me. I will not take away My favor from him as I did from the one who was before you. [14] I will assign him a place in My house and in My kingdom forever, and his throne will be established for all time.

[15] Thus, Nathan spoke to David all these words and according to all this vision.

The Prayer of David
2Sa 7:18–29

[16] Then King David came and sat before the LORD, and he said,

"Who am I, O LORD God, and what is my house that You have brought me this far? [17] This was something small in Your eyes, God, but You have spoken concerning the house of Your servant for a great while to come and have regarded me with the status of a great man, O LORD God.

[18] "What more can David *speak* to You for the honor of Your servant? For You know Your servant. [19] O LORD, for the sake of Your servant and according to Your own heart You have done all these great things and made known all these great things.

[20] "O LORD, there is none like You, and there is no god besides You as we have heard with our ears. [21] Who is like Your people Israel, a nation on earth whom God has redeemed for Himself as a people to make for Yourself a great name by great and awesome deeds in driving out nations from before Your people whom You redeemed from Egypt? [22] For You made Your people Israel for Yourself for a people forever, and You, O LORD, have become their God.

[23] "And now, LORD, the word which You have spoken concerning Your servant and concerning his house, *let it* endure forever and do just as You have spoken. [24] Let Your name endure and be magnified forever, saying, 'The LORD of Hosts, the God of Israel, is God to Israel.' And let the house of David Your servant be established before You.

[25] "For You, my God, have revealed to Your servant that You will build a house for him. Therefore Your servant has found courage to pray before You. [26] And now, O LORD, You are God, and You have promised this good *word* to Your servant. [27] Now, You have been pleased to bless the house of Your servant that it may be forever before You. For You, O LORD, have blessed it, and it shall be blessed forever."

David's Conquests
2Sa 8:1–18

18 Now it happened after this that David attacked the Philistines and subdued them, so he took Gath and its neighboring towns from Philistine control.

[2] He also defeated Moab so that the Moabites became servants to David and brought tribute.

[3] Next David struck down Hadadezer the king of Zobah toward Hamath as he marched out to establish his authority along the Euphrates. [4] David captured from him one thousand chariots, seven thousand horsemen, and twenty thousand infantry men. Then David hamstrung all the chariot *horses* except for the one hundred he spared.

[5] When the Arameans of Damascus came to help Hadadezer king of Zobah, David struck down twenty-two thousand Arameans. [6] Then David set *garrisons* in Aram of Damascus; and Arameans became subject to David, and brought tribute. The LORD gave victory to David wherever he went.

[7] So David took the shields of gold that were on the servants of Hadadezer, and brought them to Jerusalem. [8] Also from Tibhath[*f*] and Kun, cities of Hadadezer, David took a large amount of bronze; with it Solomon made the bronze Sea, the pillars, and the vessels of bronze.

[9] When Tou king of Hamath heard that David had defeated all the army of Hadadezer king of Zobah, [10] he sent his son Hadoram to King David to ask about his welfare and to bless him because he fought and defeated Hadadezer (for Hadadezer had been at war with Tou). He sent all kinds of articles of gold, silver, and bronze.

[11] King David also dedicated these to the LORD, together with the silver and gold which he had carried away from all the surrounding nations, from Edom, Moab, the Ammonites, the Philistines, and Amalek.

[12] Also Abishai the son of Zeruiah struck down eighteen thousand men of Edom in the Valley of Salt. [13] He set up garrisons in Edom, and all the Edomites became servants to David. Wherever he went, the LORD gave David victory.

David's Officials

[14] So David was king over all Israel, and he executed justice and righteousness for all his people. [15] Joab the son of Zeruiah *was* over the army, and Jehoshaphat the son of Ahilud was the historian. [16] Zadok the son of Ahitub and Abimelek the son of Abiathar *served as* priests, while Shavsha *was* scribe. [17] Benaiah the son of Jehoiada *was* over the Kerethites and the Pelethites, and the sons of David were the king's principal officials.

---

f 8 Betah in 2Sa 8:8.

David Defeats the Ammonites
2Sa 10:1–19

19 Now it happened after this that Nahash the king of the Ammonites died, and his son reigned in his place. ² Then David said, "I will show kindness to Hanun the son of Nahash, because his father showed kindness to me." So David sent messengers to comfort him concerning his father. And David's servants came to Hanun in the land of the Ammonites to comfort him.

³ But the leaders of the Ammonites said to Hanun, "Do you think that David is honoring your father because he sent consolers? Have not his servants come to you to search and to overthrow and to spy out the land?" ⁴ So Hanun took the servants of David, shaved them, cut their garments in half as far as the hip, and sent them away.

⁵ Then *some* came and told David about the men, so he sent to meet them, for the men were greatly humiliated. The king said, "Remain in Jericho until your beards grow full, and then return."

⁶ When the Ammonites saw that they had become a stench to David, Hanun and the Ammonites sent one thousand talents¹ of silver to hire chariots and horsemen from Aram Naharaim, Aram Maakah, and Zobah. ⁷ So they hired for themselves thirty-two thousand chariots, with the king of Maakah and his people. They camped before Medeba as the Ammonites gathered from their cities to go out to war.

⁸ When David heard of it, he sent Joab and all the army of the mighty men. ⁹ So the Ammonites went out and formed ranks for battle at the entrance to the city while the kings who had come were by themselves in the open country.

¹⁰ When Joab saw the battle line was drawn in front of him and behind him, he chose some of the best men in Israel and arrayed them against the Arameans. ¹¹ The rest of the people he placed in the charge of his brother Abishai, and they took up positions to engage the Ammonites. ¹² Then he said, "If the Arameans are too strong for me, then you will come help me, but if the Ammonites are too strong for you, I will come help you. ¹³ Take courage, and let us prove worthy of our people and the cities of our God. May the Lord do what seems right to Him."

¹⁴ So Joab and the people who *were* with him drew near to the Arameans for battle, and they fled before him. ¹⁵ When the Ammonites saw the Arameans fleeing, they also fled before Abishai his brother and entered the city. So Joab returned to Jerusalem.

¹⁶ When the Arameans saw that they had been defeated by Israel, they sent messengers and summoned the Arameans who were beyond the River,² and Shophak, the commander of Hadadezer's army *went* before them.

¹⁷ When David was told about it, he gathered all Israel, crossed over the Jordan, and came against them. He divided his ranks and prepared to engage the Arameans in battle, so they fought against him. ¹⁸ But the Arameans fled before Israel, and David killed seven thousand chariot drivers and forty thousand infantry men of the Arameans, and killed Shophak, the commander of the army.

¹⁹ And when the servants of Hadadezer saw that they were defeated before Israel, they negotiated peace with David and served him. So the Arameans were not willing to aid the Ammonites in battle again.

Rabbah Captured
2Sa 11:1; 12:29–31

20 Now at the beginning of the year when kings would go out *to war*, Joab led the army and devastated the land of the Ammonites. He came and besieged Rabbah. But David remained in Jerusalem. So Joab struck Rabbah and overthrew it. ² Then David took the crown of their king from his head and found it weighed about a talent³ of gold with a precious stone *set* in it. And it was placed on David's head. He also brought out a great abundance of plunder from the city. ³ He brought out the people who were in it, and put *them* to work with saws, sharp iron tools, and axes. Thus David did to all the cities of the Ammonites, and then he and all the people returned to Jerusalem.

Philistine Giants Killed
2Sa 21:15–22

⁴ Now after *this*, *when* war broke out in Gezer with the Philistines, Sibbekai of Hushah killed Sippai, who was one of the descendants of the giants, and they were humbled.

⁵ Again there was war with the Philistines, and Elhanan the son of Jair killed Lahmi, the brother of Goliath the Gittite, the shaft of whose wooden spear was like a weaver's beam.

⁶ Yet again there was war at Gath, where there was a man of great stature, who had six fingers on each hand and six toes on each foot, twenty-four in number; and he also was descended from the giants. ⁷ When he taunted Israel, Jonathan the son of Shimea, David's brother, killed him.

⁸ These were descended from the giants in Gath, and they fell by the hand of David and his servants.

The Census of Israel and Judah
2Sa 24:1–25

21 Now Satan stood against Israel and incited David to number Israel. ² Then David said to Joab and the leaders of the people, "Go count Israel from Beersheba to Dan and bring me a report, that I may know their number."

³ But Joab said, "May the Lord increase the number of His people one hundred times more. My lord the king, are not all of them my lord's servants? Why then should my lord require this? Why should it bring guilt on Israel?"

⁴ Nevertheless, the king's word prevailed against Joab, so Joab departed and went throughout all Israel. Then he returned to Jerusalem. ⁵ Joab gave the results of the census of the people to David: All Israel had one million one hundred thousand men who drew the sword, and in Judah four hundred and seventy thousand men drew the sword.

⁶ However, he did not include the Levites and Benjamin because the word of the king was abhorrent to Joab. ⁷ Now this thing was evil in the sight of God, and He struck Israel.

⁸ So David said to God, "I have sinned greatly in doing this thing. Now, please, take away the iniquity of your servant, for I have acted very foolishly."

⁹ And the Lord spoke to Gad, David's seer, saying, ¹⁰ "Go and speak to David, 'Thus says the Lord: Three things I offer you; choose one of these for yourself that I may do to you.' "

¹¹ So Gad came to David and said to him, "Thus says the Lord, 'Select for yourself, ¹² either three years of famine, or three months of being swept away before your foes while the sword of your enemy overtakes you, or three days of the sword of the Lord, even pestilence in the land, with the angel of the Lord destroying throughout all the territory of Israel.' Now then consider what answer I shall return to Him who sent me."

¹³ David replied to Gad, "I am in great distress. Let me fall into the hands of the Lord, for His mercies *are* very great, but do not let me fall into the hand of man."

¹⁴ So the Lord sent a plague throughout Israel, and seventy thousand men of Israel fell. ¹⁵ And God sent an angel to Jerusalem to destroy it, but as he prepared to destroy it, the Lord looked and relented from the calamity. And He said to the angel bringing the destruction, "It is enough. Remove your hand." The angel of the Lord was then standing by the threshing floor of Ornan the Jebusite.

¹⁶ David lifted up his eyes and saw the angel of the Lord standing between earth and heaven with his sword drawn in his hand stretched out over Jerusalem. So David and the elders, covered in sackcloth, fell on their faces.

¹⁷ David said to God, "Was it not I who gave the command to number the people? I am the one who has sinned and surely done evil. But these sheep, what have they done? O Lord my God, I pray, let Your hand be against me and my father's house, but do not let Your people be plagued."

David Builds an Altar
¹⁸ Then the angel of the Lord commanded Gad to tell David that David should go up and raise an altar to the Lord on the threshing

---

¹ 6 About 38 tons, or 34 metric tons.   ² 16 Euphrates River.   ³ 2 About 75 pounds, or 34 kilograms.

floor of Ornan the Jebusite. [19] So David went up at the word of Gad which he delivered in the name of the LORD.

[20] Now Ornan turned and saw the angel, but his four sons *who were* with him hid themselves as Ornan threshed the wheat. [21] As David came to Ornan, Ornan looked and saw David and went out from the threshing floor and bowed down before David with *his* face to the ground.

[22] Then David said to Ornan, "Give me the site of the threshing floor so that I may build an altar on it to the LORD. Sell it to me at full price so the plague on the people may be restrained."

[23] So Ornan replied to David, "Take it for yourself, and let my lord the king do whatever seems good in his eyes. Look, I will give the oxen for the burnt offerings, the threshing wagons for wood, and the wheat for the grain offering. I will give it all."

[24] Then King David said to Ornan, "No, for I will surely acquire it for the full price, for I will not take what is yours for the LORD nor offer burnt offerings that cost me nothing."

[25] So David gave Ornan six hundred shekels[1] of gold by weight for the site, [26] and David built there an altar to the LORD and offered up burnt offerings and peace offerings. He called on the LORD, and the LORD answered him by fire from heaven on the altar of burnt offering.

[27] So the LORD spoke to the angel, and he put away his sword in its sheath. [28] At that time, when David saw that the LORD had answered him at the threshing floor of Ornan the Jebusite, he sacrificed there. [29] For the tabernacle of the LORD and the altar of burnt offering that Moses had made in the wilderness *were* in the high place in Gibeon at that time. [30] But David was unable to go before it to inquire of God, because he was terrified by the sword of the angel of the LORD.

22 Then David said, "Here shall be the house of the LORD God and here the altar of the burnt offering for Israel."

Plans to Build the Temple

[2] So David gave instructions to gather together those sojourning in the land of Israel, and he appointed stonemasons to cut hewn stones for building the house of God. [3] David also provided large quantities of iron for nails for the doors of the gates and for the clamps as well as an abundance of bronze beyond measure, [4] and cedar logs without number, for the Sidonians and the Tyrians brought much cedar wood to David.

[5] Now David said, "Solomon my son *is* young and inexperienced, and the house that is to be built for the LORD *must* be exceedingly magnificent, of fame and glory throughout all the lands. Therefore I will make preparation for it now." So David made extensive preparations before his death.

[6] Then David called Solomon his son and commanded him to build a house for the LORD, the God of Israel. [7] David said to Solomon, "My son, I had it in my heart to build a house for the name of the LORD my God, [8] but the word of the LORD came to me, saying, 'You have shed much blood and waged great wars. You shall not build a house for My name because you have shed much blood on the earth before Me. [9] A son shall be born to you who shall be a man of rest. I will give him rest from all his enemies all around. Solomon will be his name, and I will give peace and tranquility to Israel in his days. [10] He will be the one to build a house for My name. He shall be a son to Me, and I will be a father to him, and I will establish the throne of his kingdom over Israel forever.'

[11] "Now, my son, may the LORD be with you, and may you have success in building the house of the LORD your God just as He has spoken concerning you. [12] Only may the LORD give you insight and understanding and give you charge over Israel so you may keep the law of the LORD your God. [13] Then you will prosper if you carefully observe the statutes and the judgments which the LORD commanded Moses for Israel. Be strong and of good courage. Do not be afraid or dismayed.

[14] "With great difficulty I have prepared for the house of the LORD one hundred thousand talents[2] of gold and one million[3] talents of silver as well as innumerable quantities of bronze and

iron, beyond measure. I have also prepared timber and stone to which you may add even more. [15] Moreover you have an abundance of workers: stonecutters, masons, carpenters, and men skilled in all *kinds of* work, [16] craftsmen in gold, silver, bronze, and iron without number. Rise up and work, and may the LORD be with you."

[17] Then David commanded all the leaders of Israel to assist Solomon his son, *saying*, [18] "Is not the LORD your God with you? Has He not given you rest all around? For He has given the inhabitants of the land into my hand, and the land is subdued before the LORD and His people. [19] Now dedicate your heart and your soul to seek the LORD your God. Rise up and build the sanctuary of the LORD God, so that you may bring the ark of the covenant of the LORD along with the holy vessels of God into the house which is to be built for the name of the LORD."

The Levites

23 Now David was old and full of days when he made Solomon his son king over Israel. [2] So he gathered together all the leaders of Israel with the priests and the Levites.

[3] The Levites from thirty years old and up were counted, and their head count of men was thirty-eight thousand. [4] Twenty-four thousand of these, David said, "shall have charge of the work in the house of the LORD; six thousand shall be officers and judges, [5] four thousand shall be gatekeepers, and four thousand shall offer praises to the LORD with the instruments that I have made for praise."

[6] David assigned them to divisions according to the sons of Levi: Gershon, Kohath, and Merari.

Gershonites

[7] From the Gershonites:
Ladan and Shimei.
[8] The sons of Ladan *were*
first Jehiel, then Zetham and Joel, three *in all.*
[9] The sons of Shimei *were*
Shelomith, Haziel, and Haran, three.
These *were* the heads of the fathers' houses of Ladan.
[10] The sons of Shimei *were*
Jahath, Zina, Jeush, and Beriah.
These four *were* the sons of Shimei.
[11] Now Jahath was the first and Ziza the second, but Jeush and Beriah did not have many sons, so they were counted as one unit for their father's house.

Kohathites

[12] The sons of Kohath *were*
Amram, Izhar, Hebron, and Uzziel, four *in all.*
[13] The sons of Amram *were*
Aaron and Moses,
but Aaron was set apart to consecrate the most holy things, he and his sons forever, to offer sacrifices before the LORD, to minister to Him, and to bless in His name forever. [14] As for Moses, the man of God, his sons were named among the tribe of Levi.
[15] The sons of Moses *were*
Gershom and Eliezer.
[16] The son of Gershom *was*
Shubael the chief.
[17] The son of Eliezer *was*
Rehabiah the chief.
Eliezer had no other sons, but the sons of Rehabiah were very many.
[18] The son of Izhar *was*
Shelomith the chief.
[19] The sons of Hebron *were*
Jeriah the first, Amariah the second, Jahaziel the third, *and* Jekameam the fourth.
[20] The sons of Uzziel *were*
Micah the first and Ishiah the second.

---

[1] 25 About 15 pounds, or 6.9 kilograms.   [2] 14 About 3,750 tons, or 3,400 metric tons.   [3] 14 About 37,500 tons, or 34,000 metric tons.

Merarites

²¹ The sons of Merari *were*
Mahli and Mushi.
The sons of Mahli *were*
Eleazar and Kish.
²² Eleazar died having no sons, but only daughters, so the sons of Kish, their brothers, took them *as wives*.
²³ The sons of Mushi were
Mahli, Eder, and Jerimoth, three.

²⁴ These *were* the sons of Levi according to their fathers' houses, the heads of the fathers' houses as they were registered by the number of their names according to their head count, those doing the work for the service of the house of the Lord, from twenty years old and up. ²⁵ For David said, "The Lord, the God of Israel, has given rest to His people, and He dwells in Jerusalem forever. ²⁶ And so the Levites no longer need to carry the tabernacle and all its implements for its service." ²⁷ For by the last words of David, the sons of Levi were numbered from twenty years old and up; ²⁸ because their duty was to help the sons of Aaron in the service of the house of the Lord, in the courts and in the chambers, with the purifying of all holy things, even the work of service of the house of God, ²⁹ and with the showbread, the fine flour for a grain offering, the wafers of unleavened bread, the baked offering, the offering mixed with oil, and all measures of quantity and size, ³⁰ to stand morning by morning to thank and praise the Lord, and likewise in the evening, ³¹ and to offer up all burnt offerings to the Lord, for Sabbaths, New Moons, and appointed feasts, by number as the judgment concerning them, continually before the Lord, ³² and that they should keep charge of the tent of meeting and the sanctuary and attend to the sons of Aaron, their brothers, for the service of the house of the Lord.

Priestly Divisions Assigned

24 Now the divisions of the sons of Aaron *were* these. The sons of Aaron: Nadab, Abihu, Eleazar, and Ithamar. ² But Nadab and Abihu died before their father, and they had no sons. So Eleazar and Ithamar served as priests. ³ Then David, along with Zadok of the sons of Eleazar and Ahimelek of the sons of Ithamar, divided them to their offices by their service. ⁴ Since the sons of Eleazar were found *to have* more chief men than the sons of Ithamar, they divided them into sixteen heads of the fathers' houses for the sons of Eleazar, and eight for the sons of Ithamar, according to their fathers' houses. ⁵ So they divided them by lots, the one as the other, for there were officers of the sanctuary and officers of God among both the sons of Eleazar and Ithamar.
⁶ Shemaiah the son of Nethanel, the Levite scribe, wrote them down in the presence of the king, the leaders, Zadok the priest, Ahimelek the son of Abiathar, and the heads of the fathers' houses of the priests and the Levites, one father's house taken for Eleazar and one for Ithamar.

⁷ The first lot fell to Jehoiarib,
the second to Jedaiah,
⁸ the third to Harim,
the fourth to Seorim,
⁹ the fifth to Malkijah,
the sixth to Mijamin,
¹⁰ the seventh to Hakkoz,
the eighth to Abijah,
¹¹ the ninth to Jeshua,
the tenth to Shekaniah,
¹² the eleventh to Eliashib,
the twelfth to Jakim,
¹³ the thirteenth to Huppah,
the fourteenth to Jeshebeab,
¹⁴ the fifteenth to Bilgah,
the sixteenth to Immer,
¹⁵ the seventeenth to Hezir,
the eighteenth to Happizzez,
¹⁶ the nineteenth to Pethahiah,
the twentieth to Jehezkel,

¹⁷ the twenty-first to Jakin,
the twenty-second to Gamul,
¹⁸ the twenty-third to Delaiah,
the twenty-fourth to Maaziah.

¹⁹ These were their appointments for their service to come into the house of the Lord according to the schedule prescribed for them by Aaron their father, as the Lord God of Israel had commanded him.

Remaining Levite Assignments

²⁰ Now for the remaining sons of Levi:
from the sons of Amram, Shubael;
from the sons of Shubael, Jehdeiah.
²¹ For Rehabiah: from the sons of Rehabiah,
the first *was* Ishiah.
²² From the Izharites, Shelomoth;
from the sons of Shelomoth, Jahath.
²³ The sons of Hebron: Jeriah *the first*, Amariah the second,
Jahaziel the third, *and* Jekameam the fourth.
²⁴ The sons of Uzziel, Micah;
from the sons of Micah, Shamir.
²⁵ The brother of Micah, Ishiah;
from the sons of Ishiah, Zechariah.
²⁶ The sons of Merari, Mahli and Mushi;
the son of Jaaziah, Beno.
²⁷ The sons of Merari:
by Jaaziah *were* Beno, Shoham, Zakkur, and Ibri.
²⁸ For Mahli: Eleazar, who had no sons.
²⁹ For Kish: the son of Kish,
Jerahmeel.
³⁰ The sons of Mushi: Mahli, Eder, and Jerimoth.

These *were* the sons of the Levites according to their fathers' houses. ³¹ These also cast lots just as their brothers, the sons of Aaron, in the presence of David the king, Zadok, Ahimelek, and the heads of the fathers' houses of the priests and of the Levites, the head of the fathers' houses as well as his younger brother.

The Musicians

25 Then David and the officers of the army also set apart for the service *some* of the sons of Asaph, and of Heman, and of Jeduthun, those who prophesied with lyres, harps, and cymbals. The number of those who did the work according to their service was:

² From the sons of Asaph:
Zakkur, Joseph, Nethaniah, and Asarelah, the sons of Asaph under the guidance of Asaph, who prophesied according to the decree of the king.
³ For Jeduthun, the sons of Jeduthun:
Gedaliah, Zeri, Jeshaiah, Hashabiah, and Mattithiah, six, under the guidance of their father Jeduthun, who prophesied with the lyre in giving thanks and praise to the Lord.
⁴ For Heman, the sons of Heman:
Bukkiah, Mattaniah, Uzziel, Shubael and Jerimoth, Hananiah, Hanani, Eliathah, Giddalti, and Romamti-Ezer, Joshbekashah, Mallothi, Hothir, Mahazioth. ⁵ All these were the sons of Heman, the king's seer, according to the words of God, to exalt him, for God gave fourteen sons and three daughters to Heman.

⁶ All these *were* under the direction of their father for the music in the house of the Lord with cymbals, harps, and lyres, for the service of the house of God by decree of the king: Asaph, Jeduthun, and Heman. ⁷ So the number of them, with their brothers, who were trained in singing to the Lord, all of whom were skillful, *was* two hundred and eighty-eight. ⁸ They cast lots for their duties, small and great, teacher and student alike.

⁹ The first lot fell for Asaph to Joseph;
the second to Gedaliah,
to him and his brothers and his sons, twelve;

¹⁰ the third to Zakkur,
  his sons and his brothers, twelve;
¹¹ the fourth to Izri,
  his sons and his brothers, twelve;
¹² the fifth to Nethaniah,
  his sons and his brothers, twelve;
¹³ the sixth to Bukkiah,
  his sons and his brothers, twelve;
¹⁴ the seventh to Jesarelah,
  his sons and his brothers, twelve;
¹⁵ the eighth to Jeshaiah,
  his sons and his brothers, twelve;
¹⁶ the ninth to Mattaniah,
  his sons and his brothers, twelve;
¹⁷ the tenth to Shimei,
  his sons and his brothers, twelve;
¹⁸ the eleventh to Azarel,
  his sons and his brothers, twelve;
¹⁹ the twelfth to Hashabiah,
  his sons and his brothers, twelve;
²⁰ for the thirteenth to Shubael,
  his sons and his brothers, twelve;
²¹ for the fourteenth to Mattithiah,
  his sons and his brothers, twelve;
²² for the fifteenth to Jerimoth,
  his sons and his brothers, twelve;
²³ for the sixteenth to Hananiah,
  his sons and his brothers, twelve;
²⁴ for the seventeenth to Joshbekashah,
  his sons and his brothers, twelve;
²⁵ for the eighteenth to Hanani,
  his sons and his brothers, twelve;
²⁶ for the nineteenth to Mallothi,
  his sons and his brothers, twelve;
²⁷ for the twentieth to Eliathah,
  his sons and his brothers, twelve;
²⁸ for the twenty-first to Hothir,
  his sons and his brothers, twelve;
²⁹ for the twenty-second to Giddalti,
  his sons and his brothers, twelve;
³⁰ for the twenty-third to Mahazioth,
  his sons and his brothers, twelve;
³¹ for the twenty-fourth to Romamti-Ezer,
  his sons and his brothers, twelve.

The Gatekeepers

26 *These were* the divisions of the gatekeepers:

from the Korahites, Meshelemiah the son of Kore, *one* of the sons of Asaph. ² Meshelemiah had sons:
  Zechariah the firstborn,
  Jediael the second,
  Zebadiah the third,
  Jathniel the fourth,
  ³ Elam the fifth,
  Jehohanan the sixth,
  and Eliehoenai the seventh.
⁴ Obed-Edom had sons:
  Shemaiah the firstborn,
  Jehozabad the second,
  Joah the third,
  Sakar the fourth,
  Nethanel the fifth,
  ⁵ Ammiel the sixth,
  Issachar the seventh,
  and Peullethai the eighth
  (for God blessed him).

⁶ Also to his son Shemaiah sons were born who ruled their fathers' houses, for they were men of great ability. ⁷ The sons of Shemaiah *were* Othni, Rephael, Obed, *and*

Elzabad, whose brothers were able men: *namely* Elihu and Semakiah. ⁸ All these were of the sons of Obed-Edom with their sons and their brothers, able men qualified for service, sixty-two of Obed-Edom. ⁹ Meshelemiah had sons and brothers, able men, eighteen *in all*.

¹⁰ Also Hosah, of the sons of Merari, had sons: Shimri the first (although he was not the firstborn, his father made him the first), ¹¹ Hilkiah the second, Tabaliah the third, Zechariah the fourth: all the sons and brothers of Hosah, thirteen.

¹² These divisions of the gatekeepers, for their chief men, had assignments to minister in the house of the Lᴏʀᴅ just as their brothers. ¹³ They cast lots, small and great alike, according to their fathers' houses, gate by gate.

¹⁴ The lot for the East Gate fell to Shelemiah. Then they cast lots for Zechariah his son, a wise counselor, and his lot came out for the North Gate; ¹⁵ to Obed-Edom the South Gate, and to his sons was allotted the storehouse. ¹⁶ For Shuppim and Hosah *the lot* came out for the West Gate, at the Shalleketh Gate on the ascending road, guard corresponding to guard.

¹⁷ On the east there were six Levites *each day*, on the north four each day, on the south four each day, as well as two and two at the storehouse. ¹⁸ For the colonnade on the west, *there were* four at the highway, and two at the colonnade.

¹⁹ These were the divisions of the gatekeepers of the sons of Korah and of the sons of Merari.

The Treasurers and Other Officials

²⁰ And of the Levites, Ahijah *was* over the treasures of the house of God, and over the treasures of the dedicated offerings.

²¹ The sons of Ladan, the sons of the Gershonites, belonging to Ladan, the heads of the fathers' houses belonging to Ladan the Gershonite: Jehieli. ²² The sons of Jehieli, Zetham, and Joel his brother, *were in charge of* the treasures of the house of the Lᴏʀᴅ.

²³ From the Amramites, the Izharites, the Hebronites, and the Uzzielites:

²⁴ Shubael the son of Gershom, the son of Moses, *was* ruler of the treasures. ²⁵ His brothers by Eliezer *were* Rehabiah his son, Jeshaiah his son, Joram his son, Zikri his son, and Shelomith his son. ²⁶ This Shelomith and his brothers *were in charge of* all the treasures of the dedicated offerings, which David the king, the heads of the fathers, the officers of the thousands and the hundreds, and the commanders of the army had dedicated. ²⁷ Some of the spoils won in battles they dedicated for the maintenance of the house of the Lᴏʀᴅ. ²⁸ Also all that Samuel the seer and Saul the son of Kish and Abner the son of Ner and Joab the son of Zeruiah had dedicated—all dedicated gifts were in the care of Shelomith and his brothers.

²⁹ From the Izharites, Kenaniah and his sons were *assigned* the outside duties for Israel, as officers and judges.

³⁰ From the Hebronites: Hashabiah and his brothers, one thousand seven hundred able men, *were* administrators of Israel on the west side of the Jordan for all the work of the Lᴏʀᴅ and for the service of the king. ³¹ Jeriah was chief of the Hebronites according to the genealogical records of his fathers. In the fortieth year of the reign of David, mighty men of valor were found in the records among the Hebronites at Jazer of Gilead, ³² and his brothers, able men, two thousand seven hundred heads of the fathers, to them King David entrusted all matters of God and of the king concerning the Reubenites, the Gadites, and the half-tribe of Manasseh.

The Military Divisions

27 Now *these are* the sons of Israel according to their number, the heads of fathers' houses, the commanders of thousands and hundreds, and their officers who ministered to the king in all matters concerning the divisions, which came and went, month by month throughout all the months of the year, to each division of twenty-four thousand:

2 Jashobeam the son of Zabdiel led the first division for the first month; in his division, twenty-four thousand. 3 He was from the sons of Perez and was the leader of all the officers of the army for the first month.
4 Dodai the Ahohite and his division led the division of the second month with Mikloth as the ruler: in his division, twenty-four thousand.
5 The third commander of the army for the third month was Benaiah the son of Jehoiada, a chief priest: in his division, twenty-four thousand. 6 Benaiah himself was the mighty man of the thirty who led the thirty: Ammizabad his son led his division.
7 The fourth for the fourth month, Asahel the brother of Joab, and Zebadiah his son after him: in his division, twenty-four thousand.
8 The fifth for the fifth month, the leader Shamhuth the Izrahite: in his division, twenty-four thousand.
9 The sixth for the sixth month, Ira the son of Ikkesh the Tekoite: in his division, twenty-four thousand.
10 The seventh for the seventh month, Helez the Pelonite, from the sons of Ephraim: in his division, twenty-four thousand.
11 The eighth for the eighth month, Sibbekai the Hushathite, of the Zerahites: in his division, twenty-four thousand.
12 The ninth for the ninth month, Abiezer the Anathothite, of the Benjamites: in his division, twenty-four thousand.
13 The tenth for the tenth month, Maharai the Netophathite, of the Zerahites: in his division, twenty-four thousand.
14 The eleventh for the eleventh month, Benaiah the Pirathonite, from the sons of Ephraim: in his division, twenty-four thousand.
15 The twelfth for the twelfth month, Heldai the Netophathite, of Othniel: in his division, twenty-four thousand.

Leaders of the Tribes
16 Over the tribes of Israel:

The chief officer over the Reubenites was Eliezer the son of Zikri;
over the Simeonites, Shephatiah the son of Maakah;
17 over the Levites, Hashabiah the son of Kemuel;
over the Aaronites, Zadok;
18 over Judah, Elihu, one of the brothers of David;
over Issachar, Omri the son of Michael;
19 over Zebulun, Ishmaiah the son of Obadiah;
over Naphtali, Jerimoth the son of Azriel;
20 over the sons of Ephraim, Hoshea the son of Azaziah;
over the half-tribe of Manasseh, Joel the son of Pedaiah;
21 over the half-tribe of Manasseh in Gilead, Iddo the son of Zechariah;
over Benjamin, Jaasiel the son of Abner;
22 over Dan, Azarel the son of Jeroham.
These were the leaders of the tribes of Israel.

23 But David did not take the number from twenty years old and under because the LORD had said He would multiply Israel as the stars of the heavens. 24 Joab the son of Zeruiah began to count them, but he did not finish. And because of this wrath came on Israel, and the number was not recorded in the account of the chronicles of King David.

Civic Officials
25 Azmaveth the son of Adiel was over the king's treasures, and Jonathan the son of Uzziah was over the storehouses in the fields, in the cities, and in the villages, and in the towers.
26 Ezri the son of Kelub was over those who did the work of the field to till the ground.
27 Shimei the Ramathite was over the vineyards, and Zabdi the Shiphmite was over what was in the vineyards for the stores of wine.

28 Baal-Hanan the Gederite was over the olive trees and the sycamore trees that were in the Shephelah, and Joash was over the stores of oil.
29 Shitrai the Sharonite was over the herds that fed in Sharon, and Shaphat the son of Adlai was over the herds that were in the valleys.
30 Obil the Ishmaelite was over the camels, and Jehdeiah the Meronothite was over the donkeys.
31 Jaziz the Hagrite was over the flocks.
All these were the overseers of King David's property.

32 Also Jonathan, David's uncle, was a counselor, a man of understanding, and a scribe; and Jehiel the son of Hakmoni was with the king's sons.
33 Now Ahithophel was the king's counselor, and Hushai the Arkite was the king's friend. 34 Jehoiada the son of Benaiah and Abiathar came after Ahithophel, and Joab was the leader of the king's army.

David's Plans for the Temple
28 Now David assembled all the leaders of Israel in Jerusalem: the leaders of the tribes, the officers of the divisions of those ministering to the king, the captains of thousands and the captains of hundreds, the stewards over all the property and livestock of the king and his sons with the eunuchs and the fighting men and all the brave warriors.
2 So King David rose to his feet and said, "Hear me, my brothers and my people. I had it in my heart to build a house of rest for the ark of the covenant of the LORD, a footstool for the feet of our God, so I prepared to build it. 3 But God said to me, 'You shall not build a house for My name because you are a man of war and have spilled much blood.'
4 "Still, the LORD God of Israel chose me from all my father's house to be king over Israel forever; for He chose Judah as leader, and in the house of Judah, the house of my father, and among the sons of my father, He took pleasure in me to make me king over all Israel. 5 Of all my sons (for the LORD has given me many sons), He has chosen my son Solomon to sit on the throne of the kingdom of the LORD over Israel. 6 For He said to me, 'Solomon your son is the one who shall build My house and My courts, for I have chosen him to be My son, and I will be his Father. 7 I will establish his kingdom forever if he is fully committed to keep My commandments and My judgments as it is this day.'
8 "Now therefore in the sight of all Israel, the assembly of the LORD, and in the hearing of our God, observe and seek out all the commandments of the LORD your God, that you may possess this good land and leave it for an inheritance for your children after you forever. 9 As for you, Solomon my son, know the God of your fathers and serve Him with a whole heart and with a willing spirit, for the LORD searches every heart and understands the intent of every thought. If you seek Him, He will be found by you, but if you forsake Him, He will abandon you forever. 10 See now that the LORD chose you to build the house for His sanctuary. Be strong and do it."
11 Then David gave to Solomon his son the building plans for the vestibule of the temple, its house, its treasury, its roof chambers, its inner rooms, and the place of the mercy seat; 12 and the plans, all of which were given to him by the Spirit, for the courts of the house of the LORD and for the surrounding rooms, the storehouses of the house of God, and the storehouses of the dedicated offerings; 13 for the divisions of the priests and the Levites for all the work of the service of the house of the LORD and for all the implements of the service of the house of the LORD; 14 the weight of gold for all the golden implements of service, the implements of silver by weight for all implements of service, 15 and the weight of the golden lampstands and their lamps, the weight of gold for each lampstand and its lamps, the weight of silver for a lampstand and its lamps according to the use of each lampstand; 16 the weight of gold for the tables of the showbread, table by table, and silver for the tables of silver; 17 and the pure gold forks, the basins, and the pitchers; for the golden bowls with the weight for each bowl; the weight of silver for each silver dish;

[18] and for the altar of incense, refined gold by weight; also his plan for the golden chariot of the cherubim that spread *their wings* and covered the ark of the covenant of the LORD.

[19] "All *this*," *said David*, "the LORD made me understand in writing by His hand upon me, all the works of this pattern."

[20] Then David said to Solomon his son, "Be strong and courageous, and take action. Do not be afraid nor be dismayed for the LORD God, my God, is with you. He will not leave you nor forsake you, until you have finished all the work of the service of the house of the LORD. [21] Now, here are the divisions of the priests and the Levites for all the service of the house of God, and all those who are willing and skillful for all the work will be with you for all the service; also the leaders and the people will be wholly at your command."

Temple Offerings

29 King David said to all the assembly, "Solomon my son, the one whom God has chosen, is young and inexperienced, and the work is great since the palace is not for a man but for the LORD God. [2] So with all my might I have prepared for the house of my God: gold for the *things of* gold, silver for the *things of* silver, bronze for the *things of* bronze, iron for the *things of* iron, and wood for the *things of* wood, *along with* onyx stones and stones for setting, stones of antimony, multicolored stones, and every precious stone, even alabaster in abundance. [3] Moreover, in my devotion to the house of my God I have offered from my own property, gold and silver, which I give for the house of my God, over and above that which I prepared for the holy dwelling place: [4] three thousand talents[1] of gold of the gold of Ophir and seven thousand talents[2] of refined silver for overlaying the walls of the house; [5] of gold for the *things of* gold and of silver for the *things of* silver, even for all the handiwork of the craftsmen. Now, who is willing to consecrate himself today to the LORD?"

[6] Then the leaders of the fathers' houses, the leaders of the tribes of Israel, the captains of thousands and hundreds, and the officials of the king's workers offered willingly. [7] Also they donated to the service of the house of God five thousand talents[3] of gold and ten thousand darics[4] of gold, ten thousand talents[5] of silver, eighteen thousand talents[6] of bronze, and one hundred thousand talents[7] of iron. [8] Whoever had *precious* stones gave them to the treasury of the house of the LORD in the custody of Jehiel the Gershonite. [9] Then the people rejoiced because they had offered willingly, for with a whole heart they had offered freely to the LORD; and King David also rejoiced greatly.

A Prayer of David

[10] So David blessed the LORD in the presence of all the assembly, and David said,

"Blessed are You, O LORD,
    the God of Israel,
    our Father forever and ever.
[11] Yours, O LORD, is the greatness, and the power,
    and the glory, and the victory, and the majesty,
    for everything in the heavens and the earth *is Yours*.
Yours is the kingdom, O LORD,
    and You exalt Yourself as head above all.

[12] Riches and honor flow from You,
    and You rule over all.
In Your hand are power and might,
    and in Your hand *it is* to make great and to strengthen all.
[13] So now, our God, we give thanks to You,
    and praise Your glorious name.

[14] "But who am I, and who are my people, that we should be able to offer so freely as this? For everything comes from You, *even* from Your own hand we have given to You. [15] For we are strangers and sojourners before You, just as all our fathers were. Our days on earth are like a shadow, and there is no hope. [16] O LORD our God, all this abundance that we have prepared to build You a house for Your holy name has come from Your hand, and all belongs to You. [17] I know, my God, that You test the heart, and with uprightness You are pleased, so in the uprightness of my heart I have offered freely all these things, and now I have seen Your people, those present here, offer freely and joyously to You. [18] O LORD, the God of Abraham, Isaac, and Israel, our fathers, keep this forever in the thoughts and intentions of the heart of Your people and direct their heart to You. [19] Grant to Solomon my son a whole heart to keep Your commandments, Your testimonies, and Your statutes, to do all *these things* and to build the palace for which I have made preparation."

[20] Then David said to all the assembly, "Bless now the LORD your God." So all the assembly blessed the LORD, the God of their fathers. They bowed down and paid homage to the LORD and the king.

Solomon, King of Israel
1Ki 1:28–53

[21] On the following day, they made sacrifices to the LORD and offered burnt offerings to the LORD: one thousand bulls, one thousand rams, *and* one thousand lambs, with their drink offerings and sacrifices in abundance for all Israel. [22] So they ate and drank before the LORD on that day with great joy.

And they made Solomon the son of David king a second time, for they anointed *him* to the LORD as a ruler and Zadok as a priest. [23] Then Solomon sat on the throne of the LORD as king instead of David his father, and he prospered, and all Israel obeyed him. [24] All the leaders and the mighty men, and also the sons of King David, pledged their allegiance to King Solomon. [25] The LORD highly exalted Solomon in the sight of all Israel and bestowed on him such royal majesty as had never been on any king in Israel before him.

The Death of David
1Ki 2:10–12

[26] Now David son of Jesse reigned over all Israel. [27] His tenure as king over Israel was forty years: In Hebron, he reigned seven years, and in Jerusalem he was king thirty-three years. [28] So he died at a good old age, full of days, riches, and honor. And Solomon his son reigned in his place.

[29] Now the acts of David the king, first to last, are written in the book of Samuel the seer, and in the book of Nathan the prophet, and in the book of Gad the seer [30] with all his reign and his might and the times that overtook him, and Israel, and all the kingdoms of the lands.

---

[1]4 About 110 tons, or 100 metric tons.   [2]4 About 260 tons, or 235 metric tons.   [3]7 About 190 tons, or 170 metric tons.
[4]7 About 185 pounds, or 84 kilograms.   [5]7 About 380 tons, or 340 metric tons.   [6]7 About 675 tons, or 610 metric tons.
[7]7 About 3,800 tons, or 3,400 metric tons.

2 Chronicles

Solomon Seeks Wisdom
1Ki 3:4–15; 10:26–29; 2Ch 9:25–28

1 Now Solomon the son of David strengthened himself over his kingdom, and the Lord his God was with him and made *Solomon* exceedingly great.

[2] And Solomon spoke to all Israel, to the commanders of thousands and of hundreds, to the judges, and to all the leaders in all Israel, the heads of fathers' houses. [3] Then they all went, Solomon and all the assembly that was with him, to the high place that was at Gibeon, because the tent of meeting with God, which Moses the servant of the Lord had made in the wilderness, was there. [4] However, David had brought up the ark of God from Kiriath Jearim to the place he had prepared, for he had pitched a tent for it in Jerusalem. [5] And the bronze altar that Bezalel the son of Uri, the son of Hur, had made was set before the tabernacle of the Lord. And Solomon and the assembly sought it out *to seek the* Lord. [6] And Solomon went up to the bronze altar before the Lord, which was before the tent of meeting, and he offered up a thousand burnt offerings on it.

[7] That night God appeared to Solomon and said to him, "Ask what I might give to you."

[8] Then Solomon said to God, "You have given a great mercy to David my father and have made me king in his place. [9] Now, Lord God, may Your word to David my father be confirmed, for You have made me king over a people numerous as the dust of the earth. [10] Now give wisdom and knowledge to me so that I might know how to go before this people, for who can judge this great people of Yours?"

[11] Then God responded to Solomon, "Because this was in your heart and you did not ask for possessions, wealth, and honor, or even the life of those who hate you, nor have you asked for many days of life, but you have asked Me for wisdom and knowledge that you might govern My people over whom I have made you king, [12] wisdom and knowledge are now given to you. Possessions, wealth, and honor I will also give to you; such has not been given to kings before you nor those who will follow after you."

[13] So Solomon came from the high place at Gibeon, before the tent of meeting, to Jerusalem, and he reigned over Israel.

[14] Solomon gathered together chariots and horses. He had one thousand four hundred chariots and twelve thousand horses, and he put them in designated cities and with the king in Jerusalem. [15] The king made silver and gold in Jerusalem as *abundant* as stones and cedar as plentiful as sycamore trees in the lowlands of the Shephelah. [16] The horses of Solomon were imported from Egypt and Kue, and the traders of the king would take them from Kue for a price. [17] They imported chariots from Egypt for six hundred shekels[1] of silver and a horse for one hundred and fifty pieces.[2] And they imported from these places to all the kings of the Hittites and Arameans.

Plans for Building the Temple
1Ki 5:1–16

2 Now Solomon wanted to build a temple for the name of the Lord and a royal house for his kingship. [2] And Solomon designated seventy thousand men to carry materials, eighty thousand men to cut stone in the hills, and three thousand six hundred supervisors to oversee these men.

[3] And Solomon sent word to Hiram[3] king of Tyre saying,

"As you did for David my father and sent him cedar trees in order to build for himself a house in which to dwell, *so deal with me.* [4] I am going to build a temple for the name of the Lord my God, sanctified for Him, for making sacrifices before Him, and for incense of fragrant spices, and for the continual showbread, for burnt offerings on both morning and evening, and for Sabbaths, New Moons, and appointed feasts of the Lord our God, as an ordinance forever for Israel.

[5] "And the house that I am building will be great because our God is greater than all other gods. [6] But who is able to build a house for Him, since the heavens and the highest heavens cannot contain Him? Who am I that I build a house for Him, except to make offerings before Him?

[7] "Now may you send to me a wise man who works with gold, silver, bronze, iron, and in purple, crimson, and violet threads and knows how to engrave, who will be with the skilled workers and me in Judah and Jerusalem, which David my father established.

[8] "And may you send me trees of cedar, cypress, and algum from Lebanon because I realize that your slaves know how to cut timber in Lebanon; and my servants will be alongside your servants, [9] to prepare an abundance of timber for me, because the temple that I will build will be great and marvelous. [10] I will provide for the woodsmen, your servants who cut timber, twenty thousand dry kors[4] of crushed wheat, twenty thousand kors[5] of barley, twenty thousand liquid baths[6] of wine, and twenty thousand liquid baths of oil."

[11] Then Hiram king of Tyre responded in a letter that he sent to Solomon,

"Because the Lord loves His people, He has made you king over them."

[12] And Hiram said,

"Blessed be the Lord God of Israel who made heaven and earth and has given King David a wise son, having insight and understanding, who is building a temple for the Lord and a royal house for his kingship. [13] And now I have sent a skilled man, endowed with understanding, Huram-Abi, [14] the son of a woman from the daughters of Dan and the son of a man of Tyre, who knows gold, silver, bronze, iron, stone, wood, and purple, violet, blue, and crimson threads, and who knows how to make all types of engravings and to devise every type of design that is given to him, with your skilled men and the skilled men of my lord David your father.

[15] "Now the wheat, the barley, the oil, and the wine that my lord has declared, may he send *these items* to his slaves. [16] And let us cut the timber from Lebanon, whatever you need, and we will bring it to you on rafts on the sea to Joppa, and you will bring it up to Jerusalem."

[17] Then Solomon numbered all the male foreigners who were in the land of Israel, after the census that David his father had taken. And there were found one hundred and fifty-three thousand six hundred. [18] And he made seventy thousand of them to carry materials, eighty thousand to cut stone in the hills, and three thousand six hundred supervisors to make the people work.

Solomon Builds the Temple
1Ki 6:1–29

3 So Solomon began to build the house of the Lord in Jerusalem on Mount Moriah, where *He* appeared to David his father, at the place that David established on the threshing floor of Ornan the Jebusite. [2] He began to build in the second month[7] on the second day during the fourth year of his reign.[8]

---

[1]17 About 15 pounds, or 6.9 kilograms. [2]17 About 3¾ pounds, or 1.7 kilograms. [3]3 Huram in the Heb. text.
[4]10 Likely about 3,600 tons, or 3,200 metric tons of wheat. [5]10 Likely about 3,000 tons, or 2,700 metric tons of barley.
[6]10 About 120,000 gallons, or 440,000 liters. [7]2 Ziv or Iyyar in the Hebrew calendar. [8]2 April or May in 966 BC.

³ These are the foundation *measurements* that Solomon used for building the house of God. The cubit¹ length in the former standard measure was sixty cubits and the width twenty cubits. ² ⁴ The porch vestibule that was in front of *the nave hall* had its length, like the width of the house, as twenty cubits, ³ and its height was one hundred and twenty cubits; ⁴ and he overlaid the inside with pure gold.

⁵ And he paneled the great house with cypress trees and then covered it with fine gold. Then he decorated it with palm trees and chain work. ⁶ And he overlaid the house with precious stones for decoration, and the gold was from Parvaim. ⁷ And he covered the house—its beams, thresholds, walls, and doors—with gold, and he engraved cherubim on the walls.

⁸ Then he made the dwelling of the Most Holy Place. Its length was as the width of twenty cubits, and its width also twenty cubits; and he covered it with fine gold, six hundred talents⁵ worth. ⁹ And the weight in gold for the nails was fifty shekels.⁶ And he covered the upper chamber in gold.

¹⁰ Then in the dwelling of the Most Holy Place, he made two cherubim that were cast metal and overlaid them with gold. ¹¹ And the wings of the cherubim were the length of twenty cubits. The wing of one cherub was five cubits, reaching the wall of the house, and the wing of the other was five cubits,⁷ reaching to the wing of the other cherub. ¹² And the wing of this cherub was five cubits, reaching to the other wall of the house, and the other wing was five cubits, touching the wing of the first cherub. ¹³ So the wings of these cherubim spread out were twenty cubits; they were upright on their feet facing inward toward the house.

¹⁴ Then he made the curtain of violet, purple, crimson, and blue thread, and he wove cherubim into it.

¹⁵ And he made two pillars in front of the house thirty-five cubits⁸ high, with a five cubit capital on the top of the pillar. ¹⁶ Then he made ornamental chain work, like in the Most Holy Place, and set it on the top of the pillars. Then he designed a hundred pomegranates and set them on the chain work. ¹⁷ He then raised the pillars in front of the temple, with one on the right *to the south* and the other on the left *to the north*, and the pillar to the south he called Jakin, and the pillar to the north he called Boaz.

The Furnishings of the Temple
1Ki 7:23–51

4 Then he made a bronze altar that was twenty cubits long, twenty cubits wide, and ten cubits⁹ high. ² And he made a cast metal sea *as a water basin*. It was round and ten cubits from edge to edge, five cubits high,¹⁰ and a line of thirty cubits¹¹ measured its circumference. ³ Figures like oxen were underneath it, going all the way around the sea basin, ten cubits¹² on each side.¹³ There were two rows of oxen that were poured as cast metal.

⁴ It stood on twelve oxen, three facing north, three facing west, three facing south, and three facing east. The sea was set on them, and their back sides were facing inward. ⁵ The thickness *of the sea* was a palm,¹⁴ and its brim was like the brim of a cup, as the flower of a lily. It held three thousand baths¹⁵ securely.

⁶ Then he made ten water basins, and he set five on the southern right side and five on the northern left side to rinse off in them the instruments of the burnt offering. And the sea basin was for the priests to wash in.

⁷ And he made ten lampstands of gold according to the specifications, and he set them in the temple, five on the southern, right side and five on the northern, left side.

⁸ Then he made ten tables and put them in the temple, five on the southern, right side and five on the northern, left side; and he made a hundred basins of gold.

⁹ Then he made the court of the priests and the great enclosure and the doors for the enclosure, and he overlaid the doors with bronze. ¹⁰ And he set the sea basin at the southeast side, opposite the southern side *of the house.*

¹¹ And Huram made the pots, shovels, and bowls.

So Huram completed the work that he did for King Solomon on the house of God: ¹² the two pillars, the bowls, and the two capitals on the top of the pillars; and the two latticeworks to cover the two bowls of the capitals that were on the top of the pillars; ¹³ and the four hundred pomegranates for the two pieces of grating, with two rows of pomegranates for each screen grate that covered the two bowl-shaped capitals on top of the pillars. ¹⁴ And he made the supporting stands and the basins on top of the stands, ¹⁵ and the sea basin and the twelve oxen underneath it; ¹⁶ the pots, shovels, utensils, and all the vessels from polished bronze, Huram-Abi made for King Solomon for the house of the Lord.

¹⁷ The king cast these *vessels* in the district of the Jordan in earthen foundries between Sukkoth and Zeredatha.¹⁶ ¹⁸ And Solomon made all of these items in a great abundance such that they did not consider the weight of the bronze.

¹⁹ So Solomon made all the vessels that were in the house of God: the gold altar and the tables displaying the showbread, ²⁰ and the finely hammered lampstands with their lamps to burn before the Most Holy Place as prescribed; ²¹ the golden flower-shaped ornaments, lamps, and tongs, of purest gold; ²² the snuffers, basins, ladles, and fire pans, of pure gold. As for the entrance to the temple: the inner doors to the Most Holy Place and the doors of the nave of the temple were of gold.

5 Thus all the work that Solomon did for the house of the Lord was finished. And Solomon brought in the things that David his father had dedicated: the silver and the gold and all the furnishings in the treasury of the house of God.

The Ark Brought to the Temple
1Ki 8:1–21

² Then Solomon assembled the elders of Israel and all the heads of the tribes and the leaders of the houses of the fathers among the sons of Israel to bring up the ark of the covenant of the Lord from the City of David, which is Zion. ³ And all the men of Israel were assembled before the king at the feast, which is the seventh month.¹⁷

⁴ All the elders of Israel came, and the Levites carried the ark. ⁵ Then they brought up the ark, and the tent of meeting, and all the holy vessels that were in the tent. So the Levitical priests brought them up. ⁶ And King Solomon and all the congregation of Israel, who were assembled with him before the ark, were sacrificing so many sheep and oxen that they could not be counted or numbered.

⁷ The priests brought the ark of the covenant of the Lord to its place—to the inner sanctuary of the temple, into the Most Holy Place, under the wings of the cherubim. ⁸ Then the cherubim wings were spread out over the place of the ark so that the cherubim covered the ark and its poles. ⁹ The poles were extended so that the ends of the poles of the ark were seen in front of the Most Holy Place, but they were not seen outside; and they are still there to this day. ¹⁰ In the ark there was nothing except the two tablets that Moses had given at Mount Horeb where the Lord made a covenant with the sons of Israel when they went out from Egypt.

¹¹ When the priests came out from the Most Holy Place—for all the priests who were present had consecrated themselves, without keeping separate divisions— ¹² and all the Levitical singers, Asaph, Heman, and Jeduthun, with their sons and relatives, all clothed in fine linen, with cymbals, harps, and lyres, stood to the east of the altar, and with them one hundred and twenty priests who were sounding with trumpets, ¹³ it happened, when the trumpet players and singers made one sound to praise and give thanks to the Lord,

---

¹ 3 The Egyptian cubit had a royal measure of 20.6 inches (52.3cm) and a commercial measure of 17.6 inches (44.7 cm). The cubit standards in Egypt and Mesopotamia were slightly different. ² 3 About 90 feet long and 30 feet wide, or 27 meters long and 9 meters wide. ³ 4 About 30 feet, or 9 meters; and in vv. 8, 11, and 13. ⁴ 4 About 180 feet, or 54 meters. ⁵ 8 About 23 tons, or 21 metric tons. ⁶ 9 About 1¼ pounds, or 575 grams. ⁷ 11 About 7½ feet, or 2.3 meters; and in v. 15. ⁸ 15 About 53 feet, or 16 meters. ⁹ 1 About 30 feet long and wide and 15 feet high, or 9 meters long and wide and 4.5 meters high. ¹⁰ 2 About 7½ feet, or 2.3 meters. ¹¹ 2 About 45 feet, or 14 meters. ¹² 3 About 18 cubits, or 45 centimeters. ¹³ 3 Or *ten oxen for a cubit*. ¹⁴ 5 About 3 inches, or 7.5 centimeters. ¹⁵ 5 About 18,000 gallons, or 66,000 liters. ¹⁶ 17 *Zarethan* in 1Ki 7:46. ¹⁷ 3 Tishri or Ethanim in the Hebrew calendar.

and when they lifted up their voice with the trumpets and cymbals and all the instruments of music and praised the LORD saying,

"For He is good
    and His mercy endures forever,"

that the house, the house of the LORD, was filled with a cloud. [14] And the priests were not able to stand in order to serve because of the cloud, for the glory of the LORD had filled the house of God.

6 Then Solomon said, "The LORD has said that He would dwell in the dark cloud. [2] But I have built for You an exalted house, even a habitation where You can continually dwell."

Solomon's Speech

[3] Then the king turned his face around, and he blessed the entire assembly of Israel while all the assembly of Israel was standing before him. [4] And he said:

"Blessed be the LORD God of Israel who spoke with David my father and fulfilled *His promise* saying, [5] 'Since the day that I brought out My people from the land of Egypt, I did not choose any city from among the tribes of Israel to build a house for My name to dwell there, nor did I select a man to be the leader over My people Israel; [6] but I have chosen Jerusalem for My name to dwell there, and I have selected David to be over My people Israel.'

[7] "And it was in the heart of David my father to build a house for the name of the LORD God of Israel. [8] But the LORD said to David my father, 'Whereas it was in your heart to build a house for My name, you did well because of what was in your heart; [9] only you will not be the one to build the house. For your son, who will be born to you, he will build a house for My name.'

[10] "The LORD has fulfilled the word that He spoke. For I have risen up in the place of David my father and sit on the throne of Israel, as the LORD spoke, and I will build the house for the name of the LORD God of Israel. [11] And there I have set the ark, in which is the covenant of the LORD that He made with the children of Israel."

Solomon's Prayer of Dedication

1Ki 8:22–53; Ps 132:8–10

[12] Then Solomon stood before the altar of the LORD before all the assembly of Israel and spread out his hands. [13] For Solomon made a bronze platform and set it in the midst of the enclosure. It was five cubits in length, five cubits in width, and three cubits in height.[1] And he stood on it and knelt down before all the assembly of Israel and spread out his hands to heaven. [14] And he said:

"O LORD God of Israel, there is no God like You in the heavens or on the earth, who keeps covenants and mercy with Your servants who walk before You with all their heart. [15] You have kept what You promised Your servant David my father. You have both spoken with Your mouth and fulfilled *it* with Your hand, as *it is* this day. [16] And now, O LORD God of Israel, keep what You promised Your servant David my father saying, 'You will not lack a man sitting on the throne of Israel before Me, if only your sons take heed to their way to walk in My law as you have walked before Me.' [17] And now, O LORD God of Israel, may Your word be confirmed which You have spoken to Your servant David.

[18] "For will God indeed dwell with man on the earth? The heavens, even the highest heavens, are not able to contain You, much less this house that I have built. [19] But respond to the prayer of Your servant and to his plea, O LORD my God, to listen to the cry and prayer of Your servant who prays before You, [20] that Your eyes might be open toward this house both day and night, to the place that You have said that You will set Your name, in order to hear the prayer of Your servant for this place. [21] And listen to the pleas of Your servant and Your people Israel when they pray toward this place. And may

You respond from heaven, the place of Your dwelling, so that You hear and forgive.

[22] "If a man sins against his companion, and the *companion* swears and puts him under a curse, and the *wronged man* comes with an oath before Your altar at this temple, [23] then You will hear from heaven, and You will act and judge Your servants, to repay the guilty one by bringing his way on his own head; and to vindicate the innocent one by rendering to him according to his righteous behavior.

[24] "If Your people Israel are struck before enemies because they have sinned against You, and they return and confess Your name and pray and seek Your favor in this house, [25] then You will hear from heaven and forgive the sin of Your people Israel, and You will bring them back to the land that You gave them and their fathers.

[26] "When the sky is shut up and there is no rain because they have sinned against You, and they pray toward this place and confess Your name and turn from their sin when You afflict them, [27] then You will hear from heaven and forgive the sin of Your servants and Your people Israel because You will teach them the good path in which they will walk, and You will send rain on the land that You have given to Your people as a possession.

[28] "When there is famine in the land or when there is pestilence, blight, mildew, winged locust, or grasshopper, or when enemies besiege them in the land up to their city gates, in whatever plague or sickness, [29] whatever prayer or plea that is made by any man or by all your people Israel, when each man knows his own affliction and his own sorrow, and stretches out his hands toward this house, [30] then You will hear from heaven, the place of the habitation of Your dwelling, and forgive, and You will render to each according to his conduct, for You know their hearts (for You alone know the heart of people), [31] so that they may fear You and walk in Your ways all the days that they live on the land that You have given to our fathers.

[32] "When foreigners are not from Your people Israel and come from a distant land, because of Your great name, mighty hand, and outstretched arm, and they come and pray toward this house, [33] then hear from heaven, from Your dwelling place, and act on everything for which the foreigner calls on You, that all the peoples of the earth may know Your name and fear You, as do Your people Israel; and that they may know that this house which I have built is called by Your name.

[34] "When Your people go out to battle against their enemies, in the way that You send them, and when they pray to You toward this city that You have chosen and the house that I have built for Your name, [35] then hear from heaven their prayer and plea and act for their cause.

[36] "When they sin against You (for there is no one who does not sin) and You are angry against them and give them to their enemies, and they are taken captive to a land, whether distant or near, [37] and they turn their hearts in the land that they have been taken captive, and they repent and seek Your favor in the land of captivity saying, 'We have sinned, done wrong, and acted wickedly,' [38] and if they turn in repentance to You with all their heart and all their soul in the land of their captivity that they were taken to, and pray toward the land that You have given to their fathers, and toward the city that You have chosen, and toward the house that I have built for Your name, [39] then hear from heaven, from Your dwelling place, their prayer and supplication, and maintain their cause, and forgive the people who have sinned against You.

[40] "Now, O my God, may Your eyes be open and Your ears attentive to the prayer *that I offer* in this place.

[41] "Now rise up, O LORD God, to Your resting place,
    both You and the ark of Your strength.
And let Your priests, O LORD God, be clothed in salvation
    and Your loyal ones rejoice in goodness.

---

[1] 13 About 7½ feet long and wide, and 4½ feet high; or 2.3 meters long and wide, and 1.4 meters high.

[42] O Lᴏʀᴅ God, do not turn Your face from Your anointed. Remember the mercies of Your servant David."

Solomon Dedicates the Temple
1Ki 8:62–66

7 And when Solomon finished praying, fire came down from the heavens and consumed the burnt offering and sacrifices, and the glory of the Lᴏʀᴅ filled the temple. [2] And the priests were not able to enter into the house of the Lᴏʀᴅ, for the glory of the Lᴏʀᴅ filled the Lᴏʀᴅ's house. [3] And all the sons of Israel saw when the fire came down and the glory of the Lᴏʀᴅ came on the temple, and they bowed their faces low to the ground on the pavement, and they worshipped confessing,

"The Lᴏʀᴅ is good,
and His mercy endures forever."

[4] Then the king and all the people were making sacrifices before the Lᴏʀᴅ. [5] King Solomon sacrificed twenty-two thousand oxen and one hundred and twenty thousand sheep. So the king and all the people dedicated the house of God. [6] The priests stood at their positions, with the Levites and all their instruments of music for the Lᴏʀᴅ that King David had made to praise the Lᴏʀᴅ—for His mercy endures forever—when David gave praise by their ministry, and the priests sounded trumpets opposite the *Levites*, and all Israel stood.

[7] And Solomon consecrated the middle of the court that was in front of the house of the Lᴏʀᴅ because there he made burnt offerings and the fat of peace offerings (because the bronze altar that Solomon made was surely not able to contain the burnt offerings, grain offerings, and fat offerings).

[8] And at the appointed time, Solomon made a feast for seven days, and all Israel—as a very great assembly—was with him, from the entrance of Lebo Hamath *in the north* to the Brook of Egypt *in the south*. [9] Then on the eighth day they made a solemn assembly because they had made a consecration of the altar for seven days and then the feast for seven days more. [10] Then on the twenty-third day of the seventh month *Solomon* sent the people away to their homes. They were joyful and good of heart because of what the Lᴏʀᴅ had done for David, Solomon, and His people Israel.

[11] Thus Solomon finished the house of the Lᴏʀᴅ and the king's house. And Solomon successfully accomplished everything that came into his heart to do in the house of the Lᴏʀᴅ and in his own house.

The Lᴏʀᴅ Appears to Solomon
1Ki 9:1–9

[12] Then the Lᴏʀᴅ appeared to Solomon at night, and He said to Solomon,

"I have heard your prayer, and I have chosen for Myself in this place a house of sacrifice. [13] "When I shut up the heaven and there is no rain, or when I command the locusts to devour the land, or send pestilence on My people, [14] if My people, who are called by My name, will humble themselves and pray, and seek My face and turn from their wicked ways, then I will hear from heaven, and will forgive their sin and will heal their land. [15] Now My eyes will be open and My ears attentive to the prayer of this place. [16] So now I have chosen and consecrated this house that My name be there continually. My eyes and heart will be there for all days. [17] "And you, if you walk before Me as David your father did to do everything that I command you to do, and you keep My statutes and judgments, [18] then I will set the throne of your kingdom as I made a covenant with David your father saying, 'You will not lack a man to rule Israel.' [19] "But if the people turn aside and abandon My statutes and commandments that I have given to you, and you walk after and serve other gods and worship them, [20] then I will uproot them from My land that I have given to them; and the house that I have consecrated for My name, I will throw it from before Me and set it as a proverb and taunt among the peoples. [21] And even though this house was majestic, it will lie desolate before all who pass by it, and they will say, 'Why did the Lᴏʀᴅ do such a thing to this land and this house?' [22] Then they will say, 'Because they abandoned the Lᴏʀᴅ, the God of their fathers who brought them up from the land of Egypt, and they took hold of other gods and worshipped and served them; therefore He has brought on them all this disaster.' "

Solomon's Other Activities
1Ki 9:10–28

8 It came that after twenty years, Solomon built the house of the Lᴏʀᴅ and his royal house, [2] and Solomon even rebuilt the cities that Hiram had given to him, and he settled the sons of Israel in them. [3] Then Solomon went to Hamath Zobah and seized it. [4] He also built Tadmor in the wilderness and all the store cities that he built in Hamath. [5] He also built the Upper and Lower Beth Horon, fortified cities with walls, gates, and bars, [6] and Baalath, and all the store cities that Solomon had, and all the cities for his chariots, the cities for his cavalry, and whatever Solomon desired to build in Jerusalem, Lebanon, and in all the land of his dominion. [7] And all the people who remained from the Hittites, Amorites, Perizzites, Hivites, and Jebusites who were not from Israel, [8] and from their descendants who remained *from these peoples* in the land and whom the sons of Israel did not finish destroying, Solomon brought them up to be forced labor, even to this day. [9] But from the sons of Israel Solomon did not make servants for his work. These were his soldiers, officers, commanders of his chariots, and horsemen. [10] And these were the two hundred and fifty chief officers for King Solomon who governed the people.

[11] And Solomon brought up the daughter of Pharaoh from the City of David to the house that he built for her, for he said, "My wife will not live in the house of David king of Israel, for the places where the ark of the Lᴏʀᴅ have been are holy."

[12] At that time Solomon offered up burnt offerings on the altar of the Lᴏʀᴅ that he built before the vestibule, [13] according to the daily duty to offer up as the commandment of Moses for Sabbaths, New Moons, and the three annual festivals: the Feast of Unleavened Bread, the Feast of Weeks, and the Feast of Tabernacles. [14] According to the ruling of David his father, he set the divisions of the priests for their service, and the Levites for their function to praise and serve before the priests according to the daily duty, and even the gatekeepers for their divisions at each gate, for this was the commandment of David the man of God. [15] And they did not turn from the commandment of the king, whether the priests or Levites, concerning any matter and concerning the treasury.

[16] So all the work of Solomon was established from the day of the foundation of the house of the Lᴏʀᴅ and until its completion; and the house of the Lᴏʀᴅ was complete.

[17] Then Solomon went to Ezion Geber and Elath at the shore of the sea in Edom. [18] And Hiram sent him ships by the hand of his servants, who knew the sea. And they went with the servants of Solomon to Ophir, and took from there four hundred and fifty talents[1] of gold, and brought them to King Solomon.

The Queen of Sheba Visits
1Ki 10:1–13

9 The queen of Sheba heard a report of Solomon, and she came to Jerusalem with a very impressive retinue—with camels carrying spices, an abundance of gold, and precious stones—to test Solomon with riddles. When she came to Solomon she shared with him everything that was on her heart. [2] Solomon declared to her everything that she asked, and there was not any matter concealed from Solomon that he did not declare to her. [3] When the queen of Sheba had observed the wisdom of Solomon, the house that he had built, [4] the food on his table, the seating of his officials, and the attendance of his servants, and their clothing, his valets, and their clothing, and his burnt offerings that he offered at the house of the Lᴏʀᴅ, there was no more spirit left in her.

---

[1] 18 About 17 tons, or 15 metric tons.

[5] Then she said to the king, "True was the report that I heard in my land concerning your words and wisdom. [6] But I did not believe their reports until I came and my eyes saw; and indeed, half the greatness of your wisdom was not declared to me. You have exceeded the report that I heard. [7] How happy your men must be! How happy these servants, those who are continually before you listening to your wisdom. [8] May the LORD your God be blessed, who has delighted in you, to set you as king on the throne of the LORD your God. Your God has loved Israel to establish them continually and has set you as king over them to perform justice and righteousness." [9] Then she gave the king one hundred and twenty talents[*] of gold and a great abundance of spices and precious stones. And there were no spices like those that the queen of Sheba gave to King Solomon.

[10] Moreover, the servants of Hiram and Solomon who brought gold from Ophir also brought algum wood and precious stones. [11] And the king used the algum wood for steps for the house of the LORD and the palace of the king, even for lyres and harps for the singers. And there had not been anything seen like these in the land of Judah.

[12] And King Solomon gave everything to the queen of Sheba in which she had pleasure, even what she asked for in addition to what she brought to the king. Then she turned and left for her own land with her servants.

The Splendor of Solomon
1Ki 10:14–29; 2Ch 1:14–17

[13] The weight of gold that came to Solomon every year was six hundred and sixty-six talents[2] of gold. [14] In addition to what the explorers and merchants brought in, all the kings of Arabia and governors of the land brought in gold and silver to Solomon.

[15] King Solomon made two hundred large shields of hammered gold, and six hundred gold pieces[3] were used for each large shield. [16] And he made three hundred shields of hammered gold; three hundred gold pieces[4] were used for each shield. And the king put them in the House of the Forest of Lebanon.

[17] And the king made a great throne of ivory, and he covered it with fine gold. [18] And there were six steps and a gold footstool attached to the throne, and on each side at the place of the seat were armrests with two lions standing beside the armrests. [19] So twelve lions stood there on the six steps, one on each side, and there was nothing like this in any kingdom. [20] Even all the drinking vessels of King Solomon were gold, and all the vessels in the House of the Forest of Lebanon were fine gold. And silver was not thought to be valuable in the days of Solomon. [21] The ships of Solomon went to Tarshish with the servants of Hiram. Once every three years the ships of Tarshish returned carrying gold, silver, ivory, apes, and peacocks.

[22] So King Solomon was greater than all the kings of the earth in wealth and wisdom. [23] All the kings of the earth sought out an audience before Solomon to hear his wisdom that God gave to his mind. [24] Every year each man brought his own tribute, vessels of silver and gold, garments, myrrh, spices, horses, and mules.

[25] Solomon had four thousand stalls for horses and chariots and twelve thousand horses, and he put them in designated cities and with him in Jerusalem. [26] He ruled over all the kings from the River[5] to the land of the Philistines and to the border of Egypt. [27] So the king made silver in Jerusalem as *abundant* as stones and cedar as plentiful as sycamore trees in the lowlands of the Shephelah. [28] The horses of Solomon were imported from Egypt and from all other lands.

The Death of Solomon
1Ki 11:41–43

[29] And the rest of the acts of Solomon, from beginning to end, are they not written in the annals of Nathan the prophet, and the prophecy of Ahijah the Shilonite, and in the visions of Iddo the seer concerning Jeroboam the son of Nebat? [30] So Solomon reigned in Jerusalem over all Israel for forty years. [31] And Solomon slept with his fathers, and they buried him in the City of David his father. And Rehoboam his son then ruled in his place.

Israel Rebels Against Rehoboam
1Ki 12:1–24

10 Rehoboam went to Shechem because all Israel journeyed to Shechem to make him king. [2] It happened that Jeroboam the son of Nebat heard this—he was in Egypt, where he fled from King Solomon—so he returned from Egypt. [3] So they sent for him and called him. And Jeroboam and all Israel came and spoke to Rehoboam saying, [4] "Your father made our yoke heavy. Now therefore, lighten your father's labor and heavy yoke that he put on us, and we will serve you."

[5] He responded, "Return again to me in three days." So the people left.

[6] Then King Rehoboam consulted with the elders who stood in the presence of Solomon his father when he was alive saying, "How do you counsel that I should give a response to this people?"

[7] They said to him, "If you are good to this people and please them and speak well to them, then they will be servants to you all your days."

[8] But he abandoned the counsel of the elders that they gave to him. And he consulted the young men who grew up and stood before him. [9] Rehoboam said to them, "What do you counsel that we give as a response to this people who have spoken to me, 'Lighten the yoke that your father placed on us'?"

[10] The young men who had grown up with him said, "So you should speak to the people who have spoken to you saying, 'Your father made our yoke heavy, but you lighten it from us.' So you will say to them, 'My little *finger* is thicker than my father's waist! [11] Whereas my father placed a heavy yoke on you, I will add to your yoke. My father chastened you with whips, but I will scourge you with scorpions.' "

[12] So Jeroboam and all the people came to Rehoboam on the third day, as the king had ordered saying, "Return to me on the third day." [13] Then the king answered them harshly. King Rehoboam rejected the advice of the elders. [14] He spoke to them with the advice of the young men, saying, "My father made your yoke heavy, but I will increase it. My father chastised you with whips, but I will chastise you with scorpions." [15] The king did not listen to the people, for the event occurred because of God, that the LORD might establish His word that He spoke through Ahijah the Shilonite to Jeroboam the son of Nebat.

[16] When all Israel saw that the king would not listen to them, the people answered the king saying,

"What portion do we have in David?
We have no inheritance in the son of Jesse.
O Israel, each man to your tent.
Now look after your own house, O David!"

Then all Israel departed to their tents. [17] The sons of Israel dwelled in the cities of Judah, and Rehoboam reigned over them. [18] Then King Rehoboam sent Hadoram, who was over the forced labor, and the sons of Israel stoned him to death. And King Rehoboam hurried to mount his chariot and to flee to Jerusalem. [19] So Israel has rebelled against the house of David until this day.

11 When Rehoboam came to Jerusalem, he called together from the house of Judah and Benjamin one hundred and eighty thousand[6] choice men to make war and to battle with Israel in order to restore the kingdom to Rehoboam. [2] But the word of the LORD came to Shemaiah the man of God saying: [3] Speak to Rehoboam, son of Solomon and king of Judah, and to all Israel in Judah and Benjamin, [4] "So says the LORD: You are not to go up and fight against your brothers. Each man must return to his house, for this event is from Me." So they obeyed the word of the LORD and turned back from attacking Jeroboam.

[*9] About 4½ tons or 4 metric tons.   [²13] About 25 tons, or 23 metric tons.   [³15] About 15 pounds, or 6.9 kilograms.   [⁴16] About 7½ pounds, or 3.5 kilograms.   [⁵26] Euphrates River.   [⁶1] From population numbers in the region at this time, the Heb. term is *division* rather than *thousand*.

Rehoboam Secures the Kingdom

[5] So Rehoboam dwelled in Jerusalem and built siege cities in Judah. [6] He built Bethlehem, Etam, Tekoa, [7] Beth Zur *in the east*, Soko, Adullam, [8] Gath, Mareshah *in the west*, Ziph, [9] Adoraim, Lachish *in the south*, Azekah, [10] Zorah, Aijalon *in the northwest*, and *central* Hebron, all of which were fortified cities in Judah and Benjamin. [11] He strengthened the fortresses and set leaders in them with stockpiles of food, oil, and wine. [12] And in all the cities he placed shields and spears, and he greatly strengthened these *places*. So he held Judah and Benjamin.

[13] And the priests and Levites in all Israel came before him from all their territories. [14] For the Levites left their pasturelands and properties, and they traveled to Judah and Jerusalem because Jeroboam and his sons excluded them from serving as priests to the Lord. [15] And he set for himself priests for the high places and for the goat and calf idols that he made. [16] And those who set their hearts to seek the Lord God of Israel followed after them from all the tribes of Israel, and they came to Jerusalem to sacrifice to the Lord God of their fathers. [17] So they strengthened the kingdom of Judah and supported Rehoboam, the son of Solomon, for three years, for they walked in the way of David and Solomon for three years.

Rehoboam's Family

[18] And Rehoboam took Mahalath for a wife, the daughter of both Jerimoth the son of David and of Abihail the daughter of Eliab the son of Jesse, [19] and she bore sons to him: Jeush, Shemariah, and Zaham. [20] Then after her he took Maakah the daughter of Absalom. And she bore to him Abijah, Attai, Ziza, and Shelomith. [21] And Rehoboam loved Maakah the daughter of Absalom more than his other wives and concubines (for he took eighteen wives and sixty concubines), and he had twenty-eight sons and sixty daughters.

[22] And Rehoboam set Abijah the son of Maakah as chief and head over his brothers for he *planned* to make him king. [23] And he was discerning and spread out all his sons to all the lands of Judah and Benjamin, even among the fortified cities, and he provided for them an abundance of provisions and wives.

Egypt Attacks Jerusalem
1Ki 14:21–31

[12] Now when the reign of Rehoboam was established and strong, he, and all of Israel with him, abandoned the law of the Lord. [2] And in the fifth year of King Rehoboam, Shishak king of Egypt went up against Jerusalem for they had acted unfaithfully against the Lord, [3] with one thousand two hundred chariots and sixty thousand horses. The people were without number who came with him from Egypt—Libyans, Sukkiktes, and Ethiopians. [4] And he captured the fortified cities that were in Judah, and he came even to Jerusalem.

[5] Then Shemaiah the prophet came to Rehoboam and the rulers of Judah who were assembled in Jerusalem before Shishak, and he said to them, "So the Lord says: You have abandoned Me, so I have abandoned you into the hand of Shishak."

[6] Then the king and the rulers of Israel humbled themselves and said, "The Lord is righteous."

[7] So when the Lord observed that they had humbled themselves, the word of the Lord came to Shemaiah, "They have humbled themselves, so I will not destroy them. I will let some of them escape, and My anger will not pour out against Jerusalem by the hand of Shishak. [8] For they will be slaves to him so that they experience My labor and the labor of the kingdoms of other lands."

[9] So Shishak king of Egypt went up against Jerusalem and took away the treasures of the house of the Lord and of the palace of the king. He took everything, even the gold shields that Solomon made. [10] And King Rehoboam made bronze shields in their place and entrusted them to the hands of the rulers of the guards, those who guarded the entrance to the king's palace. [11] And it happened that whenever the king came to the house of the Lord, the guards came and carried the *shields* and then returned them to the guardroom.

[12] And when he humbled himself, the anger of the Lord turned away from him so that there was not a complete annihilation. Moreover, there were some good things in Judah *during this time*.

The Death of Rehoboam

[13] So King Rehoboam was strong and reigned in Jerusalem. For Rehoboam was forty-one years old when he became king, and he reigned for seventeen years in Jerusalem, the city that the Lord had chosen out of all the tribes of Israel, to put His name there. His mother's name was Naamah the Ammonite. [14] And he acted evil because he did not set his heart to seek out the Lord.

[15] Now, are not the acts of Rehoboam written from beginning to end in the annals of Shemaiah the prophet and Iddo the seer, according to genealogy? And there were battles between Rehoboam and Jeroboam all their days. [16] And Rehoboam slept with his fathers and was buried in the City of David, and Abijah ruled in his place.

Abijah, King of Judah
1Ki 15:1–8

[13] In the eighteenth year of King Jeroboam, Abijah became king of Judah. [2] He reigned for three years in Judah, and his mother's name was Micaiah,[1] the granddaughter of Uriel of Gibeah.

And there was a war between Abijah and Jeroboam. [3] Abijah set the battle in order with an army of valiant men of war, four hundred thousand choice men. Jeroboam also drew up battle lines against him with an army of eight hundred thousand men, mighty men of valor.

[4] Then Abijah went up to Mount Zemaraim that is in the hills of Ephraim, and he said, "Listen to me, Jeroboam and all Israel! [5] Do you all not know that the Lord God of Israel has perpetually given the kingdom of Israel to David, even to him and to his sons with a covenant of salt? [6] And Jeroboam the son of Nebat, the servant of Solomon son of David, stood up and rebelled against his lord *Rehoboam*. [7] Then vain, worthless men gathered together around him and defied Rehoboam son of Solomon. And Rehoboam was young and timid in heart and was not strong before them.

[8] "And now you think that you can withstand before the kingdom of the Lord by the hand of the sons of David. And you all are a great multitude, and with you are the golden calves that Jeroboam has made for you to be gods. [9] Have you all not driven out the priests of the Lord, even the Levites and sons of Aaron, and made for yourselves priests from the peoples of other lands? Whoever comes to be dedicated and has in his hand a young bull or seven rams becomes a priest to what is not a god.

[10] "But for us, the Lord is our God, and we have not abandoned Him. And our priests serve the Lord and are sons of Aaron, Levites with their service. [11] They sacrifice burnt offerings to the Lord every morning and evening and put out an incense of spices. They also set the showbread in place on the ritual table and set the golden lampstand with its lamps to burn every evening. For we keep the duty of the Lord our God, but you all have abandoned Him. [12] God is with us as a leader, and His priests with their battle trumpets to call for battle against you all. O sons of Israel, do not fight against the Lord the God of your fathers because you will not find success."

[13] So Jeroboam went around them with an ambush to come from behind them. Those from Israel were in front of Judah, while the ambush was behind them. [14] Then Judah turned and saw that the battle was both in front of and behind them. Then they cried out to the Lord, and the priests sounded their trumpets. [15] Then the men from Judah shouted out; and it happened when Judah shouted out, God struck down Jeroboam and all Israel before Abijah and Judah. [16] The men of Israel fled before Judah, and God gave them into their hand. [17] Abijah and his people struck them down with a great slaughter, and the slain from Israel who fell that day were five hundred thousand choice men. [18] So the sons of Israel were subdued at that time, and the people of Judah were strong for they depended on the Lord God of their fathers.

[19] And Abijah chased after Jeroboam and captured cities from him: Bethel, Jeshanah, and Ephron with their surrounding villages. [20] And Jeroboam did not again recover his strength in the days of

---

[1]2 Maakah in 1Ki 15:2.

Abijah, and the Lord struck down Jeroboam, and he died.

²¹ So Abijah grew strong and took fourteen wives and had twenty-two sons and sixteen daughters.

²² And the remainder of the acts of Abijah, both his ways and words, are written in the story of the prophet Iddo.

14 And Abijah slept with his fathers, and they buried him in the City of David. Asa his son then reigned in his place. In his days the land was quiet for ten years.

Asa, King of Judah
1Ki 15:11–12

² Asa did what was good and right in the eyes of the Lord his God. ³ He took down the foreign altars and high places, and he shattered the pillars and cut down the images of Asherah. ⁴ Then he urged Judah to seek the Lord the God of their fathers and to keep the law and commandments. ⁵ And he also removed all the high places and incense altars in the cities in Judah. And the kingdom was at rest under Asa. ⁶ He built fortified cities in Judah because the land was quiet; and there was no war in these years, for the Lord gave peace to him.

⁷ And he said to Judah, "Let us build up these cities and let us surround them with walls, towers, gates, and bars for the land before us is still ours because we have sought after the Lord our God. We have sought Him, and He has given us peace all around." So they built and had success.

⁸ And it happened that Asa had an army from Judah carrying large shields and spears numbering three hundred thousand. And from Benjamin he had an army carrying shields and bows numbering two hundred eighty thousand. All of these were mighty men of valor.

⁹ But Zerah the Ethiopian Cushite came out against them with an army of a million men and three hundred chariots. And he came up to Mareshah. ¹⁰ Then Asa went out to engage him, and they arranged for battle in the Valley of Zephathah near Mareshah.

¹¹ And Asa cried out the Lord his God, and said, "Lord, it is nothing with You to help, whether with many or with those who have no power. Help us, O Lord our God; for we trust in You, and in Your name we come against this multitude. O Lord, You are our God. Let no man prevail against You."

¹² So the Lord struck down the Ethiopian Cushites before Asa and Judah, and the Cushites fled. ¹³ Then Asa and those with him pursued them until Gerar. And the Cushites fell till there was not one left alive because they were struck down before the Lord and His army. And those *in Judah* carried off a very great plunder. ¹⁴ And they struck down all the cities surrounding Gerar because the terror of the Lord was on them. And they plundered all the cities because there was a great amount of possessions in them. ¹⁵ And they also struck the tents holding livestock, and they carried off sheep and a great amount of camels. Then they returned to Jerusalem.

The Reforms of Asa
1Ki 15:13–16

15 Then the Spirit of God came on Azariah the son of Oded, ² and he went out to meet Asa and said to him, "Listen to me, Asa, and all Judah and Benjamin: The Lord is with you while you are with Him. If you all seek Him, He will be found with you. But if you forsake Him, He will forsake you. ³ For a long time Israel has been without the true God, and without a teaching priest and without law, ⁴ but when in their trouble they turned to the Lord God of Israel, and sought Him, He was found by them. ⁵ And at that time there was no peace to the one traveling in or out because there was a great panic on all those who dwelt in the land. ⁶ They were broken to pieces, nation against nation and city against city, because God confused them with every type of distress. ⁷ But you all must be strong and not lose heart, for there is a reward for your deeds."

⁸ And when Asa heard these words of the prophecy of *Azariah son of* Oded the prophet, he was encouraged and removed the detestable idols from the entire land of Judah and Benjamin and from the cities that he captured in the hills of Ephraim. And he repaired the altar of the Lord that was before the vestibule of the Lord.

⁹ And he gathered together all of Judah and Benjamin and those who had settled among them from Ephraim, Manasseh, and Simeon, for these had come down to him from Israel in a great number when they saw that the Lord his God was with him.

¹⁰ These were gathered in Jerusalem in the third month in the fifteenth year in the reign of Asa. ¹¹ They sacrificed to the Lord that day from the plunder that they brought in, seven hundred oxen and seven thousand sheep. ¹² And they entered into a covenant to seek the Lord God of their fathers with all their heart and soul. ¹³ But whoever would not seek the Lord God of Israel would be put to death, whether young or old, man or woman. ¹⁴ They swore an oath to the Lord in a loud voice, with shouting, trumpets, and horns. ¹⁵ And all Judah rejoiced over this oath because they swore with their whole heart and they sought Him with all their desire; and He was found by them, and the Lord gave them rest all around.

¹⁶ King Asa even removed his mother Maakah from being queen mother because she had made a detestable image for Asherah. Asa cut down her image, crushed it, and burned it in the Kidron Valley. ¹⁷ But they did not remove the high places from Israel. Nevertheless the heart of Asa was wholly committed all his days. ¹⁸ He brought into the house of God the sacred gifts of his father and his own sacred gifts—silver, gold, and utensils.

¹⁹ And there was no war until the thirty-fifth year of the reign of Asa.

Asa's Last Years
1Ki 15:17–24

16 But in the thirty-sixth year of the reign of Asa, Baasha king of Israel went up against Judah and built Ramah and did not allow anyone to come in or go out to Asa king of Judah.

² Then Asa removed silver and gold from the storehouses of the house of the Lord and palace of the king, and he sent it to Ben-Hadad king of Aram in Syria, who lived in Damascus, saying, ³ "There is a covenant between me and you as between my father and your father. I am sending you silver and gold. Go and break your covenant with Baasha king of Israel so that he might leave me."

⁴ And Ben-Hadad listened to King Asa, and he sent the commanders of his armies against the cities of Israel. They struck down Ijon, Dan, Abel Maim, and all the depot cities of Naphtali. ⁵ And it happened when Baasha heard this, that he stopped building Ramah and he ceased his work. ⁶ Then King Asa took all of Judah, and they took the stones of Ramah and its timber that Baasha had used to build, and he built with them Geba and Mizpah.

⁷ And at that time Hanani the seer came to King Asa of Judah saying, "Because you depended on the king of Aram and did not depend on the Lord your God, therefore the army of the king of Aram escaped from your hand. ⁸ Were not the Cushites and Libyans a very large army with chariots and horses, but when you depended on the Lord, He gave them to your hand. ⁹ For the eyes of the Lord move about on all the earth to strengthen the heart that is completely toward Him. You have acted foolishly in this, and from this point forward you will have wars."

¹⁰ Then Asa was angry with the seer and placed him in prison stocks, for he was enraged by these words. Asa even oppressed some of the people during this time.

The Death of Asa

¹¹ The events of Asa from beginning to end are written in the book of the kings of Judah and Israel. ¹² In the thirty-ninth year of the reign of Asa, he had a sickness in his feet until his sickness became grave. Even in his disease he did not seek after the Lord, but the physicians. ¹³ So Asa slept with his fathers; he died in the forty-first year of his reign. ¹⁴ And they buried him in the tomb that he cut for himself in the City of David. And they placed him on a place filled with all types of spices mixed with ointments, and then they burned him up with a very great conflagration.

Jehoshaphat, King of Judah

17 Then Jehoshaphat his son reigned in his place, and he grew strong against Israel. ² He put an army in all the fortified cities of Judah and set military garrisons in the land of Judah, even in the cities of Ephraim that Asa his father had captured.

³ Now the Lord was with Jehoshaphat, for he walked in the previous ways of David his father, and he did not seek out the Baal cult. ⁴ For he sought out the God of his fathers and walked in his commandments, rather than the deeds of Israel. ⁵ So the Lord made firm the kingdom in his hand, and all Judah gave a tribute to Jehoshaphat. So he had an abundance of riches and honor. ⁶ His heart was raised up for the ways of the Lord. He even removed the high places and Asherah poles from Judah.

⁷ In the third year of his reign he sent officials, Ben-Hail, Obadiah, Zechariah, Nethanel, and Micaiah, to teach in the cities of Jerusalem, ⁸ and with them were also the Levites: Shemaiah, Nethaniah, Zebadiah, Asahel, Shemiramoth, Jehonathan, Adonijah, Tobijah, and Tob-Adonijah, who were Levites. And with these were also Elishama and Jehoram, who were priests. ⁹ They taught *the people* in Judah, and they used the Book of the Law of the Lord and they traveled about all the cities of Judah and taught the people.

¹⁰ The terror of the Lord came on all the kingdoms of the land that surrounded Judah, and they did not bring war against Jehoshaphat. ¹¹ Some from the Philistine peoples brought gifts to Jehoshaphat such as silver for tribute. The Arabians even brought seven thousand seven hundred rams and seven thousand seven hundred goats to him.

¹² Jehoshaphat continued to increase in greatness, and he built citadels and storehouses in Judah. ¹³ And he had much property in the cities of Judah, and the men of war, mighty men of valor, were in Jerusalem. ¹⁴ This was their divisions by the houses of their father:

From Judah, the commanders of thousands:
Adnah the commander with three hundred thousand mighty men of valor.
¹⁵ Beside him was Jehohanan the commander with two hundred eighty thousand mighty men of war.
¹⁶ Beside him was Amasiah the son of Zikri, a volunteer for the Lord with two hundred thousand mighty men of war.
¹⁷ From Benjamin:
Eliada a mighty man of war with two hundred thousand men armed with bow and shield.
¹⁸ Beside him was Jehozabad with one hundred and eighty thousand equipped for warfare.

¹⁹ These were serving the king in addition to those the king placed in the fortified cities throughout Judah.

Micaiah Prophesies Against Ahab
1Ki 22:1–28

18 Now Jehoshaphat had great riches and honor, and he married into the family of Ahab. ² At the end of some years he went down to Ahab in Samaria. And Ahab slaughtered a great amount of sheep and oxen for Jehoshaphat and those who journeyed with him and then lured him up to Ramoth Gilead. ³ And King Ahab of Israel said to King Jehoshaphat of Judah, "Will you go up with me to Ramoth Gilead?"

And he responded, "I am as you are, and as your people also my people are. We will be with you in this war." ⁴ And Jehoshaphat further said to the king of Israel, "Inquire today the word of the Lord on this."

⁵ So the king of Israel gathered together four hundred prophets, and he inquired from them, "Should I go up to Ramoth Gilead for battle, or should I cease from this?"

They said, "Go up, for God will give this to the hand of the king." ⁶ But Jehoshaphat said, "Is there not still here another prophet for the Lord from whom we might inquire?"

⁷ Then the king of Israel responded to Jehoshaphat, "There is still one man from whom we can seek the Lord, but I hate him because he does not prophesy anything good for me but always disaster. He is Micaiah the son of Imlah."

And Jehoshaphat said, "May the king not speak like this."

⁸ So the king of Israel called to a court eunuch and said, "Hurry and bring Micaiah the son of Imlah."

⁹ And the king of Israel and Jehoshaphat the king of Judah were sitting on their own thrones, clothed in their *royal* garments, at the threshing floor at the entrance at the gate of Samaria, and all the prophets were prophesying before them. ¹⁰ Then Zedekiah the son of Kenaanah made for himself iron horns, and he said, "Thus says the Lord: With these you will thrust out the Arameans in Syria until they are finished."

¹¹ And all the prophets were prophesying the same, "Go up to Ramoth Gilead and find success, because the Lord has given the king into your hands."

¹² And the messenger who went to call Micaiah said to him, "The words of the prophets are as one voice and *only* for good to the king, so may your word be like one of them, and you speak favorably."

¹³ And Micaiah said, "As the Lord lives, whatever my God says, that will I speak."

¹⁴ When he came to the king, the king said to him, "Micaiah, should we go up to Ramoth Gilead for battle, or should I cease?"

He said, "All of you go up and be successful, and they will be given into your hands."

¹⁵ Then the king said to him, "How many times must I cause you to swear that you speak to me only truth in the name of the Lord?"

¹⁶ Then he said, "I saw all Israel scattered on the mountains like sheep that have no shepherd. The Lord said, 'There are no masters for them. Let each man return to his home in peace.' "

¹⁷ Then the king of Israel said to Jehoshaphat, "Did I not say to you that he would not prophesy good concerning me, but evil?"

¹⁸ So the *prophet* said, "Now hear the word of the Lord: I saw the Lord sitting on His throne and the heavenly assembly was standing at His right and His left. ¹⁹ And the Lord said, 'Who will deceive Ahab king of Israel so that he might go up and fall at Ramoth Gilead?'

"One was saying one thing, and another was saying something else. ²⁰ Then a spirit came out and stood before the Lord, and he said, 'I will deceive him.'

"Then the Lord said to him, 'How?'

²¹ "Then he said, 'I will go out and be a spirit of deception in the mouth of all the prophets.'

"Then the *Lord* said, 'You will deceive and find success. Go out and do this.'

²² "Now see that the Lord has put a spirit of deception in the mouth of your prophets. So the Lord has declared disaster over you."

²³ Then Zedekiah the son of Kenaanah came near to Micaiah and struck him on the cheek. And he said, "Which way then did the spirit from the Lord pass from me to speak with you?"

²⁴ Then Micaiah said, "You will see *it* on the day when you enter an inner chamber to hide yourself."

²⁵ And the king of Israel said, "Seize Micaiah and take him to Amon, the governor of the city, and to Joash the son of the king, ²⁶ and you will say, 'So says the king: Put him in a prison, and feed him a little food and water until I return in peace.' "

²⁷ Then Micaiah said, "If you certainly return in peace, then the Lord has not spoken by me. Listen, all you people!"

The Death of Ahab
1Ki 22:29–36

²⁸ So the king of Israel and Jehoshaphat the king of Judah went up to Ramoth Gilead. ²⁹ Then the king of Israel said to Jehoshaphat, "I will disguise myself and go into battle, but you will put on your clothes." So the king of Israel disguised himself, and they both entered into battle.

³⁰ And the king of Aram ordered the commanders of his chariots, "Do not wage war with the small or great but with the king of Israel alone." ³¹ And it happened when the commanders of the chariots saw Jehoshaphat they said, "It is the king of Israel." So they turned on him to wage war. But Jehoshaphat cried out, and the Lord helped him, then God drew them away from the *king*. ³² And it happened when the commanders of the chariots saw that he was not the king of Israel, then they turned away from him.

³³ But a man pulled his bow at random and struck the king of Israel between his armor scales and body armor. He said to the commander of the chariot, "Turn and remove me from the battle because I am wounded." ³⁴ And the battle continued on that day, and the king of Israel was set up in his chariot before the Arameans until evening. Then he died when the sun set.

19 But Jehoshaphat king of Judah returned to his palace in Jerusalem in peace. [2] And Jehu the son of Hanani the seer went out to meet him, and he said to King Jehoshaphat, "How do you help those who are wicked and love those who hate the LORD? Because of this, wrath has gone out against you from the LORD. [3] However, some good things are found in you for you swept away the Asherah poles from the land, and you set your heart to seek after God."

The Reforms of Jehoshaphat

[4] Jehoshaphat lived in Jerusalem, but he went out among the people from Beersheba to the hill country of Ephraim, and he brought them back to the LORD God of their fathers. [5] And he set judges in the land among all the fortified cities of Judah, one by one. [6] And he said to the judges, "Consider carefully what you do because you do not judge according to man but the LORD, and He is with you in the matter of judgment. [7] So now may the fear of the LORD be on you. Consider and act *well* because there is no injustice, partiality, or bribe taking with the LORD our God."

[8] Moreover, Jehoshaphat appointed in Jerusalem some from the Levites and the priests and some from the heads of the families of Israel, in order to render judgment and decide disputes before the LORD; and they lived in Jerusalem. [9] And he commanded them, "So you will act in the fear of the LORD, in honesty, and with a complete heart. [10] And any dispute that comes before you all from your brothers who live in their cities, concerning bloodshed or offenses against law or commandment, against statutes or judgments, you will warn them, lest they trespass against the LORD and wrath come upon you and your brothers. Do this, and you will not trespass.

[11] "Note that Amariah the chief priest is over you in all matters of the LORD; and Zebadiah the son of Ishmael, the ruler of the house of Judah, for all the king's matters; also, the Levites will be officials before you. Deal courageously, and the LORD will be with the good."

Jehoshaphat Defeats Moab and Ammon

20 After that, the Moabites and the Ammonites, together with some Meunites,[1] came against Jehoshaphat for battle. [2] And some came and declared this to Jehoshaphat, "A large multitude is coming against you from across the Dead Sea from Edom; and observe, they are in Hazezon Tamar" (that is, En Gedi). [3] Then Jehoshaphat was fearful and set himself to seek the LORD, and he called for a fast throughout all Judah. [4] And Judah was assembled to seek the LORD; even from all the cities of Judah, they came to obtain *aid* from the LORD.

[5] And Jehoshaphat stood in the midst of the assembly of Judah and Jerusalem in the house of the LORD before the new courtyard, [6] and he said:

"O LORD God of our fathers, are You not God in the heavens? And do You not rule over all the kingdoms of the nations? In Your hand are strength and might, and there is no one who can oppose You. [7] Did You not, our God, drive out those who lived in this land before Your people Israel, and You gave it perpetually to the descendants of Abraham, who was in *covenant* love with You. [8] And they have dwelled in it and have built in it for You a sanctuary for Your name saying, [9] 'If disaster comes upon us, the sword, or judgment, or pestilence, or famine, then we will stand before this temple and before You because Your name is in this temple. And we will cry out to You in our distress, and You will hear and deliver.'

[10] "Now here are the sons of Ammon and Moab and Mount Seir, whom You did not let Israel invade when they came out of the land of Egypt, when they turned away from them and did not destroy them. [11] See how they are rewarding us by coming to drive us out of Your possession, which You have given us to inherit. [12] O our God, will You not render judgment on them? For we have not strength enough to stand before this great army that is coming against us. And we do not know what we should do, but our eyes are on You."

[13] Now all of Judah was standing before the LORD, even their infants, wives, and children.

[14] And in the midst of the assembly the Spirit of the LORD came on Jahaziel the son of Zechariah, the son of Benaiah, the son of Jeiel, the son of Mattaniah, a Levite from the line of Asaph. [15] And he said, "Pay attention all Judah, and those dwelling in Jerusalem, and King Jehoshaphat: Thus says the LORD to you, 'Do not fear, nor be dismayed because of this great army, for the battle is not yours, but God's. [16] Tomorrow, go down against them. They will travel up by the Ascent of Ziz. You will find them at the back of the valley, before the Wilderness of Jeruel. [17] It will not be *necessary* for you to fight in this *conflict*. Take your positions, stand, and observe the deliverance of the LORD for you, O Judah and Jerusalem.' Do not fear or be filled with terror. Tomorrow, go out before them, and the LORD will be with you."

[18] Then Jehoshaphat bowed his face to the ground, and all Judah and those dwelling in Jerusalem fell before the LORD to worship Him. [19] And the Levites from the descendants of the Kohathites and Korahites rose up to praise the LORD God of Israel with a very loud voice.

[20] So they rose up early in the morning and went out to the Wilderness of Tekoa. And when they went out, Jehoshaphat stood and said, "Listen to me, Judah and those dwelling in Jerusalem. Believe in the LORD your God, and you will be supported. Believe His prophets, and you will succeed." [21] And he consulted with the people and then appointed singers for the LORD and those praising Him in holy attire as they went before those equipped for battle saying,

"Praise the LORD,
    for His mercy endures forever."

[22] When they began singing and praising, the LORD set ambushes against Ammon, Moab, and Mount Seir, who had come against Judah; so they were defeated. [23] Then the Ammonites and Moabites stood up against those dwelling from Mount Seir to destroy and finish them. Then when they made an end of the inhabitants of Seir, each man attacked his companion to destroy each other.

[24] And Judah came to the watchtower of the wilderness, and they turned to the vast army and saw only corpses lying on the ground. And no one was spared. [25] Then Jehoshaphat and his people came to gather their plunder, and they found among them an abundance of riches with the corpses, and precious jewelry, which they took for themselves, more than they could carry. They were gathering the plunder for three days because there was so much to carry. [26] On the fourth day they gathered at the Valley of Berakah, because there they blessed the LORD. For this reason people have called the name of this place the Valley of Berakah until this day.

[27] Then they all returned, every man from Judah and Jerusalem, with Jehoshaphat as their head, to Jerusalem with joy because the LORD made them rejoice because of the *death* of their enemies. [28] So they entered Jerusalem with harps, lyres, and trumpets to the house of the LORD.

[29] And it happened that the terror of God was on all the kingdoms of the lands who heard that the LORD had fought against the enemies of Israel. [30] So the kingdom of Jehoshaphat was quiet, because his God gave him rest on all sides.

The End of Jehoshaphat's Reign
1Ki 22:41–50

[31] And Jehoshaphat reigned over Judah. He was thirty-five years old when he began his reign, and he was king in Jerusalem for twenty-five years. The name of his mother was Azubah the daughter of Shilhi. [32] He walked in the way of his father Asa, and he did not turn aside from doing what was right in the eyes of the LORD. [33] Only the high places were not taken down. The people had yet to set their hearts to the God of their fathers.

[34] And the remainder of the acts of Jehoshaphat, from beginning to end, are written in the annals of Jehu son of Hanani, which are taken up in the book of the kings of Israel.

[35] Also, Jehoshaphat king of Judah was united with Ahaziah king of Israel, who acted wickedly. [36] Jehoshaphat joined with him to

---

[1] 1 Heb. *and others with those from the Ammonites.*

make ships to travel to Tarshish, and they made ships in Ezion Geber. [37] And Eliezer son of Dodavahu from Mareshah prophesied against Jehoshaphat saying, "Because you have joined with Ahaziah, the LORD will tear down your works." So the ships were wrecked, so that they were not able to journey to Tarshish.

21 So Jehoshaphat slept with his fathers and was buried with them in the City of David, and Jehoram his son ruled in his place. [2] And he had brothers, sons of Jehoshaphat king of Israel, Azariah, Jehiel, Zechariah, Azariahu, Michael, and Shephatiah. [3] And their father gave them great gifts of silver, gold, and excellent items, along with fortified cities in Judah, but he gave the kingdom to Jehoram because he was the firstborn.

Jehoram, King of Judah
2Ki 8:16–24

[4] Then Jehoram rose up over the kingdom of his father and he became strong. And he killed all his brothers with the sword and even some of the officials in Israel. [5] Now Jehoram was thirty-two years old when he began as king, and he reigned eight years in Jerusalem. [6] And he walked in the ways of the kings of Israel as those from the house of Ahab did, for the daughter of Ahab was the wife of Jehoram. And he did evil in the eyes of the LORD. [7] But the LORD was not willing to destroy the house of David because of the covenant that He made with David, and because He said that He would give a lamp to David and his sons for all days.

[8] In the days of Jehoram, Edom revolted from being under the hand of Judah, and they set a king for themselves. [9] So Jehoram passed over to the Edomite territory with his commanders and all his chariots, and it happened that he rose up at night and struck the Edomites, who had surrounded him and his chariot commanders. [10] So Edom revolted from being under the hand of Judah until this day.

At that time Libnah also revolted from being under their rule, because Jehoram had abandoned the LORD God of his fathers. [11] He even made high places in the hill country of Judah and caused those in Jerusalem to be like prostitutes, and he led Judah astray. [12] And a letter came to him from Elijah the prophet, saying,

"Thus says the LORD God of David your father: Because you have not walked in the ways of Jehoshaphat your father, or in the ways of Asa king of Judah, [13] but have walked in the way of the kings of Israel, and have led Judah and the inhabitants of Jerusalem into whoredom, as the house of Ahab led Israel into whoredom, and also have killed your brothers, those of your father's house, who were better than you, [14] the LORD will bring a great plague on your people, your children, your wives, and all your possessions; [15] and you will have great sickness with a disease of your intestines, until your intestines come out because of the disease, day by day."

[16] Then the LORD stirred up the spirit of the Philistines against Jehoram and also the Arabians who were near the Cushites. [17] And they went up against Judah and broke through, and they took every possession found in the palace of the king, even his sons and wives, so that no son was left with him except his youngest *Ahaziah*.

The Death of Jehoram
[18] And after all this, the LORD struck him in his entrails with an incurable disease. [19] And it happened after many days, at the end of two years, his entrails came out due to his disease, so he died by a despicable disease. And his people did not make for him a *memorial* fire like the fire for his fathers.

[20] He was thirty-two when he began to reign, and he reigned eight years in Jerusalem. And he departed with no one's regret. They buried him in the City of David, but not in the tombs of the kings.

Ahaziah, King of Judah
2Ki 8:25–29; 9:21–29

22 Then those in Jerusalem made Ahaziah, the youngest son of Jehoram, king in his place because the raiding party,

those coming with the Arabians to the camp, killed all the older sons. So Ahaziah the son of Jehoram reigned in Jerusalem.

[2] Now Ahaziah was forty-two years[1] old when he began to reign, but he only reigned one year in Jerusalem. The name of his mother was Athaliah, a granddaughter of Omri.

[3] And he also walked in the ways of the house of Ahab because his mother was the one counseling him to do evil. [4] And he also did what was evil in the eyes of the LORD, like the house of Ahab, for they served as his counselors after his father *Jehoram* died, which *led* to his destruction. [5] Even Ahaziah walked in their counsel and went with Jehoram the son of Ahab king of Israel to war against Hazael king of Aram at Ramoth Gilead. And the Arameans wounded Joram, [6] and the king returned to Jezreel to heal from the wounds that he sustained in Ramah where he fought against Hazael king of Aram.

Then Ahaziah the son of Jehoram king of Judah went down to see Joram the son of Ahab in Jezreel because he was wounded. [7] And it was from God that a downfall would happen to Ahaziah in regard to his visit with Joram. And when he arrived he went out with Joram to see Jehu the son of Nimshi, whom the LORD anointed to cut off the house of Ahab. [8] And it happened that when Jehu was acting in judgment with the house of Ahab that he found the rulers of Judah and the sons of the brothers of Ahaziah, who were serving Ahaziah, and Jehu killed them. [9] He sought out Ahaziah, and they captured him while he hid in Samaria, and they brought him to Jehu, and they put him to death. And they buried him because they said, "He is the grandson of Jehoshaphat who sought the LORD with all his heart." And there was no one from the house of Ahaziah strong enough to retain the kingdom.

Athaliah Seizes the Throne
2Ki 11:1–21

[10] So when Athaliah the mother of Ahaziah saw that her son was dead, she rose up and mounted a campaign to destroy all the royal offspring of the house of Judah. [11] But Jehoshabeath,[2] the daughter of the king, took Joash the son of Ahaziah and stole him away from the king's sons who were going to be put to death, and she placed him and his nurse in a bed chamber. So Jehoshabeath, the daughter of King Jehoram and wife of Jehoiada the priest (since she was a sister of Ahaziah), hid Joash from Athaliah. And she did not put the *royal child* to death. [12] And he was hidden away with them in the house of God for six years. And Athaliah ruled over the land.

Joash, King of Judah
23 Then in the seventh year Jehoiada strengthened himself and made a covenant with the commanders over hundreds: Azariah the son of Jeroham, Ishmael the son of Jehohanan, Azariah the son of Obed, Maaseiah the son of Adaiah, and Elishaphat the son of Zikri. [2] And they went throughout Judah and gathered the Levites from all the cities of Judah and even the heads of the fathers' houses in Israel. Then they all came to Jerusalem.

[3] So the whole assembly made a covenant with the king in the house of God, and *Jehoiada* said to them, "The king's son will reign, as the LORD has said of the sons of David. [4] And this is the thing that you all will do: A third of you all from the priests and Levites who come on the Sabbath will be gatekeepers, [5] one-third will be at the palace of the king and another third at the Foundation Gate. And all the people will be in the courts of the house of the LORD. [6] And may no one enter the house of the LORD except the priests and those Levites who are serving. Those can enter because they are holy, but all the people will keep their assigned duty of the LORD. [7] Then the Levites will surround the king, each man with his weapon in his hand, and whoever enters the house will be put to death. They will be with the king when he enters and leaves."

[8] The Levites and all Judah did everything that Jehoiada the priest commanded. Each brought his men, who were to come on duty on the Sabbath, with those who were to go off duty on the Sabbath, because Jehoiada the priest did not dismiss the divisions. [9] Then

---

[1] 2 2Ki 8:26 reads twenty-two years. [2] 11 Jehosheba in 2Ki 11:2.

Jehoiada the priest gave to the commanders of hundreds the spears and the large and small shields which had been King David's, which were in the house of God. [10] Then he set all the people around the king, each man with his weapon in hand, from the south side to the north side of the temple, from the altar to the temple.

[11] Then they brought out the son of the king and set on him the crown and the testimony and they proclaimed him as king. So Jehoiada and his sons anointed him and said, "Long live the king!"

The Death of Athaliah

[12] And when Athaliah heard the sound of the people running and praising the king, she went toward the people in the temple of the LORD. [13] And she saw the king standing by the pillar at the entrance with the officials and trumpeters next to the king, and all of the people of the land were rejoicing and blowing trumpets, and singers with their instruments with songs were offering up praise. Then Athaliah tore her garments and yelled, "Treachery! Treachery!"

[14] Then Jehoiada the priest brought out the commanders over hundreds, those entrusted over the army, and said to them, "Bring her out between the ranks, and let whoever follows her be killed with the sword." For the priest said, "Do not put her to death in the house of the LORD." [15] So they seized her, and she went to the entrance of the Horse Gate of the king's palace, and they put her to death there.

[16] And Jehoiada made a covenant between himself, the people, and the king that they would be a people *dedicated* to the LORD. [17] Then all the people went to the temple of Baal, and they tore it down along with its altars, and they shattered its images. And Mattan the priest of Baal, they killed before the altars.

[18] Then Jehoiada placed guards at the house of the LORD, under the supervision of the priests, the Levites whom David allotted for the house of the LORD to make burnt offerings to the LORD as is written in the Law of Moses, with rejoicing and music, according to the direction of David. [19] And he set the gatekeepers at the gates of the house of the LORD so that no one might enter who was in any manner unclean.

[20] Then he took the commanders over hundreds, the nobles, those in authority over the people, and all the people of the land, and they brought down the king from the house of the LORD. And they went through the Upper Gate of the palace of the king, and they brought the king to sit on the royal throne. [21] And all the people of the land rejoiced. And the city had peace when they put Athaliah to death with the sword.

Joash Repairs the Temple
2Ki 12:1–21

24 Now Joash[f] was seven years old when he started his reign, and he was king in Jerusalem for forty years. The name of his mother was Zibiah of Beersheba. [2] Joash did what was correct in the eyes of the LORD all the days of Jehoiada the priest. [3] And Jehoiada gave *Joash* two wives, and he had sons and daughters.

[4] And it happened after this that it was in the heart of Joash to restore the house of the LORD. [5] So he assembled the priests and Levites to speak with them, "Go out to the cities of Judah and collect money from all Israel to fortify the house of your God, what is necessary each year. Now hurry with this matter." But the Levites delayed.

[6] So the king called Jehoiada, who was head over this, and said to him, "Why have you not required from the Levites that they bring in from Judah and Jerusalem the tax levied by Moses, the servant of the LORD, for the congregation of Israel for the tent of the testimony?"

[7] For the sons of Athaliah, the wicked woman, had broken into the house of God and even used all the holy items of the house of the LORD for Baal *worship*.

[8] Then the king spoke, and they made a chest, and put it outside the gate of the house of the LORD. [9] And they gave a report in Judah and Jerusalem to bring in to the LORD a tax levied by Moses the servant of God on Israel in the wilderness. [10] So all the officials and people rejoiced, and they brought in *the money* and cast it into the chest until it was full. [11] And it happened that at the time the Levites brought

the chest to the guards of the king that there was a large amount of money. So the king's scribe and head priest's commissioner would bring it and empty the chest and then take it and return it to its place. They continued to do this every day and collected a great amount of money. [12] So the king and Jehoiada gave it to those doing a work of labor on the house of the LORD. And they hired masons and craftsmen to repair the house of the LORD, and even metal workers in iron and bronze to fortify the house of the LORD.

[13] So the workmen worked, and the work was completed by them. They restored the house of God to its specifications and strengthened it. [14] When they had finished, they brought the rest of the money before the king and Jehoiada, who made vessels for the house of the LORD, vessels for serving and for making burnt offerings, spoons and vessels of gold and silver. They continually offered burnt offerings in the house of the LORD all the days of Jehoiada.

[15] Then Jehoiada became old and full of days and died. He was one hundred and thirty years old when he died. [16] So they buried him in the City of David with the kings, because he had done good in Israel, both toward God and His house.

The Wickedness of Joash

[17] After the death of Jehoiada the officials of Judah came and paid homage to the king. At that time the king listened to them. [18] Then they abandoned the house of the LORD and God of their fathers, and they served the Asherah poles and idols. And *divine* wrath was on Judah and Jerusalem because of this guilt. [19] And *God* sent prophets to return them to the LORD. These warned the *people*, but they would not listen.

[20] Then the Spirit of God clothed Zechariah the son of Jehoiada the priest, and he stood above the people saying, "Thus says God: Why are you transgressing the commandments of the LORD so that you all will not be successful? Because you all have abandoned the LORD, He has abandoned you."

[21] But they plotted against him, and at the command of the king they all stoned him in the court of the house of the LORD. [22] And Joash the king did not remember the kindness that Jehoiada the father of Zechariah had shown him, but killed his son. As he was dying, he said, "May the LORD see and avenge!"

The Death of Joash

[23] And it happened that at the turn of the year the army of Aram came up against Joash. They came to Judah and Jerusalem and destroyed all the officials of the people, and they sent all their plunder to the king of Damascus. [24] Though the Aramean army came with a few men, the LORD delivered into their hand a very great Judean army because they abandoned the LORD God of their fathers. So they enacted judgment on Joash. [25] When they left him (for they abandoned him with severe wounds) his own servants plotted against him because of the blood of the son of Jehoiada the priest. So they killed him on his bed. So he died, and they buried him in the City of David, but they did not bury him in the tombs of the kings.

[26] And those who conspired against him were Zabad the son of Shimeath the Ammonite and Jehozabad the son of Shimrith the Moabite. [27] Accounts of his sons and of the many oracles against him and of the rebuilding of the house of God are written in the annals of the kings. And Amaziah his son ruled in his place.

Amaziah, King of Judah
2Ki 14:1–20

25 Amaziah was twenty-five years old when he was king, and he reigned twenty-nine years in Jerusalem. The name of his mother was Jehoaddan from Jerusalem. [2] He did what was correct in the eyes of the LORD, only not with a complete heart. [3] And it happened that when the kingdom was firmly his that he killed his servants, those who struck down his father King Joash. [4] But he did not put to death their children because, as it is written in the Law in the Book of Moses, as the LORD commanded, "You will not put to death the fathers for their children's *actions* nor the children will

you put to death for their fathers' *actions*, for every man will be put to death for his own sin."

Slaughter of the Edomites
[5] Then Amaziah assembled Judah and set over them according to the house of the fathers commanders of thousands and hundreds in all Judah and Benjamin, and he appointed men who were twenty years old and above. And they found three hundred thousand choice men fit for war and able to use a long spear and large shield. [6] And he hired out from Israel one hundred thousand mighty men of war for one hundred talents *¹* of silver.
[7] Then a man of God came to him saying, "O king, do not let the army of Israel come with you because the LORD is not with Israel or with any of the sons of Ephraim. [8] But if you go, do it. Be strong for the battle. Yet God shall make you fall before the enemy, for God has power to help and to bring down."
[9] Then Amaziah said to the man of God, "So what should I do about the one hundred talents of silver that I gave to the military party from Israel?"
And the man of God responded, "The LORD has more to give to you than this."
[10] So Amaziah dismissed the military party that came to him from Ephraim to return to their place. And they were very angry with Judah and returned to their place in a great rage.
[11] But Amaziah strengthened himself and led his people, and he journeyed to the Valley of Salt and struck down ten thousand of the people of Seir. [12] And the people of Judah took captive another ten thousand alive and brought them to the top of a cliff and threw them from the top of the rock so that they were all dashed to pieces.
[13] But the men of the military party that Amaziah turned back from going with him in battle raided the cities of Judah from Samaria to Beth Horon. They struck down three thousand *Judeans* and took a great amount of plunder.
[14] And it happened after Amaziah came back from striking down the Edomites, he brought back the gods of the people from Seir and set them up as gods for himself. He worshipped them and gave them sacrifices. [15] So the LORD was greatly angry with Amaziah, and He sent a prophet to the *king*. And he said, "Why do you seek from the gods of the people who were not even able to deliver the people from your hand?"
[16] But while the *prophet* was speaking, the *king* said, "Have we made you a counselor to the king? Stop! Why should you be struck down?"
The prophet refrained, but he said, "I know that God has determined to destroy you because you have done this and not heeded my advice."

Israel Defeats Judah
[17] Then Amaziah king of Judah received advice and sent for Jehoash *²* the son of Jehoahaz, the son of Jehu king of Israel, saying, "Come, let us meet together."
[18] So Jehoash king of Israel sent a *message* for Amaziah king of Judah saying, "A thistle in Lebanon sent for a cedar in Lebanon stating, 'Give your daughter to my son as a wife.' Then an animal of the field in Lebanon passed by and trampled the thistle. [19] You say that you have struck down Edom, and your heart lifts you up in arrogance. Now remain in your palace. Why do you provoke disaster so that you fall, you and Judah with you?"
[20] But Amaziah would not listen because this was from God so that He might give them into the hand of *Jehoash* because Amaziah had sought after the gods of Edom. [21] So Jehoash king of Israel went up, and they faced each other, he and Amaziah king of Judah, at Beth Shemesh, which is in Judah. [22] And Judah was struck down by Israel, and each man fled to his home. [23] So at Beth Shemesh, Jehoash king of Israel seized Amaziah king of Judah the son of Joash, the son of Ahaziah. And they brought him to Jerusalem and broke through the walls of the city from the Ephraim Gate to the Corner Gate, a section of four hundred cubits. *³* [24] And

Jehoash took all the gold and silver and all the vessels that were found in the house of God with Obed-Edom, even the treasures of the palace of the king and hostages. Then he returned to Samaria.

The Death of Amaziah
[25] And Amaziah, the son of Joash king of Judah, lived fifteen years more after the death of Jehoash, the son of Jehoahaz king of Israel. [26] Now the rest of the acts of Amaziah, from first to last, are they not written in the book of the kings of Judah and Israel? [27] From the time when Amaziah turned aside from the LORD, they plotted a conspiracy against him in Jerusalem, and he fled to Lachish. Then they sent for him and put him to death in Lachish. [28] They brought him on horses and buried him with his fathers in the City of David in Judah.

Uzziah, King of Judah
2Ki 14:21–22; 15:1–7

26 And all the people of Judah took Uzziah *⁴* and made him king in the place of his father Amaziah when he was sixteen years old. [2] He built Eloth and restored it to Judah after *Amaziah* the king slept with his fathers.
[3] Uzziah was sixteen years old when he began to reign, and he was king in Jerusalem for fifty-two years. The name of his mother was Jekoliah from Jerusalem. [4] And he did what was correct in the eyes of the LORD as everything his father Amaziah had done. [5] And he sought after God in the days of Zechariah, the one who instructed him in the fear of the LORD. And in the days that he sought after the LORD, God caused him to succeed.
[6] He went out to make war with the Philistines, and he broke through the walls at Gath and Jabneh and Ashdod. Then he built cities in Ashdod and among the Philistines. [7] And God brought him aid against the Philistines and Arabians, those living in Gur Baal, and the Meunites. [8] And the Ammonites gave a gift to Uzziah, and his name spread even to the border of Egypt because he became quite powerful.
[9] Uzziah built towers in Jerusalem at the Corner Gate, at the Valley Gate, and at the corner buttress; and he fortified them. [10] And he built towers in the wilderness, and he dug out many cisterns because he had a large amount of livestock, both in the lowland Shephelah and in the plain. He also had workers in the fields and vineyards in the hills and fertile orchards, for he loved agriculture.
[11] And Uzziah had an army prepared for battle, those who went out for war as companies in the number of their divisions by the appointment of Jeiel the scribe, and Maaseiah the officer, and Hananiah a commander of the king. [12] The total number of chief officers of the mighty men of valor was two thousand six hundred. [13] And under their hand was a mighty army of three hundred and seven thousand five hundred who were able to go to battle as a strong army and to help the king against his enemies. [14] And Uzziah prepared for the entire army shields, long spears, helmets, scale armor, bows, and slings for stones. [15] In Jerusalem he made war machines by skilled men to be placed on towers and corners to shoot arrows and large stones. And his name went out for a great distance. He received great help until he was even more powerful.

Uzziah's Punishment for Pride
[16] And as he grew strong, his heart grew more proud, leading to his destruction. Then he acted unfaithfully against the LORD his God, for he entered the temple main hall of the LORD to burn incense on the altar. [17] But Azariah the priest entered in after him, and with him were eighty priests of the LORD—men of valor. [18] And they stood against King Uzziah and said to him, "It is not for you, Uzziah, to burn incense to the LORD for it is for the priests, the sons of Aaron, who are consecrated to burn incense. Leave from the sanctuary because you have been unfaithful, and there will be no honor for you from the LORD God."
[19] Then Uzziah was enraged, and in his hand was a censer for incense. And when he became angry with the priests, leprosy appeared on his forehead in front of the priests in the house of the

---

16 About 3¾ tons, or 3.4 metric tons; also in v. 9.   *²17* Heb. text has *Joash*, but *Jehoash* is also given to distinguish between the Judean and Israelite kings.   *³23* About 600 feet, or 180 meters.   *⁴1* Also known as Azariah in 2Ki 15.

LORD, near the altar of incense. ²⁰ Then Azariah the head priest and all the priests turned to him, and he had leprosy on his forehead; and they hastened to remove him from there, and he also hurried to leave because the LORD had struck him.

²¹ So King Uzziah had leprosy until the day of his death. He dwelt in a separate house with his *unclean* disease because he was cut off from the house of the LORD. Then Jotham his son was over the house of the king, and he governed the people of the land.

²² Now the remainder of the acts of Uzziah, from beginning to end, Isaiah the prophet, son of Amoz, has written *them*. ²³ So Uzziah slept with his fathers, and they buried him with his fathers in the burial field belonging to the kings because they said, "He is a leper." And Jotham his son ruled in his place.

Jotham, King of Judah
2Ki 15:33–38

27 Jotham was twenty-five years old when he began as king, and he reigned sixteen years in Jerusalem. The name of his mother was Jerushah the daughter of Zadok. ² And he did what was correct in the eyes of the LORD just as his father Uzziah had done. However, he did not enter the temple of the LORD. But the people continued acting corruptly. ³ And he built the Upper Gate of the house of the LORD, and he built much on the wall of Ophel. ⁴ And he built cities in the hill country of Judah, and on the wooded heights he built citadels and towers.

⁵ He made war with the king of the Ammonites and prevailed against them. That year the Ammonites gave to him one hundred talents¹ of silver, ten thousand kors² of wheat, and ten thousand kors³ of barley. The Ammonites paid him the same amount in the second and third years as well.

⁶ So Jotham was strengthened because he established his ways before the LORD his God.

⁷ And the remainder of the acts of Jotham, all his wars and ways, are written in the book of the kings of Israel and Judah. ⁸ He was twenty-five years old when he began to reign, and he was king for sixteen years in Jerusalem. ⁹ And Jotham slept with his fathers, and they buried him in the City of David. And Ahaz his son reigned in his place.

Ahaz, King of Judah
2Ki 16:1–20

28 Ahaz was twenty years old when he began to reign, and he was king in Jerusalem for sixteen years. And he did not do what was correct in the eyes of the LORD as David his father. ² And he walked in the ways of the kings of Israel, and he cast images for Baal worship. ³ And he made sacrifices in the Valley of Ben Hinnom, and he burned his sons in the fire according to the detestable acts of the nations that the LORD had displaced before the sons of Israel. ⁴ He even made sacrifices and offered incense on the high places of the hills and under every green tree.

Judah Defeated

⁵ So the LORD his God gave him into the hand of the king of Aram. They struck *Ahaz* and took captive many prisoners and brought them to Damascus.

He was even given into the hand of the king of Israel, and he attacked *Ahaz* with a great slaughter. ⁶ And Pekah the son of Remaliah killed one hundred and twenty thousand in Judah in one day, and they were all strong men, but they abandoned the LORD God of their fathers. ⁷ And Zikri, a mighty warrior from Ephraim, killed Maaseiah the son of the king, and Azrikam the official of the palace, and Elkanah second to the king. ⁸ And the sons of Israel took captive two hundred thousand of their kin, women, sons, and daughters. They also took much plunder and brought the plunder to Samaria.

⁹ And there was a prophet there whose name was Oded, and he went out to the army as it approached Samaria and said to them, "See that the anger of the LORD God of your fathers is against Judah, and He gave them into your hand, and you all have killed them in

a rage that has reached even to heaven. ¹⁰ And now you are planning to subdue for yourselves the people of Judah and Jerusalem as male and female slaves. Do you all not surely have among you guilt before the LORD your God? ¹¹ And now listen to me. Return the captives whom you have taken captive from your relatives because the burning wrath of the LORD is on you all."

¹² And some men who were heads of the people of Ephraim rose up before those coming from the war: Azariah the son of Jehohanan, Berekiah the son of Meshillemoth, Jehizkiah the son of Shallum, and Amasa the son of Hadlai. ¹³ And they said, "You will not bring the captives here, for guilt from the LORD will be on us, and you plan to add to our sin and guilt. Our guilt is great, and there is *already* a burning anger against Israel."

¹⁴ So the soldiers left the captives and spoil before the officials and all the assembly. ¹⁵ Then the men who were designated by name took the captives *and* clothed those who were naked from the plunder. So they clothed them, gave them sandals, offered them food and drink, anointed them with oil, and led them on donkeys, even all those who stumbled. They brought them to Jericho, the city of palm trees, which was near their kinsmen. Then the *officials* returned to Samaria.

¹⁶ At that time King Ahaz sent to the king of Assyria for help. ¹⁷ The Edomites continually came and struck Judah and carried off captives. ¹⁸ Even the Philistines made raids on the cities of the lowlands of the Shephelah and the Negev of Judah. And they captured Beth Shemesh, Aijalon, Gederoth, Soko and its villages, Timnah and its villages, and Gimzo and its villages; and they settled there. ¹⁹ For the LORD humbled Judah because of Ahaz king of Judah, for he allowed depravity to spread in Judah and continually transgressed against the LORD. ²⁰ So Tiglath-Pileser king of Assyria came against him, but he brought him distress and not strength. ²¹ For Ahaz took a portion from the house of the LORD and palace of the king and the officials, and he gave it to the king of Assyria, but the king did not help Ahaz.

The Death of Ahaz

²² And at the time that he was oppressed he increased in unfaithfulness against the LORD. ²³ So he sacrificed to the gods of Damascus that had devastated him, for he said, "Because the gods of the kings of Aram have helped them, I will sacrifice to them so that they might help me." But they were his downfall *in Judah* and the downfall for all of Israel.

²⁴ And Ahaz gathered the vessels from the house of God, and he cut up the vessels. Then he shut the doors of the house of the LORD, and he made altars in every corner of Jerusalem. ²⁵ Then in every city in Judah he made high places to make offerings to other gods. So he provoked the LORD God of his fathers.

²⁶ Now the remainder of the acts and all his ways, from first to last, are written in the book of the kings of Judah and Israel. ²⁷ So Ahaz slept with his fathers, and they buried him in the city of Jerusalem because they did not bring him to the tombs of the kings of Israel. Then Hezekiah his son was king in his place.

Hezekiah, King of Judah
2Ki 18:2–3

29 Hezekiah was twenty-five years old when he began to reign, and he was king in Jerusalem for twenty-nine years. The name of his mother was Abijah⁴ the daughter of Zechariah. ² And he did what was correct in the eyes of the LORD just as his father David had done.

Hezekiah Cleanses the Temple

³ And in the first year and first month of his reign he opened the doors of the house of the LORD and restored them. ⁴ He then brought in the priests and Levites and gathered them in the square on the eastern side ⁵ and said to them, "Listen to me, Levites. Consecrate yourselves and consecrate the house of the LORD God of your fathers. And bring out the detestable things from the holy sanctuary. ⁶ For our fathers have acted unfaithfully and have done what is evil in the

---

¹⁵ About 3¾ tons, or 3.4 metric tons.   ²⁵ Likely about 1,800 tons, or 1,600 metric tons of wheat.
³⁵ Likely about 1,500 tons, or 1,350 metric tons of barley.   ⁴¹ Or Abi in 2Ki 18:2.

eyes of the LORD our God, and they have abandoned Him. They have turned their face from the sanctuary of the LORD and have turned their back. [7] They also shut the doors of the vestibule and have extinguished the lamps, nor have they burned incense or burnt offerings in the Holy Place to the God of Israel. [6] Therefore the wrath of the LORD has come on Judah and Jerusalem for a terror, horror, and scorn as you all can see with your own eyes. [9] Observe, our fathers have fallen by the sword, and now our sons, daughters, and wives are in captivity for all this. [10] Now it is in my heart to make a covenant with the LORD God of Israel so that His burning anger might turn away from us. [11] My people, do not now be negligent for the LORD has chosen you all to stand in His presence, to serve Him, and to be ministers and make sacrifices for Him."

[12] Then the Levites arose:
from the Kohathites,
    Mahath son of Amasai and Joel son of Azariah;
from the Merarites,
    Kish son of Abdi and Azariah son of Jehallelel;
from the Gershonites,
    Joah son of Zimmah and Eden son of Joah;
[13] from the descendants of Elizaphan,
    Shimri and Jeiel;
from the descendants of Asaph,
    Zechariah and Mattaniah;
[14] from the descendants of Heman,
    Jehiel and Shimei;
from the descendants of Jeduthun,
    Shemaiah and Uzziel.

[15] So they gathered their brothers together and consecrated themselves and entered in as the king commanded by the words of the LORD in order to cleanse the house of the LORD. [16] Then the priests came into the inner part of the house of the LORD to cleanse it, and they removed everything that they found that was unclean in the main hall of the temple of the LORD to the court. And the Levites took those things and brought them out to the Kidron Valley. [17] They began to consecrate themselves on the first day of the first month, and on the eighth day of the month they entered the vestibule of the LORD. They consecrated the house of the LORD for eight days. Then on the sixteenth day of the first month they completed *the task*. [18] Then they came toward Hezekiah the king and said, "We have cleaned the entire house of the LORD, the altar of burnt offerings and all its utensils, and the table for showbread and all its utensils. [19] All the vessels that King Ahaz discarded from use during his reign in his treachery we have prepared and consecrated. They are before the altar of the LORD."

Hezekiah Restores Temple Worship

[20] So King Hezekiah got up early and gathered the officials of the city and went up to the house of the LORD. [21] And he brought seven bulls, seven rams, seven lambs, and seven male goats for a sin offering for the kingdom, sanctuary, and Judah. Then he commanded the priests, the sons of Aaron, to offer them up on the altar of the LORD. [22] So they slaughtered the bulls, and the priests took their blood and sprinkled it on the altar and then slaughtered the rams and sprinkled their blood on the altar. They did the same for the lambs. [23] And they brought the male goats for a sin offering before the king and the assembly, and they placed their hands on *the goats*. [24] And the priests slaughtered them and purified the altar with their blood to provide atoning reconciliation for all Israel because the king said that the burnt offering and sin offering would be for all Israel.

[25] And he set the Levites at the house of the LORD with cymbals, harps, and lyres according to the commandment of David, and Gad the seer of the king, and Nathan the prophet. For the commandment came from the LORD through His prophets. [26] So the Levites stood with the instruments of David and the priests with the trumpets.

[27] Then Hezekiah gave the command to offer the burnt offering on the altar. When they started the burnt offering, the song of the LORD began also, with the trumpets and the instruments of David, king of Israel. [28] The entire assembly worshipped, the singers sang,

and the trumpeters sounded. All of this took place until the burnt offering was finished.

[29] When the burnt offering was finished, the king and all those with him bowed down and worshipped. [30] Then Hezekiah the king and the officials ordered the Levites to praise the LORD with the words of David and Asaph the seer. So they praised with gladness and bowed down to worship.

[31] Then Hezekiah responded, "Now you have dedicated yourselves to the LORD. Come near and bring sacrifices and thank offerings to the house of the LORD." So the assembly brought sacrifices and thank offerings, and all who had a willing heart brought burnt offerings.

[32] The number of the burnt offerings that the assembly brought was seventy bulls, one hundred rams, and two hundred lambs; all these were for a burnt offering to the LORD. [33] The consecrated animals were six hundred bulls and three thousand sheep. [34] However there were too few priests, and they were not able to skin the burnt offerings. But their brothers the Levites helped them until the work was finished and more priests consecrated themselves, for the Levites were more upright in heart to consecrate themselves than the priests. [35] Also burnt offerings were in abundance with the fat of the peace offerings and the drink offerings for the burnt offerings. So the service of the house of the LORD was set in order. [36] Then Hezekiah and all the people rejoiced that God had prepared the people, since the events happened suddenly.

Hezekiah Celebrates the Passover

30 And Hezekiah sent word to all Israel and Judah. He even wrote letters to Ephraim and Manasseh, that they come to the house of the LORD in Jerusalem to keep the Passover to the LORD God of Israel. [2] The king counseled with his officials and all the assembly in Jerusalem to have the Passover in the second month. [3] For they were not able to have it at the appropriate time *of the first month* because a sufficient amount of priests had not consecrated themselves, nor had the people assembled yet in Jerusalem. [4] And this matter was pleasing in the eyes of the king and all the assembly. [5] So they decreed to make a proclamation throughout all Israel, from Beersheba to Dan, that they come to keep the Passover to the LORD God of Israel in Jerusalem, for the *multitude of people* did not do as it was written. [6] So couriers ran throughout all Israel and Judah with a letter from the hand of the king and his officials as a command from the king:

"Sons of Israel, return to the LORD of Abraham, Isaac, and Israel that He might turn to the remnant who has escaped from the king of Assyria. [7] Do not act like your fathers and brothers who were faithless before the LORD God of their fathers, and He appointed them for horror, as you observe. [8] So now do not harden your necks as your fathers, but give yourselves to the LORD and come to the sanctuary that He has consecrated permanently. Serve the LORD your God so that His burning anger might turn away from you all. [9] Because if you return to the LORD, your brothers and children will find compassion before those who have taken them captive, in order to return you to this land. For the LORD your God is gracious and compassionate. He will not turn His face from you if you all return to Him."

[10] So the couriers ran from city to city in the land of Ephraim and Manasseh and up to Zebulun, but *the people* laughed at them and mocked them. [11] However some men from Asher, Manasseh, and Zebulun humbled themselves and journeyed to Jerusalem. [12] And even in Judah the hand of God was on them to give them one heart to do the commandment of the king and officials by the word of the LORD.

[13] And many people assembled in Jerusalem to have the Feast of Unleavened Bread in the second month. There was a very large assembly. [14] They went out and removed the altars that were in Jerusalem, and they took away all the incense altars and threw *them* into the Kidron Valley.

[15] They slaughtered the Passover lamb on the fourteenth day of the second month. The priests and Levites were ashamed, and

they consecrated themselves and brought in burnt offerings to the house of the LORD. [16] They stood at their places according to the Law of Moses, the man of God; the priests sprinkled the blood they received from the hands of the Levites. [17] For there were many in the assembly who had consecrated themselves, so the Levites slaughtered the Passover lamb for those who were not clean in order to consecrate *the people* to the LORD. [18] For a multitude of the people—many from Ephraim, Manasseh, Issachar, and Zebulun—had not purified themselves. For they ate of the Passover contrary to what was written. But Hezekiah prayed over them saying, "The LORD is good, and may He pardon [19] everyone who sets his heart to seek God, the LORD God of his fathers, but is not pure according the *rules of the* holy sanctuary." [20] So the LORD heard Hezekiah and healed the people.

[21] Then the sons of Israel present in Jerusalem kept the Feast of Unleavened Bread for seven days with great joy, and the Levites and priests praised the LORD every day, *singing* with loud instruments to the LORD.

[22] Then Hezekiah spoke encouragingly to all the Levites who taught the good knowledge of the LORD. So they ate for the appointed seven days, sacrificing peace offerings and giving thanks to the LORD God of their fathers.

[23] Then the whole assembly counseled to have the *feast* for another seven days, so they had seven more days of gladness. [24] For Hezekiah king of Judah lifted up for the assembly one thousand bulls and seven thousand sheep. And the officials offered up for the assembly one thousand bulls and ten thousand sheep. And a multitude of priests consecrated themselves. [25] So all the assembly of Judah and the priests and Levites and all the assembly who came from Israel rejoiced, even the sojourners who came from the land of Israel and those who resided in Judah. [26] And there was a great rejoicing in Jerusalem, for since the days of Solomon son of David king of Israel there had not been anything like this. [27] Then the priests and Levites went out and blessed the people, and their voices were heard. And their prayers came up to His holy habitation in the heavens.

31 And when this *celebration* was finished, all of Israel that was present went out to the cities of Judah and smashed the sacred pillars and cut down the Asherah poles and tore down the high places and the altars throughout all Judah and Benjamin, and in Ephraim and Manasseh, until everything was destroyed. Then all Israel returned to their cities, each man to his own possession.

Temple Contributions
2Ki 18:5–7

[2] And Hezekiah set up the divisions of the priests and Levites according to their divisions, each man as he worked among the priests and Levites for burnt and fellowship offerings, to serve, give thanks, and offer praise at the gates of the camp of the LORD. [3] And the portion of the king that came from his own possessions was for burnt offerings, those given in the morning and evening, and those given for Sabbaths, New Moons, and appointed feasts, as written in the Law of the LORD. [4] And he ordered those people living in Jerusalem to give a portion for the priests and Levites, in order for them to devote themselves to the Law of the LORD. [5] And when the command spread, the sons of Israel gave generously the first fruits of grain, wine, oil, honey, and all the produce of the field. And they brought in abundance a tenth portion of everything. [6] And the sons of Israel and Judah and all who dwelled in the cities of Judah also brought in a tenth portion of cattle and sheep, and a tenth portion of the consecrated items that were to the LORD their God, and brought them in and set them in great piles. [7] In the third month they began to assign the piles of contribution, and they finished in the seventh month. [8] When Hezekiah and the officials saw the contribution piles, they blessed the LORD and His people Israel.

[9] Then Hezekiah questioned the priests and Levites regarding the contribution piles. [10] Azariah the head priest from the house of Zadok said, "Since they began to bring the contributions into the house of the LORD, there has been plenty of food and a large amount left over. For the LORD has blessed His people, and this great abundance is left over."

[11] Then Hezekiah ordered them to prepare chambers in the house of the LORD, and they did this. [12] They reliably brought in the contributions, tenth portions, and consecrated items. The leader over them was Konaniah the Levite, and Shimei his brother was second to him. [13] And Jehiel, Azaziah, Nahath, Asahel, Jerimoth, Jozabad, Eliel, Ismakiah, Mahath, and Benaiah were supervisors under Konaniah and Shimei his brother by the appointment of Hezekiah the king and Azariah the leader of the house of God.

[14] And Kore the son of Imnah the Levite was gatekeeper for the East Gate and over the voluntary offerings to God, to designate the contributions of the LORD and most holy offerings. [15] Eden, Miniamin, Jeshua, Shemaiah, Amariah, and Shekaniah reliably assisted him in the cities of the priests to distribute the portions to their brothers by division, both great and small.

[16] Besides those males registered from three years old and above, they distributed to all who entered into the house of the LORD his daily portion, for their services according to their duties and their divisions. [17] The registration of the priests was according to the house of their fathers and the Levites from twenty years and above, according to their duties and their divisions. [18] They were registered with all their little children, wives, sons, and daughters for the entire assembly for they consecrated themselves in faithfulness.

[19] Also for the sons of Aaron, the priests, who were in the fields of common land of their cities, there were men in each city who were designated by name to allocate portions to every male among the priests and to everyone who was registered by genealogy among the Levites.

[20] Hezekiah did this throughout all Judah, and he did what was good and just and faithful before the LORD his God. [21] And in every deed that he undertook in the service of the house of God and with the law and commandment to seek out his God, he did this with all his heart, and he found success.

Sennacherib Threatens Jerusalem
2Ki 18:17–35; 19:35–37; Isa 36:2–20; 37:36–38

32 After these things and these acts of faithfulness, Sennacherib king of Assyria came to Judah and encamped against the fortified cities thinking that he would break through them for himself. [2] When Hezekiah observed that Sennacherib had come and that he turned to war against Jerusalem, [3] he consulted with his officials and military men to stop up the waters of the springs that were outside the city, and they helped in this. [4] So, many people assembled and worked to stop up all the springs and the stream flowing through the area. They reasoned, "Why should the king of Assyria come and find a great amount of water?" [5] He then worked hard to build up all the walls that were broken down and to raise up towers. Then he built another wall outside that one and strengthened the Millo in the City of David. And he made weapons and shields in abundance.

[6] And he designated commanders for fighting over the people, and he gathered them to himself at the open square of the gate of the city and spoke encouragingly to them saying, [7] "Be strong and brave. Do not fear or have terror before the king of Assyria or before all this army that is with him because there are more who are with us than with him. [8] With this king is a strong arm of flesh, but with us is the LORD our God who will help us and fight our battles." So the people leaned on the words of Hezekiah king of Judah.

[9] After all this Sennacherib king of Assyria sent his servants to Jerusalem—while he was at Lachish with all his military force that was with him—to Hezekiah king of Judah and to all Judah that was in Jerusalem stating,

[10] "Thus says Sennacherib king of Assyria: By what do you all trust that you remain in a besieged Jerusalem? [11] Is not Hezekiah leading you all astray to give you over to death by famine and thirst when he tells you, 'The LORD our God will deliver us from the hand of the king of Assyria'? [12] Has not Hezekiah himself taken down this god's high places and altars by ordering Judah and Jerusalem, 'You all will bow down at one altar and on it burn sacrifices'?

[13] "Do you not know what I and my fathers have done to all the peoples of other lands? Were the gods of the nations of

these lands surely able to rescue their lands from my hand? [14] Who from among all the gods of these nations that my fathers utterly destroyed was able to rescue his people from my hand? For will your god be able to rescue you all from my hand? [15] Now do not let Hezekiah trick or lead you all astray in this. And do not believe him, for no god from any nation or kingdom has been able to deliver his people from my hand or the hand of my fathers. How much less will your God deliver you from my hand?"

[16] And his servants continued to speak against the LORD God and Hezekiah his servant. [17] He also wrote letters to insult the LORD God of Israel, speaking against Him, "As the gods of the nations of other lands did not rescue their people from my hand, so the god of Hezekiah will not rescue his people from my hand." [18] And they proclaimed it also in a loud voice in the Judean language against the people of Jerusalem who were on the wall to frighten and terrify them in order to capture the city. [19] They spoke about the God of Jerusalem like the gods of the other peoples of the earth, which are only objects made by men's hands.

The Death of Sennacherib

[20] So Hezekiah the king and Isaiah the prophet son of Amoz prayed concerning this. And they called out to heaven. [21] So the LORD sent an angel and destroyed the mighty army, leaders, and officials in the camp of the king of Assyria. So the king returned in shame to his own land. When he entered the temple of his god, some of his sons fell on him there with the sword. [22] So the LORD saved Hezekiah and the inhabitants of Jerusalem from the hand of Sennacherib king of Assyria, and from the hand of all others, and gave them rest on every side. [23] Many brought tribute to the LORD in Jerusalem and choice gifts to Hezekiah king of Judah so that he was lifted up before the eyes of all the nations from then on.

Hezekiah's Pride

[24] In those days Hezekiah became ill even to the point of death, so he prayed to the LORD. He spoke to the *king* and gave him a sign. [25] But Hezekiah did not make recompense for what was given to him because his heart was proud. So *divine* anger was on him, Judah, and Jerusalem. [26] Then Hezekiah humbled himself from his arrogant heart, both he and those who lived in Jerusalem, and the anger of the LORD did not come over them in the days of Hezekiah. [27] And Hezekiah had a vast amount of riches and honor, and he made treasures for himself from silver, gold, costly stones, spices, shields, and all types of precious items. [28] He made storehouses for the produce of grain, wine, and oil; and stalls for all types of livestock and flocks. [29] He also built cities for himself and acquired numbers of flocks and herds, for God had given to him a vast amount of possessions. [30] And Hezekiah shut up the upper outlet of the waters of the Gihon and directed them downward to the western side of the City of David. And Hezekiah found success in all his works. [31] But the envoys came from the officials of Babylon who were sent to him to inquire about the sign that had been given in the land. God left him *alone* in order to test *Hezekiah*, to know what was in his heart.

The Death of Hezekiah
2Ki 20:1–21; Isa 37:21–38; 38:1–8

[32] And the remainder of the acts of Hezekiah and his kind acts, they are written in the vision of Isaiah the prophet, son of Amoz, in the book of the kings of Judah and Israel. [33] So Hezekiah slept with his fathers, and they buried him in the upper tombs of the sons of David. And all those from Judah and those living in Jerusalem paid him honor at his death. Then Manasseh his son reigned in his place.

Manasseh, King of Judah
2Ki 21:1–18

33 Manasseh was twelve years old when he became king, and he was king in Jerusalem for fifty-five years. [2] But he did evil in the sight of the LORD, according to the abominations of the nations whom the LORD *previously* cast out before the sons of Israel. [3] And he turned again to build the high places that his father Hezekiah had torn down, and he set up altars to the Baals, and made Asherah poles, and worshipped the starry assembly of heaven and served them. [4] And he built altars in the house of the LORD where the LORD said, "In Jerusalem My name will be perpetual." [5] And he built altars for the starry assembly of heaven in the two courtyards of the house of the LORD. [6] He even made his sons pass through the fire in the Valley of Ben Hinnom; and he had conjurers, and practitioners of divination and sorcery, and necromancers, and mediums. So he did a great amount of evil in the eyes of the LORD, so that God was provoked. [7] And he set the carved image of a statue that he made and put in the house of God where God said to David and to Solomon his son, "In this house and in Jerusalem where I have chosen from among all the tribes of Israel, there I have set My name perpetually. [8] And I will not again remove the foot of Israel from the ground that I have designated to your fathers, if only they will keep on doing everything that I have commanded them, the whole law, statutes, and judgments from the hand of Moses." [9] So Manasseh made Judah and those living in Jerusalem to wander and to perform more evil than the nations that the LORD destroyed from before Israel.

Manasseh's Repentance

[10] The LORD spoke to Manasseh and his people, but they did not pay attention. [11] So the LORD brought on them the officials of the army of the king of Assyria. They captured Manasseh with hooks, and they bound him in bronze chains and led him to Babylon. [12] And when he was distressed, he entreated the face of the LORD his God, and he greatly humbled himself before the God of his fathers. [13] And he prayed to *God*, and He was moved and responded to his plea and returned him to Jerusalem to his kingdom. Then Manasseh knew that the LORD was God.

[14] After this he built an outer wall for the City of David, west of Gihon, in the valley and toward the entrance of the Fish Gate, where it went around Ophel, and raised it to a very great height. Then he positioned military commanders in all the fortified cities in Judah.

[15] And he removed the foreign gods and statues from the house of the LORD, and all the altars that he built on the hill of the house of the LORD and Jerusalem, and he cast them outside the city. [16] He also restored the altar of the LORD, and he sacrificed fellowship and thanksgiving offerings, and he ordered Judah to serve the LORD God of Israel. [17] However, the people continued to sacrifice at the high places, but only to the LORD their God.

The Death of Manasseh

[18] And the remainder of the acts of Manasseh and his prayer to God and the words of the seers who spoke to him in the name of the LORD God of Israel are written in the annals of the kings of Israel. [19] And his prayer and how God received his entreaty, and all his sin and unfaithfulness, and the sites where he built high places and where he set up the Asherah poles and images before he humbled himself, indeed they are written in the sayings of Hozai. [20] So Manasseh slept with his fathers, and they buried him in his palace, and Amon his son reigned in his place.

Amon, King of Judah
2Ki 21:19–24

[21] And Amon was twenty-two years old when he began to reign, and he was king for two years in Jerusalem. [22] And he did what was evil in the eyes of the LORD as his father Manasseh had done. And Amon sacrificed to and served all the idols that Manasseh his father had made. [23] He did not humble himself before the LORD as his father humbled himself. But he increased his guilt all the more. [24] And his servants plotted against him, and they killed him in his palace. [25] Then the people of the land struck down all those who conspired against King Amon. The people of the land made Josiah his son king in his place.

Josiah, King of Judah
2Ki 22:1–7; 23:4–20

34 And Josiah was eight years old when he began to reign, and he was king for thirty-one years in Jerusalem. [2] And he did what was correct in the eyes of the LORD, and he walked in the ways of David his father and did not turn either to the right or left. [3] And in the eighth year of his reign, while he was still a young boy, he began to seek out the God of David his father; and in the twelfth year he began to cleanse Judah and Jerusalem from high places, Asherah poles, idols, and carved and cast images. [4] So they tore down the altars for the Baals, and he cut down the incense altars that were above them and smashed the Asherah poles and carved and cast images. And he crushed them to dust and scattered them before the graves of those who sacrificed to them. [5] Then he burned the bones of the priests on their altars and so cleansed Judah and Jerusalem. [6] In the cities of Manasseh, Ephraim, and Simeon, and as far as Naphtali, in their ruins all around, [7] he broke down the altars, beat Asherah poles and the images into powder, and cut down all the incense altars throughout all the land of Israel. Then he returned to Jerusalem.

[8] In the eighteenth year of his reign, when he had purged the land and the house, he sent Shaphan the son of Azaliah, Maaseiah the governor of the city, and Joah the son of Joahaz, the recorder, to repair the house of the LORD his God.

[9] When they came to Hilkiah the high priest, they delivered the money that was brought into the house of God, which the Levites, the keepers of the door, had collected from the hand of Manasseh and Ephraim, and from all the remnant of Israel, and from all Judah and Benjamin, and from the inhabitants of Jerusalem. [10] And they gave it to those appointed to do the work in the house of the LORD. And those who were doing the work on the house gave it to repair and restore the house. [11] And they gave it to the craftsmen and builders to acquire quarried stones and timber for joists and beams for the buildings that the kings of Judah had ruined.

[12] So the men did the work faithfully. Their overseers were Jahath and Obadiah the Levites, of the sons of Merari, and Zechariah and Meshullam, of the sons of the Kohathites, as supervisors. And other Levites, all skillful with musical instruments, [13] were over those laborers and supervised all those doing the work in every type of service, and other Levites were scribes, officials, and gatekeepers.

The Book of the Law Found
2Ki 22:8–20; 23:1–3

[14] When they brought out the money that had been given to the house of the LORD, Hilkiah the priest found the Book of the Law of the LORD from Moses. [15] Then Hilkiah said to Shaphan the scribe, "I have found the Book of the Law in the house of the LORD." And Hilkiah gave the book to Shaphan.

[16] Shaphan brought the book to the king and reported, "Everything that has been designated to your servants, they are doing. [17] They have given out the money that was in the house of the LORD and have allocated to those who are supervisors and those who are doing the work." [18] Then Shaphan the scribe also declared to the king, "Hilkiah the priest has given me a book." And Shaphan read from it to the king.

[19] And it happened that when the king heard the words of the Law, he tore his garments. [20] Then the king ordered Hilkiah, Ahikam the son of Shaphan, Abdon the son of Micah, Shaphan the scribe, and Asaiah the attendant of the king: [21] "Go and seek the LORD on my behalf and on the behalf of the remnant in Israel and Judah concerning what is written in the book that was found, for the wrath of the LORD that is poured out on us is great because our fathers have not kept the word of the LORD, to do everything that is written in this book."

[22] So Hilkiah and those with the king went to Huldah the prophetess, the wife of Shallum the son of Tokhath, son of Hasrah, who kept the wardrobe. She lived in Jerusalem in the Second Quarter, and they spoke to her about this.

[23] And she said to them, "So says the LORD God of Israel: Speak to the man who sent you all to Me, [24] Thus says the LORD: I am bringing disaster on this place and all who dwell in it, even all the curses that are written in the book that they read before the king of Judah.

[25] Because they have abandoned Me and offered sacrifices to other gods in order to provoke Me with everything they have made with their hands, so My rage will be poured out on this place, and it will not be quenched. [26] And the king of Judah who sent you all to seek out the LORD, so you will speak to him: So says the LORD God of Israel: The words that you have heard, [27] because your heart was tender and you humbled yourself before God when you heard His words against this place and those who dwell here, and you have brought yourself low before Me and torn your clothes and wept before Me, I have heard *you*, declares the LORD. [28] I am bringing you to be with your fathers, and you will be brought to your grave in peace, and your eyes will not see all the disaster that I am bringing on this place and on those who dwell here."

So they returned this word to the king.

Josiah Restores True Worship

[29] Then the king sent for all the elders of Judah and Jerusalem. [30] Then the king went up to the house of the LORD with men from Judah and those living in Jerusalem, even the priests and Levites and all the people from the greatest to the least, and he read within their hearing all the words of the Book of the Covenant that was found in the house of the LORD. [31] Then the king stood in his place and made a covenant before the LORD, to walk after the LORD, and to keep His commandments and His testimonies and His statutes with all his soul, to perform the words of the covenant written in this book.

[32] Then he appointed all who were in Jerusalem and Benjamin to carry this out, and those living in Jerusalem did according to the covenant of God, the God of their fathers.

[33] So Josiah took away all the detestable things from the lands that belonged to the people of Israel and caused all who were found in Israel to serve their LORD God. And all his days they did not turn away from the LORD God of their fathers.

Josiah Celebrates the Passover
2Ki 23:21–23

35 Josiah kept a Passover for the LORD in Jerusalem; they slaughtered the Passover lamb on the fourteenth day of the first month. [2] He appointed priests for their duties and encouraged them in their service to the house of the LORD. [3] And he said to the Levites who gave insight to all Israel and were consecrated to the LORD, "Set the holy ark in the house that Solomon, the son of David and king of Israel, built. You should not carry it on your shoulders. Now serve the LORD your God and His people Israel. [4] Prepare yourselves according to your fathers' houses by your divisions, as instructed in the writing of David, king of Israel, and the document of Solomon his son.

[5] "And stand in the Holy Place according to the divisions of the fathers' households of your brothers, the laypeople, and according to the Levites, by division of a father's household. [6] Then slaughter the Passover lamb and consecrate yourselves and prepare for your brothers to do according to the word of the LORD by the hand of Moses."

[7] Josiah contributed to the laypeople, as Passover *offerings* for all who were present, lambs and young goats from the flock to the number of thirty thousand, and three thousand bulls; these were from the king's possession.

[8] His officials contributed willingly to the people, to the priests, and to the Levites. Hilkiah, Zechariah, and Jehiel, the chief officers of the house of God, gave to the priests for the Passover *offerings* two thousand six hundred lambs and three hundred bulls. [9] Konaniah, his brothers Shemaiah and Nethanel, and Hashabiah, Jeiel, and Jozabad, officers of the Levites, gave to the Levites for the Passover *offerings* five thousand lambs and five hundred bulls.

[10] When the service was prepared, the priests stood in their places and the Levites in their divisions, according to the king's command. [11] And they slaughtered the Passover *offerings*, and the priests sprinkled the *blood* given to them while the Levites skinned *animals*. [12] And they set aside the burnt offering to distribute according to each house of the fathers for the people to bring near to the LORD, as written in the Book of Moses. And they did the same with the bulls. [13] And they cooked the Passover lamb

with fire according to the rule, and they cooked the holy offerings in pots, jars, bowls, and quickly brought them to all the people. 14 Afterward they prepared the *offerings* for them and the priests because the priests, the sons of Aaron, offered the burnt offering and fat portions until night. So the Levites prepared for themselves and for the priests, the sons of Aaron.

15 The singers, the sons of Asaph, were in their places according to the command of David, Asaph, Heman, and Jeduthun the king's seer. The gatekeepers were at each of the gates; they did not need to leave their service, for their brothers the Levites made preparations for them.

16 So all the service of the LORD was carried out that day to have the Passover, and to offer the burnt offerings on the altar of the LORD according to the command of King Josiah. 17 And the sons of Israel who were present had the Passover at that time and the Feast of Unleavened Bread for seven days. 18 And no Passover had been made like this in Israel since the days of Samuel the prophet. And none of the kings of Israel had performed a Passover like Josiah had done. And the priests and Levites and all Judah and Israel were present along with those living in Jerusalem. 19 In the eighteenth year of the reign of Josiah this Passover was performed.

The Death of Josiah
2Ki 23:28–30

20 After all this when Josiah had prepared the temple, Necho king of Egypt went up to war in Carchemish on the Euphrates, and Josiah went out to meet him. 21 And Necho sent messengers to him saying, "What is there between you and me, king of Judah? I am not against you this day, but *against* the house with which I am at war. And God has commanded that I hurry. Refrain from being against God who is with me so that He does not destroy you."

22 But Josiah did not turn away from him for he went to battle against him disguised. He did not listen to the words of Necho that came from the mouth of God, but he came to battle in the plain of Megiddo.

23 So the archers shot King Josiah, and the king said to his servants, "Take me away for I am severely wounded." 24 Then his servants took him from the chariot, and they set him in a second chariot, and they brought him to Jerusalem. He died and was buried in the tombs of his fathers. And all Judah and Jerusalem mourned for Josiah.

25 And Jeremiah composed a dirge for Josiah, and all the male and female singers speak of Josiah in their laments to this day. They set them as a statute over Israel. They are written in the Laments.

26 And the remainder of the acts of Josiah, his deeds and covenant faithfulness, according to what is written in the Law of the LORD, 27 and his acts from beginning to end are written in the book of the kings of Israel and Judah.

Jehoahaz, King of Judah
2Ki 23:31–34

36 Then the people of the land took Jehoahaz the son of Josiah and made him king in the place of his father in Jerusalem. 2 And Jehoahaz was twenty-three years old when he began to reign, and he reigned three months in Jerusalem. 3 Then the king of Egypt deposed him in Jerusalem and imposed on the land a tribute of a hundred talents[1] of silver and a talent[2] of gold. 4 The king of Egypt made his brother Eliakim king over Judah and Jerusalem, and changed his name to Jehoiakim. But Necho took his brother Jehoahaz and carried him to Egypt.

Jehoiakim, King of Judah
2Ki 23:36–24:6

5 Jehoiakim was twenty-five years old when he began to reign, and he was king in Jerusalem for eleven years. He did what was

evil in the eyes of the LORD his God. 6 And Nebuchadnezzar king of Babylon came up against him and bound him in bronze chains to lead him to Babylon. 7 Nebuchadnezzar also brought out some of the vessels of the house of the LORD to Babylon and put them in his temple in Babylon.

8 And the remainder of the acts of Jehoiakim, the detestable things that he did and were found against him, are written in the book of the kings of Israel and Judah. Then Jehoiachin his son reigned in his place.

Jehoiachin, King of Judah
2Ki 24:8–17

9 Jehoiachin was eighteen years old when he began to reign, and he was king in Jerusalem for three months and ten days. He did what was evil in the eyes of the LORD. 10 In the spring of that year King Nebuchadnezzar sent for him and brought him to Babylon with the precious items from the house of the LORD. Then Zedekiah his brother was king over Judah and Jerusalem.

Zedekiah, King of Judah
2Ki 24:18–20; Jer 52:1–3

11 Zedekiah was twenty-one years old when he began to reign, and he was king in Jerusalem for eleven years. 12 He did what was evil in the eyes of the LORD his God and did not humble himself before Jeremiah the prophet, who spoke from the LORD. 13 He also rebelled against King Nebuchadnezzar, who had made him swear by an oath by God. He stiffened his neck and hardened his heart against turning to the LORD God of Israel. 14 Even the officials over the priests and the people increased in their unfaithfulness in all the detestable practices of the nations, and they defiled the house of the LORD which He had consecrated in Jerusalem.

The Fall of Jerusalem
2Ki 25:1–21; Jer 52:4–27; Ezr 1:1–3

15 The LORD God of their fathers sent *warnings* to them over and over again by His messengers because He had compassion on His people and His dwelling place. 16 But they continued to jest regarding the messengers of God, despising His word and making fun of His prophets until the wrath of the LORD came up against His people, until there was no remedy. 17 So He brought up against them the king of the Chaldeans from Babylon, who killed their young men with the sword at the house of their sanctuary. He did not spare a young man or virgin, old or aged. *God* gave all of them into his hand. 18 Even all the vessels of the house of God, both large and small, and the treasures of the house of the LORD, the king, and his officials, all of this was taken to Babylon. 19 So they burned down the house of God, tore down the wall of Jerusalem, burned down all the palaces with fire, and destroyed all the precious items.

20 Then he carried into exile to Babylon the remnant, who survived the sword, and they were slaves to him and his sons until the kingdom of Persia ruled, 21 to fulfill the word of the LORD by the mouth of Jeremiah, until the land had enjoyed her Sabbaths. As long as she lay desolate, she kept Sabbath, to fulfill seventy years.

The Proclamation of Cyrus

22 In the first year of King Cyrus of Persia, that the word of the LORD spoken by the mouth of Jeremiah might be fulfilled, the LORD stirred up the spirit of King Cyrus of Persia, so that he sent a proclamation throughout all his kingdom and also declared in a written edict:

23 "Thus says King Cyrus of Persia:

"The LORD God of heaven has given me all the kingdoms of the earth, and He has commanded me to build for Him a house at Jerusalem, which is in Judah. Whoever is among you of all His people, may the LORD his God be with him. Let him go up."

---

1 3 About 3¾ tons, or 3.4 metric tons.   2 3 About 75 pounds, or 34 kilograms.

The Proclamation of Cyrus

2Ch 36:22–23

1 Now in the first year of Cyrus king of Persia, that the word of the LORD by the mouth of Jeremiah might be fulfilled, the LORD stirred up the spirit of Cyrus king of Persia, so that he issued a proclamation throughout all his kingdom, and also put it in writing, saying,

2 "Thus says Cyrus king of Persia:

"The LORD God of heaven has given me all the kingdoms of the earth, and He has charged me to build Him a house at Jerusalem, which is in Judah. 3 Whoever there is among you of all His people, may his God be with him, and may he go to Jerusalem, which is in Judah, and build the house of the LORD God of Israel. He is the God who is in Jerusalem. 4 Whoever remains in any place where he sojourns, let the men of his place help him with silver, gold, goods, and animals, along with voluntary gifts for the house of God in Jerusalem."

5 Then the heads of the households of Judah and Benjamin, and the Levitical priests, with all those whose spirits God had stirred, rose up to go up to build the house of the LORD in Jerusalem. 6 So everyone all around them strengthened their hands with vessels of silver, gold, goods, animals, and precious things, besides all that was given voluntarily. 7 Also Cyrus the king brought forth the vessels of the house of the LORD, which Nebuchadnezzar had brought from Jerusalem and had put in the house of his gods. 8 Cyrus king of Persia even brought forth more for them, by the hand of Mithredath the treasurer and had them numbered for Sheshbazzar, who was the prince of Judah.

9 This is the number of them: thirty containers of gold, one thousand containers of silver, and twenty-nine knives. 10 There were also thirty smaller bowls of gold, four hundred and ten smaller bowls of silver (of lesser value), and one thousand other various containers.

11 All the articles of gold and silver were five thousand four hundred. All these did Sheshbazzar bring up, when the exiles were brought from Babylon to Jerusalem.

The List of Returning Exiles

Ne 7:6–73

2 Now these are the people of the province who went up from the captivity of the exiles, whom Nebuchadnezzar the king of Babylon had carried away to Babylon, and came again to Jerusalem and Judah. Each returned to his own city. 2 Those who came with Zerubbabel were Joshua, Nehemiah, Seraiah, Reelaiah, Mordecai, Bilshan, Mispar, Bigvai, Rehum, and Baanah.

The number of men of the people of Israel were:

3 The sons of Parosh—two thousand one hundred and seventy-two;
4 the sons of Shephatiah—three hundred and seventy-two;
5 the sons of Arah—seven hundred and seventy-five;
6 the sons of Pahath-Moab of the sons of Jeshua and Joab—two thousand eight hundred and twelve;
7 the sons of Elam—one thousand two hundred and fifty-four;
8 the sons of Zattu—nine hundred and forty-five;
9 the sons of Zakkai—seven hundred and sixty;
10 the sons of Bani—six hundred and forty-two;
11 the sons of Bebai—six hundred and twenty-three;
12 the sons of Azgad—one thousand two hundred and twenty-two;
13 the sons of Adonikam—six hundred and sixty-six;
14 the sons of Bigvai—two thousand and fifty-six;
15 the sons of Adin—four hundred and fifty-four;
16 the sons of Ater of Hezekiah—ninety-eight;
17 the sons of Bezai—three hundred and twenty-three;
18 the sons of Jorah—one hundred and twelve;
19 the sons of Hashum—two hundred and twenty-three;
20 the sons of Gibbar—ninety-five.

21 The sons of Bethlehem—one hundred and twenty-three;
22 the men of Netophah—fifty-six;
23 the men of Anathoth—one hundred and twenty-eight;
24 the sons of Azmaveth—forty-two;
25 the sons of Kiriath Arim, Kephirah, and Beeroth—seven hundred and forty-three;
26 the sons of Ramah and Geba—six hundred and twenty-one;
27 the men of Mikmash—one hundred and twenty-two;
28 the men of Bethel and Ai—two hundred and twenty-three;
29 the sons of Nebo—fifty-two;
30 the sons of Magbish—one hundred and fifty-six;
31 the sons of the other Elam—one thousand two hundred and fifty-four;
32 the sons of Harim—three hundred and twenty;
33 the sons of Lod, Hadid, and Ono—seven hundred and twenty-five;
34 the sons of Jericho—three hundred and forty-five;
35 the sons of Senaah—three thousand six hundred and thirty.

36 *Those who came with* the priests *were:*

the sons of Jedaiah, of the house of Jeshua—nine hundred and seventy-three;

37 the sons of Immer—one thousand and fifty-two;
38 the sons of Pashhur—one thousand two hundred and forty-seven;
39 the sons of Harim—one thousand and seventeen.

40 *Those who came with* the Levites were:

the sons of Jeshua and Kadmiel, of the sons of Hodaviah—seventy-four.

41 *Those who came with* the singers were:

the sons of Asaph—one hundred and twenty-eight.

42 The sons of the gatekeepers *were*:

the sons of Shallum, the sons of Ater, the sons of Talmon, the sons of Akkub, the sons of Hatita, the sons of Shobai—in all one hundred and thirty-nine.

43 Those devoted to the temple as servants were:

the sons of Ziha, the sons of Hasupha, the sons of Tabbaoth, 44 the sons of Keros, the sons of Siaha, the sons of Padon, 45 the sons of Lebanah, the sons of Hagabah, the sons of Akkub, 46 the sons of Hagab, the sons of Shalmai, the sons of Hanan, 47 the sons of Giddel, the sons of Gahar, the sons of Reaiah, 48 the sons of Rezin, the sons of Nekoda, the sons of Gazzam, 49 the sons of Uzza, the sons of Paseah, the sons of Besai, 50 the sons of Asnah, the sons of Meunim, the sons of Nephusim, 51 the sons of Bakbuk, the sons of Hakupha, the sons of Harhur, 52 the sons of Bazluth, the sons of Mehida, the sons of Harsha,

[53] the sons of Barkos, the sons of Sisera, the sons of Temah, [54] the sons of Neziah, the sons of Hatipha.

[55] The sons of Solomon's servants were:

the sons of Sotai, the sons of Hassophereth, the sons of Peruda, [56] the sons of Jaala, the sons of Darkon, the sons of Giddel, [57] the sons of Shephatiah, the sons of Hattil, the sons of Pokereth-Hazzebaim, the sons of Ami.

[58] All those devoted to the temple as servants and the children of Solomon's servants were three hundred and ninety-two.

[59] These were the ones who came up from Tel Melah, Tel Harsha, Kerub, Addon, and Immer; but they could not prove their father's house or their descent, whether they were of Israel:

[60] the sons of Delaiah, the sons of Tobiah, and the sons of Nekoda—six hundred and fifty-two;

[61] and of the sons of the priests:

the sons of Hobaiah, the sons of Hakkoz, and the sons of Barzillai (whose ancestor married one of the daughters of Barzillai the Gileadite and was thereafter called by their name). [62] These sought their records in the genealogy register, but they were not found. Therefore, they were disqualified (as polluted) from the priesthood. [63] The governor advised them not to eat of the most holy things until a priest consulted with the Urim and Thummim. [64] The whole congregation together was forty-two thousand three hundred and sixty, [65] besides their male and female servants (these numbered seven thousand three hundred and thirty-seven); they also had two hundred singing men and women. [66] Their horses numbered seven hundred and thirty-six; their mules, two hundred and forty-five; [67] their camels, four hundred and thirty-five; and their donkeys, six thousand seven hundred and twenty.

[68] As some of the heads of households came to the house of the Lord in Jerusalem, they volunteered to erect the foundations for the house of God. [69] They gave after their ability to the treasure of the work sixty-one thousand drachmas[1] of gold, five thousand pounds[2] of silver, and one hundred priestly garments. [70] So the priests and the Levites, along with some of the people, the singers, the porters, and those donated as temple servants, lived in their cities, with the result that all Israel resettled in their cities.

Rebuilding the Altar

3 When the seventh month had come, the children of Israel *had resettled* in their cities, and the people gathered themselves together, as one man, to Jerusalem. [2] Then Joshua the son of Jozadak and his brothers the priests stood up, along with Zerubbabel the son of Shealtiel and his brothers, and they built the altar of the God of Israel in order to offer burnt offerings on it, as it had been written in the Law of Moses, the man of God. [3] They set the altar upon its foundations and, because they were living in fear of some of the peoples of the region, they offered burnt offerings on it to the Lord—morning and evening. [4] They also kept the Feast of Tabernacles, as it had been written, and offered the daily burnt offerings in accordance with the daily schedule, according to each day's custom. [5] Thereafter, *observance of* the burnt offering became a perpetual sacrifice with regard to the New Moon sacrifices and all of the appointed feasts of the Lord that had been consecrated, and all of the voluntary freewill offerings to the Lord. [6] From the first day of the seventh month they had begun to offer burnt offerings unto the Lord, but the foundation of the temple of the Lord was not yet laid.

Rebuilding the Temple

[7] They gave money to the masons and carpenters, and food, drink, and oil to the people of Sidon and to the people of Tyre so that they would bring cedar trees from Lebanon to the sea, at Joppa, according to the grant they had from Cyrus king of Persia. [8] Now in the second month of the second year of their coming to the house of God in Jerusalem, Zerubbabel the son of Shealtiel, Joshua the son of Jozadak, along with the remnant of their brothers the Levitical priests and all who had come out of captivity back to Jerusalem, began work and appointed the Levites twenty years old and older to supervise the work on the house of the Lord. [9] Then Joshua with his sons and brothers, and Kadmiel with his sons, who are the sons of Judah, along with the sons of Henadad with their sons and their brothers—all Levites—stood together to supervise the workers on the house of God.

[10] When the builders laid the foundation of the temple of the Lord, the priests in their apparel stood with trumpets and, from the Levites, the sons of Asaph *stood* with cymbals to praise the Lord, following the example of David king of Israel. [11] They sang responsively, praising and giving thanks unto the Lord,

"For He is good,
　for His mercy endures forever toward Israel."

And all the people responded with a great shout when they praised the Lord, because the foundation of the house of the Lord was laid. [12] Now many of the older Levitical priests and chiefs of the fathers' *households* who had seen the first temple wept with a loud voice as the foundation of this temple was laid before their eyes, though many others shouted exuberantly for joy. [13] As a result, the people could not distinguish the noise of the shout of joy from the noise of the weeping of the people since the people had raised such a loud noise that could be heard from afar off.

Resistance to Rebuilding

4 Now when the adversaries of Judah and Benjamin heard that the descendants of the captivity built the temple unto the Lord God of Israel, [2] they came to Zerubbabel, and to the chiefs of the fathers' households, and said to them, "Let us build with you, for, like you, we seek your God and have been sacrificing to Him since the days of Esarhaddon king of Assyria, who brought us here." [3] But Zerubbabel, and Joshua, and the rest of the chiefs of the fathers' households of Israel said to them, "*This is* not for you! It is for us to build the temple of our God, as we ourselves together will build unto the Lord God of Israel, as Cyrus the king of Persia has commanded us." [4] Then the people of the land demoralized the people of Judah and terrified them while building, [5] and hired counselors against them to frustrate their purpose, all the days of Cyrus king of Persia, even until the reign of Darius king of Persia. [6] In the reign of Ahasuerus, in the beginning of his reign, they wrote an accusation against the inhabitants of Judah and Jerusalem.

The Letter to Artaxerxes

[7] In the days of Artaxerxes, Bishlam, Mithredath, Tabeel, and the rest of their companions wrote to Artaxerxes king of Persia, and the writing of the letter was written in Aramaic, and interpreted in Aramaic. [8] Rehum the commander and Shimshai the scribe wrote a letter against Jerusalem to Artaxerxes the king in this manner:

[9] (Rehum the commander, Shimshai the scribe, and the rest of their colleagues, the judges, the officials, the officers, the Persians, the men of Uruk, and of Babylon, and of Susa—that is, the Elamites— [10] and the rest of the nations whom the great and noble Ashurbanipal deported and settled in the city of Samaria and in the rest of the province Beyond the River—and now [11] this is the copy of the letter that they sent to him)—

---

[1]69 About 1,100 pounds, or 500 kilograms.　[2]69 About 3 tons, or 2.8 metric tons.

"To Artaxerxes the king:

"Your servants the men of the province Beyond the River, and so forth.

¹² "May it be known to the king, that the Jews who came from you have come near to us at Jerusalem and that they are building the rebellious and evil city, restoring its walls, and repairing the foundations. ¹³ "Be it known now to the king, that, if this city is rebuilt and the walls set up again, then they will not pay toll, tribute, and custom, and the revenue of the kings will be impacted. ¹⁴ Now because we are under obligation to the king's palace, and it was not appropriate for us to see the king's dishonor, therefore we have sent and notified the king, ¹⁵ so that a search may be made in the book of the records of your fathers. There you will find in the book of the records and realize that this city is a rebellious city, and hurtful to kings and provinces, and that they have incited revolt within it in former times—for which cause this city was destroyed. ¹⁶ We notify the king that if this city is rebuilt and the walls repaired by this means the portion Beyond the River will no longer be yours."

¹⁷ The king sent an answer:

"To Rehum the commander, to Shimshai the scribe, to the rest of their companions that dwell in Samaria, and to the remainder Beyond the River:

"Peace, and so forth.

¹⁸ "The letter which you sent to us has been translated and read before me. ¹⁹ I commanded, and a search has been made, and it is found that this city has in the past made insurrection against kings, and that rebellion and revolt have occurred there. ²⁰ There have also been mighty kings over Jerusalem, who have ruled over the whole province Beyond the River, and toll, tribute, and custom was paid to them. ²¹ Command these men to cease now, so that this city is not built unless I give the command. ²² Take heed now that you do not fail to do this. Why should damage increase to the hurt of the king?"

²³ Now when the copy of the letter by King Artaxerxes was read before Rehum, and Shimshai the scribe, and their companions, they went up in haste to Jerusalem to the Jews and made them cease by force and power.

²⁴ Then the work of the house of God in Jerusalem ceased. So it ceased until the second year of the reign of Darius king of Persia.

Restoration of the Temple Resumed

5 Now the prophets, Haggai and Zechariah the son of Iddo, prophesied to the Jews that were in Judah and Jerusalem in the name of the God of Israel who was over them. ² Then Zerubbabel the son of Shealtiel and Joshua the son of Jozadak rose up and began to build the house of God which is at Jerusalem, and the prophets of God were with them, helping them.
³ At the same time Tattenai, governor of the province Beyond the River, and Shethar-Bozenai and their companions came to them and said to them, "Who issued a command for you to build this house and complete this structure?" ⁴ They also asked them, "What are the names of the men building this building?" ⁵ But the eye of their God was on the elders of the Jews, so that they could not cause them to cease building until a command came from Darius. Consequently, they sent a letter concerning this matter.
⁶ This is a copy of the letter that Tattenai, governor of the province Beyond the River, and Shethar-Bozenai and his colleagues, the officials who were in the province Beyond the River, sent to Darius the king.

⁷ This is the document that they sent to him, containing accordingly what follows:

"To Darius the king:

"All peace.

⁸ "May it be known to the king that we went into the province of Judah, to the temple of the great God, which is built with great stones, and timber is laid in the walls, and this work goes diligently, and prospers in their hands.
⁹ "Then we questioned those elders and said to them, 'Who issued a command for you to build this house and complete this structure?' ¹⁰ Also, we asked for their names in order to notify you and to document the names of the men that were their leaders.
¹¹ "Thus they returned us an answer, saying,

" 'We are the servants of the God of heaven and earth and are rebuilding the temple that was built these many years ago, which a great king of Israel built and completed. ¹² Afterwards, our fathers provoked the God of heaven to wrath, so He gave them into the hand of Nebuchadnezzar the king of Babylon, the Chaldean, who destroyed this temple and carried the people away into Babylon.
¹³ " 'However, in the first year of Cyrus the king of Babylon, King Cyrus made a decree to rebuild this house of God. ¹⁴ The vessels also of gold and silver of the house of God, which Nebuchadnezzar took from the temple in Jerusalem and placed them into the temple of Babylon, those Cyrus the king withdrew from the temple of Babylon and had them delivered to the one named Sheshbazzar, whom he had made governor. ¹⁵ King Cyrus said to him, 'Take these vessels, go, carry them to the temple in Jerusalem and let the house of God be built its site.'
¹⁶ " 'So that same Sheshbazzar came and laid the foundation of the house of God in Jerusalem. Since that time even until now it has been under construction, yet it is not finished.'

¹⁷ "Now therefore, if it seems good to the king, let there be search made in the king's treasure house there in Babylon to ascertain if it is so that a decree was made of Cyrus the king to build this house of God at Jerusalem. May the king send his pleasure to us concerning this matter."

The Decree of Darius

6 Then Darius the king issued a decree and a search was made in the house of records, where the treasures were stored in Babylon. ² At Ecbatana, in the provincial palace of the Medes, a scroll was found, and in it the following record was written:

³ "In the first year of Cyrus the king, the same Cyrus the king issued a decree concerning the temple of God at Jerusalem:

"Let the house be rebuilt, the place where they offered sacrifices, and let the foundations of it be strongly laid, to a height of sixty cubits,¹ and a width of sixty cubits. ⁴ *Let it consist of* three rows of great stones and a row of new timber, and let the expenses be paid from the king's treasury. ⁵ Also, let the golden and silver vessels of the house of God, which Nebuchadnezzar took from the temple in Jerusalem and brought to Babylon, be returned and brought back to their places in the temple in Jerusalem. Put them in the house of God.

⁶ "Now therefore, Tattenai, governor of the province Beyond the River, and Shethar-Bozenai, along with your colleagues, the officials who are in the province Beyond the River, stay far away from there. ⁷ Let the work of this house of God alone. Let the governor of the Jews and the elders of the Jews build this house of God in its place.

13 About 90 feet, or 27 meters.

[8] "Moreover, I issue a decree concerning what you shall do for the elders of these Jews for the rebuilding of this house of God:

"The cost is to be paid to these men, in full and without delay, from the royal revenue, the tribute of the province Beyond the River. [9] Whatever they need—whether young bulls, rams, and lambs for the burnt offerings to the God of heaven, or wheat, salt, wine, and oil, according to the appointment of the priests in Jerusalem—let it be given them daily without fail, [10] so that they may offer acceptable sacrifices to the God of heaven, as well as pray for the life of the king and of his sons.

[11] "Also, I have issued a decree that whoever shall violate this word, the timber will be pulled down from his house and arranged so that he may be hanged on it. Thus shall his house be made a dunghill for this. [12] May the God who has caused His name to dwell there overthrow all kings and people who stretch forth their hand to violate or destroy this house of God in Jerusalem.

"I, Darius, have issued the decree; so let it be done diligently."

Completion and Dedication of the Temple

[13] In compliance, Tattenai, governor of the province Beyond the River, Shethar-Bozenai, and their companions speedily accomplished what Darius the king had decreed. [14] The rebuilding by the elders of the Jews prospered through the prophesying of Haggai the prophet and Zechariah the son of Iddo. And they built, and finished it, according to the decree of the God of Israel and according to the decrees of Cyrus, Darius, and Artaxerxes king of Persia. [15] This temple was finished on the third day of the month Adar during the sixth year of the reign of Darius the king.

[16] The children of Israel, the priests and the Levites, and the rest of the descendants of the captivity kept the dedication of this house of God with joy. [17] At the dedication of this house of God, they offered a hundred bulls, two hundred rams, four hundred lambs; and as a sin offering for all Israel, they offered twelve goats (according to the number of the tribes of Israel). [18] They appointed the priests in their divisions and the Levites in their orders for the service of God in Jerusalem, as it had been written in the Book of Moses.

The Passover

[19] The children of the captivity kept the Passover on the fourteenth day of the first month. [20] Because the priests and the Levites had purified themselves together, all of them were pure. So, they slaughtered the Passover *lambs* for all the descendants of the captivity, both for their brothers the priests and for themselves. [21] Then they ate together, both the children of Israel who had come out of captivity and all those who had separated themselves from the uncleanness of the nations of the land, in order to seek the LORD God of Israel. [22] With joy they observed the Feast of Unleavened Bread for seven days because the LORD had made them joyful. He had turned the heart of the king of Assyria toward them and strengthened their hands in the work on the house of God, who is the God of Israel.

The Arrival of Ezra

7 Now after these things, in the reign of Artaxerxes king of Persia, Ezra the son of Seraiah, the son of Azariah, the son of Hilkiah, [2] the son of Shallum, the son of Zadok, the son of Ahitub, [3] the son of Amariah, the son of Azariah, the son of Meraioth, [4] the son of Zerahiah, the son of Uzzi, the son of Bukki, [5] the son of Abishua, the son of Phinehas, the son of Eleazar, the son of Aaron the high priest— [6] this Ezra went up from Babylon. He was a scribe skilled in the Law of Moses, given by the LORD God of Israel. Because the hand of the LORD his God was upon him, the king granted him all his requests. [7] Some of the children of Israel, along with some of the priests, and the Levites, the singers, the porters, and the temple servants, went up to Jerusalem in the seventh year of King Artaxerxes.

[8] Ezra arrived at Jerusalem in the fifth month, during the king's seventh year. [9] From the first day of the first month when the journey from Babylon began, until the first day of the fifth month when he arrived at Jerusalem, the good hand of his God was upon him. [10] Because Ezra had prepared his heart to seek the Law of the LORD, he was doing *so* and teaching the statutes and judgments in Israel.

The Letter of Artaxerxes to Ezra

[11] Now this is the copy of the letter that King Artaxerxes gave to Ezra the priest, who was likewise the scribe, the one responsible for the words of the commandments of the LORD and His statutes to Israel:

[12] "Artaxerxes, king of kings,

"To Ezra the priest, scribe of the law of the God of heaven:

"Perfect peace, and so forth.

[13] "I have issued a decree that all the people of Israel, and their priests, and the Levites in my realm, who are inclined to go up to Jerusalem, may go with you. [14] For you are sent by the king and his seven counselors to inquire concerning Judah and Jerusalem in accordance with the Law of your God which is in your hand, [15] and to carry the silver and gold, which the king and his counselors have freely offered to the God of Israel, whose habitation is in Jerusalem, [16] along with all the silver and gold that you can find in all the province of Babylon, plus the freewill offering of the people and priests, who are voluntarily giving for the house of their God in Jerusalem. [17] Diligently use this money to buy bulls, rams, lambs, with their grain offerings and their drink offerings, and offer them on the altar of the house of your God in Jerusalem.

[18] "Whatever seems good to you and your brothers to do with the rest of the silver and the gold, do that according to the will of your God. [19] The vessels also that are given to you for the service of the house of your God, deliver before the God of Jerusalem. [20] And whatever else is needed for the house of your God and is your responsibility to provide, use the king's treasury to pay for it.

[21] "I, even I Artaxerxes the king, issue a decree to all the treasurers of the province Beyond the River, that whatever Ezra the priest, scribe of the law of the God of heaven, should request from you, you should do it with all diligence— [22] as much as a hundred talents[1] of silver, a hundred measures[2] of wheat, a hundred baths[3] of wine, a hundred baths[4] of oil, and salt (without prescribing how much). [23] Whatever is decreed by the God of heaven, let it be zealously done for the house of the God of heaven so as to avoid there being wrath against the realm of the king and his sons. [24] Also we are informing you that with regard to all the priests, Levites, singers, doorkeepers, temple servants, or other servants of this house of God, it is not permitted to impose toll, tribute, or custom on them.

[25] "You, Ezra, according to the wisdom of your God who empowers you, appoint magistrates and judges to judge all the people of the province Beyond the River, all those who know the laws of your God and those who do not, whom you must teach. [26] Whoever will not observe the law of your God or the law of the king, let judgment be executed speedily on him, whether that be death, banishment, confiscation of goods, or imprisonment."

[27] Blessed be the LORD God of our fathers, who has put such a thing as this in the king's heart, to beautify the house of the LORD in Jerusalem, [28] and has extended mercy to me before the king, his counselors, and all the king's mighty princes. Thus I had been strengthened, because the hand of the LORD my God was upon me. As a result, I gathered together some of the chief men of Israel to go up with me.

---

[1] 22 About 3¾ tons, or 3.4 metric tons.   [2] 22 Likely about 18 tons, or 16 metric tons.
[3] 22 About 600 gallons, or 2,200 liters.   [4] 22 About 600 gallons, or 2,200 liters.

Family Leaders Returning With Ezra

8 Now these are the chiefs of the households of the fathers and the genealogical register of those who went up with me from Babylon, in the reign of King Artaxerxes:

[2] of the sons of Phinehas, Gershom; of the sons of Ithamar, Daniel; of the sons of David, Hattush, [3] a descendant of Shekaniah and a descendant of Parosh, Zechariah, plus another one hundred and fifty men registered in the genealogical register; [4] of the sons of Pahath-Moab, Eliehoenai a descendant of Zerahiah, plus two hundred other males; [5] of the sons of Zattu, Shekaniah a descendant of Jahaziel, plus three hundred other males; [6] of the sons of Adin, Ebed a descendant of Jonathan, plus fifty other males; [7] of the sons of Elam, Jeshaiah a descendant of Athaliah, plus seventy other males; [8] of the sons of Shephatiah, Zebadiah a descendant of Michael, plus eighty other males; [9] of the sons of Joab, Obadiah a descendant of Jehiel, plus two hundred and eighteen other males; [10] of the sons of Bani, Shelomith a descendant of Josiphiah, plus one hundred and sixty other males; [11] of the sons of Bebai, his son Zechariah, plus twenty-eight other males; [12] of the sons of Azgad, Johanan a descendant of Hakkatan, plus one hundred and ten other males; [13] of the last sons of Adonikam, the ones named Eliphelet, Jeuel, and Shemaiah, plus sixty other males; [14] also of the sons of Bigvai, Uthai and Zakkur, plus seventy other males.

Temple Servants

[15] I gathered them together at the river that runs to Ahava, and we camped in tents three days. As I examined the people and the priests, I discovered that none of the sons of Levi were there. [16] So I sent for Eliezer, Ariel, Shemaiah, Elnathan, Jarib, Elnathan, Nathan, Zechariah, and Meshullam, chief men; and also for Joiarib and Elnathan, discerning men. [17] I gave them orders for Iddo, chief at the place Kasiphia, and crafted exactly what they would say to Iddo, his brothers, and the temple servants at the place Kasiphia so that they would bring us ministering servants for the house of our God. [18] Because the good hand of our God was upon us, indeed they brought us a man of understanding descended from the sons of Mahli, who is a descendant of Levi, the son of Israel—Sherebiah along with his sons and his brothers, eighteen men; [19] and Hashabiah, and with him Jeshaiah of the sons of Merari, his brothers and their sons, twenty men; [20] and of the temple servants whom David and the leaders had appointed for the service of the Levites, two hundred and twenty temple servants, all of them designated by name.

[21] Then I proclaimed a fast there, at the river of Ahava, that we might humble ourselves before our God, to seek from Him a good route for us, our little ones, and all our substance. [22] For I was ashamed to ask the king for an escort of foot and horse soldiers to help us against the enemy on the way, because we had spoken to the king, saying, "The hand of our God is upon all who seek Him for good, but His power and His wrath are against all who forsake Him." [23] So we fasted and sought our God for this, and He was moved by our prayers.

Temple Gifts

[24] Then I separated twelve of the presiding priests—Sherebiah and Hashabiah, along with ten of their brothers— [25] and weighed out to them the silver, the gold, the vessels, as well as the contribution collected for the house of our God by the king, his counselors, his lords, in conjunction with what all Israel had offered. [26] I weighed out into their hand six hundred and fifty talents[1] of silver, silver articles *worth* one hundred talents,[2] one hundred

talents[3] of gold, [27] twenty gold bowls *worth* a thousand darics,[4] and two vessels of fine shining bronze, precious as gold. [28] I said to them, "You are holy to the LORD. The vessels are holy also. The silver and the gold are a freewill offering to the LORD God of your fathers. [29] Watch and guard them until you weigh them before the presiding priests and Levites, and the presiding elders of Israel at Jerusalem, for the chambers of the house of the LORD." [30] So the priests and the Levites accepted the weighed-out silver and gold, along with the vessels, to bring them to Jerusalem to the house of our God.

The Return to Jerusalem

[31] Then we began the journey from the Ahava River on the twelfth day of the first month to go to Jerusalem. The hand of our God was upon us, and He delivered us from the hand of the attacker and the ambusher along the way. [32] When we arrived at Jerusalem, we stayed there three days.

[33] Then on the fourth day the silver and the gold and the vessels were weighed out in the house of our God by the hand of Meremoth the son of Uriah the priest. With him was Eleazar the son of Phinehas as well as Jozabad the son of Jeshua, and Noadiah the son of Binnui—both Levites. [34] All of it was counted by number and by weight, and all the information was recorded at that time.

[35] Then, the children of the exile who had come out of captivity offered burnt offerings to the God of Israel. On behalf of all Israel, they offered twelve bulls, ninety-six rams, seventy-seven lambs, and twelve male goats as a sin offering. All of it was offered as a burnt offering to the LORD. [36] Finally, they delivered the king's decrees to the satraps of the king as well as to the governors of the province Beyond the River. Accordingly, they supported the people and the house of God.

Ezra Prays About Intermarriage

9 Now when these things were done, the leaders contacted me, saying, "The people of Israel, the priests, and the Levites have not separated themselves from the people of the lands. They practice the abominations of the Canaanites, the Hittites, the Perizzites, the Jebusites, the Ammonites, the Moabites, the Egyptians, and the Amorites. [2] Specifically, they have taken some of their daughters *as wives* for themselves, as well as for their sons, so that the holy seed has been mingled with the people of the lands. In fact, the involvement of the leaders and rulers has been foremost in this vile behavior."

[3] When I heard this, I tore my clothes and my robe, plucked out the hair of my head and from my beard, and sat down astonished. [4] Because of the vile behavior of those who had been in exile, every one that trembled at the words of the God of Israel gathered to me, but I sat astonished until the evening sacrifice.

[5] At the evening sacrifice I rose up from my heaviness and, despite having my clothes and my robe torn, I knelt on my knees and stretched out my hands in prayer to the LORD my God [6] and said:

"O my God, I am ashamed and embarrassed to lift up my face to You, my God, because our iniquities have expanded over our heads and our wrongdoing has grown up to the heavens. [7] Since the days of our fathers until this day, we have been in a great guilt. It is because of our iniquities that we, our kings, and our priests have been delivered—by the sword, by captivity, by spoil, and by being shamed—into the hand of the kings of the lands. This day is like that, too.

[8] "Yet now for a little while, there has been a favorable response from the LORD our God—leaving us a remnant to escape, giving us a tent peg from His holy place, having our eyes enlightened by our God, and giving us a little reviving in our bondage. [9] For though we were slaves, our God has not forsaken us in our bondage but has extended mercy to us in the sight of the kings of Persia, granting us a reviving for the rebuilding of the house of our God, for the repairing of its ruins, and for giving us a wall in Judah and in Jerusalem.

---

[1] 26 About 24 tons, or about 22 metric tons. [2] 26 About 3¾ tons, or about 3.4 metric tons. [3] 26 About 3¾ tons, or about 3.4 metric tons.
[4] 27 About ¼ ounce or 8.5 grams.

[10] "Now, O our God, what shall we say after this? For we have forsaken Your commandments, [11] which You commanded by Your servants the prophets, saying, 'The land you are going to possess, it is an unclean land with the filthiness of the people of the lands. By their abominations, it is has been filled from one end to another with their uncleanness. [12] Now, therefore, cease giving your daughters as wives to their sons, do not take their daughters to your sons, and never seek their peace or prosperity, that you might grow strong and eat the good of the land and leave it as an eternal inheritance to your children.'

[13] "After all that has come upon us because of our evil deeds and our great guilt, seeing that You our God have punished us less than our iniquities deserve and have given us such deliverance as this, [14] should we again break Your commandments and intermarry with the people of these abominations? Would You not become so completely angry with us that there would be no remnant nor any who escape? [15] O Lᴏʀᴅ God of Israel, You are righteous, for we who escaped exile yet remain to this very day. Here we stand before You in our guiltiness even though we should not stand before You because of this."

The People's Confession of Sin

10 Now while Ezra prayed and confessed, weeping and prostrating himself before the house of God, a very large congregation of men, women, and children gathered around him from Israel, for the people too wept bitterly. [2] Shekaniah the son of Jehiel, one of the sons of Elam, answered and said to Ezra, "We have acted with vile unfaithfulness against our God and have wedded foreign women from the people of the land, yet there is now hope in Israel concerning this. [3] Now therefore let us make a covenant with our God to sever relations with all the women and their children according to the counsel of my lord and those who tremble at the commandment of our God. May this be done in accordance with the law. [4] Arise, for this matter is your responsibility. But we are standing with you. Be courageous and act!"

[5] Then Ezra stood and made the presiding Levitical priests and all Israel to swear an oath to act according to this word. And they swore an oath. [6] Then Ezra stood in front of the house of God and went into the chamber of Jehohanan the son of Eliashib. When he arrived there, he ate no bread and drank no water because he was mourning over the vile unfaithfulness of the exiles.

[7] They made a proclamation throughout Judah and Jerusalem for all the children of the exile to assemble in Jerusalem. [8] Whoever would not come within three days would forfeit all his possessions, according to the counsel of the leaders and the elders, and would himself be excluded from the congregation of the exiles.

[9] Then all the men of Judah and Benjamin gathered themselves together to Jerusalem within the three days. It was the ninth month, on the twentieth day of the month. All the people sat on the grounds of the house of God, trembling about this matter and also because of the great rain. [10] Ezra the priest stood up and said to them, "You have acted unfaithfully by bringing home foreign women, adding to the guilt of Israel. [11] Now therefore make confession to the Lᴏʀᴅ God of your fathers and do what pleases Him: Sever your relationships with the people of the land, especially from the foreign women."

[12] Then all the congregation answered loudly, "As you have said to us, that we will do. [13] But there are many people, and because it is the rainy season we will not be able to set up outside. Moreover, this is not a task for a day or two since we have so grievously transgressed in this matter. [14] Let now our rulers preside over all the congregation so that, in each of our cities, all who have married foreign women, along with the elders and judges of that city, will come at appointed times, until the fierce wrath of our God for this matter is turned from us." [15] Only Jonathan the son of Asahel and Jahzeiah the son of Tikvah opposed this, with Meshullam and Shabbethai the Levite supporting them.

[16] Then the descendants of the captivity did so. Ezra the priest selected men, heads of the fathers' households, according to their families, each of them by name. They sat down in the first day of the tenth month to examine the matter, [17] and finished *dealing with* every man who had married foreign women by the first day of the first month.

Those Guilty of Intermarriage

[18] Some of the sons of the priests were discovered to have wedded foreign women,
     namely the sons of Joshua the son of Jozadak, and his
     brothers: Maaseiah, Eliezer, Jarib, and Gedaliah. [19] They
     committed to sever their relations with their women, and,
     being guilty, they offered a ram of the flock for their guilt.
[20] Likewise, of the sons of Immer,
     there were Hanani and Zebadiah.
[21] Of the sons of Harim,
     there were Maaseiah, Elijah, Shemaiah, Jehiel, and Uzziah.
[22] Of the sons of Pashhur,
     there were Elioenai, Maaseiah, Ishmael, Nethanel, Jozabad,
     and Elasah.

[23] Also, from the Levites,
     there were Jozabad, Shimei, Kelaiah, (the same is Kelita),
     Pethahiah, Judah, and Eliezer.
[24] Among the singers,
     there was Eliashib,
and from the porters,
     there were Shallum, Telem, and Uri.

[25] Further from Israel,
of the sons of Parosh,
     there were Ramiah, Izziah, Malkijah, Mijamin, Eleazar,
     Malkijah, and Benaiah.
[26] Of the sons of Elam,
     there were Mattaniah, Zechariah, Jehiel, Abdi, Jeremoth,
     and Elijah.
[27] Of the sons of Zattu,
     there were Elioenai, Eliashib, Mattaniah, Jeremoth, Zabad,
     and Aziza.
[28] Of the sons of Bebai,
     there were Jehohanan, Hananiah, Zabbai, and Athlai.
[29] Of the sons of Bani,
     there were Meshullam, Malluk, Adaiah, Jashub, Sheal,
     and Jeremoth.
[30] Of the sons of Pahath-Moab,
     there were Adna, Kelal, Benaiah, Maaseiah, Mattaniah,
     Bezalel, Binnui, and Manasseh.
[31] Of the sons of Harim,
     there were Eliezer, Ishijah, Malkijah, Shemaiah, Shimeon,
     [32] Benjamin, Malluk, and Shemariah.
[33] Of the sons of Hashum,
     there were Mattenai, Mattattah, Zabad, Eliphelet, Jeremai,
     Manasseh, and Shimei.
[34] Of the sons of Bani,
     there were Maadai, Amram, Uel, [35] Benaiah, Bedeiah,
     Keluhi, [36] Vaniah, Meremoth, Eliashib, [37] Mattaniah,
     Mattenai, and Jaasu.
[38] Of the sons of Binnui,
     there were Shimei, [39] Shelemiah, Nathan, Adaiah,
     [40] Maknadebai, Shashai, Sharai, [41] Azarel, Shelemiah,
     Shemariah, [42] Shallum, Amariah, and Joseph.
[43] Of the sons of Nebo,
     there were Jeiel, Mattithiah, Zabad, Zebina, Jaddai, Joel,
     and Benaiah.

[44] All these married foreign women, and some of them had wives that had children.

NEHEMIAH

The Prayer of Nehemiah

1 The words of Nehemiah the son of Hakaliah.

In the month Kislev, in the twentieth year, while I was in Susa the palace, [2] Hanani, one of my relatives, and some men of Judah arrived. So I asked them concerning the returning Jews who had been in captivity, and concerning Jerusalem.

[3] They said to me, "The remnant that returned from captivity is there in the province enduring great affliction and reproach. Also, the wall of Jerusalem remains broken down, and its gates have been burned with fire."

[4] When I heard these words, I sat down and wept and mourned for days. Then I fasted, and prayed before the God of heaven, [5] and said:

"I beseech You, O LORD God of heaven, the great and awesome God, who keeps covenant and mercy for those who love Him and keep His commandments. [6] Let Your ear now be attentive, and Your eyes open, that You may hear the prayer of Your servant, which I now pray before You, day and night, for the children of Israel Your servants, and confess the sins of the children of Israel, which we have sinned against You. Both my father's house and I have sinned. [7] We have acted very corruptly against You and have not obeyed the commandments, nor the statutes, nor the judgments, which You commanded Your servant Moses.

[8] "Please remember the word that You commanded Your servant Moses, saying, 'If you behave unfaithfully, then I will scatter you among the nations, [9] but if you return to Me and keep My commandments and do them, though your outcasts are under the farthest part of the heavens, I will gather them from there and bring them back to the place where I have chosen to establish My name.'

[10] "Now these are Your servants and Your people, whom You have redeemed by Your great power and by Your strong hand. [11] O Lord, I implore You, let Your ear be attentive to the prayer of Your servant, and to the prayer of Your servants who delight to revere Your name. And let Your servant prosper this day, and grant him mercy in the sight of this man."

For I was the king's cupbearer.

Nehemiah Sent to Jerusalem

2 In the month of Nisan, during the twentieth year of King Artaxerxes, when wine was before him, I took the wine and gave it to the king. Never had I been upset in his presence. [2] So the king said to me, "Why is your face troubled though you do not seem sick? This is nothing but a troubled heart."

Then I became very much afraid [3] and said to the king, "May the king live forever! Why should not my face be troubled when the city, the place of my fathers' tombs, lies waste, and its gates have been destroyed by fire?"

[4] So the king said to me, "What are you requesting about this matter?"

Immediately, I prayed to the God of heaven [5] and then said to the king, "If this pleases the king and if this might be good for your servant who is before you, then would you send me to Judah, to the city of my fathers' tombs so that I may rebuild it?"

[6] The king, with the queen sitting beside him, said to me, "How long would your journey be? And when will you return?" Because it pleased the king to send me, I established a timetable for him.

[7] I further said to the king, "If this pleases the king, may letters be given to me for the governors of the province Beyond the River so that they would allow me to pass through until I come to Judah, [8] as well as a letter to Asaph the keeper of the king's forest, that he may give me timber to make beams for the gates of the temple mount, for the city wall, and for the house into which I will enter." The king granted me these things, because the good hand of my God was upon me. [9] When I came to the governors of the province Beyond the River, I gave them the king's letters. He also sent with me commanders of foot and horse soldiers.

[10] When Sanballat the Horonite and Tobiah the Ammonite subordinate heard this, it deeply grieved them that there was a man coming to seek the welfare of the children of Israel.

Nehemiah Inspects Jerusalem's Walls

[11] When I arrived in Jerusalem, I was there three days. [12] Then I arose in the night, I and a few men who were with me; I told no one what my God had put in my heart to do for Jerusalem. There was no animal with me, except the one on which I rode.

[13] So I went out by night by the Valley Gate toward the Dragon's Well and then to the Dung Gate, because I was inspecting the broken-down walls of Jerusalem and its burned gates. [14] Next I passed by the Fountain Gate and then to the King's Pool, but there was no place for my mount to pass. [15] By going up along the riverbed at night, I inspected the wall. Then I turned back so that I could enter by the Valley Gate, and then came back again. [16] The officials did not know where I went or what I did, since I had not yet told it to the Jews, the priests, the nobles, the officials, or to any of the others who would do the work.

[17] Finally, I said to them, "You see the distress that we are in, how Jerusalem is devastated and its gates are burned with fire. Come, and let us rebuild the wall of Jerusalem so that we will no more be a reproach." [18] Then I told them that the hand of my God had been good to me and also about the king's words that he had spoken to me.

And they said, "Let us rise up and build!" So they strengthened their hands for the good work.

[19] But when Sanballat the Horonite, Tobiah the Ammonite subordinate, and Geshem the Arabian heard it, they laughed us to scorn, and despised us, and said, "What is this thing that you are doing? Are you rebelling against the king?"

[20] Then answered I them and said to them, "The God of heaven, He will enable us to prosper. Therefore we His servants will arise and build, but you will have no portion, or right, or memorial in Jerusalem."

Rebuilding the Wall

3 Then Eliashib the high priest rose up with his brothers the priests, and they built the Sheep Gate. They sanctified it and erected its doors. From the Tower of the Hundred to the Tower of Hananel, they sanctified the wall. [2] Next to him the men of Jericho built, and next to them Zakkur the son of Imri built.

[3] The sons of Hassenaah built the Fish Gate, constructing its beams, erecting its doors, and *installing* locks and bars for it. [4] Next to them Meremoth the son of Uriah, the son of Hakkoz made repairs. Next to him, Meshullam the son of Berekiah, the son of Meshezabel made repairs. Next to him Zadok the son of Baana made repairs. [5] Next to them the Tekoites made repairs, but their noblemen would not put their shoulders to the work of their Lord.

[6] Joiada the son of Paseah and Meshullam the son of Besodeiah repaired the Old Gate. They constructed its beams, erected its doors, and *installed* locks and bars for it. [7] Next to them repairs were made by Melatiah the Gibeonite and Jadon the Meronothite, the men of Gibeon and of Mizpah, places under the authority of the governor of the province Beyond the River. [8] Next to them Uzziel the son of Harhaiah, one of the goldsmiths, made repairs. Next to him Hananiah, the son of one of the apothecaries, made repairs, and they repaired Jerusalem as far as the Broad Wall. [9] Next to him Rephaiah the son of Hur, commander of half of the Jerusalem district, made repairs. [10] Next to him Jedaiah the son of Harumaph made repairs across from his house. Next to him Hattush the son of Hashabneiah made repairs. [11] Malkijah the son of Harim and Hasshub the son of Pahath-Moab repaired another section, as well as the Tower of the Furnaces. [12] Next to them Shallum the son of Hallohesh, commander of the other half of the Jerusalem district, made repairs along with his daughters.

[13] Hanun and the inhabitants of Zanoah repaired the Valley Gate. They rebuilt it, erected its doors, and *installed* locks and

bars for it, plus *repaired* one thousand cubits¹ along on the wall to the Dung Gate.

¹⁴ But the Dung Gate was repaired by Malkijah the son of Rekab, commander of the Beth Hakkerem district. He rebuilt it, and erected its doors, and *installed* the locks and bars for it.

¹⁵ Moreover, Shallun the son of Kol-Hozeh, commander of the Mizpah district, made repairs to the Fountain Gate. He rebuilt it, covered it, erected its doors, and *installed* the locks and bars for it. *He also repaired* the wall of the pool of Shelah by the king's garden as far as the steps going down from the City of David. ¹⁶ After him Nehemiah the son of Azbuk, commander of half of the Beth Zur district, made repairs as far as the area across from the Tomb of David plus to the constructed pool and to the house of the mighty.

¹⁷ After him the Levites, under Rehum the son of Bani, made repairs. Next to them Hashabiah, commander of half of the Keilah district, made repairs in his area. ¹⁸ After him their brothers, under Binnui the son of Henadad, commander of the other half of the Keilah district, made repairs. ¹⁹ Next to them Ezer the son of Jeshua, commander of Mizpah, made repairs to another section across from the ascent to the armory at the corner. ²⁰ After him Baruch the son of Zabbai zealously repaired another section, from the corner to the door of the house of Eliashib the high priest. ²¹ After him Meremoth the son of Uriah the son of Hakkoz repaired another section from the door of the house of Eliashib to the end of it.

²² After him the priests, the men of the surrounding plain, made repairs. ²³ After them Benjamin and Hasshub made repairs across from their house. After them Azariah the son of Maaseiah the son of Ananiah made repairs beside his house. ²⁴ After him Binnui the son of Henadad repaired another section from the house of Azariah as far as the corner plus the corner tower. ²⁵ Palal the son of Uzai *made repairs* across from the corner and to the tower protruding out of the king's upper house next to the courtyard of the guards. After him Pedaiah the son of Parosh *made repairs.* ²⁶ The temple servants living in Ophel *made repairs* from opposite the Water Gate eastward to the protruding tower. ²⁷ After them the Tekoites repaired another section across from the great protruding tower as far as the wall of Ophel.

²⁸ Up to the Horse Gate the priests made repairs—each one across from his house. ²⁹ After them Zadok the son of Immer repaired across from his house. After him Shemaiah the son of Shekaniah, who was keeper of the East Gate, made repairs. ³⁰ After him Hananiah the son of Shelemiah and Hanun the sixth son of Zalaph repaired another section. After them Meshullam the son of Berekiah made repairs across from his chamber. ³¹ After him Malkijah the goldsmith's son made repairs as far as the house of the temple servants and the merchants. This was across from the Mustering Gate *extending* as far as the upper room of the corner tower. ³² Between the upper room of the corner tower and the Sheep Gate, the goldsmiths and the merchants made repairs.

Opposition to the Rebuilding

4 When Sanballat heard that we were rebuilding the wall, he became angry and was greatly irritated, and he mocked the Jews. ² He spoke before his relatives and the army of Samaria and said, "What are these feeble Jews doing? Are they fortifying themselves? Will they make sacrifices? Can they complete this in a day? Can they revive the burned-up stones out of the rubbish heaps?"

³ Now Tobiah the Ammonite was beside him, and he said, "Even what they are rebuilding, if even a fox climbed it, that would break down their stone wall."

⁴ Hear, O our God, that we are despised. Turn their reproach back upon their own head, and give them as spoil in a land of captivity: ⁵ No longer cover their iniquity nor blot out their sin, which is before You since they have made insults against the builders.

⁶ So we rebuilt the wall until all of it was solidified up to half its height. The people had a passion for the work.

⁷ When Sanballat, Tobiah, the Arabians, the Ammonites, and the Ashdodites heard how the restoration of Jerusalem's walls was progressing and how the breaches had begun to be sealed, it made them extremely furious. ⁸ So they all conspired together to fight against Jerusalem in order to cause it chaos. ⁹ Nevertheless we prayed to our God, and, because of them, we set up a watch for them day and night.

¹⁰ Judah had said, "The strength of the burden bearers is failing though there is much rubble. And we ourselves are unable to rebuild the wall."

¹¹ Our adversaries said, "They will neither know nor see until we have entered in among them and slain them. Indeed, we will stop the work!"

¹² When the Jews living near them came, they told us ten times, "From every place where you turn, *they will be* against us."

¹³ Therefore I set *guards* at the lowest positions *along the wall* and just inside the wall at the unrepaired areas. I also stationed the people by families *providing them individually* their own swords, spears, and bows. ¹⁴ After I looked around, I stood up and said to the nobles, the rulers, and the rest of the people, "Stop being terrified because of them! Remember instead that the Lord is great and awesome. So fight for each other—and for your sons, your daughters, your wives, and your houses."

¹⁵ Now when our enemies heard that this had become known to us and that God had brought their counsel to nothing, then we all returned to the wall, everyone to his work.

¹⁶ After that day, half of my servants did the work while the other half handled the spears, shields, bows, and body armor. Commanders were *appointed* to support every house of Judah. ¹⁷ Those rebuilding the wall and those hauling the loads were working with one hand doing the task, but with the other hand holding the weapon. ¹⁸ For the builders, everyone had his sword bound to his side, even while rebuilding. The trumpet blower worked beside me.

¹⁹ I said to the nobles, the rulers, and to the rest of the people, "The work is vast and over a large area. Since we are spread along the wall far from each other, ²⁰ assemble to us there at the place where you hear the trumpet sounded. Our God shall fight for us."

²¹ So we labored in the work with half of them holding spears from sunrise to the rising of the stars. ²² Likewise at the same time I said to the people, "Every man and his servant must lodge within Jerusalem. By night, they may be a guard to us; by day, a *laborer for* the work." ²³ So neither I nor my brothers nor my servants nor the men of the guard who followed me took off our clothes. Each carried his weapon, *even when* washing.

Nehemiah Stops Oppression

5 Now there was a great outcry of the people and their wives against their fellow Jews. ² Some were saying, "We and our sons and our daughters are many. Therefore, let us acquire grain so that we may eat and live."

³ Others were saying, "We have mortgaged our fields, vineyards, and houses so that we might acquire grain because of hunger."

⁴ Still others were saying, "We have borrowed money for the king's tribute *against the value of* our fields and vineyards. ⁵ Now our flesh is the same as the flesh of our countrymen. Our children are like their children, but we are subjugating our sons and our daughters as servants. Indeed, some of our daughters are in bondage already, and we are powerless *to do anything* because our fields and vineyards belong to others."

⁶ I was very angry when I heard their outcry and these words. ⁷ So I contemplated about this for myself and, as a result, I rebuked the nobles and officials and said to them, "Based on the claim of each against his brother, you are exacting usury." Then I convened a great assembly against them, ⁸ and I said to them, "By whatever means we had, we purchased our Jewish countrymen who were being sold to the nations. So, will you once more sell your countrymen so that they might *again* be sold to us?" Then they kept silent, because they found nothing to answer.

⁹ Also I said, "What you are doing is not good! Should not you walk in the fear of our God because of the reproach of the nations, our enemies? ¹⁰ Moreover, I, my relatives, and my servants are loaning them money

---

¹ 13 About 1,500 feet, or about 450 meters.

and grain. So, I urge you, cease from this practice of usury. [11] Please restore to them, even this day, their fields, their vineyards, their olive groves, and their houses, along with a hundredth part of the money, the grain, the wine, and the oil that you had exacted from them."

[12] Then they said, "We will restore *it* and will require nothing of them. We will do what you have said."

Then I called the priests and made them swear an oath to keep this promise. [13] Also I shook out the front of my garment and said, "Like this, may God shake out every man from his house and from his labor who does not carry out this promise. Exactly like this, may he be shaken out and emptied."

And all the congregation said, "Amen," and praised the LORD. And the people did according to this promise.

Nehemiah's Generosity

[14] Moreover from the time that I was appointed to be their governor in the land of Judah (from the twentieth year even until the thirty-second year of King Artaxerxes) twelve years *had passed*. And my companions and I had not eaten the governor's food *allotment*. [15] The former governors preceding me had extracted a heavy burden on the people, because they took from them food and wine, besides forty shekels[1] of silver. Moreover, even their servants domineered over the people. But I myself never did so, because of the fear of God. [16] Furthermore, I stayed determined in the work on this wall. We bought no field, and all my servants were gathered there for the sake of the work.

[17] Moreover there were *regularly* at my table one hundred and fifty Jews and officials, besides those who came to us from the nations around us. [18] Daily there were one ox and six choice sheep prepared for me. Fowls were also prepared for me. Once in ten days all sorts of wine *were supplied* in abundance. Yet for all this, I never required the governor's food *allotment* because it was a heavy burden on this people.

[19] Remember me, O my God, for good, according to all that I have done for this people.

Nehemiah's Enemies

6 When Sanballat, Tobiah, Geshem the Arabian, and the rest of our enemies heard that I had rebuilt the wall and that there was not a gap in it (though at that time I had not erected the doors on the gates), [2] Sanballat and Geshem sent to me, saying, "Come, that we might meet together in one of the villages in the plain of Ono."

But they planned to do evil to me. [3] So I sent messengers to them, saying, "I am doing a great work, so I am not able to come down. Why should the work cease while I leave it and come down to you?" [4] Four more times they sent for me like this, but I answered them the same way. [5] Sanballat sent the same request a fifth time by his servant, but the letter was open in his hand. [6] In it was written,

"It is reported among the nations, and Geshem confirms it, that you and the Jews are planning to rebel; consequently you are rebuilding the wall. According to these words, you are their king. [7] You have also appointed prophets to preach on your behalf in Jerusalem, saying, 'There is a king in Judah!' According to these words, it will now be reported to the king. So come now and let us consult together."

[8] I sent him *this response*, saying, "Nothing like these reports that you are saying has occurred. From your own mind, you are inventing *them*." [9] Because they all wanted to frighten us, they thought, "They will pull their hands back from the work." But that would never be done. So now, *O God*, strengthen my hands.

[10] When I came to the house of Shemaiah the crippled son of Delaiah the son of Mehetabel, he said, "Let us meet together at the house of God, inside the temple, and then we can shut the temple doors. They are coming to kill you! Even tonight, they could come to kill you!"

[11] But I said, "Should a man like me flee? Who is there like me who would go into the temple to save his life? I would never go!" [12] Then I perceived and saw that God had not sent him, but that he pronounced the prophecy against me, because Tobiah and Sanballat had hired him. [13] He was hired for this reason: that I might become fearful, act accordingly, and sin. Then they would have an evil report by which they could reproach me.

[14] Remember, O my God, concerning Tobiah and Sanballat these deeds of theirs, as well as the prophetess Noadiah and the rest of the prophets who were trying to frighten me.

The Wall Completed

[15] The wall was finished on the twenty-fifth day of the month Elul, in fifty-two days. [16] When all our enemies heard *it* and all the surrounding nations saw *it*, they were tremendously humbled. They perceived that, because of our God, this work had been accomplished.

[17] Moreover in those days the nobles of Judah produced numerous letters in transit to Tobiah. Likewise, the letters of Tobiah came to them, [18] because so many in Judah were bound by oath to him since he was the son-in-law of Shekaniah the son of Arah, and his son Jehohanan had married the daughter of Meshullam the son of Berekiah. [19] Also they reported his good deeds in front of me and reported my words to him. Tobiah sent letters to frighten me.

7 Once the wall was rebuilt and I had erected the doors, the gatekeepers, the singers, and the Levites were appointed. [2] Over Jerusalem, I put in charge both my brother Hanani and Hananiah, the palace commander, because each was a faithful man and feared God more than many. [3] I said to them, "The gates of Jerusalem should not be opened until the sun is hot. Until *guards* are posted, the doors should be closed and bolted. Likewise, appoint guards from Jerusalem's inhabitants—each at his post, across from his own house."

[4] Now the city was large and spacious, yet the people in it were few since there had been no houses built.

The List of Returned Exiles

Ezr 2:1–70

[5] So my God put *an idea* in my mind, and I gathered the nobles, the officials, and the people together to conduct a genealogy registration. When I found the book of the genealogical register, it *contained the list* of those who first came back. I found written in it:

[6] These are the people of the province who returned from the captivity of the exiles whom King Nebuchadnezzar of Babylon had carried away, but came back to Jerusalem and to Judah, everyone to his city. [7] Those who came with Zerubbabel were Joshua, Nehemiah, Azariah, Raamiah, Nahamani, Mordecai, Bilshan, Mispereth, Bigvai, Nehum, and Baanah.

The number of the men of the people of Israel was this:

[8] The sons of Parosh, two thousand one hundred and seventy-two;
[9] the sons of Shephatiah, three hundred and seventy-two;
[10] the sons of Arah, six hundred and fifty-two;
[11] the sons of Pahath-Moab, of the sons of Jeshua and Joab, two thousand eight hundred and eighteen;
[12] the sons of Elam, one thousand two hundred and fifty-four;
[13] the sons of Zattu, eight hundred and forty-five;
[14] the sons of Zakkai, seven hundred and sixty;
[15] the sons of Binnui, six hundred and forty-eight;
[16] the sons of Bebai, six hundred and twenty-eight;
[17] the sons of Azgad, two thousand three hundred and twenty-two;
[18] the sons of Adonikam, six hundred and sixty-seven;
[19] the sons of Bigvai, two thousand and sixty-seven;
[20] the sons of Adin, six hundred and fifty-five;
[21] the sons of Ater of Hezekiah, ninety-eight;
[22] the sons of Hashum, three hundred and twenty-eight;
[23] the sons of Bezai, three hundred and twenty-four;
[24] the sons of Hariph, one hundred and twelve;
[25] the sons of Gibeon, ninety-five.

[26] The men of Bethlehem and Netophah, one hundred and eighty-eight;

---

[1] 15 About 1 pound, or 460 grams.

²⁷ the men of Anathoth, one hundred and twenty-eight;
²⁸ the men of Beth Azmaveth, forty-two;
²⁹ the men of Kiriath Jearim, Kephirah, and Beeroth, seven hundred and forty-three;
³⁰ the men of Ramah and Geba, six hundred and twenty-one;
³¹ the men of Mikmash, one hundred and twenty-two;
³² the men of Bethel and Ai, one hundred and twenty-three;
³³ the men of the other Nebo, fifty-two;
³⁴ the sons of the other Elam, one thousand two hundred and fifty-four;
³⁵ the sons of Harim, three hundred and twenty;
³⁶ the sons of Jericho, three hundred and forty-five;
³⁷ the sons of Lod, Hadid, and Ono, seven hundred and twenty-one;
³⁸ the sons of Senaah, three thousand nine hundred and thirty.

Priestly Leaders
³⁹ The priests:

the sons of Jedaiah, of the house of Jeshua, nine hundred and seventy-three;
⁴⁰ the sons of Immer, one thousand and fifty-two;
⁴¹ the sons of Pashhur, one thousand two hundred and forty-seven;
⁴² the sons of Harim, one thousand and seventeen.

⁴³ The Levites:

the sons of Jeshua, of Kadmiel, and of the sons of Hodaviah, seventy-four.

⁴⁴ The singers:

the sons of Asaph, one hundred and forty-eight.

⁴⁵ The gatekeepers:

the sons of Shallum, the sons of Ater, the sons of Talmon, the sons of Akkub, the sons of Hatita, the sons of Shobai, one hundred and thirty-eight.

⁴⁶ The temple servants:

the sons of Ziha, the sons of Hasupha, the sons of Tabbaoth, ⁴⁷ the sons of Keros, the sons of Sia, the sons of Padon, ⁴⁸ the sons of Lebana, the sons of Hagaba, the sons of Shalmai, ⁴⁹ the sons of Hanan, the sons of Giddel, the sons of Gahar, ⁵⁰ the sons of Reaiah, the sons of Rezin, the sons of Nekoda, ⁵¹ the sons of Gazzam, the sons of Uzza, the sons of Paseah, ⁵² the sons of Besai, the sons of Meunim, the sons of Nephusim, ⁵³ the sons of Bakbuk, the sons of Hakupha, the sons of Harhur, ⁵⁴ the sons of Bazluth, the sons of Mehida, the sons of Harsha, ⁵⁵ the sons of Barkos, the sons of Sisera, the sons of Temah, ⁵⁶ the sons of Neziah, the sons of Hatipha.

⁵⁷ The sons of Solomon's servants:

the sons of Sotai, the sons of Sophereth, the sons of Perida, ⁵⁸ the sons of Jaala, the sons of Darkon, the sons of Giddel, ⁵⁹ the sons of Shephatiah, the sons of Hattil, the sons of Pokereth-Hazzebaim, the sons of Amon.

⁶⁰ All the temple servants and the sons of Solomon's servants were three hundred and ninety-two.

⁶¹ These were they who came up from Tel Melah, Tel Harsha, Kerub, Addon, and Immer, but they could not show their fathers' houses nor their lineage—whether they were of Israel:

⁶² The sons of
Delaiah, the sons of Tobiah, the sons of Nekoda, six hundred and forty-two.

⁶³ Of the priests:

the sons of
Hobaiah, the sons of Hakkoz, the sons of Barzillai, who married one of the daughters of Barzillai the Gileadite, and was called by their name.

⁶⁴ These sought for their fathers' registration in the genealogical registry, but it was not found. Therefore, they were considered as unclean *and removed* from the priesthood. ⁶⁵ The magistrate said to them that they should not eat of the most holy things until there was an appointed priest with Urim and Thummim.

⁶⁶ The whole congregation together was forty-two thousand three hundred and sixty, ⁶⁷ besides their male and female servants, which numbered seven thousand three hundred and thirty-seven; and they had two hundred and forty-five male and female singers. ⁶⁸ Their horses were seven hundred and thirty-six; their mules, two hundred and forty-five; ⁶⁹ their camels, four hundred and thirty-five; the donkeys, six thousand seven hundred and twenty.

⁷⁰ Some of the chiefs of the fathers' households gave to the work. The magistrate gave to the treasury one thousand gold drachmas,¹ fifty basins, and five hundred and thirty priests' garments. ⁷¹ Others of the chiefs of the fathers' households gave to the treasury for the work twenty thousand gold drachmas² and two thousand two hundred silver minas.³ ⁷² What the rest of the people gave was twenty thousand gold drachmas, two thousand silver minas,⁴ and sixty-seven priests' garments.
⁷³ So the priests, the Levites, the gatekeepers, the singers, some of the people, the temple servants, and all Israel lived in their cities.

Ezra Reads the Law
When the seventh month came, the children of Israel were in their cities.

8 All the people gathered together as one man in the area in front of the Water Gate, and they asked Ezra the scribe to bring the Book of the Law of Moses, which the Lᴏʀᴅ had commanded to Israel. ² On the first day of the seventh month, Ezra the priest brought the Law before the congregation of men, women, and all who could listen with understanding. ³ In the area in front of the Water Gate, he read aloud from sunrise until midday to the men, women, and those who could understand. All the people listened attentively to the Book of the Law.
⁴ Ezra the scribe stood on a raised wood platform, which they had made for the purpose. Beside him stood Mattithiah, Shema, Anaiah, Uriah, Hilkiah, and Maaseiah on his right hand; and on his left hand, Pedaiah, Mishael, Malkijah, Hashum, Hashbaddanah, Zechariah, and Meshullam.
⁵ Ezra opened the book in the sight of all the people (because he was above all the people), and, as he opened it, all the people stood up. ⁶ When Ezra blessed the Lᴏʀᴅ as the great God, all the people responded "Amen, Amen!" By lifting up their hands as they bowed their heads, they worshipped the Lᴏʀᴅ with their faces to the ground.
⁷ Then Jeshua, Bani, Sherebiah, Jamin, Akkub, Shabbethai, Hodiah, Maaseiah, Kelita, Azariah, Jozabad, Hanan, Pelaiah, and the Levites, explained the Law to the people while the people stood in their place. ⁸ They read from the book, from the Law of God, with interpretation, and they gave the sense, so that the people understood the reading.
⁹ Then Nehemiah the magistrate, Ezra the priest and scribe, and the Levites who were teaching the people said to all the people, "This day is holy to the Lᴏʀᴅ your God. Stop mourning and weeping." (This was because all the people wept when they heard the words of the Law.)
¹⁰ Then he said to them, "Go your way. Eat the fat, drink the sweet *drink*, and send portions to those for whom nothing is prepared; for

---

¹ 70 About 19 pounds, or 8.4 kilograms.   ² 71 About 375 pounds, or 170 kilograms; and in v. 72.   ³ 71 About 1⅓ tons, or 1.2 metric tons.
⁴ 72 About 1¼ tons, or 1.1 metric tons.

this day is holy to our Lord. Do not be grieved, for the joy of the LORD is your strength."

¹¹ So the Levites quieted all the people, saying, "Hush! Because today is holy you should stop being so sorrowful."

¹² Then all the people went to eat, to drink, to send portions, and to enjoy a great celebration because they had understood the words declared to them.

The Feast of Tabernacles

¹³ On the second day, the chiefs of the fathers' households of all the people, the priests, and the Levites were gathered to Ezra the scribe in order to understand the words of the Law. ¹⁴ They found written in the Law where the LORD had commanded by Moses that the children of Israel should dwell in booths in the feast of the seventh month, ¹⁵ and that they should publish and proclaim in all their cities and in Jerusalem, "Go out to the hills and bring olive branches, along with wild olive branches, myrtle branches, palm branches, and other leafy branches to make booths, as it was written."

¹⁶ So the people went out and brought back *branches* and made themselves booths. Each *household did so* on its roof, in their yard, on the grounds of the house of God, in the area in front of the Water Gate, or in the area at the Gate of Ephraim. ¹⁷ All the congregation who had returned from captivity made booths and lived in them. Not since the days of Joshua the son of Nun to that day had the children of Israel done so, and there was a tremendously great feast.

¹⁸ And day by day, from the first day to the last day, he read from the Book of the Law of God. They celebrated the feast seven days, and on the eighth day there was a solemn assembly as required.

The Israelites Confess Their Sins

9 Now on the twenty-fourth day of this month the children of Israel were assembled with fasting and sackcloth, and there was dirt on them. ² The offspring of Israel separated themselves from all the foreigners and then stood and confessed their sins and the iniquities of their fathers. ³ They stood in their place and read from the Book of the Law of the LORD their God for a fourth of the day. And for another fourth, they confessed and worshiped the LORD their God. ⁴ Jeshua, Bani, Kadmiel, Shebaniah, Bunni, Sherebiah, Bani, and Kenani stood up on the stairs of the Levites and cried with a loud voice to the LORD their God. ⁵ Then the Levites, Jeshua, Kadmiel, Bani, Hashabneiah, Sherebiah, Hodiah, Shebaniah, and Pethahiah, said:

"Stand up and bless the LORD your God forever and ever! Let them bless Your glorious name, which is exalted above all blessing and praise. ⁶ You alone are the LORD. You have made heaven, the heaven of heavens, with all their host, the earth and all that is on it, the seas and all that is in them; and You preserve them all. And the host of heaven worships You.

⁷ "You are the LORD God who chose Abram and brought him out of Ur of the Chaldeans. You gave him the name Abraham ⁸ and found his heart faithful before You. And You made a covenant with him to give him the land of the Canaanites, the Hittites, the Amorites, the Perizzites, the Jebusites, and the Girgashites—to give it to his seed. Indeed, You have fulfilled Your words because You are righteous.

⁹ "When You saw the affliction of our fathers in Egypt and heard their cry by the Red Sea, ¹⁰ You enacted signs and wonders against Pharaoh, against all his servants, and against all the people of his land because You knew how arrogantly they had acted against them. Thus, You made a name for Yourself, as it is this day. ¹¹ You divided the sea before them, so they might pass through the midst of the sea on dry ground, and cast their pursuers into the deep like a stone into stormy waters. ¹² By day You led them with a pillar of cloud, and by night with a pillar of fire to light the way for them to go.

¹³ "You came down on Mount Sinai and spoke with them from heaven and gave them just requirements, true laws, good statutes and commandments. ¹⁴ You also revealed to them Your Holy Sabbath and, by the hand of Moses Your servant, set in place for them the precepts, statutes, and laws. ¹⁵ You gave them bread from heaven for their hunger and brought water out of the rock for them for their thirst. You told them to enter in order to possess the land which You had sworn to give them.

¹⁶ "But they and our fathers acted proudly and hardened their necks and did not obey Your commandments. ¹⁷ They refused to obey and were not mindful of Your wonders that You performed among them. But they hardened their necks and in their rebellion appointed a leader to return to their bondage. But You are a God ready to pardon, gracious and merciful, slow to anger and abounding in kindness, and did not forsake them.

¹⁸ "Even when they had made themselves a molded calf and said, 'This is your god that brought you out of Egypt,' and committed terrible provocations, ¹⁹ yet You in Your great mercy did not forsake them in the wilderness: The pillar of the cloud did not depart from them by day, to lead them in the way, nor the pillar of fire by night, to light for them the way they should go. ²⁰ You gave Your good Spirit to instruct them, did not withhold Your manna from their mouth, and gave them water for their thirst. ²¹ Forty years You sustained them in the wilderness, so that they lacked nothing—their clothing did not wear out nor did their feet swell.

²² "You gave them kingdoms and nations, and You divided them as boundaries. They possessed the land of Sihon, which was the land of the king of Heshbon, and the land of Og, the king of Bashan. ²³ Their descendants You increased like the stars of heaven, and You brought them into the land, which You had promised to their fathers that they would enter and possess it. ²⁴ So the descendants went in and possessed the land, and You subdued for them the inhabitants of the land, the Canaanites, and gave them into their hands—with their kings and the peoples of the land—to do with them as they would. ²⁵ They captured unassailable cities and a fertile land. They possessed houses full of all goods, wells dug, vineyards, olive groves, and fruit trees in abundance, so they ate, were filled, and became fat, and they indulged themselves in Your great goodness.

²⁶ "Nevertheless they became disobedient, and rebelled against You, and cast Your law behind their backs, and killed Your prophets who had warned them to turn back to You. But they committed terrible provocations. ²⁷ Therefore You delivered them into the hand of their enemies, who afflicted them. When they cried to You in the time of their affliction, You heard from heaven, and, according to Your abundant mercy, You gave them deliverers who delivered them out of the hand of their enemies.

²⁸ "But after they had rest, they again did evil before You. Therefore You abandoned them to the hand of their enemies, so that they had dominion over them. Yet when they turned and cried to You, You heard from heaven, and many times You delivered them according to Your mercies.

²⁹ "You warned them in order to restore them again to Your law, but they acted arrogantly and did not listen to Your commandments. They sinned against Your ordinances (which would enable a man to live, if he would do them), stubbornly turning away and becoming belligerent so that they would not hear. ³⁰ For many years You endured them and warned them by Your Spirit in Your prophets, yet they would not listen. Therefore, You gave them into the hand of the people of the lands. ³¹ Nevertheless, for the sake of Your abundant mercy, You did not completely destroy them or forsake them. Indeed, You are a gracious and merciful God.

³² "Now therefore, our God, the great, the mighty, and the awesome God, who keeps covenant and mercy, let not all the hardship, since the time of the kings of Assyria until this day, that has come on us, our kings, our princes, our priests, our prophets, our fathers, and on all Your people seem insignificant to You. ³³ You are righteous for everything that has come upon us! You have acted faithfully while we have done wickedly. ³⁴ For our kings, princes, priests, and fathers have failed to keep Your law and did not obey Your commandments and Your warnings even when You confronted them. ³⁵ For whether in their kingdom or in Your abundant goodness (that You gave them) or in the spacious and fertile land (that You set before them), they have neither served You nor turned away from their wicked deeds.

³⁶ "Here we are, slaves today. The land that You gave to our fathers was for eating its fruit and its goodness. Behold, we have become slaves on account of it, ³⁷ because its abundant produce belongs to the kings whom You have set over us due to our sins. They have control over our bodies and over our livestock, as they please. We are in great distress."

Signatories to the Agreement

[38] So on the basis of all this, we are executing a written agreement that is being sealed by our princes, Levites, and priests.

Signatories of the Covenant

10 Now *the names of* those on the sealed agreement were:

Nehemiah, the magistrate, the son of Hakaliah, and Zedekiah. [2] Next were Seraiah, Azariah, Jeremiah, [3] Pashhur, Amariah, Malkijah, [4] Hattush, Shebaniah, Malluk, [5] Harim, Meremoth, Obadiah, [6] Daniel, Ginnethon, Baruch, [7] Meshullam, Abijah, Mijamin, [8] Maaziah, Bilgai, and Shemaiah. These were the priests.

[9] The Levites were:

Jeshua the son of Azaniah, Binnui of the sons of Henadad, and Kadmiel, [10] along with their relatives Shebaniah, Hodiah, Kelita, Pelaiah, Hanan, [11] Mika, Rehob, Hashabiah, [12] Zakkur, Sherebiah, Shebaniah, [13] Hodiah, Bani, and Beninu.

[14] The leaders of the people were:

Parosh, Pahath-Moab, Elam, Zattu, Bani, [15] Bunni, Azgad, Bebai, [16] Adonijah, Bigvai, Adin, [17] Ater, Hezekiah, Azzur, [18] Hodiah, Hashum, Bezai, [19] Hariph, Anathoth, Nebai, [20] Magpiash, Meshullam, Hezir, [21] Meshezabel, Zadok, Jaddua, [22] Pelatiah, Hanan, Anaiah, [23] Hoshea, Hananiah, Hasshub, [24] Hallohesh, Pilha, Shobek, [25] Rehum, Hashabnah, Maaseiah, [26] Ahiah, Hanan, Anan, [27] Malluk, Harim, and Baanah.

Summary of the Covenant

[28] The remainder of the people, the priests, the Levites, the gate-keepers, the singers, the temple servants, and all those who on the basis of the Law of God separated themselves from the people of the lands—their wives, their sons, and their daughters, *that is,* every one *capable of* knowledge *and* understanding— [29] have decisively joined in with their countrymen and their nobles, and obligated themselves—by both a curse and an oath—to walk in the Law of God, which was given by Moses the servant of God, and to observe and do all the commandments of the LORD who is our Lord, along with His judgments and His statutes [30] so that we will not give our daughters to the people of the land nor take their daughters for our sons.

[31] If the people of the land bring merchandise or any grain on the Sabbath day to sell, we will not buy from them on the Sabbath or a holy day. We will also renounce the seventh year *harvest* and the full payment of every debt.

[32] We also establish for ourselves the ordinance to collect from ourselves annually one-third of a shekel for the service of the house of our God: [33] for the showbread, the continual grain offering, the continual burnt offering, the Sabbaths, the New Moons, the appointed feasts, the holy things, and the sin offerings to make an atonement for Israel, as well as for all the work of the house of our God.

[34] Also, we cast lots to determine *the duty* of the supply of wood that the priests, the Levites, and the people—according to the houses of our fathers, *being* set by annually appointed times— might bring to the house of our God, in order to burn *it* on the altar of the LORD our God, as it is written in the Law; [35] and, likewise, for the annual bringing of the first fruits of our ground and the first fruits of all fruit of all trees to the house of the LORD; [36] and for bringing to the priests who are ministering at the house of God, the firstborn of our sons and livestock, as it is written in the Law, plus the firstborn of our herds and flocks.

[37] Moreover, the first of our fresh dough, our contributions, the fruit of every tree, and the new wine and oil we will bring to the priests at the chambers of the house of our God, but the tithe of our crops *we will bring* to the Levites, since they themselves receive the tithes in all our agricultural cities. [38] There must be a priest, a descendant of Aaron, with the Levites when they are collecting tithes, and the Levites will offer a tenth of the tithes to the house of our God, for the chambers of the storehouse. [39] Both the children of Israel and the Levites should bring the contribution of the grain, new wine, and the fresh oil to the chambers because the vessels of the sanctuary and the ministering priests, the gatekeepers, and the singers are there.

We resolve not to forsake the house of our God.

The Residents of Jerusalem

1Ch 9:1–17

11 Now the rulers of the people lived at Jerusalem, so the rest of the people cast lots in order to bring one out of ten to stay in Jerusalem, the holy city, while the other nine *remained in other* cities. [2] The people blessed all the men who volunteered to dwell in Jerusalem. [3] Now these are the leaders of the provinces who lived in Jerusalem (though in the cities of Judah every one lived on his own property within their cities): Israel, the priests, the Levites, the temple servants, and the descendants of Solomon's servants. [4] Some of the sons of Judah and Benjamin lived in Jerusalem.

Those from Judah were:

Athaiah the son of Uzziah, the son of Zechariah, the son of Amariah, the son of Shephatiah, the son of Mahalalel—the descendants of Perez, [5] and Maaseiah the son of Baruch, the son of Kol-Hozeh, the son of Hazaiah, the son of Adaiah, the son of Joiarib, the son of Zechariah, the son of Shelah. [6] All the descendants of Perez who lived in Jerusalem were four hundred and sixty-eight valiant men.

[7] These are the sons of Benjamin:

Sallu the son of Meshullam, the son of Joed, the son of Pedaiah, the son of Kolaiah, the son of Maaseiah, the son of Ithiel, the son of Jeshaiah, [8] and after him Gabbai and Sallai, *totaling* nine hundred and twenty-eight. [9] Joel, the son of Zikri, was their overseer, and Judah the son of Hassenuah was second *to him* over the city.

[10] Of the priests there were:

Jedaiah the son of Joiarib and Jakin; [11] Seraiah the son of Hilkiah, the son of Meshullam, the son of Zadok, the son of Meraioth, the son of Ahitub, was a ruler of the house of God. [12] Their relatives performing the work of the house were eight hundred and twenty-two. There was also Adaiah the son of Jeroham, the son of Pelaliah, the son of Amzi, the son of Zechariah, the son of Pashhur, the son of Malkijah, [13] plus his relatives who were chiefs of the fathers' houses were two hundred and forty-two; and Amashsai the son of Azarel, the son of Ahzai, the son of Meshillemoth, the son of Immer, [14] and their brothers, mighty men of valor, were one hundred and twenty-eight. Their overseer was Zabdiel, the son of Haggedolim.

[15] From the Levites there were:

Shemaiah the son of Hasshub, the son of Azrikam, the son of Hashabiah, the son of Bunni; [16] plus Shabbethai and Jozabad, who as leaders of the Levites had oversight of the outside work of the house of God. [17] Mattaniah the son of Mika, the son of

Zabdi, the son of Asaph, was the first to begin the thanksgiving at prayer, Bakbukiah was the second out of his relatives, and then Abda the son of Shammua, the son of Galal, the son of Jeduthun. [18] All the Levites in the holy city were two hundred and eighty-four.

[19] Moreover, the gatekeepers, Akkub, Talmon, and their relatives who kept watch at the gates, were one hundred and seventy-two.

[20] The rest of Israel, the priests, and the Levites were in all the cities of Judah, every one *tending* to his own inheritance. [21] But the temple servants lived in Ophel, and Ziha and Gishpa were over them. [22] The overseer of the Levites in Jerusalem was Uzzi the son of Bani, the son of Hashabiah, the son of Mattaniah, the son of Mika. Some of the sons of Asaph were the singers attending to the work of the house of God, [23] for the king's regulation about them made their unity a daily issue. [24] Pethahiah the son of Meshezabel, of the sons of Zerah the son of Judah, was the king's assistant[1] in all matters concerning the people.

The Residents Outside Jerusalem
[25] For the villages *located* by their fields, some of the people of Judah lived at Kiriath Arba and its villages, *others* at Dibon and its villages, or at Jekabzeel and its villages, [26] as well as at Jeshua, at Moladah, and at Beth Pelet, [27] and at Hazar Shual, and at Beersheba and its villages, [28] and at Ziklag, at Mekonah and its villages, [29] and at En Rimmon, at Zorah, at Jarmuth, [30] Zanoah, Adullam and their villages, at Lachish and its fields, and at Azekah and its villages. So they lived from Beersheba as far as the Valley of Hinnom. [31] Some of the Benjamites settled from Geba onward, at Mikmash, Aija, and Bethel and their villages, [32] at Anathoth, Nob, Ananiah, [33] Hazor, Ramah, Gittaim, [34] Hadid, Zeboim, Neballat, [35] Lod, and Ono, the valley of craftsmen. [36] From the Levites, some divisions in Judah belonged to Benjamin.

The Priests and Levites
12 Now these are the priests and the Levites who came up with Zerubbabel the son of Shealtiel, and Joshua: Seraiah, Jeremiah, Ezra, [2] Amariah, Malluk, Hattush, [3] Shekaniah, Rehum, Meremoth, [4] Iddo, Ginnethon, Abijah, [5] Mijamin, Moadiah, Bilgah, [6] Shemaiah, and Joiarib, Jedaiah, [7] Sallu, Amok, Hilkiah, Jedaiah. These were the leaders of the priests and of their relatives in the days of Joshua.

[8] Moreover the Levites were Jeshua, Binnui, Kadmiel, Sherebiah, Judah, and Mattaniah, who was over the thanksgiving *songs*, in conjunction with his relatives. [9] There were also their relatives Bakbukiah and Unni, positioned across from each other in the watches.

[10] Joshua was the father of Joiakim, Joiakim was the father of Eliashib, Eliashib was the father of Joiada, [11] Joiada was the father of Jonathan, and Jonathan was the father of Jaddua.

[12] Now in the days of Joiakim, the priests, these were the heads of the fathers' houses:
of Seraiah, Meraiah;
of Jeremiah, Hananiah;
[13] of Ezra, Meshullam;
of Amariah, Jehohanan;
[14] of Malluk, Jonathan;
of Shebaniah, Joseph;
[15] of Harim, Adna;
of Meraioth, Helkai;
[16] of Iddo, Zechariah;
of Ginnethon, Meshullam;
[17] of Abijah, Zikri;
of Miniamin and of Moadiah, Piltai;

[18] of Bilgah, Shammua;
of Shemaiah, Jehonathan;
[19] of Joiarib, Mattenai;
of Jedaiah, Uzzi;
[20] of Sallu, Kallai;
of Amok, Eber;
[21] of Hilkiah, Hashabiah;
and of Jedaiah, Nethanel.

[22] The Levites, as well as the priests, were recorded as the chiefs of the fathers' houses in the days of Eliashib, Joiada, Johanan, and Jaddua during the reign of Darius the Persian. [23] The descendants of Levi who *served* as the chiefs of the fathers' house were recorded in the book of the chronicles until the days of Johanan the son of Eliashib. [24] The leaders of the Levites were Hashabiah, Sherebiah, and Jeshua the son of Kadmiel, with their brothers across from them, to praise and to give thanks, section opposite section, according to the commandment of David the man of God.

[25] Mattaniah, Bakbukiah, Obadiah, Meshullam, Talmon, and Akkub were gatekeepers maintaining the guard duty at the storehouse of the gates. [26] These *leaders* served during the days of Joiakim the son of Joshua, the son of Jozadak, during the days of Nehemiah the governor, and *during the days* of Ezra the priest, the scribe.

Nehemiah Dedicates the City Wall
[27] At the dedication of the wall of Jerusalem they sought to bring the Levites from all their places to Jerusalem to celebrate the dedication appropriately with thanksgiving songs and singing, accompanied by cymbals, harps, and lyres. [28] The members of choirs that assembled from the regions all around Jerusalem, from the villages of the Netophathites, [29] from Beth Gilgal, and from fields of Geba and Azmaveth, because they had built villages for themselves all around Jerusalem. [30] Then the priests and the Levites purified themselves. They also purified the people, the gates, and the wall.

[31] Then I led the commanders of Judah up to the top of the wall and appointed two great thanksgiving choirs. The first choir proceeded to the right on the wall toward the Dung Gate. [32] Behind them followed Hoshaiah, and half of the princes of Judah, [33] with Azariah, Ezra, and Meshullam, [34] Judah, Benjamin, Shemaiah, Jeremiah, [35] and some of the priests with trumpets—Zechariah, the son of Jonathan, the son of Shemaiah, the son of Mattaniah, the son of Micaiah, the son of Zakkur, the son of Asaph, [36] in conjunction with his relatives— Shemaiah, Azarel, Milalai, Gilalai, Maai, Nethanel, Judah, and Hanani, being accompanied with the musical instruments of David the man of God. Ezra the scribe went before them. [37] At the Fountain Gate, directly across from them, they ascended the steps of the City of David, following that sloped section of the wall up to the house of David, then eastward to the Water Gate.

[38] The second thanksgiving choir proceeded to the left where I followed them with the other half of the people on top of the wall, from the Tower of the Furnaces to the Broad Wall, [39] then from above the Ephraim Gate past the Old Gate, the Fish Gate, the Tower of Hananel, and the Tower of the Hundred, as far as the Sheep Gate, but they stood *still* at the Gate of the Guard.

[40] So the two thanksgiving choirs stood in the house of God, as did I and the half of the officials with me, [41] and the priests, Eliakim, Maaseiah, Miniamin, Micaiah, Elioenai, Zechariah, and Hananiah, with trumpets, [42] and Maaseiah, Shemaiah, Eleazar, Uzzi, Jehohanan, Malkijah, Elam, and Ezer. The singers sang loudly. Jezrahiah was their director. [43] On that day they offered great sacrifices and rejoiced because God had given them great cause for rejoicing. The wives and the children rejoiced, too. From far away the joyful celebration of Jerusalem was heard.

Temple Responsibilities
[44] At that time men were appointed to govern over the chambers for the treasures, for the contributions, for the first fruits, and for the tithes, so that they might gather into them out of the fields of the cities the legal portions belonging to the priests and Levites. This was because the celebration of Judah survived on the basis of the priests and the Levites [45] who, accompanied by the singers and the

---
[1] 24 Lit. *at the king's hand.*

gatekeepers, attentively preserved the practices of their God and the practices of purification, according to the commandment of David and of his son Solomon. [46] For in the former days of David and Asaph there were leaders for the singers, the songs of praise, and thanksgivings to God. [47] All Israel in the days of Zerubbabel and Nehemiah gave the singers and the gatekeepers *their* portions, as specified daily. Likewise, they consecrated what was due to the Levites, who then consecrated what was due for the descendants of Aaron.

The Reforms of Nehemiah

13 On that day they read aloud from the Book of Moses in the hearing of the people. In it there was found written that no Ammonite or Moabite should ever enter the congregation of God, [2] because they did not meet the children of Israel with bread and water, but hired Balaam to curse them. However, our God turned the curse into a blessing. [3] When they heard the Law, they separated from Israel all the racially mixed.

[4] Before this, Eliashib the priest, who had been appointed to govern the chambers of the house of our God, was related to Tobiah. [5] So, he had prepared a great chamber hall for him, where previously they had stored the contributions, the frankincense, the vessels, and the tithes of grain, new wine, and fresh oil, as required, for the Levites, the singers, the gatekeepers, and the contribution for the priests.

[6] But during this time I was not in Jerusalem, since in the thirty-second year of King Artaxerxes of Babylon I had gone to the king. At the conclusion of those days I requested a leave of the king. [7] When I came to Jerusalem and understood the evil that Eliashib did for Tobiah by preparing him a chamber in the courts of the house of God, [8] I was very grieved. So, from the chamber I threw all of the household belongings of Tobiah outside. [9] Then I commanded, and they cleansed the chambers so that I could return there the vessels of the house of God, the contributions for the offerings, and the frankincense.

[10] When I perceived that the supplies for the Levites had not been given and that the Levites and the singers doing the work had fled, everyone to his own field, [11] I confronted the officials and asked, "Why is the house of God forsaken?" So I gathered them and stationed them at their posts.

[12] Then all Judah brought the tithe of the grain, the new wine, and the fresh oil to the storehouses. [13] Overseeing the replenishing of the storehouse, I appointed Shelemiah the priest, Zadok the scribe, and Pedaiah from the Levites, and to assist them Hanan the son of Zakkur, the son of Mattaniah, for they were considered reliable, and their task was to distribute to their relatives.

[14] Remember me, O my God, concerning this. Do not blot out my good deeds that I have done for the house of my God and its workings.

[15] In those days I saw in Judah some treading winepresses on the Sabbath or hauling loads of grain or loading donkeys with wine, grapes, figs, and all manner of burdens in order to bring them to Jerusalem on the Sabbath day. So, during the day while they were selling the food goods, I warned them. [16] Men of Tyre also stayed there, having hauled in fish and all kinds of merchandise, and sold them on the Sabbath to the people of Judah, and in Jerusalem. [17] Then I confronted the nobles of Judah and asked them, "What is this evil thing that you are doing, profaning the Sabbath day? [18] Did not your fathers do likewise? Did not our God bring all this evil against us and against this city? Will you yet bring more wrath upon Israel by profaning the Sabbath?"

[19] As the gates of Jerusalem began to cast the evening shadow before the Sabbath, I commanded that the gates should be shut, and charged that they should not be opened until after the Sabbath. Some of my servants I stationed at the gates so that there would be no loads brought in on the Sabbath day. [20] Once or twice the merchants and sellers of all kind of merchandise lodged outside Jerusalem. [21] So I warned them and said to them, "Why do you spend the night next to the wall? If you do so again, I will send you away by force." From that time on they stopped coming on the Sabbath. [22] Then I commanded the Levites to purify themselves so that they could come and, as guardians of the gates, sanctify the Sabbath day.

Remember me, O my God, concerning this also, and spare me according to Your abundant mercy.

[23] Moreover, in those days I also saw Jews who had married the women of Ashdod, Ammon, and Moab. [24] Half of their children spoke in the language of Ashdod, yet none of them could recognize the language of the Jews. This was true language by language. [25] So I confronted them and cursed them. Some of the men I beat. Others, I plucked out their hair. Also, I made them swear an oath by God and said to them, "You shall neither give your daughters to their sons, nor marry their daughters to your sons or to yourselves. [26] Did not Solomon king of Israel sin by these things? Yet among many nations there was no king like him. He was loved by his God, who made him king over all Israel. Nevertheless, foreign women caused even him to sin. [27] Should we then listen to you, the ones doing all this great evil, who are behaving unfaithfully against our God by bedding foreign women?"

[28] Also, one of the sons of Joiada, the son of Eliashib the high priest, was a son-in-law to Sanballat the Horonite, so I drove him away from me.

[29] Remember them, O my God, because they have defiled the priesthood and the covenant of the priesthood and the Levites.

[30] Thus I purified them from everything foreign and appointed work crews for the priests and the Levites, each to his task, [31] and I provided the wood offering, at the appointed times, and the first fruits.

Remember me, O my God, for good.

ESTHER

Queen Vashti Deposed

1 Now in the days of Ahasuerus, *also called Xerxes*, who reigned from India to Ethiopia, over one hundred and twenty-seven provinces, [2] in those days, the palace where King Ahasuerus sat on the royal throne of his kingdom was in Susa. [3] In the third year of his reign, he prepared a feast for all his officials and his servants. So the army commanders of Persia and Media, the nobles, and the officials of the provinces were before him.

[4] He unveiled the riches of his glorious kingdom and the costly luxury of his greatness for many days, one hundred and eighty days. [5] When these days were completed, the king prepared a seven-day feast for all the people present, from the greatest to the least, in the citadel of Susa. This feast was in the courtyard garden of the king's palace [6] where white and blue linen hangings were fastened with cords of white and purple linen to silver rings and columns of marble. The gold- and silver-*plated* couches were on a mosaic pavement of porphyry, marble, mother-of-pearl, and *other* costly stones. [7] They provided drinks in golden vessels (the vessels being diverse one from another) and royal wine in abundance, by the expense of the king. [8] In accordance with the law, the drinking was not mandatory, because the king had directed all the stewards of his house to serve according to every man's pleasure.

⁹ Additionally, Vashti the queen prepared a feast for the women in the royal house of King Ahasuerus.

¹⁰ On the seventh day, when the heart of the king was merry with wine, he commanded Mehuman, Biztha, Harbona, Bigtha, Abagtha, Zethar, and Karkas, the seven eunuchs attending to the needs of King Ahasuerus, ¹¹ to bring Queen Vashti before the king with the royal crown, to unveil her beauty to the people and the officials, for she was beautiful. ¹² But Queen Vashti refused to come at the king's command delivered by his eunuchs. Therefore, the king grew very angry, and his wrath burned within him.

¹³ Then the king spoke to the wise men, who understood the times (for in this way the king would speak before all who understood law and judgment). ¹⁴ Those nearest him were Karshena, Shethar, Admatha, Tarshish, Meres, Marsena, and Memukan. *They were* the seven princes of Persia and Media and the king's closest confidants who met with the king and held the highest rank in the kingdom.

¹⁵ "According to law, what should be done about Queen Vashti because she did not obey the command of King Ahasuerus *when it was delivered* by the eunuchs?"

¹⁶ And Memukan answered before the king and the princes, "Queen Vashti has wronged not only the king but also all the princes and all the people who are in all the provinces of King Ahasuerus. ¹⁷ For should this matter of the queen spread to all wives, then they would look with contempt on their husbands when it is reported that, 'King Ahasuerus commanded Queen Vashti to be brought before him, but she never came.' ¹⁸ This very day the noble ladies of Persia and Media, who hear of the queen's act, will say the same thing to all the king's princes. Then there will be more contempt and wrath.

¹⁹ "If it pleases the king, let a royal decree be sent by him, and let it be written in the laws of the Persians and the Medes, that it may not be altered, that Vashti can never enter into the presence of King Ahasuerus, and that the king will give her royal position to another woman who is better than she. ²⁰ When the king's decree that he shall make is proclaimed throughout all his empire (for it is vast), then all the wives shall give honor to their husbands, both the prominent and lowly."

²¹ The suggestion pleased the king and the princes, so the king did according to the word of Memukan. ²² He sent letters to all the king's provinces, in the script of every province and in the language of every people group, bearing the message in the languages of his people that each man should rule over his own house.

Esther Becomes Queen

2 After these things, as the rage of King Ahasuerus abated, he became mindful of Vashti, what she had done and what was decreed against her. ² So the king's servants who attended him said, "Let beautiful young virgins be sought for the king! ³ Let the king appoint officers in all the provinces of his kingdom so that they may gather all the beautiful young virgins to the citadel of Susa, to the harem under the custody of Hegai the king's eunuch, who is in charge of the harem, and let ointments and cosmetics be given to them. ⁴ May the young woman who pleases the king be queen instead of Vashti." And the idea pleased the king, so he acted accordingly.

⁵ Now in the citadel of Susa, there was a certain Jew named Mordecai, the son of Jair, the son of Shimei, the son of Kish, a Benjamite. ⁶ He had been taken away from Jerusalem among the exiles and carried into captivity along with King Jeconiah of Judah by King Nebuchadnezzar of Babylon. ⁷ He was the guardian of Hadassah, that is Esther (who was his uncle's daughter) because she had neither father nor mother. The young woman was lovely to look at and beautiful in form. When her father and mother died, Mordecai took her as his own daughter.

⁸ When the king's notice and his decree were heard, many young women were then gathered to the citadel of Susa and *placed* under the custody of Hegai. Esther was likewise brought to the king's house and *placed* under the custody of Hegai, who was in charge of the harem. ⁹ Because the young lady appeared pleasing to him and had gained favor in his sight, he quickly gave her the ointments and cosmetics, her allotted food, and seven young chosen women from the king's palace. He also transferred her and her young women to the best place of the harem.

¹⁰ Esther had not disclosed her people or her lineage because Mordecai had charged her not to disclose it. ¹¹ Every day Mordecai walked around the courtyard of the harem to find out how Esther fared and what might be done with her.

¹² The turn came for each young woman to go in to King Ahasuerus, after being twelve months under the regulations for the women, since this was the regular period of their beautifying, six months with oil of myrrh and six months with spices and ointments for women. ¹³ When the young woman went in to the king in this way, she was given whatever she desired to take with her from the harem to take to the king's palace. ¹⁴ In the evening she went in, and in the morning she returned to the second harem in custody of Shaashgaz, the king's eunuch, who was in charge of the concubines. She did not go in to the king again unless the king delighted in her and called for her by name.

¹⁵ When the turn came for Esther, the daughter of Abihail the uncle of Mordecai, who had taken her as his own daughter, to go in to the king, she asked for nothing except what the king's eunuch Hegai, who had charge of the women, advised. Now Esther obtained favor in the sight of all who saw her. ¹⁶ So Esther was taken to King Ahasuerus at his royal house in the month of Tebeth, which is the tenth month, in the seventh year of his reign.

¹⁷ The king loved Esther more than any other woman because she had gained grace and favor in his sight more than all the virgins. So he set the royal crown on her head and made her queen instead of Vashti. ¹⁸ The king held a great feast for all his officials and servants. It was a feast for Esther. He remitted his provinces from tax payments and gave gifts according to his royal generosity.

Mordecai Uncovers a Plot

¹⁹ At the second gathering of the virgins, Mordecai was sitting at the king's gate. ²⁰ Esther had not yet disclosed her lineage or her people, since Mordecai had so commanded her. Esther followed the command of Mordecai just as she had when under his protection.

²¹ During those days when Mordecai was sitting at the king's gate, two of the king's eunuchs, Bigthan and Teresh, who served as keepers of the door, became angry and sought to attack King Ahasuerus. ²² But the matter became known to Mordecai, and he reported it to Queen Esther, and Esther reported it to the king in the name of Mordecai. ²³ When the matter was investigated and confirmed, both men were hanged on the gallows, and it was written in the book of the chronicles in the presence of the king.

Haman Plots to Destroy the Jews

3 After these things King Ahasuerus praised Haman the son of Hammedatha the Agagite, and promoted him, and set his seat above all the officials who were with him. ² All the king's servants, when they were at the king's gate, bowed or paid homage to Haman since the king had commanded it. Mordecai, however, never bowed or paid homage.

³ So the king's servants tending the king's gate said to Mordecai, "Why are you transgressing the king's commandment?" ⁴ Though they spoke to him daily, he never listened to them, so they reported it to Haman to see if the words of Mordecai would stand, for Mordecai had told them that he was a Jew.

⁵ When Haman saw that Mordecai neither bowed nor paid him homage, he was filled with rage. ⁶ But he disdained to lay hands on only Mordecai, since they had told him of the people of Mordecai. So Haman sought to destroy all the Jews throughout the whole kingdom of Ahasuerus.

⁷ In the first month, which is the month Nisan, in the twelfth year of King Ahasuerus, they cast Pur (that is, cast lots) before Haman daily, and each month, until the twelfth month, which is the month Adar, *to determine the time.*

⁸ Then Haman said to King Ahasuerus, "There exists a scattered people dispersed among the *other* peoples in all the provinces of your kingdom. Their laws are different from all others, and they are not complying with the king's laws, so there may not be a suitable reason for the king to allow them to exist. ⁹ If it pleases the king, may it be written that they are to be destroyed, and may there be ten thousand talents^f of silver deposited into the king's treasuries so that I may distribute it to the hands of those doing the work."

f 9 About 375 tons, or 340 metric tons.

[10] The king took his signet ring from his hand and gave it to Haman, the son of Hammedatha the Agagite, the enemy of the Jews. [11] The king said to Haman, "The silver has been granted to you, as have the people, so do with each as it pleases you."

[12] Then the king's scribes were summoned on the thirteenth day of the first month, and a decree was written just as Haman had commanded to the king's satraps and to the governors over each province and to the officials of all peoples and to every province according to its own script, and to every people in their language. It was written in the name of King Ahasuerus and sealed with the king's signet ring. [13] The letters were sent by mounted couriers into all the king's provinces to cause the destruction, slaughter, and annihilation of all Jews, both young and old, little children and women, in one day, the thirteenth day of the twelfth month, which is the month Adar, and even to plunder their possessions. [14] A copy of the document, issued as law in every province, was proclaimed, calling for all people to be ready for the day.

[15] The couriers went out, being hastened by the king's command. At the citadel of Susa, when the decree was issued, the king and Haman sat down to drink, but the city of Susa was in uproar.

Esther Helps the Jews

4 When Mordecai learned all that had been done, he tore his clothes and put on sackcloth with ashes, and went out into the midst of the city, and cried with a loud and bitter cry. [2] He went as far as the king's gate because no one was allowed to enter into the king's gate clothed with sackcloth. [3] In each and every province where the king's command and his decree came there was great mourning among the Jews, and fasting, and weeping, and wailing. Many lay in sackcloth and ashes.

[4] So the young women of Esther and her eunuchs came and told her of it. The queen was then seized by anguish. She sent garments to clothe Mordecai so that he could remove his sackcloth, but he would not accept them. [5] So Esther summoned Hathak, one of the king's eunuchs appointed to attend her, and commanded him concerning Mordecai to learn what this was about and why.

[6] So Hathak went out to where Mordecai was in the area of the city in front of the king's gate. [7] Mordecai told him about all that had happened to him and about the sum of silver that Haman had promised to pay to the king's treasuries for the destruction of the Jews. [8] Mordecai also gave him a copy of the written decree issued in Susa concerning their destruction so he could show Esther, tell her about it, and then charge her to go to the king in order to gain him favor with the king and to make requests in the presence of the king for her people.

[9] Hathak returned and told Esther the words of Mordecai. [10] Again Esther spoke to Hathak and ordered him *to reply* to Mordecai: [11] "All the king's servants and the people of the king's provinces know that whoever, whether man or woman, wishes to come to the king at the inner court but has not been summoned, there is one law—to put him to death—unless for some reason the king should hold out the golden scepter so that he might live. I, however, have not been summoned to come to the king for these thirty days."

[12] So all the words of Esther were told to Mordecai. [13] Then Mordecai told them to reply to Esther, "Do not think that in the king's palace you will be more likely to escape than all the other Jews. [14] For if you remain silent at this time, protection and deliverance for the Jews will be ordained from some other place, but you and your father's house shall be destroyed. And who knows if you may have attained royal position for such a time as this?"

[15] Then Esther replied, sending back to Mordecai: [16] "Go, gather all the Jews who can be found in Susa, then fast for me. Stop eating and drinking for three days, night or day. I and my young women will fast likewise. Only then would I dare go to the king since it is not allowed by law, and if I perish, I perish."

[17] So Mordecai went away and did exactly as Esther had commanded him.

Queen Esther's Banquet

5 On the third day, Esther put on her royal apparel and positioned herself in the king's palace courtyard so that she would be directly in line with the *part of* the king's throne room where the king sat facing the entrance of the room on his royal throne in the royal hall. [2] When the king saw Queen Esther standing quietly out in the courtyard, she gained favor in his sight, so the king held out the golden scepter in his hand to Esther. Esther approached and touched the top of the scepter.

[3] And the king said to her, "Queen Esther, what do you want? What is your request? Even if it is up to half of the kingdom, it will be given to you."

[4] Esther answered, "If it pleases the king, let the king and Haman come today to a feast that I have prepared for him."

[5] Then the king said, "Quickly bring Haman so that we may accept the invitation of Esther."

So the king and Haman came to the banquet that Esther had prepared. [6] While drinking wine the king said to Esther, "For whatever you ask, it shall be granted you. So, what is your request? Even if it is for as much as half of the kingdom, it shall be done."

[7] Then Esther replied and said, "This is my petition and request. [8] If I have won the king's favor, and if it pleases the king to grant my petition and fulfill my request, then let the king and Haman come to the banquet that I will prepare for them, and tomorrow I will do what the king says."

Haman's Plan to Destroy Mordecai

[9] Haman left that day joyfully and with a glad heart, but when Haman saw Mordecai at the king's gate, that he neither stood up nor trembled because of him, then Haman was full of indignation against Mordecai. [10] Nevertheless, Haman restrained himself, and when he came to his home, he sent for his friends and for his wife Zeresh.

[11] Haman recounted to them the glory of his riches, his many children, and everything about him the king had praised, and how he had promoted him over the princes and servants of the king. [12] Then Haman continued, "Indeed, Queen Esther brought to the banquet she had prepared no one but the king and me, and tomorrow I am again invited by her with the king. [13] Yet for all this, I am not satisfied whenever I see Mordecai the Jew sitting at the king's gate."

[14] Then his wife Zeresh and all his friends suggested to him, "Let a gallows fifty cubits[1] tall be constructed, and in the morning ask the king if Mordecai can be hanged on it. Then go merrily with the king to the banquet." And the suggestion pleased Haman, so he had the gallows constructed.

The King Honors Mordecai

6 During that night the king could not sleep, so he ordered that the book of memorable acts (the chronicles) be brought, and they were read before the king. [2] It was found written that Mordecai had informed on Bigthana and Teresh, the two eunuchs of the king *serving as* the keepers of the door, who had sought to assault King Ahasuerus.

[3] So the king said, "What honor or dignity has been done for Mordecai as a result of this?"

Then the king's servants attending him said, "Nothing has been done for him."

[4] So the king said, "Who is out in the courtyard?" Now Haman had just then entered from across the palace courtyard in order to speak to the king about hanging Mordecai on the gallows that he had prepared for him.

[5] The king's attendants said to him, "Haman is waiting in the court." So the king said, "Let him enter."

[6] And Haman entered. Now the king said to him, "What should be done for the man whom the king desires to honor?"

Haman thought in his heart, "Who more than me would the king desire to honor?" [7] So Haman answered the king, "For the man whom the king delights to honor, [8] let royal apparel be brought that the king himself has worn, and a horse on which the king has ridden, which has a royal insignia on its head. [9] Let the apparel and horse for this man be handled by one of the king's noble officials in order to dress the man whom the king delights to honor, as well as to lead him on horseback throughout the city. Finally, let him proclaim before him, 'Like this it shall be done for the man whom the king delights to honor.'"

[10] Then the king said to Haman, "Quickly take the apparel and the horse, as you have said, and do so for Mordecai, the Jew sitting at the king's gate. Of everything you have spoken, do not fall short of any of it."

[1] 14 About 75 feet, or 23 meters.

¹¹ So Haman took the apparel and the horse, arrayed Mordecai, led him on horseback throughout the city, and proclaimed before him, "Like this it shall be done for the man whom the king delights to honor."

¹² As Mordecai returned again to the king's gate, Haman hurried to his house, mourning with *his* head covered. ¹³ Haman recounted to his wife Zeresh and all his friends everything that had happened to him.

Then his wise friends and his wife Zeresh said to him, "If Mordecai, before whom you have begun to fall, is of Jewish lineage, then you will not be victorious over him. Rather, you will surely fall before him." ¹⁴ While they were still talking with him, the king's eunuchs arrived and rushed Haman to the banquet that Esther had prepared.

Haman Executed

7 So the king and Haman entered to feast and drink with Queen Esther. ² The king repeated to Esther what he had said on the previous day while drinking wine, "For what are you asking, Queen Esther? It shall be granted to you. Now, what is your request? Even if it is half of the kingdom, it will be done!"

³ Queen Esther replied, "If I have found favor in your sight, O king, and if it pleases the king, at my petition, let my life be given me, and my people at my request. ⁴ For we have been sold, I and my people, to be destroyed, to be slain, and to be annihilated. If only we had been sold as male and female slaves, I could have kept quiet, for that distress would not be sufficient to trouble the king."

⁵ Then King Ahasuerus answered and demanded of Queen Esther, "Who is he, and where is he, who would dare presume in his heart to do so?"

⁶ Esther said, "This wicked Haman is the adversary and enemy!"

Then Haman was seized with terror before the king and the queen. ⁷ And the king arose from the banquet of wine in his wrath and went into the palace garden. But Haman remained to plead for his life from Queen Esther, for he saw that harm was determined against him by the king.

⁸ Now the king returned from the palace garden back to the hall of the banquet as Haman was falling on the couch where Esther was. Then the king said, "Will he also violate the queen while I am in the room?"

As the shout erupted from the king's mouth, they covered the face of Haman. ⁹ Then Harbona, one of the eunuchs in the king's presence, said, "The gallows, fifty cubits¹ high, which Haman had constructed for Mordecai (who had spoken good on behalf of the king), stands at the house of Haman."

¹⁰ Then the king said, "Hang him on it!" So they hanged Haman on the gallows that he had prepared for Mordecai. Then the king's wrath was pacified.

Esther Saves the Jews

8 On that day King Ahasuerus gave Queen Esther the house of Haman, the enemy of the Jews. Mordecai came before the king because Esther disclosed who he was to her. ² The king took off his signet ring, which he had taken away from Haman, and gave it to Mordecai. Esther appointed Mordecai over the house of Haman.

³ Then Esther spoke again to the king and fell down at his feet and begged him with tears to avert the evil of Haman the Agagite, and the scheme that he had devised against the Jews. ⁴ When the king held out the golden scepter to Esther, she rose and stood before the king, ⁵ and said, "If it pleases the king, and if I have found favor in his sight, and the idea seems right before the king, and I have his approval, then let it be written to reverse the letters, devised by Haman the son of Hammedatha the Agagite, which he wrote to destroy the Jews in all the king's provinces. ⁶ For how am I able to watch the evil that will unfold against my people? How can I endure to see the destruction of my kindred?"

⁷ Then King Ahasuerus said to Queen Esther and to Mordecai the Jew, "See, I have given Esther the house of Haman, and they have hanged him on the gallows because he threatened violence against the Jews. ⁸ Now, as it suits you, write in the king's name on behalf of the Jews and seal it with the king's signet ring, because a document written in the king's name and sealed with the king's signet ring cannot be repealed."

⁹ The king's scribes were summoned at that time, in the third month, which is the month of Sivan, on the twenty-third day; and everything was written, according to all that Mordecai commanded, to the Jews, to the satraps, the governors, and the princes of the provinces from India to Ethiopia, one hundred and twenty-seven provinces, to every province in its own script, to every people in their own language, and to the Jews in their script and language. ¹⁰ He wrote in the name of King Ahasuerus, sealed it with the king's signet ring, sent letters by couriers on horseback, riding steeds bred from mares from the royal stables.

¹¹ What the king granted to the Jews in each and every city was *the right* to assemble and to defend their lives by annihilating, slaying, and destroying any army of any people or any province that would assault them, the little children and women included, and to plunder their possessions. ¹² *This would happen* on one day in all the provinces of King Ahasuerus, namely, on the thirteenth day of the twelfth month (which is the month Adar). ¹³ A copy of the edict being issued as law in each and every province was published to all people, so that the Jews could be ready for this day to avenge themselves on their enemies.

¹⁴ So the couriers riding on royal steeds went out with haste and urgency by the king's edict. The decree was given at the citadel of Susa.

¹⁵ Mordecai went out from the king's presence in royal apparel of blue and white, with a large crown of gold, and with a garment of fine linen and purple. The city of Susa erupted with shouts of rejoicing. ¹⁶ To the Jews belonged light, gladness, joy, and honor. ¹⁷ In each and every province as well as in each and every city, wherever the king's edict and his decree reached, the Jews had joy and gladness, a feast, and a holiday. Furthermore, many of the people of the land professed to be Jews because the dread of the Jews fell on them.

The Jews Destroy Their Enemies

9 Now in the twelfth month (that is, the month Adar), on the thirteenth day, when the king's edict and his decree were to be carried out on the day that the enemies of the Jews had hoped to have power over them, things were turned around. The Jews gained power over those who hated them. ² The Jews had assembled in their cities throughout all the provinces of King Ahasuerus in order to forcibly assault those seeking their injury. No man could stand before them because the dread of them had fallen on all people. ³ All the rulers of the provinces, and the satraps, and the governors, and all those doing the work of the king were helping the Jews, because the fear of Mordecai had fallen on them. ⁴ For Mordecai had become great in the king's house, and his fame went out throughout all the provinces because Mordecai grew more powerful.

⁵ So the Jews struck all their enemies by sword, slaughtering and destroying them, and doing to those who hated them as they pleased. ⁶ In the citadel of Susa, the Jews killed and destroyed five hundred men, ⁷ along with Parshandatha, Dalphon, Aspatha, ⁸ Poratha, Adalia, Aridatha, ⁹ Parmashta, Arisai, Aridai, and Vaizatha. ¹⁰ These were the ten sons of Haman the son of Hammedatha, the enemy of the Jews, whom they killed, but on their plunder none *of the Jews* attempted to take it.

¹¹ On that day the number of those who were killed in the citadel of Susa was reported before the king. ¹² The king said to Queen Esther, "The Jews have slain and destroyed five hundred men in the citadel of Susa and the ten sons of Haman. What have they done in the rest of the king's provinces? Now what is your petition? It shall be granted you! What is your request further? It shall be done!"

¹³ Then Esther said, "If it pleases the king, let it be granted to the Jews in Susa to do again tomorrow according to this day's decree. Let the ten sons of Haman be hanged on the gallows."

¹⁴ So the king commanded that it be so done, and the decree was given at Susa, and they hanged the ten sons of Haman.

¹⁵ The Jews in Susa assembled again on the fourteenth day of the month Adar and killed three hundred more there, but on the plunder no one attempted to take it.

¹⁶ But the rest of the Jews in the king's provinces assembled to defend their lives. Some had rest from their enemies, while others killed seventy-five thousand of those who hated them, but no one took the plunder. ¹⁷ Because *this occurred* on the thirteenth day of the month Adar, they rested on the fourteenth day and made it a day of feasting and rejoicing.

¹*9* About 75 feet, or 23 meters.

The Feast of Purim Established

[18] Because the Jews in Susa had assembled on the thirteenth day and the fourteenth day of Adar, then on the fifteenth day they rested and made it a day of feasting and rejoicing.

[19] Therefore, the Jews of the rural areas, who were living in the villages, made the fourteenth day of the month Adar a day of rejoicing and feasting and a special day for sending portions *of food* to one another.

[20] Mordecai recorded these events and sent letters to all the Jews throughout all the provinces of King Ahasuerus, both near and far, [21] in order to institute for them the celebration for the fourteenth day and the fifteenth day of the month of Adar, each and every year, [22] like the days when the Jews had rest from their enemies, and *like* the month when things turned around for them—*changing* from sorrow to joy and from mourning into a favorable day—so that they could celebrate a season of feasting and rejoicing and sending *food* portions to one another and gifts to the poor.

[23] So the Jews accepted what had begun *as tradition* as Mordecai had written to them. [24] Haman, the son of Hammedatha, the Agagite, the enemy of all the Jews, had plotted against the Jews to destroy them, and had cast Pur (that is, cast lots), to crush and destroy them. [25] But when Esther came before the king, he ordered by letter that the wicked plot which Haman had devised against the Jews should come upon his own head, and that he and his sons should be hanged on the gallows. [26] Therefore, they call these days Purim on the basis of the name Pur. Furthermore, based on all the information of this letter, along with what they had seen in this regard and what had happened to them, [27] the Jews instituted and accepted *as tradition* for themselves, for their descendants, and for all joining with them not to fail in observing the celebration of these two days as prescribed and as specified in each and every year. [28] These days should be remembered and celebrated throughout every generation, every family, province, and city, so that these days of Purim will not lose their significance among the Jews, and the commemoration of these days will not cease among their descendants.

[29] Then Queen Esther, the daughter of Abihail, and Mordecai the Jew wrote with all authority, to confirm this second letter about Purim. [30] He sent the letters to all the Jews, to the one hundred and twenty-seven provinces of the kingdom of Ahasuerus, with instructions for peace and truth [31] in order to confirm these days of Purim at their appointed times, as Mordecai the Jew and Queen Esther had instituted for themselves and for their offspring, with the instructions for their times of fasting and their lamenting. [32] The command of Esther confirmed these traditions of Purim, and it was written in the book.

Mordecai's Greatness

10 Then King Ahasuerus charged a tribute on the land and on the coastal lands of the sea. [2] All the deeds of his power and of his might, and the detailed record of the greatness of Mordecai, after the king promoted him, are they not written in the book of the chronicles of the kings of Media and Persia? [3] Indeed, Mordecai the Jew was second in power to King Ahasuerus. He was great among the Jews and popular with many of his countrymen, for he sought favor for his people, and spoke of peace and prosperity for all of his posterity.

JOB

The Prologue

1 There was a man in the land of Uz whose name was Job. That man was blameless and upright, fearing God and avoiding evil. [2] Seven sons and three daughters were born to him. [3] His possessions were seven thousand sheep, three thousand camels, five hundred yoke of oxen, five hundred female donkeys, and very many servants. This man was the greatest of all the people of the East.

[4] His sons used to go and make a feast in the house of each on his day, and they would send and call for their three sisters to eat and drink with them. [5] Now when the days of feasting had run their course, Job sent and sanctified them. He would rise up early in the morning, and he would offer burnt offerings according to the number of them all, because Job said: "It may be that my sons have sinned, and cursed God in their hearts." Thus Job would do always.

[6] Now there was a day when the sons of God came to present themselves before the Lord, and the Adversary also came among them. [7] And the Lord said to the Adversary, "From where have you come?"

Then the Adversary answered the Lord, saying, "From roaming on the earth, and from walking up and down on it."

[8] And the Lord said to the Adversary, "Have you considered My servant Job, that there is none like him on the earth, a blameless and an upright man, who fears God, and avoids evil?"

[9] Then the Adversary answered the Lord, saying, "Has Job feared God for nothing? [10] Have You not made a hedge around him, around his household, and around all that he has on every side? You have blessed the work of his hands, and his possessions have increased in the land. [11] But stretch out Your hand now, and touch all that he has, and he will curse You to Your face."

[12] The Lord said to the Adversary, "Look, all that he has is in your power; only do not stretch out your hand against his person."

So the Adversary departed from the presence of the Lord.

[13] So a day came when his sons and his daughters were eating and drinking wine in their eldest brother's house, [14] and a messenger came to Job and said, "The oxen were plowing, and the donkeys were feeding beside them, [15] and the Sabeans attacked them, and took them away, and they killed the servants with the edge of the sword, and only I alone have escaped to tell you."

[16] While he was still speaking, another came and said, "The fire of God fell from heaven and burned up the sheep and the servants and consumed them, and I alone have escaped to tell you."

[17] While he was still speaking, another came and said, "The Chaldeans formed three companies and made a raid on the camels and have taken them away. They killed the servants with the edge of the sword, and I alone have escaped to tell you."

[18] While he was still speaking, another came and said, "Your sons and your daughters were eating and drinking wine in their eldest brother's house, [19] and suddenly a great wind came from the wilderness and struck the four corners of the house, and it fell on the young people, and they are dead; and I alone have escaped to tell you."

[20] Then Job stood up, tore his robe, and shaved his head. He fell to the ground and worshipped. [21] He said,

"Naked I came from my mother's womb,
    and naked will I return there.
The Lord gave, and the Lord has taken away;
    blessed be the name of the Lord."

[22] In all this Job did not sin, and he did not accuse God of wrongdoing.

2 Again there was a day when the sons of God came to present themselves before the Lord, and the Adversary came also among them to present himself before the Lord. [2] The Lord said to the Adversary, "From where do you come?"

And the Adversary answered the Lord, saying, "From roaming on the earth, and from walking up and down on it."

[3] The Lord said to the Adversary, "Have you considered My servant Job, that there is none like him on the earth, a blameless and an upright

man, who fears God and avoids evil? He still holds fast his integrity, although you moved Me against him, to destroy him without cause."

⁴ The Adversary answered the Lord, saying, "Skin for skin; yes, all that a man has he will give for his life. ⁵ Put forth Your hand now and touch his bone and his flesh, and he will curse You to Your face."

⁶ The Lord said to the Adversary, "Very well, he is in your hand, but spare his life."

⁷ Therefore, the Adversary went out from the presence of the Lord, and he afflicted Job with severe sores from the sole of his foot to the top of his head. ⁸ So he took a piece of broken pottery with which to scrape himself while he was sitting among the ashes.

⁹ His wife said to him, "Are you still maintaining your integrity? Curse God and die."

¹⁰ He said to her, "You talk like one of the foolish women talks. Will we indeed accept the good from God but not accept the adversity?"

In all this Job did not sin with his lips.

¹¹ Three friends of Job heard about all this evil that had come upon him, and each one came from his own place: Eliphaz the Temanite, Bildad the Shuhite, and Zophar the Naamathite. They had agreed together to come to mourn with him and to comfort him. ¹² They saw him from a distance and did not recognize him, so they wept aloud. Each one tore his robe, and they tossed dust into the air above their heads. ¹³ Then they sat down with him on the ground seven days and seven nights. Meanwhile, no one was speaking to him at all because they saw that his pain was severe.

Job Laments His Birth

3 After this Job opened his mouth, and cursed the day of his *birth*. ² Job said:

³ "Let the day perish in which I was born
   and the night in which it was said, 'A male child is conceived.'
⁴ As for that day, let it be darkness;
   let God above not regard it;
   and let not light shine upon it.
⁵ Let darkness and the shadow of death claim it;
   let a cloud settle on it;
   let the blackness of the day terrify it.
⁶ As for that night, let darkness capture it;
   let it not rejoice among the days of the year;
   let it not come into the number of the months.
⁷ Yes, as for that night, let it be barren!
   Let no joyful cry come into it!
⁸ Let them curse it who curse any day,
   those who are prepared to rouse Leviathan.
⁹ Let its morning stars be dark;
   let it look for light, but have none;
   let it not see the rays of dawn,
¹⁰ because it did not shut the doors of my mother's womb,
   nor hide trouble from my eyes.

¹¹ "Why did I not die at birth?
   Why did I not expire when I came out of the womb?
¹² Why did *her* knees receive me?
   And why *her* breasts that I should nurse?
¹³ For now I would be lying down and would be at peace;
   I would have slept; then there would be rest for me,
¹⁴ with kings and counselors of the earth,
   who built ruins for themselves,
¹⁵ or with princes who had gold,
   who filled their houses with silver.
¹⁶ Or why was I not hidden like a stillborn child,
   like infants who never saw light?
¹⁷ There the wicked will have stopped causing trouble,
   and there the exhausted will rest.
¹⁸ Captives will relax together;
   they do not hear the voice of the oppressor.
¹⁹ The small and great, they are there,
   and the servant is free from his master.

²⁰ "Why is light given to the miserable,
   and life unto the bitter in soul,

²¹ who look for death, but it is not there;
   and they search for it more than for hidden treasures;
²² who rejoice exceedingly,
   and they are glad when they find the grave?
²³ And why is light given to a man
   whose way is hidden,
   whom God has hedged in?
²⁴ For my sighing comes before I eat,
   and my groaning pours forth like the waters.
²⁵ For the thing which I greatly feared has happened to me,
   and that which I dreaded has come to me.
²⁶ I am not at peace; I have no quiet,
   I cannot rest, and turmoil has come."

Eliphaz Speaks: Job Has Sinned

4 Then Eliphaz the Temanite answered:

² "If one attempts a word with you, will you be impatient?
   But who can keep from speaking?
³ Surely you have instructed many,
   and you have strengthened the weak hands.
⁴ Your words have raised up him who was falling,
   and you have fortified the feeble knees.
⁵ But now it comes upon you, and you are weary;
   it reaches even you, and you are terrified.
⁶ Is not your reverence your confidence?
   And the integrity of your ways your hope?

⁷ "Remember now, who being innocent ever perished?
   Or where were the upright ever wiped out?
⁸ Just like I have seen, those who plow iniquity
   and sow trouble, reap the same.
⁹ By the breath of God they perish,
   and by the blast of His anger they are destroyed.
¹⁰ The roaring of the lion, and the voice of the fierce lion,
   and the teeth of the young lions are broken.
¹¹ The old lion perishes for lack of prey,
   and the cubs of the lioness are scattered.

¹² "Now a word was brought to me secretly,
   and my ear received a whisper of it.
¹³ Amid disquieting thoughts from night visions,
   when deep sleep falls on mortals,
¹⁴ terror and trembling came to me,
   which made all my bones shake.
¹⁵ A breath of wind was passing before my face,
   and the hair on my body was standing up.
¹⁶ It stood still,
   but I could not recognize its appearance;
   a form was in front of my eyes,
   there was stillness, then I heard a voice saying:
¹⁷ 'Can a mortal be more righteous than God?
   Can a man be more pure than his Maker?
¹⁸ He does not trust in His servants,
   and He charges His angels with error;
¹⁹ Even more, those who dwell in houses of clay,
   whose foundation is in the dust,
   who are crushed before the moth.
²⁰ They are broken in pieces from morning to evening;
   they perish forever without anyone regarding it.
²¹ Are not their tent ropes plucked up,
   so they die, even without wisdom?'

Eliphaz: Job Is Chastised by God

5 "Call out now; is anyone answering you?
   And to whom among the holy ones will you turn?
² For anger slays the foolish man,
   and jealousy kills the gullible.
³ Yes, I saw the foolish taking root,
   and quickly I cursed his dwelling.
⁴ May his children be far from safety,
   and may they be crushed in the gate without a deliverer;

5 whose harvest the hungry eats up,
  and takes it even out of the thorns,
  and the thirsty captures his wealth.
6 For affliction does not come out of the dust,
  nor does trouble sprout up out of the ground;
7 but man is born to trouble,
  as the sparks fly upward.

8 "Indeed, I would appeal to God,
  and before God I would set forth my case,
9 who does the great and the inscrutable,
  wonders without number.
10 He gives rain on the surface of the earth
   and sends water on the outdoor places.
11 He sets on high those who are lowly,
   and those who mourn are lifted to safety.
12 He frustrates the schemes of the crafty,
   so that their hands cannot perform their plans.
13 He catches the wise in their own craftiness,
   and the scheme of the shrewd is swiftly stopped.
14 In the daytime they encounter darkness,
   and at noontime they grope as in the night.
15 But the needy He saves from the sword,
   from their mouth, and from the hand of the mighty.
16 So the helpless has hope,
   and injustice shuts her mouth.

17 "How happy is the man whom God corrects!
   Therefore do not despise the discipline of the Almighty,
18 for He wounds, but He applies the bandage;
   He injures, but His hands also heal.
19 In six crises He will deliver you;
   even in seven, disaster will not touch you.
20 In famine He will redeem you from death,
   and in war from the power of the sword.
21 You will be hidden from the lash of the tongue,
   and you will not fear violence when it comes.
22 You will laugh at devastation and famine,
   and you will not fear wild animals.
23 For you will have a covenant with the stones of the field,
   and the wild animals will be at peace with you.
24 You will know that your tent is peaceful,
   and you will inspect your property and find nothing missing.
25 You will know that your offspring will be many
   and your descendants as the grass of the earth.
26 You go to the grave in a full age,
   as stalks of grain are gathered up in season.

27 "Look! We have investigated all this, and it is so;
   hear it, and know for yourself."

Job Replies: My Complaint Is Just

6 But Job answered:

2 "Oh, that my grief were fully weighed,
  and my calamity laid with it on the scales!
3 For now it would be heavier than the sand of the sea;
  therefore my words are stuck in my throat.
4 For the arrows of the Almighty are within me;
  my spirit drinks in their poison;
  the terrors of God are arrayed against me.
5 Does the wild donkey bray when he has grass?
  Or the ox bellow over his fodder?
6 Is tasteless food eaten without salt?
  Or is there any taste in the white of an egg?
7 My soul refuses to touch them;
  they are like loathsome food to me.

8 "Oh, that I might have my request,
  and that God would grant me the thing that I long for!
9 That it would please God to crush me,
  that He would let loose His hand and cut me off!

10 Then I would still have comfort;
   I would revel in pain; it will not subside,
   for I have not concealed the words of the Holy One.

11 "What strength do I have, that I should hope?
   And what is my end, that I should prolong my life?
12 Is my strength the strength of stones?
   Or is my flesh made of brass?
13 Is there no help within me?
   And is success banished from me?

14 "A despairing man should be shown kindness from his friend,
   or he forsakes the fear of the Almighty.
15 My brothers have acted deceitfully like a riverbed,
   like the streams of the riverbeds that run dry;
16 which are dark because of the ice,
   and into which the snow disappears.
17 In time they are scorched; they vanish!
   When it is hot, they disappear from their place.
18 The caravans of their way turn aside;
   they go nowhere, and they perish.
19 The caravans of Tema looked,
   the travelers of Sheba hoped for them.
20 They were disappointed because they were confident;
   they arrived there and were dismayed.
21 For now you are nothing;
   you see terror and are afraid.
22 Did I say, 'Give to me'?
   Or, 'Out of your wealth, bribe me'?
23 Or, 'Deliver me from the power of the enemy'?
   Or, 'From the power of the oppressors, liberate me'?

24 "Teach me, and I will hold my tongue,
   and make me understand how I have erred.
25 How forceful are right words!
   But what does your arguing prove?
26 Do you mean to correct my words,
   and treat my desperate words as wind?
27 Yes, you cast lots for the fatherless,
   and you bargain over your friend.

28 "And now, please give me your attention,
   for surely I will not lie to you.
29 Turn, I pray, let there be no injustice!
   Yes, turn again, my righteousness still stands!
30 Is there injustice on my tongue?
   Cannot my taste discern pernicious things?

Job: My Suffering Is Endless

7 "Is there not a time of hard service for a man
      upon earth?
   Are not his days also like the days of a hired worker?
2 Like a servant, he longs for the shade,
  and like a hired worker, he looks for his wages,
3 So I have been assigned months of futility,
  and nights of trouble have been appointed to me.
4 When I lie down, I say,
  'When will I arise and the night be ended?'
  And I am full of restlessness until the dawn.
5 My flesh is covered with worms and caked with dirt;
  my skin is broken, and has become loathsome.

6 "My days fly more swiftly than a weaver's shuttle,
  and are spent without hope.
7 Oh, remember that my life is a breath!
  My eye will never again see good.
8 The eye of him who sees me will behold me no more;
  your eyes will be on me, but I will be no more.
9 As the cloud disappears and vanishes away,
  so he who goes down to Sheol will come up no more.
10 He will never return to his house,
   and his place will not recognize him anymore.

11 "Therefore, I will not restrain my mouth;
        I will speak in the anguish of my spirit;
        I will complain in the bitterness of my soul.
12 Am I the sea, or a sea monster,
        that You set a guard over me?
13 When I say, 'My bed will comfort me,
        my couch will ease my complaint,'
14 then You scare me with dreams
        and terrify me with visions,
15 so that my soul chooses strangling,
        even death rather than my life.
16 I loathe my life; I would not live forever;
        let me alone, for my days are emptiness.

17 "What is man, that You should exalt him,
        and that You should set Your heart on him,
18 and that You should visit him every morning,
        and test him every moment?
19 How long until You look away from me?
        Will You not let me alone until I swallow
            my saliva?
20 Have I sinned? What am I doing to You,
        O You watcher of men?
        Why have You set me as Your target,
        so that I am a burden to myself?
21 And why do You not pardon my transgression
        and take away my iniquity?
        For now I will lie down in the dust;
        and You will seek me diligently, but I will not be."

Bildad Speaks: Job Should Repent

8 Then Bildad the Shuhite answered:

2 "How long will you speak these things,
        and the words of your mouth be like a strong wind?
3 Does God pervert judgment?
        Or does the Almighty pervert justice?
4 If your children sinned against Him,
        He cast them away for their transgression.
5 If you yourself would seek God earnestly,
        and seek favor from the Almighty,
6 if you were pure and upright,
        surely now He would rouse Himself on your behalf,
        and He would prosper your righteous dwelling.
7 Though your beginning was small,
        your end will increase greatly.

8 "Please, ask the former generation,
        and prepare yourself for what their fathers
            searched out;
9 for we were born but yesterday and know nothing,
        because our days on earth are a shadow.
10 Will they not teach you, and tell you,
        and bring forth words out of their heart?
11 Can the papyrus grow up without a marsh?
        Can the reed grow without water?
12 While it is yet green and not cut down,
        it withers before any other plant.
13 So are the paths of all who forget God;
        and the hypocrite's hope will perish,
14 whose confidence will be cut off,
        and whose trust will be a spider's web.
15 He will lean upon his house, but it will not stand;
        he will hold it fast, but it will not endure.
16 He is green before the sun,
        and his branch shoots forth in his garden.
17 His roots are wrapped around the rock heap,
        and *he* sees the place of stones.
18 If he is uprooted from his place,
        then it will deny him, saying, 'I have not seen you.'
19 See, this is the joy of his way,
        and out of the ground others will grow.

20 "Surely, God will not cast away a perfect man,
        nor will He strengthen the evildoers,
21 until He fills your mouth with laughing,
        and your lips with rejoicing.
22 Those who hate you will be clothed with shame,
        and the dwelling place of the wicked will come
            to nothing."

Job Replies: There Is No Mediator

9 Then Job answered:

2 "Truly, I know it is so,
        but how can a man be righteous with God?
3 If one would dispute with Him,
        he cannot answer Him once in a thousand times.
4 He is wise in heart and mighty in strength.
        Who has hardened himself against Him
            and prospered?
5 He who removes mountains, and they know not,
        who overturns them in His anger.
6 He who shakes the earth out of its place,
        and its pillars tremble.
7 He who commands the sun, and it does not rise;
        he seals off the stars.
8 He who alone spreads out the heavens,
        and treads on the waves of the sea.
9 He who makes the Bear, Orion, and Pleiades,
        and the constellations of the south.
10 He who does great things, beyond discovery,
        yes, and wonders beyond number.
11 Yes, He would cross before me, and I would not see Him;
        He would pass on by, but I would not perceive Him.
12 Yes, He takes away; who can hinder Him?
        Who will say to Him, 'What are You doing?'
13 God will not withdraw His anger.
        The proud helpers bow down beneath Him.

14 "How, then, can I myself answer Him,
        and choose my words to reason with Him?
15 Even if I were righteous I could not answer;
        I would plead to my Judge for favor.
16 If I called, and He answered me,
        I would not believe that He had listened to my voice.
17 For He crushes me with a storm
        and multiplies my wounds without cause.
18 He will not allow me to get my breath,
        but fills me with bitterness.
19 If it is a matter of strength, indeed, He is strong;
        and if of justice, who will set me a time to plead?
20 Though I were righteous, my own mouth would
            condemn me;
        though I were perfect, it would prove me perverse.

21 "Though I were perfect,
        I would not know myself;
        I would despise my life.
22 It is all one thing; therefore I said,
        'He destroys both the perfect and the wicked.'
23 If the whip kills suddenly,
        He will laugh at the trial of the innocent.
24 The earth is given into the hand of the wicked.
        He covers the faces of its judges.
        If it is not He, then who is it?

25 "Now my days are swifter than a runner;
        they flee away; they see no good.
26 They pass by like reed skiffs,
        like an eagle rushing upon its prey.
27 If I say, 'I will forget my complaint,
        I will leave off my sad face and brighten up,'
28 I am afraid of all my sorrows;
        I know that You will not hold me innocent.

29 If I am guilty,
why then do I labor in vain?
30 If I wash myself with snow water
and cleanse my hands with soap,
31 yet You will plunge me into the pit,
and my own clothes will abhor me.

32 "For He is not a man as I am, that I should answer Him,
and we should come together in judgment.
33 Nor is there a mediator between us,
who may lay his hand upon us both.
34 Let Him take His rod away from me,
and let not dread of Him terrify me.
35 Then I would speak and not fear Him,
but it is not so with me.

Job: I Abhor My Life

10 "My soul loathes my life;
I will freely give my complaint,
I will speak in the bitterness of my soul.
2 I will say to God, Do not condemn me;
show me why You contend with me.
3 Is it good for You that You should oppress,
that You should despise the work of Your hands
and smile on the counsel of the wicked?
4 Do You have eyes of flesh?
Or do You see as man sees?
5 Are Your days as the days of man?
Are Your years as the days of a mortal,
6 that You inquire after my iniquity
and search after my sin?
7 You know that I am not wicked,
and there is none who can deliver out of Your hand.

8 "Your hands have shaped me and made me completely,
yet You destroy me.
9 Remember, I pray,
that You have made me as the clay.
And would You return me to dust?
10 Have You not poured me out as milk
and curdled me like cheese?
11 You have clothed me with skin and flesh,
and have knit me together with bones and sinews.
12 You have granted me life and loyal love,
and Your care has preserved my spirit.

13 "These things You have hid in Your heart.
I know that this is with You.
14 If I have sinned, then You would watch me,
and You would not acquit me from my iniquity.
15 If I am wicked, woe unto me;
and if I am righteous, yet will I not lift up my head.
I am full of shame;
look at my affliction!
16 For if *my head* is lifted up, You would hunt me like a lion,
and again You show Yourself marvelous to me.
17 You renew Your witnesses against me
and increase Your indignation upon me.
Your troops come against me.

18 "Why then did You bring me forth out of the womb?
Oh, that I had died, and no eye had seen me!
19 I should have been as though I had not been;
I should have been carried from the womb to
the grave.
20 Are not my days few? Stop then,
and leave me alone that I may cheer up a little,
21 before I go and do not return,
even to the land of darkness and the shadow of death,
22 a land of darkness, as darkness itself;
and of the shadow of death, without any order,
and where the light is as thick darkness."

Zophar Speaks: Job Is Guilty

11 Then Zophar the Naamathite answered:

2 "Should not the multitude of words be answered?
And should a man full of talk be justified?
3 Should your empty talk make men hold their peace?
And when you mock, will no one shame you?
4 For you have said, 'My teaching is pure,
And I am clean in your eyes.'
5 But oh, that God would speak
and open His lips against you,
6 and that He would show you the secrets of wisdom!
For they would double your prudence.
And know that God overlooks some of your iniquity.

7 "Can you search out the deep things of God?
Can you find out the totality of the Almighty?
8 It is as high as heaven; what can you do?
Deeper than Sheol; what can you know?
9 Its measure is longer than the earth
and broader than the sea.

10 "If He passes through, and shuts up, and gathers together
for judgment,
then who can hinder Him?
11 For He knows worthless men;
He sees wickedness also; will He not then consider it?
12 For an empty-headed man will become wise,
when a wild donkey's colt is born a man.

13 "If you prepare your heart
and stretch out your hands toward Him;
14 if iniquity is in your hand, put it far away,
and do not let wickedness dwell in your tents;
15 for then you will lift up your face without blemish;
yes, you will be steadfast and will not fear,
16 because you will forget misery,
and remember it as waters that pass away,
17 and your life will be brighter than noonday,
even your darkness will be as the morning.
18 You will trust because there is hope;
yes, you will search about you,
and you will look around and rest in safety.
19 Also you will lie down, and none will make you afraid;
yes, many will court your favor.
20 But the eyes of the wicked will fail,
and they will not escape,
and their hope will be as the giving up of breath."

Job Replies

12 And Job answered:

2 "No doubt but you are the people,
and wisdom will die with you!
3 But I have understanding as well as you;
I am not inferior to you.
Yes, who does not know such things as these?

4 "I am a laughingstock to my neighbor,
who calls upon God, and He answers him;
the righteous, upright man is a laughingstock.
5 He whose foot is unsteady
is despised in the thoughts of him who is
at ease.
6 The tents of robbers are at peace,
and those who provoke God are secure,
into whose hand they bring their own god.

7 "But now ask the beasts, and let them teach you;
and the birds of the air, and let them tell you;
8 or speak to the earth, let it teach you;
and let the fish of the sea declare to you.

⁹ Who among all these does not know
    that the hand of the Lᴏʀᴅ has done this,
¹⁰ in whose hand is the soul of every living thing
    and the breath of all mankind?
¹¹ Does not the ear test words
    and the mouth taste its food?
¹² Wisdom is with the elderly,
    and understanding comes with long life.

¹³ "With Him are wisdom and strength;
    He has counsel and understanding.
¹⁴ Surely, He tears down, and it cannot be built again;
    He imprisons a man, and there can be no release.
¹⁵ Surely, He withholds the waters, and they dry up;
    also He sends them out, and they overthrow the earth.
¹⁶ With Him are strength and wisdom.
    The deceived and the deceiver are His.
¹⁷ He leads counselors away stripped
    and makes fools of judges.
¹⁸ He has loosened the bonds imposed by kings
    and bound their waist with a belt.
¹⁹ He leads away priests stripped
    and overthrows the mighty.
²⁰ He removes speech from the trusted ones
    and takes away the understanding of the aged.
²¹ He pours contempt upon princes
    and loosens the belt of the mighty.
²² He uncovers deep things out of darkness
    and brings the shadow of death to light.
²³ He increases the nations and destroys them;
    He enlarges the nations and guides them.
²⁴ He takes away the understanding of the chiefs of the people of
    the earth,
    and causes them to wander in a wilderness where there is no way.
²⁵ They grope in the dark without light,
    and He makes them to stagger like a drunk man.

13 "Notice, my eye has seen all this;
    my ear has heard and understood it.
² What you know, I also know the same;
    I am not inferior to you.
³ Surely I would speak to the Almighty,
    and I desire to reason with God.
⁴ But you are plasterers of falsehood;
    you are all physicians of no value.
⁵ Oh, that you would altogether hold your peace,
    and it would be your wisdom!
⁶ Hear now my reasoning,
    and listen to the pleadings of my lips.
⁷ Will you speak wickedly for God?
    And talk deceitfully for Him?
⁸ Will you take His side?
    Will you plead for God?
⁹ Is it good that He would search you out?
    Or as one man mocks another, do you so mock Him?
¹⁰ He will surely rebuke you,
    if you secretly show partiality.
¹¹ Will not His excellence make you afraid,
    and the dread of Him fall upon you?
¹² Your reminders are parables made of ashes;
    your answers are answers made of clay.

¹³ "Hold your peace; leave me alone, that I may speak,
    and let come on me what may!
¹⁴ Why do I take my flesh in my teeth
    and put my life in my hand?
¹⁵ Though He slay me, yet will I trust in Him,¹
    but I will defend my own ways before Him.
¹⁶ He also will be my salvation,
    for a hypocrite could not come before Him.

¹⁷ Listen carefully to my speech,
    and to my declaration with your ears.
¹⁸ See now, I have prepared my case;
    I know that I will be justified.
¹⁹ Who is he who will plead with me?
    For now, if I hold my tongue, I will give up my breath.

²⁰ "Only grant me two things,
    then I will not hide myself from You:
²¹ Withdraw Your hand far from me,
    and let not the dread of You make me afraid.
²² Then call, and I will answer,
    or let me speak, and You answer me.
²³ How many are my iniquities and sins?
    Make known to me my transgression and my sin.
²⁴ Why do You hide Your face
    and regard me as Your enemy?
²⁵ Will You frighten a leaf driven to and fro?
    And will You pursue dry stubble?
²⁶ For You write bitter things against me
    and make me inherit the iniquities of my youth.
²⁷ You put my feet in the stocks
    and watch closely all my paths;
    You draw a line around the soles of my feet.

²⁸ "Man, as a rotten thing, decays,
    as a garment that is moth eaten.

14 "Man who is born of a woman
    is of few days and full of trouble.
² He comes forth like a flower and withers;
    he flees like a shadow and does not continue.
³ Do You open Your eyes on such a one,
    and bring me into judgment with You?
⁴ Who can bring a clean thing out of an unclean?
    There is no one.
⁵ Seeing his days are determined,
    the number of his months are with You;
    You have appointed his bounds that he cannot pass;
⁶ turn from him, that he may rest,
    until he, as a hired man, finishes his day.

⁷ "For there is hope for a tree,
    if it is cut down, that it will sprout again,
    and that its tender shoots will not cease.
⁸ Though its root may grow old in the earth,
    and its stump may die in the ground,
⁹ yet at the scent of water it will bud
    and bring forth boughs like a plant.
¹⁰ But man dies and wastes away;
    yes, man gives up his breath, and where is he?
¹¹ As the waters disappear from the sea,
    and the flood shrivels and dries up,
¹² so man lies down and does not rise;
    until the heavens are no more, he will not awake,
    nor be raised out of his sleep.

¹³ "Oh, that You would hide me in the grave,
    that You would conceal me until Your wrath is past,
    that You would appoint me a set time
    and remember me!
¹⁴ If a man dies, will he live again?
    All the days of my service I will wait,
    until my relief comes.
¹⁵ You will call, and I will answer You;
    You will long for the work of Your hands.
¹⁶ For now You number my steps;
    do You not observe my sin?
¹⁷ My transgression is sealed up in a bag,
    and You plaster over my iniquity.

¹ 15 Original Heb. *I have no hope.*

18 "Surely the mountain falling comes to nothing,
   and the rock is removed out of its place.
19 The waters wear away the stones;
   its overflow washes away the dust of the earth;
   and You destroy the hope of man.
20 You prevail forever against him, and he passes on;
   changing his countenance, You send him away.
21 His sons come to honor, and he does not know it;
   and they are brought low, but he does not perceive it.
22 But his flesh on him will have pain,
   and his soul within him will mourn."

Eliphaz Speaks: Job Does Not Fear God

15 Then Eliphaz the Temanite answered:

2 "Should a wise man reply with empty knowledge
   and fill his lungs with the east wind?
3 Should he reason with unprofitable talk
   or with speeches with which he can do no good?
4 Yes, you cast off reverence
   and hinder prayer before God.
5 For your mouth utters your iniquity,
   and you choose the tongue of the crafty.
6 Your own mouth condemns you, and not I;
   yes, your own lips testify against you.

7 "Are you the first man who was born?
   Or were you made before the hills?
8 Have you heard the counsel of God?
   And do you restrict wisdom to yourself?
9 What do you know that we do not know?
   What do you understand that is not in us?
10 Both the gray-haired and very aged are among us—
   much older than your father.
11 Are the consolations of God too small for you?
   Or the word spoken gently to you?
12 Why does your heart carry you away?
   And what do your eyes wink at,
13 that you turn your spirit against God,
   and let such words go out of your mouth?

14 "What is man that he should be pure?
   And he who is born of a woman, that he should
      be righteous?
15 Behold, He puts no trust in His holy ones,
   and the heavens are not pure in His sight.
16 How much more abhorred and corrupt is man,
   who drinks iniquity like water!

17 "I will tell you; hear me,
   and what I have seen I will declare,
18 what wise men have told,
   not hiding anything received from their fathers,
19 to whom alone the land was given,
   and no foreigner passed among them:
20 The wicked man travails with pain all his days,
   and numbered are the years stored up for the oppressor.
21 A dreadful sound is in his ears;
   in prosperity the destroyer will come upon him.
22 He does not believe that he will return from darkness,
   and a sword awaits him.
23 He wanders about for bread, saying, 'Where is it?'
   He knows that the day of darkness is ready at his hand.
24 Trouble and anguish will make him afraid;
   they will prevail against him as a king ready to the battle.
25 For he stretches out his hand against God,
   and strengthens himself against the Almighty.
26 He rushes upon Him, even on His neck,
   with his thick embossed shield.

27 "He has covered his face with his fatness
   and gathered fat upon his waist.

28 He dwells in desolate cities
   and in houses which no man inhabits,
   which are ready to become heaps.
29 He will not be rich, nor will his wealth continue,
   nor will his possessions spread over the earth.
30 He will not depart out of darkness;
   the flame will dry out his branches,
   and by the breath of His mouth he will go away.
31 Let him who is deceived not trust in futility,
   for futility will be his reward.
32 It will be accomplished before his time,
   and his branch will not be green.
33 He will shake off his unripe grape like the vine,
   and will cast off his blossom like the olive.
34 For the company of hypocrites will be desolate,
   and fire will consume the tents of bribery.
35 They conceive mischief, and give birth to futility;
   their womb prepares deceit."

Job Replies: You Are Miserable Comforters

16 Then Job answered:

2 "I have heard many such things;
   miserable comforters are you all!
3 Will windy words have an end?
   Or what provokes you that you answer?
4 I also could speak as you do,
   if your soul were in my place.
   I could heap up words against you
   and shake my head at you;
5 but I would strengthen you with my mouth,
   and the moving of my lips *would* relieve your grief.

6 "Though I speak, my grief is not relieved;
   and though I stop, how am I eased?
7 But now He has made me weary;
   You have made desolate all my company.
8 You have filled me with wrinkles, which is a witness against me;
   and my leanness has risen up and bears witness to my face.
9 He has torn me in His wrath, and He has carried a grudge
      against me.
   He has gnashed me with His teeth;
   my enemy sharpens His gaze upon me.
10 They have gaped upon me with their mouth;
   they have struck me upon the cheek with reproach;
   they have gathered themselves together against me.
11 God has delivered me to the ungodly
   and turned me over into the hands of the wicked.
12 I was at ease, but He has shattered me.
   He also has taken me by my neck, and shaken me to pieces,
   and set me up for His target.
13 His archers surround me;
   He splits open my kidneys and does not pity;
   He pours out my gall upon the ground.
14 He pierces me with thrust after thrust;
   He rushes upon me like a warrior.

15 "I have sewn sackcloth over my skin
   and thrust my horn into the dust.
16 My face is inflamed with weeping,
   and on my eyelids is the shadow of death,
17 *though* not for any violence in my hands,
   and my prayer is pure.

18 "O earth, do not cover my blood,
   and let my cry have no resting place.
19 Also now, look, my witness is in heaven,
   and my record is on high.
20 My friends scorn me;
   my eyes pour out tears unto God.
21 Oh, that one might plead for a man with God,
   as a man pleads for his neighbor!

²² "For when a few years have passed,
I will go the way from which I will not return.

Job Prays for Relief

17 "My spirit is broken,
my days are extinguished,
the grave is ready for me.
² Are not mockers with me?
And does not my eye dwell on their provocation?

³ "Now put down a pledge for me with Yourself.
Who is he who will shake hands with me?
⁴ For You have hidden their heart from understanding.
Therefore will You not exalt them.
⁵ He who speaks flattery to his friends,
even the eyes of his children will fail.

⁶ "And He has made me a byword of the people,
someone in whose face they spit.
⁷ My eye also is dim because of sorrow,
and all my members are like a shadow.
⁸ Upright men will be astonished at this,
and the innocent will stir up himself against the hypocrite.
⁹ The righteous also will hold to his way,
and he who has clean hands will be stronger and stronger.

¹⁰ "But as for you all, return and come now,
for I cannot find one wise man among you.
¹¹ My days are past, my purposes are broken off,
even the thoughts of my heart.
¹² They change the night into day;
the light is short because of darkness.
¹³ If I wait, the grave is my house;
I have made my bed in the darkness.
¹⁴ I have said to the pit, 'You are my father';
to the worm, 'You are my mother and my sister.'
¹⁵ Where now is my hope?
As for my hope, who will see it?
¹⁶ Will they go down to the gates of Sheol?
Will we descend together in the dust?"

Bildad Speaks: God Punishes the Wicked

18 Then Bildad the Shuhite answered:

² "How long will it be until you put an end to words?
Gain understanding, and afterwards we will speak.
³ Why are we counted as beasts
and regarded as stupid in your sight?
⁴ You who tear yourself in anger,
will the earth be forsaken for you?
And will the rock be removed from its place?

⁵ "Yes, the light of the wicked will be put out,
and the spark of his fire will not shine.
⁶ The light will be dark in his tent,
and his candle beside him will be put out.
⁷ The steps of his strength will be shortened,
and his own counsel will cast him down.
⁸ For he is cast into a net by his own feet,
and he walks upon a snare.
⁹ The trap will take him by the heel,
and the snare will prevail against him.
¹⁰ The snare is laid for him in the ground,
and a trap for him in the path.
¹¹ Terrors will make him afraid on every side
and will drive him to his feet.
¹² His strength will be hungry,
and destruction will be ready at his side.
¹³ It will devour the parts of his skin;
the firstborn of death will devour his limbs.
¹⁴ His confidence will be rooted out of his tent,
and it will bring him to the king of terrors.

¹⁵ They dwell in his tent who have no part with him;
brimstone will be scattered upon his habitation.
¹⁶ His roots will be dried up beneath,
and above his branch will dry up.
¹⁷ The memory of him will perish from the earth,
and he will have no name in the street.
¹⁸ He will be driven from light into darkness,
and chased out of the world.
¹⁹ He has neither descendant nor posterity among his people,
nor anyone remaining in his dwellings.
²⁰ They who come after him will be astonished at his day,
as they who went before were seized with fright.
²¹ Surely such are the dwellings of the wicked,
and this is the place of him who does not know God."

Job Replies: My Redeemer Lives

19 Then Job answered:

² "How long will you torment my soul
and break me in pieces with words?
³ These ten times you have reproached me;
you are not ashamed that you have wronged me.
⁴ And if indeed I have erred,
my error remains with me.
⁵ If indeed you exalt yourselves against me
and plead against me with my disgrace,
⁶ know now that God has bent me
and has surrounded me with His net.

⁷ "Look, I cry out concerning wrong, but I am not heard;
I cry aloud, but there is no justice.
⁸ He has fenced up my way that I cannot pass,
and He has set darkness in my paths.
⁹ He has stripped me of my glory
and taken the crown from my head.
¹⁰ He has destroyed me on every side, and I am gone;
my hope He has uprooted like a tree.
¹¹ He has also kindled His wrath against me,
and He counts me as one of His enemies.
¹² His troops come together
and build up their road against me;
they set up camp all around my tent.

¹³ "He has removed my brothers far from me,
and my acquaintances are completely estranged from me.
¹⁴ My relatives have failed,
and my close friends have forgotten me.
¹⁵ Those who dwell in my house, and my maidservants,
count me for a stranger;
I am a foreigner in their sight.
¹⁶ I called my servant, but he gave me no answer;
I begged him with my mouth.
¹⁷ My breath is offensive to my wife;
I am loathsome to the children of my own body.
¹⁸ Yes, young children despise me;
I arose, and they spoke against me.
¹⁹ All my close friends abhorred me,
and they whom I love are turned against me.
²⁰ My bones cling to my skin and to my flesh,
and I have escaped by the skin of my teeth.

²¹ "Have pity upon me, have pity upon me, O you my friends,
for the hand of God has struck me!
²² Why do you persecute me as God does,
and are not satisfied with my flesh?

²³ "Oh, that my words were written!
Oh, that they were inscribed in a book!
²⁴ That they were engraved with an iron pen
and lead in the rock forever!
²⁵ For I know that my Redeemer lives,
and He will stand at last on the earth;

26 and after my skin is destroyed,
  yet in my flesh I will see God,
27 whom I will see for myself,
  and my eyes will behold, and not another.
  How my heart yearns within me.

28 "If you should say, 'How shall we persecute him?'
  since the root of the matter is found in me,
29 be afraid of the sword for yourselves;
  for wrath brings the punishments of the sword,
  that you may know there is a judgment."

Zophar Speaks: The Wicked Will Suffer

20 Then Zophar the Naamathite answered:

2 "Therefore my thoughts cause me to answer,
  and for this I make haste.
3 I have heard the rebuke that disgraces me,
  and the spirit of my understanding causes me to answer.

4 "Do you not know this of old,
  since man was placed upon earth,
5 that the triumphing of the wicked is short,
  and the joy of the hypocrite is but for a moment?
6 Though his loftiness extends to the heavens,
  and his head reaches to the clouds,
7 yet he will perish forever like his own excrement;
  those who have seen him will say, 'Where is he?'
8 He will fly away like a dream and will not be found;
  yes, he will be chased away as a vision of the night.
9 The eye that saw him will see him no more;
  nor will his place behold him anymore.
10 His children will seek favor from the poor,
  and his hands will give back his wealth.
11 His bones are full of his youthful vigor,
  but it will lie down with him in the dust.

12 "Though evil is sweet in his mouth,
  and he hides it under his tongue,
13 though he spares it and does not forsake it,
  but keeps it in his mouth,
14 yet his food in his stomach turns sour;
  it becomes the venom of cobras within him.
15 He has swallowed down riches,
  and he will vomit them up again;
  God will cast them out of his belly.
16 He will suck the poison of cobras;
  the viper's tongue will slay him.
17 He will not see the streams, the rivers,
  the brooks of honey and butter.
18 He will give back the produce of labor and will not swallow
    it down.
  According to his wealth the restitution will be, and he will
    not rejoice in it;
19 because he has oppressed and has forsaken the poor.
  He has violently taken away a house that he did
    not build.

20 "Because he knows no quietness in his belly,
  he will not save anything he desired.
21 Nothing is left for him to eat;
  therefore his prosperity will not endure.
22 In his self-sufficiency he will be in distress;
  every hand of misery will come upon him.
23 When he is about to fill his belly,
  God will cast the fury of His wrath on him
  and will rain it on him while he is eating.
24 He will flee from the iron weapon;
  a bronze bow will pierce him through.
25 It is drawn and comes out of the body;
  yes, the glittering point comes out of his gall.
  Terrors are upon him.

26 Total darkness is stored up for his treasures.
  An unfanned fire will consume him;
  what is left in his tent will be consumed.
27 The heavens will reveal his iniquity,
  and the earth will rise up against him.
28 The increase of his house will depart,
  and his goods will flow away in the day of His wrath.
29 This is the wicked man's portion from God,
  and the inheritance appointed to him by God."

Job Replies: The Wicked Do Prosper

21 But Job answered:

2 "Listen carefully to my speech,
  and let this be your consolation.
3 Bear with me that I may speak,
  and after I have spoken, mock on.

4 "As for me, is my complaint against man?
  And if it were so, why should not my spirit be troubled?
5 Look at me and be astonished,
  and put your hand over your mouth.
6 Even when I remember I am afraid,
  and trembling takes hold of my body.
7 Why do the wicked live and become old;
  yes, become mighty in power?
8 Their descendants are established with them in their sight,
  and their offspring before their eyes.
9 Their houses are safe from fear,
  nor is the rod of God upon them.
10 Their bull breeds without failure;
  their cow gives calves without miscarriage.
11 They send forth their little ones like a flock,
  and their children dance.
12 They take up the tambourine and harp
  and rejoice at the sound of the flute.
13 They spend their days in wealth,
  and in a moment go down to Sheol.
14 Therefore they say to God, 'Depart from us,
  for we do not desire the knowledge of Your ways.
15 Who is the Almighty, that we should serve Him?
  And what profit do we have if we pray to Him?'
16 Indeed, their prosperity is not in their hand.
  The counsel of the wicked is far from me.

17 "How often is the lamp of the wicked put out?
  How often does their destruction come upon them,
  the sorrows God distributes in His anger?
18 They are like straw before the wind,
  and like chaff that a storm carries away.
19 God stores up their iniquity for their children;
  let Him reward the people themselves, and they will know it.
20 Let their eyes see their own destruction,
  and let them drink of the wrath of the Almighty.
21 For what do they care about their households after them,
  when the number of their months is cut off?

22 "Can anyone teach God knowledge,
  since He judges those who are on high?
23 One dies in his full strength,
  being wholly at ease and secure.
24 His pails are full of milk,
  and the marrow of his bones is moist.
25 Another dies in the bitterness of his soul,
  never having eaten with pleasure.
26 They will lie down alike in the dust,
  and worms will cover them.

27 "Behold, I know your thoughts,
  and the schemes with which you would wrong me.
28 For you say, 'Where is the house of the prince?
  And where are the dwelling places of the wicked?'

29 Have you not asked them who travel the road?
  And do you not know their signs?
30 For the wicked are reserved for the day of destruction;
  they will be brought forth on the day of wrath.
31 Who will declare his way to his face?
  And who will repay him for what he has done?
32 Yet will he be brought to the grave
  and will remain in the tomb.
33 The clods of the valley will be sweet unto him;
  and everyone will follow him,
  as countless have gone before.

34 "How then can you comfort me with emptiness,
  since deceit remains in your answers?"

Eliphaz Speaks: Job's Wickedness Is Great

22 Then Eliphaz the Temanite answered:

2 "Can a man be profitable to God,
  as he who is wise may be profitable to himself?
3 Is it any pleasure to the Almighty that you are righteous?
  Or is it gain to Him that you make your ways blameless?

4 "Is it because of your fear of Him that He corrects you,
  and enters into judgment with you?
5 Is not your wickedness great,
  and your iniquity infinite?
6 For you have taken a pledge from your brother for nothing,
  and stripped the naked of their clothing.
7 You have not given water to the weary to drink,
  and you have withheld bread from the hungry.
8 But as for the mighty man, he possessed the earth,
  and the honorable man lived in it.
9 You have sent widows away empty,
  and the strength of the fatherless was crushed.
10 Therefore snares are all around you,
  and sudden fear troubles you,
11 or darkness, so that you cannot see;
  and an abundance of waters covers you.

12 "Is not God in the height of heaven?
  And see the height of the stars, how high they are!
13 And you say, 'What does God know?
  Can He judge through the dark cloud?
14 Thick clouds are His covering, so He cannot see;
  and He walks above the circle of heaven.'
15 Will you keep to the old way,
  that wicked men have trod?
16 They were cut down before their time;
  their foundations were swept away by a flood.
17 They said to God, 'Depart from us,'
  and, 'What can the Almighty do to us?'
18 Yet He filled their houses with good things;
  but the counsel of the wicked is far from me.

19 "The righteous see it and are glad,
  and the innocent laugh them to scorn:
20 'Surely our adversaries are cut down,
  and the fire consumes their remnant.'

21 "Now acquaint yourself with Him and be at peace;
  thereby good will come to you.
22 Receive, I pray, the teaching from His mouth,
  and lay up His words in your heart.
23 If you return to the Almighty, you will be built up;
  you will put away iniquity far from your tents.
24 Then you will lay up gold as dust,
  and the gold of Ophir as the stones of the brooks.
25 Yes, the Almighty will be your gold
  and your precious silver;
26 for then you will delight yourself in the Almighty,
  and will lift up your face unto God.

27 You will make your prayer to Him, and He will hear you,
  and you will pay your vows.
28 You will also declare a matter, and it will be established unto you;
  and the light will shine upon your ways.
29 When men are cast down, and you say, 'There is a time
  of exaltation!'
  then He will save the humble person.
30 He will even deliver one who is not innocent;
  he will be delivered by the purity of your hands."

Job Replies: My Complaint Is Grievous

23 Then Job answered:

2 "Today also my complaint is bitter;
  my hand is heavy because of my groaning.
3 Oh, that I knew where I might find Him,
  that I might come even to His seat!
4 I would present my case before Him
  and fill my mouth with arguments.
5 I would know the words that He would answer me
  and understand what He would say to me.
6 Will He plead against me with His great power?
  No! But He would take note of me.
7 There the righteous might dispute with Him;
  so would I be delivered forever from my Judge.

8 "Look, I go forward, but He is not there,
  and backward, but I cannot perceive Him;
9 when He works on the left hand, I cannot behold Him;
  He turns to the right hand, I cannot see Him.
10 But He knows the way that I take;
  when He has tested me, I will come forth as gold.
11 My foot has held fast to His steps;
  I have kept His way and have not turned aside.
12 I have not departed from the commandment of His lips;
  I have esteemed the words of His mouth more than my
  necessary food.

13 "But He is resolute, and who can turn Him?
  And whatever His soul desires, that He does.
14 For He performs what is appointed for me,
  and many such things are with Him.
15 Therefore I am troubled at His presence;
  when I consider, I am afraid of Him.
16 For God makes my heart soft,
  and the Almighty troubles me;
17 because I was not cut off from the presence of darkness,
  nor has He covered the darkness from my face.

24 "Since times of judgment are not kept by the Almighty,
  why do they who know Him not see His days?
2 Some remove the landmarks;
  they violently take away flocks and feed on them.
3 They drive away the donkey of the orphan;
  they take the widow's ox for a pledge.
4 They turn away the needy;
  the poor of the earth are forced to hide.
5 Behold, as wild donkeys in the desert,
  they go out to their work, rising early for a prey.
  The wilderness yields food for them and for their children.
6 They gather their fodder in the field,
  and they glean in the vineyard of the wicked.
7 They cause the naked to lodge without clothing,
  and they have no covering in the cold.
8 They are wet with the showers of the mountains
  and embrace the rock for want of a shelter.
9 They snatch the fatherless from the breast
  and take a pledge from the poor.
10 They cause him to go naked without clothing,
  and they take away the sheaf from the hungry.
11 They press out oil within their walls
  and tread their winepresses, yet suffer thirst.

[12] Men groan from outside the city,
and the soul of the wounded cries out;
yet God does not charge them with wrong.

[13] "They are those who rebel against the light;
they do not know its ways
nor abide in its paths.
[14] The murderer, rising with the light, kills the poor and needy,
and in the night he is like a thief.
[15] Also the eye of the adulterer waits for the twilight,
saying, 'No eye will see me';
and he disguises his face.
[16] In the dark they break into houses,
which they had marked for themselves in the daytime;
they do not know the light.
[17] For the morning is the same to them as the shadow of death;
if someone recognizes them,
they are in the terrors of the shadow of death.

[18] "He is swift as the waters.
Their portion is cursed in the earth.
They do not turn toward the way of the vineyards.
[19] Drought and heat consume the snow waters;
so the grave consumes those who have sinned.
[20] The womb will forget him;
the worm will feed sweetly on him;
he will be remembered no more,
and wickedness will be broken like a tree.
[21] He preys on the barren who do not bear,
and does no good for the widow.
[22] But God draws the mighty away with His power;
He rises up, and no man is sure of life.
[23] He gives them security, and they rely on it;
yet His eyes are on their ways.
[24] They are exalted for a little while but are gone and brought low;
they are taken out of the way like all others
and cut off as the tops of the grain.

[25] "If it is not so, who will prove me a liar
and make my speech worth nothing?"

Bildad Speaks: Man Cannot Be Righteous

25 Then Bildad the Shuhite answered:

[2] "Dominion and fear are with Him;
He makes peace in His high places.
[3] Is there any number to His armies?
And upon whom does His light not rise?
[4] How then can man be righteous with God?
Or how can he who is born of a woman be clean?
[5] Behold, even the moon does not shine,
and the stars are not pure in His sight;
[6] how much less man, who is a maggot,
And the son of man, who is a worm?"

Job Replies: God's Majesty Is Unsearchable

26 But Job answered:

[2] "How have you helped him who is without power?
How have you saved the arm that has no strength?
[3] How have you counseled him who has no wisdom?
And how have you plentifully declared sound knowledge?
[4] To whom have you uttered words?
And whose breath came from you?

[5] "The departed spirits tremble under the waters,
and their inhabitants.
[6] The underworld is naked before Him,
and destruction has no covering.
[7] He stretches out the north over empty space,
He hangs the earth upon nothing.

[8] He binds up the waters in His thick clouds,
and the cloud is not broken under them.
[9] He covers the face of the full moon
and spreads His cloud over it.
[10] He has circled the waters with boundaries,
until the day and night come to an end.
[11] The pillars of heaven tremble
and are astonished at His reproof.
[12] He divides the sea with His power,
and by His understanding He strikes through the proud.
[13] By His breath He has made fair the heavens;
His hand has formed the fleeing serpent.
[14] Indeed, these are but a part of His ways,
and how small a whisper we hear of Him!
But the thunder of His power who can understand?"

Job's Last Words to His Friends

27 Moreover Job continued his discourse:

[2] "As God lives, who has taken away my judgment,
and the Almighty, who has made my soul bitter,
[3] all the while my spirit is in me,
and the breath of God is in my nostrils,
[4] my lips will not speak wickedness,
nor my tongue utter deceit.
[5] God forbid that I should justify you.
Until I die I will not put away my integrity from me.
[6] My righteousness I hold fast and will not let it go;
my heart will not reproach me as long as I live.

[7] "Let my enemy be like the wicked,
and he who rises up against me like the unrighteous.
[8] For what is the hope of the hypocrite,
though he may gain much, when God takes away his soul?
[9] Will God hear his cry
when trouble comes upon him?
[10] Will he delight himself in the Almighty?
Will he always call upon God?

[11] "I will teach you about the hand of God;
what is with the Almighty I will not conceal.
[12] Look, all of you have seen it;
why then have you become altogether vain?

[13] "This is the portion of a wicked man with God,
and the inheritance that oppressors receive from the Almighty:
[14] If his children are multiplied, it is for the sword,
and his offspring will not be satisfied with bread.
[15] Those who survive him will be buried in death,
and their widows will not weep.
[16] Though he heaps up silver like the dust
and piles up clothing like the clay—
[17] he may pile it up, but the just will wear it,
and the innocent will divide the silver.
[18] He builds his house like a moth,
and like a booth that the watchman makes.
[19] The rich man will lie down, but he will not be gathered;
he opens his eyes, and he is not.
[20] Terrors overtake him like floodwaters;
a tempest steals him away in the night.
[21] The east wind carries him away, and he departs;
it sweeps him out of his place.
[22] For God will cast it upon him and not spare;
he would flee from its power.
[23] Men will clap their hands at him
and will hiss him out of his place.

Interlude: Where Wisdom Is Found

28 "Surely there is a mine for the silver,
and a place where they refine gold.
[2] Iron is taken out of the earth,
and copper is smelted from the ore.

3 Man puts an end to darkness,
   and searches every extremity
   for ore in the darkness and the shadow of death.
4 He breaks open a shaft away from the inhabitants;
   in places forgotten by feet
   they hang far away from men; and they totter.
5 As for the earth, from it comes bread,
   and underneath it is turned up as by fire.
6 Its stones are the source of sapphires,
   and it has dust of gold.
7 There is a path that no bird knows,
   and that the vulture's eye has not seen;
8 the lion cubs have not trodden it,
   nor has the fierce lion passed by it.
9 He puts forth his hand upon the rock;
   he overturns the mountains by the roots.
10 He cuts out rivers among the rocks,
   and his eye sees every precious thing.
11 He prevents the floods from overflowing,
   and the thing that is hidden he brings forth
      to light.

12 "But where will wisdom be found?
   And where is the place of understanding?
13 Man does not know its price,
   nor is it found in the land of the living.
14 The depth says, 'It is not in me,'
   and the sea says, 'It is not with me.'
15 It cannot be bought for gold,
   nor can silver be weighed for its price.
16 It cannot be valued in the gold of Ophir,
   with the precious onyx or the sapphire.
17 The gold and the crystal cannot equal it,
   and it cannot be exchanged for jewels of fine gold.
18 No mention will be made of coral or of pearls,
   for the price of wisdom is above rubies.
19 The topaz of Ethiopia will not equal it,
   nor will it be valued with pure gold.

20 "From where then does wisdom come?
   And where is the place of understanding?
21 It is hidden from the eyes of all living
   and concealed from the birds of the air.
22 Destruction and Death say,
   'We have heard of its fame with our ears.'
23 God understands its way,
   and He knows its place.
24 For He looks to the ends of the earth,
   and sees under the whole heaven,
25 to make the weight of the wind,
   and He weighs the waters by measure.
26 When He made a decree for the rain,
   and a path for the lightning of the thunder,
27 then He saw it and declared it;
   He prepared it, yes, and searched it out.
28 To man He said:
   'Look, the fear of the Lord, that is wisdom;
   and to depart from evil is understanding.'"

Job's Final Defense

29 Moreover Job continued his discourse:

2 "Oh, that I were as in months past,
   as in the days when God watched over me;
3 when His lamp shone upon my head,
   and when by His light I walked through darkness;
4 as I was in the days of my autumn youth,
   when the friendly counsel of God was over my tent;
5 when the Almighty was still with me,
   when my children were around me;
6 when my steps were bathed in butter,
   and the rock poured out rivers of oil for me!

7 "When I went out to the gate of the city,
   when I took my seat in the square,
8 the young men saw me and hid themselves,
   and the aged arose and stood up.
9 The princes refrained from talking,
   and put their hand on their mouth.
10 The nobles held their peace,
   and their tongue stuck to the roof of their mouth.
11 When the ear heard, then it blessed me;
   and when the eye saw, then it approved me,
12 because I delivered the poor who cried,
   and the fatherless, and him who had none to help him.
13 The blessing of the perishing man came upon me,
   and I caused the widow's heart to sing for joy.
14 I put on righteousness, and it clothed me;
   my judgment was like a robe and a diadem.
15 I was eyes for the blind,
   and I was feet for the lame.
16 I was a father to the poor,
   and I searched out the case that I did not know.
17 I broke the jaws of the wicked
   and plucked the victim from his teeth.

18 "Then I said, 'I will die in my nest,
   and I will multiply my days as the sand.
19 My root was spread out by the waters,
   and the dew lay all night upon my branch.
20 My glory was fresh in me,
   and my bow was renewed in my hand.'

21 "Men listened to me and waited,
   and kept silence for my counsel.
22 After my words they did not speak again,
   and my speech settled on them like dew.
23 They waited for me as for the rain,
   and they opened their mouth wide as for the spring rain.
24 If I mocked at them, they did not believe it,
   and the light of my countenance they did not cast down.
25 I chose the way for them and sat as chief,
   and lived as a king in the army,
   as one who comforts mourners.

30 "But now those who are younger than I mock me,
   whose fathers I disdained to put with the dogs of my flock.
2 Yes, how does the strength of their hands profit me?
   Their vigor has perished.
3 For want and famine
   they gnawed the parched land;
   fleeing into the wilderness in former time, desolate and waste.
4 Who pluck mallow by the bushes,
   and juniper roots for their food.
5 They were driven out from among men;
   they shout after them as after a thief.
6 They had to dwell in the rocky riverbeds,
   in caves of the earth, and in the rocks.
7 Among the bushes they brayed;
   under the nettles they were gathered together.
8 They were children of fools, yes, children of vile men;
   they were scourged from the earth.

9 "Now I am their taunting song;
   yes, I am their byword.
10 They abhor me, they flee far from me;
   they do not hesitate to spit in my face.
11 Because He has loosed my bowstring and afflicted me,
   they have cast off the bridle before me.
12 At my right hand their brood arises;
   they push away my feet,
   and they raise against me their ways of destruction.
13 They tear apart my path,
   they promote my calamity;
   they have no helper.

14 They came upon me as a wide breach, with a crash
        they came;
    in the desolation they rolled themselves upon me.
15 Terrors are turned on me;
    they pursue my dignity like the wind,
    and my help passes away as a cloud.

16 "Now my soul is poured out within me;
    the days of affliction have taken hold of me.
17 My bones are pierced in me at night,
    and my sinews have no rest.
18 By the great force of my disease my garment is changed;
    it binds me about as the collar of my coat.
19 He has cast me into the mire,
    and I have become like dust and ashes.

20 "I cry unto You, but You do not hear me;
    I stand up, and You do not regard me.
21 You have become cruel to me;
    with Your strong hand You oppose me.
22 You lift me up to the wind and cause me to ride on it;
    You dissolve my success.
23 For I know that You will bring me to death,
    and to the house appointed for all living.

24 "Surely He will not stretch out His hand to the grave,
    though they cry when He destroys it.
25 Did I not weep for him who was in trouble?
    Was not my soul grieved for the poor?
26 When I looked for good, then evil disaster came upon me;
    and when I waited for light, darkness came.
27 My insides boiled and did not rest;
    the days of affliction have met me.
28 I went mourning without the sun;
    I stood up, and I cried in the congregation.
29 I am a brother of jackals
    and a companion of owls.
30 My skin is black upon me,
    and my bones are burned with fever.
31 My harp is turned to mourning,
    and my flute to the voice of those who weep.

31 "I made a covenant with my eyes;
    why then should I look upon a young woman?
2 For what portion of God is there from above?
    And what inheritance of the Almighty from on high?
3 Does not destruction belong to the wicked,
    and calamity to the workers of iniquity?
4 Does He not see my ways,
    and count all my steps?

5 "If I have walked in vanity,
    or if my foot has hurried after deceit,
6 let me be weighed in an even balance
    that God may know my integrity.
7 If my step has turned out of the path,
    and my heart has gone after my eyes,
    and if any spot has clung to my hands,
8 then let me sow, but let another eat;
    yes, let my offspring be rooted out.

9 "If my heart has been deceived by a woman,
    or if I have laid wait at my neighbor's door,
10 then let my wife grind for another,
    and let others bow down over her.
11 For this is a heinous crime;
    yes, it is an iniquity to be punished by the judges.
12 For it is a fire that consumes to destruction
    and would root out all my increase.

13 "If I have despised the cause of my male or female servant
    when they complained against me,

14 what then will I do when God rises up?
    And when He visits, what will I answer Him?
15 Did not He who made me in the womb make him?
    And did not the same One fashion us in the womb?

16 "If I have kept the poor from their desire,
    or have caused the eyes of the widow to fail,
17 or have eaten my morsel by myself,
    so that the fatherless could not eat of it
18 (but from my youth he was brought up with me, as with
        a father,
    and I have guided the widow from my mother's womb);
19 if I have seen anyone perish for lack of clothing,
    or any poor without covering;
20 if his body has not blessed me,
    and if he was not warmed with the fleece of my sheep;
21 if I have lifted up my hand against the fatherless,
    when I saw I had help in the gate;
22 then let my arm fall from my shoulder blade,
    and my arm be broken from the bone.
23 For destruction from God is a terror to me,
    and because of His highness I cannot endure.

24 "If I have made gold my hope,
    or have said to the fine gold, 'You are my confidence';
25 if I rejoiced because my wealth was great,
    and because my hand had gained much;
26 if I saw the sun when it shined,
    or the moon moving in brightness;
27 and my heart has been secretly enticed,
    or my mouth has kissed my hand;
28 this also would be an iniquity to be punished by the judge,
    for I would have denied the God who is above.

29 "If I rejoiced at the destruction of him who hated me,
    or lifted up myself when disaster found him
30 (nor have I allowed my mouth to sin
    by wishing for a curse on his soul);
31 if the men of my tent have not said,
    'Who is there who has not been satisfied with his meat?'
32 (the stranger has not lodged in the street,
    but I opened my doors to the traveler);
33 if I covered my transgressions as any man,
    by hiding my iniquity in my heart,
34 did I fear a great multitude,
    or did the contempt of families terrify me,
    so that I kept silence, and did not go out of the door?

35 "Oh, that one would hear me!
    Behold, my desire is that the Almighty would answer me,
    and that the One who contends against me had written
        a book!
36 Surely I would carry it on my shoulder
    and bind it on me like a crown.
37 I would declare to Him the number of my steps;
    like a prince I would approach Him.

38 "If my land cries out against me,
    and its furrows also weep together;
39 if I have eaten its fruit without money,
    or have caused its owners to lose their life;
40 let thistles grow instead of wheat,
    and weeds instead of barley."

The words of Job are ended.

Elihu Speaks: Job's Three Friends Rebuked

32 So these three men ceased answering Job, because he was
    righteous in his own eyes. 2 Then the wrath of Elihu the son
of Barakel the Buzite, of the family of Ram, was aroused; his wrath
was aroused against Job because he justified himself rather than God.
3 His wrath was aroused also against his three friends because they

had found no answer and yet had condemned Job. [4] Now Elihu had waited until Job had spoken because they were older than he. [5] When Elihu saw that there was no answer in the mouth of these three men, then his wrath was aroused.

[6] Elihu the son of Barakel the Buzite answered:

"I am young,
    and you are very old;
therefore I was afraid
    and dared not show you my opinion.
[7] I said, 'Age should speak,
    and multitude of years should teach wisdom.'
[8] But there is a spirit in man,
    and the breath of the Almighty gives him understanding.
[9] Great men are not always wise,
    nor do the aged always understand judgment.

[10] "Therefore I say,
    'Listen to me; I will also declare my opinion.'
[11] Indeed, I waited for your words;
    I listened to your reasons,
while you searched out what to say.
[12] Yes, I paid attention to you;
    and surely none of you convinced Job
    or answered his words.
[13] Lest you say, 'We have found wisdom';
    God *will* subdue him, not man.
[14] Now he has not directed his words against me,
    so I will not answer him with your speeches.

[15] "They are amazed; they answer no more;
    they cease speaking.
[16] And I have waited,
    (for they did not speak, but stood still and answered
        no more).
[17] I said, 'I also will answer my part;
    I too will show my opinion.'
[18] For I am full of words;
    the spirit within me compels me.
[19] See, my belly is like wine that has no vent;
    it is ready to burst like new wineskins.
[20] I will speak, that I may be refreshed;
    I will open my lips and answer.
[21] Let me not, I pray, show partiality to anyone,
    nor let me give flattering titles to man.
[22] For I do not know how to give flattering titles;
    in so doing my Maker would soon take me away.

Elihu Addresses Job

33 "Therefore, Job, I pray, hear my speeches,
    and listen to all my words.
[2] Behold, now I have opened my mouth;
    my tongue has spoken in my mouth.
[3] My words will be from the uprightness of my heart,
    and my lips will utter knowledge clearly.
[4] The Spirit of God has made me,
    and the breath of the Almighty has given me life.
[5] If you can answer me,
    set your words in order before me; stand up.
[6] Surely I am before God like you;
    I also am formed out of the clay.
[7] Indeed, no dread of me will make you afraid,
    nor will my hand be heavy upon you.

[8] "Surely you have spoken in my hearing,
    and I have heard the sound of your words, saying,
[9] 'I am clean, without transgression;
    I am innocent, nor is there iniquity in me.
[10] Behold, He finds occasions against me,
    He counts me for His enemy;
[11] He puts my feet in the stocks,
    He watches all my paths.'

[12] "Look, in this you are not just.
    I will answer you, that God is greater than man.
[13] Why do you strive against Him?
    For He does not give an accounting for any of His words.
[14] For God speaks once, yes twice,
    yet man does not perceive it.
[15] In a dream, in a vision of the night,
    when deep sleep falls upon men,
    in slumber on their beds,
[16] then He opens the ears of men,
    and seals their instruction,
[17] that He *might* turn aside man from his purpose,
    and conceal pride from man.
[18] He keeps back his soul from the pit,
    and his life from perishing by the sword.

[19] "He is also chastened with pain on his bed,
    and with strong pain in many of his bones,
[20] so that his life abhors bread,
    and his soul dainty food.
[21] His flesh is consumed away that it cannot be seen,
    and his bones that were not seen stick out.
[22] Yes, his soul draws near to the grave,
    and his life to the executioners.
[23] If there is a messenger for him,
    an interpreter, one among a thousand,
    to show to man what is right for him,
[24] then He is gracious to him, and says,
    'Deliver him from going down to the pit;
    I have found a ransom.'
[25] His flesh will be fresher than a child's;
    he will return to the days of his youth;
[26] he will pray to God, and He will be favorable unto him,
    and he will see His face with joy,
    for He will render unto man His righteousness.
[27] Then he looks at men and says,
    'I have sinned and perverted what was right,
    and it did not profit me.'
[28] He will deliver his soul from going down to the pit,
    and his life will see the light.

[29] "Behold, God works all these things,
    twice, three times with man,
[30] to bring back his soul from the pit,
    to be enlightened with the light of the living.

[31] "Pay attention, Job, listen to me;
    hold your peace, and I will speak.
[32] If you have anything to say, answer me;
    speak, for I desire to justify you.
[33] If not, listen to me; hold your peace,
    and I will teach you wisdom."

Elihu Proclaims God's Justice

34 Furthermore Elihu answered and said:

[2] "Hear my words, O you wise men;
    and give ear unto me, you that have knowledge.
[3] For the ear tests words,
    as the mouth tastes food.
[4] Let us choose justice for ourselves;
    let us know among ourselves what is good.

[5] "For Job has said, 'I am righteous,
    but God has taken away my judgment.
[6] Should I lie concerning my right?
    My wound is incurable, though I am without
        transgression.'
[7] What man is like Job,
    who drinks scorn like water,
[8] who goes in company with the workers of iniquity
    and walks with wicked men?

9 For he has said, 'It profits a man nothing
    that he should delight himself in God.'

10 "Therefore listen to me, you men of understanding:
    Far be it from God that He should do wickedness,
    and from the Almighty that He should commit iniquity.
11 He will repay a man for his work,
    and cause every man to find what is according to
      his ways.
12 Yes, surely God will not do wickedly,
    nor will the Almighty pervert judgment.
13 Who has given Him charge over the earth?
    Or who has set in order the whole world?
14 If He sets His heart on man,
    if He gathers unto Himself His Spirit and His breath,
15 all flesh will perish together,
    and man will turn again to dust.

16 "If now you have understanding, hear this;
    listen to the voice of my words:
17 Should he who hates justice govern?
    And will you condemn Him who is most just?
18 Is it fitting to say to a king, 'You are wicked'?
    And to princes, 'You are ungodly'?
19 Yet He is not partial to princes,
    nor does He regard the rich more than the poor.
    For they all are the work of His hands.
20 In a moment they will die,
    and the people will be troubled at midnight and
      pass away,
    and the mighty will be taken away without a hand.

21 "For His eyes are upon the ways of man,
    and He sees all his goings.
22 There is no darkness nor shadow of death
    where the workers of iniquity may hide themselves.
23 For He will not lay upon man more than right,
    that he should enter into judgment with God.
24 He will break in pieces mighty men without number,
    and set others in their place.
25 Therefore He knows their works,
    and He overturns them in the night
      so that they are destroyed.
26 He strikes them as wicked men
    in the open sight of others,
27 because they turned back from Him
    and would not consider any of His ways,
28 so that they cause the cry of the poor to come unto Him;
    and He hears the cry of the afflicted.
29 When He gives quietness, who then can make trouble?
    And when He hides His face, who then can behold Him,
    whether it is done against a nation or against a man only?
30   That the hypocrite should not reign,
    lest the people be ensnared.

31 "Should anyone say to God,
    'I have borne chastisement, I will offend no more;
32 teach me what I do not see;
    if I have done iniquity, I will do no more'?
33 Should it be according to your mind?
    He will repay it, whether you refuse or whether you choose,
    and not I; therefore speak what you know.

34 "Let men of understanding say to me,
    wise men who listen to me:
35 'Job has spoken without knowledge,
    and his words were without wisdom.'
36 My desire is that Job may be tried unto the end,
    because he answers like wicked men.
37 For he adds rebellion unto his sin;
    he claps his hands among us,
    and multiplies his words against God."

Elihu Condemns Self-Righteousness

35 Elihu spoke again and said:

2 "Do you think this is right,
    that you say, 'My righteousness is before God'?
3 For you said, 'What advantage will it be to me?
    What profit will I have if I am cleansed from my sin?'

4 "I will answer you,
    and your companions with you.
5 Look unto the heavens and see,
    and behold the clouds that are higher than you.
6 If you sin, what do you accomplish against Him?
    Or if your transgressions are multiplied, what does it do
      to Him?
7 If you are righteous, what does it give Him?
    Or what does He receive from your hand?
8 Your wickedness may hurt a man like you,
    and your righteousness may profit a son of man.

9 "Because of the many oppressions they cry out;
    they cry out because of the arm of the mighty.
10 But none says, 'Where is God my Maker,
    who gives songs in the night,
11 who teaches us more than the beasts of the earth,
    and makes us wiser than the birds of heaven?'
12 There they cry out, but He does not answer
    because of the pride of evil men.
13 Surely God will not hear vanity,
    nor will the Almighty regard it.
14 Although you say you do not see Him,
    yet judgment is before Him,
    and you *must* trust in Him.
15 But now, because He has not punished in His anger,
    nor taken much notice of folly,
16 therefore Job opens his mouth in vain;
    he multiplies words without knowledge."

Elihu Proclaims God's Majesty

36 Elihu continued and said:

2 "Bear with me a little, and I will show you
    that I have yet to speak on God's behalf.
3 I will bring my knowledge from afar
    and will ascribe righteousness to my Maker.
4 For truly my words will not be false;
    He who is perfect in knowledge is with you.

5 "Behold, God is mighty and despises no one;
    He is mighty in strength and wisdom.
6 He does not preserve the life of the wicked,
    but gives justice to the poor.
7 He does not withdraw His eyes from the righteous;
    but they are on the throne with kings,
    for He establishes them forever, and they are exalted.
8 If they are bound in chains
    and held in cords of affliction,
9 then He shows them their work,
    and their transgressions that they have exceeded;
10 and He opens their ear to discipline,
    and commands that they turn from iniquity.
11 If they obey and serve Him,
    they will spend their days in prosperity
    and their years in pleasures.
12 But if they do not obey,
    they will perish by the sword,
    and they will die without knowledge.

13 "But the hypocrites in heart heap up wrath;
    they do not cry out when He binds them.
14 They die in youth,
    and their life ends among the unclean.

15 He delivers the poor in their affliction,
and opens their ears in oppression.

16 "Even so He would have removed you out of distress
into a broad place where there is no restraint;
and that which was set on your table would be full of
richness.
17 But you are filled with the judgment due the wicked;
judgment and justice take hold of you.
18 Because there is wrath, beware lest He take you away with a blow;
even a great ransom cannot deliver you.
19 Will He esteem your riches?
No, not gold, nor all the force of your strength.
20 Do not desire the night,
when people are cut off in their place.
21 Take heed! Do not turn to iniquity,
for you have chosen this rather than affliction.

22 "Behold, God is exalted in His power;
who teaches like Him?
23 Who has prescribed His way for Him?
Or who can say, 'You have worked iniquity'?
24 Remember to magnify His work,
which men behold.
25 Every man may see it;
man may behold it from afar.
26 Look, God is great, and we do not know Him,
nor can the number of His years be searched out.

27 "For He draws up the drops of water;
they distill rain according to its mist,
28 which the clouds drop down,
and drip upon man abundantly.
29 Indeed, can anyone understand the spreading of clouds,
or the noise of His tent?
30 See, He spreads His light upon it
and covers the bottom of the sea.
31 For by these He judges the people;
He gives food in abundance.
32 With clouds He covers the light,
and commands it to strike the mark.
33 Its thunder declares it,
the cattle also, concerning the rising storm.

37 "At this also my heart trembles
and moves out of its place.
2 Hear attentively the thunder of His voice,
and the sound that goes out of His mouth.
3 He lets it loose under the whole heaven,
and His lightning unto the ends of the earth.
4 After it a voice roars; He thunders with His majestic voice,
and He does not restrain them when His voice is heard.
5 God thunders marvelously with His voice;
He does great things that we cannot comprehend.
6 For He says to the snow, 'Come on the earth,'
likewise to the gentle rain and to the heavy rain of His
strength.
7 He seals up the hand of every man,
that all men may know His work.
8 Then the beasts go into dens
and remain in their places.
9 Out of the south comes the whirlwind,
and cold out of the north.
10 By the breath of God frost is given,
and the broad waters are frozen.
11 Also He loads the thick clouds with moisture;
He scatters His bright clouds,
12 and they are turned about by His guidance,
that they may do whatever He commands them
upon the face of the inhabited earth.
13 He causes it to come, whether for correction,
or for His land or for mercy.

14 "Listen to this, Job; stand still
and consider the wondrous works of God.
15 Do you know when God dispatches them
and causes the light of His cloud to shine?
16 Do you know how the clouds are balanced,
the wondrous works of Him who is perfect in knowledge?
17 How your garments are warm,
when He quiets the earth by the south wind?
18 Have you, with Him, spread out the sky,
which is strong and is like a molded mirror?

19 "Teach us what we will say to Him,
for we cannot prepare our speech because of
the darkness.
20 Will it be told Him that I speak?
If a man speaks, surely he will be swallowed up.
21 Now men do not see the bright light
which is in the clouds,
but the wind passes and cleanses them.
22 Fair weather comes out of the north;
with God is terrible majesty.
23 Concerning the Almighty, we cannot find Him out;
He is excellent in power, and in judgment,
and in much righteousness He will not oppress.
24 Men therefore fear Him;
He shows no partiality to those who are wise
in heart."

The LORD Speaks to Job

38 Then the LORD answered Job out of the whirlwind and said:

2 "Who is this who darkens counsel
by words without knowledge?
3 Prepare yourself like a man;
for I will question you,
and you shall answer Me.

4 "Where were you when I laid the foundations of
the earth?
Declare, if you have understanding.
5 Who has determined its measurements, if you know?
Or who has stretched the line upon it?
6 To what are its foundations fastened?
Or who laid its cornerstone
7 when the morning stars sang together,
and all the sons of God shouted for joy?

8 "Or who shut up the sea with doors
when it broke forth and went out of the womb?
9 When I made the cloud its garment,
and thick darkness its swaddling band,
10 and broke up for it My decreed place,
and set bars and doors,
11 and said, 'This far you will come but no farther,
and here your proud waves will be stopped'?

12 "Have you commanded the morning in your days,
and caused the dawn to know its place,
13 that it might take hold of the ends of the earth,
that the wicked might be shaken out of it?
14 It is turned like clay by the seal,
and it stands out as a garment.
15 From the wicked their light is withheld,
and the high arm will be broken.

16 "Have you entered into the springs of the sea?
Or have you walked in search of the depths?
17 Have the gates of death been opened to you?
Or have you seen the doors of the shadow
of death?
18 Have you perceived the breadth of the earth?
Declare, if you know it all.

19 "Where is the path where light dwells?
    And as for darkness, where is its place,
20 that you should take it to its boundary,
    and that you should know the paths to its house?
21 Do you know it because you were born then,
    or because the number of your days is many?

22 "Have you entered the treasuries of the snow?
    Or have you seen the treasuries of the hail,
23 which I have reserved against the time of trouble,
    against the day of battle and war?
24 By what way is the light diffused,
    or the east wind scattered upon the earth?
25 Who has divided a channel for the overflowing waters,
    or a path for the thunderbolt,
26 to cause it to rain on the earth where no man is,
    on the wilderness in which there are no people,
27 to satisfy the desolate waste,
    and to cause the bud of the tender herb to spring forth?
28 Does the rain have a father?
    Or who has produced the drops of dew?
29 From whose womb came the ice?
    And the frost of heaven, who gives it birth?
30 The waters harden like stone,
    and the surface of the deep is frozen.

31 "Can you tie the cords to the Pleiades
    or loosen the belt of Orion?
32 Can you bring out the constellation in its season?
    Or can you guide the Bear with its cubs?
33 Do you know the ordinances of heaven?
    Can you set their dominion over the earth?

34 "Can you lift up your voice to the clouds,
    that abundance of waters may cover you?
35 Can you send lightning that they may go forth
    and say to you, 'Here we are'?
36 Who has put wisdom in the inward parts,
    or who has given understanding to the heart?[1]
37 Who can number the clouds by wisdom?
    Or who *can* empty out the bottles of heaven,
38 when the dust turns into hard clumps
    and the clods stick together?

39 "Will you hunt the prey for the lion?
    Or fill the appetite of the young lions,
40 when they crouch in their dens
    and lie in the thicket to wait in ambush?
41 Who provides for the raven his food
    when his young ones cry unto God,
    and they wander about for lack of food?

39

"Do you know the time when the wild mountain goats
    produce offspring?
    Or can you observe when the deer gives birth?
2 Can you number the months that they fulfill,
    or do you know the time when they bring forth?
3 They bow themselves, they bring forth their young ones,
    they get rid of their labor pains.
4 Their young ones are healthy, they grow strong with grain;
    they go forth and do not return to them.

5 "Who has sent out the wild donkey free?
    Or who has loosed the bands of the wild donkey,
6 whose home I have made the wilderness,
    and the barren land his dwelling?
7 He scorns the multitude in the city
    and does not regard the shouts of the driver.
8 The range of the mountains is his pasture,
    and he searches after every green thing.

9 "Will the wild ox be willing to serve you
    or spend the night by your manger?
10 Can you bind the wild ox in the furrow with ropes?
    Or will he plow the valleys behind you?
11 Will you trust him because his strength is great?
    Or will you leave your labor to him?
12 Will you trust him to bring home your grain
    and gather it into your barn?

13 "Did you give the beautiful wings to the peacocks?
    Or wings and feathers to the ostrich,
14 who leaves her eggs in the earth,
    and warms them in dust,
15 and forgets that a foot may crush them,
    or that the wild beast may break them?
16 She is hardened against her young ones,
    as though they were not hers;
    her labor is in vain, without concern,
17 because God has deprived her of wisdom,
    nor has He imparted understanding to her.
18 When she lifts up herself on high,
    she scorns the horse and his rider.

19 "Have you given the horse strength?
    Have you clothed his neck with thunder?
20 Can you make him afraid like a grasshopper?
    The glory of his nostrils is awesome.
21 He paws in the valley and rejoices in his strength;
    he goes on to meet the armed men.
22 He mocks at fear and is not frightened,
    nor does he turn back from the sword.
23 The quiver rattles against him,
    the glittering spear and the shield.
24 He devours the distance with fierceness and rage,
    and he does not stand still at the sound of the trumpet.
25 At the sound of the trumpet he says, 'Aha';
    he smells the battle afar off,
    the thunder of the captains, and the shouting.

26 "Does the hawk fly by your wisdom,
    and stretch her wings toward the south?
27 Does the eagle mount up at your command
    and make her nest on high?
28 She dwells and remains on the rock,
    upon the crag of the rock, and the strong place.
29 From there she seeks the prey,
    and her eyes see it from afar.
30 Her young ones also suck up blood,
    and where the slain are, there she is."

40

Moreover, the LORD answered Job and said:
2 "Will he who argues with the Almighty instruct Him?
    He who rebukes God, let him answer it."

Job Replies to the LORD
3 Then Job answered the LORD and said:

4 "Behold, I am vile; what shall I answer You?
    I will lay my hand over my mouth.
5 Once have I spoken, but I will not answer;
    yes, twice, but I will proceed no further."

The LORD Challenges Job
6 Then the LORD answered Job out of the whirlwind
and said:

7 "Prepare yourself now like a man;
    I will question you,
    and you will answer Me.

---

[1] 36 The Heb. may refer to celestial bodies.

8 "Will you indeed annul My judgment?
    Will you condemn Me, that you may be righteous?
9 Have you an arm like God?
    Or can you thunder with a voice like Him?
10 Adorn yourself now with majesty and excellence,
    and array yourself with glory and beauty.
11 Let loose the rage of your wrath,
    and look on every one who is proud and abase him;
12 look on every one who is proud and bring him low,
    and tread down the wicked in their place.
13 Hide them in the dust together,
    and imprison them in the hidden place of the grave.
14 Then I will also confess to you
    that your own right hand can save you.

15 "Look now at the behemoth
    which I made along with you;
    he eats grass like an ox.
16 See now his strength is in his hips,
    and his power is in the muscles of his belly.
17 He moves his tail like a cedar;
    the sinews of his thighs are wrapped together.
18 His bones are like strong pieces of brass;
    his bones are like bars of iron.
19 He is the first of the works of God;
    He who made him can bring near His sword.
20 Surely the mountains bring forth food for him,
    where all the beasts of the field play.
21 He lies under the shady trees,
    in the thicket of the reed and marsh.
22 The shady trees cover him with their shadow;
    the willows of the brook surround him.
23 Look, the river rages, but he is not alarmed;
    he trusts that he can draw up the Jordan into his mouth.
24 Can anyone catch it by its eyes,
    or pierce its nose with a snare?

41 "Can you draw out Leviathan with a hook[1]
    or snare his tongue with a line which you let down?
2 Can you put a cord into his nose,
    or pierce his jaw with a hook?
3 Will he make many supplications to you?
    Will he speak soft words to you?
4 Will he make a covenant with you?
    Will you take him for a servant forever?
5 Will you play with him as with a bird?
    Or will you put him on a leash for your maidens?
6 Will your companions make a banquet of him?
    Will they divide him among the merchants?
7 Can you fill his skin with harpoons
    or his head with fishing spears?
8 Lay your hand on him;
    remember the battle—you will do it no more.
9 Notice, any hope of overcoming him is in vain;
    shall not one be overwhelmed at the sight of him?
10 No one is so fierce that he dares to stir him up.
    Who then is able to stand before Me?
11 Who has preceded Me that I should repay him?
    Everything under heaven is Mine.

12 "I will not conceal his limbs,
    nor his power, nor his graceful proportions.
13 Who can remove his outer garment?
    Or who can approach him with a double bridle?
14 Who can open the jaws of his face?
    His teeth are terrible all around.
15 His scales are his pride,
    shut up tightly as with a seal.
16 One is so near to another
    that no air can come between them.

17 They are joined to each other;
    they stick together that they cannot be separated.
18 His sneezing flashes forth light,
    and his eyes are like the eyelids of the morning.
19 Out of his mouth go burning lights,
    and sparks of fire leap out.
20 Out of his nostrils goes smoke
    as out of a seething pot or cauldron.
21 His breath kindles coals,
    and a flame goes out of his mouth.
22 In his neck remains strength,
    and sorrow is turned into joy before him.
23 The folds of his flesh are joined together;
    they are firm on him; they cannot be moved.
24 His heart is as firm as a stone,
    yes, as hard as a piece of the lower millstone.
25 When he raises up himself even the gods are afraid;
    because of his crashings they are beside themselves.
26 The sword that reaches him cannot avail,
    nor does the spear, the arrow, or the javelin.
27 He counts iron as straw,
    and brass as rotten wood.
28 The arrow cannot make him flee;
    slingstones are turned into stubble by him.
29 Arrows are counted as straw;
    he laughs at the shaking of a spear.
30 Sharp stones are his underside;
    he leaves a mark in the mire like a sharp threshing sledge.
31 He makes the deep to boil like a pot;
    he makes the sea like a pot of ointment.
32 He leaves a shining wake behind him;
    one would think the deep had white hair.
33 On earth there is nothing like him,
    a creature made without fear.
34 He beholds all high things;
    he is a king over all the children of pride."

Job's Repentance

42 Then Job answered the Lord and said:

2 "I know that You can do everything,
    and that no thought can be withheld from You.
3 'Who is he who hides counsel without knowledge?'
    Therefore I have uttered what I did not understand,
    things too wonderful for me which I did not know.

4 " 'Hear, and I will speak;
    I will question you,
    and you declare to Me.'
5 I have heard of You by the hearing of the ear,
    but now my eye sees You.
6 Therefore I abhor myself,
    and repent in dust and ashes."

Epilogue

7 And so it was, that after the Lord had spoken these words to Job, the Lord said to Eliphaz the Temanite, "My wrath is kindled against you and against your two friends, for you have not spoken of Me what is right as My servant Job has. 8 And now, take for yourselves seven bulls and seven rams, and go to My servant Job, and offer up for yourselves a burnt offering; and My servant Job will pray for you. For him I will accept, lest I deal with you according to your folly, in that you have not spoken of Me the thing which is right like My servant Job." 9 So Eliphaz the Temanite, and Bildad the Shuhite, and Zophar the Naamathite went and did as the Lord had commanded them; the Lord also accepted Job.

10 And the Lord restored the fortunes of Job when he prayed for his friends, and also the Lord gave Job twice as much as he had before. 11 Then all of his brothers, and all his sisters, and all of those who had been of acquaintance before came to Job, and they ate bread with him

1 Heb. text 40:25.

in his house, and they consoled him and comforted him for all the adversity that the LORD had brought upon him. Every man also gave him a piece of money and an earring of gold.

[12] So the LORD blessed the latter days of Job more than his beginning, for he had fourteen thousand sheep, and six thousand camels, and a thousand yoke of oxen, and a thousand female donkeys. [13] He had also seven sons and three daughters. [14] He called the name of the first Jemimah; and the name of the second Keziah; and the name of the third Keren-Happuch. [15] In all the land, there were no women as beautiful as the daughters of Job, and their father gave them an inheritance along with their brothers.

[16] After this, Job lived a hundred and forty years, and saw his sons, and their sons to the fourth generation. [17] So Job died, being old and full of days.

PSALMS

BOOK ONE
Psalms 1–41

PSALM 1

[1] Blessed is the man
who walks not in the counsel of the ungodly,
nor stands in the path of sinners,
nor sits in the seat of scoffers;
[2] but his delight is in the law of the LORD,
and in His law he meditates day and night.
[3] He will be like a tree planted by the rivers of water,
that brings forth its fruit in its season;
its leaf will not wither,
and whatever he does will prosper.

[4] The ungodly are not so,
but are like the chaff
which the wind drives away.
[5] Therefore the ungodly will not stand in the judgment,
nor sinners in the congregation of the righteous.

[6] For the LORD knows the way of the righteous,
but the way of the ungodly will perish.

PSALM 2

[1] Why do the nations rage,
and the peoples plot in vain?
[2] The kings of the earth set themselves,
and the rulers take counsel together,
against the LORD
and against His anointed, saying,
[3] "Let us tear off their bonds
and cast away their ropes from us."

[4] He who sits in the heavens laughs;
the LORD ridicules them.
[5] Then He will speak to them in His wrath
and terrify them in His burning anger.
[6] "I have installed My king
on Zion, My holy hill."

[7] I will declare the decree of the LORD:

He said to me, "You are My son;
this day have I begotten you.
[8] Ask of Me,
and I will give you the nations for your inheritance,
and the ends of the earth for your possession.
[9] You will break them with a scepter of iron;
you will dash them in pieces like a potter's vessel."

[10] Now then, you kings, be wise;
be admonished, you judges of the earth.
[11] Serve the LORD with fear;
tremble with trepidation!
[12] Kiss the son, lest He become angry,
and you perish in the way,
for His wrath kindles in a flash.
Blessed are all who seek refuge in Him.

PSALM 3
A Psalm of David, when he fled
from Absalom his son.

[1] LORD, how my foes have multiplied!
Many rise up against me!
[2] Many are saying about my life,
"There is no help for him in God."   Selah[1]

[3] But You, O LORD, are a shield for me,
my glory and the One who raises up my head.
[4] I cried to the LORD with my voice,
and He answered me from His holy hill.   Selah

[5] I lay down and slept;
I awoke, for the LORD sustained me.
[6] I will not be afraid of multitudes of people
who have set themselves against me all around.

[7] Arise, O LORD;
save me, O my God!
For You have struck all my enemies on the cheek;
You have broken the teeth of the wicked.

[8] Salvation belongs to the LORD.
Your blessing is on Your people.   Selah

PSALM 4
For the Music Director. With stringed
instruments. A Psalm of David.

[1] Hear me when I call,
O God of my righteousness!
You have given me relief when I was in distress;
have mercy on me, and hear my prayer.

[2] O people, how long will you turn my glory into shame?
How long will you love vanity and seek after lies?
Selah
[3] Know that the LORD set apart the faithful for Himself;
the LORD hears when I call to Him.

---

[1] 2 Musical term for a pause or change in the music.

4 Tremble *in awe*, and do not sin.
　　Commune with your own heart on your bed,
　　and be still.　Selah
5 Offer sacrifices of righteousness,
　　and trust in the LORD.

6 Many are saying, "Who will show us any good?"
　　Lift up the light of Your face over us.
7 You have placed gladness in my heart
　　that is better than when their corn and their new wine abound.

8 I will both lie down in peace and sleep;
　　for You, LORD,
　　make me dwell safely and securely.

PSALM 5

For the Music Director. With the flutes.
A Psalm of David.

1 Give ear to my words, O LORD;
　　consider my meditation.
2 Listen to the voice of my cry,
　　my King and my God,
　　for to You will I pray.

3 O LORD, in the morning You will hear my voice;
　　in the morning I will direct my prayer to You,
　　and I will watch expectantly.
4 For You are not a God who has pleasure in wickedness,
　　nor will evil dwell with You.
5 Those who boast will not stand in Your sight;
　　You hate all workers of iniquity.
6 You will destroy those who speak lies;
　　the LORD abhors
　　the bloodthirsty and deceitful man.
7 But as for me, in the abundance of Your mercy
　　I will enter Your house;
　　in fear of You I will worship
　　at Your holy temple.

8 Lead me, O LORD, in Your righteousness
　　because of my enemies;
　　make Your way straight before me.
9 For there is no uprightness in their mouth;
　　destruction is in their midst;
　　their throat is an open tomb;
　　they flatter with their tongue.
10 Declare them guilty, O God;
　　may they fall by their own counsels;
　　cast them out in the multitude of their transgressions,
　　for they have rebelled against You.
11 But may all those who seek refuge in You rejoice;
　　may they ever shout for joy,
　　because You defend them;
　　may those who love Your name be joyful in You.

12 For You, LORD, will bless the righteous;
　　You surround him with favor like a shield.

PSALM 6

For the Music Director. With stringed instruments.
According to The Sheminith. A Psalm of David.

1 O LORD, do not rebuke me in Your anger,
　　nor discipline me in the heat of Your anger.
2 Be gracious to me, O LORD, for I am weak;
　　O LORD, heal me, for my bones are terrified.
3 My soul is greatly troubled,
　　but You, O LORD, how long?

4 Return, O LORD, rescue my soul.
　　Save me for the sake of Your lovingkindness.

5 For in death there is no remembrance of You;
　　in Sheol who will give You thanks?

6 I am weary with my groaning;
　　all night I flood my bed *with weeping*;
　　I drench my couch with my tears.
7 My eye wastes away from grief;
　　it grows weak because of all those hostile to me.

8 Depart from me, all you workers of iniquity;
　　for the LORD has heard the voice of my weeping.
9 The LORD has heard my supplication;
　　the LORD accepts my prayer.
10 May all my enemies be ashamed and greatly terrified;
　　may they turn back and be suddenly ashamed.

PSALM 7

A Shiggaion of David, which he sang to the LORD
concerning the words of Cush, a Benjamite.

1 O LORD my God, in You I put my trust;
　　save me from all those who persecute me, and deliver me,
2 lest they tear my soul like a lion,
　　rending it in pieces, while there is none to deliver.

3 O LORD my God, if I have done this,
　　if there is iniquity in the palms of my hands,
4 if I have repaid evil to him who was at peace with me,
　　or have delivered my adversary without cause;
5 then may the enemy pursue my life and overtake me;
　　may my enemy trample my life to the ground,
　　and lay my honor in the dust.　Selah

6 Arise, O LORD, in Your anger;
　　rise up because of the rage of my adversaries,
　　and awaken Yourself for me; You have commanded justice.
7 The congregation of the peoples surround You;
　　return above it to heaven's heights.
8 The LORD will judge the peoples;
　　grant me justice, O LORD, according to my righteousness,
　　and according to my integrity within me.
9 May the evil of the wicked come to an end;
　　may You vindicate the righteous one;
　　You are a righteous God who examines the minds
　　and hearts.

10 My defense depends on God,
　　who saves the upright in heart.
11 God is a righteous judge,
　　and God has indignation every day.
12 If one does not repent,
　　God will sharpen His sword;
　　He has bent His bow and made it ready.
13 He has prepared for Himself deadly weapons;
　　He makes His arrows flaming shafts.

14 The wicked man writhes in pain of iniquity;
　　he has conceived mischief and brought forth falsehood.
15 He who digs a hole and hollows it
　　will then fall into his own pit.
16 His mischief will return on his own head;
　　his violence will descend on the crown of his own head.

17 I will thank the LORD according to His righteousness,
　　and will sing praise to the name of the LORD Most High.

PSALM 8

For the Music Director. According to
The Gittith. A Psalm of David.

1 O LORD, our Lord,
　　how excellent is Your name in all the earth!

You have set Your glory
    above the heavens.
2 Out of the mouth of babes and nursing infants
    You have ordained strength
    because of Your enemies,
        to silence the enemy and the avenger.
3 When I consider Your heavens,
    the work of Your fingers,
    the moon and the stars,
    which You have established,
4 what is man that You are mindful of him,
    and the son of man that You attend to him?

5 For You have made him a little lower than the angels,
    and crowned him with glory and honor.
6 You have given him dominion over the works of Your hands;
    You have put all things under his feet,
7 all sheep and oxen,
    and also the beasts of the field,
8 the birds of the air,
    and the fish of the sea,
    and whatever travels the paths of the seas.

9 O Lord, our Lord,
    how excellent is Your name in all the earth!

PSALM 9
For the Music Director. To the melody of "The
Death of the Son." A Psalm of David.

1 I will give thanks to You, O Lord, with my whole heart;
    I will declare all Your marvelous works.
2 I will be glad and rejoice in You;
    I will sing praise to Your name, O Most High.

3 When my enemies are turned back,
    they will stumble and perish at Your presence.
4 For You have maintained my right and my cause;
    You sat on the throne judging what is right.
5 You have rebuked the nations,
    You have destroyed the wicked,
    You have wiped out their name forever and ever.
6 O you enemy, destructions have come to you for a perpetual end.
    You have destroyed cities;
    their memory perished with them.

7 But the Lord remains forever;
    He has established His throne for judgment.
8 He will judge the world in righteousness;
    He will give judgment to the peoples in uprightness.
9 The Lord also will be a refuge for the oppressed,
    a refuge in times of trouble.
10 Those who know Your name will put their trust in You,
    for You, Lord, have not forsaken those who seek You.

11 Sing praises to the Lord who dwells in Zion;
    declare His deeds among the people.
12 He who avenges deaths remembers them;
    He does not forget the cry of the humble.

13 Be gracious to me, O Lord; consider my trouble from those who
    hate me,
    O You who lifts me up from the gates of death,
14 that I may recount all Your praise
    in the gates of the daughter of Zion,
    that I may rejoice in Your salvation.

15 The nations have sunk down in the pit that they made;
    their own foot is caught in the net which they hid.
16 The Lord is known by the judgment that He executes;
    the wicked one is snared in the work of his own hands.
    Meditation. Selah

17 The wicked will be turned to Sheol,
    and all the nations that forget God.
18 For the needy will not always be forgotten,
    nor will the hope of the poor perish forever.

19 Arise, O Lord, may mortals not prevail;
    let the nations be judged in Your sight.
20 Put them in fear, O Lord,
    that the nations themselves may know they are
        mortals. Selah

PSALM 10
1 Why do You stand far off, O Lord?
    Why do You hide Yourself in times of trouble?

2 In arrogance the wicked persecutes the poor;
    let them be caught in the devices they have planned.
3 For the wicked boasts of his soul's desire;
    he blesses the greedy and despises the Lord.
4 The wicked, through the pride of his countenance, will not seek God;
    God is not in all his thoughts.
5 His ways are always prosperous;
    Your judgments are high and distant from him;
    as for all his enemies, they scoff at him.
6 He says in his heart, "I shall not be moved;
    for generations I shall not meet adversity."

7 His mouth is filled with cursing and deceit and oppression;
    under his tongue is mischief and iniquity.
8 He sits in the lurking places of the villages;
    in the secret places he murders the innocent;
    his eyes lurk against the unfortunate.
9 He lies in wait secretly as a lion in his den;
    he lies in wait to catch the poor;
    he catches the poor, drawing them into his net.
10 He crouches; he lies low,
    so that the unfortunate fall by his strength.
11 He says in his heart, "God has forgotten;
    He hides His face; He will never see it."

12 Arise, O Lord! O God, lift up Your hand!
    Do not forget the humble.
13 Why do the wicked despise God?
    He says in his heart,
    "You will require an account."
14 You have seen it, for You observe trouble and grief,
    to repay it with Your hand.
    The unfortunate one entrusts it to You;
    You are the helper of the orphan.
15 Break the arm of the wicked and the evil man;
    seek out his wickedness
    until You find none.

16 The Lord is King forever and ever;
    the nations perished from His land.
17 The desire of the humble You have heard, O Lord;
    You make their heart attentive; You bend Your ear
18 to judge the orphan and the oppressed;
    man on earth no longer trembles.

PSALM 11
For the Music Director. A Psalm of David.

1 In the Lord I seek refuge;
    how do you say to my soul,
    "Flee as a bird to your mountain,
2 for the wicked bend their bow;
    they make ready their arrow on the string,
    that they may treacherously shoot
    the upright in heart.
3 If the foundations are broken,
    what can the righteous do?"

4 The Lord is in His holy temple,
His throne is in heaven;
His eyes see,
His eyes examine mankind.
5 The Lord tests the righteous,
but the wicked and one who loves violence
His soul hates.
6 Upon the wicked He will rain
coals of fire and brimstone and a burning wind;
this will be the portion of their cup.

7 For the righteous Lord
loves righteousness;
His countenance beholds the upright.

PSALM 12

For the Music Director. According to
The Sheminith. A Psalm of David.

1 Help, Lord, for the godly man comes to an end,
for the faithful disappear from sons of men.
2 They speak empty words, each with his own neighbor;
they speak with flattering lips and a double heart.

3 The Lord will cut off all flattering lips,
and the tongue that speaks proud things,
4 who have said, "With our tongue will we prevail;
our lips are in our control, who is master over us?"

5 "Because the poor are plundered,
because the needy sigh,
now I will arise," says the Lord;
"I will place him in the safety for which he yearns."
6 The words of the Lord are pure words;
they are silver tried in an earthen furnace
refined seven times.

7 You will keep them, O Lord;
You will preserve them from this generation.
8 The wicked walk on every side,
when the worthless of mankind are exalted.

PSALM 13

For the Music Director. A Psalm of David.

1 How long, O Lord? Will You forget me for good?
How long will you hide Your face from me?
2 How long will I harbor cares in my soul
and sorrow in my heart by day?
How long will my enemy loom over me?

3 Take note and answer me, O Lord my God!
Brighten my eyes, lest I sleep the sleep of death,
4 lest my enemy say, "I have him,"
lest my foes exult when I stumble.

5 I for my part confide in Your kindness;
may my heart exult in Your salvation!
6 I will sing to the Lord,
because He has dealt bountifully with me.

PSALM 14

Ps 53:1–6
For the Music Director. A Psalm of David.

1 The fool has said in his heart,
"There is no God."
They are corrupt, they do abominable deeds,
there is none who does good.

2 The Lord looks down from heaven
on the children of men,

to see if there are any who understand,
who seek God.
3 They all turn aside,
together they become corrupt;
there is none who does good,
not even one.

4 Have all the workers of iniquity no knowledge,
who eat my people as they eat bread,
but do not call on the Lord?
5 There they were in great fear,
for God is with the generation of the righteous.
6 You shame the counsel of the poor,
but the Lord is his refuge.

7 Oh, that the salvation of Israel would come from Zion!
When the Lord turns back the captivity of His people,
Jacob will rejoice, and Israel will be glad.

PSALM 15

A Psalm of David.

1 Lord, who will abide in Your tabernacle?
Who will dwell in Your holy hill?

2 He who walks uprightly,
and does righteousness,
and speaks truth in his heart;
3 he who does not slander with the tongue
and does no evil to his neighbor,
nor bears a reproach against his friend;
4 in whose eyes a vile person is despised,
but who honors those who fear the Lord;
he who swears to avoid evil
and does not change;
5 he who does not put his money out to usury,
nor take a bribe against the innocent.

He who does these things
will never be moved.

PSALM 16

A Miktam of David.

1 Preserve me, O God,
for in You I take refuge.

2 I have said to the Lord, "You are my Lord;
my welfare has no existence outside of You."
3 For the holy ones who are in the land,
they are the majestic ones; in them is all my delight.
4 Those who chase after other *gods*,
their sorrows will be multiplied;
their drink offerings of blood I will not offer,
nor lift their names on my lips.

5 The Lord is the portion of my inheritance and of
my cup;
You support my lot.
6 The lines have fallen for me in pleasant places;
yes, an inheritance is beautiful for me.
7 I will bless the Lord who has given me counsel;
my affections also instruct me in the night seasons.
8 I have set the Lord always before me;
because He is at my right hand,
I will not be moved.

9 Therefore my heart is glad, and my glory rejoices;
my flesh also will rest in security.
10 For You will not leave my soul in Sheol,
nor will You suffer Your godly one to see corruption.
11 You will make known to me the path of life;

in Your presence is fullness of joy;
at Your right hand there are pleasures for evermore.

PSALM 17

A Prayer of David.

1 Hear a just cause, O Lord,
attend to my cry;
give ear to my prayer
that is not spoken from deceitful lips.
2 May my sentence go out from Your presence;
may Your eyes see rightly.

3 You have examined my heart; You have visited me in the night;
You have tried me and found nothing;
I have purposed that my mouth will not transgress.
4 Concerning the works of men,
by the word of Your lips
I have avoided
the paths of the violent,
5 placing my steps in Your paths,
that my footsteps do not slip.

6 I called on You, for You will answer me, O God;
incline Your ear to me, and hear my speech.
7 Show marvelously Your lovingkindness,
O Deliverer of those who seek refuge
by Your right hand from those who arise in opposition.
8 Keep me as the apple of Your eye;
hide me under the shadow of Your wings,
9 from the wicked who bring ruin to me,
from my deadly enemies who surround me.

10 They close their hard hearts;
with their mouth they speak proudly.
11 They have now encircled us in our steps;
they have set their eyes to bend down to the earth;
12 it is like a lion that is anxious to rip its prey,
and as a young lion lurking in secrecy.

13 Arise, O Lord! Confront him, cast him down!
Deliver my soul from the wicked by Your sword,
14 from men by Your hand, O Lord,
from men of the world whose portion is in this life.
You fill their belly with Your treasure;
they are satisfied with children,
and they leave their abundance to their infants.

15 As for me, I will see Your face in righteousness;
I will be satisfied when I awake with Your likeness.

PSALM 18

2Sa 22:1–51

For the Music Director. A Psalm of David the servant of
the Lord. He spoke to the Lord the words of this song on
the day that the Lord delivered him from the hand of
all his enemies, and from the hand of Saul. He said:

1 I love You, O Lord, my strength.

2 The Lord is my pillar, and my fortress, and my deliverer;
my God, my rock, in whom I take refuge;
my shield, and the horn of my salvation, my high tower.
3 I will call on the Lord, who is worthy to be praised,
and I will be saved from my enemies.
4 The cords of death encircled me,
and the torrents of destruction terrified me.
5 The cords of Sheol surrounded me;
the snares of death confronted me.

6 In my distress I called on the Lord,
and cried for help to my God;

He heard my voice from His temple,
and my cry for help came before Him to His ears.
7 Then the earth shook and quaked;
the foundations of the hills also moved;
they reeled because His anger burned.
8 Smoke went up out of His nostrils,
and fire from His mouth devoured;
coals were kindled by it.
9 He bent the heavens and came down,
and darkness was under His feet.
10 He rode on a cherub, and flew;
He flew swiftly on the wings of the wind.
11 He made darkness His secret place;
His pavilion was surrounding Him,
dark waters and thick clouds of the skies.
12 At the brightness before Him His thick clouds passed by,
hailstones and coals of fire.
13 The Lord also thundered in the heavens,
and the Most High gave His voice,
hailstones and coals of fire.
14 He sent out His arrows and scattered them,
and He shot out lightning and distressed them.
15 Then the channels of waters appeared,
and the foundations of the world were discovered
at Your rebuke, O Lord,
at the blast of the breath of Your nostrils.

16 He sent from above, He took me;
He drew me out of many waters.
17 He delivered me from my strong enemy,
and from those who hated me,
for they were too strong for me.
18 They confronted me in the day of my calamity,
but the Lord was my support.
19 He also brought me forth into a large place;
He delivered me because He delighted in me.

20 The Lord rewarded me according to my righteousness;
according to the cleanness of my hands He has
repaid me.
21 For I have kept the ways of the Lord,
and have not wickedly departed from my God.
22 For all His judgments were before me,
and I did not put away His statutes from me.
23 I was also upright before Him,
and I kept myself from my iniquity.
24 Therefore the Lord has repaid me according to my righteousness,
according to the cleanness of my hands in His view.

25 With the merciful You will show Yourself merciful;
with the blameless man You will show Yourself blameless;
26 with the pure You will show Yourself pure;
and with the crooked You will show Yourself crooked.
27 For You will save the afflicted people,
but will bring down prideful eyes.
28 For You will cause my lamp to shine;
the Lord my God will enlighten my darkness.
29 For by You I can run through a troop,
and by my God I can leap a wall.

30 As for God, His way has integrity;
the word of the Lord is proven;
He is a shield
to all those who take refuge in Him.
31 For who is God except the Lord?
Or who is a rock besides our God?
32 It is God who clothes me with strength,
and gives my way integrity.
33 He makes my feet like the feet of a deer,
and causes me to stand on my high places.
34 He trains my hands for war,
so that my arms bend a bow of bronze.

35 You have given me the shield of Your salvation,
    and Your right hand has held me up,
    and Your gentleness has made me great.
36 You have lengthened my stride under me,
    so that my feet did not slip.

37 I pursued my enemies and overtook them;
    I did not return until they were destroyed.
38 I wounded them, and they were not able to rise;
    they are fallen under my feet.
39 For You clothed me with strength for the battle;
    You subdued under me those who rose up against me.
40 You gave me the necks of my enemies,
    and I destroyed those who hate me.
41 They cried for help, but there was none to save them;
    even to the Lord, but He did not answer them.
42 Then I beat them small as the dust before the wind;
    I cast them out as the dirt in the streets.
43 You have delivered me from the hostilities of the people,
    and You have made me the head of nations;
    a people whom I have not known serve me.
44 At hearing a report, they obey me;
    foreigners come cringing to me.
45 Foreigners fade away,
    and come quaking out of their prisons.

46 The Lord lives! And blessed be my Rock!
    May the God of my salvation be exalted.
47 It is God who avenges me
    and subdues the people under me;
48 He delivers me from my enemies.
    You lift me up above those who rise up against me;
    You have delivered me from the violent man.
49 Therefore I will give thanks to You, O Lord, among
        the nations,
    and sing praises to Your name.

50 He gives great deliverance to His king,
    and shows lovingkindness to His anointed,
    to David and to his descendants for evermore.

PSALM 19
For the Music Director. A Psalm of David.

1 The heavens declare the glory of God,
    and the firmament shows His handiwork.
2 Day unto day utters speech,
    and night unto night declares knowledge.
3 There is no speech and there are no words;
    their voice is not heard.
4 Their line has gone out through all the earth,
    and their words to the end of the world.

    In them has He set a tent for the sun,
5   which is like a bridegroom coming out of his chamber;
    it rejoices as a strong man to run a race.
6 Its going forth is from one end of the heavens,
    and its circuit extends to the other end,
    and there is nothing hidden from its heat.

7 The law of the Lord is perfect,
        converting the soul;
    the testimony of the Lord is sure,
        making wise the simple;
8 the statutes of the Lord are right,
        rejoicing the heart;
    the commandment of the Lord is pure,
        enlightening the eyes;
9 the fear of the Lord is clean,
        enduring forever;
    the judgments of the Lord are true
        and righteous altogether.

10 More to be desired are they than gold,
    yes, than much fine gold;
    sweeter also than honey and the honeycomb.
11 Moreover by them is Your servant warned,
    and by keeping them comes great reward.
12 Who can understand his errors?
    Cleanse me from secret faults.
13 Keep back Your servant also from presumptuous sins;
    may they not rule over me.
    Then I will be upright
    and innocent from great transgression.

14 Let the words of my mouth and the meditation of my heart
    be acceptable in Your sight,
    O Lord, my strength and my Redeemer.

PSALM 20
For the Music Director. A Psalm of David.

1 May the Lord answer you in the day of trouble;
    may the name of the God of Jacob defend you;
2 may He send you help from the sanctuary,
    and strengthen you from Zion;
3 may He remember all your offerings,
    and accept your burnt offering.   Selah
4 May He grant you according to your own heart,
    and fulfill all your counsel.
5 We will rejoice in your salvation,
    and in the name of our God we will set up our banners;
    may the Lord fulfill all your petitions.

6 Now I know that the Lord saves His anointed;
    He will answer him from His holy heaven
    with the saving strength of His right hand.
7 Some trust in chariots, and some in horses,
    but we will remember the name of the Lord our God.
8 They are brought down and fallen,
    but we arise and stand upright.
9 Save, Lord!
    May the King answer us when we call.

PSALM 21
For the Music Director. A Psalm of David.

1 The king will rejoice in Your strength, O Lord,
    and in Your salvation how greatly will he rejoice!

2 You have given him his heart's desire,
    and have not withheld the request of his lips.   Selah
3 For You meet him with the blessings of goodness;
    You set a crown of pure gold on his head.
4 He asked life of You, and You gave it him,
    length of days forever and ever.
5 His glory is great in Your salvation;
    honor and majesty You set on him.
6 For You place blessings on him forever;
    You make him rejoice with gladness with Your presence.
7 For the king trusts in the Lord,
    and by the lovingkindness of the Most High
    he will not be moved.

8 Your hand will find out all Your enemies;
    Your right hand will find out those who hate You.
9 You will make them as a fiery oven
    in the time of Your appearance;
    the Lord will swallow them up in His wrath,
    and fire will devour them.
10 You will destroy their offspring from the earth,
    and their descendants from among the children of men.
11 For they intended evil against You;
    they devised evil thoughts they will not be able
        to accomplish.

¹² For You will make them turn their back,
    when You aim with Your bowstrings against
      their face.

¹³ Be exalted, Lord, by Your strength;
    may we sing and make music to Your might.

PSALM 22

For the Music Director. To the melody of
"The Doe of the Dawn." A Psalm of David.

¹ My God, my God, why have You forsaken me?
    Why are You so far from delivering me,
    and from my roaring words of distress?
² O my God, I cry in the daytime, but You do not answer;
    and at night, but I have no rest.

³ But You are holy,
    O You who inhabits the praises of Israel.
⁴ Our fathers trusted in You;
    they trusted, and You did deliver them.
⁵ They cried to You and were delivered;
    they trusted in You and were not put to shame.

⁶ But I am a worm, and not a man;
    a reproach of men and despised by the people.
⁷ All who see me laugh me to scorn;
    they sneer with the lip, they shake the head, saying,
⁸ "Trust in the Lord,
    let Him deliver him;
  let Him rescue him,
    seeing He delights in him."

⁹ But You are He who took me out of the womb;
    You caused me to trust
    while I was on my mother's breasts.
¹⁰ I was cast on You from birth;
    You are my God from my mother's womb.

¹¹ Be not far from me
    for trouble is near,
    for there is none to help.

¹² Many bulls encircle me;
    strong bulls of Bashan surround me.
¹³ They open their mouths against me,
    as a preying and roaring lion.
¹⁴ I am poured out like water,
    and all my bones are out of joint;
  my heart is like wax;
    it is melted inside my body.
¹⁵ My strength is dried up like a potsherd,
    and my tongue cleaves to my jaws;
    and You have set me toward the dust of death.

¹⁶ For dogs have encompassed me;
    the assembly of the wicked has enclosed me;
    like a lion they pin my hands and my feet;
¹⁷ I can count all my bones;
    they look and stare on me.
¹⁸ They part my garments among them
    and cast lots for my clothes.

¹⁹ But do not be far from me, O Lord;
    O my Help, hasten to my aid.
²⁰ Rescue my soul from the sword,
    my only life from the power of the dog.
²¹ Save me from the lion's mouth,
    and from the horns of the wild ox, answer me!

²² I will declare Your name to my community;
    in the midst of the congregation I will praise You.

²³ You who fear the Lord, praise Him;
    all you descendants of Jacob, glorify Him,
    and stand in awe of Him, all you descendants
      of Israel.
²⁴ For He has not despised nor abhorred
    the affliction of the afflicted;
  nor has He hid His face from him;
    but when he cried to Him, He heard.

²⁵ From You my praise will be in the great congregation;
    I will pay my vows before those who fear Him.
²⁶ The meek will eat and be satisfied;
    those who seek Him will praise the Lord.
    May your hearts live forever.

²⁷ All the ends of the world
    will remember and turn to the Lord,
    and all the families of the nations
      will worship before You.
²⁸ For kingship belongs to the Lord,
    and He rules among the nations.

²⁹ All the prosperous ones of the earth will eat and worship;
    all who go down to the dust will bow before Him,
    even he who cannot keep his own soul alive.
³⁰ Posterity will serve Him;
    it will be told to generations about the Lord;
³¹ they will come and declare His righteousness
    to a people yet to be born,
    that He has acted.

PSALM 23

A Psalm of David.

¹ The Lord is my shepherd; I shall not want.
²   He makes me lie down in green pastures;
  He leads me beside still waters.
³   He restores my soul;
  He leads me in paths of righteousness
    for His name's sake.
⁴ Even though I walk
    through the valley of the shadow of death,
  I will fear no evil;
    for You are with me;
  Your rod and Your staff,
    they comfort me.

⁵ You prepare a table before me
    in the presence of my enemies;
  You anoint my head with oil;
    my cup runs over.
⁶ Surely goodness and mercy shall follow me
    all the days of my life,
  and I will dwell in the house of the Lord
    forever.

PSALM 24

A Psalm of David.

¹ The earth belongs to the Lord, and its fullness,
    the world, and those who dwell in it.
² For He has founded it on the seas,
    and established it on the floods.

³ Who may ascend the hill of the Lord?
    Who may stand in His holy place?
⁴ He who has clean hands and a pure heart;
    who has not lifted up his soul unto vanity,
    nor sworn deceitfully.

⁵ He will receive the blessing from the Lord,
    and righteousness from the God of his salvation.

6 This is Jacob, the generation of those who seek Him,
    who seek Your face. Selah

7 Lift up your heads, O you gates;
    and be lifted up, you everlasting doors,
    that the King of glory may enter.
8 Who is this King of glory?
    The Lord strong and mighty,
    the Lord mighty in battle.
9 Lift up your heads, O you gates;
    lift up, you everlasting doors,
    that the King of glory may enter.
10 Who is He—this King of glory?
    The Lord of Hosts,
    He is the King of glory. Selah

PSALM 25
A Psalm of David.

1 To You, O Lord,
    do I lift up my soul.

2 O my God, I trust in You;
    may I not be ashamed;
    may my enemies not triumph over me.
3 Yes, let none who wait on You
    be ashamed;
    let them be ashamed
    who transgress without cause.

4 Make me to know Your ways, O Lord;
    teach me Your paths.
5 Lead me in Your truth and teach me,
    for You are the God of my salvation;
    on You I wait all the day.
6 Remember Your mercies, O Lord, and Your lovingkindness,
    for they are from old.
7 Do not remember the sins of my youth
    or my transgressions;
    according to Your lovingkindness remember me,
    on account of Your goodness, O Lord.

8 Good and upright is the Lord;
    therefore He will teach sinners in the way.
9 The meek will He guide in judgment,
    and the meek He will teach His way.
10 All the paths of the Lord are lovingkindness and truth,
    for those who keep His covenant and His testimonies.
11 For Your name's sake, O Lord, pardon my iniquity,
    for it is great.

12 Who is the man who fears the Lord?
    He will teach him in the way He should choose.
13 He will dwell at ease,
    and his descendants will inherit the land.
14 The counsel of the Lord is with those who fear him,
    and He will make His covenant known to them.
15 My eyes are ever toward the Lord,
    for He will lead my feet from the net.

16 Turn to me, and be gracious to me,
    for I am isolated and afflicted.
17 The troubles of my heart are enlarged;
    bring me out of my distresses.
18 Look on my pain and misery,
    and forgive all my sins.
19 Consider my enemies, for they are many,
    and they hate me with violent hatred.

20 Watch over my life, and deliver me!
    Let me not suffer shame,
    for I seek refuge in You.

21 Truth and integrity will preserve me
    while I wait for You.

22 Redeem Israel, O God,
    out of all their troubles.

PSALM 26
A Psalm of David.

1 Judge me, O Lord,
    for I have walked in my integrity.
    I have trusted in the Lord;
    I will not slip.
2 Examine me, O Lord, and test me;
    try my affections and my heart.
3 For Your lovingkindness is before my eyes,
    and I have walked in Your truth.

4 I have not sat with the worthless,
    nor will I go with hypocrites.
5 I have hated the congregation of evildoers,
    and will not sit with the wicked.
6 I will wash my hands in innocence;
    thus I will go around Your altar, O Lord,
7 that I may proclaim with the voice of thanksgiving,
    and tell of all Your wondrous works.
8 Lord, I have loved the refuge of Your house,
    and the place where Your honor dwells.
9 Do not gather my soul with sinners,
    nor my life with murderers,
10 in whose hands is wickedness,
    and their right hand is full of bribes.
11 But as for me, I will walk in my integrity;
    redeem me and be gracious to me.

12 My foot stands in an even place;
    with the congregations I will bless the Lord.

PSALM 27
A Psalm of David.

1 The Lord is my light and my salvation;
    whom will I fear?
    The Lord is the strength of my life;
    of whom will I be afraid?

2 When the wicked came against me
    to eat my flesh—
    my enemies and my foes—
    they stumbled and fell.
3 Though an army should encamp against me,
    my heart will not fear;
    though war should rise against me,
    in this will I be confident.

4 One thing I have asked from the Lord,
    that will I seek after—
    for me to dwell in the house of the Lord
    all the days of my life,
    to see the beauty of the Lord,
    and to inquire in His temple.
5 For in the time of trouble
    He will hide me in His pavilion;
    in the shelter of His tabernacle He will
    hide me;
    He will set me up on a rock.

6 Now my head will be lifted up
    above my enemies encircling me;
    therefore I will offer sacrifices of joy in
    His tabernacle;
    I will sing, yes, I will sing praises to the Lord.

7 Hear, O Lord, when I cry with my voice!
  Be gracious to me and answer me.
8 When You said, "Seek My face,"
  my heart said to You, "Your face, Lord, I will seek."
9 Do not hide Your face far from me;
  do not thrust Your servant away in anger;
  You have been my help.
  Do not leave me nor forsake me,
  O God of my salvation.
10 If my father and my mother forsake me,
   then the Lord will take me in.
11 Teach me Your way, O Lord,
   and lead me in an upright path,
   because of my enemies.
12 Do not deliver me to the will of my enemies;
   for false witnesses have risen against me,
   and they breathe out violence.

13 I believe
   I will see the goodness of the Lord
   in the land of the living.
14 Wait on the Lord;
   be strong, and may your heart be stout;
   wait on the Lord.

PSALM 28
A Psalm of David.

1 To You, O Lord, will I cry;
  my Rock, do not be silent to me;
  lest if You were silent to me,
  then I would become like those who go down
  to the pit.
2 Hear the voice of my supplications
  when I cry to You,
  when I lift up my hands
  toward Your most holy place.

3 Do not draw me away with the wicked
  and with the workers of iniquity,
  who speak peace to their neighbors,
  but mischief is in their hearts.
4 Give them according to their deeds,
  and according to the wickedness of their endeavors;
  give them according to the work of their hands;
  return to them what they deserve.

5 Because they do not regard the works of the Lord,
  nor the work of His hands,
  He will destroy them
  and not build them up.

6 Blessed be the Lord,
  because He has heard the voice of my supplications.
7 The Lord is my strength and my shield;
  my heart trusted in Him, and I was helped;
  therefore my heart rejoices,
  and with my song I will thank Him.

8 The Lord is the strength of His people,
  and He is the saving strength of His anointed.
9 Save Your people,
  and bless Your inheritance;
  feed them and lift them up forever.

PSALM 29
A Psalm of David.

1 Give to the Lord, you heavenly beings,
  give to the Lord glory and strength.
2 Give to the Lord the glory of His name;
  worship the Lord in holy splendor.

3 The voice of the Lord is over the waters;
  the God of glory thunders;
  the Lord is over many waters.
4 The voice of the Lord sounds with strength;
  the voice of the Lord—with majesty.
5 The voice of the Lord breaks the cedars;
  the Lord breaks the cedars of Lebanon.
6 He makes them skip like a calf,
  Lebanon and Sirion like a wild ox.
7 The voice of the Lord flashes
  like flames of fire.
8 The voice of the Lord shakes the wilderness;
  the Lord shakes the Wilderness of Kadesh.
9 The voice of the Lord makes the deer to give birth,
  and strips the forests bare;
  and in His temple everyone says, "Glory!"

10 The Lord sits enthroned above the flood,
   the Lord sits as King forever.
11 The Lord will give strength to His people;
   the Lord will bless His people with peace.

PSALM 30
A Psalm of David. A Song at the dedication of the temple.

1 I will extol You, O Lord, for You have drawn me up,
  and have not caused my foes to rejoice over me.
2 O Lord my God, I cried to You,
  and You healed me.
3 O Lord, You have brought up my soul from the grave;
  You have kept me alive, that I should not go down
  to the pit.

4 Sing to the Lord, O you saints of His,
  and give thanks at the remembrance of His holiness.
5 For His anger endures but a moment,
  in His favor is life;
  weeping may endure for a night,
  but joy comes in the morning.

6 In my prosperity I said,
  "I will never be moved."
7 Lord, by Your favor
  You had set me strong as a mountain;
  You hid Your face,
  and I was terrified.

8 I cried to You, O Lord,
  and to the Lord I made supplication:
9 "What profit is there in my death,
  if I go down to the pit?
  Will the dust give You thanks?
  Will it declare Your truth?
10 Hear, O Lord, and be gracious to me;
   Lord, be my helper."

11 For You have turned my mourning into dancing;
   You have put off my sackcloth and girded me with gladness,
12 so that my glory may sing praise to You and not be silent.
   O Lord my God, I will give thanks to You forever.

PSALM 31
Ps 71:1–3
For the Music Director. A Psalm of David.

1 In You, O Lord, do I seek refuge;
  may I never be ashamed;
  deliver me in Your righteousness.
2 Incline Your ear to me;
  deliver me speedily;
  be my strong rock,
  a strong fortress to save me.

³ For You are my rock and my fortress;
    for Your name's sake lead me and guide me.
⁴ Lead me out of the net that they have hidden for me,
    for You are my strength.
⁵ Into Your hand I commit my spirit;
    You have redeemed me, O Lord, God of truth.

⁶ I have hated those who regard worthless vanity,
    but I trust in the Lord.
⁷ I will be glad and rejoice in Your lovingkindness,
    for You have seen my trouble;
    You have known my soul in adversities,
⁸ and have not delivered me up into the hand of
       the enemy;
    You have set my feet in a broad place.

⁹ Be gracious to me, O Lord, for I am in trouble;
    my eye wastes away with grief,
    yes, my soul and my body.
¹⁰ For my life is spent with grief,
    and my years with sighing;
    my strength fails because of my iniquity,
    and my bones waste away.
¹¹ I became a reproach among all my enemies,
    but especially among my neighbors,
    and a dread to my acquaintances;
    those who saw me outside fled from me.
¹² I am forgotten as a dead man out of mind;
    I am like a broken vessel.
¹³ For I have heard the slander of many;
    fear was on every side;
    while they took counsel together against me,
    they planned to take away my life.

¹⁴ But I trusted in You, O Lord;
    I said, "You are my God."
¹⁵ My times are in Your hand;
    deliver me from the hand of my enemies
    and my pursuers.
¹⁶ Make Your face to shine on Your servant;
    save me by Your lovingkindness.
¹⁷ Do not let me be ashamed, O Lord,
    for I have called on You;
    let the wicked be ashamed,
    and let them be silent in the grave.
¹⁸ Let the lying lips be put to silence,
    who speak arrogantly
    in pride and contempt against the righteous.

¹⁹ Oh, how great is Your goodness,
    which You have laid up for those who fear You,
    which You have done for those
    seeking refuge in You before people!
²⁰ You will hide them in the secret of Your presence
    from conspirators;
    You will keep them secretly in a shelter
    from the strife of tongues.

²¹ Blessed be the Lord,
    for He has shown me His marvelous
       lovingkindness
    in a fortified city.
²² For I said in my haste,
    "I am cut off from before Your eyes."
    Nevertheless You heard the voice of my supplications
    when I cried to You.

²³ Oh, love the Lord, all you His saints,
    for the Lord preserves the faithful,
    but amply repays the one who acts in pride.
²⁴ Be strong, and He will strengthen your heart,
    all you who wait for the Lord.

PSALM 32
A Psalm of David. A Contemplative Maskil.

¹ Blessed is he
    whose transgression is forgiven,
    whose sin is covered.
² Blessed is the man
    against whom the Lord does not count iniquity,
    and in whose spirit there is no deceit.

³ When I kept silent,
    my bones wasted away
    through my groaning all day long.
⁴ For day and night
    Your hand was heavy on me;
    my strength was changed
    into the drought of summer.   Selah

⁵ I acknowledged my sin to You,
    and my iniquity I did not conceal.
    I said, "I will confess
    my transgressions to the Lord,"
    and You forgave
    the iniquity of my sin.   Selah

⁶ For this cause everyone who is godly will pray to You
    in a time when You may be found;
    surely in the floods of great waters
    they will not reach him.
⁷ You are my hiding place;
    You will preserve me from trouble;
    You will surround me with shouts of deliverance.   Selah

⁸ I will instruct you and teach you in the way you should go;
    I will counsel you with my eye on you.
⁹ Do not be as the horse or as the mule
    that are without understanding,
    that must be restrained with bit and bridle,
    or they will not come near you.
¹⁰ Many sorrows come to the wicked,
    but lovingkindness will surround
    the man who trusts in the Lord.

¹¹ Be glad in the Lord, and rejoice, you righteous one;
    and shout for joy, all you who are upright in heart!

PSALM 33
The Sovereignty of the Lord.

¹ Rejoice in the Lord, O you righteous,
    for praise is fitting for the upright.
² Give thanks to the Lord with the harp;
    make music to Him with an instrument of ten strings.
³ Sing to Him a new song;
    play an instrument skillfully with a joyful shout.

⁴ For the word of the Lord is upright,
    and all His work is done in truth.
⁵ He loves righteousness and justice;
    the earth is full of the lovingkindness of the Lord.

⁶ By the word of the Lord the heavens were made,
    and all their host by the breath of His mouth.
⁷ He gathers the waters of the sea together as a heap;
    He puts the depths in storehouses.
⁸ Let all the earth fear the Lord;
    let all the inhabitants of the world stand in awe of Him.
⁹ For He spoke, and it was done;
    He commanded, and it stood fast.

¹⁰ The Lord frustrates the counsel of the nations;
    He restrains the purposes of the people.

11 The counsel of the LORD stands forever,
    the purposes of His heart to all generations.

12 Blessed is the nation whose God is the LORD,
    the people whom He has chosen as His inheritance.
13 The LORD looks from heaven;
    He sees all the sons of men.
14 From the place of His habitation He gazes
    on all the inhabitants of the earth;
15 He fashions their hearts alike;
    He considers all their works.

16 No king is saved by a great army;
    a mighty man is not delivered by great strength.
17 A horse is a vain hope for safety;
    it will not deliver by its great strength.
18 The eye of the LORD is on those who fear Him,
    on those who hope in His lovingkindness,
19 to deliver their soul from death,
    and to keep them alive in famine.

20 Our soul waits for the LORD;
    He is our help and our shield.
21 For our heart will rejoice in Him,
    because we have trusted in His holy name.
22 Let Your lovingkindness, O LORD, be on us,
    just as we hope in You.

PSALM 34

*A Psalm of David, when he feigned madness before
Abimelek, who drove him away, and he departed.*

1 I will bless the LORD at all times;
    His praise will continually be in my mouth.
2 My soul will make its boast in the LORD;
    the humble will hear of it and be glad.
3 Oh, magnify the LORD with me,
    and let us exalt His name together.

4 I sought the LORD, and He answered me,
    and delivered me from all my fears.
5 They looked to Him and became radiant,
    and their faces are not ashamed.
6 This poor man cried, and the LORD heard,
    and saved him out of all his troubles.
7 The angel of the LORD camps around those who fear Him,
    and delivers them.

8 Oh, taste and see that the LORD is good;
    blessed is the man who takes refuge in Him.
9 Oh, fear the LORD, you His saints;
    for the ones who fear Him will not be in need.
10 The young lions are in want and suffer hunger,
    but the ones who seek the LORD will not lack any good thing.
11 Come, you children, listen to me;
    I will teach you the fear of the LORD.
12 Who is the man who desires life,
    and loves a long life in order to see good?
13 Keep your tongue from evil,
    and your lips from speaking deceit.
14 Turn away from evil, and do good;
    seek peace, and pursue it.

15 The eyes of the LORD are on the righteous,
    and His ears are open to their cry.
16 The face of the LORD is against the ones doing evil,
    to cut off the memory of them from the earth.

17 The *righteous* cry out, and the LORD hears,
    and delivers them out of all their troubles.
18 The LORD is near to the broken-hearted,
    and saves the contrite of spirit.

19 Many are the afflictions of the righteous,
    but the LORD delivers him out of them all.
20 A righteous one keeps all his bones;
    not one of them is broken.

21 Evil will slay the wicked,
    and those who hate the righteous will be condemned.
22 The LORD redeems the life of His servants,
    and all who take refuge in Him will not be punished.

PSALM 35

A Psalm of David.

1 Plead my cause, O LORD, with my adversaries;
    fight those who fight me.
2 Take hold of the large shield and small shield,
    and rise up for my help.
3 Draw the spear and javelin
    against those who pursue me.
    Say to my soul,
    "I am Your salvation."

4 May those who seek my life
    be ashamed and humiliated;
    may those who plan my injury
    be turned back and put to shame.
5 May they be as chaff before the wind,
    and may the angel of the LORD cast them down.
6 May their way be dark and slippery,
    and may the angel of the LORD pursue them.

7 For without cause they have hidden their net for me in a pit,
    which they have dug without cause for my soul.
8 Let destruction come on him without warning,
    and let the net that he hid ensnare him;
    let him fall into it, to his destruction.
9 My soul will be joyful in the LORD;
    it will rejoice in His salvation.
10 All my bones will say,
    "LORD, who is like You,
    who delivers the poor from a stronger one,
    the poor and the needy from the one who robs them?"

11 Witnesses intent on violence rose up;
    they accused me of things I knew nothing about.
12 They rewarded me evil for good,
    the bereavement of my soul.
13 But as for me, when they were sick, my clothing was sackcloth;
    I humbled my soul with fasting;
    and my prayer returns to my own heart.
14 I paced as though he were my friend or brother;
    I bowed down lamenting,
    as one who mourns for a mother.
15 But in my adversity they rejoiced and gathered together;
    assailants gathered together against me, though I was
    unaware;
    they tore me apart and did not stop;
16 with hypocritical mockers in feasts,
    they gnashed on me with their teeth.

17 Lord, how long will You look on?
    Rescue my soul from their destructions,
    my life from the lions.
18 I will give You thanks in the great congregation;
    I will praise You among a mighty people.
19 May my deceitful enemies
    not rejoice over me;
    nor may those who hate me without cause
    wink with their eye.
20 For they do not speak peace,
    but they devise deceitful matters
    against the restful ones in the land.

21 They opened their mouth wide against me,
   and said, "Aha, aha, our eye has seen it."

22 This You have seen, O Lord; do not be silent;
   O Lord, be not far from me.
23 Rouse Yourself and awake for my judgment,
   for my cause, my God and my Lord.
24 Judge me, O Lord my God, according to Your righteousness,
   and may they not rejoice over me.
25 May they not say in their hearts, "Ah, *we have* our soul's desire."
   May they not say, "We have swallowed him up."

26 May those who rejoice at my harm be ashamed
   and altogether put to shame;
   may they be clothed with shame and dishonor
   who magnify themselves against me.
27 May those who favor my righteous cause
   shout for joy and be glad;
   may they say continually, "The Lord be magnified,
   who delights in the peace of His servant."

28 My tongue will speak of Your righteousness
   and of Your praise all the day long.

PSALM 36

For the Music Director. A Psalm of
David, the servant of the Lord.

1 An oracle within my heart
   about the transgression of the wicked:
   There is no fear of God
   before their eyes.

2 For they flatter themselves in their own eyes,
   that their iniquity cannot be found out and hated.
3 The words of their mouth are wickedness and deceit;
   they have ceased to be wise and to do good.
4 They devise mischief on their bed;
   they set themselves on a path that is not good;
   they do not reject evil.

5 Your mercy, O Lord, is in the heavens,
   and Your faithfulness reaches to the clouds.
6 Your righteousness is like the great mountains,
   Your judgments like the great deep;
   O Lord, You preserve man and beast.
7 How excellent is Your lovingkindness, O God!
   Therefore mankind
   seeks refuge in the shadow of Your wings.
8 They will drink their fill from the abundance of Your house,
   and You will cause them to drink from the river of Your
   pleasures.
9 For with You is the fountain of life;
   in Your light we see light.

10 Oh, continue Your lovingkindness to those who know You,
   and Your righteousness to the upright in heart.
11 Do not let the foot of the arrogant come against me,
   and do not let the hand of the wicked cause me to wander.
12 There the workers of iniquity have fallen;
   they are cast down and not able to rise.

PSALM 37

A Psalm of David.

1 Do not fret because of evildoers,
   nor be jealous of those who do injustice.
2 For they will quickly wither like the grass,
   and fade like the green herbs.

3 Trust in the Lord, and do good;
   dwell in the land, and practice faithfulness.

4 Delight yourself in the Lord,
   and He will give you the desires of your heart.

5 Commit your way to the Lord;
   trust also in Him, and He will bring it to pass.
6 He will bring forth your righteousness as the light,
   and your judgment as the noonday.

7 Rest in the Lord, and wait patiently for Him;
   do not fret because of those who prosper in their way,
   because of those who make wicked schemes.

8 Let go of anger, and forsake wrath;
   do not fret—it surely leads to evil deeds.
9 For evildoers will be cut off,
   but those who hope in the Lord will inherit the earth.

10 For yet a little while, and the wicked will not be;
   you will look diligently for their place, and it will not be.
11 But the meek will inherit the earth,
   and will delight themselves in the abundance of peace.

12 The wicked plot against the righteous,
   and grind their teeth against them.
13 The Lord will laugh at him,
   for He sees that his day is coming.

14 The wicked have drawn out the sword
   and have bent their bow,
   to cast down the poor and needy,
   and to slay those on the upright path.
15 Their sword will enter into their own heart,
   and their bows will be broken.

16 Better is a little that the righteous has
   than the abundance of many wicked.
17 For the arms of the wicked will be broken,
   but the Lord supports the righteous.

18 The Lord knows the days of people of integrity,
   and their inheritance will be forever.
19 They will not be ashamed in the evil time,
   and in the days of famine they will be satisfied.

20 But the wicked will perish,
   and the enemies of the Lord will be like the glory of pastures;
   they will waste away, in smoke they will waste away.

21 The wicked borrows and does not repay,
   but the righteous is gracious and gives.
22 For those who are blessed of Him will inherit the earth,
   but those who are cursed of Him will be cut off.

23 The steps of a man are made firm by the Lord;
   He delights in his way.
24 Though he falls, he will not be hurled down,
   for the Lord supports him with His hand.

25 I have been young, and now am old;
   yet I have not seen the righteous forsaken,
   nor their offspring begging bread.
26 The righteous are gracious and lend,
   and their offspring are a source of blessing.

27 Depart from evil and do good,
   and abide forevermore.
28 For the Lord loves justice,
   and does not forsake His saints;
   they are preserved forever,
   but the descendants of the wicked will be cut off.
29 The righteous will inherit the land,
   and dwell on it forever.

30 The mouth of the righteous utters wisdom,
   and their tongue speaks justice.
31 The law of their God is in their heart;
   none of their steps will slip.

32 The wicked watch the righteous,
   and seek to kill them.
33 The Lord will not forsake them to their hand,
   nor condemn them when they are judged.

34 Hope in the Lord,
   and keep His way,
   and He will exalt you to inherit the land;
   when the wicked are cut off, you will see it.

35 I have seen the wicked in great power,
   and spreading himself like a luxuriant tree.
36 Yet he passed away, and he was not;
   I sought him, but he could not be found.

37 Mark the blameless man, and consider the upright,
   for the end of that man is peace.
38 But the transgressors will be destroyed together;
   the end of the wicked is to be cut off.

39 But the salvation of the righteous is from the Lord;
   He is their refuge in the time of distress.
40 The Lord will help them and deliver them;
   He will deliver them from the wicked,
   and save them, because they take refuge in Him.

PSALM 38
A Psalm of David. To bring remembrance.

1 O Lord, do not rebuke me in Your wrath,
   nor chasten me in Your hot displeasure.
2 For Your arrows pierce me,
   and Your hand presses down on me.
3 There is no soundness in my flesh because of Your indignation,
   nor is there health in my bones because of my sin.
4 For my iniquities have passed over my head;
   as a heavy burden they are too heavy for me.

5 My wounds grow foul and fester
   because of my foolishness.
6 I am bent, I am bowed down greatly;
   I go mourning all the day long.
7 For my sides are filled with burning,
   and there is no soundness in my flesh.
8 I am numb and completely crushed;
   I have roared because of the groaning of my heart.

9 Lord, all my desire is before You,
   and my sighing is not hidden from You.
10 My heart throbs, my strength fails me;
   as for the light of my eyes, it also is gone from me.
11 My friends and my companions stand back because of my affliction,
   and those close to me stand at a distance.
12 The people who seek my life strike at me;
   those who seek my harm speak destruction,
   and plan treacheries all the day long.

13 But I, like a deaf man, did not hear;
   and like a dumb man, did not open my mouth.
14 Thus I was as a man who does not hear,
   and in whose mouth are no reproofs.
15 For in You, O Lord, do I hope;
   You will answer, O Lord my God.
16 For I said, "Lest otherwise they should rejoice over me.
   When my foot slips, they magnify themselves
      against me."

17 For I am ready to stumble,
   and my pain is continually before me.
18 For I will declare my iniquity;
   I am anxious because of my sin.
19 But my enemies are lively, and they are strong;
   and those who wrongfully hate me are many.
20 Those also who repay evil for good are my adversaries,
   because I pursue good.

21 Do not abandon me, O Lord;
   O my God, do not be far from me.
22 Make haste to help me,
   O Lord, my salvation.

PSALM 39
For the Music Director. To Jeduthun. A Psalm of David.

1 I said, "I will take heed of my ways
   so that I do not sin with my tongue;
   I will keep my mouth muzzled
   while the wicked are before me."
2 I was speechless in silence;
   I was silent to no avail,
   but my anguish was stirred up.
3 My heart was hot within me;
   while I was musing, the fire burned,
   then I spoke with my tongue:

4 "Lord, make me to know my end,
   and what is the measure of my days,
   that I may know how transient I am.
5 Indeed, You have made my days as a handbreadth,
   and my age is as nothing before You;
   indeed every man at his best is as a breath."   Selah
6 Surely every man walks in a mere shadow;
   surely he goes as a breath;
   he heaps up riches, and does not know who will gather them.

7 Now, Lord, what do I wait for?
   My hope is in You.
8 Deliver me from all my transgressions;
   do not make me the reproach of the foolish.
9 I was speechless, I did not open my mouth,
   because You did it.
10 Remove Your blow from me;
   I am consumed by the hostility of Your hand.
11 When with rebukes You correct a man for iniquity,
   You consume like a moth what is dear to him;
   surely every man is vapor.   Selah

12 Hear my prayer, O Lord,
   and give ear to my cry;
   do not be silent at my tears,
   for I am a stranger with You,
   and a sojourner, as all my fathers were.
13 Turn Your gaze of *displeasure* from me, that I may smile,
   before I go away and am no more.

PSALM 40
Ps 70:1–5
For the Music Director. A Psalm of David.

1 I waited patiently for the Lord,
   and He turned to me, and heard my cry.
2 He also brought me up out of a horrible pit,
   out of the miry clay,
   and set my feet on a rock,
   and established my steps.
3 He has put a new song in my mouth,
   even praise to our God;
   many will see it, and fear,
   and will trust in the Lord.

4 Blessed is the man
    who places trust in the LORD,
but does not turn toward the proud,
    nor those falling away to falsehood.
5 O LORD my God,
    You have done many wonderful works,
and Your thoughts toward us
    cannot be compared;
if I would declare and speak of them,
    they are more than can be numbered.

6 Sacrifice and offering You did not desire;
    You have opened up my ears to listen.
Burnt offering and sin offering
    You have not required.
7 Then I said, "Behold, I have come;
    in the scroll of the book it is written of me,
8 I delight to do Your will, O my God;
    Your law is within my inward parts."

9 I have proclaimed righteousness in the great congregation;
    I have not held back my lips,
    O LORD, You know.
10 I have not hidden Your righteousness within my heart;
    I have declared Your faithfulness and Your salvation;
    I have not concealed Your lovingkindness and Your truth
        from the great congregation.

11 Do not withhold Your compassion from me, O LORD;
    may Your lovingkindness and Your truth always guard me.
12 For innumerable evils have surrounded me;
    my iniquities have overtaken me, so that I am not able to
        look up;
they are more than the hairs of my head
    so that my heart fails me.
13 Be pleased, O LORD, to deliver me;
    O LORD, make haste to help me.

14 May those seeking to snatch away my life
    be ashamed and confounded together;
may those who desire my harm
    be driven backward and dishonored.
15 May those who say to me "Aha, aha!"
    be appalled on account of their shame.
16 May all those who seek You
    rejoice and be glad in You;
may those who love Your salvation say continually,
    "The LORD is magnified."

17 But I am poor and needy;
    yet the LORD thinks about me.
You are my help and my deliverer;
    do not delay, O my God.

PSALM 41
For the Music Director. A Psalm of David.

1 Blessed are those who consider the poor;
    the LORD will deliver them in the day of trouble.
2 The LORD will preserve them and keep them alive,
    and they will be blessed on the earth,
    and You will not deliver them to the will of their enemies.
3 The LORD will sustain them on the sickbed;
    You will restore all his lying down in his illness.

4 I said, "LORD, be gracious to me;
    heal my soul, for I have sinned against You."
5 My enemies speak evil of me:
    "When will he die, and his name perish?"
6 And if people come to see me, they speak insincerely;
    their heart gathers iniquity to itself,
    when they go outside, they tell it.

7 All who hate me whisper together against me;
    they devise harm against me.
8 "An evil disease clings to him.
    And now that he lies down, he will not rise up again."
9 Yes, my own close friend,
    in whom I trusted, who ate of my bread,
    has lifted up the heel against me.

10 But You, O LORD, be gracious to me,
    and raise me up, that I may repay them.
11 By this I know that You favor me,
    because my enemy does not triumph over me.
12 As for me, You uphold me in my integrity,
    and set me before You forever.

13 Blessed be the LORD God of Israel
    from everlasting and to everlasting.
Amen and Amen.

BOOK TWO
Psalms 42–72

PSALM 42
For the Music Director. A Contemplative
Maskil of the sons of Korah.

1 As the deer pants after the water brooks,
    so my soul pants after You, O God.
2 My soul thirsts for God, for the living God.
    When will I come and appear before God?
3 My tears have been my food
    day and night,
while they always say to me,
    "Where is your God?"
4 When I remember these things,
    I pour out my soul within me.
For I would travel with the throng of people;
    I proceeded with them to the house of God,
with the voice of joy and thanks,
    with a multitude making a pilgrimage.

5 Why are you cast down, O my soul?
    And why are you disquieted in me?
Hope in God,
    for I will yet thank Him
    for the help of His presence.

6 O my God, my soul is cast down within me;
    therefore I will remember You
from the land of Jordan,
    and of the Hermon, from the hill of Mizar.
7 Deep calls to deep
    at the noise of Your waterfalls;
all Your waves and Your billows
    passed over me.

8 Yet the LORD will command His lovingkindness in the daytime,
    and in the night His song will be with me,
    a prayer to the God of my life.

9 I will say to God, my rock,
    "Why have You forgotten me?
Why do I go mourning
    because of the oppression of the enemy?"
10 With shattering in my bones,
    those harassing me reproach me,
when they say to me every day,
    "Where is your God?"

11 Why, my soul, are you cast down?
    Why do you groan within me?

Wait for God;
    I will yet thank Him,
    for He is my deliverance and my God.

PSALM 43

1 Vindicate me, O God,
    and plead my cause against an ungodly nation;
    deliver me from the deceitful and unjust man.
2 For You are the God of my refuge;
    why have You rejected me?
Why do I walk about mourning
    because of the oppression of the enemy?
3 Send out Your light and Your truth.
    Let them lead me;
let them bring me to Your holy hill,
    and to Your dwelling place.
4 Then I will go to the altar of God,
    to the God of my joyful gladness;
with the harp I will give thanks to You,
    O God, my God.

5 Why are you cast down, O my soul?
    And why are you disquieted within me?
Hope in God;
    for I will yet give Him thanks,
    the salvation of my countenance and my God.

PSALM 44

For the Music Director. A Contemplative
Maskil of the sons of Korah.

1 We have heard with our ears, O God,
    our fathers have told us
what work You did in their days,
    in the days of old:
2 how You drove out the nations with Your hand,
    and planted others instead;
how You afflicted peoples,
    and sent them away.
3 For they did not take possession of the land by their own sword,
    nor did their own arm save them;
but it was Your right hand, and Your arm,
    and the light of Your countenance, because You had favor
    on them.

4 You are my King, O God;
    command deliverances for Jacob.
5 Through You we will push down our opponents;
    through Your name we will trample those who rise up
    against us.
6 For I will not trust in my bow,
    nor will my sword save me.
7 But You have saved us from our opponents,
    and have put to shame those who hate us.
8 In God we boast all the day long,
    and give thanks to Your name forever.   Selah

9 But You have rejected us and put us to shame,
    and do not go out with our armies.
10 You make us to turn back from the opponent,
    and those who hate us make us their spoil.
11 You have placed us like sheep for prey,
    and have scattered us among the nations.
12 You sell Your people for nothing,
    and do not increase Your wealth by their sale.

13 You make us a reproach to our neighbors,
    a scorn and a derision to those who surround us.
14 You make us a byword among the nations,
    a shaking of the head among the people.
15 All day long my reproach is before me,
    and the shame of my face covers me,

16 from the voice of him who reproaches and reviles,
    by reason of the enemy and avenger.

17 All this is come on us,
    yet we have not forgotten You,
    nor have we dealt falsely in Your covenant.
18 Our heart is not turned back,
    nor have our steps deviated from Your way,
19 though You have crushed us in the place of jackals,
    and covered us with the shadow of death.

20 If we have forgotten the name of our God,
    or stretched out our hands to a strange god,
21 would not God search this out?
    For He knows the secrets of the heart.
22 Yes, for Your sake we are killed all the day long;
    we are considered like sheep for the slaughter.

23 Awake; why do You sleep, O Lord?
    Arise; do not reject us forever.
24 Why do You hide Your face,
    and forget our affliction and our oppression?

25 For our soul is bowed down to the dust;
    our body cleaves to the earth.
26 Arise, be our help,
    and redeem us for the sake of Your lovingkindness.

PSALM 45

For the Music Director. To the melody of "Lilies."
A Contemplative Maskil of the sons of Korah.
A love song.

1 My heart is overflowing with a good thought;
    I am speaking my works for the king;
    my tongue is the pen of a skilled scribe.

2 You are fairer than all the sons of men;
    favor is poured on your lips;
    therefore God has blessed you forever.
3 Gird your sword on your thigh, O mighty one,
    with your splendor and your majesty.
4 In your majesty ride prosperously
    because of truth and meekness and righteousness;
    and your right hand will teach you awesome things.
5 Your arrows are sharp in the heart of the king's enemies;
    peoples will fall under you.
6 Your throne, O God, is forever and ever;
    the scepter of Your kingdom is an upright scepter.
7 You love righteousness and hate wickedness;
    therefore God, your God, anointed you
    with the oil of gladness above your companions.
8 All your garments are fragrant with myrrh and aloes
    and cassia;
    from the ivory palaces stringed instruments make
    you glad.
9 Kings' daughters are among your honorable women;
    at your right hand stands the queen in gold of Ophir.

10 Listen, O daughter, consider and incline your ear;
    forget your own people, and your father's house,
11 and the king will desire your beauty.
    Since he is your lord, bow to him.
12 The daughter of Tyre will be there with a gift;
    even the rich among the people will entreat your favor.
13 The royal daughter is all glorious within *her chamber*;
    her clothing is plaited gold.
14 She shall be brought to the king in embroidered garments;
    the virgins, her companions who follow her,
    shall be brought to you.
15 With gladness and rejoicing they shall be brought;
    they shall enter into the king's palace.

16 Your sons shall succeed your fathers;
    you will make them princes in all the land.

17 I will cause your name to be remembered in all generations;
    therefore the people will praise you forever and ever.

PSALM 46
*For the Music Director. A Psalm of the sons of
Korah. According to Alamoth. A Song.*

1 God is our refuge and strength,
    a well-proven help in trouble.
2 Therefore we will not fear, though the earth be removed,
    and though the mountains be carried into the midst of the sea;
3 though its waters roar and foam,
    though the mountains shake with its swelling.   Selah

4 There is a river whose streams make glad the city of God,
    the holy dwelling place of the Most High.
5 God is in the midst of her; she will not be moved;
    God will help her in the early dawn.
6 The nations roared; the kingdoms were moved;
    He uttered His voice; the earth melted.

7 The Lord of Hosts is with us;
    the god of Jacob is our refuge.   Selah

8 Come, see the works of the Lord,
    who makes desolations in the earth.
9 He makes wars cease to the end of the earth;
    He breaks the bow and cuts off the spear;
    He burns the chariot in the fire.
10 Be still and know that I am God;
    I will be exalted among the nations,
    I will be exalted in the earth.

11 The Lord of Hosts is with us;
    the God of Jacob is our refuge.   Selah

PSALM 47
For the Music Director. A Psalm of the sons of Korah.

1 Clap your hands, all you people!
    Shout to God with a joyful voice.

2 For the Lord Most High is awesome;
    He is a great King over all the earth.
3 He subdued peoples under us,
    and nations under our feet.
4 He chose our inheritance for us,
    the excellency of Jacob whom He loved.   Selah

5 God went up with a shout,
    the Lord with the sound of a trumpet.
6 Sing praises to God, sing praises;
    sing praises to our King, sing praises.

7 For God is the King of all the earth;
    sing praises with understanding.

8 God reigns over the nations;
    God sits on His holy throne.
9 The princes of peoples are gathered together,
    even the people of the God of Abraham.
    For the shields of the earth belong to God;
    He is greatly exalted.

PSALM 48
A Song. A Psalm of the sons of Korah.

1 Great is the Lord, and greatly to be praised
    in the city of our God, in His holy mountain.

2 Beautiful in elevation,
    the joy of the whole earth,
    is Mount Zion, on the sides of the north,
    the city of the great King.
3 God is known in her citadels
    as a refuge.

4 For the kings were assembled,
    they passed by together.
5 They saw it, and so they were astounded;
    they were alarmed, they hurried away.
6 Trembling seized them there,
    and pain like a woman in labor;
7 You break the ships of Tarshish
    with an east wind.

8 As we have heard,
    so have we seen
    in the city of the Lord of Hosts,
    in the city of our God;
    God will establish it forever.   Selah

9 We have thought of Your lovingkindness, O God,
    in the midst of Your temple.
10 According to Your name, O God,
    so is Your praise to the ends of the earth;
    Your right hand is full of righteousness.
11 May Mount Zion rejoice,
    may the daughters of Judah be glad,
    because of Your judgments.

12 Walk about Zion, and go round about her;
    count her towers;
13 mark well her bulwarks;
    consider her citadels;
    that you may tell it to the generation following.

14 For this God is our God forever and ever;
    He will be our guide even to death.

PSALM 49
For the Music Director. A Psalm of the sons of Korah.

1 Hear this, all you people;
    give ear, all you inhabitants of the world,
2 both low and high,
    rich and poor together.
3 My mouth will speak wisdom,
    and the meditation of my heart will be understanding.
4 I will incline my ear to a parable;
    I will expound my riddle with a harp.

5 Why should I fear in the days of evil,
    when the iniquity of my stalkers surrounds me?
6 Those who trust in their wealth,
    and boast in the multitude of their riches,
7 none of them can by any means redeem the other,
    nor give to God a ransom for anyone,
8 for the redemption of their souls is costly;
    even so people cease to exist forever,
9 making efforts to live eternally,
    and not see the pit.
10 For one sees that wise men die,
    together the fool and the brute perish,
    and leave their wealth to others.
11 Their graves become their perpetual homes,
    and their dwelling places to all generations,
    though they call their lands after their
    own names.

12 But a man does not abide in honor;
    mankind is like the beasts that come to ruin.

13 This is their way, it is their folly;
   yet their posterity approve their sayings.   Selah
14 Like sheep they are appointed for Sheol;
   Death shall be their shepherd;
   the upright shall rule over them in the morning,
   and their form shall waste away in Sheol,
   far from their dwelling.
15 But God shall redeem my soul from the power of Sheol,
   for He shall receive me.   Selah
16 Do not fear when one is made rich,
   when the glory of his house is increased,
17 for he takes nothing away in death;
   his glory does not descend after him.
18 Though while he lives he blesses his soul—
   and men will praise you when you do well for yourself—
19 that soul will go to the generation of his fathers;
   they will never see light.

20 A man in honor, and yet without understanding,
   is like the animals that perish.

PSALM 50
A Psalm of Asaph.

1 The Mighty One, God, is the LORD;
   He has spoken and summoned the earth
   from the rising of the sun to its setting.
2 Out of Zion, the perfection of beauty,
   God has shined.
3 Our God will come, and will not keep silent;
   a fire consumes before Him,
   and a strong tempest is around Him.
4 He calls to the heavens above,
   and to the earth, that He may judge His people:
5 "Gather My faithful ones together to Me,
   those who have made a covenant with Me
   by sacrifice."
6 The heavens will declare His righteousness,
   for God Himself is judge. Selah

7 "Hear, O My people, and I will speak,
   O Israel, and I will testify against you;
   I am God, even your God.
8 I will not reprove you for your sacrifices
   or for your burnt offerings that are continually
   before Me.
9 I will take no young bull out of your house,
   nor male goats out of your folds.
10 For every wild animal of the forest is Mine,
   and the cattle on a thousand hills.
11 I know every bird of the mountains,
   and the creatures that move in the field are Mine.
12 If I were hungry, I would not tell you;
   for the world is Mine, and all its fullness.
13 Will I eat the flesh of bulls,
   or drink the blood of goats?

14 "Sacrifice a thank offering to God,
   and pay your vows to the Most High,
15 and call on Me in the day of trouble;
   I will deliver you, and you will glorify Me."

16 But to the wicked God says:

"What right have you to declare My statutes,
   or take My covenant in your mouth?
17 You hate instruction,
   and cast My words behind you.
18 When you see a thief, you are pleased,
   and have a share in those who commit adultery.
19 You let loose your mouth to evil,
   and your tongue is bound to deceit.

20 You sit and speak against your brother;
   you accuse your own mother's son.
21 These things have you done, and I kept silent;
   you thought that I was indeed like you;
   but I will reprove you
   and make a case before your eyes.

22 "Now consider this, you who forget God,
   lest I tear you in pieces, and there be none
   to deliver:
23 Whoever sacrifices a thank offering
   glorifies Me and makes a way;
   I will show him the salvation of God."

PSALM 51
For the Music Director. A Psalm of David, when Nathan the Prophet came to him, after he had gone in to Bathsheba.

1 Have mercy on me, O God,
   according to Your lovingkindness;
   according to the abundance of Your compassion,
   blot out my transgressions.
2 Wash me thoroughly from my iniquity,
   and cleanse me from my sin.

3 For I acknowledge my transgressions,
   and my sin is ever before me.
4 Against You, You only, have I sinned,
   and done this evil in Your sight,
   so that You are justified when You speak,
   and You are blameless when You judge.
5 I was brought forth in iniquity,
   and in sin my mother conceived me.
6 You desire truth in the inward parts,
   and in the hidden part You make me to
   know wisdom.

7 Purify me with hyssop, and I will be clean;
   wash me, and I will be whiter than snow.
8 Make me to hear joy and gladness,
   that the bones that You have broken may rejoice.
9 Hide Your face from my sins,
   and blot out all my iniquities.

10 Create in me a clean heart, O God,
   and renew a right spirit within me.
11 Do not cast me away from Your presence,
   and do not take Your Holy Spirit from me.
12 Restore to me the joy of Your salvation,
   and uphold me with Your willing spirit.

13 Then I will teach transgressors Your ways,
   and sinners will return to You.
14 Deliver me from blood guiltiness, O God,
   God of my salvation,
   and my tongue will sing aloud of Your
   righteousness.
15 O Lord, open my lips,
   and my mouth will declare Your praise.
16 For You do not desire sacrifice, or I would give it;
   You do not delight in burnt offering.
17 The sacrifices of God are a broken spirit;
   a broken and a contrite heart,
   O God, You will not despise.

18 Do good to Zion in Your good pleasure;
   build the walls of Jerusalem.
19 Then You will be pleased with the sacrifices of
   righteousness,
   with burnt offering and whole burnt offering;
   then they will offer young bulls on Your altar.

PSALM 52

For the Music Director. A Contemplative Maskil. A Psalm
of David, when Doeg the Edomite came and told
Saul, "David has come to the house of Ahimelek."

1 Why do you boast in evil, O mighty man?
   The goodness of God endures continually.
2 Your tongue devises calamities,
   like a sharp razor, you worker of treachery.
3 You love evil more than good,
   and lying rather than speaking righteousness. Selah
4 You love all devouring words,
   O you deceitful tongue.

5 God will likewise break you down forever;
   He will snatch you away and pluck you from your home,
   and uproot you from the land of the living. Selah
6 The righteous also will see and fear,
   and will laugh in contempt,
7 "See, this is the man
   who did not make God his refuge,
   but trusted in the abundance of riches,
   and grew strong in his own wickedness."

8 But I am like a green olive tree
   in the house of God;
   I trust in the mercy of God
   forever and ever.
9 I will give thanks to You forever, because You have acted;
   and I will wait on Your name,
   for it is good before Your saints.

PSALM 53

Ps 14:1–7
For the Music Director. According to Mahalath.
A Contemplative Maskil of David.

1 The fool has said in his heart,
   "There is no God."
   They are corrupt, and have done abhorrent injustice;
   there is none who does good.

2 God looked down from heaven
   on the children of men,
   to see if there were any who have insight,
   who seek God.
3 Every one of them has turned aside;
   they are altogether corrupt;
   there is no one who does good,
   not even one.

4 Have the workers of iniquity no knowledge,
   who eat up my people as they eat bread,
   and do not call on God?
5 There they were in fear,
   where there was nothing to fear,
   for God has scattered the bones of him who camps against you;
   you have put them to shame, because God has rejected them.

6 Oh, that the salvation of Israel would come out of Zion!
   When God brings back the captivity of His people,
   Jacob will rejoice and Israel will be glad.

PSALM 54

For the Music Director. With stringed instruments.
A Contemplative Maskil of David, when the Ziphites
went and told Saul, "Is David not hiding among us?"

1 O God, save me by Your name,
   and judge me by Your strength.
2 O God, hear my prayer;
   give ear to the words of my mouth.

3 For strangers rise up against me,
   and formidable adversaries seek my life;
   they do not set God before them. Selah

4 God is my helper;
   the Lord is with those who support my life.

5 He will repay my enemies for their evil.
   In Your faithfulness, destroy them.

6 I will sacrifice a freewill offering to You;
   I will give thanks to Your name, O LORD,
   for it is good.
7 For He has delivered me out of all trouble;
   and my eye has looked down on my enemies.

PSALM 55

For the Music Director. With stringed instruments.
A Contemplative Maskil of David.

1 Give ear to my prayer, O God,
   and do not hide Yourself from my supplication.
2 Attend to me, and answer me;
   I am restless in my complaint, and I murmur,
3 because of the voice of the enemy,
   because of the pressure of the wicked,
   for they cause trouble to drop on me,
   and in wrath they have animosity against me.

4 My heart is in pain within me,
   and the terrors of death have fallen on me.
5 Fear and trembling come into me,
   and horror has overwhelmed me.
6 I said, "Oh, that I had wings like a dove!
   For then I would fly away and be at rest.
7 Indeed, then I would wander far off,
   and remain in the wilderness. Selah
8 I would hasten my escape
   from the windy storm and tempest."

9 Confuse, O Lord, divide their tongues,
   for I have seen violence and strife in the city.
10 Day and night they go around it on its walls;
   trouble and sorrow are in its midst.
11 Destruction is in its midst;
   oppression and treachery do not depart from its streets.

12 For it is not an enemy who reproaches me;
   then I could bear it.
   Nor is it one who hates me who has exalted himself against me;
   then I could hide from him.
13 But it was you, my peer,
   my guide, and my acquaintance.
14 We took pleasant counsel together,
   and walked to the house of God in company.

15 May death surprise them,
   and may their lives go down to Sheol,
   for wickedness is in their dwellings and among them.

16 As for me, I will call on God,
   and the LORD will save me.
17 Evening and morning and at noon,
   I will make my complaint and murmur,
   and He will hear my voice.
18 He has ransomed my life in peace
   from the battle against me,
   for there were many against me.
19 God will hear and afflict them,
   even He who sits enthroned from of old. Selah
   Because they do not change,
   therefore they do not fear God.

20 My friend has set his hands against those at peace with him;
　　he has violated his covenant.
21 The words of his mouth were smoother than butter,
　　but battle was in his heart;
　his words were softer than oil,
　　yet they were drawn swords.

22 Cast your burden on the LORD,
　　and He will sustain you;
　He will never allow
　　the righteous to be moved.
23 But You, O God, will cast the wicked down
　　into the pit of destruction;
　men of blood and deceitful men
　　will not live out half their days.

But I will trust in You.

PSALM 56

For the Music Director. To the melody of "Silent Dove at a Distance." A
　Miktam of David, when the Philistines seized him in Gath.

1 Be gracious to me, O God, for man would crush me;
　　all day long he who battles oppresses me.
2 All day long my enemies would crush me,
　　for there are many who arrogantly battle against me.

3 In the day when I am afraid,
　　I will trust in You.
4 In God whose word I praise,
　　in God I have trusted; I will not fear.
　What can mere flesh do to me?

5 Every day they twist my words;
　　all their thoughts are against me for evil.
6 They stir up strife, they lurk,
　　they watch my steps,
　　when they wait for my life.
7 Should there be deliverance for them on account of wickedness?
　　In Your anger cast down the peoples, O God.

8 You take account of my wandering;
　　put my tears in Your bottle;
　　are they not in Your book?
9 In the day I cry to You,
　　then my enemies will turn back;
　　this I know, that God is for me.

10 In God whose word I praise,
　　in the LORD whose word I praise,
11 in God I trust, I will not fear;
　　what can a man do to me?

12 Your vows are on me, O God;
　　I will complete them with thank offerings to You;
13 for You have delivered my soul from death,
　　even my feet from stumbling,
　to walk before God
　　in the light of the living.

PSALM 57

Ps 108:1–5

For the Music Director. To the melody of "Do Not Destroy."
　A Miktam of David when he fled from Saul in the cave.

1 Be gracious to me, O God, be gracious to me!
　　For my soul seeks refuge in You;
　in the shadow of Your wings I will make my refuge,
　　until the ruinous storm passes by.

2 I will cry to God Most High,
　　to God who vindicates me.

3 He will send from heaven and save me
　　from the taunt of the one who crushes me.   Selah
　God will send forth His mercy and His truth.

4 My soul is among lions,
　　and I lie among the sons of men who blaze like fire,
　whose teeth are spears and arrows,
　　and their tongue a sharp sword.

5 Be exalted, O God, above the heavens;
　　may Your glory be above all the earth.

6 They have prepared a net for my steps;
　　my soul is bowed down;
　they have dug a pit before me,
　　but they have fallen into it.   Selah

7 My heart is fixed, O God,
　　my heart is fixed;
　　I will sing and give praise.
8 Awake, my glory!
　　Awake, psaltery and harp!
　　I will awake the dawn.

9 I will thank You, O Lord, among the peoples;
　　I will sing to You among the nations.
10 For Your mercy is great up to the heavens,
　　and Your truth extends to the clouds.

11 Be exalted, O God, above the heavens;
　　may Your glory be above all the earth.

PSALM 58

For the Music Director. To the melody of
　"Do Not Destroy." A Miktam of David.

1 Do you truly speak righteousness, O heavenly gods?
　　Do you judge uprightly, O earthly men?
2 Indeed, in the heart you work wickedness;
　　you weigh the violence of your hands in the earth.

3 The wicked are estranged from the womb onward;
　　those who speak lies go astray from birth.
4 Their poison is like the poison of a serpent;
　　they are like the deaf adder that plugs its ear,
5 and will not listen to the voice of charmers,
　　even the best and wisest enchanter.

6 Break their teeth in their mouth, O God;
　　break out the great teeth of the young lions, O LORD.
7 May they melt away as waters which run continually;
　　when he bends his bow to shoot his arrows, let them
　　be trodden under.
8 May they become as a snail that melts as it goes,
　　like the untimely birth of a woman, may they not
　　see the sun.

9 Before your pots can feel the thorns' heat, green or burning,
　　may He sweep them away.
10 The righteous will rejoice when he sees the vengeance;
　　he will wash his feet in the blood of the wicked;
11 and people will say,
　　"Surely there is a reward for the righteous;
　　surely there is a God who judges on the earth."

PSALM 59

For the Music Director. To the melody of "Do
　Not Destroy." A Miktam of David, when Saul sent
　men, and they watched the house to kill him.

1 Deliver me from my enemies, O my God;
　　give me refuge from those who rise up against me.

2 Deliver me from the workers of iniquity,
   and save me from bloodthirsty people.

3 For they lie in wait for my life;
   the mighty are gathered against me,
   not for my transgression, nor for my sin, O LORD.
4 For no guilt of mine, they run and prepare themselves.
   Arise to help me, and take notice.
5 You, O LORD God of Hosts, the God of Israel,
   awake to punish all the nations;
   do not be gracious to any wicked transgressors. Selah

6 They return at evening,
   they growl like a dog,
   and go around the city.
7 Indeed, they burst out with their mouth;
   swords are in their lips;
   for who listens?
8 But You, O LORD, will laugh at them;
   You will have all the nations in derision.

9 O my strength, I will wait on You;
   for God is my refuge.

10 The God of lovingkindness will go before me;
   God will cause me to look in triumph on my enemies.
11 Do not slay them,
   lest my people forget;
   scatter them by Your power,
   and bring them down, O Lord our shield.
12 For the sin of their mouth
   and the words of their lips,
   may they be snared by their pride,
   and because of curses and lies that they speak.
13   Consume them in wrath,
   consume them so they no longer exist;
   and let them know that God rules in Jacob
   to the ends of the earth. Selah

14 At evening they return,
   and growl like a dog,
   and go around the city.
15 They roam about to eat,
   and if they are not satisfied, they complain.
16 But I will sing of Your power;
   I will sing aloud of Your lovingkindness in the morning,
   for You have been my refuge
   and escape in the day of my trouble.

17 To You, O my strength, I will sing,
   for God is my refuge, and the God of my lovingkindness.

PSALM 60
Ps 108:6–13
For the Music Director. A Miktam of David to teach. To the
melody of "Lily of the Testimony," when he struggled with Aram
Naharaim and with Aram Zobah and when Joab returned from
striking down twelve thousand Edomites in the Valley of Salt.

1 O God, You have rejected us, You have scattered us;
   You have been displeased; take us back.
2 You have made the earth tremble; You have split it open;
   heal its breaches, for it shook.
3 You have shown Your people hard times;
   You have made us drink wine, causing us to stagger.
4 You have given a banner to those who fear You,
   that they may flee to it from the bow.¹ Selah

5 That Your beloved ones may be delivered,
   save with Your right hand and answer us.

6 God has spoken in His holiness:
   "I will rejoice, I will divide Shechem,
   and measure out the Valley of Sukkoth.
7 Gilead is Mine, and Manasseh is Mine;
   Ephraim also is My helmet;
   Judah is My scepter;
8 Moab is My wash basin;
   over Edom I will cast My shoe;
   shout the alarm, O Philistia, because of Me."

9 Who will bring me into the fortified city?
   Who will lead me into Edom?
10 You, O God, have You not cast us off?
   And You, O God, did not go out with our armies.
11 Give us help from trouble,
   for the help of man is worthless.
12 Through God we will do valiantly,
   for He will tread down our enemies.

PSALM 61
For the Music Director. With stringed
instruments. A Psalm of David.

1 Hear my cry, O God,
   attend to my prayer.

2 From the end of the earth I will cry to You;
   when my heart faints,
   lead me to the rock that is higher than I.
3 For You have been a refuge for me,
   and a strong tower from the enemy.

4 I will abide in Your tent forever;
   I will seek refuge in the covering of Your wings. Selah
5 For You, O God, have heard my vows;
   You have given me the heritage of those who fear
   Your name.

6 May You prolong the king's life,
   and may his years be as many generations.
7 May he sit enthroned before God forever;
   oh, prepare mercy and truth, which may preserve him.

8 Thus will I sing praise to Your name forever,
   that I may fulfill my vows day by day.

PSALM 62
For the Music Director. According to
Jeduthun. A Psalm of David.

1 My soul waits in silence on God alone;
   from Him comes my salvation.
2 He only is my rock and my salvation;
   He is my refuge; I will not be greatly shaken.

3 How long will you attack a man,
   to batter him, all of you,
   as you would a leaning wall, a tottering fence?
4 They only conspire to cast him down
   from his high position;
   they delight in lies,
   they bless with their mouth,
   but they curse inwardly. Selah

5 My soul, wait silently for God,
   for my hope is from Him.
6 He only is my rock and my salvation;
   He is my refuge; I will not be moved.
7 In God is my salvation and my glory;
   the rock of my strength, and my shelter, is in God.

---

1 4 Or for the truth.

8 Trust in Him at all times;
        you people, pour out your heart before Him;
        God is a shelter for us. Selah

9 Surely people of low degree are a breath,
        and men of high degree are a lie;
    if they are placed in the balance,
        they are altogether lighter than vapor.
10 Do not trust in oppression,
        and do not become vain in robbery;
    if riches increase,
        do not set your heart on them.

11 God has spoken once,
        twice have I heard this:
    that power belongs to God.
12   Also to You, O Lord, belongs mercy;
    for You render to each one
        according to his work.

PSALM 63

A Psalm of David, when he was
in the Wilderness of Judah.

1 O God, You are my God;
        early will I seek You;
    my soul thirsts for You,
        my flesh faints for You,
    in a dry and thirsty land
        with no water.

2 I have seen You in the sanctuary,
        to see Your power and Your glory.
3 Because Your lovingkindness is better than life,
        my lips will praise You.
4 Thus will I bless You while I live;
        I will lift up my hands in Your name.
5 My soul will be satisfied as with marrow and fatness,
        and my mouth will praise You with joyful lips.

6 When I remember You on my bed,
        and meditate on You in the night watches,
7 because You have been my help,
        therefore in the shadow of Your wings I will rejoice.
8 My soul clings hard to You;
        Your right hand upholds me.

9 But those who seek my soul to destroy it
        will go into the lower parts of the earth.
10 They will fall by the sword;
        they will be a portion for jackals.

11 But the king will rejoice in God;
        everyone who swears by Him will glory,
        because the mouth of liars will be stopped.

PSALM 64

For the Music Director. A Psalm of David.

1 Hear my voice, O God, in my complaint;
        guard my life from dread of the enemy.

2 Hide me from the secret counsel of the wicked,
        from the throng of the workers of iniquity;
3 they sharpen their tongue like a sword,
        and bend their bows to shoot their arrows—bitter words,
4 that they may shoot in secret at the blameless;
        suddenly they shoot at him and do not fear.

5 They harden themselves in an evil matter;
        they talk privately of laying snares;
        they say, "Who will see them?"

6 They devise injustice,
        saying "We have perfected a secret plot."
    Both the inward thought of man and the heart are deep.

7 But God will suddenly shoot them with an arrow;
        they will be wounded.
8 They will bring ruin on themselves
        by their own tongues;
        all who see them will flee away.
9 All people will fear,
        and declare the work of God;
        they will wisely consider His deeds.

10 The righteous will be glad in the Lord,
        and seek refuge in Him,
        and all the upright in heart will glory.

PSALM 65

For the Music Director. A Psalm of David. A Song.

1 Praise awaits You, O God, in Zion;
        and to You a vow will be fulfilled.
2 O You who hears prayer,
        to You all flesh will come.
3 Iniquities are stronger than me;
        as for our transgressions, You atone for them.
4 Blessed is the man You choose and allow to draw near;
        he will dwell in Your courts.
    We will be satisfied with the goodness of Your house,
        even Your holy temple.

5 In righteousness You will answer us gloriously,
        O God of our salvation,
    You, who are the confidence of all the ends of
            the earth,
        and of those who are afar off on the sea;
6 who established the mountains by His strength,
        being clothed with might;
7 who stills the noise of the seas,
        the noise of their waves,
        and the tumult of peoples.
8 Those who dwell in the uttermost parts
        are in awe because of Your signs;
    You make the going out of the morning
        and evening rejoice.

9 You visit the earth, and water it;
        You enrich it
    with the river of God, which is full of water;
        You prepare their grain,
        for thus You have established it.
10 You water its furrows abundantly;
        You settle its ridges;
    You soften it with showers;
        You bless its sprouting.
11 You crown the year with Your goodness,
        and Your paths drip abundance.
12 They drip on the pastures of the wilderness,
        and the hills clothe themselves with rejoicing.
13 The pastures are clothed with flocks;
        the valleys also are covered with grain;
        they shout for joy, they also sing.

PSALM 66

For the Music Director. A Song. A Psalm.

1 Shout joyfully to God, all you lands!
2   Sing out the glory of His name;
        make His praise glorious.
3 Say to God, "How awesome are Your works!
        Through the greatness of Your power
        Your enemies cringe before You.

4 All the earth will worship You
　　and will sing to You;
　　they will sing to Your name." Selah

5 Come and see the works of God;
　　He is awesome in His doings toward mankind.
6 He turned the sea into dry land;
　　they crossed the river on foot;
　　there we rejoiced in Him.
7 He rules by His power forever;
　　His eyes keep watch on the nations;
　　do not let the rebellious exalt themselves. Selah

8 Oh, bless our God, you people,
　　and make the voice of His praise to be heard,
9 who keeps our soul among the living,
　　and does not allow our feet to slip.
10 For You, O God, have proved us;
　　You have refined us, as silver is refined.
11 You brought us into the net;
　　You placed distress on our backs.
12 You have allowed people to ride over our heads;
　　we went through fire and through water;
　　but You brought us out into a well-watered place.

13 I will go into Your house with burnt offerings;
　　I will fulfill my vows to You,
14 which my lips have uttered,
　　and my mouth spoke when I was in trouble.
15 I will offer You burnt sacrifices of fat animals,
　　with the incense of rams;
　　I will offer bulls with goats. Selah

16 Come and hear, all you who fear God,
　　and I will declare what He has done for my soul.
17 I cried to Him with my mouth,
　　and He was extolled with my tongue.
18 If I regard iniquity in my heart,
　　the Lord will not hear me;
19 but certainly God has heard me;
　　He has attended to the voice of my prayer.
20 Blessed be God,
　　who has not turned away my prayer,
　　nor His mercy from me.

PSALM 67

For the Music Director. With stringed
instruments. A Psalm. A Song.

1 May God be gracious to us, and bless us,
　　and cause His face to shine on us; Selah
2 that Your way may be known on earth,
　　Your salvation among all nations.

3 Let the peoples praise You, O God;
　　let all the peoples praise You.
4 Oh, let the nations be glad and sing for joy;
　　for You will judge the people uprightly,
　　and lead the nations on earth. Selah
5 Let the peoples praise You, O God;
　　let all the peoples praise You.

6 Then will the earth yield its produce,
　　and God, our God, will bless us.
7 God will bless us,
　　and all the ends of the earth will fear Him.

PSALM 68

For the Music Director. A Psalm of David. A Song.

1 Let God arise, let His enemies be scattered;
　　let those who hate Him flee before Him.

2 As smoke is driven away,
　　You drive them away;
　　as wax melts before the fire,
　　so may the wicked perish before God.
3 But let the righteous be glad;
　　let them rejoice before God;
　　let them rejoice exceedingly.

4 Sing to God, sing praises to His name;
　　raise a song to Him who rides through the deserts—
　　His name is the LORD;
　　exult before Him.
5 A father of the fatherless, and a protector of the widows,
　　is God in His holy habitation.
6 God sets the deserted in families;
　　He brings out prisoners into prosperity,
　　but the rebellious dwell in a dry land.

7 O God, when You went forth before Your people,
　　when You marched through the wasteland, Selah
8 the earth shook;
　　the heavens also poured down *rain*
　　at the presence of God; even Sinai shook
　　at the presence of God, the God of Israel.
9 You, O God, sent plentiful rain;
　　You established Your inheritance when it was weary.
10 Your congregation has lived in it;
　　You, O God, by Your goodness have prepared for the poor.

11 The Lord gave the word;
　　great was the company of women who proclaimed it:
12 "Kings of armies flee; they flee!"
　　Even the women who were at home divided the spoil.
13 Though you sleep between the sheepfolds,
　　yet you will be like the wings of a dove overlaid
　　　　with silver,
　　and its feathers with yellow gold.
14 When the Almighty scattered kings in it,
　　it was white as snow on Mount Zalmon.

15 The mountain of God is as the mountain of Bashan;
　　a mountain of many peaks like the mountain of Bashan.
16 Why are you envious, you mountains of many peaks?
　　This is the mountain which God desires to dwell in;
　　yes, the LORD will dwell in it forever.
17 The chariots of God are twice ten thousand, even thousands
　　　　of thousands;
　　the Lord is among them, as in Sinai, in the holy place.
18 You have ascended on high,
　　You have led captivity captive;
　　You have received gifts from people,
　　yes, even from the rebellious,
　　that the LORD God might dwell among them.

19 Blessed be the Lord, who daily loads us with benefits,
　　even the God who is our salvation. Selah
20 That God is for us, the God of saving acts;
　　and to GOD the Lord belongs escape from death.
21 But God will shatter the head of His enemies,
　　and the scalp of one who walks in his trespasses.
22 The Lord said, "I will cause them to return from Bashan,
　　I will bring my people again from the depths of the sea,
23 that your foot may stomp in the blood of your enemies,
　　and the tongue of your dogs may have a portion in it."

24 They have seen Your processions, O God,
　　the processions of my God, my King, in the sanctuary.
25 The singers went before,
　　the players on instruments followed after;
　　among them were the young women playing tambourines.
26 Bless God in the congregations,
　　the LORD, from the fountain of Israel.

27 There is little Benjamin leading them,
    the princes of Judah and their throng of people,
    the princes of Zebulun, and the princes of Naphtali.

28 Your God has commanded your strength;
    strengthen, O God, what You have done for us.
29 From Your temple above Jerusalem,
    kings will bring gifts to You.
30 Rebuke the animals that live among the reeds,
    the herd of bulls, with the calves of the people,
until everyone submits himself with pieces of silver;
    scatter peoples who delight in war.
31 Ambassadors will come out of Egypt;
    Ethiopia will stretch out its hands to God.

32 Sing to God, you kingdoms of the earth;
    oh, sing praises to the Lord;   Selah
33 to Him who rides on the heavens, the ancient heavens;
    He who sends out His voice, a mighty voice.
34 Ascribe strength to God;
    His majesty is over Israel,
    and His strength is in the clouds.
35 O God, You are awesome from Your sanctuaries;
    the God of Israel is He who gives strength and power to people.

Blessed be God!

PSALM 69

For the Music Director. To the melody
of "Lilies." A Psalm of David.

1 Save me, O God!
    For the waters have come up to my throat.
2 I sink in deep mire;
    there is no standing place;
I have come into the watery depths,
    and a stream overflows me.
3 I am weary of my crying;
    my throat is parched;
my eyes fail
    while I wait for my God.
4 Those who hate me without cause
    are more than the hairs of my head;
they are mighty
    who would destroy me, being my wrongful enemies,
so that I must pay back
    what I did not steal.

5 O God, You know my folly,
    and my sins are not hidden from You.

6 May those who wait on You,
    O Lord God of Hosts,
    not be ashamed because of me;
may those who seek You
    not be humiliated because of me,
    O God of Israel.
7 Because for Your sake I have endured insult;
    humiliation has covered my face.
8 I have become estranged to my relatives,
    and a foreigner to my mother's children;
9 for the zeal of Your house has consumed me,
    and the insults of those who insulted You fell on me.
10 When I wept with fasting for my soul,
    it became an insult to me.
11 I also made sackcloth my garment,
    and I became a byword to them.
12 Those who sit in the gate speak against me,
    and I am the song of the drunkards.

13 But as for me, my prayer is to You, O Lord;
    in an acceptable time, O God,

in the abundance of Your mercy,
    answer me in the truth of Your salvation.
14 Deliver me out of the mire
    that I may not sink;
may I be delivered from those who hate me,
    and out of the watery depths.
15 May the stream not overflow me;
    neither may the deep swallow me up,
    nor the pit close its mouth on me.

16 Answer me, O Lord, for Your lovingkindness is good;
    turn Your face to me according to the abundance of Your
        tender mercies.
17 Do not hide Your face from Your servant,
    for I am in trouble; answer me quickly.
18 Draw near to my soul, and redeem it;
    deliver me because of my enemies.

19 You have known how I am insulted, and my shame and my dishonor;
    my adversaries are all before You.
20 Insults have broken my heart,
    and I am sick;
and I looked for some to take pity, but there was none;
    and for comforters, but I found none.
21 They also gave me poison for my food,
    and in my thirst they gave me vinegar to drink.

22 May their table become a snare before them,
    and may security become a trap.
23 May their eyes be darkened so they do not see,
    and make their sides shake continually.
24 Pour out Your indignation on them,
    and may Your wrathful anger overtake them.
25 May their habitation be desolate,
    and may no one dwell in their tents.
26 For they persecute him whom You have struck down,
    and they recount the pain of those You have wounded.
27 Add punishment to their iniquity,
    and do not let them come into Your righteousness.
28 Let them be blotted out of the book of the living,
    and not be written along with the righteous.

29 But I am poor and in pain;
    may Your salvation, O God, set me secure on high.

30 I will praise the name of God with a song,
    and will magnify Him with thanksgiving.
31 This also will please the Lord
    more than an ox or bull with horns and hoofs.
32 The humble will see this and be glad;
    and you who seek God, may your heart live.
33 For the Lord hears the poor,
    and does not despise His prisoners.

34 Let heaven and earth praise Him,
    the seas and everything that moves in them.
35 For God will save Zion,
    and will build the cities of Judah;
that they may dwell there, and take possession of it.
36   The descendants of His servants will inherit it;
    and those who love His name will dwell in it.

PSALM 70

Ps 40:13–17
For the Music Director. A Psalm of
David. To bring remembrance.

1 Make haste, O God, to deliver me!
    Make haste to help me, O Lord.

2 May those who seek my life
    be ashamed and confused;

may those who desire my harm
　　be driven back and humiliated.
3　May they turn back as a consequence of their shame
　　who say "Aha! Aha!"
4　May all those who seek You
　　rejoice and be glad in You;
and may those who love Your salvation continually say,
　　"God be magnified!"

5　But I am poor and needy;
　　make haste to me, O God!
You are my help and my deliverer;
　　O Lord, do not delay!

PSALM 71
Ps 31:1–4

1　In You, O Lord, I seek refuge;
　　may I never be put to shame.
2　Deliver me in Your righteousness and help me escape;
　　incline Your ear to me and save me.
3　Be my rock of refuge
　　to enter continually;
You have given commandment to save me;
　　for You are my rock and my stronghold.
4　Deliver me, O my God, out of the hand of the wicked,
　　out of the hand of the unjust and cruel man.

5　For You are my hope, O Lord God;
　　You are my confidence from my youth.
6　On You I have supported myself from the womb;
　　You took me out of my mother's womb.
　　My praise will continually be about You.
7　I am like a wondrous sign to many;
　　You are my strong refuge.
8　My mouth will be filled with Your praise
　　and with Your glory all the day.

9　Do not cast me off in the time of old age;
　　do not forsake me when my strength fails.
10　For my enemies speak against me;
　　and those who watch for my life take counsel together,
11　saying, "God has forsaken him;
　　pursue and catch him,
　　for there is none to deliver him."
12　O God, do not be far from me;
　　O my God, act quickly to help me.
13　May the adversaries of my life be ashamed and confused;
　　may those who seek my harm
　　be enveloped in scorn and dishonor.

14　But I will hope continually,
　　and will add to all Your praise.

15　My mouth will declare Your righteousness
　　and Your salvation all the day,
　　for I cannot know their numbers.
16　I will go in the strength of the Lord God;
　　I will make mention of Your righteousness, of
　　Yours only.
17　O God, You have taught me from my youth;
　　and until now I have proclaimed Your wondrous works.
18　Now also when I am old and gray,
　　O God, do not forsake me,
until I have proclaimed Your strength to this generation,
　　and Your power to everyone who is to come.

19　Your righteousness, O God, reaches to the heights;
　　You have done great deeds;
　　O God, who is like You?
20　You who have shown me great distresses and troubles
　　will revive me again,

and will bring me up again
　　from the depths of the earth.
21　You will increase my greatness,
　　and You will encircle and comfort me.

22　I will give You thanks with the harp,
　　even Your truth, O my God;
to You I will sing with the lyre,
　　O Holy One of Israel.
23　My lips will rejoice
　　when I sing to You,
　　and my soul, which You have redeemed.
24　My tongue also will speak of Your righteousness
　　all the day long;
for those who seek my harm are ashamed,
　　for they have been put to shame.

PSALM 72
A Psalm of Solomon.

1　Give the king Your judgments, O God,
　　and Your righteousness to the king's son.
2　May he judge Your people with righteousness,
　　and Your poor with justice.

3　May the mountains bring well-being to the people,
　　and the hills, in righteousness.
4　May he judge the poor of the people,
　　may he save the children of the needy,
　　and crush the oppressor.
5　May they fear You as long as the sun endures,
　　and the moon, throughout all generations.
6　May he descend like rain on the mown grass,
　　as showers dripping on the earth.
7　In his days may the righteous flourish,
　　and abundance of peace until the moon is no more.

8　May he have dominion from sea to sea,
　　and from the River to the ends of the earth.
9　May those who dwell in the wilderness bow before him,
　　and his enemies lick the dust.
10　May the kings of Tarshish and of the isles
　　bring presents;
the kings of Sheba and Seba
　　offer a gift.
11　May all kings bow down before him;
　　may all nations serve him.

12　Indeed, may he deliver the needy when he cries;
　　the poor also, and him who has no helper.
13　May he have compassion on the poor and needy,
　　and save the lives of the needy.
14　May he redeem their life from deceit and violence;
　　and may their blood be precious in his sight.

15　May he live long,
　　and may one give him the gold of Sheba;
and pray for him continually;
　　and all day long may he be blessed.
16　May there be abundance of grain in the earth
　　on the top of the mountains;
may its fruit shake like Lebanon;
　　and may those from the city flourish like grass
　　of the earth.
17　May his name endure forever;
　　may his name increase as long as the sun.

May men be blessed in him;
　　may all nations call him blessed!

18　Blessed be the Lord God, the God of Israel,
　　who alone does wondrous deeds.

¹⁹ Blessed be His glorious name forever;
     and may the whole earth be filled with His glory.
     Amen, and Amen.

²⁰ The prayers of David the son of Jesse are ended.

BOOK THREE
Psalms 73–89

PSALM 73
A Psalm of Asaph.

¹ Truly God is good to Israel,
     to the pure in heart.

² But as for me, my feet almost stumbled;
     my steps had almost slipped.
³ For I was envious at the boastful;
     I saw the prosperity of the wicked.

⁴ For there are no pains in their death;
     their bodies are fat.
⁵ They are not in trouble as other people;
     nor are they plagued like others.
⁶ Therefore pride is their necklace;
     violence covers them as a garment.
⁷ Their eyes bulge with fatness;
     they have more than a heart could wish.
⁸ They mock and speak with evil oppression;
     they speak loftily.
⁹ They set their mouth against the heavens,
     and their tongue struts through the earth.
¹⁰ Therefore people turn to them,
     and abundant waters are drunk by them.
¹¹ They say, "How does God know?
     And is there knowledge with the Most High?"

¹² Observe, these are the wicked, always at ease;
     they increase in riches.

¹³ Surely I have kept my heart pure for nothing,
     and washed my hands in innocence.
¹⁴ For all the day long I am plagued,
     and chastened every morning.

¹⁵ If I said, "I will speak thus,"
     I would have betrayed the generation of Your children.
¹⁶ When I thought to understand this,
     it was troublesome in my eyes,
¹⁷ until I went into the sanctuary of God;
     then I understood their end.

¹⁸ Surely You have set them in slippery places;
     You have brought them down to ruin.
¹⁹ How they come to desolation, as in a moment!
     They have come to an end, utterly consumed with terrors.
²⁰ As a dream when one awakes,
     so, O Lord, when You awake,
     You will despise their form.

²¹ Thus my heart was embittered,
     and I was pierced in my feelings.
²² I was a brute and did not understand;
     I was as a beast before You.

²³ Nevertheless I am continually with You;
     You have held me by my right hand.
²⁴ You will guide me with Your counsel,
     and afterward receive me to glory.
²⁵ Whom have I in heaven but You?
     And there is nothing on earth that I desire besides You.

²⁶ My flesh and my heart fails,
     but God is the strength of my heart
     and my portion forever.

²⁷ For those who are far from You will perish;
     You destroy everyone who is unfaithful to You.
²⁸ But it is good for me to draw near to God;
     I have taken my refuge in the Lord GOD,
     that I may declare all Your works.

PSALM 74
A Contemplative Maskil of Asaph.

¹ O God, why have You cast us off forever?
     Why does Your anger smoke against the sheep of Your
         pasture?
² Remember Your congregation, which You have purchased
         of old,
     the rod of Your inheritance, which You have redeemed,
     this Mount Zion, where You have lived.
³ Move Your footsteps to the perpetual desolations,
     to all the harm the enemy has done in the sanctuary.

⁴ Your enemies roar in the midst of Your meeting place;
     they set up their miracles for signs.
⁵ They seem like men who lift up axes
     on a thicket of trees.
⁶ But now they strike down its carved work altogether
     with axes and hammers.
⁷ They have cast fire into Your sanctuary;
     they have defiled the dwelling place of Your name to
         the ground.
⁸ They said in their hearts, "Let us destroy them together."
     They have burned up all the meeting places of God in
         the land.

⁹ We do not see our signs;
     there is no longer any prophet,
     nor is there among us any who knows how long.
¹⁰ O God, how long will the adversary scorn?
     Will the enemy blaspheme Your name forever?
¹¹ Why do You withdraw Your hand, Your right hand?
     Draw it out of Your bosom and destroy them!

¹² For God is my King of old,
     working salvation in the midst of the earth.
¹³ You divided the sea by Your strength;
     You broke the heads of the dragons on the waters.
¹⁴ You crushed the heads of Leviathan in pieces,
     and gave him for food to the people inhabiting
         the wilderness.
¹⁵ You split the fountain and the flood;
     You dried up ever-flowing rivers.
¹⁶ The day is Yours, the night also is Yours;
     You have prepared the light and the sun.
¹⁷ You have established all the borders of the earth;
     You have made summer and winter.

¹⁸ Remember this, that the enemy has scorned, O LORD,
     and that the foolish people have blasphemed Your name.
¹⁹ Do not give the life of Your turtledove to a wild animal;
     do not forget the life of Your poor forever.
²⁰ Have regard for the covenant;
     for the dark places of the earth are full of the habitations
         of violence.
²¹ May the oppressed not return ashamed;
     may the poor and needy praise Your name.
²² Arise, O God, plead Your own cause;
     remember how the fool insults You daily.
²³ Do not forget the voice of Your enemies,
     the tumult of those who rise up against
         You continually.

PSALM 75

For the Music Director. To the melody of "Do
Not Destroy." A Psalm of Asaph. A Song.

1 We give thanks to You, O God;
   we give thanks, and Your name is near;
   Your wondrous works declare it.

2 When I select an appointed time,
   I will judge with equity.
3 Though the earth and all its inhabitants are swaying,
   I steady its pillars. Selah
4 I said to the boastful, "Do not boast,"
   and to the wicked, "Do not lift up your horn.
5 Do not lift up your horn on high,
   or speak with an arrogant neck."

6 For neither from the east nor west,
   nor from the wilderness comes victory.
7 But God is the judge;
   He brings one low, and lifts up another.
8 For in the hand of the LORD there is a cup,
   and it is full of mixed, foaming wine,
and He pours from it;
   surely all the wicked of the earth will find and drink its dregs.

9 But I will declare forever,
   I will sing praises to the God of Jacob.
10 All the horns of the wicked I will cut off,
   but the horns of the righteous will be exalted.

PSALM 76

For the Music Director. With stringed
instruments. A Psalm of Asaph. A Song.

1 In Judah God is known;
   in Israel His name is great.
2 In Salem is His abode,
   and His dwelling place in Zion.
3 There He broke the fiery arrows of the bow,
   the shield, the sword, and the *weapons of* war. Selah

4 You are more glorious and excellent
   than the mountains of prey.
5 The strong of heart have been plundered;
   they have been put to sleep;
and none of the mighty men
   could use their hands.
6 At Your rebuke, O God of Jacob,
   both the chariot and horse lay stunned.

7 You, even You, are to be feared;
   and who may stand in Your sight from the moment of
     Your anger?
8 From the heavens You gave their judgment,
   and the earth feared and was silent,
9 when God arose to judgment,
   to save all the meek of the earth. Selah
10 Surely the wrath of people shall bring You praise;
   the remainder of wrath You shall put on.

11 Make your vows to the LORD your God, and fulfill them;
   let all who surround Him
   bring tribute to Him who is to be feared.
12 He reduces the spirit of princes,
   and is feared among the kings of the earth.

PSALM 77

For the Music Director. To Jeduthun. A Psalm of Asaph.

1 I cried out to God with my voice,
   even to God with my voice; and He listened to me.

2 In the day of my trouble I sought the Lord;
   in the night my hand is stretched out and does not weary,
   my soul refuses to be comforted.

3 I remember God, and I groan;
   I complain, and my spirit is overwhelmed. Selah
4 You hold my eyelids open;
   I am so troubled that I cannot speak.
5 I have considered the days of old,
   the years long ago.
6 May I remember my song in the night;
   may I meditate in my heart;
   my spirit made a diligent search:

7 "Will the Lord cast off forever,
   and will He be favorable no more?
8 Has His mercy ceased forever,
   and have His promises failed for all time?
9 Has God forgotten to be gracious,
   and has He in anger shut up His tender mercies?" Selah

10 Then I said, "This is my grief;
   yet I will remember the years of the right hand of the
     Most High."
11 I will remember the works of the LORD;
   surely I will remember Your wonders of old.
12 I will meditate also on all Your work
   and ponder on Your mighty deeds.

13 Your way, O God, is holiness;
   what god is as great as our God?
14 You are the God who can do wonders;
   You have declared Your strength among the nations.
15 You have with Your arm redeemed Your people,
   the children of Jacob and Joseph. Selah

16 The waters saw You, O God.
   The waters saw You; they were afraid;
   the depths also trembled.
17 The clouds poured out water;
   the skies thundered.
   Your arrows flashed about.
18 The sound of Your thunder was in the whirlwind,
   and Your lightning lit up the world;
   the earth trembled and shook.
19 Your way is through the sea,
   and Your path in the great waters,
   and your footsteps are not seen.

20 You led Your people like a flock
   by the hand of Moses and Aaron.

PSALM 78

A Contemplative Maskil of Asaph.

1 Give ear, O my people, to my teaching;
   incline your ears to the words of my mouth.
2 I will open my mouth in a parable;
   I will utter insightful sayings of old,
3 which we have heard and known,
   what our fathers have told us.
4 We will not hide them from their children,
   but will tell the coming generation
the praises of the LORD,
   and His strength, and the wonderful works that He has done.
5 For He established a rule in Jacob,
   and appointed a law in Israel,
which He commanded our fathers
   that they should make them known to their children,
6 that the generation to come might know them,
   even the children who are not yet born,
   who will arise and declare them to their children:

7 that they might set their hope in God
    and not forget the works of God,
    but keep His commandments,
8 and they might not be as their fathers,
    a stubborn and rebellious generation,
    a generation that did not set their heart steadfast,
    and whose spirit was not faithful to God.

9 The people of Ephraim, being armed with bows,
    turned back in the day of battle.
10 They did not keep the covenant of God
    and refused to walk in His law;
11 and they forgot His works
    and the wonders that He had shown them.
12 In the sight of their ancestors He did marvelous wonders
    in the land of Egypt, in the field of Zoan.
13 He divided the sea and caused them to pass through,
    and He made the waters to stand as a heap.
14 In the daytime He led them with a cloud,
    and all the night with a light of fire.
15 He split rocks in the wilderness
    and gave them abundance to drink as out of the great depths.
16 He brought streams out of the rock
    and caused waters to run down like rivers.

17 They sinned yet more against Him
    by provoking the Most High in the wilderness.
18 They tested God in their heart
    by demanding the food that they craved.
19 They spoke against God by saying,
    "Can God furnish a table in the wilderness?
20 Behold, He struck the rock, so that the waters gushed out
    and the streams overflowed.
    Can He give bread
    or provide meat for His people?"
21 Therefore the LORD heard this and was full of wrath;
    a fire was kindled against Jacob,
    and anger also came up against Israel,
22 because they did not believe in God
    nor trust in His deliverance.
23 Yet He had commanded the skies above
    and opened the doors of heaven,
24 and He rained down manna upon them to eat
    and gave them the grain of heaven.
25 Man ate the food of mighty angels;
    He sent them bread in abundance.
26 He caused an east wind to blow in the heavens,
    and by His power He brought out a south wind.
27 He rained meat on them as dust,
    and winged birds as the sand of the sea;
28 and He let them fall in the midst of their camp
    all around their habitations.
29 So they ate and were satisfied,
    for He gave them their own desire;
30 while they were not yet filled up,
    and while the meat was still in their mouths,
31 the wrath of God came upon them,
    and He killed the strongest of them
    and struck down the young men of Israel.

32 For all this they sinned still,
    and did not believe despite His wondrous works.
33 Therefore He made their days vanish like a breath,
    and their years in trouble.
34 When He killed them, then they sought Him;
    they turned back and longed for God.
35 They remembered that God was their rock,
    and the Most High God their redeemer.
36 Nevertheless they flattered Him with their mouth,
    and they lied to Him with their tongues;
37 for their heart was not devoted to Him,
    neither were they committed to His covenant.

38 But He being full of compassion
    forgave their iniquity
    and did not destroy them.
    He constantly restrained His anger,
    and did not stir up all His wrath;
39 for He remembered that they were but flesh,
    like a wind that passes away and does not return.

40 How often they provoked Him in the wilderness
    and grieved Him in the desert!
41 Yes, they tested God over and over,
    and provoked the Holy One of Israel.
42 They did not remember His power,
    nor the day when He delivered them from
        the enemy,
43 how He had performed His signs in Egypt
    and His wonders in the fields of Zoan:
44 and He turned their rivers into blood,
    so that they could not drink from their streams.
45 He sent swarms of flies among them, which devoured them,
    and frogs, which destroyed them.
46 He gave also their crops to the grasshopper
    and the fruit of their labor to the locust.
47 He destroyed their vines with hail
    and their sycamore trees with frost.
48 He gave up their cattle also to the hail
    and their flocks to thunderbolts.
49 He cast upon them the fierceness of His anger,
    wrath, indignation, and trouble,
    by sending angels bringing disaster.
50 He made a path for His anger;
    He did not spare them from death,
    but gave their lives over to the plague,
51 and struck down all the firstborn in Egypt,
    the first fruits of their strength in the tents of Ham.
52 Then He led out His own people like sheep
    and guided them in the wilderness like a flock;
53 He led them in safety, so that they were not afraid,
    but the sea overwhelmed their enemies.
54 He brought them to the border of His holy land,
    to the mountain that His right hand had acquired.
55 He cast out the nations also before them,
    and divided for them their tribal allotments,
    and made the tribes of Israel dwell in their tents.

56 Yet they tested and provoked the Most High God,
    and did not keep His commands,
57 but turned back and acted unfaithfully like their fathers;
    they turned aside like a deceitful bow.
58 For they provoked Him to anger with their high places
    and moved Him to jealousy with their graven images.
59 When God heard this, He was full of wrath
    and greatly rejected Israel
60 so that He left the tabernacle at Shiloh,
    the tent where He lived among people,
61 and delivered His strength to captivity
    and His glory into the enemy's hand.
62 He gave His people over also to the sword;
    He was enraged with His inheritance.
63 The fire consumed their young men,
    and their maidens were not given to marriage in song.
64 Their priests fell by the sword,
    and their widows made no lamentation.

65 Then the Lord awoke as one out of sleep,
    and like a mighty man who shouts because of wine.
66 He routed His enemies back,
    and He made them a perpetual reproach.
67 Moreover, He rejected the tent of Joseph,
    and He did not choose the tribe of Ephraim,
68 but chose the tribe of Judah,
    Mount Zion which He loves.

69 He built His sanctuary like the high heavens,
   like the earth that He has established perpetually.
70 He chose David His servant
   and took him from the sheepfolds;
71 from following the nursing ewes He brought him
   to shepherd Jacob His people,
   and Israel His inheritance.
72 So he shepherded them according to the integrity of
   his heart
   and guided them by the skillfulness of his hands.

PSALM 79
A Psalm of Asaph.

1 O God, the nations have come into Your inheritance;
   Your holy temple they have defiled;
   they have laid Jerusalem in ruins.
2 The dead bodies of Your servants
   they have given to the birds of the sky for food
   and the flesh of Your faithful to the animals of
   the land.
3 Their blood they have poured out like water
   all around Jerusalem,
   and there was no one to bury them.
4 We have become a reproach to our neighbors,
   a scorn and derision to those who are around us.

5 How long, O LORD? Will You be angry forever?
   Will Your jealousy burn like fire?
6 Pour out Your wrath
   upon the nations who do not know You,
   and upon the kingdoms
   who have not called upon Your name.
7 For they have devoured Jacob,
   and laid waste his dwelling place.

8 Do not choose to remember our former iniquities;
   let Your tender mercies come swiftly to us,
   for we are brought very low.
9 Help us, O God of our salvation,
   for the glory of Your name;
   deliver us, and purge away our sins,
   for Your name's sake.
10 Why should the nations say,
   "Where is their God?"

May the avenging of the shed blood of Your servants
   be known among the nations before our eyes.
11 Let the groans of the prisoners come before You;
   according to the greatness of Your power
   preserve those who are appointed to die.
12 And render unto our neighbors sevenfold into their lap
   the reproach that they have reproached You, O Lord.
13 But we are Your people, the sheep of Your pasture,
   and will give You thanks forever;
   we will declare Your praise
   to all generations.

PSALM 80
For the Music Director. To the melody of "Lilies
of the Testimony." A Psalm of Asaph.

1 Give ear, O Shepherd of Israel,
   You who lead Joseph like a flock;
   You who are enthroned between the cherubim, shine forth.
2   In the sight of Ephraim and Benjamin and Manasseh,
   stir up Your strength,
   and come and rescue us.

3 Restore us again, O God,
   and cause Your face to shine,
   and we shall be delivered.

4 O LORD God of Hosts,
   how long will You be angry
   against the prayers of Your people?
5 You have fed them with the bread of tears
   and have given them tears to drink in great measure.
6 You make us contention for our neighbors,
   and our enemies laugh among themselves.

7 Restore us again, O God of Hosts,
   and cause Your face to shine,
   and we shall be delivered.

8 You have brought a vine out of Egypt;
   You have cast out the nations and planted it.
9 You cleared the *ground* for it;
   it took deep root and filled the land.
10 The mountains were covered with its shadow
   and the mighty cedars with its branches.
11 It sent out its branches to the sea
   and its shoots to the River.

12 Why have You then broken down its walls,
   so that all those who pass by the way pluck its *fruit*?
13 The boar from the woods ravages it,
   and the insects of the field devour it.
14 Return again, O God of Hosts;
   look down from heaven, and behold,
   have regard for this vine
15   and the root that Your right hand has planted,
   and the shoots that You made strong for Yourself.

16 It is burned with fire; it is cut down;
   may they perish at the rebuke from Your presence.
17 Let Your hand be upon the man of Your right hand,
   the son of man whom You made strong for Yourself.
18 So we will not turn back from You;
   give us life, and we will call upon Your name.

19 Restore us again, O LORD God of Hosts;
   cause Your face to shine,
   and we shall be delivered.

PSALM 81
For the Music Director. According to
The Gittith. A Psalm of Asaph.

1 Sing aloud unto God our strength;
   make a joyful noise unto the God of Jacob.
2 Lift up a melody, and sound the tambourine,
   the pleasant lyre with the harp.

3 Blow the trumpet at the New Moon,
   at the full moon on our feast day.
4 For this is a statute for Israel,
   a decree of the God of Jacob.
5 This He ordained in Joseph as a decree
   when He went out against the land of Egypt.

I heard a voice that I had not known:

6 "I removed his shoulder from the burden;
   his hands were released from holding the basket.
7 You called in trouble, and I delivered you;
   I answered you in the secret place of thunder;
   I tested you at the waters of Meribah.   Selah
8 Hear, O My people, and I will testify against you.
   O Israel, if you would listen to me!
9 There shall be no strange god among you;
   neither shall you bow down to any strange god.
10 I am the LORD your God,
   who brought you out of the land of Egypt;
   open your mouth wide, and I will fill it.

11 "But My people would not listen to My voice;
    Israel would not submit to Me.
12 So I gave them up to their stubborn hearts,
    to walk in their own counsels.

13 "Oh, that My people would listen to Me,
    and Israel would follow in My ways!
14 I would soon subdue their enemies,
    and turn My hand against their adversaries.
15 Let those who hate the LORD cower before Him
    and their fate might last forever.
16 But I would feed them with the finest of wheat,
    and with honey out of the rock I would satisfy you."

PSALM 82
A Psalm of Asaph.

1 God stands among the divine council;
    He renders judgment among the gods.

2 "How long will you all judge unjustly
    and accept partiality of the wicked?   Selah
3 Defend the poor and fatherless;
    vindicate the afflicted and needy.
4 Grant escape to the abused and the destitute,
    pluck them out of the hand of the false.

5 "They have neither knowledge nor understanding;
    they walk in darkness:
    all the foundations of the earth are shaken."

6 I have said, "You are gods,
    sons of the Most High, all of you,
7 but you all shall die like men,
    and fall like a man, O princes."

8 Arise, O God, judge the earth,
    for You shall inherit all nations.

PSALM 83
A Song. A Psalm of Asaph.

1 Do not keep Your silence, O God;
    do not hold Your peace or be still, O God.
2 For, look, Your enemies make an uproar,
    and those who hate You have lifted up their heads.
3 They have given crafty counsel against Your people,
    and have consulted against Your treasured ones.
4 They have said, "Come, and let us cut them off from being
        a nation,
    that the name of Israel may be no more remembered."

5 For they have conspired together;
    they make a covenant against You—
6 the tents of Edom and the Ishmaelites,
    even Moab and the Hagrites;
7 Gebal and Ammon and Amalek,
    the Philistines with the inhabitants of Tyre;
8 Assyria also is joined with them,
    they are the strength of the descendants of Lot.   Selah

9 Do to them as You did to the Midianites,
    as to Sisera and Jabin at the river of Kishon,
10 who perished at Endor;
    they became as dung for the ground.
11 Make their nobles like Oreb and Zeeb;
    yes, all their princes as Zebah and Zalmunna,
12 who said, "Let us take for ourselves
    the pastures of God as a possession."

13 O my God, make them like a tumbleweed,
    as stubble before the wind.

14 As fire burns a forest,
    and as the flame sets the mountains ablaze,
15 so pursue them with Your storm,
    and make them afraid with Your hurricane.
16 Fill their faces with shame,
    that they may seek your name, O LORD.

17 Let them be confounded and troubled forever;
    yes, let them be put to shame and perish,
18 that they may know that You, whose name alone
        is the LORD,
    are the Most High over all the earth.

PSALM 84
For the Music Director. According to
The Gittith. A Psalm of the sons of Korah.

1 How lovely is Your dwelling place,
    O LORD of Hosts!
2 My soul longs, yes, even faints
    for the courts of the LORD;
my heart and my body cry out
    for the living God.

3 Yes, the sparrow has found a home
    and the swallow a nest for herself,
    where she may lay her young,
even at Your altars,
    O LORD of Hosts, my King and my God.
4 Blessed are those who dwell in Your house;
    they continually praise You.   Selah

5 Blessed is the man whose strength is in You,
    in whose heart are the paths to *Zion*.
6 As they pass through the Valley of Baca,
    they make it a spring;
    the early rain also covers it with pools.
7 They go from strength to strength;
    every one of them appears in Zion before God.

8 O LORD God of Hosts, hear my prayer,
    and give ear, O God of Jacob.   Selah
9 Behold, O God our shield,
    and look upon the face of Your anointed.

10 For a day in Your courts is better
    than a thousand elsewhere.
I had rather be a doorkeeper in the house of my God
    than to dwell in the tents of wickedness.
11 For the LORD God is a sun and shield;
    the LORD will give favor and glory,
for no good thing will He withhold
    from the one who walks uprightly.

12 O LORD of Hosts,
    blessed is the man who trusts in You.

PSALM 85
For the Music Director.
A Psalm of the songs of Korah.

1 LORD, You have been favorable to Your land;
    You have brought back the captivity of Jacob.
2 You have forgiven the iniquity of Your people;
    You have covered all their sin.   Selah
3 You have withdrawn all Your wrath;
    You have turned from the fierceness of Your anger.

4 Restore us, O God of our salvation,
    and put away Your indignation toward us.
5 Will You be angry with us forever?
    Will You draw out Your anger to all generations?

6 Will You not revive us again,
    that Your people may rejoice in You?
7 Show us Your mercy, O Lord,
    and grant us Your deliverance.

8 I will hear what God the Lord will speak,
    for He will speak peace to His people and to
        His saints,
    but let them not turn again to folly.
9 Surely His salvation is near to them who fear Him,
    that glory may dwell in our land.

10 Mercy and truth have met together;
    righteousness and peace have kissed.
11 Truth springs from the ground,
    and righteousness looks down from the sky.
12 Yes, the Lord gives that which is good,
    and our land shall yield its increase.
13 Righteousness shall go before Him
    and prepare a way for His footsteps.

PSALM 86
A Prayer of David.

1 Incline Your ear, O Lord, and answer me,
    for I am oppressed and needy.
2 Preserve my soul, for I am godly;
    You are my God; save Your servant
        who trusts in You.
3 Have mercy on me, O Lord,
    for to You I cry all day long.
4 Gladden the soul of Your servant,
    for to You, O Lord,
    I lift my soul.

5 For You, Lord, are good, and forgiving,
    abounding in kindness to all who call on You.
6 Give ear, O Lord, to my prayer,
    and attend to my plea for mercy.
7 In the day of my trouble I will call upon You,
    for You will answer me.

8 Among the gods there is none like You, O Lord;
    neither are there any works like Your works.
9 All nations whom You have made
    shall come and worship before You, O Lord,
    and shall glorify Your name.
10 For You are great and do wondrous deeds;
    You are God alone.

11 Teach me Your way, O Lord,
    that I will walk in Your truth;
    bind my heart
        to fear Your name.
12 I will give You thanks, O Lord my God, with all my heart,
    and I will glorify Your name forever.
13 For great is Your mercy toward me,
    and You have delivered my soul from the depths
        of Sheol.

14 O God, insolent men have risen against me,
    and bands of violent men have sought my life;
    they have not set You before them.
15 But You, O Lord, are a God full of compassion
        and gracious,
    slow to anger, and abundant in mercy and truth.
16 Turn to me and have mercy on me;
    give Your strength to Your servant,
    and save the *humble* son of Your female servant.
17 Show me a sign of Your favor,
    that those who hate me may see it and be ashamed
    because You, Lord, have helped and comforted me.

PSALM 87
A Psalm of the sons of Korah. A Song.

1 The city of His foundation is on the holy mountain.
2 The Lord loves the gates of Zion
    more than all the dwelling places of Jacob.

3 Glorious things are spoken of you,
    O city of God. Selah.
4 I will make mention of Rahab and Babylon
    to those who know Me;
    look, Philistia and Tyre with Ethiopia;
    "This man was born there."
5 But of Zion it shall be said,
    "This one and that one were born in her,"
    for the Most High shall make her secure.
6 The Lord shall count when He registers the people,
    "This one was born there." Selah

7 As well the singers and the players of instruments say,
    "All my springs are in you."

PSALM 88
For the Music Director. A Song. A Psalm of the sons
of Korah. To the melody of "Suffering of Affliction."
A Contemplative Maskil of Heman the Ezrahite.

1 O Lord, God of my salvation,
    I cry out day and night before You.
2 Let my prayer come before You;
    incline Your ear to my cry.

3 For my soul is full of troubles,
    and my life draws near to Sheol.
4 I am counted with those who go down to the grave;
    I am a man who has no strength,
5 like one who is set free among the dead,
    like the slain who lie in the grave,
    like those whom You remember no more,
    for they are cut off from Your hand.

6 You have laid me in the depths of the pit,
    in dark and deep regions.
7 Your wrath lies heavy upon me,
    and You have afflicted me with all Your waves. Selah
8 You have caused my companions to be far from me;
    You have made me an abomination to them;
    I am shut up, and I cannot escape;
9   my eye is dim from my affliction.

Lord, I call daily upon You,
    and I have stretched out my hands to You.
10 Will You show wonders to the dead?
    Shall the dead rise up to praise You? Selah
11 Shall Your lovingkindness be declared in the grave,
    or your faithfulness in Abaddon?
12 Shall Your wonders be known in the darkness
    or Your righteousness in the land of forgetfulness?

13 But unto You have I cried, O Lord,
    and in the morning my prayer comes before You.
14 O Lord, why do You cast away my soul?
    Why do You hide Your face from me?

15 I am afflicted and close to death since my youth;
    while I suffer Your terrors I am helpless.
16 Your fierce wrath sweeps over me;
    Your terrors destroy me.
17 They come around me daily like a flood;
    they encircle me together.
18 You have caused to be far from me my lovers and friends,
    and my companion is darkness.

PSALM 89

A Contemplative Maskil of Ethan the Ezrahite.

1 I will sing of the mercies of the LORD forever;
  with my mouth I will make known Your faithfulness to
    all generations.
2 For I have said, "Mercy shall be built up forever;
  Your faithfulness shall be established in the heavens."
3 You have said, "I have made a covenant with my chosen one;
  I have sworn to David my servant:
4 'Your offspring I will establish forever,
  and build up your throne for all generations.' " Selah

5 Let the heavens praise Your wonders, O LORD;
  Your faithfulness also in the assembly of the holy ones.
6 For who in the skies can be compared to the LORD?
  Who among the *heavenly* sons is like the LORD?
7 God is greatly to be feared in the assembly of the holy ones
  and awesome to all those who surround Him.
8 O LORD God of Hosts, who is a mighty LORD like You,
  with Your faithfulness all around You?

9 You rule the raging of the sea;
  when the waves arise, You still them.
10 You crushed Rahab like a corpse;
  You scattered Your enemies with Your strong arm.
11 The heavens are Yours; the earth also is Yours;
  the world and all that is in it, You have founded them.
12 The north and the south, You have created them;
  Tabor and Hermon rejoice in Your name.
13 You have a mighty arm,
  and strong is Your hand, and victorious is
    Your right hand.

14 Righteousness and justice are the foundation of Your throne;
  mercy and truth shall go before Your presence.
15 Blessed are the people who know the joyful shout.
  They walk, O LORD, in the light of Your presence.
16 In Your name they rejoice all the day,
  and in Your righteousness they shall be exalted.
17 For You are the beauty of their strength;
  by Your favor our horn is exalted.
18 For the LORD is our shield of defense,
  and the Holy One of Israel is our king.

19 Long ago You spoke in a vision
  to Your godly one and said:
"I have given help to one who is mighty;
  I have exalted one chosen from the people.
20 I have found David, My servant;
  with My holy oil I have anointed him:
21 By whom My hand shall be established;
  My arm also shall strengthen him.
22 The enemy shall not take tribute from him,
  nor the wicked humiliate him.
23 I will beat down his foes before him
  and strike down those who hate him.
24 My faithfulness and My mercy shall be with him,
  and in My name his horn shall be exalted.
25 I will set his hand on the sea
  and his right hand on the rivers.
26 He shall cry unto Me, 'You are my Father, my God,
  and the Rock of my salvation.'
27 Also I will make him my firstborn,
  the highest of the kings of the earth.
28 In My mercy I will keep him forever,
  and My covenant shall stand firm with him.
29 His offspring also I will establish forever
  and his throne as the days of heaven.

30 "If his children forsake My law
  and do not walk in My judgments,

31 if they break My statutes
  and do not keep My commandments,
32 then I will punish their transgression with the rod
  and their iniquity with lashes.
33 Nevertheless My lovingkindness I will not remove from him
  nor be false in My faithfulness.
34 My covenant I will not violate
  nor alter the word that has gone out from My lips.
35 Once and for all I have sworn by My holiness
  that I will not lie to David:
36 His offspring shall endure forever,
  and his throne as the sun before Me;
37 it shall be established forever as the moon
  and as a faithful witness in the heavens." Selah

38 But now You have cast off and rejected *him*,
  You have been wrathful with Your anointed king.
39 You have renounced the covenant with Your servant;
  You have defiled his crown by casting it to
    the ground.
40 You have broken down all his walls;
  You have brought his strongholds to ruin.
41 All who pass by the way plunder him;
  he is a reproach to his neighbors.
42 You have set high the right hand of his adversaries;
  You have made all his enemies rejoice.
43 You have also turned back the edge of his sword
  and have not made him stand in battle.
44 You have made his glory cease
  and cast his throne down to the ground.
45 The days of his youth You have shortened;
  You have covered him with shame. Selah

46 How long, O LORD? Will You hide Yourself forever?
  How long shall Your wrath burn like fire?
47 Remember how short my time is!
  Why have You made all people in such emptiness?
48 What man can live and not see death?
  Who can deliver his soul from the power of Sheol? Selah
49 Lord, where are Your former lovingkindnesses,
  which You swore to David in Your faithfulness?
50 Remember, O Lord, the reproach of Your servants
  and how I bear in my heart *the insults* of the
    many nations,
51 which Your enemies taunt, O LORD,
  with which they mock the footsteps of Your
    anointed king.

52 Blessed be the LORD forever!
  Amen and Amen.

BOOK FOUR

Psalms 90–106

PSALM 90

A Prayer of Moses, the man of God.

1 Lord, You have been our dwelling place
  in all generations.
2 Before the mountains were brought forth,
  or You had formed the earth and the world,
  even from everlasting to everlasting You are God.

3 You return man to the dust
  and say, "Return, you children of men."
4 For a thousand years in Your sight
  are but as yesterday when it is past,
  or as a night watch in the night time.
5 You carry them away as with a flood;
  they are as a dream, like renewed grass in
    the morning:

⁶ In the morning it flourishes and grows up;
   in the evening it fades and withers.

⁷ For we are consumed by Your anger,
   and by Your wrath we are terrified.
⁸ You have set our iniquities before You,
   even our secret sins in the light of Your presence.
⁹ For all our days pass away in Your wrath;
   we end our years with a groan.
¹⁰ The years of our life are seventy,
   and if by reason of strength eighty;
   yet their length is toil and sorrow,
   for they soon end, and we fly away.
¹¹ Who knows the power of Your anger?
   Or Your wrath according to Your fear?
¹² So teach us to number our days,
   that we may apply our hearts to wisdom.

¹³ Return, O Lord, how long?
   Have mercy on Your servants.
¹⁴ Satisfy us in the early morning with Your mercy,
   that we may rejoice and be glad all our days.
¹⁵ Make us glad according to the days that You have afflicted us,
   and the years that we have seen evil.
¹⁶ Let Your work be displayed to Your servants
   and Your glory to their children.

¹⁷ Let the beauty of the Lord our God be upon us,
   and establish the work of our hands among us;
   yes, establish the work of our hands.

PSALM 91

¹ He who dwells in the shelter of the Most High
   shall abide under the shadow of the Almighty.
² I will say of the Lord, "He is my refuge and my fortress,
   my God in whom I trust."

³ Surely He shall deliver you from the snare of the hunter
   and from the deadly pestilence.
⁴ He shall cover you with His feathers,
   and under His wings you shall find protection;
   His faithfulness shall be your shield and wall.
⁵ You shall not be afraid of the terror by night,
   nor of the arrow that flies by day;
⁶ nor of the pestilence that pursues in darkness,
   nor of the destruction that strikes at noonday.
⁷ A thousand may fall at your side
   and ten thousand at your right hand,
   but it shall not come near you.
⁸ Only with your eyes shall you behold
   and see the reward of the wicked.

⁹ Because you have made the Lord, who is my refuge,
   even the Most High, your dwelling,
¹⁰ there shall be no evil befall you,
   neither shall any plague come near your tent;
¹¹ for He shall give His angels charge over you
   to guard you in all your ways.
¹² They shall bear you up in their hands,
   lest you strike your foot against a stone.
¹³ You shall tread upon the lion and adder;
   the young lion and the serpent you shall trample underfoot.

¹⁴ Because he has set his love upon Me, therefore I will
   deliver him;
   I will set him on high, because he has known
   My name.
¹⁵ He shall call upon Me, and I will answer him;
   I will be with him in trouble,
   and I will deliver him and honor him.
¹⁶ With long life I will satisfy him
   and show him My salvation.

PSALM 92
A Psalm. A Song for the Sabbath day.

¹ It is good to give thanks to the Lord,
   and to sing praises unto Your name, O Most High:
² to declare forth Your lovingkindness in the morning
   and Your faithfulness in the night,
³ on a ten-stringed lute and on the harp,
   and on the lyre with a solemn sound.

⁴ For you, O Lord, have made me glad through Your work;
   I will sing joyfully at the works of Your hands.
⁵ O Lord, how great are Your works!
   Your thoughts are very deep!
⁶ A brutish man does not recognize,
   neither does the fool understand this.
⁷ Though the wicked spring up as the grass
   and all those who do iniquity flourish,
   they shall be destroyed forever:

⁸ But You, O Lord, are on high forever.

⁹ For Your enemies, O Lord,
   for Your enemies shall perish;
   all those who do iniquity shall be scattered.
¹⁰ But my horn You have exalted like the horn of the wild ox;
   You have anointed me with fresh oil.
¹¹ My eyes also shall see the downfall of my enemies,
   and my ears shall hear the doom of my wicked adversaries.

¹² The righteous shall flourish like the palm tree
   and grow like a cedar in Lebanon.
¹³ Those that are planted in the house of the Lord
   shall flourish in the courts of our God.
¹⁴ They shall still bring forth fruit in old age;
   they shall be filled with vitality and foliage,
¹⁵ to show that the Lord is upright;
   He is my rock, and there is no unrighteousness in Him.

PSALM 93

¹ The Lord reigns; He is robed in majesty;
   the Lord is robed; He has put on strength as His belt.
   Indeed, the world is established;
   it cannot be moved.
² Your throne is established of old;
   You are from everlasting.

³ The floods have lifted up, O Lord,
   the floods have lifted up their voice;
   the floods lift up their roaring waves.
⁴ The Lord on high is mightier than the noise of
   many waters,
   yes, than the mighty waves of the sea.

⁵ Your statutes are very sure;
   holiness is becoming to Your house,
   O Lord, forever.

PSALM 94

¹ O Lord God, to whom vengeance belongs;
   O God to whom vengeance belongs, shine forth.
² Rise up, O Judge of the earth;
   render to the proud what they deserve.
³ O Lord, how long shall the wicked,
   how long shall the wicked triumph?

⁴ They spew forth their arrogant words;
   all those who do iniquity boast.
⁵ They break in pieces Your people, O Lord,
   and afflict Your inheritance.
⁶ They kill the widow and the sojourner,
   and murder the fatherless.

7 Yet they say, "The Lord does not see,
  neither does the God of Jacob regard it."

8 Understand, you brutish among the people;
  fools, when will you be wise?
9 He who made the ear, shall He not hear?
  He who formed the eye, shall He not see?
10 He who chastises the nations, shall He not correct?
  He teaches people knowledge!
11 The Lord, He knows the thoughts of people,
  that they are a breath.

12 Blessed is the man whom You chasten, O Lord,
  and teach from Your law,
13 that You may give him rest from the days of adversity,
  until a pit is dug for the wicked.
14 For the Lord will not forsake His people;
  neither will He abandon His inheritance.
15 But justice shall return to those who are righteous,
  and all the upright in heart shall follow it.

16 Who will rise up for me against the wicked?
  Who will stand up for me against those who
    do iniquity?
17 Unless the Lord had been my help,
  my soul would have lived in the land of
    silent death.
18 When I said, "My foot slips,"
  Your mercy, O Lord, held me up.
19 When there is a multitude of worries within me,
  Your comforts delight my soul.

20 Shall wicked rulers, who make oppressive laws,
  align with You?
21 They conspire together against the life of the righteous
  and condemn innocent blood to death.
22 But the Lord is my defense,
  and my God is the rock of my refuge.
23 He shall bring upon them their own iniquity
  and shall cut them off for their own wickedness;
  yes, the Lord our God shall destroy them.

PSALM 95

1 O come, let us sing unto the Lord;
  let us make a joyful noise to the rock of our salvation!
2 Let us come before His presence with thanksgiving;
  let us make a joyful noise unto Him with psalms!

3 For the Lord is a great God,
  and a great King above all gods.
4 In His hand are the deep places of the earth;
  the heights of the mountains are also His.
5 The sea is His, for He made it,
  and His hands formed the dry land.

6 O come, let us worship and bow down;
  let us kneel before the Lord, our Maker.
7 For He is our God,
  and we are the people of His pasture
  and the sheep of His hand.

  Today if you hear His voice,
8 do not harden your hearts, as at Meribah,
  and as in the day of Massah in the wilderness,
9 when your fathers tested Me and tried Me,
  though they had seen My deeds.
10 For forty years I loathed that generation
  and said, "They are a people who go astray in
    their heart,
  and they have not known My ways."
11 Therefore I swore in My wrath,
  "They shall not enter into My rest."

PSALM 96
1Ch 16:23–33

1 O sing unto the Lord a new song;
  sing unto the Lord, all the earth!
2 Sing unto the Lord, bless His name;
  declare His salvation from day to day.
3 Proclaim His glory among the nations,
  His wonders among all peoples.

4 For the Lord is great, and greatly to be praised;
  He is to be feared above all gods.
5 For all the gods of the nations are worthless,
  but the Lord made the heavens.
6 Honor and majesty are before Him;
  strength and beauty are in His sanctuary.

7 Give unto the Lord, O families of the people,
  give unto the Lord glory and strength.
8 Give unto the Lord the glory due His name;
  bring an offering, and come into His courts.
9 Worship the Lord in the beauty of holiness;
  tremble before Him, all the earth.
10 Say among the nations, "The Lord reigns!
  Indeed, the world is established; it shall not be moved;
  He shall judge the peoples righteously."

11 Let the heavens rejoice, and let the earth be glad;
  let the sea roar, and all that fills it;
12 let the field be joyful, and all that is in it;
  then all the trees of the forests shall rejoice
13 before the Lord, for He comes,
  for He comes to judge the earth.
  He shall judge the world with righteousness
  and the peoples with His faithfulness.

PSALM 97

1 The Lord reigns; let the earth rejoice;
  let the many coastlands be glad!
2 Clouds and darkness are all around Him;
  righteousness and justice are the foundation of His throne.
3 A fire goes before Him
  and burns up His enemies all around.
4 His lightning bolts light up the world;
  the earth sees and shakes.
5 The mountains melt like wax at the presence of the Lord,
  at the presence of the Lord of the earth.
6 The heavens declare His righteousness,
  and all the peoples see His glory.

7 All who serve graven images are ashamed,
  who boast in worthless idols;
  worship Him, all you gods.

8 Zion hears and is glad,
  and the daughters of Judah rejoice
  because of Your judgments, O Lord.
9 For You, O Lord, are Most High above all the earth;
  You are exalted far above all gods.
10 You who love the Lord, hate evil!
  He preserves the lives of His devoted ones;
  He delivers them from the hand of the wicked.
11 Light goes out for the righteous,
  and gladness for the upright in heart.
12 Rejoice in the Lord, you righteous,
  and give thanks at the memory of His holy name.

PSALM 98
A Psalm.

1 Oh, sing to the Lord a new song,
  for He has done marvelous deeds!

His right hand and His holy arm
  have accomplished deliverance.
2 The Lord has made known His salvation;
  His righteousness He has revealed in the sight of
    the nations.
3 He has remembered His mercy
  and His faithfulness toward the house of Israel;
all the ends of the earth have seen
  the deliverance of our God.

4 Make a joyful noise unto the Lord, all the earth;
  break out in loud songs, and sing praises.
5 Sing unto the Lord with the harp,
  with the harp and the sound of melody,
6 with trumpets and sound of the horn;
  make a joyful noise before the Lord, the King.

7 Let the sea roar, and all that fills it,
  the world and those who live in it;
8 let the rivers clap their hands;
  let the hills be joyful together
9 before the Lord,
  for He is coming to judge the earth.
With righteousness He will judge the world,
  and the peoples with justice.

PSALM 99

1 The Lord reigns;
  let the peoples tremble!
 He sits enthroned between the cherubim;
  let the earth shake.
2 The Lord is great in Zion;
  He is high above all the peoples.
3 Let them praise Your great and awesome name—
  He is holy!

4 The King's strength loves justice;
  You establish righteousness,
and You execute judgment
  and fairness in Jacob.
5 Exalt the Lord our God,
  and worship at His footstool—
  He is holy!

6 Moses and Aaron were among His priests,
  even Samuel was among them who called upon His name;
they called upon the Lord,
  and He answered them.
7 He spoke to them in the pillar of cloud;
  they kept His statues and the ordinance that He gave them.

8 You answered them,
  O Lord our God;
You were a God who forgave them,
  though You took vengeance on their wrongdoing.
9 Exalt the Lord our God,
  and worship at His holy mountain;
for the Lord our God is holy!

PSALM 100
A Psalm of thanksgiving.

1 Make a joyful noise unto the Lord, all the earth!
2 Serve the Lord with gladness;
  come before His presence with singing.
3 Know that the Lord, He is God;
  it is He who has made us, and not we ourselves;
  we are His people, and the sheep of His pasture.

4 Enter into His gates with thanksgiving,
  and into His courts with praise;
  be thankful to Him, and bless His name.

5 For the Lord is good; His mercy endures forever,
  and His faithfulness to all generations.

PSALM 101
A Psalm of David.

1 I will sing of mercy and justice;
  to You, O Lord, I will sing.
2 I will consider the path that is blameless.
  When will You come to me?

I will walk within my house
  with a perfect heart.
3 I will set no wicked thing
  before my eyes.

I hate the work of those who turn aside;
  it shall not have part of me.
4 A perverted heart shall be far from me;
  I will not know anything wicked.

5 Whoever privately slanders his neighbor,
  him I will destroy;
whoever has a haughty look and a proud heart
  I will not endure.

6 My eyes shall be favorable to the faithful in
    the land,
  that they may live with me;
he who walks in a blameless manner,
  he shall serve me.

7 He who practices deceit
  shall not dwell within my house;
he who tells lies
  shall not remain in my sight.

8 Every morning I will destroy
  all the wicked in the land,
that I may cut off all wicked doers
  from the city of the Lord.

PSALM 102
A Prayer of one afflicted, when he is
overwhelmed and pours out his
complaint before the Lord.

1 Hear my prayer, O Lord,
  and let my cry come unto You.
2 Do not hide Your face from me
  in the day when I am in trouble;
incline Your ear to me;
  in the day when I call answer me quickly.

3 For my days are consumed like smoke,
  and my bones are burned as a furnace.
4 My heart is struck down and withered like grass,
  so that I forget to eat my bread.
5 Because of the sound of my groaning
  my bones cling to my skin.
6 I am like an owl of the wilderness,
  like a screech owl of the desert.
7 I stay awake and am
  as a sparrow alone upon the housetop.
8 My enemies reproach me all the day,
  and those who taunt me curse my name.
9 For I have eaten ashes like bread
  and mixed my drink with weeping,
10 because of Your indignation and Your wrath,
  for You have lifted me up, and cast me down.
11 My days are like an evening shadow that vanishes,
  and I wither away like grass.

¹² But You, O Lord, shall endure forever enthroned
    and Your reputation to all generations.
¹³ You shall arise, and have mercy upon Zion,
    for the time to favor her,
    indeed, the appointed time has come.
¹⁴ For Your servants take pleasure in her stones,
    and have pity on her dust.
¹⁵ So the nations shall fear the name of the Lord,
    and all the kings of the earth Your glory.
¹⁶ For the Lord shall build up Zion;
    He shall appear in His glory.
¹⁷ He will regard the prayer of the destitute
    and will not despise their prayer.

¹⁸ Let this be written for the generation to come,
    that a people who shall be created shall praise the Lord.
¹⁹ For He has looked down from the height of His sanctuary;
    from heaven the Lord looked down on the earth,
²⁰ to hear the groaning of the prisoners
    and to set free those who are appointed to death,
²¹ that they may declare the name of the Lord in Zion
    and His praise in Jerusalem;
²² when the peoples are gathered together,
    and the kingdoms, to serve the Lord.

²³ He has weakened my strength in my midlife;
    He has shortened my days.
²⁴ I said,
    "O my God, do not take me away in the midst of my days—
    Your years endure throughout all generations."
²⁵ From before You have laid the foundation of the earth,
    and the heavens are the work of Your hands.
²⁶ They shall perish, but You shall endure;
    indeed, all of them shall wear out like a garment;
    like a robe You shall change them,
    and they shall pass away,
²⁷ but You are the same,
    and Your years shall have no end.
²⁸ The children of Your servants shall be secure,
    and their offspring shall be established before You.

PSALM 103
A Psalm of David.

¹ Bless the Lord, O my soul,
    and all that is within me, bless His holy name.
² Bless the Lord, O my soul,
    and forget not all His benefits,
³ who forgives all your iniquities,
    who heals all your diseases,
⁴ who redeems your life from the pit,
    who crowns you with lovingkindness and tender mercies,
⁵ who satisfies your mouth with good things,
    so that your youth is renewed like the eagle's.

⁶ The Lord does righteousness
    and justice for all who are oppressed.

⁷ He made known His ways to Moses,
    His acts to the people of Israel.
⁸ The Lord is merciful and gracious,
    slow to anger, and abounding in mercy.
⁹ He will not always accuse,
    neither will He keep his anger forever.
¹⁰ He does not treat us according to our sins,
    nor repay us according to our iniquities.
¹¹ For as the heavens are high above the earth,
    so great is His mercy toward those who fear Him;
¹² as far as the east is from the west,
    so far has He removed our transgressions from us.
¹³ Like a father shows compassion to his children,
    so the Lord gives compassion to those who fear Him.

¹⁴ For He knows how we are formed;
    He remembers that we are dust.
¹⁵ As for man, his days are as grass;
    as a flower of the field he flourishes.
¹⁶ For the *hot* wind passes over it, and it is gone;
    the place where it was is not known.
¹⁷ But the mercy of the Lord
    is from everlasting to everlasting
    upon those who fear Him,
    and His righteousness to children's children,
¹⁸ to those who keep His covenant,
    and to those who remember to do His commandments.

¹⁹ The Lord has established His throne in the heavens,
    and His kingdom rules over all.

²⁰ Bless the Lord, you His angels,
    who are mighty, and do His commands,
    and obey the voice of His word.
²¹ Bless the Lord, all you His hosts;
    you servants who do His pleasure.
²² Bless the Lord, all His works,
    in all places of His dominion.

Bless the Lord, O my soul!

PSALM 104

¹ Bless the Lord, O my soul!

O Lord my God, You are very great!
    You are clothed with honor and majesty,
² covering Yourself with light as a garment,
    who stretches out the heavens like a tent curtain,
³ who lays the upper beams of His chambers on the
        waters above,
    who makes the clouds His chariot,
    who rides upon the wings of the wind,
⁴ who makes His angels as winds,
    His ministers a flaming fire.

⁵ You laid the earth on its foundations,
    so that it should never be moved.
⁶ You covered it with the deep as a garment;
    the waters stood above the mountains.
⁷ At Your rebuke they fled;
    at the sound of Your thunder they departed away.
⁸ The mountains rose up;
    the valleys went down
    to the place that You appointed them.
⁹ You set a boundary that they may not pass over,
    that they may not again cover the earth.

¹⁰ You send the springs to gush forth in the valleys,
    which flow between the hills.
¹¹ They give drink to every animal of the field;
    the wild donkeys quench their thirst.
¹² By them the birds of the heavens have their habitation;
    they sing among the branches.
¹³ You water the mountains from Your lofty chamber;
    the earth is satisfied with the fruit of Your works.
¹⁴ You cause the grass to grow for the cattle
    and plants for the cultivation of man,
    that he may bring forth food from the earth
¹⁵ and wine that makes glad the heart of man,
    and oil that makes shine his face,
    and bread that strengthens his heart.
¹⁶ The trees of the Lord are well watered,
    the cedars of Lebanon that He has planted,
¹⁷ where the birds make their nests,
    where the stork has its home in the fir trees.
¹⁸ The high mountains are for the wild goats,
    and the rocks a refuge for the badgers.

¹⁹ He set the moon to mark the appointed seasons;
    the sun knows its time for going down.
²⁰ You make darkness, and it is night,
    when all the animals of the forest go forth.
²¹ The young lions roar after their prey
    and seek their food from God.
²² When the sun arises, they gather themselves together
    and lay down in their dens.
²³ Man goes forth to his work
    and to his labor until the evening.

²⁴ O Lord, how manifold are Your works!
    With wisdom You have made them all;
    the earth is full of Your creatures—
²⁵ so is this great and wide sea,
    which is full of innumerable creatures,
    living animals both small and great.
²⁶ There go the ships,
    and there is Leviathan, which You have made
        to play in it.

²⁷ These all wait upon You,
    that You may give them their food in due season.
²⁸ When You give it to them,
    they gather it;
    when You open Your hand,
    they are filled with good food.
²⁹ When You hide Your face,
    they are troubled;
You take away their breath,
    and they die and return to their dust.
³⁰ When You send forth Your Spirit,
    they are created,
    and You renew the surface of the ground.

³¹ May the glory of the Lord endure forever;
    may the Lord rejoice in His works.
³² He looks on the earth, and it trembles;
    He touches the mountains, and they smoke.

³³ I will sing unto the Lord as long as I live;
    I will sing praise to my God while I have my being.
³⁴ May my meditation be sweet to Him,
    for I will be glad in the Lord.
³⁵ Let sinners be consumed from the earth,
    and let the wicked be no more.

Bless the Lord, O my soul!

Praise the Lord!

PSALM 105
1Ch 16:8–22

¹ Oh, give thanks unto the Lord; call upon His name;
    make known His deeds among the peoples.
² Sing unto Him, sing praises unto Him;
    proclaim all His wondrous works.
³ Glory in His holy name;
    let the heart rejoice for those who seek the Lord.
⁴ Seek the Lord and His strength;
    seek His presence continuously.

⁵ Remember His marvelous works that He has done;
    His wonders and the judgments from His mouth,
⁶ O offspring of Abraham, His servant,
    O children of Jacob, His chosen ones.
⁷ He is the Lord our God;
    His judgments are in all the earth.

⁸ He remembers His covenant forever,
    the word that He commanded, to a thousand generations,

⁹ that covenant He made with Abraham,
    and His oath to Isaac,
¹⁰ and confirmed to Jacob as a decree,
    and to Israel for an everlasting covenant,
¹¹ saying, "To you I will give the land of Canaan
    as the portion of your inheritance."

¹² When they were but a few people in number,
    indeed, very few, and strangers in it,
¹³ when they went from one nation to another,
    from one kingdom to another people,
¹⁴ He did not permit anyone to do them wrong;
    indeed, He reproved kings on their behalf,
¹⁵ saying, "Do not touch my anointed ones,
    and do no harm to my prophets."

¹⁶ Moreover He called for a famine upon the land;
    He broke the whole supply of bread.
¹⁷ He sent a man before them,
    Joseph, who was sold as a slave.
¹⁸ They hurt his feet with fetters;
    his neck was put in an iron collar.
¹⁹ Until the time that his word came to pass,
    the word of the Lord tested him.
²⁰ The king sent and released him;
    the ruler of the people let him go free.
²¹ He made Joseph lord of his house
    and ruler of all his possessions,
²² to imprison his princes at Joseph's pleasure
    and to teach his elders wisdom.

²³ Then Israel came into Egypt,
    and Jacob sojourned in the land of Ham.
²⁴ The Lord increased His people greatly
    and made them stronger than their enemies.
²⁵ He turned their hearts to hate His people,
    to deal cleverly with His servants.
²⁶ He sent Moses, His servant,
    and Aaron whom He had chosen.
²⁷ They showed His signs among them
    and wonders in the land of Ham.
²⁸ He sent darkness and made the land dark,
    and Moses and Aaron did not rebel against
        His word.
²⁹ He turned their waters into blood
    and caused their fish to die.
³⁰ Their land brought forth frogs in abundance,
    even in the chambers of their kings.
³¹ He spoke, and there came swarms of flies
    and gnats in all their country.
³² He gave them hail for rain
    and flaming lightning in their land.
³³ He struck their vines and their fig trees
    and shattered the trees of their country.
³⁴ He spoke, and the locusts came,
    and caterpillars without number,
³⁵ that devoured all the vegetation in their land,
    and ate all the fruit of their ground.
³⁶ He struck down all the firstborn in their land,
    the first fruits of all their strength.
³⁷ Then He brought them out with silver and gold,
    and no one among their tribes faltered.
³⁸ Egypt was glad when they left,
    for the fear of Israel fell upon them.

³⁹ He spread a cloud for a covering,
    and fire to give light in the night.
⁴⁰ The people asked, and He brought quail,
    and satisfied them with abundant bread
        of heaven.
⁴¹ He opened the rock, and the waters gushed out;
    they ran in the desert like a river.

42 For he recalled His holy promise
    to Abraham His servant.
43 He brought forth His people with joy,
    and His chosen ones with gladness,
44 and gave them the lands of the nations,
    and they took possession of the fruitful labor of the people,
45 that they might observe His statutes
    and keep His laws.

Praise the Lord!

PSALM 106
1Ch 16:34–36

1 Praise the Lord!

Oh, give thanks unto the Lord, for He is good,
    for His mercy endures forever.
2 Who can recount the mighty acts of the Lord
    or declare all His praise?
3 Blessed are those who keep justice
    and who do righteousness at all times.

4 Remember me, O Lord, when You give favor to Your people;
    visit me with Your deliverance,
5 that I may see the goodness over Your chosen ones,
    that I may rejoice in the gladness of Your nation,
    that I may glory with Your inheritance.

6 We have sinned with our fathers;
    we have committed iniquity; we have done wickedly.
7 Our fathers did not consider
    Your wonders in Egypt;
    they did not remember the greatness of Your mercy,
    but rebelled against Him at the sea, by the Red Sea.
8 Nevertheless He saved them for His name's sake,
    that He might make His mighty power known.
9 He rebuked the Red Sea, and it was dried up,
    so He led them through the depths as through
        the wilderness.
10 He saved them from the hand of him who hated them
    and redeemed them from the hand of the enemy.
11 The waters covered their enemies;
    there was not one of them left.
12 Then they believed His words;
    they sang His praise.

13 But they soon forgot His works;
    they did not wait for His counsel,
14 but they lusted exceedingly in the wilderness
    and tested God in the desert.
15 He gave them their request,
    but He sent a wasting disease on them.

16 They envied in the camp Moses
    and Aaron, the holy priest of the Lord.
17 The earth opened and swallowed up Dathan
    and engulfed those led by Abiram.
18 A fire broke out among their company;
    the flame burned up the wicked.
19 They made a calf at Horeb,
    and worshipped the molded image.
20 Thus they changed the glory of God
    for the image of an ox that eats grass.
21 They forgot God, their Deliverer,
    who had done great things in Egypt,
22 wondrous works in the land of Ham,
    and marvelous deeds by the Red Sea.
23 Therefore He said that He would destroy them,
    had not Moses, His chosen one,
    stood before Him to intercede,
    to turn away His wrath from destroying them.

24 Then they despised the pleasant land;
    they did not believe His promise,
25 but they grumbled in their tents,
    and did not listen to the voice of the Lord.
26 Therefore He lifted up His hand against them
    and swore to overthrow them in the wilderness,
27 and to overthrow their offspring among the nations,
    and to scatter them in the lands.

28 They joined themselves to Baal of Peor
    and ate the sacrifices given for the dead.
29 Thus they provoked Him to anger with their acts,
    and a plague broke out upon them.
30 Then Phinehas stood up and interceded,
    and so the plague ceased.
31 That was counted unto him for righteousness
    unto all generations forever.
32 They angered Him also at the waters of Meribah,
    so that Moses suffered because of them,
33 because they provoked his temper,
    so that he spoke impulsively with his lips.

34 They did not destroy the nations
    as the Lord commanded them,
35 but they mixed among the nations
    and learned their deeds;
36 they served their idols,
    which were a snare to them.
37 Yes, they sacrificed their sons
    and their daughters to demons,
38 and poured out innocent blood,
    even the blood of their sons and of their daughters,
    whom they sacrificed to the idols of Canaan,
    and the land was polluted with blood.
39 Thus were they defiled by their acts
    and acted like whores with these actions.

40 Therefore the wrath of the Lord was kindled against His people,
    and He abhorred His own inheritance.
41 He gave them into the hand of the nations,
    and those who hated them ruled over them.
42 Their enemies also oppressed them,
    and Israel was brought into subjection under their
        powerful hand.
43 Many times He delivered them,
    but they were rebellious against Him with their counsel,
    and were afflicted for their iniquity.
44 Nevertheless, He regarded their affliction,
    when He heard their cry:
45 and He remembered on their behalf His covenant
    and relented according to the greatness of His mercies.
46 He made them pitied
    among all those who held them captive.

47 Save us, O Lord our God,
    and gather us from among the nations,
    to give thanks unto Your holy name
    and to boast in Your praise.

48 Blessed be the Lord God of Israel,
    from everlasting to everlasting,
    and let all the people say, "Amen!"

Praise the Lord!

BOOK FIVE
Psalms 107–150

PSALM 107
1 Oh, give thanks unto the Lord, for He is good,
    for His mercy endures forever!

2 Let the redeemed of the Lord speak out,
whom He has redeemed from the hand of the enemy,
3 and gathered them from the lands,
from the east and from the west, from the north and from
the south.

4 They wandered in the wilderness on a deserted path;
they found no city to dwell in.
5 Hungry and thirsty,
their soul fainted in them.
6 Then they cried unto the Lord in their trouble,
and He delivered them out of their distresses.
7 He led them on a level road,
that they might go to a city to live in.
8 Let them praise the Lord for His goodness
and for His wonderful works to the people!
9 For He satisfies the longing soul
and fills the hungry soul with goodness.

10 Some sit in darkness and in the shadow of death,
being prisoners in affliction and irons,
11 because they rebelled against the words of God
and rejected the counsel of the Most High.
12 Therefore He brought down their hearts with *hard* labor;
they fell down, and there was none to help.
13 Then they cried unto the Lord in their trouble,
and He delivered them out of their distress.
14 He brought them out of darkness and the shadow of death
and broke apart their bonds.
15 Let them praise the Lord for His goodness
and for His wonderful works to the people!
16 For He has broken the gates of bronze
and cut the bars of iron in two.

17 Some were fools because of their transgressions,
and because of their iniquities they are afflicted.
18 They loathed all manner of food,
and they drew near to the gates of death.
19 Then they cried unto the Lord in their trouble,
and He saved them out of their distress.
20 He sent His word and healed them
and delivered them from their destruction.
21 Let them praise the Lord for His goodness
and for His wonderful works to the people!
22 And let them offer the sacrifices of thanksgiving
and declare His works with rejoicing.

23 Some went down to the sea in ships,
to do business in the vast waters;
24 they saw the works of the Lord
and His wonders in the deep water.
25 For He commands and raises the stormy wind,
which lifts up the sea waves.
26 The *sailors* went up to the sky, they came down to the depths;
their strength melted because of the great danger.
27 They reeled to and fro and staggered like drunken men,
and were completely confused.
28 Then they cried out to the Lord in their trouble,
and He saved them out of their distress.
29 He made the storm calm,
and the sea waves were still.
30 They were glad because the waters were quiet,
so He brought them to their desired harbor.
31 Let them praise the Lord for His goodness
and for His wonderful works to the people!
32 Let them exalt Him in the congregation of the people,
and praise him in the assembly of the elders.

33 He turns rivers into a desert,
water springs into dry ground,
34 a fruitful land into salty wasteland,
because of the wickedness of those living there.

35 He turns a wilderness into pools of water,
a parched ground into springs of water.
36 There He makes the hungry dwell,
and they prepare a city to live in;
37 they sow fields and plant vineyards,
and yield a fruitful harvest.
38 He blesses them, so that they are greatly multiplied,
and He does not let their livestock decrease.

39 But when they are diminished and brought down
through oppression, affliction, and sorrow,
40 He pours contempt upon princes,
and causes them to wander in a wilderness with
no road;
41 yet He raises up the poor from affliction
and cares for their families like flocks of sheep.
42 The righteous shall see it and rejoice,
and all evil people shall stop their mouth.

43 Whoever is wise let him observe these things;
let them consider the lovingkindness of the Lord.

PSALM 108

Ps 57:7–11; 60:5–12
A Song. A Psalm of David.

1 O God, my heart is determined;
I will sing and give praise with my whole heart.
2 Awake, O lyre and harp!
I will awake at dawn!
3 I will praise you, O Lord, among the peoples,
and I will sing praises unto You among the nations.
4 For Your mercy is great above the heavens;
Your faithfulness reaches to the clouds.
5 Be exalted, O God, above the heavens,
may Your glory be above all the earth.

6 That Your beloved ones may be delivered,
provide salvation with Your right hand and answer me.
7 God has spoken in His sanctuary:
"I will triumph and will divide up Shechem
and portion out the Valley of Sukkoth.
8 Gilead is Mine; Manasseh is Mine;
Ephraim is My helmet;
Judah is My royal scepter;
9 Moab is My washbasin;
on Edom I throw My shoe;
over Philistia I shout in triumph."

10 Who will bring me into the fortified city?
Who will lead me into Edom?
11 Have You not rejected us, O God?
You surely do not go out, O God, with our armies.
12 Grant us help against the foe,
for the help of man is worthless.
13 Through God we shall be valiant,
for He shall tread down our enemies.

PSALM 109

For the Music Director. A Psalm of David.

1 Do not remain silent,
O God of my praise!
2 For the mouth of the wicked and deceitful
are opened against me;
they have spoken against me with a lying tongue.
3 They encircled me with words of hatred
and fought against me without cause.
4 In return for my love they are my adversaries,
but I give myself to prayer.
5 They have rewarded me evil for good
and hatred for my love.

6 Set a wicked man against him,
and let an accuser stand at his right hand.
7 When he shall be judged, let him be condemned,
and let his prayer be reckoned as sin.
8 Let his days be few,
and let another take his office.
9 Let his children be fatherless
and his wife a widow.
10 Let his children be wandering beggars;
let them seek their bread far from their desolate places.
11 Let the creditor seize all that he has;
let the strangers plunder the fruit of his labor.
12 Let there be none to extend mercy unto him,
neither let there be any to pity his fatherless children.
13 Let his posterity be cut off,
and in the generation following let his name be blotted out.
14 Let the iniquity of his fathers be remembered with the Lord,
and let not the sin of his mother be blotted out.
15 Let them be before the Lord continually,
that the Lord may cut off the memory of them from
the earth.

16 For he did not remember to show kindness,
but pursued the poor and needy and broken-hearted
to their death.
17 As he loved cursing,
so let it come over him;
as he did not delight in blessing,
so let it be far from him.
18 As he clothed himself with cursing like a garment,
so let it soak into him like water,
and like oil into his bones.
19 Let it be unto him as the garment that covers him,
and a belt that he continually wears.
20 Let this be the reward of my adversaries from the Lord,
and of those who speak evil against my soul.

21 But You, O God my Lord,
work on my behalf for your name's sake;
because your mercy is good, deliver me.
22 For I am poor and needy,
and my heart is wounded within me.
23 I am gone like a shadow in the evening;
I am tossed as the locust.
24 My knees are weak through fasting,
and my body is thin with no fat.
25 I am a reproach to my accusers;
when they look upon me, they shake their heads.

26 Help me, O Lord my God!
Save me according to Your mercy,
27 that they may know that this is by Your hand,
that You, O Lord, have done it.
28 Let them curse, but You will bless;
when they arise, let them be ashamed,
but let Your servant rejoice.
29 Let my adversaries be clothed with shame,
and let them cover themselves with their own disgrace like
a cloak.

30 I will greatly praise the Lord with my mouth;
indeed, I will praise Him among the multitude.
31 For He stands at the right hand of the poor,
to save him from those who condemn his soul to death.

PSALM 110
A Psalm of David.

1 The Lord said to my lord,
"Sit at My right hand,
until I make your enemies
your footstool."

2 The Lord shall send your mighty scepter out of Zion;
rule in the midst of your enemies.
3 Your people will follow you
in the day of your battle;
on the holy mountains
at dawn of the morning,
the dew of your youth belongs to you.

4 The Lord has sworn
and will not change,
"You are a priest forever
after the order of Melchizedek."

5 The Lord is at your right hand;
He shall strike down kings in the day of His wrath.
6 He shall judge among the nations; He shall fill them with
dead bodies;
He shall scatter heads all over the land.
7 He shall drink of the brook in the path;
then He shall lift up the head.

PSALM 111

1 Praise the Lord!

I will praise the Lord with my whole heart,
in the assembly of the upright, and in the congregation.

2 The works of the Lord are great,
sought out by all who have pleasure in them.
3 His work is honorable and glorious,
and His righteousness endures forever.
4 He has made His wonderful works to be remembered;
the Lord is gracious and full of compassion.
5 He has given food to those who fear Him;
He will ever be mindful of His covenant.

6 He has shown His people the power of His works,
that He may give them the inheritance of
the nations.
7 The works of His hands are true and just;
all His commands are sure.
8 They stand forever and ever,
and are done in truth and uprightness.
9 He sent redemption to His people;
He has commanded His covenant forever;
holy and fearful is His name.

10 The fear of the Lord is the beginning of wisdom;
all who live it have insight.
His praise endures forever!

PSALM 112

1 Praise the Lord!

Blessed is the man who fears the Lord,
who delights greatly in His commandments.

2 His offspring shall be mighty in the land;
the generation of the upright shall be blessed.
3 Wealth and riches shall be in his house,
and his righteousness endures forever.
4 To the upright there arises light in the darkness;
he is gracious, and full of compassion, and righteous.
5 A good man shows generous favor, and lends;
he will guide his affairs with justice.

6 Surely the righteous man shall not be moved;
the righteous shall be in everlasting remembrance.
7 He shall not be afraid of evil tidings;
his heart is fixed, trusting in the Lord.
8 His heart is established; he shall not be afraid,
until he sees triumph upon his enemies.

9 He has given away freely; he has given to the poor;
   his righteousness endures forever;
   his horn shall be exalted with honor.

10 The wicked shall see it and be grieved;
   he shall gnash his teeth and melt away;
   the desire of the wicked shall perish.

PSALM 113

1 Praise the LORD!

 Praise, O you servants of the LORD,
   praise the name of the LORD.
2 Blessed be the name of the LORD
   from this time forth and for evermore.
3 From the rising of the sun to its going down,
   the LORD's name is to be praised.

4 The LORD is high above all nations,
   and His glory above the heavens.
5 Who is like the LORD our God,
   who dwells on high,
6 who looks down on the things
   that are in heaven and on the earth?

7 He raises up the poor out of the dust
   and lifts the needy out of the ash heap,
8 to make them sit with princes,
   even with the princes of His people.
9 He gives the barren woman a dwelling,
   making her the joyful mother of children.

 Praise the LORD!

PSALM 114

1 When Israel went out of Egypt,
   the house of Jacob from a people of strange language,
2 Judah was His sanctuary,
   and Israel His dominion.

3 The sea saw it and fled;
   the Jordan was driven back;
4 the mountains skipped like rams
   and the hills like lambs.

5 What alarmed you, O sea, that you fled,
   O Jordan, that you turned back,
6 O mountains, that you skipped like rams,
   O hills, like lambs?

7 Tremble, O earth, at the presence of the Lord,
   at the presence of the God of Jacob
8 who turned the rock into a pool of water,
   the hard stone into a spring of waters.

PSALM 115
Ps 135:15–20

1 Not unto us, O LORD, not unto us,
   but unto Your name give glory,
   for the sake of Your mercy, and for the sake of Your truth.

2 Why should the nations say,
   "Where now is their God?"
3 But our God is in the heavens;
   He does whatever He pleases.
4 Their idols are silver and gold,
   the work of men's hands.
5 They have mouths, but they cannot speak;
   eyes, but they cannot see;
6 they have ears, but they cannot hear;
   noses, but they cannot smell;

7 they have hands, but they cannot feel;
   feet, but they cannot walk;
   neither can they speak with their throat.
8 Those who make them are like them;
   so is everyone who trusts in them.

9 O Israel, trust in the LORD;
   He is their help and their shield.
10 O house of Aaron, trust in the LORD;
   He is their help and their shield.
11 You who fear the LORD, trust in the LORD;
   He is their help and their shield.

12 The LORD has been mindful of us; He will bless us;
   He will bless the house of Israel;
   He will bless the house of Aaron.
13 He will bless those who fear the LORD,
   both the small and great ones.

14 The LORD shall increase you more and more,
   you and your children.
15 You are blessed of the LORD,
   who made heaven and earth.

16 The heavens belong to the LORD,
   but the earth He has given to the children
   of men.
17 The dead do not praise the LORD,
   nor do any who go down into silence.
18 But we will bless the LORD
   from this time and for evermore.

 Praise the LORD!

PSALM 116

1 I love the LORD, because He has heard my voice
   and my supplications.
2 Because He has inclined His ear to me,
   therefore I will call upon Him as long as I live.

3 The cords of death encircled me,
   and the pains of Sheol took hold of me;
   I found trouble and sorrow.
4 Then called I upon the name of the LORD:
   "O LORD, I plead with You, deliver my soul."

5 Gracious is the LORD, and righteous;
   indeed, our God is merciful.
6 The LORD protects the simple;
   I was brought low, and He helped me.

7 Return to your rest, O my soul;
   for the LORD has vindicated you.

8 For You have delivered my soul from death,
   my eyes from tears,
   and my feet from falling.
9 I will walk before the LORD
   in the land of the living.

10 I believed, indeed I have spoken:
   "I am greatly afflicted."
11 I said in my haste,
   "All men are liars."

12 What shall I render unto the LORD
   for all His benefits toward me?

13 I will take the cup of salvation
   and call upon the name of the LORD.
14 I will pay my vows unto the LORD
   now in the presence of all His people.

¹⁵ Precious in the sight of the Lord
      is the death of His godly ones.
¹⁶ O Lord, I am Your servant;
      I am Your servant, the son of Your female servant;
      You have loosed my bonds.

¹⁷ I will offer to You the sacrifice of thanksgiving
      and will call upon the name of the Lord.
¹⁸ I will pay my vows unto the Lord
      now in the presence of all His people,
¹⁹ in the courts of the house of the Lord,
      in your midst, O Jerusalem.

Praise the Lord!

PSALM 117

¹ Praise the Lord, all you nations!
      Exalt Him, all you peoples!
² For His merciful kindness is great toward us,
      and the faithfulness of the Lord endures forever.

Praise the Lord!

PSALM 118

¹ Oh, give thanks unto the Lord, for He is good,
      because His mercy endures forever.

² Let Israel say,
      "His mercy endures forever."
³ Let the house of Aaron say,
      "His mercy endures forever."
⁴ Let those who fear the Lord say,
      "His mercy endures forever."

⁵ I called upon the Lord from my distress;
      the Lord answered me and *set me* in an open place.
⁶ The Lord is on my side; I will not fear.
      What can people do to me?
⁷ The Lord is on my side to help me;
      I shall look in triumph upon those who hate me.

⁸ It is better to trust in the Lord
      than to put confidence in man.
⁹ It is better to trust in the Lord
      than to put confidence in princes.
¹⁰ All nations encircled me,
      but in the name of the Lord I will destroy them.
¹¹ They circled me; indeed, they surrounded me,
      but in the name of the Lord I will destroy them.
¹² They circled me like bees;
      they went forth as a fire over thorns,
      but in the name of the Lord I will destroy them.
¹³ You have pushed against me, that I was falling,
      but the Lord helped me.
¹⁴ The Lord is my strength and song;
      He has become my salvation.

¹⁵ The voice of rejoicing and salvation
      is in the tents of the righteous:
      "The right hand of the Lord is valiant.
¹⁶ The right hand of the Lord is exalted;
      the right hand of the Lord is valiant."
¹⁷ I shall not die, but I shall live
      and declare the works of the Lord.
¹⁸ The Lord has severely chastened me,
      but He has not given me over unto death.
¹⁹ Open to me the gates of righteousness;
      I will go into them, and I will praise the Lord.
²⁰ This is the gate of the Lord;
      the righteous shall enter through.
²¹ I will thank You that You have heard me
      and have become my deliverance.

²² The stone that the builders rejected
      has become the cornerstone.
²³ This is what the Lord has done;
      it is marvelous in our eyes.
²⁴ This is the day that the Lord has made;
      we will rejoice and be glad in it.

²⁵ Save us, we ask You, O Lord;
      O Lord, we ask You, send now success.

²⁶ Blessed be he that comes in the name of the Lord:
      we have blessed you out of the house of the Lord.
²⁷ The Lord is God,
      and He has shown us His light;
      bind the sacrifice with cords,
      even unto the horns of the altar.

²⁸ You are my God, and I will praise You;
      You are my God, I will exalt You.

²⁹ Oh, give thanks unto the Lord, for He is good,
      for His mercy endures forever.

PSALM 119

א ALEPH

¹ Blessed are those whose way is blameless,
      who walk in the law of the Lord.
² Blessed are those who keep His testimonies,
      and who seek Him with all their heart.
³ They also do no wrong;
      they walk in His ways.
⁴ You have commanded us
      to keep Your precepts diligently.
⁵ Oh, that my ways were established
      to keep Your statutes!
⁶ Then I shall not be ashamed,
      when I have my focus on all Your commandments.
⁷ I will praise You with an upright heart,
      when I have learned Your righteous judgments.
⁸ I will keep Your statutes;
      do not completely abandon me.

ב BETH

⁹ How shall a young man keep his way pure?
      By keeping it according to Your word.
¹⁰ With my whole heart I seek You;
      do not allow me to wander from Your commandments.
¹¹ Your word I have hidden in my heart,
      that I might not sin against You.
¹² Blessed are You, O Lord;
      teach me Your statutes.
¹³ With my lips I declare
      all the decrees of Your mouth.
¹⁴ I rejoice in the way of Your testimonies,
      as much as in all riches.
¹⁵ I will meditate on Your precepts
      and keep my eyes on Your ways.
¹⁶ I will delight in Your statutes;
      I will not forget Your word.

ג GIMEL

¹⁷ Deal kindly with Your servant, that I may live
      and keep Your word.
¹⁸ Open my eyes, that I may behold
      wondrous things from Your law.
¹⁹ I am a sojourner in the land;
      do not hide Your commandments from me.
²⁰ My soul is consumed all the time
      with a longing for Your decrees.
²¹ You have rebuked the proud, those cursed,
      who depart from Your commandments.

²² Remove from me reproach and contempt,
for I have kept Your testimonies.
²³ Even if princes sit and conspire against me,
Your servant will meditate on Your statutes.
²⁴ Your testimonies are my delight
and my counselors.

ד DALETH

²⁵ My soul clings to the dust;
revive me according to Your word.
²⁶ I have declared my ways, and You heard me;
teach me Your statutes.
²⁷ Make me to understand the way of Your precepts;
then I shall contemplate on Your wondrous works.
²⁸ My soul collapses on account of grief;
strengthen me according to Your word.
²⁹ Remove from me the way of falsehood,
and graciously grant me Your law.
³⁰ I have chosen the way of faithfulness;
Your judgments I have laid before me.
³¹ I have stayed with Your testimonies, O Lord;
may I not be put to shame.
³² I will run in the way of Your commandments,
when You set my heart free.

ה HE

³³ Teach me, O Lord, the way of Your statutes,
and I shall keep it to the end.
³⁴ Give me understanding, and I shall keep Your law
and observe it with my whole heart.
³⁵ Lead me in the path of Your commandments,
for I delight in them.
³⁶ Incline my heart unto Your testimonies,
and not for unjust gain.
³⁷ Turn away my eyes from beholding worthlessness,
and revive me in Your way.
³⁸ Establish Your word to Your servant,
so that You are feared.
³⁹ Turn away my reproach that I dread,
for Your judgments are good.
⁴⁰ Behold, I have a longing for Your precepts;
revive me in Your righteousness.

ו WAW

⁴¹ Let Your mercies come to me, O Lord,
even Your deliverance according to Your word.
⁴² So I shall have an answer for him who reproaches me,
for I trust in Your word.
⁴³ Do not take the word of truth out of my mouth,
for I have hoped in Your judgments.
⁴⁴ So I shall keep Your law continually,
forever and ever.
⁴⁵ I will walk in an open space,
for I seek Your precepts.
⁴⁶ I will speak of Your testimonies also before kings
and will not be ashamed.
⁴⁷ I will delight in Your commandments,
which I have loved.
⁴⁸ My hands I will lift up unto Your commandments, which I have loved;
I will meditate on Your statutes.

ז ZAYIN

⁴⁹ Remember Your word to Your servant,
on which You have caused me to hope.
⁵⁰ This is my comfort in my affliction,
for Your word revives me.
⁵¹ The proud ones have derided me,
yet I have not forsaken Your law.
⁵² I remembered Your judgments of old, O Lord,
and I have comforted myself.
⁵³ Fury has taken hold of me because of the wicked
who forsake Your law.

⁵⁴ Your statutes have been my songs
in the house of my temporary dwelling.
⁵⁵ I have remembered Your name, O Lord, in the night,
and have kept Your law.
⁵⁶ This is my blessing,
because I have kept Your precepts.

ח HETH

⁵⁷ You are my portion, O Lord;
I have said that I would keep Your words.
⁵⁸ I seek Your favor with my whole heart;
be merciful to me according to Your word.
⁵⁹ I consider my ways,
and I turn my feet to Your testimonies.
⁶⁰ I made haste, and I did not delay
to keep Your commandments.
⁶¹ The bands of the wicked have trapped me,
but I have not forgotten Your law.
⁶² At midnight I will rise to give thanks to You,
because of Your righteous judgments.
⁶³ I am a companion of all who fear You,
and of those who keep Your precepts.
⁶⁴ The earth, O Lord, is full of Your mercy;
teach me Your statutes.

ט TETH

⁶⁵ You have been good to Your servant,
O Lord, according to Your word.
⁶⁶ Teach me good discernment and knowledge,
for I have believed Your commandments.
⁶⁷ Before I was afflicted I wandered,
but now I keep Your word.
⁶⁸ You are good and do good;
teach me Your statutes.
⁶⁹ The proud have spoken lies against me,
but I keep Your precepts with my whole heart.
⁷⁰ Their heart is as thick as fat,
but I delight in Your law.
⁷¹ It is good for me that I have been afflicted,
that I might learn Your statutes.
⁷² The law from Your mouth is better to me
than thousands of gold and silver coins.

י YODH

⁷³ Your hands have made me and fashioned me;
give me understanding, that I may learn Your
commandments.
⁷⁴ Those who fear You will be glad when they see me,
because I have hoped in Your word.
⁷⁵ I know, O Lord, that Your judgments are right,
and that You in faithfulness have afflicted me.
⁷⁶ Let Your merciful kindness comfort me,
according to Your word to Your servant.
⁷⁷ Let Your compassion come to me, that I may live,
for Your law is my delight.
⁷⁸ Let the proud be ashamed, for they have been wicked to me
in falsehood,
but I will meditate on Your precepts.
⁷⁹ Let those who fear You turn to me,
that they might know Your testimonies.
⁸⁰ Let my heart be blameless in Your statutes,
that I may not be ashamed.

כ KAPH

⁸¹ My soul longs for Your deliverance,
but I hope in Your word.
⁸² My eyes are weary for Your word,
saying, "When will You comfort me?"
⁸³ For I have become like a wineskin *dried* in the smoke,
yet I have not forgotten Your statutes.
⁸⁴ How many days are given to Your servant?
When will You provide judgment on those who persecute me?

85 The proud have dug pits for me,
and they do not live in accordance to Your law.
86 All Your commandments are faithful;
I am persecuted without cause; help me!
87 They have almost consumed me on the earth,
but I have not abandoned Your precepts.
88 Revive me according to Your lovingkindness,
that I may keep the testimony from Your mouth.

ל LAMEDH

89 Forever, O Lord, Your word
is established in heaven.
90 Your faithfulness is for all generations;
You have established the earth, and it is firm.
91 They continue this day according to Your ordinance,
for all are Your servants.
92 Unless Your law had been my delight,
I would have perished in my affliction.
93 I will never forget Your precepts,
for with them You have revived me.
94 I am Yours; deliver me,
for I have sought Your precepts.
95 The wicked have waited to destroy me,
but I will consider Your testimonies.
96 I have seen that all perfection has an end,
but Your commandment is quite broad.

מ MEM

97 Oh, how I love Your law!
It is my meditation all the day.
98 Your commandments have made me wiser than my enemies,
for they are continually with me.
99 I have more understanding than all my teachers,
for Your testimonies are my meditation.
100 I understand more than the elders,
because I keep Your precepts.
101 I have restrained my feet from every evil way,
that I might keep Your word.
102 I have not departed from Your judgments,
for You have taught me.
103 How sweet are Your words to the taste of my mouth!
Sweeter than honey to my mouth!
104 Through Your precepts I receive understanding;
therefore I hate every false way.

נ NUN

105 Your word is a lamp to my feet
and a light to my path.
106 I have sworn, and I will perform it,
that I will keep Your righteous judgments.
107 I am greatly afflicted;
revive me, O Lord, according to Your word.
108 Accept the freewill offerings of my praise, O Lord,
and teach me Your judgments.
109 My soul is continually in my hand,
yet I do not forget Your law.
110 The wicked have laid a trap for me,
yet I do not depart from Your precepts.
111 Your testimonies are my inheritance forever,
for they are the rejoicing of my heart.
112 I have inclined my heart to perform Your statutes always,
even unto the end.

ס SAMEKH

113 I hate those who are double-minded,
but I love Your law.
114 You are my hiding place and my shield,
I hope in Your word.
115 Depart from me, you who are wicked,
for I keep the commandments of my God.
116 Uphold me according to Your word, that I may live,
and let me not be ashamed with my hope.

117 Hold me up, and I shall be safe,
and I will have respect for Your statutes continually.
118 You have rejected all those who stray from Your statutes,
for their deceit is falsehood.
119 You put away all the wicked of the earth like dross;
therefore I love Your testimonies.
120 My body trembles for fear of You,
and I am afraid of Your judgments.

ע AYIN

121 I have done what is right and just;
do not abandon me to my oppressors.
122 Be true to Your servant for good;
let not the proud ones oppress me.
123 My eyes long for Your deliverance
and for the promise of Your righteousness.
124 Deal with Your servant according to Your mercy,
and teach me Your statutes.
125 I am Your servant; grant me understanding,
that I may know Your testimonies.
126 It is time for You, O Lord, to act,
for they have broken Your law.
127 Therefore I love Your commandments
above gold, even fine gold.
128 For I follow all Your precepts to be right,
and I hate every false way.

פ PE

129 Your testimonies are wonderful;
therefore my soul keeps them.
130 The giving of Your words gives light;
it grants understanding to the simple.
131 I opened my mouth and panted,
for I long for Your commandments.
132 Look upon me, and be merciful to me,
as You are for those who love Your name.
133 Order my steps according to Your word,
and let not any iniquity have dominion over me.
134 Deliver me from the oppression of man,
so I will keep Your precepts.
135 Make Your face to shine upon Your servant,
and teach me Your statutes.
136 Rivers of waters run down my eyes,
because people do not keep Your law.

צ TSADHE

137 You are righteous, O Lord,
and upright are Your judgments.
138 You have set Your testimonies in righteousness
and faithfulness.
139 My zeal has consumed me,
because my enemies have forgotten Your words.
140 Your word is pure and true;
therefore Your servant loves it.
141 I am small and despised,
yet I do not forget Your precepts.
142 Your righteousness is an everlasting righteousness,
and Your law is true.
143 Trouble and anguish have discovered me,
but Your commandments are my delight.
144 The righteousness of Your testimonies is everlasting;
grant me understanding, and I shall live.

ק QOPH

145 I cried with my whole heart; hear me, O Lord,
I will keep Your statutes.
146 I cried unto You; deliver me,
and I shall keep Your testimonies.
147 I arose before the dawn of the morning and cried for help;
I hope in Your words.
148 My eyes are awake before the night watches,
that I might meditate on Your word.

149 Hear my voice according to Your lovingkindness, O LORD;
    revive me according to Your judgment.
150 They draw close, those who persecute me with evil;
    they are far from Your law.
151 But You are near, O LORD,
    and all Your commandments are true.
152 I have known of old
    that You have established Your testimonies forever.

ר RESH

153 Consider my affliction, and deliver me,
    for I do not forget Your law.
154 Plead my cause, and defend me;
    revive me according to Your word.
155 Salvation is far from the wicked,
    for they do not seek Your statutes.
156 Great are Your compassions, O LORD;
    revive me according to Your judgments.
157 Many are my persecutors and my enemies,
    yet I do not turn from Your testimonies.
158 I behold the transgressors with disgust,
    because they have not kept Your word.
159 Consider how I love Your precepts;
    revive me, O LORD, according to Your lovingkindness.
160 Your word is true from the beginning,
    and every one of Your righteous judgments
    endures forever.

ש SIN AND SHIN

161 Princes have persecuted me without a cause,
    but my heart stands in awe of Your words.
162 I rejoice at Your word,
    as one who finds great plunder.
163 I hate and abhor lying,
    but I love Your law.
164 Seven times a day I praise You,
    because of Your righteous judgments.
165 Those who love Your law have great peace,
    and nothing shall cause them to stumble.
166 LORD, I have hoped for Your deliverance,
    and I carry out Your commandments.
167 My soul has kept Your testimonies,
    and I love them greatly.
168 I have kept Your precepts and Your testimonies,
    for all my ways are before You.

ת TAW

169 Let my cry come near before You, O LORD;
    give me understanding according to Your word.
170 Let my supplication come before You;
    deliver me according to Your word.
171 My lips shall declare praise,
    for You have taught me Your statutes.
172 My tongue shall speak of Your word,
    for all Your commandments are right.
173 Let Your hand help me,
    for I have chosen Your precepts.
174 I have longed for Your salvation, O LORD,
    and Your law is my delight.
175 Let my soul live and praise You,
    and let Your judgments come to my aid.
176 I have wandered like a lost sheep;
    seek Your servant,
    for I do not forget Your commandments.

PSALM 120
A Song of Ascents.

1 In my distress I cried unto the LORD,
    and He heard me.
2 Deliver my soul, O LORD, from lying lips
    and from a deceitful tongue.

3 What shall be given to you,
    or what shall be done to you, you false tongue?
4 Sharp arrows of the warrior,
    with coals of the broom tree!

5 Woe is me, that I have sojourned in Meshek,
    or that I have dwelled among the tents of Kedar!
6 My soul has long lived
    with those who hate peace.
7 I am for peace,
    but when I speak, they are for war!

PSALM 121
A Song of Ascents.

1 I will lift up my eyes to the hills,
    from where does my help come?
2 My help comes from the LORD,
    who made heaven and earth.

3 He will not let your foot slip;
    He who keeps you will not slumber.
4 Behold, He who guards Israel
    shall neither slumber nor sleep.

5 The LORD is your guardian;
    the LORD is your shade at your right hand.
6 The sun shall not harm you during the day,
    nor the moon during the night.

7 The LORD shall protect you from all evil;
    He shall preserve your soul.
8 The LORD shall preserve your going out and your coming in
    from now and for evermore.

PSALM 122
A Song of Ascents. Of David.

1 I was glad when they said to me,
    "Let us go into the house of the LORD."
2 Our feet shall stand
    within your gates, O Jerusalem.

3 Jerusalem is built as a city
    that is designed for a multitude,
4 where the tribes go up,
    the tribes of the LORD,
    as a decree of Israel,
    to give thanks unto the name of the LORD.
5 There are set thrones of judgment,
    the thrones of the house of David.

6 Pray for the peace of Jerusalem:
    "May they prosper who love you!
7 Peace be within your walls
    and security within your towers!"
8 For my brothers and companions' sake,
    I will now say, "Peace be within you."
9 Because of the house of the LORD our God,
    I will seek your good.

PSALM 123
A Song of Ascents.

1 To You I lift up my eyes,
    O You who dwell in the heavens.
2 Behold, as the eyes of servants look to the hand of
    their master,
    and as the eyes of a maiden to the hand of
    her mistress,
    so our eyes look upon the LORD our God,
    until He has mercy upon us.

³ Have mercy upon us, O Lord, have mercy
  upon us,
    for we have been completely filled
    with contempt.
⁴ Our soul is exceedingly filled with the ridicule
    of those who are at ease,
    and with the contempt of the proud ones.

PSALM 124
A Song of Ascents. Of David.

¹ If it had not been the Lord who was on our side,
    now may Israel say,
² if it had not been the Lord who was on our side,
    when men rose up against us,
³ then they would have swallowed us up,
    when their wrath was kindled against us;
⁴ then the flood would have overwhelmed us,
    the torrent would have passed over our lives;
⁵ then the surging waters
    would have gone over us.

⁶ Blessed be the Lord,
    who has not given us for a prey to their teeth.
⁷ We have escaped
    as a bird out of the snare of the hunters;
  the snare is broken,
    and we have escaped.
⁸ Our help is in the name of the Lord,
    who made heaven and earth.

PSALM 125
A Song of Ascents.

¹ Those who trust in the Lord shall be as Mount Zion,
    which cannot be removed, but abides forever.
² As the mountains are around Jerusalem,
    so the Lord surrounds His people,
    from now and forever.

³ For the scepter of the wicked shall not rest
    upon the land allotted to the righteous,
  lest the righteous put forth
    their hands to do iniquity.

⁴ Do good, O Lord, for those who are good,
    and to those who are upright in their hearts.
⁵ As for those who turn aside to their twisted ways,
    the Lord shall lead them away with the other workers of iniquity.

Peace be upon Israel!

PSALM 126
A Song of Ascents.

¹ When the Lord restored the captives of Zion,
    we were like those who dream.
² Then our mouth was filled with laughter,
    and our tongue with singing.
  Then they said among the nations,
    "The Lord has done great things for them."
³ The Lord has done great things for us;
    we are glad.

⁴ Restore our captives, O Lord,
    as the streams in the Negev.
⁵ Those who sow in tears
    shall reap in joy.
⁶ He who goes forth and weeps,
    bearing precious seed to sow,
  shall come home again with rejoicing,
    bringing his grain sheaves with him.

PSALM 127
A Song of Ascents. Of Solomon.

¹ Except the Lord build the house,
    those who build labor in vain; . . .
  except the Lord guards the city,
    the watchman stays awake in vain.
² It is in vain for you to rise up early,
    to stay up late,
  and to eat the bread of hard toil,
    for He gives sleep to His beloved.

³ Look, children are a gift of the Lord,
    and the fruit of the womb is a reward.
⁴ As arrows in the hand of a mighty warrior,
    so are the children of one's youth.
⁵ Happy is the man
    who has his quiver full of them;
  he shall not be ashamed
    when he speaks with the enemies at the gate.

PSALM 128
A Song of Ascents.

¹ Blessed is everyone who fears the Lord,
    who walks in His ways.
² For you shall eat the fruit of the labor of
    your hands;
    you will be happy, and it shall be well
    with you.
³ Your wife shall be as a fruitful vine
    in your house,
  your children like olive shoots
    around your table.
⁴ Behold, this man shall be blessed
    who fears the Lord.

⁵ The Lord shall bless you from Zion,
    and may you see the welfare of Jerusalem
  all the days of your life.
⁶   Indeed, may you see your children's children.
  Peace upon Israel!

PSALM 129
A Song of Ascents.

¹ "Often they have afflicted me from my youth,"
    may Israel now say,
² "often they have afflicted me from my youth,
    yet they have not prevailed against me.
³ The plowmen plowed upon my back;
    they made their furrows long."
⁴ The Lord is righteous;
    He has cut the cords of the wicked.

⁵ Let all those be shamed
    and turned back who hate Zion.
⁶ Let them be as the grass on the housetops,
    which withers before it even grows,
⁷ where the reaper is unable to fill his hand,
    or he who binds sheaves, his arms.
⁸ Neither do they who pass by say,
    "The blessing of the Lord be upon you;
    we bless you in the name of the Lord!"

PSALM 130
A Song of Ascents.

¹ From the depths I call on You, O Lord!
²   O Lord, hear my voice;
  let Your ears be attentive
    to the sound of my supplications.

3 If you, O Lord, should keep track of iniquities,
    O Lord, who shall stand?
4 For there is forgiveness with You,
    that You may be feared.

5 I wait for the Lord, with bated breath I wait;
    I long for His Word!
6 My soul waits for the Lord,
    more than watchmen for the morning,
    more than watchmen for the morning.

7 Let Israel wait for the Lord!
    For mercy is found with the Lord;
    with Him is great redemption.
8 He shall redeem Israel
    from all their iniquities.

PSALM 131
A Song of Ascents. Of David.

1 Lord, my heart is not haughty,
    my eyes are not raised too high.
    I have not striven for enormities,
    for things too wonderful for me.
2 I composed and quieted my desire,
    like a child given suck by his mother;
    like a child who sucks is my desire
    within me.

3 Let Israel hope in the Lord
    from now and forever.

PSALM 132
2Ch 6:41–42
A Song of Ascents.

1 O Lord, remember David
    and all his afflictions,
2 how he swore unto the Lord,
    and vowed unto the mighty God of Jacob:
3 "I will not come into my house,
    nor go up to my bed;
4 I will not give sleep to my eyes,
    or slumber to my eyelids,
5 until I find a place for the Lord,
    a dwelling for the mighty God of Jacob."

6 We heard of it in Ephrathah;
    we found it in the fields of Jaar.
7 "We will go to His dwelling place,
    we will worship at His footstool."
8 Arise, O Lord, go to Your resting place,
    You and the ark of Your strength.
9 Let Your priests be clothed with righteousness,
    and let Your godly ones shout for joy.

10 For Your servant David's sake,
    do not turn away Your anointed king.

11 The Lord has sworn with a sure oath to David
    that He will not turn from it:
    "From the fruit of your body
    I will set a son on your throne.
12 If your children will keep My covenant
    and My testimonies that I shall teach them,
    then their children shall also sit
    upon your throne forever."

13 For the Lord has chosen Zion;
    He has desired it for His dwelling:
14 "This is My resting place forever;
    here I will dwell, for I have chosen it.

15 I will abundantly bless her provisions;
    I will satisfy her poor with bread.
16 I will also clothe her priests with salvation,
    and her godly ones shall shout for joy.

17 "There I will make a horn sprout for David;
    I have prepared a lamp for My anointed one.
18 His enemies I will clothe with shame,
    but on him his crown will shine."

PSALM 133
A Song of Ascents. Of David.

1 Behold, how good and how pleasant it is
    for brothers to dwell together in unity!

2 It is like precious oil upon the head,
    that runs down on the beard—
    even Aaron's beard—
    and going down to the collar of his garments;
3 as the dew of Hermon,
    that descends upon the mountains of Zion,
    for there the Lord has commanded the blessing,
    even life forever.

PSALM 134
A Song of Ascents.

1 Come, bless the Lord, all you servants of the Lord,
    who by night stand in the house of the Lord.
2 Lift up your hands in the sanctuary,
    and bless the Lord.

3 May the Lord who made heaven and earth
    bless you from Zion.

PSALM 135
Ps 115:4–11

1 Praise the Lord!

    Praise the name of the Lord;
    praise Him, O servants of the Lord,
2 you who stand in the house of the Lord,
    in the courts of the house of our God!

3 Praise the Lord, for the Lord is good;
    sing praises unto His name, for it is pleasant.
4 For the Lord has chosen Jacob for Himself,
    and Israel for His special possession.

5 For I know that the Lord is great,
    and that our Lord is above all gods.
6 Whatever the Lord pleases,
    He does in heaven and on earth,
    in the seas and all the depths.
7 He causes the clouds to ascend from the ends
        of the earth;
    He makes lightning for the rain;
    He brings the wind out from His storehouses.

8 He struck down the firstborn of Egypt,
    both of man and animal.
9 He sent signs and wonders into your midst, O Egypt,
    against Pharaoh and all his servants;
10 He struck down great nations
    and slew mighty kings—
11 Sihon, king of the Amorites,
    and Og king of Bashan,
    and all the kingdoms of Canaan—
12 and gave their land for an inheritance,
    a possession to Israel His people.

¹³ Your name, O LORD, endures forever;
    and Your renown, O LORD, throughout
        all generations.
¹⁴ For the LORD will defend His people,
    and He will have compassion on His servants.

¹⁵ The idols of the nations are silver and gold,
    the work of men's hands.
¹⁶ They have mouths, but do not speak;
    they have eyes, but do not see;
¹⁷ they have ears, but do not hear;
    neither is there any breath in their mouths.
¹⁸ Those who make them are like them;
    so is everyone who trusts in them.

¹⁹ Bless the LORD, O house of Israel;
    bless the LORD, O house of Aaron.
²⁰ Bless the LORD, O house of Levi;
    you who fear the LORD, bless the LORD.
²¹ Blessed be the LORD from Zion,
    who dwells at Jerusalem.

Praise you the LORD!

PSALM 136

¹ Oh, give thanks unto the LORD, for He is good,
    for His mercy endures forever.
² Oh, give thanks unto the God of gods,
    for His mercy endures forever.
³ Oh, give thanks to the Lord of lords,
    for His mercy endures forever:

⁴ to Him who alone does great wonders,
    for His mercy endures forever;
⁵ to Him who by wisdom made the heavens,
    for His mercy endures forever;
⁶ to Him who stretched out the earth above
        the waters,
    for His mercy endures forever;
⁷ to Him who made the great *heavenly* lights,
    for His mercy endures forever;
⁸ the sun to rule over the day,
    for His mercy endures forever;
⁹ the moon and stars to rule over the night,
    for His mercy endures forever;

¹⁰ to Him who struck down in Egypt their firstborn,
    for His mercy endures forever;
¹¹ and brought out Israel from among them,
    for His mercy endures forever;
¹² with a strong hand and a stretched-out arm,
    for His mercy endures forever;

¹³ to Him who divided the Red Sea into two,
    for His mercy endures forever;
¹⁴ and made Israel to pass through the midst of it,
    for His mercy endures forever;
¹⁵ but overthrew Pharaoh and his host in the
        Red Sea,
    for His mercy endures forever;

¹⁶ to Him who led His people through the wilderness,
    for His mercy endures forever;

¹⁷ to Him who struck down great kings,
    for His mercy endures forever;
¹⁸ and slew mighty kings,
    for His mercy endures forever;
¹⁹ Sihon king of the Amorites,
    for His mercy endures forever;
²⁰ and Og king of Bashan,
    for His mercy endures forever;

²¹ and gave their land for a possession,
    for His mercy endures forever;
²² even an inheritance to Israel His servant,
    for His mercy endures forever.

²³ Who remembered us in our low place,
    for His mercy endures forever;
²⁴ and has redeemed us from our enemies,
    for His mercy endures forever;
²⁵ who gives food to all people,
    for His mercy endures forever.

²⁶ Give thanks unto the God of heaven,
    for His mercy endures forever.

PSALM 137

¹ By the rivers of Babylon, there we sat down and wept
    when we remembered Zion.
² We hung our harps
    upon the poplars.
³ For there our captors made us sing
    and our tormentors made us entertain,
    saying, "Sing us one of the songs of Zion."

⁴ How shall we sing the song of the LORD
    in a foreign land?
⁵ If I forget you, O Jerusalem,
    let my right hand forget its skill.
⁶ If I do not remember you,
    let my tongue stick to the roof of my mouth,
    if I do not have Jerusalem
    as my highest joy.

⁷ Remember, O LORD, the people of Edom
    in the day of Jerusalem,
    who said, "Raze it, raze it,
    down to its foundations."

⁸ O daughter of Babylon, who is to be destroyed,
    blessed is the one who rewards you
    as you have done to us.
⁹ Blessed is the one who takes
    and dashes your little ones against the rocks.

PSALM 138
A Psalm of David.

¹ I will praise You, O LORD, with my whole heart;
    before the gods I will sing Your praise.
² I will worship toward Your holy temple,
    and praise Your name
    for Your lovingkindness and for Your truth;
for You have exalted Your word
    above all Your name.
³ On the day I called, You answered me,
    and strengthened me in my soul.

⁴ All the kings of the earth shall praise You, O LORD,
    for they have heard the words of Your mouth.
⁵ Indeed, they shall sing of the ways of the LORD,
    for great is the glory of the LORD.

⁶ Though the LORD is exalted, yet He has concern
        for the lowly,
    but the proud one He knows from a distance.
⁷ Though I walk in the midst of trouble,
    You will preserve me;
You stretch forth Your hand against the wrath of my enemies,
    and Your right hand saves me.
⁸ The LORD will fulfill His purpose for me;
    Your mercy, O LORD, endures forever;
    do not forsake the works of Your hands.

PSALM 139
For the Music Director. A Psalm of David.

1 O Lord, You have searched me
   and known me.
2 You know when I sit down and when I get up;
   You understand my thought from far off.
3 You search my path and my lying down
   and are aware of all my ways.
4 For there is not a word on my tongue,
   but behold, O Lord, You know it fully.

5 You put Yourself behind and before me,
   and keep Your hand on me.
6 Such knowledge is too wonderful for me;
   it is lofty, and I cannot fathom it.

7 Where shall I go from Your spirit,
   or where shall I flee from Your presence?
8 If I ascend to heaven, You are there;
   if I make my bed in Sheol, You are there.
9 If I take the wings of the morning
   and dwell at the end of the sea,
10 even there Your hand shall guide me,
   and Your right hand shall take hold of me.
11 If I say, "Surely the darkness shall cover me,
   and the light shall be as night about me,"
12 even the darkness is not dark to You,
   but the night shines as the day,
   for the darkness is like light to You.

13 You brought my inner parts into being;
   You wove me in my mother's womb.
14 I will praise you, for You made me with fear and wonder;
   marvelous are Your works,
   and You know me completely.
15 My frame was not hidden from You
   when I was made in secret,
   and intricately put together in the lowest parts of
       the earth.
16 Your eyes saw me unformed,
   yet in Your book
   all my days were written,
   before any of them came into being.
17 How precious also are Your thoughts to me, O God!
   How great is the sum of them!
18 If I should count them,
   they are more in number than the sand;
   when I awake,
   I am still with You.

19 If only You would slay the wicked, O God!
   O violent men, depart from me.
20 For they speak against You with malice,
   and Your enemies take your *name* in vain.
21 Do I not hate those, O Lord, who hate You?
   And do I not abhor those who rise up against You?
22 I hate them with perfect hatred;
   I count them my enemies.

23 Search me, O God, and know my heart;
   try me, and know my concerns,
24 and see if there is any rebellious way in me,
   and lead me in the ancient way.

PSALM 140
For the Music Director. A Psalm of David.

1 Deliver me, O Lord, from evil men;
   protect me from violent men,
2 who plan evil deeds in their heart
   and continually gather together for conflicts.

3 They have tongues as sharp as a serpent;
   adders' poison is with their lips.   Selah

4 Keep me, O Lord, from the hands of the wicked;
   preserve me from the violent men
   who have planned to overthrow me.
5 The proud have hid a snare for me,
   and with cords they have spread a net;
   they have set traps for me.   Selah

6 I said to the Lord, "You are my God;
   hear the voice of my supplications, O Lord."
7 O God my Lord, the strength of my salvation,
   You have covered my head in the day of battle.
8 Grant not, O Lord, the desires of the wicked;
   do not allow his evil plot,
   lest he be raised up.   Selah

9 As for the head of those who encompass me,
   let the mischief of their own lips overwhelm them;
10 let burning coals fall upon them;
   let them be cast into the fire,
   into deep pits that they do not rise up again.
11 Let not an evil speaker be established in the land;
   let evil hunt the violent man to overthrow him!

12 I know that the Lord will maintain the cause of the afflicted
   and will give justice to the poor.
13 Surely the righteous shall give thanks unto Your name;
   the upright shall dwell in Your presence.

PSALM 141
A Psalm of David.

1 Lord, I cry unto You; make haste to me;
   give ear to my voice, when I cry unto You.
2 Let my prayer be set forth before You as incense,
   and the lifting up of my hands as the evening sacrifice.

3 Set a guard, O Lord, over my mouth;
   keep watch over the door of my lips.
4 Do not let my heart be drawn to any evil,
   to practice wicked deeds
   with men who do iniquity,
   and do not let me eat of their delights.

5 Let the righteous man strike me;
   it shall be a kindness.
   Let him rebuke me;
   it shall be oil for my head;
   let my head not refuse it.
   For my prayer is continually against their evil deeds.

6 When their judges are thrown to stony places,
   then they shall hear my words, for they are sweet.
7 As when one plows to break up the land,
   so our bones are scattered at the mouth of Sheol.

8 But my eyes are unto You, O God my Lord,
   in You is my trust; do not leave my soul defenseless.
9 Keep me from the snares that they have laid for me,
   and the traps of those who do iniquity.
10 Let the wicked fall into their own nets,
   while I pass by and escape.

PSALM 142
A Contemplative Maskil of David, when he was in the cave. A Prayer.

1 I cried unto the Lord with my voice;
   with my voice I made my supplication unto the Lord.
2 I poured out my complaint before Him;
   I declared to Him my trouble.

3 When my spirit was overwhelmed within me,
    then You knew my path.
In the way where I walk,
    they have laid a snare for me.
4 I looked on my right and noticed,
    but there was no one who would care for me;
there is no refuge for me;
    no one cares for my soul.

5 I cried unto You, O Lord;
    I said, "You are my refuge
    and my portion in the land of the living."

6 Attend to my cry,
    for I am brought very low;
deliver me from my persecutors,
    for they are stronger than me.
7 Bring my soul out of prison,
    that I may praise Your name;
the righteous shall surround me,
    for You shall deal bountifully with me.

PSALM 143
A Psalm of David.

1 Hear my prayer, O Lord,
    give ear to my supplications;
in Your faithfulness answer me,
    and in Your righteousness.
2 Enter not into judgment with Your servant,
    for in Your sight no one living is righteous.

3 For the enemy has persecuted my soul;
    he has crushed my life down to the ground;
he has made me to dwell in darkness,
    as those who have been long dead.
4 Therefore my spirit is overwhelmed within me;
    my heart within me is desolate.
5 I remember the days of old;
    I meditate on all Your works;
    I consider the work of Your hands.
6 I stretch forth my hands unto You;
    my soul thirsts after You as a thirsty land. Selah

7 Respond to me quickly, O Lord,
    my spirit fails;
do not hide Your face from me,
    lest I be like those who go down into the pit.
8 Cause me to hear Your lovingkindness in the morning;
    for in You I have my trust;
cause me to know the way I should walk,
    for I lift up my soul unto You.
9 Deliver me, O Lord, from my enemies;
    I flee unto You for my protection.
10 Teach me to do Your will,
    for You are my God;
may Your good spirit
    lead me onto level ground.

11 Revive me, O Lord, for Your name's sake,
    for Your righteousness' sake bring my soul out
        of trouble.
12 In Your mercy cut off my enemies,
    and destroy all them who afflict my soul,
    for I am Your servant.

PSALM 144
A Psalm of David.

1 Blessed be the Lord my strength,
    who prepares my hands for war,
    and my fingers to fight;

2 my goodness, and my fortress;
    my high tower, and my deliverer,
my shield, and in whom I trust;
    who subdues nations under me.

3 O Lord, who is man that You take notice of him
    or the son of a man that You make account of him?
4 Man is like a breath;
    his days are as a shadow that passes away.

5 Bow your heavens, O Lord, and come down;
    touch the mountains, and they shall smoke.
6 Cast forth lightning, and scatter them;
    shoot out Your arrows, and destroy them.
7 Send Your hand from above;
    rescue me, and deliver me
out of the great waters,
    from the hand of foreigners,
8 whose mouth speaks lies,
    and their right hand is a right hand of falsehood.

9 I will sing a new song unto You, O God,
    on a harp and an instrument of ten strings I will sing
        praises unto You;
10 it is He who gives victory to kings,
    who delivers David His servant from the cruel sword.

11 Rescue me and deliver me
    from the hand of foreigners,
whose mouths speak lies
    and whose right hand is a right hand of falsehood.

12 May our sons in their youth
    be like plants full grown,
and our daughters like cornerstones,
    cut in the similitude of a palace,
13 that our granaries may be full,
    providing all manner of produce,
that our sheep may bring forth
    thousands and ten thousands in our fields,
14   and may our cattle be strong in labor.
May there be no breaking in
    or going out,
    and no wailing in our streets.
15 Blessed are the people who have such things;
    indeed, blessed are the people whose God is the Lord.

PSALM 145
A Psalm of Praise. Of David.

1 I will exalt you, my God and King,
    and I will bless Your name forever and ever.
2 Every day I will bless You,
    and I will praise Your name forever and ever.

3 Great is the Lord, and greatly to be praised,
    and His greatness is unfathomable.
4 One generation shall praise Your works to another
    and shall declare Your mighty acts.
5 I will speak of the glorious honor of Your majesty
    and of Your wondrous works.
6 They shall speak of the might of Your awesome acts,
    and I will declare Your greatness.
7 They shall abundantly declare the fame of Your
        great goodness
    and shall sing of Your righteousness.

8 The Lord is gracious and full of compassion,
    slow to anger, and great in mercy.

9 The Lord is good to all,
    and His compassion is over all His works.

10 All Your works shall praise You, O Lord,
    and Your godly ones shall bless You.
11 They shall speak of the glory of Your kingdom
    and talk of Your power,
12 to make known to people His mighty acts,
    and the glorious majesty of His kingdom.
13 Your kingdom is an everlasting kingdom,
    and Your dominion endures throughout
      all generations.

14 The Lord upholds all who fall,
    and raises up all who are bowed down.
15 The eyes of all wait upon You,
    and You give them their food in due season.
16 You open Your hand
    and satisfy the desire of every living thing.

17 The Lord is righteous in all His ways
    and loving in all His works.
18 The Lord is near to all those who call upon Him,
    to all who call upon Him in truth.
19 He will fulfill the desire of those who fear Him;
    He also will hear their cry and will save them.
20 The Lord preserves all those who love Him,
    but all the wicked He will destroy.

21 My mouth shall speak the praise of the Lord,
    and let all people bless His holy name
      forever and ever.

PSALM 146

1 Praise the Lord!

Praise the Lord, O my soul!

2 While I live I will praise the Lord;
    I will sing praises unto my God while I have my life.
3 Do not put your trust in princes,
    nor in a son of man, in whom there is no help.
4 His breath leaves him, and he returns to the earth;
    on that very day his plans perish.

5 Blessed is he who has the God of Jacob for his help,
    whose hope is in the Lord his God,
6 who made heaven, and earth,
    the sea, and all that is in them,
    who keeps faithfulness forever,
7 who executes justice for the oppressed,
    who gives food to the hungry.
    The Lord releases the prisoners.
8   The Lord opens the eyes of the blind;
    the Lord raises those who are brought down;
    the Lord loves the righteous.
9 The Lord preserves the sojourners;
    He lifts up the fatherless and widow,
    but on the way of the wicked He brings disaster.

10 The Lord shall reign forever,
    your God, O Zion, unto all generations.

Praise you the Lord!

PSALM 147

1 Praise the Lord!

For it is good to sing praises unto our God;
    for it is pleasant, and a song of praise is fitting.

2 The Lord builds up Jerusalem;
    He gathers together the outcasts of Israel.
3 He heals the broken in heart,
    and binds up their wounds.

4 He counts the number of the stars;
    He calls them all by their names.
5 Great is our Lord and great in power;
    His understanding is without measure.
6 The Lord lifts up the meek;
    He casts the wicked down to the ground.

7 Sing unto the Lord with thanksgiving;
    sing praise upon the harp unto our God:
8 who covers the heaven with clouds,
    who provides rain for the earth,
    who makes grass to grow upon the mountains.
9 He gives food to the animals
    and to the young ravens that chirp.

10 He delights not in the strength of the horse,
    nor does He take pleasure in the legs of a man,
11 but the Lord takes pleasure in those who fear Him,
    in those who hope in His mercy.

12 Praise the Lord, O Jerusalem;
    praise your God, O Zion.

13 For He has strengthened the bars of your gates;
    He has blessed your children within you.
14 He makes peace in your borders,
    and fills you with the finest of the wheat.

15 He sends forth His commandment on the earth;
    His word goes out swiftly.
16 He gives snow like wool;
    He scatters the frost like ashes;
17 He casts forth His ice like morsels;
    who can stand before His cold?
18 He sends out His word and melts them;
    He causes His wind to blow and the
      waters flow.

19 He shows His word to Jacob,
    and His statutes and His judgments to Israel.
20 He has not dealt so with any other nation;
    they have not known His judgments.

Praise the Lord!

PSALM 148

1 Praise the Lord!

Praise the Lord from the heavens;
    praise Him in the heights.
2 Praise Him, all His angels;
    praise Him, all His heavenly hosts.
3 Praise Him, sun and moon;
    praise Him, all you stars of light.
4 Praise Him, you highest of heavens,
    and you waters that are above the skies.

5 Let them praise the name of the Lord,
    for He commanded, and they were created.
6 He has also established them forever and ever;
    He has made a decree that shall not pass away.

7 Praise the Lord from the earth,
    you great sea creatures, and all you depths,
8 fire and hail, snow and mist,
    storming wind fulfilling His word,
9 mountains and all hills,
    fruitful trees and all cedars;
10 animals and all cattle,
    creeping things and flying birds;
11 kings of the earth and all peoples,
    princes and all rulers of the earth;

[12] both young men and maidens,
    old men and children.

[13] Let them praise the name of the Lord,
    for His name alone is excellent;
    His glory is above the earth and heaven.
[14] He has raised up a *victory* horn for His people,
    praise for all His saints,
    even for the people of Israel near Him.

Praise the Lord!

PSALM 149

[1] Praise the Lord!

Sing unto the Lord a new song,
    and His praise in the assembly of the
        godly ones.

[2] Let Israel rejoice in its Maker;
    let the children of Zion be joyful in their King.
[3] Let them praise His name with dancing;
    let them sing praises unto Him with the
        tambourine and harp.
[4] For the Lord takes pleasure in His people;
    He will beautify the meek with salvation.
[5] Let the godly ones be joyful in glory;
    let them sing for joy on their beds.

[6] Let the high praises of God be in their mouths,
    and two-edged swords in their hands,
[7] to execute vengeance on the nations,
    and punishments on the peoples;
[8] to bind their kings with chains,
    and their nobles with shackles of iron;
[9] to execute upon them the written judgment;
    this is honor for all His godly ones.

Praise the Lord!

PSALM 150

[1] Praise the Lord!

Praise God in His sanctuary;
    praise Him in the firmament of His power!
[2] Praise Him for His mighty acts;
    praise Him according to His excellent greatness!
[3] Praise Him with the sound of the trumpet;
    praise Him with the lyre and harp!
[4] Praise Him with the tambourine and dancing;
    praise Him with stringed instruments and flute!
[5] Praise Him with loud cymbals;
    praise Him with the clanging cymbals!

[6] Let everything that has breath praise the Lord.

Praise the Lord!

PROVERBS

The Purpose and Theme

1 The proverbs of Solomon, the son of David, king of Israel:

[2] To know wisdom and instruction,
    to perceive the words of understanding,
[3] to receive the instruction of wisdom,
    justice, judgment, and equity;
[4] to give subtlety to the simple,
    to the young man knowledge and discretion—
[5] a wise man will hear and will increase learning,
    and a man of understanding will attain wise counsel,
[6] to understand a proverb and the interpretation,
    the words of the wise and their riddles.

[7] The fear of the Lord is the beginning of knowledge,
    but fools despise wisdom and instruction.

The Prologue: Embrace Wisdom

[8] My son, hear the instruction of your father,
    and do not forsake the teaching of your mother;
[9] for they will be a garland of grace on your head,
    and chains about your neck.

[10] My son, if sinners entice you,
    do not consent.
[11] If they say, "Come with us,
    let us lie in wait for blood;
    let us lurk secretly for the innocent without cause;
[12] let us swallow them up alive as the grave,
    and whole, as those who go down into the pit;
[13] we will find all kinds of precious possessions;
    we will fill our houses with spoil;

[14] cast in your lot among us,
    let us all have one purse"—
[15] my son, do not walk in the way with them,
    keep your foot from their path;
[16] for their feet run to evil
    and make haste to shed blood.
[17] Surely in vain the net is spread
    in the sight of any bird.
[18] They lie in wait for their own blood;
    they lurk secretly for their own lives.
[19] So are the ways of everyone who is greedy of gain,
    which takes away the life of its owners.

The Call of Wisdom

[20] Wisdom cries out in the street;
    she utters her voice in the markets.
[21] She cries at the corner of the streets, in the openings
        of the gates;
    she speaks her words in the city, saying:

[22] "How long, you simple ones, will you love simplicity?
    For the scorners delight in their scorning,
    and fools hate knowledge.
[23] Turn at my reproof;
    surely I will pour out my spirit on you;
    I will make my words known to you.
[24] Because I have called and you refused,
    I have stretched out my hand and no man regarded,
[25] because you neglected all my counsel,
    and would have none of my reproof,
[26] I also will laugh at your calamity;
    I will mock when your fear comes,

27 when your fear comes as desolation
and your destruction comes as a whirlwind,
when distress and anguish come upon you.

28 "Then they will call on me, but I will not answer;
they will seek me early, but they will not
find me.
29 Because they hated knowledge
and did not choose the fear of the LORD,
30 they would have none of my counsel
and despised all my reproof.
31 Therefore they will eat of the fruit of their own way,
and be filled with their own devices.
32 For the turning away of the simple will slay them,
and the prosperity of fools will destroy them.
33 But whoever listens to me will dwell safely,
and will be secure from fear of evil."

The Value of Wisdom

2 My son, if you will receive my words,
and hide my commandments within you,
2 so that you incline your ear to wisdom,
and apply your heart to understanding;
3 yes, if you cry out for knowledge,
and lift up your voice for understanding,
4 if you seek her as silver,
and search for her as for hidden treasures,
5 then you will understand the fear of the LORD,
and find the knowledge of God.
6 For the LORD gives wisdom;
out of His mouth come knowledge and understanding.
7 He lays up sound wisdom for the righteous;
He is a shield to those who walk uprightly.
8 He keeps the paths of justice,
and preserves the way of His saints.

9 Then you will understand righteousness and judgment
and equity, and every good path.
10 When wisdom enters your heart,
and knowledge is pleasant to your soul,
11 discretion will preserve you;
understanding will keep you,
12 to deliver you from the way of the evil man,
from the man who speaks perverse things,
13 from those who leave the paths of uprightness
to walk in the ways of darkness;
14 who rejoice to do evil,
and delight in the perversity of the wicked;
15 whose ways are crooked,
and who are devious in their paths;
16 to deliver you from the immoral woman,
even from the seductress who flatters with
her words,
17 who forsakes the guide of her youth,
and forgets the covenant of her God.
18 For her house leads down to death,
and her paths to the departed spirits;
19 none who go to her return again,
nor do they take hold of the paths of life.

20 So you may walk in the way of good men
and keep the paths of the righteous.
21 For the upright will dwell in the land,
and the innocent will remain in it;
22 but the wicked will be cut off from the earth,
and the transgressors will be rooted out of it.

The Rewards of Wisdom

3 My son, do not forget my teaching,
but let your heart keep my commandments;
2 for length of days and long life
and peace will they add to you.

3 Do not let mercy and truth forsake you;
bind them around your neck,
write them on the tablet of your heart,
4 so you will find favor and good understanding
in the sight of God and man.

5 Trust in the LORD with all your heart,
and lean not on your own understanding;
6 in all your ways acknowledge Him,
and He will direct your paths.

7 Do not be wise in your own eyes;
fear the LORD and depart from evil.
8 It will be health to your body,
and strength to your bones.

9 Honor the LORD with your substance,
and with the first fruits of all your increase;
10 so your barns will be filled with plenty,
and your presses will burst out with new wine.

11 My son, do not despise the chastening of the LORD,
nor be weary of His correction;
12 for whom the LORD loves He corrects,
even as a father the son in whom he delights.

13 Happy is the man who finds wisdom,
and the man who gets understanding;
14 for her benefit is more profitable than silver,
and her gain than *fine* gold.
15 She is more precious than rubies,
and all the things you may desire are not to be
compared with her.
16 Length of days is in her right hand,
and in her left hand riches and honor.
17 Her ways are ways of pleasantness,
and all her paths are peace.
18 She is a tree of life to those who take hold of her,
and happy is everyone who retains her.

19 The LORD by wisdom has founded the earth;
by understanding He has established the heavens;
20 by His knowledge the depths are broken up,
and the clouds drop down the dew.

21 My son, let them not depart from your eyes—
keep sound wisdom and discretion;
22 so they will be life to your soul
and grace to your neck.
23 Then you will walk safely in your way,
and your foot will not stumble.
24 When you lie down, you will not be afraid;
yes, you will lie down and your sleep will
be sweet.
25 Do not be afraid of sudden terror,
nor of trouble from the wicked when it comes;
26 for the LORD will be your confidence,
and will keep your foot from being caught.

27 Do not withhold good from those to whom it is due,
when it is in the power of your hand to do it.
28 Do not say to your neighbor,
"Go, and come again, and tomorrow I will give it,"
when you have it with you.

29 Do not devise evil against your neighbor,
seeing he dwells securely by you.
30 Do not strive with a man without cause,
if he has done you no harm.

31 Do not envy the oppressor,
and choose none of his ways;

³² for the perverse is an abomination to the LORD,
    but His secret *counsel* is with the righteous.
³³ The curse of the LORD is on the house of the wicked,
    but He blesses the habitation of the just.
³⁴ Surely He scorns the scornful,
    but He gives favor to the humble.
³⁵ The wise will inherit glory,
    but shame will be the legacy of fools.

Wisdom Is Supreme

4 Hear, O children, the instruction of a father,
    and attend to know understanding.
² For I give you good precepts;
    do not forsake my teaching.
³ For I was my father's son,
    tender and the only beloved in the sight of my mother.
⁴ He also taught me and said to me,
    "Let your heart retain my words;
    keep my commandments, and live.
⁵ Get wisdom! Get understanding!
    Do not forget it, nor turn away from the words of my mouth.
⁶ Do not forsake her, and she will preserve you;
    love her, and she will keep you.
⁷ Wisdom is principal; therefore get wisdom.
    And with all your getting, get understanding.
⁸ Exalt her, and she will promote you;
    she will bring you honor, when you embrace her.
⁹ She will place on your head an ornament of grace;
    a crown of glory she will deliver to you."

¹⁰ Hear, my son, and receive my sayings,
    and the years of your life will be many.
¹¹ I have taught you in the way of wisdom;
    I have led you in right paths.
¹² When you walk, your steps will not be hindered,
    and when you run, you will not stumble.
¹³ Take firm hold of instruction, do not let her go;
    keep her, for she is your life.
¹⁴ Do not enter the path of the wicked,
    and do not go in the way of evil men.
¹⁵ Avoid it, do not travel on it;
    turn from it and pass on.
¹⁶ For they do not sleep unless they have done mischief;
    and their sleep is taken away unless they cause some to fall.
¹⁷ For they eat the bread of wickedness
    and drink the wine of violence.

¹⁸ But the path of the just is as the shining light,
    that shines more and more unto the perfect day.
¹⁹ The way of the wicked is as darkness;
    they do not know at what they stumble.

²⁰ My son, attend to my words;
    incline your ear to my sayings.
²¹ Do not let them depart from your eyes;
    keep them in the midst of your heart;
²² for they are life to those who find them,
    and health to all their body.
²³ Keep your heart with all diligence,
    for out of it are the issues of life.
²⁴ Put away from you a deceitful mouth,
    and put perverse lips far from you.
²⁵ Let your eyes look right on,
    and let your eyelids look straight before you.
²⁶ Ponder the path of your feet,
    and let all your ways be established.
²⁷ Do not turn to the right or to the left;
    remove your foot from evil.

Warning Against Adultery

5 My son, attend to my wisdom,
    and bow your ear to my understanding,

² that you may regard discretion,
    and that your lips may keep knowledge.
³ For the lips of an immoral woman drip as
    a honeycomb,
    and her mouth is smoother than oil.
⁴ But her end is bitter as wormwood,
    sharp as a two-edged sword.
⁵ Her feet go down to death,
    her steps take hold of Sheol.
⁶ She does not ponder the path of life;
    her ways are unstable, and she does not know it.

⁷ Hear me now therefore, O children,
    and do not depart from the words of my mouth.
⁸ Remove your way far from her,
    and do not go near the door of her house,
⁹ lest you give your honor to others,
    and your years to the cruel;
¹⁰ lest strangers be filled with your wealth,
    and your labors go to the house of a stranger;
¹¹ and you mourn at the last,
    when your flesh and your body are consumed,
¹² and say, "How I have hated instruction,
    and my heart despised reproof!
¹³ And I have not obeyed the voice of my teachers,
    nor inclined my ear to those who instructed me!
¹⁴ I was almost in utter ruin
    in the midst of the congregation and assembly."

¹⁵ Drink waters out of your own cistern,
    and running waters out of your own well.
¹⁶ Should your fountains be dispersed abroad,
    streams of water in the streets?
¹⁷ Let them be only your own,
    and not for strangers with you.
¹⁸ Let your fountain be blessed,
    and rejoice with the wife of your youth.
¹⁹ Let her be as the loving deer and pleasant doe;
    let her breasts satisfy you at all times;
    and always be enraptured with her love.
²⁰ Why should you, my son, be intoxicated by an
    immoral woman,
    and embrace the bosom of a seductress?

²¹ For the ways of man are before the eyes of the LORD,
    and He ponders all his goings.
²² His own iniquities entrap the wicked himself,
    and he is snared in the cords of his sins.
²³ He will die for lack of instruction,
    and in the greatness of his folly he will go astray.

Warning Against Pledges

6 My son, if you put up a security for your friend,
    if you have shaken hands with a stranger,
² you are snared with the words of your mouth;
    you are taken with the words of your mouth.
³ Do this now, my son, and deliver yourself;
    when you have come into the hand of your friend,
    go and humble yourself;
    plead with your friend.
⁴ Give no sleep to your eyes,
    nor slumber to your eyelids.
⁵ Deliver yourself as a doe from the hand of the hunter,
    and as a bird from the hand of the fowler.

The Folly of Idleness

⁶ Go to the ant, you sluggard!
    Consider her ways and be wise.
⁷ Which, having no guide,
    overseer, or ruler,
⁸ provides her bread in the summer,
    and gathers her food in the harvest.

9 How long will you sleep, O sluggard?
     When will you arise out of your sleep?
10 Yet a little sleep, a little slumber,
     a little folding of the hands to sleep—
11 so will your poverty come upon you like a stalker,
     and your need as an armed man.

The Wicked Man

12 A wayward person, a wicked man,
     walks with a perverse mouth.
13   He winks with his eyes,
     he signals with his feet,
     he motions with his fingers;
14   perversity is in his heart,
     he devises mischief continually, he sows discord.
15 Therefore his calamity will come suddenly;
     in a moment he will be broken without remedy.

16 These six things the Lord hates,
     yes, seven are an abomination to him:
17   a proud look,
     a lying tongue,
     and hands that shed innocent blood,
18   a heart that devises wicked imaginations,
     feet that are swift in running to mischief,
19   a false witness who speaks lies,
     and he who sows discord among brethren.

Warning Against Adultery

20 My son, keep your father's commandment,
     and do not forsake the instruction of your mother.
21 Bind them continually upon your heart,
     and tie them around your neck.
22 When you go, they will lead you;
     when you sleep, they will keep you;
     and when you awake, they will speak with you.
23 For the commandment is a lamp, and the law is light;
     and reproofs of instruction are the way of life,
24 to keep you from the evil woman,
     from the flattery of the tongue of a seductress.

25 Do not lust after her beauty in your heart,
     nor let her allure you with her eyelids.

26 For by means of a harlot a man is reduced to a piece of bread,
     and the adulteress will prey upon his precious life.
27 Can a man take fire in his bosom,
     and his clothes not be burned?
28 Can one walk upon hot coals,
     and his feet not be burned?
29 So he who goes in to his neighbor's wife;
     whoever touches her will not be innocent.

30 Men do not despise a thief if he steals
     to satisfy himself when he is hungry.
31 But if he is found, he will restore sevenfold;
     he will give all the substance of his house.
32 But whoever commits adultery with a woman lacks understanding;
     he who does it destroys his own soul.
33 A wound and dishonor will he get,
     and his reproach will not be wiped away.

34 For jealousy is the rage of a man;
     therefore he will not spare in the day of vengeance.
35 He will not regard any ransom,
     nor will he rest content, though you give many gifts.

Beware of the Adulteress

7 My son, keep my words,
     and lay up my commandments within you.
2 Keep my commandments and live,
     and my teaching as the apple of your eye.

3 Bind them on your fingers;
     write them on the tablet of your heart.
4 Say to wisdom, "You are my sister,"
     and call understanding your kinswoman,
5 that they may keep you from the immoral woman,
     from the seductress who flatters with her words.

6 For at the window of my house
     I looked through my casement,
7 and saw among the simple ones,
     I discerned among the youths,
     a young man void of understanding,
8 passing through the street near her corner;
     and he went the way to her house
9 in the twilight, in the evening,
     in the black and dark night.

10 And there a woman met him,
     with the attire of a harlot, and subtle of heart.
11 She is loud and stubborn;
     her feet do not abide in her house.
12 Now she is without, now in the streets,
     and lies in wait at every corner.
13 So she caught him, and kissed him;
     and with an impudent face said to him:

14 "I have peace offerings with me;
     this day have I paid my vows.
15 Therefore I came out to meet you,
     diligently to seek your face, and I have found you.
16 I have decked my bed with coverings of tapestry,
     with carved works, with fine linen of Egypt.
17 I have perfumed my bed
     with myrrh, aloes, and cinnamon.
18 Come, let us take our fill of love until the morning;
     let us solace ourselves with love.
19 For my husband is not at home;
     he has gone on a long journey;
20 he has taken a bag of money with him,
     and will come home at the day appointed."

21 With her enticing speech she caused him to yield,
     with the flattering of her lips she seduced him.
22 He went after her straightway,
     as an ox goes to the slaughter,
     or as a fool to the correction of the stocks,
23   until a dart struck through his liver.
     As a bird hastens to the snare,
     he did not know that it would cost him his life.

24 Listen to me now therefore, O children,
     and attend to the words of my mouth:
25 do not let your heart turn aside to her ways,
     do not go astray in her paths;
26 for she has cast down many wounded,
     and many strong men have been slain by her.
27 Her house is the way to Sheol,
     going down to the chambers of death.

The Virtue of Wisdom

8 Does not wisdom cry out,
     and understanding lift up her voice?
2 She stands on the top of high places,
     by the way in the places of the paths.
3 She cries out at the gates,
     at the entry of the city, at the entrance of the doors:
4 "To you, O men, I call,
     and my voice is to the sons of men.
5 O you simple, understand wisdom,
     and you fools, be of an understanding heart.
6 Hear, for I will speak of excellent things,
     and from the opening of my lips will be right things;

7 for my mouth will speak truth,
    and wickedness is an abomination to my lips.
8 All the words of my mouth are in righteousness;
    there is nothing crooked or perverse in them.
9 They are all plain to him who understands,
    and right to those who find knowledge.
10 Receive my instruction, and not silver,
    and knowledge rather than choice gold;
11 for wisdom is better than rubies,
    and all the things that may be desired are not to be
      compared to it.

12 "I, wisdom, dwell with prudence,
    and find out knowledge and discretion.
13 The fear of the Lord is to hate evil;
    pride and arrogance
    and the evil way and the perverse mouth I hate.
14 Counsel is mine, and sound wisdom;
    I am understanding, I have strength.
15 By me kings reign,
    and princes decree justice.
16 By me princes rule,
    and nobles, even all the judges of the earth.
17 I love those who love me,
    and those who seek me early will find me.
18 Riches and honor are with me,
    yes, enduring riches and righteousness.
19 My fruit is better than gold,
    yes, than fine gold, and my revenue than choice silver.
20 I lead in the way of righteousness,
    in the midst of the paths of justice,
21 that I may cause those who love me to inherit wealth,
    and I will fill their treasuries.

22 "The Lord possessed me in the beginning of His way,
    before His works of old.
23 I was set up from everlasting,
    from the beginning, before there was ever an earth.
24 When there were no depths, I was brought forth,
    when there were no fountains abounding with water.
25 Before the mountains were settled,
    before the hills I was brought forth;
26 while as yet He had not made the earth or the fields,
    or the first dust of the world.
27 When He prepared the heavens, I was there,
    when He drew a circle on the face of the deep,
28 when He established the clouds above,
    when He strengthened the fountains of the deep,
29 when He gave to the sea His decree,
    that the waters should not pass His commandment,
    when He appointed the foundations of the earth,
30   then I was by Him, as one brought up with Him;
    and I was daily His delight,
      rejoicing always before Him,
31 rejoicing in the habitable part of His earth,
    and my delights were with the sons of men.

32 "Now therefore listen to me, O you children,
    for blessed are those who keep my ways.
33 Hear instruction, and be wise,
    and do not refuse it.
34 Blessed is the man who hears me,
    watching daily at my gates,
    waiting at the posts of my doors.
35 For whoever finds me finds life,
    and will obtain favor of the Lord;
36 but he who sins against me wrongs his own soul;
    all those who hate me love death."

The Way of Wisdom

9 Wisdom has built her house,
    she has hewn out her seven pillars;

2 she has killed her beasts, she has mixed her wine,
    she has also furnished her table.
3 She has sent out her maidens,
    she cries out from the highest places of the city,
4 "Whoever is simple, let him turn in here."
    As for him who wants understanding, she
      says to him,
5 "Come, eat of my bread,
    and drink of the wine which I have mixed.
6 Forsake foolishness and live,
    and go in the way of understanding."

7 He who reproves a scorner gets shame for himself,
    and he who rebukes a wicked man gets hurt.
8 Do not reprove a scorner, lest he hate you;
    rebuke a wise man, and he will love you.
9 Give instruction to a wise man, and he will be yet wiser;
    teach a just man, and he will increase in learning.

10 The fear of the Lord is the beginning of wisdom,
    and the knowledge of the Holy One is understanding.
11 For by me your days will be multiplied,
    and the years of your life will be increased.
12 If you are wise, you will be wise for yourself,
    but if you scorn, you alone will bear it.

The Way of Foolishness

13 A foolish woman is clamorous;
    she is simple, and knows nothing.
14 For she sits at the door of her house,
    on a seat in the high places of the city,
15 to call those who pass by
    who go right on their way:
16 "Whoever is simple, let him turn in here."
    And as for him who lacks understanding, she says to him,
17 "Stolen waters are sweet,
    and bread eaten in secret is pleasant."
18 But he does not know that the dead are there,
    and that her guests are in the depths of the grave.

The Proverbs of Solomon

10 The proverbs of Solomon.

A wise son makes a glad father,
    but a foolish son is the grief of his mother.

2 Treasures of wickedness profit nothing,
    but righteousness delivers from death.

3 The Lord will not allow the soul of the righteous to famish,
    but He casts away the desire of the wicked.

4 He becomes poor who deals with a slack hand,
    but the hand of the diligent makes rich.

5 He who gathers in summer is a wise son,
    but he who sleeps in harvest is a son who causes shame.

6 Blessings are on the head of the just,
    but violence covers the mouth of the wicked.

7 The memory of the just is blessed,
    but the name of the wicked will rot.

8 The wise in heart will receive commandments,
    but a prating fool will fall.

9 He who walks uprightly walks surely,
    but he who perverts his ways will be known.

10 He who winks with the eye causes sorrow,
    but a prating fool will fall.

11 The mouth of a righteous man is a well of life,
   but violence covers the mouth of the wicked.

12 Hatred stirs up strife,
   but love covers all sins.

13 In the lips of him who has understanding wisdom is found,
   but a rod is for the back of him who is void of understanding.

14 Wise men store up knowledge,
   but the mouth of the foolish is near destruction.

15 The rich man's wealth is his strong city;
   the destruction of the poor is their poverty.

16 The labor of the righteous tends to life,
   the fruit of the wicked to sin.

17 He who keeps instruction is in the way of life,
   but he who refuses reproof errs.

18 He who hides hatred has lying lips,
   and he who spreads slander is a fool.

19 In the multitude of words sin is not lacking,
   but he who restrains his lips is wise.

20 The tongue of the just is as choice silver;
   the heart of the wicked is worth little.

21 The lips of the righteous feed many,
   but fools die for lack of wisdom.

22 The blessing of the LORD makes rich,
   and He adds no sorrow with it.

23 To do mischief is like sport to a fool,
   but a man of understanding has wisdom.

24 The fear of the wicked will come upon him,
   but the desire of the righteous will be granted.

25 As the whirlwind passes, so is the wicked no more,
   but the righteous has an everlasting foundation.

26 As vinegar to the teeth and as smoke to the eyes,
   so is the sluggard to those who send him.

27 The fear of the LORD prolongs days,
   but the years of the wicked will be shortened.

28 The hope of the righteous will be gladness,
   but the expectation of the wicked will perish.

29 The way of the LORD is strength to the upright,
   but destruction will come to the workers of iniquity.

30 The righteous will never be removed,
   but the wicked will not inhabit the earth.

31 The mouth of the just brings forth wisdom,
   but the perverse tongue will be cut out.

32 The lips of the righteous know what is acceptable,
   but the mouth of the wicked speaks what
   is perverse.

11 A false balance is abomination to the LORD,
   but a just weight is His delight.

2 When pride comes, then comes shame;
  but with the humble is wisdom.

3 The integrity of the upright will guide them,
  but the perverseness of transgressors will destroy them.

4 Riches do not profit in the day of wrath,
  but righteousness delivers from death.

5 The righteousness of the upright will direct his way,
  but the wicked will fall by his own wickedness.

6 The righteousness of the upright will deliver them,
  but transgressors will be taken by their schemes.

7 When a wicked man dies, his expectation will perish,
  and the hope of unjust men perishes.

8 The righteous is delivered out of trouble,
  and the wicked comes in his place.

9 A hypocrite with his mouth destroys his neighbor,
  but through knowledge the just will be delivered.

10 When it goes well with the righteous, the city rejoices;
   and when the wicked perish, there is shouting.

11 By the blessing of the upright the city is exalted,
   but it is overthrown by the mouth of the wicked.

12 He who is void of wisdom despises his neighbor,
   but a man of understanding holds his peace.

13 A talebearer reveals secrets,
   but he who is of a faithful spirit conceals the matter.

14 Where there is no counsel, the people fall;
   but in the multitude of counselors there is safety.

15 He who puts up a pledge for a stranger will suffer for it,
   and he who hates being a pledge is secure.

16 A gracious woman retains honor,
   but ruthless men retain riches.

17 The merciful man does good to his own soul,
   but he who is cruel troubles his own body.

18 The wicked works a deceitful work,
   but to him who sows righteousness will be a sure reward.

19 As righteousness tends to life,
   so he who pursues evil pursues it to his own death.

20 Those who are of a perverse heart are abomination to the LORD,
   but such as are upright in their way are His delight.

21 Though be assured, the wicked will not be unpunished,
   but the posterity of the righteous will be delivered.

22 As a jewel of gold in a swine's snout,
   so is a fair woman who is without discretion.

23 The desire of the righteous is only good,
   but the expectation of the wicked is wrath.

24 There is *one* who scatters, yet increases;
   and there is *one* who withholds more than is right, but it
   leads to poverty.

25 The generous soul will be made rich,
   and he who waters will be watered also himself.

26 The people will curse him who withholds grain,
   but blessing will be upon the head of him who sells it.

27 He who diligently seeks good procures favor,
  but he who seeks mischief, it will come to him.

28 He who trusts in his riches will fall,
  but the righteous will flourish as a branch.

29 He who troubles his own house will inherit the wind,
  and the fool will be servant to the wise of heart.

30 The fruit of the righteous is a tree of life,
  and he who wins souls is wise.

31 If the righteous will be recompensed in the earth,
  how much more the wicked and the sinner.

12 Whoever loves instruction loves knowledge,
  but he who hates reproof is brutish.

2 A good man obtains favor of the LORD,
  but a man of wicked devices will He condemn.

3 A man will not be established by wickedness,
  but the root of the righteous will not be moved.

4 A virtuous woman is a crown to her husband,
  but she who brings shame is as rottenness in his bones.

5 The thoughts of the righteous are right,
  but the counsels of the wicked are deceit.

6 The words of the wicked are, "Lie in wait for blood,"
  but the mouth of the upright will deliver them.

7 The wicked are overthrown, and are not,
  but the house of the righteous will stand.

8 A man will be commended according to his wisdom,
  but he who is of a perverse heart will be despised.

9 He who is lightly esteemed and has a servant is better
  than he who honors himself and lacks bread.

10 A righteous man regards the life of his animal,
  but the tender mercies of the wicked are cruel.

11 He who tills his land will be satisfied with bread,
  but he who follows vain persons is void of understanding.

12 The wicked covet the plunder of evil men,
  but the root of the righteous yields fruit.

13 The wicked is snared by the transgression of his lips,
  but the just will come out of trouble.

14 A man will be satisfied with good by the fruit of his mouth,
  and the recompense of a man's hands will be rendered
  to him.

15 The way of a fool is right in his own eyes,
  but he who listens to counsel is wise.

16 A fool's wrath is presently known,
  but a prudent man covers shame.

17 He who speaks truth shows forth righteousness,
  but a false witness deceit.

18 There is one who speaks like the piercings of a sword,
  but the tongue of the wise is health.

19 The truthful lip will be established forever,
  but a lying tongue is but for a moment.

20 Deceit is in the heart of those who imagine evil,
  but to the counselors of peace is joy.

21 There will no evil happen to the just,
  but the wicked will be filled with mischief.

22 Lying lips are abomination to the LORD,
  but those who deal truly are His delight.

23 A prudent man conceals knowledge,
  but the heart of fools proclaims foolishness.

24 The hand of the diligent will rule,
  but the slothful will be put to forced labor.

25 Heaviness in the heart of man makes it droop,
  but a good word makes it glad.

26 The righteous is a guide to his neighbors,
  but the way of the wicked leads them astray.

27 The slothful man does not roast that which he took
      in hunting,
  but the substance of a diligent man is precious.

28 In the way of righteousness is life,
  and in its pathway there is no death.

13 A wise son heeds his father's instruction,
  but a scoffer does not listen to rebuke.

2 A man will eat well by the fruit of his mouth,
  but the soul of the transgressor will eat violence.

3 He who guards his mouth preserves his life,
  but he who opens wide his lips will have destruction.

4 The soul of the sluggard desires, and has nothing;
  but the soul of the diligent will be made fat.

5 A righteous man hates lying,
  but a wicked man is loathsome and comes to shame.

6 Righteousness keeps him who is upright in the way,
  but wickedness overthrows the sinner.

7 There is one who makes himself rich, yet has nothing;
  there is one who makes himself poor, yet has great riches.

8 The ransom of a man's life is his riches,
  but the poor does not hear rebuke.

9 The light of the righteous rejoices,
  but the lamp of the wicked will be put out.

10 Only by pride comes contention,
  but with the well-advised is wisdom.

11 Wealth gained by vanity will be diminished,
  but he who gathers by labor will increase.

12 Hope deferred makes the heart sick,
  but when the desire comes, it is a tree of life.

13 Whoever despises the word will be destroyed,
  but he who fears the commandment will be rewarded.

14 The teaching of the wise is a fountain of life,
  to depart from the snares of death.

15 Good understanding gives favor,
  but the way of transgressors is hard.

16 Every prudent man deals with knowledge,
  but a fool lays open his folly.

17 A wicked messenger falls into mischief,
  but a faithful envoy is health.

18 Poverty and shame will be to him who refuses instruction,
  but he who regards reproof will be honored.

19 The desire accomplished is sweet to the soul,
  but it is abomination to fools to depart from evil.

20 He who walks with wise men will be wise,
  but a companion of fools will be destroyed.

21 Evil pursues sinners,
  but to the righteous good will be repaid.

22 A good man leaves an inheritance to his children's children,
  and the wealth of the sinner is laid up for the just.

23 Much food is in the tillage of the poor,
  but for lack of justice it is destroyed.

24 He who spares his rod hates his son,
  but he who loves him disciplines him early.

25 The righteous eats to the satisfying of his soul,
  but the stomach of the wicked will want.

14 Every wise woman builds her house,
  but the foolish pulls it down with her hands.

2 He who walks in his uprightness fears the LORD,
  but he who is perverse in his ways despises Him.

3 In the mouth of the foolish is a rod of pride,
  but the lips of the wise will preserve them.

4 Where no oxen are, the crib is clean;
  but much increase is by the strength of the ox.

5 A faithful witness will not lie,
  but a false witness will utter lies.

6 A scorner seeks wisdom and does not find it,
  but knowledge is easy to him who understands.

7 Go from the presence of a foolish man,
  when you do not perceive in him the lips
    of knowledge.

8 The wisdom of the prudent is to understand his way,
  but the folly of fools is deceit.

9 Fools make a mock at sin,
  but among the righteous there is favor.

10 The heart knows its own bitterness,
  and a stranger does not share its joy.

11 The house of the wicked will be overthrown,
  but the tent of the upright will flourish.

12 There is a way that seems right to a man,
  but its end is the way of death.

13 Even in laughter the heart is sorrowful,
  and the end of that cheer is grief.

14 The backslider in heart will be filled with his own ways,
  but a good man will be satisfied with his.

15 The simple believes every word,
  but the prudent man considers his steps.

16 A wise man fears and departs from evil,
  but the fool rages and is self-confident.

17 He who is quick-tempered deals foolishly,
  and a man of wicked devices is hated.

18 The simple inherit folly,
  but the prudent are crowned with knowledge.

19 The evil bow before the good,
  and the wicked at the gates of the righteous.

20 The poor is hated even by his own neighbor,
  but the rich has many friends.

21 He who despises his neighbor sins,
  but he who has mercy on the poor, happy is he.

22 Do they not err who devise evil?
  But mercy and truth will be to those who
    devise good.

23 In all labor there is profit,
  but mere talk leads only to poverty.

24 The crown of the wise is their riches,
  but the foolishness of fools is folly.

25 A true witness delivers souls,
  but a deceitful witness speaks lies.

26 In the fear of the LORD is strong confidence,
  and His children will have a place of refuge.

27 The fear of the LORD is a fountain of life,
  to depart from the snares of death.

28 In the multitude of people is a king's honor,
  but in the lack of people is the destruction of a prince.

29 He who is slow to wrath is of great understanding,
  but he who is hasty of spirit exalts folly.

30 A sound heart is the life of the flesh,
  but envy the rottenness of the bones.

31 He who oppresses the poor reproaches his Maker,
  but he who honors Him has mercy on the poor.

32 The wicked is driven away in his wickedness,
  but the righteous has hope in his death.

33 Wisdom rests in the heart of him who has understanding,
  but that which is in the midst of fools is made known.

34 Righteousness exalts a nation,
  but sin is a reproach to any people.

35 The king's favor is toward a wise servant,
  but his wrath is against him who causes shame.

15 A soft answer turns away wrath,
  but grievous words stir up anger.

2 The tongue of the wise uses knowledge aright,
  but the mouth of fools pours out foolishness.

3 The eyes of the LORD are in every place,
  keeping watch on the evil and the good.

4 A wholesome tongue is a tree of life,
     but perverseness in it crushes the spirit.

5 A fool despises his father's instruction,
     but he who regards reproof is prudent.

6 In the house of the righteous is much treasure,
     but in the revenue of the wicked is trouble.

7 The lips of the wise disperse knowledge,
     but the heart of the foolish does not do so.

8 The sacrifice of the wicked is an abomination to the LORD,
     but the prayer of the upright is His delight.

9 The way of the wicked is an abomination unto the LORD,
     but He loves him who follows after righteousness.

10 Correction is grievous to him who forsakes the way,
     and he who hates reproof will die.

11 Death and destruction are before the LORD;
     so how much more the hearts of the children of men.

12 A scorner does not love one who reproves him,
     nor will he go to the wise.

13 A merry heart makes a cheerful countenance,
     but by sorrow of the heart the spirit is broken.

14 The heart of him who has understanding seeks knowledge,
     but the mouth of fools feeds on foolishness.

15 All the days of the afflicted are evil,
     but he who is of a merry heart has a continual feast.

16 Better is little with the fear of the LORD
     than great treasure with trouble.

17 Better is a dinner of herbs where love is
     than a fatted calf with hatred.

18 A wrathful man stirs up strife,
     but he who is slow to anger appeases strife.

19 The way of the slothful man is as a hedge of thorns,
     but the way of the righteous is made plain.

20 A wise son makes a father glad,
     but a foolish man despises his mother.

21 Folly is joy to him who is destitute of wisdom,
     but a man of understanding walks uprightly.

22 Without counsel, purposes are disappointed,
     but in the multitude of counselors they are established.

23 A man has joy by the answer of his mouth,
     and a word spoken in due season, how good it is!

24 The way of life leads above for the wise,
     that he may depart from Sheol below.

25 The LORD will destroy the house of the proud,
     but He will establish the border of the widow.

26 The thoughts of the wicked are an abomination to
          the LORD,
     but the words of the pure are pleasant words.

27 He who is greedy of gain troubles his own house,
     but he who hates bribes will live.

28 The heart of the righteous studies to answer,
     but the mouth of the wicked pours out evil things.

29 The LORD is far from the wicked,
     but He hears the prayer of the righteous.

30 The light of the eyes rejoices the heart,
     and a good report makes the bones healthy.

31 The ear that hears the reproof of life
     abides among the wise.

32 He who refuses instruction despises his own soul,
     but he who hears reproof gains understanding.

33 The fear of the LORD is the instruction of wisdom,
     and before honor is humility.

16 The preparations of the heart belong to man,
     but the answer of the tongue is from the LORD.

2 All the ways of a man are clean in his own eyes,
     but the LORD weighs the spirit.

3 Commit your works to the LORD,
     and your thoughts will be established.

4 The LORD has made all things for Himself,
     yes, even the wicked for the day of evil.

5 Everyone who is proud in heart is an abomination to the LORD;
     be assured, he will not be unpunished.

6 By mercy and truth iniquity is purged;
     and by the fear of the LORD men depart from evil.

7 When a man's ways please the LORD,
     He makes even his enemies to be at peace with him.

8 Better is a little with righteousness
     than great revenues with injustice.

9 A man's heart devises his way,
     but the LORD directs his steps.

10 A divine sentence is in the lips of the king;
     his mouth does not transgress in judgment.

11 A just weight and balance belong to the LORD;
     all the weights of the bag are His work.

12 It is an abomination to kings to commit wickedness,
     for the throne is established by righteousness.

13 Righteous lips are the delight of kings,
     and they love him who speaks right.

14 The wrath of a king is as messengers of death,
     but a wise man will pacify it.

15 In the light of the king's countenance is life,
     and his favor is as a cloud of the latter rain.

16 How much better to get wisdom than gold!
     And to get understanding is to be chosen rather
          than silver!

17 The highway of the upright is to depart from evil;
     he who keeps his way preserves his soul.

18 Pride goes before destruction,
     and a haughty spirit before a fall.

¹⁹ Better it is to be of a humble spirit with the lowly
  than to divide the spoil with the proud.

²⁰ He who handles a matter wisely will find good,
  and whoever trusts in the Lord, happy is he.

²¹ The wise in heart will be called prudent,
  and the sweetness of the lips increases learning.

²² Understanding is a wellspring of life to him who has it,
  but the instruction of fools is folly.

²³ The heart of the wise teaches his mouth,
  and adds learning to his lips.

²⁴ Pleasant words are as a honeycomb,
  sweet to the soul and health to the bones.

²⁵ There is a way that seems right to a man,
  but its end is the way of death.

²⁶ He who labors, labors for himself,
  for his mouth craves it of him.

²⁷ An ungodly man digs up evil,
  and in his lips there is as a burning fire.

²⁸ A perverse man sows strife,
  and a whisperer separates the best of friends.

²⁹ A violent man entices his neighbor,
  and leads him into the way that is not good.

³⁰ He shuts his eyes to devise perverse things;
  moving his lips he brings evil to pass.

³¹ The gray-haired head is a crown of glory,
  if it is found in the way of righteousness.

³² He who is slow to anger is better than the mighty,
  and he who rules his spirit than he who takes
    a city.

³³ The lot is cast into the lap,
  but the whole outcome is of the Lord.

17 Better is a dry morsel with quietness
  than a house full of sacrifices with strife.

² A wise servant will have rule over a son who causes shame,
  and will have part of the inheritance among the brothers.

³ The refining pot is for silver and the furnace for gold,
  but the Lord tries the hearts.

⁴ A wicked doer gives heed to false lips,
  and a liar gives ear to a wayward tongue.

⁵ Whoever mocks the poor reproaches his Maker,
  and he who is glad at calamities will not be unpunished.

⁶ Grandchildren are the crown of old men,
  and the glory of children are their fathers.

⁷ Excellent speech is not becoming to a fool,
  much less lying lips to a prince.

⁸ A gift is as a precious stone in the eyes of him who has it;
  wherever he turns, it prospers.

⁹ He who covers a transgression seeks love,
  but he who repeats a matter separates friends.

¹⁰ A reproof enters deeper into a wise man
  than a hundred stripes into a fool.

¹¹ An evil man seeks only rebellion;
  therefore a cruel messenger will be sent against him.

¹² Let a man meet a bear robbed of her cubs
  rather than a fool in his folly.

¹³ Whoever rewards evil for good,
  evil will not depart from his house.

¹⁴ The beginning of strife is as when one lets out water;
  therefore abandon contention before a quarrel starts.

¹⁵ He who justifies the wicked, and he who condemns the just,
  both of them are abomination to the Lord.

¹⁶ Why is there a price in the hand of a fool to get wisdom,
  seeing he has no heart for it?

¹⁷ A friend loves at all times,
  and a brother is born for adversity.

¹⁸ A man void of understanding shakes hands,
  and becomes a pledge in the presence of his friend.

¹⁹ He loves transgression who loves strife,
  and he who exalts his gate seeks destruction.

²⁰ He who has a deceitful heart finds no good,
  and he who has a perverse tongue falls
    into mischief.

²¹ He who fathers a fool does it to his sorrow,
  and the father of a fool has no joy.

²² A merry heart does good like a medicine,
  but a broken spirit dries the bones.

²³ A wicked man takes a bribe out of a hidden place
  to pervert the ways of judgment.

²⁴ Wisdom is before him who has understanding,
  but the eyes of a fool are in the ends of the earth.

²⁵ A foolish son is a grief to his father,
  and bitterness to her who bore him.

²⁶ Also to punish the just is not good,
  nor to strike princes for their uprightness.

²⁷ He who has knowledge spares his words,
  and a man of understanding is of an excellent spirit.

²⁸ Even a fool, when he holds his peace, is counted wise;
  and he who shuts his lips is esteemed a man of understanding.

18 He who separates himself seeks his own desire;
  he seeks and quarrels against all wisdom.

² A fool has no delight in understanding,
  but in expressing his own heart.

³ When the wicked comes, then comes also contempt,
  and with dishonor reproach.

⁴ The words of a man's mouth are as deep waters,
  and the wellspring of wisdom as a flowing brook.

⁵ It is not good to favor the wicked,
  or to turn aside the righteous in judgment.

⁶ A fool's lips enter into contention,
and his mouth calls for flogging.

⁷ A fool's mouth is his destruction,
and his lips are the snare of his soul.

⁸ The words of a talebearer are as wounds,
and they go down into the innermost parts of the body.

⁹ He also who is slothful in his work
is brother to him who is a great waster.

¹⁰ The name of the LORD is a strong tower;
the righteous run into it and are safe.

¹¹ The rich man's wealth is his strong city,
and as a high wall in his own conceit.

¹² Before destruction the heart of man is haughty,
and before honor is humility.

¹³ He who answers a matter before he hears it,
it is folly and shame to him.

¹⁴ The spirit of a man will sustain his infirmity,
but a wounded spirit who can bear?

¹⁵ The heart of the prudent gets knowledge,
and the ear of the wise seeks knowledge.

¹⁶ A man's gift makes room for him,
and brings him before great men.

¹⁷ He who is first in his own cause seems just,
but his neighbor comes and searches him.

¹⁸ The lot causes contentions to cease,
and keeps the mighty ones apart.

¹⁹ A brother offended is harder to be won than
a strong city,
and their contentions are like the bars
of a castle.

²⁰ A man's stomach will be satisfied with the fruit of
his mouth;
and with the increase of his lips will he be filled.

²¹ Death and life are in the power of the tongue,
and those who love it will eat its fruit.

²² Whoever finds a wife finds a good thing,
and obtains favor of the LORD.

²³ The poor *man* uses entreaties,
but the rich *man* answers roughly.

²⁴ A man who has friends must show himself friendly,
and there is a friend who sticks closer than
a brother.

19 Better is the poor who walks in his integrity
than he who is perverse in his lips and is a fool.

² Also, it is not good for the soul to be without knowledge,
and he who hastens with his feet sins.

³ The foolishness of man perverts his way,
and his heart frets against the LORD.

⁴ Wealth makes many friends,
but the poor is separated from his neighbor.

⁵ A false witness will not be unpunished,
and he who speaks lies will not escape.

⁶ Many will entreat the favor of the prince,
and every man is a friend to him who gives gifts.

⁷ All the brothers of the poor hate him;
how much more do his friends go far from him!
He pursues them with words,
yet they abandon him.

⁸ He who gets wisdom loves his own soul;
he who keeps understanding will find good.

⁹ A false witness will not be unpunished,
and he who speaks lies will perish.

¹⁰ Delight is not seemly for a fool,
much less for a servant to have rule over princes.

¹¹ The discretion of a man defers his anger,
and it is his glory to pass over a transgression.

¹² The king's wrath is as the roaring of a lion,
but his favor is as dew upon the grass.

¹³ A foolish son is the calamity of his father,
and the contentions of a wife are a continual dripping of water.

¹⁴ House and riches are the inheritance of fathers,
and a prudent wife is from the LORD.

¹⁵ Slothfulness casts into a deep sleep,
and an idle soul will suffer hunger.

¹⁶ He who keeps the commandment keeps his own soul,
but he who is careless in his ways will die.

¹⁷ He who has pity on the poor lends to the LORD,
and He will repay what he has given.

¹⁸ Chasten your son while there is hope,
and let not your soul spare for his crying.

¹⁹ A man of great wrath will suffer punishment;
for if you deliver him, yet you must do it again.

²⁰ Hear counsel and receive instruction,
that you may be wise in your latter days.

²¹ There are many plans in a man's heart,
nevertheless the counsel of the LORD will stand.

²² The desire of a man is his kindness,
and a poor man is better than a liar.

²³ The fear of the LORD tends to life,
and he who has it will abide satisfied; he will not be
visited with evil.

²⁴ A slothful man hides his hand in his bowl,
and will not so much as bring it to his mouth again.

²⁵ Smite a scorner, and the simple will beware;
and reprove one who has understanding, and he will
understand knowledge.

²⁶ He who mistreats his father and chases away his mother
is a son who causes shame and brings reproach.

²⁷ Cease, my son, to hear the instruction
that causes to err from the words of knowledge.

28 An ungodly witness scorns judgment,
and the mouth of the wicked devours iniquity.

29 Judgments are prepared for scorners,
and beatings for the back of fools.

20 Wine is a mocker, strong drink is raging,
and whoever is deceived by it is not wise.

2 The terror of a king is as the roaring of a lion;
whoever provokes him to anger sins against his own soul.

3 It is an honor for a man to cease from strife,
but every fool will be meddling.

4 The sluggard will not plow because of the cold;
therefore he will beg during harvest and have nothing.

5 Counsel in the heart of man is like deep water,
but a man of understanding will draw it out.

6 Most men will proclaim everyone his own goodness,
but who can find a faithful man?

7 The just man walks in his integrity;
his children are blessed after him.

8 A king who sits on the throne of judgment
scatters away all evil with his eyes.

9 Who can say, "I have made my heart clean,
I am pure from my sin"?

10 Diverse weights and diverse measures,
both of them alike are an abomination to the Lord.

11 Even a child is known by his doings,
whether his work is pure and whether it is right.

12 The hearing ear and the seeing eye,
the Lord has made both of them.

13 Do not love sleep, lest you come to poverty;
open your eyes, and you will be satisfied with bread.

14 "It is bad, it is bad," says the buyer;
but when he has gone his way, then he boasts.

15 There is gold and a multitude of rubies,
but the lips of knowledge are a precious jewel.

16 Take the garment of him who is a pledge for a stranger,
and hold it as a security when it is for a wayward woman.

17 Bread of deceit is sweet to a man,
but afterwards his mouth will be filled with gravel.

18 Every purpose is established by counsel,
and with good advice wage war.

19 He who goes about as a talebearer reveals secrets;
therefore do not meddle with him who flatters with
his lips.

20 Whoever curses his father or his mother,
his lamp will be put out in obscure darkness.

21 An inheritance may be gained hastily at the beginning,
but the end of it will not be blessed.

22 Do not say, "I will recompense evil";
but wait on the Lord, and He will save you.

23 Diverse weights are an abomination to the Lord,
and a false balance is not good.

24 Man's goings are of the Lord;
how can a man then understand his own way?

25 It is a snare to the man who dedicates rashly that which
is holy,
and after the vows to make inquiry.

26 A wise king sifts out the wicked,
and drives the threshing wheel over them.

27 The spirit of man is the candle of the Lord,
searching all the inward parts of the heart.

28 Mercy and truth preserve the king,
and his throne is upheld by mercy.

29 The glory of young men is their strength,
and the beauty of old men is the gray head.

30 The blows of a wound cleanse away evil,
so do stripes the inward parts of the heart.

21 The king's heart is in the hand of the Lord,
as the rivers of water; He turns it to any place He will.

2 Every way of a man is right in his own eyes,
but the Lord weighs the hearts.

3 To do justice and judgment
is more acceptable to the Lord than sacrifice.

4 A high look, a proud heart,
and the plowing of the wicked are sin.

5 The thoughts of the diligent tend only to plenty,
but of everyone who is hasty only to want.

6 The getting of treasures by a lying tongue
is a vanity tossed back and forth by those who seek death.

7 The violence of the wicked will destroy them,
because they refuse to do justice.

8 The way of a guilty man is perverse;
but as for the pure, his work is right.

9 It is better to dwell in a corner of the housetop
than with a brawling woman in a wide house.

10 The soul of the wicked desires evil;
his neighbor finds no favor in his eyes.

11 When the scorner is punished, the simple is made wise;
and when the wise is instructed, he receives knowledge.

12 The righteous man wisely considers the house of the wicked,
but God overthrows the wicked for their wickedness.

13 Whoever shuts his ears at the cry of the poor,
he also will cry himself, but will not be heard.

14 A gift in secret pacifies anger,
and a concealed bribe strong wrath.

15 It is joy to the just to do justice,
but destruction will come to the workers of iniquity.

16 The man who wanders out of the way of understanding
will remain in the congregation of the dead.

[17] He who loves pleasure will be a poor man;
      he who loves wine and oil will not be rich.

[18] The wicked will be a ransom for the righteous,
      and the transgressor for the upright.

[19] It is better to dwell in the wilderness
      than with a contentious and angry woman.

[20] There is treasure to be desired and oil in the dwelling
            of the wise,
      but a foolish man squanders it.

[21] He who follows after righteousness and mercy
      finds life, righteousness, and honor.

[22] A wise man scales the city of the mighty,
      and casts down the strength of its confidence.

[23] Whoever guards his mouth and his tongue
      keeps his soul from trouble.

[24] Proud and haughty—scorner is his name,
      who deals in proud wrath.

[25] The desire of the slothful kills him,
      for his hands refuse to labor.

[26] He covets greedily all the day long,
      but the righteous gives and does not spare.

[27] The sacrifice of the wicked is an abomination;
      how much more when he brings it with a wicked intent!

[28] A false witness will perish,
      but a man who listens will speak forever.

[29] A wicked man hardens his face,
      but as for the upright, he directs his way.

[30] There is no wisdom nor understanding nor counsel
      against the LORD.

[31] The horse is prepared against the day of battle,
      but victory is of the LORD.

22 A good name is rather to be chosen than great riches,
      and loving favor rather than silver and gold.

[2] The rich and poor have this in common,
      the LORD is the maker of them all.

[3] A prudent man foresees the evil and hides himself,
      but the simple pass on and are punished.

[4] By humility and the fear of the LORD
      are riches, and honor, and life.

[5] Thorns and snares are in the way of the perverse;
      he who guards his soul will be far from them.

[6] Train up a child in the way he should go,
      and when he is old he will not depart from it.

[7] The rich rules over the poor,
      and the borrower is servant to the lender.

[8] He who sows iniquity will reap vanity,
      and the rod of his anger will fail.

[9] He who has a bountiful eye will be blessed,
      for he gives of his bread to the poor.

[10] Cast out the scorner, and contention will go out;
      yes, strife and reproach will cease.

[11] He who loves pureness of heart, for the grace of his lips
      the king will be his friend.

[12] The eyes of the LORD preserve knowledge,
      and He overthrows the words of the transgressor.

[13] The slothful man says, "There is a lion without!
      I will be slain in the streets!"

[14] The mouth of an immoral woman is a deep pit;
      he who is detested by the LORD will fall therein.

[15] Foolishness is bound in the heart of a child,
      but the rod of correction will drive it far from him.

[16] He who oppresses the poor to increase his riches,
      and he who gives to the rich, will surely come
            to want.

Thirty Sayings of the Wise

Saying One

[17] Incline your ear and hear the words of the wise,
      and apply your heart to my knowledge;
[18] for it is a pleasant thing if you keep them within you;
      they will readily be fitted in your lips.
[19] That your trust may be in the LORD,
      I have made known to you this day, even to you.
[20] Have I not written to you excellent things
      in counsels and knowledge,
[21] that I might make you know the certainty of the words
            of truth,
      that you might answer the words of truth
      to those who send to you?

Saying Two

[22] Do not rob the poor because he is poor,
      neither oppress the afflicted in the gate;
[23] for the LORD will plead their cause,
      and spoil the soul of those who spoiled them.

Saying Three

[24] Make no friendship with an angry man,
      and with a furious man you will not go,
[25] lest you learn his ways
      and get a snare to your soul.

Saying Four

[26] Do not be one of those who shakes hands in a pledge,
      or of those who use securities for debts;
[27] if you have nothing to pay,
      why should he take away your bed from under you?

Saying Five

[28] Do not remove the ancient landmark
      which your fathers have set.

Saying Six

[29] Do you see a man diligent in his business?
      He will stand before kings;
      he will not stand before obscure men.

Saying Seven

23 When you sit to eat with a ruler,
      consider diligently what is before you;
[2] and put a knife to your throat,
      if you are a man given to appetite.
[3] Be not desirous of his delicacies,
      for they are deceptive food.

Saying Eight

4 Do not labor to be rich;
  cease from your own wisdom.
5 Will you set your eyes on that which is not?
  For riches certainly make themselves wings;
  they fly away as an eagle toward heaven.

Saying Nine

6 Do not eat the bread of him who has an evil eye,
  neither desire his delicacies;
7 for as he thinks in his heart,
  so is he.
  "Eat and drink!" he says to you,
  but his heart is not with you.
8 The morsel you have eaten, you will vomit up,
  and lose your sweet words.

Saying Ten

9 . Do not speak in the ears of a fool,
  for he will despise the wisdom of your words.

Saying Eleven

10 Do not remove the old landmark,
  nor enter the fields of the fatherless;
11 for their Redeemer is mighty;
  He will plead their cause with you.

Saying Twelve

12 Apply your heart to instruction,
  and your ears to the words of knowledge.

Saying Thirteen

13 Do not withhold correction from a child,
  for if you beat him with the rod, he will not die.
14 You shall beat him with the rod,
  and deliver his soul from death.

Saying Fourteen

15 My son, if your heart is wise,
  my heart will rejoice—even mine.
16 Yes, my inmost being will rejoice
  when your lips speak right things.

Saying Fifteen

17 Do not let your heart envy sinners,
  but continue in the fear of the Lord all day long;
18 for surely there is an end,
  and your expectation will not be cut off.

Saying Sixteen

19 Hear, my son, and be wise;
  and guide your heart in the way.
20 Do not be among winebibbers,
  among riotous eaters of meat;
21 for the drunkard and the glutton will come to poverty,
  and drowsiness will clothe a man with rags.

Saying Seventeen

22 Listen to your father who gave you life,
  and do not despise your mother when she is old.
23 Buy the truth, and do not sell it,
  also wisdom and instruction and understanding.
24 The father of the righteous will greatly rejoice,
  and he who fathers a wise child will have joy of him.
25 Your father and your mother will be glad,
  and she who bore you will rejoice.

Saying Eighteen

26 My son, give me your heart,
  and let your eyes observe my ways.
27 For a prostitute is a deep ditch,
  and a seductress is a narrow pit.

28 She also lies in wait as for a prey,
  and increases the transgressors among men.

Saying Nineteen

29 Who has woe? Who has sorrow?
  Who has contentions? Who has babbling?
  Who has wounds without cause? Who has redness of eyes?
30 Those who tarry long at the wine,
  those who go to seek mixed wine.
31 Do not look on the wine when it is red,
  when it sparkles in the cup,
  when it swirls around smoothly;
32 at the last it bites like a serpent,
  and stings like a viper.
33 Your eyes will see strange things,
  and your heart will utter perverse things.
34 Yes, you will be as he who lies down in the midst of the sea,
  or as he who lies upon the top of a mast.
35 "They have stricken me," you will say, "and I was not sick;
  they have beaten me, and I did not feel it.
  When will I awake?
  I will seek it yet again."

Saying Twenty

24 Do not be envious against evil men,
  nor desire to be with them;
2 for their heart studies destruction,
  and their lips talk of mischief.

Saying Twenty-One

3 Through wisdom is a house built,
  and by understanding it is established;
4 and by knowledge the rooms will be filled
  with all precious and pleasant riches.

Saying Twenty-Two

5 A wise man is strong;
  yes, a man of knowledge increases strength.
6 For by wise counsel you will wage your war,
  and in multitude of counselors there is safety.

Saying Twenty-Three

7 Wisdom is too high for a fool;
  he does not open his mouth in the gate.

Saying Twenty-Four

8 He who devises to do evil
  will be called a schemer of plots.
9 The thought of foolishness is sin,
  and the scorner is an abomination to men.

Saying Twenty-Five

10 If you faint in the day of adversity,
  your strength is small.
11 If you refrain to deliver those who are drawn unto death,
  and those who are ready to be slain;
12 if you say, "Surely we did not know this,"
  does not He who ponders the heart consider it?
  And He who keeps your soul, does He not know it?
  And will He not render to every man according to his works?

Saying Twenty-Six

13 My son, eat honey because it is good,
  and the honeycomb that is sweet to your taste;
14 so shall the knowledge of wisdom be to your soul;
  when you have found it, then there will be a reward,
  and your expectation will not be cut off.

Saying Twenty-Seven

15 Do not lie in wait, O wicked man, against the dwelling of
    the righteous;
  do not spoil his resting place;

16 for a just man falls seven times and rises up again,
  but the wicked will fall into mischief.

Saying Twenty-Eight

17 Do not rejoice when your enemy falls,
  and do not let your heart be glad when
    he stumbles;
18 lest the Lord see it, and it displease Him,
  and He turn away His wrath from him.

Saying Twenty-Nine

19 Do not fret because of evil men,
  nor be envious of the wicked;
20 for there will be no reward to the evil man;
  the candle of the wicked will be put out.

Saying Thirty

21 My son, fear the Lord and the king;
  and do not meddle with those who are given
    to change;
22 for their calamity will rise suddenly,
  and who knows the ruin of them both?

More Sayings of the Wise

23 These *things* also *belong* to the wise:

It is not good to show partiality in judgment.
24 He who says to the wicked, "You are righteous,"
  him the people will curse; nations will abhor him.
25 But to those who rebuke him will be delight,
  and a good blessing will come upon them.

26 Every man will kiss his lips
  that gives a right answer.

27 Prepare your work outside,
  and make it fit for yourself in the field;
  and afterwards build your house.

28 Do not be a witness against your neighbor without cause,
  and do not deceive with your lips.
29 Do not say, "I will do so to him as he has done to me;
  I will render to the man according to his work."

30 I went by the field of the slothful,
  and by the vineyard of the man void of understanding;
31 and it was all grown over with thorns,
  and nettles covered its surface,
  and the stone wall was broken down.
32 Then I saw, and considered it;
  I looked on it and received instruction:
33 Yet a little sleep, a little slumber,
  a little folding of the hands to sleep,
34 so your poverty will come like a stalker,
  and your need as an armed man.

More Proverbs of Solomon

25 These are also proverbs of Solomon, which the men of Hezekiah king of Judah copied.

2 It is the glory of God to conceal a thing,
  but the honor of kings is to search out a matter.
3 As the heaven for height, and the earth for depth,
  so the heart of kings is unsearchable.

4 Take away the dross from the silver,
  and there will come forth a vessel for the refiner.
5 Take away the wicked from before the king,
  and his throne will be established in righteousness.

6 Do not exalt yourself in the presence of the king,
  and do not stand in the place of great men;

7 for it is better that it be said to you, "Come up here,"
  than that you should be put lower in the presence
    of the prince,
  whom your eyes have seen.

8 Do not go forth hastily to strive;
  lest you do not know what to do in the end,
  when your neighbor has put you to shame.

9 Debate your cause with your neighbor himself,
  and do not disclose a secret to another;
10 lest he who hears it put you to shame,
  and your reputation be ruined.

11 A word fitly spoken
  is like apples of gold in settings of silver.
12 As an earring of gold and an ornament of fine gold,
  so is a wise reprover to an obedient ear.

13 As the cold of snow in the time of harvest,
  so is a faithful messenger to those who send him,
  for he refreshes the soul of his masters.
14 Whoever boasts himself of a false gift
  is like clouds and wind without rain.

15 By long forbearing is a prince persuaded,
  and a soft tongue breaks the bone.

16 Have you found honey? Eat only as much as is sufficient for you,
  lest you be filled with it and vomit it.
17 Withdraw your foot from your neighbor's house,
  lest he be weary of you and so hate you.

18 A man who bears false witness against his neighbor
  is like a club, a sword, and a sharp arrow.
19 Confidence in an unfaithful man in time of trouble
  is like a broken tooth and a foot out of joint.
20 As he who takes away a garment in cold weather,
  and as vinegar on soda,
  so is he who sings songs to a heavy heart.

21 If your enemy is hungry, give him bread to eat;
  and if he is thirsty, give him water to drink;
22 for you will heap coals of fire upon his head,
  and the Lord will reward you.

23 The north wind brings rain,
  and a backbiting tongue an angry countenance.

24 It is better to dwell in the corner of the housetop
  than with a brawling woman in a wide house.

25 As cold waters to a thirsty soul,
  so is good news from a far country.
26 A righteous man falling down before the wicked
  is as a troubled fountain and a corrupt spring.

27 It is not good to eat much honey;
  so for men to search their own glory is not glory.

28 He who has no rule over his own spirit
  is like a city that is broken down and without walls.

26 As snow in summer, and as rain in harvest,
  so honor is not seemly for a fool.
2 As the bird by flitting, as the swallow by flying,
  so the curse without cause will not alight.
3 A whip for the horse, a bridle for the donkey,
  and a rod for the fool's back.
4 Do not answer a fool according to his folly,
  lest you also be like unto him.
5 Answer a fool according to his folly,
  lest he be wise in his own conceit.

6 He who sends a message by the hand of a fool
    cuts off the feet and drinks violence.
7 The legs of the lame are not equal;
    so is a parable in the mouth of fools.
8 As he who binds a stone in a sling,
    so is he who gives honor to a fool.
9 As a thorn goes into the hand of a drunkard,
    so is a parable in the mouth of fools.
10 The great God who formed all things
    rewards the fool and rewards the transgressor.
11 As a dog returns to its vomit,
    so a fool returns to his folly.
12 Do you see a man wise in his own conceit?
    There is more hope for a fool than for him.

13 The slothful man says, "There is a lion in the way!
    A lion is in the streets!"
14 As the door turns upon his hinges,
    so does the slothful upon his bed.
15 The slothful buries his hand in his bowl;
    it grieves him to bring it again to his mouth.
16 The sluggard is wiser in his own conceit
    than seven men who can answer reasonably.

17 He who passes by and meddles with strife not belonging to him
    is like one who takes a dog by the ears.

18 As a madman who casts
    firebrands, arrows, and death,
19 so is the man who deceives his neighbor,
    and says, "I was only joking."

20 Where there is no wood, the fire goes out;
    so where there is no talebearer, the strife ceases.
21 As charcoal is to burning coals, and wood to fire,
    so is a contentious man to kindle strife.
22 The words of a talebearer are as wounds,
    and go down into the innermost parts of the body.

23 Burning lips and a wicked heart
    are like earthenware covered with silver dross.
24 He who hates dissembles with his lips,
    and lays up deceit within him;
25 when he speaks kindly, do not believe him,
    for there are seven abominations in his heart;
26 though his hatred is covered by deceit,
    his wickedness will be shown before the whole congregation.
27 Whoever digs a pit will fall into it,
    and he who rolls a stone, it will return upon him.
28 A lying tongue hates those who are afflicted by it,
    and a flattering mouth works ruin.

27 Do not boast about tomorrow,
    for you do not know what a day may bring forth.

2 Let another man praise you, and not your own mouth;
    a stranger, and not your own lips.

3 A stone is heavy and the sand weighty,
    but a fool's wrath is heavier than them both.

4 Wrath is cruel, and anger is outrageous,
    but who is able to stand before envy?

5 Open rebuke is better
    than secret love.

6 Faithful are the wounds of a friend,
    but the kisses of an enemy are deceitful.

7 The full soul loathes a honeycomb,
    but to the hungry soul every bitter thing is sweet.

8 As a bird that wanders from her nest,
    so is a man who wanders from his place.

9 Ointment and perfume rejoice the heart,
    so does the sweetness of a man's friend by
        hearty counsel.

10 Do not forsake your own friend or your father's friend,
    nor go into your brother's house in the day of your calamity;
    for better is a neighbor who is near than a brother far off.

11 My son, be wise, and make my heart glad,
    that I may answer him who reproaches me.

12 A prudent man foresees the evil and hides himself,
    but the simple pass on and are punished.

13 Take his garment that is security for a stranger,
    and take a pledge of him for an adulterous woman.

14 He who blesses his friend with a loud voice, rising early in
        the morning,
    it will be counted a curse to him.

15 A continual dripping on a very rainy day
    and a contentious woman are alike;
16 whoever restrains her restrains the wind,
    and grasps oil in his right hand.

17 Iron sharpens iron,
    so a man sharpens the countenance of his friend.

18 Whoever keeps the fig tree will eat its fruit;
    so he who waits on his master will be honored.

19 As in water face answers to face,
    so the heart of man to man.

20 Death and destruction are never full;
    so the eyes of man are never satisfied.

21 As the refining pot for silver, and the furnace for gold,
    so is a man to his praise.

22 Though you should grind a fool in a mortar
    among wheat with a pestle,
    yet his foolishness will not depart from him.

23 Be diligent to know the state of your flocks,
    and look well to your herds;
24 for riches are not forever,
    nor does the crown endure to every generation.
25 The hay appears, and the tender grass shows itself,
    and herbs of the mountains are gathered.
26 The lambs are for your clothing,
    and the goats are the price of the field.
27 You will have goats' milk enough
    for your food, for the food of your household,
    and for the maintenance of your maidens.

28 The wicked flee when no man pursues,
    but the righteous are bold as a lion.

2 Because of the transgression of a land, many are its princes;
    but by a man of understanding and knowledge, it shall
        be prolonged.

3 A poor man who oppresses the poor
    is like a sweeping rain that leaves no food.

4 Those who forsake instruction praise the wicked,
    but such as keep instruction contend with them.

5 Evil men do not understand justice,
   but those who seek the Lord understand all things.

6 Better is the poor who walks in his uprightness
   than he who is perverse in his ways, though he be rich.

7 Whoever keeps the law is a wise son,
   but he who is a companion of riotous men shames his father.

8 He who by usury and unjust gain increases his substance
   will gather it for him who will pity the poor.

9 He who turns away his ear from hearing instruction,
   even his prayer will be an abomination.

10 Whoever causes the righteous to go astray in an evil way,
   he himself will fall into his own pit;
   but the upright will have good things in possession.

11 The rich man is wise in his own conceit,
   but the poor who has understanding searches him out.

12 When righteous men rejoice, there is great glory;
   but when the wicked rise, a man hides himself.

13 He who covers his sins will not prosper,
   but whoever confesses and forsakes them will have mercy.

14 Happy is the man who always fears,
   but he who hardens his heart will fall into mischief.

15 As a roaring lion and a charging bear,
   so is a wicked ruler over the poor people.

16 The prince who lacks understanding is also a great oppressor,
   but he who hates covetousness will prolong his days.

17 A man burdened with bloodshed of any person
   will flee until death;
   let no man help him.

18 Whoever walks uprightly will be saved,
   but he who is perverse in his ways will fall at once.

19 He who tills his land will have plenty of bread,
   but he who follows after vain things will have
   poverty enough.

20 A faithful man will abound with blessings,
   but he who makes haste to be rich will not be innocent.

21 To show partiality is not good,
   because for a morsel of bread that man will transgress.

22 He who hastens to be rich has an evil eye,
   and does not consider that poverty will come upon him.

23 He who rebukes a man will find more favor afterward
   than he who flatters with the tongue.

24 Whoever robs his father or his mother
   and says, "It is no transgression,"
   the same is the companion of a destroyer.

25 He who is of a proud heart stirs up strife,
   but he who puts his trust in the Lord will prosper.

26 He who trusts in his own heart is a fool,
   but whoever walks wisely will be delivered.

27 He who gives to the poor will not lack,
   but he who hides his eyes will have many a curse.

28 When the wicked rise, men hide themselves;
   but when they perish, the righteous increase.

29 He who is often reproved, yet hardens his neck,
   will suddenly be destroyed, and that without remedy.

2 When the righteous are in authority, the people rejoice;
   but when the wicked rule, the people mourn.

3 Whoever loves wisdom rejoices his father,
   but he who keeps company with harlots spends
   his substance.

4 The king establishes the land by judgment,
   but he who receives bribes overthrows it.

5 A man who flatters his neighbor
   spreads a net for his feet.

6 In the transgression of an evil man there is a snare,
   but the righteous sing and rejoice.

7 The righteous considers the cause of the poor,
   but the wicked regards not to know it.

8 Scornful men bring a city into a snare,
   but wise men turn away wrath.

9 If a wise man contends with a foolish man,
   whether he rage or laugh, there is no rest.

10 The bloodthirsty hate the upright,
   but the just seek his soul.

11 A fool utters all his mind,
   but a wise man keeps it in until afterwards.

12 If a ruler listens to lies,
   all his servants are wicked.

13 The poor and the deceitful man have this in common:
   The Lord gives light to the eyes of both.

14 The king who faithfully judges the poor,
   his throne will be established forever.

15 The rod and reproof give wisdom,
   but a child left to himself brings his mother to shame.

16 When the wicked are multiplied, transgression increases;
   but the righteous will see their fall.

17 Correct your son, and he will give you rest;
   yes, he will give delight to your soul.

18 Where there is no vision, the people perish;
   but happy is he who keeps the teaching.

19 A servant will not be corrected by words,
   for though he understands he will not answer.

20 Do you see a man who is hasty in his words?
   There is more hope for a fool than for him.

21 He who delicately brings up his servant from a child
   will have him as a son in the end.

22 An angry man stirs up strife,
   and a furious man abounds in transgression.

23 A man's pride will bring him low,
   but honor will uphold the humble in spirit.

24 Whoever is partner with a thief hates his own soul;
   he hears the oath but tells nothing.

25 The fear of man brings a snare,
   but whoever puts his trust in the LORD will be safe.

26 Many seek the ruler's favor,
   but every man's judgment comes from the LORD.

27 An unjust man is an abomination to the just,
   and he who is upright in the way is an abomination to the wicked.

The Sayings of Agur

30 The words of Agur the son of Jakeh, the oracle.

The man declares to Ithiel,
   to Ithiel and Ukal:

2 Surely I am more brutish than any man,
   and have not the understanding of a man.
3 I neither learned wisdom,
   nor have the knowledge of the holy.
4 Who has ascended up into heaven, or descended?
   Who has gathered the wind in his fists?
   Who has bound the waters in a garment?
   Who has established all the ends of the earth?
   What is His name, and what is the name of His son,
   if you know?

5 Every word of God is pure;
   He is a shield to those who put their trust in Him.
6 Do not add to His words,
   lest He reprove you, and you be found a liar.

7 Two things I have required of you;
   do not deny me them before I die:
8 Remove vanity and lies far from me—
   give me neither poverty nor riches;
   feed me with food convenient for me;
9 lest I be full, and deny You,
   and say, "Who is the LORD?"
   or lest I be poor, and steal,
   and take the name of my God in vain.

10 Do not accuse a servant to his master,
   lest he curse you, and you be found guilty.

11 There is a generation that curses their father,
   and does not bless its mother.
12 There is a generation that is pure in its own eyes,
   and yet is not washed from its filthiness.
13 There is a generation—oh, how lofty are their eyes!
   And their eyelids are lifted up.
14 There is a generation whose teeth are as swords,
   and their jaw teeth as knives,
   to devour the poor from off the earth,
   and the needy from among men.

15 The leech has two daughters,
   crying, "Give, give."

There are three things that are never satisfied,
   indeed, four things never say, "It is enough":
16 the grave, the barren womb,
   the earth that is not filled with water,
   and the fire that never says, "It is enough."

17 The eye that mocks at his father,
   and despises to obey his mother,
   the ravens of the valley will pick it out,
   and the young eagles will eat it.

18 There are three things which are too wonderful for me,
   indeed, four which I do not know:
19 the way of an eagle in the air,
   the way of a serpent on a rock,
   the way of a ship in the midst of the sea,
   and the way of a man with a maid.

20 Such is the way of an adulterous woman;
   she eats and wipes her mouth,
   and says, "I have done no wickedness."

21 For three things the earth is disquieted,
   and for four which it cannot bear:
22 for a servant when he reigns,
   and a fool when he is filled with food,
23 for a hateful woman when she is married,
   and a handmaid who is heir to her mistress.

24 There are four things which are little upon the earth,
   but they are exceeding wise:
25 The ants are a people not strong,
   yet they prepare their food in the summer;
26 the badgers are but a feeble folk,
   yet they make their houses in the rocks;
27 the locusts have no king,
   yet they go forth all of them by bands;
28 the spider takes hold with her hands,
   and is in kings' palaces.

29 There are three things which go well,
   indeed, four are comely in going:
30 a lion which is strongest among beasts,
   and does not turn away for any;
31 a strutting rooster, a male goat also,
   and a king, against whom there is no rising up.

32 If you have been foolish in lifting up yourself,
   or if you have thought evil,
   put your hand on your mouth.
33 Surely the churning of milk brings forth butter,
   and the wringing of the nose brings forth blood,
   so the forcing of wrath brings forth strife.

The Sayings of King Lemuel's Mother

31 The words of King Lemuel, an oracle that his mother taught
him:

2 What, my son? And what, the son of my womb?
   And what, the son of my vows?
3 Do not give your strength to women,
   nor your ways to that which destroys kings.

4 It is not for kings, O Lemuel,
   it is not for kings to drink wine,
   nor for princes strong drink;
5 lest they drink and forget the law,
   and pervert the justice of any of the afflicted.
6 Give strong drink to him who is ready to perish,
   and wine to those who are of heavy hearts.
7 Let him drink, and forget his poverty,
   and remember his misery no more.

8 Open your mouth for the speechless
   in the cause of all such as are appointed to destruction.
9 Open your mouth, judge righteously,
   and plead the cause of the poor and needy.

Epilogue: The Virtuous Wife

10 Who can find a virtuous woman?
   For her worth is far above rubies.
11 The heart of her husband safely trusts in her,
   so that he will have no lack of gain.

¹² She will do him good and not evil
    all the days of her life.
¹³ She seeks wool and flax,
    and works willingly with her hands.
¹⁴ She is like the merchant ships,
    she brings her food from afar.
¹⁵ She also rises while it is yet night,
    and gives food to her household,
    and a portion to her maidens.
¹⁶ She considers a field and buys it;
    with the fruit of her hands she plants a vineyard.
¹⁷ She clothes herself with strength,
    and strengthens her arms.
¹⁸ She perceives that her merchandise is good;
    her candle does not go out by night.
¹⁹ She lays her hands to the spindle,
    and her hands hold the distaff.
²⁰ She stretches out her hand to the poor;
    yes, she reaches forth her hands to the needy.
²¹ She is not afraid of the snow for her household,
    for all her household are clothed with scarlet.

²² She makes herself coverings of tapestry;
    her clothing is silk and purple.
²³ Her husband is known in the gates,
    when he sits among the elders of the land.
²⁴ She makes fine linen and sells it,
    and delivers sashes to the merchant.
²⁵ Strength and honor are her clothing,
    and she will rejoice in time to come.
²⁶ She opens her mouth with wisdom,
    and in her tongue is the teaching of kindness.
²⁷ She looks well to the ways of her household,
    and does not eat the bread of idleness.
²⁸ Her children rise up and call her blessed;
    her husband also, and he praises her:
²⁹ "Many daughters have done virtuously,
    but you excel them all."
³⁰ Charm is deceitful, and beauty is vain,
    but a woman who fears the Lord, she shall
    be praised.
³¹ Give her of the fruit of her hands,
    and let her own works praise her in the gates.

Ecclesiastes

All Is Vanity

1 These are the words of the Preacher, the son of David and king in Jerusalem.

² "Vanity ¹ of vanities,"
    says the Preacher;
"vanity of vanities,
    all is vanity."

³ What benefit is there to a man in all his labors
    that he toils under the sun?
⁴ A generation comes, and a generation goes,
    but the earth continually remains.
⁵ The sun comes up, and the sun goes down,
    and hurries to the place where it rises.
⁶ It moves to the south,
    and then moves around to the north;
the wind continually travels around,
    and it keeps turning on its circuit.
⁷ All the streams flow into the sea,
    and the sea is never filled up.
And to the place where the streams flow,
    there they continually return to flow.
⁸ All matters are wearisome;
    a man is not able to speak to them.
The eye is not satisfied with what it sees,
    and the ear is not content with what it hears.
⁹ What has been is the same as what will be,
    and what has been done is the same as what will be done;
    there is nothing new under the sun.
¹⁰ Is there a matter where it is said,
    "See, this is truly new"?
Long ago in the past
    every matter has already been in our midst.
¹¹ There is not a memory for the former things,
    and moreover, there will not be
a memory for the things coming after,
    even those things that are yet to come.

The Burden of Wisdom

¹² I, the Preacher, have been king over Israel in Jerusalem. ¹³ I set my heart to seek and to investigate with wisdom everything that is done under heaven. It is a burdensome task that God has given to the sons of men, by which they may be occupied. ¹⁴ I have seen everything that is done under the sun, and indeed, all is vanity and like chasing the wind.

¹⁵ What is bent cannot be straightened,
    and what is missing cannot be counted.

¹⁶ I spoke in my heart, saying, "I have been great and increased in wisdom more than anyone else who has been before me in Jerusalem, and my heart has had great experience of wisdom and knowledge." ¹⁷ And I set my heart to know wisdom and to know the folly of ideas and to know foolish behavior, and I know that this as well is like chasing the wind.

¹⁸ For in an abundance of wisdom is an abundance of frustration,
    and he who increases in knowledge also increases in sorrow.

The Vanity of Pleasure

2 And I said in my heart, "Come, and I will test you with selfish pleasures to experience desires." And notice that this too is vanity. ² And I said of frivolous fun, "They are only senseless ideas"; and regarding selfish pleasure, "What purpose is this?" ³ I investigated how to cheer up my body with wine, while my heart was still guiding me with wisdom, in order to grasp folly until I might experience what is good for sons of men to do under heaven during the number of days that they might have life.

⁴ I accomplished great works. I built houses for myself, and planted myself vineyards. ⁵ I made for myself royal gardens and parks, and I planted in them all sorts of fruit trees. ⁶ I made for myself pools of water to irrigate the forests of growing trees. ⁷ I even bought male and female slaves; even some were born to me in my house. I had also great possessions of herds and flocks more than any who had been in Jerusalem before me. ⁸ I also gathered for myself silver and gold and treasures of kings and provinces. I obtained singers, both men and women, and the delights of the sons of men, and many concubines. ⁹ So I became

great and surpassed anyone who had been in Jerusalem before me. All the while my wisdom remained with me.

10 And everything that my eyes wanted I did not refuse them.
And I did not withhold my heart from any selfish pleasure,
for my heart was glad from all my efforts;
and this was my reward for all my efforts.
11 Then I turned to all the work that my hands had designed
and all the labor that I had toiled to make;
and notice, all of it was vanity and chasing the wind.
And there was no benefit under the sun.

The Fate of the Wise and the Fool

12 So I turned to consider wisdom,
the folly of ideas, and foolish behavior;
for what else can a man do who comes after the king?
Or what more than those have already done?
13 Then I saw that there is more benefit in wisdom than in
foolishness,
more benefit in light than in darkness.
14 A wise man has eyes in his head so he sees where he walks,
but the fool continues in darkness.
Yet I perceived
that the same fate overtakes them all.

15 Then I said in my heart,

"What happens to the fool will happen to me also.
So to what advantage is my wisdom?"
Then I said to myself,
"This also is vanity."
16 For there is no lasting memory for the wise or the fool,
by which in the coming days everyone will be forgotten.
How the wise dies just like the fool!

17 And I began to hate life for the labor that was done under the sun was contemptible to me, for all of this was vanity and chasing the wind. 18 And I despised all the toil in which I labored under the sun, which I will give up to the man who comes after me. 19 And who knows if this man will be wise or a fool? Yet he will gain power over every labor that I have toiled and *my use of* wisdom under the sun. Also this is vanity. 20 So I turned to give my heart up to despair concerning all the toil of my labors under the sun. 21 For there is a man who labors with wisdom, knowledge, and skill; yet to a man who did not labor for this, he leaves it as his inheritance. This also is vanity and a great distress. 22 For what becomes of a man with all his labor and with the striving in his heart that he toils under the sun? 23 For all his days are sorrowful, and his work is a vexation; even at night his heart finds no rest. Also this is fleeting.

24 There is nothing better for a man than to eat and drink, and find enjoyment in his labor. This also, I saw, is from the hand of God. 25 For who can even eat or have enjoyment more so than I?[1] 26 For to a man who is pleasing before Him, God gives wisdom, knowledge, and joy; but to the sinner He gives the work of gathering and collecting to give him who is pleasing before God. Also this is vanity and chasing the wind.

A Time for Everything

3 To everything there is a season,
a time for every purpose under heaven:

2 a time to be born, and a time to die;
a time to plant, and a time to uproot what is planted;
3 a time to kill, and a time to heal;
a time to break down, and a time to build up;
4 a time to weep, and a time to laugh;
a time to mourn, and a time to dance;
5 a time to cast away stones, and a time to gather stones;
a time to embrace, and a time to refrain from embracing;
6 a time to gain, and a time to lose;
a time to keep, and a time to cast away;

7 a time to tear, and a time to sew;
a time to keep silence, and a time to speak;
8 a time to love, and a time to hate;
a time of war, and a time of peace.

The God-Given Task

9 What benefit does the worker have in his toil? 10 I have seen the task that God has given to sons of men to be concerned with. 11 He has made everything beautiful in its appropriate time. He has also put obscurity in their hearts[2] so that no one comes to know the work that God has done from the beginning to the end. 12 I experienced that there is nothing better for them than to be glad and do good in their life. 13 And also that everyone should eat and drink and experience good in all their labor. This is a gift of God. 14 I have perceived that everything that God has done will be lasting. And to this there is nothing to be added, and from it there is nothing to be taken away. And God has done this so that in His presence men fear Him.

15 That which is has already been,
and what is to come has also already been;
and God seeks out what has been driven away.

The Vanity of Injustice

16 Moreover I saw what was under the sun:

In the place of justice, there was wickedness;
and in the place of righteousness, there was wickedness.

17 I thought in my heart:

God will bring judgment
to the righteous and the wicked,
for there is an appropriate time
for every matter and deed.

18 Then I thought in my heart: Regarding the account of sons of men, God is making clear to them to show that they are but animals. 19 For what befalls the sons of men befalls animals; as one dies, so dies the other. There is one breath for all of them; there is no advantage for man any more than animals, for all is vanity. 20 All go to one place: All are from the dust and all return to dust. 21 Who knows whether the spirit of man goes upward and the spirit of animals goes down to the earth?

22 So I saw that there is nothing better than that a man should rejoice in his labor, for that is his reward. For who will bring him to see what will happen after his life?

Evil Under the Sun

4 Again I saw all types of oppression that are done under the sun:

Look! The tears of the oppressed,
and no one was there to comfort them.
And there was force from the hand of the oppressors,
and no one was there to comfort them.
2 And I thought that fortunate were the dead
who had already died,
even more than the living
who were still alive.
3 And still better than both
is he who has not been,
who has not seen the evil deeds
that are done under the sun.

4 Then I saw that all toil and every skillful work come from one man's envy of another. This also is vanity and like chasing the wind.

5 The fool folds his hands
and eats his own flesh.
6 Better is a full hand of quietness
than handfuls of toil and chasing the wind.

---

[1] 25 Some Heb. and Gk. texts, *apart from Him.* [2] 11 Or *timelessness,* or *perpetuity.*

[7] Again, I saw vanity under the sun:

[8] There is a man who is alone,
   neither having son or brother,
and there is not an end to all his toil,
   and his eyes are not satisfied with riches to say,
"For whom do I labor
   and cause my life to lack good things?"
Also this is vanity
   and a burdensome task.

[9] Two are better than one,
   because there is a good reward for their labor together.
[10] For if they fall,
   then one will help up his companion.
But woe to him who is alone when he falls
   and has no one to help him up.
[11] Also if two lie down together, then they will keep warm;
   but how can one keep warm by himself?
[12] And if someone might overpower another by himself,
   two together can withstand him.
A threefold cord is not quickly broken.

The Vanity of Status

[13] Better is a poor and wise youth than an old and foolish king who will no longer be admonished. [14] For out of prison he has come to reign, even though he was born poor in the kingdom. [15] Then I saw all those who live and walk under the sun, along with the next youth who will arise in the *king's* place. [16] There is no end of all the people, to all who were before them. Yet those who come later will not rejoice in him. Surely this also is vanity and chasing the wind.

Revere God

5 Guard your steps when you enter the house of God, and draw near to listen rather than to offer the sacrifice of fools, for they do not know that they are doing evil. *[1]*

[2] Do not be quick *to speak* with your mouth,
   nor let your heart be hasty to utter a word
   before God.
For God is in heaven,
   and you are on the earth;
   therefore may your words be few.
[3] For a dream comes when there is a great burden,
   and a foolish voice when there are many words.

[4] When you make a vow to God, do not delay in fulfilling it because He has no pleasure in fools. Fulfill what you have vowed. [5] Better it is that you do not make a vow than you make a vow and not fulfill it. [6] Do not let your mouth cause you to sin, and do not say before the messenger that it was an error. Why should God be angry with your words and destroy the work of your hands? [7] For when there is an abundance of dreams and futilities, then words increase too. Therefore it is God you should fear.

The Vanity of Loving Money

[8] If you see in a district the oppression of the poor and the violent perversion of justice and righteousness, do not be astounded at the matter; for the high official is watched over by an even higher official, and there are even higher officials over them. [9] But this is an advantage to the land in every way, like a king committed to a cultivated field.

[10] He who loves money will not be satisfied with money;
   nor he who loves abundance with increase.
   This also is vanity.

[11] When there is an increase of good things,
   then there is an increase of those who devour them.
And what profit have the owners
   except to see them with their eyes?

[12] Sweet is the sleep of a laboring man,
   whether he eats a little or much;
but the abundance of the rich
   will not let him sleep.

[13] There is a grave misery that I have seen under the sun:

when riches were kept by an owner to his hurt,
[14]   and those riches were lost in a misfortunate business deal;
and although he has a son,
   there is nothing at all to put in his hand.
[15] As he came from his mother's womb,
   naked shall he return, to go as he came;
he shall take nothing from his labor
   which he may carry away in his hands.

[16] This also is a grievous evil:

Just as he came,
   so shall he go.
And what profit is there to him who toils for the wind?
[17] Moreover, in all his days he eats in darkness,
   while he is greatly irritated in sickness and anger.

[18] This is what I have seen to be good: It is fitting to eat and drink and find enjoyment in all his labor in which he toils under the sun all the days of his life, which God has given to him; for this is his reward. [19] And also everyone to whom God has given wealth and possessions, and given him power to enjoy them, and to receive his reward and to rejoice in his labor—this is the gift of God. [20] For he will not much remember the days of his life because God keeps him occupied with joy in his heart.

6 There is an evil that I have seen under the sun, and it lies heavy on mankind: [2] a man to whom God gives wealth, possessions, and honor so that there is no want in his life from among anything that he desires; yet God does not give him ability to eat from them because another man eats and enjoys from *his possessions*. This is vanity and a tormenting injustice.
[3] If a man fathers a hundred children and lives many years, so that the days of his years are many, but his soul is not satisfied with life's good things, and he has no burial, I say that a stillborn child is better off than he— [4] for it comes in vanity and departs in darkness, and in darkness its name is covered up. [5] Moreover, it has not seen the sun or known anything, yet it finds rest rather than he. [6] Though the man may live a thousand years, twice over, yet he does not see the good things. Does not everyone go to the same place?

[7] All the labor of man is for his mouth,
   yet his appetite is not satisfied.
[8] For what benefit is there for the wise
   over the fool?
And what more does the poor man know
   who walks before others?
[9] Better to be content with the sight of eyes
   than to have a wandering appetite.
This is vanity
   and like chasing the wind.

[10] Whatever happens, it has already been given a name,
   and it is known what man is;
he cannot contend with Him who is stronger than he.
[11] The more words,
   the more vanity,
   so what profit is there to mankind?

[12] For who knows what is good for man while he lives the few days of his vain life which pass like a shadow? For who can tell men what will be after them under the sun?

---

[1] [1] 4:17 in the Heb. text.

The Value of Wisdom

7 A good name is better than precious ointment,
and the day of death than the day of birth.
2 It is better to go to a house of mourning
than to go to a house of feasting,
for this is the end of all mankind;
and the living will lay it to heart.
3 Grief is better than laughter,
for with a downcast face the heart considers the good.
4 The heart of those who are wise is in the house of mourning,
but the heart of those who are foolish in the house
of feasting.
5 It is better to hear the rebuke from a wise man
than a man listen to the song of
fools.
6 For like the crackling sound of thorns under a pot,
so is the mocking laughter of fools.
And this is also vanity.

7 For oppression brings confusion to the wise man,
and a bribe destroys a man's heart.

8 The end of a matter is better than the beginning of it,
and the patient in spirit than the haughty in spirit.
9 Do not be quick in your spirit to be angry,
for irritation settles in the bosom of fools.

10 Do not say, "Why were the earlier days better than these days?"
For it is not from wisdom that you inquire this.

11 Wisdom is good with an inheritance,
and an advantage to those who see the sun.
12 For the protection of wisdom
is like the protection of money,
and the advantage of knowledge is
that wisdom preserves the life of him who has it.

13 Consider the work of God:

Who is able to make straight
what He has made crooked?
14 In the day of prosperity be joyful,
but in the day of distress consider:
God has made the one
as well as the other.
For this reason man will not be able to understand
anything that comes after him.

15 I have seen everything in my days of vanity:

There is the righteous man who dies in his righteousness,
and there is the wicked man who extends his life of evil.
16 Do not be excessively righteous,
and do not be extremely wise;
why should you destroy yourself?
17 Do not be overly wicked,
and do not be a fool;
why should you die before your time?
18 It is good that you should take hold of this,
and from the other not withhold your hand;
for he who fears God will come out from them all.

19 Wisdom strengthens the wise man
more than ten rulers who are in the city.

20 For there is not a righteous man on earth
who only does good and refrains from sin.

21 Do not give heed to everything people say,
lest you hear your servant cursing you.

22 Your heart knows
that many times you have spoken a curse against others.

23 All this I have tested by wisdom. I said,

"I will be wise,"
but it was far from me.
24 That which is, is far off,
and exceedingly deep.
Who can find it out?
25 And I turned my heart to know,
and seek and search out wisdom in how things are
and to experience wicked folly,
even foolishness and madness.

26 I find more bitter than death
the woman whose heart is snares
and nets,
and whose hands are fetters.
He who pleases God escapes her,
but the sinner is taken by her.

27 "See, this is what I found," says the Preacher,

"adding one thing to another to find the sum,
28 which my soul still seeks
but I do not find:
One man among a thousand I have found,
but a woman among all these I have not found.
29 See, this only have I found:
that God made man upright,
but they have sought out many schemes."

8 Who is like a wise man?
And who knows the interpretation of a matter?
A man's wisdom makes his face shine,
and the harshness of his face is softened.

The Value of Obedience

2 I say, "Keep the king's command, because of your oath to God. 3 Do not be hasty to leave his presence. Do not take a stand in an unpleasant matter, for he does whatever pleases him." 4 For the word of the king is powerful, and who would say to him, "What are you doing?"

5 He who keeps his command will know no evil thing;
and a wise heart will know the appropriate time and just way.
6 For to every matter there is an appropriate time and just way,
though a man's distress weighs heavily on him.

7 For he does not know what will happen;
for who can declare to him what will occur?
8 There is not a man with mastery over the wind to restrain it,
nor with power over the day of death.
And no one can discharge a battle,
nor can wickedness rescue the one possessing it.

9 All this I saw while applying my heart to every work that is done under the sun, when one man rules over another to the other's hurt.

God's Unknowable Ways

10 Then I saw the wicked buried. They used to go in and out of the holy place, and they were praised[l] in the city where they did works. This is also vanity.
11 Because the sentence against an evil deed is not executed swiftly, the heart of the sons of men is fully set to do evil. 12 Since one who sins may do evil a hundred times and extend his life, I also have experienced that it will be good for those who fear God when they have reverence before Him. 13 But it will not be well for the wicked, and he will not prolong his days, like a shadow, because he does not fear before God.

---

l 10 Or the Heb. *forgotten.*

[14] There is a vanity that takes place on the earth that there are righteous men who are treated according to the deeds of the wicked, and there are wicked men who are treated according to the deeds of the righteous. I said that this also is vanity. [15] And I commend joy, for man has nothing better under the sun than to eat and drink and be joyful; for this will go with him in his labor all the days of his life that God has given him under the sun.

[16] When I set my heart to know wisdom and to experience the affairs that are done on earth, though day and night there is no sleep for one's eyes, [17] then I saw all the work of God, that a man cannot comprehend the work that is done under the sun. Inasmuch as a man labors to seek, he will not understand. Even if a wise man claims to know, he cannot grasp it.

A Common Fate

9 For I considered all this in my heart, so that I could declare it all: that the deeds of the righteous and the wise are in the hand of God. No man knows whether love or hate awaits them; both are before him. [2] The same fate comes to all: There is one fate for the righteous and the wicked, for the good and the evil, [1] for the clean and the unclean, for him who sacrifices and him who does not sacrifice.

As is the good,
　　so is the sinner;
he who takes an oath
　　as he who fears an oath.

[3] And this is an evil in all that is done under the sun: that the same event happens to all. Truly the hearts of the sons of men are filled with evil, and folly is in their hearts while they have life, and after that they go to the dead. [4] But for him who is joined to all the living there is hope, for a living dog is better than a dead lion.

[5] 　The living know that they will die,
　　but the dead know nothing;
they have no more reward,
　　for the memory of them is forgotten.
[6] 　What they loved, hated,
　　and envied has already perished;
and there is no reward for them from long ago
　　in everything that is done under the sun.

[7] Go and eat your food with gladness, and drink your wine with a pleasant heart; for God is already pleased with your deeds. [8] At all times may your clothing be white, and let not oil ever lack on your head. [9] Enjoy life with the wife whom you love all the days of your vain life which He has given you under the sun; because that is your reward in life and in your toil because you have labored under the sun. [10] Whatever your hands find to do, do with your strength; for there is no work or planning or knowledge or wisdom in Sheol, the place where you are going.

[11] Again I saw under the sun that—

the race is not to the swift,
　　nor the battle to the strong,
nor food to the wise,
　　nor riches to the intelligent,
　　nor favor to those with knowledge;
but time and chance happen to them all.

[12] For man does not know his time:

Like fish caught in an unfortunate net,
　　like birds caught in a snare,
so the sons of men are ensnared at a tragic, yet appointed time,
　　when it suddenly falls on them.

The Excellence of Wisdom

[13] I have also seen this wisdom under the sun, and it seemed great to me: [14] There was a small city with a few men in it; and a great king came and surrounded it, and he built up great siege works against it. [15] But a poor, wise man was found there, and he himself in his wisdom delivered the city, but no one remembered that poor man. [16] Then I said, "Wisdom is better than strength; yet the poor man's wisdom is despised, and his words are not heard."

[17] 　The words of the wise heard in quietness are better
　　than the shouting of a ruler among fools.
[18] 　Wisdom is better than weapons of war,
　　but only one sinner can destroy much that is good.

10 A dead fly causes a stench in mixed anointing oil,
　　so a little folly is more weighty than wisdom and honor.
[2] 　The heart of the wise inclines to the right,
　　but the heart of a fool to the left.
[3] 　Even when a fool walks on the road,
　　he lacks sense,
　　and he shows everyone that he is a fool.
[4] 　If the anger of a ruler rises against you,
　　do not leave your post;
　　for calmness pacifies great offenses.

[5] 　There is an evil that I have seen under the sun
　　like an error that goes out from a ruler:
[6] 　Folly is set in many high places,
　　but the rich sit in a low place.
[7] 　I have seen slaves riding on horses,
　　and officials walking along the ground like slaves.

[8] 　He who digs a pit will fall into it,
　　and whoever breaks through a wall will be bitten by a serpent.
[9] 　He who quarries stones is injured by them,
　　and he who splits wood is in danger from them.

[10] 　If an iron piece is blunt
　　and there is no one to sharpen it,
　　then he must prevail with more strength;
　　but wisdom is a benefit to succeed.

[11] 　If a serpent bites before it is charmed,
　　there is no advantage to the charmer.

[12] 　The words of a wise man's mouth bring favor,
　　but the speech of a fool consumes him;
[13] 　the beginning of the words of his mouth is foolishness,
　　and the end of his talk is evil madness.
[14] 　A fool multiplies words,
　　though no man knows what is to be;
　　who can tell him what will be after him?

[15] 　The labor of the foolish makes him weary,
　　such that he does not know the way to the city!

[16] 　Woe to you, O land, when your king is a lad,
　　and your princes are feasting in the morning!
[17] 　Happy are you, O land, when your king is from nobility,
　　and your princes are feasting at the appropriate time—
　　with self-control and not drunkenness!

[18] 　The roof beams sink in with slothfulness,
　　and with the idleness of one's hands the house drips.

[19] 　They make feasts for laughter,
　　and wine gladdens life;
　　but money resolves everything.

[20] 　Even in your mind do not curse the king;
　　and in your bedchamber do not curse the rich;
for a bird in the sky may carry your voice,
　　and a winged creature may declare the matter.

---

[1] 2 *Evil* from Gk. is missing in some Heb. mss.

The Value of Diligence

11 Cast your bread upon the waters,
for you will find it after many days.
2 Give a portion to seven, or even eight,
for you do not know what calamity may happen on the earth.

3 If the clouds are full of rain,
they empty out on the land;
and if a tree falls to the north or south,
in the place that the tree falls, there it will be.
4 He who observes the wind will not sow,
and he who regards the clouds will not reap.

5 As you do not know the way of the wind,
or how the bones grow in the womb of her who is with child;
likewise you do not know the work of God
who has made everything.

6 In the morning sow your seed,
and in the evening do not let your hand rest;
because you do not know which activity will find success,
this way or that way,
or if the both will be good.

Remember Your Creator in Your Youth

7 Light is sweet,
and good for the eyes to see the sun;
8 for if a man lives many years,
may he rejoice in all of them.
But let him also remember
that the days of darkness are many.
Everything that comes is vanity.

9 Rejoice, O young man, in your youth,
and in your early years may your heart do you good;
walk in the path of your heart
and the desire of your eyes;
but know that in all these things
God will bring you into judgment.
10 Take away anger from your heart,
and remove distress from your body,
for youth and the dawn are vanity.

12 Remember your Creator
in the days of your youth,
before the difficult days come
and the years arrive when you say,
"I have no pleasure in them":

2 before the sun, light,
moon, and stars are darkened,
and the clouds leave after the rain;
3 in the day when those watching the house tremble,
and the strong men are bent over;
when the grinders cease because they are few,
and those looking through the windows have
dimmed *eyes*;
4 and the doors on the street are shut,
and the sound of grinding is low;
and one rises up at the sound of a bird,
and all the daughters of song are brought low;
5 when they are afraid of heights,
even the terrors along the road;
the almond tree blossoms,
the grasshopper drags itself along
and desire fails,
because man goes to his eternal home,
and the mourners go about the streets.

6 *Remember your Creator* before the cord of silver is snapped,
or the bowl of gold smashed,
or the jar by the spring broken
or the wheel at the cistern crushed.
7 The dust returns to the earth where it was,
and the spirit returns to God who gave it.

8 It is all vanity, says the Preacher;
all is vanity.

Epilogue

9 And in addition to being wise, the Preacher still taught the people knowledge, and he considered, sought out, and arranged many proverbs. 10 And the Preacher sought to discover words of delight, and to write in uprightness words of truth.

11 The words of the wise are like goads, and the collected sayings are like firmly embedded nails, given by one shepherd. 12 My son, beware of anything beyond these.

Of making many books there is no end, and much study is a weariness to the flesh.

13 Now all has been heard.
Let us hear the conclusion of the matter:
Fear God and keep His commandments,
for this is the whole *duty* of man.
14 For God will bring every deed into judgment,
including every secret thing,
whether good or evil.

SONGS

Introduction

1 The Song of Songs, which is Solomon's.

The Woman

2 Let him kiss me with the kisses of his mouth!
For your love is better than wine.
3 Your anointing oils are fragrant,
your name is oil poured out;
therefore the virgins love you.
4 Draw me after you, let us run.
The king has brought me into his chambers.

Friends of the Woman

We will exult and rejoice in you;
we will remember your love more than wine;
rightly do they love you.

The Woman

5 I am dark, but still lovely, O daughters of Jerusalem,
like the tents of Kedar,
like the curtains of Solomon.
6 Do not gaze at me, because I am dark,
because the sun has looked
upon me.

My mother's sons were angry with me;
    they made me the keeper of the vineyards,
  but my own vineyard I have not kept.
7 Tell me, you whom my soul loves,
    where you pasture your flock,
  where you make it lie down at noon;
      for why should I be like one who veils herself by the flocks of
        your companions?

Friends of the Woman

8 If you do not know, O fairest among women,
    follow in the tracks of the flock,
  and pasture your young goats
    beside the shepherds' tents.

The Man

9 I compare you, my love, to a mare among Pharaoh's chariots.
10 Lovely are your cheeks with ornaments,
    your neck with chains of gold.

Friends of the Woman

11 We will make you ornaments of gold,
    with studs of silver.

The Woman

12 While the king was on his couch,
    my nard gave forth its fragrance.
13 My beloved is to me a bundle of myrrh
    that lies all night between my breasts.
14 My beloved is to me a cluster of henna blossoms
    in the vineyards of En Gedi.

The Man

15 How fair you are, my love.
    How fair you are! Your eyes are doves.

The Woman

16 How fair you are, my beloved!
    Yes, pleasant!
    Our bed is verdant;
17 the beams of our house are cedar,
    and our rafters of fir.

2 I am the rose of Sharon,
    the lily of the valleys.

The Man

2 As a lily among thorns,
    so is my love among the maidens.

The Woman

3 As an apple tree among the trees of the forest,
    so is my beloved among the young men.
  In his shadow I sat with great delight,
    and his fruit was sweet to my taste.
4 He brought me to the banquet house,
    and his banner over me was love.
5 Sustain me with raisins,
    refresh me with apples;
  for I am faint with love.
6 His left hand is under my head,
    and his right hand embraces me.
7 I charge you, O daughters of Jerusalem,
    by the gazelles or the does of the field,
  do not stir up or awaken love
    until it pleases.

8 The voice of my beloved!
    Look, he comes
  leaping over the mountains,
    bounding over the hills.

9 My beloved is like a gazelle or a young stag.
    Look, he stands behind our wall, gazing through
      the windows,
    looking through the lattice.
10 My beloved speaks and says to me:
    "Rise up, my love,
    my fair one, and come away.
11 For now the winter has past;
    the rain is over and gone.
12 The flowers appear on the earth;
    the time of singing has come,
  and the voice of the turtledove is heard in our land.
13 The fig tree puts forth its green figs,
    and the vines their blossoms;
  and they give forth fragrance.
    Rise up, my love, my beautiful one, and come away.

14 O my dove, in the clefts of the rock,
    in the secret places of the cliffs,
  let me see your face,
    let me hear your voice;
  for your voice is sweet,
    and your face is lovely.
15 Catch the foxes for us,
    the little foxes
  that spoil the vineyards,
    for our vineyards are in blossom."

16 My beloved is mine, and I am his;
    he feeds *his flock* among the lilies.
17 Until the day breathes
    and the shadows flee,
  turn, my beloved,
    be like a gazelle
  or a young stag
    on the cleft mountains. [1]

3 On my bed by night I sought him
    whom my soul loves;
  I sought him, but found him not.
2 I will rise now and go about the city,
    in the streets and in the squares;
  I will seek him whom my soul loves.
  I sought him, but found him not.
3 The watchmen found me,
    as they went about the city.
    "Have you seen him whom my soul loves?"
4 Scarcely had I passed them,
    when I found him whom my soul loves.
  I held him, and would not let him go
    until I brought him to my mother's house,
    and into the chamber of her who conceived me.
5 I charge you, O daughters of Jerusalem,
    by the gazelles or does of the field,
  do not stir up or awaken love
    until it pleases.

6 Who is that coming up from the wilderness,
    like columns of smoke,
  perfumed with myrrh and frankincense,
    with all the fragrant powders of the merchant?
7 Look, it is the litter of Solomon!
    Around it are sixty mighty men,
    of the mighty men of Israel,
8 all of them holding swords
    and expert in war,
  each with his sword at his thigh,
    because of terrors by night.
9 King Solomon made himself a palanquin
    from the wood of Lebanon.

---

[1] 17 Or *mountains of Bether.*

¹⁰ He made its posts of silver,
    its back of gold,
its seat of purple;
    its interior was inlaid with love
    by the daughters of Jerusalem.
¹¹ Go forth, O daughters of Zion,
    and see King Solomon with the crown
    with which his mother crowned him
on the day of his wedding,
    on the day of the gladness of his heart.

The Man

4 How fair you are, my love!
    How very fair!
    Your eyes are doves behind your veil.
Your hair is like a flock of goats,
    streaming down the hills of Gilead.
² Your teeth are like a flock of shorn ewes
    that have come up from the washing,
all of which bear twins,
    and not one among them has lost its young.
³ Your lips are like a scarlet thread,
    and your mouth is lovely.
Your cheeks are halves of a pomegranate
    behind your veil.
⁴ Your neck is like the tower of David,
    built in rows of stone;
on it hang a thousand shields,
    all of them shields of mighty men.
⁵ Your two breasts are like two fawns,
    twins of a gazelle,
    that feed among the lilies.
⁶ Until the day breathes
    and the shadows flee,
I will go away to the mountain of myrrh
    and the hill of frankincense.
⁷ You are altogether fair, my love;
    there is no flaw in you.

⁸ Come with me from Lebanon, my bride;
    come with me from Lebanon.
Depart from the peak of Amana,
    from the peak of Senir and Hermon,
from the dens of lions,
    from the mountains of leopards.
⁹ You have ravished my heart, my sister, my bride;
    you have ravished my heart
with one *glance* of your eyes,
    with one jewel of your necklace.
¹⁰ How fair is your love, my sister, my bride!
    How much better than wine is your love,
    and the fragrance of your oils than any spice!
¹¹ Your lips drip honey, my bride;
    honey and milk are under your tongue;
    and the fragrance of your garments is like the scent of Lebanon.
¹² A garden locked is my sister, my bride,
    a fountain sealed.
¹³ Your plants are an orchard of pomegranates
    with all choicest fruits,
    henna with nard,
¹⁴   nard and saffron,
    calamus and cinnamon,
with all trees of frankincense,
    myrrh and aloes,
    with all the chief spices—
¹⁵ a garden fountain,
    a well of living water,
    and flowing streams from Lebanon.

The Woman
¹⁶ Awake, O north wind,
    and come, O south wind!

Blow upon my garden,
    that its spices may flow out.
Let my beloved come to his garden,
    and eat its choicest fruits.

The Man

5 I come to my garden, my sister, my bride;
    I gather my myrrh with my spice;
I eat my honeycomb with my honey;
    I drink my wine with my milk.

Friends of the Man
Eat, friends!
    Drink, and be drunk with love!

The Woman
² I slept, but my heart was awake.
A sound! My beloved is knocking. "Open to me, my sister, and
        my love,
    my dove, my perfect one;
for my head is wet with dew,
    my locks with the drops of the night."
³ I had taken off my garment;
    how could I put it on again?
I had bathed my feet;
    how could I soil them?
⁴ My beloved put his hand by the latch,
    and my heart yearned for him.
⁵ I rose up to open to my beloved,
    and my hands dripped with myrrh,
my fingers with liquid myrrh
    on the handles of the bolt.
⁶ I opened to my beloved,
    but my beloved had turned and was gone.
My soul failed me when he spoke.
I sought him, but found him not;
    I called him, but he gave no answer.
⁷ The watchmen found me
    as they went about the city;
they struck me, they wounded me;
    they took away my mantle,
    those watchmen of the walls.
⁸ I charge you, O daughters of Jerusalem,
    if you find my beloved,
    that you tell him I am faint with love.

Friends of the Woman
⁹ What is your beloved more than another beloved,
    O fairest among women?
What is your beloved more than another beloved,
    that you so charge us?

The Woman
¹⁰ My beloved is white and ruddy,
    distinguished among ten thousand.
¹¹ His head is the finest gold;
    his locks are wavy,
    black as a raven.
¹² His eyes are like doves
    beside rivers of water,
bathed in milk,
    fitly set.
¹³ His cheeks are like beds of spices,
    mounds of scented herbs.
His lips are lilies,
    dripping liquid myrrh.
¹⁴ His arms are rods of gold,
    set with jewels.
His body is bright ivory,
    inlaid with sapphires.
¹⁵ His legs are alabaster columns,
    set on bases of gold.

His appearance is like Lebanon,
    choice as the cedars.
16 His mouth is most sweet,
    and he is altogether desirable.
This is my beloved and this is my friend,
    O daughters of Jerusalem.

Friends of the Woman

6 Where has your beloved gone,
    O fairest among women?
Where has your beloved turned aside,
    that we may seek him with you?

The Woman

2 My beloved has gone down to his garden,
    to the beds of spices,
    to feed *his flock* in the gardens,
    and to gather lilies.
3 I am my beloved's and my beloved is mine;
    he feeds *his flock* among the lilies.

The Man

4 You are beautiful as Tirzah, my love,
    comely as Jerusalem,
    awesome as an army with banners!
5 Turn your eyes away from me,
    for they overwhelm me!
Your hair is like a flock of goats
    streaming down from Gilead.
6 your teeth are like a flock of ewes
    that have come up from the washing;
all of them bear twins; not one among them has lost its young;
7 your cheeks are like halves
    of a pomegranate behind your veil.
8 There are sixty queens
    and eighty concubines,
    and virgins without number.
9 My dove, my perfect one, is the only one,
    the only one of her mother,
    choice to her who bore her.
The maidens saw her and called her blessed;
    the queens and concubines also, and they praised her.

10 Who is this who looks forth like the dawn,
    fair as the moon, radiant as the sun,
    awesome as an army with banners?

11 I went down to the nut orchard
    to look at the blossoms of the valley,
to see whether the vines had budded,
    whether the pomegranates were in bloom.
12 Before I was aware, my soul set me in a chariot beside
    my prince.

Friends of the Woman

13 Return, return, O Shulammite![1]
    Return, return, that we may look upon you.

The Man

Why should you look upon the Shulammite,
    as upon a dance before two armies?[2]

7 How beautiful are your feet in sandals,
    O prince's daughter!
The curves of your thighs are like jewels,
    the work of a master hand.
2 Your navel is a round bowl
    that never lacks mixed wine.
Your belly is a heap of wheat,
    encircled with lilies.

3 Your two breasts are like two fawns,
    twins of a gazelle.
4 Your neck is like an ivory tower,
    your eyes pools in Heshbon,
    by the gate of Bath Rabbim.
Your nose is like a tower of Lebanon,
    overlooking Damascus.
5 Your head crowns like Carmel,
    and your flowing hair is like purple;
    a king is held captive in the tresses.
6 How fair and pleasant you are,
    O loved one, with all your delights!
7 Your stature is like a palm tree,
    and your breasts are like its clusters.
8 I say I will climb the palm tree
    and take hold of its branches.
Oh, may your breasts be like clusters of the vine,
    and the scent of your breath like apples,
9   and your mouth like the best wine.
It goes down smoothly for my beloved,
    gliding over lips and teeth.

The Woman

10 I am my beloved's,
    and his desire is for me.
11 Come, my beloved, let us go forth into the fields,
    and lodge in the villages;
12 let us go out early to the vineyards,
    and see whether the vines have budded,
whether the grape blossoms have opened
    and the pomegranates are in bloom.
There I will give you my love.
13 The mandrakes give forth fragrance,
    and at our doors are all choice fruits,
new as well as old,
    which I have laid up for you,
    my beloved.

8 Oh, that you were like a brother to me,
    who nursed at my mother's breasts!
If I found you outside,
    I would kiss you,
    and no one would despise me.
2 I would lead you and bring you
    into the house of my mother,
    she who used to instruct me.
I would give you spiced wine to drink,
    the juice of my pomegranates.
3 His left hand is under my head,
    and his right arm embraces me!
4 I charge you, O daughters of Jerusalem,
    do not stir up or awaken love
    until it pleases.

Friends of the Woman

5 Who is that coming up from the wilderness,
    leaning upon her beloved?

The Woman

Under the apple tree I awakened you.
    There your mother was in labor with you;
    there she who bore you was in labor.
6 Set me as a seal upon your heart,
    as a seal upon your arm;
for love is strong as death,
    passion fierce as the grave.
Its fires of desire are as ardent flames,
    a most intense flame.
7 Many waters cannot quench love,
    neither can floods drown it.

---

[1] 13 7:1 in the Heb. text.   [2] 13 Or *dance of Mahanaim.*

If a man offered for love
    all the wealth of his house,
    it would be utterly condemned.

Brothers of the Woman

8 We have a little sister,
    and she has no breasts.
What will we do for our sister
    on the day when she is spoken for?
9 If she is a wall,
    we will build upon her a battlement of silver;
but if she is a door,
    we will enclose her with boards of cedar.

The Woman

10 I was a wall,
    and my breasts were like towers;
then I was in his eyes

as one who finds peace.
11 Solomon had a vineyard at Baal Hamon;
    he leased the vineyard to keepers;
each man was to bring for its fruit a thousand pieces
    of silver.
12 My vineyard, my very own, is before me;
    you, O Solomon, may have the thousand,
    and the keepers of the fruit two hundred.

The Man

13 O you who dwell in the gardens,
    my companions listen for your voice;
    let me hear it!

The Woman

14 Make haste, my beloved,
    and be like a gazelle or a young stag
    on the mountains of spices!

ISAIAH

1 The vision of Isaiah the son of Amoz, which he saw concerning Judah and Jerusalem in the days of Uzziah, Jotham, Ahaz, and Hezekiah, kings of Judah.

The Wickedness of Judah

2 Hear, O heavens, and give ear, O earth.
    For the Lord has spoken:
I have nourished and brought up children,
    and they have rebelled against Me;
3 the ox knows his owner,
    and the donkey his master's crib,
but Israel does not know;
    My people do not consider.

4 Alas, sinful nation,
    a people laden with iniquity,
a brood of evildoers,
    children who deal corruptly!
They have forsaken the Lord,
    they have provoked the Holy One of Israel to anger,
    they are estranged and backward.

5 Why should you be beaten again,
    that you revolt more and more?
The whole head is sick,
    and the whole heart faint.
6 From the sole of the foot even to the head
    there is no soundness in it.
Wounds, bruises,
    and open sores;
they have not been closed,
    nor bandaged, nor soothed with oil.

7 Your country is desolate,
    your cities are burned with fire;
strangers devour your land
    in your presence;
    and it is desolate, as overthrown by strangers.
8 The daughter of Zion is left
    like a shelter in a vineyard,
like a hut in a field of melons,
    like a besieged city.

9 Unless the Lord of Hosts
    had left to us a very small remnant,
we would have been as Sodom;
    we would have been like Gomorrah.

10 Hear the word of the Lord,
    you rulers of Sodom;
listen to the law of our God,
    you people of Gomorrah:
11 For what purpose is the multitude
    of your sacrifices to Me? says the Lord.
I am full of the burnt offerings of rams,
    and the fat of fed animals.
I do not delight in the blood of bulls,
    or of lambs, or of male goats.
12 When you come to appear before Me,
    who has required this at your hand,
    to trample My courts?
13 Bring no more vain offerings;
    incense is an abomination to Me.
New Moons, Sabbaths, and convocations—
    I cannot bear with evil assemblies.
14 My soul hates
    your New Moons and your appointed feasts;
they are a burden to Me;
    I am weary of bearing them.
15 When you reach out your hands,
    I will hide My eyes from you;
even when you make many prayers,
    I will not hear.

Your hands are full of blood.

16 Wash yourselves, make yourselves clean;
    put away the evil from your deeds,
    from before My eyes.
Cease to do evil,
17 learn to do good; seek justice,
    relieve the oppressed;
judge the fatherless,
    plead for the widow.

[18] Come now, and let us reason together,
  says the LORD.
Though your sins be as scarlet,
  they shall be as white as snow;
though they be red like crimson,
  they shall be as wool.
[19] If you are willing and obedient,
  you shall eat the good of the land;
[20] but if you refuse and rebel,
  you shall be devoured with the sword;
  for the mouth of the LORD has spoken it.

The Degenerate City
[21] How the faithful city
  has become a prostitute!
She was full of justice;
  righteousness lodged in her,
  but now murderers.
[22] Your silver has become dross,
  your wine mixed with water.
[23] Your princes are rebellious
  and companions of thieves;
everyone loves a bribe
  and follows after rewards.
They do not defend the fatherless,
  nor does the cause of the widow come before them.

[24] Therefore the Lord, the LORD of Hosts,
  the Mighty One of Israel, says:
Ah, I will get relief from My adversaries,
  and avenge Myself on My enemies.
[25] And I will turn My hand against you,
  thoroughly purge away your dross,
  and take away all your impurities.
[26] I will restore your judges as at the first,
  and your counselors as at the beginning.
Afterward you shall be called
  the city of righteousness,
  a faithful town.

[27] Zion shall be redeemed with justice
  and her converts with righteousness.
[28] But the destruction of the transgressors and sinners shall be together,
  and those who forsake the LORD shall be consumed.

[29] For they shall be ashamed of the oaks
  which you have desired,
and you shall be humiliated for the gardens
  that you have chosen.
[30] For you shall be as an oak whose leaf fades,
  and as a garden that has no water.
[31] The strong shall be as tinder,
  and his work like a spark;
they will both burn together,
  and no one will quench them.

The Mountain of the LORD
Mic 4:1–3
2 The word that Isaiah the son of Amoz saw concerning Judah and Jerusalem.

[2] In the last days,

the mountain of the LORD's house shall be established
  on the top of the mountains,
and shall be exalted above the hills,
  and all nations shall flow to it.

[3] Many people shall go and say,

"Come, and let us go up to the mountain of the LORD,
  to the house of the God of Jacob,

and He will teach us of His ways,
  and we will walk in His paths."
For out of Zion shall go forth the law,
  and the word of the LORD from Jerusalem.
[4] He shall judge among the nations,
  and shall rebuke many peoples;
and they shall beat their swords into plowshares,
  and their spears into pruning hooks;
nation shall not lift up sword against nation,
  nor shall they learn war any more.

[5] O house of Jacob, come,
  and let us walk in the light of the LORD.

The Day of the LORD
[6] For You have forsaken Your people,
  the house of Jacob,
because they are replenished from the east,
  and are soothsayers like the Philistines,
  and they please themselves with the children
    of strangers.
[7] Their land also is full of silver and gold,
  and there is no end to their treasures;
their land is also full of horses,
  and there is no end to their chariots.
[8] Their land also is full of idols;
  they worship the work of their own hands,
  that which their own fingers have made.
[9] And the *common* man bows down,
  and the *great* man humbles himself;
  therefore, do not forgive them.

[10] Enter into the rock,
  and hide in the dust
from the fear of the LORD
  and from the glory of His majesty.
[11] The lofty looks of man shall be humbled,
  and the haughtiness of men shall be bowed down,
  and the LORD alone shall be exalted in that day.

[12] For the day of the LORD of Hosts shall be
  upon everything that is proud and lofty,
  and upon everything that is lifted up,
  and it shall be brought low;
[13] and *it will be* upon all the cedars of Lebanon that are high and
    lifted up,
  and upon all the oaks of Bashan,
[14] and upon all the high mountains,
  and upon all the hills that are lifted up,
[15] and upon all the high towers,
  and upon every fenced wall,
[16] and upon all the ships of Tarshish,
  and upon all pleasant sloops.
[17] The loftiness of man shall be humbled,
  and the haughtiness of men shall be brought low;
the LORD alone will be exalted in that day;
[18]   the idols He shall utterly abolish.

[19] They shall go into the holes of the rocks,
  and into the caves of the earth,
from the fear of the LORD,
  and from the glory of His majesty,
  when He shall arise to shake the earth mightily.
[20] In that day a man shall cast away
  his idols of silver and his idols of gold,
which they made for themselves to worship,
  to the moles and to the bats,
[21] to enter the caverns of the rocks,
  and into the clefts of the cliffs,
from the terror of the LORD,
  and from the glory of His majesty,
  when He arises to shake the earth mightily.

²² Cease regarding man,
　　whose breath is in his nostrils;
　for why should he be esteemed?

Judgment on Judah and Jerusalem

3 For now the Lord,
　　the LORD of Hosts,
takes away from Jerusalem and from Judah
　the stock and the store,
　the whole supply of bread, and the whole supply of water;
² 　the mighty man and the man of war,
　the judge and the prophet,
　　and the prudent and the ancient,
³ 　the captain of fifty and the honorable man,
　　the counselor and the skillful artisan, and the eloquent orator.

⁴ I will give youths to be their princes,
　　and unweaned children shall rule over them.

⁵ The people shall be oppressed,
　　every one by another, and every one by his neighbor;
　the youth shall behave himself proudly against the elder,
　　and the inferior against the honorable.

⁶ When a man shall take hold of his brother
　　in the house of his father saying,
　"You have clothing; be our ruler,
　　and let this ruin be under your power,"
⁷ in that day he shall swear saying,
　　"I will not be a healer.
　For in my house is neither bread nor clothing;
　　do not make me a ruler of the people."

⁸ For Jerusalem is ruined,
　　and Judah is fallen,
　because their tongue and their deeds are against the LORD,
　　to provoke the eyes of His glory.
⁹ The expression of their countenance witnesses against them,
　　and they declare their sin as Sodom;
　they hide it not.
　Woe to them!
　　For they have brought evil on themselves.

¹⁰ Say to the righteous that it shall be well with them,
　　for they shall eat the fruit of their deeds.
¹¹ Woe to the wicked! It shall be ill with him,
　　for the reward of his hands shall be given him.

¹² As for My people, children are their oppressors,
　　and women rule over them.
　O My people, those who lead you cause you to err,
　　and destroy the way of your paths.

¹³ The LORD stands up to plead
　　and stands to judge the people.
¹⁴ The LORD will enter into judgment
　　with the elders and the princes of His people:
　For you have eaten up the vineyard;
　　the spoil of the poor is in your houses.
¹⁵ What do you mean that you beat My people to pieces
　　and grind the faces of the poor?
　　says the Lord GOD of Hosts.

¹⁶ Moreover the LORD says:
　　Because the daughters of Zion are haughty
　and walk with outstretched necks
　　and wanton eyes,
　walking and mincing as they go,
　　and making a tinkling with their feet,
¹⁷ therefore, the Lord will strike with a scab the crown of the head of
　　the daughters of Zion,
　and the LORD will make their foreheads bare.

¹⁸ In that day the Lord will take away the finery of the ankle ornaments, and the headbands, and the crescent ornaments, ¹⁹ the chains, and the bracelets, and the veils, ²⁰ the bonnets, the leg ornaments, the sashes, perfume boxes, amulets, ²¹ the finger rings, nose rings, ²² festal robes, outer tunics, cloaks, purses, ²³ hand mirrors, and undergarments, hoods, and veils.

²⁴ Instead of sweet perfume there shall be a stench;
　　and instead of a belt, a rope;
　and instead of well-set hair, baldness;
　　and instead of fine clothes, a girding of sackcloth;
　　and branding instead of beauty.
²⁵ Your men shall fall by the sword,
　　and your mighty in the war.
²⁶ Her gates shall lament and mourn,
　　and she, being desolate, shall sit on the ground.

4 And in that day seven women
　　shall take hold of one man, saying,
　"We will eat our own bread,
　　and wear our own apparel,
　only let us be called by your name,
　　to take away our reproach."

The Branch of the LORD

² In that day the branch of the LORD shall be beautiful and glorious, and the fruit of the earth shall be excellent and comely for those of Israel who have escaped. ³ He who is left in Zion and he who remains in Jerusalem shall be called holy, even everyone who is written among the living in Jerusalem. ⁴ When the Lord has washed away the filth of the daughters of Zion and has purged the blood of Jerusalem from the midst by the spirit of justice and by the spirit of burning, ⁵ then the LORD will create upon every dwelling place of Mount Zion, and upon her assemblies, a cloud and smoke by day and the shining of a flaming fire by night. For over all the glory shall be a covering. ⁶ There shall be a tabernacle for a shadow in the daytime from the heat, and for a place of refuge, and for a shelter from storm and from rain.

The Song of the Vineyard

5 Now I will sing to my well-beloved a song of my beloved
　　concerning His vineyard:
　My well-beloved has a vineyard
　　in a very fruitful hill.
² And He fenced it, and removed its stones,
　　and planted it with the choicest vine.
　And He built a tower in the midst of it,
　　and also made a winepress in it;
　and He expected it to bring forth good grapes,
　　but it brought forth wild grapes.

³ Now, O inhabitants of Jerusalem and men of Judah,
　　judge between My vineyard and Me.
⁴ What more could have been done to My vineyard
　　that I have not done in it?
　Why, when I expected it to bring forth good grapes,
　　did it bring forth wild grapes?
⁵ So now I will tell you
　　what I will do to My vineyard:
　I will take away its hedge,
　　and it shall be consumed;
　I will break down its wall,
　　and it shall be trodden down.
⁶ And I will lay it waste:
　　It shall not be pruned or dug,
　　but briers and thorns shall come up.
　I will also command the clouds
　　that they rain no rain on it.

⁷ For the vineyard of the LORD of Hosts
　　is the house of Israel,
　and the men of Judah
　　His pleasant plant.
　Thus He looked for justice, but saw oppression;
　　for righteousness, but heard a cry.

Woes and Judgment

8 Woe to those who join house to house,
    who add field to field,
until there is no more space
    where they may live alone in the midst of the land!

9 In my ears the LORD of Hosts said:

Truly, many houses shall be desolate,
    even great and beautiful, without inhabitants.
10 For ten acres of vineyard shall yield one bath,[1]
    and the homer[2] of seed shall yield an ephah.[3]

11 Woe to those who rise up early in the morning
    that they may pursue strong drink;
who continue late in the evening
    until wine inflames them!
12 The lyre and the harp, the tambourine and pipe,
    and wine are in their feasts;
but they do not regard the deeds of the LORD,
    or consider the work of His hands.
13 Therefore My people go into captivity
    because they have no knowledge;
and their honorable men are famished,
    and their multitude dried up with thirst.
14 Therefore Sheol has enlarged itself
    and opened its mouth without measure;
so their glory, and their multitude, and their pomp,
    and he who rejoices shall descend into it.
15 The *common* man shall be brought down,
    and the *great* man shall be humbled,
    and the eyes of the lofty shall be humbled.
16 But the LORD of Hosts shall be exalted in judgment,
    and God who is holy shall be hallowed in righteousness.
17 Then the lambs shall feed in their pasture,
    and strangers shall eat *in* the waste places of
        the wealthy.

18 Woe to those who draw iniquity with cords of falsehood
    and sin as if with a cart rope,
19 who say, "Let Him make speed
    and hasten His work,
        that we may see it;
and let the counsel of the Holy One of Israel
    draw near and come,
        that we may know it!"

20 Woe to those who call evil good,
    and good evil;
who exchange darkness for light,
    and light for darkness;
who exchange bitter for sweet,
    and sweet for bitter!

21 Woe to those who are wise in their own eyes
    and prudent in their own sight!

22 Woe to those who are mighty to drink wine,
    and men of strength to mingle strong drink,
23 who justify the wicked for a reward,
    and take away the justice of the righteous from him!
24 Therefore, as the fire devours the stubble
    and the flame consumes the chaff,
so their root shall be as rottenness,
    and their blossom shall go up as dust;
because they have cast away the law of the LORD of Hosts
    and despised the word of the Holy One of Israel.
25 Therefore the anger of the LORD burns against His people,
    and He has stretched out His hand against them, and has
        stricken them,

and the hills trembled.
    Their corpses were torn in the midst of
        the streets.

For all this His anger is not turned away,
    and His hand is still stretched out.

26 He will lift up a banner to the nations from afar
    and will hiss at them from the ends of the earth;
certainly they shall come
    with speed, swiftly.
27 No one shall be weary or stumble among them;
    no one shall slumber or sleep;
neither shall the girdle of their loins be loosed,
    nor the strap of their shoes be broken;
28 their arrows are sharp
    and all their bows bent;
their horses' hooves will seem like flint,
    and their wheels like a whirlwind.
29 Their roaring shall be like a lion,
    they shall roar like young lions;
they shall roar and lay hold of the prey;
    and shall carry it away, and no one shall deliver it.
30 In that day they shall roar against them
    like the roaring of the sea.
And if one looks to the land—
    only darkness and sorrow,
    and the light is darkened by the clouds.

The Commission of Isaiah

6 In the year that King Uzziah died I saw the Lord sitting on a throne, high and lifted up, and His train filled the temple. 2 Above it stood the seraphim. Each one had six wings. With two he covered his face, and with two he covered his feet, and with two he flew. 3 One cried to another and said:

"Holy, holy, holy, is the LORD of Hosts;
    the whole earth is full of His glory."

4 The posts of the door moved at the voice of him who cried, and the house was filled with smoke. 5 And I said: "Woe is me! For I am undone because I am a man of unclean lips, and I dwell in the midst of a people of unclean lips. For my eyes have seen the King, the LORD of Hosts." 6 Then one of the seraphim flew to me with a live coal which he had taken with the tongs from off the altar in his hand. 7 And he laid it on my mouth, and said, "This has touched your lips, and your iniquity is taken away, and your sin purged." 8 Also I heard the voice of the Lord saying, "Whom shall I send, and who will go for us?"
    Then I said, "Here am I. Send me."
    9 He said, "Go, and tell this people:

'Keep on hearing, but do not understand;
    keep on seeing, but do not perceive.'
10 Make the heart of this people dull,
    and their ears heavy,
    and shut their eyes;
lest they see with their eyes,
    and hear with their ears,
    and understand with their heart,
and turn and be healed."

11 Then I said, "Lord, how long?"
And He answered:

"Until the cities are laid waste
    without inhabitants,
and the houses without man,
    and the land is utterly desolate,

---

[1] 10 About 6 gallons, or 22 liters.   [2] 10 Likely about 360 pounds, or 160 kilograms.   [3] 10 Likely about 36 pounds, or 16 kilograms.

¹² and the Lᴏʀᴅ has removed men far away,
　　and there is a great forsaking in the midst of the land.
¹³ But yet in it shall be a tenth,
　　and it shall return, and shall be burned,
　as a terebinth tree or as an oak,
　　whose stump remains when it is cut down,
　so the holy seed is its stump."

Isaiah Reassures King Ahaz

7 And it came to pass in the days of Ahaz the son of Jotham, the son of Uzziah, king of Judah, that Rezin the king of Aram, and Pekah the son of Remaliah, king of Israel, went up toward Jerusalem to war against it, but could not prevail against it. ² It was said to the house of David, "Aram is allied with Ephraim." Then his heart trembled and the heart of his people, as the trees of the wood tremble with the wind. ³ Then the Lᴏʀᴅ said to Isaiah: Go out now to meet Ahaz, you, and Shear-Jashub your son, at the end of the conduit of the upper pool in the highway of the fuller's field, ⁴ and say to him, Take heed, and be quiet. Do not fear nor be fainthearted because of the two tails of these smoking firebrands, because of the fierce anger of Rezin with Aram and of the son of Remaliah, ⁵ because Aram, Ephraim, and the son of Remaliah have taken evil counsel against you, saying, ⁶ Let us go up against Judah, and trouble it, and let us make a breach there for us, and set a king in the midst of it, even the son of Tabeel. ⁷ Thus says the Lord Gᴏᴅ:

It shall not stand,
　　nor shall it come to pass.
⁸ For the head of Aram is Damascus,
　　and the head of Damascus is Rezin.
　Now within sixty-five years
　　Ephraim shall be broken so that it is not a people.
⁹ The head of Ephraim is Samaria,
　　and the head of Samaria is the son of Remaliah.
　If you will not believe,
　　surely you shall not be established.

The Sign of Immanuel

¹⁰ Moreover the Lᴏʀᴅ spoke again to Ahaz, saying; ¹¹ Ask for a sign from the Lᴏʀᴅ your God. Make it either as deep as Sheol or as high as heaven. ¹² But Ahaz said, I will not ask, nor will I tempt the Lᴏʀᴅ. ¹³ Then he said, "Hear now, O house of David. Is it a small thing for you to weary men, but will you weary my God also? ¹⁴ Therefore the Lord Himself shall give you a sign: The virgin¹ shall conceive, and bear a son, and shall call his name Immanuel.² ¹⁵ Curds and honey he shall eat at the time that he knows enough to refuse the evil and choose the good. ¹⁶ For before the child shall know to refuse the evil and choose the good, the land that you dread shall be forsaken of both her kings. ¹⁷ The Lᴏʀᴅ shall bring upon you, and upon your people, and upon your father's house, days that have not come from the day that Ephraim departed from Judah, even the king of Assyria." ¹⁸ In that day the Lᴏʀᴅ shall whistle for the fly that is in the uttermost part of the rivers of Egypt, and for the bee that is in the land of Assyria. ¹⁹ They shall come, and all of them shall rest in the desolate valleys, and in the holes of the rocks, and on all thorns, and on all bushes. ²⁰ In that same day the Lᴏʀᴅ shall shave with a hired razor, from regions beyond the River,³ with the king of Assyria, the head, and the hair of the legs, and it shall also remove the beard. ²¹ In that day a man shall nourish a young cow and two sheep, ²² and because of the abundance of milk that they give, he shall eat curds; for everyone who is left in the land shall eat curds and honey. ²³ In that day every place where there were a thousand vines, *worth* a thousand *shekels⁴* of silver, shall become briers and thorns. ²⁴ With arrows and with bows shall men come there because all the land shall become briers and thorns. ²⁵ On all hills that used to be cultivated with the hoe, you will not go there for fear of briers and thorns. But it shall be for pasturing oxen and for sheep to tread.

The Coming Assyrian Invasion

8 Moreover the Lᴏʀᴅ said to me, Take for yourself a large book and write in it with a man's pen: "Swift is the booty, speedy is the prey."⁵ ² I will take to Myself faithful witnesses for testimony, Uriah the priest and Zechariah the son of Jeberekiah. ³ So I went in to the prophetess, and she conceived and bore a son. Then the Lᴏʀᴅ said to me, Call his name Maher-Shalal-Hash-Baz.⁶ ⁴ For before the child knows how to cry "My father" and "My mother," the riches of Damascus and the spoil of Samaria shall be taken away before the king of Assyria.

⁵ The Lᴏʀᴅ spoke to me again, saying:

⁶ Because this people refuses
　　the gently flowing waters of Shiloah
　and rejoices in Rezin
　　and the son of Remaliah,
⁷ now therefore the Lord certainly is about to bring upon them
　　the strong and plentiful waters of the River,⁷
　　even the king of Assyria and all his glory;
　and he shall come up over all his channels
　　and go over all his banks.
⁸ And he shall pass through Judah, he shall overflow and go over,
　　he shall reach even to the neck,
　and the stretching out of his wings shall fill the breadth of
　　　your land,
　O Immanuel.

⁹ Be broken, O you peoples, and be broken in pieces.
　　And give ear, all you from far countries.
　Gird yourselves, but be broken in pieces;
　　gird yourselves, but be broken in pieces.
¹⁰ Take counsel together, but it shall come to nothing;
　　speak the word, but it shall not stand
　for God is with us.

Fear God

¹¹ For the Lᴏʀᴅ spoke thus to me with a strong hand and instructed me that I should not walk in the way of this people, saying:

¹² You should not say, "It is a conspiracy,"
　　concerning all that this people calls a conspiracy,
　neither fear their threats
　　nor be afraid of them.
¹³ Sanctify the Lᴏʀᴅ of Hosts Himself,
　　and let Him be your fear,
　　and let Him be your dread.
¹⁴ He shall become a sanctuary,
　　but a stone of stumbling and a rock of offense
　to both the houses of Israel,
　　and a trap and a snare to the inhabitants of Jerusalem.
¹⁵ Many among them shall stumble
　　and fall and be broken
　　and be snared and be taken.

¹⁶ Bind up the testimony;
　　seal the law among My disciples.
¹⁷ I will wait on the Lᴏʀᴅ,
　　who hides His face from the house of Jacob,
　and I will eagerly look for Him.

¹⁸ See, I and the children whom the Lᴏʀᴅ has given me are for signs and for wonders in Israel from the Lᴏʀᴅ of Hosts who dwells in Mount Zion.

¹⁹ When they say to you, "Seek after the mediums and the wizards, who whisper and mutter," should not a people seek after their God? *Should they consult* the dead for the living? ²⁰ To the law and to the testimony; if they do not speak according to this word, it is because there is no light in them. ²¹ They shall pass through the land hard-pressed and hungry; when they are hungry, they shall be furious and curse their king and their God as they look upward. ²² Then they shall look

---

¹14 Heb. *young woman.*　²14 Or *God with us.*　³20 Euphrates River.　⁴23 About 25 pounds, or 12 kilograms.　⁵1 See v. 3.　⁶3 See v. 1.
⁷7 Euphrates River.

to the earth and see trouble and darkness, gloom of anguish. And they shall be driven away into darkness.

The Coming King

9 Nevertheless there shall be no more gloom for her who was in anguish. In the former time He contemptuously treated the land of Zebulun and the land of Naphtali, but in the latter time He shall make it glorious, by the way of the sea, beyond the Jordan, in Galilee of the nations.

2 The people who walked in darkness
  have seen a great light;
  those who dwell in the land of the shadow of death,
  upon them the light has shined.
3 You have multiplied the nation
  and increased the joy;
  they rejoice before You
  according to the joy of harvest
  and as men rejoice
  when they divide the spoil.
4 For You have broken the yoke of his burden
  and the bar of his shoulder,
  the rod of his oppressor
  as in the day of Midian's defeat.
5 For all the sandals of the tramping warriors
  and all the garments rolled in blood
  shall be burned as fuel for the fire.
6 For unto us a child is born,
  unto us a son is given,
  and the government shall be upon his shoulder.
  And his name shall be called
  Wonderful Counselor, Mighty God,
  Eternal Father, Prince of Peace.
7 Of the increase of his government and peace
  there shall be no end,
  upon the throne of David
  and over his kingdom,
  to order it and to establish it
  with justice and with righteousness,
  from now until forever.
  The zeal of the Lord of Hosts
  will perform this.

The Message Against Israel

8 The Lord sent a word against Jacob,
  and it falls upon Israel.
9 All the people shall know,
  even Ephraim and the inhabitants of Samaria,
  who say in the pride
  and stoutness of heart,
10 "The bricks are fallen down,
  but we will build with hewn stones;
  the sycamores are cut down,
  but we will replace them with cedars."
11 Therefore, the Lord shall set up the adversaries of Rezin
  against him,
  and join his enemies together.
12 The Arameans shall be before and the Philistines behind;
  and they shall devour Israel with open jaws.

For all this His anger is not turned away,
  and His hand is stretched out still.

13 For the people do not turn to Him who struck them,
  nor do they seek the Lord of Hosts.
14 Therefore the Lord will cut off from Israel head and tail,
  branch and bulrush, in one day.
15 The elder and honorable man, he is the head;
  and the prophet that teaches lies, he is the tail.
16 For the leaders of this people cause them to err,
  and those who are led by them are destroyed.
17 Therefore the Lord shall have no joy in their young men,

nor shall He have mercy on their fatherless and widows;
  for every one of them is a hypocrite and an evildoer,
  and every mouth speaks folly.

For all this His anger is not turned away,
  and His hand is stretched out still.

18 For wickedness burns as a fire;
  it shall devour the briers and thorns,
  and shall ignite in the thickets of the forest,
  and they shall mount up like rising smoke.
19 Through the wrath of the Lord of Hosts
  is the land burned up,
  and the people shall be as fuel for the fire;
  no man shall spare his brother.
20 They shall snatch on the right hand,
  but still be hungry;
  and they shall eat on the left hand,
  and shall not be satisfied;
  every man shall eat the flesh of his own arm.
21 Manasseh *consumes* Ephraim, and Ephraim, Manasseh,
  and they together shall be against Judah.

For all this His anger is not turned away,
  and His hand is stretched out still.

10 Woe to those who decree unrighteous decrees
  and who write unjust judgments which they have prescribed
2 to turn aside the needy from justice
  and to take away the right from the poor of My people,
  that widows may be their prey,
  and that they may rob the fatherless!
3 And what will you do in the day of punishment
  and in the desolation which shall come from afar?
  To whom will you flee for help,
  and where will you leave your wealth?
4 Nothing remains but to bow down among the prisoners,
  and they shall fall among the slain.

For all this His anger is not turned away,
  and His hand is stretched out still.

Judgment on Assyria

5 Woe to Assyria, the rod of My anger
  and the staff in whose hand is My indignation.
6 I will send him against an ungodly nation,
  and against the people of My wrath I will give him a command,
  to seize the plunder, to take the prey,
  and to tread them down like the mire of the streets.
7 However he does not so intend,
  nor does he plan so in his heart;
  but his purpose is to destroy
  and to cut off many nations.
8 For he says, "Are not my princes altogether kings?
9 Is not Kalno as Carchemish?
  Is not Hamath as Arpad?
  Is not Samaria as Damascus?
10 As my hand has found the kingdoms of the idols
  whose graven images were greater than those of Jerusalem
  and Samaria,
11 shall I not, as I have done to Samaria and her idols,
  so do to Jerusalem and her idols?"

12 When the Lord has performed all His work on Mount Zion and on Jerusalem, *He will say*, "I will punish the fruit of the stout heart of the king of Assyria and the glory of his high looks." 13 For he says:

"By the strength of my hand and by my wisdom,
  I have done it, for I am prudent;
  and I have removed the bounds of the people,
  and have robbed their treasures,
  and I have put down the inhabitants like a *valiant man.*

¹⁴ And my hand has found as a nest
　　the riches of the people,
　and as one gathers eggs that are left,
　　I have gathered all the earth
　and there was no one who moved the wing
　　or opened the mouth or peeped."

¹⁵ Shall the axe boast itself against him who hews with it?
　　Or shall the saw magnify itself against him who wields it?
　That is as if the rod wields itself against those who lift it up,
　　or as if the staff should lift itself up as if it were not wood.
¹⁶ Therefore the Lord, God of Hosts,
　　shall send leanness among his stout ones,
　and under his glory he shall kindle a burning
　　like the burning of a fire.
¹⁷ The light of Israel shall be a fire,
　　and his Holy One a flame,
　and it shall burn and devour
　　his thorns and his briers in one day,
¹⁸ and shall consume the glory of his forest,
　　and of his fruitful field, both soul and body;
　and it shall be as when a sick man faints.
¹⁹ The rest of the trees of his forest shall be so few
　　that a child may write them down.

The Returning Remnant of Israel

²⁰ In that day the remnant of Israel
　　and those who have escaped of the house of Jacob
　shall never again depend on him
　　who struck them,
　but shall depend on the Lord,
　　the Holy One of Israel, in truth.
²¹ The remnant shall return, even the remnant of Jacob,
　　to the mighty God.
²² For though your people, O Israel, are as the sand of the sea,
　　yet a remnant of them shall return;
　the destruction is decreed,
　　overflowing with righteousness.
²³ For the Lord God of Hosts shall make a complete destruction,
　　as decreed, in the midst of all the land.

²⁴ Therefore, thus says the Lord God of Hosts:

O My people who dwell in Zion,
　do not be afraid of the Assyrian.
He shall strike you with a rod
　and shall lift up his staff against you, after the manner
　　of Egypt.
²⁵ For yet a very little while, and the indignation shall cease,
　　and My anger will be directed to their destruction.

²⁶ The Lord of Hosts shall stir up a scourge for him
　　according to the slaughter of Midian at the rock of Oreb;
　and as His rod was over the sea, so shall He lift it up
　　after the manner of Egypt.
²⁷ In that day his burden shall be taken away from off your shoulder,
　　and his yoke from off your neck;
　and the yoke shall be destroyed
　　because of the anointing oil.

²⁸ He has come against Aiath,
　　he has passed through Migron;
　at Mikmash he has laid up his carriages.
²⁹ They are gone over the pass,
　　they have taken up their lodging at Geba.
　Ramah is afraid,
　　Gibeah of Saul has fled.
³⁰ Lift up your voice, O daughter of Gallim.
　　Listen, Laishah
　　and poor Anathoth.

³¹ Madmenah has fled,
　　the inhabitants of Gebim gather themselves to flee.
³² Yet today he shall remain at Nob;
　　he shakes his fist
　against the mount of the daughter of Zion,
　　the hill of Jerusalem.

³³ See, the Lord, the Lord of Hosts,
　　shall lop the bough with terror;
　and the tall ones of stature shall be hewn down,
　　and the haughty shall be humbled.
³⁴ He shall cut down the thickets of the forest with iron,
　　and Lebanon shall fall by the Mighty One.

The Righteous Branch of Jesse

11 And there shall come forth a shoot from the stump of Jesse,
　　and a Branch shall grow out of his roots.
² The Spirit of the Lord shall rest upon him,
　　the Spirit of wisdom and understanding,
　the Spirit of counsel and might,
　　the Spirit of knowledge and of the fear of the Lord.

³ He shall delight in the fear of the Lord,
　　and he shall not judge by what his eyes see,
　　nor reprove by what his ears hear;
⁴ but with righteousness he shall judge the poor,
　　and reprove with fairness for the meek of the earth.
　He shall strike the earth with the rod of his mouth,
　　and with the breath of his lips he shall slay the wicked.
⁵ Righteousness shall be the belt of his loins,
　　and faithfulness the belt about his waist.

⁶ The wolf also shall dwell with the lamb,
　　and the leopard shall lie down with the young goat,
　and the calf and the young lion and the fatling together;
　　and a little child shall lead them.
⁷ The cow and the bear shall graze;
　　their young ones shall lie down together;
　and the lion shall eat straw like the ox.
⁸ The nursing child shall play by the hole of the asp,
　　and the weaned child shall put his hand in the viper's den.
⁹ They shall not hurt or destroy
　　in all My holy mountain,
　for the earth shall be full of the knowledge of the Lord,
　　as the waters cover the sea.

¹⁰ In that day there shall be a Root of Jesse, who shall stand as a banner to the peoples. For him shall the nations seek. And his rest shall be glorious. ¹¹ In that day the Lord shall set His hand again the second time to recover the remnant of His people, who shall be left, from Assyria, from Egypt, from Pathros, from Cush, from Elam, from Shinar, from Hamath, and from the islands of the sea.

¹² He shall set up a banner for the nations,
　　and shall assemble the outcasts of Israel,
　and gather together the dispersed of Judah
　　from the four corners of the earth.
¹³ The envy also of Ephraim shall depart,
　　and the adversaries of Judah shall be cut off;
　Ephraim shall not envy Judah,
　　and Judah shall not harass Ephraim.
¹⁴ But they shall swoop down on the slopes of the Philistines towards
　　the west;
　they shall plunder the sons of the east together;
　they shall lay their hand on Edom and Moab,
　　and the children of Ammon shall obey them.
¹⁵ The Lord shall utterly destroy
　　the tongue of the Egyptian sea,
　and with His mighty wind He shall shake His hand
　　over the River, *ⁱ*

ⁱ 15 Euphrates River.

and shall strike it into seven streams,
    and make men walk over dry-shod.
16 There shall be a highway for the remnant of His people,
    who will be left from Assyria,
as it was for Israel
    when he came up from the land of Egypt.

Hymns of Praise

12 And in that day you shall say:

O Lord, I will praise You;
    though You were angry with me,
Your anger has turned away,
    and You comforted me.
2 Certainly God is my salvation;
    I will trust and not be afraid;
for the Lord God is my strength and my song;
    He also has become my salvation.
3 Therefore with joy you shall draw water
    out of the wells of salvation.

4 In that day you shall say:

Praise the Lord, call upon His name,
    declare His deeds among the peoples,
    make them remember that His name is exalted.
5 Sing to the Lord, for He has done excellent things;
    let this be known in all the earth.
6 Cry out and shout for joy, O inhabitant of Zion.
    For great is the Holy One of Israel in
    your midst.

A Prophecy Against Babylon

13 The burden of Babylon, which Isaiah the son of Amoz saw.

2 Lift up a banner on the high mountain,
    exalt the voice to them,
shake the hand,
    that they may go into the gates of the nobles.
3 I have commanded My sanctified ones,
    I have also called My mighty ones for My anger,
    even those who rejoice in My exaltation.

4 The noise of a multitude in the mountains,
    like as of a great people!
A tumultuous noise of the kingdoms
    of nations gathered together!
The Lord of Hosts musters
    the army for battle.
5 They come from a far country,
    from the end of heaven,
the Lord and the weapons of His indignation,
    to destroy the whole land.

6 Wail, for the day of the Lord is at hand!
    It shall come as destruction from the Almighty.
7 Therefore all hands shall be faint,
    and every man's heart shall melt,
8 and they shall be afraid.
Pangs and sorrows shall take hold of them;
    they shall be in pain as a woman who travails;
they shall be amazed one at another;
    their faces shall be as flames.

9 See, the day of the Lord comes,
    cruel, both with wrath and fierce anger,
to lay the land desolate,
    and He shall destroy its sinners out of it.
10 For the stars of heaven and their constellations
    shall not give their light;
the sun shall be dark when it rises,
    and the moon shall not cause her light to shine.

11 I will punish the world for its evil,
    and the wicked for their iniquity;
and I will cause the arrogance of the proud to cease,
    and will lay low the haughtiness of the ruthless.
12 I will make a man more rare than fine gold,
    and mankind than the golden wedge of Ophir.
13 Therefore, I will shake the heavens,
    and the earth shall be shaken out of her place
at the wrath of the Lord of Hosts
    and in the day of His fierce anger.

14 It shall be as the chased roe,
    and as a sheep that no man takes up;
every man shall turn to his own people
    and flee every one into his own land.
15 Every one who is found shall be thrust through,
    and every one who is joined to them shall fall by the sword.
16 Their children also shall be dashed to pieces before their eyes;
    their houses shall be devastated and their wives ravished.

17 See, I will stir up the Medes against them,
    who shall not regard silver;
    and as for gold, they shall not delight in it.
18 Their bows also shall dash the young men to pieces,
    and they shall have no pity on the fruit of the womb;
    their eye shall not spare children.
19 Babylon, the glory of kingdoms,
    the beauty of the Chaldean's excellency,
shall be as when God overthrew
    Sodom and Gomorrah.
20 It shall never be inhabited,
    nor shall it be lived in from generation to generation,
nor shall the Arabian pitch a tent there,
    nor shall the shepherds make their fold there.
21 But wild beasts of the desert shall lie down there,
    and their houses shall be full of owls,
ostriches also shall dwell there,
    and shaggy goats shall dance there.
22 The wild beasts of the islands shall cry in their
    desolate houses
    and jackals in their pleasant palaces.
And her time is near to come,
    and her days shall not be prolonged.

The Restoration of Judah

14 For the Lord will have mercy on Jacob,
    and will yet choose Israel,
    and set them in their own land.
Then the strangers shall be joined with them,
    and they shall cleave to the house of Jacob.
2 The people shall take them
    and bring them to their place,
and the house of Israel shall possess them
    in the land of the Lord for servants and handmaids;
and they shall take them captive, whose captives they were,
    and they shall rule over their oppressors.

The Fall of Babylon's King

3 In the day the Lord gives you rest from your sorrow, and from your fear, and from the hard bondage in which you were made to serve, 4 you shall take up this proverb against the king of Babylon, and say:

How has the oppressor ceased!
    The golden city ceased!
5 The Lord has broken the staff of the wicked,
    and the scepter of the rulers;
6 he who struck the people in wrath with unceasing strokes,
    he who ruled the nations in anger, is persecuted, and no
    one hinders.
7 The whole earth is at rest and is quiet;
    they break forth into singing.

⁸ Indeed, the fir trees rejoice at you,
  and the cedars of Lebanon, saying,
"Since you are laid down,
  no tree cutter has come up against us."

⁹ Hell from beneath is moved for you
  to meet you at your coming;
it stirs up the dead for you,
  even all the chief ones of the earth;
it has raised up from their thrones
  all the kings of the nations.
¹⁰ They all shall speak
  and say to you:
"Have you also become as weak as we have?
  Have you become like us?"
¹¹ Your pomp is brought down to Hell,
  and the noise of your harps;
maggots are spread under you,
  and the worms cover you.

¹² How are you fallen from heaven,
  O Lucifer, son of the morning!
How you are cut down to the ground,
  you who weaken the nations!
¹³ For you have said in your heart,
  "I will ascend into heaven,
I will exalt my throne
  above the stars of God;
I will sit also on the mount of the congregation,
  in the recesses of the north;
¹⁴ I will ascend above the heights of the clouds,
  I will be like the Most High."
¹⁵ Yet you shall be brought down to Hell,
  to the sides of the pit.

¹⁶ Those who see you shall stare at you
  and ponder over you:
"Is this the man who made the earth
  to tremble and shook kingdoms,
¹⁷ who made the world as a wilderness
  and destroyed its cities,
  who did not open the house of his prisoners?"

¹⁸ All the kings of the nations, even all of them, lie
    in glory,
  each one in his own tomb;
¹⁹ but you are cast out of your grave
    like an abominable branch
  and clothed with those who are slain,
    thrust through with a sword,
  who go down to the stones of the pit
    as a corpse trodden underfoot.
²⁰   You shall not be joined with them in burial
  because you have destroyed your land
    and slain your people.

The seed of evildoers
  shall never be renowned.
²¹ Prepare a place of slaughter for his children
  for the iniquity of their fathers;
they must not rise nor possess the land,
  nor fill the face of the world with cities.

²² For I will rise up against them,
    says the Lord of Hosts,
  and cut off from Babylon the name, and remnant,
    and son, and nephew,
    says the Lord.
²³ I will also make it a possession for the hedgehog
    and pools of water,
  and I will sweep it with the broom of destruction,
    says the Lord of Hosts.

An Oracle Concerning Assyria
²⁴ The Lord of Hosts has sworn, saying:

Surely as I have thought, so shall it come to pass,
  and as I have purposed, so shall it stand:
²⁵ that I will break the Assyrian in My land,
  and on My mountains tread him under foot.
Then shall his yoke depart from off them
  and his burden depart from off their shoulders.

²⁶ This is the purpose that is purposed on the whole earth,
  and this is the hand that is stretched out on all the nations.
²⁷ For the Lord of Hosts has purposed, and who shall disannul it?
  And His hand is stretched out, and who shall turn it back?

An Oracle Concerning Philistia
²⁸ In the year that King Ahaz died was this oracle:

²⁹ Rejoice not, O Philistia, all of you,
  because the rod that struck you is broken;
for out of the serpent's root shall come forth a viper,
  and his fruit shall be a fiery flying serpent.
³⁰ The firstborn of the poor shall feed,
  and the needy shall lie down in safety:
and I will kill your root with famine,
  and he shall slay your remnant.

³¹ Wail, O gate. Cry, O city.
  Melt away, O Philistia, all of you;
for smoke shall come from the north,
  and there is no straggler in his ranks.
³² What shall one then answer
  the messengers of the nation?
That the Lord has founded Zion,
  and the poor of His people shall trust in it.

A Prophecy Against Moab
Jer 48:29–36

15 The oracle of Moab.

Surely in the night Ar of Moab is laid waste
  and brought to silence,
surely in the night Kir of Moab is laid waste
  and brought to silence,
² he has gone up to the temple and to Dibon,
  the high places, to weep.
Moab shall wail over Nebo and over Medeba;
  on all their heads shall be baldness,
  and every beard cut off.
³ In their streets they shall clothe themselves with sackcloth;
  on the tops of their houses and in their streets,
everyone shall wail,
  weeping abundantly.
⁴ Heshbon shall cry, and Elealeh;
  their voice shall be heard even to Jahaz;
therefore the armed soldiers of Moab shall cry out;
  his life shall be grievous to him.

⁵ My heart shall cry out for Moab;
  his fugitives shall flee to Zoar,
  like a three-year-old heifer.
For by the Ascent of Luhith
  they shall go up with weeping;
for in the way of Horonaim
  they shall raise up a cry of destruction,
⁶ for the waters of Nimrim shall be desolate;
  surely the grass is withered away;
the grass fails,
  there is no green thing.
⁷ Therefore the abundance they have gained, and that which they
    have laid up,
  they shall carry away to the Brook of the Willows.

8 For the cry has gone all around the borders of Moab;
　　its wailing to Eglaim,
　　and its wailing to Beer Elim.
9 For the waters of Dimon shall be full of blood;
　　for I will bring more woes on Dimon,
lions on the fugitives of Moab,
　　and on the remnant of the land.

16 Send the lamb
　　to the ruler of the land
from Sela by way of the wilderness,
　　to the mount of the daughter of Zion.
2 For it shall be that as a wandering bird
　　cast out of the nest,
so the daughters of Moab shall be
　　at the fords of Arnon.

3 "Take counsel,
　　execute justice,
make your shadow as the night
　　at the height of noon.
Hide the outcasts,
　　do not betray the fugitive.
4 Let my outcasts dwell with you, Moab;
　　be a hiding place to them from the face of the destroyer."

For the extortioner has come to an end;
　　the destroyer ceases;
　　the oppressors are *consumed* out of the land.
5 In mercy the throne shall be established;
　　and one who judges and seeks justice
　　and is diligent in righteousness
shall sit on it in truth
　　in the tabernacle of David, judging.

6 We have heard of the pride of Moab;
　　he is very proud,
even of his haughtiness and his pride and his wrath;
　　but his lies shall not be so.
7 Therefore Moab shall wail for Moab;
　　everyone shall wail.
For the loss of raisin cakes of Kir Hareseth you shall mourn;
　　surely they are destroyed.
8 For the fields of Heshbon languish,
　　and the vine of Sibmah;
the lords of the nations
　　have broken down its choice plants;
they have come as far as Jazer
　　and wandered through the wilderness.
Her branches are stretched out;
　　they are passed over the sea.
9 Therefore I will weep bitterly for Jazer,
　　the vine of Sibmah;
I will water you with my tears,
　　O Heshbon and Elealeh.
For the shouting for your summer fruits
　　and for your harvest has fallen away.
10 Gladness and joy are taken away out of the plentiful field,
　　and in the vineyards there shall be no singing,
　　nor shall there be shouting;
the treaders shall tread out no wine in their presses.
　　I have made their vintage shouting to cease.
11 Therefore my heart shall sound like a harp for Moab,
　　and my inward parts for Kir Hareseth.
12 When it is seen that Moab
　　is weary on the high place,
he shall come to his sanctuary to pray;
　　but he shall not prevail.

13 This is the word that the LORD has spoken earlier concerning Moab. 14 But now the LORD has spoken, saying, Within three years, as the years of a hireling, the glory of Moab shall be brought into contempt with all his great population, and his remnant shall be very small and feeble.

An Oracle Concerning Damascus

17 The oracle of Damascus.

See, Damascus will cease from being a city;
　　it shall be a ruinous heap.
2 The cities of Aroer are forsaken;
　　they shall be for flocks, which shall lie down,
　　and no one shall make them afraid.
3 The fortress also shall cease from Ephraim,
　　and the kingdom from Damascus,
and the remnant of Aram;
　　they shall be as the glory of the sons of Israel,
　　says the LORD of Hosts.

4 In that day the glory of Jacob shall decrease,
　　and the fatness of his flesh shall grow lean.
5 It shall be as when the harvestman gathers the corn
　　and reaps the ears with his arm,
and it shall be as he who gathers ears
　　in the Valley of Rephaim.
6 Yet gleaning grapes shall be left in it,
　　as the shaking of an olive tree,
two or three berries in the top of the uppermost bough,
　　four or five in its outmost fruitful branches,
　　says the LORD God of Israel.

7 On that day a man shall look to his Maker,
　　and his eyes shall have respect for the Holy One of Israel.
8 He shall not look to the altars,
　　the work of his hands,
nor shall he respect what his fingers have made,
　　either the groves or the images.

9 In that day his strong cities shall be as a forsaken bough and an uppermost branch, which they left because of the sons of Israel; and there shall be a desolation.

10 Because you have forgotten the God of your salvation
　　and have not been mindful of the rock of your strength,
therefore you plant pleasant plants
　　and set them with vine slips of a strange god;
11 in the day that you plant it, you carefully fence it in,
　　and in the morning you make your seed to flourish;
but the harvest shall be a heap of ruins
　　in the day of grief and desperate pain.

12 Woe to the multitude of many people
　　who make a noise like the noise of the seas,
and the rushing of many peoples
　　who make a rumble like the rumbling of mighty waters!
13 The nations rumble like the rumbling of many waters;
　　but God shall rebuke them, and they shall flee far off,
and shall be chased as the chaff of the mountains before
　　　　the wind,
　　and like rolling dust before the whirlwind.
14 At evening time, sudden terror!
　　And before the morning, they are no more.
This is the portion of those who plunder us,
　　and the lot of those who rob us.

An Oracle Concerning Ethiopia

18 Woe to the land vibrating with wings,
　　which is beyond the rivers of Ethiopia,
2 which sends ambassadors by the sea,
　　even in vessels of reeds on the waters, saying,

"Go, swift messengers,
to a nation tall and smooth,
　　to a people feared far and wide,

a nation strong and oppressive,
    whose land the rivers have divided."

3 All you inhabitants of the world,
    and dwellers on the earth:
When he lifts up a banner on the mountains,
    you will see it;
and when he blows a trumpet,
    you will hear it.
4 For so the LORD said to me:
    I will look from My dwelling place quietly,
    like dazzling heat in the sunshine,
    like a cloud of dew in the heat of harvest.
5 For before the harvest, when the bud is perfect
    and the sour grape is ripening in the flower,
then He shall both cut off the sprigs with pruning hooks
    and take away and cut down the branches.
6 They shall be left together for the fowl of the mountains
    and for the beasts of the earth;
and the fowl shall spend the summer *feeding* on them,
    and all the beasts of the earth shall spend the winter
      on them.

7 In that time a present shall be brought to the LORD of Hosts

from a people tall and smooth,
    and from a people feared far and wide,
a nation strong and oppressive,
    whose land the rivers have divided,

to the place of the name of the LORD of Hosts, even Mount Zion.

An Oracle Concerning Egypt

19 The oracle of Egypt.

See, the LORD is riding on a swift cloud
    and shall come into Egypt;
and the idols of Egypt shall tremble at His presence,
    and the heart of Egypt shall melt in its midst.

2 I will set the Egyptians against the Egyptians,
    and they shall fight every one against his brother,
    and every one against his neighbor,
    city against city,
    and kingdom against kingdom.
3 The spirit of Egypt shall be discouraged in their midst,
    and I will destroy their counsel;
then they shall seek for the idols and for the charmers
    and for the mediums and the sorcerers.
4 The Egyptians I will give over
    into the hand of a cruel lord,
and a fierce king shall rule over them,
    says the Lord, the LORD of Hosts.

5 The waters from the sea shall dry up,
    and the river shall be parched and dry.
6 The canals shall emit a stench;
    the streams of Egypt shall diminish and dry up;
the reeds and rushes shall wither.
7   The papyrus reeds by the brooks,
    by the mouth of the brooks,
and everything sown by the brooks,
    shall wither, be driven away, and be no more.
8 The fishermen also shall mourn,
    and all those who cast a line into the brooks
      shall lament;
    and those who spread nets on the waters
      shall languish.
9 Moreover those who work with fine flax
    and those who weave white cloth shall be humiliated;

10 and the pillars *of Egypt* shall be crushed.
    All the hired workers shall be grieved in soul.

11 Surely the princes of Zoan are fools;
    the counsel of the wise counselors of Pharaoh has
      become stupid.
How can you say to Pharaoh,
    "I am a son of the wise,
    a son of ancient kings?"

12 Where are they? Where are your wise men?
    Let them tell you now, and let them understand
what the LORD of Hosts
    has purposed against Egypt.
13 The princes of Zoan have become fools;
    the princes of Memphis are deceived;
they have also seduced Egypt,
    even those who are the cornerstone of her tribes.
14 The LORD has mingled
    a perverse spirit in her;
so they have caused Egypt to err in her every work,
    as a drunken man staggers in his vomit.
15 Nor shall there be any work for Egypt,
    which its head or tail, its branch or bulrush, may do.

16 In that day Egypt shall become like women. And it shall be afraid and be in dread because of the shaking of the hand of the LORD of Hosts which He is about to shake over it. 17 The land of Judah shall become a terror to Egypt. Everyone to whom it is mentioned shall be in dread of it, because of the counsel of the LORD of Hosts which He has determined against it. 18 In that day five cities in the land of Egypt shall speak the language of Canaan and swear to the LORD of Hosts. One shall be called the City of Destruction.

19 In that day there shall be an altar to the LORD in the midst of the land of Egypt, and a pillar to the LORD at its border. 20 It shall be for a sign and for a witness to the LORD of Hosts in the land of Egypt. For they shall cry to the LORD because of the oppressors, and He shall send them a Savior and a Champion. And He shall deliver them. 21 The LORD shall be known to Egypt, and the Egyptians shall know the LORD in that day, and shall worship with sacrifice and offering, they shall make a vow to the LORD and perform it. 22 The LORD shall strike Egypt. He shall strike and heal it. Then they shall return to the LORD, and He shall be entreated by them and shall heal them.

23 In that day there shall be a highway out of Egypt to Assyria, and the Assyrian shall come into Egypt, and the Egyptian into Assyria, and the Egyptians shall worship with the Assyrians. 24 In that day Israel shall be the third group with Egypt and Assyria, even a blessing in the midst of the earth, 25 whom the LORD of Hosts has blessed, saying, "Blessed is Egypt My people, and Assyria the work of My hands, and Israel My inheritance."

A Prophecy Against Egypt and Ethiopia

20 In the year that the Tartan[1] came to Ashdod, when Sargon the king of Assyria sent him, and he fought against Ashdod and took it, 2 at the same time the LORD spoke by Isaiah the son of Amoz saying, "Go and loosen the sackcloth from your waist and take off your shoes from your feet." And he did so, walking naked and barefoot.

3 The LORD said, "Even as My servant Isaiah has walked naked and barefoot three years for a sign and wonder against Egypt and Ethiopia, 4 so the king of Assyria shall lead away the Egyptians as prisoners and the Ethiopians as captives, young and old, naked and barefoot, even with their buttocks uncovered, to the shame of Egypt. 5 Then they shall be dismayed and ashamed of Ethiopia their hope and Egypt their boast. 6 So the inhabitants of this coastland shall say in that day, 'Certainly such is our hope, where we flee for help to be delivered from the king of Assyria! And how shall we escape?' "

A Prophecy Against Babylon

21 The oracle of the desert of the sea.

As whirlwinds in the Negev pass through,
    so it comes from the desert,
    from a terrible land.

2 A grievous vision is declared to me;
    the treacherous one still deals treacherously, and the
        destroyer still destroys.
Go up, O Elam. Lay siege, O Media.
    All her sighing I have made to cease.

3 Therefore, my loins are filled with pain;
    pangs have taken hold of me as the pangs of a woman
        who travails.
I am so perplexed at the hearing of it;
    I am so dismayed at the seeing of it.
4 My heart panted,
    fearfulness overwhelmed me;
the night for which I longed
    has turned into trembling for me.

5 Prepare the table,
    watch in the watchtower,
    eat and drink.
Arise, you princes,
    and oil the shields.

6 For thus the Lord has said to me:

"Go, station a watchman;
    let him declare what he sees.
7 When he sees chariots
    with horsemen in pairs,
a chariot of donkeys,
    and a chariot of camels,
then let him pay close attention,
    very close attention."

8 Then the watchman called:

"O Lord, I stand continually on the watchtower in the daytime,
    and I am stationed at my guard post every night.
9 Look, here comes a chariot of men,
    horsemen in pairs."
And he answered and said,
    "Fallen, fallen is Babylon.
And all the graven images of her gods
    lie shattered on the ground."

10 O my threshed people and my afflicted of the threshing floor!
    What I have heard from the Lord of Hosts,
the God of Israel,
    I have declared to you.

A Prophecy Against Edom

11 The oracle of Dumah.

He calls to me out of Seir,
    "Watchman, how far gone is the night?
Watchman, how far gone is the night?"
12 The watchman says,
    "The morning comes and also the night.
If you would inquire, inquire;
    return again."

A Prophecy Against Arabia

13 The oracle about Arabia.

In the forest of Arabia you shall lodge,
    O traveling companies of Dedanites.

14   Bring water for the thirsty,
O inhabitants of the land of Tema;
    meet the fugitive with bread.
15 For they fled from the swords,
    from the drawn sword,
and from the bent bow,
    and from the grievousness of war.

16 For thus the Lord has said to me: Within a year, according to the years of a hireling, all the glory of Kedar shall fail. 17 And the remainder of the number of archers, the mighty men of the children of Kedar, shall be diminished, for the Lord God of Israel has spoken it.

An Oracle Concerning Jerusalem

22 The oracle of the Valley of Vision.

What ails you now,
    that you all have gone up to the housetops,
2 you who were full of noise,
    a tumultuous city, a joyous city?
Your slain are not slain with the sword,
    nor did they die in battle.
3 All your rulers have fled together;
    they are captured by the archers.
All of you who were found were taken captive together,
    although they had fled from afar.
4 Therefore, I say, "Look away from me,
    I will weep bitterly;
do not try to comfort me
    because of the destruction of the daughter of my people."

5 For it is a day of trouble and of treading down and of perplexity
    by the Lord God of Hosts
    in the Valley of Vision,
a breaking down of the walls
    and a crying to the mountains.
6 Elam took up the quiver
    with chariots of men and horsemen,
    and Kir uncovered the shield.
7 Your choicest valleys shall be full of chariots,
    and the horsemen shall set themselves in array at the gate.

8 And He shall remove the protection of Judah.
    You shall depend in that day
    on the weapons of the house of the forest;
9 you have seen also that the breaches
    of the City of David are many;
and you gathered together the waters
    of the lower pool.
10 You have numbered the houses of Jerusalem,
    and the houses you have broken down to fortify the wall.
11 You also made a reservoir between the two walls
    for the water of the old pool.
But you have not looked to its Maker,
    nor did you respect Him who fashioned it long ago.

12 In that day the Lord God of Hosts
    called you to weeping and mourning,
    and to tear your hair and wear sackcloth.
13 Yet, there is joy and gladness,
    slaying of oxen and killing of sheep,
    eating of meat and drinking wine:
"Let us eat and drink,
    for tomorrow we may die."

14 It was revealed in my hearing by the Lord of Hosts: Surely this iniquity shall not be forgiven you until you die, says the Lord God of Hosts.

15 Thus says the Lord God of Hosts:

Come, go to this treasurer,
    even to Shebna, who is over the royal household, and say:

¹⁶ What right do you have here? And whom do you have here
     that you have dug out for yourself a tomb here,
as he who hews out for himself a tomb on high,
     and who cuts a habitation for himself in a rock?

¹⁷ Indeed, the Lᴏʀᴅ is about to hurl you headlong, O man;
     He is about to seize you firmly.
¹⁸ He will surely violently turn
     and toss you like a ball into a large country;
there you shall die,
     and there the chariots of your glory shall be
     the shame of your lord's house.
¹⁹ I will drive you from your office
     and pull you down from your station.

²⁰ In that day I will call My servant Eliakim the son of Hilkiah. ²¹ And I will clothe him with your robe and tie him securely
with your sash. And I will entrust him with your authority, and
he shall be a father to the inhabitants of Jerusalem and to the
house of Judah. ²² The key of the house of David I will lay on his
shoulder. Then he shall open, and no one shall shut. And he shall
shut, and no one shall open. ²³ I will fasten him as a nail in a firm
place, and he shall become a glorious throne to his father's house.
²⁴ They shall hang on him all the glory of his father's house, the
offspring and the issue, all vessels of small quantity, from the bowls
to all the jars.

²⁵ In that day, says the Lᴏʀᴅ of Hosts, the nail that is fastened in the
firm place shall be removed, and be cut down and fall. And the load
that was on it shall be cut off, for the Lᴏʀᴅ has spoken it.

An Oracle Concerning Tyre

23 The oracle of Tyre.

Wail, O ships of Tarshish,
     for Tyre is laid waste
so that there is no house or harbor;
     from the land of Cyprus
     it is reported to them.

² Be still, you inhabitants of the coastland,
     you merchants of Sidon;
     your messengers passed over the sea,
³ and were on many waters;
     the grain of the Nile,
the harvest of the River¹ was her revenue;
     and she was the market of nations.

⁴ Be ashamed, O Sidon; for the sea has spoken,
     even the stronghold of the sea, saying,
"I have not travailed nor brought forth children;
     neither have I brought up young men nor
        raised virgins."
⁵ When the report *reaches* Egypt,
     they shall be sorely pained at the report of Tyre.

⁶ Pass over to Tarshish;
     wail, O inhabitants of the coastland.
⁷ Is this your joyous city,
     whose origin is from ancient days,
whose feet used to carry her
     to sojourn in distant locations?
⁸ Who has planned this against Tyre,
     the crowning city,
whose merchants are princes,
     whose traffickers are the honorable of the earth?
⁹ The Lᴏʀᴅ of Hosts has purposed it,
     to stain the pride of all glory
     and to bring into contempt all the honorable of
        the earth.

¹⁰ Pass through your land as the Nile,
     O daughter of Tarshish;
     there is no more restraint.
¹¹ He stretched out His hand over the sea,
     He shook the kingdoms;
the Lᴏʀᴅ has given a command against the merchant city,
     to destroy its strongholds.
¹² He said: You shall rejoice no more,
     O oppressed virgin daughter of Sidon.

Arise, pass over to Cyprus;
     there also you shall have no rest.
¹³ Look at the land of the Chaldeans;
     this was a people who was not;
Assyria founded it
     for those who dwell in the wilderness.
They set up their siege towers,
     they stripped its palaces,
     and brought it to ruin.

¹⁴ Wail, O ships of Tarshish,
     for your stronghold is laid waste.

¹⁵ In that day Tyre shall be forgotten for seventy years, according to the
days of one king. After the end of seventy years Tyre shall sing as a harlot:

¹⁶ Take your harp, go about the city,
     O forgotten harlot;
make sweet melody, sing many songs,
     that you may be remembered.

¹⁷ At the end of seventy years, the Lᴏʀᴅ will punish Tyre. Then she
shall turn to her harlot's wages and shall commit fornication with all
the kingdoms on the face of the earth. ¹⁸ Her merchandise and her
harlot's wages shall be set apart to the Lᴏʀᴅ. It shall not be treasured
nor stored up, for her merchandise shall be for those who dwell before
the Lᴏʀᴅ, to eat sufficiently, and for choice clothing.

Judgment on the Earth

24 Now the Lᴏʀᴅ makes the earth empty,
     and makes it waste,
and turns it upside down,
     and scatters its inhabitants abroad.
² It shall be:
     as with the people, so with the priest;
     as with the servant, so with his master;
     as with the maid, so with her mistress;
     as with the buyer, so with the seller;
     as with the lender, so with the borrower;
     as with the creditor, so with the debtor.
³ The land shall be utterly emptied,
     and utterly despoiled,
     for the Lᴏʀᴅ has spoken this word.

⁴ The earth mourns and fades away,
     the world languishes and fades away,
     the haughty people of the earth languish.
⁵ The earth also is defiled by its inhabitants
     because they have transgressed the laws,
violated the ordinances,
     broken the everlasting covenant.
⁶ Therefore, the curse devours the earth,
     and those who dwell in it are held guilty.
Therefore, the inhabitants of the earth are burned,
     and few men are left.
⁷ The new wine fails, the vine languishes,
     all the merry-hearted sigh.
⁸ The joy of tambourines ceases,
     the noise of those who rejoice ends,
     the joy of the harp ceases.

¹ 3 Nile River.

⁹ They shall not drink wine with song;
    strong drink shall be bitter to those who drink it.
¹⁰ The city of confusion is broken down;
    every house is shut up so that no one may come in.
¹¹ There is an outcry for wine in the streets,
    all joy is turned to gloom,
    the joyfulness of the earth is gone.
¹² Desolation is left in the city,
    and the gate is battered to destruction.
¹³ For thus it shall be in the midst of the earth
    among the peoples,
  as the shaking of an olive tree,
    and as the gleaning of grapes when the vintage
      is done.

¹⁴ They lift up their voices; they sing for the majesty of the Lord;
    they cry aloud from the west.
¹⁵ Therefore glorify the Lord in the east,
    even the name of the Lord God of Israel
    in the coastlands of the sea.
¹⁶ From the uttermost part of the earth we hear songs,
    that is, "Glory to the Righteous One."

But I say, Woe to me! Woe to me!
    Alas for me!
The treacherous deal treacherously;
    indeed, the treacherous deal very treacherously.
¹⁷ Terror and the pit and the snare are upon you,
    O inhabitant of the earth.
¹⁸ He who flees from the report of disaster
    shall fall into the pit,
and he who comes up out of the midst of the pit
    shall be taken in the snare.

For the windows from on high are open,
    and the foundations of the earth shake.
¹⁹ The earth is utterly broken down,
    the earth is split through,
    the earth is shaken violently.
²⁰ The earth reels to and fro like a drunkard,
    and it totters like a shack,
and its transgression is heavy upon it,
    and it shall fall, never to rise again.

²¹ In that day the Lord shall punish
    the host of heaven on high
    and the kings of the earth on the earth.
²² They shall be gathered together,
    as prisoners are gathered in the dungeon,
and shall be shut up in the prison,
    and after many days they shall be punished.
²³ Then the moon shall be humiliated and the sun ashamed,
    when the Lord of Hosts reigns
in Mount Zion and in Jerusalem,
    and His glory shall be before His elders.

Praise to the Lord

25 O Lord, You are my God.
    I will exalt You, I will praise Your name,
for You have done wonderful things;
    Your plans formed of old
    are faithfulness and truth.
² For You have made a city into a heap,
    a fortified city into a ruin;
a palace of strangers is a city no longer;
    it shall never be built.
³ Therefore a strong people shall glorify You;
    cities of ruthless nations shall fear You.
⁴ For You have been a defense to the poor,
    a defense to the needy in his distress,
a refuge from the storm,
    a shadow from the heat;

for the breath of the ruthless ones
    is as a storm against the wall.
⁵ You bring down the noise of strangers,
as heat in drought;
    as the heat by the shadow of a cloud,
    the song of the ruthless ones shall be brought low.

⁶ In this mountain the Lord of Hosts shall prepare
    for all people a lavish feast,
a feast of aged wines,
    choice pieces full of marrow, and refined, aged wines.
⁷ He will destroy in this mountain
    the covering which is over all peoples,
even the veil that is spread over all nations.
⁸   He will swallow up death for all time,
and the Lord God will wipe away tears
    from all faces;
and the reproach of His people He shall take away
    from all the earth,
    for the Lord has spoken it.

⁹ It shall be said in that day:

Look, this is our God
    for whom we have waited that He might save us.
This is the Lord for whom we have waited;
    we will be glad and rejoice in His salvation.

¹⁰ For in this mountain the hand of the Lord shall rest,
    and Moab shall be trodden down in his place
    as straw is trodden down in the water for the manure pile.
¹¹ He shall spread out his hands in the midst of it,
    as a swimmer spreads out *his hands* to swim,
yet *the Lord* shall bring down his pride
    together with the trickery of his hands.
¹² The unassailable fortresses of your walls
    He shall bring down, lay low,
and bring to the ground,
    even to the dust.

A Song of Victory

26 In that day this song shall be sung in the land of Judah:

We have a strong city;
    He appoints walls
    and bulwarks for security.
² Open the gates,
    that the righteous nation may enter,
    the one who remains faithful.
³ You will keep him in perfect peace,
    whose mind is stayed on You,
    because he trusts in You.
⁴ Trust in the Lord forever,
    for in God the Lord we have an everlasting rock.
⁵ For He brings down those who dwell on high,
    the lofty city; He lays it low; He lays it low,
even to the ground;
    He brings it even to the dust.
⁶ The foot shall tread it down,
    even the feet of the poor
    and the steps of the needy.

⁷ The way of the righteous is smooth;
    O Upright One, make the path of the righteous level.
⁸ In the way of Your judgments, O Lord,
    we have waited for You eagerly;
the desire of our souls is Your name,
    even Your memory.
⁹ With my soul I have desired You in the night;
    my spirit within me seeks You diligently;
for when Your judgments are in the earth,
    the inhabitants of the world learn righteousness.

10 Though favor is shown to the wicked,
    yet he will not learn righteousness;
in the land of uprightness he deals unjustly
    and does not perceive the majesty of the Lord.
11 Lord, Your hand is lifted up,
    but they do not see it.
They see Your zeal for the people and are put to shame;
    the fire of Your enemies shall devour them.

12 Lord, You will ordain peace for us,
    for You also have done all our works for us.
13 O Lord our God, other lords besides You have had dominion over us,
    but through You alone we confess Your name.
14 The dead shall not live;
    the departed spirits shall not rise.
Therefore, You have punished and destroyed them
    and made all remembrance of them to perish.
15 You have increased the nation, O Lord,
    You have increased the nation;
You are glorified;
    You have extended all the borders of the land.

16 Lord, in trouble they have sought You;
    they poured out a prayer
    when Your chastening was on them.
17 Like a woman with child, who is in pain and cries out in her
        pangs
    when she draws near the time of her delivery,
so have we been in Your sight, O Lord.
18 We have been with child, we have been in pain,
    we have, as it were, brought forth wind;
we have not accomplished any deliverance in the earth,
    nor were the inhabitants of the world born.

19 Your dead shall live,
    their corpses shall arise.
Awake and sing,
    you who dwell in dust,
for your dew is as the dew of the dawn,
    and the earth shall give birth to the departed spirits.

20 Come, my people, enter your chambers,
    and shut your doors behind you;
hide for a little while
    until the indignation is over.
21 For the Lord comes out of His place
    to punish the inhabitants of the earth for their iniquity;
the earth also shall disclose her bloodshed
    and shall cover her slain no more.

The Deliverance of Israel

27 In that day

the Lord with His fierce and great
    and strong sword shall punish
Leviathan the fleeing serpent,
    even Leviathan the twisted serpent;
and He shall slay the dragon that is in the sea.

2 In that day:

Sing of it! A vineyard of red wine.
3 I, the Lord, am its keeper;
I water it every moment;
lest anyone damage it,
    I protect it night and day.
4   I have no fury.
Should someone give Me briers and thorns in battle,
    then I would step on them,
    I would burn them fully.

5 Or let him rely on My strength;
    let him make peace with Me;
    let him make peace with Me.

6 In the days to come Jacob shall take root;
Israel shall blossom and bud
    and shall fill the whole world with fruit.

7 Has He struck them,
    as He struck those who struck them?
Or like the slaughter of His slain,
    have they been slain?
8 You fought with them by banishing them, by driving
        them away.
He has expelled them
    on the day of the east wind with His fierce wind.
9 Through this, therefore, the iniquity of Jacob shall be forgiven,
    and this will be the full price of the removal of his sin:
when he makes all the stones of the altar
    as chalkstones that are pulverized,
when the groves and incense altars
    shall not stand.
10 For the fortified city shall be desolate,
    a homestead forlorn and forsaken like a wilderness;
there the calf shall graze,
    and there it shall lie down
    and eat its branches.
11 When its boughs are withered, they are broken off;
    the women come and make a fire with them,
for they are not a people of understanding;
    therefore, their Maker will not have mercy on them,
    and their Creator will show them no grace.

12 In that day the Lord shall thresh from the channel of the River[1] to the stream of Egypt, and you shall be gathered one by one, O sons of Israel. 13 And in that day the great trumpet shall be blown, and those who were ready to perish in the land of Assyria and the outcasts in the land of Egypt shall worship the Lord in the holy mount at Jerusalem.

Woe to the Leaders of Ephraim and Judah

28 Woe to the proud crown of the drunkards of Ephraim,
    whose glorious beauty is a fading flower
which is at the head of the fertile valley
    of those who are overcome with wine!
2 See, the Lord has a mighty and strong one,
    as a tempest of hail and a destroying storm,
as a flood of mighty overflowing waters,
    He has cast it down to the earth with His hand.
3 The proud crown of the drunkards of Ephraim
    is trodden under foot;
4 and the fading flower of its glorious beauty,
    which is at the head of the fertile valley,
shall be like a first-ripe fig before the summer,
    which when one sees, while it is yet in his hand,
    he eats it up.

5 In that day the Lord of Hosts
    shall become a crown of glory
and a diadem of beauty
    to the remnant of His people,
6 a spirit of justice
    for him who sits in judgment,
and strength
    to those who turn away the battle at the gate.

7 But they also have erred through wine
    and stagger from strong drink;
the priest and the prophet have erred through strong drink,
    they are confused by wine,

---

1 12 Euphrates River.

they stagger from strong drink;
they err while having visions,
they stumble *when rendering* judgment.
8 For all the tables are full of vomit
and filthiness so that there is no *clean* place.

9 "To whom shall He teach knowledge,
and to whom shall He interpret the message?
Those just weaned from the milk
and drawn from the breasts?
10 For He says,
'Precept upon precept, precept upon precept,
line upon line, line upon line,
here a little, there a little.'"

11 For with stammering lips and foreign tongue
He will speak to this people,
12 He who said to them,
"This is the rest. Give rest to the weary,"
and, "This is repose,"
yet they would not listen.
13 So the word of the LORD will be to them,
"Precept upon precept, precept upon precept,
line upon line, line upon line,
here a little, there a little,"
that they might go and fall backward,
be broken, snared, and taken captive.

14 Therefore, hear the word of the LORD, O scoffers,
who rule this people who are in Jerusalem,
15 because you have said, "We have made a covenant
with death,
and with hell we are in agreement.
The overflowing scourge shall not come to us
when it passes through,
for we have made lies our refuge
and under falsehood we have hid ourselves."

A Cornerstone in Zion
16 Therefore, thus says the Lord GOD:

See, I lay in Zion a stone,
a tested stone,
a precious cornerstone, firmly placed;
he who believes shall not act hastily.
17 I shall make justice the measuring line
and righteousness the plummet;
then the hail shall sweep away the refuge of lies
and the waters shall overflow the hiding place.
18 Your covenant with death shall be annulled,
and your agreement with hell shall not stand;
when the overflowing scourge passes through,
then you shall be trodden down by it.
19 As often as it passes through, it shall seize you;
for morning by morning it shall pass through,
anytime by day or night.

It shall be terror only
to understand the report.
20 The bed is too short to stretch out,
and the covering is too small to wrap oneself in it.
21 For the LORD shall rise up as at Mount Perazim,
He shall be wrathful as in the Valley of Gibeon
to do His work, His unusual work,
and bring to pass His task, His exceptional task.
22 Now therefore, do not continue as mockers,
lest your bonds be made stronger;
for I have heard from the Lord GOD of Hosts
of determined destruction upon the whole earth.

23 Give ear and hear my voice;
listen and hear my speech.

24 Does the plowman plow all day to sow?
Does he continually turn and break the clods of his ground?
25 Does he not level its surface
and sow dill and scatter the cumin
and plant wheat in rows,
barley in its place
and the rye within its area?
26 For his God instructs
and teaches him appropriately.

27 For the dill is not threshed with a threshing instrument,
nor is a cartwheel driven over the cumin;
but the dill is beaten out with a staff,
and the cumin with a rod.
28 *Grain for* bread is crushed;
so he does not continue to thresh it forever,
nor break it with the wheel of his cart,
nor crush it with his horsemen.
29 This also comes from the LORD of Hosts,
who is wonderful in counsel and excellent in wisdom.

Woe to the City of David
29 Woe to Ariel, to Ariel,
the city where David lived!
Add year to year,
observe your feasts on schedule.
2 Yet I will distress Ariel,
and she shall be *a city of* lamenting and sorrow,
and she shall be as an Ariel to me.
3 I will encamp against you all around,
and will lay siege against you with a mound,
and I will raise forts against you.
4 You shall be brought down, and shall speak from the ground,
and from the dust where you are prostrate your speech
shall come;
your voice shall also be as that of a ghost from the ground;
and your speech shall whisper from the dust.

5 Moreover the multitude of your enemies shall become like
fine dust,
and the multitude of the ruthless ones as chaff which
blows away;
and it shall happen in an instant, suddenly.
6 You shall be punished from the LORD of Hosts
with thunder and earthquake and loud noise,
with storm and tempest, and the flame of a devouring fire.
7 The multitude of all the nations who fight against Ariel,
even all who fight against her and her stronghold, and who
distress her,
shall be as a dream
of a night vision.
8 It shall even be as when a hungry man dreams, and he eats;
but when he awakens, his hunger is not satisfied;
or as when a thirsty man dreams, and he is drinking;
but when he awakens, he is faint, and his thirst is not
quenched;
so shall the multitude of all the nations be
who fight against Mount Zion.

9 Be delayed and wait,
blind yourselves and be blind.
They are drunk, but not with wine.
They stagger, but not with strong drink.
10 For the LORD has poured out on you the spirit of deep sleep
and has closed your eyes, the prophets;
and He has covered your heads, the seers.

11 The whole vision will be to you as the words of a book that is
sealed, which when they deliver it to one who is learned, saying, "Read
this, please," he shall say, "I cannot, for it is sealed." 12 Then the book
shall be delivered to him who is not learned, saying, "Read this, please."
And he shall say, "I cannot read."

¹³ Therefore, the Lᴏʀᴅ said:

Because this people draw near with their mouths
    and honor Me with their lips,
    but have removed their hearts far from Me,
and their fear toward Me
    is tradition by the precept of men,
¹⁴ therefore I will once again do a marvelous work among this
        people,
    even a marvelous work and a wonder;
for the wisdom of their wise men shall perish,
    and the understanding of their prudent men shall
        be hidden.

¹⁵ Woe to those who deeply
    hide their counsel from the Lᴏʀᴅ
and whose works are done in the dark, and they say,
    "Who sees us?" and "Who knows us?"
¹⁶ Surely you turn things upside down!
    Shall the potter be esteemed as the potter's clay?
Shall what is made say to its maker,
    "He did not make me"?
Or shall the thing formed say to him who formed it,
    "He has no understanding"?

¹⁷ Is it not yet a very little while before Lebanon shall be turned into
        a fruitful field,
    and the fruitful field shall be counted as a forest?
¹⁸ And on that day the deaf shall hear the words of a book,
    and the eyes of the blind shall see
    out of obscurity and darkness.
¹⁹ The meek also shall increase their joy in the Lᴏʀᴅ,
    and the poor among men shall rejoice in the Holy One
        of Israel.
²⁰ For the ruthless shall come to nothing,
    and the scorner will be consumed,
    and all who are intent on doing iniquity shall be cut off—
²¹ those who cause a man to be indicted by a word,
    and lay a snare for him who reproves in the gate,
    and turn aside the righteous with meaningless arguments.

²² Therefore thus says the Lᴏʀᴅ, who redeemed Abraham, concerning
the house of Jacob:

Jacob shall not now be ashamed,
    nor shall his face now turn pale;
²³ but when he sees his children,
    the work of My hands, in his midst,
they shall sanctify My name
    and sanctify the Holy One of Jacob,
    and fear the God of Israel.
²⁴ Those also who err in spirit shall know the truth,
    and those who murmured shall accept instruction.

The Warning of Judah

30 Woe to the rebellious children,
    says the Lᴏʀᴅ,
who take counsel, but not from Me,
    and make an alliance, but not of My Spirit,
    in order to add sin to sin;
² they walk down to Egypt
    and have not asked from My mouth,
to strengthen themselves in the safety of Pharaoh
    and to trust in the shadow of Egypt!
³ Therefore the safety of Pharaoh shall be your shame
    and the trust in the shadow of Egypt your humiliation.
⁴ For their princes were at Zoan,
    and their ambassadors came to Hanes.
⁵ They all will be ashamed
    of a people who cannot profit them,
who are not a help or profit,
    but a shame and also a reproach.

⁶ The burden of the beasts of the Negev.

Through a land of trouble and anguish,
    from which comes the lioness and lion,
    the viper and fiery flying serpent,
they will carry their riches on the shoulders of young donkeys,
    and their treasures on the humps of camels,
to a people who shall not profit them.
⁷   For the Egyptians shall help in vain and to no purpose.
Therefore, I have called her,
    "Rahab who has been exterminated."

⁸ Now go, write it before them on a tablet,
    and note it in a book,
that it may serve in the time to come
    as a witness forever;
⁹ for this is a rebellious people, lying children,
    children who refuse to listen to the law of the Lᴏʀᴅ;
¹⁰ they say to the seers,
    "You must not see *visions*,"
and to the prophets,
    "You must not prophesy to us right things;
speak to us pleasant things,
    prophesy illusions.
¹¹ Get out of the way,
    turn aside from the path,
let us hear no more
    about the Holy One of Israel."

¹² Therefore, thus says the Holy One of Israel:

Because you despise this word
    and trust in oppression and perverseness,
    and rely on them,
¹³ therefore this iniquity shall be to you
    as a breach ready to fall, swelling up in a high wall,
    whose collapse comes suddenly, in an instant.
¹⁴ He shall break it as the breaking of the potter's vessel
    that is broken in pieces;
He shall not spare so that there shall not be found in the breaking
        of it a shard
    to take fire from the hearth
    or with which to take water out of a cistern.

¹⁵ For thus says the Lord Gᴏᴅ, the Holy One of Israel:

In returning and rest you shall be saved;
    in quietness and in confidence shall be your strength.
    Yet you were not willing,
¹⁶ and you said, "No, for we will flee on horses";
    therefore you shall flee.
"And we will ride on swift horses";
    therefore those who pursue you shall be swift.
¹⁷ One thousand *shall flee*
    at the threat of one man;
at the threat of five
    you shall flee
until you are left
    as a flag on the top of a mountain
    and as a banner on a hill.

God's Promise to Zion

¹⁸ Therefore, the Lᴏʀᴅ longs to be gracious to you,
    and therefore, He waits on high to have mercy on you;
for the Lᴏʀᴅ is a God of justice;
    how blessed are all who long for Him.

¹⁹ O people in Zion, inhabitants in Jerusalem, you shall weep no
more. He will be very gracious to you at the sound of your cry. When
He hears it, He will answer you. ²⁰ Though the Lord has given you the
bread of adversity and the water of affliction, yet He, your Teacher, will
no longer hide Himself, but your eyes shall see your Teacher. ²¹ Your

ears shall hear a word behind you, saying, "This is the way, walk in it," whenever you turn to the right hand and when you turn to the left. ²² You shall defile also your graven images overlaid with silver, and your molded images ornamented with gold. You shall scatter them as an impure thing, and say to them, "Be gone!"

²³ Then He shall give you rain for the seed which you shall sow in the ground and bread of the increase of the earth. And it shall be rich and plentiful. On that day your cattle shall feed in large pastures. ²⁴ The oxen likewise and the young donkeys that work the ground shall eat cured fodder, which has been winnowed with the shovel and fork. ²⁵ There shall be on every high mountain and on every high hill rivers and streams of waters in the day of the great slaughter, when the towers fall. ²⁶ Moreover the light of the moon shall be as the light of the sun, and the light of the sun shall be sevenfold, as the light of seven days, in the day that the LORD binds up the breach of His people and heals the wound from His blow.

Judgment on Assyria

²⁷ See, the name of the LORD comes from afar,
    burning with His anger, and its burden is heavy;
His lips are full of indignation,
    and His tongue as a devouring fire.
²⁸ And His breath is as an overflowing stream
    which reaches to the middle of the neck,
to sift the nations with the sieve of vanity;
    and there shall be a bridle in the jaws of the people,
    causing them to err.
²⁹ You shall have songs,
    as in the night when a festival is kept,
and gladness of heart,
    as when one goes with a flute
to come into the mountain of the LORD,
    to the Mighty One of Israel.
³⁰ The LORD shall cause His glorious voice to be heard,
    and shall show the descending of His arm
with the indignation of His anger, and with the flame of a
    devouring fire,
    with scattering, and cloudburst, and hailstones.
³¹ For through the voice of the LORD the Assyrian shall be
    beaten down
    when He strikes with a rod.
³² And every blow of the rod of punishment
    which the LORD shall lay on him
shall be with tambourines and harps;
    and in battles, brandishing weapons, He will fight them.
³³ For Topheth has been long prepared,
    indeed, for the king it has been prepared.
He has made it deep and large,
    a pile of fire with much wood;
the breath of the LORD,
    like a stream of brimstone,
    kindles it.

Woe to Those Who Trust Egypt

31 Woe to those who go down to Egypt for help,
    and rely on horses,
and trust in chariots because they are many,
    and in horsemen because they are very strong,
but they do not look to the Holy One of Israel
    nor seek the LORD!
² Yet He also is wise and will bring disaster
    and will not call back His words,
but will arise against the house of the evildoers
    and against the help of those who work iniquity.
³ Now the Egyptians are men and not God;
    and their horses flesh and not spirit.
When the LORD shall stretch out His hand,
    both he who helps shall fall
    and he who is helped shall fall down,
    and they all shall fail together.

⁴ For thus the LORD has spoken to me:

Like the lion, and the young lion,
    roars over his prey,
against which a multitude of shepherds
    is called out against him,
he will not be afraid of their voice,
    nor disturbed at their noise,
so shall the LORD of Hosts come down
    to fight for Mount Zion, and for its hill.
⁵ Like flying birds,
    so the LORD of Hosts will defend Jerusalem.
He will defend and deliver it;
    He will pass over and preserve it.

⁶ Turn to Him whom you have deeply betrayed, O sons of Israel. ⁷ For in that day every man shall cast away his idols of silver and his idols of gold which your own hands have made for you as a sin.

⁸ "Then the Assyrian shall fall by the sword that is not of man,
    and the sword not of man shall devour him.
So he shall not escape the sword,
    and his young men shall become forced laborers.
⁹ He shall cross over to his stronghold for fear,
    and his princes shall be afraid of the banner,"
says the LORD,
    whose fire is in Zion,
    and whose furnace is in Jerusalem.

The Kingdom of Righteousness

32 See, a king shall reign in righteousness,
    and princes shall rule justly.
² A man shall be as a hiding place from the wind,
    and a shelter from the tempest,
as rivers of water in a dry place,
    as the shadow of a great rock in a weary land.

³ The eyes of those who see shall not be blinded,
    and the ears of those who hear shall listen.
⁴ The heart also of the hasty shall understand knowledge,
    and the tongue of the stammerers shall be ready to speak
      plainly.
⁵ The vile person shall no more be called noble,
    nor the rogue be spoken of as generous;
⁶ for the vile person will speak nonsense,
    and his heart will work iniquity:
to practice hypocrisy
    and to utter error against the LORD,
to keep the hungry unsatisfied
    and to withhold drink from the thirsty.
⁷ The instruments also of the rogue are evil;
    he devises wicked schemes
to destroy the poor with lying words,
    even when the needy speaks right.
⁸ But the noble devises noble things,
    and by noble things he stands.

The Women of Jerusalem

⁹ Rise up, you women who are at ease,
    hear my voice;
you careless daughters,
    give ear to my speech.
¹⁰ Within a year and a few days
    you shall be troubled, you careless daughters;
for the vintage is ended
    and the fruit gathering shall not come.
¹¹ Tremble, you *women* who are at ease;
    be troubled, you careless *daughters*;
strip, undress,
    and put *sackcloth* on your waist.
¹² Beat your breasts for the pleasant fields,
    for the fruitful vine,

13 for the land of my people
  in which thorns and briers shall come up,
yes, for all the joyful houses
  and for the jubilant city;
14 because the palaces have been forsaken,
  the populated city is forsaken.
The forts and towers shall be caves forever,
  a joy of wild donkeys, a pasture of flocks,
15 until the Spirit is poured on us from on high,
  and the wilderness is a fruitful field,
  and the fruitful field is counted as a forest.

The Peace of God's Reign
16 Then justice shall dwell in the wilderness,
  and righteousness will abide in the fruitful field.
17 The work of righteousness shall be peace,
  and the effect of righteousness, quietness and assurance forever.
18 My people shall dwell in a peaceable habitation
  and in secure dwellings
  and in quiet resting places;
19 and it shall hail when the forest comes down,
  and the city shall be utterly laid low.
20 How blessed are you
  who sow beside all waters,
  who send out freely the ox and the donkey.

A Prophecy of Deliverance
33 Woe to you, O destroyer,
  though you were not destroyed,
and he who is treacherous,
  though others did not deal treacherously with you!
When you cease destroying,
  you shall be destroyed;
and when you finish dealing treacherously,
  others shall deal treacherously with you.

2 O LORD, be gracious to us;
  we have waited for You.
Be our strength every morning,
  our salvation also in the time of trouble.
3 At the noise of the tumult, the people flee;
  at the lifting up of Yourself, the nations scatter;
4 your spoil is gathered like the caterpillar gathers;
  as locusts rush about, men rush about on it.

5 The LORD is exalted, for He dwells on high;
  He has filled Zion with justice and righteousness.
6 He shall be the stability of your times,
  a wealth of salvation, wisdom, and knowledge;
  the fear of the LORD is His treasure.

7 Listen! Their valiant ones cry in the streets;
  the ambassadors of peace weep bitterly.
8 The highways lie waste,
  the wayfaring man ceases.
He has broken the covenant,
  he has despised the cities,
  he has no regard for man.
9 The earth mourns and languishes;
  Lebanon is ashamed and hewn down.
Sharon is like a wilderness,
  and Bashan and Carmel shake off *their fruits*.

Impending Judgment on Israel
10 "Now I will rise," says the LORD,
  "now I will be exalted,
  now I will be lifted up.
11 You have conceived chaff,
  you shall bring forth stubble;
  My breath, as fire, shall devour you.
12 The people shall be burned to lime,
  as thorns cut up are burned in the fire."

13 Hear what I have done, you who are far away;
  and you who are near, acknowledge My might.
14 The sinners in Zion are afraid;
  fearfulness has seized the hypocrites:
"Who among us can live with the continual fire?
  Who among us can live with everlasting burning?"
15 He who walks righteously
  and speaks uprightly,
he who rejects unjust gain
  and shakes his hands from holding bribes,
who stops his ears from hearing of bloodshed,
  and shuts his eyes from seeing evil:
16 He shall dwell on high;
  his place of defense shall be the impregnable rock;
his bread shall be given him,
  his waters shall be sure.

The Land of the Majestic King
17 Your eyes shall see the King in His beauty;
  they shall see the land that is very far away.
18 Your heart shall meditate on terror:
"Where is he who counts?
  Where is he who weighs?
  Where is he who counts the towers?"
19 You shall not see a fierce people any more,
  a people of unintelligible speech which no one comprehends,
  of a stammering tongue which no one understands.

20 Look upon Zion, the city of our appointed feasts;
  your eyes shall see Jerusalem,
  a quiet habitation, a tabernacle that shall not be taken down;
not one of its stakes shall ever be removed,
  nor shall any of its cords be broken.
21 But there the glorious LORD will be to us
  a place of broad rivers and streams
on which no boat with oars shall go
  and on which no gallant ship shall pass,
22 for the LORD is our judge,
  the LORD is our lawgiver,
  the LORD is our king;
  He will save us.

23 Your tackle hangs loose;
  it cannot hold the base of its mast securely,
  nor spread out the sail.
Then the prey of an abundant spoil shall be divided;
  the lame shall take the prey.
24 The inhabitant shall not say, "I am sick";
  the people who dwell there shall be forgiven
  their iniquity.

Judgment on the Nations
34 Come near, O nations, to hear;
  and listen, O peoples!
Let the earth hear, and all that is in it,
  the world, and all that comes from it.
2 For the indignation of the LORD is upon all nations
  and His fury upon all their armies;
He has utterly destroyed them,
  He has delivered them to the slaughter.
3 Their slain also shall be cast out,
  and their corpses shall emit their stench,
  and the mountains shall be drenched with their blood.
4 All the host of heaven shall be dissolved,
  and the heavens shall be rolled together as a book;
and all their host shall fall down
  as the leaf falls from the vine,
  and as a falling fig from the fig tree.

5 For My sword is filled in heaven;
  see, it shall come down for judgment on Edom,
  and on the people whom I have devoted to destruction.

6 The sword of the Lᴏʀᴅ is filled with blood,
    it is made full with fatness,
and with the blood of lambs and goats,
    with the fat of the kidneys of rams.
For the Lᴏʀᴅ has a sacrifice in Bozrah,
    and a great slaughter in the land of Edom.
7 The wild oxen shall also fall with them,
    and the young bulls with the mighty bulls;
so their land shall be soaked with blood,
    and their dust become greasy with fat.

8 For it is the day of the vengeance of the Lᴏʀᴅ,
    and the year of recompense for the cause of Zion.
9 Its streams shall be turned into pitch,
    and its dust into brimstone,
    and its land shall become burning pitch.
10 It shall not be quenched night or day;
    its smoke shall go up forever.
From generation to generation it shall lie waste;
    no one shall pass through it forever and ever.
11 But the cormorant and the hedgehog shall possess it,
    the owl also and the raven shall dwell in it.
And He shall stretch out on it
    the line of desolation,
    and the plumb line of emptiness.
12 They shall call its nobles to the kingdom, but no one
        shall be there,
    and all her princes shall be nothing.
13 Thorns shall come up in her palaces,
    nettles and brambles in the fortresses;
and it shall be a habitation of jackals
    and a home for owls.
14 The wild beasts of the desert shall also meet with the wolves,
    and the wild goat shall cry to its kind;
the screech owl also shall rest there
    and find for herself a place of rest.
15 There shall the tree snake make its nest and lay eggs,
    and it shall hatch and gather them under its protection;
yes, there shall the vultures also be gathered,
    every one with its kind.

16 Seek from the book of the Lᴏʀᴅ, and read.

Not one of these shall be missing,
    not one shall lack its mate.
For His mouth has commanded,
    and His Spirit has gathered them.
17 He has cast the lot for them,
    and His hand has divided it to them by line.
They shall possess it forever,
    from generation to generation they shall dwell in it.

The Future Glory of Zion

35 The wilderness and the solitary place shall be glad,
    and the desert shall rejoice and blossom as the rose;
2 it shall blossom abundantly
    and rejoice even with joy and singing.
The glory of Lebanon shall be given to it,
    the excellency of Carmel and Sharon.
They shall see the glory of the Lᴏʀᴅ
    and the excellency of our God.

3 Strengthen the weak hands,
    and support the feeble knees.
4 Say to those who are of a fearful heart,
    "Be strong, fear not.
Your God will come
    with vengeance,
even God with a recompense;
    He will come and save you."

5 Then the eyes of the blind shall be opened,
    and the ears of the deaf shall be unstopped.
6 Then the lame man shall leap as a deer,
    and the tongue of the mute sing for joy.
For in the wilderness waters shall break out
    and streams in the desert.
7 The parched ground shall become a pool,
    and the thirsty land springs of water;
in the habitation of jackals where each lay,
    there shall be grass with reeds and rushes.

8 A highway shall be there, a roadway,
    and it shall be called the Highway of Holiness.
The unclean shall not pass on it,
    but it shall be for the wayfaring men,
    and fools shall not wander on it.
9 No lion shall be there,
    nor any ravenous beast shall go up on it;
    these shall not be found there,
but the redeemed shall walk there,
10   and the ransomed of the Lᴏʀᴅ shall return
and come to Zion with songs
    and everlasting joy upon their heads.
They shall obtain joy and gladness,
    and sorrow and sighing shall flee away.

Sennacherib Invades Judah
2Ki 18:13–37; 2Ch 32:9–19

36 Now it came to pass in the fourteenth year of King Hezekiah that Sennacherib king of Assyria came up against all the fortified cities of Judah and took them. 2 The king of Assyria sent the Rabshakeh[1] from Lachish to Jerusalem to King Hezekiah with a great army. And he stood by the conduit of the upper pool in the highway of the fuller's field. 3 Then Eliakim came to him, the son of Hilkiah, who was over the household, and Shebna the scribe, and Joah, the son of Asaph, the recorder.
4 The Rabshakeh said to them:

"Say now to Hezekiah: Thus says the great king, the king of Assyria: What confidence is this that you have? 5 I say, Your counsel and strength for war are only empty words. Now on whom do you rely that you rebel against me? 6 You rely on the staff of this broken reed, on Egypt, on which if a man leans, it will go into his hand and pierce it. So is Pharaoh king of Egypt to all who rely on him. 7 But if you say to me, 'We trust in the Lᴏʀᴅ our God,' is it not He whose high places and whose altars Hezekiah has taken away, and said to Judah and to Jerusalem, 'You shall worship before this altar'?
8 "Now therefore, come make a bargain with my master the king of Assyria, and I will give you two thousand horses, if you are able on your part to set riders on them. 9 How then will you turn away one captain of the least of my master's servants and rely on Egypt for chariots and for horsemen? 10 Have I now come up without the approval of the Lᴏʀᴅ against this land to destroy it? The Lᴏʀᴅ said to me, Go up against this land, and destroy it."

11 Then Eliakim and Shebna and Joah said to the Rabshakeh, "Speak now to your servants in Aramaic, for we understand it. And do not speak to us in Hebrew in the ears of the people who are on the wall."
12 But the Rabshakeh said, "Has my master sent me only to your master and to you to speak these words? Has he not sent me to the men who sit on the wall, that they may eat their own dung and drink their own urine with you?"
13 Then the Rabshakeh stood and cried out with a loud voice in Hebrew, and said, "Hear the words of the great king, the king of Assyria. 14 Thus says the king, 'Do not let Hezekiah deceive you, for he shall not be able to deliver you; 15 nor let Hezekiah make you trust in the Lᴏʀᴅ, saying, The Lᴏʀᴅ will surely deliver us. This city shall not be delivered into the hand of the king of Assyria.'

---

1 2 Possibly *Commanding General*.

[16] "Do not listen to Hezekiah, for thus says the king of Assyria: 'Make your peace with me and come out to me, and eat every one of his vine and every one of his fig tree, and drink every one the waters of his own cistern, [17] until I come and take you away to a land like your own land, a land of corn and new wine, a land of bread and vineyards.

[18] " '*Beware* lest Hezekiah persuade you, saying, The Lord will deliver us. Has any one of the gods of the nations delivered his land out of the hand of the king of Assyria? [19] Where are the gods of Hamath and Arpad? Where are the gods of Sepharvaim? And when have they delivered Samaria out of my hand? [20] Who are they among all the gods of these lands that have delivered their land out of my hand, that the Lord should deliver Jerusalem out of my hand?' "

[21] But they held their peace, and answered him not a word, for the king's commandment was, "Do not answer him."

[22] Then Eliakim the son of Hilkiah, who was over the household, and Shebna the scribe, and Joah the son of Asaph, the recorder, came to Hezekiah with their clothes torn and told him the words of the Rabshakeh.

Isaiah Foretells Deliverance
2Ki 19:1–13

37 And it came to pass when King Hezekiah heard it that he tore his clothes, and covered himself with sackcloth, and went into the house of the Lord. [2] He sent Eliakim, who was over the household, and Shebna the scribe, and the elders of the priests, covered with sackcloth, to Isaiah the prophet, the son of Amoz. [3] They said to him, "Thus says Hezekiah: This day is a day of trouble, and of rebuke, and of blasphemy. For children have come to birth, and there is no strength to bring them forth. [4] Perhaps the Lord your God will hear the words of the Rabshakeh, whom the king of Assyria his master has sent to reproach the living God, and will reprove the words which the Lord your God has heard. Therefore, lift up a prayer for the remnant that is left."

[5] So the servants of King Hezekiah came to Isaiah. [6] Isaiah said to them, "Thus you shall say to your master, 'Thus says the Lord: Do not be afraid of the words that you have heard, with which the servants of the king of Assyria have blasphemed Me. [7] Listen! I will put a spirit in him so that he shall hear a rumor, and return to his own land. And I will cause him to fall by the sword in his own land.' "

[8] So the Rabshakeh returned and found the king of Assyria warring against Libnah. For he had heard that the king had left Lachish. [9] He heard them say concerning Tirhakah king of Ethiopia, "He has come out to make war with you." And when he heard it, he sent messengers to Hezekiah, saying, [10] "Thus you shall speak to Hezekiah king of Judah, saying: Do not let your God in whom you trust deceive you, saying, 'Jerusalem shall not be given into the hand of the king of Assyria.' [11] Certainly you have heard what the kings of Assyria have done to all lands by utterly destroying them. So shall you be delivered? [12] Have the gods of the nations delivered them which my fathers have destroyed, even Gozan and Harran and Rezeph and the sons of Eden who were in Tel Assar? [13] Where is the king of Hamath, and the king of Arpad, and the kings of the city of Sepharvaim, Hena, and Ivvah?"

The Prayer of Hezekiah
2Ki 19:14–19

[14] And Hezekiah received the letter from the hand of the messengers and read it. Then Hezekiah went up to the house of the Lord, and spread it before the Lord. [15] Hezekiah prayed to the Lord, saying, [16] "O Lord of Hosts, God of Israel, who dwells above the cherubim, You are the God, even You alone, of all the kingdoms of the earth. You have made heaven and earth. [17] Incline Your ear, O Lord, and hear. Open Your eyes, O Lord, and see, and hear all the words of Sennacherib, which he has sent to reproach the living God.

[18] Truly, O Lord, the kings of Assyria have laid waste all the nations and their countries, [19] and have cast their gods into the fire. For they were not gods, but the work of men's hands, wood and stone. Therefore, they have destroyed them. [20] Now, O Lord our God, save us from his hand that all the kingdoms of the earth may know that You alone, Lord, are God."

The Fall of Sennacherib
2Ki 19:20–37; 2Ch 32:20–21

[21] Then Isaiah the son of Amoz sent to Hezekiah, saying, "Thus says the Lord God of Israel: Because you have prayed to Me about Sennacherib king of Assyria, [22] this is the word which the Lord has spoken against him:

The virgin daughter of Zion
    has despised you and mocked you;
the daughter of Jerusalem
    has shaken her head at you.
[23] Whom have you reproached and blasphemed?
    And against whom have you raised your voice,
and lifted up your eyes haughtily?
    Against the Holy One of Israel!
[24] Through your servants
    you have reproached the Lord
and have said,
    'With my many chariots
I have come up to the heights of the mountains,
    to the remotest parts of Lebanon;
and I cut down its tall cedars,
    and its choice fir trees;
and I will go to its highest peak,
    its thickest forest.
[25] I have dug wells
    and drunk water,
and with the sole of my feet
    I have dried up all the rivers of Egypt.'

[26] "Have you not heard?
    Long ago I have done it,
from ancient times I have formed it.
    Now I have brought it to pass,
that you should turn fortified cities
    into ruinous heaps.
[27] Therefore, their inhabitants were short of strength;
    they were dismayed and humiliated;
they were as the grass of the field
    and as the green herb,
as the grass on the housetops
    is scorched before it is grown up.

[28] "But I know your abode,
    and your going out and your coming in,
    and your rage against Me.
[29] Because your rage against Me
    and your tumult have come up into My ears,
therefore I will put My hook in your nose,
    and My bridle in your lips,
and I will turn you back
    on the way by which you came.

[30] "This shall be a sign to you:

You shall eat this year what grows of itself,
    and the second year what springs from the same,
and in the third year sow and reap
    and plant vineyards, and eat their fruit.
[31] The surviving remnant of the house of Judah
    shall again take root downward and bear fruit upward.
[32] For from Jerusalem shall go out a remnant,
    and those who escape out of Mount Zion.
The zeal of the Lord of Hosts
    shall do this.

[33] "Therefore, thus says the Lord concerning the king of Assyria:

He shall not come into this city,
    nor shoot an arrow there,
nor come before it with shields,
    nor build a siege ramp against it.

³⁴ By the way that he came, by the same shall he return,
and shall not come into this city,
says the Lord.
³⁵ For I will defend this city to save it
for My own sake and for the sake of My servant David."

³⁶ Then the angel of the Lord went out and struck one hundred eighty-five thousand in the camp of the Assyrians. When others woke up early in the morning, these were all dead bodies. ³⁷ So Sennacherib king of Assyria departed and returned home and lived in Nineveh. ³⁸ It came to pass as he was worshipping in the house of Nisrok, his god, that Adrammelek and Sharezer, his sons, struck him with the sword, and they escaped into the land of Ararat. And Esarhaddon his son reigned in his stead.

Hezekiah's Illness
2Ki 20:1–11; 2Ch 32:24–26

38 In those days Hezekiah was mortally ill. And Isaiah the prophet, the son of Amoz, came to him and said to him, "Thus says the Lord: Set your house in order, for you shall die, and not live." ² Then Hezekiah turned his face toward the wall, and prayed to the Lord, ³ and said, "Remember now, O Lord, I beseech You, how I have walked before You in truth and with a perfect heart, and have done what is good in Your sight." And Hezekiah wept bitterly.

⁴ Then the word of the Lord came to Isaiah, saying: ⁵ "Go, and say to Hezekiah, Thus says the Lord, the God of David your father: I have heard your prayer, I have seen your tears. Surely I will add to your days fifteen years. ⁶ I will deliver you and this city out of the hand of the king of Assyria, and I will defend this city.

⁷ "This shall be a sign to you from the Lord, that the Lord will do this thing that He has spoken: ⁸ I will cause the shadow on the sundial, which has gone down with the sun on the sundial of Ahaz, to go back ten steps." So the sun's *shadow* returned ten steps on the sundial by which it had gone down.

⁹ This is the writing of Hezekiah king of Judah after his illness and recovery:

¹⁰ I said: In the middle of my days,
I shall go to the gates of Sheol;
I am to be deprived of the rest of my years.
¹¹ I said, I shall not see the Lord,
even the Lord, in the land of the living;
I shall see man no more
with the inhabitants of the world.
¹² My dwelling is pulled up
and removed from me as a shepherd's tent;
I rolled up my life like a weaver.
He cuts me off from the loom;
from day even to night You make an end of me.
¹³ I composed *my soul* until morning,
like a lion, so He breaks all my bones;
from day even to night You make an end of me.
¹⁴ Like a crane or a swallow, so I twitter;
I mourn as a dove;
my eyes look wistfully upward.
O Lord, I am oppressed; undertake for me.

¹⁵ What shall I say?
For He has spoken to me, and He Himself has done it.
I shall wander about all my years
in the bitterness of my soul.
¹⁶ O Lord, by these things men live,
and in all these things is the life of my spirit;
O restore me to health
and make me live!
¹⁷ Surely *it was* for *my own* peace
that I had great bitterness;
but You have kept my soul
from the pit of corruption,
for You have cast all my sins
behind Your back.

¹⁸ For Sheol cannot thank You,
death cannot praise You;
those who go down into the pit
cannot hope for Your faithfulness.
¹⁹ It is the living who give thanks to You,
as I do this day;
a father explains to his sons
about Your faithfulness.

²⁰ The Lord shall surely save me;
therefore, we will sing my songs to the stringed instruments
all the days of our lives
in the house of the Lord.

²¹ For Isaiah had said, "Let them take a cake of figs and lay it on the boil, and he shall recover." ²² Hezekiah also had said, "What is the sign that I shall go up to the house of the Lord?"

Envoys From Babylon
2Ki 20:12–19

39 At that time Marduk-Baladan the son of Baladan, king of Babylon, sent letters and a present to Hezekiah, for he had heard that he had been sick and had recovered. ² Hezekiah was glad and showed them the house of his precious things: the silver, and the gold, and the spices, and the precious ointment, and his whole armory, and all that was found in his treasuries. There was nothing in his house, nor in all his dominion, that Hezekiah did not show them.

³ Then Isaiah the prophet came to King Hezekiah and said to him, "What did these men say, and from where did they come to you?"

And Hezekiah said, "They have come to me from a far country, from Babylon."

⁴ Then he said, "What have they seen in your house?"

And Hezekiah answered, "All that is in my house they have seen. There is nothing among my treasures that I have not shown them."

⁵ Then Isaiah said to Hezekiah, "Hear the word of the Lord of Hosts. ⁶ The days are surely coming when all that is in your house, and that which your fathers have laid up in store until this day, shall be carried to Babylon. Nothing shall be left, says the Lord. ⁷ And some of your sons who descend from you, whom you shall father, shall be taken away. And they shall become officials in the palace of the king of Babylon."

⁸ Then Hezekiah said to Isaiah, "The word of the Lord which you have spoken is good." For he said, "For there shall be peace and truth in my days."

Comfort for God's People

40 Comfort, O comfort, My people,
says your God.
² Speak kindly to Jerusalem,
and cry to her
that her warfare has ended,
that her iniquity has been pardoned,
that she has received of the hand of the Lord
double for all her sins.

³ The voice of him who cries out,
"Prepare the way of the Lord
in the wilderness,
make straight in the desert
a highway for our God.
⁴ Let every valley be lifted up,
and every mountain and hill be made low,
and let the rough ground become a plain,
and the rough places a plain;
⁵ then the glory of the Lord shall be revealed,
and all flesh shall see it together,
for the mouth of the Lord has spoken it."

⁶ The voice said, "Cry out."
And he said, "What shall I cry out?"

All flesh is grass,
and all its loveliness is as the flower of the field.
7 The grass withers, the flower fades
because the Spirit of the LORD blows upon it;
surely the people are grass.
8 The grass withers, the flower fades,
but the word of our God shall stand forever.

9 O Zion, bearer of good news,
get yourself up onto a high mountain;
O Jerusalem, bearer of good news,
lift up your voice with strength,
lift it up, do not be afraid;
say to the cities of Judah,
"Here is your God!"
10 See, the Lord GOD will come with a strong hand,
and His arm shall rule for Him;
see, His reward is with Him,
and His recompense before Him.
11 He shall feed His flock like a shepherd;
He shall gather the lambs with His arm,
and carry them in His bosom,
and shall gently lead those that are with young.

12 Who has measured the waters in the hollow of His hand,
and meted out heaven with the span,
and calculated the dust of the earth by the measure,
and weighed the mountains in scales,
and the hills in a balance?
13 Who has directed the Spirit of the LORD,
or as His counselor has taught Him?
14 With whom did He take counsel, and who instructed Him,
and taught Him in the path of justice,
and taught Him knowledge,
and showed to Him the way of understanding?

15 Certainly the nations are as a drop in a bucket,
and are counted as the small dust of the balance;
He takes up the coastlands as a very little thing.
16 Lebanon is not sufficient to burn,
nor the beasts sufficient as a burnt offering.
17 All nations before Him are as nothing,
and they are counted by Him as less than nothing
and meaningless.

18 To whom then will you liken God?
Or what likeness will you compare to Him?
19 The workman melts a graven image,
and the goldsmith spreads it over with gold,
and casts silver chains.
20 He who is too impoverished for such an offering
chooses a tree that will not rot;
he seeks for himself a skillful workman
to prepare a graven image that shall not totter.

21 Have you not known?
Have you not heard?
Has it not been told to you from the beginning?
Have you not understood from the foundations of
the earth?
22 It is He who sits upon the circle of the earth,
and the inhabitants are as grasshoppers,
who stretches out the heavens as a curtain,
and spreads them out as a tent to dwell in.
23 He brings the princes to nothing;
He makes the judges of the earth meaningless.
24 Scarcely shall they be planted;
scarcely shall they be sown;
scarcely shall their tree take root in the earth,
when He will also blow on them,
and they will wither,
and the whirlwind will take them away as stubble.

25 To whom then will you liken Me,
that I should be equal to him? says the Holy One.
26 Lift up your eyes on high,
and see who has created these things,
who brings out their host by number;
He calls them all by name,
by the greatness of His might and the strength of
His power;
not one of them is missing.

27 Why do you say, O Jacob,
and assert, O Israel,
"My way is hidden from the LORD,
and my justice escapes the notice of my God"?
28 Have you not known?
Have you not heard,
that the everlasting God, the LORD,
the Creator of the ends of the earth,
does not faint, nor is He weary?
His understanding is inscrutable.
29 He gives power to the faint,
and to those who have no might He increases strength.
30 Even the youths shall faint and be weary,
and the young men shall utterly fall,
31 but those who wait upon the LORD
shall renew their strength;
they shall mount up with wings as eagles,
they shall run and not be weary,
and they shall walk and not faint.

The LORD Helps Israel

41 Keep silent before Me, O islands,
and let the peoples renew their strength.
Let them come near, then let them speak;
let us come near together to judgment.

2 Who raised up the righteous man from the east,
called him to His foot,
gave the nations before him,
and made him rule over kings?
He makes them as the dust with his sword,
and as driven stubble with his bow.
3 He pursued them, and passed safely,
by paths his feet have not traveled.
4 Who has performed and done this,
calling the generations from the beginning?
I, the LORD, am the first,
and with the last. I am He.

5 The coastlands saw it and feared,
the ends of the earth were afraid;
they drew near and came.
6 Every one helped his neighbor,
and every one said to his brother, "Be of good courage."
7 So the carpenter encouraged the goldsmith,
and he who smooths *metal* with the hammer
encourages him who strikes the anvil,
saying, "It is ready for the soldering";
and he fastened it with nails so that it should
not totter.

8 But you, Israel, are My servant,
Jacob whom I have chosen,
the seed of Abraham, My friend.
9 You whom I have taken from the ends of the earth,
and called from its remotest parts,
and said to you, "You are My servant;
I have chosen you and have not rejected you."
10 Do not fear, for I am with you;
do not be dismayed, for I am your God.
I will strengthen you, I will help you,
yes, I will uphold you with My righteous right hand.

11 Certainly all those who were incensed against you
    shall be ashamed and humiliated;
they shall be as nothing,
    and those who strive with you shall perish.
12 You shall seek them
    and shall not find them, even those who contended
      with you.
Those who war against you
    shall be as nothing, as a thing of nonexistence.
13 For I, the LORD your God,
    will hold your right hand,
saying to you, "Do not fear;
    I will help you."
14 Do not fear, you worm Jacob,
    and you men of Israel.
I will help you, says the LORD
    and your Redeemer, the Holy One of Israel.
15 See, I will make you a new sharp threshing instrument
    with double edges;
you shall thresh the mountains, and beat them small,
    and shall make the hills as chaff.
16 You shall fan them, and the wind shall carry them away,
    and the whirlwind shall scatter them;
and you shall rejoice in the LORD,
    and shall glory in the Holy One of Israel.

17 When the poor and needy seek water,
    and there is none,
    and their tongues fail for thirst,
I, the LORD, will hear them,
    I, the God of Israel, will not forsake them.
18 I will open rivers in high places,
    and fountains in the midst of the valleys;
I will make the wilderness a pool of water,
    and the dry land springs of water.
19 I will plant in the wilderness
    the cedar, the acacia, the myrtle, and the olive tree;
I will set in the desert
    the fir tree, and the pine, and the box tree together,
20 that they may see, and know,
    and consider, and understand together,
that the hand of the LORD has done this,
    and the Holy One of Israel has created it.

The Futility of Idols

21 Present your case, says the LORD.
    Bring forth your arguments, says the King of Jacob.
22 Let them bring them forth, and show us
    what shall happen;
let them show the former things, what they were,
    that we may consider them
    and know their outcome,
or declare to us things to come.
23   Show the things that are to come hereafter,
    that we may know that you are gods;
do good, or do evil,
    that we may be dismayed and see it together.
24 Indeed you are nothing,
    and your work amounts to nothing;
he who chooses you is an abomination.

25 I have raised up one from the north, and he shall come;
    from the rising of the sun he shall call on My name;
and he shall come on princes as on mortar,
    and as the potter treads clay.
26 Who has declared from the beginning, that we may know?
    And from former times, that we may say, "He is right!"?
There is no one who shows,
    no one who declares,
    no one who hears your words.
27 Formerly I said to Zion, "Look, here they are,"
    and to Jerusalem, "I will give one who brings good news."

28 But when I look, there is no man,
    even among them, and there is no counselor
    who, when I ask of them, could answer a word.
29 See, they all are vanity;
    their works are nothing;
    their molded images are wind and emptiness.

The Servant of the LORD

42 Here is My servant, whom I uphold,
    My chosen one, in whom My soul delights.
I have put My Spirit upon him;
    he shall bring forth justice to the nations.
2 He shall not cry out, nor lift up his voice,
    nor cause his voice to be heard in the street.
3 A bruised reed he shall not break,
    and the smoking flax he shall not quench;
he shall bring forth justice faithfully.
4   He shall not be disheartened nor be discouraged,
until he has set justice in the earth;
    and the coastlands shall wait for his law.

5 Thus says God the LORD,
who created the heavens and stretched them out,
    who spread forth the earth and that which comes out of it,
who gives breath to the people on it,
    and spirit to those who walk in it:
6 I the LORD have called You in righteousness,
    and will hold Your hand,
and will keep You and appoint You
    for a covenant of the people,
    for a light of the nations,
7 to open the blind eyes,
    to bring out the prisoners from the prison,
    and those who sit in darkness out of the prison house.

8 I am the LORD, that is My name;
    and My glory I will not give to another,
    nor My praise to graven images.
9 See, the former things have come to pass,
    and new things I declare;
before they spring forth
    I tell you of them.

A Song of Praise

10 Sing to the LORD a new song,
    and His praise from the ends of the earth,
you who go down to the sea, and all that is in it,
    the coastlands, and the inhabitants.
11 Let the wilderness and the cities lift up *their voices*,
    the villages that Kedar inhabits.
Let the inhabitants of Sela sing,
    let them shout from the top of the mountains.
12 Let them give glory to the LORD,
    and declare His praise in the islands.
13 The LORD shall go forth like a mighty man;
    He shall stir up zeal like a man of war.
He shall cry out, yes, raise a war cry;
    He shall prevail against His enemies.

The LORD's Help Is Promised

14 I have for a long time held My peace;
    I have been still and refrained Myself.
Now I will cry like a travailing woman;
    I will destroy and devour at once.
15 I will lay waste mountains and hills
    and dry up all their vegetation,
and I will make the rivers islands,
    and I will dry up the pools.
16 I will bring the blind by a way that they did not know;
    I will lead them in paths that they have not known.
I will make darkness light before them
    and crooked things straight.

These things I will do for them
   and not forsake them.
17 They shall be turned back, they shall be greatly ashamed,
   who trust in graven images,
   who say to the molded images, "You are our gods."

Israel's Disobedience

18 Hear, you deaf;
   look, you blind, that you may see.
19 Who is blind, but My servant?
   Or deaf, as My messenger whom I sent?
Who is blind as he who is at peace *with Me,*
   and blind as the servant of the LORD?
20 You have seen many things, but you do not observe them;
   your ears are open, but no one hears.
21 The LORD is well pleased
   for His righteousness' sake
   to magnify the law and make it honorable.
22 But this is a people robbed and despoiled;
   they are all snared in holes,
   and they are hidden in prison houses;
they are for a prey,
   and no one delivers,
for a spoil,
   and no one says, "Restore them."

23 Who among you will give ear to this?
   Who will listen and hear for the time to come?
24 Who gave up Jacob as spoil,
   and Israel to the robbers?
Did not the LORD,
   against whom we have sinned?
For they would not walk in His ways,
   nor were they obedient to His law.
25 Therefore, He has poured on him the fury of His anger
   and the strength of battle;
and it has set him on fire all around, yet he did not
     recognize it;
   and it burned him, yet he laid it not to heart.

The Redeemer of Israel

43 But now, thus says the LORD
   who created you, O Jacob,
   and He who formed you, O Israel:
Do not fear, for I have redeemed you;
   I have called you by your name; you are Mine.
2 When you pass through waters,
   I will be with you.
And through the rivers,
   they shall not overflow you.
When you walk through the fire,
   you shall not be burned,
   nor shall the flame kindle on you.
3 For I am the LORD your God,
   the Holy One of Israel, your Savior;
I gave Egypt for your ransom,
   Ethiopia and Seba in your place.
4 Since you were precious in My sight, you have
     been honorable,
   and I have loved you;
therefore, I will give men for you,
   and people for your life.
5 Do not fear, for I am with you;
   I will bring your descendants from the east,
   and gather you from the west;
6 I will say to the north, "Give them up,"
   and to the south, "Do not keep them back.
Bring My sons from afar,
   and My daughters from the ends of the earth,
7 even everyone who is called by My name;
   for I have created him for My glory;
   I have formed him, and I have made him."

8 Bring forth the blind people who have eyes,
   and the deaf who have ears.
9 Let all the nations be gathered together,
   and let the people be assembled.
Who among them can declare this,
   and show us former things?
Let them bring their witnesses, that they may be justified;
   or let them hear and say, "It is true."
10 You are My witnesses, says the LORD,
   and My servant whom I have chosen,
that you may know and believe Me,
   and understand that I am He.
Before Me there was no God formed,
   nor shall there be after Me.
11 I, even I, am the LORD,
   and besides Me there is no savior.
12 I have declared, and have saved, and I have shown,
   when there was no strange god among you;
therefore, you are My witnesses, says the LORD, that I am God.
13   Indeed, from eternity I am He;
there is no one who can deliver out of My hand;
   I act, and who can reverse it?

14 Thus says the LORD,
   your Redeemer, the Holy One of Israel:
For your sake I have sent to Babylon,
   and have brought down all their nobles, and the Chaldeans,
   into the ships in which they rejoice.
15 I am the LORD, your Holy One,
   the Creator of Israel, your King.

16 Thus says the LORD,
   who makes a way in the sea
   and a path in the mighty waters,
17 who brings forth the chariot and horse,
   the army and the mighty men
(they shall lie down together, they shall not rise;
   they are extinguished, they are quenched like a wick):
18 Do not remember the former things
   nor consider the things of old.
19 See, I will do a new thing,
   now it shall spring forth; shall you not be aware of it?
I will even make a way in the wilderness,
   and rivers in the desert.
20 The beast of the field shall honor Me,
   the jackals and the owls,
because I give waters in the wilderness,
   and rivers in the desert,
to give drink to My people, My chosen ones.
21   This people I have formed for Myself;
   they shall declare My praise.

Pleading With Israel

22 But you have not called upon Me, O Jacob;
   but you have been weary of Me, O Israel.
23 You have not brought Me the sheep for your burnt offerings,
   nor have you honored Me with your sacrifices.
I have not burdened you with offerings,
   nor wearied you with incense.
24 You have bought Me no sweet cane with money,
   nor have you filled Me with the fat of your sacrifices;
but you have made Me burdened with your sins,
   you have wearied Me with your iniquities.

25 I, even I, am He who blots out
   your transgressions for My own sake,
   and will not remember your sins.
26 Put Me in remembrance;
   let us plead together;
   state your *cause,* that you may be justified.
27 Your first father has sinned,
   and your teachers have transgressed against Me.

²⁸ Therefore, I have profaned the princes of the sanctuary,
and have given Jacob to the curse,
and Israel to reproaches.

God's Blessing on Jacob

44 Yet now listen, O Jacob, My servant,
and Israel, whom I have chosen.
² Thus says the LORD
who made you, and formed you from the womb,
who will help you:
Do not fear, O Jacob, My servant, and you,
Jeshurun, whom I have chosen.
³ For I will pour water on him who is thirsty,
and floods on the dry ground;
I will pour out My Spirit on your descendants,
and My blessing on your offspring;
⁴ and they shall spring up as among the grass,
as willows by the water courses.
⁵ One will say, "I am the LORD's";
another will call himself by the name of Jacob;
and another will write on his hand, "Belonging to the LORD,"
and name himself by the name of Israel.

Idolatry Condemned

⁶ Thus says the LORD the King of Israel,
and his Redeemer the LORD of Hosts:
I am the first, and I am the last;
besides Me there is no God.
⁷ Who is like Me? Let him proclaim
and declare it, and recount it in order for Me,
since I appointed the ancient people.
And let them declare to them the things that are coming,
and shall come.
⁸ Do not fear, nor be afraid;
have I not told you from of old, and declared it?
You are My witnesses!
Is there a God besides Me?
There is no Rock; I know not any.

⁹ Those who make a graven image are, all of them, vain,
and their delectable things shall not profit;
and they are their own witnesses;
they do not see nor know, that they may be ashamed.
¹⁰ Who has formed a god or molded a graven image
that is profitable for nothing?
¹¹ All his companions shall be ashamed;
and the workmen, they are mere men.
Let them all be gathered together; let them stand up,
yet they shall fear; they shall be ashamed together.

¹² The smith with the tongs
both works in the coals
and fashions it with hammers,
and works it with the strength of his arms.
He becomes hungry, and his strength fails;
He drinks no water and is faint.
¹³ The carpenter stretches out his measuring line;
he marks it out with a line;
he fits it with planes,
and he marks it out with the compass,
and makes it after the figure of a man,
according to the beauty of a man,
that it may remain in the house.
¹⁴ He hews down cedars for himself,
and takes the cypress and the oak,
which he raises for himself among the trees of the forest.
He plants a fir, and the rain makes it grow.
¹⁵ Then it shall be for a man to burn,
for he will take some of it and warm himself;
he kindles it and bakes bread;
he also makes a god and worships it;
he makes it a graven image and bows down to it.

¹⁶ He burns half of it in the fire;
over this half he eats meat;
he roasts it and is satisfied.
Also he warms himself and says,
"Aha, I am warm, I have seen the fire."
¹⁷ And the rest he makes into a god, even his carved image.
He falls down to it, and worships it,
and prays to it, and says,
"Deliver me, for you are my god."
¹⁸ They have not known nor understood;
for He has shut their eyes so that they cannot see,
and their hearts so that they cannot understand.
¹⁹ No one considers in his heart,
nor is there knowledge nor understanding to say,
"I have burned part of it in the fire;
I also have baked bread on the coals;
I have roasted meat and eaten it;
and shall I make the rest into an abomination?
Shall I fall down to a block of wood?"
²⁰ He feeds on ashes; a deceived heart has turned him aside
so that he cannot deliver his soul, nor say,
"Is there not a lie in my right hand?"

Israel Not Forgotten

²¹ Remember these things, O Jacob,
and Israel, for you are My servant;
I have formed you; you are My servant;
O Israel, you shall not be forgotten by Me.
²² I have blotted out, as a thick cloud,
your transgressions, and your sins, as a cloud.
Return to Me,
for I have redeemed you.

²³ Sing, O heavens, for the LORD has done it.
Shout joyfully, you lower parts of the earth;
break forth into singing, you mountains,
O forest, and every tree in it.
For the LORD has redeemed Jacob,
and glorified Himself in Israel.

Jerusalem to Be Inhabited

²⁴ Thus says the LORD,
your Redeemer, and He who formed you from the womb:

I am the LORD
who makes all things,
who stretches out the heavens alone,
who spreads abroad the earth by Myself,
²⁵ who frustrates the omens of the boasters
and makes fools out of diviners,
who turns wise men backward
and makes their knowledge foolish,
²⁶ who confirms the word of His servant
and performs the counsel of His messengers,

who says to Jerusalem, "You shall be inhabited,"
and to the cities of Judah, "You shall be built."
And I will raise up her ruins again;
²⁷ it is I who says to the deep, "Be dried up!"
And I will dry up your rivers;
²⁸ it is I who says of Cyrus, "He is My shepherd,
and shall perform all My desire";
and he declares to Jerusalem, "You shall be built,"
and to the temple, "Your foundation shall be laid."

Cyrus, God's Anointed

45 Thus says the LORD to Cyrus, His anointed,
whose right hand I have held—
to subdue nations before him
and to loosen the loins of kings,
to open doors before him
so that the gates will not be shut:

2 I will go before you
  and make the crooked places straight;
I will break in pieces the gates of bronze
  and shatter the bars of iron.
3 And I will give you the treasures of darkness
  and hidden riches of secret places
so that you may know that I, the LORD,
  who calls you by your name, am the God of Israel.
4 For Jacob My servant's sake
  and Israel My chosen one,
I have even called you by your name;
  I have named you,
    though you have not known Me.
5 I am the LORD and there is no other;
  there is no God besides Me.
I strengthen you,
  though you have not known Me,
6 so that they may know from the rising of the sun
  and from the west
that there is no one besides Me.
  I am the LORD, and there is no other;
7 I form the light and create darkness;
  I make peace and create calamity;
  I, the LORD, do all these things.

8 Drip down, O heavens, from above,
  and let the clouds pour down righteousness;
let the earth open up,
  and let them bring forth salvation,
and let righteousness spring up together.
  I, the LORD, have created it.

9 Woe to him who strives with his Maker,
  the potsherd with the potsherds of the earth!
Shall the clay say to the potter,
  "What are you making?"
Or the thing you are making say,
  "He has no hands"?
10 Woe to him who says to his father,
  "What are you begetting?"
Or to the woman,
  "To what are you giving birth?"

11 Thus says the LORD,
  the Holy One of Israel and his Maker:
Ask Me of things to come
  concerning My sons,
  and you shall commit to Me the work of My hands.
12 I have made the earth
  and created man on it.
I, even My hands, have stretched out the heavens,
  and I have ordained all their host.
13 I have raised him up in righteousness,
  and I will direct all his ways;
he shall build My city,
  and he shall let My captives go,
neither for price nor reward,
  says the LORD of Hosts.

The Only Savior
14 Thus says the LORD:

The products of Egypt and merchandise of Ethiopia
  and of the Sabeans—men of stature—
shall come over to you,
  and they shall be yours;
they shall come after you;
  in chains they shall come over,
and they shall fall down before you.
  They shall make supplication to you, saying,
"Surely God is with you, and there is no other;
  there is no other God."

15 Truly You are a God who hides Yourself,
  O God of Israel, the Savior.
16 They shall be ashamed and also humiliated, all of them;
  the craftsmen of idols shall go away in confusion together,
17 but Israel shall be saved by the LORD
  with an everlasting salvation;
you shall not be ashamed nor humiliated
  to all eternity.

18 For thus says the LORD,
  who created the heavens,
    who is God,
who formed the earth and made it,
    who has established it,
who did not create it in vain,
    who formed it to be inhabited:
I am the LORD,
  and there is no other.
19 I have not spoken in secret
  in a dark place of the earth;
I did not say to the descendants of Jacob,
  "Seek Me in a waste place";
I, the LORD, speak righteousness;
  I declare things that are right.

20 Assemble yourselves and come;
  draw near together, you fugitives of the nations.
They have no knowledge who set up the wood of their
    carved image,
  and pray to a god that cannot save.
21 Declare and set forth your case;
  let them take counsel together.
Who has declared this from ancient times?
  Who has told it from that time?
Have not I, the LORD?
  And there is no God besides Me,
a righteous God and Savior;
  there is no other besides Me.

22 Turn to Me and be saved,
  all the ends of the earth.
For I am God, and there is no other.
23 I have sworn by Myself,
  the word has gone out of My mouth in righteousness
  and shall not return,
that to Me every knee shall bow,
  every tongue shall take an oath.
24 Surely, one shall say, "Only in the LORD
  are righteousness and strength."
Men shall come to him,
  and all who are incensed at Him shall be ashamed.
25 In the LORD shall all the seed of Israel
  be justified and shall glory.

The Idols of Babylon
46 Bel bows down, Nebo stoops,
  their idols are appointed to the beasts and
    the cattle.
The things that you carry are burdensome;
  they are a burden to the weary beast.
2 They stoop, they bow down together;
  they could not deliver the burden,
  but themselves have gone into captivity.

3 Listen to Me, O house of Jacob,
  and all the remnant of the house of Israel,
who are borne by Me from birth
  and are carried from the womb:
4 And even to your old age I am He,
  and even to your graying years I will carry you;
I have done it, and I will bear you;
  even I will carry, and will deliver you.

5 To whom will you liken Me, and make Me equal,
  and compare Me that we may be alike?
6 They lavish gold out of the bag,
  and weigh silver on the scales;
  they hire a goldsmith, and he makes it a god;
  they fall down and worship it.
7 They lift it on the shoulder, they carry it,
  and they set it in its place, and it stands;
  from its place it does not move.
  If one shall cry to it, it cannot answer
  nor save him out of his trouble.

8 Remember this, and show yourselves men;
  bring it to mind again, O transgressors.
9 Remember the former things of old,
  for I am God, and there is no other;
  I am God, and there is no one like Me,
10 declaring the end from the beginning,
  and from ancient times the things that are not yet done, saying,
  "My counsel shall stand,
  and I will do all My good pleasure,"
11 calling a ravenous bird from the east,
  the man who executes My counsel from a far country.
  Indeed, I have spoken it; I will also bring it to pass.
  I have purposed it; I will also do it.
12 Listen to Me, you stubborn-hearted,
  who are far from righteousness;
13 I bring My righteousness near;
  it shall not be far off,
  and My salvation shall not tarry.
  And I will grant salvation in Zion,
  and My glory for Israel.

The Fall of Babylon

47 Come down, and sit in the dust,
  O virgin daughter of Babylon;
  sit on the ground; there is no throne,
  O daughter of the Chaldeans.
  For you shall no more be called
  tender and delicate.
2 Take the millstones and grind meal.
  Uncover your veil,
  strip off the skirt, uncover the leg,
  pass over the rivers.
3 Your nakedness shall be uncovered,
  and your shame shall be seen;
  I will take vengeance,
  and I will not meet you as a man.

4 As for our Redeemer, the LORD of Hosts is His name,
  the Holy One of Israel.

5 Sit silently, and go into darkness,
  O daughter of the Chaldeans;
  for you shall no more be called
  the queen of kingdoms.
6 I was angry with My people;
  I have polluted My inheritance
  and given them into your hand.
  You did not show them mercy;
  on the aged
  you have laid your yoke very heavily.
7 You said, "I shall be a queen forever,"
  but you did not take these things to heart,
  nor remember the outcome of them.

8 Therefore, now hear this, you who are given to pleasures,
  who dwell carelessly,
  who say in your heart,
  "I am, and there is no one besides me;
  I shall not sit as a widow,
  nor shall I know the loss of children";

9 but these two things shall come to you
  in a moment, in one day,
  the loss of children and widowhood.
  They shall come upon you in their fullness
  because of the multitude of your sorceries
  and for the great abundance of your enchantments.
10 For you have trusted in your wickedness;
  you have said, "No one sees me";
  your wisdom and your knowledge have perverted you;
  and you have said in your heart,
  "I am, and there is no one besides me."
11 Therefore, evil shall come upon you,
  which you shall not know from where it rises.
  And disaster shall fall upon you,
  for which you shall not be able to atone.
  And desolation shall come upon you suddenly,
  which you shall not know.

12 Stand fast now with your enchantments,
  and with the multitude of your sorceries
  in which you have labored from your youth.
  Perhaps you shall be able to profit,
  perhaps you may cause trembling.
13 You are wearied in the multitude of your counsels;
  let now the astrologers, the stargazers,
  the monthly prognosticators stand up
  and save you from these things that shall come upon you.
14 Surely they shall be as stubble,
  the fire shall burn them;
  they shall not deliver themselves
  from the power of the flame;
  it shall not be coal to be warmed by
  nor a fire to sit before.
15 Thus those shall be to you
  with whom you have labored,
  even your merchants, from your youth;
  they shall wander, everyone to his quarter.
  No one shall save you.

Israel Refined for God's Glory

48 Hear this, O house of Jacob,
  who are called by the name of Israel,
  and have come forth from the waters of Judah;
  who swear by the name of the LORD,
  and invoke the God of Israel,
  but not in truth or in righteousness;
2 for they call themselves after the holy city,
  and lean on the God of Israel;
  the LORD of Hosts is His name:
3 I have declared the former things from the beginning;
  and they went forth from My mouth, and I announced them.
  Suddenly I did them, and they came to pass.
4 Because I knew that you are obstinate,
  and your neck is an iron sinew,
  and your brow bronze;
5 I have even from the beginning declared it to you;
  before it came to pass I announced it to you,
  lest you should say,
  "My idol has done them,
  and my carved image and my molded image has
  commanded them."
6 You have heard; see all this.
  And will you not declare it?

  I have shown you new things from this time,
  even hidden things, and you did not know them.
7 They are created now and not from the beginning;
  even before the day when you did not hear them,
  lest you should say,
  "Yes, I knew them."
8 You have not heard, you have not known,
  indeed, from long ago your ear has not been open.

For I knew that you would deal very treacherously,
and that from birth you have been called a rebel.
9 For My name's sake I will defer My anger,
and for My praise I will restrain it for you
so that you are not cut off.
10 See, I have refined you, but not with silver;
I have chosen you in the furnace of affliction.
11 For My own sake, even for My own sake, I will do it;
for how can *My name* be polluted?
And I will not give My glory to another.

The Lord's Call to Israel

12 Listen to Me, O Jacob
and Israel, whom I called:
I am He;
I am the First, and I am the Last.
13 My hand also has laid the foundation of the earth,
and My right hand has spanned the heavens;
when I call to them,
they stand up together.

14 Assemble, all of you, and listen.
Who among them has declared these things?
The Lord has loved him;
he will do His pleasure on Babylon,
and His arm *shall be against* the Chaldeans.
15 I, even I, have spoken,
and I have called him;
I have brought him,
and his way will prosper.

16 Come near to Me, hear this:

I have not spoken in secret from the beginning;
from the time that it was, there I am.

And now the Lord God has sent me
and His Spirit.

17 Thus says the Lord,
your Redeemer, the Holy One of Israel:
I am the Lord your God,
who teaches you to profit,
who leads you in the way you should go.
18 Oh, that you had listened to My commandments!
Then your peace would have been as a river
and your righteousness as the waves of the sea.
19 Your descendants also would have been as the sand
and your offspring like grains of sand;
their name would not have been cut off
nor destroyed from before Me.

20 Go forth from Babylon!
Flee from the Chaldeans!
With a voice of singing declare,
proclaim this,
utter it even to the ends of the earth;
say, "The Lord has redeemed His servant Jacob."
21 They did not thirst when He led them through the deserts;
He caused the waters to flow out of the rock for them;
He also split the rock,
and the waters gushed out.

22 "There is no peace," says the Lord, "for the wicked."

The Servant of the Lord

49 Listen to me, O coastlands,
and pay attention, you peoples from afar.
The Lord called me from the womb;
from the body of my mother He named me.
2 He has made my mouth like a sharp sword;
in the shadow of His hand He has hidden me

and made me a select arrow;
in His quiver He has hidden me.
3 He said to me, "You are My servant,
Israel, in whom I will be glorified."
4 Then I said, "I have labored in vain;
I have spent my strength for nothing and vanity,
yet surely my justice due to me is with the Lord,
and my reward with my God."

5 Now says the Lord,
who formed me from the womb to be His servant,
to bring Jacob back to Him,
so that Israel might be gathered to Him
(yet I am honored in the eyes of the Lord,
and my God is my strength),
6 He says,
"It is a light thing that you should be My servant
to raise up the tribes of Jacob
and to restore the preserved ones of Israel;
I will also make you a light to the nations
so that My salvation may reach to the ends of
the earth."

7 Thus says the Lord,
the Redeemer of Israel, and his Holy One,
to the despised one, to the one whom the nation abhors,
to the servant of rulers:
"Kings shall see and arise,
princes also shall worship,
because of the Lord who is faithful
and the Holy One of Israel who has chosen you."

The Restoration of Israel

8 Thus says the Lord:

In an acceptable time I have heard you,
and in a day of salvation I have helped you;
and I will preserve you, and give you
as a covenant of the people,
to restore the earth,
to make them inherit the desolate heritages,
9 saying to the prisoners, "Go forth,"
to those who are in darkness, "Show yourselves."

They shall feed along the paths,
and their pastures shall be in all desolate heights;
10 they shall not hunger nor thirst,
neither shall the heat nor sun strike them;
for He who has mercy on them shall lead them,
even by the springs of water He shall guide them.
11 I will make all My mountains a road,
and My highways shall be raised up.
12 See, these shall come from afar;
and these *will come* from the north and from
the west,
and these from the land of Sinim.

13 Sing, O heavens!
And be joyful, O earth!
And break forth into singing, O mountains!
For the Lord has comforted His people
and will have mercy on His afflicted.

14 But Zion said, "The Lord has forsaken me,
and the Lord has forgotten me."

15 Can a woman forget her nursing child,
and have no compassion on the son of her womb?
Even these may forget,
yet I will not forget.
16 See, I have inscribed you on the palms of *My hands*;
your walls are continually before Me;

17 your builders hurry;
    your destroyers and those who devastated you shall depart
        from you.
18 Lift up your eyes and look all around;
    all these gather themselves together and come to you.
As I live, says the LORD,
    you shall surely put on all of them as ornaments
    and bind them on you as a bride does.

19 For your waste and your desolate places,
    and the land of your destruction,
shall even now be too narrow by reason of the inhabitants,
    and those who swallowed you up shall be far away.
20 The children whom you shall have,
    after you have lost the others,
shall say again in your ears,
    "The place is too cramped for me;
    make room for me that I may dwell here."
21 Then you shall say in your heart,
    "Who bore these for me,
since I have lost my children and am barren,
    a captive and a wanderer?
And who has brought these up?
I was left alone;
    from where did these come?"

22 Thus says the Lord GOD:

See, I will lift up My hand to the nations
    and set up My standard to the peoples;
and they shall bring your sons in their arms,
    and your daughters shall be carried on their shoulders;
23 kings shall be your foster fathers
    and their queens your nursing mothers;
they shall bow down to you with their faces toward the ground
    and lick up the dust of your feet.
And you shall know that I am the LORD,
    for those who wait for Me shall not be ashamed.

24 Can the prey be taken from the mighty
    or the captives of a tyrant be delivered?

25 For thus says the LORD:

Even the captives of the mighty shall be taken away,
    and the prey of the tyrant shall be delivered;
for I will contend with him who contends with you,
    and I will save your sons.
26 I will feed those who oppress you with their own flesh,
    and they shall be drunk with their own blood as with
        sweet wine.
And all flesh shall know
    that I, the LORD, am your Savior
    and your Redeemer, the Mighty One of Jacob.

The Servant, Hope of Israel

50 Thus says the LORD:

Where is the certificate of divorce
    by which I sent your mother away?
Or to which of My creditors
    did I sell you?
For your iniquities you were sold,
    and for your transgressions your mother was sent away.
2 Why, when I came, was there no man?
    When I called, was there no one to answer?
Is My hand so short that it cannot redeem?
    Or have I no power to deliver?
Indeed, at My rebuke I dry up the sea,
    I make the rivers a wilderness;
Their fish stink because there is no water,
    and die for thirst.

3 I clothe the heavens with blackness,
    and I make sackcloth their covering.

4 The Lord GOD has given me the tongue of the learned,
    that I may know how to sustain him who is weary with a
        word;
He awakens me morning by morning;
    He awakens my ear to listen as the learned.
5 The Lord GOD has opened my ear,
    and I was not rebellious,
    nor did I turn back.
6 I gave my back to those who struck me,
    and my cheeks to those who plucked out my beard;
I did not cover my face
    from shame and spitting.
7 For the Lord GOD will help me;
    therefore, I shall not be disgraced;
therefore, I have set my face like a flint,
    and I know that I shall not be ashamed.
8 He who vindicates me is near;
    who will contend with me?
Let us stand up to each other.
Who is my adversary?
    Let him come near to me.
9 Certainly the Lord GOD will help me;
    who is he who condemns me?
Indeed they all shall grow old as a garment;
    the moth shall eat them up.

10 Who among you fears the LORD,
    who obeys the voice of His servant,
who walks in darkness
    and has no light?
Let him trust in the name of the LORD,
    and rely upon his God.
11 But now, all you who kindle a fire,
    who encompass yourselves with sparks:
Walk in the light of your fire
    and among the sparks that you have ignited.
This you shall have from My hand:
    You shall lie down in sorrow.

The Eternal Salvation of Zion

51 Listen to Me, you who pursue righteousness,
    you who seek the LORD:
Look to the rock from which you were hewn
    and to the quarry from which you were dug.
2 Look to Abraham your father
    and to Sarah who bore you;
for I called him alone,
    and blessed him, and multiplied him.
3 For the LORD shall comfort Zion,
    He will comfort all her waste places;
He will make her wilderness like Eden,
    and her desert like the garden of the LORD;
joy and gladness shall be found in it,
    thanksgiving, and the voice of melody.

4 Listen to Me, O My people;
    and give ear to Me, O My nation:
for a law shall proceed from Me,
    and I will set My justice as a light of the peoples.
5 My righteousness is near,
    My salvation has gone forth,
    and My arms shall judge the peoples;
the coastlands shall wait for Me,
    and for My arm they shall expectantly wait.
6 Lift up your eyes to the heavens,
    and look on the earth beneath.
For the heavens shall vanish away like smoke,
    and the earth shall grow old like a garment,
    and those who dwell in it shall die in like manner;

but My salvation shall be forever,
and My righteousness shall not be abolished.

7 Listen to Me, you who know righteousness,
the people in whose heart is My law;
do not fear the reproach of men
nor be afraid of their revilings.
8 For the moth shall eat them up like a garment,
and the worm shall eat them like wool;
but My righteousness shall be forever
and My salvation from generation to generation.

9 Awake, awake, put on strength,
O arm of the LORD.
Awake as in the ancient days,
in the generations of old.
Was it not You who cut Rahab to pieces
and wounded the dragon?
10 Was it not You who dried up the sea,
the waters of the great deep,
who made the depths of the sea a pathway
for the ransomed to pass over?
11 Therefore, the redeemed of the LORD shall return
and come with singing to Zion,
and everlasting joy shall be upon their head.
They shall obtain gladness and joy,
and sorrow and mourning shall flee away.

12 I, even I, am He who comforts you.
Who are you that you should be afraid of a man who
shall die,
and of the son of man who shall be made
as grass,
13 and forget the LORD your maker
who has stretched out the heavens
and laid the foundations of the earth?
And have feared continually every day
because of the fury of the oppressor
as he makes ready to destroy?
Yet where is the fury of the oppressor?
14 The exile shall soon be freed,
and shall not die in the dungeon,
nor will his bread be lacking.
15 But I am the LORD your God
who divided the sea whose waves roared;
the LORD of Hosts is His name.
16 I have put My words in your mouth,
and I have covered you in the shadow of My hand
that I may plant the heavens,
and lay the foundations of the earth,
and say to Zion, "You are My people."

The Wrath of God Ceases

17 Awake, awake,
stand up, O Jerusalem,
you who have drunk at the hand of the LORD
the cup of His fury;
the cup of reeling
you have drained to the dregs.
18 There is no one to guide her
among all the sons she has brought forth;
nor is there anyone to take hold of her hand
of all the sons that she has brought up.
19 These two things have befallen you;
who shall be mournful for you?
Desolation, and destruction, and famine, and sword—
how shall I comfort you?
20 Your sons have fainted;
they lie at the head of all the streets
as an antelope in a net;
they are full of the fury of the LORD,
the rebuke of your God.

21 Therefore please hear this,
you afflicted who are drunk but not with wine.
22 Thus says your Lord, the LORD,
and your God who pleads the cause of His people:
See, I have taken out of your hand
the cup of reeling,
even the dregs of the cup of My fury;
you will never drink it again.
23 But I will put it into the hand of those who afflict you,
who have said to you,
"Lie down that we may walk over you."
And you have laid your back as the ground
and as the street for those who walk on it.

52 Awake, awake!
Put on your strength, O Zion;
put on your beautiful garments,
O Jerusalem, the holy city.
For the uncircumcised and the unclean
will no longer enter you.
2 Shake yourself from the dust;
arise, O captive Jerusalem.
Loose yourself from the bonds of your neck,
O captive daughter of Zion.

3 For thus says the LORD:

You were sold for nothing,
and you shall be redeemed without money.

4 For thus says the Lord GOD:

My people went down at the first into Egypt to sojourn
there;
then the Assyrian oppressed them without cause.

5 Now therefore, what do I have here, says the LORD,

seeing that My people have been taken away for nothing?
Those who rule over them make them wail,
says the LORD,
and My name is continually blasphemed
all day long.
6 Therefore, My people shall know My name;
therefore, they shall know in that day
that I am He who does speak:
Here I am.

7 How beautiful upon the mountains
are the feet of him who brings good news,
who proclaims peace,
who brings good news of happiness,
who proclaims salvation,
who says to Zion,
"Your God reigns!"
8 Your watchmen lift up their voices;
they sing joyfully together;
for they shall see with their own eyes
when the LORD brings Zion back.
9 Break forth into joy, sing together,
you waste places of Jerusalem.
For the LORD has comforted His people;
He has redeemed Jerusalem.
10 The LORD has bared His holy arm
in the eyes of all the nations,
and all the ends of the earth shall see
the salvation of our God.

11 Depart, depart, go out from there,
touch no unclean thing;
go out of the midst of her; be clean,
you who bear the vessels of the LORD.

12 For you shall not go out with haste
    nor go by flight.
For the Lord will go before you,
    and the God of Israel will be your rear guard.

The Suffering Servant

13 See, My servant shall deal prudently;
    he shall be exalted and extolled, and be very high.
14 Just as many were astonished at you,
    his visage was so marred, more than any man,
    and his form more than the sons of men;
15 so he shall sprinkle many nations.
    Kings shall shut their mouths at him;
for that which had not been told them they shall see,
    and that which they had not heard they
        shall consider.

53 Who has believed our report?
    And to whom has the arm of the Lord been revealed?
2 For he grew up before Him as a tender plant
    and as a root out of a dry ground.
He has no form or majesty that we should look upon him
    nor appearance that we should desire him.
3 He was despised and rejected of men,
    a man of sorrows and acquainted with grief.
And we hid, as it were, our faces from him;
    he was despised, and we did not esteem him.

4 Surely he has borne our grief
    and carried our sorrows;
Yet we esteemed him stricken,
    smitten of God, and afflicted.
5 But he was wounded for our transgressions,
    he was bruised for our iniquities;
the chastisement of our peace was upon him,
    and by his stripes we are healed.
6 All of us like sheep have gone astray;
    each of us has turned to his own way,
but the Lord has laid on him
    the iniquity of us all.

7 He was oppressed, and he was afflicted,
    yet he opened not his mouth;
he was brought as a lamb to the slaughter,
    and as a sheep before its shearers is silent,
    so he opened not his mouth.
8 By oppression and judgment he was taken away,
    and who shall declare his generation?
For he was cut off out of the land of the living;
    for the transgression of my people he was struck.
9 His grave was assigned with the wicked,
    yet with the rich in his death,
because he had done no violence,
    nor was any deceit in his mouth.

10 Yet it pleased the Lord to bruise him; He has put him
        to grief.
If he made himself as an offering for sin,
he shall see his offspring, he shall prolong his days,
    and the good pleasure of the Lord shall prosper in
        his hand.
11 He shall see of the anguish of his soul
    and be satisfied.
By his knowledge My righteous servant shall justify
        the many,
    for he shall bear their iniquities.
12 Therefore, I will divide him a portion with the great,
    and he shall divide the spoil with the strong,
because he poured out his soul to death,
    and he was numbered with the transgressors,
thus he bore the sin of many
    and made intercession for the transgressors.

The Covenant of Peace

54 Sing, O barren,
    you who did not bear a child.
Break forth into singing and cry aloud,
    you who did not travail with child.
For more are the children of the desolate
    than the children of the married wife,
    says the Lord.
2 Enlarge the place of your tent,
    and let them stretch out the curtains of your habitations;
    spare not,
lengthen your cords,
    and strengthen your stakes.
3 For you shall spread out to the right hand and to the left,
    and your descendants shall inherit the nations
    and make the desolate cities to be inhabited.

4 Do not fear, for you shall not be ashamed nor be humiliated;
    for you shall not be put to shame,
for you shall forget the shame of your youth
    and shall not remember the reproach of your widowhood
        anymore.
5 For your Maker is your husband,
    the Lord of Hosts is His name;
and your Redeemer is the Holy One of Israel;
    He shall be called the God of the whole earth.
6 For the Lord has called you
    as a woman forsaken and grieved in spirit,
and a wife of youth
    when you were refused, says your God.
7 For a small moment I have forsaken you,
    but with great mercies I will gather you.
8 In a little wrath
    I hid My face from you for a moment;
but with everlasting kindness
    I will have mercy on you,
    says the Lord your Redeemer.

9 For this is as the waters of Noah to Me;
    for as I have sworn that the waters of Noah should no longer
        cover the earth,
so I have sworn that I would not be wrathful with you
    nor rebuke you.
10 For the mountains may be removed,
    and the hills may shake,
but My kindness shall not depart from you,
    nor shall My covenant of peace be removed,
    says the Lord who has mercy on you.

11 O afflicted one, tossed with tempest and not comforted,
    I will lay your stones with fair colors
    and lay your foundations with sapphires.
12 I will make your windows of agates,
    and your gates of crystal,
    and all your borders of precious stones.
13 All your sons shall be taught of the Lord,
    and great shall be the peace of your sons.
14 In righteousness you shall be established;
you shall be far from oppression,
    for you shall not fear,
and from terror,
    for it shall not come near you.
15 Indeed they shall surely assail you fiercely, but not from Me.
    Whoever assails you shall fall for your sake.

16 See, I have created the smith
    that blows the coals in the fire
    and who brings forth an instrument for his work;
and I have created the destroyer in order to cause ruin.
17 No weapon that is formed against you shall prosper,
    and every tongue that shall rise against you in judgment, you
        shall condemn.

This is the heritage of the servants of the Lord,
   and their vindication is from Me,
   says the Lord.

The Invitation to the Waters

55 Ho! Everyone who thirsts,
   come to the waters;
   and you who have no money,
      come, buy and eat.
Come, buy wine and milk
   without money and without price.
2 Why do you spend money for that which is not bread,
   and your labor for that which does not satisfy?
Listen diligently to Me, and eat what is good,
   and let your soul delight itself in abundance.
3 Incline your ear, and come to Me.
   Listen, so that your soul may live,
and I will make an everlasting covenant with you,
   even the sure mercies of David.
4 See, I have given him as a witness to the people,
   a leader and commander to the people.
5 Surely you shall call a nation that you do not know,
   and nations that did not know you shall run to you
because of the Lord your God,
   even the Holy One of Israel;
   for He has glorified you.

6 Seek the Lord while He may be found,
   call you upon Him while He is near.
7 Let the wicked forsake his way,
   and the unrighteous man his thoughts;
and let him return to the Lord, and He will have mercy
      upon him,
   and to our God, for He will abundantly pardon.

8 For My thoughts are not your thoughts,
   nor are your ways My ways,
   says the Lord.
9 For as the heavens are higher than the earth,
   so are My ways higher than your ways,
   and My thoughts than your thoughts.
10 For as the rain comes down,
   and the snow from heaven,
and do not return there
   but water the earth
and make it bring forth and bud
   that it may give seed to the sower and bread to the eater,
11 so shall My word be that goes forth from My mouth;
   it shall not return to Me void,
but it shall accomplish that which I please,
   and it shall prosper in the thing for which I sent it.
12 For you shall go out with joy,
   and be led out with peace;
the mountains and the hills
   shall break forth into singing before you,
and all the trees of the field
   shall clap their hands.
13 Instead of the thorn shall come up the fir tree,
   and instead of the brier shall come up the myrtle tree;
and it shall be to the Lord for a memorial,
   for an everlasting sign
   that shall not be cut off.

Salvation for the Nations

56 Thus says the Lord:

Preserve justice
   and do righteousness,
for My salvation is about to come
   and My righteousness to be revealed.
2 Blessed is the man who does this,
   and the son of man who takes hold of it,

who keeps from polluting the Sabbath
   and keeps his hand from doing any evil.

3 Do not let the son of the foreigner
   who has joined himself to the Lord
speak, saying,
   "The Lord has utterly separated me from His people";
do not let the eunuch say,
   "I am only a dry tree."

4 For thus says the Lord:

To the eunuchs who keep My Sabbaths,
   and choose the things that please Me,
   and take hold of My covenant,
5 to them I will give in My house and within My walls
   a memorial, and a name
   better than that of sons and of daughters;
I will give them an everlasting name
   that shall not be cut off.
6 Also the sons of the foreigner who join themselves to the Lord
   to serve Him,
and to love the name of the Lord,
   and to be His servants,
to everyone who keeps from polluting the Sabbath
   and takes hold of My covenant,
7 even them I will bring to My holy mountain
   and make them joyful in My house of prayer.
Their burnt offerings and their sacrifices
   shall be accepted on My altar;
for My house shall be called
   a house of prayer for all people.
8 The Lord God
   who gathers the outcasts of Israel says,
Yet I will gather others to them
   besides those who already are gathered to him.

God Accuses the Wicked

9 All you beasts of the field,
   all you beasts in the forest, come to devour.
10 His watchmen are blind;
   they all are ignorant;
they all are dumb dogs,
   unable to bark;
sleepers lying down,
   who love to slumber.
11 They are greedy dogs
   which can never have enough,
and they are shepherds who cannot understand;
   they all turn to their own way,
   every one for his gain, from his territory.
12 "Come," *they say*, "let us get wine,
   and let us fill ourselves with strong drink;
and tomorrow shall be as today,
   only more so."

Israel's Futile Idolatry

57 The righteous man perishes,
   and no man lays it to heart;
and merciful men are taken away
   while no one understands,
for the righteous man is taken away
   from the evil to come.
2 He shall enter into peace;
   they shall rest in their beds,
   each one walking in his uprightness.

3 But draw near to here, you sons of a sorceress,
   offspring of an adulterer and prostitute.
4 Whom do you mock?
   Against whom do you open wide your mouth
   and stick out your tongue?

Are you not children of transgression,
 offspring of falsehood,
5 inflaming yourselves with idols
 under every green tree,
slaying the children in the valleys
 under the clefts of the rocks?
6 Among the smooth stones of the stream is your portion;
 they are your lot.
Even to them you have poured out a drink offering;
 you have offered a grain offering.
Should I relent concerning these things?
7 On a lofty and high mountain you have set your bed;
 even there you went up to offer sacrifice.
8 Behind the doors and the doorposts
 you have set up your memorial;
far removed from Me, you have uncovered yourself;
 you have enlarged your bed and made a covenant with them;
you have loved their bed,
 you have looked on their nakedness.
9 You went to the king with ointment,
 and increased your perfumes,
and sent your messengers far off,
 and made them go down to Sheol.
10 You were wearied by the length of your road;
 yet you did not say, "There is no hope."
You have found renewed strength;
 therefore, you did not faint.

11 Of whom were you afraid or fearful
 when you lied
and you did not remember Me,
 nor give Me a thought?
Have I not held My peace for a long time
 so that you do not fear Me?
12 I will declare your righteousness, and your works,
 yet they shall not profit you.
13 When you cry out,
 let your collection of idols deliver you.
But the wind shall carry them all away,
 a breath shall take them away.
But he who puts his trust in Me
 shall possess the land
 and shall inherit My holy mountain.

Healing for the Contrite

14 And it shall be said,

"Build up, build up, prepare the way,
 take up every stumbling block out of the way of My people."
15 For thus says the High and Lofty One
 who inhabits eternity, whose name is Holy:
I dwell in the high and holy place
 and also with him who is of a contrite and humble spirit,
to revive the spirit of the humble,
 and to revive the heart of the contrite ones.
16 For I will not contend forever,
 nor will I always be angry;
for the spirit would grow faint before Me,
 and the souls whom I have made.
17 For the iniquity of his unjust gain I was angry and struck him;
 I hid My face and was wrathful,
 and he went on turning away in the way of his heart.
18 I have seen his ways but will heal him;
 I will lead him and restore comfort to him and to his
  mourners,
19 by creating the fruit of the lips.
Peace, peace to him who is far off and to him who is near,
 says the LORD, and I will heal him.
20 But the wicked are like the troubled
 sea when it cannot rest,
 whose waters cast up mire and dirt.
21 There is no peace, says my God, for the wicked.

The Chosen Fast

58 Cry aloud, do not hold back;
 lift up your voice like a trumpet,
and show My people their transgression
 and the house of Jacob their sins.
2 Yet they seek Me daily
 and delight to know My ways,
as a nation that has done righteousness
 and has not forsaken the ordinance of their God.
They ask Me for the ordinances of justice;
 they take delight in approaching God.
3 "Why have we fasted
 and You do not see?
Why have we humbled ourselves
 and You take no notice?"

Certainly, on the day of your fast you find your desire
 and are exacting on all your laborers.
4 Certainly, you fast for strife and debate
 and to strike with the fist of wickedness.
You do not fast as you do this day,
 to make your voice to be heard on high.
5 Is it such a fast that I have chosen,
 a day for a man to humble himself?
Is it to bow down his head as a bulrush,
 and to spread out sackcloth and ashes under him?
Will you call this a fast
 and an acceptable day to the LORD?

6 Is not this the fast that I have chosen:
 to loose the bonds of wickedness,
 to undo the heavy burdens,
and to let the oppressed go free,
 and break every yoke?
7 Is it not to divide your bread with the hungry
 and bring the poor who are outcasts into your house?
When you see the naked, to cover him
 and not hide yourself from your own flesh?
8 Then your light shall break forth as the morning,
 and your healing shall spring forth quickly,
and your righteousness shall go before you;
 the glory of the LORD shall be your reward.
9 Then you shall call, and the LORD shall answer;
 you shall cry, and He shall say, Here I am.

If you take away the yoke from your midst,
 the pointing of the finger, and speaking wickedness,
10 and if you give yourself to the hungry
 and satisfy the afflicted soul,
then your light shall rise in obscurity,
 and your darkness shall become as the noonday.
11 And the LORD shall guide you continually,
 and satisfy your soul in drought,
 and strengthen your bones;
and you shall be like a watered garden,
 and like a spring of water, whose waters do not fail.
12 Those from among you shall rebuild the old waste places;
 you shall raise up the foundations of many generations;
and you shall be called, the Repairer of the Breach,
 the Restorer of Paths in which to Dwell.

13 If because of the Sabbath you turn away your foot
 from doing your pleasure on My holy day,
and call the Sabbath a delight,
 the holy day of the LORD honorable,
and honor it, not doing your own ways,
 nor finding your own pleasure, nor speaking your own words,
14 then you shall delight yourself in the LORD,
 and I will cause you to ride upon the high places of
  the earth,
 and feed you with the heritage of Jacob your father.
For the mouth of the LORD has spoken it.

The Consequence of Sin

59 Certainly, the hand of the LORD is not so short that it
cannot save,
nor is His ear so dull that it cannot hear.
2 But your iniquities have made a separation between
you and your God,
and your sins have hidden His face from you
so that He will not hear.
3 For your hands are defiled with blood
and your fingers with iniquity;
your lips have spoken lies,
your tongue has muttered perverseness.
4 No one calls for justice,
nor does anyone plead for truth.
They trust in vanity and speak lies;
they conceive mischief and bring forth iniquity.
5 They hatch adders' eggs
and weave the spider's web;
he who eats of their eggs dies,
and that which is crushed breaks out into a viper.
6 Their webs shall not become garments,
nor shall they cover themselves with their works;
their works are works of iniquity,
and an act of violence is in their hands.
7 Their feet run to evil,
and they make haste to shed innocent blood;
their thoughts are thoughts of iniquity;
devastation and destruction are in their paths.
8 The way of peace they do not know,
and there is no justice in their ways;
they have made their paths crooked;
whoever walks in them does not know peace.

The Confession of Sin

9 Therefore, justice is far from us,
nor does righteousness overtake us;
we wait for light, but there is darkness,
for brightness, but we walk in gloom.
10 We grope along the wall like the blind,
and we grope as if we had no eyes;
we stumble at noonday as in the night;
among those who are vigorous, we are as
dead men.
11 We all roar like bears
and mourn sadly like doves;
we look for justice, but there is none;
for salvation, but it is far from us.

12 For our transgressions are multiplied before You,
and our sins testify against us;
for our transgressions are with us.
And as for our iniquities, we know them:
13 transgressing, and lying against the LORD,
and departing away from our God,
speaking oppression and revolt,
conceiving and uttering from the heart words of falsehood.
14 Justice is turned backward,
and righteousness stands far off;
for truth is fallen in the street,
and equity cannot enter.
15 Truth is lacking,
and he who departs from evil makes himself a prey.

The Redeemer of Zion

Then the LORD saw it, and it displeased Him
that there was no justice.
16 He saw that there was no man
and was astonished that there was no intercessor;
therefore, His own arm brought salvation to Him,
and His righteousness sustained Him.
17 For He put on righteousness as a breastplate
and a helmet of salvation on His head;

He put on the garments of vengeance for clothing
and was clad with zeal as a cloak.
18 According to their deeds,
accordingly He will repay:
fury to His adversaries,
recompense to His enemies;
to the islands He will make recompense.
19 So shall they fear the name of the LORD from the west
and His glory from the rising of the sun;
when the enemy shall come in like a flood,
the Spirit of the LORD shall lift up a standard against him.

20 The Redeemer shall come to Zion
and to those who turn from transgression in Jacob,
says the LORD.

21 As for Me, this is My covenant with them, says the LORD: My Spirit
who is upon you, and My words which I have put in your mouth shall
not depart out of your mouth, nor out of the mouth of your descendants, nor out of the mouth of your descendants' descendants, says the
LORD, from this time forth and forever.

The Glory of Zion

60 Arise, shine, for your light has come,
and the glory of the LORD has risen upon you.
2 For the darkness shall cover the earth
and deep darkness the peoples;
but the LORD shall rise upon you,
and His glory shall be seen upon you.
3 The nations shall come to your light
and kings to the brightness of your rising.

4 Lift up your eyes all around, and see:
They all gather themselves together; they come to you;
your sons shall come from afar,
and your daughters shall be carried at your side.
5 Then you shall see and be radiant,
and your heart shall thrill and rejoice
because the abundance of the sea shall be converted
to you,
the wealth of the nations shall come to you.
6 The multitude of camels shall cover your *land*,
the young camels of Midian and Ephah;
all those from Sheba shall come;
they shall bring gold and incense
and shall bear good news of the praises of the LORD.
7 All the flocks of Kedar shall be gathered together to you,
the rams of Nebaioth shall minister to you;
they shall come up with acceptance on My altar,
and I will glorify My glorious house.

8 Who are these who fly as a cloud
and as the doves to their roosts?
9 Surely the coastlands shall wait for Me,
and the ships of Tarshish shall come first,
to bring your sons from afar,
their silver and their gold with them,
to the name of the LORD your God
and to the Holy One of Israel
because He has glorified you.

10 The sons of foreigners shall build up your walls,
and their kings shall minister to you;
for in My wrath I struck you,
but in My favor I have had mercy on you.
11 Therefore, your gates shall be open continually;
they shall not be shut day nor night,
so that men may bring to you the wealth of the nations,
and that their kings may be brought.
12 For the nation and kingdom that will not serve you
shall perish,
and those nations shall be utterly destroyed.

13 The glory of Lebanon shall come to you,
the fir tree, the pine tree, and the box tree together,
to beautify the place of My sanctuary;
and I will make the place of My feet glorious.
14 The sons also of those who afflicted you shall come bowing
before you,
and all those who despised you shall bow themselves down at
the soles of your feet;
and they shall call you, The City of the Lord,
the Zion of the Holy One of Israel.

15 Whereas you have been forsaken
and hated so that no man went through you,
I will make you an eternal excellency,
a joy of many generations.
16 You shall also suck the milk of the nations
and suck the breast of kings;
then you shall know that I, the Lord, am your Savior
and your Redeemer, the Mighty One of Jacob.
17 Instead of bronze I will bring gold,
and instead of iron I will bring silver;
and instead of wood, bronze;
and instead of stones, iron.
I will also make your officers peace
and your exactors righteousness.
18 Violence shall no more be heard in your land,
nor devastation or destruction within your borders;
but you shall call your walls Salvation
and your gates Praise.
19 The sun shall no longer be your light by day,
nor for brightness shall the moon give light to you;
but the Lord shall be an everlasting light to you
and your God for your glory.
20 Your sun shall no more go down,
nor shall your moon wane;
for the Lord shall be your everlasting light,
and the days of your mourning shall end.
21 Then all your people shall be righteous;
they shall inherit the land forever,
the branch of My planting,
the work of My hands,
that I may be glorified.
22 A little one shall become a thousand,
and a small one a strong nation.
I, the Lord,
will hasten it in its time.

The Lord's Favor

61 The Spirit of the Lord God is upon me
because the Lord has anointed me
to preach good news to the poor;
He has sent me to heal the broken-hearted,
to proclaim liberty to the captives,
and the opening of the prison to those who are bound;
2 to proclaim the acceptable year of the Lord
and the day of vengeance of our God;
to comfort all who mourn,
3 to preserve those who mourn in Zion,
to give to them beauty
for ashes,
the oil of joy
for mourning,
the garment of praise
for the spirit of heaviness,
that they might be called trees of righteousness,
the planting of the Lord,
that He might be glorified.

4 They shall build the old ruins;
they shall raise up the former desolations,
and they shall repair the waste cities,
the desolations of many generations.

5 Strangers shall stand and feed your flocks,
and the sons of the alien shall be your plowmen and your
vinedressers.
6 But you shall be named the priests of the Lord;
men shall call you the ministers of our God.
You shall eat the riches of the nations,
and in their glory you shall boast.

7 Instead of your shame
you shall have double honor,
and instead of humiliation
they shall rejoice over their portion.
Therefore, in their land they shall possess a double portion;
everlasting joy shall be theirs.

8 For I, the Lord, love justice,
I hate robbery in the burnt offering;
and I will faithfully give them their recompense
and make an everlasting covenant with them.
9 Their descendants shall be known among the nations
and their offspring among the peoples.
All who see them shall acknowledge them
because they are the descendants whom the Lord has blessed.

10 I will greatly rejoice in the Lord,
my soul shall be joyful in my God;
for He has clothed me with the garments of salvation,
He has covered me with the robe of righteousness,
as a bridegroom decks himself with ornaments,
and as a bride adorns herself with her jewels.
11 For as the earth brings forth her buds,
and as the garden causes the things that are sown in it to
spring forth,
so the Lord God will cause righteousness and praise
to spring forth before all the nations.

The Salvation of Zion

62 For the sake of Zion I will not keep silent,
and for the sake of Jerusalem I will not rest
until her righteousness goes forth as brightness
and her salvation as a lamp that burns.
2 The nations shall see your righteousness,
and all kings your glory.
And you shall be called by a new name,
which the mouth of the Lord shall name.
3 You shall also be a crown of glory in the hand of the Lord
and a royal diadem in the hand of your God.
4 You shall no more be termed Forsaken,
nor shall your land be termed Desolate;
but you shall be called My Delight Is In Her,
and your land Married;
for the Lord delights in you,
and your land shall be married.
5 For as a young man marries a virgin,
so your sons shall marry you;
and as the bridegroom rejoices over the bride,
so your God shall rejoice over you.

6 I have set watchmen on your walls, O Jerusalem,
who shall never hold their peace day nor night.
You who remind the Lord,
do not keep silent;
7 give Him no rest until He establishes
and makes Jerusalem a glory in the earth.

8 The Lord has sworn by His right hand
and by His strong arm:
Surely I will no longer give your grain
as food for your enemies;
and the sons of the foreigners shall not drink
your wine
for which you have labored.

9 But those who have gathered it shall eat it
 and praise the Lord;
and those who have brought it shall drink it
 in the courts of My sanctuary.

10 Go through, go through the gates.
 Prepare the way of the people;
build up, build up the highway.
 Remove the stones;
lift up a standard over the peoples.

11 The Lord has proclaimed
 to the ends of the earth:
Say to the daughter of Zion,
 "See, your salvation comes;
see, His reward is with Him,
 and His recompense before Him."
12 They shall call them The Holy People,
 the Redeemed of the Lord;
and you shall be called Sought Out,
 a City Not Forsaken.

The Revenge of God

63 "Who is this who comes from Edom
 with dyed garments from Bozrah?
This one who is glorious in His apparel,
 traveling in the greatness of His strength?"

"It is I who speak in righteousness,
 mighty to save."

2 "Why is Your apparel red,
 and Your garments like him who treads in the
 wine vat?"

3 "I have trodden the winepress alone;
 and from the peoples there was no one with Me.
For I will tread them in My anger,
 and trample them in My fury,
and their blood shall be sprinkled upon My garments,
 and I will stain all My raiment.
4 For the day of vengeance is in My heart,
 and My year of redemption has come.
5 I looked and there was no one to help,
 and I was astonished, and there was no one
 to uphold;
therefore, My own arm brought salvation to Me;
 and My fury upheld Me.
6 I will tread down the peoples in My anger
 and make them drunk in My fury,
and I will pour out their lifeblood on the earth."

The Mercy of God Remembered

7 I will mention the steadfast love of the Lord
 and the praises of the Lord,
according to all that the Lord has bestowed on us,
and the great goodness toward the house of Israel,
 which He has bestowed on them
 according to His mercy,
 and according to the multitude of His kindnesses.
8 For He said, "Surely they are My people,
 sons who will not lie."
So He became their Savior.
9 In all their affliction He was afflicted,
 and the angel of His presence saved them;
in His love and in His mercy He redeemed them;
 and He lifted them and carried them
 all the days of old.
10 But they rebelled
 and grieved His Holy Spirit;
therefore, He turned Himself to be their enemy,
 and He fought against them.

11 Then His people remembered the days of old,
 of Moses, saying:
Where is He who brought them up out of the sea
 with the shepherds of His flock?
Where is He who put
 His Holy Spirit in their midst,
12 who led them with His glorious arm
 by the right hand of Moses,
dividing the water before them,
 to make Himself an everlasting name,
13 who led them through the deep,
 as a horse in the wilderness,
 that they should not stumble?
14 As the cattle which go down into the valley,
 the Spirit of the Lord caused them to rest,
so You led Your people,
 to make Yourself a glorious name.

A Prayer of Penitence

15 Look down from heaven and see,
 from Your holy and glorious habitation.
Where are Your zeal and Your strength?
 The stirrings of Your heart and Your mercies toward me are
 restrained.
16 For You are our Father,
 though Abraham is ignorant of us
 and Israel does not recognize us.
You, O Lord, are our Father, our Redeemer;
 Your name is from everlasting.
17 O Lord, why have You made us to err from Your ways
 and hardened our heart from fearing You?
Return for Your servants' sake,
 the tribes of Your inheritance.
18 Your holy people possessed Your sanctuary for a little while;
 our adversaries have trodden it down.
19 We have become
 as those over whom You have never ruled,
 as those who were not called by Your name.

64 Oh, that You would rend the heavens and come down,
 that the mountains might shake at Your presence,
2 as when the melting fire burns,
 as the fire causes the waters to boil,
to make Your name known to Your adversaries,
 that the nations may tremble at Your presence!
3 When You did awesome things *for which* we did not look,
 You came down; the mountains quaked at Your presence.
4 For since the beginning of the world men have not heard,
 nor perceived by ear,
neither has the eye seen a God besides You,
 who acts for the one who waits for Him.
5 You meet him who rejoices in doing righteousness,
 those who remember You in Your ways.
Indeed, You were angry, for we had sinned;
 in *our sins* we remained a long time,
 and shall we be saved?
6 But we all are as an unclean thing,
 and all our righteousness is as filthy rags;
and we all fade as a leaf,
 and our iniquities, like the wind, have taken us away.
7 There is no one who calls on Your name,
 who stirs up himself to take hold of You;
for You have hidden Your face from us
 and have consumed us because of our iniquities.

8 But now, O Lord, You are our Father;
 we are the clay, and You are our potter;
 and we all are the work of Your hand.
9 Do not be wrathful beyond measure, O Lord,
 nor remember iniquity forever;
look upon us, we pray,
 we all are Your people.

[10] Your holy cities are a wilderness;
   Zion is a wilderness, Jerusalem a desolation.
[11] Our holy and beautiful house where our fathers praised You
   is burned up with fire;
   and all our precious things are laid waste.
[12] Will You refrain Yourself from these things, O Lord?
   Will You hold Your peace and afflict us beyond measure?

Judgment and Salvation

65 I was sought by those who did not ask for Me;
   I was found of those who did not seek Me.
I said, "Here I am, here I am,"
   to a nation that did not call on My name.
[2] I have spread out My hands all day
   to a rebellious people
who walk in a way that was not good,
   after their own thoughts;
[3] a people who provoke Me continually
   to My face,
presenting sacrifices in gardens
   and burning incense on altars of brick;
[4] who sit among the graves
   and lodge in the monuments;
who eat swine's flesh,
   and the broth of abominable things is in their vessels;
[5] who say, "Stand by yourself; do not come near to me,
   for I am holier than you!"
These are smoke in My nose,
   a fire that burns all day.

[6] See, it is written before Me:
   I will not keep silent, but I will recompense,
   even recompense into their bosom,
[7] your iniquities and the iniquities of your fathers together,
   says the Lord;
because they have burned incense on the mountains
   and blasphemed Me on the hills,
therefore, I will measure their former work
   into their bosom.

[8] Thus says the Lord:

As the new wine is found in the cluster,
   and one says, "Do not destroy it
   for a blessing is in it,"
so I will do for the sake of My servants
   that I may not destroy them all.
[9] I will bring forth descendants from Jacob,
   and out of Judah an inheritor of My mountains;
and My chosen ones shall inherit it,
   and My servants shall dwell there.
[10] Sharon shall be a fold of flocks,
   and the Valley of Achor a place for the herds to lie down in,
   for My people who seek Me.

[11] But you are those who forsake the Lord,
   who forget My holy mountain,
who prepare a table for Fortune,
   and who furnish the drink offering for Destiny.
[12] I will destine you for the sword,
   and you all shall bow down to the slaughter;
because when I called, you did not answer;
   when I spoke, you did not hear
but did evil before My eyes
   and chose that in which I did not delight.

[13] Therefore, thus says the Lord God:

My servants shall eat,
   but you shall be hungry;
My servants shall drink,
   but you shall be thirsty;

My servants shall rejoice,
   but you shall be ashamed;
[14] My servants shall sing for joy
   with a glad heart,
but you shall cry
   with a heavy heart
   and shall wail with grief of spirit.
[15] You shall leave your name
   for a curse to My chosen ones;
for the Lord God shall slay you,
   but My servants shall be called by another name;
[16] because he who is blessed in the earth
   shall bless himself in the God of truth;
and he who swears in the earth
   shall swear by the God of truth;
because the former troubles are forgotten
   and because they are hidden from My eyes.

The New Creation

[17] For I create
   new heavens and a new earth;
the former things shall not be remembered
   or come to mind.
[18] But be glad and rejoice forever
   in that which I create;
for I create Jerusalem for rejoicing
   and her people for joy.
[19] I will rejoice in Jerusalem
   and be glad in My people;
and the voice of weeping shall no longer be heard
   in her,
   nor the voice of crying.

[20] There shall no longer be
   an infant *who lives only a few* days
   nor an old man who has not filled out his days.
For the child shall die
   a hundred years old,
but the sinner being a hundred years old
   shall be accursed.
[21] They shall build houses and inhabit them;
   and they shall plant vineyards and eat the fruit
      of them.
[22] They shall not build and another inhabit;
   they shall not plant and another eat;
for as the days of a tree
   are the days of My people,
and My chosen ones shall long enjoy
   the work of their hands.
[23] They shall not labor in vain
   nor bring forth children for trouble;
for they are the descendants of the blessed of the Lord
   and their offspring with them.
[24] Before they call, I will answer;
   and while they are yet speaking, I will hear.
[25] The wolf and the lamb shall feed together,
   and the lion shall eat straw like the bull,
   and dust shall be the serpent's food.
They shall not hurt nor destroy
   in all My holy mountain,
   says the Lord.

True Worship

66 Thus says the Lord:

Heaven is My throne,
   and the earth is My footstool.
Where then is the house that you could build for Me?
   And where is the place of My rest?
[2] For My hand made all those things,
   thus all those things have come to be,
   says the Lord.

But to this man I will look,
　　even to him who is poor and of a contrite spirit,
　　and trembles at My word.
3 He who kills a bull
　　is as if he kills a man;
he who sacrifices a lamb,
　　as if he breaks a dog's neck;
he who offers a grain offering,
　　as if he offers swine's blood;
he who burns incense,
　　as if he blesses an idol.
They have chosen their own ways,
　　and their soul delights in their abominations;
4 I also will choose their punishments
　　and will bring their fears on them,
because when I called, no one answered;
　　when I spoke, they did not listen;
but they did evil before My eyes
　　and chose that in which I did not delight.

The Vindication of Zion
5 Hear the word of the LORD,
　　you who tremble at His word:
Your brothers who hate you,
　　who cast you out for My name's sake, said,
"Let the LORD be glorified
　　that we may see your joy."
　　Yet they shall be ashamed.
6 A voice of noise from the city,
　　a voice from the temple,
the voice of the LORD
　　who renders recompense to His enemies.

7 Before she was in labor,
　　she gave birth;
before her pain came,
　　she delivered a son.
8 Who has heard such a thing?
　　Who has seen such things?
Shall the earth be made to give birth in one day?
　　Shall a nation be born at once?
For as soon as Zion was in labor,
　　she brought forth her sons.
9 Shall I bring to the point of birth
　　and not cause delivery? says the LORD.
Shall I who cause delivery
　　shut the womb? says your God.
10 Rejoice with Jerusalem and be glad for her,
　　all you who love her;
rejoice exceedingly with her,
　　all you who mourn for her,

11 that you may feed and be satisfied
　　with her consoling breasts,
that you may feed
　　and be delighted with the abundance of her bosom.

12 For thus says the LORD:

I will extend peace to her like a river
　　and the glory of the nations like a flowing stream.
Then you shall nurse, you shall be carried on her sides,
　　and dandled on her knees.
13 As one whom his mother comforts,
　　so I will comfort you;
　　and you shall be comforted in Jerusalem.

God's Reign and Final Judgment
14 Then you shall see this, and your heart shall rejoice,
　　and your bones shall flourish like an herb;
and the hand of the LORD shall be known toward His servants,
　　and His indignation toward His enemies.
15 For the LORD shall come with fire
　　and with His chariots like a whirlwind,
to render His anger with fury
　　and His rebuke with flames of fire.
16 For by fire and by His sword on all flesh,
　　the LORD shall execute judgment;
　　and the slain of the LORD shall be many.

17 Those who sanctify themselves and purify themselves in the gardens behind one tree in the midst, eating swine's flesh, and abominable things, and mice shall be consumed together, says the LORD.
18 For I know their works and their thoughts. The time shall come to gather all nations and tongues. And they shall come and see My glory.
19 I will set a sign among them, and send from them survivors to the nations: to Tarshish, Pul, and Lud—who draw the bow—to Tubal, and Javan, to the coastlands afar off who have not heard My fame nor seen My glory. And they shall declare My glory among the nations.
20 They shall bring all your brothers out of all nations as an offering to the LORD on horses, and in chariots, and in litters, and on mules, and on swift beasts to My holy mountain Jerusalem, says the LORD, as the sons of Israel bring an offering in a clean vessel into the house of the LORD.
21 I will also take some of them for priests and for Levites, says the LORD.

22 For as the new heavens and the new earth which I will make shall remain before Me, says the LORD, so shall your descendants and your name remain. 23 From one New Moon to another, and from one Sabbath to another, all flesh shall come to worship before Me, says the LORD. 24 And they shall go forth and look on the corpses of the men who have transgressed against Me. For their worm shall not die, nor shall their fire be quenched. And they shall be an abhorrence to all flesh.

JEREMIAH

The Commission of Jeremiah

1 The words of Jeremiah the son of Hilkiah, of the priests who were in Anathoth in the land of Benjamin, ² to whom the word of the LORD came in the days of Josiah the son of Amon, king of Judah, in the thirteenth year of his reign. ³ It came also in the days of Jehoiakim the son of Josiah, king of Judah, to the end of the eleventh year of Zedekiah the son of Josiah, king of Judah, until the captivity of Jerusalem in the fifth month.

⁴ Now the word of the LORD came to me, saying,

⁵ "Before I formed you in the womb I knew you;
    and before you were born I sanctified you,
    and I ordained you a prophet to the nations."

⁶ Then I said, "Ah, Lord GOD! Truly, I cannot speak, for I am a youth." ⁷ But the LORD said to me, "Do not say, 'I am a youth.' For you shall go everywhere that I send you, and whatever I command you, you shall speak. ⁸ Do not be afraid of their faces. For I am with you to deliver you," says the LORD.

⁹ Then the LORD put forth His hand and touched my mouth. And the LORD said to me, "Now, I have put My words in your mouth. ¹⁰ See, I have this day set you over the nations and over the kingdoms, to root out and to pull down, to destroy and to throw down, to build and to plant."

The Almond Rod and Boiling Pot

¹¹ Moreover the word of the LORD came to me, saying, "Jeremiah, what do you see?"

And I said, "I see a branch of an almond tree."

¹² Then the LORD said to me, "You have seen well. For I will hasten My word to perform it."

¹³ The word of the LORD came to me the second time, saying, "What do you see?"

And I said, "I see a boiling pot, and it is facing away from the north." ¹⁴ Then the LORD said to me: Out of the north calamity will break forth on all the inhabitants of the land. ¹⁵ For I will call all the families of the kingdoms of the north, says the LORD.

And they will come and they will set each one his throne
    at the entrance of the gates of Jerusalem,
and against all the walls all around,
    and against all the cities of Judah.
¹⁶ I will utter My judgments against them
    concerning all their wickedness, whereby they have
        forsaken Me
and have burned incense to other gods,
    and have worshipped the works of their own hands.

¹⁷ You therefore gird up your loins and arise, and speak to them all that I command you. Do not be dismayed at their faces, lest I confound you before them. ¹⁸ For indeed, I have made you this day a fortified city and an iron pillar and bronze walls against the whole land, against the kings of Judah, against the officials, against the priests, and against the people of the land. ¹⁹ They will fight against you, but they will not prevail against you, for I am with you, says the LORD, to deliver you.

God Pleads With Israel to Repent

2 Moreover the word of the LORD came to me, saying, ² Go and proclaim in the ears of Jerusalem, saying,

Thus says the LORD:

I remember you, the kindness of your youth,
    the love of your espousals,
when you followed Me in the wilderness,
    in a land that was not sown.
³ Israel is holy to the LORD,
    and the first fruits of His harvest.

All who eat of it will become guilty;
    disaster will come upon them,
    says the LORD.

⁴ Hear the word of the LORD, O house of Jacob
    and all the families of the house of Israel.

⁵ Thus says the LORD:

What iniquity have your fathers found in Me,
    that they have gone far from Me,
and have walked after vanity
    and have become vain?
⁶ They did not say, "Where is the LORD
    who brought us up out of the land of Egypt,
who led us through the wilderness,
    through a land of deserts and of pits,
through a land of drought and of the shadow of death,
    through a land that no man passed through and where
        no man lived?"
⁷ And I brought you into a plentiful country
    to eat its fruit and its goodness.
But when you entered, you defiled My land
    and made My heritage an abomination.
⁸ The priests did not say,
    "Where is the LORD?"
And those who handle the law did not know Me;
    the shepherds also transgressed against Me,
and the prophets prophesied by Baal
    and walked after things that do not profit.

⁹ Therefore I will yet contend with you,
    says the LORD,
    and with your sons' sons I will contend.
¹⁰ For pass over the coastlands of Cyprus and see,
    and send to Kedar and consider diligently,
    and see if there is such a thing.
¹¹ Has a nation changed their gods,
    though they are not gods?
But My people have changed their glory
    for that which does not profit.
¹² Be astonished at this, O heavens,
    and be horribly afraid, be very desolate,
    says the LORD.
¹³ For My people have committed two evils.
They have forsaken Me,
    the fountain of living waters,
and hewed out for themselves cisterns,
    broken cisterns, that can hold no water.
¹⁴ Is Israel a servant? Is he a homeborn slave?
    Why has he been plundered?
¹⁵ The young lions roared at him
    and roared loudly,
and they made his land a waste;
    his cities have been destroyed, without inhabitant.
¹⁶ Also the men of Memphis and Tahpanhes
    have shaved the crown of your head.
¹⁷ Have you not brought this on yourself,
    in that you have forsaken the LORD your God
    when He led you in the way?
¹⁸ And now what are you doing in the way of Egypt,
    to drink the waters of the Nile?
Or what are you doing in the way of Assyria,
    to drink the waters of the River?
¹⁹ Your own wickedness will correct you,
    and your backslidings will reprove you.
Know therefore and see
    that it is an evil thing and bitter for you

to have forsaken the Lord your God,
and the fear of Me is not in you,
says the Lord God of Hosts.

20 For long ago I have broken your yoke
and burst your bonds;
and you said, "I will not serve."
For upon every high hill
and under every green tree
you wander, playing the harlot.
21 Yet I had planted you a noble vine,
a wholly faithful seed.
How then have you turned
into the degenerate plant of a strange vine to Me?
22 For though you wash yourself with lye,
and take much soap,
yet your iniquity is marked before Me,
says the Lord God.
23 How can you say, "I am not polluted,
I have not gone after the Baals"?
See your way in the valley.
Know what you have done.
You are a swift young camel
entangling her ways,
24 a wild donkey used to the wilderness
that sniffs the wind in her passion.
In the time of her heat, who can turn her away?
All those who seek her will not weary themselves;
in her month they shall find her.
25 Withhold your foot from being unshod
and your throat from thirst.
But you said, "There is no hope. No!
For I have loved strangers,
and after them I will go."

26 As the thief is ashamed when he is found,
so is the house of Israel ashamed.
They, their kings, their officials,
and their priests, and their prophets
27 say to a tree, "You are my father,"
And to a stone, "You gave birth to me."
For they have turned their back to Me,
and not their face.
But in the time of their trouble they will say,
"Arise and save us."
28 But where are your gods that you have made for yourself?
Let them arise, if they can save you
in the time of your trouble;
for according to the number of your cities
are your gods, O Judah.

29 Why will you plead with Me?
You all have transgressed against Me,
says the Lord.
30 In vain I have smitten your children;
they received no correction.
Your own sword has devoured your prophets
like a destroying lion.

31 O generation, consider the word of the Lord:

Have I been a wilderness to Israel?
A land of darkness?
Why do My people say, "We *are free* to roam.
We will come no more to You"?
32 Can a virgin forget her ornaments,
or a bride her attire?
Yet My people have forgotten Me
for days without number.
33 You prepare your way very well to seek love.
Therefore you have also taught the wicked women
your ways.

34 Also in your skirts is found
the blood of the souls of the innocent poor.
I have not found it by breaking in,
but in spite of all these things.
35 Yet you say, "Because I am innocent,
surely His anger shall turn away from me."
Now I will plead with you,
because you say, "I have not sinned."
36 Why do you go about so much
to change your way?
You also shall be ashamed of Egypt,
as you were ashamed of Assyria.
37 Indeed, you shall go forth from him
with your hands upon your head;
for the Lord has rejected those in whom you trust,
and you shall not prosper in them.

Unfaithful Israel

3 If a man divorces his wife,
and she goes from him and becomes another man's,
shall he return to her again?
Shall not that land be greatly polluted?
But you have played the harlot with many lovers;
yet return again to Me,
says the Lord.
2 Lift up your eyes to the high places,
and see! Where have you not been ravished?
In the roads you have sat for them
as the Arabian in the wilderness.
And you have polluted the land
with your harlotry and with your wickedness.
3 Therefore the showers have been withheld,
and there has been no latter rain.
And you had a harlot's forehead;
you refused to be ashamed.
4 Shall you not from this time cry to Me,
"My Father, You are the guide of my youth?
5 Shall He reserve His anger forever?
Shall He keep it to the end?"
Indeed, you have spoken
and done evil things as you could.

A Call to Repentance

6 The Lord said also to me in the days of Josiah the king: Have you seen that which backsliding Israel has done? She has gone up on every high mountain and under every green tree, and there has played the harlot. 7 I said after she had done all these things, "Turn to Me." But she did not return. And her treacherous sister Judah saw it. 8 I saw that for all the adulteries of backsliding Israel, I had put her away and given her a bill of divorce. Yet her treacherous sister Judah did not fear, but went and played the harlot also. 9 Through the lightness of her harlotry she defiled the land and committed adultery with stones and with trees. 10 Yet for all this, her treacherous sister Judah has not turned to Me with her whole heart, but feignedly, says the Lord.

God Invites Repentance

11 The Lord said to me: Backsliding Israel has proved herself more righteous than treacherous Judah. 12 Go and proclaim these words toward the north, and say:

Return, backsliding Israel, says the Lord,
and I will not cause My anger to fall on you.
For I am merciful, says the Lord,
and I will not keep anger forever.
13 Only acknowledge your iniquity,
that you have transgressed against the Lord
your God
and have scattered your ways to the strangers
under every green tree,
and you have not obeyed My voice,
says the Lord.

¹⁴ Return, O backsliding sons, says the Lord. For I am married to you. And I will take you, one from a city and two from a family, and I will bring you to Zion. ¹⁵ And I will give you shepherds according to My heart, who shall feed you with knowledge and understanding. ¹⁶ It shall come to pass when you are multiplied and increased in the land in those days, says the Lord, they will say no more, "The ark of the covenant of the Lord." And it will not come to mind, nor will they remember it, nor will they call for it, nor will it be made any more. ¹⁷ At that time they will call Jerusalem, the Throne of the Lord, and all the nations will be gathered to it, to Jerusalem, for the name of the Lord; nor will they walk any more after the stubbornness of their evil hearts. ¹⁸ In those days the house of Judah will walk with the house of Israel, and they will come together out of the land of the north to the land that I have given to your fathers for an inheritance.

¹⁹ But I said:

How can I put you among My sons
　　and give you a pleasant land,
　　the most beautiful heritage of the nations?
And I said: You shall call Me, My Father,
　　and shall not turn away from Me.
²⁰ Surely as a wife treacherously departs from her husband,
　　so you have dealt treacherously with Me, O house of Israel,
says the Lord.

²¹ A voice was heard upon the high places,
　　the weeping and the supplications of the sons of Israel,
because they have perverted their way,
　　they have forgotten the Lord their God.

²² Return, O backsliding sons,
　　and I will heal your backslidings.

"We come to You;
　　for You are the Lord our God.
²³ Truly in vain is salvation hoped for from the hills,
　　and from the multitude of mountains.
Truly, in the Lord our God
　　is the salvation of Israel.
²⁴ For shame has devoured the labor
　　of our fathers from our youth,
their flocks and their herds,
　　their sons and their daughters.
²⁵ We lie down in our shame,
　　and our humiliation covers us.
For we have sinned against the Lord our God,
　　we and our fathers,
from our youth even to this day,
　　and have not obeyed the voice of the Lord our God."

Judah Threatened With Invasion

4 If you will return, O Israel,
　　says the Lord,
　　return to Me.
And if you will put away your abominations out of My sight,
　　then you shall not be moved.
² You shall swear, "As the Lord lives,"
　　in truth, in justice, and in righteousness;
then the nations shall bless themselves in Him,
　　and in Him they shall glory.

³ For thus says the Lord to the men of Judah and Jerusalem:

Break up your fallow ground,
　　and do not sow among thorns.
⁴ Circumcise yourselves to the Lord,
　　and take away the foreskins of your heart,
　　you men of Judah and inhabitants of Jerusalem,
lest My fury come forth like fire,
　　and burn so that no one can quench it,
　　because of the evil of your deeds.

⁵ Declare in Judah and publish in Jerusalem, and say:
　　Blow the trumpet in the land.
Cry aloud and say,
　　"Assemble yourselves,
　　and let us go into the fortified cities."
⁶ Set up the standard toward Zion.
　　Seek refuge, do not delay.
For I will bring disaster from the north,
　　and a great destruction.

⁷ The lion has come up from his thicket,
　　and the destroyer of the nations is on his way.
He has gone forth from his place
　　to make your land desolate.
And your cities shall be laid waste
　　without an inhabitant.
⁸ For this gird yourself with sackcloth,
　　lament and howl.
For the fierce anger of the Lord
　　is not turned back from us.

⁹ It shall come to pass in that day, says the Lord,
　　that the heart of the king will fail and the heart of
　　　　the officials;
and the priests will be astonished
　　and the prophets will wonder.

¹⁰ Then I said, "Ah, Lord God! Surely You have greatly deceived this people and Jerusalem, saying, 'You shall have peace,' whereas the sword reaches the throat."

¹¹ At that time it will be said to this people and to Jerusalem: A dry wind of the high places in the wilderness toward the daughter of My people, not to fan or to cleanse, ¹² even a full wind from those places, will come to Me. Now also I will pronounce judgments against them.

¹³ Look! He shall come up as clouds,
　　and his chariots shall be as a whirlwind.
His horses are swifter than eagles.
　　Woe to us, for we are ruined!
¹⁴ O Jerusalem, wash your heart from wickedness, that you may
　　be saved.
How long shall your evil thoughts lodge within you?
¹⁵ For a voice declares from Dan,
　　and publishes wickedness from Mount Ephraim:
¹⁶ "Report it to the nations, now!"
　　Indeed, proclaim against Jerusalem:
"Besiegers come from a far country,
　　and lift their voices against the cities of Judah.
¹⁷ As watchmen of a field, they are against her
　　all around,
　　because she has been rebellious against Me,
says the Lord.
¹⁸ Your way and your deeds
　　have procured these things to you.
This is your wickedness.
　　How bitter it is!
　　How it touches your heart!"

Sorrow for a Doomed Nation

¹⁹ My soul, my soul!
　　I am pained at my very heart.
My heart makes a noise in me.
　　I cannot hold my peace,
because you have heard, O my soul,
　　the sound of the trumpet, the alarm of war.
²⁰ Destruction upon destruction is proclaimed,
　　for the whole land is devastated.
Suddenly are my tents devastated,
　　and my curtains in a moment.
²¹ How long shall I see the standard
　　and hear the sound of the trumpet?

22 "For My people are foolish,
 they have not known Me.
They are foolish children,
 and they have no understanding.
They are wise to do evil,
 but to do good they have no knowledge."

23 I looked on the earth,
 and it was without form and void.
And to the heavens,
 and they had no light.
24 I looked on the mountains,
 and they trembled,
 and all the hills moved to and fro.
25 I looked, and there was no man,
 and all the birds of the heavens had fled.
26 I looked, and the fruitful place was a wilderness,
 and all the cities were broken down
 at the presence of the Lord, and by His fierce anger.

27 For thus says the Lord:

The whole land shall be desolate.
 Yet I will not make a full end.
28 For this the earth shall mourn,
 and the heavens above be black,
because I have spoken it, I have purposed it,
 and will not relent, nor will I turn back from it.

29 The whole city shall flee
 for the noise of the horsemen and bowmen.
They shall go into thickets
 and climb up upon the rocks.
Every city shall be forsaken,
 and not a man dwell in it.

30 When you are devastated, what will you do?
 Though you clothe yourself with crimson,
 though you deck yourself with ornaments of gold,
though you enlarge your eyes with paint,
 in vain you will make yourself fair.
Your lovers will despise you;
 they will seek your life.

31 For I have heard a voice as of a woman in labor,
 and the anguish as of her who brings forth her
  first child,
the voice of the daughter of Zion,
 that bewails herself, that spreads her hands, saying,
"Ah, woe is me,
 for my soul is wearied because of murderers."

The Justice of God's Judgment

5 Run to and fro through the streets of Jerusalem,
 see now and know;
 seek in the open places
if you can find a man,
 if there is any who executes justice, who seeks the truth,
 that I may pardon her.
2 Though they say, "The Lord lives,"
 surely they swear falsely.

3 O Lord, are not Your eyes upon the truth?
 You have stricken them, but they have not grieved.
 You have consumed them, but they have refused to
  receive correction.
They have made their faces harder than a rock;
 they have refused to return.
4 Therefore I said, "Surely these are the poor.
 They are foolish;
for they know not the way of the Lord
 or the judgment of their God.

5 I will go to the great men
 and will speak to them,
for they have known the way of the Lord
 and the judgment of their God."
But these have altogether broken the yoke
 and burst the bonds.
6 Therefore a lion out of the forest will slay them,
 and a wolf from the deserts will destroy them;
a leopard will watch over their cities.
 Everyone who goes out from there will be torn
  in pieces,
because their transgressions are many
 and their backslidings have increased.

7 How shall I pardon you for this?
 Your children have forsaken Me
 and sworn by those who are not gods.
When I had fed them to the full,
 then they committed adultery
 and assembled themselves by troops in the harlots' houses.
8 They were as fed horses in the morning;
 everyone neighed after his neighbor's wife.
9 Shall I not punish for these things? says the Lord,
 and shall not My soul be avenged on such a nation
  as this?

10 Go up upon her walls and destroy,
 but make not a full end.
Take away her battlements.
 For they are not the Lord's.
11 For the house of Israel and the house of Judah
 have dealt very treacherously against Me,
 says the Lord.

12 They have lied about the Lord,
 and said, "Not He.
Neither shall evil come upon us,
 nor shall we see sword or famine."
13 And the prophets shall become wind,
 and the word is not in them.
 Thus it shall be done to them!

14 Therefore thus says the Lord God of Hosts:

Because you speak this word,
 indeed I will make My words in your mouth fire
 and this people wood, and it shall devour them.
15 Truly, I will bring a nation upon you from far,
 O house of Israel, says the Lord.
It is a mighty nation, it is an ancient nation,
 a nation whose language you do not know,
 nor do you understand what they say.
16 Their quiver is as an open sepulcher,
 they all are mighty men.
17 They will eat up your harvest and your bread
 which your sons and your daughters should eat.
They will eat up your flocks and your herds;
 they will eat up your vines and your fig trees;
they will impoverish your fenced cities,
 in which you trusted, with the sword.

18 Nevertheless in those days, says the Lord, I will not make a full end of you. 19 It shall come to pass when they say, "Why does the Lord our God do all these things to us?" then you shall answer them, "As you have forsaken Me and served strange gods in your land, so you will serve strangers in a land that is not yours."

20 Declare this in the house of Jacob
 and publish it in Judah, saying:
21 Hear this now, O foolish people and without understanding,
 who have eyes but do not see,
 who have ears but do not hear.

22 Do you not fear Me? says the Lord.
  Will you not tremble at My presence?
For I have placed the sand for the boundary of the sea
  by a perpetual decree so that it cannot pass over it.
And though the waves toss themselves, yet they cannot prevail;
  though they roar, yet they cannot pass over it.
23 But this people has a revolting and a rebellious heart;
  they have revolted and gone aside.
24 They do not say in their heart,
  "Let us now fear the Lord our God,
who gives rain, both the former and the latter, in its season.
He reserves for us the appointed weeks of the harvest."
25 Your iniquities have turned away these things,
  and your sins have withheld good things from you.

26 For among My people are found wicked men.
  They lie in wait, as he who sets snares;
  they set a trap, they catch men.
27 As a cage is full of birds,
  so are their houses full of deceit.
Therefore they have become great and rich.
28   They are fat, they are sleek.
Indeed, they excel in deeds of wickedness.
  They do not judge the cause of the fatherless,
so that they may prosper;
  and the right of the needy they do not defend.
29 Shall I not punish them for these things?
  says the Lord.
Shall not My soul be avenged
  on such a nation as this?

30 An appalling and horrible thing
  has been committed in the land.
31 The prophets prophesy falsely,
  and the priests rule by their own authority;
and My people love to have it so.
  Yet what will you do in the end?

Siege of Jerusalem

6 O sons of Benjamin, gather yourselves
  to flee from the midst of Jerusalem,
and blow the trumpet in Tekoa,
  and set up a sign of fire in Beth Hakkerem;
for disaster appears out of the north,
  and great destruction.
2 I have likened the daughter of Zion
  to a comely and delicate woman.
3 The shepherds with their flocks will come to her.
  They will pitch their tents against her all around.
  They will pasture each in his place.

4 "Prepare war against her;
  arise, and let us go up at noon."
"Woe to us, for the day declines,
  for the shadows of the evening are stretched out."
5 "Arise, and let us go by night
  and let us destroy her palaces."

6 For thus says the Lord of Hosts:

Hew down trees
  and build a mound against Jerusalem.
This is the city to be punished.
  She is full of oppression in her midst.
7 As a fountain casts out her waters,
  so she casts out her wickedness.
Violence and devastation are heard in her;
  before Me continually are grief and wounds.
8 Be instructed, O Jerusalem,
  lest My soul depart from you;
lest I make you desolate,
  a land not inhabited.

9 Thus says the Lord of Hosts:

They will thoroughly glean
  the remnant of Israel as a vine.
Turn back your hand
  as a grape gatherer into the baskets.

10 To whom shall I speak and give warning
  that they may hear?
See, their ears are closed,
  and they cannot listen.
Indeed, the word of the Lord is a reproach to them;
  they have no delight in it.
11 Therefore I am full of the fury of the Lord;
  I am weary with holding in.

I will pour it out upon the children in the street
  and upon the assembly of young men together;
for even the husband with the wife shall be taken,
  the aged with him who is full of days.
12 Their houses shall be turned to others,
  with their fields and wives together;
for I will stretch out My hand
  upon the inhabitants of the land,
  says the Lord.
13 For from the least of them even to the greatest of them,
  everyone is given to covetousness.
And from the prophet even to the priest,
  everyone deals falsely.
14 They have healed also the brokenness
  of the daughter of My people superficially,
saying, "Peace, peace,"
  when there is no peace.
15 Were they ashamed when they had committed abomination?
  They were not at all ashamed,
  nor could they blush.
Therefore they shall fall among those who fall;
  at the time that I punish them they shall be
      cast down,
  says the Lord.

16 Thus says the Lord:

Stand in the ways and see,
  and ask for the old paths
where the good way is and walk in it,
  and you shall find rest for your souls.
But they said, "We will not walk in it."
17 Also I set watchmen over you, saying,
  "Listen to the sound of the trumpet."
But they said, "We will not listen."
18 Therefore hear, O nations,
  and know, O congregation,
  what is among them.
19 Hear, O earth.
  I will bring calamity on this people,
  even the fruit of their thoughts,
because they have not listened to My words,
  nor to My law, but rejected it.
20 To what purpose does incense from Sheba come to Me,
  and the sweet cane from a far country?
Your burnt offerings are not acceptable,
  nor are your sacrifices sweet to Me.

21 Therefore thus says the Lord:

See, I will lay stumbling blocks before this people,
  and the fathers and the sons together will fall
      upon them.
  The neighbor and his friend will perish.

22 Thus says the Lord:

See, a people comes
    from the north country,
and a great nation will be raised
    from the remote parts of the earth.
23 They will lay hold on bow and spear;
    they are cruel and have no mercy.
Their voice roars like the sea,
    and they ride upon horses,
set in array as men for war
    against you, O daughter of Zion.

24 "We have heard the report of it;
    our hands grow feeble.
Anguish has taken hold of us,
    and pain as of a woman in labor.
25 Do not go out into the field,
    nor walk on the road.
For the sword of the enemy
    and terror is on every side."
26 O daughter of my people, gird yourself with sackcloth
    and wallow in ashes.
Mourn as for an only son,
    a most bitter lamentation;
for the destroyer
    shall suddenly come upon us.

27 I have set you as an assayer
    and fortress among My people
that you may know
    and try their way.
28 They all are stubborn rebels
    walking about practicing slander.
They are bronze and iron;
    they all are corrupters.
29 The bellows blow fiercely,
    the lead is consumed by the fire;
the founder melts in vain,
    for the wicked are not plucked away.
30 Men will call them rejected silver,
    because the LORD has rejected them.

False Trust in the Temple

7 The word that came to Jeremiah from the LORD, saying: 2 Stand in the gate of the house of the LORD and proclaim there this word: Hear the word of the LORD, all you of Judah, who enter at these gates to worship the LORD. 3 Thus says the LORD of Hosts, the God of Israel: Amend your ways and your deeds, and I will cause you to dwell in this place. 4 Do not trust in lying words, saying, "The temple of the LORD, the temple of the LORD, the temple of the LORD." 5 For if you thoroughly amend your ways and your deeds, if you thoroughly execute justice between a man and his neighbor, 6 if you do not oppress the stranger, the fatherless, and the widow, and do not shed innocent blood in this place, or walk after other gods to your harm, 7 then I will cause you to dwell in this place, in the land that I gave to your fathers, forever and ever. 8 Indeed, you trust in lying words that cannot profit.

9 Shall you steal, murder, and commit adultery, and swear falsely, and burn incense to Baal, and walk after other gods whom you do not know, 10 and come and stand before Me in this house, which is called by My name, and say, "We are delivered," so that you may do all these abominations? 11 Has this house, which is called by My name, become a den of robbers in your eyes? Certainly, even I have seen it, says the LORD.

12 But go now to My place which was in Shiloh, where I set My name at the first, and see what I did to it for the wickedness of My people Israel. 13 And now, because you have done all these works, says the LORD, and I spoke to you, rising up early and speaking, but you did not hear, and I called you, but you did not answer, 14 therefore I will do to this house, which is called by My name, in which you trust, and to the place which I gave to you and to your fathers, as I have done to Shiloh. 15 I will cast you out of My sight as I have cast out all your brothers, even the whole seed of Ephraim.

16 As for you, do not pray for this people, nor lift up a cry nor prayer for them, nor make intercession to Me, for I will not hear you. 17 Do you not see what they do in the cities of Judah and in the streets of Jerusalem? 18 The children gather wood, and the fathers kindle the fire, and the women knead their dough, to make cakes to the queen of heaven, and to pour out drink offerings to other gods, that they may provoke Me to anger. 19 Do they provoke Me to anger? says the LORD. Do they not provoke themselves to the shame of their own faces?

20 Therefore thus says the Lord GOD: My anger and My fury will be poured out upon this place, upon man and upon beast, and upon the trees of the field, and upon the fruit of the ground; and it shall burn, and shall not be quenched.

21 Thus says the LORD of Hosts, the God of Israel: Add your burnt offerings to your sacrifices and eat flesh. 22 For I spoke not to your fathers, nor commanded them in the day that I brought them out of the land of Egypt, concerning burnt offerings or sacrifices. 23 But this thing I commanded them, saying, "Obey My voice, and I will be your God, and you shall be My people. And walk in all the ways that I have commanded you, that it may be well with you." 24 But they did not listen, nor incline their ear, but walked in the counsels and in the imagination of their evil heart, and went backward and not forward. 25 Since the day that your fathers came out of the land of Egypt to this day, I have even sent to you all My servants the prophets, daily rising up early and sending them. 26 Yet they did not listen to Me, nor incline their ear, but hardened their neck. They did worse than their fathers.

27 Therefore you will speak all these words to them. But they will not listen to you. You will also call to them, but they will not answer you. 28 You shall say to them: This is a nation that does not obey the voice of the LORD their God, nor receive correction. Truth has perished, and has been cut off from their mouth.

29 Cut off your hair, O Jerusalem, and cast it away, and take up a lamentation on high places; for the LORD has rejected and forsaken the generation of His wrath.

30 For the sons of Judah have done evil in My sight, says the LORD. They have set their abominations in the house which is called by My name, to pollute it. 31 They have built the high places of Topheth, which is in the Valley of Ben Hinnom, to burn their sons and their daughters in the fire, which I did not command them, nor did it come into My heart. 32 Therefore, truly the days are coming, says the LORD, that it will no more be called Topheth, nor the Valley of Ben Hinnom, but the Valley of Slaughter; for they will bury in Topheth because there is no other place. 33 The corpses of this people shall be food for the fowl of the heaven and for the beasts of the earth; and no one will frighten them away. 34 Then I will cause to cease from the cities of Judah and from the streets of Jerusalem the voice of laughter and the voice of gladness, the voice of the bridegroom and the voice of the bride; for the land shall become desolate.

8 At that time, says the LORD, they will bring out the bones of the kings of Judah, and the bones of his officials, and the bones of the priests, and the bones of the prophets, and the bones of the inhabitants of Jerusalem out of their graves. 2 And they will spread them before the sun and the moon and all the host of heaven, whom they have loved and whom they have served, and after whom they have walked and whom they have sought, and whom they have worshipped. They will not be gathered, nor be buried. They will be as dung upon the face of the earth. 3 Death will be chosen rather than life by all the rest of those who remain of this evil family, which remains in all the places wherever I have driven them, says the LORD of Hosts.

Sin and Judgment

4 Moreover you shall say to them, Thus says the LORD:

Do men fall and not arise?
    Do they turn away and not repent?
5 Why then is this people of Jerusalem
    turned away by a perpetual backsliding?
They hold fast to deceit;
    they refuse to return.
6 I listened and heard,
    but they did not speak what is right.

No man repented of his wickedness,
    saying, "What have I done?"
Everyone turned to his course,
    as the horse rushes into the battle.
7 Indeed, the stork in the sky
    knows her appointed times.
And the turtledove and the crane and the swallow
    observe the time of their coming.
But My people do not know
    the judgment of the Lord.

8 How do you say, "We are wise,
    and the law of the Lord is with us"?
Certainly the lying pen of the scribes
    has made it into a lie.
9 The wise men are ashamed;
    they are dismayed and caught.
Indeed, they have rejected the word of the Lord,
    and what kind of wisdom do they have?
10 Therefore I will give their wives to others,
    and their fields to those who shall inherit them.
For everyone from the least even to the greatest
    is given to covetousness;
from the prophet even to the priest
    everyone deals falsely.
11 For they have healed the brokenness
    of the daughter of My people superficially,
saying, "Peace, peace,"
    when there is no peace.
12 Were they ashamed when they had committed abomination?
    They were not at all ashamed,
    nor could they blush.
Therefore they will fall among those who fall;
    in the time of their punishment they will be
        cast down,
    says the Lord.

13 I will surely consume them,
    says the Lord.
There will be no grapes on the vine
nor figs on the fig tree,
    and the leaf shall fade;
and the things that I have given them
    will pass away from them.

14 Why do we sit still?
    Assemble yourselves,
and let us enter the fortified cities
    and let us perish there.
For the Lord our God has doomed us
    and given us water of gall to drink,
    because we have sinned against the Lord.
15 We looked for peace,
    but no good came;
and for a time of health,
    but there was trouble!
16 The snorting of his horses
    was heard from Dan;
the whole land trembled
    at the sound of the neighing of his strong ones.
For they have come and have devoured
    the land and all that is in it,
    the city, and those who dwell in it.

17 See, I will send serpents against you,
    adders, which will not be charmed,
    and they will bite you,
    declares the Lord.

Jeremiah Mourns for His People
18 My sorrow is beyond healing;
    my heart is faint within me.

19 Listen! The cry of the daughter of my people
    from a far country:
"Is not the Lord in Zion?
    Is not her king in her?"

"Why have they provoked Me to anger with their graven images,
    with foreign vanities?"

20 "The harvest is past,
    the summer is ended,
    and we are not saved."

21 For the brokenness of the daughter of my people am I broken;
    I mourn; dismay has taken hold of me.
22 Is there no balm in Gilead?
    Is there no physician there?
Why then has not the health
    of the daughter of my people recovered?

Failures of Judah
9 Oh, that my head were waters
    and my eyes a fountain of tears,
that I might weep day and night
    for the slain of the daughter of my people!
2 Oh, that I had in the wilderness
    a lodging place of wayfaring men,
that I might leave my people
    and go from them!
For they all are adulterers,
    an assembly of treacherous men.

3 They bend their tongues like their bow;
    lies and not truth prevail upon the land;
for they proceed from evil to evil,
    and they do not know Me,
    says the Lord.
4 Let everyone be on guard against his neighbor,
    and do not trust in any brother;
for every brother supplants,
    and every neighbor walks about with slanders.
5 Everyone deceives his neighbor
    and does not speak the truth.
They have taught their tongue to speak lies;
    they weary themselves in committing iniquity.
6 Your habitation is in the midst of deceit;
    through deceit they refuse to know Me,
    says the Lord.

7 Therefore thus says the Lord of Hosts:

Now, I will refine them and assay them;
    for what else shall I do
    for the daughter of My people?
8 Their tongue is a deadly arrow;
    it speaks deceit.
One speaks peaceably to his neighbor with his mouth,
    but in his heart he lies in wait.
9 Shall I not punish them for these things?
    says the Lord.
Shall not My soul be avenged
    on such a nation as this?

10 For the mountains I will take up a weeping and wailing,
    and for the habitations of the wilderness a lamentation,
because they are burned up so that no one can pass
        through them;
    nor can men hear the lowing of the cattle.
Both the fowl of the heavens and the beast have fled;
    they are gone.

11 I will make Jerusalem a heap of ruins
    and a den of jackals;

and I will make the cities of Judah desolate,
　　without an inhabitant.

12 Who is the wise man who may understand this? And who is he to whom the mouth of the LORD has spoken, that he may declare it? Why is the land ruined and burned up like a wilderness, so that no one passes through? 13 And the LORD said: Because they have forsaken My law which I set before them, and have not obeyed My voice, nor walked in it, 14 but have walked after the imagination of their own heart and after the Baals, which their fathers taught them. 15 Therefore thus says the LORD of Hosts, the God of Israel: I will feed them, even this people, with wormwood and give them water of gall to drink. 16 I will scatter them also among the nations, whom neither they nor their fathers have known. And I will send a sword after them until I have consumed them.

17 Thus says the LORD of Hosts:

Consider and call for the mourning women, that they may come;
　　and send for wailing women, that they may come.
18 And let them make haste
　　and take up a wailing for us,
that our eyes may run down with tears
　　and our eyelids gush out with waters.
19 For a voice of wailing is heard out of Zion,
　　"How devastated we are!
　　We are greatly humiliated,
because we have forsaken the land,
　　because our dwellings have cast us out."

20 Yet hear the word of the LORD, O you women,
　　and let your ear receive the word of His mouth;
and teach your daughters wailing,
　　and everyone her neighbor a lamentation.
21 "For death has come up into our windows;
　　and has entered our palaces,
to cut off the children from the streets,
　　and the young men from the squares."

22 Speak, Thus says the LORD:

"The carcasses of men shall fall
　　as dung upon the open field,
and as the sheaf after the harvester,
　　and no one shall gather them."

23 Thus says the LORD:

Let not the wise man glory in his wisdom,
　　and let not the mighty man glory in his might,
　　let not the rich man glory in his riches;
24 but let him who glories glory in this,
　　that he understands and knows Me,
that I am the LORD who exercises lovingkindness,
　　justice, and righteousness in the earth.
　　For in these things I delight,
　　says the LORD.

25 The days are surely coming, says the LORD, that I will punish all who are circumcised and yet uncircumcised— 26 Egypt, Judah, Edom, the children of Ammon, Moab, and all who dwell in the wilderness who clip the hair on their temples; for all these nations are uncircumcised, and all the house of Israel are uncircumcised of heart.

The True God and Idols
Jer 51:15–19

10 Hear the word which the LORD speaks to you, O house of Israel. 2 Thus says the LORD:

Do not learn the way of the nations;
　　do not be terrified at the signs of heaven,
　　although the nations are terrified at them.

3 For the customs of the people are vain;
　　for with the axe one cuts a tree out of the forest,
　　the work of the hands of the workman.
4 They deck it with silver and with gold;
　　they fasten it with nails and with hammers
　　so that it may not move.
5 They are as a scarecrow in a cucumber field,
　　but do not speak;
they must be carried,
　　because they cannot walk.
Do not be afraid of them,
　　for they cannot do evil,
　　nor can they do good.

6 There is no one like You, O LORD.
　　You are great,
　　and Your name is great in might.
7 Who would not fear You,
　　O King of the nations?
　　Indeed, it is Your due.
For among all the wise men of the nations,
　　and in all their kingdoms,
　　there is no one like You.

8 But they are altogether unthinking and foolish;
　　the tree is a doctrine of vanities.
9 Silver spread into plates is brought from Tarshish,
　　and gold from Uphaz,
the work of the workman and of the hands of the founder;
　　blue and purple are their clothing;
　　they all are the work of skilled men.
10 But the LORD is the true God;
　　He is the living God and an everlasting King.
At His wrath the earth trembles,
　　and the nations cannot endure His indignation.

11 Thus you shall say to them: The gods that have not made the heavens and the earth, even they shall perish from the earth and from under these heavens.

12 He has made the earth by His power.
　　He has established the world by His wisdom
　　and has stretched out the heavens by His discretion.
13 When He utters His voice, there is a multitude of waters in the
　　heavens,
　　and He causes the vapors to ascend from the remote parts
　　　　of the earth;
He makes lightning with rain,
　　and brings out the wind from His storehouses.

14 Every man is stupid, without knowledge;
　　every goldsmith is put to shame by an idol;
for his molded image is false,
　　and there is no breath in them.
15 They are vain and a work of mockery;
　　in the time of their punishment they shall perish.
16 The portion of Jacob is not like them,
　　for He is the Maker of all things,
and Israel is the rod of His inheritance.
　　The LORD of Hosts is His name.

The Exile Prophesied
17 Gather up your wares out of the land,
　　O inhabitant of the fortress.
18 For thus says the LORD:
　　I will sling out
　　the inhabitants of the land at this time,
and will distress them
　　that they may be found.

19 Woe is me because of my brokenness!
　　My wound is grievous.

But I said,
    "Truly this is an illness, and I must bear it."
20 My tabernacle is devastated,
    and all my cords are broken.
My sons have gone from me and are no more.
    There is no one to spread my tent anymore,
    and to set up my curtains.
21 For the shepherds have become unthinking
    and have not sought the LORD.
Therefore they have not prospered,
    and all their flocks are scattered.
22 Listen! The sound of the report has come,
    and a great commotion out of the north country,
to make the cities of Judah desolate
    and a den of jackals.

The Prayer of Jeremiah

23 O LORD, I know that the way of man is not in himself;
    it is not in man who walks to direct his steps.
24 O LORD, correct me, but with justice,
    not in Your anger,
    lest You bring me to nothing.
25 Pour out Your fury upon the nations
    that do not know You
    and upon the families that do not call on Your name;
for they have eaten up Jacob
    and devoured him, and consumed him,
    and have made his habitation desolate.

The Broken Covenant

11 The word that came to Jeremiah from the LORD, saying: 2 Hear the words of this covenant, and speak to the men of Judah and to the inhabitants of Jerusalem. 3 And say you to them, Thus says the LORD God of Israel: Cursed is the man who does not obey the words of this covenant, 4 which I commanded your fathers in the day that I brought them out of the land of Egypt, from the iron furnace, saying, Obey My voice, and do according to all which I command you. So you shall be My people, and I will be your God, 5 that I may perform the oath which I have sworn to your fathers, to give them a land flowing with milk and honey, as it is this day.

Then I answered and said, "So be it, O LORD."

6 Then the LORD said to me: Proclaim all these words in the cities of Judah and in the streets of Jerusalem: saying, Hear the words of this covenant, and do them. 7 For I earnestly warned your fathers in the day that I brought them up out of the land of Egypt, even to this day, rising early and warning, saying, Obey My voice. 8 Yet they did not obey or incline their ear, but everyone walked in the imagination of their evil heart. Therefore I will bring upon them all the words of this covenant, which I commanded them to do, but which they did not do.

9 The LORD said to me: A conspiracy has been found among the men of Judah and among the inhabitants of Jerusalem. 10 They have turned back to the iniquities of their forefathers who refused to hear My words. And they have gone after other gods to serve them. The house of Israel and the house of Judah have broken My covenant which I made with their fathers. 11 Therefore thus says the LORD, Surely, I will bring calamity upon them which they will not be able to escape. And though they cry to Me, I will not listen to them. 12 Then the cities of Judah and inhabitants of Jerusalem will go and cry to the gods to whom they offer incense. But they will not save them at all in the time of their trouble. 13 For according to the number of your cities are your gods, O Judah. And according to the number of the streets of Jerusalem you have set up altars to that shameful thing, even altars to burn incense to Baal.

14 Therefore do not pray for this people, nor lift up a cry or prayer for them. For I will not hear them in the time that they cry to Me because of their trouble.

15 What right has My beloved in My house,
    seeing that she has done many lewd deeds?
    Can the sacrificial meat take away from you your disaster,
    so that you can rejoice while doing evil?

16 The LORD called your name,
    "A green olive tree, fair in fruit and form."
With the noise of a great tumult
    He has kindled fire upon it,
    and its branches are broken.

17 For the LORD of Hosts, who planted you, has pronounced disaster against you, because of the evil of the house of Israel and of the house of Judah, which they have done against themselves to provoke Me to anger in offering incense to Baal.

Jeremiah's Life Threatened

18 The LORD has made it known to me and I knew it; then You showed me their deeds. 19 But I was like a gentle lamb that is brought to the slaughter, and I did not know that they had devised plots against me, saying,

"Let us destroy the tree with the fruit,
    and let us cut him off from the land of the living
    so that his name may be remembered no more."
20 But, O LORD of Hosts, who judges righteously,
    who tries the feelings and the heart,
let me see Your vengeance on them,
    for to You I have revealed my cause.

21 Therefore thus says the LORD of the men of Anathoth who seek your life, saying, "Do not prophesy in the name of the LORD so that you not die by our hand." 22 Therefore thus says the LORD of Hosts: I will punish them. The young men shall die by the sword. Their sons and their daughters shall die by famine. 23 And there shall be no remnant of them, for I will bring calamity upon the men of Anathoth, even the year of their punishment.

Jeremiah's Plea

12 Righteous are You, O LORD,
    that I plead with You.
Indeed, let me talk with You about matters of justice.
    Why does the way of the wicked prosper?
    Why are all those happy who deal very treacherously?
2 You have planted them; indeed, they have taken root;
    they grow; indeed, they bring forth fruit.
You are near in their mouth,
    but far from their mind.
3 But You, O LORD, know me;
    You have seen me and tested my heart toward You.
Pull them out like sheep for the slaughter,
    and prepare them for the day of slaughter.
4 How long shall the land mourn
    and the herbs of every field wither?
For the wickedness of those who dwell in it,
    the beasts and the birds have been snatched away,
because they said,
    "He will not see our latter end."

God Answers Jeremiah

5 If you have run with the footmen,
    and they have wearied you,
    then how can you contend with horses?
And if in the land of peace in which you trusted, they wearied you,
    then how will you do in the thicket of the Jordan?
6 For even your brothers and the household of your father,
    even they have dealt treacherously with you.
    Indeed, they have cried aloud after you.
Do not believe them
    though they speak fair words to you.

7 I have forsaken My house,
    I have abandoned My heritage;
I have given the dearly beloved of My soul
    into the hand of her enemies.
8 My heritage is to Me
    as a lion in the forest.

She cries out against Me;
　　therefore I have hated her.
9 My heritage is to Me
　　as a speckled vulture;
　　the vultures all around are against her.
Come, assemble all the beasts of the field,
　　bring them to devour.
10 Many shepherds have destroyed My vineyard;
　　they have trodden My portion under foot;
　　they have made My pleasant portion
　　a desolate wilderness.
11 They have made it desolate,
　　and being desolate, it mourns to Me.
The whole land has been made desolate,
　　because no man lays it to heart.
12 The destroyers have come
　　upon all high places through the wilderness,
for the sword of the LORD shall devour
　　from the one end of the land even to the other end of the land.
No one shall have peace.
13 They have sown wheat, but reap thorns;
　　they have strained themselves, but shall not profit.
And they shall be ashamed of your harvest
　　because of the fierce anger of the LORD.

14 Thus says the LORD: Against all My evil neighbors who touch the inheritance which I have caused My people Israel to inherit, I will pluck them out of their land and pluck out the house of Judah from among them. 15 It shall come to pass that after I have plucked them out, I will again have compassion on them, and will bring them back, every man to his heritage, and every man to his land. 16 It shall come to pass if they will diligently learn the ways of My people, to swear by My name, "As the LORD lives," as they taught My people to swear by Baal, then they shall be built up in the midst of My people. 17 But if they will not obey, I will utterly pluck up and destroy that nation, says the LORD.

A Linen Sash

13 Thus says the LORD to me, "Go and buy yourself a linen waistband and put it upon your loins, and do not put it in water." 2 So I bought a waistband according to the word of the LORD and put it on my loins.

3 The word of the LORD came to me the second time, saying, 4 "Take the waistband that you have, which is upon your loins, and arise, go to the Euphrates and hide it there in a hole of the rock." 5 So I went and hid it by the Euphrates, as the LORD had commanded me.

6 After many days the LORD said to me, "Arise, go to the Euphrates and take the waistband from there, which I commanded you to hide there." 7 Then I went to the Euphrates, and dug, and took the waistband from the place where I had hidden it. But the waistband was destroyed. It was profitable for nothing.

8 Then the word of the LORD came to me: 9 Thus says the LORD: After this manner I will destroy the pride of Judah and the great pride of Jerusalem. 10 This evil people, who refuse to hear My words, who walk in the imagination of their hearts, and walk after other gods, to serve them, and to worship them, shall be even as this waistband which is good for nothing. 11 For as the waistband cleaves to the loins of a man, so I have caused the whole house of Israel and the whole house of Judah to cleave to Me, says the LORD, so that they might be to Me a people for renown, and for a praise, and for a glory; but they would not listen.

The Metaphor of Wine Bottles

12 Therefore you shall speak to them this word: Thus says the LORD God of Israel: Every bottle shall be filled with wine. And when they say to you, "Do we not certainly know that every bottle should be filled with wine?" 13 then you shall say to them: Thus says the LORD: I will fill all the inhabitants of this land—even the kings that sit on the throne of David, and the priests, and the prophets, and all the inhabitants of Jerusalem—with drunkenness. 14 I will dash them against one another, even the fathers and the sons together, says the LORD. I will not show pity nor spare nor have mercy, but will destroy them.

Exile Threatened

15 Hear and give heed;
　　do not be proud,
　　for the LORD has spoken.
16 Give glory to the LORD your God,
　　before He causes darkness
and before your feet stumble
　　on the dark mountains,
and while you look for light,
　　He turns it into the shadow of death
　　and makes it gross darkness.
17 But if you will not listen to it,
　　my soul will weep in secret places
　　for your pride;
and my eyes will weep sorely
　　and run down with tears,
because the flock of the LORD is carried away captive.

18 Say to the king and to the queen mother:
　　"Humble yourselves, sit down,
for your beautiful crown
　　shall come down from your head."
19 The cities of the Negev will be shut up,
　　and no one will open them;
all Judah will be carried away into captivity;
　　it will be wholly carried away captive.

20 Lift up your eyes and see
　　those who come from the north.
Where is the flock that was given to you,
　　your beautiful flock?
21 What will you say when He appoints over you
　　those you yourself had taught to be companions
　　　　to you?
Shall not sorrows take hold of you,
　　as a woman in labor?
22 And if you say in your heart,
　　"Why have these things come upon me?"
for the greatness of your iniquity
　　your skirts have been removed
　　and your heels made bare.
23 Can the Ethiopian change his skin
　　or the leopard his spots?
Then you also can do good,
　　who are accustomed to doing evil.

24 Therefore I will scatter them as the stubble
　　that passes away by the wind of the wilderness.
25 This is your lot,
　　the portion of your measures from Me,
　　says the LORD,
because you have forgotten Me
　　and trusted in falsehood.
26 Therefore I Myself have uncovered your skirts over your face
　　so that your shame may appear.
27 I have seen your adulteries and your *lustful* neighings,
　　the lewdness of your harlotry,
and your abominations
　　on the hills in the fields.
Woe to you, O Jerusalem!
　　How long will you remain unclean?

Drought, Famine, and Sword

14 The word of the LORD which came to Jeremiah concerning the drought:

2 Judah mourns,
　　and the gates languish;
they sit on the ground while mourning,
　　and the cry of Jerusalem has gone up.
3 Their nobles have sent their servants for water;
　　they came to the cisterns and found no water.

They returned with their vessels empty;
    they were ashamed and humiliated,
    and covered their heads.
4 Because the ground is chapped,
    for there was no rain in the earth,
    the plowmen were ashamed;
    they have covered their heads.
5 Indeed, the hind also calved in the field
    and abandoned *her young*
    because there was no grass.
6 The wild donkeys stand in the high places;
    they pant for air like jackals;
    their eyes fail
    because there is no grass.

7 O Lord, though our iniquities testify against us,
    do it for Your name's sake.
Indeed, our backslidings are many;
    we have sinned against You.
8 O the Hope of Israel,
    its Savior in time of trouble,
why should You be as a stranger in the land,
    and as a wayfaring man who turns aside to pitch his tent
        for a night?
9 Why should You be as a man dismayed,
    as a mighty man who cannot save?
Yet You, O Lord, are in our midst,
    and we are called by Your name.
    Do not forsake us!

10 Thus says the Lord to this people:

Even so they have loved to wander;
    they have not restrained their feet.
Therefore, the Lord does not accept them;
    He will now remember their iniquity
    and punish their sins.

11 Then the Lord said to me: Do not pray for the good of this people. 12 When they fast, I will not hear their cry. And when they offer a burnt offering and an oblation, I will not accept them. But I will consume them by the sword, and by the famine, and by the pestilence.

False Prophets

13 Yet I said, "Ah, Lord God! Here the prophets say to them, 'You shall not see the sword nor shall you have famine, but I will give you assured peace in this place.' "

14 Then the Lord said to me: The prophets prophesy lies in My name. I have not sent them nor have I commanded them nor have I spoken to them. They prophesy to you a false vision and divination, and emptiness, and the deceit of their heart. 15 Therefore thus says the Lord concerning the prophets who prophesy in My name though I did not send them, yet they say, "Sword and famine will not be in this land." By sword and famine those prophets will be consumed. 16 The people to whom they prophesy will be cast out in the streets of Jerusalem because of the famine and the sword. And they will have no one to bury them, not them, nor their wives, nor their sons, nor their daughters. For I will pour out their wickedness upon them.

17 Therefore you will say this word to them:

Let my eyes run down with tears
    night and day, and let them not cease;
for the virgin daughter of my people
    has been broken with a great blow,
    with a very infected wound.
18 If I go out into the field,
    I see those slain with the sword!
And if I enter the city,
    I see those who are sick with famine!
Indeed, both the prophet and the priest
    go about into a land that they do not know.

The People Ask for Mercy

19 Have You utterly rejected Judah?
    Has Your soul loathed Zion?
Why have You stricken us
    so that there is no healing for us?
We looked for peace,
    but there was nothing good;
    and for the time of healing,
    but there is trouble!
20 We acknowledge, O Lord, our wickedness
    and the iniquity of our fathers,
    for we have sinned against You.
21 Do not abhor us. For Your name's sake,
    do not disgrace Your glorious throne.
Remember and do not break
    Your covenant with us.
22 Are there any among the idols of the nations that can
        cause rain?
    Or can the heavens give showers?
Is it not You, O Lord our God?
    Therefore, we will wait upon You,
    for You have done all these things.

The Lord Will Not Relent

15 Then the Lord said to me: Even though Moses and Samuel were to stand before Me, yet My heart would not be with this people. Cast them out of My sight and let them go! 2 It shall come to pass if they say to you, "Where should we go?" then you shall tell them: Thus says the Lord:

Those destined for death, to death;
    and those destined for the sword, to the sword;
    and those destined for the famine, to the famine;
    and those destined for the captivity, to the captivity.

3 I will appoint over them four kinds of disaster, says the Lord: the sword to slay, the dogs to tear, the birds of the heaven, the beasts of the earth to devour and destroy. 4 I will cause them to be removed into all kingdoms of the earth, because of Manasseh the son of Hezekiah king of Judah, for that which he did in Jerusalem.

5 For who shall have pity on you, O Jerusalem?
    Or who shall bemoan you?
    Or who shall go aside to ask how you are doing?
6 You who have forsaken Me, says the Lord,
    you keep going backward.
Therefore I will stretch out My hand against you and destroy you.
    I am weary of relenting!
7 I will winnow them with a winnowing fork
    in the gates of the land;
I will bereave them of children. I will destroy My people,
    since they did not repent from their ways.
8 Their widows will increase before Me
    more than the sand of the seas;
I will bring against them, against the mother of a young man,
    a destroyer at noonday;
I will suddenly bring down on her
    sorrow and terrors.
9 She who has borne seven sons languishes;
    she has given up the spirit;
her sun has gone down while it was yet day;
    she has been ashamed and humiliated.
And the rest of them I will deliver to the sword
    before their enemies,
    says the Lord.

Jeremiah's Sorrow

10 Woe is me, my mother, that you have borne me
    as a man of strife and a man of contention to the whole
        earth!
I have not lent with usury, nor have men lent to me on usury,
    yet every one of them curses me!

[11] The LORD said:

Truly I will set you free for good purposes.
  Truly I will cause the enemy to entreat you
  in the time of evil and in the time of affliction.

[12] Can anyone break the northern iron
  or the bronze?

[13] Your wealth and your treasures
  I will give to the destroyer without price,
and that for all your sins,
  even within all your borders.
[14] I will make you to pass with your enemies
  into a land which you do not know;
for a fire is kindled in My anger,
  which shall burn upon you.

[15] O LORD, You who know, remember me,
  and take notice of me,
  and take vengeance on my persecutors.
  Because of your longsuffering, do not take me away.
  Know that for Your sake I have suffered rebuke.
[16] Your words were found and I ate them.
  And Your word became to me the joy and rejoicing of
    my heart,
  for I am called by Your name,
  O LORD God of Hosts.
[17] I did not sit in the assembly of mockers,
  nor did I rejoice;
I sat alone because of Your hand,
  for You have filled me with indignation.
[18] Why is my pain perpetual
  and my wound incurable, which refuses to be healed?
Shall You be altogether to me as a deceptive stream
  and as waters that fail?

The LORD Reassures Jeremiah

[19] Therefore thus says the LORD:

If you return, then I will bring you back,
  and you shall stand before Me;
and if you take out the precious from the worthless,
  you will be My spokesman.
Let them return to you,
  but do not return to them.
[20] I will make you to this people
  a fortified bronze wall;
and they shall fight against you,
  but they shall not prevail against you;
for I am with you
  to save you and to deliver you,
  says the LORD.
[21] I will deliver you out of the hand of the wicked,
  and I will redeem you out of the hand of the violent.

The Day of Disaster

16 The word of the LORD came also to me, saying: [2] You shall not take a wife, nor shall you have sons or daughters in this place. [3] For thus says the LORD concerning the sons and concerning the daughters who are born in this place, and concerning their mothers who bore them, and concerning their fathers who fathered them in this land: [4] They will die of deadly diseases. They will not be lamented, nor shall they be buried. But they will be as dung upon the face of the ground. And they will be consumed by the sword and by famine. And their carcasses will be food for the fowl of heaven and for the beasts of the earth.

[5] For thus says the LORD: Do not enter a house of mourning, nor go to lament or bemoan them; for I have taken away My peace from this people, says the LORD, even lovingkindness and mercy. [6] Both the great and the small will die in this land. They will not be buried; neither will men lament for them, cut themselves, nor make themselves bald for

them. [7] Neither will men tear themselves for them in mourning, to comfort them for the dead; nor will men give them the cup of consolation to drink for their father or for their mother.

[8] Also you shall not go into the house of feasting, to sit with them to eat and to drink. [9] For thus says the LORD of Hosts, the God of Israel: I will cause to cease out of this place, before your eyes and in your days, the voice of laughter and the voice of gladness, the voice of the bridegroom and the voice of the bride.

[10] And when you tell this people all these words, and they say to you, "Why has the LORD pronounced all this great disaster against us? Or what is our iniquity? Or what is our sin that we have committed against the LORD our God?" [11] then you shall say to them: Because your fathers have forsaken Me, says the LORD, and have walked after other gods and have served them and have worshipped them, but have forsaken Me and have not kept My law. [12] And you have done worse than your fathers, for here you are, each one walking after the imaginations of his evil heart so that they do not listen to Me. [13] Therefore I will cast you out of this land into a land that you do not know, neither you nor your fathers; and there you will serve other gods day and night because I will not show you favor.

God Will Restore Israel

[14] Therefore, surely the days are coming, says the LORD, that it will no longer be said, "As the LORD lives, who brought up the sons of Israel out of the land of Egypt," [15] but, "As the LORD lives, who brought up the sons of Israel from the land of the north and from all the lands wherever He had driven them." And I will bring them again into their land that I gave to their fathers.

[16] Now, I will send for many fishermen, says the LORD, and they shall fish for them; and afterwards I will send for many hunters, and they will hunt them from every mountain and from every hill and out of the holes of the rocks. [17] For My eyes are upon all their ways; they are not hidden from My face, nor is their iniquity hidden from My eyes. [18] First I will doubly recompense their iniquity and their sin, because they have defiled My land; they have filled My inheritance with the carcasses of their detestable and abominable things.

[19] O LORD, my strength and my fortress,
  and my refuge in the day of affliction,
  the nations will come to You
  from the remote parts of the earth, and will say:
  Surely our fathers have inherited lies, vanity,
  and things in which there is no profit.
[20] Shall a man make gods for himself,
  which are not gods?

[21] "Therefore, surely I will this once cause them to know,
  I will cause them to know
  My hand and My might;
and they shall know
  that My name is the LORD."

Judah's Sin and Punishment

17 The sin of Judah is written with an iron pen
  and with a diamond point;
  it is engraved on the tablet of their heart
  and on the horns of their altars;
[2] as they remember their children,
  so they remember their altars
  and their groves by the green trees
  on the high hills.
[3] O My mountain in the field,
  I will give your wealth
  and all your treasures to the destroyer,
  and your high places
  for sin throughout all your borders.
[4] You, even yourself, will discontinue
  from your heritage that I gave you;
  and I will cause you to serve your enemies
  in the land which you do not know;
for you have kindled a fire in My anger
  which will burn forever.

5 Thus says the Lord:

Cursed is the man who trusts in man
   and makes flesh his strength,
   and whose heart departs from the Lord.
6 For he will be like a bush in the desert
   and will not see when good comes,
but will inhabit the parched places in the wilderness,
   in a salt land and not inhabited.

7 Blessed is the man who trusts in the Lord,
   and whose hope is the Lord.
8 For he shall be as a tree planted by the waters,
   and that spreads out its roots by the river,
and shall not fear when heat comes,
   but its leaf shall be green,
and it shall not be anxious in the year of drought,
   neither shall cease from yielding fruit.

9 The heart is more deceitful than all things
   and desperately wicked;
   who can understand it?

10 I, the Lord, search the heart,
   I test the mind,
even to give to every man according to his ways,
   and according to the fruit of his deeds.

11 As the partridge sits on eggs which it has not laid,
   so is he who gets riches, but not justly;
it will forsake him in the midst of his days,
   and in the end he will be a fool.

12 A glorious high throne from the beginning
   is the place of our sanctuary.
13 O Lord, the Hope of Israel,
   all who forsake You will be ashamed.
"Those who depart from Me in the earth will be written down,
   because they have forsaken the Lord,
   the fountain of living waters."

Jeremiah Prays for Deliverance

14 Heal me, O Lord, and I will be healed;
   save me, and I will be saved,
   for You are my praise.
15 See how they say to me,
   "Where is the word of the Lord?
   Let it come now!"
16 As for me, I have not hurried away from being a shepherd
   after You,
nor have I desired the woeful day;
   You Yourself know that which came out of my lips was in
   Your presence.
17 Do not be a terror to me;
   You are my hope in the day of disaster.
18 Let those who persecute me be humiliated,
   but let me not be humiliated;
let them be dismayed,
   but let me not be dismayed.
Bring upon them the day of evil,
   and destroy them with double destruction.

Keep the Sabbath Day Holy

19 Thus the Lord said to me: Go and stand in the gate of the sons of the people whereby the kings of Judah come in and by which they go out, and in all the gates of Jerusalem. 20 And say to them: Hear the word of the Lord, kings of Judah, and all Judah and all the inhabitants of Jerusalem who enter by these gates. 21 Thus says the Lord: Take heed to yourselves, and do not bear any load on the Sabbath day nor bring anything in by the gates of Jerusalem. 22 You shall not carry a load out of your houses on the Sabbath day, nor do any work, but keep the Sabbath day holy, as I commanded your fathers. 23 But they did not obey or incline their ears, but made their neck stiff, that they might not hear nor receive instruction. 24 It shall come to pass, if you diligently listen to Me, says the Lord, to bring in no load through the gates of this city on the Sabbath day, but sanctify the Sabbath day to do no work in it, 25 then there shall enter by the gates of this city kings and officials sitting on the throne of David, riding in chariots and on horses, they, and their officials, the men of Judah, and the inhabitants of Jerusalem. And this city will be inhabited forever. 26 They will come from the cities of Judah and from the places about Jerusalem, and from the land of Benjamin, and from the plain, and from the mountains, and from the Negev, bringing burnt offerings, and sacrifices, and grain offerings, and incense, and bringing sacrifices of praise to the house of the Lord. 27 But if you will not listen to Me to sanctify the Sabbath day and not to bear a load, even entering in at the gates of Jerusalem on the Sabbath day, then I will kindle a fire in the gates and it will devour the palaces of Jerusalem and it will not be quenched.

The Potter and the Clay

18 The word which came to Jeremiah from the Lord, saying: 2 "Arise and go down to the potter's house, and there I will cause you to hear My words." 3 Then I went down to the potter's house, and there he was making something on the wheel. 4 Yet the vessel that he made of clay was spoiled in the hand of the potter; so he made it again into another vessel, as seemed good to the potter to make it.

5 Then the word of the Lord came to me, saying: 6 O house of Israel, can I not do with you as this potter? says the Lord. As the clay is in the potter's hand, so are you in My hand, O house of Israel. 7 At one moment I may speak concerning a nation and concerning a kingdom to pluck up, and to pull down, and to destroy it. 8 If that nation against which I have spoken turns from its evil, I will relent of the disaster that I thought to do to it. 9 Or at another moment I may speak concerning a nation and concerning a kingdom to build and to plant it. 10 If it does evil in My sight by not obeying My voice, then I will relent of the good with which I said I would bless it.

11 Now therefore speak to the men of Judah and to the inhabitants of Jerusalem, saying: Thus says the Lord: Look, I am shaping disaster against you and devising a plan against you. Repent now, everyone from his evil way, and make your ways and your deeds good. 12 But they say, "There is no hope! But we will walk after our own devices, and each of us will do according to the stubbornness of his evil heart."

13 Therefore thus says the Lord:

Ask now among the nations,
   who has heard such things?
The virgin of Israel
   has done a very horrible thing.
14 Shall a man leave the snow of Lebanon,
   which comes from the rock of the field?
Shall the cold flowing water that comes from another place
   be forsaken?
15 Because My people have forgotten Me,
   they have burned incense to vain gods
and they have stumbled in their ways
   from the ancient paths,
to walk in bypaths,
   not on a highway,
16 to make their land desolate,
   and a perpetual hissing;
everyone who passes by shall be astonished
   and shake his head.
17 I will scatter them before the enemy
   as with an east wind;
I will show them the back and not the face
   in the day of their calamity.

Jeremiah Persecuted

18 Then they said, "Come and let us devise plans against Jeremiah. For the law will not be lost from the priest, nor counsel from the wise, nor the word from the prophet. Come and let us strike him with the tongue, and let us not give heed to any of his words."

¹⁹ Give heed to me, O LORD,
and listen to the voice of those who contend with me.
²⁰ Shall evil be recompensed for good?
For they have dug a pit for my soul.
Remember that I stood before You
to speak good for them,
and to turn away Your wrath from them.
²¹ Therefore, deliver up their children to the famine
and pour out their blood by the power of the sword;
and let their wives be bereaved of their children and
become widows
and let their men be put to death;
let their young men be slain by the sword in battle.
²² Let a cry be heard from their houses,
when You bring a troop suddenly upon them;
for they have dug a pit to take me
and hidden snares for my feet.
²³ Yet, LORD, You know
all their counsel against me to slay me.
Do not forgive their iniquity
nor blot out their sin from Your sight;
but let them be overthrown before You;
deal thus with them in the time of Your anger.

The Broken Jar

19 Thus says the LORD: Go and buy a potter's earthen bottle, and take some of the elders of the people and some of the elders of the priests. ² Then go out to the Valley of Ben Hinnom, which is by the entry of the Potsherd Gate, and proclaim there the words that I will tell you, ³ and say: Hear the word of the LORD, O kings of Judah and inhabitants of Jerusalem. Thus says the LORD of Hosts, the God of Israel: I will bring such disaster upon this place, at which whoever hears of it, his ears shall tingle. ⁴ Because they have forsaken Me and have profaned this place by making offerings in it to other gods whom neither they, their fathers, nor the kings of Judah have known, and have filled this place with the blood of the innocent, ⁵ and have built the high places of Baal to burn their sons with fire for burnt offerings to Baal, which I did not command or decree, nor did it come into My mind— ⁶ therefore, surely the days are coming, says the LORD, when this place shall no more be called Topheth or the Valley of Ben Hinnom, but the Valley of Slaughter.

⁷ I will make void the counsel of Judah and Jerusalem in this place, and I will cause them to fall by the sword before their enemies, and by the hands of those who seek their lives. And their corpses I will give to be food for the fowl of the heaven and for the beasts of the earth. ⁸ I will make this city desolate and a hissing. Everyone who passes by will be astonished and hiss because of all the wounds. ⁹ I will cause them to eat the flesh of their sons and the flesh of their daughters, and everyone will eat the flesh of his friend in the siege and distress, with which their enemies and those who seek their lives will distress them.

¹⁰ Then you will break the bottle in the sight of the men that go with you, ¹¹ and say to them: Thus says the LORD of Hosts: Even so I will break this people and this city, as one breaks a potter's vessel that cannot be made whole again; and they will bury them in Topheth until there is no other place to bury. ¹² Thus I will do to this place and to the inhabitants, says the LORD, and even make this city as Topheth. ¹³ And the houses of Jerusalem and the houses of the kings of Judah will be defiled as the place of Topheth, because of all the houses upon whose roofs they have burned incense to all the host of heaven and have poured out drink offerings to other gods.

¹⁴ Then Jeremiah came from Topheth, where the LORD had sent him to prophesy. And he stood in the court of the house of the LORD and said to all the people: ¹⁵ Thus says the LORD of Hosts, the God of Israel: I am about to bring upon this city and upon all her towns all the disaster that I have pronounced against it, because they have stiffened their necks so that they might not heed My words.

Pashhur Strikes Jeremiah

20 Now Pashhur the son of Immer the priest, who was also chief officer in the house of the LORD, heard that Jeremiah proph-esied these things. ² Then Pashhur struck Jeremiah the prophet and put him in the stocks that were in the upper Gate of Benjamin, which was by the house of the LORD. ³ On the next day Pashhur brought Jeremiah out of the stocks. Then Jeremiah said to him, The LORD has not called your name Pashhur, but "Magor-missabib."[1] ⁴ For thus says the LORD: I will make you a terror to yourself and to all your friends. And they will fall by the sword of their enemies while your eyes will see it. Thus I will give all Judah into the hand of the king of Babylon, and he will carry them captive into Babylon and will slay them with the sword. ⁵ Moreover I will deliver all the wealth of this city, and all its produce, and all the precious things; and all the treasures of the kings of Judah I will give into the hand of their enemies who will destroy them, and take them, and carry them to Babylon. ⁶ You, Pashhur, and all who dwell in your house will go into captivity; and you will come to Babylon, and there you will die and will be buried there, you and all your friends to whom you have prophesied lies.

Jeremiah Dejected

⁷ O LORD, You have deceived me and I was deceived;
You are stronger than I and have prevailed.
I am held in derision daily;
everyone mocks me.
⁸ For each time I speak, I cry out;
I cry out, "Violence and devastation,"
because to me the word of the LORD has resulted
in reproach and derision daily.
⁹ But if I say, "I will not make mention of Him
nor speak any more in His name,"
then His word was in my heart
as a burning fire shut up in my bones;
and I was weary of forbearing it,
and I could not endure it.
¹⁰ For I heard the defaming of many,
"Terror on every side!
Denounce him. Yes, denounce him!"
All my familiar friends
who watch for my fall, say,
"Perhaps he will be enticed
so that we can prevail against him,
and we will take our revenge on him."

¹¹ But the LORD is with me as a dread mighty One.
Therefore my persecutors will stumble, and will not prevail.
They will be greatly ashamed, for they will not prosper.
Their everlasting shame will never be forgotten.
¹² But, O LORD of Hosts, who tests the righteous
and sees the mind and the heart,
let me see Your vengeance on them,
for to You I have presented my cause.

¹³ Sing to the LORD,
praise the LORD.
For He has delivered the soul of the poor
from the hand of evildoers.

¹⁴ Cursed be the day in which I was born.
Let not the day be blessed in which my mother bore me.
¹⁵ Cursed be the man who brought tidings to my father,
saying, "A baby boy has been born to you!"
and made him very glad.
¹⁶ Let that man be as the cities
which the LORD overthrew and did not relent,
and let him hear the cry in the morning
and the shout of alarm at noon,
¹⁷ because he did not kill me from the womb,
so that my mother might have been my grave,
and her womb be always pregnant.
¹⁸ Why did I come forth from the womb
to see trouble and sorrow,
so that my days are spent in shame?

Zedekiah's Request Denied

21 The word which came to Jeremiah from the Lord when King Zedekiah sent to him Pashhur the son of Malkijah, and Zephaniah the son of Maaseiah the priest, saying, ² "Please inquire of the Lord for us. For Nebuchadnezzar king of Babylon is making war against us. Perhaps the Lord will deal with us according to all His wondrous works, so that the enemy withdraws from us."

³ Then Jeremiah said to them: Thus you shall say to Zedekiah: ⁴ Thus says the Lord God of Israel: Behold, I will turn back the weapons of war that are in your hands with which you fight against the king of Babylon and against the Chaldeans who besiege you outside the walls; and I will assemble them into the midst of this city. ⁵ I Myself will fight against you with an outstretched hand and with a strong arm, even in anger, and in fury, and in great wrath. ⁶ I will strike the inhabitants of this city, both man and beast; they will die of a great pestilence. ⁷ Afterwards, says the Lord, I will deliver Zedekiah king of Judah and his servants and the people and such as are left in this city from the pestilence, from the sword, and from the famine into the hand of Nebuchadnezzar king of Babylon, and into the hand of their enemies and into the hand of those who seek their life. And he will strike them with the edge of the sword. He will not spare them or have pity or mercy.

⁸ To this people you shall say: Thus says the Lord: See, I set before you the way of life, and the way of death. ⁹ He who abides in this city will die by the sword and by the famine and by the pestilence. But he who goes out and falls away to the Chaldeans who besiege you, he will live, and he will have his own life as booty. ¹⁰ For I have set My face against this city for disaster and not for good, says the Lord. It will be given into the hand of the king of Babylon, and he will burn it with fire.

Message to the House of David

¹¹ Concerning the house of the king of Judah, say, Hear the word of the Lord, ¹² O house of David; thus says the Lord:

Execute justice each morning,
    and deliver him who has been robbed
    from the hand of the oppressor,
lest My fury go out like fire
    and burn so that no one can quench it,
    because of the evil of your deeds.
¹³ See, I am against you,
    O inhabitant of the valley,
    O rocky plain,
    says the Lord,
you men who say,
    "Who shall come down against us?
    Or who shall enter our dwellings?"
¹⁴ But I will punish you
    according to the fruit of your deeds,
    says the Lord,
and I will kindle a fire in the forest,
    and it will devour all things around it.

Impending Judgment

22 Thus says the Lord: Go down to the house of the king of Judah, and speak this word there, ² and say: Hear the word of the Lord, O king of Judah who sits on the throne of David, you and your servants and your people who enter by these gates. ³ Thus says the Lord: Execute justice and righteousness, and deliver the robbed out of the hand of the oppressor. And do no wrong or violence to the stranger, the fatherless, or the widow, neither shed innocent blood in this place. ⁴ For if you indeed do these things, then kings sitting on the throne of David will enter by the gates of this house, riding in chariots and on horses, he and his servants and his people. ⁵ But if you will not obey these words, I swear by Myself, says the Lord, that this house will become a desolation.

⁶ For thus says the Lord to the king's house of Judah:

You are Gilead to Me,
    and the peak of Lebanon;
yet surely I will make you a wilderness
    and cities which are not inhabited.
⁷ I will prepare destroyers against you,
    everyone with his weapons;

and they shall cut down your choice cedars
    and cast them into the fire.

⁸ Many nations will pass by this city, and every man will say to his neighbor, "Why has the Lord done thus to this great city?" ⁹ Then they will answer, "Because they have forsaken the covenant of the Lord their God, and worshipped other gods, and served them."

¹⁰ Do not weep for the dead nor bemoan him,
    but weep constantly for him who goes away;
for he will return no more
    nor see his native country.

¹¹ For thus says the Lord concerning Shallum the son of Josiah king of Judah, who became king instead of Josiah his father, who went from this place: He will not return any more, ¹² but will die in the place where they have led him captive and will see this land no more.

¹³ Woe to him who builds his house with unrighteousness
    and his chambers with injustice,
who uses his neighbor's services without wages,
    and gives him nothing for his work,
¹⁴ who says, "I will build myself a roomy house
    and large chambers,"
and cuts out its windows,
    paneling it with cedar
    and painting it with vermilion.

¹⁵ Do you reign
    because you compete in cedar?
Did not your father eat and drink
    and do justice and righteousness,
    and then it was well with him?
¹⁶ He judged the cause of the poor and needy;
    then it was well with him.
Is not this what it means to know Me?
    says the Lord.
¹⁷ But your eyes and your heart
    are intent only on your covetousness
and on shedding innocent blood
    and on oppression and violence.

¹⁸ Therefore thus says the Lord concerning Jehoiakim the son of Josiah, king of Judah:

They will not lament for him, saying,
    "Ah, my brother!" or, "Ah, sister!"
They will not lament for him, saying,
    "Ah, lord!" or, "Ah, his glory!"
¹⁹ He will be buried with the burial of a donkey,
    drawn and cast out
    beyond the gates of Jerusalem.

²⁰ Go up to Lebanon and cry out,
    and lift up your voice in Bashan,
and cry out from Abarim,
    for all your lovers are destroyed.
²¹ I spoke to you in your prosperity,
    but you said, "I will not listen!"
This has been your manner from your youth,
    that you have not obeyed My voice.
²² The wind will sweep away all your shepherds,
    and your lovers shall go into captivity;
surely then you will be ashamed and humiliated
    for all your wickedness.
²³ O inhabitant of Lebanon,
    who makes your nest in the cedars,
how you will groan when pangs come upon you,
    the pain as of a woman in labor!

²⁴ As I live, says the Lord, though Koniah the son of Jehoiakim king of Judah were the signet on My right hand, yet would I pluck you from

there. [25] And I will give you into the hand of those who seek your life and into the hand of those whose face you fear, even into the hand of Nebuchadnezzar king of Babylon and into the hand of the Chaldeans. [26] I will cast you and your mother that bore you out into another country where you were not born, and there you shall die. [27] But to the land where they desire to return, they will not return there.

[28] Is this man Koniah a despised broken jar?
    Is he a vessel in which is no desire?
Why are he and his seed cast out
    and thrown into a land which they had not known?
[29] O land, land, land,
    hear the word of the Lord!
[30] Thus says the Lord:
    Write down this man childless,
    a man who will not prosper in his days;
for no man of his seed shall prosper,
    sitting on the throne of David
    and ruling any more in Judah.

The Righteous Branch

23 Woe to the shepherds who destroy and scatter the sheep of My pasture! says the Lord. [2] Therefore thus says the Lord God of Israel against the shepherds that feed My people: You have scattered My flock and driven them away and have not visited them. I am about to punish you for the evil of your deeds, says the Lord. [3] I will gather the remnant of My flock out of all countries wherever I have driven them and bring them again to their folds, and they shall be fruitful and increase. [4] I will also set up shepherds over them who will feed them; and they will fear no more, nor be dismayed, nor will they be missing, says the Lord.

[5] The days are coming, says the Lord,
    that I will raise up for David a righteous Branch,
and he shall reign as king and deal wisely,
    and shall execute justice and righteousness in the earth.
[6] In his days Judah will be saved,
    and Israel will dwell safely.
And this is the name by which he will be called:

THE LORD OUR RIGHTEOUSNESS.

[7] Therefore, surely the days are coming, says the Lord, when they will no more say, "As the Lord lives who brought up the sons of Israel out of the land of Egypt," [8] but, "As the Lord lives who brought up and led the descendants of the house of Israel out of the north country and from all countries where I had driven them." Then they will dwell in their own land.

Lying Prophets

[9] My heart is broken within me,
    because of the prophets;
    all my bones shake;
I am like a drunken man,
    like a man overcome by wine,
because of the Lord,
    and because of His holy words.
[10] For the land is full of adulterers;
    for the land mourns because of the curse.
    The pleasant places of the wilderness have dried up.
And their course is evil
    and their might is not right.

[11] For both prophet and priest are profane;
    indeed, in My house I have found their wickedness,
    says the Lord.
[12] Therefore their way will be as slippery ways to them;
    they shall be driven into the darkness
    and fall in it;
for I will bring disaster upon them,
    even the year of their punishment,
    says the Lord.

[13] In addition, I have seen folly
    in the prophets of Samaria.
They prophesied by Baal
    and caused My people Israel to err.
[14] I have seen also among the prophets of Jerusalem
    a horrible thing.
They commit adultery and walk in lies.
They also strengthen the hands of evildoers,
    so that no one repents from his wickedness.
All of them are as Sodom to Me
    and her inhabitants as Gomorrah.

[15] Therefore thus says the Lord of Hosts concerning the prophets:

"I will feed them with wormwood
    and make them drink the water of gall,
for from the prophets of Jerusalem
    profaneness has gone out into all the land."

[16] Thus says the Lord of Hosts:

Do not listen to the words of the prophets who prophesy to you.
    They lead you into vanity;
they speak a vision of their own heart
    and not out of the mouth of the Lord.
[17] They still say to those who despise Me,
    "The Lord has said, 'You will have peace' ";
and they say to everyone who walks after the imagination of his
    own heart,
    "No evil will come upon you."
[18] For who has stood in the counsel of the Lord
    and has perceived and heard His word?
Who has given heed to His word and listened to it?
[19] Look, a whirlwind of the Lord
    has gone forth in fury,
a tempestuous whirlwind.
    It will fall tempestuously upon the head of the wicked.
[20] The anger of the Lord will not turn back
    until He has executed and performed
    the thoughts of His heart.
In the latter days
    you will understand it perfectly.
[21] I have not sent these prophets,
    yet they ran.
I have not spoken to them,
    yet they prophesied.
[22] But if they had stood in My counsel
    and had caused My people to hear My words,
then they would have turned them from their evil way
    and from the evil of their deeds.

[23] Am I a God who is near,
    says the Lord,
    and not a God far off?
[24] Can a man hide himself in secret places
    so that I do not see him?
    says the Lord.
Do I not fill heaven and earth?
    says the Lord.

[25] I have heard what the prophets have said who prophesy lies in My name, saying, "I had a dream, I had a dream!" [26] How long shall this be in the heart of the prophets who prophesy lies? Indeed, they are prophets of the deceit of their own heart, [27] who plan to cause My people to forget My name by their dreams, which they tell to their neighbor, as their fathers have forgotten My name for Baal. [28] The prophet who has a dream, let him tell his dream. And he who has My word, let him speak My word faithfully. What is the chaff to the wheat? says the Lord. [29] Is not My word like fire, says the Lord, and like a hammer that breaks the rock in pieces?

[30] See, therefore I am against the prophets, says the Lord, who steal My words, each from his neighbor. [31] See, I am against the prophets,

says the LORD, who use their tongues and say, "The LORD says." [32] See, I am against those who prophesy false dreams, says the LORD, and recount them and cause My people to err by their lies and reckless boasting. Yet I sent them not nor commanded them. Therefore they shall not profit this people at all, says the LORD.

False Prophecy

[33] When this people or the prophet or a priest asks you, saying, "What is the oracle of the LORD?" you shall then say to them, "What oracle? I will forsake you, says the LORD." [34] As for the prophet and the priest and the people who say, "The oracle of the LORD," I will punish that man and his house. [35] Thus each of you will say to his neighbor and to his brother, "What has the LORD answered?" and, "What has the LORD spoken?" [36] And the oracle of the LORD you shall mention no more, for every man's word will be his oracle. For you have perverted the words of the living God, of the LORD of Hosts our God. [37] Thus you will say to that prophet, "What has the LORD answered you?" and, "What has the LORD spoken?" [38] But if you say, "The oracle of the LORD"; therefore thus says the LORD: Because you say this word, "The oracle of the LORD," I have also sent to you, saying, You shall not say, "The oracle of the LORD." [39] Therefore, surely, I, even I, will utterly forget you and cast you and the city that I gave you and your fathers out of My presence. [40] And I will bring an everlasting reproach upon you and perpetual shame which shall not be forgotten.

The Good and Bad Figs

24 The LORD showed me two baskets of figs that were set before the temple of the LORD after Nebuchadnezzar king of Babylon had carried away captive Jeconiah the son of Jehoiakim, king of Judah, and the officials of Judah with the carpenters and smiths from Jerusalem and brought them to Babylon. [2] One basket had very good figs, even like the figs that are first ripe, and the other basket had very rotten figs, which were so rotten they could not be eaten.

[3] Then the LORD said to me, "What do you see, Jeremiah?"

And I said, "Figs, the good figs, very good. And the rotten, very rotten, that are so rotten they cannot be eaten."

[4] Again the word of the LORD came to me, saying: [5] Thus says the LORD the God of Israel: Like these good figs, so I will acknowledge those who are carried away captive of Judah, whom I have sent out of this place into the land of the Chaldeans for their good. [6] For I will set My eyes upon them for good, and I will bring them again to this land. And I will build them up and not pull them down. And I will plant them and not pluck them up. [7] I will give them a heart to know Me, that I am the LORD; and they will be My people, and I will be their God, for they will return to Me with their whole heart.

[8] But as the rotten figs, which cannot be eaten, they are so rotten, says the LORD, so I will forsake Zedekiah the king of Judah and his officials, and the rest of Jerusalem who remain in this land, and those who dwell in the land of Egypt. [9] And I will make them a horror and an evil to all the kingdoms of the earth, to be a reproach and a byword, a taunt and a curse, in all places wherever I shall drive them. [10] I will send the sword, the famine, and the pestilence among them until they are consumed from off the land that I gave to them and to their fathers.

Seventy Years of Captivity

25 The word that came to Jeremiah concerning all the people of Judah in the fourth year of Jehoiakim the son of Josiah, king of Judah, that was the first year of Nebuchadnezzar king of Babylon, [2] which Jeremiah the prophet spoke to all the people of Judah and to all the inhabitants of Jerusalem, saying: [3] From the thirteenth year of Josiah the son of Amon, king of Judah, even to this day, these twenty-three years the word of the LORD has come to me, and I have spoken to you, rising early and speaking, but you have not listened.

[4] The LORD has sent to you all His servants the prophets, rising early and sending them, but you have not listened nor inclined your ear to hear. [5] They said, "Turn now again everyone from his evil way and from the evil of your deeds, and dwell in the land that the LORD has given to you and to your fathers forever and ever. [6] And do not go after other gods to serve them and to worship them, and provoke Me not to anger with the works of your hands; and I will do you no harm."

[7] Yet you have not listened to Me, says the LORD, that you might provoke Me to anger with the works of your hands to your own harm. [8] Therefore thus says the LORD of Hosts: Because you have not obeyed My words, [9] I will send and take all the families of the north, says the LORD, and Nebuchadnezzar the king of Babylon, My servant, and will bring them against this land and its inhabitants, and against all these surrounding nations; I will utterly destroy them, and make them an astonishment, a hissing, and perpetual desolations. [10] Moreover I will take from them the voice of laughter and the voice of gladness, the voice of the bridegroom and the voice of the bride, the sound of the millstones and the light of the candle. [11] This whole land shall be a desolation and an astonishment, and these nations will serve the king of Babylon seventy years.

[12] It shall come to pass when seventy years are finished that I will punish the king of Babylon and that nation, says the LORD, for their iniquity, and the land of the Chaldeans, and will make it perpetual desolations. [13] I will bring upon that land all My words which I have pronounced against it, even all that is written in this book, which Jeremiah has prophesied against all the nations. [14] For many nations and great kings will make slaves of them, even them. And I will recompense them according to their deeds and according to the works of their hands.

The Cup of God's Wrath

[15] For thus says the LORD God of Israel to me: Take the wine cup of this fury at My hand and cause all the nations to whom I send you to drink it. [16] They will drink, and totter, and be mad, because of the sword that I will send among them.

[17] Then I took the cup from the hand of the LORD and made all the nations, to whom the LORD had sent me, drink: [18] Jerusalem and the cities of Judah and the kings and the officials, to make them a desolation, an astonishment, a hissing, and a curse, as it is this day; [19] Pharaoh king of Egypt, and his servants, and his officials, and all his people; [20] and all the foreign people, and all the kings of the land of Uz, and all the kings of the land of the Philistines (even Ashkelon, and Gaza, and Ekron, and the remnant of Ashdod); [21] Edom, and Moab, and the children of Ammon; [22] and all the kings of Tyre, and all the kings of Sidon, and the kings of the coastlands which are beyond the sea; [23] Dedan, and Tema, and Buz, and all who cut the corners of their hair; [24] and all the kings of Arabia, and all the kings of the foreign people who dwell in the desert; [25] and all the kings of Zimri, and all the kings of Elam, and all the kings of the Medes; [26] and all the kings of the north, far and near, one with another; and all the kingdoms of the earth which are upon the face of the earth, and the king of Sheshak shall drink after them.

[27] Therefore you shall say to them, Thus says the LORD of Hosts, the God of Israel: Drink and be drunk and spew and fall and rise no more because of the sword which I will send among you. [28] It will be, if they refuse to take the cup from your hand to drink, then you will say to them: Thus says the LORD of Hosts: You shall certainly drink! [29] For I am starting to bring calamity on the city which is called by My name, and should you be utterly unpunished? You shall not be unpunished. For I will call for a sword upon all the inhabitants of the earth, says the LORD of Hosts.

[30] Therefore prophesy against them all these words, and say to them:

The LORD will roar from on high,
    and utter His voice from His holy habitation;
    He will mightily roar against His fold.
He will give a shout, as those who tread the grapes,
    against all the inhabitants of the earth.
[31] A noise shall come even to the remote parts of the earth,
    for the LORD has a controversy with the nations;
He shall enter into judgment with all flesh.
    He shall give those who are wicked to the sword,
    says the LORD.

[32] Thus says the LORD of Hosts:

See, disaster shall go forth
    from nation to nation,
and a great whirlwind shall be raised up
    from the remote parts of the earth.

[33] The slain of the LORD on that day will be from one end of the earth even to the other end of the earth. They will not be lamented or gathered or buried. They will be as dung on the ground.

[34] Howl, you shepherds, and cry;
and wallow in the ashes, you leaders of the flock.
For the days of your slaughter and of your dispersions are accomplished;
and you will fall like a choice vessel.
[35] The shepherds will have no way to flee,
nor the leaders of the flock to escape.
[36] A voice of the cry of the shepherds
and a howling of the leaders of the flock shall be heard,
for the LORD has devastated their pasture.
[37] The peaceable habitations are cut down
because of the fierce anger of the LORD.
[38] He has left His lair as the lion;
for their land is desolate
because of the fierceness of the oppressor
and because of His fierce anger.

Jeremiah Threatened With Death

26 In the beginning of the reign of Jehoiakim the son of Josiah, king of Judah, this word came from the LORD, saying: [2] Thus says the LORD: Stand in the court of the house of the LORD, and speak to all the cities of Judah who come to worship in the house of the LORD all the words that I command you to speak to them. Do not diminish a word. [3] Perhaps they will listen and turn every man from his evil way, that I may repent of the calamity which I purpose to do to them because of the evil of their deeds. [4] You will say to them: Thus says the LORD: If you will not listen to Me, to walk in My law which I have set before you, [5] to listen to the words of My servants the prophets, whom I sent to you, both rising up early and sending them, but you have not listened, [6] then I will make this house like Shiloh and will make this city a curse to all the nations of the earth.

[7] So the priests and the prophets and all the people heard Jeremiah speaking these words in the house of the LORD. [8] And when Jeremiah had made an end of speaking all that the LORD had commanded him to speak to all the people, the priests and the prophets and all the people took hold of him, saying, "You shall surely die. [9] Why have you prophesied in the name of the LORD, saying, 'This house shall be like Shiloh, and this city shall be desolate without an inhabitant'?" And all the people were gathered against Jeremiah in the house of the LORD.

[10] When the officials of Judah heard these things, then they came up from the king's house to the house of the LORD and sat down in the entry of the New Gate of the house of the LORD. [11] Then the priests and the prophets spoke to the officials and to all the people, saying, "This man deserves to die! For he has prophesied against this city, as you have heard with your ears."

[12] Then Jeremiah spoke to all the officials and to all the people, saying, "The LORD sent me to prophesy against this house and against this city all the words that you have heard. [13] Therefore now amend your ways and your deeds, and obey the voice of the LORD your God; and the LORD will repent of the disaster that He has pronounced against you. [14] As for me, here I am in your hand. Do with me as seems good and right to you. [15] But know for certain that if you put me to death, you will surely bring innocent blood upon yourselves and upon this city and upon the inhabitants. For truly the LORD has sent me to you to speak all these words in your ears."

Jeremiah Spared From Death

[16] Then the officials and all the people said to the priests and to the prophets, "This man is not worthy of death. For he has spoken to us in the name of the LORD our God."

[17] Then certain of the elders of the land rose up and spoke to all the assembly of the people, saying: [18] "Micah of Moresheth prophesied in the days of Hezekiah king of Judah, and spoke to all the people of Judah, saying, 'Thus says the LORD of Hosts:

Zion shall be plowed like a field,
and Jerusalem shall become heaps,
and the mountain of the house as the high places of a forest.'

[19] Did Hezekiah king of Judah and all Judah put him to death? Did he not fear the LORD and entreat the LORD, and the LORD relented of the disaster which He had pronounced against them? Thus we might procure great evil against ourselves."

[20] There was also a man that prophesied in the name of the LORD, Uriah the son of Shemaiah of Kiriath Jearim, who prophesied against this city and against this land according to all the words of Jeremiah. [21] And when Jehoiakim the king, with all his mighty men and all the officials, heard his words, the king sought to put him to death. But when Uriah heard it, he was afraid and fled and went into Egypt. [22] And Jehoiakim the king sent men into Egypt: namely, Elnathan the son of Akbor and certain men with him into Egypt. [23] They brought Uriah out of Egypt and led him to Jehoiakim the king, who slew him with the sword and cast his dead body into the graves of the common people.

[24] Nevertheless the hand of Ahikam the son of Shaphan was with Jeremiah, with the result that he was not given into the hands of the people to put him to death.

Judah to Serve Nebuchadnezzar

27 In the beginning of the reign of Zedekiah the son of Josiah, king of Judah, this word came to Jeremiah from the LORD: [2] Thus says the LORD to me: Make bonds and yokes and put them on your neck, [3] and send them to the king of Edom, and to the king of Moab, and to the king of the Ammonites, and to the king of Tyre, and to the king of Sidon, by the hand of the messengers who come to Jerusalem to Zedekiah king of Judah. [4] And command them to go to their masters, saying: Thus says the LORD of Hosts, the God of Israel: Thus you shall say to your masters: [5] I have made the earth, the men, and the beasts which are on the ground by My great power and by My outstretched arm, and have given it to whom it seemed good to Me. [6] Now I have given all these lands into the hand of Nebuchadnezzar the king of Babylon, My servant. And also I have given to him the beasts of the field to serve him. [7] All nations shall serve him and his son and his son's son until the time of his own land comes; and then many nations and great kings will make him their servant.

[8] It shall come to pass that I will punish the nation and kingdom which will not serve Nebuchadnezzar the king of Babylon, and that will not put their neck under the yoke of the king of Babylon, says the LORD. I will punish that nation with the sword, and with famine, and with pestilence, until I have consumed them by his hand. [9] Therefore do not listen to your prophets, or to your diviners, or to your dreamers, or to your enchanters, or to your sorcerers who speak to you, saying, "You shall not serve the king of Babylon." [10] For they prophesy a lie to you in order to remove you far from your land. And I will drive you out, and you shall perish. [11] But the nations that bring their neck under the yoke of the king of Babylon, and serve him, those I will let remain still in their own land, says the LORD, and they shall till it and dwell in it.

[12] I spoke also to Zedekiah king of Judah according to all these words, saying: Bring your necks under the yoke of the king of Babylon and serve him and his people, and live. [13] Why will you die, you and your people, by the sword, by the famine, and by the pestilence, as the LORD has spoken against the nation that will not serve the king of Babylon? [14] Therefore do not listen to the words of the prophets who speak to you, saying, "You will not serve the king of Babylon," because they prophesy a lie to you. [15] For I have not sent them, says the LORD, yet they prophesy a lie in My name, so that I might drive you out and that you might perish, you and the prophets that prophesy to you.

[16] I also spoke to the priests and to all this people: Thus says the LORD: Do not listen to the words of your prophets that prophesy to you, saying, "The vessels of the house of the LORD will now soon be brought again from Babylon." For they prophesy a lie to you. [17] Do not listen to them; serve the king of Babylon, and live. Why should this city be laid waste? [18] But if they are prophets, and if the word of the LORD is with them, let them now make intercession to the LORD of Hosts, that the vessels which are left in the house of the LORD and in the house of the king of Judah and in Jerusalem not go to Babylon. [19] For thus says the LORD of Hosts concerning the pillars, and concerning the sea, and concerning the bases, and concerning the rest of the vessels that remain in this city, [20] which Nebuchadnezzar king of Babylon did not take when he carried away captive Jeconiah the son of Jehoiakim, king of Judah from Jerusalem to Babylon, and all the nobles of Judah and Jerusalem. [21] Indeed, thus says the LORD of Hosts, the God of Israel,

concerning the vessels that remain in the house of the Lord and in the house of the king of Judah and in Jerusalem: ²² They will be carried to Babylon and they will be there until the day that I visit them, says the Lord. Then I will bring them up and restore them to this place.

The False Prophet Hananiah

28 In that same year, at the beginning of the reign of Zedekiah king of Judah, in the fourth year and in the fifth month, Hananiah the son of Azzur, the prophet, who was from Gibeon, spoke to me in the house of the Lord in the presence of the priests and of all the people, saying, ² "Thus says the Lord of Hosts, the God of Israel: I have broken the yoke of the king of Babylon. ³ Within two full years I will bring back into this place all the vessels of the house of the Lord that Nebuchadnezzar king of Babylon took away from this place and carried to Babylon. ⁴ And I will bring back to this place Jeconiah the son of Jehoiakim, king of Judah, with all the captives of Judah who went into Babylon, says the Lord, for I will break the yoke of the king of Babylon."

⁵ Then the prophet Jeremiah said to the prophet Hananiah in the presence of the priests and in the presence of all the people that stood in the house of the Lord, ⁶ even the prophet Jeremiah said, "Amen. May the Lord do so; may the Lord perform your words which you have prophesied, to bring back the vessels of the house of the Lord and all that was carried away captive, from Babylon into this place. ⁷ Nevertheless hear now this word that I speak in your ears and in the ears of all the people. ⁸ The prophets of old who have been before me and before you prophesied both against many countries and against great kingdoms, of war and disaster and pestilence. ⁹ As for the prophet who prophesies of peace, when the word of the prophet comes to pass, then that prophet shall be known as one whom the Lord has truly sent."

¹⁰ Then Hananiah the prophet took the yoke from off the neck of the prophet Jeremiah and broke it. ¹¹ Hananiah spoke in the presence of all the people, saying, "Thus says the Lord: Even so I will break the yoke of Nebuchadnezzar king of Babylon from the neck of all the nations within the space of two full years." Then the prophet Jeremiah went his way.

¹² Then the word of the Lord came to Jeremiah the prophet, after Hananiah the prophet had broken the yoke from off the neck of the prophet Jeremiah, saying: ¹³ Go and tell Hananiah, saying, Thus says the Lord: You have broken the yokes of wood, but you have made instead of them yokes of iron. ¹⁴ For thus says the Lord of Hosts, the God of Israel: I have put a yoke of iron on the neck of all these nations, that they may serve Nebuchadnezzar king of Babylon; and they shall serve him. And I have given him the beasts of the field also.

¹⁵ Then the prophet Jeremiah said to Hananiah the prophet, "Listen now, Hananiah. The Lord has not sent you, and you make this people trust in a lie. ¹⁶ Therefore thus says the Lord: I am about to cast you from off the face of the earth. This year you shall die, because you have taught rebellion against the Lord."

¹⁷ So Hananiah the prophet died the same year in the seventh month.

Jeremiah's Letter to the Exiles

29 Now these are the words of the letter that Jeremiah the prophet sent from Jerusalem to the rest of the elders of the captivity, and the priests, and the prophets, and all the people whom Nebuchadnezzar had carried away captive from Jerusalem to Babylon. ² (This was after Jeconiah the king, and the queen, and the eunuchs, and the officials of Judah and Jerusalem, and the carpenters, and the smiths had departed from Jerusalem.) ³ It was sent by the hand of Elasah the son of Shaphan and Gemariah the son of Hilkiah (whom Zedekiah, king of Judah, sent to Babylon to Nebuchadnezzar king of Babylon), saying:

⁴ Thus says the Lord of Hosts, the God of Israel, to all who have been carried away captive whom I have caused to be carried away from Jerusalem to Babylon: ⁵ Build houses and dwell in them; and plant gardens and eat their fruit. ⁶ Take wives and beget sons and daughters; and take wives for your sons and give your daughters to husbands, so that they may bear sons and daughters; so that you may increase there and not diminish. ⁷ Seek the peace of the city where I have caused you to be carried away captive, and pray to the Lord for it; for in its peace you will have peace. ⁸ For thus says the Lord of Hosts, the God of Israel: Do not let your prophets and

your diviners who are in your midst deceive you, and do not listen to the dreams which they dream. ⁹ For they prophesy falsely to you in My name. I have not sent them, says the Lord.

¹⁰ For thus says the Lord: When seventy years have been completed for Babylon, I will visit you and perform My good word toward you, in causing you to return to this place. ¹¹ For I know the plans that I have for you, says the Lord, plans for peace and not for evil, to give you a future and a hope. ¹² Then you shall call upon Me, and you shall come and pray to Me, and I will listen to you. ¹³ You shall seek Me and find Me, when you shall search for Me with all your heart. ¹⁴ I will be found by you, says the Lord, and I will turn away your captivity and gather you from all the nations and from all the places where I have driven you, says the Lord, and I will bring you back into the place from where I caused you to be carried away captive.

¹⁵ Because you have said, "The Lord has raised up prophets for us in Babylon," ¹⁶ thus says the Lord concerning the king who sits on the throne of David, and concerning all the people who dwell in this city, your brothers who did not go out with you into exile, ¹⁷ thus says the Lord of Hosts: I will send upon them the sword, the famine, and the pestilence, and will make them like vile figs that cannot be eaten, they are so rotten. ¹⁸ I will pursue them with the sword, with famine, and with pestilence; and will make them a terror to all the kingdoms of the earth, to be a curse and an astonishment, a hissing and a reproach among all the nations where I have driven them, ¹⁹ because they have not listened to My words, says the Lord, which I sent to them by My servants the prophets, rising up early and sending them. But you would not listen, says the Lord.

²⁰ Therefore hear the word of the Lord, all you in captivity whom I have sent from Jerusalem to Babylon. ²¹ Thus says the Lord of Hosts, the God of Israel, concerning Ahab the son of Kolaiah and concerning Zedekiah the son of Maaseiah, who prophesy a lie to you in My name: I will deliver them into the hand of Nebuchadnezzar king of Babylon, and he shall slay them before your eyes. ²² And because of them a curse shall be taken up by all the captives of Judah who are in Babylon, saying, "May the Lord make you like Zedekiah and Ahab, whom the king of Babylon roasted in the fire," ²³ because they have committed folly in Israel, and have committed adultery with their neighbors' wives, and have spoken lying words in My name, which I have not commanded them. Indeed, I know and am a witness, says the Lord.

A Message to Shemaiah

²⁴ Thus you shall also speak to Shemaiah the Nehelamite, saying: ²⁵ Thus says the Lord of Hosts, the God of Israel: Because you have sent letters in your name to all the people who are in Jerusalem, and to Zephaniah the son of Maaseiah the priest, and to all the priests, saying, ²⁶ The Lord has made you priest instead of Jehoiada the priest, that you should be officers in the house of the Lord, for every man that is mad and makes himself a prophet, that you should put him in the stocks and in prison. ²⁷ Now therefore why have you not reproved Jeremiah of Anathoth who prophesies to you? ²⁸ For he has sent to us in Babylon, saying, "This captivity will be long; build houses and dwell in them, and plant gardens and eat their fruit."

²⁹ Zephaniah the priest read this letter in the ears of Jeremiah the prophet. ³⁰ Then the word of the Lord came to Jeremiah, saying: ³¹ Send to all the captives, saying, Thus says the Lord concerning Shemaiah the Nehelamite: Because Shemaiah has prophesied to you though I did not send, and he caused you to trust in a lie, ³² therefore thus says the Lord: I will punish Shemaiah the Nehelamite and his seed. He will not have a man to dwell among this people, nor will he see the good that I will do for My people, says the Lord, because he has taught rebellion against the Lord.

Israel and Judah Restored

30 The word that came to Jeremiah from the Lord, saying: ² Thus says the Lord God of Israel: Write all the words that I have spoken to you in a book. ³ For surely the days are coming, says the Lord, when I will restore the fortunes of My people Israel and Judah. The Lord says, I also will cause them to return to the land that I gave to their fathers, and they shall possess it.

⁴ These are the words that the Lord spoke concerning Israel and Judah. ⁵ For thus says the Lord:

I have heard a sound of trembling,
of fear, and not of peace.
⁶ Ask now, and see,
can a male labor with child?
Why do I see every man
with his hands on his loins, as a woman in labor,
and all faces turned pale?
⁷ Alas! for that day is great,
so that no one is like it;
it is even the time of Jacob's trouble,
but he shall be saved out of it.

⁸ For it shall come to pass in that day, says the Lord of Hosts,
that I shall break his yoke from off their neck
and tear away their bonds,
and strangers shall no longer make them their slaves.
⁹ But they shall serve the Lord their God
and David their king,
whom I will raise up for them.

¹⁰ Therefore do not fear, O My servant Jacob,
says the Lord,
nor be dismayed, O Israel;
for I will save you from afar,
and your seed from the land of their captivity.
And Jacob shall return and shall be in rest and be quiet,
and no one shall make him afraid.
¹¹ For I am with you, says the Lord,
to save you.
Although I make a full end of all nations
wherever I have scattered you,
yet I will not make a full end of you.
But I will correct you in measure
and will not leave you altogether unpunished.

¹² For thus says the Lord:

Your bruise is incurable
and your wound is severe.
¹³ There is no one to plead your cause
that you may be bound up.
You have no healing medicines.
¹⁴ All your lovers have forgotten you;
they do not seek you;
for I have wounded you with the wound of an enemy,
with the chastisement of a cruel one,
because of the multitude of your iniquities, because your sins
are numerous.
¹⁵ Why do you cry because of your affliction?
Your sorrow is incurable.
Because of the multitude of your iniquities, because your sins
are numerous,
I have done these things to you.

¹⁶ Therefore all who devour you will be devoured;
and all your adversaries, every one of them, will go into
captivity.
And those who plunder you will become plunder,
and all who prey upon you I will give for prey.
¹⁷ For I will restore health to you,
and I will heal you of your wounds,
says the Lord,
because they called you an outcast, saying,
"This is Zion whom no man cares for."

¹⁸ Thus says the Lord:

I will restore the fortunes of Jacob's tents
and have mercy on his dwelling places;

and the city will be built upon her own heap,
and the palace will remain on its rightful place.
¹⁹ Out of them will proceed thanksgiving
and the voice of those who make merry;
and I will multiply them,
and they will not be few.
I will also glorify them,
and they will not be small.
²⁰ Their children also will be as before,
and their congregation will be established before Me;
and I will punish all who oppress them.
²¹ Their leader shall be one of them,
and their ruler shall proceed from their midst;
and I will cause him to draw near and he will approach Me;
for who is this that dares
to approach Me?
says the Lord.
²² You shall be My people,
and I will be your God.

²³ Look, the whirlwind of the Lord
goes forth with fury,
a continuing whirlwind;
it will fall with pain upon the head of the wicked.
²⁴ The fierce anger of the Lord shall not return
until He has done it
and until He has performed the intentions of His heart.
In the latter days
you will understand it.

The Exiles Return

31 At that time, says the Lord, I will be the God of all the families of Israel, and they shall be My people. ² Thus says the Lord:

The people who survived the sword
found grace in the wilderness,
when I went to give Israel rest.

³ The Lord has appeared to him from afar, saying:

Indeed, I have loved you with an everlasting love;
therefore with lovingkindness I have drawn you.
⁴ Again I will build you
and you will be built, O virgin of Israel.
You will again be adorned with your tambourines
and shall go forth in the dances of those who
make merry.
⁵ You will yet plant vines
on the mountains of Samaria;
the planters will plant
and will enjoy them.
⁶ For there will be a day when the watchmen
on the hills of Ephraim will proclaim,
"Arise, and let us go up to Zion,
to the Lord our God."

⁷ For thus says the Lord:

Sing with gladness for Jacob,
and shout among the chief of the nations;
publish, praise, and say,
"O Lord, save Your people,
the remnant of Israel."
⁸ See, I will bring them from the north country,
and gather them from the remote parts of the earth,
and with them the blind and the lame,
the woman with child and her who is in labor with
child, together;
a great company will return here.
⁹ They will come with weeping,
and with supplications I will lead them.

I will cause them to walk by the rivers of waters,
in a straight way in which they shall not stumble.
For I am a Father to Israel,
and Ephraim is My firstborn.

[10] Hear the word of the LORD, O nations,
and declare it in the coastlands far off, and say,
"He who scattered Israel will gather him
and keep him, as a shepherd does his flock."
[11] For the LORD has redeemed Jacob
and ransomed him from the hand of him who was
stronger than he.
[12] Therefore they will come and sing in the height of Zion,
and will be joyful over the goodness of the LORD,
for wheat and for wine and for oil
and for the young of the flock and of the herd;
and their souls will be as a watered garden.
And they will not sorrow any more at all.
[13] Then the virgin shall rejoice in the dance,
both young men and old together;
for I will turn their mourning into joy,
and will comfort them, and make them rejoice from
their sorrow.
[14] I will satiate the soul of the priests with abundance,
and My people shall be satisfied with My goodness,
says the LORD.

[15] Thus says the LORD:

A voice is heard in Ramah,
lamentation and bitter weeping,
Rachel weeping for her children,
refusing to be comforted for her children,
because they are no more.

[16] Thus says the LORD:

Keep your voice from weeping
and your eyes from tears;
for your work shall be rewarded,
says the LORD,
and they shall come back from the land of the enemy.
[17] There is hope for your future,
says the LORD,
that your children will come back to their
own border.

[18] I have surely heard Ephraim pleading:
"You have chastised me,
and I was chastised, as an untrained calf;
turn me back and I will be turned,
for you are the LORD my God.
[19] Surely after I turned back,
I repented;
and after I was instructed,
I struck myself on my thigh;
I was ashamed and even humiliated
because I bore the reproach of my youth."
[20] Is Ephraim My dear son?
Is he a pleasant child?
For since I spoke against him,
I *surely do* remember him *still*;
therefore My heart longs for him.
I will surely have mercy on him,
says the LORD.

[21] Set up road marks,
place guideposts.
Set your heart toward the highway,
even the way by which you went.
Turn back, O virgin of Israel,
turn back to these your cities.

[22] How long will you go about,
O faithless daughter?
For the LORD has created a new thing in the earth:
A woman shall obtain a man.

[23] Thus says the LORD of Hosts, the God of Israel: Once again they shall use this speech in the land of Judah and in the cities when I restore their fortunes: "May the LORD bless you, O habitation of righteousness and mountain of holiness!" [24] And Judah and all its cities shall dwell there, the farmer and those who go out with the flocks. [25] For I satiate the weary souls and I replenish every languishing soul.

[26] Upon this I awoke and looked, and my sleep was sweet to me.

[27] Surely, the days are coming, says the LORD, when I will sow the house of Israel and the house of Judah with the seed of man and with the seed of beast. [28] It shall come to pass that as I have watched over them to pluck up, and to break down, and to throw down, and to destroy, and to afflict, so I will watch over them, to build, and to plant, says the LORD. [29] In those days they will say no more:

"The fathers have eaten sour grapes,
and the children's teeth are set on edge."

[30] But everyone will die for his own iniquity. Every man that eats the sour grape, his teeth will be set on edge.

A New Covenant

[31] Surely, the days are coming, says the LORD,
when I will make a new covenant
with the house of Israel
and with the house of Judah.
[32] It will not be according to the covenant
that I made with their fathers
in the day that I took them by the hand
to bring them out of the land of Egypt,
because they broke My covenant,
although I was a husband to them,
says the LORD.
[33] But this shall be the covenant that I will make with the house
of Israel
after those days, says the LORD:
I will put My law within them
and write it in their hearts;
and I will be their God,
and they shall be My people.
[34] They shall teach no more every man his neighbor
and every man his brother, saying, "Know the LORD,"
for they all shall know Me,
from the least of them to the greatest of them,
says the LORD,
for I will forgive their iniquity,
and I will remember their sin no more.

[35] Thus says the LORD,

who gives the sun
for a light by day
and the ordinances of the moon and of the stars
for a light by night,
who stirs up the sea
so that the waves roar,
the LORD of Hosts is His name:
[36] If those ordinances depart from before Me,
says the LORD,
then the seed of Israel also will cease
from being a nation before Me forever.

[37] Thus says the LORD:

If heaven above can be measured,
and the foundations of the earth searched out beneath,

I will also cast off all the seed of Israel
for all that they have done,
says the LORD.

[38] Surely, the days are coming, says the LORD, when the city will be built to the LORD from the Tower of Hananel to the Corner Gate. [39] The measuring line shall stretch out straight to the hill Gareb, and shall then turn to Goah. [40] The whole valley of the dead bodies and of the ashes, and all the fields to the Kidron Valley, to the corner of the Horse Gate toward the east, will be holy to the LORD. It will not be plucked up nor thrown down any more forever.

Jeremiah Buys a Field

32 The word that came to Jeremiah from the LORD in the tenth year of Zedekiah king of Judah, which was the eighteenth year of Nebuchadnezzar. [2] For then the king of Babylon's army besieged Jerusalem, and Jeremiah the prophet was shut up in the court of the prison, which was in the house of the king of Judah.

[3] For Zedekiah king of Judah had shut him up, saying, "Why do you prophesy? You say: Thus says the LORD: I am about to give this city into the hand of the king of Babylon, and he shall take it, [4] and Zedekiah king of Judah will not escape out of the hand of the Chaldeans, but will surely be delivered into the hand of the king of Babylon, and will speak with him face to face and see him eye to eye. [5] And he will lead Zedekiah to Babylon, and there he will be until I visit him, says the LORD. Though you fight against the Chaldeans, you will not succeed."

[6] So Jeremiah said, The word of the LORD came to me, saying: [7] Hanamel the son of Shallum your uncle will come to you, saying, "Buy my field that is in Anathoth. For the right of redemption is yours to buy it."

[8] So Hanamel my uncle's son came to me in the court of the prison according to the word of the LORD and said to me, "Please buy my field, that is in Anathoth, which is in the country of Benjamin; for the right of inheritance and the redemption is yours. Buy it for yourself."

Then I knew that this was the word of the LORD. [9] I bought the field of Hanamel my uncle's son, that was in Anathoth, and weighed him the money, even seventeen shekels[1] of silver. [10] I signed and sealed the deed, and summoned witnesses, and weighed the money from him in the balances. [11] So I took the deed of purchase, both that which was sealed according to the law and custom, and that which was open. [12] And I gave the deed of purchase to Baruch the son of Neriah, the son of Mahseiah, in the sight of Hanamel my uncle's son, and in the presence of the witnesses who signed the deed of purchase, before all the Jews who sat in the court of the prison.

[13] I charged Baruch in their presence, saying, [14] Thus says the LORD of Hosts, the God of Israel: Take these deeds, this sealed deed of purchase and this deed which is open, and put them in an earthen vessel that they may last many days. [15] For thus says the LORD of Hosts, the God of Israel: Houses and fields and vineyards shall be possessed again in this land.

Jeremiah Prays for Understanding

[16] Now when I had delivered the deed of purchase to Baruch the son of Neriah, I prayed to the LORD, saying:

[17] Ah Lord GOD! Truly, You have made the heavens and the earth by Your great power and outstretched arm, and there is nothing too hard for You. [18] You show lovingkindness to thousands, and recompense the iniquity of the fathers into the bosom of their children after them, O great and mighty God. The LORD of Hosts is His name, [19] great in counsel and mighty in deed, whose eyes are open to all the ways of the sons of men, to give to everyone according to his ways and according to the fruit of his deeds. [20] You have set signs and wonders in the land of Egypt, even to this day, and in Israel, and among other men, and have made Yourself a name, as it is today. [21] And You have brought your people Israel out of the land of Egypt with signs, and with wonders, and with a strong hand, and with a stretched-out arm, and with great terror. [22] And You have given them this land, which You swore to their fathers to give them, a land flowing with milk and honey. [23] And they entered and possessed it. But they did not obey Your voice or walk in Your law. They have done nothing of all that You commanded them to do; therefore You have caused all this calamity to come upon them. [24] See, the siege ramps have come to the city to take it. And the city is given into the hand of the Chaldeans who fight against it, because of the sword, and of the famine, and of the pestilence, and what You have spoken has come to pass, as You can see. [25] O Lord GOD, You have said to me, "Buy the field for money and call in witnesses," although the city is given into the hand of the Chaldeans.

God Promises the People's Return

[26] Then the word of the LORD came to Jeremiah, saying: [27] Behold, I am the LORD, the God of all flesh. Is anything too hard for Me? [28] Therefore thus says the LORD: I will give this city into the hand of the Chaldeans and into the hand of Nebuchadnezzar king of Babylon, and he shall take it. [29] And the Chaldeans who fight against this city will come and set this city on fire and burn it with the houses, upon whose roofs they have offered incense to Baal and poured out drink offerings to other gods, to provoke Me to anger.

[30] Indeed the sons of Israel and the sons of Judah have only done evil before Me from their youth. For the sons of Israel have only provoked Me to anger with the work of their hands, says the LORD. [31] Indeed this city has been to Me a provocation of My anger and My fury from the day that they built it, even to this day, so that I should remove it from before My face, [32] because of all the evil of the sons of Israel and of the sons of Judah which they have done to provoke Me to anger, they, their kings, their officials, their priests, and their prophets, and the men of Judah and the inhabitants of Jerusalem. [33] They have turned their back to Me and not their face. Though I taught them, rising up early and teaching them, yet they have not listened nor received instruction. [34] But they set their abominations in the house which is called by My name, to defile it. [35] They built the high places of Baal which are in the Valley of Ben Hinnom to cause their sons and their daughters to pass through *the fire* to Molek, which I had not commanded them, nor did it come into My mind that they should do this abomination, to cause Judah to sin.

[36] Now therefore, thus says the LORD, the God of Israel, concerning this city of which you say, "It shall be delivered into the hand of the king of Babylon by the sword, and by famine, and by pestilence": [37] See, I will gather them out of all countries wherever I have driven them in My anger, and in My fury, and in great wrath; and I will bring them again to this place, and I will cause them to dwell safely. [38] And they shall be My people, and I will be their God. [39] And I will give them one heart and one way, that they may fear Me forever, for their good and for their children after them. [40] And I will make an everlasting covenant with them that I will not turn away from them, to do them good. But I will put My fear in their hearts so that they shall not depart from Me. [41] Indeed, I will rejoice over them to do them good, and I will plant them in this land assuredly with My whole heart and with My whole soul.

[42] For thus says the LORD: Just as I have brought all this great calamity upon this people, so I will bring upon them all the good that I have promised them. [43] Fields will be bought in this land of which you say, It is desolate, without man or beast. It is given into the hand of the Chaldeans. [44] Men will buy fields for money, sign and seal deeds, and call in witnesses in the land of Benjamin, and in the places about Jerusalem, and in the cities of Judah, and in the cities of the mountains, and in the cities of the valley, and in the cities of the Negev; for I will restore their fortunes, says the LORD.

The Promise of Restoration

33 Moreover the word of the LORD came to Jeremiah the second time, while he was yet shut up in the court of the prison, saying: [2] Thus says the LORD, the Maker of the earth, the LORD who formed it to establish it; the LORD is His name: [3] Call to Me, and I will answer you, and show you great and mighty things which you do not know. [4] For thus says the LORD God of Israel concerning the houses of this city, and concerning the houses of the kings of Judah, which are thrown down *to make a defense* against the siege mounds and against the sword: [5] They come to fight with the Chaldeans, but it is to fill them with the dead bodies of men whom I have slain in My anger and in My fury, all for whose wickedness I have hidden My face from this city.

[1]9 About 7 ounces, or 200 grams.

[6] I will bring it health and healing, and I will heal them; and I will reveal to them the abundance of peace and truth. [7] I will restore the fortunes of Judah and the fortunes of Israel, and will build them as at the first. [8] I will cleanse them from all their iniquity whereby they have sinned against Me. And I will pardon all their iniquities whereby they have sinned and whereby they have transgressed against Me. [9] It will be to Me a name of joy, praise, and honor before all the nations of the earth which shall hear of all the good that I do to them; and they will fear and tremble for all the goodness and for all the prosperity that I procure for it.

[10] Thus says the Lord: Again there shall be heard in this place of which you say, "It is desolate, without man and without beast," even in the cities of Judah, and in the streets of Jerusalem, that are desolate, without man and without inhabitant, and without beast, [11] the voice of joy, and the voice of gladness, the voice of the bridegroom, and the voice of the bride, the voice of those who shall say,

> "Give thanks to the Lord of Hosts,
>   for the Lord is good;
>   for His mercy endures forever,"

and of those who bring the sacrifice of praise into the house of the Lord. For I will restore the fortunes of the land as at the first, says the Lord. [12] Thus says the Lord of Hosts: Again in this place which is desolate, without man and without beast, and in all the cities, will be a habitation of shepherds causing their flocks to lie down. [13] In the cities of the mountains, in the cities of the vale, and in the cities of the Negev, and in the land of Benjamin, and in the places about Jerusalem, and in the cities of Judah, shall the flocks pass again under the hands of him who numbers them, says the Lord.

The Davidic Covenant

[14] Surely, the days are coming, says the Lord, when I will perform that good word which I have promised to the house of Israel and to the house of Judah:

[15] In those days and at that time,
    I will cause a righteous Branch to spring up for David;
    and he shall execute justice and righteousness in the earth.
[16] In those days Judah will be saved,
    and Jerusalem will dwell safely.
And this is *the name* by which she will be called:

THE LORD OUR RIGHTEOUSNESS.

[17] For thus says the Lord: David shall never lack a man to sit on the throne of the house of Israel; [18] nor shall the Levitical priests lack a man before Me to offer burnt offerings, to kindle grain offerings, and to sacrifice continually.

[19] The word of the Lord came to Jeremiah, saying: [20] Thus says the Lord: If you can break My covenant of the day and My covenant of the night so that there should not be day and night in their season, [21] then also My covenant may be broken with David My servant, that he should not have a son to reign on his throne, and with the Levitical priests, My ministers. [22] As the host of heaven cannot be numbered nor the sand of the sea measured, so I will multiply the seed of David My servant and the Levites that minister to Me.

[23] Moreover the word of the Lord came to Jeremiah, saying: [24] Have you not considered what this people have spoken, saying, "The two families which the Lord has chosen, He has cast them off"? Thus they have despised My people, that they should be no more a nation before them. [25] Thus says the Lord: If My covenant for day and night does not stand, and if I have not appointed the ordinances of heaven and earth, [26] then I would cast away the seed of Jacob and David My servant, so that I would not take any of his seed to be rulers over the seed of Abraham, Isaac, and Jacob. Yet I will restore their fortunes and have mercy on them.

Zedekiah to Die in Exile

34 The word which came to Jeremiah from the Lord when Nebuchadnezzar king of Babylon and all his army and all the kingdoms of the earth of his dominion and all the people fought against Jerusalem and against all the cities, saying: [2] Thus says the Lord, the God of Israel: Go and speak to Zedekiah king of Judah and tell him: Thus says the Lord: I will give this city into the hand of the king of Babylon, and he will burn it with fire. [3] And you will not escape out of his hand, but will surely be taken and delivered into his hand. And you will see the king of Babylon eye to eye, and he will speak with you face to face, and you will go to Babylon.

[4] Yet hear the word of the Lord, O Zedekiah king of Judah! Thus says the Lord concerning you: You will not die by the sword. [5] But you will die in peace; and as spices were burned for your fathers, the former kings who were before you, so they burn spices for you. And they will lament for you, saying, "Alas, lord!" For I have pronounced the word, says the Lord.

[6] Then Jeremiah the prophet spoke all these words to Zedekiah king of Judah in Jerusalem, [7] when the king of Babylon's army fought against Jerusalem, and against all the cities of Judah that were left, against Lachish and Azekah, for these fortified cities remained of the cities of Judah.

Slaves to be Free

[8] This is the word that came to Jeremiah from the Lord after the king Zedekiah had made a covenant with all the people who were in Jerusalem to proclaim liberty to them: [9] that every man should let his male slave and every man his female slave, being a Hebrew man or a Hebrew woman, go free so that no one should keep them, a Jew his brother, in bondage. [10] Now when all the officials and all the people who had entered into the covenant heard that everyone should let his male slave and everyone his female slave go free, so that no one should keep them any more in bondage, then they obeyed and let them go. [11] But afterward they turned around and caused the male slaves and the female slaves whom they had set free to return, and brought them into subjection for male slaves and female slaves.

[12] Therefore the word of the Lord came to Jeremiah from the Lord, saying: [13] Thus says the Lord, the God of Israel: I made a covenant with your fathers in the day that I brought them out of the land of Egypt, out of the house of bondage, saying: [14] "At the end of seven years, each of you shall set free his Hebrew brother who has been sold to you; and when he has served you six years, you shall let him go free from you." But your fathers did not obey Me nor incline their ear. [15] You recently turned and did what was right in My sight by proclaiming liberty, every man to his neighbor; and you made a covenant before Me in the house that is called by My name. [16] But then you turned around and profaned My name when every one of you took back his male and female slaves, whom you had set free, at their pleasure, and you brought them into subjection to be your slaves.

[17] Therefore thus says the Lord: You have not obeyed Me in proclaiming liberty, everyone to his brother and every man to his neighbor. I proclaim a liberty to you, says the Lord, to the sword, to the pestilence, and to the famine; and I will make you a terror to all the kingdoms of the earth. [18] I will give the men who have transgressed My covenant, who have not performed the words of the covenant which they had made before Me, when they cut the calf in two and passed between the parts, [19] the officials of Judah and the officials of Jerusalem, the court officers, and the priests, and all the people of the land, who passed between the parts of the calf, [20] I will even give them into the hand of their enemies and into the hand of those who seek their life; and their dead bodies shall be food to the fowl of heaven and to the beasts of the earth. [21] Zedekiah king of Judah and his officials I will give into the hand of their enemies and into the hand of those who seek their life and into the hand of the king of Babylon's army, which has gone away from you. [22] I will command, says the Lord, and cause them to return to this city, and they will fight against it and take it and burn it with fire; and I will make the cities of Judah a desolation without an inhabitant.

The Rekabites' Obedience

35 The word which came to Jeremiah from the Lord in the days of Jehoiakim the son of Josiah, king of Judah, saying: [2] Go to the house of the Rekabites and speak to them, and bring them into the house of the Lord, into one of the chambers, and give them wine to drink. [3] Then I took Jaazaniah the son of Jeremiah, the son of Habazziniah, and his brothers and all his sons and the whole house of the Rekabites,

⁴ and I brought them into the house of the Lord, into the chamber of the sons of Hanan, the son of Igdaliah, a man of God, which was by the chamber of the officials, which was above the chamber of Maaseiah the son of Shallum, the keeper of the door. ⁵ Then I set before the sons of the house of the Rekabites pots full of wine and cups, and I said to them, "Drink wine."

⁶ But they said, "We will drink no wine. For Jonadab the son of Rekab our father commanded us, saying, 'You shall not drink wine, neither you nor your sons forever. ⁷ You shall not build a house, sow seed, plant a vineyard, nor own one; but all your days you shall dwell in tents so that you may live many days in the land where you sojourn.' ⁸ Thus we have obeyed the voice of Jonadab the son of Rekab, our father, in all that he has charged us, to drink no wine all our days, we, our wives, our sons, nor our daughters, ⁹ nor to build houses for us to dwell in; and we do not have vineyard, or field, or seed. ¹⁰ But we have lived in tents only and have obeyed and done according to all that Jonadab our father commanded us. ¹¹ But when Nebuchadnezzar king of Babylon came up into the land, we said, 'Come, and let us go to Jerusalem before the army of the Chaldeans and before the army of the Arameans.' So we have dwelt in Jerusalem."

¹² Then the word of the Lord came to Jeremiah, saying: ¹³ Thus says the Lord of Hosts, the God of Israel: Go and tell the men of Judah and the inhabitants of Jerusalem, Will you not receive instruction by listening to My words? says the Lord. ¹⁴ The words of Jonadab the son of Rekab, that he commanded his sons not to drink wine, are performed. For to this day they drink none, but they obey their father's commandment. However, I have spoken to you, rising early and speaking, but you did not obey Me. ¹⁵ I also have sent to you all My servants the prophets, rising up early and sending them, saying, "Return now every man from his evil way and amend your deeds, and do not go after other gods to serve them, and you will dwell in the land that I have given to you and to your fathers." But you have not inclined your ear nor obeyed Me. ¹⁶ Indeed, the sons of Jonadab the son of Rekab have performed the commandment of their father, which he commanded them, but this people has not obeyed Me.

¹⁷ Therefore thus says the Lord God of Hosts, the God of Israel: I will bring upon Judah and upon all the inhabitants of Jerusalem all the disaster that I have pronounced against them; because I have spoken to them but they have not listened, and I have called them but they have not answered.

¹⁸ Jeremiah said to the house of the Rekabites: Thus says the Lord of Hosts, the God of Israel: Because you have obeyed the commandment of Jonadab your father and kept all his precepts and done according to all that he has commanded you, ¹⁹ therefore thus says the Lord of Hosts, the God of Israel, Jonadab the son of Rekab shall not lack a man to stand before Me always.

Jeremiah's Scroll Is Burned

36 In the fourth year of Jehoiakim the son of Josiah, king of Judah, this word came to Jeremiah from the Lord, saying: ² Take a scroll of a book, and write in it all the words that I have spoken to you against Israel and against Judah and against all the nations, from the day I spoke to you, from the days of Josiah, even to this day. ³ It may be that the house of Judah will hear all the disaster which I intend to do to them, so that every man may turn from his evil way; then I will forgive their iniquity and their sin.

⁴ Then Jeremiah called Baruch the son of Neriah. And Baruch wrote on a scroll at the dictation of Jeremiah all the words of the Lord which He had spoken to him. ⁵ Jeremiah commanded Baruch, saying, "I am shut in. I cannot go into the house of the Lord. ⁶ Therefore go and read from the scroll that you have written at my dictation the words of the Lord in the hearing of the people in the house of the Lord on a fast day. And also you shall read them in the ears of all Judah who come out of their cities. ⁷ Perhaps their supplication will come before the Lord, and everyone will turn from his evil way, for great is the anger and the fury that the Lord has pronounced against this people."

⁸ Baruch the son of Neriah did according to all that Jeremiah the prophet commanded him, reading in the book the words of the Lord in the house of the Lord. ⁹ In the fifth year of Jehoiakim the son of Josiah, king of Judah, in the ninth month, they proclaimed a fast before the Lord to all the people in Jerusalem and to all the people who came from the cities of Judah to Jerusalem. ¹⁰ Then Baruch read from the book the

words of Jeremiah in the house of the Lord, in the chamber of Gemariah the son of Shaphan the scribe, in the higher court, at the entry of the New Gate of the house of the Lord, in the ears of all the people.

¹¹ When Micaiah the son of Gemariah, the son of Shaphan, had heard out of the book all the words of the Lord, ¹² then he went down to the king's house, into the scribe's chamber. And all the officials sat there, even Elishama the scribe, and Delaiah the son of Shemaiah, and Elnathan the son of Akbor, and Gemariah the son of Shaphan, and Zedekiah the son of Hananiah, and all the other officials. ¹³ Then Micaiah declared to them all the words that he had heard when Baruch read the book in the ears of the people. ¹⁴ Then all the officials sent Jehudi the son of Nethaniah, the son of Shelemiah, the son of Cushi, to Baruch, saying, "Take in your hand the scroll from which you have read in the ears of the people and come." So Baruch the son of Neriah took the scroll in his hand and came to them. ¹⁵ They said to him, "Sit down now, and read it in our ears."

So Baruch read it in their ears. ¹⁶ When they heard all the words, they turned to one another in fear and said to Baruch, "We will surely tell the king of all these words." ¹⁷ They also asked Baruch, saying, "Tell us now, how did you write all these words? Was it at his mouth?"

¹⁸ Then Baruch answered them, "He pronounced all these words to me with his mouth, and I wrote them with ink in the book."

¹⁹ Then the officials said to Baruch, "Go hide, you and Jeremiah, and let no man know where you are."

²⁰ Then they went to the king in the court, but they laid up the scroll in the chamber of Elishama the scribe, and told all the words in the ears of the king. ²¹ So the king sent Jehudi to fetch the scroll, and he took it out of Elishama the scribe's chamber. And Jehudi read it in the ears of the king and in the ears of all the officials who stood beside the king. ²² Now the king sat in the winter house in the ninth month, and there was a fire burning on the hearth before him. ²³ As Jehudi read three or four columns, the king cut it with a scribe's knife and cast it into the fire that was on the hearth, until all the scroll was consumed in the fire that was on the hearth. ²⁴ Yet they were not afraid, nor did they tear their garments, neither the king nor any of his servants who heard all these words. ²⁵ Although Elnathan and Delaiah and Gemariah entreated the king not to burn the scroll, yet he would not listen to them. ²⁶ But the king commanded Jerahmeel the son of Hammelech, and Seraiah the son of Azriel, and Shelemiah the son of Abdeel to seize Baruch the scribe and Jeremiah the prophet. But the Lord hid them.

Jeremiah and Baruch Rewrite the Scroll

²⁷ Then the word of the Lord came to Jeremiah after the king had burned the book and the words which Baruch had written at the mouth of Jeremiah, saying: ²⁸ Take again another scroll and write in it all the former words that were in the first book, which Jehoiakim the king of Judah has burned. ²⁹ You shall say to Jehoiakim king of Judah: Thus says the Lord: You have burned this book, saying, Why have you written in it that the king of Babylon will certainly come and destroy this land, and will cause man and beast to cease from here? ³⁰ Therefore thus says the Lord concerning Jehoiakim king of Judah: He shall have no one to sit on the throne of David. And his dead body shall be cast out to the heat of the day and the frost of the night. ³¹ I will also punish him and his seed and his servants for their iniquity. And I will bring upon Judah and upon the inhabitants of Jerusalem and upon the men of Judah all the disaster that I have pronounced against them; but they did not listen.

³² Then Jeremiah took another scroll and gave it to Baruch the scribe, the son of Neriah who wrote in it from the mouth of Jeremiah all the words of the book which Jehoiakim king of Judah had burned in the fire. And there were added to them many like words.

Jeremiah Warns Zedekiah

37 And King Zedekiah the son of Josiah reigned instead of Koniah the son of Jehoiakim, whom Nebuchadnezzar king of Babylon made king in the land of Judah. ² But neither he nor his servants nor the people of the land listened to the words of the Lord, which He spoke through the prophet Jeremiah.

³ But Zedekiah the king sent Jehukal the son of Shelemiah and Zephaniah the son of Maaseiah, the priest, to the prophet Jeremiah, saying, "Please pray to the Lord our God for us."

⁴ Now Jeremiah was still coming in and going out among the people, for they had not yet put him into prison. ⁵ At that time Pharaoh's army had come out of Egypt, and when the Chaldeans who were besieging Jerusalem heard the report of them, they departed from Jerusalem.

⁶ Then the word of the Lᴏʀᴅ came to the prophet Jeremiah, saying: ⁷ Thus says the Lᴏʀᴅ, the God of Israel: Thus you shall say to the king of Judah who sent you to Me to inquire of Me: Pharaoh's army which has come out to help you shall return to Egypt, to its own land. ⁸ The Chaldeans will come again and fight against this city, and take it, and burn it with fire.

⁹ Thus says the Lᴏʀᴅ: Do not deceive yourselves, saying, "The Chaldeans will surely depart from us," for they will not depart. ¹⁰ For though you had struck the whole army of the Chaldeans who fight against you and there remained but wounded men among them, yet every man would rise up in his tent and burn this city with fire.

Jeremiah Imprisoned

¹¹ Now when the army of the Chaldeans had withdrawn from Jerusalem at the approach of Pharaoh's army, ¹² Jeremiah set out from Jerusalem to go into the land of Benjamin to take possession of his property there among the people. ¹³ When he was in the Gate of Benjamin, a captain of the guard was there whose name was Irijah the son of Shelemiah, the son of Hananiah. And he seized Jeremiah the prophet, saying, "You are falling away to the Chaldeans!"

¹⁴ But Jeremiah said, "It is false! I am not falling away to the Chaldeans," but he did not listen to him. So Irijah seized Jeremiah and brought him to the officials. ¹⁵ Therefore the officials were wrathful with Jeremiah, and struck him, and put him in prison in the house of Jonathan the scribe; for they had made that the prison.

¹⁶ For Jeremiah had entered the dungeon, that is, the vaulted cell, and Jeremiah had remained there many days. ¹⁷ Then Zedekiah the king sent and took him out; and the king asked him secretly in his house, and said, "Is there any word from the Lᴏʀᴅ?"

And Jeremiah said, "There is!" Then he said, "You shall be delivered into the hand of the king of Babylon."

¹⁸ Moreover Jeremiah said to King Zedekiah, "How have I sinned against you or against your servants or against this people that you have put me in prison? ¹⁹ Where now are your prophets who prophesied to you, saying, 'The king of Babylon will not come against you, nor against this land'? ²⁰ Therefore now please listen, O my lord the king. Please let my supplication be accepted before you, that you not cause me to return to the house of Jonathan the scribe, lest I die there."

²¹ Then Zedekiah the king commanded that they should commit Jeremiah into the court of the prison and give him daily a piece of bread out of the bakers' street, until all the bread in the city was finished. Thus Jeremiah remained in the court of the prison.

Jeremiah Thrown Into a Cistern

38 Now Shephatiah the son of Mattan, and Gedaliah the son of Pashhur, and Jukal the son of Shelemiah, and Pashhur the son of Malkijah heard the words that Jeremiah had spoken to all the people, saying: ² Thus says the Lᴏʀᴅ: He who remains in this city will die by the sword, by famine, and by pestilence. But he who goes out to the Chaldeans shall live, for he shall have his life as plunder, and shall live. ³ Thus says the Lᴏʀᴅ: This city shall surely be given into the hand of the king of Babylon's army, and he will capture it.

⁴ Therefore the officials said to the king, "We beseech you, let this man be put to death, for he thus weakens the hands of the men of war who remain in this city and the hands of all the people, in speaking such words to them; for this man does not seek the welfare of this people, but their harm."

⁵ Then Zedekiah the king said, "Here he is; he is in your hand; for the king cannot do anything against you."

⁶ Then they took Jeremiah and cast him into the cistern of Malkijah the son of Hammelech that was in the court of the prison, and they let Jeremiah down with cords. And in the cistern there was no water, only mud, so Jeremiah sank in the mud.

⁷ Now Ebed-Melek the Ethiopian, one of the eunuchs who was in the king's house, heard that they had put Jeremiah in the cistern. Now the king was sitting in the Gate of Benjamin. ⁸ Ebed-Melek went forth out of the king's house and spoke to the king, saying, ⁹ "My lord the king, these men have done evil in all that they have done

to Jeremiah the prophet whom they have cast into the cistern. And he will die by hunger in the place where he is, for there is no more bread in the city."

¹⁰ Then the king commanded Ebed-Melek the Ethiopian, saying, "Take thirty men with you from here and take up Jeremiah the prophet out of the cistern before he dies."

¹¹ So Ebed-Melek took the men under his authority and went into the house of the king under the storeroom and took from there worn-out clothes and worn-out rags and let them down by cords into the cistern to Jeremiah. ¹² Then Ebed-Melek the Ethiopian said to Jeremiah, "Now put these worn-out clothes and worn-out rags under your armpits under the cords," so Jeremiah did accordingly. ¹³ Then they drew Jeremiah up with cords and took him up out of the cistern, and Jeremiah remained in the court of the prison.

Jeremiah Warns Zedekiah Again

¹⁴ Then Zedekiah the king sent and had Jeremiah the prophet brought to him at the third entrance that is in the house of the Lᴏʀᴅ. And the king said to Jeremiah, "I will ask you something; hide nothing from me."

¹⁵ Then Jeremiah said to Zedekiah, "If I declare it to you, shall you not surely put me to death? And if I give you counsel, you will not listen to me."

¹⁶ So Zedekiah the king swore secretly to Jeremiah, saying, "As the Lᴏʀᴅ lives, who made our souls, I surely will not put you to death, nor will I give you into the hand of these men who seek your life."

¹⁷ Then Jeremiah said to Zedekiah, "Thus says the Lᴏʀᴅ, the God of Hosts, the God of Israel: If you will surrender to the officers of the king of Babylon, then your soul will live and this city will not be burned with fire. Thus you and your household will live. ¹⁸ But if you do not surrender to the king of Babylon's officials, then this city will be given into the hand of the Chaldeans, and they will burn it with fire, and you will not escape out of their hand."

¹⁹ Then Zedekiah the king said to Jeremiah, "I am afraid of the Jews who have fallen over to the Chaldeans, lest they deliver me into their hand and mock me."

²⁰ But Jeremiah said, "They will not deliver you. Please obey the voice of the Lᴏʀᴅ which I speak to you, so it will be well with you and your soul will live. ²¹ But if you refuse to surrender, this is the word that the Lᴏʀᴅ has shown me: ²² Then all the women who are left in the house of the king of Judah will be brought out to the officers of the king of Babylon; and those women shall say:

'Your friends have misled
    and prevailed against you;
while your feet were sunk in the mud,
    they turned back.'

²³ "So they will bring out all your wives and your children to the Chaldeans. And you will not escape out of their hand, but will be taken by the hand of the king of Babylon; and you will cause this city to be burned with fire."

²⁴ Then Zedekiah said to Jeremiah, "Let no man know of these words, and you will not die. ²⁵ But if the officials hear that I have talked with you and they come to you and say to you, 'Declare to us now what you said to the king and what the king said to you; do not hide it from us and we will not put you to death,' ²⁶ then you will say to them, 'I presented my supplication before the king, that he would not cause me to return to the house of Jonathan, to die there.' "

²⁷ Then all the officials came to Jeremiah and asked him. And he told them according to all these words that the king had commanded; so they stopped speaking with him, for the matter was not overheard. ²⁸ So Jeremiah remained in the court of the prison until the day that Jerusalem was captured.

The Fall of Jerusalem

2Ki 25:1–12; Jer 52:4–16

39 In the ninth year of Zedekiah king of Judah, in the tenth month, Nebuchadnezzar king of Babylon and all his army came against Jerusalem and besieged it. ² In the eleventh year of Zedekiah, in the fourth month, the ninth day of the month, the city wall was broken up. ³ All the officials of the king of Babylon entered and sat in the Middle Gate: Nergal-Sharezer, Samgar-Nebo, Sarsekim the Rabsaris,[1] Nergal-Sharezer the Rabmag,[2] and all the rest of the officials of the king of Babylon. [4] When Zedekiah the king of Judah saw them and all the men of war, then they fled and went out of the city by night, by way of the king's garden, by the gate between the two walls. And he went out the way of the Arabah.

[5] But the Chaldeans' army pursued after them and overtook Zedekiah in the plains of Jericho. And when they had taken him, they brought him up to Nebuchadnezzar king of Babylon to Riblah in the land of Hamath, where he passed sentence on him. [6] Then the king of Babylon slew the sons of Zedekiah in Riblah before his eyes. Moreover, the king of Babylon slew all the nobles of Judah. [7] He also put out Zedekiah's eyes and bound him with chains to carry him to Babylon.

[8] The Chaldeans burned the king's house and the houses of the people with fire and broke down the walls of Jerusalem. [9] Then Nebuzaradan the captain of the guard carried away captive into Babylon the remnant of the people who remained in the city, and those who fell away, who fell to him, with the rest of the people who remained. [10] But Nebuzaradan the captain of the guard left behind in the land of Judah the poor people who had nothing, and gave them vineyards and fields at that time.

The LORD Delivers Jeremiah

[11] Now Nebuchadnezzar king of Babylon gave charge concerning Jeremiah to Nebuzaradan the captain of the guard, saying, [12] "Take him and look after him, and do not harm him. But do to him just as he says to you." [13] So Nebuzaradan the captain of the guard, Nebushazban the Rabsaris, Nergal-Sharezer the Rabmag, and all the chief officers of the king of Babylon [14] sent and took Jeremiah out of the court of the prison and committed him to Gedaliah the son of Ahikam, the son of Shaphan, that he should take him home. So he lived among the people.

[15] Now the word of the LORD came to Jeremiah while he was shut up in the court of the prison, saying: [16] Go and speak to Ebed-Melek the Ethiopian, saying: Thus says the LORD of Hosts, the God of Israel: I will bring My words upon this city for harm and not for good. And they shall be accomplished in that day before you. [17] But I will deliver you in that day, says the LORD, and you shall not be given into the hand of the men of whom you are afraid. [18] For I will surely deliver you, and you will not fall by the sword; but your life will be as plunder to you, because you have put your trust in Me, says the LORD.

Jeremiah With Gedaliah the Governor

40 The word that came to Jeremiah from the LORD after Nebuzaradan the captain of the guard had let him go from Ramah, when he had taken him bound in chains among all who were carried away captive of Jerusalem and Judah who were being carried away captive to Babylon. [2] The captain of the guard had taken Jeremiah, and said to him: "The LORD your God has pronounced this disaster upon this place. [3] And the LORD has brought it and done according as He has said. Because you have sinned against the LORD, and have not obeyed His voice, therefore this thing has come upon you. [4] Now look, I am loosening you this day from the chains which are on your hands. If it seems good to you to come with me to Babylon, come and I will look well after you. But if it seems bad to you to come with me into Babylon, never mind. See, all the land is before you. Go wherever it seems good and right for you to go." [5] Now while he was not yet going back, *he said*, "Go back also to Gedaliah the son of Ahikam, the son of Shaphan, whom the king of Babylon has made governor over the cities of Judah, and dwell with him among the people. Or go wherever it seems right for you to go."

So the captain of the guard gave him rations and a gift and let him go. [6] Then Jeremiah went to Gedaliah the son of Ahikam to Mizpah and lived with him among the people who were left in the land.

Gedaliah Is Assassinated

2Ki 25:22–26

[7] Now all the captains of the forces which were in the fields, they and their men, heard that the king of Babylon had made Gedaliah the son of Ahikam governor in the land and had committed men to him, and women, and children, and some of the poorest of the land

who were not carried away captive to Babylon. [8] Then they came to Gedaliah to Mizpah, even Ishmael the son of Nethaniah, and Johanan and Jonathan the sons of Kareah, and Seraiah the son of Tanhumeth, and the sons of Ephai the Netophathite, and Jezaniah the son of a Maakathite, they and their men. [9] Then Gedaliah the son of Ahikam, the son of Shaphan swore to them and to their men, saying, "Do not be afraid to serve the Chaldeans. Dwell in the land and serve the king of Babylon, and it will be well with you. [10] As for me, I will dwell at Mizpah to serve the Chaldeans who will come to us. But you, gather wine and summer fruits and oil, and put them in your vessels and dwell in your cities that you have taken."

[11] Likewise, also all the Jews who were in Moab, and among the Ammonites, and in Edom, and who were in all the countries, heard that the king of Babylon had left a remnant of Judah, and that he had set over them Gedaliah the son of Ahikam the son of Shaphan. [12] Then all the Jews returned out of all places wherever they were driven and came to the land of Judah, to Gedaliah at Mizpah, and gathered very much wine and summer fruits.

[13] Moreover Johanan the son of Kareah, and all the captains of the forces that were in the fields, came to Gedaliah at Mizpah, [14] and said to him, "Do you certainly know that Baalis, the king of the Ammonites, has sent Ishmael the son of Nethaniah to slay you?" But Gedaliah the son of Ahikam did not believe them.

[15] Then Johanan the son of Kareah spoke to Gedaliah in Mizpah secretly, saying, "Let me go, please, and I will slay Ishmael the son of Nethaniah and no man shall know it. Why should he slay you so that all the Jews who are gathered to you should be scattered and the remnant in Judah perish?"

[16] But Gedaliah the son of Ahikam said to Johanan the son of Kareah, "You shall not do this thing, for you speak falsely of Ishmael."

41 In the seventh month Ishmael the son of Nethaniah, the son of Elishama of the royal seed, and the officials of the king, even ten men with him, came to Gedaliah the son of Ahikam to Mizpah. While they were eating bread together in Mizpah, [2] Ishmael the son of Nethaniah and the ten men that were with him arose and struck Gedaliah the son of Ahikam, the son of Shaphan with the sword and slew him, whom the king of Babylon had made governor over the land. [3] Ishmael also slew all the Jews who were with him, even with Gedaliah at Mizpah, and the Chaldeans who were found there, and the men of war.

[4] On the day after he had slain Gedaliah, when no one knew it, [5] eighty men came from Shechem, from Shiloh, and from Samaria, having their beards shaven, and their clothes torn, and their bodies gashed, with offerings and incense in their hands to bring them to the house of the LORD. [6] Then Ishmael the son of Nethaniah went out from Mizpah to meet them, weeping all along as he went. As he met them, he said to them, "Come to Gedaliah the son of Ahikam!" [7] Yet it was so when they came into the midst of the city that Ishmael the son of Nethaniah, he and the men who were with him, slew them and cast them into the midst of the cistern. [8] But ten men were found among those who said to Ishmael, "Do not slay us, for we have stores in the field, of wheat and barley, and of oil and honey." So he refrained and did not slay them among their brothers. [9] Now the cistern in which Ishmael had cast all the dead bodies of the men, whom he had slain because of Gedaliah, was what Asa the king had made because of Baasha the king of Israel. And Ishmael the son of Nethaniah filled it with those who were slain.

[10] Then Ishmael carried away captive all the rest of the people who were in Mizpah, even the king's daughters, and all the people who remained in Mizpah whom Nebuzaradan the captain of the guard had committed to Gedaliah the son of Ahikam. And Ishmael the son of Nethaniah carried them away captive, and departed to go over to the Ammonites.

[11] But when Johanan the son of Kareah and all the captains of the forces that were with him heard of all the evil that Ishmael the son of Nethaniah had done, [12] then they took all the men and went to fight with Ishmael the son of Nethaniah, and found him by the great waters that are in Gibeon. [13] And when all the people who were with Ishmael saw Johanan the son of Kareah and all the captains of the forces that were with him, they were glad. [14] So all the people whom Ishmael had

carried away captive from Mizpah turned about and returned, and went to Johanan the son of Kareah. [15] But Ishmael the son of Nethaniah escaped from Johanan with eight men and went to the Ammonites.

[16] Then Johanan the son of Kareah and all the captains of the forces that were with him took all the remnant of the people whom he had recovered from Ishmael the son of Nethaniah, from Mizpah, after he had slain Gedaliah the son of Ahikam, even mighty men of war, and the women, and the children, and the eunuchs, whom he had brought back from Gibeon. [17] And they departed and lived in the habitation of Geruth Kimham, which is by Bethlehem, intending to go to Egypt, [18] because of the Chaldeans. For they were afraid of them, because Ishmael the son of Nethaniah had slain Gedaliah the son of Ahikam, whom the king of Babylon made governor in the land.

Jeremiah Warns Against Going to Egypt

42 Then all the captains of the forces, and Johanan the son of Kareah, and Jezaniah the son of Hoshaiah, and all the people from the least even to the greatest came near, [2] and said to Jeremiah the prophet, "Please let our supplication be accepted before you, and pray for us to the LORD your God, even for all this remnant. For we are left but a few out of many, as your eyes now see us. [3] Pray that the LORD your God may show us the way in which we should walk and the thing that we should do."

[4] Then Jeremiah the prophet said to them, "I have heard you. I will pray to the LORD your God according to your words. And it shall come to pass, that whatever the LORD will answer you, I will declare it to you. I will keep nothing back from you."

[5] Then they said to Jeremiah, "May the LORD be a true and faithful witness against us, if we do not act according to all things for which the LORD your God shall send you to us. [6] Whether it is good or whether it is bad, we will obey the voice of the LORD our God, to whom we send you so that it may be well with us when we obey the voice of the LORD our God."

[7] At the end of ten days the word of the LORD came to Jeremiah. [8] Then he called Johanan the son of Kareah and all the captains of the forces that were with him and all the people from the least even to the greatest, [9] and said to them, "Thus says the LORD, the God of Israel, to whom you sent me to present your supplication before Him: [10] If you will still abide in this land, then I will build you up and not pull you down, and I will plant you and not pluck you up; for I will relent of the disaster that I have brought on you. [11] Do not be afraid of the king of Babylon of whom you are now afraid. Do not be afraid of him, says the LORD. For I am with you to save you and to deliver you from his hand. [12] I will show mercies to you so that he may have mercy on you and cause you to return to your own land.

[13] "But if you say, 'We will not dwell in this land,' so as not to obey the voice of the LORD your God, [14] saying, 'No, but we will go into the land of Egypt where we shall see no war, nor hear the sound of the trumpet, nor have hunger for bread, and there we will dwell,' [15] now therefore hear the word of the LORD, O remnant of Judah. Thus says the LORD of Hosts, the God of Israel: If you wholly set your faces to enter Egypt, and go to dwell there, [16] then it shall come to pass that the sword which you feared shall overtake you there in the land of Egypt and the famine of which you were afraid shall follow close after you there in Egypt. And there you shall die. [17] So it shall be with all the men who set their faces to go into Egypt to sojourn there. They shall die by the sword, by famine, and by pestilence. And none of them shall remain or escape from the disaster that I will bring upon them. [18] For thus says the LORD of Hosts, the God of Israel: As My anger and My fury have been poured out upon the inhabitants of Jerusalem, so will My fury be poured out upon you when you go to Egypt. And you will be an execration, and an astonishment, and a curse, and a reproach. And you shall see this place no more.

[19] "The LORD has said concerning you, O remnant of Judah, Do not go into Egypt! Know certainly that I have admonished you this day. [20] For you have only deceived yourselves when you sent me to the LORD your God, saying, 'Pray for us to the LORD our God. And according to all that the LORD our God shall say, so declare to us, and we will do it.' [21] Now I have this day declared it to you. But you have not obeyed the voice of the LORD your God, or anything for which He has sent me to you. [22] Now therefore certainly know that you will die by the sword, by famine, and by pestilence, in the place wherever you desire to go and to sojourn."

Jeremiah Taken to Egypt

43 When Jeremiah had finished speaking to all the people all these words of the LORD their God, with which the LORD their God had sent him to them, [2] Azariah the son of Hoshaiah, and Johanan the son of Kareah, and all the proud men said to Jeremiah, "You speak falsely. The LORD our God has not sent you to say, 'Do not go into Egypt to sojourn there.' [3] But Baruch the son of Neriah sets you against us to deliver us into the hand of the Chaldeans, that they might put us to death and carry us away captives into Babylon."

[4] So Johanan the son of Kareah and all the captains of the forces and all the people did not obey the voice of the LORD to dwell in the land of Judah. [5] But Johanan the son of Kareah and all the captains of the forces took all the remnant of Judah who had returned from all nations wherever they had been driven to dwell in the land of Judah, [6] even men, and women, and children, and the king's daughters, and every person that Nebuzaradan the captain of the guard had left with Gedaliah the son of Ahikam, the son of Shaphan, and Jeremiah the prophet, and Baruch the son of Neriah. [7] So they came into the land of Egypt because they did not obey the voice of the LORD. Thus they entered as far as Tahpanhes.

[8] Then the word of the LORD came to Jeremiah in Tahpanhes, saying: [9] Take some large stones in your hand and hide them in the clay in the brick kiln which is at the entrance of Pharaoh's house in Tahpanhes, in the sight of the men of Judah, [10] and say to them, Thus says the LORD of Hosts, the God of Israel: I will send and take Nebuchadnezzar the king of Babylon, My servant, and will set his throne upon these stones that I have hid; and he shall spread his royal pavilion over them. [11] When he comes, he shall ravage the land of Egypt and deliver whoever is *meant* for death to death, and whoever is *meant* for captivity to captivity, and whoever is *meant* for the sword to the sword. [12] I will kindle a fire in the houses of the gods of Egypt and he shall burn them and carry them away captives. And he shall array himself with the land of Egypt, as a shepherd puts on his garment, and he shall depart from there in peace. [13] He shall also break the images of Heliopolis that is in the land of Egypt, and the houses of the gods of the Egyptians he shall burn with fire.

Idolatry Leads to Judgment

44 The word that came to Jeremiah concerning all the Jews which dwell in the land of Egypt, who dwell at Migdol, and Tahpanhes, and Memphis, and in the country of Pathros,[*f*] saying, [2] Thus says the LORD of Hosts, the God of Israel: You have seen all the calamity that I have brought upon Jerusalem and upon all the cities of Judah. Look at them; today they are a desolation, and no man dwells in them, [3] because of their wickedness, which they have committed to provoke Me to anger, in that they went to burn incense and to serve other gods, whom they did not know; they nor you nor your fathers. [4] However, I sent to you all My servants the prophets, rising early and sending them, saying, "Oh, do not do this abominable thing that I hate." [5] But they did not listen nor incline their ear to turn from their wickedness, not to burn incense to other gods. [6] Therefore My fury and My anger was poured out and was kindled in the cities of Judah and in the streets of Jerusalem; and they are ruined and desolate, as it is this day.

[7] Now thus says the LORD God of Hosts, the God of Israel: Why are you committing this great evil against your souls, to cut off from you man and woman, child and infant, out of Judah, leaving you no one to remain, [8] provoking Me to wrath with the works of your hands, burning incense to other gods in the land of Egypt, where you have gone to dwell, so that you might cut yourselves off and become a curse and a reproach among all the nations of the earth? [9] Have you forgotten the wickedness of your fathers, and the wickedness of the kings of Judah, and the wickedness of their wives, and your own wickedness, and the wickedness of your wives, which they have committed in the land of Judah and in the streets of Jerusalem? [10] They are not humbled even to this day, nor have they feared, nor have they walked in My law and My statutes that I set before you and before your fathers.

[11] Therefore thus says the LORD of Hosts, the God of Israel: I will set My face against you for disaster, and to cut off all Judah. [12] I will take the remnant of Judah who have set their faces to go into the land of Egypt to sojourn there, and they all will be consumed and fall in the

land of Egypt. They will even be consumed by the sword and by the famine. They will die, from the least even to the greatest, by the sword and by the famine; and they will be an execration, and an astonishment, and a curse, and a reproach. [13] For I will punish those who dwell in the land of Egypt, as I have punished Jerusalem; by the sword, by famine, and by pestilence. [14] So none of the remnant of Judah who have gone into the land of Egypt to sojourn there will escape or remain, with the result that they return into the land of Judah to which they have a desire to return to dwell there. For no one shall return except those who escape.

[15] Then all the men who knew that their wives had burned incense to other gods and all the women that stood by, a great multitude, even all the people who lived in the land of Egypt, in Pathros, answered Jeremiah, saying: [16] "As for the word that you have spoken to us in the name of the LORD, we will not listen to you. [17] But we will certainly do whatever we have vowed, to burn incense to the queen of heaven, and to pour out drink offerings to her, as we have done, we, and our fathers, our kings, and our officials, in the cities of Judah and in the streets of Jerusalem. For then we had plenty of food, and were well off, and saw no disaster. [18] But since we left off burning incense to the queen of heaven and pouring out drink offerings to her, we have been in want of all things and have been consumed by the sword and by the famine."

[19] *The women also said*, "When we burned incense to the queen of heaven, and poured out drink offerings to her, did we make her cakes to worship her and pour out drink offerings to her without our husbands?"

Calamity for the Jews

[20] Then Jeremiah said to all the people, to the men and to the women, and to all the people who had given him such an answer: [21] "The incense offerings that you burned in the cities of Judah and in the streets of Jerusalem, you, and your fathers, your kings, and your officials, and the people of the land, did not the LORD remember them and did they not come into His mind? [22] So the LORD could no longer bear it because of the evil of your deeds and because of the abominations which you have committed. Therefore your land is a desolation, and an astonishment, and a curse, without an inhabitant, as it is this day. [23] Because you have burned incense and because you have sinned against the LORD and have not obeyed the voice of the LORD, nor walked in His law, nor in His statutes, nor in His testimonies, therefore this calamity has happened to you, as it is this day."

[24] Moreover Jeremiah said to all the people and to all the women, "Hear the word of the LORD, all Judah who are in the land of Egypt. [25] Thus says the LORD of Hosts, the God of Israel: You and your wives have both spoken with your mouths and fulfilled with your hand, saying, 'We will surely perform our vows that we have vowed, to burn incense to the queen of heaven and to pour out drink offerings to her.'

"Proceed to accomplish your vows and surely perform your vows! [26] Yet hear the word of the LORD, all Judah who dwells in the land of Egypt: I have sworn by My great name, says the LORD, that My name shall no more be named in the mouth of any man of Judah in all the land of Egypt, saying, 'As the Lord GOD lives.' [27] I will watch over them for disaster and not for good. And all the men of Judah who are in the land of Egypt shall be consumed by the sword and by the famine until there is an end of them. [28] Yet a small number who escape the sword shall return out of the land of Egypt into the land of Judah, and all the remnant of Judah who have gone into the land of Egypt to sojourn there will know whose words will stand, Mine or theirs.

[29] "This will be a sign to you, says the LORD, that I will punish you in this place so that you may know that My words shall surely stand against you for disaster. [30] Thus says the LORD: I will give Pharaoh Hophra the king of Egypt into the hand of his enemies and into the hand of those who seek his life, just as I gave Zedekiah king of Judah into the hand of Nebuchadnezzar king of Babylon, who was his enemy, and sought his life."

A Message to Baruch

45 The word that Jeremiah the prophet spoke to Baruch the son of Neriah when he had written these words in a book at the mouth of Jeremiah, in the fourth year of Jehoiakim the son of Josiah, king of Judah, saying: [2] Thus says the LORD, the God of Israel, to you, O Baruch: [3] You said, "Alas, woe is me! For the LORD has added grief to my

sorrow. I fainted in my sighing, and I find no rest." [4] Thus you shall say to him, "Thus says the LORD: That which I have built I will break down, and that which I have planted I will pluck up, even this whole land. [5] But are you seeking great things for yourself? Do not seek them. For I will bring disaster upon all flesh, says the LORD, but I will give your life to you as booty in all the places where you go."

Judgment on Egypt

46 The word of the LORD which came to Jeremiah the prophet against the nations:

[2] Concerning Egypt, about the army of Pharaoh Necho king of Egypt, which was by the River Euphrates in Carchemish, which Nebuchadnezzar king of Babylon defeated in the fourth year of Jehoiakim the son of Josiah, king of Judah:

[3] Order the buckler and shield,
   and draw near to battle!
[4] Harness the horses;
   mount the steeds!
Take your positions
   with your helmets,
polish the spears,
   put on the armor!
[5] Why have I seen them
   dismayed and drawing back?
Their mighty ones are beaten down
   and have taken refuge in flight,
and not looking back.
   Terror is on every side!
   says the LORD.
[6] Let not the swift flee away,
   nor the mighty man escape;
they will stumble and fall
   towards the north by the River Euphrates.

[7] Who is this that comes up as the Nile,
   whose waters surge about as the rivers?
[8] Egypt rises up like the Nile,
   and his waters surge about like the rivers.
And he has said, I will go up and will cover the land.
   I will surely destroy the city and its inhabitants.
[9] Come up, O horses,
   and rage, O chariots!
And let the mighty men come forth:
   the Ethiopians and the Libyans who handle the shield,
   and the Lydians who handle and bend the bow.
[10] For this is the day of the Lord GOD of Hosts,
   a day of vengeance, so that He may avenge Himself of His
      adversaries.
And the sword will devour;
   and it will be satiated and made drunk with their blood;
for the Lord GOD of Hosts has a slaughter
   in the north country by the River Euphrates.

[11] Go up into Gilead and take balm,
   O virgin daughter of Egypt;
in vain you shall use many medicines,
   for you will not be cured.
[12] The nations have heard of your shame,
   and your cry has filled the land;
for the mighty man has stumbled over the mighty,
   and they both have fallen together.

Defeat of Egypt Foretold

[13] The word that the LORD spoke to Jeremiah the prophet, about Nebuchadnezzar king of Babylon coming to strike the land of Egypt.

[14] Declare in Egypt and publish in Migdol, .
   and publish in Memphis and in Tahpanhes;
say, "Stand fast and prepare yourself,
   for the sword will devour those about you."

15 Why have your valiant men become prostrate?
    They do not stand because the LORD has thrust them down.
16 He made many to fall.
    Indeed, each one has fallen upon another.
    Then they said, "Arise and let us go back
      to our own people and to the land of our nativity,
      away from the oppressing sword."
17 They cried there,
    "Pharaoh king of Egypt is a tumult.
    He has let the time appointed pass by!"

18 As I live, says the King
      whose name is the LORD of Hosts,
    surely as Tabor is among the mountains,
      and as Carmel by the sea, so he shall come.
19 O daughter dwelling in Egypt,
    prepare your baggage for captivity,
    for Memphis will become desolate,
      it will even be burned down without an inhabitant.

20 Egypt is like a very fair heifer,
      but destruction comes,
      it comes out of the north.
21 Also her mercenaries are in her midst
      like fat bulls,
    for they also have turned back and have fled away together.
      They did not stand their ground
    because the day of their calamity has come upon them,
      even the time of their punishment.
22 Its sound goes along like a serpent,
      for they march on as an army,
    and come against her with axes,
      as choppers of wood.
23 They have cut down her forest,
      says the LORD.
    Surely it will not be found any more,
    even though they are now more numerous than the grasshoppers,
      and are innumerable.
24 The daughter of Egypt has been humiliated;
      she has been delivered into the hand of the people of the
        north.

25 The LORD of Hosts, the God of Israel, says: See, I will punish Amon of Thebes, and Pharaoh, and Egypt, with their gods and their kings, even Pharaoh and all those who trust in him. 26 And I shall deliver them into the hand of those who seek their lives and into the hand of Nebuchadnezzar king of Babylon and into the hand of his servants. But afterwards it will be inhabited, as in the days of old, says the LORD.

God Will Save Israel

27 But do not fear, O My servant Jacob,
      and do not be dismayed, O Israel.
    For I will save you from afar off,
      and your seed from the land of their captivity;
    and Jacob shall return and be in rest and at ease,
      and no one shall make him afraid.
28 Do not fear, O Jacob My servant,
      says the LORD, for I am with you;
    for I will make a full end of all the nations
      where I have driven you.
    However, I will not make a full end of you,
    but correct you in measure,
      and I will not leave you wholly unpunished.

Judgment on the Philistines

47 The word of the LORD which came to Jeremiah the prophet against the Philistines, before Pharaoh conquered Gaza.

2 Thus says the LORD:

See, waters rise up out of the north
      and will be an overflowing flood,
    and will overflow the land, and all that is in it,
      the city and those who dwell in it.
    Then the men shall cry out
      and all the inhabitants of the land will howl
3   at the noise of the stamping of the hoofs of his strong horses,
      at the rushing of his chariots,
      and at the rumbling of his wheels.
    The fathers will not look back to their children
      because of the feebleness of their hands,
4   because of the day that comes
        to destroy all the Philistines
    and to cut off from Tyre and Sidon
        every helper that remains.
    For the LORD will destroy the Philistines,
        the remnant of the country of Caphtor.
5   Baldness has come upon Gaza;
        Ashkelon has been cut off.
    O remnant of their valley,
        how long shall you gash yourself?

6   O sword of the LORD,
        how long shall you not be quiet?
    Withdraw into your sheath,
        rest, and be still.
7   How can it be quiet,
        seeing the LORD has given it a charge
    against Ashkelon and against the sea shore?
        There He has appointed it.

Judgment on Moab
Isa 16:6–12

48 Concerning Moab:

Thus says the LORD of Hosts, the God of Israel:

Woe to Nebo, for it is devastated.
      Kiriathaim is humiliated and captured;
      Misgab[1] is humiliated and dismayed.
2   There is no more praise for Moab;
      in Heshbon they have devised evil against her:
      "Come and let us cut it off from being a nation!"
    Also you will be cut down, O Madmen.
      The sword will pursue you.
3   A sound of crying will be from Horonaim:
      "Devastation and great destruction!"
4   "Moab is destroyed";
        her little ones have caused a cry of distress to
          be heard;
5   for by the Ascent of Luhith they will go up
        with continual weeping;
    for at the descent of Horonaim
        they have heard a cry of destruction.
6   Flee, save your lives,
        and be like the juniper in the wilderness.
7   For because you have trusted in your works and in
          your treasures,
        you will also be captured;
    and Chemosh shall go forth into captivity
        together with his priests and his officials.
8   The destroyer will come upon every city,
        and no city will escape.
    The valley also will perish,
        and the plain will be destroyed,
        as the LORD has spoken.
9   Give wings to Moab,
        that she may flee and get away;
    for the cities will become desolate,
        without any to dwell in them.

1 1 Or *the stronghold.*

¹⁰ Cursed be he who does the work of the LORD negligently,
    and cursed be he who keeps back his sword from blood.

¹¹ Moab has been at ease from his youth,
    and he has also been undisturbed,
    like wine on its dregs,
and he has not been emptied from vessel to vessel,
    nor has he gone into captivity.
Therefore his taste remained in him,
    and his scent has not changed.
¹² Therefore, surely the days are coming,
    says the LORD,
when I will send to him those who tip vessels,
    and they will tip him over,
and will empty his vessels
    and break his bottles.
¹³ Moab shall be ashamed of Chemosh,
    as the house of Israel was ashamed
    of Bethel, their confidence.

¹⁴ How do you say, "We are mighty
    and strong men for the war"?
¹⁵ Moab has been devastated and gone up out of her cities,
    and her chosen young men have also gone down to the
      slaughter,
    says the King whose name is the LORD of Hosts.
¹⁶ The calamity of Moab will come soon,
    and his affliction hastens fast.
¹⁷ All you who are about him, mourn for him.
    And all you who know his name,
say, "How the strong staff has been broken,
    the beautiful rod!"

¹⁸ O daughter who inhabits Dibon,
    come down from your glory
    and sit on the parched ground,
for the destroyer of Moab
    will come upon you,
    and he will destroy your strongholds.
¹⁹ O inhabitant of Aroer,
    stand by the road and keep watch.
Ask him who flees and her who escapes,
    and say, "What has happened?"
²⁰ Moab has been humiliated, for it has been broken down.
    Howl and cry out.
Tell it in Arnon,
    that Moab has been devastated.
²¹ And judgment has come upon the plain country:
    upon Holon and Jahzah and Mephaath,
²²   and Dibon and Nebo and Beth Diblathaim,
²³   and Kiriathaim and Beth Gamul and Beth Meon,
²⁴   and Kerioth and Bozrah,
    and all the cities of the land of Moab, far and near.
²⁵ The horn of Moab has been cut off
    and his arm has been broken,
    says the LORD.

²⁶ Make him drunk,
    for he magnified himself against the LORD.
Moab also will wallow in his vomit,
    and he also will be held in derision.
²⁷ For was not Israel a derision to you?
    Or was he caught among thieves?
For each time you speak of him,
    you shake your head in scorn.
²⁸ O you who dwell in Moab,
    leave the cities and dwell in the rock,
and be like the dove that makes her nest
    in the sides of the hole's mouth.

²⁹ We have heard of the pride of Moab
    (he is very proud),

of his loftiness, and his arrogance, and his pride,
    and the haughtiness of his heart.
³⁰ I know his wrath,
    says the LORD,
but it is futile. His lies have accomplished nothing.
³¹ Therefore I will howl for Moab,
    and I will cry out for all Moab.
My heart shall mourn for the men of Kir Hareseth.
³² O vine of Sibmah,
    I will weep for you more than the weeping of Jazer.
Your plants have stretched over the sea,
    they reach even to the sea of Jazer.
The destroyer has fallen upon your summer fruits
    and upon your vintage.
³³ Joy and gladness are taken away
    from the plentiful field, even from the land of Moab,
and I have caused wine to fail from the winepresses;
    no one will tread with shouting.
    Their shouting will not be shouts of joy.

³⁴ From the outcry of Heshbon even to Elealeh, and even to Jahaz,
    they have uttered their voice,
from Zoar even to Horonaim and to Eglath Shelishiyah;
    for also the waters of Nimrim shall become desolate.
³⁵ Moreover I will cause to cease in Moab,
    says the LORD,
him who offers *sacrifice* in the high place
    and him who burns incense to his gods.

³⁶ Therefore My heart will wail for Moab like pipes,
    and My heart will wail like pipes for the men of Kir Hareseth,
    because the riches that they have gotten have perished.
³⁷ For every head will be bald
    and every beard clipped;
upon all the hands will be gashes,
    and upon the loins sackcloth.
³⁸ There will be lamentation everywhere
    upon all the housetops of Moab
    and in the streets,
for I have broken Moab
    like a vessel in which is no pleasure,
    says the LORD.
³⁹ How it is broken down! How they have wailed!
    How Moab has turned his back with shame!
So Moab will be a derision
    and a terror to all around him.

⁴⁰ For thus says the LORD:

Look, one will fly as an eagle
    and spread his wings against Moab.
⁴¹ Kerioth has been captured,
    and the strongholds have been seized,
and the mighty men's hearts in Moab in that day
    will be as the heart of a woman in her pangs.
⁴² Moab will be destroyed from being a people
    because he has magnified himself against the LORD.
⁴³ Fear and the pit and the snare will be upon you,
    O inhabitant of Moab,
    says the LORD.
⁴⁴ He who flees from the terror
    shall fall into the pit,
and he who gets up out of the pit
    will be taken in the snare;
for I will bring upon it, even upon Moab,
    the year of their punishment,
    says the LORD.

⁴⁵ The fugitives stand without strength
    under the shadow of Heshbon;
for a fire will come out of Heshbon
    and a flame from the midst of Sihon,

and will devour the forehead of Moab
  and the crown of the head of the tumultuous ones.
46 Woe to you, O Moab!
  The people of Chemosh have perished;
for your sons have been taken away captive
  and your daughters into captivity.

47 Yet I will restore the fortunes of Moab
  in the latter days,
  says the LORD.

Thus far is the judgment of Moab.

Judgment on Ammon

49 Concerning the Ammonites:

Thus says the LORD:

Does Israel have no sons?
  Or has he no heirs?
Why then does their king inherit Gad
  and his people dwell in his cities?
2 Therefore, surely the days are coming,
  says the LORD,
when I will cause an alarm of war
  to be heard in Rabbah of the Ammonites;
and it will be a desolate heap,
  and her towns will be burned with fire.
Then Israel will be heir
  to those who were his heirs,
  says the LORD.
3 Howl, O Heshbon, for Ai has been devastated!
  Cry out, O daughters of Rabbah,
gird yourselves with sackcloth and lament,
  and run to and fro inside the walls;
for their king shall go into captivity,
  and his priests and his officials together.
4 Why do you glory in the valleys,
  your flowing valley,
O backsliding daughter
  who trusts in her treasures, saying,
  "Who shall come against me?"
5 I will bring a fear upon you,
  says the Lord GOD of Hosts,
  from all those who are around you;
and each of you will be driven out headlong,
  and no one will gather together the fugitives.

6 Yet afterward I will restore the fortunes of the sons
  of Ammon,
  says the LORD.

Judgment on Edom

Ob 1–6
7 Concerning Edom.

Thus says the LORD of Hosts:

Is there no more wisdom in Teman?
  Has counsel perished from the prudent?
  Has their wisdom vanished?
8 Flee, turn back, dwell in the depths,
  O inhabitants of Dedan.
For I will bring the calamity of Esau upon him,
  the time that I punish him.
9 If grape gatherers came to you,
  would they not leave some gleaning grapes?
If thieves came by night,
  they would destroy until they had enough.
10 But I have made Esau bare,
  I have uncovered his secret places
so that he will not be able to hide himself.

His seed is devastated, and his brothers, and his neighbors,
  and he is no more.
11 Leave your fatherless children behind. I will preserve them alive;
  and let your widows trust in Me.

12 For thus says the LORD: They whose judgment was not to drink of the cup have assuredly drunk. And are you the one who shall go unpunished altogether? You will not go unpunished, but you will surely drink of it. 13 For I have sworn by Myself, says the LORD, that Bozrah will become a desolation, a reproach, a waste, and a curse. And all the cities will become perpetual wastes.

14 I have heard a message from the LORD,
  and an ambassador has been sent to the nations:
  "Gather together, and come against her,
  and rise up to the battle!"

15 For I will make you small among the nations,
  and despised among men.
16 As for the terror of you,
  the pride of your heart has deceived you,
O you who dwell in the clefts of the rock,
  who hold the height of the hill.
Though you make your nest as high as the eagle,
  I will bring you down from there,
  says the LORD.
17 Also Edom will become a desolation;
  everyone who goes by it will be astonished,
  and will hiss at all its wounds.
18 As in the overthrow of Sodom and Gomorrah
  and the neighboring cities,
  says the LORD,
no man will abide there,
  nor will a son of man dwell in it.

19 He will come up like a lion from the thickets of the Jordan
  against the perpetually watered meadow;
but I will suddenly make him run away from her.
  And I will appoint over her whomever I choose.
For who is like Me? And who will summon Me *into court*?
  Who is the shepherd who can stand against Me?

20 Therefore hear the counsel of the LORD that He has planned
  against Edom,
  and His purposes that He has purposed against the
  inhabitants of Teman:
Surely the least of the flock will drag them out;
  surely He will make their habitations desolate because of them.
21 The earth has shaken at the noise of their fall;
  there is an outcry. Its noise has been heard at the Red Sea.
22 He will mount up and fly as the eagle
  and spread his wings against Bozrah;
and in that day the hearts of the mighty men of Edom
  will be as the heart of a woman in her pangs.

Judgment on Damascus

23 Concerning Damascus:

Hamath and Arpad have been humiliated,
  for they have heard bad news.
They are faint-hearted;
  there is sorrow on the sea; it cannot be quieted.
24 Damascus has become helpless;
  she has turned away to flee,
  and panic has seized her.
Anguish and sorrows have seized her
  as a woman in labor.
25 How the city of praise has not been deserted,
  the city of My joy!
26 Therefore her young men will fall in her streets,
  and all the men of war will be cut off in that day,
  says the LORD of Hosts.

27 I will kindle a fire to the wall of Damascus,
    and it will consume the palaces of Ben-Hadad.

Judgment on Kedar and Hazor

28 Concerning Kedar, and concerning the kingdoms of Hazor, which Nebuchadnezzar king of Babylon defeated:

Thus says the LORD:

Arise, go up to Kedar,
    and destroy the men of the East.
29 Their tents and their flocks they will take away.
    They will carry away their curtains for themselves,
    and all their vessels, and their camels;
and they will call out to one another,
    "Terror is on every side!"

30 Flee, go far away,
    dwell in the depths, O inhabitants of Hazor,
    says the LORD.
For Nebuchadnezzar king of Babylon has taken counsel against
        you,
    and has conceived a purpose against you.

31 Arise, go up to the nation at ease,
    that dwells securely,
    says the LORD.
It has neither gates nor bars;
    they dwell alone.
32 Their camels will become plunder,
    and the multitude of their cattle booty.
And I will scatter into all winds those who cut the corners *of*
        their hair,
    and I will bring their calamity from all sides,
    says the LORD.
33 Hazor will become a dwelling for jackals
    and a desolation forever.
No man will abide there,
    nor any son of man dwell in it.

Judgment on Elam

34 The word of the LORD which came to Jeremiah the prophet against Elam in the beginning of the reign of Zedekiah king of Judah, saying:

35 Thus says the LORD of Hosts:

I will break the bow of Elam,
    the chief of their might.
36 Upon Elam I will bring the four winds
    from the four quarters of heaven,
and will scatter them toward all those winds.
    And there will be no nation
    where the outcasts of Elam will not go.
37 For I will cause Elam to be dismayed before their enemies,
    and before those who seek their life.
And I will bring disaster upon them,
    even My fierce anger,
    says the LORD;
and I will send the sword after them
    until I have consumed them.
38 And I will set My throne in Elam
    and will destroy from there the king and the officials,
    says the LORD.
39 But it will come to pass in the latter days
    that I will restore the fortunes of Elam,
    says the LORD.

Judgment on Babylon

Jer 10:12–16

50 The word that the LORD spoke against Babylon and against the land of the Chaldeans by Jeremiah the prophet:

2 Declare among the nations and publish,
    and set up a standard;
    do not conceal it, but say,
Babylon has been captured.
    Bel has been humiliated.
    Marduk has been broken in pieces;
    her idols have been humiliated;
    her images have been broken in pieces.
3 For out of the north there comes up a nation against her,
    which will make her land desolate,
and no one will dwell in it.
    They will wander away;
they will depart,
    both man and beast.

4 In those days and at that time,
    says the LORD,
the sons of Israel will come,
    they and the children of Judah together.
They will go along weeping as they go,
    and seek the LORD their God.
5 They will ask for the way to Zion
    with their faces in its direction.
They will come that they may join themselves to the LORD
    in a perpetual covenant
    that will not be forgotten.

6 My people have been lost sheep.
    Their shepherds have caused them to go astray;
they have turned them away on the mountains.
    They have gone from mountain to hill
    and have forgotten their resting place.
7 All who found them have devoured them,
    and their adversaries said, "We are not guilty,
because they have sinned against the LORD, the habitation
        of justice,
    even the LORD, the hope of their fathers."

8 Wander away out of the midst of Babylon,
    and go out of the land of the Chaldeans,
    and be as the male goats before the flocks.
9 For I will raise and cause to come up against Babylon
    an assembly of great nations from the north country.
And they shall set themselves in array against her;
    from there she shall be taken captive.
Their arrows *will be* like *those* of a skilled warrior;
    no one shall return empty-handed.
10 Chaldea will become plunder;
    all who destroy her will be satisfied,
    says the LORD.

11 Because you were glad, because you rejoiced,
    O you destroyers of My heritage,
because you have grown fat as the heifer at the grass,
    and bellow as bulls,
12 your mother will be sorely humiliated;
    she who bore you will be ashamed.
She will be the least of the nations,
    a wilderness, a dry land, and a desert.
13 Because of the wrath of the LORD she will not be inhabited,
    but shall be wholly desolate.
Everyone who goes by Babylon will be astonished
    and hiss at all her wounds.

14 Put yourselves in battle array against Babylon
        all around,
    all you who bend the bow;
shoot at her, spare no arrows,
    for she has sinned against the LORD.
15 Shout against her all around;
    she has given herself up, her foundations have fallen,
    her walls have been thrown down.

For this is the vengeance of the LORD.
　　Take vengeance on her;
　　as she has done, do to her.
16 Cut off the sower from Babylon,
　　and him who handles the sickle in the time of harvest.
　For fear of the oppressing sword
　　everyone will turn to his people,
　　and everyone will flee to his own land.

17 Israel is a scattered flock.
　　The lions have driven him away.
　First the king of Assyria
　　devoured him;
　and this last one who has broken his bones
　　is Nebuchadnezzar king of Babylon.

18 Therefore thus says the LORD of Hosts, the God of Israel:

　I will punish the king of Babylon and his land,
　　as I have punished the king of Assyria.
19 I will bring Israel again to his habitation,
　　and he will feed on Carmel and Bashan,
　and his soul will be satisfied
　　upon Mount Ephraim and Gilead.
20 In those days and at that time,
　　says the LORD,
　the iniquity of Israel will be sought for,
　　and there shall be none.
　And the sins of Judah,
　　but they shall not be found;
　　for I will pardon those whom I leave as a remnant.

21 Go up against the land of Merathaim, even against it,
　　and against the inhabitants of Pekod.
　Slay and utterly destroy them,
　　says the LORD,
　　and do according to all that I have commanded you.
22 A noise of battle is in the land,
　　and great destruction.
23 How the hammer of the whole earth
　　has been cut asunder and broken!
　How Babylon has become a desolation
　　among the nations!
24 I have laid a snare for you,
　　and you were also caught, O Babylon,
　　and you were not aware.
　You have been found, and also caught,
　　because you have striven against the LORD.
25 The LORD has opened His armory
　　and has brought out the weapons of His indignation,
　for this is the work of the Lord GOD of Hosts
　　in the land of the Chaldeans.
26 Come against her from the utmost border,
　　open her storehouses;
　cast her up as heaps and destroy her utterly;
　　let nothing of her be left.
27 Slay all her bulls,
　　let them go down to the slaughter.
　Woe to them! For their day has come,
　　the time of their punishment.
28 There is the sound of those who flee and escape out of the land of Babylon,
　　to declare in Zion
　the vengeance of the LORD our God,
　　the vengeance of His temple.

29 Call together the archers against Babylon.
　　All you who bend the bow,
　encamp against it all around;
　　let no one escape.
　Recompense her according to her work;
　　according to all that she has done, do to her,

for she has been proud against the LORD,
　　against the Holy One of Israel.
30 Therefore her young men shall fall in the streets,
　　and all her men of war shall be cut off in that day,
　　says the LORD.
31 I am against you, O most proud,
　　says the Lord GOD of Hosts,
　for your day has come,
　　the time when I will punish you.
32 The most proud will stumble and fall,
　　and no one will raise him up;
　and I will kindle a fire in his cities,
　　and it will devour all all around him.

33 Thus says the LORD of Hosts:

　The sons of Israel and the sons of Judah
　　were oppressed together;
　and all who took them captives held them fast;
　　they refused to let them go.
34 Their Redeemer is strong;
　　the LORD of Hosts is His name.
　He will thoroughly plead their case,
　　that He may give rest to the land,
　　but disquiet to the inhabitants of Babylon.

35 A sword is against the Chaldeans,
　　says the LORD,
　and against the inhabitants of Babylon,
　　and against her officials, and against her wise men.
36 A sword is against the oracle priests,
　　and they will become fools.
　A sword is against her mighty men,
　　and they shall be dismayed.
37 A sword is against their horses, and against their chariots,
　　and against all the foreigners who are in her midst;
　　and they will become as women.
　A sword is against her treasures,
　　and they will be robbed.
38 A drought is against her waters,
　　and they will be dried up.
　For it is the land of graven images,
　　and they are mad over their idols.

39 Therefore the wild beasts of the desert
　　with the wild beasts of the islands will dwell there,
　　and the ostriches will dwell in it.
　It will be inhabited no more forever,
　　nor will it be lived in from generation to generation.
40 As God overthrew Sodom and Gomorrah
　　and the neighboring cities,
　　says the LORD,
　so no man will abide there,
　　nor will any son of man dwell in it.

41 Look! A people shall come from the north
　　and a great nation, and many kings
　　will be raised up from the remote parts of the earth.
42 They will hold the bow and the lance;
　　they are cruel and will not show mercy.
　Their voice shall roar like the sea;
　　and they shall ride on horses,
　everyone put in array, like a man to the battle,
　　against you, O daughter of Babylon.
43 The king of Babylon has heard the report of them,
　　and his hands waxed feeble.
　Anguish took hold of him,
　　and pangs as of a woman in labor.
44 He will come up like a lion from the thicket of the Jordan
　　to the perpetually watered meadow.
　But I will make them suddenly run away from it,
　　and whoever is chosen I will appoint over it.

For who is like Me? And who will summon Me *into court?*
     And who is the shepherd that can stand before Me?

45 Therefore hear the counsel of the LORD that He has planned
     against Babylon,
     and His purposes that He has purposed against the land of
        the Chaldeans:
Surely the least of the flock will drag them out.
     Surely He will make their habitation desolate because of
        them.
46 At the shout, "Babylon has been seized!" the earth is shaken,
     and the outcry is heard among the nations.

The Destruction of Babylon

51 Thus says the LORD:

I will raise up against Babylon,
     and against those who dwell in Leb Kamai,
     the spirit of a destroyer.
2 And I will send foreigners to Babylon
     that they may winnow her and empty her land.
For in the day of trouble
     they will be against her all around.
3 Let not him who bends his bow bend it,
     and let him not rise up in his scale-armor,
and do not spare her young men;
     utterly destroy all her host.
4 Thus the slain will fall in the land of the Chaldeans,
     and those who are thrust through in her streets.
5 For Israel has not been forsaken, nor Judah,
     by his God, the LORD of Hosts,
though their land was filled with sin
     against the Holy One of Israel.

6 Flee out of the midst of Babylon,
     and each of you deliver his soul!
Do not be cut off in her punishment,
     for this is the time of the vengeance of the LORD;
     He will render to her a recompense.
7 Babylon has been a golden cup in the hand of the LORD,
     that made all the earth drunk.
The nations have drunk of her wine;
     therefore the nations are mad.
8 Babylon is suddenly fallen and destroyed.
Howl for her.
Take balm for her pain;
     perhaps she may be healed.

9 We applied healing to Babylon,
     but she is not healed.
Forsake her, and let us each go into his own country;
     for her judgment reaches to heaven
     and is lifted up even to the skies.

10 The LORD has brought forth our righteousness.
     Come, and let us declare in Zion
     the work of the LORD our God.

11 Sharpen the arrows.
     Gather the shields.
The LORD has raised up the spirit of the kings of the Medes.
     For His device is against Babylon, to destroy it;
because it is the vengeance of the LORD,
     the vengeance of His temple.
12 Set up the standard against the walls of Babylon,
     make the watch strong,
set up the watchmen,
     prepare the ambushes.
For the LORD has both devised and done
     that which He spoke against the inhabitants of Babylon.
13 O you who dwell by many waters,
     abundant in treasures,

your end has come,
     and the measure of your end.
14 The LORD of Hosts has sworn by Himself,
     saying: Surely I will fill you with men, as with locusts,
     and they will lift up shouts of victory against you.

15 He has made the earth by His power;
     He has established the world by His wisdom,
     and has stretched out the heaven by His understanding.
16 When He utters His voice, there is a multitude of waters in the
     heavens,
     and He causes the clouds to ascend from the remote parts
        of the earth;
He makes lightning with rain,
     and brings out the wind from His storehouses.

17 Every man is ignorant by His knowledge;
     every founder is humiliated by the graven image,
for his molded image is falsehood,
     and there is no breath in them.
18 They are vanity, the work of errors;
     in the time of their punishment they will perish.
19 The portion of Jacob is not like them,
     for He is the former of all things,
and Israel is the rod of His inheritance.
     The LORD of Hosts is His name.

20 *He says*: You are My battle-ax
     and weapon of war:
for with you I will break in pieces the nations,
     and with you I will destroy kingdoms;
21 and with you I will break in pieces the horse and his rider,
     and with you I will break in pieces the chariot and his rider.
22 With you also I will break in pieces man and woman;
     and with you I will break in pieces old and young;
     and with you I will break in pieces the young man and the
        young woman.
23 I will also break in pieces with you the shepherd and his flock;
     and with you I will break in pieces the farmer and his yoke
        of oxen;
     and with you I will break in pieces captains and rulers.

24 I will render to Babylon and to all the inhabitants of Chaldea
all their evil that they have done in Zion in your sight, says the LORD.

25 I am against you, O destroying mountain,
     says the LORD,
     who destroys all the earth.
And I will stretch out My hand against you,
     and roll you down from the rocks,
     and will make you a burned mountain.
26 They will not take of you a stone for a corner,
     or a stone for foundations,
but you will be desolate forever,
     says the LORD.

27 Set up a standard in the land,
     blow the trumpet among the nations,
prepare the nations against her,
     call together against her the kingdoms
     of Ararat, Minni, and Ashkenaz;
appoint a captain against her.
     Cause the horses to come up as the rough locusts.
28 Prepare against her the nations,
     the kings of the Medes,
the captains, and all the rulers,
     and every land of their dominion.
29 So the land trembles and sorrows,
     for the purposes of the LORD will be performed
        against Babylon,
to make the land of Babylon a desolation
     without an inhabitant.

³⁰ The mighty men of Babylon have ceased fighting;
　　they have remained in their strongholds.
　Their might has failed;
　　they became as women.
　They have burned her dwelling places;
　　the bars of her gates are broken.
³¹ One courier will run to meet another,
　　and one messenger to meet another,
　to show the king of Babylon
　　that his city has been captured from end *to end*,
³² and the passages have been seized,
　　and they have burned the reeds with fire,
　　and the men of war are terrified.

³³ For thus says the Lord of Hosts, the God of Israel:

The daughter of Babylon is like a threshing floor,
　it is time to thresh her;
yet a little while and the time of her harvest will come.

³⁴ "Nebuchadnezzar the king of Babylon
　　has devoured me and crushed me;
　　he has made me an empty vessel.
　He has swallowed me up like a dragon;
　　he has filled his belly with my delicacies,
　　he has cast me out.
³⁵ May the violence done to me and to my flesh be upon Babylon,"
　　the inhabitant of Zion will say;
　and, "May my blood be upon the inhabitants of Chaldea,"
　　Jerusalem will say.

³⁶ Therefore thus says the Lord:

I will plead your cause,
　and take vengeance for you.
And I will dry up her sea,
　and make her springs dry.
³⁷ Babylon will become heaps,
　a dwelling place for jackals,
an astonishment, and a hissing,
　without an inhabitant.
³⁸ They will roar together like young lions;
　they will growl as lions' whelps.
³⁹ When they become heated up,
　I will make their feasts,
　and I will make them drunk,
that they may rejoice,
　and sleep a perpetual sleep, and not awake,
　says the Lord.
⁴⁰ I will bring them down
　like lambs to the slaughter,
　like rams with male goats.

⁴¹ How Sheshak has been captured!
　And how the praise of the whole earth has been seized!
How Babylon has become an astonishment
　among the nations!
⁴² The sea has come up over Babylon;
　she has been covered with the multitude of the waves.
⁴³ Her cities have become a desolation,
　a dry land and a wilderness,
a land in which no man dwells,
　through which no son of man passes.
⁴⁴ I will punish Bel in Babylon,
　and I will bring forth from his mouth what he has
　　swallowed up;
and the nations will not flow together any more to him.
　Indeed, the wall of Babylon will fall.

⁴⁵ My people, go out of her midst,
　and deliver every man his soul
　from the fierce anger of the Lord,

⁴⁶ lest your heart grows faint, and you are afraid
　for the report that will be heard in the land—
for the report will come one year, and after that in another year
　　will come another report,
　and violence will be in the land,
　　ruler against ruler—
⁴⁷ therefore the days are coming
　when I will punish the graven images of Babylon;
and her whole land will be humiliated,
　and all her slain will fall in her midst.
⁴⁸ Then the heaven and the earth, and all that is in it,
　shall sing for joy over Babylon;
for the destroyers will come to her
　from the north,
　says the Lord.

⁴⁹ As Babylon has caused the slain of Israel to fall,
　so at Babylon the slain of all the earth will fall.
⁵⁰ You who have escaped the sword,
　go away, do not stand still.
Remember the Lord afar off,
　and let Jerusalem come into your mind.

⁵¹ We are humiliated
　because we have heard reproach.
Shame has covered our faces,
for strangers have come into
　the holy places of the house of the Lord.

⁵² Therefore, surely the days are coming, says the Lord,
　when I will punish her graven images,
and the mortally wounded shall groan
　through all her land.
⁵³ Though Babylon should mount up to heaven,
　and though she should fortify the height of her strength,
yet from Me will destroyers come to her,
　says the Lord.

⁵⁴ A sound of an outcry comes from Babylon,
　and great destruction
　from the land of the Chaldeans,
⁵⁵ because the Lord has devastated Babylon,
　and destroyed the great voice out of her.
When her waves roar like great waters,
　a noise of their voice is uttered.
⁵⁶ Because the destroyer is coming against her, even upon Babylon,
　and her mighty men will be captured,
　every one of their bows are broken.
For the Lord is a God of recompense;
　He will completely repay.
⁵⁷ I will make her officials drunk, and her wise men,
　her captains, and her rulers, and her mighty men;
and they will sleep a perpetual sleep, and not awake,
　says the King whose name is the Lord of Hosts.

⁵⁸ Thus says the Lord of Hosts:

The broad wall of Babylon will be utterly broken,
　and her high gates will be burned with fire;
and the peoples will labor in vain,
　and the nations become exhausted only for fire.

Jeremiah's Command to Seraiah

⁵⁹ The word which Jeremiah the prophet commanded Seraiah the son of Neriah, the son of Mahseiah, when he went with Zedekiah the king of Judah into Babylon in the fourth year of his reign. Now Seraiah was a quartermaster. ⁶⁰ So Jeremiah wrote in a single scroll all the evil that should come upon Babylon, even all these words that are written against Babylon. ⁶¹ Jeremiah said to Seraiah, "When you come to Babylon, then see that you read aloud all these words, ⁶² and say, 'O Lord, You have spoken against this place to cut it off, that no one will remain in it, neither man nor beast, but that it shall

be desolate forever.' [63] It will be that when you have made an end of reading this scroll that you will bind a stone to it, and cast it into the midst of the Euphrates, [64] and say, 'Thus Babylon will sink and not rise from the disaster that I will bring upon her, and they will become weary.' "

Thus far are the words of Jeremiah.

The Fall of Jerusalem Reviewed

2Ki 24:18–20; 25:1–21; 2Ch 36:11–20; Jer 39:1–10

52 Zedekiah was twenty-one years old when he began to reign, and he reigned eleven years in Jerusalem. And his mother's name was Hamutal the daughter of Jeremiah of Libnah. [2] He did what was evil in the eyes of the LORD, according to all that Jehoiakim had done. [3] Through the anger of the LORD this came to pass in Jerusalem and Judah until He had cast them out from His presence.

Then Zedekiah rebelled against the king of Babylon.

[4] In the ninth year of his reign, in the tenth month, in the tenth day of the month, Nebuchadnezzar king of Babylon came, he and all his army, against Jerusalem, and laid siege to it; they built a siege wall all around it. [5] So the city was besieged until the eleventh year of King Zedekiah.

[6] In the fourth month, in the ninth day of the month, the famine was so severe in the city that there was no bread for the people of the land. [7] Then the city was breached, and all the men of war fled and went out of the city by night by way of the gate between the two walls, which was by the king's garden, though the Chaldeans were all around the city, and they went by way of the Arabah. [8] But the army of the Chaldeans pursued after the king and overtook Zedekiah in the plains of Jericho, and all his army was scattered from him.

[9] Then they took the king and carried him up to the king of Babylon at Riblah in the land of Hamath where he passed sentence on him. [10] The king of Babylon slew the sons of Zedekiah before his eyes; he also slew all the officials of Judah in Riblah. [11] Then he put out the eyes of Zedekiah, and the king of Babylon bound him in chains and carried him to Babylon and put him in prison until the day of his death.

The Temple Burned

[12] Now in the fifth month, in the tenth day of the month, which was the nineteenth year of Nebuchadnezzar king of Babylon, Nebuzaradan the captain of the guard who served the king of Babylon came into Jerusalem, [13] and burned the house of the LORD, and the king's house, and all the houses of Jerusalem. Even all the large houses, he burned with fire. [14] And all the army of the Chaldeans who were with the captain of the guard broke down all the walls of Jerusalem all around. [15] Then Nebuzaradan the captain of the guard carried away captive some of the poorest of the people, and the rest of the people who remained in the city, and those who fell away, who fell to the king of Babylon, and the rest of the multitude. [16] But Nebuzaradan the captain of the guard left some of the poorest of the land to be vinedressers and farmers.

[17] Also the pillars of bronze that were in the house of the LORD, and the stands, and the bronze sea that was in the house of the LORD,

the Chaldeans broke and carried all their bronze to Babylon. [18] The cauldrons also, and the shovels, and the snuffers, and the bowls, and the spoons, and all the vessels of bronze with which they ministered, they took away. [19] The captain of the guard also took away the basins, and the fire pans, and the bowls, and the cauldrons, and the lampstands, and the spoons, and the cups, what was of fine gold, and what was of fine silver.

[20] The two pillars, one sea, and twelve bronze bulls that were under the bases, which King Solomon had made in the house of the LORD, the bronze of all these vessels was beyond weight. [21] Concerning the pillars: the height of one pillar was eighteen cubits, and it was twelve cubits in circumference and in thickness it was four fingers, [1] and hollow. [22] A capital of bronze was upon it, and the height of one capital was five cubits, [2] with network and pomegranates upon the capital all around, all of bronze. The second pillar also and the pomegranates were like these. [23] There were ninety-six pomegranates on the sides; all the pomegranates were a hundred upon the network all around.

The Babylonian Exile

[24] The captain of the guard took Seraiah the chief priest, and Zephaniah the second priest, and the three officers of the temple. [25] He also took out of the city one official who had charge of the men of war, and seven men of the advisers of the king who were found in the city, and the scribe of the commander of the army who mustered the people of the land, and sixty men of the people of the land who were found in the midst of the city. [26] So Nebuzaradan the captain of the guard took them and brought them to the king of Babylon to Riblah. [27] The king of Babylon struck them and put them to death in Riblah in the land of Hamath.

Thus Judah was carried away captive out of its own land. [28] These are the people whom Nebuchadnezzar carried away captive:

in the seventh year three thousand and twenty-three Jews.
[29] In the eighteenth year of Nebuchadnezzar
he carried away captive from Jerusalem eight hundred and thirty-two persons.
[30] In the twenty-third year of Nebuchadnezzar,
Nebuzaradan the captain of the guard carried away captive of the Jews seven hundred and forty-five.
All the persons were four thousand and six hundred.

Jehoiachin Released

2Ki 25:27–30

[31] In the thirty-seventh year of the captivity of Jehoiachin, king of Judah, in the twelfth month, on the twenty-fifth day of the month, Awel-Marduk, king of Babylon, in the first year of his reign lifted up the head of Jehoiachin king of Judah and brought him out of prison, [32] and spoke kindly to him, and set his throne above the throne of the kings who were with him in Babylon. [33] Therefore Jehoiachin changed his prison garments and continually ate meals before him all the days of his life. [34] For his allowance, there was a continual allowance given him by the king of Babylon, every day a portion all the days of his life until the day of his death.

---

[1]21 About 27 feet high and 18 feet in circumference, or 8.1 meters high and 5.4 meters in circumference.   [2]22 About 7½ feet, or 2.3 meters.

LAMENTATIONS

The Sorrows of Jerusalem

1 How lonely sits the city
    that was full of people!
How she has become like a widow,
    who was once great among the nations!
She who was a princess among the provinces
    has become a slave!

2 She weeps sorely in the night,
    her tears are on her cheeks;
among all her lovers
    she has none to comfort her.
All her friends have dealt treacherously with her;
    they have become her enemies.

3 Judah has gone into captivity,
    under affliction and great servitude;
she dwells among the nations,
    she finds no rest;
all her persecutors overtook her
    in the midst of distress.

4 The roads to Zion mourn
    because no one comes to the solemn feasts.
All her gates are desolate;
    her priests sigh,
her virgins are afflicted,
    and she herself suffers bitterly.

5 Her adversaries have become her masters,
    her enemies prosper;
for the LORD has afflicted her
    because of the multitude of her transgressions.
Her children have gone into captivity
    before the enemy.

6 From the daughter of Zion
    all her beauty has departed.
Her princes have become like deer
    that find no pasture;
they fled without strength
    before the pursuer.

7 In the days of her affliction and misery
    Jerusalem remembers all her pleasant things
    that she had in the days of old.
When her people fell into the hand of the enemy,
    there was no one to help her.
The adversaries saw her
    and mocked at her desolation.

8 Jerusalem has sinned grievously;
    therefore she has become vile.
All who honored her despise her,
    for they have seen her nakedness;
she herself sighs
    and turns away.

9 Her uncleanness is in her skirts;
    she took no thought of her future;
therefore her fall is astounding;
    she has no comforter.
"O LORD, look upon my affliction,
    for the enemy has triumphed!"

10 The adversary has spread his hand
    over all her precious things;
for she has seen the nations
enter her sanctuary,
those whom You commanded
    not to enter Your congregation.

11 All her people groan,
    as they search for bread;
they trade their treasures for food
    to restore their strength.
Look, O LORD, and consider,
    for I am despised.

12 Is it nothing to you, all you who pass by?
    Look and see
if there is any sorrow like my sorrow,
    which was brought upon me,
which the LORD has inflicted
    on the day of His fierce anger.

13 From on high He has sent fire into my bones,
    and it prevailed against them;
He has spread a net for my feet;
    He turned me back;
He has made me desolate
    and faint all the day long.

14 The yoke of my transgressions
    was bound; by His hand
they were fastened together; they were set upon my neck.
    He made my strength fail;
the Lord delivered me into the hands
    of those whom I am not able to withstand.

15 The Lord has trampled underfoot
    all my mighty men in my midst;
He has called an assembly against me
    to crush my young men;
The Lord has trodden the virgin daughter of Judah
    as in a winepress.

16 For these things I weep;
    my eyes flow with tears;
for the comforter, who should relieve my soul,
    is far from me.
My children are desolate
    for the enemy has prevailed.

17 Zion spreads out her hands,
    but there is no one to comfort her;
the LORD has commanded against Jacob
    that his neighbors should be his adversaries;
Jerusalem has become a filthy thing among them.

18 The LORD is in the right,
    for I have rebelled against His commandment.
Hear now, all peoples,
    and see my sorrow;
my virgins and my young men
    have gone into captivity.

19 I called for my lovers,
    but they deceived me;
my priests and my elders
    perished in the city,
while they sought food
    to restore their strength.

20 Look, O LORD, for I am in distress;
    my soul is greatly troubled;

my heart is overturned within me,
for I have grievously rebelled.
In the street the sword bereaves,
at home it is like death.

21 They have heard my groaning,
yet there is no one to comfort me.
All my enemies have heard of my trouble;
they are glad that You have done it.
Bring the day that You have announced,
that they become like me.

22 Let all their wickedness come before You,
and do to them
as You have done to me
for all my transgressions;
for my groans are many,
and my heart is faint.

The Anger of God Over Jerusalem

2 How the Lord has covered the daughter of Zion
with a cloud in His anger!
He has cast down from heaven to the earth
the beauty of Israel;
He has not remembered His footstool
in the day of His anger.

2 The Lord has swallowed up without mercy
all the habitations of Jacob;
in His wrath He has thrown down
the strongholds of the daughter of Judah;
He has brought them down to the ground;
He has profaned the kingdom and its princes.

3 He has cut off in fierce anger
all the might of Israel;
He has drawn back His right hand
from before the enemy.
He has burned against Jacob
like a flaming fire, devouring all around.

4 He has bent His bow like an enemy,
with his right hand set like an adversary;
He has killed all who were pleasant to His eye;
in the tabernacle of the daughter of Zion,
He has poured out His fury like fire.

5 The Lord has become like an enemy;
He has swallowed up Israel,
He has swallowed up all her palaces;
He has destroyed her strongholds,
and has increased mourning and lamentation
in the daughter of Judah.

6 He has violently taken away His tabernacle as if it were
a garden;
He has destroyed His place of assembly;
the Lord has caused the solemn feasts and Sabbaths
to be forgotten in Zion.
In his fierce indignation He has despised the king and the priest.

7 The Lord has scorned His altar,
He has disowned His sanctuary;
He has given up the walls of her palaces
into the hand of the enemy.
They have made a noise in the house of the Lord
as on the day of a solemn feast.

8 The Lord has purposed to destroy
the wall of the daughter of Zion.
He has stretched out a line;
He has not withdrawn His hand from destroying;

therefore He caused the rampart and the wall to lament;
they languished together.

9 Her gates have sunk into the ground;
He has destroyed and broken her bars.
Her king and her princes are among the nations;
the Law is no more,
and her prophets find
no vision from the Lord.

10 The elders of the daughter of Zion
sit on the ground in silence;
they throw dust on their heads
and gird themselves with sackcloth.
The virgins of Jerusalem
bow their heads to the ground.

11 My eyes fail with tears,
my spirit is greatly troubled;
my bile is poured on the ground
because of the destruction of the daughter of my people,
because the children and infants faint
in the streets of the city.

12 They say to their mothers,
"Where is grain and wine?"
when they faint like a wounded man
in the streets of the city,
as their life is poured out
on their mothers' bosom.

13 What can I say for you,
to what shall I liken you,
O daughter of Jerusalem?
What shall I compare with you,
that I may comfort you,
O virgin daughter of Zion?
For your devastation is great like the sea;
who can heal you?

14 Your prophets have seen for you
false and deceptive visions;
they have not revealed your iniquity,
to bring back your captives,
but have seen for you oracles
that are false and misleading.

15 All who pass by
clap their hands at you;
they hiss and shake their heads
at the daughter of Jerusalem, saying,
"Is this the city that men call
the perfection of beauty,
the joy of the whole earth?"

16 All your enemies
have opened their mouth against you;
they hiss and gnash their teeth.
They say, "We have swallowed her up!
Certainly this is the day that we longed for;
we have found it; we have seen it."

17 The Lord has done what He planned;
He has fulfilled His word
that He had commanded in the days of old.
He has thrown down and has not pitied,
and He has caused the enemy to rejoice over you;
He has exalted the power of your adversaries.

18 Their heart cried to the Lord:
O wall of the daughter of Zion,
let your tears run down like a river day and night;

give yourself no rest,
    your eyes no respite!

19 Arise, cry out in the night,
    at the beginning of the watches;
pour out your heart like water
    before the face of the Lord.
Lift your hands to Him
    for the lives of your young children,
who faint for hunger
    at the head of every street.

20 Look, O Lord, and consider!
    To whom have You done this?
Should the women eat their offspring,
    the children who were born healthy?
Should the priest and the prophet be killed
    in the sanctuary of the Lord?

21 The young and the old lie
    on the ground in the streets;
my virgins and my young men
    have fallen by the sword;
You have killed them in the day of Your anger,
    You have slaughtered and not pitied.

22 You have invited as to a feast day the terrors all around;
    in the day of the Lord's anger
no one escaped or survived;
    those whom I held and raised
    my enemy destroyed.

The Prophet's Anguish

3 I am the man who has seen affliction
    by the rod of His wrath.
2 He has driven and brought me
    into darkness without any light.
3 Surely against me has He turned His hand
    continually, the whole day long.

4 My flesh and my skin He has made waste away;
    He has broken my bones;
5 He has besieged and enveloped me
    with gall and travail.
6 He has set me in dark places,
    like the dead of long ago.

7 He has hedged me in so that I cannot get out;
    He has made my chain heavy.
8 Even when I cry for help,
    He shuts out my prayer.
9 He has blocked my ways with hewn stone;
    He has made my paths crooked.

10 He is to me a bear lying in wait,
    a lion in hiding.
11 He has turned aside my ways and torn me in pieces;
    He has made me desolate.
12 He has bent His bow
    and set me as a target for the arrow.

13 He has caused the arrows of His quiver
    to pierce my inward parts.
14 I have become the derision of all my people,
    their mocking song all the day.
15 He has filled me with bitterness,
    He has sated me with wormwood.

16 He has made my teeth grind on gravel,
    and covered me with ashes.
17 My soul is bereft of peace;
    I have forgotten prosperity.

18 So I say, "My strength and my hope
    from the Lord have perished."

19 Remember my affliction and my misery,
    the wormwood and the gall.
20 Surely my soul remembers
    and is humbled within me.
21 But this I call to mind,
    and therefore I have hope:

22 It is of the Lord's mercies that we are not consumed;
    His compassions do not fail.
23 They are new every morning;
    great is Your faithfulness.
24 "The Lord is my portion," says my soul,
    "therefore I will hope in Him."

25 The Lord is good to those who wait for Him,
    to the soul who seeks Him.
26 It is good that a man should wait quietly
    for the salvation of the Lord.
27 It is good for a man to bear the yoke
    in his youth.

28 Let him sit alone in silence
    when it is laid on him;
29 let him put his mouth in the dust—
    there may yet be hope.
30 Let him give his cheek to the one who strikes,
    and let him be filled with insults.

31 For the Lord
    will not cast off forever.
32 But though He causes grief, yet He will have compassion
    according to the abundance of His mercies.
33 For He does not afflict from His heart,
    nor grieve the sons of men.

34 To crush underfoot
    all the prisoners of the earth,
35 to turn aside the justice due a man
    in the presence of the Most High,
36 to subvert a man in his cause,
    the Lord does not approve.

37 Who is he who speaks and it comes to pass,
    unless the Lord has commanded it?
38 Is it not from the mouth of the Most High
    that good and bad proceed?
39 Why should a living man complain,
    a man for the punishment of his sins?

40 Let us search and try our ways,
    and return to the Lord!
41 Let us lift up our hearts and hands
    to God in heaven:
42 We have transgressed and rebelled;
    You have not pardoned.

43 You have covered Yourself with anger and pursued us;
    You have killed and not pitied.
44 You have covered Yourself with a cloud,
    so that no prayer should pass through.
45 You have made us filthy refuse
    in the midst of the peoples.

46 All our enemies have opened their mouths
    against us.
47 Panic and snare have come upon us,
    desolation and destruction.
48 My eyes flow with rivers of tears
    for the destruction of the daughter of my people.

⁴⁹ My eyes flow and do not cease,
    without respite,
⁵⁰ until the Lᴏʀᴅ from heaven
    looks down and sees.
⁵¹ My eyes bring suffering to my soul
    at the fate of all the daughters of my city.

⁵² My enemies chased me like a bird,
    without cause.
⁵³ They cut off my life in the pit
    and cast stones on me.
⁵⁴ Waters flowed over my head;
    I said, "I am cut off!"

⁵⁵ I called on Your name, O Lᴏʀᴅ,
    from the lowest pit.
⁵⁶ You have heard my plea:
    "Do not close Your ear to my cry for help!"
⁵⁷ You drew near on the day I called on You,
    and You said, "Do not fear!"

⁵⁸ O Lord, You have pleaded the case for my soul;
    You have redeemed my life.
⁵⁹ O Lᴏʀᴅ, You have seen the wrong done to me;
    judge my case.
⁶⁰ You have seen all their vengeance,
    all their schemes against me.

⁶¹ You have heard their reproach, O Lᴏʀᴅ,
    all their schemes against me,
⁶² the lips of my enemies and
    their devices against me all the day.
⁶³ Look at their sitting down and their rising up;
    I am their mocking song.

⁶⁴ Render to them a recompense, O Lᴏʀᴅ,
    according to the work of their hands.
⁶⁵ Give them hardness of heart;
    may Your curse be upon them!
⁶⁶ In Your anger pursue and destroy them
    from under Your heavens, O Lᴏʀᴅ!

The Punishment of Zion

4 How the gold has become dim!
    How the most fine gold has changed!
  The stones of the sanctuary lie scattered
    at the head of every street.

² The precious sons of Zion,
    comparable to fine gold,
  how they are esteemed as earthen pots,
    the work of a potter's hands!

³ Even the jackals offer the breast;
    they nurse their young,
  yet the daughter of my people has become cruel,
    like ostriches in the wilderness.

⁴ The tongue of the infant cleaves
    to the roof of his mouth for thirst;
  the children beg for bread,
    but no one divides it for them.

⁵ Those who once ate delicacies
    are desolate in the streets;
  those who were brought up in scarlet
    embrace ash heaps.

⁶ For the iniquity of the daughter of my people
    is greater than the sin of Sodom,
  which was overthrown in a moment,
    and no hands were wrung for her.

⁷ Her princes were purer than snow,
    whiter than milk;
  their bodies were more ruddy than rubies,
    their appearance like sapphire.

⁸ Their form is blacker than coal;
    they are not recognized in the streets;
  their skin cleaves to their bones,
    it has become as dry as wood.

⁹ Those killed by the sword
    are better off than those who die of hunger,
  for they pine away,
    stricken for want of the fruits of the field.

¹⁰ The hands of compassionate women
    have boiled their own children;
  they became their food in the destruction
    of the daughter of my people.

¹¹ The Lᴏʀᴅ has fulfilled His fury,
    He has poured out His fierce anger.
  He kindled a fire in Zion,
    and it has devoured its foundations.

¹² The kings of the earth, and all the inhabitants of the world,
    would not have believed
  that the adversary and the enemy could enter
    the gates of Jerusalem.

¹³ This was for the sins of her prophets
    and the iniquities of her priests,
  who poured out in her midst the blood of the righteous.

¹⁴ They wandered,
    blind, in the streets;
  they have defiled themselves with blood,
    so that no one could touch their garments.

¹⁵ They cried out to them, "Depart! Unclean!
    Depart, depart, do not touch us!"
  Therefore they fled and wandered;
    men among the nations said,
    "They shall live with us no longer."

¹⁶ The presence of the Lᴏʀᴅ scattered them;
    He will regard them no more;
  they do not respect the priests,
    nor show favor to the elders.

¹⁷ Our eyes failed us,
    watching vainly for help;
  in our watchtowers we watched
    for a nation that could not save us.

¹⁸ They tracked our steps
    so that we could not walk in our streets.
  Our end drew near; our days were numbered,
    for our end had come.

¹⁹ Our pursuers were swifter
    than the eagles of the skies.
  They pursued us on the mountains;
    they lay in wait for us in the wilderness.

²⁰ The breath of our life, the anointed king of the Lᴏʀᴅ,
    was captured in their traps,
  of whom we said, "Under his shadow
    we shall live among the nations."

²¹ Rejoice and be glad, O daughter of Edom,
    you who dwell in the land of Uz!

The cup shall also pass to you;
you shall become drunk and strip yourself bare.

22 The punishment of your iniquity, O daughter of Zion, is accomplished;
He shall exile you no longer.
He shall punish your iniquity, O daughter of Edom;
He will expose your sins!

A Prayer for Restoration

5 Remember, O Lord, what has come upon us;
look, and see our reproach!
2 Our inheritance has been turned over to strangers,
our homes to foreigners.
3 We have become orphans and fatherless;
our mothers are like widows.
4 We must pay for the water we drink;
our wood is sold to us.
5 Our pursuers are at our necks;
we labor and have no rest.
6 We have given our hand to Egypt and to Assyria,
to be satisfied with bread.
7 Our fathers sinned and are no more,
but we bear their iniquities.
8 Slaves rule over us;
there is no one to deliver us from their hand.
9 We get our bread at the peril of our lives,
because of the sword in the wilderness.

10 Our skin is hot as an oven,
because of the terrible famine.
11 They ravished the women in Zion,
the virgins in the cities of Judah.
12 Princes were hung up by their hands,
the faces of elders were not honored.
13 Young men ground at the millstones;
boys staggered under loads of wood.
14 The elders have left the city gate,
the young men stopped their music.
15 The joy of our hearts has ceased;
our dancing has turned into mourning.
16 The crown has fallen from our head;
woe to us, for we have sinned!
17 For this our heart is faint;
for these things our eyes grow dim;
18 because of Mount Zion, which is desolate,
with foxes walking upon it.

19 You, O Lord, remain forever;
Your throne endures from generation to generation.
20 Why do You forget us forever,
and forsake us for so long a time?
21 Restore us to Yourself, O Lord, that we may return!
Renew our days as of old,
22 unless You have utterly rejected us,
and are very angry with us.

EZEKIEL

The Vision of the Lord's Glory

1 In the thirtieth year, in the fourth month, on the fifth day of the month, as I was among the captives by the river of Kebar, the heavens were opened and I saw visions of God.

2 On the fifth day of the month, which was the fifth year of the captivity of King Jehoiachin, 3 the word of the Lord came expressly to Ezekiel the priest, the son of Buzi, in the land of the Chaldeans by the River Kebar. And the hand of the Lord was on him there.

4 As I looked, a whirlwind came out of the north, a great cloud with fire flashing forth continually, and a brightness was all around it, and in its midst something as glowing metal in the midst of the fire. 5 Also out of the midst came the likeness of four living creatures. And this was their appearance: They had the likeness of a man. 6 Every one had four faces, and every one had four wings. 7 Their legs were straight and the soles of their feet were like the sole of a calf's hoof. And they gleamed like the color of burnished bronze. 8 They had the hands of a man under their wings on their four sides. As for the faces and wings of the four of them, 9 their wings were joined to one another. Their *faces* did not turn when they went. Each went straight forward.

10 As for the likeness of their faces, each had the face of a man, and all four had the face of a lion on the right side, and the face of an ox on the left side, and the face of an eagle. 11 Thus were their faces. And their wings were stretched upward. Two wings of every one were joined to one another, and two covered their bodies. 12 Each went straight forward. Wherever the spirit was to go, they would go and not turn as they went. 13 As for the likeness of the living creatures, their appearance was like burning coals of fire and like the appearance of lamps. It went up and down among the living creatures. And the fire was bright, and out of the fire went forth lightning. 14 The living creatures ran to and fro as the appearance of a flash of lightning.

15 Now as I looked at the living creatures, one wheel was on the ground by the living creatures for each of the four faces. 16 The appearance of the wheels and their work was like the color of sparkling beryl. And all four of them had one likeness. And their appearance and their work was, as it were, a wheel in the middle of a wheel. 17 Whenever they went, they went in any of their four sides and did not turn as they went. 18 As for their rims, they were so high that they were dreadful. And the rims of all four of them were full of eyes all around.

19 Whenever the living creatures went, the wheels went with them. And whenever the living creatures were lifted up from the ground, the wheels also were lifted up. 20 Wherever the spirit was about to go, they would go in that direction. And the wheels rose close beside them. For the spirit of the living creatures was in the wheels. 21 Whenever these went, these went. And whenever those stood still, these stood still. And whenever those rose from the ground, the wheels rose close beside them. For the spirit of the living creatures was in the wheels.

22 The likeness of the expanse over the heads of the living creatures was as the awesome gleam of crystal, stretched out over their heads above. 23 Under the expanse their wings *were stretched out* straight, the one toward the other. Each one also had two wings which covered its body on the one side and the other. 24 When they went, I heard the noise of their wings, like the noise of abundant waters, as the voice of the Almighty, the noise of tumult as the noise of an army camp. Whenever they stood still, they let down their wings.

25 There was a voice from the expanse that was over their heads whenever they stood still and let down their wings. 26 Above the expanse that was over their heads was the likeness of a throne, as the appearance of a sapphire stone. And on the likeness of the throne was the likeness as the appearance of a man on it high up. 27 Then I saw as glowing metal, as the appearance of fire all around within it, from the appearance of His loins and upward; and from the appearance of His loins and downward I saw as it were the appearance of fire, and there was a brightness around Him. 28 As the appearance of the rainbow that is in the cloud on a day of rain, so was the appearance of the brightness all around.

This was the appearance of the likeness of the glory of the LORD. And when I saw it, I fell on my face and heard a voice of one speaking.

The Call of Ezekiel

2 Then He said to me: Son of man, stand on your feet, and I will speak to you! [2] When He spoke to me, the Spirit entered me and set me on my feet. Then I heard Him speaking to me.

[3] And He said to me: Son of man, I send you to the sons of Israel, to a rebellious nation that has rebelled against Me. They and their fathers have transgressed against Me even to this very day. [4] And as for the impudent and obstinate children, I am sending you to them. And you shall say to them, "Thus says the Lord GOD." [5] As for them, whether they listen or not (for they are a rebellious house), they shall know that there has been a prophet among them. [6] And you, son of man, do not be afraid of them or be afraid of their words, though briers and thorns be with you, and you dwell among scorpions. Do not be afraid of their words or be dismayed at their looks, for they are a rebellious house. [7] You shall speak My words to them, whether they listen or not, for they are rebellious. [8] But you, son of man, hear what I say to you. Do not be rebellious like that rebellious house. Open your mouth and eat what I give you.

[9] When I looked, a hand was sent to me. And a scroll was in it. [10] And He spread it before me. And there was writing on the inside and on the outside, and written on it were words of lamentation and mourning and woe.

3 Moreover He said to me, Son of man, eat what you find. Eat this scroll and go speak to the house of Israel. [2] So I opened my mouth, and He fed me this scroll.

[3] He said to me, Son of man, feed your stomach and fill your inward parts with this scroll that I give you. Then I ate it, and it was as honey for sweetness in my mouth.

[4] Then He said to me: Son of man, go to the house of Israel and speak with My words to them. [5] For you are not being sent to a people of foreign speech and hard language, but to the house of Israel, [6] nor to many peoples of foreign speech and hard language, whose words you cannot understand. But I have sent you to them who should listen to you. [7] But the house of Israel will not listen to you, because they will not listen to Me. For all the house of Israel is impudent and obstinate. [8] But I have made your face as hard as their faces and your forehead as hard as their foreheads. [9] As emery harder than flint, I have made your forehead. Do not be afraid of them or be dismayed at their looks, though they are a rebellious house.

[10] Moreover He said to me: Son of man, all My words that I shall speak to you receive in your heart and hear with your ears. [11] Go to the captives, to the sons of your people, and speak to them and tell them, whether they listen or not, "Thus says the Lord GOD."

[12] Then the Spirit took me up, and I heard behind me a great thundering voice: "Blessed be the glory of the LORD in His place." [13] I *heard* also the noise of the wings of the living creatures that touched one another and the noise of the wheels beside them, even a great rushing sound. [14] So the Spirit lifted me up and took me away, and I went in bitterness, in the heat of my spirit, and the hand of the LORD was strong upon me. [15] Then I came to the captives at Tel Aviv, who lived by the River Kebar, and I sat there where they sat seven days, causing consternation among them.

Ezekiel, a Watchman for Israel

[16] At the end of seven days, the word of the LORD came to me, saying, [17] Son of man, I have made you a watchman to the house of Israel. Whenever you hear the word from My mouth, then warn them from Me. [18] When I say to the wicked, "You shall surely die," and you do not warn him, nor speak to warn the wicked from his wicked way that he may live, the same wicked man shall die in his iniquity, but his blood I will require at your hand. [19] Yet if you warn the wicked and he does not turn from his wickedness or from his wicked way, he shall die in his iniquity. But you have delivered your soul.

[20] Again, when a righteous man turns from his righteousness and commits iniquity, and I lay a stumbling block before him, he shall die. Because you have not given him warning, he shall die in his sin, and his righteousness which he has done shall not be remembered.

But his blood I will require at your hand. [21] Nevertheless if you warn the righteous man that the righteous should not sin and he does not sin, he shall surely live because he took warning. And you have delivered your soul.

[22] The hand of the LORD was upon me there, and He said to me, Rise, go out into the plain, and I will talk with you there. [23] Then I arose, and went out into the plain. And the glory of the LORD stood there, as the glory which I saw by the river of Kebar, and I fell on my face.

[24] Then the Spirit entered me, and set me on my feet, and spoke with me and said to me: Go, shut yourself up within your house. [25] As for you, son of man, they shall put bands on you and shall bind you with them, so that you cannot go out among them. [26] And I will make your tongue cleave to the roof of your mouth so that you shall be mute and cannot be one to rebuke them, for they are a rebellious house. [27] But when I speak with you, I will open your mouth, and you shall say to them, "Thus says the Lord GOD." He who hears, let him hear. And he who refuses, let him refuse. For they are a rebellious house.

The Siege of Jerusalem Portrayed

4 You also, son of man, take a brick and lay it before you and inscribe a city on it, even Jerusalem. [2] Then lay siege against it, and build a fort against it, and build a mound against it; set camps and place battering rams against it all around. [3] Moreover take for yourself an iron plate and set it up for a wall of iron between you and the city. And set your face against it so that it is besieged, and lay siege against it. This shall be a sign to the house of Israel.

[4] As for you, lie down on your left side and lay the iniquity of the house of Israel upon it. According to the number of the days that you lie on it, you shall bear their iniquity. [5] For I have laid upon you the years of their iniquity according to the number of the days, three hundred and ninety days. So you shall bear the iniquity of the house of Israel.

[6] When you have accomplished them, lie again on your right side, and you shall bear the iniquity of the house of Judah forty days. I have appointed you each day for a year. [7] Therefore you shall set your face toward the siege of Jerusalem, and your arm shall be uncovered, and you shall prophesy against it. [8] I will lay bands upon you, and you shall not turn yourself from one side to another until you have ended the days of your siege.

[9] Also take for yourself wheat, and barley, and beans, and lentils, and millet, and spelt, and put them in one vessel and make bread. According to the number of the days that you lie on your side, three hundred and ninety days, you shall eat it. [10] Your food which you shall eat *shall be* by weight, twenty shekels[1] a day. From time to time you shall eat it. [11] You also shall drink water by measure, the sixth part of a hin.[2] From time to time you shall drink it. [12] You shall eat it as barley cake, having baked it in their sight with dung that comes out of man. [13] Then the LORD said, "Even so the sons of Israel shall eat their defiled bread among the nations where I drive them."

[14] Then I said, "Ah, Lord GOD! My soul has not been defiled. For from my youth up even until now I have not eaten of that which dies of itself, or is torn in pieces, nor has abominable meat come into my mouth."

[15] Then He said to me, "I have given you cow dung instead of man's dung over which you shall prepare your bread."

[16] Moreover He said to me, Son of man, I will cut off the supply of bread in Jerusalem. They shall eat bread by weight and with anxiety and drink water by measure and with horror, [17] because bread and water will be scarce, and they will be appalled with one another, and waste away for their iniquity.

A Sword Against Jerusalem

5 As for you, son of man, take a sharp sword. Take and cause it to pass upon your head and upon your beard as a barber's razor. Then take balances to weigh and divide the hair. [2] You shall burn with fire a third part in the midst of the city when the days of the siege are fulfilled. Then you shall take a third part and strike it with the sword all around the city. And a third part you shall scatter in the wind. And I will draw out a sword after them. [3] You shall also take a few in number from them and bind them in the edges of your *robes.* [4] Then take some of them again and cast them into the midst

of the fire and burn them in the fire. For a fire shall come out into all the house of Israel.

⁵ Thus says the Lord God: This is Jerusalem. I have set it in the midst of the nations, with countries that are all around her. ⁶ But she has rebelled against My judgments more wickedly than the nations, and against My statutes more than the countries that are all around her. For they have refused My judgments and My statutes, and have not walked in them.

⁷ Therefore thus says the Lord God: Because you have more turmoil than the nations that are round about you and have not walked in My statutes, or have kept My judgments, and have not even acted according to the judgments of the nations that are all around you, ⁸ therefore thus says the Lord God: Pay attention. I, even I, am against you and will execute judgments in your midst in the sight of the nations. ⁹ I will do in you what I have not done, and the like of which I will not do anymore, because of all your abominations. ¹⁰ Therefore the fathers shall eat their sons in your midst, and the sons shall eat their fathers. For I will execute judgments on you, and the whole remnant of you I will scatter into all the winds. ¹¹ Therefore, as I live, says the Lord God, surely, because you have defiled My sanctuary with all your detestable things and with all your abominations, therefore I will also diminish you, and My eye shall have no pity, nor will I spare. ¹² A third part of you shall die by pestilence or by famine; they shall be consumed in your midst. And a third part shall fall by the sword all around you. And I will scatter a third part into all the winds, and I will draw out a sword after them.

¹³ Thus My anger shall be accomplished, and I will cause My fury to rest upon them, and I will be comforted. Then they shall know that I the Lord have spoken it in My zeal when I have accomplished My fury in them.

¹⁴ Moreover I will make you a desolation and a reproach among the nations that are all around you, in the sight of all who pass by. ¹⁵ So it shall be a reproach and a taunt, a warning and an astonishment to the nations that are all around you, when I execute judgments in you in anger and in fury and in furious rebukes. I the Lord have spoken it. ¹⁶ When I send upon them the deadly arrows of famine which shall be for their destruction and which I will send to destroy you, then I will also increase the famine upon you and break your staff of bread. ¹⁷ So I will send upon you famine and wild beasts, and they shall bereave you of children. And pestilence and bloodshed shall pass through you. And I will bring the sword upon you. I the Lord have spoken it.

Judgment on Idolatrous Israel

6 And the word of the Lord came to me, saying: ² Son of man, set your face toward the mountains of Israel, and prophesy against them, ³ and say, Mountains of Israel, hear the word of the Lord God. Thus says the Lord God to the mountains, and to the hills, to the rivers, and to the valleys: Pay attention. I, even I, will bring a sword upon you, and I will destroy your high places. ⁴ Your altars shall be desolate, and your images shall be broken. And I will cast down your slain men before your idols. ⁵ I will lay the dead corpses of the sons of Israel before their idols. And I will scatter your bones all around your altars. ⁶ In all your dwelling places, the cities shall be laid waste and the high places shall be desolate so that your altars may be laid waste and made desolate, and your idols may be broken and cease, and your images may be cut down, and your works may be abolished. ⁷ The slain shall fall in your midst, and you shall know that I am the Lord.

⁸ Yet I will leave a remnant, for you will have some who escape the sword among the nations when you are scattered among the countries. ⁹ Those of you who escape shall remember Me among the nations wherever they shall be carried captive, because I am broken by their whorish heart which has departed from Me, and with their eyes which play the harlot after their idols. And they shall loathe themselves for the evils which they have committed in all their abominations. ¹⁰ They shall know that I am the Lord, and that I have not said in vain that I would bring this calamity upon them.

¹¹ Thus says the Lord God: Clap your hand, and stamp with your foot, and say, Alas for all the evil abominations of the house of Israel! For they shall fall by sword, by famine, and by pestilence. ¹² He who is far off shall die of pestilence, and he who is near shall fall by the

sword, and he who remains and is besieged shall die by famine. Thus I will accomplish My fury upon them. ¹³ Then you shall know that I am the Lord, when their slain men shall be among their idols all around their altars, on every high hill, in all the tops of the mountains, and under every green tree, and under every thick oak, the place where they offered sweet savor to all their idols. ¹⁴ So, in all their habitations I will stretch out My hand upon them and make the land desolate, indeed, more desolate than the wilderness toward Diblah. And they shall know that I am the Lord.

The Day of the Lord's Wrath

7 Moreover the word of the Lord came to me, saying: ² And you, son of man, thus says the Lord God to the land of Israel:

An end, the end is coming
　upon the four corners of the land.
³ Now the end has come upon you,
　and I will send My anger upon you,
and will judge you according to your ways,
　and will recompense upon you all your abominations.
⁴ My eye shall not spare you,
　nor will I have pity;
but I will recompense your ways upon you,
　and your abominations shall be in your midst.

And you shall know that I am the Lord!

⁵ Thus says the Lord God:

A disaster, a singular disaster,
　it is coming!
⁶ An end is coming,
　the end has come;
it watches for you;
　it has come!
⁷ Your doom has come to you,
　O inhabitant in the land;
the time has come, the day of trouble is near,
　and not the joyful shouting on the mountains.
⁸ Now I will shortly pour out My fury upon you,
　and accomplish My anger upon you;
and I will judge you according to your ways,
　and will recompense you for all your abominations.
⁹ My eye shall not spare,
　nor will I have pity;
I will recompense you according to your ways,
　and your abominations that are in your midst.

And you shall know that I am the Lord who strikes.

¹⁰ The day is coming!
　Your doom has gone out;
　the rod has blossomed,
　pride has budded.
¹¹ Violence has risen up
　into a rod of wickedness;
none of them shall remain,
　none of their people,
none of their wealth,
　nor anything eminent among them.
¹² The time has come,
　the day has drawn near.
Do not let the buyer rejoice,
　or the seller mourn,
for wrath is against all their multitude.
¹³ For the seller shall not return
　to that which is sold,
　although they both live;
for the vision concerning the whole multitude
　shall not return;
nor shall any strengthen his life
　by his iniquity.

¹⁴ They have blown the trumpet
      even to make all ready,
but none goes to the battle;
      for My wrath is against all the multitude.
¹⁵ The sword is outside,
      and the pestilence and the famine within.
He who is in the field
      shall die by the sword;
and he who is in the city,
      famine and pestilence shall devour him.
¹⁶ Even when their survivors escape,
      they shall be on the mountains
like doves of the valleys,
      all of them mourning,
      every one over his iniquity.
¹⁷ All hands shall be feeble,
      and all knees shall be weak as water.
¹⁸ They shall also gird themselves with sackcloth,
      and horror shall cover them;
and shame shall be upon all faces,
      and baldness upon all their heads.

¹⁹ They shall cast their silver in the streets,
      and their gold shall become abhorrent;
their silver and their gold
      shall not be able to deliver them
      in the day of the wrath of the Lord;
they shall not satisfy their souls,
      or fill their stomachs,
      for their iniquity has become a stumbling block.
²⁰ They transformed the beauty of His ornaments into pride,
      and made the images of their abominations
and of their detestable things with it;
      therefore I will make it an abhorrent thing to them.
²¹ I will give it into the hands of the strangers
      as plunder and to the wicked of the earth for destruction,
      and they shall pollute it.
²² My face also I will turn from them,
      and they shall pollute My secret place;
for the robbers shall enter
      and defile it.

²³ Make a chain,
      for the land is full of bloody crimes,
      and the city is full of violence.
²⁴ Therefore I will bring the worst of the nations,
      and they shall possess their houses;
I will also make the pomp of the strong to cease,
      and their holy places shall be defiled.
²⁵ When destruction comes,
      then they shall seek peace, but there shall be none.
²⁶ Mischief shall come upon mischief,
      and rumor shall be upon rumor.
Then they shall seek a vision of the prophet;
      but the law shall perish from the priest,
      and counsel from the elders.
²⁷ The king shall mourn,
      and the prince shall be clothed with desolation,
      and the hands of the people of the land shall tremble.
I will do to them according to their way,
      and according to what they deserve I will judge them.

And they shall know that I am the Lord!

Abominations in the Temple

8 In the sixth year, in the sixth month, on the fifth day of the month, as I sat in my house and the elders of Judah sat before me, the hand of the Lord God fell upon me there. ² Then I looked, and there was a likeness as the appearance of a man. From His loins and downward was the appearance of fire. And from His loins and upward was the appearance of brightness, as the appearance of glowing metal. ³ He stretched out the form of a hand and

took me by a lock of my head. And the Spirit lifted me up between the earth and the heavens, and brought me in the visions of God to Jerusalem, to the entrance of the north gate of the inner court, where the seat of the image of jealousy was, which provokes to jealousy. ⁴ The glory of the God of Israel was there, according to the vision that I saw in the plain. ⁵ Then He said to me, "Son of man, lift up your eyes now toward the north." So I lifted up my eyes toward the north, and northward at the gate of the altar was this image of jealousy in the entrance. ⁶ He said furthermore to me, "Son of man, do you see what they do, even the great abominations that the house of Israel commits here, so that I should go far off from My sanctuary? But yet you shall see still greater abominations."

⁷ Then He brought me to the door of the court. And when I looked, there was a hole in the wall. ⁸ So He said to me, "Son of man, now dig in the wall." And when I had dug in the wall, there was a door. ⁹ He said to me, "Enter and notice the wicked abominations that they do here." ¹⁰ So I went in and saw every form of creeping things, and abominable beasts, and all the idols of the house of Israel, portrayed upon the wall all around. ¹¹ There stood before them seventy men of the elders of the house of Israel, and in their midst stood Jaazaniah the son of Shaphan, with every man his censer in his hand, and a thick cloud of incense went up. ¹² Then He said to me, "Son of man, have you seen what the elders of the house of Israel do in the dark, every man in the chambers of his images? For they say, 'The Lord does not see us. The Lord has forsaken the land.'" ¹³ He also said to me, "Yet again you shall see greater abominations that they do."

¹⁴ Then He brought me to the door of the gate of the house of the Lord which was toward the north. And women sat there weeping for Tammuz. ¹⁵ Then He said to me, "Have you seen this, O son of man? Yet again you shall see greater abominations than these."

¹⁶ He brought me into the inner court of the house of the Lord, and at the door of the temple of the Lord, between the porch and the altar, were about twenty-five men with their backs toward the temple of the Lord and their faces toward the east. And they worshipped the sun toward the east.

¹⁷ Then He said to me, "Have you seen this, O son of man? Is it a light thing to the house of Judah that they commit the abominations which they commit here? For they have filled the land with violence and have continually provoked Me to anger. And they put the branch to their nose. ¹⁸ Therefore I will indeed deal in fury. My eye shall not spare, nor will I have pity. And though they cry in My ears with a loud voice, yet I will not listen to them."

The Slaughter of the Wicked

9 He cried out also in my ears with a loud voice, saying, "Cause those who have charge over the city to draw near, even every man with his destroying weapon in his hand." ² Six men came from the way of the higher gate which lies toward the north, each with his battle weapon in his hand. And one man among them was clothed with linen with a writer's case by his side. And they went in and stood beside the bronze altar.

³ Then the glory of the God of Israel ascended from the cherub on which it had been, to the threshold of the temple. And He called to the man clothed with linen who had the writer's case by his side. ⁴ And the Lord said to him, "Go through the midst of the city, through the midst of Jerusalem, and set a mark upon the foreheads of the men who sigh and groan for all the abominations that are done in its midst." ⁵ To the others He said in my hearing, "Go after him through the city and strike. Do not let your eye spare or have pity. ⁶ Utterly slay old and young, both maidens and little children, and women. But do not touch any man on whom is the mark. And begin at My sanctuary." Then they began with the elders who were before the temple.

⁷ Then he said to them, "Defile the temple, and fill the courts with the slain. Go forth!" So they went out and killed in the city. ⁸ While they were killing, I was left alone; and I fell on my face and cried out, "Ah, Lord God! Will You destroy all the rest of Israel by Your pouring out of Your fury upon Jerusalem?"

⁹ Then He said to me, "The iniquity of the house of Israel and Judah is exceedingly great, and the land is full of blood, and the city is full of perverseness. For they say, 'The Lord has forsaken the land, and the Lord

does not see.' [10] But as for Me, My eye shall not spare, nor will I have pity, but I will recompense their way upon their heads."

[11] Then the man clothed with linen who had the case by his side reported the matter, saying, "I have done just as You have commanded me."

The Glory of God Leaves the Temple

10 Then I looked, and in the expanse that was above the heads of the cherubim there appeared over them, as it were, a sapphire stone, as the appearance of the likeness of a throne. [2] And He spoke to the man clothed with linen and said, "Go in between the wheels under the cherubim and fill your hands with coals of fire from among the cherubim and scatter them over the city." And he entered in my sight. [3] Now the cherubim stood on the right side of the temple when the man went in, and the cloud filled the inner court. [4] Then the glory of the LORD went up from the cherub and stood over the threshold of the temple. And the house was filled with the cloud, and the court was full of the brightness of the glory of the LORD. [5] The sound of the wings of the cherubim was heard even in the outer court, like the voice of the Almighty God when He speaks.

[6] When He had commanded the man clothed with linen, saying, "Take fire from between the wheels, from among the cherubim," he went in and stood beside the wheel. [7] One cherub stretched out his hand from among the cherubim to the fire that was between the cherubs, and took some, and put it into the hands of him who was clothed with linen, who took it and went out. [8] There appeared among the cherubim the form of a man's hand under their wings.

[9] Then I looked, and there were the four wheels by the cherubim, one wheel by one cherub, and another wheel by another cherub. And the appearance of the wheels was as the color of a beryl stone. [10] As for their appearances, all four had one likeness, as if one wheel had been in the middle of a wheel. [11] When they went, they went on their four sides. They did not turn as they went, but they followed to the place wherever the head looked. They did not turn as they went. [12] Their whole body, and their backs, and their hands, and their wings, and the wheels that the four had were full of eyes all round. [13] As for the wheels, they were called in my hearing the whirling wheels. [14] Each one had four faces. The first face was the face of a cherub, the second face was the face of a man, the third the face of a lion, and the fourth the face of an eagle.

[15] Then the cherubim rose up. They are the living creatures that I saw by the River Kebar. [16] When the cherubim went, the wheels went by them. And when the cherubim lifted up their wings to mount up from the earth, the same wheels also would not turn from beside them. [17] When the cherubim stood, the wheels stood. And when they rose up, the wheels also rose up with them. For the spirit of the living creatures was in them.

[18] Then the glory of the LORD departed from off the threshold of the temple and stood over the cherubim. [19] The cherubim lifted up their wings and mounted up from the earth in my sight. When they went out, the wheels were beside them. They stood at the door of the east gate of the house of the LORD; and the glory of the God of Israel was above them. [20] These are the living creatures that I saw under the God of Israel by the River Kebar. So I knew that they were cherubim. [21] Every one had four faces apiece, and every one four wings. And the likeness of the hands of a man was under their wings. [22] The likeness of their faces was the same faces which I saw by the River Kebar, their appearances and themselves. Each went straight forward.

God's Judgment on Wicked Counselors

11 Moreover the Spirit lifted me up and brought me to the east gate of the house of the LORD which faces eastward. And at the door of the gate *were* twenty-five men, among whom I saw Jaazaniah the son of Azzur and Pelatiah the son of Benaiah, officials of the people. [2] Then He said to me, "Son of man, these are the men who devise mischief and give wicked counsel in this city, [3] who say, 'The time is not near to build houses. This city is the cauldron, and we are the flesh.' [4] Therefore prophesy against them; prophesy, son of man!"

[5] Then the Spirit of the LORD fell upon me, and He said to me, Say, Thus says the LORD: Thus you have said, O house of Israel, for I know the things that come into your mind, every one of them. [6] You have multiplied your slain in this city, and you have filled the streets with them.

[7] Therefore thus says the Lord GOD: Your slain whom you have laid in the midst of it, they are the flesh and this city is the cauldron. But I will bring you out of the midst of it. [8] You have feared the sword, so I will bring a sword upon you, says the Lord GOD. [9] I will bring you out of the midst of the city and deliver you into the hands of strangers and execute judgments against you. [10] You shall fall by the sword. I will judge you in the border of Israel. Then you shall know that I am the LORD. [11] This city shall not be your cauldron, nor shall you be the flesh in the midst of it, but I will judge you in the border of Israel. [12] Thus you shall know that I am the LORD. For you have not walked in My statutes, or executed My judgments, but have done after the customs of the nations all around you.

[13] Now while I was prophesying, Pelatiah the son of Benaiah died. Then fell I down upon my face and cried out with a loud voice and said, "Ah, Lord GOD! Will You make a full end of the remnant of Israel?"

The Exiles' Return Promised

[14] Again the word of the LORD came to me, saying: [15] Son of man, your brothers, your kindred, your fellow captives, and all the house of Israel, all of them, are they to whom the inhabitants of Jerusalem have said, "Go far from the LORD. This land has been given to us as a possession."

[16] Therefore say, Thus says the Lord GOD: Although I have cast them far off among the nations, and although I have scattered them among the countries, yet I will be a sanctuary to them for a little while in the countries where they have gone.

[17] Therefore say, Thus says the Lord GOD: I will gather you from the peoples and assemble you out of the countries where you have been scattered, and I will give you the land of Israel.

[18] When they come there, they shall take away all the detestable things and all the abominations from it. [19] I will give them one heart, and I will put a new spirit within them. And I will take the stony heart out of their flesh, and give them a heart of flesh, [20] that they may walk in My statutes, and keep My ordinances, and do them. And they shall be My people, and I will be their God. [21] But as for those whose hearts walk after the hearts of their detestable things and their abominations, I will recompense their way upon their own heads, says the Lord GOD.

[22] Then the cherubim lifted up their wings with the wheels beside them. And the glory of the God of Israel was over them. [23] The glory of the LORD went up from the midst of the city and stood on the mountain which is on the east side of the city. [24] Afterwards the Spirit took me up and brought me in a vision by the Spirit of God into Chaldea to those of the captivity.

So the vision that I had seen went up from me. [25] Then I spoke to those of the captivity all the things that the LORD had shown me.

Judah's Captivity Symbolized

12 The word of the LORD also came to me, saying: [2] Son of man, you dwell in the midst of a rebellious house, which has eyes to see but does not see, and ears to hear but does not hear. For they are a rebellious house.

[3] Therefore, son of man, prepare baggage for captivity and go into captivity by day in their sight. And you shall go into captivity from your place to another place in their sight. It may be that they understand, though they are a rebellious house. [4] You shall bring out your belongings by day in their sight, as baggage for exile; and you shall go out at evening in their sight, as those who go into exile. [5] Dig a hole through the wall in their sight, and go out thereby. [6] In their sight you shall bear it on your shoulders and carry it out in the twilight. You shall cover your face so that you cannot see the land. For I have set you as a sign to the house of Israel.

[7] I did so as I was commanded. I brought out my baggage by day as baggage for captivity, and in the evening I dug through the wall with my own hands. I brought it out at twilight, carrying it on my shoulder in their sight.

[8] In the morning the word of the LORD came to me, saying: [9] Son of man, has not the house of Israel, the rebellious house, said to you, "What are you doing?"

[10] Say to them, "Thus says the Lord GOD: This oracle concerns the prince in Jerusalem and all the house of Israel who are in it." [11] Say, "I am your sign.

"As I have done, so it shall be done to them. They shall go into exile, into captivity."

[12] The prince who is among them shall bear *his baggage* on his shoulder in the twilight and go out. They shall dig through the wall to carry it out thereby. He shall cover his face so that he cannot see the land with his eyes. [13] My net also I will spread upon him, and he shall be taken in My snare. And I will bring him to Babylon to the land of the Chaldeans. Yet he shall not see it, though he shall die there. [14] I will scatter toward every wind all who are about him, his helpers and all his troops. And I will draw out the sword after them.

[15] Then they shall know that I am the LORD when I scatter them among the nations and disperse them among the countries. [16] But I will spare a few men of them from the sword, from famine, and from pestilence, so that they may declare all their abominations among the nations where they go and know that I am the LORD.

[17] Moreover the word of the LORD came to me, saying: [18] Son of man, eat your bread with quaking, and drink your water with trembling and with anxiety. [19] And say to the people of the land, Thus says the Lord GOD concerning the inhabitants of Jerusalem in the land of Israel: They shall eat their bread with carefulness and drink their water with astonishment, because their land shall be desolate from all that is in it, because of the violence of all those who dwell in it. [20] The cities that are inhabited shall be laid waste, and the land shall be desolate. Then you shall know that I am the LORD.

[21] The word of the LORD came to me, saying: [22] Son of man, what is this proverb that you people have in the land of Israel, saying, "The days are prolonged, and every vision fails"? [23] Tell them therefore, "Thus says the Lord GOD: I will make this proverb cease so that they shall no more use it as a proverb in Israel." But say to them, The days are at hand and the effect of every vision. [24] For there shall be no more any vain vision or flattering divination within the house of Israel. [25] For I the LORD will speak, and the word that I speak shall come to pass. It shall be no more prolonged. For in your days, O rebellious house, I will say the word, and will perform it, says the Lord GOD.

[26] Again the word of the LORD came to me, saying: [27] Son of man, look, the house of Israel says, "The vision that he sees is for many days to come, and he prophesies of the times that are far off."

[28] Therefore say to them, Thus says the Lord GOD: There shall none of My words be prolonged anymore, but the word which I have spoken shall be done, says the Lord GOD.

False Prophets Condemned

13 And the word of the LORD came to me, saying: [2] Son of man, prophesy against the prophets of Israel who prophesy, and say to those who prophesy out of their own hearts, "Hear the word of the LORD!" [3] Thus says the Lord GOD: Woe to the foolish prophets who follow their own spirit and have seen nothing! [4] O Israel, your prophets are like the foxes in the ruins. [5] You have not gone up into the gaps, nor did you build up the hedge for the house of Israel to stand in the battle on the day of the LORD. [6] They have seen vanity and lying divination, saying, "The LORD says," when the LORD has not sent them. And they have made others to hope for the confirmation of their word. [7] Have you not seen a vain vision, and have you not spoken a lying divination when you say, "The LORD says," yet it is not I who have spoken?

[8] Therefore thus says the Lord GOD: Because you have spoken vanity and seen lies, therefore I am against you, says the Lord GOD. [9] Thus My hand shall be against the prophets who see vanity and who divine lies. They shall not have a place in the council of My people, nor shall they be written in the register of the house of Israel, nor shall they enter into the land of Israel so that you may know that I am the Lord GOD.

[10] It is surely because they have seduced My people, saying, "Peace," when there was no peace. And when anyone builds up a wall, they daub it with whitewash. [11] Say to those who daub it with whitewash that it shall fall. There shall be an overflowing shower, and you, O great hailstones, shall fall. And a stormy wind shall break it. [12] When the wall has fallen, will you not be asked, "Where is the whitewash with which you have daubed it?"

[13] Therefore thus says the Lord GOD: I will make a violent wind break out in My fury. And there shall be an overflowing shower in My anger, and hailstones in My fury to consume it. [14] So I will break down the wall that you have daubed with whitewash, and bring it down to the ground so that its foundation is laid bare. And when it falls, you shall be consumed in its midst. And you shall

know that I am the LORD. [15] Thus I will accomplish My wrath upon the wall and upon those who have daubed it with whitewash, and I will say to you, The wall is no more, nor those who daubed it, [16] *along with* the prophets of Israel who prophesy concerning Jerusalem and who see visions of peace for her when there is no peace, says the Lord GOD.

[17] Now you, son of man, set your face against the daughters of your people who prophesy out of their own heart and prophesy against them, [18] and say, Thus says the Lord GOD: Woe to the women who sew magic bands on all wrists and make veils on the heads of persons of every stature to hunt souls! Will you hunt the souls of My people but save the souls alive *of others* for yourselves? [19] And you pollute Me among My people for handfuls of barley and pieces of bread to slay the souls of those who should not die and to save the souls alive of those who should not live by your lying to My people who hear your lies.

[20] Therefore thus says the Lord GOD: I am against your magic bands with which you hunt the souls there as birds, and I will tear them from your arms, and I will let the souls go, even the souls that you hunt as birds. [21] Your veils also I will tear off and deliver My people out of your hands, and they shall be no more in your hand to be hunted. And you shall know that I am the LORD. [22] Because with lies you have made the heart of the righteous sad, whom I have not made sad, and strengthened the hands of the wicked that he should not turn from his wicked way and save his life, [23] therefore you women shall no more see vanity or practice divinations, and I will deliver My people out of your hand. Thus you shall know that I am the LORD.

Idolatrous Elders Condemned

14 Then some of the elders of Israel came to me and sat before me. [2] The word of the LORD came to me, saying: [3] Son of man, these men have set up their idols in their heart and put the stumbling block of their iniquity before their face. Should I be inquired of by them at all? [4] Therefore speak to them and say to them, Thus says the Lord GOD: Every man of the house of Israel who sets up his idols in his heart, and puts the stumbling block of his iniquity before his face, and comes to the prophet, I the LORD will answer him who comes according to the multitude of his idols, [5] in order to seize the heart of the house of Israel who are estranged from Me through all their idols.

[6] Therefore say to the house of Israel, Thus says the Lord GOD: Repent and turn away from your idols and turn away your faces from all your abominations.

[7] For every one of the house of Israel or of the stranger who sojourns in Israel who separates himself from Me, and sets up his idols in his heart, and puts the stumbling block of his iniquity before his face, and comes to the prophet to inquire of Me for himself, I the LORD will answer him by Myself. [8] And I will set My face against that man and will make him a sign and a proverb, and I will cut him off from the midst of My people. And you shall know that I am the LORD.

[9] And if the prophet is deceived when he has spoken a word, I the LORD have deceived that prophet, and I will stretch out My hand against him and will destroy him from the midst of My people Israel. [10] They shall bear *the punishment of* their iniquity. The punishment of the prophet shall be even as the punishment of him who seeks him [11] in order that the house of Israel may no more go astray from Me or be polluted anymore with all their transgressions. Thus they shall be My people, and I shall be their God, says the Lord GOD.

Jerusalem's Imminent Judgment

[12] The word of the LORD came to me again, saying: [13] Son of man, when the land sins against Me by trespassing grievously, then I will stretch out My hand against it, and break the staff of the bread, and send famine against it, and cut off man and beast from it. [14] Even though these three men, Noah, Daniel, and Job, were in it, they could deliver but their own souls by their righteousness, says the Lord GOD.

[15] If I cause wild beasts to pass through the land, and they destroy it so that it becomes desolate, that no man may pass through because of the beasts, [16] though these three men were in it, as I live, says the Lord GOD, they could deliver neither their sons nor their daughters. They alone would be delivered, but the land would be desolate.

[17] Or if I bring a sword on that land, and say, "Let the sword go through the land and cut off man and beast from it," [18] though

these three men were in it, as I live, says the Lord God, they would deliver neither their sons nor their daughters, but they alone would deliver themselves.

[19] Or *if* I send a pestilence into that land and pour out My fury on it in blood to cut off from it man and beast, [20] though Noah, Daniel, and Job were in it, as I live, says the Lord God, they would deliver neither their sons nor their daughters. They would deliver only their own souls by their righteousness.

[21] For thus says the Lord God: How much more when I send My four sore judgments on Jerusalem, the sword, and the famine, and the wild beasts, and the pestilence, to cut off man and beast from it. [22] Yet a remnant shall be left in it who shall be brought out, both sons and daughters. They shall come out to you, and you shall see their way and their deeds. Then you shall be comforted concerning the disaster that I have brought against Jerusalem, even concerning all that I have brought upon it. [23] Then they shall comfort you when you see their ways and their deeds. And you shall know that I have not done without cause all that I have done in it, says the Lord God.

Jerusalem as a Useless Vine

15 And the word of the Lord came to me, saying: [2] Son of man, how is the wood of the vine tree better than any wood of a branch which is among the trees of the forest? [3] Can wood be taken from it to do any work, or can men take a peg of it to hang any vessel on it? [4] If it has been cast into the fire for fuel and the fire has devoured both ends of it and the middle of it is burned, is it useful for any work? [5] When it was whole, it was not made into anything. How much less is it useful for any work when the fire has devoured it and it is burned!

[6] Therefore thus says the Lord God: As the wood of the vine tree among the trees of the forest, which I have given to the fire for fuel, so I will give the inhabitants of Jerusalem. [7] I will set My face against them. Though they go out from one fire, yet the fire shall devour them. Then you shall know that I am the Lord when I set My face against them. [8] I will make the land desolate, because they have committed a trespass, says the Lord God.

Jerusalem as an Adulterous Bride

16 Again the word of the Lord came to me, saying: [2] Son of man, cause Jerusalem to know her abominations, [3] and say, Thus says the Lord God to Jerusalem: Your birth and your nativity are from the land of Canaan. Your father was an Amorite, and your mother a Hittite. [4] As for your birth, on the day you were born your navel cord was not cut, nor were you washed in water to cleanse you. You were not rubbed with salt, nor wrapped in swaddling cloths. [5] No eye pitied you to do any of these to you, to have compassion on you. But you were cast out in the open field, to the loathing of your person, in the day that you were born.

[6] When I passed by you and saw you polluted in your own blood, I said to you when you were in your blood, "Live!" Indeed, I said to you when you were in your blood, "Live!" [7] I have caused you to multiply as the bud of the field, and you have increased and become tall, and you have reached the age of fine ornaments. Your breasts were fashioned and your hair had grown, yet you were naked and bare.

[8] Now when I passed by you and looked upon you, you were old enough for love. So I spread My garment over you and covered your nakedness. Indeed, I swore to you, and entered into a covenant with you, says the Lord God, and you became Mine.

[9] Then I washed you with water. Indeed, I thoroughly washed away your blood from you, and I anointed you with oil. [10] I clothed you also with embroidered work, and put sandals of porpoise skin on your feet, and girded you about with fine linen, and covered you with silk. [11] I decked you also with ornaments, and put bracelets on your hands, and a chain on your neck. [12] I put a jewel on your forehead, and earrings in your ears, and a beautiful crown on your head. [13] Thus you were decked with gold and silver. And your raiment was of fine linen, and silk, and embroidered work. You ate fine flour, and honey, and oil. And you were exceedingly beautiful and advanced to royalty. [14] Then your renown went out among the nations for your beauty. For it was perfect through My comeliness which I had put upon you, says the Lord God.

[15] But you trusted in your own beauty, and played the harlot because of your renown, and poured out your fornications on every willing passerby. [16] Of your garments you took and decked your high places with various colors and played the harlot on them, which should never come about or happen. [17] You have also taken your fair jewels made of My gold and My silver, which I had given you, and made for yourself images of men that you might commit harlotry with them. [18] Then you took your embroidered garments and covered them. And you have set My oil and My incense before them. [19] My bread also which I gave you, fine flour, and oil, and honey, with which I fed you, you have even set before them for a sweet savor. And thus it was, says the Lord God.

[20] Moreover you have taken your sons and your daughters, whom you have borne to Me, and these you have sacrificed to them to be devoured. Were your harlotries so small a matter? [21] You have slain My children and delivered them up to idols by causing them to pass through the fire. [22] Besides all your abominations and your harlotries you have not remembered the days of your youth when you were naked and bare and were polluted in your blood.

[23] After all your wickedness (Woe, woe to you! says the Lord God) [24] you also built for yourself a shrine and have made yourself a high place in every street. [25] You have built yourself a high place at the head of every street, and have made your beauty to be abhorred, and have spread your legs to every passerby to multiply your harlotries. [26] You have also committed fornication with the Egyptians, your lustful neighbors, and increased your harlotries to provoke Me to anger. [27] Therefore I have stretched out My hand against you and have diminished your ordinary food and delivered you to the will of those who hate you, the daughters of the Philistines who are ashamed of your lewd conduct. [28] You have played the harlot also with the Assyrians because you were insatiable. Indeed, you have played the harlot with them, and yet could not be satisfied. [29] You have moreover multiplied your fornication with the land of merchants, Chaldea. And yet you were not satisfied even with this.

[30] How weak is your heart, says the Lord God, seeing you do all these things, the works of an imperious harlot. [31] When you built your shrine at the head of every street and made your high place in every square, you have not been as a harlot in that you scorned payment.

[32] You have been as a wife who commits adultery, who takes strangers instead of her husband! [33] Men give gifts to all harlots. But you give your gifts to all your lovers, and hire them that they may come to you on every side for your harlotry. [34] Thus you are different from other women in your harlotries in that no one follows you to commit harlotries, because you give money, and no money is given to you. Thus you are different.

[35] Therefore, O harlot, hear the word of the Lord. [36] Thus says the Lord God, Because your filthiness was poured out and your nakedness discovered through your harlotries with your lovers, and with all the idols of your abominations, and by the blood of your children, which you gave to idols, [37] therefore I will gather all your lovers with whom you have taken pleasure and all those whom you have loved with all those whom you have hated. I will even gather them from all around against you and will reveal your nakedness to them so that they may see all your nakedness. [38] I will judge you as women who commit adultery or shed blood are judged. And I will bring on you the blood of fury and jealousy. [39] I will also give you into their hand, and they shall throw down your shrines, and shall break down your high places. They shall strip you also of your clothes, and shall take your fair jewels, and leave you naked and bare. [40] They shall also bring up a company against you, and they shall stone you with stones, and thrust you through with their swords. [41] They shall burn your houses with fire and execute judgments on you in the sight of many women. And I will cause you to cease from playing the harlot, and you also shall give no hire anymore. [42] So I will make My fury toward you to rest, and My jealousy shall depart from you, and I will be quiet, and will be angry no more.

[43] Because you have not remembered the days of your youth, but have enraged Me in all these things, I also will recompense your way upon your head, says the Lord God, so that you shall not commit this lewdness above all your other abominations.

[44] Everyone who uses proverbs shall use this proverb against you, saying, "Like mother, like daughter." [45] You are your mother's daughter who loathed her husband and her children. And

you are the sister of your sisters who loathed their husbands and their children. Your mother was a Hittite, and your father an Amorite. ⁴⁶ Now your elder sister is Samaria, she and her daughters who dwell north of you. And your younger sister who dwells south of you is Sodom and her daughters. ⁴⁷ Yet you have not walked after their ways, or done according to their abominations. But, as if that were a very little thing, you were corrupted more than they in all your ways. ⁴⁸ As I live, says the Lord God, Sodom your sister has not done, she nor her daughters, as you and your daughters have done.

⁴⁹ This was the iniquity of your sister Sodom. Pride, abundance of bread, and careless ease was in her and in her daughters, but she did strengthen the hand of the poor and needy. ⁵⁰ They were haughty and committed abominations before Me. Therefore I took them away when I saw it. ⁵¹ Moreover, Samaria did not commit half of your sins. But you have multiplied your abominations more than they and have made your sisters appear righteous in all your abominations which you have done. ⁵² Also bear your own shame in that you have made judgment favorable to your sisters. Because of your sins that you have committed more abominable than they, they are more righteous than you. Indeed, be humiliated also and bear your shame in that you have made your sisters appear righteous.

⁵³ Yet I shall restore their captivity, the captivity of Sodom and her daughters, and the captivity of Samaria and her daughters, and along with them your own captivity, ⁵⁴ in order that you may bear your own shame and may be humiliated in all that you have done in that you are a comfort to them. ⁵⁵ Your sisters, Sodom and her daughters and Samaria and her daughters, shall return to their former state, and you and your daughters shall return to your former state. ⁵⁶ As the name of your sister Sodom was not mentioned by your mouth in the day of your pride, ⁵⁷ before your wickedness was uncovered, so now you have become the reproach of the daughters of Edom and all who are around her, the daughters of the Philistines, those all around who despise you. ⁵⁸ You have borne *the punishment of* your lewdness and your abominations, says the Lord.

An Everlasting Covenant

⁵⁹ For thus, says the Lord God, I will even deal with you as you have done, you who have despised the oath by breaking the covenant. ⁶⁰ Nevertheless I will remember My covenant with you in the days of your youth, and I will establish an everlasting covenant with you. ⁶¹ Then you shall remember your ways and be ashamed when you receive your sisters, your elder and your younger. And I will give them to you as daughters, but not because of your covenant. ⁶² Thus I will establish My covenant with you, and you shall know that I am the Lord, ⁶³ in order that you may remember, and be humiliated, and never open your mouth anymore because of your shame, when I am pacified toward you for all that you have done, says the Lord God.

Two Eagles and a Vine

17 And the word of the Lord came to me, saying: ² Son of man, put forth a riddle, and speak a parable to the house of Israel, ³ and say, Thus says the Lord God: A great eagle with great wings, long-winged, full of feathers which had various colors, came to Lebanon and took away the highest branch of the cedar. ⁴ He cropped off the top of its young twigs and carried it into a land of merchants. He set it in a city of dealers. ⁵ He took also some of the seed of the land and planted it in a fruitful field. He placed it by great waters and set it as a willow tree. ⁶ It grew and became a spreading vine of low stature, whose branches turned toward him, and its roots were under it. So it became a vine, and brought forth branches, and shot forth sprigs. ⁷ There was also another great eagle with great wings and many feathers. And this vine bent its roots toward him and shot forth its branches toward him, that he might water it by the bed where it was planted. ⁸ It was planted in a good soil by many waters, that it might bring forth branches, and that it might bear fruit, that it might be a splendid vine. ⁹ Say: Thus says the Lord God: Will it thrive? Will he not pull up its roots and cut off its fruit, so that it withers, so that all its spring leaves wither? It will not take a great power or many people to pull it from its roots. ¹⁰ Though it has been planted, will it prosper? Shall

it not utterly wither when the east wind hits it? It shall wither in the furrows where it grew.

¹¹ Moreover the word of the Lord came to me, saying: ¹² Say now to the rebellious house: Do you not know what these things *mean*? Tell them: The king of Babylon came to Jerusalem, and took its king and its officials, and led them to him in Babylon. ¹³ He took one of the king's seed, and made a covenant with him, and put him under oath. He has also taken away the mighty of the land, ¹⁴ that the kingdom might be debased, that it might not lift itself up, but by the keeping of his covenant it might stand. ¹⁵ But he rebelled against him in sending his ambassadors into Egypt, that they might give him horses and much people. Shall he prosper? Shall he escape who does such things? Can he indeed break the covenant and be delivered?

¹⁶ As I live, says the Lord God, surely in the country of the king who made him king, whose oath he despised and whose covenant he broke, in the midst of Babylon he shall die. ¹⁷ Nor shall Pharaoh with his mighty army and great company help him in the war by casting up mounts and building forts to cut off many persons. ¹⁸ Seeing he despised the oath by breaking the covenant, when he had given his allegiance and has done all these things, he shall not escape.

¹⁹ Therefore thus says the Lord God: As I live, surely My oath that he has despised and My covenant that he has broken, I will inflict upon his own head. ²⁰ I will spread My net upon him, and he shall be taken in My snare, and I will bring him to Babylon and will enter into judgment with him there for his trespass that he has trespassed against Me. ²¹ All the choice men in all his troops shall fall by the sword, and those who remain shall be scattered toward all winds. And you shall know that I the Lord have spoken it.

²² Thus says the Lord God: I will also take of the highest branch of the high cedar and set it aside. I will crop off from the top of its young twigs a tender one and will plant it on a high and lofty mountain. ²³ On the mountain of the height of Israel I will plant it. And it shall bring forth boughs, and bear fruit, and be a splendid cedar. And under it all fowl of every wing shall nest. In the shadow of its branches they shall nest. ²⁴ All the trees of the field shall know that I the Lord have brought down the high tree, have exalted the low tree, have dried up the green tree, and have made the dry tree to flourish.

I, the Lord, have spoken and will do it.

The Soul Who Sins Will Die

18 The word of the Lord came to me again, saying: ² What do you mean in using this proverb concerning the land of Israel, saying:

"The fathers have eaten sour grapes,
　and the children's teeth are set on edge"?

³ As I live, says the Lord God, you shall not have occasion anymore to use this proverb in Israel. ⁴ All souls are Mine. The soul of the father, so also the soul of the son is Mine. The soul who sins shall die.

⁵ But if a man is righteous
　and does that which is lawful and right,
⁶ and has not eaten on the mountains;
　nor has he lifted up his eyes to the idols of the house of Israel,
nor has he defiled his neighbor's wife,
　nor has he approached a woman during her impurity;
⁷ and he has not oppressed anyone,
　but has restored to the debtor his pledge;
has devastated no one by violence,
　has given his bread to the hungry,
　and has covered the naked with a garment;
⁸ if he has not lent at interest,
　nor has taken any increase,
but has withdrawn his hand from iniquity,
　has executed true justice between man and man;
⁹ has walked in My statutes,
　and has kept My judgments to deal truly,
he is righteous
　and shall surely live,
　says the Lord God.

¹⁰ If he begets a son who is a robber, a shedder of blood, and who does any of these things to a brother ¹¹ (though he himself does not do any of these things),

but even has eaten on the mountain shrines
and defiled his neighbor's wife;
¹² has oppressed the poor and needy,
has devastated by violence,
has not restored the pledge,
and has lifted up his eyes to the idols,
has committed abomination,
¹³ has lent at interest, and has taken increase, shall he then live?

He shall not live. He has done all these abominations. He shall surely die. His blood shall be upon his own head.

¹⁴ Now if he begets a son who sees all his father's sins which he has done, and considering does not do likewise:

¹⁵ He has not eaten on the mountain shrines,
nor has he lifted up his eyes to the idols of the house of Israel,
has not defiled his neighbor's wife;
¹⁶ nor has he oppressed anyone,
has not withheld a pledge,
nor has he devastated by violence,
but has given his bread to the hungry,
and has covered the naked with a garment;
¹⁷ he keeps his hand from the poor,
has not received usury nor increase,
has executed My judgments, and has walked in My statutes.

He shall not die for the iniquity of his father; he shall surely live. ¹⁸ As for his father, because he cruelly oppressed, devastated his brother by violence, and did that which is not good among his people, he shall die for his iniquity.

Repent and Live

¹⁹ Yet you say, "Why should the son not bear the punishment of the iniquity of the father?" When the son has done what is lawful and right, and has kept all My statutes, and has done them, he shall surely live. ²⁰ The soul who sins shall die. The son shall not bear the punishment of the iniquity of the father, nor shall the father bear the punishment of the iniquity of the son. The righteousness of the righteous shall be upon himself, and the wickedness of the wicked shall be upon himself.

²¹ But if the wicked turns from all his sins that he has committed, and keeps all My statutes, and does that which is lawful and right, he shall surely live. He shall not die. ²² All his transgressions that he has committed, they shall not be remembered against him. Because of his righteousness that he has done, he shall live. ²³ Do I have any pleasure in the death of the wicked, says the Lord God, but rather that he should turn from his ways and live?

²⁴ But when a righteous man turns away from his righteousness, and commits iniquity, and does according to all the abominations that the wicked man does, shall he live? All his righteousness that he has done shall not be remembered; for his trespass that he has committed and in his sin that he has done. In them he shall die.

²⁵ Yet you say, "The way of the Lord is not right." Hear now, O house of Israel. Is not My way right? Are not your ways not right? ²⁶ When a righteous man turns away from his righteousness and commits iniquity, he dies in it. For his iniquity that he has done he shall die. ²⁷ Again, when the wicked turns away from his wickedness that he has committed and does that which is lawful and right, he shall save his soul. ²⁸ Because he considered and turned away from all his transgressions that he has committed, he shall surely live. He shall not die. ²⁹ Yet the house of Israel says, "The way of the Lord is not right." O house of Israel, are not My ways right? Are not your ways not right?

³⁰ Therefore I will judge you, O house of Israel, every one according to his ways, says the Lord God. Repent, and turn away from all your transgressions so that iniquity shall not be your ruin. ³¹ Cast away from you all your transgressions whereby you have transgressed, and make yourselves a new heart and a new spirit. For why will you die, O house

of Israel? ³² For I have no pleasure in the death of anyone who dies, says the Lord God. Therefore, repent and live.

A Lament for Israel's Princes

19 Moreover take up a lamentation for the officials of Israel, ² and say:

What was your mother?
A lioness among lions!
She lay down among young lions;
she nourished her whelps.
³ When she brought up one of her whelps,
he became a lion
and learned to catch his prey;
he devoured men.
⁴ The nations also heard of him;
he was taken in their pit,
and they brought him with chains
to the land of Egypt.

⁵ Now when she saw as she had waited
that her hope was lost,
then she took another of her whelps
and made him a young lion.
⁶ He went up and down among the lions;
he became a young lion,
and learned to catch the prey,
and devoured men.
⁷ He destroyed their fortified palaces,
and he laid waste their cities;
and the land and its fullness
were appalled by the noise of his roaring.
⁸ Then the nations set against him
on every side from their provinces,
and spread their net over him;
he was taken in their pit.
⁹ They put him in a cage with hooks
and brought him to the king of Babylon;
they brought him in hunting nets,
so that his voice would be heard no more
on the mountains of Israel.

¹⁰ Your mother was like a vine in your vineyard,
planted by the waters;
it was fruitful and full of branches
by reason of many waters.
¹¹ It had strong rods
for the scepters of those who rule.
And its stature
was exalted above the clouds,
so it appeared in its height
with the multitude of its branches.
¹² But it was plucked up in fury,
it was cast down to the ground,
and the east wind dried up its fruit.
Its strong rod was broken and it withered;
the fire consumed it.
¹³ Now it is planted in the wilderness,
in a dry and thirsty ground.
¹⁴ Fire has gone out from its branch;
it has devoured its shoots and fruit,
so that there is no strong rod in it,
a scepter to rule.

This is a lamentation, and has become a lamentation.

Israel's Continuing Rebellion

20 In the seventh year, in the fifth *month*, on the tenth day of the month, certain of the elders of Israel came to inquire of the Lord and sat before me.

² Then the word of the Lord came to me, saying: ³ Son of man, speak to the elders of Israel, and say to them: Thus says the Lord God:

Do you come to inquire of Me? As I live, says the Lord God, I will not be inquired of by you.

⁴ Will you judge them, son of man, will you judge them? Cause them to know the abominations of their fathers. ⁵ And say to them: Thus says the Lord God: On the day when I chose Israel, and lifted up My hand to the seed of the house of Jacob, and made Myself known to them in the land of Egypt, when I lifted up My hand to them, saying, I am the Lord your God, ⁶ on that day that I lifted up My hand to them to bring them out of the land of Egypt into a land that I had selected for them, flowing with milk and honey, which is the glory of all lands, ⁷ then I said to them: Cast away, each of you, the abominations of his eyes, and do not defile yourselves with the idols of Egypt. I am the Lord your God.

⁸ But they rebelled against Me and would not listen to Me. They did not cast away the abominations of their eyes, nor did they forsake the idols of Egypt. Then I said I will pour out My fury upon them, to accomplish My anger against them in the midst of the land of Egypt. ⁹ But I acted for My name's sake, that it should not be polluted before the nations among whom they were, in whose sight I made Myself known to them in bringing them out of the land of Egypt. ¹⁰ Therefore I caused them to go forth out of the land of Egypt and brought them into the wilderness. ¹¹ I gave them My statutes and showed them My judgments, which if a man does them, he shall live. ¹² Moreover I gave them My Sabbaths to be a sign between them and Me, that they might know that I am the Lord who sanctifies them.

¹³ But the house of Israel rebelled against Me in the wilderness. They did not walk in My statutes, and they despised My judgments, which if a man does them, he shall live. And My Sabbaths they greatly polluted. Then I said I would pour out My fury upon them in the wilderness to consume them. ¹⁴ But I acted for My name's sake, that it should not be polluted before the nations in whose sight I brought them out. ¹⁵ Also I lifted up My hand to them in the wilderness that I would not bring them into the land which I had given them, flowing with milk and honey, which is the glory of all lands, ¹⁶ because they despised My judgments and did not walk in My statutes, but polluted My Sabbaths. For their hearts went after their idols. ¹⁷ Nevertheless My eye spared them from destroying them, nor did I make an end of them in the wilderness. ¹⁸ But I said to their children in the wilderness: Do not walk in the statutes of your fathers, neither observe their judgments, nor defile yourselves with their idols. ¹⁹ I am the Lord your God: Walk in My statutes, and keep My judgments, and do them. ²⁰ And hallow My Sabbaths. And they shall be a sign between Me and you that you may know that I am the Lord your God.

²¹ Yet the children rebelled against Me. They did not walk in My statutes, nor did they keep My judgments to do them, which if a man does them, he shall live. They polluted My Sabbaths. Then I said I would pour out My fury upon them to accomplish My anger against them in the wilderness. ²² Nevertheless I withdrew My hand and acted for My name's sake, that it should not be polluted in the sight of the nations in whose sight I brought them out. ²³ I lifted up My hand to them also in the wilderness, that I would scatter them among the nations and disperse them through the countries, ²⁴ because they had not executed My judgments, but had despised My statutes and had polluted My Sabbaths, and their eyes were after their fathers' idols. ²⁵ Therefore I gave them also statutes that were not good and judgments by which they could not live. ²⁶ And I pronounced them unclean because of their gifts, in that they caused to pass through the fire all who opened the womb, that I might make them desolate in order that they might know that I am the Lord.

²⁷ Therefore, son of man, speak to the house of Israel and say to them, Thus says the Lord God: Yet in this your fathers have blasphemed Me, in that they have committed a trespass against Me. ²⁸ When I had brought them into the land for which I lifted up My hand to give it to them, then they saw every high hill and all the leafy trees, and there they offered their sacrifices, and there they presented the provocation of their offering. There also they made their sweet savor and there poured out their drink offerings. ²⁹ Then I said to them: What is the high place to which you go? And the name is called Bamah to this day.

³⁰ Therefore say to the house of Israel, Thus says the Lord God: Will you pollute yourselves after the manner of your fathers and commit harlotry after their abominations? ³¹ When you offer your gifts, when you make your sons to pass through the fire, you pollute yourselves with all your idols, even to this day. And shall I be inquired of by you, O house of Israel? As I live, says the Lord God, I will not be inquired of by you.

³² That which comes into your mind shall not come about when you say, "We will be as the nations, as the families of the countries, to serve wood and stone."

God Will Restore Israel

³³ As I live, says the Lord God, surely with a mighty hand and with a stretched-out arm and with fury poured out, I will rule over you. ³⁴ And I will bring you out from the peoples and will gather you out of the countries in which you are scattered with a mighty hand and with a stretched-out arm and with fury poured out. ³⁵ I will bring you into the wilderness of the peoples, and there I will enter into judgment with you face to face. ³⁶ As I entered into judgment with your fathers in the wilderness of the land of Egypt, so I will enter into judgment with you, says the Lord God. ³⁷ I will cause you to pass under the rod, and I will bring you into the bond of the covenant. ³⁸ And I will purge from among you the rebels and those who transgress against Me. I will bring them out of the country where they sojourn, and they shall not enter into the land of Israel. And you shall know that I am the Lord.

³⁹ As for you, O house of Israel, thus says the Lord God: Go serve every one of you his idols, but later you shall surely listen to Me. But do not pollute My holy name anymore with your gifts and with your idols. ⁴⁰ For on My holy mountain, on the mountain of the height of Israel, says the Lord God, there all the house of Israel, all of them, shall serve Me in the land. There I will accept them, and there I will seek your offerings and the first fruits of your gifts with all your holy things. ⁴¹ I will accept you with your sweet savor when I bring you out from the peoples and gather you out of the countries in which you have been scattered. And I will be sanctified among you before the nations. ⁴² You shall know that I am the Lord when I bring you into the land of Israel, into the country for which I lifted up My hand to give it to your fathers. ⁴³ There you shall remember your ways and all your deeds in which you have been defiled. And you shall loathe yourselves in your own sight for all your evils that you have committed. ⁴⁴ You shall know that I am the Lord when I have dealt with you for My name's sake, not according to your wicked ways, or according to your corrupt deeds, O house of Israel, says the Lord God.

A Prophecy Against the Negev

⁴⁵ Moreover the word of the Lord came to me, saying: ⁴⁶ Son of man, set your face toward the south, preach against the south, and prophesy against the forest land in the Negev. ⁴⁷ And say to the forest of the Negev, Hear the word of the Lord. Thus says the Lord God: I will kindle a fire in you, and it shall devour every green tree in you and every dry tree. The flaming flame shall not be quenched, and all faces from the south to the north shall be burned in it. ⁴⁸ All flesh shall see that I the Lord have kindled it. It shall not be quenched.

⁴⁹ Then I said, "Ah, Lord God! They say of me, 'Does he not speak parables?'"

Babylon, the Sword of the Lord

21 And the word of the Lord came to me, saying: ² Son of man, set your face toward Jerusalem, and speak against the holy places, and prophesy against the land of Israel, ³ and say to the land of Israel, Thus says the Lord: I am against you, and will draw My sword from its sheath, and will cut off from you the righteous and the wicked. ⁴ Seeing then that I will cut off from you the righteous and the wicked, therefore My sword shall be drawn from its sheath against all flesh from the south to the north, ⁵ that all flesh shall know that I the Lord have drawn forth My sword from its sheath. It shall not return anymore.

⁶ As for you, son of man, groan with breaking heart and bitter grief, groan before their eyes. ⁷ It shall be when they say to you, "Why do you groan?" that you shall answer, "Because of the news that is coming. And every heart shall melt, and all hands shall be feeble, and every spirit shall faint, and all knees shall be weak as water. It comes and shall be brought to pass," says the Lord God.

⁸ Again the word of the Lord came to me, saying: ⁹ Son of man, prophesy and say, Thus says the Lord! Say:

A sword, a sword is sharpened
 and also furbished!
10 It is sharpened to make a slaughter;
 it is furbished so that it may glitter like lightning.

Should we then make cheer, the rod of My son despising every tree?

11 He has given it to be furbished,
 that it may be handled;
the sword is sharpened,
 and it is furbished to give it into the hand of the slayer.
12 Cry out and howl, son of man;
 for it shall be against My people,
 it shall be against all the officials of Israel.
Terrors by reason of the sword
 shall be upon My people;
therefore strike your thigh.

13 Because it is a trial, and what if even the rod which despises shall be no more? says the Lord God.

14 You therefore, son of man, prophesy
 and clap your hands together.
And let the sword be doubled
 the third time,
the sword of the slain.
 It is the sword of the great one slain,
 which surrounds them.
15 That their hearts may faint,
 and many fall at all their gates,
 I have given the glittering sword.
Ah! It is made for striking like lightning;
 it is wrapped up for the slaughter.
16 Show yourself sharp, go to the right hand.
 Set yourself. Go to the left hand,
 wherever your edge is set.
17 I will also clap My hands together,
 and I will cause My fury to rest;
 I the Lord have spoken.

18 The word of the Lord came to me again, saying: 19 As for you, son of man, appoint two ways for the sword of the king of Babylon to come. Both of them shall come out of one land. And make a signpost. Make it at the head of the way to the city. 20 Appoint a way for the sword to come to Rabbah of the sons of Ammon and to Judah in Jerusalem the fortified. 21 For the king of Babylon stands at the parting of the way, at the head of the two ways, to use divination: He shakes the arrows, he consults the images, he looks in the liver. 22 At his right hand was the divination for Jerusalem: to appoint battering rams, to open the mouth for the slaughter, to lift up the voice with a battle shout, to appoint battering rams against the gates, to cast up a ramp, and to build a siege tower. 23 It shall be to them as a false divination in their sight, to those who have sworn oaths. But he will call to remembrance the iniquity, that they may be seized.

24 Therefore thus says the Lord God: Because you have made your iniquity to be remembered, in that your transgressions are uncovered, so that in all your deeds your sins do appear, because, I say, that you have come to remembrance, you shall be seized with the hand.

25 You, profane wicked prince of Israel, whose day has come in the time of the punishment of the end, 26 thus says the Lord God: Remove the diadem and take off the crown. This shall not be the same anymore. Exalt what is low, and abase what is high. 27 A ruin, a ruin, a ruin I shall make it. And it shall be no more until He comes whose right it is, and I shall give it to Him.

A Sword Against the Ammonites

28 You, son of man, prophesy and say: Thus says the Lord God concerning the sons of Ammon and concerning their reproach, and say,

The sword, the sword is drawn,
 furbished for the slaughter,

to cause it to consume
 that it may be like lightning,
29 while they see vanity for you,
 while they divine a lie to you
to bring you upon the necks
 of the wicked who are slain,
whose day has come
 in the time of the punishment of the end.

30 Return it to its sheath.
 I will judge you
in the place where you were created,
 in the land of your nativity.
31 I will pour out My indignation upon you;
 I will blow against you in the fire of My wrath,
and deliver you into the hand of cruel men,
 skilled in destruction.
32 You shall be fuel to the fire;
 your blood shall be in the midst of the land.
You shall be no more remembered,
 for I the Lord have spoken.

The Sins of Jerusalem

22 Moreover the word of the Lord came to me, saying: 2 Now you, son of man, will you judge, will you judge the bloody city? Indeed, you shall show her all her abominations. 3 Then say, Thus says the Lord God: The city sheds blood in her midst, that her time may come, and makes idols against herself to defile herself. 4 You have become guilty in your blood that you have shed and have defiled yourself with your idols which you have made. And you have caused your day to draw near and have come to your years. Therefore I have made you a reproach to the nations and a mocking to all countries. 5 Those who are near and those who are far from you shall mock you, you of infamy and much turmoil.

6 The princes of Israel in you, every one according to his power, have been bent on shedding blood. 7 In you they have treated father and mother lightly. In your midst they have dealt with the stranger by oppression. In you they have vexed the fatherless and the widow. 8 You have despised My holy things and have profaned My Sabbaths. 9 In you are men who carry slanders to shed blood. And in you they eat at the mountain shrines. In your midst they commit lewdness. 10 In you they have uncovered their fathers' nakedness. In you they have humbled her who was unclean in her menstrual impurity. 11 One has committed abomination with his neighbor's wife, and another has lewdly defiled his daughter-in-law. And another in you has humbled his sister, his father's daughter. 12 In you they have taken bribes to shed blood. You have taken usury and increase, and you have injured your neighbors for gain by extortion, and you have forgotten Me, says the Lord God.

13 Therefore I have struck My hand toward your dishonest gain which you have made, and toward your blood which has been in your midst. 14 Can your heart endure, or can your hands be strong in the days that I shall deal with you? I the Lord have spoken and will do it. 15 I will scatter you among the nations and disperse you in the countries and consume your filthiness out of you. 16 You shall profane yourself in the sight of the nations, and you shall know that I am the Lord.

Jerusalem as God's Furnace

17 The word of the Lord came to me, saying: 18 Son of man, the house of Israel has become dross to Me. All of them are bronze and tin and iron and lead in the midst of the furnace. They are the dross of silver. 19 Therefore thus says the Lord God: Because you all have become dross, therefore, I will gather you into the midst of Jerusalem. 20 As they gather silver and bronze and iron and lead and tin into the midst of a furnace to blow fire on it to melt it, so I will gather you in My anger and in My fury, and I will lay you there and melt you. 21 Indeed, I will gather you and blow upon you in the fire of My wrath, and you shall be melted in the midst of it. 22 As silver is melted in the midst of a furnace, so you shall be melted in the midst of it. And you shall know that I the Lord have poured out My fury upon you.

Indictment of Sinful Leaders

²³ The word of the Lᴏʀᴅ came to me, saying: ²⁴ Son of man, say to her: You are the land that is not cleansed nor rained upon in the day of indignation. ²⁵ There is a conspiracy of her prophets in her midst like a roaring lion ravening the prey. They have devoured souls. They have taken the treasure and precious things. They have made many widows in her midst. ²⁶ Her priests have violated My law and have profaned My holy things. They have made no distinction between the holy and profane, nor have they shown the difference between the unclean and the clean, and they have hidden their eyes from My Sabbaths, and I am profaned among them. ²⁷ Her officials in her midst are like wolves ravening the prey by shedding blood and destroying lives in order to obtain dishonest gain. ²⁸ Her prophets have daubed them with whitewash, seeing vanity and divining lies for them, saying, "Thus says the Lord Gᴏᴅ," when the Lᴏʀᴅ has not spoken. ²⁹ The people of the land have used oppression and exercised robbery and have vexed the poor and needy and have oppressed the sojourner wrongfully.

³⁰ I sought for a man among them who would build up the hedge and stand in the gap before Me for the land so that I would not destroy it, but I found no one. ³¹ Therefore I have poured out My indignation on them. I have consumed them with the fire of My wrath. Their own way I have recompensed on their heads, says the Lord Gᴏᴅ.

The Sins of Oholah and Oholibah

23 The word of the Lᴏʀᴅ came again to me, saying: ² Son of man, there were two women, the daughters of one mother. ³ And they committed harlotries in Egypt. They committed harlotries in their youth. There their breasts were pressed, and there their virgin bosom was handled. ⁴ Their names were Oholah the elder and Oholibah her sister. And they were mine, and they bore sons and daughters. As for their names, Samaria is Oholah, and Jerusalem is Oholibah.

Samaria

⁵ Oholah played the harlot when she was Mine. And she lusted after her lovers, on the Assyrians her neighbors, ⁶ who were clothed in purple, captains and rulers, all of them desirable young men, horsemen riding on horses. ⁷ Thus she committed her harlotries with them, with all those who were the chosen men of Assyria, and with all on whom she doted, with all their idols she defiled herself. ⁸ She did not forsake her harlotries from the time in Egypt. For in her youth they lay with her, and they handled her virgin bosom and poured their harlotry upon her.

⁹ Therefore I have delivered her into the hand of her lovers, into the hand of the Assyrians after whom she doted. ¹⁰ They uncovered her nakedness. They took her sons and her daughters and killed her with the sword. And she became a byword among women, for they had executed judgments on her.

Jerusalem

¹¹ Now her sister Oholibah saw this, but she was more corrupt in her inordinate love than she, and in her harlotries more than her sister in her harlotries. ¹² She lusted after the Assyrians her neighbors, captains and rulers clothed most gorgeously, horsemen riding on horses, all of them desirable young men. ¹³ Then I saw that she was defiled, that they both took the same way.

¹⁴ So she increased her harlotries. And she saw men portrayed on the wall, the images of the Chaldeans portrayed with vermilion, ¹⁵ girded with belts on their loins, exceeding in dyed attire on their heads, all of them looking like officials, after the manner of the Babylonians of Chaldea, the land of their nativity. ¹⁶ And as soon as she saw them with her eyes, she lusted after them and sent messengers to them into Chaldea. ¹⁷ The Babylonians came to her into the bed of love, and they defiled her with their harlotry, and she was polluted with them, and her soul became disgusted with them. ¹⁸ So she uncovered her harlotries and uncovered her nakedness. Then My soul became disgusted with her, as My soul became disgusted with her sister. ¹⁹ Yet she multiplied her harlotries while remembering the days of her youth in which she had played the harlot in the land of Egypt. ²⁰ For she lusted after their paramours, whose flesh is as the flesh of donkeys and whose issue is like the issue of horses. ²¹ Thus you longed for the lewdness of your youth when the Egyptians handled your bosom because of the breasts of your youth.

Judgment on Jerusalem

²² Therefore, O Oholibah, thus says the Lord Gᴏᴅ: I will raise up your lovers against you, from whom you were alienated, and I will bring them against you on every side: ²³ the Babylonians and all the Chaldeans, Pekod and Shoa and Koa, and all the Assyrians with them. All of them are desirable young men, captains and rulers, officers and men of renown, all of them riding on horses. ²⁴ They shall come against you with weapons, chariots and wagons, and with an assembly of peoples. They shall set themselves against you on every side with buckler and shield and helmet. And I will set the judgment before them, and they shall judge you according to their customs. ²⁵ I will set My jealousy against you, so that they deal furiously with you. They shall take away your nose and your ears. And your remnant shall fall by the sword. They shall take your sons and your daughters. And your remnant shall be devoured by the fire. ²⁶ They shall also strip you of your clothes and take away your fair jewels. ²⁷ Thus I will make your lewdness and your harlotry *brought* from the land of Egypt to cease from you so that you shall not lift up your eyes to them or remember Egypt anymore.

²⁸ For thus says the Lord Gᴏᴅ: I will deliver you into the hand of those whom you hate, into the hand of those from whom you were alienated. ²⁹ And they shall deal with you hatefully, and shall take away all your labor, and shall leave you naked and bare. And the nakedness of your harlotries shall be uncovered, both your lewdness and your harlotries. ³⁰ I will do these things to you because you have gone whoring after the nations, because you have polluted yourself with their idols. ³¹ You have walked in the way of your sister. Therefore I will give her cup into your hand.

³² Thus says the Lord Gᴏᴅ:

You shall drink of your sister's cup,
        which is deep and wide;
you shall be laughed to scorn and held in derision;
        it contains much.
³³ You shall be filled with drunkenness and sorrow,
        the cup of horror and desolation,
        the cup of your sister Samaria.
³⁴ You shall drink it and drain it,
        then you shall gnaw at its fragments
        and tear off your own breasts;

for I have spoken, says the Lord Gᴏᴅ.

³⁵ Therefore thus says the Lord Gᴏᴅ: Because you have forgotten Me and cast Me behind your back, now bear *the punishment of* your lewdness and your harlotries.

Judgment on the Sisters

³⁶ The Lᴏʀᴅ moreover said to me: Son of man, will you judge Oholah and Oholibah? Then declare to them their abominations. ³⁷ For they have committed adultery, and blood is in their hands. Thus with their idols they have committed adultery and have also caused their sons whom they bore to Me to pass through *the fire* for them as food. ³⁸ Moreover they have done this to Me: They have defiled My sanctuary in the same day and have profaned My Sabbaths. ³⁹ For when they had slain their children to their idols, then they came the same day into My sanctuary to profane it. And thus they have done in the midst of My house.

⁴⁰ Furthermore, they have even sent for men to come from afar, to whom a messenger was sent; and they came. For them you washed yourself, painted your eyes, and decked yourself with ornaments. ⁴¹ And you sat on a stately couch with a table prepared before it on which you had set My incense and My oil.

⁴² A sound of a multitude at ease was with her, and drunkards were brought from the wilderness with men of the common sort. And they put bracelets on the hands of the women and beautiful crowns on their heads. ⁴³ Then I said to her who was worn out by adulteries, "Will they now commit harlotries with her when she is so?" ⁴⁴ Yet they went in to her as they go in to a woman who plays the harlot. So they went in to Oholah and to Oholibah, the lewd women. ⁴⁵ But righteous men shall judge them after the manner of adulteresses, and after the manner of women who shed blood, because they are adulteresses, and blood is on their hands.

⁴⁶ For thus says the Lord God: Bring up a company against them and give them over to terror and devastation. ⁴⁷ The company shall stone them with stones and cut them down with their swords. They shall slay their sons and their daughters, and burn up their houses with fire. ⁴⁸ Thus I will cause lewdness to cease from the land, that all women may be warned and not commit lewdness as you have done. ⁴⁹ Your lewdness shall be recompensed upon you, and you shall bear *the punishment of worshipping* your idols. Then you shall know that I am the Lord God.

The Siege of Jerusalem

24 And in the ninth year, in the tenth month, on the tenth day of the month, the word of the LORD came to me, saying: ² Son of man, write the name of the day, this same day. The king of Babylon has laid siege to Jerusalem this same day. ³ Utter a parable to the rebellious house and say to them, Thus says the Lord God:

Put on the pot, put it on,
    and also pour water into it.
⁴ Gather the pieces into it,
    even every good piece, the thigh and the shoulder.
Fill it with the choice bones;
⁵   take the choicest of the flock,
and also pile the bones under it;
    make it boil well,
    also seethe its bones in it.

⁶ Therefore thus says the Lord God:

Woe to the bloody city,
    to the pot whose rust is in it,
    and whose rust has not gone out of it!
Take out of it piece by piece
    without choosing.

⁷   For her blood is in her midst;
    she set it on the bare rock;
she did not pour it on the ground
    to cover it with dust.
⁸   That it may cause fury to come up to take vengeance,
    I have set her blood on the bare rock,
    that it may not be covered.

⁹ Therefore thus says the Lord God:

Woe to the bloody city!
    I will also make the pile great.
¹⁰ Heap on wood,
    kindle the fire;
boil the flesh,
    and spice it well,
    and let the bones be burned.
¹¹ Then set it empty on its coals,
    so that it may be hot and its bronze may glow,
and its filthiness may be melted in it,
    and its rust may be consumed.
¹² She has wearied Me with toil,
    and her great rust has not gone from her.
    Let her rust be in the fire.

¹³ In your filthiness is lewdness. Because I *would* have purged you, yet you are not purged, you shall not be purged from your filthiness anymore until I have caused My fury to rest on you.

¹⁴ I the LORD have spoken. It shall come to pass and I will act. I will not go back, nor will I spare, nor will I be sorry. According to your ways and according to your deeds, I shall judge you, says the Lord God.

The Death of Ezekiel's Wife

¹⁵ Also the word of the LORD came to me, saying: ¹⁶ Son of man, I am about to take away from you the desire of your eyes with a stroke. Yet

you shall not mourn or weep, nor shall your tears run down. ¹⁷ Groan silently. Make no mourning for the dead. Bind on your turban and put your shoes on your feet and do not cover your mustache and do not eat the bread of men.

¹⁸ So I spoke to the people in the morning, and in the evening my wife died. And in the morning I did as I was commanded.

¹⁹ And the people said to me, "Will you not tell us what these things mean for us, that you are behaving this way?"

²⁰ Then I answered them: The word of the LORD came to me, saying: ²¹ Speak to the house of Israel, Thus says the Lord God: I will profane My sanctuary, the pride of your strength, the desire of your eyes and the delight of your soul. And your sons and your daughters whom you have left behind shall fall by the sword. ²² You shall do as I have done. You shall not cover your mustache, nor will you eat the bread of men. ²³ Your turbans shall be on your heads, and your shoes on your feet. You shall not mourn or weep. But you shall pine away for your iniquities and groan toward one another. ²⁴ Thus Ezekiel is a sign to you. According to all that he has done you shall do. And when it comes about, then you shall know that I am the Lord God.

²⁵ As for you, son of man, shall it not be on the day when I take from them their strength, the joy of their glory, the desire of their eyes, and that on which they set their minds, their sons and their daughters, ²⁶ that on that day he who escapes shall come to you to cause you to hear it with your ears? ²⁷ On that day your mouth shall be opened to him who escaped, and you shall speak and be mute no more. Thus you shall be a sign to them. And they shall know that I am the LORD.

A Prophecy Against Ammon

25 The word of the LORD came again to me, saying: ² Son of man, set your face against the sons of Ammon and prophesy against them, ³ and say to the sons of Ammon, Hear the word of the Lord God: Because you said, "Aha!" against My sanctuary when it was profaned, and against the land of Israel when it was made desolate, and against the house of Judah when they went into captivity, ⁴ therefore, I will deliver you to the men of the East for a possession, and they shall set their camps among you and make their dwellings among you. They shall eat your fruit and drink your milk. ⁵ I will make Rabbah a meadow for camels, and the sons of Ammon a couching place for flocks. Thus you shall know that I am the LORD. ⁶ For thus says the Lord God: Because you have clapped your hands and stamped your feet and rejoiced in heart with all your spite against the land of Israel, ⁷ therefore, I will stretch out My hand against you and deliver you for destruction to the nations. And I will cut you off from the peoples and cause you to perish from the countries. I will destroy you. Then you shall know that I am the LORD.

A Prophecy Against Moab

⁸ Thus says the Lord God: Because Moab and Seir say, Look, the house of Judah is like all the nations, ⁹ therefore, I will deprive the side of Moab of its cities, of its cities which are on its frontiers, the glory of the country, Beth Jeshimoth, Baal Meon, and Kiriathaim, ¹⁰ and I will give it for a possession with the Ammonites to the men of the East, so that the sons of Ammon may not be remembered among the nations. ¹¹ I will execute judgments on Moab. And they shall know that I am the LORD.

A Prophecy Against Edom

¹² Thus says the Lord God: Because Edom has acted against the house of Judah by taking vengeance and has greatly offended and revenged themselves upon them, ¹³ therefore thus says the Lord God: I will also stretch out My hand against Edom and cut off man and beast from it. And I will make it desolate. From Teman even to Dedan they shall fall by the sword. ¹⁴ I will lay My vengeance upon Edom by the hand of My people Israel. And they shall do in Edom according to My anger and according to My fury. And they shall know My vengeance, says the Lord God.

A Prophecy Against Philistia

¹⁵ Thus says the Lord God: Because the Philistines have dealt by revenge and have taken vengeance with a spiteful heart to destroy with everlasting hatred, ¹⁶ therefore thus says the Lord God: I will stretch

out My hand against the Philistines and will cut off the Kerethites and destroy the remnant of the seacoast. [17] I will execute great vengeance upon them with furious rebukes. And they shall know that I am the LORD when I lay My vengeance upon them.

A Prophecy Against Tyre

26 In the eleventh year, on the first day of the month, the word of the LORD came to me, saying: [2] Son of man, because Tyre has said against Jerusalem, "Aha, the gateway of the peoples is broken. It has opened to me. I shall be filled now that she is laid waste," [3] therefore thus says the Lord GOD: I am against you, O Tyre, and will cause many nations to come up against you, as the sea causes its waves to come up. [4] They shall destroy the walls of Tyre and break down her towers. I will also scrape her dust from her and make her a bare rock. [5] She shall be a place for the spreading of nets in the midst of the sea, for I have spoken, says the Lord GOD, and she shall become destruction to the nations. [6] Her daughters who are on the mainland shall be slain by the sword. And they shall know that I am the LORD.

[7] For thus says the Lord GOD: From the north I will bring upon Tyre Nebuchadnezzar king of Babylon, a king of kings, with horses and with chariots and with cavalry and a great army. [8] He shall slay your daughters on the mainland with the sword. And he shall set up a siege wall against you and cast up a mound against you and lift up the roof of shields against you. [9] He shall set engines of war against your walls, and with his axes he shall break down your towers. [10] By reason of the abundance of his horses, their dust shall cover you. Your walls shall shake at the noise of the horsemen and of the wagons and of the chariots when he enters your gates as men enter a city that has been breached. [11] With the hoofs of his horses he shall tread down all your streets. He shall slay your people by the sword, and your strong garrisons shall go down to the ground. [12] They shall make a spoil of your riches, and a prey of your merchandise. And they shall break down your walls and destroy your pleasant houses. And they shall lay your stones and your timber and your dust in the midst of the water. [13] I will cause the noise of your songs to cease. And the sound of your harps shall be heard no more. [14] I will make you a bare rock. You shall be a place to spread nets upon. You shall be built no more, for I the LORD have spoken, says the Lord GOD.

[15] Thus says the Lord GOD to Tyre: Shall not the coastlands shake at the sound of your fall when the wounded cry, when the slaughter is made in your midst? [16] Then all the officials of the sea shall come down from their thrones and lay away their robes and take off their embroidered garments. They shall clothe themselves with trembling. They shall sit on the ground and tremble every moment and be astonished at you. [17] They shall take up a lamentation over you and say to you:

How you are destroyed, O inhabited one of the seas,
    the renowned city,
which was strong in the sea,
    she and her inhabitants,
who caused her terror
    to be on all her inhabitants!
[18] Now the coastlands shall tremble
    on the day of your fall; indeed,
the coastlands that are by the sea
    shall be troubled at your departure.

[19] For thus says the Lord GOD: When I make you a desolate city, like the cities that are not inhabited, when I bring up the deep upon you and great waters shall cover you, [20] then I shall bring you down with those who descend into the pit, to the people of old, and make you dwell in the lower parts of the earth, in places desolate of old, with those who go down to the pit so that you will not be inhabited. But I shall set glory in the land of the living. [21] I will bring terrors on you and you shall be no more. Though you will be sought, you shall never be found again, says the Lord GOD.

A Lament for Tyre

27 The word of the LORD came again to me, saying: [2] Now you, son of man, take up a lamentation over Tyre. [3] And say to Tyre who is situated at the entrance of the sea, who is a merchant of the peoples

for many coastlands, Thus says the Lord GOD:

O Tyre, you have said,
    "I am perfect in beauty."
[4] Your borders are in the midst of the seas.
    Your builders have perfected your beauty.
[5] They have made all your ship boards
    of fir trees from Senir;
they have taken cedars from Lebanon
    to make a mast for you.
[6] Of the oaks of Bashan
    they have made your oars;
with ivory they have inlaid your deck of boxwood
    out of the coastlands of Cyprus.
[7] Fine linen with embroidered work from Egypt was your sail,
    so that it became your distinguishing sign;
blue and purple from the coastlands of Elishah
    was your awning.
[8] The inhabitants of Sidon and Arvad were your mariners;
    your wise men, O Tyre, were aboard; they were your pilots.
[9] The elders of Byblos and her wise men
    were in you repairing your seams;
all the ships of the sea with their mariners
    were in you to deal in your merchandise.

[10] They of Persia and of Lydia and of Put
    were in your army, your men of war;
they hung the shield and helmet in you;
    they set forth your comeliness.
[11] The sons of Arvad and your army
    were upon your walls all around,
and the Gammad
    were in your towers;
they hung their shields on your walls all around;
    they have made your beauty perfect.

[12] Tarshish was your merchant by reason of the multitude of all kinds of riches. With silver, iron, tin, and lead, they traded in your wares. [13] Greece, Tubal, and Meshek, they were your merchants. They traded in your market with the lives of men and vessels of bronze. [14] Those of Beth Togarmah gave horses and horsemen and mules for your wares. [15] The sons of Dedan were your merchants. Many coastlands were your merchandise. They brought you for a payment horns of ivory and ebony. [16] Aram was your merchant by reason of the multitude of your wares. They paid for your wares with emeralds, purple, embroidered work, fine linen, coral, and agate. [17] Judah and the land of Israel, they were your merchants. They traded in your market with the wheat of Minnith, cakes, honey, oil, and balm. [18] Damascus was your merchant in the multitude of your wares, because of the multitude of all *kinds of* riches, because of the wine of Helbon and white wool. [19] Dan and Javan paid for your wares from Izal. Bright iron, cassia, and sweet cane were in your market. [20] Dedan was your merchant in saddlecloths for chariots. [21] Arabia and all the officials of Kedar, they were your customers in lambs, rams, and goats. For these they were your merchants. [22] The merchants of Sheba and Raamah, they were your merchants. They paid for your wares with the best of all kinds of spices and with all kinds of precious stones and gold. [23] Harran, and Kanneh, and Eden, the merchants of Sheba, Ashur, and Kilmad, were your merchants. [24] They traded with you in choice garments, in clothes of blue and embroidered work, and in carpets of many colors and tightly wound cords, *which were* among your merchandise.

[25] The ships of Tarshish were
    the carriers for your market.
And you were filled and were very glorious
    in the midst of the seas.

²⁶ Your rowers have brought you
    into great waters;
the east wind has broken you
    in the midst of the seas.
²⁷ Your riches and your wares, your merchandise,
    your mariners and your pilots, your caulkers,
and the dealers of your merchandise, and all your men of
    war who are in you,
with all your company which is in your midst,
    shall fall into the midst of the seas
in the day of your ruin.
²⁸ The meadowlands shall shake
    at the sound of the cry of your pilots.
²⁹ All who handle the oar,
    the mariners and all the pilots of the sea,
shall come down from their ships;
    they shall stand upon the land.
³⁰ And they shall cause their voice to be heard against you,
    and shall cry bitterly,
and shall cast up dust upon their heads;
    they shall wallow in ashes.
³¹ Also they shall make themselves utterly bald for you,
    and gird themselves with sackcloth;
and they shall weep for you with bitterness of heart
    and bitter wailing.
³² Also, in their wailing
    they shall take up a lamentation for you and lament
    over you, saying,
"Who is like Tyre, like her who is silent
    in the midst of the sea?
³³ When your wares went out by sea,
    you filled many peoples;
you enriched the kings of the earth
    with the multitude of your riches and of your
    merchandise.
³⁴ Now that you are broken by the seas
    in the depths of the waters,
your merchandise and all your company
    in your midst have fallen.
³⁵ All the inhabitants of the coastlands
    shall be astonished at you,
and their kings shall be sorely afraid;
    they are troubled in countenance.
³⁶ The merchants among the peoples hiss at you;
    you shall be a terror,
and you shall cease to be forever."

A Prophecy Against the King of Tyre

28 The word of the LORD came again to me, saying: ² Son of man, say to the leader of Tyre, Thus says the Lord GOD:

Because your heart is lifted up,
    and you have said, "I am a god;
I sit in the seat of gods
    in the midst of the seas,"
yet you are a man, and not God,
    though you set your heart as the heart of God.
³ You are wiser than Daniel;
    there is no secret that is a match for you.
⁴ With your wisdom and with your understanding,
    you have obtained riches for yourself,
and have obtained gold and silver
    into your treasuries;
⁵ by your great wisdom, by your trade,
    you have increased your riches,
and your heart is lifted up
    because of your riches.

⁶ Therefore thus says the Lord GOD:

Because you have set your heart
    as the heart of God,

⁷ therefore, I will bring strangers upon you,
    the most cruel of the nations;
and they shall draw their swords against the beauty of your
    wisdom,
    and defile your brightness.
⁸ They shall bring you down to the pit,
    and you shall die the death of those who are slain
    in the midst of the seas.
⁹ Will you yet say before him who slays you,
    "I am a god,"
although you are a man and not God,
    in the hands of those who wound you?
¹⁰ You shall die the death of the uncircumcised
    by the hand of strangers;
for I have spoken! says the Lord GOD.

A Lament for the King of Tyre

¹¹ Moreover the word of the LORD came to me, saying: ¹² Son of man, take up a lamentation over the king of Tyre and say to him, Thus says the Lord GOD:

You had the seal of perfection,
    full of wisdom and perfect in beauty.
¹³ You were in Eden,
    the garden of God;
every precious stone was your covering:
    the sardius, topaz, and the diamond,
    the beryl, the onyx, and the jasper,
    the sapphire, the emerald, and the carbuncle, and gold.
The workmanship of your settings and sockets was in you;
    on the day that you were created, they were prepared.
¹⁴ You were the anointed cherub that covers,
    and I set you there;
you were upon the holy mountain of God;
    you walked up and down in the midst of the stones of fire.
¹⁵ You were perfect in your ways
    from the day that you were created,
    until iniquity was found in you.
¹⁶ By the multitude of your merchandise,
    you were filled with violence in your midst,
    and you sinned;
therefore I have cast you as profane out of the mountain of God;
    and I have destroyed you, O covering cherub,
    from the midst of the stones of fire.
¹⁷ Your heart was lifted up
    because of your beauty;
you have corrupted your wisdom
    by reason of your brightness;
I cast you to the ground,
    I lay you before kings, that they may see you.
¹⁸ You have defiled your sanctuaries
    by the multitude of your iniquities, by the iniquity of
    your trade;
therefore I have brought fire out from your midst;
    it has devoured you,
and I have turned you to ashes upon the earth
    in the sight of all those who see you.
¹⁹ All those who know you among the people
    are astonished at you;
you are a terror,
    and you shall cease to be forever.

A Prophecy Against Sidon

²⁰ Again the word of the LORD came to me, saying: ²¹ Son of man, set your face toward Sidon and prophesy against her ²² and say, Thus says the Lord GOD:

I am against you, O Sidon;
    and I will be glorified in your midst;
and they shall know that I am the LORD,
    when I execute judgments in her
    and display My holiness in her.

23 For I will send pestilence into her,
  and blood into her streets;
and the wounded shall fall in her midst
  by the sword upon her on every side;
and they shall know that I am the Lord.

24 There shall be no more a pricking brier to the house of Israel, nor any painful thorn among all who are around them, who despised them. Then they shall know that I am the Lord God.

The Future Blessing for Israel

25 Thus says the Lord God: When I gather the house of Israel from the peoples among whom they are scattered and display My holiness in them in the sight of the nations, then they shall dwell in their land that I have given to My servant Jacob. **26** They shall dwell safely in it and shall build houses and plant vineyards and dwell securely when I execute judgments on all those around them who despise them. Then they shall know that I am the Lord their God.

A Prophecy Against Egypt

29 In the tenth year, in the tenth month, on the twelfth day of the month, the word of the Lord came to me, saying: **2** Son of man, set your face against Pharaoh king of Egypt and prophesy against him and against all Egypt. **3** Speak, and say, Thus says the Lord God:

I am against you, Pharaoh king of Egypt,
  the great dragon that lies in the midst of his rivers,
which has said, "My Nile is my own,
  and I myself have made it."
4 But I will put hooks in your jaws,
  and will cause the fish of your rivers to stick to your scales,
  and will bring you up out of the midst of your rivers,
  and all the fish of your rivers shall stick to your scales.
5 I will abandon you to the wilderness,
  you and all the fish of your rivers;
you shall fall upon the open field;
  you shall not be brought together or gathered.
I have given you for food
  to the beasts of the field and to the fowl of the heavens.

6 All the inhabitants of Egypt shall know that I am the Lord, because they have been a staff of reed to the house of Israel. **7** When they took hold of you by your hand, you broke and tore all their hands. And when they leaned upon you, you broke and made all their legs shake.

8 Therefore thus says the Lord God: I will bring a sword upon you, and cut off man and beast out of you. **9** The land of Egypt shall become a desolation and waste. Then they shall know that I am the Lord.

Because you said, "The Nile is mine, and I have made it," **10** therefore, I am against you and against your rivers, and I will make the land of Egypt an utter waste and desolation, from Migdol to Syene, as far as the border of Ethiopia. **11** No foot of man shall pass through it, nor foot of beast pass through it, nor shall it be inhabited for forty years. **12** Thus I will make the land of Egypt desolate in the midst of the countries that are desolate, and her cities among the cities that are laid waste shall be desolate for forty years. And I will scatter the Egyptians among the nations and will disperse them among the countries.

13 For thus says the Lord God: At the end of forty years I will gather the Egyptians from the peoples wherever they were scattered. **14** And I will turn the fortunes of Egypt and will cause them to return into the land of Pathros, into the land of their origin, and there they shall be a debased kingdom. **15** It shall be the basest of the kingdoms, and it shall exalt itself no more above the nations. For I will diminish them so that they shall rule over the nations no more. **16** It shall be the confidence of the house of Israel no more, bringing to mind the iniquity of their having turned to Egypt. But they shall know that I am the Lord God.

Babylonia to Plunder Egypt

17 In the twenty-seventh year, in the first *month*, on the first day of the month, the word of the Lord came to me, saying: **18** Son of man, Nebuchadnezzar king of Babylon caused his army to labor hard against Tyre. Every head was made bald, and every shoulder

was peeled. Yet he and his army had no wages from Tyre for the labor that he had done against it. **19** Therefore thus says the Lord God: I will give the land of Egypt to Nebuchadnezzar king of Babylon. And he shall carry off her wealth and take her spoil and take her prey. And it shall be wages for his army. **20** I have given him the land of Egypt for his labor with which he labored against it, because they acted for Me, says the Lord God.

21 On that day I will cause the horn of the house of Israel to spring forth, and I will open your mouth in their midst. Then they shall know that I am the Lord.

A Lament for Egypt

30 The word of the Lord came to me again, saying: **2** Son of man, prophesy and say, Thus says the Lord God:

Howl,
  "Woe to the day!"
3 For the day is near,
  even the day of the Lord is near,
a cloudy day,
  it shall be the time *of doom* for the nations.
4 The sword shall come upon Egypt,
  and great pain shall be in Ethiopia,
when the slain fall in Egypt,
  they take away her wealth,
  and her foundations are broken down.

5 Ethiopia, and Libya, and Lydia, all Arabia, Kub, and the men of the land that is in league shall fall with them by the sword.
6 Thus says the Lord:

Indeed, those who uphold Egypt shall fall,
  and the pride of her power shall come down.
From Migdol to Syene
  they shall fall in her by the sword,
  says the Lord God.
7 They shall be desolate
  in the midst of the countries that are desolate,
and her cities shall be
  in the midst of the cities that are wasted.
8 They shall know that I am the Lord
  when I have set a fire in Egypt
  and when all her helpers are destroyed.

9 In that day messengers shall go forth from Me in ships to make the careless Ethiopians afraid, and great pain shall come upon them as in the day of Egypt. For it is coming!

10 Thus says the Lord God:

I will also make the multitude of Egypt to cease
  by the hand of Nebuchadnezzar king of Babylon.
11 He and his people with him, the terrible of the nations,
  shall be brought to destroy the land;
and they shall draw their swords against Egypt,
  and fill the land with the slain.
12 I will make the rivers dry,
  and sell the land into the hand of the wicked;
and I will make the land waste and all that is in it,
  by the hand of strangers.

I, the Lord, have spoken.

13 Thus says the Lord God:

I will also destroy the idols,
  and I will cause their images to cease from Memphis;
and no more shall there be a prince of the land of Egypt.
  And I will put a fear in the land of Egypt.
14 I will make Pathros desolate,
  and will set fire in Zoan,
  and will execute judgments in Thebes.

¹⁵ I will pour out My fury upon Pelusium,
the strength of Egypt;
and I will cut off the multitude of Thebes.
¹⁶ I will set fire in Egypt;
Pelusium shall have great pain,
and Thebes shall be rent asunder,
and Memphis *shall have* distresses daily.
¹⁷ The young men of Heliopolis and of Bubastis
shall fall by the sword,
and the women shall go into captivity.
¹⁸ In Tahpanhes also the day shall be darkened,
when I break there the yokes of Egypt.
And the pomp of her strength shall cease in her;
as for her, a cloud shall cover her,
and her daughters shall go into captivity.
¹⁹ Thus I will execute judgments in Egypt,
and they shall know that I am the Lord.

A Prophecy Against Pharaoh

²⁰ In the eleventh year, in the first *month*, on the seventh day of the month, the word of the Lord came to me, saying: ²¹ Son of man, I have broken the arm of Pharaoh king of Egypt. And it has not been bound up to be healed or wrapped with a bandage to make it strong to hold the sword. ²² Therefore thus says the Lord God: I am against Pharaoh king of Egypt and will break his arms, both the strong and the broken. And I will cause the sword to fall out of his hand. ²³ I will scatter the Egyptians among the nations and disperse them among the countries. ²⁴ For I will strengthen the arms of the king of Babylon and put My sword in his hand. But I will break the arms of Pharaoh so that he groans before him with the groanings of a wounded man. ²⁵ So I will strengthen the arms of the king of Babylon, but the arms of Pharaoh shall fall down. Then they shall know that I am the Lord when I put My sword into the hand of the king of Babylon and he stretches it out upon the land of Egypt. ²⁶ When I scatter the Egyptians among the nations and disperse them among the countries, then they shall know that I am the Lord.

Pharaoh to Be Slain

31 In the eleventh year, in the third *month*, on the first day of the month, the word of the Lord came to me, saying: ² Son of man, speak to Pharaoh king of Egypt, and to his multitude:

Whom are you like in your greatness?
³ Assyria was a cedar in Lebanon,
with fair branches and shade for a forest,
and high stature;
and its top was among the clouds.
⁴ The waters made it great;
the deep set it up on high.
With its rivers it continually ran
all around its plants,
and sent out its little rivers
to all the trees of the field.
⁵ Therefore its height was exalted
above all the trees of the field,
and its boughs were multiplied,
and its branches became long
because of the abundance of water, as it spread them out.
⁶ All the fowl of heaven
made their nests in its boughs;
and under its branches
all the beasts of the field gave birth;
and under its shadow
all great nations lived.
⁷ Thus it was fair in its greatness,
in the length of its branches,
for its roots were
by many waters.
⁸ The cedars in the garden of God
could not match it;
the fir trees
were not like its boughs,

and the chestnut trees
were not like its branches;
nor was any tree in the garden of God
like it in its beauty.
⁹ I made it beautiful with an abundance of branches,
so that all the trees of Eden envied it,
that were in the garden of God.

¹⁰ Therefore, thus says the Lord God: Because it is lifted up in height and has shot up its top among the clouds, and its heart is arrogant in its height, ¹¹ I therefore will deliver it into the hand of the mighty one of the nations. He shall surely deal with it. I have driven it out for its wickedness. ¹² Aliens, the tyrants of the nations have cut it off and left it. Upon the mountains and in all the valleys its branches have fallen, and its boughs have been broken by all the rivers of the land. And all the peoples of the earth have gone down from its shadow and have left it. ¹³ Upon its ruin all the fowl of the heavens shall remain, and all the beasts of the field shall be upon its *fallen* branches ¹⁴ to the end that none of all the trees by the waters exalt themselves for their height, or shoot up their tops among the clouds, or their well-watered trees stand up in their height. For they all have been delivered to death, to the nether parts of the earth in the midst of the sons of men, with those who go down to the pit.

¹⁵ Thus says the Lord God: On the day when it went down to Sheol I caused mourning. I covered the deep over it and restrained its rivers, and its many waters were stayed. And I caused Lebanon to mourn for it, and all the trees of the field fainted for it. ¹⁶ I made the nations to shake at the sound of its fall when I cast him down to Sheol with those who descend into the pit. And all the well-watered trees of Eden, the choice and best of Lebanon, were comforted in the nether parts of the earth. ¹⁷ They also went down into Sheol with it to those who were slain with the sword. And those who were its power lived under its shadow in the midst of the nations.

¹⁸ To whom are you thus like in glory and in greatness among the trees of Eden? Yet you shall be brought down with the trees of Eden to the nether parts of the earth. You shall lie in the midst of the uncircumcised with those who were slain by the sword.

This is Pharaoh and all his multitude, says the Lord God.

A Lament for Pharaoh and Egypt

32 In the twelfth year, in the twelfth *month*, on the first day of the month, the word of the Lord came to me, saying: ² Son of man, take up a lamentation for Pharaoh king of Egypt and say to him:

You likened yourself to a young lion of the nations,
but you are as the monster in the seas;
and you burst forth in your rivers,
and muddied the waters with your feet,
and made foul their rivers.

³ Thus says the Lord God:

I will therefore spread out My net over you
with a company of many peoples,
and they shall bring you up in My net.
⁴ Then I will leave you upon the land;
I will cast you out on the open field,
and I will cause all the fowl of the heavens to remain upon you.
And I will fill the beasts of the whole earth with you.
⁵ I will lay your flesh upon the mountains,
and fill the valleys with your refuse.
⁶ I will also water the land with your blood,
as far as the mountains;
and the rivers shall be full of you.
⁷ When *I* put you out, I will cover the heavens
and make their stars dark;
I will cover the sun with a cloud,
and the moon shall not give its light.
⁸ All the bright lights in the heavens
I will make dark over you,
and set darkness upon your land,
says the Lord God.

⁹ I will also vex the hearts of many peoples when I bring your destruction among the nations, into the countries which you have not known. ¹⁰ Indeed, I will make many peoples amazed at you, and their kings shall be horribly afraid for you when I brandish My sword before them. And they shall tremble at every moment, every man for his own life, on the day of your fall.

¹¹ For thus says the Lord God:

The sword of the king of Babylon
    shall come upon you.
¹² By the swords of the mighty,
    I will cause your multitude to fall.
All of them are tyrants of the nations;
    they shall destroy the pride of Egypt,
    and all its multitude shall be destroyed.
¹³ I also will destroy all the beasts
    from beside many waters;
nor shall the foot of man muddy them anymore,
    nor the hoofs of beasts muddy them.
¹⁴ Then I will make their waters settle,
    and cause their rivers to run like oil,
    says the Lord God.
¹⁵ When I make the land of Egypt desolate,
    and the country is destitute of that by which it was full,
when I smite all those who dwell in it,
    then shall they know that I am the Lord.

¹⁶ This is the lamentation, and they shall chant it. The daughters of the nations shall chant it. They shall chant it over Egypt and over all her multitude, says the Lord God.

A Dirge for Egypt

¹⁷ In the twelfth year, on the fifteenth day of the month, the word of the Lord came to me, saying: ¹⁸ Son of man, wail for the multitude of Egypt and cast it down, her and the daughters of the powerful nations, to the nether parts of the earth, with those who go down into the pit. ¹⁹ "Whom do you surpass in beauty? Descend and make your bed with the uncircumcised." ²⁰ They shall fall in the midst of those who are slain by the sword. She is delivered to the sword. They have drawn her and all her multitudes away. ²¹ The strong among the mighty shall speak to him and those who help him out of the midst of Sheol: "They have gone down, they lie still, uncircumcised, slain by the sword."

²² Assyria is there and all her company. Her graves are around her. All of them are slain, fallen by the sword, ²³ whose graves are set in the sides of the pit and her company is all around her grave. All of them are slain, fallen by the sword, who cause terror in the land of the living.

²⁴ There is Elam and all her multitude all around her grave, all of them slain, fallen by the sword, who descended uncircumcised into the nether parts of the earth, who caused their terror in the land of the living and bore their shame with those who went down to the pit. ²⁵ They have set a bed for her in the midst of the slain with all her multitude. Her graves are all around it. All of them uncircumcised, slain by the sword; though their terror was caused in the land of the living, yet they have borne their shame with those who go down to the pit. They were put in the midst of those who are slain.

²⁶ There is Meshek, Tubal, and all her multitude. Their graves are all around them. All of them uncircumcised, slain by the sword, though they caused their terror in the land of the living. ²⁷ They shall not lie with the mighty who are fallen of the uncircumcised, who have gone down to Sheol with their weapons of war and whose swords were laid under their heads. But the punishment for their iniquity rested upon their bones, though the terror of these mighty ones was once in the land of the living.

²⁸ Indeed, you shall be broken in the midst of the uncircumcised and shall lie with those who are slain with the sword.

²⁹ There is Edom also, its kings and all its officials, who for all their might are laid by those who were slain by the sword. They shall lie with the uncircumcised and with those who go down to the pit.

³⁰ There are also the officials of the north, all of them, and all the Sidonians, who in spite of the terror from their might have gone down in shame with the slain. So they lie down uncircumcised with those who are slain by the sword, and bear their shame with those who go down to the pit.

³¹ Pharaoh shall see them, and shall be comforted over all his multitude slain by the sword, even Pharaoh and all his army, says the Lord God. ³² Though I have caused a terror of him in the land of the living, yet he shall be laid in the midst of the uncircumcised with those who are slain with the sword, even Pharaoh and all his multitude, says the Lord God.

Renewal of Ezekiel's Call

33 Again the word of the Lord came to me, saying: ² Son of man, speak to the children of your people and say to them: If I bring a sword upon a land, and the people of the land take a man from among them and set him for their watchman, ³ and he sees the sword come upon the land and blows the trumpet and warns the people, ⁴ then whoever hears the sound of the trumpet and does not take warning, and a sword comes and takes him away, his blood shall be upon his own head. ⁵ He heard the sound of the trumpet yet did not take warning. His blood shall be upon himself. But he who takes warning delivers his soul. ⁶ But if the watchman sees the sword come and does not blow the trumpet and the people are not warned and a sword comes and takes a person from among them, he is taken away in his iniquity. But his blood I will require from the hand of the watchman.

⁷ Now as for you, son of man: I have set you a watchman to the house of Israel. Therefore you shall hear a word from My mouth and warn them from Me. ⁸ When I say to the wicked, "O wicked man, you shall surely die," and you do not speak to warn the wicked from his way, that wicked man shall die in his iniquity. But his blood I will require from your hand. ⁹ Nevertheless, if you on your part warn the wicked to turn from his way and he does not turn from his way, he shall die in his iniquity. But you have delivered your soul.

God's Justice and Mercy

¹⁰ Therefore as for you, son of man, say to the house of Israel: Thus you have spoken, saying, "Surely our transgressions and our sins are upon us, and we pine away in them. How should we then live?" ¹¹ Say to them: As I live, says the Lord God, I have no pleasure in the death of the wicked, but rather that the wicked turn from his way and live. Turn, turn from your evil ways! For why will you die, O house of Israel?

¹² Therefore you, son of man, say to the sons of your people: The righteousness of a righteous man shall not deliver him in the day of his transgression. As for the wickedness of the wicked, he shall not fall by it in the day that he turns from his wickedness. Nor shall the righteous be able to live for his righteousness in the day that he sins. ¹³ When I say to the righteous that he shall surely live and he so trusts in his righteousness that he commits iniquity, all his righteousness shall not be remembered. But for that iniquity of his that he has committed, he shall die. ¹⁴ Again, when I say to the wicked, "You shall surely die," and he turns from his sin and does that which is lawful and right, ¹⁵ if the wicked man restores a pledge, gives back what he had robbed, walks in the statutes of life without committing iniquity, he shall surely live. He shall not die. ¹⁶ None of his sins that he has committed shall be remembered against him. He has done what is lawful and right. He shall surely live.

¹⁷ Yet the sons of your people say, "The way of the Lord is not right," when their way is not right. ¹⁸ When the righteous turns from his righteousness and commits iniquity, he shall die by it. ¹⁹ But if the wicked turns from his wickedness and does that which is lawful and right, he shall live by them. ²⁰ Yet you say, "The way of the Lord is not right." O house of Israel, I will judge you, every one according to his ways.

The Fall of Jerusalem

²¹ In the twelfth year of our captivity, in the tenth month, on the fifth day of the month, one who had escaped out of Jerusalem came to me, saying, "The city is taken." ²² Now the hand of the Lord was upon me in the evening, before those who escaped came. And He opened my mouth at the time they came to me in the morning. Therefore my mouth was opened and I was speechless no more.

²³ Then the word of the Lord came to me, saying: ²⁴ Son of man, those who inhabit these wastes in the land of Israel are saying, "Abraham was one, yet he inherited the land. But to us who are many, the land has been given for an inheritance." ²⁵ Therefore say to

them, Thus says the Lord God: You eat *meat* with the blood in it and lift up your eyes toward your idols as you shed blood. Should you then possess the land? [26] You rely upon your sword, you work abominations, and every one of you defiles his neighbor's wife. Should you then possess the land?

[27] Thus you shall say to them, Thus says the Lord God: As I live, surely those who are in the ruins shall fall by the sword, and him who is in the open field I will give to the beasts to be devoured, and those who are in the forts and in the caves shall die of pestilence. [28] For I will make the land a desolation and a waste, and the pomp of her strength shall cease. And the mountains of Israel shall be desolate so that none shall pass through. [29] Then shall they know that I am the Lord, when I make the land a desolation and a waste because of all their abominations which they have committed.

[30] As for you, son of man, the sons of your people are talking about you by the walls and in the doorways of the houses; and they speak to one another, each saying to his brother, "Come now, and hear what the word is that comes from the Lord." [31] They come to you as people come, and they sit before you as My people, and they hear your words; but they will not do them. For they do the lustful desires in their mouth, and their heart goes after their covetousness. [32] You are to them as a sensual song of one who has a pleasant voice and can play well on an instrument. For they hear your words, but they do not do them.

[33] When this comes to pass, and it is coming to pass, then shall they know that a prophet has been among them.

A Prophecy Against Israel's Shepherds

34 And the word of the Lord came to me, saying: [2] Son of man, prophesy against the shepherds of Israel. Prophesy and say to those shepherds, Thus says the Lord God: Woe to the shepherds of Israel who feed themselves! Should not the shepherds feed the flock? [3] You eat the fat and clothe yourself with the wool; you kill those who are fed without feeding the flock. [4] The diseased you have not strengthened, nor have you healed that which was sick, nor have you bound up that which was broken, nor have you brought back that which was driven away, nor have you sought that which was lost. But with force and with cruelty you have subjugated them. [5] They were scattered because there was no shepherd. And they became meat to all the beasts of the field and were scattered. [6] My sheep wandered through all the mountains and upon every high hill. Indeed, My flock was scattered upon all the face of the earth, and no one searched or sought after them.

[7] Therefore, you shepherds, hear the word of the Lord: [8] As I live, says the Lord God, surely because My flock became a prey, and My flock even became meat to every beast of the field, because there was no shepherd, nor did My shepherds search for My flock; but the shepherds fed themselves and did not feed My flock, [9] therefore, you shepherds, hear the word of the Lord. [10] Thus says the Lord God: I am against the shepherds. And I will require My flock from their hand and cause them to cease from feeding the flock. Nor shall the shepherds feed themselves anymore, for I will deliver My flock from their mouth so that they may not be meat for them.

The True Shepherd

[11] For thus says the Lord God: I, even I, will search for My sheep and seek them out. [12] As a shepherd seeks out his flock in the day that he is among his sheep that are scattered, so I will seek out My sheep and will deliver them out of all the places where they have been scattered in a cloudy and dark day. [13] I will bring them out from the peoples, and gather them from the countries, and bring them to their own land, and feed them upon the mountains of Israel by the rivers and in all the inhabited places of the country. [14] I will feed them in a good pasture, and upon the high mountains of Israel their grazing ground shall be. There they shall lie on good grazing ground, and in a rich pasture they shall feed upon the mountains of Israel. [15] I will feed My flock, and I will cause them to lie down, says the Lord God. [16] I will seek that which was lost and bring back that which was driven away and bind up that which was broken and will strengthen that which was sick. But I will destroy the fat and the strong. I will feed them with judgment.

[17] As for you, O My flock, thus says the Lord God: I will judge between sheep and cattle, between the rams and the male goats. [18] Does it seem a small thing to you to have eaten up the good pasture, that you must tread down with your feet the rest of your pastures? Or that you should

drink of the clear waters, that you must foul the rest with your feet? [19] And as for My flock, they eat that which you have trodden with your feet, and they drink that which you have fouled with your feet. [20] Therefore thus says the Lord God to them: I, even I, will judge between the fat sheep and between the lean sheep. [21] Because you have thrust with side and with shoulder, and pushed all the diseased with your horns until you have scattered them abroad, [22] therefore I will save My flock, and they shall no more be a prey. And I will judge between one sheep and another. [23] I will set up one shepherd over them, and he shall feed them, even My servant David. He shall feed them himself and be their shepherd. [24] I the Lord will be their God, and My servant David shall be prince among them. I the Lord have spoken.

[25] I will make with them a covenant of peace and will cause the wild beasts to cease from the land so that they dwell safely in the wilderness and sleep in the woods. [26] I will make them and the places all around My hill a blessing. And I will cause the showers to come down in their season. They shall be showers of blessing. [27] The tree of the field shall yield its fruit, and the ground shall yield its increase, and they shall be safe in their land. Then they shall know that I am the Lord, when I have broken the bands of their yoke and delivered them out of the hand of those who enslaved them. [28] They shall no more be a prey to the nations, nor shall the beast of the land devour them. But they shall dwell safely and no one shall make them afraid. [29] I will raise up for them a planting place of renown, and no more shall they be consumed with hunger in the land, nor shall they bear the shame of the nations anymore. [30] Thus shall they know that I, the Lord their God, am with them, and that they, the house of Israel, are My people, says the Lord God. [31] As for you, My flock, the flock of My pasture, you are men, and I am your God, says the Lord God.

A Prophecy Against Edom

35 Moreover the word of the Lord came to me, saying: [2] Son of man, set your face against Mount Seir and prophesy against it, [3] and say to it, Thus says the Lord God: I am against you, O Mount Seir, and I will stretch out My hand against you, and I will make you a desolation and a waste. [4] I will lay your cities waste, and you shall become a desolation. Then you shall know that I am the Lord.

[5] Because you have had a perpetual hatred and have delivered the sons of Israel to the power of the sword in the time of their calamity, in the time of the punishment of the end, [6] therefore, as I live, says the Lord God, I will prepare you for bloodshed, and bloodshed shall pursue you. Since you have not hated bloodshed, therefore blood shall pursue you. [7] Thus I will make Mount Seir a desolation and a waste, and cut off from it the one who passes through and the one who returns. [8] I will fill its mountains with its slain men. On your hills and in your valleys and in all your rivers, they shall fall who are slain with the sword. [9] I will make you a perpetual desolation, and your cities shall not be inhabited. Then you shall know that I am the Lord.

[10] Because you have said, "These two nations and these two countries shall be mine, and we will possess them," whereas the Lord was there, [11] therefore, as I live, says the Lord God, I will treat you according to your anger and according to your envy, which you have showed out of your hatred against them. And I will make Myself known among them when I have judged you. [12] Then you shall know that I, the Lord, have heard all your blasphemies which you have spoken against the mountains of Israel, saying, "They are laid desolate. They are given to us to consume." [13] Thus with your mouth you have boasted against Me and have multiplied your words against Me. I have heard them. [14] Thus says the Lord God: When the whole earth rejoices, I will make you a desolation. [15] As you rejoiced at the inheritance of the house of Israel because it was desolate, so I will do to you. You shall be a desolation, O Mount Seir, and all Edom, all of it. Then they shall know that I am the Lord.

A Prophecy to the Mountains of Israel

36 As for you, son of man, prophesy to the mountains of Israel and say: O mountains of Israel, hear the word of the Lord. [2] Thus says the Lord God: Because the enemy has said against you, "Aha! Even the ancient high places are our possession," [3] therefore, prophesy and say: Thus says the Lord God: For good reason they have made you desolate and swallowed you up on every side so that you might become a possession to the rest of the nations, and you have been taken up on the lips of talkers and are an infamy of the people. [4] Therefore, O mountains of Israel, hear the word of the Lord GOD: Thus says the Lord GOD to the mountains and to the hills, to the rivers and to the valleys, to the desolate wastes and to the cities that are forsaken, which became a prey and derision to the rest of the nations that are all around; [5] therefore thus says the Lord GOD: Surely in the fire of My jealousy I have spoken against the rest of the nations and against all Edom, who have arrogated My land into their possession with the joy of all their hearts and with a spiteful soul, to cast it out for a prey. [6] Prophesy therefore concerning the land of Israel and say to the mountains and to the hills, to the rivers and to the valleys: Thus says the Lord GOD: I have spoken in My jealousy and in My fury, because you have borne the shame of the nations. [7] Therefore, thus says the Lord GOD: I have lifted up My hand that surely the nations who are about you shall themselves bear their invectives.

[8] But you, O mountains of Israel, you shall shoot forth your branches and yield your fruit for My people Israel. For they shall come soon. [9] For I am for you, and I will turn to you, and you shall be tilled and sown. [10] And I will multiply men upon you, all the house of Israel, all of it. And the cities shall be inhabited, and the waste places shall be built. [11] And I will multiply man and beast upon you. And they shall increase and bring forth fruit. And I will settle you as you were before and do better to you than at the beginning. Thus you shall know that I am the LORD. [12] Indeed, I will cause men to walk upon you, My people Israel, and they shall possess you, and you shall be their inheritance, and you shall no longer bereave them of children.

[13] Thus says the Lord GOD: Because they say to you, "You are a devourer of men and have bereaved your nation of children," [14] therefore you shall devour men no more or bereave your nation of children anymore, says the Lord GOD. [15] Nor will I cause men to hear in you the invectives of the nations anymore, nor shall you bear the reproach of the peoples anymore, nor shall you cause your nation to fall anymore, says the Lord GOD.

The Restoration of Israel

[16] Moreover the word of the LORD came to me, saying: [17] Son of man, when the house of Israel lived in their own land, they defiled it by their ways and their deeds. Their way was before Me as the uncleanness of a woman in her impurity. [18] Therefore I poured My fury upon them for the blood that they had shed upon the land and for their idols with which they had polluted it. [19] And I scattered them among the nations, and they were dispersed throughout the countries. According to their ways and according to their deeds, I judged them. [20] When they entered the nations, where they went, they profaned My holy name, because they said of them, "These are the people of the LORD and have gone out of His land." [21] But I had pity for My holy name, which the house of Israel had profaned among the nations where they went.

[22] Therefore say to the house of Israel, Thus says the Lord GOD: I do not do this for your sake, O house of Israel, but for My holy name's sake which you have profaned among the nations where you went. [23] I will vindicate the sanctity of My great name which was profaned among the nations, which you have profaned in their midst. Then the nations shall know that I am the LORD, says the Lord GOD, when I shall be sanctified among you before their eyes.

[24] For I will take you from among the nations and gather you out of all countries and will bring you into your own land. [25] Then I will sprinkle clean water upon you, and you shall be clean. From all your filthiness and from all your idols, I will cleanse you. [26] Also, I will give you a new heart, and a new spirit I will put within you. And I will take away the stony heart out of your flesh, and I will give you a heart of flesh. [27] I will put My Spirit within you and cause you to walk in My statutes, and you will keep My judgments and do them. [28] You will dwell in the land that I gave to your fathers. And you will be My people, and I will be your God. [29] I will also save you from all your uncleanness. And I will call for the grain and increase it and lay no famine upon you. [30] I will multiply the fruit of the tree and the increase of the field so that you shall receive no more reproach of famine among the nations. [31] Then you shall remember your evil ways and your deeds that were not good, and shall loathe yourselves in your own sight for your iniquities and your abominations. [32] Not for your sake am I doing this, says the Lord GOD, let it be known to you. Be ashamed and humiliated for your ways, O house of Israel!

[33] Thus says the Lord GOD: On the day that I cleanse you from all your iniquities, I will cause you to dwell in the cities, and the waste places shall be built. [34] The desolate land shall be tilled, whereas it lay desolate in the sight of all who pass by. [35] They shall say, "This land that was desolate has become like the garden of Eden. And the waste and desolate and ruined cities have become fenced and inhabited." [36] Then the nations that are left all around you shall know that I the LORD have built the ruined places and planted that which was desolate. I the LORD have spoken it, and I will do it.

[37] Thus says the Lord GOD: This also I will let the house of Israel ask Me to do for them: I will increase their men like a flock. [38] As the flock for sacrifices, as the flock of Jerusalem in her solemn feasts, so shall the waste cities be filled with flocks of men. Then they shall know that I am the LORD.

The Valley of Dry Bones

37 The hand of the LORD was upon me, and He carried me out in the Spirit of the LORD and set me down in the midst of the valley which was full of bones, [2] and He caused me to pass among them all around. And *there were* very many in the open valley. And *they were* very dry. [3] He said to me, "Son of man, can these bones live?"

And I answered, "O Lord GOD, You know."

[4] Again He said to me, "Prophesy over these bones and say to them, O dry bones, hear the word of the LORD. [5] Thus says the Lord GOD to these bones: I will cause breath to enter you so that you live. [6] And I will lay sinews upon you and will grow back flesh upon you and cover you with skin and put breath in you so that you live. Then you shall know that I am the LORD."

[7] So I prophesied as I was commanded. And as I prophesied, there was a noise and a shaking. And the bones came together, bone to its bone. [8] When I looked, the sinews and the flesh grew upon them, and the skin covered them. But there was no breath in them.

[9] Then He said to me, "Prophesy to the wind; prophesy, son of man, and say to the wind: Thus says the Lord GOD: Come from the four winds, O breath, and breathe upon these slain so that they live." [10] So I prophesied as He commanded me, and the breath came into them, and they lived and stood up upon their feet, an exceeding great army.

[11] Then He said to me, "Son of man, these bones are the whole house of Israel. They say, 'Our bones are dried up, and our hope is lost. We are cut off completely.' [12] Therefore prophesy and say to them, Thus says the Lord GOD: Pay attention, O My people, I will open your graves and cause you to come up out of your graves and bring you into the land of Israel. [13] Then you shall know that I am the LORD, when I have opened your graves, O My people, and brought you up out of your graves. [14] And I shall put My Spirit in you, and you shall live, and I shall place you in your own land. Then you shall know that I the LORD have spoken and performed it, says the LORD."

Israel and Judah Unite

[15] The word of the LORD came again to me, saying: [16] Moreover, son of man, take one stick and write on it: "For Judah and for the sons of Israel his companions." Then take another stick and write on it, "For Joseph the stick of Ephraim and for all the house of Israel his companions." [17] Then join them to one another into one stick so that they become one in your hand.

[18] When the sons of your people speak to you, saying, "Will you not show us what you mean by these things?" [19] say to them, Thus says the Lord GOD: I will take the stick of Joseph, which is in the hand of Ephraim, and the tribes of Israel his companions, and will put them with it, with the stick of Judah, and make them one stick; and they shall be one in My hand. [20] The sticks on which you write shall be in your hand before their eyes. [21] Say to them, Thus says the Lord GOD: I will take the sons of Israel from among the nations where they have gone and will gather them on every side and bring them into their own land. [22] And I will make them one nation in the land upon the mountains of Israel. And one king shall be king over them all. And they shall be two nations no more, nor shall they be divided into two kingdoms anymore. [23] Nor shall they defile themselves anymore with their idols, nor with their detestable things, nor with any of their transgressions. But I will save them out of all their dwelling places in which they have sinned and will cleanse them. So they shall be My people, and I will be their God.

[24] David My servant shall be king over them. And they all shall have one shepherd. They shall also walk in My judgments, and observe My statutes and do them. [25] They shall dwell in the land that I have given to Jacob My servant, in which your fathers lived. And they shall dwell in it, they and their sons and their son's sons forever. And My servant David shall be their prince forever. [26] Moreover I will make a covenant of peace with them. It shall be an everlasting covenant with them. And I will place them and multiply them and will set My sanctuary in their midst forevermore. [27] My tabernacle also shall be with them. Indeed, I will be their God and they shall be My people. [28] The nations shall know that I the LORD do sanctify Israel when My sanctuary is in their midst forevermore.

A Prophecy Against Gog

38 And the word of the LORD came to me, saying: [2] Son of man, set your face against Gog of the land of Magog, the prince of Rosh, Meshek and Tubal, and prophesy against him, [3] and say: Thus says the Lord GOD: I am against you, O Gog, the prince of Rosh, Meshek and Tubal. [4] And I will turn you back and put hooks into your jaws, and I will bring you out, and all your army, horses, and horsemen, all of them clothed with all sorts of armor, even a great company with buckler and shield, all of them handling swords. [5] Persia, Ethiopia, and Put with them, all of them with shield and helmet. [6] I will do so to Gomer and all its troops, Beth Togarmah of the north quarters and all its troops, and many peoples with you.

[7] Be prepared and prepare yourself, you and all your companies that are assembled to you, and be a guard to them. [8] After many days you shall be called. In the latter years you shall come into the land that is restored from the sword, *whose inhabitants* have been gathered out of many peoples, against the mountains of Israel which had been always a waste. But its people were brought out of the nations, and they, all of them, are dwelling safely. [9] You shall ascend and come like a storm; you shall be like a cloud to cover the land, you and all your troops, and many peoples with you.

[10] Thus says the Lord GOD: It shall come to pass on that day that things shall come into your mind and you shall think an evil thought, [11] and you shall say, "I will go up against the land of unwalled villages. I will go against those who are at rest, that dwell safely, all of them dwelling without walls and having neither bars nor gates," [12] to take spoil and to seize prey, to turn your hand against the desolate places that are now inhabited, and against the people who are gathered out of the nations, who have obtained livestock and goods, who dwell in the midst of the world. [13] Sheba and Dedan and the merchants of Tarshish with all its villages shall say to you, "Have you come to take spoil? Have you gathered your company to seize prey, to carry away silver and gold, to take away livestock and goods, to take great spoil?"

[14] Therefore, son of man, prophesy and say to Gog: Thus says the Lord GOD: On that day when My people of Israel dwell safely, shall you not know it? [15] And you shall come from your place out of the north parts, you and many peoples with you, all of them riding on horses, a great company and a mighty army. [16] And you shall come up against My people of Israel as a cloud to cover the land. It shall come about in the latter days that I will bring you against My land so that the nations may know Me when I shall be sanctified in you, O Gog, before their eyes.

Judgment on Gog

[17] Thus says the Lord GOD: Are you he of whom I have spoken in former days by My servants the prophets of Israel, who prophesied in those days for many years that I would bring you against them? [18] And it shall come to pass at the same time when Gog comes against the land of Israel, says the Lord GOD, that My fury shall come up in My anger. [19] For in My jealousy and in the fire of My wrath I have spoken: Surely in that day there shall be a great earthquake in the land of Israel. [20] The fish of the sea and the fowl of the heavens and the beasts of the field and all creeping things that creep upon the earth and all the men who are upon the face of the earth shall shake at My presence, and the mountains shall be thrown down, and the steep places shall fall, and every wall shall fall to the ground. [21] I will call for a sword against him on all My mountains, says the Lord GOD. Every man's sword shall be against his brother. [22] I will enter into judgment with him with pestilence and with blood. And I will rain upon him and upon his troops and upon the many peoples who are with him, an overflowing rain and hailstones, fire and brimstone. [23] Thus I will magnify Myself, and sanctify Myself, and I will be known in the eyes of many nations. Then they shall know that I am the LORD.

The Destruction of Gog's Armies

39 Moreover you, son of man, prophesy against Gog and say: Thus says the Lord GOD: I am against you, O Gog, prince of Rosh, Meshek, and Tubal. [2] And I will turn you back, drive you on, and take you up the north parts and bring you against the mountains of Israel. [3] And I will strike your bow out of your left hand and will cause your arrows to fall out of your right hand. [4] You shall fall upon the mountains of Israel, you and all your troops and the peoples who are with you. I will give you to the ravenous birds of every sort, and to the beasts of the field to be devoured. [5] You shall fall upon the open field. For I have spoken, says the Lord GOD. [6] I will send a fire on Magog and among those who dwell safely in the coastlands. Then they shall know that I am the LORD.

[7] So I will make My holy name known in the midst of My people Israel. And I will not let them pollute My holy name anymore. And the nations shall know that I am the LORD, the Holy One in Israel. [8] It is coming and it shall be done, says the Lord GOD. This is the day of which I have spoken.

[9] Those who dwell in the cities of Israel shall go and make fires with the weapons and burn them, both the shields and the bucklers, the bows and the arrows, and the war clubs and the spears, and they shall burn them with fire for seven years. [10] They shall take no wood out of the field, or cut down any out of the forests, for they shall make fires with the weapons. And they shall despoil those who despoiled them, and plunder those who plundered them, says the Lord GOD.

The Burial of Gog

[11] It shall come to pass in that day that I will give to Gog a place of graves there in Israel, the valley of the passengers on the east of the sea, and it shall stop the passengers. And there they shall bury Gog and all his multitude, and they shall call it the Valley of Hamon Gog.

[12] For seven months the house of Israel shall be burying them so that they may cleanse the land. [13] Indeed, all the people of the land shall bury them. And it shall be their renown on the day that I shall be glorified, says the Lord GOD. [14] They shall separate men who continually pass through the land to bury the passengers, even those who remain upon the face of the earth, to cleanse it.

After the end of seven months they shall search. [15] As the passengers pass through the land and anyone sees a man's bone, then he shall set up a sign by it until the buriers have buried it in the Valley of Hamon Gog. [16] Also the name of the city shall be Hamonah. Thus they shall cleanse the land.

[17] As for you, son of man, thus says the Lord GOD: Speak to every kind of fowl and to every beast of the field: Assemble and come. Gather on every side to My sacrifice that I sacrifice for you, even a great sacrifice upon the mountains of Israel, that you may eat flesh and drink blood. [18] You shall eat the flesh of the mighty and drink the blood of the officials of the earth as *though of* rams, of lambs, and of goats, of bulls, all of them fatlings of Bashan. [19] You shall eat fat until you are full and drink blood until you are drunk from My sacrifice which I have sacrificed for you. [20] Thus you shall be filled at My table with horses and chariots, with mighty men, and with all the men of war, says the Lord GOD.

[21] I will set My glory among the nations, and all the nations shall see My judgment that I have executed, and My hand that I have laid upon them. [22] So the house of Israel shall know that I am the LORD their God from that day and forward. [23] The nations shall know that the house of Israel went into captivity for their iniquity because they trespassed against Me, and I hid My face from them. And I gave them into the hand of their enemies, and all of them fell by the sword. [24] According to their uncleanness and according to their transgressions, I have done to them and hid My face from them.

The Restoration of Israel

[25] Therefore thus says the Lord GOD: Now I will restore the fortunes of Jacob and have mercy on the whole house of Israel and will be jealous for My holy name. [26] They shall forget their shame and all

their trespasses by which they have trespassed against Me when they lived safely in their land and no one made them afraid. [27] When I have brought them back from the peoples and gathered them out of the lands of their enemies, then I shall be sanctified in them in the sight of many nations. [28] Then they shall know that I am the Lord their God who caused them to be led into captivity among the nations, and then gathered them again to their own land and have left none of them there anymore. [29] Nor will I hide My face from them anymore. For I will have poured out My Spirit on the house of Israel, says the Lord God.

The Vision of the New Temple

40 In the twenty-fifth year of our captivity, in the beginning of the year, on the tenth day of the month, in the fourteenth year after the city was struck, on that very day the hand of the Lord was upon me and He brought me there. [2] In the visions of God He brought me into the land of Israel and set me upon a very high mountain, on which was as the frame of a city on the south. [3] He brought me there, and there was a man whose appearance was like the appearance of bronze, with a line of flax and a measuring reed in his hand. And he stood in the gate. [4] The man said to me, "Son of man, look with your eyes, and hear with your ears, and set your heart on all that I shall show you. For you have been brought here to show it to you. Declare all that you see to the house of Israel."

The East Gate

[5] There was a wall all around the outside of the temple. In the man's hand was a measuring reed of six cubits[1] long, each being a cubit and a handbreadth.[2] So he measured the width of the building, one reed. And the height, one reed. [6] Then he went to the gateway facing east; and he went up its stairs and measured the threshold of the gate, which was one reed wide. And the other threshold of the gate was one reed wide. [7] Every little chamber was one reed long and one reed wide. And between the little chambers were five cubits.[3] And the threshold of the gate by the vestibule of the inside gate was one reed.

[8] He measured also the vestibule of the gate within, one reed. [9] Then he measured the vestibule of the gate, eight cubits.[4] And its posts, two cubits.[5] And the vestibule of the gate was the inner end.

[10] The little chambers of the gate eastward were three on this side and three on that side. The three were of one measurement. And the posts had one measure on this side and on that side. [11] He measured the width of the entrance of the gate, ten cubits,[6] and the length of the gate, thirteen cubits.[7] [12] The space also before the little chambers was one cubit[8] on this side, and the space was one cubit on that side. And the little chambers were six cubits on this side, and six cubits on that side. [13] He measured then the gate from the roof of one little chamber to the roof of another; the width was twenty-five cubits,[9] door against door. [14] He measured the posts, sixty cubits,[10] even to the post of the court all around the gate. [15] From the face of the gate of the entrance to the face of the vestibule of the inner gate was fifty cubits.[11] [16] There were narrow windows in the little chambers and in their posts inside the gate all around, and likewise in the vestibules. And windows were all around inside. And on each post were palm tree ornaments.

The Outer Court

[17] Then he brought me into the outer court, and there were chambers and a pavement made all around the court. Thirty chambers were on the pavement. [18] The pavement was by the side of the gates, corresponding to the length of the gates; this was the lower pavement. [19] Then he measured the width from the front of the lower gate to the outer front of the inner court, a hundred cubits[12] eastward and northward.

The North Gate

[20] As for the gate of the outer court that faced north, he measured its length and its width. [21] Its little chambers, three on this side and three on that side, its posts, and its arches had the same measurements as the first gate; its length was fifty cubits, and its width twenty-five cubits. [22] Its windows, and those of its arches, and its palm trees had the same measurements as the gate facing east. Seven steps led up to it; and its arches were in front of it. [23] The gate of the inner court was opposite the gate on the north, as on the east. And he measured from gate to gate, a hundred cubits.

The South Gate

[24] After that he brought me toward the south, and there was a gate facing south. And he measured its posts and its arches according to these same measurements. [25] There were windows in it and in its arches all around like those windows. The length was fifty cubits, and the width twenty-five cubits. [26] There were seven steps to go up to it, and its arches were before them. And it had palm tree ornaments, one on this side, and another on that side on its posts. [27] There was a gate in the inner court facing south. And he measured from gate to gate toward the south, a hundred cubits.

The Inner Court

[28] He brought me to the inner court by the south gate. And he measured the south gate according to these same measurements. [29] And its little chambers and its posts and its arches were according to these same measurements. And there were windows in it and in its arches all around. It was fifty cubits long and twenty-five cubits wide. [30] The arches all around were twenty-five cubits long and five cubits wide. [31] Its arches faced the outer court. And palm tree ornaments were on its posts. And its staircase had eight steps.

[32] He brought me into the inner court facing east. And he measured the gate according to these same measurements. [33] Its little chambers and its posts and its arches were according to these same measurements. And there were windows in it and in its arches all around. It was fifty cubits[13] long and twenty-five cubits wide. [34] Its arches faced the outer court. And palm tree ornaments were on its posts, on this side and on that side. And its staircase had eight steps.

[35] He brought me to the north gate and measured it according to these same measurements; [36] its little chambers, its posts, and its arches, and it had windows all around: the length was fifty cubits, and the width twenty-five cubits. [37] Its posts faced the outer court. And palm tree ornaments were on its posts, on this side and on that side. And its staircase had eight steps.

Chambers for Washing the Sacrifice

[38] The chambers and its entrance were by the posts of the gates where they washed the burnt offering. [39] In the vestibule of the gate were two tables on this side and two tables on that side, to slay on it the burnt offering and the sin offering and the trespass offering. [40] On the outside of the *vestibule*, as one goes up to the entrance of the north gate, were two tables. And on the other side of the vestibule of the gate were two tables. [41] Four tables were on this side and four tables on that side by the side of the gate, eight tables on which they slaughtered *their sacrifices*. [42] The four tables were of hewn stone for the burnt offering, of a cubit and a half long, and a cubit and a half wide, and one cubit high.[14] On which also they laid the instruments with which they slaughtered the burnt offering and the sacrifice. [43] Within were hooks, a handbreadth wide,[15] fastened all around. And on the tables was the flesh of the offering.

Chambers for the Singers and Priests

[44] Outside the inner gate were the chambers for the singers in the inner court, one at the side of the north gate facing south, the other at

---

[1]5 About 11 feet, or 3.2 meters. The long cubit of about 21 inches, or about 53 centimeters is used throughout ch. 40–48.
[2]5 About 3 inches, or 7.5 centimeters. [3]7 About 8¾ feet, or 2.7 meters; and in v. 48. [4]9 About 14 feet, or 4.2 meters.
[5]9 About 3½ feet, or 1 meter. [6]11 About 18 feet, or 5.3 meters. [7]11 About 18 feet wide and 23 feet long, or 5.3 meters wide and 6.9 meters long.
[8]12 About 21 inches, or about 53 centimeters. [9]13 About 44 feet, or 13 meters; and in vv. 21, 25, 29, 30, 33, and 36.
[10]14 About 105 feet, or 32 meters. [11]15 About 88 feet, or 27 meters; and in vv. 21, 25, 29, 33, and 36. [12]19 About 175 feet, or 53 meters; and in vv. 23, 27, and 47. [13]33 About 88 feet, or 27 meters. [14]42 About 2⅔ feet long and wide and 21 inches high, or 80 centimeters long and wide and 53 centimeters high. [15]43 About 3½ inches, or 9 centimeters.

the side of the east gate facing north. [45] He said to me, "This chamber that faces south is for the priests who have charge of the temple. [46] The chamber that faces north is for the priests who have charge of the altar. These are the sons of Zadok among the sons of Levi, who come near to the LORD to minister to Him."

[47] So he measured the court, a hundred cubits long, and a hundred cubits wide, foursquare. And the altar was before the temple.

The Vestibule of the Temple

[48] Then he brought me to the vestibule of the temple and measured each post of the vestibule, five cubits[1] on this side, and five cubits on that side. And the width of the gate was three cubits[2] on this side and three cubits on that side. [49] The length of the vestibule was twenty cubits[3] and the width eleven cubits.[4] And he brought me by the steps whereby they went up to it. And there were pillars by the posts, one on this side and another on that side.

The Inner Temple

41 Afterward he brought me to the temple and measured the posts, six cubits[5] wide on the one side and six cubits wide on the other side, which was the width of the tabernacle. [2] The width of the door was ten cubits.[6] And the sides of the door were five cubits[7] on the one side and five cubits on the other side. And he measured its length, forty cubits, and the width, twenty cubits.[8]

[3] Then he went inward and measured the post of the door, two cubits,[9] and the door, six cubits, and the width of the door, seven cubits.[10] [4] So he measured its length, twenty cubits. And before the temple, the width was twenty cubits. And he said to me, "This is the Most Holy Place."

[5] Afterward he measured the wall of the temple, six cubits, and the width of every side chamber, four cubits,[11] all around the temple on every side. [6] The side chambers were in three stories, one above the other, thirty in each story. There were offsets all around to serve as supports for the side chambers, so that they should not be supported by the wall of the temple. [7] The side chambers became wider with each successive story going up because the structures went up all around the temple. Therefore the width of the temple increased going upwards and thus one went up from the lowest to the highest level through the middle level.

[8] I saw also the height all around the temple. The foundations of the side chambers were a full reed of six great cubits. [9] The thickness of the wall of the side chambers was five cubits. And that which was left was the place of the side chambers that were within. [10] Between the chambers was the wideness of twenty cubits all around the temple on every side. [11] The doors of the side chambers opened onto the open place, one door toward the north and another door toward the south. And the width of the open place was five cubits all around.

[12] Now the building that was facing the separate yard on the west side was seventy cubits[12] wide. And the wall of the building was five cubits thick all around, and its length ninety cubits.[13]

[13] So he measured the temple, a hundred cubits long; and the separate yard and the building with its walls, a hundred cubits long;[14] [14] also the width of the eastern face of the temple and the separate yard was a hundred cubits.

[15] Then he measured the length of the building facing the yard at the west, together with its galleries on either side, one hundred cubits with the nave of the temple and the porches of the court, [16] the doorposts and the narrow windows. The galleries all around their three stories opposite the threshold were paneled with wood from the ground to the windows (the windows were covered), [17] from the space above the door, even to the inner room, as well as outside, and on every wall all around, inside and outside, by measure. [18] It was made with cherubim and palm trees, so that a palm tree was between cherub and cherub. And every cherub had two faces, [19] so that the face of a man was toward the

palm tree on the one side, and the face of a young lion toward the palm tree on the other side. It was made throughout the temple all round. [20] From the ground to the top of the door and on the wall of the nave, cherubim and palm trees were carved.

[21] The posts of the temple and the face of the sanctuary were squared. The appearance of the one was as the appearance of the other. [22] The altar of wood was three cubits[15] high, and its length two cubits. And its corners and its length and its walls were of wood. And he said to me, "This is the table that is before the LORD." [23] The temple and the sanctuary had two doors. [24] The doors had two leaves apiece, two turning leaves. Two leaves were for the one door, and two leaves for the other door. [25] There were made on them, on the doors of the temple, cherubim and palm trees like those made on the walls. And there were thick planks on the front of the vestibule outside. [26] There were beveled windows and palm trees on both sides, on the sides of the vestibule; thus were the side chambers of the temple and the thresholds.

The Chambers for the Priests

42 Then he brought me out into the outer court, toward the north; and he brought me into the chamber that was opposite the separate yard and which was opposite the building on the north. [2] Before the length of a hundred cubits was the north door, and the width was fifty cubits.[16] [3] Opposite the twenty cubits[17] that belonged to the inner court, and opposite the pavement that belonged to the outer court, was gallery against gallery in three stories. [4] In front of the chambers was a passage on the inner side, ten cubits wide and one *hundred* cubits[18] deep; and their doors faced north. [5] Now the upper chambers were shorter. For the galleries were higher than these, than the lower and the middle ones of the building. [6] For they were in three stories, but had no pillars as the pillars of the courts. Therefore the building was set back more than the lowest and the middle ones from the ground. [7] And a wall that was outside was parallel to the chambers, toward the outer court, opposite the chambers; its length was fifty cubits. [8] For the length of the chambers that were in the outer court was fifty cubits. And the length of those before the temple was a hundred cubits. [9] From under these chambers was the entrance on the east side as one goes into them from the outer court.

[10] The chambers were in the thickness of the wall of the court toward the east, opposite the separate yard and opposite the building, [11] with a passage in front of them; they were like the appearance of the chambers which were toward the north, of the same length and width. And all their exits and arrangements were according to plan. [12] Corresponding to the doors of the chambers that were facing south was a door at the head of the passage way, the passage way directly in front of the wall toward the east.

[13] Then he said to me, "The north chambers and the south chambers, which are before the separate place, are the holy chambers where the priests who approach the LORD shall eat the most holy offerings. There they shall lay the most holy offerings—the grain offering, the sin offering, and the guilt offering—for the place is holy. [14] When the priests enter it, then they shall not go out of the holy place into the outer court, but there they shall lay their garments in which they minister, for they are holy. And they shall put on other garments, and shall approach those things which are for the people."

[15] Now when he had made an end of measuring the inner temple, he brought me out by the gate that faces east, and measured it all around. [16] He measured the east side with the measuring reed, five hundred cubits[19] with the measuring reed all around. [17] He measured the north side with the measuring reed round about, five hundred reeds. [18] He measured the south side with the measuring reed, five hundred reeds. [19] He turned about to the west side and measured five hundred reeds with the measuring reed. [20] He measured it by the four sides. It had a wall all around, five hundred reeds long and five hundred wide,[20] to make a separation between the sanctuary and the profane place.

---

[1]48 About 8.75 feet, or 2.7 meters.   [2]48 About 5¼ feet, or 1.6 meters.   [3]49 About 35 feet, or 11 meters.   [4]49 About 19.25 feet, or 5.9 meters.   [5]1 About 11 feet, or 3.2 meters; and in w. 3, 5, and 8.   [6]2 About 18 feet, or 5.3 meters.   [7]2 About 8¾ feet, or 2.7 meters; and in w. 9, 11, and 12.   [8]2 About 70 feet long and 35 feet wide, or 21 meters long and 11 meters wide.   [9]3 About 3½ feet, or 1.1 meters; and in v. 22.   [10]3 About 12 feet, or 3.7 meters.   [11]5 About 7 feet, or 2.1 meters.   [12]12 About 123 feet, or 37 meters.   [13]12 About 158 feet, or 48 meters.   [14]13 About 175 feet, or 53 meters; and in vv. 14 and 15.   [15]22 About 5¼ feet, or 1.5 meters.   [16]2 About 175 feet long and 88 feet wide, or 53 meters long and 27 meters wide.   [17]3 About 35 feet, or 11 meters.   [18]4 About 18 feet wide and 175 feet long, or 5.3 meters wide and 53 meters long.   [19]16 Five hundred cubits equal about 875 feet, or 265 meters; and in vv. 17, 18, and 19.   [20]20 Five hundred cubits equal about 875 feet, or 265 meters.

God's Glory Returns to the Temple

43 Afterward he brought me to the gate, the gate facing east. [2] And the glory of the God of Israel came from the way of the east. And His voice was like a noise of many waters. And the earth shone with His glory. [3] It was according to the appearance of the vision which I saw, even according to the vision that I saw, when He came to destroy the city. And the visions were like the vision that I saw by the River Kebar. And I fell upon my face. [4] The glory of the LORD came into the temple by the way of the gate facing east. [5] So the Spirit took me up and brought me into the inner court. And the glory of the LORD filled the temple.

[6] Then I heard one speaking to me out of the temple. And a man stood by me. [7] He said to me: Son of man, this is the place of My throne and the place of the soles of My feet, where I will dwell in the midst of the sons of Israel forever. And My holy name shall the house of Israel defile no more, nor they nor their kings by their harlotry, nor by the corpses of their kings when they die. [8] By setting their threshold by My threshold and their post by My posts and the wall between Me and them, they have even defiled My holy name by their abominations that they have committed. Therefore I have consumed them in My anger. [9] Now let them put away their harlotry and the corpses of their kings far from Me, and I will dwell in their midst forever.

[10] As for you, son of man, describe the temple to the house of Israel, that they may be ashamed of their iniquities. And let them measure the pattern. [11] If they are ashamed of all that they have done, show them the design of the temple and its fashion and exits and its entrances and all its forms and all its ordinances and all its laws. And write it in their sight so that they may keep its whole form and all its ordinances and do them.

[12] This is the law of the temple: The whole territory on the top of the mountain all around shall be most holy. This is the law of the temple.

The Altar Restored

[13] These are the measurements of the altar by cubits[1] (the cubit is a cubit and a handbreadth): The base shall be a cubit, and the width a cubit, and its border by its edge all around shall be a span.[2] And this shall be the height of the altar: [14] From the bottom on the ground even to the lower ledge shall be two cubits, and the width one cubit.[3] And from the lesser ledge even to the greater ledge shall be four cubits, and the width one cubit.[4] [15] So the altar shall be four cubits. And from the altar and upward shall be four horns. [16] The altar hearth shall be twelve cubits long by twelve wide,[5] square in its four corners. [17] The ledge shall be fourteen cubits[6] long and fourteen wide in the four squares. And the border about it shall be half a cubit.[7] And its bottom shall be a cubit all around. And its stairs shall face east.

[18] He said to me: Son of man, thus says the Lord GOD: These are the ordinances of the altar in the day when they shall make it to offer burnt offerings on it and to sprinkle blood on it. [19] You shall give to the priests the Levites that are of the seed of Zadok who approach Me to minister to Me, says the Lord GOD, a young bull as a sin offering. [20] You shall take of its blood and put it on its four horns, and on the four corners of the ledge and on the rim all around. Thus you shall cleanse and purge it. [21] You shall take the bull also of the sin offering, and it shall be burned in the appointed place of the temple, outside the sanctuary.

[22] On the second day you shall offer a male goat without blemish as a sin offering. And they shall cleanse the altar as they cleansed it with the bull. [23] When you have made an end of cleansing it, you shall offer a young bull without blemish and a ram out of the flock without blemish. [24] You shall offer them before the LORD, and the priests shall cast salt on them, and they shall offer them up as a burnt offering to the LORD.

[25] For seven days you shall prepare every day a goat as a sin offering. They shall also prepare a young bull and a ram out of the flock, without blemish. [26] For seven days they shall purge the altar and purify it. So they shall consecrate it. [27] When they have completed the days, it shall be that on the eighth day and forward, the priests shall present your burnt offerings and your peace offerings upon the altar. And I will accept you, says the Lord GOD.

The East Gate for the Prince

44 Then he brought me back to the gate of the outer sanctuary, which faces east. And it was shut. [2] Then the LORD said to me: This gate shall be shut; it shall not be opened, and no man shall enter by it. Because the LORD, the God of Israel, has entered by it, therefore it shall be shut. [3] As for the prince, he shall sit in it as prince to eat bread before the LORD. He shall enter by the way of the vestibule of the gate and shall go out by the same way.

[4] Then he brought me by the way of the north gate before the temple. And I looked, and the glory of the LORD filled the house of the LORD, and I fell upon my face.

[5] The LORD said to me: Son of man, mark well, and see with your eyes and hear with your ears all that I say to you concerning all the ordinances of the house of the LORD and all its laws. And mark well those who may enter the house, with all exits of the sanctuary. [6] You shall say to the rebellious, even to the house of Israel, Thus says the Lord GOD: O house of Israel, let all your abominations suffice; [7] you brought foreigners into My sanctuary, uncircumcised in heart and uncircumcised in flesh, to be in My sanctuary to pollute it, even My house, when you offered My food, the fat and the blood. For they have broken My covenant because of all your abominations. [8] You have not kept the charge of My holy things. But you have set foreigners to keep charge of My sanctuary. [9] Thus says the Lord GOD: No foreigner, uncircumcised in heart nor uncircumcised in flesh, shall enter into My sanctuary, of any foreigner who is among the sons of Israel.

Laws for the Priests

[10] But the Levites who have gone far from Me when Israel went astray, who went astray away from Me after their idols, they shall bear the punishment of their iniquity. [11] Yet they shall be ministers in My sanctuary, having charge at the gates of the house and ministering to the house. They shall slay the burnt offering and the sacrifice for the people, and they shall stand before them to minister to them. [12] Because they ministered to them before their idols and caused the house of Israel to fall into iniquity, therefore I have lifted up My hand against them, says the Lord GOD, that they shall bear the punishment of their iniquity. [13] They shall not come near to Me to do the office of a priest to Me, nor to come near to any of My holy things in the Most Holy Place. But they shall bear their shame and their abominations which they have committed. [14] But I will make them keepers of the charge of the temple for all its service and for all that shall be done in it.

[15] But the Levitical priests, the sons of Zadok, who kept the charge of My sanctuary when the sons of Israel went astray from Me, they shall come near to Me to minister to Me, and they shall stand before Me to offer to Me the fat and the blood, says the Lord GOD. [16] They shall enter My sanctuary, and they shall come near to My table to minister to Me, and they shall keep My charge.

[17] It shall come to pass that when they enter at the gates of the inner court, they shall be clothed with linen garments. And no wool shall come upon them while they minister in the gates of the inner court, and within. [18] They shall have linen turbans on their heads and shall have linen breeches on their loins. They shall not gird themselves with *anything that causes* sweat. [19] When they go out into the outer court, even into the outer court to the people, they shall put off their garments in which they ministered and lay them in the holy chambers, and they shall put on other garments. And they shall not sanctify the people with their garments.

[20] Nor shall they shave their heads, nor suffer their locks to grow long. They shall only trim the hair of their heads. [21] Nor shall any priest drink wine when they enter the inner court. [22] Nor shall they take for their wives a widow, nor her who has been put away. But they shall take maidens of the seed of the house of Israel, or a widow who had a priest before. [23] They shall teach My people the difference between the holy and profane, and cause them to discern between the unclean and the clean.

[24] In controversy they shall stand in judgment. And they shall judge it according to My judgments. And they shall keep My laws and My statutes in all My assemblies. And they shall hallow My Sabbaths.

---

[1] 13 About 21 inches, or 53 centimeters; and in vv. 14 and 17.   [2] 13 About 11 inches, or 27 centimeters.   [3] 14 About 3½ feet high and 1¾ feet wide, or 105 centimeters high and 53 centimeters wide.   [4] 14 About 7 feet high and 1¾ feet wide, or 2.1 meters high and 53 centimeters wide.   [5] 16 About 21 feet, or 6.4 meters.   [6] 17 About 25 feet, or 7.4 meters.   [7] 17 About 11 inches, or 27 centimeters.

25 They shall not go to a dead person to defile themselves. But for father, or for mother, or for son, or for daughter, for brother, or for sister that has had no husband, they may defile themselves. 26 After he is cleansed, they shall reckon to him seven days. 27 In the day that he goes into the sanctuary, to the inner court, to minister in the sanctuary, he shall offer his sin offering, says the Lord GOD.

28 It shall be to them for an inheritance. I am their inheritance. And you shall give them no possession in Israel. I am their possession. 29 They shall eat the grain offering and the sin offering and the guilt offering. And every dedicated thing in Israel shall be theirs. 30 The first of all the first fruits of all things and every oblation of all of every sort of your oblations shall be the priest's. You shall also give to the priest the first of your dough to cause a blessing to rest in your house. 31 The priests shall not eat any bird or beast that has died naturally or was torn to pieces.

The Holy District

45 Moreover, when you divide by lot the land for inheritance, you shall offer an allotment to the LORD, a holy portion of the land. The length shall be the length of twenty-five thousand cubits,[1] and the width shall be twenty thousand.[2] It shall be holy throughout its territory all around. 2 Of this there shall be a square plot for the sanctuary, five hundred by five hundred cubits,[3] with fifty cubits[4] for an open space around it. 3 Of this measure you shall measure the length of twenty-five thousand cubits and the width of ten thousand cubits.[5] And in it shall be the sanctuary, the Most Holy Place. 4 The holy portion of the land shall be for the priests, the ministers of the sanctuary, who shall come near to minister to the LORD. And it shall be a place for their houses and a holy place for the sanctuary. 5 An area twenty-five thousand cubits in length and ten thousand in width shall be for the Levites, the ministers of the temple, and for their possession cities in which to dwell.

6 You shall appoint the possession of the city five thousand cubits[6] wide and twenty-five thousand cubits long adjacent to the allotment of the holy portion. It shall be for the whole house of Israel.

The Portion for the Prince

7 A portion shall be for the prince on the one side and on the other side of the holy allotment and property of the city, adjacent to the holy allotment and the property of the city, from the west side westward and from the east side eastward. And the length shall correspond to one of the tribal portions, from the west border to the east border. 8 In the land shall be his possession in Israel. And My officials shall no more oppress My people. And the rest of the land they shall give to the house of Israel according to their tribes.

Laws Governing the Prince

9 Thus says the Lord GOD: Let it suffice you officials of Israel. Remove violence and destruction, and execute justice and righteousness. Take away your exactions from My people, says the Lord GOD. 10 You shall have just balances and a just ephah[7] and a just bath.[8] 11 The ephah and the bath shall be of one measure so that the bath may contain the tenth part of a homer,[9] and the ephah the tenth part of a homer. Their measure shall be after the homer. 12 The shekel[10] shall be twenty gerahs.[11] Twenty shekels, twenty-five shekels, and fifteen shekels shall be your mina.[12]

13 This is the offering that you shall offer: the sixth part of an ephah[13] of a homer of wheat, and you shall give the sixth part of an ephah[14] of a homer of barley. 14 Concerning the ordinance of oil that is the bath of oil, you shall offer the tenth part of a bath[15] out of the kor,[16] which is a homer or ten baths, for ten baths are a homer. 15 And one lamb shall be out of the flock, out of two hundred, out of the watering places of Israel, as a grain offering and as a burnt offering

and for peace offerings, to make reconciliation for them, says the Lord GOD. 16 All the people of the land shall give this offering for the prince in Israel. 17 It shall be the prince's part to give burnt offerings and grain offerings and drink offerings in the feasts and in the New Moons and in the Sabbaths, in all solemnities of the house of Israel. He shall prepare the sin offering and the grain offering and the burnt offering and the peace offerings, to make reconciliation for the house of Israel.

Observing the Feasts

18 Thus says the Lord GOD: In the first month, on the first day of the month, you shall take a young bull without blemish and cleanse the sanctuary. 19 And the priest shall take some of the blood of the sin offering and put it on the doorposts of the temple and on the four corners of the ledge of the altar and on the gateposts of the inner court. 20 So you shall do the seventh day of the month for everyone who errs and for him who is naive. So you shall make atonement for the temple.

21 In the first month, on the fourteenth day of the month, you shall have the Passover, a feast of seven days. Unleavened bread shall be eaten. 22 On that day the prince shall prepare for himself and for all the people of the land a bull as a sin offering. 23 For seven days of the feast he shall prepare a burnt offering to the LORD, seven bulls and seven rams without blemish daily for the seven days, and a male of the goats daily as a sin offering. 24 He shall prepare a grain offering of an ephah for a bull and an ephah for a ram and a hin[17] of oil for an ephah.

25 In the seventh month, on the fifteenth day of the month, he shall do the like in the feast of the seven days, according to the sin offering, according to the burnt offering, and according to the grain offering, and according to the oil.

The Prince and the Feasts

46 Thus says the Lord GOD: The gate of the inner court that faces east shall be shut the six working days. But on the Sabbath it shall be opened, and in the day of the New Moon it shall be opened. 2 The prince shall enter by the way of the vestibule of that gate from outside, and shall stand by the post of the gate, and the priests shall prepare his burnt offering and his peace offerings, and he shall worship at the threshold of the gate. Then he shall go out. But the gate shall not be shut until the evening. 3 Likewise the people of the land shall worship at the door of this gate before the LORD in the Sabbaths and in the New Moons. 4 The burnt offering that the prince shall offer to the LORD in the Sabbath day shall be six lambs without blemish and a ram without blemish. 5 The grain offering shall be an ephah[18] for a ram and the grain offering for the lambs as he shall be able to give and a hin[19] of oil to an ephah. 6 In the day of the New Moon it shall be a young bull without blemish and six lambs and a ram. They shall be without blemish. 7 He shall prepare a grain offering, an ephah[20] for a bull and an ephah for a ram, and for the lambs according as his hand shall attain to, and a hin of oil to an ephah. 8 When the prince enters, he shall go in by the way of the vestibule of that gate, and he shall go out the same way.

9 But when the people of the land shall come before the LORD in the solemn feasts, he who enters by the way of the north gate to worship shall go out by way of the south gate. And he who enters by the way of the south gate shall go out by way of the north gate. He shall not return by way of the gate by which he entered, but shall go out the opposite gate. 10 The prince shall be in their midst. When they enter, he shall enter; and when they go out, he shall go out. 11 At the feasts and the appointed festivals the grain offering shall be an ephah[21] for a bull, and an ephah for a ram, and with the lambs as much as he is able to give, together with a hin of oil for an ephah.

12 Now when the prince prepares a voluntary burnt offering or voluntary peace offering to the LORD, the gate facing east shall be opened for him; and he shall prepare his burnt offering and his peace offerings

as he did on the Sabbath day. Then he shall go out. And after he goes out, the gate shall be shut.

[13] You shall daily prepare a burnt offering to the LORD of a lamb of the first year without blemish. You shall prepare it every morning. [14] You shall prepare a grain offering for it every morning, the sixth part of an ephah,[1] and the third part of a hin[2] of oil to temper with the fine flour, a grain offering continually by a perpetual ordinance to the LORD. [15] Thus they shall prepare the lamb and the grain offering and the oil every morning as a continual burnt offering.

Inheritance Laws for the Prince

[16] Thus says the Lord GOD: If the prince gives a gift out of his inheritance to any of his sons, it will belong to his sons. It is their possession by inheritance. [17] But if he gives a gift out of his inheritance to one of his servants, it will be his until the year of liberty. Then it will revert to the prince. His inheritance will be only his sons. It will belong to them. [18] Moreover the prince shall not take of the people's inheritance by oppression to thrust them out of their possession. But he shall give his sons inheritance out of his own possession so that My people not be scattered, every man from his possession.

Preparations for the Offerings

[19] Then he brought me through the entrance, which was at the side of the gate, into the holy chambers of the priests which face toward the north. And there was a place at the extreme westward end of them. [20] Then he said to me, "This is the place where the priests shall boil the guilt offering and the sin offering, and where they shall bake the grain offering so that they not bear them out into the outer court, to sanctify the people."

[21] Then he brought me out into the outer court and caused me to pass by the four corners of the court. And in every corner of the court *there was* a court. [22] In the four corners of the court there were courts joined of forty cubits long and thirty wide.[3] These four corners were of one measurement. [23] There was a row of *masonry* all around in them, all around the four of them; and it was made with hearths at the bottom of the rows all around. [24] Then he said to me, "These are the boiling places where the ministers of the temple shall boil the sacrifices of the people."

The River Flowing From the Temple

47 Then he brought me back to the door of the temple; and water was flowing out from under the threshold of the temple eastward, for the front of the temple faced east; the water was flowing down from under from the right side of the temple, south of the altar. [2] Then he brought me out by way of the north gate, and led me around on the outside to the outer gate that faces east; and the water was coming out on the south side.

[3] When the man who had the line in his hand went eastward, he measured a thousand cubits, and he brought me through the water; the water reached the ankles. [4] Again he measured a thousand and brought me through the water. The water reached the knees. Again he measured a thousand and brought me through *the water*. The water *reached* the loins. [5] Afterward he measured a thousand. And it was a river that I could not pass over, for the water had risen, *enough* water to swim in, a river that could not be passed over. [6] He said to me, "Son of man, have you seen this?"

Then he brought me and caused me to return to the brink of the river. [7] When I had returned I saw on the bank of the river very many trees on the one side and on the other. [8] Then he said to me, "This water flows toward the eastern region and goes down into the valley, and enters the sea. When it flows into the sea, the water will become fresh. [9] Every living creature that swarms, wherever the rivers go, will live. And there shall be a very great multitude of fish, because these waters shall come there and the others become fresh. Thus everything shall live wherever the river comes. [10] It shall come to pass that the fishermen shall stand upon it. From En Gedi even to En Eglaim there shall be a place to spread out nets. Their fish shall be according to their kinds, as the fish of the *Mediterranean* Sea, exceedingly many. [11] But its miry places and its marshes shall

not be healed. They shall be given to salt. [12] By the river upon its bank, on this side and on that side, shall grow all *kinds of* trees for food, whose leaf shall not fade nor shall its fruit fail. They shall bring forth fruit according to their months, because their water issues out of the sanctuary. And their fruit shall be for food and their leaves for medicine."

The Borders of the Land

[13] Thus says the Lord GOD: This shall be the border by which you shall divide the land for an inheritance according to the twelve tribes of Israel. Joseph *shall have two* portions. [14] You shall divide it for an inheritance, one as equally as another. For I lifted up My hand to give it to your fathers, and this land shall fall to you for inheritance.

[15] This shall be the border of the land on the north: from the *Mediterranean* Sea by the way of Hethlon as men go to Zedad, [16] Hamath, Berothah, Sibraim (which lies between the border of Damascus and the border of Hamath), to Hazar Hattikon, which is on the border of Hauran. [17] The border from the sea shall be Hazar Enan at the border of Damascus, and on the north northward is the border of Hamath. And this is the north side.

[18] The east side, from Hauran and from Damascus and from Gilead and the land of Israel, shall be the Jordan. You shall measure from the northern border to the eastern sea. And this is the east side.

[19] The south side, toward the Negev, shall run from Tamar even to the waters of Meribah Kadesh, from there along the brook *of Egypt* to the *Mediterranean* Sea. This shall be the south side, toward the Negev.

[20] The west side also shall be the *Mediterranean* Sea from the *southern* border to a point opposite Lebo Hamath. This is the west side.

[21] So you shall divide this land among you according to the tribes of Israel. [22] It shall come to pass that you shall divide it by lot for an inheritance among yourselves and among the aliens who sojourn among you, who shall bear sons among you. And they shall be to you as born in the country among the sons of Israel. They shall have inheritance with you among the tribes of Israel. [23] It shall come to pass that in whatever tribe the alien sojourns, there you shall give him his inheritance, says the Lord GOD.

The Division of the Land

48 Now these are the names of the tribes: From the north end beside the way of Hethlon as one goes to Lebo Hamath, *as far as* Hazar Enan at the border of Damascus northward beside Hamath going from east to west, Dan, one portion;

[2] by the border of Dan from the east side to the west side, a portion for Asher;

[3] by the border of Asher from the east side even to the west side, a portion for Naphtali;

[4] by the border of Naphtali from the east side to the west side, a portion for Manasseh;

[5] by the border of Manasseh from the east side to the west side, a portion for Ephraim;

[6] by the border of Ephraim from the east side even to the west side, a portion for Reuben;

[7] by the border of Reuben from the east side to the west side, a portion for Judah;

[8] by the border of Judah from the east side to the west side shall be the allotment which you shall set apart, twenty-five thousand cubits[4] in width and in length as one of the other parts, from the east side to the west side. And the sanctuary shall be in the middle of it.

[9] The allotment that you shall set apart to the LORD shall be twenty-five thousand cubits in length, and ten thousand[5] in width. [10] For them, even for the priests, shall be this holy allotment, toward the north twenty-five thousand cubits in length and toward the west ten thousand in width and toward the east ten thousand in width and toward the south twenty-five thousand cubits in length. And the sanctuary of the LORD shall be in its midst. [11] It shall be for the priests who are sanctified of the sons of Zadok, who have kept My charge, who did not go astray when the sons of Israel went astray as the Levites went astray.

---

[1] 14 Likely about 6 pounds, or 2.7 kilograms.   [2] 14 About 1½ quarts, or 1.3 liters.   [3] 22 About 70 feet long and 53 feet wide, or 21 meters long and 16 meters wide.   [4] 8 About 8 miles, or 13 kilometers; and in vv. 9, 10, 13, 15, 20, and 21.   [5] 9 About 3½ miles, or 5.3 kilometer; and in vv. 10, 13, and 18.

¹² It shall be an allotment to them, a thing most holy, the allotment of the land by the border of the Levites.

¹³ Opposite the border of the priests, the Levites shall have twenty-five thousand cubits in length and ten thousand in width. All the length shall be twenty-five thousand cubits, and the width ten thousand. ¹⁴ They shall not sell of it or exchange or alienate this choice portion of the land, for it is holy to the LORD.

¹⁵ The five thousand cubits*¹* in width that remain and the twenty-five thousand in length shall be for common use for the city, for dwellings and for suburbs. And the city shall be in the midst. ¹⁶ These shall be its measurements: the north side four thousand five hundred cubits;*²* and the south side four thousand five hundred cubits; and on the east side four thousand five hundred cubits; and the west side four thousand five hundred cubits. ¹⁷ The suburbs of the city shall be: to the north, two hundred and fifty cubits;*³* to the south, two hundred and fifty cubits; to the east, two hundred and fifty cubits; and to the west, two hundred and fifty cubits. ¹⁸ The rest in length alongside the holy portion shall be ten thousand cubits eastward and ten thousand westward. And it shall be alongside the holy portion. And its increase shall be for food to those who serve the city. ¹⁹ Those who serve the city, out of all the tribes of Israel, shall cultivate it. ²⁰ All the allotment shall be twenty-five thousand by twenty-five thousand cubits. You shall set apart the holy allotment foursquare, with the property of the city.

²¹ The rest shall belong to the prince, on both sides of the holy allotment and the city property, next to the twenty-five thousand cubits of the allotment toward the eastern border, and westward next to the twenty-five thousand toward the western border, next to the portions for the prince. And the holy allotment and the sanctuary of the temple shall be in its midst. ²² Moreover excluding the property of the Levites and the property of the city, being in the midst of that which is the prince's, everything between the border of Judah and the border of Benjamin shall be for the prince.

²³ As for the rest of the tribes, from the east side to the west side, Benjamin *shall have* one portion.

²⁴ By the border of Benjamin from the east side to the west side, Simeon *shall have* one portion.

²⁵ By the border of Simeon from the east side to the west side, Issachar *shall have* one portion.

²⁶ By the border of Issachar from the east side to the west side, Zebulun *shall have* one portion.

²⁷ By the border of Zebulun from the east side to the west side, Gad *shall have* one portion.

²⁸ By the border of Gad at the south side southward the border shall be even from Tamar to the waters of Meribah Kadesh and to the brook of *Egypt* toward the *Mediterranean* Sea.

²⁹ This is the land which you shall divide by lot to the tribes of Israel for inheritance, and these are their portions, says the Lord GOD.

The Gates of the New City

³⁰ These are the exits of the city on the north side, four thousand five hundred cubits by measurement. ³¹ The gates of the city shall be named after the tribes of Israel, three gates northward: one gate of Reuben, one gate of Judah, one gate of Levi.

³² At the east side, four thousand five hundred cubits, shall be three gates: one gate of Joseph, one gate of Benjamin, one gate of Dan.

³³ At the south side, four thousand five hundred cubits*⁴* by measurement, shall be three gates: one gate of Simeon, one gate of Issachar, one gate of Zebulun.

³⁴ At the west side, four thousand five hundred cubits, shall be three gates: one gate of Gad, one gate of Asher, one gate of Naphtali.

³⁵ The circumference *shall be* eighteen thousand cubits.*⁵*

And the name of the city from that day *shall be*, The LORD Is There.

DANIEL

Daniel Taken to Babylon

1 In the third year of the reign of Jehoiakim king of Judah, Nebuchadnezzar king of Babylon came to Jerusalem and besieged it. ² The Lord gave Jehoiakim king of Judah into his hand, with part of the vessels of the house of God, and he carried them into the land of Shinar to the house of his god. And he brought the vessels into the treasure house of his god.

³ The king spoke to Ashpenaz the master of his officials that he should bring some of the sons of Israel and some of the king's descendants and some of the nobles, ⁴ youths in whom was no blemish, who were handsome and skillful in every *branch of* wisdom and gifted with understanding and discerning knowledge, and such as had ability in them to serve in the king's palace, and whom they might teach the learning and the language of the Chaldeans. ⁵ The king appointed them a daily provision of the king's food and of the wine which he drank. They were to be educated for three years, that at the end of it they might serve before the king.

⁶ Now among them were of the sons of Judah: Daniel, Hananiah, Mishael, and Azariah, ⁷ to whom the commander of the officials gave names. And he gave to Daniel the name of Belteshazzar; to Hananiah, Shadrach; to Mishael, Meshach; and to Azariah, Abednego.

⁸ But Daniel purposed in his heart that he would not defile himself with the portion of the king's food, nor with the wine which he drank. Therefore he requested of the master of the officials that he might not defile himself. ⁹ Now God had brought Daniel into favor and compassion with the master of the officials. ¹⁰ The master of the officials said to Daniel, "I fear my lord the king who has appointed your food and your drink. For why should he see your faces worse-looking than the youths who are your age? Then you would endanger my head before the king."

¹¹ Then Daniel said to the steward, whom the master of the officials had set over Daniel, Hananiah, Mishael, and Azariah, ¹² "Please test your servants for ten days, and let them give us vegetables to eat and water to drink. ¹³ Then let our countenances be looked upon before you, and the countenance of the youths who eat of the portion of the king's food. And as you see, deal with your servants." ¹⁴ So he consented to them in this matter and tested them for ten days.

¹⁵ At the end of ten days their countenances appeared fairer and fatter than all the youths who ate the portion of the king's food. ¹⁶ Thus the guard continued to take away the portion of their food and the wine that they were to drink, and gave them vegetables.

¹⁷ As for these four youths, God gave them knowledge and skill in every *branch of* learning and wisdom. And Daniel had understanding in all *kinds of* visions and dreams.

¹⁸ Now at the end of the days that the king had set for them to be brought in, the master of the officials brought them in before Nebuchadnezzar. ¹⁹ The king spoke with them, and, among them all, none was found like Daniel, Hananiah, Mishael, and Azariah. Therefore they served before the king. ²⁰ In all matters of wisdom and understanding which the king inquired of them, he found them ten times better than all the magicians and astrologers that were in all his realm.

²¹ Daniel continued even to the first year of King Cyrus.

---

¹*15* About 1⅔ miles, or 2.7 kilometers.   ²*16* About 1½ miles, or 2.4 kilometers; and in vv. 30, 32, 33, and 34.
³*17* About 440 feet, or 135 meters.   ⁴*33* About 1½ miles, or 2.4 kilometers.   ⁵*35* About 6 miles, or 9.5 kilometers.

Nebuchadnezzar's Dream

2 And in the second year of the reign of Nebuchadnezzar, Nebuchadnezzar had dreams, and his spirit was troubled and his sleep left him. [2] Then the king gave the command to call the magicians and the astrologers and the sorcerers and the Chaldeans to tell the king his dreams. So they came and stood before the king. [3] The king said to them, "I have had a dream, and my spirit is anxious to understand the dream."

[4] Then the Chaldeans spoke to the king in Aramaic,[1] "O king, live forever. Tell your servants the dream, and we will tell the interpretation."

[5] The king answered and said to the Chaldeans, "The command from me is firm: If you will not make known to me the dream with its interpretation, you shall be cut in pieces and your houses shall be made a dunghill. [6] But if you tell the dream and its interpretation, you shall receive from me gifts and rewards and great honor. Therefore tell me the dream and its interpretation."

[7] They answered again and said, "Let the king tell his servants the dream, and we will tell the interpretation."

[8] The king answered and said, "I know of certainty that you are bargaining for time, because you see that the command from me is firm: [9] If you will not make known to me the dream, there is but one decree for you. For you have agreed to speak lying and corrupt words before me until the circumstance is changed. Therefore tell me the dream so that I know that you can tell me its interpretation."

[10] The Chaldeans answered before the king and said, "There is not a man on the earth who can tell the king's matter, inasmuch as no great king or ruler has ever asked such things of any magician or astrologer or Chaldean. [11] Also, it is a rare thing that the king requires, and there is no one else who can tell it before the king, except the gods whose dwelling is not with flesh."

[12] For this cause the king was angry and very furious, and commanded to destroy all the wise men of Babylon. [13] Therefore the decree went out that the wise men should be slain. And they sought for Daniel and his companions to be slain.

[14] Then Daniel answered with discretion and wisdom to Arioch the captain of the king's guard, who had gone out to kill the wise men of Babylon. [15] He answered and said to Arioch the king's captain, "Why is the decree from the king so urgent?" Then Arioch made the thing known to Daniel. [16] Then Daniel went in and desired of the king that he would give him time in order that he could tell the king the interpretation.

[17] Then Daniel went to his house and made the thing known to Hananiah, Mishael, and Azariah, his companions, [18] so that they might ask for compassion from the God of heaven concerning this secret, so that Daniel and his companions might not perish with the rest of the wise men of Babylon.

God Reveals Nebuchadnezzar's Dream

[19] Then the secret was revealed to Daniel in a night vision. Then Daniel blessed the God of heaven. [20] Daniel answered and said:

"Blessed be the name of God forever and ever,
　for wisdom and might are His.
[21] It is He who changes the times and the seasons;
　He removes kings and sets up kings;
　He gives wisdom to the wise
　　and knowledge to those who know understanding.
[22] He reveals the deep and secret things;
　He knows what is in the darkness,
　　and the light dwells with Him.
[23] I thank and praise You, O God of my fathers;
　for You have given me wisdom and might,
　and have made known to me now what we asked of You,
　　for You have made known to us the king's matter."

Daniel Interprets the Dream

[24] Therefore Daniel went in to Arioch, whom the king had ordained to destroy the wise men of Babylon. He went and said to him: "Do not destroy the wise men of Babylon. Bring me in before the king, and I will tell the king the interpretation."

[25] Then in haste Arioch brought Daniel before the king and said thus to him, "I have found a man of the captives of Judah who can make known to the king the interpretation."

[26] The king answered and said to Daniel, whose name was Belteshazzar, "Are you able to make known to me the dream which I have seen, and its interpretation?"

[27] Daniel answered in the presence of the king and said, "The secret which the king has demanded, the wise men, the astrologers, the magicians, and the soothsayers cannot tell the king. [28] But there is a God in heaven who reveals secrets and makes known to King Nebuchadnezzar what shall be in the latter days. Your dream and the visions of your head upon your bed are these: [29] As for you, O king, your thoughts came into your mind upon your bed about what would come to pass hereafter, and He who reveals secrets makes known to you what shall come to pass. [30] But as for me, this secret is not revealed to me for any wisdom that I have more than any living man, but for the purpose of making known the interpretation to the king, and that you might understand the thoughts of your heart.

[31] "You, O king, were watching, and there was a great image. This great image, whose brightness was excellent, stood before you. And its form was awesome. [32] This image's head was of fine gold, its breast and its arms of silver, its belly and its thighs of bronze, [33] its legs of iron, its feet partly of iron and partly of clay. [34] You watched until a stone was cut out without hands which struck the image upon its feet, which were of iron and clay, and broke them to pieces. [35] Then the iron, the clay, the bronze, the silver, and the gold were broken to pieces together, and became like the chaff of the summer threshing floors. And the wind carried them away so that not a trace of them was found. But the stone that struck the image became a great mountain and filled the whole earth.

[36] "This was the dream. Now we will tell its interpretation before the king. [37] You, O king, are the king of kings. For the God of heaven has given you a kingdom, power, and strength, and glory. [38] Wherever the sons of men dwell, or the animals of the field, or the fowl of the heavens, He has given them into your hand and has made you ruler over them all. You are the head of gold.

[39] "After you, another kingdom inferior to you shall arise, and a third kingdom of bronze, which shall rule over all the earth. [40] And the fourth kingdom shall be strong as iron, for iron breaks in pieces and shatters everything; and like iron that crushes, it shall crush and shatter all these. [41] As you saw the feet and toes, partly of potters' clay and partly of iron, the kingdom shall be divided. But there shall be in it some of the strength of the iron, inasmuch as you saw the iron mixed with miry clay. [42] As the toes of the feet were partly of iron and partly of clay, so the kingdom shall be partly strong and partly broken. [43] Whereas you saw iron mixed with miry clay, they shall mingle themselves with the seed of men, but they shall not cleave to one another, even as iron does not mix with clay.

[44] "In the days of these kings the God of heaven shall set up a kingdom which shall never be destroyed. And the kingdom shall not be left to another people, but it shall break in pieces and consume all these kingdoms, and it shall stand forever. [45] Inasmuch as you saw that the stone was cut out of the mountain without hands and that it broke in pieces the iron, the bronze, the clay, the silver, and the gold, the great God has made known to the king what shall come to pass hereafter. And the dream is certain, and its interpretation sure."

The Promotion of Daniel

[46] Then King Nebuchadnezzar fell upon his face and did homage to Daniel, and commanded that they should present an offering and sweet incense to him. [47] The king answered Daniel and said, "Truly your God is a God of gods, and a Lord of kings, and a revealer of secrets, since you could reveal this secret."

[48] Then the king advanced Daniel and gave him many great gifts, and made him ruler over the whole province of Babylon and chief of the governors over all the wise men of Babylon. [49] Then Daniel requested of the king, and he set Shadrach, Meshach, and Abednego over the affairs of the province of Babylon. But Daniel sat at the court of the king.

[1] 4 2:4–7:28 is originally from the Aramaic language.

The Image of Gold

3 Nebuchadnezzar the king made an image of gold, whose height was sixty cubits and its width six cubits. [1] He set it up in the plain of Dura in the province of Babylon. [2] Then Nebuchadnezzar the king sent to gather together the officials, the governors, and the captains, the judges, the treasurers, the counselors, the sheriffs, and all the rulers of the provinces to come to the dedication of the image which Nebuchadnezzar the king had set up. [3] Then the officials, the governors, and captains, the judges, the treasurers, the counselors, the sheriffs, and all the rulers of the provinces were gathered together to the dedication of the image that Nebuchadnezzar the king had set up, and they stood before the image that Nebuchadnezzar had set up.

[4] Then a herald cried aloud: "To you it is commanded, O peoples, nations, and languages, [5] that at the time you hear the sound of the cornet, flute, harp, sackbut, psaltery, dulcimer, and all kinds of music, you should fall down and worship the golden image that Nebuchadnezzar the king has set up. [6] And whoever does not fall down and worship shall the same hour be cast into the midst of a burning fiery furnace."

[7] Therefore at that time, when all the people heard the sound of the cornet, flute, harp, sackbut, psaltery, and all kinds of music, all the peoples, the nations, and the languages fell down and worshipped the golden image that Nebuchadnezzar the king had set up.

The Fiery Furnace

[8] Therefore at that time certain Chaldeans came near and accused the Jews. [9] They spoke and said to King Nebuchadnezzar, "O king, live forever. [10] You, O king, have made a decree, that every man who hears the sound of the cornet, flute, harp, sackbut, psaltery, and dulcimer, and all kinds of music should fall down and worship the golden image. [11] And whoever does not fall down and worship should be cast into the midst of a burning fiery furnace. [12] There are certain Jews whom you have set over the affairs of the province of Babylon: Shadrach, Meshach, and Abednego. These men, O king, have not regarded you. They do not serve your gods or worship the golden image which you have set up."

[13] Then Nebuchadnezzar in his rage and fury commanded Shadrach, Meshach, and Abednego be brought. Then they brought these men before the king. [14] Nebuchadnezzar spoke and said to them, "Is it true, Shadrach, Meshach, and Abednego, that you do not serve my gods or worship the golden image which I have set up? [15] Now if you are ready at the time you hear the sound of the cornet, flute, harp, sackbut, psaltery, and dulcimer, and all kinds of music to fall down and worship the image which I have made, very well. But if you do not worship, you shall be cast the same hour into the midst of a burning fiery furnace. And who is that god who can deliver you out of my hands?"

[16] Shadrach, Meshach, and Abednego answered and said to the king, "O Nebuchadnezzar, we do not need to give you an answer in this matter. [17] If it be so, our God whom we serve is able to deliver us from the burning fiery furnace, and He will deliver us out of your hand, O king. [18] But even if He does not, be it known to you, O king, that we will not serve your gods, nor worship the golden image which you have set up."

Protection in the Fiery Furnace

[19] Then Nebuchadnezzar was full of fury, and the form of his visage was changed against Shadrach, Meshach, and Abednego. Therefore he spoke, and commanded that they should heat the furnace seven times more than it was usually heated. [20] He commanded the most mighty men in his army to bind Shadrach, Meshach, and Abednego and cast them into the burning fiery furnace. [21] Then these men were bound in their trousers, their coats, and their hats, and their other garments, and were cast into the midst of the burning fiery furnace. [22] Therefore, because the king's commandment was urgent and the furnace exceeding hot, the flame of the fire killed those men who took up Shadrach, Meshach, and Abednego. [23] These three men, Shadrach, Meshach, and Abednego, fell down bound into the midst of the burning fiery furnace.

[24] Then Nebuchadnezzar the king was astonished, and rose up in haste, and spoke, and said to his counselors, "Did we not cast three men bound into the midst of the fire?"

They answered and said to the king, "True, O king."

[25] He answered and said, "But I see four men loose and walking in the midst of the fire, and they are unharmed. And the form of the fourth is like the Son of God!"

Nebuchadnezzar Praises God

[26] Then Nebuchadnezzar came near to the mouth of the burning fiery furnace, and spoke, and said, "Shadrach, Meshach, and Abednego, you servants of the Most High God, come out and come here!"

Then Shadrach, Meshach, and Abednego came out of the midst of the fire. [27] The officials, governors, and captains, and the king's counselors, being gathered together, saw these men upon whose bodies the fire had no power, nor was a hair of their head singed, neither were their coats changed, nor had the smell of fire even come upon them.

[28] Then Nebuchadnezzar spoke and said, "Blessed be the God of Shadrach, Meshach, and Abednego, who has sent His angel and delivered His servants who trusted in Him. They have defied the king's word, and yielded their bodies, that they might not serve nor worship any god, except their own God. [29] Therefore I make a decree that every people, nation, and language which speaks anything amiss against the God of Shadrach, Meshach, and Abednego shall be cut in pieces, and their houses shall be made a dunghill, because there is no other God who can deliver in this way."

[30] Then the king promoted Shadrach, Meshach, and Abednego in the province of Babylon.

Nebuchadnezzar's Second Dream

4 Nebuchadnezzar the king,

to all peoples, nations, and languages, who dwell in all the earth:

Peace be multiplied to you.

[2] I thought it good to declare the signs and wonders that the Most High God has done for me.

[3] How great are His signs,
   and how mighty are His wonders!
His kingdom is an everlasting kingdom,
   and His dominion is from generation to generation.

[4] I, Nebuchadnezzar, was at rest in my house, and flourishing in my palace. [5] I saw a dream which made me afraid, and the thoughts upon my bed and the visions of my head troubled me. [6] Therefore I made a decree to bring in all the wise men of Babylon before me, that they might make known to me the interpretation of the dream. [7] Then came in the magicians, the astrologers, the Chaldeans, and the soothsayers, and I told the dream before them; but they did not make known to me its interpretation.

[8] But at the last Daniel came in before me, whose name was Belteshazzar according to the name of my god and in whom is the Spirit of the Holy God, and before him I told the dream, saying, [9] "Belteshazzar, master of the magicians, because I know that the Spirit of the Holy God is in you and no secret troubles you, tell me the visions of my dream that I have seen, and its interpretation. [10] Now these were the visions of my mind *while* on my bed: I saw a tree in the midst of the earth, and its height was great. [11] The tree grew and became strong, and its height reached heaven, and it was visible to the end of all the earth. [12] Its leaves were fair, and its fruit much, and in it was food for all. The animals of the field had shadow under it, and the fowl of the heavens lived in its boughs, and all flesh was fed of it.

[13] "I saw in the visions of my head upon my bed, and there was a holy watcher coming down from heaven. [14] He cried aloud and said thus: 'Hew down the tree and cut off its branches, shake off its leaves and scatter its fruit. Let the animals get away from under it, and the fowl from its branches. [15] Nevertheless leave the stump of its roots in the earth, even with a band of iron and bronze, in the tender grass of the field.

" 'And let it be wet with the dew of heaven, and let its portion be with the animals in the grass of the earth. [16] Let its heart be

---

[1] 1 About 90 feet high and 9 feet wide, or 27 meters high and 2.7 meters wide.

changed from that of a man, let him be given the heart of an animal. And let seven periods of time pass over it.

17 " 'This matter is by the decree of the watchers, and the demand by the word of the holy ones, in order that the living may know that the Most High rules over the kingdom of men and gives it to whomever He wills and sets up over it the basest of men.'

18 "This dream I, King Nebuchadnezzar, have seen. Now you, Belteshazzar, tell its interpretation to me, because all the wise men of my kingdom are not able to make known to me the interpretation. But you are able, for the Spirit of the Holy God is in you."

Daniel Interprets the Dream

19 Then Daniel, whose name was Belteshazzar, was astonished for a while, and his thoughts troubled him. The king spoke and said, "Belteshazzar, do not let the dream, or its interpretation, trouble you."

Belteshazzar answered and said, "My lord, *if only* the dream was for those who hate you, and its interpretation for your enemies! 20 The tree that you saw, which grew and became strong, whose height reached to the heavens, and was visible to all the earth, 21 and whose leaves were fair, and its fruit much, and in it was food for all, under which the animals of the field lived, and upon whose branches the fowl of the heavens had their habitation: 22 It is you, O king, who have grown and become strong. Your greatness has grown and reaches to heaven, and your dominion to the ends of the earth.

23 "Whereas the king saw a watcher and a holy one coming down from heaven and saying, 'Cut the tree down and destroy it, yet leave the stump of its roots in the ground, even with a band of iron and bronze, in the tender grass of the field. And let it be wet with the dew of heaven, and let its portion be with the animals of the field until seven periods of time pass over it'— 24 "This is the interpretation, O king, and this is the decree of the Most High, which has come upon my lord the king: 25 You shall be driven away from men, and your dwelling shall be with the wild animals. You shall be given grass to eat like oxen, and wet with the dew of heaven. And seven times shall pass over you, until you have learned that the Most High rules over the kingdom of men and gives it to whomever He chooses. 26 Inasmuch as they commanded to leave the stump of the tree roots, your kingdom shall be assured to you after you acknowledge that Heaven rules. 27 Therefore, O king, let my counsel be acceptable to you, and break off your sins by righteousness and your iniquities by showing mercy to the poor, in case there may be a lengthening of your prosperity."

The Dream Is Fulfilled

28 All this came upon King Nebuchadnezzar. 29 At the end of twelve months he walked on *the roof of* the palace of the kingdom of Babylon. 30 The king spoke, saying, "Is this not Babylon the Great that I myself have built as a royal residence by my mighty power and for the honor of my majesty?"

31 While the word was in the king's mouth, there fell a voice from heaven: "O King Nebuchadnezzar, to you it is spoken: The kingdom has departed from you! 32 And you shall be driven away from men, and your dwelling shall be with the animals of the field. You shall be given grass to eat as oxen, and seven periods of time shall pass over you until you know that the Most High rules over the kingdom of men and gives it to whomever He wills."

33 Immediately the thing was fulfilled concerning Nebuchadnezzar. And he was driven from men and ate grass as oxen, and his body was wet with the dew of heaven until his hairs were grown like eagles' *feathers* and his nails like birds' *claws*.

Nebuchadnezzar Praises God

34 But at the end of the days, I, Nebuchadnezzar, lifted up my eyes to heaven, and my understanding returned to me, and I blessed the Most High, and I praised and honored Him who lives forever:

For His dominion is an everlasting dominion,
  and whose kingdom endures from generation
    to generation.

35 And all the inhabitants of the earth
  are reputed as nothing;
and He does according to His will
  in the army of heaven
  and among the inhabitants of the earth.
And no one can stay His hand or say to Him,
  "What have You done?"

36 At the same time my reason returned to me. And for the glory of my kingdom, my honor and splendor returned to me. And my counselors and my lords sought me out. Then I was established in my kingdom, and excellent majesty was added to me. 37 Now I, Nebuchadnezzar, praise and extol and honor the King of heaven, for all His works are true and His ways just, and those who walk in pride He is able to abase.

Belshazzar's Feast

5 Belshazzar the king made a great feast for a thousand of his lords and drank wine before the thousand. 2 While he tasted the wine, Belshazzar commanded that they bring in the golden and silver vessels which his father Nebuchadnezzar had taken from the temple which was in Jerusalem, so that the king, and his officials, his wives, and his concubines might drink from them. 3 Then they brought the golden vessels that were taken out of the temple of the house of God which was at Jerusalem. And the king and his officials, his wives and his concubines drank from them. 4 They drank wine and praised the gods of gold and of silver, of bronze, of iron, of wood, and of stone.

The Writing on the Wall

5 Immediately fingers of a man's hand appeared and wrote opposite the lampstand on the plaster of the wall of the king's palace. And the king saw the back of the hand that wrote. 6 Then the king's countenance was changed, and his thoughts troubled him, so that the joints of his loins were loosed, and his knees struck against one another.

7 The king cried aloud to bring in the astrologers, the Chaldeans, and the soothsayers. And the king spoke and said to the wise men of Babylon, "Whoever shall read this writing and show me its interpretation shall be clothed with scarlet and have a chain of gold about his neck and shall be the third ruler in the kingdom."

8 Then all the king's wise men came in, but they could not read the writing, nor make known to the king its interpretation. 9 Then King Belshazzar was greatly troubled, and his countenance was changed in him, and his nobles were astonished.

10 Now the queen came into the banquet house because of the words of the king and his nobles. And the queen spoke and said, "O king, live forever. Do not let your thoughts trouble you, or let your countenance be changed. 11 There is a man in your kingdom in whom is the Spirit of the Holy God. And, in the days of your father, light and understanding and wisdom, like the wisdom of the gods, were found in him. And King Nebuchadnezzar, your father, your father the king, made him master of the magicians, astrologers, Chaldeans, and soothsayers. 12 Inasmuch as an excellent spirit and knowledge and understanding, interpreting dreams and explanation of enigmas and solving of problems, were found in the same Daniel, whom the king named Belteshazzar, now let Daniel be called, and he will give the interpretation."

Daniel Interprets the Writing

13 Then Daniel was brought in before the king. And the king spoke and said to Daniel, "Are you that Daniel who is one of the sons of the captivity of Judah, whom the king my father brought out of Judah? 14 Now I have heard of you, that the Spirit of God is in you; and that light, and understanding, and excellent wisdom have been found in you. 15 Now the wise men, the astrologers, have been brought in before me, that they should read this writing and make known to me its interpretation, but they could not give the interpretation of the matter. 16 And I have heard of you, that you can give interpretations and solve problems. Now if you can read the writing, and make known to me its interpretation, you shall be clothed with scarlet and have a chain of gold about your neck and shall be the third ruler in the kingdom."

17 Then Daniel answered and said before the king, "Let your gifts be for yourself, or give your rewards to another. Yet I will read the writing to the king and make known to him the interpretation.

[18] "O king, the Most High God gave Nebuchadnezzar your father a kingdom and majesty and glory and honor. [19] And for the majesty that He gave him, all peoples, nations, and languages trembled and feared before him. Whom he would, he slaughtered, and whom he would, he kept alive; whom he would, he set up, and whom he would, he put down. [20] But when his heart was lifted up and his mind hardened in pride, he was deposed from his kingly throne and they took his glory from him. [21] And he was driven from the sons of men, and his heart was made like the animals, and his dwelling was with the wild donkeys. He was given grass to eat like oxen, and his body was wet with the dew of heaven until he knew that the Most High God rules in the kingdom of men, and that He appoints over it whomever He wills.

[22] "Yet you, his son, O Belshazzar, have not humbled your heart, though you knew all this; [23] but have lifted up yourself against the Lord of heaven. And they have brought the vessels of His house before you, and you and your lords, your wives and your concubines, have drunk wine in them. And you have praised the gods of silver and gold, of bronze, iron, wood, and stone, which see not, nor hear, nor know. And the God in whose hand is your breath, and whose are all your ways, you have not glorified. [24] Then the hand was sent from Him, and this inscription was written.

[25] "This is the inscription that was written:

MENE, MENE, TEKEL, UPHARSIN.

[26] "This is the interpretation of the message:

MENE:[1] God has numbered your kingdom and put an end to it.

[27] TEKEL:[2] you have been weighed in the balances and are found wanting.

[28] PERES:[3] your kingdom has been divided and given to the Medes and Persians."

[29] Then Belshazzar gave the command, and they clothed Daniel with scarlet and put a chain of gold about his neck, and made a proclamation concerning him, that he should be the third ruler in the kingdom.

[30] That same night Belshazzar the king of the Chaldeans was slain. [31] Then Darius the Mede received the kingdom, being about sixty-two years old.

Daniel and the Lions' Den

6 It pleased Darius to set over the kingdom one hundred and twenty officials, so that they would be over the whole kingdom, [2] and over them three presidents, of whom Daniel was first, so that the officials might give accounts to them and the king not suffer loss. [3] Then this Daniel was preferred above the presidents and officials because an excellent spirit was in him, and the king thought to set him over the whole realm. [4] Then the presidents and officials sought to find occasion against Daniel concerning the kingdom, but they could find no occasion or fault because he was faithful; nor was there any error or fault found in him. [5] Then these men said, "We shall not find any occasion against this Daniel, unless we find it against him concerning the law of his God."

[6] Then these presidents and officials assembled together to the king, and said to him: "King Darius, live forever! [7] All the presidents of the kingdom, the governors, and the officials, the counselors, and the captains have consulted together to establish a royal statute and to make a firm decree, that whoever shall ask a petition of any god or man for thirty days, save of you, O king, shall be cast into the den of lions. [8] Now, O king, establish the decree and sign the writing, that it not be changed, according to the law of the Medes and Persians, which may not be altered." [9] Therefore King Darius signed the writing, even the decree.

[10] Now when Daniel knew that the writing was signed, he went into his house. And his windows being open in his chamber toward Jerusalem, he kneeled on his knees three times a day, and prayed, and gave thanks before his God, as he had been doing previously. [11] Then these men assembled and found Daniel praying and making supplication before his God. [12] Then they came near and spoke before the king concerning the king's decree: "Have you not signed a decree, that every man who asks a petition of any god or man within thirty days, save of you, O king, shall be cast into the den of lions?"

The king answered and said, "The thing is true, according to the law of the Medes and Persians, which may not be altered."

[13] Then they answered and said before the king, "That Daniel, who is of the sons of the captivity of Judah, does not regard you, O king, or the decree that you have signed, but makes his petition three times a day." [14] Then the king, when he heard these words, was sorely displeased with himself and set his heart on Daniel to deliver him. And he labored until sunset to deliver him.

[15] Then these men came by agreement to the king and said to the king, "Know, O king, that it is the law of the Medes and Persians that no decree or statute which the king establishes may be changed."

[16] Then the king commanded, and they brought Daniel and cast him into the den of lions. Now the king spoke and said to Daniel, "Your God whom you serve continually, He will deliver you."

Daniel Saved From the Lions

[17] A stone was brought and laid upon the mouth of the den, and the king sealed it with his own signet and with the signet of his lords so that nothing might be changed concerning Daniel. [18] Then the king went to his palace and passed the night fasting, and no instruments of music were brought before him. And his sleep fled from him.

[19] Then the king arose very early in the morning and went in haste to the den of lions. [20] When he came to the den, he cried with a voice full of sorrow to Daniel. And the king spoke and said to Daniel, "Daniel, servant of the living God, has your God whom you serve continually been able to deliver you from the lions?"

[21] Then Daniel said to the king, "O king, live forever! [22] My God has sent His angel and has shut the lions' mouths so that they have not hurt me, because innocence was found in me before Him; and also before you, O king, I have done no harm."

[23] Then the king was exceeding glad for him and commanded that they take Daniel up out of the den. So Daniel was taken up out of the den, and no manner of harm was found on him, because he believed in his God.

[24] Then the king commanded, and they brought those men who had accused Daniel, and they cast them into the den of lions—them, their children, and their wives. And the lions overpowered them and broke all their bones in pieces before they came to the bottom of the den.

[25] Then King Darius wrote:

To all peoples, nations, and languages that dwell in all the earth:

"Peace be multiplied unto you.

[26] "I make a decree that in every dominion of my kingdom men are to fear and tremble before the God of Daniel.

"For He is the living God,
    enduring forever;
His kingdom shall never be destroyed,
    and His dominion shall be forever.
[27] He delivers and rescues,
    and He works signs and wonders
    in heaven and on earth,
who has delivered Daniel
    from the power of the lions."

[28] So this Daniel prospered in the reign of Darius and in the reign of Cyrus the Persian.

Daniel's Vision of the Four Beasts

7 In the first year of Belshazzar king of Babylon, Daniel had a dream and visions of his mind *while* on his bed. Then he wrote the dream and told the sum of the matters.

[2] Daniel spoke and said: I saw in my vision by night the four winds of the heaven striving upon the *Mediterranean* Sea. [3] Four great beasts came up from the sea, diverse from one another.

[4] The first was like a lion and had eagle's wings. I watched until its wings were plucked and it was lifted up from the earth and made to stand on the feet as a man, and a man's heart was given to it.

---

[1] 26 Meaning *to number.*   [2] 27 Meaning *to weigh.*   [3] 28 Meaning *to divide.*

[5] Another beast appeared, a second, like a bear, and it raised itself up on one side, and it had three ribs in its mouth between its teeth. And they said to it, "Arise, devour much flesh." [6] After this I looked and there was another, like a leopard, which had on its back four wings of a fowl. The beast also had four heads. And dominion was given to it. [7] After this I saw in the visions at night a fourth beast, dreadful and terrible, and exceedingly strong. And it had great iron teeth. It devoured and broke in pieces, and stamped the rest with its feet. And it was different from all the beasts that were before it, and it had ten horns.

[8] I considered the horns, when there came up among them another little horn before whom three of the first horns were plucked up by the roots. And there, in this horn, were eyes like the eyes of man, and a mouth speaking great things.

The Ancient of Days Reigns
[9] I watched until

the thrones were cast down
   and the Ancient of Days was seated,
whose garment was white as snow,
   and the hair of His head like the pure wool.
His throne was like the fiery flame,
   and its wheels as burning fire.
[10] A fiery stream issued
   and came out from before Him.
A thousand thousands ministered to Him;
   and ten thousand times ten thousand stood before Him.
The judgment was set,
   and the books were opened.

[11] Then I watched because of the sound of the boastful words which the horn was speaking. I watched even until the beast was slain, and his body destroyed and given to the burning flame. [12] As for the rest of the beasts, they had their dominion taken away; yet their lives were prolonged for a season and time. [13] I saw in the night visions, and there was one like a Son of Man coming with the clouds of heaven. He came to the Ancient of Days and was presented before Him. [14] There was given to Him dominion, and glory, and a kingdom, that all peoples, nations, and languages should serve Him. His dominion is an everlasting dominion, which shall not pass away, and His kingdom that which shall not be destroyed.

The Interpretation of the Dream
[15] I, Daniel, was grieved in my spirit in the midst of my body, and the visions of my head troubled me. [16] I approached one of those who were standing by and asked him the truth of all this.

So he told me and made known to me the interpretation of these things. [17] "These great beasts, which are four, are four kings which shall arise out of the earth. [18] But the saints of the Most High shall take the kingdom and possess the kingdom forever, even forever and ever."

[19] Then I desired to know the truth of the fourth beast, which was different from all the others, exceeding dreadful, whose teeth were of iron and its nails of bronze, and which devoured, broke in pieces, and stamped the rest with its feet; [20] and of the ten horns that were in its head, and of the other which came up, and before whom three fell, even of that horn that had eyes and a mouth that spoke boastful words, whose look was more stout than its fellows. [21] I beheld, and the same horn was warring with the saints and prevailing against them [22] until the Ancient of Days came, and judgment was passed in favor of the saints of the Most High, and the time came when the saints possessed the kingdom.

[23] Thus he said: "The fourth beast shall be the fourth kingdom upon earth, which shall be different from all kingdoms, and shall devour the whole earth and shall tread it down and break it in pieces. [24] The ten horns out of this kingdom are ten kings that shall arise; and another shall rise after them, and he shall be different from the first, and he shall subdue three kings. [25] He shall speak words against the Most High and shall wear out the saints of the Most High and plan to change times and law. And they shall be given into his hand until a time and times and half a time.[1]

[26] "But the court shall sit for judgment, and they shall take away his dominion, to consume and to destroy it forever. [27] Then the kingdom and dominion, and the greatness of all the kingdoms under the whole heaven, shall be given to the people of the saints of the Most High, whose kingdom is an everlasting kingdom, and all dominions shall serve and obey Him."

[28] At this point the matter ended. As for me, Daniel, my thoughts troubled me much, and my countenance changed in me; but I kept the matter in my heart.

Daniel's Vision of a Ram and a Goat
8 In the third year of the reign of King Belshazzar a vision appeared to me, even to me Daniel, after that which appeared to me at the first. [2] I saw in the vision, and while I was looking, I was at Susa in the palace which is in the province of Elam. And I saw in the vision that I was by the canal of Ulai. [3] Then I lifted up my eyes and looked, and there stood before the river a ram which had two horns, and the two horns were high. But one was higher than the other, and the higher one came up last. [4] I saw the ram pushing westward and northward and southward, so that no animal might stand before him; nor was there any that could deliver out of his hand, but he did according to his will and became great.

[5] As I was considering this, suddenly a male goat came from the west across the face of the whole earth and did not touch the ground. And the goat had a notable horn between his eyes. [6] He came to the ram that had two horns, which I had seen standing before the river, and ran to him in the fury of his power. [7] I saw him come close to the ram, and he was moved with rage against him, and struck the ram and broke his two horns. And there was no power in the ram to stand before him, but he cast him down to the ground and stamped on him. And there was none who could deliver the ram out of his hand. [8] Therefore the male goat grew very great. And when he was strong, the great horn was broken, and four conspicuous *horns* came up in its place toward the four winds of heaven.

The Little Horn
[9] Out of one of them came a little horn, which grew exceedingly great toward the south, toward the east, and toward the Pleasant *Land*. [10] It grew great, even to the host of heaven. And it cast down some of the host and of the stars to the ground and stamped upon them. [11] Indeed, he magnified himself even to the Prince of the host, and from Him the daily sacrifice was taken away, and the place of His sanctuary was cast down. [12] Because of rebellion, an army was given *to the horn* to oppose the daily sacrifice; and it cast truth to the ground. It practiced this and prospered.

[13] Then I heard one saint speaking, and another saint said to that certain saint which spoke, "How long shall be the vision concerning the daily sacrifice and the transgression of desolation, the giving of both the sanctuary and the host to be trodden under foot?"

[14] And he said to me, "For two thousand three hundred evenings and mornings. Then the sanctuary shall be cleansed properly."

Gabriel Interprets the Vision
[15] When I, Daniel, had seen the vision, I sought for the meaning. Then there before me stood one who had the appearance of a man. [16] I heard a man's voice between *the banks of* Ulai, which called, and said, "Gabriel, make this man understand the vision."

[17] So he came near where I stood. And when he came, I was afraid and fell upon my face; but he said to me, "Understand, son of man, that the vision deals with the time of the end."

[18] Now as he was speaking with me, I was in a deep sleep with my face toward the ground. But he touched me and set me upright.

[19] He said, "Listen, I will make you know what shall be in the final period of the indignation, for the end shall be at the appointed time. [20] The ram which you saw having two horns represents the kings of Media and Persia. [21] The rough goat is the king of Greece, and the great horn that is between his eyes is the first king. [22] Now the broken horn

---

[1] 25 Or for a year, two years, and half a year.

and the four horns that stood up in its place are four kingdoms that shall stand up out of his nation, but not with his power.

23 "In the latter time of their kingdom, when the transgressors have reached their limit, a king will arise, having a fierce countenance, skilled in intrigue. 24 His power shall be mighty, but not by his own power. And he shall destroy wonderfully and shall prosper and practice his will and shall destroy the mighty men and the holy people. 25 By his cunning, he shall cause deceit to succeed under his hand, and he shall magnify himself in his heart. He shall destroy many in a time of peace. He shall also rise up against the Prince of princes; but he shall be broken, not by human hands.

26 "And the vision of the evenings and the mornings, which was told, is true. Therefore shut up the vision, for it deals with many days *in the future.*"

27 Then I, Daniel, fainted and was sick for some days. Afterward I rose up again and did the king's business. So I was astonished at the vision, but there was none to explain it.

The Prayer of Daniel

9 In the first year of Darius the son of Ahasuerus of the lineage of the Medes, who was made king over the realm of the Chaldeans, 2 in the first year of his reign, I, Daniel, observed in the books the number of the years which *were specified by* the word of the Lord to Jeremiah the prophet for the accomplishment of the desolations of Jerusalem, that is, seventy years. 3 I set my face toward the Lord God to seek by prayer and supplications with fasting and sackcloth and ashes.

4 And I prayed to the Lord my God, and made my confession, and said,

"Alas, O Lord, the great and dreadful God, keeping His covenant and mercy to those who love Him, and to those who keep His commandments. 5 We have sinned and have committed iniquity and have done wickedly and have rebelled, even by departing from Your precepts and from Your judgments. 6 We have not listened to Your servants the prophets, who spoke in Your name to our kings, our officials, and our fathers, and to all the people of the land.

7 "O Lord, righteousness belongs to You, but to us shame of face, as it is this day, to the men of Judah and to the inhabitants of Jerusalem and to all Israel, who are near and who are far off, through all the countries wherever You have driven them, because of their trespass that they have trespassed against You. 8 O Lord, to us belongs shame of face, to our kings, to our officials, and to our fathers, because we have sinned against You. 9 To the Lord our God belong mercies and forgiveness, though we have rebelled against Him. 10 We have not obeyed the voice of the Lord our God, to walk in His laws, which He set before us by His servants the prophets. 11 Indeed, all Israel has transgressed Your law, even by departing that they might not obey Your voice.

"Therefore the curse has been poured upon us, and the oath that is written in the Law of Moses the servant of God, because we have sinned against Him. 12 He has confirmed His words, which He had spoken against us and against our judges who judged us, by bringing on us great calamity. For under the whole heaven there has not been done such as has been done to Jerusalem. 13 As it is written in the Law of Moses, great calamity has come on us. Yet we have not sought the favor of the Lord our God so that we might turn from our iniquities and give attention to Your truth. 14 Therefore, the Lord has kept the disaster in store and brought it upon us. For the Lord our God is righteous in all His works which He does, but we have not obeyed His voice.

15 "Now, O Lord our God, who brought Your people out of the land of Egypt with a mighty hand, and made Yourself a name, even to this day, we have sinned, we have done wickedly. 16 O Lord, according to all Your righteousness, I beseech You, let Your anger and Your fury be turned away from Your city Jerusalem, Your holy mountain, because for our sins and for the iniquities of our fathers, Jerusalem and Your people have become a reproach to all who are around us.

17 "Now therefore, O God, hear the prayer of Your servant and his supplications, and for Your sake, O Lord, cause Your face to shine upon Your sanctuary, which is desolate. 18 O my God, incline Your ear and hear. Open Your eyes and look at our desolations and the city which is called by Your name, for we do not present our supplications before You for our righteousness, but for Your great mercies. 19 O Lord, hear! O Lord, forgive! O Lord, listen and act! Do not defer, for Your own sake, O my God. For Your city and Your people are called by Your name."

The Seventy Weeks

20 While I was speaking and praying and confessing my sin and the sin of my people Israel, and presenting my supplication before the Lord my God for the holy mountain of my God, 21 indeed, while I was speaking in prayer, the man Gabriel, whom I had seen in the vision at the beginning, being caused to fly swiftly, touched me about the time of the evening oblation. 22 He informed me and talked with me, and said, "Daniel, I have now come to give you insight and understanding. 23 At the beginning of your supplications the command went out, and I have come to tell you, for you are greatly beloved. Therefore understand the matter and consider the vision:

24 "Seventy weeks have been determined for your people and upon your holy city, to finish the transgression, and to make an end of sins, and to make atonement for iniquity, and to bring in everlasting righteousness, and to seal up the vision and prophecy, and to anoint the Most Holy *Place.*

25 "Know therefore and understand that from the going forth of the command to restore and to rebuild Jerusalem until the Prince Messiah shall be seven weeks, and sixty-two weeks. It shall be built again, with plaza and moat, even in times of trouble. 26 After the sixty-two weeks Messiah shall be cut off and shall have nothing. And the troops of the prince who shall come shall destroy the city and the sanctuary. The end of it shall come with a flood. And until the end of the war desolations are determined. 27 And he shall make a firm covenant with many for one week. But in the middle of the week he shall cause the sacrifice and the offering to cease. And on the wing of abominations shall come one who makes desolate, until the decreed destruction is poured out on the desolator."

Daniel's Vision of a Man

10 In the third year of Cyrus king of Persia a message was revealed to Daniel, whose name was called Belteshazzar, and the message was true and one of great conflict. And he understood the message and had understanding of the vision.

2 In those days I, Daniel, was mourning three full weeks. 3 I ate no tasty food, no meat or wine entered my mouth, nor did I anoint myself at all until three whole weeks were fulfilled.

4 On the twenty-fourth day of the first month, as I was by the side of the great river which is Tigris, 5 I lifted up my eyes and looked and saw a certain man clothed in linen, whose loins were girded with the fine gold of Uphaz. 6 His body also was like beryl, and his face had the appearance of lightning, and his eyes were like lamps of fire, and his arms and his feet were like the gleam of polished bronze, and the sound of his words like the sound of a tumult.

7 I, Daniel, alone saw the vision, while the men who were with me did not see the vision; but a great quaking fell upon them, so that they fled to hide themselves. 8 Therefore I was left alone and saw this great vision, and there remained no strength in me, and my countenance grew deathly pale, and I retained no strength. 9 Yet I heard the sound of his words; and while I heard the sound of his words, then I was in a deep sleep on my face with my face toward the ground.

Prophecies of Persia and Greece

10 But then a hand touched me, which set me on my knees and on the palms of my hands. 11 He said to me, "O Daniel, a man greatly beloved, understand the words that I speak to you, and stand upright, for I have been sent to you now." And when he had spoken this word to me, I stood trembling.

12 Then he said to me, "Do not be afraid, Daniel. For from the first day that you set your heart to understand this and to humble yourself before your God, your words were heard, and I have come because of your words. 13 But the prince of the kingdom of Persia withstood me for twenty-one days. So Michael, one of the chief princes, came to help me, for I had been left there with the kings of Persia. 14 Now I have come to make you understand what shall befall your people in the latter days. For the vision is yet for many days."

¹⁵ When he had spoken such words to me, I set my face toward the ground, and I became mute. ¹⁶ Then one in the likeness of the sons of men touched my lips. Then I opened my mouth and spoke and said to him who stood before me, "O my lord, because of the vision, sorrows have come upon me, and I have retained no strength. ¹⁷ How can the servant of my lord talk with you, my lord? And as for me, there remains no strength in me now, nor is there any breath left in me."

¹⁸ Then again, the one having the appearance of a man came and touched me, and he strengthened me. ¹⁹ He said, "O man, greatly beloved, do not fear. Peace be unto you. Be strong and courageous!"

When he spoke to me, I was strengthened and said, "Let my lord speak, for you have strengthened me."

²⁰ Then he said, "Do you understand why I have come to you? But now I shall return to fight against the prince of Persia, and when I have gone forth, then truly the prince of Greece will come. ²¹ But I will show you what is inscribed in the Scripture of Truth. Yet there is no one who stands firmly with me against these forces, except Michael your prince.

The Kings of the South and the North

11 "Also, in the first year of Darius the Mede, I, even I, stood to confirm and to strengthen him.

² "And now I will tell you the truth. Truly, there shall stand up yet three kings in Persia, and the fourth shall be far richer than all of them; and by his strength, through his riches, he shall stir up all against the realm of Greece. ³ A mighty king shall stand up who shall rule with great dominion and do according to his will. ⁴ When he shall stand up, his kingdom shall be broken and shall be divided toward the four winds of heaven, but not to his posterity, nor according to his dominion which he ruled. For his kingdom shall be plucked up, even for others besides them.

⁵ "The king of the South shall be strong, as well as one of his officials who shall be strong above him and have dominion. His dominion shall be a great dominion. ⁶ In the end of some years they shall join themselves together. For the king's daughter of the South shall come to the king of the North to make an agreement. But she shall not retain her position of power, and neither he nor his power shall stand. But she shall be given up with those who brought her and with him who fathered her and with him who strengthened her in those times.

⁷ "But out of a branch of her roots shall one stand up in his place, who shall come with an army and shall enter the fortress of the king of the North and shall deal against them and shall prevail. ⁸ And he shall also carry captive into Egypt their gods, with their officials, and with their precious vessels of silver and of gold. And he shall continue more years than the king of the North, ⁹ who will enter the kingdom of the king of the South, but shall return to his own land. ¹⁰ His sons shall wage war and assemble a multitude of armed forces. One shall advance like a flood and pass through, and again shall wage the war as far as his fortress.

¹¹ "The king of the South shall be moved with rage, and shall go out and fight with him, with the king of the North, who shall raise a great multitude; but that multitude shall be given into his *enemy's* hand. ¹² When he has taken away the multitude, his heart shall be lifted up; and he shall cast down many ten thousands, but he shall not be strengthened by it. ¹³ For the king of the North shall return and shall raise a multitude greater than the former, and shall certainly come after certain years with a great army and with much equipment.

¹⁴ "In those times many shall stand up against the king of the South. Also the robbers of your people shall exalt themselves to fulfill the vision, but they shall fall. ¹⁵ Then the king of the North shall come and set up a siege mound and capture a fortified city. And the forces of the South shall not withstand him; neither shall his chosen best troops have strength to resist. ¹⁶ But he who comes against him shall do according to his own will, and none shall stand before him. And he shall stand in the Pleasant Land, which shall be consumed by his hand. ¹⁷ He shall also set his face to enter with the strength of his whole kingdom, bringing with him a proposal of peace which he shall put into effect. And he shall give him the daughter of women to corrupt it. But she shall not stand on his side or be for him. ¹⁸ After this he shall turn his face to the coastlands and shall capture many. But a commander shall put a stop to his reproach against him, and he shall repay him for his reproach. ¹⁹ Then he shall turn his face toward the fortresses of his own land, but shall stumble and fall and not be found any more.

²⁰ "Then one shall stand up in his place who shall send an oppressor in the glory of his kingdom. But within a few days he shall be destroyed, but not in anger or in battle.

²¹ "In his place a vile person shall stand up, to whom they shall not give the honor of the kingdom. But he shall come in peaceably and obtain the kingdom by flatteries. ²² A flood of armies shall be swept away before him and be broken, and the prince of the covenant as well. ²³ After the league *is* made with him, he shall work deceitfully, and he shall come up and shall become strong with a small force of people. ²⁴ He shall enter peaceably even upon the richest places of the realm. And he shall do that which his fathers have not done, nor his fathers' fathers. He shall distribute among them the plunder and spoil and riches. And he shall plan his devices against the strongholds, but only for a time.

²⁵ "He shall stir up his power and his courage against the king of the South with a great army. And the king of the South shall be stirred up to battle with a very great and mighty army. But he shall not stand, for schemes shall be devised against him. ²⁶ Indeed, those who eat his choice food shall destroy him, and his army shall overflow, and many shall fall down slain. ²⁷ As for both of these kings, their hearts shall plan on mischief, and they shall speak lies to one another at one table. But it shall not prosper, for the end shall yet be at the appointed time. ²⁸ While turning back to his land with great wealth, his heart shall be against the holy covenant. He shall *wage war* and turn back to his own land.

Blasphemies of the Northern King

²⁹ "At the appointed time he shall return and come into the south, but this latter time shall not be as the former. ³⁰ For the ships of Kittim shall come against him. Therefore he shall be grieved and return and have indignation against the holy covenant and take action. He shall even return and show regard to those who forsake the holy covenant.

³¹ "His armies shall rise up and desecrate the sanctuary fortress. They shall abolish the daily sacrifice and set up the abomination that makes desolate. ³² By flatteries he will corrupt those who act wickedly toward the covenant. But the people who know their God will be strong and take action.

³³ "The wise among the people shall instruct many. Yet for many days they shall fall by the sword and by flame, by captivity and by destruction. ³⁴ Now when they fall, they shall be given a little help. But many shall cleave to them with flatteries. ³⁵ Some of the wise will fall, so that they may be purged, purified, and made white, until the time of the end, for it is still for the appointed time.

³⁶ "The king shall do according to his will. And he shall exalt himself, and magnify himself above every god, and shall speak blasphemous things against the God of gods, and shall prosper until the indignation is accomplished. For that which is determined shall be done. ³⁷ He shall regard neither the gods of his fathers, nor the desire of women, nor regard any god; for he shall magnify himself above them all. ³⁸ But instead he shall honor the god of forces, a god whom his fathers did not know. He shall honor him with gold and silver, and with precious stones, and pleasant things. ³⁹ Thus he shall do in the strongest of fortresses with a foreign god. He shall give great honor to those who acknowledge him, and shall cause them to rule over the many and shall divide the land for gain.

Conquests of the Northern King

⁴⁰ "At the time of the end the king of the South shall push at him. But the king of the North shall come against him like a whirlwind, with chariots and with horsemen and with many ships. And he shall enter the countries and shall overflow them and pass over. ⁴¹ He shall enter also the Pleasant Land, and many *countries* shall be overthrown. But these shall escape out of his hand, even Edom, and Moab, and the chief of the sons of Ammon. ⁴² Then he shall stretch out his hand against the countries, and the land of Egypt shall not escape. ⁴³ But he shall have power over the hidden treasures of gold and of silver, and over all the precious things of Egypt. And the Libyans and the Ethiopians shall be at his steps. ⁴⁴ But reports from the east and from the north shall trouble him. Therefore he shall go out with great fury to destroy

and annihilate many. ⁴⁵ He shall pitch the tabernacles of his palace between the seas in the beautiful holy mountain. Yet he shall come to his end, and no one shall help him.

The Prophecy of the End Times

12 "And at that time Michael shall stand up, the great prince who stands *guard* over the sons of your people. And there shall be a time of trouble such as never was since there was a nation even to that time. And at that time your people shall be delivered, everyone who shall be found written in the book. ² Many of those who sleep in the dust of the earth shall awake, some to everlasting life, but others to shame and everlasting contempt. ³ Those who are wise shall shine as the brightness of the expanse of heaven, and those who turn the many to righteousness as the stars forever and ever. ⁴ But you, Daniel, shut up the words and seal the book until the time of the end. Many shall run to and fro, and knowledge shall increase."

⁵ Then I, Daniel, looked, and there before me stood two others, the one on this side of the bank of the river, and the other on that side of the bank of the river. ⁶ One said to the man clothed in linen, who was above the water of the river, "How long shall it be to the end of these wonders?"

⁷ And I heard the man clothed in linen, who was over the water of the river, when he held up his right hand and his left hand to heaven, and swore by Him who lives forever that it would be for a time, times, and half a time. ^I And when they finish shattering the power of the holy people, all these things shall be finished.

⁸ As for me, I heard, but I could not understand. So I said, "My lord, what shall be the result of these things?"

⁹ And he said, "Go your way, Daniel. For these words are closed up and sealed until the time of the end. ¹⁰ Many shall be purified and made white and tried. But the wicked shall do wickedly, and none of the wicked shall understand, but the wise shall understand.

¹¹ "From the time that the daily sacrifice shall be taken away and the abomination that makes desolate set up, there shall be one thousand two hundred and ninety days. ¹² Blessed is he who waits and comes to the one thousand three hundred and thirty-five days.

¹³ "But as for you, go your way until the end. Then you shall rest and rise *again* for your lot at the end of the age."

HOSEA

1 The word of the Lord that came to Hosea son of Beeri, in the days of Uzziah, Jotham, Ahaz, and Hezekiah, kings of Judah, and in the days of Jeroboam the son of Joash, king of Israel.

Hosea's Wife and Children

² When the Lord first spoke by Hosea, the Lord said to Hosea: "Go, take for yourself a wife of harlotry and children of harlotry, for the land has committed great harlotry, departing from the Lord." ³ So he went and took Gomer the daughter of Diblaim as a wife. She conceived, and bore him a son.

⁴ The Lord said to him: "Call his name Jezreel,² for in a little while, I will punish the house of Jehu for the blood of Jezreel, and will bring to an end the kingdom of the house of Israel. ⁵ On that day, I will break the bow of Israel in the Valley of Jezreel."

⁶ Then Gomer conceived again, and bore a daughter. And the Lord said to Hosea: "Call her name Lo-Ruhamah,³ for I will no longer have mercy upon the house of Israel but will utterly sweep them away. ⁷ But I will have mercy upon the house of Judah, and will save them by the Lord their God, and will not save them by bow, or by sword, or by battle, or by horses, or by horsemen."

⁸ When Gomer had weaned Lo-Ruhamah, she conceived, and bore a son. ⁹ Then the Lord said: "Call his name Lo-Ammi,⁴ for you are not My people, and I am not your God."

¹⁰ Yet the number of the children of Israel will be as the sand of the sea, which cannot be measured nor numbered. And in the place where it was said to them, "You are not My people," there it will be said to them, "You are the children of the living God." ¹¹ Then will the Judahites and the children of Israel be gathered together, and appoint themselves one head, and they will come up out of the land, for great will be the day of Jezreel.

2 Say to your brothers, Ammi,⁵ and to your sisters, Ruhamah.⁶

Israel's Unfaithfulness Punished

² Plead with your mother, plead—
for she is not My wife,
and am I not her husband—
that she put away her harlotry from her face,
and her adultery from between her breasts,

³ lest I strip her naked
and leave her as in the day that she was born,
and turn her into a wilderness,
and turn her into a dry land,
and kill her with thirst.
⁴ I will not have mercy upon her children,
for they are children of harlotry.
⁵ For their mother has played the whore.
She that conceived them has acted shamefully.
For she said, "I will pursue my lovers,
who provide my bread and my water,
my wool and my flax, my oil and my drink."
⁶ Therefore, behold, I will hedge up your way with thorns,
and make a wall, so that she will not find her paths.
⁷ She will pursue her lovers, but she will not reach them;
and she will seek them but will not find them.
Then she will say,
"I will go and return to my first husband,
for it was better for me then than now."
⁸ But she did not know that it was I who provided her
the grain, the wine, and the oil,
and multiplied her silver and gold
that they used for Baal.

⁹ Therefore I will take back My grain in its time
and My wine in its season,
and I will recover My wool and My flax,
given to cover her nakedness.
¹⁰ Therefore I will uncover her shame
in the sight of her lovers,
and no one will deliver her from My hand.
¹¹ I will also bring to an end all her joy,
her *annual* feasts, her New Moons,
and her Sabbaths, and all her solemn
assemblies.
¹² I will destroy her vines and her fig trees,
of which she has said, "These are my rewards
that my lovers have given me."

1 7 Or a year, two years, and half a year. 2 4 That is, May God make fertile. 3 6 That is, Not pitied. 4 9 That is, Not My people.
5 1 That is, My people. 6 1 That is, Pitied.

I will make them a forest,
    and the beasts of the field will eat them.
[13] I will punish her for the days of the Baals,
    when she burned incense to them
and adorned herself with her earrings and her jewelry,
    and pursued her lovers,
    but forgot Me,
    declares the LORD.

God's Mercy on Israel

[14] Therefore, I will allure her,
    and bring her into the wilderness,
    and speak tenderly to her.
[15] From there, I will give her vineyards to her,
    and the Valley of Achor as a door of hope.
She will respond there as in the days of her youth,
    and as in the day when she came up out of the land of Egypt.

[16] On that day, declares the LORD,
    you will call Me, "My husband,"
    and will no longer call Me, "My Baal."[1]
[17] I will remove the names of the Baals from her mouth,
    and they will no longer be remembered by their name.
[18] On that day, I will make a covenant for them
    with the beasts of the field, with the fowls of heaven,
    and with the creeping things of the ground.
I will break the bow and the sword and the battle
    from the earth,
    and will make them to lie down safely.
[19] I will take you for My wife forever.
    I will take you for My wife in righteousness and in justice,
    in mercy and in compassion.
[20] I will take you for My wife in faithfulness,
    and you will know the LORD.

[21] On that day I will answer,
    declares the LORD;
I will answer the heavens,
    and they will answer the earth.
[22] The earth will answer the grain,
    the wine, and the oil;
    and they will answer Jezreel.
[23] Then I will sow her for Myself in the earth.
    I will have mercy upon Lo-Ruhamah,
and I will say to Lo-Ammi, "You are My people,"
    and they will say, "You are my God."

Hosea Redeems His Wife

3 Then the LORD said to me, "Go, again, love a woman who is loved by a lover and is committing adultery, just as the LORD loves the children of Israel, who look to other gods and love raisin cakes."
[2] So I purchased her for myself for fifteen shekels of silver, and for a homer of barley, and a half homer of barley. [3] Then I said to her, "You will remain with me many days. You will not play the whore, and you will not belong to *another* man. And also I *will be* with you."
[4] For the children of Israel will remain many days without a king and without a prince, without a sacrifice and without a standing stone, and without an ephod and teraphim. [5] Afterward the children of Israel will return and seek the LORD their God and David their king. They will come in fear to the LORD and to His goodness in the latter days.

God Accuses Israel

4 Hear the word of the LORD, O children of Israel,
    for the LORD has a dispute
    with the inhabitants of the land:
There is no truth or mercy,
    and no knowledge of God in the land.

[2] Swearing, lying, and killing,
    and stealing and adultery
break out,
    and bloodshed follows bloodshed.
[3] Therefore the land dries up,
    and everyone who lives in it withers
with the beasts of the field
    and the birds of the sky;
    even the fish of the sea disappear.

[4] Yet let no one contend,
    and let none reprove another,
for your people are like those
    that contend with a priest.[2]
[5] You will stumble in the day,
    and the prophet also will stumble with you in the night,
    and I will destroy your mother.
[6]   My people are destroyed for lack of knowledge.

Because you have rejected knowledge,
    I will reject you from being My priest.
And because you have forgotten the law of your God,
    I will also forget your children.
[7] As they increased, so they sinned against Me.
    I will change[3] their glory[4] into shame.
[8] They feed upon the sin of My people,
    and they are greedy for their iniquity.
[9] It will be like people, like priest.
    I will punish them for their ways
    and reward them for their deeds.

[10] They will eat, but not be satisfied;
    they will play the whore, but not multiply,
because they have forsaken the LORD
    by devoting themselves to [11]harlotry;
wine and new wine
    take away understanding.

The Idolatry of Israel

[12] My people seek counsel from their wood,
    and their staff informs them.
For the spirit of harlotry has led them astray,
    and they have played the whore in defiance of their God.
[13] They sacrifice upon the tops of the mountains,
    and burn incense upon the hills
under oak, poplar, and elm
    because their shade is good.
Therefore your daughters play the whore,
    and your daughters-in-law commit adultery.

[14] I will not punish your daughters
    when they play the whore,
nor your daughters-in-law
    when they commit adultery.
For the men separate themselves with whores,
    and they sacrifice with cult prostitutes.
    A people without understanding will come to ruin.

[15] Though you play the whore, O Israel,
    do not let Judah offend.

Do not come to Gilgal,
    or go up to Beth Aven,
    and do not swear, "As the LORD lives."
[16] Like a stubborn heifer,
    Israel is stubborn.
Now will the LORD feed them
    like a lamb in a wide pasture?
[17] Ephraim is joined to idols;
    let him alone.

---

[1] 16 Or *My master.*   [2] 4 Meaning of Heb. uncertain.   [3] 7 MT; Ancient Heb. tradition *They will change.*   [4] 7 MT; Ancient Heb. tradition *My glory.*

18 Their drink has soured,
    they have played the whore continually.
    Her rulers dearly love shame.
19 A wind has wrapped her in its wings,
    and they will be ashamed because of their sacrifices.

Judgment Against Israel and Judah

5 Hear this, O priests!
    Pay attention, O house of Israel!
Listen, O house of the king!
    For the judgment is for you,
because you have been a snare at Mizpah
    and a net spread over Tabor,
2 and a pit dug deep in Shittim;
    but I will discipline them all.
3 I know Ephraim,
    and Israel is not hidden from Me;
for now, O Ephraim, you have played the whore.
    Israel is defiled.

4 Their deeds do not allow them
    to return to their God;
for a spirit of harlotry is in their midst,
    and they do not know the LORD.
5 The pride of Israel testifies against him.
    Israel and Ephraim stumble in their iniquity.
    Judah also stumbles with them.
6 With their flocks and their herds they will go
    to seek the LORD,
but they will not find Him.
    He has withdrawn from them.
7 They have dealt faithlessly with the LORD,
    for they have given birth to illegitimate children.
Now the New Moon will devour them
    along with their portion.

War, Wrath, and Repentance

8 Blow the horn in Gibeah,
    and the trumpet in Ramah.
Cry aloud at Beth Aven,
    "*Look* behind you, O Benjamin!"[1]
9 Ephraim will become desolate
    in the day of punishment.
Among the tribes of Israel
    I make known that which is sure.
10 The princes of Judah have become
    like those who remove a boundary marker.
Upon them I will pour out
    My wrath like water.
11 Ephraim is oppressed
    and broken in judgment,
    because he eagerly followed after vanity.
12 Therefore I will be like pus to Ephraim
    and like rottenness to the house of Judah.

13 When Ephraim saw his sickness
    and Judah saw his wound,
then Ephraim went to Assyria,
    and sent to King Jareb.[2]
Yet he cannot cure you
    or heal your wound.
14 For I will be like a lion to Ephraim
    and like a young lion to the house of Judah.
I, Myself, will tear and go away.
    I will carry off, and no one will rescue.
15 I will again return to My place
    until they acknowledge their offense
and seek My face.
    In their affliction they will earnestly seek Me.

A Call to Repentance

6 Come, let us return to the LORD,
    for He has torn,
    and He will heal us.
He has struck,
    and He will bind us up.
2 After two days He will revive us.
    On the third day He will raise us up,
    that we may live before Him.
3 Let us know, let us press on to know the LORD.
    His appearance is as sure as the dawn.
He will come to us like the rain;
    like the spring rains He will water the earth.

Impenitence of Israel and Judah

4 What shall I do to you, O Ephraim?
    What shall I do to you, O Judah?
Your faithfulness is like a morning cloud,
    and like the early dew it goes away.
5 Therefore I have hewn them by the prophets.
    I have killed them by the words of My mouth,
    and My[3] judgments go forth like light.
6 For I desired mercy, and not sacrifice,
    and the knowledge of God more than burnt offerings.
7 But like men[4] they have transgressed the covenant.
    There they dealt faithlessly with Me.
8 Gilead is a city of evildoers,
    polluted with blood.
9 As robbers lie in wait for someone,
    so a company of priests
murder on the way to Shechem.
    They commit a shameful deed.
10 I have seen a horrible thing
    in the house of Israel.
The harlotry of Ephraim is there;
    Israel is defiled.

11 Also, O Judah, a harvest is appointed for you,
    when I restore the fortunes of My people.

7 When I would heal Israel,
    the iniquity of Ephraim is revealed,
    and the wickedness of Samaria.
For they deal deceitfully;
    the thief breaks in;
    the robbers raid outside,
2 but they did not consider in their hearts
    that I remember all their wickedness.
Now their own deeds surround them;
    they are before My face.

Corrupt and Disloyal Politics

3 They make the king glad with their wickedness,
    and the princes with their lies.
4 They are all adulterers,
    like an oven heated by a baker,
who ceases stirring *the fire*
    after kneading the dough until it is leavened.
5 On the day of our king the princes made *him* sick
    from the heat of wine.
He stretched out his hand with scorners.
6 For they are kindled[5] like an oven.
    Their heart burns within them;[6]
their anger smolders[7] all night;
    in the morning it blazes like a flaming fire.
7 They are all hot as an oven,
    and they devour their judges.
All their kings have fallen,
    and none of them calls to Me.

---

18 Or *"After you, O Benjamin!"*   2 13 Or *the great king.*   3 5 Gk. Syr.: Heb. *Your.*   4 7 Or *like/at Adam.*   5 6 Gk. Syr.: Heb. *brought near.*
6 6 Or *while they lie in wait.*   7 6 Or *Their baker sleeps.*

[8] Ephraim mixes himself with the people.
    Ephraim is a cake not turned.
[9] Foreigners devour his strength,
    but he does not know it.
Gray hairs are here and there upon him,
    but he does not know it.
[10] The pride of Israel testifies against him,
    but they do not return to the Lord their God,
    nor seek Him for all this.

[11] Ephraim is like a dove,
    silly and without sense;
they call to Egypt,
    they go to Assyria.
[12] Wherever they go, I will spread My net over them;
    I will bring them down like the birds of the sky;
I will discipline them according to
    the report to their congregation.
[13] Woe to them,
    for they have fled from Me!
Destruction to them,
    for they have rebelled against Me!
Though I would redeem them,
    yet they speak lies against Me.
[14] They do not cry to Me with their heart
    when they howl on their beds.
They gather together for grain and wine,
    they rebel against Me.
[15] Though I trained and strengthened their arms,
    yet they devise mischief against Me.
[16] They return, *but* not to the Most High.
    They are like a loose bow.
Their princes will fall by the sword
    for the rage of their tongue.
This will be their derision
    in the land of Egypt.

The Apostasy of Israel

8 Set the trumpet to your mouth!
    One like an eagle is on the house of
    the Lord,
because they have transgressed My covenant
    and rebelled against My law.
[2] Israel cries to Me,
    "My God, we know You."
[3] Israel has cast off the good;
    the enemy will pursue him.
[4] They set up kings, but not through Me;
    they made princes, but I did not know it.
With their silver and gold,
    they made idols,
    so that they will be cut off.
[5] Your calf, O Samaria, is rejected!
    My anger is kindled against them.
How long will they be incapable of innocence?
[6] For it is from Israel;
    a craftsman made it,
    and it is not God!
The calf of Samaria
    will be broken to pieces.

[7] For they sow the wind,
    and they will reap the whirlwind.
The standing grain has no head
    and will yield no flour.
If it were to yield,
    foreigners would swallow it up.
[8] Israel is swallowed up.
    Now they are among the nations
    as a vessel in which there is no pleasure.

[9] For they have gone up to Assyria
    like a wild donkey alone by itself;
    Ephraim has hired lovers.
[10] Though they hire among the nations,
    I will now gather them.
They will begin to diminish due to the burden
    of the king of princes.

[11] Because Ephraim has multiplied altars for sin,
    they have become to him altars for sinning.
[12] I have written for him the great things of My law,
    but they were regarded as a strange thing.
[13] For the sacrifices of My offerings,
    they sacrifice flesh and eat it;
    but the Lord does not accept them.
Now He will remember their iniquity
    and punish their sins.
They will return to Egypt.
[14] Israel has forgotten his Maker
    and built temples,
    and Judah has multiplied fortified cities;
so I will send a fire upon his cities,
    and it will devour his palaces.

The Punishment of Israel

9 Do not rejoice, O Israel!
    Do not exult[1] like the peoples,
for you have played the whore departing from
    your God.
You have loved a prostitute's wages
    on every threshing floor.
[2] The threshing floor and the winepress will not
    feed them,
    and the new wine will fail in her.
[3] They will not dwell in the land of the Lord;
    but Ephraim will return to Egypt,
    and they will eat unclean things in Assyria.
[4] They will not offer wine offerings to the Lord,
    and their sacrifices will not please Him.
Their sacrifices will be like the bread of mourners;
    all who eat of it will be defiled.
For their bread will be only to satisfy their own hunger;
    it will not come into the house of the Lord.

[5] What will you do on the appointed day,
    and on the day of the festival of the Lord?
[6] For indeed they are gone because of destruction.
    Egypt will gather them,
    and Memphis will bury them.
Nettles will possess their pleasant things of silver,
    and thorns will be in their tents.
[7] The days of punishment have come;
    the days of recompense have come.
Israel knows!
The prophet is a fool;
    the man of the spirit is insane,
because of your great iniquity and great hatred.
[8] The watchman of Ephraim is a prophet
    for my God;
yet a fowler's snare is on all his ways,
    and hatred in the house of his God.
[9] They have deeply corrupted themselves
    as in the days of Gibeah.
He will remember their iniquity,
    He will punish their sins.

[10] Like grapes in the wilderness,
    I found Israel.
Like the first fruit on the fig tree in its first season,
    I saw your fathers.

1 Gk.; Heb. to exultation.

But they went to Baal Peor
and consecrated themselves to *a thing of* shame,
and they became an abomination like *the thing* they loved.
[11] As for Ephraim, their glory shall fly away like a bird:
no birth, no pregnancy, no conception!
[12] Though they bring up their children,
I will bereave them until none are left.
Woe to them indeed,
when I depart from them!
[13] Just as I saw Ephraim like Tyre,
planted in a pleasant place,
so now Ephraim will bring out
his children for slaughter.

[14] Give them, O LORD—
what will You give?
Give them a miscarrying womb
and dry breasts.

[15] All their wickedness is in Gilgal,
for there I hated them.
Because of the wickedness of their deeds,
I will drive them out of My house.
I will love them no more.
All their princes are rebels.
[16] Ephraim is stricken,
their root is dried up,
they shall bear no fruit.
Even though they give birth,
I will slay the beloved offspring of their womb.

[17] My God will reject them
because they did not listen to Him,
and they will be wanderers among the nations.

Israel's Sin and Captivity

10 Israel is a fertile vine
that brings forth its fruit.
As his fruit multiplied,
so his altars increased;
as his land prospered,
so he[1] improved *his* pillars.
[2] Their heart is divided;
now they must bear their guilt.
He will break down their altars
and destroy their pillars.

[3] For now they will say,
"We have no king,
because we do not fear the LORD;
and a king, what could he do for us?"
[4] They speak mere words,
swearing falsely
in making a covenant.
Thus judgment springs up like a poisonous plant
in the furrows of the field.
[5] The inhabitants of Samaria fear
because of the calf of Beth Aven.
For its people mourn for it,
and its priests shriek for it,
because its glory has departed from it.
[6] It will be carried to Assyria
as a tribute to King Jareb.[2]
Ephraim shall be put to shame,
and Israel shall be ashamed of his idol.[3]
[7] As for Samaria, her king will perish
like a twig on the water.
[8] The high places of Aven, the sin of Israel,
will be destroyed.

Thorn and thistle will grow
on their altars.
They will say to the mountains, Cover us,
and to the hills, Fall on us.

[9] O Israel, you have sinned since the days of Gibeah.
There they have continued.[4]
Will not the war in Gibeah against evildoers
overtake them?
[10] When I desire, I will punish them.
The nations will be gathered against them
when they are disciplined[5] for their two
transgressions.
[11] Ephraim is a trained heifer
that loves to thresh grain,
but I harnessed her fair neck;
I will make Ephraim pull *a plow*.
Judah will plow;
Jacob shall furrow for himself.
[12] Sow to yourselves righteousness,
reap mercy,
break up your fallow ground;
for it is time to seek the LORD,
until He comes
and rains righteousness upon you.
[13] You have plowed wickedness.
You have reaped iniquity,
and you have eaten the fruit of lies.
Because you have trusted in your power
and in the numbers of your warriors,
[14] therefore a tumult will arise among your people,
and all your fortresses will be destroyed
as Shalman destroyed Beth Arbel in the day of battle;
mothers were dashed to pieces upon *their* children.
[15] So will it be done to you, O Bethel,
because of your great wickedness.
At dawn
the king of Israel will be utterly cut off.

God's Love for Israel

11 When Israel was a child, I loved him,
and out of Egypt I called My son.
[2] As I[6] called them,
so they went from Me.[7]
They sacrificed to the Baals
and burned incense to idols.
[3] I taught Ephraim to walk,
taking them up in My[8] arms,
but they did not know
that I healed them.
[4] I drew them with cords of human kindness,[9]
with bands of love.
I was to them as those who ease the yoke on their neck,[10]
and I bent down and fed them.

[5] He will return[11] to the land of Egypt,
and Assyria will be his king,
because they refused to return *to Me*.
[6] The sword slashes in their cities,
consumes their oracle-priests,
and devours because of their own counsels.
[7] My people are bent on backsliding from Me.
Though they called to the Most High,
none at all exalt Him.

[8] How can I give you up, Ephraim?
How can I hand you over, Israel?
How can I make you like Admah?
How can I treat you like Zeboyim?

---

[1] 1 Heb. *they.* [2] 6 Or *the great king.* [3] 6 Or *counsel.* [4] 9 Or *There they stood.* [5] 10 Gk.; Heb. *bound.* [6] 2 Gk.; Heb. *they.*
[7] 2 Gk.; Heb. *them.* [8] 3 Gk. Syr. Vulg.; Heb. *his.* [9] 4 Heb. *cords of a man.* [10] 4 Or *jaws.* [11] 5 So LXX. Heb. *He not will return.*

My heart churns within Me;
　　My compassion is stirred.
[9] I will not execute the fierceness of My anger;
　　I will not again destroy Ephraim.
For I am God, and not man,
　　the Holy One in your midst,
　　and I will not come in wrath.
[10] They will walk after the LORD,
　　who roars like a lion.
When He roars,
　　His children will come trembling from the west.
[11] They will come trembling
　　like a bird out of Egypt
　　and like a dove from the land of Assyria.
And I will let them dwell in their houses,
　　says the LORD.

God's Charge Against Ephraim
[12] Ephraim has surrounded Me with lies,
　　and the house of Israel with deceit.
But Judah still walks with God,
　　and is faithful to the Holy One.[1]

12
Ephraim feeds on the wind
　　and chases after the east wind all day long.
He multiplies lies and devastation.
They make a covenant with Assyria,
　　and oil is carried to Egypt.

A History of Rebellion
[2] The LORD has a dispute with Judah,
　　and will punish Jacob according to his ways,
　　and repay him according to his doings.
[3] In the womb, he took his brother by the heel,
　　and by his strength he strove with God.
[4] He struggled with the angel, and prevailed;
　　he wept, and sought favor from Him.
He found Him in Bethel,
　　and there He spoke with us.
[5] As for the LORD the God of Hosts,
　　the LORD is the name by which He is invoked!
[6] But as for you, return to your God,
　　hold fast to mercy and justice,
　　and wait on your God continually.

[7] A merchant, in whose hands are deceitful balances,
　　he loves to oppress.
[8] Ephraim said,
　　"Yet I am rich, I have found wealth for myself.
In all my labors, they shall find no offense in me
　　that would be sin."

[9] I am the LORD your God
　　from the land of Egypt.
I will again make you to dwell in tents,
　　as in the days of the appointed feast.
[10] I have spoken by the prophets,
　　and I have multiplied visions,
　　and through the prophets I will bring destruction.[2]

[11] In Gilead there is iniquity;
　　surely they will come to nothing.
In Gilgal they sacrifice bulls,
　　so their altars will be like stone heaps
　　in the furrows of the fields.
[12] Jacob fled to the land of Aram,
　　and Israel served for a wife,
　　and for a wife he kept *sheep*.
[13] By a prophet the LORD brought Israel up from Egypt,
　　and by a prophet he was preserved.
[14] Ephraim provoked Him to anger most bitterly,

so his Lord shall leave his bloodguilt on him
　　and repay him for his reproach.

God's Unrelenting Judgment on Israel

13
When Ephraim spoke, trembling,
　　he was exalted in Israel.
But he incurred guilt through Baal *worship* and he died.
[2] And now they continue sinning
　　and have made a cast image for themselves,
idols of their silver, according to their understanding,
　　all of them the work of craftsmen.
They say of them,
　　"Those who sacrifice[3]
　　are kissing calves!"
[3] Therefore they will be like the morning cloud,
　　or like the early dew that passes away,
like chaff blown off the threshing floor,
　　or like the smoke from a chimney.

[4] Yet I am the LORD your God
　　ever since the land of Egypt.
You know no God but Me,
　　and there is no savior besides Me.
[5] I knew[4] you in the wilderness,
　　in the land of great drought.
[6] When they had pasture, they were satisfied.
　　They were satisfied, and their heart
　　　　was exalted;
　　therefore they forgot Me.
[7] So I will be like a lion to them,
　　like a leopard I will lurk by the path.
[8] I will attack them like a bear bereaved of her cubs,
　　and will tear open their rib cage.
There I will devour them like a lion,
　　as the wild beast would tear them to pieces.

[9] O Israel, you are destroyed,[5]
　　but in Me is your help.
[10] Where now is your king
　　that he may save you in all your cities?
And where are your judges of whom you said,
　　"Give me a king and princes"?
[11] I gave you a king in My anger,
　　and took him away in My wrath.
[12] The iniquity of Ephraim is bound up;
　　his sin is stored up.
[13] The pains of childbirth come for him.
　　He is an unwise son,
for he does not present himself
　　at the opening of the womb.

[14] I will ransom them from the power of Sheol.
　　I will redeem them from Death.
O Death, where are your plagues?
　　O Sheol, where is your sting?

Compassion is hidden from My eyes.
[15] Though he be fruitful among *his* brothers,
　　the east wind will come, a wind of the LORD,
　　rising from the wilderness.
And his spring shall become dry,
　　his fountain shall be dried up.
It shall plunder *his* treasury
　　of every desirable thing.
[16] Samaria will be held guilty,
　　for she has rebelled against her God.
They will fall by the sword,
　　their infants will be dashed to pieces,
　　and their pregnant women will be
　　　　ripped open.

---

[1] 12 Or *holy ones.* [2] 10 Or *speak in parables.* [3] 2 Or *those who offer human sacrifice.* [4] 5 Or *fed.* [5] 9 Heb. *he has destroyed you.*

A Plea for Repentance

14 Return, O Israel, to the LORD your God,
for you have stumbled because of your iniquity.
2 Take words with you
and return to the LORD.
Say to Him,
"Take away all iniquity,
and accept that which is good;
and we will offer the fruit[1] of our lips!
3 Assyria will not save us,
we will not ride on horses.
We will no longer say, 'Our God,'
to the work of our hands.
In You the orphan finds mercy."

4 I will heal their backsliding;
I will love them freely,
for My anger has turned away from him.
5 I will be like the dew to Israel;
he shall grow like the lily

and shall strike his roots
like Lebanon.
6 His branches will spread out,
and his beauty shall be like the olive tree,
and his fragrance like that of Lebanon.
7 Those that dwell under his shadow will return,
they will flourish like the grain
and grow as a vine.
Their fragrance will be like the wine
of Lebanon.
8 O Ephraim, what have I to do with idols?
It is I who answer and look after him.
I am like a green fir tree;
your fruit is found in Me.

9 Whoever is wise, let him understand these things;
whoever prudent, let him know them.
For the ways of the LORD are right,
and the just will walk in them;
but the transgressors stumble in them.

JOEL

1 The word of the LORD, which came to Joel, son of Pethuel.

A Land Laid Waste

2 Hear this, elders,
and give ear, all inhabitants of the land!
Has anything like this happened in your days,
or in the days of your fathers?
3 Tell it to your children,
and let your children tell their children,
and let their children tell another
generation.
4 What the fledging locust left,
the adult locust has eaten;
what the adult locust left,
the larval locust has eaten;
what the larval locust left,
the hopper locust has eaten.

5 Awaken, drunkards, and weep!
Wail, all wine-drinkers,
because the sweet wine
has been cut off from your lips.
6 For a nation powerful and innumerable
has invaded my land;
its teeth are like the teeth of a lion,
like the fangs of a lioness.
7 It has despoiled my vine,
and splintered my fig tree;
it has stripped off its bark
and cast it away,
leaving its branches white.

8 Lament like a virgin wearing sackcloth
for the husband of her youth.
9 The grain offering and the drink offering
are cut off from the house of the LORD;
the priests mourn, who are
ministers to the LORD.

10 The field is ravaged,
the ground mourns;
for the grain is ruined,
the new wine is dried up,
and the oil dwindles.

11 Despair, fieldworkers;
wail, vinedressers,
for the wheat and the barley,
because the harvest of the field has perished.
12 The vine is dried up,
and the fig tree is withered;
pomegranate, palm, and apple—
all the trees of the field are dry;
surely joy has withered away
from the sons of men.

A Call to Repentance

13 Put on sackcloth and lament, O priests;
wail, ministers of the altar.
Come, spend the night in sackcloth,
ministers of my God,
because the grain offering and the drink offering
are withheld from the house of your God.
14 Consecrate a fast,
call a sacred assembly,
assemble the elders
and all the inhabitants of the land
to the house of the LORD your God,
and cry out to the LORD.

15 Alas, for the day!
For the day of the LORD is near,
and like devastation from the Almighty it comes.

16 Has not the food been cut off
before our eyes,
joy and gladness

---

1 2 Gk. Syr.; Heb. *bulls.*

from the house of our God?

17 The seeds have shriveled
under their shovels,
the storehouses have been deserted;
the granaries have been torn down,
because the grain has dried up.
18 How the beasts groan!
The herds of cattle are confused,
because they have no pasture;
even the flocks of sheep suffer.

19 To You, O Lord, I call,
because fire has devoured the wild pastures,
and flame has burned all the trees of the field.
20 Even the beasts of the field long for You,
because the streams of water have dried up,
and fire has devoured the wild pastures.

The Day of the Lord

2 Blow the ram's horn in Zion,
sound the alarm on My holy mountain!

All the inhabitants of the earth will tremble,
because the day of the Lord has come,
because it is near—
2 a day of darkness and gloom,
a day of clouds and thick darkness.
Like blackness spreading over the mountain,
a great and mighty army comes,
such as was never before,
and will never be again,
even through the years of all generations.

3 Before them fire devours,
and behind them a flame blazes;
the land is like the garden of Eden before them,
but behind them a desolate wasteland,
and nothing escapes them.
4 They have the appearance of horses,
and like cavalry they run.
5 As with the sound of chariots,
they leap on the mountaintops,
as with the sound of a flame of fire consuming stubble,
as a mighty army arrayed for war.

6 Before them, peoples are tormented;
every face turns pale.
7 Like mighty men they run,
like men of war they scale a wall;
each marches on his way,
they do not swerve from their paths.
8 They do not jostle one another;
each marches in his track.
Through the weapons they plunge;
they do not break rank.
9 They rush on the city,
they run on the wall;
they climb up into the houses,
they enter through the windows like thieves.

10 Before them the earth quakes,
the heavens shake;
the sun and moon darken,
and the stars withdraw their radiance.
11 The Lord has sounded His voice
before His army,
for His camp is exceedingly great;
mighty is the one who accomplishes
His word.
For great is the day of the Lord,
and very awe-inspiring.
Who can endure it?

Return to the Lord
12 Yet even now, declares the Lord,
return to Me with all your heart,
and with fasting and with weeping and
with mourning.

13 Rend your heart,
and not your garments;
return to the Lord your God,
for He is gracious and merciful,
slow to anger, and abounding in steadfast love;
and He relents from punishing.
14 Who knows? He might turn aside and relent,
and He might leave behind a blessing—
a grain offering and a food offering
for the Lord your God.

15 Blow the ram's horn in Zion,
consecrate a fast,
call a sacred assembly.
16 Gather the people,
consecrate the congregation,
assemble the elders,
gather the children
and those nursing at the breast;
let the bridegroom leave his room
and the bride her chamber.
17 Between the temple porch and the altar,
let the priests, ministers of the Lord, weep
and say,
"Have pity upon Your people,
and do not make Your heritage a disgrace,
a mockery among the nations.
Why should they say among the peoples,
'Where is their God?' "

Rescue and Restitution
18 Then the Lord became jealous for His land
and took pity upon His people.

19 So the Lord answered and said to His people,

Here! I am sending you grain, new wine,
and oil,
and you will be satisfied,
and I will never again make you
a disgrace among the nations.

20 I will remove the northerner far from you,
and I will banish him to a dry and desolate land,
those in front to the eastern sea,
and those in back to the western sea,
and his stink will rise,
and his stench will rise,
for he has done great things.

21 Do not be afraid, land;
exult and rejoice,
for the Lord has done great things!
22 Do not be afraid, beasts of the field,
because the wild pastures flourish,
because the tree bears its fruit;
the fig tree and the vine yield their abundance.
23 And children of Zion, exult
and rejoice in the Lord your God,
because He has given to you
the early rain for vindication.
He showers down rains for you,
the early rain and the latter rain, as before.
24 Then the threshing floors will be filled with grain,
and the vats will overflow with new wine
and oil.

25 And I will compensate you for the years the locusts
         have eaten—
    the larval locust, the hopper locust,
    and the fledging locust—
    My great army which I sent against you.
26 You will eat abundantly and be satisfied,
    and you will praise the name of the LORD your God,
    who has worked wonders for you;
    and My people will never again be shamed.
27 Then you will know that I am in the midst of Israel,
    that I am the LORD your God,
    and that there is no other.
And My people will never again be shamed.

The Outpouring of the Spirit

28 And it will be that, afterwards,
    I will pour out My Spirit on all flesh;
    then your sons and your daughters will prophesy,
      your old men will dream dreams,
      and your young men will see visions.
29 Even on the menservants and maidservants
    in those days I will pour out My Spirit.
30 Then I will work wonders in the heavens
      and the earth—
      blood and fire and columns of smoke.
31 The sun will be turned to darkness,
      and the moon to blood,
      before the great and awe-inspiring day of the LORD comes.
32 And it will be that everyone
    who calls on the name of the LORD will be saved.
For on Mount Zion and in Jerusalem
    there will be deliverance,
    as the LORD has said,
and among the survivors
    whom the LORD calls.

Judging the Nations

3 In those days and at that time,
    when I restore the fortunes of Judah and Jerusalem,
2 I will gather all the nations,
    and bring them down to the Valley of Jehoshaphat.
I will enter into judgment with them there
    regarding My people and My heritage Israel,
    whom they have scattered among the nations;
    they have also divided up My land.
3 They have cast lots for My people,
    and have traded a boy for a prostitute;
they have sold a girl for wine,
    that they might drink.

4 Also, what are you to Me, Tyre and Sidon and all the regions of Philistia? Are you repaying Me for something? If you are repaying Me, I will return your payment swiftly and speedily on your head. 5 For you have taken My silver and My gold, and you have carried off My finest treasures to your temples. 6 You have sold the people of Judah and Jerusalem to the Greeks in order to remove them far from their border.
    7 I am about to rouse them from the place to which you have sold them, and I will return your payment on your head. 8 I will sell your sons and your daughters into the hand of the people of Judah, and

they will sell them to the Sabeans—to a distant nation, for the LORD has spoken.

9 Proclaim this among the nations:
    Consecrate a war!
Stir up the mighty men!
    Let all the men of war draw near and rise.
10 Beat your plowshares into swords
    and your pruning hooks into spears;
let the weakling say,
    "I am a warrior!"
11 Hurry and come, all you surrounding nations,
    and gather there.

Bring down Your warriors, O LORD.

12 Let the nations be roused,
    and go up to the Valley of Jehoshaphat;
for there I will sit
    to judge all the surrounding nations.
13 Swing the sickle,
    for the harvest is ripe.
Come and tread,
    for the winepress is full.
    The wine vats overflow,
because their evil is great.

14 Multitudes, multitudes,
    in the valley of decision!
For the day of the LORD is near
    in the valley of the decision.
15 The sun and moon darken,
    and the stars withdraw their radiance.
16 The LORD roars from Zion,
    and sounds His voice from Jerusalem,
    and heaven and earth quake.
But the LORD is a refuge for His people,
    and a stronghold for the children of Israel.

The LORD Dwells in Zion

17 Then you will know that I am the LORD your God,
    who dwells in Zion, My holy mountain.
And Jerusalem will be holy,
    and invaders will never again pass through her.

18 And it will be that in that day the mountains will drip sweet wine,
    and the hills will flow with milk,
    and all the streambeds of Judah will flow with water;
a spring will proceed from the house of the LORD
    and will water the Valley of Shittim.
19 Egypt will become a desolation,
    and Edom a desolate wasteland,
because of the violence done to the people of Judah—
    they shed innocent blood in their land.
20 But Judah will be inhabited forever,
    and Jerusalem for generations and generations.
21 I will avenge their blood,
    which I have not yet avenged.

The LORD dwells in Zion!

AMOS

Judgment Against Israel's Neighbors

1 The words of Amos, who was among the shepherds of Tekoa, which he saw concerning Israel in the days of Uzziah king of Judah and in the days of Jeroboam the son of Joash king of Israel two years before the earthquake.

2 He said:

The LORD roars from Zion
and utters His voice from Jerusalem;
the pastures of the shepherds languish,
the top of Carmel withers.

3 Thus says the LORD:

For three transgressions of Damascus,
and for four, I will not revoke the punishment,
because they have threshed Gilead
with threshing sledges of iron.
4 So I will send fire against the house of Hazael,
and it will devour the fortresses of Ben-Hadad.
5 I will break the gate bar of Damascus;
from the Valley of Aven I will cut off the one enthroned,
and from Beth Eden the one who holds the scepter.
The people of Aram will go into captivity to Kir,
says the LORD.

6 Thus says the LORD:

For three transgressions of Gaza,
and for four, I will not revoke the punishment,
because they carried away into exile an entire deportation,
to deliver them up to Edom.
7 So I will send fire against the wall of Gaza,
and it will devour its fortresses.
8 From Ashdod I will cut off the one enthroned
and from Ashkelon the one who holds the scepter.
I will turn My hand against Ekron,
and the remnant of the Philistines will perish,
says the Lord GOD.

9 Thus says the LORD:

For three transgressions of Tyre,
and for four, I will not revoke the punishment,
because they delivered up an entire deportation to Edom,
and did not remember the covenant of kinship.
10 So I will send fire against the wall of Tyre,
and it will devour its fortresses.

11 Thus says the LORD:

For three transgressions of Edom,
and for four, I will not revoke the punishment,
because he pursued his brother with the sword,
and repressed all pity;
his anger tore with no ceasing,
and his wrath persisted with no end.
12 So I will send fire against Teman,
and it will devour the fortresses of Bozrah.

13 Thus says the LORD:

For three transgressions of the Ammonites,
and for four, I will not revoke the punishment,
because they ripped open the pregnant women of Gilead,
in order to enlarge their border.
14 So I will kindle a fire against the wall of Rabbah,
and it will devour its fortresses,

with a war cry on the day of battle,
with a tempest on the day of the whirlwind.
15 Their king shall go into captivity,
he and his princes together,
says the LORD.

2 Thus says the LORD:

For three transgressions of Moab,
and for four, I will not revoke the punishment,
because he burned to lime
the bones of the king of Edom.
2 So I will send fire against Moab,
and it will devour the fortresses of Kerioth;
Moab will die in uproar,
with a war cry and the alarm of the trumpet.
3 I will cut off the ruler from its midst,
and will slay all its princes with him,
says the LORD.

Judgment Against Judah

4 Thus says the LORD:

For three transgressions of Judah,
and for four, I will not revoke the punishment,
because they have rejected the law of the LORD,
and have not kept His commandments.
The lies which their fathers followed
have led them astray.
5 So I will send fire against Judah,
and it will devour the fortresses of Jerusalem.

Judgment Against Israel

6 Thus says the LORD:

For three transgressions of Israel,
and for four, I will not revoke the punishment,
because they sell the righteous for silver,
and the poor for a pair of sandals.
7 They trample the head of the poor
into the dust of the earth,
and push the oppressed out of the way.
A man and his father go in to the same woman,
profaning My holy name.
8 They recline by every altar
on garments taken in pledge,
and in the house of their gods
they drink the wine from those who have been fined.

9 Yet it was I who destroyed the Amorite before them,
whose height was like the height of the cedars.
He was strong as the oaks,
yet I destroyed his fruit above
and his roots below.

10 It was I who brought you up from the land of Egypt,
and led you forty years through the wilderness,
to possess the land of the Amorite.

11 I raised up some of your sons as prophets,
and some of your young men as Nazirites.
Is it not so, O children of Israel?
says the LORD.
12 But you made the Nazirites drink wine,
and commanded the prophets, saying, "Do not prophesy."

13 Indeed I will slow you down,
as a wagon is slowed that is full of sheaves.

14 Flight will perish from the swift,
  the strong will not retain his strength,
  nor will the warrior save his life.
15 The bowman will not stand firm,
  the swift-footed will not escape,
  nor will the horseman save his life.
16 He that is courageous among the warriors
  will flee away naked on that day,
  says the LORD.

First Pronouncement of Punishment

3 Hear this word that the LORD has spoken against you, O children of Israel, against the whole family I brought up from the land of Egypt, saying:

2 You alone have I known
  of all the families of the earth;
 therefore I will punish you
  for all your iniquities.

3 Do two people walk together,
  if they have not agreed?
4 Does a lion roar in the forest,
  if it has no prey?
 Does a young lion cry out from its den,
  if it has not caught something?
5 Does a bird fall into a trap on the ground,
  if there was no snare for it?
 Does a trap spring up from the ground,
  if it has not caught something?
6 If the trumpet blasts in the city,
  are not the people frightened?
 If there is disaster against a city,
  is it not the LORD who has done it?

7 Surely the Lord GOD does nothing
  without revealing His purpose
  to His servants the prophets.

8 The lion has roared;
  who will not fear?
 The Lord GOD has spoken;
  who can but prophesy?

9 Proclaim to the fortresses in Ashdod,
  and the fortresses in the land of Egypt, and say:
 "Assemble yourselves on the mountains of Samaria,
  and see the great disorders within her,
  and the oppression in her midst."

10 They do not know how to do right, says the LORD,
  storing up violence and destruction in their
   fortresses.

11 Therefore thus says the Lord GOD:

An enemy will surround your land;
 he will tear down your defenses,
 and your fortresses will be plundered.

12 Thus says the LORD:

As the shepherd rescues out of the mouth of
  the lion
 a pair of legs or a piece of an ear,
 so will the children of Israel be rescued,
those who live in Samaria,
 with the corner of a bed
 or a piece of a couch.

13 Hear and testify against the house of Jacob, says the Lord GOD, the God of Hosts:

14 Surely on the day I punish the transgressions of Israel,
  I will also punish the altars of Bethel;
 the horns of the altar will be cut off
  and fall to the ground.
15 I will destroy the winter house
  as well as the summer house,
 and the houses of ivory will perish;
  the great houses will come to an end,
  says the LORD.

Second Pronouncement of Punishment

4 Hear this word, you cows of Bashan, who are on the
  mountain of Samaria,
 who oppress the poor and crush the needy,
 who say to their husbands, "Bring us something
  to drink!"
2 The Lord GOD has sworn by His holiness:
  Indeed the days are coming upon you
 when they will take you away with hooks,
  the last one of you with fishhooks.
3 You will go out through breached walls,
  every one straight ahead of her;
 you will be exiled to Harmon,
  says the LORD.
4 Come to Bethel and transgress,
  to Gilgal and multiply transgression;
 bring your sacrifices every morning
  and your tithes every three days.
5 Burn leavened bread as a thank offering;
  announce your voluntary offerings loudly,
 for so you love to do, O children of Israel,
  says the Lord GOD.

6 Though I gave you cleanness of teeth in all your cities
  and lack of food in all your places,
  yet you did not return to Me,
  says the LORD.

7 I also withheld the rain from you,
  when there were still three months to the harvest.
 I would send rain on one town,
  and send no rain on another town.
 One field would receive rain,
  but another field without rain would wither.
8 So two or three towns wandered to one town to drink water,
  but they were not satisfied;
  yet you did not return to Me,
  says the LORD.

9 I struck you with blight and mildew.
  Locusts devoured your many gardens and vineyards,
 your fig trees and olive trees;
  yet you did not return to Me,
  says the LORD.

10 Pestilence like that of Egypt
  I sent against you.
 By the sword I killed your young men;
  your horses were taken captive.
 The stench of your camps I brought up into your nostrils;
  yet you did not return to Me,
  says the LORD.

11 I destroyed some of you,
  as God destroyed Sodom and Gomorrah.
 You were like a firebrand plucked out of the fire;
  yet you did not return to Me,
  says the LORD.

12 Therefore thus will I do to you, O Israel,
  and because I will do this to you,
 prepare to meet your God, O Israel!

13 The One who forms the mountains
    and creates the wind,
    who reveals His thoughts to man,
who turns the darkness into dawn
    and strides on the heights of the earth—
    the Lord, the God of Hosts, is His name.

Third Pronouncement of Punishment

5 Hear this word which I take up as a dirge against you, O house of Israel:

2 Fallen, no more to rise
    is maiden Israel;
forsaken on her land,
    with no one to raise her up.

3 For thus says the Lord God:

The city that went out with a thousand
    will be left with a hundred,
and the one that went out with a hundred
    will be left with ten for the house of Israel.

4 Indeed, thus says the Lord to the house of Israel:

Seek Me and live!
5   But do not seek Bethel,
and do not enter into Gilgal
    or cross over to Beersheba;
for Gilgal will surely go into captivity,
    and Bethel shall be no more.
6 Seek the Lord and live,
    or He will break out like fire in the house of Joseph,
and it will devour Bethel,
    with no one to quench it.

7 You who turn justice into bitterness
    and cast righteousness down to the ground!

8 The One who made the Pleiades and Orion,
    who turns the deep darkness into dawn
    and darkens the day into night,
who summons the waters of the sea
    and pours them out on the surface of the earth—
    the Lord is His name,
9 the One who flashes destruction against the strong,
    so that destruction comes against the fortress.

10 They hate the one who prosecutes at the gate,
    and abhor the one who speaks with integrity.

11 Therefore, because you trample on the poor
    and take from him a levy of wheat,
though you have built houses of hewn stone,
    you will not dwell in them;
though you have planted pleasant vineyards,
    you will not drink their wine.
12 For I know your transgressions are many
    and your sins are grievous,
you who oppress the just,
    who take a bribe and subvert the needy at the gate.
13 Therefore the prudent are silent at such a time,
    for it is an evil time.

14 Seek good and not evil,
    so that you may live;
then the Lord, the God of Hosts, will truly be with you,
    as you claim.
15 Hate evil and love good,
    and establish justice at the gate.
It may then be that the Lord God of Hosts will be gracious
    to the remnant of Joseph.

16 Therefore thus says the Lord, the God of Hosts, the Lord:

Wailing will be in all the squares,
    and in all the streets they will say, "Alas! Alas!"
They shall call the farmer to mourning,
    and to wailing those skilled in lamentation.
17 In all vineyards there shall be wailing,
    for I will pass through you,
    says the Lord.

The Day of the Lord Is Darkness

18 Woe to you that desire
    the day of the Lord!
Why do you want the day of the Lord?
    It is darkness, and not light,
19 as if someone fled away from a lion,
    but a bear attacked him,
or got into the house
    and rested his hand on the wall,
    but a snake bit him.
20 Will not the day of the Lord be darkness, and not light?
    Will it not be deep darkness, with no brightness in it?

21 I hate, I despise your festivals,
    and I am not pleased by your solemn assemblies.
22 Though you offer Me burnt offerings or your grain offerings,
    I will not accept them,
nor will I regard the offerings
    of your fattened animals.
23 Take away from Me the noise of your songs;
    I will not listen to the melody of your harps.
24 But let justice roll down like water,
    and righteousness like an ever-flowing stream.

25 Did you bring Me sacrifices and offerings
    those forty years in the wilderness, O house of Israel?
26 But you will carry away Sukkuth your king
    and Kaiwan your star-images,
    your gods that you made for yourselves,
27 as I drive you away into exile beyond Damascus,
    says the Lord, whose name is the God of Hosts.

Woe to the Complacent

6 Woe to those who are at ease in Zion,
    and to those confident on the mount of Samaria,
nobles of the first of the nations,
    to whom the house of Israel comes!
2 Cross over to Kalneh and see,
    and go from there to Hamath the great;
    then go down to Gath of the Philistines—
are you better than these kingdoms?
    Or is their territory greater than your territory?
3 You who brush off the day of disaster,
    but bring on a session of lawlessness;
4 who lie upon beds of ivory, and lounge on their couches,
    eating lambs from the flock and calves from the stall;
5 who sing to the sound of the harp
    and invent musical instruments for themselves
    like David;
6 who drink from bowls of wine
    and anoint themselves with the finest oils,
    but are not grieved over the destruction of Joseph.
7 Therefore now they will go at the head of the captives into exile,
    and the revelry of those who are lounging will vanish.

8 The Lord God hath sworn by Himself, an oracle of the Lord the God of Hosts:

I abhor the pride of Jacob
    and hate his palaces,
so I will deliver up the city
    with all that is in it.

⁹ If there remain ten people in one house, they will die. ¹⁰ And when a relative or one who prepares the bodies picks them up to carry them out of the house, and says to someone in the recesses of the house, "Is anyone else with you?" and he says, "No," he will say, "Hush!"—not to pronounce the name of the Lord.

¹¹ But indeed the Lord gives a command,
     and He will shatter the great house to bits,
     and the small house to pieces.

¹² Can horses run on a rocky crag?
     Can one plow the sea with oxen?
But you have turned justice into poison,
     and the fruit of righteousness into wormwood,
¹³ you who rejoice in Lo Debar, who say,
     "Is it not by our own strength that we captured Karnaim?"

¹⁴ Watch: I will raise up against you a nation, O house of Israel,
     says the Lord, the God of Hosts,
and they will oppress you
     from Lebo Hamath to the Wadi Arabah.

Plague of Locusts

7 This is what the Lord God showed me: He was forming a plague of locusts when the latter growth was beginning to sprout up, the latter growth after the king's reaping. ² When they had finished devouring the foliage of the land, I said, "O Lord God, please forgive. How can Jacob survive? For he is small."

³ The Lord relented concerning this:
"It shall not be," said the Lord.

Fire

⁴ This is what the Lord God showed me: The Lord God was calling for a judgment by fire. It was consuming the great deep and was devouring the fields. ⁵ I said, "O Lord God, please stop. How can Jacob survive? For he is small."

⁶ The Lord relented concerning this:
"This also shall not be," said the Lord God.

Plumb Line

⁷ This is what He showed me: The Lord was standing by a wall made using a plumb line, with a plumb line in His hand. ⁸ The Lord said to me, "Amos, what do you see?"

And I said, "A plumb line."

Then the Lord said, "See, I am putting a plumb line in the midst of My people Israel. I will forgive them no more.

⁹ The high places of Isaac will be destroyed,
     the sanctuaries of Israel will be laid waste,
     and I will rise against the house of Jeroboam with the sword."

The Priest Tries to Banish Amos

¹⁰ Then Amaziah the priest of Bethel sent a message to Jeroboam king of Israel, saying, "Amos has conspired against you at the very center of the house of Israel. The country cannot endure all his words. ¹¹ For this is what Amos said:

'Jeroboam will die by the sword,
     and Israel will surely be exiled
     away from its land.' "

¹² So Amaziah said to Amos, "O seer, go, flee back to the land of Judah. Earn your sustenance there, and prophesy there. ¹³ But do not prophesy any more at Bethel, for it is the king's sanctuary and a royal temple."

¹⁴ But Amos answered Amaziah: "I am no prophet, and I am no prophet's disciple. Rather, I am a herdsman and a dresser of sycamore trees. ¹⁵ But the Lord took me away from the flock, and the Lord said to me, 'Go, prophesy to My people Israel.' ¹⁶ Now therefore hear the word of the Lord: You say,

'Do not prophesy against Israel,
     and do not preach against the house of Isaac.'

¹⁷ "Therefore thus says the Lord:

'Your wife will be a prostitute in the city,
     your sons and daughters will fall by the sword,
and your land will be divided by measuring line;
     you yourself will die in an unclean land;
and Israel will surely go into exile
     away from its land.' "

Basket of Fruit

8 This is what the Lord God showed me: a basket of summer fruit. ² He said, "Amos, what do you see?"

And I said, "A basket of summer fruit."

Then the Lord said to me, "The end has come upon My people Israel. I will forgive them no more.

³ "The songs of the temple shall become wailings on that day," says the Lord God. "The corpses shall be many, cast down everywhere. Hush!"

Against the Greedy

⁴ Hear this, you who trample on the needy
     to make the poor of the land fail,

⁵ saying,

"When will the New Moon be over,
     so that we may sell grain?
And the Sabbath,
     that we may open the wheat sales,
making the ephah¹ too small,
     and the shekel² too heavy,
     cheating with dishonest scales,
⁶ that we may buy the poor for silver,
     the needy for a pair of sandals,
     and sell the refuse as wheat?"

⁷ The Lord has sworn by the pride of Jacob: Surely I will never forget any of their deeds.

⁸ Will not the land tremble because of this,
     and everyone mourn who lives on it?
It will all rise up like the Nile,
     and be tossed around, then sink
     like the Nile of Egypt.

⁹ On that day, says the Lord God,

I will make the sun go down at noon,
     and darken the earth in mid-daylight;
¹⁰ I will turn your feasts into mourning,
     and all your songs into dirges;
I will put sackcloth upon all loins,
     and baldness on every head;
I will make it like the mourning for an only child,
     and its end like a bitter day.

¹¹ The time is coming, says the Lord God,
     when I will send a famine on the land,
not a famine of bread, nor a thirst for water,
     but of hearing the words of the Lord.
¹² They will wander from sea to sea,
     and from north to east;
they will run back and forth to seek the word of
     the Lord,
     but they will not find it.

¹³ On that day

---

¹ 5 A dry measure of about ⅗ bushel, or 22 liters.   ² 5 About ⅖ ounce, or 12 grams.

the beautiful maidens and the young men
   will faint with thirst.
14 Those who swear by Ashimah of Samaria, and say,
   "By the life of your god, O Dan,"
   and, "By the life of the way of Beersheba"—
they shall fall
   and never rise again.

Destruction of the Sanctuary

9 I saw the Lord standing upon the altar, and He said:

Strike the capitals
   so that the thresholds shake;
break them off onto the heads of all of them.
   Those who remain I will slay with the sword.
Not one of them will get away;
   not one fugitive will survive.
2 Though they dig down to Sheol,
   from there My hand will capture them;
though they climb up to the heavens,
   from there I will bring them down;
3 though they hide on the top of Carmel,
   from there I will search and catch them;
though they hide from My sight on the bottom of the sea,
   from there I will command the serpent to bite them;
4 and though they go into captivity before their enemies,
   from there will I command the sword to slay them.

I will set My eyes upon them
   for evil and not for good.

5 The Lord God of Hosts,
   He who touches the earth and it melts,
   and all who live on it mourn;
it all rises up like the Nile,
   and subsides like the river of Egypt;
6 who builds His chambers in the heavens,
   and founds His vault over the earth;
who summons the waters of the sea,
   and pours them out upon the surface of the earth—
   the Lord is His name.

7 Are you not like the Ethiopians to Me,
   O children of Israel?
says the Lord.

Did I not bring Israel up from the land of Egypt,
   but also the Philistines from Caphtor,
   and the Arameans from Kir?

8 The eyes of the Lord God
   are upon the sinful kingdom,
and I will destroy it
   from off the face of the earth,
though I will not completely destroy
   the house of Jacob,
   says the Lord.
9 See, I am giving the command,
   and I will sift the house of Israel
   among all the nations,
as one sifts with a sieve,
   and not a pebble falls to the ground.
10 All the sinners of My people
   will die by the sword,
those who say,
   "Never will disaster reach or overtake us."

Restoration of the Davidic Kingdom

11 On that day will I raise up
   the hut of David that is fallen;
I will close up its breached walls,
   raise up its ruins,
   and rebuild it as in the days of old;
12 that they may possess the remnant of Edom,
   and of all the nations called by My name,
   says the Lord who will do this.

13 Indeed, the days are coming, says the Lord,

when the plowman will overtake the one who is reaping,
   and the treader of grapes the one who is sowing the seed;
the mountains will drip sweet wine,
   and all the hills will flow with it.
14 I will restore the fortunes of My people Israel;
   they will rebuild the ruined cities and inhabit them;
they will plant vineyards and drink their wine;
   they will make gardens and eat their fruit.
15 I will plant them upon their land,
   and no more will they be uprooted
out of their land which I have given them.
   The Lord your God has spoken.

OBADIAH

Judgment on Edom

Jer 49:9–16
   The vision of Obadiah.

Thus says the Lord God concerning Edom

(We have heard a report from the Lord
   and a messenger has been sent among the nations, saying:
"Rise up! Let us rise up against it for battle!"):

2 See, I will make you small among the nations;
   you will be greatly despised.
3 The pride of your heart has deceived you,
   you who live in the clefts of the rock,
   whose dwelling is high;

you say in your heart,
   "Who will bring me down to the ground?"
4 Though you ascend high like the eagle,
   and though you set your nest among the stars,
I will bring you down from there,
   says the Lord.

5 If thieves came to you,
   if robbers by night—
how you have been destroyed!—
   would they not steal only what they want?
If grape gatherers come to you,
   would they not leave gleanings?
6 How *the things of* Esau have been ransacked!
   How his hidden treasures hunted out!

7 All your confederates have driven you to the border;
　　your allies have deceived and prevailed against you.
　Those who eat your bread have set a trap for you.
　　You will not detect it.

8 On that day, says the LORD,
　　I will destroy the wise out of Edom,
　　and understanding out of Mount Esau.
9 Your mighty men shall be shattered, O Teman,
　　so that everyone from Mount Esau will be cut off.

Edom's Violence Against Jacob

10 For the slaughter and the violence done to your brother Jacob,
　　shame shall cover you,
　　and you shall be cut off forever.
11 On the day that you stood aside,
　　on the day that strangers carried off his wealth,
　　and foreigners entered his gates
　　and cast lots on Jerusalem,
　　you also were like one of them.
12 But you should not have gloated
　　on the day of your brother,
　　on the day of his misfortune;
　you should not have rejoiced over the children of Judah
　　on the day of their destruction;
　you should not have boasted
　　on the day of distress.
13 You should not have entered the gate of My people
　　on the day of their calamity.
　You should not have gloated over *the* disaster *of Judah*[1]
　　on the day of his calamity;
　you should not have seized his wealth
　　on the day of his calamity.
14 You should not have stood at the crossroads
　　to cut off his fugitives;
　you should not have handed over his survivors,
　　on the day of distress.

The Day of the LORD Is Near

15 For the day of the LORD is near
　　upon all the nations;
　as you have done, it shall be done to you;
　　your deeds shall return on your own head.
16 For as you have drunk on My holy mountain,
　　all the nations shall drink continually;
　they shall drink and swallow
　　and shall be as though they had never been.
17 But on Mount Zion there shall be deliverance,
　　and it shall be holy;
　and the house of Jacob shall possess
　　those who dispossessed them.[2]
18 The house of Jacob shall be a fire,
　　the house of Joseph a flame,
　but the house of Esau stubble;
　　they shall burn them and consume them,
　and there shall be no survivors
　　from the house of Esau,
　　for the LORD has spoken.

The Restoration of Israel

19 Those of the Negev shall possess
　　Mount Esau,
　and those of the Shephelah the land
　　of the Philistines.
　They shall possess the fields of Ephraim and the fields
　　of Samaria,
　　and Benjamin shall possess Gilead.
20 The exiles of this army of the sons of Israel,
　　shall inherit the land of the Canaanites as far
　　　as Zarephath,
　and the exiles of Jerusalem who are in Sepharad
　　shall inherit the cities of the Negev.
21 Saviors shall go up to Mount Zion
　　to rule Mount Esau,
　　and the kingdom shall be the LORD's.

JONAH

The Call of Jonah

1 Now the word of the LORD came to Jonah son of Amittai, saying, 2 "Get up, go to Nineveh, the great city, and cry out against it, because their wickedness has come up before Me."

3 But Jonah got up to flee to Tarshish from the presence of the LORD. He went down to Joppa and found there a ship going to Tarshish. He paid its fare and went down into it to go with them to Tarshish from the presence of the LORD.

4 But the LORD hurled a great wind upon the sea, and a mighty storm came upon the sea, so that the ship was in danger of breaking up. 5 Then the sailors were afraid, and each cried to his god. They tossed the ship's cargo into the sea in order to lighten the load.

But Jonah had gone down into the hold of the ship, had lain down, and was fast asleep. 6 The captain came to him and said, "What are you doing asleep? Get up, call to your god! Perhaps *your* god will consider us, so that we will not perish."

7 The sailors said to one another, "Come, let us cast lots that we may know on whose account this disaster has come upon us." So they cast lots, and the lot fell on Jonah.

8 Then the sailors said to Jonah, "Tell us why this disaster has come upon us. What is your occupation? Where do you come from? What is your country? And from what people are you?"

9 Jonah replied, "I am a Hebrew, and I fear the LORD, the God of heaven, who made the sea and the dry land."

10 Then the men were very afraid and said to him, "What is this you have done?" For the men knew that he was fleeing from the presence of the LORD because he had told them.

11 Then they said to Jonah, "What shall we do to you, so that the sea may quiet down for us?" For the sea was growing stormier.

12 So Jonah said to them, "Pick me up and toss me into the sea. Then the sea will quiet down for you. For I know that it is on my account this great storm has come upon you."

13 Nevertheless, the men rowed hard to bring the ship to land, but they could not do it, for the sea grew more tempestuous against them. 14 Then they cried to the LORD and said, "Please, LORD, do not let us perish for this man's life, and do not make us guilty for innocent blood, for You, LORD, have done as it pleased You." 15 So they picked up Jonah and tossed him into the sea. Then the sea ceased from its raging. 16 Therefore the men were very afraid of the LORD, and they offered a sacrifice to the LORD and made vows.

The Prayer and Deliverance of Jonah

17 Now the LORD appointed a great fish to swallow Jonah. And Jonah was in the belly of the fish three days and three nights.

---

1 13 Heb. *his.* *2* 17 Gk.; Heb. *their possessions.*

2 Then Jonah prayed to the Lord his God from the belly of the fish. [2] He said:

> "I called to the Lord out of my distress,
>   and He answered me.
> Out of the belly of Sheol I cried,
>   and You heard my voice.
> [3] You cast me into the deep,
>   into the heart of the seas,
>   and the flood surrounded me.
> All Your billows and Your waves
>   passed over me.
> [4] Then I said, 'I am cast away
>   from Your sight;
> yet I will look again
>   to Your holy temple.'
> [5] The waters encompassed me; *even* to my soul
>   the deep surrounded me;
>   weeds were wrapped around my head.
> [6] I went down to the foundations of the mountains;
>   the earth with its bars *was* around me forever;
> yet You have brought up my life from the pit,
>   O Lord my God.
>
> [7] "When my life was ebbing away,
>   I remembered the Lord;
> and my prayer came to You,
>   into Your holy temple.
>
> [8] "Those who follow vain idols
>   forsake their true loyalty.
> [9] But I will sacrifice to You
>   with the voice of thanksgiving;
> I will pay what I have vowed.
>   Salvation is of the Lord!"

[10] Then the Lord spoke to the fish, and it vomited Jonah out upon dry land.

Jonah Preaches at Nineveh

3 The word of the Lord came to Jonah a second time, saying, [2] "Get up, go to Nineveh, the great city, and proclaim to it the message that I tell you."

[3] So Jonah got up and went to Nineveh, according to the word of the Lord. Now Nineveh was an exceedingly large city, a three-day journey across. [4] Jonah began to enter the city, going a day's walk. And he cried out, "In forty days' time, Nineveh will be overthrown!" [5] So the people of Nineveh believed God, and proclaimed a fast. And everyone, great and small, put on sackcloth.

[6] When the news reached the king of Nineveh, he arose from his throne, removed his robe, covered himself in sackcloth, and sat in ashes. [7] Then he made a proclamation in Nineveh:

> "By decree of the king and his nobles:
>
> No man or animal, no herd or flock, shall taste anything. They shall not eat or drink water. [8] Both man and animals shall cover themselves with sackcloth and cry mightily to God. All shall turn from their evil ways and from the violence that is in their hands. [9] Who knows? God may relent and change His mind. He may turn from His fierce anger, so that we will not perish."

[10] When God saw their actions, that they turned from their evil ways, He changed His mind about the disaster that He had said He would bring upon them, and He did not do it.

Jonah's Anger and the Lord's Compassion

4 Now this greatly displeased Jonah, and he became angry. [2] He prayed to the Lord and said, "O Lord! Is this not what I said while I was still in my own land? This is the reason that I fled before to Tarshish, because I knew that You are a gracious God and merciful, slow to anger, abundant in faithfulness, and ready to relent from punishment. [3] Therefore, Lord, take my life from me, for it is better for me to die than to live."

[4] Then the Lord said, "Is it right for you to be angry?"

[5] So Jonah went out of the city and sat down east of the city and made for himself a booth there. He sat under it in the shade, waiting to see what would happen to the city. [6] Then the Lord God appointed a plant, and it grew up over Jonah to provide shade over his head, to provide comfort from his grief. And Jonah was very happy about the plant. [7] But at dawn the next day, God appointed a worm to attack the plant so that it withered. [8] When the sun rose, God appointed a scorching east wind, and the sun beat upon the head of Jonah so that he became faint and asked that he might die. He said, "It is better for me to die than to live."

[9] Then God said to Jonah, "Is it right for you to be angry about the plant?"

And Jonah replied, "It is right for me to be angry, even to death."

[10] The Lord said, "You are troubled about the plant for which you did not labor and did not grow. It came up in a night and perished in a night. [11] Should I not, therefore, be concerned about Nineveh, that great city, in which there are more than a hundred and twenty thousand people, who do not know their right hand from their left, and also many animals?"

MICAH

1 The word of the Lord, which came to Micah the Morashite in the days of Jotham, Ahaz, and Hezekiah, kings of Judah, which he saw regarding Samaria and Jerusalem.

> [2] Hear, all you peoples!
>   Listen, earth and everything in it,
> that the Sovereign Lord may be a witness against you,
>   the Lord from His holy temple.

Judgment Against Samaria and Jerusalem

> [3] Look! The Lord is coming out from His place,
>   so that He might come down and tread upon the high places
>   of the earth.
> [4] The mountains will melt beneath Him,
>   and the valleys split apart
> like wax before the fire,
>   like waters deluged down a slope.
> [5] All this because of the transgression of Jacob
>   and because of the sins of the house of Israel.
> What is the transgression of Jacob?
>   Is it not Samaria?
> And what is the high place of Judah?
>   Is it not Jerusalem?
>
> [6] Therefore I will make Samaria a heap in the field
>   for the planting of vineyards.

I will dump her stones into the valley
  and expose her foundations.
7 All her idols will be shattered,
  and her gifts burned with fire,
  and I will annihilate her images,
because she gathered them as the wages of a prostitute,
  and as the wages of a prostitute they will again be used.

The Lament of Micah

8 Because of this I will lament and wail,
  I will go about barefoot and naked;
I will howl like the jackals
  and moan like owlets.
9 For her wound is mortal,
  for it has come to Judah;
it has extended to the gate of my people,
  to Jerusalem.
10 Do not tell it in Gath,
  do not weep at all;
in Beth Ophrah,
  roll around in the dust.
11 Pass on your way,
  inhabitants of Shaphir, naked and ashamed;
the inhabitants of Zaanan
  have not come out.
The mourning of Beth Ezel
  has taken from you its foothold.
12 Indeed the inhabitants of Maroth
  wait anxiously for good,
because calamity has come down from the LORD
  to the gate of Jerusalem.
13 Harness the chariot to the steeds,
  inhabitants of Lachish.
It was the beginning of sin
  to the daughter of Zion,
because in you were found
  the transgressions of Israel.
14 Therefore you will give parting gifts
  to Moresheth Gath;
the houses of Akzib will be deception
  to the kings of Israel.
15 I will again bring a conqueror to you,
  inhabitants of Mareshah;
the glory of Israel
  will come to Adullam.
16 Make yourself bald and shave your head
  for the children of your delight;
make yourself as bald as the eagle,
  for they will go from you into exile.

Woe to the Wicked

2 Woe to those who conceive wickedness,
  to those who devise evil on their beds!
At morning's light they execute it,
  because it is in the power of their hand.
2 They covet fields and seize them,
  and houses and take them.
They defraud a man of his house,
  and a fellow man of his inheritance.

3 Therefore, thus says the LORD:

I am devising disaster against this family,
  from which you cannot remove your necks;
and you will not walk haughtily,
  for it will be a time of calamity.
4 In that day they will take up a taunt against you,
  and they will wail a wailing lament, and say:
"We are totally ruined!
  He diminishes the portion of my people;
how He removes it from me!
  To a traitor He reassigns our fields!"

5 Therefore you will not have anyone to apportion the land by lot
  in the assembly of the LORD.

Prophets of Deceit

6 "Do not prophesy," they say.
  "One should not prophesy about these things.
  Disgrace will not overtake us."
7 Should it be said, O house of Jacob,
  "Is the Spirit of the LORD impatient?
  Are these His deeds?"

Do not My words benefit
  him who walks uprightly?
8 But lately My people rise up
  like an enemy.
You strip off the rich robe
  from those who pass by trustingly,
  like men returning from war.
9 The women of My people you drive out
  from their delightful homes;
from their children
  you take My adornment forever.
10 Get up and go,
  for this is not the resting place,
because uncleanness ruins,
  and ruin sickens.
11 If a man, going about vapidly and deceitfully, lies,
  "I will preach for you wine and beer,"
  he would be just the preacher for this people.

The Restoration of Israel

12 I will indeed assemble Jacob—all of you;
  I will indeed gather the remnant of Israel.
I will place them together like sheep in a fold,
  like a herd in its pasture—
  thronging with people.
13 He who breaks through has gone up before them;
  they will break through and pass the gate and go out
  by it.
Then their king will pass on before them,
  the LORD at their head.

Leaders and Prophets Judged

3 Then I said:

Listen now, heads of Jacob,
  and rulers of the house of Israel.
Should you not know justice?
2 You who hate good and love evil,
who tear the skin from My people
  and the flesh from their bones;
3 you who have eaten the flesh of My people,
  and have flayed their skin from them,
  and broken their bones in pieces;
who have chopped *them* up like meat in the pot,
  and like flesh in the cauldron.

4 Then they will cry out to the LORD,
  but He will not answer them;
He will hide His face from them at that time,
  because they have wrought evil deeds.

5 Thus says the LORD:

Regarding the prophets
  who mislead My people—
the ones who have something to eat
  proclaim "Peace,"
but if one does not feed them,
  then they prepare for war against him.
6 Therefore you will have night without vision,
  and you will have darkness without divination;

the sun will set upon the prophets,
  and black upon them will be the day.
[7] The seers will be shamed
  and the diviners disgraced,
and they will all cover their beards,
  for there is no answer from God.

[8] But as for me, I am filled with power,
  with the Spirit of the LORD,
  and with justice and might,
to declare to Jacob his transgression
  and to Israel his sin.

[9] Please hear this, heads of the house of Jacob
  and rulers of the house of Israel,
who detest justice
  and warp all that is straight,
[10] who build Zion with bloodguilt
  and Jerusalem with wickedness.
[11] Her leaders judge for a bribe,
  her priests teach for a price,
  and her prophets practice divination for money.
Yet upon the LORD they lean, saying,
  "Is not the LORD in our midst?
Evil will not come upon us."
[12] Therefore, because of you,
  Zion will be plowed like a field,
Jerusalem will be mounds of ruins,
  and the mountain of the house will become wooded heights.

The Mountain of the LORD
Isa 2:1–4

4 Then it will be that in the latter days,

the mountain of the house of the LORD will be established
  as head of the mountains,
and will be lifted up above the hills;
  and people will stream to it.

[2] And many nations will come and say,

"Come, that we might go up to the mountain of the LORD,
  and to the house of the God of Jacob,
that He might teach us His ways,
  and that we might walk in His paths."
For from Zion will go forth the law,
  and the word of the LORD from Jerusalem.
[3] Then He will judge between many peoples
  and mediate for mighty nations far and wide;
they will beat their swords into plowshares,
  and their spears into pruning hooks.
Nation will not take up sword against nation,
  and they will no longer train for war.
[4] Then each man will sit under his vine
  and under his fig tree,
and no one will make them afraid;
  for the mouth of the LORD of Hosts has spoken.
[5] For all the peoples walk,
  each in the name of its god,
but we will walk in the name of the LORD
  our God forever and ever.

The Promise of Restoration
[6] In that day, declares the LORD,

I will assemble the lame
  and gather the banished
  and those whom I have afflicted;
[7] and I will make the lame into a remnant,
  and the banished into a mighty nation;
and the LORD will reign over them on Mount Zion
  from this time forth and forevermore.

[8] As for you, watchtower of the flock,
  citadel of the daughter of Zion,
to you it will come, the former dominion will come,
  kingship for the daughter of Jerusalem.

[9] Now why do you cry loudly?
  Have you no king?
Has your counselor perished,
  that agony has seized you like the woman in labor?
[10] Writhe and bring forth, daughter of Zion,
  like the woman in labor,
because now you will go forth from the city
  and reside in the field,
and you will come to Babylon.
  There you will be rescued;
there the LORD will redeem you
  from the hand of your enemies.

[11] But now many nations
  are gathered against you, saying,
"May she be defiled,
  and may our eyes gaze upon Zion."
[12] But they do not know
  the thoughts of the LORD,
and they do not understand His plan,
  that He has gathered them like sheaves to the
    threshing floor.
[13] Arise and thresh, daughter of Zion,
  for I will make your horn iron;
your hoofs I will make bronze,
  and you will shatter many peoples.
I will devote their pillage to the LORD,
  their wealth to the LORD of all the earth.

The Ruler From Bethlehem

5 Now gather yourself in troops, O daughter of troops;
  he has laid siege against us.
With a rod they will strike
  the judge of Israel on the cheek.

[2] But you, Bethlehem Ephrathah,
  although you are small among the tribes of Judah,
from you will come forth for Me
  one who will be ruler over Israel.
His origins are from of old,
  from ancient days.

[3] Therefore He will give them up,
  until the time when she who is in labor has given birth,
and the rest of his brothers will return
  to the children of Israel.

[4] He will stand and shepherd
  in the strength of the LORD,
  in the majesty of the name of the LORD his God;
then they will live securely, because now He will be great
  until the ends of the earth;
[5] and He will be their peace.

The Remnant of Jacob Delivered
When Assyria enters our land
  and treads through our palaces,
then we will raise up against him seven shepherds
  and eight commanders of men.
[6] They will shepherd the land of Assyria with the sword,
  and the land of Nimrod at her gates;
He will rescue us from Assyria,
  when he enters our land
  and when he treads within our border.

[7] Then the remnant of Jacob will be
  in the midst of many peoples,

like dew from the Lord,
  like showers upon the grass,
which do not wait for a man
  and do not linger for the sons of men.
8 The remnant of Jacob will be among the nations,
  in the midst of many peoples,
like a lion among the beasts of the forest,
  like a young lion among flocks of sheep,
which when it passes through, tramples and mauls,
  without rescuer.
9 Your hand will be lifted up over your adversaries,
  and all your enemies will be cut off.

10 And in that day, declares the Lord,

I will cut off your horses from among you,
  and I will destroy your chariots.
11 Then I will cut off the cities of your land,
  and I will overthrow your strongholds;
12 then I will cut off sorceries from your hand,
  and you will no longer have fortune-tellers.
13 Then I will cut off your idols,
  and your sacred stones from among you,
and you will no longer bow down
  to the work of your hands;
14 then I will root out your Asherah idols from among you,
  and I will annihilate your cities.
15 And in anger and wrath I will take vengeance
  on the nations that have not listened.

The Indictment of the Lord

6 Listen to what the Lord says:

Arise, plead your case before the mountains,
  that the hills may hear your voice.
2 Hear, mountains, the indictment of the Lord,
  O enduring foundations of the earth—
that the Lord has an indictment against His people,
  and against Israel He will dispute.

3 "My people, what have I done to you,
  and how have I wearied you? Answer Me!
4 For I have brought you up from the land of Egypt,
  and from the house of slaves I have redeemed you;
and I sent before you Moses,
  Aaron, and Miriam.
5 O My people, remember now
  what Balak king of Moab counseled,
  and what Balaam son of Beor answered him,
and remember what happened from Shittim to Gilgal,
  so that you might know the righteous acts of the Lord."

The Requirement of the Lord

6 "With what should I come before the Lord,
  and bow down before God on high?
Shall I come before Him with burnt offerings,
  with calves a year old?
7 Will the Lord be pleased with thousands of rams,
  with ten thousand rivers of oil?
Shall I give my firstborn for my transgression,
  the fruit of my body for the sin of my soul?"
8 He has told you, O man, what is good—
  and what does the Lord require of you,
but to do justice and to love kindness,
  and to walk humbly with your God?

The Punishment of Israel's Guilt

9 The voice of the Lord calls to the city—
  and wisdom will fear Your name:
Heed the rod and Him who has appointed it.

10 Are there still in the house of the wicked
  treasures of wickedness?
And the short ephah [†] which is accursed?
11 Should I acquit the scales of wickedness,
  and the sack of dishonest weights?
12 Her wealthy men are full of violence,
  and her inhabitants speak deception,
  and their tongue in their mouth is treachery.
13 Therefore, I have struck you a dreadful blow,
  devastating you because of your sins.
14 You will eat, but not be satisfied,
  with hunger within you.
You will set aside, but not retain;
  and what you retain I will give over to the sword.
15 You will sow, but not reap;
  you will tread olives, but not anoint yourselves
    with oil;
  you will crush grapes, but not drink wine.
16 You observe the statutes of Omri,
  and every practice of the house of Ahab,
  and you walk in their counsels.
Therefore I will give you over to destruction,
  and the inhabitants to derision.
  You will bear the contempt of My people.

Wait on the Lord

7 Woe is me!
  Because I am as the gathering of summer fruit,
  as the gleaning of grapes;
there is no cluster to eat,
  no early fig that my soul desires.
2 The godly has perished from the earth,
  and no one is upright among men.
All of them lie in wait for bloodshed;
  each hunts his brother with a net.
3 Both hands are upon evil, to do it well.
  The prince and the judge request the bribe,
the powerful asserts the craving of his very soul—
  they intertwine together.
4 The best among them is like a brier,
  the most upright among them a bramble;
the day of your watchmen,
  of your punishment, has come;
  now their confusion is at hand.
5 Do not trust in a companion,
  do not rely on a friend;
from her who lies in your embrace,
  guard the doors of your mouth.
6 For the son dishonors the father,
  the daughter rises up against her mother,
the daughter-in-law against her mother-in-law—
  the enemies of a man are members of his own household.

7 But as for me, I watch for the Lord;
  I await the God of my salvation;
  my God will hear me.

The Penitence of Israel

8 Do not rejoice over me, my enemy!
  Although I have fallen, I will rise;
although I dwell in darkness,
  the Lord is my light.
9 I will endure the rage of the Lord,
  because I have sinned against Him,
until the time when He pleads my case
  and executes judgment for me.
He will bring me out into the light;
  I will look upon His vindication.
10 Then my enemy will see,
  and shame will cover her

---

† 10 A dry measure of about ⅗ bushel, or 22 liters.

who said to me,
　"Where is the Lord your God?"
My eyes will look upon her;
　now she will be trampled
　like muck in the streets.

¹¹ A day for building your walls,
　in that day the boundary will be extended.
¹² In that day they will come to you
　from Assyria and the cities of Egypt,
and from Egypt to the River,
　from sea to sea,
　and from mountain to mountain.
¹³ The earth will become desolate because of
　its inhabitants,
　from the fruit of their deeds.

The Restoration of Israel
¹⁴ Shepherd your people with your staff,
　the flock of your inheritance,
which live alone in a forest,
　in the midst of a fertile land;
let them graze in Bashan and Gilead,
　as in the days of old.

¹⁵ As in the days when you came out of Egypt,
　I will display wonders.

¹⁶ Nations will see and be ashamed,
　despite all their might;
they will put their hand on their mouth,
　and their ears will be deaf.
¹⁷ They will lick dust like the serpent,
　like crawling creatures of the earth;
they will come shuddering from their lairs.
　They will turn in dread to the Lord our God,
　and they will be afraid of You.
¹⁸ Who is a God like You,
　bearing iniquity and passing over transgression
　for the remnant of His inheritance?
He does not remain angry forever,
　because He delights in benevolence.
¹⁹ He will again have compassion upon us.
　He will tread down our iniquities,
　and cast all of our sins into the depths of the sea.
²⁰ You will give faithfulness to Jacob
　and benevolence to Abraham,
which You swore to our fathers
　from the days of old.

NAHUM

1 An oracle for Nineveh, a writing of the vision of Nahum, the Elkoshite.

God's Anger With Nineveh
² The Lord is a jealous and avenging God;
　the Lord avenges and is furious.
The Lord takes vengeance on His enemies,
　and He reserves it for His adversaries;
³ the Lord is slow to anger and great in power,
　and the Lord will in no way acquit the guilty.
In gale winds and a storm is His way,
　and clouds are the dust of His feet.
⁴ He rebukes and dries up the sea,
　and He makes waterless all the rivers.
Bashan and Carmel wither up,
　and the sprout of Lebanon wastes away.
⁵ The mountains quake before Him,
　and the hills melt;
the land rises up before Him,
　the earth and everything that dwells on it.
⁶ Who can stand before His anger?
　Who will rise up before His burning wrath?
His heat is poured out like fire,
　and the rocks are broken up before Him.

⁷ The Lord is good,
　a stronghold in the day of distress;
and He knows those who take refuge in Him.
⁸ As a flood running forth,
He will bring to an end the distress,
　and He will pursue His adversaries into darkness.

⁹ Why do you all scheme against the Lord?
　He will bring it to an end.
　It will not rise up a second time.
¹⁰ Because they are like interwoven thorns
　and as drunkards imbibing,
　they are consumed like completely dry stubble.

¹¹ Out of you, O Nineveh, comes one,
　a worthless counselor,
　who devises evil against the Lord.

¹² So the Lord says:

"Even though they are full and many,
　they will be cut down, and it will pass away.
Even though I have afflicted you,
　I will no longer afflict you, O Judah;
¹³ now I will break apart his yoke from over you,
　and I will tear apart your bonds."

¹⁴ The Lord has given a command concerning you:
　"No longer will your name go forth.
I will cut off the carved image and metal image
　from the house of your gods.
I will prepare your grave,
　for you are despised."

¹⁵ Look, on the mountains
　come the feet of him who brings good news,
　who proclaims peace!
Make your feasts, O Judah,
　and complete your vows.
For the wicked one will never again pass through your midst;
　he is completely cut down.

The Fall of Nineveh
2 He who scatters has come to you.
　Guard the fortifications!
　Watch the road!
　Prepare yourself,
　and strengthen yourself!

² For the Lord is restoring the prominence of Jacob,
　even the prominence of Israel,

for others have certainly
    laid waste their vines.

3 The shields of his mighty men are soaked red,
    even the mighty men are clad in red.
In the day he prepares the chariots,
    they are like a fire of iron.
    The cypress spears are ready.
4 The chariots run wildly through the streets,
    they rush to and fro in the open areas;
their appearance is like torches,
    they dash to and fro like lightning.

5 He remembers his officers
    as they stumble about on the road;
they hurry on to the wall
    as the siege tower is set up.
6 The holding gates are opened wide,
    and the palace washes away.
7 It is decreed:
    She is uncovered and led away captive;
her handmaidens shall lead her as with the voice
      of doves,
    beating their chests.
8 Nineveh is like a pool
    whose waters run away.
"Halt! Halt!" they cry,
    but no one turns back.
9 "Plunder the silver!
    Plunder the gold!
There is no limit to the treasure,
    or to the wealth of every precious thing."
10 She is desolate, empty, and waste!
    Hearts melt away, and knees shake;
pain is in all the loins, and all their faces grow pale.

11 Where is the den of the lions,
    and the feeding place of the young lions,
where the lion and lioness prowl,
    and the lion's cub goes, with no one to disturb *them*?
12 The lion tore enough food for his cubs,
    and strangled prey for his lionesses;
he has filled his caves with prey,
    and his dens with flesh.

13 I am against you,
    says the Lord of Hosts,
and I will burn your chariots in smoke,
    and the sword will devour your lions.
I will cut off your prey from the earth,
and the voice of your messengers
    will be heard no more.

Woe to Nineveh

3 Woe to the bloody city!
    It is full of lies
and plunder.
    The prey never departs.
2 The noise of the whip
    and the noise of the rattling of the wheels,
galloping horses,
    and rushing chariots!
3 Horsemen charging
    with flashing sword
    and glittering spear.
Multitude of slain,
    great number of corpses,
dead bodies without end—
    they stumble on the corpses—
4 because of the countless harlotries of the seductive harlot,
    the mistress of sorceries,

who sells nations through her harlotries
    and families through her sorceries.

5 I am against you, says the Lord of Hosts;
    I will lift your skirts over your face,
and I will show the nations your nakedness,
    and the kingdoms your shame.
6 I will throw filth on you,
    and make you vile,
    and make you a spectacle.
7 All who look at you will flee from you, and say,
    "Nineveh is devastated! Who will lament for her?"
    Where shall I seek comforters for you?

8 Are you better than Thebes
    that sat by the Nile,
    with water around her,
whose rampart was the sea,
    and whose wall was the water?
9 Ethiopia and Egypt were her strength, and it was without limit;
    Put and Libya were her helpers.
10 Yet she went into exile,
    she went into captivity;
her young children were dashed to pieces
    at the head of every street;
they cast lots for her honorable men,
    and all her great men were bound in chains.
11 You also will be drunk;
    you will go into hiding;
    you will seek refuge from the enemy.

12 All your fortresses are like fig trees
    with first-ripe figs:
If they are shaken,
    they fall into the mouth of the eater.
13 Your troops
    are women in your midst!
The gates of your land
    are wide open to your enemies;
    fire has devoured your bars.

14 Draw water for the siege!
    Strengthen your forts!
Go into the clay and
    tread the mortar!
    Take hold of the brick mold!
15 There the fire will devour you,
    the sword will cut you off;
    it will eat you up like the locust.
Multiply yourselves—like the locust!
    Multiply—like the grasshopper!
16 You have multiplied your merchants
    more than the stars of heaven.
The locust plunders
    and flies away.
17 Your leaders are like grasshoppers,
    your commanders like swarms of locusts,
    which camp in the hedges on a cold day;
when the sun rises they fly away,
    and the place where they are is not known.

18 Your shepherds slumber, O king of Assyria;
    Your nobles lie *in the dust*.
Your people are scattered on the mountains,
    and no one gathers them.
19 There is no healing of your injury,
    your wound is grievous.
All who hear news about you
    clap their hands over you,
for upon whom has not your wickedness
    continually passed?

HABAKKUK

1 The oracle that Habakkuk the prophet saw.

Habakkuk's Complaint

2 O LORD, how long shall I cry,
    and You will not hear?
Or cry to You, "Violence!"
    and You will not save?
3 Why do You make me see wickedness,
    and cause me to see trouble?
Plundering and violence are before me;
    strife and contention arise.
4 Therefore the law is powerless,
    and justice never goes forth.
For the wicked surround the righteous;
    therefore injustice proceeds.

The LORD's Answer

5 Look among the nations, and watch—
    wonder and be amazed!
For I am doing a work in your days
    that you would not believe,
    though it were told you.
6 For I am raising up the Chaldeans,
    that bitter and hasty nation
which marches through the breadth of the earth,
    to possess dwelling places that are not theirs.
7 They are terrible and dreadful;
    their justice and their dignity
    proceed from themselves.
8 Their horses are swifter than leopards,
    more fierce than evening wolves.
Their horsemen charge on;
    their horsemen come from afar;
they fly like the eagle that hastens to eat.
9 They all come for violence;
    their forces advance like the east wind.
They gather captives like sand.
10 They scoff at kings,
    and they scorn rulers.
They deride every stronghold,
    for they build up siege ramps to capture it.
11 Then their mind changes,
    and they transgress and commit offense;
    their own power is their god.

Habakkuk's Second Complaint

12 Are You not from everlasting,
    O LORD my God, my Holy One? We will not die.
O LORD, You have appointed them for judgment;
    and You, O Rock, have established them for correction.
13 Your eyes are too pure to look on evil,
    and You cannot look on wickedness.
Why do You look on those who deal treacherously,
    and hold Your tongue when the wicked
devours the man who is more righteous than he?
14 You make men like fish of the sea,
    like crawling things that have no ruler.
15 They bring all of them up with a hook,
    they catch them in their net;
they gather them in their dragnet.
    Therefore they rejoice and are glad.
16 Therefore they sacrifice to their net
    and burn incense to their dragnet;
for by them their portion is extravagant,
    and their food plentiful.
17 Shall they continue to empty their net,
    and continually kill the nations while not
        sparing anyone?

2 I will stand at my watch
    and station myself on the watchtower;
and I will keep watch to see what He will say to me,
    and what I will answer when I am reproved.

The Just Shall Live by Faith

2 And the LORD answered me:

Write the vision,
    and make it plain on tablets,
    that he who reads it may run.
3 For the vision is yet for an appointed time;
    but it speaks of the end,
    and does not lie.
If it delays, wait for it;
    it will surely come, it will not delay.

4 Look, his soul is lifted up;
    it is not upright in him;
    but the just shall live by his faith.
5 Indeed, wine betrays the proud man,
    who does not stay at home.
He enlarges his appetite as Sheol,
    and like death he is never satisfied.
He gathers to himself all nations
    and collects for himself all peoples.

Woe to the Wicked

6 Shall not all these take up a taunt against him, with satire and riddles, and say,

"Woe to him who increases what is not his—how long?
    And to him who loads himself with heavy debts!"
7 Shall not your debtors rise up suddenly,
    and those awake who oppress you?
Then you will be their plunder.
8 Because you have plundered many nations,
    all the remnant of the people will plunder you,
because of the bloodshed of men and violence of the land,
    of the cities and all who live in them.

9 "Woe to him who gets evil gain for his house,
    to set his nest on high,
    to be delivered from the power of calamity!"
10 You have given shameful counsel to your house
    by cutting off many peoples,
    and forfeiting your life.
11 For the stone will cry out from the wall,
    and the beam of the woodwork will answer it.

12 "Woe to him who builds a town with bloodshed
    and establishes a city on iniquity!"
13 Is it not from the LORD of Hosts
    that the people labor to feed fire,
    and the nations weary themselves for nothing?
14 For the earth will be filled with the knowledge of the glory of
        the LORD,
    as the waters cover the seas.

15 "Woe to him who makes his neighbor drink,
    pouring out your poison until they are drunk,
    that you may look on their nakedness!"
16 You will be filled with shame instead of glory.
    You yourself—drink and show your uncircumcision!
The cup of the LORD's right hand will be turned against you,
    and utter shame will come on your glory!
17 The violence done to Lebanon will cover you,
    as will the plunder of beasts that terrified them,

because of the bloodshed of men and violence of the land,
of the cities and all who live in them.

18 What profit is a carved image when its maker has carved it,
a cast image, and a teacher of lies,
that its maker trusts in what he has shaped
when he makes mute idols?
19 Woe to him who says to the wood, "Awake!"
To the silent stone, "Arise!" Can it teach?
It is overlaid with gold and silver,
and there is no breath at all in it.

20 But the LORD is in His holy temple.
Let all the earth keep silence before Him.

The Prayer of Habakkuk

3 A prayer of Habakkuk the prophet, on Shigionoth.

2 O LORD, I have heard the report of You,
and was afraid;
O LORD, revive Your work
in the midst of the years!
In the midst of these years
make them known;
in wrath remember mercy.

3 God came from Teman,
and the Holy One from Mount Paran.   Selah
His glory covered the heavens,
and the earth was full of His praise.
4 His brightness was like the light;
rays flashed from His hand,
and there His power was hidden.
5 Pestilence went out before Him,
and plague followed His feet.
6 He stood and measured the earth;
He looked and shook the nations.
The eternal mountains were scattered,
the perpetual hills bowed.
His ways are everlasting.
7 I saw the tents of Cushan in affliction;
the curtains of the land of Midian trembled.

8 Were you displeased with the rivers, O LORD?
Was Your anger against the rivers,
and was Your wrath against the sea
when You rode on Your horses,

on Your chariots of salvation?
9 You made bare Your bow;
oaths were the arrows at Your command.   Selah
You divided the earth with the rivers.
10 The mountains saw You and trembled;
the overflowing water passed by.
The deep lifted its voice,
and lifted its hands on high.

11 The sun and moon stood still in their places;
at the light of Your arrows they went,
at the flash of Your glittering spear.
12 You marched throughout the earth in indignation;
You threshed the nations in anger.
13 You went forth to deliver Your people,
to deliver Your anointed one.
You wounded the head of the house of the wicked,
laying him bare from head to foot.   Selah
14 You pierced with his own arrows
the leaders of his villages.
They came like a whirlwind to scatter me;
their rejoicing was like devouring the poor in secret.
15 You trampled the sea with Your horses,
through the wakes of great waters.

16 I heard, and my body trembled;
my lips quivered at the sound;
rottenness entered my bones;
my legs tremble beneath me.
Yet I will wait quietly for the day
when calamity comes on the people invading us.

A Hymn of Faith

17 Though the fig tree does not blossom,
nor fruit be on the vines;
though the yield of the olive fails,
and the fields produce no food;
though the flocks are cut off from the fold,
and there be no herd in the stalls—
18 yet I will rejoice in the LORD;
I will exult in the God of my salvation.

19 The LORD God is my strength;
He will make my feet like hinds' feet,
and He will make me walk on my high places.

To the Music Director: with my stringed instruments.

ZEPHANIAH

1 The word of the LORD which came to Zephaniah the son of Cushi,
the son of Gedaliah, the son of Amariah, the son of Hezekiah, in
the days of Josiah the son of Amon, king of Judah.

The Great Day of the LORD

2 I will utterly consume all things
on the face of the earth,
says the LORD;
3 I will consume man and beast;
I will consume the birds of the heavens
and the fish of the sea,
and the stumbling blocks with the wicked.
I will cut off man from the face of the land,
says the LORD.

4 I will stretch out my hand against Judah,
and against all the inhabitants of Jerusalem.
I will cut off from this place the remnant of Baal,
and the name of the idolatrous priests along with
the priests,
5 and those who bow down on the roofs
to the host of heaven;
those who worship and swear oaths by the LORD
and yet swear by Milcom;
6 those who have turned back from following the LORD,
who have not sought the LORD nor inquired of Him.

7 Be silent before the Lord GOD!
For the day of the LORD is at hand;

the LORD has prepared the sacrifice;
 He has consecrated His guests.

8 On the day of the LORD's sacrifice,
 I will punish the officials
 and the king's sons,
and all who clothe themselves
 with foreign attire.
9 On that day I will punish
 all who step over the threshold,
who fill their masters' houses
 with violence and deceit.

10 On that day, says the LORD,
 a cry will be heard from the Fish Gate,
 a wail from the Second Quarter,
 and a loud crash from the hills.
11 Wail, you inhabitants of the Mortar!
 For all the merchants are cut down;
 all those who weigh out silver are cut off.
12 At that time I will search Jerusalem with lamps,
 and I will punish the men
 who are settled on their lees,
who say in their heart,
 "The LORD will not do good, nor will He do evil."
13 Their goods will be plundered,
 and their houses laid waste.
Though they build houses,
 they will not inhabit them;
though they plant vineyards,
 they will not drink from their wine.

The Great Day of the LORD
14 The great day of the LORD is near,
 near and hastening quickly.
The sound of the day of the LORD is bitter;
 the mighty man shall cry out there.
15 That day is a day of wrath,
 a day of trouble and distress,
  a day of ruin and desolation,
 a day of darkness and gloom,
  a day of clouds and blackness,
16 a day of trumpet and alarms
against the fortified cities
 and against the high towers.

17 I will bring distress on men,
 so that they will walk like blind men.
Because they have sinned against the LORD,
 their blood will be poured out like dust,
 and their flesh like dung.
18 Neither their silver nor their gold
 will be able to deliver them
 on the day of the LORD's wrath.

But the whole earth will be consumed
 by the fire of His jealousy,
for He will make a sudden end
 of all those who dwell on the earth.

Judgment on the Nations
2 Gather together, yes, gather together,
 O shameless nation,
2 before the decree takes effect,
 before the day passes like chaff,
before the fierce anger of the LORD comes upon you,
 before the day of the LORD's anger comes upon you.
3 Seek the LORD, all you humble of the land,
 who carry out His judgment.
Seek righteousness, seek humility.
 Perhaps you will be hidden
 on the day of the LORD's anger.

4 For Gaza will be forsaken,
 and Ashkelon a desolation;
Ashdod will be driven out at noon,
 and Ekron will be uprooted.
5 Woe to the inhabitants of the seacoast,
 the nation of Kerethites!
The word of the LORD is against you,
 O Canaan, land of the Philistines:
I will destroy you,
 so that there will be no inhabitant.
6 The seacoast will be pastures,
 with meadows for shepherds and folds for flocks.
7 The coast will be for the remnant of the house
  of Judah,
 on which they will feed.
In the houses of Ashkelon
 they will lie down at evening.
For the LORD their God will visit them
 and restore their fortunes.

8 I have heard these taunts of Moab,
 and the revilings of the Ammonites,
by which they have reproached My people,
 and made boasts against their territory.
9 Therefore, as I live,
 says the LORD of Hosts, the God of Israel,
surely Moab will be like Sodom,
 and the Ammonites like Gomorrah—
a land of weeds and salt pits,
 and a perpetual desolation.
The remnant of My people will plunder them,
 and the survivors of My nation will possess them.

10 This will they have for their pride,
 because they taunted and boasted against
 the people of the LORD of Hosts.
11 The LORD will be dreadful to them,
 for He will weaken all the gods of the earth;
men will worship Him, every one from his place,
 all the lands of the nations.

12 You also, O Ethiopians,
 will be slain by My sword.

13 And He will stretch out His hand against
  the north
 and destroy Assyria;
and He will make Nineveh a desolation,
 and dry like the desert.
14 Herds will lie down in her midst,
 beasts of every kind;
the cormorant and the bittern
 will lodge on her pillars.
Their voice will sing in the windows;
 desolation will be on the threshold;
 for He will lay bare the cedar work.
15 This is the rejoicing city
 that dwelt securely,
that said in her heart,
 "I am, and there is no one besides me."
How has she become a desolation,
 a place for beasts to lie down!
Everyone who passes by her will hiss
 and shake his fist.

Woe to Jerusalem
3 Woe to her who is rebellious and defiled,
 the oppressing city.
2 She obeys no voice,
 she receives no correction;
she does not trust in the LORD,
 she does not draw near to her God.

3 Her princes within her are roaring lions;
    her judges are evening wolves
    who leave nothing until the morning.
4 Her prophets are reckless,
    treacherous men;
    her priests have profaned the sanctuary
    and done violence to the law.
5 The LORD is righteous in her midst;
    He does no unrighteousness.
    Every morning He brings His justice to light;
    He does not fail,
    but the unjust knows no shame.

6 I have cut off nations,
    their strongholds are devastated;
    I have made their streets desolate,
    with no one passing by.
    Their cities are destroyed;
    there is no man, no inhabitant.
7 I said,
    "Surely you will fear Me;
    and you will receive correction."
    So her dwelling will not be cut off,
    according to all that I have appointed against her.
    But they were more eager
    to corrupt all their deeds.

The Conversion of the Nations

8 Therefore wait for Me, declares the LORD,
    until the day when I rise up to seize the plunder;
    for My decision is to gather nations,
    to assemble kingdoms,
    to pour on them My indignation,
    all My fierce anger;
    for all the earth will be devoured
    with the fire of My jealousy.

9 For then I will restore to the peoples a pure speech
    that all of them may call on the name of the LORD,
    to serve Him with one accord.
10 From beyond the rivers of Ethiopia
    My worshippers, the daughter of My dispersed ones,
    will bring My offering.
11 On that day you will not be ashamed
    for all your deeds by which you have transgressed against Me;
    for then I will remove from your midst

    those who rejoice in your pride,
    and you will no longer be haughty
    in My holy mountain.
12 But I will leave in your midst
    a meek and humble people,
    and they will trust in the name of the LORD.
13 The remnant of Israel will do no unrighteousness,
    nor speak lies;
    nor will a deceitful tongue be found in their mouth;
    for they will feed and lie down,
    and no one will make them afraid.

Israel's Song of Joy

14 Sing, O daughter of Zion!
    Shout, O Israel!
    Be glad and rejoice with all your heart,
    O daughter of Jerusalem!
15 The LORD has taken away your judgments,
    He has cast out your enemies.
    The King of Israel, the LORD, is in your midst;
    you will see evil no more.
16 On that day it will be said to Jerusalem:
    Fear not, O Zion;
    let not your hands be slack.
17 The LORD your God is in your midst,
    a Mighty One, who will save.
    He will rejoice over you with gladness,
    He will renew you with His love,
    He will rejoice over you with singing.

18 I will gather those who grieve
    for the appointed festival,
    which is a reproach and burden on you.
19 At that time I will deal
    with all who oppress you;
    I will save the lame
    and gather the outcast;
    I will give them praise and fame
    in every land where they have been put to shame.
20 At that time I will bring you in,
    at the time when I gather you;
    for I will make you renowned and praised
    among all peoples of the earth,
    when I restore your fortunes
    before your eyes,
    says the LORD.

HAGGAI

God's Command to Rebuild the Temple

1 In the second year of King Darius, in the sixth month, on the first day of the month, the word of the LORD came by Haggai the prophet to Zerubbabel the son of Shealtiel, governor of Judah, and to Joshua the son of Jehozadak, the high priest, saying,
2 Thus says the LORD of Hosts: These people say, The time has not yet come to rebuild the house of the LORD.
3 Then the word of the LORD came by Haggai the prophet, saying:
4 Is it time for you yourselves to live in paneled houses, while this house lies in ruins?
5 Now, therefore, thus says the LORD of Hosts: Consider your ways.
6 You have sown much, and harvested little. You eat, but you do not have enough; you drink, but you are not filled with drink; you clothe yourselves, but no one is warm; and he who earns wages earns wages to put them into a bag with holes.
7 Thus says the LORD of Hosts: Consider your ways. 8 Go up to the mountain and bring wood and rebuild the house, that I may take pleasure in it and be glorified, says the LORD. 9 You looked for much, and it came to little; and when you brought it home, I blew it away. Why? says the LORD of Hosts. Because of My house that lies in ruins while each of you runs to his own house. 10 Therefore the heavens above you have withheld the dew, and the earth has withheld its crops. 11 I called for a drought on the land and the mountains, on the grain, on the new wine, on the oil, on what the ground brings forth, on men, on livestock, and on all the labor of your hands.

The People Obey God's Command

¹² Then Zerubbabel the son of Shealtiel, and Joshua the son of Jehozadak, the high priest, with all the remnant of the people, obeyed the voice of the Lord their God, and the words of Haggai the prophet, as the Lord their God had sent him. And the people feared the Lord. ¹³ Then Haggai, the messenger of the Lord, spoke the message of the Lord to the people, saying: I am with you, says the Lord. ¹⁴ And the Lord stirred up the spirit of Zerubbabel the son of Shealtiel, governor of Judah, and the spirit of Joshua the son of Jehozadak, the high priest, and the spirit of all the remnant of the people. And they came and worked on the house of the Lord of Hosts their God, ¹⁵ on the twenty-fourth day of the sixth month, in the second year of King Darius.

The Future Glory of the Temple

2 In the seventh month, on the twenty-first day of the month, the word of the Lord came by Haggai the prophet, saying: ² Speak now to Zerubbabel the son of Shealtiel, governor of Judah, and to Joshua the son of Jehozadak, the high priest, and to all the remnant of the people, saying: ³ Who is left among you who saw this house in its former glory? How do you see it now? Is it not, in your eyes, as nothing in comparison? ⁴ Yet now be strong, O Zerubbabel, says the Lord, and be strong, O Joshua, son of Jehozadak, the high priest. Be strong all you people of the land, says the Lord. Work, for I am with you, says the Lord of Hosts. ⁵ According to the covenant that I made with you when you came out of Egypt, so My Spirit remains among you. Do not fear.

⁶ For thus says the Lord of Hosts: Once more, in a little while, I will shake the heavens and earth, the sea and dry land. ⁷ And I will shake all the nations, and they will come with the wealth of all nations, and I will fill this house with glory, says the Lord of Hosts. ⁸ The silver is mine, and the gold is Mine, says the Lord of Hosts. ⁹ The glory of this latter house will be greater than the former, says the Lord of Hosts. And in this place I will give peace, says the Lord of Hosts.

Blessings on a Defiled People

¹⁰ On the twenty-fourth day of the ninth month, in the second year of Darius, the word of the Lord came by Haggai the prophet, saying: ¹¹ Thus says the Lord of Hosts: Now ask the priests concerning the law, saying, ¹² If a man carries holy meat in the fold of his garment, and touches with his fold bread or stew, or wine or oil, or any food, will it become holy?

The priests answered, "No."

¹³ Then Haggai said, "If one who is unclean by contact with a dead body touches any of these, will it become unclean?"

The priests answered, "It will become unclean."

¹⁴ Then Haggai said, So it is with this people, and so it is with this nation before Me, says the Lord, and so with every work of their hands; and what they offer there is unclean.

¹⁵ Now consider from this day onward: from before stone was laid upon stone in the temple of the Lord, ¹⁶ from those days when one came to a heap of twenty measures, there were but ten. When one came to the wine vat to draw fifty measures, there were but twenty. ¹⁷ I struck you and all the labor of your hands with blight and mildew and hail; yet you did not turn to Me. ¹⁸ Consider from this day onward, from the twenty-fourth day of the ninth month, from the day when the foundation of the temple of the Lord was laid, consider: ¹⁹ Is the seed yet in the barn? As of yet, the vine, the fig tree, the pomegranate, and the olive tree have yielded nothing.

But from this day on I will bless you.

The Promise of God to Zerubbabel

²⁰ The word of the Lord came a second time to Haggai on the twenty-fourth day of the month: ²¹ Speak to Zerubbabel, governor of Judah, saying, I will shake the heavens and the earth. ²² I will overthrow the throne of the kingdoms. I will destroy the strength of the kingdoms of the nations. I will overthrow the chariots and their riders. The horses and their riders will come down, every one by the sword of his brother. ²³ On that day, says the Lord of Hosts, I will take you, O Zerubbabel My servant, the son of Shealtiel, says the Lord, and I will make you like a signet ring; for I have chosen you, says the Lord of Hosts.

ZECHARIAH

1 In the eighth month, during the second year of King Darius, the word of the Lord came to the prophet Zechariah, son of Berekiah, son of Iddo, saying:

A Call to Repentance

² The Lord was very angry with your fathers, ³ so you will say to them, Thus says the Lord of Hosts: Return to Me, and I will return to you, says the Lord of Hosts. ⁴ Do not be like your fathers to whom the former prophets cried, "Thus says the Lord of Hosts: Turn away from your evil ways and deeds!" But they did not listen or pay attention to Me, says the Lord. ⁵ So where are your fathers, and do the prophets live forever? ⁶ Surely My words and statutes that I commanded to My servants, the prophets, did they not persuade your fathers?

They turned back and said, "Whatever the Lord of Hosts planned to do to us according to our ways and deeds, so He has done to us."

Vision of the Horsemen

⁷ On the twenty-fourth day, in the eleventh month, which is the month Shebat, during the second year of Darius, the word of the Lord came to the prophet Zechariah, son of Berekiah, son of Iddo:

⁸ I saw during the night a man riding on a red horse. But he was standing among the myrtle trees that were in the ravine, and behind him were red, sorrel, and white horses.

⁹ And I said, "What are these, my lord?"

Then the angel who was speaking with me said, "I will show you what these are."

¹⁰ Then the man who was standing among the myrtle trees responded and said, "These are the ones whom the Lord has sent out to walk to and fro on the earth."

¹¹ They answered and said to the angel of the Lord who was standing among the myrtle trees, "We have gone to and fro on the earth, and all the earth is resting and peaceful."

¹² Then the angel of the Lord said, "How much longer, O Lord of Hosts, will You withhold mercy from Jerusalem and the cities of Judah with which You have been angry these seventy years?" ¹³ And the Lord answered the angel speaking to me with good and comforting words.

¹⁴ So the angel who spoke with me said, Cry out, saying: Thus says the Lord of Hosts: I have a great jealousy for Jerusalem and Zion. ¹⁵ And I have a great anger for those nations who are at ease, for while I was angry but a little, they helped to increase evil.

¹⁶ Therefore thus says the Lord: I have returned to Jerusalem with mercy, and My house will be built in it, says the Lord of Hosts, and a measuring line will be stretched over Jerusalem.

17 Cry out again, saying, Thus says the LORD of Hosts: Yet again My cities will overflow with goodness, and again the LORD will comfort Zion and choose Jerusalem.

The Vision of the Horns and Craftsmen
18 And I then lifted up my eyes, and I saw four horns. 19 And I said to the angel speaking to me, "What are these?"

And he answered, "These are the horns that have scattered Judah, Israel, and Jerusalem."

20 Then the LORD showed me four craftsmen. 21 And I said, "What are these coming to do?"

And he said, "These are the horns that scattered Judah after which no one could raise his head; and these four craftsmen have come to terrify and throw down the horns of the nations who lifted up their horn against the land of Judah to scatter it."

The Vision of the Man With the Measuring Line
2 And I lifted up my eyes, and I saw a man with a measuring cord in his hand. 2 And I said, "Where are you going?"

And he responded, "To measure Jerusalem and to note what is its width and length."

3 Then the angel who was speaking with me went out, and then another angel came out to meet him, 4 and said to him, "Run, say to this young man: Jerusalem will be inhabited as villages without walls, because of the multitude of men and animals in her. 5 And I will be like a wall of fire all around her, says the LORD, and I will be as glory in her midst."

Interlude: An Appeal to the Exiles
6 Up, up, flee from the northern land, says the LORD, for I have spread you abroad like the four winds of heaven, says the LORD.

7 Deliver yourself, O Zion, you who live with the daughter of Babylon. 8 For thus says the LORD of Hosts: He has sent Me after glory to the nations which plunder you, for he who touches you touches the apple of His eye. 9 For I will swing My hand against them, and they will become plunder for their servants. Then you will know well that the LORD of Hosts has sent Me.

10 Sing and rejoice, O daughter of Zion, for I am coming and will dwell in your midst, says the LORD. 11 And many nations will join themselves with the LORD in that day, and they will be My people. And I will reside in your midst, and you will know that the LORD of Hosts has sent Me to you. 12 And the LORD will possess Judah as His portion in the holy land, and He will again choose Jerusalem. 13 Be still, all flesh before the LORD, for He is stirred from His holy habitation.

The Vision of Joshua the High Priest
3 Then he showed me Joshua, the high priest, standing before the angel of the LORD, and Satan standing at his right hand to accuse him. 2 And the LORD said to Satan, "The LORD rebuke you, Satan! The LORD who has chosen Jerusalem rebukes you! Is this not a burning brand taken out of the fire?"

3 Now Joshua had on filthy garments and was standing before the angel. 4 And he said to those standing before him, "Take off his filthy garments."

Then he said, "See that I have removed from you your iniquity, and I will clothe you with rich robes."

5 And I said, "Let them place a pure turban on his head." So they put a pure turban on his head and garments on him. And the angel of the LORD was standing by.

6 And the angel of the LORD admonished Joshua, saying, 7 "Thus says the LORD of Hosts: If you walk in My ways and keep My charge, then you will judge My house and guard My courts, and I will give to you access to these who are standing here.

8 "Hear this, O Joshua the high priest, you and your friends sitting before you, for these men are a sign. I am bringing My servant, the Branch. 9 The stone that I have set before Joshua, on that single stone is seven eyes. And I will engrave an inscription, says the LORD of Hosts, and I will remove the iniquity of this land in one day.

10 "On that day, says the LORD of Hosts, each of you will invite your companion to come and sit under the vine and under the fig tree."

The Vision of the Gold Lampstand
4 And the angel who was speaking with me returned and woke me up like a man who is roused from his sleep. 2 And he said to me, "What do you see?"

And I responded, "I see a completely gold lampstand and a bowl at its top, with seven lights on it, and seven pipes on it for each lamp in order to light them. 3 And there are two olive trees next to it, one on the right of the bowl and one on the left."

4 So I answered and I asked the angel speaking with me, "What are these, my lord?"

5 Then the angel speaking with me responded, "Do you really not know what these are?"

And I said, "No, my lord."

6 And he said to me: "This is the word of the LORD to Zerubbabel, saying: Not by might nor by power, but by My Spirit, says the LORD of Hosts.

7 "Who are you, O great mountain? Before Zerubbabel you will be made level ground, and he will bring out the top stone amidst shouting of 'Grace! Grace to the stone!' "

8 Then the word of the LORD came to me, saying: 9 "The hands of Zerubbabel have established the foundation of this house, and they will even complete it. Then you will know that the LORD of Hosts has sent Me to all of you.

10 "For who has despised the day of small things? These seven will rejoice and see the plumb line in the hand of Zerubbabel. These are the eyes of the LORD, which survey to and fro throughout the earth."

11 Then I answered and I asked, "What are these two olives trees on the right and left of the lampstand?"

12 And I asked a second time, "What are these two branches of the olive trees that are next to the two golden pipes from which they pour out the gold oil?"

13 And he asked me, "Do you not know what these are?"

I responded, "No, my lord."

14 He answered, "These are the two anointed ones who stand by the Lord of all the earth."

The Vision of the Flying Scroll
5 Then I turned and lifted up my eyes and saw a flying scroll. 2 He asked me, "What do you see?"

And I responded, "I see a flying scroll with its length as twenty cubits and its width as ten cubits." 1

3 He said to me, "This is the curse going out over the surface of all the land. Everyone who steals will be purged according to the writing on one side, and everyone who swears falsely will be purged according to the writing on the other side. 4 I will send it out, says the LORD of Hosts, and it will enter the house of the thief, and the house of him who swears falsely by My name. It will remain in his house and consume it, with its timber and stones."

The Vision of the Woman in the Basket
5 Then the angel who was speaking with me came out, saying, "Now lift up your eyes and see what this is that is going forth."

6 And I asked, "What is it?"

He said, "This is the ephah basket going forth. This represents their iniquity throughout all the land."

7 The lead cover was lifted, and there was a woman sitting in the ephah basket. 8 And he said, "This is wickedness." And he threw her back into the basket and then thrust back the lead stone over its opening.

9 Then I lifted my eyes and saw coming forward two women. There was wind in their wings, and the wings were like those of a stork, and they lifted up and carried the ephah basket between heaven and earth.

10 Then I said to the angel who was speaking with me, "Where are they carrying the basket?"

11 He responded, "To build a house for it in the land of Shinar. And when the house is established, the basket will be set there on a pedestal."

---

1 2 About 30 feet long and 15 feet wide, or 9 meters long and 4.5 meters wide.

The Vision of the Four Chariots

6 And I turned around and lifted my eyes, and I saw four chariots coming out from between two mountains, which were bronze mountains. [2] The first chariot had red horses, the second black horses, [3] the third white horses, and the fourth chariot dappled horses—all of them strong. [4] Then I answered the angel speaking with me, "What are these, my lord?"

[5] The angel responded, "These are the four winds of heaven going out after standing before the Lord of all the earth. [6] The one with the black horses is going toward the north country, the white ones are going after them, while the dappled ones are going toward the south country."

[7] When the strong horses went out, they were seeking to go to and fro throughout the earth. And he said, "Go out to and fro throughout the earth." And they went out to walk to and fro throughout the earth.

[8] Then he cried out to me, "Look, the ones going out to the northern land have given rest to my Spirit in the north."

The Coronation of Joshua

[9] Then the word of the Lord came to me, saying: [10] Take from the exiles Heldai, Tobijah, and Jedaiah who have come from Babylon, and go on that day to the house of Josiah, the son of Zephaniah. [11] Take the silver and gold and make a crown, and set it on the head of Joshua, the son of Jehozadak, the high priest. [12] And say to him: Thus says the Lord of Hosts: Here is a man whose name is Branch; for he shall branch out from his place, and he shall build the temple of the Lord. [13] It is he who shall build the temple of the Lord; he shall bear the glory, and shall sit and rule on his throne. He shall be a priest on his throne, and the counsel of peace shall be between them both. [14] And the crown shall be for a memorial to Helem, Tobijah, Jedaiah, and Hen the son of Zephaniah, in the temple of the Lord. [15] And those who are far off shall come and help to build the temple of the Lord; and you all shall know that the Lord of Hosts has sent me to you. This shall happen if you diligently obey the voice of the Lord your God.

A Call for Justice and Mercy

7 And in the fourth year of King Darius, on the fourth day of the ninth month, Kislev, the word of the Lord came to Zechariah. [2] Those in Bethel sent Sharezer and Regem-Melek and their men to entreat the graces of the Lord, [3] saying to the priests and prophets of the house of the Lord of Hosts, "Should I weep and dedicate myself during the fifth month as I have done in these many years?"

[4] Then the word of the Lord came to me, saying: [5] Say to all the people in the land and to the priests: When you fasted and lamented during the fifth and seventh months for these seventy years, did you really fast for Me? [6] And when you eat and when you drink, do you not eat and drink for yourselves? [7] Were these not the very words that the former prophets proclaimed when Jerusalem dwelled with ease along with her surrounding cities, and when the Negev and the Lowland were inhabited?

Punishment for Rejecting God's Demands

[8] And the word of the Lord came to Zechariah, saying: [9] Thus says the Lord of Hosts: Execute true justice, show mercy and compassion, every man to his brother. [10] Do not oppress the widow, orphan, sojourner, or poor. And let none of you contemplate evil deeds in your hearts against his brother.

[11] But they refused to pay attention and turned a stubborn shoulder, and stopped their ears so that they should not hear. [12] They made their hearts hard like a diamond so as not to hear the instruction and words that the Lord of Hosts sent by His Spirit through the former prophets, and there was great anger from the Lord of Hosts.

[13] Therefore it happened that as I called, and they would not hear, so they called, and I would not hear, says the Lord of Hosts. [14] So I scattered them among all the nations whom they did not know, so the land was left desolate behind them with no one coming or going. And they made a desirable land desolate.

The Holy City of Peace and Prosperity

8 And the word of the Lord came, saying: [2] Thus says the Lord of Hosts: I am exceedingly jealous for Zion, and *with* great wrath I am jealous for her.

[3] Thus says the Lord: I have returned to Zion and will dwell in the midst of Jerusalem, and Jerusalem will be called a city of faithfulness and the mountain of the Lord of Hosts, the holy mountain.

[4] Thus says the Lord of Hosts: Older men and women will again sit in the streets of Jerusalem, each having a staff in his hand because of advanced age. [5] And the plazas of the city will be filled with young boys and girls playing in her open places.

[6] Thus says the Lord of Hosts: If it is marvelous in the eyes of the remnant of this people in these days, will it also be marvelous in My eyes? says the Lord of Hosts.

[7] Thus says the Lord of Hosts: I will deliver My people from the eastern lands and from the western lands. [8] And I will bring them, and they will reside in Jerusalem, and they will be for Me as a people, and I will be for them as God, with faithfulness and righteousness.

[9] Thus says the Lord of Hosts: Let your hands be strengthened, whoever is hearing these words in these days, from the mouth of the prophets who were there in the day that the house of the Lord of Hosts was founded, that the temple might be built. [10] For before those days there were no wages for a man nor any hire for an animal; and there was no peace from an enemy for him who went out or came in; for I set every man against his neighbor. [11] But now I will not be as in the former days against this remnant people, says the Lord of Hosts.

[12] For sowing will be done in peace, and the vine will produce its fruit, and the ground will provide its produce, and the heavens will give their rain. And I will cause the remnant of this people to inherit all of these benefits. [13] And as you have been like a curse among the nations, O house of Israel and house of Judah, I will deliver you, and you will be a blessing. Fear not, and strengthen your hands!

[14] Thus says the Lord of Hosts: Just as I had determined to punish you when your fathers incited Me to wrath, says the Lord of Hosts, I did not relent. [15] So again have I purposed in these days to do good to Jerusalem and to the house of Judah. Do not fear! [16] These are the things you will do: Speak truth each to his neighbor, and make judgments in your gates that are for truth, and justice, and peace. [17] Let none of you consider evil plans in your heart against your neighbor, and do not love false oaths, for I hate all these things, says the Lord.

[18] And the word of the Lord of Hosts came to me, saying:

[19] Thus says the Lord of Hosts: The fast during the fourth and fifth months, and the fasts during the seventh and tenth months, will become rejoicing and joy and pleasant feasts for the house of Judah. So love what brings truth and peace.

[20] Thus says the Lord of Hosts: Peoples will still come, even those who live in many cities. [21] Those who live in one city will journey to another, saying, "Let us surely go to seek the Lord of Hosts. I myself am going." [22] Many peoples and strong nations will seek out the Lord of Hosts in Jerusalem and to entreat the favor of the Lord.

[23] Thus says the Lord of Hosts: In those days ten men from every language of the nations will take hold of the garment of a Jew, saying, "Let us go with you, for we have heard that God is with you."

Judgment on Israel's Enemies

9 An oracle of the word of the Lord that is against the land of Hadrak,
and Damascus is the place where it will rest.
For the eyes of men and the tribes of Israel
are on the Lord.
[2] Also Hamath borders it,
even Tyre and Sidon, cities that are very wise.
[3] Tyre has built a rampart for herself
and stored up silver like it were dust,
and even gold like it were mud in the streets.
[4] The Lord will dispossess her of her possessions
and strike down her power in the sea,
and she will be devoured with fire.
[5] Ashkelon will observe this and fear;
Gaza as well and will writhe in anguish;
even Ekron, her hope will be confounded.
The king of Gaza will perish,
and no one will inhabit Ashkelon.
[6] A mongrel people will dwell in Ashdod,
and I will cut down the pride of Philistia.
[7] I will take away the bloodshed from its mouth,
and the abominations from between its teeth.

Even it will be a remnant for our God.
It will be like a tribe of a clan in Judah,
and Ekron like the Jebusites.
8 Then I will make camp at My house with a garrison,
so that no one can pass back and forth.
And no oppressor will pass through them,
for now I see with My eyes.

The Coming King of Zion

9 Rejoice greatly, O daughter of Zion!
And cry aloud, O daughter of Jerusalem!
See, your king is coming to you;
he is righteous and able to deliver,
he is humble and riding on a donkey,
a colt, the offspring of a donkey.
10 I will cut off the chariot from Ephraim
and the horse from Jerusalem;
and the bow for battle will be cut off.
He will speak peace to the nations;
and his dominion will be from one sea to another,
and from the Great River to the ends of the earth.
11 And as for you, because of the blood of your covenant,
I will send your prisoners from the empty, waterless pits.
12 Return to your stronghold, prisoners who now have hope.
Today I declare that I will return to you a double portion.
13 Because I have bent Judah as My bow
and fitted the bow with Ephraim.
I will stir up your sons, O Zion,
against your sons, O Greece,
and will set you like the sword of a warrior.

14 Then the Lord will appear over them,
and His arrow will go out like lightning.
The Lord God will sound His trumpet,
and will march forth like storm winds of southern Teman.
15 The Lord of Hosts will protect them.
They will devour up
and subdue them with stone slingers.
And they will drink and make noise as with wine;
they will be filled *with blood* as a bowl,
saturated like the corners of the altar.
16 The Lord their God will deliver them that day
like the flock of His people.
For like jewels embedded in a crown,
they will shine in His land.
17 For how great is His goodness, and how great His beauty!
There will be grain for the young men
and new wine to prosper the young women.

The Restoration of Judah and Israel

10 Ask for rain from the Lord
during the season of the latter spring rains.
And the Lord will make the storm winds;
and He will give them showers of rain;
all will have vegetation in the field.
2 For the household Teraphim idols speak wickedness,
and the diviners envision lies.
They utter false dreams,
and provide comfort that does not last.
So the people wander about like sheep;
they are afflicted because there is no shepherd.

3 My anger burns against the shepherds,
and I will visit judgment on the male goats.
For the Lord of Hosts will visit His flock, the house of Judah,
and will make them like His majestic horse in battle.
4 From him comes the cornerstone,
and from him the tent peg.
From him comes the bow for battle,
and from him every ruler goes out, all these together.
5 And they will be as mighty men,
who trample down in the muddy streets in battle.

They will fight because the Lord is with them,
and He will put to shame those riding on horses.
6 I will make strong the house of Judah,
and will deliver the house of Joseph.
I will restore them
because I have compassion on them.
They will be like
I had never rejected them;
for I am the Lord their God,
and I will respond to them.
7 Then Ephraim shall be like a mighty man,
and their hearts shall rejoice as with wine.
Their children shall see this and be glad;
their hearts shall rejoice in the Lord.
8 I will whistle to them
and gather them in,
for I have ransomed them;
they will be numerous as they were numerous before.
9 When I scatter them among the nations,
they will remember Me in the distant lands;
they will live with their children
and then return.
10 I will bring them home from the land of Egypt,
and gather them from Assyria.
I will bring them into the land of Gilead and Lebanon,
until there is no room for them.
11 He will pass through the sea of distress,
and will put down the waves in the sea:
All the depths of the Nile will be dried up;
and the arrogance of Assyria will be brought down,
and the scepter of Egypt will turn away.
12 I will make them strong in the Lord,
and they will go to and fro in His name,
says the Lord.

11 Open your doors, O Lebanon,
so the fire can consume your cedar.
2 Wail, O cypress, for the cedar has fallen;
the majestic trees are destroyed.
Wail, O oaks of Bashan,
because the unassailable forest has been brought down.
3 *There is* the sound of wailing shepherds,
because their glory is ruined.
There is the sound of roaring lions,
because the pride of Jordan is ruined.

Two Kinds of Shepherds

4 Thus says the Lord my God: Shepherd the flock of slaughter. 5 The ones who buy them then slaughter them and have no guilt, and those who sell them say, "Blessed is the Lord because I am rich." Their own shepherds do not take pity on them. 6 For I will no longer have pity on those who dwell in the land, says the Lord. But I will cause each of them to fall into the hands of his neighbor, even into the hands of his king. They will crush the land, and I will not deliver any from their hands.

7 So I shepherded the flock that was for slaughter, even the afflicted of the flock. And I took for myself two staffs. One I called Favor and the other I gave the name Union. So I pastured the flock. 8 I destroyed the three shepherds in the span of one month.

For my soul was impatient with them, and their souls detested me. 9 Then I said, "I will not shepherd you. What is to die, let it die. What is to be destroyed, let it be destroyed. Let those who are left devour each other's flesh."

10 I took the staff named Favor and cut it into pieces, to break the covenant that I made with all the peoples. 11 So it was broken that day, and the afflicted of the flock were watching me and knew that this was the word of the Lord.

12 Then I said to them, "If this is good in your eyes, then give my wages to me, but if not, then keep it." They weighed my wages at thirty pieces of silver.

13 Then the Lord said to me, "Throw it to the potter, the splendid price by which I was valued by them." So I took the thirty silver pieces

and threw them to the house of the LORD to the potter.

¹⁴ Then I cut up the second staff, Union, to break the brotherhood between Judah and Israel.

¹⁵ Then the LORD said to me: Take for yourself again the vessels carried by a foolish shepherd. ¹⁶ I am raising up a shepherd in the land who will not care for those who are perishing, nor seek the young, nor heal the broken, nor feed those who are standing still. But he will eat the flesh of the fat and tear their hoofs in pieces.

¹⁷ Woe to this worthless shepherd
    who abandons his flock.
May the sword take his arm and right eye;
    may his arm surely wither up,
    and his right eye become blind.

The Deliverance of Judah

12 The oracle of the word of the LORD against Israel.

Thus says the LORD, the One who stretches out the heavens and establishes the earth and forms the spirit of man within him: ² I am going to make Jerusalem a cup of reeling before all the surrounding nations. And when there is a siege against Judah, it is also against Jerusalem. ³ And it will be on that day that I will set Jerusalem as a weighty stone to all the peoples. All who carry it will surely gash themselves, and all the nations of the land will be gathered against it. ⁴ On that day I will strike every horse with confusion and its rider with madness, but for the house of Judah I will keep My eyes open although I will strike with blindness every horse of the peoples. ⁵ Then the clans of Judah will say in their hearts, "There is strength for us with those residing in Jerusalem by the LORD of Hosts, their God."

⁶ On that day I will set Judah like a fiery pot among wood and as a flaming torch among cut grain. And they will devour to the right and left all the surrounding peoples, while Jerusalem will still reside in her place, the place of Jerusalem.

⁷ The LORD will deliver the tents of Judah as before, so that the glory of the house of David and the glory of those dwelling in Jerusalem will not eclipse Judah. ⁸ On that day the LORD will defend those residing in Jerusalem; and even the one who stumbles among them will be as David on that day. And the house of David will be like God, like the angel of the LORD going out before them. ⁹ On that day I will seek to destroy all the nations who come out against Jerusalem.

Mourning for Him Whom They Have Pierced

¹⁰ And I will pour out on the house of David and over those dwelling in Jerusalem a spirit of favor and supplication so that they look to Me, whom they have pierced through. And they will mourn over him as one mourns for an only child and weep bitterly over him as a firstborn. ¹¹ On that day the mourning in Jerusalem will be as great as that of Hadad Rimmon in the plain of Megiddo. ¹² The land will mourn with each family by itself: the family of the house of David by themselves, and their wives by themselves; the family of the house of Nathan by themselves, and their wives by themselves; ¹³ the family of the house of Levi by themselves, and their wives by themselves; the family of Shimei by themselves, and their wives also by themselves; ¹⁴ and all the families that remain, each by itself and their wives by themselves.

The Cleansing of God's People

13 On that day there will be a spring opened up for the house of David and for the inhabitants of Jerusalem for sin and impurity. ² And on that day, says the LORD of Hosts, I will cut off the names of the idols from the land, and they will not be remembered any more. And I will also remove from the land the prophets and the unclean spirit. ³ And it will be if a man again prophesies, then his father and mother who gave birth to him will say, "You will not live because you speak deception in the name of the LORD." Then when he prophesies, his father and mother will pierce him through.

⁴ On that day each prophet will be ashamed of his vision when he prophesies. He will not put on a robe of coarse hair in order to deceive. ⁵ But he will say, "I am not a prophet. I am a man who works the ground, for a man purchased me when I was young." ⁶ If someone asks, "What are these wounds on your arms?" he will say, "I was struck in the house of my close friends."

Striking the Shepherd, Scattering the Sheep

⁷ "Awake, O sword, against My shepherd
    and the man of My association,"
    says the LORD of Hosts.
Strike the shepherd,
    and the sheep will scatter.
    I will turn My hand against the small ones.
⁸ And it will happen in all the land, says the LORD,
    that two-thirds will be cut off and die,
    and one-third will be left in the land.
⁹ And I will bring this one-third left into the fire,
    and will refine them as the refinement of silver,
    and will test them as the testing of gold.
They will call on My name,
    and I will answer them.
I will say, "They are My people";
    and they will say, "The LORD is my God."

The Day of the LORD

14 A day of the LORD is coming when your spoil will be divided in your midst.

² For I will gather all the nations against Jerusalem for battle. The city will be captured and the houses plundered and the women ravished. Half of the city will go to exile, but the remainder of the people will not be cut off from the city. ³ Then the LORD will go out and fight those nations as He fights in the day of war. ⁴ On that day His feet will stand on the Mount of Olives, which is to the east of Jerusalem. And from east to west the Mount of Olives will be split in two halves by a very great valley so that one half moves to the north and the other to the south. ⁵ And you will flee to my mountain valley, for the mountain valley will reach to Azal. You will flee just like you fled from the earthquake in the days of Uzziah king of Judah. Then the LORD my God will come and all His holy ones with you.

⁶ And on that day there will be no light. The lights will diminish. ⁷ And there will be one day known to the LORD, neither during the day nor the night, but at the evening time there will be light.

⁸ On that day living water will flow out from Jerusalem, half to the Dead Sea and the other half to the *Mediterranean* Sea. This will happen for the summer as well as the winter.

⁹ And the LORD will be king over all the earth. In that day it will be— "The LORD is one," and His name is one.

¹⁰ All the land will be turned into a plain from Geba to Rimmon to the south of Jerusalem. But Jerusalem will rise and dwell in her place from the Benjamin Gate to the place of the Old Gate, to the Corner Gate, and then from the Tower of Hananel to the winepress of the king. ¹¹ And *people* will live there, and she will never again be devoted for destruction. Jerusalem will reside in security.

¹² And this will be the pestilence with which the LORD will strike all the peoples who go to battle against Jerusalem: Their flesh will rot as they stand on their feet, their eyes will rot in their sockets, and their tongues will rot in their mouths. ¹³ Then on that day a great tumult from the LORD will come on them as each person will seize the hand of his neighbor, and the hand of one will be raised against the hand of another. ¹⁴ And even Judah will fight with Jerusalem, and the wealth of all the surrounding nations will be gathered, a great abundance of gold, silver, and garments. ¹⁵ So this plague will come to horses, mules, camels, donkeys, and any other animals that are in the camp. So will this plague be.

¹⁶ Then it will be that all the nations who have come against Jerusalem and survived will go up each year to worship the King, the LORD of Hosts, and to celebrate the Feast of Tabernacles. ¹⁷ And it will happen that if any of the families of the earth do not go up to Jerusalem to worship the King, the LORD of Hosts, then there will not be rain for them. ¹⁸ If the family of Egypt does not go up and enter in, they shall have no rain. This will be the plague with which the LORD strikes the nations that do not go up to celebrate the Feast of Tabernacles. ¹⁹ This will be the punishment of Egypt and the punishment of all the nations who do not go up to celebrate the Feast of Tabernacles.

²⁰ On that day "HOLY TO THE LORD" will be engraved on the bells of the horses. And the pots in the house of the LORD will be as the basins before the altar. ²¹ And every pot in Jerusalem and Judah will be holy to the LORD of Hosts so that all who come to sacrifice will take from those pots and boil the meat in them. And on that day there will no longer be a Canaanite in the house of the LORD of Hosts.

MALACHI

1

The oracle of the word of the Lord to Israel by Malachi.

Israel Preferred to Edom

2 I have loved you, says the Lord.

But you say, "How have You loved us?"

Was not Esau Jacob's brother? says the Lord. Yet I have loved Jacob; 3 but Esau I have hated, and I have made his mountains a desolation and left his inheritance for the jackals of the desert.

4 Whereas Edom says, "We are impoverished, but we will rebuild the ruins," thus says the Lord of Hosts: They may build, but I will tear down. They will be called the Wicked Territory, and the people against whom the Lord has indignation forever. 5 Your eyes will see this, and you will say, "Great is the Lord, beyond the border of Israel!"

Profane Offerings

6 A son honors his father, and a servant his master. If then I am a father, where is My honor? And if I am a master, where is My fear? says the Lord of Hosts to you, O priests, who despise My name.

But you say, "How have we despised Your name?"

7 You offer defiled food on My altar, but say, "How have we defiled You?"

By saying, "The table of the Lord is contemptible." 8 When you offer the blind as a sacrifice, is it not evil? When you offer the lame and sick, is it not evil? Offer it now to your governor! Would he be pleased with you, or accept you? says the Lord of Hosts.

9 But now entreat God's favor, that He may be gracious to us. With such offerings from your hands, will He accept you favorably? says the Lord of Hosts.

10 Who is there among you who would shut the doors, that you might not kindle fire on My altar in vain? I have no pleasure in you, says the Lord of Hosts, nor will I accept an offering from your hand. 11 For from the rising of the sun to its setting, My name will be great among the nations, and in every place incense will be offered to My name, and a pure offering. For My name will be great among the nations, says the Lord of Hosts.

12 But you profane it, in that you say, "The table of the Lord is defiled, and its fruit, that is, its food is contemptible." 13 You also say, "What a weariness it is," and you snort at it, says the Lord of Hosts.

You bring in what is stolen, the lame, or the sick; thus you bring an offering! Should I accept this from your hand? says the Lord. 14 But cursed be the deceiver who has in his flock a male, and vows, and yet sacrifices to the Lord what is blemished. For I am a great king, says the Lord of Hosts, and My name is to be feared among the nations.

Divine Warnings to the Priests

2

And now, O priests, this commandment is for you. 2 If you will not listen, and if you will not take it to heart to give honor to My name, says the Lord of Hosts, I will send a curse on you and I will curse your blessings. Yes, I have cursed them already, because you do not take it to heart.

3 I rebuke your descendants, and spread refuse on your faces, the refuse of your solemn feasts, and you will be taken away with it. 4 And you will know that I have sent this command to you, that My covenant with Levi may remain, says the Lord of Hosts. 5 My covenant with him was for life and peace, and I gave them to him. With awe he feared Me, and he was reverent before My name. 6 True instruction was in his mouth, and injustice was not found on his lips. He walked with Me in peace and with uprightness, and turned many away from iniquity.

7 For a priest's lips should preserve knowledge, and people should seek the law from his mouth; for he is the messenger of the Lord of Hosts. 8 But you have departed from the way. You have caused many to stumble at the law. You have violated the covenant of Levi, says the Lord of Hosts. 9 So I have made you contemptible and base before all the people, because you have not kept My ways, but have shown partiality in the law.

The Covenant Profaned

10 Have we not all one Father? Has not one God created us? Why do we deal treacherously with one another, by profaning the covenant of our fathers?

11 Judah has dealt treacherously, and an abomination has been committed in Israel and Jerusalem. For Judah has profaned the sanctuary of the Lord, which He loves, and has married the daughter of a foreign god. 12 May the Lord cut off from the tents of Jacob any descendant of the man who does this, teacher and student, yet who brings an offering to the Lord of Hosts.

13 This is the second thing you do: You cover the altar of the Lord with tears, with weeping and crying out, because He no longer regards the offering, nor receives it with good will from your hand. 14 Yet you say, "Why?" It is because the Lord has been a witness between you and the wife of your youth, against whom you have dealt treacherously. Yet she is your companion and your wife by covenant.

15 Did He not make them one, having a remnant of the Spirit? And why one? He seeks godly offspring. So take heed to your spirit, that you do not deal treacherously.

16 For the Lord, the God of Israel, says that He hates divorce; for it covers one's garment with violence, says the Lord of Hosts.

Therefore take heed to your spirit, that you do not deal treacherously.

Injustice Committed

17 You have wearied the Lord with your words.

Yet you say, "How have we wearied Him?"

When you say, "Everyone who does evil is good in the sight of the Lord, and He delights in them," or, "Where is the God of justice?"

The Coming Messenger

3

I will send My messenger, and he will prepare the way before Me. And the Lord, whom you seek, will suddenly come to His temple, even the messenger of the covenant, in whom you delight. He is coming, says the Lord of Hosts.

2 But who can endure the day of his coming, and who can stand when he appears? For he is like a refiner's fire and like fullers' soap. 3 He will sit as a refiner and purifier of silver; he will purify the sons of Levi, and refine them like gold and silver, and they will present to the Lord offerings in righteousness. 4 Then the offering of Judah and Jerusalem will be pleasant to the Lord as in the days of old and as in former years.

5 Then I will draw near to you for judgment. I will be a swift witness against the sorcerers, against the adulterers, against the perjurers, against those who oppress the hired worker in his wages, the widow and the fatherless, against those who turn aside the stranger, and do not fear Me, says the Lord of Hosts.

Withholding Tithes

6 For I am the Lord, I do not change; therefore you, O sons of Jacob, are not consumed. 7 From the days of your fathers you have gone away from My ordinances and have not kept them. Return to Me, and I will return to you, says the Lord of Hosts.

But you say, "How shall we return?"

8 Will a man rob God? Yet you have robbed Me.

But you say, "How have we robbed You?"

In tithes and offerings. 9 You are cursed with a curse, your whole nation, for you are robbing Me. 10 Bring all the tithes into the storehouse, that there may be food in My house, and test Me now in this, says the Lord of Hosts, if I will not open for you the windows of heaven and pour out for you a blessing, that *there will* not *be room* enough *to receive it*. 11 I will rebuke the devourer for your sakes, so that it will not destroy the fruit of your ground, and the vines in your field will not fail to bear fruit, says the Lord of Hosts. 12 Then all the nations will call you blessed, for you will be a delightful land, says the Lord of Hosts.

13 Your words have been hard against Me, says the Lord.

Yet you say, "What have we spoken against You?"

[14] You said, "It is vain to serve God. What profit is it that we have kept His ordinance, and that we have walked as mourners before the LORD of Hosts? [15] And now we call the proud blessed, for those who do wickedness are built up; they even test God and escape."

The Reward of the Faithful

[16] Then those who feared the LORD spoke to one another. The LORD listened and heard them, and a book of remembrance was written before Him for those who fear the LORD and who esteem His name.

[17] They shall be Mine, says the LORD of Hosts, on the day when I make up My jewels. And I will spare them as a man spares his son who serves him. [18] Then you will again discern between the righteous and the wicked, between one who serves God and one who does not serve Him.

The Great Day of the LORD

4 Surely the day is coming, burning like an oven; all the proud, yes, all evildoers will be stubble. The day that is coming will burn them up, says the LORD of Hosts, so that it will leave them neither root nor branch. [2] But for you who fear My name, the sun of righteousness will rise with healing in its wings. You will go out and grow up like calves from the stall. [3] And you will tread down the wicked, for they will be ashes under the soles of your feet, on the day when I do this, says the LORD of Hosts.

[4] Remember the Law of Moses, My servant, the statutes and judgments which I commanded him at Horeb for all Israel.

[5] See, I will send you Elijah the prophet before the coming of the great and dreaded day of the LORD. [6] He will turn the hearts of the fathers to their children, and the hearts of the children to their fathers, lest I come and strike the earth with a curse.

THE
NEW TESTAMENT

MATTHEW

The Genealogy of Jesus Christ
Lk 3:23–38

1 The book of the genealogy of Jesus Christ, the Son of David, the son of Abraham:

2 Abraham was the father of Isaac,
Isaac the father of Jacob,
and Jacob the father of Judah and his brothers.
3 Judah was the father of Perez and Zerah by Tamar,
Perez the father of Hezron,
and Hezron the father of Ram.
4 Ram was the father of Amminadab,
Amminadab the father of Nahshon,
and Nahshon the father of Salmon.
5 Salmon was the father of Boaz by Rahab,
Boaz the father of Obed by Ruth,
and Obed the father of Jesse.
6 Jesse was the father of David the king.

David the king was the father of Solomon, by her who had been the wife of Uriah.
7 Solomon was the father of Rehoboam,
Rehoboam the father of Abijah,
and Abijah the father of Asa.
8 Asa was the father of Jehoshaphat,
Jehoshaphat the father of Joram,
and Joram the father of Uzziah.
9 Uzziah was the father of Jotham,
Jotham the father of Ahaz,
and Ahaz the father of Hezekiah.
10 Hezekiah was the father of Manasseh,
Manasseh the father of Amon,
and Amon the father of Josiah.
11 Josiah was the father of Jeconiah and his brothers about the time they were exiled to Babylon.

12 And after they were brought to Babylon,
Jeconiah was the father of Shealtiel,
and Shealtiel the father of Zerubbabel.
13 Zerubbabel was the father of Abiud,
Abiud the father of Eliakim,
and Eliakim the father of Azor.
14 Azor was the father of Zadok,
Zadok the father of Akim,
and Akim the father of Eliud.
15 Eliud was the father of Eleazar,
Eleazar the father of Matthan,
and Matthan the father of Jacob.
16 And Jacob was the father of Joseph, the husband of Mary, of whom was born Jesus, who is called Christ.

17 So all the generations from Abraham to David are fourteen generations, from David until the exile to Babylon are fourteen generations, and from the exile in Babylon to Christ are fourteen generations.

The Birth of Jesus Christ
Lk 2:1–7

18 Now the birth of Jesus Christ happened this way: After His mother Mary was engaged to Joseph, before they came together, she was found with child by the Holy Spirit. 19 Then Joseph her husband, being a just man and not willing to make her a public example, had in mind to divorce her privately.
20 But while he thought on these things, the angel of the Lord appeared to him in a dream saying, "Joseph, son of David, do not be afraid to take Mary as your wife, for He who is conceived in her is of the Holy Spirit. 21 She will bear a Son, and you shall call His name JESUS, for He will save His people from their sins."
22 Now all this occurred to fulfill what the Lord had spoken through the prophet, saying, 23 "A virgin shall be with child, and will bear a Son, and they shall call His name Immanuel,"[1] which is interpreted, "God with us."
24 Then Joseph, being awakened from sleep, did as the angel of the Lord had commanded him, and remained with his wife, 25 and did not know her until she had given birth to her firstborn Son. And he called His name JESUS.

The Visit of the Wise Men

2 Now after Jesus was born in Bethlehem of Judea in the days of Herod the king, wise men came from the east to Jerusalem, 2 saying, "Where is He who was born King of the Jews? For we have seen His star in the east and have come to worship Him."
3 When Herod the king heard these things, he was troubled, and all Jerusalem with him. 4 And when he had gathered all the chief priests and scribes of the people together, he inquired of them where Christ should be born. 5 They told him, "In Bethlehem of Judea, for this is what the prophet wrote:

6   'And you, Bethlehem, in the land of Judah,
     are no longer least among the princes of Judah;
   for out of you shall come a Governor,
     who will shepherd My people Israel.'[2]"

7 Then Herod, when he had privately called the wise men, carefully inquired of them what time the star appeared. 8 And he sent them to Bethlehem and said, "Go and search diligently for the young Child, and when you have found Him, bring me word again, so that I may come and worship Him also."
9 When they heard the king, they departed. And the star which they saw in the east went before them until it came and stood over where the young Child was. 10 When they saw the star, they rejoiced with great excitement. 11 And when they came into the house, they saw the young Child with Mary, His mother, and fell down and worshipped Him. And when they had opened their treasures, they presented gifts to Him: gold, frankincense, and myrrh. 12 But being warned in a dream that they should not return to Herod, they returned to their own country by another route.

The Escape to Egypt

13 Now when they departed, the angel of the Lord appeared to Joseph in a dream, saying, "Arise, take the young Child and His mother, and escape to Egypt, and stay there until I bring you word. For Herod will seek the young Child to kill Him."
14 When he rose, he took the young Child and His mother by night, and departed into Egypt, 15 and remained there until the death of Herod, to fulfill what the Lord had spoken through the prophet, "Out of Egypt I have called My Son."[3]

The Killing of the Infants

16 Then Herod, when he saw that he had been tricked by the wise men, was utterly furious and sent forth and killed all the male children who were in Bethlehem and the surrounding region, from two years old and under, based on the time which he had diligently inquired of the wise men. 17 Then was fulfilled what was spoken by Jeremiah the prophet:

18 "In Ramah a voice was heard,
     grieving and weeping and great mourning,
   Rachel weeping for her children,
     and she would not be comforted,
   because they are no more."[4]

---

[1] 23 Isa 7:14. [2] 6 Mic 5:2. [3] 15 Hos 11:1. [4] 18 Jer 31:15.

The Return From Egypt

[19] But when Herod was dead, an angel of the Lord appeared in a dream to Joseph in Egypt, [20] saying, "Arise, take the young Child and His mother, and go into the land of Israel, for those who sought the young Child's life are dead."

[21] And he rose, took the young Child and His mother, and came into the land of Israel. [22] But when he heard that Archelaus reigned in Judea instead of his father Herod, he was afraid to go there. Nevertheless, being warned by God in a dream, he withdrew to the region of Galilee. [23] And he went and lived in a city called Nazareth, that what was spoken by the prophets might be fulfilled, "He shall be called a Nazarene."

The Preaching of John the Baptist

Mk 1:1–8; Lk 3:1–9, 15–17; Jn 1:19–28

3 In those days John the Baptist came, preaching in the wilderness of Judea, [2] and saying, "Repent, for the kingdom of heaven is at hand." [3] For this is he who was spoken of by the prophet Isaiah, saying:

"The voice of one crying in the wilderness:
'Prepare the way of the Lord;
    make His paths straight.' " [1]

[4] This same John had clothing made of camel's hair, a leather belt around his waist, and his food was locusts and wild honey. [5] Then Jerusalem, and all Judea, and all the region around the Jordan went out to him, [6] and were baptized by him in the Jordan, confessing their sins.

[7] But when he saw many of the Pharisees and Sadducees come to his baptism, he said to them, "O generation of vipers, who has warned you to escape from the wrath to come? [8] Therefore, bear fruit worthy of repentance, [9] and do not think to say within yourselves, 'We have Abraham as our father,' for I say to you that God is able from these stones to raise up children for Abraham. [10] Even now the axe is put to the tree roots. Therefore, every tree which does not bear good fruit is cut down and thrown into the fire.

[11] "I indeed baptize you with water to repentance, but He who is coming after me is mightier than I, whose shoes I am not worthy to carry. He will baptize you with the Holy Spirit and with fire. [12] His fan is in His hand, and He will thoroughly clean His floor and gather His wheat into the granary, but He will burn up the chaff with unquenchable fire."

The Baptism of Jesus

Mk 1:9–11; Lk 3:21–22

[13] Then Jesus came from Galilee to John at the Jordan to be baptized by him. [14] But John prohibited Him, saying, "I need to be baptized by You, and do You come to me?"

[15] But Jesus answered him, "Let it be so now, for it is fitting for us to fulfill all righteousness." Then he permitted Him.

[16] And when Jesus was baptized, He came up immediately out of the water. And suddenly the heavens were opened to Him, and He saw the Spirit of God descending on Him like a dove. [17] And a voice came from heaven, saying, "This is My beloved Son, in whom I am well pleased."

The Temptation of Jesus

Mk 1:12–13; Lk 4:1–13

4 Then Jesus was led up into the wilderness by the Spirit to be tempted by the devil. [2] And He had fasted for forty days and forty nights, and then He was hungry. [3] And the tempter came to Him and said, "If You are the Son of God, command that these stones be turned into bread."

[4] But He answered, "It is written, 'Man shall not live by bread alone, but by every word that proceeds out of the mouth of God.' [2] "

[5] Then the devil took Him up into the holy city, and set Him on the highest point of the temple, [6] and said to Him, "If You are the Son of God, throw Yourself down. For it is written,

'He shall give His angels charge concerning you,' [3]

and

'In their hands they shall lift you up,
    lest at any time you dash your foot against a stone.' [4] "

[7] Jesus said to him, "It is also written, 'You shall not tempt the Lord your God.' [5] "

[8] Again, the devil took Him up on a very high mountain, and showed Him all the kingdoms of the world and their grandeur, [9] and said to Him, "All these things I will give You if You will fall down and worship me."

[10] Then Jesus said to him, "Get away from here, Satan! For it is written, 'You shall worship the Lord your God, and Him only shall you serve.' [6] "

[11] Then the devil left Him, and immediately angels came and ministered to Him.

The Beginning of the Galilean Ministry

Mk 1:14–15; Lk 4:14–15

[12] Now when Jesus heard that John was put in prison, He left for Galilee. [13] And leaving Nazareth, He came and lived in Capernaum, which is by the sea, in the regions of Zebulun and Naphtali, [14] that what was spoken by Isaiah the prophet might be fulfilled, saying:

[15] "The land of Zebulun and the land of Naphtali,
    the way to the sea, beyond the Jordan,
    Galilee of the Gentiles;
[16] The people who sat in darkness
    saw great light.
And on those who sat in the land of the shadow of death,
    light has dawned." [7]

[17] From that time Jesus began to preach, saying, "Repent! For the kingdom of heaven is at hand."

The Calling of the First Disciples

Mk 1:16–20; Lk 5:1–11

[18] As Jesus walked beside the Sea of Galilee, He saw two brothers, Simon called Peter, and Andrew his brother, throwing a net into the sea, for they were fishermen. [19] And He said to them, "Follow Me, and I will make you fishers of men." [20] They immediately left their nets and followed Him.

[21] And going on from there, He saw two other brothers, James the son of Zebedee and John his brother, in a boat with Zebedee their father, mending their nets, and He called them. [22] They immediately left the boat and their father and followed Him.

Ministering to Great Crowds

Lk 6:17–19

[23] Jesus went throughout all Galilee teaching in their synagogues, preaching the gospel of the kingdom, and healing all kinds of sickness and all sorts of diseases among the people. [24] His fame went throughout all Syria. And they brought to Him all sick people who were taken with various diseases and tormented with pain, those who were possessed with demons, those who had seizures, and those who had paralysis, and He healed them. [25] Great crowds followed Him from Galilee, the Decapolis, Jerusalem, Judea, and from beyond the Jordan.

The Sermon on the Mount

(Mt 5–7)

5 Now seeing the crowds, He went up on a mountain. And when He sat down, His disciples came to Him.

The Beatitudes

Lk 6:20–23

[2] And He began speaking and taught them, saying:

---

1 3 Isa 40:3.   *2 4* Dt 8:3.   *3 6* Ps 91:11–12.   *4 6* Ps 91:12.   *5 7* Dt 6:16.   *6 10* Dt 6:13.   *7 15–16* Isa 9:1–2.

3 "Blessed are the poor in spirit,
　　for theirs is the kingdom of heaven.
4 Blessed are those who mourn,
　　for they shall be comforted.
5 Blessed are the meek,
　　for they shall inherit the earth.
6 Blessed are those who hunger and thirst for righteousness,
　　for they shall be filled.
7 Blessed are the merciful,
　　for they shall obtain mercy.
8 Blessed are the pure in heart,
　　for they shall see God.
9 Blessed are the peacemakers,
　　for they shall be called the sons of God.
10 Blessed are those who are persecuted for righteousness' sake,
　　for theirs is the kingdom of heaven.

11 "Blessed are you when men revile you, and persecute you, and say all kinds of evil against you falsely for My sake. 12 Rejoice and be very glad, because great is your reward in heaven, for in this manner they persecuted the prophets who were before you.

Salt and Light
Mk 9:50; Lk 14:34–35

13 "You are the salt of the earth. But if the salt loses its saltiness, how shall it be made salty? It is from then on good for nothing but to be thrown out and to be trampled underfoot by men.

14 "You are the light of the world. A city that is set on a hill cannot be hidden. 15 Neither do men light a candle and put it under a basket, but on a candlestick. And it gives light to all who are in the house. 16 Let your light so shine before men that they may see your good works and glorify your Father who is in heaven.

Teaching About the Law

17 "Do not think that I have come to abolish the Law or the Prophets. I have not come to abolish, but to fulfill. 18 For truly I say to you, until heaven and earth pass away, not one dot or one mark will pass from the law until all be fulfilled. 19 Whoever, therefore, breaks one of the least of these commandments and teaches others to do likewise shall be called the least in the kingdom of heaven. But whoever does and teaches them shall be called great in the kingdom of heaven. 20 For I say to you that unless your righteousness exceeds the righteousness of the scribes and Pharisees, you will in no way enter the kingdom of heaven.

Teaching About Anger

21 "You have heard that it was said by the ancients, 'You shall not murder,'¹ and 'Whoever murders shall be in danger of the judgment.' 22 But I say to you that whoever is angry with his brother without a cause shall be in danger of the judgment. And whoever says to his brother, 'Raca,' shall be in danger of the Sanhedrin. But whoever says, 'You fool,' shall be in danger of hell fire. 23 "Therefore, if you bring your gift to the altar and there remember that your brother has something against you, 24 leave your gift there before the altar and go on your way. First be reconciled to your brother, and then come and offer your gift. 25 "Reconcile with your adversary quickly, while you are on the way with him, lest your adversary deliver you to the judge, and the judge deliver you to the officer, and you be thrown into prison. 26 Truly I say to you, you will by no means come out of there until you have paid the last penny.²

Teaching About Adultery

27 "You have heard that it was said by the ancients, 'You shall not commit adultery.'³ 28 But I say to you that whoever looks on a woman to lust after her has committed adultery with her already in his heart. 29 And if your right eye causes you to sin, pluck it out and throw it away. For it is profitable that one of your members should perish, and not that your whole body be thrown into hell. 30 And if

your right hand causes you to sin, cut it off and throw it away. For it is profitable for you that one of your members should perish, and not that your whole body be thrown into hell.

Teaching About Divorce
Mt 19:9; Mk 10:11–12; Lk 16:18

31 "It was said, 'Whoever divorces his wife, let him give her a certificate of divorce.'⁴ 32 But I say to you that whoever divorces his wife, except for marital unfaithfulness, causes her to commit adultery. And whoever marries her who is divorced commits adultery.

Teaching About Oaths

33 "Again, you have heard that it was said by the ancients, 'You shall not swear falsely, but shall fulfill your oaths to the Lord.'⁵ 34 But I say to you, do not swear at all: neither by heaven, for it is God's throne; 35 nor by the earth, for it is His footstool; nor by Jerusalem, for it is the city of the great King. 36 Nor shall you swear by your head, because you cannot make one hair white or black. 37 But let your 'Yes' mean 'Yes,' and 'No' mean 'No.' For whatever is more than these comes from the evil one.

Teaching About Revenge
Lk 6:29–30

38 "You have heard that it was said, 'An eye for an eye, and a tooth for a tooth.'⁶ 39 But I say to you, do not resist an evil person. But whoever strikes you on your right cheek, turn to him the other as well. 40 And if anyone sues you in a court of law and takes away your tunic, let him have your cloak also. 41 And whoever compels you to go a mile,⁷ go with him two. 42 Give to him who asks you, and from him who would borrow from you do not turn away.

Love for Enemies
Lk 6:27–28, 32–36

43 "You have heard that it was said, 'You shall love your neighbor⁸ and hate your enemy.' 44 But I say to you, love your enemies, bless those who curse you, do good to those who hate you, and pray for those who spitefully use you and persecute you, 45 that you may be sons of your Father who is in heaven. For He makes His sun rise on the evil and on the good and sends rain on the just and on the unjust. 46 For if you love those who love you, what reward do you have? Do not even the tax collectors do the same? 47 And if you greet your brothers only, what are you doing more than others? Do not even the tax collectors do so? 48 Therefore be perfect, even as your Father who is in heaven is perfect.

Teaching About Charitable Giving

6 "Be sure that you not do your charitable deeds before men to be seen by them. Otherwise you have no reward from your Father who is in heaven.

2 "Therefore, when you do your charitable deeds, do not sound a trumpet before you as the hypocrites do in the synagogues and in the streets, that they may be honored by men. Truly I say to you, they have their reward. 3 But when you do your charitable deeds, do not let your left hand know what your right hand is doing, 4 that your charitable deeds may be in secret. And your Father who sees in secret will Himself reward you openly.

The Lord's Prayer
Lk 11:1–4

5 "When you pray, you shall not be like the hypocrites. For they love to pray standing in the synagogues and on the street corners that they may be seen by men. Truly I say to you, they have their reward. 6 But you, when you pray, enter your closet, and when you have shut your door, pray to your Father who is in secret. And your Father who sees in secret will reward you openly. 7 But when you pray, do not use vain repetitions, as the heathen do. For they think that they will be heard for their much speaking. 8 Do not be like them, for your Father knows what things you have need of before you ask Him.

---

¹21 Ex 20:13; Dt 5:17.　²26 Gk. *kodrantes*.　³27 Ex 20:14; Dt 5:18.　⁴31 Dt 24:1, 3.　⁵33 Lev 19:12; Nu 30:2; Dt 23:21.
⁶38 Ex 21:24; Lev 24:20; Dt 19:21.　⁷41 Gk. *milion*, or 1.48 kilometers.　⁸43 Lev 19:18.

[9] "Therefore pray in this manner:

Our Father who is in heaven,
  hallowed be Your name.
[10] Your kingdom come;
  Your will be done
    on earth, as it is in heaven.
[11] Give us this day our daily bread.
[12] And forgive us our debts,
  as we forgive our debtors.
[13] And lead us not into temptation,
  but deliver us from evil.
For Yours is the kingdom and the power and the
  glory forever. Amen.

[14] For if you forgive men for their sins, your heavenly Father will also forgive you. [15] But if you do not forgive men for their sins, neither will your Father forgive your sins.

Teaching About Fasting

[16] "Moreover, when you fast, do not be like the hypocrites with a sad countenance. For they disfigure their faces so they may appear to men to be fasting. Truly I say to you, they have their reward. [17] But you, when you fast, anoint your head and wash your face, [18] so that you will not appear to men to be fasting, but to your Father who is in secret. And your Father who sees in secret will reward you openly.

Treasures in Heaven
Lk 12:33–34
[19] "Do not store up for yourselves treasures on earth where moth and rust destroy and where thieves break in and steal. [20] But store up for yourselves treasures in heaven, where neither moth nor rust destroy and where thieves do not break in nor steal, [21] for where your treasure is, there will your heart be also.

The Light of the Body
Lk 11:34–36
[22] "The light of the body is the eye. Therefore, if your eye is clear, your whole body will be full of light. [23] But if your eye is unclear, your whole body will be full of darkness. Therefore, if the light that is in you is darkness, how great is that darkness!

God and Money
[24] "No one can serve two masters. For either he will hate the one and love the other, or else he will hold to the one and despise the other. You cannot serve God and money.

Care and Anxiety
Lk 12:22–34
[25] "Therefore, I say to you, take no thought about your life, what you will eat, or what you will drink, nor about your body, what you will put on. Is not life more than food and the body than clothing? [26] Look at the birds of the air, for they do not sow, nor do they reap, nor gather into barns. Yet your heavenly Father feeds them. Are you not much better than they? [27] Who among you by taking thought can add a cubit[1] to his stature? [28] "Why take thought about clothing? Consider the lilies of the field, how they grow: They neither work, nor do they spin. [29] Yet I say to you that even Solomon in all his glory was not dressed like one of these. [30] Therefore, if God so clothes the grass of the field, which today is here and tomorrow is thrown into the oven, will He not much more clothe you, O you of little faith? [31] Therefore, take no thought, saying, 'What shall we eat?' or 'What shall we drink?' or 'What shall we wear?' [32] (For the Gentiles seek after all these things.) For your heavenly Father knows that you have need of all these things. [33] But seek first the kingdom of God and His righteousness, and all these things shall be given to you. [34] Therefore, take no thought about tomorrow, for tomorrow will take thought about the things of itself. Sufficient to the day is the trouble thereof.

Judging Others
Lk 6:37–38, 41–42
7 "Judge not, that you be not judged. [2] For with what judgment you judge, you will be judged. And with the measure you use, it will be measured again for you.
[3] "And why do you see the speck that is in your brother's eye, but do not consider the plank that is in your own eye? [4] Or how will you say to your brother, 'Let me pull the speck out of your eye,' when a log is in your own eye? [5] You hypocrite! First take the plank out of your own eye, and then you will see clearly to take the speck out of your brother's eye.
[6] "Do not give what is holy to the dogs, nor throw your pearls before swine, lest they trample them under their feet and turn around and attack you.

Ask, Seek, Knock
Lk 11:9–13
[7] "Ask and it will be given to you; seek and you will find; knock and it will be opened to you. [8] For everyone who asks receives, and he who seeks finds, and to him who knocks, it will be opened.
[9] "What man is there among you who, if his son asks for bread, will give him a stone? [10] Or if he asks for a fish, will he give him a snake? [11] If you then, being evil, know how to give good gifts to your children, how much more will your Father who is in heaven give good things to those who ask Him! [12] Therefore, everything you would like men to do to you, do also to them, for this is the Law and the Prophets.

The Narrow Gate
Lk 13:24
[13] "Enter at the narrow gate, for wide is the gate and broad is the way that leads to destruction, and there are many who are going through it, [14] because small is the gate and narrow is the way which leads to life, and there are few who find it.

A Tree and Its Fruit
Lk 6:43–44
[15] "Beware of false prophets who come to you in sheep's clothing, but inwardly they are ravenous wolves. [16] You will know them by their fruit. Do men gather grapes from thorns, or figs from thistles? [17] Even so, every good tree bears good fruit. But a corrupt tree bears evil fruit. [18] A good tree cannot bear evil fruit, nor can a corrupt tree bear good fruit. [19] Every tree that does not bear good fruit is cut down and thrown into the fire. [20] Therefore, by their fruit you will know them.

I Never Knew You
Lk 13:25–27
[21] "Not everyone who says to Me, 'Lord, Lord,' shall enter the kingdom of heaven, but he who does the will of My Father who is in heaven. [22] Many will say to Me on that day, 'Lord, Lord, have we not prophesied in Your name, cast out demons in Your name, and done many wonderful works in Your name?' [23] But then I will declare to them, 'I never knew you. Depart from Me, you who practice evil.'[2]

The Two Housebuilders
Lk 6:47–49
[24] "Whoever hears these sayings of Mine and does them, I will liken him to a wise man who built his house on a rock. [25] And the rain descended, the floods came, and the winds blew and beat on that house. And it did not fall, for it was founded a rock. [26] And every one who hears these sayings of Mine and does not do them will be likened to a foolish man who built his house on the sand. [27] And the rain descended, the floods came, and the winds blew and beat on that house. And it fell. And its fall was great."

[28] When Jesus finished these sayings, the people were astonished at His teaching, [29] for He taught them as one having authority, and not as the scribes.

---

[1] 27 A cubit is about half a meter.   [2] 23 Ps 6:8.

The Cleansing of a Leper
Mk 1:40–45; Lk 5:12–16

8 When He came down from the mountains, large crowds followed Him. [2] And then a leper came and worshipped Him, saying, "Lord, if You are willing, You can make me clean." [3] Jesus reached out His hand and touched him, saying, "I will. Be clean." And immediately his leprosy was cleansed. [4] Then Jesus said to him, "See that you tell no one. But go your way, show yourself to the priest, and offer the gift that Moses commanded as a testimony to them."

The Healing of a Centurion's Servant
Lk 7:1–10; Jn 4:43–54

[5] And when Jesus entered Capernaum, a centurion[1] came to Him, entreating Him, [6] and saying, "Lord, my servant is lying at home, sick with paralysis, terribly tormented."

[7] Jesus said to him, "I will come and heal him."

[8] The centurion answered and said, "Lord, I am not worthy that You should come under my roof. But speak the word only, and my servant will be healed. [9] For I am a man under authority, having soldiers under me. And I say to this man, 'Go,' and he goes, and to another, 'Come,' and he comes, and to my servant, 'Do this,' and he does it."

[10] When Jesus heard it, He was amazed and said to those who followed, "Truly I say to you, I have not found such great faith, no, not in Israel. [11] And I say to you that many will come from the east and west and will dine with Abraham, Isaac, and Jacob in the kingdom of heaven. [12] But the sons of the kingdom will be thrown out into outer darkness. There will be weeping and gnashing of teeth."

[13] Then Jesus said to the centurion, "Go your way. And as you have believed, so let it be done for you." And his servant was healed that very moment.

The Healing of Many People
Mk 1:29–34; Lk 4:38–41

[14] When Jesus entered Peter's house, He saw his wife's mother, lying sick with a fever. [15] He touched her hand, and the fever left her. And she rose and served them.

[16] When the evening came, they brought to Him many who were possessed with demons. And He cast out the spirits with His word, and healed all who were sick, [17] to fulfill what was spoken by Isaiah the prophet,

> "He Himself took our infirmities
> and bore our sicknesses."[2]

The Would-Be Followers of Jesus
Lk 9:57–62

[18] Now when Jesus saw large crowds around Him, He gave a command to depart to the other side. [19] Then a certain scribe came and said to Him, "Teacher, I will follow You wherever You go."

[20] Jesus replied, "The foxes have holes and the birds of the air have nests, but the Son of Man has no place to lay His head."

[21] Another of His other disciples said to Him, "Lord, let me first go and bury my father."

[22] But Jesus said to him, "Follow Me, and let the dead bury their dead."

The Calming of a Storm
Mk 4:35–41; Lk 8:22–25

[23] Then He entered the boat, and His disciples followed Him. [24] Suddenly a great storm arose on the sea, so that the boat was covered with the waves. But He was asleep. [25] His disciples went to Him and awoke Him, saying, "Lord, save us! We are perishing!"

[26] He replied, "Why are you fearful, O you of little faith?" Then He rose and rebuked the winds and the sea. And there was a great calm.

[27] The men were amazed, saying, "What kind of Man is this that even the winds and the sea obey Him!"

The Healing of the Gergesene Demoniacs
Mk 5:1–20; Lk 8:26–39

[28] When He came to the other side into the country of the Gergesenes, there met Him two men possessed with demons, coming out of the tombs, extremely fierce, so that no one might pass by that way. [29] Suddenly they cried out, saying, "What have we to do with You, Jesus, Son of God? Have You come here to torment us before the time?"

[30] Now a good way off from them was a herd of many swine feeding. [31] So the demons begged Him, saying, "If You cast us out, permit us to go away into the herd of swine."

[32] He said to them, "Go!" And when they came out, they went into the herd of swine. And suddenly the whole herd of swine ran violently down a steep place into the sea, and perished in the waters. [33] Those who kept them fled, and went their ways into the city, and told everything, including what had happened to those possessed by the demons. [34] The whole city came out to meet Jesus. And when they saw Him, they begged Him to depart out of their region.

The Healing of a Paralytic
Mk 2:1–12; Lk 5:17–26

9 He entered a boat, crossed over, and came into His own city. [2] They brought to Him a man sick with paralysis, lying on a bed. And Jesus, seeing their faith, said to the paralytic, "Son, be of good cheer. Your sins are forgiven you."

[3] Then certain scribes said within themselves, "This Man blasphemes."

[4] Jesus, knowing their thoughts, said, "Why do you think evil in your hearts? [5] For which is easier, to say, 'Your sins are forgiven you' or to say, 'Arise and walk'? [6] But that you may know that the Son of Man has authority on earth to forgive sins"—then He said to the paralytic, "Arise, pick up your bed, and go into your house." [7] And he rose and departed to his house. [8] But when the crowds saw it, they were amazed and glorified God who had given such authority to men.

The Calling of Matthew
Mk 2:13–17; Lk 5:27–32

[9] As Jesus passed on from there, He saw a man named Matthew sitting at the tax collector's station. And He said to him, "Follow Me." And he rose and followed Him.

[10] While Jesus sat at supper in the house, many tax collectors and sinners came and sat down with Him and His disciples. [11] When the Pharisees saw it, they said to His disciples, "Why does your Teacher eat with tax collectors and sinners?"

[12] But when Jesus heard that, He said to them, "Those who are well do not need a physician, but those who are sick. [13] But go and learn what this means, 'I desire mercy, and not sacrifice.'[3] For I have not come to call the righteous, but sinners, to repentance."

The Question About Fasting
Mk 2:18–22; Lk 5:33–39

[14] Then the disciples of John came to Him, asking, "Why do we and the Pharisees fast often, but Your disciples do not fast?"

[15] Jesus answered, "Can the guests of the bridegroom mourn as long as the bridegroom is with them? But the days will come when the bridegroom will be taken from them, and then they will fast.

[16] "No one sews a piece of new cloth into an old garment, for that which is sewn in to fill it up pulls on the garment, and the tear is made worse. [17] Neither do men put new wine into old wineskins. Or else the wineskins burst, the wine runs out, and the wineskins perish. But they put new wine into new wineskins, and both are preserved."

The Ruler's Daughter and a Woman Healed
Mk 5:21–43; Lk 8:40–56

[18] While He was speaking these things to them, a certain ruler came and worshipped Him, saying, "My daughter is even now dead. But come and lay Your hand on her, and she will live." [19] Jesus rose and followed him, and so did His disciples.

---

[1] 5 Commander with the rank of captain over 100 soldiers.   [2] 17 Isa 53:4.   [3] 13 Hos 6:6.

[20] Then a woman, who was ill with a flow of blood for twelve years, came behind Him and touched the hem of His garment. [21] For she said within herself, "If I may just touch His garment, I shall be healed." [22] But Jesus turned around, and when He saw her, He said, "Daughter, be of good comfort. Your faith has made you well." And the woman was made well instantly. [23] When Jesus came to the ruler's house and saw the musicians and the mourners making a noise, [24] He said to them, "Depart. The girl is not dead, but is sleeping." And they laughed Him to scorn. [25] But when the people were put outside, He went in and took her by the hand, and the girl arose. [26] The news of this went out into all that land.

The Healing of Two Blind Men

[27] As Jesus departed from there, two blind men followed Him, crying out and saying, "Son of David, have mercy on us!" [28] When He entered the house, the blind men came to Him. And Jesus said to them, "Do you believe that I am able to do this?" They said to Him, "Yes, Lord." [29] Then He touched their eyes, saying, "According to your faith, let it be done for you." [30] And their eyes were opened, and Jesus strictly commanded them, saying, "See that no one knows of it." [31] But when they had departed, they spread His fame in all that region.

The Healing of a Mute Man

[32] As they went out, they brought to Him a mute man possessed with a demon. [33] And when the demon was cast out, the mute man spoke, and the crowds were amazed, saying, "This has never been seen in Israel." [34] But the Pharisees said, "He casts out demons through the ruler of the demons."

The Compassion of Jesus

[35] Jesus went throughout all the cities and villages, teaching in their synagogues, preaching the gospel of the kingdom, and healing every sickness and every disease among the people. [36] But when He saw the crowds, He was moved with compassion for them, because they fainted and were scattered, like sheep without a shepherd. [37] Then He said to His disciples, "The harvest truly is plentiful, but the laborers are few. [38] Therefore, pray to the Lord of the harvest, that He will send out laborers into His harvest."

The Mission of the Twelve Apostles
Mk 3:13–19; Lk 6:12–16

10 He called His twelve disciples to Him and gave them authority over unclean spirits, to cast them out, and to heal all kinds of sickness and all kinds of disease. [2] Now the names of the twelve apostles are these: first, Simon, who is called Peter, and Andrew, his brother; James, the son of Zebedee, and John, his brother; [3] Philip and Bartholomew; Thomas, and Matthew, the tax collector; James, the son of Alphaeus; and Lebbaeus, whose surname was Thaddaeus; [4] Simon the Zealot; and Judas Iscariot, who also betrayed Him.

The Commissioning of the Twelve Apostles
Mk 6:7–13; Lk 9:1–6

[5] These twelve Jesus sent out, and commanded them, saying, "Do not go into the way of the Gentiles, and do not enter any city of the Samaritans. [6] But go rather to the lost sheep of the house of Israel. [7] As you go, preach, saying, 'The kingdom of heaven is at hand.' [8] Heal the sick, cleanse the lepers, raise the dead, and cast out demons. Freely you have received, freely give. [9] "Provide neither gold nor silver nor copper for your purses, [10] nor bag for your journey, nor two tunics, nor shoes, nor even staffs. For the workman is worthy of his keep. [11] "In whatever city or town you enter, inquire in it who is worthy. And live there until you leave. [12] When you come into a house, greet it. [13] If the house is worthy, let your peace come upon it. But if it is not worthy, let your peace return to you. [14] Whoever will not receive you, nor hear your words, when you depart out of that house or city, shake off the dust of your feet. [15] Truly I say to you, it will be more tolerable for the land of Sodom and Gomorrah on the Day of Judgment than for that town.

Coming Persecutions
Mk 13:9–13; Lk 21:12–17

[16] "Look, I am sending you out as sheep in the midst of wolves. Therefore be wise as serpents and harmless as doves. [17] But beware of men, for they will deliver you up to the councils, and they will scourge you in their synagogues. [18] You will be brought before governors and kings for My sake, for a testimony against them and the Gentiles. [19] But when they deliver you up, take no thought of how or what you will speak. For it will be given you at that time what you will speak. [20] For it is not you who speak, but the Spirit of your Father who speaks through you. [21] "The brother will deliver up the brother to death, and the father the child. And the children will rise up against their parents and cause them to be put to death. [22] You will be hated by all men for My name's sake. But he who endures to the end will be saved. [23] But when they persecute you in this city, escape into another. For truly I say to you, you will not have gone through the cities of Israel before the Son of Man comes.

[24] "The disciple is not above his teacher, nor the servant above his master. [25] It is enough for the disciple that he be like his teacher, and the servant like his master. If they have called the master of the house Beelzebub, how much more will they call those of his household?

Whom to Fear
Lk 12:2–7

[26] "Therefore do not fear them. For nothing is covered that will not be revealed, or hidden that will not be known. [27] What I tell you in darkness, speak in the light. And what you hear in the ear, preach on the housetops. [28] Do not fear those who kill the body but are not able to kill the soul. But rather fear Him who is able to destroy both soul and body in hell. [29] Are not two sparrows sold for a penny? And not one of them will fall to the ground without your Father. [30] But the very hairs of your head are all numbered. [31] Therefore do not fear. You are more valuable than many sparrows.

Confessing and Denying Christ
Lk 12:8–9

[32] "Whoever will confess Me before men, him will I confess also before My Father who is in heaven. [33] But whoever will deny Me before men, him will I also deny before My Father who is in heaven.

Not Peace, but a Sword
Lk 12:51–53; 14:26–27

[34] "Do not think that I have come to bring peace on earth. I did not come to bring peace, but a sword. [35] For I have come to turn

'a man against his father,
    a daughter against his mother,
    and a daughter-in-law against her mother-in-law;
[36]   a man's foes will be those of his own household.'[1]

[37] "He who loves father or mother more than Me is not worthy of Me. And he who loves son or daughter more than Me is not worthy of Me. [38] And He who does not take his cross and follow after Me is not worthy of Me. [39] He who finds his life will lose it, and he who loses his life for My sake will find it.

Rewards
Mk 9:41

[40] "He who receives you receives Me, and he who receives Me receives Him who sent Me. [41] He who receives a prophet in the name of a prophet shall receive a prophet's reward. And he who receives a righteous man in the name of a righteous man shall receive a

---

[1] 35–36 Mic 7:6.

righteous man's reward. [42] And whoever gives even a cup of cold water to one of these little ones in the name of a disciple, truly I tell you, he shall in no way lose his reward."

11

When Jesus finished instructing His twelve disciples, He departed from there to teach and to preach in their cities.

The Messengers From John the Baptist
Lk 7:18–35

[2] Now when John had heard in prison the works of Christ, he sent two of his disciples, [3] and said to Him, "Are You He who should come, or should we look for another?"

[4] Jesus answered them, "Go and tell John what you hear and see: [5] The blind receive their sight and the lame walk, the lepers are cleansed and the deaf hear, the dead are raised up, and the poor have the gospel preached to them.[1] [6] Blessed is he who does not fall away because of Me."

[7] As they departed, Jesus began to say to the crowds concerning John, "What did you go out into the wilderness to see? A reed shaken by the wind? [8] If not, what did you go out to see? A man dressed in soft clothing? Indeed, those who wear soft clothing are in kings' houses. [9] Then what did you go out to see? A prophet? Yes, I say to you, and more than a prophet. [10] For this is he of whom it is written:

> 'Look, I am sending My messenger before Your face,
> who will prepare Your way before You.'[2]

[11] Truly I say to you, among those who are born of women, there has risen no one greater than John the Baptist. But he who is least in the kingdom of heaven is greater than he. [12] From the days of John the Baptist until now, the kingdom of heaven has forcefully advanced, and the strong take it by force. [13] For all the Prophets and the Law prophesied until John. [14] And if you are willing to receive it, he is Elijah, who is to come. [15] He who has ears to hear, let him hear.
[16] "But to what shall I liken this generation? It is like children sitting in the markets, calling to their friends, [17] saying:

> 'We played the flute for you,
>   and you did not dance;
> we sang a dirge to you,
>   and you did not mourn.'

[18] For John came neither eating nor drinking, and they say, 'He has a demon.' [19] The Son of Man came eating and drinking, and they say, 'Here is a gluttonous man, a drunkard, a friend of tax collectors and sinners.' But wisdom is justified by her children."

Unrepentant Cities
Lk 10:13–15

[20] Then He began to reprimand the cities where most of His mighty works were done, because they did not repent: [21] "Woe to you, Chorazin! Woe to you, Bethsaida! For if the mighty works which were done in you had been done in Tyre and Sidon, they would have repented long ago in sackcloth and ashes. [22] But I say to you, it will be more tolerable for Tyre and Sidon on the Day of Judgment than for you. [23] And you, Capernaum, who is exalted toward heaven, will be brought down to Hades. For if the mighty works which have been done in you had been done in Sodom, it would have remained until this day. [24] But I say to you that it shall be more tolerable for the land of Sodom on the Day of Judgment than for you."

Come to Me and Rest
Lk 10:21–22

[25] At that time Jesus said, "I thank You, O Father, Lord of heaven and earth, because You have hidden these things from the wise and prudent and revealed them to infants. [26] Even so, Father, for it seemed good in Your sight.

[27] "All things are delivered to Me by My Father, and no one knows the Son, except the Father. And no one knows the Father, except the Son and he to whom the Son will reveal Him.

[28] "Come to Me, all you who labor and are heavily burdened, and I will give you rest. [29] Take My yoke upon you, and learn from Me. For I am meek and lowly in heart, and you will find rest for your souls.[3] [30] For My yoke is easy, and My burden is light."

The Question About the Sabbath
Mk 2:23–28; Lk 6:1–5

12

At that time Jesus went through the grain fields on the Sabbath. And His disciples were hungry and began to pluck the heads of grain and to eat. [2] But when the Pharisees saw it, they said to Him, "Look, Your disciples are doing that which is not lawful to do on the Sabbath!"

[3] But He said to them, "Have you not read what David and those who were with him did when he was hungry, [4] how he entered the house of God and ate the ritual bread, which was not lawful for him to eat, neither for those who were with him, but only for the priests? [5] Or have you not read in the law how on the Sabbath the priests in the temple profane the Sabbath, but are blameless? [6] I say to you, in this place there is One who is greater than the temple. [7] If you had known what this meant, 'I desire mercy, and not sacrifice,' you would not have condemned the innocent. [8] For the Son of Man is Lord even of the Sabbath."

The Healing of the Withered Hand
Mk 3:1–6; Lk 6:6–11

[9] When He had departed from there, He went into their synagogue. [10] And there was a man whose hand had withered. They asked Him, "Is it lawful to heal on the Sabbath?" that they might accuse Him.

[11] He said to them, "What man is there among you who has one sheep, and if it falls into a pit on the Sabbath, will not lay hold of it and lift it out? [12] Then how much better is a man than a sheep? Therefore, it is lawful to do good on the Sabbath."

[13] Then He said to the man, "Stretch out your hand." And he stretched it out, and it was restored whole like the other. [14] Then the Pharisees went out and took counsel against Him, how they might kill Him.

The Chosen Servant

[15] But when Jesus knew it, He withdrew from there. And great crowds followed Him, and He healed them all, [16] and warned them that they should not make Him known, [17] to fulfill what was spoken by Isaiah the prophet, saying:

> [18] "Here is My Servant, whom I have chosen,
>   My Beloved, in whom My soul is well pleased;
> I will put My Spirit upon Him,
>   and He will render judgment to the Gentiles.
> [19] He shall not struggle nor cry out,
>   nor will anyone hear His voice in the streets.
> [20] A bruised reed He will not break,
>   and a smoldering wick He will not quench,
>   until He renders judgment unto victory;
> [21]   and in His name will the Gentiles trust."[4]

Jesus and Beelzebub
Mk 3:20–30; Lk 11:14–23; 12:10

[22] Then one possessed with a demon was brought to Him, blind and mute, and He healed him, so that the blind and mute man both spoke and saw. [23] All the people were amazed and said, "Is He not the Son of David?"

[24] But when the Pharisees heard it, they said, "This Man does not cast out demons, except by Beelzebub the ruler of the demons."

[25] Jesus knew their thoughts and said to them, "Every kingdom divided against itself is brought to desolation. And every city or house divided against itself will not stand. [26] If Satan casts out Satan, he is divided against himself. Then how will his kingdom stand? [27] And if I cast out demons by Beelzebub, by whom do your sons cast them out? Therefore, they shall be your judges. [28] But if I cast out demons by the Spirit of God, then the kingdom of God has come upon you.

---

[1] 5 Taken from Isa 35:5–6; 61:1.   [2] 10 Mal 3:1.   [3] 29 Jer 6:16.   [4] 18–21 Isa 42:1–4.

[29] "Or else how can one enter a strong man's house and plunder his goods unless he first binds the strong man? And then he will plunder his house.

[30] "He who is not with Me is against Me, and he who does not gather with Me scatters abroad. [31] Therefore I say to you, all kinds of sin and blasphemy will be forgiven men, but the blasphemy against the Holy Spirit will not be forgiven men. [32] Whoever speaks a word against the Son of Man will be forgiven. But whoever speaks against the Holy Spirit will not be forgiven, neither in this world, nor in the world to come.

A Tree and Its Fruit
Lk 6:43–45

[33] "Either make the tree good and its fruit good, or else make the tree corrupt and its fruit corrupt. For the tree is known by its fruit. [34] O generation of vipers, how can you, being evil, speak good things? For out of the abundance of the heart the mouth speaks. [35] A good man out of the good treasure of his heart brings forth good things. And an evil man out of the evil treasure brings forth evil things. [36] But I say to you that for every idle word that men speak, they will give an account on the Day of Judgment. [37] For by your words you will be justified, and by your words you will be condemned."

The Demand for a Sign
Mk 8:11–12; Lk 11:29–32

[38] Then some of the scribes and Pharisees said to Him, "Teacher, we wish to see a sign from You."

[39] But He answered them, "An evil and adulterous generation seeks after a sign, and no sign will be given to it except the sign of the prophet Jonah. [40] For as Jonah was three days and three nights in the belly of the great fish,[1] so will the Son of Man be three days and three nights in the heart of the earth. [41] The men of Nineveh will stand up at the judgment with this generation and will condemn it, because they repented at the preaching of Jonah.[2] And now One greater than Jonah is here. [42] The Queen of the South will rise up at the judgment with this generation and will condemn it, for she came from the ends of the earth to hear the wisdom of Solomon. And now One greater than Solomon is here.

The Return of the Unclean Spirit
Lk 11:24–26

[43] "When an unclean spirit goes out of a man, it passes through dry places seeking rest, but finds none. [44] Then it says, 'I will return to my house from which I came.' And when it comes, it finds it empty, swept, and put in order. [45] Then it goes and brings with itself seven other spirits more evil than itself, and they enter and dwell there. And the last state of that man is worse than the first. So shall it be also with this evil generation."

The Mother and Brothers of Jesus
Mk 3:31–35; Lk 8:19–21

[46] While He was still speaking to the people, right then His mother and His brothers stood outside asking to speak with Him. [47] Then one said to Him, "Look, Your mother and Your brothers are standing outside asking to speak with You."

[48] But He answered the man who told him, "Who is My mother, and who are My brothers?" [49] He stretched out His hand toward His disciples and said, "Here are My mother and My brothers! [50] For whoever does the will of My Father who is in heaven is My brother, and sister, and mother."

The Parable of the Sower
Mk 4:1–9; Lk 8:4–8

13 That same day Jesus went out of the house and sat beside the sea. [2] Great crowds assembled around Him, so that He went into a boat and sat there. And the whole assembly stood on the shore. [3] Then He told them many things in parables, saying, "Listen! A sower went out to sow. [4] While he sowed, some seeds fell beside the path, and the birds came and devoured them.

[5] But other seeds fell on rocky ground where they did not have much soil, and immediately they sprang up because they did not have deep soil. [6] But when the sun rose, they were scorched. And because they did not take root, they withered away. [7] Some seeds fell among thorns, and the thorns grew up and choked them. [8] But other seeds fell into good ground and produced grain: a hundred, sixty, or thirty times as much. [9] Whoever has ears to hear, let him hear."

The Purpose of the Parables
Mk 4:10–12; Lk 8:9–10

[10] The disciples came and said to Him, "Why do You speak to them in parables?"

[11] He answered them, "It is given to you to know the mysteries of the kingdom of heaven, but to them it is not given. [12] For to him who has, will more be given, and he will have abundance. But from him who has not, even what he has will be taken away. [13] Therefore I speak to them in parables:

'Because they look, but do not see.
    And they listen, but they do not hear, neither do they
        understand.'[3]

[14] In them is fulfilled the prophecy of Isaiah which says:

'By hearing, you will hear and shall not understand,
    and seeing, you will see and shall not perceive;[4]
[15] for this people's heart has grown dull.
    Their ears have become hard of hearing,
    and they have closed their eyes,
lest they should see with their eyes
    and hear with their ears
    and understand with their hearts,
and turn, and I should heal them.'[5]

[16] But blessed are your eyes, for they see, and your ears, for they hear. [17] For truly I say to you that many prophets and righteous men have desired to see those things which you see, and have not seen them, and to hear those things which you hear, and have not heard them.

The Parable of the Sower Explained
Mk 4:13–20; Lk 8:11–15

[18] "Therefore listen to the parable of the sower. [19] When anyone hears the word of the kingdom and does not understand it, the evil one comes and snatches away what was sown in his heart. This is the one who received seed beside the path. [20] But he who received the seed on rocky ground is he who hears the word and immediately receives it with joy, [21] yet he has no root in himself, but endures for a while. For when tribulation or persecution arises because of the word, eventually he falls away. [22] He also who received seed among the thorns is he who hears the word, but the cares of this world and the deceitfulness of riches choke the word, and he becomes unfruitful. [23] But he who received seed on the good ground is he who hears the word and understands it, who indeed bears fruit. Some produce a hundred, sixty, or thirty times what was sown."

The Parable of the Weeds

[24] He told them another parable, saying, "The kingdom of heaven is like a man who sowed good seed in his field. [25] But while men slept, his enemy came and sowed weeds among the wheat and went away. [26] But when the shoots had sprung up and produced fruit, the weeds also appeared.

[27] "So the servants of the landowner came and said to him, 'Sir, did you not sow good seed in your field? Then where did the weeds come from?'

[28] "He said to them, 'An enemy did this.'

"The servants said to him, 'Will you then have us go and gather them up?'

---

[1] 40 Jnh 1:17.   [2] 41 Jnh 3:5.   [3] 13 Dt 29:4; Isa 42:19–20; Jer 5:21; Eze 12:2.   [4] 14 Isa 6:9.   [5] 15 Isa 6:10; Ps 119:70; Zec 7:11.

²⁹ "But he said, 'No, lest while you gather up the weeds, you pull up also the wheat with them. ³⁰ Let both grow together until the harvest, and in the time of harvest I will say to the reapers: Gather up the weeds first and bind them in bundles to burn them, but gather the wheat into my barn.' "

The Parables of the Mustard Seed and the Yeast
Mk 4:30–32; Lk 13:18–21

³¹ He told them another parable, saying, "The kingdom of heaven is like a grain of mustard seed which a man took and sowed in his field. ³² This indeed is the least of all seeds, but when it has grown, it is the greatest among herbs and is a tree, so that the birds of the air come and lodge in its branches."

³³ He told them another parable: "The kingdom of heaven is like yeast which a woman took and mixed in sixty pounds¹ of meal until it had leavened the whole batch."

The Use of Parables
Mk 4:33–34

³⁴ Jesus said all these things to the crowds in parables. And without a parable He did not speak to them, ³⁵ to fulfill what was spoken by the prophet, saying:

"I will open My mouth in parables;
    I will say things which have been kept secret since the
    foundation of the world."²

The Parable of the Weeds Explained

³⁶ Then Jesus sent the crowds away and went into the house. And His disciples came to Him, saying, "Explain to us the parable of the weeds of the field."

³⁷ He answered, "He who sows the good seed is the Son of Man, ³⁸ the field is the world, and the good seed are the sons of the kingdom. But the weeds are the sons of the evil one. ³⁹ The enemy who sowed them is the devil, the harvest is the end of the world, and the reapers are the angels. ⁴⁰ "Therefore as the weeds are gathered and burned in the fire, so shall it be in the end of this world. ⁴¹ The Son of Man shall send out His angels, and they shall gather out of His kingdom all things that offend, and those who do evil, ⁴² and will throw them into a fiery furnace. There will be wailing and gnashing of teeth. ⁴³ Then the righteous will shine forth as the sun³ in the kingdom of their Father. Whoever has ears to hear, let him hear.

The Parable of the Hidden Treasure

⁴⁴ "Again, the kingdom of heaven is like treasure hidden in a field, which a man found and hid. And with joy over it he goes and sells all that he has and buys that field.

The Parable of the Pearl of Great Price

⁴⁵ "Again, the kingdom of heaven is like a merchant seeking beautiful pearls, ⁴⁶ who, on finding one pearl of great price, went and sold all that he had and bought it.

The Parable of the Net

⁴⁷ "Again, the kingdom of heaven is like a net that was cast into the sea and gathered all kinds of fish. ⁴⁸ When it was full, they drew it to shore, sat down, and gathered the good into baskets, but threw the bad away. ⁴⁹ So shall it be at the end of the world. The angels will come out and separate the evil from the righteous ⁵⁰ and throw them into the fiery furnace. There will be wailing and gnashing of teeth."

Treasures New and Old

⁵¹ Jesus said to them, "Have you understood all of these things?" They said to Him, "Yes, Lord."

⁵² Then He said to them, "Therefore every scribe who is discipled for the kingdom of heaven is like a man who is master of the household who brings out of his treasure new and old things."

The Rejection of Jesus at Nazareth
Mk 6:1–6; Lk 4:16–30

⁵³ When Jesus finished these parables, He departed from there. ⁵⁴ When He came to His own country, He taught them in their synagogue, so that they were astonished, and said, "Where did this Man get this wisdom and these mighty works? ⁵⁵ Is He not the carpenter's son? Is His mother not called Mary? And are not His brothers James and Joseph and Simon and Judas? ⁵⁶ And His sisters, are they not all with us? Where then did this Man get all these things?" ⁵⁷ And they took offense at Him.

But Jesus said to them, "A prophet is not without honor except in his own country and in his own house."

⁵⁸ And He did not do many mighty works there because of their unbelief.

The Death of John the Baptist
Mk 6:14–29; Lk 9:7–9

14 At that time Herod the tetrarch heard of the fame of Jesus, ² and said to his servants, "This is John the Baptist; he has risen from the dead. And therefore mighty works are at work in him."

³ For Herod had laid hold of John, bound him, and put him in prison for the sake of Herodias, his brother Philip's wife. ⁴ For John said to him, "It is not lawful for you to have her." ⁵ When Herod would have put him to death, he feared the crowd, because they counted him as a prophet.

⁶ But when Herod's birthday was celebrated, the daughter of Herodias danced before them and pleased Herod. ⁷ Therefore he promised with an oath to give her whatever she would ask. ⁸ Being previously instructed by her mother, she said, "Give me John the Baptist's head on a platter." ⁹ The king was sorry. Nevertheless, for the oath's sake and those who sat with him at supper, he commanded it to be given to her. ¹⁰ He sent and beheaded John in the prison. ¹¹ His head was brought on a platter and given to the girl, and she brought it to her mother. ¹² His disciples came and took up the body and buried it. And they went and told Jesus.

The Feeding of the Five Thousand
Mk 6:30–44; Lk 9:10–17; Jn 6:1–14

¹³ When Jesus heard this, He departed from there by boat for a deserted place. But when the people heard it, they followed Him on foot from the cities. ¹⁴ Jesus went ashore and saw a great assembly. And He was moved with compassion toward them, and He healed their sick.

¹⁵ When it was evening, His disciples came to Him, saying, "This is a lonely place and the day is now over. Send the crowds away to go into the villages and buy themselves food."

¹⁶ But Jesus said to them, "They do not need to depart. You give them something to eat."

¹⁷ They said to Him, "We have only five loaves here and two fish."

¹⁸ He said, "Bring them here to Me." ¹⁹ Then He commanded the crowds to sit down on the grass. He took the five loaves and the two fish, and looking up to heaven, He blessed and broke and gave the loaves to His disciples; and the disciples gave them to the crowds. ²⁰ They all ate and were filled. And they took up twelve baskets full of the fragments that remained. ²¹ Those who had eaten were about five thousand men, besides women and children.

Walking on the Water
Mk 6:45–52; Jn 6:15–21

²² Then Jesus commanded His disciples to get into the boat and go ahead of Him to the other side, while He sent the crowds away. ²³ When He sent the crowds away, He went up into a mountain by Himself to pray. And when evening came, He was there alone. ²⁴ But the boat was now in the middle of the sea, tossed by the waves, for the wind was turbulent.

²⁵ During the fourth watch of the night Jesus went to them, walking on the sea. ²⁶ But when the disciples saw Him walking on the sea, they were troubled, saying, "It is a spirit." And they cried out in fear.

---

¹33 Gk. *3 sata*, about 22 liters each.   ²35 Ps 78:2.   ³43 Da 12:3.

[27] But immediately Jesus spoke to them, saying, "Be of good cheer. It is I. Do not be afraid."

[28] Peter answered Him and said, "Lord, if it is You, bid me come to You on the water."

[29] He said, "Come."

And when Peter got out of the boat, he walked on the water to go to Jesus. [30] But when he saw the strong wind, he was afraid, and beginning to sink, he cried out, "Lord, save me!"

[31] Immediately Jesus reached out His hand and caught him, and said to him, "O you of little faith, why did you doubt?"

[32] And when they got into the boat, the wind ceased. [33] Then those who were in the boat came and worshipped Him, saying, "Truly You are the Son of God."

The Healing of the Sick in Gennesaret
Mk 6:53–56

[34] When they had crossed over, they came to the land of Gennesaret. [35] And when the men of that place recognized Him, they sent word to all the surrounding country and brought to Him all who were sick, [36] and begged Him that they might only touch the hem of His garment. And as many as touched it were made perfectly well.

The Tradition of the Elders
Mk 7:1–23

15 Then scribes and Pharisees who were from Jerusalem came to Jesus, saying, [2] "Why do Your disciples violate the tradition of the elders? For they do not wash their hands when they eat bread."

[3] But He answered them, "Why do you also violate the commandment of God by your tradition? [4] For God commanded, 'Honor your father and mother,'[1] and, 'He who speaks evil of father or mother, let him be put to death.'[2] [5] But you say, 'Whoever shall say to his father or his mother, "What you would have profited from me is a gift to God," [6] will be free from honoring his father or his mother.' So you have made the commandment of God of no effect by your tradition. [7] You hypocrites, Isaiah well prophesied of you, saying:

[8] 'These people draw near to Me with their mouth, and honor
        Me with their lips,
        but their heart is far from Me.
[9]   In vain they do worship Me,
        teaching as doctrines the precepts of men.'[3]"

[10] He called the crowds and said to them, "Hear and understand: [11] That which goes into the mouth does not defile a man, but that which comes out of the mouth, this defiles a man."

[12] Then His disciples came and said to Him, "Do You know that the Pharisees were offended after they heard this saying?"

[13] But He answered, "Every plant which My heavenly Father has not planted will be uprooted. [14] Leave them alone. They are blind leaders of the blind. And if the blind lead the blind, both will fall into the ditch."

[15] Then Peter said to Him, "Explain this parable to us."

[16] Jesus said, "Are you also still without understanding? [17] Do you not yet understand that whatever enters at the mouth goes into the stomach and is cast out into the sewer? [18] But those things which proceed out of the mouth come from the heart, and they defile the man. [19] For out of the heart proceed evil thoughts, murders, adulteries, sexual immorality, thefts, false witness, and blasphemies. [20] These are the things which defile a man. But to eat with unwashed hands does not defile a man."

The Faith of the Canaanite Woman
Mk 7:24–30

[21] Then Jesus went from there and departed into the regions of Tyre and Sidon. [22] There, a woman of Canaan came out of the same regions and cried out to Him, saying, "Have mercy on me, O Lord, Son of David. My daughter is severely possessed by a demon."

[23] But He did not answer her a word. And His disciples came and begged Him, saying, "Send her away, for she cries out after us."

[24] But He answered, "I was sent only to the lost sheep of the house of Israel."

[25] Then she came and worshipped Him, saying, "Lord, help me."

[26] But He answered, "It is not fair to take the children's bread and to throw it to dogs."

[27] She said, "Yes, Lord, yet even dogs eat the crumbs that fall from their masters' table."

[28] Then Jesus answered her, "O woman, great is your faith. Let it be done for you as you desire." And her daughter was healed instantly.

The Healing of Many People

[29] Jesus departed from there, and passed by the Sea of Galilee, and went up on a mountain and sat down there. [30] Great crowds came to Him, having with them those who were lame, blind, mute, maimed, and many others, and placed them down at Jesus' feet, and He healed them, [31] so that the crowds wondered when they saw the mute speak, the maimed made whole, the lame walk, and the blind see. And they glorified the God of Israel.

The Feeding of the Four Thousand
Mk 8:1–10

[32] Then Jesus called His disciples to Him and said, "I have compassion on the crowd, because they have remained with Me now for three days and have nothing to eat. I will not send them away hungry, lest they faint on the way."

[33] His disciples said to Him, "Where will we get enough bread in the wilderness to feed such a great crowd?"

[34] Jesus said to them, "How many loaves do you have?"

And they said, "Seven and a few little fish."

[35] He commanded the crowd to sit down on the ground. [36] He took the seven loaves and the fish, gave thanks, broke them, and gave them to His disciples, and the disciples gave them to the crowd. [37] They all ate and were filled. And they collected seven baskets full of the broken pieces that were left. [38] Those who ate were four thousand men, besides women and children. [39] He sent the crowd away, and got into the boat, and went to the region of Magdala.

The Demand for a Sign
Mk 8:11–13; Lk 12:54–56

16 The Pharisees and Sadducees came and, testing Him, asked Him to show them a sign from heaven.

[2] He answered them, "When it is evening, you say, 'It will be fair weather, for the sky is red,' [3] and in the morning, 'It will be foul weather today, for the sky is red and overcast.' O you hypocrites, you can discern the face of the sky, but you cannot discern the signs of the times. [4] A wicked and adulterous generation seeks for a sign, but no sign shall be given to it except the sign of the prophet Jonah." So He left them and departed.

The Yeast of Pharisees and Sadducees
Mk 8:14–21

[5] But when His disciples reached the other side, they had forgotten to take bread. [6] Then Jesus said to them, "Take heed and beware of the yeast of the Pharisees and Sadducees."

[7] They reasoned among themselves, saying, "It is because we have taken no bread."

[8] But when Jesus perceived it, He said to them, "O you of little faith, why reason among yourselves, that it is because you have brought no bread? [9] Do you not yet understand or remember the five loaves of the five thousand and how many baskets you collected? [10] Or the seven loaves of the four thousand and how many baskets you collected? [11] How is it that you do not understand that I spoke to you not concerning bread, but that you should beware of the yeast of the Pharisees and Sadducees?" [12] Then they understood that He did not tell them to beware of the yeast of bread, but of the teaching of the Pharisees and Sadducees.

---

1 4 Ex 20:12; Dt 5:16.   *2 4* Ex 21:17; Lev 20:9.   *3 8–9* Isa 29:13.

Peter's Declaration About Jesus
Mk 8:27–30; Lk 9:18–21

[13] When Jesus came into the region of Caesarea Philippi, He asked His disciples, "Who do men say that I, the Son of Man, am?"

[14] They said, "Some say that You are John the Baptist, others say Elijah, and others Jeremiah or one of the prophets."

[15] He said to them, "But who do you say that I am?"

[16] Simon Peter replied, "You are the Christ, the Son of the living God."

[17] Jesus answered him, "Blessed are you, Simon son of Jonah, for flesh and blood has not revealed this to you, but My Father who is in heaven. [18] And I tell you that you are Peter, and on this rock I will build My church, and the gates of Hades shall not prevail against it. [19] I will give you the keys of the kingdom of heaven, and whatever you bind on earth shall be bound in heaven, and whatever you loose on earth shall be loosed in heaven." [20] Then He commanded His disciples to tell no one that He was Jesus the Christ.

Jesus Foretells His Death and Resurrection
Mk 8:31–9:1; Lk 9:22–27

[21] From that time on, Jesus began to show His disciples that He must go to Jerusalem and suffer many things from the elders and chief priests and scribes, and be killed, and be raised on the third day.

[22] Then Peter took Him and began rebuking Him, saying, "Far be it from You, Lord! This shall not happen to You."

[23] But He turned and said to Peter, "Get behind Me, Satan! You are an offense to Me, for you are not mindful of the things that are of God, but those that are of men."

[24] Then Jesus said to His disciples, "If anyone will come after Me, let him deny himself, and take up his cross, and follow Me. [25] For whoever would save his life will lose it, and whoever loses his life for My sake will find it. [26] For what will it profit a man if he gains the whole world and loses his own soul? Or what shall a man give in exchange for his soul? [27] For the Son of Man shall come with His angels in the glory of His Father, and then He will repay every man according to his works. [28] Truly I say to you, there are some standing here who shall not taste death before they see the Son of Man coming in His kingdom."

The Transfiguration
Mk 9:2–13; Lk 9:28–36

17 After six days Jesus took Peter, James, and John his brother and brought them up to a high mountain alone, [2] and was transfigured before them. His face shone as the sun, and His garments became white as the light. [3] Suddenly Moses and Elijah appeared to them, talking with Him.

[4] Then Peter said to Jesus, "Lord, it is good for us to be here. If You wish, let us make three tabernacles here: one for You, one for Moses, and one for Elijah."

[5] While he was still speaking, suddenly a bright cloud overshadowed them, and a voice from the cloud said, "This is My beloved Son, with whom I am well pleased. Listen to Him."

[6] When the disciples heard this, they fell on their faces and were filled with awe. [7] But Jesus came and touched them and said, "Rise, and do not be afraid." [8] When they lifted up their eyes, they saw no one but Jesus only.

[9] As they came down the mountain, Jesus commanded them, "Tell the vision to no one until the Son of Man is risen from the dead."

[10] His disciples asked Him, "Why then do the scribes say that Elijah must come first?"

[11] Jesus answered, "Elijah truly does first come and will restore all things. [12] But I tell you that Elijah has already come, and they did not know him, but did to him whatever they pleased. Likewise, the Son of Man will also suffer at their hands." [13] Then the disciples understood that He was speaking to them of John the Baptist.

The Healing of a Boy with a Demon
Mk 9:14–29; Lk 9:37–43

[14] When they came to the crowd, a man came to Him and knelt before Him, saying, [15] "Lord, have mercy on my son, for he is an epileptic and suffers terribly. He often falls into the fire and often into the water. [16] I brought him to Your disciples, but they could not heal him."

[17] Then Jesus answered, "O faithless and perverse generation, how long shall I be with you? How long shall I bear with you? Bring him here to Me." [18] Jesus rebuked the demon, and he came out of him. And the child was healed instantly.

[19] Then the disciples came to Jesus privately and said, "Why could we not cast him out?"

[20] Jesus said to them, "Because of your unbelief. For truly I say to you, if you have faith as a grain of mustard seed, you will say to this mountain, 'Move from here to there,' and it will move. And nothing will be impossible for you. [21] But this kind does not go out except by prayer and fasting."

Jesus Again Foretells His Death and Resurrection
Mk 9:30–32; Lk 9:43b–45

[22] While they were staying in Galilee, Jesus said to them, "The Son of Man is about to be betrayed into the hands of men, [23] and they will kill Him, and He will be raised on the third day." And they were extremely sorrowful.

Payment of the Temple Tax

[24] When they came to Capernaum, those who collected tax money came to Peter and said, "Does your Teacher not pay the tax[1]?"

[25] He said, "Yes."

And when he came home, Jesus stopped him, saying, "What do you think, Simon? From whom do the kings of the earth take custom or taxes? From their own sons or from strangers?"

[26] Peter said to Him, "From strangers."

Jesus said to him, "Then the sons are free. [27] However, lest we offend them, go to the sea and cast a hook, and take the first fish that comes up. And when you open its mouth, you will find a coin. Take it and give it to them for you and Me."

The Greatest in the Kingdom
Mk 9:33–37; Lk 9:46–48

18 At that time the disciples came to Jesus, saying, "Who is the greatest in the kingdom of heaven?"

[2] Jesus called a little child to Him and set him in their midst, [3] and said, "Truly I say to you, unless you are converted and become like little children, you will not enter the kingdom of heaven. [4] Therefore whoever humbles himself like this little child is greatest in the kingdom of heaven. [5] And whoever receives one such little child in My name receives Me.

Temptations to Sin
Mk 9:42–48; Lk 17:1–2

[6] "But whoever misleads one of these little ones who believe in Me, it would be better for him to have a millstone hung about his neck and to be drowned in the depth of the sea. [7] Woe to the world because of temptations! For it must be that temptations come, but woe to that man by whom the temptation comes! [8] Therefore if your hand or your foot causes you to sin, cut it off and throw it away. It is better for you to enter life lame or maimed than having two hands or two feet to be thrown into eternal fire. [9] And if your eye causes you to sin, pluck it out and throw it away. It is better for you to enter life with one eye than having two eyes to be thrown into the fire of hell.

The Parable of the Lost Sheep
Lk 15:5–7

[10] "See that you do not despise one of these little ones. For I say to you that in heaven their angels always see the face of My Father who is in heaven. [11] For the Son of Man has come to save that which was lost.

---

[1] 24 Gk. 2 *drachmas*, or two days' wages.

[12] "What do you think? If a man has a hundred sheep and one of them goes astray, does he not leave the ninety-nine on the hills and go in search for the one which went astray? [13] And if he finds it, truly I say to you, he rejoices more over that sheep than over the ninety-nine which never went astray. [14] So it is not the will of your Father who is in heaven that one of these little ones should perish.

The Brother Who Sins
Lk 17:3

[15] "Now if your brother sins against you, go and tell him his fault between you and him alone. If he listens to you, you have gained your brother. [16] But if he does not listen, then take with you one or two others, that by the testimony of two or three witnesses every word may be established.[1] [17] If he refuses to listen to them, tell it to the church. But if he refuses to listen even to the church, let him be to you as a Gentile and a tax collector.

[18] "Truly I say to you, whatever you bind on earth will be bound in heaven, and whatever you loose on earth will be loosed in heaven.

[19] "Again I say to you, that if two of you agree on earth about anything they ask, it will be done for them by My Father who is in heaven. [20] For where two or three are assembled in My name, there I am in their midst."

The Parable of the Unforgiving Servant

[21] Then Peter came to Him and said, "Lord, how often shall I forgive my brother who sins against me? Up to seven times?"

[22] Jesus said to him, "I do not say to you up to seven times, but up to seventy times seven.

[23] "Therefore the kingdom of heaven is like a certain king who wanted to settle accounts with his servants. [24] When he began to settle the accounts, one was brought to him who owed him ten thousand talents.[2] [25] But since he was not able to pay, his master ordered that he be sold with his wife, their children, and all that he had, and payment to be made.

[26] "So the servant fell on his knees, pleading with him, saying, 'Master, have patience with me, and I will pay you everything.' [27] Then the master of that servant was moved with compassion, released him, and forgave him the debt.

[28] "But that same servant went out and found one of his fellow servants who owed him a hundred denarii.[3] He laid hands on him and took him by the throat, saying, 'Pay me what you owe.'

[29] "So his fellow servant fell down at his feet and entreated him, saying, 'Have patience with me, and I will pay you everything.' [30] "But he would not and went and threw him in prison until he should pay the debt. [31] So when his fellow servants saw what took place, they were very sorry and went and told their master all that had taken place.

[32] "Then his master, after he had summoned him, said to him, 'O you wicked servant! I forgave you all that debt because you pleaded with me. [33] Should you not also have had compassion on your fellow servant, even as I had pity on you?' [34] His master was angry and delivered him to the jailers until he should pay all his debt.

[35] "So also My heavenly Father will do to each of you, if from your heart you do not forgive your brother for his trespasses."

Teaching About Divorce
Mk 10:1–12

19 Now when Jesus finished these sayings, He departed from Galilee and came into the region of Judea beyond the Jordan. [2] Large crowds followed Him, and He healed them there.

[3] The Pharisees also came to Him, tempting Him and saying, "Is it lawful for a man to divorce his wife for any reason?"

[4] He answered, "Have you not read that He who made them at the beginning 'made them male and female,'[4] [5] and said, 'For this reason a man shall leave his father and mother and be joined to his wife, and the two shall become one flesh'?[5] [6] So they are no longer two, but one flesh. Therefore what God has joined together, let no man put asunder."

[7] They said to Him, "Then why did Moses command to give a certificate of divorce, and to send her away?"[6]

[8] He said to them, "Moses, for the hardness of your hearts, permitted you to divorce your wives, but from the beginning it was not so. [9] But I say to you, whoever divorces his wife, except for sexual immorality, and marries another, commits adultery. And whoever marries her who is divorced commits adultery."

[10] His disciples said to Him, "If such is the case of the man with his wife, it is not good to marry."

[11] But He said to them, "Not all men can receive this precept, but only those to whom it is given. [12] For there are some eunuchs who have been so from birth, there are some eunuchs who have been made eunuchs by men, and there are some eunuchs who have made themselves eunuchs for the sake of the kingdom of heaven. He who is able to receive this, let him receive it."

Little Children Blessed
Mk 10:13–16; Lk 18:15–17

[13] Then little children were brought to Him that He might put His hands on them and pray. But the disciples rebuked them.

[14] But Jesus said, "Let the little children come to Me, and do not forbid them. For to such belongs the kingdom of heaven." [15] He laid His hands on them and departed from there.

The Rich Young Man
Mk 10:17–31; Lk 18:18–30

[16] Now one came and said to Him, "Good Teacher, what good deed shall I do to have eternal life?"

[17] He replied to him, "Why do you call Me good? There is One who is good. But if you would enter life, keep the commandments."

[18] He said to Him, "Which ones?"

Jesus said, "You shall not murder, You shall not commit adultery, You shall not steal, You shall not bear false witness,[7] [19] Honor your father and your mother,[8] and, You shall love your neighbor as yourself.'[9]"

[20] The young man said to Him, "All these I have kept from my youth. What do I still lack?"

[21] Jesus said to him, "If you would be perfect, go and sell what you have, and give to the poor, and you will have treasure in heaven. And come, follow Me."

[22] But when the young man heard this, he went away sorrowful. For he had great possessions.

[23] Then Jesus said to His disciples, "Truly, I say to you that it will be hard for a rich man to enter the kingdom of heaven. [24] And again I say to you, it is easier for a camel to go through the eye of a needle than for a rich man to enter the kingdom of God."

[25] When His disciples heard this, they were greatly amazed, saying, "Who then can be saved?"

[26] But Jesus looked at them and said, "With men this is impossible, but with God all things are possible."

[27] Then Peter answered Him, "See, we have left everything and followed You. What then shall we have?"

[28] Jesus said to them, "Truly I say to you, in the regeneration, when the Son of Man sits on His glorious throne, you who have followed Me will also sit on twelve thrones, judging the twelve tribes of Israel. [29] And everyone who has left houses or brothers or sisters or father or mother or wife or children or fields for My name's sake shall receive a hundred times as much and inherit eternal life. [30] But many who are first will be last, and the last first."

The Workers in the Vineyard

20 "For the kingdom of heaven is like a landowner who went out early in the morning to hire laborers for his vineyard. [2] When he had agreed with the laborers for a denarius a day, he sent them into his vineyard.

[3] "Then he went out about the third hour and saw others standing idle in the marketplace, [4] and said to them, 'You also

go into the vineyard, and whatever is right I will give you.' So they went. [5] Again he went out about the sixth hour and the ninth hour and did likewise.

[6] "About the eleventh hour he went out and found others standing idle, and said to them, 'Why do you stand here idle all day?'

[7] "They said to him, 'Because no one has hired us.'

"He said to them, 'You also go into the vineyard, and whatever is right you will receive.'

[8] "So when evening came, the owner of the vineyard said to his steward, 'Call the laborers and give them their wages, beginning with the last to the first.'

[9] "When they who were hired about the eleventh hour came, they each received a denarius. [10] But when the first came, they supposed that they would receive more, but each of them likewise received a denarius. [11] When they received it, they grumbled against the landowner, [12] saying, 'These last worked only one hour, and you made them equal to us, who have borne the burden and the heat of the day.'

[13] "But he answered one of them, 'Friend, I am doing you no wrong. Did you not agree with me for a denarius? [14] Take what is yours and go your way. I will give to this last one even as I give to you. [15] Is it not lawful for me to do what I wish with my own things? Or is your eye evil because I am good?'

[16] "So the last will be first, and the first last. For many are called, but few are chosen."

A Third Time Jesus Foretells His Death and Resurrection
Mk 10:32–34; Lk 18:31–34

[17] As Jesus was going up to Jerusalem, He took the twelve disciples aside on the road and said to them, [18] "Now we are going up to Jerusalem, and the Son of Man will be betrayed to the chief priests and scribes. And they will condemn Him to death [19] and deliver Him to the Gentiles to mock, and to scourge, and to crucify Him, but on the third day He will rise."

A Mother's Request
Mk 10:35–45

[20] Then the mother of Zebedee's sons came to Him with her sons. And kneeling before Him, she asked for a certain thing.

[21] He said to her, "What do you want?"

She said to Him, "Grant that these two sons of mine may sit, one at Your right hand and one at Your left, in Your kingdom."

[22] But Jesus answered, "You do not know what you are asking. Are you able to drink from the cup that I am to drink, and to be baptized with the baptism that I am baptized with?"

They said to Him, "We are able."

[23] He said to them, "You will indeed drink from My cup and be baptized with the baptism that I am baptized with. But to sit at My right hand and at My left is not Mine to grant, but it is for those for whom it is prepared by My Father."

[24] When the ten heard it, they were moved with indignation against the two brothers. [25] But Jesus called them to Him and said, "You know that the rulers of the Gentiles lord it over them, and those who are great exercise authority over them. [26] It shall not be so among you. Whoever would be great among you, let him serve you, [27] and whoever would be first among you, let him be your slave, [28] even as the Son of Man did not come to be served, but to serve and to give His life as a ransom for many."

The Healing of Two Blind Men
Mk 10:46–52; Lk 18:35–43

[29] As they departed from Jericho, a large crowd followed Him. [30] There, two blind men sitting by the road, when they heard that Jesus was passing by, cried out, "Have mercy on us, O Lord, Son of David!"

[31] The crowd rebuked them, that they should be silent. But they cried out even more, "Have mercy on us, O Lord, Son of David!"

[32] Jesus stood still and called them, saying, "What do you want Me to do for you?"

[33] They said to Him, "Lord, let our eyes be opened."

[34] So Jesus had compassion on them and touched their eyes. Immediately their eyes received sight, and they followed Him.

The Triumphant Entry Into Jerusalem
Mk 11:1–11; Lk 19:28–38; Jn 12:12–19

21 When they drew near to Jerusalem and came to Bethphage, on the Mount of Olives, then Jesus sent two disciples, [2] saying to them, "Go over into the village opposite you, and immediately you will find a donkey tied, and a colt with her. Untie them and bring them to Me. [3] If anyone says anything to you, you shall say, 'The Lord has need of them.' And he will send them immediately."

[4] All this was done to fulfill what was spoken by the prophet, saying:

[5] "Tell the daughter of Zion,
   'Look, your King is coming to you,
humble, and sitting on a donkey,
   and on a colt, the foal of a donkey.'[1]"

[6] The disciples went and did as Jesus commanded them. [7] They brought the donkey and the colt, laid their garments on them, and He sat on them. [8] A very large crowd spread their garments on the road. Others cut down branches from the trees and spread them on the road. [9] The crowds that went before Him and that followed Him cried out:

"Hosanna to the Son of David!
'Blessed is He who comes in the name of the Lord!'[2]
Hosanna in the highest!"

[10] When He entered Jerusalem, the entire city was moved, saying, "Who is He?"

[11] The crowds said, "This is Jesus, the prophet from Nazareth of Galilee."

The Cleansing of the Temple
Mk 11:15–19; Lk 19:45–48; Jn 2:13–22

[12] Jesus went into the temple of God and drove out all those who sold and bought in the temple and overturned the tables of the moneychangers and the seats of those who sold doves. [13] He said to them, "It is written, 'My house shall be called a house of prayer,'[3] but you have made it 'a den of thieves.'[4]"

[14] The blind and the lame came to Him in the temple, and He healed them. [15] But when the chief priests and scribes saw the wonderful things that He did, and the children crying out in the temple, "Hosanna to the Son of David," they were extremely displeased [16] and said to Him, "Do You hear what these are saying?"

Jesus said to them, "Yes. Have you never read,

'Out of the mouth of children and infants
   You have perfected praise'[5]?"

[17] And He left them and went out of the city into Bethany, and He lodged there.

The Cursing of the Fig Tree
Mk 11:12–14, 20–24

[18] Now in the morning as He returned to the city, He became hungry. [19] When He saw a fig tree by the road, He went to it but found nothing on it except leaves. He said to it, "Let no fruit ever grow on you again." Immediately the fig tree withered away.

[20] When the disciples saw it, they were amazed, saying, "How did the fig tree wither away instantly?"

[21] Jesus answered them, "Truly I say to you, if you have faith and do not doubt, you will not only do what was done to the fig tree, but also, if you say to this mountain, 'Be removed, and be thrown into the sea,' it will be done. [22] And whatever you ask in prayer, if you believe, you will receive."

---

[1] 5 Zec 9:9.   [2] 9 Ps 118:26.   [3] 13 Isa 56:7.   [4] 13 Jer 7:11.   [5] 16 Ps 8:2.

The Question of Jesus' Authority
Mk 11:27–33; Lk 20:1–8

23 When He entered the temple, the chief priests and the elders of the people came up to Him as He was teaching, and said, "By what authority are You doing these things? And who gave You this authority?"

24 Jesus answered them, "I also will ask you one question. If you tell Me, I likewise will tell you by what authority I do these things. 25 Where did the baptism of John come from? From heaven or from men?"

They reasoned among themselves, saying, "If we say, 'From heaven,' He will say to us, 'Then why did you not believe him?' 26 But if we say, 'From men,' we are afraid of the people, for all hold John as a prophet."

27 So they answered Jesus, "We do not know."

Then He said to them, "Neither will I tell you by what authority I do these things.

The Parable of the Two Sons

28 "What do you think? A man had two sons. He came to the first and said, 'Son, go work today in my vineyard.'

29 "He answered, 'I will not,' but afterward he repented and went.

30 "Then he came to the second, and said likewise. He answered, 'I will go, sir,' but did not go.

31 "Which of the two did the will of his father?"

They said, "The first."

Jesus said to them, "Truly I say to you, the tax collectors and prostitutes enter the kingdom of God before you. 32 For John came to you in the way of righteousness, and you did not believe him. But the tax collectors and prostitutes believed him. And even when you saw it, you did not afterward repent and believe him.

The Parable of the Vineyard and the Vinedressers
Mk 12:1–12; Lk 20:9–19

33 "Listen to another parable: There was a certain landowner who planted a vineyard and built a wall around it. He dug a winepress in it and built a tower. Then he rented it to vinedressers and went into a distant country. 34 When the season of the fruit drew near, he sent his servants to the vinedressers to receive his fruit.

35 "The vinedressers took his servants and beat one, killed another, and stoned another. 36 Again, he sent other servants, more than the first. And they did likewise to them. 37 Last of all, he sent his son to them, saying, 'They will respect my son.'

38 "But when the vinedressers saw the son, they said to themselves, 'This is the heir. Come, let us kill him and seize his inheritance.' 39 So they caught him, threw him out of the vineyard, and killed him.

40 "Therefore, when the owner of the vineyard comes, what will he do to those vinedressers?"

41 They said, "He will severely destroy those wicked men and rent his vineyard to other vinedressers who will give him the fruits in their seasons."

42 Jesus said to them, "Have you never read in the Scriptures:

'The stone which the builders rejected
　　has become the cornerstone.
This is the Lord's doing,
　　and it is marvelous in our eyes'¹?

43 "Therefore I tell you, the kingdom of God will be taken from you and given to a nation bearing its fruits. 44 Whoever falls on this stone will be broken to pieces. But on whomever it falls, it will crush him."

45 When the chief priests and Pharisees heard His parables, they perceived that He was speaking of them. 46 But as they tried to arrest Him, they feared the crowds, because they held Him as a prophet.

The Parable of the Wedding Banquet
Lk 14:15–24

22 Jesus spoke to them again by parables, saying, 2 "The kingdom of heaven is like a certain king who arranged a marriage for his son, 3 and sent out his servants to call those who were invited to the wedding, but they would not come.

4 "Again, he sent out other servants, saying, 'Tell those who are invited: See, I have prepared my supper. My oxen and fattened calves are killed, and everything is ready. Come to the wedding banquet.'

5 "But they made light of it and went their ways, one to his farm, another to his business; 6 the rest took his servants, treated them spitefully, and killed them. 7 When the king heard about it, he was angry. He sent in his army and destroyed those murderers and burned up their city.

8 "Then he said to his servants, 'The wedding is ready, but those who were invited were not worthy. 9 Go therefore to the streets, and invite to the wedding banquet as many as you find.' 10 So those servants went out into the streets and gathered together as many as they found, both bad and good. So the wedding hall was filled with guests.

11 "But when the king came in to see the guests, he saw a man who was not wearing wedding garments. 12 He said to him, 'Friend, how did you get in here without wedding garments?' And he was speechless.

13 "Then the king told the attendants, 'Bind him hand and foot, take him away, and cast him into outer darkness, where there will be weeping and gnashing of teeth.'

14 "For many are called, but few are chosen."

The Question of Paying Taxes
Mk 12:13–17; Lk 20:20–26

15 Then the Pharisees went and took counsel to entangle Him in His words. 16 They sent their disciples to Him with the Herodians, saying, "Teacher, we know that You are truthful and teach the way of God truthfully, and are swayed by no one. For You do not regard the person of men. 17 Tell us then, what do You think? Is it lawful to pay taxes to Caesar, or not?"

18 But Jesus perceived their wickedness and said, "Why test Me, you hypocrites? 19 Show Me the tax money." They brought Him a denarius. 20 He said to them, "Whose is this image and inscription?"

21 They said to Him, "Caesar's."

Then He said to them, "Render therefore to Caesar the things that are Caesar's, and to God the things that are God's."

22 When they heard these words, they were amazed, and left Him and went on their way.

The Question About the Resurrection
Mk 12:18–27; Lk 20:27–40

23 The same day the Sadducees, who say that there is no resurrection, came to Him and asked Him, 24 "Teacher, Moses said, 'If a man dies having no children, his brother must marry his wife and raise up children for his brother.'² 25 Now there were seven brothers with us. The first died after he married and, having no children, left his wife to his brother. 26 Likewise the second and third, on to the seventh. 27 Last of all, the woman died also. 28 Therefore, in the resurrection, whose wife shall she be of the seven? For they all had her."

29 Jesus answered, "You err, not knowing the Scriptures nor the power of God. 30 For in the resurrection they neither marry nor are given in marriage, but are like the angels of God in heaven. 31 But concerning the resurrection of the dead, have you not read what was spoken to you by God, 32 'I am the God of Abraham, the God of Isaac, and the God of Jacob'³? God is not the God of the dead, but of the living."

33 When the crowds heard this, they were astonished at His teaching.

The Great Commandment
Mk 12:28–34; Lk 10:25–28

34 When the Pharisees heard that He silenced the Sadducees, they came together. 35 One of them, who was a lawyer, tested Him

¹42 Ps 118:22–23.　²24 Dt 25:5.　³32 Ex 3:6.

by asking Him, [36] "Teacher, which is the greatest commandment in the law?" [37] Jesus said to him, " 'You shall love the Lord your God with all your heart, and with all your soul, and with all your mind.'[1] [38] This is the first and great commandment. [39] And the second is like it: 'You shall love your neighbor as yourself.'[2] [40] On these two commandments hang all the Law and the Prophets."

The Question About David's Son
Mk 12:35–37; Lk 20:41–44

[41] While the Pharisees were assembled, Jesus asked them, [42] "What do you think of the Christ? Whose Son is He?"

They said to Him, "The Son of David."

[43] He said to them, "How then does David in the Spirit call Him 'Lord,' saying:

[44] 'The Lord said to my Lord,
  "Sit at My right hand,
  until I make Your enemies
    Your footstool" '[3]

[45] If David then calls Him 'Lord,' how is He his Son?" [46] No one was able to answer Him a word, nor from that day on did anyone dare to ask Him any more questions.

The Denouncing of the Scribes and Pharisees
Mk 12:38–40; Lk 11:37–52; 20:45–47

23 Then Jesus said to the crowds and to His disciples, [2] "The scribes and the Pharisees sit in Moses' seat. [3] Therefore, whatever they tell you to observe, that observe and do, but do not do their works. For they speak, but do nothing. [4] They fasten heavy loads that are hard to carry and lay them on men's shoulders, but they themselves will not move them with their finger.

[5] "They do all their works to be seen by men. They make their Scripture boxes broad and lengthen the tassels on their prayer shawls. [6] They love the places of honor at feasts, and the prominent seats in the synagogues, [7] and greetings in the marketplaces, and being called 'Rabbi' by men.

[8] "But do not be called 'Rabbi,' for you have one Teacher, the Christ, and you are all brothers. [9] And call no man on earth your father, for you have one Father, who is in heaven. [10] Nor be called teachers, for you have one Teacher, the Christ. [11] He who is greatest among you shall be your servant. [12] For he who exalts himself will be humbled, and he who humbles himself will be exalted.

[13] "Woe to you, scribes and Pharisees, hypocrites! You shut the kingdom of heaven against men. For you neither enter yourselves, nor allow those who are entering to go in. [14] Woe to you, scribes and Pharisees, hypocrites! You devour widows' houses and for pretense make long prayers. Therefore you will receive the greater condemnation.

[15] "Woe to you, scribes and Pharisees, hypocrites! You travel sea and land to make one proselyte, and when he becomes one, you make him twice as much a son of hell as yourselves.

[16] "Woe to you, blind guides, who say, 'If anyone swears by the temple, it is nothing. But if anyone swears by the gold of the temple, he is obligated.' [17] You blind fools! Which is greater, the gold or the temple that sanctifies the gold? [18] And you say, 'If anyone swears by the altar, it is nothing. But if anyone swears by the gift on it, he is obligated.' [19] You blind fools! Which is greater, the gift or the altar that sanctifies the gift? [20] Therefore he who swears by the altar, swears by it and by all things on it. [21] But he who swears by the temple, swears by it and by Him who dwells in it. [22] And he who swears by heaven, swears by the throne of God and by Him who sits on it.

[23] "Woe to you, scribes and Pharisees, hypocrites! You tithe mint and dill and cumin, but have neglected the weightier matters of the law: justice and mercy and faith. These you ought to have done without leaving the others undone. [24] You blind guides who strain out a gnat and swallow a camel!

[25] "Woe to you, scribes and Pharisees, hypocrites! You cleanse the outside of the cup and dish, but inside they are full of extortion and greed. [26] You blind Pharisee, first cleanse the inside of the cup and dish, that the outside of them may also be clean.

[27] "Woe to you, scribes and Pharisees, hypocrites! You are like whitewashed tombs, which indeed appear beautiful outwardly, but inside are full of dead men's bones and of all uncleanness. [28] So you also outwardly appear righteous to men, but inside you are full of hypocrisy and iniquity.

[29] "Woe to you, scribes and Pharisees, hypocrites! You build the tombs of the prophets, and adorn the memorials of the righteous, [30] and say, 'If we lived in the days of our fathers, we would not have partaken with them in shedding the blood of the prophets.' [31] Therefore you are witnesses against yourselves that you are sons of those who murdered the prophets. [32] Fill up, then, the measure of your fathers' *guilt*.

[33] "You serpents! You generation of vipers! How can you escape the judgment of hell? [34] Therefore I send you prophets, and wise men, and scribes. Some of them you will kill and crucify, and some you will scourge in your synagogues and persecute them from city to city, [35] that on you may come all the righteous blood shed on the earth, from the blood of righteous Abel to the blood of Zechariah son of Berekiah, whom you murdered between the temple and the altar. [36] Truly I say to you, all these things will come on this generation.

The Lament Over Jerusalem
Lk 13:34–35

[37] "O Jerusalem, Jerusalem, you who kill the prophets and stone those who are sent to you, how often I would have gathered your children together as a hen gathers her chicks under her wings, but you would not! [38] Look, your house is left to you desolate. [39] For I tell you, you shall not see Me again until you say, 'Blessed is He who comes in the name of the Lord.'[4]"

The Destruction of the Temple Foretold
Mk 13:1–2; Lk 21:5–6

24 Jesus departed from the temple and was leaving when His disciples came to show Him the temple buildings. [2] Jesus answered them, "Do you not see all these things? Truly I say to you, not one stone shall be left here upon another that shall not be thrown down."

Troubles and Persecutions
Mk 13:3–13; Lk 21:7–19

[3] As He sat on the Mount of Olives, the disciples came to Him privately, saying, "Tell us, when will these things be, and what will be the sign of Your coming and of the end of the age?"

[4] Jesus answered them, "Take heed that no one deceives you. [5] For many will come in My name, saying, 'I am the Christ,' and will deceive many. [6] You will hear of wars and rumors of wars. See that you are not troubled. For all these things must happen, but the end is not yet. [7] For nation will rise against nation, and kingdom against kingdom. There will be famines, epidemics, and earthquakes in various places. [8] All these are the beginning of sorrows. [9] "Then they will hand you over to be persecuted and will kill you. And you will be hated by all nations for My name's sake. [10] Then many will fall away, and betray one another, and hate one another. [11] And many false prophets will rise and will deceive many. [12] Because iniquity will abound, the love of many will grow cold. [13] But he who endures to the end shall be saved. [14] And this gospel of the kingdom will be preached throughout the world as a testimony to all nations, and then the end will come.

The Great Tribulation
Mk 13:14–23; Lk 21:20–24

[15] "So when you see the 'abomination of desolation,'[5] spoken of by Daniel the prophet, standing in the holy place (let the reader understand), [16] then let those who are in Judea flee to the mountains. [17] Let him who is on the housetop not go down to

take anything out of his house. [18] Let him who is in the field not return to take his clothes. [19] Woe to those who are with child and to those who nurse in those days! [20] Pray that your escape will not be in the winter or on the Sabbath. [21] For then will be great tribulation, such as has not happened since the beginning of the world until now, no, nor ever shall be.

[22] "Unless those days were shortened, no one would be saved. But for the sake of the elect those days will be shortened. [23] Then if anyone says to you, 'Look, here is the Christ,' or 'There He is,' do not believe it. [24] For false christs and false prophets will arise and show great signs and wonders to deceive, if possible, even the elect. [25] Listen, I have told you beforehand.

[26] "So, if they say to you, 'Look, He is in the desert,' do not go there; or, 'Look, He is in the private chambers,' do not believe it. [27] For as the lightning comes from the east and flashes to the west, so will be the coming of the Son of Man. [28] Wherever the carcass is, there the eagles will be gathered together.

The Coming of the Son of Man
Mk 13:24–27; Lk 21:25–28

[29] "Immediately after the tribulation of those days,

'the sun will be darkened,
　and the moon will not give its light;
the stars will fall from heaven,
　and the powers of the heavens will be shaken.'[1]

[30] "Then the sign of the Son of Man will appear in heaven, and then all the tribes of the earth will mourn, and they will see the Son of Man coming on the clouds of heaven with power and great glory. [31] And He will send His angels with a great sound of a trumpet, and they shall gather His elect from the four winds, from one end of the heavens to the other.

The Lesson of the Fig Tree
Mk 13:28–31; Lk 21:29–33

[32] "Now learn this lesson from the fig tree: When its branch becomes tender and grows leaves, you know that summer is near. [33] So also, when you shall see all these things, you know that it is near, even at the doors. [34] Truly I say to you, this generation will not pass away until all these things take place. [35] Heaven and earth will pass away, but My words will never pass away.

The Unknown Day and Hour
Mk 13:32–37; Lk 17:26–30, 34–36

[36] "Concerning that day and hour no one knows, not even the angels of heaven, but My Father only. [37] As were the days of Noah, so will be the coming of the Son of Man. [38] For as in the days before the flood, they were eating and drinking, marrying and giving in marriage, until the day Noah entered the ark, [39] and did not know until the flood came and took them all away, so will be the coming of the Son of Man. [40] Two will be in the field; one will be taken, and the other left. [41] Two women will be grinding at the mill; one will be taken, and the other left.

[42] "Watch therefore, for you do not know what hour your Lord will come. [43] But know this, that if the owner of the house had known what hour the thief would come, he would have watched and not have let his house be broken into. [44] Therefore you also must be ready, for in an hour when you least expect, the Son of Man is coming.

The Faithful or the Unfaithful Servant
Lk 12:41–48

[45] "Who then is a faithful and wise servant, whom his master has made ruler over his household to give them food at the appointed time? [46] Blessed is that servant whom his master will find so doing when he comes. [47] Truly, I say to you that he will make him ruler over all his goods. [48] But if that evil servant says in his heart, 'My master delays his coming,' [49] and begins to strike his fellow servants and eat and drink with the drunkards, [50] the

master of that servant will come on a day when he does not look for him and in an hour he is not aware of [51] and will cut him in pieces and appoint him his portion with the hypocrites, where there shall be weeping and gnashing of teeth.

The Parable of the Ten Virgins

25 "Then the kingdom of heaven shall be like ten virgins, who took their lamps and went out to meet the bridegroom. [2] Five of them were wise and five were foolish. [3] Those who were foolish took their lamps, but took no oil with them. [4] But the wise took jars of oil with their lamps. [5] While the bridegroom delayed, they all rested and slept.

[6] "But at midnight there was a cry, 'Look, the bridegroom is coming! Come out to meet him!'

[7] "Then all those virgins rose and trimmed their lamps. [8] But the foolish said to the wise, 'Give us some of your oil, for our lamps have gone out.'

[9] "The wise answered, 'No, lest there not be enough for us and you. Go rather to those who sell it, and buy some for yourselves.'

[10] "But while they went to buy some, the bridegroom came, and those who were ready went in with him to the wedding banquet. And the door was shut.

[11] "Afterward, the other virgins came also, saying, 'Lord, Lord, open the door for us.'

[12] "But he answered, 'Truly I say to you, I do not know you.'

[13] "Watch therefore, for you know neither the day nor the hour in which the Son of Man is coming.

The Parable of the Talents
Lk 19:11–27

[14] "Again, the kingdom of heaven is like a man traveling into a far country, who called his own servants and entrusted his goods to them. [15] To one he gave five talents,[2] to another two, and to another one, to every man according to his ability. And immediately he took his journey. [16] He who had received the five talents went and traded with them and made another five talents. [17] So also, he who had received two gained another two. [18] But he who had received one went and dug in the ground and hid his master's money.

[19] "After a long time the master of those servants came and settled accounts with them. [20] He who had received five talents came and brought the other five talents, saying, 'Master, you entrusted to me five talents. Look, I have gained five talents more.'

[21] "His master said to him, 'Well done, you good and faithful servant. You have been faithful over a few things. I will make you ruler over many things. Enter the joy of your master.'

[22] "He who had received two talents also came and said, 'Master, you entrusted me with two talents. See, I have gained two more talents besides them.'

[23] "His master said to him, 'Well done, you good and faithful servant. You have been faithful over a few things. I will make you ruler over many things. Enter the joy of your master.'

[24] "Then he who had received the one talent came and said, 'Master, I knew that you are a hard man, reaping where you did not sow, and gathering where you did not winnow. [25] So I was afraid, and went and hid your talent in the ground. Here you have what is yours.'

[26] "His master answered, 'You wicked and slothful servant! You knew that I reap where I have not sown, and gather where I have not winnowed. [27] Then you ought to have given my money to the bankers, and at my coming I should have received what was my own with interest.

[28] " 'So take the talent from him, and give it to him who has ten talents. [29] For to everyone who has will more be given, and he will have an abundance. But from him who has nothing, even what he has will be taken away. [30] And throw the unprofitable servant into outer darkness, where there will be weeping and gnashing of teeth.'

The Judgment of the Nations

[31] "When the Son of Man comes in His glory, and all the holy angels with Him, then He will sit on the throne of His glory.

---

[1] 29 Joel 2:10.　　[2] 15 A talent was worth several hundred pounds.

[32] Before Him will be gathered all nations, and He will separate them one from another as a shepherd separates his sheep from the goats. [33] He will set the sheep at His right hand, but the goats at the left.

[34] "Then the King will say to those at His right hand, 'Come, you blessed of My Father, inherit the kingdom prepared for you since the foundation of the world. [35] For I was hungry and you gave Me food, I was thirsty and you gave Me drink, I was a stranger and you took Me in. [36] I was naked and you clothed Me, I was sick and you visited Me, I was in prison and you came to Me.'

[37] "Then the righteous will answer Him, 'Lord, when did we see You hungry and feed You, or thirsty and give You drink? [38] When did we see You a stranger and take You in, or naked and clothe You? [39] And when did we see You sick or in prison and come to You?'

[40] "The King will answer, 'Truly I say to you, as you have done it for one of the least of these brothers of Mine, you have done it for Me.'

[41] "Then He will say to those at the left hand, 'Depart from Me, you cursed, into the eternal fire, prepared for the devil and his angels. [42] For I was hungry and you gave Me no food, I was thirsty and you gave Me no drink, [43] I was a stranger and you did not take Me in, I was naked and you did not clothe Me, I was sick and in prison and you did not visit Me.'

[44] "Then they also will answer Him, 'Lord, when did we see You hungry or thirsty or a stranger or naked or sick or in prison, and did not serve You?'

[45] "He will answer, 'Truly I say to you, as you did it not for one of the least of these, you did it not for Me.'

[46] "And they will go away into eternal punishment, but the righteous into eternal life."

The Plot to Kill Jesus
Mk 14:1–2; Lk 22:1–2; Jn 11:45–53

26 When Jesus had finished all these sayings, He said to His disciples, [2] "You know that after two days is the Passover, and the Son of Man will be betrayed to be crucified."

[3] Then the chief priests, the scribes, and the elders of the people gathered in the palace of the high priest, who was called Caiaphas, [4] and took counsel that they might take Jesus covertly and kill Him. [5] But they said, "Not on the feast day, lest there be an uproar among the people."

The Anointing at Bethany
Mk 14:3–9; Jn 12:1–8

[6] When Jesus was in Bethany in the house of Simon the leper, [7] a woman came to Him having an alabaster jar of very expensive ointment and poured it on His head as He sat at supper.

[8] When His disciples saw it, they were indignant, saying, "For what purpose is this waste? [9] This ointment might have been sold for a large sum and given to the poor."

[10] When Jesus perceived it, He said to them, "Why do you trouble the woman? She has done a good work for Me. [11] For you have the poor always with you, but you do not always have Me. [12] In pouring this ointment on My body, she did it for My burial. [13] Truly I say to you, wherever this gospel shall be preached in the whole world, what this woman has done will be told in memory of her."

Judas' Agreement to Betray Jesus
Mk 14:10–11; Lk 22:3–6

[14] Then one of the twelve, who was called Judas Iscariot, went to the chief priests [15] and said to them, "What will you give me if I hand Him over to you?" And they paid him thirty pieces of silver. [16] From that moment he searched for an opportunity to betray Him.

The Passover With the Disciples
Mk 14:12–21; Lk 22:7–14, 21–23; Jn 13:21–30

[17] On the first day of the Feast of Unleavened Bread the disciples came to Jesus, saying, "Where will You have us to prepare for You to eat the Passover?"

[18] He said, "Go into the city to a certain man, and say to him, 'The Teacher says, My time is at hand. I will keep the Passover at your house with My disciples.'" [19] The disciples did as Jesus had directed them, and they prepared the Passover.

[20] When evening came, He sat down with the twelve. [21] And as they were eating, He said, "Truly I say to you, one of you will betray Me."

[22] They were very sorrowful, and each of them began saying to Him, "Lord, is it I?"

[23] He answered and said, "He who has dipped his hand with Me in the dish will betray Me. [24] The Son of Man goes as it is written of Him, but woe to that man by whom the Son of Man is betrayed! It would have been good for that man if he had not been born."

[25] Then Judas, who betrayed Him, answered, "Master, is it I?" He said to him, "You have said it."

The Lord's Supper
Mk 14:22–26; Lk 22:15–20; 1Co 11:23–25

[26] As they were eating, Jesus took bread, blessed it and broke it, and gave it to the disciples and said, "Take and eat. This is My body." [27] Then He took the cup, and after He gave thanks, He gave it to them, saying, "Drink of it, all of you. [28] For this is My blood of the new covenant, which is shed for many for the remission of sins. [29] I say to you, I will not drink of this fruit of the vine from now on until that day when I drink it new with you in My Father's kingdom."

[30] And when they had sung a hymn, they went out to the Mount of Olives.

Peter's Denial Foretold
Mk 14:27–31; Lk 22:31–34; Jn 13:36–38

[31] Then Jesus said to them, "All of you will fall away on account of Me this night, for it is written:

'I will strike the shepherd,
and the sheep of the flock shall be scattered.'[1]

[32] But after I have risen, I will go before you to Galilee."

[33] Peter answered, "Though all men will fall away on account of You, yet I will never fall away."

[34] Jesus said to him, "Truly I say to you, this night, before the rooster crows, you will deny Me three times."

[35] Peter said to Him, "Though I should die with You, yet I will not deny You." And all the disciples spoke in this manner.

The Prayer in Gethsemane
Mk 14:32–42; Lk 22:39–46

[36] Then Jesus came with them to a place called Gethsemane and said to the disciples, "Sit here while I go and pray close by." [37] He took with Him Peter and the two sons of Zebedee and began to be sorrowful and troubled. [38] Then He said to them, "My soul is very sorrowful, even to death. Wait here, and keep watch with Me."

[39] He went a little farther, and falling on His face, He prayed, "O My Father, if it is possible, let this cup pass from Me. Nevertheless, not as I will, but as You will."

[40] Then He came to the disciples and found them sleeping, and said to Peter, "So, could you not keep watch with Me one hour? [41] Watch and pray that you enter not into temptation. The spirit indeed is willing, but the flesh is weak."

[42] He went away a second time and prayed, "O My Father, if this cup cannot pass away from Me unless I drink it, Your will be done."

[43] Again, He came and found them sleeping, for their eyes were heavy. [44] So leaving them again, He went away and prayed the third time, saying the same words.

[45] Then He came to His disciples and said to them, "Sleep on now, and take your rest. Look, the hour is near, and the Son of Man is betrayed into the hands of sinners. [46] Rise, let us be going. Look, he who betrays Me is at hand."

---

[1] 31 Zec 13:7.

The Betrayal and Arrest of Jesus
Mk 14:43–50; Lk 22:47–53; Jn 18:3–12

[47] While He was still speaking, Judas, one of the twelve, came. And with him was a great crowd with swords and clubs, from the chief priests and elders of the people. [48] Now he who betrayed Him had given him a sign, saying, "Whomever I shall kiss is the Man. Seize Him." [49] He immediately came to Jesus and said, "Hail, Rabbi!" and kissed Him.

[50] And Jesus said to him, "Friend, why have you come?"

Then they came and laid hands on Jesus and took Him. [51] Immediately, one of those who were with Jesus stretched out his hand, and drew his sword, and struck the servant of the high priest, and cut off his ear.

[52] Then Jesus said to him, "Put your sword back in its place. For all those who take up the sword will perish by the sword. [53] Do you think that I cannot now pray to My Father, and He will at once give Me more than twelve legions of angels? [54] But how then would the Scriptures be fulfilled, that it must be so?"

[55] At that same moment Jesus said to the crowds, "Have you come out as against a thief to take Me with swords and clubs? Daily I sat with you in the temple teaching, and you did not seize Me. [56] But all this was done that the Scriptures of the prophets might be fulfilled." Then all the disciples forsook Him and fled.

Jesus Before the Sanhedrin
Mk 14:53–65; Lk 22:54–55, 63–71; Jn 18:13–14, 19–24

[57] Those who had seized Jesus led Him away to Caiaphas the high priest, where the scribes and the elders had assembled. [58] But Peter followed Him from afar to the high priest's courtyard and went in, and sat with the servants to see the end.

[59] The chief priests and the elders and the entire Sanhedrin searched for false witness against Jesus to put Him to death, [60] but they found none. Yes, though many false witnesses came forward, they found none.

At last two false witnesses came forward [61] and said, "This fellow said, 'I am able to destroy the temple of God and to build it in three days.'"

[62] Then the high priest stood up and said to Him, "Do You answer nothing? What is it these men testify against You?" [63] But Jesus remained silent.

The high priest said to Him, "I adjure You by the living God, tell us whether You are the Christ, the Son of God."

[64] Jesus said to him, "You have said so. But I say to you, hereafter you will see the Son of Man seated at the right hand of Power and coming on the clouds of heaven."

[65] Then the high priest tore his clothes, saying, "He has uttered blasphemy. What further need do we have for witnesses? See, now you have heard His blasphemy. [66] What do you think?"

They answered, "He is guilty unto death."

[67] Then they spat in His face and struck Him. And others slapped Him with the palms of their hands, [68] saying, "Prophesy to us, You Christ! Who is it that struck You?"

Peter's Denial of Jesus
Mk 14:66–72; Lk 22:56–62; Jn 18:15–18, 25–27

[69] Now Peter sat outside in the courtyard. And a girl came to him, saying, "You also were with Jesus of Galilee."

[70] But he denied it before them all, saying, "I do not know what you are saying."

[71] Then when he went out onto the porch, another girl saw him and said to those who were there, "This man was also with Jesus of Nazareth."

[72] Again he denied with an oath, "I do not know the Man."

[73] After a while those who stood by came to Peter and said, "Surely you also are one of them, for your accent betrays you."

[74] Then he began to invoke a curse on himself and he swore, "I do not know the Man."

Then immediately a rooster crowed. [75] Then Peter remembered the word Jesus had spoken, "Before a rooster crows, you will deny Me three times." Then he went out and wept bitterly.

Jesus Brought Before Pilate
Mk 15:1; Lk 23:1–2; Jn 18:28–32

27 When the morning came, all the chief priests and elders of the people took counsel against Jesus to put Him to death. [2] When they had bound Him, they led Him away and handed Him over to Pontius Pilate the governor.

The Death of Judas
Ac 1:18–19

[3] When Judas, who had betrayed Him, saw that He was condemned, he repented and brought back the thirty pieces of silver to the chief priests and elders, [4] saying, "I have sinned in that I have betrayed innocent blood."

They said, "What is that to us? You must see to that."

[5] So he threw down the pieces of silver in the temple and departed. And he went and hanged himself.

[6] The chief priests took the silver pieces and said, "It is not lawful to put them into the treasury, because this is the price of blood." [7] So they took counsel, and bought with them the potter's field to bury strangers in. [8] Therefore that field has been called the Field of Blood to this day. [9] Then what was spoken by Jeremiah the prophet was fulfilled: "They took the thirty pieces of silver, the value of that the sons of Israel set on Him, [10] and gave them for the potter's field, as the Lord appointed me."[1]

Jesus Questioned by Pilate
Mk 15:2–5; Lk 23:3–5; Jn 18:33–38

[11] Jesus stood before the governor. And the governor asked Him, "Are You the King of the Jews?"

Jesus said to him, "You have said so."

[12] When He was accused by the chief priests and elders, He gave no answer. [13] Then Pilate said to Him, "Do You not hear how many things they testify against You?" [14] But He never answered him a word, so that the governor was greatly amazed.

Jesus Sentenced to Die
Mk 15:6–15; Lk 23:13–25; Jn 18:39–19:16

[15] Now at the feast, the governor was accustomed to releasing to the people a prisoner whom they chose. [16] They had then a notorious prisoner called Barabbas. [17] So when they had gathered together, Pilate said to them, "Whom do you want me to release to you—Barabbas, or Jesus who is called Christ?" [18] For he knew that they had handed Him over out of envy.

[19] When he was sitting on the judgment seat, his wife sent word to him, "Have nothing to do with that righteous Man, for I have suffered much today in a dream on account of Him."

[20] But the chief priests and elders persuaded the crowd to ask for Barabbas and kill Jesus.

[21] The governor answered, "Which of the two do you want me to release to you?"

They said, "Barabbas."

[22] Pilate said to them, "Then what shall I do with Jesus who is called Christ?"

They all said to him, "Let Him be crucified!"

[23] The governor said, "Why, what evil has He done?"

But they cried out all the more, "Let Him be crucified!"

[24] When Pilate saw that he could not prevail, but rather that unrest was beginning, he took water and washed his hands before the crowd, saying, "I am innocent of the blood of this righteous Man. See to it yourselves."

[25] Then all the people answered, "His blood be on us and on our children!"

[26] Then he released Barabbas to them. But when he had scourged Jesus, he handed Him over to be crucified.

The Soldiers Mock Jesus
Mk 15:16–20; Jn 19:2–3

[27] Then the soldiers of the governor took Jesus into the Praetorium, and gathered the whole detachment of soldiers before Him. [28] They stripped Him and put a scarlet robe on Him, [29] and when

---

[1] 9–10 Zec 11:12–13; Jer 32:6–9.

they wove a crown of thorns, they put it on His head and put a staff in His right hand. They knelt before Him and mocked Him, saying, "Hail, King of the Jews!" [30] They spit on Him, and took the staff and hit Him on the head. [31] After they had mocked Him, they took the robe off Him, put His own garments on Him, and led Him away to crucify Him.

The Crucifixion
Mk 15:21–32; Lk 23:26–43; Jn 19:17–27
[32] As they came out, they found a man of Cyrene, Simon by name. This man they compelled to bear His cross. [33] When they came to a place called Golgotha, which means The Place of the Skull, [34] they gave Him sour wine mingled with gall to drink. But when He tasted it, He would not drink it. [35] When they crucified Him, they divided His garments by casting lots to fulfill what was spoken by the prophet, "They divided My garments among themselves and for My clothing they cast lots."*[1]* [36] And sitting down, they kept watch over Him there. [37] They put His accusation over His head, which read:

THIS IS JESUS THE KING OF THE JEWS.

[38] Then two thieves were crucified with Him, one on the right and another on the left. [39] Those who passed by insulted Him, wagging their heads, [40] saying, "You who would destroy the temple and build it in three days, save Yourself! If You are the Son of God, come down from the cross." [41] Likewise the chief priests, with the scribes and elders, mocked Him, saying, [42] "He saved others. He cannot save Himself. If He is the King of Israel, let Him now come down from the cross, and we will believe Him. [43] He trusted in God. Let Him deliver Him now, if He will have Him. For He said, 'I am the Son of God.'" [44] Even the thieves who were crucified with Him insulted Him in the same way.

The Death of Jesus
Mk 15:33–41; Lk 23:44–49; Jn 19:28–30
[45] Now from the sixth hour until the ninth hour there was darkness over all the land. [46] About the ninth hour Jesus cried out with a loud voice, *"Eli, Eli, lama sabachthani?"* which means, "My God, My God, why have You forsaken Me?"*[2]*
[47] Some of those who stood there heard it and said, "This Man is calling for Elijah."
[48] Immediately one of them ran, took a sponge, filled it with wine, and put it on a stick, and gave it to Him to drink. [49] The rest said, "Leave Him alone. Let us see if Elijah will come to save Him."
[50] And Jesus, when He had cried out again with a loud voice, released His spirit.
[51] At that moment the curtain of the temple was torn in two, from the top to the bottom. And the ground shook, and the rocks split apart. [52] The graves also were opened, and many bodies of the saints who had died were raised, [53] and coming out of the graves after His resurrection, they went into the Holy City and appeared to many.
[54] When the centurion and those with him, keeping watch over Jesus, saw the earthquake and what took place, they feared greatly and said, "Truly He was the Son of God!"
[55] Many women who were there watching from afar followed Jesus from Galilee, serving Him, [56] among whom was Mary Magdalene, and Mary the mother of James and Joseph, and the mother of Zebedee's sons.

The Burial of Jesus
Mk 15:42–47; Lk 23:50–56; Jn 19:38–42
[57] When the evening came, there came a rich man of Arimathea, named Joseph, who also was a disciple of Jesus. [58] He went to Pilate and asked for the body of Jesus. Then Pilate commanded the body to be given to him. [59] When Joseph had taken the body, he wrapped it in a clean linen cloth, [60] and laid it in his own new tomb, which he had cut out of the rock. And he rolled a large stone to the door of the tomb and departed. [61] Mary Magdalene and the other Mary were there, sitting opposite the tomb.

The Guard at the Tomb
[62] The next day, following the Day of Preparation, the chief priests and Pharisees gathered before Pilate, [63] saying, "Sir, we remember that deceiver saying while He was still alive, 'After three days I will rise.' [64] Therefore command that the tomb be made secure until the third day, lest His disciples come by night and steal Him away, and tell the people, 'He has risen from the dead.' The last deception will be worse than the first."
[65] Pilate said to them, "You have a guard. Go your way. Make it as secure as you can." [66] So they went and made the tomb secure by sealing the stone and posting the guard.

The Resurrection
Mk 16:1–8; Lk 24:1–12; Jn 20:1–10
28 At the end of the Sabbath, as it began to dawn on the first day of the week, Mary Magdalene and the other Mary went to see the tomb.
[2] And then there was a great earthquake. For the angel of the Lord descended from heaven and came and rolled back the stone from the door and sat on it. [3] His countenance was like lightning, and his garments white as snow. [4] The soldiers shook for fear of him and became like dead men. [5] The angel said to the women, "Do not be afraid. For I know that you are looking for Jesus who was crucified. [6] He is not here. For He has risen, as He said. Come, see the place where the Lord lay. [7] Then go quickly and tell His disciples that He has risen from the dead, and indeed, He is going before you to Galilee. There you will see Him. Listen, I have told you."
[8] So they departed quickly from the tomb with fear and great joy, and ran to bring His disciples word. [9] As they went to tell His disciples, suddenly Jesus met them, saying, "Greetings!" They came and took hold of His feet and worshipped Him. [10] Then Jesus said to them, "Do not be afraid. Go tell My brothers to go to Galilee, and there they will see Me."

The Report of the Guard
[11] While they were going, indeed, some of the soldiers went into the city and described to the chief priests everything that had happened. [12] When the chief priests were assembled with the elders and had taken counsel, they gave much money to the soldiers, [13] saying, "You are to say, 'His disciples came by night and stole Him away while we were sleeping.' [14] If this comes to the governor's ears, we will satisfy him and keep you secure." [15] So they took the money and did as they were instructed. And this saying has been commonly reported among the Jews to this day.

The Commissioning of the Disciples
Mk 16:14–18; Lk 24:36–49; Jn 20:19–23; Ac 1:6–8
[16] Then the eleven disciples went away to Galilee, to the mountain to which Jesus had directed them. [17] When they saw Him, they worshipped Him. But some doubted. [18] Then Jesus came and spoke to them, saying, "All authority has been given to Me in heaven and on earth. [19] Go therefore and make disciples of all nations, baptizing them in the name of the Father and of the Son and of the Holy Spirit, [20] teaching them to observe all things I have commanded you. And remember, I am with you always, even to the end of the age." Amen.

---

[1] 35 Ps 22:18.   *[2]* 46 Ps 22:1.

MARK

The Preaching of John the Baptist
Mt 3:1–12; Lk 3:1–9, 15–17; Jn 1:19–28

1 The beginning of the gospel of Jesus Christ, the Son of God. [2] As it is written in the Prophets:

"Look, I am sending My messenger before Your face,
    who will prepare Your way before You." [1]
[3] "The voice of one crying in the wilderness:
'Prepare the way of the Lord,
    make His paths straight.' " [2]

[4] John came baptizing in the wilderness and preaching a baptism of repentance for the remission of sins. [5] The whole region of Judea and all the people of Jerusalem went out to him and were all baptized by him in the Jordan River, confessing their sins. [6] John was clothed with camel's hair and with a leather belt around his waist. And he ate locusts and wild honey. [7] He preached saying, "After me is coming One mightier than I, the straps of whose shoes I am not worthy to stoop down and untie. [8] I indeed have baptized you with water, but He will baptize you with the Holy Spirit."

The Baptism of Jesus
Mt 3:13–17; Lk 3:21–22

[9] In those days Jesus came from Nazareth in Galilee and was baptized by John in the Jordan. [10] Coming up out of the water, He immediately saw the heavens opened and the Spirit descending on Him like a dove. [11] And a voice came from heaven, saying, "You are My beloved Son in whom I am well pleased."

The Temptation of Jesus
Mt 4:1–11; Lk 4:1–13

[12] The Spirit immediately drove Him into the wilderness. [13] And He was there in the wilderness for forty days, tempted by Satan, and was with the wild beasts. And the angels ministered to Him.

The Beginning of the Galilean Ministry
Mt 4:12–17; Lk 4:14–15

[14] After John was put in prison, Jesus came to Galilee preaching the gospel of the kingdom of God, [15] saying, "The time is fulfilled, and the kingdom of God is at hand. Repent and believe the gospel."

The Calling of the First Disciples
Mt 4:18–22; Lk 5:1–11

[16] As He walked by the Sea of Galilee, He saw Simon and Andrew, his brother, throwing a net into the sea, for they were fishermen. [17] Jesus said to them, "Come, follow Me, and I will make you fishers of men." [18] Immediately they left their nets and followed Him.
[19] When He had gone a little farther from there, He saw James the son of Zebedee and John, his brother, who also were in the boat mending their nets. [20] Immediately He called them. And they left their father Zebedee in the boat with the hired servants and followed Him.

The Man With an Unclean Spirit
Lk 4:31–37

[21] They went to Capernaum, and immediately on the Sabbath He entered the synagogue and taught. [22] They were astonished at His teaching, for He taught them as one having authority, and not as the scribes. [23] In their synagogue there was a man with an unclean spirit. [24] And he cried out, "Leave us alone! What do You have to do with us, Jesus of Nazareth? Have You come to destroy us? I know who You are, the Holy One of God." [25] Jesus rebuked him, saying, "Be silent and come out of him!" [26] When the unclean spirit had convulsed him and cried out with a loud voice, it came out of him.

[27] They were all amazed, so that they questioned among themselves, "What is this? What new teaching is this? With authority He commands even the unclean spirits, and they obey Him." [28] Immediately His fame spread everywhere throughout the region surrounding Galilee.

The Healing of Many People
Mt 8:14–17; Lk 4:38–41

[29] When He came out of the synagogue with James and John, they went directly to the house of Simon and Andrew. [30] The mother of Simon's wife lay sick with a fever, and immediately they told Him of her. [31] So He came and took her by the hand and lifted her up, and immediately the fever left her. And she served them.
[32] In the evening, when the sun had set, they brought to Him all who were sick and those who were possessed with demons. [33] The whole city was gathered at the door, [34] and He healed many who were sick with various diseases and cast out many demons. And He did not let the demons speak, because they knew Him.

A Preaching Tour
Lk 4:42–44

[35] In the morning, rising up a great while before sunrise, He went out and departed to a solitary place. And there He prayed. [36] Simon and those who were with Him followed Him, [37] and when they found Him, they said to Him, "Everyone is searching for You."
[38] He said to them, "Let us go into the nearby towns, that I may preach there also. For that is why I have come." [39] So He preached in their synagogues throughout Galilee and cast out demons.

The Cleansing of a Leper
Mt 8:1–4; Lk 5:12–16

[40] A leper came to Him, pleading with Him and kneeling before Him, saying, "If You are willing, You can make me clean." [41] Then Jesus, moved with compassion, extended His hand and touched him, and said to him, "I will. Be clean." [42] As soon as He had spoken, the leprosy immediately departed from him, and he was cleansed.
[43] He sternly warned him, and sent him away at once, [44] saying, "See that you say nothing to anyone. But go your way, show yourself to the priest, and offer for your cleansing what Moses commanded, as a testimony to them." [45] Instead he went out and began to proclaim it widely and to spread the news around, so that Jesus could no more openly enter the city, but was out in remote places. And they came to Him from every quarter.

The Healing of a Paralytic
Mt 9:1–8; Lk 5:17–26

2 Again, He entered Capernaum after some days. And it was reported that He was in the house. [2] Immediately many were gathered together, so that there was no room to receive them, not even at the door. And He preached the word to them. [3] They came to Him bringing one sick with paralysis, who was carried by four men. [4] When they could not come near Him due to the crowding, they uncovered the roof where He was. When they had broken it open, they let down the bed on which the paralytic lay. [5] When Jesus saw their faith, He said to the paralytic, "Son, your sins are forgiven you."
[6] But some of the scribes were sitting there, reasoning in their hearts, [7] "Why does this Man speak such blasphemies? Who can forgive sins but God alone?"
[8] Immediately, when Jesus perceived in His spirit that they so reasoned within themselves, He said to them, "Why do you contemplate these things in your hearts? [9] Which is easier to say to the paralytic: 'Your sins are forgiven you,' or to say, 'Rise, take up your bed and walk'? [10] But that you may know that the Son of Man has authority on earth to forgive sins," He said to the paralytic, [11] "I say to you, rise, and take up your bed, and go your way to your house."

[1][2] Mal 3:1.   [2][3] Isa 40:3.

[12] Immediately he rose, picked up the bed, and went out in front of them all, so that they were all amazed and glorified God, saying, "We never saw anything like this!"

The Calling of Levi
Mt 9:9–13; Lk 5:27–32

[13] He went out again by the seaside, and the whole crowd came to Him, and He taught them. [14] As He passed by, He saw Levi the son of Alphaeus sitting at the tax collector's station, and He said to him, "Follow Me." And he rose and followed Him.

[15] As Jesus was at supper in his house, many tax collectors and sinners also sat together with Jesus and His disciples. For there were many, and they followed Him. [16] When the scribes and Pharisees saw Him eating with tax collectors and sinners, they said to His disciples, "How is it that He eats and drinks with tax collectors and sinners?"

[17] When Jesus heard it, He said to them, "Those who are well have no need of a physician, but those who are sick. I came not to call the righteous, but sinners to repentance."

The Question About Fasting
Mt 9:14–17; Lk 5:33–39

[18] Now the disciples of John and of the Pharisees were fasting. And people came and said to Him, "Why do the disciples of John and of the Pharisees fast, but Your disciples do not fast?"

[19] Jesus said to them, "Can the wedding guests fast while the bridegroom is with them? As long as they have the bridegroom with them, they cannot fast. [20] But the days will come when the bridegroom will be taken away from them, and then they will fast in those days.

[21] "No one sews a piece of new cloth on an old garment, or else the new piece that covered it tears away from the old, and the tear is made worse. [22] And no one pours new wine into old wineskins, or else the new wine bursts the wineskins, and the wine is spilled, and the wineskins will be marred. But new wine must be poured into new wineskins."

The Question About the Sabbath
Mt 12:1–8; Lk 6:1–5

[23] He went through the grain fields on the Sabbath. As they went, His disciples began to pluck the heads of grain. [24] The Pharisees said to Him, "Look, why are they doing on the Sabbath what is not lawful?"

[25] He said to them, "Have you never read what David did, when he and those who were with him were in need and hungry: [26] how he went into the house of God, in the days Abiathar was the high priest, and ate the ritual bread, which is lawful only for the priests to eat, and also gave it to those who were with him?"

[27] Then He said to them, "The Sabbath was made for man, and not man for the Sabbath. [28] So the Son of Man is Lord even of the Sabbath."

The Man With a Withered Hand
Mt 12:9–14; Lk 6:6–11

3 Again, He entered the synagogue, and there was a man who had a withered hand. [2] They watched Him to see whether He would heal him on the Sabbath, so that they might accuse Him. [3] He said to the man who had the withered hand, "Stand up."

[4] Then He said to them, "Is it lawful to do good or to do evil on the Sabbath, to save life or to kill?" But they kept silent.

[5] When He had looked around at them with anger, being grieved for the hardness of their hearts, He said to the man, "Stretch your hand forward." He stretched it out, and his hand was restored as whole as the other. [6] Then the Pharisees went out and immediately took counsel with the Herodians against Him, how to kill Him.

The Crowd at the Seaside
[7] Jesus withdrew with His disciples to the sea. And a great crowd followed Him from Galilee and Judea [8] and Jerusalem, and Idumea, and from beyond the Jordan. And those from Tyre and Sidon, a great crowd, when they heard what great things He did, came to Him. [9] He told the disciples to have a small boat ready for Him because

of the crowd, lest they should crush Him. [10] For He had healed many, so that all who had diseases pressed on Him to touch Him. [11] When unclean spirits saw Him, they fell down before Him, crying out, "You are the Son of God." [12] But He sternly ordered them not to make Him known.

The Choosing of the Twelve Apostles
Mt 10:1–4; Lk 6:12–16

[13] He went up into the mountain and called to Him those whom He desired, and they came to Him. [14] He ordained twelve to be with Him, and to be sent out to preach, [15] and to have authority to heal sicknesses and to cast out demons: [16] Simon, whom He named Peter; [17] James, the son of Zebedee, and John, the brother of James, whom he surnamed Boanerges (meaning Sons of Thunder); [18] Andrew, and Philip, and Bartholomew, and Matthew, and Thomas; and James the son of Alphaeus; and Thaddaeus, and Simon the Zealot; [19] and Judas Iscariot, who betrayed Him.

Jesus and Beelzebub
Mt 12:22–32; Lk 11:14–23; 12:10

[20] Then they entered a house, and the crowd came together again, so that they could not even eat bread. [21] When His family heard of it, they went out to seize Him, for they said, "He is beside Himself."

[22] And the scribes who came down from Jerusalem said, "He is possessed by Beelzebub, and by the ruler of the demons He casts out demons."

[23] So He called them to Him and said to them in parables, "How can Satan cast out Satan? [24] If a kingdom is divided against itself, that kingdom cannot stand. [25] If a house is divided against itself, that house cannot stand. [26] And if Satan rises up against himself and is divided, he cannot stand, but is coming to an end. [27] No one can enter a strong man's house and plunder his goods, unless he first binds the strong man. Then he will plunder his house. [28] Truly I say to you, all sins will be forgiven the sons of men, and whatever blasphemies they speak. [29] But he who blasphemes against the Holy Spirit never has forgiveness, but is in danger of eternal condemnation."

[30] For they said, "He has an unclean spirit."

The Mother and Brothers of Jesus
Mt 12:46–50; Lk 8:19–21

[31] Then His mother and His brothers came, and standing outside, they sent to Him, calling Him. [32] The crowd sat around Him and said to Him, "Your mother and Your brothers are outside asking for You."

[33] He answered, "Who are My mother and My brothers?" [34] Then He looked around at those who sat around Him and said, "Here are My mother and My brothers! [35] For whoever does the will of God is My brother, and My sister, and My mother."

The Parable of the Sower
Mt 13:1–9; Lk 8:4–8

4 Again He began to teach by the seaside. A large crowd was gathered before Him, so that He entered a boat and sat in it on the sea. And the whole crowd was by the sea on the land. [2] He taught them many things in parables and said to them in His teaching: [3] "Listen! And take note: A sower went out to sow. [4] As he sowed, some seed fell beside the path, and the birds of the air came and devoured it. [5] Some seed fell on rocky ground, where it did not have much soil, and soon it sprang up because it did not have deep soil. [6] But when the sun rose, it was scorched. And because it had no root, it withered away. [7] Other seed fell among thorns, and the thorns grew up and choked it, and it yielded no grain. [8] And other seed fell on good ground, and it yielded grain that sprang up and increased by thirty, sixty, or a hundred times as much." [9] Then He said to them, "He who has ears to hear, let him hear."

The Purpose of the Parables
Mt 13:10–17; Lk 8:9–10

[10] When He was alone, those who were around Him with the twelve asked Him about the parable. [11] He said to them, "To you is

given the secret of the kingdom of God, but to those who are outside, everything is said in parables, [12] so that

'seeing they may see, and not perceive,
and hearing they may hear and not understand;
lest they should turn, and their sins be forgiven them.'[1]"

The Parable of the Sower Explained
Mt 13:18–23; Lk 8:11–15

[13] Then He said to them, "Do you not understand this parable? How then will you understand all the parables? [14] The sower sows the word. [15] These are those beside the path, where the word is sown. But when they hear, Satan comes immediately and takes away the word which is sown in their hearts. [16] Others, likewise, are seed sown on rocky ground, who, when they hear the word, immediately receive it with gladness, [17] but have no root in themselves, and so endure for a time. Afterward, when affliction or persecution rises for the word's sake, immediately they fall away. [18] And others are seed sown among thorns, the ones who hear the word. [19] But the cares of this world, and the deceitfulness of riches, and the desires for other things entering in choke the word, and it proves unfruitful. [20] Still others are seed sown on good ground, those who hear the word, and receive it, and bear fruit: thirty, sixty, or a hundred times as much."

A Light Under a Basket
Lk 8:16–18

[21] He said to them, "Is a candle brought to be put under a basket or under a bed and not to be set on a candlestick? [22] For there is nothing hidden except to be revealed; neither is anything kept secret except to be proclaimed. [23] If anyone has ears to hear, let him hear."

[24] He said to them, "Take heed what you hear. The measure you give will be measured for you, and to you who hear will more be given. [25] For to him who has will more be given. And from him who has not will be taken, even what he has."

The Parable of the Growing Seed

[26] He said, "The kingdom of God is like a man who scatters seed on the ground. [27] He sleeps and rises night and day, and the seed sprouts and grows; he does not know how. [28] For the earth bears fruit by itself: first the blade, then the head, then the full seed in the head. [29] But when the grain is ripe, immediately he applies the sickle because the harvest has come."

The Parable of the Mustard Seed
Mt 13:31–32; Lk 13:18–19

[30] He said, "To what shall we liken the kingdom of God, or with what parable shall we compare it? [31] It is like a grain of mustard seed which, when it is sown in the ground, is the smallest seed on earth. [32] Yet when it is sown, it grows up and becomes greater than all shrubs, and shoots out great branches, so that the birds of the air may nest in its shade."

The Use of Parables
Mt 13:34–35

[33] With many such parables He spoke the word to them as they were able to hear it. [34] Without a parable He did not speak to them. But when they were alone, He expounded on all things to His disciples.

The Calming of a Storm
Mt 8:23–27; Lk 8:22–25

[35] That same day, when the evening came, He said to them, "Let us go cross to the other side." [36] When they had sent the crowd away, they took Him in the boat just as He was. There were also other little boats with Him. [37] A great windstorm arose, and the waves splashed into the boat, so that it was now filling the boat. [38] He was in the stern asleep on a pillow. They woke Him and said, "Teacher, do You not care that we are perishing?"

[39] He rose and rebuked the wind, and said to the sea, "Peace, be still!" Then the wind ceased and there was a great calm.

[40] He said to them, "Why are you so fearful? How is that you have no faith?"

[41] They feared greatly and said to one another, "What kind of Man is He, that even the wind and the sea obey Him?"

The Healing of the Gadarene Demoniac
Mt 8:28–34; Lk 8:26–39

5 They went to the other side of the sea to the region of the Gadarenes. [2] When He had come out of the boat, immediately a man with an unclean spirit came out of the tombs and met Him. [3] He lived among the tombs. And no one could constrain him, not even with chains, [4] because he had often been bound with shackles and chains. But he had pulled the chains apart and broken the shackles to pieces. And no one could subdue him. [5] Always, night and day, he was in the mountains and in the tombs, crying out and cutting himself with stones.

[6] But when he saw Jesus afar off, he ran up and kneeled before Him, [7] and cried out with a loud voice, "What have You to do with me, Jesus, Son of the Most High God? I adjure You by God, do not torment me." [8] For Jesus said to him, "Come out of the man, you unclean spirit!"

[9] Then He asked him, "What is your name?"

He answered, "My name is Legion. For we are many." [10] And he begged Him repeatedly not to send them away out of the country. [11] Now there was a great herd of swine feeding near the mountains. [12] All the demons pleaded with Him, asking, "Send us to the swine, so that we may enter them." [13] At once, Jesus gave them leave. Then the unclean spirits came out and entered the swine. And the herd, numbering about two thousand, ran wildly down a steep hill into the sea and were drowned in the sea.

[14] Those who fed the swine fled and reported it in the city and in the country. And people went out to see what it was that had happened. [15] They came to Jesus and saw him who had been possessed with the legion of demons sitting and clothed and in his right mind. And they were afraid. [16] Those who saw it told them how it befell him who had been possessed with the demons and also concerning the swine. [17] Then they began to plead with Him to depart out of their region.

[18] When He entered the boat, he who had been possessed with the demons prayed Him that he might be with Him. [19] Jesus did not let him, but said to him, "Go home to your friends and tell them what great things the Lord has done for you and how He has had compassion on you." [20] So he departed and began to proclaim in the Decapolis[2] what great things Jesus had done for him. And everyone was amazed.

Jairus' Daughter and the Woman Who Touched Jesus' Garment
Mt 9:18–26; Lk 8:40–56

[21] When Jesus had crossed again by boat to the other side, many people gathered to Him. And He was beside the sea. [22] One of the rulers of the synagogue, named Jairus, saw Jesus and came and fell at His feet [23] and earnestly asked Him, "My little daughter is lying at the point of death. I ask You, come and lay Your hands on her, so that she may be healed. And she will live." [24] So Jesus went with him.

And many people followed Him and pressed in on Him. [25] And a certain woman had a hemorrhage for twelve years, [26] and had suffered much under many physicians. She had spent all that she had, and was not better but rather grew worse. [27] When she had heard of Jesus, she came in the crowd behind Him and touched His garment. [28] For she said, "If I may touch His garments, I shall be healed." [29] And immediately her hemorrhage dried up, and she felt in her body that she was healed of the affliction.

[30] At once, Jesus knew within Himself that power had gone out of Him. He turned around in the crowd and said, "Who touched My garments?"

[31] His disciples said to Him, "You see the crowd pressing against You, and You say, 'Who touched Me?'"

[32] And He looked around to see her who had done it. [33] But the woman, fearing and trembling, knowing what had happened to

---

[1] 12 Isa 6:9–10.   [2] 20 The Ten Cities.

her, came and fell down before Him and told Him the entire truth. ³⁴ He said to her, "Daughter, your faith has made you well. Go in peace, and be healed of your affliction."

³⁵ While He was still speaking, some came from the house of the synagogue ruler and said, "Your daughter is dead. Why trouble the Teacher any further?"

³⁶ As soon as Jesus heard the word that was spoken, He said to the ruler of the synagogue, "Do not be afraid, only believe."

³⁷ He let no one follow Him, except Peter, and James, and John the brother of James. ³⁸ He came to the house of the ruler of the synagogue, and saw the tumult, and those who wept and wailed loudly. ³⁹ When He came in, He said to them, "Why make this uproar and weep? The girl is not dead, but sleeping." ⁴⁰ They laughed at Him in ridicule.

But when He had put them all out, He took the father and the mother of the girl and those who were with Him and entered where the girl was lying. ⁴¹ He took the girl by the hand and said to her, *"Talitha cumi,"* which means, "Little girl, I say to you, arise." ⁴² Immediately the girl arose and walked, for she was twelve years of age. And they were greatly astonished. ⁴³ He strictly ordered them to let no one know of it and directed them to give her something to eat.

The Rejection of Jesus at Nazareth
Mt 13:53–58; Lk 4:16–30

6 He went away from there and came into His own country. And His disciples followed Him. ² When the Sabbath came, He began to teach in the synagogue. And many hearing Him were astonished, saying, "Where did this Man get this? What is this wisdom that is given Him, that even miracles are done by His hands? ³ Is this not the carpenter, the Son of Mary and the brother of James and Joseph and Judas and Simon? Are not His sisters here with us?" And they took offense at Him.

⁴ Jesus said to them, "A prophet is not without honor, except in his own country, and among his own relatives, and in his own house." ⁵ He could not do any miracles there, except that He laid His hands on a few sick people and healed them. ⁶ And He was amazed because of their unbelief.

The Mission of the Twelve
Mt 10:1, 5–15; Lk 9:1–6

Then He went to the surrounding villages, teaching. ⁷ He called to Him the twelve, and began to send them out two by two, and gave them authority over unclean spirits.

⁸ He commanded them to take nothing for their journey except a staff: no bag, no bread, and no money in their purse, ⁹ but to wear sandals, and not put on two tunics. ¹⁰ He said to them, "Wherever you enter a house, remain there until you depart from that place. ¹¹ And whoever will not receive you or hear you, when you depart from there, shake the dust off your feet as a testimony against them. Truly I say to you, it will be more tolerable for Sodom and Gomorrah on the Day of Judgment than for that city."

¹² So they went out and preached that men should repent. ¹³ And they cast out many demons and anointed with oil many who were sick and healed them.

The Death of John the Baptist
Mt 14:1–12; Lk 9:7–9

¹⁴ King Herod heard of Him, for His name was spread publicly. He said, "John the Baptist has been raised from the dead, and therefore these miracles are at work in him."

¹⁵ But others said, "He is Elijah."

And yet others said, "He is the Prophet, or like one of the prophets."

¹⁶ But when Herod heard of it, he said, "It is John, whom I beheaded. He has been raised from the dead!"

¹⁷ Herod had sent and seized John and bound him in prison for the sake of Herodias, his brother Philip's wife, for he had married her. ¹⁸ For John said to Herod, "It is not lawful for you to have your brother's wife." ¹⁹ So Herodias had a grudge against him and would have killed him, but she could not, ²⁰ for Herod feared John,

knowing that he was a righteous and holy man, and protected him. When he heard him, he was greatly perplexed, but heard him gladly.

²¹ But a convenient day came when Herod on his birthday prepared a ceremonial dinner for his lords and commanding officers and leading men of Galilee. ²² When the daughter of Herodias came in and danced and pleased Herod and those who sat with him, the king said to the girl, "Ask of me whatever you desire, and I will give it to you." ²³ And he swore to her, "Whatever you ask of me, I will give you, up to half of my kingdom."

²⁴ She went out and said to her mother, "What shall I ask?"

She said, "The head of John the Baptist."

²⁵ She came in immediately with haste to the king and asked, "I want you to give me the head of John the Baptist on a platter at once."

²⁶ The king was extremely sorrowful. Yet for the sake of his oath and those who sat with him, he would not reject her. ²⁷ So the king immediately sent an executioner and commanded his head to be brought. He went and beheaded him in the prison, ²⁸ and brought his head on a platter, and gave it to the girl. And the girl gave it to her mother. ²⁹ When his disciples heard of it, they came and took up his corpse and laid it in a tomb.

The Feeding of the Five Thousand
Mt 14:13–21; Lk 9:10–17; Jn 6:1–14

³⁰ The apostles met with Jesus and told him everything, both what they had done and what they had taught. ³¹ Then He said to them, "Come away by yourselves to a remote place and rest a while," for many were coming and going, and they had no leisure even to eat.

³² So they went into a remote place privately by boat. ³³ But the people saw them departing, and many knew Him and ran there on foot out of every city. They arrived first and came together to Him. ³⁴ When Jesus came out and saw many people, He was moved with compassion on them, because they were like sheep without a shepherd. And He began to teach them many things.

³⁵ When the day was now getting late, His disciples came to Him and said, "This is a remote place, and now the time is passing. ³⁶ Send them away into the surrounding country and villages to buy themselves bread, for they have nothing to eat."

³⁷ But He answered, "You give them something to eat."

They said to Him, "Shall we go and buy two hundred denarii¹ worth of bread and give it to them to eat?"

³⁸ He said to them, "How many loaves have you? Go and see."

When they found out, they said, "Five, and two fish."

³⁹ Then He commanded them to make everyone sit down by companies on the green grass. ⁴⁰ So they sat down in ranks, by hundreds and by fifties. ⁴¹ When He had taken the five loaves and the two fish, He looked up to heaven, and blessed and broke the loaves, and gave them to His disciples to set before them. And He divided the two fish among them all. ⁴² They all ate and were filled. ⁴³ And they took up twelve baskets full of the fragments and of the fish. ⁴⁴ Those who ate of the loaves were about five thousand men.

Walking on the Water
Mt 14:22–33; Jn 6:15–21

⁴⁵ Immediately He compelled His disciples to get into the boat and to go before Him to the other side, to Bethsaida, while He sent the crowd away. ⁴⁶ When He had sent them away, He departed to a mountain to pray.

⁴⁷ When evening came, the boat was in the midst of the sea. And He was alone on the land. ⁴⁸ He saw them straining at rowing, for the wind was against them. About the fourth watch of the night He came to them, walking on the sea and would have passed by them. ⁴⁹ But when they saw Him walking on the sea, they supposed it was a ghost, and cried out. ⁵⁰ For they all saw Him and were troubled.

Immediately He spoke to them and said, "Be of good cheer, it is I. Do not be afraid." ⁵¹ Then He went up to them in the boat and the wind ceased. They were greatly astonished in themselves beyond measure, and wondered. ⁵² For they had not comprehended the miracle of the loaves, for their hearts were hardened.

---

¹37 Eight months' wages.

The Healing of the Sick in Gennesaret
Mt 14:34–36

[53] When they had crossed over, they came to the land of Gennesaret and anchored on the shore. [54] When they had come out of the boat, immediately the people recognized Him, [55] and ran throughout the surrounding region, and began to carry the sick on beds to wherever they heard He was. [56] And wherever He entered, into villages, cities, or the country, they laid the sick in the marketplaces and pleaded with Him that they might touch even the fringe of His garment. And as many as touched Him were healed.

The Tradition of the Elders
Mt 15:1–20

7 The Pharisees and certain scribes who came from Jerusalem gathered around Him. [2] When they saw some of His disciples eat bread with defiled, that is, ritually unwashed hands, they found fault. [3] For the Pharisees and all the Jews, unless they wash their hands ritually, do not eat, keeping the tradition of the elders. [4] When they come from the market, unless they wash, they do not eat. And there are many other traditions which they have received and observe, such as the washing of cups and pitchers and bronze vessels and dining couches.

[5] So the Pharisees and scribes asked Him, "Why do Your disciples not live according to the tradition of the elders, but eat bread with unwashed hands?"

[6] He answered, "Well has Isaiah prophesied of you hypocrites, as it is written:

'These people honor Me with their lips,
    but their hearts are far from Me.
[7] In vain do they worship Me,
    teaching as doctrines the precepts of men.'[1]

[8] For laying aside the commandment of God, you hold the tradition of men—the washing of pitchers and cups, and many other such things you do."

[9] And He said to them, "You full well reject the commandment of God so that you may keep your own tradition. [10] For Moses said, 'Honor your father and your mother,'[2] and, 'Whoever curses father or mother, let him be put to death.'[3] [11] But you say, 'If a man says to his father or mother, "It is Corban," that is to say, "What you would have profited from me is a gift to God," he shall be free.' [12] Then you no longer let him do anything for his father or his mother, [13] making the word of God of no effect through your tradition, which you have delivered. And you do many similar things."

[14] When He had called all the people to Him, He said, "Listen to Me, every one of you, and understand: [15] There is nothing from outside a man that by entering him can defile him. But the things which come out of the man are what defile him. [16] If anyone has ears to hear, let him hear."

[17] When He had left the people and entered the house, His disciples asked Him concerning the parable. [18] He said to them, "Are you so without understanding also? Do you not know that anything from the outside that enters a man cannot defile him, [19] because it does not enter his heart, but into his stomach, and goes out into the sewer, thus purifying all foods?"

[20] And He said, "What comes out of a man is what defiles a man. [21] For from within, out of the heart of men, proceed evil thoughts, adultery, fornication, murder, [22] theft, covetousness, wickedness, deceit, licentiousness, an evil eye, blasphemy, pride and foolishness. [23] All these evil things come from within and defile a man."

The Syrophoenician Woman's Faith
Mt 15:21–28

[24] From there He arose and went to the region of Tyre and Sidon. He entered a house and would have no one know it. Yet He could not be hidden. [25] For a certain woman, whose young daughter had an unclean spirit, heard of Him, and came and fell at His feet. [26] The woman was a Greek, a Syrophoenician by race. And she begged Him to cast the demon out of her daughter.

[27] Jesus said to her, "Let the children first be filled. For it is not fitting to take the children's bread and throw it to the dogs."

[28] She answered, "Yes, Lord. Yet the dogs under the table eat the children's crumbs."

[29] Then He said to her, "For this answer, go your way. The demon has gone out of your daughter."

[30] When she had come to her house, she found the demon had gone out, and her daughter lying on the bed.

The Deaf and Mute Man Healed
[31] Again, departing from the region of Tyre and Sidon, He came to the Sea of Galilee, through the region of the Decapolis. [32] They brought to Him one who was deaf and had difficulty speaking. And they pleaded with Him to put His hand on him.

[33] He took him aside from the crowd, and put His fingers into his ears, and spat and touched his tongue. [34] Looking up to heaven, He sighed, and said to him, *"Ephphatha,"* that is, "Be opened." [35] Immediately his ears were opened, and the impediment of his tongue was loosened, and he spoke correctly.

[36] He ordered them to tell no one. But the more He ordered them, the more they greatly proclaimed it. [37] They were astonished beyond measure, saying, "He has done all things well. He makes both the deaf to hear and the mute to speak."

The Feeding of the Four Thousand
Mt 15:32–39

8 In those days, the crowds being very great with nothing to eat, Jesus called His disciples to Him and said to them, [2] "I have compassion on the crowd, because they have now been with Me three days and have nothing to eat. [3] If I send them away fasting to their own houses, they will faint on the way, for some of them have come from afar."

[4] His disciples answered, "Where can one get bread to feed these men here in the wilderness?"

[5] He asked them, "How many loaves do you have?"

They said, "Seven."

[6] He commanded the people to sit down on the ground. Taking the seven loaves and giving thanks, He broke them and gave them to His disciples to serve. And they served the crowd. [7] And they had a few small fish. And blessing them, He commanded that these also be served them. [8] So they ate and were filled. And they collected seven baskets of the broken pieces that were left. [9] There were about four thousand who had eaten, and He sent them away. [10] He immediately entered a boat with His disciples and came to the region of Dalmanutha.

The Demand for a Sign
Mt 16:1–4

[11] The Pharisees came up and began to debate with Him, seeking from Him a sign from heaven to test Him. [12] He sighed deeply in His spirit and said, "Why does this generation look for a sign? Truly I say to you, no sign shall be given to this generation." [13] Then He left them and, entering the boat again, departed to the other side.

The Yeast of the Pharisees and of Herod
Mt 16:5–12

[14] Now the disciples had forgotten to take bread and did not have more than one loaf with them in the boat. [15] He warned them, "Take heed. Beware of the yeast of the Pharisees and the yeast of Herod."

[16] They reasoned among themselves, saying, "It is because we have no bread."

[17] Being aware of it, Jesus said to them, "Why do you reason that you have no bread? Do you still not perceive or understand? Are your hearts still hardened? [18] Having eyes, do you not see? Having ears,

---

1 6–7 Isa 29:13.   *2 10* Ex 20:12; Dt 5:16.   *3 10* Ex 21:17; Lev 20:9.

do you not hear?[1] And do you not remember? [19] When I broke the five loaves for the five thousand, how many baskets full of broken pieces did you collect?"

They said to Him, "Twelve."

[20] "And the seven among the four thousand, how many baskets full of broken pieces did you collect?"

They said, "Seven."

[21] He said to them, "Do you still not understand?"

The Healing of a Blind Man at Bethsaida

[22] He came to Bethsaida. And they brought a blind man to Him and entreated Him to touch him. [23] He took the blind man by the hand and led him out of the town. When He had spit on his eyes and put His hands on him, He asked him, "Do you see anything?"

[24] He looked up and said, "I see men as trees, walking."

[25] Then again He put His hands on his eyes and made him look up. And he was restored and saw everyone clearly. [26] He sent him home away to his house, saying, "Neither go into the town, nor tell it to anyone in the town."

Peter's Declaration About Jesus

Mt 16:13–20; Lk 9:18–21

[27] Jesus and His disciples went out into the towns of Caesarea Philippi. On the way He asked His disciples, "Who do men say that I am?"

[28] They answered, "John the Baptist, but some say, Elijah; and others, one of the prophets."

[29] He said to them, "But who do you say that I am?"

Peter answered Him, "You are the Christ."

[30] He warned them that they should tell no one about Him.

Jesus Foretells His Death and Resurrection

Mt 16:21–18; Lk 9:22–27

[31] He began to teach them that the Son of Man must suffer many things, and be rejected by the elders and the chief priests and the scribes, and be killed, and after three days rise again. [32] He said this openly. And Peter took Him and began to rebuke Him.

[33] But when He had turned around and looked at His disciples, He rebuked Peter, saying, "Get behind Me, Satan! For you are not mindful of the things of God, but the things of men."

[34] When He had called the people to Him, with His disciples, He said to them, "If any man would come after Me, let him deny himself and take up his cross and follow Me. [35] For whoever would save his life will lose it. But whoever would lose his life for My sake and the gospel's will save it. [36] For what does it profit a man if he gains the whole world and loses his own soul? [37] Or what will a man give in exchange for his soul? [38] Whoever therefore is ashamed of Me and of My words in this adulterous and sinful generation, of him will the Son of Man also be ashamed when He comes in the glory of His Father with the holy angels."

9 And He said to them, "Truly I say to you, there are some standing here who will not taste death before they see the kingdom of God come with power."

The Transfiguration

Mt 17:1–13; Lk 9:28–36

[2] After six days Jesus took with Him Peter and James and John and led them up a high mountain, alone by themselves. And He was transfigured before them. [3] His garments became shiny, extremely white as snow, such as no launderer on earth could whiten them. [4] And there appeared to them Elijah with Moses. And they were talking with Jesus.

[5] Peter said to Jesus, "Rabbi, it is good for us to be here. Let us make three sanctuaries: one for You, and one for Moses, and one for Elijah." [6] For he did not know what to say, because they were very afraid.

[7] Then a cloud overshadowed them, and a voice came out of the cloud, saying, "This is My beloved Son. Listen to Him."

[8] Suddenly, when they looked around, they no longer saw anyone with them except Jesus only.

[9] As they came down the mountain, He warned them to tell no one what they had seen, until the Son of Man had risen from the dead. [10] They kept that statement to themselves, questioning each other what the rising from the dead meant.

[11] And they asked Him, "Why do the scribes say that Elijah must first come?"

[12] He answered, "Elijah indeed comes first to restore all things. Yet how is it written of the Son of Man that He should suffer many things and be treated with contempt? [13] But I say to you that Elijah has indeed come, and they have done to him whatever they wished, as it is written of him."

The Healing of a Boy With an Unclean Spirit

Mt 17:14–20; Lk 9:37–43

[14] When He came to His other disciples, He saw a great crowd around them, and the scribes disputing with them. [15] Immediately when all the people saw Him, they were greatly amazed, and running to Him, greeted Him.

[16] He asked the scribes, "What are you debating with them?"

[17] One in the crowd answered, "Teacher, I brought You my son, who has a mute spirit. [18] Wherever it takes hold on him, it dashes him to the ground. And he foams at the mouth and gnashes with his teeth and becomes rigid. And I told Your disciples so that they would cast it out, but they could not."

[19] He answered, "O faithless generation, how long shall I be with you? How long shall I bear with you? Bring him to Me."

[20] So they brought the boy to Him. When he saw Him, immediately the spirit dashed him, and he fell on the ground and wallowed, foaming at the mouth.

[21] He asked his father, "How long has it been since it came to him?" He said, "From childhood. [22] Often it has thrown him into the fire and into the water to kill him. But if You can do anything, have compassion on us and help us."

[23] Jesus said, "If you can believe, all things are possible to him who believes."

[24] Immediately the father of the child cried out with tears, "Lord, I believe. Help my unbelief!"

[25] When Jesus saw that the people came running together, He rebuked the foul spirit, saying to it, "You mute and deaf spirit, I command you, come out of him, and enter him no more."

[26] The spirit cried out and convulsed him greatly. But it came out of him, and he was as dead, so that many said, "He is dead." [27] But Jesus took him by the hand and lifted him up, and he arose.

[28] When He had entered the house, His disciples asked Him privately, "Why could we not cast it out?"

[29] He said to them, "This kind cannot come out except by prayer and fasting."

Jesus Again Foretells His Death and Resurrection

Mt 17:22–23; Lk 9:43b–45

[30] They departed from there and passed through Galilee, and He did not want anyone to know it. [31] For He was teaching His disciples, saying, "The Son of Man will be delivered into the hands of men, and they will kill Him. After He is killed, He will rise the third day." [32] But they did not understand the teaching and were afraid to ask Him.

Who Is the Greatest?

Mt 18:1–5; Lk 9:46–48

[33] He came to Capernaum. And being in the house, He asked them, "What was it that you disputed among yourselves on the way?" [34] But they kept silent, for on the way they had disputed among themselves who was the greatest.

[35] He sat down and called the twelve. And He said to them, "If anyone desires to be first, he must be last of all and servant of all."

[36] He took a child and set him in their midst. And when He had taken him in His arms, He said to them, [37] "Whoever receives one of these children in My name receives Me. And whoever receives Me receives not Me, but Him who sent Me."

[1] 18 Jer 5:21; Isa 6:9–10.

He Who Is Not Against Us Is for Us
Lk 9:49–50

[38] John answered Him, "Teacher, we saw one who does not follow us casting out demons in Your name, and we forbade him because he was not following us."

[39] But Jesus said, "Do not forbid him, for no one who does a miracle in My name can quickly speak evil of Me. [40] For he who is not against us is for us. [41] Truly I say to you, whoever gives you a cup of water to drink in My name, because you belong to Christ, will not lose his reward.

Temptations to Sin
Mt 18:6–9; Lk 17:1–2

[42] "Whoever causes one of these little ones who believe in Me to sin, it would be better for him if a millstone were hung around his neck and he were thrown into the sea. [43] If your hand causes you to sin, cut it off. It is better for you to enter life maimed than with two hands to go into hell, into the fire that shall never be quenched, [44] where

'their worm does not die,
    and the fire is not quenched.'[1]

[45] And if your foot causes you to sin, cut it off. It is better for you to enter life lame than with two feet to be thrown into hell, into the fire that shall never be quenched, [46] where

'their worm does not die,
    and the fire is not quenched.'[2]

[47] And if your eye causes you to sin, pluck it out. It is better for you to enter the kingdom of God with one eye than with two eyes to be thrown into the fire of hell, [48] where

'their worm does not die,
    and the fire is not quenched.'[3]

[49] Everyone will be salted with fire, and every sacrifice will be salted with salt. [50] "Salt is good. But if the salt loses its saltiness, how will you season it? Have salt in yourselves, and have peace with one another."

Teaching About Divorce
Mt 19:1–12

10 He arose and went from there to the region of Judea to the other side of the Jordan, and the people came to Him again. And again, as was His custom, He taught them. [2] The Pharisees came to test Him, asking, "Is it lawful for a man to divorce his wife?"

[3] He answered them, "What did Moses command you?"

[4] They said, "Moses permitted a man to write a certificate of divorce and to divorce her."

[5] Jesus answered them, "Due to the hardness of your heart he wrote you this precept. [6] But from the beginning of the creation, God 'made them male and female.'[4] [7] 'For this cause shall a man leave his father and mother, and cleave to his wife, [8] and the two shall be one flesh.'[5] So then they are no longer two, but one flesh. [9] What therefore God has joined together, let not man put asunder."

[10] In the house His disciples asked Him concerning this matter again. [11] He said to them, "Whoever divorces his wife and marries another commits adultery against her. [12] And if a woman divorces her husband and marries another, she commits adultery."

Little Children Blessed
Mt 19:13–18; Lk 18:15–17

[13] They brought young children to Him, that He might touch them. But the disciples rebuked those who brought them. [14] But when Jesus saw it, He was very displeased and said to them, "Allow the little children to come to Me, and do not forbid them, for of such is the kingdom of God. [15] Truly I say to you, whoever does not receive the kingdom of God as a little child shall not enter it." [16] And He took them up in His arms, put His hands on them, and blessed them.

The Rich Man
Mt 19:16–30; Lk 18:18–30

[17] When He set out on His way, a man came running and knelt before Him, and asked Him, "Good Teacher, what must I do to inherit eternal life?"

[18] He said to him, "Why do you call Me good? No one is good, except God alone. [19] You know the commandments, Do not commit adultery, Do not murder, Do not steal, Do not bear false witness, Do not defraud, Honor your father and mother.[6]"

[20] He answered Him, "Teacher, all these have I observed from my youth."

[21] Then Jesus, looking upon him, loved him and said to him, "You lack one thing: Go your way, sell whatever you have and give to the poor, and you will have treasure in heaven. And come, take up the cross and follow Me."

[22] He was saddened by that word, and he went away grieving. For he had many possessions.

[23] Jesus looked around and said to His disciples, "How hard it will be for those who have wealth to enter the kingdom of God!"

[24] The disciples were astonished at His words. But Jesus answered again, "Children, how hard it is for those who trust in riches to enter the kingdom of God! [25] It is easier for a camel to go through the eye of a needle than for a rich man to enter the kingdom of God."

[26] They were astonished beyond measure, saying among themselves, "Who then can be saved?"

[27] Jesus, looking at them, said, "With men it is impossible, but not with God. For with God all things are possible."

[28] Peter began to say to Him, "Look, we have left everything and have followed You."

[29] Jesus answered, "Truly I say to you, there is no one who has left a house or brothers or sisters or father or mother or wife or children or fields, for My sake and for the gospel's sake, [30] who shall not receive a hundred times as much now in this age, houses and brothers and sisters and mothers and children and fields, with persecution, and in the age to come, eternal life. [31] But many who are first will be last, and the last first."

Jesus Foretells His Death and Resurrection a Third Time
Mt 20:17–19; Lk 18:31–34

[32] They were on the way, going up to Jerusalem, and Jesus went ahead of them. And they were amazed, and those who followed were afraid. Again, He took the twelve aside and began to tell them what would happen to Him, [33] saying, "Listen! We are going up to Jerusalem. The Son of Man will be handed over to the chief priests and the scribes, and they will condemn Him to death and hand Him over to the Gentiles. [34] They will mock Him, and scourge Him, and spit on Him, and kill Him. Then after three days He will rise."

The Request of James and John
Mt 20:20–28

[35] Then James and John, the sons of Zebedee, came to Him, saying, "Teacher, we want that whatever we may ask, You would do for us."

[36] He said to them, "What do you want Me to do for you?"

[37] They said to Him, "Grant us to sit, one at Your right hand and the other at Your left hand, in Your glory."

[38] But Jesus said to them, "You do not know what you are asking. Can you drink the cup that I drink and be baptized with the baptism with which I am baptized?"

[39] They said to Him, "We can."

Jesus said to them, "You will indeed drink the cup that I drink and be baptized with the baptism with which I am baptized. [40] But to sit at My right hand or at My left hand is not Mine to grant. It is for those for whom it has been prepared."

---

[1] *44* Isa 66:24.   [2] *46* Isa 66:24.   [3] *48* Isa 66:24.   [4] *6* Ge 1:27.   [5] *7–8* Ge 2:24.   [6] *19* Ex 20:12–16; Dt 5:16–20.

[41] When the ten heard it, they began to be very displeased with James and John. [42] But Jesus called them together, and said, "You know that those who are appointed to rule over the Gentiles lord it over them, and their great ones exercise authority over them. [43] But it shall not be so among you. Whoever would be great among you must be your servant, [44] and whoever among you would be greatest must be servant of all. [45] For even the Son of Man came not to be served, but to serve, and to give His life as a ransom for many."

The Healing of Blind Bartimaeus
Mt 20:29–34; Lk 18:35–43

[46] Then they came to Jericho. And as He went out of Jericho with His disciples and a great number of people, blind Bartimaeus, the son of Timaeus, sat along the way begging. [47] When he heard that it was Jesus of Nazareth, he began to cry out, "Jesus, Son of David, have mercy on me!"

[48] Many ordered him to keep silent. But he cried out even more, "Son of David, have mercy on me!"

[49] Jesus stood still and commanded him to be called.

So they called the blind man, saying, "Be of good comfort. Rise, He is calling you." [50] Throwing aside his garment, he rose and came to Jesus.

[51] Jesus answered him, "What do you want Me to do for you?"

The blind man said to Him, "Rabbi, that I might receive my sight."

[52] Jesus said to him, "Go your way. Your faith has made you well." Immediately he received his sight and followed Jesus on the way.

The Triumphant Entry Into Jerusalem
Mt 21:1–11; Lk 19:28–40; Jn 12:12–19

11 When they drew near Jerusalem and came to Bethphage and Bethany at the Mount of Olives, He sent out two of His disciples [2] and said to them, "Go into the village opposite you. As soon as you enter it, you will find a colt tied, on which no one has ever sat. Untie it and bring it here. [3] If anyone says to you, 'Why are you doing this?' say 'The Lord has need of it,' and immediately he will send it here."

[4] They went their way and found the colt tied by the door outside on the street. And they untied it. [5] Some of those who stood there said to them, "What are you doing untying the colt?" [6] They answered just as Jesus had commanded. And they let them go. [7] They brought the colt to Jesus and threw their garments on it. And He sat upon it. [8] Many spread their garments on the street. And others cut down branches off the trees and scattered them on the street. [9] Those who went before and those who followed cried out, saying:

"Hosanna!
'Blessed is He who comes in the name of the Lord!'[1]
[10] Blessed is the kingdom of our father David that is coming in
        the name of the Lord!
Hosanna in the highest!"

[11] Jesus entered Jerusalem and went into the temple. When He had looked around at everything, as the hour was now late, He went out to Bethany with the twelve.

The Cursing of the Fig Tree
Mt 21:18–19

[12] On the next day when they had returned from Bethany, He was hungry. [13] Seeing from afar a fig tree with leaves, He went to see if perhaps He might find anything on it. When He came to it, He found nothing except leaves, for it was not the season for figs. [14] Jesus said to it, "May no one ever eat fruit from you again." And His disciples heard it.

The Cleansing of the Temple
Mt 21:12–17; Lk 19:45–48; Jn 2:13–22

[15] And they came to Jerusalem. Jesus went into the temple and began to drive out those who sold and bought in the temple, and He overturned the tables of the moneychangers and the seats of those who sold doves. [16] And He would not allow anyone to carry any vessel through the temple. [17] And He taught them, and said, "Is it not written, 'My house shall be called a house of prayer for all nations'[2]? But you have made it a 'den of thieves.'[3] "

[18] The scribes and chief priests heard it and looked for a way to kill Him. For they feared Him, because all the people were astonished at His teaching.

[19] When evening came, He went out of the city.

The Lesson From the Fig Tree
Mt 21:20–22

[20] In the morning, as they passed by, they saw the fig tree withered from the roots. [21] Peter, calling to remembrance, said to Him, "Rabbi, look! The fig tree which You cursed has withered away."

[22] Jesus answered them, "Have faith in God. [23] For truly I say to you, whoever says to this mountain, 'Be removed and be thrown into the sea,' and does not doubt in his heart, but believes that what he says will come to pass, he will have whatever he says. [24] Therefore I say to you, whatever things you ask when you pray, believe that you will receive them, and you will have them. [25] And when you stand praying, forgive if you have anything against anyone, so that your Father who is in heaven may also forgive you your sins. [26] But if you do not forgive, neither will your Father who is in heaven forgive your sins."

The Question of Jesus' Authority
Mt 21:23–27; Lk 20:1–8

[27] They came again to Jerusalem, and as He was walking in the temple, the chief priests and the scribes and the elders came to Him, [28] and said, "By what authority are You doing these things, and who gave You this authority to do them?"

[29] Jesus answered them, "I will also ask of you one question. Answer Me, and I will tell you by what authority I do these things. [30] Was the baptism of John from heaven or from men? Answer Me."

[31] They debated among themselves, saying, "If we say, 'From heaven,' He will say, 'Why then did you not believe him?' [32] But if we say, 'From men' "—they feared the people, for everyone held John to be a real prophet.

[33] So they answered Jesus, "We do not know."

Jesus answered them, "Neither will I tell you by what authority I do these things."

The Parable of the Vineyard and the Vinedressers
Mt 21:33–46; Lk 20:9–10

12 He began to speak to them in parables. "A man planted a vineyard, and set a hedge around it, and dug a pit for the winepress, and built a tower, and rented it to vinedressers, and went to a far country. [2] At harvest time he sent a servant to the vinedressers to receive from them some of the fruit of the vineyard. [3] But they seized him and beat him and sent him away empty-handed. [4] Then he sent another servant to them. They threw stones at him, and wounded him in the head, and sent him away shamefully handled. [5] Still he sent another, and they killed him. And there were many others. Some they beat, and some they killed.

[6] "Having yet his one well-beloved son, he sent him last to them, saying, 'They will revere my son.'

[7] "But those vinedressers said among themselves, 'This is the heir. Come, let us kill him, and the inheritance will be ours.' [8] So they took him and killed him and threw him out of the vineyard.

[9] "What then will the owner of the vineyard do? He will come and kill the vinedressers and give the vineyard to others. [10] Have you not read this Scripture:

'The stone which the builders rejected
        has become the cornerstone.
[11] This was the Lord's doing,
        and it is marvelous in our eyes'[4]?"

---

[1] 9 Ps 118:26.   [2] 17 Isa 56:7.   [3] 17 Jer 7:11.   [4] 10–11 Ps 118:22–23.

¹² Then they tried to seize Him, but feared the people, for they knew that He had spoken the parable against them. So they left Him and went their way.

The Question of Paying Taxes
Mt 22:15–22; Lk 20:20–26

¹³ They sent to Him some of the Pharisees and some of the Herodians to trap Him in His words. ¹⁴ When they came to Him, they said, "Teacher, we know that You are true and swayed by no man. For You do not regard the person of men, but truthfully teach the way of God. Is it lawful to pay taxes to Caesar, or not? ¹⁵ Should we pay, or should we not pay?"

But He, knowing their hypocrisy, said to them, "Why test Me? Bring Me a denarius that I may see it." ¹⁶ They brought it, and He said to them, "Whose image and inscription is this?"

They said to Him, "Caesar's."

¹⁷ Then Jesus answered them, "Render to Caesar the things that are Caesar's, and to God the things that are God's."

And they were amazed at Him.

The Question About the Resurrection
Mt 22:23–33; Lk 20:27–40

¹⁸ Then the Sadducees, who say there is no resurrection, came to Him, saying, ¹⁹ "Teacher, Moses wrote for us that if a man's brother dies and leaves his wife behind, but leaves no children, that man must take the wife and raise up children for his brother.¹ ²⁰ Now there were seven brothers. The first took a wife, and when he died, he left no children. ²¹ The second took her and died, leaving no children, and the third likewise. ²² The seven had her and left no children. Last of all, the woman died too. ²³ In the resurrection, when they rise, whose wife will she be? For the seven had her as wife."

²⁴ Jesus answered them, "Do you not err, because you know neither the Scriptures nor the power of God? ²⁵ When they rise from the dead, they neither marry nor are given in marriage, but are like angels in heaven. ²⁶ Now concerning the dead rising, have you not read in the book of Moses, in the account about the bush, how God spoke to him, saying, 'I am the God of Abraham and the God of Isaac and the God of Jacob²? ²⁷ He is not the God of the dead, but the God of the living. You therefore do greatly err."

The Great Commandment
Mt 22:34–40; Lk 10:25–28

²⁸ One of the scribes came and heard them reasoning together. Perceiving that Jesus had answered them well, he asked Him, "Which is the first commandment of all?"

²⁹ Jesus answered him, "The first of all the commandments is, 'Hear, O Israel, the Lord our God is one Lord. ³⁰ You shall love the Lord your God with all your heart, and with all your soul, and with all your mind, and with all your strength.'³ This is the first commandment. ³¹ The second is this: 'You shall love your neighbor as yourself.'⁴ There is no other commandment greater than these."

³² The scribe said to Him, "Well said, Teacher. You have spoken the truth, that there is one God and there is no other but Him. ³³ To love Him with all the heart, and with all the understanding, and with all the soul, and with all the strength, and to love one's neighbor as oneself, is more than all burnt offerings and sacrifices."

³⁴ When Jesus saw that he answered wisely, He said to him, "You are not far from the kingdom of God." After that, no one dared to ask Him any question.

The Question About David's Son
Mt 22:41–46; Lk 20:41–44

³⁵ While Jesus taught in the temple, He said, "How can the scribes say that Christ is the Son of David? ³⁶ David himself, speaking by the Holy Spirit, declared:

'The Lord said to my Lord,
"Sit at My right hand,

until I put Your enemies
under Your feet." '⁵

³⁷ David himself calls Him 'Lord.' How then is He his Son?" And the large crowd heard him gladly.

The Denouncing of the Scribes
Mt 23:1–36; Lk 20:45–47

³⁸ He said to them in His teaching, "Beware of the scribes, who love to go about in long robes and love greetings in the marketplaces, ³⁹ and the prominent seats in the synagogues, and the places of honor at banquets, ⁴⁰ who devour widows' houses and for a pretense make long prayers. They will receive greater condemnation."

The Widow's Offering
Lk 21:1–4

⁴¹ Jesus sat opposite the treasury and saw how the people put money into the treasury. Many who were rich put in much. ⁴² But a certain poor widow came and put in two mites, which make a farthing.⁶

⁴³ He called His disciples to Him and said to them, "Truly I say to you, this poor widow has put in more than all those who are contributing to the treasury. ⁴⁴ They all contributed out of their abundance. But she, out of her poverty, put in all that she had, her entire livelihood."

The Destruction of the Temple Foretold
Mt 24:1–2; Lk 21:5–6

13 As He went out of the temple, one of His disciples said to Him, "Teacher, see what great stones and what great buildings are here."

² Jesus answered him, "Do you see these great buildings? Not one stone shall be left upon another that shall not be thrown down."

Troubles and Persecutions
Mt 24:3–14; Lk 21:7–19

³ As He sat on the Mount of Olives opposite the temple, Peter, James, John, and Andrew asked Him privately, ⁴ "Tell us, when will these things happen, and what will be the sign when all these things will be fulfilled?"

⁵ Jesus answered them, "Take heed lest anyone deceive you. ⁶ Many will come in My name, saying, 'I am He,' and will deceive many. ⁷ When you hear of wars and rumors of wars, do not be troubled. For such things must happen, but the end is still to come. ⁸ For nation will rise against nation, and kingdom against kingdom. And there will be earthquakes in various places, and there will be famines and troubles. These are the beginning of sorrows.

⁹ "But take heed. For they will hand you over to councils, and in the synagogues you will be beaten. You will be brought before rulers and kings for My sake, as a testimony to them. ¹⁰ And the gospel must first be preached to all nations. ¹¹ But when they arrest you and hand you over, take no thought beforehand, or premeditate what you should speak. But speak whatever is given you in that time, for it is not you who speaks, but the Holy Spirit. ¹² "Now a brother will betray his brother to death, and the father the son; children will rise up against their parents, and will cause them to be put to death. ¹³ You will be hated by all men for My name's sake. But he who endures to the end shall be saved.

The Great Tribulation
Mt 24:15–28; Lk 21:20–24

¹⁴ "When you see the 'abomination of desolation'⁷ spoken of by Daniel the prophet standing where it should not be (let the reader understand), then let those who are in Judea flee to the mountains. ¹⁵ Let him who is on the housetop not go down or enter the house to take anything out of his house. ¹⁶ Let him who is in the field not turn back to take his garment. ¹⁷ But woe to

---

women who are pregnant and to those who nurse in those days! [18] Pray that your escape may not be in winter. [19] For in those days there will be distress as has not been from the beginning of the creation which God created to this time, nor ever shall be. [20] "Except the Lord shortened the days, no flesh would be saved. But for the sake of the elect, whom He chose, He shortened the days. [21] Then if anyone says to you, 'Look, here is the Christ!' or 'Look, there He is!' do not believe it. [22] For false christs and false prophets will rise and show signs and wonders to deceive, if possible, even the elect. [23] But take heed. I have told you all things beforehand.

The Coming of the Son of Man
Mt 24:29–31; Lk 21:25–28

[24] "But in those days, after that distress,

'the sun will be darkened,
   and the moon will not give her light;
[25] the stars of heaven will fall,
   and the powers that are in heaven will be shaken.'[1]

[26] "Then they will see the Son of Man coming in clouds with great power and glory. [27] Then He will send His angels and gather His elect from the four winds, from the farthest part of the earth to the farthest part of heaven.

The Lesson of the Fig Tree
Mt 24:32–35; Lk 21:29–33

[28] "Now learn a parable of the fig tree: When her branch is yet tender and puts out leaves, you know that summer is near. [29] So also, when you see these things come to pass, know that it is near, even at the doors. [30] Truly I say to you, this generation will not pass away until all these things happen. [31] Heaven and earth will pass away, but My words will not pass away.

The Unknown Day and Hour
Mt 24:36–44

[32] "But concerning that day or hour no one knows, not even the angels in heaven, nor the Son, but only the Father. [33] Take heed, watch and pray. For you do not know when the time will come. [34] For the Son of Man is like a man leaving on a far journey who left his house and gave authority to his servants and to every man his work, and commanded the porter to watch. [35] "Watch therefore—for you do not know when the master of the house is coming, in the evening, or at midnight, or at the crowing of the rooster, or in the morning— [36] lest he come suddenly and find you sleeping. [37] What I say to you I say to all: Watch!"

The Plot to Kill Jesus
Mt 26:1–5; Lk 22:1–2; Jn 11:45–53

14 Now the feasts of the Passover and of Unleavened Bread were two days away. And the chief priests and the scribes looked for a way to seize Him secretly and kill Him. [2] But they said "Not on the feast day, lest there will be an uproar among the people."

The Anointing at Bethany
Mt 26:6–13; Jn 12:1–8

[3] While He was in Bethany in the house of Simon the leper, as He sat at supper, a woman came with an alabaster jar of ointment, a very costly spikenard. She broke the jar and poured the ointment on His head.
[4] There were some with indignation within themselves, saying, "Why was this ointment wasted? [5] It might have been sold for more than three hundred denarii[2] and given to the poor." And they grumbled against her.
[6] Jesus said, "Leave her alone. Why do you trouble her? She has done a good work for Me. [7] You always have the poor with you, and whenever you wish, you may do good to them. But you will not always have Me. [8] She has done what she could. She has come be-

forehand to anoint My body for burial. [9] Truly I say to you, wherever this gospel will be preached throughout the whole world, what she has done will also be spoken of as a memorial to her."

Judas' Agreement to Betray Jesus
Mt 26:14–18; Lk 22:3–6

[10] Then Judas Iscariot, who was one of the twelve, went to the chief priests to betray Him to them. [11] When they heard it, they were glad and promised to give him silver. So he looked for how he might conveniently betray Him.

The Passover With the Disciples
Mt 26:17–28; Lk 22:7–14, 21–23; Jn 13:21–30

[12] On the first day of Unleavened Bread, when they sacrificed the Passover lamb, His disciples said to Him, "Where do You want us to prepare for You to eat the Passover?"
[13] So He sent two of His disciples and said to them, "Go into the city, and a man carrying a pitcher of water will meet you there. Follow him. [14] Wherever he enters, say to the owner of the house, 'The Teacher says, Where is the guest room where I may eat the Passover with My disciples?' [15] He will show you a large upper room, furnished and ready. Make preparations for us there."
[16] His disciples went out, and came into the city, and found it as He had told them. And they prepared the Passover.
[17] In the evening He came with the twelve. [18] As they sat and ate, Jesus said, "Truly I say to you, one of you who is eating with Me will betray Me."
[19] They began to be sorrowful and to say to Him one by one, "Is it I?" and another, "Is it I?"
[20] He answered them, "It is one of the twelve, one who is dipping bread in the dish with Me. [21] The Son of Man indeed goes as it is written concerning Him, but woe to that man by whom the Son of Man is betrayed! It would have been good for that man if he had never been born."

The Lord's Supper
Mt 26:26–30; Lk 22:15–20; 1Co 11:23–25

[22] As they were eating, Jesus took bread, blessed and broke it, and gave it to them, saying, "Take and eat it. This is My body."
[23] Then He took the cup, and when He had given thanks, He gave it to them. And they all drank from it.
[24] He said to them, "This is My blood of the new covenant, which is shed for many. [25] Truly I say to you, I will drink no more of the fruit of the vine until that day when I drink it new in the kingdom of God."
[26] When they had sung a hymn, they went out to the Mount of Olives.

Peter's Denial Foretold
Mt 26:31–35; Lk 22:31–34; Jn 13:36–38

[27] Jesus said to them, "All of you will fall away on account of Me this night, for it is written:

'I will strike the shepherd,
   and the sheep will be scattered.'[3]

[28] But after I have risen, I will go before you to Galilee."
[29] Peter said to Him, "Even if all fall away, I will not."
[30] Jesus said to him, "Truly, I say to you that this day, during the night, before the rooster crows twice, you will deny Me three times."
[31] But he said more vehemently, "If I must die with You, I will not deny You." They all said the same thing.

The Prayer in Gethsemane
Mt 26:36–46; Lk 22:39–46

[32] They came to a place which was named Gethsemane. And He said to His disciples, "Sit here while I pray." [33] He took Peter and James and John with Him and began to be greatly distressed and very troubled. [34] And He said to them, "My soul is deeply sorrowful unto death. Remain here and keep watch."

---

[1] 24–25 Isa 13:10; 34:4.   [2] 5 A year's wages.   [3] 27 Zec 13:7.

[35] He went a little farther and fell on the ground and prayed that, if it were possible, the hour might pass from Him. [36] He said, *"Abba*, Father, all things are possible for You. Remove this cup from Me; yet not what I will, but what You will."

[37] Then He came and found them sleeping and said to Peter, "Simon, are you sleeping? Could you not keep watch one hour? [38] Watch and pray, lest you enter into temptation. The spirit indeed is willing, but the flesh is weak."

[39] Again He went away and prayed the same words. [40] When He returned, He again found them sleeping, for their eyes were heavy. And they did not know what to answer Him.

[41] When He returned a third time, He said to them, "Are you still sleeping and taking your rest? It is enough! The hour has come. Look, the Son of Man is betrayed into the hands of sinners. [42] Rise up, let us go. Look! He who betrays Me is at hand."

The Betrayal and Arrest of Jesus
Mt 26:47–56; Lk 22:47–53; Jn 18:3–12

[43] Immediately, while He was still speaking, Judas, one of the twelve, and with him a great crowd with swords and clubs, came from the chief priests and the scribes and the elders.

[44] Now he who betrayed Him had given them a sign, saying, "Whomever I kiss, He is the One. Seize Him and lead Him away safely." [45] So as soon as he came, he went to Him immediately and said, "Rabbi, Rabbi!" and kissed Him. [46] They laid hands on Him and seized Him. [47] Then one of those who stood by drew his sword and struck the servant of the high priest and cut off his ear.

[48] Jesus said to them, "Have you come out with swords and clubs to arrest Me as you would a thief? [49] Every day I was with you in the temple teaching, and you did not seize Me. But the Scriptures must be fulfilled." [50] Then they all deserted Him and fled.

The Young Man Who Fled

[51] A young man followed Him, wearing a linen cloth around himself. And the young men laid hold of him, [52] so he left the linen cloth, and fled from them unclothed.

Jesus Before the Sanhedrin
Mt 26:57–68; Lk 22:54–55, 63–71; Jn 10:13–14, 19–24

[53] They led Jesus away to the high priest. And all the chief priests and the elders and the scribes were assembled with him. [54] Peter followed Him at a distance into the courtyard of the high priest. He sat with the guards and warmed himself by the fire.

[55] Now the chief priests and the entire Sanhedrin requested testimony against Jesus to put Him to death, but found none. [56] Many bore false witness against Him, but their testimonies did not agree.

[57] Then some rose up and bore false witness against Him, saying, [58] "We heard Him say, 'I will destroy this temple that is made with hands, and within three days I will build another not made with hands.' " [59] But still their testimony did not agree.

[60] Then the high priest stood up in the midst and asked Jesus, "Do You answer nothing? What is it which these men testify against You?" [61] But He kept silent and answered nothing.

Again the high priest asked Him, "Are You the Christ, the Son of the Blessed One?"

[62] Jesus said, "I am. And you will see the Son of Man sitting at the right hand of Power and coming with the clouds of heaven."

[63] The high priest tore his robes, saying, "What need do we have of any further witnesses? [64] You have heard the blasphemy. What do you think?"

They all condemned Him as guilty unto death. [65] Then some began to spit on Him, and to blindfold Him, and to strike Him, saying to Him, "Prophesy!" And the guards struck Him with the palms of their hands.

Peter's Denial of Jesus
Mt 26:69–75; Lk 22:56–62; Jn 18:15–18, 25–27

[66] While Peter was below in the courtyard, one of the servant girls of the high priest came. [67] When she saw Peter warming himself, she looked at him and said, "You also were with Jesus of Nazareth."

[68] But he denied it, saying, "I neither know nor understand what you are saying." Then he went out to the porch, and a rooster crowed.

[69] The servant girl saw him again and began to say to those who stood by, "This man is one of them." [70] But again, he denied it.

A little while later, those who stood by said again to Peter, "Surely, you are one of them. For you are a Galilean, and your speech confirms it."

[71] Peter began to invoke a curse on himself, and to swear, "I do not know this Man of whom you speak."

[72] And the rooster crowed a second time. And Peter called to mind the word that Jesus said to him, "Before the rooster crows twice, you will deny Me three times." And when he thought on this, he wept.

Jesus Before Pilate
Mt 27:1–2, 11–14; Lk 23:1–5; Jn 18:28–38

15 Early in the morning the chief priests held a consultation with the elders and scribes and the whole Sanhedrin. And they bound Jesus and took Him away and handed Him over to Pilate.

[2] Pilate asked Him, "Are You the King of the Jews?"

He answered him, "You have said so."

[3] The chief priests accused Him of many things, but He answered nothing. [4] So Pilate asked Him again, "Do You answer nothing? See how many things they testify against You."

[5] But Jesus still answered nothing, so that Pilate was astonished.

Jesus Sentenced to Die
Mt 27:15–26; Lk 23:13–25; Jn 18:39–19:16

[6] Now at the feast he always released to them one prisoner, whomever they requested. [7] There was one named Barabbas, who had committed murder in the insurrection and was bound with the rebels. [8] The crowd began crying aloud, asking Pilate to do as he had always done for them.

[9] He answered them, "Do you want me to release to you the King of the Jews?" [10] For he knew that the chief priests had handed Him over out of envy. [11] But the chief priests stirred the people, so that he should instead release Barabbas to them.

[12] Pilate answered them again, "What then would you have me do to Him whom you call the King of the Jews?"

[13] They again cried out, "Crucify Him!"

[14] Pilate said to them, "Why, what evil has He done?"

But they cried out even more, "Crucify Him!"

[15] So Pilate, resolving to satisfy the people, released Barabbas to them. And when he had scourged Jesus, he handed Him over to be crucified.

The Soldiers Mock Jesus
Mt 27:27–31; Jn 19:2–3

[16] The soldiers led Him away to Praetorium Hall, and they called together the entire battalion. [17] They clothed Him with a purple robe. And they wove a crown of thorns and put it on His head, [18] and began to salute Him, "Hail, King of the Jews!" [19] They struck His head with a staff and spit on Him. And bowing their knees, they worshipped Him. [20] When they had mocked Him, they took the purple robe off of Him and put His own garments on Him. Then they led Him out to crucify Him.

The Crucifixion
Mt 27:32–44; Lk 23:26–43; Jn 19:17–27

[21] They compelled a man named Simon from Cyrene, the father of Alexander and Rufus, as he was passing through from the country, to bear Jesus' cross. [22] They brought Him to the place called Golgotha, which means, "Place of a Skull." [23] They gave Him wine mingled with myrrh to drink, but He did not take it. [24] When they had crucified Him, they divided His garments, casting lots for them, to decide what each man should take.

[25] Now it was the third hour, and they crucified Him. [26] The inscription of His accusation was written above:

THE KING OF THE JEWS.

[27] With Him they crucified two thieves, one on His right and the other on His left. [28] And the Scripture was fulfilled, which says, "He was numbered with the lawless ones." *1* [29] Those who passed by blasphemed Him, shaking their heads and saying, "Ah, You who would destroy the temple and build it in three days, [30] save Yourself, and come down from the cross!" [31] Likewise the chief priests mocked Him among themselves with the scribes and said, "He saved others, but He cannot save Himself! [32] Let the Christ, the King of Israel, descend now from the cross, that we may see and believe." Those who were crucified with Him also reviled Him.

The Death of Jesus
Mt 27:45–56; Lk 23:44–49; Jn 19:28–30

[33] When the sixth hour had come, there was darkness over the whole land until the ninth hour. [34] And at the ninth hour Jesus cried out with a loud voice, saying, *"Eloi, Eloi, lama sabachthani?"* which means, "My God, My God, why have You forsaken Me?" *2* [35] Some of those who stood by, when they heard it, said, "Listen, He is calling Elijah!" [36] One man ran and filled a sponge with vinegar, put it on a stick, and gave it to Him to drink, saying, "Leave Him alone. Let us see if Elijah will come to take Him down." [37] But Jesus cried with a loud voice and gave up the spirit. [38] And the curtain of the temple was torn in two from top to bottom. [39] When the centurion *3* who stood facing Him saw that He cried out and gave up the spirit, he said, "Truly, this Man was the Son of God." [40] There were also women looking on from a distance, among whom were Mary Magdalene, and Mary the mother of James the Less and of Joseph, and Salome. [41] They also had followed Him and had ministered to Him when He was in Galilee. And many other women who came up with Him to Jerusalem were there.

The Burial of Jesus
Mt 27:57–61; Lk 23:50–56; Jn 19:38–42

[42] When the evening had come, because it was the Day of Preparation, that is, the day before the Sabbath, [43] Joseph of Arimathea, an honorable member of the Council, who also waited for the kingdom of God, came and went in boldly to Pilate, and requested the body of Jesus. [44] Pilate wondered if He were already dead. And calling for the centurion, he asked him whether He had been dead for a while. [45] When he learned about it from the centurion, he granted the body to Joseph. [46] So he bought fine linen, and taking Him down, wrapped Him in the linen and laid Him in a tomb which had been hewn out of the rock. And he rolled a stone against the door of the tomb. [47] Mary Magdalene and Mary the mother of Joseph saw where He was laid.

The Resurrection of Jesus
Mt 28:1–8; Lk 24:1–12; Jn 20:1–10

16 When the Sabbath was past, Mary Magdalene, and Mary the mother of James, and Salome, bought spices, so that they might go and anoint Him. [2] Very early in the morning, on the first day of the week, they came to the tomb at the rising of the sun. [3] They said among themselves, "Who will roll the stone away from the door of the tomb for us?" [4] But when they looked, they saw that the stone had been rolled away. For it was very large. [5] And entering the tomb, they saw a young man sitting on the right side, clothed in a long white robe. And they were frightened. [6] He said to them, "Do not be frightened. You are looking for Jesus of Nazareth, who was crucified. He is risen. He is not here. See the place where they laid Him. [7] But go your way, tell His disciples and Peter that He is going before you to Galilee. There you will see Him, as He told you." [8] They went out quickly and fled from the tomb, for they trembled and were amazed. And they said nothing to anyone, for they were afraid.

The Appearance to Mary Magdalene
Mt 28:9–10; Jn 20:11–18

[9] Now when Jesus rose early on the first day of the week, He appeared first to Mary Magdalene, out of whom He had cast seven demons. [10] She went and told those who had been with Him as they mourned and wept. [11] When they heard that He was alive and had been seen by her, they did not believe it.

The Appearance to Two Disciples
Lk 24:13–35

[12] After that He appeared in another form to two of them as they walked and went into the country. [13] And they went and told it to the rest, but they did not believe them either.

The Commissioning of the Disciples
Mt 28:16–20; Lk 24:36–49; Jn 20:19–23; Ac 1:6–8

[14] Afterward He appeared to the eleven as they sat at supper, and He reprimanded them for their hardness of heart, because they did not believe those who had seen Him after He had risen. [15] He said to them, "Go into all the world, and preach the gospel to every creature. [16] He who believes and is baptized will be saved. But he who does not believe will be condemned. [17] These signs will accompany those who believe: In My name they will cast out demons; they will speak with new tongues; [18] they will take up serpents; if they drink any deadly thing, it will not hurt them; they will lay hands on the sick, and they will recover."

The Ascension
Lk 24:50–53; Ac 1:9–11

[19] After the Lord had spoken to them, He was received up into heaven and sat at the right hand of God. [20] Then they went forth and preached everywhere, the Lord working with them and confirming the word through the accompanying signs. Amen.

---

1 28 Isa 53:12. *2 34* Ps 22:1. *3 39* Commander with the rank of captain over 100 soldiers.

LUKE

The Prologue

1 Whereas many have undertaken to write a narrative of those things which are most surely believed among us, [2] just as they were handed down to us by those who from the beginning were eyewitnesses and ministers of the word, [3] it seemed good to me also, having accurately investigated all things from the very beginning, to write to you an orderly account, most excellent Theophilus, [4] that you might know the certainty of the things which you have been told.

The Birth of John the Baptist Foretold

[5] There was in the days of Herod, the king of Judea, a certain priest named Zechariah, of the division of Abijah. And his wife was of the daughters of Aaron, and her name was Elizabeth. [6] They were both righteous before God, walking in all the commandments and ordinances of the Lord blamelessly. [7] But they had no child, because Elizabeth was barren, and they both were now well advanced in years.

[8] Now while he served as priest before God, when his division was on duty, [9] according to the custom of the priest's office, his lot was to burn incense when he went into the temple of the Lord. [10] And the whole crowd of people were praying outside at the hour of incense.

[11] Then an angel of the Lord appeared to him, standing on the right side of the altar of incense. [12] When Zechariah saw him, he was troubled, and fear fell upon him. [13] But the angel said to him, "Do not fear, Zechariah, for your prayer has been heard, and your wife Elizabeth will bear you a son, and you shall call his name John. [14] You will have joy and gladness, and many will rejoice at his birth. [15] For he will be great in the sight of the Lord, and shall drink neither wine nor strong drink, and he will be filled with the Holy Spirit, even from his mother's womb. [16] He will turn many of the sons of Israel to the Lord their God. [17] And he will go before Him in the spirit and power of Elijah, to turn the hearts of the fathers to the children *1* and the disobedient to the wisdom of the just, to make ready a people prepared for the Lord."

[18] Zechariah said to the angel, "How shall I know this? For I am an old man and my wife well advanced in years."

[19] The angel answered him, "I am Gabriel, who stands in the presence of God. And I was sent to speak to you and to bring you this good news. [20] And now you will be silent and unable to speak until the day that these things happen, because you did not believe my words, which will be fulfilled in their season."

[21] The people waited for Zechariah, and wondered why he waited so long in the temple. [22] When he came out, he could not speak to them. They perceived that he had seen a vision in the temple, for he made signs to them and remained speechless.

[23] As soon as the days of his service were fulfilled, he departed to his own home. [24] After those days his wife Elizabeth conceived, and for five months she hid herself, saying, [25] "Thus the Lord has dealt with me in the days when He looked on me, to take away my reproach among men."

The Birth of Jesus Foretold

[26] In the sixth month the angel Gabriel was sent from God to a city of Galilee named Nazareth, [27] to a virgin betrothed to a man whose name was Joseph, of the house of David. And the virgin's name was Mary. [28] The angel came to her and said, "Greetings, you who are highly favored. The Lord is with you. Blessed are you among women."

[29] When she saw him, she was troubled by his words, and considered in her mind what kind of greeting this might be. [30] But the angel said to her, "Do not be afraid, Mary, for you have found favor with God. [31] Listen, you will conceive in your womb and bear a Son and shall call His name JESUS. [32] He will be great, and will be called the Son of the Highest. And the Lord God will give Him the throne

of His father David, [33] and He will reign over the house of Jacob forever. And of His kingdom there will be no end."

[34] Then Mary said to the angel, "How can this be, since I do not know a man?"

[35] The angel answered her, "The Holy Spirit will come upon you, and the power of the Highest will overshadow you. Therefore the Holy One who will be born will be called the Son of God. [36] Listen, your cousin Elizabeth has also conceived a son in her old age. And this is the sixth month with her who was declared barren. [37] For with God nothing will be impossible."

[38] Mary said, "I am the servant of the Lord. May it be unto me according to your word." Then the angel departed from her.

Mary Visits Elizabeth

[39] In those days Mary arose and quickly went into the hill country, to a city of Judah, [40] and entered the house of Zechariah and greeted Elizabeth. [41] When Elizabeth heard the greeting of Mary, the baby leaped in her womb. And Elizabeth was filled with the Holy Spirit. [42] She spoke out with a loud voice, "Blessed are you among women, and blessed is the fruit of your womb! [43] But why is this granted to me, that the mother of my Lord should come to me? [44] Indeed, as soon as the sound of your greeting came to my ears, the baby in my womb leaped for joy. [45] Blessed is she who believed, for there will be a completion to those things which were told her by the Lord."

The Song of Mary

[46] And Mary said:

"My soul magnifies the Lord,
[47]   and my spirit rejoices in God my Savior.
[48] For He has regarded
        the low estate of His servant;
    surely, from now on all generations will call me blessed.
[49] For He who is mighty has done great things for me,
        and holy is His name.
[50] His mercy is on those who fear Him
        from generation to generation.
[51] He has shown strength with His arm;
        He has scattered the proud in the imagination of their
            hearts.
[52] He has pulled down the mighty from their thrones
        and exalted those of low degree.
[53] He has filled the hungry with good things,
        and the rich He has sent away empty.
[54] He has helped His servant Israel,
        in remembrance of His mercy,
[55] as He spoke to our fathers,
        to Abraham and to his descendants forever." *2*

[56] Mary remained with her about three months and returned to her own house.

The Birth of John the Baptist

[57] Now Elizabeth's time had come to give birth, and she gave birth to a son. [58] Her neighbors and cousins heard how the Lord had shown her great mercy, and they rejoiced with her.

[59] On the eighth day they came to circumcise the child. And they were calling him Zechariah, after the name of his father. [60] But his mother answered, "Not so! He shall be called John."

[61] They said to her, "There is no one among your relatives who is called by this name."

[62] They made signs to his father, asking what he would have him called. [63] He asked for a writing tablet and wrote, "His name is John." And they all were amazed. [64] Immediately his mouth was opened and his tongue was loosed, and he spoke and

---

1 17 Mal 4:5–6.   *2 46–55* 1Sa 2:1–10; Mic 7:20; Ge 17:7; 18:18; 22:17.

praised God. [65] Fear came on all who lived around them. And all these facts were talked about throughout all the hill country of Judea. [66] All those who heard them laid them up in their hearts, saying, "What kind of child will he be?" For the hand of the Lord was with him.

The Prophecy of Zechariah

[67] His father Zechariah was filled with the Holy Spirit and prophesied, saying,

[68] "Blessed be the Lord God of Israel,
    for He has visited and redeemed His people,
[69] and has raised up a horn of salvation for us
    in the house of His servant David,
[70] as He spoke by the mouth of His holy prophets of long ago,
[71] that we should be saved from our enemies
    and from the hand of all who hate us,
[72] to perform the mercy promised to our fathers
    and to remember His holy covenant,
[73]   the oath which He swore to our father Abraham,
[74] to grant us that we, being delivered out of the hand of our
    enemies,
    might serve Him without fear,
[75]   in holiness and righteousness before Him all the days of
    our lives.

[76] "And you, child, will be called the prophet of the Highest;
    for you will go before the face of the Lord to prepare
    His ways,
[77] to give knowledge of salvation to His people
    by the remission of their sins,
[78] through the tender mercy of our God,
    whereby the sunrise from on high has visited us;
[79] to give light to those who sit in darkness
    and in the shadow of death,
    to guide our feet into the way of peace."

[80] And the child grew and became strong in spirit, and he remained in the wilderness until the day of his appearance to Israel.

The Birth of Jesus
Mt 1:18–25

2 In those days a decree went out from Caesar Augustus that the entire inhabited earth should be taxed. [2] This taxation was first made when Quirinius was governor of Syria. [3] And everyone went to his own city to be taxed.

[4] So Joseph also departed from the city of Nazareth in Galilee to the City of David which is called Bethlehem, in Judea, because he was of the house and lineage of David, [5] to be taxed with Mary, his betrothed wife, who was with child. [6] So while they were there, the day came for her to give birth. [7] And she gave birth to her firstborn Son, and wrapped Him in strips of cloth, and laid Him in a manger, because there was no room for them in the inn.

The Shepherds and the Angels

[8] And in the same area there were shepherds living in the fields, keeping watch over their flock by night. [9] And then an angel of the Lord appeared to them, and the glory of the Lord shone around them, and they were very afraid. [10] But the angel said to them, "Listen! Do not fear. For I bring you good news of great joy, which will be to all people. [11] For unto you is born this day in the City of David a Savior, who is Christ the Lord. [12] And this will be a sign to you: You will find the Baby wrapped in strips of cloth, lying in a manger."

[13] Suddenly there was with the angel a company of the heavenly host praising God and saying,

[14] "Glory to God in the highest,
    and on earth peace, and good will toward men."

[15] When the angels went away from them into heaven, the shepherds said to each other, "Let us now go to Bethlehem and see what has happened, which the Lord has made known to us."

[16] So they came hurrying and found Mary and Joseph, and the Baby lying in a manger. [17] When they had seen Him, they made widely known the word which was told them concerning this Child. [18] And all those who heard it marveled at what the shepherds told them. [19] But Mary kept all these things and pondered them in her heart. [20] The shepherds returned, glorifying and praising God for all the things they had heard and seen, as it had been told them.

The Presentation of Jesus in the Temple

[21] When eight days had passed and the Child was circumcised, He was named JESUS, the name given by the angel before He was conceived in the womb.

[22] When the days of her purification according to the Law of Moses were completed, they brought Him to Jerusalem to present Him to the Lord [23] (as it is written in the law of the Lord, "Every firstborn male shall be called holy to the Lord"[1]) [24] and to offer a sacrifice according to what is said in the law of the Lord, "a pair of turtledoves, or two young pigeons."[2]

[25] Now there was a man in Jerusalem whose name was Simeon, and this man was righteous and devout, waiting for the consolation of Israel, and the Holy Spirit was upon him. [26] It was revealed to him by the Holy Spirit that he would not die before he had seen the Lord's Christ. [27] Led by the Spirit, he came into the temple. And when the parents brought in the Child Jesus, to do for Him according to the custom of the law, [28] he received Him in his arms and blessed God and said:

[29] "Lord, now let Your servant depart in peace,
    according to Your word;
[30] for my eyes have seen Your salvation
[31]   which You have prepared in the sight of all people,
[32] a light for revelation to the Gentiles,
    and the glory of Your people Israel."

[33] Joseph and His mother were amazed at those things which were spoken about Him. [34] Then Simeon blessed them and said to Mary His mother, "Listen, this Child is destined to cause the fall and rising of many in Israel and to be a sign which will be spoken against, [35] so that the thoughts of many hearts may be revealed. And a sword will pierce through your own soul also."

[36] And there was Anna a prophetess, a daughter of Phanuel, of the tribe of Asher. She was of a great age and had lived with her husband seven years from her virginity. [37] And she was a widow of about eighty-four years of age who did not depart from the temple, but served God with fasting and prayer night and day. [38] Coming at that moment she gave thanks to the Lord and spoke of Him to all those who looked for the redemption of Jerusalem.

The Return to Nazareth

[39] When they had performed everything according to the law of the Lord, they returned to Galilee, to their own city of Nazareth. [40] And the Child grew and became strong in spirit, filled with wisdom. And the grace of God was upon Him.

The Boy Jesus in the Temple

[41] Now His parents went to Jerusalem every year at the Feast of the Passover. [42] When He was twelve years old, they went up to Jerusalem according to the custom of the feast. [43] When the days of the feast were complete, as they returned, the Child Jesus remained behind in Jerusalem. And Joseph and His mother did not know of it. [44] But supposing Him to be in their company, they went a day's journey. Then they searched for Him among their relatives and acquaintances. [45] When they did not find Him, they returned to Jerusalem, searching for Him. [46] After three days they found Him in the temple, sitting in the midst of the teachers, listening

---

[1] 23 Ex 13:2, 12; Nu 3:13; 8:17.   [2] 24 Lev 5:11; 12:8.

to them and asking them questions. [47] All who heard Him were astonished at His understanding and His answers. [48] When they saw Him, they were amazed. And His mother said to Him, "Son, why have You dealt with us like this? Look, Your father and I have anxiously searched for You."

[49] He said to them, "How is it that you searched for Me? Did you not know that I must be about My Father's business?" [50] But they did not understand the word which He spoke to them.

[51] Then He went down with them and came to Nazareth and was obedient to them. But His mother kept all these words in her heart. [52] And Jesus increased in wisdom and in stature and in favor with God and men.

The Preaching of John the Baptist
Mt 3:1–12; Mk 1:1–8; Jn 1:19–28

3 In the fifteenth year of the reign of Caesar Tiberius, Pontius Pilate was governor of Judea, Herod was tetrarch of Galilee, his brother Philip was tetrarch of Iturea and the region of Traconitis, and Lysanias was the tetrarch of Abilene. [2] Annas and Caiaphas being the high priests, the word of God came to John the son of Zechariah in the wilderness. [3] He came into the region surrounding the Jordan, preaching the baptism of repentance for the remission of sins. [4] As it is written in the book of the words of Isaiah the prophet, saying:

"The voice of one crying in the wilderness:
'Prepare the way of the Lord;
    make His paths straight.
[5] Every valley shall be filled
    and every mountain and hill shall be brought low;
and the crooked shall be made straight
    and the rough ways shall be made smooth;
[6] and all flesh shall see the salvation of God.' "[1]

[7] Then he said to the crowds that came out to be baptized by him, "You children of vipers! Who warned you to flee from the wrath to come? [8] Therefore bear fruit worthy of repentance, and do not begin to say to yourselves, 'We have Abraham as our father.' For I say to you that God is able from these stones to raise up children for Abraham. [9] Even now the axe is put to the root of the trees. Every tree therefore which does not bear good fruit is cut down and thrown into the fire."

[10] The people asked him, "What then must we do?"

[11] John answered, "He who has two tunics, let him give to him who has none. And he who has food, let him do likewise."

[12] Then tax collectors also came to be baptized and said to him, "Teacher, what must we do?"

[13] He said to them, "Collect no more than what is appointed you."

[14] Then the soldiers likewise demanded of him, "And what must we do?"

He said to them, "Do no violence to anyone nor accuse any falsely, and be content with your wages."

[15] As the people were in expectation, and everyone reflected in their hearts upon John, whether he might be the Christ or not, [16] John answered them all, "I indeed baptize you with water. But One mightier than I is coming, the strings of whose shoes I am not worthy to untie. He will baptize you with the Holy Spirit and with fire. [17] His fan is in His hand, and He will thoroughly cleanse His threshing floor, and will gather the wheat into His granary. But He will burn the chaff with unquenchable fire." [18] Then he preached many other things in his exhortation to the people.

[19] But Herod the tetrarch, being rebuked by him because of Herodias, his brother Philip's wife, and for all the evils which Herod had done, [20] added also this above them all: He locked John up in prison.

The Baptism of Jesus
Mt 3:13–17; Mk 1:9–11

[21] Now when all the people were baptized, and when Jesus also had been baptized and was praying, the heavens were opened,

[22] and the Holy Spirit descended in a bodily form like a dove on Him, and a voice came from heaven which said, "You are My beloved Son. In You I am well pleased."

The Genealogy of Jesus
Mt 1:1–17

[23] Now Jesus Himself began His ministry at about thirty years of age, being, as was supposed, the son of Joseph,

who was the son of Heli, [24] who was the son of Matthat,
who was the son of Levi, who was the son of Melchi,
who was the son of Jannai, who was the son of Joseph,
[25] who was the son of Mattathias, who was the son of Amos,
who was the son of Nahum, who was the son of Esli,
who was the son of Naggai, [26] who was the son of Maath,
who was the son of Mattathias, who was the son of Semein,
who was the son of Josech, who was the son of Joda,
[27] who was the son of Joanan, who was the son of Rhesa,
who was the son of Zerubbabel, who was the son of Shealtiel,
who was the son of Neri, [28] who was the son of Melchi,
who was the son of Addi, who was the son of Cosam,
who was the son of Elmadam, who was the son of Er,
[29] who was the son of Joshua, who was the son of Eliezer,
who was the son of Jorim, who was the son of Matthat,
who was the son of Levi, [30] who was the son of Simeon,
who was the son of Judah, who was the son of Joseph,
who was the son of Jonan, who was the son of Eliakim,
[31] who was the son of Melea, who was the son of Menna,
who was the son of Mattatha, who was the son of Nathan,
who was the son of David, [32] who was the son of Jesse,
who was the son of Obed, who was the son of Boaz,
who was the son of Salmon, who was the son of Nahshon,
[33] who was the son of Amminadab, who was the son of Ram,
who was the son of Hezron, who was the son of Perez,
who was the son of Judah, [34] who was the son of Jacob,
who was the son of Isaac, who was the son of Abraham,
who was the son of Terah, who was the son of Nahor,
[35] who was the son of Serug, who was the son of Reu,
who was the son of Peleg, who was the son of Eber,
who was the son of Shelah, [36] who was the son of Cainan,
who was the son of Arphaxad, who was the son of Shem,
who was the son of Noah, who was the son of Lamech,
[37] who was the son of Methuselah, who was the son
    of Enoch,
who was the son of Jared, who was the son of Mahalalel,
who was the son of Cainan, [38] who was the son of Enosh,
who was the son of Seth, who was the son of Adam,
who was the son of God.

The Temptation of Jesus
Mt 4:1–11; Mk 1:12–13

4 Jesus, being filled with the Holy Spirit, returned from the Jordan and was led by the Spirit into the wilderness, [2] being tempted by the devil for forty days. During those days He ate nothing. And when they were ended, He was hungry.

[3] The devil said to Him, "If You are the Son of God, command this stone to become bread."

[4] Jesus answered him, "It is written, 'Man shall not live by bread alone, but by every word of God.' [2]"

[5] The devil, taking Him up onto a high mountain, showed Him all the kingdoms of the world in a moment of time. [6] And the devil said to Him, "I will give You all this power and their glory, for it has been delivered to me. And I give it to whomever I will. [7] If You, then, will worship me, all will be Yours."

[8] And Jesus answered him, "Get behind Me, Satan! For it is written, 'You shall worship the Lord your God, and Him only shall you serve.' [3]"

[9] He brought Him to Jerusalem, set Him on the pinnacle of the temple, and said to Him, "If You are the Son of God, throw Yourself down from here. [10] For it is written:

---

[1] 4–6 Isa 40:3–5.   [2] 4 Dt 8:3.   [3] 8 Dt 6:13.

'He shall give His angels charge concerning you,
  to preserve you,'

[11] and

'In their hands they shall hold you up,
  lest you strike your foot against a stone.'[1]"

[12] Jesus answered him, "It is said, 'You shall not tempt the Lord your God.'[2]"
[13] When the devil had ended all the temptations, he departed from Him until another time.

The Beginning of the Galilean Ministry
Mt 4:12–17; Mk 1:14–15

[14] Jesus returned in the power of the Spirit to Galilee. And His fame went throughout the surrounding region. [15] He taught in their synagogues, being glorified by everyone.

The Rejection of Jesus at Nazareth
Mt 13:53–58; Mk 6:1–6

[16] He came to Nazareth, where He had been brought up. And as His custom was, He went to the synagogue on the Sabbath day. And He stood up to read. [17] The scroll of the prophet Isaiah was handed to Him. When He had unrolled the scroll, He found the place where it was written:

[18] "The Spirit of the Lord is upon Me,
  because He has anointed Me
  to preach the gospel to the poor;
He has sent Me to heal the broken-hearted,
  to preach deliverance to the captives
  and recovery of sight to the blind,
  to set at liberty those who are oppressed;
[19]   to preach the acceptable year of the Lord."[3]

[20] Then He rolled up the scroll, and He gave it back to the attendant, and sat down. The eyes of all those who were in the synagogue were fixed on Him. [21] And He began to say to them, "Today this Scripture is fulfilled in your hearing."
[22] All bore witness to Him, and wondered at the gracious words which came from His mouth. Then they said, "Is this not Joseph's son?"
[23] He said to them, "You will surely say to Me this proverb, 'Physician, heal Yourself. Whatever we have heard done in Capernaum, do also here in Your country.'"
[24] He also said, "Truly, I say to you, no prophet is accepted in his own country. [25] But I tell you truthfully, many widows were in Israel in the days of Elijah, when the heavens were closed for three years and six months, when great famine was throughout all the land. [26] Yet to none of them was Elijah sent except to Zarephath, a city of Sidon, to a woman who was a widow. [27] And many lepers were in Israel in the time of Elisha the prophet. But none of them was cleansed except Naaman the Syrian."
[28] All those in the synagogue, when they heard these things, were filled with wrath. [29] They rose up and thrust Him out of the city and led Him to the brow of the hill on which their city was built, that they might throw Him down headlong. [30] But passing through the midst of them, He went His way.

The Man With an Unclean Spirit
Mk 1:21–28

[31] Then He went down to Capernaum, a city of Galilee, and was teaching them on the Sabbaths. [32] They were astonished at His teaching, for His word was with authority.
[33] In the synagogue there was a man who had the spirit of an unclean demon. And he cried out with a loud voice, [34] "Leave us alone! What have You to do with us, Jesus of Nazareth? Have You come to destroy us? I know who You are—the Holy One of God!"

[35] Jesus rebuked him, saying, "Be silent, and come out of him!" When the demon had thrown him down in their midst, he came out of him and did not hurt him.
[36] They were all amazed and said among themselves, "What a word this is! For with authority and power He commands the unclean spirits, and they come out." [37] And His fame went out to every place in the surrounding countryside.

The Healing of Many People
Mt 8:14–17; Mk 1:29–34

[38] He went out of the synagogue and entered Simon's house. Now Simon's mother-in-law was taken ill with a high fever, and they asked Him about her. [39] So He stood over her and rebuked the fever, and it left her. And immediately she rose and served them.
[40] Now when the sun was setting, all those who had anyone sick with various diseases brought them to Him. And He laid His hands on every one of them and healed them. [41] And demons came out of many, crying out, "You are the Christ, the Son of God!" But He rebuked them and did not permit them to speak, because they knew that He was the Christ.

Preaching in the Synagogues
Mk 1:35–39

[42] When it was day He departed and went into a remote place. And searching for Him, the people came to Him and tried to prevent Him from leaving them. [43] But He said to them, "I must preach the kingdom of God to other cities also, for this is why I was sent." [44] And He was preaching in the synagogues of Galilee.

The Calling of the First Disciples
Mt 4:18–22; Mk 1:16–20

5 As the people pressed upon Him to hear the word of God, He stood by the Lake of Gennesaret [2] and saw two boats beside the lake. But the fishermen had gone out of them and were washing their nets. [3] He entered one of the boats, which was Simon's, and asked him to thrust it out a little from the land. Then He sat down and taught the people from the boat.
[4] When He had finished speaking, He said to Simon, "Launch out into the deep and let down your nets for a catch."
[5] Simon answered Him, "Master, we have worked all night and have caught nothing. But at Your word I will let down the net."
[6] When they had done this, they caught a great number of fish, and their net was tearing. [7] So they signaled to their partners in the other boat to come and help them. And they came and filled both boats, so that they began to sink.
[8] When Simon Peter saw it, he fell down at Jesus' knees, saying, "Depart from me, for I am a sinful man, O Lord." [9] For he and all who were with him were astonished at the catch of fish which they had taken, [10] and so were James and John, the sons of Zebedee, who were partners with Simon.
Then Jesus said to Simon, "Do not fear. From now on you will catch men." [11] So when they had brought their boats to land, they left everything and followed Him.

The Cleansing of a Leper
Mt 8:1–4; Mk 1:40–45

[12] When He was in a certain city, a man full of leprosy, upon seeing Jesus, fell on his face and begged Him, "Lord, if You will, You can make me clean."
[13] He reached out His hand and touched him, saying, "I will. Be clean." And immediately the leprosy left him.
[14] Then He commanded him to tell no one, "But go and show yourself to the priest and make an offering for your cleansing, as Moses commanded, as a testimony to them."
[15] Yet even more so His fame went everywhere. And great crowds came together to hear and to be healed by Him of their infirmities. [16] But He withdrew to the wilderness and prayed.

---

[1]11 Ps 91:11–12.   [2]12 Dt 6:16;   [3]18–19 Isa 61:1–2.

The Healing of a Paralytic

Mt 9:1–8; Mk 2:1–12

[17] On a certain day, as He was teaching, Pharisees and teachers of the law were sitting nearby, who had come from every town of Galilee and Judea and from Jerusalem. And the power of the Lord was present to heal the sick. [18] Now some men brought in a bed a man who was paralyzed. They searched for ways to bring him in and lay him before Him. [19] When they could not find a way to bring him in, because of the crowd, they went up on the roof and let him down through the tiles with his bed into their midst before Jesus. [20] When He saw their faith, He said to him, "Man, your sins are forgiven you." [21] The scribes and the Pharisees began to question, "Who is He who speaks blasphemies? Who can forgive sins but God alone?" [22] When Jesus perceived their thoughts, He answered them, "Why question in your hearts? [23] Which is easier, to say, 'Your sins are forgiven you,' or to say, 'Rise up and walk'? [24] But that you may know that the Son of Man has authority on earth to forgive sins," He said to the paralyzed man, "I say to you, rise, take up your bed, and go to your house." [25] Immediately he rose before them, and took up that on which he lay, and departed to his own house, glorifying God. [26] They were all amazed, and they glorified God and were filled with fear, saying, "We have seen wonderful things today."

The Calling of Levi

Mt 9:9–13; Mk 2:13–17

[27] After these things He went out and saw a tax collector, named Levi, sitting at the tax collector's station. He said to him, "Follow Me." [28] And he left everything, rose up, and followed Him.

[29] Then Levi made Him a great feast in his house. And there was a group of many tax collectors and others who sat down with them. [30] But their scribes and Pharisees murmured against His disciples, saying, "Why do you eat and drink with tax collectors and sinners?" [31] Jesus answered them, "Those who are well do not need a physician, but those who are sick. [32] I have not come to call the righteous, but sinners to repentance."

The Question About Fasting

Mt 9:14–17; Mk 2:18–22

[33] They said to Him, "Why do the disciples of John fast often and offer prayers, and likewise the disciples of the Pharisees, but Yours eat and drink?" [34] He said to them, "Can you make the attendants of the bridegroom fast while the bridegroom is with them? [35] But the days will come when the bridegroom will be taken away from them. Then in those days they will fast."

[36] He told them a parable also: "No one sews a piece of a new material on an old one. Otherwise the new would tear, for the new piece does not match the old. [37] And no one puts new wine into old wineskins. Otherwise the new wine will burst the wineskins, and it will be spilled, and the wineskins will be destroyed. [38] But new wine must be put into new wineskins, and both are preserved. [39] And no one, having drunk old wine, immediately desires new. For he says, 'The old is better.' "

Plucking Grain on the Sabbath

Mt 12:1–8; Mk 2:23–28

6 On the second Sabbath after the first, He went through the grain fields, and His disciples plucked and ate the heads of grain, rubbing them in their hands. [2] Some of the Pharisees said to them, "Why are you doing what is not lawful to do on the Sabbath?" [3] Jesus answered them, "Have you not read what David did when he and those who were with him were hungry? [4] He went into the house of God, and took and ate the ritual bread, and also gave it to those who were with him. This was not lawful, but for the priests only to eat." [5] Then He said to them, "The Son of Man is Lord even of the Sabbath."

The Man With a Withered Hand

Mt 12:9–14; Mk 3:1–6

[6] On another Sabbath, when He entered the synagogue and taught, there was a man whose right hand had withered. [7] The scribes and the Pharisees watched Him to see whether He would heal on the Sabbath, so that they might find an accusation against Him. [8] But He knew their thoughts, and He said to the man who had the withered hand, "Rise and stand in front." So he rose and stood in front.

[9] Then Jesus said to them, "I will ask you one thing: Is it lawful on the Sabbath to do good or to do evil, to save life or to destroy it?" [10] Then looking around at them all, He said to the man, "Stretch out your hand." He did so, and his hand was restored as whole as the other. [11] But they were filled with madness and discussed with each other what they might do to Jesus.

The Choosing of the Twelve Apostles

Mt 10:1–4; Mk 3:13–19

[12] In these days He went out to the mountain to pray and continued all night in prayer to God. [13] When it was day, He called for His disciples, and of them He chose twelve, whom He named apostles: [14] Simon, whom He named Peter, and Andrew his brother, and James and John, and Philip and Bartholomew, [15] and Matthew and Thomas, and James the son of Alphaeus, and Simon called the Zealot, [16] and Judas the son of James, and Judas Iscariot, who became a traitor.

Ministering to a Great Crowd

Mt 4:23–25

[17] He came down with them and stood on a level place with a crowd of His disciples and a great crowd of people from all Judea and Jerusalem, and from the seacoast of Tyre and Sidon, who came to hear Him and be healed of their diseases, [18] including those who were vexed by unclean spirits. And they were healed. [19] The whole crowd tried to touch Him, for power went out from Him and healed them all.

Blessings and Woes

Mt 5:1–12

[20] He lifted up His eyes on His disciples, and said:

"Blessed are you poor,
for yours is the kingdom of God.
[21] Blessed are you who hunger now,
for you shall be filled.
Blessed are you who weep now,
for you shall laugh.
[22] Blessed are you when men hate you,
and when they separate you from their company and
insult you,
and cast out your name as evil,
on account of the Son of Man.

[23] "Rejoice in that day, and leap for joy, for indeed, your reward is great in heaven. For in like manner their fathers treated the prophets.

[24] "But woe to you who are rich,
for you have received your consolation.
[25] Woe to you who are filled,
for you shall hunger.
Woe to you who laugh now,
for you shall mourn and weep.
[26] Woe to you, when all men speak well of you,
for so their fathers spoke of the false prophets.

Love for Enemies

Mt 5:38–48

[27] "But I say to you who hear, love your enemies, do good to those who hate you, [28] bless those who curse you, and pray for those who spitefully use you. [29] To him who strikes you on the one cheek, offer also the other. And from him who takes away your cloak, do not withhold your tunic as well. [30] Give to everyone who asks of you. And of him who takes away your goods, do not ask for them back. [31] Do unto others as you would have others do unto you.

32 "For if you love those who love you, what thanks do you receive? For even sinners love those who love them. 33 And if you do good to those who do good to you, what thanks do you receive? For even sinners do the same. 34 And if you lend to those from whom you hope to receive, what thanks do you receive? Even sinners lend to sinners, to receive as much in return. 35 But love your enemies, and do good, and lend, hoping for nothing in return. Then your reward will be great, and you will be the sons of the Highest. For He is kind to the unthankful and the evil. 36 Be therefore merciful, even as your Father is merciful.

Judging Others
Mt 7:1–5

37 "Judge not, and you shall not be judged. Condemn not, and you will not be condemned. Forgive, and you shall be forgiven. 38 Give, and it will be given to you: Good measure, pressed down, shaken together, and running over will men give unto you. For with the measure you use, it will be measured unto you."

39 He spoke a parable to them: "Can the blind lead the blind? Will they not both fall into the ditch? 40 The disciple is not above his teacher, but everyone who is trained will be like his teacher.

41 "Why do you see the speck that is in your brother's eye, but do not see the beam that is in your own eye? 42 How can you say to your brother, 'Brother, let me remove the speck that is in your eye,' when you yourself do not see the beam that is in your own eye? You hypocrite! First remove the beam from your own eye, and then you will see clearly to remove the speck that is in your brother's eye.

A Tree and Its Fruit
Mt 7:17–20

43 "A good tree does not bear corrupt fruit, nor does a corrupt tree bear good fruit. 44 Each tree is known by its own fruit. Men do not gather figs from thorns, nor do they gather grapes from a wild bush. 45 A good man out of the good treasure of his heart bears what is good, and an evil man out of the evil treasure of his heart bears what is evil. For of the abundance of the heart his mouth speaks.

The Two Housebuilders
Mt 7:24–27

46 "Why do you call Me, 'Lord, Lord,' and not do what I say? 47 Whoever comes to Me and hears My words and does them, I will show whom he is like: 48 He is like a man who built a house, and dug deep, and laid the foundation on rock. When the flood arose, the stream beat vehemently against that house, but could not shake it, for it was founded on rock. 49 But he who hears and does not obey is like a man who built a house on the ground without a foundation, against which the stream beat vehemently. Immediately it fell, and the ruin of that house was great."

The Healing of a Centurion's Servant
Mt 8:5–13; Jn 4:43–54

7 When He had completed all His words in the hearing of the people, He entered Capernaum. 2 Now a centurion's¹ servant, who was dear to him, was sick and ready to die. 3 When he heard of Jesus, he sent the elders of the Jews to Him, asking Him to come and heal his servant. 4 When they came to Jesus, they asked Him earnestly, saying, "You should do this for him for he is worthy, 5 for he loves our nation, and he has built us a synagogue." 6 So Jesus went with them.

When He was not far from the house, the centurion sent friends to Him, saying, "Lord, do not trouble Yourself, for I am not worthy to have You come under my roof. 7 Likewise, I did not think myself worthy to come to You. But say the word, and my servant will be healed. 8 For I myself am a man placed under authority, having soldiers under me. I say to one, 'Go,' and he goes, and to another, 'Come,' and he comes, and to my servant, 'Do this,' and he does it." 9 When Jesus heard these words, He marveled at him, and turned and said to the people who followed Him, "I tell you, I have not found such great faith even in Israel." 10 Then those who were sent, returning to the house, found the servant well who had been sick.

The Raising of the Widow's Son

11 The following day He went into a city called Nain, and many of His disciples and a large crowd went with Him. 12 When He came near the gate of the city, a man who had died was being carried out, the only son of his mother, and she was a widow. And a large crowd from the city was with her. 13 When the Lord saw her, He had compassion on her and said to her, "Do not weep."

14 Then He came and touched the coffin, and those who carried it stood still. He said, "Young man, I say to you, arise." 15 He who was dead sat up and began to speak. And He gave him to his mother.

16 Fear came on everyone. And they glorified God, saying, "A great prophet has risen up among us!" and "God has visited His people!" 17 This rumor of Him went throughout all Judea and the surrounding region.

The Messengers From John the Baptist
Mt 11:2–19

18 The disciples of John told him of all these things. 19 John, calling for two of his disciples, sent them to Jesus, saying, "Are You the One who is coming, or shall we look for another?"

20 When the men had come to Him, they said, "John the Baptist has sent us to You, saying, 'Are You the One who is coming, or shall we look for another?'"

21 In that same hour He cured many of their infirmities and afflictions and evil spirits. And to many who were blind He gave sight. 22 So Jesus answered them, "Go and tell John what you have seen and heard: that the blind see, the lame walk, the lepers are cleansed, the deaf hear, the dead are raised, and the gospel is preached to the poor. 23 Blessed is he who does not fall away on account of Me."

24 When the messengers of John had departed, He began to speak to the crowd concerning John: "What did you go out into the wilderness to see? A reed shaken by the wind? 25 If not, what did you go out to see? A man dressed in fine clothes? Now those who are splendidly clothed and live luxuriously are in royal palaces. 26 What then did you go out to see? A prophet? Yes, I say to you, and much more than a prophet. 27 This is he of whom it is written:

'Look, I am sending My messenger before Your face,
    who shall prepare Your way before You.'²

28 I say to you, among those who are born of women there is no greater prophet than John the Baptist. Yet he who is least in the kingdom of God is greater than he."

29 All the people who heard Him, including the tax collectors, justified God, having been baptized with the baptism of John. 30 But the Pharisees and lawyers rejected the counsel of God for themselves, not having been baptized by John.

31 Then the Lord said, "To what then shall I compare the men of this generation, and what are they like? 32 They are like children sitting in the marketplace, calling to each other, saying:

'We played the flute for you,
    and you did not dance;
we mourned to you,
    and you did not weep.'

33 For John the Baptist came neither eating bread nor drinking wine. But you say, 'He has a demon.' 34 The Son of Man has come eating and drinking. But you say, 'Look, a glutton and a drunkard, a friend of tax collectors and sinners!' 35 But wisdom is justified by all her children."

A Sinful Woman Forgiven

36 One of the Pharisees asked Him to eat with him. So He went to the Pharisee's house and sat down for supper. 37 There, a woman of the city who was a sinner, when she learned that Jesus was sitting for supper in the Pharisee's house, brought an alabaster jar of ointment, 38 and stood behind Him at His feet, weeping, and began to wash His feet with tears, and wiped them

---

¹ 2 Commander with the rank of captain over 100 soldiers. ² 27 Mal 3:1.

with the hair of her head, and kissed His feet, and anointed them with the ointment.

[39] Now when the Pharisee who had invited Him saw it, he said to himself, "If this Man were a prophet, He would have known who and what kind of woman she is who is touching Him, for she is a sinner."

[40] Jesus answered him, "Simon, I have something to say to you." He said, "Teacher, say it."

[41] "A creditor had two debtors. The one owed five hundred denarii,[1] and the other fifty. [42] When they had no money to pay, he freely forgave them both. Tell Me, therefore, which of them will love him more?"

[43] Simon answered, "I suppose he whom he forgave more." He said to him, "You have judged rightly."

[44] Then He turned to the woman and said to Simon, "Do you see this woman? I entered your house. You gave Me no water for My feet, but she has washed My feet with her tears and wiped them with the hair of her head. [45] You gave Me no kiss, but this woman, since the time I came in, has not ceased to kiss My feet. [46] You did not anoint My head with oil, but this woman has anointed My feet with ointment. [47] Therefore I say to you, her sins, which are many, are forgiven, for she loved much. But he who is forgiven little loves little."

[48] Then He said to her, "Your sins are forgiven."

[49] Those who sat at supper with Him began to say to themselves, "Who is He who even forgives sins?"

[50] He said to the woman, "Your faith has saved you. Go in peace."

Women Who Accompany Jesus

8 Afterward, He went throughout every city and village, preaching and bringing the good news of the kingdom of God. With Him were the twelve [2] and some women who had been healed of evil spirits and infirmities: Mary, called Magdalene, from whom seven demons had come out, [3] and Joanna, the wife of Chuza, Herod's steward, and Susanna, and many others, who supported Him with their possessions.

The Parable of the Sower
Mt 13:1–9; Mk 4:1–9

[4] When a large crowd had gathered together and people were coming to Him from every city, He told this parable: [5] "A sower went out to sow his seed. As he sowed, some fell along the path and was trampled down, and the birds of the air devoured it. [6] Some fell on a rock. And as soon as it sprang up, it withered away, because it lacked moisture. [7] Yet some fell among thorns. And the thorns sprang up with it and choked it. [8] And other seed fell on good ground and sprang up and yielded a hundred times the amount sown."

When He had said these things, He cried out, "He who has ears to hear, let him hear."

The Purpose of the Parables
Mt 13:10–17; Mk 4:10–12

[9] His disciples asked Him, "What might this parable mean?" [10] He said, "To you it has been given to know the secrets of the kingdom of God, but to others they are in parables, so that

'seeing they may not see,
and hearing they may not understand.'[2]

The Parable of the Sower Explained
Mt 13:18–23; Mk 4:13–20

[11] "Now the parable means this: The seed is the word of God. [12] Those along the path are those who hear. Then comes the devil, who takes away the word from their hearts, lest they should believe and be saved. [13] Those on the rock are the ones who, when they hear the word, receive it with joy. But these have no root, for they believe for a while, then in the time of temptation fall away. [14] That which fell among thorns are those who, when they have heard, go out and are choked with the cares and riches and pleasures of this life, and bring no fruit to maturity. [15] But the seed on the good ground are those who, having heard the word, keep it in an honest and good heart and bear fruit with patience.

A Light Under a Vessel
Mk 4:21–25

[16] "No one, when he lights a candle, covers it with a vessel or puts it under a bed, but sets it on a candlestick, that those who enter may see the light. [17] For nothing is secret that will not be revealed, nor anything hidden that will not be known and revealed. [18] Take heed therefore how you hear. For whoever has, to him will be given. And whoever has not, from him will be taken even what he thinks he has."

The Mother and Brothers of Jesus
Mt 12:46–50; Mk 3:31–35

[19] Then His mother and His brothers came to Him, but could not reach Him because of the crowd. [20] Someone told Him, "Your mother and Your brothers are standing outside, desiring to see You."

[21] He answered them, "My mother and My brothers are these who hear the word of God and do it."

The Calming of a Storm
Mt 8:23–27; Mk 4:35–41

[22] One day He went into a boat with His disciples, and He said to them, "Let us go over to the other side of the lake." So they launched out. [23] As they sailed, He fell asleep. Then a windstorm came down on the lake, and they were filling with water, and were in danger.

[24] They came to Him and awoke Him, saying, "Master, Master, we are perishing!"

Then He arose and rebuked the wind and the raging of the water. And they ceased, and there was a calm. [25] He said to them, "Where is your faith?"

Being afraid, they marveled, saying to each other, "Who then is this Man? He commands even the winds and water, and they obey Him."

The Healing of the Gadarene Demoniac
Mt 8:28–34; Mk 5:1–20

[26] They sailed to the country of the Gadarenes, which is across from Galilee. [27] When He stepped out on land, a man from the city who had demons for a long time met Him. He wore no clothes, nor did he live in a house but in the tombs. [28] When he saw Jesus, he cried out and fell down before Him, and with a loud voice said, "What have You to do with me, Jesus, Son of the Most High God? I plead with You, do not torment me." [29] For He had commanded the unclean spirit to come out of the man. It often had seized him, and he was kept under guard, bound with chains and shackles. But he broke the shackles and was driven by the demon into the wilderness.

[30] Jesus asked him, "What is your name?"

He said, "Legion," because many demons had entered him. [31] And they begged Him not to command them to go out into the abyss.

[32] There was a large herd of swine feeding on the mountain. They begged Him to permit them to enter them, and He permitted them. [33] Then the demons went out of the man and entered the swine, and the herd ran violently down the steep bank into the lake and was drowned.

[34] When those who fed them saw what had happened, they fled and reported it in the city and in the country. [35] Then they went out to see what had happened, and came to Jesus, and found the man from whom the demons had departed sitting at the feet of Jesus, clothed, and in his right mind. And they were afraid. [36] Those who had seen it told them how he who had been possessed by demons was healed. [37] Then the whole crowd from the surrounding country of the Gadarenes asked Him to depart from them, for they were seized with great fear. So He went into the boat and returned.

[38] Now the man from whom the demons had departed asked Him if he could stay with Him. But Jesus sent him away, saying,

---

[1] 41 Gk. *denarius*, a coin worth about a day's wage.   [2] 10 Isa 6:9.

[39] "Return to your own house, and tell what great things God has done for you." So he went his way and proclaimed throughout the whole city what great things Jesus had done for him.

Jairus' Daughter and the Woman Who Touched Jesus' Garment
Mt 9:18–26; Mk 5:21–43

[40] When Jesus returned, the crowd gladly received Him, for they were all waiting for Him. [41] Then a man named Jairus, who was a ruler of the synagogue, came and fell down at Jesus' feet, and begged Him to come to his house, [42] for he had an only daughter, about twelve years of age, and she was dying.

As He went, the people crowded Him. [43] And a woman having a hemorrhage for twelve years, who had spent all her living on physicians, but could not be healed by anyone, [44] came behind Him, and touched the fringe of His garment. And immediately her hemorrhage dried up.

[45] Jesus said, "Who touched Me?"

When everyone denied it, Peter and those who were with Him said, "Master, the crowds are pressing against You, and You say, 'Who touched Me?' "

[46] But Jesus said, "Someone touched Me, for I perceive that power has gone out from Me."

[47] When the woman saw that she was not hidden, she came trembling. And falling down before Him, she declared to Him before all the people why she had touched Him and how she was healed immediately. [48] Then He said to her, "Daughter, be of good cheer. Your faith has made you well. Go in peace."

[49] While He was still speaking, someone from the synagogue ruler's house came, saying to Jairus, "Your daughter is dead. Do not trouble the Teacher."

[50] But when Jesus heard it, He answered him, "Do not fear. Only believe, and she will be made well."

[51] When He came into the house, He permitted no one to go in except Peter, John and James, and the father and mother of the girl. [52] All wept and mourned for her. But He said, "Do not weep. She is not dead but sleeping."

[53] They laughed at Him, knowing that she was dead. [54] But He put them all outside and took her by the hand and called, saying, "Little girl, arise." [55] Her spirit returned, and she arose immediately. And He told them to give her food. [56] Her parents were astonished, but He commanded them to tell no one what had happened.

The Mission of the Twelve Apostles
Mt 10:1, 5–15; Mk 6:7–13

9 Then He called His twelve disciples together and gave them power and authority over all demons and to cure diseases. [2] And He sent them to preach the kingdom of God and to heal the sick. [3] He said to them, "Take nothing for your journey: no staff, no bag, no bread, no money. And do not take two tunics apiece. [4] Whatever house you enter, stay there, and from there depart. [5] Whoever will not receive you, when you go out of that city, shake off the very dust from your feet as a testimony against them." [6] So they departed and went through the towns, preaching the gospel and healing everywhere.

Herod's Anxiety
Mt 14:1–12; Mk 6:14–29

[7] Now Herod the tetrarch heard of all that was done by Him. And he was perplexed, because it was said by some that John had risen from the dead, [8] and by some that Elijah had appeared, and by others that one of the old prophets had risen. [9] But Herod said, "I have beheaded John. But who is this of whom I hear such things?" And he tried to see Him.

The Feeding of the Five Thousand
Mt 14:13–21; Mk 6:30–44; Jn 6:1–14

[10] When the apostles returned, they told Jesus all that they had done. Then He took them and went aside privately into a deserted place belonging to the city called Bethsaida. [11] But when the crowds knew it, they followed Him. And He welcomed them and spoke to them about the kingdom of God, and healed those who had need of healing.

[12] When the day began to end, the twelve came and said to Him, "Send the crowds away, so they can go into the towns and surrounding countryside and lodge and get food. For we are in a deserted place here."

[13] He said to them, "You give them something to eat."

They said, "We have no more than five loaves and two fish, unless we go and buy food for all these people." [14] There were about five thousand men.

But He said to His disciples, "Make them sit down in groups of fifty." [15] They did so, and made them all sit down. [16] Then He took the five loaves and the two fish, and looking up to heaven, He blessed them, and broke them, and gave them to the disciples to set before the crowd. [17] They all ate and were filled, and twelve baskets of broken pieces that remained were collected.

Peter's Declaration About Jesus
Mt 16:13–19; Mk 8:27–29

[18] As He was alone praying, His disciples were with Him. And He asked them, "Who do the people say that I am?"

[19] They answered, "John the Baptist. But some say Elijah. And others say that one of the old prophets has risen."

[20] He said to them, "But who do you say that I am?"

Peter answered, "The Christ of God."

Jesus Foretells His Death and Resurrection
Mt 16:20–28; Mk 8:30–9:1

[21] Jesus strictly commanded them to tell no one of this, [22] saying, "The Son of Man must suffer many things, and be rejected by the elders and chief priests and scribes, and be killed, and be raised the third day."

[23] Then He said to them all, "If anyone will come after Me, let him deny himself, and take up his cross daily, and follow Me. [24] For whoever will save his life will lose it, but whoever loses his life for My sake will save it. [25] For what does it profit a man if he gains the whole world, yet loses or forfeits himself? [26] For whoever is ashamed of Me and My words, of him will the Son of Man be ashamed when He comes in His own glory and in the glory of His Father and of the holy angels.

[27] "But I tell you truly, there are some standing here who shall not taste death before they see the kingdom of God."

The Transfiguration
Mt 17:1–8; Mk 9:2–8

[28] About eight days after these sayings, He took Peter and John and James and went up onto a mountain to pray. [29] As He prayed, the appearance of His countenance was altered, and His clothing was white and glistening. [30] And suddenly two men were talking with Him, who were Moses and Elijah, [31] who appeared in glory and spoke of His departure which He was to accomplish in Jerusalem. [32] Peter and those who were with him were heavy with sleep. But waking thoroughly, they saw His glory and the two men who stood with Him. [33] As they departed from Him, Peter said to Jesus, "Master, it is good for us to be here. Let us make three sanctuaries: one for You, and one for Moses, and one for Elijah," not knowing what he said.

[34] While he was speaking, a cloud came and overshadowed them. And they were afraid as they entered the cloud. [35] A voice came from out of the cloud, saying, "This is My beloved Son. Listen to Him." [36] When the voice had spoken, Jesus was found alone. They kept silent and told no one in those days anything they had seen.

The Healing of a Boy With an Unclean Spirit
Mt 17:14–18; Mk 9:14–27

[37] The next day, when they came down from the mountain, a great crowd met Him. [38] Suddenly a man cried out from the crowd, saying, "Teacher, I beg You, look upon my son, for he is my only child. [39] A spirit seizes him, and he suddenly cries out. It convulses him until he foams at the mouth, and bruises him, and scarcely leaves him. [40] I begged Your disciples to cast it out, but they could not."

[41] Jesus said, "O faithless and perverse generation, how long shall I be with you and bear with you? Bring your son here." [42] While he was coming, the demon threw him down and convulsed him. But Jesus rebuked the unclean spirit, and healed the child, and returned him to his father. [43] And they were all amazed at the mighty power of God.

Jesus Foretells His Death a Second Time
Mt 17:22–23; Mk 9:30–32

But while everyone marveled at all the things Jesus did, He said to His disciples, [44] "Let these words sink down into your ears, for the Son of Man is about to be betrayed into the hands of men." [45] But they did not understand this statement, and it was hidden from them, so that they did not perceive it. And they were afraid to ask Him about this statement.

Who Is the Greatest?
Mt 18:1–5; Mk 9:33–37

[46] A dispute arose among them as to which of them was the greatest. [47] Jesus, perceiving the thought of their heart, took a child and put him by Him, [48] and said to them, "Whoever receives this child in My name receives Me, and whoever receives Me receives Him who sent Me. For he who is least among you all will be great."

He Who Is Not Against You Is for You
Mk 9:38–40

[49] John answered, "Master, we saw a man casting out demons in Your name and we forbade him, because he does not follow with us." [50] Jesus said, "Do not forbid him, for he who is not against you is for you."

A Samaritan Village Refuses to Receive Jesus

[51] When the time came for Him to be received up, He was steadfastly set to go to Jerusalem, [52] and sent messengers ahead of Him. They went and entered a village of the Samaritans to make things ready for Him, [53] but they did not receive Him, because He was set to go to Jerusalem. [54] When His disciples James and John saw this, they said, "Lord, do You want us to command fire to come down from heaven and consume them, even as Elijah did?" [55] But He turned and rebuked them and said, "You do not know what kind of spirit you are of. [56] For the Son of Man did not come to destroy men's lives but to save them." And they went to another village.

The Would-Be Followers of Jesus
Mt 8:19–22

[57] As they went along the way, a man said to Him, "Lord, I will follow You wherever You go." [58] Jesus said to him, "Foxes have holes and birds of the air have nests. But the Son of Man has no place to lay His head." [59] He said to another man, "Follow Me."

But he said, "Lord, let me first go and bury my father." [60] Jesus said to him, "Leave the dead to bury their own dead. But you go and preach the kingdom of God." [61] Yet another said, "Lord, I will follow You, but let me first go bid farewell to those at my house." [62] Jesus said to him, "No one who puts his hand to the plow and looks back at things is fit for the kingdom of God."

The Mission of the Seventy

10 After this the Lord appointed seventy others, and sent them two by two ahead of Him into every city and place where He Himself was about to come. [2] He said to them, "The harvest truly is plentiful, but the laborers are few. Pray therefore the Lord of the harvest to send out laborers into His harvest. [3] Go your ways. Listen, I am sending you out as lambs among wolves. [4] Carry no purse, no bag, no shoes, and greet no one on the road.

[5] "When you enter a house, first say, 'Peace be to this house.' [6] If a son of peace is there, your peace will rest upon him; but if not, it will return upon you. [7] Remain in the same house, eating and drinking what they give, for the laborer is worthy of his hire. Do not go from house to house.

[8] "When you enter a city and they receive you, eat what is set before you. [9] Heal the sick who are there and say to them, 'The kingdom of God has come near to you.' [10] But when you enter a city and they do not receive you, go your way out into their streets and say, [11] 'Even the dust of your city which clings to us, we wipe off against you. Yet be sure of this, that the kingdom of God has come near to you.' [12] But I say to you, it will be more tolerable on that Day for Sodom than for that city.

Unrepentant Cities
Mt 11:20–24

[13] "Woe to you, Chorazin! Woe to you, Bethsaida! For if the mighty works had been done in Tyre and Sidon which have been done for you, they would have repented long ago, sitting in sackcloth and ashes. [14] But it will be more tolerable for Tyre and Sidon at the judgment than for you. [15] And you, Capernaum, will you be exalted to heaven? You will be thrust down to hell.

[16] "He who listens to you listens to Me, he who rejects you rejects Me, and he who rejects Me rejects Him who sent Me."

The Return of the Seventy

[17] The seventy returned with joy, saying, "Lord, even the demons are subject to us through Your name." [18] He said to them, "I saw Satan as lightning fall from heaven. [19] Look, I give you authority to trample on serpents and scorpions, and over all the power of the enemy. And nothing shall by any means hurt you. [20] Nevertheless do not rejoice that the spirits are subject to you, but rather rejoice that your names are written in heaven."

The Rejoicing of Jesus
Mt 11:25–27; 13:16–17

[21] At that time Jesus rejoiced in the Holy Spirit and said, "I thank You, O Father, Lord of heaven and earth, because You have hidden these things from the wise and intelligent and revealed them to infants. Yes, Father, for it was Your good pleasure. [22] "All things have been handed over to Me by My Father. And no one knows who the Son is but the Father, and who the Father is but the Son and he to whom the Son desires to reveal Him." [23] Then He turned to His disciples and said privately, "Blessed are the eyes which see what you see. [24] For I tell you, many prophets and kings have desired to see what you see, and have not seen it, and to hear what you hear, and have not heard it."

The Good Samaritan

[25] Now, a lawyer stood up and tested Him, saying, "Teacher, what must I do to inherit eternal life?" [26] He said to him, "What is written in the law? How do you read?" [27] He answered, " 'You shall love the Lord your God with all your heart, and with all your soul, and with all your strength, and with all your mind' [1] and 'your neighbor as yourself.' [2] " [28] He said to him, "You have answered correctly. Do this, and you will live."

[29] But he, desiring to justify himself, said to Jesus, "And who is my neighbor?" [30] Jesus answered, "A man went down from Jerusalem to Jericho and fell among thieves, who stripped him of his clothing and wounded him and departed, leaving him half dead. [31] By chance a priest came down that way. And when he saw him, he passed by on the other side. [32] So likewise a Levite, when he came to that place, looked at him and passed by on the other side. [33] But a Samaritan, as he journeyed, came where he was. And when he saw him, he had compassion on him, [34] and came to him and bound up his wounds, pouring in oil and wine. Then he set him on his own donkey and brought him to an inn, and took care of him. [35] The next day when he departed, he took out two denarii [3] and gave them

---

[1] 27 Dt 6:5. [2] 27 Lev 19:18. [3] 35 Gk. *denarius*, a coin worth about a day's wage.

.to the innkeeper and said to him, 'Take care of him. I will repay you whatever else you spend when I return.'

[36] "Now which of these three do you think was a neighbor to him who fell among the thieves?"

[37] He said, "The one who showed mercy on him."

Then Jesus said to him, "Go and do likewise."

Visiting Martha and Mary

[38] As they went, He entered a village. And a woman named Martha welcomed Him into her house. [39] She had a sister called Mary, who also sat at Jesus' feet and listened to His teaching. [40] But Martha was distracted with much serving, and she came to Him and said, "Lord, do You not care that my sister has left me to serve alone? Then tell her to help me."

[41] Jesus answered her, "Martha, Martha, you are anxious and troubled about many things. [42] But one thing is needed. And Mary has chosen the good part, which shall not be taken from her."

Teaching About Prayer

Mt 6:9–15; 7:7–11

11 He was praying in a certain place, and when He ceased, one of His disciples said to Him, "Lord, teach us to pray, as John also taught his disciples."

[2] He said to them, "When you pray, say:

Our Father, who is in heaven,
hallowed be Your name.
Your kingdom come;
Your will be done
    on earth, as it is in heaven.
[3] Give us each day our daily bread.
[4] And forgive us our sins,
    for we also forgive everyone who is indebted to us.
And lead us not into temptation,
    but deliver us from evil."

[5] Then He said to them, "Which of you has a friend and shall go to him at midnight and say to him, 'Friend, lend me three loaves, [6] for a friend of mine on his journey has come to me, and I have nothing to set before him'; [7] and he will answer from within, 'Do not trouble me; the door is now shut, and my children are with me in bed; I cannot rise and give you anything'? [8] I say to you, though he will not rise and give him anything because he is his friend, yet because of his persistence he will rise and give him as much as he needs.

[9] "And I tell you, ask, and it will be given to you; seek, and you will find; knock, and it will be opened to you. [10] For everyone who asks receives, and he who seeks finds, and to him who knocks it will be opened.

[11] "If a son asks for bread from any of you who is a father, will you give him a stone? Or if he asks for a fish, will you give him a serpent instead of a fish? [12] Or if he asks for an egg, will you offer him a scorpion? [13] If you then, being evil, know how to give good gifts to your children, how much more will your heavenly Father give the Holy Spirit to those who ask Him?"

Jesus and Beelzebub

Mt 12:22–30; Mk 3:20–27

[14] He was casting out a demon, and it was mute. When the demon had gone out, the mute man spoke, and the crowd marveled. [15] But some of them said, "He casts out demons through Beelzebub, the ruler of the demons." [16] Others, testing Him, asked Him for a sign from heaven.

[17] But He, knowing their thoughts, said to them, "Every kingdom divided against itself is made desolate. And a house divided against itself falls. [18] If Satan also is divided against himself, how will his kingdom stand? For you say that I cast out demons through Beelzebub. [19] Now if I cast out demons by Beelzebub, by whom do your sons cast them out? Therefore they will be your judges. [20] But if I cast out demons with the finger of God, no doubt the kingdom of God has come upon you.

[21] "When a strong man, fully armed, guards his own palace, his goods are peacefully kept. [22] But when a stronger man than he attacks and overpowers him, he seizes all the armor in which the man trusted and divides his spoils.

[23] "He who is not with Me is against Me, and he who does not gather with Me scatters.

The Return of the Unclean Spirit

Mt 12:43–45

[24] "When an unclean spirit goes out of a man, it goes through dry places seeking rest. Finding none, it says, 'I will return to my house, from which I came.' [25] When it comes, it finds it swept and furnished. [26] Then it goes and brings seven other spirits more wicked than itself, and they enter and dwell there. And the last state of that man is worse than the first."

True Blessedness

[27] As He spoke these things, a woman from the crowd raised her voice and said to Him, "Blessed is the woman who gave You birth and nursed You."

[28] But He said, "Indeed, blessed are those who hear the word of God and keep it."

The Demand for a Sign

Mt 12:38–42; Mk 8:12

[29] When the crowds pressed upon Him, He began to say, "This is an evil generation. It looks for a sign, but no sign will be given it except the sign of Jonah the prophet. [30] For as Jonah was a sign to the Ninevites, so will the Son of Man be to this generation. [31] The Queen of the South will rise up in the judgment with the men of this generation and condemn them, for she came from the ends of the earth to hear the wisdom of Solomon. And now one greater than Solomon is here. [32] The men of Nineveh will rise up in the judgment with this generation and will condemn it, for they repented at the preaching of Jonah. And now one greater than Jonah is here.

The Light of the Body

Mt 5:15; 6:22–23

[33] "No one, when he has lit a candle, puts it in a secret place or under a basket, but on a candlestick, that those who come in may see the light. [34] The eye is the lamp of the body. Therefore when your eye is good, your whole body also is full of light. But when your eye is bad, your body also is full of darkness. [35] Take heed therefore lest the light which is in you is darkness. [36] If your whole body, then, is full of light, no part being dark, the whole body will be full of light, as when the shining candle gives you light."

The Denouncing of the Pharisees and Lawyers

Mt 23:1–36; Mk 12:38–40; Lk 20:45–47

[37] As He spoke, a Pharisee asked Him to dine with him. So He went in and sat down to eat. [38] When the Pharisee saw it, he marveled that He had not first washed before dinner.

[39] Then the Lord said to him, "Now you Pharisees clean the outside of the cup and the dish. But inside you are full of extortion and wickedness. [40] You fools! Did not he who made the outside make the inside also? [41] But give alms from what is within. And then all things are clean to you.

[42] "Woe to you, Pharisees! For you tithe mint and rue and every herb and pass over justice and the love of God. These you ought to have done, without leaving the others undone.

[43] "Woe to you, Pharisees! For you love the prominent seats in the synagogues and greetings in the marketplaces.

[44] "Woe to you, scribes and Pharisees, hypocrites! For you are like unseen graves, and the men who walk over them are not aware of them."

[45] One of the lawyers answered, "Teacher, by saying these things You insult us also."

[46] He said, "Woe to you also, you lawyers! For you load men with burdens difficult to carry, and you yourselves do not touch the burdens with one of your fingers.

[47] "Woe to you! For you build the tombs of the prophets, and your fathers killed them. [48] So you are witnesses and entirely approve the deeds of your fathers, because they killed them, and you build their tombs. [49] Therefore also the wisdom of God said, 'I will send them prophets and apostles, and some of them they will kill and persecute,' [50] that the blood of all the prophets, shed since the beginning of the world, may be required from this generation, [51] from the blood of Abel to the blood of Zechariah, who was killed between the altar and the sanctuary. Yes, I tell you, it shall be required from this generation.

[52] "Woe to you, lawyers! For you have taken away the key of knowledge. You did not enter yourselves, and you hindered those who were entering."

[53] As He said these things to them, the scribes and the Pharisees began to incite Him vehemently and angrily draw Him out concerning many things, [54] lying in wait for Him and seeking to catch something out of His mouth, that they might accuse Him.

A Warning Against Hypocrisy

12 Meanwhile, when thousands of the crowd were assembled, so as to trample on one another, He began to say to His disciples first, "Beware of the yeast of the Pharisees, which is hypocrisy. [2] For there is nothing covered that will not be revealed, or hidden that will not be known. [3] Therefore what you have said in the darkness will be heard in the light. And what you have whispered in the ear in private rooms will be proclaimed on the housetops.

Whom to Fear
Mt 10:28–31

[4] "I say to you, My friends, do not be afraid of those who kill the body, and after that can do no more. [5] But I will warn you whom you shall fear: Fear Him who, after He has killed, has power to cast into hell. Yes, I say to you, fear Him. [6] Are not five sparrows sold for two pennies[1]? Yet not one of them is forgotten by God. [7] Indeed, even the hairs of your head are all numbered. Therefore do not fear. You are more valuable than many sparrows.

Confessing Christ Before Men
Mt 10:19–20, 32–33; 12:32

[8] "I say to you, whoever confesses Me before men, him will the Son of Man also confess before the angels of God. [9] But he who denies Me before men will be denied before the angels of God. [10] And everyone who speaks a word against the Son of Man will be forgiven, but he who blasphemes against the Holy Spirit will not be forgiven.

[11] "When they bring you to the synagogues, rulers, and authorities, do not be anxious how you will answer or what you will say. [12] For the Holy Spirit will teach you at that time what you should say."

The Parable of the Rich Fool

[13] Someone in the crowd said to Him, "Teacher, tell my brother to divide the inheritance with me."

[14] Jesus said to him, "Man, who appointed Me a judge or an arbitrator between you?" [15] Then He said to them, "Take heed and beware of covetousness. For a man's life does not consist in the abundance of his possessions."

[16] And He told a parable to them, saying, "The land of a rich man produced plentifully. [17] He thought to himself, 'What shall I do, for I have no room to store my crops?'

[18] "Then he said, 'This I will do: I will pull down my barns and build greater ones, and there I will store all my grain and my goods. [19] And I will say to my soul, Soul, you have many goods laid up for many years. Take rest. Eat, drink, and be merry.'

[20] "But God said to him, 'You fool! This night your soul will be required of you. Then whose will those things be which you have provided?'

[21] "So is he who stores up treasure for himself, and is not rich toward God."

Care and Anxiety
Mt 6:25–34, 19–21

[22] Then He said to His disciples, "Therefore I say to you, do not be anxious for your life, what you will eat, nor for your body, what you will wear. [23] Life is more than food, and the body is more than clothes. [24] Consider the ravens: They neither sow nor reap, they have neither storehouses nor barns. Yet God feeds them. How much more valuable are you than birds? [25] Who of you by worrying can add one cubit[2] to his height? [26] If you then cannot do what is least, why are you anxious about the other things?

[27] "Consider how the lilies grow. They neither spin nor weave. Yet I say to you that Solomon in all his glory was not arrayed like one of these. [28] If God so clothes the grass, which today is in the field and tomorrow is thrown into the oven, how much more will He clothe you, O you of little faith? [29] And do not seek what you will eat or what you will drink, nor be of an anxious mind. [30] For the nations of the world seek all these things, and your Father knows that you need them. [31] But seek the kingdom of God, and all these things shall be given to you.

[32] "Do not be afraid, little flock, for it is your Father's good pleasure to give you the kingdom. [33] Sell your possessions and give alms. Provide yourselves purses that do not grow old, an unfailing treasure in the heavens, where no thief comes near and no moth destroys. [34] For where your treasure is, there will your heart be also.

Watchful Servants
Mt 24:45–51

[35] "Let your waist be girded and your lights be burning, [36] and you be like men waiting for their master to return from the wedding banquet, so that they may open the door immediately for him when he comes and knocks. [37] Blessed are those servants whom the master will find watching when he comes. Truly I say to you, he will dress himself and have them sit down to dine, and he will come and serve them. [38] If he comes in the second watch, or comes in the third watch, and finds them so, blessed are those servants. [39] But know this: If the owner of the house had known at what hour the thief was coming, he would have watched and not have allowed his house to be broken into. [40] Therefore be ready, for the Son of Man is coming at an hour you do not expect."

[41] Peter said to Him, "Lord, are You telling this parable to us, or to everyone?"

[42] The Lord said, "Who then is the faithful and wise steward, whom his master will make ruler over his house servants, to give them their portion of food at the proper time? [43] Blessed is that servant whom his master will find so doing when he comes. [44] Truly, I say to you, he will appoint him over all his possessions. [45] But if that servant says in his heart, 'My master delays his coming,' and begins to beat the house servants, both men and women, and to eat and drink and get drunk, [46] the master of that servant will come on a day when he does not look for him, and at an hour when he is not aware, and will cut him to pieces and will appoint him his portion with the unbelievers.

[47] "That servant who knew his master's will, but did not prepare himself or do according to his will, shall be beaten with many stripes. [48] But he who unknowingly committed acts worthy of punishment shall be beaten with few stripes. For to whom much is given, of him much shall be required. And from him to whom much was entrusted, much will be asked.

Jesus the Cause of Division
Mt 10:34–36

[49] "I have come to send fire upon the earth and wish that it were already kindled! [50] But I have a baptism to be baptized with, and how pressed I am until it is accomplished! [51] Do you suppose that I have come to give peace on earth? No, I tell you, but rather division. [52] For there will be from now on five divided in one house, three against two and two against three. [53] They will be divided, father against son and son against father, mother against daughter and daughter against mother, and mother-in-law against her daughter-in-law and daughter-in-law against her mother-in-law."

---

[1] 6 Gk. *2 assaria. An assarion* was worth 1⁄16 of a denarius, which was a day's wage.   [2] 25 A cubit is about half a meter.

Discerning the Appointed Time
Mt 16:2–3

⁵⁴ Then He said to the crowd: "When you see a cloud rise out of the west, immediately you say, 'A shower is coming,' and so it is. ⁵⁵ And when a south wind blows, you say, 'There will be heat,' and it happens. ⁵⁶ You hypocrites! You can discern the face of the sky and of the earth. But why do you not know how to discern this time?

Settling With Your Accuser
Mt 5:25–26

⁵⁷ "Why even among yourselves do you not judge what is right? ⁵⁸ When you go with your adversary to the magistrate, as you are on the way, diligently try to settle matters with him, lest he drag you to the judge, and the judge will hand you over to the officer, and the officer will throw you into prison. ⁵⁹ I tell you, you shall not come out from there until you have paid the very last penny." *²*

Repent or Perish

13 There were present at that time some who told Him of the Galileans whose blood Pilate had mingled with their sacrifices. ² Jesus answered, "Do you suppose that these Galileans were worse sinners than all the other Galileans, because they suffered such things? ³ I tell you, no! But unless you repent, you will all likewise perish. ⁴ Or those eighteen, upon whom the tower in Siloam fell and killed them, do you think that they were worse offenders than all men living in Jerusalem? ⁵ I tell you, no! But unless you repent, you will all likewise perish."

The Parable of the Barren Fig Tree

⁶ Then He told this parable: "A man had a fig tree planted in his vineyard. He came and looked for fruit on it and found none. ⁷ So he said to the vinedresser of his vineyard, 'Now these three years I have come looking for fruit on this fig tree, and I find none. Cut it down. Why should it deplete the soil?'

⁸ "He answered him, 'Sir, leave it alone this year also, until I dig around it and fertilize it. ⁹ And if it bears fruit, well. But if not, after that you shall cut it down.' "

Healing a Woman on the Sabbath

¹⁰ He was teaching in one of the synagogues on the Sabbath. ¹¹ And there was a woman who had a spirit of infirmity for eighteen years and was bent over and could not straighten herself up. ¹² When Jesus saw her, He called her and said to her, "Woman, you are loosed from your infirmity." ¹³ Then He laid His hands on her, and immediately she was made straight and glorified God.

¹⁴ But the ruler of the synagogue answered with indignation, because Jesus had healed on the Sabbath, and said to the people, "There are six days in which men ought to work. Therefore come and be healed on those days, but not on the Sabbath day."

¹⁵ The Lord answered him, "You hypocrite! Does not each one of you on the Sabbath untie his ox or his donkey from the stall and lead it away to water it? ¹⁶ Then should not this woman, being a daughter of Abraham whom Satan has bound these eighteen years, be loosed from this bondage on the Sabbath?"

¹⁷ When He said this, all His adversaries were ashamed. And all the people rejoiced for all the glorious things that were done by Him.

The Parables of the Mustard Seed and the Yeast
Mt 13:31–33; Mk 4:30–32

¹⁸ Then He said, "What is the kingdom of God like? To what shall I compare it? ¹⁹ It is like a grain of mustard seed which a man took and planted in his garden. It grew and became a large tree, and the birds of the air nested in its branches."

²⁰ Again He said, "To what shall I compare the kingdom of God? ²¹ It is like yeast, which a woman took and hid in sixty pounds *²* of meal until all of it was leavened."

The Narrow Gate
Mt 7:13–14, 21–23

²² Then He went through the cities and villages, teaching, and journeying toward Jerusalem. ²³ Someone said to Him, "Lord, will those who are saved be few?"

He said to them, ²⁴ "Strive to enter through the narrow gate. For many, I tell you, will try to enter and will not be able. ²⁵ Once the Master of the house has risen up and shut the door, and you begin to stand outside and knock at the door, saying, 'Lord, Lord, open for us,' He will answer you, 'I do not know where you come from.'

²⁶ "Then you will begin to say, 'We ate and drank in your presence, and you taught in our streets.'

²⁷ "But He will say, 'I tell you, I do not know you, or where you come from. Depart from Me, all you workers of iniquity.'

²⁸ "There will be weeping and gnashing of teeth when you see Abraham, and Isaac, and Jacob, and all the prophets in the kingdom of God, and you yourselves thrust out. ²⁹ They will come from the east and from the west and from the north and from the south and will sit down to dine in the kingdom of God. ³⁰ Listen, there are the last who will be first, and the first who will be last."

The Lament Over Jerusalem
Mt 23:37–39

³¹ On the same day certain Pharisees came, saying to Him, "Get out and depart from here, for Herod wants to kill You."

³² He said to them, "Go and tell that fox, 'Look, I cast out demons. And I perform healings today and tomorrow, and on the third day I shall be perfected.' ³³ Nevertheless I must travel today and tomorrow and the day following. For it cannot be that a prophet should perish outside Jerusalem.

³⁴ "O Jerusalem, Jerusalem, which kills the prophets and stones those who are sent to you! How often would I have gathered your children together, as a hen gathers her chicks under her wings, and you were not willing! ³⁵ Look, your house is forsaken. Truly I say to you, you shall not see Me until the time comes when you say, 'Blessed is He who comes in the name of the Lord.'³"

The Healing of the Man With Edema

14 On the Sabbath they watched Him as He went into the house of one of the leaders of the Pharisees to eat bread. ² There before Him was a man who had edema. *⁴* ³ Jesus said to the lawyers and Pharisees, "Is it lawful to heal on the Sabbath?" ⁴ But they remained silent. So He took him and healed him, and let him go.

⁵ Then He said, "Which of you having a donkey or an ox that has fallen into a pit will not immediately pull him out on the Sabbath day?" ⁶ And they could not answer Him regarding these things.

A Lesson to Guests and a Host

⁷ When He marked how they chose the seats of honor, He told a parable to those who were invited, saying to them, ⁸ "When you are invited by any man to a wedding banquet, do not sit down in a seat of honor, lest a more honorable man than you be invited by him; ⁹ and he who invited you both will come and say to you, 'Give this man the seat,' and then you will begin with shame to take the lowest seat. ¹⁰ But when you are invited, go and sit down in the lowest seat, so that when he who invited you comes, he may say to you, 'Friend, go up higher.' Then you will have respect in the presence of those who sit at dinner with you. ¹¹ For whoever exalts himself will be humbled, and he who humbles himself will be exalted."

¹² Then He said also to the one who invited Him, "When you prepare a dinner or a supper, do not call your friends or your brothers or your kinsmen or your rich neighbors, lest they also invite you in return, and you be repaid. ¹³ But when you prepare a banquet, call the poor, the maimed, the lame, the blind, ¹⁴ and you will be blessed, for they cannot repay you. You shall be repaid at the resurrection of the just."

---

¹ 59 Gk. *lepton*, the smallest coin circulated, means "small" or "thin."   *² 21* Gk. *3 sata*, or 27 kilograms.   *³ 35* Ps 118:26.   *⁴ 2* Or *dropsy*.

The Parable of the Great Banquet
Mt 22:1–10

[15] When one of those who sat at dinner with Him heard this, he said to Him, "Blessed is he who shall eat bread in the kingdom of God!"

[16] Then He said to him, "A man prepared a banquet and invited many, [17] and sent his servant at supper time to say to those who had been invited, 'Come, for everything is now prepared.'

[18] "But they all with one mind began to make excuses. The first said to him, 'I have bought a piece of land, and I must go and see it. I ask you to excuse me.'

[19] "Another said, 'I have bought five yoke of oxen, and I am going to prove them. I ask you to excuse me.'

[20] "Still another said, 'I have married a wife, and therefore I cannot come.'

[21] "The servant came and reported this to his master. Then the master of the house in anger said to his servant, 'Go out quickly into the streets and lanes of the city, and bring in here the poor and the maimed and the lame and the blind.'

[22] "The servant said, 'Master, what you commanded has been done, and yet there is room.'

[23] "Then the master said to the servant, 'Go out to the highways and hedges, and compel them to come in, so that my house may be filled. [24] For I tell you, none of those men who were invited shall taste my supper.' "

The Cost of Discipleship
Mt 10:37–38

[25] Large crowds went with Him. And He turned and said to them, [26] "If anyone comes to Me and does not hate his father and mother and wife and children and brothers and sisters, yes, and even his own life, he cannot be My disciple. [27] And whoever does not bear his cross and follow Me cannot be My disciple.

[28] "For who among you, intending to build a tower, does not sit down first and count the cost to see whether he has resources to complete it? [29] Otherwise, perhaps, after he has laid the foundation and is not able to complete it, all who see it will begin to mock him, [30] saying, 'This man began to build and was not able to complete it.'

[31] "Or what king, going to wage war against another king, does not sit down first and take counsel whether he is able with ten thousand to meet him who comes against him with twenty thousand? [32] Otherwise, while the other is yet at a distance, he sends a delegation and requests conditions of peace. [33] So likewise, any of you who does not forsake all that he has cannot be My disciple.

Tasteless Salt
Mt 5:13; Mk 9:50

[34] "Salt is good. But if the salt has lost its saltiness, how shall it be made salty? [35] It is fit neither for the land nor for the manure pile. So men throw it out.

"He who has ears to hear, let him hear."

The Parable of the Lost Sheep
Mt 18:12–14

15 Now all the tax collectors and sinners drew near to Him to hear Him. [2] But the Pharisees and scribes murmured, saying, "This Man receives sinners and eats with them."

[3] So He told them this parable, saying, [4] "What man among you having a hundred sheep and losing one of them does not leave the ninety-nine in the wilderness and go after the one which is lost until he finds it? [5] And when he has found it, he places it on his shoulders, rejoicing. [6] Then when he comes home, he calls together his friends and neighbors, saying to them, 'Rejoice with me, for I have found my sheep which was lost.' [7] Likewise, I tell you, there will be more joy in heaven over one sinner who repents than over ninety-nine righteous men who need no repentance.

The Parable of the Lost Coin
[8] "Or what woman, having ten silver coins[1] and losing one, does not light a candle and sweep the house and search diligently until she finds it? [9] And when she has found it, she calls together her friends and neighbors, saying, 'Rejoice with me, for I have found the coin which I had lost.' [10] Likewise, I tell you, there is joy in the presence of the angels of God over one sinner who repents."

The Parable of the Prodigal Son
[11] Then He said, "A man had two sons. [12] The younger of them said to his father, 'Father, give me the share of the property that falls to me.' So he divided his estate between them.

[13] "Not many days later, the younger son gathered everything together, and journeyed to a distant country, and there squandered his possessions in prodigal living. [14] When he had spent everything, there came a severe famine in that country, and he began to be in want. [15] So he went and hired himself to a citizen of that county, who sent him into his fields to feed swine. [16] He would gladly have filled his stomach with the husks that the swine were eating, but no one gave him any.

[17] "When he came to himself, he said, 'How many of my father's hired servants have an abundance of bread, and here I am perishing with hunger! [18] I will arise and go to my father, and I will say to him, "Father, I have sinned against heaven and before you. [19] I am no longer worthy to be called your son. Make me like one of your hired servants." ' [20] So he arose and came to his father.

"But while he was yet far away, his father saw him and was moved with compassion, and ran and embraced his neck and kissed him.

[21] "The son said to him, 'Father, I have sinned against heaven and before you. I am no longer worthy to be called your son.'

[22] "But the father said to his servants, 'Bring out the best robe and put it on him. And put a ring on his hand and shoes on his feet. [23] Bring here the fattened calf and kill it, and let us eat and be merry. [24] For this son of mine was dead, and is alive again; he was lost, and is found.' So they began to be merry.

[25] "Now his older son was in the field. As he came and drew near the house, he heard music and dancing. [26] So he called one of the servants and asked what this meant. [27] He said to him, 'Your brother has come, and your father has killed the fattened calf, because he has received him safe and sound.'

[28] "He was angry and would not go in. Therefore his father came out and entreated him. [29] But he answered his father, 'Look! These many years have I served you. Nor have I ever transgressed your commands, yet never have you given me a goat, so that I might be merry with my friends. [30] But when this son of yours came, who has devoured your living with harlots, you killed the fattened calf for him.'

[31] "He said to him, 'Son, you are always with me, and all that I have is yours. [32] But it was fitting to be merry and be glad, for this brother of yours was dead and is alive again; he was lost and is found.' "

The Parable of the Dishonest Steward
16 He told His disciples: "There was a rich man who had a steward who was accused to the man of wasting his resources. [2] So he called him and said, 'How is it that I hear this about you? Give an account of your stewardship, for you may no longer be steward.'

[3] "Then the steward said to himself, 'What shall I do, for my master is taking away the stewardship from me? I cannot dig. I am ashamed to beg. [4] I know what to do so that, when I am removed from the stewardship, others may receive me into their houses.'

[5] "So he called each of his master's debtors, and said to the first, 'How much do you owe my master?'

[6] "He said, 'Eight hundred gallons[2] of oil.'

"He said to him, 'Take your bill, and sit down quickly and write four hundred.'

[7] "Then he said to another, 'And how much do you owe?'

"He said, 'One thousand bushels[3] of wheat.'

"He said to him, 'Take your bill, and write eight hundred.'

[8] "The master commended the dishonest steward, because he had acted prudently. For the sons of this world are wiser in their

---

1 8 Gk. *drachmas*, each worth about a day's wage.   2 6 Gk. *100 batous*, or 3 kiloliters.   3 7 Gk. *100 korous*, or 35 kiloliters.

own generation than the sons of light. [9] I say to you, make friends for yourself by means of unrighteous wealth, so that when you fall short, they may receive you into eternal dwellings.

[10] "He who is faithful in what is least is faithful also in much. And he who is dishonest in the least is dishonest also in much. [11] So if you have not been faithful in the unrighteous wealth, who will commit to your trust the true riches? [12] And if you have not been faithful in that which is another man's, who will give you that which is your own?

[13] "No servant can serve two masters. Either he will hate the one and love the other, or he will be loyal to the one and despise the other. You cannot serve God and wealth."

The Law and the Kingdom of God
Mt 11:12–13

[14] The Pharisees, who were lovers of money, heard all these things and derided Him. [15] He said to them, "You are those who justify yourselves before men, but God knows your hearts. For that which is highly esteemed before men is an abomination before God.

[16] "The Law and the Prophets were preached until John. Since then the kingdom of God has been preached, and everyone is pressing into it. [17] It is easier for heaven and earth to pass away than for one stroke of the law to fail.

[18] "Whoever divorces his wife and marries another commits adultery, and whoever marries her who is divorced by her husband commits adultery.

The Rich Man and Lazarus

[19] "There was a rich man who was clothed in purple and fine linen and fared sumptuously every day. [20] There was also a beggar named Lazarus, covered with sores, who had been placed at his gate, [21] desiring to be fed the crumbs falling from the rich man's table. Moreover the dogs came and licked his sores.

[22] "It came to pass that the beggar died and was carried by the angels to Abraham's presence. The rich man also died and was buried. [23] In Hades, being in torment, he lifted up his eyes and saw Abraham from a distance and Lazarus in his presence. [24] So he cried out, 'Father Abraham, have mercy on me, and send Lazarus to dip the tip of his finger in water and cool my tongue. For I am tormented in this flame.'

[25] "But Abraham said, 'Son, remember that you in your lifetime received your good things, and Lazarus in like manner evil things. But now he is comforted and you there are tormented. [26] And besides all this, between us and you there is a great gulf, so that those who would pass from here to you cannot, nor can those from there pass to us.'

[27] "He said, 'Then I pray you, father, to send him to my father's house, [28] for I have five brothers, to testify to them, lest they also come to this place of torment.'

[29] "Abraham said to him, 'They have Moses and the Prophets. Let them hear them.'

[30] "He said, 'No, father Abraham. But if someone from the dead goes to them, they will repent.'

[31] "He said to him, 'If they do not hear Moses and the Prophets, neither will they be persuaded if someone should rise from the dead.' "

Some Sayings of Jesus
Mt 18:6–7, 21–22; Mk 9:42

17 Then He said to the disciples, "It is impossible except that offenses will come. But woe to him through whom they come! [2] It would be better for him if a millstone were hung around his neck and he was thrown into the sea, than to offend one of these little ones. [3] Take heed to yourselves.

"If your brother sins against you, rebuke him. And if he repents, forgive him. [4] If he sins against you seven times in a day, and seven times in a day turns to you, saying, 'I repent,' you must forgive him."

[5] The apostles said to the Lord, "Increase our faith."

[6] The Lord said, "If you had faith as a grain of mustard seed, you could say to this mulberry tree, 'Be uprooted and be planted in the sea,' and it would obey you.

[7] "Which of you, having a servant plowing or herding sheep, will say to him when he has come in from the field, 'Come now and sit down for dinner'? [8] Will he not rather say to him, 'Prepare my supper, and dress yourself and serve me until I eat and drink. And afterward you will eat and drink'? [9] Does he thank the servant because he did what was commanded? I think not. [10] So you also, when you have done everything commanded you, say, 'We are unprofitable servants. We have done our duty.' "

The Cleansing of Ten Lepers

[11] As Jesus went to Jerusalem, He passed between Samaria and Galilee. [12] As He entered a village, there met Him ten men who were lepers, who stood at a distance. [13] They lifted up their voices, saying, "Jesus, Master, have pity on us!"

[14] When He saw them, He said to them, "Go, show yourselves to the priests." And as they went, they were cleansed.

[15] One of them, when he saw that he was healed, returned with a loud voice glorifying God, [16] and fell down on his face at His feet, giving Him thanks. And he was a Samaritan.

[17] Jesus said, "Were not the ten cleansed? Where are the nine? [18] Were there not any found to return and give glory to God except this foreigner?" [19] Then He said to him, "Rise, go your way. Your faith has made you well."

The Coming of the Kingdom
Mt 24:23–28, 37–41

[20] When He was asked by the Pharisees when the kingdom of God would come, He answered them, "The kingdom of God does not come with observation. [21] Nor will they say, 'Here it is!' or 'There it is!' For remember, the kingdom of God is within you."

[22] Then He said to the disciples, "The days will come when you will desire to see one of the days of the Son of Man, but you will not see it. [23] They will say to you, 'Look here,' or 'Look there!' Do not follow after them. [24] For as the lightning flashes and lights up the heavens from one side to the other, so will the Son of Man be in His day. [25] But first He must suffer many things and be rejected by this generation.

[26] "Just as it was in the days of Noah, so will it be in the days of the Son of Man. [27] They were eating, drinking, marrying, and were given in marriage until the day when Noah entered the ark. Then the flood came and destroyed them all.

[28] "Likewise as it was in the days of Lot: They ate, they drank, they bought, they sold, they planted, they built. [29] But on the day that Lot departed from Sodom, fire and brimstone rained from heaven and destroyed them all.

[30] "So will it be on the day when the Son of Man is revealed. [31] On that day let him who is on the housetop, with his goods in the house, not come down to take them away. And likewise let him who is in the field not return to the things behind. [32] Remember Lot's wife. [33] Whoever seeks to save his life will lose it, and whoever loses his life will preserve it. [34] I tell you, on that night two men will be in one bed; the one will be taken and the other will be left. [35] Two women will be grinding grain together; the one will be taken and the other will be left. [36] Two men will be in the field; the one will be taken and the other will be left."

[37] They asked, "Where, Lord?"

He replied, "Where the body is, there the eagles will be gathered together."

The Parable of the Widow and the Judge

18 He told them a parable to illustrate that it is necessary always to pray and not lose heart. [2] He said: "In a city there was a judge who did not fear God or regard man. [3] And a widow was in that city. She came to him, saying, 'Avenge me against my adversary.'

[4] "He would not for a while. Yet afterward he said to himself, 'Though I do not fear God or respect man, [5] yet because this widow troubles me, I will avenge her, lest by her continual coming she will weary me.' "

[6] And the Lord said, "Hear what the unjust judge says. [7] And shall not God avenge His own elect and be patient with them, who cry day and night to Him? [8] I tell you, He will avenge them

speedily. Nevertheless, when the Son of Man comes, will He find faith on the earth?"

The Parable of the Pharisee and the Tax Collector

[9] He told this parable to some who trusted in themselves, as though they were righteous, and despised others: [10] "Two men went up to the temple to pray, the one a Pharisee and the other a tax collector. [11] The Pharisee stood and prayed these things about himself, 'God, I thank You that I am not like other men: extortioners, unjust, adulterers, or even like this tax collector. [12] I fast twice a week, and I tithe of all that I earn.'

[13] "But the tax collector, standing at a distance, would not even lift his eyes to heaven, but struck his chest, saying, 'God, be merciful to me a sinner.'

[14] "I tell you, this man went down to his house justified rather than the other. For everyone who exalts himself will be humbled, and he who humbles himself will be exalted."

Little Children Blessed
Mt 19:13–15; Mk 10:13–16

[15] They also brought infants to Him that He might touch them. When the disciples saw it, they rebuked them. [16] But Jesus called them to Him and said, "Permit the little children to come to Me, and do not hinder them. For to such belongs the kingdom of God. [17] Truly, I say to you, whoever will not receive the kingdom of God as a little child will in no wise enter it."

The Rich Ruler
Mt 19:16–30; Mk 10:17–31

[18] A certain ruler asked Him, "Good Teacher, what must I do to inherit eternal life?"

[19] Jesus said to him, "Why do you call Me good? No one is good, except God alone. [20] You know the commandments: Do not commit adultery, Do not murder, Do not steal, Do not bear false witness, Honor your father and your mother.[1]"

[21] He said, "All these I have kept since my youth."

[22] When Jesus heard this, He said to him, "Yet you lack one thing. Sell all that you have and distribute to the poor, and you will have treasure in heaven. And come, follow Me."

[23] When he heard this he became very sorrowful, for he was very rich. [24] When Jesus saw that he became very sorrowful, He said, "How hard it is for those who have riches to enter the kingdom of God! [25] For it is easier for a camel to go through the eye of a needle than for a rich man to enter the kingdom of God."

[26] Those who heard this said, "Who then can be saved?"

[27] He said, "What is impossible with men is possible with God."

[28] Peter said, "Look, we have left everything and followed You."

[29] He said to them, "Truly, I tell you, there is no man who has left his home or parents or brothers or wife or children, for the sake of the kingdom of God, [30] who shall not receive many times more in this age and, in the age to come, eternal life."

Jesus Foretells His Death and Resurrection a Third Time
Mt 20:17–19; Mk 10:32–34

[31] Taking the twelve, He said, "Listen! We are going up to Jerusalem, and everything that is written by the prophets concerning the Son of Man will be accomplished, [32] for He will be handed over to the Gentiles and will be mocked and insulted and spit upon. [33] They will scourge Him and put Him to death, and on the third day He will rise again."

[34] They understood none of these things. This saying was hidden from them, and they did not comprehend what was spoken.

The Healing of a Blind Beggar Near Jericho
Mt 20:29–34; Mk 10:46–52

[35] As He was drawing near Jericho, a certain blind man sat along the way begging. [36] Hearing a crowd passing by, he asked what it meant. [37] They told him that Jesus of Nazareth was passing by.

[38] He cried out, "Jesus, Son of David, have mercy on me!"

[39] Those who went in front rebuked him, so that he would keep quiet. But he cried out much more, "Son of David, have mercy on me!"

[40] Jesus stood and commanded him to be brought to Him. When he came near, He asked him, [41] "What do you want Me to do for you?"

He said, "Lord, grant that I may receive my sight."

[42] Jesus said to him, "Receive your sight. Your faith has saved you." [43] Immediately he received his sight and followed Him, glorifying God. When all the people saw it, they gave praise to God.

Jesus and Zacchaeus

19 Jesus entered and passed through Jericho. [2] A man was there named Zacchaeus who was a chief tax collector, and he was rich. [3] He tried to see who Jesus was, but was not able from the crowd, because he was little in stature. [4] So he ran ahead and climbed up into a sycamore tree to see Him, for He was to pass that way.

[5] When Jesus came to the vicinity, He looked up and saw him, and said to him, "Zacchaeus, hurry and come down, for today I must remain at your house." [6] So he hurried and came down, and received Him joyfully.

[7] When they saw it, they all murmured, saying, "He has gone to be the guest of a man who is a sinner."

[8] But Zacchaeus stood and said to the Lord, "Look, Lord, I give half of my possessions to the poor. And if I have taken anything from anyone by false accusation, I will repay him four times as much."

[9] Jesus said to him, "Today salvation has come to this house, because he also is a son of Abraham. [10] For the Son of Man has come to seek and to save that which was lost."

The Parable of the Ten Pounds
Mt 25:14–30

[11] As they heard these things, He continued and told them a parable, because He was near Jerusalem and because they thought the kingdom of God would immediately appear. [12] Therefore He said, "A nobleman went to a distant country to receive a kingdom and to return. [13] So he called his ten servants and entrusted to them ten pounds[2] and said to them, 'Trade until I come.'

[14] "But his citizens hated him and sent a delegation after him, saying, 'We do not want this man to reign over us.'

[15] "When he returned, having received the kingdom, he summoned these servants, to whom he had entrusted the money, that he might know what everyone gained by trading.

[16] "The first came, saying, 'Master, your pound has made ten pounds more.'

[17] "He said to him, 'Well done, good servant! Because you have been faithful in very little, take authority over ten cities.'

[18] "The second came, saying, 'Master, your pound has made five pounds more.'

[19] "He said in like manner to him, 'You, take authority over five cities.'

[20] "Then another came, saying, 'Master, look, here is your pound, which I have kept put away in a napkin. [21] For I feared you, because you are an exacting man. You collect what you did not deposit, and reap what you did not sow.'

[22] "He said to him, 'Out of your own mouth will I judge you, you wicked servant. You knew that I was an exacting man, collecting what I did not deposit and reaping what I did not sow. [23] Why then did you not deposit my money in the bank, so that at my coming I might have collected it with interest?'

[24] "Then he said to those who stood by, 'Take the pound from him and give it to him who has ten pounds.'

[25] "They said to him, 'Master, he has ten pounds.'

[26] " 'I tell you that to everyone who has will be given. But from him who has not, even what he has will be taken away from him. [27] But as for those enemies of mine, who would not let me reign over them, bring them here and slay them before me.' "

---

[1] 20 Ex 20:12–16; Dt 5:16–20.   [2] 13 Gk. *mina*, worth about 3 months' wages.

The Triumphant Entry in Jerusalem
Mt 21:1–11; Mk 11:1–11; Jn 12:12–19

[28] When He had said this, He went before them, ascending up to Jerusalem. [29] When He came near to Bethphage and Bethany, at the mountain called the Mount of Olives, He sent two of His disciples, [30] saying, "Go over into the village opposite you, where, as you enter, you will find a colt tied, on which no one has ever yet sat. Untie it and bring it here. [31] If anyone asks you, 'Why are you untying it?' you shall say to him, 'Because the Lord has need of it.' "

[32] Those who were sent went and found it just as He had told them. [33] As they were untying the colt, its owners said to them, "Why are you untying the colt?"

[34] They said, "The Lord has need of it."

[35] They brought it to Jesus. And they threw their garments on the colt, and they set Jesus on it. [36] As He went, they spread their clothes in the street.

[37] When He was coming near the descent of the Mount of Olives, the whole crowd of the disciples began to rejoice and praise God with loud voices for all the mighty works that they had seen, [38] saying:

> " 'Blessed is the King who comes in the name of the Lord!'[1]
> Peace in heaven and glory in the highest!"

[39] Some of the Pharisees from the crowd said to Him, "Teacher, rebuke Your disciples."

[40] He answered them, "I tell you, if these should be silent, the stones would immediately cry out."

[41] When He came near, He beheld the city and wept over it, [42] saying, "If you, even you, had known even today what things would bring you peace! But now they are hidden from your eyes. [43] For the days will come upon you when your enemies will build an embankment around you and surround you, and press you in on every side. [44] They will dash you, and your children within you, to the ground. They will not leave one stone upon another within you, because you did not know the time of your visitation."

The Cleansing of the Temple
Mt 21:12–17; Mk 11:15–19; Jn 2:13–22

[45] Then He entered the temple and began to drive out those who sold and bought in it, [46] saying to them, "It is written, 'My house will be a house of prayer,'[2] but you have made it 'a den of thieves.'[3]"

[47] He taught daily in the temple. But the chief priests, the scribes, and the leaders of the people tried to kill Him. [48] Yet they could not find a way to do it, for all the people were very attentive to hear Him.

The Question of Jesus' Authority
Mt 21:23–27; Mk 11:27–33

20 One day, as He taught the people in the temple and preached the gospel, the chief priests and the scribes with the elders came up to Him, [2] and said to Him, "Tell us, by what authority are You doing these things? Who is he who gave You this authority?"

[3] He answered them, "I will also ask you one thing. Answer Me: [4] Was the baptism of John from heaven or from men?"

[5] They debated with themselves, saying, "If we say, 'From heaven,' He will say, 'Why then did you not believe him?' [6] But if we say, 'From men,' all the people will stone us, for they are persuaded that John was a prophet."

[7] So they answered that they did not know where it was from.

[8] Jesus said to them, "Neither will I tell you by what authority I do these things."

The Parable of the Vineyard and the Vinedressers
Mt 21:33–46; Mk 12:1–12

[9] He began to tell the people this parable: "A man planted a vineyard, and leased it to vinedressers, and went to a distant country for a long time. [10] At harvest time he sent a servant to the vinedressers so they might give him some fruit of the vineyard. But the vinedressers beat him and sent him away empty-handed. [11] Again, he sent another servant. But they beat him also, and treated him shamefully, and sent him away empty-handed. [12] Once again, he sent a third. And they wounded him also and drove him out.

[13] "Then the owner of the vineyard said, 'What shall I do? I will send my beloved son. Perhaps they will respect him when they see him.'

[14] "But when the vinedressers saw him, they debated among themselves, saying, 'This is the heir. Come, let us kill him, that the inheritance may be ours.' [15] So they drove him out of the vineyard and killed him.

"What then will the owner of the vineyard do to them? [16] He will come and kill these vinedressers and will give the vineyard to others."

When they heard this, they said, "May it not be so!"

[17] He looked at them and said, "What then is this that is written:

> 'The stone which the builders rejected
> has become the cornerstone'[4]?

[18] Whoever falls on that stone will be broken. But he on whom it falls will be crushed to powder."[5]

[19] The chief priests and the scribes tried to lay their hands on Him that same hour, but they feared the people. For they perceived that He had told this parable against them.

The Question of Paying Taxes
Mt 22:18–22; Mk 12:13–17

[20] They watched Him and sent out spies who pretended to be righteous men, that they might seize Him in His words to hand Him over to the power and authority of the governor. [21] So they asked Him, "Teacher, we know that You speak and teach rightly. And You do not show partiality, but You truly teach the way of God. [22] Is it lawful for us to pay taxes to Caesar, or not?"

[23] He perceived their craftiness and said to them, "Why do you test Me? [24] Show Me a denarius.[6] Whose image and inscription does it have?"

They said, "Caesar's."

[25] He said to them, "Then render to Caesar what is Caesar's, and to God what is God's."

[26] They could not catch Him in His words before the people. And they marveled at His answer and were silent.

The Question About the Resurrection
Mt 22:23–33; Mk 12:18–27

[27] Some of the Sadducees, who deny that there is any resurrection, came to Him and asked Him, [28] "Teacher, Moses wrote for us that if a man's brother dies, having a wife but no children, then this man should take the wife and raise up children for his brother.[7] [29] Now there were seven brothers. The first took a wife and died childless. [30] The second took her as wife, and he died childless. [31] And then the third took her, and in like manner, all seven died and left no children. [32] Last of all, the woman died also. [33] Therefore in the resurrection whose wife will she be? For the seven had her as a wife."

[34] Jesus answered them, "The sons of this age marry and are given in marriage. [35] But those who are counted worthy to attain that age, and the resurrection from the dead, neither marry nor are given in marriage. [36] For they cannot die any more, for they are equal to the angels and are the sons of God, being sons of the resurrection. [37] Now, at the bush, even Moses pointed out that the dead are raised when he called the Lord 'the God of Abraham, and the God of Isaac, and the God of Jacob.'[8] [38] For He is not the God of the dead, but of the living. For to Him all live."

[39] Some of the scribes said, "Teacher, You have spoken well." [40] After that they dared not ask Him any question at all.

---

[1] 38 Ps 118:26.   [2] 46 Isa 56:7.   [3] 46 Jer 7:11.   [4] 17 Ps 118:22.   [5] 18 Isa 8:14–15.   [6] 24 Gk. *denarius*, a coin worth about a day's wage.
[7] 28 Dt 25:5–6.   [8] 37 Ex 3:6.

The Question About David's Son
Mt 22:41–46; Mk 12:35–37

[41] Then Jesus said to them, "How do they say that Christ is David's Son? [42] David himself says in the Book of Psalms,

'The Lord said to my Lord,
   "Sit at My right hand,
[43] until I make Your enemies
   Your footstool." *¹*

[44] David therefore calls Him 'Lord.' How is He then his Son?"

The Denouncing of the Scribes
Mt 23:1–36; Mk 12:38–40; Lk 11:37–54

[45] Then as all the people heard, He said to His disciples, [46] "Beware of the scribes who desire to walk in long robes and who love greetings in the marketplaces and the prominent seats in the synagogues and the seats of honor at banquets, [47] who devour widows' houses and for a pretense make long prayers. They will receive greater condemnation."

The Widow's Offering
Mk 12:41–44

21 He looked up and saw the rich putting their gifts in the treasury. [2] He also saw a poor widow putting in two mites, *²* [3] and He said, "Truly I tell you, this poor widow has put in more than all of them. [4] For all these out of their abundance have put in their gifts for God. But she out of her poverty has put in all the living she had."

The Destruction of the Temple Foretold
Mt 24:1–2; Mk 13:1–2

[5] As some spoke of how the temple was adorned with beautiful stones and gifts, [6] "As for these things which you see, the days will come when not one stone shall be left on another that will not be thrown down."

Signs and Persecutions
Mt 24:3–14; Mk 13:3–13

[7] They asked Him, "Teacher, when will these things be, and what will be the sign when this is about to happen?"

[8] He said, "Beware lest you be deceived. For many will come in My name, saying, 'I am He,' and 'The time has drawn near.' Therefore do not go after them. [9] When you hear of wars and commotions, do not be afraid. For these things must first take place, but the end will not be at hand."

[10] Then He said to them, "Nation will rise against nation, and kingdom against kingdom. [11] Great earthquakes will occur in various places, and there will be famines and pestilence. And there will be terrors and great signs from heaven.

[12] "But before all these things, they will seize you and persecute you, delivering you up to the synagogues and prisons, and you will be brought before kings and governors for My name's sake. [13] It will turn out as a testimony for you. [14] Therefore resolve in your hearts beforehand not to practice your defense. [15] For I will give you a mouth and wisdom, which all your opponents will be able to neither refute nor resist. [16] You will be betrayed by parents and brothers and relatives and friends. And they will put some of you to death. [17] You will be hated by all men for My name's sake, [18] but not a hair of your head shall perish. [19] In your endurance you will gain your souls.

The Destruction of Jerusalem Foretold
Mt 24:15–21; Mk 13:14–19

[20] "When you see Jerusalem surrounded by armies, then you know that its desolation has drawn near. [21] Then let those who are in Judea flee to the mountains, and let those who are in the city depart, and let not those who are in the country enter it. [22] For

these are the days of vengeance, that all things which are written may be fulfilled. [23] But woe to those who are pregnant and to those who nurse in those days! For there will be great distress in the land and wrath upon this people. [24] They will fall by the edge of the sword and will be led away captive to all nations. And Jerusalem will be trampled on by the Gentiles until the times of the Gentiles are fulfilled.

The Coming of the Son of Man
Mt 24:29–31; Mk 13:24–27

[25] "There will be signs in the sun and the moon and the stars; and on the earth distress of nations, with perplexity, the sea and the waves roaring; [26] men fainting from fear and expectation of what is coming on the inhabited earth. For the powers of heaven will be shaken. [27] Then they will see the Son of Man coming in a cloud with power and great glory. [28] When these things begin to happen, look up and lift up your heads, for your redemption is drawing near."

The Lesson of the Fig Tree
Mt 24:32–35; Mk 13:28–31

[29] He told them this parable: "Look at the fig tree, and all the trees. [30] When they are sprouting leaves already, you see and know for yourselves that summer is now near. [31] So in like manner, when you see these things happening, you know that the kingdom of God is near. [32] Truly, I tell you, this generation will not pass away until all these things are fulfilled. [33] Heaven and earth will pass away, but My words will not pass away.

Exhortation to Watch

[34] "Take heed to yourselves, lest your hearts become burdened by excessiveness and drunkenness and anxieties of life, and that Day comes on you unexpectedly. [35] For as a snare it will come on all those who dwell on the face of the whole earth. [36] Therefore watch always and pray that you may be counted worthy to escape all these things that will happen and to stand before the Son of Man."

[37] Each day He was teaching in the temple, and each night He went out and stayed on the mountain called the Mount of Olives. [38] And all the people came early in the morning to hear Him in the temple.

The Plot to Kill Jesus
Mt 26:1–5, 14–16; Mk 14:1–2, 10–11; Jn 11:45–53

22 Now the Feast of Unleavened Bread, which is called the Passover, drew near. [2] And the chief priests and scribes were seeking how to kill Jesus, for they feared the people. [3] Then Satan entered into Judas, called Iscariot, who was one of the twelve. [4] He went and discussed with the chief priests and captains how he might betray Him to them. [5] They were glad and agreed to give him money. [6] He fully consented and searched for an opportunity to betray Him to them apart from the crowds.

The Preparation of the Passover
Mt 26:17–25; Mk 14:12–21; Jn 13:21–30

[7] Then the Day of Unleavened Bread came, when the Passover lamb must be killed. [8] He sent Peter and John, saying, "Go and prepare the Passover for us to eat it."

[9] They said to Him, "Where will You have us prepare it?"

[10] He said to them, "Now, as you enter the city, a man carrying a pitcher of water will meet you. Follow him into the house which he enters, [11] and say to the owner of the house, 'The Teacher says to you, "Where is the guest room where I may eat the Passover with My disciples?" ' [12] He will show you a large furnished upper room. Prepare there."

[13] They went and found it as He had told them. So they prepared the Passover.

---

¹43 Ps 110:1.   *²2* Gk. *2 lepta*. A *lepton*, meaning "small" or "thin," is a fraction of a penny and about ¹⁄₁₂₈ of a *denarius*, which was a day's wage. A Jewish bronze or copper coin, it was the smallest coin circulated.

The Lord's Supper
Mt 26:26–30; Mk 14:22–26; 1Co 11:23–25

[14] When the hour had come, He and the twelve apostles with Him sat down. [15] And He said to them, "I have earnestly desired to eat this Passover with you before I suffer. [16] For I tell you, I will never eat it again until it is fulfilled in the kingdom of God."

[17] And He took the cup and gave thanks and said, "Take this and divide it among yourselves. [18] For I tell you, I will not drink of the fruit of the vine until the kingdom of God comes."

[19] Then He took the bread, and when He had given thanks, He broke it and gave it to them, saying, "This is My body which is given for you. Do this in remembrance of Me."

[20] In like manner, He took the cup after supper, saying, "This cup is the new covenant in My blood which is shed for you. [21] But see the hand of him who betrays Me is with Me at the table. [22] Indeed, the Son of Man goes as it has been determined. But woe to that man by whom He is betrayed!" [23] They began to inquire among themselves which of them it was who would do this.

The Dispute About Greatness

[24] There was also rivalry among them concerning which of them was to be counted the greatest. [25] He said to them, "The kings of the Gentiles exercise lordship over them, and those who exercise authority over them are called benefactors. [26] But you are not so. Instead, let him who is greatest among you be as the younger, and he who rules as he who serves. [27] For who is greater: he who sits at the table, or he who serves? Is it not he who sits at the table? But I am among you as He who serves. [28] You are those who have continued with Me in My trials. [29] And I appoint to you a kingdom as My Father has appointed one to Me, [30] so that you may eat and drink at My table in My kingdom, and sit on thrones judging the twelve tribes of Israel."

Peter's Denial Foretold

[31] Then the Lord said, "Simon, Simon, listen! Satan has demanded to have you to sift you as wheat. [32] But I have prayed for you that your faith may not fail. And when you have repented, strengthen your brothers."

[33] He said to Him, "Lord, I am ready to go with You to prison and to death."

[34] He said, "I tell you, Peter, before the rooster crows today, you will deny three times that you know Me."

Purse, Bag, and Sword

[35] Then He said to them, "When I sent you without purse or bag or sandals, did you lack anything?"

They said, "Nothing."

[36] He said to them, "But now, let him who has a purse take it and also a bag. And let him who has no sword sell his garment and buy one. [37] For I tell you, what is written must yet be accomplished in Me, 'And He was numbered with the transgressors.'[1] Indeed, what is written concerning Me has a fulfillment."

[38] They said, "Lord, look, here are two swords."

He said to them, "It is enough."

The Prayer on the Mount of Olives
Mt 26:36–46; Mk 14:32–42

[39] According to His custom, He came out and went to the Mount of Olives. And His disciples followed Him. [40] When He came there, He said to them, "Pray that you may not fall into temptation." [41] He withdrew from them about a stone's throw, and He knelt down and prayed, [42] "Father, if You are willing, remove this cup from Me. Nevertheless not My will, but Yours, be done." [43] An angel from heaven appeared to Him, strengthening Him. [44] And being in anguish, He prayed more earnestly. And His sweat became like great drops of blood falling down to the ground.

[45] When He rose from prayer and had come to His disciples, He found them sleeping from sorrow. [46] He said to them, "Why do you sleep? Rise and pray, lest you fall into temptation."

The Betrayal and Arrest of Jesus
Mt 26:47–56; Mk 14:43–50; Jn 18:3–11

[47] While He was yet speaking, a crowd came. And he who was called Judas, one of the twelve, was leading them. He drew near to Jesus to kiss Him. [48] But Jesus said to him, "Judas, do you betray the Son of Man with a kiss?"

[49] When those who were around Him saw what would follow, they said, "Lord, shall we strike with the sword?" [50] And one of them struck the servant of the high priest and cut off his right ear.

[51] But Jesus said, "This is enough!" And He touched his ear and healed him.

[52] Then Jesus said to the chief priests, and captains of the temple guard, and the elders who had come for Him, "Have you come out with swords and clubs as against a rebel? [53] Daily, while I was with you in the temple, you did not lay hands on Me. But this is your hour, and the power of darkness!"

Peter's Denial of Jesus
Mt 26:57–58, 69–75; Mk 14:53–54, 66–72; Jn 18:12–18, 25–27

[54] Then they arrested Him, and led Him away, and brought Him into the high priest's house. Peter followed at a distance. [55] But when they had kindled a fire in the middle of the courtyard and sat down together, Peter sat among them. [56] Then a servant girl saw him as he sat near the fire, and gazed at him, and said, "This man was with Him."

[57] But he denied Him, saying, "Woman, I do not know Him.".

[58] A little later someone else saw him and said, "You also are one of them."

Peter said, "Man, I am not!"

[59] About an hour later another man firmly declared, "Certainly, this man also was with Him, for he is a Galilean."

[60] Peter said, "Man, I do not know what you are saying." Immediately, while he was yet speaking, the rooster crowed. [61] The Lord turned and looked at Peter. Then Peter remembered the word of the Lord, how He had told him, "Before the rooster crows, you will deny Me three times." [62] And Peter went outside and wept bitterly.

The Mocking and Whipping of Jesus
Mt 26:67–68; Mk 14:65

[63] The men who guarded Jesus mocked Him and whipped Him. [64] When they had blindfolded Him, they struck Him on the face and asked Him, "Prophesy! Who struck You?" [65] And many other things they blasphemously spoke against Him.

Jesus Before the Council
Mt 26:59–66; Mk 14:55–64; Jn 18:19–24

[66] When day came, the assembly of the elders of the people, both the chief priests and scribes, came together and led Him away to their council, saying, [67] "Are You the Christ? Tell us!"

He said to them, "If I tell you, you will not believe. [68] And if I also question you, you will not answer Me or release Me. [69] From now on the Son of Man will be seated at the right hand of the power of God."

[70] They all said, "Are You then the Son of God?"

He said to them, "You truly say that I am."

[71] Then they said, "What further testimony do we need? We have heard it from His own mouth."

Jesus Brought Before Pilate
Mt 27:1–2, 11–14; Mk 15:1–5; Jn 18:28–38

23 Then the whole assembly rose and led Him to Pilate. [2] And they began to accuse Him, saying, "We found this Man perverting our nation, and forbidding us to pay taxes to Caesar, and saying that He Himself is Christ a King."

[3] So Pilate asked Him, "Are You the King of the Jews?"

He answered, "You truly say so."

[4] Then Pilate said to the chief priests and to the people, "I find no fault in this Man."

[5] But they insisted, saying, "He stirs up the people, teaching throughout all Judea, beginning from Galilee to here."

---

[1] 37 Isa 53:12.

Jesus Before Herod

[6] When Pilate heard of Galilee, he asked whether the Man was a Galilean. [7] When he learned that He belonged to Herod's jurisdiction, he sent Him to Herod, who was also in Jerusalem at that time. [8] When Herod saw Jesus, he greatly rejoiced, for he had desired to see Him for a long time, because he had heard many things of Him, and he was hoping to see some miracle performed by Him. [9] He questioned Him with many words, but He gave no answer. [10] The chief priests and the scribes stood by, vehemently accusing Him. [11] Then Herod with his soldiers despised Him, and mocked Him, and dressed Him in a fine robe, and sent Him back to Pilate. [12] On the same day Pilate and Herod became friends with each other, having previously been at enmity with each other.

Jesus Sentenced to Die
Mt 27:15–26; Mk 15:6–15; Jn 18:39–19:16

[13] Pilate called together the chief priests and the rulers and the people, [14] and said to them, "You have brought this Man to me as one who incites the people. And truly, I, having examined Him before you, have found no fault in this Man concerning those things of which you accuse Him. [15] No, neither has Herod, for he sent him back to us. Look, nothing worthy of death has been done by Him. [16] I will therefore chastise Him and release Him." [17] For he was obligated to release one man to them at the feast. [18] But they all cried out at once saying, "Take this Man away and release Barabbas to us!" [19] This man had been thrown in prison for an insurrection in the city and for murder. [20] Therefore Pilate spoke to them again, desiring to release Jesus. [21] But they cried out, "Crucify Him! Crucify Him!" [22] He said to them a third time, "Why, what evil has He done? I have found in Him no cause worthy of death. I will therefore chastise Him and release Him." [23] But they insisted with loud voices, asking that He be crucified. And the voices of these men and of the chief priests prevailed. [24] So Pilate gave the sentence as they demanded. [25] He released to them the man who was thrown in prison for insurrection and murder, whom they asked for. But he sentenced Jesus according to their will.

The Crucifixion
Mt 27:32–44; Mk 15:21–32; Jn 19:17–27

[26] As they led Him away, they seized Simon of Cyrene, who was coming from the country, and they laid the cross on him to carry it behind Jesus. [27] A large number of people followed Him, including women who mourned and lamented Him. [28] Jesus turned to them, saying, "Daughters of Jerusalem, weep not for Me, but weep for yourselves and for your children. [29] Listen, the days are coming when they will say, 'Blessed are the barren, who never bore and never nursed!' [30] Then

they will begin to say to the mountains, 'Fall on us,'
and to the hills, 'Cover us.'

[31] For if men do these things when the tree is green, what will happen when it is dry?" [32] Two different men, who were criminals, also were led with Him to be killed. [33] When they came to the place which is called The Skull, there they crucified Him and the criminals, one on the right and one on the left. [34] Jesus said, "Father, forgive them, for they know not what they do." And they divided His clothes by casting lots.

[35] The people stood by watching. But the rulers with them scoffed, saying, "He saved others. Let Him save Himself if He is the Christ, the Chosen One of God." [36] And the soldiers also mocked Him, coming to Him and offering Him sour wine, [37] saying, "If You are the King of the Jews, save Yourself." [38] An inscription was written over Him in letters of Greek and Latin and Hebrew:

THIS IS THE KING OF THE JEWS.

[39] One of the criminals who were hanged blasphemed Him, saying, "If You are the Christ, save Yourself and us!" [40] But the other rebuked him, saying, "Do you not fear God, seeing you are under the same sentence? [41] And we indeed, justly. For we are receiving the due reward of our deeds. But this Man has done nothing amiss." [42] Then he said to Jesus, "Lord, remember me when You come into Your kingdom." [43] Jesus said to him, "Truly, I tell you, today you will be with Me in Paradise."

The Death of Jesus
Mt 27:45–56; Mk 15:33–41; Jn 19:28–30

[44] It was now about the sixth hour, and darkness came over all the land until the ninth hour, [45] while the sun was darkened. And the veil of the temple was torn in the middle. [46] And Jesus cried out with a loud voice, "Father, into Your hands I commit My spirit." Having said this, He gave up the spirit. [47] When the centurion saw what had happened, he glorified God and said, "Certainly, this was a righteous Man." [48] All the crowds who came together to that sight, witnessing what occurred, struck their chests and returned. [49] But all those who knew Him and the women accompanying Him from Galilee stood at a distance, seeing these things.

The Burial of Jesus
Mt 27:57–61; Mk 15:42–47; Jn 19:38–42

[50] Now there was a man named Joseph, a member of the Council, who was a good and just man. [51] He had not consented to their counsel and deed. He was from Arimathea, a city of the Jews, and he himself was also waiting for the kingdom of God. [52] This man went to Pilate and asked for the body of Jesus. [53] Then he took Him down, and wrapped Him in linen, and placed Him in a hewn tomb, where no one had ever been buried. [54] It was the Day of Preparation, and the Sabbath was drawing near. [55] The women who came with Him from Galilee followed, and saw the tomb and how His body was placed. [56] Then they returned and prepared spices and ointments. On the Sabbath they rested according to the commandment.

The Resurrection of Jesus
Mt 28:1–10; Mk 16:1–8; Jn 20:1–10

24 Now on the first day of the week, very early in the morning, they, and certain other women with them, came to the tomb bringing the spices they had prepared. [2] They found the stone rolled away from the tomb. [3] But when they entered, they did not find the body of the Lord Jesus. [4] While they were greatly perplexed concerning this, suddenly two men stood by them in shining garments. [5] As they were afraid and bowed their faces to the ground, they said to them, "Why do you seek the living among the dead? [6] He is not here, but has risen! Remember how He spoke to you while He was still in Galilee, [7] saying, 'The Son of Man must be delivered into the hands of sinful men, and be crucified, and on the third day rise again.'" [8] Then they remembered His words.

[9] And they returned from the tomb and reported all these things to the eleven and to all the rest. [10] It was Mary Magdalene and Joanna, Mary the mother of James, and other women with them, who told these things to the apostles. [11] But their words seemed like fables to them, and they did not believe them. [12] But Peter rose and ran to the tomb. Stooping down, he saw the linen clothes lying by themselves. He departed, wondering in himself what had happened.

The Walk to Emmaus
Mk 16:12–13

[13] Now that same day two of them were going to a village called Emmaus, about seven miles *[1]* from Jerusalem. [14] They were talking with each other about all these things that had happened. [15] While they communed and reasoned together, Jesus Himself drew near

---

[1] 13 Gk. *60 stadia,* or 11 kilometers.

and went with them. [16] But their eyes were kept from recognizing Him.

[17] He said to them, "What kind of communication are you sharing with one another while you are walking and are sad?"

[18] One of them, named Cleopas, answered Him, "Are You the only foreigner in Jerusalem who does not know what has happened there in these days?"

[19] He said to them, "What things?"

They said to Him, "Concerning Jesus of Nazareth, who was a prophet, powerful in deed and word before God and all the people, [20] and how our chief priests and rulers handed Him over to be sentenced to death and crucified Him. [21] But we were hoping that it was He who was to redeem Israel. Moreover, today is the third day since these things happened. [22] Even some women from among us, who arrived early at the tomb, surprised us. [23] When they did not find His body, they returned saying that they had even seen a vision of angels, who said that He was alive. [24] Then some of those who were with us went to the tomb and found it just as the women had said. But they did not see Him."

[25] He said to them, "O fools! And slow of heart to believe what the prophets have spoken! [26] Was it not necessary for the Christ to suffer these things and to enter His glory?" [27] And beginning with Moses and all the Prophets, He explained to them the things concerning Himself in all the Scriptures.

[28] They drew near the village where they were traveling, and He seemed to be going farther. [29] But they urged Him, saying, "Stay with us. For it is nearly evening and the day is far spent." So He went in to stay with them.

[30] As He sat at supper with them, He took the bread, blessed it and broke it, and gave it to them. [31] Then their eyes were opened, and they recognized Him. And He vanished out of their sight. [32] They said to each other, "Did not our hearts burn within us while He talked to us on the way and while He opened the Scriptures to us?"

[33] They rose up and returned to Jerusalem at once. And they found the eleven and those who were with them assembled together, [34] saying, "The Lord has risen indeed, and has appeared to Simon!"

[35] Then they reported what had happened on the way, and how He was recognized by them in the breaking of the bread.

The Appearance to the Disciples
Mt 28:16–20; Mk 16:14–18; Jn 20:19–23; Ac 1:6–8

[36] As they were saying this, Jesus Himself stood among them and said to them, "Peace be unto you."

[37] They were terrified and frightened, and supposed that they saw a spirit. [38] He said to them, "Why are you troubled, and why do doubts arise in your hearts? [39] See My hands and My feet, that it is I Myself. Feel Me and see. For a spirit does not have flesh and bones as you see that I have."

[40] When He said this, He showed them His hands and His feet. [41] And while they yet disbelieved for joy and wondered, He said to them, "Do you have any food here?" [42] They gave Him a piece of broiled fish and some honeycomb. [43] And He took it and ate it before them.

[44] He said to them, "These are the words which I spoke to you while I was still with you, that all things must be fulfilled which were written in the Law of Moses and in the Prophets and in the Psalms concerning Me."

[45] Then He opened their minds to understand the Scriptures. [46] He said to them, "Thus it is written, and accordingly it was necessary for the Christ to suffer and to rise from the dead the third day, [47] and that repentance and remission of sins should be preached in His name to all nations, beginning at Jerusalem. [48] You are witnesses of these things. [49] And look, I am sending the promise of My Father upon you. But wait in the city of Jerusalem until you are clothed with power from on high."

The Ascension
Mk 16:19–20; Ac 1:9–11

[50] Then He led them out as far as Bethany, and He lifted up His hands and blessed them. [51] While He blessed them, He parted from them and was carried up into heaven. [52] Then they worshipped Him, and returned to Jerusalem with great joy, [53] and were continually in the temple, praising and blessing God. Amen.

JOHN

The Word Became Flesh

1 In the beginning was the Word, and the Word was with God, and the Word was God. [2] He was in the beginning with God. [3] All things were created through Him, and without Him nothing was created that was created. [4] In Him was life, and the life was the light of mankind. [5] The light shines in darkness, but the darkness has not overcome it.

[6] There was a man sent from God whose name was John. [7] This man came as a witness in order to testify concerning the Light, that all men through Him might believe. [8] He was not this Light, but was sent in order to testify concerning the Light.

[9] The true Light, which enlightens everyone, was coming into the world. [10] He was in the world, and the world was created through Him, yet the world did not know Him. [11] He came to His own, and His own people did not receive Him. [12] Yet to all who received Him, He gave the power to become sons of God, to those who believed in His name, [13] who were born not of blood, nor of the will of the flesh, nor of the will of man, but of God.

[14] The Word became flesh and dwelt among us, and we saw His glory, the glory as the only Son of the Father, full of grace and truth.

[15] John bore witness of Him and cried out, "This was He of whom I said, 'He who comes after me is preferred before me, for He was before me.' " [16] We have all received from His fullness grace upon grace. [17] For the law was given through Moses; grace and truth came through Jesus Christ. [18] No one has seen God at any time. The only Son, who is at the Father's side, has made Him known.

The Testimony of John the Baptist
Mt 3:1–12; Mk 1:2–8; Lk 3:15–17

[19] Now this is the testimony of John, when the Jews sent priests and Levites from Jerusalem to ask him, "Who are you?" [20] He confessed, and did not deny, but confessed, "I am not the Christ."

[21] They asked him, "Who then? Are you Elijah?"

He said, "I am not."

"Are you the Prophet?"

He answered, "No."

[22] They said to him then, "Who are you? Tell us so that we may give an answer to those who sent us. What do you say concerning yourself?"

[23] John said, "I am the voice of one crying out in the wilderness, 'Make straight the way of the Lord,'[1] just as the prophet Isaiah said."

---

[1] 23 Isa 40:3.

[24] Now those who were sent were from the Pharisees. [25] They asked him, "Why do you baptize then, if you are not the Christ, nor Elijah, nor the Prophet?" [26] John answered them, "I baptize with water, but One stands among you, whom you do not know. [27] This is He who comes after me, who is preferred before me, the strap of whose sandal I am not worthy to untie." [28] These things took place in Bethany beyond the Jordan, where John was baptizing.

The Lamb of God

[29] The next day John saw Jesus coming toward him and said, "Look, the Lamb of God, who takes away the sin of the world. [30] This is He of whom I said, 'After me comes a Man who is preferred before me, for He was before me.' [31] I did not know Him, but for this reason I came baptizing with water: so that He might be revealed to Israel." [32] Then John bore witness, saying, "I saw the Spirit descending from heaven like a dove, and it remained on Him. [33] I did not know Him, but He who sent me to baptize with water said to me, 'The One on whom you see the Spirit descending and remaining, this is He who baptizes with the Holy Spirit.' [34] I have seen and have borne witness that He is the Son of God."

The First Disciples

[35] Again, the next day John was standing with two of his disciples. [36] Looking upon Jesus as He walked, he said, "Look, the Lamb of God!" [37] The two disciples heard him speak, and they followed Jesus. [38] Then Jesus turned, saw them following, and said to them, "What do you seek?"

And they said to Him, "Rabbi" (which means Teacher), "where are You staying?"

[39] Jesus said to them, "Come and see." So they came and saw where He stayed and remained with Him that day, for it was about the tenth hour. [40] One of the two who heard John speak, and followed Him, was Andrew, Simon Peter's brother. [41] He first found his own brother Simon, and said to him, "We have found the Messiah" (which means the Christ). [42] Then he brought him to Jesus.

When Jesus saw him, He said, "You are Simon the son of John. You shall be called Cephas" (which means Peter).

The Calling of Philip and Nathanael

[43] The next day Jesus wanted to go to Galilee, and He found Philip, and said to him, "Follow Me." [44] Now Philip was from Bethsaida, the city of Andrew and Peter. [45] Philip found Nathanael and said to him, "We have found Him of whom Moses in the law, as well as the prophets, wrote, Jesus of Nazareth, the son of Joseph." [46] Nathanael said to him, "Can any good thing come out of Nazareth?"

Philip said to him, "Come and see." [47] Jesus saw Nathanael coming to Him and said concerning him, "Here is an Israelite indeed, in whom is no guile."

[48] Nathanael said to Him, "How do You know me?"

Jesus answered him, "Before Philip called you, when you were under the fig tree, I saw you." [49] Nathanael answered Him, "Rabbi, You are the Son of God! You are the King of Israel!" [50] Jesus answered him, "Because I said to you, 'I saw you under the fig tree,' do you believe? You will see greater things than these." [51] And He said to him, "Truly, truly I say to you, hereafter you shall see heaven opened and the angels of God ascending and descending upon the Son of Man."

The Wedding at Cana

2 On the third day there was a wedding in Cana of Galilee. The mother of Jesus was there. [2] Both Jesus and His disciples were invited to the wedding. [3] When the wine ran out, the mother of Jesus said to Him, "They have no wine."

[4] Jesus said to her, "Woman, what does this have to do with Me? My hour has not yet come."

[5] His mother said to the servants, "Whatever He says to you, do it."

[6] Six water pots made of stone were sitting there, used for ceremonial cleansing by the Jews, containing twenty to thirty gallons[1] each.

[7] Jesus said to them, "Fill the water pots with water." And they filled them up to the brim.

[8] Then He said to them, "Now draw some out, and take it to the master of the feast."

And they took it. [9] When the master of the feast tasted the water that had been turned into wine, and did not know where it came from (though the servants who drew the water knew), the master of the feast called the bridegroom, [10] and he said to him, "Every man serves the good wine first, and after men have drunk freely, then the poor wine is served. But you have kept the good wine until now."

[11] This, the first of His signs, Jesus did in Cana of Galilee, and He revealed His glory, and His disciples believed in Him.

[12] After this He, and His mother, and His brothers, and His disciples went down to Capernaum. They remained there a few days.

The Cleansing of the Temple
Mt 21:12–17; Mk 11:15–17; Lk 19:45–48

[13] The Passover of the Jews was at hand, and Jesus went up to Jerusalem. [14] In the temple He found those who were selling oxen and sheep and doves, and the moneychangers sitting there. [15] When He had made a whip of cords, He drove them all out of the temple, with the sheep and oxen. He poured out the changers' money and overturned the tables. [16] He said to those who sold doves, "Take these things away! Do not make My Father's house a house of merchandise!" [17] His disciples remembered that it was written, "Zeal for Your house will consume Me."[2]

[18] Then the Jews said to Him, "What sign do You show us, seeing that You do these things?"

[19] Jesus answered them, "Destroy this temple, and in three days I will raise it up."

[20] Then the Jews said, "It has taken forty-six years to build this temple, and will You raise it up in three days?" [21] But He was speaking concerning the temple of His body. [22] Therefore, when He was raised from the dead, His disciples remembered that He had said this to them. And they believed the Scripture and the word which Jesus had spoken.

Jesus Knows All Men

[23] Now when He was in Jerusalem at the Passover Feast, many believed in His name when they saw the signs which He did. [24] But Jesus did not entrust Himself to them, because He knew all men, [25] and did not need anyone to bear witness of man, for He knew what was in man.

Jesus and Nicodemus

3 There was a man of the Pharisees named Nicodemus, a ruler of the Jews. [2] He came to Jesus by night and said to Him, "Rabbi, we know that You are a teacher who has come from God. For no one can do these signs that You do unless God is with him."

[3] Jesus answered him, "Truly, truly I say to you, unless a man is born again,[3] he cannot see the kingdom of God."

[4] Nicodemus said to Him, "How can a man be born when he is old? Can he enter a second time into his mother's womb and be born?"

[5] Jesus answered, "Truly, truly I say to you, unless a man is born of water and the Spirit, he cannot enter the kingdom of God. [6] That which is born of the flesh is flesh, and that which is born of the Spirit is spirit. [7] Do not marvel that I said to you, 'You must be born again.' [8] The wind blows where it wishes, and you hear its sound, but you do not know where it comes from or where it goes. So it is with everyone who is born of the Spirit."

[9] Nicodemus said to Him, "How can this be?"

[10] Jesus answered him, "Are you the teacher of Israel, but you do not know these things? [11] Truly, truly I say to you, We speak of what

---

[1] 6 Gk. 2 to 3 metretes, or 75 to 115 liters.   [2] 17 Ps 69:9.   [3] 3 Or born from above.

We know and bear witness of what We have seen, but you do not receive Our testimony. [12] If I have told you earthly things and you do not believe, how will you believe if I tell you heavenly things? [13] No one has ascended to heaven except He who descended from heaven, even the Son of Man who is in heaven. [14] Just as Moses lifted up the serpent in the wilderness, even so must the Son of Man be lifted up, [15] that whoever believes in Him should not perish, but may have eternal life.

[16] "For God so loved the world that He gave His only begotten Son, that whoever believes in Him should not perish, but have eternal life. [17] For God did not send His Son into the world to condemn the world, but that the world through Him might be saved. [18] He who believes in Him is not condemned. But he who does not believe is condemned already, because he has not believed in the name of the only begotten Son of God. [19] This is the verdict, that light has come into the world, and men loved darkness rather than light, because their deeds were evil. [20] For everyone who does evil hates the light and does not come to the light, lest his deeds should be exposed. [21] But he who does the truth comes to the light, that it may be revealed that his deeds have been done in God."

Jesus and John the Baptist

[22] After these things Jesus and His disciples came into the land of Judea. He remained with them there and baptized. [23] John also was baptizing in Aenon toward Salim, because much water was there. And people came and were baptized. [24] For John had not yet been put in prison. [25] Then a dispute arose between some of John's disciples and the Jews about ceremonial cleansing. [26] They came to John and said to him, "Rabbi, He who was with you beyond the Jordan, to whom you bore witness, look, He is baptizing, and everyone is going to Him."

[27] John answered, "A man can receive nothing unless it has been given to him from heaven. [28] You yourselves bear witness of me, that I said, 'I am not the Christ,' but 'I have been sent before Him.' [29] He who has the bride is the bridegroom. But the friend of the bridegroom, who stands and hears him, rejoices greatly at the bridegroom's voice. Therefore this joy of mine is fulfilled. [30] He must increase, but I must decrease."

He Who Comes From Heaven

[31] He who comes from above is above all. He who is of the earth is earthly and speaks of the earth. He who comes from heaven is above all. [32] He bears witness of what He has seen and heard, yet no one receives His testimony. [33] He who has received His testimony has certified that God is true. [34] For He whom God has sent speaks the words of God, for God gives the Spirit without measure to Him. [35] The Father loves the Son, and has placed all things into His hand. [36] He who believes in the Son has eternal life. He who does not believe the Son shall not see life, but the wrath of God remains on him.

Jesus and the Samaritan Woman

4 Now when the Lord learned that the Pharisees had heard that Jesus was making and baptizing more disciples than John [2] (though Jesus Himself did not baptize, but His disciples), [3] He left Judea and departed again to Galilee.

[4] Now it was necessary that He go through Samaria. [5] So He came to a city of Samaria which is called Sychar, near the plot of ground that Jacob gave to his son Joseph. [6] Jacob's well was there. Jesus, therefore, being exhausted from His journey, sat down by the well. It was about the sixth hour.

[7] A woman of Samaria came there to draw water. Jesus said to her, "Give Me a drink." [8] For His disciples had gone away into the city to buy food.

[9] Then the woman of Samaria said to Him, "How is it that You, being a Jew, ask a drink from me, a woman of Samaria?" For Jews have no dealings with Samaritans.

[10] Jesus answered her, "If you knew the gift of God, and who it is who is saying to you, 'Give Me a drink,' you would have asked Him, and He would have given you living water."

[11] The woman said to Him, "Sir, You have nothing to draw with, and the well is deep. Where then do You get that living water? [12] Are You greater than our father Jacob, who gave us the well and drank from it himself, along with his sons and his livestock?"

[13] Jesus said to her, "Everyone who drinks of this water will thirst again, [14] but whoever drinks of the water that I shall give him will never thirst. Indeed, the water that I shall give him will become in him a well of water springing up into eternal life."

[15] The woman said to Him, "Sir, give me this water, so that I will not thirst, nor come here to draw."

[16] Jesus said to her, "Go, call your husband, and come here."

[17] The woman answered, "I have no husband."

Jesus said to her, "You are right in saying, 'I have no husband,' [18] for you have had five husbands, and he whom you now have is not your husband. So you have spoken truthfully."

[19] The woman said to Him, "Sir, I perceive that You are a prophet. [20] Our fathers worshipped on this mountain, but you all say that in Jerusalem is the place where men ought to worship."

[21] Jesus said to her, "Woman, believe Me, the hour is coming when neither on this mountain nor in Jerusalem will you worship the Father. [22] You worship what you do not know; we know what we worship, for salvation is of the Jews. [23] Yet the hour is coming, and is now here, when the true worshippers will worship the Father in spirit and truth. For the Father seeks such to worship Him. [24] God is Spirit, and those who worship Him must worship Him in spirit and truth."

[25] The woman said to Him, "I know that Messiah is coming" (who is called Christ). "When He comes, He will tell us all things."

[26] Jesus said to her, "I who speak to you am He."

[27] Then His disciples came. They marveled that He talked with a woman. Yet no one said, "What do You seek?" or, "Why are You talking with her?"

[28] The woman then left her water pot, went her way into the city, and said to the men, [29] "Come, see a Man who told me all things that I ever did. Could this be the Christ?" [30] They went out of the city and came to Him.

[31] Meanwhile His disciples urged Him, saying, "Rabbi, eat."

[32] But He said to them, "I have food to eat of which you do not know."

[33] Therefore the disciples said one to another, "Has anyone brought Him anything to eat?"

[34] Jesus said to them, "My food is to do the will of Him who sent Me, and to finish His work. [35] Do you not say, 'There are yet four months, and then comes the harvest'? Listen! I say to you, lift up your eyes and look at the fields, for they are already white for harvest. [36] He who reaps receives wages, and gathers fruit that leads to eternal life, that both he who sows and he who reaps may rejoice together. [37] For in this is the saying true, 'One sows, and another reaps.' [38] I sent you to reap a crop for which you did not labor. And you have benefited from their labor."

[39] Many of the Samaritans of that city believed in Him because of the word of the woman who testified, "He told me all that I ever did." [40] So when the Samaritans came to Him, they asked Him to remain with them. And He stayed there two days. [41] And many more believed because of His word.

[42] They said to the woman, "Now we believe, not because of what you said, for we have heard for ourselves and know that this Man is indeed the Christ, the Savior of the world."

The Healing of the Nobleman's Son
Mt 8:5–13; Lk 7:1–10

[43] After the two days He departed from there and went to Galilee. [44] For Jesus Himself testified that a prophet has no honor in his own country. [45] Then, when He came to Galilee, the Galileans welcomed Him, having seen all the things He did at Jerusalem at the feast. For they had also gone to the feast.

[46] So Jesus came again to Cana of Galilee where He had made the water wine. And there was a certain nobleman whose son was sick in Capernaum. [47] When he heard that Jesus had come out of Judea into Galilee, he went to Him, pleading that He would come down and heal his son, for he was at the point of death.

[48] Then Jesus said to him, "Unless you see signs and wonders, you will not believe."

[49] The nobleman said to Him, "Sir, come down before my child dies."

[50] Jesus said to him, "Go your way. Your son lives." And the man believed the word that Jesus spoke to him, and he went his way. [51] While he was going down, his servants met him and told him, "Your son lives!" [52] When he inquired of them the hour when he began to heal, they answered, "Yesterday at the seventh hour the fever left him."

[53] Then the father knew that it was at the same hour in which Jesus said to him, "Your son lives." So he and his whole household believed.

[54] This was the second sign that Jesus did when He had come from Judea to Galilee.

The Healing at the Pool

5 After this there was a feast of the Jews, and Jesus went up to Jerusalem. [2] Now in Jerusalem by the Sheep Gate there is a pool, which in Hebrew is called Bethesda, having five porches. [3] In these lay a great crowd of invalids, blind, lame, and paralyzed, waiting for the moving of the water. [4] For an angel went down at a certain time into the pool and stirred up the water. After the stirring of the water, whoever stepped in first was healed of whatever disease he had. [5] A certain man was there who had an illness for thirty-eight years. [6] When Jesus saw him lying there, and knew that he had been in that condition now a long time, He said to him, "Do you want to be healed?"

[7] The sick man answered Him, "Sir, I have no one to put me into the pool when the water is stirred. But while I am coming, another steps down before me."

[8] Jesus said to him, "Rise, take up your bed and walk." [9] Immediately the man was healed, took up his bed, and walked.

That day was the Sabbath. [10] The Jews therefore said to him who was cured, "It is the Sabbath day. It is not lawful for you to carry your bed."

[11] He answered them, "He who healed me said to me, 'Take up your bed and walk.' "

[12] So they asked him, "Who is the Man who said to you, 'Take up your bed and walk'?"

[13] Now the man who was healed did not know who it was, for Jesus had withdrawn, as there was a crowd in that place.

[14] Afterward Jesus found him in the temple, and said to him, "See, you have become whole. Sin no more lest something worse happens to you." [15] The man departed and told the Jews that it was Jesus who had healed him.

[16] So the Jews persecuted Jesus and sought to kill Him, because He had done these things on the Sabbath day. [17] Jesus answered them, "My Father is working still, and I am working." [18] So the Jews sought even more to kill Him, because He not only had broken the Sabbath, but also said that God was His Father, making Himself equal with God.

The Authority of the Son

[19] Then Jesus said to them, "Truly, truly I say to you, the Son can do nothing of Himself, but what He sees the Father do. For whatever He does, likewise the Son does. [20] For the Father loves the Son and shows Him all things that He Himself does. And He will show Him greater works than these so that you may marvel. [21] For as the Father raises the dead and gives them life, even so the Son gives life to whom He will. [22] The Father judges no one, but has committed all judgment to the Son, [23] that all men should honor the Son, just as they honor the Father. He who does not honor the Son does not honor the Father who sent Him.

[24] "Truly, truly I say to you, whoever hears My word and believes in Him who sent Me has eternal life and shall not come into condemnation, but has passed from death into life. [25] Truly, truly I say to you, the hour is coming, and is now here, when the dead will hear the voice of the Son of God, and those who hear will live. [26] For as the Father has life in Himself, so He has given to the Son to have life in Himself, [27] and has given Him authority to execute judgment also, because He is the Son of Man.

[28] "Do not marvel at this. For the hour is coming in which all who are in the graves will hear His voice [29] and come out—those who have done good to the resurrection of life, and those who have done evil to the resurrection of judgment. [30] I can do nothing of Myself. As I hear, I judge. My judgment is just, because I seek not My own will, but the will of the Father who sent Me.

Witnesses to Jesus

[31] "If I bear witness of Myself, My testimony is not true. [32] There is another who bears witness of Me, and I know that the testimony which He bears of Me is true.

[33] "You sent to John, and he bore witness of the truth. [34] I do not receive testimony from man, but I say these things that you may be saved. [35] He was a burning and a shining lamp, and you were willing for a season to rejoice in his light.

[36] "I have greater testimony than that of John. The works which the Father has given Me to finish, the very works that I do, bear witness of Me, that the Father has sent Me. [37] The Father Himself, who has sent Me, has borne witness of Me. You have neither heard His voice at any time, nor seen His form. [38] You do not have His word abiding in you, for you do not believe the One He has sent. [39] You search the Scriptures, because you think in them you have eternal life. These are they who bear witness of Me. [40] Yet you are not willing to come to Me that you may have life.

[41] "I do not receive honor from men. [42] But I know you, that you do not have the love of God in you. [43] I have come in My Father's name, but you do not receive Me. If another comes in his own name, you will receive him. [44] How can you believe, who receive glory from one another and do not seek the glory that comes from the only God?

[45] "Do not think that I shall accuse you to the Father. There is one who accuses you—Moses, in whom you trust. [46] For if you believed Moses, you would believe Me, for he wrote of Me. [47] But if you do not believe his writings, how will you believe My words?"

The Feeding of the Five Thousand
Mt 14:13–21; Mk 6:30–44; Lk 9:10–17

6 After these things Jesus went across the Sea of Galilee, which is the Sea of Tiberias. [2] And a great crowd followed Him, because they saw His signs which He did for the sick. [3] Then Jesus went up on a mountain, and He sat there with His disciples. [4] Now the Passover, the feast of the Jews, was near.

[5] When Jesus looked up and saw a great crowd coming to Him, He said to Philip, "Where shall we buy bread that these may eat?" [6] He said this to test him, for He Himself knew what He would do.

[7] Philip answered Him, "Two hundred denarii¹ worth of bread is not sufficient for each of them to receive but a little."

[8] One of His disciples, Andrew, Simon Peter's brother, said to Him, [9] "There is a boy here who has five barley loaves and two small fish. But what are they among so many?"

[10] Jesus said, "Make the people sit down." Now there was much grass in the place. So the men sat down, numbering about five thousand. [11] Jesus then took the loaves, and when He had given thanks, He distributed them to the disciples, and the disciples to those who were sitting down; and likewise, they distributed the fish, as much as they wanted.

[12] When they were filled, He told His disciples, "Collect the fragments that remain, that nothing may be lost." [13] So they collected them and filled twelve baskets with the fragments of the five barley loaves which were left over by those who had eaten.

[14] When those men saw the sign which He had done, they then said, "This is truly the Prophet who is to come into the world." [15] Therefore, knowing that they would come and take Him by force to make Him king, Jesus departed again to a mountain by Himself alone.

Walking on the Water
Mt 14:22–27; Mk 6:45–52

[16] Now when evening came, His disciples went down to the sea. [17] They got into a boat and went across the sea toward Capernaum.

---

1 7 Eight months' wages.

It was now dark, and Jesus had not come to them. [18] The sea was stirred up because a strong wind was blowing. [19] So when they had rowed about three or four miles,[1] they saw Jesus walking on the sea and coming near the boat. And they were afraid. [20] But He said to them, "It is I. Do not be afraid." [21] Then they gladly received Him into the boat, and immediately the boat was at the land to which they were going.

Jesus the Bread of Life

[22] The following day the people who stood on the other side of the sea saw that there was no other boat there, except the one which His disciples had entered, and that Jesus had not entered the boat with His disciples, but that His disciples had gone away alone. [23] However, other boats came from Tiberias near the place where they ate bread when the Lord had given thanks. [24] When the people therefore saw that neither Jesus nor His disciples were there, they also got into boats and came to Capernaum, looking for Jesus.

[25] When they found Him on the other side of the sea, they said to Him, "Rabbi, when did You come here?"

[26] Jesus answered them, "Truly, truly I say to you, you seek Me not because you saw signs, but because you ate of the loaves and were filled. [27] Do not work for the food which perishes, but for that food which endures to eternal life, which the Son of Man will give you. For God the Father has set His seal on Him."

[28] Then they asked Him, "What shall we do that we may work the works of God?"

[29] Jesus answered them, "This is the work of God, that you believe in Him whom He has sent."

[30] Therefore they said to Him, "What sign do You show then, that we may see and believe You? What work will You perform? [31] Our fathers ate manna in the desert. As it is written, 'He gave them bread from heaven to eat.'[2]"

[32] Then Jesus said, "Truly, truly I say to you, Moses did not give you the bread from heaven, but My Father gives you the true bread from heaven. [33] For the bread of God is He who comes down from heaven and gives life to the world."

[34] Then they said to Him, "Lord, give us this bread always."

[35] Jesus said to them, "I am the bread of life. Whoever comes to Me shall never hunger, and whoever believes in Me shall never thirst. [36] But I told you that you have seen Me, and yet do not believe. [37] All whom the Father gives Me will come to Me, and he who comes to Me I will never cast out. [38] For I came down from heaven, not to do My own will, but the will of Him who sent Me. [39] This is the will of the Father who has sent Me, that of all whom He has given Me, I should lose nothing, but should raise it up at the last day. [40] This is the will of Him who sent Me, that everyone who sees the Son and believes in Him may have eternal life, and I will raise him up on the last day."

[41] The Jews then murmured about Him, because He said, "I am the bread which came down from heaven." [42] They said, "Is this not Jesus, the son of Joseph, whose father and mother we know? How is it then that He says, 'I have come down from heaven'? "

[43] Jesus therefore answered them, "Do not murmur among yourselves. [44] No one can come to Me unless the Father who has sent Me draws him. And I will raise him up on the last day. [45] It is written in the Prophets, 'They shall all be taught by God.'[3] Therefore everyone who has heard and has learned of the Father comes to Me. [46] Not that anyone has seen the Father, except He who is from God. He has seen the Father. [47] Truly, truly I say to you, whoever believes in Me has eternal life. [48] I am the bread of life. [49] Your fathers ate manna in the wilderness, and they died. [50] This is the bread which comes down from heaven, that one may eat of it and not die. [51] I am the living bread which came down from heaven. If anyone eats of this bread, he will live forever. The bread which I shall give for the life of the world is My flesh."

[52] The Jews therefore quarreled among themselves, saying, "How can this Man give us His flesh to eat?"

[53] Jesus said to them, "Truly, truly I say to you, unless you eat the flesh of the Son of Man and drink His blood, you have no life in you.

[54] Whoever eats My flesh and drinks My blood has eternal life. And I will raise him up on the last day. [55] For My flesh is food indeed, and My blood is drink indeed. [56] Whoever eats My flesh and drinks My blood remains in Me, and I in him. [57] As the living Father sent Me, and I live because of the Father, so whoever feeds on Me also will live because of Me. [58] This is the bread which came down from heaven, not as your fathers ate manna and died. He who eats this bread will live forever." [59] He said these things in the synagogue, as He taught in Capernaum.

The Words of Eternal Life

[60] When they heard this, many of His disciples said, "This is a hard saying. Who can listen to it?"

[61] Knowing in Himself that His disciples murmured about it, Jesus said to them, "Does this offend you? [62] Then what if you see the Son of Man ascend to where He was before? [63] It is the Spirit who gives life. The flesh profits nothing. The words that I speak to you are spirit and are life. [64] But there are some of you who do not believe." For Jesus knew from the beginning who they were who did not believe, and who it was who would betray Him. [65] Then He said, "For this reason I have said to you that no one can come to Me unless it were given him by My Father."

[66] From that time many of His disciples went back and walked no more with Him.

[67] So Jesus said to the twelve, "Do you also want to go away?"

[68] Simon Peter answered Him, "Lord, to whom shall we go? You have the words of eternal life. [69] We have believed and have come to know that You are the Christ, the Son of the living God."

[70] Jesus answered them, "Have I not chosen you, the twelve, and yet one of you is a devil?" [71] He spoke of Judas Iscariot, the son of Simon. For it was he who would betray Him, being one of the twelve.

The Unbelief of Jesus' Brothers

7 After these things Jesus walked in Galilee. He would not walk in Judea, because the Jews were seeking to kill Him. [2] Now the Jews' Feast of Tabernacles was at hand. [3] His brothers therefore said to Him, "Depart from here and go into Judea, that Your disciples also may see the works that You do. [4] For no one does anything in secret, while he himself seeks to be known openly. If You do these things, reveal Yourself to the world." [5] For even His brothers did not believe in Him.

[6] Therefore Jesus told them, "My time has not yet come, but your time is always fitting. [7] The world cannot hate you. But it hates Me, because I testify concerning it, that its works are evil. [8] You go up to this feast. I am not going up to this feast yet, because My time has not yet fully come." [9] Having said these things to them, He remained in Galilee.

Jesus at the Feast of Tabernacles

[10] However, after His brothers had gone up to the feast, then He also went up, not publicly, but secretly. [11] Then the Jews looked for Him at the feast, and said, "Where is He?"

[12] There was much complaining among the people concerning Him. For some said, "He is a good Man."

Others said, "No, He deceives the people." [13] Yet no one spoke openly of Him for fear of the Jews.

[14] Now about the middle of the feast Jesus went up into the temple and began teaching. [15] The Jews marveled, saying, "How has this Man become educated, having never been taught?"

[16] Jesus answered them, "My teaching is not Mine, but His who sent Me. [17] If any man desires to do His will, he shall know whether the teaching is from God or whether I speak on My own authority. [18] He who speaks on his own authority seeks his own glory. But He who seeks the glory of Him who sent Him is true, and no unrighteousness is in Him. [19] Did Moses not give you the law, and yet none of you keeps the law? Why do you seek to kill Me?"

[20] The people answered and said, "You have a demon. Who is seeking to kill You?"

---

[1] 19 Gk. *25 to 30 stadia*, or 5 or 6 kilometers.   [2] 31 Ex 16:4, 15; Ne 9:15; Ps 78:24–25.   [3] 45 Isa 54:13.

[21] Jesus answered them, "I did one work, and you all marvel. [22] Yet, because Moses gave you circumcision, you circumcise a man on the Sabbath day (although it did not come from Moses, but from the Patriarchs). [23] If a man receives circumcision on the Sabbath day, so that the Law of Moses should not be broken, are you angry at Me because I completely healed a man on the Sabbath day? [24] Do not judge according to appearance, but practice righteous judgment."

Is He the Christ?

[25] Then some of them from Jerusalem said, "Is this not He whom they seek to kill? [26] Look! He speaks publicly, and they say nothing to Him. Do the rulers indeed know that this is really the Christ? [27] But we know where this Man is from. When the Christ comes, no one will know where He is from."

[28] Then Jesus, still teaching in the temple, cried out, "You know Me and you likewise know where I am from. I have not come on My own authority, but He who sent Me is true, whom you do not know. [29] But I know Him, for I am from Him, and He sent Me."

[30] So they tried to seize Him, but no one laid hands on Him, because His hour had not yet come. [31] Still, many of the people believed in Him and said, "When the Christ comes, will He do more signs than these which this Man has done?"

Officials Sent to Arrest Jesus

[32] The Pharisees heard the people murmuring these things concerning Him. So the Pharisees and the chief priests sent officers to arrest Him. [33] Then Jesus said to them, "I shall be with you a little while longer, and then I go to Him who sent Me. [34] You will look for Me and you will not find Me. And where I am, you cannot come."

[35] The Jews said among themselves, "Where does He intend to go that we shall not find Him? Does He intend to go to the Dispersion among the Greeks and teach the Greeks? [36] What kind of saying is this which He said, 'You will look for Me and you will not find Me. And where I am, you cannot come'?"

Rivers of Living Water

[37] On the last and greatest day of the feast, Jesus stood and cried out, "If anyone is thirsty, let him come to Me and drink. [38] He who believes in Me, as the Scripture has said, out of his heart shall flow rivers of living water." [39] By this He spoke of the Spirit, whom those who believe in Him would receive. For the Holy Spirit was not yet given, because Jesus was not yet glorified.

Division Among the People

[40] Therefore when they heard these words, many of the people said, "Truly, this is the Prophet."

[41] Others said, "This is the Christ."

But some said, "Will the Christ come out of Galilee? [42] Has the Scripture not said that the Christ comes from the seed of David, out of the town of Bethlehem where David was?" [43] So there was a division among the people because of Him. [44] Some of them wanted to arrest Him, but no one laid hands on Him.

The Unbelief of Those in Authority

[45] Then the officers came to the chief priests and Pharisees, who said to them, "Why did you not bring Him?"

[46] The officers answered, "No man has ever spoken like this Man."

[47] Then the Pharisees answered them, "Are you also deceived? [48] Have any of the rulers or the Pharisees believed in Him? [49] Not at all. This crowd who does not know the law is accursed."

[50] Nicodemus, being one of them who came to Jesus by night, said to them, [51] "Does our law judge a man before it hears him and knows what he is doing?"

[52] They answered him, "Are you also from Galilee? Search and see that no prophet arises out of Galilee."

The Woman Caught in Adultery

[53] Then everyone went to his own house. [1]

8 But Jesus went to the Mount of Olives. [2] Early in the morning He returned to the temple. All the people came to Him, and He sat down and taught them. [3] The scribes and Pharisees brought a woman caught in adultery. When they had put her in the middle, [4] they said to Him, "Teacher, this woman was caught in the very act of adultery. [5] Now Moses in the law commanded us to stone such, but what do You say?" [6] They said this, testing Him, that they might have something of which to accuse Him.

But Jesus stooped down and wrote on the ground with His finger, as though He did not hear them. [7] So when they continued asking Him, He stood up and said to them, "Let him who is without sin among you be the first to throw a stone at her." [8] Again He stooped down and wrote on the ground.

[9] Being convicted by their conscience, those who heard it went out one by one, beginning with the eldest even to the last. Jesus was left alone, and the woman standing in the midst. [10] When Jesus had stood up and saw no one but the woman, He said to her, "Woman, where are your accusers? Did no one condemn you?"

[11] She said, "No one, Lord."

Jesus said to her, "Neither do I condemn you. Go and sin no more."

Jesus the Light of the World

[12] Again, Jesus spoke to them, saying, "I am the light of the world. Whoever follows Me shall not walk in the darkness, but shall have the light of life."

[13] The Pharisees therefore said to Him, "You bear witness of Yourself. Your testimony is not true."

[14] Jesus answered them, "Though I bear witness of Myself, My testimony is true. For I know where I came from and where I am going. But you do not know where I came from or where I am going. [15] You judge according to the flesh. I judge no one. [16] Yet if I do judge, My judgment is true. For I am not alone, but I am with the Father who sent Me. [17] Even in your law it is written that the testimony of two men is true. [18] I am One who bears witness of Myself, and the Father that sent Me bears witness of Me."

[19] Then they said to Him, "Where is Your Father?"

Jesus answered, "You know neither Me nor My Father. If you knew Me, you would know My Father also." [20] Jesus spoke these words in the treasury, as He taught in the temple. No one arrested Him, for His hour had not yet come.

Where I Am Going You Cannot Come

[21] Again, Jesus said to them, "I am going away, and you will seek Me, and you will die in your sins. Where I am going, you cannot come."

[22] So the Jews said, "Will He kill Himself? For He said, 'Where I am going, you cannot come.'"

[23] He said to them, "You are from below; I am from above. You are of this world; I am not of this world. [24] Therefore I said to you that you will die in your sins. For unless you believe that I am He, you will die in your sins."

[25] They said to Him, "Who are You?"

Jesus said to them, "Just who I have been telling you from the beginning. [26] I have many things to say and to judge concerning you, but He who sent Me is true. So I tell the world what I heard from Him."

[27] They did not understand that He spoke to them of the Father. [28] So Jesus said to them, "When you lift up the Son of Man, then you will know that I am He, and I do nothing of Myself. But I speak these things as My Father taught Me. [29] He who sent Me is with Me. The Father has not left Me alone, for I always do those things that please Him." [30] As He spoke these words, many believed in Him.

The Truth Will Set You Free

[31] Then Jesus said to those Jews who believed Him, "If you remain in My word, then you are truly My disciples. [32] You shall know the truth, and the truth shall set you free."

[33] They answered Him, "We are Abraham's seed and have never been in bondage to anyone. Why do You say, 'You shall be set free'?"

[34] Jesus answered them, "Truly, truly I say to you, whoever commits sin is a slave of sin. [35] Now a slave does not remain in the house forever, but a son remains forever. [36] Therefore if the Son sets you free, you shall be free indeed. [37] I know that you are Abraham's seed. But you seek to kill Me, because My word has no place in you. [38] I am telling what I have seen with My Father, and you are doing what you have seen with your father."

Your Father the Devil

[39] They answered Him, "Abraham is our father."

Jesus said to them, "If you were Abraham's children, you would do the works of Abraham. [40] But now you seek to kill Me, a Man who has told you the truth which I heard from God. Abraham did not do this. [41] You are doing the works of your father."

Then they said to Him, "We were not born of sexual immorality. We have one Father: God."

[42] Jesus said to them, "If God were your Father, you would love Me, for I came from God and proceeded into the world. I did not come of My own authority, but He sent Me. [43] Why do you not understand My speaking? Because you cannot bear to hear My word. [44] You are of your father the devil, and you want to do the desires of your father. He was a murderer from the beginning, and does not stand in the truth, because there is no truth in him. When he lies, he speaks from his own nature, for he is a liar and the father of lies. [45] Yet because I tell the truth, you do not believe Me. [46] Which of you convicts Me of sin? If I speak the truth, why do you not believe Me? [47] He who is of God hears God's words. Therefore, you do not hear them, because you are not of God."

The Preexistence of Jesus

[48] The Jews answered Him, "Do we not rightly say that You are a Samaritan and have a demon?"

[49] Jesus answered, "I do not have a demon. But I honor My Father, and you dishonor Me. [50] I do not seek glory for Myself. There is One who seeks it and judges. [51] Truly, truly I say to you, if anyone keeps My word, he shall never see death."

[52] Then the Jews said to Him, "Now we know that You have a demon. Abraham and the prophets died, and You say, 'If a man keeps My word, he shall never taste death.' [53] Are You greater than our father Abraham, who died? The prophets are dead! Who do You make Yourself out to be?"

[54] Jesus answered, "If I glorify Myself, My glory is nothing. It is My Father who glorifies Me, of whom you say that He is your God. [55] Yet you have not known Him, but I know Him. If I say, 'I do not know Him,' I shall be a liar like you. But I know Him and keep His word. [56] Your father Abraham rejoiced to see My day. He saw it and was glad."

[57] Then the Jews said to Him, "You are not yet fifty years old. Have You seen Abraham?"

[58] Jesus said to them, "Truly, truly I say to you, before Abraham was born, I AM." [59] Then they took up stones to throw at Him. But Jesus hid Himself and went out of the temple. Going through their midst, He passed by.

The Healing of a Man Born Blind

9 As Jesus passed by, He saw a man blind from birth. [2] His disciples asked Him, "Rabbi, who sinned, this man or his parents, that he was born blind?"

[3] Jesus answered, "Neither this man nor his parents sinned. But it happened so that the works of God might be displayed in him. [4] I must do the works of Him who sent Me while it is day. Night is coming when no one can work. [5] While I am in the world, I am the light of the world."

[6] When He had said this, He spat on the ground and made clay with the saliva. He anointed the eyes of the blind man with the clay, [7] and said to him, "Go, wash in the pool of Siloam" (which means "Sent"). So he went away and washed, and returned seeing.

[8] The neighbors and those who had previously seen that he was blind said, "Is this not he who sat and begged?" [9] Some said, "This is he."

Others said, "He is like him."

But he said, "I am he."

[10] So they said to him, "How were your eyes opened?"

[11] He answered, "A Man called Jesus made clay, anointed my eyes, and said to me, 'Go to the pool of Siloam and wash.' So I went away and washed, and I received my sight."

[12] They said to him, "Where is He?"

He said, "I do not know."

The Pharisees Investigate the Healing

[13] They brought the man who had been blind to the Pharisees. [14] Now it was a Sabbath day when Jesus made the clay and opened his eyes. [15] Therefore the Pharisees also asked him how he received his sight. He said to them, "He put clay on my eyes, and I washed, and I see."

[16] Some of the Pharisees said, "This Man is not from God, because He does not keep the Sabbath day."

Others said, "How can a man who is a sinner do such signs?" So there was division among them.

[17] Then they said to the blind man again, "What do you say about Him, since He opened your eyes?"

He said, "He is a prophet."

[18] But the Jews did not believe concerning him, that he had been blind and received his sight, until they called the parents of the one who had received his sight. [19] They asked them, "Is this your son, whom you say was born blind? How then does he now see?"

[20] His parents answered them, "We know that this is our son and that he was born blind. [21] But how he now sees, we do not know, or who opened his eyes, we do not know. He is of age. Ask him. He will speak for himself." [22] His parents said this, because they feared the Jews. For the Jews had already agreed that if anyone confessed that He was the Christ, he would be put out of the synagogue. [23] Therefore his parents said, "He is of age. Ask him."

[24] So again they called the man who was blind and said to him, "Give glory to God. We know that this Man is a sinner."

[25] He said, "I do not know if He is a sinner. I know one thing: I was blind, but now I see."

[26] Then they said to him again, "What did He do to you? How did He open your eyes?"

[27] He answered them, "I told you already, and you did not listen. Why do you want to hear it again? Do you also want to become His disciples?"

[28] Then they insulted him and said, "You are His disciple, but we are Moses' disciples. [29] We know that God has spoken to Moses. As for this fellow, we do not know where He is from."

[30] The man answered, "Well, here is an amazing thing! You do not know where He is from, and yet He opened my eyes. [31] We know that God does not listen to sinners. But if anyone is a worshipper of God and does His will, He hears him. [32] Since the world began, it has never been heard that anyone opened the eyes of someone born blind. [33] If this Man were not from God, He could do nothing."

[34] They answered him, "You were completely born in sin. Are you teaching us?" And they threw him out.

Spiritual Blindness

[35] Jesus heard that they had thrown him out, and when He found him, He said, "Do you believe in the Son of God?"

[36] He answered, "Who is He, Lord, that I may believe in Him?"

[37] Jesus said to him, "You have seen Him, and it is He who speaks with you."

[38] Then he said, "Lord, I believe." And he worshipped Him.

[39] Jesus said, "I came into this world for judgment, that those who do not see may see, and that those who see may become blind."

[40] Some Pharisees who were with Him heard these words, and said to Him, "Are we also blind?"

[41] Jesus said, "If you were blind, you would have no sin. But now you say, 'We see.' Therefore your sin remains.

The Parable of the Shepherd

10 "Truly, truly I say to you, he who does not enter by the door into the sheepfold, but climbs up some other way, is a thief and a robber. [2] But he who enters by the door is the shepherd of the sheep. [3] To him the doorkeeper opens, and the sheep hear his voice. He calls his own sheep by name, and he leads them out. [4] When he brings out his own sheep, he goes before them. And the sheep follow him, for they know his voice. [5] Yet they will never follow a stranger, but will run away from him. For they do not know the voice of strangers." [6] Jesus told them this parable, but they did not understand what He was telling them.

Jesus the Good Shepherd

[7] Then Jesus said to them again, "Truly, truly I say to you, I am the door of the sheep. [8] All who came before Me are thieves and robbers, but the sheep did not listen to them. [9] I am the door. If anyone enters through Me, he will be saved and will go in and out and find pasture. [10] The thief does not come, except to steal and kill and destroy. I came that they may have life, and that they may have it more abundantly.

[11] "I am the good shepherd. The good shepherd lays down His life for the sheep. [12] But he who is a hired hand, and not a shepherd, who does not own the sheep, sees the wolf coming, and leaves the sheep, and runs away. So the wolf catches the sheep and scatters them. [13] The hired hand runs away because he is a hired hand and does not care about the sheep.

[14] "I am the good shepherd. I know My sheep and am known by My own. [15] Even as the Father knows Me, so I know the Father. And I lay down My life for the sheep. [16] I have other sheep who are not of this fold. I must also bring them, and they will hear My voice. There will be one flock and one shepherd. [17] Therefore My Father loves Me, because I lay down My life that I may take it up again. [18] No one takes it from Me, but I lay it down Myself. I have power to lay it down, and I have power to take it up again. I received this command from My Father."

[19] Therefore there was a division again among the Jews because of these sayings. [20] Many of them said, "He has a demon and is insane. Why do you listen to Him?" [21] Others said, "These are not the words of one who has a demon. Can a demon open the eyes of the blind?"

Jesus Rejected by the Jews

[22] The Feast of the Dedication[f] was at Jerusalem, and it was winter. [23] Jesus walked in the temple in Solomon's Porch. [24] Then the Jews surrounded Him, saying, "How long will You keep us in suspense? If You are the Christ, tell us plainly." [25] Jesus answered them, "I told you, and you did not believe. The works that I do in My Father's name bear witness of Me. [26] But you do not believe, because you are not of My sheep, as I said to you. [27] My sheep hear My voice, and I know them, and they follow Me. [28] I give them eternal life. They shall never perish, nor shall anyone snatch them from My hand. [29] My Father, who has given them to Me, is greater than all. No one is able to snatch them from My Father's hand. [30] My Father and I are one."

[31] Again the Jews took up stones to stone Him. [32] Jesus answered them, "I have shown you many good works from My Father. For which of those works do you stone Me?" [33] The Jews answered Him, "We are not stoning You for a good work, but for blasphemy, and because You, being a Man, claim to be God." [34] Jesus answered them, "Is it not written in your law, 'I said, "You are gods"'?[g] [35] If He called them 'gods,' to whom the word of God came, and the Scripture cannot be broken, [36] do you say of Him, whom the Father has sanctified and sent into the world, 'You blaspheme,' because I said, 'I am the Son of God'? [37] If I am not doing the works of My Father, do not believe Me. [38] But if I do them, though you do not believe Me, believe the works, that you may know and believe that the Father is in Me, and I in Him." [39] Again they tried to seize Him, but He escaped from their hands.

[40] Then He went away again beyond the Jordan into the place where John was baptizing at first, and He remained there. [41] Many came to Him and said, "John did no sign. But everything that John said about this Man was true." [42] And many believed in Him there.

The Death of Lazarus

11 Now a man was sick, Lazarus from Bethany, the village of Mary and her sister Martha. [2] This was Mary who anointed the Lord with ointment and wiped His feet with her hair, whose brother Lazarus was sick. [3] So the sisters sent word to Him, saying, "Lord, he whom You love is sick." [4] When Jesus heard this, He said, "This sickness is not unto death, but for the glory of God, that the Son of God may be glorified by it." [5] Now Jesus loved Martha, and her sister, and Lazarus. [6] So when He heard that he was sick, He remained where He was two more days. [7] Then after this He said to the disciples, "Let us go into Judea again."

[8] His disciples said to Him, "Rabbi, the Jews were just trying to stone You. Are You going there again?" [9] Jesus answered, "Are there not twelve hours in the day? If anyone walks during the day, he does not stumble, because he sees the light of this world. [10] But if anyone walks during the night, he stumbles, because the light is not in him." [11] After He said this, He said to them, "Our friend Lazarus has fallen asleep. But I am going that I may awaken him from sleep." [12] Then His disciples said, "Lord, if he is sleeping, he will be well." [13] Jesus had spoken of his death. But they thought that He was speaking of getting rest through sleep. [14] So then Jesus plainly told them, "Lazarus is dead. [15] And I am glad for your sakes that I was not there, so that you may believe. Nevertheless let us go to him." [16] Then Thomas, who is called Didymus, said to his fellow disciples, "Let us go also, that we may die with Him."

Jesus the Resurrection and the Life

[17] When Jesus arrived, He found that he had been in the tomb four days already. [18] Now Bethany was near Jerusalem, less than two miles away.[h] [19] Many of the Jews had come to Martha and Mary, to comfort them concerning their brother. [20] When Martha heard that Jesus was coming, she went and met Him, but Mary remained in the house.

[21] Martha said to Jesus, "Lord, if You had been here, my brother would not have died. [22] But even now I know that whatever You may ask of God, God will give You." [23] Jesus said to her, "Your brother will rise again." [24] Martha said to Him, "I know that he will rise again in the resurrection on the last day." [25] Jesus said to her, "I am the resurrection and the life. He who believes in Me, though he may die, yet shall he live. [26] And whoever lives and believes in Me shall never die. Do you believe this?" [27] She said to Him, "Yes, Lord, I believe that You are the Christ, the Son of God, who is to come into the world."

Jesus Weeps

[28] When she had said this, she went her way and secretly called her sister Mary, saying, "The Teacher has come and is calling for you." [29] When she heard this, she rose quickly and went to Him. [30] Now Jesus had not yet entered the village, but was in the place where Martha met Him. [31] When the Jews who were with Mary in the house, comforting her, saw that she quickly rose up and went out, they followed her, saying, "She is going to the tomb to weep there." [32] When Mary came to where Jesus was, and saw Him, she fell down at His feet, saying to Him, "Lord, if You had been here, my brother would not have died." [33] When Jesus saw her weeping, and the Jews who came with her weeping, He groaned in the spirit and was troubled. [34] He said, "Where have you laid him?" They said to Him, "Lord, come and see." [35] Jesus wept. [36] Then the Jews said, "See how He loved him." [37] But some of them said, "Could not this Man, who opened the eyes of the blind man, have also kept this man from dying?"

[f] 22 Or *Hanukkah.*   [g] 34 Ps 82:6.   [h] 18 Gk. 15 *stadia,* or about 3 kilometers.

Lazarus Brought to Life

[38] Then Jesus, again groaning within Himself, came to the tomb. It was a cave, and a stone was lying against it. [39] Jesus said, "Take away the stone."

Martha, the sister of him who was dead, said to Him, "Lord, by this time there is a stench, for he has been dead four days."

[40] Jesus said to her, "Did I not tell you that if you believed, you would see the glory of God?"

[41] So they took away the stone from the place where the dead man was lying. Jesus lifted up His eyes and said, "Father, I thank You that You have heard Me. [42] I know that You always hear Me. But because of the people standing around, I said this, that they may believe that You sent Me."

[43] When He had said this, He cried out with a loud voice, "Lazarus, come out!" [44] He who was dead came out, his hands and feet wrapped with grave clothes, and his face wrapped with a cloth.

Jesus said to them, "Unbind him, and let him go."

The Plot to Kill Jesus

Mt 26:1–5; Mk 14:1–2; Lk 22:1–2

[45] Therefore many of the Jews who came to Mary, and saw what Jesus had done, believed in Him. [46] But some of them went away to the Pharisees and told them what Jesus had done. [47] Then the chief priests and the Pharisees assembled the Sanhedrin and said, "What shall we do? This Man is performing many signs. [48] If we leave Him alone like this, everyone will believe in Him, and the Romans will come and take away both our temple and our nation."

[49] Then one of them named Caiaphas, who was the high priest that year, said to them, "You know nothing at all, [50] nor do you consider that it is expedient for us that one man should die for the people, that the whole nation should not perish."

[51] He did not say this on his own authority. But being the high priest that year, he prophesied that Jesus would die for the nation, [52] and not for the nation only, but that He might also gather together in unity the children of God who were scattered abroad. [53] So from that day forward they planned to put Him to death.

[54] Therefore Jesus no longer walked openly among the Jews, but went away from there to the country near the wilderness, into a city called Ephraim, and remained there with His disciples.

[55] Now the Passover of the Jews was at hand. Many went up to Jerusalem from the country before the Passover to purify themselves. [56] Then they searched for Jesus and said among themselves as they stood in the temple, "What do you think, that He will not come to the feast?" [57] Now both the chief priests and the Pharisees had given orders that if anyone knew where He was, he should report it, that they might seize Him.

The Anointing at Bethany

Mt 26:6–13; Mk 14:3–9

12 Six days before the Passover Jesus came to Bethany, where Lazarus was, who had been dead, whom He had raised from the dead. [2] They prepared a supper for Him there. Martha served, but Lazarus was one of those who sat at the table with Him. [3] Then Mary took a pint[1] of very costly ointment made from pure nard, and anointed the feet of Jesus, and wiped His feet with her hair. The house was filled with the fragrance of the ointment.

[4] But one of His disciples, Judas Iscariot, Simon's son, who would betray Him, said, [5] "Why was this ointment not sold for three hundred denarii[2] and given to the poor?" [6] He said this, not because he cared for the poor, but because he was a thief. And having the money box, he used to steal what was put in it.

[7] But Jesus said, "Leave her alone. She has kept this for the day of My burial. [8] For you always have the poor with you, but you do not always have Me."

The Plot Against Lazarus

[9] When many of the Jews learned that He was there, they came, not for Jesus' sake only, but that they might also see Lazarus, whom He had raised from the dead. [10] So the chief priests planned to put Lazarus to death also, [11] because on account of him many of the Jews went away and believed in Jesus.

The Triumphant Entry into Jerusalem

Mt 21:1–11; Mk 11:1–11; Lk 19:28–40

[12] On the next day a great crowd that had come to the feast heard that Jesus was coming to Jerusalem. [13] They took branches of palm trees, and went out to meet Him, and cried out:

"Hosanna!
'Blessed is He who comes in the name of the Lord!'[3]
The King of Israel!"

[14] Then Jesus, having found a young donkey, sat on it. As it is written:

[15] "Fear not, daughter of Zion;
   see, your King is coming,
     sitting on a donkey's colt."[4]

[16] His disciples did not understand these things at first. But when Jesus was glorified, they remembered that these things were written about Him and that they had done these things to Him.

[17] Now the crowd that was with Him when He called Lazarus out of the tomb and raised him from the dead bore witness. [18] The crowd went and met Him for this reason: They heard that He had performed this sign. [19] So the Pharisees said among themselves, "See, you are gaining nothing! Look, the world has followed Him!"

Some Greeks Seek Jesus

[20] Now there were some Greeks among those who went up to worship at the feast. [21] They came to Philip, who was from Bethsaida of Galilee, and asked him, "Sir, we want to see Jesus." [22] Philip came and told Andrew, and in turn Andrew and Philip told Jesus.

[23] Jesus answered them, "The hour has come for the Son of Man to be glorified. [24] Truly, truly I say to you, unless a grain of wheat falls into the ground and dies, it remains alone. But if it dies, it bears much fruit. [25] He who loves his life will lose it. And he who hates his life in this world will keep it for eternal life. [26] If anyone serves Me, he must follow Me. Where I am, there will My servant be also. If anyone serves Me, the Father will honor him.

The Son of Man Must Be Lifted Up

[27] "Now My soul is troubled. What shall I say? 'Father, save Me from this hour'? Instead, for this reason I came to this hour. [28] Father, glorify Your name."

Then a voice came from heaven, saying, "I have glorified it, and will glorify it again." [29] The crowd that stood by and heard it said that it had thundered. Others said, "An angel has spoken to Him."

[30] Jesus answered, "This voice came not for My sake, but for your sakes. [31] Now judgment is upon this world. Now the ruler of this world will be cast out. [32] And if I be lifted up from the earth, I will draw all men to Myself." [33] He said this to signify by what kind of death He would die.

[34] The crowd answered Him, "We have heard from the law that the Christ remains forever. Why do You say, 'The Son of Man must be lifted up'? Who is this Son of Man?"

[35] Then Jesus said to them, "Yet a little while the light is with you. Walk while you have the light, lest darkness overtake you. He who walks in darkness does not know where he is going. [36] While you have light, believe in the light that you may become sons of light." Jesus said these things, and departed and hid Himself from them.

The Unbelief of the Jews

[37] Though He had done so many signs before them, yet they did not believe in Him. [38] This fulfilled the word spoken by Isaiah the prophet:

"Lord, who has believed our report,
   and to whom has the arm of the Lord been revealed?"[5]

---

[1]3 Gk. a litra, or half a liter.   *[2]5 About a year's wages.*   *[3]13 Ps 118:25–26.*   *[4]15 Zec 9:9.*   *[5]38 Isa 53:1.*

[39] Therefore they could not believe. For Isaiah said again:

[40] "He has blinded their eyes
and hardened their hearts,
lest they should see with their eyes
and perceive with their hearts and turn,
and I would heal them."[1]

[41] Isaiah said this when he saw His glory and spoke of Him. [42] Yet many of the rulers also believed in Him. But because of the Pharisees they did not confess Him, lest they be put out of the synagogue. [43] For they loved the praise of men more than the praise of God.

Judgment by Jesus' Word

[44] Jesus cried out, "He who believes in Me believes not only in Me, but in Him who sent Me. [45] He who sees Me sees Him who sent Me. [46] I have come as a light into the world, that whoever believes in Me should not remain in darkness.

[47] "If anyone hears My words and does not believe, I do not judge him. For I did not come to judge the world, but to save the world. [48] He who rejects Me, and does not receive My words, has that which judges him. The word I have spoken will judge him on the last day. [49] For I have not spoken on My own authority, but the Father who sent Me gave Me a command, what I should say and what I should speak. [50] I know that His command is eternal life. Therefore what I say, I say as the Father tells me."

Washing the Disciples' Feet

13 Now before the Passover Feast, Jesus knew that His hour had come to depart from this world to the Father. Having loved His own who were in the world, He loved them to the end.

[2] Now supper being concluded, the devil had put into the heart of Judas Iscariot, Simon's son, to betray Him. [3] Jesus, knowing that the Father had given all things into His hands and that He came from God and was going to God, [4] rose from supper, laid aside His garments, and took a towel and wrapped Himself. [5] After that, He poured water into a basin and began to wash the disciples' feet and to wipe them with the towel with which He was wrapped.

[6] Then He came to Simon Peter, and Peter said to Him, "Lord, are You washing my feet?"

[7] Jesus answered him, "You do not understand what I am doing now. But later you will understand."

[8] Peter said to Him, "You shall never wash my feet!"

Jesus answered him, "If I do not wash you, you have no part with Me."

[9] Simon Peter said to Him, "Lord, not my feet only, but also my hands and my head!"

[10] Jesus said to him, "He who is bathed needs only to wash his feet, but is completely clean. You are clean, but not all of you." [11] For He knew who would betray Him. Therefore He said, "Not all of you are clean."

[12] So when He had washed their feet, and put on His garments, and sat down again, He said to them, "Do you know what I have done to you? [13] You call Me Teacher and Lord. You speak accurately, for so I am. [14] If I then, your Lord and Teacher, have washed your feet, you also ought to wash one another's feet. [15] For I have given you an example, that you should do as I have done to you. [16] Truly, truly I say to you, a servant is not greater than his master, nor is he who is sent greater than he who sent him. [17] If you know these things, blessed are you if you do them.

[18] "I do not speak concerning all of you. I know whom I have chosen, but that the Scripture may be fulfilled, 'He who eats bread with Me has lifted up his heel against Me.'[2]

[19] "Now I tell you before it happens, that when it does happen, you may believe that I am He. [20] Truly, truly I say to you, he who receives whomever I send receives Me. And he who receives Me receives Him who sent Me."

Jesus Foretells His Betrayal
Mt 26:20–25; Mk 14:17–21; Lk 22:21–23

[21] When Jesus had said this, He was troubled in spirit, and testified, "Truly, truly I say to you that one of you will betray Me."

[22] The disciples looked at one another, uncertain of whom He spoke. [23] Now there was leaning against Jesus' bosom one of His disciples whom Jesus loved. [24] Therefore Simon Peter motioned to him to ask who it was of whom He spoke.

[25] Leaning back against Jesus' bosom, he said to Him, "Lord, who is it?"

[26] Jesus answered, "It is he to whom I shall give a piece of bread when I have dipped it." When He had dipped the bread, He gave it to Judas Iscariot, the son of Simon. [27] After receiving the piece of bread, Satan entered him.

Then Jesus said to him, "What you are going to do, do quickly." [28] But no one at the table knew why He said this to him. [29] Since Judas had the moneybox, some thought that Jesus said to him, "Buy what we need for the feast," or that he should give something to the poor. [30] Having received the piece of bread, he then left immediately. And it was night.

The New Commandment

[31] When he had gone out, Jesus then said, "Now is the Son of Man glorified, and in Him God is glorified. [32] If God is glorified in Him, God will also glorify Him in Himself and will immediately glorify Him.

[33] "Little children, yet a little while I am with you. You will seek Me. And as I said to the Jews, so now I tell you, 'Where I am going, you cannot come.'

[34] "A new commandment I give to you, that you love one another, even as I have loved you, that you also love one another. [35] By this all men will know that you are My disciples, if you have love for one another."

Peter's Denial Foretold
Mt 26:31–35; Mk 14:27–31; Lk 22:31–34

[36] Simon Peter said to Him, "Lord, where are You going?"

Jesus answered him, "Where I am going, you cannot follow Me now. But you shall follow Me afterward."

[37] Peter said to Him, "Lord, why can I not follow You now? I will lay down my life for Your sake."

[38] Jesus answered Him, "Will you lay down your life for My sake? Truly, truly I say to you, the rooster shall not crow until you have denied Me three times.

Jesus the Way to the Father

14 "Let not your heart be troubled. You believe in God. Believe also in Me. [2] In My Father's house are many dwelling places. If it were not so, I would have told you. I am going to prepare a place for you. [3] And if I go and prepare a place for you, I will come again and receive you to Myself, that where I am, you may be also. [4] You know where I am going, and you know the way."

[5] Thomas said to Him, "Lord, we do not know where You are going. How can we know the way?"

[6] Jesus said to him, "I am the way, the truth, and the life. No one comes to the Father except through Me. [7] If you had known Me, you would have known My Father also. From now on you do know Him and have seen Him."

[8] Philip said to Him, "Lord, show us the Father, and that is sufficient for us."

[9] Jesus said to him, "Have I been with you such a long time, and yet you have not known Me, Philip? He who has seen Me has seen the Father. So how can you say, 'Show us the Father'? [10] Do you not believe that I am in the Father and the Father is in Me? The words that I say to you I do not speak on My own authority. But the Father who lives in Me does the works. [11] Believe Me that I am in the Father, and the Father is in Me. Or else believe Me on account of the works themselves. [12] Truly, truly I say to you, he who believes in Me will do the works that I do also. And he will do greater works than these, because I am going to My Father. [13] I will do whatever

you ask in My name, that the Father may be glorified in the Son. [14] If you ask anything in My name, I will do it.

The Promise of the Spirit

[15] "If you love Me, keep My commandments. [16] I will pray the Father, and He will give you another Counselor, that He may be with you forever: [17] the Spirit of truth, whom the world cannot receive, for it does not see Him, neither does it know Him. But you know Him, for He lives with you, and will be in you. [18] I will not leave you fatherless. I will come to you. [19] Yet a little while and the world will see Me no more. But you will see Me. Because I live, you will live also. [20] On that day you will know that I am in My Father, and you are in Me, and I am in you. [21] He who has My commandments and keeps them is the one who loves Me. And he who loves Me will be loved by My Father. And I will love him and will reveal Myself to him."

[22] Then Judas (not Iscariot) said to Him, "Lord, how is it that You will reveal Yourself to us, but not to the world?"

[23] Jesus answered him, "If a man loves Me, he will keep My word. My Father will love him, and We will come to him, and make Our home with him. [24] He who does not love Me does not keep My words. The word which you hear is not Mine, but the Father's who sent Me.

[25] "I have spoken these things to you while I am still with you. [26] But the Counselor, the Holy Spirit, whom the Father will send in My name, will teach you everything and remind you of all that I told you. [27] Peace I leave with you. My peace I give to you. Not as the world gives do I give to you. Let not your heart be troubled, neither let it be afraid.

[28] "You have heard Me say to you, 'I am going away and am returning to you.' If you loved Me, you would rejoice because I said, 'I am going to the Father,' for My Father is greater than I. [29] Now I have told you before it happens so that, when it happens, you may believe. [30] After this I will not speak much with you, for the ruler of this world is coming. He has no power over Me. [31] But I do as the Father has commanded Me so that the world may know that I love the Father.

"Rise, let us go from here.

Jesus the True Vine

15 "I am the true vine, and My Father is the vinedresser. [2] Every branch in Me that bears no fruit, He takes away. And every branch that bears fruit, He prunes, that it may bear more fruit. [3] You are already clean through the word which I have spoken to you. [4] Remain in Me, as I also remain in you. As the branch cannot bear fruit by itself, unless it remains in the vine, neither can you, unless you remain in Me.

[5] "I am the vine, you are the branches. He who remains in Me, and I in him, bears much fruit. For without Me you can do nothing. [6] If a man does not remain in Me, he is thrown out as a branch and withers. And they gather them and throw them into the fire, and they are burned. [7] If you remain in Me, and My words remain in you, you will ask whatever you desire, and it shall be done for you. [8] My Father is glorified by this, that you bear much fruit; so you will be My disciples.

[9] "As the Father loved Me, I also loved you. Remain in My love. [10] If you keep My commandments, you will remain in My love, even as I have kept My Father's commandments and remain in His love. [11] I have spoken these things to you, that My joy may remain in you, and that your joy may be full. [12] This is My commandment: that you love one another, as I have loved you. [13] Greater love has no man than this: that a man lay down his life for his friends. [14] You are My friends if you do whatever I command you. [15] I no longer call you servants, for a servant does not know what his master does. But I have called you friends, for everything that I have heard from My Father have I made known to you. [16] You did not choose Me, but I chose you, and appointed you, that you should go and bear fruit, and that your fruit should remain, that the Father may give you whatever you ask Him in My name. [17] This I command you: that you love one another.

The World's Hatred

[18] "If the world hates you, you know that it hated Me before it hated you. [19] If you were of the world, the world would love you as its own. But because you are not of the world, since I chose you out of the world, the world therefore hates you. [20] Remember the word that I said to you: 'A servant is not greater than his master.' If they persecuted Me, they will also persecute you. If they kept My words, they will keep yours also. [21] But all these things they will do to you for My name's sake, because they do not know Him who sent Me. [22] If I had not come and spoken to them, they would not have had sin. But now they have no excuse for their sin. [23] He who hates Me hates My Father also. [24] If I had not performed among them the works which no one else did, they would have no sin. But now have they seen and hated both My Father and Me. [25] But that the word which is written in their law might be fulfilled, 'They hated Me without a cause.'[1]

[26] "But when the Counselor comes, whom I shall send to you from the Father, the Spirit of truth who proceeds from the Father, He will bear witness of Me. [27] And you also will bear witness, because you have been with Me from the beginning.

16 "I have spoken these things to you so that you will not fall away. [2] They will put you out of the synagogues. Yes, the time is coming that whoever kills you will think that he is offering a service to God. [3] They will do these things to you, because they have not known the Father nor Me. [4] I have told you these things, so that when the time comes, you may remember that I told you about them.

The Work of the Spirit

"I did not tell you these things at the beginning, because I was with you. [5] But now I am going to Him who sent Me, and none of you asks Me, 'Where are You going?' [6] Rather, sorrow has filled your heart because I have told you these things. [7] Nevertheless I tell you the truth: It is expedient for you that I go away. For if I do not go away, the Counselor will not come to you. But if I go, I will send Him to you. [8] When He comes, He will convict the world of sin and of righteousness and of judgment: [9] of sin, because they do not believe in Me; [10] of righteousness, because I am going to My Father, and you will see Me no more; [11] and of judgment, because the ruler of this world stands condemned.

[12] "I have yet many things to tell you, but you cannot bear them now. [13] But when the Spirit of truth comes, He will guide you into all truth. For He will not speak on His own authority. But He will speak whatever He hears, and He will tell you things that are to come. [14] He will glorify Me, for He will receive from Me and will declare it to you. [15] All that the Father has is Mine. Therefore I said that He will take what is Mine and will declare it to you.

Sorrow Will Turn Into Joy

[16] "In a little while you will not see Me. And then after a little while you will see Me, because I am going to the Father."

[17] Then some of His disciples said among themselves, "What is this He is telling us: 'In a little while you will not see Me; and then after a little while you will see Me,' and, 'because I am going to the Father'?" [18] Then they said, "What is this He is telling us: 'In a little while'? We do not know what He is saying."

[19] Then Jesus knew that they wanted to ask Him. So He said to them, "Do you inquire among yourselves concerning what I said: 'In a little while you will not see Me; and then after a little while you will see Me'? [20] Truly, truly I say to you that you will weep and lament, but the world will rejoice. You will be sorrowful, but your sorrow will be turned into joy. [21] When a woman is giving birth, she has pain, because her hour has come. But as soon as she delivers the child, she no longer remembers the anguish for joy that a child is born into the world. [22] Therefore you now have sorrow. But I will see you again, and your heart will rejoice, and no one will take your joy from you. [23] On that day you will ask Me nothing. Truly, truly I say to you, whatever you ask the Father in My name, He will give it to you. [24] Until now you have asked nothing in My name. Ask, and you will receive, that your joy may be full.

[1] 25 Ps 35:19; 69:4.

I Have Overcome the World

25 "I have told you these things in proverbs. But the time is coming when I will no longer speak to you in proverbs, for I will speak to you plainly about the Father. 26 On that day you will ask in My name. I am not saying to you that I shall ask the Father on your behalf. 27 For the Father Himself loves you, because you have loved Me, and have believed that I came from God. 28 I came from the Father and have come into the world. As I said, I am leaving the world and am going to the Father."

29 His disciples said to Him, "Yes! Now You are speaking plainly and with no figure of speech. 30 Now we know that You know everything and do not need anyone to question You. By this we believe that You came from God."

31 Jesus answered them, "Do you now believe? 32 Listen, the hour is coming. Yes, it has now come that you will be scattered, each to his own home, and will leave Me alone. Yet I am not alone, for the Father is with Me.

33 "I have told you these things so that in Me you may have peace. In the world you will have tribulation. But be of good cheer. I have overcome the world."

The Prayer of Jesus

17 When Jesus spoke these words, He lifted His eyes toward heaven and said:

"Father, the hour has come. Glorify Your Son, that Your Son may also glorify You. 2 As You have given Him authority over all flesh, He will give eternal life to all whom You have given Him. 3 This is eternal life: that they may know You, the only true God, and Jesus Christ, whom You have sent. 4 I have glorified You on the earth. I have finished the work You have given Me to do. 5 And now, O Father, glorify Me in Your own presence with the glory which I had with You before the world existed.

6 "I have revealed Your name to the men whom You have given Me out of the world. They were Yours, and You gave them to Me, and they have kept Your word. 7 Now they know that all things You have given Me are from You. 8 For I have given them the words which You gave Me. They have received them and certainly know that I came from You, and they have believed that You sent Me. 9 I pray for them. I do not pray for the world, but for those whom You have given Me. For they are Yours. 10 All that are Mine are Yours, and all that are Yours are Mine. And I am glorified in them. 11 I am to be no longer in the world, though these are in the world, for I am coming to You. Holy Father, through Your name keep those whom You have given Me, that they may be one as We are one. 12 While I was with them in the world, I kept them in Your name. I have kept those whom You have given Me. And none of them is lost except the son of perdition, that the Scripture might be fulfilled.

13 "But now I am coming to You, and I say these things in the world, that they may have My joy fulfilled in themselves. 14 I have given them Your word. And the world has hated them because they are not of the world, just as I am not of the world. 15 I do not pray that You should take them out of the world, but that You should keep them from the evil one. 16 They are not of the world even as I am not of the world. 17 Sanctify them by Your truth. Your word is truth. 18 As You sent Me into the world, so I sent them into the world. 19 For their sakes I sanctify Myself, that they also may be sanctified by the truth.

20 "I do not pray for these alone, but also for those who will believe in Me through their word, 21 that they may all be one, as You, Father, are in Me, and I in You. May they also be one in Us, that the world may believe that You have sent Me. 22 I have given them the glory which You gave Me, that they may be one even as We are one: 23 I in them and You in Me, that they may be perfect in unity, and that the world may know that You have sent Me, and have loved them as You have loved Me.

24 "Father, I desire that they also, whom You have given Me, be with Me where I am, that they may see My glory which You have given Me. For You loved Me before the creation of the world.

25 "O righteous Father, the world has not known You, but I have known You, and these have known that You sent Me. 26 I have declared Your name to them, and will declare it, that the love with which You loved Me may be in them, and I in them."

The Betrayal and Arrest of Jesus
Mt 26:47–56; Mk 14:43–50; Lk 22:47–53

18 When Jesus had spoken these words, He went out with His disciples across the Kidron Valley. There was a garden which He and His disciples entered.

2 Now Judas, who betrayed Him, also knew the place, for Jesus often met there with His disciples. 3 So Judas, having taken a detachment of soldiers and officers from the chief priests and Pharisees, came there with lanterns and torches and weapons.

4 Jesus therefore, knowing everything that would happen to Him, went forward and said to them, "Whom do you seek?"

5 They answered Him, "Jesus of Nazareth."

Jesus said to them, "I am He." And Judas, who betrayed Him, was standing with them. 6 When He said, "I am He," they drew back and fell to the ground.

7 Again Jesus asked them, "Whom do you seek?"

They said, "Jesus of Nazareth."

8 Jesus answered, "I told you that I am He. So then let these go their way if you are looking for Me." 9 This was to fulfill the word which He had spoken, "I have lost none of those whom You have given Me."

10 Then Simon Peter, having a sword, drew it and struck the high priest's servant, and cut off his right ear. The servant's name was Malchus.

11 Then Jesus said to Peter, "Put your sword into the sheath. Shall I not drink the cup which My Father has given Me?"

Jesus Before the High Priest
Mt 26:57–58; Mk 14:53–54; Lk 22:54

12 Then the detachment of soldiers and the commander and the officers of the Jews arrested Jesus and bound Him. 13 First they led Him to Annas, for he was the father-in-law to Caiaphas, who was the high priest that year. 14 Now it was Caiaphas who advised the Jews that it was expedient that one man should die for the people.

Peter's Denial of Jesus
Mt 26:69–70; Mk 14:66–68; Lk 22:55–57

15 Simon Peter followed Jesus, and so did another disciple. That disciple was known to the high priest and went with Jesus into the courtyard of the high priest. 16 But Peter stood at the door outside. Then the other disciple, who was known to the high priest, went out and spoke to the doorkeeper and brought Peter in.

17 Then the servant girl, being the doorkeeper, said to Peter, "Are you not also one of this Man's disciples?"

He said, "I am not."

18 Now the servants and officers stood there and warmed themselves, having made a fire of coals, for it was cold. Peter also stood with them and warmed himself.

The High Priest Questions Jesus
Mt 26:59–66; Mk 14:55–64; Lk 22:66–71

19 The high priest then asked Jesus about His disciples and His teaching.

20 Jesus answered him, "I spoke openly to the world. I always taught in the synagogue and in the temple, where the Jews always meet, and I said nothing in secret. 21 Why do you ask Me? Ask those who heard Me and what I have said to them. Certainly they know what I said."

22 When He had said this, one of the officers who stood by struck Jesus with the palm of his hand, saying, "Is that how You answer the high priest?"

23 Jesus answered him, "If I have spoken evil, bear witness of the evil; but if well, why do you strike me?" 24 Then Annas sent Him bound to Caiaphas the high priest.

Peter Denies Jesus Again
Mt 26:71–75; Mk 14:69–72; Lk 22:58–62

[25] Meanwhile Simon Peter was standing and warming himself. So they said to him, "Are you not also one of His disciples?"

He denied it and said, "I am not!"

[26] One of the servants of the high priest, being a relative of the man whose ear Peter cut off, said, "Did I not see you in the garden with Him?" [27] Peter then denied it again, and immediately a rooster crowed.

Jesus Before Pilate
Mt 27:1–2, 11–14; Mk 15:1–5; Lk 23:1–5

[28] Then they led Jesus from Caiaphas to the Praetorium. It was early. Yet they themselves did not enter the Praetorium, so that they might not be defiled, but might eat the Passover. [29] Pilate then went out to them and said, "What accusation do you bring against this Man?"

[30] They answered him, "If He were not an evildoer, we would not have handed Him over to you."

[31] Then Pilate said, "Take Him and judge Him according to your law."

The Jews said to him, "It is not lawful for us to put anyone to death," [32] that the saying of Jesus might be fulfilled which He spoke, signifying what death He would die.

[33] Again Pilate entered the Praetorium, called Jesus, and said to Him, "Are You the King of the Jews?"

[34] Jesus answered him, "Are you speaking of your own accord, or did others tell you about Me?"

[35] Pilate answered, "Am I a Jew? Your own nation and the chief priests handed You over to me. What have You done?"

[36] Jesus answered, "My kingdom is not of this world. If My kingdom were of this world, then My servants would fight, that I would not be handed over to the Jews. But now My kingdom is not from here."

[37] Therefore Pilate said to Him, "Then are You a king?"

Jesus answered, "You say correctly that I am a king. For this reason I was born, and for this reason I came into the world, to bear witness to the truth. Everyone who is of the truth hears My voice."

[38] Pilate said to Him, "What is truth?" When he had said this, he went out again to the Jews and said to them, "I find no guilt in Him at all.

Jesus Sentenced to Die
Mt 27:15–31; Mk 15:6–20; Lk 23:13–25

[39] "But you have a custom, that I should release someone to you at the Passover. Do you therefore want me to release to you the King of the Jews?"

[40] They all shouted again, "Not this Man, but Barabbas!" Now Barabbas was a robber.

19 Then Pilate took Jesus and flogged Him. [2] The soldiers twisted a crown of thorns and put it on His head, and they put a purple robe on Him. [3] They said, "Hail, King of the Jews!" And they hit Him with their hands.

[4] Again Pilate went out and said to them, "Look, I am bringing Him out to you, that you may know that I find no guilt in Him." [5] Then Jesus came out, wearing the crown of thorns and the purple robe. Pilate said to them, "Here is the Man!"

[6] When the chief priests and officers saw Him, they cried out, "Crucify Him! Crucify Him!"

Pilate said to them, "Take Him yourselves and crucify Him, for I find no guilt in Him."

[7] The Jews answered him, "We have a law, and by our law He ought to die, because He made Himself the Son of God!"

[8] When Pilate heard these words, he was more afraid, [9] and entered the Praetorium again, and said to Jesus, "Where are You from?" But Jesus gave him no answer. [10] Pilate said to Him, "Are You not speaking to me? Do You not know that I have power to release You, and power to crucify You?"

[11] Jesus answered, "You would have no power at all over Me, unless it were given to you from above. Therefore he who handed Me over to you has the greater sin."

[12] From then on, Pilate tried to release Him. But the Jews cried out, "If you release this Man, you are not Caesar's friend. Whoever makes himself a king speaks against Caesar!"

[13] When Pilate heard these words, he brought Jesus out and sat down on the judgment seat at a place called The Pavement (which in Hebrew is Gabbatha). [14] It was the Day of Preparation of the Passover and about the sixth hour.

He said to the Jews, "Here is your King!"

[15] But they shouted, "Away with Him! Away with Him! Crucify Him!"

Pilate said to them, "Shall I crucify your King?"

The chief priests answered, "We have no king but Caesar!"

[16] Then he handed Him over to them to be crucified.

The Crucifixion
Mt 27:32–44; Mk 15:21–32; Lk 23:26–43

So they took Jesus and led Him away. [17] He went out, carrying His own cross, to a place called The Place of a Skull, which in Hebrew is called Golgotha. [18] There they crucified Him, and two others with Him, one on either side, and Jesus in the middle.

[19] Pilate wrote a title and put it on the cross. The writing was:

JESUS OF NAZARETH, THE KING OF THE JEWS.

[20] Many of the Jews read this title, for the place where Jesus was crucified was near the city. And it was written in Hebrew, in Greek, and in Latin. [21] The chief priests of the Jews said to Pilate, "Do not write, 'The King of the Jews,' but 'He said, I am King of the Jews.' "

[22] Pilate answered, "What I have written, I have written."

[23] When the soldiers had crucified Jesus, they took His garments and divided them into four parts, a part for each soldier; and also His tunic. Now the tunic was seamless, woven from top to bottom. [24] So they said to one another, "Let us not tear it, but cast lots for it to decide whose it shall be."

This happened to fulfill the Scripture which says:

"They divided My garments among them,
    and for My clothing they cast lots." [1]

Therefore the soldiers did these things. [25] But standing by the cross of Jesus were His mother, and His mother's sister, Mary the wife of Clopas, and Mary Magdalene. [26] When Jesus saw His mother and the disciple whom He loved standing nearby, He said to His mother, "Woman, here is your son." [27] Then He said to the disciple, "Here is your mother." From that time, this disciple took her to his own home.

The Death of Jesus
Mt 27:45–56; Mk 15:33–41; Lk 23:44–49

[28] After this, Jesus, knowing that everything was now accomplished, that the Scripture might be fulfilled, said, "I thirst." [29] A bowl full of sour wine was placed there. So they put a sponge full of sour wine on hyssop and held it to His mouth. [30] When Jesus had received the sour wine, He said, "It is finished." And He bowed His head and gave up His spirit.

The Piercing of Jesus' Side
[31] Since it was the Day of Preparation, to prevent bodies from remaining on the cross on the Sabbath day (for that Sabbath day was a high day), the Jews asked Pilate that their legs might be broken, and that they might be taken away. [32] Therefore the soldiers came and broke the legs of the first and of the other who was crucified with Him. [33] But when they came to Jesus and saw that He was dead already, they did not break His legs. [34] However, one of the soldiers pierced His side with a spear, and immediately blood and water came out. [35] He who saw it has testified, and his testimony is true. He knows that he is telling the truth, that you may believe. [36] For

these things happened so that the Scripture should be fulfilled, "Not one of His bones shall be broken," [1] [37] and again another Scripture says, "They shall look on Him whom they have pierced." [2]

The Burial of Jesus
Mt 27:57–61; Mk 15:42–47; Lk 23:50–56

[38] After this, Joseph of Arimathea, being a disciple of Jesus, but secretly for fear of the Jews, asked Pilate that he might take away the body of Jesus. Pilate gave him permission. So he came and took away His body. [39] Nicodemus, who at first came to Jesus by night, also came, bringing a mixture of myrrh and aloes, weighing about seventy-five pounds. [3] [40] Then they took the body of Jesus and wrapped it in linen cloths with the spices, as is the burial custom of the Jews. [41] Now in the place where He was crucified there was a garden, and in the garden was a new tomb in which no one had ever been buried. [42] So because of the Jewish Day of Preparation, and since the tomb was nearby, they buried Jesus there.

The Resurrection of Jesus
Mt 28:1–10; Mk 16:1–8; Lk 24:1–12

20 Early on the first day of the week, Mary Magdalene went to the tomb while it was still dark and saw that the stone had been taken away from the tomb. [2] So she came running to Simon Peter and to the other disciple whom Jesus loved, and said to them, "They have taken the Lord out of the tomb, and we do not know where they have put Him."

[3] So Peter came out with the other disciple and they went toward the tomb. [4] They both ran together, and the other disciple outran Peter and came to the tomb first. [5] Stooping down and looking in, he saw the linen cloths lying. Yet he did not enter. [6] Then Simon Peter came, following him, and went inside the tomb. He saw the linen cloths lying there, [7] and the cloth that was around His head, not lying with the linen cloths, but wrapped in a place by itself. [8] Then the other disciple, who came first to the tomb, went in also. He saw and believed. [9] For as yet they did not know the Scripture, that He must rise from the dead. [10] Then the disciples went away again to their own homes.

The Appearance of Jesus to Mary Magdalene
Mk 16:9–11

[11] But Mary stood outside at the tomb weeping. As she wept, she stooped down and looked into the tomb, [12] and she saw two angels in white sitting where the body of Jesus had lain, one at the head and one at the feet.

[13] They said to her, "Woman, why are you weeping?"

She said to them, "Because they have taken away my Lord, and I do not know where they have put Him." [14] When she had said this, she turned around and saw Jesus standing, but she did not know that it was Jesus.

[15] Jesus said to her, "Woman, why are you weeping? Whom are you seeking?"

Supposing Him to be the gardener, she said to Him, "Sir, if You have carried Him away, tell me where You have put Him, and I will take Him away."

[16] Jesus said to her, "Mary."

She turned and said to Him, "Rabboni!" (which means Teacher).

[17] Jesus said to her, "Stop holding on to Me, for I have not yet ascended to My Father. But go to My brothers and tell them, 'I am ascending to My Father and your Father, to My God and your God.' "

[18] Mary Magdalene came and told the disciples that she had seen the Lord and that He had said these things to her.

The Appearance of Jesus to His Disciples
Mt 28:16–20; Mk 16:14–18; Lk 24:36–49

[19] On the evening of that first day of the week, the doors being locked where the disciples were assembled, for fear of the Jews, Jesus came and stood in their midst, and said to them,

"Peace be with you." [20] When He had said this, He showed them His hands and His side. The disciples were then glad when they saw the Lord.

[21] So Jesus said to them again, "Peace be with you. As My Father has sent Me, even so I send you." [22] When He had said this, He breathed on them and said to them, "Receive the Holy Spirit. [23] If you forgive the sins of anyone, they are forgiven them. If you retain the sins of anyone, they are retained."

Jesus and Thomas

[24] But Thomas, one of the twelve, called The Twin, was not with them when Jesus came. [25] So the other disciples told him, "We have seen the Lord!"

But he said to them, "Unless I see the nail prints in His hands, and put my finger in the nail prints, and put my hand in His side, I will not believe."

[26] After eight days His disciples were again inside with the doors shut, and Thomas was with them. Jesus came and stood among them, and said, "Peace be with you." [27] Then He said to Thomas, "Put your finger here, and look at My hands. Put your hand here and place it in My side. Do not be faithless, but believing."

[28] Thomas answered Him, "My Lord and my God!"

[29] Jesus said to him, "Thomas, because you have seen Me, you have believed. Blessed are those who have not seen, and have yet believed."

The Purpose of the Book

[30] Jesus performed many other signs in the presence of His disciples, which are not written in this book. [31] But these are written that you might believe that Jesus is the Christ, the Son of God, and that believing you may have life in His name.

The Appearance of Jesus to the Seven Disciples

21 After this, Jesus revealed Himself again to the disciples at the Sea of Tiberias. He revealed Himself this way: [2] Simon Peter; Thomas, called The Twin; Nathanael of Cana in Galilee; the sons of Zebedee; and two more of His disciples were together. [3] Simon Peter said to them, "I am going fishing." Then they said to him, "We will go with you." They went out and immediately entered the boat. But that night they caught nothing.

[4] When the morning came, Jesus stood on the shore. But the disciples did not know that it was Jesus.

[5] Jesus said to them, "Children, do you have any fish?"

They answered Him, "No."

[6] He said to them, "Throw the net on the right side of the boat, and you will find some." So they threw it, and now they were not able to draw it in because of the abundance of fish.

[7] Then the disciple whom Jesus loved said to Peter, "It is the Lord!" When Simon Peter heard that it was the Lord, he put on his outer garment, for he had taken it off, and jumped into the sea. [8] The other disciples came in the little boat, dragging the net full of fish. For they were not far from land, but about three hundred feet away. [4] [9] When they came to land, they saw a charcoal fire there with fish lying on it, and bread.

[10] Jesus said to them, "Bring some of the fish which you have just caught." [11] Simon Peter went up and dragged the net, full of one hundred and fifty-three large fish, to land. Although there were so many, the net was not torn. [12] Jesus said to them, "Come and eat breakfast." None of the disciples dared ask, "Who are You?" They knew it was the Lord. [13] Jesus came and took the bread and gave it to them, and likewise the fish. [14] This was now the third time that Jesus was revealed to His disciples after He was raised from the dead.

Jesus and Peter

[15] So when they had eaten breakfast, Jesus said to Simon Peter, "Simon, son of John, do you love Me more than these?"

He said to Him, "Yes, Lord. You know that I love You."

He said to him, "Feed My lambs."

[1] 36 Ex 12:46; Nu 9:12; Ps 34:20.   [2] 37 Zec 12:10.   [3] 39 Gk. *a hundred litrai* or 34 kilograms.   [4] 8 About 200 cubits, or 90 meters.

[16] He said to him again a second time, "Simon, son of John, do you love Me?"

He said to Him, "Yes, Lord. You know that I love You."

He said to him, "Tend My sheep."

[17] He said to him the third time, "Simon, son of John, do you love Me?"

Peter was grieved because He asked him the third time, "Do you love Me?" He said to Him, "Lord, You know everything. You know that I love You."

Jesus said to him, "Feed My sheep. [18] Truly, truly I say to you, when you were young, you dressed yourself and walked where you desired. But when you are old, you will stretch out your hands, and another will dress you and carry you where you do not want to go." [19] He said this, signifying by what kind of death he would glorify God. When He had said this, He said to him, "Follow Me."

Jesus and the Beloved Disciple

[20] Peter turned and saw following them the disciple whom Jesus loved, who also leaned against His bosom at the supper and had said, "Lord, who is it that is going to betray You?" [21] When Peter saw him, he said to Jesus, "Lord, what about this man?"

[22] Jesus said to him, "If it is My will that he remain until I come, what is that to you? Follow Me!" [23] The saying went out among the brothers that this disciple would not die. Yet Jesus did not say to him that he would not die, but, "If it is My will that he remain until I come, what is that to you?"

[24] This is the disciple who testifies about these things, and wrote these things. We know that his testimony is true.

[25] There are also many other things which Jesus did. Were every one of them to be written, I suppose that not even the world itself could contain the books that would be written. Amen.

ACTS

The Promise of the Holy Spirit

1 The former treatise have I made, O Theophilus, concerning all that Jesus began both to do and teach, [2] until the day when He was taken up, after He had given commandments through the Holy Spirit to the apostles whom He had chosen, [3] to whom He presented Himself alive after His passion by many infallible proofs, appearing to them for forty days, and speaking concerning the kingdom of God. [4] Being assembled with them, He commanded them, "Do not depart from Jerusalem, but wait for the promise of the Father, of which you have heard from Me.[1] [5] For John baptized with water, but you shall be baptized with the Holy Spirit not many days from now."

The Ascension

[6] So when they had come together, they asked Him, "Lord, will You at this time restore the kingdom to Israel?"

[7] He said to them, "It is not for you to know the times or the dates, which the Father has fixed by His own authority. [8] But you shall receive power when the Holy Spirit comes upon you. And you shall be My witnesses in Jerusalem, and in all Judea and Samaria, and to the ends of the earth."

[9] When He had spoken these things, while they looked, He was taken up. And a cloud received Him from their sight.

[10] While they looked intently toward heaven as He ascended, suddenly two men stood by them in white garments. [11] They said, "Men of Galilee, why stand looking toward heaven? This same Jesus, who was taken up from you to heaven, will come in like manner as you saw Him go into heaven."

Judas' Successor

[12] Then they returned to Jerusalem from the Mount of Olives, which is a Sabbath day's walk[2] from Jerusalem. [13] When they had entered, they went up into the upper room, where they were staying: Peter, James, John, and Andrew; Philip and Thomas; Bartholomew and Matthew; James the son of Alphaeus and Simon the Zealot; and Judas the son of James. [14] These all continued with one accord in prayer and supplication, with the women and Mary the mother of Jesus, and with His brothers.

[15] In those days Peter stood up among the disciples (the number of people together was about a hundred and twenty), and said, [16] "Brothers, this Scripture had to be fulfilled, which the Holy Spirit previously spoke by the mouth of David concerning Judas, who

became the guide to those who seized Jesus. [17] For he was numbered with us and took part in this ministry."

[18] (Now this man purchased a field with the reward of iniquity. And falling headlong, he burst asunder in the middle and all his organs spilled out. [19] It became known to all the residents of Jerusalem. So this field is called in their dialect Akeldama, that is, Field of Blood.)

[20] "For it is written in the Book of Psalms,

'Let his habitation become desolate,
    and let no one live in it,'[3]

and,

'Let another take his office.'[4]

[21] Therefore, of these men who have accompanied us while the Lord Jesus went in and out among us, [22] beginning from the baptism of John until the very day that He was taken up from us, one of these men must become with us a witness of His resurrection."

[23] So they proposed two, Joseph, called Barsabbas, who was surnamed Justus, and Matthias. [24] Then they prayed, "You, Lord, who knows the hearts of all men, show which of these two You have chosen [25] to take the place in this ministry and apostleship, from which Judas by transgression fell, to go to his own place." [26] Then they cast lots, and the lot fell on Matthias. So he was numbered with the eleven apostles.

The Coming of the Holy Spirit

2 When the day of Pentecost had come, they were all together in one place. [2] Suddenly a sound like a mighty rushing wind came from heaven, and it filled the whole house where they were sitting. [3] There appeared to them tongues as of fire, being distributed and resting on each of them, [4] and they were all filled with the Holy Spirit and began to speak in other tongues, as the Spirit enabled them to speak.

[5] Now dwelling in Jerusalem were Jews, devout men, from every nation under heaven. [6] When this sound occurred, the crowd came together and were confounded, because each man heard them speaking in his own language. [7] They were all amazed and marveled, saying to each other, "Are not all these who are speaking Galileans? [8] How is it that we hear, each in our

---

[1]4 Lk 24:49.   [2]12 About half a mile.   [3]20 Ps 69:25.   [4]20 Ps 109:8.

own native language? [9] Parthians, Medes and Elamites, residents of Mesopotamia, Judea and Cappadocia, Pontus and Asia, [10] Phrygia and Pamphylia, Egypt and the regions of Libya near Cyrene, and visitors from Rome, both Jews and proselytes, [11] Cretans and Arabs—we hear them speaking in our own languages the mighty works of God." [12] They were all amazed and perplexed, saying to each other, "What does this mean?"

[13] Others mocking said, "These men are full of new wine."

Peter's Speech at Pentecost

[14] But Peter, standing up with the eleven, lifted up his voice and said to them, "Men of Judea and all you who dwell in Jerusalem, let this be known to you, and listen to my words. [15] For these are not drunk, as you suppose, since it is the third hour of the day. [16] But this is what was spoken by the prophet Joel:

[17] 'In the last days it shall be,' says God,
    'that I will pour out My Spirit on all flesh;
    your sons and your daughters shall prophesy,
      your young men shall see visions,
      and your old men shall dream dreams.
[18] Even on My menservants and maidservants
    I will pour out My Spirit in those days;
    and they shall prophesy.
[19] And I will show wonders in heaven above
    and signs on the earth below:
      blood, and fire, and vapor of smoke.
[20] The sun shall be turned into darkness,
    and the moon into blood,
    before that great and glorious day of the Lord comes.
[21] And whoever calls
    on the name of the Lord shall be saved.'[1]

[22] "Men of Israel, hear these words: Jesus of Nazareth was a man attested to you by God with powerful works and wonders and signs, which God did through Him in your midst, as you yourselves know. [23] You have taken Him, who was handed over to you by the ordained counsel and foreknowledge of God, and by lawless hands have crucified and killed Him, [24] whom God raised up by loosening the pull of death, because it was not possible that He should be held by it. [25] For David says concerning Him:

'I foresaw the Lord always before me,
    for He is at my right hand,
    that I may not be shaken.
[26] Therefore my heart was glad, and my tongue rejoiced;
    moreover my flesh will dwell in hope.
[27] For You will not abandon my soul to Hades,
    nor will You allow Your Holy One to see corruption.
[28] You have made known to me the ways of life;
    You will make me full of joy with Your presence.'[2]

[29] "Brothers, I may speak confidently to you concerning the patriarch David, that he both died and was buried, and his tomb is with us to this day. [30] But being a prophet, and knowing that God had sworn with an oath to him, that of his seed according to the flesh, He would raise up the Christ to sit on his throne, [31] he foresaw this and spoke concerning the resurrection of the Christ, that His soul was not abandoned to Hades, nor did His flesh see corruption. [32] God raised up this Jesus, of which we all are witnesses. [33] Therefore being exalted to the right hand of God, and having received from the Father the promise of the Holy Spirit, He has poured out this which you now see and hear. [34] For David has not ascended to the heavens, yet he says:

'The Lord said to my Lord,
    "Sit at My right hand,
[35] Until I make Your enemies
    Your footstool." '[3]

[36] "Therefore, let all the house of Israel assuredly know that God has made this Jesus, whom you have crucified, both Lord and Christ."

[37] When they heard this, they were stung in the heart and said to Peter and to the rest of the apostles, "Brothers, what shall we do?"

[38] Peter said to them, "Repent and be baptized, every one of you, in the name of Jesus Christ for the forgiveness of sins, and you shall receive the gift of the Holy Spirit. [39] For the promise is to you, and to your children, and to all who are far away, as many as the Lord our God will call."

[40] With many other words he testified and exhorted them, saying, "Be saved from this perverse generation." [41] Then those who gladly received his word were baptized, and that day about three thousand souls were added to them.

Life Among the Believers

[42] They continued steadfastly in the apostles' teaching and fellowship, in the breaking of bread and in the prayers. [43] Fear came to every soul. And many wonders and signs were done through the apostles. [44] All who believed were together and had all things in common. [45] They sold their property and goods and distributed them to all, according to their need. [46] And continuing daily with one mind in the temple, and breaking bread from house to house, they ate their food with gladness and simplicity of heart, [47] praising God and having favor with all the people. And the Lord added to the church daily those who were being saved.

The Lame Man Healed at the Temple Gate

3 Now Peter and John went up together to the temple at the ninth hour, the hour of prayer. [2] A man lame from birth was being carried, whom people placed daily at the gate of the temple called Beautiful to ask alms from those who entered the temple. [3] Seeing Peter and John about to go into the temple, he asked for alms. [4] Peter, gazing at him with John, said, "Look at us." [5] So he paid attention to them, expecting to receive something from them.

[6] Then Peter said, "I have no silver and gold, but I give you what I have. In the name of Jesus Christ of Nazareth, rise up and walk." [7] He took him by the right hand and raised him up. Immediately his feet and ankles were strengthened. [8] Jumping up, he stood and walked and entered the temple with them, walking and jumping and praising God. [9] All the people saw him walking and praising God. [10] They knew that it was he who sat for alms at the Beautiful Gate of the temple. And they were filled with wonder and amazement at what happened to him.

Peter's Speech at Solomon's Porch

[11] As the lame man who was healed held on to Peter and John, all the people ran together to them in the entrance that is called Solomon's Porch, greatly amazed. [12] When Peter saw it, he answered the people: "Men of Israel, why do you marvel at this man? Or why do you stare at us, as if by our own power or piety we had made him walk? [13] The God of Abraham and Isaac and Jacob, the God of our fathers, has glorified His Son Jesus, whom you handed over and denied in the presence of Pilate, when he had decided to release Him. [14] You denied the Holy and Righteous One and asked for a murderer to be granted to you, [15] and you killed the Creator of Life, whom God has raised from the dead, of which we are witnesses. [16] And His name, by faith in His name, has made this man strong, whom you see and know. And faith which comes through Him has given him perfect health in your presence.

[17] "Now brothers, I know that you acted in ignorance, as did also your rulers. [18] But what God foretold through all the prophets, that His Christ should suffer, He thus fulfilled. [19] Therefore repent and be converted, that your sins may be wiped away, that times of refreshing may come from the presence of the Lord, [20] and that He may send the One who previously was preached to you, Jesus Christ, [21] whom the heavens must receive until the time of restoring what God spoke through all His holy prophets since the world began. [22] For Moses indeed said to the fathers, 'The Lord your God will raise up for you a prophet like me from your brothers. You

shall hear whatever He may say to you. [23] And it shall be that every soul who will not hear that prophet shall be utterly eliminated from the people.'[1]

[24] "Indeed, all the prophets since Samuel and those who follow, as many as have spoken, have likewise foretold these days. [25] You are the sons of the prophets and of the covenant which God made with our fathers, saying to Abraham, 'And in your seed shall all the families of the earth be blessed.'[2] [26] God, having raised up His Son Jesus, sent Him to you first, to bless you in turning every one of you from your iniquities."

Peter and John Before the Sanhedrin

4 As they spoke to the people, the priests, the captain of the temple, and the Sadducees came upon them, [2] being greatly troubled because they taught the people and preached through Jesus the resurrection from the dead. [3] And they seized them and put them in custody until the next day, for it was already evening. [4] But many of those who heard the word believed, and the number of the men grew to about five thousand.

[5] On the next day their rulers and elders and scribes [6] were assembled at Jerusalem with Annas the high priest, and Caiaphas, and John and Alexander, and all who were of the family of the high priest. [7] When they had stood them in the midst, they asked, "By what power or by what name have you done this?"

[8] Then Peter, filled with the Holy Spirit, said to them, "Rulers of the people and elders of Israel: [9] If we today are being examined concerning a good deed done to a crippled man, how this man has been healed; [10] be it known to you all, and to all the people of Israel, that by the name of Jesus Christ of Nazareth, whom you crucified, whom God raised from the dead, by Him this man stands before you whole. [11] He is

'the stone you builders rejected,
    which has become the cornerstone.'[3]

[12] There is no salvation in any other, for there is no other name under heaven given among men by which we must be saved."

[13] When they saw the boldness of Peter and John and perceived that they were illiterate and uneducated men, they marveled. And they recognized that they had been with Jesus. [14] But seeing the man who was healed standing with them, they had nothing to say against it. [15] So when they had commanded them to go outside of the Sanhedrin, they conferred among themselves, [16] saying, "What shall we do to these men? For, indeed, that an acknowledged miracle has been done through them is revealed to all who dwell in Jerusalem, and we cannot deny it. [17] But lest it spread further among the people, let us threaten them that they no longer speak to anyone in this name."

[18] Then they called them and commanded them not to speak or teach at all in the name of Jesus. [19] But Peter and John answered them, "Whether it is right in the sight of God to listen to you more than to God, you judge. [20] For we cannot help but declare what we have seen and heard."

[21] When they had further threatened them, they let them go, finding no way to punish them, because of the people. For all glorified God for what was done, [22] for the man on whom this miracle of healing was performed was over forty years old.

The Believers Pray for Boldness

[23] On being released, they went to their own people and reported what the chief priests and elders had said to them. [24] When they heard this, they lifted their voices in unity to God and prayed, "Lord, You are God, who has made the heaven and the earth and the sea and everything in them, [25] and who by the mouth of Your servant David said:

'Why did the nations rage,
    and the people devise vain things?
[26] The kings of the earth came,
    and the rulers were assembled together

against the Lord
    and against His Christ.'[4]

[27] Indeed, both Herod and Pontius Pilate, with the Gentiles and the people of Israel, were assembled together against Your holy Son Jesus whom You have anointed, [28] to do what Your hand and Your counsel had foreordained to be done. [29] Now, Lord, look on their threats and grant that Your servants may speak Your word with great boldness, [30] by stretching out Your hand to heal and that signs and wonders may be performed in the name of Your holy Son Jesus."

[31] When they had prayed, the place where they were assembled together was shaken. And they were all filled with the Holy Spirit and spoke the word of God with boldness.

All Things in Common

[32] All the believers were of one heart and one soul, and no one said that what he possessed was his own. But to them all things were in common. [33] With great power the apostles testified to the resurrection of the Lord Jesus, and great grace was on them all. [34] There was no one among them who lacked, for all those who were owners of land or houses sold them, and brought the income from what was sold, [35] and placed it at the apostles' feet. And it was distributed to each according to his need.

[36] Joseph, whom the apostles called Barnabas (which means, Son of Encouragement), a Levite from the land of Cyprus, [37] sold a field he owned, and brought the money and placed it at the apostles' feet.

Ananias and Sapphira

5 Now a man named Ananias, with his wife Sapphira, sold a piece of property. [2] He kept back part of the proceeds with his wife's knowledge, and brought a part of it and placed it at the apostles' feet.

[3] Then Peter said, "Ananias, why has Satan filled your heart to deceive the Holy Spirit and keep back part of the proceeds of the land? [4] While it remained unsold, was it not your own? And when it was sold, was it not under your authority? Why have you conceived this deed in your heart? You did not lie to men, but to God."

[5] On hearing these words, Ananias fell down and died. And great fear came on all those who heard these things. [6] The young men rose and wrapped him up and carried him out and buried him.

[7] About three hours later his wife came in, not knowing what had happened. [8] Peter said to her, "Tell me whether you sold the land for this amount?"

She said, "Yes, for that much."

[9] Peter said to her, "How is it that you have agreed together to test the Spirit of the Lord? Look! The feet of those who have buried your husband are at the door, and they will carry you out."

[10] At once she fell down at his feet and died. Upon entering, the young men found her dead and carried her out and buried her beside her husband. [11] Great fear came on the entire church and on all those who heard these things.

Signs and Wonders

[12] Many signs and wonders were performed among the people by the hands of the apostles. And they were all together in Solomon's Porch. [13] No one else dared join them, but the people respected them. [14] Believers were increasingly added to the Lord, crowds of both men and women, [15] so that they even brought the sick out into the streets and placed them on beds and mats, that at least the shadow of Peter passing by might touch some of them. [16] Crowds also came out of the cities surrounding Jerusalem, bringing the sick and those who were afflicted by evil spirits, and they were all healed.

Persecution of the Apostles

[17] Then the high priest and all those who were with him (that is, the sect of the Sadducees) rose up and were filled with jealousy. [18] They seized the apostles and put them in the common prison. [19] But during the night an angel of the Lord opened the prison doors

---

[1] 23 Dt 18:15, 18–19.   [2] 25 Ge 22:18; 26:4.   [3] 11 Ps 118:22.   [4] 25–26 Ps 2:1–2.

and led them out, and said, [20] "Go, stand and speak in the temple to the people all the words of this life."

[21] Having heard this, they entered the temple at dawn and taught. But the high priest and those who were with him came and called together the Sanhedrin and the senate of all the sons of Israel, and sent to the prison to have them brought out. [22] But when the officers came and did not find them in the prison, they returned and reported, [23] "We found the prison securely shut and the guards standing outside before the doors. But when we opened it, we found no one inside." [24] Now when the high priest, the captain of the temple, and the chief priests heard these things, they were in doubt of what might become of this.

[25] Then one came and told them, "Look, the men whom you put in prison are standing in the temple and teaching the people." [26] Then the captain with his escorts went and brought them, without force lest they should be stoned, for they feared the people.

[27] When they had brought them, they stood them before the Sanhedrin. And the high priest questioned them, [28] saying, "Did we not strictly command you not to teach in this name? Yet now you have filled Jerusalem with your teaching, and you intend to bring on us this Man's blood."

[29] Peter and the other apostles answered, "We must obey God rather than men. [30] The God of our fathers raised Jesus, whom you killed by hanging on a tree. [31] God exalted this Man to His right hand to be a Ruler and a Savior, to give repentance to Israel and forgiveness of sins. [32] We are His witnesses to these words, as is the Holy Spirit whom God has given to those who obey Him."

[33] When they heard this, they were cut to the heart and took counsel to kill them. [34] But a Pharisee in the Sanhedrin named Gamaliel, a teacher of the law honored by all the people, stood and ordered the apostles to be put outside for a little while. [35] Then he said to them, "Men of Israel, take heed to yourselves what you intend to do concerning these men. [36] For in previous days Theudas rose up, boasting to be somebody, to whom a number of about four hundred men joined themselves. He was killed, and all who obeyed him were dispersed and came to nothing. [37] After Theudas, Judas the Galilean rose up in the days of the census and drew away many people after him. This man also perished, and all who obeyed him were scattered. [38] Now I tell you, keep away from these men and leave them alone, because if this intention or this activity is of men, it will come to nothing. [39] But if it is of God, you will not be able to overthrow them, lest perhaps you be found even fighting against God."

[40] They agreed with him. When they had called in the apostles, they beat them, and commanded them not to speak in the name of Jesus, and released them.

[41] Then they departed from the presence of the Sanhedrin, rejoicing that they were counted worthy to suffer shame for His name. [42] Daily, in the temple and from house to house, they did not cease to teach and preach Jesus Christ.

The Seven Helpers

6 Now in those days, as the disciples were multiplied, there was murmuring among the Hellenists against the Hebrews, because their widows were overlooked in the daily distribution. [2] So the twelve called the multitude of disciples together and said, "It is not reasonable for us to leave the word of God and serve tables. [3] Brothers, look among yourselves for seven men who are known to be full of the Holy Spirit and of wisdom, whom we will appoint over this duty. [4] But we will give ourselves continually to prayer and to the ministry of the word."

[5] And what was said pleased the whole multitude, and they chose Stephen, who was a man full of faith and of the Holy Spirit, and Philip, and Procorus, and Nicanor, and Timon, and Parmenas, and Nicolas, a proselyte from Antioch, [6] whom they presented before the apostles. And when they had prayed, they placed their hands on them.

[7] So the word of God spread, and the number of the disciples grew rapidly in Jerusalem, and a great number of the priests were obedient to the faith.

The Arrest of Stephen

[8] Now Stephen, full of faith and power, did great wonders and miracles among the people. [9] Then some men rose up from what is called the Synagogue of the Freedmen (Cyrenians, Alexandrians, and those from Cilicia and of Asia), disputing with Stephen. [10] But they were not able to withstand the wisdom and the Spirit by which he spoke.

[11] Then they secretly instigated men who said, "We have heard him speak blasphemous words against Moses and God."

[12] So they stirred up the people and the elders and the scribes, and came upon him and seized him and led him to the Sanhedrin, [13] and set up false witnesses who said, "This man does not cease to speak blasphemous words against this holy place and the law. [14] For we have heard him say that this Jesus of Nazareth will destroy this place, and will change the customs which Moses handed down to us."

[15] All who sat in the Sanhedrin, gazing at him, saw his face as the face of an angel.

Stephen's Speech

7 Then the high priest said, "Are these things so?"
[2] He said, "Brothers and fathers, listen! The God of glory appeared to our father Abraham, before he was in Mesopotamia, before he lived in Harran, [3] and said to him, 'Leave your country and your relatives, and come to the land which I will show you.'[1]

[4] "Then he departed from the land of the Chaldeans and lived in Harran. When his father died, He removed him from there to this land in which you now live. [5] He gave him no inheritance in it, nor a foothold, and promised to give it to him as a possession and to his descendants after him while he had no child. [6] God spoke in this way, 'Your descendants shall be sojourners in a land belonging to others, who will enslave them and mistreat them four hundred years.'[2] And I will judge the nation to whom they will be enslaved,'[3] said God. 'After that they shall come out and worship Me in this place.'[4] [8] Then He gave him the covenant of circumcision. And Abraham became the father of Isaac and circumcised him on the eighth day. And Isaac became the father of Jacob, and Jacob of the twelve patriarchs.

[9] "The patriarchs, moved with envy, sold Joseph into Egypt. But God was with him, [10] and delivered him out of all his afflictions, and gave him favor and wisdom before Pharaoh, king of Egypt, who appointed him governor over Egypt and all his house.

[11] "Then a famine came over all Egypt and Canaan with great affliction, and our fathers found no sustenance. [12] But when Jacob heard that there was grain in Egypt, he sent out our fathers the first time. [13] During the second time Joseph was made known to his brothers, and Joseph's family became known to Pharaoh. [14] Then Joseph sent and called for his father Jacob and all his kindred, seventy-five souls. [15] Then Jacob went down into Egypt. And he and our fathers died, [16] and were carried to Shechem and put in the tomb that Abraham had bought for a price of silver from the sons of Hamor, the father of Shechem.

[17] "When the time of the promise drew near, which God had sworn to Abraham, the people grew and multiplied in Egypt [18] until another king rose up who did not know Joseph.[5] [19] He dealt deceitfully with our people and mistreated our fathers, forcing them to put out their young children, that they might not live.

[20] "At that time Moses was born, and was fair in the sight of God. And he was reared for three months in his father's house. [21] When he was put out, Pharaoh's daughter took him up and reared him as her own son. [22] Moses was educated in all the wisdom of the Egyptians and was powerful in words and in deeds.

[23] "When he was forty years old, it came to his heart to visit his brothers, the sons of Israel. [24] But seeing one being wronged, he defended him, and avenged him who was oppressed, and struck the Egyptian. [25] He supposed that his brothers would understand that God would deliver them by his hand, but they did not understand. [26] On the next day he appeared to them as they fought and tried to reconcile them in peace, saying, 'Men, you are brothers. Why do you wrong each other?'[6]

---

[1] Ge 12:1. [2] Ge 15:13. [3] Ge 15:14. [4] Ex 3:12. [5] Ex 1:8. [6] Ex 2:13.

27 "But the one wronging his neighbor pushed him away, saying, 'Who appointed you a ruler and a judge over us? 28 Will you kill me as you killed the Egyptian yesterday?'[1] 29 Moses fled at this word and became a sojourner in the land of Midian,[2] where he became the father of two sons.

30 "When forty years had passed, an angel of the Lord appeared to him in the wilderness of Mount Sinai, in a flame of fire in a bush.[3] 31 When Moses saw it, he marveled at the sight. As he drew near to look at it, the voice of the Lord came to him, saying, 32 'I am the God of your fathers, the God of Abraham and the God of Isaac and the God of Jacob.'[4] Moses trembled and dared not look.

33 "Then the Lord said to him, 'Take off the shoes from your feet, for the place where you are standing is holy ground.[5] 34 I have indeed seen the oppression of My people who are in Egypt. I have heard their groaning, and I have come down to deliver them. Now come, I will send you to Egypt.'[6]

35 "This Moses, whom they rejected, saying, 'Who appointed you a ruler and a judge?'[7] God sent as both ruler and redeemer by the hand of the angel who appeared to him in the bush. 36 He led them out after he had shown wonders and signs in the land of Egypt, and at the Red Sea, and for forty years in the wilderness.

37 "This is the Moses who said to the sons of Israel, 'The Lord your God will raise up for you a prophet like me from your brothers. Him you shall hear.'[8] 38 This is he who was in the congregation in the wilderness with the angel who spoke to him on Mount Sinai, and with our fathers, who received living oracles to give to us, 39 whom our fathers would not obey, but thrust away. And in their hearts they turned back to Egypt, 40 saying to Aaron, 'Make for us gods to go before us. For we do not know what has become of this Moses, who led us out of the land of Egypt.'[9] 41 So they made a calf in those days, and offered a sacrifice to the idol, and rejoiced in the works of their hands. 42 But God turned and gave them up to worship the host of heaven, as it is written in the book of the Prophets:

'O House of Israel, have you offered to Me slain animals and sacrifices
    for forty years in the wilderness?
43 Yes, you even raised the shrine of Moloch,
    and the star of your god Remphan,
    idols which you made to worship;
therefore I will exile you beyond Babylon.'[10]

44 "Our fathers had the tabernacle of witness in the wilderness, telling Moses to make it as He had commanded, according to the pattern that he had seen, 45 which our fathers, having received it, brought with Joshua into the land possessed by the Gentiles, whom God drove out in front of our fathers until the days of David, 46 who found favor in the presence of God and asked to find a tabernacle for the God of Jacob. 47 But Solomon built Him a house.

48 "However, the Most High does not dwell in houses made with hands. As the prophet says:

49 'Heaven is My throne,
    and the earth is My footstool.
What house will you build for Me? says the Lord,
    or what is the place of My rest?
50 Has not My hand made all these things?'[11]

51 "You stiff-necked people, uncircumcised in heart and ears! You always resist the Holy Spirit. As your fathers did, so do you. 52 Which of the prophets have your fathers not persecuted? They have even killed those who foretold the coming of the Righteous One, of whom you have now become the betrayers and murderers, 53 who have received the law by the disposition of angels, but have not kept it."

The Stoning of Stephen
54 When they heard these things, they were cut to the heart, and they gnashed their teeth at him. 55 But being full of the Holy Spirit, he gazed into heaven and saw the glory of God, and Jesus standing at the right hand of God, 56 and said, "Look! I see the heavens opened and the Son of Man standing at the right hand of God."

57 Then they cried out with a loud voice, closed their ears, and rushed at him in unison. 58 And they threw him out of the city and stoned him. The witnesses laid down their garments at the feet of a young man named Saul.

59 They stoned Stephen as he was calling on God, praying, "Lord Jesus, receive my spirit." 60 Then he knelt down and cried with a loud voice, "Lord, do not hold this sin against them." Having said this, he fell asleep.

8 And Saul was consenting to his death.

Saul Persecutes the Church
On that day a great persecution broke out against the church in Jerusalem. And they were all scattered throughout the regions of Judea and Samaria, except the apostles. 2 Devout men carried Stephen to his burial and made great lamentation over him. 3 But Saul ravaged the church, entering house by house and dragging out both men and women and committing them to prison.

The Gospel Preached in Samaria
4 Therefore those who were scattered went everywhere preaching the word. 5 Philip went down to the city of Samaria and preached Christ to them. 6 When the crowds heard Philip and saw the miracles which he did, they listened in unity to what he said. 7 For unclean spirits, crying with a loud voice, came out of many who were possessed. And many who were paralyzed or lame were healed. 8 So there was much joy in that city.

Simon the Sorcerer Believes
9 Now a man named Simon was previously in the city practicing sorcery and astonishing the nation of Samaria, saying he was someone great, 10 to whom they all listened, from the least to the greatest, saying, "This man is the great power of God." 11 They listened to him, because for a long time he had astonished them by his sorceries. 12 But when they believed Philip preaching about the kingdom of God and the name of Jesus Christ, both men and women were baptized. 13 Even Simon himself believed. And when he was baptized, he continued with Philip and was amazed as he watched the miracles and signs which were done.

Samaritans Receive the Holy Spirit
14 Now when the apostles who were at Jerusalem heard that Samaria had received the word of God, they sent Peter and John to them. 15 When they came down, they prayed for them that they might receive the Holy Spirit, 16 for still He had come on none of them. They were only baptized in the name of the Lord Jesus. 17 Then they laid their hands on them, and they received the Holy Spirit.

18 When Simon saw that through the laying on of the apostles' hands the Holy Spirit was given, he offered them money, 19 saying, "Give me also this power, that whomever I lay hands on may receive the Holy Spirit." 20 Peter said to him, "May your money perish with you, because you thought you could purchase the gift of God with money! 21 You have neither part nor share in this matter, for your heart is not right before God. 22 Therefore repent of your wickedness, and ask God if perhaps the intention of your heart may be forgiven you. 23 For I see that you are in the gall of bitterness and in the bond of iniquity."

24 Then Simon answered, "Pray to the Lord for me that nothing you have spoken may come upon me."

25 When they had testified and preached the word of the Lord, they returned to Jerusalem and preached the gospel in many villages of the Samaritans.

Philip and the Ethiopian Eunuch
26 Now an angel of the Lord said to Philip, "Rise up and go toward the south on the way that goes down from Jerusalem to Gaza." This is desert. 27 So he rose up and went. And there was a man of

---

1 28 Ex 2:14.   2 29 Ex 2:11–15.   3 30 Ex 3:1–4.   4 32 Ex 3:6.   5 33 Ex 3:5.   6 34 Ex 3:7, 10.   7 35 Ex 2:14.   8 37 Dt 18:15.   9 40 Ex 32:1, 23.   10 42–43 Am 5:25–27.   11 49–50 Isa 66:1–2.

Ethiopia, a eunuch of great authority under Candace, queen of the Ethiopians, who was in command of her entire treasury. He had come to Jerusalem to worship. [28] He was returning, sitting in his chariot and reading the book of Isaiah the prophet. [29] The Spirit said to Philip, "Go to this chariot and stay with it."

[30] Then Philip ran to him, and heard him read the book of Isaiah the prophet, and said, "Do you understand what you are reading?" [31] He said, "How can I, unless someone guides me?" So he invited Philip to come up and sit with him.

[32] The passage of Scripture which he was reading was this:

"He was led as a sheep to slaughter;
    and as a lamb before its shearer is silent,
    so He opened not His mouth.
[33] In His humiliation justice was denied Him;
    who will speak of His generation?
For His life is taken from the earth."[1]

[34] The eunuch said to Philip, "I ask you, of whom does the prophet speak, of himself or of someone else?" [35] Then Philip spoke, beginning with the same Scripture, and preached Jesus to him.

[36] As they went on their way, they came to some water. And the eunuch said, "Look, here is water. What hinders me from being baptized?" [37] Philip said, "If you believe with all your heart, you may." He answered, "I believe that Jesus Christ is the Son of God." [38] And he commanded the chariot to halt. Then both Philip and the eunuch went down into the water, and he baptized him. [39] When they came up out of the water, the Spirit of the Lord took Philip away. And the eunuch saw him no more, and he went his way rejoicing. [40] But Philip was found at Azotus. And passing through, he preached the gospel in all the cities until he came to Caesarea.

The Conversion of Saul
Ac 22:6–16; 26:12–18

9 Saul, still breathing out threats and murder against the disciples of the Lord, went to the high priest, [2] and requested letters from him to the synagogues of Damascus, so that if he found any there of the Way, either men or women, he might bring them bound to Jerusalem. [3] As he went he drew near Damascus, and suddenly a light from heaven shone around him. [4] He fell to the ground and heard a voice saying to him, "Saul, Saul, why do you persecute Me?"

[5] He said, "Who are You, Lord?"

The Lord said, "I am Jesus, whom you are persecuting. It is hard for you to kick against the goads." [6] Trembling and astonished, he said, "Lord, what will You have me do?" The Lord said to him, "Rise up and go into the city, and you will be told what you must do."

[7] The men traveling with him stood speechless, hearing the voice, but seeing no one. [8] Saul rose up from the ground. And when his eyes were opened, he saw nothing. So they led him by the hand and brought him into Damascus. [9] For three days he was without sight, and neither ate nor drank.

[10] A disciple named Ananias was in Damascus. The Lord said to him in a vision, "Ananias."

He said, "Here I am, Lord."

[11] The Lord said to him, "Rise and go to Straight Street, and inquire at Judas' house for someone named Saul of Tarsus, for he is praying, [12] and has seen in a vision a man named Ananias coming in and putting his hand on him, so that he may see again."

[13] Ananias answered, "Lord, I have heard from many about this man, how many evil things he has done to Your saints at Jerusalem. [14] And here he has authority from the chief priests to bind all who call on Your name."

[15] But the Lord said to him, "Go your way. For this man is a chosen vessel of Mine, to bear My name before the Gentiles and their kings, and before the sons of Israel. [16] For I will show him how much he must suffer for My name's sake."

[17] Then Ananias went his way and entered the house. Putting his hands on him, he said, "Brother Saul, the Lord Jesus, who appeared to you on the way as you came, has sent me so that you may see

again and be filled with the Holy Spirit." [18] Immediately something like scales fell from his eyes, and he could see again. And he rose up and was baptized. [19] When he had eaten, he was strengthened.

Saul Preaches in Damascus

For several days Saul was with the disciples in Damascus. [20] Immediately he preached in the synagogues that the Christ is the Son of God. [21] All who heard him were amazed and said, "Is not this he who killed those who called on this name in Jerusalem, and came here with that intent, to bring them bound to the chief priests?" [22] Yet Saul increased all the more with power and confounded the Jews living in Damascus, proving that this One is the Christ.

Saul Escapes from the Jews

[23] After many days had passed, the Jews arranged to kill him. [24] But their scheme was known by Saul. They watched the gates day and night to kill him. [25] But the disciples took him by night, and lowered him in a basket through the wall.

Saul in Jerusalem

[26] When Saul had come to Jerusalem, he tried to join the disciples. But they all feared him, not believing he was a disciple. [27] But Barnabas took him, and led him to the apostles, and declared to them how on the road he had seen the Lord, and that He had spoken to him, and how he had boldly preached in Damascus in the name of Jesus. [28] So he stayed with them while coming in and going out of Jerusalem. [29] And he spoke boldly in the name of the Lord Jesus and disputed against the Hellenists. But they tried to kill him. [30] When the brothers learned this, they brought him down to Caesarea, and sent him off to Tarsus.

[31] Then the churches throughout all Judea and Galilee and Samaria had peace and were built up. And walking in the fear of the Lord and in the comfort of the Holy Spirit, they were multiplied.

The Healing of Aeneas

[32] As Peter passed through every region, he came down also to the saints who lived in Lydda. [33] There he found a man named Aeneas, who had been bedridden for eight years and was paralyzed. [34] Peter said to him, "Aeneas, Jesus the Christ heals you. Rise up and make your bed." And immediately he rose up. [35] All those who lived in Lydda and Sharon saw him and turned to the Lord.

Dorcas Restored to Life

[36] In Joppa there was a disciple named Tabitha, which is translated Dorcas. This woman was full of good works and almsgiving. [37] In those days she became ill and died. And when they had washed her, they placed her in an upper room. [38] Since Lydda was near Joppa, the disciples, hearing that Peter was there, sent two men to him, pleading, "Do not delay to come to us."

[39] Peter rose up and went with them. When he arrived, they led him into the upper room. All the widows stood by him weeping, and showing the tunics and garments which Dorcas had made while she was with them.

[40] Peter put them all outside and knelt down and prayed. And turning to the body he said, "Tabitha, arise." She opened her eyes, and when she saw Peter she sat up. [41] He gave her his hand and lifted her up. And when he had called the saints and widows, he presented her alive. [42] It became known throughout all Joppa, and many believed in the Lord. [43] He remained in Joppa for many days with Simon, a tanner.

Peter and Cornelius

10 In Caesarea there was a man named Cornelius, the centurion[2] of a band of soldiers called the Italian Detachment, [2] a devout man and one who feared God with all his household, who gave many alms to the people and continually prayed to God. [3] About the ninth hour of the day he saw clearly in a vision an angel of God coming in and saying to him, "Cornelius."

[4] When he looked at him he was afraid, and said, "What is it, Lord?"

---

[1] 32–33 Isa 53:7–8.   [2] 1 Commander with the rank of captain over 100 soldiers.

He said to him, "Your prayers and your alms have come up as a memorial before God. [5] Now send men to Joppa, and bring back Simon whose surname is Peter. [6] He is lodging with Simon, a tanner, whose house is by the sea. He will tell you what you must do."

[7] When the angel who spoke to him had departed, Cornelius called two of his household servants and a devout soldier from among those who continually waited on him. [8] When he had explained everything to them, he sent them to Joppa.

[9] The next day as they went on their journey and drew near the city, Peter went up on the housetop to pray about the sixth hour. [10] He became very hungry and desired to eat. But while they prepared a meal, he fell into a trance [11] and saw heaven opened, and a vessel like a great sheet, tied at the four corners, descending to him, and let down to the earth. [12] In it were all kinds of four-footed animals of the earth and wild beasts and reptiles and birds of the air. [13] Then a voice came to him, "Rise, Peter; kill and eat."

[14] Peter said, "Not at all, Lord. For I have never eaten anything that is common or unclean."

[15] The voice spoke to him a second time: "What God has cleansed, do not call common."

[16] This happened three times. And again the vessel was taken up into heaven.

[17] Now while Peter wondered what this vision which he had seen might mean, the men who were sent by Cornelius had inquired for Simon's house and stood at the gate, [18] and called and asked whether Simon, who was surnamed Peter, was lodging there.

[19] While Peter thought about the vision, the Spirit said to him, "Three men are looking for you. [20] So rise and go down, and go with them, doubting nothing. For I have sent them."

[21] Then Peter went down to the men who were sent to him by Cornelius and said, "Here I am, the one you are seeking. Why have you come?"

[22] They said, "Cornelius, a centurion, a man who is righteous and fears God and is of good report throughout the nation of the Jews, was directed by a holy angel to summon you to his house to hear your words." [23] Then he invited them in and gave them lodging.

The next day Peter went with them, and some brothers from Joppa accompanied him. [24] And the next day they entered Caesarea. Cornelius was waiting for them and had called together his relatives and close friends. [25] As Peter entered the house, Cornelius met him and fell down at his feet and worshipped him. [26] But Peter lifted him up, saying, "Stand up. I myself am a man."

[27] As he talked with him, he went in and found many who had come together. [28] He said to them, "You know how unlawful it is for a Jew to visit or approach a foreigner. But God has shown me not to call any man common or unclean. [29] So when I was sent for, I came without question. Therefore I ask why you have sent for me."

[30] Cornelius said, "Four days ago I was fasting until this hour. At the ninth hour I prayed in my house, and suddenly a man stood before me in bright clothing, [31] and said, 'Cornelius, your prayer has been heard, and your alms are remembered before God. [32] Therefore send to Joppa for Simon, whose surname is Peter. He is lodging in the house of Simon, a tanner, by the sea. When he comes, he will speak to you.' [33] So immediately I sent for you, and you have done well to come. Now therefore we are all here, present before God, to hear everything the Lord has commanded you."

Peter Speaks in Cornelius' House

[34] Then Peter began to speak, saying, "Truthfully, I perceive that God is no respecter of persons. [35] But in every nation he who fears Him and works righteousness is accepted by Him. [36] The word which He sent to the children of Israel, preaching peace through Jesus Christ, who is Lord of all, [37] the word, which you know, that was proclaimed throughout all Judea, beginning from Galilee after the baptism which John preached: [38] how God anointed Jesus of Nazareth with the Holy Spirit and with power, who went about doing good and healing all who were oppressed by the devil, for God was with Him.

[39] "We are witnesses of all that He did both in the land of the Jews and in Jerusalem, whom they killed by hanging on a tree.

[40] But God raised Him on the third day and presented Him publicly, [41] not to all the people, but to witnesses previously chosen by God, to us who ate and drank with Him after He rose from the dead. [42] He commanded us to preach to the people and to testify that it is He who was ordained by God to be the Judge of the living and the dead. [43] To Him all the prophets bear witness that whoever believes in Him will receive remission of sins through His name."

Gentiles Receive the Holy Spirit

[44] While Peter was still speaking these words, the Holy Spirit fell on all those who heard the word. [45] All the believers of the circumcision who had come with Peter were astonished, because the gift of the Holy Spirit had been poured out even on the Gentiles. [46] For they heard them speaking in other tongues and magnifying God.

Then Peter continued, [47] "Can anyone forbid water for baptizing these, who have received the Holy Spirit as we have?" [48] So he commanded them to be baptized in the name of the Lord. Then they asked him to stay a few days.

Peter's Report to the Church in Jerusalem

11 The apostles and the brothers throughout Judea heard that the Gentiles also had received the word of God. [2] So when Peter went up to Jerusalem, those who were circumcised disputed with him, [3] saying, "You went in and ate with uncircumcised men!"

[4] Peter began explaining it to them in order, saying, [5] "I was in the city of Joppa praying. And in a trance I saw a vision: A vessel like a great sheet was descending, let down from heaven by four corners, and it came to me. [6] I considered what I had observed and saw four-footed creatures and wild beasts and reptiles and birds of the air. [7] Then I heard a voice saying to me, 'Rise, Peter; kill and eat.'

[8] "I said, 'Not at all, Lord. For nothing common or unclean has at any time entered my mouth.'

[9] "The voice answered from heaven a second time, 'What God has cleansed, do not call common.' [10] This happened three times. And again everything was taken up into heaven.

[11] "And immediately three men sent from Caesarea to me came to the house where I was. [12] The Spirit told me to go with them without hesitation. Moreover these six brothers came with me, and we entered the man's house. [13] He told us how he had seen an angel in his house, who stood and said to him, 'Send men to Joppa, and call for Simon whose surname is Peter. [14] He will speak words to you by which you and all your household will be saved.'

[15] "As I began to speak, the Holy Spirit fell on them, as He fell on us at the beginning. [16] Then I remembered the word of the Lord, how He said, 'John indeed baptized with water, but you shall be baptized with the Holy Spirit.'[1] [17] If then God gave them the same gift as He gave us when we believed in the Lord Jesus Christ, who was I to be able to hinder God?"

[18] When they heard these things, they were silent. And they glorified God, saying, "Then God has granted to the Gentiles also repentance unto life."

The Church in Antioch

[19] Now those who were scattered by the persecution that arose over Stephen traveled as far as Phoenicia and Cyprus and Antioch, preaching the word to no one except Jews. [20] Some of them were men of Cyprus and Cyrene, who, when they had come to Antioch, spoke to the Hellenists, preaching the Lord Jesus. [21] The hand of the Lord was with them, and a great number believed and turned to the Lord.

[22] News of these things came to the ears of the church which was in Jerusalem, and they sent Barnabas to Antioch. [23] When he arrived and saw the grace of God, he rejoiced and exhorted them all to remain with the Lord with a loyal heart. [24] For he was a good man, full of the Holy Spirit and of faith. And many people were added to the Lord.

---

[1] 16 Ac 1:5.

²⁵ Then Barnabas went to Tarsus to look for Saul. ²⁶ When he had found him, he brought him to Antioch. For a whole year they met with the church and taught a considerable crowd. And the disciples were first called Christians in Antioch.

²⁷ In these days prophets came down from Jerusalem to Antioch. ²⁸ One of them, named Agabus, stood up and prophesied by the Spirit that there would be a great famine throughout all the world, which came to pass in the days of Claudius Caesar. ²⁹ Then every disciple, according to his ability, determined to send relief to the brothers who lived in Judea. ³⁰ Indeed they did, and sent it to the elders by the hands of Barnabas and Saul.

James Killed and Peter Imprisoned

12 About that time King Herod extended his hands to harm certain ones from the church. ² He killed James the brother of John with the sword. ³ Seeing that it pleased the Jews, he proceeded further to arrest Peter also. This happened during the Days of Unleavened Bread. ⁴ When he had seized him, he put him in prison and handed him over to four squads of soldiers to guard him, intending to bring him before the people after the Passover.

⁵ So Peter was kept in prison. But the church prayed to God without ceasing for him.

Peter Delivered From Prison

⁶ The very night when Herod would have brought him out, Peter was sleeping between two soldiers, bound with two chains. And the guards before the door were securing the prison. ⁷ And suddenly an angel of the Lord approached him, and a light shone in the prison. He struck Peter on the side and woke him up, saying, "Rise up, quickly." And the chains fell off his hands.

⁸ Then the angel said to him, "Dress yourself and put your sandals on." And he did so. Then he said to him, "Wrap your cloak around you and follow me." ⁹ He went out and followed him, and did not know that what was done by the angel was real, but thought he was seeing a vision. ¹⁰ When they had passed the first and the second guards, they came to the iron gate leading to the city, which opened to them by itself. And they went out and went forward one street. And immediately the angel left him.

¹¹ When Peter had come to himself, he said, "Now I certainly know that the Lord has sent His angel and delivered me from the hand of Herod and from all that the Jewish people were expecting."

¹² Realizing this, he came to the house of Mary, the mother of John, whose other name was Mark, where many were gathered together praying. ¹³ As Peter knocked at the door of the porch, a servant girl named Rhoda came to answer. ¹⁴ When she recognized Peter's voice, from joy she did not open the door, but ran in and announced that Peter was standing at the door.

¹⁵ They said to her, "You are insane." But she insisted that it was really so. So they said, "It is his angel."

¹⁶ But Peter continued knocking. And when they opened the door and saw him, they were astonished. ¹⁷ Motioning to them with his hand to be quiet, he described to them how the Lord had led him out of the prison. And he said, "Go, tell these things to James and to the brothers." Then he departed and went to another place.

¹⁸ Now when day came, there was a great disturbance among the soldiers about what had become of Peter. ¹⁹ When Herod had searched for him and did not find him, he examined the guards and commanded that they should be put to death.

Then he went down from Judea to Caesarea, and stayed there.

The Death of Herod

²⁰ Now Herod was very angry with the people of Tyre and Sidon. But they came to him in unity, and having made Blastus, the king's personal servant, their friend, they asked for peace, because their country was fed by the king's country.

²¹ On an appointed day, Herod, dressed in royal apparel, sat on his throne and gave a public speech to them. ²² The mob shouted, "It is the voice of a god, and not of a man!" ²³ Immediately an angel of the Lord struck him, because he did not give God the glory. And he was eaten by worms and died.

²⁴ But the word of God spread and increased.

²⁵ When Barnabas and Saul had fulfilled their ministry, they returned from Jerusalem and took with them John, whose surname was Mark.

Barnabas and Saul Commissioned

13 In the church that was in Antioch there were prophets and teachers: Barnabas, Simeon who was called Niger, Lucius of Cyrene, Manaen who had been brought up with Herod the tetrarch, and Saul. ² As they worshipped the Lord and fasted, the Holy Spirit said, "Set apart for Me Barnabas and Saul for the work to which I have called them." ³ Then after fasting and praying, they laid their hands on them and sent them off.

The Apostles Preach in Cyprus

⁴ So, being sent out by the Holy Spirit, they went down to Seleucia, and from there they sailed to Cyprus. ⁵ When they arrived at Salamis, they preached the word of God in the synagogues of the Jews. And they had John as an assistant.

⁶ When they had gone through the whole island to Paphos, they found a certain sorcerer, a Jewish false prophet, whose name was Bar-Jesus, ⁷ who was with the proconsul, Sergius Paulus, an intelligent man. This man called for Barnabas and Saul and sought to hear the word of God. ⁸ But Elymas the sorcerer (which is his name by interpretation) opposed them, trying to divert the proconsul from the faith. ⁹ Then Saul, who also is called Paul, filled with the Holy Spirit, stared at him and said, ¹⁰ "You son of the devil, enemy of all righteousness, full of deceit and of all fraud, will you not cease perverting the right ways of the Lord? ¹¹ Now, look! The hand of the Lord is against you, and you shall be blind, not seeing the sun for a time."

Immediately mist and darkness fell on him, and he went about seeking someone to lead him by the hand. ¹² When the proconsul saw what had happened, he believed and was astonished at the doctrine of the Lord.

Paul and Barnabas in Antioch of Pisidia

¹³ Now when Paul and his companions set sail from Paphos, they came to Perga in Pamphylia. And John departed from them and returned to Jerusalem. ¹⁴ But they departed from Perga and came to Antioch in Pisidia. And they went into the synagogue on the Sabbath day and sat down. ¹⁵ After the reading from the Law and the Prophets, the rulers of the synagogue sent word to them, saying, "Brothers, if you have any word of exhortation for the people, say it."

¹⁶ Then Paul stood up, and motioning with his hand said: "Men of Israel, and you who fear God, listen. ¹⁷ The God of this people of Israel chose our fathers, and exalted the people when they lived as foreigners in the land of Egypt, and with great power He led them out of it. ¹⁸ For about forty years He endured their conduct in the desert. ¹⁹ When He had destroyed seven nations in the land of Canaan, He gave them their land as an inheritance by lot.

²⁰ "After about four hundred and fifty years, God gave them judges until Samuel the prophet. ²¹ Then they requested a king. And God gave them Saul the son of Kish, a man of the tribe of Benjamin, for forty years. ²² When He had removed him, He raised up David to be their king, of whom He testified, saying, 'I have found David¹ the son of Jesse, a man after My own heart, who will fulfill My entire will.'²

²³ "From this man's descendants God has raised a Savior for Israel, Jesus, according to His promise. ²⁴ Before His coming John had preached a baptism of repentance to all the people of Israel. ²⁵ As John was fulfilling his course, he said, 'Who do you think I am? I am not He. But look! He is coming after me, the sandals of whose feet I am not worthy to untie.'³

²⁶ "Brothers, sons of the family of Abraham, and those of you who fear God, the word of this salvation has been sent to us. ²⁷ Because those who live in Jerusalem, and their rulers, did not know Him, in condemning Him they have fulfilled the voices of the Prophets which are read every Sabbath. ²⁸ Though they found in Him no

cause worthy of death, yet they asked Pilate to have Him killed. [29] When they had fulfilled all that was written of Him, they took Him down from the tree and placed Him in a tomb. [30] But God raised Him from the dead, [31] and for many days He appeared to those who came up with Him from Galilee to Jerusalem, who are now His witnesses to the people.

[32] "We preach to you good news: The promise which was made to the fathers, [33] God has fulfilled to us, their children, raising Jesus. As it is written in the second Psalm:

'You are My Son;
　　today I have become Your Father.'[1]

[34] That He raised Him from the dead, no more to return to corruption, He has spoken in this way:

'I will give You the holy and sure blessings of David.'[2]

[35] So He says in another Psalm:

'You will not let Your Holy One see decay.'[3]

[36] "For after David had served by the counsel of God in his own generation, he fell asleep, was buried with his fathers, and saw decay. [37] But He whom God raised up saw no decay. [38] "Therefore, brothers, let it be known to you that through this Man forgiveness of sins is proclaimed to you, [39] and by Him everyone who believes is justified from everything from which you could not be justified by the Law of Moses. [40] Therefore beware, lest what is spoken of in the prophets come upon you:

[41] 'Look, you scoffers,
　　marvel and perish!
For I will perform a work in your days
　　which you will never believe,
　　even if someone declares it to you.'[4]"

[42] When Paul and Barnabas went out of the synagogue, the Gentiles asked that these words might be preached to them the next Sabbath. [43] When the congregation was dismissed, many of the Jews and devout proselytes followed Paul and Barnabas, who spoke to them and urged them to continue in the grace of God. [44] On the next Sabbath almost the whole city assembled to hear the word of God. [45] But when the Jews saw the crowds, they were filled with jealousy, blaspheming and contradicting what Paul was saying. [46] Then Paul and Barnabas boldly said, "It was necessary that the word of God should be spoken to you first. But seeing you reject it, and judge yourselves unworthy of eternal life, we are turning to the Gentiles. [47] For thus has the Lord commanded us:

'I have established you to be a light of the Gentiles,
　　that you may bring salvation to the ends of the earth.'[5]"

[48] When the Gentiles heard this, they were glad and glorified the word of the Lord. And all who were ordained to eternal life believed. [49] The word of the Lord was spread throughout the entire region. [50] But the Jews stirred up the devout and honorable women and the chief men of the city, and raised up persecution against Paul and Barnabas, and drove them from their region. [51] So they shook off the dust of their feet against them and went to Iconium. [52] And the disciples were filled with joy and with the Holy Spirit.

Paul and Barnabas in Iconium

14 At Iconium they entered the synagogue of the Jews together and so spoke that a great crowd of both Jews and Greeks believed. [2] But the unbelieving Jews stirred up the Gentiles and embittered their minds against the brothers. [3] So they continued there a long time, speaking boldly for the Lord, who bore witness to His gracious word, granting signs and wonders to be done by

their hands. [4] But the people of the city were divided. Some sided with the Jews, and others with the apostles. [5] When an assault was planned by both Gentiles and Jews, with their leaders, to attack them and to stone them, [6] they learned of it and fled to Lystra and Derbe, cities of Lycaonia, and to the surrounding region. [7] And there they preached the gospel.

Paul and Barnabas in Lystra

[8] In Lystra there sat a man, crippled in his feet, who had never walked and was lame from birth. [9] He heard Paul speaking, who looked intently at him and perceived that he had faith to be healed [10] and said with a loud voice, "Stand upright on your feet." And he jumped up and walked.

[11] When the crowds saw what Paul had done, they lifted up their voices, saying in Lycaonian, "The gods have come down to us in the likeness of men!" [12] Barnabas they called Zeus, and Paul they called Hermes, because he was the main speaker. [13] The priest of Zeus, who was in front of the city, brought bulls and garlands to the gates to offer sacrifices with the crowds.

[14] But when the apostles Barnabas and Paul heard this, they tore their clothes and rushed out into the crowd, crying out, [15] "Men, why are you doing this? We also are men, of like nature with you, preaching to you to turn from these vain things to the living God, who made the heaven and the earth and the sea, and everything that is in them, [16] who in times past allowed all nations to walk in their own ways. [17] Yet He did not leave Himself without witness, for He did good and gave us rain from heaven and fruitful seasons, satisfying our hearts with food and gladness." [18] With these words they scarcely restrained the crowds from sacrificing to them.

[19] Then some Jews from Antioch and Iconium came there and persuaded the crowds. They stoned Paul and dragged him out of the city, supposing he was dead. [20] But as the disciples gathered around him, he rose up and went into the city. The next day he departed with Barnabas for Derbe.

The Return to Antioch in Syria

[21] When they had preached the gospel to that city and had made many disciples, they returned to Lystra and to Iconium and to Antioch, [22] strengthening the minds of the disciples and exhorting them to continue in the faith, to go through many afflictions and thus enter the kingdom of God. [23] When they had appointed elders for them in every church, with prayer and fasting, they commended them to the Lord in whom they believed. [24] Then they passed throughout Pisidia and came to Pamphylia, [25] and when they had preached the word in Perga, they went down into Attalia. [26] From there they sailed to Antioch, where they had been commended to the grace of God for the work which they had completed. [27] When they arrived and had assembled the church, they reported what God had done through them and how He had opened the door of faith to the Gentiles. [28] And there they stayed a long time with the disciples.

The Council in Jerusalem

15 Some men came down from Judea and were teaching the brothers, "Unless you are circumcised in the tradition of Moses, you cannot be saved." [2] Therefore when Paul and Barnabas had no small dissension and dispute with them, they determined that Paul and Barnabas, and certain others among them, should go up to Jerusalem to the apostles and elders about this question. [3] So being sent on their way by the church, they passed through Phoenicia and Samaria, declaring the conversion of the Gentiles, and they brought great joy to all the brothers. [4] When they arrived in Jerusalem, they were welcomed by the church and the apostles and the elders, and they declared what God had done through them.

[5] Then some believers of the sect of the Pharisees rose up, saying, "It is necessary to circumcise them, and to command them to keep the Law of Moses."

[6] The apostles and elders assembled to consider this matter. [7] After much disputing, Peter rose up and said to them, "Brothers, you

---

[1] 33 Ps 2:7.　[2] 34 Isa 55:3.　[3] 35 Ps 16:10.　[4] 41 Hab 1:5.　[5] 47 Isa 42:6; 49:6.

know that some time ago God decided among us, that by my mouth the Gentiles should hear the word of the gospel and believe. [8] God, who knows the heart, approved of them, giving them the Holy Spirit just as He did to us, [9] and made no distinction between them and us, and purified their hearts by faith. [10] Now then, why test God by putting a yoke upon the neck of the disciples, which neither our fathers nor we have been able to bear? [11] But we believe that through the grace of the Lord Jesus Christ we shall be saved, even as they."

[12] The entire assembly remained silent and listened to Barnabas and Paul declaring what signs and wonders God had done through them among the Gentiles. [13] After they had become silent, James answered, "Brothers, listen to me. [14] Simon has declared how God first visited the Gentiles to take from among them a people for His name. [15] With this the words of the prophets agree. As it is written:

[16] 'After this I will return,
       and I will rebuild the tabernacle of David,
           which has fallen;
       I will rebuild its ruins,
           and I will set it up;[1]
[17] that the rest of men may seek the Lord,
       and all the Gentiles who are called by My name,[2]
   says the Lord who does all these things.'[3]
[18]   Known to God are all His works since the beginning
           of the world.

[19] "Therefore my judgment is that we should not trouble those of the Gentiles who are turning to God, [20] but that we write to them to abstain from food offered to idols, from sexual immorality, from strangled animals, and from blood. [21] For Moses has had in every city since early generations those who preach him, being read in the synagogues every Sabbath."

The Reply of the Council
[22] Then it pleased the apostles and the elders, with the whole church, to send chosen men from among them to Antioch with Paul and Barnabas, namely, Judas called Barsabas, and Silas, leading men among the brothers. [23] They wrote this letter by their hand:

The apostles and the elders and the brothers,

To the brothers who are of the Gentiles in Antioch and Syria and Cilicia:

Greetings.

[24] Since we have heard that some of us, whom we did not commission, have gone out and have troubled you with words, unsettling your minds, saying, "You must be circumcised and keep the law," [25] it seemed good to us, being assembled in unity, to send chosen men to you with our beloved Barnabas and Paul, [26] men who have risked their lives for the name of our Lord Jesus Christ. [27] Therefore we have sent Judas and Silas, who will also speak to you, saying the same things. [28] For it seemed good to the Holy Spirit and to us to put on you no greater burden than these necessary things: [29] Abstain from food offered to idols, from sexual immorality, from strangled animals, and from blood. If you keep yourselves from these, you will do well.

Farewell.

[30] So when they were dismissed, they went down to Antioch. And when they had assembled the congregation, they delivered the letter. [31] When they had read it, they rejoiced over the exhortation. [32] Judas and Silas, being prophets themselves, exhorted the brothers with many words and strengthened them. [33] After they had remained there for a time, they were sent off in peace by the brothers to the apostles. [34] But it seemed good to Silas to remain there. [35] And Paul and Barnabas remained in Antioch, teaching and preaching the word of the Lord, with many others also.

Paul and Barnabas Separate
[36] After some days Paul said to Barnabas, "Let us return and visit our brothers in every city where we preached the word of the Lord and see how they are doing." [37] Barnabas determined to take with them John, who was called Mark. [38] But Paul thought it was not good to take with them one who had withdrawn from them in Pamphylia and had not gone with them to the work. [39] Then there arose a sharp contention, so that they separated from each other. Barnabas took Mark and sailed to Cyprus, [40] but Paul chose Silas and departed, being commended by the brothers to the grace of God. [41] And he went through Syria and Cilicia, strengthening the churches.

Timothy Accompanies Paul and Silas
16 Then he came to Derbe and then to Lystra. A disciple was there, named Timothy, the son of a Jewess who believed, but his father was a Greek. [2] He was well spoken of by the brothers who were at Lystra and Iconium. [3] Paul wanted him to travel with him. So he took him and circumcised him because of the Jews who were in those places, for they all knew that his father was a Greek. [4] As they went through the cities, they delivered to them the decrees to observe, that were set forth by the apostles and elders at Jerusalem. [5] So the churches were strengthened in the faith, and increased in number daily.

Paul's Vision of the Macedonian
[6] They went through the region of Phrygia and Galatia and were forbidden by the Holy Spirit to speak the word in Asia. [7] When they came near Mysia, they tried to go into Bithynia, but the Spirit did not allow them. [8] So they passed by Mysia and went down to Troas. [9] During the night a vision appeared to Paul: A man of Macedonia stood and pleaded with him, saying, "Come over to Macedonia and help us." [10] After he had seen the vision, immediately we sought to go into Macedonia, concluding that the Lord had called us to preach the gospel to them.

The Conversion of Lydia
[11] From Troas we set sail on a straight course to Samothrace and the next day to Neapolis, [12] and from there to Philippi, which is the main city of that part of Macedonia, and a colony. We stayed in this city several days. [13] On the Sabbath we went out of the city to a riverside, where prayer was customarily offered. And we sat down and spoke to the women who had assembled. [14] A woman named Lydia, a seller of purple fabric of the city of Thyatira, who worshipped God, heard us. The Lord opened her heart to acknowledge what Paul said. [15] When she and her household were baptized, she entreated us, saying, "If you have judged me to be faithful to the Lord, come to my house and remain there." And she persuaded us.

The Imprisonment in Philippi
[16] On one occasion, as we went to the place of prayer, a servant girl possessed with a spirit of divination met us, who brought her masters much profit by fortune-telling. [17] She followed Paul and us, shouting, "These men are servants of the Most High God, who proclaim to us the way of salvation." [18] She did this for many days. But becoming greatly troubled, Paul turned to the spirit and said, "I command you in the name of Jesus Christ to come out of her." And it came out at that moment.

[19] When her masters saw that the hope of their profits was gone, they seized Paul and Silas, and dragged them into the marketplace to the rulers. [20] And they brought them to the magistrates, saying, "These men, being Jews, greatly trouble our city [21] and teach customs which are not lawful for us, being Romans, to receive or observe."

[22] The crowd rose up together against them. And the magistrates tore the garments off them and gave orders to beat them. [23] After they had laid many stripes on them, they threw them into prison, commanding the jailer to guard them securely. [24] Having received such an order, he threw them into the inner prison and fastened their feet in the stocks.

---

[1] 16 Am 9:11; Jer 12:15.   [2] 17 Am 9:12; Dt 28:10; Isa 63:19; Jer 14:9; Da 9:19.   [3] 17 Am 9:11–12.

25 At midnight Paul and Silas were praying and singing hymns to God, and the prisoners were listening to them. 26 Suddenly there was a great earthquake, so that the foundations of the prison were shaken. And immediately all the doors were opened and everyone's shackles were loosened. 27 When the jailer awoke and saw the prison doors open, he drew his sword and would have killed himself, supposing that the prisoners had escaped. 28 But Paul shouted, "Do not harm yourself, for we are all here."

29 He called for lights and rushed in, trembling, and fell down before Paul and Silas. 30 He then led them out and asked, "Sirs, what must I do to be saved?"

31 They said, "Believe in the Lord Jesus Christ, and you and your household will be saved." 32 And they spoke the word of the Lord to him and to all who were in his household. 33 In that hour of the night he took them and washed their wounds. And immediately he and his entire household were baptized. 34 Then he brought them up to his house and set food before them. And he rejoiced with his entire household believing in God.

35 When it was day, the magistrates sent the sergeants, saying, "Release those men." 36 The prison guard reported these words to Paul, saying, "The magistrates have sent to release you. Now therefore depart, and go in peace."

37 But Paul said to them, "They have publicly beaten us, who are uncondemned Romans, and have thrown us into prison. And now do they secretly throw us out? Certainly not! Let them come themselves and bring us out."

38 The sergeants reported these words to the magistrates, and they were afraid when they heard that they were Romans. 39 So they came and entreated them. And they brought them out, asking them to leave the city. 40 They went out of the prison and entered the house of Lydia. When they had seen the brothers, they exhorted them and departed.

The Uproar in Thessalonica

17 When they had traveled through Amphipolis and Apollonia, they came to Thessalonica, where there was a synagogue of the Jews. 2 According to his custom, Paul went in, and on three Sabbaths he lectured to them from the Scriptures, 3 explaining and proving that the Christ had to suffer and to rise from the dead, and saying, "This Jesus, whom I preach to you, is the Christ." 4 Some of them were persuaded and joined with Paul and Silas, including a great crowd of devout Greeks and many leading women.

5 But the Jews who did not believe became jealous and, taking some evil men from the marketplace, gathered a crowd, stirred up the city, and attacked the house of Jason, trying to bring them out to the mob. 6 But when they did not find them, they dragged Jason and some brothers to the city officials, crying out, "These men who have turned the world upside down have come here also, 7 and Jason has received them. They are all acting contrary to the decrees of Caesar, saying that there is another king, Jesus." 8 They troubled the crowd and the city officials when they heard these things. 9 When they had taken a bail payment from Jason and the rest, they released them.

The Apostles in Berea

10 The brothers immediately sent Paul and Silas away by night to Berea. When they arrived, they went into the synagogue of the Jews. 11 These were more noble than those in Thessalonica, for they received the word with all eagerness, daily examining the Scriptures, to find out if these things were so. 12 Therefore many of them believed, including honorable Greek women and many Greek men.

13 But when the Jews of Thessalonica learned that the word of God was preached by Paul at Berea, they came there also, stirring up the crowds. 14 The brothers immediately sent Paul away to the sea. But Silas and Timothy remained there. 15 Those who escorted Paul brought him to Athens and departed with instructions for Silas and Timothy to come to him quickly.

Paul in Athens

16 While Paul waited for them in Athens, his spirit was provoked within him as he saw that the city was full of idols. 17 Therefore he disputed in the synagogue with the Jews and the devout persons, and in the marketplace daily with those who happened to be there. 18 Then some of the Epicurean and Stoic philosophers encountered him. And some said, "What will this babbler say?" Others said, "He seems to be a proclaimer of foreign gods," because he preached Jesus and the resurrection to them. 19 They took hold of him and led him to the Areopagus, saying, "May we know what this new doctrine is of which you speak? 20 For you are bringing strange things to our ears. Therefore we want to know what these things mean." 21 For all the Athenians and foreigners who lived there spent their time in nothing else, but either telling or hearing something new.

22 Then Paul stood in the middle of the Areopagus, and said: "Men of Athens, I perceive that in all things you are very religious. 23 For as I passed by and looked up at your objects of worship, I found an altar with this inscription:

TO THE UNKNOWN GOD.

Whom you therefore unknowingly worship, Him I proclaim to you. 24 "God who made the world and all things in it, being Lord of heaven and earth, does not live in temples made by hands. 25 Nor is He served by men's hands, as though He needed anything, since He gives all men life and breath and all things. 26 He has made from one blood every nation of men to live on the entire face of the earth, having appointed fixed times and the boundaries of their habitation, 27 that they should seek the Lord so perhaps they might reach for Him and find Him, though He is not far from each one of us. 28 'For in Him we live and move and have our being.' As some of your own poets have said, 'We are His offspring.'

29 "Therefore since we are the offspring of God, we ought not to suppose that the Deity is like gold or silver or stone or an engraved work of art or an image of the reflection of man. 30 God overlooked the times of ignorance, but now He commands all men everywhere to repent. 31 For He has appointed a day on which He will judge the world in righteousness by a Man whom He has appointed, having given assurance of this to all men by raising Him from the dead."

32 When they heard of the resurrection of the dead, some scoffed. But others said, "We will hear you again concerning this matter." 33 So Paul departed from them. 34 However, some men joined him and believed. Among them were Dionysius the Areopagite, and a woman named Damaris, and others with them.

Paul in Corinth

18 After this, Paul left Athens and went to Corinth. 2 He found a Jew named Aquila, a native of Pontus, who had recently come from Italy with his wife Priscilla, because Claudius had commanded all the Jews to leave Rome. And he went to them. 3 And because he was of the same trade, he remained with them and worked, for they were tentmakers by trade. 4 He lectured in the synagogue every Sabbath and persuaded Jews and Greeks.

5 When Silas and Timothy came from Macedonia, Paul was pressed by the Spirit and testified to the Jews that Jesus was the Christ. 6 But when they opposed him and blasphemed, he shook out his garments and said to them, "Your blood be upon your heads. I am innocent. From now on I will go to the Gentiles."

7 Then he departed from there and entered the house of a man named Justus, one who worshipped God, whose house was next door to the synagogue. 8 Crispus, the ruler of the synagogue, believed in the Lord with his entire household. And many of the Corinthians, who heard, believed and were baptized.

9 The Lord spoke to Paul in the night through a vision, "Do not be afraid, but speak and do not be silent. 10 For I am with you, and no one shall attack you and hurt you, for I have many people in this city." 11 So for a year and six months he sat among them, teaching the word of God.

12 When Gallio was proconsul of Achaia, the Jews in unity attacked Paul and brought him to court, 13 saying, "This man is persuading men to worship God contrary to the law."

14 When Paul was about to speak, Gallio said to the Jews, "O Jews, if it were a matter of a misdemeanor or serious crime, I would rightly bear with you. 15 But if it is a question of words and names and your law, look into it yourselves. For I do not intend to be a judge of these matters." 16 So he drove them out of court.

[17] Then all the Greeks seized Sosthenes, the ruler of the synagogue, and beat him before the judgment seat. But none of these things mattered to Gallio.

Paul's Return to Antioch

[18] Yet Paul remained many days. He had his hair cut in Cenchrea, for he had taken a vow. Then, bidding farewell to the brothers, he sailed to Syria, and Priscilla and Aquila were with him. [19] He arrived at Ephesus and left them there. But he himself went into the synagogue and lectured the Jews. [20] When they asked him to remain for a while longer, he did not consent, [21] but, bidding farewell, said, "I must by all means attend this upcoming feast in Jerusalem, but I will return to you if God wills." And he set sail from Ephesus. [22] When he had landed at Caesarea, he went up and greeted the church and then went down to Antioch.

[23] After spending some time there, he departed and passed through the entire region of Galatia and Phrygia in sequence, strengthening all the disciples.

Apollos Preaches in Ephesus

[24] Meanwhile a Jew named Apollos, born in Alexandria, who was an eloquent man and powerful in the Scriptures, came to Ephesus. [25] This man was instructed in the way of the Lord, knowing only the baptism of John, but being fervent in spirit, he accurately spoke and taught the things concerning the Lord. [26] He began to speak boldly in the synagogue. When Aquila and Priscilla heard him, they took him and explained the way of God more accurately.

[27] When Apollos intended to pass into Achaia, the brothers wrote to encourage the disciples to welcome him. On arriving, he greatly helped those who had believed through grace. [28] For he vehemently refuted the Jews publicly, proving from the Scriptures that Jesus was the Christ.

Ephesians Receive the Holy Spirit

19 While Apollos was at Corinth, Paul passed through the upper regions and came to Ephesus. He found some disciples [2] and said to them, "Have you received the Holy Spirit since you believed?"

They said to him, "No, we have not even heard that there is a Holy Spirit."

[3] He said to them, "Into what then were you baptized?"

They said, "Into John's baptism."

[4] Paul said, "John indeed baptized with the baptism of repentance, telling the people that they should believe in the One coming after him, that is, in Christ Jesus." [5] When they heard this, they were baptized in the name of the Lord Jesus. [6] When Paul had laid his hands on them, the Holy Spirit came on them, and they spoke in other tongues and prophesied. [7] There were about twelve men in all.

[8] He went into the synagogue and spoke boldly for three months, lecturing and persuading concerning the kingdom of God. [9] But when some were hardened and did not believe, but spoke evil of the Way before the crowd, he withdrew from them and took the disciples, lecturing daily in the school of Tyrannus. [10] This continued for two years, so that all who lived in Asia heard the word of the Lord Jesus, both Jews and Greeks.

The Sons of Sceva

[11] God worked powerful miracles by the hands of Paul. [12] So handkerchiefs or aprons he had touched were brought to the sick, and the diseases left them, and the evil spirits went out of them. [13] Then some of the itinerant Jewish exorcists invoked the name of the Lord Jesus over those who had evil spirits, saying, "We command you to come out in the name of Jesus whom Paul preaches." [14] There were seven sons of a Jewish high priest named Sceva doing this. [15] The evil spirit answered, "I know Jesus, and I know Paul, but who are you?" [16] Then the man in whom the evil spirit was jumped on them, overpowered them, and prevailed against them, so that they fled from that house naked and wounded.

[17] This became known to all Jews and Greeks living in Ephesus. And fear fell on them all, and the name of the Lord Jesus was magnified. [18] Many who believed came confessing and telling their deeds. [19] Many who practiced magic brought their books together and burned them before everyone. They calculated their value, which equaled fifty thousand drachmas. [1] [20] So the word of the Lord powerfully grew and spread.

The Riot in Ephesus

[21] After these things happened, Paul determined in his spirit to pass through Macedonia and Achaia and go to Jerusalem, saying, "After I have been there, I must also see Rome." [22] He sent two who ministered to him, Timothy and Erastus, into Macedonia, but he delayed in Asia for a season.

[23] About that time great trouble arose about the Way. [24] For a silversmith named Demetrius, who made silver shrines for Artemis, brought much business to the craftsmen. [25] He gathered them together with the workmen of similar trades and said, "Men, you know that by this trade we have our wealth. [26] And you see and hear, not only at Ephesus, but almost throughout all Asia, that this Paul has persuaded and turned away many people, saying that these things made by hands are not gods. [27] Now not only is our trade in danger of coming into disrepute, but also the temple of the great goddess Artemis, whom all Asia and the world worship, may be discredited and her magnificence destroyed."

[28] When they heard this, they were full of anger and cried out, "Great is Artemis of the Ephesians!" [29] The city was filled with confusion. And in unison they seized Gaius and Aristarchus, Paul's traveling companions from Macedonia, and rushed into the theater. [30] When Paul intended to go in among the crowd, the disciples would not let him. [31] Even some of the rulers of Asia, who were his friends, sent to him begging him not to venture into the theater.

[32] The assembly was confused. Therefore some cried out one thing and some another, and most of them did not know why they had come together. [33] The Jews pushed Alexander to the front as the crowd prompted him. Alexander motioned with his hand, wishing to make his defense to the mob. [34] But when they learned that he was a Jew, for about two hours they all with one voice cried out, "Great is Artemis of the Ephesians!"

[35] The city clerk quieted the crowd and said, "Men of Ephesus, what man is there who does not know that the city of the Ephesians is the guardian of the temple of the great Artemis and of the image which fell from heaven? [36] Seeing then that these things are undeniable, you ought to be quiet and do nothing rash. [37] For you have brought these men here who are neither temple robbers nor blasphemers of your goddess. [38] So if Demetrius and the craftsmen who are with him have a complaint against anyone, the courts are open and there are proconsuls. Let them press charges against one another. [39] If you seek anything further, it shall be settled in the legal assembly. [40] For we are in danger of being charged with rioting today, since there is no reason we may give to account for this uproar." [41] When he had said this, he dismissed the assembly.

Paul's Journey to Macedonia and Greece

20 After the uproar ceased, Paul summoned the disciples and embraced them and departed for Macedonia. [2] When he had gone through that region and had greatly exhorted them, he arrived in Greece, [3] and stayed there three months. When the Jews plotted against him as he was about to sail to Syria, he decided to return through Macedonia. [4] Accompanying him to Asia were Sopater of Berea, and Aristarchus and Secundus of Thessalonica, Gaius of Derbe, and Timothy, and Tychicus and Trophimus of Asia. [5] These men went forward and waited for us at Troas. [6] But we sailed away from Philippi after the Days of Unleavened Bread, and after five days we came to them at Troas, where we stayed for seven days.

Paul's Farewell Visit to Troas

[7] On the first day of the week, when the disciples came together to break bread, Paul, ready to leave the next day, preached to them and continued his message until midnight. [8] There were many lamps in the upper room where they were assembled. [9] A young man named Eutychus sat in the window, falling into a deep sleep as Paul spoke

---

[1] 19 A drachma was worth about a day's wage.

for a longer time. Being overcome by sleep, he fell down from the third floor and was taken up dead. [10] Paul went down and leaned over him, and embracing him said, "Do not be troubled, for he is alive." [11] When he had gone up and had broken bread and eaten, he conversed for a long while until dawn and departed. [12] They took the lad in alive and were greatly comforted.

The Voyage From Troas to Miletus

[13] We went ahead to the ship and sailed to Assos, intending to take Paul on board there. For he had arranged this, intending to go on foot. [14] When he met us at Assos, we took him on board and went to Mitylene. [15] The day after sailing from there we arrived off Chios. And the next day we crossed over to Samos and stayed at Trogyllium, and the following day we came to Miletus. [16] Paul had decided to sail by Ephesus, to avoid spending time in Asia. For he was hurrying so he could be in Jerusalem, if possible, on the day of Pentecost.

Paul Speaks to the Ephesian Elders

[17] From Miletus he sent to Ephesus for the elders of the church. [18] When they came to him, he said to them, "You know how I always lived among you from the first day that I came to Asia, [19] serving the Lord with all humility and with many tears and trials which befell me through the plots of the Jews. [20] I did not keep from declaring what was beneficial to you, and teaching you publicly and from house to house, [21] testifying to both Jews and Greeks of repentance toward God and of faith in our Lord Jesus Christ.

[22] "Now, compelled by the Spirit, I am going to Jerusalem, not knowing what shall befall me there, [23] except that the Holy Spirit testifies to me in every city that imprisonment and afflictions await me. [24] But none of these things deter me. Nor do I count my life of value to myself, so that I may joyfully finish my course and the ministry which I have received from the Lord Jesus, to testify to the gospel of the grace of God.

[25] "Now I know that all you, among whom I went proclaiming the kingdom of God, will see my face no more. [26] Therefore I testify to you this day that I am innocent of the blood of all men. [27] For I did not keep from declaring to you the whole counsel of God. [28] Therefore take heed to yourselves and to the entire flock, over which the Holy Spirit has made you overseers, to shepherd the church of God which He purchased with His own blood. [29] For I know that after my departure, dreadful wolves will enter among you, not sparing the flock. [30] Even from among you men will arise speaking perverse things, to draw the disciples away after them. [31] Therefore watch, remembering that for three years night and day I did not cease to warn everyone with tears.

[32] "Now, brothers, I commend you to God and to the word of His grace, which is able to build you up and give you an inheritance among all who are sanctified. [33] I have not coveted anyone's silver or gold or clothing. [34] Yes, you yourselves know that these hands have provided for my necessities and for those who were with me. [35] In all things I have shown you how, working like this, you must help the weak, remembering the words of the Lord Jesus, how He said, 'It is more blessed to give than to receive.'"

[36] Having said these things, he knelt down with all of them and prayed. [37] They all wept much and embraced Paul's neck and kissed him, [38] grieving most over the words he spoke, that they were to see his face no more. Then they escorted him to the ship.

Paul's Journey to Jerusalem

21 When we had withdrawn from them and set sail, we went on a straight course to Cos, the next day to Rhodes, and from there to Patara. [2] We found a ship crossing over to Phoenicia, went aboard, and set sail. [3] Having come in sight of Cyprus, we passed to the south of it and sailed to Syria, and landed at Tyre, for there the ship's cargo was to be unloaded. [4] When we found the disciples, we remained there seven days. They told Paul through the Spirit not to go up to Jerusalem. [5] But when our days were over, we parted and traveled on. Everyone, with wives and children, escorted us until we were outside the city. And we knelt on the shore and

prayed. [6] After bidding farewell to one another, we boarded the ship, and they returned home.

[7] We finished the voyage from Tyre when we landed at Ptolemais, where we greeted the brothers and stayed with them for one day. [8] The next day we who were Paul's companions departed, and arrived at Caesarea, and entered the house of Philip the evangelist, who was one of the seven, and stayed with him. [9] He had four virgin daughters who prophesied. [10] While we stayed there many days, a prophet named Agabus came down from Judea. [11] When he had arrived, he took Paul's belt and bound his own hands and feet, saying, "The Holy Spirit says, 'In this manner the Jews at Jerusalem shall bind the man who owns this belt and deliver him into the hands of the Gentiles.'"

[12] When we heard these things, both we and the residents implored him not to go up to Jerusalem. [13] Then Paul answered, "What are you doing, weeping and breaking my heart? For I am ready not only to be imprisoned, but also to die in Jerusalem for the name of the Lord Jesus." [14] When he would not be persuaded, we kept silent and said, "Let the will of the Lord be done."

[15] After those days we got ready and went up to Jerusalem. [16] Some of the disciples from Caesarea went with us and brought with them Mnason of Cyprus, an early disciple, with whom we should lodge.

Paul Visits James

[17] When we had come to Jerusalem, the brothers received us gladly. [18] On the next day Paul went with us to James, and all the elders were present. [19] He greeted them and recounted one by one what God had done among the Gentiles through his ministry. [20] When they heard this, they glorified the Lord. Then they said to him, "You see, brother, how many thousands of Jews there are who believe, and they are all zealous for the law. [21] They have been informed concerning you that you teach all the Jews who are among the Gentiles to forsake Moses, telling them not to circumcise their children nor to observe the customs. [22] What then shall be done? The assembly will certainly meet, for they will hear that you have come. [23] Therefore do what we tell you. We have four men who have taken a vow. [24] Take these men and be purified with them, and pay their expenses so that they may have their heads shaved. Then all will know that what they were told concerning you is nothing, but that you yourself live in observance of the law. [25] As for the Gentiles who believe, we have written and concluded that they should observe no such thing, except that they abstain from food offered to idols, from sexual immorality, from strangled animals, and from blood."

[26] Then on the next day, Paul took the men and purified himself with them. And he went into the temple, announcing when the days of purification would be complete and an offering would be given for each one of them.

Paul Arrested in the Temple

[27] When the seven days were nearly concluded, the Jews from Asia saw him in the temple, stirred up all the people, and laid hands on him, [28] crying out, "Men of Israel, help! This is the man teaching all men everywhere against the people and the law and this place. He even brought Greeks into the temple and has defiled this holy place." [29] For they had previously seen Trophimus the Ephesian in the city with him, whom they supposed Paul had brought into the temple. [30] Then the whole city was provoked, and the people ran together. They seized Paul and dragged him out of the temple. And immediately the doors were shut. [31] While they were trying to kill him, news came up to the commander[1] of the battalion of soldiers that all Jerusalem was in an uproar. [32] He at once took soldiers and centurions, and ran down to them. When they saw the commander and the soldiers, they stopped beating Paul. [33] Then the commander came and arrested him, and ordered that he be bound with two chains. Then he asked who he was and what he had done. [34] Some in the crowd shouted one thing, some another. As he could not learn the truth because of the uproar, he commanded that he be brought into the barracks.

---

[1] 31 Gk. *chiliarch*, a battalion commander with the rank of lieutenant colonel over 1,000 soldiers.

35 When he came onto the stairs, he was carried by the soldiers because of the violence of the people. 36 For the mob of people followed, crying out, "Away with him!"

Paul Defends Himself

37 As Paul was about to be brought into the barracks, he said to the commander, "May I speak to you?"

He replied, "Do you know how to speak Greek? 38 Are you not the Egyptian who in past days caused an uproar and led the four thousand men of the Sicarii *¹* out into the wilderness?"

39 Paul said, "I am a Jew, from Tarsus of Cilicia, a citizen of no common city. I beg of you, permit me to speak to the people."

40 When he had given him permission, Paul stood on the stairs and motioned with his hand to the people. When there was great silence, he addressed them in the Hebrew language, saying,

22 "Brothers and fathers, hear my defense which I now make to you."

2 When they heard that he addressed them in the Hebrew language, they became even more quiet.

Then he said, 3 "I am a Jew, born in Tarsus of Cilicia, but brought up in this city. At the feet of Gamaliel I was trained in the strict tradition of the law of the fathers, being zealous toward God as you all are today. 4 I persecuted this Way to the death, arresting and imprisoning both men and women, 5 as even the high priest and the council of elders bear witness of me. From them I received letters to the brothers in Damascus, where I went to take even those who were there and lead them in chains to Jerusalem to be punished.

Paul Tells of His Conversion

Ac 9:1–19; 26:12–18

6 "As I journeyed and came near Damascus, about noon suddenly a great light from heaven shone around me. 7 I fell to the ground and heard a voice saying to me, 'Saul, Saul, why do you persecute Me?'

8 "I answered, 'Who are You, Lord?'

"He said to me, 'I am Jesus of Nazareth, whom you are persecuting.' 9 Those who were with me saw the light and were afraid, but they did not hear the voice of Him who was speaking to me.

10 "I said, 'What shall I do, Lord?'

"The Lord said to me, 'Rise and go into Damascus. There you will be told what you have been appointed to do.' 11 Since I was blinded by the glory of that light, those who were with me led me by the hand into Damascus.

12 "Ananias, a devout man according to the law, who was well spoken of by all the Jews living there, 13 came and stood by me, and said, 'Brother Saul, receive your sight.' And at that moment I looked up at him.

14 "Then he said, 'The God of our fathers has appointed you to know His will and to see the Just One and to hear His voice, 15 for you will be His witness to all men of what you have seen and heard. 16 And now why do you wait? Rise, be baptized and wash away your sins, and call on the name of the Lord.'

Paul Sent to the Gentiles

17 "When I returned to Jerusalem and was praying in the temple, I fell into a trance 18 and saw Him saying to me, 'Hurry! Get out of Jerusalem immediately, for they will not receive your testimony concerning Me.'

19 "I said, 'Lord, they know that I imprisoned and beat those who believed in You in every synagogue. 20 And when the blood of Your martyr Stephen was shed, I was standing by consenting to his death, guarding the clothes of those who killed him.'

21 "Then He said to me, 'Depart, for I will send you far away to the Gentiles.' "

Paul and the Roman Commander

22 They listened to him up to this word, and then they lifted up their voices and said, "Away with such a man from the earth, for he is not fit to live!"

23 As they shouted and threw off their garments and threw dust into the air, 24 the commander ordered him to be brought into the barracks and examined with scourging, so that he might learn what crime they were alleging against him. 25 As they stretched him forward with straps, Paul said to the centurion standing by, "Is it legal for you to flog an uncondemned Roman citizen?"

26 On hearing this, the centurion reported to the commander, saying, "What are you doing? This man is a Roman citizen."

27 The commander came and said to him, "Tell me, are you a Roman citizen?"

He said, "Yes."

28 The commander answered, "I bought my citizenship for a large sum."

So Paul said, "But I was born a citizen."

29 Therefore those who were about to examine Paul immediately backed away from him. And the commander feared, knowing that he was a Roman citizen and because he had bound him.

Paul Before the Sanhedrin

30 On the next day, desiring to know exactly why he was accused by the Jews, he released him and ordered the chief priests and all the Sanhedrin to assemble, and he brought Paul down to stand before them.

23 Paul looked at the Sanhedrin and said, "Brothers, I have lived in all good conscience before God until this day." 2 The high priest Ananias ordered those who stood by him to strike him on the mouth. 3 Then Paul said to him, "God will strike you, you whitewashed wall! Do you sit judging me according to the law, yet order me to be struck contrary to the law?"

4 Those who stood by said, "Do you criticize God's high priest?"

5 Paul said, "Brothers, I did not know that he was the high priest. For it is written, 'You shall not speak evil of the ruler of your people.' *²*"

6 Then Paul, knowing that one sect were Sadducees and the other Pharisees, cried out among the Sanhedrin, "Brothers, I am a Pharisee, a son of a Pharisee. I am being judged for my hope in the resurrection of the dead." 7 When he had said this, dissension arose between the Pharisees and the Sadducees, and the assembly was divided. 8 For the Sadducees say that there is no resurrection, nor angel, nor spirit. But the Pharisees acknowledge them all.

9 There was a great outcry. The scribes that were from the sect of Pharisees stood up and argued, "We find no evil in this man. But if a spirit or an angel has spoken to him, let us not fight against God." 10 When much dissension arose, fearing that Paul would be torn to pieces by them, the commander ordered the soldiers to go down and take him from them by force and bring him into the barracks.

11 The following night the Lord stood by him and said, "Take courage, Paul. For as you have testified about Me in Jerusalem, so you must also testify at Rome."

The Plot Against Paul's Life

12 At daybreak some of the Jews conspired under oath, saying they would neither eat nor drink until they had killed Paul. 13 There were more than forty who had conspired. 14 They went to the chief priests and elders and said, "We have bound ourselves under oath not to eat until we have killed Paul. 15 So now, with the Sanhedrin, tell the commander to bring him down to you tomorrow, pretending to inquire further concerning him. We are ready to kill him before he arrives."

16 But when the son of Paul's sister heard of the treachery, he went and entered the barracks and told Paul.

17 Then Paul called one of the centurions over and said, "Take this young man to the commander, for he has something to tell him." 18 So he took him to the commander and said, "Paul the prisoner sent for me and asked me to bring you this young man who has something to tell you."

19 Then the commander took him by the hand, went aside privately, and asked him, "What is it you have to tell me?"

20 The boy said, "The Jews have agreed to ask you to bring Paul down tomorrow to the Sanhedrin, pretending to inquire further concerning him. 21 Do not trust them. More than forty men, who

---

¹ 38 Or men of the Assassins.   ² 5 Ex 22:28.

have bound themselves with an oath to neither eat nor drink until they have killed him, are waiting for him. And now they are ready, waiting for your promise."

[22] The commander dismissed the young man and ordered him, "Tell no one that you have reported these things to me."

Paul Sent to Felix the Governor

[23] Then he summoned two centurions and said, "Prepare two hundred infantrymen, seventy mounted soldiers, and two hundred light infantrymen with spears to go to Caesarea at the third hour of the night. [24] And provide mounts so Paul may ride and take him safely to Felix the governor."

[25] He wrote a letter that went like this:

[26] Claudius Lysias,

To His Excellency Governor Felix:

Greetings.

[27] This man was seized by the Jews and was about to be killed by them. When I learned that he was a Roman citizen, I came with soldiers and rescued him. [28] Being minded to learn what crime they alleged, I took him to their Sanhedrin. [29] I found him being accused of controversial matters about their law, but charged with nothing worthy of death or imprisonment. [30] When it was revealed to me that there was a plot against the man, at once I sent him to you and ordered the accusers to state before you their charges against him.

Farewell.

[31] So the soldiers, according to their orders, took Paul by night to Antipatris. [32] The next day they let the cavalry depart with him and they returned to the barracks. [33] When they arrived in Caesarea and delivered the letter to the governor, they presented Paul also to him. [34] Upon reading the letter, the governor asked what province he was from. When he learned that he was from Cilicia, [35] he said, "I will hear you when your accusers also arrive." And he ordered that he be guarded in Herod's Praetorium.

The Case Against Paul

24 After five days Ananias the high priest arrived with some of the elders and a lawyer named Tertullus. They brought before the governor their charges against Paul. [2] When he was summoned, Tertullus began to accuse him, saying, "Since through you we enjoy much peace, and your foresight is bringing reforms to this nation, [3] with all thankfulness, most excellent Felix, we always welcome it everywhere. [4] But not to detain you further, I beg you to briefly hear us in your patience.

[5] "We have found this man a troublemaker, instigating riots among all the Jews throughout the world, and a ringleader of the sect of the Nazarenes. [6] He even tried to profane the temple. So we seized him and wanted to judge him according to our law. [7] But the commander, Lysias, came to us and forcefully took him out of our hands, [8] ordering his accusers to come before you. By examining him yourself you will be able to learn about all these things concerning which we accuse him."

[9] The Jews assented, alleging these things to be true.

Paul's Defense Before Felix

[10] After the governor motioned to him to speak, Paul answered, "Knowing that for many years you have been a judge over this nation, I cheerfully defend myself. [11] You may verify that it is no more than twelve days since I went up to Jerusalem to worship. [12] They did not find me in the temple or in the synagogues or in the city disputing with anyone or stirring up a crowd. [13] They cannot prove the things concerning which they now accuse me. [14] However, I affirm that in accordance with the Way, which they call a sect, I worship the God of my fathers and believe everything written in the Law and in the Prophets. [15] I have hope in God that there will be a resurrection of the dead, both of the just and the unjust, which they

also expect. [16] In this do I always strive to have a clear conscience toward God and toward men.

[17] "Now after many years I came to bring alms and offerings to my nation, [18] when some Jews from Asia found me purified in the temple, neither with a crowd nor an uproar. [19] They ought to be here before you to accuse me if they have any charges. [20] Or let these men say what crime they found in me when I stood before the Sanhedrin, [21] unless it is concerning this one statement which I cried out while standing among them, 'Concerning the resurrection of the dead, I am being judged by you this day.' "

[22] When Felix, who had more exact knowledge concerning the Way, had heard this, he adjourned the proceedings and said, "When Lysias the commander arrives, I will decide your case." [23] Then he ordered the centurion to guard Paul, and to let him have liberty, and to forbid none of his own people from attending to him.

Paul Held in Custody

[24] After several days, when Felix arrived with his wife Drusilla, who was a Jewess, he sent for Paul and heard him speak concerning faith in Christ. [25] As he lectured about righteousness, self-control, and the coming judgment, Felix was afraid and answered, "For now, leave! When time permits, I will send for you." [26] At the same time he hoped that money would be given him by Paul, that he might release him. So he sent for him more often and conversed with him.

[27] But after two years Porcius Festus succeeded Felix. And Felix, desiring to do the Jews a favor, left Paul imprisoned.

Paul Appeals to Caesar

25 Now three days after Festus had come into the province, he went from Caesarea up to Jerusalem. [2] The high priest and the elders of the Jews spoke to him against Paul. And they begged him, [3] asking as a favor against him, that he would summon him to Jerusalem, plotting to kill him along the way. [4] Festus said that Paul should be kept at Caesarea and that he himself intended to go there shortly. [5] He also said, "Let the men in authority go down with me. If there is anything wrong in the man, let them accuse him."

[6] Having stayed among them more than ten days, he went down to Caesarea. And the next day he sat on the judgment seat and ordered that Paul be brought in. [7] When he arrived, the Jews who had come down from Jerusalem stood around him and brought many serious charges against him which they could not prove, [8] while he defended himself, saying, "Neither against the law of the Jews, nor against the temple, nor against Caesar have I sinned at all."

[9] Desiring to do the Jews a favor, Festus answered, "Are you willing to go up to Jerusalem to be judged concerning these charges before me?"

[10] Paul said, "I am standing before Caesar's judgment seat, where I ought to be judged. I have done no wrong to the Jews, as you know very well. [11] If I am doing wrong or have done anything worthy of death, I do not refuse to die. But if these are empty charges of which these men accuse me, no one may deliver me to them. I appeal to Caesar."

[12] When Festus had conferred with the council, he then answered, "To Caesar you have appealed. To Caesar you shall go."

Paul Before Agrippa and Bernice

[13] After several days King Agrippa and Bernice arrived at Caesarea to welcome Festus. [14] When they had been there many days, Festus stated Paul's case to the king, saying, "There is a man left as a prisoner by Felix. [15] When I was at Jerusalem, the chief priests and the elders of the Jews informed me about him, asking for a sentence against him.

[16] "I answered, 'It is not the custom of the Romans to deliver any man to die before he who is accused meets the accusers face to face and has the opportunity to make his defense concerning the charge brought against him.' [17] So when they assembled here, without delay I sat on the judgment seat the next day and ordered that the man be brought in. [18] When the accusers stood up, they brought no accusation against him of such crimes as I had supposed. [19] But they had disagreements with him about their own religion and

about a Man named Jesus, who had died, but whom Paul asserted was alive. [20] Being perplexed about such questions, I asked if he would be willing to go to Jerusalem and be tried there concerning these charges. [21] But when Paul had appealed to be under guard for the decision of Caesar, I ordered that he be secured until I could send him to Caesar."

[22] Then Agrippa said to Festus, "I would like to hear the man myself."

He said, "Tomorrow you shall hear him."

[23] The next day Agrippa and Bernice came with great pomp, and they entered the hall with the commanders and the leading men of the city. When Festus gave the order, Paul was brought in. [24] Festus said, "King Agrippa, and all the men who are present with us, you see this man, concerning whom the whole assembly of the Jews petitioned me, both at Jerusalem and here, shouting that he ought not to live any longer. [25] I found that he had committed nothing worthy of death. But when he himself appealed to Caesar, I decided to send him. [26] But I have nothing to write to His Majesty concerning him. Therefore I have brought him before you, and especially before you, King Agrippa, so that upon examination, I might have something to write. [27] For it seems unreasonable to me to send a prisoner without signifying the charges against him."

Paul's Defense Before Agrippa

26 Then Agrippa said to Paul, "You are permitted to speak for yourself."

So Paul stretched out his hand and made his defense: [2] "King Agrippa, I consider myself fortunate that today I shall make my defense before you against all the accusations of the Jews, [3] especially because you are an expert in all customs and controversies of the Jews. Therefore I beg you to patiently listen to me.

[4] "My manner of life from my youth, spent from the beginning in my own nation and at Jerusalem, is known by all the Jews. [5] They knew me from the beginning and could testify, if they wished, how according to the strictest sect of our religion I lived as a Pharisee. [6] And now I stand on trial for hope in the promise made by God to our fathers, [7] to which our twelve tribes hope to attain, by earnestly serve God day and night. Concerning this hope, King Agrippa, I am accused by the Jews. [8] Why is it judged incredible by you that God raises the dead?

[9] "I, too, thought that I must do many things contrary to the name of Jesus of Nazareth, [10] which I indeed did in Jerusalem and locked up many of the saints in prison by authority from the chief priests. And when they were killed, I cast my vote against them. [11] I punished them often in every synagogue and compelled them to blaspheme. And being extremely enraged against them, I persecuted them even to foreign cities.

Paul Tells of His Conversion

Ac 9:1–19; 22:6–16

[12] "So I went to Damascus with authority and a commission from the chief priests. [13] At midday, O King, I saw along the way a light from heaven, brighter than the sun, shining around me and those who journeyed with me. [14] When we had all fallen to the ground, I heard a voice saying to me in the Hebrew language, 'Saul, Saul, why do you persecute Me? It is hard for you to kick against the goads.'

[15] "I said, 'Who are You, Lord?'

"He said, 'I am Jesus whom you are persecuting. [16] But rise and stand on your feet. For I have appeared to you for this purpose, to appoint you as a servant and a witness both of what you have seen and of what I will yet reveal to you. [17] I will deliver you from your people and from the Gentiles to whom I now send you, [18] to open their eyes and to turn them from darkness to light, and from the power of Satan to God, that they may receive forgiveness of sins and an inheritance among those who are sanctified by faith in Me.'

Paul's Testimony to Jews and Gentiles

[19] "Therefore, King Agrippa, I was not disobedient to the heavenly vision, [20] but declared first to those at Damascus, then at Jerusalem

and throughout all the region of Judea, and also to the Gentiles, that they should repent and turn to God and do works proving their repentance. [21] For these reasons the Jews seized me in the temple and tried to kill me. [22] Therefore having obtained help from God, I continue to this day, testifying both to small and great, saying nothing but what the prophets and Moses said would happen: [23] that the Christ must suffer, that He would be the first who would rise from the dead, and would announce light to His own people and to the Gentiles."

Paul Appeals to Agrippa to Believe

[24] So as he made his defense, Festus said with a loud voice, "Paul, you are mad. Much learning is turning you to madness."

[25] Paul said, "I am not mad, most excellent Festus. I speak the words of truth and reason. [26] The king, before whom I also speak freely, knows about these things. For I am persuaded that none of this is hidden from him, for this was not done in a corner. [27] King Agrippa, do you believe the prophets? I know that you believe."

[28] Then Agrippa said to Paul, "You almost persuade me to be a Christian."

[29] Paul said, "I pray to God that not only you, but all who hear me this day, might become not only almost, but thoroughly and altogether, what I am, except for these chains."

[30] When he had said this, the king rose, as well as the governor and Bernice and those who sat with them. [31] When they had gone aside, they said to one another, "This man is doing nothing deserving death or imprisonment."

[32] And Agrippa said to Festus, "This man could have been set free if he had not appealed to Caesar."

Paul Sails for Rome

27 When it was decided that we should sail into Italy, they handed Paul and some other prisoners over to a centurion of the Augustan Regiment, named Julius. [2] Boarding a ship from Adramyttium, we put out to sea, meaning to sail along the coasts of Asia. Aristarchus, a Macedonian of Thessalonica, was with us.

[3] The next day we landed at Sidon. And Julius treated Paul kindly and gave him leave to go to his friends and be given care. [4] From there we put out to sea and sailed under the lee of Cyprus, because the winds were against us. [5] Sailing across the sea off of Cilicia and Pamphylia, we came to Myra, a city of Lycia. [6] There the centurion found a ship of Alexandria sailing to Italy, and he put us on board. [7] We sailed slowly for many days, and arrived with difficulty off Cnidus, and as the wind did not allow us to proceed, we sailed under the lee of Crete off Salmone. [8] Sailing past it with difficulty, we came to a place called Fair Havens, near the city of Lasea.

[9] As much time had been lost and as the voyage was now dangerous, because the Day of Atonement was already over, Paul advised them, [10] saying, "Men, I perceive that this voyage will be with injury and much loss, not only of the cargo and ship, but also of our lives." [11] But the centurion was persuaded more by the captain and the owner of the ship than by what Paul said. [12] Since the harbor was not suitable to winter in, the majority decided to sail on from there, if somehow we might reach Phoenix, a harbor in Crete, facing southwest and northwest, and winter there.

The Storm at Sea

[13] When a south wind blew gently, supposing that they had obtained the necessary conditions, they weighed anchor and sailed along the shore of Crete. [14] But soon afterward a tempestuous wind swept through, called the Euroclydon.[*1*] [15] When the ship was overpowered and could not head into the wind, we let her drift. [16] Drifting under the lee of an island called Cauda, we could scarcely secure the rowboat. [17] When they had hoisted it aboard, they used ropes to undergird the ship. And fearing that they might run aground on the sand of Syrtis, they let down the mast, and so were driven. [18] We were violently tossed by the storm. The next day they threw cargo overboard. [19] On the third day we threw the tackle of the ship overboard with our own hands. [20] When neither sun nor

---

14 Or Northeaster.

stars appeared for many days, and no small storm was upon us, all hope that we should be saved was lost.

[21] After they had long abstained from food, Paul stood in their midst and said, "Men, you should have listened to me and not have set sail from Crete, incurring this injury and loss. [22] But now I advise you to take courage, for there will be no loss of life among you, but only of the ship. [23] For there stood by me this night the angel of God to whom I belong and whom I serve, [24] saying, 'Do not be afraid, Paul. You must stand before Caesar. And, look! God has given you all those who sail with you.' [25] Therefore, men, take courage, for I believe God that it will be exactly as it was told to me. [26] Nevertheless, we must be shipwrecked on a certain island."

[27] When the fourteenth night came, while we were drifting in the Adriatic Sea, about midnight the sailors supposed that they were approaching land. [28] They took soundings and found the water to be one hundred and twenty feet deep.[1] When they had gone a little farther, they took soundings again and found it to be ninety feet deep.[2] [29] Fearing that we might run aground on the rocks, they dropped four anchors from the stern and prayed for day to come. [30] When the sailors strove to abandon ship and lowered the rowboat into the sea, under the pretext of lowering anchors out of the bow, [31] Paul said to the centurion and to the soldiers, "Unless these sailors remain in the ship, you cannot be saved." [32] Then the soldiers cut away the ropes of the rowboat and let her fall off.

[33] As day was about to dawn, Paul asked them all to eat, saying, "Today is the fourteenth day you have waited and continued without food, having eaten nothing. [34] So I urge you to eat. This is for your preservation, for not a hair shall fall from your head." [35] When he had said this, he took some bread and gave thanks to God in the presence of them all. And when he had broken it he began to eat. [36] Then they were all encouraged, and they also ate food themselves. [37] In all we were two hundred and seventy-six persons on the ship. [38] When they had eaten enough, they lightened the ship and threw the wheat into the sea.

The Shipwreck

[39] When it was day, they did not recognize the land. But they noticed a bay with a shore, into which they were determined to run the ship if possible. [40] Casting off the anchors, they left them in the sea while loosening the ropes that secured the rudders. Then they hoisted the mainsail to the wind and made for shore. [41] But striking a sandbar where two seas met, they ran the ship aground. The bow stuck and remained immovable, but the stern was broken up by the violent surf.

[42] The soldiers' plan was to kill the prisoners, lest any of them should swim away and escape. [43] But the centurion, wanting to save Paul, prevented them from their intent and ordered those who could swim to abandon ship first and get to land, [44] and the rest on planks or on pieces of the ship. And in this way they all escaped safely to land.

Paul in Malta

28 When they had escaped, they learned that the island was called Malta. [2] The natives showed extraordinary kindness, for they kindled a fire and welcomed us all, because of the rain and the cold. [3] When Paul had gathered a bundle of sticks and put them on the fire, a viper driven out by the heat fastened on his hand. [4] When the natives saw the creature hanging from his hand, they said to one another, "Surely this man is a murderer. Though he has escaped from the sea, justice does not allow him to live." [5] But he shook off the creature into the fire and suffered no harm. [6] They expected him to swell up or suddenly fall down dead. But while they waited and saw no harm befall him, they changed their minds and said that he was a god.

[7] In that area was an estate of the chief man of the island, named Publius, who had welcomed us and courteously housed us for three days. [8] It happened that the father of Publius lay sick with a fever and dysentery. Paul visited him and, placing his hands on him, prayed and healed him. [9] When this happened, the rest on the island who had diseases also came and were healed. [10] They honored us in many ways. And when we sailed, they provided us with necessary supplies.

Paul Arrives in Rome

[11] After three months we sailed in an Alexandrian ship whose figurehead was the Twin Brothers, which had wintered at the island. [12] Landing at Syracuse, we waited there for three days. [13] From there we circled around and sailed to Rhegium. After one day the south wind blew, and the next day we arrived at Puteoli. [14] There we found brothers, and were invited to remain with them for seven days. And so we went to Rome. [15] From there, when the brothers heard of us, they traveled as far as the Forum of Appius[3] and the Three Taverns[4] to meet us. When Paul saw them, he thanked God and took courage. [16] When we arrived at Rome, the centurion handed the prisoners over to the captain of the guard. But Paul was allowed to remain by himself with the soldier who guarded him.

Paul Preaches in Rome

[17] After three days Paul called the leaders of the Jews together. When they had assembled, he said to them, "Brothers, having done nothing contrary to our people or the customs of our fathers, I was delivered as a prisoner from Jerusalem into the hands of the Romans. [18] When they had examined me, they were determined to release me, because there was no charge against me deserving death. [19] But when the Jews objected, I was compelled to appeal to Caesar, not that I had any charge to bring against my nation. [20] For this reason I have asked to see you and speak with you, because I am bound with this chain for the hope of Israel."

[21] They said to him, "We have not received any letters from Judea concerning you, and none of the brothers that have come here reported or spoken any evil of you. [22] But we think it is proper to hear from you what you think. For concerning this sect, we know that it is spoken against everywhere."

[23] When they had arranged a day to be with him, many came to him at his residence. From morning until evening he explained and solemnly testified of the kingdom of God to them, persuading them concerning Jesus from both the Law of Moses and the Prophets. [24] Some believed what was said, but some did not believe. [25] Being in disagreement with one another, they were dismissed after Paul had said one word: "The Holy Spirit accurately spoke to our fathers through Isaiah the prophet,

[26] 'Go to this people and say:
     You shall certainly hear, but never understand;
         and you shall certainly see, but never perceive;
[27] for the heart of this people has grown dull.
         Their ears are hard of hearing,
         and they have closed their eyes,
     lest they should see with their eyes
         and hear with their ears
         and understand with their heart
     and turn, and I would heal them.[5]'

[28] "Therefore let it be known to you that the salvation of God has been sent to the Gentiles. They will hear it!"

[29] When he had said these words, the Jews departed and disputed greatly among themselves. [30] Paul remained two whole years in his own rented house. He welcomed all who came to him, [31] boldly and freely preaching the kingdom of God and teaching those things which concern the Lord Jesus Christ.

---

[1] 28 Gk. 20 orguias, about 37 meters.   [2] 28 Gk. 15 orguias, about 27 meters.   [3] 15 A town on the Appian Way about 55 miles from Rome.
[4] 15 Or Three Inns, also on the Appian Way and about 10 miles closer to Rome.   [5] 26–27 Isa 6:9–10.

ROMANS

Salutation

1 Paul, a servant of Jesus Christ, called to be an apostle and set apart for the gospel of God, [2] which He promised beforehand through His prophets in the Holy Scriptures, [3] concerning His Son, Jesus Christ our Lord, who was born of the seed of David according to the flesh [4] and declared to be the Son of God with power, according to the Spirit of holiness, by the resurrection from the dead. [5] Through Him we have received grace and apostleship for the obedience of faith among all nations for His name, [6] among whom you also are called by Jesus Christ:

[7] To all who are in Rome, beloved of God, called to be saints:

Grace to you and peace from God our Father and the Lord Jesus Christ.

Paul's Desire to Visit Rome

[8] First, I thank my God through Jesus Christ for you all, because your faith is spoken of throughout the whole world. [9] For God is my witness, whom I serve with my spirit in the gospel of His Son, that without ceasing, I mention you always in my prayers, [10] making request of, by any means, now at last I might find a way in the will of God to come to you.

[11] For I long to see you, that I may impart to you some spiritual gift, so that you may be strengthened. [12] This is so that I may be encouraged together with you by each other's faith, both yours and mine. [13] Now I would not have you unaware, brothers, that I often intended to come to you (but was prevented until now), that I might have a harvest among you also, even as among the other Gentiles.

[14] I am a debtor both to the Greeks and to the barbarians, both to the wise and to the unwise. [15] So, as much as is in me, I am ready to preach the gospel to you also who are in Rome.

The Definition of the Gospel

[16] For I am not ashamed of the gospel of Christ. For it is the power of God for salvation to everyone who believes, to the Jew first, and also to the Greek. [17] For in it the righteousness of God is revealed from faith to faith. As it is written, "The just shall live by faith."[1]

The Guilt of Mankind

[18] The wrath of God is revealed from heaven against all ungodliness and unrighteousness of men, who suppress the truth through unrighteousness. [19] For what may be known about God is clear to them since God has shown it to them. [20] The invisible things about Him—His eternal power and deity—have been clearly seen since the creation of the world and are understood by the things that are made, so that they are without excuse.

[21] Because, although they knew God, they did not glorify Him or give thanks to Him as God, but became futile in their imaginations, and their foolish hearts were darkened. [22] Claiming to be wise, they became fools. [23] They changed the glory of the incorruptible God into an image made like corruptible man, birds, four-footed beasts, and creeping things.

[24] Therefore God gave them up to uncleanness through the lusts of their hearts, to dishonor their own bodies among themselves. [25] They turned the truth of God into a lie and worshipped and served the creature rather than the Creator, who is blessed forever. Amen.

[26] For this reason God gave them up to dishonorable passions. Their women exchanged the natural function for what is against nature. [27] Likewise the men, leaving the natural function of the woman, burned in their lust toward one another, men with men doing that which is shameful, and receiving in themselves the due penalty of their error.

[28] And since they did not see fit to acknowledge God, God gave them over to a debased mind, to do those things which are not proper. [29] They were filled with all unrighteousness, sexual immorality, wickedness, covetousness, maliciousness; full of envy, murder, strife, deceit. They are gossips, [30] slanderers, God-haters, insolent, proud, boastful, inventors of evil things, and disobedient toward parents, [31] without understanding, covenant breakers, without natural affection, calloused, and unmerciful, [32] who know the righteous requirement of God, that those who commit such things are worthy of death. They not only do them, but also give hearty approval to those who practice them.

The Righteous Judgment of God

2 Therefore you are without excuse, O man, whoever you are who judges, for when you judge another, you condemn yourself, for you who judge do the same things. [2] But we know that the judgment of God is according to truth against those who commit such things. [3] Do you think, O man, who judges those who do such things, and who does the same thing, that you will escape the judgment of God? [4] Do you despise the riches of His goodness, tolerance, and patience, not knowing that the goodness of God leads you to repentance?

[5] But because of your hardness and impenitent heart, you are storing up treasures of wrath against yourself on the day of wrath when the righteous judgment of God will be revealed, [6] and He "will render to every man according to his deeds."[2] [7] To those who by patiently doing good seek for glory and honor and immortality will be eternal life. [8] But to those who are contentious and do not obey the truth, but obey unrighteousness, indignation and wrath, [9] will be tribulation and anguish, upon every soul of man who does evil, to the Jew first, and then to the Gentile. [10] But glory, honor, and peace will be to every man who does good work—to the Jew first, and then to the Gentile, [11] for there is no partiality with God.

[12] As many as have sinned without the law will also perish without the law, and as many as have sinned under the law will be judged by the law, [13] for the hearers of the law are not justified before God, but the doers of the law will be justified. [14] For when Gentiles, who do not have the law, do by nature the things contained in the law, these, not having the law, are a law unto themselves, [15] who show the work of the law written in their hearts, their conscience also bearing witness, while their conflicting thoughts accuse or even excuse them, [16] in the day when, according to my gospel, God will judge the secrets of men through Jesus Christ.

The Jews and the Law

[17] Indeed you are called a Jew, and rest in the law, and make your boast in God. [18] You know His will and approve the things that are more excellent, because you are instructed in the law. [19] You are confident that you are a guide to the blind, a light to those who are in darkness, [20] an instructor of the foolish, and a teacher of babes, who have the full content of knowledge and truth in the law: [21] You, therefore, who teach another, do you not teach yourself? You who preach not to steal, do you steal? [22] You who say not to commit adultery, do you commit adultery? You who abhor idols, do you rob temples? [23] You who boast in the law, do you dishonor God through breaking the law? [24] As it is written, "The name of God is blasphemed among the Gentiles because of you."[3]

[25] Circumcision indeed has merit, if you keep the law, but if you are a breaker of the law, your circumcision becomes uncircumcision. [26] Therefore, if an uncircumcised man keeps the righteousness of the law, will not his uncircumcision be counted as circumcision? [27] Will the uncircumcised one who is righteous by nature, if he fulfills the law, not judge you who, by the letter of the law and circumcision, violate the law?

[28] He is not a Jew who is one outwardly, nor is circumcision that which is external in the flesh. [29] But he is a Jew who is one inwardly.

---

[1] 17 Hab 2:4.   [2] 6 Ps 62:12; Pr 24:12.   [3] 24 Isa 52:5; Eze 36:22.

And circumcision is of the heart, by the Spirit, and not by the letter. His praise is not from men, but from God.

3 What advantage then does the Jew have? Or what profit is there in circumcision? [2] Much in every way! Chiefly because the oracles of God were entrusted to them.

[3] What if some did not believe? Would their unbelief nullify the faithfulness of God? [4] God forbid! Let God be true, and every man a liar. As it is written:

"That You may be justified in Your words,
    and may prevail in Your judging."[1]

[5] But if our unrighteousness demonstrates the righteousness of God, what shall we say? Is God unrighteous in taking vengeance? (I am speaking in human terms.) [6] God forbid! For then how could God judge the world? [7] If through my lie the truth of God has abounded more to His glory, why am I still being judged as a sinner? [8] Why not rather say, "Let us do evil that good may come," as we are slanderously accused and as some claim that we say? Their condemnation is just.

There Is None Righteous

[9] What then? Are we better than they? No, not at all. For we have already charged that both Jews and Gentiles are all under sin. [10] As it is written:

"There is none righteous, no, not one;[2]
[11]   there is no one who understands;
    there is no one who seeks after God.[3]
[12] They have all turned aside;
    together they have become worthless;
there is no one who does good,
    no, not one."[4]
[13] "Their throats are an open grave;
    with their tongues they have used deceit";
"the poison of vipers is under their lips";[5]
[14]   "their mouths are full of cursing and bitterness."[6]
[15] "Their feet are swift to shed blood;[7]
[16]   destruction and misery are in their paths;[8]
[17] and they do not know the way of peace."[9]
[18]   "There is no fear of God before their eyes."[10]

[19] Now we know that whatever the law says, it says to those who are under the law, so that every mouth may be silenced, and all the world may become accountable to God. [20] Therefore by the works of the law no flesh will be justified in His sight, for through the law comes the knowledge of sin.

Righteousness Through Faith

[21] But now, apart from the law, the righteousness of God is revealed, being witnessed by the Law and the Prophets. [22] This righteousness of God comes through faith in Jesus Christ[11] to all and upon all who believe, for there is no distinction. [23] For all have sinned and come short of the glory of God, [24] being justified freely by His grace through the redemption that is in Christ Jesus, [25] whom God has set forth to be a propitiation through faith, in His blood, for a demonstration of His righteousness, because in His forbearance God had passed over the sins previously committed, [26] to prove His righteousness at this present time so that He might be just and be the justifier of him who has faith in Jesus.

[27] Where is boasting then? It is excluded. By what law? Of works? No, but by the law of faith. [28] Therefore we conclude that a man is justified by faith without the works of the law. [29] Is He the God of the Jews only? Is He not also the God of the Gentiles? Yes, of the Gentiles also, [30] seeing it is one God, who shall justify the circumcised by faith, and the uncircumcised through faith. [31] Do we then make the law void through faith? God forbid! Instead, we establish the law.

The Example of Abraham

4 What then shall we say that Abraham, our father according to the flesh, has found? [2] If Abraham was justified by works, he has something to boast about, but not before God. [3] What does the Scripture say? "Abraham believed God, and it was credited to him as righteousness."[12]

[4] Now to him who works, wages are not given as a gift, but as a debt. [5] But to him who does not work, but believes in Him who justifies the ungodly, his faith is credited as righteousness. [6] Even David describes the blessedness of the man to whom God credits righteousness without works:

[7] "Blessed are those
    whose iniquities are forgiven,
    and whose sins are covered;
[8]   blessed is the man
    to whom the Lord shall not impute sin."[13]

[9] Does this blessedness then come upon the circumcised only, or upon the uncircumcised also? We are saying that faith was credited to Abraham as righteousness. [10] How then was it credited? When he was in circumcision? Or in uncircumcision? Not in circumcision, but in uncircumcision. [11] And he received the sign of circumcision, a seal of the righteousness of the faith that he had while being uncircumcised, so that he might be the father of all those who believe, though they are uncircumcised, that righteousness might be credited to them also, [12] and the father of circumcision to those who are not of the circumcision only, but who also walk in the steps of the faith of our father Abraham, which he had while still being uncircumcised.

The Promise Received Through Faith

[13] It was not through the law that Abraham and his descendants received the promise that he would be the heir of the world, but through the righteousness of faith. [14] For if those who are of the law become heirs, faith would be made void and the promise nullified, [15] because the law produces wrath, for where there is no law, there is no sin.

[16] Therefore the promise comes through faith, so that it might be by grace, that the promise would be certain to all the descendants, not only to those who are of the law, but also to those who are of the faith of Abraham, who is the father of us all [17] (as it is written, "I have made you a father of many nations"[14]) before God whom he believed, and who raises the dead, and calls those things that do not exist as though they did.

[18] Against all hope, he believed in hope, that he might become the father of many nations according to what was spoken, "So shall your descendants be."[15] [19] And not being weak in faith, he did not consider his own body to be dead (when he was about a hundred years old), nor yet the deadness of Sarah's womb. [20] He did not waver at the promise of God through unbelief, but was strong in faith, giving glory to God, [21] and being fully persuaded that what God had promised, He was able to perform. [22] Therefore "it was credited to him as righteousness."[16] [23] Now the words, "it was credited to him," were not written for his sake only, [24] but also for us, to whom it shall be credited if we believe in Him who raised Jesus our Lord from the dead, [25] who was delivered for our transgressions, and was raised for our justification.

Results of Justification

5 Therefore, since we have been justified by faith, we have peace with God through our Lord Jesus Christ, [2] through whom we also have access by faith into this grace in which we stand, and so we rejoice in hope of the glory of God. [3] Not only so, but we also boast in tribulation, knowing that tribulation produces patience, [4] patience produces character, and character produces hope. [5] And hope does not disappoint, because the love of God is shed abroad in our hearts by the Holy Spirit who has been given to us.

---

[1] 4 Ps 51:4.   [2] 10 Ps 14:1; 53:1.   [3] 11 Ps 14:2; 53:2.   [4] 12 Ps 14:3; 53:3.   [5] 13 Ps 5:9; 140:3.   [6] 14 Ps 10:7.   [7] 15 Pr 1:16; Isa 59:7.   [8] 16 Isa 59:7.   [9] 17 Isa 59:8.   [10] 18 Ps 36:1.   [11] 22 Or *through the faith of Jesus Christ*.   [12] 3 Ge 15:6.   [13] 7–8 Ps 32:1–2.   [14] 17 Ge 17:5.   [15] 18 Ge 15:5.   [16] 22 Ge 15:6.

[6] While we were yet weak, in due time Christ died for the ungodly. [7] Rarely for a righteous man will one die. Yet perhaps for a good man some would even dare to die. [8] But God demonstrates His own love toward us, in that while we were yet sinners, Christ died for us.

[9] How much more then, being now justified by His blood, shall we be saved from wrath through Him. [10] For if while we were enemies, we were reconciled to God by the death of His Son, how much more, being reconciled, shall we be saved by His life. [11] Furthermore, we also rejoice in God through our Lord Jesus Christ, through whom we have now received reconciliation.

Adam and Christ

[12] Therefore as sin came into the world through one man and death through sin, so death has spread to all men, because all have sinned.

[13] For until the law, sin was in the world. But sin is not counted when there is no law. [14] Nevertheless death reigned from Adam to Moses, even over those who had not sinned in the likeness of Adam's sin, who was a type of Him who was to come.

[15] But the free gift is not like the trespass. For if through the trespass of one man many died, then how much more has the grace of God and the free gift by the grace of the one Man, Jesus Christ, abounded to many. [16] The gift is not like the result that came through the one who sinned. For the judgment from one sin led to condemnation, but the free gift, which came after many trespasses, leads to justification. [17] For if by one man's trespass death reigned through him, then how much more will those who receive abundance of grace and the gift of righteousness reign in life through the One, Jesus Christ.

[18] Therefore just as through the trespass of one man came condemnation for all men, so through the righteous act of One came justification of life for all men. [19] For just as through one man's disobedience the many were made sinners, so by the obedience of One the many will be made righteous.

[20] But the law entered, so that sin might increase, but where sin increased, grace abounded much more, [21] so that just as sin reigned in death, grace might reign through righteousness unto eternal life through Jesus Christ our Lord.

Dead to Sin but Alive in Christ

6 What shall we say then? Shall we continue in sin that grace may increase? [2] God forbid! How shall we who died to sin live any longer in it? [3] Do you not know that we who were baptized into Jesus Christ were baptized into His death? [4] Therefore we were buried with Him by baptism into death, that just as Christ was raised up from the dead by the glory of the Father, even so we also should walk in newness of life.

[5] For if we have been united with Him in the likeness of His death, so shall we also be united with Him in the likeness of His resurrection, [6] knowing this, that our old man has been crucified with Him, so that the body of sin might be destroyed, and we should no longer be slaves to sin. [7] For the one who has died is freed from sin.

[8] Now if we died with Christ, we believe that we shall also live with Him, [9] knowing that Christ, being raised from the dead, will never die again; death has no further dominion over Him. [10] For the death He died, He died to sin once for all, but the life He lives, He lives to God.

[11] Likewise, you also consider yourselves to be dead to sin, but alive to God through Jesus Christ our Lord. [12] Therefore do not let sin reign in your mortal body, that you should obey it in its lusts. [13] Do not yield your members to sin as instruments of unrighteousness, but yield yourselves to God, as those who are alive from the dead, and your bodies to God as instruments of righteousness. [14] For sin shall not have dominion over you, for you are not under the law, but under grace.

Slaves of Righteousness

[15] What then? Shall we sin because we are not under the law but under grace? God forbid! [16] Do you not know that to whom you yield yourselves as slaves to obey, you are slaves of the one whom you obey, whether of sin leading to death, or of obedience leading to righteousness? [17] But thanks be to God, for you were slaves of sin, but you have obeyed from the heart that form of teaching to which you were entrusted, [18] and having been freed from sin, you became the slaves of righteousness.

[19] I speak in human terms because of the weakness of your flesh, for just as you have yielded your members as slaves to impurity and iniquity leading to more iniquity, even so now yield your members as slaves to righteousness unto holiness. [20] For when you were the slaves of sin, you were free from righteousness. [21] What fruit did you have then from the things of which you are now ashamed? The result of those things is death. [22] But now, having been freed from sin and having become slaves of God, you have fruit unto holiness, and the end is eternal life. [23] For the wages of sin is death, but the gift of God is eternal life through Jesus Christ our Lord.

An Analogy From Marriage

7 Do you not know, brothers (for I speak to those who know the law), that the law has dominion over a man as long as he lives? [2] For the woman who has a husband is bound by the law to her husband so long as he lives. But if her husband dies, she is released from the law regarding her husband. [3] So then, she will be called an adulteress if she marries another man while her husband lives. But if her husband dies, she is free from that law, so that she would not be an adulteress if she marries another man.

[4] So, my brothers, you also have died to the law through the body of Christ, so that you may be married to another, to Him who has been raised from the dead, so that we may bear fruit for God. [5] When we were in the flesh, the passions of sin, through the law, worked in our members to bear fruit leading to death. [6] But now we are delivered from the law, having died to things in which we were bound, so that we may serve in newness of the Spirit, and not in the oldness of the letter of the law.

The Problem of Indwelling Sin

[7] What shall we say then? Is the law sin? God forbid! But I did not know sin, except through the law. I would not have known coveting if the law had not said, "You shall not covet "[1] [8] But sin, taking opportunity through the commandment, produced in me all kinds of coveting. For apart from the law sin is dead. [9] I was alive without the law once, but when the commandment came, sin revived, and I died. [10] And the commandment, which was intended for life, proved to be death in me. [11] For sin, taking opportunity through the commandment, deceived and killed me through it. [12] So then, the law is holy and the commandment is holy and just and good.

[13] Therefore has that which is good become death unto me? God forbid! Rather, sin, that it might be shown to be sin, was working death in me through that which is good, so that sin through the commandment might become exceedingly sinful.

[14] We know that the law is spiritual, but I am carnal, sold under sin. [15] For what I am doing, I do not understand, for I do not practice what I will to do, but I do the very thing I hate. [16] But if I practice what I do not will to do, I agree with the law that it is good. [17] So now it is no longer I that do it, but sin that dwells in me. [18] For I know that in me (that is, in my flesh) dwells no good thing, for the will to do what is right is present with me, but how to perform what is good I do not find. [19] For the good I desire to do, I do not do, but the evil I do not want is what I do. [20] Now if I do what I do not want, it is no longer I who does it, but sin that lives in me.

[21] I find then a law that when I desire to do good, evil is present with me. [22] For I delight in the law of God according to the inner man, [23] but I see another law in my members, warring against the law of my mind and bringing me into captivity to the law of sin which is in my members. [24] O wretched man that I am! Who will deliver me from the body of this death? [25] I thank God through Jesus Christ our Lord.

So then, with my mind, I serve the law of God, but with my flesh, the law of sin.

---

[1] 7 Ex 20:17; Dt 5:21.

Life in the Spirit

8 There is therefore now no condemnation for those who are in Christ Jesus, who walk not according to the flesh, but according to the Spirit. [2] For the law of the Spirit of life in Christ Jesus has set me free from the law of sin and death. [3] For what the law could not do, in that it was weak through the flesh, God did by sending His own Son in the likeness of sinful flesh, and concerning sin, He condemned sin in the flesh, [4] in order that the righteous requirement of the law might be fulfilled in us, who walk not according to the flesh but according to the Spirit.

[5] For those who live according to the flesh set their minds on the things of the flesh, but those who live according to the Spirit, the things of the Spirit. [6] To be carnally minded is death, but to be spiritually minded is life and peace, [7] for the carnal mind is hostile toward God, for it is not subject to the law of God, nor indeed can it be, [8] and those who are in the flesh cannot please God.

[9] You, however, are not in the flesh but in the Spirit, if indeed the Spirit of God lives in you. Now if any man does not have the Spirit of Christ, he does not belong to Him. [10] And if Christ is in you, though the body is dead because of sin, the Spirit is alive because of righteousness. [11] But if the Spirit of Him who raised Jesus from the dead lives in you, He who raised Christ from the dead will also give life to your mortal bodies through His Spirit that lives in you.

[12] Therefore, brothers, we are debtors not to the flesh, to live according to the flesh. [13] For if you live according to the flesh, you will die, but if through the Spirit you put to death the deeds of the body, you will live.

[14] For as many as are led by the Spirit of God, these are the sons of God. [15] For you have not received the spirit of slavery again to fear. But you have received the Spirit of adoption, by whom we cry, "Abba, Father." [16] The Spirit Himself bears witness with our spirits that we are the children of God, [17] and if children, then heirs: heirs of God and joint-heirs with Christ, if indeed we suffer with Him, that we may also be glorified with Him.

The Glory That Is to Be

[18] For I consider that the sufferings of this present time are not worthy to be compared with the glory which shall be revealed to us. [19] The eager expectation of the creation waits for the appearance of the sons of God. [20] For the creation was subjected to futility, not willingly, but by the will of Him who subjected it, in hope [21] that the creation itself also will be set free from its slavery to corruption into the glorious freedom of the children of God.

[22] We know that the whole creation groans and travails in pain together until now. [23] Not only that, but we also, who have the first fruits of the Spirit, groan within ourselves while eagerly waiting for adoption, the redemption of our bodies. [24] For we are saved through hope, but hope that is seen is not hope, for why does a man still hope for what he sees? [25] But if we hope for what we do not see, we wait for it with patience.

[26] Likewise, the Spirit helps us in our weaknesses, for we do not know what to pray for as we ought, but the Spirit Himself intercedes for us with groanings too deep for words. [27] He who searches the hearts knows what the mind of the Spirit is, because He intercedes for the saints according to the will of God.

[28] We know that all things work together for good to those who love God, to those who are called according to His purpose. [29] For those whom He foreknew, He predestined to be conformed to the image of His Son, so that He might be the firstborn among many brothers. [30] And those whom He predestined, He also called; and those whom He called, He also justified; and those whom He justified, He also glorified.

The Love of God

[31] What then shall we say to these things? If God is for us, who can be against us? [32] He who did not spare His own Son, but delivered Him up for us all, how shall He not with Him also freely give us all things? [33] Who shall bring a charge against God's elect? It is God who justifies. [34] Who is he who condemns? It is Christ who died, yes, who is risen, who is also at the right hand of God, who also intercedes for us. [35] Who shall separate us from the love of Christ? Shall tribulation, or distress, or persecution, or famine, or nakedness, or peril, or sword? [36] As it is written:

> "For Your sake we are killed all day long;
> we are counted as sheep for the slaughter." [1]

[37] No, in all these things we are more than conquerors through Him who loved us. [38] For I am persuaded that neither death nor life, neither angels nor principalities nor powers, neither things present nor things to come, [39] neither height nor depth, nor any other created thing, shall be able to separate us from the love of God, which is in Christ Jesus our Lord.

God's Election of Israel

9 I am speaking the truth in Christ, I am not lying; my conscience testifies with me in the Holy Spirit, [2] that I have great sorrow and continual anguish in my heart. [3] For I could wish that I myself were accursed from Christ for my brothers, my kinsmen by race, [4] who are Israelites, to whom belong the adoption, the glory, the covenants, the giving of the law, the service of God, and the promises, [5] to whom belong the patriarchs, and from whom, according to the flesh, is Christ, who is over all, God forever blessed. Amen.

[6] It is not as though the word of God has failed. For they are not all Israel who are descended from Israel, [7] nor are they all children because they are descendants of Abraham, but "In Isaac shall your descendants be called." [2] [8] So those who are the children of the flesh are not the children of God, but the children of the promise are counted as descendants. [9] For this is the word of promise, "At this time I will come, and Sarah shall have a son." [3]

[10] Not only that, but Rebekah also had conceived by one man, our father Isaac. [11] For before the children had been born, having done neither evil nor good, so that the purpose of God according to election might stand, not of works, but through Him who calls, [12] it was said to her, "The elder shall serve the younger." [4] [13] As it is written, "Jacob I have loved, but Esau I have hated." [5]

[14] What shall we say then? Is there unrighteousness with God? God forbid! [15] For He says to Moses,

> "I will have mercy on whom I have mercy,
> and I will have compassion on whom I have
> compassion." [6]

[16] So then it is not of him who wills, nor of him who runs, but of God who shows mercy. [17] For the Scripture says to Pharaoh, "For this very purpose I have raised you up, that I may show My power in you, and that My name may be proclaimed in all the earth." [7] [18] Therefore He has mercy on whom He wills, and He hardens whom He wills.

Wrath and Mercy of God

[19] You will then say to me, "Why does He yet find fault? For who can resist His will?" [20] Rather, O man, who are you to answer back to God? Shall the thing formed say to him who formed it, "Why have you made me like this?" [21] Does the potter not have power over the clay to make from the same lump one vessel for honor and another for dishonor?

[22] What if God, willing to show His wrath and to make His power known, endured with much patience the vessels of wrath prepared for destruction, [23] in order to make known the riches of His glory on the vessels of mercy, which He previously prepared for glory, [24] even us, whom He has called, not from the Jews only, but also from the Gentiles? [25] As indeed He says in Hosea:

> "I will call those who were not My people, 'My people,'
> and her who was not beloved, 'Beloved,' " [8]

---

[1] 36 Ps 44:22.   [2] 7 Ge 21:12.   [3] 9 Ge 18:10.   [4] 12 Ge 25:23.   [5] 13 Mal 1:2.   [6] 15 Ex 33:19.   [7] 17 Ex 9:16.   [8] 25 Hos 2:23.

[26] and,

> "In the place where it was said to them,
> 'You are not My people,'
> there they shall be called 'sons of the living God.' "[1]

[27] Isaiah also cries out concerning Israel:

> "Though the number of the children of Israel be like the sand
> of the sea,
> a remnant shall be saved.[2]
[28] For He will finish the work, and cut it short in righteousness,
> because the Lord will make a quick work upon the
> earth."[3]

[29] And as Isaiah previously said:

> "Unless the Lord of Hosts
> had left us a seed,
> we would have become like Sodom,
> and been made like Gomorrah."[4]

Israel and the Gospel

[30] What shall we say then? The Gentiles, who did not pursue righteousness, have attained righteousness, even the righteousness which is by faith, [31] but Israel, pursuing the law of righteousness, did not attain the law of righteousness. [32] Why not? Because they did not seek it by faith, but by the works of the law. For they stumbled over the stumbling stone. [33] As it is written:

> "Look! I lay in Zion a stumbling stone
> and rock of offense,
> and whoever believes in Him will not be ashamed."[5]

10 Brothers, my heart's desire and prayer to God for Israel is that they may be saved. [2] For I testify about them that they have a zeal for God, but not according to knowledge. [3] For, being ignorant of God's righteousness and seeking to establish their own righteousness, they did not submit to the righteousness of God. [4] Christ is the end of the law unto righteousness for every one who believes.

Salvation for All

[5] For Moses writes about the righteousness which is based on the law: "The man who does those things shall live by them."[6] [6] But the righteousness which is based on faith says, "Do not say in your heart, 'Who will ascend into heaven?'"[7] (that is, to bring Christ down), [7] "or, 'Who will descend into the deep?'"[8] (that is, to bring Christ up from the dead). [8] But what does it say? "The word is near you, in your mouth and in your heart.[9] This is the word of faith that we preach: [9] that if you confess with your mouth Jesus is Lord, and believe in your heart that God has raised Him from the dead, you will be saved, [10] for with the heart one believes unto righteousness, and with the mouth confession is made unto salvation. [11] For the Scripture says, "Whoever believes in Him will not be ashamed."[10] [12] For there is no distinction between Jew and Greek, for the same Lord over all is generous toward all who call upon Him. [13] For, "Everyone who calls on the name of the Lord shall be saved."[11] [14] How then shall they call on Him in whom they have not believed? And how shall they believe in Him of whom they have not heard? And how shall they hear without a preacher? [15] And how shall they preach unless they are sent? As it is written: "How beautiful are the feet of those who preach the gospel of peace, who bring good news of good things!"[12] [16] But they have not all obeyed the gospel. For Isaiah says, "Lord, who has believed our report?"[13] [17] So then faith comes by hearing, and hearing by the word of God. [18] But I say, have they not heard? Yes, indeed:

> "Their voice went into all the earth,
> and their words to the ends of the world."[14]

[19] But I say, did Israel not know? First, Moses says:

> "I will make you jealous by those who are not a nation,
> and by a foolish nation I will anger you."[15]

[20] And Isaiah is very bold and says:

> "I was found by those who did not seek Me;
> I revealed myself to those who did not ask for Me."[16]

[21] But to Israel He says:

> "All day long I have stretched out My hands
> to a disobedient and contrary people."[17]

The Remnant of Israel

11 I say then, has God rejected His people? God forbid! For I also am an Israelite, a descendant of Abraham, of the tribe of Benjamin. [2] God has not rejected His people whom He foreknew. Do you not know what the Scripture says of Elijah? How he pleads with God against Israel, saying, [3] "Lord, they have killed Your prophets and destroyed Your altars. I alone am left, and they seek my life"?[18] [4] But what is the divine reply to him? "I have kept for Myself seven thousand men, who have not bowed the knee to Baal."[19] [5] So then at this present time there is a remnant according to the election of grace. [6] And if by grace, then it is no longer by works; otherwise grace would no longer be grace. But if it is by works, then is it no longer by grace; otherwise work would no longer be work. [7] What then? Israel has not obtained what it was seeking. But the elect obtained it, and the rest were hardened. [8] As it is written:

> "God has given them a spirit of slumber,
> eyes that would not see
> and ears that would not hear,
> to this very day."[20]

[9] And David says:

> "Let their table become a snare and a trap,
> a stumbling block and a retribution to them.
[10] Let their eyes be darkened, so that they may not see,
> and always bow down their backs."[21]

The Salvation of the Gentiles

[11] I say then, have they stumbled that they should fall? God forbid! But through their transgression salvation has come to the Gentiles, to make them jealous. [12] Now if their transgression means riches for the world, and their failure means riches for the Gentiles, how much more will their fullness mean?

[13] For I am speaking to you Gentiles. Inasmuch as I am the apostle to the Gentiles, I magnify my ministry, [14] if somehow I may make my kinsmen jealous and may save some of them. [15] For if their rejection means the reconciliation of the world, what will their acceptance mean but life from the dead? [16] If the first portion of the dough is holy, the batch is also holy. And if the root is holy, so are the branches.

[17] But if some of the branches were broken off, and you, being a wild olive shoot, were grafted in among them and became a partaker with them of the root and richness of the olive tree, [18] do not boast against the branches. If you boast, remember you do not sustain the root, but the root sustains you. [19] You will say then, "The branches were broken off, so that I might be grafted in." [20] This is correct. They were broken off because of unbelief, but you stand by faith. Do not be arrogant, but fear. [21] For if God did not spare the natural branches, neither will He spare you.

---

[1]26 Hos 1:10. [2]27 Isa 10:22. [3]28 Isa 10:23. [4]29 Isa 1:9. [5]33 Isa 8:14; 28:16. [6]5 Lev 18:5. [7]6 Dt 30:12. [8]7 Dt 30:13.
[9]8 Dt 30:14. [10]11 Isa 28:16. [11]13 Joel 2:32. [12]15 Isa 52:7. [13]16 Isa 53:1. [14]18 Ps 19:4. [15]19 Dt 32:21. [16]20 Isa 65:1.
[17]21 Isa 65:2. [18]3 1Ki 19:10. [19]4 1Ki 19:18. [20]8 Isa 29:10. [21]10 Ps 69:22–23.

[22] Therefore consider the goodness and severity of God—severity toward those who fell, but goodness toward you, if you continue in His goodness. Otherwise, you also will be cut off. [23] And these also, if they do not remain in unbelief, will be grafted in, for God is able to graft them in again. [24] For if you were cut out of the olive tree which is wild by nature, and were grafted contrary to nature into a cultivated olive tree, how much more will these, who are the natural branches, be grafted into their own olive tree?

The Restoration of Israel

[25] For I do not want you to be ignorant of this mystery, brothers, lest you be wise in your own estimation, for a partial hardening has come upon Israel until the fullness of the Gentiles has come in. [26] And so all Israel will be saved, as it is written:

"The Deliverer will come out of Zion,
　　and He will remove ungodliness from Jacob";[1]
[27] "for this is My covenant with them,
　　when I shall take away their sins."[2]

[28] As concerning the gospel, they are enemies for your sake, but as regarding the election, they are beloved for the sake of the patriarchs. [29] For the gifts and calling of God are irrevocable. [30] For just as you once were disobedient to God, but have now received mercy through their disobedience, [31] so these also have now been disobedient, that they also may receive mercy by the mercy shown to you. [32] For God has imprisoned them all in disobedience, so that He might be merciful to all.

[33] O the depth of the riches and wisdom and knowledge of God!
　　How unsearchable are His judgments
　　and unfathomable are His ways!
[34] "For who has known the mind of the Lord?
　　Or who has become His counselor?"[3]
[35] "Or who has first given to Him,
　　and it shall be repaid to him?"[4]
[36] For from Him and through Him and to Him are all things.
　　To Him be glory forever! Amen.

The New Life in Christ

12 I urge you therefore, brothers, by the mercies of God, that you present your bodies as a living sacrifice, holy, and acceptable to God, which is your reasonable service of worship. [2] Do not be conformed to this world, but be transformed by the renewing of your mind, that you may prove what is the good and acceptable and perfect will of God.

[3] For I say, through the grace given to me, to everyone among you, not to think of himself more highly than he ought to think, but to think with sound judgment, according to the measure of faith God has distributed to every man. [4] For just as we have many parts in one body, and not all parts have the same function, [5] so we, being many, are one body in Christ, and all are parts of one another. [6] We have diverse gifts according to the grace that is given to us: if prophecy, according to the proportion of faith; [7] if service, in serving; he who teaches, in teaching; [8] he who exhorts, in exhortation; he who gives, with generosity; he who rules, with diligence; he who shows mercy, with cheerfulness.

Rules of the Christian Life

[9] Let love be without hypocrisy. Hate what is evil. Cleave to what is good. [10] Be devoted to one another with brotherly love; prefer one another in honor, [11] do not be lazy in diligence, be fervent in spirit, serve the Lord, [12] rejoice in hope, be patient in suffering, persevere in prayer, [13] contribute to the needs of the saints, practice hospitality.

[14] Bless those who persecute you; bless, and do not curse. [15] Rejoice with those who rejoice, and weep with those who weep. [16] Be of the same mind toward one another. Do not be haughty, but associate with the lowly. Do not pretend to be wiser than you are.

[17] Repay no one evil for evil. Commend what is honest in the sight of all men. [18] If it is possible, as much as it depends on you, live peaceably with all men. [19] Beloved, do not avenge yourselves, but rather give place to God's wrath, for it is written: "Vengeance is Mine. I will repay,"[5] says the Lord. [20] Therefore

"If your enemy is hungry, feed him;
　　if he is thirsty, give him a drink;
　　for in doing so you will heap coals of fire on his head."[6]

[21] Do not be overcome by evil, but overcome evil with good.

Subjection to Authorities

13 Let every person be subject to the governing authorities, for there is no authority except from God, and those that exist are appointed by God. [2] Therefore whoever resists the authority resists what God has appointed, and those who resist will incur judgment. [3] Rulers are not a terror to good works, but to evil works. Do you wish to have no fear of the authority? Do what is good, and you will have praise from him, [4] for he is the servant of God for your good. But if you do what is evil, be afraid, for he does not bear the sword in vain, for he is the servant of God, an avenger to execute wrath upon him who practices evil. [5] So it is necessary to be in subjection, not only because of wrath, but also for the sake of conscience.

[6] For this reason you also pay taxes, for they are God's servants, devoting themselves to this very thing. [7] Render to all what is due them: taxes to whom taxes are due, respect to whom respect is due, fear to whom fear is due, and honor to whom honor is due.

Brotherly Love

[8] Owe no one anything, except to love one another, for he who loves another has fulfilled the law. [9] For the commandments, "You shall not commit adultery, You shall not murder, You shall not steal, You shall not give false testimony, You shall not covet,"[7] and if there are any other commandments, are summed up in this saying, "You shall love your neighbor as yourself."[8] [10] Love works no evil to a neighbor. Therefore love is the fulfillment of the law.

The Approach of the Day of Christ

[11] Furthermore, knowing the time, now is the moment to awake from sleep. For now our salvation is nearer than when we believed. [12] The night is far spent, the day is at hand. Therefore let us take off the works of darkness and put on the armor of light. [13] Let us behave properly, as in the day, not in carousing and drunkenness, not in immorality and wickedness, not in strife and envy. [14] But put on the Lord Jesus Christ, and make no provision for the flesh to fulfill its lusts.

Do Not Judge Your Brother

14 Welcome him who is weak in faith, but not for the purpose of arguing over opinions. [2] For one has faith to eat all things, but he who is weak eats only vegetables. [3] Do not let him who eats despise him who does not eat, and do not let him who does not eat judge him who eats, for God has welcomed him. [4] Who are you to judge another man's servant? To his own master he stands or falls. And he will stand, for God is able to make him stand.

[5] One man judges one day above another; another judges every day alike. Let each one be fully persuaded in his own mind. [6] He who observes the day observes it for the Lord, and he who does not observe the day, to the Lord he does not observe it. He who eats, eats in honor of the Lord, for he gives thanks to God; and the one who does not eat, in honor of the Lord he does not eat, and gives thanks to God. [7] For none of us lives for himself, and no one dies for himself. [8] For if we live, we live for the Lord. And if we die, we die for the Lord. So, whether we live or die, we are the Lord's. [9] For to this end Christ died and rose and lived again, so that He might be Lord of both the dead and living.

---

[1] 26 Isa 59:20.　[2] 27 Isa 59:20–21; Jer 31:31–34.　[3] 34 Isa 40:13.　[4] 35 Job 35:7; 41:11.　[5] 19 Dt 32:35.　[6] 20 Pr 25:21–22.　[7] 9 Ex 20:13–15, 17; Dt 5:17–19, 21.　[8] 9 Lev 19:18.

[10] So why do you judge your brother? Or why do you despise your brother? For we shall all stand before the judgment seat of Christ. [11] For it is written:

"As I live, says the Lord,
every knee shall bow to Me,
and every tongue shall confess to God."[1]

[12] So then each of us shall give an account of himself to God.

Do Not Make Your Brother Stumble

[13] Therefore let us no longer pass judgment on one another, but rather determine not to put a stumbling block or an obstacle in a brother's way. [14] I know and am persuaded by the Lord Jesus that nothing is unclean in itself, but to him who considers anything to be unclean, to him it is unclean. [15] If your brother is grieved because of your food, you are no longer walking in love. Do not destroy with your food one for whom Christ died. [16] So do not let what is good to you be spoken of as evil. [17] For the kingdom of God does not mean eating and drinking, but righteousness and peace and joy in the Holy Spirit. [18] For he who serves Christ in these things is acceptable to God and approved by men.

[19] Therefore let us pursue the things which produce peace and the things that build up one another. [20] Do not destroy the work of God for the sake of food. All things indeed are clean, but it is evil for the man who causes someone to fall by what he eats. [21] It is good neither to eat meat nor drink wine, nor do anything whereby your brother stumbles or is offended or is made weak.

[22] The faith that you have, have as your own conviction before God. Happy is he who does not condemn himself in what he approves. [23] But he who doubts is condemned if he eats, because it is not from faith, for whatever is not from faith is sin.

Please Others, Not Yourself

15 We who are strong ought to bear the weaknesses of the weak and not please ourselves. [2] Let each of us please his neighbor for his good, leading to edification. [3] For even Christ did not please Himself. But as it is written, "The insults of those who insulted You fell on Me."[2] [4] For whatever was previously written was written for our instruction, so that through perseverance and encouragement of the Scriptures we might have hope.

[5] Now may the God of perseverance and encouragement grant you to live in harmony with one another in accordance with Christ Jesus, [6] so that together you may with one voice glorify the God and Father of our Lord Jesus Christ.

The Gospel for Jews and Gentiles Alike

[7] Therefore welcome one another, just as Christ also welcomed us, for the glory of God. [8] Now I say that Jesus Christ has become a servant to the circumcised on behalf of the truth of God, to confirm the promises made to the patriarchs, [9] and that the Gentiles might glorify God for His mercy, as it is written:

"For this reason I will acknowledge You among the Gentiles,
and I will sing praises to Your name."[3]

[10] He also says:

"Rejoice, O Gentiles, with His people!"[4]

[11] And again:

"Praise the Lord, all you Gentiles;
let all the peoples praise Him."[5]

[12] And again Isaiah says:

"There shall be a root of Jesse;
He who shall rise to reign over the Gentiles,
in Him shall the Gentiles hope."[6]

[13] Now may the God of hope fill you with all joy and peace in believing, so that you may abound in hope, through the power of the Holy Spirit.

Paul's Missionary Commission

[14] Now I myself am persuaded concerning you, my brothers, that you also are full of goodness, filled with all knowledge, and also able to instruct one another. [15] Nevertheless, brothers, I have written even more boldly to you on some points, to remind you, because of the grace that is given to me from God, [16] that I might be a minister of Jesus Christ to the Gentiles, in the priestly service of the gospel of God, so that the offering of the Gentiles might be acceptable, being sanctified by the Holy Spirit.

[17] In Christ Jesus therefore I have reason to boast in my service to God. [18] For I will not dare to speak of anything except what Christ has accomplished through me, to make the Gentiles obedient, by word and deed, [19] by the power of signs and wonders, by the power of the Spirit of God, so that from Jerusalem and as far around as Illyricum, I have fully preached the gospel of Christ. [20] So I have strived to preach the gospel, not where Christ was named, so that I should not build on another man's foundation. [21] But as it is written:

"To whom He was not announced, they shall see;
and those who have not heard shall understand."[7]

Paul's Plan to Visit Rome

[22] For this reason also I was often hindered from coming to you. [23] But now, no longer having a place in these regions, and having a great desire for many years to come to you, [24] whenever I go to Spain, I shall come to you, for I hope to see you when I pass through and to be helped on my way there by you, when I have first enjoyed your company for a little while. [25] But now I am going to Jerusalem to minister to the saints. [26] For Macedonia and Achaia were pleased to make some contribution for the poor among the saints who are in Jerusalem. [27] It has pleased them indeed, and they are their debtors. For if the Gentiles have been partakers of their spiritual things, they also ought to minister to them in material things. [28] Therefore, when I have completed this and have given this blessing to them, I shall come by way of you to Spain, [29] and I know that when I come to you, I shall come in the fullness of the blessing of the gospel of Christ.

[30] Now I ask you, brothers, through the Lord Jesus Christ and through the love of the Spirit, to strive together with me in your prayers to God on my behalf, [31] that I may be delivered from the unbelievers in Judea, and that my ministry for Jerusalem may be acceptable to the saints, [32] so that I may come to you with joy by the will of God, and may be refreshed together with you. [33] Now the God of peace be with you all. Amen.

Personal Greetings

16 I commend to you our sister Phoebe, who is a servant[8] of the church at Cenchrea, [2] that you welcome her in the Lord in a manner worthy of the saints, and that you assist her in whatever matter she may have need of you, for she has been a helper of many and of myself as well.

[3] Greet Priscilla and Aquila, my fellow workers in Christ Jesus, [4] who risked their own necks for my life, to whom not only I, but also all the churches of the Gentiles, give thanks. [5] Likewise greet the church that is in their house. Greet my beloved Epaenetus, who is the first convert of Achaia for Christ. [6] Greet Mary, who labored much for us. [7] Greet Andronicus and Junia, my kinsmen and fellow prisoners, who are noteworthy among the apostles, who also came to Christ before me. [8] Greet Ampliatus, my beloved in the Lord. [9] Greet Urbanus, our fellow worker in Christ, and my beloved Stachys.

---

[1] 11 Isa 45:23.   [2] 3 Ps 69:9.   [3] 9 Ps 18:49.   [4] 10 Dt 32:43.   [5] 11 Ps 117:1.   [6] 12 Isa 11:10.   [7] 21 Isa 52:15.   [8] 1 Or *deacon*.

[10] Greet Apelles, who is approved in Christ.
Greet those who are of the household of Aristobulus.
[11] Greet Herodion, my kinsman.
Greet those who are of the household of Narcissus, who are in the Lord.
[12] Greet Tryphena and Tryphosa, who labor in the Lord.
Greet the beloved Persis, who also labored much in the Lord.
[13] Greet Rufus, chosen in the Lord, and his mother, who is like a mother to me.
[14] Greet Asyncritus, Phlegon, Hermes, Patrobas, Hermas, and the brothers who are with them.
[15] Greet Philologus, Julia, Nereus and his sister, and Olympas, and all the saints who are with them.
[16] Greet one another with a holy kiss.
The churches of Christ greet you.

[17] Now I urge you, brothers, to closely watch those who cause divisions and offenses, contrary to the teaching which you have learned, and avoid them. [18] For such people do not serve our Lord Jesus Christ, but their own appetites, and through smooth talk and flattery they deceive the hearts of the unsuspecting.

[19] Your obedience has become known to all men. Therefore I am glad on your behalf. Yet I want you to be wise to that which is good, and innocent to that which is evil. [20] The God of peace will soon crush Satan under your feet. The grace of our Lord Jesus Christ be with you. [21] Timothy, my fellow worker, and Lucius, Jason, and Sosipater, my kinsmen, greet you. [22] I, Tertius, who wrote this epistle, greet you in the Lord. [23] Gaius, who is host to me and to the whole church, greets you. Erastus, who is the city treasurer, and our brother Quartus greet you. [24] The grace of our Lord Jesus Christ be with you all. Amen.

Doxology

[25] Now to Him who has power to establish you according to my gospel and the preaching of Jesus Christ, according to the revelation of the mystery, which was kept secret for long ages past, [26] but now is revealed by the prophetic Scriptures according to the commandment of the everlasting God, made known to all the Gentiles for the obedience of faith, [27] to the only wise God, through Jesus Christ, to whom be glory forever. Amen.

1 CORINTHIANS

Greeting and Thanksgiving

1 Paul, called to be an apostle of Jesus Christ through the will of God, and Sosthenes, our brother,

[2] To the church of God which is at Corinth, to those who are sanctified in Christ Jesus, called to be saints, with all who in every place call on the name of Jesus Christ our Lord, both their Lord and ours:

[3] Grace to you and peace from God our Father and the Lord Jesus Christ. [4] I thank my God always on your behalf for the grace of God which has been given to you through Jesus Christ. [5] By Him you are enriched in everything, in all speech and in all knowledge, [6] even as the testimony of Christ was confirmed in you, [7] so that you are not lacking in any gift while waiting for the revelation of our Lord Jesus Christ. [8] He will strengthen you to the end, so that you may be blameless on the day of our Lord Jesus Christ. [9] God is faithful, and by Him you were called to the fellowship of His Son, Jesus Christ our Lord.

Divisions in the Church

[10] Now I ask you, brothers, by the name of our Lord Jesus Christ, that you all speak in agreement and that there be no divisions among you. But be perfectly joined together in the same mind and in the same judgment. [11] For it has been declared to me concerning you, my brothers, by those who are of the house of Chloe, that there are contentions among you. [12] Now this is what I mean: Every one of you is saying, "I am of Paul," or "I am of Apollos," or "I am of Cephas," or "I am of Christ."

[13] Is Christ divided? Was Paul crucified for you? Or were you baptized in the name of Paul? [14] I thank God that I baptized none of you except Crispus and Gaius, [15] lest any should say that I had baptized in my own name. [16] I also baptized the household of Stephanas. Besides them, I do not know whether I baptized any other. [17] For Christ did not send me to baptize, but to preach the gospel, not with eloquent words, lest the cross of Christ should be made of no effect.

Christ the Power and Wisdom of God

[18] For to those who are perishing, the preaching of the cross is foolishness, but to us who are being saved it is the power of God. [19] For it is written:

"I will destroy the wisdom of the wise,
    and will bring to nothing the understanding of the prudent."[1]

[20] Where is the wise? Where is the scribe? Where is the debater of this age? Has God not made the wisdom of this world foolish? [21] For since, in the wisdom of God, the world through its wisdom did not know God, it pleased God through the foolishness of preaching to save those who believe. [22] For the Jews require a sign, and the Greeks seek after wisdom. [23] But we preach Christ crucified, a stumbling block to the Jews and foolishness to the Greeks. [24] But to those who are called, both Jews and Greeks, we preach Christ as the power of God and the wisdom of God. [25] For the foolishness of God is wiser than men, and the weakness of God is stronger than men.

[26] For observe your calling, brothers. Among you, not many wise men according to the flesh, not many mighty men, and not many noble men were called. [27] But God has chosen the foolish things of the world to confound the wise. God has chosen the weak things of the world to confound the things which are mighty. [28] And God has chosen the base things of the world and things which are despised. Yes, and He chose things which did not exist to bring to nothing things that do, [29] so that no flesh should boast in His presence. [30] But because of Him you are in Christ Jesus, whom God made unto us wisdom, righteousness, sanctification, and redemption. [31] Therefore, as it is written, "Let him who boasts, boast in the Lord."[2]

Proclaiming Christ Crucified

2 Brothers, when I came to you, I did not come with superiority of speech or wisdom, declaring to you the testimony of God. [2] For I determined not to know anything among you except Jesus Christ and Him crucified. [3] I was with you in weakness and in fear and in much trembling. [4] My speech and my preaching was not

---

[1] 19 Isa 29:14.   [2] 31 Jer 9:24.

with enticing words of man's wisdom, but in demonstration of the Spirit and of power, [5] so that your faith should not stand in the wisdom of men, but in the power of God.

The Revelation by God's Spirit

[6] Yet we speak wisdom among those who are mature, although not the wisdom of this age, nor of the rulers of this age, who are coming to nothing. [7] But we speak the wisdom of God in a mystery, the hidden wisdom, which God ordained before the ages for our glory. [8] None of the rulers of this age knew it. For had they known it, they would not have crucified the Lord of glory. [9] But as it is written,

"Eye has not seen,
nor ear heard,
nor has it entered into the heart of man
the things which God has prepared for those who love Him." [1]

[10] But God has revealed them to us by His Spirit.

For the Spirit searches all things, yes, the deep things of God. [11] For what man knows the things of a man, except the spirit of man which is in him? Likewise, no one knows the things of God, except the Spirit of God. [12] Now we have received not the spirit of the world, but the Spirit which is of God, so that we might know the things that are freely given to us by God. [13] These things also we proclaim, not in the words which man's wisdom teaches, but which the Holy Spirit teaches, comparing spiritual things with spiritual. [14] But the natural man does not receive the things of the Spirit of God, for they are foolishness to him; nor can he know them, because they are spiritually discerned. [15] But he who is spiritual judges all things. Yet he himself is not judged by anyone. [16] For

"who has known the mind of the Lord
that he may instruct Him?" [2]

But we have the mind of Christ.

Fellow Servants of God

3 Brothers, I could not speak to you as to spiritual men, but as to worldly, even as to babes in Christ. [2] I have fed you with milk and not with solid food. For to this day you were not able to endure it. Nor are you able now, [3] for you are still worldly. Since there is envy, strife, and divisions among you, are you not worldly and behaving as mere men? [4] For while one says, "I am of Paul," and another, "I am of Apollos," are you not worldly?

[5] Who then is Paul, and who is Apollos, but ministers by whom you believed, even as the Lord gave to each one? [6] I have planted, Apollos watered, but God gave the increase. [7] So then neither is he who plants nor he who waters anything, but God who gives the increase. [8] Now he who plants and he who waters are one, and each one will receive his own reward according to his own labor. [9] For we are laborers together with God: You are God's vineyard; you are God's building.

[10] According to the grace of God which has been given to me, as a wise master builder, I have laid the foundation, but another builds on it. Now let each one take heed how he builds on it. [11] For no one can lay another foundation than that which was laid, which is Jesus Christ. [12] Now if anyone builds on this foundation with gold, silver, precious stones, wood, hay, or stubble, [13] each one's work will be revealed. For the Day will declare it, because it will be revealed by fire, and the fire will test what sort of work each has done. [14] If anyone's work which he has built on the foundation endures, he will receive a reward. [15] If anyone's work is burned, he will suffer loss. But he himself will be saved, still going through the fire.

[16] Do you not know that you are the temple of God, and that the Spirit of God dwells in you? [17] If anyone defiles the temple of God, God will destroy him. For the temple of God is holy. And you are His temple.

[18] Let no one deceive himself. If anyone among you seems to be wise in this world, let him become a fool that he may be wise. [19] For

the wisdom of this world is foolishness with God. For it is written, "He catches the wise in their own craftiness," [3] [20] and again, "The Lord knows the thoughts of the wise, that they are vain." [4] [21] Therefore let no one boast in men. For all things are yours: [22] whether Paul or Apollos or Cephas or the world or life or death or things present or things to come, all are yours, [23] and you are Christ's, and Christ is God's.

The Ministry of the Apostles

4 Let a man so regard us as the ministers of Christ and stewards of the mysteries of God. [2] Moreover it is required in stewards that a man be found faithful. [3] But with me it is a very small thing that I should be judged by you or by man's judgment. I do not even judge myself. [4] For I know nothing against myself. Yet I am not justified by this. But He who judges me is the Lord. [5] Therefore judge nothing before the appointed time until the Lord comes. He will bring to light the hidden things of darkness and will reveal the purposes of the hearts. Then everyone will have commendation from God.

[6] Brothers, I have figuratively applied these things to myself and to Apollos for your sakes, so that you may learn from us not to think of men above that which is written, and that not one of you would be arrogant for one against another. [7] For who makes you differ from another? And what do you have that you did not receive? Now if you received it, why do you boast as if you had not received it?

[8] Now you are full, now you are rich; you have begun reigning as kings without us, and I wish to God you reigned, so that we also might reign with you. [9] For I think that God has exhibited us, the apostles, last, as if we were sentenced to death. For we have been made a spectacle to the world, to angels and to men. [10] We are fools for Christ's sake, but you are wise in Christ. We are weak, but you are strong. You are honorable, but we are despised. [11] Even to this present hour we both hunger and thirst, and are poorly clothed and beaten and homeless. [12] We labor, working with our own hands. Being reviled, we bless. Being persecuted, we endure. [13] Being slandered, we encourage. We are made as the filth of the world, and are the refuse of all things to this day.

[14] I do not write these things to shame you, but as my beloved sons I warn you. [15] For if you were to have ten thousand instructors in Christ, yet you do not have many fathers. In Christ Jesus I have become a father to you through the gospel. [16] So I implore you, be followers of me. [17] Therefore I have sent Timothy to you. He is my beloved son and is faithful in the Lord. He will remind you of my ways which are in Christ, as I teach everywhere in every church.

[18] Now some are arrogant, as though I were not coming to you. [19] But I will come to you shortly if the Lord wills. And I will know not only what those who are arrogant are saying, but also their power. [20] For the kingdom of God is not in word, but in power. [21] What do you desire? Shall I come to you with a rod, or in love and in the spirit of meekness?

Judgment Against Immorality

5 It is actually reported that there is sexual immorality among you, and such immorality as is not even named among the Gentiles, that a man has his father's wife. [2] But you are arrogant. Instead you should have mourned, so that he who has done this deed might be removed from among you. [3] For indeed, though absent in body but present in spirit, I have already, as if I were present, judged him who has done this deed, [4] in the name of our Lord Jesus Christ. When you are assembled, along with my spirit, in the power of our Lord Jesus Christ, [5] deliver him to Satan for the destruction of the flesh, so that the spirit may be saved on the day of the Lord Jesus.

[6] Your boasting is not good. Do you not know that a little yeast leavens the whole batch? [7] Therefore purge out the old yeast, that you may be a new batch, since you are unleavened. For even Christ, our Passover, has been sacrificed for us. [8] Therefore let us keep the feast, not with old yeast, nor with the yeast of malice and wickedness, but with the unleavened bread of sincerity and truth.

[9] I wrote to you in my letter not to keep company with sexually immoral people. [10] Yet I did not mean the sexually immoral people of this world, or the covetous and extortioners, or the idolaters, since you would then need to go out of the world. [11] But I have written to you not to keep company with any man who is called a brother, who is sexually immoral, or covetous, or an idolater, or a reviler, or a drunkard, or an extortioner. Do not even eat with such a person.

[12] For what have I to do with judging those also who are outside? Do you not judge those who are inside? [13] But God judges those who are outside. Therefore "put away from among yourselves that wicked person."[1]

Going to Law Before Unbelievers

6 Dare any of you, having a matter against another, go to the law before the unrighteous, and not before the saints? [2] Do you not know that the saints will judge the world? If the world will be judged by you, are you unworthy to judge the smallest matters? [3] Do you not know that we shall judge angels? How much more the things that pertain to this life? [4] If then you have judgments dealing with matters of this life, do you appoint as judges those who are least esteemed in the church? [5] I speak to your shame. Is it true that there is not even one wise man among you who shall be able to judge between his brothers? [6] But brother goes to the law against brother, and before unbelievers, at that.

[7] Now therefore it is already an utter failure for you that you go to law against one another. Why not rather be wronged? Why not rather be defrauded? [8] But you yourselves do wrong and defraud, and do this to your brothers. [9] Do you not know that the unrighteous will not inherit the kingdom of God? Do not be deceived. Neither the sexually immoral, nor idolaters, nor adulterers, nor male prostitutes, nor homosexuals, [10] nor thieves, nor covetous, nor drunkards, nor revilers, nor extortioners will inherit the kingdom of God. [11] Such were some of you. But you were washed, you were sanctified, and you were justified in the name of the Lord Jesus by the Spirit of our God.

Glorify God in Your Body

[12] "All things are lawful to me," but not all things are helpful. "All things are lawful for me," but I will not be brought under the power of anything. [13] "Food is for the belly, and the belly is for food," but God will destroy both of them. Now the body is not for sexual immorality, but for the Lord, and the Lord is for the body. [14] God has raised up the Lord and will also raise us up by His own power. [15] Do you not know that your bodies are the parts of Christ? Shall I then take the parts of Christ and make them the parts of a harlot? God forbid! [16] What? Do you not know that he who is joined to a harlot is one body with her? For "the two," He says, "shall become one flesh."[2] [17] But he who is joined to the Lord becomes one spirit with Him.

[18] Escape from sexual immorality. Every sin that a man commits is outside the body. But he who commits sexual immorality sins against his own body. [19] What? Do you not know that your body is the temple of the Holy Spirit, who is in you, whom you have received from God, and that you are not your own? [20] You were bought with a price. Therefore glorify God in your body and in your spirit, which are God's.

Questions About Marriage

7 Now concerning the things about which you wrote to me: "It is good for a man not to touch a woman." [2] Nevertheless, because of sexual immorality, let every man have his own wife, and let every woman have her own husband. [3] Let the husband render to the wife due affection, and likewise the wife to the husband. [4] The wife does not have authority over her own body, but the husband does. Likewise, the husband does not have authority over his own body, but the wife does. [5] Do not deprive one another except with consent for a time, that you may give yourselves to fasting and prayer. Then come together again, so that Satan does not tempt you for lack of self-control. [6] I speak this as a concession and not

as a command. [7] For I would that all men were even as I myself. But every man has his proper gift from God, one after this manner and another after that.

[8] I say to the unmarried and widows that it is good for them if they live even as I am. [9] But if they cannot restrain themselves, let them marry. For it is better to marry than to burn with passion.

[10] Now to the married I command, not I, but the Lord, do not let the wife depart from her husband. [11] But if she departs, let her remain unmarried or be reconciled to her husband. And do not let the husband divorce his wife.

[12] To the rest I speak, not the Lord: If any brother has an unbelieving wife who consents to live with him, he should not divorce her. [13] And if the woman has an unbelieving husband who consents to live with her, she should not divorce him. [14] For the unbelieving husband is sanctified by the wife, and the unbelieving wife is sanctified by the husband. Otherwise, your children would be unclean. But now they are holy.

[15] But if the unbeliever departs, let that one depart. A brother or a sister is not bound in such cases. God has called us to peace. [16] For how do you know, O wife, whether you will save your husband? Or how do you know, O husband, whether you will save your wife?

Living as God Called You

[17] But as God has given to every man and as the Lord has called every man, so let him walk. This I command in all churches. [18] Is any man called while circumcised? Let him not become uncircumcised. Is any man called while uncircumcised? Let him not be circumcised. [19] Circumcision is nothing, and uncircumcision is nothing, but the keeping of the commandments of God is everything. [20] Let each man remain in the same condition in which he was called.

[21] Were you called while a servant? Do not worry about it. But if you may become free, do so. [22] For he who is called in the Lord while a servant is the Lord's freeman. Likewise, he who is called while free is Christ's servant. [23] You were bought at a price. Do not be the servants of men. [24] Brothers, let every man, in whatever condition he is called, remain there with God.

The Unmarried and Widows

[25] Now concerning virgins, I have no command from the Lord. Yet I will give my judgment as one who has obtained mercy from the Lord to be faithful. [26] I suppose therefore that this is good because of the present distress, that it is good for a man to remain as he is. [27] Are you committed to a wife? Do not seek to be uncommitted. Are you free from a wife? Do not seek a wife. [28] But if you marry, you have not sinned. And if a virgin marries, she has not sinned. Nevertheless they will have trouble in this life, but I would spare you that.

[29] But this I say, brothers, the time is short. It remains that those who have wives should be as though they had none; [30] those who weep, as though they did not weep; those who rejoice, as though they did not rejoice; those who buy, as though they possessed nothing; [31] and those who use this world, as though they did not make full use of it. For the form of this world is passing away.

[32] But I prefer that you have no concern. He who is unmarried cares for the things of the Lord, how he may please the Lord. [33] But he who is married cares for the things of the world, how he may please his wife. [34] There is a difference between a wife and a virgin. The unmarried woman cares for the things of the Lord, that she may be holy in body and in spirit. But she who is married cares for the things of the world, how she may please her husband. [35] I say this for your own benefit, not to put any restraint upon you, but for what is proper, and that you may serve the Lord without distraction.

[36] If any man thinks that he is behaving improperly toward his virgin,[3] and if she is past the flower of her youth, and passions so require, let him do what he will. He does not sin. Let them marry. [37] Nevertheless he who stands steadfast in his heart without necessity, and has power over his own will, and has so decreed in his heart that he will keep his virgin, does well.

---

[1] 13 Dt 17:7; 19:19; 21:21; 22:21; 24:7.   [2] 16 Ge 2:24.   [3] 36 Some versions translate this word as "virgin daughters," others translate it as "fiancée." Since the Greek text itself remains unclear, the editors have chosen to keep the literal translation.

[38] So then he who gives her in marriage does well, but he who gives her not in marriage does better.

[39] The wife is bound by the law as long as her husband lives. But if her husband dies, she is at liberty to be married to whom she will, but only in the Lord. [40] But in my judgment she is happier if she so remains as she is. And I think that I have the Spirit of God.

Food Offered to Idols

8 Now as concerning food offered to idols: We know that "we all have knowledge." Knowledge produces arrogance, but love edifies. [2] So if anyone thinks that he knows anything, he knows nothing yet as he ought to know. [3] But if anyone loves God, this one is known by Him.

[4] So concerning the eating of foods that are offered in sacrifice to idols, we know that an idol is nothing in the world, and that there is no other God but one. [5] For there are those who are called gods, whether in heaven or in earth, as there are many gods and many lords. [6] But for us there is but one God, the Father, from whom are all things and for whom we exist. And there is one Lord Jesus Christ, through whom are all things and through whom we exist.

[7] However, not everyone has this knowledge. Some, being accustomed to the idol until now, eat the food as a thing offered to an idol. So their weak conscience is defiled. [8] But food does not commend us to God. Neither if we eat are we the better, nor if we do not eat are we the worse.

[9] But take heed, lest by any means this liberty of yours becomes a stumbling block to those who are weak. [10] For if anyone sees you, who have knowledge, eating in the idol's temple, shall the conscience of him who is weak not be emboldened to eat those things which are offered to idols, [11] and by your knowledge shall the weak brother perish, for whom Christ died? [12] When you thus sin against the brothers, wounding their weak conscience, you sin against Christ. [13] Therefore, if food causes my brother to stumble, I will never eat meat, lest I cause my brother to stumble.

The Rights of an Apostle

9 Am I not an apostle? Am I not free? Have I not seen Jesus Christ our Lord? Are you not my work in the Lord? [2] If I am not an apostle to others, yet indeed I am to you. For you are the seal of my apostleship in the Lord.

[3] This is my answer to those who examine me. [4] Do we have no right to eat and to drink? [5] Do we not have the right to take along a believing wife as do other apostles, the brothers of the Lord, and Cephas? [6] Or is it only Barnabas and I who have no right to refrain from working?

[7] Who goes to war at any time at his own expense? Who plants a vineyard, but does not eat of its fruit? Or who feeds a flock, but does not drink of the flock's milk? [8] Do I say these things as a man? Or does the law not say the same thing also? [9] For it is written in the Law of Moses, "You shall not muzzle the mouth of the ox while it treads out the grain."[1] Is God concerned about oxen? [10] Or does He say it completely for our sake? For our sake, no doubt, this is written so that he who plows should plow in hope, and that he who threshes in hope should partake of his hope. [11] If we have sown for you spiritual things, is it a great thing if we shall reap your material things? [12] If others partake of this right over you, should not we instead?

Nevertheless, we have not used this right, but suffer all things, lest we might hinder the gospel of Christ.

[13] Do you not know that those who minister unto holy things live from the things of the temple? And do you not know that those who wait at the altar partake of the altar? [14] In the same way, the Lord has ordained that those who preach the gospel should live from the gospel.

[15] But I have used none of these rights, nor have I written these things that it should be so done to me. For it would be better for me to die than allow anyone to make my boasting void. [16] Though I preach the gospel, I have nothing to boast of, for the require-

ment is laid upon me. Yes, woe unto me if I do not preach the gospel! [17] So if I do this willingly, I have a reward, but if against my will, I have been entrusted with a commission. [18] What is my reward then? Truly that when I preach the gospel, I may present the gospel of Christ without charge, so that I may not abuse my authority in the gospel.

[19] For though I am free from all men, I have made myself servant to all, that I might win even more. [20] To the Jews, I became as a Jew, that I might win the Jews; to those who are under the law, as under the law, that I might win those who are under the law; [21] to those who are outside the law, as outside the law (being not without God's law, but under Christ's law) that I might win those who are outside the law. [22] To the weak, I became as weak, that I might win the weak. I have become all things to all men, that I might by all means save some. [23] This I do for the gospel's sake, that I might partake of it with you.

[24] Do you not know that all those who run in a race run, but one receives the prize? So run, that you may obtain it. [25] Everyone who strives for the prize exercises self-control in all things. Now they do it to obtain a corruptible crown, but we an incorruptible one. [26] So, therefore, I run, not with uncertainty. So I fight, not as one who beats the air. [27] But I bring and keep my body under subjection, lest when preaching to others I myself should be disqualified.

Warning Against Idolatry

10 I would not want you to be unaware that all our fathers were under the cloud, and all passed through the sea, [2] and all were baptized into Moses in the cloud and in the sea; [3] all ate the same spiritual food; [4] and all drank the same spiritual drink, for they drank of that spiritual Rock that followed them, and that Rock was Christ. [5] But with many of them God was not well pleased, and they were overthrown in the wilderness.

[6] Now these things were our examples to the intent that we should not lust after evil things as they lusted. [7] Neither be idolaters as were some of them. As it is written, "The people sat down to eat and drink and rose up to revel."[2] [8] Neither let us commit sexual immorality as some of them committed, when twenty-three thousand fell in one day. [9] Neither let us tempt Christ, as some of them also tempted and were destroyed by serpents. [10] Neither murmur, as some of them also murmured and were destroyed by the destroyer.

[11] Now all these things happened to them for examples. They are written as an admonition to us, upon whom the end of the ages has come. [12] Therefore let him who thinks he stands take heed, lest he fall. [13] No temptation has taken you except what is common to man. God is faithful, and He will not permit you to be tempted above what you can endure, but will with the temptation also make a way to escape, that you may be able to bear it.

[14] So, my beloved, flee from idolatry. [15] I speak as to wise men. Judge for yourselves what I say. [16] The cup of blessing which we bless, is it not the communion of the blood of Christ? The bread which we break, is it not the communion of the body of Christ? [17] For we, being many, are one bread and one body, for we are all partakers of that one bread.

[18] Consider Israel after the flesh: Are not those who eat of the sacrifices partakers of the altar? [19] What am I saying then, that the idol is anything or that which is offered in sacrifice to idols is anything? [20] But I say that the things which the Gentiles sacrifice, they sacrifice to demons, and not to God. I do not want you to have fellowship with demons. [21] You cannot drink the cup of the Lord and the cup of demons. You cannot be partakers of the Lord's table and of the table of demons. [22] Do we provoke the Lord to jealousy? Are we stronger than He?

Do All to the Glory of God

[23] "All things are lawful for me," but not all things are helpful. "All things are lawful for me," but not all things edify. [24] Let no one seek his own, but each one the other's well-being.

[25] Eat whatever is sold in the meat market, asking no question for the sake of conscience, [26] for "The earth is the Lord's, and everything in it."[3]

---

[1]9 Dt 25:4. [2]7 Ex 32:6. [3]26 Ps 24:1.

[27] If any of those who do not believe invite you to a feast, and you desire to go, eat whatever is set before you, asking no question for the sake of conscience. [28] But if anyone says to you, "This was offered in sacrifice to idols," do not eat it for the sake of him that mentioned it and for the sake of conscience, for "The earth is the Lord's, and everything in it."[1] [29] Conscience, I say, not your own, but that of the other. For why is my liberty judged by another man's conscience? [30] If I partake with thankfulness, why am I slandered concerning that for which I give thanks?

[31] Therefore, whether you eat, or drink, or whatever you do, do it all to the glory of God. [32] Give no offense, neither to the Jews, nor to the Gentiles, nor to the church of God, [33] just as I try to please all men in all things, not seeking my own profit, but the profit of many, that they may be saved.

11 Follow me as I follow Christ.

Covering the Head in Worship

[2] I praise you, brothers, that you remember me in all things and keep the traditions as I delivered them to you. [3] But I would have you know that the head of the woman is the man, the head of every man is Christ, and the head of Christ is God. [4] Every man praying or prophesying having his head covered dishonors his head, [5] but every woman who prays or prophesies with her head uncovered dishonors her head, for that is the same as if she were shaved. [6] For if the woman is not covered, let her also cut off her hair. But if it is a shame for a woman to have her hair cut off or shaved, let her be covered.

[7] For a man indeed ought not to cover his head, because he is the image and glory of God. But the woman is the glory of the man. [8] The man is not from the woman, but the woman from the man. [9] The man was not created for the woman, but the woman for the man. [10] For this reason the woman ought to have a veil of authority over her head, because of the angels. [11] Nevertheless, neither is the man without the woman, nor the woman without the man in the Lord. [12] For just as the woman came from the man, so the man comes through the woman, but all things come from God.

[13] Judge for yourselves. Is it proper for a woman to pray to God uncovered? [14] Does even nature itself not teach you that if a man has long hair it is a shame to him? [15] But if a woman has long hair, it is a glory to her, for her hair is given her for a covering. [16] But if anyone seems to be contentious, we have no such custom, nor have the churches of God.

Abuses at the Lord's Supper

[17] Now in what I have to say to you, I do not praise you. You have come together not for the better, but for the worse. [18] First of all, when you come together as the church, I hear that there are divisions among you, and in part I believe it. [19] For there must also be factions among you so that those who are genuine may become evident among you. [20] Therefore when you come together into one place, it is not to eat the Lord's Supper. [21] For in eating, each one eats his own supper ahead of others. One goes hungry, and another becomes drunk. [22] What? Do you not have houses to eat and to drink in? Or do you despise the church of God and shame those who have nothing? What shall I say to you? Shall I praise you in this? I do not praise you.

The Lord's Supper

Mt 26:26–29; Mk 14:22–25; Lk 22:14–20

[23] I have received of the Lord that which I delivered to you: that the Lord Jesus, on the night in which He was betrayed, took bread. [24] When He had given thanks, He broke it and said, "Take and eat. This is My body which is broken for you. Do this in remembrance of Me."[2] [25] In the same manner He took the cup after He had supper, saying, "This cup is the new covenant in My blood. Do this, as often as you drink it, in remembrance of Me."[3] [26] As often as you eat this bread and drink this cup, you proclaim the Lord's death until He comes.

Partaking of the Supper Unworthily

[27] Therefore whoever eats this bread and drinks this cup of the Lord unworthily will be guilty of the body and blood of the Lord. [28] Let a man examine himself, and so eat of the bread and drink of the cup. [29] For he who eats and drinks unworthily, eats and drinks damnation to himself, not discerning the Lord's body. [30] For this reason many are weak and unhealthy among you, and many die. [31] If we would judge ourselves, we would not be judged. [32] But when we are judged, we are disciplined by the Lord, so that we would not be condemned with the world.

[33] So, my brothers, when you come together to eat, wait for one another. [34] If anyone hungers, let him eat at home, so that you may not come together into condemnation.

I will set the rest in order when I come.

Spiritual Gifts

12 Now concerning spiritual gifts, brothers, I do not want you to be ignorant. [2] You know that you were Gentiles, carried away to these dumb idols, however you were led. [3] Therefore I make known to you that no one speaking by the Spirit of God says, "Jesus be cursed!" And no one can say, "Jesus is the Lord," except by the Holy Spirit.

[4] There are various gifts, but the same Spirit. [5] There are differences of administrations, but the same Lord. [6] There are various operations, but it is the same God who operates all of them in all people. [7] But the manifestation of the Spirit is given to everyone for the common good. [8] To one is given by the Spirit the word of wisdom, to another the word of knowledge by the same Spirit, [9] to another faith by the same Spirit, to another gifts of healings by the same Spirit, [10] to another the working of miracles, to another prophecy, to another discerning of spirits, to another various kinds of tongues, and to another the interpretation of tongues. [11] But that one and very same Spirit works all these, dividing to each one individually as He will.

One Body With Many Members

[12] For as the body is one and has many parts, and all the many parts of that one body are one body, so also is Christ. [13] For by one Spirit we are all baptized into one body, whether we are Jews or Gentiles, whether we are slaves or free, and we have all been made to drink of one Spirit. [14] The body is not one part, but many.

[15] If the foot says, "Because I am not the hand, I am not of the body," is it therefore not of the body? [16] And if the ear says, "Because I am not the eye, I am not of the body," is it therefore not of the body? [17] If the whole body were an eye, where would the hearing be? If the whole body were hearing, where would the sense of smell be? [18] But now God has established the parts, every one of them, in the body as it has pleased Him. [19] If they were all one part, where would the body be? [20] So there are many parts, yet one body.

[21] The eye cannot say to the hand, "I have no need of you," nor the head to the feet, "I have no need of you." [22] No, those parts of the body which seem to be weaker are necessary. [23] And those parts of the body which we think are less honorable, upon these we bestow more abundant honor. And our less respectable parts are treated with much more respect, [24] whereas our more respectable parts have no need of this. But God has composed the body, having given more abundant honor to that part which lacks it, [25] so that there should be no division in the body, but that the parts should have the same care for one another. [26] If one part suffers, all the parts suffer with it, and if one part is honored, all the parts rejoice with it.

[27] Now you are the body of Christ and members individually. [28] God has put these in the church: first apostles, second prophets, third teachers, after that miracles, then gifts of healings, helps, governments, and various tongues. [29] Are all apostles? Are all prophets? Are all teachers? Are all workers of miracles? [30] Do all have the gifts of healings? Do all speak with tongues? Do all interpret? [31] But earnestly covet the greater gifts.

---

[1] 28 Ps 24:1. [2] 24 Mt 26:26; Mk 14:22; Lk 22:19. [3] 25 Mt 26:27–28; Mk 14:24; Lk 22:20.

Love

Yet I show you a more excellent way.

13 If I speak with the tongues of men and of angels, and have not love, I have become as sounding brass or a clanging cymbal. [2] If I have the gift of prophecy, and understand all mysteries and all knowledge, and if I have all faith, so that I could remove mountains, and have not love, I am nothing. [3] If I give all my goods to feed the poor, and if I give my body to be burned, and have not love, it profits me nothing.

[4] Love suffers long and is kind; love envies not; love flaunts not itself and is not puffed up, [5] does not behave itself improperly, seeks not its own, is not easily provoked, thinks no evil; [6] rejoices not in iniquity, but rejoices in the truth; [7] bears all things, believes all things, hopes all things, and endures all things.

[8] Love never fails. But if there are prophecies, they shall fail; if there are tongues, they shall cease; and if there is knowledge, it shall vanish. [9] For we know in part, and we prophesy in part. [10] But when that which is perfect comes, then that which is imperfect shall pass away. [11] When I was a child, I spoke as a child, I understood as a child, and I thought as a child. But when I became a man, I put away childish things. [12] For now we see as through a glass, dimly, but then, face to face. Now I know in part, but then I shall know, even as I also am known.

[13] So now abide faith, hope, and love, these three. But the greatest of these is love.

Tongues and Prophecy

14 Follow after love and desire spiritual gifts, but especially that you may prophesy. [2] For he who speaks in an unknown tongue does not speak to men, but to God. For no one understands him, although in the spirit, he speaks mysteries. [3] But he who prophesies speaks to men for their edification and exhortation and comfort. [4] He who speaks in an unknown tongue edifies himself, but he who prophesies edifies the church. [5] I desire that you all speak in tongues, but even more that you prophesy. For greater is he who prophesies than he who speaks in tongues, unless he interprets, so that the church may receive edification.

[6] Now, brothers, if I come to you speaking in tongues, what shall I profit you, unless I speak to you by revelation or knowledge or prophesying or doctrine? [7] Even when things without life give sound, whether flute or harp, how will it be known what is played unless they give a distinction in the sounds? [8] If the trumpet makes an uncertain sound, who will prepare himself for the battle? [9] So also you, unless with the tongue you speak words easy to understand, how will it be known what is spoken? For you shall speak into the air. [10] There are, it may be, so many kinds of languages in the world, and none of them is without significance. [11] Therefore, if I do not know the meaning of the speech, I shall be a barbarian to him who speaks, and he who speaks will be a barbarian to me. [12] So, seeing that you are zealous of spiritual gifts, seek that you may excel to the edifying of the church.

[13] Let him who speaks in an unknown tongue pray that he may interpret. [14] For if I pray in an unknown tongue, my spirit prays, but my understanding is unfruitful. [15] What is it then? I will pray with the spirit, and I will pray with the understanding. I will sing with the spirit, and I will sing with the understanding. [16] Otherwise, when you bless with the spirit, how will he who occupies the place of the unlearned say "Amen" at your giving of thanks, seeing he does not understand what you say? [17] For you indeed give thanks well, but the other is not edified.

[18] I thank my God that I speak in tongues more than you all. [19] Yet in the church I had rather speak five words with my understanding, that by my voice I might teach others also, than ten thousand words in an unknown tongue.

[20] Brothers, do not be children in your thinking; rather be infants in evil, but in your thinking be mature. [21] In the law it is written:

"With men of other tongues
    and other lips

I will speak to this people;
    but even then they will not hear Me," [1]
    says the Lord.

[22] So tongues are for a sign, not to believers, but to unbelievers. But prophesying does not serve unbelievers, but believers. [23] Therefore if the whole church assembles in one place and all speak with tongues, and those who are unlearned or unbelievers come in, will they not say that you are out of your mind? [24] But if all prophesy and there comes in one who does not believe or one unlearned, he is convinced by all and judged by all. [25] Thus the secrets of his heart are revealed. And so falling down on his face, he will worship God and report that God is truly among you.

All Things to Be Done in Order

[26] How is it then, brothers? When you come together, every one of you has a psalm, a teaching, a tongue, a revelation, and an interpretation. Let all things be done for edification. [27] If anyone speaks in an unknown tongue, let it be by two, or at the most by three, and each in turn, and let one interpret. [28] But if there is no interpreter, let him remain silent in the church, and let him speak to himself and to God.

[29] Let two or three prophets speak, and let the others judge. [30] If anything is revealed to another that sits by, let the first keep silent. [31] For you may all prophesy one by one, that all may learn and all may be encouraged. [32] The spirits of the prophets are subject to the prophets. [33] For God is not the author of confusion, but of peace, as in all churches of the saints.

[34] Let your women remain silent in the churches. For they are not permitted to speak. They are commanded to be under obedience, as the law also says. [35] If they will learn anything, let them ask their husbands at home, for it is a shame for women to speak in the church.

[36] What? Did the word of God come from you? Or did it come to you only? [37] If anyone thinks himself to be a prophet or spiritual, let him acknowledge that what I am writing you is a command of the Lord. [38] But if anyone is ignorant, let him be ignorant.

[39] Therefore, brothers, eagerly desire to prophesy, and do not forbid speaking in tongues. [40] Let all things be done decently and in order.

The Resurrection of Christ

15 Now, brothers, I declare to you the gospel which I preached to you, which you have received, and in which you stand. [2] Through it you are saved, if you keep in memory what I preached to you, unless you have believed in vain.

[3] For I delivered to you first of all that which I also received: how Christ died for our sins according to the Scriptures, [4] was buried, rose again the third day according to the Scriptures, [5] and was seen by Cephas, and then by the twelve. [6] Then He was seen by over five hundred brothers at once, of whom the greater part remain to this present time, though some have passed away. [7] Then He was seen by James and then by all the apostles. [8] Last of all, He was seen by me also, as by one born at the wrong time.

[9] For I am the least of the apostles and am not fit to be called an apostle, because I persecuted the church of God. [10] But by the grace of God I am what I am. And His grace toward me was not in vain. I labored more abundantly than all of them, yet not I, but the grace of God which was with me. [11] Therefore, whether it was I or they, so we preach and so you believed.

The Resurrection of the Dead

[12] Now if Christ is preached that He rose from the dead, how can some of you say that there is no resurrection of the dead? [13] If there is no resurrection of the dead, then Christ has not risen. [14] If Christ has not risen, then our preaching is vain, and your faith is also vain. [15] Yes, and we would then be found false witnesses of God, because we have testified that God raised up Christ, whom He did not raise up, if in fact the dead do not rise. [16] For if the dead do not rise, then Christ has not been raised. [17] If Christ is not raised, your

faith is vain; you are still in your sins. [18] Then they also who have fallen asleep in Christ have perished. [19] If in this life only we have hope in Christ, we are of all men most miserable.

[20] But now is Christ risen from the dead and become the first fruits of those who have fallen asleep. [21] For since death came by man, by man came also the resurrection of the dead. [22] For as in Adam all die, even so in Christ shall all be made alive. [23] But every man in his own order: Christ the first fruits; afterward, those who are Christ's at His coming. [24] Then comes the end when He will deliver up the kingdom to God the Father, when He puts an end to all rule and all authority and power. [25] For He will reign until He has put all enemies under His feet. [26] The last enemy that will be destroyed is death. [27] For He "has put all things under His feet."[1] But when He says, "all things are put under Him," it is revealed that He, who has put all things under Him, is the exception. [28] When all things are subjected to Him, then the Son Himself will also be subject to Him who put all things under Him, that God may be all in all.

[29] Otherwise, what will they do who are baptized for the dead, if the dead do not rise at all? Why are they then baptized for the dead? [30] And why do we stand in danger every hour? [31] I affirm, by the boasting in you which I have in Christ Jesus our Lord, I die daily. [32] If, in the manner of men, I have fought with beasts at Ephesus, what advantage is it to me if the dead do not rise?

> "Let us eat and drink,
>   for tomorrow we die."[2]

[33] Do not be deceived: "Bad company corrupts good morals." [34] Awake to righteousness and do not sin, for some do not have the knowledge of God. I say this to your shame.

The Resurrection Body

[35] But someone will say, "How are the dead raised up? With what body do they come?" [36] You fool! What you sow is not made alive unless it dies. [37] When you sow, you do not sow the body that shall be, but a bare kernel, perhaps of wheat or of some other grain. [38] Then God gives it a body as He pleases, and to each seed its own body. [39] All flesh is not the same flesh. There is one kind of flesh of men, another flesh of beasts, another of fish, and another of birds. [40] There are also celestial bodies and terrestrial bodies. The glory of the celestial is one, and the glory of the terrestrial is another. [41] There is one glory of the sun, and another glory of the moon, and another glory of the stars. One star differs from another star in glory.

[42] So also is the resurrection of the dead. *The body* is sown in corruption; it is raised in incorruption. [43] It is sown in dishonor, it is raised in glory. It is sown in weakness, it is raised in power. [44] It is sown a natural body, it is raised a spiritual body.

There is a natural body, and there is a spiritual body. [45] So it is written, "The first man Adam was made a living soul."[3] The last Adam was made a life-giving spirit. [46] However, that which is spiritual is not first, but the natural, and then the spiritual. [47] The first man was of the earth, made of dust; the second man was the Lord from heaven. [48] As was the man of dust, so are those who are of dust; and as is the man of heaven, so are those who are of heaven. [49] As we have borne the image of the man of dust, we shall also bear the image of the man of heaven.

[50] Now this I say, brothers, that flesh and blood cannot inherit the kingdom of God, nor does corruption inherit incorruption. [51] Listen, I tell you a mystery: We shall not all sleep, but we shall all be changed. [52] In a moment, in the twinkling of an eye, at the last trumpet, for the trumpet will sound, the dead will be raised incorruptible, and we shall be changed. [53] For this corruptible will put on incorruption, and this mortal will put on immortality. [54] When this corruptible will have put on incorruption, and this mortal will have put on immortality, then the saying that is written shall come to pass: "Death is swallowed up in victory."[4]

[55] "O death, where is your sting?
   O grave, where is your victory?"[5]

[56] The sting of death is sin, and the strength of sin is the law. [57] But thanks be to God, who gives us the victory through our Lord Jesus Christ!

[58] Therefore, my beloved brothers, be steadfast, unmovable, always abounding in the work of the Lord, knowing that your labor in the Lord is not in vain.

The Contribution for the Saints

16 Now concerning the collection for the saints, as I have given instruction to the churches of Galatia, so even you must do. [2] On the first day of the week let every one of you lay in store, as God has prospered him, so that no collections be made when I come. [3] And when I come, I will send whomever you approve with your letters to take your generous gifts to Jerusalem. [4] If it is fitting that I go also, they will go with me.

Paul's Plans for Travel

[5] Now I will come to you after I pass through Macedonia. For I will pass through Macedonia. [6] It may be that I will remain, of course, and spend the winter with you, that you may send me on my journey wherever I go. [7] For I do not wish to see you now in passing. Instead, I trust to remain a while with you, if the Lord permits. [8] But I will remain at Ephesus until Pentecost. [9] For a great and effective door has opened to me, and there are many adversaries.

[10] Now if Timothy comes, see that he may remain with you without fear, for he does the work of the Lord, as I also do. [11] Therefore let no one despise him. But send him on his way in peace, that he may come to me. I am expecting him with the brothers.

[12] As for our brother Apollos, I greatly wanted him to come to you with the brothers. But he was not willing at all to come at this time. However, he will come when he has a convenient time.

[13] Watch, stand fast in the faith, be bold like men, and be strong. [14] Let all that you do be done with love.

[15] You know the house of Stephanas, that it is the first fruits of Achaia, and that they have devoted themselves to the ministry of the saints. So I ask you, brothers, [16] that you submit yourselves to such people, and to everyone who helps and labors with us. [17] I am happy about the arrival of Stephanas, Fortunatus, and Achaicus, for they supplied what was lacking on your part. [18] They have refreshed my spirit and yours. Therefore acknowledge these men.

Final Request and Greetings

[19] The churches of Asia greet you. Aquila and Priscilla greet you heartily in the Lord, with the church that is in their house. [20] All the brothers greet you. Greet one another with a holy kiss.

[21] I, Paul, write this greeting with my own hand.

[22] If anyone does not love the Lord Jesus Christ, let him be accursed. Come, O Lord!

[23] The grace of our Lord Jesus Christ be with you.

[24] My love be with you all in Christ Jesus. Amen.

---

[1] 27 Ps 8:6. [2] 32 Isa 22:13. [3] 45 Ge 2:7. [4] 54 Isa 25:8. [5] 55 Hos 13:14.

2 CORINTHIANS

Salutation

1 Paul, an apostle of Jesus Christ by the will of God, and Timothy our brother,

To the church of God which is at Corinth, with all the saints who are in all Achaia:

[2] Grace to you and peace from God our Father and from the Lord Jesus Christ.

Paul's Thanksgiving After Affliction

[3] Blessed be God, the Father of our Lord Jesus Christ, the Father of mercies, and the God of all comfort, [4] who comforts us in all our tribulation, that we may be able to comfort those who are in any trouble by the comfort with which we ourselves are comforted by God. [5] As the sufferings of Christ abound in us, so our consolation also abounds through Christ. [6] If we are afflicted, it is for your consolation and salvation, which is effective in enduring the same sufferings which we also suffer. Or if we are comforted, it is for your consolation and salvation. [7] Our hope for you is steadfast, knowing that as you partake in the sufferings, so also you will partake of the consolation.

[8] For we would not, brothers, have you ignorant of our troubles which came to us in Asia. We were pressured beyond measure, above strength, so that we despaired even of life. [9] We had the sentence of death in ourselves, so that we would not trust in ourselves, but in God who raises the dead. [10] He delivered us from so great a death and does deliver us. In Him we trust that He will still deliver us, [11] as you help together by praying for us, so that thanks may be given by many on our behalf for the gift bestowed upon us by means of many persons.

Paul's Travel Plans Change

[12] For our rejoicing is this: The testimony of our conscience is that we conducted ourselves in the world, and more abundantly toward you, in simplicity and godly sincerity, not with fleshly wisdom, but by the grace of God. [13] For we write nothing else to you than what you read or understand. And I trust you will understand even to the end, [14] as you have understood us in part, that we are yours, boasting even as you are ours on the day of the Lord Jesus.

[15] In this confidence I planned to come to you before, that you might have a second benefit: [16] to visit you while going to Macedonia, and to come again to you from Macedonia, and then be sent by you on my way to Judea. [17] Therefore, when I was planning this, did I do this lightly? Or the things that I plan, do I plan according to the flesh, so that I would tell you "Yes, yes" and "No, no"?

[18] But as God is true, we did not tell you "Yes" and "No." [19] For the Son of God, Jesus Christ, who was preached among you by us, even by Silas, Timothy, and me, was not "Yes" and "No." In Him it was "Yes." [20] For all the promises of God in Him are "Yes," and in Him "Amen," to the glory of God through us. [21] Now He who establishes us with you in Christ and has anointed us is God, [22] who also has sealed us and established the guarantee with the Spirit in our hearts.

[23] Moreover I call God as a witness upon my soul, that it is to spare you that I have not yet gone to Corinth. [24] Not that we have dominion over your faith, but we are fellow workers for your joy, for by faith you stand.

2 But I determined this for myself, that I would not come again to you in sorrow. [2] For if I make you sorrowful, who then will there be to make me rejoice, but the one whom I have made sorrowful? [3] I wrote concerning this matter to you, so that when I came, I would not be grieved by those in whom I ought to rejoice, having confidence in you all, that my joy is your joy. [4] For out of much affliction and anguish of heart I wrote to you with many tears, not that you should be grieved, but that you might know the love which I have more abundantly for you.

Forgiveness for the Offender

[5] But if anyone has caused grief, he has not grieved me, but to some extent all of you, not to put it too severely. [6] This punishment which was inflicted by many on such a man is sufficient. [7] So on the contrary, you ought to forgive him and comfort him, lest perhaps he might be swallowed up with excessive sorrow. [8] Therefore I ask you to confirm your love toward him. [9] For to this end I also wrote, so that I might know that you are proving yourselves by whether you are being obedient in all things. [10] Whomever you forgive anything, I also forgive. For if I forgave someone anything, for your sakes I forgave it in Christ, [11] lest Satan should take advantage of us. For we are not ignorant of his devices.

Paul's Anxiety in Troas

[12] Furthermore, when I came to Troas to preach Christ's gospel, and a door was opened to me by the Lord, [13] I had no rest in my spirit, because I did not find Titus my brother. So taking my leave of them, I went from there into Macedonia.

[14] Now thanks be to God who always causes us to triumph in Christ and through us reveals the fragrance of His knowledge in every place. [15] For we are to God a sweet fragrance of Christ among those who are saved and among those who perish. [16] To the one we are the fragrance of death, which brings death, and to the other the fragrance of life, which brings life. Who is sufficient for these things? [17] For we are not as many are who peddle the word of God. Instead, being sent by God, we sincerely speak in Christ in the sight of God.

Ministers of the New Covenant

3 Do we begin again to commend ourselves? Or do we need, as some others, letters of commendation to you, or letters of commendation from you? [2] You are our letter written in our hearts, known and read by all men. [3] For you are prominently declared to be the letter of Christ, prepared by us, written not with ink but with the Spirit of the living God, not on tablets of stone but on human tablets of the heart.

[4] We have such trust through Christ toward God, [5] not that we are sufficient in ourselves to take credit for anything of ourselves, but our sufficiency is from God, [6] who has made us able ministers of the new covenant, not of the letter but of the Spirit. For the letter kills, but the Spirit gives life.

[7] If the ministry that brought death, written and engraved on stones, was glorious, so that the children of Israel could not look intently at the face of Moses because of the glory of his countenance, the glory which was to fade away, [8] how will the ministry of the Spirit not be more glorious? [9] For if the ministry of condemnation is glorious, the ministry of righteousness much more exceeds it in glory. [10] Even that which was made glorious had no glory in comparison to the glory that excels. [11] For if that which fades was glorious, that which remains is much more glorious.

[12] Seeing then that we have such hope, we speak with great boldness, [13] not as Moses, who put a veil over his face, so that the children of Israel could not look intently at the end of what was fading away. [14] Instead, their minds were blinded. For until this day the same veil remains unlifted in the reading of the old covenant, the veil which was done away with in Christ. [15] But even to this day, when Moses is read, the veil is in their hearts. [16] Nevertheless when anyone turns to the Lord, the veil is removed. [17] Now the Lord is the Spirit. And where the Spirit of the Lord is, there is liberty. [18] But we all, seeing the glory of the Lord with unveiled faces, as in a mirror, are being transformed into the same image from glory to glory by the Spirit of the Lord.

Treasure in Earthen Vessels

4 Therefore, since we have this ministry through the mercy we have received, we do not lose heart. [2] But we have renounced the secret things of shame, not walking in craftiness nor handling the word of God deceitfully, but by expressing the truth and commending ourselves to every man's conscience in the sight of

God. [3] But if our gospel is hidden, it is hidden to those who are lost. [4] The god of this world has blinded the minds of those who do not believe, lest the light of the glorious gospel of Christ, who is the image of God, should shine on them. [5] For we do not preach ourselves, but Christ Jesus the Lord, and ourselves your servants for Jesus' sake. [6] For God, who commanded the light to shine out of darkness, has shone in our hearts to give the light of the knowledge of the glory of God in the face of Jesus Christ.

[7] But we have this treasure in earthen vessels, the excellency of the power being from God and not from ourselves. [8] We are troubled on every side, yet not distressed; we are perplexed, but not in despair; [9] persecuted, but not forsaken; cast down, but not destroyed; [10] and always carrying around in the body the death of the Lord Jesus, that also the life of Jesus might be expressed in our bodies. [11] For we who live are always delivered to death for Jesus' sake, that also the life of Jesus might be manifested in our mortal flesh. [12] So then, death works in us, but life in you.

[13] We have the same spirit of faith. As it is written, "I believed, and therefore I have spoken."[1] So we also believe and therefore speak, [14] knowing that He who raised the Lord Jesus will also raise us through Jesus and will present us with you. [15] All these things are for your sakes, so that the abundant grace through the thanksgiving of many might overflow to the glory of God.

Living by Faith

[16] For this reason we do not lose heart: Even though our outward man is perishing, yet our inward man is being renewed day by day. [17] Our light affliction, which lasts but for a moment, works for us a far more exceeding and eternal weight of glory, [18] while we do not look at the things which are seen, but at the things which are not seen. For the things which are seen are temporal, but the things which are not seen are eternal.

5 We know that if our earthly house, this tent, were to be destroyed, we have an eternal building of God in the heavens, a house not made with hands. [2] In this one we groan, earnestly desiring to be sheltered with our house which is from heaven. [3] Thus being sheltered, we shall not be found unsheltered. [4] For we who are in this tent groan, being burdened, not because we wish to be unclothed, but to be further clothed, so that what is mortal might be swallowed up by life. [5] Now He who has created us for this very thing is God, who also has given to us the guarantee of the Spirit.

[6] Therefore we are always confident, knowing that while we are at home in the body, we are absent from the Lord. [7] For we walk by faith, not by sight. [8] Instead, I say that we are confident and willing to be absent from the body and to be present with the Lord. [9] So whether present or absent, we labor that we may be accepted by Him. [10] For we must all appear before the judgment seat of Christ, that each one may receive his recompense in the body, according to what he has done, whether it was good or bad.

The Ministry of Reconciliation

[11] Therefore, knowing the fear of the Lord, we persuade men. But we are revealed to God, and I trust we are also revealed in your consciences. [12] For we are not commending ourselves again to you. Instead, we give you occasion to boast on our behalf, that you may have something to answer those who boast in appearance and not in heart. [13] If we are beside ourselves, it is for God; if we are in our right mind, it is for you. [14] For the love of Christ constrains us, because we thus judge: that if one died for all, then all have died. [15] And He died for all, that those who live should not from now on live for themselves, but for Him who died for them and rose again.

[16] So from now on we do not regard anyone according to the flesh. Yes, though we have known Christ according to the flesh, yet we do not regard Him as such from now on. [17] Therefore, if any man is in Christ, he is a new creature. Old things have passed away. Look, all things have become new. [18] All this is from God, who has reconciled us to Himself through Jesus Christ and has given to us the ministry of reconciliation, [19] that is, that God was

in Christ reconciling the world to Himself, not counting their sins against them, and has entrusted to us the message of reconciliation. [20] So we are ambassadors for Christ, as though God were pleading through us. We implore you in Christ's stead: Be reconciled to God. [21] God made Him who knew no sin to be sin for us, that we might become the righteousness of God in Him.

6 As workers together with God, we ask you not to receive the grace of God in vain. [2] For He says:

"In an acceptable time I have listened to you,
and in the day of salvation I have helped you."[2]

Look, now is the accepted time; look, now is the day of salvation. [3] We give no offense in anything, that our service may not be blamed. [4] But in all things we commend ourselves as servants of God: in much patience, in afflictions, in necessities, in distress, [5] in stripes, in imprisonments, in tumults, in labors, in sleeplessness, and in hunger; [6] by purity, by knowledge, by patience, by kindness, by the Holy Spirit, by genuine love, [7] by the word of truth, by the power of God, by the armor of righteousness on the right hand and on the left, [8] by honor and dishonor, by evil report and good report; as deceivers, and yet true; [9] as unknown, and yet well known; as dying, and look, we live; as punished, but not killed; [10] as sorrowful, yet always rejoicing; as poor, yet making many rich; and as having nothing, and yet possessing all things.

[11] O Corinthians, we have spoken frankly to you; our heart is opened wide. [12] You are not restrained by us, but you are restrained in your own affections. [13] In return (I speak as to my children) you also be open.

The Temple of the Living God

[14] Do not be unequally yoked together with unbelievers. For what fellowship has righteousness with unrighteousness? What communion has light with darkness? [15] What agreement has Christ with Belial? Or what part has he who believes with an unbeliever? [16] What agreement has the temple of God with idols? For you are the temple of the living God. As God has said:

"I will live in them
and walk in them.
I will be their God,
and they shall be My people."[3]

[17] Therefore,

"Come out from among them
and be separate,
says the Lord.
Do not touch what is unclean,
and I will receive you."[4]

[18] "I will be a Father to you,
and you shall be My sons and daughters,
says the Lord Almighty."[5]

7 Since we have these promises, beloved, let us cleanse ourselves from all filthiness of the flesh and spirit, perfecting holiness in the fear of God.

Paul's Joy at the Church's Repentance

[2] Accept us. We have wronged no one, we have corrupted no one, and we have defrauded no one. [3] I do not say this to condemn you, for I have said before that you are in our hearts, so that we would die or live with you. [4] Great is my boldness of speech toward you; great is my boasting of you. I am filled with comfort, and I am exceedingly joyful in all our tribulation.

[5] For when we came to Macedonia, our bodies had no rest, and we were troubled on every side. On the outside were conflicts; on the inside were fears. [6] Nevertheless God, who comforts the downcast, comforted us through the coming of Titus, [7] and not only by his

coming, but also by the comfort with which he was comforted in you, when he told us about your sincere desire, your mourning, and your zeal toward me, so that I rejoiced even more. [8] Though I caused you sorrow by my letter, I do not regret it, though I did regret it. For I perceive that this same letter has caused you sorrow, though only for a while. [9] Now I rejoice, not that you were made sorrowful, but that your sorrow led to repentance. For you were made sorrowful in a godly way, that you might not suffer loss in any way through us. [10] Godly sorrow produces repentance that leads to salvation and brings no regret, but the sorrow of the world produces death. [11] For observe this very thing, which you sorrowed in a godly way: What carefulness it produced in you, what vindication of yourselves, what indignation, what fear, what intense desire, what zeal, what avenging of wrong! In all things you have proven yourselves to be innocent in this matter. [12] So though I wrote to you, I did it not because of him who had done the wrong, nor because of him who suffered wrong, but that our care for you in the sight of God might be evident to you. [13] Therefore we were comforted in your comfort.

Yes, and we were exceedingly the more joyful for the sake of Titus, because his spirit was refreshed by you all. [14] So I am not ashamed if I have boasted of anything to him regarding you. But as we spoke all things to you in truth, even our boasting in the presence of Titus is found to be true. [15] Now his affection abounds all the more toward you, as he remembers the obedience of you all, how with fear and trembling you received him. [16] Therefore I rejoice that I have confidence in you in everything.

Liberal Giving

8 Moreover, brothers, we want you to experience the grace of God bestowed on the churches of Macedonia, [2] how in a great trial of affliction, the abundance of their joy and their deep poverty overflowed toward the riches of their generous giving. [3] For I bear record that according to their means, and beyond their means, they freely gave, [4] begging us with much urgency that we would receive the gift and the fellowship of ministering to the saints. [5] This they did, not as we expected. First, they gave themselves to the Lord, and then to us by the will of God. [6] So we urged Titus, that as he had begun, so he would also complete this gracious deed for you. [7] But as you abound in everything—in faith, in utterance, in knowledge, in all diligence, and in your love to us—see that you abound in this grace also.

[8] I say this not as a command, but to prove through the authenticity of others, the sincerity also of your love. [9] For you know the grace of our Lord Jesus Christ, that though He was rich, yet for your sakes He became poor, that through His poverty you might be rich. [10] And in this matter I give my advice. It is appropriate for you, who began last year not only to give, but also to willingly give. [11] Now therefore complete the task, so that, as there was a willingness to do so, there may be a performance of it according to your means. [12] For if there is a willing mind first, the gift is accepted according to what a man possesses and not according to what he does not possess.

[13] I do not mean that other men have relief, and you be burdened, [14] but for equality, that your abundance now at this time may supply their need, and their abundance may supply your need—that there may be equality. [15] As it is written, "He who gathered much had no excess. And he who gathered little had no lack."[1] [16] But thanks be to God, who placed the same sincere care in the heart of Titus for you. [17] For indeed he accepted the exhortation. But being more zealous, he went to you of his own accord. [18] And we have sent with him the brother whose praise is in the gospel throughout all the churches. [19] And not only that, but he was also chosen by the churches to travel with us with this gift, which we administer to the glory of the same Lord, and to declare your willing mind, [20] to prevent any man from blaming us in administering this abundant gift, [21] providing for honest things, not only in the sight of the Lord but also in the sight of men.

[22] Furthermore, we have sent with them our brother whom we have frequently proved diligent in many things, but now is much more diligent, due to the great confidence which he has in you. [23] If anyone inquires about Titus, he is my partner and fellow helper concerning you. Or if our brothers are inquired about, they are the messengers of the churches, and the glory of Christ. [24] Therefore show to them, and before the churches, the proof of your love and of our boasting on your behalf.

The Offering for the Saints

9 It is redundant for me to write to you concerning the ministry to the saints. [2] I know your willingness, for which I boast of you to those in Macedonia, that Achaia was ready a year ago, and your zeal has stirred up most of them. [3] Yet I have sent the brothers, lest our boasting of you might be in vain in this case, that, as I said, you may be ready; [4] and lest if any Macedonians come with me and find you unprepared, we (not to mention you) should be ashamed of this confident boasting. [5] Therefore I thought it necessary to exhort the brothers to go ahead to you and arrange beforehand your bountiful gift you previously promised, that it might be prepared as a gift, not as a matter of greed.

[6] But this I say: He who sows sparingly will also reap sparingly, and he who sows bountifully will also reap bountifully. [7] Let every man give according to the purposes in his heart, not grudgingly or out of necessity, for God loves a cheerful giver. [8] God is able to make all grace abound toward you, so that you, always having enough of everything, may abound to every good work. [9] As it is written:

"He has dispersed abroad, He has given to the poor;
His righteousness remains forever."[2]

[10] Now He who supplies seed to the sower and supplies bread for your food will also multiply your seed sown and increase the fruits of your righteousness. [11] So you will be enriched in everything to all bountifulness, which makes us give thanks to God. [12] For the administration of this service not only supplies the need of the saints, but is abundant also through many thanksgivings to God. [13] Meanwhile, through the performance of this ministry, they glorify God for the profession of your faith in the gospel of Christ and for your liberal sharing with them and with all others. [14] And in their prayer for you, they long for you because of the surpassing grace of God in you. [15] Thanks be to God for His indescribable gift.

Paul Defends His Ministry

10 Now I, Paul, who am lowly in presence among you but bold toward you while absent, appeal to you by the meekness and gentleness of Christ. [2] I beg you that when I am present, I might not have to be bold with that confidence by which I intend to be bold against some, who think of us as if we walked according to the flesh. [3] For though we walk in the flesh, we do not war according to the flesh. [4] For the weapons of our warfare are not carnal, but mighty through God for the pulling down of strongholds, [5] casting down imaginations and every high thing that exalts itself against the knowledge of God, bringing every thought into captivity to the obedience of Christ, [6] and being ready to punish all disobedience when your obedience is complete.

[7] Do you look at things from the outward appearance? If any man trusts that he is Christ's, let him consider again that, as he is Christ's, even so are we Christ's. [8] For even if I should boast somewhat more of our authority, which the Lord has given us for edification and not for your destruction, I shall not be ashamed, [9] lest I appear to frighten you by my letters. [10] "For his letters," they say, "are weighty and powerful, but his bodily presence is weak, and his speech contemptible." [11] Let such a person consider this: that as we are in word by letters when we are absent, we will also be in deed when we are present.

[12] For we dare not count or compare ourselves with those who commend themselves. They who measure themselves by one another and compare ourselves with one another are not wise. [13] But we will not boast beyond measure, but within the boundaries

which God has appointed us, which reach even you. [14] For we are not overextending ourselves as though we did not reach you, since we have come to you, preaching the gospel of Christ. [15] We are not boasting of things beyond our measure in other men's labors. But we have hope that when your faith is increased, our region shall be greatly enlarged by you, [16] to preach the gospel in the regions beyond you and not to boast in another man's accomplishments. [17] But, "Let him who boasts, boast in the Lord."[1] [18] For it is not he who commends himself who is approved, but he whom the Lord commends.

Paul and the False Apostles

11 I would to God you could bear with me a little in my folly. Indeed, bear with me. [2] For I am jealous over you with godly jealousy. For I have espoused you to one husband, that I may present you as a chaste virgin to Christ. [3] But I fear that somehow, as the serpent deceived Eve through his trickery, so your minds might be led astray from the simplicity that is in Christ. [4] For if he who comes preaches another Jesus, whom we have not preached, or if you receive another spirit, which you have not received, or another gospel, which you have not accepted, you might submit to it readily enough.

[5] For I think I am not in any way inferior to the most eminent of the apostles. [6] Even though I am unpolished in speech, yet I am not in knowledge. All things about us have been thoroughly revealed to you. [7] Did I commit a sin in abasing myself that you might be exalted, because I preached to you the gospel of God free of charge? [8] I robbed other churches by accepting wages from them to serve you. [9] Furthermore, when I was present with you and was lacking, I was a burden to no one. For the brothers who came from Macedonia supplied what I lacked. In all things I have kept myself from being burdensome to you, and so will I keep myself. [10] As the truth of Christ is in me, no one shall stop me from this boasting in the regions of Achaia. [11] Why? Because I do not love you? God knows.

[12] And I will continue doing what I am doing, that I may cut off the opportunity from those who desire an opportunity to be found equal to us in what they boast about. [13] For such are false apostles and deceitful workers, disguising themselves as apostles of Christ. [14] And no wonder! For even Satan disguises himself as an angel of light. [15] Therefore it is no great thing if his ministers also disguise themselves as ministers of righteousness, whose end will be according to their works.

Paul's Sufferings as an Apostle

[16] I say again, let no one think that I am a fool. Otherwise, at least receive me as a fool, so that I also may boast a little. [17] What I speak, I speak not according to the Lord, but as it were foolishly, in this confidence of boasting. [18] Seeing that many boast according to the flesh, I also will boast. [19] For you tolerate fools gladly, seeing you yourselves are wise. [20] For you permit it if a man brings you into bondage, if a man devours you, if a man takes from you, if a man exalts himself, or if a man strikes you on the face. [21] I say to my reproach that we were too weak for that.

But whenever anyone is bold (I speak foolishly), I am bold also. [22] Are they Hebrews? So am I. Are they Israelites? So am I. Are they the seed of Abraham? So am I. [23] Are they servants of Christ? I speak as a fool. I am more: in labors more abundant, in stripes above measure, in prisons more frequently, in deaths often. [24] Five times I received from the Jews forty lashes minus one. [25] Three times I was beaten with rods; once I was stoned; three times I suffered shipwreck; a night and a day I have been in the deep; [26] in journeys often, in perils of waters, in perils of robbers, in perils by my own countrymen, in perils by the Gentiles, in perils in the city, in perils in the wilderness, in perils in the sea, in perils among false brothers; [27] in weariness and painfulness, in sleeplessness often, in hunger and thirst, in fastings often, and in cold and nakedness. [28] Beside the external things, the care of all the churches pressures me daily. [29] Who is weak, and I am not weak? Who is led into sin, and I am not distressed?

[30] If I must boast, I will boast of the things which concern my weakness. [31] The God and Father of our Lord Jesus Christ, who is blessed forevermore, knows that I am not lying. [32] In Damascus the governor under King Aretas secured the city of the Damascenes with a garrison, desiring to arrest me. [33] But I was let down by the wall through a window in a basket and escaped his hands.

Visions and Revelations

12 Doubtless it is not profitable for me to boast. So I will move on to visions and revelations of the Lord. [2] I knew a man in Christ over fourteen years ago—whether in the body or out of the body I cannot tell, God knows—such a one was caught up to the third heaven. [3] And I knew that such a man—whether in the body or out of the body I cannot tell, God knows—[4] was caught up into paradise and heard inexpressible words not permitted for a man to say. [5] Of such a person, I will boast. Yet of myself I will not boast, except in my weaknesses. [6] For if I desire to boast, I will not be a fool, for I will be speaking the truth. But now I resist, lest anyone should think of me above that which he sees me to be or hears from me. [7] And lest I should be exalted above measure by the abundance of revelations, a thorn was given me in the flesh, a messenger of Satan, to torment me, lest I be exalted above measure. [8] I asked the Lord three times that this thing might depart from me. [9] But He said to me, "My grace is sufficient for you, for My strength is made perfect in weakness." Therefore most gladly I will boast in my weaknesses, that the power of Christ may rest upon me. [10] So I take pleasure in weaknesses, in reproaches, in hardships, in persecutions, and in distresses for Christ's sake. For when I am weak, then I am strong.

Paul's Concern for the Corinthian Church

[11] I have become a fool in boasting. You have compelled me, for I ought to have been commended by you, for I am in no way inferior to the leading apostles, though I am nothing. [12] Truly the signs of an apostle were performed among you in all patience, in signs and wonders, and mighty deeds. [13] For in what respect were you inferior to other churches, unless it be that I myself was not burdensome to you? Forgive me this wrong!

[14] I am ready to come to you this third time. And I will not be burdensome to you, for I do not seek what is yours, but you. For the children ought not to lay up for the parents, but the parents for the children. [15] And I will very gladly spend and be spent for you. If I love you more, am I to be loved less? [16] But be that as it may. I did not burden you. Nevertheless, being crafty, I caught you with deceit. [17] Did I take advantage of you by any of those whom I sent to you? [18] I urged Titus to go, and with him I sent a brother. Did Titus take advantage of you? Did we not walk in the same spirit? Did we not walk in the same steps?

[19] Again, do you think that we are defending ourselves to you? We speak before God in Christ. We do all things, beloved, for your edifying. [20] For I fear that when I come, I shall not find you such as I wish, and that I shall be found by you such as you do not wish. I fear there are debates, envying, wrath, strife, backbiting, whispering, arrogance, and disorder. [21] And I fear that when I come again, my God will humble me among you, and that I shall mourn for many who have sinned already, who have not repented of uncleanness, sexual immorality, and lasciviousness which they have committed.

Final Warnings and Greetings

13 This is the third time I am coming to you. "In the mouth of two or three witnesses shall every word be established."[2] [2] I told you before, and foretell as if I were present the second time. And being absent now, I write to those who have sinned before, and to all the others, that if I come again, I will not spare *anyone*, [3] since you seek proof of Christ speaking through me, who toward you is not weak, but is mighty in you. [4] For though He was crucified through weakness, yet He lives by the power of God. So also we are weak in Him, but we shall live with Him by the power of God serving you.

---

[1] 17 Jer 9:24.   [2] 1 Dt 19:15.

⁵ Examine yourselves, seeing whether you are in the faith; test yourselves. Do you not know that Jesus Christ is in you?—unless indeed you are disqualified. ⁶ I trust that you will know that we are not disqualified. ⁷ Now I pray to God that you do no evil, not that we should appear approved, but that you should do that which is honorable, whether or not we may seem disqualified. ⁸ For we can do nothing against the truth, but only for the truth. ⁹ For we are glad when we are weak, and you are strong. We wish even your perfection. ¹⁰ Therefore I write these things being absent, lest being present I should be sharp, according to the authority which the Lord has given me for edification and not for destruction.

¹¹ Finally, brothers, farewell. Be perfect, be of good comfort, be of one mind, and live in peace, and the God of love and peace will be with you.

¹² Greet one another with a holy kiss. ¹³ All the saints greet you.

¹⁴ The grace of the Lord Jesus Christ, and the love of God, and the communion of the Holy Spirit be with you all. Amen.

GALATIANS

Salutation

1 Paul, an apostle (not from men nor through man, but through Jesus Christ and God the Father, who raised Him from the dead), ² and all the brothers who are with me,

To the churches of Galatia:

³ Grace to you and peace from God our Father and the Lord Jesus Christ, ⁴ who gave Himself for our sins, that He might deliver us from this present evil age, according to the will of our God and Father, ⁵ to whom be glory forever and ever. Amen.

There Is No Other Gospel

⁶ I marvel that you are turning away so soon from Him who called you in the grace of Christ to a different gospel, ⁷ which is not a gospel. But there are some who trouble you and would pervert the gospel of Christ. ⁸ Although if we or an angel from heaven preach any other gospel to you than the one we have preached to you, let him be accursed. ⁹ As we said before, so I say now again: If anyone preaches any other gospel to you than the one you have received, let him be accursed.

¹⁰ For am I now seeking the approval of men or of God? Or am I trying to please men? For if I were still trying to please men, I would not be the servant of Christ.

How Paul Became an Apostle

¹¹ But I reveal to you, brothers, that the gospel which was preached by me is not according to man. ¹² For I neither received it from man, neither was I taught it, except by a revelation of Jesus Christ.

¹³ For you have heard of my former life in Judaism, how I persecuted the church of God beyond measure and tried to destroy it, ¹⁴ and progressed in Judaism above many of my equals in my own heritage, being more exceedingly zealous for the traditions of my fathers. ¹⁵ But when it pleased God, who set me apart since I was in my mother's womb and called me by His grace, ¹⁶ to reveal His Son in me, that I might preach Him among the nations, I did not immediately confer with flesh and blood, ¹⁷ nor did I go up to Jerusalem to those who were apostles before me. But I went into Arabia, and returned again to Damascus.

¹⁸ After three years I went up to Jerusalem to see Peter and stayed with him for fifteen days. ¹⁹ I saw none of the other apostles except James, the Lord's brother. ²⁰ In what I am writing to you, before God, I do not lie!

²¹ Then I went into the regions of Syria and Cilicia ²² and was unknown by face to the churches of Judea which were in Christ. ²³ They had heard only, "He who persecuted us in times past now preaches the faith which he once destroyed." ²⁴ And they glorified God because of me.

Paul Accepted by the Other Apostles

2 Then after fourteen years I went up again to Jerusalem with Barnabas and also took Titus with me. ² I went up in response to a revelation and communicated to them the gospel which I preach among the Gentiles. But privately I communicated to those who were of reputation, in case I might be running, or had run, in vain. ³ But even Titus, who was with me, though he was a Greek, was not compelled to be circumcised. ⁴ This happened because false brothers were secretly brought in, who sneaked in to spy out our liberty, which we have in Christ Jesus, that they might bring us into bondage. ⁵ We did not yield to subjection to them, not for an hour, that the truth of the gospel might continue with you.

⁶ But of these who seemed to be something—whatever they were, it makes no difference to me; God shows no partiality to anyone—for those who seemed to be something added nothing to me. ⁷ On the contrary, they saw that I was entrusted with the gospel to the uncircumcised, as the gospel to the circumcised was to Peter. ⁸ For He who worked effectively in Peter for the apostleship to the circumcised worked effectively in me toward the Gentiles. ⁹ When James, Cephas, and John, who seemed to be pillars, understood the grace that was given to me, they gave to Barnabas and me the right hand of fellowship, that we should go to the Gentiles and they to the circumcised. ¹⁰ Only they requested that we should remember the poor, which I also was eager to do.

Paul Rebukes Peter in Antioch

¹¹ But when Peter came to Antioch, I withstood him face to face, because he stood condemned. ¹² Before certain men came from James, he ate with the Gentiles. But when they came, he withdrew and separated himself, fearing those who were of the circumcision. ¹³ And the other Jews, likewise, joined together in hypocrisy with him, so that even Barnabas was carried away by their hypocrisy.

¹⁴ But when I saw that they were not straightforward about the truth of the gospel, I said to Peter before them all, "If you, being a Jew, live like a Gentile and not like a Jew, why do you compel the Gentiles to live like Jews?" ¹

Jews, Like Gentiles, Are Saved by Faith

¹⁵ We are Jews by nature, and not Gentile sinners, ¹⁶ yet we know that a man is not justified by the works of the law, but through faith in Jesus Christ. Even we have believed in Christ Jesus, so that we might be justified by faith in Christ, rather than by the works of the law. For by the works of the law no flesh shall be justified.

¹⁷ If, while we seek to be justified by Christ, we ourselves also are found to be sinners, is Christ therefore the minister of sin? God forbid! ¹⁸ For if I build again the things which I destroyed, I make myself a transgressor.

---

¹ 14 Some interpreters hold that the quotation extends into the following paragraph.

[19] For through the law I am dead to the law, that I might live for God. [20] I have been crucified with Christ. It is no longer I who live, but Christ who lives in me. And the life I now live in the flesh, I live by faith in the Son of God,[1] who loved me and gave Himself for me. [21] I do not nullify the grace of God. For if righteousness comes by the law, then Christ died in vain.

Law or Faith

3 O foolish Galatians! Who has bewitched you that you should not obey the truth? Before your eyes Jesus Christ was clearly portrayed among you as crucified. [2] I want to learn only this from you: Did you receive the Spirit through the works of the law, or by hearing with faith? [3] Are you so foolish? Having begun in the Spirit, are you now being perfected by the flesh? [4] Have you endured so many things for nothing, if indeed it was for nothing? [5] Does God give you the Spirit and work miracles among you by the works of the law, or by hearing with faith? [6] Even Abraham "believed God, and it was credited to him as righteousness."[2] [7] Therefore know that those who are of faith are the sons of Abraham. [8] And the Scripture, foreseeing that God would justify the Gentiles by faith, preached the gospel in advance to Abraham, saying, "In you shall all the nations be blessed."[3] [9] So then those who are of faith are blessed with faithful Abraham.

[10] For all who rely on the works of the law are under the curse. For it is written, "Cursed is everyone who does not continue in all things which are written in the Book of the Law, to do them."[4] [11] Now it is evident that no man is justified by the law in the sight of God, for "The just shall live by faith."[5] [12] But the law is not of faith, for "The man who does them shall live by them."[6] [13] Christ has redeemed us from the curse of the law by being made a curse for us—as it is written, "Cursed is everyone who hangs on a tree"[7]— [14] so that the blessing of Abraham might come on the Gentiles through Jesus Christ, that we might receive the promise of the Spirit through faith.

The Law and the Promise

[15] Brothers, I am speaking in human terms: Though it is only a man's covenant, yet if it is ratified, no one annuls or adds to it. [16] Now the promises were made to Abraham and his Seed. He does not say, "and to seeds," meaning many, but "and to your Seed,"[8] meaning one, who is Christ. [17] And this I say, that the law, which came four hundred and thirty years later, does not annul the covenant that was ratified by God in Christ, so as to nullify the promise. [18] For if the inheritance comes from the law, it no longer comes from the promise. But God gave it to Abraham through a promise.

[19] What purpose then does the law serve? It was added because of transgressions, until the Seed should come to whom the promise was made. And it was ordained through angels by the hand of a mediator. [20] Now a mediator is not a mediator for only one party, but God is one.

Slaves and Sons

[21] Is the law then contrary to the promises of God? God forbid! For if there had been a law given which could have given life, righteousness would indeed come through the law. [22] But the Scripture has confined all things under sin, that the promise through faith in Jesus Christ[9] might be given to those who believe.

[23] But before faith came, we were imprisoned under the law, kept for the faith which was later to be revealed. [24] So the law was our tutor to bring us to Christ, that we might be justified by faith. [25] But now that faith has come, we are no longer under a tutor.

[26] You are all sons of God by faith in Christ Jesus. [27] For as many of you as have been baptized into Christ have put on Christ. [28] There is neither Jew nor Greek, there is neither slave nor free, and there is neither male nor female, for you are all one in Christ Jesus. [29] If you are Christ's, then you are Abraham's seed, and heirs according to the promise.

4 Now I say that as long as the heir is a child, he does not differ from a servant though he is lord of all. [2] But he is under tutors and governors until the time appointed by the father. [3] So when we were children, we were in bondage to the elements of the world. [4] But when the fullness of time came, God sent forth His Son, born from a woman, born under the law, [5] to redeem those who were under the law, that we might receive the adoption as sons. [6] And because you are sons, God has sent forth into our hearts the Spirit of His Son, crying, "Abba, Father!" [7] Therefore you are no longer a servant, but a son, and if a son, then an heir of God through Christ.

Paul's Concern for the Galatians

[8] Previously, when you did not know God, you served those who by nature are not gods. [9] But now, after you have known God, or rather are known by God, how do you turn again to the weak and beggarly elemental forces to which you desire again to be in bondage? [10] You observe days and months and seasons and years. [11] I am afraid for you, lest I have worked for you in vain.

[12] Brothers, I ask you, become as I am, for I also have become as you are. You have done me no wrong. [13] You know that it was because of an infirmity of the flesh that I first preached the gospel to you. [14] Though my infirmity was a trial to you, you neither despised nor rejected me, but received me as an angel of God, even as Christ Jesus. [15] So where is your blessing? For I bear witness of you that, if it had been possible, you would have plucked out your own eyes and given them to me. [16] Have I therefore become your enemy because I tell you the truth?

[17] They would zealously influence you, but not favorably. Yes, they would exclusively control you, so that you might consult them. [18] But it is good to be zealous in a good manner always and not only when I am present with you. [19] My little children, of whom I labor in birth again until Christ is formed in you, [20] I desire to be present with you now and to change my tone, for I am displeased with you.

The Allegory of Hagar and Sarah

[21] Tell me, you who desire to be under the law, do you not hear the law? [22] For it is written that Abraham had two sons, the one by a slave woman, the other by a free woman. [23] But he who was of the slave woman was born according to the flesh, but he of the free woman through the promise.

[24] These things are an allegory, for these are the two covenants. The one is from Mount Sinai, which gives birth to bondage; she is Hagar. [25] Now this Hagar is Mount Sinai in Arabia, and represents the present Jerusalem, and is in bondage with her children. [26] But the Jerusalem which is above is free, which is our mother. [27] For it is written:

"Rejoice, barren woman
  who does not bear;
break forth and shout,
  you who have no labor pains!
For the desolate has many more children
  than she who has a husband."[10]

[28] Now we, brothers, like Isaac, are the children of promise. [29] But as it was then, he who was born after the flesh persecuted him who was born after the Spirit, so it is now also. [30] Nevertheless what does the Scripture say? "Cast out the slave woman and her son, for the son of the slave woman shall not be heir with the son of the free woman."[11] [31] So then, brothers, we are not children of the slave woman, but of the free woman.

5 For freedom Christ freed us. Stand fast therefore and do not be entangled again with the yoke of bondage.

Christian Freedom

[2] Indeed I, Paul, say to you that if you become circumcised, Christ will profit you nothing. [3] I testify again to every man who is circumcised that he is obligated to keep the whole law. [4] You have been cut off from Christ, whoever of you are justified by law; you

---

[1] 20 Or *by the faith of the Son of God.*   [2] 6 Ge 15:6.   [3] 8 Ge 12:3; 18:18; 22:18.   [4] 10 Dt 27:26.   [5] 11 Hab 2:4.   [6] 12 Lev 18:5.
[7] 13 Dt 21:23.   [8] 16 Ge 12:7; 13:15; 24:7.   [9] 22 Or *through the faith of Jesus Christ.*   [10] 27 Isa 54:1.   [11] 30 Ge 21:10.

have fallen from grace. [5] For we, through the Spirit, by faith, eagerly wait for the hope of righteousness. [6] For in Christ Jesus neither circumcision nor uncircumcision means anything, but faith which works through love.

[7] You were running well. Who hindered you from obeying the truth? [8] This persuasion does not come from Him who calls you. [9] A little yeast leavens the whole batch. [10] I have confidence in you through the Lord that you will not think otherwise. But he who is troubling you shall bear his judgment, whoever he is. [11] Brothers, if I am still preaching circumcision, why do I still suffer persecution? Then the offense of the cross has ceased. [12] I wish that those who are troubling you would castrate themselves!

[13] You, brothers, have been called to liberty. Only do not use liberty to give an opportunity to the flesh, but by love serve one another. [14] For the entire law is fulfilled in one word, even in this: "You shall love your neighbor as yourself."[1] [15] But if you bite and devour one another, take heed that you are not consumed by one another.

Spiritual Fruit and Fleshly Works

[16] I say then, walk in the Spirit, and you shall not fulfill the lust of the flesh. [17] For the flesh lusts against the Spirit, and the Spirit against the flesh. These are in opposition to one another, so that you may not do the things that you please. [18] But if you are led by the Spirit, you are not under the law.

[19] Now the works of the flesh are revealed, which are these: adultery, sexual immorality, impurity, lewdness, [20] idolatry, sorcery, hatred, strife, jealousy, rage, selfishness, dissensions, heresies, [21] envy, murders, drunkenness, carousing, and the like. I warn you, as I previously warned you, that those who do such things shall not inherit the kingdom of God.

[22] But the fruit of the Spirit is love, joy, peace, patience, gentleness, goodness, faith, [23] meekness, and self-control; against such there is no law. [24] Those who are Christ's have crucified the flesh with its passions and lusts. [25] If we live in the Spirit, let us also walk in the Spirit. [26] Let us not be conceited, provoking one another and envying one another.

Bear One Another's Burdens

6 Brothers, if a man is caught in any transgression, you who are spiritual should restore such a one in the spirit of meekness, watching yourselves, lest you also be tempted. [2] Bear one another's burdens, and so fulfill the law of Christ. [3] For if someone thinks himself to be something when he is nothing, he deceives himself. [4] But let each one examine his own work, and then he will have rejoicing in himself alone, and not in another. [5] For each one shall bear his own burden. [6] Let him who is taught in the word share all good things with him who teaches.

[7] Be not deceived. God is not mocked. For whatever a man sows, that will he also reap. [8] For the one who sows to his own flesh will from the flesh reap corruption, but the one who sows to the Spirit will from the Spirit reap eternal life. [9] And let us not grow weary in doing good, for in due season we shall reap, if we do not give up. [10] Therefore, as we have opportunity, let us do good to all people, especially to those who are of the household of faith.

Final Warning and Benediction

[11] You see what large letters I have written to you with my own hand.

[12] It is those who desire to make a good showing in the flesh that try to compel you to be circumcised, only that they may not be persecuted for the cross of Christ. [13] For they themselves who are circumcised do not keep the law. But they desire to have you circumcised, so that they may boast in your flesh. [14] God forbid that I should boast, except in the cross of our Lord Jesus Christ, by whom the world is crucified to me, and I to the world. [15] For in Christ Jesus neither circumcision nor uncircumcision means anything, but a new creation. [16] Peace and mercy be on all who walk according to this rule and upon the Israel of God.

[17] From now on let no one trouble me, for I bear in my body the marks of the Lord Jesus.

[18] Brothers, the grace of our Lord Jesus Christ be with your spirit. Amen.

EPHESIANS

Salutation

1 Paul, an apostle of Jesus Christ by the will of God,

To the saints who are at Ephesus and to the faithful in Christ Jesus:

[2] Grace to you and peace from God our Father and the Lord Jesus Christ.

Spiritual Blessings in Christ

[3] Blessed be the God and Father of our Lord Jesus Christ, who has blessed us with every spiritual blessing in the heavenly places in Christ [4] just as He chose us in Him before the foundation of the world, to be holy and blameless before Him in love; [5] He predestined us to adoption as sons to Himself through Jesus Christ according to the good pleasure of His will, [6] to the praise of the glory of His grace which He graciously bestowed on us in the Beloved. [7] In Him we have redemption through His blood and the forgiveness of sins according to the riches of His grace, [8] which He lavished on us in all wisdom and insight, [9] making known to us the mystery of His will, according to His good pleasure, which He purposed in Himself, [10] as a plan for the fullness of time, to unite all things in Christ, which are in heaven and on earth.

[11] In Him also we have received an inheritance, being predestined according to the purpose of Him who works all things according to the counsel of His own will, [12] that we, who were the first to hope in Christ, should live for the praise of His glory. [13] In Him you also, after hearing the word of truth, the gospel of your salvation, and after believing in Him, were sealed with the promised Holy Spirit, [14] who is the guarantee of our inheritance until the redemption of the purchased possession, to the praise of His glory.

Paul's Prayer

[15] Therefore I also, after hearing of your faith in the Lord Jesus and your love toward all the saints, [16] do not cease giving thanks for you, mentioning you in my prayers, [17] so that the God of our Lord Jesus Christ, the Father of glory, may give you the Spirit of wisdom and revelation in the knowledge of Him, [18] that the eyes of your understanding may be enlightened, that you may know what is the hope of His calling and what are the riches of the glory of His inheritance among the saints, [19] and what is the surpassing greatness of His power toward us who believe, according to the working of His mighty power, [20] which He performed in Christ when He raised Him from the dead

---

[1] 14 Lev 19:18.

and seated Him at His own right hand in the heavenly places, [21] far above all principalities, and power, and might, and dominion, and every name that is named, not only in this age but also in that which is to come. [22] And He put all things in subjection under His feet and made Him the head over all things for the church, [23] which is His body, the fullness of Him who fills all things in all ways.

From Death to Life

2 And you were dead in your trespasses and sins, [2] in which you formerly walked according to the age of this world and according to the prince of the power of the air, the spirit who now works in the sons of disobedience, [3] among them we all also once lived in the lusts of our flesh, doing the desires of the flesh and of the mind, and we were by nature children of wrath, even as the rest. [4] But God, being rich in mercy, because of His great love with which He loved us, [5] even when we were dead in sins, made us alive together with Christ (by grace you have been saved), [6] and He raised us up and seated us together in the heavenly places in Christ Jesus, [7] so that in the coming ages He might show the surpassing riches of His grace in kindness toward us in Christ Jesus. [8] For by grace you have been saved through faith, and this is not of yourselves. It is the gift of God, [9] not of works, so that no one should boast. [10] For we are His workmanship, created in Christ Jesus for good works, which God prepared beforehand, so that we should walk in them.

One in Christ

[11] Therefore remember that formerly you, the Gentiles in the flesh, who are called the "uncircumcision" by the so-called "circumcision" in the flesh by human hands, [12] were at that time apart from Christ, alienated from the citizenship of Israel and strangers to the covenants of promise, without hope and without God in the world. [13] But now in Christ Jesus you who were formerly far away have been brought near by the blood of Christ.

[14] For He is our peace, who has made both groups one and has broken down the barrier of the dividing wall, [15] by abolishing in His flesh the enmity, that is, the law of the commandments contained in ordinances, that in Himself He might make the two into one new man, thus making peace, [16] and that He might reconcile both to God into one body through the cross, thereby slaying the enmity. [17] And He came and preached peace to you who were far away and peace to those who were near. [18] For through Him we both have access by one Spirit to the Father.

[19] Now, therefore, you are no longer strangers and foreigners, but are fellow citizens with the saints and members of the household of God, [20] having been built upon the foundation of the apostles and prophets, Jesus Christ Himself being the chief cornerstone, [21] in whom the entire building, tightly framed together, grows into a holy temple in the Lord, [22] in whom you also are being built together into a dwelling place of God through the Spirit.

Paul's Ministry to the Gentiles

3 For this reason I, Paul, am the prisoner of Jesus Christ for you Gentiles. [2] You may have heard of the administration of the grace of God which was given me for you, [3] how by revelation He made known to me the mystery, as I have written briefly already, [4] by which, when you read it, you may understand my knowledge of the mystery of Christ, [5] which in other generations was not made known to the sons of men, as it is now revealed to His holy apostles and prophets by the Spirit, [6] how the Gentiles are fellow heirs, and fellow members, and partakers of the promise in Christ by the gospel. [7] Of this I was made a minister, according to the gift of the grace of God given to me by the effective working of His power. [8] To me, the very least of all saints, this grace was given, to preach to the Gentiles the incomprehensible riches of Christ, [9] and to reveal for all people what is the fellowship of the mystery, which from the beginning of the ages has been hidden in God, who created all things through Jesus Christ, [10] so that now the manifold wisdom of God might be made known by the church to the principalities and powers in the heavenly places, [11] according to the eternal purpose which He completed in

Christ Jesus our Lord, [12] in whom we have boldness and confident access through faith in Him. [13] Therefore I ask you not to lose heart at my tribulations for you, which is your glory.

To Know the Love of Christ

[14] For this reason I bow my knees to the Father of our Lord Jesus Christ, [15] from whom the whole family in heaven and earth is named, [16] that He would give you, according to the riches of His glory, power to be strengthened by His Spirit in the inner man, [17] and that Christ may dwell in your hearts through faith; that you, being rooted and grounded in love, [18] may be able to comprehend with all saints what is the breadth and length and depth and height, [19] and to know the love of Christ which surpasses knowledge; that you may be filled with all the fullness of God.

[20] Now to Him who is able to do exceedingly abundantly beyond all that we ask or imagine, according to the power that works in us, [21] to Him be the glory in the church and in Christ Jesus throughout all generations, forever and ever. Amen.

Unity of the Body

4 I, therefore, the prisoner of the Lord, exhort you to walk in a manner worthy of the calling with which you were called. [2] With all humility, meekness, and patience, bearing with one another in love, [3] be eager to keep the unity of the Spirit in the bond of peace. [4] There is one body and one Spirit, even as you were called in one hope of your calling, [5] one Lord, one faith, one baptism, [6] one God and Father of all, who is above all, and through all, and in you all.

[7] But grace was given to each one of us according to the measure of the gift of Christ. [8] Therefore He says:

"When He ascended on high,
He led captivity captive,
and gave gifts to men."[1]

[9] (In saying, "He ascended," what does it mean but that He also descended first into the lower parts of the earth? [10] He who descended is also He who ascended far above all the heavens that He might fill all things.) [11] He gave some to be apostles, prophets, evangelists, pastors, and teachers, [12] for the equipping of the saints, for the work of service, and for the building up of the body of Christ, [13] until we all come into the unity of the faith and of the knowledge of the Son of God, into a complete man, to the measure of the stature of the fullness of Christ, [14] so we may no longer be children, tossed here and there by waves and carried about with every wind of doctrine by the trickery of men, by craftiness with deceitful scheming. [15] But, speaking the truth in love, we may grow up in all things into Him, who is the head, Christ Himself, [16] from whom the whole body is joined together and connected by every joint and ligament, as every part effectively does its work and grows, building itself up in love.

The Old Life and New Life

[17] Therefore this I say and testify in the Lord, that from now on you walk no as other Gentiles walk, in the vanity of their minds, [18] having their understanding darkened, excluded from the life of God through the ignorance that is within them, due to the hardness of their hearts. [19] Being calloused they have given themselves over to sensuality for the practice of every kind of impurity with greediness.

[20] But you did not learn about Christ in this manner, [21] if indeed you have heard Him and have been taught by Him, as the truth is in Jesus: [22] that you put off the former way of life in the old nature, which is corrupt according to the deceitful lusts, [23] and be renewed in the spirit of your mind; [24] and that you put on the new nature, which was created according to God in righteousness and true holiness.

Rules for the New Life

[25] Therefore, putting away lying, let every man speak truthfully with his neighbor, for we are members of one another. [26] Be angry

---

[1]8 Ps 68:18.

but do not sin. Do not let the sun go down on your anger. [27] Do not give place to the devil. [28] Let him who steals steal no more. Instead, let him labor, working with his hands things which are good, that he may have something to share with him who is in need.

[29] Let no unwholesome word proceed out of your mouth, but only that which is good for building up, that it may give grace to the listeners. [30] And do not grieve the Holy Spirit of God, in whom you are sealed for the day of redemption. [31] Let all bitterness, wrath, anger, outbursts, and blasphemies, with all malice, be taken away from you. [32] And be kind one to another, tenderhearted, forgiving one another, just as God in Christ also forgave you.

5 Therefore be imitators of God as beloved children. [2] Walk in love, as Christ loved us and gave Himself for us as a fragrant offering and a sacrifice to God.

[3] And do not let sexual immorality, or any impurity, or greed be named among you, as these are not proper among saints. [4] Let there be no filthiness, nor foolish talking, nor coarse joking, which are not fitting. Instead, give thanks. [5] For this you know, that no sexually immoral or impure person, or one who is greedy, who is an idolater, has any inheritance in the kingdom of Christ and of God.

Walk as Children of Light

[6] Let no one deceive you with empty words, for because of these things the wrath of God is coming upon the sons of disobedience. [7] Therefore do not be partakers with them.

[8] For you were formerly darkness, but now you are light in the Lord. Walk as children of light— [9] for the fruit of the Spirit is in all goodness and righteousness and truth— [10] proving what is pleasing to the Lord. [11] And do not have fellowship with the unfruitful works of darkness; instead, expose them. [12] For it is shameful even to speak of those things which are done by them in secret. [13] But all things are exposed when they are revealed by the light, for everything that becomes visible is light. [14] Therefore He says:

"Awake, you who sleep,
    arise from the dead,
and Christ will give you light."

[15] See then that you walk carefully, not as fools, but as wise men, [16] making the most of the time because the days are evil. [17] Therefore do not be unwise, but understand what the will of the Lord is. [18] Do not be drunk with wine, for that is reckless living. But be filled with the Spirit. [19] Speak to one another in psalms, hymns, and spiritual songs, singing and making melody in your heart to the Lord. [20] Give thanks always for all things to God the Father in the name of our Lord Jesus Christ, [21] being submissive to one another in the fear of God.

Wives and Husbands

[22] Wives, be submissive to your own husbands as unto the Lord. [23] For the husband is the head of the wife, just as Christ is the head and Savior of the church, which is His body. [24] But as the church submits to Christ, so also let the wives be to their own husbands in everything.

[25] Husbands, love your wives, just as Christ also loved the church and gave Himself for it, [26] that He might sanctify and cleanse it with the washing of water by the word, [27] and that He might present to Himself a glorious church, not having spot, or wrinkle, or any such thing, but that it should be holy and without blemish. [28] In this way men ought to love their wives as their own bodies. He who loves his wife loves himself. [29] For no one ever hated his own flesh, but nourishes and cherishes it, just as the Lord cares for the church. [30] For we are members of His body, of His flesh and of His bones. [31] "For this reason a man shall leave his father and mother and shall be joined to his wife, and the two shall be one flesh." [1] [32] This is a great mystery, but I am speaking about Christ and the church. [33] However, let each one of you love his wife as himself, and let the wife see that she respects her husband.

Children and Parents

6 Children, obey your parents in the Lord, for this is right. [2] "Honor your father and mother," which is the first commandment with a promise, [3] "so that it may be well with you and you may live long on the earth." [2]

[4] Fathers, do not provoke your children to anger, but bring them up in the discipline and instruction of the Lord.

Servants and Masters

[5] Servants, obey those who are your masters according to the flesh, with fear and trembling, in sincerity of your heart, as to Christ, [6] not serving when eyes are on you, but as pleasing men as the servants of Christ, doing the will of God from the heart, [7] with good will doing service, as to the Lord, and not to men, [8] knowing that whatever good thing any man does, he will receive the same from the Lord, whether he is enslaved or free.

[9] And masters, do the same things for them, no longer threatening, knowing that your Master also is in heaven, and there is no partiality with Him.

The Battle Against Evil

[10] Finally, my brothers, be strong in the Lord and in the power of His might. [11] Put on the whole armor of God that you may be able to stand against the schemes of the devil. [12] For our fight is not against flesh and blood, but against principalities, against powers, against the rulers of the darkness of this world, and against spiritual forces of evil in the heavenly places. [13] Therefore take up the whole armor of God that you may be able to resist in the evil day, and having done all, to stand. [14] Stand therefore, having your waist girded with truth, having put on the breastplate of righteousness, [15] having your feet fitted with the readiness of the gospel of peace, [16] and above all, taking the shield of faith, with which you will be able to extinguish all the fiery arrows of the evil one. [17] Take the helmet of salvation and the sword of the Spirit, which is the word of God.

[18] Pray in the Spirit always with all kinds of prayer and supplication. To that end be alert with all perseverance and supplication for all the saints. [19] Pray for me, that the power to speak may be given to me, that I may open my mouth boldly to make known the mystery of the gospel, [20] for which I am an ambassador in chains, that I may speak boldly as I ought to speak.

Final Greetings

[21] Now that you also may know my activities and how I am doing, Tychicus, a beloved brother and faithful minister in the Lord, will make everything known to you. [22] I have sent him to you for this very purpose, that you might know our activities and that he might comfort your hearts.

[23] Peace be to the brothers, and love with faith, from God the Father and the Lord Jesus Christ. [24] Grace be with all those who love our Lord Jesus Christ in sincerity. Amen.

---

[1] 31 Ge 2:24. [2] 2–3 Dt 5:16.

PHILIPPIANS

Salutation

1 Paul and Timothy, servants of Jesus Christ,

To all the saints in Christ Jesus who are at Philippi, with the overseers and deacons:

[2] Grace to you and peace from God our Father and the Lord Jesus Christ.

Paul's Prayer for the Philippians

[3] I thank my God for every reminder of you. [4] In every prayer of mine for you all, I have always made requests with joy, [5] due to your fellowship in the gospel from the first day until now. [6] I am confident of this very thing, that He who began a good work in you will perfect it until the day of Jesus Christ.

[7] It is right for me to think this of you all because I have you in my heart, since both in my imprisonments and in the defense and confirmation of the gospel, you all are fellow partakers of my grace. [8] For God is my witness, how I long after you all with the affection of Jesus Christ.

[9] And this I pray, that your love may abound yet more and more in knowledge and in all discernment, [10] that you may approve things that are excellent so that you may be pure and blameless for the day of Christ, [11] being filled with the fruit of righteousness, which comes through Jesus Christ, for the glory and praise of God.

To Live Is Christ

[12] But I want you to know, brothers, that the things which happened to me have resulted in advancing the gospel, [13] so that my imprisonments in Christ have become known throughout the entire palace guard and to all the rest. [14] And a great many of the brothers in the Lord, having become confident because of my incarcerations, have dared to speak the word without fear.

[15] Some indeed are preaching Christ out of envy and strife, and some also from good will. [16] The former preach Christ out of contention, not sincerely, intending to add trouble to my circumstance. [17] But the latter preach out of love, knowing that I am appointed for the defense of the gospel. [18] What then? Only that in every way, whether in pretense or in truth, Christ is preached. And in this I rejoice.

Indeed, I will rejoice. [19] For I know that through your prayer and the support of the Spirit of Jesus Christ, this will result in my deliverance. [20] Accordingly, it is my earnest expectation and my hope that I shall be ashamed in nothing, but that with all boldness as always, so now also, Christ will be magnified in my body, whether it be by life or by death. [21] For to me, to continue living is Christ, and to die is gain. [22] But if I am to live on in the flesh, this will mean fruitful labor to me. Yet I do not know what I shall choose. [23] I am in a difficult position between the two, having a desire to depart and to be with Christ, which is far better. [24] Nevertheless, to remain in the flesh is more needful for your sake. [25] Having this confidence, I know that I shall remain and continue with you all for your joyful advancement of the faith, [26] so that your rejoicing for me may be more abundant in Jesus Christ when I am in your presence again.

[27] Only let your conduct be worthy of the gospel of Christ, that whether or not I come and see you, I may hear of your activities, that you are standing fast in one spirit, with one mind, striving together for the faith of the gospel. [28] Do not be frightened by your adversaries. This is a sign to them of their destruction, but of your salvation, and this from God. [29] For to you it was granted on behalf of Christ not only to believe in Him, but also to suffer for His sake, [30] having the same conflict which you saw in me and now hear is in me.

Christian Humility and Christ's Humility

2 If there is any encouragement in Christ, if any comfort of love, if any fellowship of the Spirit, if any compassion and mercy, [2] then fulfill my joy and be like-minded, having the same love, being in unity with one mind. [3] Let nothing be done out of strife or conceit, but in humility let each esteem the other better than himself. [4] Let each of you look not only to your own interests, but also to the interests of others.

[5] Let this mind be in you all, which was also in Christ Jesus,

[6] who, being in the form of God,
did not consider equality with God something to
be grasped.
[7] But He emptied Himself,
taking upon Himself the form of a servant,
and was made in the likeness of men.
[8] And being found in the form of a man,
He humbled Himself
and became obedient to death,
even death on a cross.
[9] Therefore God highly exalted Him
and gave Him the name which is above every name,
[10] that at the name of Jesus every knee should bow,
of those in heaven and on earth and under the earth,
[11] and every tongue should confess that Jesus Christ is Lord,
to the glory of God the Father.[1]

Shining as Lights in the World

[12] Therefore, my beloved, as you have always obeyed, not only in my presence, but so much more in my absence, work out your own salvation with fear and trembling. [13] For God is the One working in you, both to will and to do His good pleasure.

[14] Do all things without murmuring and disputing, [15] that you may be blameless and harmless, sons of God, without fault, in the midst of a crooked and perverse generation, in which you shine as lights in the world. [16] Hold forth the word of life that I may rejoice on the day of Christ that I have not run in vain or labored in vain. [17] Yes, and even if I am offered upon the sacrifice and service of your faith, I take delight and rejoice with you all. [18] For this reason you also take delight and rejoice with me.

Timothy and Epaphroditus

[19] I trust in the Lord Jesus to send Timothy shortly to you, that I also may be of good comfort when I get word concerning you. [20] For I have no one like-minded, who will sincerely care for your welfare. [21] For all seek their own, not the things of Christ Jesus. [22] But you know of his proven worth, that as a son with a father, he has served with me in the gospel. [23] Therefore I hope to send him soon after my situation is resolved. [24] But I trust in the Lord that I, myself, shall also come shortly.

[25] Yet I thought it necessary to send to you Epaphroditus, who is my brother and companion in labor, fellow soldier, your messenger, and he who ministered to my necessity. [26] For he longed after you all and was filled with heaviness, because you heard that he was sick. [27] Indeed he was sick, near death. But God had mercy on him, and not only on him, but also on me, lest I should have had sorrow upon sorrow. [28] Therefore I sent him the more eagerly, that when you see him again, you may rejoice and I may be less sorrowful. [29] So receive him in the Lord with all joy. And hold such ones in high regard, [30] because for the work of Christ he was near death, not regarding his life, endeavoring to make up for your lack of service toward me.

The True Righteousness

3 Finally, my brothers, rejoice in the Lord. To write the same things to you is no trouble to me, and it is reassuring for you.

[16–11] A hymn about Jesus' attitude of servanthood.

[2] Watch out for dogs, watch out for evil workers, watch out for those who practice mutilation. [3] For we are the circumcision who worship God in the Spirit, and boast in Christ Jesus, and place no trust in the flesh, [4] though I also have confidence in the flesh.

If any other man thinks that he has reason to trust in the flesh, I have more: [5] I was circumcised the eighth day, of the stock of Israel, of the tribe of Benjamin, and a Hebrew of Hebrews; as concerning the law, a Pharisee; [6] concerning zeal, persecuting the church; and concerning the righteousness which is in the law, blameless.

[7] But what things were gain to me, I have counted these things to be loss for the sake of Christ. [8] Yes, certainly, I count everything as loss for the excellence of the knowledge of Christ Jesus my Lord, for whom I have forfeited the loss of all things and count them as rubbish that I may gain Christ, [9] and be found in Him, not having my own righteousness which is from the law, but that which is through faith in Christ, [1] the righteousness which is of God on the basis of faith, [10] to know Him, and the power of His resurrection, and the fellowship of His sufferings, being conformed to His death, [11] if somehow I might make it to the resurrection of the dead.

Pressing Toward the Mark

[12] Not that I have already attained or have already been perfected, but I follow after it so that I may lay hold of that for which I was seized by Christ Jesus. [13] Brothers, I do not count myself to have attained, but this one thing I do, forgetting those things which are behind and reaching forward to those things which are ahead, [14] I press toward the goal to the prize of the high calling of God in Christ Jesus.

[15] Therefore let those of us who are mature be thus minded. And if you think differently in any way, God will reveal even this to you. [16] Nevertheless, according to what we have already attained, let us walk by the same rule, let us be of the same mind.

[17] Brothers, become fellow imitators with me and observe those who walk according to our example. [18] For many are walking in such a way that they are the enemies of the cross of Christ. I have told you of them often and tell you again, even weeping. [19] Their destination is destruction, their god is their appetite, their glory is in their shame, their minds are set on earthly things. [20] But our citizenship is in heaven, from where also we await for our Savior, the Lord Jesus Christ, [21] who will transform our body of humiliation, so that it may be conformed to His glorious body, according to the working of His power even to subdue all things to Himself.

4 Therefore, my beloved and longed-for brothers, my joy and crown, so stand fast in the Lord, my beloved.

Exhortations

[2] I exhort Euodia and Syntyche to be of the same mind in the Lord. [3] I ask you also, true companion, help those women who labored with me in the gospel, with Clement also, and with my other fellow laborers, whose names are in the Book of Life.

[4] Rejoice in the Lord always. Again I will say, rejoice! [5] Let everyone come to know your gentleness. The Lord is at hand. [6] Be anxious for nothing, but in everything, by prayer and supplication with gratitude, make your requests known to God. [7] And the peace of God, which surpasses all understanding, will protect your hearts and minds through Christ Jesus.

[8] Finally, brothers, whatever things are true, whatever things are honest, whatever things are just, whatever things are pure, whatever things are lovely, whatever things are of good report, if there is any virtue, and if there is any praise, think on these things. [9] Do those things which you have both learned and received, and heard and seen in me, and the God of peace will be with you.

Acknowledgment of the Philippians' Gift

[10] I rejoiced in the Lord greatly that now at last you have revived your concern for me. Regarding this, you did care, but you lacked opportunity. [11] I do not speak because I have need, for I have learned in whatever state I am to be content. [12] I know both how to face humble circumstances and how to have abundance. Everywhere and in all things I have learned the secret, both to be full and to be hungry, both to abound and to suffer need. [13] I can do all things because of Christ who strengthens me.

[14] Nevertheless you did well having shared in my affliction. [15] Now you Philippians know also, that in the beginning of the gospel when I departed from Macedonia, no church shared with me in the matter of giving and receiving, except you alone. [16] Even in Thessalonica, you sent aid once and again for my necessity, [17] not because I desired a gift, but I desire fruit that accumulates to your account. [18] But I have everything and abound. I have been filled, having received from Epaphroditus the things which were sent from you, like a sweet fragrance, an acceptable sacrifice, well pleasing to God. [19] But my God shall supply your every need according to His riches in glory by Christ Jesus.

[20] Now to God and our Father be glory forever and ever. Amen.

Final Greetings

[21] Greet every saint in Christ Jesus. The brothers who are with me greet you. [22] All the saints greet you, especially those who are of Caesar's household.

[23] The grace of our Lord Jesus Christ be with you all. Amen.

COLOSSIANS

Salutation

1 Paul, an apostle of Jesus Christ, by the will of God, and Timothy our brother,

[2] To the saints and faithful brothers in Christ who are at Colosse:

Grace to you and peace from God our Father and the Lord Jesus Christ.

Thankfulness for the Colossians

[3] We give thanks to God and the Father of our Lord Jesus Christ, praying always for you. [4] For we heard of your faith in Christ Jesus and your love for all the saints, [5] because of the hope which is laid up for you in heaven, of which you have already heard in the word of the truth of the gospel, [6] which has come to you, as it has in all the world, and brings forth fruit, as it has also in you, since the day you heard it and knew the grace of God in truth. [7] And you also learned of Epaphras, our dear fellow servant, who is a faithful minister of Christ for you, [8] who also declared to us your love in the Spirit.

The Person and Work of Christ

[9] For this reason we also, since the day we heard it, do not cease to pray for you and to ask that you may be filled with the knowledge of His will in all wisdom and spiritual understanding; [10] that you may walk in a manner worthy of the

1 9 Or through the faith of Christ.

Lord, pleasing to all, being fruitful in every good work, and increasing in the knowledge of God, [11] strengthened with all might according to His glorious power, enduring everything with perseverance and patience joyfully, [12] giving thanks to the Father, who has enabled us to be partakers in the inheritance of the saints in light. [13] He has delivered us from the power of darkness and has transferred us into the kingdom of His dear Son, [14] in whom we have redemption through His blood, the forgiveness of sins.

[15] He is the image of the invisible God and the firstborn of every creature. [16] For by Him all things were created that are in heaven and that are in earth, visible and invisible, whether they are thrones, or dominions, or principalities, or powers. All things were created by Him and for Him. [17] He is before all things, and in Him all things hold together. [18] He is the head of the body, the church. He is the beginning, the firstborn from the dead, so that in all things He may have the preeminence. [19] For it pleased the Father that in Him all fullness should dwell, [20] and to reconcile all things to Himself by Him, having made peace through the blood of His cross, by Him, I say—whether they are things in earth, or things in heaven.

[21] And you, who were formerly alienated and enemies in your mind by wicked works, yet now He has reconciled [22] in the body of His flesh through death, to present you holy and blameless and above reproach in His sight, [23] if you continue in the faith, grounded and settled, and are not removed from the hope of the gospel, which you have heard, and which was preached to every creature which is under heaven, and of which I, Paul, have become a servant.

Paul's Ministry to the Church

[24] Now I rejoice in my sufferings for your sake and fill up in my flesh that which is lacking in the afflictions of Christ, for the sake of His body, which is the church. [25] I have been made a servant of it according to the commission of God, which has been given to me for you, to fulfill the word of God, [26] even the mystery which has been hidden from past ages and generations, but now is revealed to His saints. [27] To them God would make known what is the glorious riches of this mystery among the nations. It is Christ in you, the hope of glory, [28] whom we preach, warning everyone and teaching everyone in all wisdom, so that we may present them perfect in Christ Jesus. [29] In this I labor, striving according to His power, which effectively works in me.

2 I would like you to know what a great struggle I am having for you, and for those at Laodicea, and for everyone who has not seen my face in the flesh, [2] that their hearts may be comforted, being knit together in love, and receive all the riches and assurance of full understanding, and knowledge of the mystery of God, both of the Father and of Christ, [3] in whom are hidden all the treasures of wisdom and knowledge. [4] Now this I say lest anyone beguile you with enticing words. [5] For though I am absent in the flesh, yet I am with you in spirit, rejoicing and seeing your orderliness and the steadfastness of your faith in Christ.

Fullness of Life in Christ

[6] As you have received Christ Jesus the Lord, so walk in Him, [7] rooted and built up in Him and established in the faith, as you have been taught, and abounding with thanksgiving.

[8] Beware lest anyone captivate you through philosophy and vain deceit, in the tradition of men and the elementary principles of the world, and not after Christ. [9] For in Him lives all the fullness of the Godhead bodily. [10] And you are complete in Him, who is the head of all authority and power. [11] In Him you were also circumcised with the circumcision made without hands, by putting off the body of the sins of the flesh, by the circumcision of Christ, [12] buried with Him in baptism, in which also you were raised with Him through the faith of the power of God, who has raised Him from the dead. [13] And you, being dead in your sins and the uncircumcision of your flesh, He has resurrected together with Him, having forgiven you all sins. [14] He blotted out the handwriting of ordinances that was against us and contrary to us, and He took it out of the way,

nailing it to the cross. [15] And having disarmed authorities and powers, He made a show of them openly, triumphing over them by the cross.

[16] Therefore let no one judge you regarding food, or drink, or in respect of a holy day or new moon or sabbath days. [17] These are shadows of things to come, but the substance belongs to Christ. [18] Do not let anyone cheat you of your reward by delighting in false humility and the worship of angels, dwelling on those things which he has not seen, vainly arrogant due to his unspiritual mind, [19] and not supporting the head, from which the entire body, nourished and knit together by joints and sinews, grows as God gives the increase.

The New Life in Christ

[20] Therefore, if you died with Christ to the elementary principles of the world, why, as if you were living in the world, do you subject yourself to legalistic rules? [21] "Do not touch! Do not taste! Do not handle!" [22] These all are to perish with use and are aligned with the commandments and doctrines of men. [23] These things have indeed a show of wisdom in self-imposed worship and humility and neglecting of the body, but are worthless against the indulgence of the flesh.

3 If you then were raised with Christ, desire those things which are above, where Christ sits at the right hand of God. [2] Set your affection on things above, not on things on earth. [3] For you are dead, and your life is hidden with Christ in God. [4] When Christ who is our life shall appear, then you also shall appear with Him in glory.

[5] Therefore put to death the parts of your earthly nature: sexual immorality, uncleanness, inordinate affection, evil desire, and covetousness, which is idolatry. [6] Because of these things, the wrath of God comes on the sons of disobedience. [7] You also once walked in these, when you lived in them. [8] But now you must also put away all these: anger, wrath, malice, blasphemy, and filthy language out of your mouth. [9] Do not lie one to another, since you have put off the old nature with its deeds, [10] and have embraced the new nature, which is renewed in knowledge after the image of Him who created it, [11] where there is neither Greek nor Jew, circumcision nor uncircumcision, barbarian, Scythian, slave nor free, but Christ is all and in all.

[12] So embrace, as the elect of God, holy and beloved, a spirit of mercy, kindness, humbleness of mind, meekness, and longsuffering. [13] Bear with one another and forgive one another. If anyone has a quarrel against anyone, even as Christ forgave you, so you must do. [14] And above all these things, embrace love, which is the bond of perfection. [15] Let the peace of God, to which also you are called in one body, rule in your hearts. And be thankful. [16] Let the word of Christ dwell in you richly in all wisdom, teaching and admonishing one another in psalms and hymns and spiritual songs, singing with grace in your hearts to the Lord. [17] And whatever you do in word or deed, do all in the name of the Lord Jesus, giving thanks to God the Father through Him.

Social Duties of the New Life

[18] Wives, submit yourselves to your own husbands, as it is fitting in the Lord.

[19] Husbands, love your wives, and do not be bitter toward them.

[20] Children, obey your parents in all things, for this is well pleasing to the Lord.

[21] Fathers, do not provoke your children to anger, lest they be discouraged.

[22] Servants, obey your masters in all things according to the flesh, serving not only when they are watching, as the servants of men, but in singleness of heart, fearing God. [23] And whatever you do, do it heartily, as for the Lord and not for men, [24] knowing that from the Lord you will receive the reward of the inheritance. For you serve the Lord Christ. [25] But he who does wrong will receive for the wrong which he has done, and there is no partiality.

4 Masters, give to your servants that which is just and fair, knowing that you also have a Master in heaven.

Exhortations

² Continue in prayer, and be watchful with thanksgiving, ³ while praying also for us, that God would open to us a door of utterance to speak the mystery of Christ, for which I am also in chains, ⁴ that I may reveal it clearly, as I ought to speak. ⁵ Walk in wisdom toward those who are outside, wisely using the opportunity. ⁶ Let your speech always be with grace, seasoned with salt, that you may know how you should answer everyone.

Final Greetings

⁷ Tychicus, who is a beloved brother and a faithful minister and fellow servant in the Lord, will tell you all the news about me. ⁸ I have sent him to you for this very purpose, that he might know your circumstances and comfort your hearts, ⁹ with Onesimus, a faithful and beloved brother, who is one of you. They will make known to you everything which is happening here.

¹⁰ Aristarchus my fellow prisoner greets you, with Mark, the cousin of Barnabas (concerning whom you received instructions: If he comes to you, receive him), ¹¹ and Jesus, who is called Justus. These are my only fellow workers for the kingdom of God who are of the circumcision. They have been a comfort to me. ¹² Epaphras greets you. He is one of you, a servant of Christ, always laboring fervently for you in prayers, that you may stand mature and complete in the entire will of God. ¹³ I bear witness of him, that he has a great zeal for you, those who are in Laodicea, and those in Hierapolis. ¹⁴ Luke, the beloved physician, and Demas greet you. ¹⁵ Greet the brothers who are in Laodicea, and Nympha, and the church which is in his house.

¹⁶ When this epistle is read among you, ensure that it is read also in the church of the Laodiceans, and that you, likewise, read the epistle from Laodicea.

¹⁷ Tell Archippus, "Make sure that you fulfill the ministry which you have received in the Lord."

¹⁸ I, Paul, write this greeting with my own hand. Remember my chains. Grace be with you. Amen.

1 THESSALONIANS

Salutation

1 Paul, Silas, and Timothy,

To the church of the Thessalonians which is in God the Father and in the Lord Jesus Christ:

Grace to you and peace from God our Father and the Lord Jesus Christ.

The Thessalonians' Faith and Example

² We give thanks to God always for you all, mentioning you in our prayers, ³ remembering without ceasing your work of faith, labor of love, and patient hope in our Lord Jesus Christ in the sight of God and our Father.

⁴ For we know, beloved brothers, your election by God. ⁵ For our gospel did not come to you in word only, but also in power, and in the Holy Spirit, and in much assurance, just as you know what kind of men we were among you for your sake. ⁶ You became followers of us and the Lord, having received the word in much affliction, with joy of the Holy Spirit. ⁷ Therefore you were examples to all who believe in Macedonia and Achaia. ⁸ For the word of the Lord sounded out from you not only in Macedonia and Achaia, but also in every place your faith in God has gone forth, so that we do not need to say anything. ⁹ For they themselves declare how we were received by you, and how you turned to God from idols, to serve the living and true God, ¹⁰ and to wait for His Son from heaven, whom He raised from the dead—Jesus, who delivered us from the wrath to come.

Paul's Ministry in Thessalonica

2 You yourselves know, brothers, that our visit to you was not in vain. ² But even after we had previously suffered and were shamefully treated at Philippi, as you know, we were bold in our God to declare to you the gospel of God amid much opposition. ³ For our exhortation was not from deceit, nor from uncleanness, nor in guile. ⁴ But as we were allowed by God to be entrusted with the gospel, even so we speak, not to please men, but God, who examines our hearts. ⁵ For neither at any time did we come with flattering words, as you know, nor with a pretext for greed. God is our witness. ⁶ Nor did we seek glory from men, either from you, or from others, even though we might have made demands as the apostles of Christ.

⁷ But we were gentle among you, like a nurse caring for her own children. ⁸ So having great love toward you, we were willing to impart to you not only the gospel of God but also our own lives, because you were dear to us. ⁹ For you remember, brothers, our labor and toil. Laboring night and day so as not to be an expense to any of you, we preached to you the gospel of God. ¹⁰ You and God are witnesses of how pure, upright, and blameless we ourselves behaved among you who believe. ¹¹ As you know, we exhorted, comforted, and commanded every one of you, as a father does his own children, ¹² that you would walk in a manner worthy of God, who has called you to His kingdom and glory.

¹³ For this reason we thank God without ceasing because, when you received the word of God, which you heard from us, you received it not as the word of men, but as it truly is, the word of God, which effectively works also in you who believe. ¹⁴ For you, brothers, became followers of the churches of God, which in Judea are in Christ Jesus. You also have suffered the same things from your own countrymen, as they have from the Jews, ¹⁵ who both killed the Lord Jesus and their own prophets and have persecuted us. They do not please God and are contrary to all men, ¹⁶ forbidding us to speak to the Gentiles that they might be saved. In this way they are always piling up their sins, but wrath has come upon them to the extreme.

Paul's Desire to Visit Again

¹⁷ But we, brothers, being taken from you for a short time, in presence, not in heart, endeavored all the more abundantly to see your face with great desire. ¹⁸ Therefore we wished to come to you—even I, Paul, once and again—but Satan hindered us. ¹⁹ For what is our hope, or joy, or crown of rejoicing? Will it not even be you in the presence of our Lord Jesus Christ at His coming? ²⁰ You are our glory and joy.

3 Therefore, when we could no longer endure it, we thought it good to be left at Athens alone. ² We sent Timothy, who is our brother and minister of God and our fellow laborer in the gospel of Christ, to establish and comfort you with regard to your faith, ³ so that no one would be shaken by these afflictions. For you know that we are appointed to this. ⁴ Indeed, we told you before when we were with you that we would suffer tribulation, just as it came to pass, as you well know. ⁵ For this reason, when I could no longer endure it, I sent to inquire about your faith, lest by some means the tempter might have tempted you, and our labor might have been in vain.

⁶ But just now Timothy has come from you to us and brought us good news of your faith and love, and that you always have good memories of us, desiring greatly to see us, as we also desire to see

you. [7] Therefore, brothers, during all our afflictions and distress, we have been encouraged about you through your faith. [8] For now we live, if you stand strong in the Lord. [9] For what thanks can we render to God for you, for all the joy with which we rejoice for your sakes before our God, [10] night and day praying earnestly that we might see your face and might perfect that which is lacking in your faith?

[11] Now may our God and Father Himself, and our Lord Jesus Christ, direct our way to you. [12] And may the Lord make you increase and abound in love for one another and for all men, even as we do for you. [13] To this end may He establish your hearts to be blameless in holiness before our God and Father at the coming of our Lord Jesus Christ with all His saints.

A Life Pleasing to God

4 Finally, brothers, we urge and exhort you by the Lord Jesus, that as you have learned from us how you ought to walk and to please God, you should excel more and more. [2] For you know what commands we gave you through the Lord Jesus.

[3] For this is the will of God, your sanctification: that you should abstain from sexual immorality, [4] that each one of you should know how to possess his own vessel in sanctification and honor, [5] not in the lust of depravity, even as the Gentiles who do not know God, [6] and that no man take advantage of and defraud his brother in any matter, because the Lord is the avenger in all these things, as we also have forewarned you and testified. [7] For God has not called us to uncleanness, but to holiness. [8] Therefore he that despises does not despise man, but God, who has also given us His Holy Spirit.

[9] As concerning brotherly love, you do not need me to write to you. For you yourselves are taught by God to love one another. [10] And indeed, you do have love for all the brothers who are in all Macedonia. But we urge you, brothers, that you increase more and more. [11] Learn to be calm, and to conduct your own business, and to work with your own hands, as we commanded you, [12] so that you may walk honestly toward those who are outsiders and that you may lack nothing.

The Lord's Coming

[13] But I would not have you ignorant, brothers, concerning those who are asleep, that you may not grieve as others who have no hope. [14] For if we believe that Jesus died and arose again, so God will bring with Him those who sleep in Jesus. [15] For this we say to you by the word of the Lord, that we who are alive and remain until the coming of the Lord will not precede those who are asleep. [16] For the Lord Himself will descend from heaven with a shout, with the voice of the archangel, and with the trumpet call of God. And the dead in Christ will rise first. [17] Then we who are alive and remain shall be caught up together with them in the clouds to meet the Lord in the air. And so we shall be forever with the Lord. [18] Therefore comfort one another with these words.

5 Concerning the times and the seasons, brothers, you have no need that I write to you. [2] For you know perfectly that the day of the Lord will come like a thief in the night. [3] When they say, "Peace and safety!" then sudden destruction will come upon them as labor upon a woman with child, and they shall not escape.

[4] But you, brothers, are not in darkness so that this Day should overtake you as a thief. [5] You are all the sons of light and the sons of the day. We are not of the night nor of darkness. [6] Therefore let us not sleep as others do. But let us be alert and sober. [7] For those who sleep, sleep at night, and those who get drunk, are drunk at night. [8] But let us, who are of the day, be sober, putting on the breastplate of faith and love, and as a helmet, the hope of salvation. [9] For God has not appointed us to wrath, but to obtain salvation by our Lord Jesus Christ, [10] who died for us, so that whether we are awake or asleep, we should live together with Him. [11] So comfort yourselves together, and edify one another, just as you are doing.

Final Exhortations and Greetings

[12] We ask you, brothers, to acknowledge those who labor among you, and are appointed over you in the Lord, and instruct you. [13] Esteem them very highly in love for their work's sake. And be at peace among yourselves. [14] Now we exhort you, brothers, warn those who are unruly, comfort the faint-hearted, support the weak, and be patient toward everyone. [15] See that no one renders evil for evil to anyone. But always seek to do good to one another and to all. [16] Rejoice always. [17] Pray without ceasing. [18] In everything give thanks, for this is the will of God in Christ Jesus concerning you. [19] Do not quench the Spirit. [20] Do not despise prophecies. [21] Examine all things. Firmly hold onto what is good. [22] Abstain from all appearances of evil.

[23] May the very God of peace sanctify you completely. And I pray to God that your whole spirit, soul, and body be preserved blameless unto the coming of our Lord Jesus Christ. [24] Faithful is He who calls you, who also will do it.

[25] Brothers, pray for us. [26] Greet all the brothers with a holy kiss. [27] I command you by the Lord that this letter be read to all the holy brothers. [28] The grace of our Lord Jesus Christ be with you. Amen.

2 THESSALONIANS

Salutation

1 Paul, and Silas, and Timothy,

To the church of the Thessalonians in God our Father and the Lord Jesus Christ:

[2] Grace to you and peace from God our Father and the Lord Jesus Christ.

The Judgment at Christ's Coming

[3] We are bound to thank God always for you, brothers, as it is fitting, because your faith is growing abundantly, and the love of every one of you abounds toward each other. [4] So we boast about you in the churches of God for your patience and faith in all your persecutions and tribulations that you are enduring.

[5] This is evidence that God's judgment, being righteous, will count you worthy of the kingdom of God for which you are suffering. [6] It is a righteous matter with God to repay with tribulation those who trouble you, [7] and to give you who are troubled rest with us when the Lord Jesus is revealed from heaven with His mighty angels, [8] in flaming fire taking vengeance on those who do not know God and do not obey the gospel of our Lord Jesus Christ. [9] They shall be punished with eternal destruction, isolated from the presence of the Lord and from the glory of His power, [10] when He comes, in that Day, to be glorified in His saints and to be marveled at by all those who believe, because our testimony among you was believed.

[11] Therefore we always pray for you that our God would count you worthy of this calling and with power fulfill all your good desires and works done by faith, [12] so that the name of our Lord

Jesus Christ may be glorified in you, and you in Him, according to the grace of our God and the Lord Jesus Christ.

The Man of Lawlessness

2 Now, brothers, concerning the coming of our Lord Jesus Christ, and concerning our gathering together unto Him, we ask you [2] not to let your mind be quickly shaken or be troubled, neither in spirit nor by word, nor by letter coming as though from us, as if the day of Christ is already here. [3] Do not let anyone deceive you in any way. For that Day will not come unless a falling away comes first, and the man of sin is revealed, the son of destruction, [4] who opposes and exalts himself above all that is called God or is worshipped, so that he sits as God in the temple of God, showing himself as God.

[5] Do you not remember that when I was still with you, I told you these things? [6] Now you know what restrains him that he might be revealed in his time. [7] For the mystery of lawlessness is already working. Only He who is now restraining him will do so until He is taken out of the way. [8] Then the lawless one will be revealed, whom the Lord will consume with the breath of His mouth, and destroy with the brightness of His presence, [9] even him, whose coming is in accordance with the working of Satan with all power and signs and false wonders, [10] and with all deception of unrighteousness among those who perish, because they did not receive the love for the truth that they might be saved. [11] Therefore God will send them a strong delusion, that they should believe the lie: [12] that they all might be condemned who did not believe the truth but had pleasure in unrighteousness.

Chosen for Salvation

[13] But we are bound to give thanks to God for you always, beloved brothers of the Lord, because God has from the beginning called you to salvation through sanctification by the Spirit and belief of the truth. [14] To this He called you by our gospel, to obtain the glory of our Lord Jesus Christ.

[15] Therefore, brothers, stand firm and hold the traditions which you have been taught, whether by word or by our letter.

[16] Now may our Lord Jesus Christ Himself, and God our Father, who has loved us and has given us eternal consolation and good hope through grace, [17] comfort your hearts and establish you in every good word and work.

Pray for Us

3 Finally, brothers, pray for us, that the word of the Lord may quickly spread and be glorified, even as it did with you. [2] And pray that we may be delivered from unreasonable and wicked men, for not all men have faith. [3] But the Lord is faithful, who will establish you and guard you from the evil one. [4] We have confidence in the Lord concerning you, that you are doing and will do the things which we command you. [5] May the Lord direct your hearts to the love of God and to the steadfastness of Christ.

Warning Against Idleness

[6] Now we command you, brothers, in the name of our Lord Jesus Christ, that you withdraw yourselves from every brother who walks in idleness and not according to the tradition that he received from us. [7] For you know how you should follow us. For we were not idle among you, [8] neither did we eat anyone's bread without paying for it, but we worked tirelessly and toiled night and day that we might not be a burden to any of you. [9] We did this, not because we did not have that right, but to make ourselves an example for you to follow. [10] For when we were with you, we commanded you that if any will not work, neither shall he eat.

[11] For we hear that there are some among you who live in idleness, mere busybodies, not working at all. [12] Now, concerning those who are such, we command and exhort by our Lord Jesus Christ that they quietly work and eat their own bread. [13] But you, brothers, do not be weary in doing good.

[14] If anyone does not obey our word in this letter, note that man, and do not socialize with him, so that he may be ashamed. [15] Still, do not count him as an enemy, but admonish him as a brother.

Benediction

[16] Now may the Lord of peace Himself give you peace always in every way. The Lord be with you all.

[17] I, Paul, write this greeting with my own hand, and this is the distinguishing mark in every letter. So I write.

[18] The grace of our Lord Jesus Christ be with you all. Amen.

1 TIMOTHY

Salutation

1 Paul, an apostle of Jesus Christ by the command of God our Savior, and of the Lord Jesus Christ, our hope,

[2] To Timothy, my true son in the faith:

Grace, mercy, and peace, from God our Father and Jesus Christ our Lord.

Warning Against False Doctrine

[3] As I urged you when I went into Macedonia, continue to remain at Ephesus so that you might command some to teach no other doctrine, [4] nor pay attention to fables and endless genealogies, which cause debates rather than godly edifying, which is in faith. [5] Now the goal of this command is love from a pure heart, and from a good conscience, and from sincere faith. [6] From this, some have lost their way and turned aside to empty talk, [7] desiring to be teachers of the law, and understanding neither what they say nor what they affirm.

[8] But we know that the law is good if someone uses it lawfully. [9] And we know that the law is not given for a righteous person, but for the lawless and disobedient, for the ungodly and for sinners, for the unholy and the profane, for those who kill their fathers and mothers, for murderers, [10] for the sexually immoral, for sodomites, for slave traders, for liars, for perjurers, and for anything else that is contrary to sound doctrine, [11] according to the glorious gospel of the blessed God, which was committed to my trust.

Thankfulness for Mercy

[12] I thank Christ Jesus our Lord, who has enabled me, because He counted me faithful and appointed me to the ministry. [13] I was previously a blasphemer, and a persecutor, and an insolent man. But I was shown mercy, because I did it ignorantly in unbelief. [14] The grace of our Lord overflowed with the faith and love which is in Christ Jesus.

[15] This is a faithful saying and worthy of all acceptance, that Christ Jesus came into the world to save sinners, of whom I am the worst. [16] But I received mercy for this reason, that in me, first, Jesus Christ might show all patience, as an example to those who were to believe in Him for eternal life. [17] Now to the eternal, immortal, invisible King, the only wise God, be honor and glory forever. Amen.

[18] This command I commit to you, my son Timothy, according to the prophecies that were previously given to you, that by

them you might fight a good fight, [19] keeping faith and a good conscience, which some have rejected and suffered shipwreck in regard to their faith. [20] Among these are Hymenaeus and Alexander, whom I have delivered to Satan that they may learn not to blaspheme.

Instructions Concerning Prayer

2 Therefore I exhort first of all that you make supplications, prayers, intercessions, and thanksgivings for everyone, [2] for kings and for all who are in authority, that we may lead a quiet and peaceful life in all godliness and honesty, [3] for this is good and acceptable in the sight of God our Savior, [4] who desires all men to be saved and to come to the knowledge of the truth. [5] There is one God and one mediator between God and men, the Man Christ Jesus, [6] who gave Himself as a ransom for all. This was the testimony given at the proper time. [7] For this I was appointed a preacher and an apostle (I speak the truth in Christ and do not lie), a teacher of the Gentiles in faith and truth.

[8] Therefore I desire that the men pray everywhere, lifting up holy hands, without wrath or contentiousness. [9] In like manner also, that women clothe themselves in modest clothing, with decency and self-control, not with braided hair, gold, pearls, or expensive clothing, [10] but with good works, which is proper for women professing godliness.

[11] Let a woman learn in silence with all obedience. [12] I do not permit a woman to teach or to usurp authority over a man, but to be silent. [13] For Adam was formed first, then Eve. [14] And Adam was not deceived, but the woman, being deceived, fell into sin. [15] Yet she will be saved in childbearing if they continue in faith, love, and holiness, with self-control.

Qualifications of Overseers

3 This is a faithful saying: If a man desires the office of an overseer, he desires a good work. [2] An overseer then must be blameless, the husband of one wife, sober, self-controlled, respectable, hospitable, able to teach; [3] not given to drunkenness, not violent, not greedy for money, but patient, not argumentative, not covetous; [4] and one who manages his own house well, having his children in submission with all reverence. [5] For if a man does not know how to manage his own house, how will he take care of the church of God? [6] He must not be newly converted, so that he does not become prideful and fall into the condemnation of the devil. [7] Moreover he must have a good reputation among those who are outsiders, so that he does not fall into reproach and the snare of the devil.

Qualifications of Deacons

[8] Likewise deacons must be serious, not insincere, not given to much wine, not greedy, [9] keeping the mystery of the faith in a pure conscience. [10] And let them first be tested; then, being found blameless, let them serve as deacons.

[11] Likewise, their wives must be serious, not slanderers, sober, and faithful in all things.

[12] Let the deacons be the husbands of one wife, managing their children and their own houses well. [13] For those who have served well in the office of deacon purchase for themselves good standing and great boldness in the faith, which is in Christ Jesus.

The Mystery of Our Religion

[14] I am writing these things to you, hoping to come to you shortly, [15] but if I am delayed, you might know how you ought to conduct yourself in the house of God, which is the church of the living God, the pillar and foundation of the truth. [16] Without question, great is the mystery of godliness:

God was revealed in the flesh,
    justified in the Spirit,
seen by angels,
    preached to the Gentiles,
believed on in the world,
    taken up into glory.

Prediction of Apostasy

4 Now the Spirit clearly says that in the last times some will depart from the faith and pay attention to seducing spirits and doctrines of devils, [2] speaking lies in hypocrisy, having their consciences seared with a hot iron, [3] forbidding to marry, and commanding to abstain from foods, which God has created to be received with thanksgiving by those who believe and know the truth. [4] For everything created by God is good, and not to be refused if it is received with thanksgiving, [5] for it is sanctified by the word of God and prayer.

A Good Minister of Christ Jesus

[6] If you remind the brothers of these things, you will be a good minister of Jesus Christ, nourished by the words of faith and of good doctrine, which you have followed closely. [7] But refuse profane and foolish myths. Instead, exercise in the ways of godliness. [8] For bodily exercise profits a little, but godliness is profitable in all things, holding promise for the present life and also for the life to come. [9] This is a faithful saying and worthy of all acceptance. [10] For to this end we both labor and suffer reproach, because we trust in the living God, who is the Savior of all men, especially of those who believe.

[11] Command and teach these things. [12] Let no one despise your youth, but be an example to the believers in speech, in conduct, in love, in spirit, in faith, and in purity. [13] Until I come, give attention to reading, exhortation, and doctrine. [14] Do not neglect the gift that is in you, which was given to you by prophecy, with the laying on of hands by the elders.

[15] Meditate on these things. Give yourself completely to them, that your progress may be known to everyone. [16] Take heed to yourself and to the doctrine. Continue in them, for in doing this you will save both yourself and those who hear you.

Duties Toward Others

5 Do not rebuke an elder, but exhort him as a father, the younger men as brothers, [2] the elder women as mothers, and the younger women as sisters, with complete purity.

[3] Honor widows that are widows indeed. [4] But if any widow has children or grandchildren, let them learn first to show piety at home and to repay their parents. For this is good and acceptable before God. [5] Now she who is a widow indeed, and desolate, trusts in God, and continues in supplications and prayers night and day. [6] But she who lives in pleasure is dead while she lives. [7] And these things command, that they may be blameless. [8] But if any do not care for their own, and especially for those of their own house, they have denied the faith and are worse than unbelievers.

[9] Do not let a widow be counted unless she is over sixty years old, has been the wife of one man, [10] is well attested in good works, if she has brought up children, has lodged strangers, has washed the saints' feet, has relieved the afflicted, and has diligently followed every good work.

[11] But refuse the younger widows, for when their sensual desires have drawn them away from Christ, they want to marry, [12] and bring judgment on themselves, because they have cast off their first pledge. [13] Besides that, they learn to be idle, and not only idle, wandering around from house to house, but also gossips and busybodies, saying what they ought not. [14] Therefore I desire that the younger women marry, bear children, manage the house, and give no occasion to the adversary to speak reproachfully. [15] For some have already turned aside after Satan.

[16] If any believing man or woman has widows, let those assist them. Do not let the church be charged, so that it may relieve those who are widows indeed.

[17] Let the elders who rule well be counted worthy of double honor, especially those who labor in the word and doctrine. [18] For the Scripture says, "You shall not muzzle the ox that treads out the grain,"[1] and, "The laborer is worthy of his reward."[2] [19] Do not receive an accusation against an elder, except before two or three witnesses. [20] Rebuke in the presence of everyone those who sin, that the rest also may fear. [21] I command you before God and the

[1] 18 Dt 25:4.   [2] 18 Lk 10:7.

Lord Jesus Christ and the elect angels that you observe these things without prejudice, doing nothing by partiality. [22] Do not lay hands suddenly on anyone, and do not partake of other men's sins. Keep yourself pure.

[23] No longer drink only water, but use a little wine for your stomach's sake and your frequent illnesses.

[24] Some men's sins are evident, pointing to judgment, but other men's sins are revealed later. [25] Likewise, the good works of some are evident, but those that are not cannot be hidden.

6 Let as many servants as are under the yoke of slavery count their own masters worthy of all honor, so that the name of God and His doctrine may not be slandered. [2] Let those who have believing masters not despise them, because they are brothers. Instead, let them serve as slaves, because those who receive their service are faithful and beloved.

False Teaching and True Wealth

Teach and command these things. [3] Anyone who teaches otherwise and does not consent to wholesome words, to the words of our Lord Jesus Christ, and to godly doctrine [4] is conceited and knows nothing. He has a morbid disposition for controversy and verbal disputes, from which come envy, strife, blasphemies, evil speculations, [5] constant disputes by men of corrupt minds, being destitute of the truth, and supposing that financial gain is godliness. Withdraw yourself from such men.

[6] But godliness with contentment is great gain. [7] For we brought nothing into this world, and it is certain that we can carry nothing out. [8] If we have food and clothing, we shall be content with these things. [9] But those who desire to be rich fall into temptation and a snare and into many foolish and harmful lusts, which drown men in ruin and destruction. [10] For the love of money is the root of all evil. While coveting after money, some have strayed from the faith and pierced themselves through with many sorrows.

The Good Fight of Faith

[11] But you, O man of God, escape these things, and follow after righteousness, godliness, faith, love, patience, and gentleness. [12] Fight the good fight of faith. Lay hold on eternal life, to which you are called and have professed a good profession before many witnesses. [13] I command you, in the sight of God, who gives life to all things, and in the sight of Christ Jesus, who testified a good confession before Pontius Pilate, [14] to keep this commandment without blemish, blameless until the appearing of our Lord Jesus Christ, [15] which He, who is the blessed and only Ruler, the King of kings and Lord of lords, will reveal at the proper time. [16] He alone has immortality, living in unapproachable light, whom no one has seen, nor can see. To Him be honor and everlasting power. Amen.

[17] Command those who are rich in this world that they not be conceited, nor trust in uncertain riches, but in the living God, who richly gives us all things to enjoy. [18] Command that they do good, that they be rich in good works, generous, willing to share, [19] and laying up in store for themselves a good foundation for the coming age, so that they may take hold of eternal life.

[20] O Timothy, guard that which is committed to your trust. Avoid profane babblings and opposing views from so-called knowledge. [21] By professing it, some have erred concerning the faith.

Grace be with you. Amen.

2 TIMOTHY

Salutation

1 Paul, an apostle of Jesus Christ by the will of God, according to the promise of life which is in Christ Jesus,

[2] To Timothy, my beloved son:

Grace, mercy, and peace, from God the Father and Christ Jesus our Lord.

Loyalty to the Gospel

[3] I thank God, whom I serve with a pure conscience as my forefathers did, as I continually remember you in my prayers night and day, [4] greatly desiring to see you, remembering your tears, that I may be filled with joy, [5] remembering the genuine faith that first lived in your grandmother Lois and your mother Eunice and that I am persuaded lives in you also. [6] Therefore I remind you to stir up the gift of God, which is in you by the laying on of my hands. [7] For God has not given us the spirit of fear, but of power, and love, and self-control. [8] So do not be ashamed of the testimony of our Lord, nor of me, His prisoner. But share in the sufferings of the gospel by the power of God, [9] who has saved us and called us with a holy calling, not by our works, but by His own purpose and grace, which was given us in Christ Jesus before the world began, [10] but is now revealed by the appearing of our Savior, Jesus Christ, who has abolished death and has brought life and immortality to light through the gospel, [11] for which I was appointed a preacher, an apostle, and a teacher of the Gentiles. [12] For these things I suffer, but I am not ashamed, for I know whom I have believed, and am persuaded that He is able to keep that which I have committed to Him until that Day.

[13] Follow the pattern of sound teaching which you have heard from me in the faith and love that is in Christ Jesus. [14] Guard the treasure that was committed to you through the Holy Spirit who lives in us.

[15] You know that all those who are in Asia have turned away from me, including Phygelus and Hermogenes. [16] May the Lord grant mercy to the house of Onesiphorus, for he often refreshed me and was not ashamed of my chains. [17] But when he arrived in Rome, he searched me out very diligently and found me. [18] May the Lord grant that he may find mercy from the Lord on that Day. You know very well how many ways he ministered to me at Ephesus.

A Good Soldier of Christ Jesus

2 So you, my son, be strong in the grace that is in Christ Jesus [2] Share the things that you have heard from me in the presence of many witnesses with faithful men who will be able to teach others also. [3] Endure hard times as a good soldier of Jesus Christ. [4] No soldier on active duty entangles himself with civilian affairs, that he may please the enlisting officer. [5] Anyone who competes as an athlete is not rewarded without competing legally. [6] The farmer who labors should be first to partake of the crops. [7] Consider what I am saying, and may the Lord grant you understanding in all things.

[8] Remember Jesus Christ, raised from the dead, descended from David, according to my gospel, [9] in which I suffer trouble like a criminal, even with chains. But the word of God is not bound. [10] Therefore I endure all things for the sake of the elect, that they also may obtain the salvation which is in Christ Jesus with eternal glory.

[11] This is a faithful saying:

If we die with Him,
    we shall also live with Him.
[12] If we endure,
    we shall also reign with Him.
If we deny Him,
    He also will deny us.
[13] If we are faithless,
    He remains faithful;
    He cannot deny Himself.

An Approved Workman

[14] Remind them of these things, commanding them before the Lord that they not argue about words, which leads to nothing of value and to the destruction of those who hear them. [15] Study to show yourself approved by God, a workman who need not be ashamed, rightly dividing the word of truth. [16] But avoid profane foolish babblings, for they will increase to more ungodliness, [17] and their word will spread like gangrene: Among them are Hymenaeus and Philetus, [18] who have erred concerning the truth, saying that the resurrection has already occurred, and who overthrow the faith of some. [19] But the firm foundation of God stands, having this seal, "The Lord knows those who are His," and, "Let everyone who calls on the name of Christ depart from iniquity."

[20] In a large house there are not only gold and silver vessels, but also those of wood and clay; some are for honor, and some for dishonor. [21] One who cleanses himself from these things will be a vessel for honor, sanctified, fit for the Master's use, and prepared for every good work.

[22] So flee youthful desires and pursue righteousness, faith, love, and peace, with those who call on the Lord out of a pure heart. [23] But avoid foolish and unlearned debates, knowing that they create strife. [24] The servant of the Lord must not quarrel, but must be gentle toward all people, able to teach, patient, [25] in gentleness instructing those in opposition. Perhaps God will grant them repentance to know the truth, [26] and they may escape from the snare of the devil, after being captured by him to do his will.

The Last Days

3 Know this: In the last days perilous times will come. [2] Men will be lovers of themselves, lovers of money, boastful, proud, blasphemers, disobedient to parents, unthankful, unholy, [3] without natural affection, trucebreakers, slanderers, unrestrained, fierce, despisers of those who are good, [4] traitors, reckless, conceited, lovers of pleasures more than lovers of God, [5] having a form of godliness, but denying its power. Turn away from such people.

[6] Those of this nature creep into houses and captivate silly women who are burdened with sins and led away with various desires, [7] always learning, but never able to come to the knowledge of the truth. [8] Now as Jannes and Jambres resisted Moses, so these also resist the truth, men of corrupt minds and worthless concerning the faith. [9] But they shall proceed no further, for their folly will be revealed to everyone, as theirs also was.

Last Charge to Timothy

[10] But you have observed my doctrine, manner of life, purpose, faith, tolerance, love, patience, [11] persecutions, and afflictions, which came to me at Antioch, Iconium, and Lystra—what persecutions I endured! But the Lord delivered me out of them all. [12] Yes, and all who desire to live a godly life in Christ Jesus will suffer persecution. [13] But evil men and seducers will grow worse and worse, deceiving and being deceived. [14] But continue in the things that you have learned and have been assured of, knowing those from whom you have learned them, [15] and that since childhood you have known the Holy Scriptures, which are able to make you wise unto salvation through the faith that is in Christ Jesus. [16] All Scripture is inspired by God and is profitable for teaching, for reproof, for correction, and for instruction in righteousness, [17] that the man of God may be complete, thoroughly equipped for every good work.

4 I charge you therefore before God and the Lord Jesus Christ, who will judge the living and the dead at His appearing and His kingdom: [2] Preach the word, be ready in season and out of season, reprove, rebuke, and exhort, with all patience and teaching. [3] For the time will come when people will not endure sound doctrine, but they will gather to themselves teachers in accordance with their own desires, having itching ears, [4] and they will turn their ears away from the truth and turn to myths. [5] But be self-controlled in all things, endure afflictions, do the work of an evangelist, and prove your ministry.

[6] For I am already being poured out as a drink offering, and the time of my departure has come. [7] I have fought a good fight, I have finished my course, and I have kept the faith. [8] From now on a crown of righteousness is laid up for me, which the Lord, the righteous Judge, will give me on that Day, and not only to me but also to all who have loved His appearing.

Personal Instructions

[9] Diligently try to come to me soon. [10] Demas has forsaken me, having loved this present world, and has departed to Thessalonica, Crescens to Galatia, and Titus to Dalmatia. [11] Only Luke is with me. Get Mark, and bring him with you, for he is profitable to me for the ministry. [12] I sent Tychicus to Ephesus. [13] When you come, bring with you the cloak that I left at Troas with Carpus, and the books, but especially the parchments.

[14] Alexander the coppersmith did me much evil. May the Lord reward him according to his works. [15] Beware of him, for he has greatly opposed our words.

[16] At my first defense no one stood with me, but everyone forsook me. May it not be charged against them. [17] But the Lord stood with me and strengthened me, so that through me the preaching might be fully known, and that all the Gentiles might hear. And I was delivered out of the mouth of the lion. [18] The Lord will deliver me from every evil work and will preserve me for His heavenly kingdom, to whom be glory forever and ever. Amen.

Final Greetings

[19] Greet Priscilla and Aquila and the household of Onesiphorus. [20] Erastus remained at Corinth, and I have left Trophimus ill in Miletus. [21] Diligently try to come before winter. Eubulus greets you, and so do Pudens, Linus, Claudia, and all the brothers.

[22] The Lord Jesus Christ be with your spirit. Grace be with you. Amen.

TITUS

Salutation

1 Paul, a servant of God and an apostle of Jesus Christ, according to the faith of God's elect and the knowledge of the truth which leads to godliness, [2] in hope of eternal life which God, who cannot lie, promised before the world began, [3] and has in due time revealed His word through preaching, with which I was entrusted according to the command of God our Savior,

[4] To Titus, my own son in the common faith:

Grace, mercy, and peace, from God the Father and the Lord Jesus Christ our Savior.

Titus' Work in Crete

[5] For this reason I left you in Crete, that you should set in order the things that are lacking, and appoint elders in every city, as I commanded you: [6] any man who is blameless, the husband of one wife, having faithful children who are not accused of being wild or unruly. [7] For an overseer must be blameless, as a steward of God, not self-willed, not easily angered, not given to drunkenness, not violent, not greedy for dishonest gain, [8] but hospitable, a lover of what is good, self-controlled, just, holy, temperate, [9] holding firmly the trustworthy word that is in accordance with the teaching, that he may be able both to exhort with sound doctrine and to convince those who oppose it.

[10] For there are many unruly men, empty talkers and deceivers, especially those of the circumcision, [11] who must be silenced, who subvert whole houses by teaching for dishonest gain things they ought not teach. [12] One of them, a prophet of their own, said, "The Cretans are always liars, evil beasts, and idle gluttons!" [13] This witness is true. So rebuke them sharply that they may be sound in the faith, [14] not paying attention to Jewish myths and commandments of men who reject the truth. [15] To the pure, all things are pure. But to those who are defiled and unbelieving, nothing is pure. Even their minds and consciences are defiled. [16] They profess that they know God, but in their deeds they deny Him, being abominable, disobedient, and worthless for every good work.

The Teaching of Sound Doctrine

2 But as for you, teach what is fitting of sound doctrine: [2] Older men should be sober, serious, temperate, sound in faith, in love, in patience.

[3] Likewise, older women should be reverent in behavior, and not be false accusers, not be enslaved to much wine, but teachers of good things, [4] that they may teach the young women to love their husbands, to love their children, [5] and to be self-controlled, pure, homemakers, good, obedient to their own husbands, that the word of God may not be dishonored.

[6] Likewise, exhort young men to be self-controlled, [7] in all things presenting yourself as an example of good works: in doctrine showing integrity, gravity, incorruptibility, [8] and sound speech that cannot be condemned, so that the one who opposes you may be ashamed, having nothing evil to say of you.

[9] Exhort servants to be obedient to their own masters, to please them well in everything, not answering back, [10] or stealing, but showing complete fidelity, so that they may exemplify the doctrine of God our Savior in all things.

[11] For the grace of God that brings salvation has appeared to all men, [12] teaching us that, denying ungodliness and worldly desires, we should live soberly, righteously, and in godliness in this present world, [13] as we await the blessed hope and the appearing of the glory of our great God and Savior Jesus Christ, [14] who gave Himself for us, that He might redeem us from all lawlessness and purify for Himself a special people, zealous of good works.

[15] Teach these things, exhort, and rebuke with all authority. Let no one despise you.

Maintain Good Deeds

3 Remind them to be subject to rulers and authorities, to obey them, to be ready for every good work, [2] to speak evil of no one, not to be contentious, but gentle, showing all humility toward everyone.

[3] We also were once foolish, disobedient, deceived, serving various desires and pleasures, living in evil and envy, filled with hatred and hating each other. [4] But when the kindness and the love of God our Savior toward mankind appeared, [5] not by works of righteousness which we have done, but according to His mercy He saved us, through the washing of rebirth and the renewal of the Holy Spirit, [6] whom He poured out on us abundantly through Jesus Christ our Savior, [7] so that, being justified by His grace, we might become heirs according to the hope of eternal life. [8] This is a faithful saying, and these things I want you constantly to affirm, so that those who have believed in God might be careful to maintain good works. These things are good and profitable to everyone.

[9] But avoid foolish debates, genealogies, contentions, and arguments about the law, for they are unprofitable and useless. [10] Reject a divisive man after a first and second admonition, [11] knowing that such a man is perverted and is sinning, being self-condemned.

Personal Instructions and Greetings

[12] When I send Artemas or Tychicus to you, be diligent to come to me in Nicopolis, for I have decided to spend the winter there. [13] Diligently send Zenas the lawyer and Apollos on their journey. See that they lack nothing. [14] And let our people also learn to continue doing good works to meet urgent needs, that they may not be unproductive.

[15] All who are with me greet you. Greet those who love us in the faith.

Grace be with you all. Amen.

Philemon

Salutation

Paul, a prisoner of Christ Jesus, and Timothy our brother,

To Philemon, our beloved fellow laborer, [2] and to beloved Apphia, and to Archippus our fellow soldier, and to the church in your house:

[3] Grace to you and peace from God our Father and the Lord Jesus Christ.

Philemon's Love and Faith

[4] I thank my God, always mentioning you in my prayers, [5] whenever I hear of your love and faith, which you have toward the Lord Jesus and for all the saints, [6] that the sharing of your faith may be most effective by the acknowledgment of every good thing which is in you from Christ Jesus. [7] For we have great joy and encouragement on account of your love, because the hearts of the saints are refreshed through you, brother.

Paul Pleads for Onesimus

[8] Therefore, though I might be very bold in Christ to command you to do that which is proper, [9] yet for love's sake I rather appeal to you—I, Paul, an old man, and now also a prisoner of Jesus Christ— [10] I appeal to you on behalf of my son Onesimus, whose father I have become in my imprisonment, [11] who in the past was unprofitable to you, but now he is profitable to you and to me. [12] I have sent him back. Therefore receive him as my own heart. [13] I wanted to keep him with me, so that in your place he might serve me during my imprisonment for the gospel. [14] But without your consent I would do nothing, so that your goodness would not be forced, but given willingly. [15] Perhaps this was why he departed for a while, that you might receive him forever, [16] no longer as a slave but more than a slave, a beloved brother, especially to me but how much more to you, both in the flesh and in the Lord.

[17] If then you consider me a partner, receive him as you would me. [18] If he wronged you or owes you anything, charge this to my account. [19] I, Paul, have written this with my own hand. I will repay it—not to mention that you owe me even your own self. [20] Yes, brother, help me rejoice in the Lord, refresh my heart in the Lord. [21] Being convinced of your obedience, I write to you, knowing that you will also do more than I say.

[22] But, in addition, prepare also lodging for me, for I hope that through your prayers I shall be graciously restored to you.

Final Greetings

[23] Epaphras, my fellow prisoner in Christ Jesus, greets you, [24] as do Mark, Aristarchus, Demas, and Luke, my fellow laborers.

[25] The grace of our Lord Jesus Christ be with your spirit. Amen.

Hebrews

God Has Spoken by His Son

1 God, who at various times and in diverse ways spoke long ago to the fathers through the prophets, [2] has in these last days spoken to us by His Son, whom He has appointed heir of all things, and through whom He made the world. [3] He is the brightness of His glory, the express image of Himself, and upholds all things by the word of His power. When He had by Himself purged our sins, He sat down at the right hand of the Majesty on high. [4] He was made so much better than the angels as He has inherited a more excellent name than they.

The Son Superior to Angels

[5] For to which of the angels did He at any time say:

"You are My Son;
today I have become Your Father"[1]?

Or again,

"I will be a Father to Him,
and He shall be a Son to Me"[2]?

[6] And again, when He brings the firstborn into the world, He says:

"Let all the angels of God worship Him."[3]

[7] Of the angels He says:

"He makes His angels spirits,
and His servants a flame of fire."[4]

[8] But to the Son He says:

"Your throne, O God, lasts forever and ever;
a scepter of righteousness is the scepter of Your kingdom.[5]
[9] You have loved righteousness and hated wickedness;
therefore God, Your God, has anointed You
with the oil of gladness more than Your companions."[6]

[10] And,

"You, Lord, laid the foundation of the earth in the beginning,
and the heavens are the works of Your hands.
[11] They will perish, but You remain;
and they all will wear out like a garment;
[12] as a cloak You will fold them up,
and they will be changed.
But You are the same,
and Your years will not end."[7]

[13] But to which of the angels did He at any time say:

"Sit at My right hand,
until I make Your enemies
Your footstool"[8]?

---

[1] 5 Ps 2:7. [2] 5 2Sa 7:8, 14. [3] 6 Ps 97:7. [4] 7 Ps 104:4. [5] 8 Ps 45:6. [6] 9 Ps 45:7; Isa 61:1, 3. [7] 10–12 Ps 102:25–27.
[8] 13 Ps 110:1.

[14] Are they not all ministering spirits sent out to minister to those who will inherit salvation?

The Great Salvation

2 Therefore we should be more attentive to what we have heard, lest we drift away. [2] For if the word spoken by angels was true, and every sin and disobedience received a just recompense, [3] how shall we escape if we neglect such a great salvation, which was first declared by the Lord, and was confirmed to us by those who heard Him? [4] God also bore them witness with signs and wonders and diverse miracles and with gifts of the Holy Spirit distributed according to His own will.

The Pioneer of Salvation

[5] For it was not to the angels that He has subjected the world to come, of which we are speaking. [6] But someone in a certain place testified, saying:

"What is man that You are mindful of him,
    or the son of man that You care for him?
[7] You made him a little lower than the angels;
    You crowned him with glory and honor,
    and set him over the works of Your hands.
[8]   You have put all things in subjection under his feet." [1]

For in subjecting all things under him, He left nothing that is not subjected to him. Yet now we do not see all things subject to him. [9] But we see Jesus, who was made a little lower than the angels to suffer death, crowned with glory and honor, so that He, by the grace of God, should experience death for everyone.

[10] For it was fitting for Him, for whom and by whom all things exist, in bringing many sons to glory, to make the Author of their salvation perfect through suffering. [11] For both He who sanctifies and those who are sanctified are all of One. For this reason He is not ashamed to call them brothers, [12] saying:

"I will declare Your name to My brothers;
    in the midst of the congregation I will sing praise
        to You." [2]

[13] And again:

"I will put My trust in Him." [3]

And again:

"Here am I and the children whom God has given Me." [4]

[14] So then, as the children share in flesh and blood, He likewise took part in these, so that through death He might destroy him who has the power of death, that is, the devil, [15] and deliver those who through fear of death were throughout their lives subject to bondage. [16] For surely He does not help the angels, but He helps the seed of Abraham. [17] Therefore, in all things it was necessary for Him to be made like His brothers, so that He might be a merciful and faithful High Priest in the things pertaining to God, to make atonement for the sins of the people. [18] For since He Himself suffered while being tempted, He is able to help those who are being tempted.

Jesus Superior to Moses

3 Therefore, holy brothers, partakers in a heavenly calling, consider the Apostle and High Priest of our profession, Jesus Christ, [2] who was faithful to Him who appointed Him, as Moses was faithful in all His house. [3] For the One was counted worthy of more glory than Moses, in that He who builds the house has more honor than the house itself. [4] For every house is built by someone, but the One who builds all things is God. [5] Moses was faithful in all God's house as a servant, testifying about those things that were to

be spoken later. [6] But Christ is faithful over God's house as a Son, whose house we are if we hold fast the confidence and the rejoicing of our hope firm to the end.

A Rest for God's People

[7] Therefore, as the Holy Spirit says:

"Today, if you hear His voice,
[8]   do not harden your hearts
    as in the rebellion,
        on the day of temptation in the wilderness,
[9]   where your fathers tested Me and tried Me
        and saw My works for forty years.
[10] Therefore I was angry with that generation,
    and said, 'They always go astray in their heart,
    and they have not known My ways.'
[11] So I swore in My wrath,
    'They shall not enter My rest.' " [5]

[12] Be attentive, brothers, lest there be in any of you an evil, unbelieving heart, and you depart from the living God. [13] But exhort one another daily, while it is called "Today," lest any of you be hardened through the deceitfulness of sin. [14] For we have become partakers of Christ if we hold the beginning of our confidence firmly to the end, [15] while it is said:

"Today, if you will hear His voice,
    do not harden your hearts
    as in the rebellion." [6]

[16] For who were they who heard and rebelled? Was it not all of those who came out of Egypt, led by Moses? [17] And with whom was He grieved for forty years? Was it not with those who had sinned, whose bodies fell in the wilderness? [18] And to whom did He swear that they would not enter His rest, but to those who disobeyed? [19] So we see that they could not enter because of unbelief.

4 Therefore, since the promise of entering His rest remains, let us fear lest any of you should seem to come short of it. [2] For the gospel was preached to us as well as to them. But the word preached did not benefit them, because it was not mixed with faith in those who heard it. [3] For we who have believed have entered this rest, as He has said,

"As I have sworn in My wrath,
    'They shall not enter My rest.' " [7]

However, His works have been finished since the creation of the world. [4] For He spoke somewhere about the seventh day like this: "And God rested on the seventh day from all His works." [8] [5] And again in the present passage He said, "They shall not enter My rest." [9]

[6] Since therefore it remains for some to enter it, and they to whom it was first preached did not enter due to unbelief, [7] again He establishes a certain day, "Today," saying through David, after so long a time, as it has been said:

"Today, if you will hear His voice,
    do not harden your hearts." [10]

[8] For if Joshua had given them rest, He would not have later spoken of another day. [9] Therefore a rest remains for the people of God. [10] For whoever enters His rest will also cease from his own works, as God did from His. [11] Let us labor therefore to enter that rest, lest anyone fall by the same pattern of unbelief.

[12] For the word of God is alive, and active, and sharper than any two-edged sword, piercing even to the division of soul and spirit, of joints and marrow, and able to judge the thoughts and intents of the heart. [13] There is no creature that is not revealed in His sight,

---

[1] 6–8 Ps 8:4–6. [2] 12 Ps 22:22. [3] 13 Isa 12:2. [4] 13 Isa 8:18. [5] 7–11 Ps 95:7–11. [6] 15 Ps 95:7–8. [7] 3 Ps 95:11. [8] 4 Ge 2:2.
[9] 5 Ps 95:11. [10] 7 Ps 95:7–8.

for all things are bare and exposed to the eyes of Him to whom we must give account.

Jesus the Great High Priest

[14] Since then we have a great High Priest who has passed into the heavens, Jesus the Son of God, let us hold firmly to our confession. [15] For we do not have a High Priest who cannot sympathize with our weaknesses, but One who was in every sense tempted like we are, yet without sin. [16] Let us then come with confidence to the throne of grace, that we may obtain mercy and find grace to help in time of need.

5 For every high priest chosen from among men is appointed to represent men in things pertaining to God, that he may offer both gifts and sacrifices for sins. [2] He is able to have compassion on the ignorant and on those who are wayward, for he himself is also subject to weakness. [3] Because of this he must offer sacrifices for his own sins, just as he does for the people. [4] No man takes this honor for himself, but he who is called by God receives it, just as Aaron did.

[5] So also Christ did not glorify Himself to be made a High Priest, but it was He who said to Him:

"You are My Son;
   today I have become Your Father." [1]

[6] As He also says in another place:

"You are a priest forever
   in the order of Melchizedek." [2]

[7] In the days of His flesh, Jesus offered up prayers and supplications with loud cries and tears to Him who was able to save Him from death. He was heard because of His godly fear. [8] Though He was a Son, He learned obedience through the things that He suffered, [9] and being made perfect, He became the source of eternal salvation for all those who obey Him, [10] being designated by God a High Priest according to the order of Melchizedek.

Warning Against Apostasy

[11] Concerning this we have much to say that is hard to explain, since you have become hard of hearing. [12] For though by now you should be teachers, you need someone to teach you again the first principles of the oracles of God and have come to need milk rather than solid food. [13] Everyone who lives on milk is unskilled in the word of righteousness, for he is a baby. [14] But solid food belongs to those who are mature, for those who through practice have powers of discernment that are trained to distinguish good from evil.

6 Therefore, leaving the elementary principles of the doctrine of Christ, let us go on to maturity, not laying again a foundation of repentance from dead works and of faith toward God, [2] of instruction about washings, the laying on of hands, the resurrection of the dead, and eternal judgment. [3] This we will do if God permits.

[4] For it is impossible for those who were once enlightened, who have tasted the heavenly gift, who shared in the Holy Spirit, [5] and have tasted the good word of God and the powers of the age to come, [6] if they fall away, to be renewed once more to repentance, since they again crucify to themselves the Son of God and subject Him to public shame. [7] For land that drinks in the rain that often falls upon it and bears a crop useful to those for whom it is cultivated receives a blessing from God. [8] But land that bears thorns and thistles is rejected and near to being cursed. Its destiny is to be burned.

[9] But though we speak in this manner, we are persuaded of better things for you, things that accompany salvation, [10] for God is not unjust so as to forget your work and labor of love that you have shown for His name, in that you have ministered to the saints and continue ministering. [11] We desire that every one of you show the same diligence for the full assurance of hope to the end, [12] so that you may not be lazy, but imitators of those who through faith and patience inherit the promises.

Sure Promise of God

[13] For when God made a promise to Abraham, because He could vow by no one greater, He vowed by Himself, [14] saying, "Surely I will bless you, and surely I will multiply you." [3] [15] So after Abraham had patiently endured, he obtained the promise.

[16] For men indeed swear by a greater authority than themselves, and for them an oath of confirmation ends all dispute. [17] So God, wanting to show more abundantly the immutability of His counsel to the heirs of promise, confirmed it by an oath. [18] So that by two immutable things, in which it was impossible for God to lie, we who have fled for refuge might have strong encouragement to hold fast to the hope set before us. [19] We have this hope as a sure and steadfast anchor of the soul, which enters the Inner Place behind the veil. [20] This is where Jesus has entered for us as a forerunner, since He has become the everlasting High Priest in the order of Melchizedek.

The Priestly Order of Melchizedek

7 For this Melchizedek, king of Salem, priest of the Most High God, met Abraham returning from the slaughter of the kings and blessed him. [2] To him Abraham also gave a tenth part of everything. In the first place, his name is translated "king of righteousness," and then also he is king of Salem, which means "king of peace." [3] Without father, without mother, without descent, having neither beginning of days nor end of life, but made like the Son of God, he continually remains a priest.

[4] Now consider how great this man was, to whom even the patriarch Abraham gave a tenth of the spoils. [5] Surely the sons of Levi, who receive the office of the priesthood, have a command to take tithes of the people according to the law, that is, from their brothers, though they also come from the seed of Abraham. [6] But this man, whose descent is not numbered among them, received tithes from Abraham and blessed him who had the promises. [7] Without question, the inferior is blessed by the superior. [8] In the one case mortal men receive tithes, but in the other he of whom it is witnessed that he is alive receives them. [9] One might say that Levi also, who receives tithes, paid tithes through Abraham, [10] for he was still in the loins of his father when Melchizedek met Abraham.

[11] If perfection were attained through the Levitical priesthood (for through it the people received the law), what further need was there that another priest should rise in the order of Melchizedek, rather than established in the order of Aaron? [12] For a change in the priesthood necessitates a change in the law. [13] For the One concerning whom these things are spoken pertains to another tribe, from which no man served at the altar. [14] For it is evident that our Lord descended from Judah, a tribe concerning which Moses said nothing about priests. [15] This is far more evident when another priest arises in the likeness of Melchizedek, [16] who becomes a priest not by a law pertaining to ancestry, but by the power of an endless life. [17] For He testifies:

"You are a priest forever,
   in the order of Melchizedek." [4]

[18] For there is then an annulling of the previous commandment due to its weakness and uselessness. [19] For the law made nothing perfect, but now a better hope is introduced, by which we draw near to God.

[20] And He was not made a priest without an oath. [21] (Other priests were made without an oath, but this One with an oath by the One who said to Him:

"The Lord has sworn
   and will not relent,
'You are a priest forever, in the order of Melchizedek.'" [5])

[22] Through this oath Jesus became the guarantor of a better covenant.

[23] And the former priests were numerous because they were hindered from serving because of death. [24] But He, because He lives

---

[15] Ps 2:7.   [2 6] Ps 110:4.   [3 14] Ge 22:17.   [4 17] Ps 110:4.   [5 21] Nu 23:19; 1Sa 15:29; Ps 110:4.

forever, has an everlasting priesthood. [25] Therefore He is able to save to the uttermost those who come to God through Him, because He at all times lives to make intercession for them.

[26] For such a High Priest was fitting for us, for He is holy, innocent, undefiled, separate from sinners, and is higher than the heavens. [27] Unlike those high priests, He does not need to offer daily sacrifices—first for His own sins and then for the people's, for He did this once for all when He offered up Himself. [28] For the law appoints men who are weak as high priests, but the word of the oath, which came after the law, appoints a Son who is made perfect forever.

Jesus Our High Priest

8 Now this is the main point of the things that we are saying: We have such a High Priest, who is seated at the right hand of the throne of the Majesty in the heavens, [2] a minister in the sanctuary and the true tabernacle, which the Lord, not man, set up.

[3] For every high priest is appointed to offer gifts and sacrifices. Therefore it is necessary that this priest also have something to offer. [4] For if He were on earth, He would not be a priest, since there are priests that offer gifts according to the law. [5] They serve in a sanctuary that is an example and shadow of the heavenly one, as Moses was instructed by God when he was about to make the tabernacle, "See that you make all things according to the pattern shown you on the mountain." [1] [6] But now He has obtained a more excellent ministry, because He is the Mediator of a better covenant, which was established on better promises.

[7] For if that first covenant had been faultless, then no occasion would have been sought for a second. [8] For finding fault with them, God says:

"Surely the days are coming, says the Lord,
when I will make a new covenant
with the house of Israel
and with the house of Judah,
[9] not according to the covenant
that I made with their fathers
in the day when I took them by the hand
to lead them out of the land of Egypt;
because they did not continue in My covenant,
and I rejected them, says the Lord.
[10] This is the covenant that I will make with the house of Israel
after those days, says the Lord:
I will put My laws into their minds
and write them on their hearts;
and I will be their God,
and they shall be My people.
[11] No longer shall every man teach his neighbor,
and every man his brother, saying, 'Know the Lord,'
for all shall know Me,
from the least of them to the greatest. [2]
[12] For I will be merciful toward their unrighteousness,
and their sins and their lawless deeds I will remember
no more." [3]

[13] In speaking of a new covenant He has made the first one old. Now that which is decaying and growing old is ready to vanish away.

The Earthly and Heavenly Sanctuaries

9 Then indeed, the first covenant had ordinances for divine services and an earthly sanctuary. [2] A tabernacle was made. In the first part of the tabernacle, called the Holy Place, were the candlestick, the table, and the showbread. [3] Behind the second veil was the second part of the tabernacle called the Most Holy Place, [4] which contained the golden censer and the ark of the covenant overlaid with gold, containing the golden pot holding the manna, Aaron's rod that budded, and the tablets of the covenant. [5] Above the ark were the cherubim of glory overshadowing the mercy seat. Concerning these things we cannot now speak in detail.

[6] Now when these things were thus ordained, the priests would regularly go into the first part, conducting the services of God. [7] But only the high priest went into the second part once a year, not without blood, which he offered for himself and for the sins of the people, committed in ignorance. [8] The Holy Spirit was signifying through this that the way into the Most Holy Place was not yet revealed, because the first part of the tabernacle was still standing. [9] This is an illustration for the present time, showing that the gifts and sacrifices offered could not perfect the conscience of those who worshipped, [10] since they are concerned only with foods and drinks, ceremonial cleansings, and fleshly ordinances imposed until the time of reformation.

[11] But Christ, when He came as a High Priest of the good things to come, by a greater and more perfect tabernacle, not made with hands, that is to say, not of this creation, [12] neither by the blood of goats and calves, but by His own blood, He entered the Most Holy Place once for all, having obtained eternal redemption. [13] For if the blood of bulls and goats, and the ashes of a heifer, sprinkling the unclean, sanctifies so that the flesh is purified, [14] how much more shall the blood of Christ, who through the eternal Spirit offered Himself without blemish to God, cleanse your conscience from dead works to serve the living God?

[15] For this reason He is the Mediator of a new covenant, since a death has occurred for the redemption of the sins that were committed under the first covenant, so that those who are called might receive the promise of eternal inheritance.

[16] For where there is a will, there must also of necessity be the death of the testator. [17] For a will has force after men are dead, since it has no force at all while the testator lives. [18] So not even the first covenant was inaugurated without blood. [19] For when Moses had taught every precept to all the people according to the law, he took the blood of calves and goats, with water, scarlet wool, and hyssop, and sprinkled both the book and all the people, [20] saying, "This is the blood of the covenant that God has commanded you to keep." [4] [21] Likewise he sprinkled both the tabernacle and all the vessels of worship with blood. [22] And according to the law almost everything must be cleansed with blood; without the shedding of blood there is no forgiveness.

Christ's Sacrifice Takes Away Sin

[23] It was therefore necessary that the replicas of heavenly things be cleansed with these sacrifices, but that the heavenly things themselves be cleansed with better sacrifices than these. [24] For Christ did not enter holy places made with hands, which are patterned after the true one, but into heaven itself, now to appear in the presence of God for us. [25] Nor did He enter to offer Himself often, as the high priest enters the Most Holy Place every year with blood that is not His own. [26] For then He would have had to suffer repeatedly since the world was created, but now He has appeared once at the end of the ages to put away sin by sacrificing Himself. [27] As it is appointed for men to die once, but after this comes the judgment, [28] so Christ was offered once to bear the sins of many, and He will appear a second time, not to bear sin but to save those who eagerly wait for Him.

10 For the law is a shadow of the good things to come, and not the very image of those things. It could never by the same sacrifices, which they offer continually year after year, perfect those who draw near. [2] Otherwise, would they not have ceased to be offered, since the worshippers, once purified, would no longer be conscious of sins? [3] But in those sacrifices there is an annual reminder of sins. [4] For it is not possible for the blood of bulls and goats to take away sins.

[5] Therefore, when He came into the world, He said:

"Sacrifices and offerings You did not desire,
but a body You have prepared for Me.
[6] In burnt offerings and sacrifices for sin
You have had no pleasure.

---

[1] 5 Ex 25:40.   [2] 11 Isa 54:13.   [3] 8–12 Isa 43:25; Jer 31:31–34; 50:20; Mic 7:18–19.   [4] 20 Ex 24:8.

[7] Then I said, 'See, I have come to do Your will, O God,' as it is
      written of Me
      in the volume of the book.'" [1]

[8] Previously when He said, "You did not desire sacrifices and offerings. You have had no pleasure in burnt offerings and sacrifices for sin," [2] which are offered in accordance with the law, [9] then He said, "See, I have come to do Your will, O God." [3] He takes away the first that He may establish the second. [10] By this will we have been sanctified through the offering of the body of Jesus Christ once for all.

[11] But every priest stands daily ministering and repetitively offering the same sacrifices, which can never take away sins. [12] But this Man, after He had offered one sacrifice for sins forever, sat down at the right hand of God. [13] Since that time He has been waiting for His enemies to be made His footstool. [14] For by one offering He has forever perfected those who are sanctified.

[15] The Holy Spirit also witnesses to us about this. For after saying,

[16] "This is the covenant that I will make with them
      after those days, says the Lord:
  I will put My laws into their hearts,
      and in their minds I will write them," [4]

[17] then He adds,

  "Their sins and lawless deeds
      will I remember no more." [5]

[18] Now where there is forgiveness of these, there is no longer an offering for sin.

Exhortation and Warning

[19] Therefore, brothers, we have confidence to enter the Most Holy Place by the blood of Jesus, [20] by a new and living way that He has opened for us through the veil, that is to say, His flesh, [21] and since we have a High Priest over the house of God, [22] let us draw near with a true heart in full assurance of faith, having our hearts sprinkled to cleanse them from an evil conscience, and our bodies washed with pure water. [23] Let us firmly hold the profession of our faith without wavering, for He who promised is faithful. [24] And let us consider how to spur one another to love and to good works. [25] Let us not forsake the assembling of ourselves together, as is the manner of some, but let us exhort one another, especially as you see the Day approaching.

[26] For if we willfully continue to sin after we have received the knowledge of the truth, there no longer remains a sacrifice for sins, [27] but a fearful expectation of judgment and fiery indignation, which will devour the adversaries. [28] Anyone who despised Moses' law died without mercy in the presence of two or three witnesses. [29] How much more severe a punishment do you suppose he deserves, who has trampled under foot the Son of God, and has regarded the blood of the covenant that sanctified him to be a common thing, and has insulted the Spirit of grace? [30] For we know Him who said, "Vengeance is Mine," says the Lord, "I will repay." [6] And again He says, "The Lord will judge His people." [7] [31] It is a fearful thing to fall into the hands of the living God.

[32] Remember the former days, after you were enlightened, in which you endured a great struggle of afflictions. [33] In part you were made a spectacle both by reproaches and afflictions. And in part you became companions of those who were so abused. [34] For you had compassion on me in my chains and joyfully endured the confiscation of your property, knowing that you have in heaven a better and an enduring possession for yourselves. [35] Therefore do not throw away your confidence, which will be greatly rewarded.

[36] For you need patience, so that after you have done the will of God, you will receive the promise. [37] For,

"In yet a little while,
      He who is to come will come, and will not wait.
[38] Now the just shall live by faith;
      but if anyone draws back,
      My soul shall have no pleasure in him." [8]

[39] But we are not of those who draw back to destruction, but of those who have faith to the saving of the soul.

Faith

11 Now faith is the substance of things hoped for, the evidence of things not seen. [2] For by it the men of old obtained a good report.

[3] By faith we understand that the universe was framed by the word of God, so that things that are seen were not made out of things which are visible.

[4] By faith Abel offered to God a more excellent sacrifice than Cain offered. Through this he was approved as righteous, with God testifying concerning his gifts. He still speaks through his faith, though he is dead.

[5] By faith Enoch was taken to heaven so that he would not see death. He was not found, because God took him away. For before he was taken, he had this commendation, that he pleased God. [6] And without faith it is impossible to please God, for he who comes to God must believe that He exists and that He is a rewarder of those who diligently seek Him.

[7] By faith Noah, being divinely warned about things not yet seen, moved with godly fear, prepared an ark to save his family, by which he condemned the world and became an heir of the righteousness that comes by faith.

[8] By faith Abraham obeyed when he was called to go out into a place which he would later receive as an inheritance. He went out not knowing where he was going. [9] By faith he dwelt in the promised land, as in a foreign land, dwelling in tents with Isaac and Jacob, the heirs of the same promise, [10] for he was looking for a city which has foundations, whose builder and maker is God. [11] By faith Sarah herself also received the ability to conceive seed, and she bore a child when she was past the age, because she judged Him faithful who had promised. [12] Therefore from one man, who was as good as dead, sprang so many, a multitude as the stars of the sky and innumerable as the sand by the seashore.

[13] These all died in faith not having received the promises, but having seen them from afar were assured of them, embraced them, and confessed that they were strangers and pilgrims on the earth. [14] Those who say such things declare plainly that they are looking for a homeland. [15] And certainly, if they had been thinking of the country out of which they came, they might have had the opportunity to return. [16] But they desired a better country, that is, a heavenly one. Therefore God is not ashamed to be called their God, for He has prepared a city for them.

[17] By faith Abraham, when he was tested, offered up Isaac, and he who had received the promises offered up his only begotten son. [18] Of him God said, "Through Isaac shall your seed be named." [9] [19] He reasoned that God was able to raise him up, even from the dead, from which he indeed received him in a figurative sense.

[20] By faith Isaac blessed Jacob and Esau concerning things to come.

[21] By faith Jacob, when he was dying, blessed each of the sons of Joseph and worshipped while leaning on the top of his staff.

[22] By faith Joseph, when he was dying, mentioned the exodus of the children of Israel and gave instructions concerning his bones.

[23] By faith Moses, when he was born, was hidden by his parents for three months, because they saw he was a beautiful child, and they were not afraid of the king's command.

[24] By faith Moses, when he became of age, refused to be called the son of Pharaoh's daughter, [25] choosing rather to suffer affliction with the people of God than to enjoy the pleasures of sin for a time. [26] He esteemed the reproach of Christ as greater riches than the treasures in Egypt, for he looked to the reward. [27] By faith he

---

[1] 5–7 Ps 40:6–8.   [2] 8 Ps 40:6.   [3] 9 Ps 40:8.   [4] 16 Jer 31:33.   [5] 17 Jer 31:34.   [6] 30 Dt 32:35.   [7] 30 Dt 32:36.   [8] 37–38 Hab 2:3–4.   [9] 18 Ge 21:12.

forsook Egypt, not fearing the wrath of the king. He endured by looking to Him who is invisible. [28] By faith he kept the Passover and the sprinkling of blood, lest the one who destroys the firstborn touch them.

[29] By faith they passed through the Red Sea as on dry land, which the Egyptians attempted to do, but were drowned.

[30] By faith the walls of Jericho fell down after they were encircled for seven days.

[31] By faith the prostitute Rahab, when she received the spies with peace, did not perish with those who did not believe.

[32] And what more shall I say? For time would fail me to tell of Gideon, Barak, Samson, Jephthah, of David and Samuel and the prophets, [33] who through faith subdued kingdoms, administered justice, obtained promises, stopped the mouths of lions, [34] quenched the violence of fire, escaped the edge of the sword, out of weakness were made strong, became valiant in fighting, and turned the armies of foreign enemies to flight. [35] Women received their dead raised to life again. Others were tortured and did not accept deliverance, so that they might obtain a better resurrection. [36] Still others had trials of mocking and scourging, and even chains and imprisonment. [37] They were stoned, they were sawn in two, were tempted, were slain with the sword. They wandered around in sheepskins and goatskins, while destitute, afflicted, and tormented. [38] The world was not worthy of them. They wandered in deserts and mountains, in dens and caves of the earth.

[39] These all have obtained a good report through faith, but they did not receive the promise. [40] For God provided something better for us, so that with us they would be made perfect.

The Discipline of the Lord

12 Therefore, since we are encompassed with such a great cloud of witnesses, let us also lay aside every weight and the sin that so easily entangles us, and let us run with endurance the race that is set before us. [2] Let us look to Jesus, the author and finisher of our faith, who for the joy that was set before Him endured the cross, despising the shame, and is seated at the right hand of the throne of God. [3] For consider Him who endured such hostility from sinners against Himself, lest you become weary and your hearts give up.

[4] You have not yet resisted to bloodshed while striving against sin. [5] And you have forgotten the exhortation addressed to you as sons:

"My son, do not despise the discipline from the Lord,
　nor grow weary when you are rebuked by Him;
[6] for whom the Lord loves He disciplines,
　and scourges every son whom He receives." [1]

[7] Endure discipline; God is dealing with you as with sons. For what son is there whom a father does not discipline? [8] If you are without discipline, of which everyone has partaken, then you are illegitimate children and not sons. [9] Furthermore, we have had human fathers, and they corrected us, and we gave them reverence. Shall we not much more be subject to the Father of spirits and live? [10] For they indeed disciplined us for a short time according to their own judgment, but He does so for our profit, that we may partake of His holiness. [11] Now no discipline seems to be joyful at the time, but grievous. Yet afterward it yields the peaceful fruit of righteousness in those who have been trained by it.

[12] Therefore lift up your tired hands, and strengthen your weak knees. [13] Make straight paths for your feet, lest that which is lame go out of joint, but rather be healed.

Warning Against Rejecting God's Grace

[14] Pursue peace with all men, and the holiness without which no one will see the Lord, [15] watching diligently so that no one falls short of the grace of God, lest any root of bitterness spring up to cause trouble, and many become defiled by it, [16] lest there be any sexually immoral or profane person, as Esau, who for one morsel of food sold his birthright. [17] For you know that afterward, when he wanted to inherit the blessing, he was rejected.

For he found no place for repentance, though he sought it diligently with tears.

[18] You have not come to a mountain that can be touched and that burned with fire, and to blackness and darkness and storm, [19] and to the sound of a trumpet and to a voice speaking words, such that those who heard them begged that the word not be spoken to them anymore. [20] For they could not endure that which was commanded: "If so much as a beast touches the mountain, it must be stoned or thrust through with a spear." [2] [21] So terrible was the sight that Moses said, "I am terrified and trembling." [3]

[22] But you have come to Mount Zion and to the city of the living God, the heavenly Jerusalem, and to an innumerable company of angels; [23] to the general assembly and church of the firstborn, who are enrolled in heaven; to God, the Judge of all; and to the spirits of the righteous ones made perfect; [24] and to Jesus, the Mediator of a new covenant; and to the sprinkled blood that speaks better than that of Abel.

[25] See that you do not refuse Him who is speaking. For if they did not escape when they refused Him who spoke on earth, much less shall we escape if we turn away from Him who speaks from heaven. [26] At that time His voice shook the earth, but now He has given us a promise, saying, "Yet once more I will shake not only the earth but also heaven." [4] [27] And this statement, "Yet once more," signifies the removal of those things that can be shaken, things that are created, so that only those things that cannot be shaken will remain.

[28] Therefore, since we are receiving a kingdom that cannot be moved, let us be gracious, by which we may serve God acceptably with reverence and godly fear. [29] For our God is a consuming fire.

Service That Pleases God

13 Let brotherly love continue. [2] Do not forget to entertain strangers, for thereby some have entertained angels unknowingly. [3] Remember those who are in chains, as if imprisoned with them, and those who are ill treated, since you are also in the body.

[4] Marriage is to be honored among everyone, and the bed undefiled. But God will judge the sexually immoral and adulterers. [5] Let your lives be without love of money, and be content with the things you have. For He has said:

"I will never leave you,
　nor forsake you." [5]

[6] So we may boldly say:

"The Lord is my helper; I will not fear.
　What can man do to me?" [6]

[7] Remember those who rule over you, who have proclaimed to you the word of God. Follow their faith, considering the results it has produced in their lives. [8] Jesus Christ is the same yesterday, and today, and forever.

[9] Do not be carried away with diverse and strange doctrines. It is a good thing that the heart be strengthened with grace, not with foods, which have not profited those who have been occupied with them. [10] We have an altar from which those who serve in the tabernacle have no right to eat.

[11] For the bodies of those beasts, whose blood is brought into the sanctuary by the high priest on account of sin, are burned outside the camp. [12] Therefore Jesus also, so that He might sanctify the people with His own blood, suffered outside the gate. [13] Therefore let us go forth to Him outside the camp, bearing the reproach that He bore. [14] For here we have no continuing city, but we seek one to come.

[15] Through Him, then, let us continually offer to God the sacrifice of praise, which is the fruit of our lips, giving thanks to His name. [16] But do not forget to do good and to share. For with such sacrifices God is well pleased.

---

1 5–6 Pr 3:11–12.　*2* 20 Ex 19:12–13.　*3* 21 Dt 9:19.　*4* 26 Hag 2:6.　*5* 5 Dt 31:6, 8; Jos 1:5.　*6* 6 Ps 118:6.

[17] Obey your leaders and submit to them, for they watch over your souls as those who must give an account. Let them do this with joy and not complaining, for that would not be profitable to you.

[18] Pray for us. For we trust that we have a good conscience and in all things are willing to live honestly. [19] But I implore you to pray, that I may be restored to you very soon.

Benediction and Final Greetings

[20] Now may the God of peace, who through the blood of the eternal covenant brought again from the dead our Lord Jesus, the Great Shepherd of the sheep, [21] make you perfect in every good work to do His will, working in you that which is pleasing in His sight, through Jesus Christ, to whom be glory forever and ever. Amen.

[22] I implore you, brothers, to heed this word of exhortation, for I have written to you in few words. [23] Know that our brother Timothy has been set free, with whom I shall see you if he comes soon.

[24] Greet all those who rule over you and all the saints. Those from Italy greet you.

[25] Grace be with you all. Amen.

JAMES

Salutation

1 James, a servant of God and of the Lord Jesus Christ,

To the twelve tribes which are scattered abroad:

Greetings.

Faith and Wisdom

[2] My brothers, count it all joy when you fall into diverse temptations, [3] knowing that the trying of your faith develops patience. [4] But let patience perfect its work, that you may be perfect and complete, lacking nothing. [5] If any of you lacks wisdom, let him ask of God, who gives to all men liberally and without criticism, and it will be given to him. [6] But let him ask in faith, without wavering. For he who wavers is like a wave of the sea, driven and tossed with the wind. [7] Let not that man think that he will receive anything from the Lord. [8] A double-minded man is unstable in all his ways.

Poverty and Riches

[9] Let the brother of low degree rejoice in that he is exalted, [10] but the rich in that he is made low, because as the flower of the grass he will pass away. [11] For the sun rises with a burning heat and it withers the grass, and its flowers fall, and its beauty perishes. So will the rich man wither away in his ways.

Trial and Temptation

[12] Blessed is the man who endures temptation, for when he is tried, he will receive the crown of life, which the Lord has promised to those who love Him. [13] Let no man say when he is tempted, "I am tempted by God," for God cannot be tempted with evil; neither does He tempt anyone. [14] But each man is tempted when he is drawn away by his own lust and enticed. [15] Then, when lust has conceived, it brings forth sin; and when sin is finished, it brings forth death.

[16] Do not err, my beloved brothers. [17] Every good gift and every perfect gift is from above and comes down from the Father of lights, with whom is no change or shadow of turning. [18] Of His own will He brought us forth with the word of truth, that we should be a kind of first fruits of His creatures.

Hearing and Doing the Word

[19] Therefore, my beloved brothers, let every man be swift to hear, slow to speak, and slow to anger, [20] for the anger of man does not work the righteousness of God. [21] Therefore lay aside all filthiness and remaining wickedness and receive with meekness the engrafted word, which is able to save your souls.

[22] Be doers of the word and not hearers only, deceiving yourselves. [23] For if anyone is a hearer of the word and not a doer, he is like a man viewing his natural face in a mirror. [24] He views himself, and goes his way, and immediately forgets what kind of man he was. [25] But whoever looks into the perfect law of liberty, and continues in it, and is not a forgetful hearer but a doer of the work, this man will be blessed in his deeds.

[26] If anyone among you seems to be religious and does not bridle his tongue, but deceives his own heart, this man's religion is vain. [27] Religion that is pure and undefiled before God, the Father, is this: to visit the fatherless and widows in their affliction and to keep oneself unstained by the world.

Warning Against Partiality

2 My brothers, have faith in our Lord Jesus Christ, the Lord of glory, without partiality. [2] For if a man with a gold ring, in fine clothing, comes into your assembly, and also a poor man in ragged clothing comes in, [3] and you have respect for him who wears the fine clothing and say to him, "Sit here in a good place," and say to the poor, "Stand there," or "Sit here under my footstool," [4] have you not then become partial among yourselves and become judges with evil thoughts?

[5] Listen, my beloved brothers. Has God not chosen the poor of this world to be rich in faith and heirs of the kingdom which He has promised to those who love Him? [6] But you have despised the poor. Do not rich men oppress you and drag you before the judgment seats? [7] Do they not blaspheme that worthy name by which you are called?

[8] If you fulfill the royal law according to the Scripture, "You shall love your neighbor as yourself,"[1] you are doing well. [9] But if you show partiality, you are committing sin and are convicted by the law as sinners. [10] For whoever shall keep the whole law and yet offend in one point is guilty of breaking the whole law. [11] For He who said, "Do not commit adultery,"[2] also said, "Do not kill."[3] Now if you do not commit adultery, yet you kill, you have become a lawbreaker.

[12] So speak and so do as those who will be judged by the law of liberty. [13] For he who has shown no mercy will have judgment without mercy, for mercy triumphs over judgment.

Faith and Works

[14] What does it profit, my brothers, if a man says he has faith but has no works? Can faith save him? [15] If a brother or sister is naked and lacking daily food, [16] and one of you says to them, "Depart in peace, be warmed and filled," and yet you give them nothing that the body needs, what does it profit? [17] So faith by itself, if it has no works, is dead.

[18] But a man may say, "You have faith and I have works."

Show me your faith without your works, and I will show you my faith by my works. [19] You believe that there is one God; you do well. The demons also believe and tremble.

---

[1] 8 Lev 19:18.   *[2] 11* Ex 20:14; Dt 5:18.   *[3] 11* Ex 20:13; Dt 5:17.

[20] But do you want to be shown, O foolish man, that faith without works is dead? [21] Was not Abraham our father justified by works when he offered his son Isaac on the altar? [22] Do you see how faith worked with his works, and by works faith was made perfect? [23] The Scripture was fulfilled which says, "Abraham believed God, and it was reckoned to him as righteousness,"[1] and he was called the friend of God. [24] You see then how by works a man is justified, and not by faith only.

[25] Likewise, was not Rahab the prostitute justified by works when she received the messengers and sent them out another way? [26] As the body without the spirit is dead, so faith without works is dead.

The Tongue

3 My brothers, not many of you should become teachers, knowing that we shall receive the greater judgment. [2] We all err in many ways. But if any man does not err in word, he is a perfect man and able also to control the whole body.

[3] See how we put bits in the mouths of horses that they may obey us, and we control their whole bodies. [4] And observe ships. Though they are so great and are driven by fierce winds, yet they are directed with a very small rudder wherever the captain pleases. [5] Even so, the tongue is a little part of the body and boasts great things. See how great a forest a little fire kindles. [6] The tongue is a fire, a world of evil. The tongue is among the parts of the body, defiling the whole body, and setting the course of nature on fire, and it is set on fire by hell.

[7] All kinds of beasts, and birds, and serpents, and things in the sea are tamed or have been tamed by mankind. [8] But no man can tame the tongue. It is an unruly evil, full of deadly poison.

[9] With it we bless the Lord and Father, and with it we curse men, who are made in the image of God. [10] Out of the same mouth proceed blessing and cursing. My brothers, these things ought not to be so. [11] Does a spring yield at the same opening sweet and bitter water? [12] Can the fig tree, my brothers, bear olives, or a vine, figs? So no spring can yield both salt water and fresh water.

The Wisdom From Above

[13] Who is wise and understanding among you? Let him show his works by his good life in the meekness of wisdom. [14] But if you have bitter envying and strife in your hearts, do not boast and do not lie against the truth. [15] This wisdom descends not from above, but is earthly, unspiritual, and devilish. [16] For where there is envying and strife, there is confusion and every evil work.

[17] But the wisdom that is from above is first pure, then peaceable, gentle, open to reason, full of mercy and good fruits, without partiality, and without hypocrisy. [18] And the fruit of righteousness is sown in peace by those who make peace.

Friendship With the World

4 Where do wars and fights among you come from? Do they not come from your lusts that war in your body? [2] You lust and do not have, so you kill. You desire to have and cannot obtain. You fight and war. Yet you do not have, because you do not ask. [3] You ask, and do not receive, because you ask amiss, that you may spend it on your passions.

[4] You adulterers and adulteresses, do you not know that the friendship with the world is enmity with God? Whoever therefore will be a friend of the world is the enemy of God. [5] Do you think that the Scripture says in vain, "He yearns jealously for the spirit that lives in us"?[2] [6] But He gives more grace. For this reason it says:

"God resists the proud,
    but gives grace to the humble."[3]

[7] Therefore submit yourselves to God. Resist the devil, and he will flee from you. [8] Draw near to God, and He will draw near to you. Cleanse your hands, you sinners, and purify your hearts, you double-minded. [9] Grieve and mourn and weep. Let your laughter be turned to mourning, and your joy to dejection. [10] Humble yourselves in the sight of the Lord, and He will lift you up.

Judging a Brother

[11] Do not speak evil of one another, brothers. He who speaks evil of his brother and judges his brother speaks evil of the law and judges the law. If you judge the law, you are not a doer of the law, but a judge. [12] There is one Lawgiver who is able to save and to destroy. Who are you to judge another?

Warning Against Boasting

[13] Come now, you who say, "Today or tomorrow we will go into this city, spend a year there, buy and sell, and make a profit," [14] whereas you do not know what will happen tomorrow. What is your life? It is just a vapor that appears for a little while and then vanishes away. [15] Instead you ought to say, "If the Lord wills, we shall live and do this or that." [16] But now you are rejoicing in your boastings. All such rejoicing is evil. [17] Therefore, to him who knows to do good and does not do it, it is sin.

Warning to the Rich

5 Come now, you rich men, weep and howl for your miseries that shall come upon you. [2] Your riches are corrupted and your garments are moth-eaten. [3] Your gold and silver are corroded, and their corrosion will be a witness against you and will eat your flesh like fire. You have stored up treasures for the last days. [4] Indeed the wages that you kept back by fraud from the laborers who harvested your fields are crying, and the cries of those who harvested have entered into the ears of the Lord of Hosts. [5] You have lived in pleasure on the earth and have been wayward. You have nourished your hearts as in a day of slaughter. [6] You have condemned and killed the righteous man who does not resist you.

Patience and Prayer

[7] Therefore be patient, brothers, until the coming of the Lord. Notice how the farmer waits for the precious fruit of the earth and is patient with it until he receives the early and late rain. [8] You also be patient. Establish your hearts, for the coming of the Lord is drawing near. [9] Do not grumble against one another, brothers, lest you be condemned. Look, the Judge is standing at the door.

[10] My brothers, take the prophets, who spoke in the name of the Lord, as an example of suffering and patience. [11] Indeed we count them happy who endure. You have heard of the patience of Job and have seen the purpose of the Lord, that the Lord is very gracious and merciful.

[12] But above all things, my brothers, do not swear, either by heaven or by the earth or by any other oath. But let your "Yes" be "Yes" and your "No" be "No," that you do not fall into condemnation.

[13] Is anyone among you suffering? Let him pray. Is anyone merry? Let him sing psalms. [14] Is anyone sick among you? Let him call for the elders of the church, and let them pray over him, anointing him with oil in the name of the Lord. [15] And the prayer of faith will save the sick, and the Lord will raise him up. And if he has committed any sins, he will be forgiven. [16] Confess your faults to one another and pray for one another, that you may be healed. The effective, fervent prayer of a righteous man accomplishes much.

[17] Elijah was a man subject to natural passions as we are, and he prayed earnestly that it might not rain, and it did not rain on the earth for three years and six months. [18] And he prayed again, and the sky gave rain, and the earth brought forth its fruit.

[19] Brothers, if any one of you strays from the truth and someone corrects him, [20] let him know that he who converts the sinner from the error of his way will save a soul from death and will cover a multitude of sins.

---

[1] 23 Ge 15:6.   [2] 5 The source of this quotation is uncertain.   [3] 6 Pr 3:34.

1 PETER

Salutation

1 Peter, an apostle of Jesus Christ,

To the refugees scattered throughout Pontus, Galatia, Cappadocia, Asia, and Bithynia, [2] elect according to the foreknowledge of God the Father, through sanctification by the Spirit, for obedience and sprinkling with the blood of Jesus Christ:

Grace to you and peace be multiplied.

A Living Hope

[3] Blessed be the God and Father of our Lord Jesus Christ, who according to His abundant mercy has given us a new birth into a living hope through the resurrection of Jesus Christ from the dead, [4] to an incorruptible and undefiled inheritance that does not fade away, kept in heaven for you, [5] who are protected by the power of God through faith for a salvation ready to be revealed in the last time. [6] In this you greatly rejoice, even though now, if for a little while, you have had to suffer various trials, [7] in order that the genuineness of your faith, which is more precious than gold that perishes, though it is tried by fire, may be found to result in praise, glory, and honor at the revelation of Jesus Christ, [8] whom, having not seen, you love; and in whom, though you do not see Him now, you believe and you rejoice with joy unspeakable and full of glory, [9] receiving as the result of your faith the salvation of your souls. [10] Concerning this salvation, the prophets who prophesied of the grace that should come to you have inquired and searched diligently, [11] seeking the events and time the Spirit of Christ, who was within them, signified when He foretold the sufferings of Christ and the glories to follow. [12] It was revealed to them that they were not serving themselves but you, concerning the things which are now reported to you by those who have preached the gospel to you through the Holy Spirit, who was sent from heaven—things into which the angels desire to look.

A Call to Holy Living

[13] Therefore guard your minds, be sober, and hope to the end for the grace that is to be brought to you at the revelation of Jesus Christ. [14] As obedient children do not conduct yourselves according to the former lusts in your ignorance. [15] But as He who has called you is holy, so be holy in all your conduct, [16] because it is written, "Be holy, for I am holy." [1]

[17] And if you address as Father the One who impartially judges according to each one's work, conduct yourselves in fear during the time of your sojourning. [18] For you know that you were not redeemed from your vain way of life inherited from your fathers with perishable things, like silver or gold, [19] but with the precious blood of Christ, as of a lamb without blemish and without spot. [20] He was foreordained before the creation of the world, but was revealed in these last times for you. [21] Through Him you believe in God who raised Him up from the dead and gave Him glory, so that your faith and hope might be in God.

[22] Since your souls have been purified by obedience to the truth through the Spirit unto a genuine brotherly love, love one another deeply with a pure heart, [23] for you have been born again, not from perishable seed, but imperishable, through the word of God which lives and abides forever. [24] For

"All flesh is as grass,
    and all the glory of man as the flower of grass.
The grass withers, and its flower falls away,
[25]   but the word of the Lord endures forever." [2]

This is the word that was preached to you.

The Living Stone and the Holy Nation

2 Therefore put away all wickedness, deceit, hypocrisy, envy, and all evil speaking. [2] As newborn babies, desire the pure milk of the word, that by it you may grow, [3] if it is true that you have experienced that the Lord is good.

[4] Coming to Him as to a living stone who is rejected by men, but chosen by God and precious, [5] you also, as living stones, are being built up into a spiritual house as a holy priesthood to offer up spiritual sacrifices that are acceptable to God through Jesus Christ. [6] For also it is contained in the Scripture,

"Look! I lay in Zion
    a chief cornerstone, elect, precious,
and he who believes in Him
    shall never be put to shame." [3]

[7] Therefore, to you who believe, He is precious. But to those who are disobedient,

"The stone that the builders rejected
    has become the cornerstone," [4]

[8] and,

"A stone of stumbling,
    and a rock of offense." [5]

They stumble because they are disobedient to the word, to which also they were appointed. [9] But you are a chosen race, a royal priesthood, a holy nation, a people for God's own possession, so that you may declare the goodness of Him who has called you out of darkness into His marvelous light. [10] In times past, you were not a people, but now you are the people of God. You had not received mercy, but now you have received mercy.

Live as Servants of God

[11] Dearly beloved, I implore you as aliens and refugees, abstain from fleshly lusts, which wage war against the soul. [12] Live your lives honorably among the Gentiles, so that though they speak against you as evildoers, they shall see your good works and thereby glorify God in the day of visitation.

[13] Submit yourselves to every human authority for the Lord's sake, whether it be to the king, as supreme, [14] or to governors, as sent by him for the punishment of evildoers and to praise those who do right. [15] For it is the will of God that by doing right you may put to silence the ignorance of foolish men. [16] As free people, do not use your liberty as a covering for evil, but live as servants of God. [17] Honor all people. Love the brotherhood. Fear God. Honor the king.

The Example of Christ's Suffering

[18] Servants, be submissive to your masters with all fear, not only to the good and gentle, but also to the harsh. [19] For this is commendable, if because of conscience toward God a person endures grief, suffering unjustly. [20] For what credit is it if when you are being beaten for your sins you patiently endure? But if when doing good and suffering for it, you patiently endure, this is favorable before God. [21] For to this you were called, because Christ suffered for us, leaving us an example, that you should follow His steps:

[22] "He committed no sin,
    nor was deceit found in His mouth." [6]

[23] When He was reviled, He did not revile back; when He suffered, He did not threaten, but He entrusted Himself to Him who judges

---

[1] 16 Lev 11:44; 19:2; 20:7.   [2] 24–25 Isa 40:6–8.   [3] 6 Isa 28:16.   [4] 7 Ps 118:22.   [5] 8 Isa 8:14.   [6] 22 Isa 53:9.

righteously. [24] He Himself bore our sins in His own body on the tree, that we, being dead to sins, should live unto righteousness. "By His wounds you were healed."[1] [25] For you were as sheep going astray, but now have been returned to the Shepherd and Guardian of your souls.

Wives and Husbands

3 Likewise you wives, be submissive to your own husbands, so that if any do not obey the word, they may be won without a word by the conduct of their wives, [2] as they see the purity and reverence of your lives. [3] Do not let your adorning be the outward adorning of braiding the hair, wearing gold, or putting on fine clothing. [4] But let it be the hidden nature of the heart, that which is not corruptible, even the ornament of a gentle and quiet spirit, which is very precious in the sight of God. [5] For in this manner, in the old times, the holy women, who trusted in God, adorned themselves, being submissive to their own husbands, [6] even as Sarah obeyed Abraham, calling him lord. You are her children as long as you do right and are not afraid with any terror.

[7] Likewise, you husbands, live considerately with your wives, giving honor to the woman as the weaker vessel, since they too are also heirs of the grace of life, so that your prayers will not be hindered.

Suffering for Righteousness' Sake

[8] Finally, be all of one mind, be loving toward one another, be gracious, and be kind. [9] Do not repay evil for evil, or curse for curse, but on the contrary, bless, knowing that to this you are called, so that you may receive a blessing. [10] For

"He who would love life
and see good days,
let him keep his tongue from evil,
and his lips from speaking deceit.
[11] Let him turn away from evil and do good;
let him seek peace and pursue it.
[12] For the eyes of the Lord are on the righteous,
and His ears are open to their prayers;
but the face of the Lord is against those who do evil."[2]

[13] Who is he who will harm you if you follow that which is good? [14] But even if you suffer for the sake of righteousness, you are blessed. "Do not be afraid of their terror, do not be troubled."[3] [15] But sanctify the Lord God in your hearts. Always be ready to give an answer to every man who asks you for a reason for the hope that is in you, with gentleness and fear. [16] Have a good conscience so that evildoers who speak evil of you and falsely accuse your good conduct in Christ may be ashamed. [17] For it is better, if it is the will of God, that you suffer for doing good than for doing evil. [18] For Christ also has once suffered for sins, the just for the unjust, so that He might bring us to God, being put to death in the flesh, but made alive by the Spirit, [19] by whom He also went and preached to the spirits in prison, [20] who in times past were disobedient, when God waited patiently in the days of Noah while the ark was being prepared, in which a few, that is, eight souls, were saved through water. [21] Figuratively this is like baptism, which also saves us now. It is not washing off the dirt from the body, but a response to God from a good conscience through the resurrection of Jesus Christ, [22] who has gone into heaven and is at the right hand of God, with angels and authorities and powers being made subject to Him.

Good Stewards of God's Grace

4 Therefore, since Christ has suffered for us in the flesh, arm yourselves likewise with the same mind, for he who has suffered in the flesh has ceased from sin, [2] so that he no longer should live the rest of his time in the flesh serving human desires, but the will of God. [3] For in earlier times of our lives it may have sufficed us to do what the Gentiles like to do, when we walked in immorality: lusts, drunkenness, carousing, debauchery, and abominable idolatries. [4] They are surprised that you do not join them in the same excess of wild living, and so they speak evil of you. [5] They will give account to Him who is ready to judge the living and the dead.

[6] For this reason the gospel was preached also to those who are dead, so that even though they might be judged according to men in the flesh, they might live according to God in the spirit.

[7] The end of all things is near. Therefore be solemn and sober so you can pray. [8] Above all things, have unfailing love for one another, because love covers a multitude of sins. [9] Show hospitality to one another without complaining. [10] As everyone has received a gift, even so serve one another with it, as good stewards of the manifold grace of God. [11] If anyone speaks, let him speak as the oracles of God. If anyone serves, let him serve with the strength that God supplies, so that God in all things may be glorified through Jesus Christ, to whom be praise and dominion forever and ever. Amen.

Suffering as a Christian

[12] Beloved, do not be surprised at the fiery ordeal that is taking place among you to test you, as though some strange thing happened to you. [13] But rejoice insofar as you share in Christ's sufferings, so that you may rejoice and be glad also in the revelation of His glory. [14] If you are reproached because of the name of Christ, you are blessed, because the Spirit of glory and of God rests upon you. On their part He is blasphemed, but on your part He is glorified. [15] Let none of you suffer as a murderer, or a thief, or an evildoer, or even as a busybody. [16] Yet if anyone suffers as a Christian, let him not be ashamed, but let him glorify God because of it. [17] For the time has come for judgment to begin at the house of God, and if it begins first with us, what shall the end be for those who do not obey the gospel of God? [18] And

"If the righteous one is scarcely saved,
where shall the ungodly and the sinner appear?"[4]

[19] So then, let those who suffer according to the will of God entrust their souls to a faithful Creator, while continuing to do good.

Tending the Flock of God

5 I exhort the elders who are among you, as one who is also an elder and a witness of the sufferings of Christ as well as a partaker of the glory that shall be revealed: [2] Shepherd the flock of God that is among you, take care of them, not by constraint, but willingly, not for dishonest gain, but eagerly. [3] Do not lord over those in your charge, but be examples to the flock. [4] And when the chief Shepherd appears, you will receive a crown of glory that will not fade away.

[5] Likewise you younger ones, submit yourselves to the elders. Yes, all of you be submissive one to another and clothe yourselves with humility, because

"God resists the proud,
but gives grace to the humble."[5]

[6] Humble yourselves under the mighty hand of God, that He may exalt you in due time. [7] Cast all your care upon Him, because He cares for you.

[8] Be sober and watchful, because your adversary the devil walks around as a roaring lion, seeking whom he may devour. [9] Resist him firmly in the faith, knowing that the same afflictions are experienced by your brotherhood throughout the world.

[10] But after you have suffered a little while, the God of all grace, who has called us to His eternal glory through Christ Jesus, will restore, support, strengthen, and establish you. [11] To Him be glory and dominion forever and ever. Amen.

Final Greetings

[12] With the help of Silas, whom I consider to be a faithful brother to you, I have written briefly, exhorting you and testifying that this is the true grace of God in which you stand.

[13] The church that is at Babylon, elect together with you, greets you, and so does Mark, my son. [14] Greet one another with a kiss of love.

Peace be with all you who are in Christ Jesus. Amen.

---

[1] 24 Isa 53:5.   [2] 10–12 Ps 34:12–16.   [3] 14 Isa 8:12.   [4] 18 Pr 11:31.   [5] 5 Pr 3:34.

2 PETER

Salutation

1 Simon Peter, a servant and apostle of Jesus Christ,

To those who have received a faith as precious as ours through the righteousness of our God and Savior Jesus Christ.

[2] Grace and peace be multiplied to you through the knowledge of God and of Jesus our Lord.

The Christian's Call and Election

[3] His divine power has given to us all things that pertain to life and godliness through the knowledge of Him who has called us by His own glory and excellence, [4] by which He has given to us exceedingly great and precious promises, so that through these things you might become partakers of the divine nature and escape the corruption that is in the world through lust.

[5] For this reason make every effort to add virtue to your faith; and to your virtue, knowledge; [6] and to your knowledge, self-control; and to your self-control, patient endurance; and to your patient endurance, godliness; [7] and to your godliness, brotherly kindness; and to your brotherly kindness, love. [8] For if these things reside in you and abound, they ensure that you will neither be useless nor unfruitful in the knowledge of our Lord Jesus Christ. [9] But the one who lacks these things is blind and shortsighted because he has forgotten that he was cleansed from his former sins.

[10] Therefore, brothers, diligently make your calling and election sure. For if you do these things, you will never stumble. [11] For in this way the entrance into the eternal kingdom of our Lord and Savior Jesus Christ will be abundantly provided for you.

[12] Therefore I will not be negligent to always remind you of these things, though you know them and are established in the truth that is present with you. [13] I consider it right, as long as I live in this body, to stir you up by reminding you, [14] knowing that soon I will take off this body, even as our Lord Jesus Christ has shown me. [15] And I will also be diligent to make sure that after my death you will always remember these things.

Christ's Glory and the Prophetic Word

[16] For we have not followed cleverly devised myths when we made known to you the power and coming of our Lord Jesus Christ, but we were eyewitnesses of His majesty. [17] For He received honor and glory from God the Father when a voice came to Him from the majestic glory, saying, "This is My beloved Son, in whom I am well pleased." [1] [18] And we ourselves heard this voice, which came from heaven, when we were with Him on the holy mountain.

[19] And we have a more reliable word of prophecy, which you would do well to follow, as to a light that shines in a dark place, until the day dawns and the morning star arises in your hearts. [20] But know this first of all, that no prophecy of the Scripture is a matter of one's own interpretation. [21] For no prophecy at any time was produced by the will of man, but holy men moved by the Holy Spirit spoke from God.

False Prophets and Teachers
Jude 4–13

2 But there were also false prophets among the people, just as there will be false teachers among you, who will secretly bring in destructive heresies, even denying the Lord who bought them, bringing swift destruction upon themselves. [2] And many will follow their destructive ways, because of whom the way of truth will be blasphemed. [3] And in their greed they will exploit you with deceptive words. Their judgment, made long ago, does not linger, and their destruction does not slumber.

[4] For if God did not spare the angels that sinned, but cast them down to hell and delivered them into chains of darkness to be kept for judgment; [5] and if He did not spare the ancient world, but saved Noah, a preacher of righteousness, with seven others, when He brought a flood upon the world of the ungodly; [6] and if He condemned the cities of Sodom and Gomorrah to destruction by reducing them to ashes, making them an example to those afterward who would live ungodly lives; [7] and if He delivered righteous Lot, who was distressed by the filthy conduct of the wicked [8] (for that righteous man lived among them, and what he saw and heard of their lawless deeds tormented his righteous soul day after day); [9] then the Lord knows how to rescue the godly from trial, and to keep the unrighteous under punishment for the Day of Judgment, [10] especially those who walk after the flesh in pursuit of unclean desires, and despise authority.

They are presumptuous and arrogant, and are not afraid to slander the angelic beings. [11] Whereas angels, who are greater in power and might, do not bring slanderous accusations against them before the Lord. [12] But these people are like irrational animals, born to be captured and destroyed. They speak evil of the things that they do not understand, and in their corruption they will be destroyed.

[13] They shall receive the wages of unrighteousness. They count it a pleasure to carouse in the daytime. They are blots and blemishes who revel in their own deception while they carouse together with you. [14] They have eyes full of adultery that cannot cease from sin. They entice unstable souls. Their hearts are trained in greed. They are cursed children! [15] They have forsaken the right way and have gone astray. They follow the way of Balaam the son of Beor, who loved the wages of wickedness; [16] but who was rebuked for his iniquity. The mute donkey speaking with a man's voice constrained the madness of the prophet.

[17] These men are wells without water and clouds that are carried by a storm, for whom the gloom of darkness has been reserved forever. [18] For when they speak arrogant words of vanity, they entice by the lusts of the flesh and by depravity those who barely escaped from those who live in error. [19] Although they promise them freedom, they themselves are slaves of corruption, for by that which a man is overcome, to this he is enslaved. [20] For if after they have escaped the defilements of the world through the knowledge of the Lord and Savior Jesus Christ, and they are again entangled in them and are overcome, the latter end is worse for them than the beginning. [21] For it would have been better for them not to have known the way of righteousness than to have known it and then turn back from the holy commandment that was delivered to them. [22] But it has happened to them according to the true proverb, "The dog returns to his own vomit," [2] and "the sow that was washed to her wallowing in the mud."

The Promise of the Lord's Coming

3 This is now, beloved, the second epistle I am writing to you, in which I am stirring up your sincere minds by way of reminder, [2] that you should remember the words that were spoken previously by the holy prophets and the commandment of our Lord and Savior spoken through us, the apostles.

[3] Know this first, that there shall come scoffers in the last days who walk after their own lusts, [4] and say, "Where is the promise of His coming? For since the fathers fell asleep, all things have continued as they were since the beginning of the creation." [5] For they willingly ignore that, by the word of God the heavens existed long ago, and the earth was formed standing out of the water and in the water, [6] by which the world that then existed was flooded with water and perished. [7] But by the same word, the heavens and the earth that now exist are being reserved for fire, kept for the Day of Judgment and destruction of the ungodly.

[8] But, beloved, do not be ignorant of this one thing, that with the Lord one day is as a thousand years, and a thousand years as one day. [9] The Lord is not slow concerning His promise, as some count

slowness. But He is patient with us, because He does not want any to perish, but all to come to repentance.

[10] But the day of the Lord will come like a thief in the night, in which the heavens will pass away with a loud noise, and the elements will be destroyed with intense heat. The earth also and the works that are in it will be burned up.

[11] Seeing then that all these things are to be destroyed, what sort of people ought you to be in holy conduct and godliness, [12] while you are waiting for and desiring the coming of the day of God, in which the heavens will be destroyed by fire and the elements will be consumed by intense heat? [13] But, according to His promise, we are waiting for new heavens and a new earth, in which righteousness dwells.

[14] Therefore, beloved, since you are waiting for these things, be diligent that you may be found by Him in peace, spotless and blameless. [15] Keep in mind that the patience of our Lord means salvation, even as our beloved brother Paul has also written to you according to the wisdom given to him. [16] As in all his letters, he writes about these things, in which some things are hard to understand, which the unlearned and unstable distort, as they also do the other Scriptures, to their own destruction.

[17] You therefore, beloved, since you know these things beforehand, beware lest you also fall from your own firm footing, being led away by the deception of the wicked. [18] But grow in the grace and knowledge of our Lord and Savior Jesus Christ. To Him be glory, both now and forever. Amen.

1 JOHN

The Word of Life

1 That which was from the beginning, which we have heard, which we have seen with our eyes, which we have looked upon, and our hands have touched, concerning the Word of life— [2] the life was revealed, and we have seen it and testify to it, and announce to you the eternal life, which was with the Father and was revealed to us— [3] we declare to you that which we have seen and heard, that you also may have fellowship with us. And our fellowship is with the Father and with His Son Jesus Christ. [4] We are writing these things to you so that our joy may be complete.

God Is Light

[5] This then is the message which we have heard from Him and declare to you: God is light, and in Him is no darkness at all. [6] If we say that we have fellowship with Him, yet walk in darkness, we lie and do not practice the truth. [7] But if we walk in the light as He is in the light, we have fellowship one with another, and the blood of Jesus Christ His Son cleanses us from all sin.

[8] If we say that we have no sin, we deceive ourselves, and the truth is not in us. [9] If we confess our sins, He is faithful and just to forgive us our sins and cleanse us from all unrighteousness. [10] If we say that we have not sinned, we make Him a liar and His word is not in us.

Christ Our Advocate

2 My little children, I am writing these things to you, so that you do not sin. But if anyone does sin, we have an Advocate with the Father, Jesus Christ the Righteous One. [2] He is the atoning sacrifice for our sins, and not for ours only, but also for the sins of the whole world.

[3] By this we know that we know Him, if we keep His commandments. [4] Whoever says, "I know Him," and does not keep His commandments is a liar, and the truth is not in him. [5] But whoever keeps His word truly has the love of God perfected in him. By this we know we are in Him. [6] Whoever says he remains in Him ought to walk as He walked.

The New Commandment

[7] Brothers, I am writing no new commandment to you, but an old commandment which you have had from the beginning. The old commandment is the word which you have heard from the beginning. [8] Yet a new commandment I am writing to you, which holds true in Him and in you, because the darkness is passing away, and the true light is already shining.

[9] Whoever says he is in the light but hates his brother is in darkness even until now. [10] Whoever loves his brother lives in the light, and in him there is no cause for stumbling. [11] But whoever hates his brother is in darkness, and walks in darkness, and does not know where he is going, because the darkness has blinded his eyes.

[12] I am writing to you, little children,
    because your sins are forgiven for His name's sake.
[13] I am writing to you, fathers,
    because you have known Him who is from the beginning.
I am writing to you, young men,
    because you have overcome the evil one.

I am writing to you, little children,
    because you have known the Father.
[14] I have written to you, fathers,
    because you have known Him who is from the beginning.

I have written to you, young men,
    because you are strong,
    and the word of God lives in you,
    and you have overcome the evil one.

[15] Do not love the world or the things in the world. If anyone loves the world, the love of the Father is not in him. [16] For all that is in the world—the lust of the flesh, the lust of the eyes, and the pride of life—is not of the Father, but is of the world. [17] The world and its desires are passing away, but the one who does the will of God lives forever.

The Antichrist

[18] Little children, it is the last hour. As you have heard that the antichrist will come, even now there are many antichrists. By this we know that it is the last hour. [19] They went out from us, but they were not of us, for if they had been of us, they would no doubt have remained with us. But they went out, revealing that none of them were of us.

[20] But you have an anointing from the Holy One, and you know all things. [21] I have written to you, not because you do not know the truth, but because you know it, and because no lie is of the truth. [22] Who is a liar but the one who denies that Jesus is the Christ? Whoever denies the Father and the Son is the antichrist. [23] No one who denies the Son has the Father; the one who confesses the Son has the Father.

[24] Let that which you have heard from the beginning remain in you. If that which you have heard from the beginning remains in you, you also will remain in the Son and in the Father. [25] And this is the promise that He has promised us—eternal life.

[26] I have written these things to you concerning those who deceive you. [27] But the anointing which you have received from

Him remains in you, and you do not need anyone to teach you. For as the same anointing teaches you concerning all things, and is truth, and is no lie, and just as it has taught you, remain in Him.

Children of God

28 And now, little children, remain in Him, so that when He appears, we may have confidence and not be ashamed before Him when He comes.

29 If you know that He is righteous, you know that everyone who does righteousness is born of Him.

3 Consider how much love the Father has given to us, that we should be called children of God. Therefore the world does not know us, because it did not know Him. 2 Beloved, now are we children of God, and it has not yet been revealed what we shall be. But we know that when He appears, we shall be like Him, for we shall see Him as He is. 3 Everyone who has this hope in Him purifies himself, just as He is pure.

4 Whoever practices sin breaks the law, for sin is lawlessness. 5 You know that He was revealed to take away our sins, and in Him there is no sin. 6 Whoever remains in Him does not sin. Whoever sins has not seen Him and does not know Him.

7 Little children, let no one deceive you. The one who does righteousness is righteous, just as Christ is righteous. 8 Whoever practices sin is of the devil, for the devil has been sinning from the beginning. For this purpose the Son of God was revealed, that He might destroy the works of the devil. 9 Whoever has been born of God does not practice sin, for His seed remains in him. And he cannot keep on sinning, because he has been born of God. 10 In this the children of God and the children of the devil are revealed: Whoever does not live in righteousness is not of God, nor is the one who does not love his brother.

Love One Another

11 For this is the message that you heard from the beginning: We should love one another, 12 not like Cain, who was of the wicked one and murdered his brother. And why did he murder him? Because his own works were evil, and his brother's works were righteous. 13 Do not marvel, my brothers, if the world hates you. 14 We know that we have passed from death to life, because we love the brothers. Whoever does not love his brother remains in death. 15 Whoever hates his brother is a murderer, and you know that no murderer has eternal life remaining in him.

16 By this we know the love of God: that He laid down His life for us, and we ought to lay down our lives for the brothers. 17 Whoever has the world's goods and sees his brother in need, but closes his heart of compassion from him, how can the love of God remain in him? 18 My little children, let us love not in word and speech, but in action and truth.

Confidence Before God

19 By this we know that we are of the truth, and shall reassure our hearts before Him. 20 For if our heart condemns us, God is greater than our heart and knows everything. 21 Beloved, if our heart does not condemn us, then we have confidence before God. 22 And whatever we ask, we will receive from Him, because we keep His commandments and do the things that are pleasing in His sight. 23 And this is His commandment: that we should believe on the name of His Son Jesus Christ and love one another as He commanded us. 24 Now the one who keeps His commandments remains in Him, and He in him. And by this we know that He remains in us, through the Spirit whom He has given us.

Test the Spirits

4 Beloved, do not believe every spirit, but test the spirits to see whether they are from God, because many false prophets have gone out into the world. 2 This is how you know the Spirit of God: Every spirit that confesses that Jesus Christ has come in the flesh is from God, 3 and every spirit that does not confess that

Jesus Christ has come in the flesh is not from God. This is the spirit of the antichrist, which you have heard is coming and is already in the world.

4 You are of God, little children, and have overcome them, because He who is in you is greater than he who is in the world. 5 They are of the world, and therefore they speak from the world, and the world listens to them. 6 We are of God, and whoever knows God listens to us. Whoever is not of God does not listen to us. This is how we know the spirit of truth and the spirit of error.

God Is Love

7 Beloved, let us love one another, for love is of God, and everyone who loves is born of God and knows God. 8 Anyone who does not love does not know God, for God is love. 9 In this way the love of God was revealed to us, that God sent His only begotten Son into the world, that we might live through Him. 10 In this is love: not that we loved God, but that He loved us and sent His Son to be the atoning sacrifice for our sins. 11 Beloved, if God so loved us, we must also love one another. 12 No one has seen God at any time. If we love one another, God dwells in us, and His love is perfected in us.

13 We know that we live in Him, and He in us, because He has given us His Spirit. 14 And we have seen and testify that the Father sent the Son to be the Savior of the world. 15 Whoever confesses that Jesus is the Son of God, God lives in him, and he in God. 16 And we have come to know and to believe the love that God has for us.

God is love. Whoever lives in love lives in God, and God in him. 17 In this way God's love is perfected in us, so that we may have boldness on the Day of Judgment, because as He is, so are we in this world. 18 There is no fear in love, but perfect love casts out fear, because fear has to do with punishment. Whoever fears is not perfect in love.

19 We love Him because He first loved us. 20 If anyone says, "I love God," and hates his brother, he is a liar. For whoever does not love his brother whom he has seen, how can he love God whom he has not seen? 21 We have this commandment from Him: Whoever loves God must also love his brother.

Overcoming the World

5 Whoever believes that Jesus is the Christ is born of God, and everyone who loves the Father loves the one born of the Father. 2 By this we know that we love the children of God: when we love God and keep His commandments. 3 For this is the love of God, that we keep His commandments. And His commandments are not burdensome, 4 for whoever is born of God overcomes the world, and the victory that overcomes the world is our faith. 5 Who is it that overcomes the world, but the one who believes that Jesus is the Son of God?

The Witness Concerning the Son

6 This is He who came by water and blood—Jesus Christ. He did not come by water only, but by water and blood. It is the Spirit who bears witness, because the Spirit is the truth. 7 There are three who testify in heaven: the Father, the Word, and the Holy Spirit, and three are one. 8 There are three that testify on earth: the Spirit, the water, and the blood, and the three are toward the one.[7] 9 If we receive the testimony of men, the testimony of God is greater; for this is the testimony of God which He has given concerning His Son. 10 Whoever believes in the Son of God has this witness in himself. Whoever does not believe God has made Him out to be a liar, because he does not believe the testimony that God gave about His Son. 11 And this is the testimony: that God has given us eternal life, and this life is in His Son. 12 Whoever has the Son has life, and whoever does not have the Son of God does not have life.

Purpose of Writing

13 I have written these things to you who believe in the name of the Son of God, that you may know that you have eternal life, and that you may continue to believe in the name of the Son

---

[7] 7–8 The earliest Greek manuscripts lack in heaven: the Father, the Word, and the Holy Spirit, and the three are one. There are three that testify on earth.

of God. [14] This is the confidence that we have in Him, that if we ask anything according to His will, He hears us. [15] So if we know that He hears whatever we ask, we know that we have whatever we asked of Him.

[16] If anyone sees his brother commit a sin which does not lead to death, he shall ask, and He shall give him life. This is for those whose sin does not lead to death. There is a sin that leads to death. I do not say that he should pray for it. [17] All wrongdoing is sin, but there is a sin that does not lead to death.

[18] We know that whoever is born of God does not keep on sinning. But whoever has been born of God guards himself, and the wicked one cannot touch him. [19] We know that we are of God, and the whole world lies in wickedness. [20] And we know that the Son of God has come and has given us understanding, so that we may know Him who is true, and we are in Him who is true—His Son Jesus Christ. He is the true God and eternal life.

[21] Little children, keep yourselves from idols. Amen.

2 JOHN

Salutation

The elder,

To the elect lady and her children, whom I love in the truth, and not I only, but also all those who know the truth, [2] for the sake of the truth, which remains in us, and will be with us forever:

[3] Grace, mercy, and peace will be with you from God the Father and from the Lord Jesus Christ, the Son of the Father, in truth and love.

Truth and Love

[4] I greatly rejoiced that I found some of your children walking in truth as we were commanded by the Father. [5] And now I ask you, lady, not as though I wrote a new commandment to you, but that which we have had from the beginning, that we love one another. [6] And this is love: that we walk according to His commandments. This is the commandment, that as you have heard from the beginning,

you should walk in it.

[7] For many deceivers, who do not confess that Jesus Christ has come in the flesh, have gone out into the world. Each one is a deceiver and an antichrist. [8] Watch yourselves, so that we do not lose those things for which we have worked, but that we receive a full reward. [9] Whoever transgresses and does not remain in the teaching of Christ does not have God. Whoever remains in the teaching of Christ has both the Father and the Son. [10] If anyone comes to you and does not bring this teaching, do not receive him into your house, nor greet him. [11] For whoever greets him takes part in his evil deeds.

Final Greetings

[12] I have many things to write to you, but I prefer not to write with paper and ink. Instead, I hope to come to you and speak face to face that our joy may be complete.

[13] The children of your elect sister greet you. Amen.

3 JOHN

Salutation

The elder,

To the beloved Gaius, whom I love in the truth:

[2] Beloved, I pray that all may go well with you and that you may be in good health, even as your soul is well. [3] For I greatly rejoiced when brothers came and testified of the truth that is in you, just as you walk in the truth. [4] I have no greater joy than to hear that my children walk in truth.

Working Together

[5] Beloved, you are faithful in all you do for the brothers and for strangers, [6] who have testified of your love before the church. You will do well to send them along on their journey in a manner worthy of God. [7] For His name's sake they went out, receiving no help from the Gentiles. [8] Therefore we ought to receive such men, that we might be fellow workers for the truth.

[9] I wrote to the church, but Diotrephes, who loves to put himself first among them, did not accept us. [10] Because of this, if I come, I will bring up what kinds of works he does: ranting against us with malicious words. Not content with that, he does not accept the brothers, and stops those who want to, and throws them out of the church.

[11] Beloved, do not imitate that which is evil, but that which is good. Whoever does good is from God, but whoever does evil has not seen God. [12] Demetrius receives good reports from everyone and from the truth itself. Yes, and we also testify, and you know that our testimony is true.

Final Greetings

[13] I had many things to write, but I would rather not write to you with pen and ink. [14] Instead, I hope to see you soon, and we shall speak face to face.

Peace be to you. The friends greet you. Greet the friends by name.

JUDE

Salutation

Jude, a servant of Jesus Christ and a brother of James,

To those who are sanctified and called by God the Father and preserved in Jesus Christ:

[2] May mercy, peace, and love be multiplied to you.

Judgment on False Teachers

2Pe 2:1–17

[3] Beloved, while I diligently tried to write to you of the salvation we have in common, I found it necessary to write and appeal to you to contend for the faith which was once delivered to the saints. [4] For there are some men who secretly crept in, who were marked long ago for this condemnation. They are ungodly men, who pervert the grace of our God into immorality and deny the only Lord God and our Lord Jesus Christ.

[5] Now I want to remind you, though you already know, that the Lord saved the people out of the land of Egypt and afterward destroyed those who did not believe. [6] Likewise, the angels who did not keep to their first domain, but forsook their own dwelling, He has kept in everlasting chains under darkness for the judgment of the great day. [7] Just as Sodom and Gomorrah, and the surrounding cities in like manner, gave themselves to immorality and went after different flesh, they serve as an example by suffering the punishment of eternal fire.

[8] Likewise, these ungodly dreamers defile the flesh, reject authority, and slander celestial beings. [9] Yet Michael the archangel, when contending with the devil in a dispute about the body of Moses, did not dare to pronounce upon him a railing judgment. But he said, "The Lord rebuke you!" [10] But these men slander those things that they do not understand. But they destroy themselves in those things that, like unreasoning animals, they know by instinct.

[11] Woe to them! For they have gone in the way of Cain, have run greedily after the error of Balaam for a reward, and perished in the rebellion of Korah.

[12] These are the ones who are stains on your love feasts as they feast with you irreverently and care only for themselves. They are clouds without water, carried along by winds; autumn trees without fruit, twice dead, uprooted; [13] raging waves of the sea, which are foaming up their own shame; wandering stars for whom the gloom of darkness has been kept forever.

[14] Enoch, the seventh generation from Adam, also prophesied of these men, saying, "Look! The Lord is coming with ten thousand of His holy ones, [15] to execute judgment on everyone, and to convict all who are godless of all their wicked deeds that they have committed, and of all the terrible words that godless sinners have spoken against Him." [16] These men are grumblers, complainers, who walk after their own lusts. Their mouths speak arrogant words, and they flatter others to gain profit.

Warnings and Exhortations

[17] But, beloved, remember the words that were previously spoken by the apostles of our Lord Jesus Christ. [18] They said to you, "In the last days there will be scoffers who will walk after their own ungodly desires." [19] These are the men who cause divisions, sensual, devoid of the Spirit.

[20] But you, beloved, build yourselves up in your most holy faith. Pray in the Holy Spirit. [21] Keep yourselves in the love of God while you are waiting for the mercy of our Lord Jesus Christ, which leads to eternal life.

[22] On some have compassion, using discernment. [23] And others save with fear while pulling them out of the fire, hating even the garment stained by the flesh.

Benediction

[24] Now to Him who is able to keep you from falling and to present you blameless before the presence of His glory with rejoicing, [25] to the only wise God our Savior, be glory and majesty, dominion and power, both now and forever. Amen.

REVELATION

Introduction and Salutation

1 The Revelation of Jesus Christ, which God gave to Him to show to His servants things which must soon take place. He sent and signified it by His angel to His servant John, [2] who bears record of the word of God, and of the testimony of Jesus Christ, and of all things that he saw. [3] Blessed is he who reads and those who hear the words of this prophecy and keep those things which are written in it, for the time is near.

[4] John,

To the seven churches which are in Asia:

Grace to you and peace from Him who is and who was and who is to come and from the seven Spirits who are before His throne, [5] and from Jesus Christ, who is the faithful witness, the firstborn from the dead, and the ruler of the kings of the earth.

To Him who loved us and washed us from our sins in His own blood, [6] and has made us kings and priests to His God and Father, to Him be glory and dominion forever and ever. Amen.

[7] Look! He is coming with clouds,
    and every eye will see Him,
even those who pierced Him.
    And all the tribes of the earth will mourn because
        of Him.
Even so, Amen.

[8] "I am the Alpha and the Omega, the Beginning and the End," says the Lord, "who is and who was and who is to come, the Almighty."

A Vision of Christ

[9] I, John, both your brother and companion in the tribulation and kingdom and patience of Jesus Christ, was on the isle that is called Patmos on account of the word of God and the testimony of Jesus Christ. [10] I was in the Spirit on the Lord's Day, and I heard behind me a great voice like a trumpet, [11] saying, "I am the Alpha and the Omega, the First and the Last," and "What you see, write in a book, and send it to the seven churches which are in Asia: to Ephesus, Smyrna, Pergamum, Thyatira, Sardis, Philadelphia, and Laodicea."

[12] I turned to see the voice that spoke with me. And when I turned, I saw seven golden candlesticks, [13] and in the midst of the seven candlesticks was one like a Son of Man, clothed with a garment down to the feet and with a golden sash wrapped around the chest. [14] The hair on His head was white like wool, as white as snow. His eyes were like a flame of fire. [15] His feet were like fine brass, as if refined in a furnace, and His voice as the sound of many waters. [16] He had in His right hand seven stars, and out of His mouth went a sharp two-edged sword. His appearance was like the sun shining brightly.

[17] When I saw Him, I fell at His feet as though I were dead. Then He laid His right hand on me, saying to me, "Do not be afraid. I am the First and the Last. [18] I am He who lives, though I was dead. Look! I am alive forevermore. Amen. And I have the keys of Hades and of Death.

[19] "Write the things which you have seen, and the things which are, and the things which will take place after this. [20] The mystery of the seven stars which you saw in My right hand, and the seven golden candlesticks: The seven stars are the angels of the seven churches, and the seven candlesticks which you saw are the seven churches.

The Message to Ephesus

2 "To the angel of the church of Ephesus write:

"He who holds the seven stars in His right hand, who walks in the midst of the seven golden candlesticks, says these things: [2] I know your works, your labor and your patience, and that you cannot bear those who are evil. And you have tested those who say they are apostles, but are not, and have found them to be liars. [3] You have endured, and have been patient, and for My name's sake have labored and have not grown weary.

[4] "But I have something against you, that you have abandoned the love you had at first. [5] Remember therefore from where you have fallen. Repent, and do the works you did at first, or else I will come to you quickly and remove your candlestick from its place, unless you repent. [6] But this you have: You hate the works of the Nicolaitans, which I also hate.

[7] "He who has an ear, let him hear what the Spirit says to the churches. To him who overcomes I will give permission to eat of the tree of life, which is in the midst of the Paradise of God.

The Message to Smyrna

[8] "To the angel of the church in Smyrna write:

"The First and the Last, who was dead and came to life, says these things: [9] I know your works and tribulation and poverty (but you are rich). And I know the blasphemy of those who say they are Jews and are not, but are a synagogue of Satan. [10] Do not fear any of those things which you are about to suffer. Look, the devil is about to throw some of you into prison, that you may be tried, and you will have tribulation for ten days. Be faithful unto death, and I will give you the crown of life.

[11] "He who has an ear, let him hear what the Spirit says to the churches. He who overcomes shall not be hurt by the second death.

The Message to Pergamum

[12] "To the angel of the church in Pergamum write:

"He who has the sharp two-edged sword says these things: [13] I know your works and where you live, where Satan's throne is. Yet you hold firmly to My name, and did not deny My faith even in the days of Antipas, My faithful martyr, who was killed among you, where Satan dwells.

[14] "But I have a few things against you: You have there those who hold the teaching of Balaam, who taught Balak to cast a stumbling block before the children of Israel, to eat things sacrificed to idols and to commit sexual immorality. [15] So you also have those who hold the teaching of the Nicolaitans. [16] Repent, or else I will come to you quickly and will war against them with the sword of My mouth.

[17] "He who has an ear, let him hear what the Spirit says to the churches. To him who overcomes I will give the hidden manna to eat. And I will give him a white stone, and on the stone a new name written, which no one knows except he who receives it.

The Message to Thyatira

[18] "To the angel of the church in Thyatira write:

"The Son of God, who has eyes like a flame of fire, and whose feet are like fine brass, says these things: [19] I know your works, love, service, faith, and your patience, and that your last works are more than the first.

[20] "But I have a few things against you: You permit that woman Jezebel, who calls herself a prophetess, to teach and seduce My servants to commit sexual immorality and eat food sacrificed to idols. [21] I gave her time to repent of her sexual immorality, but she did not repent. [22] Look! I will throw her onto a sickbed, and those who commit adultery with her into great tribulation, unless they repent of their deeds. [23] I will put her children to death, and all the churches shall know that I am He who searches the hearts and minds. I will give to each one of you according to your deeds.

[24] "Now to you I say, and to the rest in Thyatira, as many as do not have this teaching, who have not known what some call the 'depths of Satan,' I will put on you no other burden. [25] But hold firmly what you have until I come.

[26] "To him who overcomes and keeps My works to the end, I will give authority over the nations—

[27] He 'shall rule them with a rod of iron;
    like the vessels of a potter they shall be broken in
        pieces' [1]—

even as I myself have received authority from My Father. [28] And I will give him the morning star. [29] He who has an ear, let him hear what the Spirit says to the churches.

The Message to Sardis

3 "To the angel of the church in Sardis write:

"He who has the seven Spirits of God and the seven stars says these things: I know your works, that you have a reputation of being alive, but you are dead. [2] Be watchful, and strengthen the things which remain but are ready to die, for I have not found your works perfected before God. [3] Remember therefore how you have received and heard; hold fast and repent. Therefore if you will not watch, I will come upon you as a thief, and you will not know what hour I will come upon you.

[4] "You have a few names even in Sardis who have not soiled their garments. They shall walk with Me in white, for they are worthy. [5] He who overcomes shall be clothed in white garments. I will not blot his name out of the Book of Life, but I will confess his name before My Father and before His angels. [6] He who has an ear, let him hear what the Spirit says to the churches.

The Message to Philadelphia

[7] "To the angel of the church in Philadelphia write:

"He who is holy, He who is true, He who has the key of David, He who opens and no one shuts, and shuts and no one opens, says these things: [8] I know your works. Look! I have set before you an open door, and no one can shut it. For you have a little strength, and have kept My word, and have not denied My name. [9] Listen! I will make them of the synagogue of Satan, who say they are Jews and are not, but lie. Listen! I will make them come and worship before your feet and to know that I have loved you. [10] Because you have kept My word of patience, I also

---

[1] 27 Ps 2:9.

will keep you from the hour of temptation which shall come upon the entire world, to test those who dwell on the earth.

[11] "Look, I am coming quickly. Hold firmly what you have, so that no one may take your crown. [12] He who overcomes will I make a pillar in the temple of My God, and he shall go out no more. I will write on him the name of My God and the name of the city of My God, the New Jerusalem, which comes down out of heaven from My God, and My own new name. [13] He who has an ear, let him hear what the Spirit says to the churches.

The Message to Laodicea

[14] "To the angel of the church of the Laodiceans write:

"The Amen, the Faithful and True Witness, the Beginning of the creation of God, says these things: [15] I know your works, that you are neither cold nor hot. I wish you were cold or hot. [16] So then, because you are lukewarm, and neither cold nor hot, I will spit you out of My mouth. [17] For you say, 'I am rich, and have stored up goods, and have need of nothing,' yet do not realize that you are wretched, miserable, poor, blind, and naked. [18] I counsel you to buy from Me gold refined by fire, that you may be rich, and white garments, that you may be dressed, that the shame of your nakedness may not appear, and anoint your eyes with eye salve, that you may see. [19] "Those whom I love, I rebuke and discipline. Therefore be zealous and repent. [20] Listen! I stand at the door and knock. If anyone hears My voice and opens the door, I will come in and dine with him, and he with Me. [21] "To him who overcomes will I grant to sit with Me on My throne, as I also overcame and sat down with My Father on His throne. [22] He who has an ear, let him hear what the Spirit says to the churches."

The Heavenly Worship

4 After this I looked. And there was an open door in heaven. The first voice I heard was like a trumpet speaking with me, saying, "Come up here, and I will show you things which must take place after this." [2] Immediately I was in the Spirit. And there was a throne set in heaven with One sitting on the throne! [3] And He who sat there appeared like a jasper and a sardius stone. There was a rainbow around the throne, appearing like an emerald. [4] Twenty-four thrones were around the throne. And I saw twenty-four elders sitting on the thrones, clothed in white garments. They had crowns of gold on their heads. [5] Lightnings and thunderings and voices proceeded from the throne. Seven lamps of fire were burning before the throne, which are the seven Spirits of God. [6] Before the throne was a sea of glass like crystal.

In the midst of the throne, and around the throne, were four living creatures covered with eyes in front and in back. [7] The first living creature was like a lion, the second living creature like a calf, the third living creature had a face like a man, and the fourth creature was like a flying eagle. [8] The four living creatures had six wings each, and they were covered with eyes all around. All day and night, without ceasing, they were saying:

"'Holy, holy, holy,
Lord God Almighty,'[1]
who was, and is, and is to come."

[9] When the living creatures give glory and honor and thanks to Him who sits on the throne, who lives forever and ever, [10] the twenty-four elders fall down before Him who sits on the throne, and worship Him, who lives forever and ever. Then they cast their crowns before the throne, saying,

[11] "You are worthy, O Lord,
　to receive glory and honor and power;
for You have created all things,
　　and by Your will they exist
　　and were created."

The Scroll and the Lamb

5 Then I saw in the right hand of Him who sat on the throne a scroll written within and on the back, sealed with seven seals. [2] And I saw a strong angel proclaiming with a loud voice, "Who is worthy to open the scroll and to break its seals?" [3] But no one in heaven or on earth or under the earth was able to open the scroll or to look in it. [4] I began to weep loudly, because no one was found worthy to open and read the scroll, or to look in it. [5] Then one of the elders said to me, "Do not weep. Look! The Lion of the tribe of Judah, the Root of David, has triumphed. He is able to open the scroll and to loose its seven seals."

[6] I saw a Lamb in the midst of the throne and of the four living creatures, and in the midst of the elders, standing as though it had been slain, having seven horns and seven eyes, which are the seven Spirits of God, sent out into all the earth. [7] He came and took the scroll out of the right hand of Him who sat on the throne. [8] When He had taken the scroll, the four living creatures and the twenty-four elders fell down before the Lamb, each one having a harp, and golden bowls full of incense, which are the prayers of saints. [9] And they sang a new song, saying:

"You are worthy to take the scroll,
　and to open its seals;
for You were slain,
　and have redeemed us to God by Your blood
　out of every tribe and tongue and people and nation,
[10] and have made us kings and priests unto our God;
　and we shall reign on the earth."

[11] Then I looked, and I heard around the throne and the living creatures and the elders the voices of many angels, numbering ten thousand times ten thousand, and thousands of thousands, [12] saying with a loud voice:

"Worthy is the Lamb who was slain,
　to receive power and riches and wisdom and strength
　and honor and glory and blessing!"

[13] Then I heard every creature which is in heaven and on the earth and under the earth and in the sea, and all that are in them, saying:

"To Him who sits on the throne and to the Lamb
　be blessing and honor and glory and power,
　　forever and ever!"

[14] The four living creatures said, "Amen." And the twenty-four elders fell down and worshipped Him who lives forever and ever.

The Seals

6 I saw when the Lamb opened one of the seals. Then I heard one of the four living creatures saying, with voice like thunder, "Come and see." [2] And I looked, and there before me was a white horse. He who sat on it had a bow. And a crown was given to him, and he went forth conquering that he might overcome.

[3] When He opened the second seal, I heard the second living creature say, "Come and see." [4] Then another horse that was red went forth. Power was given to him who sat on it to take peace from the earth, causing people to kill one another. Then a great sword was given to him.

[5] When He opened the third seal, I heard the third living creature say, "Come!" I looked, and there was a black horse, and he who sat on it had a pair of scales in his hand. [6] Then I heard a voice in the midst of the four living creatures saying, "A quart[2] of wheat for a day's wages, and three quarts of barley for a day's wages,[3] and do not harm the oil and the wine."

[7] When He opened the fourth seal, I heard the voice of the fourth living creature say, "Come!" [8] So I looked, and there was a pale horse, and the name of him who sat on it was Death, and Hades followed him. Power over a fourth of the earth was given to them,

---

[1]8 Isa 6:3.　　[2]6 Gk. *choenix*, or a kilogram.　　[3]6 Gk. *denarius*.

to kill with sword, with hunger, with death, and by the beasts of the earth.

⁹ When He opened the fifth seal, I saw under the altar the souls of those who had been slain for the word of God and for the testimony they had held. ¹⁰ They cried out with a loud voice, "How long, O Sovereign Lord, holy and true, until You judge and avenge our blood on those who dwell on the earth?" ¹¹ Then a white robe was given to each of them, and they were told to rest a little longer, until the number of their fellow servants and brothers should be completed, who would be killed as they were.

¹² I watched as He opened the sixth seal. And suddenly there was a great earthquake. The sun became black, like sackcloth made from goat hair, and the moon became like blood. ¹³ And the stars of heaven fell to the earth, as a fig tree drops its unripe figs when it is shaken by a strong wind. ¹⁴ Then the heavens receded like a scroll when it is rolled up, and every mountain and island was removed from its place.

¹⁵ Then the kings of the earth and the great men and the rich men and the commanding officers and the strong and everyone, slave and free, hid themselves in the caves and in the rocks of the mountains. ¹⁶ They said to the mountains and rocks, "Fall on us, and hide us from the face of Him who sits on the throne, and from the wrath of the Lamb, ¹⁷ for the great day of His wrath has come. Who is able to withstand it?"¹

The 144,000 of Israel Sealed

7 Then I saw four angels standing at the four corners of the earth, holding the four winds of the earth, that the wind would not blow on the earth or on the sea or on any tree. ² And I saw another angel ascending from the east, having the seal of the living God. He cried out with a loud voice to the four angels who had been given power to harm the earth and the sea, ³ saying, "Do not harm the earth or the sea or the trees, until we have sealed the servants of our God on their foreheads." ⁴ Then I heard the number of those who were sealed, one hundred and forty-four thousand out of every tribe of the children of Israel:

⁵ Twelve thousand from the tribe of Judah were sealed, twelve thousand from the tribe of Reuben were sealed, twelve thousand from the tribe of Gad were sealed, ⁶ twelve thousand from the tribe of Asher were sealed, twelve thousand from the tribe of Naphtali were sealed, twelve thousand from the tribe of Manasseh were sealed, ⁷ twelve thousand from the tribe of Simeon were sealed, twelve thousand from the tribe of Levi were sealed, twelve thousand from the tribe of Issachar were sealed, ⁸ twelve thousand from the tribe of Zebulun were sealed, twelve thousand from the tribe of Joseph were sealed, and twelve thousand from the tribe of Benjamin were sealed.

The Multitude From Every Nation

⁹ Then I looked. And there was a great multitude which no one could count, from all nations and tribes and peoples and tongues, standing before the throne and before the Lamb, clothed with white robes, with palm branches in their hands. ¹⁰ They cried out with a loud voice:

"Salvation belongs to our God
who sits on the throne,
and to the Lamb!"

¹¹ All the angels stood around the throne and the elders and the four living creatures and fell on their faces before the throne and worshipped God, ¹² saying:

"Amen!
Blessing and glory
and wisdom and thanksgiving and honor
and power and might
be to our God forever and ever!
Amen."

¹³ Then one of the elders asked me, "Who are these clothed in white robes, and where did they come from?"

¹⁴ I said to him, "Sir, you know."

He said to me, "These are those who came out of great tribulation and washed their robes and made them white in the blood of the Lamb. ¹⁵ Therefore,

they are before the throne of God,
and serve Him day and night in His temple.
And He who sits on the throne
will dwell among them.
¹⁶ 'They shall neither hunger any more,
nor shall they thirst any more;
the sun shall not strike them,'²
nor any scorching heat;
¹⁷ for the Lamb who is in the midst of the throne
will shepherd them
and 'He will lead them to springs of living water.'³
'And God will wipe away every tear from their eyes.'⁴"

The Seventh Seal

8 When He opened the seventh seal, there was silence in heaven for about half an hour.

² And I saw the seven angels who stand before God, and seven trumpets were given to them.

³ Another angel, having a golden censer, came and stood at the altar. He was given much incense to offer with the prayers of all the saints on the golden altar which was before the throne. ⁴ The smoke of the incense, with the prayers of the saints, ascended before God from the angel's hand. ⁵ Then the angel took the censer, filled it with fire from the altar, and threw it onto the earth. And there were noises, thundering, lightning, and an earthquake.

The Trumpets

⁶ Then the seven angels who had the seven trumpets prepared themselves to sound them.

⁷ The first angel sounded, and there followed hail and fire mixed with blood, and they were thrown upon the earth. A third of the trees and all the green grass were burned up.

⁸ Then the second angel sounded, and something like a great mountain, burning with fire, was thrown into the sea. A third of the sea became blood, ⁹ a third of the living creatures in the sea died, and a third of the ships were destroyed.

¹⁰ The third angel sounded, and a great star from heaven, burning like a torch, fell on a third of the rivers and on the springs of waters. ¹¹ The name of this star is Wormwood. A third of the waters became wormwood, and many men died from the waters, because they were made bitter.

¹² The fourth angel sounded, and a third of the sun was struck, and a third of the moon, and a third of the stars, so that a third of them were darkened. A third of the day had no light, and likewise a third of the night.

¹³ Then I watched, and I heard an angel flying through the midst of heaven, saying with a loud voice, "Woe, woe, woe to the inhabitants of the earth, because of the other trumpet blasts of the three angels, who are yet to sound!"

9 The fifth angel sounded, and I saw a star fallen from heaven to the earth. The star was given the key to the bottomless pit. ² He opened the bottomless pit, and smoke ascended from the pit, like the smoke of a great furnace. The sun and the air were darkened by the smoke from the pit. ³ And out of the smoke locusts came upon the earth. Power was given them as the scorpions of the earth have power. ⁴ They were commanded not to harm the grass of the earth, or any green thing, or any tree, but only those men who did not have the seal of God on their foreheads. ⁵ They were given authority, not to kill them, but to torment them for five months. Their torment was like the torment of a scorpion when it stings a man. ⁶ In those days men will seek death but will not find it. They will desire to die, but death will elude them.

---

¹ 17 Ho 10:8.   ² 16 Isa 49:10.   ³ 17 Isa 49:10.   ⁴ 17 Isa 25:8.

[7] The shape of the locusts was like horses prepared for battle. On their heads were something like crowns of gold, and their faces were like faces of men. [8] They had hair like the hair of women, and their teeth were like the teeth of lions. [9] They had breastplates like breastplates of iron, and the sound of their wings was like the sound of chariots with many horses running to battle. [10] They had tails like scorpions and stings in their tails. Their power was to hurt men for five months. [11] They had as king over them the angel of the bottomless pit, whose name in Hebrew is Abaddon, and in Greek his name is Apollyon.[1]

[12] The first woe is past. Now, two more woes are yet to come.

[13] The sixth angel sounded, and I heard a voice from the four horns of the golden altar which is before God, [14] saying to the sixth angel who had the trumpet, "Release the four angels who are bound at the great Euphrates River." [15] And the four angels, who had been prepared for the hour and day and month and year, were released to kill a third of mankind. [16] The army of horsemen numbered two hundred million. I heard their number.

[17] Thus I saw the horses in the vision: Those who sat on them had breastplates of fiery red, hyacinth blue, and sulfur yellow. The heads of the horses were like the heads of lions, and out of their mouths came fire and smoke and brimstone. [18] A third of mankind was killed by these three plagues—by the fire and by the smoke and by the brimstone, which came out of their mouths. [19] The power of the horses is in their mouths and in their tails. For their tails are like serpents, with heads by which they inflict injury.

[20] The rest of mankind, who were not killed by these plagues, did not repent of the works of their hands. They did not cease to worship demons, and idols of gold, silver, brass, stone, and wood, which cannot see nor hear nor walk. [21] Nor did they repent of their murders or their magical arts or their sexual immorality or their thefts.

The Angel and the Little Scroll

10 Then I saw another mighty angel coming down from heaven, clothed with a cloud and a rainbow on his head. His face was like the sun, and his feet like pillars of fire. [2] He had a little scroll open in his hand. He set his right foot on the sea and his left foot on the land, [3] and cried out with a loud voice, like a lion roaring. When he cried out, seven thunders sounded their voices. [4] And when the seven thunders sounded their voices, I was about to write, but I heard a voice from heaven saying to me, "Seal up those things which the seven thunders said, and do not write them." [5] The angel whom I saw standing on the sea and on the earth lifted up his hand to heaven [6] and swore by Him who lives forever and ever, who created heaven and the things that are in them, and the earth and the things that are in it, and the sea and the things that are in it, that there should be no more delay. [7] But in the days when the seventh angel is about to sound, the mystery of God will be fulfilled, as He has declared to His servants the prophets.

[8] Then the voice which I heard from heaven spoke to me again and said, "Go, take the little scroll which is open in the hand of the angel who is standing on the sea and on the earth." [9] So I went to the angel and said to him, "Give me the little scroll." He said to me, "Take it and eat it. It will turn your stomach sour, but in your mouth it will be as sweet as honey.'[2]" [10] I took the little scroll from the angel's hand and ate it. It was as sweet as honey in my mouth, but when I had eaten it, my stomach turned sour. [11] Then he said to me, "You must prophesy again about many peoples and nations and tongues and kings."

The Two Witnesses

11 I was given a reed like a measuring rod. The angel stood, saying, "Rise and measure the temple of God and the altar, and those who worship in it. [2] But exclude the court which is outside the temple, and do not measure it, for it has been given to the nations. They will trample on the Holy City for forty-two months. [3] And I will give power to my two witnesses, and they will prophesy for one thousand two hundred and sixty days, clothed in sackcloth." [4] These are the two olive trees and the two candlesticks standing before the God of the earth.[3] [5] If anyone desires to harm them, fire proceeds out of their mouth and devours their enemies. If anyone desires to harm them, he must be killed in this way. [6] They have power to shut heaven, that it may not rain during the days of their prophecy. They have power over waters to turn them into blood and to strike the earth with every plague as often as they desire.

[7] When they have finished their testimony, the beast that ascends from the bottomless pit will wage war against them and overcome them and kill them. [8] Their dead bodies will lie in the street of the great city, which spiritually is called Sodom and Egypt, where also our Lord was crucified. [9] Those from every people and tribe and tongue and nation will see their dead bodies for three and a half days, and will not allow their dead bodies to be put in graves. [10] Those who dwell on the earth will rejoice over them and make merry and send gifts to one another, because these two prophets tormented those who dwell on the earth.

[11] After the three and a half days, the breath[4] of life from God entered them, and they stood on their feet, and great fear fell on those who saw them. [12] Then they heard a loud voice from heaven saying to them, "Come up here!" And they ascended to heaven in a cloud, while their enemies watched them.

[13] At that same hour there was a great earthquake, and a tenth of the city fell. Seven thousand men were killed in the earthquake, and the remnant were frightened and gave glory to the God of heaven.

[14] The second woe is past. Listen, the third woe is coming quickly.

The Seventh Trumpet

[15] The seventh angel sounded, and there were loud voices in heaven, saying:

"The kingdoms of the world have become
    the kingdoms of our Lord, and of His Christ,
    and He shall reign forever and ever."

[16] And the twenty-four elders, who sat before God on their thrones, fell on their faces and worshipped God, [17] saying:

"We give You thanks, O Lord God Almighty,
    who is and was and who is to come,
because You have taken Your great power
    and begun to reign.
[18] The nations were angry,
    and Your wrath has come,
and the time has come for the dead to be judged,
    and to reward Your servants the prophets
and the saints and those who fear Your name,
    small and great,
and to destroy those who destroy the earth."

[19] Then the temple of God was opened in heaven, and the ark of His covenant was seen in His temple. And there came lightning, noises, thundering, an earthquake, and great hail.

The Woman and the Dragon

12 A great sign appeared in heaven: a woman clothed with the sun, with the moon under her feet, and on her head a crown of twelve stars. [2] She was with child and cried out in labor and in pain to give birth. [3] Then another sign appeared in heaven: There was a great red dragon with seven heads and ten horns, and seven diadems on his heads. [4] His tail drew a third of the stars of heaven, and threw them to the earth. The dragon stood before the woman who was ready to give birth, to devour her Child as soon as He was born. [5] She gave birth to a male Child, "who was to rule all nations with an iron scepter."[5] And her Child was caught up to God and to His throne. [6] The woman fled into the wilderness where she has a place prepared by God, that they may nourish her there for one thousand two hundred and sixty days.

[7] Then war broke out in heaven. Michael and his angels fought against the dragon, and the dragon and his angels fought, [8] but they did not prevail, nor was there a place for them in heaven any longer. [9] The great dragon was cast out, that ancient serpent called the Devil

---

[1] 11 Or *Destroyer*.   [2] 9 Eze 3:3.   [3] 4 Zec 4:3, 11, 14.   [4] 11 Eze 37:5–14.   [5] 5 Ps 2:9.

and Satan, who deceives the whole world. He was cast down to the earth, and his angels were cast down with him.

[10] Then I heard a loud voice in heaven, saying:

"Now the salvation and the power and the kingdom of our God
    and the authority of His Christ have come,
for the accuser of our brothers,
who accused them before our God day and night,
    has been cast down.
[11] They overcame him
    by the blood of the Lamb
    and by the word of their testimony,
and they loved not their lives
    unto the death.
[12] Therefore rejoice, O heavens,
    and you who dwell in them!
Woe unto the inhabitants of the earth and the sea!
    For the devil has come down to you
        in great wrath,
    because he knows that his time is short."

[13] When the dragon saw that he was cast down to the earth, he persecuted the woman who gave birth to the male Child. [14] The woman was given two wings of a great eagle, that she might fly into the wilderness to her place, where she is to be nourished for a time and times and half a time, from the presence of the serpent. [15] Then the serpent spewed water out of his mouth like a flood after the woman, that he might cause her to be carried away by the flood. [16] But the earth helped the woman. The earth opened its mouth and swallowed the flood which the dragon spewed out of his mouth. [17] Then the dragon was angry with the woman, and he went to wage war with the remnant of her offspring, who keep the commandments of God and have the testimony of Jesus Christ.

The Two Beasts

13 I stood on the sand of the sea. And I saw a beast rising out of the sea, having seven heads and ten horns, with ten crowns on his horns, and blasphemous names on his heads. [2] The beast which I saw was like a leopard. His feet were like those of a bear, and his mouth like the mouth of a lion. The dragon gave him his power and his throne and great authority. [3] I saw one of his heads as if it was mortally wounded, but his deadly wound was healed, and the whole world marveled and followed the beast. [4] They worshipped the dragon who gave authority to the beast. And they worshipped the beast, saying, "Who is like the beast? Who is able to wage war with him?"

[5] He was given a mouth speaking great things and blasphemies. And he was given authority to wage war for forty-two months. [6] He opened his mouth to speak blasphemies against God, to blaspheme His name and His tabernacle and those who dwell in heaven. [7] It was granted to him to wage war with the saints and to overcome them. And authority was given him over every tribe and tongue and nation. [8] All who dwell on the earth will worship him, all whose names have not been written in the Book of Life of the Lamb who was slain from the foundation of the world.

[9] If anyone has an ear, let him hear:

[10] "He who is to be taken captive,
    into captivity he shall go;
he who kills with the sword,
    with the sword he must be killed."[1]

Here is a call for the patience and the faith of the saints.

[11] Then I saw another beast rising out of the earth. He had two horns like a lamb and he spoke like a dragon. [12] He exercises all the authority of the first beast in his presence and causes the earth and those who dwell on it to worship the first beast, whose deadly wound was healed. [13] He performs great signs, making fire come down from heaven on the earth in the sight of men. [14] He deceives those who dwell on the earth by the signs which he was granted to do in the presence of the beast, telling those who dwell on the earth to make an image to the beast who was wounded by a sword and lived. [15] He was allowed to give breath to the image of the beast, that the image of the beast should both speak and cause as many as would not worship the image of the beast to be killed. [16] He causes all, both small and great, both rich and poor, both free and slave, to receive a mark on their right hand or on their forehead, [17] so that no one may buy or sell, except he who has the mark or the name of the beast or the number of his name.

[18] Here is a call for wisdom: Let him who has understanding calculate the number of the beast. It is the number of a man. His number is six hundred and sixty-six.

The Lamb and the 144,000

14 Then I looked. The Lamb was standing on Mount Zion and with Him one hundred and forty-four thousand having His Father's name written on their foreheads. [2] And I heard a sound from heaven, like the sound of many waters and like the sound of a great thunder. I heard the sound of harpists playing their harps. [3] They sang a new song before the throne and before the four living creatures and the elders. No one could learn that song except the one hundred and forty-four thousand who were redeemed from the earth. [4] These are those who were not defiled with women, for they are virgins. These are those who follow the Lamb wherever He goes. These were redeemed from among men, as first fruits to God and to the Lamb. [5] No lie was found in their mouths, for they are without fault before the throne of God.

The Messages of the Three Angels

[6] Then I saw another angel flying in the midst of heaven, having the eternal gospel to preach to those who dwell on the earth, to every nation and tribe and tongue and people. [7] He said with a loud voice, "Fear God and give Him glory, for the hour of His judgment has come. Worship Him who made heaven and earth, the sea and the springs of water."

[8] Another angel followed, saying, " 'Fallen! Fallen is Babylon, that Great City,'[2] because she made all the nations drink of the wine of the wrath of her sexual immorality."

[9] A third angel followed them, saying with a loud voice, "If anyone worships the beast and his image and receives his mark on his forehead or on his hand, [10] he also shall drink of the wine of the wrath of God, which is poured out in full strength into the cup of His anger. He shall be tormented with fire and brimstone in the presence of the holy angels and in the presence of the Lamb. [11] The smoke of their torment will ascend forever and ever. They have no rest day or night, who worship the beast and his image and whoever receives the mark of his name." [12] Here is the patience of the saints; here are those who keep the commandments of God and the faith of Jesus.

[13] Then I heard a voice from heaven saying to me, "Write: Blessed are the dead who die in the Lord from now on."

"Yes," says the Spirit, "that they may rest from their labors, for their works follow them."

The Harvest of the Earth

[14] I looked. And there was a white cloud, and on the cloud sat One like a Son of Man, having on his head a golden crown, and in His hand a sharp sickle. [15] Then another angel came out of the temple, crying with a loud voice to Him who sat on the cloud, "Thrust in Your sickle and reap. The time has come for You to reap, for the harvest of the earth is ripe." [16] So He who sat on the cloud thrust His sickle on the earth, and the earth was harvested.

[17] Another angel came out of the temple which is in heaven. He also had a sharp sickle. [18] Yet another angel who had authority over fire came out from the altar. He cried with a loud voice to him who had the sharp sickle, saying, "Thrust in your sharp sickle and gather the clusters of the vine of the earth, for her grapes are fully ripe." [19] The angel thrust his sickle into the earth and gathered the vintage of the earth, and threw it into the great winepress of the wrath of God. [20] The winepress was trampled outside the city, and

---

[1] 10 Jer 15:2.   [2] 8 Isa 21:9.

blood came out of the winepress, up to the horses' bridles, for one hundred and eighty-six miles. [1]

The Angels With the Last Plagues

15 I saw another great and marvelous sign in heaven: seven angels having the seven last plagues, for in them the wrath of God is complete. [2] And I saw what looked like a sea of glass mixed with fire, and those who have the victory over the beast, over his image and over his mark and over the number of his name, standing on the sea of glass, having harps of God. [3] They sang the song of Moses, the servant of God, and the song of the Lamb, saying:

"Great and marvelous are Your works,
    Lord God Almighty!
Just and true are Your ways,
    O King of saints!
[4] Who shall not fear You, O Lord,
    and glorify Your name?
For You alone are holy.
All nations shall come
    and worship before You,
    for Your judgments have been revealed." [2]

[5] After this I looked. And now the temple of the tabernacle of the testimony in heaven was opened. [6] The seven angels came out of the temple with the seven plagues. They were clothed in pure, bright linen, having their chests wrapped with golden sashes. [7] Then one of the four living creatures gave to the seven angels seven golden bowls full of the wrath of God, who lives forever and ever. [8] And the temple was filled with smoke from the glory of God and from His power. No one was able to enter the temple until the seven plagues of the seven angels were completed.

The Seven Bowls of God's Wrath

16 Then I heard a loud voice from the temple saying to the seven angels, "Go, pour out the bowls of the wrath of God on the earth."
[2] The first went and poured out his bowl on the earth, and foul and grievous sores came on the men who had the mark of the beast and those who worshipped his image.
[3] The second angel poured out his bowl on the sea. It became like the blood of a dead man, and every living creature in the sea died.
[4] The third angel poured out his bowl on the rivers and springs of water, and they became blood. [5] Then I heard the angel of the waters saying:

"You are righteous, O Lord,
    who is and was and who is to be,
    because You have judged these things.
[6] For they have shed the blood of saints and prophets,
    and You have given them blood to drink. It is what
        they deserve!"

[7] And I heard another from the altar saying:

"Yes, Lord God Almighty,
    true and righteous are Your judgments."

[8] The fourth angel poured out his bowl on the sun, and power was given to him to scorch men with fire. [9] Men were scorched with great heat, and they blasphemed the name of God who has power over these plagues, and they did not repent and give Him glory.
[10] The fifth angel poured out his bowl on the throne of the beast, and his kingdom was filled with darkness. They gnawed their tongues because of the anguish, [11] and blasphemed the God of heaven because of their pains and their sores, and did not repent of their deeds.
[12] The sixth angel poured out his bowl on the great Euphrates River, and its water was dried up, to prepare the way for the kings from the East. [13] Then I saw three unclean spirits like frogs

coming out of the mouth of the dragon, out of the mouth of the beast, and out of the mouth of the false prophet. [14] For they are spirits of demons, performing signs, who go out to the kings of the earth and of the whole world, to gather them to the battle of that great day of God Almighty.

[15] "Look, I am coming as a thief. Blessed is he who watches and keeps his garments on, lest he walk naked and his shame be exposed."

[16] They gathered them together to the place which in Hebrew is called Armageddon.
[17] The seventh angel poured out his bowl into the air, and a loud voice came out of the temple of heaven, from the throne, saying, "It is done!" [18] And there were noises and thundering and lightning and a great earthquake, such a mighty and great earthquake, as had never occurred since men were on the earth. [19] The great city was divided into three parts, and the cities of the nations fell. Babylon the Great was remembered before God, to give to her the cup of the wine of the fierceness of His wrath. [20] Every island fled away, and the mountains were not found. [21] Great hail, about the weight of a hundred pounds, [3] fell from heaven upon man. Men blasphemed God because of the plague of the hail, because that plague was so severe.

The Great Harlot and the Beast

17 One of the seven angels who had the seven bowls came and talked with me, saying to me, "Come, I will show you the judgment of the great prostitute who sits on many waters, [2] with whom the kings of the earth committed adultery, and the inhabitants of the earth were made drunk with the wine of her sexual immorality."
[3] Then he carried me away in the Spirit into the wilderness. I saw a woman sitting on a scarlet beast which was full of blasphemous names, having seven heads and ten horns. [4] The woman was arrayed in purple and scarlet, and adorned with gold and precious stones and pearls, having in her hand a golden cup full of abominations and the filth of her sexual immorality. [5] On her forehead a name was written:

MYSTERY,
BABYLON THE GREAT,
THE MOTHER OF PROSTITUTES
AND OF THE ABOMINATIONS
OF THE EARTH.

[6] I saw the woman, drunk with the blood of the saints and with the blood of the martyrs of Jesus.
When I saw her, I marveled greatly. [7] Then the angel said to me, "Why do you marvel? I will tell you the mystery of the woman and of the beast that carries her, which has the seven heads and the ten horns. [8] The beast, which you saw, was, and is not, and is to ascend out of the bottomless pit and go to destruction. Those who dwell on the earth whose names are not written in the Book of Life from the foundation of the world will marvel when they see the beast that was, and is not, and is to come.
[9] "Here is the mind which has wisdom: The seven heads are seven mountains on which the woman sits. [10] They are also seven kings. Five have fallen, one is, the other has not yet come; and when he comes, he must remain a little while. [11] Concerning the beast who was, and is not, he is the eighth, and is of the seven, and is going to destruction.
[12] "The ten horns which you saw are ten kings who have received no kingdom yet, but they will receive authority as kings for one hour with the beast. [13] These are of one mind and will give their power and authority to the beast. [14] These will wage war with the Lamb, but the Lamb will overcome them, for He is Lord of lords and King of kings. Those who are with Him are called and chosen and faithful."
[15] Then he said to me, "The waters which you saw, where the prostitute sits, are peoples and multitudes and nations and tongues.

---

[1] 20 Gk. 1,600 stadia or 300 kilometers.   [2] 3–4 Phrases from Ps 111:2–3; Dt 32:4; Jer 10:7; Ps 86:9; 98:2.   [3] 21 Or 45 kilograms.

[16] These ten horns and the beast which you saw will hate the prostitute; they will make her desolate and naked, and devour her flesh, and burn her with fire. [17] For God has put in their hearts to fulfill His will, and to be of one mind, and to give their kingdom to the beast, until the words of God are fulfilled. [18] The woman whom you saw is that great city, which reigns over the kings of the earth."

The Fall of Babylon

18 After this I saw another angel coming down from heaven, having great authority, and the earth was illuminated with his glory. [2] He cried out mightily with a loud voice, saying:

" 'Fallen! Fallen is Babylon the Great!'[1]
　　She has become a dwelling place of demons,
　a haunt for every unclean spirit,
　　and a haunt for every unclean and hateful bird.
[3] For all the nations have drunk
　　of the wine of the wrath of her sexual immorality,
　the kings of the earth have committed adultery with her,
　　and the merchants of the earth have become rich
　　　　through the
　　　　abundance of her luxury."

[4] Then I heard another voice from heaven saying:

" 'Come out of her, my people,'[2]
　　lest you partake in her sins,
　　and lest you receive her plagues.
[5] For her sins have reached up to heaven,
　　and God has remembered her iniquities.
[6] Render to her as she has rendered to you,
　　and repay her double for her deeds;
　　in the cup which she has mixed, mix a double
　　　　portion for her.
[7] To the extent that she glorified herself and lived luxuriously,
　　so give her torment and sorrow;
　for in her heart she says,
　　'I sit as a queen, and am no widow,
　　and will see no sorrow.'[3]
[8] Therefore her plagues will come in one day—
　　death and mourning and famine.
And she will be utterly burned with fire,
　　for strong is the Lord God who judges her.

[9] "The kings of the earth, who have committed adultery and lived luxuriously with her, will weep and mourn over her when they see the smoke of her burning. [10] Standing far off for the fear of her torment, they will say:

'Alas, alas for that great city,
　　that mighty city, Babylon!
In one hour your judgment has come.'

[11] "The merchants of the earth will weep and mourn over her, for no one buys their merchandise anymore: [12] the merchandise of gold, silver, precious stones and pearls, fine linen, purple, silk and scarlet, all kinds of scented wood, all artifacts of ivory, all merchandise of costly wood, bronze, iron, and marble; [13] and cinnamon and incense, myrrh and frankincense, wine, oil, fine flour and wheat, cattle and sheep, horses and chariots, and slaves and souls of men.

[14] 'The fruit that your soul lusted after
　　has departed from you,
　and all the things which graceful and exquisite
　　have departed from you,
　　and you shall never find them.'

[15] "The merchants of these things, who gained wealth by her, will stand far off for fear of her torment, weeping and wailing, [16] and saying:

'Alas, alas, that great city,
　　that was arrayed in fine linen, in purple and scarlet,
　　and decked with gold and precious stones and pearls!
[17] In one hour such great riches came to nothing!'

"All sea captains and seafaring men, sailors and all who trade by sea, stood far off, [18] and cried out when they saw the smoke of her burning, saying, 'What city is like this great city?' [19] They threw dust on their heads and cried out, weeping and wailing, and saying:

'Alas, alas, that great city,
　　in which all who had ships in the sea
　　grew rich from her wealth!
In one hour she has been laid waste!'

[20] "Rejoice over her, O heaven
　　and saints and apostles and prophets,
　for God has avenged you against her."

[21] Then a mighty angel took up a stone like a great millstone and threw it into the sea, saying:

"With such violence
　　shall that great city Babylon be thrown down,
　　and shall be found no more.
[22] The sound of harpists and musicians, flute players
　　　　and trumpeters,
　　shall not be heard in you any more.
No craftsman of any craft
　　shall be found in you any more,
　and the sound of a millstone
　　shall not be heard in you any more.
[23] The light of a lamp
　　shall shine in you no more,
　and the voice of bridegroom and of bride
　　shall be heard in you no more.
For your merchants were the great men of the earth,
　　and all nations were deceived by your sorcery.
[24] In her was found the blood of prophets and of saints
　　and of all who were slain on the earth."

19 After these things I heard a great sound of many people in heaven, shouting:

"Alleluia!
Salvation and glory and honor and power belong to the
　　　　Lord our God!
[2] 　For true and righteous are His judgments,
because He has judged the great prostitute
　　who corrupted the earth with her sexual immorality;
and He has avenged on her the blood of His servants."

[3] Again they said:

"Alleluia!
Her smoke rises forever and ever."

[4] The twenty-four elders and the four living creatures fell down and worshiped God who sat on the throne, saying:

"Amen! Alleluia!"

The Marriage Supper of the Lamb

[5] Then a voice came from the throne, saying:

"Praise our God,
　　all you His servants
　and those who fear Him,
　　both small and great!"

[6] Then I heard something like the sound like a great multitude, as the sound of many waters and as the sound of mighty thunderings, saying:

"Alleluia!
    For the Lord God Omnipotent reigns!
[7] Let us be glad and rejoice
    and give Him glory,
for the marriage of the Lamb has come,
    and His wife has made herself ready.
[8] It was granted her to be arrayed in fine linen,
    clean and white."
Fine linen is the righteous deeds of the saints.

[9] Then he said to me, "Write: Blessed are those who are invited to the marriage supper of the Lamb." And he said to me, "These are the true sayings of God."

[10] I fell at his feet to worship him. But he said to me, "See that you not do that. I am your fellow servant, and of your brothers who hold the testimony of Jesus. Worship God! For the testimony of Jesus is the spirit of prophecy."

The Rider on the White Horse

[11] I saw heaven opened. And there was a white horse. He who sat on it is called Faithful and True, and in righteousness He judges and wages war. [12] His eyes are like a flame of fire, and on His head are many crowns. He has a name written, that no one knows but He Himself. [13] He is clothed with a robe dipped in blood. His name is called The Word of God. [14] The armies in heaven, clothed in fine linen, white and clean, followed Him on white horses. [15] Out of His mouth proceeds a sharp sword, with which He may strike the nations. "He shall rule them with an iron scepter."[1] He treads the winepress of the fury and wrath of God the Almighty. [16] On His robe and on His thigh He has a name written:

KING OF KINGS
AND LORD OF LORDS.

[17] And I saw an angel standing in the sun, and he cried with a loud voice to all the birds flying in the midst of heaven, "Come and gather for the supper of the great God, [18] to eat the flesh of kings, the flesh of commanders, the flesh of strong men, the flesh of horses and their riders, and the flesh of all men, both free and slave, both small and great!"

[19] Then I saw the beast and the kings of the earth with their armies gathered to wage war against Him who sat on the horse and against His army. [20] But the beast was captured and with him the false prophet who worked signs in his presence, by which he deceived those who received the mark of the beast and those who worshipped his image. These two were thrown alive into the lake of fire that burns with brimstone. [21] The remnant were slain with the sword which proceeded out of the mouth of Him who sat on the horse. And all the birds gorged themselves with their flesh.

The Thousand Years

20 And I saw an angel coming down out of heaven, having the key to the bottomless pit and a great chain in his hand. [2] He seized the dragon, that ancient serpent, who is the Devil and Satan, and bound him for a thousand years. [3] He cast him into the bottomless pit, and shut him up, and set a seal on him, that he should deceive the nations no more, until the thousand years were ended. After that he must be set free for a little while.

[4] I saw thrones, and they sat on them, and the authority to judge was given to them. And I saw the souls of those who had been beheaded for their witness of Jesus and for the word of God. They had not worshipped the beast or his image, and had not received his mark on their foreheads or on their hands. They came to life and reigned with Christ for a thousand years. [5] The rest of the dead did not come to life until the thousand years were ended. This is the first resurrection. [6] Blessed and holy is he who takes part in the first resurrection. Over these the second death has no power, but they shall be priests of God and of Christ and shall reign with Him a thousand years.

The Defeat of Satan

[7] When the thousand years are ended, Satan will be set free from his prison [8] and will go out to deceive the nations which are in the four corners of the earth, Gog and Magog, to gather them for battle. Their number is like the sand of the sea. [9] They traveled the breadth of the earth and surrounded the camp of the saints and the beloved city. But fire came down from God out of heaven and devoured them. [10] The devil, who deceived them, was cast into the lake of fire and brimstone where the beast and the false prophet were. They will be tormented day and night forever and ever.

The Great White Throne Judgment

[11] Then I saw a great white throne and Him who was seated on it. From His face the earth and the heavens fled away, and no place was found for them. [12] And I saw the dead, small and great, standing before God. Books were opened. Then another book was opened, which is the Book of Life. The dead were judged according to their works as recorded in the books. [13] The sea gave up the dead who were in it, and Death and Hades delivered up the dead who were in them. And they were judged, each one by his works. [14] Then Death and Hades were cast into the lake of fire. This is the second death. [15] Anyone whose name was not found written in the Book of Life was cast into the lake of fire.

The New Heaven and the New Earth

21 Then I saw "a new heaven and a new earth."[2] For the first heaven and the first earth had passed away, and there was no more sea. [2] I, John, saw the Holy City, the New Jerusalem, coming down out of heaven from God, prepared as a bride adorned for her husband. [3] And I heard a loud voice from heaven, saying, "Look! The tabernacle of God is with men, and He will dwell with them. They shall be His people, and God Himself will be with them and be their God. [4] God shall wipe away all tears from their eyes. There shall be no more death.[3] Neither shall there be any more sorrow nor crying nor pain, for the former things have passed away."

[5] He who was seated on the throne said, "Look! I am making all things new." Then He said to me, "Write, for these words are faithful and true."

[6] He said to me, "It is done. I am the Alpha and the Omega, the Beginning and the End. I will give of the spring of the water of life to him who thirsts. [7] He who overcomes shall inherit all things, and I will be his God and he shall be My son.[4] [8] But the cowardly, the unbelieving, the abominable, the murderers, the sexually immoral, the sorcerers, the idolaters, and all liars shall have their portion in the lake which burns with fire and brimstone. This is the second death."

The New Jerusalem

[9] One of the seven angels who had the seven bowls full of the seven last plagues came to me and said to me, "Come, I will show you the bride, the wife of the Lamb." [10] And he carried me away in the Spirit to a great and high mountain, and showed me the Holy City, Jerusalem, descending out of heaven from God, [11] having the glory of God, her light like a most precious jewel, like a jasper, clear as crystal. [12] It had a great, high wall, with twelve gates, and at the gates twelve angels, and on the gates the names of the twelve tribes of the sons of Israel were written: [13] three gates on the east, three gates on the north, three gates on the south, and three gates on the west. [14] The wall of the city had twelve foundations, and on them were the names of the twelve apostles of the Lamb.

[15] He who talked with me had a golden rod to measure the city and its gates and wall. [16] The city lies as a square, its length as long as its width. He measured the city with the rod: one thousand four hundred miles.[5] Its length and breadth and height are equal. [17] He then measured its wall: two hundred feet[6] by the

---

[1]15 Ps 2:9.   [2]1 Isa 65:17.   [3]4 Isa 25:8.   [4]7 2Sa 7:14; Ps 89:26.   [5]16 Gk. 12,000 stadia, or 2,200 kilometers.   [6]17 144 cubits, or 65 meters.

measurement of a man, that is, of an angel. [18] The wall was built of jasper and the city was pure gold, as clear as glass. [19] The foundations of the wall of the city were garnished with all kinds of precious jewels. The first foundation was jasper; the second, sapphire; the third, chalcedony; the fourth, emerald; [20] the fifth, sardonyx; the sixth, sardius; the seventh, chrysolite; the eighth, beryl; the ninth, topaz; the tenth, chrysoprase; the eleventh, jacinth; and the twelfth, amethyst. [21] The twelve gates were twelve pearls, each of the gates made of a single pearl, and the street of the city was pure gold, transparent as glass.

[22] I saw no temple in the city, for the Lord God Almighty and the Lamb are its temple. [23] The city has no need of sun or moon to shine in it, for the glory of God is its light, and its lamp is the Lamb. [24] And the nations of those who are saved shall walk in its light, and the kings of the earth shall bring their glory and honor into it. [25] Its gates shall never be shut by day, for there shall be no night there. [26] They shall bring into it the glory and the honor of the nations. [27] No unclean thing shall ever enter it, nor shall anyone who commits abomination or falsehood, but only those whose names are written in the Lamb's Book of Life.

22 Then he showed me a pure river of the water of life, clear as crystal, flowing from the throne of God and of the Lamb [2] in the middle of its street. On each side of the river was the tree of life, which bore twelve kinds of fruit, yielding its fruit each month. The leaves of the tree were for the healing of the nations. [3] There shall be no more curse. The throne of God and of the Lamb shall be in it, and His servants shall serve Him. [4] They shall see His face, and His name shall be on their foreheads. [5] Night shall be no more. They need no lamp nor the light of the sun, for the Lord God will give them light. And they shall reign forever and ever.

The Coming of Christ

[6] The angel said to me, "These words are faithful and true. The Lord God of the holy prophets sent His angel to show to His servants the things which must soon take place."

[7] "Look, I am coming soon. Blessed is he who keeps the words of the prophecy of this book."

[8] I, John, am he who saw and heard these things. When I heard and saw them, I fell down to worship at the feet of the angel who showed me these things. [9] But he said to me, "See that you not do that. For I am your fellow servant, and of your brothers the prophets, and of those who keep the words of this book. Worship God!"

[10] Then he said to me, "Do not seal the words of the prophecy of this book, for the time is at hand. [11] He who is unjust, let him be unjust still. He who is filthy, let him be filthy still. He who is righteous, let him be righteous still. He who is holy, let him be holy still."

[12] "Look, I am coming soon! My reward is with Me to give to each one according to his work. [13] I am the Alpha and the Omega, the Beginning and the End, the First and the Last."

[14] Blessed are those who do His commandments, that they may have the right to the tree of life, and may enter through the gates into the city. [15] Outside are dogs and sorcerers and the sexually immoral and murderers and idolaters and everyone who loves and practices a lie.

[16] "I, Jesus, have sent My angel to you with this testimony for the churches. I am the Root and the Offspring of David, the Bright and Morning Star."

[17] The Spirit and the bride say, "Come." Let him who hears say, "Come." Let him who is thirsty come. Let him who desires take the water of life freely.

[18] I testify to everyone who hears the words of the prophecy of this book: If anyone adds to these things, God shall add to him the plagues that are written in this book. [19] And if anyone takes away from the words of the book of this prophecy, God shall take away his part out of the Book of Life and out of the Holy City and out of the things which are written in this book.

[20] He who testifies to these things says, "Surely I am coming soon."

Amen. Even so, come Lord Jesus!

[21] The grace of our Lord Jesus Christ be with you all. Amen.

FELLOWSHIP LOST, FELLOWSHIP RESTORED

It is possible that this Bible was given to you by a church, a friend, or a family member, or you may have purchased it at your local bookstore or online. Whatever the means of its delivery, we trust and know that it was ordained and planned by God.

You see, beloved, what you hold in your hand is the greatest book ever written. It was penned or written down by men, but God through the Holy Spirit is the ultimate writer. God's Word is true, and it is "alive, and active" according to Hebrews 4:12. Our God is not silent; He has spoken.

The Bible story is a story of what was created, what was lost, but what was ultimately recovered through the person and work of Jesus Christ. It is a story that tells of fellowship lost, but also fellowship restored.

What Was Created

Genesis (the book of beginnings) tells the story of a loving God who, because of His love, begins to create. He creates light, plants, fruit trees, water, animals, and His crowning creation who was made in "His own image" (Genesis 1:27)—man. God breathed life into man (Adam and Eve), and God called everything that He had made "good." It was good because God made it. There was nothing that this loving God had not provided for man, and even more importantly than what was provided for man, man had fellowship with the Provider, namely God.

Everything was as it should be; it was perfect and would continue to be that way if man loved and obeyed God. However, man did not.

What Was Lost

As Genesis unfolds, we see that everything goes bad (Genesis 3). God's loving commands are not obeyed but are disregarded, and fellowship with God due to man's sin appears to be lost. Willful obedience is replaced by willful disobedience, and the human race descends into the chaos that is characteristic of our present broken world. Man sinned against God, and the curse that we see in the garden is the curse we see in our world today.

Sin is serious; it kills (Romans 6:23) and affects everything. The Book of Romans tells us, "Therefore as sin came into the world through one man and death through sin, so death has spread to all men, because all have sinned" (Romans 5:12). You see, because we are all part of the same family, the human race, sin is a problem we all share. The saying really is true: "Your actions affect other people." And how true it is when it comes to sin. We know this as a result of us being connected to Adam, but we also know this when we look at our lives; none of us are without sin. Adam sinned against a holy, loving, and perfect God, and so have we. However, God was not without a plan.

God knows everything. And since He knows everything, He knew man would sin; therefore He designed the perfect rescue plan to redeem and restore the fellowship that man through sin severed and lost. God had a plan to bring us back home.

What Is Recovered

God's plan of recovery, redemption, and restoration was announced in the garden—the place where it all seemed to unravel. It was first announced to

628

the serpent who deceived God's creation, but then it was heralded to the rest of creation as well (Genesis 3:15). God would restore, God would redeem, and it would be God who would provide the way for man to come back home to fellowship with Him.

God restored man and creation by coming to earth as a man. That man is Jesus. Jesus is the Son of God. It would be Jesus who would "bruise" the head of the serpent and would defeat sin and death and provide the way back to God. He would come to earth, obey and love God perfectly and completely, and pave the way for the rest of us.

Jesus is the only way back to God (John 14:6). Thank God for providing a way! It is through trusting in what Jesus has done through His death, burial, and resurrection that we are saved. We cannot earn salvation through our works; we must trust in the work He has done, for "it is finished"!

The whole of Scripture tells this one story: fellowship lost, but ultimately fellowship restored—and it is restored through Jesus. The debt we owed because of sin has been satisfied through Jesus. The Bible is all about Jesus, and it is through Jesus that we are welcomed into God's presence once again and will one day be with Him forever when He returns (1 Thessalonians 4:13–18).

It is God's will for you to be saved. If you've never received Jesus as your Savior, then you've never received the benefits of what He did for you on the cross, and you're still in a sinful state. You can receive Him today. It is not hard. The Bible says:

If you confess with your mouth Jesus is Lord, and believe in your heart that God has raised Him from the dead, you will be saved, for with the heart one believes unto righteousness, and with the mouth confession is made unto salvation. For the Scripture says, "Whoever believes in Him will not be ashamed." For there is no distinction between Jew and Greek, for the same Lord over all is generous toward all who call upon Him. For, "Everyone who calls on the name of the Lord shall be saved."
—Romans 10:9–13

All of God's blessings and the benefits of salvation can be yours if you receive Him into your heart. You can do this by praying this prayer:

Dear God, I come to You admitting that I am a sinner. I believe that Your Son, Jesus, died on the cross to take away my sins. I also believe He rose from the dead so I could be justified and made righteous through faith in Him. I call upon the name of Jesus Christ for Him to be the Savior and Lord of my life. Jesus, thank You for washing away my sin. I choose to follow You. I declare right now that I am a born-again child of God. I am free from sin, and I am the righteousness of God in Christ. I am saved, in Jesus's name. Amen.

Congratulations, and welcome to the family of God! Until He returns, we commend two things to you:

Become part of a church
The apostle Paul wrote several New Testament letters (1 and 2 Corinthians, Galatians, Ephesians, Philippians, Colossians, 1 and 2 Thessalonians) that are mostly to churches. It is in the context of community that we grow in God and are nourished. God through Christ has established the church (Ephesians 4:11–16) as a means to growing in Christ likeness, which is the goal of every believer as it is God's design (Romans 8:28–30).

We are not to forsake the call to community (Hebrews 10:25) but to embrace it. Your growth is tied to community; find a local Bible-believing, Christ-exalting, Spirit-embracing church. A perfect church does not exist, but one that seeks to honor God, exalts Christ, embraces the Spirit, and loves people does.

Read the Word
This Bible was given to you with the intention that you would read it. God has chosen to reveal Himself or show us who He is through creation (what is made) and through His revelation (what is written), or the Scriptures. It is through God's truth that we learn of God, learn of Christ, and learn to live a life that pleases God.

Brother or sister, "let the word of Christ dwell in you richly" (Colossians 3:16), and by it be changed and tell others.

WELCOME HOME,
THE PASSIO FAMILY

Genesis 3

Renew our minds / to change our
old selves!

2 Chor 2:10 & 11

The mind / Thinking / Forgiveness

Power over our minds

Satan wants to make us not
understand & destroy us!
No power over me/his schemes

He wants us to focus on everyone
else, gives him authority & access
over our lives! It's really him
who tries to destroy us! Depression &
negative thoughts
Chapt. 10:4 / Prone to fear & anxiety,
jealous, keep in to destroy our lives
Scheme to do harm in her life

John 10:10 Satan is the thief
→ Satan continues to bring these
things up! Pulling down
Way of thinking (receiving information
We believe his lies (Stronghold)
Faith to deal w/ these things
Conflict w/ what God says!
Think in our minds there is no way
to overcome these beliefs: Depression
Addiction, family
Old things Have passed away
& all things have become New — Good!